S0-AGZ-389

UNIVERSITY CASEBOOK SERIES

CASES AND MATERIALS

FAMILY LAW

FIFTH EDITION

by

JUDITH AREEN
Paul Regis Dean Professor of Law
Georgetown University Law Center

MILTON C. REGAN, JR.
Professor of Law
Georgetown University Law Center

FOUNDATION PRESS

2006

THOMSON
WEST

395 Hudson Street
New York, NY 10014
Phone Toll Free 1–877–888–1330
Fax (212) 367–6799
foundation–press.com
Printed in the United States of America

ISBN–13: 978–1–58778–877–2
ISBN–10: 1–58778–877–2

J.C.A.

For my parents, Gordon and Pauline Areen

M.C.R.

For three generations of family: Sylvia, Nancy, Rebecca, and Ben

*

PREFACE TO THE FIFTH EDITION

This is the first co-authored edition of the book. As with earlier editions, this book is first and foremost designed for use in the classroom. It is structured to introduce students to the major issues in the field with a particular emphasis on 21st century case law and statutes.

Two especially significant changes in family law and family life in recent years have shaped the material we have included in this book and how it is organized. First, while traditional gender roles continue to have influence in subtle ways, law for the most part has abandoned reliance on the assumption that men have primary responsibility for economic support and women for domestic tasks. In 1979, for instance, the United States Supreme Court in Orr v. Orr (p. 174) first held unconstitutional a state alimony statute that authorized alimony for needy wives but not for needy husbands. The Court criticized the traditional model of family, explaining "[n]o longer is the female destined solely for the home and the rearing of the family and only the male for the marketplace and the world of ideas."

Second, recent years have seen challenges to both the prominence and meaning of marriage. Marriage has become less central to the organization of intimate relationships. Non-marital cohabitation has become more common and subject to less stigma over the past generation or so. Related to this trend, marriage and parenthood have become less closely linked. Married couples will not necessarily have children, and couples who have children will not necessarily marry. In addition, same-sex couples have pressed for the elimination of long-standing barriers to their ability to marry.

These developments make it necessary to rethink most aspects of the field of family law. This edition, for instance, devotes considerable space to the issues raised by nontraditional relationships. There is a separate section on same-sex marriage in the chapter on marriage, sections on the rights and obligations of unmarried partners in the custody and financial awards chapters, a section on the developing concept of "parenthood" in the chapter on reproduction, and a new first chapter on how society should determine what constitutes a family, and the legal implications that follow from that determination.

As previous editions have done, this book draws on a variety of sources in order to emphasize the powerful emotional and psychological dynamics of family life that law may find it difficult to influence. The book includes material on what occurred after the decision in a number of cases in order to highlight the strengths and weaknesses of judicial intervention in family matters. Material from history and the social sciences is also included in order to provide students with a broader perspective on major issues. In addition to traditional appellate opinions, the books includes a custody trial transcript and follow-up court opinions designed to enable students to understand the limits of the best interest of the child standard, and the strengths and weaknesses of reliance on experts. The book also includes a series of court opinions interpreting a single state domestic violence statute in order to illustrate the practical and interpretive challenges that legislation dealing with intimate relationships can present..

The materials in the book have been selected to develop several key themes that tend to recur across topics. Perhaps most important is the tension between private ordering and state supervision of family life. In the late 20th century, private ordering increased dramatically with the adoption in all fifty states of no-fault grounds for divorce. At the same time, the disadvantages of private ordering became more apparent, including the economic burden imposed by divorce on many wives and children. One response has been significant growth in federal laws designed to establish minimum standards for calculating and enforcing child support orders. In addition, subjects such as reproductive technology, premarital contracts, separation agreements, and open adoption all raise questions about the appropriate balance between private ordering and state regulation.

A second theme is the growing importance of constitutional law in family matters. The Supreme Court has tightened constitutional protection for everything from access to marriage, to the rights of the juveniles who commit serious offenses. Regulation of the family traditionally has been premised in many instances on deeply-rooted assumptions and values that do not easily admit of empirical proof. What will be the fate of such regulation if the state is required both to articulate a compelling state interest and to demonstrate that the law in question is narrowly tailored to achieve that interest? Can a prohibition on polygamy, for instance, satisfy this standard?

A third theme is to focus on the larger context in which family law matters arise. The family, after all, is an institution both older and more universal than the corporation, and at least as fundamental to human life as the law of real property.

Finally, gender issues are inescapable in any discussion of family law. An important question in analyzing any topic is whether the consequences of a legal rule are likely to be different for men and women. In addition, are there differences between men and women that the law should take into account? Does it depend on whether we believe those differences are mainly biological or social in origin? How should the law treat changes in gender presented by transsexuals? These and other questions about gender underscore that family law often requires that we consider the complexity of ideals such as equality and autonomy.

Deletions from excerpted material are marked except when the omitted material consists only of citations or footnotes.

We are indebted to the many colleagues and students whose probing questions and suggestions over the years have helped to shape these materials, particularly Patricia King, Marc Spindelman, and Herma Hill Kay. We also wish to thank Laurie Kohn and Deborah Epstein for their valuable suggestions on the section of Chapter Three that deals with Domestic Violence. Georgetown law students Flora Ahn, Emily Fisher, Michael Glover and Kalah Paisley provided outstanding research assistance in the preparation of this edition. Anna Selden organized the manuscript and Jennifer Locke Davitt coordinated both the copyright permissions and a portion of the research assistance. Our thanks go to all of you and to our families for their inspiration and support.

JUDITH AREEN
MILTON C. REGAN, JR.

Washington D.C.

February, 2006

*

ACKNOWLEDGMENTS

We wish to thank the following authors and copyright holders for granting permission to reprint excerpts from the following copyrighted works:

Albrandt, Note, Turning in the Client: Mandatory Child Abuse Reporting Requirements and the Criminal Defense of Battered Women, 81 Texas L. Rev. 655 (2002). Copyright 2002 by the Texas Law Review Association. Reprinted by permission.

Amato, Commentary: Good Enough Marriages: Parental Discord, Divorce and Children's Long-Term Well Being, 9 Va. J. Soc. Pol'y & L. 71 (2001).

American Families: A Documentary History by Donald M. Scott and Bernard Wishy. Copyright 1982 by Donald M. Scott and Bernard Wishy. Reprinted by permission of HarperCollins Publishers.

American Law Institute, Principles of the Law of Family Dissolution (2002).

Andrews, The Justice of Parental Accountability: Hypothetical Disinterested Citizens and Real Victims' Voices in the Debate over Expanded Parental Liability, 75 Temp. L. Rev. 375 (2002). Reproduced with the permission of Temple Law Review Volume 75. Copyright 2002 Temple University of the Commonwealth System of Higher Education.

Areen, Intervention Between Parent and Child: A Reappraisal of the State's Role in Child Neglect and Abuse Cases, 63 Geo.L.J. 887 (1975). Reprinted with permission of the publisher; copyright 1975 by the Georgetown Law Journal.

Banks, The Color of Desire: Fulfilling Adoptive Parents' Racial Preferences Through Discriminatory State Action, 107 Yale L.J. 875 (1998). Reprinted by permission of The Yale Law Journal Company and William S. Hein Company from The Yale Law Journal, Vol. 107, pages 875-964.

Barlow, Divorce Child Custody Mediation: In Order to Form a More Perfect Disunion?, 52 Clev. St. L. Rev. 499 (2004-2005).

Bartlett, Comparing Race and Sex Discrimination in Custody Cases, 28 Hofstra L. Rev. 877 (2000). Reprinted with the permission of the Hofstra Law Review Association.

Basch, Framing American Divorce: From the Revolutionary Generation to the Victorians (1999). Copyright 1999 by the University of California Press. Reproduced with permission of the University of California Press via the Copyright Clearance Center.

Benedetto, An Ounce of Prevention: A Foster Youth's Substantive Due Process Right to Proper Preparation for Emancipation, 9 U.C. Davis J. Juv. L & Pol'y 381 (2005). This work was originally published in 9 U.C. Davis J. Juv. L & Pol'y 381 (2005), copyright 2005 by the Regents of the University of California. Reprinted with permission. All rights reserved.

Bohannan, Divorce Chains, Households of Remarriage and Multiple Divorces in Divorce and After (1970). Copyright 1970 by Paul Bohannan. Used by permission of Doubleday & Company, Inc.

Braver, Ellman & Fabricius, Relocation of Children after Divorce and Children's Best Interests: New Evidence and Legal Considerations, 17 J. Fam. Psychol. 206 (2003).

Carbone and Brinig, Rethinking Marriage: Feminist Ideology, Economic Change, and Divorce Reform, 65 Tulane Law Review 953, 954, 957–961, 988–1010 (1991). Reprinted with permission of Tulane Law Review.

Coltrane, Family Man: Fatherhood, Housework, and Gender Equity (1996). Copyright 1996 by Oxford University Press, Inc. Used by permission of Oxford University Press, Inc.

Cott, Public Vows: A History of Marriage and the Nation 1-2 (2000). Reprinted by permission of the publisher, Cambridge, Mass.: Harvard University Press, Copyright (c) 2000 by the President and Fellows of Harvard College.

Demos, Images of the American Family, Then and Now in Changing Images of the Family 43–60 (V. Tufte & B. Myerhoft eds. 1979). Reprinted with permission of Yale University Press.

DiFonzo, Customized Marriage, 75 Indiana Law Journal 875 (2000). Copyright 2000 by the Trustees of Indiana University. Reprinted with permission.

Ellman and Sugarman, Spousal Emotional Abuse as a Tort? 55 Md. L. Rev. 1268 (1996). Reprinted with permission of the authors.

Elmer, Human Genomics: Toward a New Paradigm for Equal Protection Jurisprudence, Part II, 50 Rhode Island Bar Journal 11 (2002). Reprinted by permission.

Elster, Solomonic Judgments: Against the Best Interest of the Child, 54 U. Chi. L. Rev. 1 (1986). Copyright 1986 by the University of Chicago Law School. Reproduced with permission of the University of Chicago Law School via the Copyright Clearance Center.

Folberg, Divorce Mediation—A Workable Alternative. Reprinted by permission of Jay Folberg, Professor of Law, Lewis and Clark Law School.

Friedman, A History of American Law 179–184 (1973).

Galston, Marriage - Just a Piece of Paper? (2002). Copyright 2002 William B. Eerdmans Publishing Co.

Ginsburg, Gender and the Constitution, 44 U.Cinn.L.Rev. 1, 2–4 (1975).

Ginsburg, Some Thoughts on Autonomy and Equality in Relation to Roe V. Wade, 63 N.C.L.Rev., 375, 379-84 (1985).

Glendon, Marriage and the State: The Withering Away of Marriage, 62 Va. L.Rev. 663, 677–82 (1976).

Hartman, Adolescent Autonomy: Clarifying an Ageless Conundrum, 51 Hastings L.J. 1265 (2000). Copyright 2000 by University of California, Hastings College of the Law. Reprinted from Hastings Law Journal, Volume 51, Number 6, August 2000, 1265, by permission.

Hartog, Man and Wife in America: A History (2000). Reprinted by permission of the publisher, Cambridge, Mass.: Harvard University Press, Copyright (c) 2000 by the President and Fellows of Harvard College.

Harvey, Adolescent Competency and the Refusal of Medical Treatment, 13 Health Matrix: J. L. & Medicine 297 (2003). Copyright 2003 by Case Western Reserve University Law. Reproduced with permission of Case Western Reserve University Law via Copyright Clearance Center.

Hasday, Contest and Consent: A Legal History of Marital Rape, 88 Calif. L. Rev. 1375, 1375-1523 (2000). Copyright 2000 by the California Law Review. Reprinted by permission of the California Law Review and Jill Elaine Hasday.

Karlan, Foreword: Loving Lawrence, 102 Mich. L. Rev. 1447 (2004).

Kay, From the Second Sex to the Joint Venture: An Overview of Women's Rights and Family Law in the United States During the Twentieth Century, 88 Calif. L. Rev. 2017 (2000). Copyright 2000 by the California Law Review. Reprinted by permission of the California Law Review.

Kay, Equality and Difference: A Perspective on No-Fault Divorce and its Aftermath, 56 U. Cin. L. Rev. 1 (1987). Copyright 1987 by University of Cincinnati Law Review. Reprinted by permission.

LaFemina, Note, The Lawyer's Role in the Independent Adoption Process: Parental Consent and Best Interests of the Child, 3 Touro L. Rev. 283 (1987).

LaFollette, Licensing Parents, 9 Philosophy and Public Affairs 182–97 (Winter 1980). Copyright by Princeton University Press. Reprinted by permission of Princeton University Press.

Levi-Strauss, The Family in Man, Culture and Society, edited by Harry L. Shapiro. Copyright 1956, 1971 by Oxford University Press, Inc. Reprinted by permission.

Mead, Anomalies in American Post-Divorce Relationships in Divorce and After. Copyright 1970 by Paul Bohannan. Used by permission of Doubleday & Company, Inc.

Miller, The Making of a Confused Middle-Class Husband, 2 Social Policy 33, 34, 36–39 (1971). Reprinted by permission of the publisher, Social Policy Corporation, New York, N.Y. 10036.

Mnookin, Child-Custody Adjudication: Judicial Functions in the Face of Indeterminacy, 39 Law and Contemporary Problems 226 (1975). Reprinted with permission from a symposium on children and law appearing in 39 Law and Contemporary Problems, summer, 1975, published by the Duke University School of Law, Durham, North Carolina. Copyright 1975 by Duke University. Article copyright 1976 by the author.

Mnookin and Kornhauser, Bargaining in the Shadow of the Law: the Case of Divorce. Reprinted by permission of the Yale Law Journal Co. and Fred B. Rothman & Co. from 88 Yale Law Journal 954.

Mundy, Fault Line, Washington Post, October 26, 1997, at W08. Copyright 1997, The Washington Post. Reprinted with permission.

Murdock, Sterilization of the Retarded: A Problem as a Solution, 62 Cal.L.Rev. 918, 928–30 (1970). Copyright 1974, California Law Review, Inc. Reprinted by permission.

Nader, The Law Versus Plural Marriages, 31 Harvard Law Record 10 (1960). Reprinted with permission.

National Conference of Commissioners on Uniform State Laws;

— The Uniform Adoption Act

— The Uniform Child Custody Jurisdiction Act

— The Uniform Marriage and Divorce Act (both 1971 and 1974 editions)

— The Uniform Premarital Agreement Act

— The Uniform Reciprocal Enforcement of Support Act (1968). Reprinted with permission.

Note, Black Market Adoptions, 22 Cath. Lawyer 48 (1976).

Pauling, Forward, Reflections on the New Biology, 15 U.C.L.A.L.Rev. 267, 269 (1968). Reprinted with permission.

Perry, The Transracial Adoption Controversy: An Analysis of Discourse and Subordination, 21 N.Y.U. Rev. L. & Soc. Change 33 (1994). Reprinted with permission.

Posner, Sex and Reason (1992). Reprinted by permission of the publisher, Cambridge, Mass.: Harvard University Press, Copyright (c) 1992 by the President and Fellows of Harvard College.

Pound, Individual Interests in Domestic Relations, 14 Mich.L.Rev. 177 (1961). Reprinted with permission.

Ramsey, Ethics at the Edge of Life 192–95, 201–03, 212–15, 218–19. Reprinted with permission of the Yale University Press.

Regan, Double Identity: Law and the Meanings of Marriage (1999). Copyright Oxford University Press, Ltd. Used by permission of Oxford University Press, Inc.

Ring, Comment, Personal Jurisdiction and Child Support: Establishing the Parent-Child Relationship as Minimum Contacts, 89 Calif. L. Rev. 1125 (2001). Copyright 2001 by the California Law Review, Inc. Reprinted by permission.

Ross, Revealing Confidential Secrets: Will it Save Our Children?, 28 Seton Hall L. Rev. 963, 967-68 (1998). Reprinted by permission.

Santorum, It Takes a Family: Conservatism and the Common Good 6-7 (2005). Copyright 2005 by ISI Books. Reprinted by permission.

Scott & Wishy, America's Families: A Documentary History 70-72 (1982). Copyright 1982 by Donald M. Scott and Bernard Wishy. Reprinted by permission of HarperCollins Publishers.

Spaht, Covenant Marriage Seven Years Later: Its as Yet Fulfilled Promise, 65 La. L. Rev. 605 (2005). Reprinted by permission.

Spindelman, Surviving *Lawrence v. Texas*, 102 Mich. L. Rev. 1615 (2004). Reprinted with permission of the author.

Tesler, Collaborative Family Law, 4 Pepp. Disp. Resol. L.J. 317 (2004). Copyright 2004 by Pepperdine University School of Law. Reprinted by permission.

Wexler, Husbands and Wives: The Uneasy Case for Antinepotism Rules, 62 B.U.L.Rev. 75, 76–87, 141–42 (1982). Reprinted with permission.

Weitzman, Legal Regulation of Marriage: Tradition and Change, 62 Cal.L.Rev. 1169 (1974). Reprinted by permission of the author.

Zainaldin, The Emergence of a Modern American Family Law: Child Custody, Adoption and the Courts, 1796–1851, 73 Nw.U.L.Rev. 1038 (1979). Reprinted by permission.

*

SUMMARY OF CONTENTS

*

TABLE OF CONTENTS

PART II. CHILDREN, PARENTS AND THE STATE

CHAPTER 8. Parents and Children 1017

TABLE OF CASES

Principal cases are in bold type. Non-principal cases are in roman type. References are to Pages.

*

FAMILY LAW

*

PART I

Husbands, Wives and Lovers

CHAPTER 1

What Is A Family?

Family Law deals with "families," of course, but defining this term is as much a normative as a descriptive exercise. What relationships should we regard as families? There is considerable controversy about which kinds of intimate relationships Family Law should recognize, as well as about the rights, benefits, and obligations that should flow from that recognition.

This controversy exists in large measure because of some distance between legal form and lived experience. All areas of the law must struggle with this distance to varying degrees. The challenge is especially acute, however, in Family Law. Perhaps more than in any other subject, Family Law attempts to impose some measure of coherence and rationality upon an inherently unruly and often irrational domain of life. As people meet, become intimately involved, intertwine their lives, raise children, become estranged, attempt reconciliation, and decide to part, the legal forms available to address these experiences may be responsive and useful or insensitive and even harmful. People act partly within the structures that the law provides, but also may feel the need to ignore, transform, or destroy them in order to live their lives as they wish.

As the material in this casebook will describe, some believe that the distance between form and substance in Family Law has widened considerably over the past generation or so. Marriage may be a less central legal form for organizing intimate relationships, as unmarried cohabitation increases and births outside of marriage are more common. Similarly, advances in reproductive technology call into question the relevance of traditional legal definitions of parenthood. As a result of these and other developments, there is some sentiment for less reliance on legal form, and greater attention to the substance of relationships, as a conceptual basis for Family Law. The concern is that in too many cases, adhering strictly to legal form seems to lead to unfair results.

Considering the invitation to formulate Family Law in this way raises important and difficult questions. What characteristics do we have in mind when we say that an arrangement is "in substance" a family relationship? Are those features the same across all types of relationships, or do they differ depending on whether adults, children, or some combination of the two are involved?

If there are such core characteristics, should we expand legal status to encompass them, or grant them legal recognition without requiring any formalities such as marriage or adoption? If we expand our legal categories to encompass a wider range of relationships, how inclusive should we be? Should we permit anyone who wants it to assume a particular legal status, or should we impose certain requirements for being able to do so?

If we decide instead to disregard legal form, there are other issues to confront. Are we prepared for courts and agencies to conduct in-depth examinations of intimate relationships to identify those that have the essential characteristics of a family? Will such case-by-case determinations provide enough predictability for the parties involved and those who deal with them? If legal form no longer plays an important role in ordering intimate life, will society lose one important way of both shaping and expressing a set of common values?

The material in this Chapter raises these questions in the course of examining different types of relationships in which there is some tension between form and substance. They provide a short preview of the issues that we will cover in much more depth in the remainder of this book. Ideally, they will allow you to analyze each of those issues with a keener sense of the complex challenges of Family Law.

A. Adult-Child Relationships

Matthew M. Kavanagh, Rewriting the Legal Family: Beyond Exclusivity to a Care-Based Standard

16 Yale J. L. & Feminism 83 (2004).

Introduction: Negotiating the Post-Modern Family

The immediate family in which I grew up began with two adults and their two biological sons. During my childhood, however, it included (at various times) two households, shared custody, lesbian mothers, heterosexual stepparents, a foster child, and three stepsiblings, all in the same small town. I have ex-step-grandparents. A typical day when I was ten might have begun in the home of my mother or my father, who shared equal custody of my brother and me. If that day began at my mother's house, we would have risen early so that my mother, a teacher, could head to work across the river. My mother's female partner, Lisa, who was one of our three parents, would have driven my brother, me, and our foster brother to my father's house across town. There, because my father did not have to go to work until later, we would eat breakfast and board the bus to school. After school we would head back to my mother's house and stay with a neighbor until my mother or Lisa got home. If we were staying at my father's house that week, our foster brother (who lived with my mother) would be dropped off in the morning to join us for breakfast and, in the evening, my father would pick us up from my mother's after he got off of work.

Our family also included a community of adults on whom the children in the family could and did regularly rely for care, support, and guidance—who stood in various relationships to various children. Some were close family members who provided direct care, while others were more peripheral. Christmas in my family was always a joyous family occasion, with the dinner table set for 20 or more—almost none of whom were blood relatives, but many of whom were close members of our family network.

Our family changed during my childhood—homes moved, stepparents and children were added and subtracted, and new adults came into our lives. It was not always easy in our family—there were difficult times and difficult relationships, as in any family. What remained stable, however, was the abundance of care provided to children by different adults—through interwoven, supportive connections. Mine was a family, built on changing relationships, that provided the children with an incredibly supportive and healthy environment in which to grow, learn, and become adults.

My family is surely unrecognizable to many Americans, given all of the rules about gender, sexuality, and number of caregivers it has broken. Nonetheless, my family represents a combination of the real-life, post-modern family constructions that are increasingly common throughout the United States—stepparents, gay parents, and caregivers whose bonds with children are not based on adult sexual relationships.

The American legal system, however, has its own narrative of what a family looks like. Had my family come in contact with that system, our story would have been drastically re-written. From a cast of several children, multiple parents, and innumerable other caregiving adults, the state would have stepped in to rewrite my family's story to meet its formal model. We would have been a family with two children and two divorced parents.

Our current family law and politics would prescribe that my two (and only two) parents of opposite sexes assume full responsibility for the care of their own children. If there were ever a dispute about custody, several of the caregivers in our lives would have held no legal standing. Attempts by my mother's partner to enroll me in school or bring my brother to the doctor might have met official suspicion and requirements that the legal parents be present. My brother and I would have had to sit silently by as policymakers, lawyers, judges, and our "rights-bearing" parents argued about the constituent relationships of our lives.

This is the rule of the "exclusive" family and is a central problem in family law in the United States.

. . .

I. Writing The Family in Law & Politics

A. Current Constructions of Family

Parenting and caregiving in the United States is too often understood as work to be done in isolation and in private. Mainstream political discussions locate the care for children largely in the private, two-parent nuclear family. Here, our discourse suggests that all care is to be given and all responsibility is to rest. Our society's gender norms further assign most of this care and responsibility to women—mothers—who do the majority of our caring work. Sometimes middle and upper-class women are able to hire others to do this caring work, but the mother is most often the one who does the hiring and oversees the caregiving. Since caring work is not generally valued in our society, the people hired to care for children are usually women, often poor women, women of color, or migrant women from the global south who are paid comparatively little for their labor. Thus, caring work is simply shifted from white, upper-class women to women with less class, race, or geographic privilege. Working-class parents, for their part, have no choice but to work outside the home. All the care and authority needed by their children is nonetheless presumed to be provided exclusively by them, unless they are fortunate enough to find affordable day-care programs.

Positioning care as a "private" concern suggests that the family is outside the purview of the state. In many legal instances, a doctrine of privacy is both right and realistic.... In our tradition the State is not omnipresent in the home. And there are other spheres of our lives and existence, outside the home, where the State should not be a dominant presence.

. . .

When it comes to issues of family construction and child custody, however, the state can and does intrude into "private" family relationships. When it does so, it regularly uses a values-based standard of family to frame some forms of family as right and others as wrong. As I will discuss below, the results of state intrusion are directly related to how closely a family fits the state-imposed vision of family.

As Katharine Bartlett identified in 1984, a legal doctrine of "exclusivity" pervades family law in the United States. Under this doctrine, legal families have two defining features. First, children have two, and only two, parents. These parents preferably are married and are, almost without exception, of opposite sexes. Second, adults stand in relation to children either as full legal parents or as strangers. Parents generally have exclusive control over and access to children, without the possibility of some access or limited control or input.

Justice Sandra O'Connor [has written that] "the interest of parents in the care, custody, and control of their children . . . is perhaps the oldest of the fundamental liberty interests recognized by this Court." Instead of translating this into a doctrine that includes a variety of family forms, many courts, including the Supreme Court, have translated this fundamental interest into an exclusive status. Decisions under this doctrine are made in reference to the fundamental rights of these two parents in relation to their children.

This exclusive family model provides the basis for much of the states' interaction with, protection of, and intrusion into the family. Courts arbitrate and enforce the rights of the child's two-and-only-two parents in matters of custody. Government agencies enforce the rights of children's exclusive parents to make medical, educational, religious, legal and other choices for their children. Police agencies apprehend and return runaway children to their parents, even against the child's wishes.

Parents are given the affirmative duty to care for and support their children. Courts step in to require that even non-custodial parents provide child support and intercede to ensure that parents do not mistreat their children.

. . .

All of these decisions base state intrusion on beliefs by the state about what a family should look like and the rights and the responsibilities of just two members of that family. Nowhere is there space for the voices or relationships of those who are not one of the two parents. Nowhere are the constituent relationships of children's lives given full protection or the voices of these children fully heard. Procedurally, much attention is paid to the best interests of the child, but hardly ever may those best interests include relationships not included in the exclusive family.

B. Insider Families: The Right Side of the Law

Today, nearly one-third of first marriages end within ten years. One in three women giving birth is unmarried. Only sixty-nine percent of children in the United States live in two-parent families. Conservative estimates suggest these families include over six million stepchildren, meaning the exclusive biological family represents the lives of less than sixty percent of children in the United States. At least seventy-five thousand same-sex couples in the United States have children in their homes.

Twenty-eight million children in the United States grow up in families in which care is not provided exclusively by two heterosexual opposite-sex parents. Instead caregivers increasingly include gay and lesbian families, single parent or "cohabitating" parent families, families with grandparents (either as primary caregivers or in addition to primary caregivers), and various other formations.

We can clearly disagree about whether these aspects of family life in the United States are good, bad, or mixed, but refusing to recognize them legally will not help matters. Despite the reality that US families take a great many forms, we continue to base our legal decision-making on a model that is not reality for a huge proportion of the affected population.

. . .

The idea . . . that . . . exclusive families are successful and independent units for the provision of care to children is truly a myth. As a practical matter, most nuclear families simply cannot provide complete care for children by themselves. The family wage has never been a reality for most families and the idea of the working father and stay-at-home mother is equally fictitious for all but an upper-class, largely white minority. Today, less than one fifth of American children live with a "stay-at-home" parent of either gender. Most families rely on outside caregivers, be they family, friends, neighbors, hired help, or day-care programs. In 1999 over two thirds of pre-school children in the United States were cared for in regular arrangements with people other than their parents. On average these children spent thirty-seven hours a week in the care of others. Many social scientists have found that this contact with caregivers, including those outside the exclusive, nuclear family, is important and beneficial to children.

There is an important state interest in assuring that children's care will be handled in an orderly way—making sure that the messiness of the twenty-first century American family does not result in gaps in children's care or in chaos. Some argue that the exclusive family is the best way to assure this. Without this construction, a free-for-all would ensue, overburdening the state with arbitration and failing to assure that children have caregivers who possess the necessary legal authority and who the state can easily identify. To this end, exclusivity does not simply function to enforce existing nuclear families. Even after divorce, parental death and other interruptions of nuclear families, legal exclusivity is generally preserved and works to assure that children have no more than two parents and that those two parents have complete control and access. This is seen as a continuation of the state interest in easy, orderly identification of family authority. After nuclear family interruption, and until it can be restored, it is in the state's and family's best interests to continue exclusivity.

The reality that families do have multiple outside caregivers cannot and should not be ignored. When stepparents, grandparents, gay and lesbian parents, and a variety of other caregivers and potential caregivers are written out of the legal narrative of family, they are discouraged or prevented from making and maintaining positive relationships with the children. If the goal is to decrease the burden on the state and maximize the care available to children, this would hardly seem helpful.

. . .

C. Learning from Outsider Families

. . .

As researcher Froma Walsh writes:

> Family cultures and structures are becoming increasingly diverse and fluid. Over an extended family life-cycle, adults and their children are moving in and out of increasingly complex family configurations, each transition posing new adaptational challenges. Amid social, economic, and political upheavals worldwide . . . many families are showing remarkable resilience in creatively reworking their family life.

In so doing, they often also provide children with a depth and diversity of relationships that prepares them for the increasingly diverse communities and experiences that await them in the United States. Families that provide children with deep relationship pools—from which children can pull the support needed for new and different challenges—ensure that conflict or abuse in a single relationship will not leave children without support. These families model relationships that will equip children well for a globalizing world in which the ability to adapt is an essential life skill. New family forms, however, currently leave families open to interactions with the legal system that distort their lives and fail to protect the relationships that are created to meet that family's individual needs.

. . .

III. Beyond Exclusivity

. . .

B. Moving Toward

. . .

I agree that we need to empower and protect parent-child relationships from unwarranted and potentially damaging outside infringement. We can do this, however, while imagining fully inclusive families. The basis for this, as I will show below, is an element not explicitly included in other analyses—care. If care and caregiving relationships are central to the lives of children, then this care should be clearly at the center of decisions—legal and political—about their lives. The assumption that parenthood per se bestows legal rights regarding their children should be replaced with the idea that rights flow from relationships between caregivers and children. If a conception of care is moved to the center of our legal analysis, we will see that exclusivity cannot continue and more comprehensive alternatives will become available.

. . .

IV. Creating a Care–Based Theory for Children and Custody

. . .

B. Bringing Care into Custody

. . .

Individuals should not be assumed to be outside the family structure, nor should they be assumed part of the family. Instead, individuals should be required to show relationships based on the acts they perform and given privileges and rights based on those actions. Such a design encourages care and requires that the legal system grant support to care where it occurs.

An ethic of care points us to needs as the best basis for judging an individual's actions. Who has needs for care and who is able and prepared to provide for those needs are central questions. For our discussion, the main questions that arise concern the needs of children and the adults who are available to meet those needs. We should also ask, however, about the needs of caregivers—for help in meeting child's needs and for help in meeting their own needs so that they actually can be available to care for the child.

This basis in the concrete stands in opposition to the "parents' rights" talk engaged in by parents, lawyers, judges, and lawmakers. In case after case, as we have seen, the needs of all involved were subordinated to the "rights" of parents. Unmarried fathers, birth mothers, grandmothers, and other caregivers must argue that they have rights, rather than seeking recognition and support for the actual relationships and the ways they have provided for the needs of children and families. Rather than my child, a new approach would allow center on the child with whom I stand in a caregiving relationship.

. . .

D. A Care–Based Standard

Moving beyond the "best interests" standard, a new principle should guide our decision-making with respect to children and their custody. I propose that both legal decision-making and legislation be based on a new principle:

Mutual caregiving relationships, in which an adult provides for the needs of a child, should be legally recognized. The level of legal protection accorded should be appropriate for, reflective of, and limited to that which is beneficial and necessary to protect and support the established caregiving relationship. Further, the legal protection accorded should be granted in accordance with the protection for practical parental decision-making authority necessary for life of each child.

. . .

Recognition & Standing

This test is based firmly in the concrete and connectional. It uses the language of needs, rather than of interests or rights to establish legal recognition and standing. It also rests on a demonstrable question: the provision of care—when and in what ways did the person actually give care and provide for needs?

The requirement that the relationship be mutual would establish that the bond is "real." I do not use the word mutual to mean that caregiving in the relationship occurs equally—which should certainly not be the case in a caregiver-child relationship. Instead, I use mutual to signify a relationship that is understood to be an important caregiving relationship by both parties—the caregiver and the child. This would, necessarily, involve the direct consideration of the child's point of view, where that child was old enough. Listening to the story of family, as told by the child, would be central to determining if the relationship is mutual. The best test—would be exactly how the child understands the relationship—as parental, as auxiliary, as non-family, etc.—thus, recognizing the child's real-life family. This will take tailored attention to how children construct narratives and caution must be used to assure the child does not become a pawn for parents. I believe, however, that this can happen and, in listening to children, that we can do justice to their caring relationships.

Second, in a mutual caregiving relationship, the caregiver chooses to do the work out of her or his connection to the person, for non-selfish reasons, and with the object of providing for their needs. . . . Thus, the requirement of mutuality would mean that paid caregivers and other self-interested parties would not warrant legal recognition.

While excluding those who have not given care toward meeting children's needs, or who have done so for selfish reasons, this new principle would include all those who have done this important work. The channeling function of law, described by Carl Schneider, could be used, not to limit options, but instead to encourage creative family formations that maximize care. This principle would channel adults into caregiving roles instead of channeling families into rigid forms.

This principle would recognize the caregivers in children's lives, regardless of their number and regardless of their gender, sexuality, blood relationship, or socially assumed role. This would move the ideas of mother and father away from exclusive concepts with culturally and politically embedded sex roles and toward, as in some other cultures, a linguistically gendered word that includes many people and varying forms of caregiving.

Perhaps most importantly, this would not invest rights in parents. Instead, it would invest relationships and caregiving with right-generating power.

. . .

Conclusion: Expanded Families, Webs of Care

Families should have the right to create caregiving relationships that best meet their needs. We know that children grow up healthiest when they have attentive, involved, and dependable caregivers in their lives. When families provide such an environment to children by including people other than a child's two exclusive parents, the law should recognize and respect these relationships.

. . .

Basing our understanding of family on networks of care means that families are not centrally about individual rights, but are instead about relationships. The needs and relationships of children should be the center of our understanding of the family, and there are ways, even within the legal system, to act upon this understanding. The proposals made here help us to shift our analysis away from recognizing the assertions of individual adults of their rights to children and toward recognizing caregiver-child relationships and the recognition and protection such relationships are due. This also allows us to move away from . . . notions of ownership within the family and the tendency to view children as "property." Instead, by bringing children to the very center of our analysis, we can build law and politics based on the needs of their day-to-day lives.

. . .

In my family—to take just one example of a family with real needs—we created a variety of caregiving relationships to fit those needs. This new vision of family and a care-based, non-exclusive legal principle would recognize those needs. Through co-guardianship orders, my parents could have taken proactive steps to assure that all of the parents had equal access and responsibility for the children in their family. We also would not have been left to wonder if, because we had transgressed imagined boundaries, we were vulnerable to intrusion. In reality, though, had one or the other of my parents died, Lisa (my mother's partner) could have been written out of the picture despite years of primary caregiving. In contrast, my grandparents, who were never significant caregivers in our lives, might have been able to demand custody and visitation. Under the new construction I have described, this sort of intrusion would not have been a worry, and we all would have been more secure.

NOTES

1. How easy would it be to apply a "care-based" standard that focused on the various caregiving relationships in which a child was involved? Should there be a threshold showing of a relationship of sufficient significance before acknowledging any right to continued contact with the child? Or should the court use a sliding scale, and seek to preserve contact between adult and child in proportion to the existing pattern of contact?

2. Cavanaugh would exclude from consideration persons who provide care in return for financial compensation. If the focus should be on the significance of the relationship to the child, however, why is that relevant? Can't children develop close attachments to paid caregivers?

B. ADULT RELATIONSHIPS

1. CONJUGAL

Baker v. State

Vermont Supreme Court, 1999.
170 Vt. 194, 744 A.2d 864.

... [T]he marriage laws transform a private agreement into a source of significant public benefits and protections. While the laws relating to marriage have undergone many changes during the last century, largely toward the goal of equalizing the status of husbands and wives, the benefits of marriage have not diminished in value. On the contrary, the benefits and protections incident to a marriage license under Vermont law have never been greater. They include, for example, the right to receive a portion of the estate of a spouse who dies intestate and protection against disinheritance through elective share provisions, under 14 V.S.A. §§ 401–404, 551; preference in being appointed as the personal representative of a spouse who dies intestate, under 14 V.S.A. § 903; the right to bring a lawsuit for the wrongful death of a spouse, under 14 V.S.A. § 1492; the right to bring an action for loss of consortium, under 12 V.S.A. § 5431; the right to workers' compensation survivor benefits under 21 V.S.A. § 632; the right to spousal benefits statutorily guaranteed to public employees, including health, life, disability, and accident insurance, under 3 V.S.A. § 631; the opportunity to be covered as a spouse under group life insurance policies issued to an employee, under 8 V.S.A. § 3811; the opportunity to be covered as the insured's spouse under an individual health insurance policy, under 8 V.S.A. § 4063; the right to claim an evidentiary privilege for marital communications, under V.R.E. 504; homestead rights and protections, under 27 V.S.A. §§ 105–108, 141–142; the presumption of joint ownership of property and the concomitant right of survivorship, under 27 V.S.A. § 2; hospital visitation and other rights incident to the medical treatment of a family member, under 18 V.S.A. § 1852; and the right to receive, and the obligation to provide, spousal support, maintenance, and property division in the event of separation or divorce, under 15 V.S.A. §§ 751–752.

Pamela Smock & Wendy Manning, Living Together Unmarried in the United States: Demographic Perspectives and Implications for Family Policy

26 Law & Policy 87, 87–92, 96–98, 108–109 (2004).

I. INTRODUCTION

The last few decades have ushered in significant changes in family patterns—in union formation, union dissolution, childbearing and attitudes about a range of family issues. After a brief period characterized by early marriage and low levels of divorce after World War II (i.e., the Baby Boom), recent decades have been marked by lower levels of childbearing, higher divorce rates, increases in the average age at marriage, rising nonmarital childbearing and . . . rising levels of cohabitation.

Although most Americans still marry at some point and the vast majority express strong desires to marry, unmarried cohabitation has dramatically transformed the marriage process. Today, the majority of marriages and remarriages begin as cohabiting relationships. Most young men and women have cohabited or will cohabit, cohabitation has increased in all age groups and cohabitation is increasingly becoming a context for childbearing and childrearing; it is estimated that two-fifths of children born in the early 1990s will spend time in a cohabiting-parent family Clearly, cohabitation has become a widely-experienced, even normative, phenomenon in recent decades.

II. TRENDS IN UNION FORMATION AND DISSOLUTION

One of the key changes in the union formation process has been a postponement in marriage since the Baby Boom (approximately 1947–1963). [F]or women, age at marriage hovered around 21–22 years between 1890 and 1950, declined significantly during the Baby Boom, and began rising thereafter, reaching slightly over 25 years in 2000. Patterns for men are somewhat different, with a general decline in age at marriage between 1890 and the Baby Boom. Like women, however, age at marriage for men began rising after the Baby Boom, and, in the year 2000, is higher than at any time in the past century (nearly 27).

At the same time that marriage is being postponed, unmarried cohabitation has increased. . . . In 1960, the number [of opposite-sex cohabiting couples] was estimated at less than half a million; at the 2000 census, there were nearly five million such households. In fact, research suggests that this postponement in marriage has, by and large, been offset by the increase in cohabitation. In other words, while the pace of entering marriage has slowed, [one study has indicated] that unmarried cohabitation compensated for over 80% of the decline in marriage by age 25 over recent cohorts for blacks and 61% for whites.

Other indicators of the rapidly growing prominence of cohabitation are, first, that the percentage of marriages preceded by cohabitation rose from about 10% for those marrying between 1965 and 1974 to well over 50% for those marrying between 1990 and 1994. Second, the percentage of women in their late thirties who report having cohabited at least once rose from 30% in 1987 to 48% in 1995.

Cohabitations in general are of short duration with many ending as marriages (roughly 50%) and others dissolving without marriage. Moreover, over 50% of cohabiting unions in the U.S., whether or not they are eventually legalized by marriage, end by separation within five years compared to roughly 20% for marriages. In addition, research suggests that marriages that begin as cohabitations, a growing proportion of marriages, are more likely to dissolve than those that do not. In fact, one of the key distinctions between cohabitation and marriage is the duration of the relationship, with some arguing that the underlying "contract" of cohabitation is substantially more fragile than that of marriage.

The prominence of cohabitation is echoed in the beliefs of the American people. An ongoing survey of high school seniors asks whether living together is a good idea before marriage to determine compatibility; the percent of young women agreeing with this statement rose from 33% to 60% between the late 1970s and the late 1990s, and from 47% to 67% for young men. Another survey, this one focusing on a cohort of white children born in 1961 in the Detroit area, asked respondents in 1993 (when they were in their early thirties) whether living together is acceptable even if there are no plans to marry; 64% and 72% of women and men agreed, respectively. Moreover, 74% of the women and 78% explicitly *disagreed* with the statement "a young couple should not live together unless they are married." While it remains unclear precisely how these shifting attitudes are related to behavioral changes in cohabitation, the two are probably mutually reinforcing: changes in behavior may set the stage for changes in attitudes and shifts in attitudes may follow changes in behavior.

At the same time, while recently stabilizing, levels of union instability have increased over the past century or so, most studies suggest that the chance of marital disruption now stands at about 50%.

. . .

. . . [C]ohabitation is intertwined with important changes in fertility and represents a family form increasingly experienced by children. This has made it of concern to a broader audience due to possible implications for child well-being.

. . . As is by now well-known, a substantial proportion of births in the U.S., as well as Canada and many European countries, are now occurring outside of marriage: in the U.S. that proportion is approximately one-third. . . . [A] large share of these nonmarital births are occurring in the context of cohabitation. Recent estimates suggest that this percentage is almost 40% overall. . . .

In terms of trends, the percentage of children born in cohabiting unions doubled between 1980–84 and 1990–94, now accounting for nearly one in eight births. Further, the share of births to unmarried mothers who were cohabiting increased substantially more between the early 1980s and early 1990s than did the share to single mothers living without a partner. This pace of change is suggestive of a possible further increase in cohabitation as a setting for childbearing in the future.

. . .

Further, while earlier work demonstrated that in response to a pregnancy, single women rarely cohabited, nowadays single women who become pregnant are as likely to cohabit as to marry. Taken together, these results are suggestive that, for some couples, a cohabiting union is an acceptable context for childbearing and raising a family and this may be increasingly so.

. . .

While today cohabitation is common throughout the socioeconomic spectrum, there is evidence that its role may vary by social class. Overall, cohabitation appears to play a more prominent role in family life among those with fewer economic resources.

First, people with less education appear somewhat more likely to have experienced cohabitation at some point. [One study reports] that in 1995, nearly 60% of women ages 19–44 without high school degrees had ever cohabited compared to less than 40% among those with a college education. This is consistent with levels of educational attainment among currently cohabiting couples compared to married couples; in the year 2000, approximately 30% of husbands and 25% of wives were college graduates compared to 18% and 17% among cohabiting men and women, respectively.

Second, cohabitors tend to have lower incomes and higher poverty rates than married couples. In the year 2000, for example, approximately 27% of married men had earnings over $50,000 compared to 14.6% of cohabiting men. Conversely, only 6% of husbands had earnings of $10,000 or less compared to 12% of cohabiting men.... [R]oughly 30% of children in cohabiting families are poor compared to 9% for those in married couple households. Also, cohabitors' levels of unemployment are more than twice as high as those of married men and women.

Third, there is evidence that good economic prospects enhance the likelihood of marriage among cohabiting couples. Studies suggest that the male partners' economic well-being (e.g., as measured by indicators such as earnings, education, or employment) are positively associated with the transition to marriage among cohabitors. Consistent with this, there is some evidence that marriage is perceived as requiring better economic circumstances than cohabitation.

. . .

IV. CLASS, RACE, AND COHABITATION

Marriage and childbearing ... appear to be more "de-coupled" among blacks than whites, with roughly a third of first births among white women now occurring before marriage compared to 77% among black women.... [The literature on] racial and ethnic variation in cohabitation [indicates first that] whites, blacks and Hispanics report similar *levels* of cohabitation experience, suggesting that cohabitation is commonplace in all these groups. Second, and however, there may be some differences in regard to the role played by cohabitation in family formation. For example, while cohabitation has become an increasingly prominent feature of the lives of American children, this is especially so for minority children.... [C]hildren are more likely to be present in black and Hispanic cohabiting couple households (54% and 59% respectively) than in white cohabiting households (35%). Further, estimates suggest that about half (55%) of black children, two-fifths (40%) of Hispanic children and three-tenths (30%) of white children are expected to experience a cohabiting-parent family, with black and Hispanic children expected to spend more time in such a family.

. . .

Correspondingly, there are racial and ethnic differentials in the proportion of children being born to cohabiting parents. Among whites, only about one in ten children are now born into cohabiting-parent families compared to nearly one in five black and Hispanic children.

Further, [one study] shows that Hispanic and black women are 77% and 69%, respectively, more likely than white women to conceive a child while cohabiting. Among those who do become pregnant, Hispanics are twice as likely and blacks three times as likely to remain cohabiting with their partner, rather than marry, when their child is born. . . .

Other findings suggestive of racial and ethnic variation in the role of cohabitation include, first, that greater proportions of Hispanics and blacks than whites select cohabitation as their first union. In fact, the black–white differential in union formation (including both cohabitation and marriage) is about half that of the gap in marriage (Raley 1996). Second, blacks more commonly separate from, rather than marry, their cohabiting partners, and cohabiting whites move into marriage more quickly than Hispanics. . . .

In sum, evidence suggests that cohabitation is less central to childbearing and family formation among whites. However, it is very difficult to disentangle these patterns from economic status. In the U.S., there is a correlation between social class and race and ethnicity, with whites being the most privileged economically. Non–Hispanic whites enjoy, on average, the highest incomes and lowest levels of poverty. . . . [G]iven the correlation between race/ethnicity and economic status, and good economic prospects and marriage, it is not surprising that cohabitation appears to play a more prominent role in the family lives of the less advantaged, who are more likely to be people of color in the U.S.

. . .

VI. CONCLUDING THOUGHTS

. . . In combination with concerns about its possible effects on child well-being, cohabitation is considered an important phenomenon to understand because it has been linked, directly or indirectly, to the more general issue of the decreasing centrality of marriage in the United States. In fact, arguably the first prominent debate about the significance of cohabitation was whether it represents a stage in the marriage process (i.e., a form of engagement that culminates in marriage) or is a substitute form of marriage. According to the first view, marriage as an institution is not threatened by cohabitation, and cohabitation plays much the same role as engagement. The second view—that cohabitation is an alternative kind of marriage—implies that marriage as an institution is threatened and losing its centrality in the United States. A third view . . . is that cohabitation is more appropriately viewed as an alternative to singlehood than to marriage. This argument is that cohabitation represents an extension of dating and sexual relationships. Most recently, however, there has been recognition that cohabitation may represent all of these for different couples and at different points in the life course.

Our second observation is that the data suggest to us that cohabitation is not going away, and will most likely become a more prominent feature of family patterns, even among the advantaged. While the pace of growth in cohabiting households seems to have slowed during the 1990s, it is still growing.

Third, we think the proportion of children exposed to cohabitation (either by being born into one or by entering a quasi-stepfamily) will also continue to increase. As we noted earlier, this is a trend of great concern to policymakers due to its implications for child well-being, not least of which have to do with the effects of family structure instability on children.

Finally, our reading of the policy and social science research on family structure, economic well-being and child well-being, leads us to conclude that promoting or strengthening marriage will not go far over the long haul in alleviating poverty and improving child well-being unless equal attention is paid to improving access to other resources that undergird marriage (e.g., stable, well-paying jobs, good schools for children, safe communities). In this regard, we are struck by the economic and racial stratification in the likely impact of the "case for marriage" on individual lives. While in some respects the marriage movement has been a broad conversation, it is important to recognize that it is largely the disadvantaged (poor people, minorities) whose family lives are being interpreted as needing change.

Braschi v. Stahl Associates Company

Court of Appeals of New York, 1989.
74 N.Y.2d 201, 544 N.Y.S.2d 784, 543 N.E.2d 49.

■ TITONE, JUDGE.

In this dispute over occupancy rights to a rent-controlled apartment, the central question to be resolved on this request for preliminary injunctive relief is whether appellant has demonstrated a likelihood of success on the merits by showing that, as a matter of law, he is entitled to seek protection from eviction under New York City Rent and Eviction Regulations 9 NYCRR 2204.6(d). That regulation provides that upon the death of a rent-control tenant, the landlord may not dispossess "either the surviving spouse of the deceased tenant or some other member of the deceased tenant's family who has been living with the tenant" (emphasis supplied). Resolution of this question requires this court to determine the meaning of the term "family" as it is used in this context.

Appellant, Miguel Braschi, was living with Leslie Blanchard in a rent-controlled apartment located at 405 East 54th Street from the summer of 1975 until Blanchard's death in September of 1986. In November of 1986, respondent, Stahl Associates Company, the owner of the apartment building, served a notice to cure on appellant contending that he was a mere licensee with no right to occupy the apartment since only Blanchard was the tenant of record. In December of 1986 respondent served appellant with a notice to terminate informing appellant that he had one month to vacate the apartment and that, if the apartment was not vacated, respondent would commence summary proceedings to evict him.

Appellant then initiated an action seeking a permanent injunction and a declaration of entitlement to occupy the apartment. By order to show cause appellant then moved for a preliminary injunction, pendente lite, enjoining respondent from evicting him until a court could determine whether he was a member of Blanchard's family within the meaning of 9 NYCRR 2204.6(d). After examining the nature of the relationship between the two men, the Supreme Court concluded that appellant was a "family member" within the meaning of the regulation and, accordingly, that a preliminary injunction should be issued. The court based this decision on its finding that the long-term interdependent nature of the 10-year relationship between appellant and Blanchard "fulfills any definitional criteria of the term 'family.' "

The Appellate Division reversed, concluding that section 2204.6(d) provides non-eviction protection only to "family members within traditional, legally recognized familial relationships." Since appellant's and Blanchard's relationship was not one given formal recognition by the law, the court held that appellant could not seek the protection of the noneviction ordinance. After denying the motion for preliminary injunctive relief, the Appellate Division granted leave to appeal to this court, certifying the following question of law: "Was the order of this Court, which reversed the order of the Supreme Court, properly made?" We now reverse.

. . .

The present dispute arises because the term "family" is not defined in the rent-control code and the legislative history is devoid of any specific reference to the non-eviction provision. All that is known is the legislative purpose underlying the enactment of the rent-control laws as a whole.

legislative purpose

Rent control was enacted to address a "serious public emergency" created by "an acute shortage in dwellings," which resulted in "speculative, unwarranted and abnormal increases in rents" (L.1946 ch. 274, codified, as amended, at McKinney's Uncons.Laws of N.Y. § 8581 et seq.). These measures were designed to regulate and control the housing market so as to "prevent exactions of unjust, unreasonable and oppressive rents and rental agreements and to forestall profiteering, speculation and other disruptive practices tending to produce threats to the public health . . . [and] to prevent uncertainty, hardship and dislocation." Although initially designed as an emergency measure to alleviate the housing shortage attributable to the end of World War II, "a serious public emergency continues to exist in the housing of a considerable number of persons." Consequently, the Legislature has found it necessary to continually reenact the rent-control laws, thereby providing continued protection to tenants.

To accomplish its goals, the Legislature recognized that not only would rents have to be controlled, but that evictions would have to be regulated and controlled as well. Hence, section 2204.6 of the New York City Rent and Eviction Regulations (9 NYCRR 2204.6), which authorizes the issuance of a certificate for the eviction of persons occupying a rent-controlled apartment after the death of the named tenant, provides, in subdivision (d), noneviction protection to those occupants who are either the "surviving spouse of the deceased *tenant or some other member of the deceased tenant's family* who has been living with the tenant [of record]" (emphasis supplied). The manifest intent of this section is to restrict the landowners' ability to evict a narrow class of occupants other than the tenant of record. The question presented here concerns the scope of the protections provided. Juxtaposed against this intent favoring the protection of tenants, is the over-all objective of a gradual "transition from regulation to a normal market of free bargaining between landlord and tenant." One way in which this goal is to be achieved is "vacancy decontrol," which automatically makes rent-control units subject to the less rigorous provisions of rent stabilization upon the termination of the rent-control tenancy.

Emphasizing the latter objective, respondent argues that the term "family member" as used in 9 NYCRR 2204.6(d) should be construed, consistent with this State's intestacy laws, to mean relationships of blood, consanguinity and adoption in order to effectuate the overall goal of orderly succession to real property. Under this interpretation, only those entitled to inherit under the laws of intestacy would be afforded noneviction protection. Further, as did the Appellate Division, respondent [maintains] that since the relationship between appellant and Blanchard has not been accorded legal status by the Legislature, it is not entitled to the protections of section 2204.6(d), which, according to the Appellate Division, applies only to "family members within traditional, legally recognized familial relationships."

. . .

However, as we have continually noted, the rent-stabilization system is different from the rent-control system in that the former is a less onerous burden on the property owner, and thus the provisions of one cannot simply be imported into the other.

. . .

We . . . reject respondent's argument that the purpose of the noneviction provision of the rent-control laws is to control the orderly succession to real property in a manner similar to that which occurs under our State's intestacy laws. The noneviction provision does not concern succession to real property but rather is a means of protecting a certain class of occupants from the sudden loss of their homes. The regulation does not create an alienable property right that could be sold, assigned or otherwise disposed of and, hence, need not be construed as coextensive with the intestacy laws. Moreover, such a construction would be inconsistent with the purposes of the rent-control system as a whole, since it would afford protection to distant blood relatives who actually had but a superficial relationship with the deceased tenant while denying that protection to unmarried lifetime partners.

. . .

[W]e conclude that the term family, as used in 9 NYCRR 2204.6(d), should not be rigidly restricted to those people who have formalized their relationship by obtaining, for instance, a marriage certificate or an adoption order. The intended protection against sudden eviction should not rest on fictitious legal distinctions or genetic history, but instead should find its foundation in the reality of family life. In the context of eviction, a more realistic, and certainly equally valid, view of a family includes two adult lifetime partners whose relationship is long term and characterized by an emotional and financial commitment and interdependence. This view comports both with our society's traditional concept of "family" and with the expectations of individuals who live in such nuclear units. In fact, Webster's Dictionary defines "family" *first* as "a group of people united by certain convictions or common affiliation." Hence, it is reasonable to conclude that, in using the term "family," the Legislature intended to extend protection to those who reside in households having all of the normal familial characteristics. Appellant Braschi should therefore be afforded the opportunity to prove that he and Blanchard had such a household.

This definition of "family" is consistent with both of the competing purposes of the rent-control laws: the protection of individuals from sudden dislocation and the gradual transition to a free market system. Family members, whether or not related by blood or law, who have always treated the apartment as their family home will be protected against the hardship of eviction following the death of the named tenant, thereby furthering the Legislature's goals of preventing dislocation and preserving family units which might otherwise be broken apart upon eviction. This approach will foster the transition from rent control to rent stabilization by drawing a distinction between those individuals who are, in fact, genuine family members, and those who are mere roommates or newly discovered relatives hoping to inherit the rent-controlled apartment after the existing tenant's death.

The determination as to whether an individual is entitled to noneviction protection should be based upon an objective examination of the relationship of the parties. In making this assessment, the lower courts of this State have looked to a number of factors, including the exclusivity and longevity of the relationship, the level of emotional and financial commitment, the manner in which the parties have conducted their everyday lives and held themselves out to society, and the reliance placed upon one another for daily family services (see, e.g., Athineos v. Thayer, N.Y.L.J., Mar. 25, 1987, at 14, col. 4 [Civ.Ct., Kings County], affd. N.Y.L.J., Feb. 9, 1988, at 15, col. 4 [App.Term, 2d Dept.] [orphan never formally adopted but lived in family home for 34 years]; 2–4 Realty Assocs. v. Pittman, 137 Misc.2d 898, 902, 523 N.Y.S.2d 7 [two men living in a "father-son" relationship for 25 years]; Zimmerman v. Burton, 107 Misc.2d 401, 404, 434 N.Y.S.2d 127 [unmarried heterosexual life partner]; Rutar Co. v. Yoshito, No. 53042/79 [Civ.Ct., N.Y. County] [unmarried heterosexual life partner]; Gelman v. Castaneda, NYLJ, Oct. 22, 1986, at 13, col. 1 [Civ.Ct., N.Y. County] [male life partners]). These factors are most helpful, although it should be emphasized that the presence or absence of one or more of them is not dispositive since it is the totality of the relationship as evidenced by the dedication, caring and self-sacrifice of the parties which should, in the final analysis, control. Appellant's situation provides an example of how the rule should be applied.

Appellant and Blanchard lived together as permanent life partners for more than 10 years. They regarded one another, and were regarded by friends and family, as spouses. The two men's families were aware of the nature of the relationship, and they regularly visited each other's families and attended family functions together, as a couple. Even today, appellant continues to maintain a relationship with Blanchard's niece, who considers him an uncle.

In addition to their interwoven social lives, appellant clearly considered the apartment his home. He lists the apartment as his address on his driver's license and passport, and receives all his mail at the apartment address. Moreover, appellant's tenancy was known to the building's superintendent and doormen, who viewed the two men as a couple.

Financially, the two men shared all obligations including a household budget. The two were authorized signatories of three safe-deposit boxes, they maintained joint checking and savings accounts, and joint credit cards. In fact, rent was often paid with a check from their joint checking account. Additionally, Blanchard executed a power of attorney in appellant's favor so that appellant could make necessary decisions—financial, medical and personal—for him during his illness. Finally, appellant was the named beneficiary of Blanchard's life insurance policy, as well as the primary legatee and coexecutor of Blanchard's estate. Hence, a court examining these facts could reasonably conclude that these men were much more than mere roommates.

Inasmuch as this case is before us on a certified question, we conclude only that appellant has demonstrated a likelihood of success on the merits, in that he is not excluded, as a matter of law, from seeking noneviction protection. Since all remaining issues are beyond this court's scope of review, we remit this case to the Appellate Division so that it may exercise its discretionary powers in accordance with this decision.

Accordingly, the order of the Appellate Division should be reversed and the case remitted to that court for a consideration of undetermined questions. The certified question should be answered in the negative.

. . .

■ Simons, Judge (dissenting).

I would affirm. The plurality has adopted a definition of family which extends the language of the regulation well beyond the implication of the words used in it. In doing so, it has expanded the class indefinitely to include anyone who can satisfy an administrator that he or she had an emotional and financial "commitment" to the statutory tenant. Its interpretation is inconsistent with the legislative scheme underlying rent regulation, goes well beyond the intended purposes of 9 NYCRR 2204.6(d), and produces an unworkable test that is subject to abuse.

NOTE

Braschi involves two issues that can be distinguished from one another. One is the extent to which the law should treat same-sex couples as conjugal family members; the other is whether law should extend such recognition to unmarried conjugal partners more generally.

The debate over same-sex marriage reflects consideration of the first issue. Chapter 3, Section A–4 discusses this debate in some detail, as well as alternative forms of recognition for same-sex couples, such as civil unions and domestic partner registration programs.

The second issue requires that we decide whether the absence of marriage should preclude treating any conjugal couple as a family. Some of these couples will have deliberately chosen not to marry; should that preclude recognizing any familial rights, benefits, or obligations in such instances? What if a couple is unable to marry because their state does not permit same-sex marriage? Is there a stronger or a weaker case for treating the partners as family members?

If we believe that formal marital status is not the prerequisite for treating conjugal partners as a family, which relationships are entitled to recognition and what benefits and responsibilities should result? Should we take the approach of the court in *Braschi*, and determine whether the parties' relationship seems in substance to resemble marriage? Does that risk imposing a conventional model of intimacy that a couple may not wish to adopt? If deference to the parties' preferences is our goal, should the law limit itself to enforcing any agreements that the parties enter into about their rights and obligations? What about letting the couple choose from a "menu" of options and register as a domestic partnership?

These questions are especially salient in determining whether unmarried intimate partners should have any financial claims on one another when the relationship ends. Chapter 5, Section B–4 examines them in some detail in that context. For now, keep in mind the potential costs and benefits of recognizing unmarried partners as family members, and, if we choose to do so, the complex considerations that we must take into account in deciding which approach is the best way of accomplishing this.

2. Non-Conjugal

Law Commission of Canada, Beyond Conjugality: Recognizing and Supporting Close Personal Adult Relationships

2001.

. . .

Chapter One: The Diversity of Personal Adult Relationships

Canadians have always formed a diverse range of adult personal relationships. Caring relationships are formed by married and common-law couples, relatives or friends sharing a household, and care recipients and caregivers, to name a few. Recognizing and supporting caring personal adult relationships is an important state objective. The diversity of personal adult relationships poses significant challenges to governments as they seek to align state policy with social facts. Before we discuss the ways in which the law has responded to the diversity of relationships, we will briefly describe what some of the available demographic data tells us about the nature of Canadians' personal relationships. In this Chapter, we will also present some of the significant demographic shifts that have occurred over the last few decades.

A majority of Canadian households have long consisted of married couples or other conjugal couples living together with or without children. Alongside the nuclear family centred on the conjugal couple, a variety of other living arrangements have been enduring features of Canadian society. There have always been, for example, significant numbers of adult siblings living together, widows and widowers forming blended families with new partners, adult children living with their parents and multi-generational households. In the past, because of shorter life expectancy and the loss of life during wartime, it was not uncommon for children to lose a parent or for spouses to become widowed. Often widows or widowers would form new relationships, and the new partner would become a parent to any dependent children living in the household.

Over the course of recent decades, particularly since the mid–1960s, a number of major, inter-related demographic shifts have occurred in the nature of Canadian adults' close personal relationships. As is the case in many other countries, domestic relationships in Canada appear to have become even more diverse in the past 30 years.

. . .

Almost all adult Canadians form a conjugal union at some point in their lives. A clear majority of Canadians—over 60 percent—were married or cohabiting in a conjugal relationship at the time of the 1996 census.

It remains the case that a strong majority of opposite-sex conjugal unions are marital relationships. However, the marriage rate has declined steadily since 1971, while the number of opposite-sex couples choosing to live in common-law relationships outside of marriage has increased steadily since they were first recorded in 1981. Rates of opposite-sex cohabitation are highest among young never-married adults, although growth rates in non-marital cohabitation are highest among older adults, many of whom were previously married. Opposite-sex cohabitation—whether as an alternative to marriage, as a prelude to marriage, or as a sequel to marriage—is a growing phenomenon that now has widespread social acceptance.

There is as yet no census data or reliable studies on the number of lesbian and gay couples living together in Canada. While same-sex couples were included in the census questionnaire for the first time in 2001, it will take some time before the data is compiled and available for analysis.... A number of smaller-scale studies of the lesbian and gay population in urban Canada suggest that gays and lesbians form enduring conjugal relationships in numbers comparable to the population as a whole. Based on the available data, it appears that a significant minority of Canadian households consist of same-sex couples.

People today have more options in choosing whether to form a conjugal relationship and, if so, what type of conjugal relationship they wish to have. Once subject to punitive social and legal sanctions, both opposite-sex and same-sex common-law partners now enjoy much greater social acceptance and have many of the legal rights and obligations that attach to married spouses.

The ways in which individuals who form conjugal relationships are structuring their lives have also changed dramatically. The average age of marriage has increased. There are significant numbers of step-families, including blended families where children of different unions are raised in the same household. An increasing number of adults are delaying having children until their late twenties or early thirties, or are deciding not to have children at all. Those who decide to become parents are having fewer children than previous generations.

Women's participation in the paid labour force increased steadily from the 1950s to the 1990s. As a result, a declining minority of Canadian families rely on a sole male breadwinner for economic support. In 1996, the dual earnings of mothers and fathers supported 68 percent of married or opposite-sex common-law couples with children. Even when young children are in the home, both parents are employed in a strong majority of families. Women's participation in the labour force has become essential to the living standards of families. Indeed, economic necessity has been an important driving force behind the emergence of more dual earner families than ever before.

Non–Conjugal Households and Non–Conjugal Relationships

While 60 percent of adult Canadians live in a conjugal relationship, and the majority of Canadian households consist of conjugal couples living with or without children, a substantial minority of households involve adults living alone, lone-parent families or adults living together in non-conjugal relationships. And within households centred around conjugal relationships, often other adults are present, having non-conjugal ties to other members of the household. Non-conjugal relationships may be with unrelated friends or they may be with relatives other than spouses or minor children.

Non-Conjugal Relationships Between Relatives

Adult children are remaining at home longer and also leaving home and then moving back in increasing numbers. As a result, it is now common for adult children to live with their middle-aged parents. It appears that adult children return home or stay at home mainly because of financial constraints imposed by difficulties in obtaining adequate employment or the need to complete their education; this allows them to benefit from the sharing of income and wealth within the household.

Many Canadians who are not defined by Statistics Canada as belonging to a census or nuclear family nevertheless live with relatives in what have been called "economic families." While a census family includes couples or parents with never-married children, an economic family is a broader concept that encompasses all relatives living in the same household, regardless of how they are related. For example, it would include an older woman living with her married children, or adult siblings sharing a home.

In 1996, 3 percent of the population in private households lived with relatives (other than a spouse or never-married children), a proportion that remained stable compared with the previous two decades. Domestic relationships between adult siblings form the largest component of economic families. There is reason to believe that sibling relationships will increase in importance in the future. The high birthrate of the 1950s and the aging population mean that within the next 20 to 30 years, older adults will have substantially more siblings alive as compared with older adults today. This may mean that in the future more siblings will care for each other in old age.

Non-Conjugal Relationships Between Non–Relatives

Another 3.5 percent of the population lived with non-relatives in 1996. Since same-sex couples were not counted in the census prior to 2001, by default they would have been included as households composed of non-relatives. Thus, same-sex conjugal relationships and non-conjugal relationships would together comprise unknown portions of this 3.5 percent of Canadians.

We know little about the characteristics of non-conjugal relationships between unrelated persons since it is a topic that has rarely been investigated. We do know that kinship relations between unrelated persons can be experienced as the equivalent of biological or legal ties. We also know that within gay and lesbian communities, individuals are more likely to form families of friends. If biological family members do not support an individual's sexual orientation or family decisions, then forming kinship relations with friends becomes a particularly important replacement or supplement to the family of origin.

"Families of friends" also appear to be particularly important to older adults. One recent study of older people in Ontario found that 4 percent of non-widowed and 8 percent of widowed individuals include a friend in their description of family. Friends are also particularly important in the lives of older women.

Caregiving Relationships

People with disabilities have the same range of close personal relationships as other Canadians. They are spouses, friends, lovers, parents, children, aunts, uncles, cousins, grandchildren, grandparents and so on. Many people with disabilities are also in close personal relationships that are characterized at least in part by personal care or support that is related to their disabilities. Caregiving relationships involve the provision or exchange of a number of different kinds of care necessary to maintain or enhance the care recipients' independence. The research suggests that there is frequently interdependence or reciprocity—an exchange of personal and social supports—in the personal relationships of people with disabilities. The kinds of care provided or exchanged include social and emotional support; assistance with the physical activities of daily living such as shopping, cleaning and cooking; and assistance with personal or medical aspects of daily living such as dressing, bathing and taking medications. The literature distinguishes between formal care provided by paid professionals and informal care provided without pay by family and friends.

Over 90 percent of persons with disabilities live in their own homes. The vast majority must develop relationships of support with paid and non-paid caregivers for their basic survival and well-being. In 1991, among the 1.8 million persons with disabilities residing in households and aged 15 or over who were in need of supports, almost 900,000 obtained those supports exclusively from family members. Almost 100,000 persons with disabilities rely on friends only for personal supports, while another 53,000 rely on friends in combination with family and an agency.

Persons with permanent disabilities are not the only Canadians whose relationships are characterized by the provision or exchange of personal care and supports. Everyone needs this kind of care at some point in their lives. The need for care, perhaps surprisingly, is not closely tied to age. Similar proportions of persons receive personal care across age groups. Over half of persons over the age of 65 say that they get some help with household chores and personal tasks. Half also say that they provide care to others.

The available data show that women continue to provide the bulk of caregiving on an unpaid basis and spend more time than men in providing care. For the most part, caregivers provide care willingly and as a reciprocal aspect of rewarding relationships. However, numerous studies have shown that supports to individuals with disabilities and their families are often insufficient. The demands placed on informal caregiving have been increased by an aging population, reductions in public services and deinstutionalization. Many people are discharged from hospital while still requiring complex and skilled care. This situation puts stress on family members who are expected to compensate for gaps in formal care in their unpaid role as caregivers. The extent of their caregiving responsibilities can take a major toll on caregivers' economic security and physical, emotional and psychological health. Inadequate social support for caregiving has a negative impact on caregivers and care-receivers, and on the quality of their relationships.

Conclusion

Canadians have always formed a diverse array of personal adult relationships. While about half of the adult population is married, significant numbers of Canadians are choosing to form same-sex unions or non-marital opposite-sex conjugal unions. In addition, there are significant numbers of blended families, lone-parent families, non-conjugal domestic relationships and families with adult children living at home. Families with a sole male breadwinner are becoming rare. Large numbers of older adults and persons with disabilities rely on family and friends for personal care and support.

Recognizing and supporting personal adult relationships that involve caring and interdependence is an important state objective. In the past, many policies were framed to apply only to married persons. Governments have taken important steps forward in recent years by extending rights and obligations to persons who are living with same-sex partners or with a person of the opposite-sex outside of marriage. But this extension of rights and obligations has maintained the legal focus on conjugal relationships. A more principled and comprehensive approach is needed to consider not just the situation of spouses and common-law partners, but also the needs of persons in non-conjugal relationships, including caregiver relationships. . . .

Chapter Four: The Legal Organization of Personal Relationships

. . . What should the state's role be in relation to committed relationships? What is the nature of the state's obligation in providing legal mechanisms to support relationships and to assist in the legal organization of such relationships?

The Role of the State

Many people long for stability and certainty in their personal relationships just as they do in other areas of their lives, at work or in business. The state does have a role in providing legal mechanisms for people to be able to achieve such private understandings. It must provide an orderly framework in which people can express their commitment to each other and voluntarily assume a range of legal rights and obligations.

. . .

For a long time, the state has focused on marriage as the vehicle of choice for adults to express their commitment. Marriage provides parties with the ability to state publicly and officially their intentions toward one another. It is entered voluntarily. It also provides for certainty and stability since the marriage cannot be terminated without legal procedures. Marriage as a legal tool demonstrates characteristics of voluntariness, stability, certainty and publicity that made it attractive as a model to regulate relationships.

But it is no longer a sufficient model to respond to the variety of relationships that exist in Canada today. Whether we look at older people living with their adult children, adults with disabilities living with their caregivers, or siblings cohabiting in the same residence, the marriage model is inadequate. Some of these other relationships are also characterized by emotional and economic interdependence, mutual care and concern and the expectation of some duration. All of these personal adult relationships could also benefit from legal frameworks to support people's need for certainty and stability.

Throughout our consultations, it became clear that simply allowing people the option to enter into private contracts, such as cohabitation agreements or caregiving arrangements, was insufficient because it did not always have the official or public aspect that was needed, nor did it offer sufficient guarantee of certainty. In addition, the lack of official record of such private arrangements prevents the efficient administration of laws and programs where relationships could be relevant. . . .

We must therefore examine ways for the state to offer all Canadians appropriate legal frameworks that respond to their needs for certainty and stability in their personal relationships. This role of providing sufficient legal mechanisms for people to carry out their private and personal commitments is an important one. It is just as important as insuring that the corporate world has the legal tools to respond to its needs for stability and certainty. These legal frameworks must keep pace with the ways in which adults organize their lives.

It is in this context that one must look at the mechanisms currently developed to allow Canadians to organize their private lives.

Legal Frameworks for Personal Relationships

In this section, we review four legal models of regulation of personal relationships. The first, the private law model, is one that operates by default. When governments do not provide any legal framework, parties resort to traditional private law concepts to organize their lives. This is the current case for non-conjugal relationships in Canada in which people may choose to be regulated privately. For conjugal relationships, there are three models to regulate personal relationships that have been used around the world: ascription [i.e., treating unmarried cohabitants as if they were married, without their having taken any positive action to be legally recognized], registration and marriage . . .

Private Law

People are always at liberty to express their commitments through contracts. Whether written or oral, contracts do regulate personal relationships. Expressly or implicitly, people who reside together, who help each other or who have an intimate relationship organize their lives around shared expectations that are more or less well defined. When such expectations are not fulfilled, they may seek remedy in court under various theories of private law, unjust enrichment, constructive trust, or the creation of an implicit partnership, to name a few.

Parties may choose to state explicitly in a written document their shared expectations and demand execution of such a contractual arrangement through the civil courts. The ability to forge one's own contractual regime and negotiate the terms of one's commitment is a valued tool in a free society and one which must always be available.

But it is a tool beyond the reach of many people. Leaving the parties to design their own contractual or private law arrangements imposes too high a burden on people who do not have time, energy or the requisite knowledge to do so. The possible involvement of a lawyer to design such arrangements is also too costly or inconvenient for the majority of people. Furthermore, there is also a concern that the stronger or wealthier party may impose unfavourable terms on the poorer or weaker party.

Although contracts will continue to remain an important method for individuals to determine their mutual rights and obligations, they are not a sufficient remedy in and of themselves.

Ascription

. . .

Ascription is generally heralded as a way for governments to prevent the risks of exploitation inherent in a contractual model. It imposes a set of obligations on people in conjugal relationships which are presumed to correspond to the expectations of the majority of people. It has hence allowed governments to respond to the changes in Canadian society, particularly with respect to the regulation of the relationships of unmarried conjugal relationships. It also supplies a default arrangement for couples who have not provided for any arrangements and who would otherwise have to resort to cumbersome traditional private law models.

However, ascription as a model has limits. First, it is a blunt policy tool in that it treats all conjugal relationships alike, irrespective of the level of emotional or economic interdependency that they may present. Second, it infringes upon the value of autonomy. Although people may opt out of certain statutory provisions governing their relationships, they are not always aware of this possibility. In addition, ascription is not the best way to respond to the needs of non-conjugal relationships. It would be inappropriate to presume that all older parents living with their adult children have the same needs or that adults with disabilities have equally similar patterns of caring and support. Although ascription may serve the particular purpose of preventing exploitation, it is a tool that must be used sparingly, where there is evidence of exploitation. Governments should continue to use the model of ascription but they should also provide Canadians with appropriate tools to define for themselves the terms of their relationships.

It is in that context that governments should look at a system that would affirm the capacity of people to establish for themselves the terms of their relationships while providing models for doing so. Registration models would serve that purpose.

Registration

Recently, there has been a move toward the creation of a new status, often called registered partnership (or Registered Domestic Partnership or RDP).

. . .

The objective of . . . registration schemes is to provide an alternative way for the state to recognize and support close personal relationships. When people register their relationships, they are then included within a range of rights and responsibilities often similar to marriage. It is a regime that has begun to develop as a parallel to marriage, in which the state is promoting a similar set of objectives in the recognition and support of personal relationships.

. . .

. . . [A] registration scheme is worthy of consideration because it would enable a broader range of relationships to be recognized. It would therefore provide both conjugal and non-conjugal unions with a way to formalize their relationship and to voluntarily assume rights and responsibilities toward each other. In this way, a registration system would promote the equality of non-conjugal relationships. The second major advantage of a registration scheme is that it affirms the autonomy and choices of Canadians in their close personal relationships. There is value in encouraging people to make their relationship commitments clear and in recognizing the choices that people make in their close personal relationships. A registration scheme provides a way in which a broad range of relationships, including non-conjugal relationships, can be recognized, while also promoting and respecting the value of autonomy. A registration scheme has a number of advantages specifically related to the value of autonomy and choice. In such a scheme, rights and responsibilities are based on the mutual and voluntary decisions of the individuals in the relationship. It thereby avoids many of the problems with functional definitions that impose relationship status on individuals whether or not they so desire.

A registration scheme could play an important role in broadening the range of options available for people (conjugal and non-conjugal alike) to voluntarily assume rights and responsibilities. The ability to formalize a relationship through a public declaration of commitment is important to Canadians. A registration scheme provides a way in which individuals in close personal relationships can choose to make such a public declaration of commitment, which would then be respected by government.

A registration system may also promote the values of equality and autonomy within relationships without compromising the value of privacy. The ascription model described above, if it were to use more functional definitions, would require that governments examine individual relationships to decide whether they fit the definition. It is an approach that necessarily involves some degree of invasion of privacy. A registration scheme, on the other hand, by leaving the choice entirely up to the individuals within relationships and then respecting that choice, provides a way of recognizing conjugal and non-conjugal relationships without ... subject[ing] the relationship to [state] scrutiny. Ascription, however, should continue to be used where there is evidence of exploitation.

Designing a Registration Scheme

There are many challenging questions that governments will have to address in deciding how a registration scheme should be designed and implemented. In this section, we review some of these questions and, drawing on the insights that can be gleaned from developments in other jurisdictions, we suggest how a registration system should be designed.

Formal Attributes

The first question that must be addressed in designing a registration scheme involves its formal attributes, that is, who may register? Should there be any limits on who may register?

One of the greatest advantages of a registration scheme is that it provides an opportunity to recognize the formal commitment of individuals in any relationship. There is no reason for governments to restrict a registration scheme to conjugal couples or to same-sex couples or, indeed, only to couples.... [T]here [also] is no reason to impose a residential requirement on registrations. There is no similar restriction on marriage: married couples do not have to live together for the marriage to be valid. There is, then, no compelling reason to impose such a restriction on registered relationships.

Another question that governments will have to address is how registrations should be terminable; that is, how can partners decide to end their registration? In our view, registrations should be terminable by mutual agreement. Registered partners should be able to make a mutual declaration that their partnership has ended. Furthermore, given that married spouses can end their marriage unilaterally by making an application for divorce after living separate and apart for one year, it would not be justifiable to impose a more rigorous standard on domestic partners. Partners in a registered relationships should similarly be able to register a dissolution of their registration.

In addition, the regulation of the dissolution of registrations must ensure that the legal obligations between the registrants are respected upon relationship breakdown. Restructuring financial relationships on relationship breakdown remains an important state objective. The state should ensure that the reasonable expectations of partners are not undermined on the breakdown of the relationship.

Legal Implications of Registrations

. . .

Governments could enact a registration regime based on this model, whereby people could formally enter into a registration and then be entitled to predetermined rights and responsibilities. The possibility of choosing the same rights and responsibilities as spouses or common-law partners could be offered. It might also be possible to design more flexible arrangements that may respond better to the variety of caregiving relationships that exist.

Models of caregiving arrangements could be proposed which parties could modify, if they so wish.

The legal consequences of registration might be limited to the private rights and responsibilities within the relationship. It could involve such issues as property and support obligations both during and after the relationship. It could involve determinations for care arrangements, consent to treatment or other aspects of the relationship. The commitment of entering into a registration would be about the voluntary assumption of mutual responsibilities. It would be about clarifying this commitment of mutual responsibility in law, both for the parties themselves and for potentially interested third parties.

Recommendation:

> Parliament and provincial/territorial legislatures should pass laws enabling adults to register their relationship.

Considerations:

> —The registration should not be restricted only to conjugal relationships.
>
> —It should provide for a set of commitments, which could include caring arrangements, consent to treatment dispositions, support and sharing in property from which the parties may opt out.

NOTES

1. The Law Commission's report suggests that registration may be a valuable way of promoting the state's objective of "recognizing and supporting personal adult relationships that involve caring and interdependence" outside of marriage. Should such a registration system displace marriage, so that the law recognizes a variety of relationships without privileging any one of them?

2. For thoughtful discussions of the possibility of replacing marriage with a legal regime that focuses on caregiving relationships, see Martha Albertson Fineman, The Neutered Mother, the Sexual Family, and Other Twentieth-Century Tragedies (1995); Elizabeth S. Scott, Marriage, Cohabitation, and Collective Responsibility for Dependency, 2004 U. Chi. Legal F. 225; Linda C. McClain, Intimate Affiliation and Democracy, 32 Hofstra L. Rev. 379 (2003); Nancy D. Polikoff, Ending Marriage As We Know It, 32 Hofstra L. Rev. 201 (2003).

C. GROUPS

Village of Belle Terre v. Boraas

Supreme Court of the United States, 1974.
416 U.S. 1, 94 S.Ct. 1536, 39 L.Ed.2d 797.

■ JUSTICE DOUGLAS delivered the opinion of the Court.

Belle Terre is a village on Long Island's north shore of about 220 homes inhabited by 700 people. Its total land area is less than one square mile. It has restricted land use to one-family dwellings excluding lodging houses, boarding houses, fraternity houses, or multiple dwelling houses. The word "Family" as used in the ordinance means "One or more persons related by blood, adoption, or marriage, living and cooking together as a single housekeeping unit, exclusive of household servants. A number of persons but not exceeding two (2) living and cooking together as a single housekeeping unit though not related by blood, adoption, or marriage shall be deemed to constitute a family."

Appellees (Dickmans) are owners of a house in the village and leased it in December, 1971 for a term of 18 months to Michael Truman. Later Bruce Boraas became a colessee. Then Anne Parish moved into the house along with three others. These six are students at nearby State University at Stony Brook and none is related to the other by blood, adoption, or marriage....

This case brings to this Court a different phase of local zoning regulations than we have previously reviewed. Euclid v. Ambler Realty Co., 272 U.S. 365, involved a zoning ordinance classifying land use in a given area into six categories....

The Court sustained the zoning ordinance under the police power of the State, saying that the line "which in this field separates the legitimate from the illegitimate assumption of power is not capable of precise delimitation...."

The main thrust of the case in the mind of the Court was in the exclusion of industries and apartments and as respects that it commented on the desire to keep residential areas free of "disturbing noises"; "increased traffic"; the hazard of "moving and parked automobiles"; the "depriving children of the privilege of quiet and open spaces for play, enjoyed by those in more favored localities." Id., at 394. The ordinance was sanctioned because the validity of the legislative classification was "fairly debatable" and therefore could not be said to be wholly arbitrary.

. . .

The present ordinance is challenged on several grounds: that it interferes with a person's right to travel; that it interferes with the right to immigrate to and settle within a State; that it bars people who are uncongenial to the present residents; that the ordinance expresses the social preferences of the residents for groups that will be congenial to them; that social homogeneity is not a legitimate interest of government; that the restriction of those whom the neighbors do not like trenches on the newcomers' rights of privacy; that it is of no rightful concern to villagers whether the residents are married or unmarried; that the ordinance is antithetical to the Nation's experience, ideology and self-perception as an open, egalitarian, and integrated society.

We find none of these reasons in the record before us. It is not aimed at transients. It involves no procedural disparity inflicted on some but not on others. It involves no "fundamental" right guaranteed by the Constitution.... We deal with economic and social legislation where legislatures have historically drawn lines which we respect against the charge of violation of the Equal Protection Clause if the law be "reasonable, not arbitrary" and bears "a rational relationship to a [permissible] state objective." Reed v. Reed, 404 U.S. 71, 76.

It is said, however, that if two unmarried people can constitute a "family," there is no reason why three or four may not. But every line drawn by a legislature leaves some out that might well have been included. That exercise of discretion, however, is a legislative not a judicial function.

It is said that the Belle Terre ordinance reeks with an animosity to unmarried couples who live together. There is no evidence to support it; and the provision of the ordinance bringing within the definition of a "family" two unmarried people belies the charge.

The ordinance places no ban on other forms of association, for a "family" may, so far as the ordinance is concerned, entertain whomever they like.

The regimes of boarding houses, fraternity houses, and the like present urban problems. More people occupy a given space; more cars rather continuously pass by; more cars are parked; noise travels with crowds.

A quiet place where yards are wide, people few, and motor vehicles restricted are legitimate guidelines in a land use project addressed to family needs. ... The police power is not confined to elimination of filth, stench, and unhealthy places. It is ample to lay out zones where family values, youth values, and the blessings of quiet seclusion, and clean air make the area a sanctuary for people.

. . .

Reversed.

■ JUSTICE MARSHALL, dissenting.

... In my view, the disputed classification burdens the students' fundamental rights of association and privacy guaranteed by the First and Fourteenth Amendments. Because the application of strict equal protection scrutiny is therefore required, I am at odds with my brethren's conclusion that the ordinance may be sustained on a showing that it bears a rational relationship to the accomplishment of legitimate governmental objectives.

. . .

My disagreement with the Court today is based upon my view that the ordinance in this case unnecessarily burdens appellees' First Amendment freedom of association and their constitutionally guaranteed right to privacy. Our decisions establish that the First and Fourteenth Amendments protect the freedom to choose one's associates. Constitutional protection is extended not only to modes of association that are political in the usual sense, but also to those that pertain to the social and economic benefit of the members. The selection of one's living companions involves similar choices as to the emotional, social, or economic benefits to be derived from alternative living arrangements.

The freedom of association is often inextricably entwined with the constitutionally guaranteed right of privacy. The right to "establish a home" is an essential part of the liberty guaranteed by the Fourteenth Amendment. Meyer v. Nebraska, 262 U.S. 390, 399 (1923). And the Constitution secures to an individual a freedom "to satisfy his intellectual and emotional needs within the privacy of his own home." Constitutionally protected privacy is, in Mr. Justice Brandeis' words, "as against the government, the right to be let alone ... the right most valued by civilized man." Olmstead v. United States, 277 U.S. 438, 478 (1928) (dissenting opinion). The choice of household companions—of whether a person's "intellectual and emotional needs" are best met by living with family, friends, professional associates or others—involves deeply personal considerations as to the kind and quality of intimate relationships within the home.

The instant ordinance discriminates on the basis of just such a personal lifestyle choice as to household companions. It permits any number of persons related by blood or marriage, be it two or twenty, to live in a single household, but it limits to two the number of unrelated persons bound by profession, love, friendship, religious or political affiliation or mere economics who can occupy a single home. Belle Terre imposes upon those who deviate from the community norm in their choice of living companions significantly greater restrictions than are applied to residential groups who are related by blood or marriage, and comprise the established order with the community. The town has, in effect, acted to fence out those individuals whose choice of lifestyle differs from that of its current residents.

This is not a case where the Court is being asked to nullify a township's sincere efforts to maintain its residential character by preventing the operation of rooming houses, fraternity houses or other commercial or high-density residential uses. Unquestionably, a town is free to restrict such uses. Moreover, as a general proposition, I see no constitutional infirmity in a town limiting the density of use in residential areas by zoning regulations which do not discriminate on the basis of constitutionally suspect criteria. This ordinance, however, limits the density of occupancy of only those homes occupied by unrelated persons. It thus reaches beyond control of the use of land or the density of population and undertakes to regulate the way people choose to associate with each other within the privacy of their own homes.

. . .

A variety of justifications have been proffered in support of the village's ordinance. It is claimed that the ordinance controls population density, prevents noise, traffic and parking problems, and preserves the rent structure of the community and its attractiveness to families. As I noted earlier, these are all legitimate and substantial interests of government. But I think it clear that the means chosen to accomplish these purposes are both over- and under-inclusive, and that the asserted goals could be as effectively achieved by means of an ordinance that did not discriminate on the basis of constitutionally protected choices of life style. The ordinance imposes no restriction whatsoever on the number of persons who may live in a house, as long as they are related by marital or sanguinary bonds—presumably no matter how distant their relationship. Nor does the ordinance restrict the number of income earners who may contribute to rent in such a household, or the number of automobiles that may be maintained by its occupants. In that sense the ordinance is under-inclusive. On the other hand, the statute restricts the number of unrelated persons who may live in a home to no more than two. It would therefore prevent three unrelated people from occupying a dwelling even if among them they had but one income and no vehicles. While an extended family of a dozen or more might live in a small bungalow, three elderly and retired persons could not occupy the large manor house next door. Thus the statute is also grossly over-inclusive to accomplish its intended purposes.

There are some 220 residences in Belle Terre occupied by about 700 persons. The density is therefore just above three per household. The village is justifiably concerned with density of population and the related problems of noise, traffic, and the like. It could deal with those problems by limiting each household to a specified number of adults, two or three perhaps, without limitation on the number of dependent children. The burden of such an ordinance would fall equally upon all segments of the community. It would surely be better tailored to the goals asserted by the township than the ordinance before us today, for it would more realistically restrict population density and growth and their attendant environmental costs. Various other statutory mechanisms also suggest themselves as solutions to Belle Terre's problems—rent control, limits on the number of vehicles per household, and so forth, but, of course, such schemes are matters of legislative judgment and not for this Court. Appellants also refer to the necessity of maintaining the family character of the village. There is not a shred of evidence in the record indicating that if Belle Terre permitted a limited number of unrelated persons living together, the residential, familial character of the community would be fundamentally affected.

By limiting unrelated households to two persons while placing no limitation on households of related individuals, the village has embarked upon its commendable course in a constitutionally faulty vessel. I would find the challenged ordinance unconstitutional. But I would not ask the village to abandon its goal of providing quiet streets, little traffic, and a pleasant and reasonably priced environment in which families might raise their children. Rather, I would commend the town to continue to pursue those purposes but by means of more carefully drawn and even-handed legislation.

Penobscot Area Housing Development Corp. v. City of Brewer

Supreme Judicial Court of Maine, 1981.
434 A.2d 14.

■ Nichols, Justice.

. . .

The Penobscot Area Housing Development Corporation is a private, nonprofit Maine corporation, recently organized to provide housing for retarded citizens. For that purpose it has negotiated a purchase and sale agreement to acquire a house and lot in a district of the City of Brewer which is zoned for low density single family residential use under the City's zoning ordinance. The Corporation applied to the City's code enforcement officer for an occupancy certificate and described the proposed use as "group home for six adults or older minors, which group home would be licensed as a Boarding Home by the State." The Corporation intended to use the property as a group home for six retarded persons who would be supervised by "approximately two" full-time employees. The Brewer Code Enforcement Officer, William L. Wetherbee, denied the occupancy permit because he concluded the Corporation's proposed use did "not meet the terms of the City of Brewer's zoning ordinance as a single family." . . . [T]he Corporation appealed to the City's Board of Appeals. The Board of Appeals . . . affirmed Wetherbee's decision that the proposed use could not be classified as a single family use under the ordinance.

From the Board of Appeal's decision, the Corporation sought review of that decision by the Superior Court (Kennebec County). . . .

The Plaintiffs . . . challenge the Superior Court's affirmance of the Board's construction and application of a section of the Brewer Zoning Ordinance providing for districts in which low density, single family residential uses were favored. Brewer Zoning Ordinance, Art. 3, § 302. Another section of the ordinance explicitly defined family:

> "FAMILY" is a single individual doing his own cooking, and living upon the premises as a separate housekeeping unit, or a collective body of persons doing their own cooking and living together upon the premises as a separate housekeeping unit in a domestic relationship based upon

> birth, marriage or other domestic bond as distinguished from a group occupying a boarding house, lodging house, club, fraternity or hotel.

Brewer Zoning Ordinance, Art. 1, § 101. After a hearing, the Brewer Board of Appeals concluded that the proposed group home for retarded persons did not meet the definition of family in the ordinance....

Construction of zoning ordinances is a legal determination. On appeal ..., the reviewing court's function is to determine only whether the decision of the Board of Appeals was unlawful, arbitrary, capricious, or unreasonable. In reviewing the ordinance before us, we note at the threshold that relationships other than those based on blood or law, i.e., founded on birth or marriage, are included in the definition of family. Relationships based upon "other domestic bond[s]" satisfy the ordinance as well.

The Plaintiffs' principal argument appears to be that the interpretation of the ordinance by the Board and its affirmance by the Superior Court placed undue emphasis on the role of the staff and ignored the fact that the plain purpose of the group home was to create a family environment for the residents. The requirement of a domestic bond, the Plaintiffs argue, would have been met by the relationship forged among the residents themselves as they lived and worked together. As authority for their position, the Plaintiffs cite several decisions from other jurisdictions in which similar definitions of family have been construed to include group homes. We reject the Plaintiffs' argument. Read in context with the definition as a whole, the concept of "domestic bond" implies the existence of a traditional family-like structure of household authority. Such a structure would include one or more resident authority figures charged with the responsibility of maintaining a separate housekeeping unit and regulating the activity and duties of the other residents. In so doing, this resident authority figure serves legitimate zoning interests of a community by stabilizing and coordinating household activity in a way that is consistent with family values and a family style of life.

Concerning the structure of authority at the proposed group home as it relates to the existence of a domestic bond, the Board found that although a staff would be employed by the Corporation for the purposes of maintaining a home for six retarded adults, staff members would not necessarily reside at the home; rather, the Board's findings suggested the staff would serve on a rotating basis. Thus, a central figure of authority residing on the premises similar to a parent or parents in a traditional family setting was clearly absent in the group home proposal tendered by these Plaintiffs.

As the Superior Court observed, the absence of a resident authority figure in the Corporation's proposal clearly distinguishes this case from cases cited by the Plaintiffs in which the definition of family was held to include group homes. See Oliver v. Zoning Commission of Town of Chester, [31 Conn.Sup. 197, 326 A.2d 841 (1974)] (resident houseparents for 10 retarded adolescents); Group House of Port Washington, Inc. v. Board of Zoning, [45 N.Y.2d 266, 380 N.E.2d 207, 408 N.Y.S.2d 377 (1978)] (resident surrogate parents for seven children). As such, evidence of a central component of the domestic bond concept was deficient. Indeed, where the domestic bond is not based on a biological or legal relationship among the residents, the importance of a relatively permanent, resident authority figure to the existence of a domestic bond may be particularly significant.

Like relationships founded on marriage or birth, the notion of domestic bond also connotes a quality of cohesiveness and permanence in the relationship of residents greater than that which typically exists among boarders, members of a fraternity or club, or hotel guests. The language of the definition itself clearly suggests the comparison is appropriate. Relevant to the potential for cohesiveness and permanence in the relationships developed at the home, the Board of Appeals found that the residents would not control "the choice of who the incoming residents would be nor when other residents would leave." Some residents would ultimately be transferred to foster homes. The Board of Appeals further found that the average stay of a resident would be one to one and one-half years. These facts are not consistent with the development of permanent and cohesive relationships among the residents, especially in the absence of a resident authority figure. Accordingly, the bond between the residents may well more resemble the relationship among boarders, club or fraternity members, whose exclusion from single family districts has been upheld in other jurisdictions.

Finally, the definition of family further specifies that the persons comprising the collective should not only be living together in a relationship founded on a domestic bond but should be "doing their *own* cooking and living together upon the premises as a *separate* housekeeping unit." Brewer Zoning Ordinance, Art. 1 § 101 (emphasis supplied). The Board found that the Corporation and its rotating staff would plan and manage the activities of the residents. Further, staff members were to be responsible for preparing meals and providing "some cleaning and other services." The Board of Appeals could reasonably have concluded that such an arrangement would not comply with the requirement of the ordinance that the residents do their own cooking as a separate housekeeping unit. Indeed, as the decisions of other courts suggest, extensive outside aid in the management and operation of a household detracts from the family nature of the home.

In light of the definitional specifications of the Brewer ordinance reviewed above, we conclude that the decision rendered by the Board of Appeals and affirmed by the Superior Court was clearly reasonable and adequately supported by factual findings of record. The Board could reasonably have decided not only that the Corporation's proposal failed to meet the definitional criteria of a domestic bond but that it failed to satisfy more concrete specifications of the ordinance as well. While the purpose of such homes is laudable and, while the promise they hold for the retarded is heartening we decline to interpret and apply local zoning ordinances by abandoning relatively objective standards of evaluation in favor of a judicial approach that requires an intimate evaluation of a home's purpose and effect in each case. If, as these Plaintiffs contend, the problem of locating group homes is pervasive in this state, legislative, not judicial, action may be most appropriate.

Borough of Glassboro v. Vallorosi

Supreme Court of New Jersey, 1990.
117 N.J. 421, 568 A.2d 888.

■ PER CURIAM.

The narrow issue presented in this case is whether a group of ten unrelated college students living in defendants' home constitutes a "family" within the definition of a restrictive zoning ordinance. The Borough of Glassboro concedes that a primary purpose of the ordinance was to prevent groups of unrelated college students from living together in the Borough's residential districts. The ordinance limits residence in such districts to stable and permanent "single housekeeping units" that constitute either a "traditional family unit" or its functional equivalent. The Chancery Division concluded that the relationship among this group of students and their living arrangements within the home demonstrated the "generic character" of a family, and denied the Borough injunctive relief. The Appellate Division affirmed. We now affirm the judgment of the Appellate Division.

In July 1986, the Borough amended its zoning ordinance, apparently in response to a rowdy weekend celebration by Glassboro State College students. The amendment applied to the Borough's residential districts and limited the use and occupancy of "detached dwellings" and structures with "two dwelling units" to "families" only. The ordinance defined a "family" as

> one or more persons occupying a dwelling unit as a single non-profit housekeeping unit, who are living together as a stable and permanent living unit, being a traditional family unit or the functional equivalency [sic] thereof. [Glassboro, N.J., Code § 107–3 (1986).]

The amendment included a statement of purpose that plainly reflected the Borough's intention to confine college students either to the dormitories provided by Glassboro State College or to the other zoning districts that permit apartments and townhouses. . . .

In June 1986, defendants purchased a home located in the restricted residential zone. The purchase was intended to provide a college home for Peter Vallorosi, the brother of defendant Diane Vallorosi and the son of two partners in S & V Associates, a real-estate investment partnership. (Under the partnership agreement, S & V Associates acquired equitable title to the premises when defendants purchased the home.) It was contemplated that nine of Peter's friends would share the house with him while the group attended Glassboro State College. Seven of the ten students renting the house were sophomores at the time their lease took effect. They were all between the ages of eighteen and twenty. All ten students entered into separate, renewable leases for a semester-long period of four months. At the end of each semester, a student could renew the lease for another term "if the house is found to be in order at [the] end of [the preceding] term."

The students moved into their new home in early September 1986. The house had one large kitchen, which was shared by all ten students. The students often ate meals together in small groups, cooked for each other, and generally shared the household chores, grocery shopping, and yard work. A common checking account paid for food and other bills. They shared the use of a telephone. Although uncertain of living arrangements after graduation, the students intended to remain tenants as long as they were enrolled at Glassboro State College.

The Borough commenced this action in September 1986, seeking an injunction against the use and occupancy of the house by the students. The complaint alleged that the occupants did not constitute a "family" as defined in the Borough's ordinance. Defendants contended that the amendment to the zoning ordinance was not authorized by the Municipal Land Use Law, N.J.S.A. 40:55D–1 to –112, and violated the New Jersey Constitution in that it regulated a class of people rather than a use of property. . . .

The Chancery Division upheld the constitutionality of the ordinance, but . . . concluded that the relationship among the students "shows stability, permanency and can be described as the functional equivalent of a family." The Appellate Division affirmed on the basis of the trial court's analysis.

. . .

The legal principles determinative of this appeal are clear and well-settled. The courts of this state have consistently invalidated zoning ordinances intended "to cure or prevent ... anti-social conduct in dwelling situations." Kirsch Holding Co. v. Borough of Manasquan, 59 N.J. 241, 253–54 (1971)....

In Kirsch Holding Co. v. Borough of Manasquan, we invalidated ordinances in two shore communities that restrictively defined "family" and prohibited seasonal rentals by unrelated persons. We held that the challenged ordinances "preclude so many harmless dwelling uses ... that they must be held to be so sweepingly excessive, and therefore legally unreasonable, that they must fall in their entirety." ...

In Berger v. State, 71 N.J. 206, we expressed our agreement with the principle that "[t]he concept of a one family dwelling is based upon its character as a single housekeeping unit." A significant issue in *Berger* was the validity of a restrictive zoning ordinance limiting the definition of family to "persons related by blood, marriage or adoption...." The challenged use was a group home for eight to twelve multi-handicapped, pre-school children who would reside in a twelve-room ocean-front house with a married couple experienced as foster parents. Staff hired by the New Jersey Department of Institutions and Agencies would provide support services but would not reside on the premises. We concluded that the State's proposed use of the premises was reasonable and thus immune from regulation by the local zoning ordinance. We also found the ordinance invalid by virtue of N.J.S.A. 40:55–33.2 (since repealed and replaced by N.J.S.A. 40:55D–66c), which prohibited municipalities from discriminating in zoning ordinances between children related to occupants of single-family dwellings by blood, marriage, or adoption, and children residing in such dwellings by virtue of placement in a "group home." Finally, we held that an ordinance limiting the term "family" to persons related by blood, marriage, or adoption cannot "satisfy the demands of due process." Such an ordinance

> so narrowly delimits the persons who may occupy a single family dwelling as to prohibit numerous potential occupants who pose no threat to the style of family living sought to be preserved.

Accordingly, we expressed our clear preference for zoning provisions that equated the term "single family" with a "single housekeeping unit."

. . .

Thus, our cases preclude municipalities from adopting zoning regulations that unreasonably distinguish between residential occupancy by unrelated persons in comparison with occupancy by individuals related by blood, marriage, or adoption. Our decisions permit zoning regulations to restrict uses in certain residential zones to single housekeeping units. But the standard for determining whether a use qualifies as a single housekeeping unit must be functional, and hence capable of being met by either related or unrelated persons.

. . .

Although the Public Advocate, as *amicus,* challenges the constitutionality of the Glassboro ordinance, we need not consider that issue, nor the issues raised in the cross-petition, in the context of this record. The narrow issue before us is whether there is sufficient credible evidence in this record to sustain the trial court's factual finding that the occupancy of defendants' dwelling by these ten college students constituted a single housekeeping unit as defined by the Glassboro ordinance.

In view of the unusual circumstances of this case, we find adequate evidence to uphold the Law Division's ruling. The uncontradicted testimony reflects a plan by ten sophomore college students to live together for three years under conditions that correspond substantially to the ordinance's requirement of a "stable and permanent living unit." To facilitate the plan, the house had been purchased by relatives of one of the students. The students ate together, shared household chores, and paid expenses from a common fund. Although the students signed four-month leases, the leases were renewable if the house was "in order" at the end of the term. Moreover, the students testified to their intention to remain in the house throughout college, and there was no significant evidence of defections up to the time of trial. As noted above, the students' occupancy ended in September 1988 because of Peter Vallorosi's post-trial withdrawal from college.

It is a matter of common experience that the costs of college and the variables characteristic of college life and student relationships do not readily lead to the formation of a household as stable and potentially durable as the one described in this record. On these facts, however, we cannot quarrel with the Law Division's conclusion that the occupancy at issue here "shows stability, permanency and can be described as the functional equivalent of a family."

It also bears repetition that noise and other socially disruptive behavior are best regulated outside the framework of municipal zoning. As we observed in State v. Baker, 81 N.J. at 111:

> Other legitimate municipal concerns can be dealt with similarly. Traffic congestion can appropriately be remedied by reasonable, evenhanded limitations upon the number of cars which may be maintained at a given residence. Moreover, area-related occupancy restrictions will, by decreasing density, tend by themselves to reduce traffic problems. Disruptive behavior—which, of course, is not limited to unrelated households—may properly be controlled through the use of the general police power. As we stated in *Kirsch v. Borough of Manasquan*, supra:
>
> Ordinarily obnoxious personal behavior can best be dealt with officially by vigorous and persistent enforcement of general police power ordinances and criminal statutes.... Zoning ordinances are not intended and cannot be expected to cure or prevent most anti-social conduct in dwelling situations. [59 N.J. at 253–54.]

Judgment affirmed.

NOTES

1. What distinguished the ten college students from the Penobscot group home for retarded adults? Are any of these distinctions relevant to the purposes of the zoning statutes? The Penobscot court emphasized the lack of any permanent, resident authority figure in the community home who would act in the role of a parent. Do you think it should be relevant that a group is organized under a single "head"? That they are held together by a common purpose? Do most traditional families fit these descriptions? Consider Crane Neck Association v. NYC/Long Island County Services Group, 92 A.D.2d 119, 460 N.Y.S.2d 69 (1983), where the court ruled that the establishment of a community residence for mentally disabled adults living with a full-time staff who set up programs and taught basic skills, similar to the program in Penobscot, did not violate zoning provisions limiting use to single family dwellings.

2. The membership turnover in the Penobscot group home appears to have influenced the court's decision. Is the stability of a group arrangement relevant? If so, could a community exclude young couples because they have the highest rate of divorce?

3. In Kirsch v. Prince George's County, 331 Md. 89, 626 A.2d 372 (1993), the Court of Appeals of Maryland held that a zoning ordinance imposing stricter requirements on landlords renting to college students than to others denied the students equal protection of laws under the Fourteenth Amendment. The court's reasoning relied in part on the precedent provided by *Belle Terre.*

Rosabeth Moss Kanter, Commitment and Community: Communes and Utopias in Sociological Perspective

1–4 (2005).

Utopia is the imaginary society in which humankind's deepest yearnings, noblest dreams, and highest aspirations come to fulfillment, where all physical, social, and spiritual forces work together, in harmony, to permit the attainment of everything people find necessary and desirable. In the imagined utopia, people work and live together closely and cooperatively, in a social order that is self-created and self-chosen rather than externally imposed, yet one that also operates according to a higher order of natural and spiritual laws. Utopia is held together by commitment rather than coercion, for in utopia what people want to do is the same as what they have to do; the interests of the individuals are congruent with the interests of the group; and personal growth and freedom entail responsibility for others. Underlying the vision of utopia is the assumption that harmony, cooperation, and mutuality of interests are natural to human existence, rather than conflict, competition, and exploitation, which arise only in imperfect societies. By providing material and psychological safety and security, the utopian social order eliminates the need for divisive competition or self-serving actions which elevate some people to the disadvantage of others; it ensures instead the flowering of mutual responsibility and trust, to the advantage of all.

Utopia, then, represents an ideal of the good, to contrast with the evils and ills of existing societies. The idea of utopia suggests a refuge from the troubles of this world as well as a hope for a better one. Utopian plans are partly an escape, as critics maintain, and partly a new creation, partly a flight *from* and partly a seeking *for*; they criticize, challenge, and reject the established order, then depart from it to seek the perfect human existence.

At a number of times in history, groups of people have decided that the ideal can become reality, and they have banded together in communities to bring about the fulfillment of their own utopian aspirations. Generally the idea of utopia has involved a way of life shared with others—and shared in such a way that the benefit of all is ensured.

. . .

The ideal of social unity has led to the formation of numerous communes and utopian communities. These are voluntary, value-based, communal social orders. Because members choose to join and choose to remain, conformity within the community is based on commitment—on the individual's own desire to obey its rules—rather than force or coercion . . . A commune seeks self-determination, often making its own laws and refusing to obey some of those set by the larger society. It is identifiable as an entity, for it has a physical location and a way of distinguishing between members and nonmembers. It intentionally implements a set of values, having been planned in order to bring about the attainment of certain ideals, and its operating decisions are made in terms of those values. All other goals are secondary and related to ends involving harmony, brotherhood, mutual support, and value expression. These ideals give rise to the key communal arrangement, the sharing of resources and finances.

. . .

The United States, in particular, has been the site for the founding of hundreds—possibly thousands—of utopian communities, from religious sects that retreated to the wilderness as early as 1680, to the vast numbers of communes today.

. . .

The religious utopians criticized the evil and immorality of the surrounding society, which placed barriers between man and God, holding that a perfect society, in close touch with fundamental truths, was immediately possible for believers.... A major theme was the possibility of human perfection through conversion to the more spiritual life offered by the utopia. John Humphrey Noyes began a group in Putney, Vermont in the late 1830s dedicated to Perfectionist ideals, which were to be implemented through complete sharing of beliefs, property, and sexual life; this group grew into the Oneida Community (1848–1881) [in New York state]. He believed that the individual soul could come into direct contact with God and that through conversion it could free itself from the sins of the existing world.

William M. Kephart, The Family, Society and the Individual

121–141 (1977).

. . .

Starting ... as a small group—no more than 20 or 30 persons in all—the Oneida Colony was barely able to survive the first few winters. The original members were primarily farmers and mechanics, and while their collectivist economy had certain advantages, they found it difficult to support a growing community solely from their land yields. Fortunately, one of their members, Sewell Newhouse, invented a steel trap, which turned out to be peerless in design. Demand for the product grew, and soon the major part of the Oneida economy came to be based on the manufacture of the now-famous traps. Thereafter, the group was without financial worry.

SOCIAL ORGANIZATION

What was there, in terms of social organization, that held the Oneida Community together in the face of both internal problems and external pressures? One integrating element was the fact that practically the entire membership was housed under one roof. Although, over the years, there were six different branches and hundreds of members, the Perfectionists' home base was at Oneida, New York. It was there that the original communal home was built in 1849, to be replaced in 1862 by a spacious brick building known as the Mansion House. In subsequent years, as the membership grew, wings were added as needed. The building still stands, a striking architectural form internally as well as externally....

Although each adult had a small room of his or her own, the building was designed to encourage a feeling of togetherness, hence the inclusion of a communal dining hall, recreation rooms, library, concert hall, outdoor picnic area, etc. It was in the Big Hall of the Mansion House that John Humphrey Noyes gave his widely quoted home talks. It was here that musical concerts, dramas, readings, dances, and other forms of socializing were held. Community members were interested in the arts and were able to organize such activities as symphony concerts, glee club recitals, and Shakespearean plays, even though practically all the talent was drawn from the membership.

Occasionally, outside artists were invited, but on a day-to-day basis the Community was more or less a closed group, with members seldom straying very far from home. What might be called their reference behavior related entirely to the group. The outside community was, figuratively and literally, "outside" and was always referred to as The World. It was this system of *cultural enclosure,* sustained over several decades, that served as a primary solidifying force.

It should not be thought that life in the old Community was a continual round of entertainment. The Oneidans built their own home, raised their own food, made all their own clothes (including shoes!), did their own laundry, ran their own school, and performed countless other collective tasks. . . .

Additionally adults were subject to self-imposed deprivations whenever they felt the group welfare threatened, and by modern standards "group welfare" was given a most liberal interpretation. For example, although the Perfectionists ate well, meat was served sparingly, pork not at all. Alcoholic beverages were prohibited, as were tea and coffee. Smoking also came to be taboo. The reasoning behind these prohibitions is not always clear, but presumably the Oneidans were dead set against informal distractions of an "anti-family" nature. Thus, dancing was permitted, since it was a social activity, while coffee-drinking and smoking were condemned on the ground that they were individualistic and appetitive in nature. One of the descendants of the Oneida Community—in an interview with the writer—spoke as follows:

> I imagine the prohibitions were pretty well thought out. They didn't just spring up, but developed gradually. I know there were some differences of opinion, but the main thing was that certain practices were felt to be bad for group living.
>
> Remember, they were trying to create a spiritual and social brotherhood, and they spent much more time in the art of developing relationships than we do. They had to. After all, hundreds of them were living together as a family, and they worked at it day after day. They were successful, too, for they held together for almost two generations without a major quarrel.

Their unique social organization was not the only thing that held the Oneida Colony together. As the membership increased, three basic principles of Noyes' teaching combined to form the very heart of Perfectionist life style: (1) economic communism; (2) mutual criticism; and (3) complex marriage.

ECONOMIC COMMUNISM

Members of the Oneida Community held equal ownership of all property, their avowed aim being to eliminate competition for the possession of material things. The needs of individual members were taken care of, but there was simply no concept of private ownership, even in the realm of personal belongings such as clothes, trinkets, and children's toys.

Writing of his boyhood, Pierrepont Noyes, a son of John Humphrey, states that "throughout my childhood, the private ownership of anything seemed to me a crude artificiality to which an unenlightened Outside still clung. For instance, we were keen for our favorite sleds, but it never occurred to me that I could possess a sled to the exclusion of the other boys. So it was with all Children's House property." With respect to clothing, the same author writes that "going-away clothes for grown folks, as for children, were common property. Any man or woman preparing for a trip was fitted out with one of the suits kept in stock for that purpose."

In addition to the manufacture of traps, the Oneidans found a ready market for their crops, which they put up in glass jars and cans and which became known for their uniform quality. As their business know-how (and their prosperity!) increased, it became necessary to hire outside help, and eventually the Perfectionists were employing several hundred local workers.

Starting in 1877, the Oneidans embarked on the manufacture of silverware. This venture proved so successful that, when the Community was disbanded, the silverware component was perpetuated as a joint-stock company (Oneida Ltd.), whose product is still widely used today.

How much of the economic success of the group was due to the communistic methods employed, and how much was due to the fortuitous invention of the trap, is difficult to say. On the one hand, collectivist methods probably had certain advantages over competing private enterprise. In tracing the economic history of the Oneidans, for instance, Edmonds notes that "to meet the deadline on an order, the whole Community—including the children—turned out."

On the other hand, the fact remains that the Perfectionists were rapidly becoming bankrupt until Sewell Newhouse's trap, figuratively and literally, "caught on." . . .

It is debatable whether the subsequent Oneida industries—including that of silverware—would ever have developed had it not been for the financial windfall brought about by Sewell Newhouse's timely invention. Some idea of the magnitude of the business can be seen from the fact that, in a good year, the Community would turn out close to 300,000 traps!

The economic aspects of [the Oneidans has] been mentioned in some detail, since most of the other communistic experiments then under way in America (and there were scores of them) became defunct either partly or largely because of economic difficulties.

Insofar as possible, the various jobs within the Community were rotated from year to year in order to eliminate feelings of discrimination. Members were quick to point out that at one time or another almost everyone took a turn at the necessary menial tasks. Nevertheless, while the jobs were generally rotated, individual variations in ability were recognized, and members were not placed in positions beyond their innate capacities. At the same time, social differentiation by occupational status was played down. If people did their work well, they presumably had equal status whether they were farm laborers or plant superintendents. It was work, rather than a specific type of job, that was held in high regard. As a matter of fact, one of the Perfectionists' most successful innovations was their employment of the cooperative enterprise or *bee*.

The latter was an ordinance exactly suited to Community life. A bee would be announced at dinner or perhaps on the bulletin board: "A bee in the kitchen to pare apples"; or "A bee to pick strawberries at five o'clock tomorrow morning"; or "A bee in the Upper Sitting Room to sew bags."

It should be mentioned that there was seldom any trouble with idlers. On the contrary, a major difficulty was to screen out most of those who made application to join the Community. Relatively few new members were admitted, and those who were accepted had to undergo a long and severe probationary period.

In their efforts to promote equality, all Perfectionists were required to eat the same kind of food, wear the same type of clothing, and live in the same home. For both sexes, dress was uniformly simple, with jewelry and adornments tabooed.

. . .

MUTUAL CRITICISM

The Oneida Community had neither laws nor law-enforcing officers, and there was little need for them, major infractions being all but unknown. In any organization, however, no matter how closely knit, conduct problems are bound to occur, and while the Oneidans considered themselves to be Perfectionists, they acknowledged that individual foibles did exist. "Mutual criticism" was the method by which such problems were handled. The system had its inception at Putney, where the original followers of Noyes would subject themselves periodically to a searching criticism by the rest of the group. At Oneida the system was perpetuated—with remarkably successful results.

Whenever a member was found to be deviating from group norms, or whenever a personality or character weakness manifested itself, a committee of peers would meet with the offender to discuss the matter. "The criticisms," according to Edmonds, "were administered in a purely clinical spirit. The subject sat in complete silence while each member of the committee in turn assessed his good points as well as his bad. In cases of unusual seriousness, perhaps involving the violation of a fundamental tenet of their common philosophy, the committee would be expanded to include the entire Community."

From the accounts of the individuals who had undergone criticism, it is evident that, while the experience itself was often an ordeal, the end result was that of a catharsis, or spiritual cleansing. The success of the system probably hinged on the subjects' willingness to accept analysis and also on the fact that, though the criticisms were penetrating, they were offered in a frank, impersonal manner.

. . .

Although the Perfectionists had their share of internal strife, as we shall see, the conflicts were over policy and had nothing to do with deviant behavior. The harmonious living enjoyed by the group and the virtual lack of pernicious behavior attest to the effectiveness of mutual criticism as an instrument of social control. In fact, as the Colony grew in membership, the technique of mutual criticism came to be employed not so much with errant members but with those who volunteered for purposes of self-improvement.

. . .

COMPLEX MARRIAGE

The world does not remember the Oneidans for their economic communism or their mutual criticism, but for their system of complex marriage. Rightly or wrongly, just as the term "Rappites" signifies celibacy, so the name "Oneida" conjures up thoughts about the unique sex practices of the Community. Noyes himself coined the term "free love," although he seems to have preferred the phrase "complex marriage," or occasionally "pantogamy." Realistically, the Oneida marital system can best be described as a combination of communitarian living and group marriage.

. . . John Humphrey Noyes had no time for romantic love or monogamous marriage. Such practices were to him manifestations of selfishness and personal possession. Romantic love, or "special love" as it was called in the Community, was believed to give rise to jealousy and hypocrisy and, according to Perfectionist doctrine, made spiritual love impossible to attain.

Accordingly, Noyes promulgated the idea of complex marriage: since it was natural for all men to love all women and all women to love all men, it followed that every adult should consider himself or herself married to every other adult of the opposite sex. This collective spiritual union of men and women also included the right to sexual intercourse.

The Perfectionist leader felt strongly that "men and women find universally that their susceptibility to love is not burnt out by one honeymoon, or satisfied by one lover. On the contrary, the secret history of the human heart will bear out the assertion that it is capable of loving any number of times and any number of persons. Variety is, in the nature of things, as beautiful and useful in love as in eating and drinking. . . . We need love as much as we need food and clothing; and if we trust God for those things, why not for love?"

John Humphrey Noyes was a devout person, and the Oneida Perfectionists were a deeply religious group; any assessment of their sexual practices must take these factors into consideration. Insofar as the available information indicates, the Community abided by the doctrine of complex marriage not for reasons of lust, as was sometimes charged, but because of the conviction that they were following God's word.

In practice, since most of the adult men and women lived in the Mansion House, sex relations were easy to manage. There was, however, one requirement that was adhered to: a man could not have sexual intercourse with a woman unless the latter gave her consent. Procedurally, if a man desired sex relations, he would transmit the message to a Central Committee, who would thereupon make his request known to the woman in question. The actual go-between was usually an older female member of the Committee.

The system was inaugurated, as Parker points out, so that the women members "might, without embarrassment, decline proposals that did not appeal to them. No member should be obliged to receive at any time, under any circumstances, the attention of those they had not learned to love. . . . Every woman was to be free to refuse any, or every, man's attention." Although the procedure varied somewhat over the years, if the Central Committee granted approval and the woman in question assented, then the man simply went to the woman's room at bedtime and spent an hour or so with her before retiring to his own quarters.

It must be admitted, apropos of complex marriage, that many of the operational details were never disclosed, and that some writers—both past and present—have taken a questioning look at the sex practices of the Oneidans. Webber, for instance, writes as follows:

> "It was commonly declared that a committee of men and women received applications from those desiring certain persons; that if they considered the pairing suitable they arranged the meetings or obtained a refusal which was relayed to the applicant.... Thus if there was a refusal there was less embarrassment than if the proposal were made directly.
>
> So much for the rule. One may suspect that it was honored largely, as it were, in the breach. Men and women constantly associated and were free to visit in each other's rooms. It seems unlikely that a burst of romantic feeling might be interrupted while someone trotted off to find a go-between.
>
> Whether, in fact, the Central Committee or the go-between were frequently by-passed must remain a matter of conjecture. One should remember that the Oneidans were a devout group, and that their sexual practices were part of an overall religious system. It is difficult, therefore, for outsiders to assess the sexual motivations of individual Community members.
>
> It is known that Oneidans were presumed to act like ladies and gentlemen at all times. Inappropriate behavior, suggestive language, overt displays of sexuality—such actions were not tolerated. As a matter of fact, sexual behavior was not openly discussed within the Community, and it is doubtful whether the subject of 'Who was having relations with whom?' ever became common knowledge. One male member who became too inquisitive on this score was literally thrown out of the Community, an act which represented the only physical expulsion in the group's history."

ROLE OF WOMEN

There is no doubt that John Humphrey Noyes had a special place in his heart for the Oneida women—and in this respect he was years ahead of his time. He saw to it that they played an integral part in the day-to-day operations of the Community. The following remarks, made to the writer, provide a good example.

> One thing that most people have overlooked is that Noyes delegated a lot more responsibility to the women here than they ever would have received on the outside. Every committee had women on it. It made a difference, too. All the old folks will tell you it made both men and women respect each other.

In the sexual sphere, also, the Perfectionist leader had advanced ideas about the role of women.... [H]e rejected the idea that sex was simply a "wifely duty," that is, an act tolerated by the female at the pleasure of the male. Later on, he incorporated his beliefs in the Oneida *Handbook,* as the following passage indicates:

> "The liberty of monogamous marriage, as commonly understood, is the liberty of a man to sleep habitually with a woman, liberty to please himself alone in his dealings with her, liberty to expose her to child-bearing without care or consultation.
>
> The term Free Love, as understood by the Oneida Community, does *not* mean any such freedom of sexual proceedings. The theory of sexual

> interchange which governs all the general measures of the Community is that which in ordinary society governs the proceedings in *courtship.* It is the theory that love *after* marriage should be what it is *before* marriage—a glowing attraction on both sides, and not the odious obligation of one party, and the sensual selfishness of the other."

Although rumors a-plenty were carried by the outsiders, there is unfortunately no published record of the extent to which requested sexual liaisons were vetoed by the Central Committee or refused by the women themselves. All the evidence is fragmentary. Some individuals, naturally, were more in demand than others. Carden, who has done research on the subject, believes that the women often had more than four different sex partners a month.

> A physician who interviewed a number of ex-members after the break-up, reported that women had intercourse every two to four days. Another report, also by a physician, quoted an obviously discontented older woman who had left the Community. She complained that young girls would be called upon to have intercourse as often as seven times in a week and oftener.

On the other hand, that there was some rejection can be inferred from Parker's finding—based on a lengthy study—that "this entire freedom of the women to accept or reject the advances of their lovers kept men as alert as during more conventional courtships. Men sought, as always, to prove themselves worthy of the favor of their sweethearts; and that made their life, they confessed, one continuous courtship."

THE EUGENICS PROGRAM

Child-rearing occupied a special place in the Perfectionist scheme of things. Having familiarized himself with the principles of Charles Darwin and Francis Galton, Noyes was convinced of the feasibility of applying scientific methods to the propagation of the race. He felt that the only people who should have children were those who possessed superior physical and mental abilities. A clear statement of his position appeared in the Oneida Circular.

> Why should not beauty and noble grace of person and every other desirable quality of men and women, internal and external, be propagated and intensified beyond all former precedent—by the application of the same scientific principles of breeding that produce such desirable results in the case of sheep, cattle, and horses?

Although the term "eugenics" had not yet been coined, a eugenics program—in which specially chosen adults would be utilized for breeding purposes—was exactly what John Humphrey Noyes had in mind. And, of course, what more logical place to put eugenic principles into actual practice than the Oneida Community? Noyes called his program "stirpiculture" (from the Latin *stirps,* meaning root or stock), and it was not long before the scientific world was discussing the implications of the unique experiment being conducted in central New York State.

For 20 years after founding their Community, the Oneidans had largely refrained from bearing children. They reasoned that procreation should be delayed until such time as the group had the facilities for proper child care. The first two decades, so to speak, merely served the purpose of laying the groundwork for the future growth of the Colony. The birth control technique advocated by Noyes was *coitus reservatus,* i.e., sexual intercourse up to, but not including, ejaculation on the part of the male. Until they had learned the necessary coital control, younger males in the Community were required to limit their sex relations to women who had passed the menopause. Although the technique was claimed by many writers to be incapable of attainment, the record contradicts them.

In any case, by 1869 the group was ready to embark upon its pioneer eugenics program. Couples desirous of becoming parents (stirps) made formal application before a cabinet composed of key members of the Community, Noyes apparently holding the deciding vote. The cabinet, after assessing the physical and mental qualities of the applicants, would either approve or disapprove the requests. The stirpiculture program was in effect for about a decade before the Community disbanded, and during this 10-year period 58 children were born. Noyes himself fathered upwards of a dozen children, so that evidently he was not averse to self-selection.

Children remained in their mothers' care up to the age of 15 months, whereupon they were gradually transferred to a special section of the Mansion House. Henceforth they would spend most of their childhood in age-graded classes. Although the children were treated with kindness by their parents, sentimentalizing was frowned upon, the feeling being that under Perfectionism all adults should love all children and vice versa.

By their own reports, the children were evidently well adjusted. Recreation, schooling, medical care—all were provided in keeping with accepted child-rearing practices. As a group, the children were remarkably healthy. Mortality comparisons indicated that the products of stirpiculture had a significantly lower death rate than children born outside the Community.

That most of the youngsters had a happy childhood can be seen from the following comments, made to the writer:

> I was born in the old Community, and the times we used to have! I don't think kids today have the kind of fun we did. There was a ready-made play group all the time, with something always going on. There was some activity in the Big Hall almost every night—plays, musical concerts, entertainment of all kinds. As children, there was always something to look forward to.
>
> . . .
>
> You knew you were loved because it was like a big family. Also, there were so many activities for the youngsters, so many things to do, well—believe me—we were happy children.
>
> . . .
>
> We were happy youngsters, and we lived in a remarkable group. Unfortunately, they broke up when I was quite young. I wish I could have lived my whole life with them.
>
> . . .

In late 1879, after fearlessly defying public opinion for almost half a century, Noyes sent a message to the Community (from Canada) proposing that they abolish complex marriage and revert to the accepted marital practices. Soon afterward the group disbanded, many of the members becoming formally married. Economically, a joint-stock company was organized and the stock (worth about $600,000) was then divided among the members. Last-ditch efforts to salvage some communal type of family organization failed, thus ending—in rather pathetic fashion—what was probably the most radical social experiment in America.

NOTE

1. A recent book by Spencer Klaw entitled Without Sin, explores the Oneida Community and the personal experiences of those who lived there. Through excerpts from the diaries and letters of many Oneida members, Klaw creates an intimate portrait of life in the community, and of the internal conflict and external pressure that toppled the most successful utopian commune in American history. Spencer Klaw, Without Sin (1993).

2. Was the Oneida community a family? If not, what characteristics was it missing? Could it be a family for some legal purposes but not others?

D. LEGAL FORM AND FAMILY LAW

Carl E. Schneider, The Channelling Function in Family Law

20 Hofstra L. Rev. 495 (1992).

I. THE THEORY OF THE CHANNELLING FUNCTION

A. What is the Channelling Function?

... I propose to explor[e] a function of family law that I believe is basic, that underlies much of family law, that resonates with the deepest purposes of culture but that is rarely addressed expressly—namely, what I call the "channelling function." As I will soon explain at length, in the channelling function the law recruits, builds, shapes, sustains, and promotes social institutions.

. . .

Family law has, I think, five functions. The first is the protective function. One of law's most basic duties is to protect citizens against harms done them by other citizens. This means protecting people from physical harm, as the law of spouse and child abuse attempts to do, and from non-physical harms, especially economic wrongs and psychological injuries. Law's second function is to help people organize their lives and affairs in the ways they prefer. Family law performs this "facilitative" function by offering people the law's services in entering and enforcing contracts, by giving legal effect to their private arrangements. Family law's third function is to help people resolve disputes. The law of divorce exemplifies family law's "arbitral" function, since today's divorce courts primarily adjudicate conflicting claims to marital property, alimony, and child custody.

. . .

Finally, in the channelling function the law creates or (more often) supports social institutions which are thought to serve desirable ends. "Social institution" I intend broadly: "In its formal sociological definition, an institution is a pattern of expected action of individuals or groups enforced by social sanctions, both positive and negative."[1] ... Generally, the channelling function does not specifically require people to use these social institutions, although it may offer incentives and disincentives for their use. Primarily, rather, it is their very presence, the social currency they have, and the governmental support they receive which combine to make it seem reason-

1. Robert N. Bellah, et al., The Good Society 10 (1991).

able and even natural for people to use them. Thus people can be said to be channelled into them.

. . .

. . . [H]ow might family law be said to support social institutions and to channel people into them?

. . .

. . . I will . . . try to describe two broad social institutions which I will use to illustrate the working of family law's channelling function. These two institutions are "marriage" and "parenthood." . . . I have no doubt that both these institutions have somewhat different meanings for different people, that they have changed over time and are still changing, and that they do not monopolize intimate life in modern America. However, a legislator might plausibly identify a core of ideas which have enough social support to justify the term "institution" and which the legislator might conclude the law should try to support, to shape, and to channel people into.

Our legislator might, then, posit a normative model of "marriage" with several fundamental characteristics. It is monogamous, heterosexual, and permanent. It rests on love. Husbands and wives are to treat each other affectionately, considerately, and fairly. They should be animated by mutual concern and willing to sacrifice for each other.

. . .

In the same way, our legislator might posit an institution of "parenthood" with several key normative characteristics. Parents should be married to each other. They are preferably the biological father and mother of their child. They have authority over their children and can make decisions for them. However, like spouses, parents are expected to love their children and to be affectionate, considerate, and fair. They should support and nurture their children during their minority. They should assure them a stable home, particularly by staying married to each other, so that the child lives with both parents and knows the comforts of security.

Obviously, these two normative models are not and never were descriptions of any universal empirical reality, and I will soon examine recent changes in social practice that might affect them. Nor are they the only models the channelling function might be recruited to serve. Nevertheless, they do describe ideals which have won and retained substantial allegiance in American life. I will thus use these models to illustrate how the channelling function can work. How, then, might out legislator interpret the law as supporting these two institutions and channelling people into them?

Our legislator might see family law as setting a framework of rules, one of whose effects is to shape, sponsor, and sustain the model of marriage I described above: It writes standards for entry into marriage, standards which prohibit polygamous, incestuous, and homosexual unions. It seeks to encourage marital stability by inhibiting divorce (although it pursues this goal much less vigorously than it once did). It tries to improve marital behavior both directly and indirectly: It imposes a few direct obligations during marriage, like the duty of support. Less directly, it has invented special categories of property . . . to reflect and reinforce the special relationship of marriage. It indirectly sets some standards for marital behavior through the law of divorce. Fault-based divorce does so by describing behavior so egregious that it justifies divorce. Marital-property law implicitly sets standards for the financial conduct of spouses. Finally, prohibitions against non-marital sexual activity and discouragements against quasi-marital arrangements in principle confine sexual life to marriage.

. . .

Similarly, our legislator might see a framework of laws molding and promoting the institution of parenthood. Laws criminalizing fornication, cohabitation, adultery, and bigamy in principle limit parenthood to married couples, and those legal disadvantages that still attach to illegitimacy make it wise to confine parenthood to marriage. Laws restricting divorce make it likelier that a child will be raised by both parents. The law buttresses parents' authority over children. Parents may use reasonable force in disciplining their children. They may decide whether their children should have medical treatment. They may choose their child's school. Parents of "children in need of supervision" can summon up the state's coercive power. However, the law also tries, directly and indirectly, to shape parental behavior. It requires parents to support their children. It penalizes the "abuse" or "neglect" of children and obliges many kinds of people to report evidence of it. It obliges parents to send their children to school. Custody law obliquely sets standards for parental behavior and emphasizes the centrality of children's interests. Finally, some states further elaborate the relationship between parent and child by obliging adult children to support their indigent parents.

These sketches suggest how the law can be seen as performing the first task of the channelling function, namely, to create—or more often, to recruit—social institutions and to mold and sustain them. The function's second task is to channel people into institutions. It can perform these two tasks in several ways. First, it does so simply by recognizing and endorsing institutions, thus giving them some aura of legitimacy and permanence. Recognition may be extended, for instance, through formalized, routinized, and regulated entry and exit to an institution, as with marriage: "By the authority vested in me by the State of Michigan, I now pronounce you man and wife."

A second channelling technique is to reward participation in an institution. Tax law, for instance, may offer advantages—like the marital deduction—to married couples that it denies the unmarried. Similarly, Social Security offers spouses benefits it refuses lovers. These advantages are enhanced if private entities consult the legal institution in allocating benefits, as when private employers offer medical insurance only to "family members" as the law defines that term. In a somewhat different vein, the law of alimony and marital property offers spouses—but generally not "cohabitants"—protections on divorce.

Third, the law can channel by disfavoring competing institutions. Sometimes competitors are flatly outlawed, as by laws prohibiting sodomy, bigamy, adultery, and prostitution. Bans on fornication and cohabitation mean (in principle) that, to have sexual relations, one must marry. Sometimes competing institutions are merely disadvantaged. For instance, the rule making contracts for meretricious consideration unenforceable traditionally denied unmarried couples the law's help in resolving some disputes. Similarly, nonparents are presumptively disadvantaged in custody disputes with parents. Finally, restrictive divorce laws impede re-entry to the alternative institution of singleness.

. . .

By and large, then, the channelling function does not primarily use direct legal coercion. People are not forced to marry. One can contract out (formally or informally) of many of the rules underlying marriage. One need not have children, and one is not forced to treat them lovingly. Rather, the function forms and reinforces institutions which have significant social support and which, optimally, come to seem so natural that people use them almost unreflectively. It relies centrally but not exclusively on social approval of the institution, on social rewards for its use, and on social disfavor of its alternatives.

. . .

B. What Purposes Does the Channelling Function Serve?

. . .

... [F]amily law's channelling function is partly a specialized way of performing its protective, facilitative, and arbitral functions. For instance, marriage variously serves the protective function. Law does not just (in conjunction with other social forces) create a shell of an institution; it builds (again with much help) institutions with norms. The institution of marriage which the law recruits and shapes attempts to induce in spouses a sense of an obligation to treat each other well—to love and honor each other. At the elemental level of physical violence, the law has tried to reinforce this socially imposed obligation by making cruelty a ground for divorce, by taking cruelty into account in settling the spouses' economic affairs, and by criminalizing and (increasingly aggressively in some jurisdictions) prosecuting spouse abuse. At the level of economic life, the law has tried to supervise the fairness of antenuptial agreements and the distribution of the spouses' assets on divorce. And marriage protects children by making it likelier that both parents will care for them throughout their minority.

The channelling function also assists the facilitative function. The latter function furnishes people mechanisms that help them organize their lives and affairs as they wish. Family law's institutions offer people models for organizing their lives. These models have been developed over time and have presumably worked for many other people. They become part of a menu of social choice. Further, marriage offers people a kind of relationship with social and legal advantages which are primarily available precisely because the law gives marriage a special status. Finally, marriage serves the dispute-resolution function by providing rules and a forum in which to adjudicate the disputes which flock around divorce like remoras around a shark. In addition, it provides norms of behavior which may help the parties resolve some of their disputes privately.

But the channelling function is more than a specialized means of performing family law's other functions. Like the corporation, marriage and parenthood serve some broad social purposes. These are crucial, but they are also so familiar they hardly need elaboration. Sixty years ago Karl Llewellyn discerned thirteen such purposes in marriage. They included the regulation of sexual behavior, the reduction of sexual conflict, the orderly perpetuation of the species, the "building and reinforcement of an economic unit," the regulation of wealth, and the "development of individual personality." And a large body of writing argues that the present happiness and future well-being of children depend on their growing up in something like the kind of institution I described above.

Less grandly ... channelling's institutions spare people having to invent the forms of family life *de novo.* Imagine two nineteen-year-olds living in a state of nature who find themselves in love. Without established social institutions, they would have to work out afresh how to express that love, how to structure their relationship, and what to expect of each other. The same couple in, say, the United States of the mid-twentieth century would find a set of answers to those questions in the institution of marriage. To be sure, they would see other answers presented by other institutions. They would hear criticisms of marriage. They would not be compelled to marry. But marriage would seem natural to them because most of the adults they knew partook of it, because society and the law supported it, and because they had to some extent internalized its values ... The institution, that is, would be part of a comfortable social vocabulary, a vocabulary that would save our lovers from having to invent their own language.

. . .

The channelling function does not just relieve people of the burden of working out afresh how to organize their lives. Even if one could satisfactorily invent modes of living for oneself, they probably could not be lived alone, but would have to be lived with others. People need to understand and predict what other people will think and do so that they can readily and safely deal and cooperate with each other. Social institutions help serve that need. As Martin Krygier writes, "There are many social situations where our decisions are strategically interdependent [with the decisions of other people].... [I]n such situations, *norms* will be generated which provide 'some *anchorage;* some preeminently conspicuous indication as to what action is likely to be taken by (most of) the others....' " Social institutions and the norms they embody, then, help us count on, cope with, and cooperate with other people.

More concretely, for example, the institution of marriage helps people to plan for the future even before becoming engaged and to reach easier understandings with their fiances and spouses about their married lives. People dealing with married couples benefit as well. Mundanely, they know that when they say, "Can you come for dinner on the sixteenth?," the invitation will be taken as including both husband and wife. Less banally and more consequentially, a wedding ring warns anyone attracted to its wearer not to contemplate an intimate relationship.

The kind of "anchorage" of which Krygier speaks may be particularly important to families, for in the complex and long-term intimate relationships that characterize family life, reliance and trust are specially needed. A central source of that reliance and trust is of course a faith in the love and steadfastness of one's family members. But that faith may be more comfortably sustained, and reciprocating love more easily given, where personal feelings are reinforced (and known to be reinforced) by social institutions. As Norval Glenn suggests, even people "who still strongly adhere to the ideal of marital permanence may be afraid to commit strongly to their marriages if they perceive a general weakening of the ideal."

. . .

We can summarize these workings of the channelling function by imagining two people looking for recreation, who live in a world without tennis, and who are given three balls, two rackets, and one net. They could no doubt find some way of amusing themselves with these toys. But tennis is a good game partly because it developed over many centuries, and our couple could not easily invent as good a game. Further, where tennis is a social institution, the two will readily find people with whom to enjoy their recreation, to improve their game, to relish their successes, and to lament their failures. And part of the pleasure of tennis lies in knowing its past glories and following its current progress. Tennis, in other words, succeeds because it is a shared and well-established social institution. Marriage and parenthood benefit from that same fact.

. . .

II. PROBING THE CHANNELLING FUNCTION

. . .

A. Limitations of the Channelling Function

. . .

In the last few decades, family law has been transformed, and perhaps the family has too. It is often said that families increasingly live in non-traditional arrangements and that even when they don't their internal relations have vitally changed. Arland Thornton, for instance sees a "decreased emphasis upon conformity to a set of behavioral standards in the family arena and an increased emphasis on individual freedom...." In recent decades, more specifically, the divorce rate has risen impressively. There are more unmarried cohabitants. Non-marital sexual activity has increased. Homosexuality has lost some of its stigma. Single parents are more numerous. More broadly, one hears that families "are becoming internally deinstitutionalized," that is, their individual members are more autonomous and less bound by the group[,] and the domestic group as a whole is less cohesive.... Are these changes so extensive that the family has become wholly "deinstitutionalized"? Has it grown unreasonable to speak of the family in terms of social institutions? Has the channelling function thus been put out of business in family law?

Certainly family law has changed. "No-fault" divorce is now everywhere available, which both makes it easier to leave marriages and inhibits setting norms for marital behavior. Prohibitions on non-marital sexual activity have largely been repealed, found unconstitutional, or fallen into desuetude. Laws disadvantaging illegitimate children have yielded to dissatisfied legislatures and courts. There has been some (partial) movement toward the "atomizing" of family law, toward seeing people not as family members, but rather as individuals dealing with other individuals. As Justice Brennan wrote in a telling and often retold phrase, "[I]f the right of privacy means anything, it is the right of the *individual*, married or single, to be free ... to bear or beget a child." By 1989, Justice Brennan could cite a string of cases he believed indicated that "we have declined to respect a State's notion, as manifested in its allocation of privileges and burdens, of what the family should be."

[In addition], one noteworthy feature of recent legal change is the occasional governmental recognition of "functional equivalents" of the family.

Can the channelling function have any role in our changed new world? I believe so ... I will readily grant that [marriage and parenthood] may well have changed in recent decades. But I will suggest reasons to doubt that even in the rather traditional terms in which I have described those institutions, they can be dismissed as objects of the channelling function.

Much less, then, can it be said that the family has been so thoroughly deinstitutionalized that the channelling function has become irrelevant.

First, the world may not have changed quite so much and so simply as people—and courts—sometimes seem, rather casually, to assume. Social change is as monolithic and complete as we perceive it to be.

. . .

I am not arguing that society has not changed. Rather, I am suggesting that we should be much more cautious than we usually are in approaching claims of radical social change and much more alive to the complexity and unscrutability of social life. For one thing, data are absurdly hard to acquire and analyze. For another, social change is too often "proved" by arguments that the number of people doing something has increased by a large percentage. But the size of the percentage may be misleading where, as often happens, only a few people were involved at the first point in time. For yet another thing, it can be extremely difficult to distinguish short-term trends from genuine secular change. Further, impressions of social change are easily distorted. Both journalists and scholars, for instance, are more beguiled by the thrilling heterodox than the boring orthodox. And, for instance, we too easily see the behavior of our own class as typical of the country at large.

Even if social behavior has changed dramatically, social norms may not have. Even if, for example, families less often consist of a married couple and their biological offspring, that grouping may still represent a powerful cultural norm. Or, to take another example, it is often observed that "[m]ost divorced people remarry, usually soon after their divorces, suggesting that their divorce experience could be interpreted more as dissatisfaction with a specific spouse than as rejection of marriage as an institution." Further, many of the specific norms respecting marriage and parenthood could change without destroying their core institutional principles. I am not suggesting that there have been no changes in social attitudes about the family or in family life. But it seems to me quite possible that the social institutions I described earlier may still retain the social strength necessary to the channelling function even if they have changed in some respects and are statistically less common.

. . .

In sum, the channelling function's reach is always limited by the degree of social support the function's institutions receive. Today, "marriage" and "parenthood" appear to be changing institutions, and they appear to be under more pressure than they have been in recent memory. But this may mean no more than that these institutions are continuing to develop as they have been developing for centuries. That they are developing does not mean that their normative core will disappear. And even if it does, it seems likely that new institutions will have been created, so that the channelling function will continue to do its work. In short, I doubt that so far, at least, the American family has become so deinstitutionalized that the channelling function is no longer useful or relevant to family law. But this does not mean, of course, that every use of the function is justifiable. What is needed, rather, is to ask case by case whether the channelling function can plausibly be said to work effectively.

A second limitation of the channelling function is that its technique of promoting one institution by disadvantaging the alternatives can be troubling.... Even if unmarried cohabitation, for example, is immoral, should it be discouraged by denying its practitioners the law's services in resolving their disputes? Doing so may in practice allow one miscreant actually to profit by taking advantage of another. And in at least one situation—illegitimacy—those who suffered most from the channelling function's operation—illegitimate children—were also those who were morally blameless.

In thinking about this second limitation on the channelling function, we need to consider its complexity: Some ways of making an alternative institution less attractive are maximally coercive, as when they invoke criminal sanctions; others will hardly be coercive at all, as when they simply withhold the state's expression of approval. The costs of the technique importantly depend on the degree of coercion it employs. A sharp example of the more coercive end of the spectrum is prohibiting homosexual conduct. Such a prohibition not only invokes the law's strongest weapon—the criminal law; it also tends to exclude homosexuals from what the twentieth century considers a preeminent part of life—sexual relations.

On the other hand, ending the practice of disadvantaging competing institutions altogether would have its own costs. The channelling function helps tell the people involved in an institution, the world in general, and the law in particular that those people stand in a particular relation to each other. When people marry, they, the world, and the law know that they have assumed special obligations to each other. When a child is born in wedlock, the parents, the child (eventually), the world, and the law know that the parents have taken on special responsibilities to their child. "Functional equivalence" approaches serve this end less well.

. . .

Channelling can surely be misused, and people can reasonably disagree about what "misuse" means. However, this is not a reason for abandoning the function. For all the function's uncertainties, inadequacies, and costs, the goals it can be used to promote are both substantial and hard to achieve in other ways. And here I should emphasize yet again that the specific goals I have used as examples are not the only ones channelling can promote. Channelling is not inherently confined to any single set of social ends. Rather, it may be recruited to serve whatever ends seem appropriate.

. . .

For example, over the last several decades we have seen systematic and ambitious attempts to restructure "marriage" and "parenthood" in order to change the way people think and act regarding gender.

Indeed, many recent reforms of family law—made and proposed—can be understood in terms of a desire to employ the channelling function to change the institutional basis of family life in order to change gender relations in American society.

. . .

The[se] reforms . . . have had a variety of goals. Many of those goals are straightforward enough and have to do with directly ameliorating the condition of women in particular contexts. But a central purpose of these reforms can be understood to be altering the institutional situation in which men and women find themselves. I suspect that doing so is crucial if the larger goals that reformers ultimately want to reach are to be achieved. Those goals—which [Susan] Okin describes as changing the "way we divide the labor and responsibilities in our personal lives"—cannot readily be achieved through direct legislation. Rather, social institutions must be structured and sustained so that "all will be likely to choose this mode of life."

. . .

III. CONCLUSION

. . .

In discussions of the channelling function, I have found people most troubled by what I think is the sense that it violates the principle that the state should be neutral among visions of the good. The function's institutions necessarily have normative components and thus to some degree favor one such vision over the rest. More, the function seeks, however obliquely, to shape people's thoughts and acts in an area of life in which freedom is widely and properly prized.

. . .

[One] response to the claim that the channelling function is improper because it violates some visions of state neutrality is that, in an important sense, one *cannot* abolish the channelling function in family law. Family law's goals—particularly those goals represented by the protective, arbitral, and facilitative functions—are so central that they are unlikely to be abandoned. As long as we pursue those goals, we will be creating, building on, and shaping social institutions and channelling people into them. The most obvious way to try to escape doing so is by expanding the facilitative function, by turning family law into contract law. That venture could not entirely succeed, of course, if only because family law centrally involves children, and children (particularly the young children about whom we worry most) cannot make contracts. But even if the venture succeeded, it would create a new institution. Contract, after all, has its own social structures, its own assumptions, its own consequences. Indeed, these are at the heart of the resistance to contract law's incursion into the sphere of family life.

Channelling, then, cannot be escaped. It arises because we are social beings whose relations with those around us shape institutions that in turn shape us. It arises because we are imperfect people who without institutions behave in ways that injure our fellows. It arises because we see the faults of the institutions around us and seek to perfect them, because we value the aspirations those institutions embody and hope to achieve them. Channelling, like any social tool, may be and has been used badly and used to bad purposes. But it is also one of the ways we try to use law to soften the harshness of life.

NOTES

1. Why does Professor Schneider believe that insisting on compliance with legal form is likely to create more stable social institutions than a legal system in which the state simply ratifies whatever intimate arrangements people want to make?

2. Does a divorce rate close to 50% and a higher incidence of unmarried cohabitation indicate that the effort to channel people toward marriage is becoming less effective? If so, should we try to strengthen the channeling function or abandon it? Is there an argument that these social trends reflect the continued emotionally privileged position of marriage?

3. Is it necessary to channel persons into marriage in order to provide social support for the importance of "a sense of an obligation to treat each other well—to love and honor each other"? Is the long tradition and cultural resonance of marriage more likely to do this than unmarried cohabitation? Or does marriage have other less salutary connotations that make the meaning of the institution more mixed?

4. If it is appropriate for law to channel couples into marriage, what benefits, rights, or obligations that spouses have should be denied to unmarried partners in order to reinforce this social preference? For an exploration of the complex considerations that may inform decisions whether to treat married and unmarried couples alike in various circumstances, see Milton C. Regan, Jr., Calibrated Commitment: The Legal Treatment of Marriage and Cohabitation, 76 Notre Dame L. Rev. 1435 (2001).

CHAPTER 2

Marrying

Should society regulate marriage? If so, what restrictions are appropriate? In answering the basic questions posed in this Chapter, it is important to consider the purpose of marriage. Is it merely an institution to promote personal happiness and emotional well being, or is it the very foundation of society? Does society have a stake in promoting marriages? In promoting sound marriages? If so, should there be any limits imposed on the power of society to regulate marriage? Is it appropriate, for example, to regulate the minimum age of the parties to a marriage? Their gender? Their wedding ceremony?

In evaluating restrictions, it is useful to consider their effects. If society lacks the ability to control fertility, for example, prohibiting some couples from marrying will not prevent them from having children out of wedlock. Marriage restrictions may also have the effect of denying to couples who are forbidden to marry some of the privileges and protections that are attached to marital status, such as income tax benefits. Are these results desirable? Harmful?

If it is decided that there should be restrictions placed on who may marry, which branch of government should be empowered to make the rules? Legislatures? Courts? What if conflicts between states arise? If State A has fewer restrictions on marriage than State B, should State B have the ability to deny recognition to the marriage of two of its citizens who travel to State A to be married?

What limits are placed on the power of states to regulate marriage by the United States Constitution? By state constitutions?

Finally, who should enforce the rules? The clerk at the license bureau? The Internal Revenue Service? Parents? Potential heirs? If two individuals manage to marry despite restrictions designed to prohibit their liaison, and continue to live together happily, perhaps bearing children, should anyone have the power to void the marriage if the parties choose not to do so?

Nancy F. Cott, Public Vows: A History of Marriage and the Nation

1–2 (2000).

Marriage is like the sphinx—a conspicuous and recognizable monument on the landscape, full of secrets. To newcomers the monument seems awesome, even marvelous, while those in the vicinity take its features for granted. In assessing matrimony's wonders or terrors, most people view it as a matter of private decision-making and domestic arrangements. The monumental public character of marriage is generally its least noticed aspect. Even Mae West's joke, "Marriage is a great institution.... but I ain't ready for an institution yet," likened it to a private asylum. Creating families and kinship networks and handing down private property, marriage certainly does design the architecture of private life. It influences individual identity and determines circles of intimacy. It can bring solace or misery—or both....

At the same time that any marriage represents personal love and commitment, it participates in the public order. Marital status is just as important to one's standing in the community and state as it is to self-understanding. Radiating outward, the structure of marriage organizes community life and facilitates the government's grasp on the populace. To *be* marriage, the institution requires public affirmation....

In the marriage ceremony, the public recognizes and supports the couple's reciprocal bond, and guarantees that this commitment (made in accord with the public's requirements) will be honored as something valuable not only to the pair but to the community at large. Their bond will be honored even by public force. This is what the public vows, when the couple take their own vows before public witnesses....

A. Restrictions on Who May Marry

1. Constitutionality of Marriage Restrictions

Loving v. Virginia

Supreme Court of the United States, 1967.
388 U.S. 1, 87 S.Ct. 1817, 18 L.Ed.2d 1010.

■ CHIEF JUSTICE WARREN delivered the opinion of the Court.

This case presents a constitutional question never addressed by this Court: whether a statutory scheme adopted by the State of Virginia to prevent marriages between persons solely on the basis of racial classifications violates the Equal Protection and Due Process Clauses of the Fourteenth Amendment....

In June 1958, two residents of Virginia, Mildred Jeter, a Negro woman, and Richard Loving, a white man, were married in the District of Columbia pursuant to its laws. Shortly after their marriage, the Lovings returned to Virginia and established their marital abode in Caroline County. At the October Term, 1958, of the Circuit Court of Caroline County, a grand jury issued an indictment charging the Lovings with violating Virginia's ban on interracial marriages. On January 6, 1959, the Lovings pleaded guilty to the charge and were sentenced to one year in jail; however, the trial judge suspended the sentence for a period of 25 years on the condition that the Lovings leave the State and not return to Virginia together for 25 years. He stated in an opinion that:

> "Almighty God created the races white, black, yellow, malay and red, and he placed them on separate continents. And but for the interference with his arrangement there would be no cause for such marriages. The fact that he separated the races shows that he did not intend for the races to mix."

After their convictions, the Lovings took up residence in the District of Columbia. On November 6, 1963, they filed a motion in the state trial court to vacate the judgment and set aside the sentence on the ground that the statutes which they had violated were repugnant to the Fourteenth Amendment.... On January 22, 1965, the state trial judge denied the motion to vacate the sentences, and the Lovings perfected an appeal to the Supreme Court of Appeals of Virginia. . . .

The Supreme Court of Appeals upheld the constitutionality of the antimiscegenation statutes and, after modifying the sentence, affirmed the convictions. The Lovings appealed this decision, and we noted probable jurisdiction on December 12, 1966, 385 U.S. 986.

The two statutes under which appellants were convicted and sentenced are part of a comprehensive statutory scheme aimed at prohibiting and punishing interracial marriages. The Lovings were convicted of violating § 20–58 of the Virginia Code:

> "*Leaving State to evade law.*—If any white person and colored person shall go out of this State, for the purpose of being married, and with the intention of returning, and be married out of it, and afterwards return to and reside in it, cohabiting as man and wife, they shall be punished as provided in § 20–59, and the marriage shall be governed by the same law as if it had been solemnized in this State. The fact of their cohabitation here as man and wife shall be evidence of their marriage."

Section 20–59, which defines the penalty for miscegenation, provides:

> "*Punishment for marriage.*—If any white person intermarry with a colored person, or any colored person intermarry with a white person, he shall be guilty of a felony and shall be punished by confinement in the penitentiary for not less than one nor more than five years."

Other central provisions in the Virginia statutory scheme are § 20–57, which automatically voids all marriages between "a white person and a colored person" without any judicial proceeding, and §§ 20–54 and 1–14 which, respectively, define "white persons" and "colored persons and Indians" for purposes of the statutory prohibitions.[4] The Lovings have never disputed in the course of this litigation that Mrs. Loving is a "colored person" or that Mr. Loving is a "white person" within the meanings given those terms by the Virginia statutes.

Virginia is now one of 16 States which prohibit and punish marriages on the basis of racial classifications.[5] Penalties for miscegenation arose as an

4. Section 20–54 of the Virginia Code provides:

"*Intermarriage prohibited; meaning of term 'white persons.'*—It shall hereafter be unlawful for any white person in this State to marry any save a white person, or a person with no other admixture of blood than white and American Indian. For the purpose of this Chapter, the term 'white person' shall apply only to such person as has no trace whatever of any blood other than Caucasian; but persons who have one-sixteenth or less of the blood of the American Indian and have no other non-Caucasic blood shall be deemed to be white persons. All laws heretofore passed and now in effect regarding the intermarriage of white and colored persons shall apply to marriages prohibited by this chapter." Va. Code Ann. § 20–54 (1960 Repl. Vol.).

The exception for persons with less than one-sixteenth "of the blood of the American Indian" is apparently accounted for, in the words of a tract issued by the Registrar of the State Bureau of Vital Statistics, by "the desire of all to recognize as an integral and honored part of the white race the descendants of John Rolfe and Pocahontas. . . ." Plecker, The New Family and Race Improvement, 17 Va. Health Bull., Extra No. 12, at 25–26 (New Family Series No. 5, 1925), cited in Wadlington, The *Loving* Case: Virginia's Anti-Miscegenation Statute in Historical Perspective, 52 Va. L. Rev. 1189, 1202, n. 93 (1966). . . .

5. After the initiation of this litigation, Maryland repealed its prohibitions against interracial marriage, Md. Laws 1967, c. 6, leaving Virginia and 15 other States with statutes outlawing interracial marriage: Alabama, Ala. Const., Art. 4, § 102, Ala. Code, Tit. 14, § 360 (1958); Arkansas, Ark. Stat. Ann. § 55–104 (1947); Delaware, Del. Code Ann., Tit. 13, § 101 (1953); Florida, Fla. Const., Art. 16, § 24, Fla. Stat. § 741.11 (1965); Georgia, Ga. Code Ann. § 53–106 (1961); Kentucky, Ky. Rev. Stat. Ann. § 402.020 (Supp. 1966); Louisiana, La. Rev. Stat. § 14:79 (1950); Mississip-

incident to slavery and have been common in Virginia since the colonial period.... The central features of ... current Virginia law, are the absolute prohibition of a "white person" marrying other than another "white person," a prohibition against issuing marriage licenses until the issuing official is satisfied that the applicants' statements as to their race are correct, certificates of "racial composition" to be kept by both local and state registrars, and the carrying forward of earlier prohibitions against racial intermarriage.

In upholding the constitutionality of these provisions in the decision below, the Supreme Court of Appeals of Virginia referred to its 1955 decision in Naim v. Naim, 197 Va. 80, 87 S.E.2d 749, as stating the reasons supporting the validity of these laws. In *Naim*, the state court concluded that the State's legitimate purposes were "to preserve the racial integrity of its citizens," and to prevent "the corruption of blood," "a mongrel breed of citizens," and "the obliteration of racial pride," obviously an endorsement of the doctrine of White Supremacy. The court also reasoned that marriage has traditionally been subject to state regulation without federal intervention, and, consequently, the regulation of marriage should be left to exclusive state control by the Tenth Amendment.

While the state court is no doubt correct in asserting that marriage is a social relation subject to the State's police power, Maynard v. Hill, 125 U.S. 190 (1888), the State does not contend in its argument before this Court that its powers to regulate marriage are unlimited notwithstanding the commands of the Fourteenth Amendment.... Instead, the State argues that the meaning of the Equal Protection Clause, as illuminated by the statements of the Framers, is only that state penal laws containing an interracial element as part of the definition of the offense must apply equally to whites and Negroes in the sense that members of each race are punished to the same degree. Thus, the State contends that, because its miscegenation statutes punish equally both the white and the Negro participants in an interracial marriage, these statutes, despite their reliance on racial classifications, do not constitute an invidious discrimination based upon race. The second argument advanced by the State assumes the validity of its equal application theory. The argument is that, if the Equal Protection Clause does not outlaw miscegenation statutes because of their reliance on racial classifications, the question of constitutionality would thus become whether there was any rational basis for a State to treat interracial marriages differently from other marriages. On this question, the State argues, the scientific evidence is substantially in doubt and, consequently, this Court should defer to the wisdom of the state legislature in adopting its policy of discouraging interracial marriages.

Because we reject the notion that the mere "equal application" of a statute containing racial classifications is enough to remove the classifications

pi, Miss. Const., Art. 14, § 263, Miss. Code Ann. § 459 (1956); Missouri, Mo. Rev. Stat. § 451.020 (Supp. 1966); North Carolina, N.C. Const., Art. XIV, § 8, N. C. Gen. Stat. § 14–181 (1953); Oklahoma, Okla. Stat., Tit. 43, § 12 (Supp. 1965); South Carolina, S.C. Const., Art. 3, § 33, S.C. Code Ann. § 20–7 (1962); Tennessee, Tenn. Const., Art. 11, § 14, Tenn. Code Ann. § 36–402 (1955); Texas, Tex. Pen. Code, Art. 492 (1952); West Virginia, W. Va. Code Ann. § 4697 (1961).

Over the past 15 years, 14 States have repealed laws outlawing interracial marriages: Arizona, California, Colorado, Idaho, Indiana, Maryland, Montana, Nebraska, Nevada, North Dakota, Oregon, South Dakota, Utah, and Wyoming.

The first state court to recognize that miscegenation statutes violate the Equal Protection Clause was the Supreme Court of California. Perez v. Sharp, 32 Cal. 2d 711, 198 P. 2d 17 (1948).

from the Fourteenth Amendment's proscription of all invidious racial discriminations, we do not accept the State's contention that these statutes should be upheld if there is any possible basis for concluding that they serve a rational purpose. The mere fact of equal application does not mean that our analysis of these statutes should follow the approach we have taken in cases involving no racial discrimination. . . .

. . .

The State finds support for its "equal application" theory in the decision of the Court in Pace v. Alabama, 106 U.S. 583 (1883). In that case, the Court upheld a conviction under an Alabama statute forbidding adultery or fornication between a white person and a Negro which imposed a greater penalty than that of a statute proscribing similar conduct by members of the same race. The Court reasoned that the statute could not be said to discriminate against Negroes because the punishment for each participant in the offense was the same. However, as recently as the 1964 Term, in rejecting the reasoning of that case, we stated "*Pace* represents a limited view of the Equal Protection Clause which has not withstood analysis in the subsequent decisions of this Court." McLaughlin v. Florida, [379 U.S. 184, 188 (1964)]. As we there demonstrated, the Equal Protection Clause requires the consideration of whether the classifications drawn by any statute constitute an arbitrary and invidious discrimination. The clear and central purpose of the Fourteenth Amendment was to eliminate all official state sources of invidious racial discrimination in the States.

There can be no question but that Virginia's miscegenation statutes rest solely upon distinctions drawn according to race. The statutes proscribe generally accepted conduct if engaged in by members of different races. Over the years, this Court has consistently repudiated "[d]istinctions between citizens solely because of their ancestry" as being "odious to a free people whose institutions are founded upon the doctrine of equality." Hirabayashi v. United States, 320 U.S. 81, 100 (1943). At the very least, the Equal Protection Clause demands that racial classifications, especially suspect in criminal statutes, be subjected to the "most rigid scrutiny," Korematsu v. United States, 323 U.S. 214, 216 (1944), and, if they are ever to be upheld, they must be shown to be necessary to the accomplishment of some permissible state objective, independent of the racial discrimination which it was the object of the Fourteenth Amendment to eliminate. . . .

There is patently no legitimate overriding purpose independent of invidious racial discrimination which justifies this classification. The fact that Virginia prohibits only interracial marriages involving white persons demonstrates that the racial classifications must stand on their own justification, as measures designed to maintain White Supremacy. We have consistently denied the constitutionality of measures which restrict the rights of citizens on account of race. There can be no doubt that restricting the freedom to marry solely because of racial classifications violates the central meaning of the Equal Protection Clause.

These statutes also deprive the Lovings of liberty without due process of law in violation of the Due Process Clause of the Fourteenth Amendment. The freedom to marry has long been recognized as one of the vital personal rights essential to the orderly pursuit of happiness by free men.

Marriage is one of the "basic civil rights of man," fundamental to our very existence and survival. Skinner v. Oklahoma, 316 U.S. 535, 541 (1942). To deny this fundamental freedom on so unsupportable a basis as the racial classifications embodied in these statutes, classifications so directly subversive of the principle of equality at the heart of the Fourteenth Amendment, is surely to deprive all the State's citizens of liberty without due process of law. The Fourteenth Amendment requires that the freedom of choice to marry not be restricted by invidious racial discriminations. Under our Constitution, the freedom to marry, or not marry, a person of another race resides with the individual and cannot be infringed by the State.

These convictions must be reversed.

NOTES

1. Consider Derrick Bell, 99 Harv. L. Rev. 4, 62 (1985), the 1984 Term: Foreward: The Civil Rights Chronicles:

> . . . I will bet few law students know, and even fewer law scholars remember, that only a few months after *Brown*, the Court refused to review the conviction under an Alabama antimiscegenation law of a black man who married a white woman.[1] Many of us do remember, of course, and remember too the procedural contortions that the Court used one year after *Brown* to avoid deciding another challenge to a state law barring interracial marriages.[2]

Does this history shed light on the question of why the Supreme Court issued a full opinion in *Loving*?

2. Mildred Loving was interviewed in 1992. A widow, with three grown children, her church had presented her with a plaque and compared her to Rosa Parks. "I don't feel like that. Not at all. What happened, we really didn't intend for it to happen. What we wanted, we wanted to come home." She was 17 when she married Richard, who was 24. She did not know the marriage was illegal. Their ordeal began at 2 a.m. one day in July, 1958, when a Caroline County, Va., sheriff roused the Lovings from sleep and took them to the Bowling Green jail. After they moved to the District, Mildred wrote for help to then-U.S. Attorney General Robert F. Kennedy. Bernard Cohen, an ACLU lawyer took on their case. Reflecting on the case, Cohen observed that it was full of ironies. "It was ironical that her husband was killed in an auto accident just a few years after they finally got peace. And the irony that the justice of the Virginia Supreme Court who wrote the decision upholding the constitutionality of the law [became the chief justice of the court.]" Lynne Duke, Intermarriage Broken Up By Death, Wash. Post, June 12, 1992, at A3.

3. *Loving* was the first case in which the Supreme Court held unconstitutional a state restriction on marrying. In its wake, courts have overturned numerous other restrictions, as the next cases in this section illustrate. Indeed, now the question is whether *any* restrictions on marriage are constitutional. Could restrictions based on affinity or consanguinity be successfully challenged in light of *Loving* and its progeny? Age restrictions? Mandatory counseling restrictions?

Zablocki v. Redhail

Supreme Court of the United States, 1978.
434 U.S. 374, 98 S.Ct. 673, 54 L.Ed.2d 618.

■ JUSTICE MARSHALL delivered the opinion of the Court.

At issue in this case is the constitutionality of a Wisconsin statute, Wis.Stat. §§ 245.10(1), (4), (5) (1973), which provides that members of a

1. Jackson v. Alabama, 37 Ala.App. 519, 72 So.2d 114 (1954)

2. In Naim v. Naim, 197 Va. 80, 87 S.E.2d 749, *remanded*, 350 U.S. 891 (1955), *aff'd* 197 Va. 734, 90 S.E.2d 849, *appeal dismissed*, 350 U.S. 985 (1956), the Supreme Court remanded the case after oral argument for development of the record regarding the parties' domicil. After the state court refused to comply with the mandate, claiming that no state procedure existed for reopening the case, the Supreme Court dismissed the appeal, finding that the state court ruling left the case devoid of a substantial federal question. Professor Wechsler remarked that this dismissal was "wholly without basis in law."

certain class of Wisconsin residents may not marry, within the State or elsewhere, without first obtaining a court order granting permission to marry. The class is defined by the statute to include any "Wisconsin resident having minor issue not in his custody and which he is under obligation to support by any court order or judgment." The statute specifies that court permission cannot be granted unless the marriage applicant submits proof of compliance with the support obligation and, in addition, demonstrates that the children covered by the support order "are not then and are not likely thereafter to become public charges." No marriage license may lawfully be issued in Wisconsin to a person covered by the statute, except upon court order; any marriage entered into without compliance with § 245.10 is declared void; and persons acquiring marriage licenses in violation of the section are subject to criminal penalties.

After being denied a marriage license because of his failure to comply with § 245.10, appellee brought this class action . . . challenging the statute as violative of the Equal Protection and Due Process Clauses of the Fourteenth Amendment and seeking declaratory and injunctive relief. The United States District Court for the Eastern District of Wisconsin held the statute unconstitutional under the Equal Protection Clause and enjoined its enforcement. 418 F.Supp. 1061 (1976). We . . . now affirm.

Appellee Redhail is a Wisconsin resident who, under the terms of § 245.10, is unable to enter into a lawful marriage in Wisconsin or elsewhere so long as he maintains his Wisconsin residency. . . . In January 1972, when appellee was a minor and a high school student, a paternity action was instituted against him in Milwaukee County Court, alleging that he was the father of a baby girl born out of wedlock on July 5, 1971. After he appeared and admitted that he was the child's father, the court entered an order on May 12, 1972, adjudging appellee the father and ordering him to pay $109 per month as support for the child until she reached 18 years of age. From May 1972 until August 1974, appellee was unemployed and indigent, and consequently was unable to make any support payments.

On September 27, 1974, appellee filed an application for a marriage license with appellant Zablocki, the County Clerk of Milwaukee County, and a few days later the application was denied on the sole ground that appellee had not obtained a court order granting him permission to marry, as required by § 245.10. Although appellee did not petition a state court thereafter, it is stipulated that he would not have been able to satisfy either of the statutory prerequisites for an order granting permission to marry. First, he had not satisfied his support obligations to his illegitimate child, and as of December 1974 there was an arrearage in excess of $3,700. Second, the child had been a public charge since her birth, receiving benefits under the Aid to Families with Dependent Children program. It is stipulated that the child's benefit payments were such that she would have been a public charge even if appellee had been current in his support payments.

On December 24, 1974, appellee filed his complaint in the District Court, on behalf of himself and the class of all Wisconsin residents who had been refused a marriage license pursuant to § 245.10(1) by one of the county clerks in Wisconsin. . . . The complaint alleged, among other things, that appellee and the woman he desired to marry were expecting a child in March 1975 and wished to be lawfully married before that time. . . .

. . .

The leading decision of this Court on the right to marry is Loving v. Virginia, 388 U.S. 1 (1967). . . .

Although *Loving* arose in the context of racial discrimination, prior and subsequent decisions of this Court confirm that the right to marry is of fundamental importance for all individuals. Long ago, in Maynard v. Hill, 125 U.S. 190 (1888), the Court characterized marriage as "the most important relation in life," and as "the foundation of the family and of society, without which there would be neither civilization nor progress." . . .

More recent decisions have established that the right to marry is part of the fundamental "right of privacy" implicit in the Fourteenth Amendment's Due Process Clause. [See] Griswold v. Connecticut, [Chapter 3, Section D].

. . .

It is not surprising that the decision to marry has been placed on the same level of importance as decisions relating to procreation, childbirth, child rearing, and family relationships. As the facts of this case illustrate, it would make little sense to recognize a right of privacy with respect to other matters of family life and not with respect to the decision to enter the relationship that is the foundation of the family in our society. The woman whom appellee desired to marry had a fundamental right to seek an abortion of their expected child, see Roe v. Wade, [410 U.S. 113 (1973)] or to bring the child into life to suffer the myriad social, if not economic, disabilities that the status of illegitimacy brings, see Trimble v. Gordon, 430 U.S. 762, 768–770, and n. 13 (1977); Weber v. Aetna Casualty & Surety Co., 406 U.S. 164, 175–176 (1972). Surely, a decision to marry and raise the child in a traditional family setting must receive equivalent protection. And, if appellee's right to procreate means anything at all, it must imply some right to enter the only relationship in which the State of Wisconsin allows sexual relations legally to take place.

By reaffirming the fundamental character of the right to marry, we do not mean to suggest that every state regulation which relates in any way to the incidents of or prerequisites for marriage must be subjected to rigorous scrutiny. To the contrary, reasonable regulations that do not significantly interfere with decisions to enter into the marital relationship may legitimately be imposed. See Califano v. Jobst, [434 U.S. 47, 48 (1977)]. The statutory classification at issue here, however, clearly does interfere directly and substantially with the right to marry.

Under the challenged statute, no Wisconsin resident in the affected class may marry in Wisconsin or elsewhere without a court order, and marriages contracted in violation of the statute are both void and punishable as criminal offenses. Some of those in the affected class, like appellee, will never be able to obtain the necessary court order, because they either lack the financial means to meet their support obligations or cannot prove that their children will not become public charges. These persons are absolutely prevented from getting married. Many others, able in theory to satisfy the statute's requirements, will be sufficiently burdened by having to do so that they will in effect be coerced into forgoing their right to marry. And even those who can be persuaded to meet the statute's requirements suffer a serious intrusion into their freedom of choice in an area in which we have held such freedom to be fundamental.[12]

12. The directness and substantiality of the interference with the freedom to marry distinguish the instant case from Califano v. Jobst, [434 U.S. 47]. In *Jobst*, we upheld sec-

When a statutory classification significantly interferes with the exercise of a fundamental right, it cannot be upheld unless it is supported by sufficiently important state interests and is closely tailored to effectuate only those interests. . . . Appellant asserts that two interests are served by the challenged statute: the permission-to-marry proceeding furnishes an opportunity to counsel the applicant as to the necessity of fulfilling his prior support obligations; and the welfare of the out-of-custody children is protected. We may accept for present purposes that these are legitimate and substantial interests, but, since the means selected by the State for achieving these interests unnecessarily impinge on the right to marry, the statute cannot be sustained.

There is evidence that the challenged statute, as originally introduced in the Wisconsin Legislature, was intended merely to establish a mechanism whereby persons with support obligations to children from prior marriages could be counseled before they entered into new marital relationships and incurred further support obligations. Court permission to marry was to be required, but apparently permission was automatically to be granted after counseling was completed. The statute actually enacted, however, does not expressly require or provide for any counseling whatsoever, nor for any automatic granting of permission to marry by the court, and thus it can hardly be justified as a means for ensuring counseling of the persons within its coverage. Even assuming that counseling does take place—a fact as to which there is no evidence in the record—this interest obviously cannot support the withholding of court permission to marry once counseling is completed.

With regard to safeguarding the welfare of the out-of-custody children, appellant's brief does not make clear the connection between the State's interest and the statute's requirements. At argument, appellant's counsel suggested that, since permission to marry cannot be granted unless the applicant shows that he has satisfied his court-determined support obligations to the prior children and that those children will not become public charges, the statute provides incentive for the applicant to make support payments to his children. This "collection device" rationale cannot justify the statute's broad infringement on the right to marry.

First, with respect to individuals who are unable to meet the statutory requirements, the statute merely prevents the applicant from getting married, without delivering any money at all into the hands of the applicant's prior children. More importantly, regardless of the applicant's ability or willingness to meet the statutory requirements, the State already has numerous other means for exacting compliance with support obligations, means that are at least as effective as the instant statute's and yet do not impinge upon the right to marry. Under Wisconsin law, whether the children are from a prior marriage or were born out of wedlock, court-determined

tions of the Social Security Act providing for termination of a dependent child's benefits upon marriage to an individual not entitled to benefits under the Act. As the opinion for the Court expressly noted, the rule terminating benefits upon marriage was not "an attempt to interfere with the individual's freedom to make a decision as important as marriage." [434 U.S. at 54]. The Social Security provisions placed no direct legal obstacle in the path of persons desiring to get married, and . . . there was no evidence that the laws significantly discouraged, let alone made "practically impossible," any marriages. Indeed, the provisions had not deterred the individual who challenged the statute from getting married, even though he and his wife were both disabled. See Califano v. Jobst, [434 U.S., at 48]. See also [434 U.S., at 57 n. 17] (because of availability of other federal benefits, total payments to the Jobsts after marriage were only $20 per month less than they would have been had Mr. Jobst's child benefits not been terminated).

support obligations may be enforced directly via wage assignments, civil contempt proceedings, and criminal penalties. And, if the State believes that parents of children out of their custody should be responsible for ensuring that those children do not become public charges, this interest can be achieved by adjusting the criteria used for determining the amounts to be paid under their support orders.

There is also some suggestion that § 245.10 protects the ability of marriage applicants to meet support obligations to prior children by preventing the applicants from incurring new support obligations. But the challenged provisions of § 245.10 are grossly underinclusive with respect to this purpose, since they do not limit in any way new financial commitments by the applicant other than those arising out of the contemplated marriage. The statutory classification is substantially over-inclusive as well: Given the possibility that the new spouse will actually better the applicant's financial situation, by contributing income from a job or otherwise, the statute in many cases may prevent affected individuals from improving their ability to satisfy their prior support obligations. And, although it is true that the applicant will incur support obligations to any children born during the contemplated marriage, preventing the marriage may only result in the children being born out of wedlock, as in fact occurred in appellee's case. Since the support obligation is the same whether the child is born in or out of wedlock, the net result of preventing the marriage is simply more illegitimate children.

The statutory classification created by §§ 245.10(1), (4), (5) thus cannot be justified by the interests advanced in support of it. The judgment of the District Court is, accordingly,

Affirmed.

■ JUSTICE POWELL, concurring in the judgment.

I concur in the judgment of the Court that Wisconsin's restrictions on the exclusive means of creating the marital bond, erected by Wis.Stat. §§ 245.10(1), (4), and (5) (1973), cannot meet applicable constitutional standards. I write separately because the majority's rationale sweeps too broadly in an area which traditionally has been subject to pervasive state regulation. The Court apparently would subject all state regulation which "directly and substantially" interferes with the decision to marry in a traditional family setting to "critical examination" or "compelling state interest" analysis. Presumably, "reasonable regulations that do not significantly interfere with decisions to enter into the marital relationship may legitimately be imposed." The Court does not present, however, any principled means for distinguishing between the two types of regulations. Since state regulation in this area typically takes the form of a prerequisite or barrier to marriage or divorce, the degree of "direct" interference with the decision to marry or to divorce is unlikely to provide either guidance for state legislatures or a basis for judicial oversight.

On several occasions, the Court has acknowledged the importance of the marriage relationship to the maintenance of values essential to organized society....

Thus, it is fair to say that there is a right of marital and familial privacy which places some substantive limits on the regulatory power of government. But the Court has yet to hold that all regulation touching upon marriage implicates a "fundamental right" triggering the most exacting judicial scrutiny.[1]

The principal authority cited by the majority is Loving v. Virginia, 388 U.S. 1 (1967).... [But] *Loving* involved a denial of a "fundamental freedom" on a wholly unsupportable basis—the use of classifications "directly subversive of the principle of equality at the heart of the Fourteenth Amendment...." It does not speak to the level of judicial scrutiny of, or governmental justification for, "supportable" restrictions on the "fundamental freedom" of individuals to marry or divorce.

In my view, analysis must start from the recognition of domestic relations as "an area that has long been regarded as a virtually exclusive province of the States." Sosna v. Iowa, 419 U.S. 393, 404 (1975). The marriage relation traditionally has been subject to regulation, initially by the ecclesiastical authorities, and later by the secular state. As early as Pennoyer v. Neff, 95 U.S. 714, 734–735 (1878), this Court noted that a State "has absolute right to prescribe the conditions upon which the marriage relation between its own citizens shall be created, and the causes for which it may be dissolved." The State, representing the collective expression of moral aspirations, has an undeniable interest in ensuring that its rules of domestic relations reflect the widely held values of its people.... State regulation has included bans on incest, bigamy, and homosexuality, as well as various preconditions to marriage, such as blood tests. Likewise, a showing of fault on the part of one of the partners traditionally has been a prerequisite to the dissolution of an unsuccessful union. A "compelling state purpose" inquiry would cast doubt on the network of restrictions that the States have fashioned to govern marriage and divorce.

State power over domestic relations is not without constitutional limits. The Due Process Clause requires a showing of justification "when the government intrudes on choices concerning family living arrangements" in a manner which is contrary to deeply rooted traditions. Moore v. East Cleveland, 431 U.S. 494, 499, 503–504 (1977) (plurality opinion). Due process constraints also limit the extent to which the State may monopolize the process of ordering certain human relationships while excluding the truly indigent from that process. Boddie v. Connecticut, 401 U.S. 371 (1971). Furthermore, under the Equal Protection Clause the means chosen by the State in this case must bear " 'a fair and substantial relation' " to the object of the legislation. Reed v. Reed, 404 U.S. 71, 76 (1971), quoting Royster Guano Co. v. Virginia, 253 U.S. 412, 415 (1920).

The Wisconsin measure in this case does not pass muster under either due process or equal protection standards. Appellant identifies three objectives which are supposedly furthered by the statute in question: (i) a counseling function; (ii) an incentive to satisfy outstanding support obligations; and (iii) a deterrent against incurring further obligations. The opinion of the Court amply demonstrates that the asserted counseling objective bears no relation to this statute....

The so-called "collection device" rationale presents a somewhat more difficult question. I do not agree with the suggestion in the Court's opinion that a State may never condition the right to marry on satisfaction of existing

1. Although the cases cited in the text indicate that there is a sphere of privacy or autonomy surrounding an existing marital relationship into which the State may not lightly intrude, they do not necessarily suggest that the same barrier of justification blocks regulation of the conditions of entry into or the dissolution of the marital bond. See generally Henkin, Privacy and Autonomy, 74 Colum.L.Rev. 1410, 1429–1432 (1974).

support obligations simply because the State has alternative methods of compelling such payments. To the extent this restriction applies to persons who are able to make the required support payments but simply wish to shirk their moral and legal obligation, the Constitution interposes no bar to this additional collection mechanism. The vice inheres, not in the collection concept, but in the failure to make provision for those without the means to comply with child support obligations. I draw support from Mr. Justice Harlan's opinion in Boddie v. Connecticut. In that case, the Court struck down filing fees for divorce actions as applied to those wholly unable to pay, holding "that a State may not, consistent with the obligations imposed on it by the Due Process Clause of the Fourteenth Amendment, pre-empt the right to dissolve this legal relationship without affording all citizens access to the means it has prescribed for doing so." 401 U.S., at 383. The monopolization present in this case is total, for Wisconsin will not recognize foreign marriages that fail to conform to the requirements of § 245.10.

The third justification, only obliquely advanced by appellant, is that the statute preserves the ability of marriage applicants to support their prior issue by preventing them from incurring new obligations. The challenged provisions of § 245.10 are so grossly underinclusive with respect to this objective, given the many ways that additional financial obligations may be incurred by the applicant quite apart from a contemplated marriage, that the classification "does not bear a fair and substantial relation to the object of the legislation." Craig v. Boren, [429 U.S. 190, 211 (1976)] (Powell, J., concurring).

The marriage applicant is required by the Wisconsin statute not only to submit proof of compliance with his support obligation, but also to demonstrate—in some unspecified way—that his children "are not then and are not likely thereafter to become public charges." This statute does more than simply "fail to alleviate the consequences of differences in economic circumstances that exist wholly apart from any state action." Griffin v. Illinois, 351 U.S. 12, 34 (1956) (Harlan, J., dissenting). It tells the truly indigent, whether they have met their support obligations or not, that they may not marry so long as their children are public charges or there is a danger that their children might go on public assistance in the future. Apparently, no other jurisdiction has embraced this approach as a method of reducing the number of children on public assistance. Because the State has not established a justification for this unprecedented foreclosure of marriage to many of its citizens solely because of their indigency, I concur in the judgment of the Court.

■ Justice Stevens, concurring in the judgment.

. . .

When a State allocates benefits or burdens, it may have valid reasons for treating married and unmarried persons differently. Classification based on marital status has been an accepted characteristic of tax legislation, Selective Service rules, and Social Security regulations. As cases like *Jobst* demonstrate, such laws may "significantly interfere with decisions to enter into the marital relationship." That kind of interference, however, is not a sufficient reason for invalidating every law reflecting a legislative judgment that there are relevant differences between married persons as a class and unmarried persons as a class.[1]

1. In *Jobst,* we pointed out that "it was rational for Congress to assume that marital status is a relevant test of probable dependency. . . ." We had explained:

A classification based on marital status is fundamentally different from a classification which determines who may lawfully enter into the marriage relationship.[2] The individual's interest in making the marriage decision independently is sufficiently important to merit special constitutional protection. It is not, however, an interest which is constitutionally immune from evenhanded regulation. Thus, laws prohibiting marriage to a child, a close relative, or a person afflicted with venereal disease, are unchallenged even though they "interfere directly and substantially with the right to marry." This Wisconsin statute has a different character.

Under this statute, a person's economic status may determine his eligibility to enter into a lawful marriage. A noncustodial parent whose children are "public charges" may not marry even if he has met his court-ordered obligations. Thus, within the class of parents who have fulfilled their court-ordered obligations, the rich may marry and the poor may not. This type of statutory discrimination is, I believe, totally unprecedented,[4] as well as inconsistent with our tradition of administering justice equally to the rich and to the poor.

The statute appears to reflect a legislative judgment that persons who have demonstrated an inability to support their offspring should not be permitted to marry and thereafter to bring additional children into the world.[6] Even putting to one side the growing number of childless marriages and the burgeoning number of children born out of wedlock, that sort of reasoning cannot justify this deliberate discrimination against the poor.

The statute prevents impoverished parents from marrying even though their intended spouses are economically independent. Presumably, the Wisconsin Legislature assumed (a) that only fathers would be affected by the legislation, and (b) that they would never marry employed women. The first assumption ignores the fact that fathers are sometimes awarded custody,[7] and the second ignores the composition of today's work force. To the extent that the statute denies a hardpressed parent any opportunity to prove that

"Both tradition and common experience support the conclusion that marriage is an event which normally marks an important change in economic status. Traditionally, the event not only creates a new family with attendant new responsibilities, but also modifies the pre-existing relationships between the bride and groom and their respective families. Frequently, of course, financial independence and marriage do not go hand in hand. Nevertheless, there can be no question about the validity of the assumption that a married person is less likely to be dependent on his parents for support than one who is unmarried." [434 U.S. at 53].

2. *Jobst* is in the former category; Loving v. Virginia, 388 U.S. 1, is in the latter.

4. The economic aspects of a prospective marriage are unquestionably relevant to almost every individual's marriage decision. But I know of no other state statute that denies the individual marriage partners the right to assess the financial consequences of their decision independently. I seriously question whether any limitation on the right to marry may be predicated on economic status, but that question need not be answered in this case.

6. The "public charge" provision, which falls on parents who have faithfully met their obligations, but who are unable to pay enough to remove their children from the welfare rolls, obviously cannot be justified by a state interest in assuring the payment of child support. And, of course, it would be absurd for the State to contend that an interest in providing paternalistic counseling supports a total ban on marriage.

7. The Wisconsin Legislature has itself provided:

> "In determining the parent with whom a child shall remain, the court shall consider all facts in the best interest of the child and shall not prefer one parent over the other solely on the basis of the sex of the parent." Wis.Stat. § 247.24(3) (1977).

an intended marriage will ease rather than aggravate his financial straits, it not only rests on unreliable premises, but also defeats its own objectives.

These questionable assumptions also explain why this statutory blunderbuss is wide of the target in another respect. The prohibition on marriage applies to the noncustodial parent but allows the parent who has custody to marry without the State's leave. Yet the danger that new children will further strain an inadequate budget is equally great for custodial and noncustodial parents, unless one assumes (a) that only mothers will ever have custody and (b) that they will never marry unemployed men.

Characteristically, this law fails to regulate the marriages of those parents who are least likely to be able to afford another family, for it applies only to parents under a court order to support their children. Wis.Stat. § 245.10(1). The very poorest parents are unlikely to be the objects of support orders. If the State meant to prevent the marriage of those who have demonstrated their inability to provide for children, it overlooked the most obvious targets of legislative concern.

In sum, the public charge provision is either futile or perverse insofar as it applies to childless couples, couples who will have illegitimate children if they are forbidden to marry, couples whose economic status will be improved by marriage, and couples who are so poor that the marriage will have no impact on the welfare status of their children in any event. Even assuming that the right to marry may sometimes be denied on economic grounds, this clumsy and deliberate legislative discrimination between the rich and the poor is irrational in so many ways that it cannot withstand scrutiny under the Equal Protection Clause of the Fourteenth Amendment.[10]

■ JUSTICE REHNQUIST, dissenting.

I substantially agree with my Brother Powell's reasons for rejecting the Court's conclusion that marriage is the sort of "fundamental right" which must invariably trigger the strictest judicial scrutiny. I disagree with his imposition of an "intermediate" standard of review, which leads him to conclude that the statute, though generally valid as an "additional collection mechanism" offends the Constitution by its "failure to make provision for those without the means to comply with child support obligations." For similar reasons, I disagree with my Brother Stewart's conclusion that the statute is invalid for its failure to exempt those persons who "simply cannot afford to meet the statute's financial requirements." I would view this legislative judgment in the light of the traditional presumption of validity. I think that under the Equal Protection Clause the statute need pass only the "rational basis test," and that under the Due Process Clause it need only be shown that it bears a rational relation to a constitutionally permissible objective. The statute so viewed is a permissible exercise of the State's power to regulate family life and to assure the support of minor children, despite its possible imprecision in the extreme cases envisioned in the concurring opinions.

. . .

10. Neither the fact that the appellee's interest is constitutionally protected, nor the fact that the classification is based on economic status is sufficient to justify a "level of scrutiny" so strict that a holding of unconstitutionality is virtually foreordained. On the other hand, the presence of these factors precludes a holding that a rational expectation of occasional and random benefit is sufficient to demonstrate compliance with the constitutional command to govern impartially. See Craig v. Boren, 429 U.S. 190, 211 (Stevens, J., concurring).

. . . Because of the limited amount of funds available for the support of needy children, the State has an exceptionally strong interest in securing as much support as their parents are able to pay. Nor does the extent of the burden imposed by this statute so differentiate it from that considered in Jobst as to warrant a different result. In the case of some applicants, this statute makes the proposed marriage legally impossible for financial reasons; in a similar number of extreme cases, the Social Security Act makes the proposed marriage practically impossible for the same reasons. I cannot conclude that such a difference justifies the application of a heightened standard of review to the statute in question here. In short, I conclude that the statute, despite its imperfections, is sufficiently rational to satisfy the demands of the Fourteenth Amendment.

NOTE

What is the constitutional status of marriage regulations after Redhail? The majority opinion holds that "reasonable regulations that do not significantly interfere with decisions to enter into the marital relationship" are constitutional. But surely state laws barring incestuous marriages "significantly interfere" for couples who are so related. Does the majority opinion mean that such state laws are unconstitutional?

Justice Stevens in his concurring opinion asserts there is a difference between classifications based on marital status and those that determine who may lawfully marry. Is the asserted difference simply a reflection of the fact that restrictions on married couples are by definition "indirect" restrictions, and thus constitutional? Compare Mapes v. United States, 217 Ct.Cl. 115, 576 F.2d 896 (1978), cert. denied, 439 U.S. 1046 (1978) (upholding different income tax rates for married and single taxpayers resulting in a "marriage penalty"); Druker v. Commissioner, 697 F.2d 46 (2d Cir.1982) (accord). The same constitutional rationale has been used to support marriage subsidies. See Peden v. State Dep't of Revenue, 261 Kan. 239, 930 P.2d 1 (1996) (upholding a tax schedule with individual rates higher than the highest possible rate for a married couple filing jointly).

Turner v. Safley

Supreme Court of the United States, 1987.
482 U.S. 78, 107 S.Ct. 2254, 96 L.Ed.2d 64.

■ JUSTICE O'CONNOR delivered the opinion of the Court.

This case requires us to determine the constitutionality of regulations promulgated by the Missouri Division of Corrections relating to inmate marriages. . . .

The challenged marriage regulation, which was promulgated while this litigation was pending, permits an inmate to marry only with the permission of the superintendent of the prison, and provides that such approval should be given only "when there are compelling reasons to do so." The term "compelling" is not defined, but prison officials testified at trial that generally only a pregnancy or the birth of an illegitimate child would be considered a compelling reason. Prior to the promulgation of this rule, the applicable regulation did not obligate Missouri Division of Corrections officials to assist an inmate who wanted to get married, but it also did not specifically authorize the superintendent of an institution to prohibit inmates from getting married.

. . .

In support of the marriage regulation, petitioners first suggest that the rule does not deprive prisoners of a constitutionally protected right. They concede that the decision to marry is a fundamental right under Zablocki v. Redhail and Loving v. Virginia, but they imply that a different rule should obtain "in . . . a prison forum." Petitioners then argue that even if the regulation burdens inmates' constitutional rights, the restriction should be tested under a reasonableness standard. They urge that the restriction is reasonably related to legitimate security and rehabilitation concerns.

We disagree with petitioners that *Zablocki* does not apply to prison inmates. It is settled that a prison inmate "retains those [constitutional] rights that are not inconsistent with his status as a prisoner or with the legitimate penological objectives of the corrections system." The right to marry, like many other rights, is subject to substantial restrictions as a result of incarceration. Many important attributes of marriage remain, however, after taking into account the limitations imposed by prison life. First, inmate marriages, like others, are expressions of emotional support and public commitment. These elements are an important and significant aspect of the marital relationship. In addition, many religions recognize marriage as having spiritual significance; for some inmates and their spouses, therefore, the commitment of marriage may be an exercise of religious faith as well as an expression of personal dedication. Third, most inmates eventually will be released by parole or commutation, and therefore most inmate marriages are formed in the expectation that they ultimately will be fully consummated. Finally, marital status often is a precondition to the receipt of government benefits (e.g., Social Security benefits), property rights (e.g., tenancy by the entirety, inheritance rights), and other, less tangible benefits (e.g., legitimation of children born out of wedlock). These incidents of marriage, like the religious and personal aspects of the marriage commitment are unaffected by the fact of confinement or the pursuit of legitimate corrections goals.

Taken together, we conclude that these remaining elements are sufficient to form a constitutionally protected marital relationship in the prison context. Our decision in Butler v. Wilson, 415 U.S. 953 (1974), summarily affirming Johnson v. Rockefeller, 365 F.Supp. 377 (S.D.N.Y.1973), is not to the contrary. That case involved a prohibition on marriage only for inmates sentenced to life imprisonment; and, importantly, denial of the right was part of the punishment for crime. . . .

Petitioners have identified both security and rehabilitation concerns in support of the marriage prohibition. The security concern emphasized by petitioners is that "love triangles" might lead to violent confrontations between inmates. With respect to rehabilitation, prison officials testified that female prisoners often were subject to abuse at home or were overly dependent on male figures, and that this dependence or abuse was connected to the crimes they had committed. The superintendent at Renz, petitioner William Turner, testified that in his view, these women prisoners needed to concentrate on developing skills of self-reliance, and that the prohibition on marriage furthered this rehabilitative goal. Petitioners emphasize that the prohibition on marriage should be understood in light of Superintendent Turner's experience with several ill-advised marriage requests from female inmates.

We conclude that on this record, the Missouri prison regulation, as written, is not reasonably related to these penological interests. No doubt legitimate security concerns may require placing reasonable restrictions upon an inmate's right to marry, and may justify requiring approval of the superintendent. The Missouri regulation, however, represents an exaggerated response to such security objectives. There are obvious, easy alternatives to the Missouri regulation that accommodate the right to marry while imposing a *de minimis* burden on the pursuit of security objectives. See, e.g., 28 CFR § 551.10 (1986) (marriage by inmates in federal prison generally permitted, but not if warden finds that it presents a threat to security or order of institution, or to public safety). We are aware of no place in the record where prison officials testified that such ready alternatives would not fully satisfy their security concerns. Moreover, with respect to the security concern emphasized in petitioners' brief—the creation of "love triangles"—petitioners have pointed to nothing in the record suggesting that the marriage regulation was viewed as preventing such entanglements. Common sense likewise suggests that there is no logical connection between the marriage restriction and the formation of love triangles: surely in prisons housing both male and female prisoners, inmate rivalries are as likely to develop without a formal marriage ceremony as with one. Finally, this is not an instance where the "ripple effect" on the security of fellow inmates and prison staff justifies a broad restriction on inmates' rights—indeed, where the inmate wishes to marry a civilian, the decision to marry (apart from the logistics of the wedding ceremony) is a completely private one.

Nor, on this record, is the marriage restriction reasonably related to the articulated rehabilitation goal. First, in requiring refusal of permission absent a finding of a compelling reason to allow the marriage, the rule sweeps much more broadly than can be explained by petitioners' penological objectives. Missouri prison officials testified that generally they had experienced no problem with the marriage of male inmates, and the District Court found that such marriages had routinely been allowed as a matter of practice at Missouri correctional institutions prior to adoption of the rule. The proffered justification thus does not explain the adoption of a rule banning marriages by these inmates. Nor does it account for the prohibition on inmate marriages to civilians. Missouri prison officials testified that generally they had no objection to inmate-civilian marriages, and Superintendent Turner testified that he usually did not object to the marriage of either male or female prisoners to civilians. The rehabilitation concern appears from the record to have been centered almost exclusively on female inmates marrying other inmates or ex-felons; it does not account for the ban on inmate-civilian marriages.

Moreover, although not necessary to the disposition of this case, we note that on this record the rehabilitative objective asserted to support the regulation itself is suspect. Of the several female inmates whose marriage requests were discussed by prison officials at trial, only one was refused on the basis of fostering excessive dependency. The District Court found that the Missouri prison system operated on the basis of excessive paternalism in that the proposed marriages of all female inmates were scrutinized carefully even before adoption of the current regulation—only one was approved at Renz in the period from 1979–1983—whereas the marriages of male inmates during the same period were routinely approved. That kind of lopsided rehabilitation concern cannot provide a justification for the broad Missouri marriage rule.

It is undisputed that Missouri prison officials may regulate the time and circumstances under which the marriage ceremony itself takes place. On this record, however, the almost complete ban on the decision to marry is not reasonably related to legitimate penological objectives. We conclude, therefore, that the Missouri marriage regulation is facially invalid.

NOTES

1. In Langone v. Coughlin, 712 F.Supp. 1061 (N.D.N.Y.1989), plaintiff brought a successful class action suit challenging the constitutionality of a New York law and its implementing directive that barred prisoners sentenced to life imprisonment from entering into a marriage until paroled. The court followed the *Turner* intermediate standard of "whether the regulation bears a reasonable relationship to legitimate penological interests." It reviewed the four factors that bear on the reasonableness determination. First, the court determined that there was no rational relationship between the prohibition of life inmates' rights to marry and the governmental interests put forth to justify it. Second, the court found that there were no alternative means available to plaintiffs that would allow them to exercise the right to marry. Third, although acknowledging that deference should be given to the judgments of corrections officials, the court found that accommodating the inmates' right to marry would not jeopardize the security of fellow inmates or prison staff. Finally, the court agreed with the inmates' assertion that there was no ready alternative to the fundamental right to marry.

2. In Akers v. McGinnis, 352 F.3d 1030 (6th Cir. 2003), the court upheld a correctional facility rule barring employees from intimate associations with prisoners, visitors, or family of inmates under a rational basis test. The court found that preventing inmate/correctional worker intimate relations was a legitimate penological interest and that barring relations with inmates' visitors and family was reasonably related to that interest. The court dismissed arguments made by the plaintiffs concerning First Amendment assembly and association rights and compared the rule to the anti-fraternization and anti-nepotism rules that abound in the private sector. For more on anti-nepotism rules see Chapter 3, Section C.

Michael H. v. Gerald D.

Supreme Court of the United States, 1989.
491 U.S. 110, 109 S.Ct. 2333, 105 L.Ed.2d 91.

■ JUSTICE SCALIA announced the judgment of the Court and delivered an opinion, in which THE CHIEF JUSTICE joins, and in all but note 6 of which JUSTICE O'CONNOR and JUSTICE KENNEDY join.

. . .

The facts of this case are, we must hope, extraordinary. On May 9, 1976, in Las Vegas, Nevada, Carole D., an international model, and Gerald D., a top executive in a French oil company, were married. The couple established a home in Playa del Rey, California in which they resided as husband and wife when one or the other was not out of the country on business. In the summer of 1978, Carole became involved in an adulterous affair with a neighbor, Michael H. In September 1980, she conceived a child, Victoria D., who was born on May 11, 1981. Gerald was listed as father on the birth certificate and has always held Victoria out to the world as his daughter. Soon after delivery of the child, however, Carole informed Michael that she believed he might be the father.

In the first three years of her life, Victoria remained always with Carole, but found herself within a variety of quasi-family units. In October 1981, Gerald moved to New York City to pursue his business interests, but Carole chose to remain in California. The end of that month, Carole and Michael had blood tests of themselves and Victoria, which showed a 98.07% probability that Michael was Victoria's father. In January 1982, Carole visited Michael in St. Thomas, where his primary business interests were based. There Michael held Victoria out as his child. In March, however, Carole left Michael and returned to California, where she took up residence with yet another man, Scott K. Later that spring, and again in the summer, Carole and Victoria spent time with Gerald in New York City, as well as on vacation in Europe. In the fall, they returned to Scott in California.

In November 1982, rebuffed in his attempts to visit Victoria, Michael filed a filiation action in California Superior Court to establish his paternity and right to visitation. In March 1983, the court appointed an attorney and guardian ad litem to represent Victoria's interests. Victoria then filed a cross-complaint asserting that if she had more than one psychological or *de facto* father, she was entitled to maintain her filial relationship, with all of the attendant rights, duties, and obligations, with both. In May 1983, Carole filed a motion for summary judgment. During this period, from March through July of 1983, Carole was again living with Gerald in New York. In August, however, she returned to California, became involved once again with Michael, and instructed her attorneys to remove the summary judgment motion from the calendar.

For the ensuing eight months, when Michael was not in St. Thomas he lived with Carole and Victoria in Carole's apartment in Los Angeles, and held Victoria out as his daughter. In April 1984, Carole and Michael signed a stipulation that Michael was Victoria's natural father. Carole left Michael the next month, however, and instructed her attorneys not to file the stipulation. In June 1984, Carole reconciled with Gerald and joined him in New York, where they now live with Victoria and two other children since born into the marriage.

In May 1984, Michael and Victoria, through her guardian ad litem, sought visitation rights for Michael *pendente lite*. To assist in determining whether visitation would be in Victoria's best interests, the Superior Court appointed a psychologist to evaluate Victoria, Gerald, Michael, and Carole. The psychologist recommended that Carole retain sole custody, but that Michael be allowed continued contact with Victoria pursuant to a restricted visitation schedule. The court concurred and ordered that Michael be provided with limited visitation privileges *pendente lite*.

Michael wants visitation

On October 19, 1984, Gerald, who had intervened in the action, moved for summary judgment on the ground that under Cal.Evid.Code § 621 there were no triable issues of fact as to Victoria's paternity. This law provides that "the issue of a wife cohabiting with her husband, who is not impotent or sterile, is conclusively presumed to be a child of the marriage." The presumption may be rebutted by blood tests, but only if a motion for such tests is made, within two years from the date of the child's birth, either by the husband or, if the natural father has filed an affidavit acknowledging paternity, by the wife.

Gerald's summary judgment

On January 28, 1985, having found that affidavits submitted by Carole and Gerald sufficed to demonstrate that the two were cohabiting at conception and birth and that Gerald was neither sterile nor impotent, the Superior Court granted Gerald's motion for summary judgment, rejecting Michael's and Victoria's challenges to the constitutionality of § 621. The court also denied their motions for continued visitation pending the appeal.... [T]he California Court of Appeal affirmed the judgment of the Superior Court and upheld the constitutionality of the statute....

. . .

Michael contends as a matter of substantive due process that because he has established a parental relationship with Victoria, protection of Gerald's and Carole's marital union is an insufficient state interest to support termination of that relationship. This argument is, of course, predicated on the assertion that Michael has a constitutionally protected liberty interest in his relationship with Victoria.

. . . In an attempt to limit and guide interpretation of the [Due Process] Clause, we have insisted not merely that the interest denominated as a "liberty" be "fundamental" (a concept that, in isolation, is hard to objectify), but also that it be an interest traditionally protected by our society. As we have put it, the Due Process Clause affords only those protections "so rooted in the traditions and conscience of our people as to be ranked as fundamental." Our cases reflect "continual insistence upon respect for the teachings of history [and] solid recognition of the basic values that underlie our society. . . ." Griswold v. Connecticut, (Harlan, J., concurring in judgment).

This insistence that the asserted liberty interest be rooted in history and tradition is evident, as elsewhere, in our cases according constitutional protection to certain parental rights. Michael reads the landmark case of Stanley v. Illinois [Chapter 4, Section I] and the subsequent cases of *Quilloin v. Walcott, Caban v. Mohammed,* and *Lehr v. Robertson,* as establishing that a liberty interest is created by biological fatherhood plus an established parental relationship—factors that exist in the present case as well. We think that distorts the rationale of those cases. As we view them, they rest not upon such isolated factors but upon the historic respect—indeed, sanctity would not be too strong a term—traditionally accorded to the relationships that develop within the unitary family.[5] In *Stanley,* for example, we forbade the destruction of such a family when, upon the death of the mother, the state had sought to remove children from the custody of a father who had lived with and supported them and their mother for 18 years. As Justice Powell stated for the plurality in Moore v. East Cleveland: "Our decisions establish that the Constitution protects the sanctity of the family precisely because the institution of the family is deeply rooted in this Nation's history and tradition."

Thus, the legal issue in the present case reduces to whether the relationship between persons in the situation of Michael and Victoria has been treated as a protected family unit under the historic practices of our society, or whether on any other basis it has been accorded special protection. We think it impossible to find that it has. In fact, quite to the contrary, our traditions have protected the marital family (Gerald, Carole, and the child they acknowledge to be theirs) against the sort of claim Michael asserts.

The presumption of legitimacy was a fundamental principle of the common law. Traditionally, that presumption could be rebutted only by proof that a husband was incapable of procreation or had had no access to his wife during the relevant period. As explained by Blackstone, nonaccess could only be proved "if the husband be out of the kingdom of England (or, as the law somewhat loosely phrases it, *extra quatuor maria* [beyond the four seas]) for above nine months. . . ." 1 Blackstone's Commentaries 456 (Chitty

5. Justice Brennan asserts that only "a pinched conception of 'the family'" would exclude Michael, Carole and Victoria from protection. We disagree. The family unit accorded traditional respect in our society, which we have referred to as the "unitary family," is typified, of course, by the marital family, but also includes the household of unmarried parents and their children. Perhaps the concept can be expanded even beyond this, but it will bear no resemblance to traditionally respected relationships—and will thus cease to have any constitutional significance—if it is stretched so far as to include the relationship established between a married woman, her lover and their child, during a three-month sojourn in St. Thomas, or during a subsequent 8-month period when, if he happened to be in Los Angeles, he stayed with her and the child.

ed. 1826). And, under the common law both in England and here, "neither husband nor wife [could] be a witness to prove access or nonaccess." The primary policy rationale underlying the common law's severe restrictions on rebuttal of the presumption appears to have been an aversion to declaring children illegitimate, thereby depriving them of rights of inheritance and succession, and likely making them wards of the state. A secondary policy concern was the interest in promoting the "peace and tranquility of States and families," a goal that is obviously impaired by facilitating suits against husband and wife asserting that their children are illegitimate. Even though, as bastardy laws became less harsh, "[j]udges in both [England and the United States] gradually widened the acceptable range of evidence that could be offered by spouses, and placed restraints on the 'four seas rule' . . . [,] the law retained a strong bias against ruling the children of married women illegitimate."

We have found nothing in the older sources, nor in the older cases, addressing specifically the power of the natural father to assert parental rights over a child born into a woman's existing marriage with another man. Since it is Michael's burden to establish that such a power (at least where the natural father has established a relationship with the child) is so deeply embedded within our traditions as to be a fundamental right, the lack of evidence alone might defeat his case. But the evidence shows that even in modern times—when, as we have noted, the rigid protection of the marital family has in other respects been relaxed—the ability of a person in Michael's position to claim paternity has not been generally acknowledged. . . .

Moreover, even if it were clear that one in Michael's position generally possesses, and has generally always possessed, standing to challenge the marital child's legitimacy, that would still not establish Michael's case. As noted earlier, what is at issue here is not entitlement to a state pronouncement that Victoria was begotten by Michael. It is no conceivable denial of constitutional right for a State to decline to declare facts unless some legal consequence hinges upon the requested declaration. What Michael asserts here is a right to have himself declared the natural father *and thereby to obtain parental prerogatives*. What he must establish, therefore, is not that our society has traditionally allowed a natural father in his circumstances to establish paternity, but that it has traditionally accorded such a father parental rights, or at least has not traditionally denied them. Even if the law in all States had always been that the entire world could challenge the marital presumption and obtain a declaration as to who was the natural father, that would not advance Michael's claim. Thus, it is ultimately irrelevant, even for purposes of determining *current* social attitudes towards the alleged substantive right Michael asserts, that the present law in a number of States appears to allow the natural father—including the natural father who has not established a relationship with the child—the theoretical power to rebut the marital presumption, see Note, Rebutting the Marital Presumption: A Developed Relationship Test, 88 Col.L.Rev. 369, 373 (1988). What counts is whether the States in fact award substantive parental rights to the natural father of a child conceived within and born into an extant marital union that wishes to embrace the child. We are not aware of a single case, old or new, that has done so. This is not the stuff of which fundamental rights qualifying as liberty interests are made.[6]

. . .

6. Justice Brennan criticizes our methodology in using historical traditions specifically relating to the rights of an adulterous natural father, rather than inquiring more

We do not accept Justice Brennan's criticism that this result "squashes" the liberty that consists of "the freedom not to conform." It seems to us that reflects the erroneous view that there is only one side to this controversy—that one disposition can expand a "liberty" of sorts without contracting an equivalent "liberty" on the other side. Such a happy choice is rarely available. Here, to *provide* protection to an adulterous natural father is to *deny* protection to a marital father, and vice versa. If Michael has a "freedom not to conform" (whatever that means), Gerald must equivalently have a "freedom to conform." One of them will pay a price for asserting that "freedom"—Michael by being unable to act as father of the child he has adulterously begotten, or Gerald by being unable to preserve the integrity of the traditional family unit he and Victoria have established. Our disposition does not choose between these two "freedoms," but leaves that to the people of California. Justice Brennan's approach chooses one of them as the constitutional imperative, on no apparent basis except that the unconventional is to be preferred.

generally "whether parenthood is an interest that historically has received our attention and protection." There seems to us no basis for the contention that this methodology is "nove[l],". For example, in Bowers v. Hardwick, we noted that at the time the Fourteenth Amendment was ratified all but 5 of the 37 States had criminal sodomy laws, that all 50 of the States had such laws prior to 1961, and that 24 States and the District of Columbia continued to have them; and we concluded from that record, regarding that very specific aspect of sexual conduct, that "to claim that a right to engage in such conduct is 'deeply rooted in this Nation's history and tradition' or 'implicit in the concept of ordered liberty' is, at best, facetious." In Roe v. Wade, we spent about a fifth of our opinion negating the proposition that there was a long-standing tradition of laws proscribing abortion.

We do not understand why, having rejected our focus upon the societal tradition regarding the natural father's rights vis-à-vis a child whose mother is married to another man, Justice Brennan would choose to focus instead upon "parenthood." Why should the relevant category not be even more general—perhaps "family relationships"; or "personal relationships"; or even "emotional attachments in general"? Though the dissent has no basis for the level of generality it would select, we do: We refer to the most specific level at which a relevant tradition protecting, or denying protection to, the asserted right can be identified. If, for example, there were no societal tradition, either way, regarding the rights of the natural father of a child adulterously conceived, we would have to consult, and (if possible) reason from, the traditions regarding natural fathers in general. But there is such a more specific tradition, and it unqualifiedly denies protection to such a parent.

One would think that Justice Brennan would appreciate the value of consulting the most specific tradition available, since he acknowledges that "[e]ven if we can agree ... that 'family' and 'parenthood' are part of the good life, it is absurd to assume that we can agree on the content of those terms and destructive to pretend that we do." Because such general traditions provide such imprecise guidance, they permit judges to dictate rather than discern the society's views. The need, if arbitrary decision-making is to be avoided, to adopt the most specific tradition as the point of reference—or at least to announce, as Justice Brennan declines to do, some other criterion for selecting among the innumerable relevant traditions that could be consulted—is well enough exemplified by the fact that in the present case Justice Brennan's opinion and Justice O'Connor's opinion, which disapproves this footnote, *both* appeal to tradition, but on the basis of the tradition they select reach opposite results. Although assuredly having the virtue (if it be that) of leaving judges free to decide as they think best when the unanticipated occurs, a rule of law that binds neither by text nor by any particular, identifiable tradition, is no rule of law at all.

Finally, we may note that this analysis is not inconsistent with the result in cases such as Griswold v. Connecticut, or Eisenstadt v. Baird. None of those cases acknowledged a longstanding and still extant societal tradition withholding the very right pronounced to be the subject of a liberty interest and then rejected it. Justice Brennan must do so here. In this case, the existence of such a tradition, continuing to the present day, refutes any possible contention that the alleged right is "so rooted in the traditions and conscience of our people as to be ranked as fundamental," or "implicit in the concept of ordered liberty."

We have never had occasion to decide whether a child has a liberty interest, symmetrical with that of her parent, in maintaining her filial relationship. We need not do so here because, even assuming that such a right exists, Victoria's claim must fail. Victoria's due process challenge is, if anything, weaker than Michael's. Her basic claim is not that California has erred in preventing her from establishing that Michael, not Gerald, should stand as her legal father. Rather, she claims a due process right to maintain filial relationships with both Michael and Gerald. This assertion merits little discussion, for, whatever the merits of the guardian ad litem's belief that such an arrangement can be of great psychological benefit to a child, the claim that a State must recognize multiple fatherhood has no support in the history or traditions of this country. Moreover, even if we were to construe Victoria's argument as forwarding the lesser proposition that, whatever her status vis-à-vis Gerald, she has a liberty interest in maintaining a filial relationship with her natural father, Michael, we find that, at best, her claim is the obverse of Michael's and fails for the same reasons.

. . .

The judgment of the California Court of Appeal is

Affirmed.

■ JUSTICE O'CONNOR, with whom JUSTICE KENNEDY joins, concurring in part.

I concur in all but footnote 6 of JUSTICE SCALIA's opinion. This footnote sketches a mode of historical analysis to be used when identifying liberty interests protected by the Due Process Clause of the Fourteenth Amendment that may be somewhat inconsistent with our past decisions in this area. On occasion the Court has characterized relevant traditions protecting asserted rights at levels of generality that might not be "the most specific level" available. I would not foreclose the unanticipated by the prior imposition of a single mode of historical analysis.

. . .

■ [JUSTICE STEVENS concurred in the judgment.]

■ JUSTICE BRENNAN, with whom JUSTICE MARSHALL and JUSTICE BLACKMUN join, dissenting.

In a case that has yielded so many opinions as has this one, it is fruitful to begin by emphasizing the common ground shared by a majority of this Court. Five Members of the Court refuse to foreclose "the possibility that a natural father might ever have a constitutionally protected interest in his relationship with a child whose mother was married to and cohabiting with another man at the time of the child's conception and birth." (STEVENS, J., concurring in judgment). Five Justices agree that the flaw inhering in a conclusive presumption that terminates a constitutionally protected interest without any hearing whatsoever is a *procedural* one. See (WHITE, J., dissenting); (STEVENS, J., concurring in judgment). Four Members of the Court agree that Michael H. has a liberty interest in his relationship with Victoria, see (WHITE, J., dissenting), and one assumes for purposes of this case that he does, see (STEVENS, J., concurring in judgment).

In contrast, only two Members of the Court fully endorse Justice Scalia's view of the proper method of analyzing questions arising under the Due Process Clause. See (O'CONNOR, J., concurring in part). Nevertheless, because the plurality opinion's exclusively historical analysis portends a significant and unfortunate departure from our prior cases and from sound constitutional decisionmaking, I devote a substantial portion of my discussion to it.

. . .

Once we recognized that the "liberty" protected by the Due Process Clause of the Fourteenth Amendment encompasses more than freedom from bodily restraint, today's plurality opinion emphasizes, the concept was cut loose from one natural limitation on its meaning. This innovation paved the way, so the plurality hints, for judges to substitute their own preferences for those of elected officials. Dissatisfied with this supposedly unbridled and uncertain state of affairs, the plurality casts about for another limitation on the concept of liberty.

It finds this limitation in "tradition." Apparently oblivious to the fact that this concept can be as malleable and as elusive as "liberty" itself, the plurality pretends that tradition places a discernible border around the Constitution. The pretense is seductive; it would be comforting to believe that a search for "tradition" involves nothing more idiosyncratic or complicated than pouring through dusty volumes on American history. Yet, as Justice White observed in his dissent in Moore v. East Cleveland: "What the deeply rooted traditions of the country are is arguable." Indeed, wherever I would begin to look for an interest "deeply rooted in the country's traditions," one thing is certain: I would not stop (as does the plurality) at Bracton, or Blackstone, or Kent, or even the American Law Reports in conducting my search. Because reasonable people can disagree about the content of particular traditions, and because they can disagree even about which traditions are relevant to the definition of "liberty," the plurality has not found the objective boundary that it seeks.

Even if we could agree, moreover, on the content and significance of particular traditions, we still would be forced to identify the point at which a tradition becomes firm enough to be relevant to our definition of liberty and the moment at which it becomes too obsolete to be relevant any longer. The plurality supplies no objective means by which we might make these determinations. Indeed, as soon as the plurality sees signs that the tradition upon which it bases its decision (the laws denying putative fathers like Michael standing to assert paternity) is crumbling, it shifts ground and says that the case has nothing to do with that tradition, after all. "What is at issue here," the plurality asserts after canvassing the law on paternity suits, "is not entitlement to a state pronouncement that Victoria was begotten by Michael." But that is precisely what is at issue here, and the plurality's last-minute denial of this fact dramatically illustrates the subjectivity of its own analysis.

It is ironic that an approach so utterly dependent on tradition is so indifferent to our precedents. Citing barely a handful of this Court's numerous decisions defining the scope of the liberty protected by the Due Process Clause to support its reliance on tradition, the plurality acts as though English legal treatises and the American Law Reports always have provided the sole source for our constitutional principles. They have not. Just as common-law notions no longer define the "property" that the Constitution protects, see Goldberg v. Kelly, neither do they circumscribe the "liberty" that it guarantees. On the contrary, " '[l]iberty' and 'property' are broad and majestic terms. They are among the '[g]reat [constitutional] concepts ... purposely left to gather meaning from experience.... [T]hey relate to the whole domain of social and economic fact, and the statesmen who founded this Nation knew too well that only a stagnant society remains unchanged.' "

It is not that tradition has been irrelevant to our prior decisions. Throughout our decisionmaking in this important area runs the theme that certain interests and practices—freedom from physical restraint, marriage, childbearing, childrearing, and others—form the core of our definition of "liberty." Our solicitude for these interests is partly the result of the fact that the Due Process Clause would seem an empty promise if it did not protect them, and partly the result of the historical and traditional importance of these interests in our society. In deciding cases arising under the Due Process Clause, therefore, we have considered whether the concrete limitation under consideration impermissibly impinges upon one of these more generalized interests.

Today's plurality, however, does not ask whether parenthood is an interest that historically has received our attention and protection; the answer to that question is too clear for dispute. Instead, the plurality asks whether the specific variety of parenthood under consideration—a natural father's relationship with a child whose mother is married to another man—has enjoyed such protection.

If we had looked to tradition with such specificity in past cases, many a decision would have reached a different result. Surely the use of contraceptives by unmarried couples, Eisenstadt v. Baird, or even by married couples, Griswold v. Connecticut, the freedom from corporal punishment in schools, Ingraham v. Wright, the freedom from an arbitrary transfer from a prison to a psychiatric institution, Vitek v. Jones, and even the right to raise one's natural but illegitimate children, Stanley v. Illinois, were not "interest[s] traditionally protected by our society," at the time of their consideration by this Court. If we had asked, therefore, in Eisenstadt, Griswold, Ingraham, Vitek, or Stanley itself whether the specific interest under consideration had been traditionally protected, the answer would have been a resounding "no." That we did not ask this question in those cases highlights the novelty of the interpretive method that the plurality opinion employs today.

The plurality's interpretive method is more than novel; it is misguided. It ignores the good reasons for limiting the role of "tradition" in interpreting the Constitution's deliberately capacious language. In the plurality's constitutional universe, we may not take notice of the fact that the original reasons for the conclusive presumption of paternity are out of place in a world in which blood tests can prove virtually beyond a shadow of a doubt who sired a particular child and in which the fact of illegitimacy no longer plays the burdensome and stigmatizing role it once did. Nor, in the plurality's world, may we deny "tradition" its full scope by pointing out that the rationale for the conventional rule has changed over the years, as has the rationale for Cal.Evid.Code Ann. § 621 (West Supp.1989); instead, our task is simply to identify a rule denying the asserted interest and not to ask whether the basis for that rule—which is the true reflection of the values undergirding it—has changed too often or too recently to call the rule embodying that rationale a "tradition." Moreover, by describing the decisive question as whether Michael and Victoria's interest is one that has been "traditionally *protected by* our society," rather than one that society traditionally has thought important (with or without protecting it), and by suggesting that our sole function is to "*discern* the society's views," the plurality acts as if the only purpose of the Due Process Clause is to confirm the importance of interests already protected by a majority of the States. Transforming the protection afforded by the Due Process Clause into a redundancy mocks those who, with care and purpose, wrote the Fourteenth Amendment.

In construing the Fourteenth Amendment to offer shelter only to those interests specifically protected by historical practice, moreover, the plurality ignores the kind of society in which our Constitution exists. We are not an assimilative, homogeneous society, but a facilitative, pluralistic one, in which we must be willing to abide someone else's unfamiliar or even repellant practice because the same tolerant impulse protects our own idiosyncracies. Even if we can agree, therefore, that "family" and "parenthood" are part of the good life, it is absurd to assume that we can agree on the content of those terms and destructive to pretend that we do. In a community such as ours, "liberty" must include the freedom not to conform. The plurality today squashes this freedom by requiring specific approval from history before protecting anything in the name of liberty.

. . .

The evidence is undisputed that Michael, Victoria, and Carole did live together as a family; that is, they shared the same household, Victoria called Michael "Daddy," Michael contributed to Victoria's support, and he is eager to continue his relationship with her. Yet they are not, in the plurality's view, a "unitary family," whereas Gerald, Carole, and Victoria do compose such a family. The only difference between these two sets of relationships, however, is the fact of marriage. The plurality, indeed, expressly recognizes that marriage is the critical fact in denying Michael a constitutionally protected stake in his relationship with Victoria: no fewer than six times, the plurality refers to Michael as the "*adulterous* natural father." . . . However, the very premise of *Stanley* and the cases following it is that marriage is not decisive in answering the question whether the Constitution protects the parental relationship under consideration. These cases are, after all, important precisely because they involve the rights of *unwed* fathers. It is important to remember, moreover, that in *Quilloin, Caban,* and *Lehr,* the putative father's demands would have disrupted a "unitary family" as the plurality defines it; in each case, the husband of the child's mother sought to adopt the child over the objections of the natural father. Significantly, our decisions in those cases in no way relied on the need to protect the marital family. Hence the plurality's claim that *Stanley, Quilloin, Caban,* and *Lehr* were about the "unitary family," as that family is defined by today's plurality, is surprising indeed.

The plurality's exclusive rather than inclusive definition of the "unitary family" is out of step with other decisions as well. This pinched conception of "the family," crucial as it is in rejecting Michael and Victoria's claim of a liberty interest, is jarring in light of our many cases preventing the States from denying important interests or statuses to those whose situations do not fit the government's narrow view of the family. From *Loving v. Virginia,* and *Glona v. American Guarantee & Liability Ins. Co.,* and from *Gomez v. Perez,* to *Moore v. East Cleveland,* we have declined to respect a State's notion, as manifested in its allocation of privileges and burdens, of what the family should be. Today's rhapsody on the "unitary family" is out of tune with such decisions.

The plurality's focus on the "unitary family" is misdirected for another reason. It conflates the question whether a liberty interest exists with the question what procedures may be used to terminate or curtail it. It is no coincidence that we never before have looked at the relationship that the unwed father seeks to disrupt, rather than the one he seeks to preserve, in determining whether he has a liberty interest in his relationship with his child. To do otherwise is to allow the State's interest in terminating the relationship to play a role in defining the "liberty" that is protected by the Constitution. According to our established framework under the Due Process Clause, however, we first ask whether the person claiming constitutional protection has an interest that the Constitution recognizes; if we find that she does, we next consider the State's interest in limiting the extent of the procedures that will attend the deprivation of that interest. . . .

The plurality's premature consideration of California's interests is evident from its careful limitation of its holding to those cases in which "the mother is, at the time of the child's conception and birth, married to and cohabitating with another man, *both of whom wish to raise the child as the offspring of their union.*" . . . The highlighted language suggests that if Carole or Gerald alone wished to raise Victoria, or if both were dead and the State wished to raise her, Michael and Victoria might be found to have a liberty interest in their relationship with each other. But that would be to say that whether Michael and Victoria have a liberty interest varies with the State's interest in recognizing that interest for it is the State's interest in protecting the marital family—and not Michael and Victoria's interest in their relationship with each other—that varies with the status of Carole and Gerald's relationship. It is a bad day for due process when the State's interest in terminating a parent-child relationship is reason to conclude that that relationship is not part of the "liberty" protected by the Fourteenth Amendment.

The plurality has wedged itself between a rock and a hard place. If it limits its holding to those situations in which a wife and husband wish to raise the child together, then it necessarily takes the State's interest into account in defining "liberty"; yet if it extends that approach to circumstances in which the marital union already has been dissolved, then it may no longer rely on the State's asserted interest in protecting the "unitary family" in denying that Michael and Victoria have been deprived of liberty.

. . .

NOTES

1. After losing in the United States Supreme Court, Michael H. founded Equality Nationwide for Unwed Fathers (ENUF) and successfully lobbied (along with the California Joint Custody Association) to change California law so that an unwed father could petition the courts for visitation and joint or sole custody when the mother is married to another man. Marcia Coyle, After the Gavel Comes Down, The National Law Journal, Feb. 25, 1991, vol. 13—No. 25, p. 1.

2. Compare Smith v. Cole, 553 So.2d 847 (La.1989) (alleged biological father who lived with child and mother as a family for several years had support obligations even though mother's husband at time of child's birth was presumed to be father).

2. Traditional Restrictions

a. INCEST

Singh v. Singh

Supreme Court of Connecticut, 1990.
213 Conn. 637, 569 A.2d 1112.

■ Arthur H. Healey, Associate Justice.

This is an appeal from the trial court's denial of the plaintiff's and the defendant's motion to open the 1984 judgment of annulment of their 1983 marriage in Connecticut. . . . We find no error.

... The parties, David Singh (husband) and Seoranie Singh (wife), were married on January 13, 1983, in Hartford. In their complaint, seeking an annulment, they alleged that their 1983 marriage was entered into "upon the mistaken belief by both parties that they were not related," but "they [had only] recently discovered that they are uncle and niece." There were no issue of this marriage. In 1984, the [trial] court ... rendered judgment of annulment declaring the marriage null and void after finding, inter alia, that "[t]he marriage was entered into upon the mistaken belief by both parties that they were legally qualified to marry," but that "[both parties] have recently discovered that they are uncle and niece."

Thereafter, in November, 1988, both parties filed a motion to open the judgment. That motion alleged that, although the judgment found that they were uncle and niece and, therefore, not legally qualified to marry, in fact, since the wife's mother is the husband's half sister, the wife is the husband's half niece and not his niece. The parties also maintained that they sought the annulment only because of the advice of counsel that their marriage was, "without question," incestuous and void under our statutory scheme. See General Statutes §§ 46b–21,[1] 53a–191.[2] In view of the fact that our statute concerning kindred who may not marry does not mention "half nieces" or "half uncles" and no Connecticut decision extends the scope of the law's prohibition to relatives of the half blood, the parties claimed that the marriage "might well be deemed lawful and valid." They further alleged that they were remarried in August, 1988, in California where, citing People v. Baker, 69 Cal.2d 44, 442 P.2d 675, 69 Cal.Rptr. 595 (1968), they assert that the California Supreme Court has determined that marriages between uncles and nieces of the half blood are not proscribed by that state's incest statute.[3]

. . .

The issue to be decided is whether a marriage between persons related to one another as half uncle and half niece is incestuous under our statutory scheme and, therefore, void.

The issue to be decided is whether a marriage between persons related to one another as half uncle and half niece is incestuous under our statutory scheme and, therefore, void. The parties maintain that such a marriage is

1. General Statutes § 46b–21 provides: "(Formerly Sec. 46–1.) KINDRED WHO MAY NOT MARRY. No man may marry his mother, grandmother, daughter, granddaughter, sister, aunt, niece, stepmother or stepdaughter, and no woman may marry her father, grandfather, son, grandson, brother, uncle, nephew, stepfather or stepson. Any marriage within these degrees is void."

2. General Statutes § 53a–191 provides: "INCEST: CLASS D FELONY. (a) A person is guilty of incest when such person marries a person whom such person knows to be related to such person within any of the degrees of kindred specified in section 46b–21.

"(b) Incest is a class D felony."

3. Despite this second marriage, the parties went on to contend in their motion to open that they would still face a "painful two year separation" unless the annulment judgment was opened. The reasons they advanced to support this latter claim of the two year delay was, they claim, due to certain amendments in November, 1986, to the Immigration and Nationality Act. The wife was a citizen of Guyana when she remarried her husband. She had been cited by the immigration authorities for exclusion as an "overstay" and was therefore precluded from applying for an "adjustment status" to permanent residency based on that marriage. Consequently, she will have to return to Guyana and cannot initiate an "adjustment status" application until she has completed two years of residence outside the United States. They emphasize ... that "their relationship has nothing in common with so-called 'green-card marriages.'"

not incestuous under our statutory law. The attorney general, who appeared as an amicus curiae, argued to the contrary. The determination of this question involves the interrelation and judicial interpretation of two statutes, §§ 46b–21 and 53a–191. This case, unlike State v. Skinner, 132 Conn. 163, 43 A.2d 76 (1945), or State v. Moore, 158 Conn. 461, 262 A.2d 166 (1969), to which counsel have referred, does not come before us on appeal from a conviction of the crime of incest. These cases, however, are instructive on the issue to be resolved in this case.

Historically, marriage between certain relatives "has been disfavored by all nations during all ages." F. Keezer, Marriage and Divorce (3d Ed.1923) § 170; 1 C. Vernier, American Family Laws (1931) § 37; 1 H. Clark, Law of Domestic Relations in the United States (2d Ed.1987) § 2.9; see Gould v. Gould, 78 Conn. 242, 244, 61 A. 604 (1905). Although incest was punished by the ecclesiastical courts in England, it was not an indictable offense at common law and punishment was left entirely to the ecclesiastical courts. "The ecclesiastical courts followed the interdiction of Levitical law which prohibited marriages between persons more closely related than fourth cousins unless a dispensation was procured from the Church of Rome; no distinction was made between persons related by affinity or consanguinity." People v. Baker, supra, 69 Cal.2d at 49, 442 P.2d 675, 69 Cal.Rptr. 595; see Butler v. Gastrill, Gilbert's Rep. 156, 156–57, 25 Eng.Rep. 110 (1721). In 1540, during the reign of Henry VIII, a statute was passed regulating the degrees of relationship within which marriage was illegal. See 32 Henry 8, c. 38. That statute limited the prohibitions against marriage to relatives closer than first cousins, and although the ecclesiastical courts approved of the statute, the courts continued to make no distinction between relatives by consanguinity or affinity. People v. Baker, supra . . .; The Queen v. St. Giles in the Fields, 11 Q.B. 173, 116 Eng.Rep. 441 (1847). . . .

The initial departure of the American jurisdictions from the English law was to declare incest a crime. The crime of incest is purely statutory, and most states have a statute making it a crime. The statutes delineating incestuous relationships departed from the ecclesiastical law in two respects. The majority of states extended the criminal prohibitions to first cousins and beyond while other states imposed criminal penalties only where the relationship was that of consanguinity. As will be seen, Connecticut's incest statute followed the former course. While these statutes may vary in detail, they generally define incest as marriage or sexual intercourse between persons too closely related in consanguinity or affinity to be entitled to marry legally.

In Connecticut, incest has been a crime since the incest statute was enacted in 1702 as part of "An Act to prevent Incestuous Marriages." General Statutes (1702–1733), p. 74; see Catalano v. Catalano, 148 Conn. 288, 290, 170 A.2d 726 (1961). . . .

Initially, the parties claim that the trial court erred by adhering to a line of cases dating from the interpretations of the incest statute during the reign of Henry VIII citing to the English statute of 32 Henry 8, c. 38. They concede that "[d]espite notable changes in sexual mores and in the very conditions which underlie the incest taboo itself, which have intervened since the time of Henry VIII, most Courts considering [the] question have been satisfied to mechanically reproduce the precedents of several hundred years ago." They, nevertheless, urge "a more modern approach to the construction of our incest statute" and maintain that they "rely upon a line of cases placing more emphasis on the rights of criminal defendants, and the importance of preserving bona fide marriages against the undue extension of statutory categories." They claim that there are several compelling reasons for the statutory construction that they urge: (1) the plain language of § 46b–21 favors the construction allowing uncle-niece marriages between relatives of the half blood; (2) undue judicial extension of the prohibitions contained in § 46b–21 may lead to unfair prosecutions for the crime of incest under § 53a–191; (3) an unwarranted extension of the incest prohibition to include uncles and nieces of the half blood is inconsistent with proper respect for the preservation of bona fide marriages; and (4) since the prohibition of "uncle-niece marriages, especially those between relatives of half blood, are not the object of universal condemnation, the Court will not be at odds with 'natural law' if it adopts the construction [advocated] by [the parties]." We are not persuaded by any of these claims.

It is clear that § 46b–21 does not contain any language that expressly distinguishes between relatives of the whole blood and the half blood. It is also clear that although § 46b–21 is a civil statute, its interrelationship with § 53a–191, the criminal statute prohibiting incest, is such that both statutes may fairly be said to be in pari materia and so § 46b–21 is to be construed in this case in harmony with the law of which it forms a part. The infusion into § 53a–191 of the degrees of relationship set out in § 46b–21 as the predicate for the commission of the crime of incest invokes the rule of strict construction that is applied to criminal statutes. . . .

In our analysis, it is proper to explore further the state of the law as it was at the time that our incest statute was enacted in 1702. The fundamental case explicating the ecclesiastical law as it was deemed at the time was Butler v. Gastrill, supra. That case, which was decided in 1722, said: "And when we consider who are prohibited to marry by the Levitical Law, we must not only consider the mere Words of the Law itself, but what, from a just and fair Interpretation, may be deduced from it." Id., 158. On the basis of early English cases discussing the prohibition of marriage within certain degrees, Halsbury said: "In reference to the prohibited degrees, relationship by the half blood is a bar to marriage equally with relationship by the whole blood." 16 Halsbury's Laws of England p. 284. Another noted text writer wrote: "The relationship by half blood is the same in [the consanguinity cases] as by whole blood; so that, for example, it is incestuous for a man to marry the daughter of his brother of the half blood, or the daughter of his half-sister." 1 J. Bishop, Marriage, Divorce and Separation § 748. It is fair to assume that, when the incest statute was enacted in 1702, the framers were aware of and adopted the interpretation of the ecclesiastical law as it then existed in England, thus treating the relation of the half blood like that of the whole blood.

There has been no substantive change since that time in our incest statute insofar as the degree of consanguinity within which marriage is proscribed. That is not without significance. Indeed, implicating the issue before us, in 1961, we said: "It has been the declared public policy of this state continuously since 1702 to prohibit marriages of uncle and niece and declare them void." Catalano v. Catalano, supra, 148 Conn. at 290, 170 A.2d 726. Our decisional law under the incest statute has been sparse. In Catalano, we held invalid a marriage between an uncle and a niece under our statutory scheme although the marriage was valid in Italy where it was performed. In that case, we noted that the "generally accepted rule" was that a marriage valid where the ceremony was performed was valid everywhere. We pointed out, however, that there were certain exceptions to the rule, including one which regarded as invalid incestuous marriages between persons so closely related that their marriage was contrary to the strong public policy of the domicil. In that context, we said: "That exception may be expressed in the terms of a statute or by necessary implication."

Besides *Catalano*, two other cases merit discussion. In State v. Skinner we held that the relationship of brother and half-sister was comprehended within the degrees of relationship forbidding marriage under the incest statute. In that case, we rejected the defendant brother's claim that the relationship of half-sister did not come within the statutory prohibition. In doing so, we pointed out that the defendant "admitted in his brief that all the cases which [his counsel] have found are to the contrary and that public policy would indicate that relationship of the half blood should be included in the prohibition of the incest statute." After referring to several cases from other jurisdictions that directly held that "brother" includes a brother of the half blood and that "sister" includes a sister of the half blood, we said: "In view of the purpose of the statute . . . its language, and the soundness of the decisions we have cited, we hold that the word sister, as used in the statute, applies to and includes a half sister."[11] Id.

In State v. Moore, the defendant had been found guilty of incest where the parties involved were the defendant and the nineteen year old daughter of the defendant's brother-in-law, that is, the daughter of the defendant's wife's brother. In reversing the incest conviction in *Moore*, we observed that the trial court "extended the meaning of § 46–1 (now § 46b–21) beyond its fair import." In doing so, we referred to *Skinner*, pointing out that the relationship in that case contained the element of consanguinity and we also noted that that element appeared in all the relationships enumerated in § 46–1 (now § 46b–21) except the relationship of stepmother or stepdaughter and stepfather or stepson. *Moore* then goes on to say: "The question at once arises as to why, in its enumeration of relationships which do not include the element of consanguinity, the General Assembly saw fit to include only those of stepparent or a stepchild. In the application of the criminal law, it would be an unwarranted extension and presumption to assume that by specifying those relationships the legislature has intended to include others which lack the element of consanguinity. Had the legislative intent been to include what, in this case, would commonly be called a relationship of niece-in-law and uncle-in-law, it would have been a simple matter to say." Therefore, the *Moore* court opined that, absent such a declaration, the trial court's construction "amounted to an unwarranted extension of its expressed meaning and intent."

The parties stress that *Moore* is very supportive of their position. We do not agree for several reasons. First, the fact pattern in *Moore* was different from that in both *Skinner* and *Catalano*, as in the latter two cases, unlike *Moore*, a blood relationship was involved. Second, in *Moore*, we referred to *Skinner*, noting that, in *Skinner*, we not only pointed out that the relationship in that case "is embraced within the meaning of the statute" but also that in that relationship there was the element of consanguinity. In *Moore*, the element of consanguinity was absent but that of affinity was present. Moreover, in *Moore*, we did not qualify our holding in *Skinner* but acknowledged

11. Long ago, albeit in a different context (the construction of a statute as to who would take in the event of a "lapsed" devise or legacy under a will) the only issue was whether the word "brother" or "sister" as used in that statute included half brothers. Seery v. Fitzpatrick, 79 Conn. 562, 65 A. 964 (1907). In *Seery*, we said: "In England it has long been settled that whenever the word 'brother' or 'sister' is used in a statute without limitation [as in the statute in *Seery*], it includes half-brothers or half-sisters respectively." Id., at 563, 65 A. 964.

its viability. Finally, in *Moore*, we were not called upon to decide whether the statute proscribed marriage between two persons where each was a relative of the half blood although *Skinner*, fairly read, was a step in that direction.

Nor do we overlook, in reaching our conclusion, those cases that the parties urge us to rely upon in reaching "a more modern approach" to the construction of our incest statute. . . .

The parties place the greatest stress on People v. Baker, supra. A close reading of that case demonstrates that it is clearly inapposite. That case was an incest prosecution against Baker who had had sexual relations with his niece who was related to him by the half blood; that is, her mother was the defendant's half sister. The trial court found him guilty of incest. His principal claim on appeal was that the prohibition in California Penal Code § 285 against fornication by an uncle and his niece did not apply where they were related by the half blood. That statute provided in part: "Persons being within the degrees of consanguinity within which marriages are declared by law to be incestuous and void . . . who commit fornication . . . with each other . . . are punishable by imprisonment. . . ." California Civil Code § 59 provided: "Marriages between parents and children, ancestors and descendants of every degree, and between brothers and sisters *of the half as well as the whole blood*, and between uncles and nieces or aunts and nephews, are incestuous, and void from the beginning, whether the relationship is legitimate or illegitimate." (Emphasis added.) The *Baker* court reversed the conviction. In doing so, it reasoned that the phrase "of the half as well as the whole blood" obviously referred to brothers and sisters and could not be interpreted also to modify "uncles and nieces" under established tenets of statutory construction. Moreover, by including relationships between brothers and sisters of the half blood and not so specifying as to more distant relatives, the *Baker* court reasoned that the legislature evinced the intention to exclude such persons from the statutory prohibition. In recognizing that various state statutes differ, it acknowledged that the more common type of statute extended the prohibition to uncles and nieces of the half blood even where half blood relationships were not mentioned. The manifest dissimilarity of the California statute in *Baker* from our statutes affords little support for the claims of the parties in this case. Indeed, *Baker* itself expressly points this up when, after stating that incest is governed by specific statutes in the various states, it says that "the relevant decisions must be considered in the context of the statutory scheme peculiar to the particular state." Id., 69 Cal.2d 47, 442 P.2d 675, 69 Cal.Rptr. 595. We agree.

. . .

Connecticut has its statutory scheme in place to implement its policy of delineating the relationships between persons under our jurisdiction who may properly enter into marriage. It has been for many years and still remains the declared public policy of the state. The degrees of relationship within which marriages are prohibited are not, from what we have already said, words of art. Fairly read, the prohibition against intermarriage of those related by consanguinity can be understood to extend to those of the half blood as well as of the whole blood. In *Skinner*, which predated the case before us by a generation, we held that the words "brother" and "sister" included those of the half blood. "According to the common meaning of the word ['uncle'], it includes the half-brother of the [mother] and there is no distinction between the whole and half blood." 90 C.J.S. 1025. We believe that the same can be said of the term "niece," that is, that it comprehends the half blood as well as the whole blood. In doing so, we accord to each word its common meaning without frustrating legislative intent but rather enhancing it. Other courts have had no difficulty concluding that their statutes, although silent on the half blood matter, comprehend that relationship in "uncle-niece" incest cases. See, e.g., State v. Lamb, 209 Iowa 132, 227 N.W. 830 (1929); Commonwealth v. Ashey, [248 Mass. 259, 260, 142 N.E. 788, 788 (1924)]. In giving a statute its full meaning where that construction is in harmony with the context and policy of the statute, "there is no canon against using common sense in construing laws as saying what they obviously mean." Roschen v. Ward, 279 U.S. 337, 339 (1929); Donnelley v. United States, 276 U.S. 505(1928). We will attempt no encompassing definition of a "bona fide marriage" in the incest context. The parties have advanced none. We submit, however, that, given the common meaning of uncle and niece, as we have discussed it, what would constitute a "bona fide marriage" in the incest context should be decided on a case-by-case basis against the background of authority we have set out above. Therefore, contrary to the parties' claim, our interpretation of the statutory scheme does not constitute an "unwarranted extension" of the incest prohibition that "is inconsistent with proper respect for the preservation of bona fide marriages."

In conclusion, a marriage between persons related to one another as half-uncle and half-niece is void under General Statutes §§ 46b–21 and 53a–191 as incestuous.

. . .

Back v. Back

Supreme Court of Iowa, 1910.
148 Iowa 223, 125 N.W. 1009.

■ McCLAIN, J.

. . . In 1890 William Back, the decedent, married a widow, one Mrs. Dirke, who then had living a daughter by her former husband, which child is the plaintiff in this case. In 1900, the wife obtained a divorce from said William Back, and four years later he married the plaintiff. No children were born to William Back by his first marriage, but as a result of his marriage to plaintiff four children were born, all of whom survive him. About two years after the second marriage, the divorced wife, mother of the plaintiff, died, and thereafter plaintiff and the decedent continued to live together as husband and wife until his death in 1906. The resistance of defendant to plaintiff's application as widow to have . . . property set apart to her was on the ground that the marriage was incestuous and void under the provisions of Code, [§]4936, which within the definition of "incest" includes marriage between a man and his wife's daughter, and prohibits such marriage. The trial court ruled . . . that the marriage to plaintiff was void in its inception and continued to be void after the death of plaintiff's mother and until the death of decedent, and that, therefore, plaintiff is not the widow of decedent. . . .

. . .

. . . [W]hether the marriage of plaintiff to decedent was within any of the prohibitions of Code, [§]4936 . . . depends upon the construction of the words "wife's daughter" in that section. . . . If the statute purported to be a definition only of degrees of relation within which marriage is prohibited, it might perhaps be argued with some plausibility that, as a man could not marry his wife's daughter while his wife was living and undivorced without committing bigamy, the object of including wife's daughter among those to whom a marriage is declared invalid was to prohibit such marriage after the death or divorce of the mother of such daughter; but, as the primary purpose of the statute apparent on its face is to punish carnal knowledge as between persons having the specified relationships as well as to punish marriage between them, it is quite evident that the enumeration of relationships is simply a method of stating more definitely what are the degrees of consanguinity or affinity rendering marriage or carnal knowledge between persons of the relationships named criminal....

Holding: We reach the conclusion, therefore, that the relationship of affinity between the decedent and plaintiff which existed during the continuance of the marriage relation between decedent and plaintiff's mother terminated when the latter procured a divorce from decedent, and after that time plaintiff was not the daughter of decedent's wife, and the marriage between them was valid.

. . .

Claude Levi–Strauss, The Family, in Man, Culture and Society

261, 276–78 (Shapiro ed. 1956).

... The universal prohibition of incest specifies, as a general rule, that people considered as parents and children, or brother and sister, even if only by name, cannot have sexual relations and even less marry each other....

The space at our disposal is too short to demonstrate that ... there is no natural ground for the custom. Geneticists have shown that while consanguineous marriages are likely to bring ill effects in a society which has consistently avoided them in the past, the danger would be much smaller if the prohibition had never existed, since this would have given ample opportunity for the harmful hereditary characters to become apparent and be automatically eliminated through selection: as a matter of fact this is the way breeders improve the quality of their subjects. Therefore, the dangers of consanguineous marriages are the outcome of the incest prohibition rather than actually explaining it. Furthermore, since very many primitive peoples do not share our belief in biological harm resulting from consanguineous marriages, but have entirely different theories, the reason should be sought elsewhere, in a way more consistent with the opinions generally held by mankind as a whole.

The true explanation should be looked for in a completely opposite direction, and what has been said concerning the sexual division of labor may help us to grasp it. This has been explained as a device to make the sexes mutually dependent on social and economic grounds, thus establishing clearly that marriage is better than celibacy. Now, exactly in the same way that the principle of sexual division of labor establishes a mutual dependency between the sexes, compelling them thereby to perpetuate themselves and to found a family, the prohibition of incest establishes a mutual dependency between families, compelling them in order to perpetuate themselves, to give rise to new families....

We now understand why it is so wrong to try to explain the family on the purely natural grounds of procreation, motherly instinct, and psychological feelings between man and woman and between father and children. None of these would be sufficient to give rise to a family, and for a reason simple enough: for the whole of mankind, the absolute requirement for the creation of a family is the previous existence of two other families, one ready to provide a man, the other one a woman, who will through their marriage start a third one, and so on indefinitely. To put it in other words: what makes man really different from the animal is that, in mankind, a family could not exist if there were no society: i.e. a plurality of families ready to acknowledge that there are other links than consanguineous ones, and that the natural process of filiation can only be carried on through the social process of affinity.

How this interdependency of families has become recognized is another problem which we are in no position to solve because there is no reason to believe that man, since he emerged from his animal state, has not enjoyed a basic form of social organization, which, as regards the fundamental principles, could not be essentially different from our own. Indeed, it will never be sufficiently emphasized that, if social organization had a beginning, this could only have consisted in the incest prohibition since, as we have just shown, the incest prohibition is, in fact, a kind of remodeling of the biological conditions of mating and procreation (which know no rule, as can be seen from observing animal life) compelling them to become perpetuated only in an artificial framework of taboos and obligations. It is there, and only there, that we find a passage from nature to culture, from animal to human life, and that we are in a position to understand the very essence of their articulation.

. . . [T]he ultimate explanation is probably that mankind has understood very early that, in order to free itself from a wild struggle for existence, it was confronted with the very simple choice of "either marrying-out or being killed-out." The alternative was between biological families living in juxtaposition and endeavoring to remain closed, self-perpetuating units, over-ridden by their fears, hatreds, and ignorances, and the systematic establishment, through the incest prohibition, of links of intermarriage between them, thus succeeding to build, out of the artificial bonds of affinity, a true human society, despite, and even in contradiction with, the isolating influence of consanguinity. . . .

Margaret Mead, Anomalies in American Post–Divorce Relationships, in Divorce and After

104–108 (Bohannan ed., 1970).

Our present frequency of divorce has coincided with the development of a new set of attitudes and beliefs about incest. Incest taboos are among the essential mechanisms of human society, permitting the development of children within a setting where identification and affection can be separated from sexual exploitation, and a set of categories of permitted and forbidden sex can be established. Once these are established by the usually implicit but heavily charged learning of early childhood, the boy or girl is prepared to establish close relationships with others, of both a sexual and an asexual but affectional nature. The permissible sex partner, who may be one of a narrowly defined group of cousins, or any appropriately aged member of another village, or any age mate in the village who is not a relative, is sharply identified. The forbidden sex partners, a category which includes parents, aunts and uncles, brothers and sisters, nephews and nieces, and sometimes a wider group of all cousins, or all members of the clan or the community, are equally sharply distinguished. Close ties may be formed with forbidden sex partners without the intrusion of inappropriate sexuality; trust and affection, dependence and succorance, can exist independently of a sexual tie. Grown to manhood and womanhood, individuals are thus equipped to mate, and to continue strong, affectional ties with others than their own mates.

Where such incest categories are not developed, there are certain kinds of social consequences. Groups that can only absorb a non-member by establishing a sexual tie to a member, like the Kaingang of South America, have a limited capacity to form wider alliances. In parts of Eastern Europe, where the father-in-law may pre-empt the daughter-in-law in his son's absence, for example, on military service, certain inevitable suspicions and antagonisms exist between fathers and sons. The complications that may result from a mother-in-law's attraction to a young son-in-law—complications that were ruled out in the case of a juvenile own son, no matter how loved—are so ubiquitous, that mother-in-law taboos placing limitations on any social relationships between son-in-law and mother-in-law are the commonest and most stringent avoidance taboos in the world. The complementary taboo, between brother and sister, is also found in many parts of the world....

If the incest taboos are seen to make an essential contribution to the rearing of children within a situation where their own immature emotions are respected, and where they are at the same time prepared for both sexual and non-sexual relationships as adults, it is then obvious that the taboo must be extended to include all members of the household. No matter what the size of the household, sex relations must be rigorously limited to the sets of marital couples—parents, grandparents, married aunts and uncles—who live within its confines. When these rigorous limitations are maintained, the children of both sexes can wander freely, sitting on laps, pulling beards, and nestling their heads against comforting breasts—neither tempting nor being tempted beyond their years....

In England, until fairly recent times, the dangerous possibilities of attraction to the wife's sister, were considered so great that there was a compensatory legal rule which specifically forbade marriage with a deceased wife's sister. This device was designed to at least interrupt daydreaming and acting out during the wife's lifetime, since membership in the same household was possible after her death. In non-monogamous societies, marriage with the wife's sister is a common and often congenial type of marriage, especially in the cases where a sister may be given to complete a household into which her childless older sister is married.

Traditionally, within the Christian usages of the past, forbidden degrees of marriage have dealt more or less successfully with the problem of protecting those who live together in a single household. Stepbrotherhood and stepsisterhood are included within the impediments to marriage in the Roman Catholic Church.

However, imperceptibly and almost unremarked, the sanctions which protect members of a common household, regardless of their blood relationships, have been eroded in the United States. About all that remains today is the prohibition of sex in consanguineous relationships—a prohibition supported by the popular belief that the offspring of close relatives are defective. Stated baldly, people believe the reason that sex relationships between any close kin, father-daughter, mother-son, brother-sister, sometimes first cousins, uncle-niece and aunt-nephew, are forbidden, is simply that such unions would result in an inferior offspring—feeble-minded, deformed, handicapped in some way. This belief is a sufficient protection against incest so long as the two-generation nuclear family is the rule of residence, and the original marriage remains intact. In such households, neither aunts nor uncles are welcome as residents, cousins are members of other households, and even boarders and domestic servants are now regarded as undesirable. The small family, united by blood ties, can thus safely indulge in intimacy and warmth between biologically related parents and children. It can be pointed out that this sanction is based on a misunderstanding of the biological principles which govern the inheritance of specific genes which are more likely to appear in closely consanguineous matings. But a more serious limitation of this sanction is that it does not provide for a household which includes a stepparent, a stepchild, stepsiblings, or adopted children.

We rear both men and women to associate certain kinds of familiarity, in dress, bathing, and relaxation, with carefully defined incest taboos in which the biological family and the single household are treated as identical. We provide little protection when individuals are asked to live in close contact within a single, closed household, with members of the opposite sex to whom they have no consanguineous relationships. This leads to enormous abuses—girls are seduced by stepbrothers and stepfathers, men are seduced by precocious stepdaughters. It also leads to a kind of corruption of the possibilities of trust and affection, confusing the children's abilities to distinguish between mates and friends, whether of the same age, or among those of another generation. If the girl is below the age of consent, seduction which takes place between a stepfather and a stepdaughter, however initiated, is treated as a sex offense against a minor rather than as incest. Moreover, there is increasing evidence of the connivance of a consanguineous member of the family in such intrigues. The consenting minor may or may not be damaged psychologically, as she would be certain to be in a relationship with her own father or brother, which is experienced as incest. In fact, there is some evidence that where the biological mother connives in a sexual relationship between a father and daughter, the daughter has not been damaged psychologically. This finding may be interpreted as a sign that there is no natural or instinctive aversion to incest. But it may also be seen as a final weakening of incest taboos in our society, as the rationale has shifted from taboos governing the relationships of persons of opposite sex and different generations in close domestic contact, to a mere precaution against defective offspring, when offspring are not in any event the purpose of such liaisons.

As the number of divorces increases, there are more and more households in which minor children live with stepparents and stepsiblings, but where the inevitable domestic familiarity and intimacy are not counterbalanced by protective, deeply felt taboos. At the very least, this situation produces confusion in the minds of growing children; the stepfather, who is seen daily but is not a taboo object, is contrasted with the biological father, who is seen occasionally and so is endowed with a deeper aura of romance. The multiplication of such situations may be expected to magnify the difficulties young people experience in forming permanent-mating relationships, as well as in forming viable relationships with older people. They may also be expected to magnify the hazards of instructor-student intrigues, of patient-doctor complications, and of employer-employee exploitation. It may even be that the emergence of the very peculiar form of sex behavior in which couples unknown to each other, arrange to meet secretly and exchange sex partners may be an expression of the kind of object confusion that has grown up in our present much-divorced, much remarried society—a society in which, however, the ideal of the biologically related, two-generation, exclusive nuclear family is still preserved.

NOTES

1. All states and the District of Columbia prohibit marriages between parent and child, brother and sister, and aunt and nephew (or uncle and niece). By 2005, twenty states and the District of Columbia permitted marriages between first cousins.[1]

A recent study reported that although married cousins are more likely than unrelated couples to have children with a birth defect, significant mental retardation, or serious genetic disease, the risk is smaller than many thought. For an unrelated couple, the risk of having a child with one of the listed problems is 3 to 4 percent. For close cousins, the risk jumps between 1.7 and 2.8 percent. Robin Bennett et al., Genetic Counseling and Screening of Consanguineous Couples and Their Offspring: Recommendations of the National Society of Genetic Counselors, 11 J. Genet. Couns. 97 (2002).

There is an organization working to overturn restrictions on cousin marriage: Cousins United to Defeat Discriminating Laws Through Education. See www.cousin-couples.com. A recent news report described the difficulties faced by two cousins who married in March, 2005. Although they were able to avoid a state prohibition on cousin marriage by traveling to another state, social sanctions were not as easily circumvented:

> Their families recoiled at the news. When the two began living together, her family disowned her for a time. She was no longer welcome at Sunday dinners. They refused to take her phone calls. Friends dredged up Bible passages to scold them.

Frederick Kunkle, Pa. Cousins Try to Overcome Taboo of "I Do," Wash. Post, April 25, 2005 at B1.

2. In light of the justifications for incest prohibitions advanced by Levi–Strauss and Mead, should statutory bars on marriages be held to apply to marriages between a parent and an adopted child? Consider State v. Lee, 196 Miss. 311, 17 So.2d 277 (1944) (father who married adopted daughter not guilty of incest), which was subsequently repudiated by the state legislature. Miss.Code Ann. § 93–1–1. Cf. Israel v. Allen, 195 Colo. 263, 577 P.2d 762 (1978) (statute prohibiting marriage between brother and sister by adoption held unconstitutional). But see In re MEW and MLB, 4 Pa.D. & C.3d 51 (C.P. Allegheny 1977) (man may not marry sister by adoption).

Four state statutes concerning incestuous marriages specifically apply to adopted children: Mass.Gen.Laws Ann. ch. 210, § 5c; Miss.Code Ann. § 93–1–1; Minn.Stat. Ann. § 517; Vernon's Tex.Fam.Code Ann. § 2.21.

Compare Section 207 of the Uniform Marriage & Divorce Act:

"(a) The following marriages are prohibited: . . .

"(2) a marriage between an ancestor and a descendant, or between a brother and a sister, whether the relationship is by the half or the whole blood, or by adoption;

"(3) a marriage between an uncle and a niece or between an aunt and a nephew, whether the relationship is by the half or the whole blood, except as to marriages permitted by the established customs of aboriginal cultures."

3. Most courts have reached the same conclusion as the court in *Back* that, in the absence of a contrary statutory provision, all affinity relationships cease upon termination of the marriages that produced them. As the opinion indicates, however, a few courts have exempted situations involving children of the original marriage.

1. Alabama, California, Colorado, Connecticut, Florida, Georgia, Hawaii, Maine (Maine requires a certificate of genetic counseling for first cousins to marry), Maryland, Massachusetts, New Jersey, New Mexico, New York, North Carolina, Rhode Island, South Carolina, Tennessee, Texas, Vermont, Virginia. In addition, Wisconsin permits such marriages if the woman is over 55 or if either party is sterile, Indiana allows them if both parties are over 65, Illinois does if both parties are over 50 or if either party is sterile, and Utah does if either both parties are 65 or older or both are 55 or older and either party is sterile.

b. AGE

Moe v. Dinkins

United States District Court, Southern District of New York, 1981.
533 F.Supp. 623, affirmed 669 F.2d 67 (2d Cir.1982).

MEMORANDUM OPINION

■ MOTLEY, DISTRICT JUDGE.

Plaintiffs Maria Moe, Raoul Roe and Ricardo Roe seek a judgment declaring unconstitutional, and enjoining the enforcement of, the parental consent requirement of New York Domestic Relations Law §§ 15.2 and 15.3 (Section 15). Section 15.2 provides that all male applicants for a marriage license between ages 16 and 18 and all female applicants between ages 14 and 18 must obtain "written consent to the marriage from both parents of the minor or minors or such as shall then be living...." Section 15.3 requires that a woman between ages 14 and 16 obtain judicial approval of the marriage, as well as the parental consent required by Section 15.2.

This action is now before the court on plaintiffs' motion for summary judgment declaring Section 15 unconstitutional and enjoining its enforcement....

. . .

The plaintiff class consists of:

> persons who wish to marry in New York State but cannot obtain a marriage license or judicial approval to obtain a marriage license because they, or the persons whom they seek to marry, lack parental consent as required by New York Dom.Rel.Law §§ 15.2 and 15.3.

The plaintiff class is represented by Maria Moe and Raoul Roe.

The defendant class consists of:

> all town and city clerks in New York State.
>
> All such clerks as are required by New York State law to enforce the parental consent provisions of New York Dom.Rel.Law §§ 15.2 and 15.3.

The defendant class is represented by David Dinkins, City Clerk of New York City....

Plaintiff Raoul Roe was eighteen years old when this action was commenced. Plaintiff Maria Moe was fifteen years old. Plaintiff Ricardo Roe is their one year old son who was born out of wedlock. Plaintiffs live together as an independent family unit. In late November, 1978, Maria became pregnant by Raoul and in April, 1979, they moved into an apartment together. Maria requested consent from her mother, a widow, to marry Raoul, but Mrs. Moe refused, allegedly because she wishes to continue receiving welfare benefits for Maria. Maria and Raoul continue to be prevented from marrying because of Mrs. Moe's failure to give consent to the marriage as required by Section 15. Maria and Raoul allege that they wish to marry in order to cement their family unit and to remove the stigma of illegitimacy from their son, Ricardo.

. . .

Plaintiffs contend that Section 15 of the New York Domestic Relations Law, requiring parental consent for the marriage of minors between the ages of fourteen and eighteen, deprives them of the liberty which is guaranteed to them by the Due Process Clause of the Fourteenth Amendment to the Federal Constitution.

A review of Supreme Court decisions defining liberties guaranteed by the Fourteenth Amendment reveals that activities relating to child-rearing and education of children, procreation, abortion, family relations, contraception, and, most recently, marriage, Zablocki v. Rehail, 434 U.S. 374 (1978), are constitutionally protected rights of individual privacy embodied within the concept of liberty which the Due Process Clause of the Fourteenth Amendment was designed to protect.

However, neither *Zablocki* nor its predecessors arose in the context of state regulation of marriages of minors. In that respect, this is a case of first impression.

While it is true that a child, because of his minority, is not beyond the protection of the Constitution, the Court has recognized the State's power to make adjustments in the constitutional rights of minors. Ginsberg v. New York, 390 U.S. 629 (1968) (criminal statute prohibiting the sale of obscene material to minors whether or not obscene to adults upheld despite First Amendment challenge); Prince v. Massachusetts, 321 U.S. 158 (1944) (child labor law prohibiting minors from selling merchandise on the streets upheld despite Jehovah Witness' challenge based on religious freedom). "The power of the State to control the conduct of children reaches beyond the scope of authority over adults." This power to adjust minors' constitutional rights flows from the State's concern with the unique position of minors. In Bellotti v. Baird, 443 U.S. 622 (1979), the Court noted "three reasons justifying the conclusion that the constitutional rights of children cannot be equated with those of adults: the peculiar vulnerability of children; their inability to make critical decisions in an informed and mature manner; and the importance of the parental role in child-rearing." Likewise, marriage occupies a unique position under the law. It has been the subject of extensive regulation and control, within constitutional limits, in its inception and termination and has "long been regarded as a virtually exclusive province of the State." Sosna v. Iowa, 419 U.S. 393, 404 (1975).

While it is evident that the New York law before this court directly abridges the right of minors to marry, *in the absence of parental consent,* the question is whether the State interests that support the abridgement can overcome the substantive protection of the Constitution. The unique position of minors and marriage under the law leads this court to conclude that Section 15 should not be subjected to strict scrutiny, the test which the Supreme Court has ruled must be applied whenever a state statute burdens the exercise of a fundamental liberty protected by the Constitution. Applying strict scrutiny would require determination of whether there was a compelling state interest and whether the statute had been closely tailored to achieve that state interest. The compelling state purpose necessitated by application of the strict scrutiny test "would cast doubt on a network of restrictions that the States have fashioned to govern marriage and divorce." Zablocki v. Redhail, 434 U.S. at 399 (Powell, J., concurring). It is this court's view that Section 15 should be looked at solely to determine whether there exists a rational relation between the means chosen by the New York legislature and the legitimate state interests advanced by the State. Section 15 clearly meets this test.

The State interests advanced to justify the parental consent requirement of Section 15 include the protection of minors from immature decision-making and preventing unstable marriages. The State possesses paternalistic power to protect and promote the welfare of children who lack the capacity to act in their own best interest. The State interests in mature decision-making and in preventing unstable marriages are legitimate under its *parens patriae* power.

An age attainment requirement for marriage is established in every American jurisdiction. The requirement of parental consent ensures that at least one mature person will participate in the decision of a minor to marry. That the State has provided for such consent in Section 15 is rationally related to the State's legitimate interest in light of the fact that minors often lack the "experience, perspective and judgment" necessary to make "important, affirmative choices with potentially serious consequences." Bellotti v. Baird, supra, 443 U.S. at 635–36.

Yet, plaintiffs fault the parental consent requirement of Section 15 as possibly arbitrary, suggesting that courts, as non-interested third parties, are in a better position to judge whether a minor is prepared for the responsibilities that attach to marriage. Although the possibility for parents to act in other than the best interest of their child exists, the law presumes that the parents "possess what the child lacks in maturity" and that "the natural bonds of affection lead parents to act in the best interest of their children." Parham v. J.R., 442 U.S. 584, 610 (1979) (procedure for voluntary commitment of children under eighteen to state hospitals by their parents held constitutional). "That the governmental power should supercede parental authority in all cases because some parents" may act in other than the best interest of their children is "repugnant to the American tradition." Id. at 602–03.

Plaintiffs also contend that Section 15 denied them the opportunity to make an individualized showing of maturity and denies them the only means by which they can legitimize their children and live in the traditional family unit sanctioned by law. On the other hand, New York's Section 15 merely delays plaintiffs' access to the institution of marriage. Cf. Sosna v. Iowa, 419 U.S. at 406 (durational residency requirement of one year for divorce proceedings held constitutional). Moreover, the prohibition does not bar minors whose parents consent to their child's marriage. Assuming arguendo that the illegitimacy of plaintiff Moe's child . . . is a harm, it is not a harm inflicted by Section 15. It is merely an incidental consequence of the lawful exercise of State power. The illegitimacy of plaintiffs' children, like the denial of marriage without parental consent, is a temporary situation at worst. A subsequent marriage of the parents legitimatizes the child, thereby erasing the mark of illegitimacy. The rights or benefits flowing from the marriage of minors are only temporarily suspended by Section 15. . . .

The fact that the State has elected to use a simple criterion, age, to determine probable maturity in the absence of parental consent, instead of requiring proof of maturity on a case by case basis, is reasonable, even if the rule produces seemingly arbitrary results in individual cases. "Simply because the decision of a parent is not agreeable to a child or because there is a [possible stigmatization of the child] does not automatically transfer power to make the decision from parents to some other agency or officer of the state." Parham v. J.R., 442 U.S. at 603.

. . .

This court concludes that Section 15's requirement of parental consent is rationally related to the State's legitimate interests in mature decision-making with respect to marriage by minors and preventing unstable marriages. It is also rationally related to the State's legitimate interest in supporting the fundamental privacy right of a parent to act in what the parent perceives to be the best interest of the child free from state court scrutiny. Section 15, therefore, does not offend the constitutional rights of minors but represents a constitutionally valid exercise of state power.

Accordingly, plaintiff's motion for summary judgment in their favor is denied and summary judgment is entered in favor of defendants.

NOTES

1. At common law, children were considered capable of consenting to marriage at age seven, although the marriage was voidable by the underage party until he or she reached the "age of discretion," the presumptive age at which the marriage could be consummated, which was twelve for girls and fourteen for boys.

By 2005, Mississippi was the only state that did not set 18 as the minimum age for marriage without parental consent. Mississippi requires parental permission only if the male is under 17 or the female is under 15. Any "interested party" (presumably including parents) has three days in which to object to the issuance of a marriage license. A court must then order denial of the license if either of the parties is under 21, the age of majority in the state, and "not of mature discretion" or "not capable of assuming responsibilities of marriage." Miss. Code Ann. §§ 93–1–5, 93–1–7, 1–3–27.

Most states permit 16 or 17 year olds to marry with parental consent. New Hampshire appears to have the lowest formal minimum: females may marry there with parental consent at age 13. Many states also allow judges to override either parental consent or refusal to consent below the age of majority. See, e.g., Cal. Fam. Code § 302 (for persons under 18, court order permitting marriage required in addition to parental consent); Smith–Hurd's 750 Ill. Comp. Stat. Ann. 5/201, 203 and 208 (court can order issuance of marriage license to minor despite a lack of parental consent "if the court finds that the underaged party is capable of assuming the responsibilities of marriage and the marriage will serve his best interest.") In addition, statutory minimums need not be followed when certain exceptional circumstances exist, with pregnancy being the most common. See, e.g., A.C.A. § 9–11–102. See generally Lynn D. Wardle, Rethinking Martial Age Restrictions, 21 J. Fam. L. 1 (1983).

What should be the minimum age for marriage, if any? Would you make an exception, as some states do, if the wife-to-be is pregnant?

2. Child marriages are also discouraged through child neglect proceedings, a topic explored in Chapter 10. See People v. Benu, 87 Misc.2d 139, 385 N.Y.S.2d 222 (1976) (father convicted of endangering the welfare of his 13–year-old daughter by arranging her marriage); In Interest of Flynn, 22 Ill.App.3d 994, 318 N.E.2d 105 (1974) (couple found unfit parents after they "sold" their 12–year-old daughter into marriage with a relative stranger for $28,000).

3. The divorce rate for teenage marriages is much higher than for other marriages. The 1970 census found that 25.2% of the white women married between the ages of 14 and 17 in the first half of the 1960s had their marriages dissolved by 1970. For women who married at 18 or 19, the figure was 17.3%. The rate fell to 10% for women who married in their twenties. For white men, the divorce rate for those married under age 19 was 20%, with a corresponding decrease as the age at marriage rose. Similar figures were recorded for non-whites, but the drop-off in divorces was not as dramatic. As many as half of these marriages were complicated by pre-marital pregnancy.

By 1995, the divorce rate within the first five years for women married between the ages of 15 and 17 had grown to nearly 50% and for women married between the ages of 17 and 19 to over 35%. See Abma et al., Fertility, Family Planning, and Women's Health: New Data From the 1995 National Survey of Family Growth, 23 Vital Health & Statistics 19 (1997).

In the 1970s, most teenagers giving birth were married. Since 1990, most teenagers giving birth have been unmarried. By 2001, barely 20% of pregnant teens were married. See Martin et al., Births: Final Data For 2001, 51 National Vital Statistics Reports, No. 5 (2002). Fewer than 5% of 15 to 19–year-olds were married in 1994, compared with 14% in 1970. Health Care Strategic Management, February 1, 1997. By the 2000 Census, the rate remained below 4.5%. See U.S. Census Bureau data available at http://factfinder.census.gov.

To combat the high divorce rate of young marriages, Arizona, California, and Utah require some premarital counseling. A.R.S. § 25–102; Cal. Fam. Code § 304; Utah Code Ann. 30–1–30 to 39. Arizona requires both parties to undergo premarital counseling, if one party is under 16, before a court can approve the marriage. California authorizes the courts to order premarital counseling for all couples in which one of the parties is under 18. Utah authorizes the county commissioners to require counseling for couples in which one partner is either under 19 or divorced. Should such barriers to "easy" marriage be encouraged? Are they constitutional? Does your answer depend on who is doing the counseling or how much is required?

c. POLYGAMY

Bronson v. Swensen

United States District Court for the District of Utah, Central Division.
2005 WL 1310482.

■ TED STEWART, DISTRICT JUDGE.

Before the Court are Plaintiffs' Motion for Summary Judgment and Defendant's Cross Motion for Summary Judgment. The opposing motions address the same issue: the constitutionality of Utah Code Ann. § 76–7–101, Utah Constitution, Article III, § 1, and the Utah Enabling Act.[1] These statutes prohibit the religious practice of polygamy by outlawing bigamy or "polygamous or plural marriages."

Plaintiffs Cook are husband and wife. Plaintiff G. Lee Cook seeks a marriage license to marry Plaintiff J. Branson. Plaintiff D. Cook consents to such marriage. Defendant [Sherrie Swensen, Salt Lake County Clerk] refuses to issue a marriage license for the marriage of G. Lee Cook and J. Bronson, citing Utah law.

Plaintiffs assert that plural marriage is a deeply held religious belief and that Defendant's refusal to permit a legal marriage deprives them of their constitutional rights to free exercise of their religious beliefs, right of association and their right to privacy, as protected by the First, Fourteenth, and other Amendments to the Constitution of the United States.

The facts in this case are not disputed. Plaintiffs assert that it is their sincere and deeply held religious belief that the doctrine of plural marriage—that is, that a man have more than one wife—is a belief that is ordained of God and is to be practiced and encouraged. Plaintiffs characterize their belief to be similar to the practice of polygamy by the Church of Jesus Christ of Latter–Day Saints (Mormons) prior to 1890.

In order to practice their religious belief, Plaintiffs sought a license to permit G. Lee Cook and J. Bronson to marry. On December 22, 2003, Plaintiffs sought a marriage license by filling out the required application and tendering the license fee. When G. Lee Cook revealed to Defendant that he was already married, both by indicating such on the application and then

1. Utah Enabling Act, ch. 138, § 3, 28 Stat. 107, 108 (1894).

orally, and that he sought to marry a second wife, Defendant refused to issue the marriage license.

Utah Code Ann. § 76–7–101 prohibits polygamy in Utah by outlawing bigamy:

> (1) A person is guilty of bigamy when, knowing he has a husband or wife or knowing the other person has a husband or wife, the person purports to marry another person or cohabits with another person.

Id. Polygamy is also prohibited by the Utah Constitution, Article III, § 1:

> Perfect toleration of religious sentiment is guaranteed. No inhabitant of the State shall ever be molested in person or property on account of his or her mode of religious worship; but polygamous or plural marriages are forever prohibited.

Id.

This language of the [Utah] Constitution is required by the Enabling Act[2] which permitted Utah to join the Union, but with certain conditions, including a proscription of polygamy. This language provides, "That polygamous or plural marriages are forever prohibited."

. . .

The question of the constitutionality of Utah's laws prohibiting the practice of polygamy is not a new question before the courts. . . .

In the case Potter v. Murray City, 760 F.2d 1065 (10th Cir. 1985), the court affirmed a district court decision rejecting a claim that the laws in question were in violation of Plaintiffs right to free exercise of religion as follows:

> We are in agreement with the district court that the State of Utah beyond the declaration of policy and public interest implicit in the prohibition of polygamy under criminal sanction, has established a vast and convoluted network of other laws clearly establishing its compelling state interest in and commitment to a system of domestic relations based exclusively upon the practice of monogamy as opposed to plural marriage.
>
> Monogamy is inextricably woven into the fabric of our society. It is the bedrock upon which our culture is built. Cf. Zablocki v. Redhail, 434 U.S. 374, 384 (1978) (marriage is foundation of family and society; "a bilateral loyalty"). In light of these fundamental values, the State is justified, by a compelling interest, in upholding and enforcing its ban on plural marriage to protect the monogamous marriage relationship.

Id. at 1070 (quoting Potter v. Murray City, 585 F. Supp. 1126, 1138 (D. Utah 1984)).

. . .

Instructive for purposes of this order is the fact that the court in *Potter* analyzed the continuing validity of Reynolds v. United States, 98 U.S. 145 (1878), in which the Supreme Court upheld the criminal conviction of a Mormon for practicing polygamy, and rejected the argument that a prohibition on polygamy violated the right to the free exercise of religion. The *Potter* court relied on the fact that *Reynolds* continued to be cited with approval by the Supreme Court in subsequent decisions, including cases

2. Utah Enabling Act, Ch. 138, § 3.

cited by the defendant in *Potter* for the proposition that *Reynolds* was no longer controlling, as clear evidence that it was still the law of the land.

The Plaintiff in *Potter* also raised the right to privacy:

> Plaintiff argues that his constitutional right to privacy prohibits the State of Utah from sanctioning him for entering into a polygamous marriage. Again we disagree. We find no authority for extending the constitutional right of privacy so far that it would protect polygamous marriages. We decline to do so.

Potter, 760 F.2d at 1070–1071.

As recently as 2002, the Tenth Circuit rejected a challenge to the constitutionality of Utah's prohibition against polygamy. In the unpublished decision in White v. Utah, 41 Fed. Appx. 325 (10th Cir. 2002), the Circuit rejected a plaintiffs constitutional challenge to the prosecution of another individual for practicing polygamy, citing *Reynolds* and *Potter.*

In State v. Green, 2004 UT 76, 99 P.3d 820 (2004), the Utah Supreme Court noted the continuing validity of *Reynolds*, and further held that even if it were "to extend its reasoning beyond *Reynolds,* Utah's bigamy statute would survive a federal free exercise of religion challenge under the most recent standards enunciated by the United States Supreme Court." 99 P.3d at 827.

Plaintiffs seem to face an insurmountable hurdle. Not only does it appear that *Reynolds* is still the law of the land on the issue of polygamy and the free exercise of religion, but in this Circuit it has been held that the State of Utah has a compelling state interest in protecting monogamous marriage.

The only question, therefore, is whether more recent rulings by the Supreme Court have undermined *Reynolds* or the above-cited Tenth Circuit cases as controlling authority.

Plaintiffs cite several recent Supreme Court decisions. However, the Court finds none of them to be helpful to Plaintiffs' position. Plaintiffs rely on Employment Division, Department of Human Resources of Oregon v. Smith, 494 U.S. 872 (1990), in which the Supreme Court considered the constitutionality of an Oregon prohibition of the use of peyote, including its usage for religious or sacramental purposes. In finding such a prohibition was not an unconstitutional infringement on the free exercise clause of the First Amendment, the Court cited the *Reynolds* case as authority for its holding.

Another example is the 1993 decision of Church of the Lukumi Babalu Aye, Inc. v. City of Hialeah, 508 U.S. 520 (1993). The Supreme Court held that city ordinances that burdened a religious practice need not be justified by a compelling state interest if the ordinance is neutral and of general applicability. If not neutral or of general applicability, the government must show both a compelling governmental interest and that the laws were narrowly tailored to advance that interest.... In its opinion, the Supreme Court cited *Reynolds* as an example of the following proposition: "To be sure, adverse impact will not always lead to a finding of impermissible targeting. For example, a social harm may have been a legitimate concern of government for reasons quite apart from discrimination." Id. at 535.

Clearly, *Reynolds* retained its vitality as recently as 1993.

Even if this court were to ignore such fact, and were to find that either *Smith* or *Lukumi,* or both, could be construed to allow this court to find that the Utah laws prohibiting polygamy were to be subject to a strict scrutiny,

Tenth Circuit precedent in *Potter* dictates the finding that there is a compelling state interest in the protection of monogamous marriage. Plaintiffs have not made a convincing argument that the statutes and constitutional provisions in question are not narrowly tailored to meet that compelling state interest.

Plaintiffs also cite the recent decision of the Supreme Court of Lawrence v. Texas, 539 U.S. 558 (2003) [set forth in Chapter 3, Section D]. In *Lawrence*, the Supreme Court ruled that the State of Texas could not criminalize the petitioner's private sexual conduct of sodomy. The Court held that such conduct was a protected liberty interest and that the State of Texas had failed to establish a rational basis for criminalizing such conduct. Plaintiffs herein assert that *Lawrence* is to be read to require the state to sanction their polygamous marriage.

It is important to note what the Court in *Lawrence* did and did not do. As the majority opinion states, "The present case does not involve minors. It does not involve persons who might be injured or coerced or who are situated in relationships where consent might not easily be refused. It does not involve public conduct. . . . It does not involve whether the government must give formal recognition to any relationship that homosexual persons seek to enter. The case does involve two adults who, with full and mutual consent from each other, engaged in sexual practices common to a homosexual lifestyle."

Giving the required deference to the Supreme Court's own stated limitations of its *Lawrence* holding, this court cannot hold that *Lawrence* can be read to require the State of Utah to give formal recognition to a public relationship of a polygamous marriage. Contrary to Plaintiffs' assertion, the laws in question here do not preclude their private sexual conduct. They do preclude the State of Utah from recognizing the marriage of Plaintiff G. Lee Cook to Plaintiff J. Branson as a valid marriage under the laws of the State of Utah.

Plaintiffs refer to the dissent of Justice Scalia in *Lawrence,* where he contends that the majority's ruling will call into question state laws against bigamy, among other statutes that are based upon moral choices. That is likely to be true. But the Tenth Circuit and Supreme Court precedents cited above remain controlling law for this Court. It is therefore

ORDERED that Plaintiffs' Motion for Summary Judgment is DENIED.

Wiley S. Maloney, Arizona Raided Short Creek—Why?

Colliers 30–31 (November 13, 1953).

For years the whispers had been heard in Arizona, Utah, Idaho, and other Western states: somewhere in each of those states was a cult of practicing polygamists, men with as many as six or seven wives and literally dozens of children: fundamentalist Mormons, still adhering to the concept of plural marriage that was outlawed by the U.S. Supreme Court and the heads of the Mormon Church in 1890.

In Fredonia, Arizona, and Hurricane, Utah, there were more than whispers; there were hard facts. Midway between those towns was the parched, ramshackle, almost inaccessible border community of Short Creek, situated in a remote area first explored in 1860 by the frontier scouts of Brigham Young, great leader of the Latter-Day Saints. The practice of polygamy had never ceased in Short Creek. In 1935, the State of Arizona had raided the community and had obtained three convictions for "open and notorious misconduct." In 1944, the Federal Bureau of Investigation had raided the town again (along with several other places in Utah, Idaho, and Arizona); there had been a few more convictions. Nevertheless, visitors reported, there were still men in Short Creek with more than one wife and many children, and the community was growing larger every year.

In Kingman, Arizona, seat of Mohave County, Superior Court Judge J.W. Faulkner collected some of the facts. County officials reported that in hard times welfare requests would pour in from the isolated little village, and often a number of women applying for relief would list the same man as their husband.

There was another, more disquieting, report: some of the wives were youngsters 13 to 15 years old. In Arizona, the age of consent is 18. Parents may permit their daughters to marry at 16, but no younger, even if the child is pregnant. Pregnancy at that age is presumptive evidence of statutory rape.

Deeply disturbed, Judge Faulkner brought his facts to the attention of Governor Howard Pyle in March 1951. He pointed out that the residents of Short Creek, living a cooperative communal life, considered themselves a "charitable and philanthropic organization" under the law, and were paying no property taxes, yet were demanding expanded school facilities to take care of the community's rapid growth. The population was increasing not only from normal causes but through a vigorous recruitment program. Even more troubling were reports that Short Creek was not a unique community; there were other groups of fundamentalist Mormons in Utah, Colorado, Idaho, Mexico, and Canada.

To Judge Faulkner, plural marriage was lawless, immoral and, if allowed to continue, dangerous, no matter how sincerely religious in intent. He was concerned about the children: Might they not become the victims of this archaic doctrine?

Aroused, the governor asked the state legislature for funds to conduct an investigation. The state lawmakers appropriated $10,000, and the Burns Detective Agency in Los Angeles was hired for the job. For several months after that, the people of Short Creek, always hard pressed for cash, were cheered by the prospect of finding work as movie extras: Film scouts had appeared in town, asking questions, taking photographs, and talking of using the region as the scene of a Western thriller.

. . .

Early [in 1953] Governor Pyle and Attorney General Ross F. Jones felt that the time had come for action. In the two years that had elapsed since Judge Faulkner had spoken to them, Short Creek's population had risen to 368. The community was fast becoming the second largest in Mohave County; residents were predicting a population of 2,000 in another couple of years, which would put Short Creek almost in a class with Kingman, the county seat. And the larger the village grew, the harder it would be to break up the cult.

The Short Creek raid was planned for months in strictest secrecy, lest the families of the community learn about it and thwart arrest by drifting across the state line to Utah (they learned anyhow, but did nothing). The $50,000 appropriation required to finance the operation was embodied in an omnibus appropriation bill and listed as part of the governor's emergency fund; only a few leaders of the legislature knew what the money was for. At one point, a bill actually was drafted appropriating the money for "grasshopper control."

The governor and attorney general of Utah were informed of Arizona's plan, and so were the leaders of the Mormon Church in Salt Lake City, which had long been embarrassed by the activities of the Fundamentalists.

[On] July 1, Arizona's governor quietly transferred the $50,000 fund to the attorney general's office and declared that a state of insurrection existed in Short Creek, the necessary legal step to justify taking action.

There was one big problem: There is no legal penalty for polygamy in Arizona. Both Arizona and Utah had been specifically required to outlaw multiple marriage as a condition of statehood, back around the turn of the century, but when Arizona's code of laws was written, a statute covering penalties for polygamy was somehow omitted. Attorney General Jones had to find other grounds for prosecuting the Short Creek group. After some study, he concluded that the community constituted a conspiracy against the state.

NOTES

1. Ralph Nader, The Law v. Plural Marriages, 31 Harv.L.Rec. 10 (1960):

> ... The Short Creek raid proved itself a costly failure. By 1955 when the children were released from state custody, after expenses of $110,000 were incurred for their care, the colony slowly resumed its normal life and now is prospering once again. No further enforcement is planned by either county or state officials. Nor did anything materialize out of the hearings held at Short Creek in 1955 by the Senate Subcommittee to Investigate Juvenile Delinquency....
>
> Why have law enforcement efforts generally failed? First, in eradicating fundamentalist polygamy, it is necessary to break the hold of strong religious commitment, not masculine concupiscence. Judge Tuller of the Superior Court of Pima County, Arizona, told a group of violators: "You have an unshakeable belief that it is the rest of the world that is out of step.... Nothing short of life imprisonment would prevent you from committing the same crime in the future." He added that confronted by such immutable beliefs, punishment would neither deter nor rehabilitate the offenders. The separation principle was probably based, to a degree, on a common-sense recognition of the law's limitations in the area of religious persuasions.
>
> The cost of caring for children of these marriages, after their parents have been convicted, can be very costly and even prohibitive to many counties. Caring for the Short Creek children amounted to a year's budget for Mohave County, had it paid the entire bill.
>
> . . .
>
> In our monogamous system that admits of no exceptions, the solution of the problem of polygamy may require more than legal control or enforcement attempts. These but inspire greater furtiveness and vigilance by the sects. A more sophisticated use of informal social approaches may succeed where attempts at enforcement have failed.

2. After leading the botched raid in 1953, Governor Pyle lost the Mormon vote in 1954 and was then denied the Republican renomination. See Lou Cannon, Plural Marriages Flourish Out West, Wash. Post, Aug. 8, 1977, at A.14.

3. In May of 2001, Tom Green, the first defendant charged with bigamy in Utah in almost fifty years, was convicted of four counts of bigamy and one count of criminal nonsupport. Green lived with five wives and twenty-five children, and publicized his arrangement in the media, stating that he chose to obey God rather than the law. Kevin Cantera and Michael Vigh, Green Guilty on All Counts; Jury Takes Less Than

Three Hours to Reach Verdict, Salt Lake Tribune, May 19, 2001, at A1. Green appealed his conviction, but lost and was then denied certiorari by the Supreme Court on his claim that his religious freedom was being denied. In 2002, Green was charged with the additional count of rape for impregnating one of his wives at the age of 13, convicted, and sentenced to from five years to life imprisonment (the minimum possible sentence). See Michael Janofsky, Mormon Leader Is Survived by 33 Sons and a Void, N.Y. Times, Sep. 15, 2002, at 22.

On June 10, 2005, Mark Shurtleff, the Utah Attorney General, announced that Warren Jeffs, the leader of the Fundamentalist Church of Jesus Christ of Latter Day Saints, had been indicted by a grand jury for child sex abuse on two felony counts of sexual conduct with a minor. Despite its name, the sect is not part of the Church of Jesus Christ of the Latter-day Saints, or Mormons, which banned polygamy in 1890 when Utah became a state. Jeffs is accused of arranging a marriage in 2002 between a 28-year-old man and a 16–year-old girl. Authorities in Arizona and Utah have also removed Jeffs from control of the sect's multimillion dollar trust in a civil action. The assets in the trust include most of the property, businesses and homes in the border towns of Hildale, Utah, and Colorado City (formerly Short Creek), Arizona, where as many as 5,000 sect members live. Warren Jeffs became head of the sect when his father and former sect leader Rulon Jeffs died in 2002. Jeffs has barred his followers from watching television, using the Internet, reading newspapers, having contact with outsiders and other access to the world that might corrupt the faithful. Deborah Frazier and Gwen Florio, Rocky Mountain News, July 16, 2005, at 23A.

4. It has been estimated that a much larger proportion of American men and women have more than one spouse during a lifetime than adults in most polygamous societies, where typically not more than one out of ten or twenty can afford the polygamous state. See Paul Landis, Sequential Marriage, 42 J.Home Econ. 625, 628 (1950). The absolute difference is strikingly sex-based. Although polyandry (more than one husband) is much rarer than polygyny (more than one wife), American women in theory have as much freedom to remarry as do men.

Is our "sequential polygamy" better or worse than concurrent polygamy? If the goal is to provide the best home life for children, would polygamy provide them with a more stable environment? Which is better for wives? For husbands? For parents?

Sanderson v. Tryon

Supreme Court of Utah, 1987.
739 P.2d 623.

■ HALL, CHIEF JUSTICE:

This case emanates from a child custody dispute between parents formerly maintaining a polygamous relationship. Jennifer L. Sanderson appeals a district court judgment awarding Robert L. Tryon custody of their three children on the ground that plaintiff was currently and continuingly engaged in the practice of plural marriage.

Sanderson and Tryon are the natural parents of three children, two of which were born during the parties' polygamous relationship from June 1975 to April 1982. In April 1982, the parties separated and Sanderson took the children. Their third child was born approximately nine months later. Since the parties were never legally married, no divorce was sought.

After leaving the polygamous relationship with Tryon, Sanderson joined the "Allred Church." This religious group openly taught and engaged in the practice of polygamy. Subsequently, plaintiff unlawfully "married" Bill Bowles; no marriage license was obtained, and Bowles was already living in a polygamous relationship with two other women. Contrastingly, Tryon has apparently abandoned the practice of polygamy since the parties' separation in April 1982.

. . .

In April 1985, the matter came to trial.... [T]he court and counsel agreed that the central issue was "whether children may be taken from an otherwise fit and proper parent solely for the reason that the parent practices plural marriage." The court allowed that issue to be presented by both parties in the form of motions for summary judgment. Subsequently, custody was awarded to defendant.

In February 1986, the trial judge signed and filed findings of fact and conclusions of law which in pertinent part provided:

. . .

> 14. [Since May 6, 1983,] Plaintiff and Mr. Bowles have cohabited and continued to cohabit as polygamous husband and wife.
>
> . . .
>
> 26. While the Sanderson/Tryon children attend public schools and otherwise receive proper maintenance and care, the law *presumes that because of their practice of polygamy,* that Bill Bowles and Jennifer L. Sanderson have each knowingly failed and neglected to provide for the Sanderson/Tryon children the proper maintenance, care, training and education contemplated and required by both law and morals.
>
> 27. The Bill Bowles/Jennifer L. Sanderson home in or near Cedar City, Utah, is an immoral environment for the rearing of the Sanderson/Tryon children by reason of its practice of polygamy in violation of Utah state law, and its tolerance and approbation of violation of state law regarding polygamy.
>
> . . .
>
> 29. After the separation of the parties in April of 1982, Defendant Robert L. Tryon was waivering in his adherence to the doctrine of "plural marriage." Defendant has since his separation from Plaintiff in April of 1982 forsaken and abandoned the teaching and practice of plural marriage....
>
> 30. The court finds that save and except for the matters already mentioned above, Plaintiff would be a fit and proper custodial parent for the Sanderson/Tryon children. Defendant Robert L. Tryon is a fit and proper person to be awarded the care, custody and control of the Sanderson/Tryon children. *Absent the influence of the doctrine of "plural marriage",* and in light of the posture of these proceedings, the court *makes no finding concerning whether the best interests of the children would be served by leaving them with Plaintiff or be [sic] awarding their custody to Defendant.*
>
> 31. Primary bonding of the children has occurred with Plaintiff, their mother. Nevertheless, both the public welfare and the welfare of the Tryon children, ... require that the right of custody and control of said children be removed from Jennifer L. Sanderson and awarded to and place [sic] in Defendant [Robert] L. Tryon.
>
> . . .

CONCLUSIONS OF LAW

1. The care, custody and control of the Sanderson/Tryon children should be removed from Plaintiff Jennifer L. Sanderson and placed in the awarded [sic] to Defendant Robert L. Tryon, subject to reasonable rights of visitation in Plaintiff, said rights of reasonable visitation to be restricted in that Plaintiff should not be permitted to exercise visitation with the children in the presence of Bill Bowles, her polygamous "husband," or overnight in the presence of any unrelated, adult member of the opposite sex, to whom she is not legally and lawfully married.

No specific finding was made as to the relative parenting abilities of the parties or the best interests of the children. Sanderson argues that the finding that she practices polygamy is alone insufficient to support the custody award or to permit meaningful review on appeal. We agree.

Utah Code Ann. § 30–3–10 (1984) provides:

Custody of Children. In any case of separation of husband and wife having minor children, or whenever a marriage is declared void or dissolved, the court shall make such order for the future care and custody of the minor children as it may deem just and proper. In determining custody, the court shall consider the *best interests of the child and* the past conduct and demonstrated moral standards of each of the parties. The court may inquire of the children and take into consideration the children's desires regarding the future custody; however, such expressed desires shall not be controlling and the court may, nevertheless, determine the children's custody otherwise.

(emhasis added).

This statute was amended in 1969, deleting a provision which permitted awarding custody to the father upon finding that the mother was immoral, incompetent, or otherwise an improper person.

... [A] custody decision must be supported by written findings and conclusions. These findings should refer to the specific factors pertinent to the decision of what placement is in the best interests of the child, "including the particular needs of [each] child and the ability of each parent to meet those needs."[6]

In the instant case, the court found that defendant Tryon was a fit and proper person to be awarded custody and that plaintiff Sanderson would be a fit and proper person to be awarded custody except that she continues to live in a plural marriage relationship. Moreover, the court specifically stated that it made no findings regarding whether the best interests of the children would be served by leaving them with Sanderson or awarding custody to Tryon, "absent the influence of ... 'plural marriage.' " Therefore, except for Sanderson's practice of polygamy, there were no findings to support the conclusion that Tryon's custody would best serve the children's interests; nor were there findings of fact "which deal with one parent or the other being the better, more nurturing parent."

Nevertheless, Tryon relies upon this Court's decision in In re Black [3 Utah 2d 315, 383 P.2d 887 (plurality opinion), cert. *denied*, 350 U.S. 923 (1955)] to argue that the finding that plaintiff practices polygamy is sufficient to support his custody award. We are not persuaded.

6. Martinez v. Martinez, 728 P.2d 994, 995 (Utah 1986).

First, the instant case is distinguishable from the decision in *Black*. *Black* involved the termination of parental rights. Therein, this Court addressed the issue of whether the parents' practice of a polygamous lifestyle justified the trial court's determination that the children were "neglected" as that term was defined in Utah Code Ann. § 55–10–6 (1953). In the plurality opinion, this Court affirmed that parental rights should be terminated pursuant to section 55–10–32 because the parents through their polygamous lifestyle had neglected to provide the proper maintenance, education, and training required by law and morals. However, the standard governing actions for termination of parental rights is not applicable to child custody disputes.

Second, when *Black* was decided in 1955, section 55–10–32 provided:

> No child as defined in this Chapter shall be taken from the custody of its parents or legal guardian without the consent of such parents or legal guardian, unless the court shall find from the evidence introduced in the case that such parent or legal guardian is incompetent, or has knowingly failed and neglected to provide for such child the proper maintenance, care, training, and education contemplated and required by both law and morals....

This section was repealed in 1965, and under the current provision in section 78–3a–48, moral references have been deleted from the grounds for termination of parental rights. Therefore, the trial judge improperly utilized this language and standard from *Black* in developing his findings. Accordingly, the analysis and ruling in *Black* do not apply.

Finally, a determination of the children's best interests turns on numerous factors, each of which may vary in importance according to the facts in the particular case. Moral character is only one of a myriad of factors the court may properly consider in determining a child's best interests. In this regard, we have previously held that a parent's extramarital sexual relationship alone is insufficient to justify a change in custody. Accordingly, we similarly hold that the trial court's finding that a parent practices polygamy is alone insufficient to support a custody award or to permit meaningful review on appeal.[16] Instead, Sanderson's polygamous practices should only be considered as one among many other factors regarding the children's best interests.

... Accordingly, we vacate the order entered below and remand this case to the district court to enter further findings of fact and judgment in accordance with this opinion.

NOTE

In many jurisdictions, legal presumptions are used to avoid potentially bigamous situations. In Gordon v. Railroad Retirement Board, 696 F.2d 131 (D.C.Cir.1983), for example, the Court of Appeals for the D.C. Circuit was faced with a dispute between two women, each claiming to be the widow of the same man and seeking to claim retirement benefits available under the Railroad Retirement Act. Each had proof of marriage. The widow from the second marriage, however, had found no proof that there had been a divorce from the first wife. The Retirement Act provides that the law of the place of domicile at the time of death controls. In this instance, the District of Columbia was the domicile at death. The Court of Appeals, id. at 132, held:

16. By our determination in this case, we do not minimize the importance of a positive, constructive, moral, and emotional home environment as one factor to be considered in custody matters.

> The District of Columbia courts have consistently recognized a strong presumption that the most recent marriage is valid. "While the presumption is not conclusive, it is one of the strongest in law, and it is settled that the party attacking the second marriage has the burden of rebutting the presumption by strong, distinct, satisfactory, and conclusive evidence." This presumption is so strong that the District of Columbia courts have stated that in a "clash" between "the [presumption] favoring the continuance of a valid ceremonial marriage [and] the other favoring the validity of the last marriage, it is generally held that the first must give way to the second."

Because the burden was on the first wife to disprove the validity of the second marriage, the pension went to the second wife.

d. SAME-SEX MARRIAGE

Goodridge v. Department of Pub. Health

Supreme Judicial Court of Massachusetts, 2003.
440 Mass. 309, 798 N.E.2d 941.

■ Marshall, C.J.

Marriage is a vital social institution. The exclusive commitment of two individuals to each other nurtures love and mutual support; it brings stability to our society. For those who choose to marry, and for their children, marriage provides an abundance of legal, financial, and social benefits. In return it imposes weighty legal, financial, and social obligations. The question before us is whether, consistent with the Massachusetts Constitution, the Commonwealth may deny the protections, benefits, and obligations conferred by civil marriage to two individuals of the same sex who wish to marry. We conclude that it may not. The Massachusetts Constitution affirms the dignity and equality of all individuals. It forbids the creation of second-class citizens. In reaching our conclusion we have given full deference to the arguments made by the Commonwealth. But it has failed to identify any constitutionally adequate reason for denying civil marriage to same-sex couples.

We are mindful that our decision marks a change in the history of our marriage law. Many people hold deep-seated religious, moral, and ethical convictions that marriage should be limited to the union of one man and one woman, and that homosexual conduct is immoral. Many hold equally strong religious, moral, and ethical convictions that same-sex couples are entitled to be married, and that homosexual persons should be treated no differently than their heterosexual neighbors. Neither view answers the question before us. Our concern is with the Massachusetts Constitution as a charter of governance for every person properly within its reach....

Whether the Commonwealth may use its formidable regulatory authority to bar same-sex couples from civil marriage is a question not previously addressed by a Massachusetts appellate court. It is a question the United States Supreme Court left open as a matter of Federal law in Lawrence [v. Texas, 539 U.S. 558, 578 (2003), Chapter 3, Section D] where it was not an issue. There, the Court affirmed that the core concept of common human dignity protected by the Fourteenth Amendment to the United States Constitution precludes government intrusion into the deeply personal realms of consensual adult expressions of intimacy and one's choice of an intimate partner. The Court also reaffirmed the central role that decisions whether to marry or have children bear in shaping one's identity. The Massachusetts Constitution is, if anything, more protective of individual liberty and equality than the Federal Constitution; it may demand broader protection for fundamental rights; and it is less tolerant of government intrusion into the protected spheres of private life.

Barred access to the protections, benefits, and obligations of civil marriage, a person who enters into an intimate, exclusive union with another of the same sex is arbitrarily deprived of membership in one of our community's most rewarding and cherished institutions. That exclusion is incompatible with the constitutional principles of respect for individual autonomy and equality under law.

The plaintiffs are fourteen individuals from five Massachusetts counties. . . .

Each plaintiff attests a desire to marry his or her partner in order to affirm publicly their commitment to each other and to secure the legal protections and benefits afforded to married couples and their children.

The Department of Public Health (department) is charged by statute with safeguarding public health. Among its responsibilities, the department oversees the registry of vital records and statistics (registry), which "enforces all laws" relative to the issuance of marriage licenses and the keeping of marriage records. . . .

In March and April, 2001, each of the plaintiff couples attempted to obtain a marriage license from a city or town clerk's office. . . . In each case, the clerk either refused to accept the notice of intention to marry or denied a marriage license to the couple on the ground that Massachusetts does not recognize same-sex marriage. . . .

On April 11, 2001, the plaintiffs filed suit in the Superior Court against the department and the commissioner seeking a judgment that "the exclusion of the plaintiff couples and other qualified same-sex couples from access to marriage licenses, and the legal and social status of civil marriage, as well as the protections, benefits and obligations of marriage, violates Massachusetts law." See G. L. c. 231A. The plaintiffs alleged violation of the laws of the Commonwealth, including but not limited to their rights under arts. 1, 6, 7, 10, 12, and 16, and Part II, c. 1, § 1, art. 4, of the Massachusetts Constitution.[7] The department, represented by the Attorney General, admitted to a

7. Article 1, as amended by art. 106 of the Amendments to the Massachusetts Constitution, provides: "All people are born free and equal and have certain natural, essential and unalienable rights; among which may be reckoned the right of enjoying and defending their lives and liberties; that of acquiring, possessing and protecting property; in fine, that of seeking and obtaining their safety and happiness. Equality under the law shall not be denied or abridged because of sex, race, color, creed or national origin."

Article 6 provides: "No man, nor corporation, or association of men, have any other title to obtain advantages, or particular and exclusive privileges, distinct from those of the community, than what arises from the consideration of services rendered to the public. . . ."

Article 7 provides: "Government is instituted for the common good; for the protection, safety, prosperity, and happiness of the people; and not for the profit, honor, or private interest of any one man, family or class of men: Therefore the people alone have an incontestable, unalienable, and indefeasible right to institute government; and to reform, alter, or totally change the same, when their protection, safety, prosperity and happiness require it."

Article 10 provides, in relevant part: "Each individual of the society has a right to be protected by it in the enjoyment of his life, liberty and property, according to standing laws. . . ."

Article 12 provides, in relevant part: "[N]o subject shall be . . . deprived of his property, immunities, or privileges, put out of the protection of the law . . . or deprived of his life, liberty, or estate, but by the judgment of his peers, or the law of the land."

Article 16, as amended by art. 77 of the Amendments, provides, in relevant part: "The right of free speech shall not be abridged."

policy and practice of denying marriage licenses to same-sex couples. It denied that its actions violated any law or that the plaintiffs were entitled to relief. The parties filed cross motions for summary judgment.

A Superior Court judge ruled for the department.... [T]he plaintiffs appealed. Both parties requested direct appellate review, which we granted.

Although the plaintiffs refer in passing to "the marriage statutes," they focus, quite properly, on G. L. c. 207, the marriage licensing statute, which controls entry into civil marriage....

... The plaintiffs argue that because nothing in that licensing law specifically prohibits marriages between persons of the same sex, we may interpret the statute to permit "qualified same sex couples" to obtain marriage licenses, thereby avoiding the question whether the law is constitutional. This claim lacks merit.

We interpret statutes to carry out the Legislature's intent, determined by the words of a statute interpreted according to "the ordinary and approved usage of the language." The everyday meaning of "marriage" is "the legal union of a man and woman as husband and wife," Black's Law Dictionary 986 (7th ed.1999), and the plaintiffs do not argue that the term "marriage" has ever had a different meaning under Massachusetts law. This definition of marriage, as both the department and the Superior Court judge point out, derives from the common law. Far from being ambiguous, the undefined word "marriage," as used in G. L. c. 207, confirms the General Court's intent to hew to the term's common-law and quotidian meaning concerning the genders of the marriage partners.

The intended scope of G. L. c. 207 is also evident in its consanguinity provisions. Sections 1 and 2 of G. L. c. 207 prohibit marriages between a man and certain female relatives and a woman and certain male relatives, but are silent as to the consanguinity of male-male or female-female marriage applicants. The only reasonable explanation is that the Legislature did not intend that same-sex couples be licensed to marry. We conclude, as did the judge, that G. L. c. 207 may not be construed to permit same-sex couples to marry.[11]

The larger question is whether, as the department claims, government action that bars same-sex couples from civil marriage constitutes a legitimate exercise of the State's authority to regulate conduct, or whether, as the plaintiffs claim, this categorical marriage exclusion violates the Massachusetts Constitution. We have recognized the long-standing statutory understanding, derived from the common law, that "marriage" means the lawful union of a woman and a man. But that history cannot and does not foreclose the constitutional question.

Part II, c. 1, § 1, art. 4, as amended by art. 112, provides, in pertinent part, that "full power and authority are hereby given and granted to the said general court, from time to time, to make, ordain, and establish all manner of wholesome and reasonable orders, laws, statutes, and ordinances, directions and instructions, either with penalties or without; so as the same be not repugnant or contrary to this constitution, as they shall judge to be for the good and welfare of this Commonwealth."

11. We use the terms "same sex" and "opposite sex" when characterizing the couples in question, because these terms are more accurate in this context than the terms "homosexual" or "heterosexual," although at times we use those terms when we consider them appropriate. Nothing in our marriage law precludes people who identify themselves (or who are identified by others) as gay, lesbian, or bisexual from marrying persons of the opposite sex. See Baehr v. Lewin, 74 Haw. 530, 543 n.11, 547 n.14, 852 P.2d 44 (1993).

The plaintiffs' claim that the marriage restriction violates the Massachusetts Constitution can be analyzed in two ways. Does it offend the Constitution's guarantees of equality before the law? Or do the liberty and due process provisions of the Massachusetts Constitution secure the plaintiffs' right to marry their chosen partner? . . . [T]he two constitutional concepts frequently overlap, as they do here. . . .

We begin by considering the nature of civil marriage itself. Simply put, the government creates civil marriage. In Massachusetts, civil marriage is, and since pre-Colonial days has been, precisely what its name implies: a wholly secular institution. No religious ceremony has ever been required to validate a Massachusetts marriage.

In a real sense, there are three partners to every civil marriage: two willing spouses and an approving State. While only the parties can mutually assent to marriage, the terms of the marriage—who may marry and what obligations, benefits, and liabilities attach to civil marriage—are set by the Commonwealth. Conversely, while only the parties can agree to end the marriage (absent the death of one of them or a marriage void ab initio), the Commonwealth defines the exit terms.

Without question, civil marriage enhances the "welfare of the community." It is a "social institution of the highest importance." Civil marriage anchors an ordered society by encouraging stable relationships over transient ones. It is central to the way the Commonwealth identifies individuals, provides for the orderly distribution of property, ensures that children and adults are cared for and supported whenever possible from private rather than public funds, and tracks important epidemiological and demographic data.

Marriage also bestows enormous private and social advantages on those who choose to marry. Civil marriage is at once a deeply personal commitment to another human being and a highly public celebration of the ideals of mutuality, companionship, intimacy, fidelity and family. . . . Because it fulfills yearnings for security, safe haven, and connection that express our common humanity, civil marriage is an esteemed institution, and the decision whether and whom to marry is among life's momentous acts of self-definition.

. . .

The benefits accessible only by way of a marriage license are enormous, touching nearly every aspect of life and death. . . . [W]e note that some of the statutory benefits conferred by the Legislature on those who enter civil marriage include as to property: joint Massachusetts income tax filing, tenancy by the entirety . . .; extension of the benefits of the homestead protection (securing up to $300,000 in equity from creditors) to one's spouse and children; automatic right to inherit the property of a deceased spouse who does not leave a will; . . . the right to share the medical policy of one's spouse; . . . financial protections for the spouses of certain Commonwealth employees (fire fighters, police officers, prosecutors, among others) killed in the performance of duty; the equitable division of marital property on divorce; temporary and permanent alimony rights; and the right to bring claims for wrongful death and loss of consortium, and for funeral and burial expenses. . . .

. . .

Where a married couple has children, their children are also directly or indirectly, but no less auspiciously, the recipients of special legal and economic protections obtained by civil marriage. Notwithstanding the Commonwealth's strong public policy to abolish legal distinctions between marital and nonmarital children ..., the fact remains that marital children reap a measure of family stability and economic security based on their parents' legally privileged status that is largely inaccessible, or not as readily accessible, to nonmarital children. Some of these benefits are social, such as the enhanced approval that still attends the status of being a marital child. Others are material, such as the greater ease of access to family-based State and Federal benefits that attend the presumption of one's parentage.

It is undoubtedly for these concrete reasons, as well as for its intimately personal significance, that civil marriage has long been termed a "civil right." See, e.g., Loving v. Virginia, 388 U.S. 1 (1967). The United States Supreme Court has described the right to marry as "of fundamental importance for all individuals" and as "part of the fundamental 'right of privacy' implicit in the Fourteenth Amendment's Due Process Clause." Zablocki v. Redhail, 434 U.S. 374 (1978).

Without the right to marry—or more properly, the right to choose to marry—one is excluded from the full range of human experience and denied full protection of the laws for one's "avowed commitment to an intimate and lasting human relationship." Baker v. State [170 Vt. 194, 229 (1999)]. Because civil marriage is central to the lives of individuals and the welfare of the community, our laws assiduously protect the individual's right to marry against undue government incursion. Laws may not "interfere directly and substantially with the right to marry." Zablocki v. Redhail, supra at 387. See Perez v. Sharp, 32 Cal. 2d 711, 714, 198 P.2d 17 (1948) ("There can be no prohibition of marriage except for an important social objective and reasonable means").[15]

Unquestionably, the regulatory power of the Commonwealth over civil marriage is broad, as is the Commonwealth's discretion to award public benefits. Individuals who have the choice to marry each other and nevertheless choose not to may properly be denied the legal benefits of marriage. But that same logic cannot hold for a qualified individual who would marry if she or he only could.

For decades, indeed centuries, in much of this country (including Massachusetts) no lawful marriage was possible between white and black Americans. That long history availed not when the Supreme Court of California held in 1948 that a legislative prohibition against interracial marriage violated the due process and equality guarantees of the Fourteenth Amendment, Perez v. Sharp, 32 Cal.2d 711, 728, 198 P.2d 17 (1948), or when, nineteen years later, the United States Supreme Court also held that a statutory bar to interracial marriage violated the Fourteenth Amendment, Loving v. Virginia, 388 U.S. (1967). As both *Perez* and *Loving* make clear the right to marry means little if it does not include the right to marry the

15. The department argues that this case concerns the rights of couples (same sex and opposite sex), not the rights of individuals. This is incorrect. The rights implicated in this case are at the core of individual privacy and autonomy. See, e.g., Loving v. Virginia, 388 U.S. 1(1967) ("Under our Constitution, the freedom to marry or not marry, a person of another race resides with the individual and cannot be infringed by the State"); Perez v. Sharp, 32 Cal.2d 711, 716, 198 P.2d 17 (1948) ("The right to marry is the right of individuals, not of racial groups"). See also A.Z. v. B.Z., 431 Mass. 150, 162, 725 N.E.2d 1051 (2000), quoting Moore v. East Cleveland, 431 U.S. 494, 499 (1977) (noting "freedom of personal choice in matters of marriage and family life"). While two individuals who wish to marry may be equally aggrieved by State action denying them that opportunity, they do not "share" the liberty and equality interests at stake.

person of one's choice, subject to appropriate government restrictions in the interests of public health, safety, and welfare. See Perez v. Sharp, supra at 717 ("the essence of the right to marry is freedom to join in marriage with the person of one's choice"). In this case, as in *Perez* and *Loving,* a statute deprives individuals of access to an institution of fundamental legal, personal, and social significance—the institution of marriage—because of a single trait: skin color in *Perez* and *Loving*, sexual orientation here. As it did in *Perez* and *Loving*, history must yield to a more fully developed understanding of the invidious quality of the discrimination.

The Massachusetts Constitution protects matters of personal liberty against government incursion as zealously, and often more so, than does the Federal Constitution, even where both Constitutions employ essentially the same language. . . .

. . .

The Massachusetts Constitution requires, at a minimum, that the exercise of the State's regulatory authority not be "arbitrary or capricious." Under both the equality and liberty guarantees, regulatory authority must, at very least, serve "a legitimate purpose in a rational way"; a statute must "bear a reasonable relation to a permissible legislative objective." Any law failing to satisfy the basic standards of rationality is void.

. . .

The department argues that no fundamental right or "suspect" class is at issue here, and rational basis is the appropriate standard of review. For the reasons we explain below, we conclude that the marriage ban does not meet the rational basis test for either due process or equal protection. Because the statute does not survive rational basis review, we do not consider the plaintiffs' arguments that this case merits strict judicial scrutiny.

The department posits three legislative rationales for prohibiting same-sex couples from marrying: (1) providing a "favorable setting for procreation"; (2) ensuring the optimal setting for child rearing, which the department defines as "a two-parent family with one parent of each sex"; and (3) preserving scarce State and private financial resources. We consider each in turn.

The judge in the Superior Court endorsed the first rationale, holding that "the state's interest in regulating marriage is based on the traditional concept that marriage's primary purpose is procreation." This is incorrect. Our laws of civil marriage do not privilege procreative heterosexual intercourse between married people above every other form of adult intimacy and every other means of creating a family. General Laws c. 207 contains no requirement that the applicants for a marriage license attest to their ability or intention to conceive children by coitus. Fertility is not a condition of marriage, nor is it grounds for divorce. People who have never consummated their marriage, and never plan to, may be and stay married. See Franklin v. Franklin, 154 Mass. 515, 516, 28 N.E. 681 (1891) ("The consummation of a marriage by coition is not necessary to its validity").[22] People who cannot

22. Our marriage law does recognize that the inability to participate in intimate relations may have a bearing on one of the central expectations of marriage. Since the earliest days of the Commonwealth, the divorce statutes have permitted (but not required) a spouse to choose to divorce his or her impotent mate. See St. 1785, c. 69, § 3. While infertility is not a ground to void or terminate a marriage, impotency (the inability to engage in sexual intercourse) is, at the election of the disaffected spouse. See G. L. c.

stir from their deathbed may marry. While it is certainly true that many, perhaps most, married couples have children together (assisted or unassisted), it is the exclusive and permanent commitment of the marriage partners to one another, not the begetting of children, that is the sine qua non of civil marriage.[23]

. . .

The "marriage is procreation" argument singles out the one unbridgeable difference between same-sex and opposite-sex couples, and transforms that difference into the essence of legal marriage. Like "Amendment 2" to the Constitution of Colorado, which effectively denied homosexual persons equality under the law and full access to the political process, the marriage restriction impermissibly "identifies persons by a single trait and then denies them protection across the board." Romer v. Evans, 517 U.S. 620, 633 (1996). In so doing, the State's action confers an official stamp of approval on the destructive stereotype that same-sex relationships are inherently unstable and inferior to opposite-sex relationships and are not worthy of respect.

The department's first stated rationale, equating marriage with unassisted heterosexual procreation, shades imperceptibly into its second: that confining marriage to opposite-sex couples ensures that children are raised in the "optimal" setting. Protecting the welfare of children is a paramount State policy. Restricting marriage to opposite-sex couples, however, cannot plausibly further this policy. "The demographic changes of the past century make it difficult to speak of an average American family. The composition of families varies greatly from household to household." Troxel v. Granville, 530 U.S. 57, 63 (2000). Massachusetts has responded supportively to "the changing realities of the American family," and has moved vigorously to strengthen the modern family in its many variations. Moreover, we have repudiated the common-law power of the State to provide varying levels of protection to children based on the circumstances of birth. The "best interests of the child" standard does not turn on a parent's sexual orientation or marital status. See e.g., Doe v. Doe, 16 Mass. App. Ct. 499, 503, 452 N.E.2d 293 (1983) (parent's sexual orientation insufficient ground to deny

207, § 14 (annulment); G. L. c. 208, § 1 (divorce). Cf. Martin v. Otis, 233 Mass. 491, 495, 124 N.E. 294 (1919) ("impotency does not render a marriage void, but only voidable at the suit of the party conceiving himself or herself to be wronged"); Smith v. Smith, 171 Mass. 404, 408, 50 N.E. 933 (1898) (marriage nullified because husband's incurable syphilis "leaves him no foundation on which the marriage relation could properly rest"). See also G. L. c. 207, § 28A. However, in Hanson v. Hanson, 287 Mass. 154, 191 N.E. 673 (1934), a decree of annulment for nonconsummation was reversed where the wife knew before the marriage that her husband had syphilis and voluntarily chose to marry him. We held that, given the circumstances of the wife's prior knowledge of the full extent of the disease and her consent to be married, the husband's condition did not go "to the essence" of the marriage. Id. at 159.

23. It is hardly surprising that civil marriage developed historically as a means to regulate heterosexual conduct and to promote child rearing, because until very recently unassisted heterosexual relations were the only means short of adoption by which children could come into the world, and the absence of widely available and effective contraceptives made the link between heterosexual sex and procreation very strong indeed. Punitive notions of illegitimacy, see Powers v. Wilkinson, 399 Mass. 650, 661, 506 N.E.2d 842 (1987), and of homosexual identity, see Lawrence, supra at [567–7], further cemented the common and legal understanding of marriage as an unquestionably heterosexual institution. But it is circular reasoning, not analysis, to maintain that marriage must remain a heterosexual institution because that is what it historically has been. As one dissent acknowledges, in "the modern age," "heterosexual intercourse, procreation, and childcare are not necessarily conjoined." Post at 382, [798 N.E. 2d at 995–996] (Cordy, J., dissenting).

custody of child in divorce action). See also E.N.O. v. L.M.M., [429 Mass. 824] at 829–830 (best interests of child determined by considering child's relationship with biological and de facto same-sex parents); Silvia v. Silvia, 9 Mass. App. Ct. 339, 341, 400 N.E.2d 1330 & n.3 (1980) (collecting support and custody statutes containing no gender distinction).

. . .

The third rationale advanced by the department is that limiting marriage to opposite-sex couples furthers the Legislature's interest in conserving scarce State and private financial resources. The marriage restriction is rational, it argues, because the General Court logically could assume that same-sex couples are more financially independent than married couples and thus less needy of public marital benefits, such as tax advantages, or private marital benefits, such as employer-financed health plans that include spouses in their coverage.

An absolute statutory ban on same-sex marriage bears no rational relationship to the goal of economy. First, the department's conclusory generalization—that same-sex couples are less financially dependent on each other than opposite-sex couples—ignores that many same-sex couples, such as many of the plaintiffs in this case, have children and other dependents (here, aged parents) in their care. The department does not contend, nor could it, that these dependents are less needy or deserving than the dependents of married couples. Second, Massachusetts marriage laws do not condition receipt of public and private financial benefits to married individuals on a demonstration of financial dependence on each other; the benefits are available to married couples regardless of whether they mingle their finances or actually depend on each other for support.

The department suggests additional rationales for prohibiting same-sex couples from marrying, which are developed by some amici. It argues that broadening civil marriage to include same-sex couples will trivialize or destroy the institution of marriage as it has historically been fashioned. Certainly our decision today marks a significant change in the definition of marriage as it has been inherited from the common law, and understood by many societies for centuries. But it does not disturb the fundamental value of marriage in our society.

Here, the plaintiffs seek only to be married, not to undermine the institution of civil marriage. They do not want marriage abolished. They do not attack the binary nature of marriage, the consanguinity provisions, or any of the other gate-keeping provisions of the marriage licensing law. Recognizing the right of an individual to marry a person of the same sex will not diminish the validity or dignity of opposite-sex marriage, any more than recognizing the right of an individual to marry a person of a different race devalues the marriage of a person who marries someone of her own race.[28] If anything, extending civil marriage to same-sex couples reinforces the importance of marriage to individuals and communities. That same-sex couples are willing to embrace marriage's solemn obligations of exclusivity, mutual

28. Justice Cordy suggests that we have "transmuted the 'right' to marry into a right to change the institution of marriage itself," because marriage is intimately tied to the reproductive systems of the marriage partners and to the "optimal" mother and father setting for child rearing. Id. That analysis hews perilously close to the argument, long repudiated by the Legislature and the courts, that men and women are so innately and fundamentally different that their respective "proper spheres" can be rigidly and universally delineated. An abundance of legislative enactments and decisions of this court negate any such stereotypical premises.

support, and commitment to one another is a testament to the enduring place of marriage in our laws and in the human spirit.[29]

It has been argued that, due to the State's strong interest in the institution of marriage as a stabilizing social structure, only the Legislature can control and define its boundaries.... The Massachusetts Constitution requires that legislation meet certain criteria and not extend beyond certain limits. It is the function of courts to determine whether these criteria are met and whether these limits are exceeded. In most instances, these limits are defined by whether a rational basis exists to conclude that legislation will bring about a rational result. The Legislature in the first instance, and the courts in the last instance, must ascertain whether such a rational basis exists. To label the court's role as usurping that of the Legislature is to misunderstand the nature and purpose of judicial review. We owe great deference to the Legislature to decide social and policy issues, but it is the traditional and settled role of courts to decide constitutional issues.

. . .

Several amici suggest that prohibiting marriage by same-sex couples reflects community consensus that homosexual conduct is immoral. Yet Massachusetts has a strong affirmative policy of preventing discrimination on the basis of sexual orientation. See G. L. c. 151B (employment, housing, credit, services); G. L. c. 265, § 39 (hate crimes); G. L. c. 272, § 98 (public accommodation); G. L. c. 76, § 5 (public education). See also, e.g., Commonwealth v. Balthazar, 366 Mass. 298, 318 N.E.2d 478 (1974) (decriminalization of private consensual adult conduct); Doe v. Doe, 16 Mass. App. Ct. 499, 503, 452 N.E.2d 293 (1983) (custody to homosexual parent not per se prohibited).

. . .

The marriage ban works a deep and scarring hardship on a very real segment of the community for no rational reason. The absence of any reasonable relationship between, on the one hand, an absolute disqualification of same-sex couples who wish to enter into civil marriage and, on the other, protection of public health, safety, or general welfare, suggests that the marriage restriction is rooted in persistent prejudices against persons who are (or who are believed to be) homosexual. "The Constitution cannot control such prejudices but neither can it tolerate them. Private biases may be outside the reach of the law, but the law cannot, directly or indirectly, give them effect." Palmore v. Sidoti, 466 U.S. 429, 433 (1984) (construing Fourteenth Amendment). Limiting the protections, benefits, and obligations of civil marriage to opposite-sex couples violates the basic premises of individual liberty and equality under law protected by the Massachusetts Constitution.

. . .

In their complaint the plaintiffs request only a declaration that their exclusion and the exclusion of other qualified same-sex couples from access

29. We are concerned only with the withholding of the benefits, protections, and obligations of civil marriage from a certain class of persons for invalid reasons. Our decision in no way limits the rights of individuals to refuse to marry persons of the same sex for religious or any other reasons. It in no way limits the personal freedom to disapprove of, or to encourage others to disapprove of, same-sex marriage. Our concern, rather, is whether historical, cultural, religious, or other reasons permit the State to impose limits on personal beliefs concerning whom a person should marry.

to civil marriage violates Massachusetts law. We declare that barring an individual from the protections, benefits, and obligations of civil marriage solely because that person would marry a person of the same sex violates the Massachusetts Constitution. We vacate the summary judgment for the department. We remand this case to the Superior Court for entry of judgment consistent with this opinion. Entry of judgment shall be stayed for 180 days to permit the Legislature to take such action as it may deem appropriate in light of this opinion.

■ Spina, J. (dissenting, with whom Sosman and Cordy, JJ., join).

What is at stake in this case is not the unequal treatment of individuals or whether individual rights have been impermissibly burdened, but the power of the Legislature to effectuate social change without interference from the courts.... The power to regulate marriage lies with the Legislature, not with the judiciary. Today, the court has transformed its role as protector of individual rights into the role of creator of rights, and I respectfully dissent.

. . .

Equal protection. The court concludes ... that G. L. c. 207 unconstitutionally discriminates against the individual plaintiffs because it denies them the "right to marry the person of one's choice" where that person is of the same sex. To reach this result the court relies on Loving v. Virginia, 388 U.S. 1, 12 (1967), and transforms "choice" into the essential element of the institution of marriage. The *Loving* case did not use the word "choice" in this manner, and it did not point to the result that the court reaches today. In *Loving*, the Supreme Court struck down as unconstitutional a statute that prohibited Caucasians from marrying non-Caucasians. It concluded that the statute was intended to preserve white supremacy and invidiously discriminated against non-Caucasians because of their race. The "choice" to which the Supreme Court referred was the "choice to marry," and it concluded that with respect to the institution of marriage, the State had no compelling interest in limiting the choice to marry along racial lines. The Supreme Court did not imply the existence of a right to marry a person of the same sex. To the same effect is Perez v. Sharp, 32 Cal.2d 711, 198 P.2d 17 (1948), on which the court also relies.

Unlike the *Loving* and *Sharp* cases, the Massachusetts Legislature has erected no barrier to marriage that intentionally discriminates against anyone. Within the institution of marriage, anyone is free to marry, with certain exceptions that are not challenged. In the absence of any discriminatory purpose, the State's marriage statutes do not violate principles of equal protection. This court should not have invoked even the most deferential standard of review within equal protection analysis because no individual was denied access to the institution of marriage.

Due process. The marriage statutes do not impermissibly burden a right protected by our constitutional guarantee of due process.... There is no restriction on the right of any plaintiff to enter into marriage. Each is free to marry a willing person of the opposite sex. Cf. Zablocki v. Redhail, 434 U.S. 374 (1978).

■ Sosman, J. (dissenting, with whom Spina and Cordy, JJ., join).

. . .

... Based on our own philosophy of child rearing, and on our observations of the children being raised by same-sex couples to whom we are personally close, we may be of the view that what matters to children is not the gender, or sexual orientation, or even the number of the adults who raise them, but rather whether those adults provide the children with a nurturing, stable, safe, consistent, and supportive environment in which to mature. Same-sex couples can provide their children with the requisite nurturing, stable, safe, consistent, and supportive environment in which to mature, just as opposite-sex couples do. It is therefore understandable that the court might view the traditional definition of marriage as an unnecessary anachronism, rooted in historical prejudices that modern society has in large measure rejected and biological limitations that modern science has overcome.

It is not, however, our assessment that matters. Conspicuously absent from the court's opinion today is any acknowledgment that the attempts at scientific study of the ramifications of raising children in same-sex couple households are themselves in their infancy and have so far produced inconclusive and conflicting results. . . .

. . .

More importantly, it is not our confidence in the lack of adverse consequences that is at issue, or even whether that confidence is justifiable. The issue is whether it is rational to reserve judgment on whether this change can be made at this time without damaging the institution of marriage or adversely affecting the critical role it has played in our society. Absent consensus on the issue (which obviously does not exist), or unanimity amongst scientists studying the issue (which also does not exist), or a more prolonged period of observation of this new family structure (which has not yet been possible), it is rational for the Legislature to postpone any redefinition of marriage that would include same-sex couples until such time as it is certain that that redefinition will not have unintended and undesirable social consequences. Through the political process, the people may decide when the benefits of extending civil marriage to same-sex couples have been shown to outweigh whatever risks—be they palpable or ephemeral—are involved. However minimal the risks of that redefinition of marriage may seem to us from our vantage point, it is not up to us to decide what risks society must run, and it is inappropriate for us to arrogate that power to ourselves merely because we are confident that "it is the right thing to do."

. . .

NOTES

1. In 2003, the Massachusetts Senate submitted a bill that would have established civil unions, instead of same-sex marriage, for same-sex couples. In Opinions of the Justices to the Senate, 440 Mass. 1201, 802 N.E.2d 565 (2004), the court held that the bill, if enacted into law, would violate the equal protection and due process requirements of the Constitution of the Commonwealth and the Massachusetts Declaration of Rights. The court explained:

> We have been asked to render an advisory opinion on Senate No. 2175, which creates a new legal status, "civil union," that is purportedly equal to "marriage" yet separate from it. . . . The same defects of rationality evident in the marriage ban considered in *Goodridge* are evident in, if not exaggerated by, Senate No. 2175. Segregating same-sex unions from opposite sex unions cannot possibly be held rationally to advance or "preserve" what we stated in *Goodridge* were the Commonwealth's legitimate interests in procreation, child rearing, and the conservation of resources. Because the proposed law by its express terms

forbids same-sex couples entry into civil marriage, it continues to relegate same-sex couples to a different status. The holding in *Goodridge*, by which we are bound, is that group classification based on unsupportable distinctions, such as that embodied in the proposed bill, are invalid under the Massachusetts Constitution.

Massachusetts remains the only state where same-sex marriages are legal. On September 7, 2005, the California legislature passed legislation that approved same-sex marriage, but it was vetoed by the Governor on September 29, 2005. See John Pomfret, Schwarzenegger Vetoes Bill Allowing Same–Sex Marriage, Wash. Post, Sept. 30, 2005, at A3.

2. Consider Susan Frelich Appleton, Missing in Action? Searching for Gender Talk in the Same–Sex Marriage Debate, 16 Stan. Law & Pol'y Rev. 97, 105, 119–120 (2005);

> [I]n 1993 ... a plurality of the Hawaii Supreme Court in Baehr v. Lewin, [852 P.2d 44 (Haw. 1993), rev'd as moot sub nom., Baehr v. Milke, 92 Haw. 634, 994 P.2d 566 (1999)] declared Hawaii's sex-based classification for marriage presumptively unconstitutional under the state's ERA. ... The *Baehr* plurality cited Loving v. Virginia to explain why the mere existence of a sex-based classification constitutes prohibited discrimination, notwithstanding the "equal application" of the restriction to men and women alike. In other words, *Loving's* treatment of the racial classifications in Virginia's marriage law ... explains why laws that prohibit women from marrying women and men from marrying men nonetheless discriminate on the basis of sex.[1]
>
> . . .
>
> ... [F]amily law increasingly treats men and women alike even in matters of procreation and parentage. ... Yet, in the public debate, no one seems to be talking about same-sex marriage in this way—as the culmination of gender neutralization of family law and perhaps a final step to equal treatment for all men and women, straight and gay alike.

For a more detailed discussion of the history of same-sex unions and their benefits see William N. Eskridge, Jr., The Case for Same–Sex Marriage: From Sexual Liberty to Civilized Commitment (1996). See generally Symposium: Same–Sex Couples: Defining Marriage in the Twenty–First Century 16 Stan. L. and Pol'y Rev. 1 (2005).

3. Several states have passed laws that provide some of the benefits of marriage to same-sex couples. In 1996, for example, Hawaii adopted a reciprocal beneficiaries statute, HRS § 572C (–1 through –7). The status is reserved for certain couples who cannot marry under Hawaii law, including same-sex couples as long as both parties are at least eighteen years old.

In Baker v. State, 170 Vt. 194, 744 A.2d 864 (1999), the Vermont Supreme Court held that under the Vermont State Constitution same-sex couples are entitled "to obtain the same benefits and protections afforded by Vermont law to married opposite-sex couples." Id. at 886. The *Baker* court left it to the state legislature to decide whether to distribute these benefits and protections to same-sex couples by extending them the right to marry or by creating an alternate "civil union" regime. In 1999, the legislature settled on the latter. Vt. Stat. Ann. Tit. 15, ch. 23 (2001).

In 1999, California adopted a domestic partnership statute, which was expanded in 2001 and again in 2003, under which domestic partners are granted most of the rights of married couples. The status is available only for same-sex couples, and for opposite-sex couples when one partner is over 62. Cal. Fam. §§ 297–299.

1. After the decision in Baehr v. Miike discussed in Note 2, both houses of the Hawaii legislature approved a proposed amendment to the Hawaii Constitution authorizing the legislature to limit marriage to opposite-sex couples. In 1998, the amendment was approved by voters. See Baehr v. Miike, 92 Haw. 634, 994 P.2d 566 (1999).

In 2004, New Jersey passed a domestic partnership statute. N.J. Stat. § 26:8A–1 through –12. See David M. Strauss, The End or Just the Beginning For Gay Rights Under the New Jersey Constitution?: The New Jersey Domestic Partnership Act, Lewis v. Harris, and the Future of Gay Rights in New Jersey, 36 Rutgers L. J. 289 (2004).

In 2005, Connecticut became the second state to approve civil unions. although it was the first such statute passed without any pressure from the courts. It provides the same rights and benefits as the Vermont statute and recognizes civil unions entered into in Vermont. The Connecticut statute also includes a provision that defines marriage as between a man and a woman. That provision is part of the reason the bill passed relatively easily (polls show that Connecticut residents favored civil unions and were against gay marriage). See William Yardley, Connecticut Approves Civil Unions For Gays, N.Y. Times, Apr. 21, 2005, at B5.

4. In Brause v. Bureau of Vital Statistics, 1998 WL 88743 (Alaska Super. 1998), an Alaska Superior Court found in the privacy provision of the Alaska Constitution a fundamental right to choose one's life partner. The court also held that the state must show a compelling interest for refusing to issue a marriage license to same-sex couples. On November 3, 1998, voters in Alaska amended the state constitution to define marriage as the union of one man and one woman. State Ballot Initiatives: Among Top Ballot Issues Decided Tuesday, Wash. Post, Nov. 5, 1998, at A46.

Since 1998, 16 states have passed constitutional amendments barring recognition of same-sex marriages. Nebraska and Nevada passed amendments in 2000 and 13 states (Arkansas, Georgia, Kentucky, Louisiana, Michigan, Missouri, Mississippi, Utah, Montana, North Dakota, Ohio, Oklahoma, and Oregon) followed suit in 2004, immediately following the Massachusetts Supreme Court ruling in *Goodridge*. Kansas passed its amendment in 2005. Most other states have passed marriage recognition laws defining marriage as being between a man and a woman. Only Massachusetts, New Jersey, New Mexico, New York, Rhode Island, and Wisconsin have neither a constitutional nor a statutory definition of marriage as being between a man and a woman.

In 2005, the Nebraska constitutional amendment was held unconstitutional in Citizens for Equal Prot. v. Bruning, 368 F.Supp.2d 980 (D.Neb.2005). The court found that the amendment both violated the Equal Protection Clause and constituted a Bill of Attainder.

5. In 2004, the Supreme Court of Canada held that the Parliament of Canada had authority to approve same-sex marriage. Reference re Same–Sex Marriage, 3 S.C.R. 698. On July 20, Canada legalized same-sex marriage nationwide. Civil Marriage Act, 2005 S.C., c.33 (Can.).

6. Canada's decision to allow same-sex marriage follows a growing trend in Western Europe. Scandinavia began the change with five countries passing domestic partnership laws. (Norway in 1993, Sweden in 1995, Iceland in 1996, Denmark in 1999, and Finland in 2002). In 2001, the Netherlands legalized same-sex marriage. Since 2001, Belgium has also legalized same-sex marriage (although same-sex couples do not have all the same rights that heterosexual couples do), Germany has approved a life partnership registry, and France has recognized civil pacts of solidarity. See Kees Waaldijk, The Introduction of Marriage, Quasi–Marriage, and Semi–Marriage For Same–Sex Couples in European Countries, 38 New Eng. L. Rev. 569 (2004). Spain became the third country in Europe to approve same-sex marriage on June 30, 2005. Ley 13/2005, de 1 de Julio, por la que se modifica el Codigo Civil en material de derecho a contraer matrimonio, Boletin Oficial del Estado (July 2, 2005, 23632). Great Britain followed suit at the end of the year. Civil Partnership Act, 2004, 52 Eliz. 2, c. 33, sched. 1 (Eng. [effective Dec. 5, 2005]).

Wilson v. Ake

United States District Court for the Middle District of Florida, Tampa Division, 2005.
354 F.Supp.2d 1298.

■ James S. Moody, Jr.

. . .

Plaintiffs Nancy Wilson and Paula Schoenwether allege that they are a lesbian couple who reside together in the Middle District of Florida. According to the Complaint, Plaintiffs were legally married in the State of Massachusetts and possess a valid marriage license from that State. Plaintiffs allege that they personally presented their Massachusetts marriage license to a Deputy Clerk at the Clerk of the Circuit Court's Office in Hillsborough County, Florida, asking for "acceptance of the valid and legal Massachusetts marriage license." Plaintiffs allege that "their demand was refused by Defendant Ake, whose Deputy Clerk stated that according to Federal and Florida law, the Clerk is not allowed to recognize, for marriage purposes, the Massachusetts marriage license, because Federal and Florida law prohibit such recognition."

Plaintiffs have filed a Complaint for Declaratory Judgment asking this Court to declare the Federal Defense of Marriage Act ("DOMA"), 1 U.S.C. § 7; 28 U.S.C. § 1738C,[1] and Florida Statutes § 741.212,[2] unconstitutional and to enjoin their enforcement. Plaintiffs have sued, in their official capacities, Richard L. Ake, Clerk of the Circuit Court in Hillsborough County, Florida, and United States Attorney General John Ashcroft.

Plaintiffs allege that the two statutes violate the Full Faith and Credit Clause, the Due Process clause of the Fourteenth Amendment, the Equal Protection Clause of the Fourteenth Amendment, the Privileges and Immunities Clause, and the Commerce Clause of the United States Constitution.

Plaintiffs assert that Florida is required to recognize Plaintiffs' valid Massachusetts marriage license because DOMA exceeds Congress' power under the Full Faith and Credit Clause. Plaintiffs also argue that twelve United States Supreme Court cases (which Plaintiffs label "The Dynamite Dozen"), beginning with Brown v. Board of Education, 347 U.S. 483 (1954), and ending with Lawrence v. Texas, 539 U.S. 558 (2003), demonstrate a

1. The Defense of Marriage Act ("DOMA") provides:

> No State, territory, or possession of the United States, or Indian tribe, shall be required to give effect to any public act, record, or judicial proceeding of any other State, territory, possession, or tribe respecting a relationship between persons of the same sex that is treated as a marriage under the laws of such other State, territory, possession, or tribe, or a right or claim arising from such relationship.

28 U.S.C. § 1738C.

. . .

In determining the meaning of any Act of Congress, or of any ruling, regulation, or interpretation of the various administrative bureaus and agencies of the United States, the word "marriage" means only a legal union between one man and one woman as husband and wife, and the word "spouse" refers only to a person of the opposite sex who is a husband or a wife. 1 U.S.C. § 7.

2. Florida Statutes § 741.212, Marriages between persons of the same sex, provides:

> (1) Marriages between persons of the same sex entered into in any jurisdiction, whether within or outside the State of Florida, the United States, or any other jurisdiction, either domestic or foreign, or any other place or location, or relationships between persons of the same sex which are treated as marriages in any jurisdiction, whether within or outside the State of Florida, the United States, or any other jurisdiction, either domestic or foreign, or any other place or location, are not recognized for any purpose in this state.
>
> (2) The state, its agencies, and its political subdivisions may not give effect to any public act, record, or judicial proceeding of any state, territory, possession, or tribe of the United States or of any other jurisdiction, either domestic or foreign, or any other place or location respecting either a marriage or relationship not recognized under subsection (1) or a claim arising from such a marriage or relationship.
>
> (3) For purposes of interpreting any state statute or rule, the term "marriage" means only a legal union between one man and one woman as husband and wife, and the term "spouse" applies only to a member of such a union.

recent trend by the United States Supreme Court to expand "the fundamental liberty of personal autonomy in connection with one's intimate affairs and family relations." Plaintiffs urge this Court to expand on "The Dynamite Dozen" by finding that the right to enter into a same-sex marriage is protected by the Constitution.

Defendant Ashcroft has moved to dismiss Plaintiffs' Complaint ... on the grounds that the Complaint fails to state a claim upon which relief can be granted....

. . .

Plaintiffs' Complaint asserts that DOMA conflicts with the Constitution's Full Faith and Credit Clause. Article IV, Section I of the Constitution provides:

> Full Faith and Credit shall be given in each State to the public Acts, Records, and Judicial Proceedings of every other State; And the Congress may by general Laws prescribe the Manner in which such Acts, Records and Proceedings shall be proved, and the Effect thereof.

Plaintiffs argue that "[o]nce Massachusetts sanctioned legal same-gender marriage, all other states should be constitutionally required to uphold the validity of the marriage." Plaintiffs believe that the differences in individuals' rights to enter into same-sex marriages among the States, such as Florida and Massachusetts, is exactly what the Full Faith and Credit Clause prohibits. They also assert that DOMA is beyond the scope of Congress' legislative power under the Full Faith and Credit Clause because Congress may only regulate what effect a law may have, it may not dictate that the law has no effect at all.

This Court disagrees with Plaintiff's interpretation of the Full Faith and Credit Clause. Congress' actions in adopting DOMA are exactly what the Framers envisioned when they created the Full Faith and Credit Clause. DOMA is an example of Congress exercising its powers under the Full Faith and Credit Clause to determine the effect that "any public act, record, or judicial proceeding of any other State, territory, possession, or tribe respecting a relationship between persons of the same sex that is treated as a marriage" has on the other States. Congress' actions are an appropriate exercise of its power to regulate conflicts between the laws of two different States, in this case, conflicts over the validity of same-sex marriages.

Adopting Plaintiffs' rigid and literal interpretation of the Full Faith and Credit would create a license for a single State to create national policy. The Supreme Court has clearly established that "the Full Faith and Credit Clause does not require a State to apply another State's law in violation of its own legitimate public policy." Florida is not required to recognize or apply Massachusetts' same-sex marriage law because it clearly conflicts with Florida's legitimate public policy of opposing same-sex marriage.

The United States argues that this Court is bound by the United States Supreme Court's decision in Baker v. Nelson, 291 Minn. 310, 191 N.W.2d 185 (1971), *appeal dismissed*, 409 U.S. 810 (1972). In Baker v. Nelson, two adult males' application for a marriage license was denied by the Clerk of the Hennepin County District Court because the petitioners were of the same sex. The plaintiffs, following the quashing of a writ of mandamus directing the clerk to issue a marriage license, appealed to the Minnesota Supreme Court. Plaintiffs argued that Minnesota Statute § 517.08, which did not authorize marriage between persons of the same sex, violated the First, Eighth, Ninth and Fourteenth Amendments of the United States Constitution. The Minnesota Supreme Court rejected plaintiffs' assertion that "the right to marry without regard to the sex of the parties is a fundamental right of all persons" and held that § 517.08 did not violate the Due Process Clause or Equal Protection Clause.

The plaintiffs then appealed the Minnesota Supreme Court's ruling to the United States Supreme Court pursuant to 28 U.S.C. § 1257(2).[7] Under 28 U.S.C. § 1257(2), the Supreme Court had no discretion to refuse to adjudicate the case on its merits. Hicks v. Miranda, 422 U.S. 332, 344 (1975). The Supreme Court dismissed the appeal "for want of a substantial federal question."

Plaintiffs assert that Baker v. Nelson is not binding upon this Court because the Supreme Court did not issue a written opinion and because the case was decided thirty-two years ago, before the "current civil rights revolution." This Court disagrees. A dismissal for lack of a substantial federal question constitutes an adjudication on the merits that is binding on lower federal courts. As Justice White noted, the Court was "not obligated to grant the case plenary consideration ... but [the Court was] required to deal with its merits."

Although Baker v. Nelson is over thirty years old, the decision addressed the same issues presented in this action and this Court is bound to follow the Supreme Court's decision.

The Supreme Court's holding in *Lawrence* does not alter the dispositive effect of *Baker*. The Supreme Court has not explicitly or implicitly overturned its holding in *Baker* or provided the lower courts, including this Court, with any reason to believe that the holding is invalid today. Accordingly, Baker v. Nelson is binding precedent upon this Court and Plaintiffs' case against Attorney General Ashcroft must be dismissed.

Recent Eleventh Circuit precedent also constrain this Court to rule contrary to Plaintiffs' position. Plaintiffs argue that their right to marry someone of the same sex is a fundamental right that is guaranteed by the Fourteenth Amendment's Due Process Clause....

The Supreme Court has defined fundamental rights as those liberties that are "implicit in the concept of ordered liberty, such that neither liberty nor justice would exist if they were sacrificed." The Court observed that the Due Process clause "specially protects those fundamental rights and liberties which are, objectively, 'deeply rooted in this Nation's history and tradition.' "

Although the Supreme Court has held that marriage is a fundamental right, no federal court has recognized that this right includes the right to marry a person of the same sex. Plaintiffs urge this Court to interpret the Supreme Court's decision in Lawrence v. Texas as establishing a fundamental right to private sexual intimacy. Plaintiffs argue that this Court should expand the fundamental right recognized in *Lawrence* to include same-sex marriages.

. . .

7. At the time, 28 U.S.C. § 1257(2) provided:

> Final judgments or decrees rendered by the highest court of a State in which a decision could be had, may be reviewed by the Supreme Court as follows:
>
> (2) by appeal, where is drawn in question the validity of a statute of any state on the ground of its being repugnant to the Constitution, treaties or laws of the United States, and the decision is in favor of its validity.

This appeal as of right was eliminated by the Supreme Court Case Selections Act (Public Law 100–352), which became law on June 27, 1988.

But the Supreme Court's decision in *Lawrence* cannot be interpreted as creating a fundamental right to same-sex marriage. First, the Eleventh Circuit disagrees with Plaintiffs' assertion that *Lawrence* created a fundamental right in private sexual intimacy and this Court must follow the holdings of the Eleventh Circuit. See Lofton v. Sec. of Dept. of Children and Family Servs., 358 F.3d 804, 817 (11th Cir.), reh'g en banc denied by, 377 F.3d 1275 (2004), and cert. denied, 543 U.S. ___, 125 S.Ct. 869, 160 L. Ed. 2d 825 (2005) [set forth in Chapter 11, Section C.]. ("We conclude that it is a strained and ultimately incorrect reading of *Lawrence* to interpret it to announce a new fundamental right."); Williams v. Attorney General of Alabama, 378 F.3d 1232, 1238 (11th Cir. 2004). The Court in *Lawrence* did not find private sexual conduct between consenting adults to be a fundamental right. *Lawrence*, 539 U.S. at 586 (Scalia, J., dissenting) ("nowhere does the Court's opinion declare that homosexual sodomy is a 'fundamental right' under the Due Process Clause; nor does it subject the Texas law to the standard of review that would be appropriate (strict scrutiny) if homosexual sodomy *were* a 'fundamental right.' "). Rather, the Court determined that the Texas statute failed under the rational basis analysis.

Second, the majority in *Lawrence* was explicitly clear that its holding did not extend to the issue of same-sex marriage, stating that the case "does not involve whether the government must give formal recognition to any relationship that homosexual persons seek to enter." *Lawrence*, 539 U.S. at 578. It is disingenuous to argue that the Supreme Court's precise language in *Lawrence* established a fundamental right to enter into a same-sex marriage.

Moreover, this Court is not inclined to elevate the ability to marry someone of the same sex to a fundamental right. Although the Court recognizes the importance of a heterosexual or homosexual individual's choice of a partner, not all important decisions are protected fundamental rights....

The Eleventh Circuit has also noted that once a right is elevated to a fundamental right, it is "effectively removed from the hands of the people and placed into the guardianship of unelected judges. We are particularly mindful of this fact in the delicate area of morals legislation." Williams, 378 F.3d at 1250 (internal citations omitted). "Of course, the Court may in due course expand *Lawrence's* precedent ... but for us preemptively to take that step would exceed our mandate as a lower court." Williams, 378 F.3d at 1238; see also *Lofton* (the "legislature is the proper forum for this debate, and we do not sit as a superlegislature 'to award by judicial decree what was not achievable by political consensus.' ") quoting Thomasson v. Perry, 80 F.3d 915, 923 (4th Cir. 1996). Therefore, the Court finds that the right to marry a person of the same sex is not a fundamental right under the Constitution.

Plaintiffs also argue that this Court should apply strict scrutiny in determining the constitutionality of DOMA because it violates the Equal Protection Clause of the Fourteenth Amendment.[11] The Eleventh Circuit has held that homosexuality is not a suspect class that would require subjecting DOMA to strict scrutiny under the Equal Protection Clause of the Fourteenth Amendment or the equal protection component of the Fifth Amendment's Due Process Clause. Moreover, DOMA does not discriminate on the basis of sex because it treats women and men equally. Therefore this Court

11. The Court again notes that the Fourteenth Amendment only applies to the states and that Plaintiffs' equal protection claims should have been brought pursuant to the equal protection component of the Due Process Clause of the Fifth Amendment.

must apply rational basis review to its equal protection analysis of the constitutionality of DOMA.

. . .

The United States asserts that DOMA is rationally related to two legitimate governmental interests. First, the government argues that DOMA fosters the development of relationships that are optimal for procreation, thereby encouraging the "stable generational continuity of the United States." DOMA allegedly furthers this interest by permitting the states to deny recognition to same-sex marriages performed elsewhere and by adopting the traditional definition of marriage for purposes of federal statutes. Second, DOMA "encourage[s] the creation of stable relationships that facilitate the rearing of children by both of their biological parents." The government argues that these stable relationships encourage the creation of stable families that are well suited to nurturing and raising children.

Plaintiffs offer little to rebut the government's argument that DOMA is rationally related to the government's proffered legitimate interests. Rather, Plaintiffs repeatedly urge the Court to apply the more rigid strict scrutiny analysis.

Although this Court does not express an opinion on the validity of the government's proffered legitimate interests, it is bound by the Eleventh Circuit's holding that encouraging the raising of children in homes consisting of a married mother and father is a legitimate state interest. DOMA is rationally related to this interest. Moreover, Plaintiffs have failed to satisfy their burden of establishing that DOMA fails rational basis review. See Lofton, 358 F.3d at 818–19.[12] Accordingly, the United States' motion to dismiss is granted.

NOTE

Does DOMA extend—or undermine—state authority to regulated marriage? Both? For additional anlysis of whether DOMA is constitutional, see generally Mark Strasser, Essay: Ex Post Facto Laws, Bills of Attainder, and The Definition of Punishment: On DOMA, The Hawaii Amendments, and Federal Constitutional Contraints, 48 Syracuse L. Rev. 227 (1998); Jon–Peter Kelly, Note, An Act of Infidelity: Why the Defense of Marriage Act is Unfaithful to the Constitution, 7 Cornell J. L. & Pub. Pol'y 203 (1997); Scott Ruskay–Kidd, Note, The Defense of Marriage Act and the Overreaction of Congressional Authority, 97 Colum. L. Rev. 1435 (1997).

e. TRANSSEXUALS AND MARRIAGE

M.T. v. J.T.

Superior Court of New Jersey, Appellate Division, 1976.
140 N.J.Super. 77, 355 A.2d 204.

■ HANDLER, J.A.D.

. . .

The case started inauspiciously enough when plaintiff M.T. filed a simple complaint in the Juvenile and Domestic Relations Court for support

12. Moreover, despite Justice Scalia's fears in *Lawrence,* the Eleventh Circuit has recently reiterated that the "furtherance of public morality [is] a legitimate state interest." *Williams,* 378 F.3d at 1238 n.8. "One would expect the Supreme Court to be manifestly more specific and articulate than it was in *Lawrence* if now such a traditional and significant jurisprudential principal has been jettisoned wholesale (with all due respect to Justice Scalia's ominous dissent notwithstanding)." *Id.*

and maintenance. The legal issue sharpened dramatically when defendant J.T. interposed the defense that M.T. was a male and that their marriage was void. Following a hearing the trial judge determined that plaintiff was a female and that defendant was her husband, and there being no fraud, ordered defendant to pay plaintiff $50 a week support. Notice of appeal was then filed by defendant.

... M.T. testified that she was born a male. While she knew that she had male sexual organs she did not know whether she also had female organs. As a youngster she did not participate in sports and at an early age became very interested in boys. At the age of 14 she began dressing in a feminine manner and later began dating men. She had no real adjustment to make because throughout her life she had always felt that she was a female.

Plaintiff first met defendant in 1964 and told him about her feelings about being a woman. Sometime after that she began to live with defendant. In 1970 she started to go to Dr. Charles L. Ihlenfeld to discuss the possibility of having an operation so that she could "be physically a woman." In 1971, upon the doctor's advice, she went to a surgeon who agreed to operate. In May of that year she underwent surgery for the removal of male sex organs and construction of a vagina. Defendant paid for the operation. Plaintiff then applied to the State of New York to have her birth certificate changed.

On August 11, 1972, over a year after the operation, plaintiff and defendant went through a ceremonial marriage in New York State and then moved to Hackensack. They lived as husband and wife and had intercourse. Defendant supported plaintiff for over two years when, in October 1974, he left their home. He has not supported plaintiff since.

Dr. Ihlenfeld, plaintiff's medical doctor with a specialty in gender identity, was accepted as an expert in the field of medicine and transsexualism. A transsexual, in the opinion of this expert, was "a person who discovers sometime, usually very early in life, that there is a great discrepancy between the physical genital anatomy and the person's sense of self-identity as a male or as a female.... [T]he transsexual is one who has a conflict between physical anatomy and psychological identity or psychological sex." Usually sexual anatomy was "normal" but for some reason transsexuals did not see themselves as members of the sex their anatomy seemed to indicate. According to Dr. Ihlenfeld, there are different theories to explain the origin of that conflict. There was, however, "very little disagreement" on the fact that gender identity generally is established "very, very firmly, almost immediately, by the age of 3 to 4 years." He defined gender identity as "a sense, a total sense of self as being masculine or female ..."; it "pervades one's entire concept of one's place in life, of one's place in society and in point of fact the actual facts of the anatomy are really secondary...."

... Dr. Ihlenfeld diagnosed [plaintiff] as a transsexual. He knew of no way to alter her sense of her own feminine gender identity in order to agree with her male body, and the only treatment available to her was to alter the body to conform with her sense of psych[ic] gender identity. That regimen consisted of hormone treatment and sex reassignment surgery. Dr. Ihlenfeld recommended such an operation and treated plaintiff both before and after it.

The examination of plaintiff before the operation showed that she had a penis, scrotum and testicles. After the operation she did not have those organs but had a vagina and labia which were "adequate for sexual intercourse" and could function as any female vagina, that is, for "traditional penile/vaginal intercourse." The "artificial vagina" constructed by such surgery was a cavity, the walls of which are lined initially by the skin of the penis, often later taking on the characteristics of normal vaginal mucosa; the vagina, though at a somewhat different angle, was not really different from a natural vagina in size, capacity and "the feeling of the walls around it." Plaintiff had no uterus or cervix, but her vagina had a "good cosmetic appearance" and was "the same as a normal female vagina after a hysterectomy." Dr. Ihlenfeld had seen plaintiff since the operation and she never complained to him that she had difficulty having intercourse. So far as he knew, no one had tested plaintiff to find out what chromosomes she had. He knew that plaintiff had had silicone injections in her breasts; he had treated her continuously with female hormones to demasculinize her body and to feminize it at the same time. In the doctor's opinion plaintiff was a female; he no longer considered plaintiff to be a male since she could not function as a male sexually either for purposes of "recreation or procreation."

. . .

Defendant called as an expert witness Dr. T, a medical doctor who was defendant's adoptive father. Over plaintiff's objection he was allowed to testify as an expert. Dr. T classified sex at birth according to sexual anatomy. He described a female as "a person who has female organs in an anatomical sense, who has a vagina and uterus and ovaries or at least has had them." The witness had heard all of the prior testimony and he said that in his opinion plaintiff was still a male because she did not have female organs. . . .

The trial judge made careful findings of fact on this evidential record. . . .

. . . The judge ruled that plaintiff was of the female psychic gender all her life and that her anatomical change through surgery required the conclusion that she was a female at the time of the marriage ceremony. He stated:

> It is the opinion of the court that if the psychological choice of a person is medically sound, not a mere whim, and irreversible sex reassignment surgery has been performed, society has no right to prohibit the transsexual from leading a normal life. Are we to look upon this person as an exhibit in a circus side show? What harm has said person done to society? The entire area of transsexualism is repugnant to the nature of many persons within our society. However, this should not govern the legal acceptance of a fact. . . .

. . .

We accept—and it is not disputed—as the fundamental premise in this case that a lawful marriage requires the performance of a ceremonial marriage of two persons of the opposite sex, a male and a female. . . .

. . .

The issue must then be confronted whether the marriage between a male and a postoperative transsexual, who has surgically changed her external sexual anatomy from male to female, is to be regarded as a lawful marriage between a man and a woman.

An English case, Corbett v. Corbett, 2 W.L.R. 1306, 2 All E.R. 33 (P.D.A.1970) appears to be the only reported decision involving the validity of marriage of a true postoperative transsexual and a male person. The judge there held that the transsexual had failed to prove that she had changed her sex from male to female. The court subscribed to the opinion of the medical witnesses that "the biological sexual constitution of an individual is fixed at birth (at the latest), and cannot be changed, either by the natural development of organs of the opposite sex, or by medical or surgical means. The respondent's operation, therefore, cannot affect her true sex." ...

. . .

The English court believed, we feel incorrectly, that an anatomical change of genitalia in the case of a transsexual cannot "affect her true sex." Its conclusion was rooted in the premise that "true sex" was required to be ascertained even for marital purposes by biological criteria. In the case of a transsexual following surgery, however, according to the expert testimony presented here, the dual tests of anatomy and gender are more significant. On this evidential demonstration, therefore, we are impelled to the conclusion that for marital purposes if the anatomical or genital features of a genuine transsexual are made to conform to the person's gender, psyche or psychological sex, then identity by sex must be governed by the congruence of these standards.

Implicit in the reasoning underpinning our determination is the tacit but valid assumption of the lower court and the experts upon whom reliance was placed that for purposes of marriage under the circumstances of this case, it is the sexual capacity of the individual which must be scrutinized. Sexual capacity or sexuality in this frame of reference requires the coalescence of both the physical ability and the psychological and emotional orientation to engage in sexual intercourse as either a male or a female.

Other decisions touching the marital status of a putative transsexual are not especially helpful. Anonymous v. Anonymous, 67 Misc.2d 982, 325 N.Y.S.2d 499 (Sup.Ct.1971), cited by defendant, held a marriage a nullity, but there the two persons had never had sexual intercourse and had never lived together. Although it was claimed that respondent was a transsexual and had had an operation to remove his male organs after the marriage, there was no medical evidence of this. In B. v. B., [78 Misc.2d 112, 355 N.Y.S.2d 712 (1974)] a female transsexual had had a hysterectomy and mastectomy but had not received any male organs and was incapable of performing sexually as a male. He had then married a normal female who later sued for an annulment on the ground that he had defrauded her by not informing her of his transsexualism and of the operation. The judge there held that even if defendant were a male and trapped in the body of a female, his attempted sex reassignment surgery had not successfully released him from that body.

Anonymous v. Weiner, 50 Misc.2d 380, 270 N.Y.S.2d 319 (Sup.Ct.1966), sustained the refusal by the New York City Board of Health to amend a sex designation on a birth certificate. The court acquiesced in the view of the administrative agency that "male-to-female transsexuals are still chromosomally males while ostensibly females" and that the desire of the transsexual for "concealment of a change of sex ... is outweighed by the public interest for protection against fraud." 270 N.Y.S.2d at 322. To reiterate, the chromosomal test of sex in this context is unhelpful. The potential for fraud, feared by the court, moreover, is effectively countered by the apt observation of the trial judge here: "The transsexual is not committing a fraud upon the public. In actuality she is doing her utmost to remove any false facade." Further, we note the Weiner case was sharply criticized in In re Anonymous, supra, which ordered a change to a female name for a postoperative transsexual.

The court concluded that the chromosomal test recommended by the New York Academy of Medicine and adopted by the court in Weiner was unrealistic and inhumane....

. . .

In sum, it has been established that an individual suffering from the condition of transsexualism is one with a disparity between his or her genitalia or anatomical sex and his or her gender, that is, the individual's strong and consistent emotional and psychological sense of sexual being. A transsexual in a proper case can be treated medically by certain supportive measures and through surgery to remove and replace existing genitalia with sex organs which will coincide with the person's gender. If such sex reassignment surgery is successful and the postoperative transsexual is, by virtue of medical treatment, thereby possessed of the full capacity to function sexually as a male or female, as the case may be, we perceive no legal barrier, cognizable social taboo, or reason grounded in public policy to prevent that person's identification at least for purposes of marriage to the sex finally indicated.

. . .

... The judgment of the court is therefore affirmed.

NOTES

1. The opinion in M.T. v. J.T. indicates that plaintiff's capacity to perform sexually as a female was crucial to the court's decision. Does this mean that if a male is impotent or castrated, he should not be permitted to contract a valid marriage with a female?

All states except Ohio and Tennessee now recognize a change in legal sex status following a sex change operation based on a doctor's sworn statement. See John A. Fisher, Sex Determination For Federal Purposes: Is Transsexual Immigration Via Marriage Permissible Under the Defense of Marriage Act?, 10 Mich. J. Gender & L. 237 (2004). But not all of them recognize the change for purposes of marriage. See, e.g., Littleton v. Prange, 9 S.W.3d 223 (Tex. App. 1999).

2. For further discussion of transsexualism and analysis of its legal ramifications, see Terry S. Kogan, Transsexuals, Intersexuals, and Same–Sex Marriage, 18 BYU J. Pub. L. 371 (2004); Sherrie L. Kopka, The Legal Status of the Postoperative Transsexual, 28 Med. Tr. T. Q. 456 (1982); Jerold Taitz, Judicial Determination of the Sexual Identity of Post-operative Transsexuals: A New Form of Sex Discrimination, 13 Am. J.L. & Med. 53 (1987); Megan Bell, Comment, Transsexuals and the Law, 98 Nw. U.L. Rev. 1709 (2004); L. Anita Richardson, Note, The Challenge of Transsexuality: Legal Responses to an Assertion of Rights, 4 N. Ill. U.L. Rev. 119 (1983).

f. OTHER RESTRICTIONS ON MARRYING (OR NOT MARRYING)

Mental incapacity remains a widely accepted restriction on who may marry. As of 1997, thirty-three states and the District of Columbia restricted marriage by people with mental retardation (although many of the states chose cruder terms such as "feeble-minded" or "idiot"). In twelve of the states and D.C., such marriages were void *ab initio*. In the other twenty-one states, such marriages are voidable if a court finds that one of the parties was either a person with mental retardation or lacked the mental capacity to contract to marry. The legal standards for defining such disabilities, legal processes for voiding marriages, and the standing of particular individuals to seek to void a marriage (the person with mental retardation, their guardian, or their spouse usually) vary from state to state. See Brooke Pietrzak, Marriage Laws and People With Mental Retardation: A Continuing History of Second Class Treatment, 17 Dev. Men. H. L. 1 (UVA 1997). Could similar restrictions be placed on individuals with serious physical disabilities? Those with genetic disorders? Alcoholics?

NOTES

1. Lord Devlin, an English judge, observed that although it makes little sense to force partners who believe their marriage is over to stay together, it might be wise to limit the right to marry a second (or third) time. Specifically, he suggested that when a marriage has failed, society should "claim the right to demand proofs of sincerity before it licenses another." P. Devlin, The Enforcement of Morals 79 (1965).

Do you agree? Would such a restriction be constitutional?

2. Private restraints on marriage in wills or contracts have been held to be illegal in some states, see, e.g., Cal. Civ. Code § 1669 ("Every contract in restraint of the marriage of any person, other than a minor, is void") and, at least in theory, are disfavored by courts as being against public policy. Partial restraints are generally permitted, however, as long as they are not "unreasonable." See, e.g., Gordon v. Gordon, 332 Mass. 197, 124 N.E.2d 228 (1955) (upholding will provision requiring children to marry a person of the "Hebrew faith"); Shapira v. Union Nat'l Bank, 39 Ohio Misc. 28, 315 N.E.2d 825 (Ohio Com.Pl.1974) (accord).

3. This Chapter has focused primarily on state restrictions on who may marry. It is only fair to note that state laws also sometimes pressure unwilling parties to marry. It is clear that private citizens cannot force a marriage, because shotgun weddings have long been held voidable for want of consent.[1] But by making marriage a defense to prosecutions for fornication,[2] or rape,[3] state policy has at times accomplished what a shotgun could not. As Professor Wadlington has observed, such decisions are conceptually at odds with a growing recognition in divorce proceedings that a marriage ended in fact should be terminable at law.[4]

4. Breach of promise actions once forced people into unwanted matrimony, but today they are no longer much of a threat.

The earliest breach of promise to marry suits were based on tort principles. The plaintiff sued to recover money paid in reliance on the (false) promise of marriage. Thus, in 1452 in England, Margaret and Alice Gardyner sued John Keche to recover the 22 marks they paid him to marry Alice. Sometime between 1504 and 1515, John James, a rebuffed law student, sought to recover in a slightly more ambitious suit not only the tokens of affection he had bestowed on Elizabeth Morgan, but also the expenses he had incurred in going to visit her. Some Early Breach of Promise Cases, 3 The Green Bag 3, 5 (1891).

By the seventeenth century, the suits began to resemble contract actions, with breach of promise the injury, and only the tort measure of damages retained to indicate the earlier history. See Stretch v. Parker, Mich. 12 Car.Rot. 21 (1639); Holcroft v. Dickenson, Cart. 233, 124 Eng.Rep. 933 (Ct.Com.Pleas 1672). Homer Clark has suggested that this change arose because marriage in seventeenth-century England was largely a property transaction, entered into for material reasons as much

1. See, e.g., Burney v. State, 111 Tex. Crim. 599, 13 S.W.2d 375 (1929). See generally Walter Wadlington, Shotgun Marriage by Operation of Law, 1 Ga.L.Rev. 183 (1967).

2. See, e.g., O.C.G.A. § 16–6–18; Minn. Stat. § 609.34; Idaho Code § 18–6603.

3. Although many states have repealed the common law marital rape exemption, marriage can still be used as a defense to statutory rape in some jurisdictions. See Kelly C. Connerton, Comment, The Resurgence of the Marital Rape Exemption: The Victimization of Teens By Their Statutory Rapists, 61 Alb. L. Rev. 237 (1997).

4. Wadlington, supra note 1, at 204.

as for sentimental ones. Breach of promise to marry thus was recognized as a legal injury at roughly the same time as breach of commercial contracts. Homer Clark, Domestic Relations § 1.1 (1968).

The American colonies permitted recovery for breach of promise to marry as early as 1633, when a colonial court fined Joyce Bradwicke 20 shillings for not performing her promise to marry Alex Becke. Becke v. Bradwicke, Records of the Court of Assistants, II Colony of Mass.Bay 1630–92 at 32. In 1661, John Sutton won 15 pounds plus costs when Mary Russell became engaged to another, and Richard Silvester collected 20 pounds for his daughter when John Palmer failed to marry her as promised. VII Plymouth Colony Records, 1636–92, Judicial Acts 101.

By 2005, twenty-seven states and the District of Columbia had abolished the action of breach of promise to marry;[5] several others had sharply limited its use.[6] More significantly, in the twenty-three jurisdictions where such actions are still possible, only a handful have been reported in the last twenty years.[7]

Breach of promise actions, in short, are almost extinct. Actions for damage to reputation or lost prospects are rarely successful, moreover, probably as a result of both the improving opportunities for rejected women, and the increase in divorce (and remarriage). With divorce such a likely outcome, breach of promise is generally viewed as a minor injury. See generally Jeffrey D. Kobar, Note, Heartbalm Statutes and Deceit Actions, 83 Mich.L.Rev. 1770 (1985).

What remain are suits to recover gifts or money given in contemplation of the marriage. Plaintiffs have recovered on a number of legal theories ranging from conditional gift,[8] and fraud,[9] to unjust enrichment.[10] A few states even regulate the return of engagement gifts by statute.[11]

B. Restrictions on the Procedure for Marrying

Rappaport v. Katz

United States District Court, Southern District of New York, 1974.
380 F.Supp. 808.

■ POLLACK, DISTRICT JUDGE.

This is an attempted federal suit against the City Clerk of the City of New York, cast in the mold of a suit for violation of Civil Rights, 42 U.S.C.A.

5. Alabama, California, Colorado, Connecticut, Delaware, District of Columbia, Florida, Indiana, Kansas, Maine, Massachusetts, Michigan, Minnesota, Montana, Nevada, New Hampshire, New Jersey, New York, North Dakota, Ohio, Pennsylvania, Texas, Utah, Vermont, Virginia, West Virginia, Wisconsin, and Wyoming. See, e.g., Cal. Civ. Code § 43.4; Burns Ind. Code Ann. § 34–12–2–1. Utah is the only state that has abolished the action through a judicial ruling. Jackson v. Brown, 904 P.2d 685 (Utah 1995).

6. See, e.g., 740 ILCS 15/1 to 15/9 (limiting damages to actual damages and implementing strict time restrictions); Md. Family Law Code Ann. § 3–102 (limiting use of breach of promise to marry actions to pregnant women who have corroboration for their claim).

7. See e.g., Finch v. Dasgupta, 251 Ga. App. 637, 555 S.E.2d 22 (2001); Menhusen v. Dake, 214 Neb. 450, 334 N.W.2d 435 (1983); Phillips v. Blankenship, 251 Ga.App. 235, 554 S.E.2d 231 (2001); Sanders v. Gore, 95–660 (La.App. 3 Cir. 7/10/96), 676 So.2d 866 (1996); Schwalb v. Wood, 288 Ill.App.3d 498, 680 N.E.2d 773, 223 Ill.Dec. 823 (1997); Wagener v. Papie, 242 Ill.App.3d 354, 609 N.E.2d 951, 182 Ill.Dec. 417 (1993).

8. See, e.g., Glass v. Wiltz, 551 So.2d 32 (La. App. 1989); Lindh v. Surman, 702 A.2d 560 (Pa. Super. 1997); Patterson v. Blanton, 109 Ohio App.3d 349, 672 N.E.2d 208 (1996). This theory has even worked in the case of an annulled marriage. LaVigne v. Wise, 43 Pa. D. & C. 4th 225 (1999).

9. Morgan v. Morgan, 193 Ga.App. 302, 388 S.E.2d 2 (1989); see Pine v. Price, 2002 WL 31168905.

10. See, e.g., Bruno v. Guerra, 146 Misc.2d 206, 549 N.Y.S.2d 925 (1990); Dixon v. Smith, 119 Ohio App.3d 308, 695 N.E.2d 284 (3d 1997); Siegel v. Siegel, 1996 WL 222140 (Conn. Super.).

11. See Cal. Civ. Code § 1590; N.Y. CLS Civ. R § 80–b.

§ 1983 [,] seeking an injunction and damages. Both sides have moved for summary judgment. . . .

The plaintiffs are two couples, one having been married by the defendant City Clerk on November 2, 1973 and one who has been planning marriage and is looking forward to a ceremony to be performed by the City Clerk. They complain that they were subjected (or are to be subjected) to dress guidelines promulgated by the City Clerk to be observed for wedding ceremonies at City Hall, including the exchange of a ring or rings. These guidelines are said to deprive them of due process of law in violation of their constitutional rights. . . .

The questioned guidelines are customarily handed to persons when they receive their marriage licenses if they request the City Clerk or his deputy to officiate at the wedding. Among other things the guidelines say that:

(9) Every couple should be properly attired, the bride must wear a dress or skirt and blouse—no slacks—and the groom must wear a coat and tie.

(10) One or two rings must be exchanged.

An office policy accepts in lieu of a tie, a turtleneck shirt or other shirts or jackets that do not require a tie. The ring requirement may be satisfied by the exchange of any other tangible item; the plaintiffs are not pressing any claim herein in regard to this requirement or its substitutes.

Plaintiff Rappaport wished to wear pants to her wedding but was told to present herself in a skirt. She did, but was unhappy that she did not wear her green velvet pants suit for her wedding. Plaintiff Dibbell states that she wishes to wear pants to her wedding, and she and her intended spouse say they do not wish to exchange either one or two rings as part of their wedding ceremony. The couple to be married are a free lance journalist and a music critic. The bride-to-be says: "I find dressing in pants . . . protects me from much of the sex-role stereotyping to which women continue to be subjected both professionally and socially." The groom-to-be says: "Because marriage has traditionally been an unequal yoke, it is essential to me that my marriage ceremony emphasize the equality of the partnership. For this reason, our dress at this ceremony must be virtually identical." The plaintiffs charge that defendant's guidelines put them to the choice between their statutory right to be married by the City Clerk and their fundamental right to marry free of unwarranted governmental intrusion on their privacy and with free expression.

. . .

The ruling herein, dismissing this suit, is not based upon or any reflection upon the merit of this complaint or the alleged justification for such guidelines and their relation to the statutory command to the Clerk—those have not been considered. While federal courts have accepted the case of a policeman's beard because "choice of personal appearance is an ingredient of an individual's personal liberty, and that any restriction on that right must be justified by a legitimate state interest reasonably related to the regulation," Dwen v. Barry, 483 F.2d 1126, 1130 (2d Cir. 1973), it does not seem to this Court that the institutional cases, the school and police cases, reach to the extent of federal cognizance of marriage decorum in City halls.

The threshold question here presented and decided is not the merit of the clothes guideline, but whether the federal courts should supervise marriage forms and procedures in City Clerk's offices. A line for acceptable issues must be drawn somewhere. The defendant's is a locally prescribed and directed function in an area fundamentally of state concern. Plaintiffs concede that some decorum is appropriate but draw the line at skirts, an accoutrement of diminishing use for many. Non constat, the forms and the degree of decorum at weddings in the City Clerk's office do not sufficiently justify provoking a federal-state conflict. Federal judges have too much to do to become involved in this type of dispute which is best and most appropriately resolved by the State of New York and the New York City Council to whom the defendant is responsible. This is a class of case where, certainly, "the state tribunals will afford full justice, subject, of course, to Supreme Court review." H.J. Friendly, Federal Jurisdiction: A General View (1973) p. 95.

Complaint dismissed.

NOTES

1. "The *Rappaport* case was appealed to the Second Circuit, but before the appeal was perfected, Herman Katz was indicted for padding the payroll. (The indictment was dismissed last week because the statute of limitations had run). The new City Clerk was more reasonable and the case was settled by stipulation. The new regulations suggest, but specifically do not require, any particular form of dress for marrying couples, and the exchange of rings requirement has been dropped." Letter from Eve Cary, attorney for the plaintiffs (Feb. 24, 1976).

2. Mary Ann Glendon, Marriage and the State: The Withering Away of Marriage, 62 Va.L.Rev. 663, 677–82 (1976):

> The preliminaries required by a legal system before marriage can take place are revealing indications of the degree to which the State is actively regulating marriage formation, as opposed to contenting itself with promulgating rules that describe ideal behavior but have no real sanctions....
>
> All states and the Uniform Act require a license before formal marriage, and the majority of states impose a waiting period (usually three days as in the UMDA) between the application for the license and its issuance. The licensing statutes usually require that the parties state under oath their names, ages, any relationship between them, whether they have been previously married, and if so how their marriages were terminated. If the statements of the parties do not reveal any irregularities, the license is issued. The licensing official need not make any investigation on his own. The Uniform Marriage and Divorce Act has followed this pattern. The UMDA draftsmen have stated that premarital regulation has been reduced to a minimum and that, as to this minimum, "substantial compliance" is enough. The UMDA does not require documentary evidence of eligibility to marry. In fact, it rejected the suggestion of the Family Law Section of the American Bar Association that, following the practice of some states, a copy of any divorce decree should be required in addition to the simple declaration of the parties regarding the termination of previous marriages. Many states require a physician's certificate stating that each party is free from venereal disease before a marriage license will be issued, but the requirement is easily evaded by marrying in another state, and a marriage contracted in violation of the requirement is not invalid. The draftsmen of the UMDA concluded that this requirement need not be preserved, but did include an optional section for those states that wanted to preserve their medical examination law.
>
> A critical feature of this scheme of regulation is the fact that nearly every aspect of a particular state's plan of regulation can be avoided by going to another state whose law does not happen to include that aspect. There has been

a great deal of sentiment in the United States in favor of a longer waiting period, but the ease of evading this or any other change making marriage more difficult has discouraged any such reforms. Compulsory counselling, waiting periods, restraints on remarriage, and consent requirements are being rejected or abandoned by the states at least as much out of despair as on principle or under the influence of recent constitutional interpretations. The law as a whole is not constructed to enforce effectively existing marriage impediments. For instance, the law lacks any system of registration that would facilitate checks on whether impediments exist in a given case.

State laws have, however, begun to manifest new and distinctively modern types of State interest in premarital preliminaries. This is apparent in the increasing number of states requiring that birth control information be dispensed to all applicants for marriage licenses. Another type of interest is manifested in requests on license application forms for information concerned not with revealing impediments to the marriage but with gathering data to study family life. This innovation poses a problem for reformers torn between the desire to protect privacy and the desire to have information in order to make better laws. ...

. . .

While the laws concerning marriage preliminaries are indicators of the degree to which various marriage restrictions are in fact policed, the laws establishing certain formalities for the actual celebration of the marriage reveal an entirely different aspect of State involvement in marriage regulation: the extent to which marriage rituals, usually religious or customary in origin, have been juridified and made uniform for all groups of the population....

The distinctive feature of American law, in contrast to that of England, France and West Germany, is that there are practically no required formalities for the celebration of marriage. In a few states a couple can form a legal marriage simply by agreeing to be husband and wife and holding themselves out as such.... Although every state requires marriage licenses and records marriage certificates, a wide variety of civil and religious officials are authorized to perform marriages, and states do not impose any particular form of ceremony.

... [I]t is not too much of an exaggeration to say that the present legal regulation of marriage in the United States is already just a matter of licensing and registration....

. . .

3. Contrary to popular belief, the captain of a ship has no authority to marry a couple. Marriages performed on the high seas have been recognized, but only if the law of the state governing the marriage recognizes common law marriages. The real issue, therefore, is what state law governs. Courts have looked to the domicile of either the ship owner, Fisher v. Fisher, 250 N.Y. 313, 165 N.E. 460 (1929), or the parties, Norman v. Norman, 121 Cal. 620, 54 P. 143 (1898). Probably the best explanation of these seemingly disparate rulings is that the courts tend to bend over backwards to sustain such marriages if possible. Comment, Law Governing Marriages on the High Seas, 22 Cal.L.Rev. 661 (1934). The exception to this pattern involves situations in which a couple attempts to circumvent the law of their domicile by marrying on the high seas, as was the case in *Norman*.

C. State of Mind Restrictions

Lester v. Lester

Domestic Relations Court of New York, 1949.
195 Misc. 1034, 87 N.Y.S.2d 517.

■ Panken, Justice.

. . .

A marriage procured in consequence of coercion or fraud will be regarded ab initio as if the marriage had not been entered into at all.

Marriages procured by coercion or in consequence of fraud may in a court having jurisdiction be annulled. An annulment of a marriage is a determination that the conventional relationship of man and wife had not been established despite and in face of a marriage ceremony.

Marriage presumably is a relationship into which two individuals enter upon freely and voluntarily. Environmental influences, and that means education, conventions at a given time and in a given place, and economic status of the parties sometimes control the character of the freedom and the voluntary attitudes of the parties entering into the marriage relationship. To that extent the freedom exercised in a marriage contract is limited.

. . .

The state and the community are interested in and concerned with the institution which marriage creates. Man enters a marital relationship to perpetuate the species. The family is the result of marital relationship. It is the institution which determines in a large measure the environmental influences, cultural backgrounds, and even economic status of its members. It is the foundation upon which society rests and is the basis for the family and all of its benefits.

The character of the culture and civilization, the morals, conventions, law and relationship in the life of a community are what man develops. The community, man, has a vital interest in the marriage institution, for the present generation is father to the succeeding one, and that generation will be the determinant as to the advance of civilization, morals, law and relationships of the future. The character of the succeeding generation is influenced by the permanence and decency of the family institution. Public policy enlists and commands the need of regulation of marriage and the course that the family institution is to pursue. Though marriage is a free institution to be entered into freely and voluntarily because of the community's interest in that institution, the state has a right to regulate and insist upon decency and morals in its maintenance.

Agreements entered into ante-nuptially between parties which do violence to the accepted conventions and laws of the state and the community are unenforceable as a matter of public policy.

The petitioner and the respondent were married according to law. The respondent claims that no valid marriage was entered into; that it was never intended to be a real marriage. He introduced in evidence two documents bearing upon his claim. One exhibited in part reads, "Know all men by these presents that whereas C.L. can no longer bear to continue her relationship with N.C.L. in the same way as in the past, but at the same time is not willing to give him up; and whereas she is desirous of reestablishing herself in the good graces of her relatives and friends; and whereas, considering all things, this cannot be done unless said relatives and friends are given the impression that N.C.L. has married her; and whereas, for personal reasons, she can no longer continue staying with her sister, B.G., but must seek a place of her own; for these and other reasons important only to herself, . . ." and then the document proceeds to set forth that that was the reason and purpose for the marriage between the parties. Another portion of the same document reads, "N.C.L. hereby states, and C.L. hereby admits, that the pretended and spurious marriage contract and ceremonies, and simulated marriage relationship, is taking place against N.C.L.'s wishes, and only because of serious and dire threats of all types made against him and against herself by C.L.; and because of the understanding that the relationship being thus established is only for the benefit of C.L., and hence is not to be interpreted under any conditions as an actual marriage; and that the said relationship involves no obligations of any kind whatsoever, now or at any time in the future, on the part of N.C.L. . . ." Upon those grounds the respondent bases his claim that the marriage is not valid and the obligations which naturally flow from a marriage relationship in favor of the petitioner do not exist. He accepted the benefits of that relationship. He cannot blow hot and cold.

The other exhibit in part reads that both the petitioner and the respondent "do hereby declare that the marriage ceremony we went through at Elkton, Maryland, is in pursuance of our agreement and contract of August 27, 1938," (the date of the other exhibit) "and we therefore consider the marriage ceremony and contract performed between us at Elkton, Maryland, null and void in all its parts and implications whatsoever, ab initio."

. . .

Issue:

Has the marriage contract entered into between the parties before me been the result of coercion, threat, force, fraud or other taint? . . .

. . .

Holding:

The testimony as well as the documentary evidence submitted herein negatives the assertion that this marriage was entered upon as the result of threat or coercion.

Private individuals may not by agreement set aside the law of the land. They may not declare that which is valid in law null and void. . . . Persons may not enter upon a marital relationship in conformity with the law and then dissolve that marriage in violation of law. As a matter of public policy the regulation of divorce is as important as is that of marriage. The parties hereto did sign a paper which is in evidence that they both declared their marriage to be "null and void" in all its parts and implications whatsoever "ab initio". What they have signed and sealed after they have entered into a marriage relationship is not enforceable as a matter of law when the purport of that agreement runs counter to the established law and to the morals and mores and conventions of the society in which they live.

The respondent's claim of coercion or threat seems to be unfounded in the light of his relationship for about ten years with the petitioner subsequent to the agreements upon which he rests his claim to invalidity of the marital relationship.

. . .

In the course of the hearing before me it was testified by the respondent repeatedly that he had been under duress during the entire period of their marital relationship. He testified, for instance, that he had had intimate relations with her, sexually, under duress. In other words he was coerced by her to have sexual relations with her. His explanation when asked what the duress was which she exercised, was "The constant fear of committing suicide and leaving me, blackening my name at the College and blackening my name so that I would lose my employment." The respondent before me is a teacher in some college and oddly he teaches the law of family relations. Evidently he thought himself familiar with the law when he caused the petitioner to sign the two documents above referred to. It is quite odd. He prepared the documents in anticipation of a claim by him that the marriage was entered into by him because of coercion and threat.

I find as a matter of fact and as a matter of law for all purposes that the petitioner has established by fair preponderance the allegations in her petition [for support]. She is the wife of the respondent and continues to be such until the marriage is annulled by a court of competent jurisdiction, if at all. In this case the respondent claims that there has been no marriage and the only method in which he might be relieved of his obligation as the petitioner's husband is by an annulment of the marriage. It is very questionable indeed whether he could possibly prevail. Indeed, I think he could not.

. . .

NOTE

Duress and other causes of action to void a marriage on the ground that the partners lacked either the capacity or the intent to contract are rarely relied on now that it has become easier to obtain a divorce in most jurisdictions.

Insanity had been the most widely recognized basis for holding that one of the partners did not have the capacity to consent to marriage. Many states specifically provide that insanity is a ground for divorce or annulment, although a few have made it a defense to such actions. The statutes use a variety of undefined terms such as "idiocy" and "lunacy," which are applied to both people with mental retardation and people with mental illness. Courts in some jurisdictions construe such statutes quite strictly, however, in keeping with a general resistance to marriage dissolution. See, e.g., Larson v. Larson, 42 Ill.App.2d 467, 192 N.E.2d 594 (1963) (annulment based on wife's insanity denied despite proof that she had a history of mental illness). Others have broadly construed such statutes in the pursuit of equity. See, e.g., In re Acker, 48 Pa. D. & C. 4th 489 (2000) (voiding the recent marriage of an elderly man with an unstable mental condition despite the fact that no party had sought an annulment).

Johnston v. Johnston

Court of Appeal, Fourth District, 1993. California
18 Cal.App.4th 499, 22 Cal.Rptr.2d 253.

■ SONENSHINE, ASSOCIATE JUSTICE.

Donald R. Johnston appeals a judgment annulling his marriage to Brenda Johnston.

After a 20-month marriage, Brenda sought to have her marriage to Donald annulled. Donald agreed the marriage should be terminated but requested a judgment of dissolution be entered.

At the trial, Brenda testified she was unaware of Donald's severe drinking problem until after the marriage and she was upset to discover this and disappointed in his refusal to seek help. She knew before the nuptials that he was unemployed, but did not realize he would refuse to work thereafter. She stated their sex life after marriage was unsatisfactory and that he was dirty and unattractive. In short, he turned from a prince into a frog.

Donald testified to the contrary, but to no avail. The trial court believed Brenda. "There is a conflict in the testimony as to what happened in this marriage. But the court tends to believe [Brenda] has told the truth when she's described the events of the marriage and what occurred before."

The court found Brenda's consent had been fraudulently obtained and annulled the marriage. Donald appeals.

Donald complains the evidence is insufficient to support a finding of fraud. He is correct.

Civil Code section 4425, subdivision (d) delineates the grounds for a voidable marriage: "A marriage is voidable and may be adjudged a nullity if . . . (d) The consent of either party was obtained by fraud, unless such party afterwards, with full knowledge of the facts constituting the fraud, freely cohabited with the other as husband or wife." There was no fraud.

Civil Code section 1710 defines deceit as "either: 1. The suggestion, as a fact, of that which is not true, by one who does not believe it to be true; 2. The assertion, as a fact, of that which is not true, by one who has no reasonable ground for believing it to be true; 3. The suppression of a fact, by one who is bound to disclose it, or who gives information of other facts which are likely to mislead for want of communication of that fact; or, 4. A promise, made without any intention of performing it."

Brenda testified Donald told her "he wanted to get a job and with my help in his life, maybe I could help him get himself back together and get his feet on the ground and go out and get a job. And he wanted to get married to me, to have a nice life with me." She also explained that prior to the marriage she saw him regularly and "he was just very polite. Very nice. Very respectful to me. Clean-shaven. Bathed. Just very nice." But after they were wed he "never treated me with respect after the marriage, that is correct. And on many occasions[,] unshaven."

Even if Brenda's testimony was believed by the trial court, she presented insufficient grounds for an annulment.[2] The concealment of "incontinence, temper, idleness, extravagance, coldness or fortune inadequate to representations" cannot be the basis for an annulment. (Marshall v. Marshall (1931) 212 Cal. 736, 740, 300 P. 816.) If a shoe salesman's false representation that he owned his own shoe store fell short of "fraud sufficient to annul a marriage" in Mayer v. Mayer (1929) 207 Cal. 685, 694–695, 279 P. 783, or a future husband's statement that he was a "man of means" (when he was really "impecunious") was not enough in Marshall v. Marshall, *supra,* 212 Cal. at pages 737–738, 300 P. 816, how much less so are the grounds here, where the husband turned out to be, in the eyes of his wife, a lazy, unshaven disappointment with a drinking problem.[3] In California, fraud must go to

2. We therefore need not discuss whether Donald knew they were false when he made them or whether Brenda relied upon them in marrying him.

3. In *Mayer,* the Supreme Court reversed an annulment where the marriage had not even been consummated and the parties had never lived together as husband or wife. By contrast, here the court recognized the parties consummated their marriage but found Brenda's disappointment with the quantity and quality of the relationship as further grounds for the annulment. "Well, first of all, the court finds that especially in second marriages or in later in life marriages as opposed to early marriages, the parties are entitled to certain expectations. And foremost among them is a loving relationship, a loving, nurturing relationship. And that absent some very powerful financial considerations, which may be part of a lot of cases but are not a part of this case, is the basic reason for wanting to be married. In addition to that, any reasonably normal person, normal mature person, is entitled to be able to seek and have sexual satisfaction. And in the days where AIDS is a life threatening reality, people are certainly entitled to be able to look within a marriage for that satisfaction, both for fidelity and that type of satisfaction, because it's just too dangerous not to. Those things morally, theoretically have always been a consideration, but especially for the last 40 or 50 years, at least, that's not been a major item. I think it's a new ball game today, and I think that that's entirely within the expectations of a person in getting married."

the *very essence* of the marital relation before it is sufficient for an annulment. Thus, the trial court erred in granting the annulment.

Brenda testified that during the marriage she executed an inter-spousal deed, transferring title to real property she owned prior to the marriage to her name and Donald's. The trial judge, after finding the marriage void, declared the deed null and void based upon the failure of consideration. In other words, she deeded the property to Donald because they were married. If the marriage is void, then so is the deed. Because we find the court erred in declaring the marriage void, we must also conclude this portion of the judgment must be reversed.

Donald appealed only the judgment of nullity and the disposition of the real property. Brenda did not file a protective cross-appeal, although the judgment includes several other orders.[4] Moreover, we note the parties stipulated the value of the real property as of June 1992 was $139,000, the purchase price in January 1988 was $101,200 and Brenda's down payment was $19,400; the loan balance at the date of marriage was $82,459 and at the date of separation it was $81,392.56. The parties also stipulated "the negative on the property from October 1989 through June 1992 was $2,384."

Neither the reversal of the portion of the judgment regarding the real property nor the reversal of the judgment of nullity requires a reversal of the stipulation or other orders. Upon remand, the stipulation and the court's other orders shall remain.

The granting of a nullity of the marriage is reversed and a judgment of dissolution shall be entered. The parties' respective property rights in the real property shall be determined based on their previous stipulations. In all other respects, the judgment is affirmed. Donald shall receive his costs on appeal.

NOTES

1. As *Johnston* suggests, most courts have required a stronger showing of fraud to void a marriage contract than to void other contracts. What policy, if any, is served by this tradition?

2. Professor Max Rheinstein noted that "the tendency [of American courts] has been . . . to limit essentiality to those facts which relate to the sex aspects of the marriage, such as affliction with venereal disease, false representation by the woman that she is pregnant by her partner, concealed intent not to consummate the marriage or not to have intercourse likely to produce progeny, also concealed intent not to go through with a promise to follow the secular conclusion of the marriage with a religious ceremony considered by the other party essential to relieve intercourse from the stigma of sin. Annulments have rarely been granted for fraudulent misrepresentations of character, past life, or social standing and hardly ever for misrepresentations on matters of property or income." M. Rheinstein, Marriage Stability, Divorce and Law 95 (1972). Case law largely supports this analysis. See Stepp v. Stepp, 2004 Ohio 1617 (disallowing annulment based on fraudulent portrayal of assets); Adler v. Adler 805 So.2d 952 (Fla. App. 2001) (lying about past marriages was not grounds for annulment). Even fraud concerning the sexual aspects of marriage will not make the marriage voidable once the marriage has been consummated. See Blair v. Blair, 147

4. The court found the money that was in the bank and the tax refund to be Brenda's separate property. "The court also [found] that [Donald] paid $9,000 for the boat and that whether or not [Brenda's] name was on the title at one time, that the boat, . . . , [was Donald's] separate property. As to the check, as to the funds for the sale of the previous boat, the court [found] that there was a fair distribution at the time; that each party got what they put into it and is not going to rule further on that."

S.W.3d 882 (Mo. App. 2004) (lying about paternity of children born during marriage did not support a claim for annulment). The primary exceptions to Rheinstein's observations are incest and bigamy, which have nothing to do with sex and render marriages void, not simply voidable, in most jurisdictions.

D. COMMON LAW MARRIAGE

In re Estate of Love

Court of Appeals of Georgia, 2005.
274 Ga.App. 316, 618 S.E.2d 97.

■ MIKELL, JUDGE.

In this will dispute, a jury determined that Darryl Arnold was the common law husband of Barbara J. Love by virtue of a marriage entered into prior to January 1, 1997,[1] and remained so until the time of her death. Bertrand Love, the decedent's son, appeals the judgment entered on the verdict. In addition to challenging the sufficiency of the evidence, Love argues that the trial court committed several errors by: (1) admitting certain medical records; (2) refusing to charge the jury that a common law marriage may not be partial or periodic; (3) denying appellant's motion in limine to exclude evidence regarding the relationship between Arnold and the decedent after January 1, 1997; (4) refusing to permit a rebuttal witness to testify; and (5) allowing Arnold's counsel to question the appellant about his criminal history. For the reasons stated below, we affirm.

"[I]f there is any evidence to support [the finding of a common law marriage], an appellate court should so construe the evidence to uphold the verdict."[2] So construed, the evidence shows that Arnold and the decedent met in or about 1991. Arnold testified that the decedent was widowed when they met and that he was divorced; that they moved in together in 1992; that they operated the decedent's business together; that they had a sexual relationship and shared a bedroom; that in August 1994, they entered an agreement to be married and the decedent accepted a ring from him; and that she wore the ring daily until her last hospitalization. Arnold introduced several pictures of the decedent wearing the ring, and recalled that two of them were taken in 1996 and 1997, respectively. Arnold also testified that he gave the decedent greeting cards, which referred to her as his wife.

Arnold and the decedent opened a joint checking account on July 17, 1998, obtained certificates of deposit in 1998, and opened additional accounts at a different financial institution in 2002. They shared household expenses, and both contributed monies to the joint accounts. They also opened separate IRAs, designating each other as sole beneficiaries. Arnold explained that they did not indicate that they were married on the IRAs because they did not have the legal documentation to that effect, which was the same reason that they did not file joint tax returns. The beneficiary designations remained unchanged at the decedent's death.

1. Pursuant to *OCGA § 19-3-1.1*, "[n]o common-law marriage shall be entered into in this state on or after January 1, 1997." This case, however, concerns a common law marriage that allegedly took place prior to January 1, 1997. The statute provides that "[o]therwise valid common-law marriages entered into prior to January 1, 1997, shall not be affected by this Code section and shall continue to be recognized in this state."

2. (Citation omitted.) Waddill v. Waddill, 143 Ga. App. 806, 809 (240 S.E.2d 129) (1977).

Arnold further testified that he and the decedent incurred debt together. In 1998, they purchased a utility vehicle. In 1999, they purchased a lot, which was titled in both of their names, on which they planned to build their dream home. Arnold introduced several exhibits that were related to that real estate transaction. They hired an architect to draw the plans for the new home and obtained an estimate, dated May 11, 2000, which was introduced into evidence. Because the lot could not accommodate the home they planned to build, Arnold and the decedent found another lot. They did not purchase the second lot because the decedent became ill in December 2001.

Arnold testified that during the decedent's final hospital stay, which began on April 3, 2003, he signed the consent forms for her treatment, which were admitted into evidence. On one occasion, however, the appellant signed the consent form because the hospital would not accept Arnold's common law status. Arnold was with the decedent when she died on June 15, 2003.

Numerous witnesses testified regarding the relationship between Arnold and the decedent. Paul Haws, a friend and business associate of the decedent, testified that in 1994, the decedent introduced Arnold to him over the telephone as her husband. Betty Johnson, Arnold and the decedent's housekeeper, testified that the decedent referred to Arnold as her husband. Nicole Witherspoon, the social worker responsible for formulating the decedent's home care plan, testified that in April 2003, the decedent told her that Arnold was her husband of seven years. One of the nurses who cared for the decedent testified that the appellant told her that he considered Arnold to be his mother's husband.

Appellant offered evidence to show that the decedent and Arnold had not entered a common law marriage. The decedent's sister, Joanne Walker, testified that the decedent said that she would not marry Arnold because she thought he was being unfaithful to her; and that the decedent authored their sister's obituary in which she referred to Arnold as her "special friend." Further, Love testified that on a warranty deed executed on December 3, 1999, the decedent referred to herself as a single female. Love also offered evidence that in medical records dated January 2001, she referred to Arnold as her fiance; that in 1998 and 2003, she indicated that she was widowed on medical forms; and that in 2003, she listed Arnold as "relative number 1" on a medical form but gave him the designation of "other."

1. Love argues that the jury verdict must be set aside because there was no evidence presented to support it. We have held that whether a woman and a man have entered into a common law marriage is a question of fact, and the factfinder's determination shall not be disturbed on appeal if there is any evidence to support it. Because there was evidence to support the verdict, we reject Love's argument.

Evidence tending to show the existence of a common law marriage may include "such circumstances as the act of living together as man and wife, holding themselves out to the world as such, and repute in the vicinity and among neighbors and visitors that they are such, and indeed all such facts as usually accompany the marriage relation and indicate the factum of marriage." The jury is the final arbiter of credibility and conflicts. While the evidence here is conflicting, the jury was authorized to conclude that a common law marriage existed. We reject Love's argument that because there were documents reflecting that the decedent and Arnold did not hold themselves out as married, there was no common law marriage.[8]

2. Love argues that the trial court erroneously admitted medical records that referred to Arnold as the decedent's husband because the status of their relationship was not pertinent to her medical diagnosis. The trial court's decision to admit or exclude evidence is reviewed under an abuse of discretion standard. We find no abuse here.

"On an issue of marriage vel non the declarations of the parties that they were or were not married, made ante litem motam, are admissible evidence of the fact declared."[10] [10] Additionally, we find that the medical records constitute original evidence, pursuant to *OCGA § 24–3–2*, which provides that "[w]hen, in a legal investigation, information, conversations, letters and replies, and similar evidence are facts to explain conduct and ascertain motives, they shall be admitted in evidence not as hearsay but as original evidence." The documents about which appellant now complains were not admitted for the purpose of proving that Arnold was the decedent's husband, but to explain Arnold and the decedent's conduct, which was relevant to the issue of whether they held themselves out as married. Moreover, even if the records should have been excluded on hearsay grounds, they were simply cumulative of other testimony in the case. Thus, this error fails.

3. Next, Love argues that the trial court erred by refusing to charge the jury that a common law marriage may not be partial or periodic and that Arnold was required to prove that his illicit relationship with the decedent had ended and a marriage contract had been entered into. "In reviewing a claim of error for refusal to charge, we must determine whether the request was entirely correct and accurate, adjusted to the pleadings, law, and evidence, and not otherwise covered in the general charge." Because we find that the substance of the requested charges was covered in the correct instructions of the court, we find no error.

The trial court refused Love's request to charge no. 27, which included the statement that the relationship could not be partial or periodic. However, the trial court charged the jury as follows:

> To constitute a valid marriage in this state, there must be—number one; parties able to contract. Number two; an actual contract and number three; consummation according to law. By common law and the law of this state, a mutual agreement to be husband and wife by parties able to contract followed by cohabitation is recognized as a valid marriage, as long as the marriage was established prior to January 1, 1997. ... For purposes of proving common law marriage, the fact that the parties agreed to live together as man and wife and consummated the agreement may be inferred from proof of cohabitation that the parties held themselves out to the world as husband and wife and such proof may be

8. See Wright [v. Goss, 229 Ga. App. 393, 395 (1997)] ("It is not true that if there is any undisputed evidence that they held themselves out as unmarried (loan applications, tax returns, etc.), then as a matter of law that precludes the element that they must agree to live together as husband and wife. A person might say on government and business documents that he or she is single, in order to reduce taxes or obtain welfare or for some other personal purpose such as not wanting certain persons to know they are married, and actually be common law married.").

10. Whigby v. Burnham, 135 Ga. 584, 586 (69 S.E. 1114) (1911). "Ante litem motam" means when the declarant had no motive to distort the truth. Black's Law Dictionary (5th ed. 1979), p. 84.

> made by general repute among neighbors and others in a position to know the facts.

This charge was in accordance with the law of this state [and] adequately covered the charge requested by the appellant.

. . .

5. Love argues that the trial court erred when it refused to permit Tracie Miller to testify as a rebuttal witness to the testimony of Betty Johnson. We disagree.

Johnson, the decedent and Arnold's housekeeper, denied that she told Miller, who had interviewed her a week before trial, that the decedent and Arnold had traveled to Las Vegas to get married and that the decedent got "cold feet." Love attempted to call Miller to testify to her conversation with Johnson. The trial court excluded Miller from testifying because the rule of sequestration had been invoked, and Miller had been present in the courtroom during the trial. "[D]ecisions regarding exceptions to the rule of sequestration in order to facilitate the orderly presentation of evidence are a matter within the discretion of the trial court." Though the trial court had the authority to allow Miller to testify, the fact that it chose not to do so did not amount to an abuse of discretion.

6. In his final enumeration of error, Love argues that the trial court erroneously permitted Arnold's counsel to question him about his criminal history without laying a proper foundation. . . . Appellant has not shown that he suffered any harm as a result of this alleged error. Accordingly, this error, too, fails.

■ Judgment affirmed. ANDREWS, P. J., and PHIPPS, J., concur.

NOTE

At the beginning of the twentieth century, two-thirds of the states recognized common law marriages. Today only ten states and the District of Columbia do.[1] The legal change in many respects reflects demographic changes. A practice that was almost a necessity when the population was scarce and scattered, and ministers or justices of the peace few and far between, became increasingly unacceptable as society grew and became more complex. Moral objections also grew. O.E. Koegel, for example, argued that common law marriages "invite impulsive, impure and secret unions." Common Law Marriage and its Development in the United States 167 (1922). A growing concern with eugenics was a third factor in tightening the procedure for contracting a legal marriage. Blood tests and prohibitions on the marriage of mentally ill individuals also embodied this concern.

Recently, however, the trend toward abolishing common law marriage has abated somewhat. For one thing, it has been recognized that those jurisdictions that do not recognize common law marriage often have to resort to other devices to achieve the same end. Most jurisdictions, for example, have adopted a presumption in favor of the validity of a second marriage when one spouse was previously married

1. Alabama, Colorado, Iowa, Kansas, Montana, Oklahoma, Pennsylvania, Texas (called "informal marriage"), Rhode Island, and South Carolina plus the District of Columbia follow the traditional common law marriage requirements. Georgia, Idaho, and Ohio have grandfather clauses recognizing common law marriages prior to certain years (1997, 1996, and 1991 respectively). New Hampshire recognizes common law marriages solely for purposes of probate (at the death of one spouse). Utah allows common law marriage of a sort, but has extra requirements beyond the traditional standard and adds a need for a court determination to validate the marriage.

(the burden of proving that the first marriage was still in existence lies with the party attacking the legitimacy of the second marriage).[2]

There are three different situations to consider: (1) instances in which both parties believed in good faith they were formally married, but in fact they were not (e.g., the person who officiated had no authority to marry them, or there was a technical flaw in the license); (2) instances in which one party believed in good faith that he or she was formally married (e.g., one spouse lied and concealed the fact that he or she was still married to someone else); and (3) instances in which both knew they were not formally married, but believed they were nonetheless legally wed. Legal recognition of the marriage or other appropriate relief seems clearly justified for both spouses in instance one, and for the innocent spouse in example two. Any decision to abolish common law marriage in a jurisdiction should therefore at least consider adopting other forms of protection for innocent parties in instances one and two. California, for example, has adopted the putative spouse doctrine in its Family Code:

> § 2251. Status of putative spouse; division of quasi-marital property
>
> (a) If a determination is made that a marriage is void or voidable and the court finds that either party or both parties believed in good faith that the marriage was valid, the court shall:
>
> (1) Declare the party or parties to have the status of a putative spouse.
>
> (2) If the division of property is in issue, divide ... that property acquired during the union.... This property is known as "quasi-marital property."
>
> § 2254. Support of putative spouse
>
> The court may, during the pendency of a proceeding for nullity of marriage or upon judgment of nullity of marriage, order a party to pay for the support of the other party in the same manner as if the marriage had not been void or voidable if the party for whose benefit the order is made is found to be a putative spouse.

It is important to note, however, that a putative marriage is not a marriage. For example, there is no need to seek an annulment or divorce to terminate a putative marriage. See generally, Christopher Blakesley, The Putative Marriage Doctrine, 60 Tul.L.Rev. 1 (1985).

2. It is consequently very difficult to tally exactly how many states recognize some form of common law marriage, particularly if a functional definition is used. Tennessee, for example, has formally abolished common law marriage, but reachieved almost the same result by presumption. See Emmit v. Emmit, 174 S.W.3d 248 (Tenn.App.2005); Richard T. Doughtie, Note, Use of Presumptions in Proving the Existence of Marriage Relationships in Tennessee, 5 Mem.St.U.L.Rev. 409 (1975).

CHAPTER 3

MARRIAGE

A. THE TRADITIONAL MODEL OF MARRIAGE

1. MARITAL PRIVACY

McGuire v. McGuire

Supreme Court of Nebraska, 1953.
157 Neb. 226, 59 N.W.2d 336.

■ MESSMORE, JUSTICE.

The plaintiff, Lydia McGuire, brought this action in equity in the district court for Wayne County against Charles W. McGuire, her husband, as defendant, to recover suitable maintenance and support money, and for costs and attorney's fees. Trial was had to the court and a decree was rendered in favor of the plaintiff.

The district court decreed that the plaintiff was legally entitled to use the credit of the defendant and obligate him to pay for certain items in the nature of improvements and repairs, furniture, and appliances for the household in the amount of several thousand dollars; required the defendant to purchase a new automobile with an effective heater within 30 days; ordered him to pay travel expenses of the plaintiff for a visit to each of her daughters at least once a year; that the plaintiff be entitled in the future to pledge the credit of the defendant for what may constitute necessaries of life; awarded a personal allowance to the plaintiff in the sum of $50 a month; awarded $800 for services for the plaintiff's attorney; and as an alternative to part of the award so made, defendant was permitted, in agreement with plaintiff, to purchase a modern home elsewhere.

. . .

The record shows that the plaintiff and defendant were married in Wayne, Nebraska, on August 11, 1919. . . . The plaintiff had been previously married. Her first husband died in October 1914, leaving surviving him the plaintiff and two daughters. He died intestate, leaving 80 acres of land in Dixon County. The plaintiff and each of the daughters inherited a one-third interest therein. At the time of the marriage of the plaintiff and defendant the plaintiff's daughters were 9 and 11 years of age. By working and receiving financial assistance from the parties to this action, the daughters received a high school education in Pender. . . . Both . . . are married and have families of their own.

On April 12, 1939, the plaintiff transferred her interest in the 80-acre farm to her two daughters. The defendant signed the deed.

At the time of trial plaintiff was 66 years of age and the defendant nearly 80 years of age. No children were born to these parties. The defendant had no dependents except the plaintiff.

The plaintiff testified that she was a dutiful and obedient wife, worked and saved, and cohabited with the defendant until the last 2 or 3 years. She worked in the fields, did outside chores, cooked, and attended to her household duties such as cleaning the house and doing the washing. For a number of years she raised as high as 300 chickens, sold poultry and eggs, and used the money to buy clothing, things she wanted, and for groceries. She further testified that the defendant was the boss of the house and his word was law; that he would not tolerate any charge accounts and would not inform her as to his finances or business; and that he was a poor companion. The defendant did not complain of her work, but left the impression to her that she had not done enough. On several occasions the plaintiff asked the defendant for money. He would give her very small amounts, and for the last 3 or 4 years he had not given her any money nor provided her with clothing, except a coat about 4 years previous. The defendant had purchased the groceries the last 3 or 4 years, and permitted her to buy groceries, but he paid for them by check. There is apparently no complaint about the groceries the defendant furnished. The defendant had not taken her to a motion picture show during the past 12 years. They did not belong to any organizations or charitable institutions, nor did he give her money to make contributions to any charitable institutions. . . . For the past 4 years or more, the defendant had not given the plaintiff money to purchase furniture or other household necessities. Three years ago he did purchase an electric, wood-and-cob combination stove which was installed in the kitchen, also linoleum floor covering for the kitchen. The plaintiff further testified that the house is not equipped with a bathroom, bathing facilities, or inside toilet. The kitchen is not modern. She does not have a kitchen sink. Hard and soft water is obtained from a well and cistern. She has a mechanical Servel refrigerator, and the house is equipped with electricity. There is a pipeless furnace which she testified had not been in good working order for 5 or 6 years, and she testified she was tired of scooping coal and ashes. She had requested a new furnace but the defendant believed the one they had to be satisfactory. She related that the furniture was old and she would like to replenish it, at least to be comparable with some of her neighbors; that her silverware and dishes were old and were primarily gifts, outside of what she purchased; that one of her daughters was good about furnishing her clothing, at least a dress a year, or sometimes two; that the defendant owns a 1929 Ford coupe equipped with a heater which is not efficient, and on the average of every 2 weeks he drives the plaintiff to Wayne to visit her mother; and that he also owns a 1927 Chevrolet pickup which is used for different purposes on the farm. The plaintiff was privileged to use all of the rent money she wanted to from the 80–acre farm, and when she goes to see her daughters, which is not frequent, she uses part of the rent money for that purpose, the defendant providing no funds for such use. The defendant ordinarily raised hogs on his farm, but the last 4 or 5 years has leased his farm land to tenants, and he generally keeps up the fences and the buildings. At the present time the plaintiff is not able to raise chickens and sell eggs. She has about 25 chickens. The plaintiff has had three abdominal operations for which the defendant has paid. She selected her own doctor, and there were no restrictions placed in that respect. When she has requested various things for the home or personal effects, defendant has informed her on many occasions that he did not have the money to pay for the same. She would like to have a new car. She visited one daughter in Spokane, Washington, in March 1951 for 3 or 4 weeks, and visited the other daughter living in Fort Worth, Texas, on three occasions for 2 to 4 weeks at a time. She had visited one of her daughters when she was living in Sioux City some weekends. The plaintiff further testified that she had very little funds, possibly $1,500 in the bank which was chicken money and money which her father furnished her, he having departed this life a few years ago; and that use of the telephone was restricted, indicating that defendant did not desire that she make long distance calls, otherwise she had free access to the telephone.

It appears that the defendant owns 398 acres of land with 2 acres deeded to a church, the land being of the value of $83,960; that he has bank deposits in the sum of $12,786.81 and government bonds in the amount of $104,500; and that his income, including interest on the bonds and rental for his real estate, is $8,000 or $9,000 a year. . . . The plaintiff has a bank account of $5,960.22. This account includes deposits of some $200 and $100 which the court required the defendant to pay his wife as temporary allowance during the pendency of these proceedings. One hundred dollars was withdrawn on the date of each deposit.

The facts are not in dispute.

. . .

In the case of Earle v. Earle, 27 Neb. 277, 43 N.W. 118, 20 Am.St.Rep. 667, the plaintiff's petition alleged, in substance, the marriage of the parties, that one child was born of the marriage, and that the defendant sent his wife away from him, did not permit her to return, contributed to her support and maintenance separate and apart from him, and later refused and ceased to provide for her support and the support of his child. The wife instituted a suit in equity against her husband for maintenance and support without a prayer for divorce or from bed and board. The question presented was whether or not the wife should be compelled to resort to a proceedings [sic] for a divorce, which she did not desire to do, or from bed and board. On this question, in this state the statutes are substantially silent and at the present time there is no statute governing this matter. The court stated that it was a well-established rule of law that it is the duty of the husband to provide his family with support and means of living—the style of support, requisite lodging, food, clothing, etc., to be such as fit his means, position, and station in life—and for this purpose the wife has generally the right to use his credit for the purchase of necessaries. The court held that if a wife is abandoned by her husband, without means of support, a bill in equity will lie to compel the husband to support the wife without asking for a decree of divorce.

In the case of Cochran v. Cochran, 42 Neb. 612, 60 N.W. 942, Mrs. Cochran was a school teacher in Wisconsin. Her husband came to Nebraska and decided to get a divorce. He did, secretly and fraudulently on the theory that his wife abandoned him. The court held: "A court of equity will entertain an action brought for alimony alone, and will grant the same, although no divorce or other relief is sought, where the wife is separated from the husband without her fault."

. . .

In the case of Brewer v. Brewer, 79 Neb. 726, 113 N.W. 161, 13 L.R.A., N.S., 222, the plaintiff lived with her husband and his mother. The mother dominated the household. The plaintiff went to her mother. She stated she would live in the same house with her husband and his mother if she could have control of her part of the house. The defendant did not offer to accede to these conditions. The court held that a wife may bring a suit in equity to secure support and alimony without reference to whether the action is for divorce or not; that every wife is entitled to a home corresponding to the circumstances and condition of her husband over which she may be permitted to preside as mistress; and that she does not forfeit her right to maintenance by refusing to live under the control of the husband's mother.

. . .

It becomes apparent that there are no cases cited by the plaintiff and relied upon by her from this jurisdiction or other jurisdictions that will sustain the action such as she has instituted in the instant case.

. . .

In the instant case the marital relation has continued for more than 33 years, and the wife has been supported in the same manner during this time without complaint on her part. The parties have not been separated or living apart from each other at any time. In the light of the cited cases it is clear, especially so in this jurisdiction, that to maintain an action such as the one at bar, the parties must be separated or living apart from each other.

The living standards of a family are a matter of concern to the household, and not for the courts to determine, even though the husband's attitude toward his wife, according to his wealth and circumstances, leaves little to be said in his behalf. As long as the home is maintained and the parties are living as husband and wife it may be said that the husband is legally supporting his wife and the purpose of the marriage relation is being carried out. Public policy requires such a holding. It appears that the plaintiff is not devoid of money in her own right. She has a fair-sized bank account and is entitled to use the rent from the 80 acres of land left by her first husband, if she so chooses.

. . .

Reversed and remanded with directions to dismiss.

■ Yeager, Justice (dissenting).

. . .

There is and can be no doubt that, independent of statutes relating to divorce, alimony, and separate maintenance, if this plaintiff were living apart from the defendant she could in equity and on the facts as outlined in the record be awarded appropriate relief.

. . .

In the light of what the decisions declare to be the basis of the right to maintain an action for support, is there any less reason for extending the right to a wife who is denied the right to maintenance in a home occupied with her husband than to one who has chosen to occupy a separate abode?

If the right is to be extended only to one who is separated from the husband equity and effective justice would be denied where a wealthy husband refused proper support and maintenance to a wife physically or mentally incapable of putting herself in a position where the rule could become available to her.

It is true that in all cases examined which uphold the right of a wife to maintain an action in equity for maintenance the parties were living apart, but no case has been cited or found which says that separation is a condition precedent to the right to maintain action in equity for maintenance. Likewise none has been cited or found which says that it is not.

In primary essence the rule contemplates the enforcement of an obligation within and not without the full marriage relationship. The reasoning contained in the opinions sustaining this right declare that purpose.

In Earle v. Earle, supra, it was said:

> "The question is, whether or not the plaintiff shall be compelled to resort to a proceeding for a divorce, which she does not desire to do, and which probably she is unwilling to do, from conscientious convictions, or, in failing to do so, shall be deprived of that support which her husband is bound to give her."

. . .

If there may not be resort to equity in circumstances such as these then as pointed out in the following statement from Earle v. Earle, *supra*, a dim view must be taken of the powers of a court of equity: "As we have already said in substance, there is not much to commend an alleged principle of equity which would hold that the wife, with her family of one or more children to support, must be driven to going into court for a divorce when such a proceeding is abhorrent to her, or, in case of her refusal so to do, being compelled to submit to a deprivation of the rights which equity and humanity clearly give her; that, in order to obtain that to which she is clearly entitled, she must institute her action for a divorce, make her grievances public, which she would otherwise prefer to keep to herself, and finally liberate a husband from an obligation of which he is already tired, but from which he is not entitled to be relieved."

. . .

I conclude therefore that the conclusion of the decree that the district court had the power to entertain the action was not contrary to law.

I think however that the court was without proper power to make any of the awards contained in the decree for the support and maintenance of the plaintiff except the one of $50 a month.

. . .

I am of the opinion that the power of the court in such instances as this should not be extended beyond the allowance of sufficient money to provide adequate support and maintenance.

. . .

NOTES

1. "In my opinion, Mr. and Mrs. McGuire were very much alike, both being very cautious when it came to money. Mrs. McGuire was not poor in any respect, and of course, he was quite wealthy for those times. They never did separate, but continued to live together as husband and wife until Mr. McGuire's death. At the time the case was pending we had a number of motions to argue before the Court. They would come together in their old Model A car during the winter with no heater to the Courthouse. As soon as they got to the lobby of the Courthouse she would immediately meet with her attorney, Mr. H.D. Addison, and he would meet with me and we would discuss the various aspects of the case. After the hearings they would immediately get in their car and go back home.

Incidentally, while the case was pending in the Supreme Court, Mr. McGuire did comply with the District Court's orders and bought a used car with a heater and made some payments to her and if my memory serves me right, modernized the farm home, all of which he resented doing." Letter from Charles McDermott, attorney for the defendant (April 18, 1977).

2. Consider Hendrik Hartog, Man & Wife in America: A History 11 (2000):

> To understand the decision in *McGuire*, we might begin by describing where and when the decision was made: the United States of America as it was between the 1790s and the last forty years of the twentieth century....
>
> The first thing to notice about the United States in this period ... was that the public officials, the authoritative legal voices, were all male. Judges, legislators, juries, treatise writers, all of them. By the early twentieth century, it was theoretically possible for a woman to become a lawyer, and by the 1920s there would be a sprinkling of women who were judges and a number of women who wrote texts (although not authoritative treatises) on family law. As late as the 1950s, however, women were a miniscule fraction of the lawmakers. One of the many "unique" aspects of McGuire v. McGuire was that the lower court judge who had recognized Lydia's right to a remedy, the judge reversed by the Nebraska Supreme Court, was a woman.

3. Does the doctrine of family privacy (which might also be termed the principle of not intervening in ongoing marriages) promote marital harmony? Does your answer depend, as the dissent in *McGuire* suggests, on whether or not the dispute at issue concerns only monetary support? Should a court, for example, attempt to enforce a wife's traditional duty of "services"? If not, is it appropriate to enforce the husband's traditional duty of support?

4. Third parties have long been entitled, in theory at least, to enforce a husband's duty of support by suing him for any "necessaries" sold to his wife. But due to the burden of litigating to enforce this duty, most merchants have not been willing to extend credit for the purchase of even obvious "necessaries" to a wife without the prior approval of her husband. Because a wife cannot enforce her right to support directly, as *McGuire* demonstrates, does a wife's alleged right to support in fact exist? Conversely does a husband really have a right to services? What kind of marital arrangements are promoted by the doctrine of "family privacy"?

2. Gender Roles

Graham v. Graham

United States District Court, Eastern District of Michigan, 1940.
33 F.Supp. 936.

■ Tuttle, District Judge.

This is a suit by a man against his former wife upon the following written agreement alleged to have been executed September 17, 1932, by the parties:

> "This agreement made this 17th day of September, 1932, between Margrethe Graham and Sidney Graham, husband and wife. For valuable consideration Margrethe Graham hereby agrees to pay to Sidney Graham the sum of Three Hundred ($300.00) Dollars per month each and every month hereafter until the parties hereto no longer desire this arrangement to continue. Said Three Hundred ($300.00) Dollars per month to be paid to Sidney Graham by said Margrethe Graham directly to said Sidney Graham.
>
> "This agreement is made to adjust financial matters between the parties hereto, so that in the future there will be no further arguments as to what money said Sidney Graham shall receive."

The parties were divorced on July 11, 1933. While the writing itself recites no consideration but merely states that it is made to prevent future arguments as to the amount of money the husband is to receive from his wife, the complaint alleges that the plaintiff had quit his job in a hotel at the solicitation of the defendant who wanted him to accompany her upon her travels, she paying his expenses, and that he was desirous of returning to work but that the defendant in order to induce him not to do so entered into this agreement. The total amount claimed until November 7, 1939, is $25,500, with interest at five per cent per annum from the time each monthly installment of $300 became due....

. . .

A ... question is presented as to whether the complaint sets forth any consideration for the alleged contract.... However, ... it is unnecessary to decide this question, since I am convinced that even if the consideration is what counsel claims, and the plaintiff did agree to refrain from work and accompany his wife on her travels, the contract was not a competent one for married persons to enter into.

In the first place, it is highly doubtful if the alleged contract is within the capacity of a married woman to make under Michigan law. The degree of emancipation of married women with respect to contract and property rights varies widely in the different states. However, it has been repeatedly stated by the Michigan Supreme Court that under the Michigan statutes a married woman has no general power to contract, but can contract only in relation to her separate property....

. . .

However, I do not rest my decision on this ground, but rather upon the broader ground that even if the contract is otherwise within the contractual power of the parties it is void because it contravenes public policy. Under the law, marriage is not merely a private contract between the parties, but creates a status in which the state is vitally interested and under which certain rights and duties incident to the relationship come into being, irrespective of the wishes of the parties. As a result of the marriage contract, for example, the husband has a duty to support and to live with his wife and the wife must contribute her services and society to the husband and follow him in his choice of domicile. The law is well settled that a private agreement between persons married or about to be married which attempts to change the essential obligations of the marriage contract as defined by the law is contrary to public policy and unenforceable. While there appears to be no Michigan decision directly in point, the principle is well stated in the Restatement of the Law of Contracts, as follows:

"Sec. 587. Bargain to Change Essential Obligations of Marriage

"A bargain between married persons or persons contemplating marriage to change the essential incidents of marriage is illegal.

"Illustrations:

"1. A and B who are about to marry agree to forego sexual intercourse. The bargain is illegal.

"2. In a state where the husband is entitled to determine the residence of a married couple, A and B who are about to marry agree that the wife shall not be required to leave the city where she then lives. The bargain is illegal."

Thus, it has been repeatedly held that a provision releasing the husband from his duty to support his wife in a contract between married persons, or those about to be married, except in connection with a pre-existing or contemplated immediate separation, makes the contract void. Garlock v. Garlock, 1939, 279 N.Y. 337, 18 N.E.2d 521; 120 A.L.R. 1331; French v. McAnarney, 1935, 290 Mass. 544, 195 N.E. 714.... Even in the states with the most liberal emancipation statutes with respect to married women, the law has not gone to the extent of permitting husbands and wives by agreement to change the essential incidents of the marriage contract.

The contract claimed to have been made by the plaintiff and defendant in the case at bar while married and living together falls within this prohibition. Under its terms, the husband becomes obligated to accompany his wife upon her travels; while under the law of marriage the wife is obliged to follow the husband's choice of domicile. Indeed, it is argued by the plaintiff's attorney that this relinquishment by the husband of his rights constitutes consideration for the promise of his wife; but, by the same token it makes the contract violative of public policy. The situation is virtually identical with that set forth in Illustration 2 of Section 587 of the Restatement quoted above. The contract, furthermore, would seem to suffer from a second defect by impliedly releasing the husband from his duty to support his wife, and thereby making it fall directly within the rule of the cases cited supra holding that a contract between married persons living together which contains such a release is void. The present contract does not expressly contain such a release, but if the husband can always call upon his wife for payments of $300 per month he is in practical effect getting rid of his obligation to support his wife. The plaintiff seems to place this construction on the contract since his claim makes no deduction from the promised $300 per month for support of his wife. It is unnecessary to consider in detail the second alleged basis of consideration, namely, the promise of the husband to refrain from working, but it would seem again that a married man should have the right to engage in such work as he sees fit to do, unrestrained by contract with his wife.

The law prohibiting married persons from altering by private agreement the personal relationships and obligations assumed upon marriage is based on sound foundations of public policy. If they were permitted to regulate by private contract where the parties are to live and whether the husband is to work or be supported by his wife, there would seem to be no reason why married persons could not contract as to the allowance the husband or wife may receive, the number of dresses she may have, the places where they will spend their evenings and vacations, and innumerable other aspects of their personal relationships. Such right would open an endless field for controversy and bickering and would destroy the element of flexibility needed in making adjustments to new conditions arising in marital life. There is no reason of course, why the wife cannot voluntarily pay her husband a monthly sum or the husband by mutual understanding quit his job and travel with his wife. The objection is to putting such conduct into a binding contract, tying the parties' hands in the future and inviting controversy and litigation between them. The time may come when it is desirable and necessary for the husband to cease work entirely, or to change to a different occupation, or move to a different city, or, if adversity overtakes the parties, to share a small income. It would be unfortunate if in making such adjustments the parties should find their hands tied by an agreement between them entered into years before.

It is important to note that the contract here was entered into between parties who were living together at the time and who obviously contemplated a continuance of that relationship. The case is to be distinguished in this respect from those cases which hold that a contract made after separation or in contemplation of an immediate separation which takes place as contemplated is legal, if the contract is a fair one, even though it contains a release of the husband's duty of support....

NOTES

1. The court bases its holding in part on the view that allowing spouses to arrange their own marriage contract would "open an endless field for controversy." Is this correct? Is it not equally plausible that court enforcement of some private agreements might eliminate a major irritant, thereby heading off a divorce? Moreover, it is not likely that the mere *availability* of relief might deter conduct deleterious to otherwise harmonious marriages? See generally Note, Litigation Between Husband and Wife, 79 Harv.L.Rev. 1650 (1966).

2. The traditional marriage model has been widely criticized for its adverse consequences for women. See, e.g., Kenneth Davidson, Ruth Bader Ginsburg, & Herma Hill Kay, Cases and Materials on Sex–Based Discrimination 140–44 (1974): "The support laws embody the legal view that a married woman is an economically nonproductive person dependent upon others for the necessities of life. That almost three-fifths of the 33 million women in the labor force as of 1972 were married ... indicates the gross inaccuracy of this view. [In addition] the wife's work in the home continues to be seen as a service she owes to the husband, rather than as a job deserving the dignity of economic return. [Finally,] the housewife cannot provide for her old age." See generally Linda L. Ammons, What's God Got to Do With It? Church and State Collaboration in the Subordination of Women and Domestic Violence, 51 Rutgers L. Rev. 1207 (1999).

For discussion of the traditional marriage model's adverse consequences for men, see Scott Coltrane, Family Man: Fatherhood, Housework, and Gender Equity (1996); Nancy E. Dowd, Redefining Fatherhood (2000); but compare Steven L Nock, Marriage in Men's Lives (1998).

Bradwell v. Illinois

Supreme Court of the United States, 1873.
83 U.S. (16 Wall.) 130, 21 L.Ed. 442.

[The petitioner, Myra Bradwell, sought admission to the bar of Illinois after being denied admission because she was a woman. The Supreme Court upheld the denial in a brief opinion. Justice Bradley, in his concurring opinion, explained:]

... [T]he civil law, as well as nature herself, has always recognized a wide difference in the respective spheres and destinies of man and woman. Man is, or should be, woman's protector and defender. The natural and proper timidity and delicacy which belongs to the female sex evidently unfits it for many of the occupations of civil life. The constitution of the family organization, which is founded in the divine ordinance, as well as in the nature of things, indicates the domestic sphere as that which properly belongs to the domain and functions of womanhood. The harmony, not to say identity, of interests and views which belong, or should belong, to the family institution is repugnant to the idea of a woman adopting a distinct and independent career from that of her husband....

It is true that many women are unmarried and not affected by any of the duties, complications, and incapacities arising out of the married state, but these are exceptions to the general rule. The paramount destiny and mission of woman are to fulfill the noble and benign offices of wife and mother. This is the law of the Creator. And the rules of civil society must be adapted to the general constitution of things, and cannot be based upon exceptional cases.

. . .

B. Other Views on Marriage and the Family

John Demos, Images of the American Family, Then and Now

in Changing Images of the Family 43–60 (Virginia Tufte and Barbara Myerhoff eds. 1979).

Within the past twenty years professional historians in several countries have directed special attention and considerable energy to the study of family life. "Family history" has become for the first time a legitimate branch of scholarly research. The entering wedge of this research was, and remains, demographic; by now we know more about the history of such circumstances as mean household size and median age of marriage than reasonable people may *want* to know. But investigation has also been moving ahead on other, more "qualitative," tracks. . . .

Meanwhile, the contemporary experience of families has also come under increasingly intense scrutiny. There is a diffuse sense of "crisis" about our domestic arrangements generally—a feeling that the family as we have traditionally known it is under siege, and may even give way entirely. . . .

. . . [W]hat light can a historian throw on the current predicament in family life? For one thing he is tempted right away to strike a soothing note of reassurance. The core structure of the family has evolved and endured over a very long period of Western history, and it is extremely hard to imagine a sudden reversal of so much weighty tradition. Moreover, for at least a century now the American family in particular has been seen as beleaguered, endangered, and possibly on the verge of extinction. The sense of crisis is hardly new; with some allowance for periodic ebb and flow, it seems an inescapable undercurrent of our modern life and consciousness.

Is this, in fact, reassuring? And does such reassurance *help,* in any substantial way? Somehow I feel that historians must try to do better.

. . .

. . . I shall propose a three-part model of family history as a way of periodizing the field. In choosing to deal with images of family life I am giving my argument an implicit social and economic bias, for such images have been created largely by people of Anglo–Saxon origin in the more comfortable layers of our social system—in short, by middleclass WASPs. . . . But . . . Americans of every color, every creed, and every economic position have been drawn toward the cultural middle. And embedded just there are the very images we must now try to examine.

THE FAMILY AS COMMUNITY

Let us begin with the settlement phase of American history, carving out—as the first part of our sequential model—a period of time lasting into the nineteenth century. It should be recognized, incidentally, that this inquiry does not lend itself to precise chronological markings. . . . And if, for the first stage, we assign a terminal date of 1820, we mean to indicate only a midpoint in that transition. . . . When we seek to approach the colonial

American family, one thing we notice immediately is that the "image" itself is rather thinly sketched. In short, people of that rather distant time and culture did not have a particularly self-conscious orientation to family life; their ideas, their attitudes in this connection, were far simpler than would ever be the case for later generations of Americans. Family life was something they took largely for granted. It was no doubt a central part of their experience, but not in such a way as to require special attention. This does not mean that they lacked ideas of what a "good family" should be and do—or, for that matter, a "bad" one—just that such notions carried a rather low charge in comparison with other areas of social concern.[3]

. . . Here is a particularly resonant statement, taken from an essay by a "Puritan" preacher in the early seventeenth century:

> A family is a little church, and a little commonwealth, at least a lively representation thereof, whereby trial may be made of such as are fit for any place of authority, or of subjection, in church or commonwealth. Or rather, it is as a school wherein the first principles and grounds of government are learned; whereby men are fitted to greater matters in church and commonwealth.

Two aspects of this description seem especially important. First, the family and the wider community are joined in a relation of profound reciprocity; one might almost say they are continuous with one another. (This is, incidentally, a general premodern pattern—in no sense specific to American life and conditions—which was analyzed first and most incisively by Philippe Airès, in his path-breaking study of twenty years ago published in English under the title *Centuries of Childhood.*) To put the matter in another way: individual families are the building blocks out of which the larger units of social organization are fashioned. Families and churches, families and governments, belong to the same world of experience. Individual people move back and forth between these settings with little effort or sense of difficulty.

The membership of these families was not fundamentally different from the pattern of our own day: a man and woman joined in marriage, and their natural-born children. The basic unit was therefore a "nuclear" one, contrary to a good deal of sociological theory about premodern times. However, non-kin could, and did, join this unit—orphans, apprentices, hired laborers, and a variety of children "bound out" for a time in conditions of fosterage. Usually designated by the general term "servants," such persons lived as regular members of many colonial households; and if they were young, the "master" and "mistress" served *in loco parentis.* Occasionally, convicts and indigent people were directed by local authorities to reside in particular families. Here the master's role was to provide care, restraint, and even a measure of rehabilitation for those involved; they, in turn, gave him their service. Thus did the needs of the individual householders intersect the requirements of the larger community.

. . .

There is one more vital aspect of colonial family life which deserves at least to be mentioned. Since the functions of the household and the wider society were so substantially interconnected, the latter might reasonably intervene when the former experienced difficulty. Magistrates and local

3. On the colonial family, see John Demos, A Little Commonwealth: Family Life in Plymouth Colony (New York: Oxford University Press, 1970), and Edmund S. Morgan, The Puritan Family, rev. ed. (New York: Harper & Row, 1966).

officials would thus compel a married couple "to live more peaceably together" or to alter and upgrade the "governance" of their children. This, too, is the context of the famous "stubborn child" laws of early New England, which prescribed the death penalty for persistent disobedience to parents. Such extreme sanctions were never actually invoked, but the statutes remained on the books as a mark of society's interest in orderly domestic relations.

. . .

THE FAMILY AS REFUGE

. . . [I]t is hard to say just how and when this colonial pattern began to break down; but by the early decades of the nineteenth century at least some American families were launched on a new course, within a very different framework of experience. For the most part these were urban families, and distinctly middle-class; and while they did not yet constitute anything like a majority position in the country at large, they pointed the way to the future.

Here, for the first time, American family life acquired an extremely sharp "image"—in the sense of becoming something *thought* about in highly self-conscious ways, *written* about at great length and by many hands, and *worried* about in relation to a host of internal and external problems. Among other things, there was a new sense that the family had a history of its own—that it was not fixed and unchanging for all time. And when some observers, especially "conservative" ones, pondered the direction of this history, they reached an unsettling conclusion: the family, they believed, was set on a course of decline and decay. From a stable and virtuous condition in former times, it had gradually passed into a "crisis" phase. After mid-century, popular literature on domestic life poured out a long litany of complaints: divorce and desertion were increasing; child-rearing had become too casual and permissive; authority was generally disrupted; the family no longer did things together; women were more and more restless in their role as homemakers. Do these complaints have a somewhat familiar ring even now? In fact, it is from this period, more than one hundred years ago, that one of our most enduring images of the family derives—what might be called the image, or the myth, of the family's golden past. It seems to me that too many around us continue to believe that there is some ideal state of domestic life which we have tragically lost. . . .

. . . [H]ow shall we characterize the main line of ideas and attitudes which were increasingly coming to the fore in this period? One point is immediately striking. The nineteenth-century family—far from joining and complementing other social networks, as in the earlier period—seemed to stand wholly apart. Indeed its relation to society at large had been very nearly reversed, so as to become a kind of adversary relation.

The brave new world of nineteenth-century America was, in some respects, a dangerous world—or so many people felt. The new egalitarian spirit, the sense of openness, the opportunities for material gain, the cult of the "self-made man": all this was new, invigorating, and liberating at *one* level—but it also conveyed a deep threat to traditional values and precepts. In order to seize the main chance and get ahead in the ongoing struggle for success, a man had to summon energies and take initiatives that would at the very least exhaust him and might involve him in terrible compromises. At the same time he would need to retain some place of rest, of harmony—some emblem of the personal and moral regime that he was otherwise leaving behind.[11]

Within this matrix of ideas the family was sharply redefined. Henceforth the life of the individual home, on the one hand, and the wider society, on the other, represented for many Americans entirely different spheres ("spheres" was indeed the customary term they used in conceptualizing their varied experiences). The two were separated by a sharply delineated frontier; different strategies and values were looked for on either side.

. . . Home—and the word itself became highly sentimentalized—was pictured as a bastion of peace, of repose, of orderliness, of unwavering devotion to people and principles beyond the self. Here the woman of the family, and the children, would pass most of their hours and days—safe from the grinding pressures and dark temptations of the world at large; here, too, the man of the family would retreat periodically for refreshment, renewal, and inner fortification against the dangers he encountered elsewhere.

Pulling these various themes together, we can reasonably conclude that the crucial function of the family had now become a *protective* one. And two kinds of protection were implied here: protection of the ways and values of an older America that was fast disappearing and protection also for the individual people who were caught up in the middle of all this change. . . . Perhaps we may now adopt, for the nineteenth century, the image of "the family as refuge."

This imagery had, in fact, particular features which deserve careful notice. For one thing, it embraced the idea of highly differentiated roles and statuses *within* the family—for the various individual family members. The husband-father undertook an exclusive responsibility for productive labor. He did this in one of a variety of settings well removed from the home-hearth, in offices, factories, shops, or wherever. So it was that family life was wrenched apart from the world of work—a veritable sea-change in social history. Meanwhile, the wife-mother was expected to confine herself to domestic activities; increasingly idealized in the figure of the "True Woman," she became the centerpiece in a developing cult of Home. Intrinsically superior (from a moral standpoint) to her male partner, the True Woman preserved Home as a safe, secure, and "pure" environment.[14] The children of this marital pair were set off as distinctive creatures in their own right. Home life, from their point of view, was a sequence of preparation in which they armored themselves for the challenges and difficulties of the years ahead.[15] The children, after all, carried the hopes of the family into the future; their lives later on would reward, or betray, the sacrifices of their parents. Taken altogether, and compared with the earlier period, these notions conveyed the sense of a family carefully differentiated as to individual task and function, but unalterably *united* as to overall goals and morale. Like other institutions in the "Machine Age," the family was now seen as a system of highly calibrated, interlocking parts.

It is clear enough that such a system conformed to various *practical* needs and circumstances in the lives of many Americans—the adaptation to urban life, the changing requirements of the workplace, the gathering

11. See Jeffrey, "Family as Utopian Retreat." Also Barbara Welter, "The Cult of True Womanhood: 1820–1860," American Quarterly 18 (1966): 151–74.

14. See Welter, "Cult of True Womanhood."

15. See Bernard Whishy, The Child and the Republic: The Dawn of Modern American Child Nurture (Philadelphia: University of Pennsylvania Press, 1972).

momentum of technology. But it must have answered to certain *emotional* needs as well. In particular, I believe, the cult of Home helped people to release the full range of aggressive and assertive energies so essential to the growth and development of the country—helped them, that is, to still anxiety and to ward off guilt about their own contributions to change. At the same time there were costs and difficulties that we cannot fail to see. The demands inherent in each of the freshly articulated family roles were sometimes literally overwhelming.

The husband-father, for example, was not just the breadwinner for the entire family; he was also its sole representative in the world at large. His "success" or "failure"—terms which had now obtained a highly personal significance—would reflect directly on the other members of the household. And this was a grievously heavy burden to carry. For anyone who found it *too* heavy, for anyone who stumbled and fell while striving to scale the heights of success, there was a bitter legacy of self-reproach—not to mention the implicit or explicit reproaches of other family members whose fate was tied to his own.

Meanwhile, the lady of the house experienced another set of pressures—different, but no less taxing. The conventions of domestic life had thrown up a model of the "perfect home"—so tranquil, so cheerful, so pure, as to constitute an almost impossible standard. And it was the exclusive responsibility of the wife to try to meet this standard. Moreover, her behavior must in all circumstances exemplify the selflessness of the True Woman. Her function was effectively defined as one of service and giving to others; she could not express needs or interests of her own. This suppression of self exacted a crushing toll from many nineteenth-century women. Few complained outright—though modern feminism dates directly from this era. But there were other, less direct forms of complaint—the neurasthenias, the hysterias, indeed a legion of "women's diseases," which allowed their victims to opt out of the prescribed system.[16]

The system also imposed new difficulties on the younger members of the household. In the traditional culture of colonial America the process of growth from child to adult had been relatively smooth and seamless. The young were gradually raised, by a sequence of short steps, from subordinate positions within their families of origin to independent status in the community at large.[17] In the nineteenth century, by contrast, maturation became disjunctive and problematic. As the condition of childhood was ever more sharply articulated, so the transition to adulthood became longer, lonelier, more painful.[18] And there was also another kind of transition to negotiate. For those who absorbed the imagery of Home the moment of *leaving* was charged with extraordinary tension. To cross the sacred threshold from inside to outside was to risk unspeakable dangers. The nostalgia, the worries, the guilt which attended such crossings are threaded through an enormous mass of domestic fiction from the period. Marriage itself was experienced as the sudden exchange of one family for another—with a little of the flavor of a blind leap.[19]

16. See Ann Douglas Wood, " 'The Fashionable Diseases': Women's Complaints and Their Treatment in Nineteenth-Century America," Journal of Interdisciplinary History 4 (1973): 25–52.

17. Demos, A Little Commonwealth, chap. 10.

18. Joseph Kett, Rites of Passage: Adolescence in America, 1790 to the Present (New York: Basic Books, 1977).

19. See, for example, the marriages described in [the novel by Catherine Maria] Sedgewick, Home [(1854)]. This theme is explored by Ellen K. Rothman in "A Most In-

In sum, the "ideal family" of the nineteenth century comprised a tightly closed circle of reciprocal obligations. And the entire system was infused with a strain of dire urgency. If the family did not function in the expected ways, there were no other institutions to back it up. If one family member fell short of prescribed ways and standards, all the others were placed in jeopardy. There is a short story by T.S. Arthur—an immensely popular author during the middle of the century—which makes this point very clearly.[20] A young couple marry and set up housekeeping. The husband is an aspiring businessman, with every prospect of "success." His wife shares his ambitions and means to become an effective "helpmeet"; however, her management of the household is marred by a certain inefficiency. The husband regularly returns from his office for lunch (an interesting vestige of premodern work rhythms), but soon a problem develops. The wife cannot hold to a firm schedule in preparing these meals, and often her husband is kept waiting. Earnest conversations and repeated vows of improvement bring no real change. Finally, one particular delay causes the husband to miss a crucial appointment—and the consequences for his business are devastating.

Domestic fiction played out similar themes in the relation of parents and children. Only the most careful and moral "rearing" would bring the young out safe in later life; anything less might imperil their destiny irrevocably. Conversely, the well-being of parents depended in large measure on their offspring. If the latter, having grown to adulthood, were to stray from the paths of virtue, the old folks might feel so "heartbroken" that they would sicken and die. Here the stakes of domestic bonding attained an aspect of life-threatening finality.

THE FAMILY AS ENCOUNTER GROUP

To some degree the image of "the family as refuge" remains with us today....

And yet for some time the tide has been running in another direction.... We have moved, it seems, from the "jungle" of the nineteenth century to the "rat race" (or the "grind") of our own day. This progression expresses clearly a lessened sense of *threat*—and also a growing feeling of monotony and meaninglessness.

The implications for family life—specifically, for images and expectations of family life—are profound. As the threat is tempered, the wish for *protection,* for armoring, wanes. Or rather it shades gradually into something else. Home is less a bunker amidst the battle than a place of "rest and recuperation" (pursuing the military analogy). According to this standard, families should provide the interest, the excitement, the stimulation missing from other sectors of our experience. If we feel that "we aren't going anywhere" in our work, we may load our personal lives—especially our family lives—with powerful compensatory needs. We wish to "grow" in special ways through our relations with family partners; a familiar complaint in counseling centers nowadays is the sense of blocked opportunities for growth. We want our spouses, our lovers, even our children, to help us feel alive and invigorated—to brighten a social landscape that otherwise seems unrelievedly gray. Again, some contrasts with the earlier setting may be

teresting Event: Marriage-Making in Nineteenth-Century America," unpublished paper (Brandeis University, 1975).

20. T.S. Arthur, "Sweethearts and Wives," in The Root of Bitterness, ed. Nancy F. Cott (New York: Dutton, 1972).

helpful. *Then* Home was to be a place of quiet, of repose. *Now* it must generate some excitement. *Then* the True Woman served as the appointed guardian of domestic values; as such she was "pure," steady, in all ways self-effacing. *Now* there is the figure of the "Total Woman"—who, to be sure, keeps an orderly house and seeks consistently to help her man, but who is also sensual and assertive within limits.

Indeed an entire spectrum of roles and responsibilities within the family is increasingly in question. No longer can we automatically accept that principle of differentiation which, in the nineteenth century, assigned to each household member a "sphere" deemed appropriate to his or her age and gender. Some families now advocate an *opposite* principle, which exalts the diffusion and mixing of roles. Mother must do her share of the "breadwinning," Father must do his share of the household chores, and so forth and so on. Much of this, of course, comes directly from the Women's Movement, and involves a long-overdue effort to right the balance of opportunity between the sexes. However, that is not the whole story. If Father is urged nowadays to help with the children or wash the dishes or take care of the laundry, this is not just in order to lighten the burdens that have traditionally fallen on Mother. There is also a feeling that such activities are *good for him.* Somehow his sensibilities will be expanded and his personal growth advanced—just as Mother expands and grows through her work outside the home. As a further benefit of these rearrangements the couple discovers new highways and byways of marital communication. Since they share so much more, they understand each other better; and their relation to one another is "deepened" accordingly. Even children are invited to join in this celebration of openness and reciprocity. The parents believe that they must listen carefully and at all times to their children, even that they can *learn* from their children—ideas which would, I think, have seemed quite preposterous just a few generations ago.

If all goes well—if reality meets expectation and conforms to image—Home becomes a bubbling kettle of lively, and mutually enhancing, activity. But, alas, all does *not* invariably go well; so we also have, for the first time in American history, a negative image—an "anti-image"—of the family. Seen from this viewpoint, domestic relationships look dangerously like an encumbrance, if not a form of bondage, inhibiting the quest for a full experience of self. Monogamous marriage is liable to become boring and stultifying; in other things, after all, variety is "the spice of life." Moreover, responsibility for children only compounds the problem. The needs and requirements of the young are so pressing, so constant, as to leave little space for adults who must attend to them. "Spice" and "space": these are, in fact, the qualities for which we yearn most especially. And the family severely limits our access to either one.

I wish to reemphasize, in closing, the distortion introduced by any discrete model of family history. The problem is not simply one of arbitrary chronological boundaries; there is also a risk of failing to see the cumulative element in all historical process. "Stage three," we have noted, retains a good part of "stage two"—and even some traces of "stage one." (We continue, after all, to see individual families as the "building blocks" of the nation as a whole.) Thus our present arrangements are best construed as a complex and heavily layered precipitate of our entire social history.

Two points about this history deserve some final underscoring. In both the second and the third of our major stages the family has been loaded with the most urgent of human needs and responsibilities. Indeed I would say *over*loaded. In each case the prevalent imagery conjures up a *compensatory* function: the family must supply what is vitally needed, but missing, in social arrangements generally. It must protect its individual constituents against imminent and mortal danger, or it must fill a void of meaninglessness. To put the matter in another way: the family is not experienced in its own right but essentially in its relation to other circumstances and other pressures. It is for this reason, I believe, that we have become so extraordinarily self-conscious about family life—and, more, have broached it for so long from an attitude of crisis.

There is a concomitant of this attitude which also has deep historical roots. Briefly, we have isolated family life as the primary setting—if not, in fact, the only one—for *caring* relations between people. The nineteenth-century images made an especially powerful contribution here: each family would look after its own—and, for the rest, may the best man win. Relationships formed within the world of work—which meant, for a long time, relationships between men—would not have an emotional dimension. Nineteenth-century women seem, on the evidence of very recent scholarship, to have maintained "networks" of affection which did cross family boundaries, but even this pattern recedes as we follow the trail toward the present.

Much of the same viewpoint has survived into our own time, and it underlies certain continuing tensions in our national experience. The United States stands almost alone among Western industrialized countries in having no coherent "family policy." More particularly, our inherited habits and values—our constricted capacity for extrafamilial caring—partly explain public indifference to the blighted conditions in which many families even now are obliged to live. The results are especially tragic as they affect children, and they leave us with a terrible paradox. In this allegedly most child-centered of nations, we find it hard to care very much or very consistently about *other people's children*. The historian may think that he understands such a predicament; he does not, however, know how to change it.

NOTES

1. Consider John Borneman and Laurie Kain Hart, An Elastic Institution, Wash. Post, April 14, 2004, at A25:

> The cult of romantic love in companionate marriage is a recent innovation in the history of marriage. While romantic passion has existed in all societies, only in a few has this unstable emotion been elaborated and intensified culturally and considered the basis for the social institution of marriage. Indeed, marriage has traditionally been more concerned with—and successful in—regulating property relations and determining lineage or inheritance rights than with confining passion and sexual behavior.

2. Alexis de Toqueville, a young French aristocrat who visited the United States in 1831, made a number of interesting observations about family life in his book Democracy in America (Henry Reeve trans., Schocken Books 1964)(1840):

> It has been universally remarked, that in our time the several members of a family stand upon an entirely new footing towards each other; that the distance which formerly separated a father from his sons has been lessened; and that paternal authority, if not destroyed, is a least impaired.
>
> Something analogous to this, but even more striking, may be observed in the United States. . . .
>
> It may perhaps not be without utility to show how these changes which take place in family relations, are closely connected with the social and political

revolution which is approaching its consummation under our own observation. . . .

In countries which are aristocratically constituted with all the gradations of rank, the government never makes a direct appeal to the mass of the governed: as men are united together, it is enough to lead the foremost, —the rest will follow. This is equally applicable to the family. . . .

. . .

Although the legislation of an aristocratic people should grant no peculiar privileges to the heads of families, I shall not be the less convinced that their power is more respected and more extensive than in a democracy.

. . .

. . . In aristocracies, the father is not only the civil head of the family, but the oracle of its traditions, the expounder of its customs, the arbiter of its manners. He is listened to with deference, he is addressed with respect, and the love which is felt for him is always tempered with fear.

. . .

In a democratic family the father exercises no other power than that with which men love to invest the affection and the experience of age; his orders would perhaps be disobeyed, but his advice is for the most authoritative.

. . .

In aristocratic families, the eldest son, inheriting the greater part of the property, and almost all the rights of the family, becomes the chief, and to a certain extent, the master of his brothers. Greatness and power are for him, —for them, mediocrity and dependence. . . .

Democracy also binds brothers to each other, but by very different means. Under democratic laws all the children are perfectly equal, and consequently independent: nothing brings them forcibly together, but nothing keeps them apart; . . . and as no peculiar privilege distinguishes or divides them, the affection and youthful intimacy of early years easily springs up between them.

. . .

Among almost all Protestant nations young women are far more the mistresses of their own actions than they are in Catholic countries. This independence is still greater in Protestant countries like England, which have retained or acquired the right of self-government; the spirit of freedom is then infused into the domestic circle by political habits and by religious opinions. In the United States the doctrines of Protestantism are combined with great political freedom and a most democratic state of society; and nowhere are young women surrendered so early or so completely to their own guidance.

. . .

In a country in which a woman is always free to exercise her power of choosing, and in which education has prepared her to choose rightly, public opinion is inexorable to her faults. The rigour of the Americans arises in part from this cause. They consider marriages as a covenant which is often onerous, but every condition of which the parties are strictly bound to fulfill, because they knew all these conditions beforehand, and were perfectly free not to have contracted them.

In aristocratic countries the object of marriage is rather to unite property than persons; hence the husband is sometimes at school and the wife at nurse when they are betrothed. It cannot be wondered at if the conjugal tie which holds the fortunes of the pair united allows their hearts to rove; this is the natural result of the nature of the contract. . . .

Second Part, Third Book, Chapters VIII, IX and XI.

3. The link between revolution and divorce is further developed in Norma Basch, Framing American Divorce: From the Revolutionary Generation to the Victorians 21–23 (1999);

> The United States was not alone in recognizing divorce in the age of revolution, a time when the sources of legitimate authority were directly contested and indelibly transformed. The first French Republic, which went from upholding the complete indissolubility of marriage to instituting the most permissive divorce code in the Western world, provides a stellar example of the late eighteenth-century confluence of revolution and divorce....
>
> . . .
>
> The terms on which Americans recognized divorce were rather more modest and, as a result of state-by-state variations, somewhat eclectic. Still, the impress of the Revolution was unmistakable. No sooner, it seems, did Americans create a rationale for dissolving bonds of empire than they set about creating rules for dissolving bonds of matrimony. Divorce ... had been available in New England before the advent of independence; Connecticut had provided for it on such liberal terms that it granted almost a thousand decrees between 1670 and 1799. By comparison, those states that relegated divorce to a legislative decision after the Revolution instituted a highly restrictive divorce policy. And yet, even in such restrictive jurisdictions, a complete divorce with the concomitant right to remarry became a legal possibility for the first time. Though American divorce policy paled before the robust liberality of the French counterpart, it assumed much more radical dimensions in an Anglo–American context. By 1800 fault divorce, as we have come to call it in our era of no-fault, was a legal concept that departed significantly from the parliamentary and ecclesiastical precedents on which it was based. In its gender-neutral approach to fault, in the completeness of its dissolutions and in the access it afforded litigants, American divorce already diverged dramatically from its principal English roots.
>
> The timing of this development was as telling as its substance. Concern with providing for formal divorce arose simultaneously with the political turmoil of the 1770s. With the notable exception of the Puritan jurisdictions, Britain's North American colonies did not challenge English divorce policy in a collective or sustained way until that time, nor did England attend to those challenges that were in fact made. ... As late as 1769, a barrister representing the Board of Trade and Plantations declared the Pennsylvania legislative divorce of Curtis and Anne Grub to be "not repugnant to the Laws of England." But confronted by a similar Pennsylvania decree three years later, the board found that it represented a dangerous power "rarely and recently assumed in your Majesty's colonies in America." An extended ruling by the Privy Council in 1773 designated "Acts of Divorce in the Plantations" as "either Improper or Unconstitutional." Subsequent divorce bills from New Hampshire and New Jersey were also disallowed....
>
> Thomas Jefferson, a proponent of legitimating divorce, may very well have had this prohibition in mind when he drafted the section of the Declaration of Independence denouncing the British monarchy's refusal to "Assent to Laws, the most wholesome and necessary for the public good." More important, his notes supporting divorce anticipated the rational he employed to justify independence: "No partnership," he declared, "can oblige continuance in contradiction to its end and design." ...

4. Divorce has never been the only way to end a marriage in the United States as Hendrik Hartog cautions in Man & Wife in America 20, 22–23 (2000):

> American mobility is the oldest and most durable cliché of post-Revolutionary American historiography. Families moving together across the great American wilderness. Families moving north to the cities to escape first slavery and then the Jim Crow south....

Yet the image of families moving together was often an illusion. People moved for many reasons, and not only to improve the well-being of their families. Frequently they moved to leave unhappy marriages or to find a jurisdiction to authorize a union that was not possible where they and their (prior) family were known. Though such conduct would always be construed as bad, as morally reprehensible, it was also understood as legal, as part of the range of legal improvisations that American federalism made available to American citizens. . . .

Too many men went to the Gold rush, leaving wife and children, and never returned. Sometimes men left for the West intending to return, but they or their wives changed in the interim. Sometimes they left, meaning to abandon. Meanwhile, wives went to cities, took jobs in domestic service or factory work or opened boarding houses. They were widows, they told people around them, and then they remarried. Andrew Jackson's beloved wife Rachel lived one of those narratives. She and her first husband parted; they went their separate ways, to different jurisdictions. Then she met Andrew Jackson and married him—except she was still married. During much of the nineteenth century, the divorce laws of a few states forbade the party at fault in a divorce from remarrying during the lifetime of the faultless party. Did that stop people from remarrying? Of course not. But it did require them to go somewhere else, usually to another state, to do their marrying business.

. . .

Europeans and other non-Americans saw the American marital regimes, their freedoms, their possibilities for remaking identities, and they were drawn to come. This was one, usually unspoken, feature of the American ideal, of the freedom that America offered. At the same time, for many Americans, especially for many poor and vulnerable women, marital life in the multi-jurisdictional landscape of the United States, was filled with dangers. The search for work, for land, for economic survival, split many couples apart as they moved across the United States. While men were away-looking for new land, at the Gold Rush, on a whaling expedition—houses burned down, inheritances were lost, children became ill and sometimes died, mortgages were foreclosed. Meanwhile, husbands changed their minds about returning to their marriages; they found new loves; they "remarried" in new jurisdictions, they never came back. Some wives looked for poor relief from towns that had no obligation to provide it, since inherited legal rules declared that a wife could only receive poor relief from her husband's "settlement," his legal residence. Other wives claimed rights as wives—to support, to marital assets, to child custody—against abandoned husbands and their estates. These wives too often found that they had no rights; they could only sue where they were "domiciled," and that turned out to be (at least under the inherited rules) wherever their husbands might be, not where they were.

Milton C. Regan, Jr., Alone Together: Law and the Meanings of Marriage

6–11 (1999).

One might claim that marriage . . . is of declining significance in a culture that emphasizes emotional rather than formal legal bonds. For support, an advocate of this position might point to our relatively high divorce rate, declining rate of marriage, increasing percentage of couples living together without marriage, and growing rate of childbearing outside of marriage. A critic also could take note of the suggestion by at least one set of family scholars that we take the "sexually based primary relationship," rather than marriage or conventional family boundaries, as the basic unit of analysis in what hitherto has been called "family studies."[26]

. . .

Marriage, however, still has powerful cultural power as the paradigm of intimate commitment. The companionate model of marriage that has become pervasive over the last two hundred years or so has created high expectations that marriage will serve as a source of personal fulfillment. In her book on divorce, Catherine Riessman notes, "The companionate ideal is stronger than it ever was. Recent evidence shows that the spouses' reliance on one another—both for emotional reassurance and for companionship in leisure—is much greater now than even a generation ago.[27] As some have suggested, the very data that supposedly document the decline of marriage may in fact reflect its power. Some divorce scholars suggest, for instance, that a relatively high divorce rate may indicate that people have high expectations for emotional support from marriage and are unwilling to settle for anything less."[28]

Furthermore, a lower marriage rate and higher unmarried cohabitation rate may reflect the perception that marriage involves a qualitatively greater commitment than an informal intimate relationship. Certainly, marriage is a far less dramatic *legal* step than it used to be. Getting married in the modern age now has fewer significant legal consequences in itself, and obtaining a divorce is relatively easy. Those who eschew marriage nowadays thus are likely to be expressing the view that marriage is an important *emotional* step for which they are not prepared. Unmarried cohabitation, for instance, may reflect the desire for a "trial" marriage that will provide greater assurance that an eventual formal marriage will meet the high expectations that accompany it. Lower marriage rates and higher divorce rates may attest to the gravity, rather than the indifference, with which marriage is regarded. This suggests that, even for those who are not married, marriage may cast a large shadow on the psychological landscape.

Marriage thus is worthy of attention because of its continuing power as a symbol of enduring rather than transitory attachment. While we must confront the question of how to deal with relationships that are not organized around marriage, this should not obscure the fact that marriage continues to hold a distinctive place in the cultural imagination. In short, as David Chambers has put it, "after thousands of years of human history, the union of two people in a relationship called 'marriage' is almost certainly here to stay[.]"[29]

A second criticism of focusing on marriage might be that marriage historically has been closely associated with patriarchy, and therefore should be deemphasized as an element of family life. Much of the momentum for treating marriage and family life as a realm of choice rather than ascription has come from feminist critiques of the ways in which marriage has constructed and reinforced hierarchical relations between men and women.

26. John Scanzoni, Karen Polonkoa, Jay Teachman, & Linda Thompson, The Sexual Bond: Rethinking Families and Close Relationships (1989).

27. Catherine Kohler Riessman, Divorce Talk 67 (1990).

28. *See* William O'Neill, The Road to Reno (1962); Roderick Phillips, Putting Asunder: A History of Divorce in Western Society 640 (1988); Glenda Riley, Divorce: An American Tradition 185 (1991).

29. David Chambers, What If? The Legal Consequences of Marriage and the Legal Needs of Lesbian and Gay Male Couples, 95 Mich. L. Rev. 447, 448 (1996).

The ways in which a marriage-based family law contributed to this system are numerous. Under the doctrine of coverture, women lost their legal identity when they married. This deprived them of basic rights to own property and to enter into contracts. Married women had no protection against sexual assault by their husbands because a man could not be liable for raping his wife. Law enforcement authorities declined to respond to domestic violence on the ground that this would constitute unwarranted intervention into the privacy of the marriage. Furthermore, the doctrine of interspousal tort immunity effectively prevented a wife from bringing a private lawsuit to redress injuries suffered at the hands of her husband. Women generally were legally eligible to marry at an earlier age than men, based on the view that marriage and economic dependence on a man was the typical career path for women. All these disabilities rested on the more general notion that a married woman's destiny was to be confined to the domestic sphere, subject to the authority of her husband. Given this legal history, those who are sympathetic to feminism may be suspicious of family law scholarship that takes marriage as its focus. They may argue that sensitivity to women's concerns should lead us to emphasize individuals rather than husbands and wives, and relationships rather than marriages.

This argument, however, seems to assume that marriage has an essential unalterable character that inevitably is disadvantageous to women. It ignores the tremendous change in the law and in social attitudes toward gender roles over the past generation. The Supreme Court, for instance, has struck down a host of legal provisions on the ground that they reflect the view that a woman's place is solely within the home and not the wage labor force. Furthermore, the argument ignores the trend that is the basis for the first criticism above—that marriage now is seen far more than before as an arena of choice. Powerful cultural assumptions still shape the opportunities of men and women and the sets of choices that they have. Nonetheless, there is more negotiation between husbands and wives about the division of labor and other terms of marriage than traditionally has been the case.

Ironically, one might argue that married couples have more freedom to order their relationship as they wish than do unmarried couples who desire some legal recognition of their intimate bond. Once a couple marries, they need conform to no particular model of behavior in order to receive the legal protections of that status. By contrast, those who are unmarried generally must act in a way that a court will regard as the substantive equivalent of marriage in order for any rights or obligations to flow from the relationship.

. . .

A final criticism is that directing attention to marriage artificially isolates it from the complex interdependence of family life. If we think about marriage in the broader family context, we will realize that our concerns about marriage flow primarily from the fact that is usually involves children. On this view, we have a social interest in marriage not for its own sake, but because marriage traditionally is the institution in which procreation has occurred.

Thus, for instance, some commentators suggest a two-tiered divorce system: relatively easy divorce for childless couples but more difficult dissolution for marital partners with children. Others argue that the law of divorce awards is misguided in implicitly focusing on marriage rather than parenthood as the basis for financial allocations. At least one scholar has suggested that the law should abandon the married couple as its fundamental unit and substitute in its stead the relationship between mother and child.[34]

. . .

This suggests that the third criticism is not so much that marriage is not a coherent topic of analysis, but that we have little legal interest in it when it doesn't overlap with parenthood. The assumption that underlies this contention is that marriage is a relationship of choice whose purpose is to provide personal fulfillment for spouses. As such, it is essentially a private matter between husbands and wives. Thus, for instance, while we may have an interest in making divorce more difficult for spouses with children, divorce for childless couples ought to be relatively quick and easy. . . .

There is a certain irony in this criticism, which illuminates why marriage in fact is of significant analytic interest. Historically, marriage has been regarded as the cornerstone of family life and thus as the basis for numerous ascribed rights and duties. Now, however, it serves as an exemplar of a family relationship of choice, in which members are bound together by emotion and volition.

Marriage has been seen as a consensual relationship for quite some time, of course. Indeed, more than three hundred years ago John Locke characterized marriage as a "voluntary compact between man and woman."[38] For many years, however, religious belief in the sanctity of marriage and marriage's close association with parenthood obscured this feature. Locke, for instance, suggested that the reason why the partnership between humans tends to last longer than that of other creatures is the helplessness of human infants. Marriage, he argued, ought to last "so long as it is necessary to the nourishment and support of the young ones, who are to be sustained by those that got them till they are able to shift and provide by themselves." Once the responsibilities of parenthood are discharged, however, "it would give one reason to inquire why this compact . . . may not be made determinable either by consent, or at a certain time, or upon certain conditions, as well as any other voluntary compacts, there being no necessity in the nature of thing, nor to the ends of it, that is should always be for life."

. . .

[H]ow are we to accommodate two aspirations of family life that are in some tension? On the one hand, there is an intense desire that family relationships provide emotional support, unconditional acceptance, and steadfast commitment. On the other hand, there is a strong belief that family relationships must rest on personal satisfaction, individual choice, and freely assumed obligation. If we can no longer rely on ascription as the central principle of family life, to what extent can variable and contingent individual sentiment serve as the basis for the self-restraint, sacrifice, and forbearance that enduring relationships require?

In raising such issues, modern marriage may be of broader social interest as well. . . .

Marriage . . . has served as a way of channeling powerful and volatile drives for sexual gratification and individual fulfillment into an arrangement that furthers interests in procreation and social stability. As such it has

34. See Martha Fineman, The Neutered Mother, the Sexual Family and other Twentieth–Century tragedies (1995).

38. John Locke, Two Treatises of Government 155 (Peter Lazlett ed. 1988) (3d ed. 1698).

carried significance as "the reconciliation of law and spontaneity" for at least the last century and a half. This reconciliation is inherently unstable, however, given the urgency of both the felt social needs and the individual passions that it must accommodate. ... Regarded at once as the most important source of adult intimate happiness and as the cornerstone of society, marriage crystallizes the tensions that we face as both distinct individuals and as members of a shared community. How the law seeks to accommodate these dimensions of marriage thus may offer instruction in how to manage the inevitable dilemma of our dual existence.

NOTES

1. Consider Rick Santorum, It Takes a Family: Conservatism and the Common Good 6–7 (2005);

> Who are [the] big, powerful forces upon which so many rely to shape our economy, culture, society, values, and learning? They are what I call the "Bigs"—big news media, big entertainment, big universities and public schools, some big businesses and some big national labor unions, and of course, the biggest Big of all, the federal government.
>
> . . .
>
> The people who run the Bigs I like to call the "village elders." They are the liberal elite who think they know what is best for individual Americans and how best to order (or rather, re-order) our society along the lines of their ideological abstractions. They see any institution that stands between the Bigs and the isolated individual as an annoyance or hindrance. In fact, in the view of the Bigs, it is often just these intermediary associations that are responsible for what the Bigs understand to be our social problems. The liberal answer to the "problem" of intermediary institutions is to "liberate" individuals from them—whether individuals want that or not.
>
> "And what are these problem-creating associations that liberals believe harm people?" They are the "Littles": local government, civic and fraternal associations, clubs, small businesses, neighborhoods, local school districts, churches and church ministries—and of course, the greatest offender of all and the greatest thorn in the liberals' side, the iconoclastic traditional family. ...
>
> So where do we conservatives look for answers to the social issues of such widespread concern to Americans today? Why, to the very associations that the village elders distrust. And we ought to start with what has been the foundation of every successful civilization in history: the traditional family.

2. Compare William Galston's essay in Marriage—Just a Piece of Paper? 323–325 (2002):

> The debate over the American family in the early 1990s was sharply polarized ... between liberals and conservatives, between people who celebrated the cultural changes that began in the late 1960s and those who deplored them. It was caught between those who focused on economic factors and those who focused on moral issues, between those who believed that family structure was an important element of family functioning, and those who denied that.
>
> There are lots of dissenters all around. But there is a broad middle of the political spectrum in the United States today, which I think is at the level of mass public opinion as well as political elites in public policy and activists. The consensus is that family structure is important for family functioning and child outcomes; that, for example, teen pregnancy, out-of-wedlock births, millions of kids being raised by young, single mothers is not a good idea either for the kids or for the young mothers or for the absent fathers or for society as a whole. There is an increased disposition to believe that keeping families together is a good idea whenever possible, whenever the costs are not too high.
>
> There is a very interesting turn in opinion among the youngest Americans, teenagers and young adults, people who are disproportionately the children of

divorce. As you examine the public opinion surveys focused on that generation, Generation X and Generation Y, you'll see that they are much more conservative than their parents were on questions of family integrity and marital stability. In fact, many of them vociferously blame their parents for breaking up marriages that in the judgment of the children, although that's necessarily a one-sided judgment, could have been maintained and should have been preserved.

. . .

. . . Take two groups of children. In the first group, the parents are high school graduates who got married before they had their first child and they waited until they were out of their teens to have that child. In that group, about 8 percent of the children are living in poverty. . . . Now take the second group, where the parents did none of those three things. They didn't graduate from high school, they didn't get married, and they didn't wait until they were out of their teens to have a child. In that second group, 79 percent of the children are living in poverty. . . .

So there are three simple things that young people can do to give their kids a better chance: they can stay in school until they're at least high school graduates, they can get married before they have their first child, and they can wait until they're out of their teens to have that child. . . .

3. Contemporary claims that marriage is in crisis often point to the rising divorce rate. See, e.g., The Marriage Movement: A Statement of Principles, http://www.marriagemovement.org (2000):

Over the last two generations, marriage as a social institution has weakened. Since 1960, the crude divorce rate has doubled. . . .

In fact, after more than a century of rising divorce rates in the United States, the rates abruptly stopped going up around 1980. Dan Hurley, Divorce Rate: It's Not as High as You Think, N.Y.Times, April 19, 2005 at D7. The decrease has a generational component. For people born in 1955 or later, "the proportion ever divorced actually declined compared to those who were born earlier." Rose M. Kreider, Number, Timing and Duration of Marriages and Divorces: 2001, Current Population Reports, U.S. Census Bureau, U.S. Dep't of Commerce 4 (February 2005). The highest rate of divorce was 41 percent for men between the ages of 50 to 59.

There is also an education "divorce divide" according to Professor Stephen P. Martin of the University of Maryland who reports that since 1980, women college graduates have a divorce rate of only 16 percent while women without an undergraduate degree have a divorce rate of around 35 percent. If the historic pattern holds that roughly 60 percent of all marriages that eventually end in divorce do so within the first 10 years, then the ultimate divorce rate for women will be around 25 percent for college graduates and 50 percent for the others. Hurley, *supra*.

One problem with divorce data in the United States is that the National Center for Health Statistics in 1996 stopped collecting detailed data from the states on divorced people. *Id.*

C. Challenges to the Traditional Marriage Model

1. The Changing Status of Women

a. Economic and Social Changes

National Commission on Children, Beyond Rhetoric: A New American Agenda for Children and Families

21–23 (1991).

Perhaps the most dramatic social change of the past 20 years has been the steady march of mothers into the paid labor force (see Figure 2–4).

Between 1970 and 1990, the proportion of mothers with children under age six who were working or looking for work outside their homes rose from 32 percent to 58 percent. Today, approximately 10.9 million children under age six, including 1.7 million babies under one year and 9.2 million toddlers and preschoolers, have mothers in the paid labor force. Mothers of school-age children are even more likely to be in the labor force. In 1990 over 74 percent of women whose youngest child was between the ages of 6 and 13 were working or looking for paid work. Approximately 17.4 million children, more than 65 percent of all children in the latter age group, had working mothers in 1990. Among employed mothers, nearly 70 percent whose youngest child is under six and more than 74 percent whose youngest child is school age work full time.

FIGURE 2-4

Mothers in the Paid Labor Force, 1970-1990

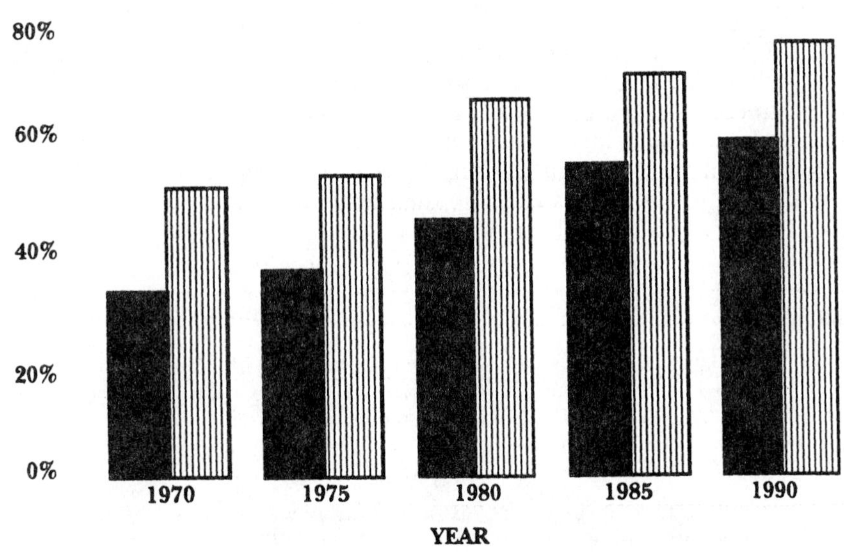

AGE OF CHILDREN ■ Less than 6 ▥ 6-17

SOURCE: US Department of Labor, Bureau of Labor Statistics, *Handbook of Labor Statistics*, bull. 2340 (Washington, DC: Government Printing Office, 1989), p. 244, tables 56 and 57; US Department of Labor, Bureau of Labor Statistics, unpublished data from March 1990 Current Population Survey.

[78A]

Historically, unmarried mothers have been far more likely to work than married mothers. Yet the sharpest increase in labor force participation among mothers over the past 20 years has been among married mothers, especially those with very young children. More than 66 percent of married mothers are now working or looking for work outside their homes. In past generations, most of these women would have quit their jobs and stayed at home when they married or had children, but today they are remaining at work. Women who wait to have their first baby until after age 25 and women with four or more years of college are more likely to continue working than are younger mothers and those who fail to complete high school.

The reasons that individual mothers decide to go to work or stay in the labor force undoubtedly vary from one family to another. On an aggregate level, however, complex social, cultural, and economic factors have fueled this trend in the United States and most other developed countries. Increases in the number of available jobs, especially in the service sector; successful legal efforts to expand women's access to the workplace; the continued influence of the women's movement; and the mechanization of many household tasks have all undoubtedly contributed. The declining income and employment opportunities of young men, especially those who lack skills, and the difficulty of maintaining a secure standard of living on one income have also added momentum.

Changing patterns of mothers' employment represent more than a mere shift in American attitudes or fluctuations in short-term macroeconomic conditions, although these have clearly played a part. Over the past generation, the opportunity costs of staying at home, primarily in the form of foregone earnings, have increased for mothers. Some scholars call for a return to the single-earner "family wage" system of the 1940s. Others, however, suggest that the movement of mothers into the paid work force is likely to become even stronger in the future as projected labor shortages make women increasingly essential to the shrinking labor pool. To date, social adjustments—in the workplace, in communities, and even in families—have been rather slow to take root. Over the coming years, society's ability to adapt to the changing needs of working fathers, working mothers, and their children will be increasingly essential to the health and vitality of families and to the well-being of their children.

NOTES

1. In 2002, the labor force participation rate of women with children under 18 peaked at 72.2 percent. By 2004 it declined to 70.1 percent for women with children under 18, and to 62.2 percent for women with children under 6. Bureau of Labor Statistics, Dep't of Labor, Employment Status of Women By Presence and Age of Youngest Child, 19740–2004, http//www.bls.gov/cps/wlf-databook2005.htm.

Women continue to trail men in terms of earning power, earning 79 percent of men's median weekly earnings in 2003 and 80 percent in 2004. Bureau of Labor Statistics, U.S. Dep't of Labor, Weekly Earnings Data Table 37: Median Weekly Earnings of Full–Time and Salary Workers By Selected Characteristics (data compiled by the Current Population Survey [CPS] at the Bureau of the Census), available at http://www.bls.gov/cps/home.htm.

2. Families headed by women constituted roughly half of all families below the poverty level in 2002 and 2003 (50 and 51 percent respectively). In 2003, women maintained 74 percent of poor Black families, 37 percent of poor Hispanic families and 41 percent of poor White non-Hispanic families. Bureau of the Census, Table POV02: People in Families by Family Structure, Age, and Sex, Iterated by Income-to-Poverty Ratio and Race (data from the CPS 2004 Annual Social and Economic Supplement), available at http://www.pubdb3.census.gov/macro/032004/pov/toc.htm.

b. CONSTITUTIONAL LIMITS ON SEX DISCRIMINATION

Ruth Ginsburg, Gender and the Constitution

44 Cin.L.Rev. 1–4 (1975).

. . .

Two themes dominate Anglo–American literature and case reports.

Their strains are echoed even to this day.[6] First, women's place in a world controlled by men is divinely ordained; second, the law's differential treatment of the sexes operates benignly in women's favor. As to the first theme, Gunnar Myrdal, in his classic study of racism in the United States, noted:

> In the earlier common law, women and children were placed under the jurisdiction of the paternal power. When a legal status had to be found for the imported Negro servants ... the nearest and most natural analogy was the status of women and children. The ninth commandment—linking together women, servants, mules and other property—could be invoked, as well as a great number of other passages of Holy Scripture.[7]

Discrimination as "benign preference" was Blackstone's justification for laws that denied the married woman legal capacity to hold property, contract or bring suit in her own name: "[T]he disabilities which the wife lies under are for the most part intended for her protection and benefit: so great a favourite is the female sex of the laws of England."[8]

During the long debate over women's suffrage the prevailing view of the natural subordination of women to men was rehearsed frequently in the press and in legislative chambers. For example, an 1852 New York Herald editorial asked:

> How did women first become subject to man as she now is all over the world? By her nature, her sex, just as the negro, is and always will be, to the end of time, inferior to the white race, and therefore, doomed to subjection; but happier than she would be in any other condition, just because it is the law of her nature. The women themselves would not have this law reversed....[9]

Mid–19th century feminists, many of them diligent workers in the cause of abolition, looked to Congress after the Civil War for an express guarantee of equal rights for men and women. Viewed in historical perspective, their expectations appear unrealistic. A problem of far greater immediacy faced the nation. Overcoming the legacy of slavery was the burning issue of the day and it eclipsed all others. The text of the fourteenth amendment occasioned particular concern among feminists, for the second section of that amendment placed in the Constitution for the first time the word "male." Threefold use of the word "male," always in conjunction with the term "citizens,"[11] generated apprehension that the grand phrases of the first section of the fourteenth amendment—"privileges and immunities of citizens of the United States," guarantees to all persons of "due process of law" and "the equal protection of the laws"—would have, at best, qualified application to women.[12]

6. See, e.g., 116 Cong.Reg. 29,670, 29,-672 (1970) (statement of Senator Ervin); Senate Comm. on the Judiciary, Equal Rights for Men and Women, S.Rep.No. 92–689, 92d Cong., 2d Sess. 48–49 (1972); Johnston, Jr. & Knapp, Sex Discrimination by Law: A Study in Judicial Perspective, 46 N.Y.U.L.Rev. 675 (1971).

7. G. Myrdal, An American Dilemma 1073 (2d ed. 1962).

8. 1 W. Blackstone, Commentaries 445 (3d ed. 1768).

9. The Woman's Rights Convention—The Last Act of the Drama, N.Y. Herald, Sept. 12, 1852, quoted in A. Kraditor, Up from the Pedestal 190 (1968).

11. The section provides for reduction of the number of Representatives where a state denies "male citizens" the right to vote. The intent was to assure the franchise to black men. See also 2 U.S.C. § 6 (1927).

12. See E. Flexner, Century of Struggle 142–55 (1959).

For more than a century after the adoption of the fourteenth amendment, the judiciary, with rare exception, demonstrated utmost deference to sex lines drawn by the legislature. In the nation's highest tribunal, until 1971, no legislatively drawn sex line, however sharp, failed to survive constitutional challenge.[13] . . .

Orr v. Orr

Supreme Court of the United States, 1979.
440 U.S. 268, 99 S.Ct. 1102, 59 L.Ed.2d 306.

■ JUSTICE BRENNAN delivered the opinion of the Court.

The question presented is the constitutionality of Alabama alimony statutes which provide that husbands, but not wives, may be required to pay alimony upon divorce.

. . .

In authorizing the imposition of alimony obligations on husbands, but not on wives, the Alabama statutory scheme "provides that different treatment be accorded . . . on the basis of . . . sex; it thus establishes a classification subject to scrutiny under the Equal Protection Clause." Reed v. Reed, 404 U.S. 71, 75 (1971). The fact that the classification expressly discriminates against men rather than women does not protect it from scrutiny. Craig v. Boren, 429 U.S. 190 (1976). "To withstand scrutiny" under the equal protection clause, " 'classifications by gender must serve important governmental objectives and must be substantially related to achievement of those objectives.' " Califano v. Webster, 430 U.S. 313, 316–317 (1977). We shall, therefore, examine the three governmental objectives that might arguably be served by Alabama's statutory scheme.

Appellant views the Alabama alimony statutes as effectively announcing the State's preference for an allocation of family responsibilities under which the wife plays a dependent role, and as seeking for their objective the reinforcement of that model among the State's citizens. We agree, as he urges, that prior cases settle that this purpose cannot sustain the statutes. Stanton v. Stanton, 421 U.S. 7, 10 (1975), held that the "old notion" that "generally it is the man's primary responsibility to provide a home and its essentials," can no longer justify a statute that discriminates on the basis of gender. "No longer is the female destined solely for the home and the rearing of the family, and only the male for the marketplace and world of ideas," id., at 14–15. See also Craig v. Boren, 429 U.S., at 198. If the statute is to survive constitutional attack, therefore, it must be validated on some other basis.

The opinion of the Alabama Court of Civil Appeals suggests other purposes that the statute may serve. Its opinion states that the Alabama statutes were "designed" for "the wife of a broken marriage who needs financial assistance," 351 So.2d, at 905. This may be read as asserting either of two legislative objectives. One is a legislative purpose to provide help for needy spouses, using sex as a proxy for need. The other is a goal of compensating women for past discrimination during marriage, which assert-

13. The Court initially invalidated laws setting minimum wages for women, principally because the legislation interfered with liberty of contract, as that doctrine was then viewed. Adkins v. Children's Hosp., 261 U.S. 525 (1923), overruled, West Coast Hotel Co. v. Parrish, 300 U.S. 379 (1937). . . .

edly has left them unprepared to fend for themselves in the working world following divorce. We concede, of course, that assisting needy spouses is a legitimate and important governmental objective. We have also recognized "[r]eduction of the disparity in economic condition between men and women caused by the long history of discrimination against women . . . as . . . an important governmental objective," Califano v. Webster, [430 U.S.,] at 317. It only remains, therefore, to determine whether the classification at issue here is "substantially related to achievement of those objectives." Ibid.

Ordinarily, we would begin the analysis of the "needy spouse" objective by considering whether sex is a sufficiently "accurate proxy," Craig v. Boren, 429 U.S., at 204, for dependency to establish that the gender classification rests " 'upon some ground of difference having a fair and substantial relation to the object of the legislation,' " Reed v. Reed, 404 U.S., at 76. Similarly, we would initially approach the "compensation" rationale by asking whether women had in fact been significantly discriminated against in the sphere to which the statute applied a sex-based classification, leaving the sexes "*not* similarly situated with respect to opportunities" in that sphere. Schlesinger v. Ballard, 419 U.S. 498, 508 (1975). . . .

But in this case, even if sex were a reliable proxy for need, and even if the institution of marriage did discriminate against women, these factors still would "not adequately justify the salient features of" Alabama's statutory scheme. Craig v. Boren, [429 U.S.,] at 202. Under the statute, individualized hearings at which the parties' relative financial circumstances are considered *already* occur. There is no reason, therefore, to use sex as a proxy for need. Needy males could be helped along with needy females with little if any additional burden on the State. In such circumstances, not even an administrative convenience rationale exists to justify operating by generalization or proxy. Similarly, since individualized hearings can determine which women were in fact discriminated against vis à vis their husbands, as well as which family units defied the stereotype and left the husband dependent on the wife, Alabama's alleged compensatory purpose may be effectuated without placing burdens solely on husbands. Progress toward fulfilling such a purpose would not be hampered, and it would cost the State nothing more, if it were to treat men and women equally by making alimony burdens independent of sex. "Thus, the gender-based distinction is gratuitous; without it the statutory scheme would only provide benefits to those men who are in fact similarly situated to the women the statute aids." Weinberger v. Wiesenfeld, 420 U.S., at 653, and the effort to help those women would not in any way be compromised.

Moreover, use of a gender classification actually produces perverse results in this case. As compared to a gender-neutral law placing alimony obligations on the spouse able to pay, the present Alabama statutes give an advantage only to the financially secure wife whose husband is in need. Although such a wife might have to pay alimony under a gender-neutral statute, the present statutes exempt her from that obligation. Thus, "[t]he [wives] who benefit from the disparate treatment are those who were . . . nondependent on their husbands." Califano v. Goldfarb, 430 U.S. 199, 221 (1977) (Stevens, J., concurring). They are precisely those who are not "needy spouses" and who are "least likely to have been victims of . . . discrimination," by the institution of marriage. A gender-based classification which, as compared to a gender-neutral one, generates additional benefits only for those it has no reason to prefer cannot survive equal protection scrutiny.

Legislative classifications which distribute benefits and burdens on the basis of gender carry the inherent risk of reinforcing stereotypes about the "proper place" of women and their need for special protection. Cf. United Jewish Organizations v. Carey, 430 U.S. 144, 173–174 (1977) (concurring opinion). Thus, even statutes purportedly designed to compensate for and ameliorate the effects of past discrimination must be carefully tailored. Where, as here, the State's compensatory and ameliorative purposes are as well served by a gender-neutral classification as one that gender-classifies and therefore carries with it the baggage of sexual stereotypes, the State cannot be permitted to classify on the basis of sex. And this is doubly so where the choice made by the State appears to redound—if only indirectly—to the benefit of those without need for special solicitude.

. . .

Reversed and remanded.

■ JUSTICE BLACKMUN, concurring.

On the assumption that the Court's language concerning discrimination "in the sphere" of the relevant preference statute does not imply that society-wide discrimination is always irrelevant, and on the further assumption that that language in no way cuts back on the Court's decision in Kahn v. Shevin, 416 U.S. 351 (1974), I join the opinion and judgment of the Court.

[Justice Powell dissented on the ground that there were unresolved issues of state law relevant to deciding whether the Court had jurisdiction to hear the case. In his view the case should have been remanded first to resolve these issues. Justice Rehnquist, joined by the Chief Justice, also found problems with jurisdiction, but would have dismissed the appeal rather than remanding the case].

NOTE

In Kahn v. Shevin, the Court upheld a state property tax exemption for widows that was intended to offset past economic discrimination against women. Is it possible to reconcile *Kahn* and *Orr* as asserted by Justice Blackmun? Consider the dissent of Justice Brennan, joined by Justice Marshall, in *Kahn:*

> I agree that, in providing special benefits for a needy segment of society long the victim of purposeful discrimination and neglect, the statute serves the compelling state interest of achieving equality for such groups. No one familiar with this country's history of pervasive sex discrimination against women can doubt the need for remedial measures to correct the resulting economic imbalances.... By providing a property tax exemption for widows, § 196.01(7) assists in reducing that disparity for a class of women particularly disadvantaged by the legacy of economic discrimination.... The statute nevertheless fails to satisfy the requirements of equal protection, since the State has not borne its burden of proving that its compelling interest could not be achieved by a more precisely tailored statute or by use of feasible, less drastic means. Section 196.191(7) is plainly overinclusive, for the $500 property tax exemption may be obtained by a financially independent heiress as well as by an unemployed widow with dependent children.

416 U.S. at 358–60.

United States v. Virginia

Supreme Court of the United States, 1996.
518 U.S. 515, 116 S.Ct. 2264, 135 L.Ed.2d 735.

■ JUSTICE GINSBURG delivered the opinion of the Court.

Virginia's public institutions of higher learning include an incomparable military college, Virginia Military Institute (VMI). The United States maintains that the Constitution's equal protection guarantee precludes Virginia from reserving exclusively to men the unique educational opportunities VMI affords. We agree.

Founded in 1839, VMI is today the sole single-sex school among Virginia's 15 public institutions of higher learning. VMI's distinctive mission is to produce "citizen-soldiers," men prepared for leadership in civilian life and in military service. VMI pursues this mission through pervasive training of a kind not available anywhere else in Virginia. Assigning prime place to character development, VMI uses an "adversative method" modeled on English public schools and once characteristic of military instruction. VMI constantly endeavors to instill physical and mental discipline in its cadets and impart to them a strong moral code. The school's graduates leave VMI with heightened comprehension of their capacity to deal with duress and stress, and a large sense of accomplishment for completing the hazardous course.

VMI has notably succeeded in its mission to produce leaders; among its alumni are military generals, Members of Congress, and business executives. The school's alumni overwhelmingly perceive that their VMI training helped them to realize their personal goals. VMI's endowment reflects the loyalty of its graduates; VMI has the largest per-student endowment of all public undergraduate institutions in the Nation.

. . .

VMI today enrolls about 1,300 men as cadets. ... In contrast to the federal service academies, institutions maintained "to prepare cadets for career service in the armed forces," VMI's program "is directed at preparation for both military and civilian life"; "[o]nly about 15% of VMI cadets enter career military service."

VMI produces its "citizen-soldiers" through "an adversative, or doubting, model of education" which features "[p]hysical rigor, mental stress, absolute equality of treatment, absence of privacy, minute regulation of behavior, and indoctrination in desirable values." As one Commandant of Cadets described it, the adversative method "dissects the young student," and makes him aware of his "limits and capabilities," so that he knows "how far he can go with his anger, ... how much he can take under stress, ... exactly what he can do when he is physically exhausted."

VMI cadets live in spartan barracks where surveillance is constant and privacy nonexistent; they wear uniforms, eat together in the mess hall, and regularly participate in drills. Entering students are incessantly exposed to the rat line, "an extreme form of the adversative model," comparable in intensity to Marine Corps boot camp. Tormenting and punishing, the rat line bonds new cadets to their fellow sufferers and, when they have completed the 7–month experience, to their former tormentors.

VMI's "adversative model" is further characterized by a hierarchical "class system" of privileges and responsibilities, a "dyke system" for assigning a senior class mentor to each entering class "rat," and a stringently enforced "honor code," which prescribes that a cadet " 'does not lie, cheat, steal nor tolerate those who do.' "

VMI attracts some applicants because of its reputation as an extraordinarily challenging military school, and "because its alumni are exceptionally close to the school." "[W]omen have no opportunity anywhere to gain the benefits of [the system of education at VMI]."

In 1990, prompted by a complaint filed with the Attorney General by a female high-school student seeking admission to VMI, the United States sued the Commonwealth of Virginia and VMI, alleging that VMI's exclusively male admission policy violated the Equal Protection Clause of the Fourteenth Amendment.

. . .

The District Court ruled in favor of VMI. . . .

The Court of Appeals for the Fourth Circuit disagreed and vacated the District Court's judgment. . . .

In response to the Fourth Circuit's ruling, Virginia proposed a parallel program for women: Virginia Women's Institute for Leadership (VWIL). The 4–year, state-sponsored undergraduate program would be located at Mary Baldwin College, a private liberal arts school for women, and would be open, initially, to about 25 to 30 students. Although VWIL would share VMI's mission—to produce "citizen-soldiers"—the VWIL program would differ, as does Mary Baldwin College, from VMI in academic offerings, methods of education, and financial resources.

. . .

Virginia returned to the District Court seeking approval of its proposed remedial plan, and the court decided the plan met the requirements of the Equal Protection Clause.

. . .

A divided Court of Appeals affirmed the District Court's judgment.

. . .

We note, the core instruction of this Court's pathmarking decisions in J.E.B. v. Alabama ex rel. T.B., 511 U.S. 127, 136–137, and n. 6 (1994), and Mississippi Univ. for Women, 458 U.S. 718, 724 (1982): Parties who seek to defend gender-based government action must demonstrate an "exceedingly persuasive justification" for that action.

Today's skeptical scrutiny of official action denying rights or opportunities based on sex responds to volumes of history. As a plurality of this Court acknowledged a generation ago, "our Nation has had a long and unfortunate history of sex discrimination." Frontiero v. Richardson, 411 U.S. 677, 684 (1973). Through a century plus three decades and more of that history, women did not count among voters composing "We the People";[5] not until 1920 did women gain a constitutional right to the franchise. And for a half century thereafter, it remained the prevailing doctrine that government, both federal and state, could withhold from women opportunities accorded men so long as any "basis in reason" could be conceived for the discrimination.

In 1971, for the first time in our Nation's history, this Court ruled in favor of a woman who complained that her State had denied her the equal protection of its laws. Reed v. Reed, 404 U.S. 71, 73 (holding unconstitution-

5. As Thomas Jefferson stated the view prevailing when the Constitution was new:

> "Were our State a pure democracy ... there would yet be excluded from their deliberations ... women, who, to prevent depravation of morals and ambiguity of issue, should not mix promiscuously in the public meetings of men." Letter from Thomas Jefferson to Samuel Kercheval (Sept. 5, 1816), in 10 Writings of Thomas Jefferson 45–46, n. 1 (P. Ford ed. 1899).

al Idaho Code prescription that, among " 'several persons claiming and equally entitled to administer [a decedent's estate], males must be preferred to females' "). Since *Reed*, the Court has repeatedly recognized that neither federal nor state government acts compatibly with the equal protection principle when a law or official policy denies to women, simply because they are women, full citizenship stature—equal opportunity to aspire, achieve, participate in and contribute to society based on their individual talents and capacities.

Without equating gender classifications, for all purposes, to classifications based on race or national origin, the Court, in post-*Reed* decisions, has carefully inspected official action that closes a door or denies opportunity to women (or to men). To summarize the Court's current directions for cases of official classification based on gender: Focusing on the differential treatment or denial of opportunity for which relief is sought, the reviewing court must determine whether the proffered justification is "exceedingly persuasive." The burden of justification is demanding and it rests entirely on the State.

The State must show "at least that the [challenged] classification serves 'important governmental objectives and that the discriminatory means employed' are 'substantially related to the achievement of those objectives.' " The justification must be genuine, not hypothesized or invented *post hoc* in response to litigation. And it must not rely on overbroad generalizations about the different talents, capacities, or preferences of males and females.

The heightened review standard our precedent establishes does not make sex a proscribed classification. Supposed "inherent differences" are no longer accepted as a ground for race or national origin classifications. See Loving v. Virginia, 388 U.S. 1 (1967). Physical differences between men and women, however, are enduring: "[T]he two sexes are not fungible; a community made up exclusively of one [sex] is different from a community composed of both." Ballard v. United States, 329 U.S. 187, 193 (1946).

"Inherent differences" between men and women, we have come to appreciate, remain cause for celebration, but not for denigration of the members of either sex or for artificial constraints on an individual's opportunity. Sex classifications may be used to compensate women "for particular economic disabilities [they have] suffered," Califano v. Webster, 430 U.S. 313, 320 (1977) (*per curiam*), to "promot[e] equal employment opportunity," see California Federal Sav. & Loan Assn. v. Guerra, 479 U.S. 272, 289 (1987), to advance full development of the talent and capacities of our Nation's people.[7] But such classifications may not be used, as they once were, to create or perpetuate the legal, social, and economic inferiority of women.

Measuring the record in this case against the review standard just described, we conclude that Virginia has shown no "exceedingly persuasive justification" for excluding all women from the citizen-soldier training af-

7. Several *amici* have urged that diversity in educational opportunities is an altogether appropriate governmental pursuit and that single-sex schools can contribute importantly to such diversity. Indeed, it is the mission of some single-sex schools "to dissipate, rather than perpetuate, traditional gender classifications." See Brief for Twenty-Six Private Women's Colleges as *Amici Curiae* 5. We do not question the State's prerogative evenhandedly to support diverse educational opportunities. We address specifically and only an educational opportunity recognized by the District Court and the Court of Appeals as "unique," an opportunity available only at Virginia's premier military institute, the State's sole single-sex public university or college. Cf. Mississippi Univ. for Women v. Hogan, 458 U.S. 718, 720, n. 1 (1982) ("Mississippi maintains no other single-sex public university or college. Thus, we are not faced with the question of whether States can provide 'separate but equal' undergraduate institutions for males and females.").

forded by VMI. We therefore affirm the Fourth Circuit's initial judgment, which held that Virginia had violated the Fourteenth Amendment's Equal Protection Clause. Because the remedy proffered by Virginia—the Mary Baldwin VWIL program—does not cure the constitutional violation, i.e., it does not provide equal opportunity, we reverse the Fourth Circuit's final judgment in this case.

. . .

Virginia ... asserts two justifications in defense of VMI's exclusion of women. First, the Commonwealth contends, "single-sex education provides important educational benefits," and the option of single-sex education contributes to "diversity in educational approaches,". Second, the Commonwealth argues, "the unique VMI method of character development and leadership training," the school's adversative approach, would have to be modified were VMI to admit women. We consider these two justifications in turn.

. . .

Neither recent nor distant history bears out Virginia's alleged pursuit of diversity through single-sex educational options. In 1839, when the State established VMI, a range of educational opportunities for men and women was scarcely contemplated. Higher education at the time was considered dangerous for women;[9] reflecting widely held views about women's proper place, the Nation's first universities and colleges—for example, Harvard in Massachusetts, William and Mary in Virginia—admitted only men. VMI was not at all novel in this respect: In admitting no women, VMI followed the lead of the State's flagship school, the University of Virginia, founded in 1819.

"[N]o struggle for the admission of women to a state university," a historian has recounted, "was longer drawn out, or developed more bitterness, than that at the University of Virginia." 2 T. Woody, A History of Women's Education in the United States 254 (1929) (History of Women's Education). In 1879, the State Senate resolved to look into the possibility of higher education for women, recognizing that Virginia " 'has never, at any period of her history,' " provided for the higher education of her daughters, though she " 'has liberally provided for the higher education of her sons.' " Despite this recognition, no new opportunities were instantly open to women.

. . .

9. Dr. Edward H. Clarke of Harvard Medical School, whose influential book, Sex in Education, went through 17 editions, was perhaps the most well-known speaker from the medical community opposing higher education for women. He maintained that the physiological effects of hard study and academic competition with boys would interfere with the development of girls' reproductive organs. See E. Clarke, Sex in Education 38–39, 62–63 (1873); id. at 127 ("identical education of the two sexes is a crime before God and humanity, that physiology protests against, and that experience weeps over"); see also H. Maudsley, Sex in Mind and in Education 17 (1874) ("It is not that girls have not ambition, nor that they fail generally to run the intellectual race [in coeducational settings], but it is asserted that they do it at a cost to their strength and health which entails life-long suffering, and even incapacitates them for the adequate performance of the natural functions of their sex."); C. Meigs, Females and Their Diseases 350 (1848) (after five or six weeks of "mental and educational discipline," a healthy woman would "lose ... the habit of menstruation" and suffer numerous ills as a result of depriving her body for the sake of her mind).

Ultimately, in 1970, "the most prestigious institution of higher education in Virginia," the University of Virginia, introduced coeducation and, in 1972, began to admit women on an equal basis with men. . . .

Virginia describes the current absence of public single-sex higher education for women as "an historical anomaly." But the historical record indicates action more deliberate than anomalous: First, protection of women against higher education; next, schools for women far from equal in resources and stature to schools for men; finally, conversion of the separate schools to coeducation. The state legislature, prior to the advent of this controversy, had repealed "[a]ll Virginia statutes requiring individual institutions to admit only men or women." And in 1990, an official commission, "legislatively established to chart the future goals of higher education in Virginia," reaffirmed the policy "of affording broad access" while maintaining "autonomy and diversity." Significantly, the Commission reported:

> " 'Because colleges and universities provide opportunities for students to develop values and learn from role models, it is extremely important that they deal with faculty, staff, and students without regard to sex, race, or ethnic origin.' "

This statement, the Court of Appeals observed, "is the only explicit one that we have found in the record in which the Commonwealth has expressed itself with respect to gender distinctions."

Our 1982 decision in *Mississippi Univ. for Women* prompted VMI to reexamine its male-only admission policy. Virginia relies on that reexamination as a legitimate basis for maintaining VMI's single-sex character. A Mission Study Committee, appointed by the VMI Board of Visitors, studied the problem from October 1983 until May 1986, and in that month counseled against "change of VMI status as a single-sex college." Whatever internal purpose the Mission Study Committee served—and however well-meaning the framers of the report—we can hardly extract from that effort any state policy evenhandedly to advance diverse educational options. As the District Court observed, the Committee's analysis "primarily focuse[d] on anticipated difficulties in attracting females to VMI," and the report, overall, supplied "very little indication of how th[e] conclusion was reached."

In sum, we find no persuasive evidence in this record that VMI's male-only admission policy "is in furtherance of a state policy of 'diversity.' " No such policy, the Fourth Circuit observed, can be discerned from the movement of all other public colleges and universities in Virginia away from single-sex education. That court also questioned "how one institution with autonomy, but with no authority over any other state institution, can give effect to a state policy of diversity among institutions." A purpose genuinely to advance an array of educational options, as the Court of Appeals recognized, is not served by VMI's historic and constant plan—a plan to "affor[d] a unique educational benefit only to males." However "liberally" this plan serves the State's sons, it makes no provision whatever for her daughters. That is not *equal* protection.

Virginia next argues that VMI's adversative method of training provides educational benefits that cannot be made available, unmodified, to women. Alterations to accommodate women would necessarily be "radical," so "drastic," Virginia asserts, as to transform, indeed "destroy," VMI's program. Neither sex would be favored by the transformation, Virginia maintains: Men would be deprived of the unique opportunity currently available to them; women would not gain that opportunity because their participation would "eliminat[e] the very aspects of [the] program that distinguish [VMI] from . . . other institutions of higher education in Virginia."

The District Court forecast from expert witness testimony, and the Court of Appeals accepted, that coeducation would materially affect "at least these three aspects of VMI's program—physical training, the absence of privacy, and the adversative approach." And it is uncontested that women's admission would require accommodations, primarily in arranging housing assignments and physical training programs for female cadets. It is also undisputed, however, that "the VMI methodology could be used to educate women." The District Court even allowed that some women may prefer it to the methodology a women's college might pursue. "[S]ome women, at least, would want to attend [VMI] if they had the opportunity," the District Court recognized, and "some women," the expert testimony established, "are capable of all of the individual activities required of VMI cadets". The parties, furthermore, agree that "*some* women can meet the physical standards [VMI] now impose[s] on men." In sum, as the Court of Appeals stated, "neither the goal of producing citizen soldiers," VMI's *raison dêtre,* "nor VMI's implementing methodology is inherently unsuitable to women."

. . .

It may be assumed, for purposes of this decision, that most women would not choose VMI's adversative method. As Fourth Circuit Judge Motz observed, however, in her dissent from the Court of Appeals' denial of rehearing en banc, it is also probable that "many men would not want to be educated in such an environment." (On that point, even our dissenting colleague might agree.) Education, to be sure, is not a "one size fits all" business. The issue, however, is not whether "women—or men—should be forced to attend VMI"; rather, the question is whether the State can constitutionally deny to women who have the will and capacity, the training and attendant opportunities that VMI uniquely affords.

The notion that admission of women would downgrade VMI's stature, destroy the adversative system and, with it, even the school, is a judgment hardly proved, a prediction hardly different from other "self-fulfilling prophec[ies]," once routinely used to deny rights or opportunities. When women first sought admission to the bar and access to legal education, concerns of the same order were expressed. For example, in 1876, the Court of Common Pleas of Hennepin County, Minnesota, explained why women were thought ineligible for the practice of law. Women train and educate the young, the court said, which

> "forbids that they shall bestow that time (early and late) and labor, so essential in attaining to the eminence to which the true lawyer should ever aspire. It cannot therefore be said that the opposition of courts to the admission of females to practice . . . is to any extent the outgrowth of . . . 'old fogyism[.]' . . . [I]t arises rather from a comprehension of the magnitude of the responsibilities connected with the successful practice of law, and a desire to *grade up* the profession." In re Application of Martha Angle Dorsett to Be Admitted to Practice as Attorney and Counselor at Law (Minn.C.P. Hennepin Cty., 1876), in The Syllabi, Oct. 21, 1876, pp. 5, 6 (emphasis added).

A like fear, according to a 1925 report, accounted for Columbia Law School's resistance to women's admission, although

> "[t]he faculty . . . never maintained that women could not master legal learning. . . . No, its argument has been . . . more practical. If women

were admitted to the Columbia Law School, [the faculty] said, then the choicer, more manly and red-blooded graduates of our great universities would go to the Harvard Law School!" The Nation, Feb. 18, 1925, p. 173.

. . .

Women's successful entry into the federal military academies, and their participation in the Nation's military forces, indicate that Virginia's fears for the future of VMI may not be solidly grounded.[15] The State's justification for excluding all women from "citizen-soldier" training for which some are qualified, in any event, cannot rank as "exceedingly persuasive," as we have explained and applied that standard.

Virginia and VMI trained their argument on "means" rather than "end," and thus misperceived our precedent. Single-sex education at VMI serves an "important governmental objective," they maintained, and exclusion of women is not only "substantially related," it is essential to that objective. By this notably circular argument, the "straightforward" test *Mississippi Univ. for Women* described, was bent and bowed.

The State's misunderstanding and, in turn, the District Court's, is apparent from VMI's mission: to produce "citizen-soldiers," individuals

> " 'imbued with love of learning, confident in the functions and attitudes of leadership, possessing a high sense of public service, advocates of the American democracy and free enterprise system, and ready ... to defend their country in time of national peril.' " 766 F.Supp., at 1425 (quoting Mission Study Committee of the VMI Board of Visitors, Report, May 16, 1986).

Surely that goal is great enough to accommodate women, who today count as citizens in our American democracy equal in stature to men. Just as surely, the State's great goal is not substantially advanced by women's categorical exclusion, in total disregard of their individual merit, from the State's premier "citizen-soldier" corps.[16] Virginia, in sum, "has fallen far short of establishing the 'exceedingly persuasive justification,' " *Mississippi Univ. for Women,* 458 U.S., at 731, that must be the solid base for any gender-defined classification.

. . .

Virginia chose not to eliminate, but to leave untouched, VMI's exclusionary policy. For women only, however, Virginia proposed a separate program, different in kind from VMI and unequal in tangible and intangible facilities....

15. Inclusion of women in settings where, traditionally, they were not wanted inevitably entails a period of adjustment. As one West Point cadet squad leader recounted: "[T]he classes of '78 and '79 see the women as women, but the classes of '80 and '81 see them as classmates." U.S. Military Academy, A. Vitters, Report of Admission of Women (Project Athena II) 84 (1978)

16. VMI has successfully managed another notable change. The school admitted its first African-American cadets in 1968. See The VMI Story 347–349 (students no longer sing "Dixie," salute the Confederate flag or the tomb of General Robert E. Lee at ceremonies and sports events). As the District Court noted, VMI established a Program on "retention of black cadets" designed to offer academic and social-cultural support to "minority members of a dominantly white and tradition-oriented student body." The school maintains a "special recruitment program for blacks" which the District Court found, "has had little, if any, effect on VMI's method of accomplishing its mission."

VWIL affords women no opportunity to experience the rigorous military training for which VMI is famed. . . .

VWIL students participate in ROTC and a "largely ceremonial" Virginia Corps of Cadets, but Virginia deliberately did not make VWIL a military institute. The VWIL House is not a military-style residence and VWIL students need not live together throughout the 4-year program, eat meals together, or wear uniforms during the school day. VWIL students thus do not experience the "barracks" life "crucial to the VMI experience," the spartan living arrangements designed to foster an "egalitarian ethic." "[T]he most important aspects of the VMI educational experience occur in the barracks," the District Court found, yet Virginia deemed that core experience nonessential, indeed inappropriate, for training its female citizen-soldiers.

VWIL students receive their "leadership training" in seminars, externships, and speaker series, episodes and encounters lacking the "[p]hysical rigor, mental stress, . . . minute regulation of behavior, and indoctrination in desirable values" made hallmarks of VMI's citizen-soldier training. Kept away from the pressures, hazards, and psychological bonding characteristic of VMI's adversative training, VWIL students will not know the "feeling of tremendous accomplishment" commonly experienced by VMI's successful cadets.

Virginia maintains that these methodological differences are "justified pedagogically," based on "important differences between men and women in learning and developmental needs," "psychological and sociological differences" Virginia describes as "real" and "not stereotypes." The Task Force charged with developing the leadership program for women, drawn from the staff and faculty at Mary Baldwin College, "determined that a military model and, especially VMI's adversative method, would be wholly inappropriate for educating and training *most women*." The Commonwealth embraced the Task Force view, as did expert witnesses who testified for Virginia.

As earlier stated, generalizations about "the way women are," estimates of what is appropriate for *most women*, no longer justify denying opportunity to women whose talent and capacity place them outside the average description. Notably, Virginia never asserted that VMI's method of education suits *most men*. It is also revealing that Virginia accounted for its failure to make the VWIL experience "the entirely militaristic experience of VMI" on the ground that VWIL "is planned for women who do not necessarily expect to pursue military careers." 852 F.Supp., at 478. By that reasoning, VMI's "entirely militaristic" program would be inappropriate for men in general or *as a group*, for "[o]nly about 15% of VMI cadets enter career military service." See 766 F.Supp., at 1432.

In contrast to the generalizations about women on which Virginia rests, we note again these dispositive realities: VMI's "implementing methodology" is not "inherently unsuitable to women," 976 F.2d, at 899; "some women . . . do well under [the] adversative model," 766 F.Supp., at 1434 (internal quotation marks omitted); "some women, at least, would want to attend [VMI] if they had the opportunity," *id.*, at 1414; "some women are capable of all of the individual activities required of VMI cadets," *id.*, at 1412, and "can meet the physical standards [VMI] now impose[s] on men," 976 F.2d, at 896. It is on behalf of these women that the United States has instituted this suit, and it is for them that a remedy must be crafted,[19] a remedy that will end their exclusion from a state-supplied educational opportunity for which they are fit, a decree that will "bar like discrimination in the future." *Louisiana*, 380 U.S., at 154.

In myriad respects other than military training, VWIL does not qualify as VMI's equal. VWIL's student body, faculty, course offerings, and facilities hardly match VMI's. Nor can the VWIL graduate anticipate the benefits associated with VMI's 157-year history, the school's prestige, and its influential alumni network.

Mary Baldwin College, whose degree VWIL students will gain, enrolls first-year women with an average combined SAT score about 100 points lower than the average score for VMI freshmen. The Mary Baldwin faculty holds "significantly fewer Ph.D.'s," and receives substantially lower salaries.

Mary Baldwin does not offer a VWIL student the range of curricular choices available to a VMI cadet. VMI awards baccalaureate degrees in liberal arts, biology, chemistry, civil engineering, electrical and computer engineering, and mechanical engineering. VWIL students attend a school that "does not have a math and science focus," they cannot take at Mary Baldwin any courses in engineering or the advanced math and physics courses VMI offers.

For physical training, Mary Baldwin has "two multi-purpose fields" and "[o]ne gymnasium." VMI has "an NCAA competition level indoor track and field facility; a number of multi-purpose fields; baseball, soccer and lacrosse fields; an obstacle course; large boxing, wrestling and martial arts facilities; an 11-laps-to-the-mile indoor running course; an indoor pool; indoor and outdoor rifle ranges; and a football stadium that also contains a practice field and outdoor track."

Although Virginia has represented that it will provide equal financial support for in-state VWIL students and VMI cadets, and the VMI Foundation has agreed to endow VWIL with $5.4625 million, the difference between the two schools' financial reserves is pronounced. Mary Baldwin's endowment, currently about $19 million, will gain an additional $35 million based on future commitments; VMI's current endowment, $131 million—the largest per-student endowment in the Nation—will gain $220 million.

The VWIL student does not graduate with the advantage of a VMI degree. Her diploma does not unite her with the legions of VMI "graduates [who] have distinguished themselves" in military and civilian life. "[VMI] alumni are exceptionally close to the school," and that closeness accounts, in part, for VMI's success in attracting applicants. A VWIL graduate cannot assume that the "network of business owners, corporations, VMI graduates and non-graduate employers ... interested in hiring VMI graduates," will be equally responsive to her search for employment.

Virginia, in sum, while maintaining VMI for men only, has failed to provide any "comparable single-gender women's institution." Instead, the Commonwealth has created a VWIL program fairly appraised as a "pale

19. Admitting women to VMI would undoubtedly require alterations necessary to afford members of each sex privacy from the other sex in living arrangements, and to adjust aspects of the physical training programs. See Brief for Petitioner 27–29. Experience shows such adjustments are manageable. See U.S. Military Academy, A. Vitters, N. Kinzer, & J. Adams, Report of Admission of Women (Project Athena I–IV) (1977–1980) (4-year longitudinal study of the admission of women to West Point); Defense Advisory Committee on Women in the Services, Report on the Integration and Performance of Women at West Point 17–18 (1992).

shadow" of VMI in terms of the range of curricular choices and faculty stature, funding, prestige, alumni support and influence.

Virginia's VWIL solution is reminiscent of the remedy Texas proposed 50 years ago, in response to a state trial court's 1946 ruling that, given the equal protection guarantee, African Americans could not be denied a legal education at a state facility. See Sweatt v. Painter, 339 U.S. 629 (1950). Reluctant to admit African Americans to its flagship University of Texas Law School, the State set up a separate school for Herman Sweatt and other black law students. As originally opened, the new school had no independent faculty or library, and it lacked accreditation. Nevertheless, the state trial and appellate courts were satisfied that the new school offered Sweatt opportunities for the study of law "substantially equivalent to those offered by the State to white students at the University of Texas."

Before this Court considered the case, the new school had gained "a faculty of five full-time professors; a student body of 23; a library of some 16,500 volumes serviced by a full-time staff; a practice court and legal aid association; and one alumnus who ha[d] become a member of the Texas Bar." This Court contrasted resources at the new school with those at the school from which Sweatt had been excluded. The University of Texas Law School had a full-time faculty of 16, a student body of 850, a library containing over 65,000 volumes, scholarship funds, a law review, and moot court facilities.

More important than the tangible features, the Court emphasized, are "those qualities which are incapable of objective measurement but which make for greatness" in a school, including "reputation of the faculty, experience of the administration, position and influence of the alumni, standing in the community, traditions and prestige." Facing the marked differences reported in the *Sweatt* opinion, the Court unanimously ruled that Texas had not shown "substantial equality in the [separate] educational opportunities" the State offered. Accordingly, the Court held, the Equal Protection Clause required Texas to admit African Americans to the University of Texas Law School. In line with *Sweatt,* we rule here that Virginia has not shown substantial equality in the separate educational opportunities the State supports at VWIL and VMI.

The Fourth Circuit plainly erred in exposing Virginia's VWIL plan to a deferential analysis, for "all gender-based classifications today" warrant "heightened scrutiny." Valuable as VWIL may prove for students who seek the program offered, Virginia's remedy affords no cure at all for the opportunities and advantages withheld from women who want a VMI education and can make the grade. In sum, Virginia's remedy does not match the constitutional violation; the State has shown no "exceedingly persuasive justification" for withholding from women qualified for the experience premier training of the kind VMI affords.

. . .

For the reasons stated, the initial judgment of the Court of Appeals is affirmed, the final judgment of the Court of Appeals, is reversed, and the case is remanded for further proceedings consistent with this opinion.

It is so ordered.

JUSTICE THOMAS took no part in the consideration or decision of this case.

■ JUSTICE SCALIA, dissenting.

I shall devote most of my analysis to evaluating the Court's opinion on the basis of our current equal-protection jurisprudence, which regards this Court as free to evaluate everything under the sun by applying one of three tests: "rational basis" scrutiny, intermediate scrutiny, or strict scrutiny. These tests are no more scientific than their names suggest, and a further element of randomness is added by the fact that it is largely up to us which test will be applied in each case. Strict scrutiny, we have said, is reserved for state "classifications based on race or national origin and classifications affecting fundamental rights," Clark v. Jeter, 486 U.S. 456, 461 (1988). It is my position that the term "fundamental rights" should be limited to "interest[s] traditionally protected by our society," but the Court has not accepted that view, so that strict scrutiny will be applied to the deprivation of whatever sort of right we consider "fundamental." We have no established criterion for "intermediate scrutiny" either, but essentially apply it when it seems like a good idea to load the dice. So far it has been applied to content-neutral restrictions that place an incidental burden on speech, to disabilities attendant to illegitimacy, and to discrimination on the basis of sex. See, e.g., Turner Broadcasting System, Inc. v. FCC, 512 U.S. 622, ___, 114 S.Ct. 2445, 2469 (1994); Mills v. Habluetzel, 456 U.S. 91, 98–99 (1982); Craig v. Boren, 429 U.S. 190, 197 (1976).

. . .

To reject the Court's disposition today, however, it is not necessary to accept my view that the Court's made-up tests cannot displace longstanding national traditions as the primary determinant of what the Constitution means. It is only necessary to apply honestly the test the Court has been applying to sex-based classifications for the past two decades. It is well settled, as Justice O'Connor stated some time ago for a unanimous Court, that we evaluate a statutory classification based on sex under a standard that lies "[b]etween th[e] extremes of rational basis review and strict scrutiny." Clark v. Jeter, 486 U.S., at 461. We have denominated this standard "intermediate scrutiny" and under it have inquired whether the statutory classification is "substantially related to an important governmental objective."

... Notwithstanding our above-described precedents and their " 'firmly established principles,' " the United States urged us to hold in this case "that strict scrutiny is the correct constitutional standard for evaluating classifications that deny opportunities to individuals based on their sex." (This was in flat contradiction of the Government's position below, which was, in its own words, to "stat[e] *unequivocally* that the appropriate standard in this case is 'intermediate scrutiny.' ") The Court, while making no reference to the Government's argument, effectively accepts it.

Although the Court in two places recites the test as stated in *Hogan,* which asks whether the State has demonstrated "that the classification serves important governmental objectives and that the discriminatory means employed are substantially related to the achievement of those objectives," the Court never answers the question presented in anything resembling that form. When it engages in analysis, the Court instead prefers the phrase "exceedingly persuasive justification" from *Hogan.* The Court's nine invocations of that phrase, and even its fanciful description of that imponderable as "the core instruction" of the Court's decisions in J.E.B. v. Alabama ex rel. T.B., 511 U.S. 127 (1994), and *Hogan,* supra, would be unobjectionable if the Court acknowledged that *whether* a "justification" is "exceedingly persuasive" must be assessed by asking "[whether] the classification serves important governmental objectives and [whether] the discriminatory means employed are substantially related to the achievement of those objectives." Instead, however, the Court proceeds to interpret "exceedingly persuasive justification" in a fashion that contradicts the reasoning of *Hogan* and our other precedents.

That is essential to the Court's result, which can only be achieved by establishing that intermediate scrutiny is not survived if there are *some* women interested in attending VMI, capable of undertaking its activities, and able to meet its physical demands.

. . .

Intermediate scrutiny has never required a least-restrictive-means analysis, but only a "substantial relation" between the classification and the state interests that it serves. Thus, in Califano v. Webster, 430 U.S. 313 (1977) (*per curiam*), we upheld a congressional statute that provided higher Social Security benefits for women than for men. We reasoned that "women . . . as such have been unfairly hindered from earning as much as men," but we did not require proof that each woman so benefited had suffered discrimination or that each disadvantaged man had not; it was sufficient that even under the former congressional scheme "women *on the average* received lower retirement benefits than men." The reasoning in our other intermediate-scrutiny cases has similarly required only a substantial relation between end and means, not a perfect fit. In Rostker v. Goldberg, 453 U.S. 57 (1981), we held that selective-service registration could constitutionally exclude women, because even "assuming that a small number of women could be drafted for noncombat roles, Congress simply did not consider it worth the added burdens of including women in draft and registration plans." . . . There is simply no support in our cases for the notion that a sex-based classification is invalid unless it relates to characteristics that hold true in every instance.

Not content to execute a *de facto* abandonment of the intermediate scrutiny that has been our standard for sex-based classifications for some two decades, the Court purports to reserve the question whether, even in principle, a higher standard (*i.e.*, strict scrutiny) should apply. "The Court has," it says, "*thus far* reserved most stringent judicial scrutiny for classifications based on race or national origin . . . ,"; and it describes our earlier cases as having done no more than decline to "equat[e] gender classifications, *for all purposes*, to classifications based on race or national origin." The wonderful thing about these statements is that they are not actually false—just as it would not be actually false to say that "our cases have thus far reserved the 'beyond a reasonable doubt' standard of proof for criminal cases," or that "we have not equated tort actions, for all purposes, to criminal prosecutions." But the statements are misleading, insofar as they suggest that we have not already categorically *held* strict scrutiny to be inapplicable to sex-based classifications. See, e.g., Heckler v. Mathews, 465 U.S. 728 (1984) (*upholding* state action after applying *only* intermediate scrutiny); Michael M. v. Superior Court of Sonoma Cty., 450 U.S. 464 (1981) (same) (plurality and both concurring opinions); Califano v. Webster, 430 U.S. 313 (1977) (same) (*per curiam*). And the statements are irresponsible, insofar as they are calculated to destabilize current law. Our task is to clarify the law—not to muddy the waters, and not to exact over-compliance by intimidation. The States and the Federal Government are entitled to know *before they act* the standard to which they will be held, rather than be compelled to guess about the outcome of Supreme Court peek-a-boo.

The Court's intimations are particularly out of place because it is perfectly clear that, if the question of the applicable standard of review for sex-based classifications were to be regarded as an appropriate subject for reconsideration, the stronger argument would be not for elevating the standard to strict scrutiny, but for reducing it to rational-basis review. The latter certainly has a firmer foundation in our past jurisprudence: Whereas no majority of the Court has ever applied strict scrutiny in a case involving sex-based classifications, we routinely applied rational-basis review until the 1970's, see, e.g., Hoyt v. Florida, 368 U.S. 57 (1961); Goesaert v. Cleary, 335 U.S. 464 (1948). And of course normal, rational-basis review of sex-based classifications would be much more in accord with the genesis of heightened standards of judicial review, the famous footnote in United States v. Carolene Products Co., 304 U.S. 144 (1938), which said (intimatingly) that we did not have to inquire in the case at hand

> "whether prejudice against discrete and insular minorities may be a special condition, which tends seriously to curtail the operation of those political processes ordinarily to be relied upon to protect minorities, and which may call for a correspondingly more searching judicial inquiry." Id., at 152–153, n. 4.

It is hard to consider women a "discrete and insular minorit[y]" unable to employ the "political processes ordinarily to be relied upon," when they constitute a majority of the electorate. And the suggestion that they are incapable of exerting that political power smacks of the same paternalism that the Court so roundly condemns. Moreover, a long list of legislation proves the proposition false. See, e.g., Equal Pay Act of 1963, 29 U.S.C. § 206(d); Title VII of the Civil Rights Act of 1964, 42 U.S.C. § 2000e–2; Title IX of the Education Amendments of 1972, 20 U.S.C. § 1681; Women's Business Ownership Act of 1988, Pub.L. 100–533, 102 Stat. 2689; Violence Against Women Act of 1994, Pub.L. 103–322, Title IV, 108 Stat. 1902.

With this explanation of how the Court has succeeded in making its analysis seem orthodox—and indeed, if intimations are to be believed, even overly generous to VMI—I now proceed to describe how the analysis should have been conducted. The question to be answered, I repeat, is whether the exclusion of women from VMI is "substantially related to an important governmental objective."

It is beyond question that Virginia has an important state interest in providing effective college education for its citizens. That single-sex instruction is an approach substantially related to that interest should be evident enough from the long and continuing history in this country of men's and women's colleges. But beyond that, as the Court of Appeals here stated: "That single-gender education at the college level is beneficial to both sexes is a *fact established in this case*." 44 F.3d 1229, 1238 (C.A.4 1995) (emphasis added).

The evidence establishing that fact was overwhelming—indeed, "virtually uncontradicted" in the words of the court that received the evidence, 766 F.Supp. 1407, 1415 (W.D.Va.1991). As an initial matter, Virginia demonstrated at trial that "[a] substantial body of contemporary scholarship and research supports the proposition that, although males and females have significant areas of developmental overlap, they also have differing developmental needs that are deep-seated." While no one questioned that for many students a coeducational environment was nonetheless not inappropriate, that could not obscure the demonstrated benefits of single-sex colleges. For example, the District Court stated as follows:

"One empirical study in evidence, not questioned by any expert, demonstrates that single-sex colleges provide better educational experiences than coeducational institutions. Students of both sexes become more academically involved, interact with faculty frequently, show larger increases in intellectual self-esteem and are more satisfied with practically all aspects of college experience (the sole exception is social life) compared with their counterparts in coeducational institutions. Attendance at an all-male college substantially increases the likelihood that a student will carry out career plans in law, business and college teaching, and also has a substantial positive effect on starting salaries in business. Women's colleges increase the chances that those who attend will obtain positions of leadership, complete the baccalaureate degree, and aspire to higher degrees." Id., at 1412.

. . .

Virginia did not make this determination regarding the make-up of its public college system on the unrealistic assumption that no other colleges exist. Substantial evidence in the District Court demonstrated that the Commonwealth has long proceeded on the principle that " '[h]igher education resources should be viewed as a whole—public and private' "—because such an approach enhances diversity and because " 'it is academic and economic waste to permit unwarranted duplication.' " Id., at 1420–1421 (quoting 1974 Report of the General Assembly Commission on Higher Education to the General Assembly of Virginia). It is thus significant that, whereas there are "four all-female private [colleges] in Virginia," there is only "one private all-male college," which "indicates that the private sector is providing for th[e] [former] form of education to a much greater extent that it provides for all-male education." In these circumstances, Virginia's election to fund one public all-male institution and one on the adversative model—and to concentrate its resources in a single entity that serves both these interests in diversity—is substantially related to the State's important educational interests.

. . .

In the course of this dissent, I have referred approvingly to the opinion of my former colleague, Justice Powell, in Mississippi Univ. for Women v. Hogan, 458 U.S. 718 (1982). Many of the points made in his dissent apply with equal force here—in particular, the criticism of judicial opinions that purport to be "narro[w]" but whose "logic" is "sweepin[g]." But there is one statement with which I cannot agree. Justice Powell observed that the Court's decision in *Hogan,* which struck down a single-sex program offered by the *Mississippi University for Women,* had thereby "[l]eft without honor . . . an element of diversity that has characterized much of American education and enriched much of American life." Today's decision does not leave VMI without honor; no court opinion can do that.

. . .

NOTE

Six members of the Court joined the majority opinion. Chief Justice Rehnquist concurred in the judgment. Only Justice Scalia dissented. Justice Thomas took no part in the decision.

c. FEDERAL STATUTORY LIMITS ON SEX DISCRIMINATION

Hopkins v. Price Waterhouse

United States Court of Appeals, District of Columbia Circuit, 1990.
920 F.2d 967.

■ HARRY T. EDWARDS, CIRCUIT JUDGE:

This case, before this court for the second time, arises from a decision by appellant Price Waterhouse to deny partnership to one of its employees, appellee Ann B. Hopkins. We are again asked to review a finding by the District Court that Price Waterhouse's denial of partnership to Ms. Hopkins violated Title VII of the Civil Rights Act of 1964, 42 U.S.C. §§ 2000e *et seq.* (1988), and to assess its shaping of an appropriate remedy.

In Hishon v. King & Spalding, 467 U.S. 69 (1984), the Supreme Court clearly established that "partnership consideration may qualify as a term, condition, or privilege of a person's employment" such that Title VII will provide a cause of action if partnership is denied because of sex discrimination. . . .

It is undisputed that, for professional employees like Ms. Hopkins, Price Waterhouse held out the prospect of admission to partnership as a privilege of employment. . . . Moreover, decisions concerning admission to partnership were to be based exclusively on merit, taking into account a range of job-related considerations—"from practice development and technical expertise to interpersonal skills and participation in civic activities." The trial court found, however, that Ann Hopkins was denied partnership at Price Waterhouse in part because of sexual stereotyping, which is a form of sex discrimination under Title VII. We upheld that finding, as did the Supreme Court, see 109 S.Ct. at 1791, 1793 (plurality opinion); id. at 1802, 1805 (O'Connor, J., concurring in the judgment).

The Supreme Court, while agreeing that Price Waterhouse had been motivated in part by discriminatory stereotyping, remanded the case for reconsideration of Price Waterhouse's claim that the decision to deny partnership to Ms. Hopkins would have remained the same even in the absence of the proscribed discrimination. During the first trial before the District Court, Price Waterhouse was given an opportunity to show that it would have reached the same decision regarding Ms. Hopkins even absent any discrimination; however, both the trial court and this court required Price Waterhouse to make this showing by clear and convincing evidence. In reversing on this point, the Supreme Court ruled that the District Court must determine whether, on the record before it, Price Waterhouse had shown by a *preponderance of the evidence,* that it would have denied partnership to Ms. Hopkins in any event for nondiscriminatory reasons. . . .

On remand, the District Court . . . reviewed that evidence and found that Price Waterhouse failed to carry the burden placed upon it by the Supreme Court. Having found appellant liable under Title VII, the District Court ordered Price Waterhouse to admit Ann Hopkins into the firm's partnership and to pay her $371,000 in back pay. On this appeal, Price Waterhouse challenges both the District Court's finding of liability and its remedial order that Ms. Hopkins be made a partner. We can find no merit in either of these challenges.

Price Waterhouse's argument that Title VII does not authorize a court to order elevation to partnership rests ultimately upon the untenable suggestion that *Hishon* conferred only a cause of action for the discriminatory denial of partnership and never meant to imply a corresponding remedy. We find it inconceivable, however, that the Supreme Court intended to open up a partnership's admission decisions to judicial scrutiny while placing them beyond effective judicial remedy. On this point, it is important to note that this case involves only an employee's *elevation* to partnership; it does *not* involve a party's retention of partnership or the regulation of the relationship *among* partners. Thus, we are not confronted by the concerns expressed in Justice Powell's concurring opinion in *Hishon,* in which he emphasized that the Court in *Hishon* did not reach the question whether Title VII would protect employees after they became partners, see 467 U.S. at 79 (Powell, J., concurring); we emphasize the same point today, for we have no occasion to decide this question.

Finding no error in either the trial court's finding of liability or in its shaping of an appropriate remedy, we affirm the judgment of the District Court.

Ann Hopkins joined Price Waterhouse in 1978, as a member of the professional staff in the firm's Office of Government Services ("OGS") in Washington, D.C. In this position, Ms. Hopkins was responsible for helping the firm to win and carry out management consulting contracts with federal agencies. She enjoyed a successful career in OGS and, in 1982, was proposed for partnership. In keeping with the firm's established personnel procedures, all partners who had worked with Ms. Hopkins were asked to submit written comments to the firm's Admissions Committee. These evaluations were written on so-called "long forms" by those partners who knew Ms. Hopkins well, and on "short forms" by those who had had only passing contact with her. The evaluations covered a range of considerations, including both technical skills and personal interactions. The Admissions Committee was then responsible for sorting through these forms, summarizing the various comments, and submitting recommendations to the firm's Policy Board. The Policy Board, in turn, was to decide whether to reject the candidate outright, "hold" her candidacy for another year or submit the candidate for a vote by the full partnership. See 618 F.Supp. at 1111–12 (recounting partnership review process).

Ms. Hopkins' record at the firm documented outstanding accomplishments as a senior manager. At the first trial in this case, the District Court found that Ms. Hopkins "played a key role in Price Waterhouse's successful effort to win a multi-million dollar contract with the Department of State." Moreover,

> [s]he had no difficulty dealing with clients and her clients appear to have been very pleased with her work. None of the other partnership candidates at Price Waterhouse that year had a comparable record in terms of successfully securing major contracts for the partnership. . . . She was generally viewed as a highly competent project leader who worked long hours, pushed vigorously to meet deadlines and demanded much from the multidisciplinary staffs with which she worked.

A number of the comments submitted by partners, however, also criticized Ms. Hopkins' "interpersonal skills," suggesting that she was sometimes overbearing and abrasive. Some of these comments went further in suggesting that these defects were especially inappropriate because Hopkins was a woman. As the Supreme Court noted in its review of this case:

> One partner described her as "macho"; another suggested that she "overcompensated for being a woman"; a third advised her to take "a

course at charm school." Several partners criticized her use of profanity; in response, one partner suggested that those partners objected to her swearing only "because it[']s a lady using foul language." Another supporter explained that Hopkins "ha[d] matured from a tough-talking somewhat masculine hard-nosed mgr to an authoritative, formidable, but much more appealing lady ptr candidate."

In March 1983, Price Waterhouse's Policy Board voted not to admit Ms. Hopkins as a partner. Rather than dismiss her outright, however, the Board decided to "hold" her candidacy, with the possibility that she might be reconsidered the following year. "When [Hopkins] consulted with the head partner at OGS, who was her strongest supporter and responsible for telling her what problems the Policy Board had identified with her candidacy, *she was advised to walk more femininely, talk more femininely, dress more femininely, wear make-up, have her hair styled, and wear jewelry.*"

Ms. Hopkins remained at Price Waterhouse but then ran into conflicts with some of the partners. Donald Epelbaum, one of the partners in appellee's home office, accused Ms. Hopkins of misrepresenting a conversation she had had with Price Waterhouse's managing partner concerning her partnership prospects. These conflicts culminated in a decision not to repropose Ms. Hopkins for partnership the following year. Ms. Hopkins then resigned and later brought this suit.

Following the first trial in 1985, the District Court held that Ms. Hopkins had proved that sex stereotyping had infected the decisionmaking process among Price Waterhouse's partners and that Price Waterhouse could avoid equitable relief only if it could show, by clear and convincing evidence, that it would have reached the same negative decision regarding Ms. Hopkins' candidacy even absent the sex stereotyping. The trial court went on, however, to hold that Price Waterhouse's subsequent decision not to renominate Ms. Hopkins was nondiscriminatory, and that Ms. Hopkins' resignation was not a constructive discharge. Consequently, the trial court held that Ms. Hopkins was not entitled to back pay for the period following her resignation.

. . .

Following our initial review of this case, the Supreme Court granted certiorari and considered the case. The Court upheld the District Court's finding that sex discrimination had tainted Price Waterhouse's decisionmaking. See 109 S.Ct. at 1791, 1793 (plurality opinion); id. at 1802, 1805 (O'Connor, J., concurring in the judgment). It agreed that "a number of the partners' comments showed sex stereotyping at work," and stated forcefully that "we are beyond the day when an employer could evaluate employees by assuming or insisting that they matched the stereotype associated with their group." The Court then ruled that Price Waterhouse could avoid liability if it could show—by a preponderance of the evidence—that it would have reached the same decision absent any discrimination. Because the District Court had not evaluated the evidence by that standard, the Court remanded the case for reconsideration pursuant to the proper evidentiary standard.

. . .

Price Waterhouse raises two objections to the District Court's finding of liability. First, it asserts that the trial court did not carry out the Supreme Court's instruction that it reevaluate the evidence pursuant to the preponderance standard. ... Second, it asserts that, even if the trial court did reweigh the evidence, it committed clear error in not being persuaded by Price Waterhouse's showing. We disagree on both counts.

[A] fair reading of Judge Gesell's opinion shows that he *did* in fact "reweigh" the evidence and that he simply found it unpersuasive. ...

. . .

Price Waterhouse also asserts that the District Court had no authority to order admission to partnership to remedy a Title VII violation. Price Waterhouse's argument is apparently that while Title VII extends far enough to protect an employee against discrimination in partnership consideration, it comes to an abrupt halt once a violation has been found, leaving the employee with the promise of fair consideration for partnership but no effective means of enforcing it. This argument seems absurd in the light of the Supreme Court's decision in Hishon v. King & Spalding, 467 U.S. 69 (1984), in which the Court held that "nothing in the change in status that advancement to partnership might entail means that partnership consideration falls outside the terms of [Title VII]." Given the Court's judgment in *Hishon,* and after careful review of Title VII, its legislative history and the case law interpreting it, we find that the District Court clearly acted within the bounds of the remedial authority conferred by the statute.

. . .

It is also noteworthy that the EEOC, the agency to which we owe deference in construing Title VII, agrees with our construction of the remedial reach of Title VII. This is significant because Congress has recognized "the importance of administrative expertise relating to the resolution of problems of employment discrimination." S.Rep. No. 415, 92d Cong., 1st Sess. 18 (1971). In explaining Congress' decision to grant the EEOC administrative enforcement powers, the Senate Committee on Labor and Public Welfare observed that "[m]any of the Title VII proceedings involve complex labor relations and business operations issues *particularly in the fashioning of the remedies for eliminating discrimination.* The Equal Employment Opportunity Commission would be expected to develop an important reservoir of expertise in these matters, expertise which would not readily be available to a widespread court system."

The EEOC has applied its expertise to the question before us and has concluded that Title VII authorizes court-ordered elevation to partnership as a remedy for the discriminatory denial of partnership. The EEOC's view reinforces our own independent reading of the statute.

. . .

Although all signposts in the statute, its legislative history and the case law point strongly toward affirming the District Court's judgment to order partnership, thereby vindicating "[t]he 'make whole' purpose of Title VII,", Price Waterhouse urges that there are several countervailing considerations weighing against this conclusion. We consider them in turn.

1. *Freedom of Association*

Price Waterhouse argues that a court order forcing it to accept Ann Hopkins as a partner would violate its partners' constitutional rights of free association. This argument is entirely unpersuasive. Even assuming *arguendo* that a large business partnership such as Price Waterhouse has cognizable associational rights, they must yield to the compelling national interest in eradicating discrimination. See, e.g., New York State Club Ass'n v. City of

New York, 487 U.S. 1, 12–13 (1988); Board of Directors of Rotary Int'l v. Rotary Club of Duarte, 481 U.S. 537, 549 (1987) ("Even if [the forced admission of women members] does work some slight infringement on Rotary members' right of expressive association, that infringement is justified because it serves the State's compelling interest in eliminating discrimination against women."); Roberts v. United States Jaycees, 468 U.S. 609, 623 (1984); Runyon v. McCrary, 427 U.S. 160, 175–76 (1976).

It is difficult to differentiate between the constitutional argument Price Waterhouse advances here and the one rejected in a nearly identical setting in *Hishon*. There, King & Spalding, a large law partnership, had similarly insisted that "application of Title VII in [its] case would infringe constitutional rights of expression or association." 467 U.S. at 78. The Supreme Court brushed aside the argument, noting that " '[i]nvidious private discrimination may be characterized as a form of exercising freedom of association protected by the First Amendment, but it has never been accorded affirmative constitutional protections.' " Id.

On the basis of the foregoing authorities, we reject Price Waterhouse's suggestion that its claimed freedom of association precludes the court from ordering partnership as a Title VII remedy.

2. *Principles of Contract Law*

Price Waterhouse also points out that courts have traditionally been reluctant to order the creation of a partnership as an equitable remedy for breach of contract, and urges that this contract principle be carried over into the realm of antidiscrimination law. It is true that in common law contract cases the courts have hesitated to compel persons to work together or to enforce other ongoing human relationships, including partnerships. ...

Title VII makes expressly clear, however, that this common law rule does not limit a court's power to fashion equitable remedies for employment discrimination in violation of the statute. Price Waterhouse concedes, as it must, that the "plain language" of Title VII contemplates judicial authority to order reinstatement and hiring of employees. Thus, even under appellant's analysis, it is plain that there is no merit to the argument that common law principles of contract law serve to limit Title VII's remedial reach.

3. *The Equities of this Case*

Lastly, Price Waterhouse argues that even if the District Court was empowered under Title VII to order partnership as a remedy, it was an abuse of discretion for the court to do so on the facts of this case. Specifically, appellant argues that Ms. Hopkins' own alleged misconduct[13] following the March 1983 decision to defer her candidacy made her eventual elevation to partnership impossible and precludes the court from now making Ms. Hopkins a partner. We do not agree.

The misconduct to which Price Waterhouse refers occurred only after Price Waterhouse's own illegal sex discrimination had intervened to deny Ms. Hopkins her place in the partnership. Given the findings of sex discrimination committed by appellant's partners, there is a certain hint of irony in the moral indignation with which Price Waterhouse protests the

13. The District Court found that Ms. Hopkins had "misstated the substance of a meeting ... between herself and Joseph E. Connor, the Chairman and Senior Partner of Price Waterhouse, regarding her partnership prospects. Ms. Hopkins misleadingly implied that Mr. Connor had disparaged certain partners who opposed her candidacy and that he had warned of the adverse consequences his partners might experience for opposing her the next year." 737 F.Supp. at 1213.

prospect of having to offer partnership to a person who allegedly misstated the substance of a conversation. We also note that Price Waterhouse does *not* claim that, if Ms. Hopkins had been admitted to partnership in March 1983, her subsequent alleged misconduct would have justified her dismissal from partnership.

Yet, with these observations aside, we find that the District Court expressly considered Ms. Hopkins' alleged misconduct in the shaping of its equitable remedy, deducting from her back pay award any "claim for the fiscal year 1983–1984." We review this judgment under the highly deferential abuse-of-discretion standard, and, on the record before us, we can find no basis to overturn the trial court's decision. For us to reject the District Court's judgment on this issue would be a flagrant disregard of the obvious limits of the abuse-of-discretion standard.

Judge Gesell not only limited back pay, he was careful to consider whether there existed too much hostility between the parties to permit an effective working relationship; he found there did not. He also considered alternative remedies, such as front pay, and concluded that it would be impossible to tailor a prospective remedy so that Ms. Hopkins truly would be made whole. Finally, he considered and rejected Price Waterhouse's contention that Ms. Hopkins is entitled only to reconsideration for partnership by Price Waterhouse, finding that ordering reconsideration in this case would be "futile and unjust." We find no abuse of discretion by Judge Gesell in ordering a partnership based on the facts of the case before him.

E. *Calculation of Back Pay*

Finally, we find no error or abuse of discretion in the District Court's calculation of Ms. Hopkins' back pay award. In particular, we find that Judge Gesell properly accounted for Ms. Hopkins' inadequate mitigation in formulating the award.

. . .

For all of the foregoing reasons, the judgment of the District Court is affirmed.

NOTE

In Rene v. MGM Grand Hotel, 305 F.3d 1061 (9th Cir. 2002) (en banc), cert. denied, 538 U.S. 922 (2003), a plurality of the court held that Title VII protects against same-sex offensive physical conduct in the work place. The plaintiff-employee in the case alleged that his co-workers whistled and blew kisses at him, grabbed his crotch and poked fingers in his anus.

Nevada Dept. of Human Resources v. Hibbs

Supreme Court of the United States, 2003.
538 U.S. 721, 123 S.Ct. 1972, 155 L.Ed.2d 953.

■ Chief Justice Rehnquist delivered the opinion of the Court.

The Family and Medical Leave Act of 1993 (FMLA or Act) entitles eligible employees to take up to 12 work weeks of unpaid leave annually for any of several reasons, including the onset of a "serious health condition" in an employee's spouse, child, or parent. 29 U.S.C. § 2612(a)(1)(C). The Act creates a private right of action to seek both equitable relief and money damages "against any employer (including a public agency) in any Federal or State court of competent jurisdiction," should that employer "interfere with, restrain, or deny the exercise of" FMLA rights. We hold that employees of the State of Nevada may recover money damages in the event of the State's failure to comply with the family-care provision of the Act.

Petitioners include the Nevada Department of Human Resources (Department) and two of its officers. Respondent William Hibbs (hereinafter respondent) worked for the Department's Welfare Division. In April and May 1997, he sought leave under the FMLA to care for his ailing wife, who was recovering from a car accident and neck surgery. The Department granted his request for the full 12 weeks of FMLA leave and authorized him to use the leave intermittently as needed between May and December 1997. Respondent did so until August 5, 1997, after which he did not return to work. In October 1997, the Department informed respondent that he had exhausted his FMLA leave, that no further leave would be granted, and that he must report to work by November 12, 1997. Respondent failed to do so and was terminated.

... The District Court awarded petitioners summary judgment on the grounds that the FMLA claim was barred by the Eleventh Amendment and that respondent's Fourteenth Amendment rights had not been violated. Respondent appealed. The Ninth Circuit reversed.

We granted certiorari to resolve a split among the Courts of Appeals on the question whether an individual may sue a State for money damages in federal court....

For over a century now, we have made clear that the Constitution does not provide for federal jurisdiction over suits against nonconsenting States, Board of Trustees of Univ. of Ala. v. Garrett, 531 U.S. 356, 363 (2001).

Congress may, however, abrogate such immunity in federal court if it makes its intention to abrogate unmistakably clear in the language of the statute and acts pursuant to a valid exercise of its power under § 5 of the Fourteenth Amendment. See *Garrett, supra,* at 363. The clarity of Congress' intent here is not fairly debatable. ... This case turns, then, on whether Congress acted within its constitutional authority when it sought to abrogate the States' immunity for purposes of the FMLA's family-leave provision.

In enacting the FMLA, Congress relied on two of the powers vested in it by the Constitution: its Article I commerce power and its power under § 5 of the Fourteenth Amendment to enforce that Amendment's guarantees. Congress may not abrogate the States' sovereign immunity pursuant to its Article I power over commerce. Seminola Tribe of Fla. V. Fla. [517 U.S. 44 (1994)]. Congress may, however, abrogate States' sovereign immunity through a valid exercise of its § 5 power, for "the Eleventh Amendment, and the principle of state sovereignty which it embodies, are necessarily limited by the enforcement provisions of § 5 of the Fourteenth Amendment." Fitzpatrick v. Bitzer, 427 U.S. 445, 456 (1976).

... Section 5 [of the Fourteenth Amendment] grants Congress the power "to enforce" the substantive guarantees of § 1—among them, equal protection of the laws—by enacting "appropriate legislation." Congress may, in the exercise of its § 5 power, do more than simply proscribe conduct that we have held unconstitutional. Congress may enact so-called prophylactic legislation that proscribes facially constitutional conduct, in order to prevent and deter unconstitutional conduct.

. . .

The FMLA aims to protect the right to be free from gender-based discrimination in the workplace. We have held that statutory classifications that distinguish between males and females are subject to heightened scrutiny. . . .

The history of the many state laws limiting women's employment opportunities is chronicled in—and, until relatively recently, was sanctioned by—this Court's own opinions. For example, in Bradwell v. State, 16 Wall. 130, 21 L Ed 442 (1873) (Illinois), and Goesaert v. Cleary, 355 U.S. 464 (1948) (Michigan) the Court upheld state laws prohibiting women from practicing law and tending bar, respectively. State laws frequently subjected women to distinctive restrictions, terms, conditions, and benefits for those jobs they could take. In Muller v. Oregon, 208 U.S. 412, 419, n. 1 (1908), for example, this Court approved a state law limiting the hours that women could work for wages, and observed that 19 States had such laws at the time. Such laws were based on the related beliefs that (1) woman is, and should remain, "the center of home and family life," Hoyt v. Florida, 368 U.S. 57, 62 (1961) and (2) "a proper discharge of [a woman's] maternal functions—having in view not merely her own health, but the well-being of the race—justifies legislation to protect her from the greed as well as the passion of man," *Muller, supra.* Until our decision in Reed v. Reed, 404 U.S. 71 (1971), "it remained the prevailing doctrine that government, both federal and state, could withhold from women opportunities accorded men so long as any 'basis in reason' "—such as the above beliefs—"could be conceived for the discrimination."

Congress responded to this history of discrimination by abrogating States' sovereign immunity in Title VII of the Civil Rights Act of 1964, 42 U.S.C. § 2000e–2(a), and we sustained this abrogation in *Fitzpatrick.* But state gender discrimination did not cease. "It can hardly be doubted that . . . women still face pervasive, although at times more subtle, discrimination . . . in the job market." . . . Frontiero v. Richardson, 411 U.S. 677, 686 (1973). According to evidence that was before Congress when it enacted the FMLA, States continue to rely on invalid gender stereotypes in the employment context, specifically in the administration of leave benefits. Reliance on such stereotypes cannot justify the States' gender discrimination in this area. *Virginia, supra.* The long and extensive history of sex discrimination prompted us to hold that measures that differentiate on the basis of gender warrant heightened scrutiny; here, as in *Fitzpatrick*, the persistence of such unconstitutional discrimination by the States justifies Congress' passage of prophylactic § 5 legislation.

As the FMLA's legislative record reflects, a 1990 Bureau of Labor Statistics (BLS) survey stated that 37 percent of surveyed private-sector employees were covered by maternity leave policies, while only 18 percent were covered by paternity leave policies. The corresponding numbers from a similar BLS survey the previous year were 33 percent and 16 percent, respectively. While these data show an increase in the percentage of employees eligible for such leave, they also show a widening of the gender gap during the same period. Thus, stereotype-based beliefs about the allocation of family duties remained firmly rooted, and employers' reliance on them in establishing discriminatory leave policies remained widespread.

Congress also heard testimony that "parental leave for fathers . . . is rare. Even . . . where child-care leave policies do exist, men, *both in the public and private sectors*, receive notoriously discriminatory treatment in their requests for such leave." Many States offered women extended "maternity" leave that far exceeded the typical 4–to 8–week period of physical disability due to pregnancy and childbirth, but very few States granted men a parallel benefit: Fifteen States provided women up to one year of extended maternity leave, while only four provided men with the same. This and other differential leave policies were not attributable to any differential physical needs of men and women, but rather to the pervasive sex-role stereotype that caring for family members is women's work.

Finally, Congress had evidence that, even where state laws and policies were not facially discriminatory, they were applied in discriminatory ways. It was aware of the "serious problems with the discretionary nature of family leave," because when "the authority to grant leave and to arrange the length of that leave rests with individual supervisors," it leaves "employees open to discretionary and possibly unequal treatment." Testimony supported that conclusion, explaining that "the lack of uniform parental and medical leave policies in the work place has created an environment where [sex] discrimination is rampant." 1987 Senate Labor Hearings, pt. 2, at 170 (testimony of Peggy Montes, Mayor's Commission on Women's Affairs, City of Chicago).

In spite of all of the above evidence, Justice Kennedy argues in dissent that Congress' passage of the FMLA was unnecessary because "the States appear to have been ahead of Congress in providing gender-neutral family leave benefits," . . . However, it was only "since Federal family leave legislation was first introduced" that the States had even "begun to consider similar family leave initiatives."

Furthermore, the dissent's statement that some States "had adopted some form of family-care leave" before the FMLA's enactment, glosses over important shortcomings of some state policies. First, seven States had child-care leave provisions that applied to women only. Indeed, Massachusetts required that notice of its leave provisions be posted only in "establishments in which females are employed." These laws reinforced the very stereotypes that Congress sought to remedy through the FMLA. Second, 12 States provided their employees no family leave, beyond an initial childbirth or adoption, to care for a seriously ill child or family member. Third, many States provided no statutorily guaranteed right to family leave, offering instead only voluntary or discretionary leave programs. Three States left the amount of leave time primarily in employers' hands. Congress could reasonably conclude that such discretionary family-leave programs would do little to combat the stereotypes about the roles of male and female employees that Congress sought to eliminate. Finally, four States provided leave only through administrative regulations or personnel policies, which Congress could reasonably conclude offered significantly less firm protection than a federal law. Against the above backdrop of limited state leave policies, no matter how generous petitioner's own may have been, Congress was justified in enacting the FMLA as remedial legislation.

In sum, the States' record of unconstitutional participation in, and fostering of, gender-based discrimination in the administration of leave benefits is weighty enough to justify the enactment of prophylactic § 5 legislation.

. . . Because the standard for demonstrating the constitutionality of a gender-based classification is more difficult to meet than our rational-basis test—it must "serve important governmental objectives" and be "substantially related to the achievement of those objectives,"—it was easier for Congress to show a pattern of state constitutional violations. Congress was similarly successful in South Carolina v. Katzenbach, 383 U.S. 301, 308 (1966), where we upheld the Voting Rights Act of 1965: Because racial classifications are presumptively invalid, most of the States' acts of race discrimination violated the Fourteenth Amendment.

The impact of the discrimination targeted by the FMLA is significant. Congress determined:

> "Historically, denial or curtailment of women's employment opportunities has been traceable directly to the pervasive presumption that women are mothers first, and workers second. This prevailing ideology about women's roles has in turn justified discrimination against women when they are mothers or mothers-to-be."

Stereotypes about women's domestic roles are reinforced by parallel stereotypes presuming a lack of domestic responsibilities for men. Because employers continued to regard the family as the woman's domain, they often denied men similar accommodations or discouraged them from taking leave. These mutually reinforcing stereotypes created a self-fulfilling cycle of discrimination that forced women to continue to assume the role of primary family caregiver, and fostered employers' stereotypical views about women's commitment to work and their value as employees. Those perceptions, in turn, Congress reasoned, lead to subtle discrimination that may be difficult to detect on a case-by-case basis.

We believe that Congress' chosen remedy, the family-care leave provision of the FMLA, is "congruent and proportional to the targeted violation." Congress had already tried unsuccessfully to address this problem through Title VII and the amendment of Title VII by the Pregnancy Discrimination Act, 42 U.S.C. § 2000e(k). Here, as in *Katzenbach,* Congress again confronted a "difficult and intractable problem," where previous legislative attempts had failed. See *Katzenbach* at 313 (upholding the Voting Rights Act). Such problems may justify added prophylactic measures in response.

By creating an across-the-board, routine employment benefit for all eligible employees, Congress sought to ensure that family-care leave would no longer be stigmatized as an inordinate drain on the workplace caused by female employees, and that employers could not evade leave obligations simply by hiring men. By setting a minimum standard of family leave for *all* eligible employees, irrespective of gender, the FMLA attacks the formerly state-sanctioned stereotype that only women are responsible for family caregiving, thereby reducing employers' incentives to engage in discrimination by basing hiring and promotion decisions on stereotypes.

. . .

The dissent characterizes the FMLA as a "substantive entitlement program" rather than a remedial statute because it establishes a floor of 12 weeks' leave. In the dissent's view, in the face of evidence of gender-based discrimination by the States in the provision of leave benefits, Congress could do no more in exercising its § 5 power than simply proscribe such discrimination. But this position cannot be squared with our recognition that Congress "is not confined to the enactment of legislation that merely parrots the precise wording of the Fourteenth Amendment," but may prohibit "a somewhat broader swath of conduct, including that which is not itself forbidden by the Amendment's text." . . .

We also find significant the many other limitations that Congress placed on the scope of this measure. . . . The FMLA requires only unpaid leave, and applies only to employees who have worked for the employer for at least one year and provided 1,250 hours of service within the last 12 months. Employees in high-ranking or sensitive positions are simply ineligible for FMLA leave; of particular importance to the States, the FMLA expressly excludes from coverage state elected officials, their staffs, and appointed policymakers. Employees must give advance notice of foreseeable leave, and employers may require certification by a health care provider of the need for leave. In choosing 12 weeks as the appropriate leave floor, Congress chose "a middle ground, a period long enough to serve 'the needs of families' but not so long that it would upset 'the legitimate interests of employers.'" ... Moreover, the cause of action under the FMLA is a restricted one: The damages recoverable are strictly defined and measured by actual monetary losses, and the accrual period for backpay is limited by the Act's 2-year statute of limitations (extended to three years only for willful violations).

The judgment of the Court of Appeals is therefore affirmed.

■ JUSTICE KENNEDY, with whom JUSTICE SCALIA and JUSTICE THOMAS join, dissenting.

. . .

The Court acknowledges that States have adopted family leave programs prior to federal intervention, but argues these policies suffered from serious imperfections. Even if correct, this observation proves, at most, that programs more generous and more effective than those operated by the States were feasible. That the States did not devise the optimal programs is not, however, evidence that the States were perpetuating unconstitutional discrimination. Given that the States assumed a pioneering role in the creation of family leave schemes, it is not surprising these early efforts may have been imperfect. This is altogether different, however, from purposeful discrimination.

. . .

Stripped of the conduct which exhibits no constitutional infirmity, the Court's "extensive and specific ... record of unconstitutional state conduct," boils down to the fact that three States, Massachusetts, Kansas, and Tennessee, provided parenting leave only to their female employees, and had no program for granting their employees (male or female) family leave. ... [T]he evidence related to the parenting leave is simply too attenuated to support a charge of unconstitutional discrimination in the provision of family leave. Nor, as the Court seems to acknowledge, does the Constitution require States to provide their employees with any family leave at all. A State's failure to devise a family leave program is not, then, evidence of unconstitutional behavior.

Considered in its entirety, the evidence fails to document a pattern of unconstitutional conduct sufficient to justify the abrogation of States' sovereign immunity....

NOTE

Justices O'Connor, Souter, Ginsburg and Breyer joined the majority opinion. Justice Stevens concurred in the judgment.

2. REALLOCATION OF DUTIES WITHIN MARRIAGE

a. BY PRIVATE CONTRACT

Edwardson v. Edwardson

Supreme Court of Kentucky, 1990.
798 S.W.2d 941.

■ LAMBERT, JUSTICE.

Almost seventy-five years ago this Court declared "the law will not permit parties contemplating marriage to enter into a contract providing for, and looking to, future separation after marriage." Stratton v. Wilson, 170 Ky. 61, 185 S.W. 522, 523 (1916).... This Court granted appellant's motion for discretionary review to reconsider the position taken in *Stratton*....

Prior to their marriage to each other, both parties had been married previously. In the divorce decree dissolving her prior marriage, appellant was awarded the sum of seventy-five dollars ($75.00) per week as maintenance, the payment of which was to be terminated upon her remarriage. Appellant and appellee executed an agreement prior to the time their marriage was solemnized which contained, *inter alia*, the following provision:

> "In the event that the marriage of the parties shall be dissolved or the parties become legally separated, to the extent permitted under Kentucky law or the state of residence where said action is filed, the Party of the First Part shall receive SEVENTY-FIVE DOLLARS ($75.00) per week as maintenance (alimony) from the Party of the Second Part for her life, or until her remarriage. Furthermore, Party of the Second Part shall maintain medical/hospitalization insurance for the Party of the First Part for her life or her remarriage, which insurance program shall have benefits substantially similar to those presently held by the Party of the First Part through the ROTHROCK INSURANCE SERVICE. Other than as provided in this paragraph, neither party shall have any obligation to the other for alimony or support, and neither party shall have any claim against the property of the other nor any claim thereto by reason of the marriage or the manner or cause thereto by reason of the marriage or the manner or cause of dissolution thereof, it being the intent hereof that the parties, each having adequate separate estates on the date of marriage, shall each retain their separate estates, any increase in the value thereof and accretions thereto, free of any and all claims or interest in property or other rights which may come into existence or arise by reason of the marriage of the parties hereto, except as stated herein."

After about two and a half years of marital turbulence, the parties finally separated. In the divorce action which followed, appellant sought enforcement of the agreement. Enforcement was denied in the trial court and on appeal the judgment of the trial court was affirmed. . . .

. . . The . . . issue before the Court is whether any antenuptial agreement which contemplates divorce and provides for the payment of maintenance and the disposition of property upon subsequent dissolution of the marriage is enforceable.

. . .

In unmistakable terms, the Court in *Stratton* held the portion of the agreement which provided for payment of alimony in the event of separation or divorce to be void. The decision was based on the view that such an agreement was destabilizing to the marital relationship and might promote or encourage marital breakup.

It is an indisputable fact that since rendition of our decision in *Stratton*, the incidence of divorce in Kentucky has followed the national experience and risen steadily. Further, the Kentucky General Assembly has abandoned the fault-based system of allowing dissolution of marriage which prevailed prior to 1972 and adopted portions of the Uniform Marriage and Divorce Act which is substantially a "no-fault" marriage dissolution system. A legislative determination has been made that abandoning the necessity of proving fault would, *inter alia*, "[s]trengthen and preserve the integrity of marriage and safeguard family relationships." KRS 403.110(1). While the rising incidence of divorce and the existence of profound legislative changes do not *per se* render the *Stratton* rule invalid, neither do they support its continuation. . . .

A number of other jurisdictions have confronted the question before this Court and abandoned or modified the prohibition against enforcement of antenuptial agreements which contemplate divorce. In a leading decision, Posner v. Posner, 233 So.2d 381 (Fla.1970), the Supreme Court of Florida reviewed a number of authorities and noted a "clearly discernible" trend in favor of enforcing antenuptial agreements. The Court observed that in some circumstances, the existence of an antenuptial agreement might actually promote the continuation of marriage rather than its dissolution and further noted the widespread enforcement of antenuptial agreements to settle property rights upon the death of a spouse. Abandoning its prior rule, the Court held that such agreements should no longer be void *ab initio*, but should be measured by the stringent standards prescribed in Del Vecchio v. Del Vecchio, 143 So.2d 17 (Fla.1962), for agreements which settle property rights on the death of a spouse, and the additional requirement that it not appear the agreement promoted procurement of the divorce. In another leading case, Scherer v. Scherer, 249 Ga. 635, 292 S.E.2d 662 (1982), the Supreme Court of Georgia overruled its prior decisions holding antenuptial agreements in contemplation of divorce invalid. As grounds for its decision, the Court recognized that divorce is a commonplace fact of life, that state law and public policy permit married persons to obtain divorces, and the absence of empirical evidence to show that antenuptial agreements in contemplation of divorce actually encourage or incite divorce. . . .

While the foregoing cases present differing factual circumstances and subtle differences in the legal issues addressed and answered, a common theme may be found throughout. The notion that divorce is promoted by an antenuptial agreement which contemplates such a possibility has been rejected and the right of parties to enter into appropriate agreements has been upheld. We concur with this view.

Finally, we observe that the legal status of marriage partners is vastly different today than it was when *Stratton v. Wilson* was decided. At that time the Nineteenth Amendment to the Constitution of the United States had not yet been ratified, married women's property acts were not yet in existence or were in their infancy, and in general the status of women in this society was decidedly second class. In 1916 it may have been entirely logical to restrict the nature of agreements available to persons contemplating marriage in an effort to avoid marital instability. Subsequent changes in society and seventy-five years of experience have rendered such restrictions inappropriate. . . .

. . .

The first limitation upon parties to an antenuptial agreement is the requirement of full disclosure. Before parties should be bound by agreements which affect their substantial rights upon dissolution of marriage, it should appear that the agreement was free of any material omission or misrepresentation. The second limitation to be observed is that the agreement must not be unconscionable at the time enforcement is sought. Regardless of the terms of the agreement and regardless of the subsequent acquisition or loss of assets, at the time enforcement is sought, the court should be satisfied that the agreement is not unconscionable.[2] Upon a finding of unconscionability, the trial court entertaining such an action may modify the parties' agreement to satisfy the necessary standard, but should otherwise give effect to the agreement as nearly as possible providing the agreement was not procured by fraud or duress.

While it may go without saying, we observe that antenuptial agreements may apply only to disposition of property and maintenance. Questions of child support, child custody and visitation are not subject to such agreements; and unless the parties otherwise agree, non-marital property retains its character as such.

We recognize that this opinion may raise a number of questions. No effort has been made to write a comprehensive treatise which answers all the questions likely to arise. The ingenuity of persons contemplating marriage to fashion unusual agreements, particularly with the assistance of counsel, cannot be overestimated. We will observe the tradition whereby the law develops on a case by case basis. It should be recognized, however, that trial courts have been vested with broad discretion to modify or invalidate antenuptial agreements. Parties and their counsel should be admonished to refrain from entering into agreements lacking mutuality and without a rational basis. Courts reviewing antenuptial agreements and faced with a claim of unconscionability should not overlook the wisdom, which is fully applicable to both spouses, expressed in this Court's decision rendered in Clark v. Clark, 301 Ky. 682, 192 S.W.2d 968, 970 (1946):

> "A separation agreement will be closely scrutinized by a court of equity,. . . . It must appear that the husband exercised the utmost good faith; that there was a full disclosure of all material facts, including the husband's circumstances and any other fact which might affect the terms of the contract; and that the provisions made in the agreement . . . were fair, reasonable, just, equitable, and adequate in view of the conditions and circumstances of the parties. . . ."

For the reasons stated, we reverse and remand this cause to the Jefferson Circuit Court for further proceedings consistent herewith.

Simeone v. Simeone

Supreme Court of Pennsylvania, 1990.
525 Pa. 392, 581 A.2d 162.

■ FLAHERTY, JUSTICE.

At issue in this appeal is the validity of a prenuptial agreement executed between the appellant, Catherine E. Walsh Simeone, and the appellee, Frederick A. Simeone. At the time of their marriage, in 1975, appellant was a twenty-three year old nurse and appellee was a thirty-nine year old neurosurgeon. Appellee had an income of approximately $90,000 per year, and appellant was unemployed. Appellee also had assets worth approximately $300,000. On the eve of the parties' wedding, appellee's attorney presented appellant with a prenuptial agreement to be signed. Appellant, without the benefit of counsel, signed the agreement. Appellee's attorney had not ad-

2. Upon review of a post-nuptial separation agreement entered into pursuant to KRS 403.180, the trial court must determine whether the agreement is unconscionable. A number of Kentucky decisions have addressed the construction of this term and we need not attempt further refinement in this opinion. The concept of unconscionability is familiar to circuit courts by virtue of KRS 403.180 and KRS 403.250.

vised appellant regarding any legal rights that the agreement surrendered. The parties are in disagreement as to whether appellant knew in advance of that date that such an agreement would be presented for signature. Appellant denies having had such knowledge and claims to have signed under adverse circumstances, which, she contends, provide a basis for declaring it void.

The agreement limited appellant to support payments of $200 per week in the event of separation or divorce, subject to a maximum total payment of $25,000. The parties separated in 1982, and, in 1984, divorce proceedings were commenced. Between 1982 and 1984 appellee made payments which satisfied the $25,000 limit. In 1985, appellant filed a claim for alimony *pendente lite*. A master's report upheld the validity of the prenuptial agreement and denied this claim. Exceptions to the master's report were dismissed by the Court of Common Pleas of Philadelphia County. The Superior Court affirmed.

We granted allowance of appeal because uncertainty was expressed by the Superior Court regarding the meaning of our plurality decision in Estate of Geyer, 516 Pa. 492, 533 A.2d 423 (1987) (Opinion Announcing Judgment of the Court). The Superior Court viewed *Geyer* as permitting a prenuptial agreement to be upheld if it *either* made a reasonable provision for the spouse *or* was entered after a full and fair disclosure of the general financial positions of the parties and the statutory rights being relinquished. Appellant contends that this interpretation of *Geyer* is in error insofar as it requires disclosure of statutory rights *only* in cases where there has not been made a reasonable provision for the spouse. Inasmuch as the courts below held that the provision made for appellant was a reasonable one, appellant's efforts to overturn the agreement have focused upon an assertion that there was an inadequate disclosure of statutory rights. Appellant continues to assert, however, that the payments provided in the agreement were less than reasonable.

The statutory rights in question are those relating to alimony *pendente lite*. Other statutory rights, such as those pertaining to alimony and equitable distribution of marital property, did not exist in 1975. Those rights arose under the Divorce Code of 1980, and the Code expressly provides that marital agreements executed prior to its effective date are not affected thereby. Certainly, at the time the present agreement was executed, no disclosure was required with respect to rights which were not then in existence. The present agreement did expressly state, however, that alimony *pendente lite* was being relinquished. It also recited that appellant "has been informed and understands" that, were it not for the agreement, appellant's obligation to pay alimony *pendente lite* "might, as a matter of law, exceed the amount provided." Hence, appellant's claim is not that the agreement failed to disclose the particular right affected, but rather that she was not adequately informed with respect to the nature of alimony *pendente lite*.

. . .

There is no longer validity in the implicit presumption that supplied the basis for *Geyer* and similar earlier decisions. Such decisions rested upon a belief that spouses are of unequal status and that women are not knowledgeable enough to understand the nature of contracts that they enter. Society has advanced, however, to the point where women are no longer regarded as the "weaker" party in marriage, or in society generally. Indeed, the stereotype that women serve as homemakers while men work as breadwinners is no longer viable. Quite often today both spouses are income earners.

Nor is there viability in the presumption that women are uninformed, uneducated, and readily subjected to unfair advantage in marital agreements. Indeed, women nowadays quite often have substantial education, financial awareness, income, and assets.

Accordingly, the law has advanced to recognize the equal status of men and women in our society. See, e.g., Pa. Const. art. 1, § 28 (constitutional prohibition of sex discrimination in laws of the Commonwealth). Paternalistic presumptions and protections that arose to shelter women from the inferiorities and incapacities which they were perceived as having in earlier times have, appropriately, been discarded. It would be inconsistent, therefore, to perpetuate the standards governing prenuptial agreements that were described in *Geyer* and similar decisions, as these reflected a paternalistic approach that is now insupportable.

Further, *Geyer* and its predecessors embodied substantial departures from traditional rules of contract law, to the extent that they allowed consideration of the knowledge of the contracting parties and reasonableness of their bargain as factors governing whether to uphold an agreement. Traditional principles of contract law provide perfectly adequate remedies where contracts are procured through fraud, misrepresentation, or duress. Consideration of other factors, such as the knowledge of the parties and the reasonableness of their bargain, is inappropriate. Prenuptial agreements are contracts, and, as such, should be evaluated under the same criteria as are applicable to other types of contracts. Absent fraud, misrepresentation, or duress, spouses should be bound by the terms of their agreements.

Contracting parties are normally bound by their agreements, without regard to whether the terms thereof were read and fully understood and irrespective of whether the agreements embodied reasonable or good bargains. Based upon these principles, the terms of the present prenuptial agreement must be regarded as binding, without regard to whether the terms were fully understood by appellant. *Ignorantia non excusat.*

Accordingly, we find no merit in a contention raised by appellant that the agreement should be declared void on the ground that she did not consult with independent legal counsel. To impose a *per se* requirement that parties entering a prenuptial agreement must obtain independent legal counsel would be contrary to traditional principles of contract law, and would constitute a paternalistic and unwarranted interference with the parties' freedom to enter contracts.

Further, the reasonableness of a prenuptial bargain is not a proper subject for judicial review. *Geyer* and earlier decisions required that, at least where there had been an inadequate disclosure made by the parties, the bargain must have been reasonable at its inception. Some have even suggested that prenuptial agreements should be examined with regard to whether their terms remain reasonable at the time of dissolution of the parties' marriage.

By invoking inquiries into reasonableness, however, the functioning and reliability of prenuptial agreements is severely undermined. Parties would not have entered such agreements, and, indeed, might not have entered their marriages, if they did not expect their agreements to be strictly enforced. If parties viewed an agreement as reasonable at the time of its inception, as evidenced by their having signed the agreement, they should be foreclosed from later trying to evade its terms by asserting that it was not in fact reasonable. Pertinently, the present agreement contained a clause reciting that "each of the parties considers this agreement fair, just and reasonable...."

Further, everyone who enters a long-term agreement knows that circumstances can change during its term, so that what initially appeared desirable might prove to be an unfavorable bargain. Such are the risks that contracting parties routinely assume. Certainly, the possibilities of illness, birth of children, reliance upon a spouse, career change, financial gain or loss, and numerous other events that can occur in the course of a marriage cannot be regarded as unforeseeable. If parties choose not to address such matters in their prenuptial agreements, they must be regarded as having contracted to bear the risk of events that alter the value of their bargains.

We are reluctant to interfere with the power of persons contemplating marriage to agree upon, and to act in reliance upon, what *they* regard as an acceptable distribution scheme for their property. A court should not ignore the parties' expressed intent by proceeding to determine whether a prenuptial agreement was, in the court's view, reasonable at the time of its inception or the time of divorce. These are exactly the sorts of judicial determinations that such agreements are designed to avoid. Rare indeed is the agreement that is beyond possible challenge when reasonableness is placed at issue. Parties can routinely assert some lack of fairness relating to the inception of the agreement, thereby placing the validity of the agreement at risk. And if reasonableness at the time of divorce were to be taken into account an additional problem would arise. Virtually nonexistent is the marriage in which there has been absolutely no change in the circumstances of either spouse during the course of the marriage. Every change in circumstance, foreseeable or not, and substantial or not, might be asserted as a basis for finding that an agreement is no longer reasonable.

In discarding the approach of *Geyer* that permitted examination of the reasonableness of prenuptial agreements and allowed inquiries into whether parties had attained informed understandings of the rights they were surrendering, we do not depart from the longstanding principle that a full and fair disclosure of the financial positions of the parties is required. Absent this disclosure, a material misrepresentation in the inducement for entering a prenuptial agreement may be asserted. Parties to these agreements do not quite deal at arm's length, but rather at the time the contract is entered into stand in a relation of mutual confidence and trust that calls for disclosure of their financial resources. It is well settled that this disclosure need not be exact, so long as it is "full and fair." In essence therefore, the duty of disclosure under these circumstances is consistent with traditional principles of contract law.

If an agreement provides that full disclosure has been made, a presumption of full disclosure arises. If a spouse attempts to rebut this presumption through an assertion of fraud or misrepresentation then this presumption can be rebutted if it is proven by clear and convincing evidence.

The present agreement recited that full disclosure had been made, and included a list of appellee's assets totalling approximately $300,000. Appellant contends that this list understated by roughly $183,000 the value of a classic car collection which appellee had included at a value of $200,000. The master, reviewing the parties' conflicting testimony regarding the value of the car collection, found that appellant failed to prove by clear and convincing evidence that the value of the collection had been understated. The courts below affirmed that finding. We have examined the record and find ample basis for concluding that the value of the car collection was fully disclosed. Appellee offered expert witnesses who testified to a value of approximately $200,000. Further, appellee's disclosure included numerous cars that appellee did not even own but which he merely hoped to inherit from his mother at some time in the future. Appellant's contention is plainly without merit.

Appellant's final contention is that the agreement was executed under conditions of duress in that it was presented to her at 5 p.m. on the eve of her wedding, a time when she could not seek counsel without the trauma, expense, and embarrassment of postponing the wedding. The master found this claim not credible. The courts below affirmed that finding, upon an ample evidentiary basis.

Although appellant testified that she did not discover until the eve of her wedding that there was going to be a prenuptial agreement, testimony from a number of other witnesses was to the contrary. Appellee testified that, although the final version of the agreement was indeed presented to appellant on the eve of the wedding, he had engaged in several discussions with appellant regarding the contents of the agreement during the six month period preceding that date. Another witness testified that appellant mentioned, approximately two or three weeks before the wedding, that she was going to enter a prenuptial agreement. Yet another witness confirmed that, during the months preceding the wedding, appellant participated in several discussions of prenuptial agreements. And the legal counsel who prepared the agreement for appellee testified that, prior to the eve of the wedding, changes were made in the agreement to increase the sums payable to appellant in the event of separation or divorce. He also stated that he was present when the agreement was signed and that appellant expressed absolutely no reluctance about signing. It should be noted, too, that during the months when the agreement was being discussed appellant had more than sufficient time to consult with independent legal counsel if she had so desired. Under these circumstances, there was plainly no error in finding that appellant failed to prove duress.

Hence, the courts below properly held that the present agreement is valid and enforceable. Appellant is barred, therefore, from receiving alimony *pendente lite*.

Order affirmed.

■ McDERMOTT files a dissenting opinion which is joined by LARSEN, J.

■ PAPADAKOS, JUSTICE, concurring.

Although I continue to adhere to the principles enunciated in Estate of Geyer, 516 Pa. 492, 533 A.2d 423 (1987), I concur in the result because the facts fully support the existence of a valid and enforceable agreement between the parties and any suggestion of duress is totally negated by the facts. The full and fair disclosure, as well as the lack of unfairness and inequity, standards reiterated in *Geyer* are supported by the facts in this case so that I can concur in the result.

However, I cannot join the opinion authored by Mr. Justice Flaherty, because, it must be clear to all readers, it contains a number of unnecessary and unwarranted declarations regarding the "equality" of women. Mr. Justice Flaherty believes that, with the hard-fought victory of the Equal Rights Amendment in Pennsylvania, all vestiges of inequality between the sexes have been erased and women are now treated equally under the law. I fear my colleague does not live in the real world. If I did not know him better I would think that his statements smack of male chauvinism, an attitude that "you women asked for it, now live with it." If you want to know about equality of women, just ask them about comparable wages for comparable work. Just ask them about sexual harassment in the workplace. Just ask them about the sexual discrimination in the Executive Suites of big business. And the list of discrimination based on sex goes on and on.

I view prenuptial agreements as being in the nature of contracts of adhesion with one party generally having greater authority than the other who deals in a subservient role. I believe the law protects the subservient party, regardless of that party's sex, to insure equal protection and treatment under the law.

The present case does not involve the broader issues to which the gratuitous declarations in question are addressed, and it is injudicious to offer declarations in a case which does not involve those issues. Especially when those declarations are inconsistent with reality.

NOTES

1. Although it is true that marriage contracts contemplating separation or divorce were not recognized before 1970, marriage contracts contemplating termination of the marriage by death were common much earlier. Consider the marriage contract of John French and Eleanor Veazie:

> A covenant of marriage being purposed and intended between John French and Eleanor Veazie of Braintree in New England, made and concluded this eighth day of July, Anno Domini one thousand six hundred and eighty three, doe witness that the said John French doth preengage unto the said Eleanor Veazie not to meddle with or take into his hand any part of her estate wherein she is invested by her former husband William Veazie or any otherwise, nor any wise weakening her right or claim to the same. The said John French doth hereby engage and covenant to pay to the said Eleanor Veazie after my decease four pounds per annum, annually, to be paid each year immediately insuing after the said John French's decease, by his lawful Administrators, Executors or Assigns, at her dwelling house, the specie of which payment shall be paid in cord wood, porke, beefe, malt or corne proportionably of each at price current. And that shee the said Eleanor Veazie shall have, hold, possess and enjoy the new end of the dwelling house, in which the said French now dwelleth with the cellar appertaining, during the time of her widowhood. But the four pound annuity to bee and continue to her and her heirs or assigns during the terme of her natural life. To the true performance whereof the said John French doth hereunto set hand this eighth day of July Anno Domini one thousand six hundred eighty three. Before signing. And she shall have apples what she pleases for spending and a place for a garden plot.
>
> Signed and concluded on before us
> Samuel Thompson
> Ben. Tompson

America's Families: A Documentary History 70–72 (Donald M. Scott & Bernard Wishy eds. 1982).

Compare the agreement between Henry Blackwell and Lucy Stone, written in 1855:

> While acknowledging our mutual affection by publicly assuming the relationship of husband and wife, yet in justice to ourselves and a great principle, we deem it a duty to declare that this act on our part implies no sanction of, nor promise of voluntary obedience to such of the present laws of marriage, as refuse to recognize the wife as an independent, rational being, while they confer upon the husband an injurious and unnatural superiority, investing him with legal

powers which no honorable man would exercise, and which no man should possess.

We protest especially against the laws which give to the husband:

1. The custody of the wife's person.

2. The exclusive control and guardianship of their children.

3. The sole ownership of her personal property, and use of her real estate, unless previously settled upon her, or placed in the hands of trustees, as in the case of minors, lunatics, and idiots.

4. The absolute right to the product of her industry.

5. Also against laws which give to the widower so much larger and more permanent an interest in the property of his deceased wife, than they give to the widow in that of the deceased husband.

6. Finally, against the whole system by which "the legal existence of the wife is suspended during marriage," so that in most States, she neither has a legal part in the choice of her residence, nor can she make a will, nor sue or be sued in her own name, nor inherit property.

We believe that personal independence and equal human rights can never be forfeited, except for crime; that marriage should be an equal and permanent partnership, and so recognized by law; that until it is so recognized, married partners should provide against the radical injustice of present laws, by every means in their power.

We believe that where domestic difficulties arise, no appeal should be made to legal tribunals under existing laws, but that all difficulties should be submitted to the equitable adjustment of arbitrators mutually chosen.

Thus reverencing law, we enter our protest against rules and customs which are unworthy of the name, since they violate justice, the essence of law.

(Signed) Henry B. Blackwell

Lucy Stone

2. Consider the contracts proposed by Lenore Weitzman in Legal Regulation of Marriage: Tradition and Change, 62 Cal.L.Rev. 1169 (1974). Which provisions, if any, are enforceable in court?

1. TRADITIONAL MARRIAGE—PARTNERSHIP OF DOCTOR AND HOUSEWIFE

David, a medical student, and Nancy, an aspiring dancer, agree to a contract under which Nancy will give up her potential career as a dancer and support David through medical school in return for a comfortable life as a doctor's wife and a guarantee of financial compensation if the relationship dissolves.

a. Aims and expectations

Both parties want to state their goals and future expectations at the time this contract is signed. Nancy is entering into the relationship with the expectation that she will enjoy the usual benefits of being a doctor's wife. In return for the assurance of a future in which she will be supported in comfort, she is willing to give up her dancing career and to support David until he completes his internship. While she supports David she realizes that she will have to work hard and make do with very little money. Further, she realizes that David's studies will be very time-consuming, and that he will be less than an ideal companion. Since she will be making a very significant contribution toward David's career, she expects to have a future interest in it. Once David becomes a doctor she will enjoy the social benefits of being a doctor's wife. Nancy expects to have a beautiful home and summer home, expensive clothing, vacations in Europe, child care and private schools for her children, and a housekeeper.

David understands that Nancy's efforts will make it possible for him to obtain his medical education in a fairly comfortable fashion. Her support will ensure that he will not have to drop out of school to earn money and he will not have to spend any time on part-time jobs or housework. He will be able to devote all his time to his studies. In return, he wants to guarantee Nancy a share in his future career.

Both parties feel that they are making a life-time contract and are building a community from which they will both benefit. Both parties feel that they are equal partners in this community and that income, property, and other gains that may accrue to the income-earning partner are the result of the joint efforts of both parties—and therefore belong equally to both parties.

b. Property

Any property of the parties shall be jointly owned as community property. Nancy will manage and control the community property and will take care of all other household business matters.

c. Support

Nancy will work as a secretary in order to support David until he has finished medical school and an internship. David will support the family from then on; he will take a (paying) residency, or begin to practice medicine. Nancy will not work outside the home after David's career has commenced.

d. Domicile

The location of the family domicile will be decided by David; the main consideration in making such a decision will be the best interests of David's career.

e. Name

Both parties will use David's surname.

f. Housekeeping responsibilities

Nancy will be responsible for maintaining the household with the assistance of a full-time housekeeper.

g. Birth control

Since the most efficient contraceptives currently available are female contraceptives, Nancy will assume the responsibility for birth control for the present. However, if a male oral contraceptive or other safe and effective male contraceptive is perfected, David agrees to use it.

h. Other responsibilities

Nancy agrees to further David's career by entertaining, serving on medical auxiliary committees, and maintaining good social relations with other doctors' wives. She will also participate actively in church and country club activities in order to maintain good contacts with potential patients and physicians. David agrees to accompany Nancy to the ballet at least once a month. He also agrees to schedule at least two two-week vacations with her each year, at least one of them in Europe.

i. Children

Children will be postponed until David's education is completed. If Nancy should become pregnant prior to that time, she will have an abortion. Nancy will have full responsibility for the care of the children; financial responsibility will be assumed by David.

j. Termination

This partnership may be dissolved by either party, at will, upon six months notice to the other party.

If this partnership is terminated by either party prior to the completion of David's education, Nancy's obligation to support him will cease. Moreover, once

David's career is begun, he will have the obligation of supporting Nancy at the rate of $12,000 a year (1974 rate to be adjusted for inflation and cost of living) for as many years as she supported him. If necessary, David will secure a loan to repay Nancy for her support. If Nancy prefers a lump sum settlement equal to the value of this support, David will arrange a loan to provide it. Both parties agree to treat Nancy's original support of David as a loan of the value specified above. David's obligation to repay this loan has the standing of any other legal debt.

If the partnership is terminated after David's career has begun, Nancy will be entitled to one-fourth of his net income for as many years as the partnership lasted. David will purchase insurance or a bond to guarantee this payment. It is agreed that this payment is not alimony, and that it shall be continued unmodified regardless of her earning capacity or remarriage. The parties consider this Nancy's reimbursement for helping David's career. It is agreed that her efforts will have helped to make his success possible and he will therefore owe her this compensation.

David also agrees to pay Nancy the fixed sum of $15,000 if their marriage terminates within 15 years, as liquidated damages for the pain and suffering she will experience from the change in her expectations and life plans.

David also agrees to pay for Nancy's medical expenses or to provide her with adequate insurance at the rate of one year of coverage for every year of marriage. It is explicitly agreed that psychiatric and dental bills be included in the above.

Community property will be divided equally upon termination. If there are children, Nancy will have custody of the children. David will have full responsibility for their support, as well as the responsibility for compensating Nancy for her services in caring for them (at the then current rate for private nurses). Suitable visiting arrangements will be made.

k. Death

Both parties agree to make wills stipulating the other partner the sole legatee. After termination of this agreement this obligation will not continue; however, David is obliged to make sure any continuing support obligations toward Nancy and the children are reflected in his will.

2. YOUNG, DUAL-CAREER, PROFESSIONAL COUPLE

Susan, an aspiring lawyer, and Peter, an aspiring social worker, have devised the following contract to maximize both career opportunities and their personal relationship.

a. Educational and living expenses

Susan and Peter decide that they will take turns going to school, so that the nonstudent partner can support the other until he or she receives a degree. Because Susan will earn more money as an attorney, they decide that they will maximize their joint income if Susan goes to school first. They therefore agree that Peter will be solely responsible for Susan's educational expenses and support for three full years. Susan will assume these same responsibilities for the following two years. If their partnership should dissolve at any time during these first five years, their contract stipulates that each shall have the following financial obligations to the other: (1) If dissolution occurs during the first three years, Peter will pay Susan's remaining tuition (which may be up to three full years' tuition in graduate school) and pay her $4,200 a year for living expenses. (2) Thereafter, Susan will pay Peter's remaining tuition (up to two full years of tuition in a school of social work) and pay him $4,200 a year in living expenses. All living expenses will be paid at the rate of $350 a month. This amount will be tied to the cost-of-living index to allow for automatic increases.

b. Domicile

Susan and Peter agree to maintain a joint domicile for the first five years of their relationship, location to be determined by the student partner to maximize educational opportunity.

After the first five years, Susan and Peter will make decisions regarding domicile jointly, with no presumption that the career of either is of greater importance in making the decision. However, if they cannot agree on where to live, the decision will be Susan's—for a period of three years. Peter will then have the right to choose the location for the following three years. They will continue to rotate the domicile decision on a three-year basis. As both parties realize that their career opportunities may not coincide with this prearranged schedule, they may decide to exchange the right of decision for any given period or make another equitable agreement which would then be incorporated into this contract. Further, both parties will always retain the option of establishing a temporary separate residence, at their own expense, if this is necessary for their careers.

c. Property

During the first five years all income and property, excluding gifts and inheritances, shall be considered community property. The income-earning partner shall have sole responsibility for its management and control.

After the first five years an inventory will be taken of all community property. Thereafter each party's earnings, as well as any gifts or bequests or the income from any property held, shall be her or his separate property. Neither party will have any rights in any present or future property of the other. A list will be kept of all household items in order to keep track of their ownership; in the event Susan and Peter decide to make a joint purchase, this will be noted on the list. Any joint purchase of items of value over $100 will be covered by a separate agreement concerning its ownership. Each party will manage and control her or his separate property, and will maintain a separate bank account.

d. Household expenses

(This part of the agreement shall go into effect five years hence.)

Household expenses will consist of rent, utilities, food, and housekeeping expenses. Susan and Peter will each contribute 50 percent of their gross income to household expenses. Their contributions will be made in monthly installments of equal amounts, and placed in a joint checking account. Responsibility for the joint account and for paying the above expenses will be rotated, with each having this responsibility for a three-month period. Each partner will be responsible for his or her own cleaning expenses, and for food and entertainment outside of the household. Each will maintain a separate car and a separate phone and will take care of these expenses separately. If money in the joint account is not exhausted by household expenses, it may be used for joint leisure activities.

Both parties recognize that Susan's income is likely to be higher than Peter's and that 50 percent of her income will allow her more money for separate expenses. The parties therefore agree to review this arrangement six months after it goes into effect. If it seems that the arrangement places an unfair burden on Peter, they will change the second line above to read: Each party's contribution to household expenses shall be as follows: Susan shall contribute 55 percent of her gross income; Peter shall contribute 40 percent of his gross income.

e. Housekeeping responsibilities

Housework will be shared equally. All necessary tasks will be divided into two categories. On even-numbered months Susan will be responsible for category 1 and Peter for category 2; and vice versa on odd-numbered months. Each party will do her or his own cooking and clean up afterwards for breakfast and lunch, as well as keeping her or his own study clean. Dinner cooking and clean up will be considered part of the housework to be rotated as specified above. In the event that one party neglects to perform any task, the other party can perform it and charge the nonperforming partner $15 per hour for his or her labor, or agree to be repaid in kind.

f. Sexual relations

Sexual relations are subject to the consent of both parties. Responsibility for birth control will be shared equally. Susan will have this responsibility for the first six months of the year, Peter for the second six months.

g. Surname

Both parties will retain their own surnames.

h. Children

While the parties have decided to have two children at some time in the future, birth control will be practiced until a decision to have a child has been reached. Since the parties believe that a woman should have control over her own body, the decision of whether or not to terminate an accidental pregnancy before then shall be Susan's alone. If Susan decides to have an abortion, the party who had responsibility for birth control the month that conception occurred will bear the cost of the abortion. This will include expenses not covered by insurance, and any other expenses or loss of pay incurred by Susan. However, if Susan decides to have the child and Peter does not agree, Susan will bear full financial and social responsibility for the child. In that event, Susan also agrees to compensate Peter should he be required to support the child. If the parties agree to have a child and Susan changes her mind after conception has occurred, she will pay for the abortion. If Peter changes his mind after conception has occurred and Susan agrees to an abortion, he will pay for it. If she does not agree, Peter will share the social and financial responsibility for the child, just as if he had not changed his mind.

When the parties decide to have a child, the following provisions will apply: Susan and Peter will assume equal financial responsibility for the child. This will include the medical expenses connected with the birth of the child as well as any other expenses incurred in preparation for the child. If it is necessary for Susan to take time off from work in connection with her pregnancy or with the birth of the child, Peter will pay her one-half of his salary to compensate for the loss. If either party has to take time off from work to care for the child, the other party will repay that party with one-half of his or her salary. All child-care, medical, and educational expenses will be shared equally.

Since Peter expects to become a psychiatric social worker specializing in preschool children, he will have the primary child-care responsibility. He will take a paternity leave after the birth in order to care for the child full-time, until day-care arrangements can be made. Susan will compensate him at the rate of one-half of her salary. Responsibility for caring for the child on evenings and weekends will be divided equally.

Any children will take the hyphenated surname of both parties.

i. Dissolution

If there are children, both parties agree to submit to at least one conciliation session prior to termination. In addition, if a decision to dissolve the partnership is made, both parties agree to submit to binding arbitration if they are unable to reach a mutual decision regarding the issues of child custody, child support, and property division. A list of mutually agreeable arbitrators is attached to this agreement. While both agree that custody should be determined according to the best interests of the child, a presumption exists in favor of Peter, since he will have had superior training in the rearing of children. Each party agrees to assume half of the financial burden of caring for the child.

If there are no children, this household agreement can be terminated by either party for any reason upon giving the other party 60 days' notice in writing. Upon separation, each party will take his or her separate property and any jointly owned property will be divided equally. Neither party will have any financial or other responsibility toward the other after separation and division of property.

3. The Uniform Premarital Agreement Act, approved by the American Bar Association in 1984, provides in pertinent part:

§ 1. Definitions

As used in this Act:

(1) "Premarital agreement" means an agreement between prospective spouses made in contemplation of marriage and to be effective upon marriage.

(2) "Property" means an interest, present or future, legal or equitable, vested or contingent, in real or personal property, including income and earnings.

§ 2. Formalities

A premarital agreement must be in writing and signed by both parties. It is enforceable without consideration.

§ 3. Content

(a) Parties to a premarital agreement may contract with respect to:

(1) the rights and obligations of each of the parties in any of the property of either or both of them whenever and wherever acquired or located;

(2) the right to buy, sell, use, transfer, exchange, abandon, lease, consume, expend, assign, create a security interest in, mortgage, encumber, dispose of, or otherwise manage and control property;

(3) the disposition of property upon separation, marital dissolution, death, or the occurrence or nonoccurrence of any other event;

(4) the modification or elimination of spousal support;

(5) the making of a will, trust, or other arrangement to carry out the provisions of the agreement;

(6) the ownership rights in and disposition of the death benefit from a life insurance policy;

(7) the choice of law governing the construction of the agreement; and

(8) any other matter, including their personal rights and obligations, not in violation of public policy or a statute imposing a criminal penalty.

(b) The right of a child to support may not be adversely affected by a premarital agreement.

§ 4. Effect of Marriage

A premarital agreement becomes effective upon marriage.

§ 5. Amendment, Revocation

After marriage, a premarital agreement may be amended or revoked only by a written agreement signed by the parties. The amended agreement or the revocation is enforceable without consideration.

§ 6. Enforcement

(a) A premarital agreement is not enforceable if the party against whom enforcement is sought proves that:

(1) that party did not execute the agreement voluntarily; or

(2) the agreement was unconscionable when it was executed and, before execution of the agreement, that party:

(i) was not provided a fair and reasonable disclosure of the property or financial obligations of the other party;

(ii) did not voluntarily and expressly waive, in writing, any right to disclosure of the property or financial obligations of the other party beyond the disclosure provided; and

(iii) did not have, or reasonably could not have had, an adequate knowledge of the property or financial obligations of the other party.

(b) If a provision of a premarital agreement modifies or eliminates spousal support and that modification or elimination causes one party to the agreement to be eligible for support under a program of public assistance at the time of separation or marital dissolution, a court, notwithstanding the terms of the agreement, may require the other party to provide support to the extent necessary to avoid that eligibility.

(c) An issue of unconscionability of a premarital agreement shall be decided by the court as a matter of law.

4. By 2003, twenty-six states and the District of Columbia had adopted the Uniform Premarital Agreement Act. See Kathy T. Graham, The Uniform Marital Property Act: A Solution for Common Law Property Systems?, 48 S.D. L. Rev. 455, 465 (2003).

5. Should marriage contracts be encouraged even if they will not be enforced by the courts? Consider Karl Fleischmann, Marriage by Contract: Defining the Terms of Relationship, 8 Fam.L.Q. 27, 31 (1974): "The most traditional sort of marriage counseling involves the attempt to resolve disputes between people whose marriages have become troubled. But before a marriage reaches the stage where it is in serious trouble there will usually be a period during which conflicts are arising but go unresolved. These conflicts may be generated by problems peculiar to the marriage or may be significantly involved with the change in value structure presently taking place in the United States: wives becoming uncertain about the role they should play in their marriage, older spouses seeking the sexual freedom of the young.

If there were an established and recognized opportunity for married couples to discuss with professional assistance the sources of conflict between them with the hope of resolving them by contract, such disputes might be more easily and frequently resolved."

If this fairly describes a major purpose of such contracts, should they be drafted by lawyers or professionals trained in therapy or counseling?

b. BY PUBLIC POLICY

(1) Recognition of the Working Wife . . .

McCourtney v. Imprimis Technology, Inc.

Court of Appeals of Minnesota, 1991.
465 N.W.2d 721.

■ KALITOWSKI, JUDGE.

Relator Diane McCourtney seeks review of a decision by the Commissioner of Jobs and Training which denied her claim for unemployment compensation benefits. McCourtney argues her persistent absences due to a sick baby did not constitute disqualifying misconduct. McCourtney also challenges the Commissioner's decision on equal protection grounds. . . . We reverse the Commissioner's decision denying benefits.

. . .

McCourtney was employed by Imprimis as a full-time accounts payable clerk for over 10 ½ years. McCourtney's ending salary was $1,360 per month. Her scheduled hours were 6:30 a.m. to 3:00 p.m. Monday through Friday.

McCourtney was an excellent employee, and until January 1990 she had no attendance problems.

On September 30, 1989, McCourtney gave birth to an infant who suffered from numerous illnesses. The baby's father and other members of McCourtney's family were unable to assist her with child care.

Due to her baby's illnesses, McCourtney was frequently absent from work between January and May 1990. She was absent 71% of the time between January 1 and February 25; 36% of the time between February 25 and March 11; 31% of the time between March 12 and March 25; and 13% of the time between March 26 and April 8. Between April 9 and April 12 she was absent for four straight days, and during that same two-week pay period, she missed another eight hours. When she missed 10 ½ hours of work the following week, she was suspended pending termination. Imprimis issued McCourtney two written warnings before finally discharging her for excessive absenteeism.

McCourtney does not challenge her employer's right to terminate her due to absenteeism. McCourtney applied for unemployment compensation benefits, but the Department of Jobs and Training denied her claim. McCourtney appealed to a Department referee, who conducted a hearing.

The evidence at the hearing demonstrated 99.9% of McCourtney's absences were due to her sick baby. Although each of McCourtney's absences was excused, Imprimis issued a written warning in February requiring McCourtney to develop a written plan to solve her child care problem.

In response to this warning, McCourtney prepared a memo to her manager, discussing two possible options for care of her baby when she was unable to take him to her regular baby sitter: (1) professional in-home care; and (2) back-up day care facilities. McCourtney agreed to determine what services were available in her community.

McCourtney looked through the yellow pages, contacted Hennepin County, and called family members. She investigated the possibility of hiring a nanny, but could not afford the cost.

McCourtney contacted ten local child care facilities, and discovered that "Tender Care" was the only provider which would care for sick infants on short notice. However, Tender Care could not guarantee a caregiver would always be available, and would not allow McCourtney to interview a caregiver before he or she entered her home. Other problems with Tender Care services included the cost and the caregiver's inflexible starting time.

Following the hearing, the referee concluded McCourtney was discharged for misconduct because she had some control over her absences and her conduct constituted a violation of behavior which Imprimis had a right to expect of its employees. McCourtney appealed, and the Commissioner's representative affirmed the referee's decision. McCourtney filed this writ of certiorari, seeking review of the decision of the Commissioner's representative.

An individual who is discharged for misconduct is disqualified from receiving unemployment compensation benefits. Minn.Stat. § 268.09, subd. 1(b) (Supp.1989). The Minnesota Supreme Court has adopted the following definition of "misconduct":

> The intended meaning of the term "misconduct" is limited to conduct evincing such wilful or wanton disregard of an employer's interests as is found in deliberate violations or disregard of standards of behavior which the employer has the right to expect of his employee, or in carelessness or negligence of such degree or recurrence as to manifest equal culpability, wrongful intent or evil design, or to show an intentional and substantial disregard of the employer's interests or of the employee's duties and obligations to his employer. On the other hand mere inefficiency, unsatisfactory conduct, failure in good performance as the result of inability or incapacity, inadvertencies or ordinary negligence in isolated instances, or good-faith errors in judgment or discretion are not to be deemed misconduct.

In re Claim of Tilseth, 295 Minn. 372, 374–75, 204 N.W.2d 644, 646 (1973) (citation omitted). . . .

An employer has the burden of proving by the greater weight of the evidence that an employee was discharged for disqualifying misconduct. On appeal, our review of the Commissioner's decision involves mixed questions of fact and law. The Commissioner's factual findings should not be overturned unless the evidence in the record does not reasonably tend to support those findings. The Commissioner's legal conclusions, however, do not deserve similar deference; this court is "free to exercise its independent judgment."

The unemployment compensation statutes are "humanitarian in nature and are liberally construed." Group Health Plan, Inc. v. Lopez, 341 N.W.2d 294, 296 (Minn.App.1983). The intent of the unemployment compensation statutes is to assist those who are unemployed "through no fault of their own." Minn.Stat. § 268.03 (1988). The issue is not whether an employer was justified in discharging an employee, but rather, whether the employee committed "misconduct" disqualifying the employee from receiving benefits.

Each of McCourtney's absences was excused and was due to circumstances beyond her control. Cf. Winkler v. Park Refuse Service, Inc., 361 N.W.2d 120, 124 (Minn.App.1985) ("Absence from work under circumstances *within the control of the employee* has been determined to be misconduct sufficient to deny benefits. . . . The critical factor is whether the employee's behavior caused his failure to report to work.") (emphasis added). McCourtney made substantial efforts to find care for her child so she could work. Respondents argue McCourtney could have utilized the services of Tender Care. We disagree. The hours offered by Tender Care personnel were incompatible with McCourtney's work schedule.

In light of McCourtney's good faith efforts, her inability to find care for her child is not "misconduct" within the meaning of Minn.Stat. § 268.09, subd. 1(b). McCourtney's actions were motivated by a willful regard for her child's interests and not a wanton disregard of her employer's interest or lack of concern for her job.

We recognize that in some circumstances misconduct may be demonstrated by excessive absenteeism alone. Where the circumstances do not overwhelmingly demonstrate that an employee's absences are deliberate, willful, or equally culpable, we may also examine the employee's history, conduct, and underlying attitude. While McCourtney's absences were undeniably excessive, her work history and good faith attempts to find care for her child weigh against a determination that her absences demonstrated the culpability required by *Tilseth*.

We conclude that under the specific facts and circumstances of this case, Imprimis has failed to meet its burden of proving McCourtney's actions constitute misconduct as intended by the legislature and further defined by *Tilseth*. Therefore, McCourtney is entitled to unemployment compensation benefits. The economic burden this conclusion places on the employer is a necessary cost of the legislature's humanitarian concern for the welfare of persons unemployed through no fault of their own.

. . .

Reversed.

NOTE

The Supreme Court of Mississippi followed *McCourtney* in Mississippi Employment Security Commission v. Bell, 584 So.2d 1270 (Miss.1991), when it granted Bell unemployment compensation benefits after she was discharged for excessive absenteeism. The court reasoned that Bell was a victim of circumstances. It determined that she was a good employee for 13 years, and that conflicts arose only after her work schedule changed and seriously interfered with her parental responsibilities. See also Garden View Care Center, Inc. v. Labor and Industrial Relations Commission of Missouri, 848 S.W.2d 603 (Mo.App.1993) (absences due to illness or family emergency are not the fault of the employee and as such cannot serve to disqualify from unemployment compensation benefits.)

Fathers have also received protection from denial of unemployment benefits when their job loss was the result of family responsibility. In Tutwiler v. Fin–Clair Corp., a Missouri court of appeals held that a father who had been fired for absenteeism was still entitled to unemployment benefits because two of his three absences were due to family illness and did not constitute misconduct. 995 S.W.2d 497 (Mo. Ct. App. 1999). In Prickett v. Circuit Science, Inc., the Supreme Court of Minnesota held that a father's absence from the job because of his inability to find child care for his son on short notice did not constitute misconduct. 518 N.W.2d 602 (Minn.1994). Similarly, in Foote v. Unemployment Appeals Commission, a Florida father's three day absence to take care of his four children and wife after her emergency surgery was found not to be misconduct. 659 So.2d 1232 (Fla.App.1995).

Vaughn v. Lawrenceburg Power Sys.

United States Court of Appeals for the Sixth Circuit, 2001.
269 F.3d 703.

■ BOGGS, CIRCUIT JUDGE.

Plaintiffs Keith Vaughn and Jennifer Vaughn, former employees of defendant Lawrenceburg Power System ("LPS"), filed an action in Tennessee state court alleging that their terminations from LPS in February 1998 violated their rights under the United States Constitution, pursuant to 42 U.S.C. § 1983, and under the Tennessee Human Rights Act (THRA), Tenn. Code Ann. § 4–21–101 et seq. Specifically, the Vaughns objected to LPS's "anti-nepotism" policy, which requires the resignation of one spouse in the event two employees marry. They claim this policy is unconstitutional under either rational basis or strict scrutiny review. They also asserted claims of retaliatory discharge under the THRA and the First Amendment. The magistrate judge initially evaluating their complaint recommended dismissing all claims.... We affirm in part, but reverse as to one issue.

Keith Vaughn began work for LPS in 1987, and has worked there in several capacities over a ten-year period. In 1997, he was responsible for maintaining LPS's grounds and buildings. Jennifer Vaughn, nee Paige, began working at LPS while in high school, and after her graduation in 1996, started a full-time job as a cashier. During the spring and summer of 1997, Keith and Jennifer became romantically involved. In September 1997, they became engaged.

Unfortunately for the Vaughns, their marriage was against power system policy. The "employment of relatives" or "anti-nepotism" portion of the LPS manual, which it is undisputed that both Vaughns received, reads as follows:

> It is the policy of the System to employ only one member of a family. No immediate relatives of employees, officers, members of the city governing body, by blood, marriage or adoption, shall be employed for permanent positions at the Lawrenceburg Power System. For purposes of this policy, said relatives are as follows: Spouse, parent, child, brother, sister, grandparent, grandchild, son-in-law, daughter-in-law, father-in-law, mother-in-law, brother-in-law, and sister-in-law.
>
> *When two employees working for the Lawrenceburg Power system are subsequently married, one must terminate employment.*

(Emphasis added.) The Vaughns ran afoul of the second part of this section forbidding marriages within the system, which may be termed LPS's rule of "exogamy."

It soon became common knowledge that the Vaughns were to be married. In late September, LPS Superintendent Ronald Cato met with Keith Vaughn, and pointed out the relevant language just quoted. Over the course of that autumn, Cato met with the Vaughns several times to inform them of the policy and to request that they decide which one of them was going to leave LPS. Cato told them he would need a decision before the marriage took place; he also told them that if they remained unmarried and merely lived together there would be no problem with the exogamy rule. The Vaughns were reluctant to pursue this option, in large part because Jennifer had become pregnant that fall with Keith's son, who was born the following July.

The Vaughns disagreed with the policy's applicability to their situation. Mr. Vaughn knew of three other groups of relatives working at LPS, two brother-in-law/sister-in-law dyads, and a father-in-law/son-in-law pair. Keith Vaughn interpreted the overall anti-nepotism policy as being contravened by the presence of these related co-workers.[1] He states that he so informed Michael Meek, the Administrative Services Manager, who Vaughn claims told him that the other employees were "grandfathered in" and that Vaughn also "should be" grandfathered in. Despite urging from Cato, neither of the Vaughns indicated they would resign. Instead, they took their case to a meeting of the Power Board in mid-December 1998, where Keith argued he should be "treated like everybody else." The Power Board was not convinced by the Vaughns' interpretation, apparently distinguishing between the first part of the employment of relatives policy, which does not mandate termination, and the second part, the exogamy rule dealing specifically with employee intermarriage, which does. The Board also refused to change the

1. Vaughn particularly focused on the case of Delton Perry and his son-in-law Steve Inman. Perry was a long-time employee, but Inman had started at LPS only in 1984, after the adoption of the policy in 1980. He had married Perry's daughter Anita, although apparently after Inman had already begun his employment. Vaughn interpreted the rule that no more than one relative be "employed" as implicitly requiring Inman to leave.

rule or make an exception, as Cato informed the Vaughns in late December, when he again demanded a decision.

Jennifer and Keith's wedding day was January 16, 1998. Keith had met with Cato the previous day and said "okay" in response to Cato's request for a decision. But Keith did not then tell Cato whether he or Jennifer would leave LPS. When the couple arrived back from their honeymoon, they found a letter suspending both of them for minium of two weeks, until February 9, 1998 (or until they reached a decision). If during that time they came to a decision, they were to let Cato know. On February 6, 1998, Keith Vaughn met with Ron Cato and told him the couple planned to have Keith, who was paid more than Jennifer, continue working at LPS while Jennifer resigned. According to Mr. Vaughn, Cato responded by asking for a letter of resignation from Mrs. Vaughn, which apparently had not previously been requested. Vaughn states that he told Cato he didn't know anything about a letter, and had just come by to inform Cato of the long-awaited decision. To this, Cato allegedly said "okay."

The following Monday, February 9, Keith Vaughn, but not Jennifer Vaughn, arrived at LPS at 8 A.M. to begin work. Cato called Vaughn and Michael Meek into his office. Fifteen to thirty minutes later, when Vaughn left Cato's office, he had been fired.[2] The parties dispute exactly what was said during the fateful meeting.

According to Vaughn, Cato asked him for a letter from Jennifer, which Vaughn did not have. Vaughn states that he asked Cato whether he needed the letter "for personal reasons or legal reasons." Cato responded: "I take it you don't fully agree with our policy." Vaughn claims that he responded, "No, sir. I don't fully agree with it, but I accept it because I've got to support—you know, I've got to work and support my family." After this speech, Cato then mentioned the Tennessee right-to-work law, and fired Keith Vaughn.

Cato's contrasting version is that when told again on February 9 of the couple's decision, he said, "I really need to hear it from her." Vaughn offered to call his wife, but Cato states that he refused to accept this and said, "I'd really rather have a letter." Cato then claims to have asked Vaughn: "Would you consider yourself a disgruntled employee?" Cato states that Vaughn replied in the affirmative. Cato then agrees that he mentioned the right-to-work law. Vaughn supposedly asked if he was fired. Cato states that it was only then that he said: "If you're going to be disgruntled and upset, you are." Vaughn supposedly responded, "I am, then." Mike Meek remembers Cato's ultimatum as being, "If you're disgruntled to the point that you don't feel like you can carry out your duties, yes, you're fired."

Cato claims that when he mentioned Tennessee law, he was thinking Vaughn would respond differently. According to Cato, "I thought he was going to say, 'Yeah, I can put it behind me, go and do my job.'" Cato had a planned response: "I was setting him up to say, 'Yeah, but we are going to be watching you every day to make sure you are doing your job. . . .'" Cato claims that he did not want Vaughn to quit, but that "I guess I had gotten to

2. At certain points in its brief, LPS asserts that Mr. Vaughn "voluntarily quit his employment at LPS." (LPS Br. at 20). The very next page, however, notes that "Mr. Vaughn was terminated for insubordination." There is persistent equivocation in the appellee's brief on this point. Compare "Mr. Vaughn voluntarily quit his employment" with "Mr. Cato terminated Mr. Vaughn for insubordination. . . ." As we must construe the facts in favor of the Vaughns, and in light of the documentary evidence and party admissions of termination, it will be assumed that Keith Vaughn, in any event, left involuntarily.

where his attitude about this, I thought, he was just trying to push me over it. Felt like I did what I had to do." Cato explained that the issue was that Keith "had a problem with authority. He had a problem accepting this policy." Outside of the policy, Cato had no problem with the Vaughns.

Vaughn, however, flatly denies that he ever said he was a "disgruntled employee" or that he remembers this phrase being used until he saw it in a letter he received after his termination. This letter, dated February 9, explained that the Vaughns had not "fully accepted" the policy, and terminated Keith Vaughn for "insubordination." For good measure, it terminated Jennifer for the same reason, Cato writing that because he did not "yet have a written resignation[,] I have no choice[.]"[3]

In January 1999, shortly before their first anniversary, the Vaughns filed a lawsuit against LPS in the Circuit Court for Lawrence County. The complaint alleged violations of 42 U.S.C. § 1983 based on "the fundamental right of marriage and freedom of association. . . ." The complaint made specific allegations regarding the termination of Keith Vaughn, claiming that such action "constituted a denial of rights, privileges and immunities including freedom of speech under the constitutional laws of the United States." It also alleged that Vaughn had been terminated in violation of the THRA for "opposing a practice declare [sic] unlawful by the Act."

LPS removed the case to federal court and it was referred to Magistrate Judge Griffin. The magistrate judge found the policy not materially distinguishable from the one upheld in Montgomery v. Carr, 101 F.3d 1117, 1124 (6th Cir. 1996), and also found that "Vaughn's objections to the defendant's no-spouse policy were personal in nature" and were therefore not protected under the First Amendment. Under the same subsection of the report, "D. Retaliation Claim," the magistrate judge also found that Keith Vaughn was not protected by the THRA because he was not opposing a discriminatory practice, but one that was in fact legitimate.

The plaintiffs objected to the magistrate judge's report. . . .

Following plaintiffs' objections, the district court, in a one-page order, adopted the magistrate judge's report and recommendation. . . .

. . .

We must first decide at what "level of scrutiny" to evaluate the challenged provision in the LPS manual. In order to trigger heightened constitutional scrutiny, the challenged portion of the anti-nepotism policy, the exogamy rule requiring termination of employment, must be shown to place "a 'direct and substantial' burden on the right of marriage." *Montgomery*, 101 F.3d at 1124. Our analysis of the case law in *Montgomery* indicated that we would find direct and substantial burdens only where a large portion of those affected by the rule are absolutely or largely prevented from marrying, or where those affected by the rule are absolutely or largely prevented from marrying a large portion of the otherwise eligible population of spouses. See id. at 1124–25 (quoting Zablocki v. Redhail, 434 U.S. 374, 387 (1978), which found such burdens when " 'some of those in the affected class . . . are absolutely prevented from getting married[,]' " and citing Loving v. Virginia, 388 U.S. 1, 12 (1967), for the proposition that a burden exists if a rule absolutely prevents individuals to marry members of another race).

3. During discovery, plaintiffs uncovered a separate draft of this letter. It differs in describing Keith Vaughn's February 9 "attempt to comply with the policy" as his "*grudging* attempt to comply with the policy." (emphasis added).

All societies structure the fundamental social fact of marriage, restricting to a lesser or greater extent who may marry whom, and these restrictions often have force of law. "Marriage, as creating the most important relation in life, as having more to do with the morals and civilization of a people than any other institution, has always been subject to the control of the legislature. That body prescribes the age at which parties may contract to marry, the procedure or form essential to constitute marriage, the duties and obligations it creates, its effects upon the property rights of both, present and prospective, and the acts which may constitute grounds for its dissolution." Maynard v. Hill, 125 U.S. 190, 205 (1888).

As a general matter, marriage as it was recognized by the common law is constitutionally protected, but this protection has not been extended to forms of marriage outside the common-law tradition.

This case is potentially distinguishable from *Montgomery* in that LPS's exogamy rule requires termination, and the plaintiff-teachers in *Montgomery* were merely required to have one spouse transfer to a different school within the school system. However, this does not change the essential fact that the policy did not bar Jennifer or Keith from getting married, nor did it prevent them marrying a large portion of population even in Lawrence County. It only made it economically burdensome to marry a small number of those eligible individuals, their fellow employees at LPS. Once Jennifer and Keith decided to marry one another, LPS's policy became onerous for them, but *ex ante*, it did not greatly restrict their freedom to marry or whom to marry. As a consequence, the exogamy rule in itself must be considered a non-oppressive burden on the right to marry, and so subject only to rational basis review by this court.

. . .

In order to satisfy rational basis scrutiny, a rule interfering with the right of marital association under the First Amendment must advance a legitimate governmental interest and must not be an unreasonable means of advancing that legitimate governmental interest. See *Montgomery*, 101 F.3d at 1130. LPS asserts that its rule exists to (1) prevent one employee from assuming the role of "spokesperson" for both, (2) to avoid involving or angering a second employee when an employee is reprimanded, (3) and to avoid marital strife or fraternization in the workplace. (LPS Br. at 14). These interests resemble those put forward by the defendant in *Montgomery* and found satisfactory. We specifically noted that a government employer may have a legitimate concern about the inherent loyalty that one spouse will show to another, making discipline more difficult. Therefore, we conclude LPS has demonstrated its exogamy rule advances a legitimate governmental interest.

The Vaughns claim that the rule, even if advancing a legitimate interest, is an unreasonable means of doing so. They point out that the rule does not affect those willing to merely to cohabitate (which in their case would have also involved the bearing of an out-of-wedlock child); the Vaughns note that cohabitating couples may well show a similar degree of loyalty and create the same problems the rule seeks to avoid. However, we rejected the same argument in *Montgomery* at 1131. There is, no doubt, wide variation in the nature and intensity of the relationships one finds among both married and unmarried couples. Yet there is good reason to believe that the level of commitment signified by marriage—and its attendant legal, moral, and financial obligations—marks those relationships in which, on average, there is likely to be intense loyalty.. Whatever the situation may be *de facto*, married and unmarried couples are not the same *de jure*; the law treats them differently, and LPS may do so as well.

The Vaughns raise a better argument by noting again that the consequences to them are inherently more severe than those affecting the couple in the *Montgomery* case. There, one of the married employees was transferred. Here, both the Vaughns were terminated, and the policy mandated this for, at least, one of them. Although the Montgomerys were forced to bear the economic costs of commuting, the immediate effect there was less than the loss of one spouse's income. In response, LPS points out that they simply do not have the option of having a transfer policy, because LPS is an operation of only 50 to 70 employees, and further separation between the spouses than already existed would not be possible.

Apparently, before relations between Cato and the Vaughns deteriorated, there had been discussion of placing one of them on non-permanent status until they could obtain work elsewhere. The Vaughns do not describe how they believe LPS could have implemented its policy in a less burdensome way. In these circumstances, the rule, once admitted not to interfere directly with the right of marriage, and to advance a legitimate interest, does not seem unreasonable. Therefore, the rule of exogamy in LPS's anti-nepotism policy does not violate the fundamental right of marriage, and summary judgment is appropriate as to the Vaughns' claims advanced on that basis.

NOTES

1. A good overview of nepotism is Joan Wexler, Husbands and Wives: The Uneasy Case for Antinepotism Rules, 62 B.U.L.Rev. 75 (1982). Dean Wexler reports:

> Nepotism was commonplace in the secular world at least from the outset of the Industrial Revolution. In industrial nations during the nineteenth century the sons of entrepreneurs were expected to succeed their fathers at the helm of the family business. In practice, however, such scions often played an absentee role and left the actual management of the business to others. Consequently, their competence rarely became an issue.
>
> In the United States, nepotistic practices developed in both private and public enterprise. The founders of large corporations and other businessmen often followed the English practice of keeping management "in the family," believing that an important purpose of a prosperous business was to provide employment for sons and other kin. Indeed, even today nepotism continues to play a notable role in the business world.[10]
>
> Public officials in this country also have not been averse to hiring or appointing their relatives. Nepotism played a particularly important role in nineteenth-century politics. For example, President Lincoln rewarded Republican members of Congress, Republican governors of Union states, and Vice–President Hamlin by appointing many of their relatives to government positions. In fact, at least one family member of each Lincoln Cabinet officer either was

10. ... Many family dynasties in America come readily to mind. Leadership of the Ford Company has passed from Henry to Edsel to grandsons Benson, Henry II, and William. In 1957, the Ford grandsons refused to discuss nepotism, saying that "it would not be in good taste." Founder Oscar Mayer of the Chicago meat packing company died in 1956, leaving six Mayer relatives on the board of directors. In a 1951 agreement, Joseph Magnin, the head of a chain of women's clothing stores, bequeathed his stock to his son Cyril and provided that Cyril had to vote his stock to elect at least two of his children to the company board of directors. The Son Also Rises, Wall St.J., Apr. 1, 1964, at 1. Other corporate families include the Bronfmans (Distillers Corp. Seagrams Ltd.), the Firestones (Firestone Tire & Rubber Co.), and the Lukes (West Virginia Pulp & Paper Corp.).

placed on the federal payroll or received military promotions during the Civil War. In more recent times, President Johnson, during his Senate tenure, put both his brother and his brother's wife on the public payroll; and President Kennedy appointed his brother to be United States Attorney General.

Although it is difficult to pinpoint the time when the pendulum of opinion began to swing against nepotistic practices in business and politics, by the mid-1950's a number of corporations had adopted "antinepotism" rules. According to a survey conducted by the American Institute of Management in 1955, seven percent of the 379 companies it rated "excellently managed" had written policies banning or restricting the hiring of relatives; a "somewhat larger" number had unwritten rules. By 1963, twenty-eight percent of the 530 companies the Institute surveyed had written antinepotism policies and thirty-six percent had unwritten ones.

Such rules were, for the most part, directed at the hiring of incompetent male relatives, the abuse that gave rise to the pejorative connotation of nepotism. Undoubtedly because women did not constitute a significant part of the professional or managerial workforce twenty to thirty years ago, such rules had minimal effect on daughters, nieces, female cousins, or wives. In recent years, however, women have begun to enter the workforce in unprecedented numbers. Consequently, rules against nepotism are now applied in situations not contemplated by their drafters—for example, when employees at the same workplace marry, a husband or wife seeks employment at the place where his or her spouse already works, or a married couple applies jointly for employment with the same employer.

. . .

[. . . T]he fact remains that antinepotism policies, which were established with other concerns in mind, are now impeding the efforts of women to find and keep jobs. This effect is both direct and subtle. When a rule requires that one spouse leave the workplace, or not be invited in, for various reasons that spouse in all likelihood will be the female. Furthermore, because women generally enter the labor market on a permanent basis later than men, a policy which limits the employment of spouses necessarily favors men over women. Although these restrictions on employment may appear to be de minimis since they leave the spouse free to work elsewhere, that option is frequently not available. In addition, by enhancing the interests of one spouse at the other's expense, antinepotism rules may be causing more friction in the home than they prevent in the workplace.

. . .

2. What justifications are there for nepotism rules? Is it appropriate to distinguish between situations in which one spouse is in a position to influence the hiring or promotion of the other from situations in which such influence is not at issue? Is it appropriate to distinguish between situations where the parties are married before the second seeks a job in the same office and situations where the marriage occurs after both are already employed? Is it appropriate to apply nepotism rules only to spouses and not to other family members? What of people who live together? Who date one another? Who play golf with each other?

Jones v. Jones

Supreme Court of Georgia, 1988.
258 Ga. 353, 369 S.E.2d 478.

■ GREGORY, JUSTICE.

The appellee, Norma Jones, retained Diane Zimmerman to represent her in a divorce action against appellant, Larry Jones. Subsequently Larry Jones retained Charles Bond to represent him in the divorce action. Bond and Zimmerman have been married at all times applicable to this litigation. Bond and Zimmerman negotiated a settlement regarding temporary custody of the minor children and alimony which was made the judgment of the court. Zimmerman's law firm then filed a motion to disqualify Bond on the ground that Bond had a conflict of interest in the case by virtue of his marriage to Zimmerman. In this motion Mrs. Jones expressed her "fear" that confidences she had divulged to Zimmerman "will be conveyed" to Bond. While this motion was pending Zimmerman's law firm withdrew from the case concluding it had a conflict of interest due to an earlier representation of Mr. Jones.[1] Mrs. Jones retained new counsel who pursued the motion to disqualify Bond.

Following a hearing the trial court granted the motion to disqualify Bond. The trial court found no evidence of impropriety or breach of confidences by either Bond or Zimmerman. The court determined, however, that this case is factually distinguishable from Blumenfeld v. Borenstein, 247 Ga. 406, 276 S.E.2d 607 (1981) in that Bond and Zimmerman had "gone head-to-head" on the issues of temporary alimony and child custody.[2] The trial court concluded that in this case there was the appearance of impropriety coupled with a jeopardy to a client's confidences, and therefore under *Blumenfeld* disqualification of Bond was mandated for the protection of Mrs. Jones. We granted Mr. Jones's application for interlocutory appeal.

In *Blumenfeld* we held that "[a]bsent a showing that special circumstances exist which prevent the adequate representation of the client, disqualification based solely on marital status is not justified." The court noted that "[w]hile we cannot disagree with the proposition that the marital relationship may be the most intimate relationship of a person's life, it does not follow that professional people allow this intimacy to interfere with professional obligations. If this court endorsed a rule imputing professional wrongdoing to an attorney on the basis of marital status alone, it would be difficult to avoid the extension of that rule to other relationships as well." 247 Ga. at 408–9, 276 S.E.2d 607. Rather, this court held that the issue of attorney disqualification exists on a continuum.

> "At one end of the scale where disqualification is always justified and indeed mandated, even when balanced against a client's right to an attorney of choice, is the appearance of impropriety coupled with a conflict of interest or jeopardy to a client's confidences. In these instances, it is clear that the disqualification is necessary for the protection of the client. Somewhere in the middle of the continuum is the appearance of impropriety based on conduct on the part of the attorney. As discussed above, this generally has been found insufficient to outweigh the client's interest in counsel of choice. This is probably so because absent danger to the client, the nebulous interest of the public at large in the propriety of the Bar is not weighty enough to justify disqualification. Finally, at the opposite end of the continuum is the appearance of impropriety based not on conduct but on status alone. This is an

1. According to the record Mr. Jones retained a member of Zimmerman's law firm to represent him in the divorce action at the same time Mrs. Jones retained Zimmerman to represent her in the divorce action. Apparently, none of the individuals involved was aware of this conflict until some time later. Mr. Jones thereafter sought the representation of Mr. Bond.

2. In *Blumenfeld* the married attorneys were associated with law firms which were on opposing sides of the case, but only the wife/attorney actively participated in the handling of the case.

insufficient ground for disqualification." 247 Ga. at 409–410, 276 S.E.2d 607.

Thus, under *Blumenfeld,* there is no *per se* rule of disqualification based on marital status. A finding by the trial court of no actual impropriety on the part of the attorneys puts the inquiry at an end. Marital status is of no legal consequence under *Blumenfeld.* Marital status may be of some factual consequence in that it affords the *opportunity* for impropriety, e.g., communication of confidences, but opportunity for impropriety exists among lawyers who are not married. Neither would we disqualify a lawyer because opposing counsel is the lawyer's parent, child, sibling or other close relative.

We have found no authority, and none has been cited to us, for the proposition that married lawyers who are involved in active litigation on opposing sides of a case must be disqualified. To the contrary, Formal Opinion 340 (September 23, 1975) issued by the Committee on Ethics and Professional Responsibility of the American Bar Association holds that:

> "It is not necessarily improper for husband-and-wife lawyers who are practicing in different offices or firms to represent differing interests. No disciplinary rule expressly requires a lawyer to decline employment if a husband, wife, son, daughter, brother, father or other close relative represents the opposing party in negotiation or litigation. Likewise, it is not necessarily improper for a law firm having a married partner or associate to represent clients whose interests are opposed to those of other clients represented by another law firm with which the married lawyer's spouse is associated as a lawyer.
>
> A lawyer whose husband or wife is also a lawyer must, like every other lawyer, obey all disciplinary rules, for disciplinary rules apply to all lawyers without distinction as to marital status. We cannot assume that a lawyer who is married to another lawyer necessarily will violate any particular disciplinary rule, such as those that protect a client's confidences, that prescribe neglect of a client's interest, and that forbid representation of differing interests."[3]

As the trial court found no evidence of actual impropriety on the part of either Zimmerman or Bond, the disqualification was based on the appearance of impropriety which attached to their marital status. Under *Blumenfeld* this was error.

. . .

Judgment reversed.

NOTE

For more on the conflicts of interest that may arise when two lawyers marry see Deena L. Buchanan, Note, Strange Bedfellows? Married Lawyers and Conflicts of Interest, 11 Geo. J. Legal Ethics 753 (1998).

In People v. Jackson, 167 Cal.App.3d 829, 213 Cal.Rptr. 521 (1985), defendant's conviction for assault with intent to commit rape was reversed on the ground that defense counsel failed to inform the defendant of counsel's sustained dating relation-

3. See also ABA Model Rules of Professional Conduct, 1.8(i) which provides, "A lawyer related to another lawyer as parent, child, sibling or spouse shall not represent a client in a representation directly adverse to a person who the lawyer knows is represented by the other lawyer except upon consent by the client after consultation regarding the relationship." The comments to paragraph (i) state that the disqualification "is personal and is not imputed to members of firms with whom the lawyers are associated."

ship with the prosecutor throughout the course of the case. See generally, Note, Lawyers as Lovers: How Far Should Ethical Restrictions on Dating or Married Attorneys Extend?, 1 Geo.J.Leg.Ethics 433 (1987).

(2) . . . and the Nurturing Husband

Knussman v. Maryland

United States Court of Appeals for the Fourth Circuit, 2001.
272 F.3d 625.

■ Traxler, Circuit Judge:

Howard Kevin Knussman, a trooper in the Maryland State Police, brought an action alleging that the State of Maryland and several individual employees of the Maryland State Police (collectively "the defendants") unlawfully discriminated against him on the basis of his gender, for which he sought recourse under 42 U.S.C.A. § 1983 (West Supp. 2000); and that the defendants violated his rights under the Family and Medical Leave Act of 1993 (FMLA), see 29 U.S.C.A. §§ 2601–2654 (West 1999), for which he sought recourse under § 1983 and directly under the FMLA. Following a jury trial and various post-trial motions, judgment in the amount of $375,000 was entered against only one of the defendants—Jill Mullineaux, a civilian employee of the Maryland State Police.

In 1994, Knussman learned that his wife Kimberly was pregnant. At the time, Knussman held the rank of trooper first class and served as a paramedic on medevac helicopters in the Aviation Division of the Maryland State Police ("MSP"). Unfortunately, Kim's pregnancy was difficult and ultimately resulted in her confinement to bed rest in the latter stages prior to delivery. In October 1994, Knussman submitted a written request to his supervisor asking that Knussman be permitted to take four to eight weeks of paid "family sick leave" to care for his wife and spend time with his family following the birth of his child.[1] Eventually, Knussman was informed by the MSP Director of Flight Operations, First Sergeant Ronnie P. Creel, that there was "no way" that he would be allowed more than two weeks. Creel testified that, at the time of Knussman's request, the Aviation Division was understaffed. According to Knussman, Creel misinformed him that if he wanted more leave, he would be forced to take unpaid leave because the FMLA did not entitle him to further paid leave. Knussman testified that he was unfamiliar with the FMLA because the MSP had failed to provide proper notice to its employees about their rights under the FMLA.

In early December, shortly before the Knussmans' daughter was born, Jill Mullineaux, manager of the medical leave and benefit section of the MSP Personnel Management Division, notified all MSP employees of a new Maryland statutory provision that allowed the use of paid sick leave by a state employee to care for a newborn. The statute permitted "primary care givers" to "use, without certification of illness or disability, up to 30 days of accrued sick leave to care for a child . . . immediately following . . . the birth of the employee's child." Md. Code Ann., State Pers. & Pens. § 7–508(a)(1). A "primary care giver" was defined as "an employee who is primarily responsi-

1. Maryland law permitted a state employee to use paid sick leave for reasons other than the employee's own illness, including "for death, illness, or disability in the employee's immediate family." Md. Code Ann., State Pers. & Pens. § 7–502(b)(2) (1994). The statute was later amended and reorganized; however, Maryland law still permits this particular use of a state employee's sick leave. See Md. Code Ann., State Pers. & Pens. § 9–501(b)(2) (1996).

ble for the care and nurturing of a child." By contrast, a "secondary care giver," i.e., "an employee who is secondarily responsible for the care and nurturing of a child," might use up to 10 days of accrued sick leave without providing proof of illness or disability.[2] In contrast to "family sick leave," which required an employee to provide verification of a family member's illness, the new "nurturing leave" provision permitted an employee to use paid sick leave without providing any medical documentation, since this type of leave was not actually related to the illness or disability of the employee or the employee's family.[3]

Believing that this "nurturing leave" might afford him more paid leave than he would receive from his request for "family sick leave," Knussman contacted Mullineaux for additional information about using his accrued sick leave under § 7–508. Specifically, he wanted to know whether he could qualify as a primary care giver under § 7–508(a)(1) and take 30 days of paid sick leave. According to Knussman, Mullineaux informed him that only birth mothers could qualify as primary care givers; fathers would only be permitted to take leave as secondary care givers since they "couldn't breast feed a baby." Mullineaux, who testified that she was merely passing along the Maryland Department of Personnel's (DOP) view of "primary care giver," denied adopting such a categorical interpretation.[4] In any case, Knussman's superior officers in the Aviation Division, having consulted Mullineaux about the untested nurturing leave provision, granted him 10 days of paid sick leave as the secondary care giver under § 7–508(b).

The Knussmans' daughter was born on December 9, 1994. Kimberly Knussman, however, continued to experience health problems. Before his authorized 10–day leave expired, Knussman contacted Sergeant J.C. Collins, one of his supervisors, and inquired whether his status could be changed to that of primary care giver and his paid sick leave extended to 30 days under section 7–508(a). Knussman explained to Collins that he was the primary care giver for the child because, given his wife's condition following delivery, he was performing the majority of the essential functions such as diaper changing, feeding, bathing and taking the child to the doctor.

David Czorapinski, the Assistant Commander for the Aviation Division during this time, learned of Knussman's inquiry and, unable to reach Mullineaux, gathered some preliminary information on the new law himself. Czorapinski learned that the Maryland DOP intended to take the position that the mother was the primary care giver and the father was secondary. Czorapinski passed this information down the chain-of-command and Knussman was told that it was unlikely that his paid sick leave would be extended under section 7–508(a).

2. Section 7–508 has been amended and recodified, and it now provides for the use of up to an aggregate of 40 days of accrued sick leave if two state employees are responsible for the care of a newborn. See Md. Code Ann., State Pers. & Pens. § 9–505(b)(1) (1996). Section 7–508(b)(1), had it been in effect at the time, apparently would have applied to the Knussmans, who were both state employees.

3. For ease of reference, we adopt the term "nurturing leave." This term, however, does not appear in the statute.

4. Mullineaux testified that she never told Knussman that fathers were, as a class, ineligible for primary care giver status. Rather, Mullineaux's version was that she told Knussman, based on information provided by the state Department of Personnel, "that the birth mother was presumed to be the primary care giver and if he wanted to qualify as the primary care giver, he could, if he could provide [supporting] information."

On the day before Knussman was scheduled to return to work, Knussman made a final attempt at obtaining additional sick leave. Sergeant Carl Lee, one of Knussman's immediate superiors, had earlier informed Knussman that although nurturing leave as a primary care giver was probably not an option, Knussman might be eligible for additional paid leave under the family sick leave provision as long as he could demonstrate that it was medically necessary for him to care for his wife. Knussman contacted Mullineaux to find out what information he needed to supply for family sick leave.[5] During this conversation, Knussman again discussed his eligibility for nurturing leave as a primary care provider under section 7–508(a) with Mullineaux, who explained that "God made women to have babies and, unless [he] could have a baby, there is no way [he] could be primary care [giver]" and that his wife had to be "in a coma or dead" for Knussman to qualify as the primary care giver.

Mullineaux denied Knussman's request for paid sick leave under § 7–508(a) as a primary care giver. Knussman returned to work as ordered and immediately filed an administrative grievance on the grounds that he had been improperly denied primary care giver status under § 7–508(a). He did not seek review of Mullineaux's denial of his request for family sick leave under section 7–502(b)(2). Once the grievance process was underway, Knussman's claim went up the MSP chain-of-command and Mullineaux's involvement ceased.

Knussman's grievance was denied at each stage of the four-level grievance procedure. . . . Essentially, Czorapinski believed that Kimberly Knussman, who was also a state employee, was enjoying the benefits of nurturing leave as a primary care giver because, following delivery, she took sick leave for a 30–day period—the same amount of time afforded a primary care giver under § 7–508(a). Thus, Czorapinski was concerned that both Knussmans were attempting to qualify as the primary care giver for their daughter when the statute indicated only one person could qualify. At trial, Knussman presented evidence that, prior to the step two grievance conference, Mullineaux and Czorapinski were made aware of the fact the Kimberly Knussman was, in fact, on sick leave for her own disability resulting from the difficult pregnancy. Following Czorapinski's decision, Knussman pursued his complaint through the two remaining steps of the internal grievance procedure without success.

Knussman then filed a three-count action in federal court. In Count I, Knussman sought relief under § 1983, claiming that his leave request under § 7–508(a) was denied as a result of gender discrimination in violation of the Equal Protection Clause of the Fourteenth Amendment to the United States Constitution. . . . He named as defendants the State of Maryland, the MSP, and several employees of the MSP, in both their individual and official capacities: Mullineaux, Czorapinski, Creel, and Colonel David B. Mitchell, Superintendent of the MSP.

After a period of discovery, the defendants moved for summary judgment on the grounds that they were entitled to qualified immunity and that

5. Knussman subsequently submitted a letter from Kimberly Knussman's doctor in support of his request for family sick leave; however, Mullineaux concluded that the letter was insufficient to justify family sick leave because "it [did not] say what care [Knussman was] going to provide, and it [did not] say that [Knussman] needed to be home . . . like it's [Knussman's] choice and not the doctor's requirement." Although Czorapinski suggested to Knussman that the deficiencies could be easily corrected, Knussman refused "to pursue this option any further."

Knussman could not prove an equal protection violation in the first place. With respect to Knussman's equal protection claim under § 1983 (Count I), the court concluded that the facts, viewed in the light most favorable to Knussman, indicated that the defendants applied a gender-based presumption that the birth mother was the primary care giver, which would amount to an equal protection violation. See Knussman v. State of Maryland, 16 F. Supp. 2d 601, 611–12 (D. Md. 1998) ("Knussman II"). The district court further concluded that the defendants were not entitled to qualified immunity because it was well-established at the time that gender discrimination in employment was prohibited under the Fourteenth Amendment:

> Although the Maryland leave law had been amended effective less than one month before [Knussman] requested leave and the DOP had not issued any guidelines regarding application of the amended law, the right to equal protection is a well-established principle. It is also clear that gender discrimination violates the equal protection clause. Discriminatory application of a gender neutral state law is patently illegal and defendants should have known at least this much.

Thus, the case went to trial on portions of both counts in the complaint. As for Count I, Knussman's § 1983 equal protection claim remained intact against the State of Maryland (but only for declaratory and injunctive relief) and the defendants in their individual capacities. At the close of the evidence, the court submitted the question of qualified immunity to the jury as well as the ultimate question of liability. . . . The jury concluded that each defendant denied Knussman's request for leave because of his gender; however, the jury also found that every defendant except Mullineaux was entitled to qualified immunity. Knussman does not challenge this conclusion on appeal. . . . The jury awarded Knussman the sum of $375,000 in damages.

. . .

On appeal, Mullineaux contends that she was entitled to qualified immunity on Knussman's equal protection claim under § 1983. She also challenges, on multiple grounds, the jury's verdict as well as the court's jury instructions.

. . .

We first consider the issue of whether the evidence adduced at trial is sufficient to establish that Mullineaux committed a constitutional violation under the law as it currently stands. In a nutshell, Knussman's contention is that Mullineaux applied a facially neutral statute unequally solely on the basis of a gender stereotype in violation of the Equal Protection Clause of the Fourteenth Amendment. The only distinction created by the statute was between "primary care givers" and "secondary care givers," the former being entitled to 30 days of accrued sick leave to care for a newborn and the latter being entitled to 10 days of accrued sick leave. The statute made no reference to gender. Rather, the gender classification was created in the application of § 7–508. Viewed in the light most favorable to Knussman, Mullineaux, based on the comments of an administrative assistant to the DOP's Director of Legislation, took the position that only mothers could qualify for additional paid leave as primary care givers under § 7–508(a). Essentially, Mullineaux applied an irrebutable presumption that the mother is the primary care giver, and therefore entitled to greater employment benefits.

We agree with Knussman that Mullineaux's conduct violated his rights under the Equal Protection Clause. Government classifications drawn on the basis of gender have been viewed with suspicion for three decades. . . .

In particular, justifications for gender-based distinctions that are rooted in "overbroad generalizations about the different talents, capacities, or preferences of males and females" will not suffice. VMI, 518 U.S. at 533. Thus, gender classifications that appear to rest on nothing more than conventional notions about the proper station in society for males and females have been declared invalid time and again by the Supreme Court. . . .

Gender classifications based upon generalizations about typical gender roles in the raising and nurturing of children have met a similar fate.

The defendants have not even attempted to explain how an irrebuttable presumption in favor of the mother under § 7-508 relates to an important state interest. We conclude that the presumption employed by Mullineaux here was not substantially related to an important governmental interest and, therefore, was not permissible under the Equal Protection Clause.

We next must decide whether Mullineaux's actions contravened "clearly established statutory or constitutional rights of which a reasonable person would have known." Harlow v. Fitzgerald, 457 U.S. 800, 818 (1982).

. . .

Mullineaux contends that the law was not clear because the Supreme Court had determined on a number of occasions that equal protection principles permit government officials to distribute employment-related benefits pursuant to gender-based classifications. In the decisions cited by Mullineaux, however, the gender-based classification was linked to something other than a sexual stereotype. For example, Mullineaux relies on Geduldig v. Aiello, 417 U.S. 484. In our view, *Geduldig* does not cloud the issue. In *Geduldig*, the Court upheld a California insurance statute that excluded pregnancy-related disabilities from coverage against an equal protection challenge, observing that the exclusion of disabilities relating to normal childbirth (as well as other short-term disabilities not related to pregnancy) represented a permissible policy choice aimed at maintaining the solvency of the insurance program. . . .

The authority cited by Mullineaux actually underscores our conclusion regarding the clarity of the law in December 1994. Mullineaux's distribution of sick leave benefits under § 7-508 was a by-product of traditional ideas about a woman's role in rearing a child, which was clearly impermissible under the Equal Protection Clause of the Fourteenth Amendment at the time in question.

. . .

In sum, we hold that Mullineaux was not entitled to qualified immunity against Knussman's equal protection claim under § 1983 and affirm the judgment as to liability, but we conclude that the jury's award of $375,000 was excessive. Accordingly, we vacate the jury's award and remand for a new trial on damages with respect to Knussman's equal protection claim (Count I). Knussman is entitled to be compensated for emotional distress caused by Mullineaux's constitutional violation but not for any emotional distress associated with the litigation of this action or his employer's general internal grievance process.

S.M. Miller, The Making of a Confused Middle Class Husband

2 Soc. Pol'y 33 (July/August 1971).

. . .

. . . In the left-wing ambience of New York City in the '40s and '50s, "male supremacy" and "male chauvinism" were frequently discussed. True, my male friends and I discussed the issues with our female friends and then often proceeded to exploit them, but a dexterous awareness we did have. (But I add, in order to avoid a reassuring self-debasement, that we did encourage our women friends and wives to think and to develop themselves; and I even believe that I was less exploitative than most.)

Yet I am dogged by the feeling expressed in the notion "If you're so smart, how come you're not rich?" Where is the egalitarian family life one would reasonably expect from my sophistication about women's issues and my personal experience with them in my younger manhood?

. . .

Probably the most important factor in accounting for the direction my wife and I took was our amazing naïveté about the impact of having children—a naïveté, incidentally, that I see today having a similarly devastating effect on many young parents. We just had no idea how much time and emotion children captured, how they simply changed a couple's lives, even when the wife's working made it possible, as it did in our case, to afford a housekeeper.

The early years of child rearing were very difficult. Our first son was superactive and did not sleep through the night. We were both exhausted. My wife insisted that I not leave everything to her; she fought with me to get me to participate in the care of our son and apartment. I took the 2 A.M. and 6 A.M. feedings and changings, for our ideology would not allow me just to help out occasionally: I had to "share," "really participate," in the whole thing. I resented that degree of involvement; it seemed to interfere terribly with the work I desperately wanted to achieve in. Indeed, I have always felt put upon because of that experience of many months.

To make matters worse, I did not know of other work-oriented husbands who were as involved as I with their children. True, I realized that my sons and I had become much attached to each other and that a lovely new element had entered my life; but I resented the time and exhaustion, particularly since I was struggling to find my way in my work. I did not consider myself productive and was in the middle of struggling to clarify my perspective. I looked at the problem largely in terms of the pressure of my job, which required a lot of effort, and, more importantly, in terms of my personality and my inability to work effectively. Although I wrote memoranda with great ease, I wasn't writing professional articles and books.

In retrospect, I think that it was the influence of the McCarthy and Eisenhower years that was more significant in my lack of development. My outlook and interests were not what social science and society were responding to. That changed later, and I was able to savor in the '60s that infrequent exhilaration of having my professional work and citizen concerns merge and of gaining both a social-science and a popular audience and constituency. But I did not know in the 1950s that this would unfold, and I felt resentment.

What I experienced was that, unlike my friends, I was working hard to make things easier for my wife, and I did not see rewards. Yes, she told me she appreciated my effort; but my activities were never enough, my sharing was never full, in the sense that I equally planned and took the initiative in the care of child and house. She was tired, too, and irritated by child care; and, in turn, I was irritated by what seemed to be her absorption in taking care of the children.

. . .

I guess what dismays me and makes me see my marriage and family as unfortunately typically upper-middle-class collegial, pseudo-egalitarian American—especially in light of my own continuing commitment to an egalitarian, participatory ethos—is that I assume no responsibility for major household tasks and family activities. True, my wife has always worked at her profession (she is a physician), even when our sons were only some weeks old. True, I help in many ways and feel responsible for her having time to work at her professional interests. But I do partial, limited things to free her to do her work. I don't do the basic thinking about the planning of meals and housekeeping, or the situation of the children. Sure, I will wash dishes and "spend time" with the children; I will often do the shopping, cook, make beds, "share" the burden of most household tasks; but that is not the same thing as direct and primary responsibility for planning and managing a household and meeting the day-to-day needs of children.

It is not that I object in principle to housekeeping and child rearing. I don't find such work demeaning or unmasculine—just a drain of my time, which could be devoted to other, "more rewarding" things. (Just as I don't like to shop for clothes for myself, even though I like clothes.) My energies are poised to help me work on my professional-political concerns, and I resist "wasting time" on other pursuits, even those basic to managing a day-to-day existence.

The more crucial issue, I now think, is not my specific omissions and commissions, but the atmosphere that I create. My wife does not expect much of me, which frees me for work and lessens the strain I produce when I feel blocked from working. Even our sons have always largely respected my efforts to work, feeling much freer to interrupt their mother at her work. The years have been less happy than they would have been if I had been more involved and attentive and my wife had not lowered her ambitions.

Outstanding academically from an early age, a "poor girl" scholarship winner to a prestige college and medical school, excelling in her beginning professional work, my wife expected, and was expected, to do great things. But with children, she immediately reduced her goals. Of course, medical schools don't pay much attention to faculty members who are part-time or female, and the combination of the two almost guarantees off-hand treatment.

She is now realizing fuller professional development. I have always felt guilty about her not achieving more, so I have nagged her to publish, though I have not provided the circumstances and climate that would make serious work much easier. I have had the benefit of feeling relieved that I was "motivating" her by my emphasis on her doing more, but I have not suffered the demands on my time and emotions that making more useful time available to her would have required. In the long run, I have undoubtedly lost more by limited involvement, because she has been distressed by the obstacles to her professional work. But the long run is hard to consider when today's saved and protected time helps meet a deadline.

What are the lessons of this saga of a well-meaning male?

One is that equality or communality is not won once and for all, but must continually be striven for. Backsliding and easy accommodation to the male (because it is less troublesome) are likely to occur unless there is, at least occasionally, effort to bring about or maintain true communality rather than peaceful adjustment.

From this it follows that women must struggle for equality—that it will not easily be won or rewon. (A male is not likely to bestow it—in more than surface ways. Some women are arguing that it is not worth the effort to have equality with men in close personal relations and that they should not bother with men, but equality and communality among women will not be automatic, either.) The struggle does not necessarily mean nastiness, but it does require the perceptiveness and willingness to engage issues not only of prejudice and discrimination but also of subtle practices requiring female accommodation to males.

I know that the point I am about to make is often misused, and will open me to much criticism; but let me try to make it. A third lesson is that the bringing up of children must be changed, and that many women are lagging in this respect, although present day-care concerns suggest a possible change. For all of male reluctance, resistance and avoidance, many women, particularly when they have young children, end up structuring life so that it is difficult to achieve a partner relationship. Indeed, the concentration on, nay, absorption with, children makes even a low-level decent relationship, let alone an egalitarian one, difficult. Yes, I realize that the subordinate group is never the main source of difficulty, that men make women embrace the mother-house-mother syndrome; but cultural and personal history are involved as well as direct or more covert husbandly pressure and unwillingness to be a full partner. Overinvolvement with children may operate to discourage many husbands from full participation because they do not accept the ideology of close attention to children.

... What is needed is a reconsideration of what is required in parenthood and in running a household.

Let me consider the household care first. The easy notion that in the right atmosphere housework is not so bad seems wrong to me. A lot of jobs can be stomached, treated as routine; that is the best one can say of them—that they are manageable, "doable." But they are not exciting, stimulating or satisfying except to the extent that they are completed or "accomplished," i.e., gotten rid of for the moment. This is especially so when one's other interests are high, for then these tasks become highly competitive with other ways of using one's time and thus are dissatisfying. Housework can be a full-time job if it is not guarded against. Some agreement on a minimum, satisfactory level of household care and some efficiency and sharing in performing it are important for a couple.

I have mentioned, verbally at least, the desirability of "salutary neglect" (before Moynihan, incidentally). But it has been difficult for my generation, whose adolescence and early twenties were stirred by Freud and who have wallowed in the guilt of parental omniscience and ethnic parental concern, to erase the sense of responsibility and guilt for how our children develop. What if one's son doesn't graduate from college or becomes a bomb-thrower ... —isn't it the parents' fault? When a son or daughter is eighteen or twenty, it seems easier to deny the responsibility, since so many youths are also in troubled times that it is difficult to talk of Freudian acting-out rather than of a generational change in consciousness. But at earlier ages it is much more difficult to shake the feeling of responsibility for how a child is developing. Obviously I don't advocate callous neglect; but some less constraining and demanding views of parenthood—and probably some additional institutional aids like day care—are needed.

The problem is not always in the mothers' attitudes. Some studies show that working-class women are very interested in working, but that their husbands feel that it is important to the children for their mothers to be home. The issue is not so much that the mother or father is lagging but how to move toward new views on child development and new institutions to further these views.

But all these "implications" are minor, except for the importance of struggle. *What strikes me as the crucial concern, at least for the occupationally striving family, is the male involvement in work, success and striving.* This is the pressure that often molds the family. Accommodation to it is frequently the measure of being a "good wife"—moving when the male's "future" requires it, regulating activities so that the male is free to concentrate on his work or business. It isn't sexism or prejudice against women that is at work here—although they are contributing factors—but the compulsive concentration upon the objective of achievement and the relegating of other activities to secondary concern. Egalitarian relationships cannot survive if people are not somewhat equally involved with each other and if the major commitment is to things outside the relationship that inevitably intrude upon it.

So long as success or achievement burns bright for the male, it is going to be difficult to change drastically the situation of the family and the woman.

However, although I am strongly of the mind that success drives should be banked and other more humanitarian urges encouraged, I don't accept that all of the drive for success or achievement is pernicious or undesirable. This drive is exciting, and can be fulfilling. But it is a great danger to be avoided when it becomes all-embracing or when the success is without a content that is both personally and socially satisfying or beneficial.

To do interesting and useful things, to feel a sense of accomplishment, should be made easier. As in military strategy, a "sufficient level" of achievement rather than a "maximum level" of security or position should be sought. Being "number one" should not be the goal; rather, high competence should be enough for both men and women. . . .

If women accept "success" to the same extent and in the same way that many men do, the problems will be enormous. If women simply adopt the "number-one-ism" that dominates the workplace, the drive for achievement will probably lead them into the same narrowing and unpromising obsessions that destroy many men.

A more egalitarian society in terms of the distribution of income and social respect would, of course, make it easier to escape "number-one-ism." But, meanwhile, we shall have to struggle with the values that surround us and corrode true equality in the home.

Finally, men have to feel some gain in the growing equality in their relationship with women. Over the long run there may well be greater satisfaction for males in egalitarian relationships, but in the short run the tensions and demands may not lead to enjoyment and satisfaction. Some short-term gains for males will be important in speeding up the road to equality. But such gains are not easily or automatically forthcoming. That is why I made the first points about the inevitability of struggle. Successful struggle requires modes of living and relationships to which the male can accommodate without total loss, which is hard to achieve without women's falling back again to accommodating to men.

I recognize that I concentrate upon the upper middle class and upon the experience of one male. I don't think either is the world—I really don't. But I do perceive that some of my experiences and interpretations are not solipsist pieces of life, that with things changing, others are experiencing similar shocks and stresses. I wonder whether the egalitarian changes I see in some young families will mean permanent changes, or "lapsed egalitarianism" once again. My hope is that the future will be different.

NOTE

Consider Steven L. Nock, Marriage in Men's Lives 40 (1998):

> If husband and wives *are* economically rational, one might expect that wives would perform more housework if they are economically dependent on their husbands. ... In general ... wives' housework time appears to vary with the degree of economic dependency on their husbands. ... One researcher showed that a husband's dependency on his wife does *not* translate into greater shares of housework....
>
> Why would economically dependent husbands do *less* housework ...? The answer is that housework and the time required to do it are more than simple economic commodities. The details of routine household life ... carry enormous symbolic meaning. "Men's" work means providing for the family and being the "breadwinner," whereas "women's" work means caring for the home and children. The associations are part of the culture and embedded in institutions. They are widely believed by American men and women and are reinforced by economic, religious, and educational institutional arrangements. ... [A] dependent husband departs from traditional assumptions about marriage. Were he to respond by doing more housework he would deviate even more. When he does even *less* housework, therefore, he is compensating for his departure from normative associations by being more traditional in whatever ways he can.

and Scott Coltrane, Family Man: Fatherhood, Housework, and Gender Equity 232 (1996):

> Fathers who take on responsibility for child care often report that the experience makes them more complete people. That is, fathering provides them opportunities to develop the more caring and emotional sides of themselves. To survive the daily trials and tribulations of child care, many parents find that they must develop clarity about what is most important, patience with the uneven pace of children's development, and sensitivity to subtle differences in feelings and actions. What's more, good parenting strikes a balance between guidance and service. Aloof, authoritarian, and judgmental styles of interaction do not work well in baby care, and tend to create more problems than they solve. Because men cannot rely on no-nonsense, directive, "masculine" styles of interaction, they are forced to develop more gentle and expressive ways of relating. In fact, some of the new fathers I interviewed told me that infant care forced them to recognize, label and talk about their own and their children's feeling.
>
> ... This is a profound experience for many men.... In their own words, it begins to "open them up" to various expressive possibilities, including sadness and loss surrounding their relationships with their own fathers....

D. Encroachments on the Doctrine of Family Privacy

1. The Constitutional Right to Privacy

Griswold v. Connecticut

Supreme Court of the United States, 1965.
381 U.S. 479, 85 S.Ct. 1678, 14 L.Ed.2d 510.

■ JUSTICE DOUGLAS delivered the opinion of the Court.

Appellant Griswold is Executive Director of the Planned Parenthood League of Connecticut. Appellant Buxton [was] . . . Medical Director for the League at its Center in New Haven—a center open . . . from November 1 to November 10, 1961, when appellants were arrested.

They gave information, instruction, and medical advice to *married persons* as to the means of preventing conception. . . . Fees were usually charged, although some couples were serviced free.

The statutes whose constitutionality is involved in this appeal are §§ 53–32 and 54–196 of the General Statutes of Connecticut (1958 rev.). The former provides:

> "Any person who uses any drug, medicinal article or instrument for the purpose of preventing conception shall be fined not less than fifty dollars or imprisoned not less than sixty days nor more than one year or be both fined and imprisoned."
>
> Section 54–196 provides:
>
> "Any person who assists, abets, counsels, causes, hires or commands another to commit any offense may be prosecuted and punished as if he were the principal offender."

The appellants were found guilty as accessories and fined $100 each, against the claim that the accessory statute as so applied violated the Fourteenth Amendment. . . .

. . .

Coming to the merits, we are met with a wide range of questions that implicate the Due Process Clause of the Fourteenth Amendment. Overtones of some arguments suggest that Lochner v. State. of New York, 198 U.S. 45 [(1905)] should be our guide. But we decline that invitation. . . . We do not sit as a super-legislature to determine the wisdom, need, and propriety of laws that touch economic problems, business affairs, or social conditions. This law, however, operates directly on an intimate relation of husband and wife and their physician's role in one aspect of that relation.

The association of people is not mentioned in the Constitution nor in the Bill of Rights. The right to educate a child in a school of the parents' choice—whether public or private or parochial—is also not mentioned. Nor is the right to study any particular subject or any foreign language. Yet the First Amendment has been construed to include certain of those rights.

By Pierce v. Society of Sisters, [Chapter 8, Section D, 2], the right to educate one's children as one chooses is made applicable to the States by the force of the First and Fourteenth Amendments. By Meyer v. State of

Nebraska, [262 U.S. 390], the same dignity is given the right to study the German language in a private school. In other words, the State may not, consistently with the spirit of the First Amendment, contract the spectrum of available knowledge....

In NAACP v. State of Alabama, 357 U.S. 449, 462 [(1958)] we protected the "freedom to associate and privacy in one's associations," noting that freedom of association was a peripheral First Amendment right.... In other words, the First Amendment has a penumbra where privacy is protected from governmental intrusion. In like context, we have protected forms of "association" that are not political in the customary sense but pertain to the social, legal, and economic benefit of the members. NAACP v. Button, 371 U.S. 415, 430–431 [(1963)].

...

The foregoing cases suggest that specific guarantees in the Bill of Rights have penumbras, formed by emanations from those guarantees that help give them life and substance. Various guarantees create zones of privacy. The right of association contained in the penumbra of the First Amendment is one, as we have seen. The Third Amendment in its prohibition against the quartering of soldiers "in any house" in time of peace without the consent of the owner is another facet of that privacy. The Fourth Amendment explicitly affirms the "right of the people to be secure in their persons, houses, papers, and effects, against unreasonable searches and seizures." The Fifth Amendment in its Self-Incrimination Clause enables the citizen to create a zone of privacy which government may not force him to surrender to his detriment. The Ninth Amendment provides: "The enumeration in the Constitution, of certain rights, shall not be construed to deny or disparage others retained by the people."

...

The present case, then concerns a relationship lying within the zone of privacy created by several fundamental constitutional guarantees. And it concerns a law which, in forbidding the use of contraceptives rather than regulating their manufacture or sale, seeks to achieve its goals by means having a maximum destructive impact upon that relationship. Such a law cannot stand in light of the familiar principle ... that a "governmental purpose to control or prevent activities constitutionally subject to state regulation may not be achieved by means which sweep unnecessarily broadly and thereby invade the area of protected freedoms." Would we allow the police to search the sacred precincts of marital bedrooms for telltale signs of the use of contraceptives? The very idea is repulsive to the notions of privacy surrounding the marriage relationship.

We deal with a right of privacy older than the Bill of Rights—older than our political parties, older than our school system. Marriage is a coming together for better or for worse, hopefully enduring, and intimate to the degree of being sacred. It is an association that promotes a way of life, not causes; a harmony in living, not political faiths; a bilateral loyalty, not commercial or social projects. Yet it is an association for as noble a purpose as any involved in our prior decisions.

Reversed.

■ JUSTICE GOLDBERG, whom THE CHIEF JUSTICE and JUSTICE BRENNAN join, concurring.

. . . I do agree that the concept of liberty protects those personal rights that are fundamental, and is not confined to the specific terms of the Bill of Rights. My conclusion . . . is supported both by numerous decisions of this Court . . . and by the language and history of the Ninth Amendment. . . .

. . .

This Court, in a series of decisions, has held that the Fourteenth Amendment absorbs and applies to the States those specifics of the first eight amendments which express fundamental personal rights. The language and history of the Ninth Amendment reveal that the Framers of the Constitution believed that there are additional fundamental rights, protected from governmental infringement, which exist alongside those fundamental rights specifically mentioned in the first eight constitutional amendments.

The Ninth Amendment reads, "The enumeration in the Constitution, of certain rights, shall not be construed to deny or disparage others retained by the people." The Amendment is almost entirely the work of James Madison. It was introduced in Congress by him and passed the House and Senate with little or no debate and virtually no change in language. It was proffered to quiet expressed fears that a bill of specifically enumerated rights could not be sufficiently broad to cover all essential rights and that the specific mention of certain rights would be interpreted as a denial that others were protected.

. . .

. . . To hold that a right so basic and fundamental and so deep-rooted in our society as the right of privacy in marriage may be infringed because that right is not guaranteed in so many words by the first eight amendments to the Constitution is to ignore the Ninth Amendment and to give it no effect whatsoever. . . .

. . .

■ Justice White, concurring in the judgment.

In my view this Connecticut law as applied to married couples deprives them of "liberty" without due process of law. . . .

. . .

intent of the statute

. . . [T]he statute is said to serve the State's policy against all forms of promiscuous or illicit sexual relationships, be they premarital or extramarital, concededly a permissible and legitimate legislative goal.

Without taking issue with the premise that the fear of conception operates as a deterrent to such relationships in addition to the criminal proscriptions Connecticut has against such conduct, I wholly fail to see how the ban on the use of contraceptives by married couples in any way reinforces the State's ban on illicit sexual relationships. . . .

. . .

. . . A statute limiting its prohibition on use to persons engaging in the prohibited relationship would serve the end posited by Connecticut. . . . I find nothing in this record justifying the sweeping scope of this statute. . . .

■ Justice Black, with whom Justice Stewart joins, dissenting.

. . .

One of the most effective ways of diluting or expanding a [constitutional] . . . right is to substitute for the crucial word or words of a constitutional guarantee another word or words.... This fact is well illustrated by the use of the term "right of privacy" as a comprehensive substitute for the Fourth Amendment's guarantee against "unreasonable searches and seizures." ... I like my privacy as well as the next one, but I am nevertheless compelled to admit that government has a right to invade it unless prohibited by some specific constitutional provision....

This brings me to [the due process and Ninth Amendment arguments.] [O]n analysis they turn out to be the same thing—merely using different words to claim for this Court ... power to invalidate any legislative act which the judges find irrational, unreasonable or offensive.

. . .

... The Due Process Clause ... was liberally used by this Court to strike down economic legislation in the early decades of this century, threatening, many people thought, the tranquility and stability of the Nation. That formula, based on subjective considerations of "natural justice," is no less dangerous when used to enforce this Court's views about personal rights than those about economic rights....

Eisenstadt v. Baird

Supreme Court of the United States, 1972.
405 U.S. 438, 92 S.Ct. 1029, 31 L.Ed.2d 349.

■ JUSTICE BRENNAN delivered the opinion of the Court.

Appellee William Baird was convicted at a bench trial in the Massachusetts Superior Court ... for exhibiting contraceptive articles in the course of delivering a lecture on contraception to a group of students at Boston University and ... for giving a young woman a package of Emko vaginal foam at the close of his address. The Massachusetts Supreme Judicial Court unanimously set aside the conviction for exhibiting contraceptives on the ground that it violated Baird's First Amendment rights, but by a four-to-three vote sustained the conviction for giving away the foam....

Massachusetts General Laws Ann., c. 272, § 21, under which Baird was convicted, provides a maximum five-year term of imprisonment for "whoever ... gives away ... any drug, medicine, instrument or article whatsoever for the prevention of conception," except as authorized in § 21A. Under § 21A, "[a] registered physician may administer to or prescribe for any married person drugs or articles intended for the prevention of pregnancy or conception. [A] registered pharmacist actually engaged in the business of pharmacy may furnish such drugs or articles to any married person presenting a prescription from a registered physician." ...

. . .

... The question for our determination in this case is whether there is some ground of difference that rationally explains the different treatment accorded married and unmarried persons under Massachusetts General Laws Ann., c. 272, §§ 21 and 21A. For the reasons that follow, we conclude that no such ground exists.

. . .

[First] [i]t would be plainly unreasonable to assume that Massachusetts has prescribed pregnancy and the birth of an unwanted child as punishment for fornication, which is a misdemeanor under Massachusetts General Laws Ann., c. 272, § 18. Aside from the scheme of values that assumption would attribute to the State, it is abundantly clear that the effect of the ban on distribution of contraceptives to unmarried persons has at best a marginal relation to the proffered objective....

. . .

[Second.] If health were the rationale of § 21A, the statute would be both discriminatory and overbroad ... in view of the federal and state laws *already* regulating the distribution of harmful drugs. See Federal Food, Drug, and Cosmetic Act, § 503, 52 Stat. 1051, as amended, 21 U.S.C.A. § 353; Mass.Gen.Laws Ann., c. 94, § 187A, as amended. We conclude, accordingly, that, despite the statute's superficial earmarks as a health measure, health, on the face of the statute, may no more reasonably be regarded as its purpose than the deterrence of premarital sexual relations.

Third. If the Massachusetts statute cannot be upheld as a deterrent to fornication or as a health measure, may it, nevertheless, be sustained simply as a prohibition on contraception? ...

. . .

... We need not and do not, however, decide that important question in this case because, whatever the rights of the individual to access to contraceptives may be, the rights must be the same for the unmarried and the married alike.

If under *Griswold* the distribution of contraceptives to married persons cannot be prohibited, a ban on distribution to unmarried persons would be equally impermissible. It is true that in *Griswold* the right of privacy in question inhered in the marital relationship. Yet the marital couple is not an independent entity with a mind and heart of its own, but an association of two individuals each with a separate intellectual and emotional makeup. If the right of privacy means anything, it is the right of the *individual*, married or single, to be free from unwarranted governmental intrusion into matters so fundamentally affecting a person as the decision whether to bear or beget a child. See Stanley v. Georgia, 394 U.S. 557 (1969). See also Skinner v. Oklahoma ex rel. Williamson, 316 U.S. 535 (1942); Jacobson v. Massachusetts, 197 U.S. 11, 29 (1905).

On the other hand, if *Griswold* is no bar to a prohibition on the distribution of contraceptives, the State could not, consistently with the Equal Protection Clause, outlaw distribution to unmarried but not to married persons. In each case the evil, as perceived by the State, would be identical, and the underinclusion would be invidious....

... We hold that by providing dissimilar treatment for married and unmarried persons who are similarly situated, Massachusetts General Laws Ann., c. 272, §§ 21 and 21A, violate the Equal Protection Clause. The judgment of the Court of Appeals is affirmed.

. . .

NOTE

Does *Eisenstadt* make it unconstitutional for a state to favor married individuals over nonmarried? If so, consider the observations of John Noonan, Jr. in The Family and the Supreme Court, 23 Cath. U. L. Rev. 255, 273 (1973):

[*Eisenstadt, Stanley* and their progeny] are not justified by a principle of elementary justice. They are not explicable by the invocation of Equal Protection or the right of privacy. They cannot be explained by viewing marriage as an impermissible religious category, when marriage has social purpose in our society. They are, then, wrong—wrong in using the Equal Protection Clause on behalf of the unmarried parent and the unmarried spouse, wrong in extending the right of procreative privacy to the unmarried person. They are wrong in subverting the privileged status of marriage, contrary to the teaching of Loving v. Virginia . . ., contrary to the place of marriage in American experience. The vital personal right recognized by Loving v. Virginia is not the right to a piece of paper issued by a city clerk. It is not the right to exchange magical words before an agent authorized by the state. It is the right to be immune to the legal disabilities of the unmarried and to acquire the legal benefits accorded to the married. Lawful marriage in the society's hierarchy of values recognized by Boddie v. Connecticut and in the host of laws yet unchallenged—the tax law, the common law of property, the law of evidence—is a constellation of these immunities and privileges. To say that legal immunities and legal benefits may not depend upon marriage is to deny the vital right. To say that Equal Protection requires the equal treatment of the married and the unmarried in all respects is to deny the hierarchy of values of our society.

Is this too broad a reading of *Eisenstadt?*

Lawrence v. Texas

Supreme Court of the United States, 2003.
539 U.S. 558, 123 S.Ct. 2472, 156 L.Ed.2d 508.

■ JUSTICE KENNEDY delivered the opinion of the Court.

. . .

The question before the Court is the validity of a Texas statute making it a crime for two persons of the same sex to engage in certain intimate sexual conduct.

In Houston, Texas, officers of the Harris County Police Department were dispatched to a private residence in response to a reported weapons disturbance. They entered an apartment where one of the petitioners, John Geddes Lawrence, resided. The right of the police to enter does not seem to have been questioned. The officers observed Lawrence and another man, Tyron Garner, engaging in a sexual act. The two petitioners were arrested, held in custody over night, and charged and convicted before a Justice of the Peace.

The complaints described their crime as "deviate sexual intercourse, namely anal sex, with a member of the same sex (man)." The applicable state law is Tex. Penal Code Ann. § 21.06(a) (2003). It provides: "A person commits an offense if he engages in deviate sexual intercourse with another individual of the same sex." The statute defines "deviate sexual intercourse" as follows:

"(A) any contact between any part of the genitals of one person and the mouth or anus of another person; or

"(B) the penetration of the genitals or the anus of another person with an object."

. . . The petitioners, having entered a plea of nolo contendere, were each fined $200 and assessed court costs of $141.25.

The Court of Appeals for the Texas Fourteenth District considered the petitioners' federal constitutional arguments under both the Equal Protection and Due Process Clauses of the Fourteenth Amendment. After hearing the case en banc the court, in a divided opinion, rejected the constitutional arguments and affirmed the convictions. The majority opinion indicates that the Court of Appeals considered our decision in Bowers v. Hardwick, 478 U.S. 186 (1986), to be controlling on the federal due process aspect of the case. Bowers then being authoritative, this was proper.

We granted certiorari to consider three questions:

"1. Whether Petitioners' criminal convictions under the Texas 'Homosexual Conduct' law—which criminalizes sexual intimacy by same-sex couples, but not identical behavior by different-sex couples—violate the Fourteenth Amendment guarantee of equal protection of laws?

"2. Whether Petitioners' criminal convictions for adult consensual sexual intimacy in the home violate their vital interests in liberty and privacy protected by the Due Process Clause of the Fourteenth Amendment?

"3. Whether Bowers v. Hardwick, 478 U.S. 186 (1986), should be overruled?"

The petitioners were adults at the time of the alleged offense. Their conduct was in private and consensual.

We conclude the case should be resolved by determining whether the petitioners were free as adults to engage in the private conduct in the exercise of their liberty under the Due Process Clause of the Fourteenth Amendment to the Constitution. For this inquiry we deem it necessary to reconsider the Court's holding in *Bowers*. . . .

. . .

The Court began its substantive discussion in *Bowers* as follows: "The issue presented is whether the Federal Constitution confers a fundamental right upon homosexuals to engage in sodomy and hence invalidates the laws of the many States that still make such conduct illegal and have done so for a very long time." That statement, we now conclude, discloses the Court's own failure to appreciate the extent of the liberty at stake. To say that the issue in *Bowers* was simply the right to engage in certain sexual conduct demeans the claim the individual put forward, just as it would demean a married couple were it to be said marriage is simply about the right to have sexual intercourse. The laws involved in *Bowers* and here are, to be sure, statutes that purport to do no more than prohibit a particular sexual act. Their penalties and purposes, though, have more far-reaching consequences, touching upon the most private human conduct, sexual behavior, and in the most private of places, the home. The statutes do seek to control a personal relationship that, whether or not entitled to formal recognition in the law, is within the liberty of persons to choose without being punished as criminals.

This, as a general rule, should counsel against attempts by the State, or a court, to define the meaning of the relationship or to set its boundaries absent injury to a person or abuse of an institution the law protects. It suffices for us to acknowledge that adults may choose to enter upon this relationship in the confines of their homes and their own private lives and still retain their dignity as free persons. When sexuality finds overt expression in intimate conduct with another person, the conduct can be but one element in a personal bond that is more enduring. The liberty protected by the Constitution allows homosexual persons the right to make this choice.

Having misapprehended the claim of liberty there presented to it, and thus stating the claim to be whether there is a fundamental right to engage in consensual sodomy, the *Bowers* Court said: "Proscriptions against that conduct have ancient roots." ... [T]he following considerations counsel against adopting the definitive conclusions upon which Bowers placed such reliance.

At the outset it should be noted that there is no longstanding history in this country of laws directed at homosexual conduct as a distinct matter. Beginning in colonial times there were prohibitions of sodomy derived from the English criminal laws passed in the first instance by the Reformation Parliament of 1533. The English prohibition was understood to include relations between men and women as well as relations between men and men. Nineteenth-century commentators similarly read American sodomy, buggery, and crime-against-nature statutes as criminalizing certain relations between men and women and between men and men.... Thus early American sodomy laws were not directed at homosexuals as such but instead sought to prohibit nonprocreative sexual activity more generally. This does not suggest approval of homosexual conduct. It does tend to show that this particular form of conduct was not thought of as a separate category from like conduct between heterosexual persons.

. . .

It was not until the 1970's that any State singled out same-sex relations for criminal prosecution, and only nine States have done so. Post-*Bowers* even some of these States did not adhere to the policy of suppressing homosexual conduct. Over the course of the last decades, States with same-sex prohibitions have moved toward abolishing them.

In summary, the historical grounds relied upon in *Bowers* are more complex than the majority opinion and the concurring opinion by Chief Justice Burger indicate. Their historical premises are not without doubt and, at the very least, are overstated.

It must be acknowledged, of course, that the Court in *Bowers* was making the broader point that for centuries there have been powerful voices to condemn homosexual conduct as immoral. The condemnation has been shaped by religious beliefs, conceptions of right and acceptable behavior, and respect for the traditional family. For many persons these are not trivial concerns but profound and deep convictions accepted as ethical and moral principles to which they aspire and which thus determine the course of their lives. These considerations do not answer the question before us, however. The issue is whether the majority may use the power of the State to enforce these views on the whole society through operation of the criminal law....

Chief Justice Burger joined the opinion for the Court in *Bowers* and further explained his views as follows: "Decisions of individuals relating to homosexual conduct have been subject to state intervention throughout the history of Western civilization. Condemnation of those practices is firmly rooted in Judeao–Christian moral and ethical standards." As with Justice White's assumptions about history, scholarship casts some doubt on the sweeping nature of the statement by Chief Justice Burger as it pertains to private homosexual conduct between consenting adults. In all events we think that our laws and traditions in the past half century are of most relevance here. These references show an emerging awareness that liberty gives substantial protection to adult persons in deciding how to conduct their private lives in matters pertaining to sex....

This emerging recognition should have been apparent when *Bowers* was decided. In 1955 the American Law Institute promulgated the Model Penal Code and made clear that it did not recommend or provide for "criminal penalties for consensual sexual relations conducted in private." ALA, Model Penal Code § 213.2, Comment 2, p. 372 (1980). It justified its decision on three grounds: (1) The prohibition undermined respect for the law by penalizing conduct many people engaged in; (2) the statutes regulated private conduct not harmful to others; and (3) the laws were arbitrarily enforced and thus invited the danger of blackmail ALI, Model Penal Code, Commentary 277–280 (Tent. Draft No. 4, 1955). In 1961 Illinois changed its laws to conform to the Model Penal Code. Other States soon followed.

. . .

The sweeping references by Chief Justice Burger to the history of Western civilization ... did not take account of other authorities pointing in an opposite direction. A committee advising the British Parliament recommended in 1957 repeal of laws punishing homosexual conduct. The Wolfenden Report: Report of the Committee on Homosexual Offenses and Prostitution (1963). Parliament enacted the substance of those recommendations 10 years later.

Of more importance, almost five years before *Bowers* was decided the European Court of Human Rights considered a case with parallels to *Bowers* and to today's case. An adult male resident in Northern Ireland alleged he was a practicing homosexual who desired to engage in consensual homosexual conduct. The laws of Northern Ireland forbade him that right. He alleged that he had been questioned, his home had been searched, and he feared criminal prosecution. The court held that the laws proscribing the conduct were invalid under the European Convention on Human Rights. Dudgeon v. United Kingdom, 45 Eur. Ct. H. R. (1981) ¶ 52 Authoritative in all countries that are members of the Council of Europe (21 nations then, 45 nations now) the decision is at odds with the premise in *Bowers* that the claim put forward was insubstantial in our Western civilization.

In our own constitutional system, the deficiencies in *Bowers* became even more apparent in the years following its announcement. The 25 States with laws prohibiting the relevant conduct referenced in the *Bowers* decision are reduced now to 13, of which 4 enforce their laws only against homosexual conduct. In those States where sodomy is still proscribed, whether for same-sex or heterosexual conduct, there is a pattern of nonenforcement with respect to consenting adults acting in private....

. . .

As an alternative argument in this case, counsel for the petitioners and some amici contend that [Romer v. Evans, 517 U.S. 620 (1996)] provides the basis for declaring the Texas statute invalid under the Equal Protection Clause. That is a tenable argument, but we conclude the instant case requires us to address whether Bowers itself has continuing validity. Were we to hold the statute invalid under the Equal Protection Clause some might question whether a prohibition would be valid if drawn differently, say, to prohibit the conduct both between same-sex and different-sex participants.

Equality of treatment and the due process right to demand respect for conduct protected by the substantive guarantee of liberty are linked in important respects, and a decision on the latter point advances both interests. If protected conduct is made criminal and the law which does so remains unexamined for its substantive validity, its stigma might remain even if it were not enforceable as drawn for equal protection reasons. When homosexual conduct is made criminal by the law of the State, that declaration in and of itself is an invitation to subject homosexual persons to discrimination both in the public and in the private spheres. The central holding of *Bowers* has been brought in question by this case, and it should be addressed. Its continuance as precedent demeans the lives of homosexual persons.

. . .

Bowers was not correct when it was decided, and it is not correct today. It ought not to remain binding precedent. Bowers v. Hardwick should be and now is overruled.

The present case does not involve minors. It does not involve persons who might be injured or coerced or who are situated in relationships where consent might not easily be refused. It does not involve public conduct or prostitution. It does not involve whether the government must give formal recognition to any relationship that homosexual persons seek to enter. The case does involve two adults who, with full and mutual consent from each other, engaged in sexual practices common to a homosexual lifestyle. The petitioners are entitled to respect for their private lives. The State cannot demean their existence or control their destiny by making their private sexual conduct a crime.... The Texas statute furthers no legitimate state interest which can justify its intrusion into the personal and private life of the individual.

■ JUSTICE O'CONNOR, concurring in the judgment:

The Court today overrules Bowers v. Hardwick. I joined *Bowers*, and do not join the Court in overruling it. Nevertheless, I agree with the Court that Texas' statute banning same-sex sodomy is unconstitutional. Rather than relying on the substantive component of the Fourteenth Amendment's Due Process Clause, as the Court does, I base my conclusion on the Fourteenth Amendment's Equal Protection Clause.

. . .

The statute at issue here makes sodomy a crime only if a person "engages in deviate sexual intercourse with another individual of the same sex." Tex. Penal Code Ann. § 21.06(a) (2003). Sodomy between opposite-sex partners, however, is not a crime in Texas. That is, Texas treats the same conduct differently based solely on the participants. Those harmed by this law are people who have a same-sex sexual orientation and thus are more likely to engage in behavior prohibited by § 21.06.

The Texas statute makes homosexuals unequal in the eyes of the law by making particular conduct—and only that conduct—subject to criminal sanction....

And the effect of Texas' sodomy law is not just limited to the threat of prosecution or consequence of conviction. Texas' sodomy law brands all homosexuals as criminals, thereby making it more difficult for homosexuals to be treated in the same manner as everyone else....

Texas attempts to justify its law, and the effects of the law, by arguing that the statute satisfies rational basis review because it furthers the legitimate governmental interest of the promotion of morality. In *Bowers*, we held that a state law criminalizing sodomy as applied to homosexual couples did not violate substantive due process. We rejected the argument that no rational basis existed to justify the law, pointing to the government's interest in promoting morality. The only question in front of the Court in *Bowers* was whether the substantive component of the Due Process Clause protected a right to engage in homosexual sodomy. *Bowers* did not hold that moral disapproval of a group is a rational basis under the Equal Protection Clause to criminalize homosexual sodomy when heterosexual sodomy is not punished.

This case raises a different issue than *Bowers*: whether, under the Equal Protection Clause, moral disapproval is a legitimate state interest to justify by itself a statute that bans homosexual sodomy, but not heterosexual sodomy. It is not. Moral disapproval of this group, like a bare desire to harm the group, is an interest that is insufficient to satisfy rational basis review under the Equal Protection Clause. Indeed, we have never held that moral disapproval, without any other asserted state interest, is a sufficient rationale under the Equal Protection Clause to justify a law that discriminates among groups of persons.

Moral disapproval of a group cannot be a legitimate governmental interest under the Equal Protection Clause because legal classifications must not be "drawn for the purpose of disadvantaging the group burdened." Texas' invocation of moral disapproval as a legitimate state interest proves nothing more than Texas' desire to criminalize homosexual sodomy. But the Equal Protection Clause prevents a State from creating "a classification of persons undertaken for its own sake." And because Texas so rarely enforces its sodomy law as applied to private, consensual acts, the law serves more as a statement of dislike and disapproval against homosexuals than as a tool to stop criminal behavior. The Texas sodomy law "raises the inevitable inference that the disadvantage imposed is born of animosity toward the class of persons affected."

. . .

A State can of course assign certain consequences to a violation of its criminal law. But the State cannot single out one identifiable class of citizens for punishment that does not apply to everyone else, with moral disapproval as the only asserted state interest for the law. The Texas sodomy statute subjects homosexuals to "a lifelong penalty and stigma. A legislative classification that threatens the creation of an underclass ... cannot be reconciled with" the Equal Protection Clause.

Whether a sodomy law that is neutral both in effect and application, would violate the substantive component of the Due Process Clause is an issue that need not be decided today. I am confident, however, that so long as the Equal Protection Clause requires a sodomy law to apply equally to the private consensual conduct of homosexuals and heterosexuals alike, such a law would not long stand in our democratic society....

That this law as applied to private, consensual conduct is unconstitutional under the Equal Protection Clause does not mean that other laws distinguishing between heterosexuals and homosexuals would similarly fail under rational basis review. Texas cannot assert any legitimate state interest here, such as national security or preserving the traditional institution of marriage. Unlike the moral disapproval of same-sex relations—the asserted state interest in this case—other reasons exist to promote the institution of marriage beyond mere moral disapproval of an excluded group.

A law branding one class of persons as criminal solely based on the State's moral disapproval of that class and the conduct associated with that class runs contrary to the values of the Constitution and the Equal Protection Clause, under any standard of review. I therefore concur in the Court's judgment that Texas' sodomy law banning "deviate sexual intercourse" between consenting adults of the same sex, but not between consenting adults of different sexes, is unconstitutional.

■ JUSTICE SCALIA, with whom THE CHIEF JUSTICE and JUSTICE THOMAS join, dissenting:

. . . .

I turn now to the ground on which the Court squarely rests its holding: the contention that there is no rational basis for the law here under attack. This proposition is so out of accord with our jurisprudence—indeed, with the jurisprudence of any society we know—that it requires little discussion.

The Texas statute undeniably seeks to further the belief of its citizens that certain forms of sexual behavior are "immoral and unacceptable,"—the same interest furthered by criminal laws against fornication, bigamy, adultery, adult incest, bestiality, and obscenity. *Bowers* held that this *was* a legitimate state interest. The Court today reaches the opposite conclusion. The Texas statute, it says, "furthers *no legitimate state interest* which can justify its intrusion into the personal and private life of the individual." ([E]mphasis added.) The Court embraces instead Justice Stevens' declaration in his Bowers dissent, that "the fact that the governing majority in a State has traditionally viewed a particular practice as immoral is not a sufficient reason for upholding a law prohibiting the practice." This effectively decrees the end of all morals legislation. If, as the Court asserts, the promotion of majoritarian sexual morality is not even a *legitimate* state interest, none of the above-mentioned laws can survive rational-basis review.

Finally, I turn to petitioners' equal-protection challenge, which no Member of the Court save Justice O'Connor embraces: On its face § 21.06(a) applies equally to all persons. Men and women, heterosexuals and homosexuals, are all subject to its prohibition of deviate sexual intercourse with someone of the same sex. To be sure, § 21.06 does distinguish between the sexes insofar as concerns the partner with whom the sexual acts are performed: men can violate the law only with other men, and women only with other women. But this cannot itself be a denial of equal protection, since it is precisely the same distinction regarding partner that is drawn in state laws prohibiting marriage with someone of the same sex while permitting marriage with someone of the opposite sex.

The objection is made, however, that the antimiscegenation laws invalidated in Loving v. Virginia, 388 U.S. 1 (1967), similarly were applicable to whites and blacks alike, and only distinguished between the races insofar as the *partner* was concerned. In *Loving*, however, we correctly applied heightened scrutiny, rather than the usual rational-basis review, because the Virginia statute was "designed to maintain White Supremacy." A racially discriminatory purpose is always sufficient to subject a law to strict scrutiny, even a facially neutral law that makes no mention of race. See Washington v. Davis, 426 U.S. 229 (1976). No purpose to discriminate against men or women as a class can be gleaned from the Texas law, so rational-basis review applies. That review is readily satisfied here by the same rational basis that satisfied it in *Bowers*—society's belief that certain forms of sexual behavior are "immoral and unacceptable," 478 U.S., at 196. This is the same justification that supports many other laws regulating sexual behavior that make a distinction based upon the identity of the partner—for example, laws against adultery, fornication, and adult incest, and laws refusing to recognize homosexual marriage.

Justice O'Connor argues that the discrimination in this law which must be justified is not its discrimination with regard to the sex of the partner but its discrimination with regard to the sexual proclivity of the principal actor.

> "While it is true that the law applies only to conduct, the conduct targeted by this law is conduct that is closely correlated with being homosexual. Under such circumstances, Texas' sodomy law is targeted at more than conduct. It is instead directed toward gay persons as a class."

Of course the same could be said of any law. A law against public nudity targets "the conduct that is closely correlated with being a nudist," and hence "is targeted at more than conduct"; it is "directed toward nudists as a class." But be that as it may. Even if the Texas law *does* deny equal protection to "homosexuals as a class," that denial *still* does not need to be justified by anything more than a rational basis, which our cases show is satisfied by the enforcement of traditional notions of sexual morality.

Justice O'Connor simply decrees application of "a more searching form of rational basis review" to the Texas statute. The cases she cites do not recognize such a standard, and reach their conclusions only after finding, as required by conventional rational-basis analysis, that no conceivable legitimate state interest supports the classification at issue. See Romer v. Evans, 517 U.S., at 635; Cleburne v. Cleburne Living Center, Inc., 473 U.S. 432, 448–450 (1985); Department of Agriculture v. Moreno, 413 U.S. 528, 534–538 (1973). Nor does Justice O'Connor explain precisely what her "more searching form" of rational-basis review consists of. It must at least mean, however, that laws exhibiting " 'a . . . desire to harm a politically unpopular group,' " are invalid *even though* there may be a conceivable rational basis to support them.

This reasoning leaves on pretty shaky grounds state laws limiting marriage to opposite-sex couples. Justice O'Connor seeks to preserve them by the conclusory statement that "preserving the traditional institution of marriage" is a legitimate state interest. But "preserving the traditional institution of marriage" is just a kinder way of describing the State's *moral disapproval* of same-sex couples. Texas's interest in § 21.06 could be recast in similarly euphemistic terms: "preserving the traditional sexual mores of our society." In the jurisprudence Justice O'Connor has seemingly created, judges can validate laws by characterizing them as "preserving the traditions of society" (good); or invalidate them by characterizing them as "expressing moral disapproval" (bad).

. . .

Let me be clear that I have nothing against homosexuals, or any other group, promoting their agenda through normal democratic means. Social perceptions of sexual and other morality change over time, and every group has the right to persuade its fellow citizens that its view of such matters is the best. That homosexuals have achieved some success in that enterprise is attested to by the fact that Texas is one of the few remaining States that criminalize private, consensual homosexual acts. But persuading one's fellow citizens is one thing, and imposing one's views in absence of democratic majority will is something else. I would no more require a State to criminalize homosexual acts—or, for that matter, display any moral disapprobation of them—than I would forbid it to do so. What Texas has chosen to do is well within the range of traditional democratic action, and its hand should not be stayed through the invention of a brand-new "constitutional right" by a Court that is impatient of democratic change. It is indeed true that "later generations can see that laws once thought necessary and proper in fact serve only to oppress," and when that happens, later generations can repeal those laws. But it is the premise of our system that those judgments are to be made by the people, and not imposed by a governing caste that knows best.

NOTE

Consider Pamela S. Karlan, Forward: Loving *Lawrence*, Colloquium: The Boundaries of Liberty after Lawrence v. Texas, 102 Mich. L. Rev. 1447, 1449–1450 (2004):

> *Loving* drew a clear distinction between rationality review and heightened scrutiny. *Lawrence*, by contrast, sidesteps this conventional doctrinal framework. *Loving* reflected the emergence of strict scrutiny under both the Equal Protection and the Due Process Clauses; *Lawrence*, however, does to due process analysis something very similar to what the Court's previous gay-rights decision, Romer v. Evans, did to equal protection analysis: it undermines the traditional tiers of scrutiny altogether. This approach reflects more than simply the fact that the two opinions share the same author. Both *Lawrence* and Romer v. Evans express an "analogical crisis." Gay rights cases "just can't be steered readily onto the strict scrutiny or the rationality track," let alone onto the due process/conduct or the equal protection/status track. Cases about race created the modern framework of heightened scrutiny; cases about sexual orientation may transform it.

Consider also Marc Spindelman, Surviving Lawrence v. Texas, 102 Mich. L. Rev. 1615, 1633–35 (2004);

> Anyone who is seriously dedicated to equality between the sexes has to acknowledge the historic breakthrough for lesbian and gay rights that *Lawrence* represents. The elimination of discrimination against lesbians and gay men, integral to sexual hierarchy and the positioning of men and women within it, is indispensable to sexual equality's realization. As an affirmation of lesbian and gay rights, then, sex-equality theorists have some reason to be pleased about Lawrence. I, for one, am.
>
> But there is more to the evaluation of a judicial text than a simple assessment of, or reaction to, its ostensible ends. Looking beyond what seems to be *Lawrence's* bottom line, its like-straight reasoning—especially its uncritical solicitude for heterosexuality, and the corresponding notion, reflected in its protection of a right to sexual intimacy, that heterosexuality is entitled to constitutional protections, in its intimacies above all—is cause for serious concern.
>
> To begin, empirical investigations into the conditions of sex inequality have demonstrated that heterosexuality is hardly as unproblematic as the Court's opinion in *Lawrence* may make it seem. These investigations have shown, for instance, that the institution of heterosexuality has largely been defined in male-supremacist terms—terms that include both the massive production and the massive denial of the sexual abuse and violence that women suffer at men's hands, along with the sexualized dimensions of the homophobic violence lesbians and gay men suffer at the hands of presumptively heterosexual men. The commonplace that sexual intimacy of the sort *Lawrence* approves should be heralded as the measure of non-violation has been uncovered as a myth, a way of ignoring and protecting the widespread abuses, including sexual assault, domestic violence, and sexual abuse of children, by more powerful partners in intimate relationships, typically, though not exclusively, men. When sexual intimacy is thought to be normatively good, the basis for relationships "more enduring," as it is in *Lawrence*, how can it (also) be a prison of abuse? Can it be? What about when, not if, in actuality, it is?

See generally Colloquium: The Boundaries of Liberty After Lawrence v. Texas, 102 Mich. L. Rev. 1447 (2004); Symposium: Gay Rights after Lawrence v. Texas, 88 Minn. L. Rev. 1017 (2004); Symposium: Equality, Privacy and Lesbian and Gay Rights after Lawrence v. Texas, 65 Ohio. St. L.J. 1057 (2004).

Roe v. Wade

Supreme Court of the United States, 1973.
410 U.S. 113, 93 S.Ct. 705, 35 L.Ed.2d 147.

■ JUSTICE BLACKMUN delivered the opinion of the Court.

This Texas federal appeal and its Georgia companion, Doe v. Bolton, present constitutional challenges to state criminal abortion legislation....

. . .

The Texas statutes that concern us here ... make it a crime to "procure an abortion," as therein defined, or to attempt one, except with respect to "an abortion procured or attempted by medical advice for the purpose of saving the life of the mother." Similar statutes are in existence in a majority of the States.

. . .

Three reasons have been advanced to explain historically the enactment of criminal abortion laws in the 19th century and to justify their continued existence.

It has been argued occasionally that these laws were the product of a Victorian social concern to discourage illicit sexual conduct. Texas, however, does not advance this justification in the present case....

A second reason is concerned with abortion as a medical procedure. When most criminal abortion laws were first enacted, the procedure was a hazardous one for the woman. This was particularly true prior to the development of antisepsis. Antiseptic techniques, of course, were based on discoveries by Lister, Pasteur, and others first announced in 1867, but were not generally accepted and employed until about the turn of the century. Abortion mortality was high. Even after 1900, and perhaps until as late as the development of antibiotics in the 1940's, standard modern techniques such as dilation and curettage were not nearly so safe as they are today. Thus it has been argued that a State's real concern in enacting a criminal abortion law was to protect the pregnant woman, that is, to restrain her from submitting to a procedure that placed her life in serious jeopardy.

Modern medical techniques have altered this situation. Appellants and various *amici* refer to medical data indicating that abortion in early pregnancy, that is, prior to the end of the first trimester, although not without its risk, is now relatively safe. Mortality rates for women undergoing early abortions, where the procedure is legal, appear to be as low as or lower than the rates for normal childbirth. ... Of course, important state interests in the area of health and medical standards do remain. The State has a legitimate interest in seeing to it that abortion, like any other medical procedure, is performed under circumstances that insure maximum safety for the patient. This interest obviously extends at least to the performing physician and his staff, to the facilities involved, to the availability of after-care, and to adequate provision for any complication or emergency that might arise. The prevalence of high mortality rates at illegal "abortion mills" strengthens, rather than weakens, the State's interest in regulating the conditions under which abortions are performed. Moreover, the risk to the woman increases as her pregnancy continues. Thus the State retains a definite interest in protecting the woman's own health and safety when an abortion is proposed at a late stage of pregnancy.

The third reason is the State's interest—some phrase it in terms of duty—in protecting prenatal life. Some of the argument for this justification rests on the theory that a new human life is present from the moment of conception. . . . In assessing the State's interest, recognition may be given to the less rigid claim that as long as at least *potential* life is involved, the State may assert interests beyond the protection of the pregnant woman alone.

. . .

The Constitution does not explicitly mention any right of privacy [but] the Court has recognized that a right of personal privacy, or a guarantee of certain areas or zones of privacy, does exist under the Constitution. . . .

. . .

This right of privacy, whether it be founded in the Fourteenth Amendment's concept of personal liberty and restrictions upon state action, as we feel it is, or, as the District Court determined, in the Ninth Amendment's reservation of rights to the people, is broad enough to encompass a woman's decision whether or not to terminate her pregnancy. The detriment that the State would impose upon the pregnant woman by denying this choice altogether is apparent. Specific and direct harm medically diagnosable even in early pregnancy may be involved. Maternity, or additional offspring, may force upon the woman a distressful life and future. Psychological harm may be imminent. Mental and physical health may be taxed by child care. There is also the distress, for all concerned, associated with the unwanted child, and there is the problem of bringing a child into a family already unable, psychologically and otherwise, to care for it. In other cases, as in this one, the additional difficulties and continuing stigma of unwed motherhood may be involved. All these are factors the woman and her responsible physician necessarily will consider in consultation.

On the basis of elements such as these, appellants and some *amici* argue that the woman's right is absolute and that she is entitled to terminate her pregnancy at whatever time, in whatever way, and for whatever reason she alone chooses. With this we do not agree. . . . The Court's decisions recognizing a right of privacy also acknowledge that some state regulation in areas protected by that right is appropriate. . . .

We therefore conclude that the right of personal privacy includes the abortion decision, but that this right is not unqualified and must be considered against important state interests in regulation.

. . .

The appellee and certain *amici* argue that the fetus is a "person" within the language and meaning of the Fourteenth Amendment. In support of this they outline at length and in detail the well-known facts of fetal development. If this suggestion of personhood is established, the appellant's case, of course, collapses, for the fetus' right to life is then guaranteed specifically by the Amendment. . . .

The Constitution does not define "person" in so many words. Section 1 of the Fourteenth Amendment contains three references to "person." The first, in defining "citizens," speaks of "persons born or naturalized in the

United States." The word also appears both in the Due Process Clause and in the Equal Protection Clause. "Person" is used in other places in the Constitution: in the listing of qualifications for representatives and senators. Art. I, § 2, cl. 2, and § 3, cl. 3; in the Apportionment Clause, Art. I, § 2, cl. 3; in the Migration and Importation provision, Art. I, § 9, cl. 1; in the Emolument Clause, Art. I, § 9, cl. 8; in the Electors provisions, Art. II, § 1, cl. 2, and the superseded cl. 3; in the provision outlining qualifications for the office of President, Art. II, § 1, cl. 5; in the Extradition provisions, Art. IV, § 2, cl. 2, and the superseded Fugitive Slave cl. 3; and in the Fifth, Twelfth, and Twenty-second Amendments as well as in §§ 2 and 3 of the Fourteenth Amendment. But in nearly all these instances, the use of the word is such that it has application only postnatally. None indicates, with any assurance, that it has any possible prenatal application.

All this, together with our observation that throughout the major portion of the 19th century prevailing legal abortion practices were far freer than they are today, persuades us that the word "person," as used in the Fourteenth Amendment, does not include the unborn....

. . .

The pregnant woman cannot be isolated in her privacy. She carries an embryo and, later, a fetus, if one accepts the medical definitions of the developing young in the human uterus. See Dorland's Illustrated Medical Dictionary, 478–479, 547 (24th ed. 1965). The situation therefore is inherently different from marital intimacy, or bedroom possession of obscene material, or marriage, or procreation, or education, with which *Eisenstadt, Griswold, Stanley, Loving, Skinner, Pierce,* and *Meyer* were respectively concerned. As we have intimated above, it is reasonable and appropriate for a State to decide that at some point in time another interest, that of health of the mother or that of potential human life, becomes significantly involved. . . .

Texas urges that, apart from the Fourteenth Amendment, life begins at conception and is present throughout pregnancy, and that, therefore, the State has a compelling interest in protecting that life from and after conception. We need not resolve the difficult question of when life begins. When those trained in the respective disciplines of medicine, philosophy, and theology are unable to arrive at any consensus, the judiciary, at this point in the development of man's knowledge, is not in a position to speculate as to the answer.

It should be sufficient to note briefly the wide divergence of thinking on this most sensitive and difficult question. There has always been strong support for the view that life does not begin until live birth. This was the belief of the Stoics. It appears to be the predominant, though not the unanimous, attitude of the Jewish faith. It may be taken to represent also the position of a large segment of the Protestant community, insofar as that can be ascertained; organized groups that have taken a formal position on the abortion issue have generally regarded abortion as a matter for the conscience of the individual and her family. As we have noted, the common law found greater significance in quickening. Physicians and their scientific colleagues have regarded that event with less interest and have tended to focus either upon conception or upon live birth or upon the interim point at which the fetus becomes "viable," that is, potentially able to live outside the mother's womb, albeit with artificial aid. Viability is usually placed at about seven months (28 weeks) but may occur earlier, even at 24 weeks. The Aristotelian theory of "mediate animation," that held sway throughout the

Middle Ages and the Renaissance in Europe, continued to be official Roman Catholic dogma until the 19th century, despite opposition to this "ensoulement" theory from those in the Church who would recognize the existence of life from the moment of conception. The latter is now, of course, the official belief of the Catholic Church. . . .

In areas other than criminal abortion [such as tort law and inheritance] the law has been reluctant to endorse any theory that life, as we recognize it, begins before live birth or to accord legal rights to the unborn except in narrowly defined situations and except when the rights are contingent upon live birth. . . .

In view of all this, we do not agree that, by adopting one theory of life, Texas may override the rights of the pregnant woman that are at stake. We repeat, however, that the State does have an important and legitimate interest in preserving and protecting the health of the pregnant woman, whether she be a resident of the State or a nonresident who seeks medical consultation and treatment there, and that it has still *another* important and legitimate interest in protecting the potentiality of human life. These interests are separate and distinct. Each grows in substantiality as the woman approaches term and, at a point during pregnancy, each becomes "compelling."

With respect to the State's important and legitimate interest in the health of the mother, the "compelling" point, in the light of present medical knowledge, is at approximately the end of the first trimester. This is so because of the now established medical fact that until the end of the first trimester mortality in abortion is less than mortality in normal childbirth. It follows that, from and after this point, a State may regulate the abortion procedure to the extent that the regulation reasonably relates to the preservation and protection of maternal health. Examples of permissible State regulation in this area are requirements as to the qualifications of the person who is to perform the abortion; as to the licensure of that person; as to the facility in which the procedure is to be performed, that is, whether it must be a hospital or may be a clinic or some other place of less-than-hospital status; as to the licensing of the facility; and the like.

This means, on the other hand, that, for the period of pregnancy prior to this "compelling" point, the attending physician, in consultation with his patient, is free to determine, without regulation by the State, that in his medical judgment the patient's pregnancy should be terminated. If that decision is reached, the judgment may be effectuated by an abortion free of interference by the State.

With respect to the State's important and legitimate interest in potential life, the "compelling" point is at viability. This is so because the fetus then presumably has the capability of meaningful life outside the mother's womb. State regulation protective of fetal life after viability thus has both logical and biological justifications. If the State is interested in protecting fetal life after viability, it may go so far as to proscribe abortion during that period except when it is necessary to preserve the life or health of the mother.

Measured against these standards, Art. 1196 of the Texas Penal Code, in restricting legal abortions to those "procured or attempted by medical advice for the purpose of saving the life of the mother," sweeps too broadly. The statute makes no distinction between abortions performed early in pregnancy and those performed later, and it limits to a single reason, "saving" the mother's life, the legal justification for the procedure. The statute, therefore, cannot survive the constitutional attack made upon it here.

. . .

To summarize and to repeat:

1. A state criminal abortion statute of the current Texas type, that excepts from criminality only a *life saving* procedure on behalf of the mother, without regard to pregnancy stage and without recognition of the other interests involved, is violative of the Due Process Clause of the Fourteenth Amendment.

(a) For the stage prior to approximately the end of the first trimester, the abortion decision and its effectuation must be left to the medical judgment of the pregnant woman's attending physician.

(b) For the stage subsequent to approximately the end of the first trimester, the State, in promoting its interest in the health of the mother, may, if it chooses, regulate the abortion procedure in ways that are reasonably related to maternal health.

(c) For the stage subsequent to viability the State, in promoting its interest in the potentiality of human life, may, if it chooses, regulate, and even proscribe, abortion except where it is necessary, in appropriate medical judgment, for the preservation of the life or health of the mother.

2. The State may define the term "physician," as it has been employed in the preceding numbered paragraphs of this Part XI of this opinion, to mean only a physician currently licensed by the State, and may proscribe any abortion by a person who is not a physician as so defined.

. . .

This holding, we feel, is consistent with the relative weights of the respective interests involved, with the lessons and example of medical and legal history, with the lenity of the common law, and with the demands of the profound problems of the present day. . . .

■ [CHIEF JUSTICE BURGER and JUSTICES DOUGLAS and STEWART each filed a concurring opinion. JUSTICES REHNQUIST and WHITE each filed a dissenting opinion.]

NOTES

1. Consider the alternative rationale for *Roe* set forth by Ruth Bader Ginsburg in Some Thoughts on Autonomy and Equality in Relation to Roe v. Wade, 63 N. Car. L. Rev. 375, 379–84 (1985):

> *Roe v. Wade,* in contrast to decisions involving explicit male/female classification, has occasioned searing criticism of the Court, over a decade of demonstrations, a stream of vituperative mail addressed to Justice Blackmun (the author of the opinion), annual proposals for overruling *Roe* by constitutional amendment, and a variety of measures in Congress and state legislatures to contain or curtail the decision. In 1973, when *Roe* issued, abortion law was in a state of change across the nation. There was a distinct trend in the states, noted by the Court, "toward liberalization of abortion statutes." Several states had adopted the American Law Institute's Model Penal Code approach setting out grounds on which abortion could be justified at any stage of pregnancy; most significantly, the Code included as a permissible ground preservation of the woman's physical

or mental health. Four states—New York, Washington, Alaska, and Hawaii—permitted physicians to perform first-trimester abortions with virtually no restrictions. This movement in legislative arenas bore some resemblance to the law revision activity that eventually swept through the states establishing no-fault divorce as the national pattern.

. . .

[I]n my judgment, *Roe* ventured too far in the change it ordered. The sweep and detail of the opinion stimulated the mobilization of a right-to-life movement and an attendant reaction in Congress and state legislatures. In place of the trend "toward liberalization of abortion statutes" noted in *Roe,* legislatures adopted measures aimed at minimizing the impact of the 1973 rulings, including notification and consent requirements, prescriptions for the protection of fetal life, and bans on public expenditures for poor women's abortions.

Professor Paul Freund explained where he thought the Court went astray in *Roe,* and I agree with his statement. The Court properly invalidated the Texas proscription, he indicated, because "[a] law that absolutely made criminal all kinds and forms of abortion could not stand up; it is not a reasonable accommodation of interests." If *Roe* had left off at that point and not adopted what Professor Freund called a "medical approach," physicians might have been less pleased with the decision, but the legislative trend might have continued in the direction in which it was headed in the early 1970s. "[S]ome of the bitter debate on the issue might have been averted," Professor Freund believed; "[t]he animus against the Court might at least have been diverted to the legislative halls." Overall, he thought that the *Roe* distinctions turning on trimesters and viability of the fetus illustrated a troublesome tendency of the modern Supreme Court under Chief Justices Burger and Warren "to specify by a kind of legislative code the one alternative pattern that will satisfy the Constitution."

... Academic criticism of *Roe,* charging the Court with reading its own values into the due process clause, might have been less pointed had the Court placed the woman alone, rather than the woman tied to her physician, at the center of its attention....

I do not pretend that, if the Court had added a distinct sex discrimination theme to its medically oriented opinion, the storm *Roe* generated would have been less furious. I appreciate the intense divisions of opinion on the moral question and recognize that abortion today cannot fairly be described as nothing more than birth control delayed. The conflict, however, is not simply one between a fetus' interests and a woman's interests, narrowly conceived, nor is the overriding issue state versus private control of a woman's body for a span of nine months. Also in the balance is a woman's autonomous charge of her full life's course—as Professor Karst put it [Foreward, Equal Citizenship Under the Fourteenth Amendment, 91 Harv. L. Rev. 1, 57–59 (1977)], her ability to stand in relation to man, society, and the state as an independent self sustaining, equal citizen.

2. In Planned Parenthood of Central Missouri v. Danforth, 428 U.S. 52 (1976), the Court, in an opinion by Justice Blackmun, held unconstitutional a requirement that the father must consent to any abortion, explaining:

> We recognize, of course, that when a woman, with the approval of her physician but without the approval of her husband, decides to terminate her pregnancy, it could be said that she is acting unilaterally. The obvious fact is that when the wife and the husband disagree on this decision, the view of only one of the two marriage partners can prevail. Since it is the woman who physically bears the child and who is more directly and immediately affected by the pregnancy, as between the two, the balance weighs in her favor.

Id. at 71.

Planned Parenthood v. Casey

Supreme Court of the United States, 1992.
505 U.S. 833, 112 S.Ct. 2791, 120 L.Ed.2d 674.

■ JUSTICE O'CONNOR, JUSTICE KENNEDY and JUSTICE SOUTER announced the judgment of the Court and delivered the opinion of the Court with respect to Parts I, II, III, V–A, V–C, and VI, an opinion with respect to Part V–E, in which JUSTICE STEVENS joins, and an opinion with respect to Parts IV, V–B, and V–D.

[This suit challenged five provisions of the Pennsylvania Abortion Control Act of 1982 on their face: § 3205, which requires that a woman seeking an abortion give her informed consent prior to the abortion procedure, and specifies that she be provided with certain information at least 24 hours before the abortion is performed; § 3206, which mandates the informed consent of one parent for a minor to obtain an abortion but provides for a judicial bypass option if the minor does not wish to or cannot obtain a parent's consent; § 3209, which requires that, unless certain exceptions apply, a married woman seeking an abortion must sign a statement indicating that she has notified her husband of her intended abortion; § 3203, which defines a "medical emergency" that will excuse compliance with the foregoing requirements; and §§ 3207(b), 3214(a), and 3214(f), which impose certain reporting requirements on facilities that provide abortion services. The trial court held all the provisions unconstitutional. The appeals court struck down the husband notification provision but upheld the others.]

I

Liberty finds no refuge in a jurisprudence of doubt. Yet 19 years after our holding that the Constitution protects a woman's right to terminate her pregnancy in its early stages, Roe v. Wade, 410 U.S. 113 (1973), that definition of liberty is still questioned. Joining the respondents as *amicus curiae*, the United States, as it has done in five other cases in the last decade, again asks us to overrule *Roe*. . . .

. . .

After considering the fundamental constitutional questions resolved by *Roe*, principles of institutional integrity, and the rule of *stare decisis*, we are led to conclude this: the essential holding of Roe v. Wade should be retained and once again reaffirmed.

It must be stated at the outset and with clarity that *Roe*'s essential holding, the holding we reaffirm, has three parts. First is a recognition of the right of the woman to choose to have an abortion before viability and to obtain it without undue interference from the State. Before viability, the State's interests are not strong enough to support a prohibition of abortion or the imposition of a substantial obstacle to the woman's effective right to elect the procedure. Second is a confirmation of the State's power to restrict abortions after fetal viability, if the law contains exceptions for pregnancies which endanger a woman's life or health. And third is the principle that the State has legitimate interests from the outset of the pregnancy in protecting the health of the woman and the life of the fetus that may become a child. These principles do not contradict one another; and we adhere to each.

II

Constitutional protection of the woman's decision to terminate her pregnancy derives from the Due Process Clause of the Fourteenth Amendment. . . .

It is also tempting ... to suppose that the Due Process Clause protects only those practices, defined at the most specific level, that were protected against government interference by other rules of law when the Fourteenth Amendment was ratified. See Michael H. v. Gerald D., 491 U.S. 110, 127–128, n.6 (1989) (opinion of SCALIA, J.). But such a view would be inconsistent with our law. It is a promise of the Constitution that there is a realm of personal liberty which the government may not enter. We have vindicated this principle before. Marriage is mentioned nowhere in the Bill of Rights and interracial marriage was illegal in most States in the 19th century, but the Court was no doubt correct in finding it to be an aspect of liberty protected against state interference by the substantive component of the Due Process Clause in Loving v. Virginia, 388 U.S. 1, 12 (1967) (relying, in an opinion for eight Justices, on the Due Process Clause). ...

Neither the Bill of Rights nor the specific practices of States at the time of the adoption of the Fourteenth Amendment marks the outer limits of the substantive sphere of liberty which the Fourteenth Amendment protects. ...

Men and women of good conscience can disagree, and we suppose some always shall disagree, about the profound moral and spiritual implications of terminating a pregnancy, even in its earliest stage. Some of us as individuals find abortion offensive to our most basic principles of morality, but that cannot control our decision. Our obligation is to define the liberty of all, not to mandate our own moral code. The underlying constitutional issue is whether the State can resolve these philosophic questions in such a definitive way that a woman lacks all choice in the matter, except perhaps in those rare circumstances in which the pregnancy is itself a danger to her own life or health, or is the result of rape or incest.

. . .

These considerations begin our analysis of the woman's interest in terminating her pregnancy but cannot end it, for this reason: though the abortion decision may originate within the zone of conscience and belief, it is more than a philosophic exercise. Abortion is a unique act. It is an act fraught with consequences for others: for the woman who must live with the implications of her decision; for the persons who perform and assist in the procedure; for the spouse, family, and society which must confront the knowledge that these procedures exist, procedures some deem nothing short of an act of violence against innocent human life; and, depending on one's beliefs, for the life or potential life that is aborted. Though abortion is conduct, it does not follow that the State is entitled to proscribe it in all instances. That is because the liberty of the woman is at stake in a sense unique to the human condition and so unique to the law. The mother who carries a child to full term is subject to anxieties, to physical constraints, to pain that only she must bear. That these sacrifices have from the beginning of the human race been endured by woman with a pride that ennobles her in the eyes of others and gives to the infant a bond of love cannot alone be grounds for the State to insist she make the sacrifice. Her suffering is too intimate and personal for the State to insist, without more, upon its own vision of the woman's role, however dominant that vision has been in the course of our history and our culture. The destiny of the woman must be shaped to a large extent on her own conception of her spiritual imperatives and her place in society.

It should be recognized, moreover, that in some critical respects the abortion decision is of the same character as the decision to use contraception, to which Griswold v. Connecticut, Eisenstadt v. Baird, and Carey v.

Population Services International, afford constitutional protection. We have no doubt as to the correctness of those decisions. . . .

III

. . .

Although *Roe* has engendered opposition, it has in no sense proven "unworkable," representing as it does a simple limitation beyond which a state law is unenforceable.

. . .

No evolution of legal principle has left *Roe's* doctrinal footings weaker than they were in 1973. No development of constitutional law since the case was decided has implicitly or explicitly left *Roe* behind as a mere survivor of obsolete constitutional thinking.

It will be recognized, of course, that *Roe* stands at an intersection of two lines of decisions, but in whichever doctrinal category one reads the case, the result for present purposes will be the same. The *Roe* Court itself placed its holding in the succession of cases most prominently exemplified by Griswold v. Connecticut, 381 U.S. 479 (1965). When it is so seen, *Roe* is clearly in no jeopardy, since subsequent constitutional developments have neither disturbed, nor do they threaten to diminish, the scope of recognized protection accorded to the liberty relating to intimate relationships, the family, and decisions about whether or not to beget or bear a child. See, *e.g.*, Carey v. Population Services International, 431 U.S. 678 (1977); Moore v. East Cleveland, 431 U.S. 494 (1977).

Roe, however, may be seen not only as an exemplar of *Griswold* liberty but as a rule (whether or not mistaken) of personal autonomy and bodily integrity, with doctrinal affinity to cases recognizing limits on governmental power to mandate medical treatment or to bar its rejection. If so, our cases since *Roe* accord with *Roe's* view that a State's interest in the protection of life falls short of justifying any plenary override of individual liberty claims. Cruzan v. Director, Mo. Dept. of Health, 497 U.S. 261, 278 (1990); cf., *e.g.*, Riggins v. Nevada, 504 U.S. 127 (1992); Washington v. Harper, 494 U.S. 210 (1990); see also, *e.g.*, Rochin v. California, 342 U.S. 165 (1952); Jacobson v. Massachusetts, 197 U.S. 11 (1905).

. . .

Finally, one could classify *Roe* as *sui generis*. If the case is so viewed, then there clearly has been no erosion of its central determination. . . .

. . .

We have seen how time has overtaken some of *Roe's* factual assumptions: advances in maternal health care allow for abortions safe to the mother later in pregnancy than was true in 1973 and advances in neonatal care have advanced viability to a point somewhat earlier. But these facts go only to the scheme of time limits on the realization of competing interests, and the divergences from the factual premises of 1973 have no bearing on the validity of *Roe's* central holding, that viability marks the earliest point at which the State's interest in fetal life is constitutionally adequate to justify a legislative ban on nontherapeutic abortions. The soundness or unsoundness of that constitutional judgment in no sense turns on whether viability occurs at approximately 28 weeks, as was usual at the time of *Roe*, at 23 to 24 weeks, as it sometimes does today, or at some moment even slightly earlier in pregnancy, as it may if fetal respiratory capacity can somehow be enhanced in the future. Whenever it may occur, the attainment of viability may continue to serve as the critical fact, just as it has done since *Roe* was decided; which is to say that no change in *Roe's* factual underpinning has left its central holding obsolete, and none supports an argument for overruling it.

The sum of the precedential enquiry to this point shows *Roe's* underpinnings unweakened in any way affecting its central holding. While it has engendered disapproval, it has not been unworkable. An entire generation has come of age free to assume *Roe's* concept of liberty in defining the capacity of women to act in society, and to make reproductive decisions; no erosion of principle going to liberty or personal autonomy has left *Roe's* central holding a doctrinal remnant; *Roe* portends no developments at odds with other precedent for the analysis of personal liberty; and no changes of fact have rendered viability more or less appropriate as the point at which the balance of interests tips. Within the bounds of normal *stare decisis* analysis, then, and subject to the considerations on which it customarily turns, the stronger argument is for affirming *Roe's* central holding, with whatever degree of personal reluctance any of us may have, not for overruling it.

In a less significant case, *stare decisis* analysis could, and would, stop at the point we have reached. But the sustained and widespread debate *Roe* has provoked calls for some comparison between that case and others of comparable dimension that have responded to national controversies and taken on the impress of the controversies addressed. Only two such decisional lines from the past century present themselves for examination, and in each instance the result reached by the Court accorded with the principles we apply today.

The first example is that line of cases identified with Lochner v. New York, 198 U.S. 45(1905), which imposed substantive limitations on legislation limiting economic autonomy in favor of health and welfare regulation, adopting, in Justice Holmes's view, the theory of laissez-faire. . . . The *Lochner* decisions were exemplified by Adkins v. Children's Hospital of District of Columbia, 261 U.S. 525 (1923), in which this Court held it to be an infringement of constitutionally protected liberty of contract to require the employers of adult women to satisfy minimum wage standards. Fourteen years later, West Coast Hotel Co. v. Parrish, 300 U.S. 379 (1937), signaled the demise of *Lochner* by overruling *Adkins*. In the meantime, the Depression had come and, with it, the lesson that seemed unmistakable to most people by 1937, that the interpretation of contractual freedom protected in *Adkins* rested on fundamentally false factual assumptions about the capacity of a relatively unregulated market to satisfy minimal levels of human welfare. As Justice Jackson wrote of the constitutional crisis of 1937 shortly before he came on the bench: "The older world of *laissez faire* was recognized everywhere outside the Court to be dead." The Struggle for Judicial Supremacy 85 (1941). The facts upon which the earlier case had premised a constitutional resolution of social controversy had proven to be untrue, and history's demonstration of their untruth not only justified but required the new choice of constitutional principle that *West Coast Hotel* announced. Of course, it was true that the Court lost something by its misperception, or its lack of prescience, and the Court-packing crisis only magnified the loss; but the clear demonstration that the facts of economic life were different from those previously assumed warranted the repudiation of the old law.

The second comparison that 20th century history invites is with the cases employing the separate-but-equal rule for applying the Fourteenth Amendment's equal protection guarantee. They began with Plessy v. Ferguson, 163 U.S. 537 (1896), holding that legislatively mandated racial segregation in public transportation works no denial of equal protection, rejecting the argument that racial separation enforced by the legal machinery of American society treats the black race as inferior. The *Plessy* Court considered "the underlying fallacy of the plaintiff's argument to consist in the assumption that the enforced separation of the two races stamps the colored race with a badge of inferiority. If this be so, it is not by reason of anything found in the act, but solely because the colored race chooses to put that construction upon it." Whether, as a matter of historical fact, the Justices in the *Plessy* majority believed this or not, this understanding of the implication of segregation was the stated justification for the Court's opinion. But this understanding of the facts and the rule it was stated to justify were repudiated in Brown v. Board of Education, 347 U.S. 483 (1954) (Brown I). As one commentator observed, the question before the Court in *Brown* was "whether discrimination inheres in that segregation which is imposed by law in the twentieth century in certain specific states in the American Union. And that question has meaning and can find an answer only on the ground of history and of common knowledge about the facts of life in the times and places aforesaid." Black, The Lawfulness of the Segregation Decisions, 69 Yale L. J. 421, 427 (1960).

The Court in *Brown* addressed these facts of life by observing that whatever may have been the understanding in *Plessy's* time of the power of segregation to stigmatize those who were segregated with a "badge of inferiority," it was clear by 1954 that legally sanctioned segregation had just such an effect, to the point that racially separate public educational facilities were deemed inherently unequal. Society's understanding of the facts upon which a constitutional ruling was sought in 1954 was thus fundamentally different from the basis claimed for the decision in 1896. While we think *Plessy* was wrong the day it was decided, we must also recognize that the *Plessy* Court's explanation for its decision was so clearly at odds with the facts apparent to the Court in 1954 that the decision to reexamine *Plessy* was on this ground alone not only justified but required.

West Coast Hotel and *Brown* each rested on facts, or an understanding of facts, changed from those which furnished the claimed justifications for the earlier constitutional resolutions. Each case was comprehensible as the Court's response to facts that the country could understand, or had come to understand already, but which the Court of an earlier day, as its own declarations disclosed, had not been able to perceive. As the decisions were thus comprehensible they were also defensible, not merely as the victories of one doctrinal school over another by dint of numbers (victories though they were), but as applications of constitutional principle to facts as they had not been seen by the Court before. In constitutional adjudication as elsewhere in life, changed circumstances may impose new obligations, and the thoughtful part of the Nation could accept each decision to overrule a prior case as a response to the Court's constitutional duty.

Because the cases before us present no such occasion it could be seen as no such response. Because neither the factual underpinnings of *Roe's* central holding nor our understanding of it has changed (and because no other indication of weakened precedent has been shown), the Court could not pretend to be reexamining the prior law with any justification beyond a present doctrinal disposition to come out differently from the Court of 1973. To overrule prior law for no other reason than that would run counter to the view repeated in our cases, that a decision to overrule should rest on

No overruling for Roe

some special reason over and above the belief that a prior case was wrongly decided. . . .

The examination of the conditions justifying the repudiation of *Adkins* by *West Coast Hotel* and *Plessy* by *Brown* is enough to suggest the terrible price that would have been paid if the Court had not overruled as it did. In the present cases, however, as our analysis to this point makes clear, the terrible price would be paid for overruling. Our analysis would not be complete, however, without explaining why overruling *Roe's* central holding would not only reach an unjustifiable result under principles of *stare decisis*, but would seriously weaken the Court's capacity to exercise the judicial power and to function as the Supreme Court of a Nation dedicated to the rule of law. . . .

The root of American governmental power is revealed most clearly in the instance of the power conferred by the Constitution upon the Judiciary of the United States and specifically upon this Court. As Americans of each succeeding generation are rightly told, the Court cannot buy support for its decisions by spending money and, except to a minor degree, it cannot independently coerce obedience to its decrees. The Court's power lies, rather, in its legitimacy, a product of substance and perception that shows itself in the people's acceptance of the Judiciary as fit to determine what the Nation's law means and to declare what it demands.

. . .

. . . Where, in the performance of its judicial duties, the Court decides a case in such a way as to resolve the sort of intensely divisive controversy reflected in *Roe* and those rare, comparable cases, its decision has a dimension that the resolution of the normal case does not carry. It is the dimension present whenever the Court's interpretation of the Constitution calls the contending sides of a national controversy to end their national division by accepting a common mandate rooted in the Constitution.

The Court is not asked to do this very often, having thus addressed the Nation only twice in our lifetime, in the decisions of *Brown* and *Roe*. But when the Court does act in this way, its decision requires an equally rare precedential force to counter the inevitable efforts to overturn it and to thwart its implementation. Some of those efforts may be mere unprincipled emotional reactions; others may proceed from principles worthy of profound respect. But whatever the premises of opposition may be, only the most convincing justification under accepted standards of precedent could suffice to demonstrate that a later decision overruling the first was anything but a surrender to political pressure, and an unjustified repudiation of the principle on which the Court staked its authority in the first instance. So to overrule under fire in the absence of the most compelling reason to reexamine a watershed decision would subvert the Court's legitimacy beyond any serious question. . . .

. . .

. . . A decision to overrule *Roe's* essential holding under the existing circumstances would address error, if error there was, at the cost of both profound and unnecessary damage to the Court's legitimacy, and to the Nation's commitment to the rule of law. It is therefore imperative to adhere to the essence of *Roe's* original decision, and we do so today.

IV

. . . We conclude that the basic decision in *Roe* was based on a constitutional analysis which we cannot now repudiate. The woman's liberty is not so unlimited, however, that from the outset the State cannot show its concern for the life of the unborn, and at a later point in fetal development the State's interest in life has sufficient force so that the right of the woman to terminate the pregnancy can be restricted.

. . .

We conclude the line should be drawn at viability, so that before that time the woman has a right to choose to terminate her pregnancy. We adhere to this principle for two reasons. First, as we have said, is the doctrine of *stare decisis*. . . . The second reason is that the concept of viability, as we noted in *Roe*, is the time at which there is a realistic possibility of maintaining and nourishing a life outside the womb, so that the independent existence of the second life can in reason and all fairness be the object of state protection that now overrides the rights of the woman. . . .

The woman's right to terminate her pregnancy before viability is the most central principle of Roe v. Wade. It is a rule of law and a component of liberty we cannot renounce.

On the other side of the equation is the interest of the State in the protection of potential life. . . .

. . . [I]t must be remembered that Roe v. Wade speaks with clarity in establishing not only the woman's liberty but also the State's "important and legitimate interest in potential life." That portion of the decision in *Roe* has been given too little acknowledgement and implementation by the Court in its subsequent cases. . . .

We reject the trimester framework, which we do not consider to be part of the essential holding of *Roe*. Measures aimed at ensuring that a woman's choice contemplates the consequences for the fetus do not necessarily interfere with the right recognized in *Roe*, although those measures have been found to be inconsistent with the rigid trimester framework announced in that case. A logical reading of the central holding in *Roe* itself, and a necessary reconciliation of the liberty of the woman and the interest of the State in promoting prenatal life, require, in our view, that we abandon the trimester framework as a rigid prohibition on all previability regulation aimed at the protection of fetal life. The trimester framework suffers from these basic flaws: in its formulation it misconceives the nature of the pregnant woman's interest; and in practice it undervalues the State's interest in potential life, as recognized in *Roe*.

As our jurisprudence relating to all liberties save perhaps abortion has recognized, not every law which makes a right more difficult to exercise is, *ipso facto*, an infringement of that right. . . .

. . . Not all governmental intrusion is of necessity unwarranted; and that brings us to the other basic flaw in the trimester framework: even in *Roe*'s terms, in practice it undervalues the State's interest in the potential life within the woman.

. . . *Not all burdens on the right to decide whether to terminate a pregnancy will be undue. In our view, the undue burden standard is the appropriate means of reconciling the State's interest with the woman's constitutionally protected liberty.*

. . .

A finding of an undue burden is shorthand for the conclusion that a state regulation has the purpose or effect of placing a substantial obstacle in the path of a woman seeking an abortion of a nonviable fetus. A statute with this purpose is invalid because the means chosen by the State to further the interest in potential life must be calculated to inform the woman's free choice, not hinder it. And a statute which, while furthering the interest in potential life or some other valid state interest, has the effect of placing a substantial obstacle in the path of a woman's choice cannot be considered a permissible means of serving its legitimate ends. ... Understood another way, we answer the question, left open in previous opinions discussing the undue burden formulation, whether a law designed to further the State's interest in fetal life which imposes an undue burden on the woman's decision before fetal viability could be constitutional. The answer is no.

Some guiding principles should emerge. What is at stake is the woman's right to make the ultimate decision, not a right to be insulated from all others in doing so. Regulations which do no more than create a structural mechanism by which the State, or the parent or guardian of a minor, may express profound respect for the life of the unborn are permitted, if they are not a substantial obstacle to the woman's exercise of the right to choose. Unless it has that effect on her right of choice, a state measure designed to persuade her to choose childbirth over abortion will be upheld if reasonably related to that goal. Regulations designed to foster the health of a woman seeking an abortion are valid if they do not constitute an undue burden.

Even when jurists reason from shared premises, some disagreement is inevitable. That is to be expected in the application of any legal standard which must accommodate life's complexity. We do not expect it to be otherwise with respect to the undue burden standard. We give this summary:

(a) To protect the central right recognized by Roe v. Wade while at the same time accommodating the State's profound interest in potential life, we will employ the undue burden analysis as explained in this opinion. An undue burden exists, and therefore a provision of law is invalid, if its purpose or effect is to place a substantial obstacle in the path of a woman seeking an abortion before the fetus attains viability.

(b) We reject the rigid trimester framework of Roe v. Wade. To promote the State's profound interest in potential life, throughout pregnancy the State may take measures to ensure that the woman's choice is informed, and measures designed to advance this interest will not be invalidated as long as their purpose is to persuade the woman to choose childbirth over abortion. These measures must not be an undue burden on the right.

(c) As with any medical procedure, the State may enact regulations to further the health or safety of a woman seeking an abortion. Unnecessary health regulations that have the purpose or effect of presenting a substantial obstacle to a woman seeking an abortion impose an undue burden on the right.

(d) Our adoption of the undue burden analysis does not disturb the central holding of Roe v. Wade, and we reaffirm that holding. Regardless of whether exceptions are made for particular circumstances, a State may not prohibit any woman from making the ultimate decision to terminate her pregnancy before viability.

(e) We also reaffirm *Roe*'s holding that "subsequent to viability, the State in promoting its interest in the potentiality of human life may, if it chooses, regulate, and even proscribe, abortion except where it is necessary, in appropriate medical judgment, for the preservation of the life or health of the mother." Roe v. Wade, 410 U.S., at 164–165.

These principles control our assessment of the Pennsylvania statute, and we now turn to the issue of the validity of its challenged provisions.

V

. . .

A

Because it is central to the operation of various other requirements, we begin with the statute's definition of medical emergency. Under the statute, a medical emergency is

> "[t]hat condition which, on the basis of the physician's good faith clinical judgment, so complicates the medical condition of a pregnant woman as to necessitate the immediate abortion of her pregnancy to avert her death or for which a delay will create serious risk of substantial and irreversible impairment of a major bodily function." 18 Pa.Cons.Stat. (1990). § 3203.

Petitioners argue that the definition is too narrow, contending that it forecloses the possibility of an immediate abortion despite some significant health risks. If the contention were correct, we would be required to invalidate the restrictive operation of the provision, for the essential holding of *Roe* forbids a State from interfering with a woman's choice to undergo an abortion procedure if continuing her pregnancy would constitute a threat to her health.

The District Court found that there were three serious conditions which would not be covered by the statute: preeclampsia, inevitable abortion, and premature ruptured membrane. Yet, as the Court of Appeals observed, it is undisputed that under some circumstances each of these conditions could lead to an illness with substantial and irreversible consequences. While the definition could be interpreted in an unconstitutional manner, the Court of Appeals construed the phrase "serious risk" to include those circumstances. It stated: "we read the medical emergency exception as intended by the Pennsylvania legislature to assure that compliance with its abortion regulations would not in any way pose a significant threat to the life or health of a woman." . . . [W]e have said that we will defer to lower court interpretations of state law unless they amount to "plain" error. . . . We adhere to that course today, and conclude that, as construed by the Court of Appeals, the medical emergency definition imposes no undue burden on a woman's abortion right.

B

We next consider the informed consent requirement. Except in a medical emergency, the statute requires that at least 24 hours before performing an abortion a physician inform the woman of the nature of the procedure, the health risks of the abortion and of childbirth, and the "probable gestational age of the unborn child." The physician or a qualified nonphysician must inform the woman of the availability of printed materials published by the State describing the fetus and providing information about medical assistance for childbirth, information about child support from the father, and a list of agencies which provide adoption and other services as alternatives to abortion. An abortion may not be performed unless the woman certifies in writing that she has been informed of the availability of these printed materials and has been provided them if she chooses to view them.

Our prior decisions establish that as with any medical procedure, the State may require a woman to give her written informed consent to an abortion. In this respect, the statute is unexceptional. Petitioners challenge the statute's definition of informed consent because it includes the provision of specific information by the doctor and the mandatory 24-hour waiting period. The conclusions reached by a majority of the Justices in the separate opinions filed today and the undue burden standard adopted in this opinion require us to overrule in part some of the Court's past decisions, decisions driven by the trimester framework's prohibition of all previability regulations designed to further the State's interest in fetal life.

In *Akron I, 462 U.S. 416 (1983),* we invalidated an ordinance which required that a woman seeking an abortion be provided by her physician with specific information "designed to influence the woman's informed choice between abortion or childbirth." *Id., at 444.* As we later described the *Akron I* holding in Thornburgh v. American College of Obstetricians and Gynecologists, 476 U.S. at 762, there were two purported flaws in the Akron ordinance: the information was designed to dissuade the woman from having an abortion and the ordinance imposed "a rigid requirement that a specific body of information be given in all cases, irrespective of the particular needs of the patient. . . ." *Ibid.*

To the extent *Akron I* and *Thornburgh* find a constitutional violation when the government requires, as it does here, the giving of truthful, nonmisleading information about the nature of the procedure, the attendant health risks and those of childbirth, and the "probable gestational age" of the fetus, those cases go too far, are inconsistent with *Roe's* acknowledgment of an important interest in potential life, and are overruled. [We have recognized] a substantial government interest justifying a requirement that a woman be apprised of the health risks of abortion and childbirth. It cannot be questioned that psychological well-being is a facet of health. Nor can it be doubted that most women considering an abortion would deem the impact on the fetus relevant, if not dispositive, to the decision. In attempting to ensure that a woman apprehend the full consequences of her decision, the State furthers the legitimate purpose of reducing the risk that a woman may elect an abortion, only to discover later, with devastating psychological consequences, that her decision was not fully informed. If the information the State requires to be made available to the woman is truthful and not misleading, the requirement may be permissible.

We also see no reason why the State may not require doctors to inform a woman seeking an abortion of the availability of materials relating to the consequences to the fetus, even when those consequences have no direct relation to her health. . . . We conclude . . . that informed choice need not be defined in such narrow terms that all considerations of the effect on the fetus are made irrelevant. As we have made clear, we depart from the holdings of *Akron I* and *Thornburgh* to the extent that we permit a State to further its legitimate goal of protecting the life of the unborn by enacting legislation aimed at ensuring a decision that is mature and informed, even when in so doing the State expresses a preference for childbirth over abortion. In short, requiring that the woman be informed of the availability of information relating to fetal development and the assistance available should she decide to carry the pregnancy to full term is a reasonable measure to ensure an informed choice, one which might cause the woman to choose childbirth over abortion. This requirement cannot be considered a substantial obstacle to obtaining an abortion, and, it follows, there is no undue burden.

. . .

Our analysis of Pennsylvania's 24–hour waiting period between the provision of the information deemed necessary to informed consent and the performance of an abortion under the undue burden standard requires us to reconsider the premise behind the decision in *Akron I* invalidating a parallel requirement. In *Akron I* we said: "Nor are we convinced that the State's legitimate concern that the woman's decision be informed is reasonably served by requiring a 24–hour delay as a matter of course." We consider that conclusion to be wrong. The idea that important decisions will be more informed and deliberate if they follow some period of reflection does not strike us as unreasonable, particularly where the statute directs that important information become part of the background of the decision. The statute, as construed by the Court of Appeals, permits avoidance of the waiting period in the event of a medical emergency and the record evidence shows that in the vast majority of cases, a 24–hour delay does not create any appreciable health risk. In theory, at least, the waiting period is a reasonable measure to implement the State's interest in protecting the life of the unborn, a measure that does not amount to an undue burden.

Whether the mandatory 24–hour waiting period is nonetheless invalid because in practice it is a substantial obstacle to a woman's choice to terminate her pregnancy is a closer question. The findings of fact by the District Court indicate that because of the distances many women must travel to reach an abortion provider, the practical effect will often be a delay of much more than a day because the waiting period requires that a woman seeking an abortion make at least two visits to the doctor. The District Court also found that in many instances this will increase the exposure of women seeking abortions to "the harassment and hostility of anti-abortion protestors demonstrating outside a clinic." As a result, the District Court found that for those women who have the fewest financial resources, those who must travel long distances, and those who have difficulty explaining their whereabouts to husbands, employers, or others, the 24–hour waiting period will be "particularly burdensome."

These findings are troubling in some respects, but they do not demonstrate that the waiting period constitutes an undue burden. We do not doubt that, as the District Court held, the waiting period has the effect of "increasing the cost and risk of delay of abortions," but the District Court did not conclude that the increased costs and potential delays amount to substantial obstacles. Rather, applying the trimester framework's strict prohibition of all regulation designed to promote the State's interest in potential life before viability, the District Court concluded that the waiting period does not further the State "interest in maternal health" and "infringes the physician's discretion to exercise sound medical judgment." Yet, as we have stated, under the undue burden standard a State is permitted to enact persuasive measures which favor childbirth over abortion, even if those measures do not further a health interest. And while the waiting period does limit a physician's discretion, that is not, standing alone, a reason to invalidate it. In light of the construction given the statute's definition of medical emergency by the Court of Appeals, and the District Court's findings, we cannot say that the waiting period imposes a real health risk.

We also disagree with the District Court's conclusion that the "particularly burdensome" effects of the waiting period on some women require its invalidation. A particular burden is not of necessity a substantial obstacle. Whether a burden falls on a particular group is a distinct inquiry from whether it is a substantial obstacle even as to the women in that group. And the District Court did not conclude that the waiting period is such an obstacle even for the women who are most burdened by it. Hence, on the record before us, and in the context of this facial challenge, we are not convinced that the 24-hour waiting period constitutes an undue burden.

We are left with the argument that the various aspects of the informed consent requirement are unconstitutional because they place barriers in the way of abortion on demand. Even the broadest reading of *Roe,* however, has not suggested that there is a constitutional right to abortion on demand. Rather, the right protected by *Roe* is a right to decide to terminate a pregnancy free of undue interference by the State. Because the informed consent requirement facilitates the wise exercise of that right it cannot be classified as an interference with the right *Roe* protects. The informed consent requirement is not an undue burden on that right.

C

Section 3209 of Pennsylvania's abortion law provides, except in cases of medical emergency, that no physician shall perform an abortion on a married woman without receiving a signed statement from the woman that she has notified her spouse that she is about to undergo an abortion. The woman has the option of providing an alternative signed statement certifying that her husband is not the man who impregnated her; that her husband could not be located; that the pregnancy is the result of spousal sexual assault which she has reported; or that the woman believes that notifying her husband will cause him or someone else to inflict bodily injury upon her. A physician who performs an abortion on a married woman without receiving the appropriate signed statement will have his or her license revoked, and is liable to the husband for damages.

The District Court heard the testimony of numerous expert witnesses, and made detailed findings of fact regarding the effect of this statute.

. . .

... "Studies suggest that from one-fifth to one-third of all women will be physically assaulted by a partner or ex-partner during their lifetime." AMA Council on Scientific Affairs, Violence Against Women 7 (1991). Thus on an average day in the United States, nearly 11,000 women are severely assaulted by their male partners. Many of these incidents involve sexual assault. In families where wife-beating takes place, moreover, child abuse is often present as well.

... Psychological abuse, particularly forced social and economic isolation of women, is also common. L. Walker, The Battered Woman Syndrome 27–28 (1984). Many victims of domestic violence remain with their abusers, perhaps because they perceive no superior alternative. Many abused women who find temporary refuge in shelters return to their husbands, in large part because they have no other source of income. Returning to one's abuser can be dangerous. Recent Federal Bureau of Investigation statistics disclose that 8.8% of all homicide victims in the United States are killed by their spouse. Thirty percent of female homicide victims are killed by their male partners. Domestic Violence: Terrorism in the Home, Hearing before the Subcommittee on Children, Family, Drugs and Alcoholism of the Senate Committee on Labor and Human Resources, 101st Cong., 2d Sess., 3 (1990).

The limited research that has been conducted with respect to notifying one's husband about an abortion, although involving samples too small to be representative, also supports the District Court's findings of fact. The vast majority of women notify their male partners of their decision to obtain an abortion. In many cases in which married women do not notify their husbands, the pregnancy is the result of an extramarital affair. Where the husband is the father, the primary reason women do not notify their husbands is that the husband and wife are experiencing marital difficulties, often accompanied by incidents of violence. Ryan & Plutzer, When Married Women Have Abortions: Spousal Notification and Marital Interaction, 51 J. Marriage & the Family 41, 44 (1989).

This information and the District Court's findings reinforce what common sense would suggest. In well-functioning marriages, spouses discuss important intimate decisions such as whether to bear a child. But there are millions of women in this country who are the victims of regular physical and psychological abuse at the hands of their husbands. Should these women become pregnant, they may have very good reasons for not wishing to inform their husbands of their decision to obtain an abortion. Many may have justifiable fears of physical abuse, but may be no less fearful of the consequences of reporting prior abuse to the Commonwealth of Pennsylvania. Many may have a reasonable fear that notifying their husbands will provoke further instances of child abuse; these women are not exempt from § 3209's notification requirement. Many may fear devastating forms of psychological abuse from their husbands, including verbal harassment, threats of future violence, the destruction of possessions, physical confinement to the home, the withdrawal of financial support, or the disclosure of the abortion to family and friends. These methods of psychological abuse may act as even more of a deterrent to notification than the possibility of physical violence, but women who are the victims of the abuse are not exempt from § 3209's notification requirement. And many women who are pregnant as a result of sexual assaults by their husbands will be unable to avail themselves of the exception for spousal sexual assault, § 3209(b)(3), because the exception requires that the women have notified law enforcement authorities within 90 days of the assault, and her husband will be notified of her report once an investigation begins. § 3128(c). If anything in this field is certain, it is that victims of spousal sexual assault are extremely reluctant to report the abuse to the government; hence, a great many spousal rape victims will not be exempt from the notification requirement imposed by § 3209.

The spousal notification requirement is thus likely to prevent a significant number of women from obtaining an abortion. It does not merely make abortions a little more difficult or expensive to obtain; for many women, it will impose a substantial obstacle. We must not blind ourselves to the fact that the significant number of women who fear for their safety and the safety of their children are likely to be deterred from procuring an abortion as surely as if the Commonwealth had outlawed abortion in all cases.

Respondents attempt to avoid the conclusion that § 3209 is invalid by pointing out that it imposes almost no burden at all for the vast majority of women seeking abortions. They begin by noting that only about 20 percent of the women who obtain abortions are married. They then note that of these women about 95 percent notify their husbands of their own volition. Thus, respondents argue, the effects of § 3209 are felt by only one percent of the women who obtain abortions. Respondents argue that since some of these women will be able to notify their husbands without adverse consequences or will qualify for one of the exceptions, the statute affects fewer than one percent of women seeking abortions. For this reason, it is asserted, the statute cannot be invalid on its face. We disagree with respondents' basic method of analysis.

The analysis does not end with the one percent of women upon whom the statute operates; it begins there. Legislation is measured for consistency with the Constitution by its impact on those whose conduct it affects. . . . The proper focus of constitutional inquiry is the group for whom the law is a restriction, not the group for whom the law is irrelevant.

. . . The unfortunate yet persisting conditions we document above will mean that in a large fraction of the cases in which § 3209 is relevant, it will operate as a substantial obstacle to a woman's choice to undergo an abortion. It is an undue burden, and therefore invalid.

This conclusion is in no way inconsistent with our decisions upholding parental notification or consent requirements. Those enactments, and our judgment that they are constitutional, are based on the quite reasonable assumption that minors will benefit from consultation with their parents and that children will often not realize that their parents have their best interests at heart. We cannot adopt a parallel assumption about adult women.

. . . If this case concerned a State's ability to require the mother to notify the father before taking some action with respect to a living child raised by both, therefore, it would be reasonable to conclude as a general matter that the father's interest in the welfare of the child and the mother's interest are equal.

Before birth, however, the issue takes on a very different cast. It is an inescapable biological fact that state regulation with respect to the child a woman is carrying will have a far greater impact on the mother's liberty than on the father's. The effect of state regulation on a woman's protected liberty is doubly deserving of scrutiny in such a case, as the State has touched not only upon the private sphere of the family but upon the very bodily integrity of the pregnant woman. Cf. Cruzan v. Director, Missouri Dept. of Health, 497 U.S., at 281. The Court has held that "when the wife and the husband disagree on this decision, the view of only one of the two marriage partners can prevail. Inasmuch as it is the woman who physically bears the child and who is the more directly and immediately affected by the pregnancy, as between the two, the balance weighs in her favor." This conclusion rests upon the basic nature of marriage and the nature of our Constitution: "[T]he marital couple is not an independent entity with a mind and heart of its own, but an association of two individuals each with a separate intellectual and emotional makeup. If the right of privacy means anything, it is the right of the *individual,* married or single, to be free from unwarranted governmental intrusion into matters so fundamentally affecting a person as the decision whether to bear or beget a child." The Constitution protects individuals, men and women alike, from unjustified state interference, even when that interference is enacted into law for the benefit of their spouses.

. . .

. . . For the great many women who are victims of abuse inflicted by their husbands, or whose children are the victims of such abuse, a spousal notice requirement enables the husband to wield an effective veto over his wife's decision. Whether the prospect of notification itself deters such women from seeking abortions, or whether the husband, through physical force or psychological pressure or economic coercion, prevents his wife from obtaining an abortion until it is too late, the notice requirement will often be tantamount to the veto found unconstitutional in *Danforth*. The women most affected by this law—those who most reasonably fear the consequences of notifying their husbands that they are pregnant—are in the gravest danger.

The husband's interest in the life of the child his wife is carrying does not permit the State to empower him with this troubling degree of authority over his wife.

. . . A State may not give to a man the kind of dominion over his wife that parents exercise over their children.

Section 3209 embodies a view of marriage consonant with the common-law status of married women but repugnant to our present understanding of marriage and of the nature of the rights secured by the Constitution. Women do not lose their constitutionally protected liberty when they marry. The Constitution protects all individuals, male or female, married or unmarried, from the abuse of governmental power, even where that power is employed for the supposed benefit of a member of the individual's family. These considerations confirm our conclusion that § 3209 is invalid.

D

We next consider the parental consent provision. Except in a medical emergency, an unemancipated young woman under 18 may not obtain an abortion unless she and one of her parents (or guardian) provides informed consent as defined above. If neither a parent nor a guardian provides consent, a court may authorize the performance of an abortion upon a determination that the young woman is mature and capable of giving informed consent and has in fact given her informed consent, or that an abortion would be in her best interests.

. . . Our cases establish, and we reaffirm today, that a State may require a minor seeking an abortion to obtain the consent of a parent or guardian, provided that there is an adequate judicial bypass procedure. . . .

The only argument made by petitioners respecting this provision and to which our prior decisions do not speak is the contention that the parental consent requirement is invalid because it requires informed parental consent. For the most part, petitioners' argument is a reprise of their argument with respect to the informed consent requirement in general, and we reject it for the reasons given above. . . .

. . .

VI

Our Constitution is a covenant running from the first generation of Americans to us and then to future generations. It is a coherent succession. Each generation must learn anew that the Constitution's written terms embody ideas and aspirations that must survive more ages than one. We accept our responsibility not to retreat from interpreting the full meaning of the covenant in light of all of our precedents. We invoke it once again to define the freedom guaranteed by the Constitution's own promise, the promise of liberty.

. . .

■ JUSTICE BLACKMUN, concurring in part, concurring in the judgment in part, and dissenting in part.

I join Parts I, II, III, V–A, V–C, and VI of the joint opinion of Justices O'Connor, Kennedy and Souter, *ante*.

Three years ago, in Webster v. Reproductive Health Services, 492 U.S. 490 (1989), four Members of this Court appeared poised to "cast into darkness the hopes and visions of every woman in this country" who had come to believe that the Constitution guaranteed her the right to reproductive choice. See *id.*, at 499 (plurality opinion of Rehnquist, C. J., joined by White and Kennedy, JJ.); *id.*, at 532 (Scalia, J., concurring in part and concurring in judgment). All that remained between the promise of *Roe* and the darkness of the plurality was a single, flickering flame. Decisions since *Webster* gave little reason to hope that this flame would cast much light. See, *e. g.*, Ohio v. Akron Center for Reproductive Health, 497 U.S. 502, 524 (1990) (Blackmun, J., dissenting). But now, just when so many expected the darkness to fall, the flame has grown bright.

I do not underestimate the significance of today's joint opinion. Yet I remain steadfast in my belief that the right to reproductive choice is entitled to the full protection afforded by this Court before *Webster*. And I fear for the darkness as four Justices anxiously await the single vote necessary to extinguish the light.

■ JUSTICE SCALIA, with whom THE CHIEF JUSTICE, JUSTICE WHITE, and JUSTICE THOMAS join, concurring in the judgment in part and dissenting in part.

... The States may, if they wish, permit abortion-on-demand, but the Constitution does not *require* them to do so. The permissibility of abortion, and the limitations upon it, are to be resolved like most important questions in our democracy: by citizens trying to persuade one another and then voting....

... I reach that conclusion not because of anything so exalted as my views concerning the "concept of existence, of meaning, of the universe, and of the mystery of human life." Rather, I reach it for the same reason I reach the conclusion that bigamy is not constitutionally protected—because of two simple facts: (1) the Constitution says absolutely nothing about it, and (2) the longstanding traditions of American society have permitted it to be legally proscribed.

. . .

... [A]pplying the rational basis test, I would uphold the Pennsylvania statute in its entirety....

The emptiness of the "reasoned judgment" that produced *Roe* is displayed in plain view by the fact that, after more than 19 years of effort by some of the brightest (and most determined) legal minds in the country, after more than 10 cases upholding abortion rights in this Court, and after dozens upon dozens of *amicus* briefs submitted in this and other cases, the best the Court can do to explain how it is that the word "liberty" *must* be thought to include the right to destroy human fetuses is to rattle off a collection of adjectives that simply decorate a value judgment and conceal a political choice. The right to abort, we are told, inheres in "liberty" because it is among "a person's most basic decisions"; it involves a "most intimate and personal choic[e]"; it is "central to personal dignity and autonomy"; it "originate[s] within the zone of conscience and belief"; it is "too intimate and personal" for state interference; it reflects "intimate views" of a "deep, personal character"; it involves "intimate relationships," and notions of "personal autonomy and bodily integrity"; and it concerns a particularly " 'important decisio[n]' ". But it is obvious to anyone applying "reasoned judgment" that the same adjectives can be applied to many forms of conduct that this Court . . . has held are *not* entitled to constitutional protection—because, like abortion, they are forms of conduct that have long been criminalized in American society. Those adjectives might be applied, for example, to homosexual sodomy, polygamy, adult incest, and suicide, all of which are equally "intimate" and "deep[ly] personal" decisions involving "personal autonomy and bodily integrity," and all of which can constitutionally be proscribed because it is our unquestionable constitutional tradition that they are proscribable. It is not reasoned judgment that supports the Court's decision; only personal predilection. . . .

. . . [T]he joint opinion announces that "it is important to clarify what is meant by an undue burden." I certainly agree with that, but I do not agree that the joint opinion succeeds in the announced endeavor. To the contrary, its efforts at clarification make clear only that the standard is inherently manipulable and will prove hopelessly unworkable in practice.

The joint opinion explains that a state regulation imposes an "undue burden" if it "has the purpose or effect of placing a substantial obstacle in the path of a woman seeking an abortion of a nonviable fetus." An obstacle is "substantial," we are told, if it is "calculated[,] [not] to inform the woman's free choice, [but to] hinder it." This latter statement cannot possibly mean what it says. *Any* regulation of abortion that is intended to advance what the joint opinion concedes is the State's "substantial" interest in protecting unborn life will be "calculated [to] hinder" a decision to have an abortion. It thus seems more accurate to say that the joint opinion would uphold abortion regulations only if they do not *unduly* hinder the woman's decision. That, of course, brings us right back to square one: Defining an "undue burden" as an "undue hindrance" (or a "substantial obstacle") hardly "clarifies" the test. Consciously or not, the joint opinion's verbal shell game will conceal raw judicial policy choices concerning what is "appropriate" abortion legislation.

The ultimately standardless nature of the "undue burden" inquiry is a reflection of the underlying fact that the concept has no principled or coherent legal basis. As The Chief Justice points out, *Roe*'s strict-scrutiny standard "at least had a recognized basis in constitutional law at the time *Roe* was decided," while "[t]he same cannot be said for the 'undue burden' standard, which is created largely out of whole cloth by the authors of the joint opinion." The joint opinion is flatly wrong in asserting that "our jurisprudence relating to all liberties save perhaps abortion has recognized" the permissibility of laws that do not impose an "undue burden." It argues that the abortion right is similar to other rights in that a law "not designed to strike at the right itself, [but which] has the incidental effect of making it more difficult or more expensive to [exercise the right,]" is not invalid. I agree, indeed I have forcefully urged, that a law of general applicability which places only an incidental burden on a fundamental right does not infringe that right, but that principle does not establish the quite different (and quite dangerous) proposition that a law which *directly* regulates a fundamental right will not be found to violate the Constitution unless it imposes an "undue burden." It is that, of course, which is at issue here: Pennsylvania has *consciously and directly* regulated conduct that our cases have held is constitutionally protected. The appropriate analogy, therefore, is that of a state law requiring purchasers of religious books to endure a 24-hour waiting period, or to pay a nominal additional tax of 1 [cent]. The joint opinion cannot possibly be correct in suggesting that we would uphold such legislation on the ground that it does not impose a "substantial obstacle" to the exercise of First Amendment rights. The "undue burden" standard is not at all the generally applicable principle the joint opinion pretends it to be; rather, it is a unique concept created specially for this case, to preserve some judicial foothold in this ill-gotten territory. In claiming otherwise, the three Justices show their willingness to place all constitutional rights at risk in an effort to preserve what they deem the "central holding in *Roe*."

. . .

To the extent I can discern *any* meaningful content in the "undue burden" standard as applied in the joint opinion, it appears to be that a State may not regulate abortion in such a way as to reduce significantly its incidence. The joint opinion repeatedly emphasizes that an important factor in the "undue burden" analysis is whether the regulation "prevent[s] a significant number of women from obtaining an abortion," whether a "significant number of women ... are likely to be deterred from procuring an abortion," and whether the regulation often "deters" women from seeking abortions. We are not told, however, what forms of "deterrence" are impermissible or what degree of success in deterrence is too much to be tolerated. For example, if a State required a woman to read a pamphlet describing, with illustrations, the facts of fetal development before she could obtain an abortion, the effect of such legislation might be to "deter" a "significant number of women" from procuring abortions, thereby seemingly allowing a district judge to invalidate it as an undue burden. Thus, despite flowery rhetoric about the State's "substantial" and "profound" interest in "potential human life," and criticism of *Roe* for undervaluing that interest, the joint opinion permits the State to pursue that interest only so long as it is not too successful....

I am certainly not in a good position to dispute that the Court *has saved* the "central holding" of *Roe,* since to do that effectively I would have to know what the Court has saved, which in turn would require me to understand (as I do not) what the "undue burden" test means. I must confess, however, that I have always thought, and I think a lot of other people have always thought, that the arbitrary trimester framework, which the Court today discards, was quite as central to *Roe* as the arbitrary viability test, which the Court today retains. It seems particularly ungrateful to carve the trimester framework out of the core of *Roe,* since its very rigidity (in sharp contrast to the utter indeterminability of the "undue burden" test) is probably the only reason the Court is able to say, in urging *stare decisis,* that *Roe* "has in no sense proven 'unworkable' ". I suppose the Court is entitled to call a "central holding" whatever it wants to call a "central holding"—which is, come to think of it, perhaps one of the difficulties with this modified version of *stare decisis*....

The Court's description of the place of *Roe* in the social history of the United States is unrecognizable. Not only did *Roe* not, as the Court suggests, *resolve* the deeply divisive issue of abortion; it did more than anything else to nourish it, by elevating it to the national level where it is infinitely more difficult to resolve. National politics were not plagued by abortion protests, national abortion lobbying, or abortion marches on Congress, before Roe v. Wade was decided. Profound disagreement existed among our citizens over the issue—as it does over other issues, such as the death penalty—but that disagreement was being worked out at the state level. As with many other issues, the division of sentiment within each State was not as closely balanced as it was among the population of the Nation as a whole, meaning not only that more people would be satisfied with the results of state-by-state resolution, but also that those results would be more stable. Pre–*Roe,* moreover, political compromise was possible.

Roe's mandate for abortion-on-demand destroyed the compromises of the past, rendered compromise impossible for the future, and required the entire issue to be resolved uniformly, at the national level. At the same time, *Roe* created a vast new class of abortion consumers and abortion proponents by eliminating the moral opprobrium that had attached to the act. ("If the Constitution *guarantees* abortion, how can it be bad?"—not an accurate line of thought, but a natural one.) Many favor all of those developments, and it is not for me to say that they are wrong. But to portray *Roe* as the statesmanlike "settlement" of a divisive issue, a jurisprudential Peace of Westphalia that is worth preserving, is nothing less than Orwellian. *Roe* fanned into life an issue that has inflamed our national politics in general, and has obscured with its smoke the selection of Justices, to this Court in particular, ever since. And by keeping us in the abortion-umpiring business, it is the perpetuation of that disruption, rather than of any *pax Roeana,* that the Court's new majority decrees.

. . .

. . . I am as distressed as the Court is . . . about the "political pressure" directed to the Court: the marches, the mail, the protests aimed at inducing us to change our opinions. How upsetting it is, that so many of our citizens (good people, not lawless ones, on both sides of this abortion issue, and on various sides of other issues as well) think that we Justices should properly take into account their views, as though we were engaged not in ascertaining an objective law but in determining some kind of social consensus. The Court would profit, I think, from giving less attention to the *fact* of this distressing phenomenon, and more attention to the *cause* of it. That cause permeates today's opinion: a new mode of constitutional adjudication that relies not upon text and traditional practice to determine the law, but upon what the Court calls "reasoned judgment," which turns out to be nothing but philosophical predilection and moral intuition. . . .

What makes all this relevant to the bothersome application of "political pressure" against the Court are the twin facts that the American people love democracy and the American people are not fools. As long as this Court thought (and the people thought) that we Justices were doing essentially lawyers' work up here—reading text and discerning our society's traditional understanding of that text—the public pretty much left us alone. Texts and traditions are facts to study, not convictions to demonstrate about. But if in reality our process of constitutional adjudication consists primarily of making *value judgments;* if we can ignore a long and clear tradition clarifying an ambiguous text, as we did, for example, five days ago in declaring unconstitutional invocations and benedictions at public-high-school graduation ceremonies, Lee v. Weisman, 505 U.S. 577 (1992); if, as I say, our pronouncement of constitutional law rests primarily on value judgments, then a free and intelligent people's attitude towards us can be expected to be (*ought* to be) quite different. The people know that their value judgments are quite as good as those taught in any law school—maybe better. If, indeed, the "liberties" protected by the Constitution are, as the Court says, undefined and unbounded, then the people *should* demonstrate, to protest that we do not implement *their* values instead of *ours.* Not only that, but confirmation hearings for new Justices *should* deteriorate into question-and-answer sessions in which Senators go through a list of their constituents' most favored and most disfavored alleged constitutional rights, and seek the nominee's commitment to support or oppose them. Value judgments, after all, should be voted on, not dictated; and if our Constitution has somehow accidently committed them to the Supreme Court, at least we can have a sort of plebiscite each time a new nominee to that body is put forward. . . .

We should get out of this area, where we have no right to be, and where we do neither ourselves nor the country any good by remaining.

NOTES

1. Compare the dissent below of Judge Alito:

> . . . I do not believe that Section 3209 has been shown to impose an undue burden as that term is used in the relevant Supreme Court opinions. . . .
>
> . . .
>
> . . . First, as the district court found, the "vast majority" of married women voluntarily inform their husbands before seeking an abortion. Indeed, in the trial testimony on which the district court relied, the plaintiffs' witness stated that in her experience 95% of married women notify their husbands. Second, the overwhelming majority of abortions are sought by unmarried women. Thus, it is immediately apparent that Section 3209 cannot affect more than about 5% of married women seeking abortions or an even smaller percentage of all women desiring abortions.
>
> The plaintiffs failed to show even roughly how many of the women in this small group would actually be adversely affected by Section 3209. . . . Section 3209 contains four significant exceptions. These exceptions apply if a woman certifies that she has not notified her husband because she believes that (1) he is not the father of the child, (2) he cannot be found after diligent effort, (3) the pregnancy is the result of a spousal sexual assault that has been reported to the authorities, or (4) she has reason to believe that notification is likely to result in the infliction of bodily injury upon her. If Section 3209 were allowed to take effect, it seems safe to assume that *some* percentage of the married women seeking abortions without notifying their husbands would qualify for and invoke these exceptions. The record, however, is devoid of evidence showing how many women could or could not invoke an exception.
>
> Of the potentially affected women who could not invoke an exception, it seems safe to assume that *some* percentage, despite an initial inclination not to tell their husbands, would notify their husbands without suffering substantial ill effects. Again, however, the record lacks evidence showing how many women would or would not fall into this category. Thus, the plaintiffs did not even roughly substantiate how many women might be inhibited from obtaining an abortion or otherwise harmed by Section 3209. At best, the record shows that Section 3209 would inhibit abortions " 'to some degree' " or that "some women [would] be less likely to choose to have an abortion by virtue of the presence" of Section 3209. . . . Consequently, the plaintiffs failed to prove that Section 3209 would impose an undue burden.
>
> Needless to say, the plight of any women, no matter how few, who may suffer physical abuse or other harm as a result of this provision is a matter of grave concern. It is apparent that the Pennsylvania legislature considered this problem and attempted to prevent Section 3209 from causing adverse effects by adopting the four exceptions noted above. Whether the legislature's approach represents sound public policy is not a question for us to decide. Our task here is simply to decide whether Section 3209 meets constitutional standards. The first step in this analysis is to determine whether Section 3209 has been shown to create an undue burden under Supreme Court precedent, and for the reasons just explained it seems clear that an undue burden has not been established.

2. In Stenberg v. Carhart, 530 U.S. 914 (2000), set forth in Chapter 7, Section A., the Supreme Court held unconstitutional a Nebraska ban on partial birth abortions.

Ayotte v. Planned Parenthood

Supreme Court of the United States, 2006.
___ U.S. ___, 126 S.Ct. 961.

■ JUSTICE O'CONNOR delivered the opinion of the Court.

We do not revisit our abortion precedents today, but rather address a question of remedy: If enforcing a statute that regulates access to abortion would be unconstitutional in medical emergencies, what is the appropriate judicial response? We hold that invalidating the statute entirely is not always necessary or justified, for lower courts may be able to render narrower declaratory and injunctive relief.

In 2003, New Hampshire enacted the Parental Notification Prior to Abortion Act. N. H. Rev. Stat. Ann. §§ 132:24–132:28 (Supp. 2004). The Act prohibits physicians from performing an abortion on a pregnant minor (or a woman for whom a guardian or conservator has been appointed) until 48 hours after written notice of the pending abortion is delivered to her parent or guardian. § 132:25(I). Notice may be delivered personally or by certified mail. §§ 132:25(II), (III). Violations of the Act are subject to criminal and civil penalties. § 132:27.

The Act allows for three circumstances in which a physician may perform an abortion without notifying the minor's parent. First, notice is not required if "the attending abortion provider certifies in the pregnant minor's record that the abortion is necessary to prevent the minor's death and there is insufficient time to provide the required notice." § 132:26(I)(a). Second, a person entitled to receive notice may certify that he or she has already been notified. § 132:26(I)(b). Finally, a minor may petition a judge to authorize her physician to perform an abortion without parental notification. The judge must so authorize if he or she finds that the minor is mature and capable of giving informed consent, or that an abortion without notification is in the minor's best interests. § 132:26(II). These judicial bypass proceedings "shall be confidential and shall be given precedence over other pending matters so that the court may reach a decision promptly and without delay," and access to the courts "shall be afforded [to the] pregnant minor 24 hours a day, 7 days a week." §§ 132:26(II)(b), (c). The trial and appellate courts must each rule on bypass petitions within seven days. *Ibid.*

The Act does not explicitly permit a physician to perform an abortion in a medical emergency without parental notification.

Respondents are Dr. Wayne Goldner, an obstetrician and gynecologist who has a private practice in Manchester, and three clinics that offer reproductive health services. ... Before the Act took effect, respondents brought suit under 42 U.S.C. § 1983, alleging that the Act is unconstitutional because it fails "to allow a physician to provide a prompt abortion to a minor whose health would be endangered" by delays inherent in the Act. Respondents also challenged the adequacy of the Act's life exception and of the judicial bypass' confidentiality provision.

The District Court declared the Act unconstitutional, see 28 U.S.C. § 2201(a), and permanently enjoined its enforcement. ... The Court of Appeals for the First Circuit affirmed. ... We granted certiorari, 544 U.S. ___, 125 S.Ct. 2294 (2005), to decide whether the courts below erred in invalidating the Act in its entirety because it lacks an exception for the preservation of pregnant minors' health. We now vacate and remand for the Court of Appeals to reconsider its choice of remedy.

As the case comes to us, three propositions—two legal and one factual—are established. First, States unquestionably have the right to require parental involvement when a minor considers terminating her pregnancy, because of their "strong and legitimate interest in the welfare of [their] young citizens, whose immaturity, inexperience, and lack of judgment may sometimes impair their ability to exercise their rights wisely." Hodgson v. Minnesota, 497 U.S. 417, 444–445 (1990) (opinion of STEVENS, J.).[1] Accordingly, we have long upheld state parental involvement statutes like the Act before us, and we cast no doubt on those holdings today. *See, e.g.*, Lambert v. Wicklund, 520 U.S. 292 (1997) (*per curiam*); *Casey* at 899 (joint opinion); Ohio v. Akron Center for Reproductive Health, 497 U.S. 502, 510–519 (1990). . . .[2]

Second, New Hampshire does not dispute, and our precedents hold, that a State may not restrict access to abortions that are " 'necessary, in appropriate medical judgment, for preservation of the life or health of the mother.' " *Casey*, 505 U.S., at 879 (plurality opinion) (quoting *Roe*, 410 U.S., at 164–165); see also Thornburgh v. American College of Obstetricians and Gynecologists, 476 U.S. 747, 768–769 (1986); Planned Parenthood Ass'n v. Ashcroft, 462 U.S. 476 (1983) (opinion of Powell, J.); Planned Parenthood of Central Mo. v. Danforth, 428 U.S. 52, 79 (1976).

Third, New Hampshire has not taken real issue with the factual basis of this litigation: In some very small percentage of cases, pregnant minors, like adult women, need immediate abortions to avert serious and often irreversible damage to their health.

New Hampshire has maintained that in most if not all cases, the Act's judicial bypass and the State's "competing harms" statutes should protect both physician and patient when a minor needs an immediate abortion. See N. H. Rev. Stat. Ann. § 627:3(I) (1996) (for criminal liability, "conduct which the actor believes to be necessary to avoid harm to . . . another is justifiable if the desirability and urgency of avoiding such harm outweigh, according to ordinary standards of reasonableness, the harm sought to be prevented by the statute defining the offense charged"); § 627:1 (similar for civil liability). But the District Court and Court of Appeals found neither of these provisions to protect minors' health reliably in all emergencies. 296 F. Supp. 2d, at 65–66; 390 F.3d at 61-62. And New Hampshire has conceded that, under our cases, it would be unconstitutional to apply the Act in a manner that subjects minors to significant health risks.

We turn to the question of remedy: When a statute restricting access to abortion may be applied in a manner that harms women's health, what is the appropriate relief? Generally speaking, when confronting a constitutional flaw in a statute, we try to limit the solution to the problem. We prefer, for

1. Forty-four States, including New Hampshire, have parental involvement (that is, consent or notification) laws. Thirty-eight of those laws have explicit exceptions for health or medical emergencies. . . .

2. It is the sad reality, however, that young women sometimes lack a loving and supportive parent capable of aiding them "to exercise their rights wisely." *Hodgson*, 497 U.S., at 444 (holding unconstitutional a statute requiring notification of both parents, and observing that "the most common reason" young women did not notify a second parent was that the second parent "was a child- or spouse-batterer, and notification would have provoked further abuse"). See also Department of Health and Human Services, Administration on Children, Youth and Families, Child Maltreatment 2003, p. 63 (2005) (parents were the perpetrators in 79.7% of cases of reported abuse or neglect).

example, to enjoin only the unconstitutional applications of a statute while leaving other applications in force, see United States v. Raines, 362 U.S. 17, 20–22, (1960), or to sever its problematic portions while leaving the remainder intact, United States v. Booker, 543 U.S. 220, 227–229 (2005).

Three interrelated principles inform our approach to remedies. First, we try not to nullify more of a legislature's work than is necessary, for we know that "[a] ruling of unconstitutionality frustrates the intent of the elected representatives of the people." Regan v. Time, Inc., 468 U.S. 641, 652 (1984) (plurality opinion). It is axiomatic that a "statute may be invalid as applied to one state of facts and yet valid as applied to another." Dahnke–Walker Milling Co. v. Bondurant, 257 U.S. 282, 289 (1921). Accordingly, the "normal rule" is that "partial, rather than facial, invalidation is the required course," such that a "statute may . . . be declared invalid to the extent that it reaches too far, but otherwise left intact." Brockett v. Spokane Arcades, Inc., 472 U.S. 491, 504 (1985).

Second, mindful that our constitutional mandate and institutional competence are limited, we re-strain ourselves from 'rewriting state law to conform it to constitutional requirements' even as we strive to salvage it. Our ability to devise a judicial remedy that does not entail quintessentially legislative work often depends on how clearly we have already articulated the background constitutional rules at issue and how easily we can articulate the remedy. . . .

Third, the touchstone for any decision about remedy is legislative intent, for a court cannot "use its remedial powers to circumvent the intent of the legislature." After finding an application or portion of a statute unconstitutional, we must next ask: Would the legislature have preferred what is left of its statute to no statute at all? All the while, we are wary of legislatures who would rely on our intervention, for "it would certainly be dangerous if the legislature could set a net large enough to catch all possible offenders, and leave it to the courts to step inside" to announce to whom the statute may be applied. United States v. Reese, 92 U.S. 214 (1876). "This would, to some extent, substitute the judicial for the legislative department of the government." *Ibid.*

In this case, the courts below chose the most blunt remedy—permanently enjoining the enforcement of New Hampshire's parental notification law and thereby invalidating it entirely. That is understandable, for we, too, have previously invalidated an abortion statute in its entirety because of the same constitutional flaw. In *Stenberg*, we addressed a Nebraska law banning so-called "partial birth abortion" unless the procedure was necessary to save the pregnant woman's life. We held Nebraska's law unconstitutional because it lacked a health exception. 530 U.S., at 930 (lack of a health exception was an "independent reason" for finding the ban unconstitutional). But the parties in Stenberg did not ask for, and we did not contemplate, relief more finely drawn.

In the case that is before us, however, we agree with New Hampshire that the lower courts need not have invalidated the law wholesale. Respondents, too, recognize the possibility of a modest remedy: They pleaded for any relief "just and proper," and conceded at oral argument that carefully crafted injunctive relief may resolve this case. Only a few applications of New Hampshire's parental notification statute would present a constitutional problem. So long as they are faithful to legislative intent, then, in this case the lower courts can issue a declaratory judgment and an injunction prohibiting the statute's unconstitutional application.

There is some dispute as to whether New Hampshire's legislature intended the statute to be susceptible to such a remedy. New Hampshire notes that the Act contains a severability clause providing that "if any provision of this subdivision or the application thereof to any person or circumstance is held invalid, such invalidity shall not affect the provisions or applications of this subdivision which can be given effect without the invalid provisions or applications." § 132:28. Respondents, on the other hand, contend that New Hampshire legislators preferred no statute at all to a statute enjoined in the way we have described. Because this is an open question, we remand for the lower courts to determine legislative intent in the first instance.

Either an injunction prohibiting unconstitutional applications or a holding that consistency with legislative intent requires invalidating the statute *in toto* should obviate any concern about the Act's life exception. We therefore need not pass on the lower courts' alternative holding. Finally, if the Act does survive in part on remand, the Court of Appeals should address respondents' separate objection to the judicial bypass' confidentiality provision. The judgment of the Court of Appeals is vacated, and the case is remanded for further proceedings consistent with this opinion.

2. DOMESTIC VIOLENCE

a. TRADITIONAL IMMUNITY AND EXEMPTION

The assumption of marital unity that characterized the traditional model of marriage for many years precluded states from "intervening" in a marriage to prevent or punish violence by one spouse against the other. In practical terms, this meant that husbands were not legally accountable for abusing their wives. The doctrine of interspousal tort immunity was one means by which this was accomplished, and the exemption of a husband from rape liability was another. Most states have now abolished interspousal tort immunity. This has enabled victims to bring actions against their abusers for such torts as assault, battery, intentional infliction of emotional distress, and even false imprisonment. See generally Claire Dalton & Elizabeth Schneider, Battered Women and the Law 816–845 (2001).

As the following article indicates, elimination of the marital rape exemption has progressed more slowly. As you read the excerpt, consider whether the asserted rationales for preserving some distinction between married and unmarried partners are distinguishable from those that underlay interspousal tort immunity.

Jill Elaine Hasday, Contest and Consent: A Legal History of Marital Rape

88 Calif. L. Rev. 1375, 1482–1523 (2000).

At common law, husbands were exempt from prosecution for raping their wives. Over the past quarter century, this law has been modified somewhat, but not entirely. A majority of states still retain some form of the common law regime: they criminalize a narrower range of offenses if committed within marriage, subject the marital rape they do recognize to less serious sanctions, and/or create special procedural hurdles for marital rape prosecutions. The current state of the law represents a confusing mix of victory and defeat for the exemption's contemporary feminist critics. Virtually every state legislature has revisited the marital rape exemption over the last twenty-five years, but most have chosen to preserve the exemption in some substantial manifestation. With rare exception, moreover, courts have not invalidated state laws protecting marital rape. Political protest and legislative action, rather than any clear judicial statement of constitutional norms, [have] driven the partial and uneven modification of the common law rule.

. . .

The first sustained contest over marital rape was coterminous with the life span of the first woman's rights movement in the United States. Begun almost immediately upon the organization of nineteenth-century feminism, it dissipated when the movement disbanded. It was not until the last quarter of the twentieth century that the legal status of marital rape was again subject to significant attack, led this time by the second organized women's movement. Here too, however, the resulting reform has been partial and uneven.

. . .

Reform of the criminal exemption has also been fragmentary. A majority of states still retain some form of the rule exempting a husband from prosecution for raping his wife. Some states require a couple to be separated at the time of the injury (and sometimes extend the exemption to cover unmarried cohabitants). Some only recognize marital rape if it involves physical force and/or serious physical harm. Some provide for vastly reduced penalties if a rape occurs in marriage, or create special procedural requirements for marital rape prosecutions. Almost all of this law, moreover, is the product of political advocacy and legislative action, rather than constitutional adjudication, so that the nature and continued path of change is insecure. Enforcement of the existing statutes recognizing some forms of marital rape has certainly been very infrequent.

. . .

The first prominent modern argument for the marital rape exemption, the claim from privacy, posits that there is something inherent in the nature of the relationship between husband and wife that makes legal intervention inappropriate, misguided, and ultimately self-defeating. It contends that the marital relation depends on intimacy protected from outside scrutiny, intimacy that could not survive if the law intervened to investigate and prosecute marital rape charges.

Contemporary defenders of the marital rape exemption do not articulate this privacy claim in sex-specific terms, or as a balancing test in which gains must be set against losses. They do not seek to explain why it is important to protect men's privacy in marriage through a marital rape exemption, even if women's interests may suffer. They make no mention of the possibility that marital rape or the absence of criminal remediation might inflict injury on wives. To the contrary, the exemption's modern defenders speak about protecting the privacy of the marital relationship that husband and wife share, of benefitting both. Consider, for instance, how a Florida state representative explained his support for a marital rape exemption: " 'The State of Florida has absolutely no business intervening into the sexual relationship between a husband and a wife.... We don't need Florida invading the sanctity and the intimacy of a relationship.' " The drafters of the Model Penal Code, who recommend an absolute marital rape exemption, similarly note that the exemption "avoids [an] unwarranted intrusion of the penal law into the life of the family." Along the same lines, the Pennsylvania Superior Court interpreted a recent legislative modification of the exemption narrowly in order to stop the state from invading "the privacy of the marital bedroom for the purpose of supervising the manner in which marital relationships are consummated." The crucial claim of this privacy defense for the marital rape exemption is that keeping the judicial system away from disputes over marital rape serves the interests that a husband and wife both have in maintaining their joint privacy, that the exemption protects the intimacy that they have established with each other and from which each benefit unambiguously. Marriage here is envisioned as a necessarily harmonious relation, and legal intervention as the first, unwelcome introduction of antagonism and injury.

The other prominent modern claim articulated in favor of the marital rape exemption, that it facilitates marital reconciliation, similarly explains the exemption as promoting the shared interests of wives and husbands. Building on the proposition that marital intimacy is destroyed by outside observation, this argument contends that the legal system should not be able to investigate or prosecute marital rape because such intervention will make reconciliation between husband and wife significantly less likely. Once the state appears on the scene, the exemption's supporters suggest, the delicate shoots of love, trust, and closeness in a marriage will be trampled in a way unlikely ever to be undone. In contrast, if the exemption remains in place, this argument asserts that many married couples will be able to reconcile after what would otherwise be considered a marital rape.

Here again, the central premise of the argument is that private reconciliation and the return to regular married life leave both wife and husband better off than they would have been if the state had been empowered to prosecute a marital rape. Supporters do not justify the exemption by explaining why the advantages to husbands of reconciliation without prosecution outweigh the potential costs to wives. They do not suggest that the interests of husband and wife might diverge like that. Modern defenders of the marital rape exemption do not even phrase their claim as a contention that a wife should sacrifice her own interests for the sake of her children, who may benefit from their parents' reconciliation, or for the sake of the broader societal benefits associated with marital stability. Their argument never acknowledges that the exemption inflicts an injury on wives that might (potentially) be justified by the benefits conferred on those around them.

Indeed, supporters go further than that and state that married couples are able to reconcile so completely after a rape that their relationship becomes essentially indistinguishable from other marriages, affirmatively denying the proposition that marital rape causes any lasting injury at all. In the view of the Colorado Supreme Court, "the marital exception may remove a substantial obstacle to the resumption of normal marital relations." The Model Penal Code similarly emphasizes the normality of the reconciliation process possible after a marital rape. As the Code's drafters note, "the problem with abandoning the [marital] immunity in many such situations ['of rape by force or threat'] is that the law of rape, if applied to spouses, would thrust the prospect of criminal sanctions into the ongoing process of adjustment in the marital relationship."

A less prominent contemporary defense of the marital rape exemption might be called the "vindictive wife" argument. This claim contends that the exemption should be preserved in order to prevent wives from pursuing false charges of marital rape, especially to gain leverage in a divorce suit.

The line of reasoning openly recognizes the possibility of marital antagonism (at least at the end of a relationship), placing it in some tension with the more prominent claims for the exemption from privacy and reconciliation. But there is a long, distinct tradition in Anglo–American law, traceable . . . to Hale's seminal treatise, advocating the particular disbelief of rape victims. Hale famously warned that rape was "an accusation easily to be made and hard to be proved, and harder to be defended by the party accused, tho never so innocent." The vindictive wife argument for preserving the marital rape exemption accords well with this tradition. There is, after all, no empirical evidence to support the proposition that wives are prone to make false charges of marital rape. To the contrary, the evidence available from states that allow marital rape prosecutions suggests that the incidents that women report to law enforcement officials tend to be very brutal, and relatively easy to prove.

More fundamentally, the vindictive wife defense of the marital rape exemption recognizes marital discord in a very particular, and limited, way. In this vision, the antagonistic and harmful act to be feared in marriage is not the possibility of an actual marital rape. The argument never suggests that the marital rape exemption may be shielding and facilitating injurious conduct inflicted by husbands on wives. To the contrary, it envisions the exemption as a check on self-interestedness within marriage, a legal rule that keeps one spouse from unjustifiably betraying the other (or, described more precisely, that keeps wives from betraying their husbands). As one state legislator explains the theory, "since society is already burdened with these kinds of women [vengeful wives], . . . the last thing we need is a law making it illegal for a husband to sexually assault his wife."

This mode of argument in defense of the marital rape exemption has been very successful. Granted, the law of marital rape has changed more notably in the late twentieth century than in the nineteenth. At the end of a half-century's effort by the first organized woman's rights movement, the only alteration apparent in the legal treatment of marital rape consisted of a marginal liberalization in the divorce law. In contrast, over the past quarter century, a minority of states have eliminated the exemption and many more have modified its reach. Yet the marital rape exemption survives in some substantial form in a majority of states, in an era in which almost every other aspect of women's legal subordination at common law (including a husband's right to assault his wife nonsexually) has been formally repudiated. The modern feminist campaign against marital rape, like its nineteenth-century predecessor, has encountered tremendous resistence and had much less of an impact on the law than it aimed for or achieved in other arenas.

Although not explicitly phrased this way, the contemporary feminist argument against the marital rape exemption, like that of the nineteenth-century woman's rights movement, is an effort to establish that marriage is a potentially antagonistic and dangerous relation, in which women need and deserve legal rights to protect themselves from the serious harms caused by unwanted sex in marriage. Modern feminists, for instance, have a radically different understanding of what privacy arguments for the marital rape exemption are safeguarding. In this view, the use of privacy rationales to justify nonintervention in cases of marital rape protects and exacerbates the current distribution of power within a marriage. Feminists take this distribution to be markedly imbalanced, noting that men are disproportionately richer, stronger, and bigger than their wives. They contend that privacy arguments for the marital rape exemption keep the state from acting to equalize relations in the wife's interest and add state sanction to the power that husbands exercise. On this account, the interests of husband and wife are very much unaligned on the question of legal remediation for marital rape, and the overriding function of the privacy defense of the exemption is not to shelter shared intimacy. Instead, the privacy claim gives husbands safety in committing highly injurious conduct that the law would otherwise consider felonious, while simultaneously disabling wives from summoning state resources for their own protection.

The feminist response to the marital reconciliation argument similarly stresses the divergent interests of husbands and wives, and the lasting harm that marital rape inflicts on married women. Feminists acknowledge that men who rape their wives will systematically favor a legal regime that permits them to avoid prosecution so that they can attempt to reconcile with their wives on private terms. But they contend that the exemption does not serve women's interests equally well. In this vision, what irreparably destroys marital harmony—from the wife's perspective—is not state prosecution, but the marital rape itself. Even with the exemption from prosecution firmly in place, a wife may have little interest in marital reconciliation after her husband has raped her. Marital rape causes women severe and abiding injury, feminists explain, and there is good reason for a wife to conclude that she will be better off if she does not reconcile with a husband who has raped her. Feminists argue that if a wife would be willing to cooperate in her husband's prosecution, the law should not second-guess her assessment of her own interests, even if that assessment diverges from her husband's preferred resolution.

In these feminist arguments, the injury ignored or denied by the exemption's modern defenders is presented in stark relief. The modern feminist rendering of the wound that marital rape inflicts upon women is somewhat different from the account that the nineteenth-century woman's rights movement provided, reflecting an evolving set of commitments. But contemporary feminists, like their nineteenth-century predecessors, emphasize that marital rape causes women serious harm.

First, modern feminists oppose marital rape on the ground that it deprives women of control over their reproductive capacity. This argument is the closest present-day equivalent to the nineteenth-century focus on control over the work of motherhood. Reproductive concerns, however, are far less prominent in modern feminist advocacy against marital rape, perhaps because contemporary feminism accepts contraception and abortion as alternate means of limiting fertility. Modern feminists also concentrate more on the physiological aspects of motherhood (like conception and gestation), than on the child rearing that occupied the nineteenth-century movement, a possible manifestation of the contemporary feminist decision to contest women's disproportionate responsibility for raising children.

More frequently, modern feminists argue that marital rape denies women the right to control their sexuality and their chances for sexual pleasure.... The first woman's rights movement, operating in an era that understood female sexuality to be weaker than its male counterpart, was more occupied by its effort to limit the downside risks of marital intercourse for women. Modern feminists, in contrast, tend (like contemporary Americans generally) to be more optimistic about and interested in the possibilities of sexual intercourse, which has implications for their understanding of the injury that marital rape inflicts. Their account of harm often notes that a marital rape victim loses the ability to determine her sexual "actions, pleasures, and desires free from external influence." From this perspective, "the damage occasioned by [marital rape exemptions] is the subordination, and in many cases the annihilation, of the psychic, physical, emotional, and erotic female self." On a related note, modern feminists also attack marital rape as a violation of women's bodily integrity, never a focus of nineteenth-century feminism. The marital rape exemption, in these terms, "manifests disregard for women's bodily integrity and autonomy and, instead, sanctions their vulnerability in marriage."

The difficulties that the contemporary feminist campaign against marital rape has encountered are particularly remarkable because the modern empirical evidence on marital rape supports the feminists' sex-specific analysis in many ways, delineating how the interests of men and women differ and revealing the trauma that marital rape inflicts upon women. All available evidence, for instance, indicates that marital rape is virtually always committed by husbands on wives. Indeed, I have been able to locate just a handful of cases in which women may have come to the attention of American law enforcement authorities for raping adult men. Only a few more examples of female-on-male rape have been reported in the psychiatric literature. It is possible to predict with almost perfect accuracy that marital rape cases will involve the husband as rapist and the wife as victim. The more lopsided the factual circumstances, the easier it is to differentiate the consequences that a marital rape exemption has for men as opposed to women. Within approximately the past twenty-five years, almost all state exemptions have been revised in a gender-neutral idiom, so that they now regulate the rape of one "spouse" by the other. But it is not the case that wives routinely, or even occasionally, benefit from their immunity from prosecution. Just as a factual matter, husbands experience the marital rape exemption by enjoying immunity from prosecution. Wives experience the marital rape exemption as the person who does not receive the protection of the criminal law for acts that would otherwise be considered serious crimes.

Contemporary empirical research also casts valuable light on the extent and nature of the injury that marital rape causes wives, adding support to the feminist argument that marital rape and the exemption inflict serious harm on women. The best available evidence suggests that approximately one out of every seven or eight married women has been subject to what in the absence of the exemption would be considered to be rape or attempted rape by their husbands. Sociological studies of marital rape victims have concluded, moreover, that rape can be more traumatic within marriage than outside of it. As one research team explained, these "victims suffer from many of the same traumas as victims of other rape—the humiliation, the physical injuries, the guilt and self-reproach. But they suffer some special traumas, too—betrayal, entrapment, and isolation." "The kind of violation they have experienced is much harder to guard against [than rape by a stranger], short of a refusal to trust any man. It touches a woman's basic confidence in forming relationships and trusting intimates."

. . .

Despite the availability of [a] dramatic record of injury, the modern feminist attempt to explain the marital rape exemption in terms of the divergent, even antagonistic, interests of husbands and wives has not been particularly effective.

. . .

If the fate of the nineteenth-century campaign against a husband's conjugal prerogatives illuminates anything, it is that society's reluctance to acknowledge that marriage is a potentially antagonistic and dangerous relation by giving women legal rights against their husbands is long-standing, well-entrenched, and extremely resistant to feminist opposition, especially where marital sex and reproduction are directly implicated. Even the nineteenth-century prescriptive authors who expounded at length on the harm that marital rape was inflicting on wives were unwilling to translate that social recognition into support for granting women legal entitlements. Where feminists made a rights claim advancing women's interests as they were distinct from and defined in opposition to those of men, the prescriptive literature put forth a series of suggested strategies for marital harmony and happiness. Authoritative legal sources, in turn, absolutely refused to alter a husband's exemption from prosecution for raping his wife. After a half-century of writing and advocacy (feminist and otherwise) exploring sexual abuse in marriage, the only change in the legal status of marital rape consisted of a marginal amelioration in the terms on which divorce was available to (privileged) women.

Phrased another way, then, one reason that people are so attracted to the consensual account of the history of marital rape in the first place is that we greatly prefer to envision marital relations as loving, mutually supportive, and harmonious, rather than loathsome, abusive, and conflict-ridden—even though, as a practical matter, we encounter evidence all the time that the latter state of affairs characterizes some relationships. That cultural denial helps explain, for instance, the studies finding that even people who know current divorce rates believe that the possibility that they will divorce is negligible and fail to plan rationally for the contingency.

. . .

The cultural need to understand marital relations as consensual and harmonious also helps explain another phenomenon of approximately the last quarter-century. During this period, dozens of states revisited their marital rape exemptions, but decided to retain them in substantial form nonetheless. One result of this review was that states modified the scope of their exemptions. Another result was that virtually every one of these states rewrote its marital rape exemption in gender-neutral terms, in contrast to the explicit and enthusiastic gender-specificity of the common law formulation. This latter, linguistic change has almost no practical consequences, given the accuracy with which one can predict that marital rapes will be committed by husbands on wives. But as a matter of modern equal protection doctrine, it is very important. Statutes that explicitly classify by sex are automatically subject to heightened scrutiny under the Equal Protection Clause, which relatively few statutes have managed to survive. Once a statute has been made formally gender-neutral, however, it is subject to heightened scrutiny only if a plaintiff can establish the equivalent of legislative malice: that the gender-neutral statute was enacted "at least in part 'because of,' not merely 'in spite of,' its adverse effects upon" women. This is precisely the sort of malignant motivation that is least likely to be uttered in the constitutionally conscious age in which we live. So, as a practical matter, modern marital rape exemptions are subject to rational basis review. Although a small number of state courts have found exemptions unconstitutional on a rational basis analysis, a marital rape exemption is likely to survive this relatively unrigorous level of constitutional scrutiny, which asks only whether the legislature has articulated one reason for the exemption that the court is willing to accept as rational.

. . .

The effect of the current equal protection doctrine on gender-neutrality is to treat men and women as occupying interchangeable roles, in all cases except where the text of the statute or explicit legislative statements of malicious intent force the court to do otherwise. It is a doctrinal methodology for disregarding evidence about gender-specific consequences that suggests the possibility that the interests of men and women may be unaligned, differentially affected, even antagonistically opposed to one another, and not interchangeable at all. Marital rape exemptions are not the only statutes with disproportionate consequences for women to have undergone recent revision into a gender-neutral idiom. Child custody and alimony laws are now almost uniformly gender-neutral, and wife beating statutes now regulate "spousal abuse." Indeed, this impulse substantially predates modern equal protection law: State interspousal tort immunity doctrines, first developed when married women gained the right to sue in their own names in the middle of the nineteenth century, were phrased in gender-neutral terms from the outset. Yet the strength of the yearning to insist within the law that the interests of men and women always harmoniously coincide is nowhere more apparent than with the marital rape exemption, where the sex-specificity of the underlying conduct and injury is extraordinarily pronounced, but equal protection doctrine nonetheless treats husbands and wives as though they occupy unassigned positions.

. . .

There is no easy path upon which contemporary feminists might proceed, given the profound and long-lived societal reluctance—particularly where marital intercourse and reproduction are at issue—to formulate women's legal rights around the understanding that marital relations are potentially antagonistic and dangerous. There is, however, a very pertinent difference between the arena in which the first organized woman's rights movement operated and the contemporary environment, which suggests that the future fate of the modern feminist campaign against marital rape need not track the historical record.

In the latter half of the nineteenth century, the proposition that marital rape inflicted severe harm upon married women was widely acknowledged. The prescriptive literature described this harm in great detail. Authoritative legal sources, moreover, never denied the proposition, and courts occasionally remarked upon it themselves while deciding divorce cases later in the century.... [F]or instance, ... when a New Jersey court wanted to underscore the weakness of Abby English's divorce petition for sexual cruelty, it cited medical testimony that, "although there would be pain" whenever English was forced to have intercourse, "a large proportion of married women assent under exactly those circumstances." In an age that still accepted and endorsed a vast range of legal structures explicitly subordinating women to men, this recognition of injury was not enough to persuade either popular experts on marriage or lawmakers to repudiate a husband's legal right to rape his wife.

The modern defenders of the marital rape exemption, in contrast, submerge and deny the harm that the rule causes women. This has been good strategy for a reason. It is much more difficult to justify the harm that marital rape inflicts upon wives, and explain the absence of legal remediation, in a nation now formally committed to women's legal equality and the undoing of women's subjection at common law. The historical record helps make this harm concrete, revealing the ways in which it is buried by the contemporary defense of the marital rape exemption. If the injury that marital rape inflicts were more systematically put at issue, and arguments presuming that marital relations never cause women harm were more systematically resisted, it might be harder for the legal system to continue to shelter a husband's prerogatives.

b. BATTERED WOMEN'S SYNDROME

(1) Self–Defense

People v. Humphrey

Supreme Court of California, 1996.
13 Cal.4th 1073, 56 Cal.Rptr.2d 142, 921 P.2d 1.

■ CHIN, J.

. . .

During the evening of March 28, 1992, defendant [Evelyn Humphrey] shot and killed Albert Hampton in their Fresno home. Officer Reagan was the first on the scene. A neighbor told Reagan that the couple in the house had been arguing all day. Defendant soon came outside appearing upset and with her hands raised as if surrendering. She told Officer Reagan, "I shot him. That's right, I shot him. I just couldn't take him beating on me no more." She led the officer into the house, showed him a .357 magnum revolver on a table, and said, "There's the gun." Hampton was on the kitchen floor, wounded but alive.

A short time later, defendant told Officer Reagan, "He deserved it. I just couldn't take it anymore. I told him to stop beating on me." "He was beating on me, so I shot him. I told him I'd shoot him if he ever beat on me again." A paramedic heard her say that she wanted to teach Hampton "a lesson." Defendant told another officer at the scene, Officer Terry, "I'm fed up. Yeah, I shot him. I'm just tired of him hitting me. He said, 'You're not going to do nothing about it.' I showed him, didn't I? I shot him good. He won't hit anybody else again. Hit me again; I shoot him again. I don't care if I go to jail. Push come to shove, I guess people gave it to him, and, kept hitting me. I warned him. I warned him not to hit me. He wouldn't listen."

Officer Terry took defendant to the police station, where she told the following story. The day before the shooting, Hampton had been drinking. He hit defendant while they were driving home in their truck and continued hitting her when they arrived. He told her, "I'll kill you," and shot at her. The bullet went through a bedroom window and struck a tree outside. The day of the shooting, Hampton "got drunk," swore at her, and started hitting her again. He walked into the kitchen. Defendant saw the gun in the living room and picked it up. Her jaw hurt, and she was in pain. She pointed the gun at Hampton and said, "You're not going to hit me anymore." Hampton said, "What are you doing?" Believing that Hampton was about to pick something up to hit her with, she shot him. She then put the gun down and went outside to wait for the police.

Hampton later died of a gunshot wound to his chest. The neighbor who spoke with Officer Reagan testified that shortly before the shooting, she heard defendant, but not Hampton, shouting. The evening before, the neighbor had heard a gunshot. Defendant's blood contained no drugs but had a blood-alcohol level of .17 percent. Hampton's blood contained no drugs or alcohol.

Defendant claimed she shot Hampton in self-defense. To support the claim, the defense presented first expert testimony and then nonexpert testimony, including that of defendant herself.

Dr. Lee Bowker testified as an expert on battered women's syndrome. The syndrome, he testified, "is not just a psychological construction, but it's a term for a wide variety of controlling mechanisms that the man or it can be a woman, but in general for this syndrome it's a man, uses against the woman, and for the effect that those control mechanisms have."

Dr. Bowker had studied about 1,000 battered women and found them often inaccurately portrayed "as cardboard figures, paper-thin punching bags who merely absorb the violence but didn't do anything about it." He found that battered women often employ strategies to stop the beatings, including hiding, running away, counterviolence, seeking the help of friends and family, going to a shelter, and contacting police. Nevertheless, many battered women remain in the relationship because of lack of money, social isolation, lack of self-confidence, inadequate police response, and a fear (often justified) of reprisals by the batterer. "The battering man will make the battered woman depend on him and generally succeed at least for a time." A battered woman often feels responsible for the abusive relationship, and "she just can't figure out a way to please him better so he'll stop beating her." In sum, "It really is the physical control of the woman through economics and through relative social isolation combined with the psychological techniques that make her so dependent."

Many battered women go from one abusive relationship to another and seek a strong man to protect them from the previous abuser. "[W]ith each successful victimization, the person becomes less able to avoid the next one." The violence can gradually escalate, as the batterer keeps control using ever more severe actions, including rape, torture, violence against the woman's loved ones or pets, and death threats. Battered women sense this escalation. In Dr. Bowker's "experience with battered women who kill in self-defense their abusers, it's always related to their perceived change of what's going on in a relationship. They become very sensitive to what sets off batterers. They watch for this stuff very carefully. . . . Anybody who is abused over a period of time becomes sensitive to the abuser's behavior and when she sees a change acceleration begin in that behavior, it tells them something is going to happen. . . ."

Dr. Bowker interviewed defendant for a full day. He believed she suffered not only from battered women's syndrome, but also from being the child of an alcoholic and an incest victim. He testified that all three of defendant's partners before Hampton were abusive and significantly older than she.

Dr. Bowker described defendant's relationship with Hampton. Hampton was a 49–year-old man who weighed almost twice as much as defendant. The two had a battering relationship that Dr. Bowker characterized as a "traditional cycle of violence." The cycle included phases of tension building, violence, and then forgiveness-seeking in which Hampton would promise not to batter defendant any more and she would believe him. During this period, there would be occasional good times. For example, defendant told Dr. Bowker that Hampton would give her a rose. "That's one of the things that hooks people in. Intermittent reinforcement is the key." But after a while, the violence would begin again. The violence would recur because "basically . . . the woman doesn't perfectly obey. That's the bottom line." For example, defendant would talk to another man, or fail to clean house "just so."

The situation worsened over time, especially when Hampton got off parole shortly before his death. He became more physically and emotionally abusive, repeatedly threatened defendant's life, and even shot at her the night before his death. Hampton often allowed defendant to go out, but she was afraid to flee because she felt he would find her as he had in the past. "He enforced her belief that she can never escape him." Dr. Bowker testified that unless her injuries were so severe that "something absolutely had to be treated," he would not expect her to seek medical treatment. "That's the pattern of her life. . . ."

Dr. Bowker believed defendant's description of her experiences. In his opinion, she suffered from battered women's syndrome in "about as extreme a pattern as you could find."

Defendant confirmed many of the details of her life and relationship with Hampton underlying Dr. Bowker's opinion. She testified that her father forcefully molested her from the time she was seven years old until she was fifteen. She described her relationship with another abusive man as being like "Nightmare on Elm Street." Regarding Hampton, she testified that they often argued and that he beat her regularly. Both were heavy drinkers. Hampton once threw a can of beer at her face, breaking her nose. Her dental plates hurt because Hampton hit her so often. He often kicked her, but usually hit her in the back of the head because, he told her, it "won't leave bruises." Hampton sometimes threatened to kill her, and often said she "would live to regret it." Matters got worse towards the end.

The evening before the shooting, March 27, 1992, Hampton arrived home "very drunk." He yelled at her and called her names. At one point when she was standing by the bedroom window, he fired his .357 magnum revolver at her. She testified, "He didn't miss me by much either." She was "real scared."

The next day, the two drove into the mountains. They argued, and Hampton continually hit her. While returning, he said that their location would be a good place to kill her because "they wouldn't find [her] for a while." She took it as a joke, although she feared him. When they returned, the arguing continued. He hit her again, then entered the kitchen. He threatened, "This time, bitch, when I shoot at you, I won't miss." He came from the kitchen and reached for the gun on the living room table. She grabbed it first, pointed it at him, and told him "that he wasn't going to hit [her]." She backed Hampton into the kitchen. He was saying something, but she did not know what. He reached for her hand and she shot him. She believed he was reaching for the gun and was going to shoot her.

Several other witnesses testified about defendant's relationship with Hampton, his abusive conduct in general, and his physical abuse of, and threats to, defendant in particular. This testimony generally corroborated defendant's. A neighbor testified that the night before the shooting, she heard a gunshot. The next morning, defendant told the neighbor that Hampton had shot at her, and that she was afraid of him. After the shooting, investigators found a bullet hole through the frame of the bedroom window and a bullet embedded in a tree in line with the window. Another neighbor testified that shortly before hearing the shot that killed Hampton, she heard defendant say, "Stop it, Albert. Stop it."

Defendant was charged with murder with personal use of a firearm. At the end of the prosecution's case-in-chief, the court granted defendant's motion under *Penal Code section 1118.1* for acquittal of first degree murder.

The court instructed the jury on second degree murder and both voluntary and involuntary manslaughter. It also instructed on self-defense, explaining that an actual and reasonable belief that the killing was necessary was a complete defense; an actual but unreasonable belief was a defense to murder, but not to voluntary manslaughter. In determining reasonableness, the jury was to consider what "would appear to be necessary to a reasonable person in a similar situation and with similar knowledge."

The court also instructed:

"Evidence regarding Battered Women's Syndrome has been introduced in this case. Such evidence, if believed, may be considered by you only for the purpose of determining whether or not the defendant held the necessary subjective honest [belief] which is a requirement for both perfect and imperfect self-defense. However, that same evidence regarding Battered Women's Syndrome may not be considered or used by you in evaluating the objective reasonableness requirement for perfect self-defense.

"Battered Women's Syndrome seeks to describe and explain common reactions of women to that experience. Thus, you may consider the evidence concerning the syndrome and its effects only for the limited purpose of showing, if it does show, that the defendant's reactions, as demonstrated by the evidence, are not inconsistent with her having been physically abused or the beliefs, perceptions, or behavior of victims of domestic violence."

During deliberations, the jury asked for and received clarification of the terms "subjectively honest and objectively unreasonable." It found defendant guilty of voluntary manslaughter with personal use of a firearm. The court sentenced defendant to prison for eight years, consisting of the lower term of three years for manslaughter, plus the upper term of five years for firearm use. The Court of Appeal remanded for resentencing on the use enhancement, but otherwise affirmed the judgment.

We granted defendant's petition for review.

... Evidence Code section 1107, subdivision (a), makes admissible in a criminal action expert testimony regarding "battered women's syndrome, including the physical, emotional, or mental effects upon the beliefs, perceptions, or behavior of victims of domestic violence...." Defendant presented the evidence to support her claim of self-defense ... The only issue is to what extent defendant established its "relevancy." To resolve this question we must examine California law regarding self-defense.

For killing to be in self-defense, the defendant must actually and reasonably believe in the need to defend. If the belief subjectively exists but is objectively unreasonable, there is "imperfect self-defense," i.e., "the defendant is deemed to have acted without malice and cannot be convicted of murder," but can be convicted of manslaughter. In re Christian S. (1994) 7 Cal. 4th 768, 783 [30 Cal. Rptr. 2d 33, 872 P.2d 574].) To constitute "perfect self-defense," i.e., to exonerate the person completely, the belief must also be objectively reasonable. As the Legislature has stated, "[T]he circumstances must be sufficient to excite the fears of a reasonable person...." *Pen. Code, § 198.* Moreover, for either perfect or imperfect self-defense, the fear must be of imminent harm. "Fear of future harm—no matter how great the fear and no matter how great the likelihood of the harm—will not suffice. The defendant's fear must be of *imminent* danger to life or great bodily injury."

Although the belief in the need to defend must be objectively reasonable, a jury must consider what "would appear to be necessary to a reasonable person in a similar situation and with similar knowledge...."

CALJIC No. 5.50. It judges reasonableness "from the point of view of a reasonable person in the position of defendant...." To do this, it must consider all the " 'facts and circumstances ... in determining whether the defendant acted in a manner in which *a reasonable man* would act in protecting his own life or bodily safety.' As we stated long ago, ... a defendant is entitled to have a jury take into consideration all the elements in the case which might be expected to operate on his mind...."

With these principles in mind, we now consider the relevance of evidence of battered women's syndrome to the elements of self-defense.

Battered women's syndrome "has been defined as 'a series of common characteristics that appear in women who are abused physically and psychologically over an extended period of time by the dominant male figure in their lives.' " State v. Kelly (1984) 97 N.J. 178, 193.

The trial court allowed the jury to consider the battered women's syndrome evidence in deciding whether defendant actually believed she needed to kill in self-defense. The question here is whether the evidence was also relevant on the reasonableness of that belief. Two Court of Appeal decisions have considered the relevance of battered women's syndrome evidence to a claim of self-defense.

People v. Aris [215 Cal. App. 3d 1178, 264 Cal. Rptr. 167 (1989)] applied "the law of self-defense in the context of a battered woman killing the batterer while he slept after he had beaten the killer and threatened serious bodily injury and death when he awoke." There, unlike here, the trial court refused to instruct the jury on perfect self-defense, but it did instruct on imperfect self-defense. The appellate court upheld the refusal, finding that "defendant presented no substantial evidence that a reasonable person under the same circumstances would have perceived imminent danger and a need to kill in self-defense."

. . .

Although the trial court did not instruct on perfect self-defense, the appellate court first concluded that battered women's syndrome evidence is not relevant to the reasonableness element. "[T]he questions of the reasonableness of a defendant's belief that self-defense is necessary and of the reasonableness of the actions taken in self-defense do not call for an evaluation of the defendant's subjective *state of mind*, but for an objective evaluation of the defendant's assertedly defensive *acts*. California law expresses the criterion for this evaluation in the objective terms of whether *a reasonable person*, as opposed to the *defendant*, would have believed and acted as the defendant did. We hold that expert testimony about a defendant's state of mind is not relevant to the reasonableness of the defendant's self-defense."

The court then found the evidence "highly relevant to the first element of self-defense—defendant's actual, subjective perception that she was in danger and that she had to kill her husband to avoid that danger.... [P] The relevance to the defendant's actual perception lies in the opinion's explanation of how such a perception would reasonably follow from the defendant's experience as a battered woman. This relates to the prosecution's argument that such a perception of imminent danger makes no sense when the victim is asleep and a way of escape open and, therefore, she did not actually have that perception." The trial court thus erred in not admitting the testimony to show "how the defendant's particular experiences as a battered woman affected her perceptions of danger, its imminence, and what actions were necessary to protect herself."

Concerned "that the jury in a particular case may misuse such evidence to establish the reasonableness requirement for perfect self-defense, for which purpose it is irrelevant," the *Aris* court stated that, "upon request whenever the jury is instructed on perfect self-defense, trial courts should instruct that such testimony is relevant only to prove the honest belief requirement for both perfect and imperfect self-defense, not to prove the reasonableness requirement for perfect self-defense." The trial court gave such an instruction here, thus creating the issue before us.

In People v. Day (1992) 2 Cal. App. 4th 405 the defendant moved for a new trial following her conviction of involuntary manslaughter. Supported by an affidavit by Dr. Bowker, she argued that her attorney should have presented evidence of battered women's syndrome to aid her claim of self-defense. Relying on *Aris,* the appellate court first found that the evidence would not have been relevant to show the objective reasonableness of the defendant's actions. It also found, however, that the evidence would have been admissible to rehabilitate the defendant's credibility as a witness. Finding that counsel's failure to present the evidence was prejudicial, the court reversed the judgment.

The Attorney General argues that *Aris* and *Day* were correct that evidence of battered women's syndrome is irrelevant to reasonableness. We disagree. Those cases too narrowly interpreted the reasonableness element. *Aris* and *Day* failed to consider that the jury, in determining objective reasonableness, must view the situation from the *defendant's perspective.* Here, for example, Dr. Bowker testified that the violence can escalate and that a battered woman can become increasingly sensitive to the abuser's behavior, testimony relevant to determining whether defendant reasonably believed when she fired the gun that this time the threat to her life was imminent. Indeed, the prosecutor argued that, "from an objective, reasonable man's standard, there was no reason for her to go get that gun. This threat that she says he made was like so many threats before. There was no reason for her to react that way." Dr. Bowker's testimony supplied a response that the jury might not otherwise receive. As violence increases over time, and threats gain credibility, a battered person might become sensitized and thus able reasonably to discern when danger is real and when it is not. "[T]he expert's testimony might also enable the jury to find that the battered [woman] . . . is particularly able to predict accurately the likely extent of violence in any attack on her. That conclusion could significantly affect the jury's evaluation of the *reasonableness* of defendant's fear for her life." State v. Kelly (1984) 97 N.J. 178.

. . .

Contrary to the Attorney General's argument, we are not changing the standard from objective to subjective, or replacing the reasonable "person" standard with a reasonable "battered woman" standard. Our decision would not, in another context, compel adoption of a " 'reasonable gang member' standard." *Evidence Code section 1107* states "a rule of evidence only" and makes "no substantive change." Evid. Code, § 1107, subd. (d). The jury must consider defendant's situation and knowledge, which makes the evidence relevant, but the ultimate question is whether a reasonable *person,* not a reasonable battered woman, would believe in the need to kill to prevent imminent harm. Moreover, it is the *jury,* not the expert,that determines whether defendant's belief and, ultimately, her actions, were objectively reasonable.

Battered women's syndrome evidence was also relevant to defendant's credibility. It "would have assisted the jury in objectively analyzing [defendant's] claim of self-defense by dispelling many of the commonly held misconceptions about battered women." People v. Day, supra, 2 Cal. App. 4th at p. 416. For example, in urging the jury not to believe defendant's testimony that Hampton shot at her the night before the killing, the prosecutor argued that "if this defendant truly believed that [Hampton] had shot at her, on that night, I mean she would have left.... [P] If she really believed that he had tried to shoot her, she would not have stayed." Dr. Bowker's testimony " 'would help dispel the ordinary lay person's perception that a woman in a battering relationship is free to leave at any time. The expert evidence would counter any "common sense" conclusions by the jury that if the beatings were really that bad the woman would have left her husband much earlier. Popular misconceptions about battered women would be put to rest....' " (People v. Day, supra, 2 Cal. App. 4th at p. 417, quoting State v. Hodges (1986) 239 Kan. 63).

. . .

We do not hold that Dr. Bowker's entire testimony was relevant to both prongs of perfect self-defense. Just as many types of evidence may be relevant to some disputed issues but not all, some of the expert evidence was no doubt relevant only to the subjective existence of defendant's belief. Evidence merely showing that a person's use of deadly force is scientifically explainable or empirically common does not, in itself, show it was objectively reasonable. To dispel any possible confusion, it might be appropriate for the court, on request, to clarify that, in assessing reasonableness, the question is whether a reasonable person in the defendant's circumstances would have perceived a threat of imminent injury or death, and not whether killing the abuser was reasonable in the sense of being an understandable response to ongoing abuse; and that, therefore, in making that assessment, the jury may not consider evidence merely showing that an abused person's use of force against the abuser is understandable.

We also emphasize that, as with any evidence, the jury may give this testimony whatever weight it deems appropriate in light of the evidence as a whole. The ultimate judgment of reasonableness is solely for the jury. We simply hold that evidence of battered women's syndrome is generally *relevant* to the reasonableness, as well as the subjective existence, of defendant's belief in the need to defend, and, to the extent it is relevant, the jury may *consider* it in deciding both questions. The court's contrary instruction was erroneous. We disapprove of People v. Aris, supra, 215 Cal. App. 3d 1178, and People v. Day, supra, 2 Cal. App. 4th 405, to the extent they are inconsistent with this conclusion.

R. v. Malott

Supreme Court of Canada, 1998.
1998 WL 1714234.

■ L'HEUREUX-DUBE J. [concurring]:

I have read the reasons of my colleague Justice Major, and I concur with the result that he reaches. However, given that this Court has not had the opportunity to discuss the value of evidence of "battered woman syndrome" since R. v. Lavallee, [1990] 1 S.C.R. 852, and given the evolving discourse on "battered woman syndrome" in the legal community, I will make a few comments on the importance of this kind of evidence to the just adjudication of charges involving battered women.

. . .

... [T]he majority of the Court in *Lavallee* ... implicitly accepted that women's experiences and perspectives may be different from the experiences and perspectives of men. It accepted that a woman's perception of what is reasonable is influenced by her gender, as well as by her individual experience, and both are relevant to the legal inquiry. This legal development was significant, because it demonstrated a willingness to look at the whole context of a woman's experience in order to inform the analysis of the particular events. But it is wrong to think of this development of the law as merely an example where an objective test—the requirement that an accused claiming self-defence must reasonably apprehend death or grievous bodily harm—has been modified to admit evidence of the subjective perceptions of a battered woman. More important, a majority of the Court accepted that the perspectives of women, which have historically been ignored, must now equally inform the "objective" standard of the reasonable person in relation to self-defence.

When interpreting and applying *Lavallee*, these broader principles should be kept in mind. In particular, they should be kept in mind in order to avoid a too rigid and restrictive approach to the admissibility and legal value of evidence of a battered woman's experiences. Concerns have been expressed that the treatment of expert evidence on battered women syndrome, which is itself admissible in order to combat the myths and stereotypes which society has about battered women, has led to a new stereotype of the "battered woman."

It is possible that those women who are unable to fit themselves within the stereotype of a victimized, passive, helpless, dependent, battered woman will not have their claims to self-defence fairly decided. For instance, women who have demonstrated too much strength or initiative, women of colour, women who are professionals, or women who might have fought back against their abusers on previous occasions, should not be penalized for failing to accord with the stereotypical image of the archetypal battered woman. Needless to say, women with these characteristics are still entitled to have their claims of self-defence fairly adjudicated, and they are also still entitled to have their experiences as battered women inform the analysis. Professor Grant warns against allowing the law to develop such that a woman accused of killing her abuser must either have been "reasonable like a man" or "reasonable like a battered woman". I agree that this must be avoided. The "reasonable woman" must not be forgotten in the analysis, and deserves to be as much a part of the objective standard of the reasonable person as does the "reasonable man."

How should the courts combat the "syndromization," as Professor Grant refers to it, of battered women who act in self-defence? The legal inquiry into the moral culpability of a woman who is, for instance, claiming self-defence must focus on the reasonableness of her actions in the context of her personal experiences, and her experiences as a woman, not on her status as a battered woman and her entitlement to claim that she is suffering from "battered woman syndrome".... By emphasizing a woman's "learned helplessness," her dependence, her victimization, and her low self-esteem, in order to establish that she suffers from "battered woman syndrome", the legal debate shifts from the objective rationality of her actions to preserve her own life to those personal inadequacies which apparently explain her failure to flee from her abuser. Such an emphasis comports too well with society's stereotypes about women. Therefore, it should be scrupulously avoided because it only serves to undermine the important advancements achieved by the decision in *Lavallee.*

There are other elements of a woman's social context which help to explain her inability to leave her abuser, and which do not focus on those characteristics most consistent with traditional stereotypes. As Wilson J. herself recognized in *Lavallee,* at p. 887, "environmental factors may also impair the woman's ability to leave—lack of job skills, the presence of children to care for, fear of retaliation by the man, etc. may each have a role to play in some cases." To this list of factors I would add a woman's need to protect her children from abuse, a fear of losing custody of her children, pressures to keep the family together, weaknesses of social and financial support for battered women, and no guarantee that the violence would cease simply because she left. These considerations necessarily inform the reasonableness of a woman's beliefs or perceptions of, for instance, her lack of an alternative to the use of deadly force to preserve herself from death or grievous bodily harm.

How should these principles be given practical effect in the context of a jury trial of a woman accused of murdering her abuser? To fully accord with the spirit of *Lavallee,* where the reasonableness of a battered woman's belief is at issue in a criminal case, a judge and jury should be made to appreciate that a battered woman's experiences are both individualized, based on her own history and relationships, as well as shared with other women, within the context of a society and a legal system which has historically undervalued women's experiences. A judge and jury should be told that a battered woman's experiences are generally outside the common understanding of the average judge and juror, and that they should seek to understand the evidence being presented to them in order to overcome the myths and stereotypes which we all share. Finally, all of this should be presented in such a way as to focus on the reasonableness of the woman's actions, without relying on old or new stereotypes about battered women.

NOTE

1. In Nicholson v. Scoppetta, 3 N.Y.3d 357, 787 N.Y.S.2d 196, 820 N.E.2d 840 (2004), the New York Court of Appeals considered whether a mother who is a victim of domestic violence fails to exercise a "minimum degree of care," and thus leaves her child neglected, if she fails to prevent the child from witnessing such violence. The court said that a determination of what constitutes minimum care under the circumstances must take into account:

> risks attendant to leaving, if the batterer has threatened to kill her if she does; risks attendant to staying and suffering continued abuse; risks attendant to seeking assistance through government channels, potentially increasing the danger to herself and her children; risks attendant to criminal prosecution against the abuser; and risks attendant to relocation. Whether a particular mother in these circumstances has actually failed to exercise a minimum degree of care is necessarily dependent on facts such as the severity and frequency of the violence, and the resources and options available to her.

Id. at 846. For a lengthier excerpt from the *Nicholson* opinion that discusses the standards for removing a child from a home in which the mother is the victim of domestic violence, see Chapter 10, Section A.

(2) *Tort Liability*

Giovine v. Giovine

Superior Court of New Jersey, Appellate Division, 1995.
284 N.J.Super. 3, 663 A.2d 109.

■ KLEINER, J.A.D.

. . .

Plaintiff and defendant were married on May 1, 1971. Three children were born of this marriage on August 17, 1975, July 5, 1979, and July 7, 1983.

On approximately December 31, 1978, defendant separated from plaintiff. In May 1980, he filed a complaint seeking to establish visitation rights with the two children of the marriage. On August 1, 1980, defendant filed a complaint for divorce, asserting a cause of action for dissolution of marriage predicated upon eighteen consecutive months of separation. Plaintiff filed an answer and counterclaim for divorce, alleging habitual drunkenness and extreme cruelty as alternative grounds for divorce. Additionally, that counterclaim contained three counts for damages predicated upon the following torts: a specific act of assault and battery in March 1972 and a final act of assault and battery on December 28, 1978; infliction of emotional distress based upon the same acts of assault and battery; and "a continuous and unbroken wrong commencing on or about March 1972 and continuing down until December 28, 1978."

Defendant filed an answer to the counterclaim and amended his complaint for divorce, adding a cause of action for divorce based upon acts of extreme cruelty.

In July 1982, while their matrimonial action was pending, the parties reconciled and resumed living together. On July 26, 1982, both parties directed their respective attorneys to discontinue the litigation. The proceedings were dismissed by a stipulation of dismissal with prejudice dated October 25, 1982. The couple separated again in September 1993. As noted, plaintiff filed her present complaint on July 1, 1994. Defendant filed an answer and counterclaim asserting a cause of action for divorce based upon extreme cruelty.

On August 8, 1994, defendant filed a motion to strike certain causes of action contained within plaintiff's complaint and to strike plaintiff's demand for a jury trial on counts three through eleven. On September 20, 1994, the motion judge granted defendant's motion, striking all tortious claims occurring prior to June 30, 1992 based upon the applicable statute of limitations, *N.J.S.A. 2A:14–2*, and limiting plaintiff's proofs on her claims for emotional distress or negligence to those acts alleged to have occurred after June 30, 1992. The motion judge also determined that plaintiff did not have a constitutional right to a jury trial. We granted plaintiff's motion seeking leave to appeal those rulings.... We now affirm in part and reverse in part.

. . .

Interspousal tort immunity no longer exists to bar the suit of one spouse against another for injuries sustained by one spouse due to the tortious conduct of the other....

The abolition of the doctrine pertained to tortious conduct generally encompassing not only conventional negligence but also intentional acts, as well as other forms of excessive behavior such as gross negligence, recklessness, wantonness, and the like. The only kind of marital conduct excepted from the abolition was that involving marital or nuptial privileges, consensual acts and simple, common domestic negligence, to be defined and developed on a case-by-case approach.

... On appeal, plaintiff contends that the motion judge erred in refusing to follow the decision in Cusseaux v. Pickett, 279 N.J. Super. 335, 652 A.2d 789 (Law Div. 1994), which concluded that "battered-woman's syndrome is the result of a continuing pattern of abuse and violent behavior that causes continuing damage." As such, "it must be treated in the same way as a continuing tort." Battered woman's syndrome would therefore be an exception to *N.J.S.A. 2A:14–2*, that "every action at law for an injury to the person caused by the wrongful act, neglect or default of any person within this state shall be commenced within 2 years next after the cause of any such action shall have occurred." The decision in *Cusseaux* substantially relied upon State v. Kelly, 97 N.J. 178, 478 A.2d 364 (1984).

In *Kelly*, the Supreme Court, relying in part on the research of Lenore E. Walker, The Battered Woman (1979), noted that battered woman's syndrome is a recognized medical condition. By definition, a battered woman is one who is repeatedly physically or emotionally abused by a man in an attempt to force her to do his bidding without regard for her rights. According to experts, in order to be a battered woman, the woman and her abuser must go through the "battering cycle" at least twice....

Cusseaux v. Pickett recognized for the first time in this state, that a woman who suffers from the medically diagnosable condition of battered woman's syndrome is entitled to seek compensation for the physical and emotional injuries attributable to the abusive conduct during the course of the relationship. The trial judge found that:

> Because the battered-woman's syndrome is the result of a continuing pattern of abuse and violent behavior that causes continuing damage, it must be treated in the same way as a continuing tort. It would be contrary to the public policy of this State, not to mention cruel, to limit recovery to only those individual incidents of assault and battery for which the applicable statute of limitations has not yet run. The mate who is responsible for creating the condition suffered by the battered victim must be made to account for his actions—all of his actions. Failure to allow affirmative recovery under these circumstances would be tantamount to the courts condoning the continued abusive treatment of women in the domestic sphere. This the courts cannot and will never do.

Cusseaux established a four-part test to state a cause of action for battered woman's syndrome:

> 1) involvement in a marital or marital-like intimate relationship; and 2) physical or psychological abuse perpetrated by the dominant partner to the relationship over an extended period of time; and 3) the aforestated abuse has caused recurring physical or psychological injury over the course of the relationship; and 4) a past or present inability to take any action to improve or alter the situation unilaterally.

We agree with the premise espoused in *Cusseaux* and conclude that a wife diagnosed with battered woman's syndrome should be permitted to sue her spouse in tort for the physical and emotional injuries sustained by continuous acts of battering during the course of the marriage, provided there is medical, psychiatric, or psychological expert testimony establishing that the wife was caused to have an "inability to take any action to improve or alter the situation unilaterally." In the absence of expert proof, the wife cannot be deemed to be suffering from battered woman's syndrome, and each act of abuse during the marriage would constitute a separate and distinct cause of action in tort, subject to the statute of limitations.

Our disagreement with *Cusseaux* is predicated upon semantics. *Cusseaux* classifies battered woman's syndrome as a continuous tort. The concept of "continuous tort" has been recognized in this state.

. . .

We do not adopt the conclusion in *Cusseaux* that battered woman's syndrome is itself a continuous tort. Battered woman's syndrome is more correctly the medical condition resulting from continued acts of physical or psychological misconduct. Because the resulting psychological state, composed of varied but identifiable characteristics, is the product of at least two separate and discrete physical or psychological acts occurring at different times, to overcome the statute of limitations, it is imperative that the tortious conduct giving rise to the medical condition be considered a continuous tort. As noted in *Kelly*:

> The combination of all of these symptoms—resulting from sustained psychological and physical trauma compounded by aggravating social and economic factors—constitutes the battered-woman's syndrome. Only by understanding these unique pressures that force battered women to remain with their mates, despite their long-standing and reasonable fear of severe bodily harm and the isolation that being a battered woman creates, can a battered woman's state of mind be accurately and fairly understood.

. . .

In Kyle v. Green Acres at Verona, Inc., 44 N.J. 100, 207 A.2d 513 (1965), the Supreme Court held that *N.J.S.A. 2A:14–21* "foreclosed a tolling of the running of [the limitations period] unless plaintiff was [insane] at the time the cause of action accrued. . . ." The Court carved out an equitable exception, however, where defendant's "negligent act brings about [a] plaintiff's insanity." Applying equitable considerations, the Court concluded:

> If plaintiff's insanity was caused by defendant's wrongful act, it may be said that such act was responsible for plaintiff's failure or inability to institute her action prior to the running of the statute of limitations. We feel that justice here requires us to carve out an equitable exception to the general principle that there is no time out for the period of time covered by the disability if the disability accrued at or after the cause of action accrued. Thus, a defendant whose negligent act brings about plaintiff's insanity should not be permitted to cloak himself with the protective garb of the statute of limitations.
>
> The Court added:
>
> The equitable approach should mandate the following: A trial court shall itself without a jury hear and determine (1) whether insanity developed on or subsequent to the date of the alleged act of defendant and within the period of limitation and if so, whether that insanity resulted from the defendant's acts; and (2) whether plaintiff's suit was started within a reasonable time after restoration of sanity . . .

"Insane," as used in *N.J.S.A. 2A:14–21,* means "such a condition of mental derangement as actually prevents the sufferer from understanding his [or her] legal rights or instituting legal action." Id.

In Jones v. Jones, 242 N.J. Super. 195, 576 A.2d 316 (App. Div.), cert. denied, 122 N.J. 418 (1990), we applied equitable considerations to abrogate the running of the statute of limitations against an incest victim. We noted the victim's emotional condition as a justification for tolling the statute of limitations, as well as the fact that the victim plaintiff was placed under physical and psychological duress by the defendant. Plaintiff's expert psychologist opined that "individuals subjected to childhood sexual abuse often find it impossible to communicate and describe such misconduct." Jones likened plaintiff's condition to the condition of insanity, which tolls the statute of limitations in *N.J.S.A. 2A:14–21* and provides in part:

> If any person entitled to any of the actions or proceedings specified in sections 2A:14–1 to 2A:14–8 or sections 2A:14–16 to 2A:14–20 . . . is or shall be, at the time of any such cause of action or right or title accruing,under the age of 21 years, or insane, such person may commence such action . . . after his coming to or being of full age or of sane mind.

We are able to draw an analogy between the status of the plaintiff in *Jones* to the status of a victim of repeated violence within the marital setting, who may "sink into a state of psychological paralysis and become unable to take any action at all to improve or alter the situation."

Jones also determined that duress may toll the statute of limitations when "it is either an element of or inherent in the underlying cause of action." We prefaced that conclusion with this admonition:

> We do not suggest that the decisions we have cited should be applied uncritically whenever a plaintiff claims that his or her failure to initiate suit in a timely fashion was caused by a defendant's wrongful act. We are, nevertheless, of the view that, within certain limits, a prospective defendant's coercive acts and threats may rise to such a level of duress as to deprive the plaintiff of his freedom of will and thereby toll the statute of limitations.

. . .

It will be incumbent upon plaintiff to establish pretrial, by medical, psychiatric or psychological evidence, that she suffers from battered woman's syndrome, which caused an inability to take any action to improve or alter the circumstances in her marriage unilaterally, so as to warrant a conclusion by the trial judge that the statute of limitations should be tolled.

We construe the clear legislative statement in the preamble to *N.J.S.A. 2C:25–18* as justification for the decision we reach: "the Legislature encourages . . . the broad application of the remedies available under this act in the civil and criminal courts of this State." [A]s we now subscribe to the concept articulated in *Cusseaux,* we reverse the motion judge's decision and direct that plaintiff shall be entitled to present proof that she has the medically diagnosed condition of battered woman's syndrome. Plaintiff shall be entitled to sue her husband for damages attributable to his continuous tortious conduct resulting in her present psychological condition, provided she has medical, psychiatric, or psychological expert proof to establish that she was caused to have an inability "to take any action at all to improve or alter the situation."

. . .

Obviously, in order to prove the medical condition of battered woman's syndrome, plaintiff must be permitted to prove all acts of physical or psychological misconduct. This proof will also encompass the first beating in March 1972. The medical condition is attributable to more than one act of battering. Although plaintiff may be barred from recovering damages for certain marital torts ... those acts and others may be relevant in plaintiff's proofs presented to establish plaintiff's claim of emotional distress.... It was error for the court to bar all evidence of abuse occurring prior to June 30, 1992. Some or all evidence of pre–1992 events may be relevant to proving plaintiff's causes of action framed in terms of infliction of emotional distress or negligence. Rulings which exclude proffered evidence are best made at trial, where the court is best able to evaluate "the logical connection between the proffered evidence and a fact in issue."

. . .

It is therefore clear that plaintiff must be permitted to present proofs of all acts of cruelty which occurred during the course of her marriage to defendant. Those prior acts may be offered to prove plaintiff's cause of action for divorce predicated on the grounds of extreme cruelty, or they may be offered as relevant evidence in conjunction with plaintiff's claim for damages attributable to battered woman's syndrome, intentional infliction of emotional distress and negligence.

. . .

The component of the order striking all tortious claims occurring prior to June 30, 1992, based upon *N.J.S.A. 2A:14–2,* is modified. Plaintiff is barred from pursuing a claim for damages for assault and battery on any battery occurring prior to June 30, 1992, but she is permitted to assert a claim for battered woman's syndrome attributable to acts occurring after October 25, 1982, when plaintiff's prior counterclaim for divorce was dismissed with prejudice. Our modification of the motion judge's order is without prejudice to defendant's right to again move to strike plaintiff's claim of continuous tort resulting in battered woman's syndrome, should plaintiff fail to amend her complaint to allege specifically the acts of continuous violence occurring after October 25, 1982, which she contends resulted in the condition described as battered woman's syndrome.

. . .

■ SKILLMAN, J.A.D., concurring and dissenting.

I see no need for the creation of a new tort cause of action for "battered woman's syndrome."

. . .

"It is inadvisable to create new causes of action in tort in advance of any necessity for doing so in order to achieve a just result." Neelthak Dev. Corp. v. Township of Gloucester, 272 N.J. Super. 319, 325, 639 A.2d 1141 (App. Div. 1994). Consequently, this court should consider whether existing tort causes of action provide an adequate remedy for conduct that may result in battered woman's syndrome before undertaking to create any new cause of action.

Any person who is a victim of violence, or the threat of violence, may recover money damages for assault and/or battery. A person may be liable for battery if "he acts intending to cause a harmful or offensive contact ... or an imminent apprehension of such contact" and a "harmful" or "offensive" contact "directly or indirectly results." 1 Restatement (Second) of Torts §§ 13, 18 (1965). A person who acts with the same intent may be liable for assault even if no contact actually results if the victim is placed in "imminent apprehension" of a harmful or offensive contact. Consequently, any woman who is the victim of an act of battering, or a threat of battering, can bring a tort action against her assailant for each of those acts. Moreover, a battered woman would be entitled to recover not only for any economic losses resulting from those acts, such as medical expenses and lost wages, but also for pain and suffering and disability which would include the psychological sequelae of any act of battering.

. . .

The majority opinion suggests that a primary objective of creating a new tort cause of action for battered woman's syndrome is to avoid the normal application of the statute of limitations to bar marital tort claims. If that is the underlying reason for the creation of this new tort, it is a classic case of the tail being allowed to wag the dog. If defendant's alleged marital misconduct could be properly characterized as "continuous" or if plaintiff's mental state could be shown to constitute "insanity," the running of the statute of limitations could be tolled regardless of whether plaintiff's cause of action were labeled assault and battery, intentional infliction of emotional distress, or the amorphous new tort of battered woman's syndrome. To state the point another way, it seems to me that the elements that a plaintiff must prove to establish a cause of action should be analyzed separately from the question whether the plaintiff has made the kind of showing required to toll the statute of limitations.

. . .

The majority's discussion of the question whether battered woman's syndrome is a continuous tort is confusing and contradictory. On the one hand, the majority states that "we disagree with *Cusseaux* insofar as *Cusseaux* classifies battered woman's syndrome as a continuous *tort" and that "we do not adopt the conclusion in Cusseaux* that battered woman's syndrome is a continuous tort." (On the other hand, the majority asserts that "to overcome the statute of limitations, it is imperative that the tortious conduct giving rise to the medical condition be considered a continuous tort." The majority never undertakes to explain how these seemingly inconsistent statements can be reconciled. Moreover, the majority later states that "plaintiff shall be entitled to sue her husband for damages attributable to his continuous tortious conduct resulting in her present psychological condition, provided she has medical, psychiatric, or psychological expert proof to establish that she was caused to have an inability 'to take any action at all to improve or alter the situation.' " Therefore, it appears that despite its prior contrary statements, the majority views the newly created tort of "battered woman's syndrome" as a "continuous tort" for which there is no operative statute of limitations.

In support of this theory, the majority relies primarily upon two cases that involved the application of *N.J.S.A. 2A:14–21*, which provides that a cause of action shall not accrue if the aggrieved party is "insane." In Kyle v. Green Acres at Verona, Inc., 44 N.J. 100, 207 A.2d 513 (1965), the Court held that even though *N.J.S.A. 2A:14–21* does not literally apply where an injured party becomes insane subsequent to the accident that is the subject of his complaint, a defendant may be foreclosed on equitable grounds from invoking the statute of limitations if the defendant's wrongful acts were the cause of plaintiff's insanity. The Court also indicated that insanity "means such a condition of mental derangement as actually prevents the sufferer from understanding his legal rights or instituting legal action." It was undisputed that the plaintiff in *Kyle*, who was "officially committed as 'insane' " for a period of five years qualified under this definition as insane.

In Jones v. Jones we held that the mental trauma resulting from a pattern of incestuous sexual abuse may constitute insanity under *N.J.S.A. 2A:14–21*, so as to toll the statute of limitations, if a plaintiff can demonstrate that she lacks "the ability and capacity, due to mental affliction allegedly caused by defendants' conduct, to assert her lawful rights." We concluded that the plaintiff's submission in opposition to the defendant's motion to dismiss, which included the treatment notes of her psychologist and the affidavit of another psychologist, raised genuine issues of material fact as to whether she suffered from such incapacity.

In contrast, plaintiff presented absolutely no evidence that she now suffers or has suffered in the past from the kind of mental affliction that could be found to constitute insanity. Plaintiff not only failed ... to allege acts of battering that could provide a factual foundation for a finding that she suffers from battered woman's syndrome, but also failed to submit any doctor's certification or report or any other medical evidence that she suffered from a "mental derangement" that was so disabling it would have prevented her "from understanding [her] legal rights or instituting legal action." Therefore, even assuming that under appropriate circumstances the condition of battered woman's syndrome could justify postponement of the accrual of a cause of action for assault, battery, or intentional infliction of emotional distress, plaintiff failed to present a prima facie case for postponing the accrual of her marital tort claims.

NOTE

The court in *Giovine* suggests that a battered woman suffers from a form of incapacity similar to a person who is insane. Does framing the syndrome in this way pose the danger described by Justice L'Heureux–Dube in *Malott* that "[i]t is possible that those women who are unable to fit themselves within the stereotype of a victimized, passive, helpless, dependent, battered woman will not have their claims to self-defence fairly decided"? That is, will women who take the initiative to leave for a time, or to resist their abuser, be unable to obtain admission of the syndrome because they presumably do not suffer from it? Even if they are able to present testimony about the syndrome, will a jury nonetheless conclude that it does not apply to them?

Rather than positing a universal battered women's experience, would relying on individualized evidence about a woman's particular experience avoid this risk? Or does the jury need evidence about the syndrome in order to counter any preconceptions they bring to the process of determining the conduct of a "reasonable" person?

c. LEGAL RESPONSES TO VIOLENCE

(1) Civil Protective Orders

ANNOTATED LAWS OF MASSACHUSETTS
PART II. REAL AND PERSONAL PROPERTY AND DOMESTIC RELATIONS

TITLE III. DOMESTIC RELATIONS
CHAPTER 209A. ABUSE PREVENTION

ALM GL ch. 209A, § 1–§ 4, 2005.

§ 1. Definitions.

As used in this Chapter the following words shall have the following meanings:

"Abuse", the occurrence of one or more of the following acts between family or household members:

(a) attempting to cause or causing physical harm;

(b) placing another in fear of imminent serious physical harm;

(c) causing another to engage involuntarily in sexual relations by force, threat or duress.

"Family or household members", persons who:

(a) are or were married to one another;

(b) are or were residing together in the same household;

(c) are or were related by blood or marriage;

(d) having a child in common regardless of whether they have ever married or lived together; or

(e) are or have been in a substantive dating or engagement relationship, which shall be adjudged by district, probate or Boston municipal courts consideration of the following factors:

> (1) the length of time of the relationship; (2) the type of relationship; (3) the frequency of interaction between the parties; and (4) if the relationship has been terminated by either person, the length of time elapsed since the termination of the relationship.

. . .

"Vacate order", court order to leave and remain away from a premises and surrendering forthwith any keys to said premises to the plaintiff. The defendant shall not damage any of the plaintiff's belongings or those of any other occupant and shall not shut off or cause to be shut off any utilities or mail delivery to the plaintiff. In the case where the premises designated in the vacate order is a residence, so long as the plaintiff is living at said residence, the defendant shall not interfere in any way with the plaintiff's right to possess such residence, except by order or judgment of a court of competent jurisdiction pursuant to appropriate civil eviction proceedings, a petition to partition real estate, or a proceeding to divide marital property. A vacate order may include in its scope a household, a multiple family dwelling and the plaintiff's workplace.

. . .

§ 3. Persons Suffering From Abuse; Complaint Requesting Protection From Abuse; Custody and Visitation of Child With Abusive Parent.

A person suffering from abuse from an adult or minor family or household member may file a complaint in the court requesting protection from such abuse, including, but not limited to, the following orders:

(a) ordering the defendant to refrain from abusing the plaintiff, whether the defendant is an adult or minor;

(b) ordering the defendant to refrain from contacting the plaintiff, unless authorized by the court, whether the defendant is an adult or minor;

(c) ordering the defendant to vacate forthwith and remain away from the household, multiple family dwelling, and workplace.... [A]n order to vacate shall be for a fixed period of time, not to exceed one year, at the expiration of which time the court may extend any such order upon motion of the plaintiff, with notice to the defendant, for such additional time as it deems necessary to protect the plaintiff from abuse;

(d) awarding the plaintiff temporary custody of a minor child; provided, however, that in any case brought in the probate and family court a finding by such court by a preponderance of the evidence that a pattern or serious incident of abuse ... toward a parent or child has occurred shall create a rebuttable presumption that it is not in the best interests of the child to be placed in sole custody, shared legal custody or shared physical custody with the abusive parent. Such presumption may be rebutted by a preponderance of the evidence that such custody award is in the best interests of the child. For the purposes of this section, an "abusive parent" shall mean a parent who has committed a pattern of abuse or a serious incident of abuse.

. . .

§ 4. Temporary Orders. Upon the filing of a complaint under this Chapter, the court may enter such temporary orders as it deems necessary to protect a plaintiff from abuse, including relief as provided in section three. Such relief shall not be contingent upon the filing of a complaint for divorce, separate support, or paternity action.

If the plaintiff demonstrates a substantial likelihood of immediate danger of abuse, the court may enter such temporary relief orders without notice as it deems necessary to protect the plaintiff from abuse and shall immediately thereafter notify the defendant that the temporary orders have been issued. The court shall give the defendant an opportunity to be heard on the question of continuing the temporary order and of granting other relief as requested by the plaintiff no later than ten court business days after such orders are entered.

Notice shall be made by the appropriate law enforcement agency as provided in section seven.

If the defendant does not appear at such subsequent hearing, the temporary orders shall continue in effect without further order of the court.

Mitchell v. Mitchell

Appeals Court of Massachusetts, 2005.
62 Mass.App.Ct. 769, 821 N.E.2d 79.

■ Duffly, J.

Six months after Mary Mitchell obtained a *G. L. c. 209A* abuse prevention order against her husband, James Mitchell, a judge of the Probate Court vacated the order on the husband's motion seeking to reconsider or vacate it. We consider in this appeal by the wife the appropriate standard for deciding a motion to reconsider or vacate a *c. 209A* order, and whether the husband's evidence was sufficient to support the judge's decision. We conclude that it was not and, therefore, that it was error to vacate the order.

After suffering from more than ten years of verbal and physical abuse inflicted by the husband, the wife, on December 20, 2001, filed a complaint for protection from abuse under *c. 209A*, supported by her affidavit and three police reports.[1] An ex parte abuse prevention order was issued that same day directing the husband to (among other things) refrain from abusing or contacting the wife. The husband appeared pro se at a hearing on January 3, 2002, the date on which the initial order was fixed to expire, and after hearing, the order was extended for one year, to January 3, 2003. The husband did not appeal from the extended order.

On June 20, 2002, the husband filed a verified motion requesting the court "to reconsider or vacate" the order dated January 3, 2002; in the motion he stated that the wife had contacted him repeatedly by telephone since the issuance of the order and had spent time with him in Los Angeles while attending the funeral of his mother.[2] In the husband's view, the wife's repeated "contacts" with him and her "successful requests" to spend time alone with him while they were in Los Angeles "clearly indicate that she does not fear physical or verbal abuse from [him] and did not fear such abuse in the past." The husband requested that the abuse prevention order be vacated retroactive to January 3, 2002.

A hearing, at which no testimony was taken, was conducted by the same judge who had issued the order of January 3, 2002. The judge had before her the husband's affidavit, the wife's verified opposition to the husband's motion,[3] and an affidavit of the husband's sister filed by the wife which, in

1. We accept as fact the wife's averments in her affidavit, including that the husband had kicked and hit her, pulled her hair, and threatened to kill her if she attempted to "get anything" through separation or divorce or if she divulged to the court certain information concerning the parties' finances, and that she was terrified of the husband and feared for her life.

2. More specifically, the husband averred that he and the wife had engaged in numerous conversations which included both "chit chat" and discussions concerning the parties' pets (all of whom were in the husband's care and needed medical attention) and various civil litigation matters in which the parties were involved. The husband also averred that following the death of his mother in Los Angeles on May 15, 2002, the wife asked him if she could attend the funeral and proposed that they fly to California together; between May 18 and May 25, 2002, while in Los Angeles, he and the wife spent time alone (attending a movie and riding in an automobile) and with others (including at his mother's memorial service, burial, and a reception), often at the wife's request; he had dinner with the wife and his sister on May 19, 2002.

3. In her opposition, the wife denied or otherwise challenged the husband's averments or his characterizations of events and stated that she continued to be in fear of him. She said, among other things, that she had not voluntarily initiated contact with the husband other than to check on the medical condition of the parties' pets. As for the trip to Los Angeles following the death of the husband's mother, the wife stated that upon receiving an invitation from the husband to attend the services, she consulted with the husband's sister, brother-in-law, and father, who invited her to attend, as they considered her to be part of the family. The husband's family also assured the wife that steps would be taken to ensure her safety. This included paying for a separate flight for her to attend the funeral; arranging for the husband to stay at a hotel while she stayed with members of the husband's family; and attempting to keep the parties separated as much as possible within the circumstances of attending the funeral and related family events. Continuing, the wife stated that there were only two occasions when she was physically alone with the husband (at a movie she had planned to attend with the husband's sister, who backed out at the last moment, and during an automobile ride after the husband's sister sent the husband to pick her up) and that on neither occasion did she choose to be alone with him. The wife said that she was in fear of the husband during the movie and was afraid that the husband would harm her during the automobile ride because he blamed her for getting lost, drove at high rates of speed, and raised his voice at her.

large part, corroborated the wife's description of events and statements concerning her fear of the husband.[4]

. . .

The standard for extending a *c. 209A* order does not require a showing of new abuse. Were the wife to apply anew without the support of further incidents of abuse (and without the benefit of an appellate court decision concluding that the prior order should not have been vacated), a judge acting on her application would quite possibly feel bound by the findings implicit in the vacating of the prior order, that then-existing evidence did not warrant continuing it. Moreover, although relief on an initial *c. 209A* complaint is limited to one year, "at a renewal hearing, a judge's discretion is broad." *Crenshaw v. Macklin, 430 Mass. 633, 635, 722 N.E.2d 458 (2000).*

"Preservation of the fundamental human right to be protected from the devastating impact of family violence" is the public policy of this Commonwealth, reflected in numerous statutes addressing the problem of domestic violence.

General Laws c. 209A sets out a statutory scheme intended to protect victims of abuse, as defined by the statute, through the issuance of abuse prevention orders. . . .

Section 3 of *c. 209A* contemplates the possibility of modification of such orders "at any subsequent time upon motion of either party." It also refers to the vacating of orders, but provides that the fact abuse has not occurred during the pendency of an order shall not, in itself, constitute sufficient grounds for allowing an order to be vacated.

. . . The husband . . . asserts in his motion that the wife's actions and conduct during the pendency of the *c. 209A* order indicate that she is not presently in fear of him, showing that there is no ongoing need for the order, which should, accordingly, be terminated. Such an assertion seeks prospective relief from the *c. 209A* order.

. . . *Chapter 209A* does not, however, articulate any standard relative to requests to modify, vacate, or terminate an abuse prevention order. . . .

. . .

The husband's motion construed as a request for relief from prospective application of the abuse prevention order . . . falls generally into that category of cases invoking the court's power to modify or prospectively to terminate an abuse prevention order . . . [T]hat power finds expression in *c. 209A, § 3*, and is also embodied in the last section of *Mass.R.Dom.Rel.P. 60(b)(5)* (1975), which authorizes a judge to relieve a party from a final order if "it is no longer equitable that the [order] should have prospective application."

There is scant authority discussing the specific standard for modifying or terminating provisions of a *c. 209A* order. In determining the appropriate standard applicable to such determinations, we look to cases interpreting the statute and also seek guidance from the rules of procedure and statutes and decisions in related areas of the law.

4. In her affidavit, the husband's sister stated that the wife did not wish to be alone with the husband when she arrived in Los Angeles, that the wife asked that the husband be put up in a hotel so that he would not be in the same home with her, that the wife was "shaken" and "upset" after the two instances she was alone with the husband, and that she (the husband's sister) made sure that the wife was not alone with the husband during the remainder of the wife's stay. In addition, the husband's sister stated that, in her view, the wife's fears for her safety if the restraining order were lifted were "not unfounded."

We have said that "in deciding whether to modify or renew an abuse prevention order, a judge's discretion is 'broad.'" In Kraytsberg v. Kraytsberg, 441 Mass. 1021, 808 N.E.2d 1242 (2004), the Supreme Judicial Court ... summarized an unpublished Rule 1:28 memorandum and order in which we said that the appellant "neither articulated any reasons why the [abuse prevention] order should be vacated nor suggested that anything of substance had occurred since the order was issued that would have allowed the District Court judge to decide to vacate her order."

Statutes governing divorce and children born out of wedlock provide that certain orders, including those pertaining to alimony and custody, may be modified upon a showing respectively, of a "substantial" or a "material and substantial" change in circumstances (and, in certain child-related matters, upon an additional finding that the modification will be in the child's best interests).

The provision in *Mass.R.Dom.Rel.P. 60(b)(5)* authorizing a judge to relieve a party from a final judgment if it is "no longer equitable that the judgment have prospective application" is identical to that in *Fed.R.Civ.P. 60(b)(5)* and derives from the traditional power of a court of equity to modify its decree in light of changed circumstances. In United States v. Swift & Co., 286 U.S. 106, 119 (1932) (a case predating the Federal Rules of Civil Procedure), the United States Supreme Court said, regarding a request to modify an injunction contained in a consent decree: "The inquiry for us is whether the changes are so important that dangers, once substantial, have become attenuated to a shadow.... Nothing less than a clear showing of grievous wrong evoked by new and unforeseen conditions should lead us to change what was decreed...." In the years after *Swift* was decided, the "grievous wrong" standard was frequently cited as the test for determining whether relief should be granted where "it is no longer equitable that the judgment should have prospective application."

More recently, the United States Supreme Court has indicated that the "grievous wrong" language in *Swift* "was not intended to take on a talismanic quality," Rufo v. Inmates of Suffolk County Jail, 502 U.S. 367, 380, (1992), and stated that *Fed.R.Civ.P. 60(b)(5)* permits a "less stringent, more flexible standard." The Court held that, under this flexible standard, "a party seeking modification of a consent decree must establish that a significant change in facts or law warrants revision of the decree...."

In the Court of Appeals for the First Circuit, commenting on *Swift* and *Rufo*, observed that the two cases distinguish between decrees protecting "'rights fully accrued upon facts so nearly permanent as to be substantially impervious to change' and decrees [that] involve 'the supervision of changing conduct or conditions and are thus provisional and tentative.' ... *Swift* illustrates the former and *Rufo* the latter. We view this not as a limited dualism but as polar opposites of a continuum...." The Federal *rule 60(b)(5)*, the court in *Alexis Lichine & Cie.* stated, "sets forth the umbrella concept of 'equitable' that both *Swift* and *Rufo* apply to particular, widely disparate fact situations."

We draw on the foregoing principles to reach our conclusion that the standard for determining whether prospective relief from a *c. 209A* order is warranted must be a flexible one. The level of impact on the underlying risk from harm that a *c. 209A* order seeks to protect against will vary from case to case; a flexible approach that incorporates the "continuum" paradigm set out in *Alexis Lichine & Cie.* is necessary to enable a court to deal effectively with the myriad circumstances that may arise during the pendency of an abuse prevention order. A request to modify a provision of the order that bears only tangentially on the safety of the protected party (e.g., certain orders for visitation or support) will fall at one end of the continuum, whereas a defendant's request to terminate an abuse prevention order in its entirety will fall at the other end. The greater the likelihood that the safety of the protected party may be put at risk by a modification, the more substantial the showing the party seeking relief must make.

In deciding whether to grant or deny a party's request for relief, the basis on which the order was initially issued is not subject to review or attack. Rather, the court must consider the nature of the relief sought keeping in mind the primary purpose of a *c. 209A* order: to protect a party from harm or the fear of imminent serious harm.

The husband's claims amounted to a collateral attack on an abuse prevention order that, at least for the one-year period of its duration, was final. Such an abuse prevention order, entered after a hearing that satisfies due process requirements, should be set aside only in the most extraordinary circumstances and where it has been clearly and convincingly established that the order is no longer needed to protect the victim from harm or the reasonable fear of serious harm. Furthermore, if the judge determines that it is appropriate to allow a motion to vacate or terminate a *c. 209A* order, the decision should be supported by findings of fact.

Taking as true the admissible averments of fact in the husband's verified motion, the evidence that the wife might have acquiesced in some contact with the husband (occasioned, in large part, by the unusual circumstance of the husband's mother's funeral) does not suffice to meet the husband's heavy burden of demonstrating that the order was no longer needed to protect the wife. Whether measured against a clear and convincing standard of proof, or proof by some lesser standard, the evidence was insufficient to establish that the order was no longer needed to protect the former wife from harm or reasonable fear of serious harm, and it was therefore error to terminate the order.

As we have stated, the abuse prevention order issued against the husband was to expire on January 3, 2003. Had the order not been vacated (erroneously) on July 11, 2002, the wife would have had the opportunity to seek an extension of the order on the date it was set to expire upon a showing of "continued need" for the order and without a showing of new abuse. She should be afforded the same opportunity now.

The order allowing the motion to reconsider and vacate the abuse prevention order is reversed. The wife may, within thirty days of the issuance of the rescript, seek a new order under *c. 209A*, the issuance of which shall be dependent upon the wife's sustaining her burden of demonstrating a continued need for the order. The judge may consider evidence subsequent to January 3, 2003.

So ordered.

C.O. v. M.M.

Supreme Judicial Court of Massachusetts, 2004.
442 Mass. 648, 815 N.E.2d 582.

■ COWIN, J.

The defendant appealed from the issuance against him of an abuse prevention order pursuant to *G. L. c. 209A, § 4*. We transferred the case to this court from the Appeals Court on our own motion. The defendant asks that we vacate the *G. L. c. 209A* abuse prevention order on the bases that: (1) the plaintiff failed to meet her burden of establishing the existence of a "substantive dating or engagement relationship" as required by *G. L. c. 209A, § 1(e)*; and (2) the District Court judge violated the defendant's due process rights by not permitting him to call any witnesses on his behalf or otherwise to challenge the evidence presented by the plaintiff during the hearing on the question of continuing the temporary order. After reviewing the parties' briefs and hearing oral argument, this court issued an order vacating the abuse prevention order. This opinion addresses the reasons for that order.

We summarize the relevant and undisputed facts of this case as set forth in the parties' briefs and pleadings. The defendant, M.M., is a seventeen year old high school student accused of having sexually assaulted a fifteen year old schoolmate. The plaintiff in this case, C.O., is the mother of the young woman who was allegedly abused ("daughter"). Shortly after the alleged incident, the plaintiff filed a complaint and supporting affidavit on behalf of her daughter and obtained an ex parte abuse prevention order against the defendant pursuant to *G. L. c. 209A, § 4*. The plaintiff's affidavit alleges that the defendant offered to drive the daughter home from school and, along the way, stopped at his house, invited the young woman inside, and then forcibly sexually assaulted her in his bedroom. The defendant contests the occurrence of the incident.

One day after an ex parte emergency temporary abuse prevention order was issued, see *G. L. c. 209A, § 4*, the defendant was arrested on charges arising from the alleged assault. The defendant was arraigned on these charges and subsequently released on bail. He was suspended from high school as a result of the arrest.

After a hearing during which both parties were represented by counsel, a judge of the Brockton District Court extended the abuse prevention order for a period of one year.

. . .

We first consider whether the plaintiff's daughter and the defendant were engaged in a "substantive dating relationship" as defined in *G. L. c. 209A, § 1*.

. . .

General Laws c. 209A, § 3, provides a range of protections and remedies for those "persons suffering from abuse from an adult or minor family or household member. . . ." Included within the definition of "family or household members" are those individuals who are or have been engaged in a "substantive dating or engagement relationship."

The defendant maintains that the plaintiff failed to show the existence of a "substantive dating relationship" between him and the plaintiff's daughter, and that, consequently, the abuse prevention order against him was improperly issued and extended. The defendant further asks this court to clarify the meaning of "substantive dating relationship" in *G. L. c. 209A, § 1*. Because the statute enumerates four factors to be considered in determining the existence of a "substantive dating relationship," there is sufficient language in the statute to enable judges to make informed and consistent determinations. We need not add to this language by interpretation.

. . .

Rather than establishing a rigid test to be applied to all relationships, the statute directs courts to "adjudge[]" the existence of substantive dating relationships by considering four factors: "(1) the length of time of the relationship; (2) the type of relationship; (3) the frequency of interaction between the parties; and (4) if the relationship has been terminated by either person, the length of time elapsed since the termination of the relationship." *G. L. c. 209A, § 1(e)(1)–(4)*. The Legislature thus anticipated that the existence or absence of a "substantive dating relationship" would be determined on a case-by-case basis. It is not our role to impose additional constraints on the interpretive instructions provided by the Legislature.

. . .

This court has had only one prior opportunity to consider the meaning of "substantive dating relationship" within *G. L. c. 209A, § 1(e)*. See Brossard v. West Roxbury Div. of the Dist. Court Dep't, 417 Mass. 183, 185, 629 N.E.2d 295 (1994) (person may be in more than one "substantive dating relationship" at any given time). In acknowledging the possibility of simultaneous "substantive dating relationships," we recognized the need for flexibility in applying the statute. Also instructive is our analysis in Turner v. Lewis in which we broadly interpreted "related by blood," as set forth in *G. L. c. 209A, § 1(c)*. In *Turner*, we recognized the changing nature of the concept of "family," as well as the Legislature's clear intent to extend protections to victims who experience violence beyond the context of the traditional "family." The Legislature intended to encompass a variety of relationships within *G. L. c. 209A*. It would not accord with this intent to restrict the statute beyond its terms in the present case.

While the four statutory factors enumerated in *G. L. c. 209A, § 1(e)(1)–(4)*, are the primary guidance for courts when making case-specific determinations about the existence of a "substantive dating relationship," courts should also consider the underlying purpose of *G. L. c. 209A*. The Legislature intended to address violence stemming from relationships which may not be considered traditional "family or household" associations. See Turner v. Lewis, *supra* at 334, quoting C.P. Kindregan, Jr. & M.L. Inker, Family Law and Practice § 57.5 (2d ed. 1996). The judicial guidelines on abuse prevention thus properly instruct courts to "give broad meaning to the term 'substantive dating relationship' to assure that the protective purposes of the statute are achieved." Guidelines for Judicial Practice: Abuse Prevention Proceedings § 3:02 commentary (Dec. 2000) (hereinafter, "Judicial Guidelines").

On the other hand, *G. L. c. 209A* is denominated a "domestic relations" statute within the General Laws. See Part II, Title III of the General Laws, entitled "Domestic Relations" (including, inter alia, marriage, divorce, and child custody statutes). The Legislature did not intend the statute to apply to acquaintance or stranger violence, nor did it intend to cover the myriad of relationships that exist or even to all those which might be considered "dating" relationships. The statutory language clearly requires something more—a "substantive dating or engagement relationship."

Dating is inherently personal and idiosyncratic, and relationships exist in endless variety. It would be unproductive to place a numerical quota on the number of "dates" that constitute a "substantive dating relationship," just as it would be inappropriate to mandate a minimum duration for a relationship to fall within *G. L. c. 209A*. Furthermore, any attempt by this court to elaborate on the meaning of "substantive dating relationship" by adding adjectives to an already well-designed statutory definition would be counterproductive. Such an effort might spawn additional litigation and result in unnecessary intrusions by courts into the precise nature of parties' interactions. See Judicial Guidelines § 1:01 commentary ("any attempt to explore the nature of the underlying relationship between the parties can inappropriately shift the focus of the proceedings away from the issue of protection. Such a shift of focus can weaken the plaintiff's resolve to seek protection . . .").

The plaintiff bears the burden of proving by a preponderance of the evidence that the parties were engaged in a "substantive dating relationship" within the meaning of *G. L. c. 209A, § 1*. Here, the plaintiff failed to sustain her burden. During the hearing on the question of continuing the temporary order, the plaintiff testified that the defendant had "been over to the house and he had taken [the daughter] to the movies." When asked about the nature of the relationship, the mother testified that she was "really not sure. They did, you know, go out." Plaintiff's counsel asserts that the plaintiff's uncertainty related only to the then-existing state of the dating relationship, not its past existence. Even so, the judge's finding of a past "boyfriend/girlfriend" relationship is not supported by the plaintiff's testimony, and the relationship between the parties does not meet the statutory standard of a "substantive dating relationship." The plaintiff's counsel also contends that the judge properly made a credibility assessment of the plaintiff, who was the sole witness at the hearing, that this court should not disturb. We do not contest the judge's assessment of the plaintiff's credibility in the present case, but rather his misapplication of the standards set forth in *G. L. c. 209A, § 1*.

The judge committed an error of law in relying on improper factors as the basis for his finding that the parties were engaged in a "substantive dating relationship." *General Laws c. 209A, § 1(e)(1)–(4)*, directs judges to consider four factors. The judge in this case ignored these factors and instead improperly relied upon judicially constructed factors, including "the fact that a criminal matter [sic] has issued," and "the age of the alleged victim." According to the judge, the determination was based "primarily" on the fact that a criminal case was pending. There was no testimony as to the length of time of the relationship or the frequency of the parties' interactions, as required by *G. L. c. 209A, § 1(e)(1), (3)*. The plaintiff contends that the judge properly exercised his broad discretion in according weight to these nonstatutory factors. While judicial discretion and flexibility are appropriate in applying the statutory definition of "substantive dating relationship," they do not relieve a court of its obligation to apply the legislative criteria.

Although the plaintiff asserts that the judge could draw an adverse inference from the defendant's failure to testify, this alone does not cure the defects in the judge's analysis. "An inference adverse to a defendant may be properly drawn . . . from his or her failure to testify in a civil matter such as this, even if criminal proceedings are pending. . . . However, inference cannot alone meet the plaintiff's burden. . . . [A] defendant's failure to testify cannot be used to justify the issuance of an abuse prevention order until a case is presented on other evidence."

Since there is insufficient evidence in the record to support a finding of a "substantive dating relationship" between the defendant and the plaintiff's daughter, the abuse prevention order is vacated. . . .

Turner v. Lewis

Supreme Judicial Court of Massachusetts, 2001.
434 Mass. 331, 749 N.E.2d 122.

■ Ireland, J.

This appeal raises the question whether the paternal grandparent of a child whose parents were not married is related by blood to the child's mother, and thus, has a right to invoke protection from domestic abuse under *G. L. c. 209A*. We answer yes.

The plaintiff in this case is the paternal grandmother of a ten year old child, whose parents were never married. The grandmother has custody of the child, and the child resides with her. The child's mother presently has visitation rights with the child, although she does not pay child support to the grandmother.

The grandmother makes the following allegations. On September 2, 1999, the mother entered the grandmother's home unannounced and without permission while the grandmother and the child were upstairs. The mother, who appeared "obviously high," yelled for the child and demanded that she come downstairs. The grandmother told her that the child was not at home. When the grandmother then attempted to descend the stairs, the mother blocked her, and punched and pushed her, saying, "You know what I want to do to you, don't you?" The mother then punched the grandmother again and pushed her up against the wall, causing the grandmother's head to hit a windowsill. After hitting the grandmother once more, the mother fled the scene in a van. The grandmother telephoned the police.

The grandmother subsequently filed a pro se complaint against the mother for protection from abuse under *G. L. c. 209A*. Although a Probate and Family Court judge granted the grandmother an emergency protective order, another Probate and Family Court judge declined to extend that order, because she found that the "parties are [not] related by blood, marriage or household membership" as required by the statute. The grandmother filed a timely notice of appeal and also filed a motion for reconsideration, which was denied. She appealed that denial as well. We granted her application for direct appellate review, as well as her motion to consolidate her appeal from the denial of the motion to reconsider with her initial appeal. Because we conclude that the parties are "related by blood," we vacate the Probate and Family Court judge's decision denying an extension of the protective order, as well as the denial of her motion for reconsideration, and remand for an order consistent with this opinion.

. . .

The question in this case is whether the abuse was perpetrated by a "family or household member." Under *G. L. c. 209A, § 1*, "family or household members" include persons who, among other categories, see note 1, supra, "(c) are or were related by blood or marriage or (d) have a child in common regardless of whether they have ever married or lived together." The grandmother claims that the parties are "related by blood" and have a "child in common," and thus, she qualifies for protection under the statute.

Because we conclude that the parties are "related by blood" for the purposes of the statute, we need not reach the question whether they have a "child in common."

. . .

In interpreting the term "related by blood," we recognize that "[a] general term in a statute ... takes meaning from the setting in which it is employed." We also bear in mind the importance of "giving broad meaning to the words 'related by blood,' " and considering "whether the relationship puts the parties into contact with one another, even though they might not otherwise seek or wish for such contact." Commentary to § 3:02 of the Guidelines for Judicial Practice: Abuse Prevention Proceedings (Dec. 2000).

Here we conclude that the parties are "related by blood." The paternal grandmother, through her son, is "related by blood" to the child. Likewise, the child and her mother are "related by blood." Thus, the child is "related by blood" to both parties, making the mother and grandmother "related by blood" through that child.

Interpreting the term "related by blood" to include the relationship between the grandmother and the mother would be consistent with the Legislature's purpose in enacting *c. 209A*. We note first that, in light of the grandmother's custody of the child and the mother's visitation rights with the child, there will likely be significant, albeit unwanted, contact between the mother and the grandmother, a fact particularly evidenced by the events that precipitated this appeal. The "main object to be accomplished" by c. 209A, was the prevention of violence in the family setting. Violence brought on by, or exacerbated by, familial relationships was the "mischief or imperfection to be remedied" by *c. 209A*. Moreover, *c. 209A* has always reflected "[a] significant decision by the legislature ... to broaden the definition of persons eligible to seek protection from abuse and domestic violence beyond the 'family' and to also include other persons having some 'family-like' connection." C.P. Kindregan, Jr., & M.L. Inker, Family Law and Practice, supra at § 57.5.

Our conclusion is supported by sound public policy. We take judicial notice of the social reality that the concept of "family" is varied and evolving and that, as a result, different types of "family" members will be forced into potentially unwanted contact with one another. The recent increases in both single parent and grandparent headed households are two examples of this trend.

With respect to the increase in single parent headed households, "children under age [eighteen] are considerably more likely to be living with only one parent today than two decades ago." Marital Status and Living Arrangements: March 1994, Bureau of the Census, United States Department of Commerce (Feb. 1996). See Marital Status and Living Arrangements: March 1998 (Update) Bureau of the Census (Dec. 1998) (between 1970 and 1998, proportion of children under age of eighteen years living with single parent grew from twelve per cent to 27.7 per cent). "High levels of divorce and postponement of first marriage are among the changes that have reshaped the living arrangements of children and adults since the 1970's." Id. In the majority of these cases, women are the head of the household. Id. (eighty-four per cent of children who lived with single parent in 1998 lived with mother). The often contentious nature of custody arrangements necessitates the protection of these single parents through legislation like G. L. c. 209A.

Likewise, as the amicus brief adverts, there has been a growing phenomenon of grandparents raising their grandchildren in the past thirty years:

> "Between 1992 and 1997, the greatest growth has occurred among grandchildren living with grandparents with no parents present. The increase in grandchildren in these 'skipped generation' living arrangements has been attributed to the growth in drug use among parents, teen pregnancy, divorce, the rapid rise of single-parent households, mental and physical illness, AIDS, crime, child abuse and neglect, and incarceration of parents." Coresident Grandparents and Grandchildren, Current Population Reports 1, Bureau of the Census, United States Department of Commerce (May, 1999) (75% increase in number of children residing in households headed by grandparents from 1970–1997).

See M. Minkler, Intergenerational Households Headed by Grandparents: Demographic and Sociological Contexts, in Grandparents and Other Relatives Raising Children (Generations United ed. 1998).

When grandparents are charged with the responsibility of caring for their grandchildren, they must often face "the biological parents' frequent resentment of the grandparental custody, and/or their jealousy of the attention being paid by their parents to their offspring." Id. at 13, 749 N.E.2d 122. Because of the parental hostility that may accompany grandparental custody, it is imperative that caregivers like the grandmother in this case be protected from such domestic abuse by *c. 209A*.

These trends require that "domestic violence statutes [such as *G. L. c. 209A*] offer coverage to a wide range of extended family relationships to fully reflect the reality of American family life [and] . . . the definition of 'family members' embraced by civil protection order statutes must be equally applicable to all concepts of family as they exist in the reality of our diverse family relationships." The relationship here meets the definition of "family," carrying with it all the risks and problems inherent in domestic violence. It is within that familial setting that this grandmother was exposed to violence and the threat of future violence.

For these reasons, we conclude that the grandmother and the defendant are "related by blood," and that the Probate and Family Court's ruling contravenes "the Commonwealth's public policy against domestic abuse—preservation of the fundamental human right to be protected from the devastating impact of family violence." Accordingly, we vacate the denial of the extension of the protective order, and the denial of the motion for reconsideration, and remand these cases to the Probate and Family Court for an order consistent with this opinion.

So ordered.

■ COWIN, J. (dissenting, with whom SOSMAN, J., joins). I respectfully dissent. In my view, the legislative history indicates that the phrase "related by blood" was not intended to encompass persons such as the paternal grandmother and mother in this case.

The court's decision ignores legislative history and bases its decision on social policy. *General Laws c. 209A* was enacted in 1978. St. 1978, c. 447, § 2. At that time a family or household member was defined as a "household member, a spouse, former spouse or their minor children or blood relative." Id. § 2. In 1986, the definition of a family or household member was amended to include a "blood relative or person who, though unrelated by blood or marriage, is the parent of the plaintiff's minor child" (emphasis supplied). St. 1986, c. 310, § 15. Pursuant to this change, two unmarried parents were considered family or household members because of their status as parents, not because of their blood connection to the child. By this definition, the Legislature expressly indicated that in its view the parents of a child were "unrelated by blood," despite any blood connection they have to their child (i.e., the father is related by blood to the child, and the mother is related by blood to the child, but, according to the statute, the father and mother are "unrelated by blood" to each other). Thus, if a father is "unrelated by blood" to the child's mother, then, a fortiori, a paternal grandmother also would be "unrelated by blood" to the child's mother.

In 1990, the definition of family or household member was amended again to its current version. The definition now includes, among others, persons "related by blood" and persons "having a child in common regardless of whether they have ever married or lived together." *G. L. c. 209A*, as appearing in St. 1990, c. 403, § 2, and as amended through St. 1996, c. 450, § 232. The statute continues to define unmarried parents as family members because of their status as parents, not because of a "blood" connection through their mutual child. Again, if the natural parents of a child would not be considered "related by blood," then the paternal grandmother is not "related by blood" to the child's mother.[1]

I recognize that each amendment of the definition of family or household member has broadened the categories of persons eligible for a protective order. However, the language and history of the statute do not support the court's interpretation on the present issue. Consequently, the court attempts to compensate by resorting to "the social reality that the concept of 'family' is varied and evolving." In identifying this "social reality," the court relies on reports from the United States Bureau of the Census as evidence of changes in family composition. These reports were issued subsequent to the 1990 amendment to the statute; there is no basis for concluding that the Legislature was aware of the information; or, if aware, that it would have based the Commonwealth's policy thereon.

Further, the court recognizes a "trend" in "single parent and grandparent headed households." According to the court, this trend "requires" that the protection offered under *G. L. c. 209A* extend to custodial grandparents, such as the grandmother here, in order "to fully reflect the reality of American family life." The role of the judiciary is to construe a statute "so that the enactment considered as a whole shall constitute a consistent and harmonious statutory provision capable of effectuating the presumed intention of the Legislature." The language of the statute "is the principal source of insight into the legislative purpose." I do not believe that it is the court's function to interpret a statute in accordance with the most recent "trend" or judicial perception of what "is best" as a matter of social policy, particularly when such interpretation is not consistent with the statutory language. "Whether a statute is wise or effective is not within the province of courts." Commonwealth v. Leno, 616 N.E.2d 453 (1993). I recognize that the violence alleged in this case would, in common parlance, be viewed as a form of "domestic" violence, and that the unique remedies of *G. L. c. 209A* would seem suitable to the situation. However, it is not for this court to engraft *G.*

1. Additionally, although not addressed by the court, I do not believe that the paternal grandmother and mother in this case would fall within the category of persons "having a child in common." The phrase "having a child in common" is modified by the clause "regardless of whether they have ever married or lived together," which indicates that the Legislature contemplates this phrase to encompass persons who could have married or cohabited, but who did not do so.

L. c. 209A onto any dispute that is, in some sense, a "domestic" dispute. The appropriate procedure for protecting a person such as the paternal grandmother in this case is by legislative, not judicial, amendment to *G. L. c. 209A*.

Ba v. United States

D.C. Court of Appeals, 2002.
809 A.2d 1178.

■ REID, ASSOCIATE JUDGE:

Appellant Alassane Ba was convicted of violating a civil protection order (CPO) under *D.C. Code §§ 16–1004, –1005* (2001) at a bench trial. On June 9, 2002, this court issued an opinion affirming Mr. Ba's conviction. Subsequently, after receiving petitions for rehearing or rehearing en banc, the court vacated its opinion; granted rehearing; requested new briefing directed at the following issue: "Under the circumstances of appellant's case, was consent a defense to the Civil Protection Order"; and scheduled the matter for oral argument. On rehearing, Mr. Ba continues to contend that his reconciliation with the complainant after the issuance of the CPO effectively vacated that order and provided him with a valid defense, or at least precluded a finding that he wilfully violated the CPO.... We affirm appellant's conviction, holding that on the facts of this case, the government proved beyond a reasonable doubt that Mr. Ba willfully violated the CPO.

The record before us reveals that in December 1999, Ms. Lashance Howard filed a petition and affidavit for a CPO against her ex-boyfriend of four years, Mr. Ba. On December 29, 1999, Mr. Ba signed a Consent CPO Without Admissions, which was effective for a twelve-month period. The CPO ordered Mr. Ba not to "assault, threaten, harass, or physically abuse [Ms. Howard] in any manner," to "stay at least 100 feet away from [Ms. Howard], [her] home [and her] workplace[,]" and prohibited him from contacting her "in any manner." The CPO further explicitly warned that: "Any and every failure to comply with this order is punishable as criminal contempt and/or as a criminal misdemeanor and may result in imprisonment for up to six months, a fine of up to $1,000, or both."

Subsequently, Mr. Ba was charged with one count of violation of a CPO, which allegedly occurred on May 13, 2000. A hearing on this charge took place on July 14, 2000.

. . .

Ms. Howard's direct, cross and redirect examination revealed that sometime after December 29, 1999, she and Mr. Ba lived together while the CPO still was in effect, and when they were attempting to work out problems in their relationship. During this period, Ms. Howard and Mr. Ba sometimes stayed at his place of residence and sometimes at Ms. Howard's home. The two continued to reside together until March 2000. Mr. Ba's testimony confirmed that he and Ms. Howard reconciled after the CPO took effect on December 29, 1999. He testified that he and Ms. Howard lived together, at times, from January 2000 to late March 2000.

Ms. Howard stated that: "As of March, the end of March, [Mr. Ba] knew [their relationship] was completely over." She also pinpointed the moment the relationship ended as "mid-March."

. . .

Ms. Howard's testimony addressed the specific incident which led to the one count charge against Mr. Ba, alleging his violation of the CPO dated December 29, 1999. That event occurred on May 13, 2000. On that day, Ms. Howard received a phone call at approximately 2:20 a.m. The caller hung up without speaking. Ms. Howard's caller identification box informed her that the call came from a pay phone; she then "beeped" Officer Wayne David who had previously responded to her complaint about Mr. Ba. When Officer David returned her call, she "asked him if he would, on his way off duty, . . . stop by [her] home just to make sure everything was okay." While she was waiting for Officer David, she looked out of a window of her residence and observed a car that resembled Mr. Ba's; she "saw a male in the car."

Ms. Howard continued recounting the events of May 13, saying that: "After maybe 20 or 30 minutes had passed with nothing . . . well, I saw a black car drive up to the driveway. And I peered out of the window again, and the person just sat in the car." The person in the unmarked car was Officer David. Ms. Howard went outside when she recognized the officer as he illuminated his unmarked vehicle, and told him that she thought she saw Mr. Ba's car, but "had heard nothing from him for the last 20 minutes or so."

After Officer David left, and as Ms. Howard "was putting the key in the lock of the gate" to re-enter, Mr. Ba appeared, approached and came "within six feet" of Ms. Howard. As Ms. Howard "tried to get in the door," Officer David returned and inquired whether the man standing near Ms. Howard was Mr. Ba. When Ms. Howard "replied yes," the officer "pulled out his weapon." At that time, Mr. Ba was about "ten feet, twelve feet" from Ms. Howard. Officer David arrested him.

Mr. Ba [testified that] . . . [h]e went to Ms. Howard's residence on May 13, 2000, "just to talk to her. . . ." When he "walked toward her . . ., and [said], how you can do this[,] . . . she started screaming." At that point, the officer intervened and arrested him.

The trial judge [found] Mr. Ba guilty beyond a reasonable doubt of violating the CPO [and sentenced him to 90 days in jail]. . . .

Mr. Ba primarily contends that Ms. Howard consented to the violation of the CPO when they reconciled shortly after the CPO was issued against him. Thus, he asserts, the CPO no longer had legal effect when he entered her property in May. Furthermore, he maintains that Ms. Howard's consent is a valid defense to all subsequent violations of the December 29, 1999, CPO. . . . The Public Defender Service ("PDS") as amicus . . . contends that in this case:

> Because the petitioner's consensual reconciliation over several months with Mr. Ba constructively and permanently modified the protection order, consent was available to Mr. Ba as a defense to the CPO violation charge regardless of whether he and the petitioner eventually broke off their relationship in March 2000.

The government argues that this court need not reach the "consent" issue essentially because Mr. Ba and Ms. Howard "could not, by their own conduct, void the CPO." However, the government asserts that if the court reaches the issue, "it should reject consent as a defense" to the CPO for a variety of reasons, including the need to "enforce the authority of the court that issued the order[,]" the difficulty of "determining whether consent to renewed contact has been freely given[,]" and "the incentive" that the subject of a CPO "would have ... to contact the complainant indirectly or even to risk direct contact in the hope of gaining an agreement to reconcile."

Under *D.C. Code § 16–1005(f)*, violation of a CPO is punishable as criminal contempt.... To establish the elements of a CPO violation, the government must present evidence proving ... that defendant engaged in: (1) wilfull disobedience (2) of a protective court order.

. . .

The purpose of the CPO proceeding is to protect the moving party, rather than to punish the offender. From this premise, as the trial court recognized, Mr. Ba arguably had a valid defense of consent when he and Ms. Howard reconciled between January and March 2000, particularly since Ms. Howard testified that there were times when she would stay at Mr. Ba's residence after the CPO was entered. The parties and amicus raise serious and complex issues regarding the consent defense and the frustration of the CPO by a party who seeks the order. We need not address those issues in this case, however, because we are satisfied that on the facts of this case, any consent by Ms. Howard during the January to March 2000 period would not establish her consent after late March 2000. Indeed, the evidence establishes, beyond a reasonable doubt, that Ms. Howard revoked her consent to violation of the CPO. As of late March, Ms. Howard and Mr. Ba had no consensual contact. In fact, according to the undisputed evidence, Mr. Ba tried to approach Ms. Howard at work and she reacted by calling the police. At this point, Ms. Howard's consent to the violation of the CPO, if such consent was possible, was effectively revoked. Moreover, Mr. Ba unsuccessfully sought to vacate the CPO in March. Thus, when he approached Ms. Howard on May 13, he clearly knew that the one-year CPO had not been vacated.

Finally, Mr. Ba's contention that there was insufficient evidence to establish his violation of the CPO is unpersuasive under the circumstances of this case. The trial court found that notwithstanding the earlier reconciliation from January to March, 2000, Mr. Ba's conduct in violation of the CPO in the early hours of May 13, 2000, was willful, and resulted in a violation of the CPO ... The CPO ordered Mr. Ba to "stay at least 100 feet away from [Ms. Howard], [her] home, [and her] workplace." In the early hours of May 13, 2000, Mr. Ba stood within at least ten or twelve feet of Ms. Howard, a clear violation of the CPO. In addition, even though the CPO ordered Mr. Ba not to contact Ms. Howard "in any manner," he went to her home and spoke with her on May 13, 2000, another clear violation of the CPO.

Accordingly, for the foregoing reasons, we affirm the judgment of the trial court.

NOTES

1. The *Ba* case raises several difficult issues. Should consent based on the behavior of the beneficiary of a Civil Protective Order be a defense to prosecution for violation of the order? Does this undercut the categorical force of the order and subject the behavior of the victim to unduly intrusive scrutiny? Or does the availability of such a defense take account of the complexity of intimate relationships and prevent unfairness to a party subject to the order? Should the order be deemed to be in force unless the victim officially requests that it be withdrawn? If the victim makes such a request, should the court scrutinize it to determine if it is genuinely voluntary?

2. If a victim allows someone subject to protective order to have contact with him or her, can he or she be liable for aiding and abetting the violation of the order? In

Henley v. District Court, 533 N.W.2d 199 (Iowa 1995), the court said that she can, referring to authority holding that contempt orders may be enforced against anyone who acts with knowledge of the protective order and in concert with the person subject to it. By contrast, the court in Ohio v. Lucas, 100 Ohio St.3d 1, 795 N.E.2d 642 (2003) held that the beneficiary of an order cannot be prosecuted for aiding and abetting its violation. The court said, "If petitioners for protection orders were liable for criminal prosecution, a violator of a protection order could create a real chill on the reporting of the violation by simply threatening to claim that an illegal visit was the result of an illegal invitation." *Id.* at 647.

(2) Mandatory Arrest Policy

Attorney General's Task Force on Family Violence 22–24

(1984)

Consistent with state law, the chief executive of every law enforcement agency should establish arrest as the preferred response in cases of family violence.

. . .

During the sixties, police trainers relied on the literature of psychologists and social scientists who believed that arrest was inappropriate because it exacerbated the violence, broke up families, and caused the abuser to lose his job. Consequently, mediation was the preferable solution to most family violence incidents. This method of response was based on assumptions that were neither closely examined nor adequately tested. Rather than emphasize the victim's right to safety and protection against future assaults, the mediation model moved away from law enforcement into social services. The shift to non-arrest was accepted by police officers who were attempting to provide help but did not have solid policy guidance. They welcomed this new intervention technique because it had the professional support and endorsement of the social scientists and did not, in and of itself, expose the officer to physical resistance.

Consequently, law enforcement officers have generally attempted to resolve incidents of family violence through the expeditious techniques of sending one party away from the home or superficially mediating the dispute. This arrest avoidance policy, based on incorrect social science assumptions, is emphasized by all segments of the criminal justice system. It starts with initial training in the police academy which teaches the officer that arrest is usually inadvisable. This is reenforced by the actions of the prosecuting attorney who generally does not issue criminal charges or routinely prosecute these cases. Many judges also act in ways to discourage arrest by setting low bail or releasing the assailant on his own recognizance, or upon conviction, failing to impose a meaningful sanction. Finally, the officers are confronted with anecdotal vignettes about victims themselves posting the assailant's bail, or refusing to appear to testify against the abuser, thereby frustrating the efforts of the most dedicated of officers.

Although called upon to stop the violence, law enforcement has not been encouraged by any component of the criminal justice or social service systems to intervene with a formal arrest. Clearly, officers regularly classify serious assaults between strangers as felonies and make appropriate arrests. Yet when the same level of injury occurs between family members, officers have been inclined to treat the crime as, at most, a misdemeanor and failed to make an arrest. They have instead tended to require the victim to initiate a citizen's arrest. By shifting the burden of arrest, police believe the credibility of the charges will be increased and their personal liability decreased. But it is precisely this burden of a citizen's arrest that often results in the victim's reluctant participation in mediation conducted by the responding officer.

However, mediation is most often an equally inappropriate law enforcement response in family violence incidents. Mediation may assume that the parties involved are of equal culpability in the assault even though one has a visible injury and the other does not, or it may assume that the underlying cause of violence can be resolved without arrest. But an abusive relationship is generally demonstrably one sided. The abuser is usually physically superior and the victim is injured and fearful of further harm.

Mediation not only fails to hold the offender accountable for his criminal actions but, worse yet, gives the abuser no incentive to change his behavior. Rather than stopping the violence and providing protection for the victim, mediation may inadvertently contribute to a dangerous escalation of violence.

The original shift by law enforcement to mediation was done for the most commendable reasons. They were responding to early assumptions of psychologists and sociologists and to signals from prosecutors and judges. But a recent research experiment is challenging these traditional beliefs that mediation is the appropriate law enforcement response. The results of the research demonstrated that arrest and overnight incarceration are the most effective interventions to reduce the likelihood of subsequent acts of family violence. A victim's chance of future assault was nearly two and a half times greater when officers did not make an arrest. Attempting to counsel both parties or sending the assailant away from home for several hours were found to be considerably less effective in deterring future violence. The research further indicated that the interaction between the officer and the victim also has significant impact on the likelihood that the abuser will commit further violence. When officers take time to listen to the victim, before making the arrest, and the offender is aware of this, the likelihood of recurring assaults declines significantly. Researchers suggest that the assaulter views the enhanced stature of the victim and subsequent arrest and overnight incarceration as a judgment that his behavior is criminal.

Because mediation is most often an inappropriate law enforcement response and because arrest and overnight incarceration have been shown to be an effective deterrent against household assault, arrest must be the presumed response in cases of family violence.... This policy of preferred arrest for household assaults puts the abuser on notice that family violence is a crime with serious consequences. It also helps the community appreciate the criminal nature of family violence.

NOTES

1. The conclusions of the Attorney General's Task Force have been called into question by more recent studies:

> The principal investigators in the original police arrest experiment concluded that their study "strongly suggest[ed] that police should use arrest in domestic violence cases," because arrest was most highly correlated with low recidivism rates. But when six replication studies were conducted in different jurisdictions, the findings ranged from arrest having no effect, to a deterrent effect, to an escalation effect. And even within the same jurisdiction, the effect of arrest often varied based on the length of detention and certain offender characteristics, such as employment and other ties to the community.

> What these studies ignored was the possibility that the procedures employed by the police might have affected the results. In 1997, researchers revisited the data from all seven studies to determine whether "the *manner* in which sanctions are imposed has an independent and more powerful effect on spouse assault than the sanction outcome itself." They found that perceptions of procedural justice have a statistically significant impact. The frequency of recidivist domestic abuse was lower for those perpetrators given only a warning than for those who were arrested, in cases where the arrested offenders perceived that they had been treated in a procedurally unfair manner. The frequency of subsequent abuse was far lower, however, when arrestees believed they had been treated fairly.

Deborah Epstein, Effective Intervention in Domestic Violence Cases: Rethinking the Roles of Prosecutors, Judges, and the Court System, 11 Yale J. L. & Feminism 3 (1999).

2. The debate about mandatory arrest policies and their effect on escalation of violence and recidivism continues. Many jurisdictions have put such policies into effect. Mandatory arrest appears to be successful in some jurisdictions and harmful in others. There is nothing approaching a consensus on the topic. See, e.g., Barbara Fedders, Lobbying for Mandatory-arrest Policies: Race, Class, and the Politics Of the Battered Women's Movement, 23 N.Y.U. Rev. L. Soc. Change 281 (1997); Erin L. Han, Note, Mandatory Arrest and No–Drop Policies: Victim Empowerment in Domestic Violence Cases, 23 B.C. Third World L.J. 159 (2004).

3. One study of the impact of mandatory arrest policies in six cities concluded:

> *Arrest reduces domestic violence among employed people but increases it among unemployed people* (emphasis in original). Mandatory arrest policies thus protect working-class women but cause greater harm to those who are poor. Conversely, not making arrests may hurt working women but reduce violence against economically poor women. Similar trade-offs may exist on the basis of race, marriage, education and neighborhood. Thus, even in cities where arrest reduces domestic violence overall, as an unintended side effect it may increase violence against the poorest victims.

Janell D. Schmidt & Lawrence W. Sherman, Does Arrest Deter Domestic Violence? in Do Arrests and Restraining Orders Work? 43 (E.S. Buzawa & C.G. Buzawa, eds. 1996).

Liza Mundy, Fault Line

Washington Post Magazine, October 26, 1997, at W8.

"This is not your decision. This is my decision," the thin young corn-blond cop is saying.

Early evening. A deserted parking lot in an office complex in Annandale. The humid aftermath of a rush-hour rainstorm. The cop stands talking to a middle-aged man of average height and average weight, a man who has sandy hair that's turning gray, and glasses, and a pink face, and a white shirt and blue pants and a diamond-patterned blue-and-white tie, and the glazed, unhappy look of a well-controlled professional in a situation that has spun horribly out of his control. Somewhere behind both of them, the man's wife is waiting in a second-floor office.

Domvio. Domestic violence. That's what the dispatcher's message said when it flashed on the computer screens of Fairfax County police squad cars. "Estranged wife has destroyed office/w/f/ . . . white T-shirt, pink shorts—hung up phone when I was talking," the message read, and now one, two, three cops have arrived to see what's going on, and one of them, Mike Tucker, is talking to the man, who was waiting on the sidewalk when they arrived, tucking his shirt into his pants. The man tells Tucker that earlier in the day his wife came to his office, bringing along a separation agreement for him to sign. He objected to some of the wording, and his wife got angry and pushed him. So, hoping a police report might be something he could use in a custody dispute, he called the cops.

Are you injured? Tucker asks.

No, says the man, whose name is Tom.

Tucker goes inside to talk to the wife, whose name is Judy. But Judy, still angry and combative, refuses to tell him anything. So Tucker talks to a witness who heard Tom say, "Stop pushing me!" and then goes outside to talk to Tom again.

All this is taking place a month after a domestic violence law went into effect throughout Virginia on July 1. The new law says that police must make an arrest whenever they have probable cause to believe a domestic assault has occurred. What constitutes probable cause? Tucker considers this question as he inspects a small tear in the breast pocket of Tom's shirt. Then, after consulting with another officer, he conveys the news to Tom: The pocket is enough. Judy must be arrested.

Tom is horrified. "Can I go on record that I don't want to press charges right now?" he asks, and Tucker says yes, he can go on record, but even so, pressing charges is not his decision, it is the decision of the commonwealth of Virginia, which is exactly what Tucker was just explaining, because that's what police are now trained to tell victims of domestic violence.

"Oh God, oh God!" Tom says while Tucker goes upstairs to make the arrest. Moments later he emerges from the doorway with a diminutive panicked woman in pink running shorts and a white "New York" T-shirt and, behind her back, handcuffs. The wife. Judy. Who has short soft brown hair, tied back, and a suntan. "Tom," she calls as she's led past her husband, "do you know they're arresting me? Tom, please! Tom, did I push you? Tom, please! Call my mother! Call our attorney!"

"Is this the Gestapo or what?" Tom says. "I just wanted documentation in a custody dispute. I certainly didn't want this!"

Tucker puts Judy in the back of his squad car and drives her to the Fairfax County Adult Detention Center, where she is charged with domestic assault and battery under Virginia's criminal code, section 18.2-57.2. The new law directs Tucker to request an emergency protective order to protect Tom from further acts of abuse, and so Tucker does, and the order is granted, directing Judy to stay away from her husband—specifically, his office—for three days, except for "incidental contact to assure welfare of children."

A $750 bond is set to guarantee she shows up for trial.

Her name is entered into the Virginia crime information network, so that if she violates the stay-away order, her existing criminal charge will be readily available.

She is fingerprinted and her mug shot is taken.

Asked if she has any scars, marks or tattoos, she says no.

Asked her occupation, she says, "Flutist."

Meanwhile, back at the office complex, the two remaining officers, T.J. Rogers and Ben Ferdinand, try to calm her husband—counseling the victim, as the new law also directs. "We don't have discretion," Ferdinand explains, gently, for the third time. "You're not pressing charges. It's Officer Tucker who's pressing charges." When Judy's court date comes up, they suggest, she probably won't get any jail time; more likely she'll be ordered to seek counseling. A good thing, perhaps. The two officers stand there in the suburban dusk, earnestly encouraging the man before them to look at the events of today, the argument and the pushing and the 911 call and the police arrival and the arrest and the handcuffs and the new law and the workings of Fairfax County's criminal justice system as, in Officer Ferdinand's words, a "positive step" for him and his family.

"There shall be an arrest. It's not may, if or should; it's shall, and in Virginia, 'shall' means there will be."

Fairfax County Police Chief M. Douglas Scott can be forgiven the pride he evinces when describing the language of Virginia's new domestic violence law, under which Judy and thousands of others have been arrested since it took effect. Variously known as "warrantless arrest," "pro-arrest" and "mandatory arrest," the law takes a single-minded approach to domestic violence, requiring that an arrest be made if there's any evidence an assault was committed. The law was fashioned by a commission that included Lt. Gov. Donald S. Beyer Jr. and James S. Gilmore III, the Democratic and Republican candidates in Virginia's gubernatorial election; it passed the General Assembly without a dissenting vote; and Scott is proud because the law was modeled, in part, on similar policies already in effect in Fairfax County and several urban Virginia jurisdictions.

"I can tell you that in my discussions with some of the rural chiefs and sheriffs, the mind set is still the old mind set: You know, old Charlie's a good guy, yeah, he got a little drunk Friday night, then he went home and slapped his wife around, so what's the problem here?" says Scott, who helped persuade cops around the state to change that Neanderthal way of thinking. He urged them to embrace the new law, convincing them that it wouldn't sap their resources or tie up their officers. What it would do, he told them, is cut down on a chronic law enforcement problem: the problem not only of domestic violence itself, but also of victims who out of love or fear or economic dependency or cultural isolation or all of the above are unwilling to press charges against their batterers, and batterers who, as a result, get away with their abuse.

"The goal is to send enough of a message to the violator that this behavior is not going to be tolerated, that it's serious, you can go to jail for it," is how Scott puts it.

The new approach represents a huge change, both practically and philosophically—and a huge victory for advocates on behalf of domestic violence victims. "We've done a fabulous job convincing the legislature that it is a highly criminal act to maim or abuse a spouse," says Judith Mueller of the Vienna-based Women's Center, who was among those lobbying for the bill. Similar victories have been won around the country: According to the Family Violence Project of the National Council of Juvenile and Family Court Judges, seven states plus the District of Columbia have mandatory arrest policies, and 26 others, including Maryland, have "presumptive arrest" policies that give officers a bit of discretion but still encourage them to make an arrest. Another 12 have laws that blend the two approaches. The thinking is that it's a lot easier on battered victims—and prosecutors—when the responsibility is taken off them and assumed by the state.

But a look at some of the arrests made in Fairfax County shortly after the law passed—arrests made by officers who are well trained and already familiar with an aggressive arrest policy—suggests that chronic abusers are by no means the only ones arrested under mandatory laws. As intended, the law has helped women—and men—who are in genuine danger from first-time and habitual batterers. But in other cases it may have created a new category of victim, indeed rendered the word so diffuse as to be meaningless.

"A lot of times, I think arrests are being made when they shouldn't be," says Kenneth E. Noyes, staff attorney and coordinator of the domestic violence project for Legal Services of Northern Virginia.

"I am stunned, quite frankly, because that was not the intention of the law. It was to protect people from predictable violent assaults, where a history occurred, and the victim was unable for whatever reason to press charges," says Mueller. "It's disheartening to think that it could be used punitively and frivolously. Frivolously being the operative word."

But in most cases, the police officers are not acting frivolously. They're acting conscientiously and in good faith, doing exactly what the law requires. And what the law requires is a rigid, inflexible response to a set of situations that are limitlessly vast. The river of human misery runs broad and deep; there are—as Tolstoy pointed out—all sorts of unhappy families, and all manner of domestic disputes. What do you do—for example—when a man calls 911 to report that his wife has destroyed his Mercedes with a ball-peen hammer and he would like her, please, arrested?

What do you do when a father calls to say that his son threw food at him, and now he would like the kid, please, arrested?

When a husband calls 911 to say that his wife slapped him with an open hand and he would like her, please, arrested?

What do you do when you have cast a net for sharks into waters that are brimming with all kinds of fish? "We didn't intend to catch minnows," Mueller says. "So, what do you do when the net brings in species or varieties for which you weren't casting?"

Alternatively: What do you do when a set of keys is flying through the air?

The keys belong to a dark-haired, dark-eyed, clear-skinned, soft-voiced young woman named Lora, who is 21. She has flung them out of fury and desperation and anger and disbelief. Her mother—her own mother!—has called the cops on Lora's boyfriend. Called the cops when her boyfriend wasn't even doing anything, in Lora's view; he just came over to visit on a Sunday morning, as he often does, except that Lora's mother, who doesn't much like him, wasn't in a visiting mood. Words were exchanged, there was an argument over a newspaper that somebody left on the floor, the argument escalated until Lora's mom threatened to call 911. Lora assumed she was kidding.

Of course she was kidding—she would never call the police.

Even so, her boyfriend thought it was a good idea to leave. Lora, too, was planning to go to a friend's house so everybody could cool off. As she was walking to the car, though, here came Officer M.A. Swain. Her mother had really done it, really called! Lora couldn't believe it—she lost her temper and flung an empty water bottle and her car keys. The water bottle, she's pretty sure, landed on the steps, but the officer said the keys went whizzing near her mother.

To Lora, the sight of the officer was shocking; to Swain, the sight of an angry mother and daughter must have been tediously familiar. Wife-beating—the old term for domestic violence—is still seen, dismayingly often, by cops. But it's by no means the only form of domestic violence or even the most common. In the fractious fractured families of the 1990s, domestic violence comprises so many kinds of behavior, and so many kinds of relationships, that it's more commonly known as "family violence," a term that embraces—to name a few—a fight between two lovers who live together, between the divorced parents of a child, between gay partners, between grandparents and grandchildren, between parents and kids.

In the course of two ordinary weekdays, for example, Fairfax County 911 dispatchers take calls from a Navy captain saying that his 21-year-old daughter is "kicking and hitting me," a woman saying that her 9-year-old daughter "hit me in the back with a shoe," a little girl complaining that her grandmother struck her on the hand and wrist with a kitchen strainer, and a woman who quickly retracts her complaint about "a little sister-to-sister fight over $50." Each call is coded as "domestic"—domestic dispute if there doesn't seem to be an assault taking place, domestic violence if there does—and the police are sent to investigate.

In other situations, cops have a great deal of discretion over how and whether to make an arrest. But in domestics—barring extraordinary circumstances such as an assailant who is quite young or mentally ill, or both—there's now just one thing that matters.

Was there an assault, or wasn't there?

In Lora's case, there really is no question. In the eyes of the law, you don't have to hit somebody to commit assault—all you have to do is try to hit them. Strictly speaking, assault is the attempt to commit "unwanted touching," while battery is the unwanted touching itself. In Fairfax, the two are treated as part of the same continuum; while the new domestic violence law says "assault and battery," this is not a distinction that the police, or the courts, stop to make. Before she knows it, Lora has handcuffs on her and is being led to a squad car and taken to the station, where she is fingerprinted and photographed.

"Is this your first time locked up?"

"Yes," Lora says.

"Have you ever tried to kill yourself?"

"No," Lora says.

"In the case of emergency, who should I contact?"

"My mom," Lora says, giving her mom's name and number. And now Swain is taking Lora before the magistrate, who says to Lora, "You're being charged with domestic assault. . . . When you threw the keys at your mother, that was the act of aggression that indicated your intent to assault her." The magistrate asks Lora where she works, and she gives the name of a firm where she was recently hired as a secretary, her first job, a job she loves. The magistrate asks how long Lora has lived at her current address, and she says 16 years. The magistrate asks whether there are ongoing problems between her mom and her boyfriend, whom, it turns out, Lora has been dating since high school, and who is not Lebanese, which, Lora suspects, is the main reason her mom doesn't like him, though her mom will later say that it's just that Lora is a sweet girl, a beautiful girl, who can do better than this particular guy.

Does this sort of argument happen a lot between you and your mother? the magistrate asks.

"Not that often."

"Once a month? Once every other week?"

"Sometimes when he comes over, she doesn't get mad," Lora says. "We go ahead and we eat and everything, and she doesn't get mad."

The magistrate sets a trial date and tells Lora that she's being released on her own recognizance—i.e., she's free to go. But she cannot have any contact with her mother for three days. Lora calls a friend to pick her up, and during the next three days her mom calls the friend's house, asking whether she's mad, whether she's going to move out. Last year Lora's dad died after an expensive and lingering bout with cancer, and if Lora moves out her mother will be alone and, probably, unable to afford the apartment. But Lora won't move out. "I would never leave my mom," she says, "until I get married."

Departing the station, Officer Mike Twomey, who assisted in the arrest, remarks that in the old days, the proper response would have been to say, hey, ladies, cool it. Now, arrest is the only option. For his part, Twomey sympathizes with the two women, but he doesn't think arrest is a bad thing, because sometimes it's the only way to help people figure out how to behave differently:

"Most of the time you feel you should drive around in one of the black-and-white shirts that referees wear, and stand in the middle, and yell, 'Foul! You're offsides!' "

Many officers, like Twomey, are comfortable with the law even as they understand the limits it places on them. That's because they know that arguments tend to recur in emotional relationships, particularly bad ones, and even if the first domestic call doesn't involve much injury—most don't—the second is likely to be worse. That's the whole point of the law: Intervene early, because otherwise, you're going to be going back and back and back.

"I'd rather have it nol-prossed in court than have something else happen, and go back and find a dead body," says Officer John Vickery.

"It does give us less discretion," says Officer Ben Ferdinand, "but it takes some of the liability off us too." That's literally true. Thanks to mandatory arrest, police departments are less likely to face a lawsuit for false arrest, or for leaving a scene where violence breaks out again.

"Elaine," the man is saying into the telephone, while nearby a 3-year-old boy is saying, "Mommy! Mommy! Mommy!"

The man, Jesse, has opened the door of his apartment to see a police officer. He doesn't seem surprised, though he does seem a little dazed. He is a fit young dark-haired Navy man wearing khaki shorts and a purple shirt. Behind him is an Ansel Adams poster; in the living room is a television with Jesse's martial arts trophies atop it. The apartment is immaculate except for, on the kitchen floor, a half-empty jar of Jif.

Jesse is on the phone with his wife, Elaine, who has called him from the jail. Earlier that day, Jesse got home from his morning job and Elaine wanted to talk to him about day-care problems that were interfering with her new job at a hospital. But Jesse didn't want to talk; instead, he went to the kitchen and began making a peanut-butter-and-jelly sandwich for the boy. Elaine, frustrated by his silence, snatched the peanut butter jar and flung it toward the sink. Jesse called 911. When the officer arrived, Jesse said Elaine had tried to shove him away from the phone. Elaine said that it was Jesse who had shoved her away when he was talking to the dispatcher. There was no injury, no evidence of who was telling the truth.

Such mutual charges are common, and they are another reason domestics have traditionally been so hard for the law to handle. At the magistrate's office, for example, a sort of bad-checks list is kept containing the names of people who are known to swear out domestic warrants for reasons that seem less than legit: anger, perhaps, or jealousy, or revenge. "Warrant should NOT be issued to either of these individuals without a police investigation," one magistrate wrote on an application he denied, noting that the couple were cross-filing, or trying to have each other arrested. Recognizing the confusion of many domestic disputes, the new law contains a clause dealing with mutual accusation and mutual assault. When possible, officers are directed to identify the "primary aggressor" and arrest that person.

Some officers think this part of the law is weighted against men, since part of the definition of primary aggressor is the person who has the potential to commit greater violence. In this case, though, Officer Fred Kessel arrested Elaine, based solely on her angry demeanor and the fact that "I actually believed him more than her."

And now, two hours after the arrest, Elaine in jail, here is another officer, Mark Dale, waiting while Jesse hands the phone to the toddler. Dale presents Jesse with an emergency protective order that will give him even more protection from his wife. Under the new law, officers are required to seek an EPO, barring the assailant from contact with the victim for at least three days, to prevent acts of retaliation. Dale has brought a copy of the document to Jesse, to make sure he's aware of the stay-away directive. This is important because it's a sad fact of human relationships that often, after an arrest has been made, the victim lets the assailant right back in the door.

And indeed here is Jesse, taking the phone back from his son, standing in front of the police officer, talking to his wife.

"She is asking me to get her out," he says.

"She's not supposed to have any contact with you," Dale explains, and Jesse stands there looking at the piece of paper that explicitly forbids precisely the sort of contact that's going on now.

It's not the first time Jesse has had his wife arrested. Months earlier, before the new law went into effect, Jesse went to the magistrate and swore out a warrant against her, charging that she struck him during an argument in their car. When the case got to court, however, Jesse dropped charges. Subsequent to her own arrest, Elaine sought a Legal Services lawyer who helped her file a civil restraining order against Jesse—civil restraining orders being a way to get protection from somebody without having the person arrested. As she described it, Jesse was the one who struck her; when he forced her out of the car, she accidentally hit him in self-defense.

Since the couple met and married four years ago, they have had a tangled and unhappy history of breakups and reconciliation. "This is not me at all; my life totally changed when I met my husband," Elaine, a 27-year-old woman with long black hair, says in an interview later, pointing to a scar on her foot that she says she got when Jesse threw her into a couch during an argument. Jesse, who has a black belt in the martial art of kenpo, denies that he has hit Elaine, though he says he has "held onto her" to restrain her. She's the one who's always coming after him, he says; when she threw the peanut butter, he was afraid she'd pick up a knife. "I'm afraid of her," he says.

Who is the real victim? In arguing that Elaine is, counselors who have worked with her point to what they call classic abuse symptoms. A native of Hawaii whose first language is Tagalog, she is isolated from her family and culture, unemployed, without her own car, dependent on her husband for income. Kenneth Noyes, the Legal Services attorney who has helped her in a custody suit for her son, believes that her husband has learned to work the system against her. Jesse, for his part, says that Elaine has learned to use the system against him, specifically the Navy's family advocacy program, where she has sought counseling. Elaine and Jesse resolved their earlier charges, Noyes says, by signing an agreement that there would be no further acts of abuse by either.

But what, exactly, is abuse? Refusing to talk to your wife? Picking up the phone to have your spouse arrested? In the eyes of the law, the Jif jar is what matters. When the officer leaves, Jesse is still on the phone with Elaine, who spends the night in jail. She is released the next day and picked up—by Jesse.

Who later says that you'd think now, after all this, Elaine would be a little nicer to him.

"If she's there, I can't go there?" asks Carl, incredulous. "I own the place! Her name is not on anything! It's my house and I can't go there?"

It should be made clear that not all cases are murky and confusing. Despite all the permutations, all the amorphous forms that family violence can take, all the mutual squabbles and dubious 911 alarms and couples racing to beat each other to the telephone or the warrant office, there are plenty of cases that are both clear and egregious. Physical abuse does happen, real violence does happen, has just happened, in fact, late on a Sunday in Mount Vernon south of Alexandria. In the police station, a couple of sheriff's deputies and police officers are in the processing room, along with a middle-aged drunk wearing socks but no shoes. Also there is Carl, a truck driver who has just been arrested for hitting his girlfriend, bruising her arm and cutting her lip and breaking her eardrum.

The 911 call came from the victim's son, who was standing in the road waving the police down when they arrived. The son told the police that Carl had come home to find dirty dishes in the sink, and the dishes made him mad, and in his anger he woke up the boy's mother, Helen, and hit her, and kept hitting her. By the time the police showed up, Helen was bruised and cut on her face and feet. Even so, she begged the officer not to arrest Carl—a classic victim's reaction.

"Back off," the officer advised, telling her to step out the door or she might go to jail, too.

And now here is Carl, absorbing the unbelievable fact that not only has he been arrested but an emergency protective order has been issued, something he's never heard of, and thanks to this thing, he cannot return to his own trailer! Even though his name is on the lease! "Everything I own is there!" he says to the drunk beside him.

"I realize you are the one who purchased the home," the magistrate tells him when he is brought before her to be charged, "but you allowed her to move in, you and she are cohabiting, so I'm allowing her to use your trailer for 72 hours."

Meanwhile, Helen has been taken off in an ambulance. In the emergency room of Mount Vernon Hospital, she is having her jaw X-rayed and her foot swabbed. A doctor shoots a painkiller directly into a cut and asks her if it hurts. Helen politely says no. Helen is a tiny longhaired woman wearing a T-shirt and shorts. She now cannot hear out of one ear. Later, the doctor will give her an antibiotic to ward off infection and tell her that basically the eardrum is going to have to heal itself.

"Are you allergic to anything?"

"Codeine," Helen says. She is frank and friendly and, for somebody who has just been beaten up, calm. "I threw an antique chamber pot right through the front door," she says, explaining how the fight started. That was after Carl came home and started getting on her about the dishes. He's a finicky person, she says, constantly picking at her son in particular, getting on him when he flushes the toilet wrong or holds the refrigerator open. This time, when he started in on the dishes, Helen had just had it, and so she threw the chamber pot, she readily admits that. She threw the chamber pot, which was hers, part of a set. Then she upended a table. Then he really came at her, hitting her so hard that she doesn't remember what came afterward, just that now her head hurts and her backside hurts and she can't hear out of one ear.

She acknowledges that she tried to dissuade the arresting officer—"When you see them going off in handcuffs, it just seems so cruel"—but now she's glad the arrest has been made. She's glad the law exists.

Carl, presumably, is not. "I don't have my reading glasses," he says unhappily when presented with the EPO, an aging man with gray hair flying wildly above his head, and no shirt, and a crucifix around his neck, and black laceless loafer-type tennis shoes. The officer explains the EPO to him one more time, and with that, Carl sits down, predicts that Helen will steal his stuff and says, to the drunk beside him, "It's a strange world we live in, Master Jack."

Helen does not steal his stuff. What she does is, she shows up the next morning at the trailer with her son and her sister and cleans the trailer until it's spotless. Then she packs stuff into boxes, but only stuff she's sure is hers. She even leaves the pictures on the wall because, though they are her pictures, they are Carl's frames. While her sister and son carry out a mattress and dresser, she sits down at the table and thinks through the months ahead: storing her stuff, living with her sister, trying to find a place she can afford.

Because she is leaving. She is definitely leaving. She's been beaten before, not by Carl, she says, but by another man, and she's not going to be beaten again. The law has given her the time and space to make this decision. It's not an easy one, and the subsequent weeks aren't going to be easy, either. She's going to have to go to the doctor about her eardrum so many times that she finally must tell her boss what happened, and she's going to see Carl on the road while she's driving, and she's going to wonder how he's doing and why he hasn't called to say he loves her or, at the very least, that he's sorry. She's going to have to find out where the courthouse is and get the day off and meanwhile, she freely admits, she still has feelings for the man who cut her lip and broke her eardrum.

"Most of the time I feel like I'm doing fine, I don't need this jerk, then I think about the good times and how much I love him," she says. "But I don't like him anymore."

"Without," says Lora, whose car keys are safely stowed, this day, in her purse.

"Without," says a defendant named Crystal, who has a baby with her.

"I would like an attorney," says a defendant named Anna, and the next defendant, Debbie, says, "I don't wish to have an attorney," and a defendant named Richard rises and says, "No counsel."

The list of names goes on and on, names of people who have been arrested for domestic assault, names of women and men and sons and daughters and parents, people young and old, wealthy and poor. They are standing and sitting in a cavernous courtroom on the second floor of the Fairfax County juvenile and domestic relations court-house, a rambling two-story brick structure that, in its old-fashioned, restful, gracious, faintly Jeffersonian design, seems an incongruous contrast to the teeming chaos within. Here, every Thursday morning, assailants and victims gather precisely at 9 o'clock, showing up sometimes in their Sunday best, sometimes in sweats, sometimes separately, often together. They cram into benches while a bailiff tells them not to talk or chew gum or read. There are so many people—hundreds, each week—that latecomers inevitably have to stand against the wall.

When the cases are heard by judges, a number of things can happen. In Virginia, domestic assault is a misdemeanor, in the same class with trespassing, shoplifting an amount under $200, owning a still. The maximum penalty is 12 months in jail and a $2,500 fine, but cops often grumble that many cases result in "suspended disposition": Charges are dropped if the assailant commits no further violation for a set period of time. Often, if it's a first-time offense, the assailant is assigned to seek counseling in, say, a men's anger program. Sometimes assailants are fined. Less frequently, they're jailed.

All have the right to an attorney. At the outset of proceedings, the defendants' names are called out, and the presiding judge asks whether they have arrived with a private lawyer, whether they would like to request a public defender, or whether they waive their right to counsel. Once the entire list has been called—it takes quite a while—the cases are divvied up and heard in smaller courtrooms. On the day Lora's key-throwing case has come to trial, it's taken early, because judges handle the easier ones—the ones without lawyers—first. It's a curious fact of the Fairfax County system that victims do not, necessarily, have the right to an attorney. That's because, in Virginia, the commonwealth's attorney is not obliged to prosecute any misdemeanors, so the Fairfax office has fashioned a somewhat strange compromise: The state will prosecute if the defendant has a lawyer.

But if the defendant has waived the right to counsel—as defendants often do—then the victim doesn't get a lawyer either. Instead, the whole thing is sorted out before the judge based on the testimony of the two parties, the police officer, and witnesses if there are any. With the bizarre result that a daughter is sometimes obliged to cross-examine her own mother, a husband to field queries from his wife—assuming she has the nerve to ask them.

Only in Lora's case, nobody else has shown up: not her mother, not Officer Swain. "The case is dismissed and you're free to go," says the judge, and she leaves, looking miserable. Though she wasn't convicted, she will have an arrest permanently on her record.

Judy, the flutist, the pocket tearer, is lucky enough to get her case dismissed, too. Though she has hired a private lawyer, Tom requests that charges be dropped, and the commonwealth's attorney, somewhat uncharacteristically, agrees. Judy will also have an arrest record from now on.

Elaine is less fortunate. By the time her court date rolls around, Jesse is again willing to drop charges for the assault with the peanut butter jar. They are still living together, although they have just signed an agreement giving Elaine custody of their son for the next two years. She plans to leave Jesse and return to Hawaii, but first this case must be disposed of. When Jesse says he wants to drop charges, the commonwealth's attorney declines. Instead, he offers Elaine a plea bargain: If she agrees to plead guilty, he'll agree to a 60–day suspended jail sentence.

Elaine refuses. She doesn't want a conviction on her record. "It's his word against mine," she tells her public defender. "If a murder was committed, would they find a person guilty based on no evidence?" The day drags on until the case is called that afternoon. Jesse takes the stand; when Elaine's lawyer asks him if there was an argument going on, Jesse says just "the argument that's been going on for years." Then Elaine takes the stand and explains that she threw the peanut butter to get it out of the way and force her husband to talk to her. The kitchen is so small, she points out, that if she'd wanted to hit him, she easily could have. Under cross-examination, the commonwealth's attorney adroitly paints a picture of her as a hectoring wife, chasing her husband from room to room, picking a fight.

"It's an offensive touching; it's an assault," he says, and the judge agrees, and to her amazement Elaine is found guilty, and sits there, sobbing.

"What would you like the court to do?" the judge asks Jesse.

"Um," says Jesse. "I don't wish any jail time, or fine, or anything like that. I just don't wish it to happen again."

"Too bad there's not a women's anger program," the commonwealth's attorney remarks.

The judge fines her and suspends the fine. "Go back to Hawaii," he advises wearily. When they leave the courtroom together, Jesse complains that he's the one who has to pay the court fees.

Which leaves Carl and his now-ex-girlfriend, Helen, who still cannot hear well out of one ear. "She'll go back to him," one officer predicted after leaving Helen in the hospital. The cynicism is not gratuitous. Often, couples have reunited by the time an arrest comes to trial. Often the victim comes to court with the assailant, sits with him, tells the judge that she provoked the fight ("I'd thrown Coke on him the night before," one victim tells a judge one morning, rationalizing why her boyfriend threw a Buddha statue at her). Often victims say that things are better now that they're in counseling, often victims beg for mercy.

Equally often, victims don't show up at all.

Helen shows up. She doesn't beg for mercy. Although she has had thoughts about getting back together with Carl, she hasn't done so, not so far; in fact, she hasn't seen him since his arrest. She has gotten her hair cut, and she has put on a pink suit and sheer hose and white flats, and she has arrived early, flanked by her sister and her son and a victim counselor provided by the police department. She's freaked, a nervous wreck. After Carl's name is called in the courtroom, she goes into the bathroom to calm down. It has taken all her courage to show up and confront Carl, who is wearing jeans and cowboy boots and accompanied by a private lawyer.

Helen has done one other thing. On her own initiative, she has taken photos of her injuries. Armed with these, and with her hospital records, she tells her story to the commonwealth's attorney, who decides to make a plea offer. If Carl will plead guilty, he'll get a 180–day jail sentence, of which he will have to serve only five days, and a $100 fine, and he'll have to pay Helen's hospital costs of almost $600. Carl takes the plea, and then the plea agreement is presented to the judge, and this is done so quickly that in moments Carl is handcuffed and hustled out of the courtroom. Helen reaches out to comfort Carl's mother, and Carl's mother shrinks away.

And so Elaine, who threw the peanut butter, and Carl, who broke a woman's eardrum, are forever placed in the same category: convicted domestic abuser.

Both, when applying for jobs, will have to acknowledge the conviction.

Both, under a new federal domestic violence statute, are forbidden to possess or carry a firearm.

And maybe this is a good thing. Maybe it's a good thing to have a law so tough, so evenhanded, so inflexible that a relatively minor assault is treated much the same as a severe one. Maybe it's a good thing to have a law that tilts against a popular culture that embraces violence, celebrates violence, glamorizes violence. Certainly, the new law is a far cry from the days when husbands and wives regularly duked it out in sitcoms and Hollywood movies.

The law is a far cry, too, from the days when police officers either ignored domestic violence, or laughed it off, or were expected to solve it through touchy-feely sociological techniques. And there's no doubt that the law makes a difference. Since Fairfax County adopted the domestic violence policy that's now in effect throughout Virginia, arrests have soared. Back in 1988, only 8 percent of "family fights"—as they were quaintly known—resulted in arrest. By 1994, that number had climbed to 34 percent. And it keeps rising. In 1995, Fairfax County dispatchers received 3,105 domestic calls that resulted in 1,267 arrests. In 1996, there were 3,327 calls and 1,441 arrests, or 43 percent.

But every law can have unintended consequences. Despite the rise in arrests, some cops and dispatchers fear that some of the most serious cases may getting away from them—that mandatory arrest may fuel "underground abuse." That is, they worry that a zero-tolerance stance may make serious abuse victims more reluctant than ever to call, for the age-old reason that they don't want to see their assailant arrested.

"These situations are more complex than any of us would like to believe," says Harriet Russell, executive director of the Commission on Family Violence Prevention, which helped write the law. Russell says she understands that people are getting arrested for what appear to be minor assaults, that women are being arrested, and so are parents, and so, in some cases, are sons and daughters. But violence is violence. And so the solution that's been chosen, to these very complex situations, is a very simple law.

A good law?

A bad law?

A tough law.

A mercilessly consistent law.

"Let's assume that this is the first argument between these people that led to a violent act, and to everybody's surprise, the person who was violent is led away in handcuffs," says Russell. "The hope is there will never be a violent act between these people again. By either. That's the intent."

And this is the reality.

Another argument. Another public place. Not a parking lot, this time. A high school baseball diamond.

A 16-year-old boy comes to say hello to his dad, Rodney, who is in the dugout coaching a Babe Ruth All-Stars game. As will be explained later in court, Rodney can tell that the boy has been drinking, and the son—who has in fact consumed a couple of beers and some vodka—vehemently denies the accusation. Rodney, who is not fooled, asks his son to go sit in the bleachers until the game is over. The boy obeys, but the next inning he's back in the dugout, and Rodney confronts him again about his drinking, and this goes on and on until the son starts to leave and Rodney realizes that the son has the family car and is probably going to pick up Rodney's wife from work. So Rodney vaults over the dugout and runs to catch up with his son, and when he does, his son gets belligerent.

Leading up to this moment: Already this year, Rodney's son has driven the family car into a batting cage, and another time he and another kid were toilet-papering somebody's yard, and the homeowner came out with a gun and pumped some bullets into the car, and there has also been some unpleasant behavior toward the boy's mother, Rodney's wife. A difficult adolescence, in short, nothing extraordinary but nothing pleasant either, and now here the boy is drunk, in public, embarrassing them both, and suddenly Rodney, a military man practiced in self-control, in discipline, just snaps. He opens his hand and slaps his son once, twice, and his son falls to the ground.

Which is when he realizes that the game has stopped. The crowd's attention has shifted—to them. "There's been enough embarrassment," he tells his son quietly, and starts to walk away, but his son gets up and yells at Rodney and hits him in the back. Rodney keeps walking, he goes back to the dugout and gets his bag of baseballs and his fungo bat and starts to leave, but then he sees that his son has taken off running through the woods, and so Rodney takes off after him, both of them running and running, getting scratched by trees and brambles.

When Rodney finally catches his son, he cradles the boy's head between his own two hands, like a father holding a baby, and says all he can think to say: "Why are you doing this?"

What 16-year-old can explain why he does anything? Rodney returns to the ball field, where, by now, the police are waiting. Citizens have called 911. A man has struck his son!

"If the issue is did I strike my son, I did. I struck him this way and that way with an open hand," Rodney says to the officer, prepared to explain everything. But there's no need. The officer checks with his supervisor, and Rodney hears something about a new law, and suddenly Rodney learns that he must be arrested. "You're kidding," he says.

Down at the station, the officers take photos of the boy's face, which is slightly red, and of the scratches on his legs from the brambles. They take maybe 10 or 15 photos: from the front, from the side, photos of the chest, photos of the face, photos of the legs. Since the boy is a minor, the police call Fairfax County Child Protective Services, which launches an investigation into whether child abuse has occurred. Since Rodney works for the Marine Corps, Child Protective Services calls the Marines' family advocacy program, which launches its own investigation into what happened. And, since Rodney has a top-secret security clearance, a third inquiry is launched by the Marine Corps criminal investigation unit. On top of which, Rodney is barred from his home for the weekend.

"These are really hard cases for me," says Judge Sandra Havrilak after listening to Rodney's testimony in court. Havrilak is an attorney and substitute judge who often hears cases in juvenile and domestic relations court. She says later that she does not favor the mandatory arrest law, which, she believes, only forces officers to make more arrests.

But as long as an arrest was being made, she asks the officer, why wasn't the son arrested, too, since he clearly pushed his father?

"Our directives are to determine who the primary aggressor is and arrest that person," the officer replies.

Do you have anything to say? the judge asks the son.

"It was a one-time thing; it hasn't happened again," says the son, a tall youth who is dressed, like his father, in pants and a soft sports shirt and who admits to Judge Havrilak that he was in fact drinking that day, but now he doesn't drink anymore. He has sought counseling. His father has sought counseling. The incident at the ball field, he says, wasn't the big deal that everybody's making it out to be.

It's a big deal now, though. "I believe you're honest and sincere, I believe your son provoked you," the judge tells Rodney. "I'm not going to find you guilty, but I've got to continue the case for six months. If there are no further violations, it will be dismissed." So for the next six months Rodney will have a charge pending, and even if the charge is dismissed, the mere fact of arrest will cause him problems in his next security review, and, knowing this, Judge Havrilak urges him to try and have the arrest expunged from his record, something that in Virginia is very difficult to do.

Now Judge Havrilak turns her attention to the boy. "This could have cost your father his job," she tells him, and she repeats her opinion that he provoked his father into slapping him and suggests that "you give serious thought to what happened, because I believe you're just as culpable." Only the law doesn't permit her to do anything about the son's assault except just this, a stern lecture, and now the two men are leaving together, father and son, making their way through the crowded hallway of the courthouse, where scores of other victims and scores of other assailants are waiting, a hallway that's always so crowded, so teeming, more and more people showing up each week, that on another day in the same hallway, an astonished passerby, looking at all the faces, is moved to say, "Are all these domestic violence cases?"

"Yeah," says one officer, waiting for his arrest to come to trial. "They used to call it love."

Town of Castle Rock v. Gonzales

Supreme Court of the United States, 2005.
___ U.S. ___, 125 S.Ct. 2796, 162 L.Ed.2d 658.

■ JUSTICE SCALIA delivered the opinion of the Court.

Issue:

We decide in this case whether an individual who has obtained a state-law restraining order has a constitutionally protected property interest in having the police enforce the restraining order when they have probable cause to believe it has been violated.

The horrible facts of this case are contained in the complaint that respondent Jessica Gonzales filed in Federal District Court. Respondent alleges that petitioner, the town of Castle Rock, Colorado, violated the Due

Process Clause of the Fourteenth Amendment to the United States Constitution when its police officers, acting pursuant to official policy or custom, failed to respond properly to her repeated reports that her estranged husband was violating the terms of a restraining order.

The restraining order had been issued by a state trial court several weeks earlier in conjunction with respondent's divorce proceedings. The original form order, issued on May 21, 1999, and served on respondent's husband on June 4, 1999, commanded him not to "molest or disturb the peace of [respondent] or of any child," and to remain at least 100 yards from the family home at all times. 366 F.3d 1093, 1143 (CA10 2004) (en banc) (appendix to dissenting opinion of O'Brien, J.). The bottom of the preprinted form noted that the reverse side contained "IMPORTANT NOTICES FOR RESTRAINED PARTIES AND LAW ENFORCEMENT OFFICIALS." The preprinted text on the back of the form included the following "WARNING":

> "A KNOWING VIOLATION OF A RESTRAINING ORDER IS A CRIME. . . . A VIOLATION WILL ALSO CONSTITUTE CONTEMPT OF COURT. YOU MAY BE ARRESTED WITHOUT NOTICE IF A LAW ENFORCEMENT OFFICER HAS PROBABLE CAUSE TO BELIEVE THAT YOU HAVE KNOWINGLY VIOLATED THIS ORDER."

The preprinted text on the back of the form also included a "NOTICE TO LAW ENFORCEMENT OFFICIALS," which read in part:

> "YOU SHALL USE EVERY REASONABLE MEANS TO ENFORCE THIS RESTRAINING ORDER. YOU SHALL ARREST, OR, IF AN ARREST WOULD BE IMPRACTICAL UNDER THE CIRCUMSTANCES, SEEK A WARRANT FOR THE ARREST OF THE RESTRAINED PERSON WHEN YOU HAVE INFORMATION AMOUNTING TO PROBABLE CAUSE THAT THE RESTRAINED PERSON HAS VIOLATED OR ATTEMPTED TO VIOLATE ANY PROVISION OF THIS ORDER AND THE RESTRAINED PERSON HAS BEEN PROPERLY SERVED WITH A COPY OF THIS ORDER OR HAS RECEIVED ACTUAL NOTICE OF THE EXISTENCE OF THIS ORDER."

On June 4, 1999, the state trial court modified the terms of the restraining order and made it permanent. The modified order gave respondent's husband the right to spend time with his three daughters (ages 10, 9, and 7) on alternate weekends, for two weeks during the summer, and, " 'upon reasonable notice,' " for a mid-week dinner visit " 'arranged by the parties' "; the modified order also allowed him to visit the home to collect the children for such "parenting time."

According to the complaint, at about 5 or 5:30 p.m. on Tuesday, June 22, 1999, respondent's husband took the three daughters while they were playing outside the family home. No advance arrangements had been made for him to see the daughters that evening. When respondent noticed the children were missing, she suspected her husband had taken them. At about 7:30 p.m., she called the Castle Rock Police Department, which dispatched two officers. The complaint continues: "When [the officers] arrived . . . , she showed them a copy of the TRO and requested that it be enforced and the three children be returned to her immediately. [The officers] stated that there was nothing they could do about the TRO and suggested that [respondent] call the Police Department again if the three children did not return home by 10:00 p.m."

At approximately 8:30 p.m., respondent talked to her husband on his cellular telephone. He told her "he had the three children [at an] amusement park in Denver." She called the police again and asked them to "have someone check for" her husband or his vehicle at the amusement park and "put out an [all points bulletin]" for her husband, but the officer with whom she spoke "refused to do so," again telling her to "wait until 10:00 p.m. and see if "her husband returned the girls.

At approximately 10:10 p.m., respondent called the police and said her children were still missing, but she was now told to wait until midnight. She called at midnight and told the dispatcher her children were still missing. She went to her husband's apartment and, finding nobody there, called the police at 12:10 a.m.; she was told to wait for an officer to arrive. When none came, she went to the police station at 12:50 a.m. and submitted an incident report. The officer who took the report "made no reasonable effort to enforce the TRO or locate the three children. Instead, he went to dinner."

At approximately 3:20 a.m., respondent's husband arrived at the police station and opened fire with a semiautomatic handgun he had purchased earlier that evening. Police shot back, killing him. Inside the cab of his pickup truck, they found the bodies of all three daughters, whom he had already murdered.

On the basis of the foregoing factual allegations, respondent brought an action under Rev. Stat. § 1979, 42 U.S.C. § 1983, claiming that the town violated the Due Process Clause because its police department had "an official policy or custom of failing to respond properly to complaints of restraining order violations" and "tolerated the non-enforcement of restraining orders by its police officers." The complaint also alleged that the town's actions "were taken either willfully, recklessly or with such gross negligence as to indicate wanton disregard and deliberate indifference to" respondent's civil rights.

Before answering the complaint, the defendants filed a motion to dismiss under Federal Rule of Civil Procedure 12(b)(6). The District Court granted the motion, concluding that, whether construed as making a substantive due process or procedural due process claim, respondent's complaint failed to state a claim upon which relief could be granted.

A panel of the Court of Appeals affirmed the rejection of a substantive due process claim, but found that respondent had alleged a cognizable procedural due process claim. On rehearing en banc, a divided court reached the same disposition, concluding that respondent had a "protected property interest in the enforcement of the terms of her restraining order" and that the town had deprived her of due process because "the police never 'heard' nor seriously entertained her request to enforce and protect her interests in the restraining order." We granted certiorari.

The Fourteenth Amendment to the United States Constitution provides that a State shall not "deprive any person of life, liberty, or property, without due process of law." Congress has created a federal cause of action for "the deprivation of any rights, privileges, or immunities secured by the Constitution and laws." Respondent claims the benefit of this provision on the ground that she had a property interest in police enforcement of the restraining order against her husband; and that the town deprived her of this property without due process by having a policy that tolerated nonenforcement of restraining orders.

. . .

The procedural component of the Due Process Clause does not protect everything that might be described as a "benefit": "To have a property interest in a benefit, a person clearly must have more than an abstract need or desire" and "more than a unilateral expectation of it. He must, instead, have a legitimate claim of entitlement to it." Board of Regents of State Colleges v. Roth, 408 U.S. 564 (1972). Such entitlements are " 'of course, ... not created by the Constitution. Rather, they are created and their dimensions are defined by existing rules or understandings that stem from an independent source such as state law.' " Paul v. Davis, 424 U.S. 693 (1976) (quoting *Roth, supra,* at 577); see also Phillips v. Washington Legal Foundation, 524 U.S. 156 (1998).

Our cases recognize that a benefit is not a protected entitlement if government officials may grant or deny it in their discretion. See, *e.g.*, Kentucky Dep't of Corrections v. Thompson, 490 U.S. 454, 462–463 (1989). The Court of Appeals in this case determined that Colorado law created an entitlement to enforcement of the restraining order because the "court-issued restraining order ... specifically dictated that its terms must be enforced" and a "state statute commanded" enforcement of the order when certain objective conditions were met (probable cause to believe that the order had been violated and that the object of the order had received notice of its existence). Respondent contends that we are obliged "to give deference to the Tenth Circuit's analysis of Colorado law on" whether she had an entitlement to enforcement of the restraining order. We will not, of course, defer to the Tenth Circuit on the ultimate issue: whether what Colorado law has given respondent constitutes a property interest for purposes of the Fourteenth Amendment. ... *focus*

. . .

We do not believe that ... provisions of Colorado law truly made enforcement of restraining orders *mandatory*. A well established tradition of police discretion has long coexisted with apparently mandatory arrest statutes.

In each and every state there are long-standing statutes that, by their terms, seem to preclude nonenforcement by the police.... However, for a number of reasons, including their legislative history, insufficient resources, and sheer physical impossibility, it has been recognized that such statutes cannot be interpreted literally.... They clearly do not mean that a police officer may not lawfully decline to make an arrest. As to third parties in these states, "the full-enforcement statutes simply have no effect, and their significance is further diminished." 1 ABA Standards for Criminal Justice 1–4.5, commentary, pp. 1–124 to 1–125 (2d ed. 1980) (footnotes omitted).

. . .

... [A] true mandate of police action would require some stronger indication from the Colorado Legislature than "shall use every reasonable means to enforce a restraining order" (or even "shall arrest ... or ... seek a warrant"), 18–6–803.5(3)(a), (b). That language is not perceptibly more mandatory than the Colorado statute which has long told municipal chiefs of police that they "shall pursue and arrest any person fleeing from justice in any part of the state" and that they "shall apprehend any person in the act of committing any offense ... and, forthwith and without any warrant, bring such person before a ... competent authority for examination and trial." Colo. Rev. Stat. § 31–4–112 (Lexis 2004). ...

The dissent correctly points out that, in the specific context of domestic violence, mandatory-arrest statutes have been found in some States to be more mandatory than traditional mandatory-arrest statutes. The Colorado statute mandating arrest for a domestic-violence offense is different from but related to the one at issue here, and it includes similar though not identical phrasing. See Colo. Rev. Stat. § 18-6-803.6(1) (Lexis 1999) ("When a peace officer determines that there is probable cause to believe that a crime or offense involving domestic violence . . . has been committed, the officer shall, without undue delay, arrest the person suspected of its commission . . ."). Even in the domestic-violence context, however, it is unclear how the mandatory-arrest paradigm applies to cases in which the offender is not present to be arrested. As the dissent explains, much of the impetus for mandatory-arrest statutes and policies derived from the idea that it is better for police officers to arrest the aggressor in a domestic-violence incident than to attempt to mediate the dispute or merely to ask the offender to leave the scene. Those other options are only available, of course, when the offender is present at the scene. See Hanna, No Right to Choose: Mandated Victim Participation in Domestic Violence Prosecutions, 109 Harv. L. Rev. 1849, 1860 (1996) ("The clear trend in police practice is to arrest the batterer *at the scene* . . . ." (emphasis added)).

As one of the cases cited by the dissent recognized, "there will be situations when no arrest is possible, *such as when the alleged abuser is not in the home*." *Donaldson,* 65 Wn. App., at 674, 831 P. 2d, at 1105 (emphasis added). That case held that Washington's mandatory-arrest statute required an arrest only in "cases where the offender is on the scene," and that it "did not create an on-going mandatory duty to conduct an investigation" to locate the offender. *Id.*, at 675, 831 P. 2d, at 1105. Colorado's restraining-order statute appears to contemplate a similar distinction, providing that when arrest is "impractical"—which was likely the case when the whereabouts of respondent's husband were unknown—the officers' statutory duty is to "seek a warrant" rather than "arrest." § 18-6-803.5(3)(b).

Respondent does not specify the precise means of enforcement that the Colorado restraining-order statute assertedly mandated—whether her interest lay in having police arrest her husband, having them seek a warrant for his arrest, or having them "use every reasonable means, up to and including arrest, to enforce the order's terms," Such indeterminacy is not the hallmark of a duty that is mandatory. Nor can someone be safely deemed "entitled" to something when the identity of the alleged entitlement is vague. Even if the statute could be said to have made enforcement of restraining orders "mandatory" because of the domestic-violence context of the underlying statute, that would not necessarily mean that state law gave *respondent* an entitlement to *enforcement* of the mandate. Making the actions of government employees obligatory can serve various legitimate ends other than the conferral of a benefit on a specific class of people. See, *e.g.*, Sandin v. Conner, 515 U.S. 472, 482 (1995) (finding no constitutionally protected liberty interest in prison regulations phrased in mandatory terms, in part because "such guidelines are not set forth solely to benefit the prisoner"). The serving of public rather than private ends is the normal course of the criminal law because criminal acts, "besides the injury [they do] to individuals, . . . strike at the very being of society; which cannot possibly subsist, where actions of this sort are suffered to escape with impunity." 4 W. Blackstone, Commentaries on the Laws of England 5 (1769); see also Huntington v. Attrill, 146 U.S. 657, 668 (1892). This principle underlies, for example, a Colorado district attorney's discretion to prosecute a domestic assault, even though the victim withdraws her charge. See People v. Cunefare, 102 P. 3d 302, 311–312 (Colo. 2004) (Bender, J., concurring in part, dissenting in part, and dissenting in part to the judgment).

. . .

The creation of a personal entitlement to something as vague and novel as enforcement of restraining orders cannot "simply go without saying." We conclude that Colorado has not created such an entitlement.

Even if we were to think otherwise concerning the creation of an entitlement by Colorado, it is by no means clear that an individual entitlement to enforcement of a restraining order could constitute a "property" interest for purposes of the Due Process Clause. Such a right would not, of course, resemble any traditional conception of property. Although that alone does not disqualify it from due process protection, as *Roth* and its progeny show, the right to have a restraining order enforced does not "have some ascertainable monetary value," as even our "*Roth*-type property-as-entitlement" cases have implicitly required. Merrill, The Landscape of Constitutional Property, 86 Va. L. Rev. 885, 964 (2000). Perhaps most radically, the alleged property interest here arises *incidentally,* not out of some new species of government benefit or service, but out of a function that government actors have always performed—to wit, arresting people who they have probable cause to believe have committed a criminal offense.

The indirect nature of a benefit was fatal to the due process claim of the nursing-home residents in O'Bannon v. Town Court Nursing Center, 447 U.S. 773 (1980). We held that, while the withdrawal of "direct benefits" (financial payments under Medicaid for certain medical services) triggered due process protections, the same was not true for the "indirect benefits" conferred on Medicaid patients when the Government enforced "minimum standards of care" for nursing-home facilities. "An indirect and incidental result of the Government's enforcement action ... does not amount to a deprivation of any interest in life, liberty, or property." In this case, as in *O'Bannon,* "the simple distinction between government action that directly affects a citizen's legal rights ... and action that is directed against a third party and affects the citizen only indirectly or incidentally, provides a sufficient answer to" respondent's reliance on cases that found government-provided services to be entitlements. The *O'Bannon* Court expressly noted that the distinction between direct and indirect benefits distinguished Memphis Light, Gas & Water Div. v. Craft, 436 U.S. 1 (1978), one of the government-services cases on which the dissent relies.

We conclude, therefore, that respondent did not, for purposes of the Due Process Clause, have a property interest in police enforcement of the restraining order against her husband. It is accordingly unnecessary to address the Court of Appeals' determination that the town's custom or policy prevented the police from giving her due process when they deprived her of that alleged interest.

. . .

The judgment of the Court of Appeals is Reversed.

■ JUSTICE SOUTER, with whom JUSTICE BREYER joins, concurring.

I agree with the Court that Jessica Gonzales has shown no violation of an interest protected by the Fourteenth Amendment's Due Process Clause, and I join the Court's opinion.... Gonzales's claim of a property right thus runs up against police discretion in the face of an individual demand to enforce, and discretion to ignore an individual instruction not to enforce (because, say, of a domestic reconciliation); no one would argue that the beneficiary of a Colorado order like the one here would be authorized to control a court's contempt power or order the police to refrain from arresting. These considerations argue against inferring any guarantee of a level of protection or safety that could be understood as the object of a "legitimate claim of entitlement," Board of Regents of State Colleges v. Roth, 408 U.S. 564, 577 (1972), in the nature of property arising under Colorado law. Consequently, the classic predicate for federal due process protection of interests under state law is missing.

. . .

... [I]n every instance of property recognized by this Court as calling for federal procedural protection, the property has been distinguishable from the procedural obligations imposed on state officials to protect it. Whether welfare benefits, Goldberg v. Kelly, 397 U.S. 254 (1970), attendance at public schools, Goss v. Lopez, 419 U.S. 565 (1975), utility services, Memphis Light, Gas & Water Div. v. Craft, 436 U.S. 1 (1978), public employment, Perry v. Sindermann, 408 U.S. 593 (1972), professional licenses, Barry v. Barchi, 443 U.S. 55 (1979), and so on, the property interest recognized in our cases has always existed apart from state procedural protection before the Court has recognized a constitutional claim to protection by federal process. To accede to Gonzales's argument would therefore work a sea change in the scope of federal due process, for she seeks federal process as a substitute simply for state process. (And she seeks damages under Rev. Stat. § 1979, 42 U.S.C. § 1983, for denial of process to which she claimed a federal right.) There is no articulable distinction between the object of Gonzales's asserted entitlement and the process she desires in order to protect her entitlement; both amount to certain steps to be taken by the police to protect her family and herself. Gonzales's claim would thus take us beyond *Roth* or any other recognized theory of Fourteenth Amendment due process, by collapsing the distinction between property protected and the process that protects it[.]

The procedural directions involved here are just that. They presuppose no enforceable substantive entitlement, and *Roth* does not raise them to federally enforceable status in the name of due process.

■ JUSTICE STEVENS, with whom JUSTICE GINSBURG joins, dissenting.

The issue presented to us is much narrower than is suggested by the far-ranging arguments of the parties and their *amici*. Neither the tragic facts of the case, nor the importance of according proper deference to law enforcement professionals, should divert our attention from that issue. That issue is whether the restraining order entered by the Colorado trial court on June 4, 1999, created a "property" interest that is protected from arbitrary deprivation by the Due Process Clause of the Fourteenth Amendment.

It is perfectly clear, on the one hand, that neither the Federal Constitution itself, nor any federal statute, granted respondent or her children any individual entitlement to police protection. See DeShaney v. Winnebago County Dep't of Social Servs., 489 U.S. 189 (1989). Nor, I assume, does any Colorado statute create any such entitlement for the ordinary citizen. On the other hand, it is equally clear that federal law imposes no impediment to the creation of such an entitlement by Colorado law. Respondent certainly could have entered into a contract with a private security firm, obligating the firm to provide protection to respondent's family; respondent's interest in such a contract would unquestionably constitute "property" within the meaning of the Due Process Clause. If a Colorado statute enacted for her benefit, or a valid order entered by a Colorado judge, created the functional equivalent of such a private contract by granting respondent an entitlement to mandatory individual protection by the local police force, that state-created right would also qualify as "property" entitled to constitutional protection.

. . .

The central question in this case is therefore whether, as a matter of Colorado law, respondent had a right to police assistance comparable to the right she would have possessed to any other service the government or a private firm might have undertaken to provide. See *Board of Regents of State Colleges* v. *Roth,* 408 U.S. 564 (1972) ("Property interests, of course, are not created by the Constitution. Rather, they are created and their dimensions are defined by existing rules or understandings that stem from an independent source such as state law—rules or understandings that secure certain benefits and that support claims of entitlement to those benefits").

. . .

Three flaws in the Court's rather superficial analysis of the merits highlight the unwisdom of its decision to answer the state-law question *de novo*. First, the Court places undue weight on the various statutes throughout the country that seemingly mandate police enforcement but are generally understood to preserve police discretion. As a result, the Court gives short shrift to the unique case of "mandatory arrest" statutes in the domestic violence context; States passed a wave of these statutes in the 1980's and 1990's with the unmistakable goal of eliminating police discretion in this area. Second, the Court's formalistic analysis fails to take seriously the fact that the Colorado statute at issue in this case was enacted for the benefit of the narrow class of persons who are beneficiaries of domestic restraining orders, and that the order at issue in this case was specifically intended to provide protection to respondent and her children. Finally, the Court is simply wrong to assert that a citizen's interest in the government's commitment to provide police enforcement in certain defined circumstances does not resemble any "traditional conception of property," *ante,* at 17; in fact, a citizen's property interest in such a commitment is just as concrete and worthy of protection as her interest in any other important service the government or a private firm has undertaken to provide.

. . .

. . . [W]hen Colorado passed its statute in 1994, it joined the ranks of 15 States that mandated arrest for domestic violence offenses and 19 States that mandated arrest for domestic restraining order violations. See Developments in the Law, 106 Harv. L. Rev., at 1537, n. 68 (noting statutes in 1993); N. Miller, Institute for Law and Justice, A Law Enforcement and Prosecution Perspective 7, and n. 74, 8, and n. 90 (2003), http://www.ilj.org/dv/dvvawa2000.htm (as visited June 24, 2005, and available in Clerk of Court's case file) (listing Colorado among the many States that currently have mandatory arrest statutes).

Given the specific purpose of these statutes, there can be no doubt that the Colorado Legislature used the term "shall" advisedly in its domestic restraining order statute. While "shall" is probably best read to mean "may" in other Colorado statutes that seemingly mandate enforcement, cf. Colo. Rev. Stat. § 31–4–112 (Lexis 2004) (police "*shall suppress* all riots, disturbances or breaches of the peace, *shall apprehend* all disorderly persons in the city. . . ." (emphases added)), it is clear that the elimination of police discretion was integral to Colorado and its fellow States' solution to the problem of underenforcement in domestic violence cases. Since the text of Colorado's statute perfectly captures this legislative purpose, it is hard to imagine what the Court has in mind when it insists on "some stronger indication from the Colorado Legislature."

While Colorado case law does not speak to the question, it is instructive that other state courts interpreting their analogous statutes have not only held that they eliminate the police's traditional discretion to refuse enforcement, but have also recognized that they create rights enforceable against the police under state law. . . .

Indeed, the Court fails to come to terms with the wave of domestic violence statutes that provides the crucial context for understanding Colorado's law. The Court concedes that, "in the specific context of domestic violence, mandatory-arrest statutes have been found in some States to be more mandatory than traditional mandatory-arrest statutes," but that is a serious understatement. The difference is not a matter of degree, but of kind. Before this wave of statutes, the legal rule was one of discretion; as the Court shows, the "traditional," general mandatory arrest statutes have always been understood to be "mandatory" in name only. The innovation of the domestic violence statutes was to make police enforcement, not "more mandatory," but simply *mandatory*. If, as the Court says, the existence of a protected "entitlement" turns on whether "government officials may grant or deny it in their discretion," the new mandatory statutes undeniably create an entitlement to police enforcement of restraining orders.

Perhaps recognizing this point, the Court glosses over the dispositive question—whether the police enjoyed discretion to deny enforcement—and focuses on a different question—which "precise means of enforcement" were called for in this case. But that question is a red herring. The statute directs that, upon probable cause of a violation, "a peace officer shall arrest, or, if an arrest would be impractical under the circumstances, seek a warrant for the arrest of a restrained person." Colo. Rev. Stat. § 18–6–803.5(3)(b) (Lexis 1999).

Given that Colorado law has quite clearly eliminated the police's discretion to deny enforcement, respondent is correct that she had much more than a "unilateral expectation" that the restraining order would be enforced; rather, she had a "legitimate claim of entitlement" to enforcement. Recognizing respondent's property interest in the enforcement of her restraining order is fully consistent with our precedent. This Court has "made clear that the property interests protected by procedural due process extend well beyond actual ownership of real estate, chattels, or money." Thus, our cases have found "property" interests in a number of state-conferred benefits and services, including welfare benefits, Goldberg v. Kelly, 397 U.S. 254 (1970); disability benefits, Mathews v. Eldridge, 424 U.S. 319 (1976); public education, Goss v. Lopez, 419 U.S. 565 (1975). . . .

Police enforcement of a restraining order is a government service that is no less concrete and no less valuable than other government services, such as education. The relative novelty of recognizing this type of property interest is explained by the relative novelty of the domestic violence statutes creating a mandatory arrest duty; before this innovation, the unfettered discretion that characterized police enforcement defeated any citizen's "legitimate claim of entitlement" to this service. Novel or not, respondent's claim finds strong support in the principles that underlie our due process jurisprudence. In this case, Colorado law *guaranteed* the provision of a certain service, in certain defined circumstances, to a certain class of beneficiaries, and respondent reasonably relied on that guarantee. As we observed in *Roth*, "it is a purpose of the ancient institution of property to protect those claims upon which people rely in their daily lives, reliance that must not be arbitrarily undermined." Surely, if respondent had contracted with a private security firm to provide her and her daughters with protection from her husband, it would be apparent that she possessed a property interest in such a contract. Here, Colorado undertook a comparable obligation, and respondent—with restraining order in hand—justifiably relied on that undertaking. Respondent's claim of entitlement to this promised service is no less legitimate than the other claims our cases have upheld, and no less concrete than a hypothetical agreement with a private firm. The fact that it is based on a statutory enactment and a judicial order entered for her special protection, rather than on a formal contract, does not provide a principled basis for refusing to consider it "property" worthy of constitutional protection.

Because respondent had a property interest in the enforcement of the restraining order, state officials could not deprive her of that interest without observing fair procedures. Her description of the police behavior in this case and the department's callous policy of failing to respond properly to reports of restraining order violations clearly alleges a due process violation. ...

Accordingly, I respectfully dissent.

NOTE

In addition to mandatory arrest laws, many jurisdictions also have adopted "no-drop" prosecution policies that provide that once the prosecutor's office has brought charges, it will not drop them at the request of the complainant. For a discussion of the issues that these policies raise, compare Cheryl Hanna, No Right to Choose: Mandated Victim Participation in Domestic Violence Prosecutions, 109 Harv. L. Rev. 1849 (1996) (supporting "no-drop" policies) with Linda G. Mills, Killing Her Softly: Intimate Abuse and the Violence of State Intervention, 113 Harv. L. Rev. 550, 554 (arguing that "no-drop" policies replicate the dynamics of the battering relationship).

3. PROPERTY LAW

a. THE COMMON LAW SYSTEM

Most states follow common law principles when resolving property disputes between spouses. At common law, once a woman married, her personal property (except for paraphernalia or "pin money") became her husband's property and her real property became subject to his control,[1] at least for the duration of the marriage.[2] The harshness of this system was ameliorated somewhat in the 19th century with the passage of the Married Women's Property Acts.[3]

1. His interest was termed an estate jure uxoris.

2. If the couple had a child, the husband also acquired "curtesy" or the right to control his wife's property until his death (if she died first, that is). The wife, by contrast was entitled to "dower", or an interest in ⅓ of his real property until her death if he died first, whether or not they had a child.

3. England did not give married women control of their earnings until 1870, 33–34 Vict., c. 93, probably because the wealthy had long used equity to arrange their affairs suitably. See Mary Ann Glendon, Matrimonial Property: A Comparative Study of Law and Social Change, 49 Tul.L.Rev. 21 (1974).

Mississippi passed the first such act in 1839. Apparently Mrs. T.J.D. Hadley, a Mississippi woman who had visited Louisiana and learned about their civil law system of marital property, played a major role in passing the legislation. While all the facts are not known, it is clear that she ran a boarding house that catered to many state senators and representatives, and that her husband was both a member of the state senate and spendthrift. The act that was passed read in pertinent part:

> Section 1. *Be it enacted, by the Legislature of the State of Mississippi,* That any married woman may become seized or possessed of any property, real or personal, by direct bequest, demise, gift, purchase, or distribution, in her own name, and as of her own property: *Provided,* the same does not come from her husband after coverture. Section 2. *And be it further enacted,* That hereafter when any woman possessed of a property in slaves, shall marry, her property in such slaves and their natural increase shall continue to her, notwithstanding her coverture; and she shall have, hold, and possess the same, as her separate property, exempt from any liability for the debts or contracts of the husband. Section 3. *And be it further enacted,* That when any woman, during coverture, shall become entitled to, or possessed of, slaves by conveyance, gift, inheritance, distribution, or otherwise, such slaves, together with their natural increase, shall enure and belong to the wife, in like manner as is above provided as to slaves which she may possess at the time of marriage. Section 4. *And be it further enacted,* That the control and management of all such slaves, the direction of their labor, and the receipt of the productions thereof, shall remain to the husband, agreeably to the laws heretofore in force.

This rather dubious "advance" in the property rights of women, marked the start of a trend that led eventually to the nearly universal acceptance of the right of a married woman (1) to her own earnings, (2) to contract and carry on a business and (3) to transfer property without her husband's consent. Because most married women did not work until well into the 20th century, the reforms of the 19th century were generally of theoretical importance only.

Cheshire Medical Center v. Holbrook

Supreme Court of New Hampshire, 1995.
140 N.H. 187, 663 A.2d 1344.

■ Johnson, Justice.

This [case] poses several questions relating to the common law doctrine of necessaries, under which a husband is bound to pay for necessary medical services furnished to his wife. We hold that a husband or wife is not liable for necessary medical expenses incurred by his or her spouse unless the resources of the spouse who received the services are insufficient to satisfy the debt.

The facts are not in dispute. In March 1993, the defendants, Rachel R. Holbrook and Robert W. Holbrook, were married and shared a residence. During this time, Mrs. Holbrook received medical services from the plaintiff, Cheshire Medical Center. Cheshire Medical Center charged her $7,080.40

for her treatment. Mrs. Holbrook, who was subsequently incarcerated, could not pay the amount due. She offered to pay the medical center ten dollars each month until her release from prison in 1996, at which time she would "make more substantial payments, provided [she is] in good health and working."

Dissatisfied with this proposed payment schedule, Cheshire Medical Center filed a petition to attach real property owned by Mrs. Holbrook's husband. During a superior court hearing on the matter, her husband questioned whether the "doctrine of necessaries" remains the law of New Hampshire. The superior court approved a motion by both parties to transfer the issue without ruling to this court.

The ... questions of law are: (1) whether the necessaries doctrine as articulated in our common law violates the equal protection clauses of the New Hampshire and United States Constitutions, N.H. CONST. pt. I, art. 2; U.S. CONST. amend. XIV, § 1; and if so, (2) whether the doctrine should be abolished; and if not, (3) whether the liability imposed under the doctrine is sole, joint and several, or primary and secondary. We find that as traditionally formulated, the necessaries doctrine is unconstitutional, and should be revised to impose reciprocal responsibilities upon husbands and wives. We also hold that the spouse who receives the necessary goods or services is primarily liable for payment; however, the other spouse is secondarily liable.

At common law, upon marriage a woman forfeited her legal existence and became the property of her husband:

> A man has as good a right to his wife, as to the property acquired under a marriage contract; and to divest him of that right without his default, and against his will, would be as flagrant a violation of the principles of justice as the confiscation of his estate.

Drew's Appeal, 57 N.H. 181, 183 (1876) (quotation omitted); *see* Fremont v. Sandown, 56 N.H. 300, 303 (1876). "[P]ersonal chattels in possession which belonged to the wife at the time of the marriage, or which fell to her afterwards, became instantly the absolute property of the husband, ... her choses in action became his ... by his asserting title to them and reducing them to possession." Hoyt v. White, 46 N.H. 45, 46–47 (1865). Moreover, "[t]he services and earnings of the wife belong[ed] to the husband, as much as his own; in law, they [were] his own." *Id.* at 47. As she had no legal identity, "the married woman's contracts were absolutely void,—not merely voidable, like those of infants and lunatics." Dunlap v. Dunlap, 84 N.H. 352, 353, 150 A. 905, 906 (1930) (quotation omitted).

Because the wife could not contract for food, clothing, or medical needs, *see id.*, her husband was obligated to provide her with such "necessaries," *cf.* Harris v. Webster, 58 N.H. 481, 482 (1878) (at common law, married woman could not contract because marriage extinguished her "legal personality"; married woman was "under the protection and influence" of her husband). If the husband failed to do so, the doctrine of necessaries made him legally liable for essential goods or services provided to his wife by third parties. Ott v. Hentall, 70 N.H. 231, 232, 47 A. 80, 80 (1900); Morrison v. Holt, 42 N.H. 478, 479–80 (1861); Tebbets v. Hapgood, 34 N.H. 420, 421 (1857). The husband's liability did not exceed his reasonable ability to pay. *See Ott,* 70 N.H. at 232, 47 A. at 80; *Fremont,* 56 N.H. at 303.

In the mid-nineteenth century, the enactment of the married woman's act partly dissipated the marital disabilities of women, *cf.* RSA chapter 460

(1992). The common law preventing married women from retaining their earnings and owning property was abolished. *See* Cooper v. Alger, 51 N.H. 172, 174–75 (1871); Houston v. Clark, 50 N.H. 479, 481–82 (1871). In 1951, the legislature finally accorded married women the unrestricted right to contract that they possess today. *See* Laws 1951, 78:1. In 1955, the legislature enacted RSA 546–A:2, which imposes a gender-neutral obligation of spousal support. Laws 1955, 206:1. Despite these developments, the common law rule of necessaries has endured.

Our constitution guarantees that "[e]quality of rights under the law shall not be denied or abridged by this state on account of . . . sex." N.H. CONST. pt. I, art. 2. In order to withstand scrutiny under this provision, a common law rule that distributes benefits or burdens on the basis of gender must be necessary to serve a compelling State interest. *See LeClair v. LeClair,* 137 N.H. 213, 222, 624 A.2d 1350, 1355 (1993).

We find no compelling justification for the gender bias embodied in the traditional necessaries doctrine.

> [T]he old notion that generally it is the man's primary responsibility to provide a home and its essentials can no longer justify a [law] that discriminates on the basis of gender. No longer is the female destined solely for the home and the rearing of the family, and only the male for the marketplace and the world of ideas.

Orr v. Orr, 440 U.S. 268, 279–80 (1979). The traditional formulation of the necessaries doctrine, predicated on anachronistic assumptions about marital relations and female dependence, does not withstand scrutiny under the compelling interest standard.

Because we find that the common law doctrine violates our State Constitution, we need not engage in a separate federal examination. *See* State v. Ball, 124 N.H. 226, 232, 471 A.2d 347, 351 (1983).

Having determined that the gender bias in the necessaries rule violates our constitution's equal protection guarantees, we must determine whether the doctrine should be abolished or revised. Compare Schilling v. Bedford Cty. Memorial Hosp., 225 Va. 539, 303 S.E.2d 905, 908 (1983) (leaving to legislature decision whether to modify necessaries doctrine) with Memorial Hospital v. Hahaj, 430 N.E.2d 412, 415–16 (Ind.Ct.App.1982) (extending necessaries doctrine).

We conclude that imposing a reciprocal obligation on both parties to the marital contract is consistent with the policy underlying New Hampshire's gender-neutral support laws. *See* RSA 546–A:2; RSA 458:19 (1992). Accordingly, we hereby expand the common law doctrine to apply to all married individuals equally, regardless of gender. We also hold that a medical provider must first seek payment from the spouse who received its services before pursuing collection from the other spouse.

Remanded.

NOTES

1. States with family expense statutes have taken widely differing positions on the extent of a wife's liability. Compare R.R.S. Neb. § 42–201 (exempts 90% of the wife's wages) with ALM GL ch. 209 § 7 (wife liable only up to $100 and only if she has property worth $2000 or more.)

2. Compare the decision of the Court of Civil Appeals of Oklahoma in Account Specialists & Credit Collections v. Jackman, 970 P.2d 202 (Okla.Civ.App.1998), overturning the common law Doctrine of Necessaries, as codified at 43 O.S. 1991 § 209, as an unconstitutional gender-based classification. See also Emanuel v. McGriff, 596 So.2d 578 (Ala.1992) (holding that the doctrine of necessaries should either be applied to neither spouse or to both spouses because of Equal Protection, applying it to neither in the case at hand, and leaving it to the legislature to decide whether to apply a gender-neutral version of the rule or abrogate it. [They chose the latter]).

3. In the fall of 1979, the National Conference of Commissioners on Uniform State Laws established a committee to draft a proposed uniform act dealing with marital property. The Uniform Marital Property Act (UMPA) was promulgated in 1983 and approved by the ABA in August, 1984. See generally William Cantwell, The Uniform Marital Property Act: Origin and Intent, 68 Marq. L. Rev. 383 (1985).

Professor William Reppy, Jr., has described the UMPA as "a community property act with a good premise: spouses should share extensively in property acquired during marriage." William Reppy, The Uniform Marital Property Act: Some Suggested Revisions for a Basically Sound Act, 21 Houston L.Rev. 679 (1984). He adds:

> The Act does not, however, mimic the typical American community property regime. By directing that all of the rents and profits accrued during marriage from separate property, called "individual property" in the Act, be co-owned by the spouses, the Act provides for greater sharing by married persons than any other American community property scheme.

Id.

A version of the Act has been adopted only in Wisconsin. Wis. Stat. § 766.001 et seq. See generally Daniel Furrh, Divorce and the Marital Property Act, 62 Wis. Law. 23 (1989). See also Howard S. Erlanger & June M. Weisberger, From Common Law Property to Community Property: Wisconsin's Marital Property Act Four Years Later, 1990 Wis. L. Rev. 769 (1990); and Palma Maria Forte, Comment, The Wisconsin Marital Property Act: Sections in Need of Reform, 79 Marq. L. Rev. 859 (1996) for a comparison between the WMPA and UMPA and a discussion of problems arising under the WMPA.

b. COMMUNITY PROPERTY

The Evolution of Community Property

Nine states have community property systems.[1] Three (Louisiana, Texas and California) have always done so, reflecting their French or Spanish origins; six (Nevada, New Mexico, Arizona, Washington, Idaho and Wisconsin) adopted their systems after first trying the common law approach.

The discussion that occurred at the California Constitutional Convention of 1849 on whether to retain the community property system is particularly revealing of the debate. One delegate called upon his fellow bachelors to support community property on the theory that it would attract rich, marriageable women to California.[2] Another altruistically asked the convention not to impose the "despotic provisions" of the common law on wives. Delegate Lippit argued for the common law system by pointing to France where, he alleged, two thirds of the married couples were living apart because the civil law had turned the wife into an equal, raising her from being "head clerk to partner." Delegate Botts concurred, pointing out that the community property system was contrary to nature, and supported by the "mental hermaphrodites" who supported women's rights.

1. In 1998, Alaska, a common law state, enacted a statute that enables spouses to elect to hold their property as a community. Alaska Stat. 34.77.030 (Michie 2005).

2. This discussion is drawn from Judith Younger, Community Property, Women and the Law School Curriculum, 48 N.Y.U.L.Rev. 211 (1973) and William Reppy & William Defuniak, Community Property in the United States (2d ed. 1982).

In fact, married women found they were not appreciably better situated in community property states than in common law jurisdictions because, at least until very recently, husbands were authorized to control all of the community property. Male control of community property has now been eliminated in all the community property states. In Kirchberg v. Feenstra, 450 U.S. 455 (1981), the Supreme Court held unconstitutional the Louisiana Code provision designating the husband as "head and master" of the community and giving him exclusive power to administer the community estate. The Court held that the provision violated the equal protection clause as interpreted in *Orr* and other cases. By the time the Court ruled, the Louisiana legislature had in fact changed its law, but the change came too late to moot the issue in *Feenstra.*

Today sole or individual management is the rule in Texas for community property derived from personal earnings, revenue from separate property and recoveries for personal injuries. All other community property (including commingled separate property) is subject to dual management, requiring the concurrence of both spouses. See Tex. Fam. Code § 3.102 (2005).

The other community property states also provide for sole management of some property and joint management of some. But they also provide for "equal" management of the rest. Consider for example:

New Mexico Stat.Ann. § 40–3–14:

A. Except as provided in Subsections B and C of this section, either spouse alone has full power to manage, control, dispose of and encumber the entire personal property.

B. Where only one [1] spouse is:

(1) named in a document evidencing ownership of community personal property; or

(2) named or designated in a written agreement between that spouse and a third party as having sole authority to manage, control, dispose of or encumber the community personal property which is described in or which is the subject of the agreement, ... only the spouse so named may manage, control, dispose of or encumber the community personal property described in such a document evidencing ownership or in such a written agreement.

C. Where both spouses are:

(1) named in a document evidencing ownership of community personal property; or

(2) named or designated in a written agreement with a third party as having joint authority to dispose of or encumber the community personal property which is described in or the subject of the agreement, ... both spouses must join to dispose of or encumber such community personal property where the names of the spouses are joined by the word "and". Where the names of the spouses are joined by the word "or", or by the words "and/or", either spouse alone may dispose of or encumber such community personal property.

4. Health Care

Skylarsky v. New Hope Guild Center

Supreme Court of New York, Kings County, 2005.
9 Misc. 3d 1108A, 806 N.Y.S. 2d 448.

■ GERARD H. ROSENBERG, J.

This is an action alleging psychiatric malpractice. Plaintiff alleges that the decedent, Sofia Skylarsky, was under the care and treatment of the defendants/third-party plaintiffs from January 5, 2000 until June 6, 2000 when decedent committed suicide. [Defendants] claim that evidence was adduced during the course of continuing discovery which reveals "culpable conduct by plaintiff Alexander Skylarsky in failing to obtain emergency medical services for his wife and in further failing to follow explicit instruction to him by the defendants to take his wife (the decedent) to a hospital emergency room to be evaluated. Mr. Skylarsky's intervening negligence was a direct and proximate cause of Mrs. Skylarsky's death."

Mr. Skylarsky testified that his wife's condition began to deteriorate approximately 1 1/2 months after her second discharge from Coney Island Hospital. Then, toward the end of May and beginning of June 2000 the deterioration of decedent's mental condition began to accelerate. [He further] testified that on Monday June 5, 2000 his wife was running around frantically and speaking nonsense, and he found a suicide note which his wife had written. Mr. Skylarsky telephoned Dr. Galea at approximately 5:00–6:00 p.m., and described his wife's behavior. While Mr. Skylarsky remembered that Dr. Galea refused his request that she see his wife at the New Hope Center that evening, as it was not her scheduled appointment, he did not recall whether Dr. Galea advised him to take the decedent to a hospital.

Mr. Skylarsky then received a telephone call from the decedent's social worker, Ruth Stein, who "strongly recommended" that he take his wife to the emergency room. Mr. Skylarsky testified that his wife had been in this condition "for this terrible three days," that he didn't know what to do, that he made several calls to his daughter, and that he decided that "we will tomorrow morning we will go, we will go" to the hospital.

Dr. Galea testified that she had first seen decedent at New Hope Guild Center on January 10, 2000. She diagnosed decedent as having a psychotic disorder and prescribed anti-psychotic medication. She next saw decedent on February 21, 2000, after decedent's discharge from her second admission at Coney Island Hospital. Decedent was still delusional and was treated with anti-psychotic medications and Valium. By May 1, 2000 decedent was no longer delusional, was going on her own to the clinic, had an improved demeanor and was discussing returning to work. On May 16, 2000 Dr. Galea saw decedent in an unscheduled visit. Her condition had deteriorated—she was paranoid, having flat affect, and was anxious and depressed. Dr. Galea last saw decedent on May 30, 2000. She testified that the decedent was doing worse, was very anxious and depressed, but testified that the decedent denied any hallucinations or homicidal or suicidal ideations. Decedent also continued to express a desire to return to work. Dr. Galea increased decedent's anti-psychotic medication, prescribed additional medications, and scheduled a followup appointment in three weeks.[26]

Dr. Galea testified that she did not think that the decedent needed to be committed at that time. Her condition was fluctuating, the course of her illness was that "she could get better, she could get worse," so the medication was changed and decedent was given some time to see how she was doing. Dr. Galea's version of the telephone conversation with Mr. Skylarsky on June 5, 2000 was that she advised Mr. Skylarsky to take his wife to the emergency room in order to address Mr. Skylarsky's complaints of his wife's inability to sleep and his desire to change his wife's medication. Dr. Galea stated that she

26. Dr. Galea claims that she wanted a followup visit in one week, but that three weeks was chosen, as that was the earliest time that the decedent was available.

could not change medication over the phone and that the decedent needed to be seen by a psychiatrist. Dr. Galea told Mr. Skylarsky that it was possible that his wife would not have to be admitted to the hospital. Also, being aware that Mr. Skylarsky felt that he had endured a bad experience with Coney Island Hospital during the wife's previous admissions, Dr. Galea advised him that he could take his wife to Maimonides Medical Center (which was closer to the Skylarsky residence), that Dr. Galea knew personally physicians at Maimonides, and that Mr. Skylarsky could ask the doctor to call Dr. Galea. She testified that Mr. Skylarsky said to Dr. Galea that "I see you don't want to help me" and hung up. He then called back, and after a similar conversation, hung up again.

Dr. Galea then notified Ms. Stein, the decedent's social worker, of this conversation and told her to followup with Mr. Skylarsky. At the end of the day she consulted with Ms. Stein, who advised Dr. Galea that she had spoken to Mr. Skylarsky and that he was going to take his wife to the hospital.

Dr. Galea explained that the reason she advised Mr. Skylarsky to take his wife to a hospital was that New Hope Guild Center was an outpatient clinic, not equipped to deal with an emergency, with no medications and no means to restrain a patient. She also stated that the inability to sleep is not an emergency, and that she did not detect and the decedent did not manifest any suicidal or homicidal ideations during her treatment of the decedent.

Ultimately, Mr. Skylarsky remained at home with his wife the evening of June 5–6, 2000. Early the next morning, some eight hours after his last conversation with Ms. Stein, the decedent fell from the fourth floor fire escape outside her apartment window in an apparent suicide.

. . .

The affidavit of Michael S. Aronoff, M.D., a physician Board Certified in General Psychiatry and Forensic Psychiatry, indicates that he has reviewed the pertinent medical records and deposition transcripts. Dr. Aronoff states that it is his opinion as a psychiatrist that Mr. Skylarsky possessed sufficient cognitive ability to comprehend the instructions from Dr. Galea and Ms. Stein to take his wife to the hospital on June 5, 2000, based on Dr. Aronoff's assessment of Alexander Skylarsky's testimony, immigration history, gainful employment, his having two daughters, including one who was a pharmacist, and his ability to testify responsively throughout his deposition in English. Dr. Aronoff notes that both Mr. Skylarsky's and Ms. Stein's testimony reflect that Mr. Skylarsky agreed to take his wife to the hospital, and that his wife's condition was an emergency.

Dr. Aronoff additionally opines that it is in keeping with the custom and practice of the psychiatric community to instruct and rely upon the assent of a patient's spouse to take the patient to the hospital in an emergency. The records indicate that Mr. Skylarsky assisted his wife in obtaining psychiatric treatment, and in Dr. Aronoff's opinion, the defendants/third-party plaintiffs reasonably expected Mr. Skylarsky to take his wife to the hospital, and such expectation is in keeping with the standard of care of the psychiatric community. Had she been taken to the hospital, it is Dr. Aronoff's opinion that the decedent would have received an emergency psychiatric evaluation and her risk of suicide and need for involuntary commitment would have been assessed.

To charge plaintiff Alexander Skylarsky with negligence, [defendants] must establish that Mr. Skylarsky had a legal duty, that he breached that duty, and that Mr. Skylarsky's alleged intervening negligence was a direct and proximate cause of Mrs. Skylarsky's death. This duty proposed by [defendants] is one to obtain emergency medical services for his wife, and/or to follow explicit instruction to him by the defendants to take his wife to a hospital emergency room to be evaluated. While it cannot be gainsaid that Mr. Skylarsky had a moral duty to so act, the question which must be determined is whether there was a legal duty to so act which, if breached, constituted negligence.

Generally, [defendants cite] cases where the amount of damages which the plaintiff may receive were reduced to the degree that the plaintiff's own negligence increased the extent of injury, by, for example, failing to keep appointments (Heller v. Medina, 50 A.D.2d 831, 377 N.Y.S.2d 100) or by failing to return to the hospital (Quinones v. City of New York, 49 A.D.2d 889, 373 N.Y.S.2d 224). [Defendants] additionally point to one New York criminal case, and several sister state holdings which [they] claim delineate a common law duty which Mr. Skylarsky was required to perform. In People v. Robbins, 83 A.D.2d 271, 443 N.Y.S.2d 1016 (1981), a woman who had suffered with diabetes and epilepsy for many years was required to take certain medications in order to control her diseases. Her husband, the defendant, had on many prior occasions summoned an ambulance or himself taken his wife to the emergency room when she lapsed into diabetic coma. This husband and wife were deeply religious "born again" Christians who met a self-proclaimed minister, the co-defendant, who convinced the husband and wife that if she had sufficient faith, God would cure all illnesses. After the wife stated that she had a revelation, the three discussed its significance and all agreed that the wife would stop taking her medications. She then suffered multiple seizures, lapsed into diabetic coma, and died.

In upholding the dismissal of the indictment charging the husband with criminally negligent homicide for failing to summon medical aid for his wife, the Appellate Division, Fourth Department recognized that "unquestionably, there is a common-law marital duty to provide medical attention to one's spouse but we must examine when, and under what circumstances, the breach of duty will result in criminal culpability". The Court noted that in New York a competent adult has a right to determine whether or not to undergo medical treatment (Matter of Storar, 52 N.Y.2d 363, 420 N.E.2d 64, 438 N.Y.S.2d 266; Schloendorff v. Society of NY Hosp., 211 N.Y. 125, 105 N.E. 92). As a result, the Court found that "it would be an unwarranted extension of the spousal duty of care to impose criminal liability for failure to summon medical aid for a competent adult spouse who has made a rational decision to eschew medical assistance" (*id, at 275*). Notably, the Court pointed out that the indictment "was defective for failure to state that [the deceased] was incapacitated or otherwise unable to make a rational decision and indeed the evidence would not support such claim" (*id., at 276*).

In a Pennsylvania case, Commonwealth v. Konz, 498 Pa. 639, 450 A.2d 638 (1982), Reverend Konz was a diabetic who self-administered insulin. After an encounter with a visiting evangelist speaker, the Reverend publicly announced his desire to discontinue insulin treatment in reliance on his belief that God would heal his diabetic condition. He assured others that he would carefully monitor his condition and, if necessary, take insulin.

During the next two weeks Reverend Konz administered insulin only one or two times. Then the Reverend and a person named Erikson, one of his students, formed a pact to pray together to enable Reverend Konz to resist the temptation to take any further insulin. The Reverend's wife was informed of this prayer pact and joined with Erikson one day in the

Reverend's home to take steps to prevent the Reverend from accessing his insulin, including concealing the insulin, physically blocking his attempts to access it, and forcing him into a bedroom where they prevented the Reverend from telephoning the police and temporarily rendered the telephone inoperable.

Following these confrontations, the three returned to an amicable relationship and Reverend Konz indicated to his aunt who resided in the house that "it's all settled now." He then proceeded with normal activities, including driving his wife to an institution having hospital facilities to pick up a close friend who was a practical nurse. While there he manifested symptoms of a lack of insulin. However, the Reverend, who appeared rational, conversant and cognizant of his environs, never requested insulin. When he returned home, the Reverend's condition worsened. While his wife and Erikson administered cracked ice to him, they never summoned medical aid. Reverend Konz died shortly thereafter of diabetic ketoacidosis.

Following the convictions of Mrs. Konz and Erikson for involuntary manslaughter, the Supreme Court of Pennsylvania noted that the determinative issue on appeal was whether Mrs. Konz had a duty to seek medical attention for her spouse. Under the circumstances of the case, the court found no such duty to have been present, and reversed the criminal convictions. The court recognized that there are exceptions to "the longstanding common law rule that one human being is under no *legal* compulsion to take action to aid another human being," such as the duty imposed on a parent for a child. This is based on the inherent dependency of a child upon the parent to obtain medical aid—the incapacity of a child to evaluate his condition and summon aid by himself, supports imposition of such a duty upon the parent.

However, an adult spouse does not generally suffer the same incapacity as do children with respect to the ability to comprehend their states of health and obtain medical assistance. The court noted that recognition of an unrestricted duty for one spouse to summon medical aid whenever the other is in a serious or immediate need of medical attention would place lay persons in peril of criminal prosecution while compelling them to medically diagnose the seriousness of their spouses' illnesses and injuries. It would additionally impose an obligation for a spouse to take action at a time when the stricken individual competently chooses not to receive assistance.

The Pennsylvania Supreme Court cited cases in two other states where the marital relationship was sufficient, in itself, to invoke a limited duty for one spouse to seek medical care for another. In Westrup v. Commonwealth, 123 Ky. 95, 93 S.W. 646, 29 Ky. L. Rptr. 519 (1906) the defendant's pregnant wife insisted that she did not want medical aid for the birth of her child. Soon after giving birth she developed complications, and her husband summoned a physician, who was at that point unable to prevent the death of the defendant's wife. The husband's conviction for involuntary manslaughter was reversed, the court finding that the husband had acted in good faith and at his wife's competent request.

The court stated:

> Where the husband neglects to provide necessaries for his wife, or medical attention in case of her illness, he will be guilty of involuntary manslaughter, provided it appears that she was in a *helpless state and unable to appeal elsewhere for aid*, and that the death, though not intended nor anticipated by him, was the natural and reasonable consequence of his negligence.

In State v. Mally, 139 Mont. 599, 366 P.2d 868 (1961), defendant's wife was in poor physical condition prior to an occurrence which left her with two fractured arms. After the accident, defendant permitted his wife to lay in a semi-comatose condition while she decried the need for aid for two days before he summoned a physician. This delay caused her death. In this case the conviction for involuntary manslaughter was affirmed, the court stating:

> We are aware that the large majority of homicide cases involving a failure to provide medical aid involve a parent-child relationship. This is undoubtedly due to the fact that a person of mature years is not generally in a helpless condition. However, fact situations do arise, such as the instant case, wherein it is apparent *that an adult is a helpless as a newborn.* The record is replete with evidence that [decedent] could not have *consciously or rationally denied medical aid.*

Thus, New York, in the *Robbins* case, Kentucky, in the *Westrup* case, and Montana, in the *Mally* case, recognize that a common law duty may exist for a person to summon medical assistance for a spouse where the spouse, by reason of being "incapacitated or otherwise unable to make a rational decision" (*People v. Robbins*), or in a "*helpless state and unable to appeal elsewhere for aid*" (*Westrup v. Commonwealth*), or "wherein it is apparent *that an adult is a helpless as a newborn*" (*State v. Mally*).

These cases establish that under the circumstances presented in this case, [defendants have] demonstrated that Mr. Skylarsky had a common-law duty to provide medical aid to his wife by calling emergency medical services to her assistance, and/or by taking her to a hospital as instructed....

In the case at bar, the decedent was arguably not able to make a rational decision to eschew medical assistance. At the time of the telephone conversations with Dr. Galea and Ruth Stein, Dr. Galea testified that decedent's condition had deteriorated from May 16, 2000, when decedent was paranoid, having flat affect, and was anxious and depressed, to where the decedent was doing worse, and was very anxious and depressed when Dr. Galea last saw decedent on May 30, 2000. While Dr. Galea testified that the decedent denied any hallucinations or homicidal or suicidal ideations as of May 30, 2000, Dr. Galea did increase decedent's anti-psychotic medication, prescribe additional medications, and attempt to schedule a followup appointment in one week. These symptoms and illnesses constitute the type of diminished, incapacitated, helpless state contemplated by the cases just cited.

Decedent's husband, having experienced "for this terrible three terrible days" of his wife's frantic behavior and speaking nonsense, and knowing that his wife had written a suicide note, was admittedly advised by Ruth Stein to get his wife to the hospital, and was also so advised by Dr. Galea, according to Dr. Galea's testimony. Mr. Skylarsky chose to wait for at least eight hours to take his wife to the hospital, and during this delay his wife was able to climb out of a window in the apartment and fall to her death in an apparent suicide. The affidavit of Dr. Aronoff indicates his opinion as a psychiatrist that Mr. Skylarsky possessed sufficient cognitive ability to comprehend the instructions from Dr. Galea and Ms. Stein to take his wife to the hospital on June 5, 2000, and that his wife's condition was an emergency.

. . .

Accordingly, the motion [for] adding a counterclaim against plaintiff Alexander Skylarsky for contribution and indemnity is granted....

NOTES

1. In Cruzan v. Director, Missouri Department of Health, 497 U.S. 261 (1990), Chief Justice Rehnquist writing for the majority of the Court held that there was not clear and convincing evidence that Nancy Cruzan, who was in a persistent vegetative state as a result of a car accident, would want hydration and nutrition withdrawn. In her concurrence, Justice O'Connor noted that the decision meant only that a state may require clear and convincing evidence. Thus States are free to develop other approaches for protecting an incompetent individual's liberty interest in refusing medical treatment, such as relying on family members and friends. The Cruzan family continued to pursue their goal of allowing Ms. Cruzan to die a dignified death. Citing new evidence of Ms. Cruzan's wishes, the family's lawyer sought a new trial. Family Yet Hopes "to Set her Free," N.Y. Times, June 26, 1990, at A18. In response, the State of Missouri, which had previously opposed the removal of the feeding tube, requested that it be permitted to withdraw from the new proceedings. Belkin, "Missouri Seeks to Quit Case of Comatose Patient," N.Y. Times, Oct. 12, 1990, at A15. The State's withdrawal left no remaining party to object to the removal of the feeding tube. On November 1, 1990, three friends of Ms. Cruzan testified to specific conversations with her in which she said she would never want to live "like a vegetable" on medical machines. Malcolm, "Missouri Family Renews Battle Over Right to Die," N.Y. Times, Nov. 2, 1990, at A14. On Dec. 14, 1990, Judge Charles E. Teel Jr., a county probate judge, authorized the Cruzan family to stop Ms. Cruzan's feeding by tube. The judge ruled that clear and convincing evidence existed of Ms. Cruzan's intent to terminate her feeding; there was no evidence that she would desire to continue in her present state; and that her parents were authorized to direct the removal of nutrition and hydration from Ms. Cruzan. Malcolm, Judge Allows Feeding–Tube Removal, N.Y. Times, Dec. 15, 1990, at 1. Ironically, Judge Teel had also presided over the family's original request to withdraw their daughter's nutritional support in 1987. His earlier decision to grant their request had been overturned by the Supreme Court. With her family at her bedside, Nancy Beth Cruzan died on December 16, 1990. Lewin, Nancy Cruzan Dies, Outlived by a Debate Over the Right to Die, N.Y. Times, Dec. 27, 1990, at A1. See generally William H. Colby, Long Goodbye: The Deaths of Nancy Cruzan (2002).

2. In 2005, national attention was focused on the case of Terri Schiavo. Mrs. Schiavo suffered extensive brain damage in 1990 after an incident diagnosed as a "potassium imbalance" that may have been a byproduct of bulimia, which left her brain without oxygen for many minutes. Abby Goodnough, Schiavo Dies, Ending Bitter Case Over Feeding Tube, NY Times, Apr. 1, 2005, at A1. Under Florida law her husband became her guardian. In 1992 he won a malpractice suit in her favor to help cover medical (and later litigation) costs. Terri's parents, the Schindler's, sought custody beginning in 1993, but were unsuccessful. In 1998 Terri's husband sought permission to remove her feeding tube. After a trial, a Florida guardianship court found that Terri was in a persistent vegetative state and that she would want treatment discontinued if she could make her own decision. The court ordered the discontinuance of artificial life support. The order was upheld on appeal. 780 So.2d 177 (Fla. 2d DCA 2001). The Schindlers continued to challenge the order, but it was later reaffirmed, 851 So.2d 183 (2003), and her feeding tube was removed. After the tube had been out for 6 days in October of 2003, the Florida legislature passed "Terri's Law," which authorized Florida's Governor Jeb Bush to stay the removal of the feeding tube pending appeals by Terri's parents to have the tube reinserted. In 2004, the Florida Supreme Court held that "Terri's Law" was unconstitutional. Bush v. Schiavo, 885 So.2d 321 (Fla. 2004). Jeb Bush appealed but the Supreme Court denied certiorari. Bush v. Schiavo, ___ U.S. ___, 125 S.Ct. 1086 (2005). The feeding tube was removed for the final time on March 18, 2005. Terri's parents continued with a flurry of motions and appeals, including an attempt to file for divorce on Terri's behalf (which would have made her parents guardians if successful), until her death on March 31. Goodnough, supra. An exhaustive autopsy later found that her brain had withered to half the normal size and that no treatment could have improved her condition. Goodnough, Shiavo Autopsy Says Brain, Withered, Was Untreatable, N.Y. Times, June 16, 2005, at A1.

CHAPTER 4

DIVORCE

A. TRADITIONAL FAULT GROUNDS AND DEFENSES

1. BACKGROUND

Lawrence Friedman, A History of American Law

204–08 (2d ed. 1985).

England had been a "divorceless society," and remained that way until 1857. There was no way to get a judicial divorce. The very wealthy might squeeze a rare private bill of divorce out of Parliament.... For the rest, unhappy husbands and wives had to be satisfied with annulment (no easy matter) or divorce from bed and board ..., a form of legal separation, which did not entitle either spouse to marry again. The most common solutions, of course, when a marriage broke down, were adultery and desertion.

In the colonial period, the South was generally faithful to English tradition. Absolute divorce was unknown, divorce from bed and board very rare. In New England, however, courts and legislatures occasionally granted divorce....

After Independence, the law and practice of divorce began to change, but regional differences remained quite strong. In the South, divorce continued to be unusual. The extreme case was South Carolina.... There was no such thing as an absolute divorce in South Carolina, throughout the 19th century. In other Southern states, legislatures dissolved marriages by passing private divorce laws....

North of the Mason–Dixon line, courtroom divorce became the normal mode, rather than legislative divorce. Pennsylvania passed a general divorce law in 1785, Massachusetts one year later. Every New England state had a divorce law before 1800, along with New York, New Jersey, and Tennessee. Grounds for divorce varied somewhat from state to state. New York's law of 1787 permitted absolute divorce only for adultery. Vermont, on the other hand, allowed divorce for impotence, adultery, intolerable severity, three years' willful desertion, and long absence with presumption of death....

This efflorescence of divorce laws must reflect real increase in demand for legal divorce. The size of the demand doomed the practice of divorce by statute. Like corporate charters, private divorce bills became a nuisance, a pointless drain on the legislature's time. At the end of the period, some states still granted legislative divorce; but others had abolished them. Later in the century, private divorce laws became extinct.

... What was the source of this sudden desire for a simpler way to divorce? The divorce rate in the 19th century, of course, was the merest trickle in comparison to the rate in more recent times. Still, it was noticeable, and it was growing; to some self-appointed guardians of national morals, it was an alarming fire bell in the night, a symptom of moral dry rot, and a cause in itself of still further moral decay. President Timothy Dwight of Yale [, for instance,] called the rise in divorces "dreadful beyond conception" ... and [warned that the] "whole community could be thrown into a general prostitution."

This apocalyptic vision never really came to pass. Nor was the rising divorce rate so obviously a sign that the family was breaking down. The family was indeed changing. There were new strains on marital relationships. William O'Neill put it this way: "when families are large and loose, arouse few expectations, and make few demands, there is no need for divorce." That need arises when "families become the center of social organization." At this point, "their intimacy can become suffocating, their demands unbearable, and their expectations too high to be easily realizable. Divorce then becomes the safety valve that makes the system workable." ... Easy divorce laws grew out of the needs of the middle-class mass. The smallholder had to have some way to stabilize and legitimize relationships, to settle doubts about ownership of family property. It was the same general impulse that lay behind the common-law marriage. Divorce was simplest to obtain and divorce laws most advanced in those parts of the country—the West especially—least stratified by class.

. . .

Since there were strong opinions on both sides, it was only natural that neither side got its way completely. Divorce laws were a kind of compromise. In general, the law never recognized full, free consensual divorce. It became simpler to get a divorce than in the past; but divorce was not routine or automatic. In form, divorce was an adversary proceeding. A divorce decree was, in theory, a reward for an innocent and virtuous spouse, victimized by an evil partner. Defendant had to be at fault; there had to be "grounds" for the divorce. Otherwise, divorce was legally impossible. Eventually, of course, the collusive or friendly divorce became the normal case. By the time divorce reached the courtroom, both partners wanted it, or at least had given up on the marriage; in any event, the real issues had all been hammered out beforehand. What went on in court became a show, a charade, an afterthought.

NOTE

For accounts of divorce in the eighteenth and nineteenth centuries in the United States, see Norma Basch, Framing American Divorce: From the Revolutionary Generation to the Victorians (2001); Richard Chused, Private Acts in Public Places: A Social History of Divorce in the Formative Era of American Family Law (1994).

2. Fault-Based Grounds for Divorce

By the 20th century, the pressure for easier divorce led not only to widespread tolerance of collusion (in New York where adultery was the only permissible ground until 1966, it was discovered that the "other woman" named in a number of suits was the secretary of a prominent divorce lawyer) but also to increasingly broad judicial interpretations of the available statutory grounds. The result was, in the words of Max Rheinstein, a "dual law of divorce:"[1] a strict law on the books that provided divorce only as punishment

1. Marriage Stability, Divorce and the Law 51 (1972). For more of the history of divorce see Herbert Jacob, Silent Revolution: The Transformation of Divorce Law in the

for grave marital misconduct; a liberal one in practice that amounted to divorce by consent.

Reliance on judicial discretion to ease the rising demand for divorce meant, however, that individual plaintiffs were often very much at the mercy of the judge who heard their case. It was difficult to predict when you might encounter a strict construction of the divorce law.

As you study the materials in this section, consider how you would explain the scope of the available grounds and defenses to a client. Consider also how a fault-based system might affect the bargaining power of spouses. Notice that the traditional fault system grants a divorce only to an "innocent" spouse. Does this comport with your understanding of most marriage relationships? Of any?

a. CRUELTY

Benscoter v. Benscoter

Superior Court of Pennsylvania, 1963.
200 Pa.Super. 251, 188 A.2d 859.

■ ERVIN, JUDGE.

In this case the husband filed a complaint in divorce on the ground of indignities to the person. The master recommended that a divorce be granted; however the court below, after reviewing the matter, dismissed the complaint. . . .

. . .

We . . . have arrived at an independent conclusion that the husband is not entitled to a divorce.

The parties were married on August 21, 1946 in West Nanticoke, Pennsylvania. Four sons were born as a result of the marriage. . . . At the time of the hearing in January 1962 the plaintiff was 39 years of age and the defendant was 37 and she was suffering from multiple sclerosis.

The main indignity of which the husband complains is that the wife expressed her disappointment in failing to have a female child and that she verbally abused him and blamed him for this failure. The wife's alleged misconduct was sporadic in nature and did not constitute a course of conduct as required by law. It must be pointed out that the parties lived together for 15 years and it was not until August of 1961 that the plaintiff complained about the defendant. Therefore, the plaintiff's condition could not have been as intolerable nor his life so burdensome as he now alleges.

In August of 1958 the defendant-wife was stricken with the incurable disease, multiple sclerosis. As a result of this disease she has double vision, slurred speech, weakness of the muscles and she cannot walk without the assistance of another person or a cane. She falls down frequently. She lost weight and at the time of the hearing weighed only 86 pounds. She is subject to the frustrations that are attendant to this progressive disease. Even the plaintiff testified that in September of 1961 the defendant attempted to commit suicide three times. These circumstances cannot be blindly disre-

United States (1988); Roderick Phillips, Putting Asunder: A History of Divorce in Western Society (1988); Lawrence Stone, Road to Divorce: England 1530–1987 (1990).

garded. Ill health both explains and excuses a wife's conduct and the acts of a spouse resulting from ill health do not furnish a ground for divorce.

During the summer of 1961 the defendant noticed that the plaintiff was taking more pride in his appearance, shaving every other day, using deodorants and changing clothes more frequently. Defendant's suspicions of another woman were aroused when she found prophylactics in the plaintiff's wallet and stains on his underclothes. Plaintiff offered a unique explanation of the presence of the prophylactics by stating that as game commissioner he used them for making turkey calls. The evidence clearly is that the plaintiff did accompany the other woman while trapping wild game and that he went swimming with her. We agree with the court below that plaintiff's interest in the other woman was above and beyond the call of duty. While the defendant was not able to prove adultery, certainly, under such circumstances, her suspicions were not unfounded. It was incumbent upon the plaintiff to show clearly and indubitably his status as the injured and innocent spouse. We do not believe that the plaintiff was the innocent and injured spouse.

The parties to a marriage take each other for better or for worse, in sickness and in health. The conclusion is inescapable that the plaintiff did not become dissatisfied with his wife until she became ill with multiple sclerosis. He cannot now discard her.

Hughes v. Hughes

Court of Appeals of Louisiana, Second Circuit, 1976.
326 So.2d 877.

■ PRICE, JUDGE.

This appeal concerns the sufficiency of evidence presented to sustain a finding by the trial court that the defendant, Clifford Carey Hughes, was guilty of cruel treatment toward his wife, Marilyn Elizabeth Hughes, to entitle her to a separation from bed and board.

Mrs. Hughes filed this action in April 1974, alleging in her original and amended pleadings that defendant had treated her coldly and indifferently, was habitually intemperate, and that on an occasion in December 1971, he had ordered her from the family home and threatened to do her bodily harm. She further alleges they separated after this incident until November of 1972, at which time she returned to the domicile on defendant's promises to correct his behavior. Further allegations are made that after approximately one month, defendant returned to his general course of abusive treatment of plaintiff, including cursing and physical threats toward her making it necessary that she again separate from defendant on December 18, 1973, and file this suit for a separation from bed and board.

Defendant denied plaintiff's accusations and reconvened for a separation in his favor contending the action of plaintiff in leaving the domicile on December 18th was without cause and constituted an abandonment.

We consider it to be in the best interest of both parties to discuss in as little detail as possible their personal marital difficulties in this appellate opinion.

As we understand defendant's argument on this appeal, he contends that although he was guilty of causing the initial separation in December 1971, the record does not contain any reliable proof of his having continued the course of cruel treatment after the reconciliation in November of 1972, and therefore plaintiff has not met her burden of proof.

In his reasons for judgment, the trial judge relied on the testimony of the only child of the marriage to resolve the conflicting testimony of the parties and to find plaintiff had proven her entitlement to a separation. This daughter who had married at the time of trial, was a college student during the troubled years of her parent's marriage but was present in the home on a number of occasions when there was discord between her parents. Her testimony confirmed her mother's allegations concerning the continuation of the cruel treatment by her father.

The trial judge construed her testimony to relate to the actions of defendant after the reconciliation in November 1972, and found the testimony sufficiently convincing to establish that defendant cursed his wife on many occasions and declared that he did not love either his wife or his daughter. The court found this conduct to constitute mental harassment sufficient to render the continued living together insupportable.

From our examination of the record, we find this conclusion to be supported by the evidence and to be in accord with the prior jurisprudence.

NOTES

1. Can you explain the difference in outcome in *Hughes* and *Benscoter?* Did the sex of the plaintiffs make a difference? Was the ill health of Mrs. Benscoter the determining factor? Was the alleged adultery of Mr. Benscoter the determining factor? If Mr. Benscoter came to your office to ask whether there is now any way for him to divorce Mrs. Benscoter, what would you advise? Should he move to Louisiana?

2. Cruelty originally was limited to bodily harm or a reasonable apprehension of bodily harm. Evans v. Evans, 1 Hagg.Cong. 35, 161 Eng.Rep. 466 (Consistory Ct. of London, 1790). Today, however, most courts consider psychological harm sufficient to grant a divorce for cruelty or its statutory variant, indignities to the person. Even where "physical" harm is required, it may be met by such evidence as weight loss, or nervousness. When there has been physical harm, most courts have held that one episode is not enough to justify a divorce, unless it was a particularly serious or shocking incident.

b. ADULTERY

Arnoult v. Arnoult

Louisiana Court of Appeal, 1997.
690 So.2d 101.

■ THOMAS F. DALEY, JUDGE.

Patricia Arnout appeals a judgment of the trial court finding she was guilty of post separation adultery. For the reasons that follow, we affirm.

Patricia and Elden Arnoult were married on August 13, 1966 and physically separated on March 10, 1995. On March 13, 1995, Patricia filed a Petition for Divorce and Incidental Matters. On March 14, 1995, Elden filed an Answer and Reconventional Demand. Both petitions requested a divorce under the provisions of C.C. Art. 102. Thereafter, on August 25, 1995, Elden amended his petition and alleged Patricia was guilty of adultery. The matter came for trial on May 3, 1996 and the trial court found Patricia was in fact guilty of adultery.

Five witnesses testified at trial, Patricia Arnoult; Patricia Arnoult's alleged paramour, Whitney Duplantis; Elden B. Arnoult, Jr.; and two private investigators, Don Satullo and Raymond Leferve, hired by Elden B. Arnoult, Jr. The investigators testified that two incidents occured during the period of surveillance relative to the issues before us. The first occurred on May 13, 1995 wherein Duplantis and Patricia Arnoult were observed leaving the Bengal Lounge in Metairie at about 3:50 a.m. The couple were observed leaning against Patricis Arnoult's car hugging and kissing. After about 35 minutes, they moved inside the car and continued embracing until about 5:55 a.m. Both investigators testified both heads would occasionally disappear from view. When Duplantis exited the vehicle, he was buttoning his shirt and rearranging his clothes.

On May 21, 1995, another incident occurred at the Bengal. Duplantis and Patricia were in the bar dancing and kissing before leaving at about 2:10 a.m. After 2:10 a.m. they got in Patricia Arnoult's car and were kissing in the car for about 45 minutes. Thereafter, Patricia Arnoult followed Whitney Duplantis to his house in Harahan. The investigators testified they arrived around 3:20 a.m., parked in the street, walked down the driveway and entered the house toward the rear. Both investigators testified they saw no lights come on in the house at any time during the surveillance. No one else either entered or exited the house. At about 5:30 a.m., Patricia Arnoult exited the house alone and returned to her apartment.

Patricia Arnout and Whitney Duplantis both testified concerning the May 21 incident. They testified that upon leaving the Bengal Lounge Whitney Duplantis was hungry and they went to Taco Bell to get something to eat. While there, they were asked to leave because Whitney Duplantis entered the store with a beer can in his hand. They returned to where he was parked near the Bengal Lounge and began to eat. Because he did not have a drink, they left to go to his house. Patricia Arnoult followed him to be sure he made it home as Whitney Duplantis had been drinking. Once there, both testified that lights were turned on, the food was eaten and they began to watch television. Whitney Duplantis began falling asleep while watching television, so Patricia Arnoult left. Both maintain that they never had intercourse or oral sex on either occasion.

The trial court found the circumstantial evidence sufficient to prove Patricia committed adultery. The trial court's factual determination is entitled to great weight on appeal and will not be disturbed unless manifest error is shown. Tablada v. Tablada, 590 So. 2d 1357 (5th Cir.1991), citing Pearce v. Pearce, 348 So. 2d 75 (La. 1977); Stewart v. Stewart, 422 So. 2d 1370 (1st Cir. 1982).

The nature of the act of adultery requires that circumstantial evidence will most likely be used to sustain the proponent's burden of proof. A prima facia case of adultery can be made out by showing facts or circumstances that lead fairly and necessarily to the conclusion that adultery has been committed. Coston v. Coston, 196 La. 1095, 200 So. 474 (1941). Courts must look with caution to the testimony of an investigator hired by one spouse to watch the other spouse, and this evidence ordinarily should be corroborated by the facts and circumstances in evidence and/or by direct testimony of other witnesses. McCartan e can be made where the only evidence presented is the testimony of hired investigators. See Hermes v. Hermes, 287 So. 2d 789 (La. 1973).

In the case at bar, the trial court found from the totality of the evidence presented that Patricia Arnout had committed adultery. Mrs. Arnoult admitted to hugging and kissing Mr. Duplantis. Although Mrs. Arnoult denies committing adultery and disputes some of the facts as testified to by the investigators surrounding the events of May 21, she admits going to Mr. Duplantis' house at 3:30 a.m. After observing the demeanor of the witnesses and the totality of the evidence submitted, the trial court found the testimony of the investigators more credible than Mrs. Arnoult and Mr. Duplantis concerning the events of May 21 and concluded that Mrs. Arnoult did in fact commit adultery. Given the facts that Mrs. Arnoult and Dr. Duplantis were clearly engaged in sexual foreplay prior to returning to Mr. Duplantis' residence at 3:30 a.m. on the morning of May 21st and the trial court's ability to evaluate the credibility of their denial of additional sexual conduct, we cannot say that the trial court's factual findings were manifestly erroneous.

Accordingly, for the reasons assigned, the trial court judgment granting Elden Arnoult Jr. a divorce from Patricia Arnoult on grounds of adultery is affirmed. Patricia Arnoult to bear all costs of this appeal.

NOTE

As the main case illustrates, adultery is normally proven by circumstantial evidence. Alternatively, one can attempt to show that the wife has borne a child that is not the child of her husband. One problem with this approach is that in 1777 Lord Mansfield ruled that there is a presumption that the child of a married woman is that of her husband. Goodright v. Moss, 98 Eng.Rep. 1257 (Ct.Ch. 1777). Although Lord Mansfield's rule was considered irrebuttable in the past, it has come under increasing attack in recent times and has been abolished in a number of jurisdictions. In some jurisdictions, the burden of proof that the wife's child is not her husband's can be met by showing (a) that the husband did not have access to the wife during the period of conception; (b) that he was impotent or sterile at that time, or (c) that blood tests exclude him as a possible father of the child. A fourth alternative, accepted in some jurisdictions, is to show that a spouse has been convicted of adultery, rape or prostitution.

In Michael H. v. Gerald D., Chapter 3, Section C, 2, the United States Supreme Court affirmed the constitutionality of a California statute providing that "the issue of a wife cohabiting with her husband, who is not impotent or sterile, is conclusively presumed to be a child of the marriage."

c. DESERTION

Crosby v. Crosby

Court of Appeals of Louisiana, 1983.
434 So.2d 162.

■ GAUDIN, JUDGE.

This is an appeal by Lois Pitre Crosby from a judgment of the 24th Judicial District Court denying her permanent alimony. The trial judge found that Mrs. Crosby ". . . failed to show that she was free from fault . . ." as required by LSA–C.C. art. 160, which reads, in pertinent part:

> "When a spouse has not been at fault and has not sufficient means for support, the court may allow that spouse, out of the property and earnings of the other spouse, permanent periodic alimony. . . ."

Rule

We have very carefully reviewed the record of this two-day hearing, and the *only* testimony tending to show legal fault on Mrs. Crosby's part concerned her refusal to follow Mr. Crosby when he changed domiciles. This failure runs afoul of LSA–C.C. art. 120, which states:

> "The wife is bound to live with her husband and to follow him wherever he chooses to reside; the husband is obligated to receive her and to furnish her with whatever is required for the convenience of life, in proportion to his means and condition."

For reasons following, we find Art. 120 unconstitutional in that it discriminates against women on the sole basis of gender by arbitrarily forcing them to follow husbands wherever they choose to live, in clear violation of the equal protection clauses of the federal and state constitutions.

. . .

The very wording of Art. 120 denies women equal protection of the laws. In striking down an Alabama statute because different treatment was accorded men and women on the basis of sex, the United States Supreme Court, in Orr v. Orr, 440 U.S. 268, 279, 99 S.Ct. 1102, 1111, 59 L.Ed.2d 306 pointed out:

> "To withstand scrutiny under the equal protection clause, classification by gender must serve important governmental objectives and must be substantially related to those objectives."

We cannot envision any "important governmental objectives" served by Art. 120.

. . .

On appeal, Mrs. Crosby contends that Art. 120 is unconstitutional and also that she was free from fault. The Crosbys were married for 18 years and had two children, and Mrs. Crosby testified that she had valid reasons for refusing to move to Harvey. As we agree with Mrs. Crosby on the constitutional issue, we have no reason to comment on her second contention.

NOTES

1. A rehearing was granted by the Court of Appeals. After oral argument, but before a decision was made, the parties settled. 442 So.2d 1248 (1983).

2. Desertion, like cruelty, has been applied to a wide variety of actions, particularly in states that recognize "constructive desertion." Constructive desertion operates in some respects like a defense. It is in this sense analogous to the concept "provocation" in criminal law. But unlike other divorce defenses, which can only defeat a spouse's suit for divorce, constructive desertion if proven both defeats the spouse's cause of action and serves as an alternate ground for divorce.

It has been held that refusal to have intercourse without contraceptives constitutes constructive desertion. Kreyling v. Kreyling, 20 N.J.Misc. 52, 23 A.2d 800 (1942). Is this judicial "interpretation" or usurpation of the powers of the legislature? Does *Kreyling* embody a wise civil definition of marriage? Is it constitutional in light of *Griswold,* Chapter 3, Section D, 1?

3. Traditional Defenses

a. RECRIMINATION

Rankin v. Rankin

Superior Court of Pennsylvania, 1956.
181 Pa.Super. 414, 124 A.2d 639.

■ Wright, Judge.

On February 3, 1953, Michael J. Rankin instituted an action in divorce against his wife, Edith L. Rankin. The parties were at that time aged 58 and

43 years, respectively. The complaint originally alleged cruel and barbarous treatment and indignities to the person, but was subsequently amended to include a charge of desertion. . . .

. . .

Considering first the question of cruel and barbarous treatment, we note that the master was "of the opinion that this ground has been established by clear and satisfactory evidence." However, the lower court said: "We have some doubt as to whether there is sufficient [evidence] in the case to sustain the cause of cruel and barbarous treatment." The term cruel and barbarous treatment comprises actual personal violence or a reasonable apprehension thereof, or such a course of treatment as endangers life or health and renders cohabitation unsafe. A single instance of cruelty may be so severe, and with such attending circumstances of atrocity, as to justify a divorce. The master bases his recommendation solely upon an incident which allegedly occurred when the parties were riding together in an automobile. As related in the master's report: "On one occasion while they were riding in a car with defendant driving, she stated: 'I am going to kill you, you son of a bitch', and proceeded to drive the car at a high rate of speed. On this occasion plaintiff succeeded in slowing down the car by turning the ignition key, following which he jumped from the car; thereupon defendant attempted to run him down." This circumstance was categorically denied by appellant, was entirely uncorroborated, and is utterly improbable in the light of appellee's testimony that he "jerked the key out to slow the car down," that he got out of the car, and that appellant then "turned the car" and endeavored "to get me along the road."

Next considering the question of indignities, the findings of the master which the lower court deemed important may be thus summarized: Appellant's "attitude toward plaintiff was one of marked antipathy; she called him vile and opprobrious names without provocation"; she refused to have children; she "had the furniture, with the exception of the box springs and mattress, removed from plaintiff's bedroom"; she "was frequently absent from the home without explanation . . . spit in his face and tried to strike him with a chair; that she threw hot water on plaintiff; and another time threatened him with a butcher knife." The lower court also considered the alleged incident in the automobile in connection with the charge of indignities, citing Phipps v. Phipps, 368 Pa. 291, 81 A.2d 523. Appellee testified that his wife had him arrested "a lot of times" for assault and battery. It should be here noted that much of appellee's testimony consisted of similar general expressions and was vague and indefinite throughout. Sidney A. Grubbs testified that, at the insistence of appellee, he went to see appellant in an effort to effect a reconciliation, but appellant said "there was no use to try to get along with that dumb hunky". Mollie M. Leathers testified that she frequently heard appellant use profanity and remark that she hated to see her husband come home. Harry Hickman testified concerning the removal of the bedroom furniture, and the use of profanity by appellant. Nora Stambaugh testified that appellant once took the keys to the truck, denied having them, but finally threw them on the floor.

As we pointed out in our opinion filed this day in Moyer v. Moyer, Pa.Super., 124 A.2d 632, 637: "In a proceeding for divorce on the grounds of indignities, it must clearly appear from the evidence that the plaintiff was the injured and innocent spouse". . . .

In her testimony appellant admitted using profanity and calling her husband names. By way of explanation, she alleged that she had acquired her knowledge of profanity from appellee, and that, in calling her husband "a dumb hunky", she was only repeating his own words. She flatly denied that she ever threw hot water on him, or threatened him with a butcher knife. With regard to the removal of the bedroom furniture, she testified that she and her husband had purchased a new bedroom suite. In anticipation of its delivery she and Mrs. Hickman removed the furniture, excepting the mattress and springs, from one bedroom. Before the suite could be delivered appellee cancelled the purchase. The outstanding incident about which appellant testified was a quarrel which took place while the Hickmans were living in the Rankin home. Appellant's story is that she fell to the floor, whereupon her husband stepped upon her, applying his full weight to her back. This is corroborated by Mrs. Hickman who testified that she was in the kitchen when she heard a commotion upstairs and appellant ran downstairs with her husband in pursuit. As appellant came into the kitchen she fell and appellee "kicked her and stepped on her." The witness went to call her husband and, when she returned, appellant was sitting on a chair and appellee was hitting her on the head with a belt. The master apparently chose to treat this entire incident as a fabrication, despite the fact that corroboration came, inter alia, from two unimpeachable sources. The one was James Morrison, the minister neighbor of the parties. The other was Dr. John A. Krosnoff, appellant's family physician, who testified that he treated appellant for multiple bruises, particularly of the left side of the face, a large swelling on the head, and bruises of the hip and back. When appellant's condition failed to improve, the doctor advised an x-ray examination which disclosed the herniated disc. A surgeon then performed an operation on appellant's spine which did not cure her condition. She is still undergoing treatment and is unable to work. On another occasion appellee pulled appellant from her chair and threw her out of the house. Appellant thereupon called the police and had appellee arrested for assault and battery. The charge was subsequently dropped. In answer to appellee's charge that she refused to have children, appellant testified that in 1949 it was necessary for her to undergo a hysterectomy. This was corroborated by Dr. Krosnoff, who referred appellant to Dr. Fisher for the operation. Catherine Reeves and Florence Mills, two other witnesses for appellant, testified that appellee frequently used vile language toward his wife. Both testified that appellant was a good cook and a good housekeeper, and that she tried to get along with her husband. As already noted, several witnesses testified that appellee threatened to kill his wife. When asked if he had not said that he "would like to shoot that God Damn Crummy," appellee's reply was: "I don't know if I did nor not."

The fact that married people do not get along well together does not justify a divorce. Testimony which proves merely an unhappy union, the parties being high strung temperamentally and unsuited to each other and neither being wholly innocent of the causes which resulted in the failure of their marriage, is insufficient to sustain a decree. If both are equally at fault, neither can clearly be said to be the innocent and injured spouse, and the law will leave them where they put themselves. At the very best, appellee's evidence might establish such a situation. A less favorable view of the evidence indicates that appellee was the principal offender, and that appellant was actually the innocent and injured spouse. In neither event has appellee established his right to a divorce on the ground of indignities.

. . .

NOTES

1. History. Although divorce proceedings are exclusively governed by statute in the United States, many courts have resurrected defenses used by the ecclesiastical courts in England without statutory authorization. Some of these defenses were designed primarily to provide economic protection for wives in a society in which unattached women could not easily survive. They were never meant to bar divorce. Does use of the defense of recrimination make sense as a state policy today?

2. Scope. Recrimination has been expressly limited or abolished by statute in 17 states. In other states the concept has been limited by: (1) granting a divorce to both spouses; (2) requiring that recrimination must be pleaded by a party rather than raised by the court; and (3) adopting the doctrine of comparative rectitude, see Hendricks v. Hendricks, 123 Utah 178, 257 P.2d 366 (1953).

The *Hendricks* court explained comparative rectitude as follows:

> [N]o good purpose, either social, moral, ethical or legal could be served by refusing to grant a divorce.... It would be but a mockery of the true concept of matrimony to thus purport to compel these two people, clearly ill-suited and maladjusted to each other to continue to retain the legal relationship of husband and wife.
>
> In view of the fact that neither spouse is accused of the commission of a felony, adultery or any other heinous offense but the reciprocal claims rest upon various acts and omissions alleged to constitute cruelty to the other, the trial court would best perform its function in the administration of justice by determining which party was least at fault, granting a divorce and adjusting their rights.... [Id. at 180–81, 257 P.2d at 367.]

b. CONNIVANCE

Sargent v. Sargent

Court of Chancery of New Jersey, 1920.
114 A. 428.

[Donald J. Sargent filed a petition for divorce charging his wife with having committed adultery with Charles Simmons, a chauffeur in his employ.]

■ FIELDER, ADV. M. ... Petitioner ... had reason to suspect [his wife] of an inclination for illicit relations with Simmons, and, suspecting, he should have taken the step which lay within his power to keep Simmons away from his home, namely, discharge him and warn him never to come to his house again. Instead, he retained Simmons in his employ. Thus he gave Simmons the chance to be with his wife frequently in the automobile and also an excuse for and opportunity to be at his house at all times during the day when petitioner was absent at his business, and petitioner purposely, on at least two occasions between May 22nd and July 11, absented himself from home for a night or nights, and he did all this, if not believing that defendant would commit adultery, at least to facilitate it. He placed detectives in his home, suborned his servants, received reports from his spies as to the progress of events. ... He threw no protection around his wife. He did not even warn her against intimacy with Simmons, but he left her in danger, and did nothing whatever to withdraw her from Simmons' evil influence. ...

Our courts have said that it is undoubtedly true that a man may watch his wife without warning her of his intention to do so, but it is equally true that he may not actually participate in a course of action leading to her downfall. He may not, with his eyes open, do that which may in some degree conduct to it. If he sees what a reasonable man could not permit and makes no effort to avert the danger, he must be supposed to see and mean the result.

If defendant committed adultery on the night of July 11, . . . if consent or willingness that the wife should commit adultery is a mental state and is to be inferred from conduct, it seems impossible to resist the conclusion that petitioner did desire his wife to commit the offense, and that, helping as he did to afford the opportunity which brought the desired result, he was consenting thereto.

c. CONDONATION

Willan v. Willan

Court of Appeal for England and Wales, 1960.
2 All E.R. 463.

■ WILLMER, L.J. . . . This is an appeal by a husband . . . [whose] petition for dissolution of his marriage [was denied] on the ground that the cruelty had been condoned. . . .

The relevant facts lie within a comparatively small compass. The parties were married on June 2, 1925, and there are two children of the marriage, one born shortly after the marriage and the other born soon after the war in 1946. The husband was away on military service during the war, but cohabitation was resumed on his demobilization, and he continued to live with his wife until the morning of Sept. 29, 1958.

Facts

The husband's case against the wife is that throughout the marriage, and more particularly in the latter part of it, she frequently and persistently assaulted him and showed violence to him and that she was immensely jealous of his relations with other women; and it was also said that she habitually used offensive and obscene language, calling him by horrible names and so forth. It is also alleged—and this is the real gravamen of the charge—that she frequently demanded sexual intercourse with him at times when he did not wish to have it, obliging him to conform to her wishes by indulging in various types of violence in order to bend his will to hers. In particular, it was said that she would pull his hair, catch hold of him by the ears, and shake his head violently to and fro; and, at any rate on one occasion, it was said that she kicked him on his injured leg, causing him great pain. She would also pester him far into the night to have sexual intercourse, so that eventually he was compelled to comply as the only means of getting his rest. That is the nature of the husband's case of cruelty which, as I have said, was found in his favour. I have referred to the details of it only because the alleged act of condonation is very largely bound up with the kind of conduct which is complained of by the husband as cruelty on the part of his wife.

It appears that for some time before the final separation the parties were on bad terms, although sexual intercourse was continuing in the circumstances which I have described. The husband at least was for some time in the hands of solicitors, and we know that on or about Aug. 13, 1958, the solicitors wrote on his behalf to his wife, complaining of her cruel conduct and informing her that the husband would be obliged to leave her. Even after that, however, life went on very much as before, the husband continuing to reside in the matrimonial home with his wife, and continuing to share the same bed with her. . . . It is not without significance, I think, that even after the solicitors' letter was written the husband is still found to be willingly and voluntarily having intercourse with his wife.

It is said (and this much is common ground between the parties) that, on the night of Sept. 28/29, i.e., the night before the husband left for the last time, an act of sexual intercourse took place between the parties. The husband says that that act, like many other acts previously, was induced by the wife pestering him far into the night, showing some degree of violence to him, pulling his hair and so forth and, finally, as I understand it, rolling on top of him, so that eventually, towards the small hours of the morning, and for the sake of peace, he did have intercourse with her. Thereafter, the parties appear to have gone straight to sleep, and the next thing that happened was the alarm clock going off at a quarter to six in the morning. The husband promptly got up, dressed and left the house at six o'clock in order to go to work. He kissed his wife and said goodbye, all in accordance with his usual procedure, the wife saying good-bye to him. I mention those facts as to what took place after the last act of intercourse because it was at one time suggested that, if that act of intercourse did amount to condonation, conduct subsequent thereto on the part of the wife was sufficient to bring about a revival. Clearly, however, on the evidence there never could have been any merit in that suggestion. . . .

When the case came on ultimately in this court . . . the first ground . . . was in the following terms:

> "That the learned commissioner misdirected himself in law in that the last act of intercourse which occurred between the parties on the night of Sept. 28, 1958, could not have constituted condonation by reason of the fact that it constituted an important element of the cruelty complained of, and/or by reason of the fact that it took place when the petitioner was under duress and/or was not a free agent."

So stated, that ground of appeal runs two or three arguments together, and I will do my best to keep them separate. In the first place, it is said that this act of intercourse on the part of the husband could not be held to amount to condonation, because it was one and the same with an act which was of itself relied on as part of the cruelty alleged. . . . Certainly there is no finding by the learned commissioner that the last act of intercourse relied on as condonation was one with the cruelty alleged by the husband against the wife. Furthermore, as it seems to me, and as I indicated during the argument, the contention is really the result of muddled thinking, because it confuses the actual act of sexual intercourse, which constitutes the evidence of condonation, with the prior conduct complained of on the part of the wife, whereby she induced the act of intercourse. I can well understand that pestering in such circumstances on the part of the wife, in such a way as to deny the husband sleep, more particularly if accompanied by the pulling of his hair, might very well be capable of amounting to cruelty. But, whether that be so or not, I find it impossible to say that the subsequent action of the wife in submitting herself to an act of sexual intercourse could in any circumstances amount to an act of cruelty against the husband. . . .

Then it was said that this act of intercourse was induced by duress on the part of the wife, and that the husband was not to be regarded as a free agent. It is well established that, whatever may be the position of a wife, in the case of a husband the fact of having intercourse with the wife, with full knowledge of the matrimonial offence of which complaint is made, is conclusive evidence of condonation by the husband of the wife. It is conclusive evidence because it is the best possible way of showing that the wife has been reinstated as a wife. Only one exception to that rule was accepted by the House of Lords ... and that is the case where the act of intercourse is induced by fraud on the part of the wife. Subject to that ... intercourse by a husband with his wife after knowledge of the matters complained of is conclusive evidence of condonation.

. . .

All that has been proved in this case is that the wife used means, to which exception may well be taken, for the purpose of persuading her husband to have intercourse with her. He was free to submit or to resist. He was free, I suppose, to have run away, but in the end he decided that the best course to take was to submit to her wishes. I dare say he did show unwillingness, but to say that he showed unwillingness is not to say that he acted involuntarily. It might be otherwise in the case of a wife; but in the case of a husband who has sexual intercourse it can only be said of him that what he does he does on purpose, and that sexual intercourse with his wife must be a voluntary act on his part.

. . .

NOTES

1. Can this defense be squared with the interest society may have in encouraging attempts at reconciliation? This tension between condonation and reconciliation may explain why courts have differed so much as to what is required to establish condonation. See, e.g., Bush v. Bush, 135 Ark. 512, 205 S.W. 895 (1918) (verbal forgiveness suffices); Lowensten v. Lowensten, 79 N.J.Super. 124, 190 A.2d 882 (1963) (renewal of sexual relations is essential); Seiferth v. Seiferth, 132 So.2d 471 (Fla.App.1961) (renewal of sexual relations creates a rebuttable presumption of forgiveness).

2. Glass v. Glass, 175 Md. 693, 2 A.2d 443, 447 (1938): "Condonation, say the books, with respect to a woman, is held not to bear so strictly, 'because it is not improper she should for a time show a patient forbearance [and] [s]he may have no means of support except under his roof' [quoting Bowic v. Bowic, 3 Md.Ch. 51, 55 (1850)]."

Could the *Glass* test today be successfully challenged as an unconstitutional gender-based standard?

d. COLLUSION

Fuchs v. Fuchs

Supreme Court of New York, Special Term, Kings County, 1946.
64 N.Y.S.2d 487.

■ DALY, JUSTICE.

The final judgment of divorce was rendered on April 15, 1946, in favor of the plaintiff on defendant's default. Prior to the commencement of this action the plaintiff had commenced a previous action on August 30, 1945, in which action defendant appeared and denied the material allegations of the complaint. In a motion made in that action defendant alleged that the plaintiff was then living with a woman (whom he has married since the decree in this action became final) and had been having relations with her for four years prior thereto. Thereafter the first action for divorce was discontinued and this action was commenced on October 30, 1945. Defendant claims that the plaintiff stated he wanted a divorce and if she would permit him to obtain it he would give her full, absolute and complete custody of the child. Defendant states that she was interested only in the custody of her child and that on plaintiff's assurance that she would always have custody, she was willing to allow him the divorce he sought. She entered into an agreement with the plaintiff, by the terms of which the custody of the child was to remain with her and as soon as this agreement was made defendant advised her attorney not to contest the divorce action. She denies ever having committed adultery with anyone.

Where a party has deliberately and intentionally suffered a default, the motion to vacate will be denied. "It is deemed in such case that there is, in fact, no default, but an abandonment of the cause and a submission to the entry of judgment." Since a party cannot consent to the entry of a decree of divorce, it is obvious why the rule is different in divorce cases. As pointed out in 9 Carmody N.Y.Prac., Sec. 160, p. 242, "The strict rules relating to opening defaults is (sic) not applied to actions for divorce, because of the well known vigilance of the courts to prevent collusion, and because of the general interest of the people of the state in the preservation of the matrimonial status of its citizens."

... This case is analogous to Jacoby v. Jacoby, 245 App.Div. 763, 280 N.Y.S. 611, 612, where it appeared "that defendant may have a good defense and was induced to refrain from answering the complaint by plaintiff's false promises to continue his payments of $40 a week during the life of the defendant, and by his threat to discontinue such payments if she defended the action." The Appellate Division, Second Department, reversed an order denying her motion to open her default and granted her leave to appear and answer. A threat to deprive a mother of her child would be an even more compelling inducement to persuade her to default in a divorce action. ...

. . .

Even though the defendant may be tainted with fraud herself, in that she was willing to permit a fraud upon the court and thus does not come into court with clean hands, the state has an interest in the matrimonial status of its citizens and the two guilty spouses are not the only parties in interest.

The defendant's right to open the default and defend the action is not affected by the fact that the plaintiff has remarried. In each of the cited cases, the plaintiff had remarried but the court set aside the default and permitted the defendant to defend, allowing the decree to stand until the trial and determination of the issue between the plaintiff and defendant and providing in the order that, if the defense were sustained, the decree should be set aside and the complaint dismissed, but if the defendant were defeated, the decree should stand in full force for the protection of the second wife. The rights of all concerned will best be served by making a similar order in this case. Accordingly, defendant's motion to set aside her default is granted, and the defendant will be permitted to answer the complaint herein within ten days after the service of a copy of the order to be entered hereon with notice of entry. The decree may stand until the trial. If the defense be sustained, the decree shall be vacated and the complaint dismissed; but if plaintiff prevail, the decree shall remain in full force for the protection of plaintiff's second wife.

. . .

NOTE

Compare *Fuchs* with Fender v. Crosby, 209 Ga. 896, 76 S.E.2d 769 (1953) (husband who alleged he was induced to agree to a collusive divorce by wife who claimed she needed it for her health, denied the chance to overturn the decree on grounds of estoppel even though wife had lied and immediately married another man).

e. INSANITY

Anonymous v. Anonymous

Supreme Court of New York, Nassau County, 1962.
37 Misc.2d 773, 236 N.Y.S.2d 288.

■ BERNARD S. MEYER, JUSTICE.

Involved in this divorce action is the question under what circumstances does the mental condition of an erring spouse constitute a defense. . . . [New York] has enacted no statute fixing criteria for responsibility for conduct in violation of marital obligations. New York case law has recognized that an insane wife is incapable of abandoning her husband and refused a divorce to a husband whose wife committed adultery while suffering from dementia praecox (Laudo v. Laudo, 188 App.Div. 699, 177 N.Y.S. 396). Some of those cases emphasize the marital obligation to provide support, including medical assistance, to an afflicted spouse; in none was it necessary to consider the degree of affliction that would excuse infidelity.

Should the standard be that advanced in M'Naghten's Case, 10 Cl. & F. 200, and now embodied in Penal Law, § 1120: ability to distinguish right from wrong or to understand the nature and quality of the act? . . . Or should the criteria of responsibility be that suggested as a revision of the criminal rule in Durham v. United States, 94 U.S.App.D.C. 228, 214 F.2d 862, and expanded upon in Carter v. United States, 102 U.S.App.D.C. 227, 252 F.2d 608 under which the defense is established by showing (a) a mental disease or defect, and (b) that the act in question was the product or result of the disease or defect; that is—that the defendant would not have committed the act if he had not been diseased as he was. . . . While at first blush the conclusion of the American Bar Foundation's study of "The Mentally Disabled and the Law" appears contrary to use of Durham–Carter standards in matrimonial cases, its suggestion (at p. 203) that "serious thought should be given to the use [in divorce cases] of standards defining civil hospitalization" of necessity refers only to the presence of a mental disease or defect and is not understood as excluding causal relationship in matrimonial cases, although causal connection has no bearing on civil hospitalization.

. . . In the present case, however, it is not necessary for the court to choose between the possible standards, for whichever is applied, the Court's conclusion is that plaintiff is entitled to judgment of divorce.

The burden of proving mental condition relieving defendant of responsibility is on defendant. Her sanity is presumed and the presumption must be overcome by a contrary showing. . . . To overcome the presumption defendant offered the testimony of her psychiatrist and the record of her hospitalization at Meadowbrook a few days after the incident which is the basis of this action. The psychiatrist testified that defendant had been under his care since September 1960; that she was even now highly unstable; that he had first diagnosed her as a character disorder, but later concluded that she was schizophrenic-affective type; . . . that prior to the incident she was aware that she was being followed since plaintiff had told her in the presence of the psychiatrist that as a result of prior infidelities he intended to have her followed; that defendant had discussed the rendezvous with the witness three days before it occurred and told him that she had sought to dissuade her paramour from going through with it and had told the paramour that he might be involved in a lawsuit; that defendant nonetheless felt compelled to go ahead with the meeting; that she was motivated by emotionality rather than rational thinking and felt justified in what she was going to do; that she was unable to determine that it was a wrong act; that it was for her primarily a means of getting even with her father, and to a lesser degree with plaintiff, both of whom considered her a "bad" person; that in his opinion she was unable to control her actions and in poor contact with reality at the time of the incident, and was then unable to distinguish the true nature of the act she was committing or to differentiate right from wrong. . . .

On the other side of the scale is the testimony of plaintiff's psychiatrist that in his opinion while defendant has had psychiatric difficulty and was emotionally unstable and in need of treatment, she was sufficiently intact to be able to use the ordinary standards of right and wrong; that she behaved in a manner which indicated that she was aware of those factors; that she knew at the time of the incident that she was committing adultery and that it was wrong; that she is not schizophrenic and that her stating to him that she had no recollection of the incident but being able quickly and accurately to supply data unrelated to the incident indicated to him that she was lying in an attempt to evade discussion of the incident with him. . . .

The court concludes that defendant has not sustained the burden of proof. Had she testified the impressions gained by the court during her testimony would have supported the opinion of one or the other of the psychiatrists. At the base of the differing opinions of the experts is their differing views of her credibility. Her credibility is also the central issue in this case. Deprived of the opportunity of forming first hand impressions concerning defendant's credibility, the court can choose between the experts' views only on the basis of the consistency of those views with the evidence as a whole. The inconsistency between the conclusion that defendant was driven into acts of adultery by an irrational necessity to get even with her father and with plaintiff and, on the one hand, the homosexual overtures at the hospital, and, on the other, the implication in defendant's affidavit that the acts of adultery resulted from the necessity of proving herself a woman, suggests to the court that the hospital overtures and the affidavit's contention are afterthoughts contrived by defendant to escape the consequences of her act. That defendant went ahead with her tryst notwithstanding she had been warned she was being followed can be interpreted as irrational but might also indicate either disbelief that plaintiff would take action or a rational conclusion on her part that her relationship with plaintiff had so far deteriorated that she didn't care whether the marriage continued or not. While her statement to her psychiatrist that she tried to talk the paramour out of going ahead with their plans is consistent with irrationality, her actions when caught and thereafter, as demonstrated by word and deed, suggest a realization of the nature of her conduct and a desire to avoid its consequences. On all of the evidence the court concludes that defendant has not demonstrated by a preponderance of the credible evidence that she was, as pleaded in her separate defense, "suffering from mental and emotional disorders so as to make her incompetent and irresponsible for the acts charged against her in the complaint."

Plaintiff is, therefore, awarded judgment of divorce. . . .

NOTES

1. What policy, if any, is served by making insanity a defense to divorce actions?

2. In 1847, in Matchin v. Matchin, 6 Pa. 332, 47 Am.Dec. 466, a Pennsylvania court held that insanity was not a defense to a divorce on adultery grounds, on the theory that allowing such a defense might result in imposing a spurious offspring on the husband. In 1960, however, in Manley v. Manley, 193 Pa.Super. 252, 264, 164 A.2d 113, 120 (1960), the court declined to follow the *Matchin* rule explaining: "[T]here is authority for our ignoring an ancient higher court rule which is unreasonable and unjust by all known standards, and which has frequently been examined and universally rejected by legal authorities and by courts in other jurisdictions."

B. No-Fault Divorce

With California leading the way in 1969, every state by 1985 had adopted, at least in part, a "no-fault" approach to divorce.[1] This section will examine the main arguments for and against eliminating fault from divorce proceedings. Chapters 4 and 5 cover the related issues of whether fault should bear on child custody or alimony decisions.

According to the American Bar Association Section on Family Law, as of November 2004 fourteen states (Alaska, Arizona, California, Colorado, Florida, Iowa, Kentucky, Michigan, Minnesota, Montana, Nebraska, Oregon, Washington, Wisconsin) and the District of Columbia had statutes allowing only for no fault divorce, with fault-based divorce unavailable.

By contrast, as of the same date, thirty-three states had divorce statutes that permitted spouses to seek divorce on either fault or no-fault grounds.

New York, Mississippi, and Tennessee have mixed fault and no-fault divorce regimes, with one key difference. The no-fault provisions in these three states contain a requirement of mutual consent. For example, New York's divorce provision states:

> Action for divorce. An action for divorce may be maintained by a husband or wife to procure a judgment divorcing the parties and dissolving the marriage on any of the following grounds:
>
> . . .
>
> (6) The husband and wife have lived separate and apart pursuant to a written agreement of separation, subscribed by the parties thereto and acknowledged or proved in the form required to entitle a deed to be recorded, for a period of one or more years after the execution of such agreement and satisfactory proof has been submitted by the plaintiff that he or she has substantially performed all the terms and conditions of such agreement . . .

N.Y. Domestic Relations Law § 170. By requiring that both parties sign a separation agreement, New York forces spouses to resolve all issues between them, including property distribution, custody, and support payments. In marriages where one spouse wants out of the marriage and the other does

1. No-fault grounds first appeared in the 19th century. In 1850, Kentucky authorized divorce for couples who had been living apart for five years. Ch. 498 [1950] Ky.Laws 54–55. Thus although California was the first jurisdiction to adopt an exclusively no-fault approach to divorce, no-fault grounds (which typically were modeled on the Kentucky "living apart" test) were *added* to fault grounds in some states much earlier.

not, these consent agreements can stand as a substantial barrier to divorce where no fault ground exists.[2]

Though supporters of mutual consent provisions argue that the laws protect the sanctity of marriage, there has also been substantial criticism. In her 2005 State of the Judiciary address, Chief Judge of the New York Court of Appeals Judith S. Kaye called on the state legislature to pass a no-fault provision that allows one party to invoke divorce unilaterally. Judge Kaye stated that, "requiring strict 'fault' grounds may well simply intensify the bitterness between the parties—wasting resources, hurting children, driving residents to other states for a divorce and delaying the inevitable dissolution of the marriage."[3]

California's reforms were the impetus for the eventual adoption of no-fault grounds for divorce in every jurisdiction. Evidence indicates, however, that many supporters of the reforms saw no-fault divorce as a way to reduce the incidence of divorce, rather than simply as a means for spouses easily to walk away from their marriages. The material in the next section discusses some of this evidence. Take note of how the California no-fault statute's failure to include lengthy separation as a ground for divorce arguably reflects this aim, and how it contrasts with the Uniform Marriage and Divorce Act no-fault divorce provisions. Consider also how the California experience provides an example of how reforms can be adopted, implemented, and perceived in ways that may be inconsistent with the aims of those who originally propose them.

1. THE CALIFORNIA REFORMS

Herma Hill Kay, Equality and Difference: A Perspective on No-Fault Divorce and Its Aftermath

56 U. Cin. L. Rev. 1 (1987).

. . .

In order to assess adequately the impact of the California [no-fault divorce] law, we must take a fresh and fuller look at the often contradictory goals of its proponents and framers.

. . .

On May 11, 1966, Governor Edmund G. Brown appointed his Commission on the Family, a body heavily weighted with lawyers. Fourteen of the twenty-two persons named to serve as co-chairs or members had legal training; of the remaining eight, five were physicians, of whom three were psychiatrists. Governor Brown charged the Commission to formulate specific proposals that could become the basis for legislation introduced during the 1967 Session, and he identified four topics of concern. These were broadly conceived, and included substantive revision of the laws relating to the family, including marriage and divorce, alimony, division of property, and custody of children; the possibility of developing family life education courses to be given in the public schools; the desirability of establishing a

2. Fault grounds for divorce in New York are limited to cruel and inhuman treatment; abandonment for at least a year; adultery; or imprisonment for at least three years. N.Y. Domestic Relations Law § 170(1)–(4).

3. See Patrick D. Healey, *Chief Judge Asks Legislature to Consider No-Fault Divorce*, N.Y. Times, June 8, 2005, at B8.

national standard for residence for marriage and divorce; and finally, and in the Governor's words, "perhaps most important," the establishment of a Family Court.

The Governor's Commission firmly linked its suggestion to eliminate fault from all aspects of marriage dissolution to its proposal for a Family Court. It viewed the existing fault-based divorce system as inextricably rooted in an adversary procedure. Families on the verge of marital breakdown were forced to appear in court as adversaries before judges who were limited to taking testimony on the existence of matrimonial misconduct that might have little to do with the personal dynamics of the relationship. Spouses in marriages that had broken down in fact might not qualify for legal termination if the "right" acts of misconduct had not occurred, while marriages that might still be viable could be ended at the suit of an "innocent" party determined to claim vindication. The role of the court was limited to an artificial inquiry into fault. The Commission believed that meaningful reform could not be attained unless both parts of the existing system were changed.

The proposed Family Court would be staffed by experienced family law judges who would receive special training and who would sit on the Court for a minimum period of two years. The judges would be assisted by trained professional staff capable of helping divorcing couples clarify the conflicts in their marriages by inquiring into the day-to-day problems they were experiencing, rather than into the existence of marital fault. The staff would provide an initial evaluation for all divorcing couples, followed either by reconciliation counseling for those couples who desired to try to save their marriages, or dissolution counseling for those couples who felt no reconciliation was likely. Dissolution counseling covered all aspects of separation and divorce, including financial issues and questions of child custody and support. The counselor would prepare a report, after consultation with the attorneys for each party, informing the court of the parties' circumstances, the matters on which they were in agreement, those issues remaining to be resolved, and a recommendation as to the viability of the marriage. A clear line separated the responsibilities of the counselor and those of the attorneys and the judge. The counselor's function was to investigate the circumstances of the marriage and to ascertain the extent of continued disagreement between the parties. The lawyers remained responsible for negotiating disputed issues and for litigating those that could not be resolved. The judge was responsible for the final adjudication and order.

The Commission gave the Family Court its highest priority. It viewed the elimination of fault from the substantive law as a change needed to further the work of the Family Court, not the other way around. The Family Court's searching inquiry into the real causes of marital breakdown would be hampered by the need to assign fault and to declare one party "innocent" and the other "guilty" of specific misconduct as the basis for dissolution. Instead of identifying marital fault, the Commission proposed that the Family Court dissolve only those marriages that had broken down in fact. Its suggested standard tied the judicial finding of a no-fault ground firmly to the factual inquiry conducted by the counselor: "[A]n order shall be made by the court dissolving the marriage if the court, after having read and considered the counselor's report and any other evidence presented by the parties, makes a finding that the legitimate objects of matrimony have been destroyed and that there is no reasonable likelihood that the marriage can be saved."

. . .

The compromise measure that emerged from the California legislature in 1969 resulted in the enactment of a far more radical law than the Governor's Commission had proposed. Its chief features were a provision permitting the dissolution of marriage on either of two grounds: "irreconcilable differences which have caused the irremediable breakdown of the marriage"; or "incurable insanity." The Family Law Act further defined "irreconcilable differences" as "those grounds which are determined by the court to be substantial reasons for not continuing the marriage and which make it appear that the marriage should be dissolved."

. . .

The California Family Law Act of 1969 was quite a different document from the Family Court Act proposed in 1966 by the Governor's Commission on the Family. The Family Law Act's statement of the no-fault ground, "irreconcilable differences, which have caused the irremediable breakdown of the marriage," focuses on the conflict between the parties, and its further reference to a court determination of "grounds ... which make it appear that the marriage should be dissolved," harks back to the fault approach. The Commission's proposed factual inquiry into the question whether "the legitimate objects of matrimony have been destroyed and that there is no reasonable likelihood that the marriage can be saved" was more neutral, and carried the connotation that both parties had contributed to the breakdown of their marriage. The deletion of the Family Court from the Family Law Act made difficult, if not impossible, any attempt to secure a consistent application of the no-fault provisions throughout the state. Without the training in the no-fault philosophy that the Commission envisaged for the specialist judges, and deprived of the assistance of trained staff, the California trial court judges were left to puzzle out the statutory language for themselves....

California Governor's Commission on the Family, Report

(1966).

. . .

... [T]he marital fault doctrine forces the Court to concentrate upon superficial aspects of the relationship of the parties before it, and it regards each of the "grounds" and the acts or situations they represent as having precisely the same significance in each marriage. We have concluded that this is unrealistic.... As a recent study by a Church of England Commission put it, the retention of specific fault grounds leads to needless divorce and "invests with spurious objectivity acts [whose] real significance varies widely" with the varied marriage relationships that provide their setting.[4]

We believe that it is personally tragic and socially destructive that the Court should be absolutely required, upon proof of a single act of adultery or "extreme cruelty"—perhaps regretted as soon as committed—to end a marriage which may yet contain a spark of life. Under present law, the Court

4. Report of the Mortimer Commission of the Church of England, Putting Asunder: A Divorce Law for Contemporary Society 29 (1966).

cannot go beyond this technical fault and reach the essential question: namely, has this particular marriage relationship so far broken down that the legitimate objects of matrimony have been destroyed and there remains no reasonable likelihood that this marriage can be saved?

It is precisely this question that we believe the Family Court must deal with, and our studies upon this point have led us to one conclusion: If the Family Court is to function at all, it must be by a procedure which permits and requires dissolution of a family only upon a finding of irremediable breakdown of the marriage. The marital relationship is a deep and complex one, and should not be sundered by the law unless the Court finds that the legitimate objects of the marriage have been irretrievably lost.

California Family Code

(2005).

§ 2310. Grounds for dissolution or legal separation

Dissolution of the marriage or legal separation of the parties may be based on either of the following grounds, which shall be pleaded generally:

(a) Irreconcilable differences, which have caused the irremediable breakdown of the marriage.

(b) Incurable insanity.

§ 2311. Irreconcilable differences

Irreconcilable differences are those grounds which are determined by the court to be substantial reasons for not continuing the marriage and which make it appear that the marriage should be dissolved.

§ 2333. Court finding and order where grounds is irreconcilable differences

Subject to Section 2334, if from the evidence at the hearing the court finds that there are irreconcilable differences which have caused the irremediable breakdown of the marriage, the court shall order the dissolution of the marriage or a legal separation of the parties.

§ 2334. Continuance for reconciliation

(a) If it appears that there is a reasonable possibility of reconciliation, the court shall continue the proceeding for the dissolution of the marriage or for a legal separation of the parties for a period not to exceed 30 days.

(b) During the period of the continuance, the court may make orders for the support and maintenance of the parties, the custody of the minor children of the marriage, the support of children for whom support may be ordered, attorney's fees, and for the preservation of the property of the parties.

(c) At any time after the termination of the period of the continuance, either party may move for the dissolution of the marriage or a legal separation of the parties, and the court may enter a judgment of dissolution of the marriage or legal separation of the parties.

§ 2335. Evidence of specific acts of misconduct

Except as otherwise provided by statute, in a pleading or proceeding for dissolution of marriage or legal separation of the parties, including depositions and discovery proceedings, evidence of specific acts of misconduct is improper and inadmissible.

NOTE

If the proposed Family Court had been created by the California legislation as originally proposed, do you think it could have achieved the goals laid out for it?

2. UNIFORM MARRIAGE AND DIVORCE ACT

SECTION 302. Dissolution of Marriage; Legal Separation

(a) The court shall enter a decree of dissolution of marriage if:

(1) the court finds that one of the parties, at the time the action was commenced, was domiciled in this State, or was stationed in this State while a member of the armed services, and that the domicile or military presence has been maintained for 90 days next preceding the making of the findings;

(2) the court finds that the marriage is irretrievably broken, if the finding is supported by evidence that

(i) the parties have lived separate and apart for a period of more than 180 days next preceding the commencement of the proceeding, or

(ii) there is serious marital discord adversely affecting the attitude of one or both of the parties toward the marriage;

(3) the court finds that the conciliation provisions of Section 305 either do not apply or have been met;

(4) to the extent it has jurisdiction to do so, the court has considered, approved, or provided for child custody, the support of any child entitled to support, the maintenance of either spouse, and the disposition of property; or has provided for a separate later hearing to complete these matters.

(b) If a party requests a decree of legal separation rather than a decree of dissolution of marriage, the court shall grant the decree in that form unless the other party objects.

. . .

Uniform Marriage and Divorce Act

SECTION 305. Irretrievable Breakdown

(a) If both of the parties by petition or otherwise have stated under oath or affirmation that the marriage is irretrievably broken, or one of the parties has so stated and the other has not denied it, the court, after hearing, shall make a finding whether the marriage is irretrievably broken.

(b) If one of the parties has denied under oath or affirmation that the marriage is irretrievably broken, the court shall consider all relevant factors, including the circumstances that gave rise to filing the petition and the prospect of reconciliation, and shall:

(1) make a finding whether the marriage is irretrievably broken; or

(2) continue the matter for further hearing not fewer than 30 or more than 60 days later, or as soon thereafter as the matter may be reached on the court's calendar, and may suggest to the parties that they seek counseling. The court, at the request of either party shall, or on its own motion may,

order a conciliation conference. At the adjourned hearing the court shall make a finding whether the marriage is irretrievably broken.

(c) A finding of irretrievable breakdown is a determination that there is no reasonable prospect of reconciliation.

3. ADJUDICATING NO-FAULT DIVORCE

In re Marriage of Dennis D. Kenik

Appellate Court of Illinois, 1989.
181 Ill.App.3d 266, 129 Ill.Dec. 932, 536 N.E.2d 982.

■ HARTMAN, J.

[We are asked to determine whether the circuit court erred in finding proper grounds existed to enter a judgment of dissolution of marriage.]

. . .

Did the circuit court err in granting the judgment of dissolution where, admittedly, the parties physically did not live "separate and apart" continuously for two years as required by section 401(a)(2) of the [Illinois Marriage and Dissolution of Marriage Act (IMDMA)]? . . . There was uncontradicted testimony at the January 21, 1988, hearing that Dennis and Irene resided in the same house until August or September of 1986.

Illinois courts have yet to construe "separate and apart" within the context of section 401(a)(2). Susceptibility of the phrase to discordant readings justifies consideration of extrinsic evidence to resolve its meaning.

Legislative debates surrounding the statute's enactment clearly reveal its sponsors intended an expansive reading of the provision. State Senator William A. Marovitz declared that a court could exercise its discretion in determining whether parties exist "separate and apart":

> "If the judge determines that living separate and apart they have to be living in separate households, so be it. If the judge determines that living . . . apart . . . they can be living under the same roof but there is [*sic*] no conjugal visits, they . . . are living in separate bedrooms, they are doing . . . their own laundry, their own meals, whatever, that's up to the judge and that's . . . what the case law is today." (83d Ill. Gen. Assem., Senate Proceedings, November 3, 1983, at 60).

This interpretation finds support in *In re Marriage of Uhls* . . . , where the court, construing a no-fault divorce provision similar to the Illinois statute, held "separate and apart" to mean "separate lives" as opposed to "separate roofs." . . . The *Uhls* court found the parties lived "separate and apart" for several years, although they shared the same home, because they ceased marital relations four years before filing the petition for divorce, maintained separate bedrooms and ate meals at different times. The parties also took separate vacations, did their laundry in different washing machines and avoided "[all] conversation or other communication." . . .

Here:

Testimony adduced in the case *sub judice* revealed Dennis and Irene not only ended all marital relations a year before Dennis filed his petition for dissolution of marriage, but also that they used separate bedrooms and had "no meaningful communication" with each other. Irene swore as well that she exhausted her credit union account to meet household expenses, to which Dennis contributed nothing. Though Dennis responds he donated whatever he was "able to give," the record demonstrates that the circuit court entered an order in February 1986, pursuant to Irene's petition for temporary support and maintenance, establishing a detailed schedule of financial obligations for each party. Dennis was ordered to pay "one-half of all average monthly expenses of the parties and minor child (except for food and telephone)," and for Scott's food when caring for him. Dennis could receive incoming calls on the home telephone, but was forbidden to make outgoing calls. Each party, further, was responsible for individual personal expenses such as "clothing, grooming, medical, ... work ... commuting, social obligations, vacations and automobile."

Dennis mistakenly relies on *Smith v. Aaron, Aaron, Schimberg & Hess* ... and *In re Marriage of Eltrevoog* ..., where the courts were called upon to interpret the phrase "separate abode" in the pre–1982 section 402 of the IMDMA.... As noted in *Rich v. Rich* ..., furthermore, "separate and apart" must be construed in the context in which it is used: if the theory animating the dissolution claim is, for instance, desertion, physical separation of the parties is an inherent element of the cause of action. Under the no-fault provisions of section 401(a)(2), dissolution is predicated upon a finding of "irretrievable breakdown" of the marriage due to "irreconcilable differences." ... In our opinion, this is a state which can be realized without physical distance between the parties.

Equally unavailing to Dennis' claim are cases he cites from foreign jurisdictions. In *Pangallo v. Pangallo* ..., the parties occupied the same farm compound but were rarely in their marital residence simultaneously, and the court expressly reserved for "another day" the question of whether persons occupying the same home live "separate and apart." ... The court in *Wife v. Husband* ... denied the possibility that nonconjugal cohabitants of a single house lived "separate and apart"; however, the petitioner sought a divorce on the grounds of "voluntary separation," which, under the reasoning of *Rich v. Rich*, could not be achieved while the parties occupied the same dwelling.

No error arose from the finding in the present case that the parties lived "separate and apart."

4. Contractual Divorce

James Herbie Difonzo, Customized Marriage

75 Ind. L. J. 875 (2000).

. . .

III. Of Covenants and Supervows: Contracts at the Altar

The debate about divorce policy and legislative options to strengthen marriage has fired across a landscape in which an increasing number of couples have taken marital law literally into their own hands by drafting prenuptial agreements to fix their legal rights and obligations vis-a-vis each other and the state. This Part focuses on the prospects and perils of privatizing the marriage contract. Both the theory of precommitment restrictions and its odd outcropping, the incipient Covenant Marriage movement, represent a paradigmatic shift in the divorce counterrevolution. Both seek to foster stronger marriages through alternative state-sanctioned prenuptial contracts.

. . .

A. Save Us from Our (Later) Selves: Ulysses and the Sirens

In a landmark 1990 article, Professor Elizabeth S. Scott advanced "precommitment theory" as a "framework for legal transformation of the conception of marriage from a 'nonbinding' and transitory bond to a more enduring relationship." By adopting precommitment restrictions, a couple could set out in a prenuptial agreement the particularized dissolution grounds for their marriage. These options might range from a legally enforceable commitment "till death do us part" to milder obstacles to divorce, such as conditioning a decree on economic penalties or mandating a delay prior to the award of any divorce. Under Scott's rationale, for example, prospective spouses could decide that only marital fault—as they defined it—would render their marriage amenable to divorce proceedings. But the fulcrum of Scott's analysis is that the couple could only adopt measures to limit future options, never to expand them. Thus, precommitment strategies are a major theoretical prop of the divorce counterrevolution, "represent[ing] a conscious attempt to reduce one's future options because subsequent preferences may be impulsive or contrary to one's long-term interests." In Scott's scheme, these long-term interests always encompass the continuation of the marriage.

. . .

C. Covenant Marriage Laws: Enacting the Freedom To Make a Binding Commitment

Bills introduced in various state houses in the 1990s proposed a version of Scott's contract marriage option for couples who desired to enter into connubial relationships impervious to unilateral no-fault divorce. These bills aimed, in the words of an Illinois measure, at differentiating between two types of state-sanctioned unions, a "marriage of commitment" and a "marriage of compatibility." Termed the "Marriage Contract Act," the Illinois bill would have allowed couples to enter into binding contracts providing that the "marriage of the parties shall not be dissolved or otherwise modified except by mutual consent of the parties or upon a showing by a preponderance of the evidence by one party of the fault of the other party." While these measures did not purport to offer couples the broad contractual freedom encompassed by the precommitment rationale, they create an opening for a variable marriage contract.

Steven Nock, a University of Virginia sociology professor who will spend the next five years tracking the phenomenon for the National Science Foundation, observed that "we are on the front end of a covenant marriage boom that could sweep across the nation." The first marriage contract bill to achieve passage was Louisiana's "covenant marriage" law of 1997. This statute created an entirely new class of marriage, defined as a union between "one male and one female who understand and agree that the marriage between them is a lifelong relationship." The new law precludes couples who have chosen "covenant marriages" from access to the state's liberal living-apart divorce ground, which grants divorce after only a six-month separation. The new law mandates counseling for parties seeking to choose this marital option, and it ostensibly seeks to reestablish the fault basis of divorce jurisprudence: "Only when there has been a complete and total breach of the marital covenant commitment may the non-breaching party seek a declaration that the marriage is no longer legally recognized." In 1998, Arizona became the second state to adopt a covenant marriage option. A bevy of covenant marriage bills have been proposed in states throughout the country.

Covenant marriage laws represent the most recent thrust of the movement to undo the excesses of the no-fault revolution. The proponents of this marital alternative aim fundamentally to reshape the discourse of domestic relations. The new law not only defines covenant marriage as a "lifelong relationship," it explicitly requires the spouses making such a commitment to "solemnly declare that marriage is a covenant between a man and a woman who agree to live together as husband and wife for so long as they both may live." The statute is awash with requirements for specific party acknowledgment of these refitted traditional terms of marital obligation. Not only must the prospective covenant partners declare their intention to pledge their everlasting troth on their marriage license application, they must each execute and file a separate "declaration of intent to contract a covenant marriage." This recitation "to love, honor, and care for one another as husband and wife for the rest of our lives" contains statutorily-prescribed terms which resemble the full disclosure requirements of prenuptial contracting:

> We have chosen each other carefully and disclosed to one another everything which could adversely affect the decision to enter into this marriage. We have received premarital counseling on the nature, purposes, and responsibilities of marriage. We have read the Covenant Marriage Act, and we understand that a Covenant Marriage is for life. If we experience marital difficulties, we commit ourselves to take all reasonable efforts to preserve our marriage, including marital counseling.

The parties must also submit an affidavit affirming their completion of premarital counseling from a member of religious clergy or from a marriage counselor. The required counseling must include:

> a discussion of the seriousness of covenant marriage, communication of the fact that a covenant marriage is a commitment for life, a discussion of the obligation to seek marital counseling in times of marital difficulties, and a discussion of the exclusive grounds for legally terminating a covenant marriage by divorce or by divorce after a judgment of separation from bed and board.

The parties must also submit a notarized attestation from the counselor specifying that the parties were counseled in the manner prescribed by the statute and that they received from the counselor the state attorney general's informational pamphlet which reiterates the terms of the Covenant Marriage Act.

The statute thus imposes two different counseling requirements. Initially, the couple must have received premarital counseling focused on covenant marriage's emphasis on lifelong unions and on the provisions of the statute itself. Although the statute requires a "discussion" of these various aims, it prescribes no particular form for this pre-entry counseling. Thus, an informational session in which the key points of the statute are simply summarized would apparently comply with this unspecific "counseling" requirement. The second mandatory counseling facet of the covenant marriage statute involves the couple's expressed commitment to avail themselves of counseling in the event of problems during marriage. The couple's declaration of intent states: "[W]e commit ourselves to take all reasonable efforts to preserve our marriage, including marital counseling."

. . .

Given the significant reintrusion of the state into the more intimate details of the marriage contract which the covenant marriage bills propose, it seems paradoxical to suggest that covenant marriage may prove a gateway for increased privatization of the marital institution. Yet covenant marriage crosses a new line in family law, one whose significance may not be properly appreciated amid the publicity surrounding the question whether covenant marriage will strengthen marriage and promote a decline in the divorce rate. For the first time in American history, the nature of the marriage contract has been rendered variable by direct state action. In other words, before the advent of covenant marriage, the married couple in the basement apartment always had exactly the same marriage contract as the married couple upstairs.

. . .

Legislative sanction of covenant marriage serves to validate the heart of prenuptial bargaining, that the couple knows best. What covenant marriage adds to the already well-established movement favoring prenuptial agreements, however, is an emphasis on shifting divorce grounds and on regulating the behavior of the parties during the marriage. The terms of the "declaration of intent to contract a covenant marriage" specify the detailed commitments of the parties to each other, and provide the framework for satisfying the contractual prerequisites for enforceability. Indeed, the construction of a divorce scheme limited to covenant spouses delineates the state's method of enforcing this form of prenuptial agreement.

. . .

D. The New Paternalism in the Guise of Free Bargaining

Particularly in the face of the damage suffered by the children of failed marriages, it seems quite reasonable to "permit people to really bind themselves to a permanent and exclusive marriage, by reinforcing the personal commitment with the force of law." Moreover, entirely apart from the societal interest in preserving and strengthening marriage, the attraction of permitting couples to bind themselves as tightly as they wish lies in the pull of contractual freedom. Contract is, after all, a prime tool for channeling expectations to enhance planning in personal and structural terms. Why should contractual flexibility be excluded from the ambit of marital affairs, some argue, since "even intimate interaction can be predicted and explained by concepts such as reciprocity, cost/benefit analysis, outcome maximization, and interpersonal equity."

. . .

[Covenant marriage] accentuate[s] the paradox at the heart of contract. The individualist impulse collides with the desire to limit future individualism. Contractual understandings allow for greater individual scope of action, but still "[e]very contract reduces freedom." When extended to family governance, the full panoply of judicially enforceable duties and consequences appropriate in a business setting distorts the fundamentals of family life, because commercial remedies are simply too blunt or ill-suited to the task of structuring intimacy. What Carol Weisbrod termed the "skeptical position" in this domestic dialogue asserts that "there are radical and finally insurmountable tensions between the ideas represented by contract and family."

The promises made at the altar are better understood as moral obligations rather than contractual undertakings. To insist on the business nature of marriage vows not only demeans their importance, but emphasizes enforcement at the cost of the very trust most beneficial to the fulfillment of those vows. It is in the nature of contract to depend on remedies, but wedging this perspective too tightly into the family unfortunately converts marriage into an increasingly commercial undertaking, and ironically exacerbates the effacement of moral discourse from conjugal life. Entering into a contract, particularly one regulating an intimate association, has a catalyzing effect. The marriage whose terms are intended to be merely enshrined by the prenuptial bargain is itself altered by the process of reducing the marital obligations into enforceable provisions. Contracting has a price, and "approaching marriage as a bargained-for relationship undermines the cooperative goals of marriage." Prenuptial contracts may sabotage the "trust, hope, and faith the parties have in each other," and weaken the psychological underpinnings of marriage as reliance is thrust onto external provisions. A prenuptial contract may begin as a bilateral document, but enforcement is always an individualistic enterprise: "A marriage contract may glorify independence and self-interest. This will undermine the sense of partnership and equality that is necessary in a successful marriage."

. . .

[In addition,] the net effect of private contracting may be pressure to restore customary gender roles in marriage. "[T]he advocates of covenant marriage want to use freedom of contract to enhance security of contract in the context of marriage.... they want to throw off the traditional limits of private ordering in marriage as a means of returning to traditional marriage." Some of these new paternalists aim to reform marriage in ways which will result in the reinvigoration of traditional gender roles. Professors Rasmussen and Stake emphasize that no-fault divorce destabilized marital expectations, so that "[d]evoting time and energy to producing assets useful to the marriage became riskier. A career became a safer bet for either party." Professor Brinig similarly promotes covenant marriage because it will result in "greater investment in the sorts of things that make marriages better but that are bad investments in the less permanent world of no-fault." But what are those "assets useful to the marriage" and "sorts of things that make marriages better"? There is no mystery here. When the new paternalists criticize "selfish career building at the expense of family" and call for "idiosyncratic specialization within household production,"they aim, whether directly or indirectly, at recreating the gendered division of labor characterized by husbands in the labor force and wives specializing in domestic production. Although they make obeisance to nonsexist linguistic norms, they give pride of place to the "traditional roles" in family life.

Their argument claims to repudiate sexism as it asserts the primacy of women as homemakers. For example, Professor Stake acknowledges his "own prejudices" in assuming that his daughters Laura and Allison would make better lawyers than whomever they will marry. I also assume that they would make much better nurturers and homemakers than whomever they will marry. The principle of comparative advantage teaches that because Laura is so much better at nurturing, she and her husband (not to mention her children) may be collectively better off if she stays home even though she could earn more than he could on the market. It is, therefore, not only from a sexist viewpoint that I might wish for her to stay home with her children until they are grown, and maybe beyond.

Professor Brinig acknowledged the strength of the objection that these counterrevolutionary divorce reforms "will particularly support traditional marriages in which the man works in the paid labor force while his wife shuns labor force participation in favor of domesticity." But she responded that the "social gains from movements toward covenant marriage (or any other regimes that increase marriage stability) will far outweigh the social costs."

In sum, marriage stability is being purchased at a cost which is unacceptable, unnecessary, and unknowable. The cost is unacceptable because it seeks to burden both sexes with outdated role assumptions. It is unnecessary because our shift into a culture of divorce has ebbed; the lessons of harm to children and the punctured illusion of freedom in serial marriages have had their sizable impact. Ultimately, the cost of the grand venture into legally customized marriage is unknowable. . . . We need legislatures to withhold the legal imprimatur from radical domestic experimentation, and we need courts to continue to monitor these agreements for reasonableness, particularly in the emerging area of prenuptial bargains that oh-so-confidently rely on romantic desire to deny future freedom. Couples always have and ever will customize their own marriages. The formal legal system should honor both the freedom of domestic partners to make good decisions and their legal capacity to unmake bad ones.

. . .

Conclusion: Do–It–Yourself Marriage and Divorce?

It is difficult to make divorce more difficult to obtain. The past generation has witnessed two movements seeking to make divorce rarer: the no-fault revolution and now the divorce counterrevolution. Both movements combined legal and social elements with the aim of improving family life by dissuading dissolution-minded spouses. No-fault divorce failed. So will the counterrevolution. The attempt to restore culpability analysis to center stage in divorce proceedings will, if it passes substantial political hurdles, succeed only in rendering divorces more antagonistic.

Covenant marriage is the newest weapon of the divorce counterrevolution. Some couples will, indeed, agree to the more restrictive divorce provisions now available. Others may take counsel in the state's shredding of the unitary conception of marriage contracts and devise their own marriage schemes. But the cozy assumption that private marriage contracts will limit access to divorce court is untested and likely unfounded. On the contrary, a far more likely reading of the evidence agrees with Katharine Fullerton Gerould's judgment, rendered three-quarters of a century ago, that "the perfect marriage is perhaps more worth fighting for than the imperfect marriage is worth protecting."

NOTE

1. In 1997, Louisiana Governor Mike Foster signed into law the Covenant Marriage Law. The law created a two-track system: couples in Louisiana could choose between traditional marriages, with few barriers to formation and the option of no-fault divorce, or covenant marriage, which imposes restriction on both the formation and the dissolution of the marriage. Katherine Shaw Spaht described these differences in her article, "Covenant Marriage Seven Years Later: Its as Yet Unfulfilled Promise," 65 La. L. Rev. 605, 612–15 (2005):

> A Louisiana covenant marriage differs in three principal respects from other legally recognized "standard" marriages: 1) mandatory pre-marital counseling; 2) the legal obligation to take all reasonable steps to preserve the couple's marriage if marital difficulties arise; and 3) restricted grounds for divorce consisting of

> *fault* on the part of the other spouse or two years living separate and apart. Each of the three components addresses John Witte's observation in *From Sacrament to Contract* that restricting exit rules of marriage by reforming divorce law requires complementary legal restrictions on entry into marriage. Covenant marriage restricts entry into and exit from marriage for those who choose it and attempts to strengthen the marriage itself by imposing a legal obligation upon the covenant spouses which they agree to in advance of their marriage—taking *reasonable* steps to preserve their marriage if difficulties arise.
>
> The mandatory pre-marital counseling under the covenant marriage statute must contain counsel about the seriousness of marriage, the intent of the couple that it be lifelong, and the agreement that the couple will take all reasonable steps to preserve the marriage. Any minister, priest, rabbi, or the secular alternative of a professional marriage counselor is permitted to provide the counseling and sign an attestation form. Of course, many religious counselors require considerably more, especially if they have signed a Community Marriage Covenant (CMC) or Agreement. The CMC, signed by community clergy, ordinarily requires a minimum of counseling sessions with the minister (four, for example), a pre-marital inventory such as PREPARE or FOCCUS, and the guarantee of a mentoring couple assigned to the engaged couple. In those cities that now have Community Marriage Agreements, the clergy signatories provide counseling that is far more extensive than the covenant marriage legislation requires.
>
> At the end of the mandatory pre-marital counseling, the prospective spouses sign a document called a Declaration of Intent that contains the content of their *covenant*, which includes the agreement to seek counseling if difficulties arise as well as their agreement to be bound by the Louisiana law of covenant marriage (choice of law clause). Both spouses sign the agreement and then execute an affidavit, signed by a notary, attesting to having had counseling as the law requires and having read the Covenant Marriage Act, the pamphlet prepared by the Attorney General that explains the differences between a covenant marriage and a standard marriage, including comparative grounds for divorce. The Declaration of Intent is in essence a special *contract* authorized by the state (Louisiana, Arizona, or Arkansas) that contains legal obligations similar to those in ordinary contracts. Most importantly, it is the agreement of the covenant spouses in advance to take reasonable steps to preserve their marriage which constitutes a legal obligation, the second distinguishing component of a covenant marriage. This obligation to take reasonable steps to preserve the marriage begins at the moment the marital difficulties arise and "should continue" until rendition of the judgment of divorce, the one exception being "when the other spouse has physically or sexually abused the spouse seeking the divorce or a child of one of the spouses."
>
> Lastly, a spouse in a covenant marriage may obtain a divorce only if she can prove adultery, conviction of a felony, abandonment for one year, or physical or sexual abuse of her or a child of the parties. Otherwise, the spouses must live separate and apart for two years. A comparison of the grounds for divorce in a Louisiana "standard" marriage reveals that a covenant marriage commits the spouses in advance to a relinquishment of the easy exit rules in favor of more stringent, morally based exit rules. In a "standard" marriage a spouse may seek a divorce for adultery, conviction of a felony, or living separate and apart for *six months* either before *or* after a suit for divorce is filed . . .

Since the Louisiana's adoption of covenant marriage, only two other states, Arkansas and Arizona, have enacted similar legislation. Approximately thirty other states have proposed covenant marriage statutes, but the bills have failed to become law. See Spaht, 65 La. L. Rev. at 605.

Louisiana's adoption of covenant marriage was, and continues to be, controversial. Proponents argue that it "bolster[s] the institution of marriage" by forcing couples to contemplate the seriousness of both marriage and divorce. Opponents of the law worry that it fails to protect victims of domestic violence and lacks provisions to ensure that participants understand the ramifications of entering into a covenant marriage. Some object to the role of clergy and other religious advisors in the premarital counseling stage. Still others have raised constitutional questions about the law's affect on individual liberty interests. For a thorough discussion of these and other viewpoints, see "Comment: Louisiana's Covenant Marriage Law: A First Step Toward a More Robust Pluralism in Marriage and Divorce Law?", 47 Emory L.J. 929, 953–58 (1998).

Although covenant marriage is not statutorily available in most states, some couples have attempted to accomplish some of the same goals by developing agreements that limit the availability of divorce. In the event of divorce, courts are forced to decide whether or not they can enforce these agreements.

2. An ongoing study of covenant marriages suggests that only 1–2% of new marriages are covenant marriages in those states in which this option is available. One reason for this may be that fewer than half the population in covenant marriage states are aware of this alternative. The best estimate at this point is that covenant couples have about 55% the divorce rate of couples in standard marriages. Determining the impact of covenant versus regular marriage on marital stability poses a challenge, however, in light of the possibility that those who choose the former may already be more disposed to stay in marriages than those who forgo the covenant option.

One feature of covenant marriage that may have some effect is the requirement of premarital counseling. Preliminary evidence indicates that men are more likely to attend marriage counseling in times of marital trouble if they had premarital counseling. Covenant marriage thus may be one way to address the traditional difficulty in persuading men to participate in marital counseling. Correspondence with Professor Steven L. Nock, University of Virginia, November 8, 2005.

Massar v. Massar

Superior Court of New Jersey, Appellate Division, 1995.
279 N.J.Super. 89, 652 A.2d 219.

■ OPINION BY JUDGE CUFF.

This appeal arises from an order enforcing an agreement between a husband and wife which limited the grounds for a complaint for divorce to eighteen months continuous separation.

This is the second marriage for both parties. Prior to their marriage on November 25, 1988, Jacqueline Massar and Cyril Massar signed a prenuptial agreement. In April 1993, the marriage had deteriorated to the point that the parties discussed separation and eventual divorce. In an agreement signed April 30, 1993, Mr. Massar agreed to vacate the marital home, and Mrs. Massar agreed not to seek termination of the marriage for any reason other than eighteen months continuous separation. Pursuant to this agreement, Mr. Massar moved out of the marital home.

However, contrary to the agreement, on October 1, 1993, Mrs. Massar filed a complaint for divorce on the grounds of extreme cruelty. Mr. Massar filed a motion to dismiss the complaint and to enforce the prenuptial agreement. After oral argument, Hon. Thomas Dilts, J.S.C. upheld the agreement and dismissed the complaint. He also denied without prejudice Mr. Massar's motion to enforce the prenuptial agreement citing the need for a plenary hearing. Finally, he ruled that Mrs. Massar could file a complaint for separate maintenance pursuant to *N.J.S.A.* 2A:34–24. . . . Mrs. Massar appeals from that portion of the order enforcing the agreement to seek a divorce solely on "no fault" grounds.

In enforcing this agreement, Judge Dilts found that the agreement was clear, unequivocal and supported by consideration. He also found that Mrs.

Massar had failed to present facts which would lead him to conclude that the agreement was executed under duress. At most, she submitted facts to support that she wanted Mr. Massar out of the house. Furthermore, Mrs. Massar was represented by an attorney who was representing solely her interests. Moreover, Judge Dilts found that public policy did not prohibit such agreements. In fact, he concluded that public policy requires that agreements which restrict the grounds on which a divorce shall be obtained to the no-fault eighteen months continuous separation should be recognized. He reasoned that such an agreement should be encouraged by the State since it can give a couple a period of time to assess their relationship and determine whether a reconciliation is possible.

On appeal, Mrs. Massar argues that a complaint for divorce on the grounds of extreme cruelty does not violate the intent of the agreement. She further argues that the agreement violates public policy and is unenforceable. Finally, she argues that a plenary hearing was required. We disagree and affirm the order entered by Judge Dilts substantially for the reasons set forth in his oral decision of December 10, 1993 as supplemented by his letter opinion dated December 13, 1993. We add only the following comments.

This State has a strong public policy favoring enforcement of agreements. Marital agreements are essentially consensual and voluntary and as a result, they are approached with a predisposition in favor of their validity and enforceability. Marital agreements, however, are enforceable only if they are fair and equitable. Any marital agreement which is unconscionable or is the product of fraud or overreaching by a party with power to take advantage of a confidential relationship may be set aside. In fact, the law affords particular leniency to agreements made in the domestic arena and similarly allows judges greater discretion when interpreting these agreements. Such discretion is based on the premise that, although marital agreements are contractual in nature, "contract principles have little place in the law of domestic relations." Nevertheless, the contractual nature of such agreements has long been recognized and principles of contract interpretation have been invoked particularly to define the terms of the agreement and divine the intent of the parties. In interpreting the agreement, the court will not draft a new agreement for the parties.

In this case, Mr. Massar agreed to vacate the marital home. Mrs. Massar agreed as follows:

> [W]aives any claim that she may have against the husband in any action to dissolve, nullify, or terminate their marriage for desertion *or any other cause of action, except no-fault divorce based upon living separate and apart for a period of 18 months or more* based upon the husband's vacating the marital premises pursuant to this agreement. (emphasis added).

We agree with Judge Dilts that this language is clear and unequivocal and that Mrs. Massar surrendered her right to seek a divorce on any other than a no-fault basis. We also agree that the certifications submitted by Mrs. Massar establish nothing more than that she wished Mr. Massar out of the house; they certainly did not create a fact issue concerning duress. Similarly, we concur that this agreement is supported by consideration. Not only did Mr. Massar leave a house in which he had as much right to reside as Mrs. Massar, but also he had to undertake the additional expense of establishing a separate residence. Finally, we also agree with Judge Dilts that there is insufficient evidence to suggest that this waiver was not a knowing and voluntary act by Mrs. Massar, and a plenary hearing was not warranted.

Mrs. Massar urges us to adopt a per se rule that agreements confining a spouse to a particular cause of action for dissolution of a marriage are against public policy and are unenforceable. We have declined, however, to adopt a per se rule of enforceability of negotiated provisions in agreements between spouses. Rather, we have reviewed the enforceability of these provisions on a case-by-case basis to determine if the application of the provision is fair and just according to the circumstances of the particular case.

The State has certainly adopted a public policy through *N.J.S.A.* 2A:34–1 *et seq.* that the citizens of this state shall have liberal grounds to disengage themselves from marriages which are not viable. On the other hand, this State does not promote divorce and has always had a strong public interest in promoting marriage. Indeed, the no-fault provision requiring an eighteen-month continuous separation was adopted in part to allow divorcing spouses the time to reflect and discern if divorce is the appropriate action for them. As observed by Judge Dilts, there is good reason to encourage a cooling off period for spouses to assess their relationship and calmly reflect whether dissolution of their marriage is the course they wish to take.

Accordingly, we decline to adopt a per se rule. We can envision many circumstances where it may be in the best interests of the parties and any children born of the marriage to dissolve a marriage without the assertion of allegations of emotional or physical abandonment, substance abuse, or certain allegations that pass for extreme cruelty. Similarly, we can envision many instances in which such an agreement may not be enforceable because it may serve to hide from the court actions of an abusive spouse or substance dependent spouse which may endanger the physical and emotional welfare of the other spouse and any children.

But that is not the situation in this case. Indeed, based on the certifications before Judge Dilts it appears that Mr. Massar realized that a physical separation was appropriate given the state of his marriage. However, he was concerned that such a separation might be interpreted as a financial abandonment of his wife. Similarly, he was concerned about his continuing ability to function as a deacon in his church. These concerns became real because upon the filing of the complaint for divorce alleging extreme cruelty he was temporarily suspended from his position in his church. Furthermore, the record before Judge Dilts suggests that Mrs. Massar filed the complaint for divorce only when her initial proposal for equitable distribution was not instantly embraced by Mr. Massar.

The parties entered this agreement presumably with full knowledge of the conduct of each during the marriage which could form the basis for a cause of action for divorce. We do not suggest that the parties could enter an agreement which would preclude seeking a judgment of divorce on a ground other than eighteen months separation based on conduct which occurred after the execution of the agreement.

We emphasize that there is no suggestion in this record of any physical or mental abuse. The certifications submitted by Mrs. Massar reveal no more than a couple engaging in verbal confrontations in the context of a disintegrating marriage. Two intelligent adults should be able to agree concerning the framework and timetable for the dissolution of their troubled marriage and have that agreement enforced, if that agreement is fair and equitable to both parties under the unique circumstances of their case.

Accordingly, the December 14, 1993 Order entered by Judge Dilts is affirmed.

Diosdado v. Diosdado

Court of Appeal of California, 2002.
97 Cal.App.4th 470, 118 Cal.Rptr.2d 494.

■ EPSTEIN, ACTING P. J.

In this case we conclude that a contract entered into between a husband and wife, providing for payment of liquidated damages in the event one of them is sexually unfaithful to the other, is unenforceable.

. . .

Donna and Manuel Diosdado were married in November 1988. In 1993, Manuel had an affair with another woman. When Donna learned of this, the parties separated but did not divorce. Instead, they entered into a written "Marital Settlement Agreement" (hereafter the agreement) intended to "preserve, protect and assure the longevity and integrity of an amicable and beneficial marital relationship between them."

. . .

Section 2 is labeled "Obligation of Fidelity," and provides: "It is further acknowledged that the parties' marriage is intended to be an exclusive relationship between Husband and Wife that is premised upon the values of emotional and sexual fidelity, and mutual trust. The parties hereto are subject to a legal obligation of emotional and sexual fidelity to the other. It shall be considered a breach of such obligation of fidelity to volitionally engage in any act of kissing on the mouth or touching in any sexual manner of any person outside of said marital relationship, as determined by a trier of fact. The parties acknowledge their mutual understanding that any such breach of fidelity by one party hereto may cause serious emotional, physical and financial injury to the other."

Section 3 is labeled "Liquidated Damages." It provides:

> "In the event it is shown by a preponderance of the evidence in a court of competent jurisdiction that either party has engaged in any breach of the obligation of sexual fidelity as defined hereinabove ... and, additionally, that election is made by one or both parties to commence an action to terminate the marriage by divorce because of said breach, the following terms and conditions shall become effective:
>
> "(a) The party shown to have committed the breach shall vacate the family residence immediately upon the completion of a showing of breach as defined above;
>
> "(b) The party shown to have committed the breach will be solely responsible for all attorney fees and court costs incurred as a result of or in connection with the litigation of any issue surrounding or relating to said breach;
>
> "(c) The party shown to have committed the breach will pay the other party (hereinafter, the 'recipient') liquidated damages for said breach in the sum of $50,000, said sum to be paid over and above, and irrespective of, any property settlement and/or support obligation imposed by law as a result of said divorce proceeding. Said damages shall be due and payable on a date that is no later than six (6) months following entry of judgment of dissolution of marriage by a court of competent jurisdiction. Said damages shall become the sole and separate property of the recipient, except that, should said recipient remarry at

any time following such payment, said damages shall be fully and completely refunded to the party shown to have committed the breach. Said refund shall be due and payable on a date no later than six (6) months following the date of the recipient's remarriage.

"(d) Both parties shall cooperate in the negotiation and execution of a reasonable property settlement and support agreement for the resolution of said divorce proceeding so as to minimize the emotional and financial expense of said litigation."

The agreement was drafted by Manuel's attorney, and both Donna and Manuel signed it voluntarily in December 1993. They resumed living together.

In 1998, Manuel again had an affair with another woman. When Donna learned of it, she confronted Manuel, who denied it. Donna obtained independent verification from a witness who saw Manuel kissing this other woman. The parties separated in August 1998, and thereafter divorced.

Donna then brought this action for breach of contract in February 2000, seeking to enforce the liquidated damages clause of the agreement. On the first day of trial, the trial court, on its own motion, granted a judgment on the pleadings in favor of Manuel. Donna appeals from the judgment.

The only question before this court is whether the agreement is enforceable. The trial court found that it was not because it was contrary to the public policy underlying California's no-fault divorce laws. That reasoning is sound.

In 1969, California enacted Civil Code section 4506 (now Fam. Code, § 2310), providing for dissolution of marriage based on irreconcilable differences which have caused the irremediable breakdown of the marriage. This change was explained in *In re Marriage of Walton* . . . : "After thorough study, the Legislature, for reasons of social policy deemed compelling, has seen fit to change the grounds for termination of marriage from a fault basis to a marriage breakdown basis."

With certain exceptions (such as child custody matters or restraining orders), "evidence of specific acts of misconduct is improper and inadmissible" in a pleading or proceeding for dissolution of marriage. . . . Fault is simply not a relevant consideration in the legal process by which a marriage is dissolved. Recovery in no-fault dissolution proceedings "is basically limited to half the community property and appropriate support and attorney fee orders—no hefty premiums for emotional angst." . . .

Contrary to the public policy underlying California's no-fault divorce laws, the agreement between Donna and Manuel attempts to impose just such a premium for the "emotional angst" caused by Manuel's breach of his promise of sexual fidelity.[1] The agreement expressly states the parties' "mutual understanding that any such breach of fidelity by one party hereto may cause serious emotional, physical and financial injury to the other." The agreement then imposes a penalty on the breaching party, in the event either party chooses to terminate the marriage "because of said breach." This penalty includes "liquidated damages for said breach in the sum of $50,000," over and above any property settlement or support obligations imposed in the dissolution proceeding.

1. Donna made an offer of proof that she suffered emotional harm as a result of the breach, that it caused her a great deal of emotional upset and trauma and that she suffered actual emotional damages as a result of the breach.

The family law court may not look to fault in dissolving the marriage, dividing property, or ordering support. Yet this agreement attempts to penalize the party who is at fault for having breached the obligation of sexual fidelity, and whose breach provided the basis for terminating the marriage. This penalty is in direct contravention of the public policy underlying no-fault divorce.

To be enforceable, a contract must have a "lawful object." ... A contract is unlawful if it is contrary to an express provision of law, contrary to the policy of express law, or otherwise contrary to good morals.... Here, where the agreement attempts to impose a penalty on one of the parties as a result of that party's "fault" during the marriage, it is contrary to the public policy underlying the no-fault provisions for dissolution of marriage.... For that reason, the agreement is unenforceable.

Donna claims a different result is required, based on two Supreme Court cases. We find these cases inapplicable.

In the first, *In re Marriage of Bonds* ..., the court addressed the enforceability of a premarital agreement....

[In *Bonds*, the court drew a distinction] between the freedom of contract found in ordinary commercial contracts and the existence of limitations in marital agreements. The court recognized that "marriage itself is a highly regulated institution of undisputed social value, and there are many limitations on the ability of persons to contract with respect to it, or to vary its statutory terms, that have nothing to do with maximizing the satisfaction of the parties or carrying out their intent.... These limitations demonstrate further that freedom of contract with respect to marital arrangements is tempered with statutory requirements and case law expressing social policy with respect to marriage." ... *Bonds* does not support Donna's position.

Donna finds no greater support in the second case, *In re Marriage of Pendleton and Fireman*.... In *Pendleton*, the Supreme Court held that a premarital agreement waiving spousal support does not violate public policy, and is not per se unenforceable.... That decision provides no authority for enforceability of an agreement between spouses to pay damages in the event one party engages in sexual infidelity.

Judgment on the pleadings was properly granted in this case.

5. Tort Claims

Twyman v. Twyman

Supreme Court of Texas, 1993.
855 S.W.2d 619.

■ Cornyn, Justice.

In this case we decide whether a claim for infliction of emotional distress can be brought in a divorce proceeding. Because the judgment of the court of appeals is based on negligent infliction of emotional distress, and cannot be affirmed on that or any other basis, we reverse the judgment of that court and remand this cause for a new trial in the interest of justice. We deem a new trial appropriate because of our recent decision that no cause of action for negligent infliction of emotional distress exists in Texas. Today, however, we expressly adopt the tort of intentional infliction of emotional distress, and hold that such a claim can be brought in a divorce proceeding.

Sheila and William Twyman married in 1969. Sheila filed for divorce in 1985. She later amended her divorce petition to add a general claim for emotional harm without specifying whether the claim was based on negligent or intentional infliction of emotional distress. In her amended petition, Sheila alleged that William "intentionally and cruelly" attempted to engage her in "deviate sexual acts."[1] Following a bench trial, the court rendered judgment dissolving the marriage, dividing the marital estate, awarding conservatorship of the children to Sheila, ordering William to pay child support, and awarding Sheila $15,000 plus interest for her claim for emotional distress. William appealed that portion of the judgment based on emotional distress, contending that interspousal tort immunity precluded Sheila's recovery for negligent infliction of emotional distress. The court of appeals affirmed the judgment, holding that Sheila could recover for William's negligent infliction of emotional distress. 790 S.W.2d 819.

While this case has been pending, we have refused to adopt the tort of negligent infliction of emotional distress. See Boyles v. Kerr, 855 S.W.2d 593 (Tex.1993). Thus the judgment of the court of appeals cannot be affirmed. We consider, therefore, whether the court of appeals' judgment may be affirmed on alternative grounds. Because Sheila's pleadings alleging a general claim for emotional harm are broad enough to encompass a claim for intentional infliction of emotional distress, we consider whether the trial court's judgment may be sustained on that legal theory.

While this court has never expressly recognized the tort of intentional infliction of emotional distress, we found no reversible error in the court of appeals' opinion in Tidelands Automobile Club v. Walters, which did so. 699 S.W.2d 939 (Tex.App.—Beaumont 1985, writ ref'd n.r.e.). There, the court of appeals adopted the elements of the tort as expressed in the Restatement (Second) of Torts § 46 (1965). The Restatement elements of intentional infliction of emotional distress are: 1) the defendant acted intentionally or recklessly, 2) the conduct was extreme and outrageous, 3) the actions of the defendant caused the plaintiff emotional distress, and 4) the emotional distress suffered by the plaintiff was severe. Id. According to the Restatement, liability for outrageous conduct should be found "only where the conduct has been so outrageous in character, and so extreme in degree, as to go beyond all possible bounds of decency, and to be regarded as atrocious, and utterly intolerable in a civilized community." Id. cmt. d. Of the forty-six states that have recognized this tort, forty-three have adopted this Restatement formulation. The other three states, although not adopting the Restatement definition, require the equivalent of "outrageous" conduct. Today we become the forty-seventh state to adopt the tort of intentional infliction of emotional distress as set out in § 46(1) of the Restatement (Second) of Torts.

We do not, however, adopt this tort only because of its broad acceptance in jurisdictions throughout the United States. As distinguished from the tort of negligent infliction of emotional distress, we believe the rigorous legal standards of the Restatement formulation of intentional infliction of emotional distress help to assure a meaningful delineation between inadvertence and intentionally or recklessly outrageous misconduct. The requirements of

1. At trial, Sheila testified that William pursued sadomasochistic bondage activities with her, even though he knew that she feared such activities because she had been raped at knife-point before their marriage. The trial court found that William "attempted to emotionally coerce [Sheila] in 'bondage' on an ongoing basis. . . ." and "engaged in a continuing course of conduct of attempting to coerce her to join in his practices of 'bondage' by continually asserting that their marriage could be saved only by [Sheila] participating with him in his practices of 'bondage.' "

intent, extreme and outrageous conduct, and severe emotional distress before liability can be established will, we think, strike a proper balance between diverse interests in a free society. That balance, at minimum, must allow freedom of individual action while providing reasonable opportunity for redress for victims of conduct that is determined to be utterly intolerable in a civilized community.

. . .

We now consider whether the cause of action for intentional infliction of emotional distress may be brought in a divorce proceeding.[13] In *Bounds v. Caudle*, this court unanimously abolished the doctrine of interspousal immunity for intentional torts. 560 S.W.2d 925 (Tex.1977). Ten years later, we abrogated interspousal immunity "completely as to any cause of action," including negligence actions for personal injuries. Price v. Price, 732 S.W.2d 316, 319 (Tex.1987). Under the rules established in *Caudle* and *Price*, there appears to be no legal impediment to bringing a tort claim in a divorce action based on either negligence or an intentional act such as assault or battery.

The more difficult issue is when the tort claim must be brought and how the tort award should be considered when making a "just and right" division of the marital estate. See Tex.Fam.Code § 3.63(b). Of the states that have answered this question, several have held that the tort case and the divorce case must be litigated separately.

We believe that the best approach lies between these two extremes. As in other civil actions, joinder of the tort cause of action should be permitted, but subject to the principles of res judicata.[17] Of course, how such claims are ultimately tried is within the sound discretion of the trial court. But joinder of tort claims with the divorce, when feasible, is encouraged. Resolving both the tort and divorce actions in the same proceeding avoids two trials based at least in part on the same facts, and settles in one suit "all matters existing between the parties."

When a tort action is tried with the divorce, however, it is imperative that the court avoid awarding a double recovery. When dividing the marital estate, the court may take into account several factors, including the fault of the parties if pleaded. The trial court may also consider "such factors as the spouses' capacities and abilities, benefits which the party not at fault would have derived from continuation of the marriage, business opportunities, education, relative physical conditions, relative financial condition and obligations, disparity of ages, size of separate estates, and the nature of the property." Id. However, a spouse should not be allowed to recover tort damages and a disproportionate division of the community estate based on the same conduct. Therefore, when a factfinder awards tort damages to a divorcing spouse, the court may not consider the same tortious acts when dividing the marital estate. Contrary to CHIEF JUSTICE PHILLIPS' con-

13. CHIEF JUSTICE PHILLIPS, and JUSTICES HECHT and ENOCH rue the court's decision to permit the tort of intentional infliction of emotional distress to be brought in divorce proceedings. But it appears that much of what they disapprove of is related to the consequences of recognizing *any* tort action between divorcing spouses. Their criticisms would seem to be better directed at the court's earlier decisions to abrogate the doctrine of interspousal tort immunity in Bounds v. Caudle, 560 S.W.2d 925 (Tex.1977), and Price v. Price, 732 S.W.2d 316 (Tex.1987).

17. We anticipate that most tort cases between spouses will be joined with the divorce proceeding, however, situations may exist in which the facts supporting the tort action will be different from those supporting a petition for divorce.

tention, an award for tortious conduct does not replace an analysis of the remaining factors to be considered when the trial court divides the marital estate. The court may still award a disproportionate division of property for reasons other than the tortious conduct. To avoid the potential problem of double recovery, the factfinder should consider the damages awarded in the tort action when dividing the parties' property. If a jury is used to render an advisory division of the parties' estate, the judge should limit, by appropriate instruction, the jury's consideration of the alleged tortious acts and later consider the award of damages in determining a just and right division of the marital estate.[20]

Sheila Twyman cannot recover based on the findings of fact made by the trial court in this case.[21] It is likely, however, that this case proceeded on a theory of negligent infliction of emotional distress in reliance on this court's holding in St. Elizabeth Hospital v. Garrard, 730 S.W.2d 649 (Tex.1987), which we recently overruled. See Boyles v. Kerr, 855 S.W.2d 593 (Tex.1993). As we noted in *Boyles,* this court has broad discretion to remand for a new trial in the interest of justice when it appears that a case proceeded under the wrong legal theory, and when it appears that the facts when developed on retrial may support recovery on an alternative theory. When, as here, a party presents her case in reliance on precedent that has been recently overruled, remand is appropriate. Therefore, in the interest of justice, we reverse the judgment of the court of appeals and remand this cause to the trial court for a new trial.

. . .

■ Phillips, Chief Justice, concurring and dissenting.

I join in the Court's recognition of the tort of intentional infliction of emotional distress. . . .

In recognizing this tort, however, I would not extend it to actions between spouses or former spouses for conduct occurring during their marriage. . . .

Married couples share an intensely personal and intimate relationship. When discord arises, it is inevitable that the parties will suffer emotional distress, often severe. In the present case, for example, Ms. Twyman testified that she suffered "utter despair" and "fell apart" upon learning that her husband was seeing another woman. She further testified that "[t]he mental anguish was unbelievable to realize, hoping every time, when he went off to Houston, that he was just going to fly and not be with her." Yet Ms. Twyman seeks no recovery for this distress, and apparently cannot do so under Texas

20. In Texas, recovery for personal injuries of a spouse, including pain and suffering, is the separate property of that spouse. Tex. Fam.Code § 5.01(a)(3); Graham v. Franco, 488 S.W.2d 390, 396 (Tex.1972). Therefore, an award to one spouse from the other does not add to the marital estate, and raises no possibility that the tort award becomes "self-offsetting." See Barbara H. Young, Interspousal Torts and Divorce: Problems, Policies, Procedures, 27 J.Fam.L. 489, 511 (1989).

21. . . . The trial court made no findings of outrageous behavior or severe emotional distress, and the judgment was based specifically and exclusively on negligent infliction of emotional distress. The divorce decree recites:

After considering the pleadings, the evidence, and the arguments of the attorneys, the Court finds the facts and law support judgment for Petition [sic] in her tort for negligent infliction of emotional distress upon Petitioner.

Additionally, the trial court made a disproportionate property division based on William's cruel treatment and adultery. It appears that such an award may allow Sheila a double recovery based on the same conduct. A new trial conducted in accordance with the principles announced in this decision should rectify this problem.

law. In such circumstances, the fact finder is left to draw a virtually impossible distinction between recoverable and disallowed injuries.

Furthermore, recognition of this tort in the context of a divorce unnecessarily restricts the trial court's discretion in dividing the marital estate. Prior to today's opinion, the trial court could, but was not required to, consider fault in dividing the community property. The court had broad discretion to weigh any fault along with other appropriate factors, such as relative financial condition, disparity of ages, and the needs of the children. Now, however, where fault takes the form of "outrageous" conduct intentionally or recklessly inflicted, it becomes a dominant factor that must be considered at the expense of the other factors. Unlike battery, fraud, or other torts resting on more objective conduct, a colorable allegation of intentional infliction of emotional distress could arguably be raised by one or both parties in most intimate relationships. As the court noted in Chiles v. Chiles, 779 S.W.2d 127, 131 (Tex.App.—Houston [14th Dist.] 1989, writ denied):

> While we recognize the trial court may consider fault in the distribution of community property, we believe permitting such separate damages [for intentional infliction of emotional distress] in divorce actions would result in evils similar to those avoided by the legislature's abrogation of fault as a ground for divorce.

See also Henriksen v. Cameron, 622 A.2d 1135, 1151 (Me.1993) (Glassman, J., dissenting) (recognizing the common-law tort of intentional infliction of emotional distress in the marriage context skews "a carefully constructed scheme of legislation governing the marriage relationship").

Perhaps because of these difficulties, the tort of intentional infliction of emotional distress has not been generally recognized in the marital context. Although most states, like Texas, have abolished interspousal immunity, it appears that, until today, only two state supreme courts have expressly held that intentional infliction of emotional distress may be applied to marital conduct. See *Henriksen,* supra; Davis v. Bostick, 282 Or. 667, 580 P.2d 544 (1978). Moreover, these two decisions do not appear to represent typical actions for the recovery of emotional distress damages. In *Henriksen,* the husband inflicted on his wife not only verbal abuse but also physical attacks, including multiple assaults and rapes. 622 A.2d at 1139. Similarly in *Bostick,* the husband broke his wife's nose, choked her, and threatened her with a loaded pistol. 580 P.2d at 545–46. To the extent that emotional distress results from a physical attack or threat of attack, it is already compensable under tort theories previously recognized in Texas. The court in *Henriksen* apparently recognized the risk of spurious claims in the divorce context, noting that "to protect defendants from the possibility of long and intrusive trials on meritless claims, motions for summary judgment should . . . be viewed sympathetically in interspousal cases." 622 A.2d at 1139. By contrast, it is far from clear that Texas' strict summary judgment standard will allow our trial courts to use this procedure in weeding out meritless or trivial claims.

. . .

Just as I join the Court's decision to recognize a tort now available in nearly every American jurisdiction, I depart from the Court's decision to extend that tort to a type of dispute where it is not generally applied in other states. I fail to understand how, lexigraphically or logically, it can be "medieval" or "archaic" to decline to adopt a position which has been expressly embraced by only two other state supreme courts. I therefore would reverse the judgment of the court of appeals and render judgment that Sheila Twyman take nothing on her tort claim.

■ HECHT, JUSTICE, concurring and dissenting.

. . .

. . . The plurality opinion gives little indication that it has considered, or why it has rejected, the arguments against adopting this tort. It bases its decision solely on the fact that the high courts of almost all the other states have at one time or another recognized a tort of intentional infliction of emotional distress in some context, and on the conclusion that this tort is more manageable than negligent infliction of emotional distress. While a consensus of our sister courts on a proposition may be some indication of its merit, that circumstance alone has not always been, and should never be, reason enough to justify our concurrence. . . .

Slight though the foundation is for today's decision, its effects are far-reaching. There is little doubt that the new tort will be asserted in many if not most contested divorce cases. The Family Law Section of the State Bar of Texas has filed a brief as amicus curiae assessing the impact of spouses' suing one another for intentional infliction of emotional distress, discussing the arguments for and against allowing such an action without taking a position on the issue, and urging us to exercise caution in considering these arguments. The plurality opinion makes no mention of the family bar's arguments. . . . Nor has the Court considered the burden of additional jury trials in divorce cases on the judicial system. This Court, as steward of the common law, possesses the power to recognize new causes of action, but the mere existence of that power cannot justify its exercise. There must be well-considered, even compelling grounds for changing the law so significantly. Where, as here, no such grounds are given, the decision is more an exercise of will than of reason.

In my view, intentional or reckless infliction of emotional distress is too broad a rubric to describe actionable conduct, as this case illustrates. Accordingly, I dissent from the Court's decision to remand this case for trial on such a cause of action. I concur only in the reversal of the court of appeals' judgment allowing recovery for negligent infliction of emotional distress.

. . .

The standard of outrageousness is certainly no easier to apply in the marital context than in other contexts, as the facts of this case illustrate. Sheila Twyman's claim of intentional infliction of emotional distress is based upon the following testimony at trial, which was mostly undisputed. William, a Navy pilot, and Sheila, a college graduate with a degree in nursing, were married in 1969. In 1975, on two or three occasions at William's suggestion, the couple engaged in what they referred to as "light bondage"—tying each other to the bed with neckties during their sexual relations. Sheila testified that William did not force her to participate in these activities. After the last occasion Sheila told William she did not like this activity and did not want to participate in it further. She revealed to him that she associated the activities with the horrible experience of having been raped at knifepoint earlier in her life. William never again suggested that she engage in the activities, nor was the subject discussed again for ten years. In 1985 Sheila inadvertently discovered that William was consulting with a psychologist. When she asked him why, he told her that he was involved with another woman. William told Sheila that if she could only have done bondage, nothing else would have mattered. For the remainder of the year the couple sought counseling. At times during this period William made derogatory remarks to Sheila about her sexual ability, comparing her to his girl friend. On their counselor's advice, William and Sheila discussed William's bondage fantasies, and Sheila again tried to participate in bondage activities with William. But she found the activity so painful and humiliating that she could not continue it. Their last encounter, which did not include bondage activities, was so rough that she was injured to the point of bleeding. At one point Sheila was distressed to discover that their ten-year-old son had found magazines William kept hidden, which portrayed sadomasochistic activities. Eleven months after she first learned of William's affair, Sheila separated from him and filed for divorce. Throughout that period, Sheila testified, she experienced utter despair, devastation, pain, humiliation and weight loss because of William's affair and her feelings that the marriage could have survived if only she had engaged in bondage activities.

To recover damages Sheila must prove that William's conduct was outrageous—that is, "extreme," "beyond all possible bounds of decency," "atrocious," and "utterly intolerable in a civilized community." Although outrageousness is, according to the plurality opinion and the Restatement, a question for the court in the first instance, this Court refuses to say whether William's conduct was or was not outrageous. If it was not, as a matter of law, then there is no need to remand this case for further proceedings. If William's conduct was outrageous, or if that issue must be decided by a jury, then it is unclear what components of the conflict between Sheila and William were actionable. There is no question from the record that Sheila claims to have suffered bitterly, but there appear to have been three causes: William's affair, his interest in bondage, and the breakup of the marriage. If the first or last causes constitute outrageous behavior, then there a tort claim may be urged successfully in most divorces. Allowing recovery based upon the first cause of Sheila's emotional distress is simply to revive the old action for alienation of affections abolished by the Legislature. Tex.Fam.Code § 4.06. I doubt whether the Court intends this result. If William's outrageous conduct was attempting to interest Sheila in sexual conduct which he considered enjoyable but she, in her words, "did not like," then again, this tort may be very broad indeed.

The sexual relationship is among the most intimate aspects of marriage. People's concepts of a beneficial sexual relationship vary widely, and spouses may expect that some accommodation of each other's feelings will be necessary for their mutual good. *Any* breach of such an intimate and essential part of marriage may be regarded as outrageous by the aggrieved spouse and will often be the cause of great distress. There are many other aspects of marriage which are likewise sensitive. How money is to be spent, how children are to be raised, and how time is to be allocated are only a few of the many areas of conflict in a marriage. Not infrequently disagreements over these matters are deep and contribute to the breakup of the marriage. If all are actionable, then tort claims will be commonplace in divorce cases, and judges and juries with their own deeply felt beliefs about what is proper in a marital relationship will face the hard task of deciding whether one spouse or another behaved outrageously with no standards but their own to guide.

The inquiry which must be made to determine whether a spouse's conduct is outrageous entails too great an intrusion into the marital relationship. Although courts are already called upon to consider fault in divorce actions, allowance of tort claims requires a more pervasive inspection of spouses' private lives than should be permissible. In this case the parties were called to testify in detail and at length about the most private moments of their marriage. If the court's only concern were the degree to which a spouse's fault had contributed to the demise of the marriage, the inquiry into each spouse's conduct need not have been so detailed. To recover damages, however, Sheila was required to testify at length before a jury, and to rebut her claim, William was obliged to answer in equal detail. The prospect of such testimony in many divorces is too great an invasion of spouses' interests in privacy, and promises to make divorce more acrimonious and injurious than it already is.

The plurality opinion's justification for allowing the tort of intentional infliction of emotional distress between spouses is that this represents a middle ground among the various positions taken by Members of this Court. But being in the middle does not equate to being right. Certainly the Court is not in the middle of the views of other state courts; rather, it is to one extreme.

. . .

For all the foregoing reasons, I dissent from the opinion and judgment of the Court.

■ SPECTOR, JUSTICE, dissenting.

Over five years ago, a trial court issued a divorce decree that included an award to Sheila Twyman of $15,000 for the years of abuse she had suffered at the hands of her husband. At the time, the award was consistent with prevailing Texas law. Today, the plurality sets aside the trial court's award and sends Sheila Twyman back to start the process over in a new trial. Because justice for Sheila Twyman has been both delayed and denied, I dissent.

. . .

The trial court found that William "engaged in a continuing course of conduct of attempting to coerce [Sheila] to join in his practices of 'bondage' by continually asserting that [their] marriage could be saved only by [Sheila] participating with [William] in his practices of 'bondage.'" The trial court also determined that Sheila's suffering was certainly foreseeable from William's continuing course of conduct, "in light of his existing knowledge of her long-existing emotional state, which was caused by her having been forcibly raped prior to their marriage." Finally, the trial court found that Sheila's mental anguish was a direct proximate result of William's sexual practices.

Based on the pleadings, evidence, and arguments, the trial court concluded that the facts and the law supported Sheila's recovery of $15,000 for William's negligent infliction of emotional distress. The court of appeals, in an opinion by Justice Gammage, affirmed the trial court's judgment under prevailing tort law and noted that this court had expressly approved the recovery of damages on a negligence claim in a divorce action.

This court, however, has now rejected Texas law established to provide redress for injuries of the kind inflicted by William Twyman. While allowing some tort claims to be brought in a divorce action, the plurality forbids recovery for negligent infliction of emotional distress, and insists that Sheila Twyman proceed on a theory of intentional infliction of emotional distress.

Today's decision is handed down contemporaneously with the overruling of the motion for rehearing in Boyles v. Kerr, 855 S.W.2d 593 (Tex. 1993), in which this court reversed a judgment in favor of a woman who was surreptitiously videotaped during intercourse, then subjected to humiliation and ridicule when the tape was displayed to others. In *Boyles*, as in this case, a majority of this court has determined that severe, negligently-inflicted emotional distress does not warrant judicial relief—no matter how intolerable the injurious conduct. The reasoning originally articulated in *Boyles*, and now implied in this case, is that "[t]ort law cannot and should not attempt to provide redress for every instance of rude, insensitive, or distasteful behavior"; providing such relief, the *Boyles* majority explained, "would dignify most disputes far beyond their social importance." 36 Tex.S.Ct.J. 231, 233–234 (Dec. 2, 1992).[1]

Neither of these cases involves "rude, insensitive, or distasteful behavior"; they involve grossly offensive conduct that was appropriately found to warrant judicial relief. The decision in *Boyles* overturns well-reasoned case law, and I strongly agree with the dissenting opinion in that case. For the same reasons, I strongly disagree with the plurality here; the rule embodied in *Boyles* is no less objectionable when applied to the facts of this case. Sheila Twyman is entitled to recover the amount awarded by the trial court for the injuries inflicted by her husband.

It is no coincidence that both this cause and *Boyles* involve serious emotional distress claims asserted by women against men. From the beginning, tort recovery for infliction of emotional distress has developed primarily as a means of compensating women for injuries inflicted by men insensitive to the harm caused by their conduct. In "[t]he leading case which broke through the shackles,"[2] a man amused himself by falsely informing a woman that her husband had been gravely injured, causing a serious and permanent shock to her nervous system. Wilkinson v. Downton, 2 Q.B.D. 57 (1897). Similarly, in the watershed Texas case, a man severely beat two others in the presence of a pregnant woman, who suffered a miscarriage as a result of her emotional distress. Hill v. Kimball, 76 Tex. 210, 13 S.W. 59 (1890). By World War II, the pattern was well-established: one survey of psychic injury claims found that the ratio of female to male plaintiffs was five to one. Hubert Winston Smith, Relation of Emotions to Injury and Disease: Legal Liability for Psychic Stimuli, 30 Va.L.Rev. 193 (1944).

Even today, when emotional distress claims by both sexes have become more widely accepted, women's claims against men predominate. Of the thirty-four Texas cases cited by the plurality—all decided since 1987—women's claims outnumbered men's by a ratio of five to four; and only four of the thirty-four involved any female defendants. Of those cases involving relations between two individuals—with no corporations involved—five involved a woman's claim against a man; none involved a man's claim against a woman.

I do not argue that women alone have an interest in recovery for emotional distress. However, since the overwhelming majority of emotional distress claims have arisen from harmful conduct by men, rather than women, I do argue that men have had a disproportionate interest in downplaying such claims.

1. On rehearing, the *Boyles* majority has reworded slightly its discussion but reiterated its reasoning and result. The majority's overriding concern there has remained the avoidance of relief for "merely rude or insensitive behavior." 855 S.W.2d 593, 602.

2. William L. Prosser, Insult and Outrage, 44 Cal.L.Rev. 40, 42 (1956).

Like the struggle for women's rights, the movement toward recovery for emotional distress has been long and tortuous. See Peter A. Bell, The Bell Tolls: Toward Full Tort Recovery for Psychic Injury, 36 U.Fla.L.Rev. 333, 336–40 (1984). In the judicial system dominated by men, emotional distress claims have historically been marginalized:

> The law of torts values physical security and property more highly than emotional security and human relationships. This apparently gender-neutral hierarchy of values has privileged men, as the traditional owners and managers of property, and has burdened women, to whom the emotional work of maintaining human relationships has commonly been assigned. The law has often failed to compensate women for recurring harms—serious though they may be in the lives of women—for which there is no precise masculine analogue.

Martha Chamallas and Linda K. Kerber, Women, Mothers, and the Law of Fright: A History, 88 Mich.L.Rev. 814 (1990). Even Prosser recognizes the role of gender in the historical treatment of claims like that involved in Hill v. Kimball:

> It is not difficult to discover in the earlier opinions a distinctly masculine astonishment that any woman should ever allow herself to be frightened or shocked into a miscarriage.

W. Page Keeton et al., Prosser and Keeton on the Law of Torts § 12, at 55–56 (5th ed. 1984).

Displaying a comparable "masculine astonishment," the dissenting opinion by Justice Hecht insists that, with a few possible exceptions, women have played no distinct part in the development of tort recovery for emotional distress. As a general matter, Justice Hecht questions how a legal system dominated by men could develop a tort to compensate women even while marginalizing women's claims. The answer is amply illustrated by the present case: to provide some appearance of relief for Sheila Twyman, the court recognizes the tort of intentional infliction of emotional distress; but in doing so, it restricts her to a theory which, as Justice Hecht observes, is "seldom successful." 855 S.W.2d at 631.

Justice Hecht acknowledges that in the early cases, recovery for emotional distress "frequently involved female plaintiffs." 855 S.W.2d at 631. However, rather than viewing this phenomenon as an indication of actual, serious injuries, Justice Hecht suggests that it may have been due to a patronizing attitude on the part of the courts.

There is little doubt that some of the case law in this area, as in any other, reflects a patronizing view of women. More often, though, the case law reflects the logical application of existing law to a wide range of claims. For example, in the only case cited by Justice Hecht to illustrate an arguably patronizing view of women, there was evidence that men employed by a railroad had humiliated a man's ten-year-old daughter by subjecting her to obscene language; but there was no evidence that the language had humiliated the father. Fort Worth & Rio Grande Ry. Co. v. Bryant, 210 S.W. 556 (Tex.Civ.App.—Fort Worth 1918, writ ref'd). There is nothing patronizing about holding a railroad company responsible for the harm caused by its employees' conduct.

I would group *Bryant* with the many other common carrier cases that were decided, in Justice Hecht's terms, "without particular regard for gender." 855 S.W.2d at 639. Neither the Fort Worth Court of Appeals, nor any of the other courts at the time were primarily concerned with protecting women's rights. But in *Bryant,* as in so many of the other cases, the evolution of the law regarding emotional distress claims did enable a female to recover for emotional harm inflicted by men. This fact does not reflect a charitable desire to help women; it reflects the fact that the serious emotional distress claims usually involved injuries inflicted by men upon women.

Given this history, the plurality's emphatic rejection of infliction of emotional distress claims based on negligence is especially troubling. Today, when the widespread mistreatment of women is being documented throughout the country—for instance, in the areas of sexual harassment and domestic violence—a majority of this court takes a step backward and abolishes one way of righting this grievous wrong.

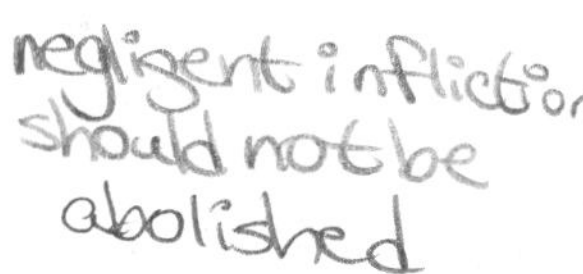
negligent infliction
should not be
abolished

NOTE

The question of intentional infliction of emotional distress was not resolved because *Twyman* was never retried. Sheila and William Twyman settled rather than endure another trial. Telephone Interview with Douglas M. Becker, Counsel for William Twyman (Aug. 19, 1996); Telephone Interview with Edwin J. Terry, Counsel for Sheila Twyman (Aug. 19, 1996).

Ira Mark Ellman and Stephen D. Sugarman, Spousal Emotional Abuse as a Tort?

55 Md. L. Rev. 1268 (1996).

Introduction

Should "spousal emotional abuse" be a tort? More precisely, should states recognize a cause of action by one spouse against another for intentional infliction of emotional distress as set out in section 46 of the Restatement (Second) of Torts?[1] In recent years, courts have been asked to apply this tort of "outrageous" conduct to the marital setting in more than a handful of cases in which the plaintiff was not claiming a physical beating. Some judges have now allowed divorcing spouses to bring such fault-based tort suits, a remarkable development if one considers the historical trend toward no-fault divorce that is relentlessly squeezing out fault as a consideration in resolving family law disputes. Are such cases an aberration, or do they suggest a new and improved approach to considering fault in divorce? In this Article we describe and evaluate this new development . . .

V. Is Spousal Emotional Abuse a Judicially Administrable Concept?

At several points in our discussion of the desirability of recognizing a tort of spousal emotional abuse, we have mentioned the importance of

1. *Restatement (Second) of Torts 46* (1965). Section 46, titled "Outrageous Conduct Causing Severe Emotional Distress," states:

(1) One who by extreme and outrageous conduct intentionally or recklessly causes severe emotional distress to another is subject to liability for such emotional distress, and if bodily harm to the other results from it, for such bodily harm.

(2) Where such conduct is directed at a third person, the actor is subject to liability if he intentionally or recklessly causes severe emotional distress

(a) to a member of such person's immediate family who is present at the time, whether or not such distress results in bodily harm, or

(b) to any other person who is present at the time, if such distress results in bodily harm.

establishing a clear standard for what constitutes outrageous conduct. We now deal directly with this issue . . .

B. The New Section 46 Cases: The Standard Fact Patterns

We turn now to the decided IIED cases that have prompted our inquiry into whether there should be a tort action for spousal emotional abuse . . .

1. *The Bully.*—Here we highlight two cases that we believe treated similar facts quite differently. In Hakkila v. Hakkila, the spouses separated in 1985 after ten years of marriage. When the husband filed a petition for dissolution, the wife, who had a history of depression, counterclaimed for IIED. It appears the divorce and tort cases were tried together before a judge, who made factual findings to support his award of tort damages to the wife. Although apparently there was no separate claim for battery, the trial court supported the IIED verdict in part with a general finding that the husband had "assaulted and battered" the wife. The finding was supported in the record, according to the appeals court, by evidence of "several" incidents.

The New Mexico appellate court in Hakkila cautiously concluded that while spousal IIED claims might be valid in other settings, the facts of this case were inadequate as a matter of law to demonstrate such a tort. Hence it reversed the judgment for the wife. Indeed, the court expressed concern that the husband was subjected to a six-day trial on these claims, and urged trial courts to make more liberal use of summary judgments if similar IIED cases arise in the future.

In Massey v. Massey, the wife claimed that her husband, a bank president, denied her any independent access to funds and doled out money to her in small amounts, belittled her in front of others, had outbursts that sometimes included property destruction and that caused her to experience "intense anxiety and fear," and threatened to tell her children and friends of her extramarital affair and take custody of her youngest daughter from her. The wife's psychologist testified that the wife dealt with the husband by "walking on egg shells so as not to trigger [his] rage." The wife made no claim of personal physical violence, and the jury ultimately found that the husband "had not assaulted [the wife] by threat of imminent injury nor acted with malice." Although the husband portrayed most facts differently than his wife, he conceded that he often used threats in both his business and his marriage "to get his way." The husband claimed that the wife was an alcoholic, and that he had been devastated by her extramarital affair. The parties had been married for twenty-two years. The distress claim, tried with the divorce action, resulted in a judgment against the husband for $362,000 in compensatory damages, with no punitive damages award. A Texas appeals court affirmed the award . . .

Massey is troubling to us for two reasons. First, it seems wrongly decided and thereby portends further inappropriate decisions if the tort of spousal emotional abuse is unleashed. Second, the way the appellate court in Massey envisioned how "outrageousness" is to be determined in individual cases seems ultimately misguided.

In rejecting the arguments that the husband's conduct was outrageous as a matter of law, the appeals court in Massey approved the following instruction that the trial judge had given the jury:

> "The bounds of decency vary from legal relationship to legal relationship. The marital relationship is highly subjective and constituted by

> mutual understandings and interchanges which are constantly in flux, and any number of which could be viewed by some segments of society as outrageous. Conduct considered extreme and outrageous in some relationships may be considered forgivable in other relationships. In your deliberation on the questions, definitions and instructions that follow, you shall consider them only in the context of the marital relationship of the parties to this case."

In short, by accepting the proposition that the "bounds of decency vary" among marital relationships, the court seemed thereby drawn to the conclusion that the same acts could be found "outrageous" in the context of one marriage but not in another. Put differently, the court approved a jury instruction that seeks to avoid imposing fixed societal standards of conduct on intimate personal relationships, asking the jury, in effect, to apply the couple's own standards. The instruction tells the jurors not to focus on what they would find outrageous in their own marriage, nor to search for some community consensus as to what marital behavior is completely out of bounds. Rather, they are to decide whether the complaining spouse can fairly label as "outrageous" the complained of acts in the setting of her own marriage.

The policy issue here—shall the outrageousness of spousal conduct be judged by external or internal standards—seems fundamental. The apparent justification for the choice expressed by the approved jury instruction is that the imposition of external standards on an intimate relationship may risk inappropriate, and possibly even unconstitutional intrusion on marital privacy. But while we agree that such intrusion should be avoided, we doubt that Massey's resort to internal standards offers a promising solution.

Presumably, any effort to judge a spouse's conduct by the couple's own standards must look for those standards in the parties' understanding at the time their marriage began, or as they mutually adjusted it at some later time, rather than in the unilateral expressions of one party after the marriage has fallen apart. Consider, then, some possible interpretations of the Massey facts. On the one hand, the opinion portrays the husband as an insensitive, domineering bully in his personal relations, a man whose conduct might be judged to fit precisely the classic fault-divorce standard of mental cruelty. Yet his marriage lasted over twenty years, and perhaps close scrutiny would have shown that during much of the marriage his wife enjoyed compensating benefits in her relationship with him. Possibly his behavior became more extreme during the course of the marriage. Or possibly when they first married both were poorly socialized and incapable of "normal" relationships, but later the wife matured. Still, their earlier understanding, even if "unhealthy," functioned for two decades or more, perhaps meeting each other's needs as well as either of them could. On this last understanding of the couple's marriage, the court's jury instruction would seem to require a verdict for the defendant.

Consider also the husband's claim in Massey that his wife was an alcoholic and that he had been devastated by her extramarital affair. Although Ruprecht tells us that the wife's affair would not give the husband an IIED action for her violation of her marital vows, under the approved jury instruction ought not the wife's adultery and excessive drinking in Massey, if proved, at least provide a context in which his behavior, even if still wrongful, should not be deemed outrageous? Indeed, on close examination, this couple's "mutual understanding" might well have condemned adultery more than the husband's behavior of which the wife complained.

What is going on here? In the first place, it appears that the kind of close examination of the couple's entire marriage history called for by the judge's instruction did not actually take place in Massey. Indeed, we find it highly questionable whether it is either realistic or desirable to ask the jury to make such an inquiry in order to determine exactly what standards the parties had set for themselves. To do so requires a great deal of nuanced detective work at a time when the parties have every incentive to cast earlier words and actions in an altogether false light. Moreover, to successfully make the inquiry requires a deep intrusion into the spouses' intimate affairs, thereby flying in the face of a central argument in favor of the internal standard in the first place—that it is supposed to respect their privacy by refraining from imposing outside standards on them.

It appears, then, that despite what both courts said, the jury and both levels of the judiciary are doing something different than what is called for by the appellate court's legal reasoning. Rather, it seems the jurors were permitted to deem the husband's conduct unacceptable for whatever reasons of their own they might have had, and, following the trial court, the reviewing court simply shrank from overturning that verdict as a matter of law. At the appellate level this means either that the court, applying its own values, decided that the husband's behavior was outrageous despite the wife's adultery and drinking, or that, by approving the internal standard, the court put itself in a position where appellate reversal of the jury determination becomes all but impossible.

The most disturbing implication for us is that standardless instructions combined with toothless appellate review add up to enormous jury discretion to impose on the couple just about any decision they wish. This not only threatens uneven justice and unpredictable outcomes, but also invites virtually all discontented, divorcing spouses to try their chance at the lottery . . .

Even if a jury wanted to be faithful to the Massey instruction, the implementation difficulties with internal standards seem irremediable. All too often it will be hopeless to derive internal marital standards from a postmarriage investigation of the typically informal and unarticulated understandings that once existed in the now-defunct relationship . . .

We conclude, therefore, that the approach to these cases envisioned by the Massey appeals court is misguided, and that if section 46 of the Restatement were made applicable to interspousal claims, one would at least have to start with external standards. Yet we also agree that the Massey court was emphasizing an important consideration. Because marital understandings do vary, important privacy norms can be violated if tort law were to impose liability after the marriage for conduct that was within the bounds of the marriage as the spouses then understood it. This means that the external standard only should reach conduct that is highly unlikely to have been part of any couple's mutual understanding, or in any event is sufficiently malevolent to justify overriding these privacy norms. Indeed, one might argue that the outrage standard is meant to incorporate this very idea: marital conduct crosses the line into outrageousness at just the point when it becomes so extreme that it is not credible to think it was part of any reasonable couple's marital understanding.

The preeminent example of such conduct is battery. In holding spouses liable for the physical injuries they intentionally inflict on one another, a court has no occasion to remind the jury that "bounds of decency vary from marital relationship to marital relationship." We normally do not believe that couples meaningfully agree that one may batter the other in return for, say, providing financial support; and the social norm against spousal beating is sufficiently strong that we are prepared to condemn it anyway, notwithstanding any alleged mutual understanding of the couple.

This approach would serve, in addition, to exclude from recovery claims by spouses who had marital relationships that were extrasensitive to matters of sexual fidelity or honesty, as illustrated in the hypotheticals described earlier involving fundamentalist religious objections to adultery and written promises to tell the truth at all cost.

But what alleged spousal emotional abuse, if any, would be included? There's the rub. In contrast to battery, it is much more difficult to establish satisfactory standards to identify when emotional mistreatment is completely out of bounds. First of all, intimate relationships often involve complex emotional bargains that make no sense to third parties with different needs or perceptions. People often remain in marriages that look to others to be unhealthy. Although staying married is sometimes the result of coercion or delusion, often what may seem to outsiders as, say, intolerably extreme verbal harshness, is instead a feature of the particular relationship with which the parties, at least on balance, are content. In short, in many matters some couples arrive at solutions that depart from the social conventions that govern most of their acquaintances. Because those who sufficiently dislike their spouse's behavior can seek a divorce, it becomes more difficult to justify the conclusion that their marital relationship was so unacceptably uncivilized as to require tort damages when they wait many years to do so.

For example, was Mrs. Massey the victim of an extremely cruel husband who fiendishly exploited her personal insecurity in order to keep her trapped in an abusive relationship? Or was she someone who willingly accepted verbal unkindness and a loss of independence in return for relief from many ordinary responsibilities, who later changed her mind and wants compensation? . . . The upshot is that while we are content to tell the batterer that he acts at his peril, we feel much less comfortable with a legal regime that says the same to Mr. Massey.

Turning away from the peculiarities of any specific couple, and looking generally at marital conduct that can be emotionally distressing, it is critical to recognize that by requiring "outrageous" conduct the Restatement clearly means to exclude from liability the common incivilities of everyday life. The idea is that such rude, insensitive, or mean-spirited behavior is better regulated, at least in the usual case, by social mechanisms or through self-help resort to divorce rather than through tort law. Although one reason for seeking to restrict recovery to extreme cases is to prevent a flood of litigation, surely another reason for a high threshold is the disparity between our aspirations and our conduct. Few if any of us consistently can avoid violating the norms of appropriate, sensitive social conduct that we endorse. The gap between societal aspiration and individual reality may be especially great in marital relations.

Yet, without clear guidelines as to what meets the threshold, the risk is that at least some juries will measure outrageousness against an ideal standard of marital relations—in effect lowering the threshold. This tendency is facilitated if outrageousness is left a flexible, open-ended concept. In this way, the outrage standard could yield liability for a much wider swath of marital conduct than for conduct by employers toward their employees, creditors toward their debtors, and landlords toward their tenants.

We concede that some commentators explicitly have urged the use of tort law as a tool for reforming intimate relations between the genders—by threatening to hold individuals to aspirational standards. But this strategy flies in the face of most modern family law reform that has acknowledged the need to conform the law to a social reality that traditional rules did not accept. Hence, applying tort law to claims of spousal emotional abuse risks a reprise of this very problem . . .

NOTE

Is Professors Ellman's and Sugarman's proposal the best way to ensure that marital tort claims are based on a relative consensus about the culpability of the behavior in question? Should tort law try to take account of the purely emotional or psychological injuries that spouses may inflict on one another?

6. RELIGIOUS RESTRICTIONS

Aflalo v. Aflalo

Superior Court of New Jersey, Chancery Division, Family Part, Monmouth County, 1996.
295 N.J.Super. 527, 685 A.2d 523.

■ FISHER, J.S.C.

This case requires the court to visit an issue that has previously troubled our courts in matrimonial actions involving Orthodox Jews—a husband's refusal to provide a "get."[1]

Here, the parties were married on October 13, 1983 in Ramle, Israel, and have one child, Samantha. Plaintiff Sondra Faye Aflalo ("Sondra") has filed a complaint seeking a dissolution of the marriage. Defendant Henry Arik Aflalo ("Henry") has answered the complaint. The matter is on the court's active trial list and should be reached for trial in the very near future. Henry does not want a divorce and has taken action with The Union of Orthodox Rabbis of the United States and Canada in New York City (the "Beth Din"[2]) to have a hearing on his attempts at reconciliation.

The issues at hand came to critical mass when the parties engaged in a settlement conference on February 14, 1996, while awaiting trial in this court. At that time the court was advised by counsel that the matter was "98% settled" but that Henry had placed what Sondra viewed as an insurmountable obstacle to a complete resolution: he refused to provide a "get." Unlike what the court faced in *Segal v. Segal,* 278 *N.J.Super.* 218, 650 A.2d 996 (App.Div.1994) and *Burns v. Burns,* 223 *N.J.Super.* 219, 538 A.2d 438 (Ch.Div.1987), Henry was not using his refusal to consent to the "get" as a means of securing a more favorable resolution of the issues before this court. That type of conduct the *Burns* court rightfully labelled "extortion". On the contrary, Henry's position (as conveyed during the settlement conference) was that regardless of what occurs in this court he will not consent to a Jewish divorce.

Henry's position spun off an unexpected problem; it caused his attorney to move to be relieved as counsel. Arguing that since he, too, is a practicing Orthodox Jew, Henry's counsel claims that he would "definitely have a

1. A "get" is a bill of divorce which the husband gives to his wife to free her to marry again. The word "get" apparently signifies the number 12, the "get" being a twelve-lined instrument. The word is a combination of "gimel" (which has a value of three) together with "tet" (which has a value of nine).

2. The "Beth Din" is a rabbinical tribunal having authority to advise and pass upon matters of traditional Jewish law.

religious problem representing a man who at the conclusion of a divorce proceeding refused, without reason, to give his wife a Get."

This motion was heard on an expedited basis. At oral argument on February 20, 1996, Henry's counsel expanded on his position and indicated, upon questioning from the court, that *his* religious quandary comes not from Henry's use of his consent to a Jewish divorce as leverage in negotiations (which was not occurring), but in the blanket refusal of his client to give a "get" without reason.

Henry opposed his attorney's motion. He stated under oath that he seeks a reconciliation and that Sondra had been summoned to appear before the Beth Din for this purpose. The court was also advised during oral argument that should reconciliation fail the Beth Din could recommend that Henry give Sondra a "get"; Henry stated under oath that while he desires a reconciliation he would follow the recommendations of the Beth Din and give the "get" if that was the end result of those proceedings. The court finds Henry both credible and sincere in this regard; his position clearly eliminates his counsel's stated concerns.

The problem, however, festers since Sondra appears unwilling to settle this case without a "get." Accordingly, this court must now lay to rest whether any order may be entered which would impact on Sondra's securing of a Jewish divorce.

Sondra claims that this court, as part of the judgment of divorce which may eventually be entered in this matter, may and should order Henry to cooperate with the obtaining of a Jewish divorce upon pain of Henry having limited or supervised visitation of Samantha or by any other coercive means. She claims that *Minkin v. Minkin,* 180 *N.J.Super.* 260, 434 A.2d 665 (Ch.Div. 1981) authorizes this court to order Henry to consent to the Jewish divorce. That trial court decision certainly supports her view. This court, however, believes that to enter such an order violates Henry's First Amendment rights and refuses to follow the course outlined in *Minkin.*

Prior to the adoption of our Nation's constitution, attempts were made in some colonies to legislate on matters of religion, including the governmental establishment of religion and the raising of taxes for the support of certain religions. Punishments were prescribed for the failure to attend religious services and for entertaining heretical opinions. In 1784 the Virginia legislature attempted to enact a bill "establishing provision for teachers of the Christian religion." This brought to bear the determined and eloquent opposition of Thomas Jefferson and James Madison. Madison responded in his "Memorial and Remonstrance" that "religion, or the duty we owe the Creator" was not within the cognizance of civil authority. The next session of the Virginia legislature led to the defeat of the aforementioned bill and the passage of a bill drafted by Jefferson which established "religious freedom" and declared that "to suffer the civil magistrate to intrude his powers into the field of opinion, and to restrain the profession or propagation of principles on supposition of their ill tendency, is a dangerous fallacy which at once destroys all religious liberty."

Not long after the adoption of the Constitution and the Bill of Rights, Jefferson made clear the meaning and intent of the First Amendment in his famous "reply" to the Danbury Baptist Association:

> Believing with you that religion is a matter which lies solely between man and his God; that he owes account to none other for his faith or his worship; that the legislative powers of the Government reach actions

> only, and not opinions, I contemplate with sovereign reverence that act of the whole American people which declared that their Legislature should "make no law respecting an establishment of religion or prohibiting the free exercise thereof," thus building a wall of separation between Church and State. Adhering to this expression of the supreme will of the Nation in behalf of the rights of conscience, I shall see, with sincere satisfaction, the progress of those sentiments which tend to restore man to all his natural rights, convinced he has no natural right in opposition to his social duties.

Since then the dimensions of this "wall of separation between Church and State" have been robustly debated and described frequently by our Nation's highest court.

The "Free Exercise Clause" of the First Amendment applies to the states through the Fourteenth Amendment's Due Process Clause. Not only does it bar a state's legislature from making a law which prohibits the free exercise of religion but it likewise inhibits a state's judiciary.

In the first instance, the Free Exercise Clause prohibits governmental regulation of religious beliefs but does not absolutely prohibit religious conduct. Second, to pass constitutional muster, a law must have both a secular purpose and a secular effect. That is, a law must not have a sectarian purpose; it must not be based upon a disagreement with a religious tenet or practice and must not be aimed at impeding religion.

Only when state action passes these threshold tests is there a need to balance the competing state and religious interests. The court is to engage in such balancing when the conduct or action sought to be regulated has "invariably posed some substantial threat to public safety, peace or order." Here, the relief Sondra seeks from this court so obviously runs afoul of the threshold tests of the Free Exercise Clause that the court need never reach the delicate balancing normally required in such cases.

The court will first endeavor to describe precisely what it is that Sondra seeks. And, while it seems beyond doubt, the court will then indicate why it cannot and certainly will not provide that relief.

"When a man takes a wife and possesses her, if she fails to please him because he finds something obnoxious about her, then he writes her a bill of divorcement, hands it to her, and sends her away from his house." *Deuteronomy* 24:1–4. From this biblical verse, the Jewish law and tradition that the "power of divorce rests exclusively with the husband" has its genesis. Wigoder, *The Encyclopedia of Judaism* (1989) 210.

The "get" is written almost entirely in Aramaic on parchment, and is drawn up by a "sofer" (a scribe), upon the husband's instruction to write "for him, for her, and for the purpose of a divorce," 6 *The Encyclopedia Judaica* (1971) 131. The materials used in the creation of the "get" must belong to the husband; the "sorer" presents them as a gift to the husband before the "get" is written. The spelling and the form of the document "are enumerated in minute detail in halakhic literature" and acknowledged by two witnesses. The rabbi who presides retains the "get"; he cuts it "in criss-cross fashion so that it cannot be used again," and to "avoid any later suspicion that it was not absolutely legal," *Encyclopedia Judaica, supra* at 132. The wife is given another document ("petor") which proves that she has been divorced and the "get" is filed away in its torn state. Wigoder, *supra* at 211.

Without such a divorce, the wife remains an "agunah" (a "tied" woman) and may not remarry in the eyes of Jewish law. Wigoder, *supra* at 211. If she remarries without a "get" she is considered to be an adulteress because she is still halakhically married to her first husband; any subsequent children are considered to be "mamzerim" (illegitimate) and may not marry other Jews. Himelstein, *The Jewish Primer* (1990) 161.

The court is not unsympathetic to Sondra's desire to have Henry's cooperation in the obtaining of a "get." She, too, is sincere in her religious beliefs. Her religion, at least in terms of divorce, does not profess gender equality. But does that mean that she can obtain the aid of this court of equity to alter this doctrine of her faith? That the question must be answered negatively seems so patently clear that the only surprising aspect of Sondra's argument is that it finds some support in the few cases on the subject.

In *Minkin,* the trial court requested the testimony of several distinguished rabbis. The court viewed the issue as whether a state court could order specific performance of the "ketubah." The "ketubah" is the marriage contract in which the couple is obligated to comply with the laws of Moses and Israel. It contains the promise of the husband "to honor and support thee and provide for thy needs, even as Jewish husbands are required to do *by our religious law* and tradition." *See, e.g., Avitzur v. Avitzur,* 58 N.Y.2d 108, 459 N.Y.S.2d 572, 576, 446 N.E.2d 136 (1983) (emphasis added), cert. denied 464 *U.S.* 817 (1983). The "ketubah" also contains the parties' agreement "to recognize the Beth Din . . . as having authority to counsel us in the light of Jewish tradition . . . and to summon either party at the request of the other. . . ." 459 N.Y.S.2d at 576, 446 N.E.2d at 140.

In determining that it could specifically enforce the "ketubah," *Minkin* relied on a New York decision which stated:

> Defendant has also contended that a decree of specific performance would interfere with his freedom of religion under the Constitution. Complying with his agreement would not compel the defendant to practice any religion, not even the Jewish faith to which he still admits adherence (paragraph Second of the complaint not denied in the answer). His appearance before the Rabbinate to answer questions and give evidence needed by them to make a decision is not a profession of faith. Specific performance herein would merely require the defendant to do what he voluntarily agreed to do.

[*Koeppel v. Koeppel,* 138 N.Y.S.2d 366, 373 (Sup.Ct.1954).] Analyzing the case against the test used to determine whether state action violates the Establishment Clause which is set forth in *Committee for Public Education and Religious Liberty v. Nyquist,* 413 U.S. 756, 772–773 (1973), the *Minkin* court said:

> Relying upon credible expert testimony that the acquisition of a *get* is not a religious act, the court finds that the entry of an order compelling defendant to secure a *get* would have the clear secular purpose of completing a dissolution of the marriage. Its primary effect neither advances nor inhibits religion since it does not require the husband to participate in a religious ceremony or to do acts contrary to his religious beliefs. Nor would the order be an excessive entanglement with religion.

Also, in reliance upon the expert testimony found credible, the *Minkin* court concluded that an order compelling a husband to acquire a "get" is "not a religious act." *Id.* The court apparently relied on one of the rabbis who testified "that Jewish law cannot be equated with religious law, but instead is comprised of two components—one regulating a man's relationship with God and the other regulating the relationship between man and man. The *get,* which has no reference to God but which does affect the relationship between two parties, falls into the latter category and is, therefore, civil and not religious in nature." 180 *N.J.Super.* at 265–266, 434 A.2d 665.

Minkin's approach that the "ketubah" may be specifically enforced without violating the First Amendment is in accord with the decisional law of New York, Illinois, and Delaware, and at odds with Arizona, and, now, this court. *Minkin* and its followers (including the New Jersey trial court in *Burns*)[4] are not persuasive for a number of reasons.

First, it examined the problem against the backdrop of the Establishment Clause and not the Free Exercise Clause. The Establishment Clause prohibits government from placing its support behind a particular religious belief. The Free Exercise Clause, obviously implicated here, prohibits government from interfering or becoming entangled in the practice of religion by its citizens.

Second, the conclusion that an order requiring the husband to provide a "get" is not a religious act nor involves the court in the religious beliefs or practices of the parties is not at all convincing. It is interesting that the court was required to choose between the conflicting testimony of the various rabbis[7] to reach this conclusion. The one way in which a court may become entangled in religious affairs, which the court in *Minkin* did not recognize, was in becoming an arbiter of what is "religious." As Justice Brennan observed in *Serbian Eastern Orthodox Diocese v. Milivojevich,* 426 *U.S.* 696, 709 (1976):

> [W]here resolution of the disputes cannot be made without extensive inquiry by civil courts into religious law and polity, the First and Fourteenth Amendments mandate that civil courts shall not disturb the decisions of the highest ecclesiastical tribunal within a church of hierarchical polity, but must accept such decisions as binding on them, in their application to the religious issues of doctrine or polity before them.

Accordingly, civil courts may not override a decision of a religious tribunal or interpret religious law or canons. Of course, religious parties and organizations are entitled to the adjudication in our civil courts of "secular legal questions." But in doing so the civil court cannot decide any disputed questions of religious doctrine. That is exactly what the *Minkin* court did when it sifted among the rabbinical testimony to find the most credible version.

Third, the conclusion that its order concerned purely civil issues is equally unconvincing. In determining to specifically enforce the "ketubah," the court recognized that "[w]ithout compliance [the wife] cannot marry in accordance with her religious beliefs." 180 *N.J.Super.* at 263, 434 A.2d 665. As noted earlier the later children of a wife who remarries without a "get" are prohibited from marrying other Jews. No matter how one semantically

4. *Burns* is equally unpersuasive, although the wife's position therein is even more sympathetic. There, the parties were divorced years earlier and the husband had remarried. However, he refused to provide his ex-wife with a "get" unless she invested $25,000 in an irrevocable trust for the benefit of their daughter. 223 *N.J.Super.* at 222, 538 A.2d 438. Relying upon *Minkin* and its broad equity powers, the court in *Burns* ordered the husband to "submit to the jurisdiction of the 'Bet Din' to initiate the proceedings for a 'get'." 223 *N.J.Super.* at 226, 538 A.2d 438. In the alternative, the court permitted the husband "to execute the prepared document, ... authorizing the preparation and presentation of the 'get' to the defendant by an agent on his behalf and forego the actual appearance before the 'Bet Din'." *Id.*

7. One rabbi testified that the acquisition of a "get" was a religious act. 180 *N.J.Super.* at 266, 434 A.2d 665.

phrases what was done in *Minkin,* the order directly affected the religious beliefs of the parties. By entering the order, the court empowered the wife to remarry in accordance with her religious beliefs and also similarly empowered any children later born to her. The mere fact that the "get" does not contain the word "God," which the *Minkin* court found significant, is hardly reason to conclude otherwise. Nor is it sound to argue that religion involves only one's relation to the creator and not one's relation to other persons, as may be obligated by religious traditions or teachings. *Minkin* might as well have said that a civil court may order a Christian to comply with the Second Great Commandment[8] but not the First.[9] The concept of "religion" certainly does have reference to one's relation to the creator but it also has relation to one's obedience to the will of the creator. In one's pursuit to comply with the creator's will one is certainly engaged in religious activity. While engaging in such conduct, one may also be subjected to civil authority but that does not remove that conduct from the scope of religious activity. *Minkin* draws too fine a line in its rejection of the latter as an area constituting "religion" to command this court's assent to its holding.

Fourth, *Minkin* fails to recognize that coercing the husband to provide the "get" would not have the effect sought. The "get" must be phrased and formulated in strict compliance with tradition, according to the wording given in the Talmud. 6 *Encyclopedia Judaica* (1971) 131. The precisely worded "get" states that the husband does "willingly consent, being under no restraint, to release, to set free, and put aside thee, my wife. . . ." *Id.* Accordingly, in giving his wife a "get" a husband must "act without constraint." Wigoder, *supra* at 210. Indeed, during the proceeding the husband is asked "whether he ordered [the 'get'] of his own free will." Singer, *The Jewish Encyclopedia* at 647. What value then is a "get" when it is ordered by a civil court and when it places the husband at risk of being held in contempt should he follow his conscience and refuse to comply? Moreover, why should this court order such relief when that is something which the Beth Din will not do? If a "get" is something which can be coerced then it should be the Beth Din which does the coercing. In coercing the husband, the civil court is, in essence, overruling or superseding any judgment which the Beth Din can or will enter, contrary to accepted First Amendment principles.

Avitzur suggests a more indirect way of providing relief to the wife. A majority of the New York Court of Appeals found that the wording of the "ketubah" suggested an agreement of the marital partners to appear before the Beth Din and held that such an agreement could be enforced by the civil court without running afoul of First Amendment law. The majority was careful in recognizing that it was not called upon to order the husband to provide a "get," noting that "plaintiff is not attempting to compel defendant to obtain a Get or to enforce a religious practice arising solely out of principles of religious law." 459 N.Y.S.2d at 574, 446 N.E.2d at 138. An order requiring defendant to appear before the Beth Din was found to be available because the majority viewed the role of the civil court as enforcing "nothing more than an agreement to refer the matter of a religious divorce to a nonjudicial forum." *Id.* The three members of the court which dissented, however, in this court's view correctly ascertained that even the limited relief which the majority of four approved required "inquiry into and resolution of questions of Jewish religious law and tradition" and thus inappropriately

8. "Thou shalt love thy neighbor as thyself."

9. "Thou shalt love the Lord thy God with thy whole heart, and with thy whole soul, and with thy whole mind, and with thy whole strength."

entangled the civil court in the wife's attempts to obtain a religious divorce. *Id.* at 577–578, 446 N.E.2d at 141–142.

Even if the majority opinion in *Avitzur* were followed by this court, the circumstances of this case do not support the relief endorsed in *Avitzur.* The "ketubah" only states the parties' recognition of the Beth Din as "having authority to counsel" them and "to summon either party at the request of the other. . . ." Here, Sondra has never sought relief in the Beth Din and in fact has not appeared in response to the summons forwarded to her by the Beth Din regarding Henry's pursuit of reconciliation. Even *Avitzur,* it is suspected, would not enforce any attempt by Sondra to compel Henry to appear before the Beth Din when she has not honored a similar request.[11]

Minkin ultimately conjures the unsettling vision of future enforcement proceedings. Should a civil court fine a husband for every day he does not comply or imprison him for contempt for following his conscience? Apparently so, according to New York law. Or, as suggested by Sondra, should visitation of Samantha be limited pending Henry's cooperation? That argument finds no support anywhere. Unlike *Minkin* (where a judgment of divorce had already been entered), Henry seeks the intervention of the Beth Din in order to effect a reconciliation with his wife.[12] Should this court enjoin Henry—no matter how imperfect he may be pursuing it—from moving for reconciliation in that forum and order other relief which the Beth Din apparently cannot give? This court should not, and will not, compel a course of conduct in the Beth Din no matter how unfair the consequences. The spectre of Henry being imprisoned or surrendering his religious freedoms because of action by a civil court is the very image which gave rise to the First Amendment.

It may seem "unfair" that Henry may ultimately refuse to provide a "get."[13] But the unfairness comes from Sondra's own sincerely-held religious beliefs. When she entered into the "ketubah" she agreed to be obligated to the laws of Moses and Israel. Those laws apparently include the tenet that if Henry does not provide her with a "get" she must remain an "agunah." That was Sondra's choice and one which can hardly be remedied by this court. This court has no authority—were it willing—to choose for these parties which aspects of their religion may be embraced and which must be rejected. Those who founded this Nation knew too well the tyranny of religious persecution and the need for religious freedom. To engage even in a "well-intentioned" resolution of a religious dispute requires the making of a choice which accommodates one view and suppresses another. If that is permitted, it readily follows that less "well-intentioned" choices may be made in the future by those who, as Justice Jackson once observed, believe "that all thought is divinely classified into two kinds—that which is their own and that which is false and dangerous." *American Communications Ass'n v. Douds,* 339 *U.S.* 382, 438 (1950) (dissenting opinion).

The tenets of Sondra's religion would be debased by this court's crafting of a short-cut or loophole through the religious doctrines she adheres to;[14]

11. During a brief hearing via telephone on February 22, 1996, Sondra's counsel indicated that Sondra had responded in writing to the summons from the Beth Din but has never provided a copy of that response to this court.

12. Apparently, however, Henry has not paid the necessary fee and the matter now sits moribund at the Beth Din level.

13. That Sondra has not cooperated with the summons of the Beth Din regarding Henry's attempts at reconciliation could also be viewed as "unfair."

14. New York's legislature has provided

and the dignity and integrity of the court and its processes would be irreparably injured by such misuse. The First Amendment was designed to protect both institutions against such unwarranted, unwanted and unlawful steps over the "wall of separation between Church and State." This court will not assist Sondra in her attempts to lower that wall. As Justice Frankfurter said, "[i]f nowhere else, in the relation between Church and State, 'good fences make good neighbors.' " *McCollum v. Board of Education,* 333 *U.S.* 203, 232 (1948) (dissenting opinion).

For these reasons, the court has denied the motion to be relieved as counsel. Further, any relief sought by either party with respect to any proceedings either currently being maintained or contemplated in the Beth Din is denied. The parties are directed to engage in a four-way conference within seven (7) days of this date and attempt to amicably resolve the issues that are actually before this court. Thereafter, they will forthwith report any results back to the court.

Henry's consent, or refusal to consent, to the providing of a "get," and Sondra's consent, or refusal to consent, to appear before the Beth Din for proceedings relating to Henry's attempts at reconciliation, are matters which are not to be bargained for or against. *Accord, Segal, supra.* The parties are urged, having previously resolved "98%" of the case, to resolve the remaining 2% for their own sake and, most importantly, for Samantha's sake.[15]

C. ACCESS TO DIVORCE

Boddie v. Connecticut

Supreme Court of the United States, 1971.
401 U.S. 371, 91 S.Ct. 780, 28 L.Ed.2d 113.

■ JUSTICE HARLAN delivered the opinion of the Court.

Appellants, welfare recipients residing in the State of Connecticut, brought this action in the Federal District Court for the District of Connecticut on behalf of themselves and others similarly situated, challenging, as applied to them, certain state procedures for the commencement of litigation, including requirements for payment of court fees and costs for service

such a short-cut. New York Domestic Relations Law § 253 requires that where a marriage has been solemnized by a clergyman, a party who commences a matrimonial action must verify that he or she has acted to remove all "barriers to remarriage." It has been held that this requirement places an obligation on a husband of the Jewish faith to provide his wife with a "get". *Megibow v. Megibow,* 161 Misc.2d 69, 612 N.Y.S.2d 758, 760 (Sup.Ct.1994). In fact, that seems to have been the precise purpose of that statute. The then Governor of New York made the following statement upon passage of the statute:

> This bill was overwhelmingly adopted by the State Legislature because it deals with a tragically unfair condition that is almost universally acknowledged.
>
> The requirement of a get is used by unscrupulous spouses who avail themselves of our civil courts and simultaneously use their denial of a get vindictively or as a form of economic coercion.
>
> Concededly this use of our civil courts unfairly imposes upon one spouse, usually the wife, enormous anguish.

[*Perl v. Perl,* 126 A.D.2d 91, 94–95, 512 N.Y.S.2d 372, 375 (1987).] This statute does not appear to have yet been challenged on First Amendment grounds.

15. Sondra's request for the issuance of a bench warrant due to Henry's alleged failure to timely make support payments shall be held in abeyance pending the four-way conference.

of process, that restrict their access to the courts in their effort to bring an action for divorce.

It appears from the briefs and oral argument that the average cost to a litigant for bringing an action for divorce is $60. Section 52–259 of the Connecticut General Statutes provides: "There shall be paid to the clerks of the supreme court or the superior court, for entering each civil cause, forty-five dollars...." An additional $15 is usually required for the service of process by the sheriff, although as much as $40 or $50 may be necessary where notice must be accomplished by publication.

There is no dispute as to the inability of the named appellants in the present case to pay either the court fees required by statute or the cost incurred for the service of process....

. . .

... As this Court on more than one occasion has recognized, marriage involves interests of basic importance in our society. It is not surprising, then, that the States have seen fit to oversee many aspects of that institution. Without a prior judicial imprimatur, individuals may freely enter into and rescind commercial contracts, for example, but we are unaware of any jurisdiction where private citizens may covenant for or dissolve marriages without state approval. Even where all substantive requirements are concededly met, we know of no instance where two consenting adults may divorce and mutually liberate themselves from the constraints of legal obligations that go with marriage, and more fundamentally the prohibition against remarriage, without invoking the State's judicial machinery.

Thus, although they assert here due process rights as would-be plaintiffs, we think appellants' plight, because resort to the state courts is the only avenue to dissolution of their marriages, is akin to that of defendants faced with exclusion from the only forum effectively empowered to settle their disputes. Resort to the judicial process by these plaintiffs is no more voluntary in a realistic sense than that of the defendant called upon to defend his interests in court. For both groups this process is not only the paramount dispute-settlement technique, but, in fact, the only available one. In this posture we think that this appeal is properly to be resolved in light of the principles enunciated in our due process decisions that delimit rights of defendants compelled to litigate their differences in the judicial forum.

. . .

Prior cases establish, first, that due process requires, at a minimum, that absent a countervailing state interest of overriding significance, persons forced to settle their claims of right and duty through the judicial process must be given a meaningful opportunity to be heard....

Our cases further establish that a statute or a rule may be held constitutionally invalid as applied when it operates to deprive an individual of a protected right although its general validity as a measure enacted in the legitimate exercise of state power is beyond question....

No less than these rights, the right to a meaningful opportunity to be heard within the limits of practicality, must be protected against denial by particular laws that operate to jeopardize it for particular individuals.

. . .

... Just as a generally valid notice procedure may fail to satisfy due process because of the circumstances of the defendant, so too a cost requirement, valid on its face, may offend due process because it operates to foreclose a particular party's opportunity to be heard. The State's obligations under the Fourteenth Amendment are not simply generalized ones; rather, the State owes to each individual that process which, in light of the values of a free society, can be characterized as due.

Drawing upon the principles established by the cases just canvassed, we conclude that the State's refusal to admit these appellants to its courts, the sole means in Connecticut for obtaining a divorce, must be regarded as the equivalent of denying them an opportunity to be heard upon their claimed right to a dissolution of their marriages, and, in the absence of a sufficient countervailing justification for the State's action, a denial of due process.

The arguments for this kind of fee and cost requirement are that the State's interest in the prevention of frivolous litigation is substantial, its use of court fees and process costs to allocate scarce resources is rational, and its balance between the defendant's right to notice and the plaintiff's right to access is reasonable.

In our opinion, none of these considerations is sufficient to override the interest of these plaintiff-appellants in having access to the only avenue open for dissolving their allegedly untenable marriages. Not only is there no necessary connection between a litigant's assets and the seriousness of his motives in bringing suit, but it is here beyond present dispute that appellants bring these actions in good faith. Moreover, other alternatives exist to fees and cost requirements as a means for conserving the time of courts and protecting parties from frivolous litigation, such as penalties for false pleadings or affidavits, and actions for malicious prosecution or abuse of process, to mention only a few. In the same vein we think that reliable alternatives exist to service of process by a state-paid sheriff if the State is unwilling to assume the cost of official service. This is perforce true of service by publication which is the method of notice least calculated to bring to a potential defendant's attention the pendency of judicial proceedings. We think in this case service at defendant's last known address by mail and posted notice is equally effective as publication in a newspaper.

. . .

NOTE

Lee Lynk, while serving a life sentence in an Indiana prison, unsuccessfully filed for divorce in state court. Although conviction of a felony is a ground for divorce in Indiana, the state court refused to issue a writ of habeas corpus *ad testificandum* to enable Lynk to appear for the scheduled hearing. Lynk then filed suit in federal court under section 1 of the Civil Rights Act of 1871, 42 U.S.C. § 1983. On appeal, the Seventh Circuit held, in an opinion written by Judge Posner:

> It can hardly matter in this case whether the right to marry and the right to divorce stand on the same footing so far as the constitutional power of the states is concerned. We shall not try to add to the scholarly discussion of this question in Murillo v. Bambrick, 681 F.2d 898, 902–03 (3d Cir.1982), beyond noting the simple point that all civilized societies recognize a right to marry, and not all a right to divorce.... While ... there may be no constitutional right to divorce ... if the right to marry and divorce is among the liberties encompassed by the due process clause the state can deprive a person of the right only if the state does so in accordance with due process of law. This conclusion was the necessary foundation of the *Boddie* decisions, and survives, we believe, the *Sosna* decision.

Lynk v. LaPorte Superior Court, 789 F.2d 554, 566–67 (7th Cir.1986). The court directed Lynk to dismiss his divorce suit "voluntarily," and then refile the suit "in the hope that by refiling his petition for divorce he can clear the roadblocks to action on it." Id. at 568.

Sosna v. Iowa

Supreme Court of the United States, 1975.
419 U.S. 393, 95 S.Ct. 553, 42 L.Ed.2d 532.

■ JUSTICE REHNQUIST delivered the opinion of the Court.

Appellant Carol Sosna married Michael Sosna on September 5, 1964, in Michigan. They lived together in New York between October 1967 and August 1971, after which date they separated but continued to live in New York. In August 1972, appellant moved to Iowa with her three children, and the following month she petitioned the District Court of Jackson County, Iowa, for a dissolution of her marriage. Michael Sosna, who had been personally served with notice of the action when he came to Iowa to visit his children, made a special appearance to contest the jurisdiction of the Iowa court. The Iowa court dismissed the petition for lack of jurisdiction, finding that Michael Sosna was not a resident of Iowa and appellant had not been a resident of the State of Iowa for one year preceding the filing of her petition. In so doing the Iowa court applied the provisions of Iowa Code § 598.6 requiring that the petitioner in such an action be "for the last year a resident of the state."

. . .

The durational residency requirement under attack in this case is a part of Iowa's comprehensive statutory regulation of domestic relations, an area that has long been regarded as a virtually exclusive province of the States. Cases decided by this Court over a period of more than a century bear witness to this historical fact. In Barber v. Barber, 62 U.S. (21 How.) 582, 584 (1859), the Court said that "[w]e disclaim altogether any jurisdiction in the courts of the United States upon the subject of divorce. . . ." In Pennoyer v. Neff, 95 U.S. 714, 734–735 (1877), the Court said: "The State . . . has absolute right to prescribe the conditions upon which the marriage relation between its own citizens shall be created, and the causes for which it may be dissolved," and the same view was reaffirmed in Simms v. Simms, 175 U.S. 162, 167 (1899).

. . .

The imposition of a durational residency requirement for divorce is scarcely unique to Iowa, since 48 States impose such a requirement as a condition for maintaining an action for divorce.[15] As might be expected, the periods vary among the States and range from six weeks to two years. The one-year period selected by Iowa is the most common length of time prescribed.

Appellant contends that the Iowa requirement of one year's residence is unconstitutional . . . because it establishes two classes of persons and discriminates against those who have recently exercised their right to travel to Iowa, thereby contravening the Court's holdings in Shapiro v. Thompson, 394 U.S. 618 (1969), Dunn v. Blumstein, 405 U.S. 330 (1972), and Memorial Hospital v. Maricopa County, 415 U.S. 250 (1974). . . .

15. Louisiana and Washington are the exceptions. . . .

State statutes imposing durational residency requirements were of course invalidated when imposed by States as a qualification for welfare payments, *Shapiro,* supra, for voting, *Dunn,* supra, and for medical care, *Maricopa County,* supra. But none of those cases intimated that the States might never impose durational residency requirements, and such a proposition was in fact expressly disclaimed. What those cases had in common was that the durational residency requirements they struck down were justified on the basis of budgetary or record-keeping considerations which were held insufficient to outweigh the constitutional claims of the individuals. But Iowa's divorce residency requirement is of a different stripe. Appellant was not irretrievably foreclosed from obtaining some part of what she sought, as was the case with the welfare recipients in *Shapiro,* the voters in *Dunn,* or the indigent patient in *Maricopa County.* She would eventually qualify for the same sort of adjudication which she demanded virtually upon her arrival in the State. Iowa's requirement delayed her access to the courts, but, by fulfilling it, a plaintiff could ultimately obtain the same opportunity for adjudication which she asserts ought to be hers at an earlier point in time.

... A decree of divorce is not a matter in which the only interested parties are the State as a sort of "grantor," and a plaintiff such as appellant in the role of "grantee." Both spouses are obviously interested in the proceedings, since it will affect their marital status and very likely their property rights. Where a married couple has minor children, a decree of divorce would usually include provisions for their custody and support. With consequences of such moment riding on a divorce decree issued by its courts, Iowa may insist that one seeking to initiate such a proceeding have the modicum of attachment to the State required here.

Such a requirement additionally furthers the State's parallel interests in both avoiding officious intermeddling in matters in which another State has a paramount interest, and in minimizing the susceptibility of its own divorce decrees to collateral attack. A State such as Iowa may quite reasonably decide that it does not wish to become a divorce mill for unhappy spouses who have lived there as short a time as appellant had when she commenced her action in the state court after having long resided elsewhere. ...

Affirmed.

. . .

■ JUSTICE MARSHALL, with whom JUSTICE BRENNAN joins, dissenting.

. . .

... Iowa's residency requirement, the Court says, merely forestalls access to the courts; applicants seeking welfare payments, medical aid, and the right to vote, on the other hand, suffer unrecoverable losses throughout the waiting period. This analysis, however, ignores the severity of the deprivation suffered by the divorce petitioner who is forced to wait a year for relief. The injury accompanying that delay is not directly measurable in money terms like the loss of welfare benefits, but it cannot reasonably be argued that when the year has elapsed, the petitioner is made whole. The year's wait prevents remarriage and locks both partners into what may be an intolerable, destructive relationship. Even applying the Court's argument on its own terms, I fail to see how the *Maricopa County* case can be distinguished. A potential patient may well need treatment for a single ailment. Under Arizona statutes he would have had to wait a year before he could be treated. Yet the majority's analysis would suggest that Mr. Evaro's claim for nonemergency medical aid is not cognizable because he would "eventually qualify for the same sort of [service]". . . . The Court cannot mean that Mrs. Sosna has not suffered any injury by being foreclosed from seeking a divorce in Iowa for a year. It must instead mean that it does not regard that deprivation as being very severe.

D. REFORM AND COUNTERREFORM

The trend toward making no-fault divorce available in all states over the last three decades has drawn criticism in some quarters. One charge is that no-fault divorce has contributed to higher divorce rates because it has lessened commitment to marriage. While the data are not definitive, most studies have concluded that the greater availability of no-fault divorce has reflected, rather than caused, changing social attitudes that attach less stigma to divorce.[1] One study that analyzed every state, for instance, found that in most states increases in divorce rates occurred before the adoption of no-fault divorce.[2]

A second concern is that no-fault divorce in many cases has resulted in economic disparities between men and women after divorce. It is true that in many marriages, particularly when couples have children, husbands have greater earning power than wives. If no economic adjustments were made between husbands and wives at divorce, men consistently would tend to end up in better financial shape than women after divorce. This suggests, however that the relative position of spouses after divorce is a function mainly of the rules governing financial distributions, rather than of the grounds for divorce.

One argument that the grounds for divorce matter is that fault-based divorce gives women a bargaining chip at divorce that enables them to demand adequate compensation for assuming primary responsibility for raising children.[3] No-fault divorce, the argument goes, permits a man to pursue his career, enjoy the benefits of having his wife assume primary domestic responsibility, and then leave over his wife's objection. If divorce is available only for fault, the husband effectively will have to obtain his wife's consent to the divorce, which gives her greater bargaining leverage on matters such as financial awards.

Fault-based divorce will not, however, inevitably benefit women. If a wife is determined to be at fault, as the "guilty" spouse she may be entitled to little if any financial support under a strict fault system. One might also argue that if bargaining power is the concern, property and alimony rules could address that by establishing an adequate level of financial entitlement that would not depend on–and would in fact shape—bargaining between the spouses. These and others issues are addressed in Chapter 5, which deals with Property, Alimony, and Child Support.

1. *See, e.g.*, Andrew Cherlin, Marriage, Divorce, Remarriage 48 (1992); Ira Mark Ellman, Divorce Rates, Marriage Rates, and the Problematic Persistence of Traditional Marital Roles, 34 Fam. L. Q. 1 (2000); Norval D. Glenn, Further Discussion of the Effects of No–Fault Divorce on Divorce Rates, 61 J. Marr. & Fam. 800 (1999). For contrary views, however, see Leora Friedberg, Did Unilateral Divorce Raise Divorce Rates? 88 Am. Econ. Rev. 608 (1998); Margaret F. Brinig & F.H. Buckley, No–Fault Divorce Laws and At–Fault People, 18 Int'l J. L. Pol'y & Fam. 225 (1997).

2. Ira Mark Ellman & Sharon L. Lohr, Dissolving the Relationship Between Divorce Rates and Divorce Laws, 18 Int'l. Rev. L. & Econ. 341 (1998).

3. Margaret F. Brinig & Steven M. Crafton, Marriage and Opportunism, 23 J. Leg. Stud. 869 (1994).

Finally, concerns have been voiced about the effects of divorce on children. The most that one can say, however, seems to be that it is unwise to make sweeping general statements on this issue.[4] Some children of divorce improve on some measures of well-being, some adjust without many ill-effects, some experience short-term stress but eventually rebound, and still others suffer adverse long-term consequences. Researchers are still attempting to tease out the variables that make the most difference. At this point, however, important factors seem to be the pre-divorce level of conflict in the household and the degree of post-divorce cooperation between the parents. Chapter 4 addresses these and other concerns in its discussion of child custody.

The debate over the widespread availability of no-fault divorce is far from over. The material below discusses some features of the debate in more detail, and describes some of the proposals that have been advanced to address various concerns. Keep these issues in mind as well when you study Chapter 4 on Custody and Chapter 5 on Property, Alimony, and Child Support arrangements at divorce.

James Herbie Difonzo, Customized Marriage

75 Ind. L. J. 875 (2000).

Introduction: American Marriage and Divorce at the Dawn of the Twenty-First Century

Americans have always taken their pursuit of happiness to the altar, and the frequent failures of our marital enterprises have diminished neither our efforts nor our expectations. In a 1930 essay entitled Romantic Divorce, Katharine Fullerton Gerould identified "the American habit of acting promptly on our marital dissatisfactions," a predilection stemming from "our seeing marriage as an intensely personal and an intensely romantic affair." Connubial individualism has a lengthy pedigree. The legal theory of marriage insisted that once wife and husband wed, the legal status of their marriage was placed almost exclusively in the state's hands. But this formulation was honored only in the breach and in the halcyon rhetoric of appellate opinions. For at least a hundred years, argued Gerould, Americans "have envisaged marriage as a purely individual, not at all as a social, contract, and have refused to consider any marriage successful that did not maintain, for both parties, a high romantic satisfaction." We pay a price in this quest for "white-hot emotional perfection," of course. And Gerould judged the matter correctly, for her generation as for its successors: "As long as personal happiness is made the only desideratum in marriage, the divorce courts will be full."

But even the equable Gerould would likely have been astonished had she lived to see just how full divorce courts became in the wake of the no-

4. *See generally* Robert E. Emery, Marriage, Divorce, and Children's Adjustment (2d ed. 1999); The Post-Divorce Family: Children, Parenting, and Society (R.A. Thompson & Paul R. Amato eds. 1999); Paul R. Amato, Children and Divorce in the 1990's: An Update of the Amato and Keith (1991) Meta-Analysis, 15 J. Fam. Psychol. 355 (2001); Yongmin Sun, Family Environment and Adolescents' Well-Being Before and After Parents' Marital Disruption: A Longitudinal Analysis, 63 J. Marr. & Fam. 697 (2001); Alan Booth & Paul R. Amato, Parental Predivorce Relations and Offspring Postdivorce Well-Being, 63 J. Marr. & Fam. 197 (2001); Andrew Cherlin, P. Lindsay Chase-Lansdale & Christine McRae, Effects of Parental Divorce on Mental Health Throughout the Life Course, 63 Am. Sociol. Rev. 239 (1998).

fault divorce revolution. Between 1970 and 1996, the number of divorced Americans more than quadrupled, from 4.3 million to 18.3 million. Although the divorce rate declined slightly after its peak in the mid–1980s, we still fail at marriage almost as often as we succeed, and critics see a drift into a "divorce culture" whose goal is "the abolition of marriage," to cite the titles of two recent popular broadsides.

In reaction to the perceived excesses of no-fault divorce, a movement has crystallized to reduce the incidence of divorce in America. Reminiscent of the outraged reaction against Victoria Woodhull's "war upon marriage" a century ago, one recent indictment charged that "increased abuse and other undesirable behavior is a natural consequence of the fact that in some states the marriage contract cannot be enforced." Iowa Governor Terry Branstad criticized no-fault divorce for "transform[ing] marriage into an arrangement of convenience rather than an act of commitment." The Michigan Family Forum referred to marriage in the age of no-fault as "notarized dating." A critical analysis identified characteristics of no-fault divorce culture which nurture divorce-related violence. There are also some indications that no-fault divorce litigation is becoming more acrimonious, with the litigative fire transferred from conflicts over divorce grounds to those over children and property issues. Indeed, some harms may be self-inflicted: David Larson, for many years a research psychiatrist at the National Institutes of Health, cites the greatly increased risk of psychiatric and physical disease attributable to the process of marital dissolution:

Being divorced and a non-smoker is only slightly less dangerous than smoking a pack or more of cigarettes and staying married. Divorced men are twice as likely to die from heart disease, stroke, hypertension, and cancer as married men in any given year. Divorced women are two to three times as likely to die from various forms of cancer.

The consensus on current domestic relations stresses that the legal structure of marriage and divorce has fallen into a "state of disarray."

. . .

Counterrevolutionary legal proposals on divorce include a range of overlapping options: restoration of fault as the exclusive dissolution ground; raising the bar of divorce for couples with children; delaying the process of obtaining divorces; and mandating or encouraging anti-divorce counseling and education at both the prenuptial and pre-divorce stages. These legal experiments constitute the juridical counterpart to the popular sallies against no-fault divorce, and are best seen within the larger cultural shift away from irresponsible marital behavior, particularly in families with children. Both the legal and popular transformations also constitute a refocusing of the family dilemma from one of achieving an easy divorce to one of maintaining a good marriage.

. . .

I. The Persistent Shadow of Fault in No–Fault Divorce

A generation ago, California led the way in the most radical transformation of divorce law in American history. This divorce law "revolution" spectacularly succeeded in removing marital fault as the primary legal principle for dissolving marriages. And today the no-fault divorce reforms are also spectacularly misunderstood. Indeed, the current widespread conviction that no-fault divorce has destroyed marriage is a historical irony, as critics often mistakenly assert that the reforms were intended to expand the freedom to divorce. But the history of no-fault divorce illustrates the gulf between founding intentions and achieved effects: the major family law reforms on both sides of the Atlantic in the 1960s and 1970s were carefully considered efforts aimed at reinforcing the family and lowering the rate of divorce.

. . .

C. "The Final Stage in the Evolution of Divorce?"

. . .

At the dawn of the no-fault divorce era, expectations were high that the process of marital dissolution had been transformed not only into a more rational process, but also into one focused on vouchsafing the traditional values of maintaining the American family. Noted family law scholar Brigitte Bodenheimer predicted a smooth transition into this responsible divorce framework in her 1968 comment that "[e]ntirely unilateral divorce at the option of either spouse, without conditions, is seldom advocated today." To the contrary, another critic observed, "under the no-fault concept there is even a greater chance that the devoted spouse may save the marriage through required conciliation." The California legislature that framed modern no-fault relied on its view that the divorce court would now "sit as an overseeing participant to do its utmost to effect a healing of the marital wounds." The goals of no-fault divorce were not only clear, they seemed easily within grasp: "By requiring the consideration of the marriage as a whole and making the possibility of reconciliation the important issue, the intent is to induce a conciliatory and uncharged atmosphere which will facilitate resolution of the other issues and perhaps effect a reconciliation." America was nearing the "final stage in the evolution of divorce." The reformers believed that they had clarified and sanitized divorce, and that through their efforts the flood of divorces had been held in check. Unfortunately, the dam soon burst.

II. The Divorce Counterrevolution

"On September 5, 1969, with a stroke of his pen, California governor Ronald Reagan wiped out the moral basis for marriage in America." Thus begins the revisionist history of the divorce counterrevolution. The mid to late 1960s have been described as the "cultural fault line, the B.C. and A.D. of American divorce."

After that decade, the legal and social systems no longer considered divorce a concern involving "multiple stakeholders." Divorce abruptly became a solo voyage, often characterized as an immoral flight from responsibility. The legal system rejected the culpability-ground-turned-entitlement theory of divorce. But enacting the marital breakdown standard never resulted in a searching judicial inquiry into the state of each marriage, as many no-fault divorce reformers had hoped. Irreconcilable differences simply were not justiciable. As Mary Ann Glendon later reported, "the virtually universal understanding . . . is that the breakdown of a marriage is irretrievable if one spouse says it is." No-fault divorce became naked divorce.

. . .

But in the generation since the creation of no-fault divorce, a strong argument has emerged that the "happiness principle embedded in the no-fault ground has dealt a devastating blow to the durability of marriages." Contemporary scholarly accounts are rife with calls for an end to a divorce process seen as facilitating individual irresponsibility at the expense of mutuality and the welfare of children. Many accounts in the popular press have also taken a cudgel to no-fault divorce, professing that "a whole generation . . . has placed its marital future in a [no-fault] law that favors the unfaithful, the uncommitted, the selfish and the immature. . . . 'Till death do us part' was replaced by 'as long as I'm happy.' "

. . .

B. A Comeback for Culpability?

The campaign to reverse the perceived evils of the no-fault revolution has yielded a wide variety of counter-reform measures in legislatures, the academy, and the popular press. These proposals to eliminate or raise the threshold of no-fault divorce range from rewriting the constitution to enforcing pre-commitment restrictions on divorce, and include a variety of counseling and educational requirements, both mandatory and hortatory. The once-unthinkable return of a culpability hurdle for divorce has not only been thought, it has appeared in state house bills attempting to undo the no-fault revolution root and branch.

In 1991, social critic Christopher Lasch proposed the "most draconian proposal of the burgeoning divorce-buster movement," a constitutional amendment banning divorce for married couples with minor children:

> Marriage should be undertaken only by those who view it as a lifelong commitment and are prepared to accept the consequences, foreseeable and unforeseeable, of such a commitment. No state shall pass laws authorizing divorce for any but the weightiest reasons. In the case of couples with children under the age of twenty-one, divorce is hereby forbidden.

. . .

[I]n articulating a difference between marriages based on the presence of children, Lasch anticipated another wing of counter-revolutionary thought. Grounded in the belief that divorce harms children, who are the innocent victims of their parents' quest for individualized happiness, reformers have called for treating marriages with children significantly different than those without. Many proposals to change our legal structure assert society's interest in preserving intact nuclear families and aim at deterring or delaying divorces in families with children.

. . .

C. "Children First"

. . .

The 1990s have seen a growing legislative effort to focus on children of divorce. In the most widely discussed bid, Michigan State Representative Jessie F. Dalman introduced in 1995 an eleven-bill package heralded as "the state of the art on divorce policy." Dalman's proposals would have established a two-tier divorce system. In families without children, or in which the children were all emancipated, the couple could obtain a divorce upon mutual consent. But in families with minor children, or where one spouse objected to the dissolution, the divorce-seeking spouse would have to prove the marital fault of the other. The reinvigorated fault grounds were the historically familiar ones of adultery, desertion, and extreme cruelty, which would have to be established by a "preponderance of the evidence." Additionally, parents seeking divorce would be required to undergo counseling about the potential effects of divorce.

Other states have attempted similar measures. A 1997 Texas bill would have allowed divorce "without regard to fault" when the marriage becomes "insupportable because of discord or conflict of personalities that destroys the legitimate ends of the marriage relationship and prevents any reasonable expectation of reconciliation." But divorce on this ground would be available only to childless couples who had passed their first wedding anniversary. A measure introduced in Virginia in 1998 would have prohibited no-fault divorce if the parties have a minor child and either party files a written objection to the initial pleading within 21 days of service. A Hawaii bill would have required a one-year waiting period and mandatory counseling after a divorce filing in cases with minor children. Counseling sessions specifically including all children aged six to sixteen would have been mandated by a Pennsylvania measure. An Illinois bill would have limited no-fault divorce actions to couples who experienced a separation period, and-if the couple had a dependent child, the marriage were of ten or more years' duration, or the wife was pregnant-mutual consent. These laws were broadly aimed at authorizing courts " 'to consider what's best for the entire family, instead of being required to grant the desire of only one spouse who wants out.' "

Scholarly critics have kept pace with their legislative counterparts, and have often inspired or helped shape the reform proposals. William Galston has called for the elimination of unilateral no-fault divorce in marriages with minor children. Parents who seek divorce would, in Galston's scheme, either have to establish a fault ground against their spouse, or wait to get divorced until they had been separated for five years.

NOTE

Would it be desirable to have a "two-tier" divorce system, in which it was more difficult for a couple to obtain a divorce if they have minor children?

Paul R. Amato, Commentary: Good Enough Marriages: Parental Discord, Divorce, and Children's Long-Term Well Being

9 Va. J. Soc. Pol'y & L. 71, 92–94 (2001).

. . .

Some people may question the efficacy of marriage counseling for divorcing couples. After all, they might argue, by the time couples apply for divorce, the marriage has deteriorated to a point where it cannot be salvaged. But the research described here suggests otherwise. Many, perhaps most, divorces are *not* preceded by severe, chronic, destructive levels of discord. Indeed, some of these marriages seem to be functioning reasonably well as little as a year prior to divorce. There is much to build on in these marriages. Furthermore, the knowledge that children are more likely to be harmed than benefited when a "good enough" marriage ends in divorce could provide an additional incentive for these couples to attempt a reconciliation. These considerations suggest that screening for low-discord couples prior to marital dissolution and targeting this group for education and counseling could be useful strategies for preventing the divorces that are most damaging to children.

Rather than addressing the problem on a case-by-case basis, it would be easier to lower the divorce rate legislatively by making marital dissolution more difficult to obtain, perhaps by returning to fault-based grounds for divorce. The research described in this paper, however, does not support this idea. Although divorce harms some children, it benefits others. If we make divorce more difficult to obtain, then we are likely to benefit some children in low-discord marriages, but we also are likely to harm some children in high-discord marriages. These tradeoffs do not make this strategy appealing as a method for protecting children.

If we accept that it would be useful to lower the rate of divorce among low-discord couples, for the sake of the children, then this raises the question of whether we should try to do something for children living with parents in discordant but stable marriages. Should we attempt to *increase* the rate of divorce in these families? Although it seems like a harsh and unpopular policy to encourage some couples to divorce, it might be advisable in cases where violence or abuse is present in the marriage. More realistically, it would seem prudent not to put barriers in the way of these couples when they seek divorce, and to allow these dissolutions to occur as expeditiously as possible.

This line of reasoning raises another interesting question: If we could distribute a minimum number of divorces to couples every year in a way that maximizes children's well-being, then what effect would that have on the current level of divorce in our society? Would the overall divorce rate go down, go up, or remain unchanged? Although very speculative, one could use the data described above to provide a first step toward an answer. Currently, about 40% of marriages with children are projected to end in divorce. Further analysis of our data suggests that about half of children are harmed by divorce and about half of children are helped by divorce.

Cutting the divorce population in half would reduce projected divorces among couples with children from 40% to 20%. In addition, we might also want to facilitate divorce among truly troubled couples [estimated at 10% of all couples] . . . Encouraging these couples to end their marriages would increase the divorce projection to 26% (20% + [.10 × 60]). These admittedly simple calculations suggest that the current divorce rate is higher than it should be, and that a reduction of about 35% in the number of marriages ending in dissolution would provide an optimal level of divorce in American society, at least as far as children are concerned. Of course, this reasoning is based on the assumption of no increase in the availability or success of marriage education, counseling, and therapy. If we could find ways to lower the level of discord in marriages with children, then the divorce rate could be safely lowered even more . . .

Herma Hill Kay, From the Second Sex to the Joint Venture: An Overview of Women's Rights and Family Law in the United States During the Twentieth Century

88 Calif. L. Rev. 2017 (2000).

. . .

K. Fixing No-Fault: The ALI's "Principles of Family Dissolution"

In contrast to the criticism of no-fault divorce by some feminists and conservatives, the American Law Institute [has] sought to build on, clarify, and complete the earlier reforms. In 1989, it reopened the family law reform effort by commencing a project called The Principles of the Law of Family Dissolution. Noting that the law of family dissolution had undergone fundamental revision in the previous two decades, the ALI spelled out the scope of its proposed project:

> These evolving legal developments generally have dealt incompletely with issues, have overlapped one another, and sometimes have resulted in internal conflict in the law itself. The resulting uncertainty suggests a need to examine the present state of legal development, to clarify underlying principles, and to suggest the future direction for public policy.

The ALI did not plan to revisit the grounds for divorce. Instead, it accepted the nationwide adoption of no-fault divorce, and undertook to complete that reform by drafting provisions dealing with the process of dissolution and the substantive standards relevant to child support, spousal support, property division, and custody of children. Under the current leadership of Chief Reporter Ira Mark Ellman and Co-Reporters Grace Ganz Blumberg and Katharine T. Bartlett, the ALI project received final approval from the Institute in May 2000.

The Principles are both imaginative and practical. The property division sections offer a redefinition of "marital" and "separate" property for use at dissolution that generally follows community property concepts. They steer a middle course between the "equitable division" and "equal division" states by calling for a presumptive equal division of marital property subject to specified exceptions. They also provide for the gradual recharacterization in lengthy marriages of a portion of separate property into marital property.

"Maintenance" is renamed "Compensatory Spousal Payments" in the Principles, and the draft draws on Professor Ira Mark Ellman's earlier work on alimony in seeking to allocate financial losses that arise at the dissolution of marriage according to specified principles rather than simply basing income transfers on need and ability to pay. Five categories of compensable loss are recognized: (1) those arising from the loss of a higher living standard by the spouse with less wealth or earning capacity at the end of a marriage of significant duration; (2) those arising from the loss of earning capacity during marriage and continuing after dissolution because of one spouse's undertaking a disproportionate share of the care of children; (3) those arising from the loss of earning capacity during marriage and continuing after dissolution because of one spouse's caring for a sick, elderly, or disabled third party in fulfillment of a joint moral obligation; (4) those arising from the loss incurred by either spouse when the marriage is dissolved before that spouse "realizes a fair return from his or her investment in the other spouse's earning capacity"; and (5) an "unfairly disproportionate disparity between the spouses in their respective abilities to recover their pre-marital living standard after the dissolution of a short marriage." Some of the policy choices reflected in the draft have been criticized, but they are important advances beyond present law.

The ALI child custody recommendations seek to avoid the "best interests of the child" standard, criticizing it as too subjective to produce predictable results. Instead, the Principles rely on private ordering, requiring that each party who seeks "a judicial allocation of custodial responsibility or decisionmaking responsibility" file a parenting plan. If the parents agree to one or more provisions of a parenting agreement, the court should enforce the agreement unless it finds either that the agreement is not "knowing or voluntary" or that "the plan would be harmful to the child." If the parents are unable to agree, the draft allocates custodial responsibility "so that the proportion of custodial time the child spends with each parent approximates the proportion of time each parent spent performing caretaking functions for the child prior to the parents' separation."

. . .

Chapter Six extends most of the provisions governing financial claims between spouses to domestic partners, defined as "two persons of the same or opposite sex, not married to one another, who for a significant period of time share a primary residence and a life together as a couple." Persons who maintain a common household with their common child for a specified continuous period of time are deemed to be domestic partners; if these circumstances are not present, the person claiming benefits must prove that the parties met the definition. Domestic partners may contract out of these provisions.

Chapter Seven undertakes to reformulate and clarify the law relating to premarital agreements, marital agreements, and separation agreements. They are tailored to the substantive provisions of the draft. While the Principles are still a work in progress at the century's end, it is apparent that, after nearly ten years of development and refinement, the ALI's Family Law Project has achieved its goal of clarifying the underlying principles relevant to family dissolution and offering a sound basis for future public policy making. Family breakdown is accepted as a given, and an appropriate, basis for dissolution, and the legal framework surrounding the Project's implementation is oriented towards fair treatment that is nonpunitive, nonsexist, nonpaternalistic, and designed as far as possible to facilitate positive outcomes for each of the individuals involved. The means chosen to achieve these ends are practical and predictable. Furthermore, they avoid undue deference to the often subjective discretion of judges to a larger extent than do the compromises imposed on both the Family Law Act and the UMDA. Fortunately, the American Law Institute approved the Principles without subjecting them to similar compromises. Now that the Principles have won approval, they deserve serious and sympathetic consideration from twenty-first century lawmakers, for they have responded to the major criticisms of no-fault divorce.

NOTE

As we will see in Chapters 5 and 6, the law is still working through the implications of no-fault divorce for custody and financial distribution decisions, respectively. The ALI Principles represent one effort to address these implications in a systematic way, as well as to take account of issues that arise when unmarried cohabitants separate. Chapters 5 and 6 will include excerpts from these Principles.

CHAPTER 5

Custody of Children

Obtaining a divorce is often the easiest part of a marital dissolution. Contests over custody of children and money, by contrast, which are the subject of this Chapter and the next, are often not only more intensely fought but may continue for years after the divorce decree is rendered. As you review the material in this Chapter, consider what changes in the legal standards employed or the process followed might discourage such continued feuding between former spouses. Consider also the impact of different custody standards on bargaining between the parties at the time of divorce.

A. Bargaining Over Custody

Most custody arrangements are the result of agreements between the divorcing parties rather than the outcome of litigation. The rules governing custody and visitation, however, provide an important backdrop against which bargaining occurs. Furthermore, litigation dealing with those rules often serves as an occasion for considering broader social issues, such as the respective roles of men and women, racial and ethnic identity, religious commitments, rights and obligations in non-marital intimate relationships, and sexual orientation.

The following influential article discusses some of the dynamics that operate when parties engage in bargaining over custody, as well as the potential impact of legal rules on that process. Keep these insights in mind as we move on in the remainder of the Chapter to the legal provisions that govern the variety of issues that arise with respect to custody and visitation.

Robert Mnookin and Lewis Kornhauser, Bargaining in the Shadow of the Law: The Case of Divorce

88 Yale L.J. 950, 951, 954–957 (1979).

. . .

Available evidence concerning how divorce proceedings actually work suggests that a reexamination from the perspective of private ordering is timely. "Typically, the parties do not go to court at all, until they have worked matters out and are ready for the rubber stamp." Both in the United States and in England, the overwhelming majority of divorcing couples resolve distributional questions concerning marital property, alimony, child support, and custody without bringing any contested issue to court for adjudication.

The parties' power to determine the consequences of divorce depends on the presence of children. When the divorcing couple has no children, the law generally recognizes the power of the parties upon separation or divorce to make their own arrangements concerning marital property and alimony . . .

In families with minor children, existing law imposes substantial doctrinal constraints. For those allocational decisions that directly affect children—that is, child support, custody, and visitation—parents lack the formal power to make their own law. Judges, exercising the state's *parens patriae power*, are said to have responsibility to determine who should have custody and on what conditions. Private agreements concerning these matters are possible and common, but agreements cannot bind the court, which, as a matter of official dogma, is said to have an independent responsibility for determining what arrangement best serves the child's welfare. Thus, the court has the power to reject a parental agreement and order some other level of child support or some other custodial arrangement it believes to be more desirable.

. . .

On the other hand, available evidence on how the legal system processes undisputed divorce cases involving minor children suggests that parents actually have broad powers to make their own deals. Typically, separation agreements are rubber stamped even in cases involving children.

. . .

The parents' broad discretion is not surprising for several reasons. First, getting information is difficult when there is no dispute. The state usually has very limited resources for a thorough and independent investigation of the family's circumstances. Furthermore, parents may be unwilling to provide damaging information that may upset their agreed arrangements. Second, the applicable legal standards are extremely vague and give judges very little guidance as to what circumstances justify overriding a parental decision. Finally, there are obvious limitations on a court's practical power to control the parents once they leave the courtroom. For all these reasons, it is not surprising that most courts behave as if their function in the divorce process is dispute settlement, not child protection. When there is no dispute, busy judges or registrars are typically quite willing to rubber stamp a private agreement, in order to conserve resources for disputed cases.

. . . There are obvious and substantial savings when a couple can resolve distributional consequences of divorce without resort to courtroom adjudication. The financial cost of litigation, both private and public, is minimized. The pain of a formal adversary proceeding is avoided. Recent psychological studies indicate that children benefit when parents agree on custodial arrangements. Moreover, a negotiated agreement allows the parties to avoid the risks and uncertainties of litigation, which may involve all-or-nothing consequences. Given the substantial delays that often characterize contested judicial proceedings, agreement can often save time and allow each spouse to proceed with his or her life. Finally, a consensual solution is by definition more likely to be consistent with the preferences of each spouse, and acceptable over time, than would a result imposed by a court.

. . .

Legal doctrine separates the potential consequences of divorce into four distributional questions: (1) how should the couple's property—the stock of existing wealth owned separately or together—be divided? (marital property law); (2) what ongoing claims should each spouse have on the future earnings of the other (alimony law); (3) what on-going claims should a child have for a share of the earnings or wealth of each of his parents? (child-support law); and (4) how should the responsibilities and opportunities of child rearing be divided in the future? (child-custody and visitation law).

. . .

[Examining the bargaining from the perspective of spouses who are negotiating their own divorce settlements suggests that] the money and custody issues are inextricably linked.

. . .

CUSTODY

. . . By varying the time the child spends with each parent, and by assigning particular child-rearing tasks to one parent or the other, a divorce settlement may divide prerogatives in many different ways. At the extreme, one parent may be entirely responsible for the child all the time, with the other spouse spending no time with the child. Or, divorcing parents may agree to share child-rearing responsibilities equally after divorce through joint custody. For example, the child may live with each parent one-half of the time, with the parents together deciding where and how the child should be educated, who the pediatrician should be, etc. Between these extremes, many other alternatives are often possible.

THE RELATIONSHIP OF CUSTODY AND MONEY

. . .

[T]o a considerable degree, it is possible to reduce the concerns of divorce bargaining into two elements: money and custody. From a bargaining perspective, even these two elements are inextricably linked for two reasons: over some range of alternatives, each parent may be willing to exchange custodial rights and obligations for income or wealth, and parents may tie support duties to custodial prerogatives as a means of enforcing their rights without resort to court.

Economic analysis suggests that a parent may, over some range, trade custodial rights for money. Although this notion may offend some, a contrary assertion would mean that a parent with full custody would accept no sum of money in exchange for slightly less custody, even if the parent were extremely poor. Faced with such alternatives, most parents would prefer to see the child a bit less and be able to give the child better housing, more food, more education, better health care, and some luxuries. Suggesting the possibility of such trade-offs does not mean that the parent would be willing to relinquish all time with the child for a sufficiently large sum of money. Indeed, with a minimum level of resources, a parent may have a parallel minimum of custodial rights for the reduction of which no additional payment, however large, could be adequate compensation.

The negotiating process itself provides many opportunities for the parties to link money and custody issues. The most obvious opportunity exists in the context of enforcement of support or visitation. The legal system does not permit these connections in most states: in a suit brought to collect overdue support payments, a father cannot defend on the ground that his ex-wife did not permit visitation. Nor have courts permitted a custodial parent to cut off visitation because of a failure to pay support. Nevertheless, it is often time-consuming and expensive to enforce promises in court. There can be substantial advantages, therefore, from the perspective of one or both bargainers, in having piecemeal bargains that spread support payments over time and, as a practical matter, link the custody issue (especially visitation) with the financial issues. If a father who values visitation fails to make support payments, then, quite apart from the mother's ability to enforce his promise in court (which may often be too slow and expensive to be effective), the mother may believe that she can retaliate by informally cutting off the father's visitation or making it more difficult. Even though this tactic has no legal validity, it is nevertheless likely to be faster, cheaper, and more effective than court enforcement. Similarly, a father may believe that his ability to cut off support will ensure that the mother will keep her word concerning visitation.

HOW LEGAL RULES CREATE BARGAINING ENDOWMENTS

Divorcing parents do not bargain over the division of family wealth and custodial prerogatives in a vacuum; they bargain in the shadow of the law. The legal rules governing alimony, child support, marital property, and custody give each parent certain claims based on what each would get if the case went to trial. In other words, the outcome that the law will impose if no agreement is reached gives each parent certain bargaining chips—an endowment of sorts.

A simplified example may be illustrative. Assume that in disputed custody cases the law flatly provided that all mothers had the right to custody of minor children and that all fathers only had the right to visitation two weekends a month. Absent some contrary agreement acceptable to both parents, a court would order this arrangement. Assume further that the legal rules relating to marital property, alimony, and child support gave the mother some determinate share of the family's economic resources. In negotiations under this regime, neither spouse would ever consent to a division that left him or her worse off than if he or she insisted on going to court. The range of negotiated outcomes would be limited to those that leave both parents as well off as they would be in the absence of a bargain.

If private ordering were allowed, we would not necessarily expect parents to split custody and money the way a judge would if they failed to agree. The father might well negotiate for more child-time and the mother for less. This result might occur either because the father made the mother better off by giving her additional money to compensate her for accepting less child-time, or because the mother found custody burdensome and considered herself better off with less custody. Indeed, she might agree to accept less money, or even to pay the father, if he agreed to relieve her of some child-rearing responsibilities. In all events, because the parents' tastes with regard to the trade-offs between money and child-time may differ, it will often be possible for the parties to negotiate some outcome that makes both better off than they would be if they simply accepted the result a court would impose.

PRIVATE ORDERING AGAINST A BACKDROP OF UNCERTAINTY

Legal rules are generally not as simple or straightforward as is suggested by the last example. Often, the outcome in court is far from certain, with any number of outcomes possible. Indeed, existing legal standards governing custody, alimony, child support, and marital property are all striking for their lack of precision and thus provide a bargaining backdrop clouded by uncertainty.

. . .

Analyzing the effects of uncertainty on bargaining is an extremely complicated task. It is apparent, however, that the effects in any particular case will depend in part on the attitudes of the two spouses toward risk—what economists call "risk preferences." This can be illustrated by considering a mechanism suggested in Beyond the Best Interests of the Child for resolving custody disputes between equally acceptable spouses: they would draw straws, with the winner getting full custodial rights and the loser none.

Because drawing straws, like flipping a coin, gives each parent a fifty percent chance of receiving full custody, economic theory suggests that for each parent the "expected" outcome is half-custody. We cannot, however, simply assume that each parent will bargain as if receiving half of the child's time were certain. Attitudes toward risk may be defined by asking a parent to compare two alternatives: (1) a certainty of having one-half of the child's time; or (2) a gamble in which the "expected" or average outcome is one-half of the child's time. By definition, a parent who treats these alternatives as equally desirable is risk-neutral. A parent who would accept a certain outcome of less than half-custody in order to avoid the gamble—the chance of losing the coin flip and receiving no custody—is risk-averse. Other parents may be risk preferrers: they would rather take the gamble and have a fifty percent chance of winning full custody than accept the certain outcome of split custody.

STRATEGIC BEHAVIOR

The actual bargain that is struck through negotiations—indeed, whether a bargain is struck at all—depends on the negotiation process. During this process, each party transmits information about his or her own preferences to the other. This information may be accurate or intentionally inaccurate; each party may promise, threaten, or bluff. Parties may intentionally exaggerate their chances of winning in court in the hope of persuading the other side to accept less. Or they may threaten to impose substantial transaction costs—economic or psychological—on the other side. In short, there are a variety of ways in which the parties may engage in strategic behavior during the bargaining process.

Opportunities for strategic behavior exist because the parties often will not know with certainty (1) the other side's true preferences with regard to the allocational outcomes; and (2) the other spouse's preferences or attitudes towards risk; and (3) what the outcome in court will be, or even what the actual odds in court are. Although parents may know a great deal about each other's preferences for money and children, complete knowledge of the other spouse's attitudes is unlikely.

How do the parties and their representatives actually behave during the process? Two alternative models are suggested by the literature: (1) a Strategic Model, which would characterize the process as "a relatively norm-free process centered on the transmutation of underlying bargaining strength into agreement by the exercise of power, horse-trading, threat, and bluff"; and (2) a Norm–Centered Model, which would characterize the process by elements normally associated with adjudication—the parties and their representatives would invoke rules, cite precedents, and engage in reasoned elaboration. Anecdotal observation suggests that each model captures part of the flavor of the process. The parties and their representatives do make appeals to legal and social norms in negotiation, but they frequently threaten and bluff as well.

Given the advantages of negotiated settlements, why do divorcing spouses ever require courtroom adjudication of their disputes? There are a variety of reasons why some divorce cases will be litigated:

1. *Spite.* One or both parties may be motivated in substantial measure by a desire to punish the other spouse, rather than simply to increase their own net worth.

2. *Distaste for Negotiation.* Even though it costs more, one or both parties may prefer the adjudicative process (with third-party decision) to any process that requires a voluntary agreement with the other spouse. Face-to-face contact may be extremely distasteful, and the parties may not be able to negotiate—even with lawyers acting as intermediaries—because of distrust or distaste.

3. *Calling the Bluff—The Breakdown of Negotiations.* If the parties get heavily engaged in strategic behavior and get carried away with making threats, a courtroom battle may result, despite both parties' preference for a settlement. Negotiations may resemble a game of "chicken" in which two teenagers set their cars on a collision course to see who turns first. Some crack-ups may result.

4. *Uncertainty and Risk Preferences.* The exact odds for any given outcome in court are unknown, and it has been suggested that litigants typically overestimate their chances of winning. To the extent that one or both of the parties typically overestimate their chances of winning, more cases will be litigated than in a world in which the outcome is uncertain but the odds are known. In any event, when the outcome is uncertain, settlement prospects depend on the risk preferences of the two spouses.

5. *No Middle Ground.* If the object of dispute cannot be divided into small enough increments—whether because of the law, the practical circumstances, or the nature of the subject at issue—there may be no middle ground on which to strike a feasible compromise. Optimal bargaining occurs when, in economic terminology, nothing is indivisible.

These points can be illustrated through a simple example. Assume a divorcing couple has no children and the only issue is how they will divide 100 shares of stock worth $10,000. Let us further assume that it would cost each spouse $1,000 to have a court decide this issue, and that each spouse must pay his own litigation costs.

If the outcome in court were entirely certain, would the parties ever litigate? Suppose it were clear that a court would inevitably award one-half of the stock to each spouse because it would be characterized as community property. If the issue were litigated, each spouse would end up with only $4,000. A spouse would therefore never accept a settlement offer of less than $4,000. One might expect that the parties would normally simply settle for $5,000, and save the costs of litigation. Taking the issue to court would substitute an expensive mode of dispute resolution—adjudication—for a cheaper mode—negotiation.

Even when the outcome in court is certain, litigation is still possible. A spouse might engage in strategic behavior and threaten to litigate in order to get more than half. Suppose the husband threatened to litigate unless the wife agreed to accept a settlement of $4,500. The wife might accept $4,500 but only if she believed the threat. She would know with proper legal advice that her husband would only end up with $4,000 if he litigated. Therefore the threat ordinarily would not be credible. She might call his bluff and tell him to sue. If the wife were convinced, however, that her husband was motivated by spite and in fact preferred to litigate rather than accept less than $5,500, she might accept $4,500. If the outcome in court is certain, then, absent spite, strategic behavior, or a distaste for negotiations, adjudication should not generally occur; litigation would impose an expensive mode of dispute settlement when a less expensive alternative could achieve the same result.

What about cases in which the result in court is uncertain? Assume, for example, that there is a fifty percent chance that the husband will get all $10,000, and a fifty percent chance that the wife will get all $10,000. Settlement in these circumstances obviously depends on the risk preferences of the two spouses. If both are risk-neutral, then both will negotiate the same way as they would if they knew for certain that a court would award each of them $5,000—the "expected" value of the litigation in this case.

To the extent that the parties are both risk-averse—each is prepared to accept less than $5,000 to avoid the risks of litigation—the parties have a broader range of possible settlements that both would prefer to the risks of litigation. This may facilitate agreement.

Conversely, if both parties are risk preferrers—each prefers the gamble to an offer of the expected value of $5,000—all cases are likely to be litigated. When one party is a risk preferrer and the other is risk-averse, it is difficult to predict the effect on the rate of litigation. In any negotiated outcome, a risk preferrer will have an advantage over the party who is risk-averse.

NOTE

1. Courts are authorized to scrutinize parental agreements dealing with custody more stringently than agreements on matters that concern other aspects of separation or divorce. Thus, a court may reject a custody agreement not only on standard contract grounds such as lack of voluntariness, but on the ground that it is not in the best interest of the child. *See, e.g.*, Ohio Rev. Code Ann. § 3109.04(D)(1)(a)(i) (2001); Wis. Stat. Ann. § 767.11(12)(a) (2000). Some states, however, require a court to adopt a custody agreement unless it makes findings on the record that support a conclusion that the agreement is not in the child's best interest. See, e.g., Mass. Ann. Laws ch. 208, § 31 (2000). In Michigan, the court must determine by "clear and convincing evidence" that the custody arrangement is not in the best interest of the child. Mich. Comp. Laws Ann. § 722.27a(2) (2001).

Reporter's Notes to the American Law Institute's Principles of the Law of Family Dissolution, however, declare, "Despite judicial rhetoric about the reviewability of [custody] agreements, agreements are rarely rejected on any grounds." American Law Institute, Principles of the Law of Family Dissolution, Chapter 2, Topic 2, § 2.06, Reporter's Notes, comment a, at 163 (2002). The ALI itself recommends that a court should accept the provisions of a plan agreed to by the parents unless it is not knowing or voluntary, or it would be harmful to the trial. ALI Principles, § 2.06(1).

2. Agreements on custody sometimes are the product of mediation. Reporter's Notes to the ALI Principles indicate that about one-fourth of the states require mediation for custody and visitation issues, somewhat fewer than half explicitly allow the court to use its discretion to require mediation for such issues, and that a few states have a voluntary mediation process. American Law Institute, Principles of the Law of Family Dissolution, Chapter 2, Topic 2, § 2.07, Reporter's Notes, comment b, at 171 (2002). In most states, mediation is prohibited in cases involving domestic violence. *Id.* For thoughtful appraisals of the use of mediation in custody matters, see Connie J.A. Beck & Bruce D. Sales, A Critical Reappraisal of Divorce Mediation Research and Policy, 6 Psychol. Pub. Pol'y L. 898 (2000); Joan B. Kelly, Psychological and Legal Interventions for Parents and Children in Custody and Access Disputes: Current Research and Practice, 10 Va. J. Soc. Pol'y & L. 129 (2002).

B. THE BEST INTEREST STANDARD

State statutes typically direct courts to make custody decisions in accordance with the best interest of the child. Uniform Marriage and Divorce Act § 402 provides an example of the considerations that a court is to take into account when making this determination.

Uniform Marriage and Divorce Act
SECTION 402. Best Interest of Child

The court shall determine custody in accordance with the best interest of the child. The court shall consider all relevant factors including:

(1) the wishes of the child's parent or parents as to his custody;

(2) the wishes of the child as to his custodian;

(3) the interaction and interrelationship of the child with his parent or parents, his siblings, and any other person who may significantly affect the child's best interest;

(4) the child's adjustment to his home, school, and community; and

(5) the mental and physical health of all individuals involved.

The court shall not consider conduct of a proposed custodian that does not affect his relationship to the child.

COMMENT

This section, excepting the last sentence, is designed to codify existing law in most jurisdictions. It simply states that the trial court must look to a variety of factors to determine what is the child's best interest. The five factors mentioned specifically are those most commonly relied upon in the appellate opinions; but the language of the section makes it clear that the judge need not be limited to the factors specified. Although none of the familiar presumptions developed by the case law are mentioned here, the language of the section is consistent with preserving such rules of thumb. The preference for the mother as custodian of young children when all things are equal, for example, is simply a shorthand method of expressing the best interest of children—and this section enjoins judges to decide custody cases according to that general standard. The same analysis is appropriate to the other common presumptions: a parent is usually preferred to a nonparent; the existing custodian is usually preferred to any new custodian because of the interest in assuring continuity for the child; preference is usually given to the custodian chosen by agreement of the parents. In the case of modification, there is also a specific provision designed to foster Continuity of custodians and discourage change. See Section 409.

The last sentence of the section changes the law in those states which continue to use fault notions in custody adjudication. There is no reason to encourage parties to spy on each other in order to discover marital (most commonly, sexual) misconduct for use in a custody contest. This provision makes it clear that unless a contestant is able to prove that the parent's behavior in fact affects his relationship to the child (a standard which could seldom be met if the parent's behavior has been circumspect or unknown to the child), evidence of such behavior is irrelevant.

C. Rose v. Rose

1. The Trial

DRAMATIS PERSONAE[1]

For the Plaintiff

Diane Winter Rose, plaintiff

Doctor Samuel Winter, her father

Amanda Winter, her mother

Polly Winter)
) her sisters
Nancy Winter)

Doug and Deborah Nathan, her friends and former neighbors

Mr. Fisk, her lawyer

For the Defendant

Steven Rose, defendant

Harold Rose, his father

Alice Rose, his mother

Keith Bennett, his friend

Mr. Mellon, his lawyer

SETTING

A Courtroom in the State of Washington Spring, 1985

THE COURT: Okay, gentlemen, we're ready to proceed on the matter of Rose versus Rose, I understand.

MR. FISK: That's correct, Your Honor.

MR. MELLON: Yes, Your Honor.

THE COURT: Okay, you may proceed.

1. George Mitchell, M.D.—For the Plaintiff

a. Direct Examination by Mr. Fisk.

Q. Doctor, are you a licensed physician? **A.** Yes, I'm licensed.

Q. In what state are you licensed? **A.** I'm licensed in the State of Maryland and in the State of Texas.

Q. Where do you practice? **A.** I practice in Kensington, Maryland.

[Dr. Mitchell next outlines his professional qualifications. He has board certification in psychiatry and neurology, and graduated from the Washington Psychoanalytic Institute. He has been a psychiatrist since 1952.]

Q. Can you tell the Court when you first saw Diane Rose and under what circumstances? **A.** Well, I first saw Diane on April the 7th, 1984.

1. This transcript is derived from an actual proceeding. Most names and identifying features have been changed to protect the privacy of participants.

Q. You were aware that she had made a suicide attempt? **A.** Yes, she had made a suicidal attempt by leaping from an eighth-story window, but had landed in a tree which had obstructed her fall and she survived it.

Q. Was she in the hospital when you first saw her? **A.** Yes, I saw her in the hospital on April the 7th. That was a Sunday morning, at about seven-thirty in the morning.

Q. Now, before you actually saw her did you have occasion to meet the husband, Steven Rose, or his mother, Alice Rose? **A.** I met them both. I met Steve and Alice at the—on the north end of the building on the first floor by the elevator.

Q. How did you happen to meet them there? **A.** Well, they were waiting there for me.

Q. Okay. Would you just tell the Court what happened? **A.** Well, they—I felt that they put me under great pressure to adopt their viewpoint of the case.

MR. MELLON: I'm going to object to that as a conclusion, Your Honor. He can state what happened. I move to strike that.

MR. FISK: Counsel would prefer you say what they told you and—

THE COURT: I'm going to overrule the objection at any rate.

A. They told me that Diane Rose was unable to love and, therefore, could not take care of her baby and was, therefore, too uncomfortable to live with the child. They told me that she was—that her mother was cold and that her father was far withdrawn from his children. I felt literally accosted. I tried to make some remarks that Diane Rose had to learn to take this responsibility and understand this move that she had made; and that I didn't think that anyone should be blamed right offhand. But I heard much blaming and—

Q. By the elevator you mean? **A.** Yes.

Q. Now, Doctor, is this a usual way that you interview one of your proposed patients, by the elevator, or do you usually go and interview the patients themselves—or herself? **A.** I usually see that patient first and then talk with the relatives, if they wish, and if the patient permits me to.

Q. All right. Then subsequent to being approached by Alice and Steve Rose, did you then go talk to Diane Rose? **A.** Yes, I talked to Diane Rose that morning of April the 7th.

Q. Who was there besides Diane, if anyone? **A.** Well, Diane had a nurse, and there was—the hospital—the ward nurse was there. And they very kindly provided me with a room where I could talk with Diane.

Q. In private? **A.** In private. And I talked with her in private for around an hour. And at this time Diane had some signs of organic brain damage. Her speech was somewhat garbled and her gait was scissory, and she seemed to be slow in her responses and to have an ironing-out of the facial musculature.

I tried to move slowly and find out about her psychological state. At that time she was not psychotic. She appeared very frightened and very tense and under great stress. She seemed to have only one thing in mind, and that was to whitewash her marital life, which I tried to ask her about and tried to find out what had obtained at the time in January of 1984. I didn't get very far and I tried not to pressure her for this information, but she did say that she loved her mother, she loved her father, she loved her sister, and she named each one; and that she loved Steve and she loved Alice and that she loved the baby. And it was—it was really a paucity of thought or a limitation of thought in her reporting to me, but I did find out that she didn't have loss of memory or sensory deficits that I could measure simply through an interview. I judged that she was guarding and the thoughts that she gave me were rather in direct opposition to the thoughts that I had had at the foot of the elevator when I first came into the building and that I had heard from Steve and Alice Rose.

When I left Diane, I arranged an appointment with her or told her that I would call her and arrange an appointment, I can't remember just how this came about.

Q. Anyway, a further appointment was arranged? **A.** Yes, a further appointment was arranged for three weeks later. I believe it was—April the 27th when I next saw her. But when I left the building, Steve and his mother were still waiting—

Q. And did they—**A.**—and still pressured me with the same kind of demand, that I listen to their theory of their case. I felt much disrespect to my professional stance and I felt this was a very hostile act toward the patient and her family to intercede in this way.

Q. Did they appear hostile towards Diane to you?

A. Well,—

MR. MELLON: I'm going to object—

A. —they said that Diane—

THE COURT: I'm sorry.

MR. MELLON: I object to that, Your Honor. I think—

MR. FISK: The doctor can testify.

THE COURT: I'm going to overrule it.

A. They said that—they said that Diane could not love; that Diane could not take care of the baby; and that it was for this reason that she jumped. And this was a—I felt that the force and insistence with which they brought these thoughts to me indicated that they had to have it that way.

Q. All right. Now, you saw her again three weeks later? **A.** Yes, I saw her again on April the 27th.

Q. Where did you see her at this time? **A.** I saw her in my office in Kensington, Maryland.

Q. And did someone bring her there? **A.** Yes. She was brought there by her nurse, who sat in the Waiting Room. And I understand that her husband drove them out there, but he went somewhere on his own business and came back and picked her up an hour later.

Q. Okay. Then did you see her on subsequent occasions? **A.** I saw her at that time, and I saw her eight more times during the month of May. During this time, she began to—slowly began to talk to me more freely about her marital life and premarital life with Steve and his mother, and she—I couldn't tell that she was making strides or improvements at that time, but she was—she did become more communicative. There was still—she would still block and become unable to say anything much more when it came to her marital life.

Q. And on each of these occasions did you find that she had some difficulty expressing herself about her marital relationship? **A.** Yes. She tended to deny the feeling side of her life at that time. She tended to call this suicidal attempt an accident and so on.

Q. Doctor, did you have any more contact with Steve Rose? **A.** Yes. There was a telephone call from Steve Rose in which he—he began by asking me how his wife was doing. And I told him that I didn't want to communicate with him about his wife. And he said, "Well, I'm her husband and I'm entitled to know."

And I said, "Yeah, well then, if she will bring you in, fine, but I'm not going to discuss this case with [you] behind her back." And I told him that he was too damned nosy about this, and that what Diane needed more than anything else was a place to express her own feelings, particularly about the people whom she loved, and that I was trying to provide this atmosphere.

The conversation ended with his telling me that I was sitting there on my fat ass collecting money at the expense of mental patients, and that the thing that was going on these days was family therapy, and that by and large I didn't know what the hell I was doing.

Q. He set himself up as a greater expert in this matter? **A.** Well,—

MR. MELLON: That's a conclusion,—

A. —that's what he told me.

MR. MELLON:—Your Honor.

THE COURT: I'll sustain the objection.

A. And before that there had been a similar call from his mother, a couple days before that, in which I refused to talk to her, but—

Q. What was Alice's reaction to that? **A.** She accepted it.

Q. Okay. In spite of his call, did you see Diane after that? **A.** I saw her on two more occasions. She remarked very candidly that I had been rude to her husband, and I thought that was true. And she didn't—I was—she didn't stop. And I asked her what was going on about that. And she said that her doctors, I believe it was Drs. Grant and Cooper, at the hospital had told her to keep coming, but the treatment was stopped on May the 28th.

Q. Now, did you see her a month or two or three later? **A.** Well, I next saw her—I next saw her late in October. I think that's the date. May I refer to my card?

THE COURT: Yes.

A. (Pause—referring.) I saw her October the 27th. I sat with her for three hours at that time.

Q. Did you take an interim history, what she had been doing and what all in the meantime? **A.** Yes. During that time she had been discharged from the hospital on June the 1st and had gone home to care for her baby, but she was very concerned at this time that she was being treated as though she were a bad influence on the baby; and she was never allowed to be alone with the baby, and was very much criticized, and was concerned about this. And she felt that her husband was quite dissatisfied with her care of the baby. And I asked her in what respect. And she told me that if—if she fed the baby when the baby cried, that this would—that she was breaking up the baby's schedule; but if the baby was allowed to cry, she said she was criticized by Alice and Steve for not loving the baby. And then she tried to somersault the baby and chuck him around, which children of that age find very helpful, and she was told she was being too rough; so if she stopped, then she was ignoring the child. And so it went. I mean, her mothering was picked to pieces and she was treated as though she was some kind of a noxious influence. This is the way she described it to me.

Q. She advised you that she had since separated from her husband? **A.** Well, she said that in August—I think it was in August, maybe late in August, that she had—August 8th and 9th, she had moved out with the Nathans for a while and then tried to move back in; and then that Steve and Alice Rose had departed the house and moved to Silver Springs, which is another suburb of—adjacent to Bethesda, and adjacent to Kensington, too. They're all crowded in around there. But—

Q. Where was the baby at this time? Did she tell you? **A.** The baby was with Steve and Alice. And she found it very difficult to visit the baby, that she—she was not—she didn't feel welcome and this concerned her. She was—she had made remarkable strides and improvement in her mental status. She was quite verbal and she seemed to be very, very occupied in the business of trying to exert herself as a mother. And I certainly thought that it would be good for her to do so, good for the baby and good for her. She seemed concerned that this child would grow up to regard its mother as a dangerous and bad influence. At no time during either of these sections of time at which she visited me did I find her to be psychotic.

Q. Doctor, in people that have depression there are two general classifications, are there not? **A.** Yes.

Q. You mentioned psychotic. That's one type, is it not? **A.** Well, there are a number of different types. The psychotic types are the psychotic depression and circular insanity. And then, there is a situational type or reactive type in which there are strong stress factors playing on the subject.

Q. Now, in which category did you feel that Diane Rose was when she had made this suicide attempt? **A.** I didn't know. I didn't have enough information. I was trying to find out. It was very difficult to treat and diagnose her. You had the feeling like you're trying to take—to examine a fine Swiss watch, but somebody is stirring the parts around while you try to look at it. And I couldn't—I didn't know at that time what the situation was, but when October came and I saw her then, and I have talked on the telephone several times since, and I saw her last night for about three hours, and I find that she describes a situation which was very bleak, very critical of her in which multiple dissatisfactions were expressed with her behavior and her motives. And I think there are very, very strong situational factors in this case.

Q. Well, would you say then the depression that she was suffering was a situational type? **A.** Yes, I would diagnose it as a reactive depression.

Q. Now, since that situation has been removed, how do you find her? **A.** Well, she is very active and very involved in this case and very interested to be with her child. She made a significant remark to me in October. She said, "Well," she said, "I left in August and went to the Nathans' house." She said, "This time I did it legitimately," which I thought was a piece of growth. She didn't go out the window, but she walked out the door and removed herself from the marital discomfort.

Q. Doctor, on the basis of your examinations and treatment of Diane Rose, have you been able to form an opinion as to whether or not she is suicidal? **A.** I do not regard her as suicidal.

Q. And would you explain the basis on which you make that conclusion, Doctor? **A.** Well, I make that conclusion on the observations that I made in October and now, and on the basis that there are strong situational factors, and that she has improved markedly since removing herself from the marriage, and that she has improved markedly in the influence of her warm and gracious home here in Seattle since she moved here.

Q. Now Doctor,—**A.** I think she's also improved because she's exerting her energies toward the care of this child.

Q.—a claim is made in connection with this matter that she poses a danger to this child. I assume by that is meant she somehow threatens him. In your opinion, is there any danger whatsoever to this child for him to be—for her to have the care, custody and control of him? **A.** None whatsoever.

Q. Now, in your opinion, would custody of the child be beneficial to Diane Rose herself? **A.** Yes, I think so.

Q. And conversely, would it be beneficial to the child? **A.** I think that the child should—yes, should have its mother.

b. Cross Examination by Mr. Mellon.

Q. Dr. Mitchell, what experience have you had in treating suicidal patients? **A.** Oh, I've had really quite a bit.

Q. Have you ever had any occasion to treat a person, a highly—who had made a highly-lethal attempt at suicide and was unsuccessful? **A.** Yes, I've worked on the program with many of these people at the—

Q. Well now, just specifically let me ask you this. Have you ever had occasion, Doctor, to treat a person who jumped out of a high-story window and survived, like the eighth floor or higher? **A.** No, I've never heard of such a case before.

Q. You never heard of such a case before? **A.** No, I haven't.

Q. It's rare, isn't it? **A.** I would think so.

Q. Doctor, before you came out here—Or first let me ask you this. Did you keep a record of all your consultations with Mrs. Rose? **A.** Yes, I have notes that I took.

Q. What type of notes did you take? **A.** Well, the type of notes that I take are a word here and there that I regard as a key word significant in her makeup.

Q. Did you take a history? **A.** Oh, yes, I took a history, best as I could get a history.

Q. Did you make tests? **A.** No, I made no tests.

Q. Now, you saw her on eight occasions, as I recall, in May of last year. **A.** That's right.

Q. Then you saw her again, you say, in October one time? **A.** Yes, I saw her for three hours in October. I had—

Q. Did you ever see her again after that? **A.** Yes, I saw her last night.

Q. All right. I mean in Washington, did you ever see her after October? **A.** No.

Q. And you never saw her again until last night? **A.** No, I didn't see her again.

Q. Did you get any information, Doctor, when you were attempting to get a history of this girl, of prior suicide attempts? **A.** There was not a prior suicide attempt. She thought of jumping from a window at a party in which she had smoked hash and she had felt very much out of place with a group of people. And she—I think she told me that she had mentioned this to her husband at that time.

Q. Doctor, this event that you have told us about that she told you about that happened at the University of Washington antedated her marriage, didn't it? **A.** Yes. That's what she said.

Q. And, thus, the feelings that caused her to consider suicide at that time had nothing to do, of course, with any marriage on her part. Do you consider that those feelings were the same feelings that she had when she did actually jump out the eighth-story window? **A.** I don't know that they are exactly the same feelings. They were related at the time. She told me, I recall, that she—that her husband chose her friends for her and that she felt was not given a voice, and she felt—

Q. Well, Doctor, you're not answering my question. I asked you if in your opinion the same feelings motivated her at the time she did jump out of the eighth-story window that motivated her when she was considering suicide at the University of Washington? **A.** I said, "not exactly," and I went ahead to tell you what the feelings were as she reported them to me then, and I think that my statements are germane to your question, sir.

Q. Did she ever tell you, Doctor, about a time that she was looking for sleeping pills that she could take in the house? **A.** She told me that she had taken some sleeping pills in January, I thought it was the 13th, but it's probably the 15th, which was the evening before she leapt from the window. That's the only story she told me. She didn't tell me that until in October or over the phone in November.

Q. That's the first time you heard about that she took some sleeping pills? **A.** Yes, the night before. It was not possible to get a history from her in—in a very orderly way. I didn't try to get it. I let her talk to me as best she could.

Q. How many sleeping pills did she say she took, Doctor? **A.** I don't remember. Something that was less than a bottle from when she had a preeclamptic condition. I think it was Phenobarbital.

Q. Was this in itself a suicide attempt? **A.** I don't know. She didn't say whether it was or not. She was very upset.

Q. Did you attempt to find out how many sleeping pills she took? **A.** I may have asked her. I don't remember how many.

Q. Did she indicate that she took anything else with the sleeping pills? **A.** I hadn't heard that, not yet.

Q. You didn't hear that she also took wine with it? **A.** No. I didn't hear that she took wine. Doesn't surprise me.

Q. What is the effect of taking alcohol or liquor with Phenobarbital? **A.** They enhance each other. They're very enhancing drugs, alcohol and Phenobarbital.

Q. In other words, if you take Phenobarbital and then add alcohol, like wine, to it, it takes less pills to kill you. Is that right? **A.** Yeah, and less wine.

Q. And less wine. So if she had taken wine along with the Phenobarbital, Doctor, that would be a further indication that she was attempting to commit suicide at that point, wouldn't it? **A.** Well, that depends on how much wine, and I didn't hear about any wine, not yet, not until you told me. May I speak to you about what I was trying to do with this woman?

Q. Well, we'll come to that, Doctor, but let me ask you this. Assuming that this girl did take wine or alcohol with the Phenobarbital, would that impress you as being a more serious attempt at suicide than even you had understood up to that time? **A.** It would depend on how much of either or both.

Q. And also in expressing an opinion at the present time, it would affect your opinion now as to what should be done regarding this girl, would it not? Wouldn't all that be important, the fact that she had done all of these things at that time? **A.** Its importance becomes less as it fades into the past. And as she works her level best to re-establish herself as a mother, and as she continues in therapy with Dr. Grant, and as she attempts to re-establish the relationships with her family, which were practically nil at the time I first saw her, that becomes less and less important and her recovery becomes more important.

Q. Now, Doctor, to what did you attribute or to what cause did you attribute as being the reason or reasons that Mrs. Rose made the suicide attempts that she did on the night of—in January of last year? **A.** I think it was because of her husband, and I think it was because of his attitude that he—the stance he took with her when he was her boy friend. I don't think that that's absolutely all there is to it, but I think that's 99 percent of it. Now, I think that before they were married it was a disjunctive love relationship in which he was often dissatisfied with her, her performance and the friends she selected, and it was the same thing after the baby was born, only after the baby was born it was a very—very much more serious proposition.

Q. Well, do you blame—**A.** I mean, this hits a woman where it hurts, when she—

Q. Do you blame her husband for being the cause of her either attempting or seriously considering suicide at the University of Washington? She wasn't married at—**A.** I don't blame. I think he was deeply involved and he did not back off with his expression of dissatisfaction with her.

Q. Doctor, what did she tell you, if anything, about the relationship that she had with her family, that is, her own parental family? **A.** She told me the—just about the same thing, almost exactly word for word, what was said in the hall by Alice and Steve Rose, plus a statement that she loved all of them very dearly, which was much like her suicide note.

Q. Did Diane Rose say anything to you about having received a letter from her mother recently, prior to jumping out the window, that caused her great upset? **A.** No, she didn't describe a letter from her mother.

Q. Did she say anything about—**A.** She spoke of a camera, and she said that Alice Rose had become enraged with her family because the family didn't buy her a movie camera at Christmas to take pictures of the baby.

Q. Doctor, isn't it a fact that Mr. Rose wanted to buy a camera and the Winters didn't want him to because it cost too much money? Isn't that the fact of the matter? **A.** The Winters didn't buy the camera, the Roses did.

Q. Did she say anything to you about having received the letter from her mother within the past few weeks prior to the night she attempted suicide? **A.** She could tell me almost nothing for—really for the whole month—all—the only—for that first section of time in which I treated her, there was very little information. There was an attitude struck by her that her family had been depriving of her, but that she loved them anyway. This is essentially what she said over and over again. This is the paucity of thought that I referred to.

Q. Didn't she refer, in rather bitter terms, and blame her family for having deprived her of a great many things during the time she was growing up, and that this had caused her a great deal of unhappiness, and that this was what was bothering her? Did she ever indicate that to you? **A.** She indicated in a general sort of a way, without specification, which I tried to get from her and was not able to get at that time, that her family had deprived her. In October I went over that same area with her and it was no longer there.

Q. Are you a child psychiatrist, Doctor? **A.** No.

Q. Are you familiar with the book entitled "Beyond the Best Interests of the Child"—**A.** No.

Q. —written by Goldstein, Freud and Solnit? **A.** No.

Q. Have you ever seen—You say you've never seen Mrs. Rose with the child. Have you ever seen Mr. Rose with the child? **A.** No, I have not.

Q. And, of course, you haven't seen both of them together with the child? **A.** No, I've had no occasion to see them.

Q. Do you feel under the circumstances—not having seen the child or having seen Mrs. Rose with the child and Mr. Rose with the child, how can you make an assessment as to what would be in the best interests of the child? **A.** I make my assessment on the best basis of what the patient told me. I make my assessment on the basis of a rather obvious and vast improvement in her condition since the end of May.

Q. You say that you're not a child psychiatrist, Doctor. Do you have any information concerning the desirability or the undesirability of continuity of care of a child under, say, two years of age? **A.** Oh, I think it's very important to have continuity of care. I think it's a very sad thing that this child has been kept away from its mother during a good part of its sixteenth to eighteenth month.

Q. What do you mean, Doctor, that he's been kept away from his mother? **A.** Well, the mother has been treated as an unwanted person, according to her statements to me. They moved out of the house and took the baby, and then they moved out here to the West Coast and she's followed them out here to the West Coast. The way she tells me is that she was unwanted, and that she was treated like a—I forget how she put it, a leper or a Nazi or something like that. So I think that the maternal care has been interrupted by herself and by her husband and mother-in-law.

2. Steven Rose—Defendant Called as Adverse Witness

MR. FISK: Your name is Steven Rose?

A. Yes.

Q. And you are the husband of Diane Winter Rose? **A.** Yes.

Q. And you are presently a medical student? **A.** Yes.

Q. Now, following the suicide attempt of your wife and following her release from the hospital, you insisted that your wife and all the relatives have a family-consultation session with a Dr. Bower, did you not? **A.** No. Dr. Bower insisted and I agreed.

Q. All right. In any event, you made the arrangements? **A.** Dr. Bower made the arrangements.

Q. Now, what was the purpose of this family get-together with Dr. Bower? **A.** The purpose was to explore the feelings, there were a lot of angry feelings expressed, and to explore these feelings amongst the members of the family.

Q. Who attended that conference? **A.** I attended the conference, Nancy, Diane, my mother, and Mr. and Mrs. Nathan and their child, Dr. Bower, and Dr. Grant, Diane's therapist.

Q. Now, was the purpose of that conference to try and commit your wife? **A.** No.

Q. Now, at that conference, I'm going to ask you if it isn't a fact that Dr. Bower stated that, "You are trying to commit her," meaning your wife, "but you are the most vicious people I've ever run into"? **A.** Yes, Dr. Bower said that about the group.

Q. Now, I'm talking about you and your mother. **A.** No. He said that including the group.

Q. Now, I'm going to ask you if Dr. Bower didn't say that there was a very unhealthy relationship between you and your mother. **A.** No, he didn't say that.

Q. He did not? **A.** No.

Q. You deny that? **A.** Yes.

Q. I'm going to ask you if he didn't say that your mother was mentally sleeping with you. **A.** Mentally sleeping with me?

Q. With you. **A.** With me?

Q. With you. **A.** I can't recall, though Diane did say I was sleeping with my mother.

Q. No, I'm talking about Dr. Bower. **A.** Yes.

Q. Let's answer the question. **A.** I'm trying to answer it as best I can. I don't recall her saying she was mentally sleeping with me. I don't recall.

Q. Is Dr. Bower a woman? **A.** No, Dr. Bower's a man.

Q. All right. I'm talking about a him, a man. **A.** Right. I don't recall if he said that.

Q. But he could have said it? **A.** I don't recall.

Q. Now, I'm going to ask you if he didn't say that you and your mother and the whole bunch of you needed treatment. **A.** Yes, he did say that.

Q. I want to ask you if he didn't say that your mother, Alice, should come back to Seattle and get out of your—the life of yourself and your wife. **A.** He said, "What are you doing here?"

Q. To Alice? **A.** To Alice. That's what he said, "What are you doing here?" He said, "Why don't you go back to Seattle?" He posed it as a question, as I remember.

Q. At this session did Alice, your mother, admit she had a poor husband-wife relationship with your father? **A.** I don't recall that. A poor husband-and-wife relationship with my father?

Q. Right, right. **A.** I believe she did say the relationship was strained. She had been living in Washington since Diane jumped out of the eight-story window, and my father had lived in Seattle and made a couple visits, and, yes, she said that it was—it was difficult.

Q. And I want to ask you if Dr. Bower didn't say to your mother that she had mentally castrated your father. **A.** I'm not sure if he said those words, but he did—

Q. Well, words to that effect? **A.** That she mentally castrated him? I believe when he spoke to us, he posed them in questions, if she did this. He said a lot of things at that session. He could have said that.

Q. He could have said that? **A.** Yes.

Q. And I want to ask you if it isn't a fact that he told her what she needed was a damned good lay. **A.** Yes. He said—that's what he did—that's what he said. I don't think he said it in that—quite that way. He didn't say "a damn good" one.

Q. Now, following these remarks to yourself and to your mother, even you refused to have any more sessions with Dr. Bower, did you not? **A.** Not so.

Q. Not so? **A.** No.

Q. Okay. **A.** I went to see Dr. Bower again.

Q. Did you ever take Diane to see him anymore? **A.** No, but he discussed Diane with me.

Q. I see. **A.** If you'd like to hear anything about that?

Q. We'll get to it a little bit more later. **A.** All right.

MR. FISK: That's all I wanted to ask of this witness at this time.

MR. MELLON: No questions.

3. Deborah Nathan—For the Plaintiff

a. Direct Examination by Mr. Fisk

THE WITNESS: I just wanted to clarify one thing,—

MR. FISK: Just—Mrs. Nathan, now we'll give you a chance to clarify everything. I'll ask you some questions, okay?

THE WITNESS: I just want to tell you that he thinks—my husband and I weren't included as being vicious with Dr. Bower.

MR. FISK: We'll get to that.

Q. Your name is Deborah Nathan? **A.** Right.

Q. And, Mrs. Nathan, where do you live? **A.** In Washington, D.C.

Q. And are you acquainted with Diane Rose and her husband, Steven? **A.** Yes.

Q. How did you get acquainted with them? **A.** I met Diane through a mutual friend before Diane was pregnant, or she might have been pregnant and I didn't know that she was pregnant at the time. It might have—you know, it might have been the first or second month.

Q. All right. Were you and your husband friends of the Roses? **A.** I'd say casual acquaintances.

Q. Now, did there come an occasion when Diane Rose left the apartment where she was living with Steve and his mother following her release from the hospital and came to your home? **A.** Yes.

Q. How did she arrive at your home? **A.** Well, my husband picked her up. She called me up on the phone and she was very upset. She said she had to get out; she couldn't stay there and could she stay with us for a few days; could she come the next morning.

Q. Now, was there some reluctance on your part to let her come and stay with you? **A.** Yes. Well, Diane had just been released from the hospital in June and I had only seen her once during that time, and I had heard from people that I know through—this is just strictly hearsay, from not seeing her, that Diane had to be watched every minute, that she was a mental midget, you know, she was a vegetable. And it meant, since I have a baby, that meant me having two babies on my hands, Diane and my own baby.

Q. But nevertheless, you took her in on this occasion? **A.** Right.

Q. How long did she stay with you? **A.** I'd say about a month and a week.

Q. All right. Now, during the time she stayed with you, how did she get along? **A.** Very well. She—it turned out that she was a tremendous help. She took care of my baby. She did the cooking. She helped with the housework. She did everything.

Q. And within a few days did you find that she was competent to handle and take care of your own child? **A.** Yes. It was great having her there, "cause it was less work for me."

Q. Now, during this month, I want to ask you whether she babysat for you on numerous occasions. **A.** Yes.

Q. And did you go away and leave your own child with her? **A.** Yes.

Q. And would she feed him, change him, bathe him,—**A.** Everything.

Q. —the whole bit? Did she cook, keep house? **A.** Yes.

Q. Did she appear perfectly competent to you to handle and take care of a child? **A.** More than competent. It was sad because she was giving my baby the love that she should have been giving her baby.

Q. How old was your child at that time? **A.** My baby, there's two months difference between them, so she was 14 months.

Q. All right. Now then, were you asked to attend the conference with Dr. Bower? **A.** Well, I was threatened to it, but then Steve called up my husband and insulted him and told him that we had to go, seven o'clock in the morning we had to be there at Dr. Bower's, at a place that was an hour away, so it meant with our baby, because nobody would babysit for us at five o'clock in the morning, having to drag our baby and get her up, feed her, take her to this session where—expose her to all this viciousness, shouting, a very frightening experience for her.

Q. Well, the arrangements were made by Steve Rose. Is that what you're saying? **A.** For us it was.

Q. Now, by this time had Diane returned to the apartment or was she still with you? **A.** She was still with me. She couldn't return to the apartment.

Q. Now, who was at this session with Dr. Bower? **A.** Nancy, Steve, Diane, Mrs. Rose, Dr. Grant, my husband, Dr. Bower and myself.

Q. Now,—**A.** And my daughter, Susan.

Q. Now, at this session, I want you to state whether or not Dr. Bower said that Steve and his mother were the most vicious people he'd ever seen, or words to that effect. **A.** It wasn't just Steve and his mother. It was Steve—

MR. MELLON: I'm going to object to this, your Honor, as being very leading.

MR. FISK: I'm going to—

MR. MELLON: She can tell what Dr. Bower said, but counsel is putting words in her mouth.

MR. FISK: I'll withdraw the question.

THE COURT: Agreed.

MR. FISK: I'll rephrase it.

Q. (Continuing) Would you state what, if anything, Dr. Bower said about the people there attending that conference, if he had anything specific to say with reference to any particular people? **A.** Well, he said about Nancy Winter, Steve Rose and Alice Rose, that they were the most vicious people that he had ever seen; that they're the most self-righteous people and unforgiving people; and he couldn't blame Diane for doing what she had done; if she had lived—if he had lived in those circumstances, he'd probably do the same thing.

Q. And this was said in Steve Rose and Alice Rose's presence? **A.** Yes.

Q. And I'll ask you whether or not he told Alice Rose that she had an unhealthy relationship with—

MR. MELLON: I am going to object to this, Your Honor.

THE COURT: Sustained.

Q. What did she say—**A.** I can tell you what he said. The thing where Steve said—'cause I was listening carefully, that they were mentally sleeping together. He said they were literally sleeping together. He did mention that. He did say that they had an unhealthy relationship, because, you see, the way that whole meeting went, we thought they were out to commit Diane into an institution. The night before I had met with Dr. Grant and he said they were there to determine reality, Steve's reality, his mother's reality, and what was—what prescription as far as what was to be done with them. And he wanted Steve and his mother to go into therapy. He felt they both needed it. He thought Alice should go back home to Seattle to get help there; Steve should stay there and go see Dr. Bower. Nancy agreed to treatment with Dr. Bower, and I don't know what happened to them. It's really a shame she didn't continue with the treatment, because I worry for Nancy.

Q. Now, was anything said by Dr. Bower with reference to whether this was a kind of a commitment hearing?

MR. MELLON: I object again, Your Honor. Counsel is putting words in her mouth.

THE COURT: Overrule the objection.

A. We were sitting there with Dr. Grant the night—well, the night before we were there. Dr. Grant had thought we were all there for Diane's commitment. And I think, in a moment of anger, while they were screaming at each other, he said, "You know," that, "you want to commit her and look at the way you—" you know, "You are the ones." It was—I can't remember his exact words, but "You're the ones that need the treatment, not her. She's getting the therapy. She's still—"

THE COURT: Was this the night before?

THE WITNESS: No, this was in the group-therapy session. I had two sessions, one with Dr. Grant—

THE COURT: Where was that?

THE WITNESS: In Dr. Grant's office, Diane's psychiatrist.

THE COURT: Where is that?

THE WITNESS: In Washington, D.C.

THE COURT: Okay. Where is Dr. Bower's—

THE WITNESS: Dr. Bower, I think, is in Potomac, Maryland.

b. Cross Examination by Mr. Mellon

Q. How many meetings did you have in Dr. Bower's office? **A.** One, and that was enough.

Q. About how long did it last? **A.** Well, we were there—we got there early and—'cause we thought it was going to take longer to get out there than it did. We got there around six-thirty and we left around twelve, one o'clock, and it was still going on.

Q. Dr. Bower apparently tends to strong language. **A.** Well, so do Steve and his mother.

Q. Well, I didn't ask you that. I said, "Dr. Bower tends to strong language," is that right? **A.** Well, not—well, you can say he tends to strong language and he also tends to soft-soap, so, you know, it depends on how you approach it. He was very sweet to my husband and myself.

Q. What do you mean "soft-soap"? **A.** Well, I meant, you know, he's soft, he's very nice and very gentle.

Q. But he can also get very rough? **A.** Well, so can Steve and his mother.

Q. I didn't ask you that. Are you out here to harpoon Steve and his mother? **A.** No, what I'm saying, you're trying to harpoon Dr. Bower. The thing is that Steve and his mother shouted at him and he shouted back to them. And when Steve and his mother were polite to him, then he was polite back to them.

Q. Did Dr. Bower also say—Well, first let me say: Were you there with Dr. Bower from seven o'clock in the morning until twelve-thirty? **A.** Uh-huh (affirmative response).

Q. Did Dr. Bower also say, as you left, "Now, don't you have compassion for Steve and his painful situation?" **A.** No.

Q. You didn't hear that? **A.** No.

Q. Well, you were gone, you left before the session ended? **A.** Right. Most of the time when we were there he just said that he wanted—he was mostly working out trying to get Steve and his mother and Nancy into therapy, trying to talk them into it.

Q. When did you come out here? **A.** Excuse me?

Q. When did you come to Seattle? **A.** Yesterday.

Q. Did you come out here just to testify in this case? **A.** Yes.

Q. Who's paying your expenses? **A.** Mr.—Dr. Winter.

Q. Did Dr. Winter contact you and ask you to come out here? **A.** Yes, he did.

4. Steven Rose—Defendant As Adverse Witness II

a. Direct Examination by Mr. Fisk

Q. Mr. Rose, would you tell us when you first met your wife? **A.** I first met my wife when she came over to my house with a friend, Carrie Wallenberg, when I must have been in about the eighth grade.

Q. When did you first start going with her? **A.** I first dated Diane in 1976 in the summer. I didn't start going steady with her till about on her birthday when I pinned her with my college fraternity pin in May of—that would be 1977.

Q. Okay. Now, were you both at college, University of Washington, at that time? **A.** Yes.

Q. Now, this would probably be a good time to discuss this so-called first suicide attempt. This occasion was in the room of Polly Winter, was it not? **A.** Yes.

Q. And you'd had a party or something? **A.** Well, it wasn't a party. It was a get-together between just a couple of people, one was her sister Polly, her sister's boy friend John, Diane's roommate Anita, Diane and myself. I don't—we just got together.

Q. Were you smoking hashish at that time? **A.** No.

Q. You weren't? **A.** No, I wasn't.

Q. Did you insist that Diane eat some hashish? **A.** No.

Q. You deny that? **A.** I deny that.

Q. Did she have some hashish? **A.** Yes.

Q. Where did she get it? **A.** She got it from her sister Polly, who had them baked in a brownie. I might say that I did have some hashish the night before. Her sister Polly gave me a brownie and said, "Here." And I—I put it in my mouth and then I spit some of it out in the sink because it tasted horrible. That night, the next night, Diane told me that she wanted to try some and she did.

Q. Now, did she become quite ill? **A.** Well, I don't know if you'd call it ill. She sat in the chair in this room. It was—it was in John Moss' room, Polly's boy friend, and she sat in the chair and didn't move, occasionally looked up and smiled. I asked her what was wrong and she just smiled.

Q. Now, actually she was lying on the bed, wasn't she? **A.** No.

Q. She didn't lie on the bed? **A.** No, she sat in the chair in the corner.

Q. All right. What happened? **A.** She stayed that way for approximately an hour or two. I didn't know what was wrong, and then I finally said to her, "Diane why don't you—why don't I escort you to Polly's room so you can lay down and go to sleep?"

Q. Oh, that's where she was on the bed? **A.** Right.

Q. Okay. Then she went to Polly's room? **A.** Right. When she laid down on the bed, I sat in one corner of the room and had one of the—one of the lamp lights on and was sitting in the chair. Then Diane opened the window—

Q. Well now, wait a minute. She's on the bed; the bed is by the window? **A.** The bed—right next to the window, yes.

Q. Okay. **A.** Diane opened the window and started to crawl out.

Q. What did you do? **A.** I went over and I had to grab her around the waist. Her head was already out the window. And I pulled her back in, slammed the window shut and stayed with her all night.

Q. Okay. Did she get okay the next day? **A.** She said—well, she said she was—felt a little funny. She said to me the next day, she says, "if you wouldn't have been there, I would have died." We talked about that incident many times.

Q. All right. Now then, what year was this that happened? **A.** Well, this was—I believe it was the winter term of 1979.

Q. So that is what? A year and a half before you got married? **A.** Sure. I was a senior in college and she was a junior.

Q. Now, you actually got married after she got out of college, did you not, she'd graduated from college? **A.** Right. We were engaged the spring before she graduated college.

Q. All right. What did you do when you first got out of college? **A.** Well, I had been accepted to Karl Franzen University in Graz, Austria, which was associated with the University of Vienna Medical School. Diane and I planned to go over there. I was going over to study medicine in Austria with two fellow dental students. I had been in dental school for one year.

Q. Mr. Rose, I think you're getting a little bit ahead of me. **A.** Okay. Well, we—

Q. You got out of college—**A.** Sure.

Q. —and you started dental school, didn't you? **A.** Right.

Q. Okay. Now then, you decided to go and try and go to medical school in Austria, right? **A.** Yes.

Q. Had you decided to get married at that time? **A.** No. Diane wanted to—Diane said to me, she said, "I would like to go with you to Austria." She says, "I think it's about time we got married." She said, "If you don't marry me, then I'll come over with you to live."

Q. Now, she was going to come and live with you whether you married her or not? **A.** Yes.

Q. And in effect she's the one that proposed to you, not the other way around? **A.** Well, it wasn't that I was opposed to being married to Diane, because I loved her very much.

Q. Well, originally hadn't you intended to go without her? **A.** We had set—we had talked about—

Q. Would you just answer my question? **A.** Okay. This is what I'm trying to say. We had talked about marriage and actually reserved the Synagogue in December before I was accepted. I had applied to the Austrian Medical School and we had reserved the Synagogue, but we had not been formally engaged when—for the—for the next few months, but she had the Synagogue date reserved.

Q. Now, when Diane suggested you ought to get married, did you have to seek some advice on that? **A.** No. I wanted to think about it.

Q. Well, isn't it a fact you told her you had to go home and ask your mother? **A.** No.

Q. Didn't you in fact go ask your mother and get her approval before you would say "yes" or "no"? **A.** No. My mother loved Diane. I knew that she—

Q. Now, just answer my question. Didn't you—**A.** No.

Q. —have to go and get Alice's approval? **A.** No.

Q. You didn't tell her that,—**A.** No.

Q. Now then, I want to ask you if one of the reasons that you thought you might marry Diane was that you thought that Dr. Winter's connections might help get you in medical school? **A.** There is no possible way I could have thought that. Do you want me to give you a reason?

Q. Yes. **A.** Dr. Winter has no academic standing at the University of Washington other than an associate clinical professor, which is—which is really the lowest person at the University.

Q. Lowest man on the totem pole there? **A.** Sort of.

Q. Now, Mr. Rose, you got married on July the 5th, 1980, right? **A.** Yes.

Q. And originally you had planned to go to the Winter's condominium for a honeymoon, had you not? **A.** Yes.

Q. And you changed those plans so you could be near your mother, did you not? **A.** No.

Q. No? **A.** No.

Q. Where did you stay on your wedding night? **A.** We stayed at Farley's.

Q. At Farley's? **A.** Yes.

Q. In Seattle? **A.** Yes.

Q. And the very next morning you got up and went to visit your mother, didn't you? **A.** Yes, the very next morning we had breakfast at Farley's. Mr. and Mrs. Martin Finch and their family—

Q. That isn't the question I asked you, Mr. Rose. **A.** The question is—

Q. Did you go visit your mother—**A.** Yes.

Q. —on the morning of July the 6th? **A.** We went over to our house, yes.

MR. MELLON: Now, Your Honor, Counsel should allow him to explain, if he desires.

MR. FISK: Well, I'll be happy to have him explain, but he should answer the question.

THE COURT: I think he is.

THE WITNESS: Yes. When we were having breakfast with Mr. and Mrs. Martin Finch at Farley's we saw these two people that came from New York who had come to our wedding. Diane had told me early in the morning that she didn't want to go down to the condominium at the beach. She said that we only had a couple more days until we were flying off to Austria and that she wanted to be close to her parents and the people that had come to see us.

Q. Now, as a medical student, you know the meaning of an Oedipal complex, do you not? **A.** Of course.

Q. And would you explain what it is? **A.** It's a fascination or desire to-love for your mother, not in a son-mother relationship, but in a lover relationship.

Q. Now, that's one of the things that Dr. Bower stated about your relationship with your mother, is it not, at this meeting that you had in Washington, D.C.? **A.** Dr. Bower did not mention that.

Q. He did not? **A.** He did not say "an Oedipal complex," no.

Q. You deny that? **A.** I deny that.

Q. Now, you went off to Austria, how long did you stay? **A.** We stayed in Austria, I believe, approximately six weeks.

Q. So that turned out to be an expensive fiasco, did it? **A.** Yes, it did, but there were circumstances surrounding that. We were taking German classes every day, twice a day. Diane refused to go to many of the German classes. Diane cried and became very depressed. She would not go with me, as the other wives did to these German classes. She told me she wanted to go home and she didn't want to live in Austria, that she hated Graz. I told her that this may be my last chance to be an M.D. She continued to cry. She wouldn't listen to me and we had an argument.

Q. Mr. Rose, during these German classes you repeatedly told your wife how stupid she was, did you not? **A.** No.

Q. You deny that? **A.** Yes.

Q. During all the time you went with her, as a matter of fact, you constantly told her she was stupid, didn't you, inadequate and (pause) **A.** Oh, when we got in arguments or something like that, she would call me something. I would say, "Oh you're so stupid," or something of that nature yes.

Q. Didn't you tell her on numerous occasions your friends couldn't understand why you did anything—had anything to do with her because you were so far above her intellectually? **A.** No.

Q. You didn't say that? **A.** No.

Q. Did you feel you were? **A.** Far above her intellectually?

Q. Yes. **A.** I thought—I thought I was more intelligent than she.

Q. And you didn't hesitate to tell her so? **A.** No, I didn't tell her so. Possibly in an argument I may say something, in—when you are in the heat of an emotional state, I may—you know, you may blurt out something that you—that you don't mean,—

Q. Well,—**A.**—but I don't recall.

Q. Okay. Finally you were admitted to George Washington University Medical School, were you not? **A.** Yes.

Q. Your wife worked at George Washington Hospital, did she not? **A.** Yes.

Q. And your wife and her earnings and what you got from the Winters is what financed your education. Isn't that true? **A.** No.

Q. Okay. Were you disturbed when Diane got pregnant? **A.** No. Happy.

Q. Did you have a feeling that this would interfere with her ability to work and send you to school? **A.** No.

Q. Didn't bother you? **A.** No.

Q. What was your wife doing at the hospital? **A.** She was a—she was a clerk-typist in Orthopedics my first—my first year, and the second year she was a typist for Radiology.

Q. In other words, she was what you would call a medical secretary? **A.** No. She was a clerk-typist. A medical secretary—she didn't answer a phone.

What she did was type from the dictaphone. The doctors would read X-rays in Radiology and she was—she would just transcribe the tapes.

Q. Did she work for two different doctors? **A.** Well, she worked with—for many doctors, for Radiology, for whoever was the resident or the attendants who were reading the X-rays, and then in Orthopedics I think there were four people, four orthopedists in the clinic that she worked for.

Q. Jason was born April, 1983? **A.** Yes.

Q. That suddenly eliminated this source of income for you, didn't it? **A.** Yes.

Q. Did your wife work right up till the day of the delivery? **A.** Yes. Diane wasn't expected to deliver for at least another five weeks. Jason was born April—

Q. The answer to the question is "yes"? **A.** Yes. Jason wasn't expected until five weeks. In fact, May 25th was his due date. He was born April 21st.

Q. That suddenly put you in a position where you needed money, did it not? **A.** We had some money saved. We were going back to Seattle for the summer.

Q. Now, did you ask your father for money? **A.** I never had to ask my father for money.

Q. Well, let me ask you this. Did you go to the—or ask your wife to go to the Winters for money? **A.** No.

Q. Did she go to the Winters for money? **A.** In the summer of that year she did go to her father. She said for the first time in her life she was going to ask them for money for—for the following year.

Q. Now, if you were getting the support from your parents, why did she need to do that? **A.** She did—she said to me, she said, "I don't want your parents to carry the full burden of our—our money, the money that we need in Washington, D.C.," she said, "so I'm going to ask him for some of the money out of my trust fund that I have." She said, "So I won't be taking it really out of his pocket, but just taking it out of the trust fund." So, she said, "I'll ask him for $5,000."

Q. I want to ask you if it isn't a fact that you wanted her to ask for the entire trust fund. **A.** No.

Q. So you got a check from Dr. Winter for $5,000? **A.** Yes.

Q. Now, along about this time you were becoming extremely critical of the Winters, were you not? **A.** No.

Q. Specifically, weren't you upset with Dr. Winter because you thought he wasn't contributing enough? **A.** No.

Q. Weren't you upset with Dr. Winter because he was indiscreet enough on one occasion to mention what a nice young medical student Judge Green's son was; you took offense at that? **A.** No. What he did say, in front of my presence and to my face, I think after he gave the check or after Diane asked him, he said, "Mike Green's a wonderful guy." He says, "You know, he doesn't ask his dad for a penny," that, "He joined the service to finance his way through medical school and he worked through medical school."

Q. Now, shortly after that you decided, among other things, you needed a movie camera, did you not? **A.** No, not shortly after that, no.

Q. When? **A.** Before. What happened with that was, I wanted to get a movie camera because Jason was now starting to move around a little bit, roll on the ground, smile. I wanted to capture him in movies and so get an 8-millimeter movie camera. I had asked my mother-in-law if she would come back and visit us during my junior year, and she said—she refused because it cost too much money. So Diane and I thought that a good idea would be to have a movie camera and we could send the movie film to Seattle to show them pictures of Jason and also keep a good record of Jason.

Q. Who was going to buy this movie camera? **A.** We were.

Q. You and Polly—or, and Diane? I'm sorry. **A.** Yes, me and Diane. We had just thought about it. We weren't purchasing it.

Q. Okay. So what caused the big problem? **A.** Amanda got into a fight with my mother. She said, "You always run away from your troubles. We can't run away from our troubles." And she said, "Steve gets his spendthrift attitudes from you. Why, he even wants to buy a movie camera."

Q. And with that, your mother took her leave and—**A.** She says, "I'm—" yes. I think she said, "You've insulted me," and she left.

Q. After the baby was born there was nothing that his mother could do that suited you. Isn't that so? **A.** No. I told Diane many times that I thought she was doing a good job.

Q. I'll ask you if it isn't a fact that you criticized her about the way she fed the baby, how she bathed the baby, how she handled him; everything she did—**A.** No.

Q.—was incorrect? **A.** There were a couple episodes, and if I could illustrate that, I was not Diane's only critic at times. Her father was, too. One which upset me was when Diane would lie Jason, who was only a couple months old, on their living room floor.

Q. Would she lie with him there? **A.** No, she would lie Jason on the floor and go into the kitchen and do some cooking or something like that rather than put him in the crib. And her father made the observation and brought it to my attention that occasionally dogs got into their house when the door was open, namely, one that—the Frank's dog, which is a big black dog, and he said that—he's told her once, "Diane, that dog was sniffing at Jason's head." He said, "All he'd have to do is make one lunge and he could dangerously harm Jason."

Q. But you deny that you generally criticized everything she did with the child? **A.** Of course I deny that.

Q. Now, your mother came back to Washington around Christmas or New Years, 1983, right? **A.** Yes.

Q. And how long did she stay? **A.** Two weeks, something like that.

Q. She was there up until about a week before the suicide attempt, wasn't she? **A.** No.

Q. How long? **A.** She was—she left a couple of weeks before.

Q. So she left around the first of the year? **A.** Before the first of the year.

Q. Now, during that period of time, isn't it true that your mother was very critical of your wife and the Winters? **A.** I'll tell you the truth, that I was on a clinical rotation in medicine at the hospital center in Washington, D.C.; that I didn't know what they talked about during the day, and Diane never told me. They seemed very happy and amicable when I got home and when I talked to them. So I don't know anything that went on.

Q. All right. After the suicide attempt you called Dr. Winter in Seattle, did you not? **A.** Yes, I called him. He was at, I believe, Hathaway Park Hospital. First—I called her mother first and told her what had happened, and she—her mother said she'd get in touch with my father-in-law, but I—I decided to call him anyway. I had some medical questions for him; Diane was very sick.

Q. And Amanda Winter came early in the day and Dr. Winter arrived there that evening. Is that true? **A.** No. Amanda Winter came later that evening. If I can tell you, I called up my parents first and told them what had happened. They told me immediately that they would come out in the first plane they could get. I called up my mother-in-law and told her, and she said, "Oh Steve" she says, "I just talked to Diane last night."

So I said,—I told her that she was in critical condition, and she says, "Oh,"—

Q. Mr. Rose, I hate to interrupt you,—**A.** I just want to tell—Okay, I just want to tell you the background.

Q. I know, you want to tell me everything I don't ask you. **A.** I told Amanda Winter to come out, yes, and she came out later that evening, I believe on the same plane as my mother and father.

Q. Okay. And when Dr. Winter arrived, you met him at the hospital, did you not? **A.** Yes.

Q. Now, at that time, that very night, I'm going to ask you if it isn't a fact you told Dr. Winter, "I've made some terrible mistakes for which I'm sorry and I just hope that I get a second chance." **A.** I told him, I said, "I pray for a second chance with Diane." I don't remember saying, "I've made terrible mistakes." I felt—I felt terrible about this. I had been up for—for now almost 48—

Q. My question is if you made this statement to Dr. Winter. **A.** I remember him—

Q. Can you answer a question without making a speech? **A.** Yes. I remember—I remember saying that I wanted a second chance.

Q. Okay. That was the question. **A.** Diane was in critical condition at the time. She was decerebrate and her pupils were unequal.

Q. Now, is this in answer to whether you—**A.** Yes.

Q. —asked for a second chance? **A.** Yes. I was praying for a second chance. This was the most terrible time of my life.

Q. Okay. Now, within a couple days your whole attitude changed, had it not? **A.** No.

Q. No? **A.** No.

Q. Within a couple days it become suddenly all the Winters' fault. Isn't that true? **A.** No. In fact, my father-in-law, when he left five days later, hugged me and wished me good luck.

Q. But shortly thereafter you were telling Amanda Winter, "It's all your fault,"—**A.** No.

Q. —isn't that so? **A.** No.

Q. Now, you haven't lived with Diane since about September 9, 1984, correct? **A.** No, since August 12, 1984.

Q. All right, August 12,—**A.** Right. I did ask Diane to come back.

Q. Beg pardon? **A.** I did ask Diane to come back several times.

Q. Now, have you been having an affair with her sister? **A.** No.

Q. Are you sure of that? **A.** Positive.

Q. Do you know any reason why your suitcase would be in her apartment in Washington, D.C.? **A.** Yes. My—I had belongings—I had some of my things, my books at Nancy's where I stored it, and I have some at a former next-door neighbors where I stored it in her locker, too. She's about a 60–year–old woman.

Q. When you were up at Silver Spring, Maryland, did Nancy come up there? **A.** Yes, she came over.

Q. Did she stay overnight? **A.** Yes.

Q. Numerous occasions? **A.** On weekends she would come over and stay, and I would sleep on the couch and my mom and—and Nancy would sleep in the two twin beds, and Jason had his own room.

Q. The night that Mr. Nathan came and got your wife and took her to his apartment—**A.** Yes.

Q. —there was an argument between Alice Rose and your wife, correct? **A.** Yes, there was.

Q. Now, at that time and in your presence did Alice Rose say to your wife, "Why do you think you should have this baby merely because you spread your legs?" **A.** I don't remember her saying that.

Q. You don't remember that? **A.** No.

Q. I see. And you deny that your wife said to you, "Are you going to let your mother talk to me like that?" and you said that you were not going to do anything or say anything about that? **A.** I deny that.

Q. You deny that. Now, at that same time in that same place do you deny that you told your wife you were going to have her committed? **A.** I deny that.

MR. MELLON: I'll reserve questioning until our case, Your Honor.

5. Samuel Winter, M.D.—For the Plaintiff

a. Direct Examination by Mr. Fisk

Q. Your name is Samuel Winter? **A.** Yes, sir.

Q. And you are a licensed physician and surgeon in the State of Washington, are you? **A.** I am.

Q. And do you have a specialty? **A.** Yes, sir.

Q. And what is your specialty? **A.** Orthopedic surgery.

Q. How long have you been an orthopedic surgeon? **A.** Since 1949.

Q. Now, Doctor, you are the father of the respondent, Diane Rose, are you not? **A.** I am.

Q. And you also have two other children,—**A.** I do.

Q. —Polly and Nancy. Is that correct? **A.** Yes, sir.

Q. And in connection with these three children of yours, did they have everything so far as physical things that you can reasonably want? **A.** I think so. I think so. The girls were all sent to music school, music lessons. Most of them didn't want to continue it, but they went. They were given classes in skiing. They were—all of them were sent to take lessons in tennis, if they wanted. Some of them did, some of them didn't.

Q. Purchased ski equipment for them to go skiing? **A.** Yes.

Q. What was the atmosphere around your home? **A.** I thought it was good. My wife is a taciturn type of person. She's quiet, but—she certainly didn't belong to any organizations. She seldom left the house and she was always with the children. There was never a time—she never played bridge, never went out to play bridge. There was never any time I called that she wasn't there during the day. I think she was as good a wife as anybody could be.

Q. Okay. Now, did your girls all grow up and go to college? **A.** Yes. They all went to high school and went to college.

Q. And did Nancy go to the University of Washington? **A.** She did.

Q. And then she started going with Steve Rose the petitioner in this case? Is that correct? **A.** You're saying Diane, not Nancy.

Q. I'm sorry. Diane started going with Steve Rose? **A.** Yes, sir.

Q. And how long did they go together, to your knowledge? **A.** Well, I think Diane met him the first year in college. I'm—she may have met him with another girl friend earlier. It's possible. I didn't know. She went out with several other boys and she went with Steve.

Q. Okay. And then they got married in 1980. Is that correct? **A.** That's right, sir.

Q. When did they go to Washington, D.C.? **A.** I think it was in 1981.

Q. And he was admitted there to medical school? **A.** Yes, sir.

Q. Were you approached by any member of his family in connection with a contribution to get him into school? **A.** Yes.

Q. By whom? **A.** By Mr. Harold Rose.

Q. Who is Mr. Harold Rose? **A.** Steve's father.

Q. And what was the story you got from him?

MR. MELLON: I'm going to object to this, Your Honor. I think that's pure hearsay, any conversation between Harold Rose and Mr.—and Dr. Winter.

MR. FISK: This is one of the parties that will end up with this child if it's left where it is, and I think—

MR. MELLON: That's not true.

THE COURT: Well, I don't know whether it's true or not, and that remains to be seen, I'm sure. I'm going to overrule the objection.

A. Mr. Rose told me he'd made a pledge to the University of $10,000, and that he needed some money and would I pay half of it.

Q. Did you do that? **A.** I did.

Q. And then did he later come back and change that story? **A.** Yes.

Q. What did he say the second time around? **A.** He said it wasn't $10,000, it was more than $10,000. I said to him, "Harold, how much was it?"

He said, "Oh it was a lot more than that." He said, "Can you give another $5,000?"

And I said, "I cannot give $5,000 at the moment, but I will give the—half of it now and half of it in a few months," which I did.

Q. Okay. And so how much total did you contribute on this pledge that Harold Rose had made to the University? **A.** $12,000.

Q. Did you know anything whatsoever about this pledge in advance? **A.** I did not.

Q. Now then, did your daughter go to work back in Washington, to your knowledge? **A.** She did.

Q. Did you give them any more money? **A.** Yes, I did.

Q. And can you tell us—give us an idea how much you gave them? **A.** I wrote to Steve and Diane—or in Diane's name or Steve and Diane's name $19,000 worth of checks.

Q. Over what period of time? **A.** Over a period of time from about 1981 to 1983 or '4. Then I—in '85 there were about $3,000 worth of checks—

Q. All right. Now, what was the first knowledge you had about her attempted suicide? **A.** I just had finished an operation. I was walking out of the Operating Room. I didn't even have my gloves off. And the Chief of Operating Service walked over to me and said, "Dr. Winter, there's a telephone—long-distance call." And on the other end of the line was Steve's voice crying, telling me something terrible had happened. I just didn't know what he meant. I said, "Who was it, for God's sake, Steve? Was it Jason?" He said—because someone fell.

He said, "No, it was Diane,"

And I said, "Where is she?"

He said, "She's in the Emergency Room at the Arlington Hospital." I think it was Arlington. And he said, "What can I do?"

I said, "Steve, do you have a neurosurgeon present?"

"Yes."

"Does she have an airway?" An "airway" means tracheal breathing.

"Yes."

I said then, "Did you get a urologist to be sure that she has kidney function?"

And he said, "Yes—no," he said, "No, I didn't get one, but that's a good suggestion."

I said, "Well, get that, please, Steve." I said, "I don't know what to—God, I don't know anything more to tell you now, Steve. I'm in the midst of an operation. There's a lady out in the hallway to go into the operating room. As soon as I finish it, I'll call you back."

Q. And did you do that? **A.** I did. No, I didn't call Steve back. I went over and, in between cases, I called Alice—rather, I called the Rose house. I didn't know whether I could do this operation, this next operation coming up, because the lady had already had her preoperative medication, the anesthetist was standing by, and she had been moved in the operating room. And I said—Alice answered the telephone. I said, "Alice, I am so sorry." She put the phone down and Harold picked up the phone and, in the distance—Harold said, "Hello." And I heard someone say, "Don't you talk to that son-of-a-bitch." And Harold said, "Alice, would you please get out of this room?"

And then I said, "Harold, it's the most critical situation," or, "a dire situation. I don't know what else to do at the moment."

He said to me, "Sam she's your daughter. We're going right back."

I said, "Harold, I know very well she's my daughter and I intend to go back sometime today, but I can't go back when you go back."

Q. Well, you went back that evening? **A.** I did.

Q. Now, Doctor, who met you at the hospital? **A.** Well, he didn't meet me. I saw Steve at the hospital. He was sobbing and he said to me, "If I can only have another chance. I've made so many mistakes. If I can only have another chance."

I put my arm around him and I said, "Steve, I am sure we're going to do our best. Everything is being done that's possible. Don't castigate yourself."

Q. Okay. Now then, did that attitude change shortly? **A.** Well, I don't know, because that was Wednesday night and I—we all stayed up Wednesday night, all of us, I mean all of us who were at the—in the hospital. I slept—everybody slept on couches. I had a razor and shaving—

Q. Doctor,—**A.** But I left. I was there Wednesday night. Thursday, Friday, Saturday, Sunday. I left Monday morning. I rode in the ambulance from the Arlington Hospital to the George Washington University Intensive Care. I stayed there. I think she went over Saturday. I stayed Saturday, Sunday, and I left Monday morning back to Seattle. No, I didn't see any great difference.

Q. Now, while you were there, did you have a discussion the very next day or so with Harold Rose about the child? **A.** Yes.

Q. Proceed, Doctor. **A.** Harold said to me "Sam, you know Diane is in dangerous condition."

"And if anything happens to Diane, Alice would like to have the baby."

I said to him, "Harold,—I can't think of anything. The baby is being well taken care of. At the moment I can't think of anything but Diane's condition now." I said, "You know, if something happens to Diane, and God forbid that should take place, Amanda loves the baby, too, Harold." That was the extent of that conversation.

Q. Well, that's the main thing we want to develop. Now, how long were you here before you went back again, Doctor? **A.** One month, three-and-a-half weeks, something like that.

Q. Now, when you were back on this occasion, was there any change in Steve Rose's attitude towards yourself? **A.** Yes.

Q. In what way? **A.** He was more distant. He was irritated with me. He talked to me, but only in a perfunctory way.

b. Cross Examination by Mr. Mellon

Q. Dr. Winter, you have three children, don't you? **A.** Yes, sir.

Q. They're three daughters; the oldest one is Diane, and then—**A.** Polly.

Q. —and then Nancy's the youngest? **A.** That's correct.

Q. Now then, when you saw Nancy in July, at some point along the line you said something about her being in love with Steve Rose? **A.** Yes.

Q. And what was her reply? **A.** "Yes, I am, but not the way you think."

Q. Is that all she said about it? **A.** Yes.

Q. Have you had any conversations with her since then? **A.** No, I've never been able to—to say anything more than "Hello, Nancy" or—we talked a little bit. We talked when she was working this summer and we talked together, and we wrote—she wrote me a letter after two letters that I wrote her. Then I wrote her back two letters, but I have not received any reply from them. One of the letters that I—the last letter I got was Steve's letter and not Nancy's.

Q. She says, "I'm in love with Steve, but not the way you think"? **A.** "Not in the way you think," yes.

Q. Now, the way you thought was that it was love in the usual sense? **A.** I thought she was in love with him, that she wants to—she wants to marry Steve,—

Q. When she said,—**A.**—that she wants to—that she wants—she feels the baby isn't adequate in Diane's care, that she feels Steve is absolutely right about this whole thing.

Q. When she said "but not in the way you think," did you ask her what she meant by that? **A.** She didn't want to talk any more about it.

Q. I'm loath in a way to bring this up, Dr. Winter, but let me ask you this. Are you attempting to charge that your daughter, Nancy is having an improper—some kind of an improper relationship with Steve Rose? **A.** Yes, I am.

Q. Do you have any evidence to back up your statement? **A.** No, except for the feeling that I have.

Q. It's just a feeling? **A.** Nancy was always a loving daughter to me, I thought so. I thought we were close. I felt that we were together. She wrote letters to my wife and myself how much she loved us and how close she was to us. And then after this incident happened with Diane, Nancy began to drift away. And so this wasn't a—this wasn't anything that happened as you make it sound, on the day that she called me about Dr. Bower. This was mostly before that I couldn't communicate with Nancy no matter what I did or said. In fact, she berated me on my second visit to say to me, "How long have you practiced, Dad? Can't you give up your practice and stay here?"

And I said, "Nancy, I can't do that. I've got patients who are ill. I must go back. You've got your mother here, you've got your sister here." And this began to take place. She was supposed to have loved her sister, but she didn't seem to feel any closeness to Diane. It began to slip. Now, this—these are assumptions.

MR. MELLON: All right. I have nothing further, Doctor.

6. Amanda Winter—For the Plaintiff

   a. Direct Examination by Mr. Fisk

Q. You're the wife of Dr. Samuel Winter? **A.** Yes.

Q. And you are, of course, the mother of the three Winter girls? **A.** Yes.

Q. Now, Mrs. Winter, did you go back to Washington, D.C., after your daughter Diane jumped from the—**A.** Yes.

Q. And what day did you go back there? **A.** January 16th.

Q. And what was your daughter's condition at that time? **A.** Diane was in the hospital, in intensive care in the Arlington Hospital, alive, but that's about all I knew.

Q. Okay. And I assume that she was in no condition to be visited at that time. **A.** No.

Q. How long were you in Washington, D.C.? **A.** From the time we moved to the apartment that I had found in Washington until about the middle of April.

Q. Now, when did you get an apartment? **A.** After Diane was transferred to Washington, Polly and I went out to find an apartment there because the Arlington apartment was a one-bedroom apartment.

Q. Where they'd been living you mean? **A.** Where Diane and Steve lived before Diane jumped from the window. I couldn't bear the thought of going to that apartment, so Polly and I went out and found a two-bedroom apartment in Washington, D.C., close to where Nancy lived. Nancy wanted it to be close to her, so we looked only in that neighborhood.

Q. Now, did Steve Rose and his mother move into that apartment? **A.** Yes.

Q. When? **A.** Must have been sometime toward the end of January when we moved over there. I'm not certain whether it was toward the end of January or the first of February. Dates were unimportant to me at that time. The only thing I was thinking of was Diane.

Q. And who paid for that apartment? **A.** I did.

Q. Okay. Where was the baby at that time? **A.** The baby was with Mrs. Rose in Arlington, in the Arlington apartment, until they moved over to Washington.

Q. Okay. Now, who took care of the baby? **A.** Who took care of the baby? Q. Yes. **A.** I never saw the baby at all until they moved over to Washington, because I was with Diane and finding the apartment in Washington and cleaning that apartment to move into.

Q. Now, did you take care of the baby when Alice would go to the hospital? **A.** Yes, after they moved to Washington, Alice went to the hospital almost every night and—and Polly and I took care of the baby until Polly left, and then I took care of the baby.

Q. Now, when Alice was there, who took care of the baby? **A.** Alice took care of the baby when she was there.

Q. And would she permit anyone else to take care of the baby? **A.** No, she made it very unpleasant for anyone else to take care of the baby. She went one time to get her hair done and came in when I was feeding the baby, and she immediately said, "He likes his bottle between bites."

And I said, "I've offered him the bottle and he has rejected it." And she snatched in front of my face and grabbed the bottle and she said, "He sometimes changes his mind." And he put the bottle in his mouth and then began to cry. And she said, "Oh, he doesn't want it now," and she put it down. And then she got toys and began dangling them in front of his face. So I got up and walked away. I didn't think it took two of us to feed the baby.

Q. And did she get real physical if anyone else tried to take care of the baby?

MR. MELLON: This is leading.

A. Yes.

MR. MELLON: This is leading, Your Honor.

A. Yes.

THE COURT: Sustained.

A. When I would change his diaper, she would come and push me aside and she would take over and I would just let her do it. Even when I slept in the room with the baby and he would wake in the night and I would get up to tend to him, she would come in and—and so I—I never tried very long to take care of the baby when she was there, because it took all the joy out of it. I enjoyed him thoroughly when she was not there.

Q. Now, what was Steve's attitude toward you during the time you were there helping them? **A.** Steve was very hostile toward me all the time.

Q. How would he—**A.** It was a—sort of a strained living-under-the-same-roof condition.

Q. Well, in what way was he hostile? **A.** In the first family meeting with Dr. Grant which was, I think, when Diane was still in intensive care in Washington, he stated that I didn't even know what my—what my husband made. And said something about, "Did you folks think that when we—our son married the famous Dr. Winter's daughter that our financial problems with schooling were ended?" And there were many statements like that.

Q. Eventually you came home in April, did you not? **A.** Yes, I came home in April.

Q. And how did that come about? **A.** As I visited Diane daily during the day back there, she grew more and more hostile toward me and there were indications in family meetings that her father and I were to blame for all of her problems. And she was agreeing with this. And I would go to the hospital and visit her during the day and hear her reiterate to me things that she could not have known were happening unless Alice or Steve were telling them to her, that were more and more hostile toward her father and me. And finally I said, "Diane, do you think the pressure would be off if I went home?"

And she said, "Yes. I think you should go home."

Q. As a result of that you did go home? **A.** I went home. And Dr. Cooper had asked that no one do anything until—without letting him know. So I went to Dr. Cooper and told him I was going home. He said, "Diane is more disturbed than she knows or you know at sending you home."

And I said, "I know that, Dr. Cooper but unless I go home and she can learn to hate us she doesn't have a snowball's chance in hell."

b. Cross Examination by Mr. Mellon

Q. Now, just a couple of questions and then I'm through. Dr. Winter originally came from Baltimore, didn't he? **A.** Yes.

Q. And you and he lived back there for awhile, did you not?

A. Yes.

Q. After you were married? **A.** Yes.

Q. And did you leave your husband in Baltimore? **A.** Yes.

Q. And was this—were you not accepted back there? **A.** I was accepted, but it was a very strained relationship and I decided if our marriage was going to survive, we had to live away and out of the influence of my husband's family. And he chose to leave his family and make our family ours and leave the other families out of it.

Q. One of the difficulties back in Baltimore was the fact that you were non-Jewish. Isn't that it? **A.** Yes, they were—they were an Orthodox family and they had objected to him marrying a non-Jewish girl, however, I had converted.

Q. Yes. **A.** That didn't make any difference to an Orthodox family.

Q. Dr. Winter described you as taciturn. **A.** As what?

Q. Taciturn. Do you know what that word means? **A.** Yes.

Q. Would you say that that correctly describes you? **A.** I think so.

Q. And your relationship with your daughters? **A.** I think so. I think—I always assumed that if anybody had anything to tell me, they'd tell me, and I never probed and questioned them a great deal.

MR. MELLON: That's all.

7. Polly Winter—For the Plaintiff

a. Direct Examination by Mr. Fisk

Q. Where do you live? **A.** I live with my folks.

Q. And you are the sister, of course, of Diane and Nancy. **A.** Yes, I am.

Q. Now, yesterday Steve Rose testified that when they were down at college and the time some of the youngsters were eating hashish, that you had baked the cookies. Is there any truth to that? **A.** No, there isn't.

Q. Would you tell us what the facts are? **A.** Yes. A friend of my boy friend at that time had baked the cookies and given them to my boy friend. And Steve knew that they were there and he made arrangements with my boy friend when they would take it, and he said that he would try it the night before, and that if he thought it was all right, Diane would try it the next night.

Q. And did Steve take—eat the cookies both nights? **A.** Yes, he did.

Q. You weren't in your room when this problem arose as to—**A.** No, I wasn't. Steve wanted to be alone with Diane and he wanted to stay with the—the night with her because she was in such physical pain.

Q. Now, you were around Diane and Steve occasionally when they were going together before they were married? **A.** Yes, I was.

Q. What was Steve's attitude toward Diane? **A.** Well, before they were married, once he told me that his friends had told him that Diane was not quite smart enough for him and below him.

Q. What terminology did he use in describing her? **A.** Little dumb.

Q. Okay. You went back to Washington, D.C., after Diane attempted—or did jump—**A.** I went back on the 16th.

Q. That was that same day? **A.** Same day.

Q. For the most part, could you tell us who took care of Jason, the boy? **A.** There's not doubt about it. It was Alice Rose.

Q. Did Alice object to anyone else taking care of him if he was—if she was there? **A.** She sure did.

Q. How long did you stay? **A.** In Washington?

Q. Yes. **A.** Until March.

Q. What was the attitude of Alice Rose towards your father? **A.** She hated him.

Q. Would you tell the Court what, if anything, she had to say about him? **A.** She told my mother and myself that he was dirt, and she would never consider him anything else. And at one time I overheard her talking with my little sister, Nancy, and my little sister was spilling her guts out to her, saying that she used to be able to laugh at my father, but now she couldn't it wasn't funny anymore. And Alice said, "I know, Nancy it's unforgivable."

Q. Did she ever use any epithets for him? **A.** She called him a son-of-a-bitch. She was talking to her brother on the telephone and she was saying "Diane is simply going to have to learn to live with the fact that her father is a son-of-a-bitch."

Q. What was Alice Rose's attitude toward yourself? **A.** She hated me.

Q. Now then, you are presently living at your parents' home, are you? **A.** Yes.

Q. Do you have any long-range plans? **A.** Yes, I do. When this whole matter is straightened out, my sister and I have plans of getting an apartment sooner or later.

8. Nancy Winter—For the Plaintiff

a. Direct Examination by Mr. Fisk

Q. Where do you live, Nancy? **A.** I—well, I live—I presently am staying at the Roses'.

Q. Okay. Now, you attended some of those family sessions, [in Washington] did you not? **A.** Yes, I did.

Q. And at some of those family sessions did you express some hostility towards your parents? **A.** Yes, I did.

Q. And would you tell us what it was that brought out this—brought on this hostility? **A.** Well, it was a number of things. It was that—a lot of it had to do with the way we were brought up as children and the way that we—that Diane and I jointly—Diane and I had many discussions, the way we jointly felt that my parents did not—did not get involved with our childhood, and that they were never really there when we really needed them.

Q. Had there been some sudden change in your thinking? **A.** No. I always—I always understood my parents and I—and I did in fact search out for other—other—my other friends' families and I spent a lot of time at my other—at friends' families, because I didn't—I didn't particularly feel that—I have to say I didn't really have any—very many problems as a child, and I—and I didn't I hadn't really gone through the same things that my older sisters had gone through with—in dealing with my parents. I had a relationship with them, yes.

Q. Well, I want to ask you, Nancy, if up until about Christmas-time, 1973, you thought you loved your parents very much and could hardly stand to be away from them. **A.** I did, yes. I really—I did love them.

Q. Nancy, apparently you feel somewhat estranged from your parents at the present time. **A.** Yes, I do.

Q. Now, would you tell the Court what your parents have done to you since the time of these letters, when you couldn't wait to get home for Christmas, that has caused you to take your present attitude towards your parents? **A.** All right. Well, since Diane's suicide attempt, I—it was a very distressing time for everybody, obviously, and I would—I had—I received a phone call from my father when he returned from Seattle—after about five days after he had come back, he returned to Seattle, he called me and he informed me that I must not stand on the sidelines any longer, that I must get involved in what my parents—in what my parents were disagreeing over and what—you know, this schism between the Roses and the Winters. I told him that I—I didn't want—I didn't want to get involved in this; I felt that it was—it was—you know, was completely irrelevant and that my mother was making a mountain out of a molehill about this idea about Mrs. Rose being very, very over—overly, you know, protective of the child.

Q. You didn't believe that? **A.** No, of course I didn't, because I was there.

9. Diane Rose, Plaintiff

a. Direct Examination by Mr. Fisk

Q. How old are you, Diane? **A.** Twenty-six.

Q. Would you tell us a little bit about your educational background? **A.** I am a graduate from college, graduated with a B.S. Degree.

Q. How did you do scholastically in college? **A.** 3–point.

Q. How about your high school grades? **A.** I graduated in the Honor Society. I'm not stupid.

Q. Now, when did you first start going with Steve Rose more or less steady? **A.** I was 18, right before I went to college.

Q. Did you go more less steadily with him up until the time you were married? **A.** Yes, four years.

Q. Now, you got married on July the 5th, 1980, did you not? **A.** Yes.

Q. At the time you got married did you have any honeymoon plans? **A.** Yes, we had planned to go to the beach for three days.

Q. Whereabouts at the beach now? **A.** At our condominium.

Q. You mean your parents' condominium? **A.** My parents' condominium, yes.

Q. Okay. Now, what happened to those plans? **A.** Steve didn't want to go, so we went to see his mother the next day.

Q. Where did you spend your wedding night then? **A.** Right near his home.

Q. Motel there? **A.** That was our honeymoon, so-called.

Q. Now, how did you come to get married to start with? **A.** Well, Steve was planning to go to Austria for medical school and it was two months before he was to leave, about two months. I didn't want to be separated from him for five or six years.

Q. Were you very much in love at that time? **A.** Very much, yes.

Q. Okay. And so what happened? **A.** I asked him to marry me, and he said he didn't know, that he had to ask his mother.

Q. And did he go ask his mother? **A.** Yes, he did. He came back the next day and he said, "She said it was okay," that she wanted him to marry me, so he said he thought that that was okay.

Q. And so then the wedding came off? **A.** Yes.

Q. Now, how was your trip to Europe financed? **A.** My father.

Q. Why did you return? **A.** Because Steve wanted to. We found that it was going to be eight or nine years and originally he had thought it was five or six. And he never dropped out of dental school.

Q. Now, during the time that you were going together and while you were in Germany, what was Steve's attitude towards you from an intellectual standpoint, if you can tell us? **A.** That I was stupid, that—German was a hard language, and whenever I didn't know an answer, he—he would laugh at me, and so I decided that I wouldn't try anymore because he was just laughing at me and saying I was stupid.

Q. Well, had he made remarks along those lines even before you were married? **A.** Yes, he sure did; I was stupid.

Q. How did you happen to marry him with that type of attitude on his part? **A.** I was in love with him and I was blind, and he did compliment me. He told me I was pretty.

Q. But stupid? **A.** But stupid, yes.

Q. Did you and Steve eventually go to Washington, D.C. then? **A.** Yes.

Q. Did you get a job there? **A.** Yes, I did.

Q. And would you tell Judge Hoover what the job was that you had? **A.** I was a medical secretary in Orthopedics and then in Radiology.

Q. And because of that fact, did Steve get a break in his tuition? **A.** He got it half off, and I paid for every monthly expense we had.

Q. Out of your salary? **A.** Yes.

Q. Did you get any money from home at that time from your parents. **A.** My father had helped us and we had come home for summers and he paid for that, of course.

Q. Now, when was the—you had been there, what, roughly a year and a half when the baby was born? **A.** Yes.

Q. Am I correct that his birthday is April 21st? **A.** 1983, uh-huh.

Q. Now, would you tell the Court whether or not you in truth and in fact worked right up to the day this boy was born? **A.** Yes, I did. It wasn't planned that way, but Jason was five weeks early, yeah.

Q. Now then, who took care of this baby? **A.** I did.

Q. You did? **A.** Yes.

Q. Did you have any babysitters? **A.** No. I loved doing it myself, yes.

Q. Well, and did you do it? **A.** Yes, I did.

Q. Now, is it true that you took care of the child from the time he was born right up until the time—**A.** Absolutely, yes.

Q. —until you—**A.** Yes.

Q. —jumped out the window? **A.** Yes. I loved doing it, m-hm.

Q. During all this time did Steve have really anything whatsoever to do with taking care of him? **A.** Absolutely nothing.

Q. Now, with your income cut off, was it necessary that you have some other money? **A.** Yes, it was.

Q. And how was that arranged then? What did you do? **A.** My father supported us.

Q. Now, during this period of time, would you tell the Court whether or not Steve was becoming increasingly critical of yourself? **A.** Yes, he certainly was.

MR. MELLON: If the Court please, counsel is assuming facts not in evidence. He can ask what the relationship was between she and Steve and so on, but—

THE COURT: Agreed.

Q. How was your relationship with Steve during this period of time? **A.** He was very critical of me. He had always told me how stupid I was, but—with the baby he said how I was inadequate. Quite a number of times he told me that a babysitter could do a better job than I could, and of course it upset me because I loved him very much.

Q. And was this a once-in-awhile or constant-daily thing? **A.** It was a daily thing.

Q. Did Alice Rose come back to visit you about—**A.** Yes, about December. I don't remember the exact date, but it was probably about the 15th, and she left a week prior to my suicide attempt.

Q. Okay. How long did she stay there? **A.** About three weeks.

Q. Now, during this period of time what was the relationship between yourself and Alice Rose? **A.** Well, she told—she would say to me that I couldn't feed the baby right, I couldn't change his diapers right, I couldn't dress him right, I couldn't bathe him right, I didn't put him down for his nap at the right time. And Steve was his mother's supporter.

Q. Now, was the baby healthy? **A.** Yes, he was.

Q. Was he getting along fine? **A.** Yes.

Q. Did Steve ever support you when his mother would criticize you? **A.** Never.

Q. Now, Diane, can you tell us the problems that—so far as how you reacted to the things that were bothering you that led up to this suicide attempt? What things were there that were—Were you depressed at that time? **A.** I was down. I don't know if you'd say I was depressed.

Q. Okay. **A.** I had been convinced that my parents did not love me by Steve and Alice. And Alice had just been back there telling me everything I was doing wrong. Steve was his mother's supporter. And he told me quite a few times that a babysitter could do a better job than I could. And I was very distraught, of course, because I loved him very much.

Q. You're talking about the baby or Steve or both? **A.** Both.

Q. All right. And before you made this suicide attempt what was the last thing that you did? **A.** I called down to the lobby for someone to come up and hold my baby.

Q. Now, of course, you don't remember too much that happened, I take it, during the first few weeks you were in the hospital. **A.** I remember nothing.

Q. Okay. About what's the first time that you began to remember? **A.** Oh, I'd say I started remembering spotty things in April, but didn't start to really remember from day to night until about, oh, June or July.

Q. You attended some—did you go to those early family sessions in March,—**A.** No.

Q. —late March? Or do you remember? **A.** When did I start? I can't remember if I started to go to them in March or April. I don't know.

Q. In the hospital records there's various quotes of your—what you had told the doctors and the nurses and so on. **A.** M-hm.

Q. For the most part, do you remember any of those for the first month or two, to say the least? **A.** No. No. Didn't even start to have a memory in late March or April or (pause)

Q. Okay. You were eventually released—**A.** June 1st.

Q. Okay. I'll ask you whether or not—Was there any pressure on you to leave the hospital actually before you left—before you did leave? **A.** Steve wanted me to come home because the problem was getting too close to home.

Q. And did Steve actually take you home from the hospital personally? **A.** He and Nancy did.

Q. Oh, Nancy was with him? **A.** Yes.

Q. Did Nancy visit you while you were in the hospital? **A.** Yes, daily.

Q. And did she come with Steve most of the time? **A.** Most of the time. And when she didn't come with Steve, she came with Alice or by herself and immediately called Steve up and had him come up.

Q. Now, when you got back to the apartment in Washington, D.C., who was living there? **A.** When do you mean? Oh, when—Okay.

Q. After the hospital. **A.** Steve, Alice. And I was going back to the same situation as Dr. Cooper didn't want me to.

Q. So you returned to Steve and Alice against his advice? **A.** Yes. I wanted to become reacquainted with my baby and I loved my husband.

Q. Now, what was the relationship after you got home from the hospital? **A.** Well, it was the same thing again. Everything that I was doing with Jason was wrong. I tried to do things, but Alice took over. And one of—the day I returned I was holding Jason and Steve said, "Diane, put him down. You will hurt him." So I could have no physical contact with him and it was terrible.

Q. Did Alice stay there all the time? **A.** She sure did.

Q. And was there anyone else there besides you three that were living there? **A.** Hm-m, hm-m (negative response).

Q. Did Nancy come over? **A.** Yes.

Q. How often did she come? **A.** Oh, two or three times a week. I really can't remember. She was close by, walking distance.

Q. All right. Now, you eventually left the apartment that you were sharing there in Washington, D.C., sometime in August. Is that correct? **A.** August 5th.

Q. So the Bower session was after you'd gone and were staying with the Nathans? **A.** Yes, uh-huh.

Q. All right. Can you tell us what led up to your leaving the apartment with Steve and Alice. **A.** That day I had seen Dr. Bower—Dr. Grant, I'm sorry, and he said to me, "Diane, how are you getting along with Alice."

And I said, "Well, she still grabs Jason away from me when he cries, and she won't let me do any—she won't let me finish anything."

And so he said to me, "Diane, you have to be consistent. You have to tell her off because Jason senses you are the child." So I returned home that day and I was bound and determined to be the only one to care for my child, and I was determined to give Jason his last bottle and put him to bed. Well, he wouldn't take it from me, and I had taken him in the bedroom away from anyone else, and I had tried out—tried to give him the bottle and he wouldn't take it. I had put him on my lap and things like that.

Alice walked into the room and she said to me, "Diane, he is not a doll." And she took him away. And I went to call the Nathans.

I said, "Debbie, I have to get away." And so she said that Doug would come and get me in about an hour or so.

Q. Was there an actual physical confrontation? **A.** Yes. Okay, I'll tell—I'll explain. In the meantime, Steve and I were talking and Alice had put Jason to bed. And Steve started to yell and woke Jason up. And Alice went to get him and Jason threw his arms out to me and I took him. I took him away from all the tension in the other room. Jason started to cry. Alice came in and grabbed Jason away from me and I was really mad. I scratched her arm. I have a maternal instinct.

And Steve came in the room and he said, "You're going to drive me crazy."

And Alice said to Steve, "She threw the baby to me."

And I said, "Quit arguing like Steve."

Q. So then you went to the Nathans? **A.** Yes. And I left Alice and Steve Rose. I was driven from my baby. I left this time legitimately.

Q. Now, Diane, how long did you stay at the—**A.** About a month.

Q. No, how long did you stay at the Nathans? **A.** About a month.

Q. Now, during the month that you were there, did you call Steve about some visitation with the baby? **A.** I called him every day and I begged him to bring Jason to see me.

Q. And did he bring him? **A.** He finally brought him three weeks later. No—well, two or three weeks later. Once he brought him with Nancy.

Q. Okay. Now, during the time that you lived with the Nathans did you care for the Nathan child? **A.** Always, yes.

Q. And what did you do for her child? **A.** Well, I fed her and I dressed her. I changed her diapers. I put her down for naps and bed and I loved her.

Q. What happened next? **A.** I returned to my—the apartment that I had left on September 9th. And I had said to Steve—Alice was gone with the baby and Steve returned a couple of hours later, was surprised to see me. And I said, "Steve, I'm back to stay."

And he said, "I'm leaving then." So he picked up a few clothes and a suitcase that I had later found in Nancy's room, and he said to me, "Diane, you're so inadequate. You couldn't even kill yourself." Then he called my doctor and told him I would be alone that night, and he said, "Fine."

Q. What doctor did he call? **A.** Grant. And he called my parents to tell them. And he said, "If anything happens to her, you are to blame."

Q. You heard this conversation? **A.** Yes, I did.

Q. When you came to Seattle, were you having difficulty with visitation then after you came here? **A.** I certainly was. I was to see the baby four times a week in Seattle without a Rose, and they wouldn't allow it, and this was for three weeks they wouldn't allow it, until I filed a custody hearing. Then they suddenly came up with a third neutral party, well, competent, and I could see Jason three times a week. Before it was two times a week and I could not see Jason without Steve.

Q. Now, the visitations you've had since this proceeding was started, how successful have they been? **A.** Well they have had not one but two and three watchdogs. They have them follow me from room to room. Everything I do with my baby is—I'm on display. Let's see. Many times I've gone there Jason has been very tired. They've said he missed his nap. And on one occasion he slept in my arms the whole night—the whole day, the whole visit. And they asked me to put him down for him to sleep and I said, "No, I want to hold my baby."

Q. Has he been—would you state whether or not he's been obviously tired on the occasions you've been there? **A.** Many times, yes.

Q. Where are you living now? **A.** At my parents.

Q. And your sister Polly lives there? **A.** Yes.

Q. Are you doing any work? **A.** Yes.

Q. What kind of work are you doing? **A.** I'm working at a church answering the phone. And when I'm not doing that, when I am free, I practice my typing, I'm a very good typist.

Q. Now, your mother has raised three children? **A.** M-hm.

Q. She knows how to wash a baby and feed him and that type of thing, does she? **A.** M-hm, yes.

Q. And if you're granted custody of this child, do you propose to keep him at the Winters temporarily? **A.** M-hm.

Q. And what are your long-range plans? **A.** Well, I am planning to move out in an apartment with my sister, and I will have a part-time job, and I'm going to put Jason in nursery school and work when he's in school, and that's what I'll do.

Q. Now, so far as the immediate future is concerned, do you have some money left in your trust account? **A.** Yes. I don't know how much, but yes.

Q. And your father is willing to help you financially? **A.** He has always been willing to help me.

Q. Do you have a good relationship with your parents at this time? **A.** Yes, I do.

b. Cross Examination by Mr. Mellon

Q. You and Steve were happily married, weren't you? **A.** I thought so. I always hid my sad feelings. That's why I tried to commit suicide, because I had realized he didn't love me and I wouldn't admit it to myself.

Q. When did you realize that? **A.** Well, I guess I—well, quite a few months it had been.

Q. Pardon? **A.** Quite a few—quite a few—a few months, but I wouldn't bring it to my conscious.

Q. You wouldn't do what? **A.** It was so conscious, I'm sorry. I wanted Steve to love me and—and he not only didn't love me, he wants me dead. That's what I found out when I went to find—I went to see Nancy and his suitcase was in her room. And he told me that I was so inadequate, I couldn't even kill myself.

Q. Now, when did you find Steve's suitcase in your room—I mean in Nancy's room? **A.** About September 13th.

Q. Yes. Well, you didn't know anything about any suitcase in Nancy's room at the time you jumped out the window, did you? **A.** No.

Q. And you and Steve were living a happy, normal life at the time of—that you jumped out the window? **A.** I thought we were happy. I wanted—I hoped to God that we were happy. I was—I loved him. I wanted him to love me, but he didn't.

Q. When you were in the hospital, Mrs. Rose, you didn't say one word against Alice Rose. **A.** I thought she was great.

Q. You thought she was great? **A.** Yes, I was brainwashed, just like Nancy is now.

Q. And you didn't say anything in the hospital against your husband, did you? **A.** No, I thought he was great, too.

Q. But you didn't think he was great when you jumped? **A.** I wouldn't admit it to myself consciously. I wouldn't admit my sad feelings.

Q. All during the time that you were in the hospital you never said anything derogatory about Steve or about his mother, did you? **A.** Not that I remember.

Q. But you said a lot of derogatory things about your parents? **A.** I sure did. I was acting just like Alice.

Q. What do you mean by that? **A.** I loved my husband, but I had to act just like Alice to keep him. That's what I mean.

Q. You mean you had to act just like Alice to keep your husband? **A.** Yes, I had to hate my parents for her, uh-huh, and I tried to, believe me. I tried to.

Q. And is that the only reason that you kept saying in the hospital how you blamed your parents—**A.** Yes.

Q. —for what had happened? **A.** That is exactly right.

Q. So that you could keep Steve? **A.** You hit it right on the nose.

Q. And you felt in order to keep Steve that you had to say that you hated your parents, that you'd had a bad upbringing? **A.** That's right.

Q. And that they were the ones that were responsible, because of the way they brought you up, for you being unhappy and depressed,—**A.** Yes, that's right.

Q. —and requiring and making you jump out the window? **A.** That's right. Yes.

Q. You did that just so you could keep Steve? **A.** Well, my mother is—yes. My mother is a very quiet woman. She never worked. She was always with the kids. And I began to misperceive her love for me.

Q. You say that you were very depressed at the time of the—that you jumped out of the window. And you say that—you say it wasn't because of your background and all that sort of thing. You say it was because of Steve. **A.** M-hm.

Q. Well, why didn't you just sue him for divorce? **A.** Because he would make me—made me feel so inferior, and I loved him and I thought that he was the best I could ever get. That's why.

Q. Well, you wanted your baby, didn't you? **A.** Yes, I did, but I thought that—I thought I was doing the best job I could as a mother, and I thought that it wasn't good enough. He made me feel that way, yes. I tried to kill myself for my baby actually.

Q. You tried to kill yourself for your baby? **A.** Because I felt I was a burden for him.

Q. For the baby? **A.** I felt I was a bad mother, yes.

Q. So you felt that divorce wouldn't be adequate, that you had to do away with yourself? **A.** I thought I couldn't do any better. Steve would not allow me to be myself and I—and I hadn't realized—I hadn't realized why. I loved him so much that I just thought there was nothing else I could do but to get rid of myself for him and my baby.

Q. Did you feel that by jumping out of the window you would in that way hurt Steve? **A.** Oh, no. No, I thought I was—I thought I was relieving him.

10. David Greenburg, M.D.—For the Plaintiff

a. Direct Examination by Mr. Fisk

Q. And are you a licensed doctor? **A.** Yes. [The Doctor is next qualified as an expert in psychiatry who has specialized in suicide.]

Q. All right. Now, Doctor, at my request, did you do a psychiatric examination of Diane Rose? **A.** Yes, I did.

Q. And when did you do that? **A.** June 8th, 1985.

Q. Okay. Now Doctor, when you examined her, were you able to form an opinion as to whether or not she was suicidal? **A.** Yes.

Q. What was your opinion? **A.** My opinion was that she was not suicidal at that time. I would put her in the lowest lethality group. And that is not to say that it would be absolutely impossible for her to make a suicide attempt, because in my way of thinking, I doubt that I would say that about any person that I have ever met. But that she certainly was in the low group.

Q. Now, do you know a suicidologist or psychiatrist, named Theodor Dorpat? **A.** Yes, I do know him, and I know of his work.

Q. And has he made a study of this same problem? **A.** Dr. Dorpat has written a number of articles and done some research, original research on suicide. He published an article in 1986 called "The Relationship Between Attempted Suicide and Committed Suicide." One of the points that he dealt with in this article was a list of thirteen factors which have been found to be associated with a high probability or risk of subsequent completed suicide, among those who have attempted suicide. Number one, age, older more than younger; number two, sex, men more than women; number three, serious suicide intent in the attempt; four, multiple prior suicide attempts; number five, unmarried marital status, unmarried could be single, widowed, divorced, or separated; number six, living alone; seven, poor physical health; eight, psychosis; nine, a lethal method used in the attempt of suicide; ten, a suicide note; number eleven, infrequent use of health agencies; number twelve—unemployed or retired; and number thirteen, from a broken home.

Q. (By Mr. Fisk) Now Doctor, of that list of thirteen, Diane Rose would fit in four categories, would she not?

MR. MELLON: I'm going to object to counsel testifying.

Q. (By Mr. Fisk) Well, how many would she fit in, Doctor? **A.** Out of this list of thirteen, I scored Diane Rose as pointing toward suicide on four of the thirteen issues. Now, there was one which I sort of have a question mark about, which is this: Number twelve says unemployed or retired. There is a question there, because although Diane Rose is not receiving any payment, it is my understanding that she has a regular agency at which she works, or a number of agencies at which she works. My prejudice would be to count that as against suicide, but it is a question.

Q. Well, assuming whether she's unemployed or not, now, assuming she fits four, is that in the low scale, or how would you rate that? **A.** That would put her at the, just speaking from this group, at four out of twelve, or four out of thirteen would, generally speaking, put her in the lower third of serious, in the spectrum of lethality.

Q. Now Doctor, up to now, we've been speaking of the statistical data, and I want to talk to you about Diane Rose as a person, and ask you, forgetting about all of those tables, how do you find her as a person, and how do you rate her? **A.** I rate Diane Rose as at the present time being of low lethality, and of continuing to move in a direction which will make her of lower lethality. Now I say this with all circumspection, that is, there are things that could happen to her. There are things that could happen to any one of us, which we cannot predict, and which turn us toward suicide or toward any other kind of untoward circumstance. But these are the reasons, as I see it, why I judge Diane Rose, at the present time, to be of low lethality.

In the first place, I think that one of the features of a suicidal person is the issue of their having a kind of an all-or-none philosophy; that is, there are one or two or whatever number of things that are very important to that person. And their feeling is—feelings of these extremely suicidal people are that if they cannot get that thing, then life is not worthwhile, and they will kill themselves.

Now, from this standpoint, I was unable to determine that there was that general kind of psychology in Diane Rose at this time. And I made a number of attempts, both to observe whether it was present, and even to ask her specific questions about it. Some of the specific questions that I remember were these: What will you do if you do not win custody of your child? Her answer, in essence, was that she would be disappointed and unhappy, but she had plans to do some other things. She was considering either going to school, or going to work, or a combination of both of them. So that seemed to me a striking thing.

Now, another issue—now I'll switch to another area, and that is, that the question of her passive personality is an extremely important one in my opinion in this case. And it is for this reason: My feeling is that the suicide attempt can best be described as a combination of an environmental stress with a particular kind of personality which tended to be subservient and to defer to authority, which also looked for authorities to whom to relate herself. Now, I think that she—a person in such a situation might have relatively good luck, and might get involved in a situation in which the authorities did not put her under stress, did not put her under states of extreme tension. That is a possibility. On the other hand, it is a possibility that the opposite could occur, and that is what I think happened in Diane Rose's case. So now, the problem, one of the problems with a passive personality is that they are caught in a severe kind of what you might call a double bind. That is, on the one hand, in order to get along with the authority who they fear and/or respect, and/or love, it is necessary for them to go along with whatever that person wants. However, at the same time, that person may be asking the passive person to do certain other things which the passive person doesn't want to do. For example, to—well, when I think of Mrs. Rose's case, to sever relations, or to have some—to decrease the intensity of her relationship with her parents, to give up her own opportunity, her own desire to treat her child as she wished. So—and there may be some other things, but I picked these as two examples that I think I remember from her history. So that in that kind of situation, the passive person's own passivity makes him vulnerable. Now, I think that Diane Rose, even prior to the time of the suicide attempt, was making some attempts to change this part of her personality. For example, I think that her marriage itself, and the resolve to utilize that as a way to move away from home, may have been part of that situation.

I believe that she is moving in that direction for some of the reasons that I cited, and I think that therefor makes the contribution to the possibility of suicide from her own passivity less. And it is for these reasons that I think that she is of less lethality, of low lethality, and that probably that this trend will continue. One other thing that I think I should add at this time is that Diane Rose, again in connection with the issue of turning—blaming herself for all kinds of things, now has changed in another way, and that is, that she has come to the conclusion that having someone, namely a professional person, namely a psychiatrist, work with her at times of stress, is a good idea. As far as I could tell, she has been working with a psychiatrist. She feels that, and I would concur, that she has made some advances. She feels that she has improved at this point, but that it is possible that she may have difficulties in the future. And that if she does, her intention is to resume more intense psychotherapeutic work. That, too, is something that I think is both an indication of less lethality, and an indication that should she have future difficulties, as all people are bound to have, that if she gets to the point where she feels it beyond her, she will seek help for them.

Q. Now, Doctor, all of this leads up to the question as to the care and custody and control of the minor child. Mr. Rose has testified that if he's awarded custody of the child, he intends to go to U.C.L.A. where he is starting a residency in internal medicine, where his hours will be eight or nine to five every day. With every fourth night, he'll have twenty-four-hour duty. I'll ask you to assume that for the past several months as you're aware, his mother has been largely responsible for taking care of the child while Mr. Rose has attended the University of Washington Medical School.

I'll ask you to assume that Diane Rose, and for the first eight months of the child's life, or thereabouts, before the suicide attempt, was, of course, a person that cared for him mostly, and his father, the child's father, was going to medical school at George Washington at that time. That since they've been out here in Washington, she did not have much visitation up until February or—January or February of this year, at which time the Court ordered visitation of four hours twice weekly, plus every other weekend, which she's enjoyed since that time.

Ask you to assume that the child views both his father and his mother as psychological as well as biological parents. Ask you to assume that either of them could provide an adequate physical facility; that if Diane gets the custody of the child, she will live with her parents, and she will devote full time to the child until he's old enough at least to be put in a nursery school or something of that kind, at which time she will probably work short hours while he was in the nursery school.

If Mr. Rose gets custody of the child, he proposes to take the child to Los Angeles; his mother proposes to go with him and stay there indefinitely until such time as he can get what is thought to be a suitable live-in person to take care of the child when he's not available.

Now, with those alternatives, and considering the welfare of the child, I'll ask you who, in your opinion, should be awarded the permanent care and custody of this child. **A.** I would say that with the knowledge that I now have, and given the particular question, that I would say that Mrs. Rose would be a superior parent to Mr. Rose. And I base that statement, I believe, on two ideas. The first one is that it is a general postulate in Western society that the mother is a more important parent than the father. And the second one is that I think at this young time in a child's life, a time when a child traditionally needs more intimate and attentive care from a parent, it also—it is possible for Mrs. Rose to supply this intimate and constant attention to a greater degree than Mr. Rose. That's my answer.

b. Cross Examination by Mr. Mellon

Q. You feel that the mother is a more important parent than the father, even with the male child with the father? **A.** Yes.

Q. Are you familiar with the law [of this state] on this subject? **A.** No.

Q. Are you familiar with the fact that the Washington law is that no parent shall be favored by reason of the fact that that parent happens to be the mother? **A.** No.

Q. Do you agree with that? **A.** No.

Q. You do not agree with the Washington law? **A.** No.

Q. As I understand it, Doctor, you have never seen this child, or have you? **A.** I have never seen the child.

Q. And you've never seen Steve Rose, you assume he's sitting on my left, but that's the only time you've ever seen him? **A.** That is correct.

Q. And you saw Diane Rose down in Los Angeles—was it in Los Angeles? **A.** Yes, it was.

Q. For how long? **A.** An hour and fifteen minutes.

Q. And is that the only time you saw her until you came up here today? **A.** That's correct.

Q. Did you see her prior to coming to the courtroom today? **A.** No.

Q. And you feel comfortable in making the assertion, Doctor, that with what you know about your visit of an hour and fifteen minutes, with never having seen the child, and never having seen Steve Rose with the child, never having observed Steve Rose with child, and how they get along, and never having observed Diane with the child, and how they get along, you feel comfortable in sitting up there and saying that you think she should have the custody of this child? **A.** Yes, I do. And I did want to remind you that I did say that I thought those issues were important ones, and that I was making—I was giving my impression without having that kind of information available.

Q. Now, are you familiar with the work of Goldstein, Freud, and Solnit, Beyond the Best Interests of the Child? **A.** No, I am not.

Q. Have you ever heard of it? **A.** I've heard of Solnit. Is the "Freud," Anna Freud?

Q. Yes. **A.** Yes. I've heard of those two people.

Q. Those are well-known people who enjoy excellent reputations, are they not? **A.** Yes.

Q. Are you familiar with the fact that their work has been cited with approval by the appellate courts in California? **A.** No, I am not.

c. Redirect Examination by Mr. Fisk

Q. [D]octor, counsel asked you some questions about the Winter family, and placing the child there, and so on; now, I want you to assume this: In this case, there is evidence and testimony that in some of these family sessions, the doctor who was conducting the session, indicated that Steve Rose and his mother both needed psychiatric treatment; that Alice Rose, the mother, was mentally sleeping with her son, Steve; that she had emasculated her own husband, mentally; that both she and Steve were in need of psychiatric treatment. He went so far as to say that what Alice Rose needed was a "good lay."

Now, with that background, would that buttress the opinion you have previously expressed? **A.** Well, of course, I can't pass—

Q. Assuming that's the facts. **A.** If that were the fact, then I think that would be further supportive of the position that I stated.

MR. FISK: Thank you, Doctor. That's all.

d. Re-cross by Mr. Mellon

Q. If you want to enter into that type of speculation, Doctor, assume that this same doctor told Diane Rose that her father was a stuffy son of a bitch; and that he should have thrown her out of the window a long time ago. Is that the sort of thing that is going to alter your opinion one way or the other? **A.** If it is true, then it mitigates against the recommendation that I made.

MR. MELLON: That's all.

MR. FISK: Thank you, Doctor.

THE COURT: Thank you. You may step down.

11. Constance Howe, Psychologist—For the Plaintiff

a. Direct Examination by Mr. Fisk

Q. Now, your name is Constance Howe? **A.** That's correct.

[Dr. Howe is next qualified as a clinical psychologist who has specialized in child development].

Q. Will you describe your current work? **A.** What I do is both in a service sense to the citizens of the State and in a research sense, I'm attempting to conduct a program that takes parents who have extreme difficulties in dealing and interacting with their children, and then apply an approach to this pair, call it a "parent-child pair," that entails observation of parent and child interacting in what we call a "standardized," if you will, laboratory, playroom setting.

One circumstance is what might best be known as an absence of parent control. We call it the "Child's Game." The mother is instructed to just go along and play with the child. It's his game, his activity, his time to do as he wishes. You just go play along with him until we communicate with you again. We'll tap on the one-way mirror.

That used to go on for thirty minutes at a time, although now, we don't have to observe that long. At the end of ten minutes, we'll rap on the window, and instructions are now reversed, and we have the necessity for a parent-control time. We call it "Mother's Game." The instructions are somewhat the same, with just one variation, "All right, Mrs. Rose, now it's time for your game, and your rules. You get Jason to play in whatever game or activity you wish. It's your game, your rules, and you keep him at it." And we will observe again for ten minutes. We also, just to wind this up, we also should we not observe the problem behavior in either of those two circumstances, which is very rare, but should we not observe the behavior, we then have other circumstances that we have the child and mother engage in. Perhaps we have had reports that the child is out of control or unmanageable when the parents have company. We would proceed to put several people in the room with the mother, for example, to try to simulate mother occupied with other people, or father occupied with other people, and watch, and observe again how a child will function.

Q. Well, before we get to this, now for a moment—you referred to "we," you are talking about yourself, or—**A.** All right. I train students. I train psychiatric residents, I train medical students, and when I say "we," we have a team of people who are lined up to receive training in this very approach.

Q. How many students do you have under you? **A.** I would have as many as seven at a time.

Q. Is this the type of thing you've been doing for the last thirteen years? **A.** I developed this approach, yes. It took me about five years to develop it. And then—I have been doing it for thirteen years.

Q. Now Doctor, what can you say with reference to whether or not this is something unique and different than has been put forward in the past, at the time you were taking training, for example? **A.** The contribution, I hope, which will come over time with this, to all kinds of community agencies, is that it will assist in the decision-making process, based on the giving of relatively solid, reliable information, observed or obtained standardly over time. In contrast to opinion-giving, based perhaps on one encounter where the conditions aren't even defined, you might—for example, you might say—my own colleagues do this, it's still in the field—where a person says, "Well, I saw Mrs. Smith, Johnny Jones"—whoever it is—"I saw them in my office, and we had a discussion, and I came to a conclusion based on that. I'm a competent person."

The problem is ... we know that clinical inference-making is very unreliable unless we have relatively repeatable data that we can bring to bear on that. We can't replicate what went on. The kinds of circumstances I've tried to describe in these observation sessions could be replicated in Atlanta, Georgia, or in Ottawa, Ontario.

Q. In other words, you've tried to standardize these? **A.** That's right.

Q. All right. Now, Doctor, I'll ask you if you were requested to do some of your specialized testing on Diane Rose and her son Jason. **A.** Yes, I was.

Q. And specifically, would you tell the Court, what were you to find out? **A.** The referral question that was posed to me was, "would you be willing to help us determine the competency of a young mother to mother her child? Would you be willing to do this?"

Q. When was the first date that you saw her? **A.** May I look at my—I don't remember all these dates.

Q. Sure. If you need to refer to your notes, please do so. **A.** Yes. I just have the initial interview. The first date—2-25.

Q. How did she do? **A.** All right. Supposing we keep in mind three categories. Diane and Jason as one category. Another category, a sample of twenty excellent moms, moms judged to be excellent by professional people, physicians, social workers, occupational therapists, psychiatrists, they all helped get the sample of good mothers.

So Diane is being compared with twenty mothers who are good moms, and twenty mothers who are poor moms. And then average moms, those who are in the middle. So we have the categories. Diane, if you take a look—if I give you numbers, it's just like trying to remember numbers, nobody is going to remember them.

First, on these mother behaviors, Diane scored in—Now, I'm going to try not to be technical, this is going to be a problem. I don't want to make it cloudy for people. When a child is doing his own thing, if you could think in terms of any human beings, when any two people want to be, or are together, just to enjoy each other, the goal there is that—neither of them, or certainly one of them, doesn't take over and command or control. That it's a kind of enjoyable thing.

And in the mother-child circumstance, it would be a condition where the mother wouldn't do what all poor mothers do. They tend to teach. "What's this, what's that, what are you doing," that's poor behavior in that circumstance. But Diane and the good moms do not—or did not do that. In other words, we have what we call a behavior called "attending," where you can just note what's going on, and what another person is doing, and make comments about it. Appreciative comments.

Q. Yes. And how did she score? **A.** The average for the three sessions, for the good mother sample, those mothers would attend to their child for 49 out of a possible 60 seconds. Diane attended for 36 seconds, and poor moms attend for 15.

Q. Okay. **A.** 15, 36, 49. Average moms attended for 38 seconds, and the 2 points, one way or the other, makes no difference. I mean you don't fix it exactly.

Q. Now, did I understand you correctly that in this particular category she came out high? **A.** She came out with the good moms.

Q. Okay. **A.** Now, the second test gives us a clue in a way, how it goes between a mother and a child when there is no need for the mother to force the child to come to me, or to do this or that.

In the good moms sample, their children interacted with that mother out of a possible 50 seconds a minute, their children interacted 46.8, forty-seven seconds a minute. Diane—or Jason, interacted 38 seconds a minute, and poor moms' children interacted 26.9—make it 27 seconds a minute. And the average moms 39, so again, on their children interaction with them, Diane and the average moms are absolutely together, and certainly nowhere near, you know, poor parenting.

Q. Taking into consideration your own observations of Diane interacting with the child, and I'm going to ask you if you have an opinion as to the—considering the welfare of the child, who should be awarded the custody? **A.** My opinion is that Diane should be awarded custody, period. I don't know if you want reasons.

Q. All right. Now, if she's awarded custody, and do you see some plusses for the child, looking at it from the child's standpoint? **A.** In terms of the hypothetical—

Q. Psychological development of a child? **A.** In terms of the hypothetical points that you've put to me, it would seem that there is a continuing stable relationship provided in the mother-child situation. Not because she's just the mother, but because of the one-to-one, and absence of other individuals. There's a stability in that situation that I think—and given the fact that she has the competencies to do it, which is my—I'm satisfied with that data. I would see no reason why she should not be awarded the custody of this child.

b. Cross Examination by Mr. Mellon

Q. Now Dr. Howe, you testified yesterday, as I understand it, that you'd had no M.D. training? **A.** No, I do not. I'm a Ph.D. psychologist.

Q. You say that you have a Master's in education and psychology. And you had a Ph.D in what? **A.** Psychology.

Q. Now, your training that you had was not with children, was it? **A.** Absolutely it was, yes.

Q. Pardon? **A.** It was. It's with both, but with a good bit of emphasis on work with children.

Q. When did you get this training? **A.** The City College in New York, and also at the—

Q. That was your Master's Degree? **A.** That was at the Master's level, and then at the Ph.D., not only in the practicum work that went on, but in the post-doctoral work I took here at the University of Washington Medical School, it's another level of training, I forgot that one, beyond the Ph.D., I took a year's post-doctoral work with children.

Q. Ph.D. was obtained where? **A.** Pennsylvania State University.

Q. Incidentally, Dr. Howe, are you married? **A.** I'm not.

Q. Have you ever been? **A.** I have not been.

Q. And have you—not going to ask if you've had any children, naturally, but have you had occasion to raise any children, have you adopted any children? **A.** No. I haven't, and that brings a very interesting point that I would like to discuss with you, and that is, that at one point in my life, this is my own personal matter, but at one point in my life, I made a decision, Mr. Mellon, that I could not carry out the kind of what I hoped would be competent professional life and rear a child and conduct a family the way I thought it should be done. I could not personally do both of those things, so you ought to know that I made that decision.

Q. Now, I also understand all of your reference was to the good moms and the average moms and the poor moms, and I believe you said that your dealing is almost primarily with mothers; is that right? **A.** Yes. For the data collection, because we can't get enough fathers to come. But whenever in our work a father can come, we work directly with him. We'll stay until six and seven at night to do so.

Q. Do I understand your testimony is, though, that the great bulk of your work is with mothers, and not fathers? **A.** Yes. I would say that has to be the case.

Q. Now Dr. Howe, have you in connection with the work that you've been doing, do I understand that you have had no publications that have been printed in any of the periodicals? **A.** That is correct. And it's correct as I tried to indicate yesterday, because I wanted to wait until we had the followup work as well, which we do now have.

Q. So, go ahead. **A.** We have parents who have participated in the program between five and seven years. You see, it's easy to get followup data after two months, for example, and then you can rapidly publish, and say, "You see, our findings show that the same thing prevails, or it doesn't," but five or seven years later, to me, seemed to be a far better time. That's what I wanted to do.

Q. You've written no texts on the subject? **A.** No, I have not.

Q. And you've had no publications? **A.** That's right.

Q. And so the data that you have, or the system that you use, that you have developed yourself, has not been submitted in any of the periodicals? **A.** Or has not been subject to peer review, your thinking?

Q. Yes. **A.** In the formal sense of periodicals, no; in the sense of national requests to do what I do because it is working, that would not be the case; but for formal publications, you are correct.

12. Harvey Pyle, M.D.—For the Defense

a. Direct Examination by Mr. Mellon

Q. Dr. Pyle, where do you come from? **A.** Washington, D.C., Metropolitan area.

Q. And what is your occupation? **A.** I'm a psychiatrist.

Q. Do you practice in Washington or in Maryland or in both? **A.** I'm licensed to practice in Washington and Maryland. [Dr. Pyle is next qualified as an expert on suicide]

Q. And have you had occasion, Dr. Pyle, at my suggestion to read over the hospital records, of Diane Rose? **A.** I have.

Q. Do you have an opinion as to what this young lady was suffering from at the time of her attempted suicide? **A.** I do.

Q. Would you explain it, please? **A.** I feel that this young lady was suffering from a severe depressive reaction.

Q. Now, could you explain that? **A.** By "severe" I mean it was out of her ability to control her feelings, her reactions and her behaviors.

Q. Now, do you have, Doctor, any opinion as to what the likelihood is of a repeat as far as this young lady is concerned in the future? **A.** Yes, I do.

Q. What is your opinion? **A.** My opinion is that it will be likely that this lady will make another suicidal attempt.

Q. Now, how do you arrive at that conclusion, Doctor? **A.** I arrive at that conclusion from several sources. My first source is my clinical experience in which I have treated over a hundred patients who have made highly lethal attempts from which they have survived only by chance. This young lady survived by the chance of having a shrub break her fall, but there are any number of lethal overdoses that you can survive by chance. These people, by definition, have been followed in our Suicide Study Unit at the National Institute of Mental Health and we've studied them in depth, and we find that they are depressed, seriously depressed and chronically depressed; that their ability to handle stress is very, very greatly impaired; that they are subject to going into precipitous and somewhat unpredictable depressive episodes from which they are likely to have great difficulty to emerge without adequate professional help or adequate support systems, support-system help, too.

Q. Now, do you have an opinion, Doctor, based upon what you've seen and heard concerning the—and your experience and learning, on what—whether or not the child in this case would be in any danger.—

A. I do.

Q. —if she were given custody of the child? **A.** I do.

Q. What is your opinion? **A.** I believe that the child is at risk of sustaining both psychological trauma and physical trauma, and that the psychological trauma could be considered both as an immediate trauma and also considered as a future trauma. By that I mean to say that the psychological trauma that happens to a child when it is separated from its mother by any forceful circumstances, by a suicidal attempt, as this was, has indeed affected that child. The circumstances, I believe, are likely to occur again, thus exposing this child to another psychological separation and trauma.

There is a psychological phenomenon involving children who tend to personalize or who feel that there is something wrong with them when a parent abandons them. The future implication is that people who go to make suicidal attempts themselves have often been exposed to suicidal behavior, so that by continuing the child in an environment where suicidal behavior is likely, there is more exposure.

The second aspect of my answer has to do with physical.

Q. With the physical, yes. **A.** A study by—by Reznick, who reviewed the infanticides in this country, show that there were two characteristics of the mothers who killed their children that were very significant. Seventy-one percent of the mothers who killed their children has a history of diagnosed depression. A third of the mothers who killed their children had a history of prior suicide attempt. I find these both present.

b. Cross Examination by Mr. Fisk

Q. Now, you put Diane in the high risk category in part because she had chronic depression? **A.** Yes.

Q. And yet all the people who have seen her, all experts and colleagues of yours, have stated that she is not depressed at this time. You heard that testimony? **A.** Yes.

Q. And yet you placed her in the chronic depressive category. **A.** I did.

Q. Now, all of your testimony is based just upon some statistical studies and has nothing to do with any examination of this particular person? **A.** It's not based on solely statistical studies. It's also based on my review of the record,—

Q. All right. **A.**—the information and my having sat in this courtroom today.

Q. But not involving any examination of Diana Rose? **A.** That's correct.

Q. Now, Doctor, as a psychiatrist, do you feel that rearing a child in the Rose home, Steve Rose and Alice Rose, in view of the admissions by Steve Rose, is healthy for this child? **A.** Excuse me. In view of the what by—

Q. All right. I'll ask you to assume that Dr. Bower is correct in his assessment that they needed therapy. **A.** Are you going to ask me to assume that Dr. Bower is a competent practitioner of psychiatry?

Q. Right. **A.** I will not assume that.

Q. You will not assume that? Well, I will ask the Court to instruct you to assume it.

THE COURT: This is a hypothetical question he's asking.

THE WITNESS: M-hm.

MR. MELLON: Could I ask the witness one question, Your Honor?

THE COURT: All right, go ahead.

MR. MELLON: Do you know Dr. Bower?

THE WITNESS: I do not know Dr. Bower. I've only heard about his practices in the treatment of this—

MR. MELLON: Now, this is a Dr. Bower in Washington, D.C., not Dr. Bower here in Seattle we're talking about.

THE WITNESS: Oh. Oh. I know Dr. Bower by reputation in Washington, D.C.

MR. FISK: But you don't know him personally?

THE WITNESS: I do not know him personally.

Q. Does he enjoy a good reputation? **A.** Not amongst the people that I've talked with.

Q. Doctor, I'll ask you to assume that Dr. Bower was correct in his assessment that Alice Rose, Nancy Winter and Steve Rose all needed psychotherapy, and ask you if under those circumstances you think that is the type of home that this child should be reared in. **A.** I think that people can undergo psychotherapy and have psychotherapy, many people do, and still have proper and appropriate homes in which to rear children.

Q. So you wouldn't think there was anything that was contraindicated so far as custody of the child concerned? **A.** No, no. I don't think that psychotherapy and custody are incompatible.

Q. Doctor, who's paying your expenses for coming here and testifying? **A.** My arrangements are with counsel.

Q. And what are your arrangements? **A.** My arrangements are my expenses, my transportation and my fee for testifying.

Q. Now then, your fee for coming out and reciting these statistics is several thousand dollars, is it not? **A.** I think it will come to that.

Q. And specifically, it's in the area of seven-or $8,000, is it not? **A.** I don't believe so.

Q. Well now, you know what it is. You've made the arrangements. Will you tell the Court what you're being paid to recite these statistics?

MR. MELLON: I'm going to object to the form of the question. He isn't being paid anything to come out and recite statistics, Your Honor.

THE COURT: Sustained.

Q. Would you tell the Court what you're being paid to come here and testify? What's your professional fee? What has Mr. Mellon agreed that his clients would pay you? Now, that's clear enough, isn't it? **A.** Right. A thousand dollars a day.

Q. A thousand dollars a day. And does that include your travel time here and back? **A.** Yes, yes.

Q. And when did you come? **A.** I arrived last night at nine p.m.

Q. Last night at nine p.m. And so you'll have at least two days or three days, depending when you get back? **A.** No, I'm leaving tonight at ten-thirty p.m. I had to make extensive rearrangements to be able to do this.

Q. Are you sure it isn't more than that, Doctor? **A.** More than what?

Q. More than a thousand dollars a day. **A.** For my testimony here?

Q. No, that isn't what I asked you. I'm asking you if you're testifying under oath that all you're getting for testifying here is $1,000. Now, you recognize the penalty for perjury, do you not?

MR. MELLON: I object to that, Your Honor. There's no point—

MR. FISK: I'm just simply—

MR. MELLON:—in making it appear as though he's going to be up for perjury. He's—

MR. FISK: I think we ought to have the truth and I just want to be sure we're getting it.

MR. MELLON: You're getting the truth.

THE COURT: Well, I understand, and you can go ahead and answer the question. Overrule the objection.

A. In addition to this, I am being paid for the compensatory time that I have had to cancel my patients in my office schedule.

Q. Are you being paid also for consultation with Mr. Mellon and Mr. Rose and so on? **A.** I am.

Q. Now, can you give us an idea what all of this amounts to, how many thousand dollars? **A.** About $4,000.

Q. Plus your travel time—**A.** M-hm (affirmative response).

Q. —or traveling expenses? **A.** M-hm, around—in that neighborhood.

MR. FISK: Thank you very much, Doctor.

13. Kenneth Piller, M.D.—For the Defense

a. Direct Examination by Mr. Mellon

Q. Doctor, you have already stated that you are an M.D. What is your specialty? **A.** Psychiatry.

Q. And are you in the general practice of psychiatry in Seattle? **A.** I am.

Q. All right. Now, in connection with your practice of psychiatry, Doctor, did you have occasion to talk to Steve Rose in the recent past? **A.** I did.

Q. All right, Doctor, would you go ahead and tell us what happened with Mr. Rose. **A.** Yes. Now, in going to the biologic or the biologic-medical area, I was the one who directed the entire interview by asking specific questions to get information, such as, he told me that his birth was normal. I asked him about family history of illness, both psychiatric and medical. He told me his grandmother had cancer. Continuing, he told me that he had no significant childhood illnesses, but as an adult had infectious mononucleosis. He practically drinks no alcohol now, but in college he did. He doesn't smoke. And he denied use of marijuana and hallucinogenic agents.

The only major accident was in the fourth grade, a skating accident, with a fracture of the right forearm.

His weight is 145 and stable. Appetite: good. Sleeps without difficulty. That led me to the next area, which is the social. He was born in Seattle, Washington, and raised in this general area. I asked him about his mother, age 46. His feeling about her, quote, "I respect her and I love her, and I often disagree with her. She's giving, she's honest. She's opinionated." Later I asked him about her health and he said that she's in good health. And then he said, quote, "She's been a strong influence on my life morally and spiritually."

Father is 50, Vice President of a tool and die company. Good health except for some bile stones. Quote, the feeling was "I love him very much. He's very warm, intelligent and forceful," unquote.

Sisters: Julie, 19. And perhaps you might notice that I definitely asked for feelings, because I'm searching to see if an individual uses feelings, such as glad, sad, warm, good, versus opinions, such as, "I feel that so-and-so," because I need to know if a patient can distinguish feelings from opinions as they talk in interpersonal communication.

"How do you feel towards your sister Julie?"

"I love Julie very much." Diane, 23, feeling—

Q. That's his sister Diane? **A.** Diane, another sister, 23, married, who lives in Ashland. His feeling: With love.

Then, "How were you raised?"

He said, "Jewish."

"How do you feel about being raised Jewish?"

Answer: "Good." Conservative synagogue he attends.

Then I got on to his marriage. He described his wife Diane, as 26, having been pregnant once and having given birth to one living child or fetus. They were together for under four years prior to marriage. He said, quote, "I loved her. She was an honest—or is an honest and loving person." Sex was okay. He told me that she worked as an orthopedic secretary and a radiology secretary the first and second years of his attendance at medical school. They've been married about four-and-a-half years. The baby is about twenty-and-a-half months old. She has a Bachelor of Science Degree from Seattle State University. He commented that there were two suicide attempts. One he thought was about 1979, the other January of 1984. I asked him if he knew why the second attempt, and he said, "One, feelings of inadequacy with the child; and, two, feeling of abandonment by her parents."

Now she lives with her parents in Seattle. The two families are about eight minutes apart by car. He has some relatives, three aunts and three uncles, and he is distant toward them.

The next area is the vocational area. He worked for his father-in-law, the first and second summers of medical school. At age 16 he worked in a supermarket. In college he worked for a pipe and casing company. One summer he sold insurance. He's never been fired. And for the future, he would like to go into academic internal medicine.

The next area is the avocation or the recreational area. He reads for pleasure. He enjoys basketball, plays the piano. He likes movies and television.

The fifth area is the learning area. He graduated high school, graduated four years of college, had two years of dental school. Now, I could slip back to the social area in this sense, although it still relates to the learning area, that in 1980, after one year of dental school, he and his wife went to Austria, and spent some days in England also, because he wanted to see about the possibility of attending medical school in Austria. He told me that his wife was with him, but was upset because of not being near her parents. He returned and finished his second year of dental school and was accepted to George Washington School of Medicine, currently is in his fourth year, taking an elective here in Seattle and can graduate without necessarily returning to Washington, D.C. He would like to go into oncology, which is the study of cancer and diseases of that nature.

The sixth area is the emotional area. In this case it is how an individual might handle his or her major emotions. With anger to his wife he at times was sarcastic and at times he would express it straightforwardly, with anger to community personnel, such as clerks, gas station attendants and so forth, he would be open. With depression he replied, quote, "I try physical exercise and I also will tell people."

There was no history of suicidal ideation. I asked him how he handled anxiety, and it was similar to the above, physical exercise or telling friends that he was anxious.

I gave him a brief IQ test. He knew the date. He told me his birthdate as June 25th, 1957. He knew the current president, current vice president, he knew the first vice president, the number of colonies, the current number of states, the capitals of Oregon, China. He got the wrong answer for Spain, saying it was Barcelona. He knew the three largest cities in the United States. I had him do serial 7 subtractions and made him go the whole way and he got them all right. He knew the difference between "idle" i-d-l-e, and "lazy." And he had recent recall for three unrelated words: "Table, red" and "Broadway" after a few minutes. And I asked him to interpret two fairly difficult proverbs: "A rolling stone gathers no moss," and "The golden hammer opens the iron door," and both were abstract, were interpreted in an abstract, correct manner. My impression then would be above average IQ, no evidence of organic brain damage and no evidence from this of schizophrenic process. So that my final diagnosis was: no mental disorder.

Q. What is your opinion as to whether or not then Mr. Rose is what you would call a normal human being? **A.** My opinion is that he is.

Q. And did you observe any possible reason why he could not make a good father to a young son? **A.** I did not.

MR. MELLON: That's it, thank you.

b. Cross Examination by Mr. Fisk

Q. You knew that Steve Rose was a smart medical student and you found him to be such, did you not? **A.** Correct.

Q. Now, you specifically inquired of him about his mother, and he told you he loved his mother, often disagreed with her? **A.** Correct.

Q. Now, suppose that you were advised that that was an out-and-out fabrication, that he never disagrees with her. How would that affect your judgment? **A.** Well, I wouldn't get that information—

Q. No, just—if you—I'm asking you a question. If you found that the statement that he often disagrees with his mother was not true,—**A.** If I were told that he were dominated by his mother, after having done a complete evaluation, I would ask his mother to come in to see me, because it doesn't jibe.

Q. I see. Now, have you ever examined his mother? **A.** I have not.

Q. Now then, did Mr. Rose advise you that he had attended some family counseling sessions in Washington, D.C.? **A.** I believe so. And I was just looking at my notes from the first session. (Pause—referring.) I don't see a note on here specifically relating to your question.

Q. Now, I'm still not quite clear in my own mind whether or not Steve Rose told you that in the late fall of '84 he'd been to a family counseling session with a psychiatrist in Washington, D.C. **A.** Well, my notes do not indicate that.

Q. Well, do you know a Dr. Bower in New York—or excuse me, in Washington, D.C., a psychiatrist there? **A.** I know a Dr. Bower, a psychiatrist in Seattle, but not in Washington, D.C.

Q. You don't know—I think the one in Washington is a brother. You don't know him? **A.** No.

Q. Doctor, if you were advised that Dr. Bower saw Steve Rose, Alice Rose and a bunch of relatives in a family session, and told Steve Rose that his mother was emotionally sleeping with him, would that surprise you? **A.** I would be surprised. I'd be curious.

Q. You have a medical term for that, do you not? **A.** Yes.

Q. Would you tell us what it is? **A.** The Oedipus complex.

Q. And would you be surprised to find out that Dr. Bower said that's what the problem was in Steve Rose's case? **A.** Yes, I would be surprised.

Q. Now, Doctor, if in truth and in fact Alice Rose is caring for this child, as distinguished from its natural mother, and she has an Oedipus complex for her son, and she is vicious person, would that—and that she dominates her son, would that contraindicate her caring for this child. **A.** Well, in using—

Q. No, Doctor. Would you answer my question? Explain it any way you want. **A.** I'd like to answer your question.

Q. All right. **A.** In using my review of areas, I would have to make an assumption. Physically meaning the biomedical area Mrs. Rose is competent and intact physically because she's in the role of mother to a grandson.

Q. Right. **A.** Okay. Socially you're talking about an Oedipal complex toward her son.

Q. Right. **A.** And jumping over to the emotional area, you're saying that she handles her emotions viciously. I don't know—

Q. I'm asking you to assume that. **A.** But I don't know if you mean viciously with her mouth, viciously with her hands,—

Q. Both. **A.** I would want the grandmother in the role of motherhoo-dery to have some psychotherapy as soon as possible, if she's handling her feelings viciously and has an Oedipus complex.

Q. You'd want some psychotherapy for her? **A.** Yes, I would.

Q. And why would you want that, Doctor? **A.** Because if she were to physically strike a twenty-and-a-half-month-old baby, it might lead to damage physically; and if she has outbursts emotionally, that could also create a shy, withdrawn little baby.

Q. You know Dr. Samuel Winter, do you not, Doctor? **A.** On an impersonal basis.

Q. Well, I don't mean you're social friends, but you know who he is? **A.** Yes.

Q. And he's a highly-respected member of the medical community, isn't he, as far as you know?

MR. MELLON: I'm going to object to that, Your Honor. That has nothing to do with the issues in this case.

THE COURT: I don't know whether it does or not. I'll allow him to answer.

A. He has a good reputation and he is highly respected in the community.

MR. FISK: Thank you, Doctor.

c. Re-direct by Mr. Mellon

Q. Doctor, do you know anything about Alice Rose at all? **A.** I do not.

Q. Have you ever seen her? **A.** I don't think I have. I hope this isn't "Candid Camera."

(Laughter.)

Q. Do you have any evidence of any kind of viciousness on the part of Steve Rose? **A.** Nothing came through to me on the evaluation that Mr. Rose had a vicious handling of his emotions.

d. Re-cross by Mr. Fisk

Q. Just one further question: Did Steve Rose tell you that his mother considered her own father a psychopath? **A.** This was not told to me.

Q. Did he tell you that at one time his mother beat the hell out of her father with a belt? **A.** This was not told to me.

Q. Did Steve tell you that during married life every time there was a family argument, he would say, quote, "I attack and she withdraws"? **A.** His marriage or his parents' marriage?

Q. No, his own marriage, his relationship with his wife. **A.** This information was not given to me.

Q. So the things that were given to you were pretty much what we might call ginger and spice? **A.** Is that a question?

Q. Yes. **A.** The things which were given to me were what I told the Court.

Q. But none of these things that I have mentioned were told to you? **A.** Correct.

MR. FISK: Thank you, Doctor.

14. Steven Rose—Defendant

a. Direct Examination by Mr. Mellon

Q. Now, Mr. Rose, there's been testimony in this case, about you going to Austria as a medical student and that, of course, you returned after a relatively short period of time. Was that because you wanted to return or was there some other reason? **A.** Not at all. I—I acquiesced to my wife's desire to come home.

Q. What was the problem? **A.** When we went to Austria, we had planned to stay for the—the five to six years. And we knew that it was going to be hard, that we were going to take German classes twice a day and to study the language. In fact, the German classes, there were—there was no English spoken, only German, and it was very difficult. There were two dental students who had applied along with me to Karl Franzen University in Graz, Austria, to attend medical school.

THE COURT: I'll sustain the objection.

Q. Well, what I, of course, want you to tell us, Mr. Rose, is—and I think that's what you were doing, is as to why you gave up your chance to go to medical school in Austria. Was it your idea or was it—

MR. FISK: He's already said it was Diane's idea.

MR. MELLON: It was hers, and now he's explaining, which I think he's entitled to do. I think he's entitled to tell exactly what happened, because—

MR. FISK: I object to any more testimony on this point. Your Honor.

THE COURT: Is that the question you want to ask him?

MR. MELLON: Yes.

THE COURT: Okay.

A. And Diane cried and said that she wanted to go home. There was another—we had other people there and we talked back and forth whether to go home. And I—I wanted to stay. And I told Diane that, "This may be my last chance for medical school." I had applied before and was not accepted in the United States. And I said that all I had was dental school, which I did not tell them that I was going to leave dental school. And so after—after awhile and after the pressure, I told her we'd come back. I had ambivalent feelings about leaving Austria, but finally I—I left. Diane and I left and we went to London for a week and New York for a few days and then went home.

Q. So when you left Austria, did you have at that time any hope of ever getting into any other medical school? **A.** Well, I always had the hope of getting into medical school, and I—

Q. Did you have any knowledge of any place you could possibly get into? **A.** No, because if there was, medical school took six years over there, it would be a lot easier to go to dental school and then—then four years to medical school, if I had a shoo-in.

Q. Well, did you know of any medical school in the United States at the time you left Austria that you could possibly get into? **A.** None.

Q. Had you attempted, exhausted the possibilities before you went over there? **A.** Yes, yes. I—well, there's over a hundred medical schools. I'd applied at a number of them and was not accepted, so my—you know, my hopes weren't high.

Q. And now do you recall a letter Diane received from her mother just before her suicide attempt? **A.** Generally I do.

Q. All right. Would you just—First, let me ask you: How long a letter was it? **A.** It was maybe ten pages typed.

Q. Would you, as best you can recall, state what the content of that letter was? **A.** Well, it was a very castigating letter against myself, both my parents and Diane, and told how we were like little children and that I—how we didn't need a car, that they never had a car when they were first married, that I should have taken the bus; and that I didn't need a camera; that I—we should not have lived in—in Virginia, we should have lived in Washington, D.C. And it talked about all the terrible times that she went through with my father-in-law; and that—that since they went through it, we should—we should go through it, too.

And one thing, what I thought was probably the lowest blow and really hurt me the most, is a reference in the letter to a physician in Seattle who had recently passed away by an unknown cause. It was Dr. Fall, and he was a very renowned thoracic surgeon. I used to have political discussions and we would argue. . . . And she said in the letter, she said, "Charley Fall now lies dead in his grave and it was you who argued with him."

And the whole letter was that she was—she said that my parents were—were like children, that they spent too much money on luxuries; the camera was just their inbreeding on me, and I was doing this to Diane; and that then she talked about Diane being like a child and she shouldn't be acting this way. And that was the general attitude of the letter.

Q. All right. Now,—**A.** She also said that we could never come home again; and to never tell Daddy, she said, that she ever wrote the letter because she would be so upset.

Q. Because he would be so upset? **A.** Because he would be so upset with her.

Q. Oh. Well, did you say that she said you could never come home again? **A.** Right.

Q. Well, what effect did this have on your wife, if any? **A.** I read the letter first and I said, "Diane, we got a letter from your mother."

And she looked at it and she said, "I don't want to read it." So I read it. Then she sat at the kitchen—at the dining room table and started to read it. And she was totally fractured after she read the letter.

She—she just said, "I can't believe it. I can't believe she's saying these things to me." She said, "I don't—I don't know what's wrong."

Q. All right. What, if anything, did she do about this after that? Did she contact her mother, anything—**A.** Well, we talked—we talked about it that evening, and then she said she was going to call her father and tell him. She—she then called her father.

Q. The day you got the letter, the evening you got the letter? **A.** I really can't remember the time sequence, but she called him shortly after she got the letter.

Q. And were you present during the conversation? **A.** Yes.

Q. What did you hear as far as the conversation was concerned? **A.** Well, my conversation was only one-sided, because I only heard Diane, and I—I did not talk to my father-in-law.

Q. How long did the conversation last? **A.** Oh, 45 minutes to an hour.

Q. Forty-five minutes to an hour? **A.** Yes.

Q. And did you discuss the conversation after it was over with— **A.** Oh, yes.

Q. —with your wife? **A.** Diane—Diane would intermittently yell and get upset, and she—

Q. You mean during the conversation— **A.** Yes.

Q. —with her father? **A.** Yes. And I was—I was holding Jason at the time and would walk out of the room. I didn't listen to all of the conversation. I'd walk out of the room and back in the room with him. And she—and she was very upset, and she said "Don't you believe me? Don't you believe me that she wrote that?"

And afterwards she told me that he said, "Your mother couldn't write something like this. I can't believe she would write it." And Diane said, "She wrote it. I would—I have it here. I would like you to see it. I'm telling you what's in the letter."

Q. Did she report anything further to you after the conversation was over that her father had said to her? **A.** Just that he couldn't believe that my mother-in-law would write such a thing.

Q. On the night of the 15th of January, 1984, were you home at the apartment? **A.** No.

Q. Where were you? **A.** I was at the Veterans Hospital in Washington, D.C. I'd been on 24—I was on 24–hour duty starting Tuesday morning and was on all night.

Q. When did you leave—when did you last see your wife? **A.** I last actually saw my—I last talked to my wife Monday evening. I last saw her Tuesday. She was sleeping when I—when I left the apartment.

Q. Now, between that time and the next time you saw her in the hospital, did you have any occasion to talk to her by telephone? **A.** Yes.

Q. When did you talk to her? **A.** I spoke to her at, oh, six or seven o'clock in the evening.

Q. Is that on the 15th? **A.** Yes.

Q. All right. **A.** I called her up, and she knew I was—I was a little upset because I—I really didn't like the Veterans Hospital. There was a lot of work there. And she—she sounded a little funny to me, because she said—she told me, "Don't call back because I'm very tired and I'm going to go to bed early." She never said that to me.

I said, "Well, what if I get a little depressed? Can I call you?"

She said, "Sure." But she mentioned to me that she was going to call her folks and then go to sleep.

Q. Is that the last time then that you talked to her? **A.** Yes.

Q. When you were away from home like that on duty, did you or did you not attempt to call her usually during the course of the day or the evening? **A.** I always called Diane. I called her in the day and I called her in the evening. And she had my phone number if she ever needed me.

Q. How did you hear—how did you get the word that she had jumped out the window? **A.** I was on the ward at the Veterans Hospital, having been up the full 24 hours. I was just going in to see a patient who was in sickle-cell crisis, and they said, "There's a phone call for Steve Rose." I thought it was just somebody saying it was a library book overdue, and I got to the telephone and it was a Mrs. Jenkins who was our—our landlady. And she said, "I have some bad news for you."

And so I said, "What is it?"

And she said, "Your wife jumped out of the window." And I—I—a nurse must have seen my expression or something and she grabbed me and she—and then Mrs. Jenkins said, "What do you want me to do with your baby?"

And I started to cry, and I said, "Hold him there." I said, "Where is she?"

She said, "She's alive and she's at Arlington Hospital."

Q. Arlington Hospital? **A.** Yes.

Q. That's Arlington, Virginia, Hospital? **A.** Yes.

Q. What did you do then? **A.** I—well, there were a lot of people around me at that time, and then people would—one guy wanted to give me an injection of Valium, and I remember throwing a chair across the—the hallway. And another medical student of mine who—friend of mine said he was going to take me, because he worked at Arlington on the weekends and he—he could get me there. So that's how I found out.

Q. Well, what did you do then after that? **A.** Well, we drove through every red light and every stop sign to get to Arlington. It took about a half an hour. And I went right to the Emergency Room where Diane was lying.

Q. And what was being done for her at that time? **A.** At that time nothing had been done. They said that X-rays had been taken and they were awaiting the results. I said, "Is there a neurosurgeon or a neurologist?"

And they said, "There's a neurosurgeon who has been called."

And I said, "Where is—"

Q. Was she actually in the—**A.** She was in the—

Q. —Emergency Room? **A.** She was in the Emergency Room on the table when I saw her there, and she was decerebrate, and she was—she was barely moving. And I went in and saw her just lying there in this decerebrate posture, and emotionally I was just destroyed.

Q. So what did you do? **A.** Well, they escorted me out of her room and said the neurosurgeon was coming. And then I—I called my parents and told them. Then they said that they'd—they would come on the—the next plane. They were very upset as well. And then I called my mother-in-law and said that, "Something terrible has happened," that, "Diane—Diane jumped out the window and she's in critical—critical condition at the hospital," and I really didn't know what to do and it looked just terrible to me.

And she said, "Oh my." She said, "What shall I do?" She said, "Are your parents coming back?"

And I said, "Yes."

So then she said, "Well, at least you'll have your parents." And then she said, "I'll call—I'll call Father. He's at the hospital."

But I didn't wait for her to call him. I—well, I—I didn't call him immediately, but I went up to the Intensive Care Unit, where they said they were going to be bringing her up. I talked to her neurosurgeon, Dr. Bortnik, and he said, "I've seen a case like this, something like this before;" that, "There was a girl in an automobile accident that was decerebrate and comatose for six months and now she's riding horses in England."

So I said, "Well, what are the chances? Does she have any real chance?"

So he said, "Well, I've seen it before. It's happened once before." He said, "It can happen again."

I said, "But does it look bad?"

He said, "Well, of course, it's bad." He says, "I'm going to start her on Asmatrol drip," that's to relieve the edema from the brain.

And I called—tried to get in touch with a neurologist who I'd been working with just a month previously.

Then I called my father-in-law after Diane had come up to the floor and I saw her, and—in a special room, just right outside the main room of the Intensive Care Unit. I was very upset. I called him and—

MR. FISK: Is this witness answering some question, Your Honor? I've lost track, it's been so long.

MR. MELLON: I asked him what he did, Your Honor, and I think he's entitled to tell what he did.

THE COURT: Go ahead.

A. I called him on the phone and I said—and I told him—I guessed he had not got the message. And he said, "Hello." And I told him that—that Diane had attempted suicide, she'd jumped out the window, and I didn't know what to do. And I said, "What—" I said, "What do you think I can do?" And he asked me if I had a neurosurgeon. And then he said, "Well,—" I told him that she had taken Phenobarbital, that the police had found Phenobarbital there. And he said, "Well, get a urologist and maybe we should have the urine alkalinized because that would get rid of more Phenobarb in the blood stream." And I told him that was a good idea, and I said, "I don't know what to do;" he said, "Neither do I." I said, "I've got to go back in."

He said, "I'll call you back." So he called me back. I went in to see Diane. By this time the whole right side of her face was swollen. I thought she had a broken jaw. I called the neurosurgeon who had left the hospital, and I told him about this, and I said, "Did you realize that her face was swollen?" And he said, "No." So I ordered ice packs on her face. The Asmatrol drip had not started, so I got the nurses to—to start an I.V. They called one of the residents to start an I.V. She was not being cardiovas—did not have a cardiovascular monitor, so I ordered a monitor on her. And I asked her to be moved out of this room where they came in every 15 minutes, to be moved to the main room where she could be seen at all times by the staff, by the nursing staff.

Q. She wasn't in Intensive Care then? **A.** She was in Intensive Care, but she was in a room right next to the main room of the Intensive Care Unit. The Intensive Care Unit had about eight beds, but there was one room that was right next to it which had a door and Diane was in that room, and the nurses would come in every 15 minutes to watch her and take vital signs.

Q. So you had her moved to the main room? **A.** Yes.

Q. Now, as a medical student, were you entitled to give any orders in that hospital? **A.** No.

Q. But you did anyhow? **A.** Yes, because she—Dr. Bortnik told me that she was going to have the Asmatrol drip. Her orders hadn't come up from the—from the Emergency Room. Diane was decerebrate, which showed that this may be fatal. Her pupils weren't equal. Her pulse was irregular and I honestly thought that she was going to die at any time.

Q. All right. Now, did her condition improve any or did it get worse, or what? **A.** Her condition stabilized that—that evening, and in the morning, on Thursday, Dr. Bortnik had his associate come. And he said, "Well, she looks better than yesterday." On Friday morning she took a turn for the worse. Her pulse became irregular. She started with Cheyne–Stokes respirations. She—her pupils became unequal again and one was not reacting to light, and she became decerebrate again. Her respirations became irregular, as the Cheyne–Stokes respirations, and her heart rate dropped to around 40, showing that there was possible herniation of her brain into the spinal canal, and this scared the hell out of me.

And I—I called—I wanted Dr. Bortnik to know and start this Asmatrol drip again, he did over the phone, but we couldn't get—we didn't see him in person. Diane did not seem to be improving, so I—I really panicked. My Dean had called the hospital before. I had not talked to him, someone else did. So I called up the Dean, to ask him for help. He told me that the best neurosurgeon in the city, Washington, D.C., was Dr. Raymond. So they gave me Dr. Raymond's number. I called him and they said Dr. Raymond was in a meeting and couldn't be reached at that time.

Q. Now, did you have any discussion with Dr. Winter at that time or about that time concerning getting Dr. Raymond? **A.** Yes. I remember that we were—he knew I wanted to get Dr. Raymond and I—I was—I left a message for him to call, to come over to Arlington Hospital. And we were in the Intensive Care Unit with one of the nurses, and he said to me, "Don't you think that this is the best, all we can do?"

And I told him, "I don't know." I said, "Dr. Raymond is supposed to be the best." I said, "If Diane dies and I don't get the best man over here, I'll blame myself forever, if there's something he could do."

Dr. Bortnik had been a student of Dr. Raymond I later found. Dr. Raymond—Dr. Bortnik was not at the hospital at that time and we couldn't reach him on the phone.

Q. And did you get Dr. Raymond over there? **A.** Yes.

Q. Did you ever have any discussion with Dr. Winter concerning the measures that you had taken that you described the first day—or the first—yes, the first day that she jumped? **A.** No, the only discussion that we had is—was—we were in the hall and I—I said I wanted another chance with Diane. I told him I shouldn't have gone to medical school, that it may have been too much of a strain on her for me to be away; that I knew Diane wanted me to be home more. And I—I told him that if she came through, that I would think about quitting. And I—I didn't want to have anything more to do, I was so upset. I told the other medical students who came later that, "I just don't think that I can go on," and that, "I should have stayed in dental school and not tried to be an M.D."

Q. Did Dr. Winter ever commend you for the emergency measures that you had taken in Diane's behalf? **A.** A few days later, at Howard Johnson's Motel—Hotel across from the Watergate, we were—we were—we went to bed—we went to sleep in the same bed and we were talking about the first day and the circumstances, and he said—and I told him what happened and—Diane's you know,—the ice packs and everything. He said, "Well, Steve if Diane pulls through," he says, "you'll be—you're to be a great part of her help."

Q. What kind of a person is Dr. Bower? **A.** Oh, he's very hostile sometimes, very affectionate other times. He—he's sort of like a Don Rickles, I think, of psychiatry. He hits you with a shock before you even mention a word and then will sort of make up to you at the end, and then he'll hit you with a few more shocks, then will walk out of the room saying he refuses to talk to you people anymore, then come back in and sort of smile and then say, "I'm going to present you my bill right now. I'm finished talking to you people." Then he'll—he'll sit—he'll laugh a little bit and then talk to you in a—with respect. And it's—it's a different—I've never experienced anybody like him. He'll hit you with everything. So he brought up things about everybody.

Q. All right. Now, did he in any way—he did accuse you of certain things, did he not? Q. Oh, yes.

Q. Did he say to the effect—to the group as a whole something to the effect that, "You're the most—"

MR. FISK: I'll object to counsel's leading questions, Your Honor.

MR. MELLON: Well, Your Honor, these questions—these things have been brought out by counsel.

THE COURT: You can refer him to the incident.

Q. Well, this was a five-hour get-together, wasn't it? **A.** Yes.

Q. —would you tell us everything that was said? **A.** I can't tell you everything that was said, but I can tell you some things. He said, "You're the most vicious group of people I've ever met." This is before we had a chance to even speak. Then he—then he said about me, he said I needed therapy. He said—he said my mother needed therapy. He said, "Nancy needs therapy." He needs—he said, "Diane, if I—if I were her husband, I would have thrown her out the window." He says, "She's a spook. She scares the hell out of me. She's incompetent." She said—he said to Nancy—these are the castigating things he said. He said to Nan—about my father-in-law, he says, "I talked to him on the phone and I know what an s.o.b. he is." He says, "Nancy, you're worse than—than fatherless." He says, "Anybody who would have a man like that," he said, "this man's in medicine," and he went on and said things of that flavor. Then he asked me a little later to explain myself and my feelings, and which he did let me have a chance to expound.

Q. Your feelings about what? **A.** About what I went through during this tragedy. And I told him—I told him how I felt. And then he came over and put his arm around me, and Diane's therapist, Dr. Grant shook my hand. And before Doug Nathan left he also shook my hand and—and told me he misjudged me. Everybody in the room at that time was crying except Diane.

Q. Was there anything said about any relationship between you and your mother? A. No.

Q. By Dr. Bower or anyone else? A. No.

Q. There was something said about your mother needing certain type of treatment? A. Yes.

Q. Could you give the context in which that statement was made? A. Well, he said—he said it on two different planes of thought. Once—once he said, "You need treatment." He says, "God, how can you take this?" He said, "This is just a terrible situation that you're in. You're not getting any support from anybody." So then he said—then at the end, I know what you're referring to, he said,—this is as he closed the meeting, he says—he sat back in his chair, he says, "What you need, Alice," he says, "you need a lay," he says, "not that I'm offering my services." So that—that sort of ended the meeting. He said to the four of us that we should go out—he says, "There's been enough things said on this day. Go out and have an outing together," he says, "do something nice." And I told him that was a very good idea. We all said that was a good idea and we left to plan an outing.

Q. Wasn't anything said about what your mother had done to your father supposedly? A. Certain things were said. I—I'm not sure of the specifics. He mentioned everybody and he said everybody was sick at one time, but I'm not—I'm not sure what specifically was said.

Q. Now, after the Bower incident Diane was still living away from— A. Yes.

Q. —the apartment, wasn't she? A. Yes.

Q. Did she ever come back? A. Well, I asked Diane to come back on several occasions. I told Diane that I wanted her to see Jason and I wanted to see her. And I told her at one time that I would pick her up, bring her over; my mother wouldn't be around and just the three of us would be there, and she refused. Diane rarely called. And then finally I talked her into—to coming over. And so on several occasions I picked her up and we visited with Jason on a couple—I think the Nathan's dropped her off one or two times.

Q. Now, what comes next as far as your progress in the medical field is concerned? A. I have been accepted by the matching program to the University of California at Los Angeles, and a residency program in internal medicine for the upcoming year, to commence on June 23rd.

Q. I believe that the testimony before was that you had stated your preferences for your residency program prior to the trouble that has arisen, that gave rise to this case? A. Yes, I did. And then after this case in Seattle, I notified my dean, and the matching program, which takes care of the residencies in the United States for the American hospitals—and placed the University of Washington—the number one position—was not chosen by the University of Washington in the match, and was chosen—I was taken by my second choice, U.C.L.A.

Q. Incidentally, you say you're graduating from George Washington? A. Yes.

Q. Is it with honors? A. Yes.

Q. What's the meaning of that? A. Well, a certain amount of people are chosen out of a class of a hundred and thirty who graduate with distinction, and nine this year graduated with distinction, and I'm one of those. The minimum criteria that they set is to have half of all courses to be honors, we are on honors, pass-fail system.

Q. Is that the highest you can graduate with, with distinction? **A.** Yes.

Q. All right. Now, when are you due to go to U.C.L.A.? **A.** I'm to start—our orientation is on June 23rd.

Q. Have you been down there and looked over the situation? **A.** Yes. I went down to U.C.L.A. twice. Once to talk to Dr. Richards, who is the head of the house staff training, that's all the residents, all the people training at the hospital, and talked to him and discussed my difficulties with him. And then I went down on another occasion and secured an apartment and furniture that was four blocks away from U.C.L.A. Hospital.

Q. Now, you say you've discussed your situation with Dr. Richards? **A.** Yes.

Q. And what situation are you talking about? **A.** I informed Dr. Richards that I had received temporary custody of my son, Jason; that I would be coming down to U.C.L.A., and would be the only parent; so I asked him for special privileges, to grant me special privileges, so that I would be able to spend as much time as possible with my son. And he responded by giving me the easiest rotation at U.C.L.A. in internal medicine, of the twenty-seven that they give. He also said he would do everything in his power—

MR. FISK: Just a moment, your Honor. This is all hearsay; it's self-serving, and I'm going to object to it.

THE COURT: Sustain the objection.

MR. MELLON: Well, your Honor, could I be heard just a moment on that?

THE COURT: Go ahead.

MR. MELLON: I think this is vital as far as—or maybe not vital, but I think it's important as to what arrangements he's going to make down there, what arrangements he is able to make. I don't know how else he can get it before the Court, unless he reports to the Court what arrangements have been made, and what he's been informed as to what the situation will be, and what hours he'll have to work, and so on. It's the only way that the information can be gotten to the Court.

MR. FISK: I would suggest counsel can secure a sworn affidavit that Mr. Rose is getting these special privileges. We might be willing to let that go in evidence.

THE COURT: Maybe, Mr. Mellon, you could then, on that suggestions, if you wish to take it up, maybe you could make a call to Mr. Richards and arrange for that, but I still sustain the objection. The fact that it would be helpful doesn't get it over the evidentiary objection. It makes alternate means more attractive, is all.

Q. (By Mr. Mellon) All right. Have you checked, Mr. Rose, generally what your duties will be at U.C.L.A.? **A.** Yes.

Q. And would you just tell the Court what you will be doing? **A.** Okay. The on-call schedule is usually every fourth night. What we do is we rotate through different services. I have chosen to rotate through the emergency room for three months, which is a twelve-hour on shift, and will be able to take nights, seven to seven. So I'll be working at night for three months, seven to seven, and be home in the day.

The rest of the months will be one month of vacation, one month of adolescent medicine, two months of what they call the Wilson Pavillion, which is their private service, and also one of the easier services.

Q. What do you mean, "their private service?" **A.** Private service is they already have their private doctor who has already seen to it that they have their diagnosis. It's their private service—the residents don't do all the work. The private doctor is the one that's in charge of taking care of the patient. We just act as ancillary help there; and then the respiratory care, and cardiac care unit. And that's more or less what my duties will be, and one month of elective time. So what generally is the case, is I will be on every fourth night.

Q. From when to when? **A.** Well, for the twenty-four hours that you're on, and you come in the morning, and then you go from eight to eight. I might add that if you live close by, you can take night call from home.

Q. In other words, you just sit there in the house, and if the phone rings, then— **A.** Right. They call you, yes.

Q. Then you go over there? **A.** Yes.

Q. Approximately how many hours a week would you be working? **A.** On the days that I am not on duty, I'll be home from five o'clock on. The days that I am on duty, you're allowed to leave in the afternoon and come back and be on call from six o'clock till the next morning, so you're able to go home in the afternoon. So I'd be able to go home for three or four hours in the afternoon, and come on call at night again. Take calls from home. It all depends on the emergencies at the hospital, how much I would have to be there, living right next to the campus, next to the hospital.

Q. Now, what arrangements have you made as far as the actual physical care of Jason is concerned? **A.** Immediately, I have contacted Dr. Kenneth Talbot, through Dr. Bower, from Seattle who is the head of the in-patient child psychiatry unit at U.C.L.A. He said that he will work with me—he said that—

MR. FISK: Just a moment. Object to all of this hearsay testimony, your Honor.

THE COURT: Sustained.

Q. (By Mr. Mellon) Have you made any advances, or have you made any inquiries to determine whether or not competent people are available to act as housekeepers, in-housekeepers? **A.** I have.

Q. And what's the situation? **A.** Situation is that they're available.

Q. And is it your intention to have this woman there part time or full time? **A.** Full time.

Q. And what would be her duties? **A.** To take care of Jason while I'm at the hospital.

Q. What are your intentions when you go down to Los Angeles the end of this month, or within ten days or so, with Jason, if the Court awards you the care, custody, and control of Jason? **A.** My intentions are to take Jason with me, and my mother, and for her—for me to screen available women to live in, and to have them live in, and then my mother to go home after a certain period of time, when Jason feels comfortable and adjusts to another face.

Q. You said "them." Are you talking about getting more than one woman? **A.** No. Just one woman.

Q. And is it your intention to have this woman there part time or full time? **A.** Full time.

Q. And what would be her duties? **A.** To take care of Jason while I'm at the hospital, to see that he gets his recreation, and his sleep, and his meals, when I'm not there. And to provide affection and care for him.

Q. Do you have any doubt at all, Mr. Rose, as to whether or not you will be able to provide good and adequate care for Jason while you're down there? **A.** I have no doubt that I can.

b. Cross examination by Mr. Fisk.

MR. FISK: Now, the person that's been taking care of this child for the most part continues to be your mother, isn't that right? **A.** Incorrect.

Q. Oh? **A.** Myself.

Q. Yourself? **A.** Yes.

Q. You've been carrying on full-time duties at the hospital, and doing most of the care yourself? **A.** I've been—during Jason's waking hours, I've been there approximately five and a half—on the weekdays—five and a half hours of his nine hours awake-time, and during that time, which is almost two-thirds, I have been the one who takes care of Jason.

Q. Now, if you are permitted to take the child to California, your mother is going to go with you, just the same as she spent eight months back in Washington with you, or six, or whatever it was? **A.** She's going to go with me for a certain length of time for adjustment.

Q. Well, if you were the one that's been taking care of him, why does he need to be adjusted away from your mother? **A.** Well, because number one, he's known my mother for a year and a half. She lives at our house; she's a familiar face, and she has taken care of Jason when I'm not there.

Now, I don't know how much study you've done on the subject of a child in a separation anxiety—

MR. FISK: Just a moment, your Honor. I didn't ask for any lectures from this witness. I'm just asking him questions.

THE COURT: That's correct. I'm not sure that's an answer. That's going quite a bit further than what he called for.

A. (Continuing) The reason is that Jason has known my mother for a year and a half, is going to get a new caretaker, and I want to have her broken in slowly. You don't suddenly throw a child against somebody new to take care of them for a prolonged period of time.

Q. Well, I take it this is going to be a dramatic change for the child if this happens? **A.** No. Not a dramatic change.

Q. I didn't say "traumatic", dramatic. **A.** I said not a dramatic change. But there would be a change in any child's life; this change to them is more dramatic than to you or I, and I want to smooth the change for Jason's sake.

Q. Now, how long is your intern or residency program? **A.** Your first year is—you sign a year contract, then you're able to practice medicine in general medicine anywhere, if you pass the national boards. I've taken two parts of three parts of the national boards, and then you can practice medicine as a general practitioner.

Q. Now, some of those residency programs last as much as four years, don't they? **A.** Not my residency program. Surgery lasts five years. If you want to be a thoracic surgeon, then you go seven years. You can go ad infinitum, what you want to do, subspecialize, and then sub-subspecialize.

Q. I understand. But on internal medicine, now, is it your testimony that your program, you can be a specialist in internal medicine in one year? **A.** No. I didn't say that. I said you could be a G.P. in one year.

Q. I beg your pardon? **A.** You can be a general practitioner in one year.

Q. But you said you wanted to be an internist. **A.** I want to do internal medicine, practice internal medicine, yes.

Q. I gather you want to be a specialist in internal medicine? **A.** That takes three years.

Q. Three years? **A.** Yes. Takes three years of training, doesn't make any difference when you do it.

Q. Now, Mr. Rose, where did you propose to practice medicine at the end of three years, or have you thought that far ahead? **A.** No. I haven't.

Q. I beg your pardon? **A.** I haven't thought that far ahead. I have always thought to come back to Seattle.

Q. But if you get down in California and like it, you might stay? **A.** I haven't thought that far ahead. I will be applying to the University of Washington for my second year of residency next year.

Q. Well now, if the Court should permit you to take that child to California, then I assume that it would be a physical impossibility for Diane to continue on anywhere near her present visitation. **A.** Of the way we have it set up now, yes. That would be impossible to fly him up or fly her down on Tuesday and Thursday for four hours, that would be very difficult.

Q. Well now, what would be your solution to that?—assuming for the moment that you were awarded the custody of the child. **A.** There could be a couple of solutions to that. One is I have a vacation which consists of a month length of time. My home base will still be Seattle, Washington; this is the town that—this is the city that I was raised in and born in. I'll be up here visiting, probably in two-week blocks.

Q. Two-week blocks, you say? **A.** Yeah, during that time. Also, provide the money for Diane to fly down to Los Angeles to visit.

Q. How many times, once a week? **A.** No. Whatever the Court felt would be proper.

15. Keith Bennett—For the Defense

a. Direct Examination by Mr. Mellon

Q. Your name is Keith Bennett. Where do you live? **A.** I live in Bloomington, Indiana.

Q. Are you acquainted with and a friend of both Mr. and Mrs. Rose? **A.** Yes.

Q. Where did you first meet them? **A.** In Graz, Austria.

Q. Were you a beginning medical student over there as well as Mr. Rose? **A.** Technically I wasn't—I was there to go to the medical school program, yes.

Q. Did you actually go to medical school there? **A.** No, I did not.

Q. Now, you've seen Mr. Rose with Jason, have you not? **A.** Yes, yes.

Q. Would you just describe how—what you've observed about how he and Jason get along? **A.** Well, I think they get along famously. Steve's always—oh, he's taught Jason a couple little dance things that he does. He's taught him how to slap 5, like basketball players do. When Steve comes in, he says, "Hey, Jason, give me 5," and he slaps his hand. He's taught Jason to pretend he's dribbling down the floor and stuffing a basketball. Steve's a basketball fan. They're very entertaining together and they get along very well.

Q. Did Steve visit you in Indiana? **A.** Yeah, yeah.

Q. When was that? **A.** That was, I think,—I believe it was just before Thanksgiving.

Q. What, if anything, did he say about Jason? **A.** Well, Steve called Jason "Little Man" a lot, and it seemed whenever Steve and I had ran out of things to say or—or when we'd just—there's a lull in the conversation or anything like that, Steve would always say, "Man, I can't wait to get out to Seattle and see the little man again, 'cause, God, I miss the little—Jason so much." He was very anxious to get back out. He mentioned that—I can't remember exactly how long he'd left Jason, but I think it was seven days or something like that, and he said, "It's only been seven days and I miss my little man so much." So he appeared very anxious to see him.

MR. MELLON: I believe that's all.

16. Joseph Goldstein, Professor of Law—For the Defense

a. Direct Examination by Mr. Mellon

Q. Your name is Joseph Goldstein? **A.** Yes.

Q. You come from the state of Connecticut, do you not? **A.** Yes, sir.

Q. What is your present occupation? **A.** I'm a professor of law at Yale Law School.

Q. How long have you been connected with Yale Law School? **A.** Let's see, I think I joined the faculty in 1966 or seven, something like that, not quite certain of that date.

Q. Now, perhaps you could give the Court a little bit of your educational background. **A.** I hold a bachelor's degree from Dartmouth College, and a doctoral degree from the London School of Economics and Political Science, and a law degree from Yale Law School, and I'm a graduate of the Western New England Psychoanalytic Institute, which is a credited institute of the American Psychoanalytic Association.

Q. All right, sir. Now, do I call you Professor Goldstein, or Mr.— **A.** Mr. is fine with me. I think that's easiest.

Q. Perhaps you could give the Court, so the Court will have an idea of your knowledge and qualifications, a little bit of your background and experience, Mr. Goldstein. **A.** Well, if I focus primarily on work with regard to families and children, I have been the Yale Law School Professor of Family Law, for, oh, I guess fifteen of those seventeen or eighteen years that I've been there.

During that time, I developed a course with a psychoanalyst, Dr. Jay Katz, which focused primarily on the relationship of the law to children, and which resulted in a casebook which is called The Family and the Law, which has been out for about ten years. And in the preparation of that casebook and in giving seminars, we did, over a period of years, invite Anna Freud, from England, to join us in the presentation of work to the students in the law school, and then ultimately with joint seminars in the medical school for residents in child psychiatry and for social workers who were doing related work.

And during that period, I've spent periods up to three months at the Hampstead Child Therapy Clinic in London, working with Anna Freud, and over the years met with her three to four times a year for periods of a week, working on materials and writing together, which resulted in the book Beyond the Best Interests of the Child, which was done also in collaboration with Dr. Albert Solnit, who's the head of our children's center, Child Study Center, at Yale University, and the former president of the American Psychoanalytic Association.

Q. Are you a married man? **A.** Yes, I am.

Q. How long have you been married? **A.** Twenty-seven or twenty-eight years.

Q. To the same wife? **A.** To the same wife.

Q. And you have children? **A.** Four children, three will be in college next fall.

Q. Three boys and a girl? **A.** Three boys and a girl, that's right.

Q. Referring to this book Beyond the Best Interests of the Child, has that been cited as authority by any courts in the United States? **A.** It has. I've not done a survey, but there's come to my attention cases from the Appellate Court of this state, from the state of Connecticut, Pennsylvania, and I know of at least one case in California—and I don't know, did I say New York State?

Q. I don't think you mentioned New York. **A.** I think New York State. I know there's at least one case that's cited the volume.

Q. When was the book first published? **A.** I believe it was the late fall of '83, but I would have to look. I'm terrible on dates, I'm quick to acknowledge that.

Q. Now, Mr. Goldstein, you have a fair idea what this case is about, do you not? **A.** Yes, I have.

Q. You understand that this case involves primarily—the reason you're testifying, or we asked you to testify in this case is it involves—or this is a dissolution of marriage case that involves—particularly the matter that we're talking to you about, involves the care, custody, and control of a boy who was born to this couple in April of 1983, so at the present time, he's about twenty-six months old.

The evidence in the case shows . . . [Mr. Mellon here recapitulates the defendant's case.]

Now, Mr. Goldstein, with the background of information, which I'll ask you to assume is correct, I assume counsel will ask you to assume other things, but this Court will be determining at the end of the case which parent, Mr. or Mrs. Rose, should have the care, custody, and control of this child, Jason. I'm going to ask you what, in your opinion, should the Court do in this regard. **A.** Accepting the facts as you've presented them, and focusing on certain ones which I think are critical, as opposed to a number of details which I don't think are particularly relevant to my answer, I would say for a child of Jason's age, which I gather is two years plus—

Q. Two years, two months. **A.**—two years and two months, who at the age of what was it, six months, that in effect he lost contact with his mother for a period of almost six months—

Q. He was about eight months old. **A.** Eight and a half months old. And for a child of that age who's had a continuing relationship with his father, it would be my expectation that that child has begun to internalize and incorporate as a psychological parent in a very substantial sense, the father, and in a much less substantial sense, the mother.

Clearly the first six or eight months of the child's life, and the visits, have contributed to what might be called a psychological parent-child tie. But it's one that's been substantially, I would expect, though I have not examined the child, substantially damaged and bruised by the very long separation, from the child's point of view, from a child's sense of time, that took place after the unpleasant events that you describe, and also by the separations that occur weekly between visits, so that I would say that the child has been substantially scarred. And a child of that age who doesn't know the reasons for absences, clearly has experienced a sense of what might be called abandonment, not in legal terms, but in psychological terms. A sense of rejection and distrust about the external world that's represented by mother, and at the same time, has experienced a sense of continuing and growing security of the tie between himself and the father.

And from the facts as you give them, and in terms just of the passage of time for a child as young as Jason and it's much more significant for a youngster that age than it is for older children, but even for older children, this would be, I think, a separation that would strain dramatically the tie between parent and child, unless extraordinary efforts are made to keep those relationships viable. That from the child's vantage point, which is the only way I can really look at this, I would say it would be least harmful—we say least detrimental to the child—to allow the child to continue in the custody of his father, and his father making whatever arrangements he feels are necessary in order to protect the child's well-being during his absences.

By "psychological parent," we're talking about a person who has assumed responsibility and continuity of care on a daily basis. That doesn't mean an hour-to-hour or minute-by-minute basis, but it means someone to whom the child can turn in times of need and frustration, someone whom the child can find a source of affection and a source of control. And that in terms of the prior experience of this youngster, it seems clear from the facts as you've stated them that the only person with whom Jason has had a chance to develop that relationship is his father, but stressed, I think by the tie that must have begun to develop between Jason and his paternal grandmother, if I understand the facts correctly.

So I would conclude that custody should remain with the father because to do otherwise, and that's really what one is thinking about, what the alternative is, is only to subject the child to another shattering experience. It would mean, I gather, since the father will be going to leave the city for study, it would mean breaking the continuous tie with the father, it would mean interrupting what apparently is a nourishing and meaningful tie with the grandmother, and can only make the child, to the extent one can put oneself inside the child, who's two, feel that the external environment doesn't offer him the security which allows him over time to develop a sense of trust in himself, because he's been let down.

He will have been let down more than once at a crucial time in which he's coming to terms with his own impulses, with the internal struggle that helps develop his identity, and all of that internal turmoil requires as much stability as is possible from the external world, and that's what we're talking about when we say maintaining a continuity of relationship.

But we're also recognizing that there's no perfect solution here. This is a family that is torn apart, so you're looking for the least harmful, or at least from our vantage point, looking for the least harmful alternative for the child. Now I think one—

MR. FISK: Your Honor, he asked him a question ten minutes ago. Are we going to have a lecture all day?

THE COURT: I'm going to overrule the objection. Implicit in the question is an explanation of why he feels the way he does, which I think he's got a right to do.

A. (Continuing) I'll try and be more brief.

The only thing I would like to add at this time, had the child Jason been placed with some third party at this length of time, at his age, and separated from both parents, except for the visits, I would expect that sufficiently new ties were developing that it would be a terrible thing to break those ties, assuming that there's nothing like abuse or neglect in the current situation, and that the child is doing well.

We originally were going to call the book, as a kind of advice, to the legal system, "Leave Well Enough Alone". We start with very strong presumption that if a child is thriving or developing well in a family constellation, whether it's a total unit or one that's been partially interrupted, that that child should not be moved.

Now, I am not saying that to move the child would necessarily bring the world to an end for that child, but it would be as if one intentionally broke a child's arm with the knowledge that certainly we have ways of putting arms in casts and expecting them to be healed. I have no question that to move the child now, just on the basis of short-term expectations, could only scar the child doubly, both in terms of the very substantial tie with the father, and what I expect is a very meaningful tie with the grandmother.

Q. When you say "move," you're talking about moving custody, not moving physically from— **A.** No. I'm not talking about a geographical move. I think they're more for older children who begin to establish very meaningful ties with playmates and peers and elementary school and high school. There is a substantial part of the continuity concept which favors leaving the child, if possible, all of the things being equal, in the geographical area in which it finds itself, but to weigh that against the very complex and delicate fabric of the psychological relationships that exist, that it's far more important that the child's ties be made continuously viable. A child and an adult, too, can cope with moves better if there's the security of the external support that comes from having a parent present with the move, then if it's a complete move without those ties.

If I were a parent in a situation like this, I would try to mitigate the extent of the impact of the move by carrying with me the kinds of items the child associates with his room, his crib, his blankets, favorite toys, maybe his potty, whatever it is, I would try and keep the continuity of objects that exist here, available there. And in the same way, I would anticipate that the father must ultimately judge when it is that a phasing out of the relationship with the grandmother and child can take place without too much difficulty for the child; hopefully those relationships being kept alive by visits and the like so the child doesn't feel there's been a rejection.

Q. Assume that Diane Rose, that's the wife, was available at all times. Now, the hypothesis I stated to you, or the facts as I stated them to you, indicated that she intended to work, or be away from the home a substantial period of time. But let's just assume that she was available all the time to care for this child, as contrasted with Dr. Rose and his medical-training schedule, as I generally indicated it to you. Would that change your view any at all, Mr. Goldstein? **A.** No. Even assuming the mother could spend full time and was in perfect health, it would be like saying, "Well, all right, let's give the child a handicap and see if he can make it during those first six or eight crucial years," because what you will be doing, I would anticipate, is making the child, in his own docile, incoherent way, suffer the idea that the world out there can't take care of him, that familiar objects can disappear at will without his understanding, and, that over time, he will find it difficult to establish a new relationship.

Each time you break a tie abruptly, you make it more difficult for the next relationship. This is an experience we've had with foster care children. They move them from one family to another, and then it becomes harder and harder for those children to have enough confidence in themselves to establish meaningful relationships. So even to move the child to a setting that is ideal by any standard, would put the child, at this stage, at a disadvantage because it would be much more difficult the next time around to establish new and meaningful relationships. It casts another very dark shadow on that child's sense of what adults have to offer him, so I would be very reluctant.

Q. You have taken into consideration, I assume, in answering as you have, that Mr. Rose will be by necessity away from the child during periods of time when he's going to have to be on training at the school, and that during those periods of time, that he will be under the care of a competent woman, or possibly even a babysitter at times, or some child-care center. You realize that, do you not? **A.** Yes. I realize that no parent can spend every minute with a child, and in fact, I think it probably would be detrimental to the well-being of the child if every minute was spent with the child.

One of the things that we're talking about when we talk about psychological parent is what is beginning to be internalized by the child about the outside world and its reliability. That's how kids are able to go to school and go to nursery school and spend time away from their parents; they begin to internalize the parent. The parent becomes a part of them, because there's an experience that the child grows on of the parent always coming back. And so the experience as you've described it that Jason has had, is that his father is always coming back, even though he's out of the house from time to time. And that he's there night after night after night, or day after day, even though it's not every hour or every minute. So it's that inner strength that's being built, which permits a child over time to develop the independence that we all want for each of our kids, to be able to walk alone in the world, but that they're carrying within them, if the relationship has been substantial, a rather substantial hunk of what their parents had to offer.

Q. What would you anticipate would be the effect on Jason if custody were transferred from his father to his mother? **A.** Well, as I tried to say, it would be putting him at an enormous handicap. It wouldn't be out of his best interests. It might be out of the best interests of the parent who wants the child, to do that. And it may be that, in fact, I would hope and would want everyone to give as much assistance as possible for a child to survive that experience, but it would be as I suggested, like doing some damage to a child to establish that medicine somehow can do a half-way decent repair job.

I just find it hard to contemplate, under the facts as you present them and the length of time of prior separations and the age of this particular child, to contemplate submitting him to that kind of abrupt termination of a relationship. I would think unless one could establish that the child is not thriving, not doing well, or has been abused or neglected by his current custodians, that one should be very reluctant to make a move or to break those relationships.

Q. Assume, Mr. Goldstein, that you have a parent, I'm just asking you to make this assumption, not based particularly on the facts of this case, but assume that you have a parent that for some reason is not everything a parent should be, he may be a drinker or have some sort of defect of some sort, but you have the situation where he has had or she has had a continuous relationship with the child, and the child seems to be getting along well. And on the other hand, you have the other parent who has not had the care, custody, and control, who doesn't have these defects. What would be your attitude on a change of custody in that situation? **A.** If we keep as given the statement of facts about the length of time?

Q. Yes. **A.** I without hesitancy would say that there's no reason to move the child. One of the problems that we try to confront in examining these issues generally is the absence of what I think a lot of us attribute to law, a kind of magic that this is an opportunity to make things perfect and beautiful and give a guarantee for the child. It's just not in the cards. I don't know of any perfect parent. In fact, a perfect parent might be an impossible one for a child to live with.

But I would say unless there are indications which justify moving that constitute neglect or abuse, that there must be in that relationship that you hypothesize, some very important strengths that are communicated between that parent, the custodial parent, and the child, which ought not to be tampered with, because you don't know what the next situation has to offer. You have a prior experience to build on that has proved reliable for the child, and you are speculating about a new experience, if everything were as perfect as the model that you describe as the alternative.

b. Cross Examination by Mr. Fisk

Q. Mr. Goldstein, you were given a little background about this case, and I want you to assume that the reason for this suicide attempt in the first place was because of pressure put upon Diane Rose by her husband and his mother, specifically with reference to permitting her to care for her own child, things of that nature. Now, assuming that to be a fact, would that make any difference in what you're testifying today? **A.** Not really.

Q. You think that's okay? **A.** If you're asking me to make a judgment about that kind of interpersonal relationship, it isn't something that I would favor, but if you're asking me in terms of how that event can be perceived or digested by the child, whatever the reason for the suicide attempt, whatever the reason for the period of absence for by the child, even if it were for the best of reasons.

Q. All right. Now, you place great emphasis, I take it, on what you refer to as "continuity of care"? **A.** Yes, continuity of relationships, yes.

Q. Now, let's take a situation. Suppose people are always snatching up a child and taking off with him. And let's assume that that happens, and a person takes the child and disappears with him, has him for several months before anybody locates him, or so on, and during the interim, the child gets a real attachment to the person that has him. **A.** Yes.

Q. Now, under that kind of a situation, do you think the person doing that should profit by their own wrong? **A.** No. I don't think the person doing that should profit by his own wrong, nor do I think that the reward or punishment should be translated in the terms of altering the custodial relationship of the child. We do have, when people are harmed in our society, a form of responding either in terms of money damages, or if there's been a violation of the criminal law, to invoke the criminal law. While I do not condone the kidnapping that you're describing, I would ultimately not want to use the child, which is always the object that's looked at, as the reward or punishment.

Q. Well, that's not what I'm asking you. Under the situation I've described, I'm asking you if you think a court under that situation ought to leave the child with the parent who stole him away, on the theory that it would be bad to give him back to the proper person. **A.** If a new and meaningful relationship had developed over sufficient period of time, I would be very reluctant, from the child's point of view, to move that child, and I think I am responding to your question, because to move the child in order to protect the State's policy with regard to kidnapping, is to use the child as chattel, which is what we're moving away from.

Q. So if I understand you, you'd leave him there? **A.** If the facts were as you suggest, that he's thriving under those circumstances. If I may, I could give you a—

Q. Just answer the question, if you will. **A.** All right, certainly.

Q. And your answer is that you would leave him there? **A.** My answer is if the child is thriving, and a substantial period of time has gone by where the old ties have begun to dissolve or break down, and new meaningful ties have developed, that I would, from the child's vantage point, I would leave him there.

Q. Now, you have no information whatsoever as to the relationship of this child with his real mother, do you? **A.** With the biological mother?

Q. Yes. **A.** Right.

Q. Now, I'm going to ask you to assume that in the period of roughly six months since we established the visitation arrangement of four hours twice a week, plus every other weekend, that the mother has had this child, and this child is extremely fond of her, will hardly let her out of his sight when she has visitation privileges, that so far as the child is concerned, this is not only the biological mother, but the psychological mother, and that he enjoys himself. **A.** What I would take it as is evidence that there must be a very healthy relationship that exists in the regular day to day caring for the child, so that the child is able to manage these visits successfully. And so my answer would be the same in the sense, to the extent the observation or the facts you give are in fact correct, it would support my expectation that a more meaningful relationship could develop with the mother over time, if the child continued in a setting where it's thriving.

Q. Now, Professor Goldstein, I'm going to ask you to assume that the father has—by evidence on official records and by other evidence which we have—has a very hostile attitude toward the parents of the mother, and against Mrs. Rose herself, and that he has done everything that's possible that he can think of to attempt to influence or alienate the child away from the mother. And I'll ask you if you think that is a good thing from the standpoint of the child? **A.** If the child is being alienated from the mother at the, I guess, instigation, you're saying—

Q. That's right, right. **A.**—of the father, it's not something that I think is particularly beneficial for the child.

Q. To put it another way, it's detrimental, isn't it? **A.** Well, we're talking about alternatives, unfortunately, because we don't have a whole family here. Ultimately, from the child's interest as far as we're concerned, the custodial parent has to deal with the child and the child's relationships with others in a way that is comfortable for that parent. That's the only way that a strong and meaningful tie can develop with the parent. We want to at least preserve one for this child's well-being.

From the vantage point of continuity, which is what we were stressing, if the father came to me for counseling, I would urge him to try to come to terms with his antagonism, and to work out in a flexible way, as I suggested in my original testimony, opportunities for the child to see the absent parent. But I'd say it's much more significant that that kind of relationship be encouraged for children who are much older, where there was a real tie. Say the family had remained together for ten years, and we're talking about children nine and eight, there you have a long-standing relationship—

Q. Professor—**A.**—that might be more significant.

Q. Excuse me for interrupting you. You've written so many articles it takes you all day to answer a simple question.

MR. MELLON: I object to counsel's remarks.

THE WITNESS: I apologize, I'm sorry.

THE COURT: I'm going to sustain the objection. If you ask him a question, I think you'll have to wait until he finishes answering, or—

MR. FISK: I'm willing to do that, your Honor.

THE COURT:—or object to his answer without trying to cover him over. It's going to be difficult for the court reporter to report that, among other things.

Q. (By Mr. Fisk) Now, let me ask you again, Professor. **A.** Yes, sir.

Q. The question was whether it was good for the child, or detrimental, or what, for one parent to attempt to alienate the child from another. That's a simple thing, I would think, as much experience as you've had, you ought to be able to answer it. **A.** Well, one of the problems is we're talking about very complex and delicate interpersonal relationships, and that it's not as easy to say an answer as I guess you would like. We're talking about alternatives.

Q. Is it yes or no? **A.** It's neither yes or no.

Q. Well, when I ask you this way—**A.** Certainly.

Q.—that you condone that sort of thing? **A.** As a parent, I don't condone one parent playing another parent against the other, to the child.

Q. That's detrimental, is it not? **A.** It can be very harmful to the child, yes.

Q. Now, I want you to assume that almost all of the care of this child, since Mr. Rose took off with the child—has been by Mr. Rose's mother. I want you to assume that. **A.** Okay.

Q. And now, then, he's testified here today that he's going to, if he gets the child in this custody hearing, he's going to take him to Los Angeles, and he's going to have a babysitter or a live-in housekeeper to take care of the child, in place of his mother.

Now, if that happens, then there's going to be an interruption in this continuity of care that you've referred to, isn't there? **A.** There's going to be an interruption with regard to part of the continuity of care that I was talking about. I relied very substantially, unless you alter the facts—

Q. I did alter the facts. **A.**—well, on the continuity of the relationship with the father. See—

Q. I ask you to assume that the paternal grandmother, for all practical purposes, has had the care of this child. Now she's, according to the present plans, she's not going to do that anymore, except for a transition period. Now, if that happens, you don't have this continuity of care that you've been talking about, do you? **A.** You have to the extent you haven't taken away the responsibility of the father to make arrangements for the child during the periods when he's at work. To the extent that that still remains, you have the continuity of the tie with the father. To the extent that you break both ties between father and grandmother, in order to place the child with the "absent parent," you're just scarring the child twice over.

Now, the expectation, as I heard it, was that this was not to be an abrupt change, but to be something that was done over time.

Q. I understand. But you're not going to have a continuity of the same care? **A.** Oh, one never has the continuity of the same care. One has the continuity of the relationship with primarily one, and hopefully, two, parents. So, yes, there is going to be for the child some transition which that child can manage better if it's got a father that it can rely on continuously, as there's a shift from the grandmother to someone else.

Q. Well, why couldn't the child rely on its mother? **A.** Well, I gather the child could; had the facts been reversed, and the child been with the mother all this time, and not with the father, clearly that would be the way it ought to be. But to break and scar the child by terminating in an abrupt fashion, a relationship with both grandmother and father, is probably as harsh a thing as you can conceive of, and as great a handicap as you can impose on that child, other than that both of those parties die unfortunately in a tragic airplane accident.

Q. Professor, you don't claim to be a child psychiatrist, do you? **A.** No, I don't. I'm not a psychiatrist. I'm a psychoanalyst.

Q. Well, isn't that a kind of a subspecialty of psychiatry? **A.** No, I think you'll find that most psychiatrists are required to have a medical degree. I have no medical degree. And my training is primarily in psychoanalysis.

Q. Now, earlier in this case, we had a child psychologist, and he testified that as between giving the custody to a babysitter and to the mother, there's no question the best interest of the child was to go to the mother; do you agree with that?

MR. MELLON: No, just a moment, your Honor. I'm going to object. He was not a child psychologist.

THE COURT: Psychiatrist, I think.

MR. MELLON: He was a psychiatrist.

MR. FISK: I'm sorry. I meant "psychiatrist," if I had inadvertently used "psychologist".

MR. MELLON: And in the second place, counsel is stating that this individual testified so and so. I recall no such testimony. He's stating it as a fact that that's the way he testified.

THE COURT: I'll overrule the objection. He was a psychiatrist, however.

MR. FISK: That's right.

THE WITNESS: Could you just restate your question, please?

Q. (By Mr. Fisk) A child psychiatrist was here to testify, right where you are and he testified in response to a direct question that as between giving the custody of this child to a new babysitter or housekeeper, whatever term you want to use, on the one hand, and giving it to the mother on the other, that there wasn't any question. The child would be better off with the mother.

MR. MELLON: I'm going to object to that, because that was assuming also that the father would be completely out of the picture.

THE WITNESS: I'd be willing to answer that if you want.

THE COURT: Overruled.

A. If by "custody," you mean give the custody to some unknown figure that hasn't yet been identified, or to the mother who currently has some relationship, no matter how tenuous, with the child, if those are your only choices, then certainly you would favor giving the custody, which I gather is the control and care of the child, to the mother. That isn't what I understand the facts to be.

Q. Now, we've got a practical consideration, Mr. Goldstein. If custody was to go to the father, and he carries out his plans to go to Los Angeles, obviously it's going to be impractical for the mother to see the child except on rare occasions. Now, isn't that in and of itself detrimental to the child? **A.** To the extent they're meaningful ties, it's detrimental. To the extent of choosing between what is the least detrimental, it's less detrimental to tamper with those tenuous ties than it is with the real ties that have developed over a two-year plus period with the one adult the child has been able to rely on.

MR. FISK: Thank you.

c. Redirect by Mr. Mellon

Q. Let me ask you just one other question. When you are faced with a problem like we've been discussing here this morning, from whose standpoint do you attempt to always solve that problem, from the parents' standpoint, the father's standpoint, the mother's standpoint, or the child's standpoint? **A.** I try to examine the question from the child's vantage point, and if I am allowed to elaborate—

Q. Yes, please do. **A.**—I would give an illustration how time often alters a position that we take. In a case in Connecticut, where a group of us, including Dr. Solnit and some—

MR. FISK: I'm going to object to this, your Honor. We don't care about his Connecticut case. I object to it.

THE COURT: I'll overrule it, because I think it explains his position.

A. (Continuing) I'll try to be very brief.

It involved a child who had been placed with a foster mother fairly early in its life, something like three or four months old, and remained with the foster mother for almost two years, at which time the court abruptly took the child, literally, the court official moved the child from the arms of the mother while sleeping in the courtroom, that is the foster mother, and returned it to the natural biological mother.

The court—and this was over the objection of all of the psychiatrists in the Child Study Center, which said that so many ties had developed with this foster parent, who wanted to adopt, that the child shouldn't be moved.

The case was in litigation for almost, I think, two years, and by the time the court again had to consider the factual issue, we felt that the new relationship that the child had begun to develop after this trauma, was such that it would be terribly damaging to move the child once again, to have it develop a sense that there isn't anything permanent in his life. That our staff had to conclude otherwise and advise the judge, "Now, look, you have to leave the child where it is," even though we thought at the time we made the judgment, it was a mistake. And it clearly was, it scarred the child. But to do it again after a two-years' lapse, we felt was terribly harmful for the child.

Now, we're constantly confronted with having to deal with our own blind spots, and it's just that kind of case, it makes us force into view for ourselves, but it's the child's interests we're concerned about, not any particular adult party, and that's the way we had to respond in that case.

17. Alice Rose—For the Defense

a. Direct Examination by Mr. Mellon

Q. You're the mother of Steve Rose, are you not? **A.** Yes.

Q. Mrs. Rose, as soon as you heard about the events of a year ago, that is, when Diane jumped out of the window, did you go right back to Washington? **A.** Right.

Q. And what, if anything, did you try to do about that situation? **A.** Well, we more or less almost started to panic. Everything, her heart rate, everything, all her vital signs looked like this was going to be it. And I felt that I wanted to do everything she—you know, that was possible, because otherwise you'd never forgive yourself. And so I called Dr. Allen a friend and distinguished surgeon in town and I told him in desperation, I said I—I just didn't want to hear about professional ethics, I wanted to—and I compared her with the Kennedys or Wallace when they were shot, that teams of doctors forgot about professional ethics and with just one thought in mind, to save the patient. And I felt that I wanted this for Diane and I felt that Washington, D.C., was an area that had so many medical facilities and experts that they don't have anywhere else in the country that there had to be someone there that was a top neurosurgeon that we could call in. And so he said to me—I called him from a pay phone at the—in the Waiting Room, and he said, "I'll get right back to you." And then he called in five minutes and he said, "I'm taking Dr. Hugo Raymond out of a meeting and I'll be right over." And they came over within a half an hour.

Q. Dr. Allen and Dr. Raymond. **A.** M-hm

Q. Now, at about this time, Mrs. Rose, did you make any statement to the effect that if Diane died, that you wanted to have—that you wanted to raise Jason, or that you wanted to have his custody. **A.** That is so ridiculous.

Q. —or something like that? **A.** That is—that is—in the first place, I have raised my family.

Q. Well, did you have any—or was there any conversation with Dr. Mitchell at the hospital before you went up to see Diane the next morning? **A.** Well, Steve spent a few minutes trying to give him some background inasmuch as just—just the pertinent facts that—you know, that they were married and they had a small child, and that she had taken an overdose of Phenobarbital and gone out an eight-story window, and that she was alive.

And he gave her physical condition and that he wanted to have him possibly as a therapist.

Q. All right. And did you get a chance to go up and see Diane that morning? **A.** No, they wouldn't let us up there.

Q. So then did you see Dr. Mitchell? **A.** Yes.

Q. —when he left the hospital also? **A.** Yes. He came down and he mentioned that Diane was—all she could talk about was how she hated her parents. And he said, "I'd like to try to tone that down."

And so I said, "Thank you very much," because nobody had ever told us how to talk to her. You know, she was constantly berating them and we didn't know what to say to her, because we didn't know whether to just let her talk or say—you know, quiet her up or—or what.

Q. Did you attempt to follow his advice? **A.** Yes. In fact, many times after that I—I would bring up the point that, "Diane, you are a parent now and it's more important for you to think of getting well and being a mother to Jason."

Q. Now, when Diane came home from the hospital, you were, of course, still there, were you not? **A.** Yes.

Q. And now, Mrs. Rose, let me go back a little bit here. How long have you known Diane? Do you recall approximately? **A.** Well, she went with Steve for four years before they were married.

Q. They were married in 1980, so you've known her about eight years— **A.** Yes.

Q. And what sort of relationship did you have with Diane? **A.** Well, it was unusual for a mother-in-law and daughter-in-law.

Q. I mean, even before, even before she became your daughter-in-law, what type of relationship did you have? **A.** All right. Well, like, for the first three years she was just a real sweet girl that my son went with, and then for the year before they were married we became very close and it was like a mother-and-daughter relationship. She brought her problems to me. I don't think that I would have given her a "no" in the world unless it was just totally impossible.

Q. Would she stay weekends at your place? **A.** Oh yes, yes. In fact, it was—it was the opposite. Usually when a boy goes with a girl, the boy's always at the girl's house and in this case she was always at our house.

b. Cross Examination by Mr. Fisk

Q. Now, Mrs. Rose, I'm going to ask you a few questions about this problem at the Winters' in September, October, whatever it was, of 1983. You remember that well, I take it. **A.** Yes.

Q. Well, what led to a discussion of money where—with reference to the camera incident then, if you can tell us? **A.** That was brought up by Amanda out of the blue.

Q. But if I understand correctly, she stated that (quoting Amanda Winter) that, "They're just spendthrifts like your kids," or something like that. **A.** Well, like our family.

Q. Yes. **A.** Actually she said like me. She was more specific, yes.

Q. Like you? **A.** "Your son—your son gets his spendthrift habits from you."

Q. Okay. And with that you flew into a rage, said that you and your son had been insulted, and stormed out of the house? **A.** No. She went on to explain that my son that summer had talked about buying a movie camera. That's when I said, "I'm highly insulted," and I left.

Q. Now, what we just talked about is all that occurred that made you feel that you were so highly insulted? **A.** No. There were a few more remarks—

Q. All right. **A.**—that were made.

Q. Would you tell us everything there that caused you to feel that you were insulted? **A.** Well, she started out by saying that, when I mentioned that—she, "That's the way you handle your problems. When you have a problem, you get out of town." And I asked her to explain herself, and she mentioned that when Steve and Diane and Jason went back to Washington, D.C., I left that same day for Las Vegas. That started it.

Q. Well, was there any truth in that statement? **A.** Yeah, I went to Las Vegas. I can't see the similarity. I don't—wasn't running away from problems.

Q. Were you a compulsive gambler? **A.** You want an answer?

Q. Well, if you can answer it. **A.** I'm not a compulsive gambler. (Laughing.)

Q. But you don't go down to Las Vegas by yourself? **A.** I met a—girl from New York.

Q. All right. Now, the very next day is when you called Dr. Winter. Is that right? **A.** No.

Q. All right. When did you call him? **A.** Well, I waited several days because I felt that possibly there would be some acknowledgment of the unfairness of—of any type of a misunderstanding and that I would get a call. Well, when I didn't, I felt really that I was entitled to some explanation, and so I called Dr. Winter at his office.

Q. You told him he was no better than his goddamn brother, didn't you? **A.** No, I didn't say that at all. No.

Q. Did you tell him you should have beat the shit out of Amanda before you left? **A.** No.

18. Jonathan Bower, M.D.—For the Defense

a. Direct Examination by Mr. Mellon

Q. And you are a licensed physician in the State of Washington are you? **A.** I am.

Q. What is your specialty, Doctor? **A.** I'm considered to have perhaps three or four.

Q. Well, that's fine. Tell us about all of them. **A.** I'm a pediatrician and I'm a professor of Pediatrics at the University of Washington Medical School. I'm a general psychiatrist and I'm a professor of Psychiatry at the University of Washington Medical School. I'm a child psychiatrist and that is the major work I do at the Medical School right now.

Q. Child psychiatry? **A.** That's right, a psychiatrist for children. And I'm a psychoanalyst.

Q. Now, Dr. Bower, there's been talk in this courtroom or testimony in this courtroom about another Dr. Bower, David Bower, in Washington, D.C. He's your brother, is he not? **A.** Yes, we are brothers.

Q. Now, have you had occasion to examine Diane Rose? **A.** Yes. I examined Diane.

Q. All right. Now, did you also have occasion to examine Jason Rose? **A.** I examined Jason Rose on perhaps five different occasions in my office, in the company of his father, and I examined Jason Rose once again in the Rose home, when Mrs. Rose and Steve Rose were present.

Q. Which Mrs. Rose? **A.** I'm sorry, Mrs. Harold Rose. And then I did still another examination of Jason in my office last week, in the presence of his mother, Mrs. Diane Rose.

Q. All right. And then you've had—did you examine Steve Rose also? **A.** I can't say that I've done a precise, formal psychiatric evaluation on Steve Rose, but I think I can venture a psychiatric opinion about him, since I've seen him in about eight different times in different circumstances.

Q. Now, I'm going to ask you, Dr. Bower, if you would just tell the Court, or give the Court the results of your examination of these three people. **A.** I'll have to take a moment to organize my thinking about that. In the first place, with Steve Rose, there was never a formal psychiatric examination, since that was never requested. I have seen him alone several times, in discussing the issues of care and custody of Jason, and in the planning for some of the examinations and my testimony here. I have also seen him in his home. My psychiatric opinion about him is that he is an intelligent, ordinary, aggressive, young man who has capable powers of organization, who is distraught and preoccupied by what I consider distressing circumstances.

THE COURT: Are you referring to the circumstances of this case?

THE WITNESS: Yes, I am.

THE COURT: Okay.

A. (Continuing) My opinion about his intellectual functioning is that he's at least of normal intelligence. My opinion about his so-called emotional or mental functioning, his ability to manage severe stresses under less than optimum conditions, is that he is of at least ordinary capability. So I would call him a psychologically normal person.

Q. (By Mr. Mellon) All right. Now—**A.** You want me to go ahead?

Q. Yes, go ahead. **A.** I examined Diane Rose last week in a one-hour psychiatric examination. I had some knowledge of Diane's condition ahead of time, because I had reviewed page by page the hospital record of her hospitalization, and my opinion—some of this may be distressing to Mrs. Rose, but my opinion is that she does not function in an ordinary, intact, normal manner. Without—

Q. How did you arrive at that? **A.** Well, by doing a rather formal, orthodox, clear psychiatric examination, which is rather standard. The procedure that I follow is most closely described in one of the standard textbooks, Daniel Freedman's Textbook of Psychiatry. The stimulus during the examination is the office, the physical setting, the psychiatrist in person, and in addition, questions and comments which ordinary enough, by themselves, are brought in mainly to attempt to determine the patient's mode of thinking, their response to ordinary human events. Through this, it's possible to make a professional guess about the patient's ability to withstand stresses of various kinds, the ability to follow a straight line of thinking, the ability to be aware of the world around them. That's how I do it.

Q. All right. Now, did you give her a mental status examination? **A.** I did.

Q. Do you have one called the "proverbs"? **A.** Yes. In an ordinary psychiatric examination, there is one section called the proverb test. The usual mode of administering it is to ask the patient what the people ordinarily mean when they say, and then you ask a proverb such as, "What do people ordinarily mean when they say, 'Don't close the barn door after the horses are out,' or, 'People in glass houses should not throw stones.' " It's a stimulus somewhat like an ink blot. There is no exact proper answer. But one can make a guess, an educated guess, by watching how a patient's thinking can stay anchored in reality, can remain unconfused, and can remain relevant to the task at hand.

Mrs. Rose's performance on the proverb test leads me to believe that under pressure, and under continued pressure, not of a terribly severe type, she becomes confused in her—her thinking becomes loose and loses the point.

Q. I don't believe you told us what your actual conclusions are. **A.** My conclusion is that from her behavior, which was not limited to watching her response to the proverb test, but watching her behavior in what is a standard setting, that is, my office, by watching and thinking about her responses to the questioning, by watching her ability to reconstitute herself after she has some difficulty in thinking, my conclusion is that she does have a disturbance in her thinking. I cannot be crystal clear at this point, since I don't have my own information of her thinking and her behavior before the suicide. So my conclusion at this point, must be that it's consistent with a personality disorder, and I use that word in the sense of the standard psychiatric nomenclature. It is also consistent with evidence of brain damage, and that comes from the manner in which she thinks and the kinds of stresses which will disorganize her, as well as observations of actual physical behavior and neurological functioning, such as the difficulty she has using her tongue and controlling her mouth movements.

THE COURT: You're going to have to tell me what personality disorder is, because I've heard over the years a lot of definitions of that.

THE WITNESS: Well, your Honor, the problem in psychiatric diagnosis is that we don't have a blueprint, and yet we have a need to communicate with others about what we see in something less than verbatim accounts, or—of our observations.

Sometime after World War II, the World Health Organization attempted to develop a world-wide diagnostic scheme. Recognizing the difficulties in that, and nevertheless trying to make—feeling that any scheme that could be agreed to by everyone, even though it was a bad one, would be preferable to no scheme. And so the standard psychiatric nomenclature was developed and was made part of an international classification scheme of diseases.

This standard nomenclature was developed in part by the American Psychiatric Association, under the World Health Organization's auspices. It's basically a very simple scheme. The major tasks are between separating the organic illnesses from the so-called psychogenic illnesses, and the major task within those is an attempt to separate the so-called psychoses from the so-called neuroses, and that's like separating ice and water. Because in real life, with real people, you add one degree of heat with one degree of lack of heat, and you suddenly have ice, or you suddenly have water. And so often, even in the best category, the best scheme, you end up with having slush.

The scheme is really very simple. It makes certain assumptions, right or wrong. It assumes that for the psychogenic diseases, they are expressions, as of this moment, of a human being's ability to manage stress, large or small. They attempt to say very little about the past or the future. The other assumption they make, which is terribly important, is that there are only four ways open to human beings to respond to stress. Psychological stress, I'm talking about, not stress of the everyday world, but the stress that's perceived.

One is to transmute it psychologically, and displace it onto a body part, usually the so-called autonomic nervous system. And those are called psychosomatic disorders, and the common everyday representatives of this are gastrointestinal disorders like stomach ulcers, although there are other kinds, migraine headaches, in the olden days, hysterical paralysis, but again the notion is, one way is to take the stress and pretend it's not a psychological stress, but one that belongs to your body.

Another way to deal with the psychological stress is to transmute it through the ordinary, normal mechanisms of thinking. That is, denial, identification, repression, sublimation, introjection, reaction formation, and that's—one example of that is seen every day with adolescents. With the stress of being an adolescent, one adolescent might identify with the ordinary stress of adolescence, being, you don't know who in the world you are at the moment, and you don't know where you're going. One adolescent might identify with a hero, a positive hero, one might identify with a negative hero.

Some of these psychological mechanisms are more adaptive to reality and to continued functioning in the rest of life, and some aren't. A surgeon who does things to people, draws blood, and things like that, that's a much more adaptive mechanism than simply destroying things. These are the so-called neuroses, and they use the ordinary so-called neurotic mechanisms of dealing with life stresses, severe or mild.

One is to displace it onto a body part, one is to deal with it purely psychologically, and to use ordinary neurotic mechanisms. The third method is to take action, to do things, to move. Sometimes this is adaptive and sometimes it isn't.

In that category, the so-called character disorders and the so-called personality disorders. The character disorders take actions that seem or prove to be more adaptive through one's life. The personality disorders are those that have a lifetime history of being maladaptive and being exceedingly brittle. They follow quite rapidly, and they reconstitute rapidly. And they are pulled into play under ordinary life stresses, rather than severe stresses.

The fourth method is a pattern of regression, disorganization, and denial of reality. Those are called the psychoses. In a proper psychiatric diagnosis, one is really not allowed to use a name alone, because that's like a swear word. One is supposed to say something about the stress that called the defense into play. And therefore, you have some idea of the severity of what that human being is dealing with at the moment. You have an idea of the stress, you have an idea of the responses of which they're capable.

You're also supposed to say something, if at all possible, about the predominant life pattern. I named these, except for the psychophysiologic reactions, in order of decreasing adaptability and capability with an ordinary human life. That is, the neuroses are generally less debilitating, and the psychoses are most debilitating. A personality disturbance is a descriptive term that applies to a human being, who for most of their life, responds to even minimal stresses with a pattern of action for behavior, attempting to get away from what's happening, rather than actually dealing with it head on.

Some of the personality disturbances are the psychopath, the sociopath, the borderline psychotic; but you must recognize that in this scheme, there are lots of borders and combinations.

That's a long answer, and I hope it helped.

Q. (By Mr. Mellon) What, Dr. Bower, is the treatment for a personality disorder, or a borderline personality?—particularly a borderline personality. **A.** You have to—you have to do a careful examination first. You have to decide—

Q. First, could I interrupt you just a minute. What is the meaning of the word "borderline," borderline with what, between what? **A.** It's generally used as a borderline between a psychosis and something that is not a psychosis, that is in touch with reality, but not functioning so well, or out of touch with reality and functioning in a very unadaptive way. You have to do a careful evaluation of what the patient's present functioning is reacting to at that moment, because they can change in time.

If the stress is an internal one, that comes from associations, memories, things, or one's own actual physical state, then you attempt to provide reality to that, as well as support to that, through providing a reliable, trustworthy listener; or, if there's a physical state that's involved, by attempting to moderate the physical disease that's causing the stress, such as a diabetic who's out of diabetic control.

So you attempt to provide internal support. If the stresses seem to be coming from outside the thinking of that human being, you attempt to provide support and strength and regularities and predictabilities in that person's world. If the stress seems to be of anxiety, it is possible nowadays to moderate or ameliorate or take the edge off anxiety, using the so-called tranquilizer. You tend then to modify the importance or the hierarchy of your treatment scheme according to where you think your patient is.

Q. Are borderline personality problems ever—or usually cleared up, or do they last throughout the person's lifetime? **A.** Borderline personality, or if we can stick to one diagnostic scheme, and I prefer, although I don't like the scheme, I find fault with it, it's the best one around, I prefer to stick with the standard psychiatric nomenclature, that is, that personality disorders are never cured. They are like a diabetic. They are like my own myopia, my nearsightedness. One doesn't cure them, one manages them. They are subject to disturbance throughout one's life, depending on both the severity of the stress perceived by the patient, and the state of their own defenses, both internal and external defenses.

For instance, if one moves away from home, certain external supports are withdrawn. For instance, if one's body changes through illness, there are other kinds of stresses. It's difficult to predict then, exactly what will happen to the so-called personality disorder, because you can't predict life's accidents. All you can do is attempt to provide a relatively benign, ordinary existence, that pays attention only to the external events.

It's almost impossible to predict what will go on internally. A more direct answer to your question, it is a disturbance, or a deficiency, or a style of thinking which is never cured, only managed.

Q. Is a manic-depressive illness a psychosis? **A.** Well, that's one of those slush items in that darn diagnostic manual.

Q. Now, Dr. Bower, let me ask you first, you are a board certified child psychiatrist, among other things, are you not? Did you find anything wrong at all with Jason this time, or when you examined him? **A.** Well, when you ask the question, did I find anything wrong, I prefer to say what I found right. Jason, in my opinion, is an ordinarily well-functioning child, a toddler who is extraordinarily susceptible to the feelings and the confusions and the intentions of the adults around him. He is exquisitely tuned to the wishes of the grownups with whom he is with at that time.

Q. Now, Doctor, do you have an opinion as to who should have the—between these two parents, who should have the care, custody, and control over Jason? **A.** Yes, I do.

Q. And what is your opinion? **A.** I came to the opinion last week after examining Mrs. Rose, and after examining her with Jason in my office. My—in my opinion, the custody should go to Mr. Steven Rose.

Q. All right. Now then, I'll ask you to explain why you have come to that conclusion. **A.** At the simplest level, I came to that conclusion because Mr. Rose manages stresses in an adaptive, continuously functioning way.

During my examination, Mrs. Rose did not. As tension would mount, as it became more and more necessary for her to provide decisions based on her own thinking, her thinking collapsed and became confused.

In part, my decision is based upon the history as I know it, that is a suicide attempt, and a history of brain damage. In my examination of Mrs. Rose, the brain damage also was interfering with her ability to think and to continue to force her thinking past the mere simple responses. As she attempted to do that, her thinking collapsed.

And then finally, my opinion is based upon my observations of Mr. Rose tending his son, compared with my observations of Mrs. Rose tending her son in the same examining situation.

Q. Do you want to go into— **A.** I can if you wish.

Q. Is there anything in particular—I don't want you to go into any great detail, but can you explain that just a little bit? **A.** I can touch on the predominant themes. I might have to explain them in more detail.

Q. Well, I don't want to take too much time doing this. **A.** The predominant theme is that Mrs. Rose was unable to continue dealing with stressful incidents of ordinary life with a child beyond a certain point. Secondly, during the examination, she tended more to her own needs, to her own thinking, rather than those of the child.

For example, at one point during the interview, I asked Mrs. Rose to direct Jason to a large uncomfortable wooden chair. It's an inappropriate chair for a child. It was purposely a stress-inducing instruction on my part. She was unable to give Jason, in my opinion, clear direct instructions. Rather, she begged, she cajoled, she offered rewards. I continued my insistence that she make Jason comply. Obviously, Jason did not want to comply. Mrs. Rose then attempted to lift Jason up by the seat of his pants, head first into a large chair, which is a terribly inappropriate way to deal with the child. Most people turn a child around, lift him up by the armpits, and put him down.

After I released both of them from this obviously unhappy situation, Jason went about his business, Mrs. Rose relaxed into what was her characteristic posture during both her examination alone with me, as well as with Jason, what would at first sight be a modest, naive, attentive attention, was really a relatively wooden, immobile, introspective posture. There was little recognition of the rather intense discomfort that Jason had gone through.

This was one example. There were others. It confirmed Mrs. Rose's behavior during the hour-long examination that I had with her alone.

Q. Are you familiar with the term "psychological parent"? **A.** I am.

Q. In your opinion, from what you've observed, seen, and so on, in this matter, who is the psychological parent of this child? **A.** Well, I wish you wouldn't put the question that way, because it's possible to have—

Q. All right. Is there— **A.**—many important people in one's life.

Q. Yes. All right. Let me put it this way: Does the child, in your opinion, have at least one psychological parent? **A.** The child has indeed at least one psychological parent, that is, one adult to whom the child turns to for care, for restitution from pain, for love, yes.

Q. All right. Does Jason have one or more psychological parents? **A.** Jason has at least two: Steve Rose; he has Mrs. Harold Rose; and to some, but much less a degree he has a third, and that is Mrs. Diane Rose.

Q. Are you familiar with the book by Goldstein, Freud, and Solnit, Beyond the Best Interests of the Child? **A.** I am.

Q. Do you consider it to be authoritative in the field? **A.** Yes. Although I don't—the book—book's primary intent was not to provide a final authority. The book intended to raise questions, provide discussion and close examination of important issues; but when it does touch on issues where authority is important, it is authoritative.

Q. Now, are you familiar with the fact that Steve Rose is going to be leaving the end of this month to take up his residency at U.C.L.A. Medical Center? **A.** He has told me that.

Q. Did you take that into consideration when you were expressing the opinion to the Court as to who should have the care, custody, and control of Jason, the fact that he's going to be leaving for U.C.L.A.? **A.** I suppose I did, but not at a very high level of priority.

Q. Who do you mean by that? **A.** The highest level of priority of my considerations was the present mental functioning of the two parties whom I examined. My assumption then being that given ordinary powers of thinking and pursuing problem-solving, and reacting to stress without confusion or breakdown, one will make the best of life's situations.

Q. Just one more question, Dr. Bower. There has been testimony concerning your brother in Washington, D.C., and a visit that—or two that he had with members of both families some time back. Are you and your brother considerably different or are you about the same? **A.** I said we are brothers.

(Laughter.)

We shared the same parents, I believe.

(Laughter.)

He is ten years older than I am, ten years and one month older than I am. I'm the baby of the family. So we share many things and then there are many things we do not share. Some of these are by virtue of the different genetic basket that we got from our parents. Some of these have to do with different lives. The infant of the family does not live the same life that the firstborn does. He came into our family at a time of prosperity. I came into our family at a time of depression. So there are these accidents of life. Then in addition there are those things that people do to themselves.

So in many ways I constructed my life in a different way, almost as a reaction to my own brother much—sometimes the way some people do in reaction to their fathers. And looking back on it, I think some of my wandering around, avoiding a certain career, had to do with avoiding confusion created in my mind and my parents' mind and my brother's mind between my brother and myself.

We're also different not only personally, we are different psychologically and we are different professionally. I'm a psychoanalyst. People have strong feelings positively and negatively about psychoanalysts. My brother is not. I feel strongly about institutions, certifications, all that kind of proper thing; my brother does not. In my professional life I tend to find some pleasure and some usefulness in zeroing in on things with precision; my brother, and I think validly, tries to deal with things globally. My brother tends to do things like family therapy, group therapy; I don't, because it's invalid. We are different people and yet we're quite close.

THE WITNESS: Does that answer your question, Mr. Mellon?

MR. MELLON: I think so. Thank you, Doctor.

NOTES AND QUESTIONS

1. If you were representing Steve Rose, the defendant, how would you have presented his case to the court?

2. If you were the judge who had presided over the Rose hearing, to which parent would you now grant custody? As you read the material in the next section on how courts have applied the "best interests" standard, consider how useful it is as a guide for making your decision. Is there a preferable standard?

2. THE TRIAL COURT DECIDES

■ SANGSTER, J.

This case has taken us quite a long time to complete, and it took me quite a bit of time last night to wrestle around with it and come up with what I wanted to say. I don't think it will be too long, but I have several things that need to be said. I appreciate, of course, all those of you who have been witnesses, and friends and family, who have been here to give your support, and of course, Steve and Diane have gone through a lot; and the lawyers, I want to thank you for your preparation and presentation. Those people who hired you I think can be pleased with your work. You presented the best case that I've ever heard, on the bench or off of it.

Now, we've had sixteen days of trial, and so it shouldn't surprise anybody that I have found that there are irreconcilable differences which have arisen and have caused the irremediable breakdown of the marriage relation, and I'm therefore going to decree the dissolution of the marriage.

Now, the thing that you are all concerned with has to do with what's going to happen to Jason. Of the . . . factors mentioned in the relevant case law, I found that really only two are relevant here, the others either don't apply or they weigh equally on both parties, obviously. The two things that I think that we have questions about are number one, . . . the moral, emotional, and physical fitness of the parties; and the second one that applies here is the desirability of continuing an existing relationship and environment.

I find some substantial changes in circumstances from the hearing [I held in January to make a temporary decision on custody.] I now find that Diane is not suicidal. I was not convinced of this in January, and that played a large part in my judgment at that point. I find that Diane is now much improved physically and mentally. In January, I didn't feel that she was quite ready for the possibility of full-time care. Now, if she is given custody, she would be able to handle it.

Diane is now viewed as a psychological parent to some degree. This was certainly not true in January. And I've found that she has now proven that she can take care of the child. In January I felt I was taking a justifiable risk, nonetheless, in allowing the frequent visitation, or at least more frequent and different kind of visitation than had been the case previously. She's now demonstrated her ability to care for Jason: in short, my reason for awarding Steve temporary custody in January was that Steve was able to care for Jason, and I felt that Diane was not. I now find that they are both fit physically and mentally to care for Jason.

Now the testimony from January and from June, taken together, has convinced me that Diane had a passive-dependent personality disorder, which, when combined with what some people have described as a demeaning husband, meddling in-laws, and parents trying to push independence on her, created a situation where she, in her depressed state, jumped from that eighth-story window. I believe that she was mentally ill at the time she was attempting suicide. I think her depression can best be described as a reaction to the situation in which she found herself. I think she's now free of that situation; I'm mindful that she meets some of the criteria for potential future suicides; however, it's now clear to me that these factors only consider past events and do not consider the person as we find her today. The mere fact that renowned psychiatrists have appeared here in this case, that those psychiatrists, even in the sub-speciality of suicidology, have disagreed as to her potential, should be enough to bring us back to more of a human consideration. I find she is not now suicidal, and not likely to be a significant risk in the future.

To the . . . factors of moral, emotional, and physical fitness, I've added, as you have seen, kind of a special consideration for this case, of mental fitness to care for the child. They're both, of course, morally fit to care for Jason. I will return to the relative emotional fitness of the parties, as it appears, and to the best interests of Jason, but first I want to talk about continuity of care. A great deal has been made of this during this trial, and rightfully so. We have all been subjected to a good deal of testimony concerning continuity of care and how it applies here. Does it apply in favor of Steve because he has had the major custody the past year and a half? Or does it apply toward Diane because she would have more time to give to Jason in the future? Or does it mean I should favor Steve because he's viewed as a primary psychological parent? Or should I go in favor of Diane because she will be here in Jason's home area with continued contact with her, her parents, Steve's parents, and Jason's playmates?

Now, I've read and reviewed all of the testimony from both hearings concerning continuity of care, and I find that both parents have valid and favorable and reasonable claims which would favor them in that consideration. I guess I gave a slight edge to Diane here, as I feel she would be continually available, and on a long-term basis. Mr. Fisk's suggestion that medicine is a consuming mistress has some merit here.

I would like finally, then, to return to the emotional factors mentioned previously. This is possibly the most difficult for me to verbalize in this case. Diane is still a bit immature, and certainly tending to excessive sarcasm, though I noticed this much less now than I did in January. Steve has progressed much faster academically than socially and emotionally. It's obvious to me that he is able to apply himself to the science of medicine and do superior work.

So, I come now to the part that's difficult to, for me, to really put into words. I'm going to give my impressions, because I think it's important for you all to know the basis for my judgments in this particular area. I have heard a great deal about Steve Rose from him and a great many witnesses, but I've also had the opportunity to watch him on the witness stand here, and down there at counsel table, for almost sixteen days now. It appears to me that he's a very demeaning person; he's prone to criticize and quick to demonstrate some kind of intellectual superiority. I got the impression that he felt that he was smarter than a good many of the experts who testified here. And in considering the emotional makeup of the parties, the things they will pass on to their child, and in subtle ways, I have given a large preference here to Diane.

Accordingly, I find that the best interests of Jason lie in his care, custody, and control by Diane Rose, subject to the reasonable and seasonable visitation by his father. I will enter an order requiring the petitioner to contribute $150 per month to the support of Jason. Further, the Court will make no award of alimony, attorneys' fees, or costs to either party. I feel that each party is able to handle these from existing assets or resources. Counsel are requested to discuss the transfer of custody and provisions for visitation, and report to me as soon as you've either agreed or find that you can't reach an agreement. And if there are any matters that I've not ruled on that I should, or any matters upon which you are unclear, I'll be able to talk with you about that today, also, or at any other time. I'll be on a jury trial, but I'll have some recesses, and I'll be glad to take up any of these matters at that time.

NOTE

If you were Steve Rose's attorney, on what grounds would you argue for reversal on appeal?

3. The Appeals Court Decides

■ Thornton, J.

Husband appeals from that portion of a dissolution of marriage decree which awarded custody of the couple's only child, a two and one-half year old boy, to the wife.

Husband alleges error on two bases. First, that the trial court erred in not awarding him custody since he, contends husband, is the sole psychological parent of the child, the mother having little contact with the child since her unsuccessful suicide attempt of January 1984. Secondly, that the wife should not have been awarded custody because of her suicidal tendencies and because of the brain damage incurred in the suicide attempt.

The trial lasted 16 days and the record contains nearly 2,500 pages of testimony. Both the husband and the wife called an imposing array of expert witnesses to the stand to testify on behalf of each party. They could agree on very little. Additionally, there was a tremendous amount of lay testimony regarding the conduct of each party and the fitness of each for custody. This testimony, too, was in hopeless conflict.

Considering the first basis, we do not agree that the husband is the sole psychological parent; both the husband and wife are psychological parents. The record reveals that even while in the hospital recovering from her attempted suicide the wife remained in frequent contact with her child. And after her release from the hospital in June of 1984 we find that she has spent a great deal of time with her son. At all times she has remained a psychological parent.

After reviewing all the medical testimony we agree with the trial judge that the wife is not now or prospectively suicidal and that she is a fit person, both physically and psychologically, to be awarded custody. Regarding the question of her possible brain damage, we conclude that she has no significant damage.

Where, as here, the issues are ones of fact and the testimony conflicts, the believability of the witnesses becomes crucial and the decision of the trial court must be given great weight.

Having considered the entire record de novo, we believe that the trial court reached the correct result.

Affirmed. Costs to respondent-wife.

NOTE

Consider the assessment of Judge Sangster set forth in Joseph Goldstein, Anna Freud, Albert Solnit and Sonja Goldstein, In the Best Interests of the Child 23–26 (1986):

> The judge assumed a professional role for which he was not qualified. He acted as a psychologist by using his own courtroom observations to determine the emotional makeup of Steven and Diane. As a judge he was authorized to take into account his personal observations of the witnesses' behavior on the stand for purposes of evaluating the veracity of their testimony. Here, however, he used these observations not for such an authorized purpose but to assess the emotional and social maturity of two adults. He assumed the role of expert in child development by relating his findings about "the emotional makeup of the parties" to "the things they will pass on to their child . . . in subtle ways." Presumably deciding that Steven would "pass on" detrimental traits to Jason, he gave "a large preference" to Diane as the better parent. He reached this conclusion despite guidance from statutory and case law that "continuing an existing relationship and environment" is usually in the child's best interest and despite uncontroverted expert evidence that Jason had thrived in Steven's custody.
>
> . . .
>
> Had the judge in the Rose case realized that he was about to venture beyond what ordinary knowledge, his own training, the statutory guides or the testimony of the experts in the case qualified him to do, he might have acted differently. He might have asked counsel for both parties to present evidence on whether Steven's personality would be harmful to Jason's development and, if so, whether that harm would be greater than the harm that would result from uprooting the child and disrupting his relationship with his father. But the judge made his

finding without explicitly posing such questions. He thus denied himself the opportunity to learn from experts that they cannot make subtle comparisons between two fit parents and that they are unable to assess the relevance of a parent's "arrogance" or "immaturity" to a child's future well-being.

D. APPLYING THE BEST INTEREST STANDARD

1. FITNESS

In re Marriage of Carney

Supreme Court of California, 1979.
24 Cal.3d 725, 157 Cal.Rptr. 383, 598 P.2d 36.

OPINION:

Appellant father (William) appeals from that portion of an interlocutory decree of dissolution which transfers custody of the two minor children of the marriage from himself to respondent mother (Ellen).

In this case of first impression we are called upon to resolve an apparent conflict between two strong public policies: the requirement that a custody award serve the best interests of the child, and the moral and legal obligation of society to respect the civil rights of its physically handicapped members, including their right not to be deprived of their children because of their disability. As will appear, we hold that upon a realistic appraisal of the present-day capabilities of the physically handicapped, these policies can both be accommodated. The trial court herein failed to make such an appraisal, and instead premised its ruling on outdated stereotypes of both the parental role and the ability of the handicapped to fill that role. Such stereotypes have no place in our law. Accordingly, the order changing custody on this ground must be set aside as an abuse of discretion.

William and Ellen were married in New York in December 1968. Both were teenagers. Two sons were soon born of the union, the first in November 1969 and the second in January 1971. The parties separated shortly afterwards, and by written agreement executed in November 1972 Ellen relinquished custody of the boys to William. For reasons of employment he eventually moved to the West Coast. In September 1973 he began living with a young woman named Lori Rivera, and she acted as stepmother to the boys. In the following year William had a daughter by Lori, and she proceeded to raise all three children as their own.

In August 1976, while serving in the military reserve, William was injured in a jeep accident. The accident left him a quadriplegic, i.e., with paralyzed legs and impaired use of his arms and hands. He spent the next year recuperating in a veterans' hospital; his children visited him several times each week, and he came home nearly every weekend.[2] He also bought a van, and it was being fitted with a wheelchair lift and hand controls to permit him to drive.

In May 1977 William filed the present action for dissolution of his marriage. Ellen moved for an order awarding her immediate custody of both boys. It was undisputed that from the date of separation (Nov. 1972) until a few days before the hearing (Aug. 1977) Ellen did not once visit her young

2. He was scheduled to be discharged shortly after the trial proceedings herein.

sons or make any contribution to their support. Throughout this period of almost five years her sole contact with the boys consisted of some telephone calls and a few letters and packages. Nevertheless the court ordered that the boys be taken from the custody of their father, and that Ellen be allowed to remove them forthwith to New York State.[3] Pursuant to stipulation of the parties, an interlocutory judgment of dissolution was entered at the same time. William appeals from that portion of the decree transferring custody of the children to Ellen.

William contends the trial court abused its discretion in making the award of custody. Several principles are here applicable. (2) First, since it was amended in 1972 the code no longer requires or permits the trial courts to favor the mother in determining proper custody of a child "of tender years." Civil Code section 4600 now declares that custody should be awarded "To either parent according to the best interests of the child." Regardless of the age of the minor, therefore, fathers now have equal custody rights with mothers; the sole concern, as it should be, is "the best interests of the child."

Next, those "best interests" are at issue here in a special way: this is not the usual case in which the parents have just separated and the choice of custody is being made for the first time. In such instances the trial court rightly has a broad discretion. Here, although this is the first actual court order on the issue, we deal in effect with a complete *change* in custody: after the children had lived with William for almost five years—virtually all their lives up to that point—Ellen sought to remove them abruptly from the only home they could remember to a wholly new environment some 3,000 miles away.

It is settled that to justify ordering a change in custody there must generally be a persuasive showing of changed circumstances affecting the child. And that change must be substantial: a child will not be removed from the prior custody of one parent and given to the other "unless the material facts and circumstances occurring subsequently are of a kind to render it essential or expedient for the welfare of the child that there be a change." The reasons for the rule are clear: "It is well established that the courts are reluctant to order a change of custody and will not do so except for imperative reasons; that it is desirable that there be an end of litigation and undesirable to change the child's established mode of living."

Moreover, although a request for a change of custody is also addressed in the first instance to the sound discretion of the trial judge, he must exercise that discretion in light of the important policy considerations just mentioned. For this reason appellate courts have been less reluctant to find an abuse of discretion when custody is changed than when it is originally awarded, and reversals of such orders have not been uncommon.

Finally, the burden of showing a sufficient change in circumstances is on the party seeking the change of custody. In attempting to carry that burden Ellen relied on several items of testimony given at the hearing; even when these circumstances are viewed in their totality, however, they are insufficient for the purpose.

First, Ellen showed that although she had been unemployed when William was given custody in 1972, at the time of trial she had a job as a

3. The court also imposed substantial financial obligations on William. He was ordered to pay all future costs of transporting his sons back to California to visit him, plus $400 a month for child support, $1,000 for Ellen's attorney's fees, $800 for her travel and hotel expenses, and $750 for her court costs.

medical records clerk in a New York hospital. But her gross income from that job was barely $500 per month, and she admitted she would not be able to support the boys without substantial financial assistance from William. By contrast, at the time of the hearing William's monthly income from a combination of veteran's disability compensation payments and social security benefits had risen to more than $1,750 per month, all tax-free.

Ellen next pointed to the fact that William's relationship with Lori might be in the process of terminating. From this evidence Ellen argued that if Lori were to leave, William would have to hire a baby-sitter to take care of the children. On cross-examination, however, Ellen admitted that if custody were transferred to her she would likewise be compelled because of her job to place the children "in a child care center under a baby-sitter nine hours a day," and she intended to do so. During that period, of course, the children would not be under her supervision; by contrast, William explained that because he is not employed he is able to remain at home "to see to their upbringing during the day as well as the night."

Additional claims lacked support in the record. Thus Ellen impliedly criticized William's living arrangements for the boys, and testified that if she were given custody she intended to move out of her one-bedroom apartment into an apartment with "at least" two bedrooms. Yet it was undisputed that the boys were presently residing in a private house containing in effect four bedrooms, with a large living room and a spacious enclosed back yard; despite additional residents, there was no showing that the accommodations were inadequate for the family's needs. Ellen further stated that in her opinion the older boy should be seen by a dentist; there was no expert testimony to this effect, however, and no evidence that the child was not receiving normal dental care. She also remarked that the younger boy seemed to have a problem with wetting his bed but had not been taken to a doctor about it; again there was no evidence that medical intervention in this matter was either necessary or desirable. We obviously cannot take judicial notice of the cause of, or currently recommended cure for, childhood enuresis.

In short, if the trial court had based its change of custody order on the foregoing circumstances alone, it would in effect have revived the "mother's preference" rule abrogated by the Legislature in 1972. The record discloses, however, that the court gave great weight to another factor—William's physical handicap and its presumed adverse effect on his capacity to be a good father to the boys. Whether that factor will support the reliance placed upon it is a difficult question to which we now turn.

Ellen first raised the issue in her declaration accompanying her request for a change of custody, asserting that because of William's handicap "it is almost impossible for [him] to actually care for the minor children," and "since [he] is confined to a hospital bed, he is never with the minor children and thus can no longer effectively care for the minor children or see to their physical and emotional needs." When asked at the hearing why she believed she should be given custody, she replied inter alia, "Bill's physical condition." Thereafter she testified that according to her observations William is not capable of feeding himself or helping the boys prepare meals or get dressed; and she summed up by agreeing that he is not able to do "anything" for himself.

The trial judge echoed this line of reasoning throughout the proceedings. Virtually the only questions he asked of any witness revolved around William's handicap and its physical consequences, real or imagined. Thus although William testified at length about his present family life and his future plans, the judge inquired only where he sat when he got out of his wheelchair, whether he had lost the use of his arms, and what his medical prognosis was. Again, when Lori took the stand and testified to William's good relationship with his boys and their various activities together, the judge interrupted to ask her in detail whether it was true that she had to bathe, dress, undress, cook for and feed William. Indeed, he seemed interested in little else.

The final witness was Dr. Jack Share, a licensed clinical psychologist specializing in child development, who had visited William's home and studied his family. Dr. Share testified that William had an IQ of 127, was a man of superior intelligence, excellent judgment and ability to plan, and had adapted well to his handicap. He observed good interaction between William and his boys, and described the latter as self-disciplined, sociable, and outgoing. On the basis of his tests and observations, Dr. Share gave as his professional opinion that neither of the children appeared threatened by William's physical condition; the condition did not in any way hinder William's ability to be a father to them, and would not be a detriment to them if they remained in his home; the present family situation in his home was a healthy environment for the children; and even if Lori were to leave, William could still fulfill his functions as father with appropriate domestic help.

Ellen made no effort on cross-examination to dispute any of the foregoing observations or conclusions, and offered no expert testimony to the contrary. The judge then took up the questioning, however, and focused on what appears to have been one of his main concerns in the case—i.e., that because of the handicap William would not be able to participate with his sons in sports and other physical activities. Thus the court asked Dr. Share, "It's very unfortunate that he's in this condition, but when these boys get another two, three years older, would it be better, in your opinion, if they had a parent that was able to actively go places with them, take them places, play Little League baseball, go fishing? Wouldn't that be advantageous to two young boys?" Dr. Share replied that "the commitment, the long-range planning, the dedication" of William to his sons were more important, and stated that from his observations William was "the more consistent, stable part of this family regardless of his physical condition at this point." The judge nevertheless persisted in stressing that William "is limited in what he can do for the boys," and demanded an answer to his question as to "the other activities that two growing boys should have with a natural parent." Dr. Share acknowledged William's obvious physical limitations, but once more asserted that "On the side dealing with what I have called the stability of the youngsters, which I put personally higher value on, I would say the father is very strong in this area." Finally, when asked on redirect examination what effect William's ability to drive will have, Dr. Share explained, "this opens up more vistas, greater alternatives when he's more mobile such as having his own van to take them places. . . ."

We need not speculate on the reasons for the judge's ensuing decision to order the change of custody, as he candidly stated them for the record. First he distinguished a case cited by William, emphasizing "There was no father there or mother that was unable to care for the children because of physical disabilities. . . ." Next he found William and Ellen to be "both good, loving parents," although he strongly chided the latter for failing to visit her sons for five years, saying "She should have crawled on her hands and knees out here if she had to to get the children. . . ." The judge then returned to the theme of William's physical inability to personally take care of the children: speculating on Lori's departure, the judge stressed that in such event "a housekeeper or a nursery" would have to be hired—overlooking the admitted fact that Ellen would be compelled to do exactly the same herself for nine hours a day. And he further assumed "There would have to be pick up and probably delivery of the children even though [William] drives his van"—a non sequitur revealing his misunderstanding of the purpose and capabilities of that vehicle.

More importantly, the judge conceded that Dr. Share "saw a nice, loving relationship, and that's absolutely true. There's a great relationship between [William] and the boys...." Yet despite this relationship the judge concluded "I think it would be detrimental to the boys to grow up until age 18 in the custody of their father. *It wouldn't be a normal relationship between father and boys.*" And what he meant by "normal" was quickly revealed: "It's unfortunate [William] has to have help bathing and dressing and undressing. *He can't do anything for the boys himself except maybe talk to them and teach them, be a tutor, which is good, but it's not enough.* I feel that it's in the best interests of the two boys to be with the mother even though she hasn't had them for five years." (Italics added.)

Such a record approaches perilously close to the showing in *Adoption of Richardson* (1967) *supra, 251 Cal. App. 2d 222.* There the trial court denied a petition to adopt an infant boy because of the physical handicap of the proposed adoptive parents, who were deaf-mutes. As here, professional opinions were introduced—and remained uncontradicted—stating that the petitioners had adjusted well to their handicap and had a good relationship with the child, and that their disability would have no adverse effects on his physical or emotional development. Nevertheless, in language strangely similar to that of the judge herein, the trial court reasoned: " 'Is this a normally happy home? There is no question about it, it is a happy home, but is it a normal home? I don't think the Court could make a finding that it is a normal home when these poor unfortunate people, they are handicapped, and what can they do in the way of bringing this child up to be the type of citizen we all want him to be.' " The Court of Appeal there concluded from this and other evidence that the trial judge was prejudiced by a belief that no deaf-mute could ever be a good parent to a "normal" child. While recognizing the rule that the granting or denial of a petition for adoption rests in the discretion of the judge, the appellate court held that such discretion had been abused and accordingly reversed the judgment.

While it is clear the judge herein did not have the totally closed mind exhibited in *Richardson*, it is equally plain that his judgment was affected by serious misconceptions as to the importance of the involvement of parents in the purely physical aspects of their children's lives. We do not mean, of course, that the health or physical condition of the parents may not be taken into account in determining whose custody would best serve the child's interests. In relation to the issues at stake, however, this factor is ordinarily of minor importance; and whenever it is raised—whether in awarding custody originally or changing it later—it is essential that the court weigh the matter with an informed and open mind.

In particular, if a person has a physical handicap it is impermissible for the court simply to rely on that condition as prima facie evidence of the person's unfitness as a parent or of probable detriment to the child; rather, in all cases the court must view the handicapped person as an individual and the family as a whole. To achieve this, the court should inquire into the person's actual and potential physical capabilities, learn how he or she has adapted to the disability and manages its problems, consider how the other members of the household have adjusted thereto, and take into account the special contributions the person may make to the family despite—or even because of—the handicap. Weighing these and all other relevant factors together, the court should then carefully determine whether the parent's condition will in fact have a substantial and lasting adverse effect on the best interests of the child.

The record shows the contrary occurred in the case at bar. To begin with, the court's belief that there could be no "normal relationship between father and boys" unless William engaged in vigorous sporting activities with his sons is a further example of the conventional sex-stereotypical thinking that we condemned in another context in *Sail'er Inn v. Kirby (1971) 485 P.2d 529.* For some, the court's emphasis on the importance of a father's "playing baseball" or "going fishing" with his sons may evoke nostalgic memories of a Norman Rockwell cover on the old Saturday Evening Post. But it has at last been understood that a boy need not prove his masculinity on the playing fields of Eton, nor must a man compete with his son in athletics in order to be a good father: their relationship is no less "normal" if it is built on shared experiences in such fields of interest as science, music, arts and crafts, history or travel, or in pursuing such classic hobbies as stamp or coin collecting. In short, an afternoon that a father and son spend together at a museum or the zoo is surely no less enriching than an equivalent amount of time spent catching either balls or fish.

Even more damaging is the fact that the court's preconception herein, wholly apart from its outdated presumption of proper gender roles, also stereotypes William as a person deemed forever unable to be a good parent simply because he is physically handicapped. Like most stereotypes, this is both false and demeaning. On one level it is false because it assumes that William will never make any significant recovery from his disability. There was no evidence whatever to this effect. On the contrary, it did appear that the hearing was being held only one year after the accident, that William had not yet begun the process of rehabilitation in a home environment, and that he was still a young man in his twenties. In these circumstances the court could not presume that modern medicine, helped by time, patience, and determination, would be powerless to restore at least some of William's former capabilities for active life.

Even if William's prognosis were poor, however, the stereotype indulged in by the court is false for an additional reason: it mistakenly assumes that the parent's handicap inevitably handicaps the child. But children are more adaptable than the court gives them credit for; if one path to their enjoyment of physical activities is closed, they will soon find another. Indeed, having a handicapped parent often stimulates the growth of a child's imagination, independence, and self-reliance. Today's urban youngster, moreover, has many more opportunities for formal and informal instruction than his isolated rural predecessor. It is true that William may not be able to play tennis or swim, ride a bicycle or do gymnastics; but it does not follow that his children cannot learn and enjoy such skills, with the guidance not only of family and friends but also the professional instructors available through schools, church groups, playgrounds, camps, the Red Cross, the YMCA, the Boy Scouts, and numerous service organizations. As Dr. Share pointed out in his testimony, ample community resources now supplement the home in these circumstances.

In addition, it is erroneous to presume that a parent in a wheelchair cannot share to a meaningful degree in the physical activities of his child, should both desire it. On the one hand, modern technology has made the handicapped increasingly mobile, as demonstrated by William's purchase of a van and his plans to drive it by means of hand controls. In the past decade the widespread availability of such vans, together with sophisticated and reliable wheelchair lifts and driving control systems, have brought about a quiet revolution in the mobility of the severely handicapped. No longer are they confined to home or institution, unable to travel except by special vehicle or with the assistance of others; today such persons use the streets and highways in ever-growing numbers for both business and pleasure. Again as Dr. Share explained, the capacity to drive such a vehicle "opens more vistas, greater alternatives" for the handicapped person.

At the same time the physically handicapped have made the public more aware of the many unnecessary obstacles to their participation in community life. Among the evidence of the public's change in attitude is a growing body of legislation intended to reduce or eliminate the physical impediments to that participation, i.e., the "architectural barriers" against access by the handicapped to buildings, facilities, and transportation systems used by the public at large.

While there is obviously much room for continued progress in removing these barriers, the handicapped person today need not remain a shut-in. Although William cannot actually play on his children's baseball team, he may nevertheless be able to take them to the game, participate as a fan, a coach, or even an umpire—and treat them to ice cream on the way home. Nor is this companionship limited to athletic events: such a parent is no less capable of accompanying his children to theaters or libraries, shops or restaurants, schools or churches, afternoon picnics or long vacation trips. Thus it is not true that, as the court herein assumed, William will be unable "to actively go places with [his children], take them places . . ."

On a deeper level, finally, the stereotype is false because it fails to reach the heart of the parent-child relationship. Contemporary psychology confirms what wise families have perhaps always known—that the essence of parenting is not to be found in the harried rounds of daily carpooling endemic to modern suburban life, or even in the doggedly dutiful acts of "togetherness" committed every weekend by well-meaning fathers and mothers across America. Rather, its essence lies in the ethical, emotional, and intellectual guidance the parent gives to the child throughout his formative years, and often beyond. The source of this guidance is the adult's own experience of life; its motive power is parental love and concern for the child's well-being; and its teachings deal with such fundamental matters as the child's feelings about himself, his relationships with others, his system of values, his standards of conduct, and his goals and priorities in life. Even if it were true, as the court herein asserted, that William cannot do "anything" for his sons except "talk to them and teach them, be a tutor," that would not only be "enough"—contrary to the court's conclusion—it would be the most valuable service a parent can render. Yet his capacity to do so is entirely unrelated to his physical prowess: however limited his bodily strength may be, a handicapped parent is a whole person to the child who needs his affection, sympathy, and wisdom to deal with the problems of growing up. Indeed, in such matters his handicap may well be an asset: few can pass through the crucible of a severe physical disability without learning enduring lessons in patience and tolerance.

No expert testimony was necessary to establish these facts. As the Court of Appeal correctly observed in a somewhat different context, "It requires no detailed discussion to demonstrate that the support and, even more, the control of the child is primarily a mental function to which soundness of mind is a crucial prerequisite. It is also well known that physical handicaps generally have no adverse effect upon mental functions.... It is also a matter of common knowledge that many persons with physical handicaps have demonstrated their ability to adequately support and control their children and to give them the benefits of stability and security through love and attention."

We agree, and conclude that a physical handicap that affects a parent's ability to participate with his children in purely physical activities is not a changed circumstance of sufficient relevance and materiality to render it either "essential or expedient" for their welfare that they be taken from his custody. This conclusion would be obvious if the handicap were heart dysfunction, emphysema, arthritis, hernia, or slipped disc; it should be no less obvious when it is the natural consequence of an impaired nervous system. Accordingly, pursuant to the authorities cited above the order changing the custody of the minor children herein from William to Ellen must be set aside as an abuse of discretion.

Both the state and federal governments now pursue the commendable goal of total integration of handicapped persons into the mainstream of society: the Legislature declares that "It is the policy of this state to encourage and enable disabled persons to participate fully in the social and economic life of the state...." Thus far these efforts have focused primarily on such critical areas as employment, housing, education, transportation, and public access. No less important to this policy is the integration of the handicapped into the responsibilities and satisfactions of family life, cornerstone of our social system. Yet as more and more physically disabled persons marry and bear or adopt children—or, as in the case at bar, previously nonhandicapped parents become disabled through accident or illness—custody disputes similar to that now before us may well recur. In discharging their admittedly difficult duty in such proceedings, the trial courts must avoid impairing or defeating the foregoing public policy. With the assistance of the considerations discussed herein, we are confident of their ability to do so.

. . .

The portion of the interlocutory decree of dissolution transferring custody of appellant's minor children to respondent is reversed.

NOTE

1. When the case was retried, the father was given custody of the children. Telephone conversation with Lawrence Buchanan, attorney for Ellen Carney (March 18, 1985).

2. If the case involved an initial award of custody rather than a request to modify an existing award, who should receive custody?

2. Weighing Multiple Factors

Hollon v. Hollon

Supreme Court of Mississippi, 2001.
784 So.2d 943.

■ Diaz, Justice.

This matter arises from a divorce action decided by the Chancery Court of Jackson County, wherein Timothy Paul Hollon (Tim) and Dorothy

Elisabeth Hollon (Beth) were granted a divorce on the grounds of irreconcilable differences. The only disputed issues argued before the trial court involved child custody, child support, and the assessment of court costs. . . .

On December 20, 1999, a final judgment nunc pro tunc was entered granting Tim and Beth a divorce. The chancellor also granted Tim custody of Zach, but reserved visitation rights for Beth. . . . Beth appeals the chancellor's decision to award custody of their son to Tim . . .

FACTS

Tim and Beth were married on April 9, 1994, in Jackson County, Mississippi. During the course of the marriage, Zachary Thomas Hollon was born on July, 16, 1996. In addition to Zach, Tyler Watson, Beth's child from a previous marriage lived with Tim and Beth. The family resided in Bonaparte Square Apartment complex in Pascagoula, where Beth served as the on-site manager. The apartment complex owners provided Beth and Tim with a rent-free apartment as part of her compensation package. Tim served the City of Moss Point as a police officer.

Soon after Zach's birth, Tim and Beth's marriage began to deteriorate. They separated in January of 1997, for approximately eight weeks. After reconciling, their marriage again drifted into troubled waters leading to a second separation on January 11, 1998. Tim moved out of the marital apartment and into his parents' home, leaving Zach and Tyler in Beth's care. In an effort to alleviate the financial strain placed upon her during her separation, Beth took in a roommate, Beth Dukes (Dukes). Prior to this arrangement, Bonaparte Square Apartment complex also provided Dukes, an officer with the Pascagoula Police department, with a rent-free apartment in exchange for her service as a "courtesy officer." Dukes performed minimal security duties and fulfilled much of her obligation to the owners by simply serving as a police officer while residing at the apartment complex. Dukes lived with her son, Seth Holder, a child from her previous marriage.

. . . At the time, five people inhabited Beth's three-bedroom apartment; Beth and her two children, Tyler and Zach, as well as Dukes and her son Seth. Tyler, a teenager, was given his own bedroom, while Seth and Zach shared a bedroom as they were both under the age of five. Beth and Dukes shared the third bedroom.

At trial, Beth freely admitted that she and Dukes slept in the same bed. However, she vehemently denied any sexual relationship existed between her and Dukes, continually characterizing their relationship as platonic. Donna Mauldin, a friend of Beth's, testified that Beth told her that she and Dukes were engaged in a sexual relationship. Mauldin further testified that Beth wanted her to deny, if asked, that she ever admitted having a sexual relationship with Dukes. Mauldin refused to do so.

During the separation, while Beth and Dukes were sharing the apartment at Bonaparte Square, Tim heard the surfacing allegations surrounding Beth and Dukes' relationship. In order to investigate, Tim borrowed a key to the apartment, his former marital residence, from Donna Mauldin. While Beth and Dukes were away, Tim and Calvin Hutchins entered the apartment without permission and made a photographic record of things Tim felt were "inappropriate." These photographs and rumors led him to become concerned with "the environment that [Zach] would be raised in." Among other things, Tim took photographs of Dukes' clothing and police equipment in the shared bedroom, beer bottles in the refrigerator and wastebasket, liquor bottles on the counter, and one red light bulb in a ceiling fixture. These photographs were admitted into evidence over Beth's objection.

. . .

Tim and Beth each testified that the other was a good parent and had only Zach's best interests at heart. Both testified that their parents would serve as supplemental care givers to Zach when they were at work or unable to fulfill their parental obligations. Tim admitted that the only problem he had with Beth retaining permanent custody of Zach was his belief that she engaged in homosexual activity.

Tim lives with his parents in their four-bedroom house and pays them fifty dollars a month in rent. During the trial, Beth moved out of the apartment complex with her two children and into her parents' five-bedroom house. She initiated this move during the break in the trial because she felt the judge disapproved of her living situation. Beth's plan to reside with her parents is temporary. She and Tyler will move into a newly remodeled three bedroom house provided, in part, by her new job as the rental property manager for R.J. Homes. Beth no longer lives with Dukes and her son, although they remain friends.

STANDARD OF REVIEW

Our familiar standard holds that, absent an abuse of discretion, we will uphold the decision of the chancellor. . . .

LEGAL ANALYSIS

. . .

factors:

The polestar consideration in child custody cases is the best interest and welfare of the child. The . . . factors used to determine what is, in fact, in the "best interests" of a child in regard to custody are as follows: 1) age, health and sex of the child; 2) determination of the parent that had the continuity of care prior to the separation; 3) which has the best parenting skills and which has the willingness and capacity to provide primary child care; 4) the employment of the parent and responsibilities of that employment; 5) physical and mental health and age of the parents; 6) emotional ties of parent and child; 7) moral fitness of parents; 8) the home, school and community record of the child; 9) the preference of the child at the age sufficient to express a preference by law; 10) stability of home environment and employment of each parent; and 11) other factors relevant to the parent-child relationship. It should further be noted that marital fault should not be used as a sanction in custody awards, nor should differences in religion, personal values and lifestyles be the sole basis for custody decisions.

In order to determine whether or not the chancellor was manifestly wrong, clearly erroneous or abused his discretion in applying the Albright factors, we review the evidence and testimony presented at trial under each factor to ensure his ruling was supported by record.

1) The age, health and sex of the child

Although this Court has weakened the "tender years" doctrine in recent years, there is still a presumption that a mother is generally better suited to raise a young child. Chancellor Watts began his analysis of the case with the statement that the child was barely three years old at the time the trial ended. He pointed out that the tender years doctrine had been weakened and found Zach to be a healthy male child, with no physical or mental impairments who could be cared for equally well by both parties. The chancellor did not explicitly say that this factor favored one party over another. This factor favors Beth because the legal presumption, although weakened, still favors the mother to raise a very small child.

2) The determination of which parent had continuous care of the child prior to the separation

Chancellor Watts was mindful of the fact that since the parties separated, the mother retained primary care of the child, with the father retaining visitation privileges. The chancellor failed to note that Tim did not have custody of Zach during the previous separation, nor express any interest in becoming the custodial parent until the allegations of homosexuality arose. The chancellor did not point out that Tim rarely exercised his visitation rights, nor did he make a specific finding that this favored one parent over the other. Clearly, this factor weighs in favor of Beth.

3) The determination of which parent has the best parenting skills as well as the willingness and capacity to provide primary child care

After scrutinizing the evidence presented under this factor, the chancellor found that

> [B]oth parties cared equally for the child prior to their separation, and that both parties are found to have contributed equally to the continuity of care of the child prior to their separation. . . . [T]he Court finds that either party—that neither parties [sic] parenting skills, willingness and capacity to take care of the child, is greater than the other.

This finding is not entirely supported by Tim's testimony and is directly contradicted by Beth's testimony. Tim admitted that he had not paid his child support obligations regularly, forcing Beth to garnish his wages. He also admitted not visiting Zach for approximately two months during the final separation. Beth further testified that Tim failed to pay any child support for Zach for four months during the separation.

Prior to the separation, Beth testified that she had the primary responsibility of caring for her two children. She estimated that she provided approximately ninety percent of the direct care for Zach, such as changing, feeding, and supervising him, as well as doing laundry and other housework. Beth shared cooking duties with Tim. Tim testified that he helped change and feed Zach, but qualified his testimony adding that he provided said care in the evenings or on his days off. Tim's work schedule prohibits consistent, in depth care of the child.

The chancellor found that neither parent held an advantage over the other here. From the entirety of the record, it is clear that Beth provided primary child care and if from familiarity or practice alone, holds an advantage over Tim in this area.

4) The employment of the parent and responsibilities of that employment

. . . Although [the chancellor] did not cite a preference for either parent in the record, it is obvious that Beth's working situation is far more conducive to caring for a young child. Tim serves the public as a police officer and thus logs eighty-four hours on duty during his two-week shift. The schedule follows a two days on, two days off, three days on, two days off, two days on, three days off pattern with Tim on duty twelve hours each working day, rotating from a day shift to a night shift every twenty-eight days.

favors Beth

Beth works approximately thirty-five hours a week as a rental property manager in an office environment. Her position requires her to work only during the day, never on weekends and never during the holidays. This is in stark contrast to the regimented schedule that Tim must adhere to, regardless of weekends, holidays, or the hour of the day. . . . Without question, this factor weighs heavily in Beth's favor.

5) The physical and mental health and age of the parents

equal

. . . Although not specifically stated by the trial judge, this factor balances equally between Beth and Tim.

6) The emotional ties of parent and child

Commenting on the emotional ties of Zach to his parents, the trial court held that no testimony was presented that showed Zach exhibited a stronger attachment to one parent over the other. Despite this finding, the trial court noted that Zach has been in Beth's continual care throughout both separations and subsequent divorce proceedings. The trial court implied that this factor also balanced equally between Tim and Beth, again never specifying for the record who, if anyone, benefitted from this factor.

7) The moral fitness of the parents

The seventh factor, moral fitness, took the lion's share of the chancellor's attention and is essentially what Beth argues dealt the fatal blow to her attempt to retain custody of Zach. Chancellor Watts noted that neither parent attended church regularly, which was "disturbing to the Court to some degree" . . .

The chancellor then dove into the allegations of the homosexual affair. Chancellor Watts found Beth's testimony regarding this issue to be untrustworthy. In fact, because Beth's testimony denying her relationship with Dukes directly contradicted Donna Mauldin's testimony confirming it, he asked the District Attorney's office to consider conducting an investigation into whether or not Beth committed perjury by denying she had a homosexual relationship with Dukes. The chancellor further noted that he ought to have confidence that the custodial parent is a truthful, forthright person, and he stated that he lacked that confidence in Beth. Accordingly, he found that this factor weighed heavily in Tim's favor.

Chancellor Watts also noted that evidence of a homosexual relationship is not, per se, a basis to determine that child custody should be denied.[4] He then went on to rehash, in detail, all of the testimony regarding Beth's alleged sexual relationship with Dukes. This Court has held that:

> In divorce actions, as distinguished from proceedings for modification of custody, sexual misconduct on the part of the wife is not per se grounds for denial of custody. A husband may upon proof of his wife's adultery be granted an absolute divorce on that grounds and yet in the same case custody of the children may be awarded to the mother. Our cases well recognize that it may be in the best interest of a child to remain with its mother even though she may have been guilty of adultery.

Cheek v. Ricker, 431 So.2d 1139, 1144–45 n. 3 (Miss.1983).

. . .

4. This Court has held that it is of no consequence that a mother was having an affair with a woman rather than a man. Plaxico v. Michael, 735 So.2d 1036, 1039–40 (Miss. 1999).

The trial court never found the mother unfit to care for Zach, and no evidence was presented regarding any detrimental effects the child may have suffered as a result of living with his mother. The chancellor failed to mention that Tim admitted drinking a couple of beers every other day, that he drank to the point of being under the influence in the past, and formerly gambled every other week, but had not gambled recently because he did not have the money to do so. Beth also admitting to drinking to the point of intoxication in the past, but admitted that she gambled only once every six months.

While this factor is as important as any other and should be given its due consideration, it appears that the allegations offered under this heading were far and away the most scrutinized among the evidence reviewed at trial.

can't weigh
this factor
too heavily

. . .

10) The stability of home environment and employment of each parent

The chancellor found, after considering the stability of the home environment and employment of each parent, that this factor favored Tim. This reasoning is inexplicable. Beth's current employment situation, discussed above, is clearly more favorable to child-rearing than Tim's schedule.

By the time the second day of the trial arrived, both Tim and Beth lived with their parents, although Beth stated her intention to move into a house of her own. The trial court seemed to hold this relocation and change in employment against her, although a less than subtle warning offered by the chancellor was the sole reason that Beth initiated the change in living situations.

. . .

11) Other factors relevant to the parent-child relationship

Under this heading, the trial judge noted that the pictures submitted as evidence portrayed a messy house with empty beer bottles on the counter. The court acknowledged that Tim admitted taking clothes out of the closet and rearranging them in the bedroom to take the picture, and that drinking is "done almost everyday by everyone." Again, no reference was made to Tim's admitted drinking.

After considering all of the evidence and weighing the enumerated factors, the trial judge found that it would be in the best interest of the child to be relocated to Tim's care. A cursory glance at the above analysis reveals that the evidence supports a finding that more factors weigh in favor of Beth than Tim. The chancellor found otherwise. While the chancellor did cover each . . . factor, he rarely did anything but restate some of the pertinent evidence to be considered under each factor, only once or twice actually ruling that a factor favored one party over the other.

This Court has held that although it could not be said that the chancellor's conclusion regarding the application of the . . . factors was so lacking in evidentiary support as to be manifest error, the absence of specific findings prevented affirming the lower court with the confidence. A similar situation presents itself today. While the chancellor analyzed the applicable factors, he did not do so with specificity, assigning very few to a particular parent. If . . . one factor should not outweigh another, the chancellor erred by determining the case on the basis of Beth's moral fitness, when upon review, Beth clearly wound up with more factors weighing in her favor.

... It is clear from the record that the chancellor's defining consideration in determining custody of Zach centered on the allegations of Beth's homosexual affair. In doing so, the chancellor committed reversible error.

. . .

Within his analysis of the ... factors, the chancellor abused his discretion by placing too much weight upon the "moral fitness" factor and ignoring the voluminous evidence presented under the remaining factors supporting Beth as the preferred custodial parent. Therefore, we reverse the decision of the Chancery Court of Jackson County and award Beth custody of Zach and remand the case for a determination of Tim's visitation rights and further proceedings not inconsistent with the dictates of this opinion.

. . .

3. RACE AND ETHNICITY

Palmore v. Sidoti

Supreme Court of the United States, 1984.
466 U.S. 429.

■ CHIEF JUSTICE BURGER delivered the opinion of the Court.

We granted certiorari to review a judgment of a state court divesting a natural mother of the custody of her infant child because of her remarriage to a person of a different race.

When petitioner Linda Sidoti Palmore and respondent Anthony J. Sidoti, both Caucasians, were divorced in May 1980 in Florida, the mother was awarded custody of their three-year-old daughter.

In September 1981 the father sought custody of the child by filing a petition to modify the prior judgment because of changed conditions. The change was that the child's mother was then cohabiting with a Negro, Clarence Palmore, Jr., whom she married two months later. Additionally, the father made several allegations of instances in which the mother had not properly cared for the child.

After hearing testimony from both parties and considering a court counselor's investigative report, the court noted that the father had made allegations about the child's care, but the court made no findings with respect to these allegations. On the contrary, the court made a finding that "there is no issue as to either party's devotion to the child, adequacy of housing facilities, or respect[a]bility of the new spouse of either parent."

The court then addressed the recommendations of the court counselor, who had made an earlier report "in [another] case coming out of this circuit also involving the social consequences of an interracial marriage. Niles v. Niles, 299 So.2d 162." From this vague reference to that earlier case, the court turned to the present case and noted the counselor's recommendation for a change in custody because "[t]he wife [petitioner] has chosen for herself and for her child, a life-style unacceptable to her father *and to society. . . . The child . . . is, or at school age will be, subject to environmental pressures not of choice.*" *Record 84 (emphasis added).*

The court then concluded that the best interests of the child would be served by awarding custody to the father. The court's rationale is contained in the following:

"The father's evident resentment of the mother's choice of a black partner is not sufficient to wrest custody from the mother. It is of some significance, however, that the mother did see fit to bring a man into her home and carry on a sexual relationship with him without being married to him. Such action tended to place gratification of her own desires ahead of her concern for the child's future welfare. This Court feels that despite the strides that have been made in bettering relations between the races in this country, it is inevitable that Melanie will, if allowed to remain in her present situation and attains school age and thus more vulnerable to peer pressures, suffer from the social stigmatization that is sure to come."

. . .

The judgment of a state court determining or reviewing a child custody decision is not ordinarily a likely candidate for review by this Court. However, the court's opinion, after stating that the "father's evident resentment of the mother's choice of a black partner is not sufficient" to deprive her of custody, then turns to what it regarded as the damaging impact on the child from remaining in a racially-mixed household. This raises important federal concerns arising from the Constitution's commitment to eradicating discrimination based on race.

The Florida court did not focus directly on the parental qualifications of the natural mother or her present husband, or indeed on the father's qualifications to have custody of the child. The court found that "there is no issue as to either party's devotion to the child, adequacy of housing facilities, or respect[a]bility of the new spouse of either parent." This, taken with the absence of any negative finding as to the quality of the care provided by the mother, constitutes a rejection of any claim of petitioner's unfitness to continue the custody of her child.

The court correctly stated that the child's welfare was the controlling factor. But that court was entirely candid and made no effort to place its holding on any ground other than race. Taking the court's findings and rationale at face value, it is clear that the outcome would have been different had petitioner married a Caucasian male of similar respectability.

A core purpose of the Fourteenth Amendment was to do away with all governmentally-imposed[1] discrimination based on race. Classifying persons according to their race is more likely to reflect racial prejudice than legitimate public concerns; the race, not the person, dictates the category. Such classifications are subject to the most exacting scrutiny; to pass constitutional muster, they must be justified by a compelling governmental interest and must be "necessary ... to the accomplishment" of its legitimate purpose, McLaughlin v. Florida, 379 U.S. 184, 196 (1964).

The State, of course, has a duty of the highest order to protect the interests of minor children, particularly those of tender years. In common with most states, Florida law mandates that custody determinations be made in the best interests of the children involved. Fla.Stat. § 61.13(2)(b)(1) (1983). The goal of granting custody based on the best interests of the child is indisputably a substantial governmental interest for purposes of the Equal Protection Clause.

1. The actions of state courts and judicial officers in their official capacity have long been held to be state action governed by the Fourteenth Amendment. Shelley v. Kraemer, 334 U.S. 1 (1948); Ex parte Virginia, 100 U.S. 339, 346–347 (1880).

It would ignore reality to suggest that racial and ethnic prejudices do not exist or that all manifestations of those prejudices have been eliminated. There is a risk that a child living with a step-parent of a different race may be subject to a variety of pressures and stresses not present if the child were living with parents of the same racial or ethnic origin.

The question, however, is whether the reality of private biases and the possible injury they might inflict are permissible considerations for removal of an infant child from the custody of its natural mother. We have little difficulty concluding that they are not. The Constitution cannot control such prejudices but neither can it tolerate them. Private biases may be outside the reach of the law, but the law cannot, directly or indirectly, give them effect. "Public officials sworn to uphold the Constitution may not avoid a constitutional duty by bowing to the hypothetical effects of private racial prejudice that they assume to be both widely and deeply held." Palmer v. Thompson, 403 U.S. 217, 260–261 (1971) (White, J., dissenting).

This is by no means the first time that acknowledged racial prejudice has been invoked to justify racial classifications. In Buchanan v. Warley, 245 U.S. 60 (1917), for example, this Court invalidated a Kentucky law forbidding Negroes from buying homes in white neighborhoods.

"It is urged that this proposed segregation will promote the public peace by preventing race conflicts. Desirable as this is, and important as is the preservation of the public peace, this aim cannot be accomplished by laws or ordinances which deny rights created or protected by the Federal Constitution." Id., at 81.

Whatever problems racially-mixed households may pose for children in 1984 can no more support a denial of constitutional rights than could the stresses that residential integration was thought to entail in 1917. The effects of racial prejudice, however real, cannot justify a racial classification removing an infant child from the custody of its natural mother found to be an appropriate person to have such custody.

The judgment of the District Court of Appeal is reversed.

It is so ordered.

NOTE

By the time the Supreme Court announced its decision, the father and his new wife had moved with Melanie to Texas. He immediately initiated proceedings in Texas to obtain custody. Noting that the Supreme Court did not direct a reinstatement of the original custody degree, Florida Court of Appeals in 1985 upheld the decision of a Florida trial court to decline jurisdiction in favor of Texas. Palmore v. Sidoti, 472 So.2d 843.

Jones v. Jones

Supreme Court of South Dakota, 1996.
542 N.W.2d 119.

■ Johns, Circuit Judge

Dawn R. Jones (Dawn) appeals from a decree of divorce awarding custody of the parties three minor children to Kevin Mark Jones (Kevin). Dawn also appeals the amount of rehabilitative alimony awarded. We affirm.

FACTS

Dawn and Kevin Jones were married on March 11, 1989 in Britton, South Dakota. Kevin was thirty years old at time of trial and is an enrolled member of the Sisseton–Wahpeton Dakota Nation. He was adopted at age seven by Maurice and Dorothy Jones. Dawn was twenty-five years old at time of trial and is Caucasian. The parties have three children, Lyndra, Elias and Desiree. Lyndra was born to Dawn prior to her marriage to Kevin.[6] She was subsequently adopted by Kevin.

During the marriage, the parties resided in a trailer house on the farm of Kevin's parents. Kevin is a minority shareholder in and works for Penrhos Farms. Penrhos is a close family farm corporation, owned primarily by Kevin's father and his three uncles. The Jones are an extremely close-knit and supportive family. In fact, Kevin often takes the children to work with him, as this is a family tradition. However, farm safety is very important and is stressed by all members of the family.

Kevin works predominantly in construction and in the feeding of the cattle on the Penrhos farm. His net earnings for child support purposes are approximately $1,880.00 a month. During the marriage, Dawn was a homemaker for a time and also held various jobs. She is currently enrolled in a nursing program at the Sisseton–Wahpeton Community College.

Kevin is a recovering alcoholic who, while drinking, exhibited a behavior of violence towards Dawn and a somewhat casual indifference to the children. He has been sober since December 1992 and regularly attends and presents Alcoholics Anonymous meetings.[7] Dawn suffers from depression and low self-esteem but is seeking counseling at this time.

Deterioration of the marriage is attributed to Kevin's alcoholism, Dawn's depression, financial problems and a lack of communication. Both parties were granted a divorce based upon mental cruelty. They were also granted joint legal custody of the children with primary physical custody being awarded to Kevin.[8] The court awarded Dawn rehabilitative alimony to allow her to finish the nursing program. She was awarded the cost of two years tuition, $10,680.00, with a monthly payment of $445.00, to commence when she returns to school.

ISSUES

Three main [issues] errors have been [raised] by Dawn in this appeal ... [The second is] whether the trial court wrongfully considered race when determining the best interests of the children ...

ANALYSIS

. . .

Dawn argues that the trial court awarded the children to Kevin for the principal reason that, as a Native American, he has suffered prejudice and will therefore be able to better deal with the needs of the children when they are discriminated against because, although they are biracial, they have Native American features. She contends that the trial court impermissibly considered the matter of race when determining the custody of the children

6. Lyndra's natural father is also of Native American descent.

7. The trial court stressed the importance of Kevin remaining alcohol-free in its decision to award him custody.

8. The trial court granted Kevin primary physical custody of the children during the pendency of the action after hearing the testimony of the parties.

and thereby violated her right to equal protection of the laws as found in Section One of the Fourteenth Amendment to the United States Constitution.

In support of her arguments, Dawn cites to the decision of the United States Supreme Court in *Palmore v. Sidoti, 466 U.S. 429 (1984)*. . . . [In *Palmore*, the Court] recognized that, while the child may well experience prejudice because she lived in a biracial home and that her best interests might be served by a change of custody, "the effects of racial prejudice, however real, cannot justify a racial classification removing an infant child from the custody of its natural mother found to be an appropriate person to have such custody." *466 U.S. at 434*. The rationale for this holding was that although the constitution cannot control racial and other ethnic prejudices, "neither can it tolerate them." Private biases may be outside the reach of the law, but the law cannot, directly or indirectly, *104 S. Ct. at 1882, 80 L. Ed. 2d at 426*.

Albeit the trial court did not cite to *Palmore* in either its memorandum opinion (which was incorporated into its findings and conclusions) or in the findings of fact and conclusions of law, the court was apparently aware of its holding and scrupulously honored it. The trial court wrote in the memorandum opinion:

> Plaintiff addressed the issue of racial discrimination and Native American culture in his testimony. He states that all three children would be discriminated against as Native Americans if they left Penrhos farm to live. He wants for them the same loving, non-discriminatory upbringing that he received as a child at Penrhos. Plaintiff also wants to continue to make the children aware of their culture and heritage and participate in Tribal functions.
>
> This is an example of the Plaintiff's concern for the totality of the upbringing of his children. However, this Court's determination of custody must be made on a racially neutral basis as far as concerning itself with the effects of any potential discrimination. . . .

Also in finding number 27 of the findings of fact and conclusions of law prepared by Kevin's counsel, the trial court deleted the portion that stated that the children would be subject to discrimination if they were raised away from Penrhos Farms and handwrote that "custody determinations are to be made on a racially neutral basis." . . .

While the trial court was not blind to the racial backgrounds of the children, we are satisfied that it did not impermissibly award custody on the basis of race. As noted, Kevin showed a sensitivity to the need for his children to be exposed to their ethnic heritage. All of us form our own personal identities, based in part, on our religious racial and cultural backgrounds. To say, as Dawn argues, that a court should never consider whether a parent is willing and able to expose to and educate children on their heritage, is to say that society is not interested in whether children ever learn who they are. *Palmore does* not require this, nor do the constitutions of the United States or the State of South Dakota. We hold that it is proper for a trial court, when determining the best interests of a child in the context of a custody dispute between parents, to consider the matter of race as it relates to a child's ethnic heritage and which parent is more prepared to expose the child to it.

Furthermore we refuse to second guess, as Dawn argues, the trial court's mental processes. The trial court said it decided custody on a racially neutral basis and we accept its statements as the record does not clearly impel us to do otherwise.

In summary, the trial court's decision is not clearly against the laws of this country or state. There was no abuse of discretion.

. . .

Katharine T. Bartlett, Comparing Race and Sex Discrimination in Custody Cases

28 Hofstra L. Rev. 877, 879–894 (2000).

. . .

This Lecture focuses on a topic in family law—child custody—as a starting point for a more detailed assessment of the similarities and differences between sex and race discrimination. It was Professor John DeWitt Gregory who first challenged me to think more deeply about this issue. One of the provisions I drafted as a Reporter for the American Law Institute ("ALI") Principles of Family Dissolution Project,[7] on which Professor Gregory was an Adviser, is a "non-discrimination" provision that prohibits courts from considering in custody cases any of the usual factors: race, ethnicity, sex, religion, or sexual orientation. Professor Gregory, early on in the project, questioned me about lumping all of these non-discrimination factors together. "They are different, aren't they?" he insisted. "Shouldn't there be a separate provision for each, reflecting the differences?" I resisted at first, but his questions eventually led me to try to think more comparatively about these separate factors.

This Lecture focuses on the operation of, and attempts to eliminate, race and sex discrimination in child custody law. . . .

I. Discrimination and Role Policing

I first consider Palmore v. Sidoti, . . .

. . .

No case so clearly prohibits consideration of sex in custody cases. It should be noted, however, that there was a potential gender issue in Palmore that received no attention from the Supreme Court. It appears that Linda began cohabiting with Clarence before they were married. According to the trial court, the mother's " 'seeing fit to bring a man into her home and carrying on a sexual relationship with him without being married to him' " showed that she " 'tended to place gratification of her own desires ahead of her concern for the child's future welfare.' " Nothing more seems to have been made of this factor, either by the trial court or on review, but some courts have since noticed that mothers who cohabit outside of marriage tend to be penalized in ways fathers who cohabit outside of marriage are not, and have concluded that differential treatment constitutes sex discrimination.

Practitioners, scholars, and, increasingly, appellate courts have identified and sought to eradicate a double standard based on sex in custody disputes. Criticized, for example, are cases that appear to attach a different significance to employment by mothers outside the home than they attach to employment by fathers. In these cases, courts seem to expect fathers to work

7. American Law Institute, Principles of the Law of Family Dissolution: Analysis and Recommendations, 2.14 (Tentative Draft No. 3, Part I, 1998).

outside the home, and respect them for their employment success. In contrast, mothers, although they also usually work outside the home, are expected to make compromises in their careers for their children, and are penalized when they do not. One South Carolina appellate court, for example, affirmed an award of custody to the father, who was an oilman, based in part on an analysis of how much time the mother, who was an obstetrician, would have to be away from home and what caretaking arrangements she would have for the child; no such analysis of the father's work schedule or baby-sitting arrangements is mentioned in the opinion.[26] . . .

Similarly, caretaking by mothers sometimes is taken for granted by courts in custody cases, whereas when fathers "help out," their contributions tend to be highly exaggerated. An at-home father in an Iowa case, for example, was credited with having "relieved" the mother of numerous child raising problems that occurred during her working hours, even though she worked from 5:30 a.m. to 2:00 p.m., and performed all the responsibilities for the family during her nonworking hours.[30]

. . . [T]here are far more appellate custody cases that raise issues of sex than there are those that raise issues of race. One explanation might be that expectations about parents are determined more by their sex than by their race; another is that sex is more conceptually central to one's identity than race. But it may be as simple as that parents fighting for custody are far more likely to be of different sexes than they are of different races, making it possible to observe a double standard within a single case—at least when both parents have had affairs, or worked the same number of hours outside the home and performed identical parenting roles.

Although there are more sex discrimination cases than race discrimination ones, both are enabled by the open-ended best-interests test applied in custody cases, which invites bias of all types. The best-interests test is an empty vessel, to be filled by the subjective views of judges about what is good for children, including views about sex and race. . . .

There are a handful of reported modification cases that involve white mothers losing custody after having affairs with black men. Every one of these cases affirms the change of custody on grounds that there were other legal justifications for the modification besides race, such as the fact that the mother lied about the affair, or that her sexual activity displayed bad moral judgment. . . .

A close look at the fundamentals of sex discrimination cases might help us better to identify cases of race discrimination. What we can observe in the sex cases is that discrimination serves to reinforce conventional roles—to keep mother in her place as sexually faithful, totally dedicated to her children and family, and to keep father in his place as primary provider. . . . Rethinking [Palmore] in terms of the possibility of role policing, one may wonder if the trial court's concern was, instead, that there is something improper about a family consisting of different races. In other words, for the trial court, the threat to Melanie may not have been a problem of peers no one could control, but rather parents—a white mother and black stepfather who crossed the line—straying too far from their appropriate racial tracks.

26. See *Richmond v. Tecklenberg*, 396 S.E.2d 111, 114 (S.C. Ct. App. 1990).

30. See *In re Marriage of Fennell, 485 N.W.2d 863, 864 (Iowa Ct. App. 1992).*

In this regard, I note that the Supreme Court in Palmore refers approvingly to its 1917 decision in Buchanan v. Warley,[40] overturning a Kentucky law that forbade whites and "Negroes" from buying houses in each other's neighborhoods. What is interesting about Buchanan is that it disapproved of a series of offered purposes for the Kentucky statute, including the purpose of "'preventing conflict and ill-feeling between the white and colored races[,] ... preserving the public peace,'" and protecting property values from depreciating on account of a breakdown in the racial integrity of a neighborhood. ... However, a fourth rationale—that of preserving racial purity—was handled differently. Rather than dismissing the motive as illegitimate, the Court went to some trouble to redefine the issue of the case so as to avoid having to commit itself one way or the other on this motive. The case, the Court explained, "*does not deal* with an attempt to prohibit the *amalgamation* of the races," but rather with the "civil right of a white man to dispose of his property if he saw fit to do so to a person of color and of a colored person to make such disposition to a white person."[48] This resistance to confronting the impulse to protect racial purity suggests that there may have been some sympathy with the fear of racial amalgamation. Could this sympathy remain in some form? ... [C]onsider whether the trial court in Palmore would have been equally concerned about Melanie if Mrs. Sidoti was African American, and her second marriage was to a white man. If the justification was really the stigma of living in a mixed-race household, one would expect the same concern. But if racial purity was the objective—given the historical context in which the white race is the only race with a perceived purity to protect—one would not expect the addition of a white parent to a black parent's home to raise the same fears about a child's welfare.

II. Discrimination and Disparate Effects

Another set of discrimination claims concerns the complaint of fathers that the sex-based double standard works against them, not in their favor. The evidence offered is circumstantial, but rather impressive: women obtain custody in eighty to ninety percent of cases. What is one to make of this disparity? In other contexts in which women, or minorities, receive an end of the stick that is this short, suspicions would be high indeed.

One needs to look more carefully at exactly what is being claimed here. The claim assumes that sex equality demands equal results for men and women but, if this is the case, how should such equal results be measured? One possibility is that mothers and fathers be awarded custody an equal percentage of the time. Another is that both parents be awarded equal time with the child at divorce in each case, i.e., joint physical custody. One might protest that such approaches ignore the child's best interests, but if the child's interests do not justify race-based custody decision-making, arguably neither are they sufficient to trump society's interest in avoiding sex discrimination.

... The better analysis questions the claimed analogy between the father's claim and the sex and race claims examined thus far. What occurred in Palmore was, by stipulation, race discrimination; the question posed by the case was whether it was justified. The statistical disparity for mother custody, in contrast, proves only disparate results, not that discrimination has actually occurred; and one cannot get to the question of whether sex discrimination

40. 245 U.S. 60 (1917).

48. *Id. at 81* (emphasis added).

is justified until it is determined whether or not sex discrimination has occurred.

Here, I would distinguish between two possibilities. On the one hand, some of the disparity in favor of mothers may be because courts evaluate claims by fathers with a bias against them, based on the belief, conscious or otherwise, that mothers are better parents. While this type of discrimination—like the examples given earlier of a double standard against women in custody cases—is not easy to identify, it is sex discrimination when it occurs and should be prohibited.

On the other hand, disparate results against men could be the result of the neutral application of custody standards meant to protect the best interests of the child. Child custody standards tend to stress past caretaking and emotional bonds which are generally generated through caretaking relationships, because it is thought that these are the best measures of the best interests of the child. To state an obvious social fact, mothers are, on average, more actively engaged than fathers, on average, in the caretaking of their children before divorce. . . . Note that, while the average woman invests more in her children, the average man invests more in his education and career, works longer hours, and builds up more extensive work experience. Given these social realities, one should be no more surprised by the fact that women most often get custody at divorce than by the fact that men, on average, earn more than women.

Yet again one might protest: women's rights advocates complain about earning less than men. Are not fathers' rights complaints in this context of the same order, deserving of the same recognition? To be sure, neither men nor women should have it both ways in this debate. But it is important to define what constitutes nondiscriminatory treatment in each context. When the father's qualifications are judged differently than the qualifications of the mother, under the same standard, this is sex discrimination, just as it is sex discrimination when women are evaluated by different criteria than men in the workplace. Also, when the criteria for determining a child's best interests have been stacked—for example, when undue weight is given to certain factors because those factors are associated with women, and thus tend to favor them—this is sex discrimination . . . When neither of these things is going on, however, and when the criteria used are designed appropriately to serve the legitimate purpose of protecting the child's best interests, the problem, if there is one, is not one of sex discrimination—at least not sex discrimination in custody decision-making.

. . . Men should not be awarded custody more often just to equalize results for fathers and mothers. Society may wish to alter cultural expectations that make caretaking an activity governed by gender, just as society may choose to alter the expectations that lead men to disproportionately invest their labor in market employment. If either of these social revolutions succeed and men assume more caretaking responsibility for children, women are likely to earn more money, and men are likely to fare better in custody cases. Before they succeed, however, men (and women) will have to put up with a disparate impact in custody cases.

. . .

This prolonged discussion of fathers' rights claims reveals a significant difference between race and sex discrimination in custody cases. Societal differences between mothers and fathers with respect to the practices and expectations of childrearing should lead one to expect that custody cases would be skewed in favor of mothers. Also, it gives further support to the proposition that parenting is governed more by gender than by race. I say this tentatively, and only because I know of no differences between whites and blacks or other racial groups that would be thought reasonably to bear on custody decisions and that are comparable to those that exist with respect to differences between mothers and fathers. If I am right, the fact that custody is skewed as to sex is only to be expected, under current social circumstances, while skewed results as to race is not.

III. Discrimination and Benign Motives

Next consider the case of a mixed race couple, Sarah, who is white, and Bob, who is black. Their biological, biracial son, Ralph, perceives himself, and is perceived by others, as black. At the divorce of Sarah and Bob, Bob uses this fact to argue that Ralph should live with him.

This case might seem like a harder case than Palmore. If it does, this is probably because the benign purpose of furthering the child's positive racial identity seems more persuasive, and more genuine—in other words, less of a pretext—than the racial stigma argument offered in Palmore. Ralph will live in a world in which he will almost certainly face discrimination as a result of being perceived as black, and because Bob shares this experience, it may be thought that he has more to teach Ralph on the subject than Sarah does. . . .

Consider, however, the same claims made in the context of gender role modeling. Sam is twelve. His parents, Dave and Marge, each want primary custody at divorce. Dave argues that he should have primary custody of Sam, even though Marge has been Sam's primary caretaker throughout the marriage, because Sam is entering adolescence and figuring out what it means to be a man. Marge could make the same arguments in her own favor, if their child were twelve-year-old Doris.

There is at least one interesting difference between these two examples. While the case for matching as to both race and sex could be viewed as helping children deal with adverse social circumstances, the argument for race modeling only runs one way. One would not expect white parents to make this argument based on the need of their white children for a healthy race identity, and if they did, you would not expect them to succeed. Gender role modeling arguments, however, run both ways: in favor of fathers seeking custody of their boys and mothers seeking custody of their girls. . . .

Despite this difference, the role modeling arguments with respect to both race and sex are equally and profoundly unpersuasive, for reasons that are again most apparent when one moves back and forth between sex and race. The most obvious problem is the reinforcement of damaging stereotypes. The fact that stereotypes damage both boys and girls does not make the damage less serious. It might be tempting to claim that the gender role modeling argument is based on biology and thus not a social construct. It is also possible, however, that the biological difference makes the reinforcement of damaging gender stereotypes more, not less, of a problem, since biological difference gives an aura of scientific legitimacy to gender roles—just as the science of race differences was used at one time to legitimize the subordination of racial minorities. In fact, both race and gender role modeling represent adaptations to social realities that intentionally, not just incidentally, are designed to fit into and recreate the realities to which they adapt.

The role modeling argument with respect to race draws on a non-biological justification; in fact, nowhere is the non-biological character of race more apparent than when one classifies a child whose parents are black and white, as black. This classification thereby more noticeably participates in the process of racial subordination and, thus, is troubling on that account. Does it help that, like other affirmative actions which many do not oppose, society participates in this process only in order to take account of and address a child's problems in living in a racially discriminatory society? Palmore would seem to say no—that taking account of racial prejudice is not a sufficient basis for race discrimination.

Whatever the reach of Palmore, there are other defects in role modeling arguments that are fatal and apply equally to race and sex. First, these arguments assume that there is some ideal identity of gender or race: the "something" that one parent, on account of his or her sex or race, is presumed to do better. But, how would is this something ever to be defined? For girls, is it to put being a wife and mother above all else? To attract boys? To compete hard at sports? To excel at school? To camp, fish, and use a gun? How should an appropriate race identity be defined? What behaviors, or attitudes, does this entail?

Even if it was possible to say from which model of "identity" a child would benefit—requiring judgments that are obviously perilous, at best—it cannot be reliably assumed that a parent of the same sex and race as the child will be better able to model that identity than that the other parent. . . .

Finally, both race-matching and sex-matching arguments assume that a child whose parents do not live together will be parented by only one residential parent. Ordinarily, however, it is expected that a child will have some continuing contact with both parents, even if more time is spent with one parent than the other. Both parents remain role models. The intact, nuclear family does not require a child to choose between role models. Family dissolution should not require this either.

IV. The Non–Discrimination Principle

Hopefully, I have persuaded you that looking at issues of race and sex discrimination in custody decision-making side-by-side reveals complexities that help one to understand each better. . . .

. . . [T]his analysis strengthens the case for applying the same non-discrimination standards for race and sex in custody cases. In the remainder of this Lecture, I outline in very broad terms what these standards should be. . . .

First, discrimination should be categorically prohibited. The ALI principles prohibit consideration of the race, ethnicity, or sex of the parent or the child, in exactly the same terms. . . . [N]othing should be presumed about a parent's ability based on his or her race or sex. This is, for the most part, the current state of the law with respect to race, and it prohibits the preference some jurisdictions still allow for a parent of the same sex as the child especially during or right before adolescence.

Second, custody standards to determine what is in a child's best interests should be more determinate. The ALI standards offer determinacy by presuming that custody will be allocated to parents in proportion to the share of caretaking each parent undertook before the divorce. Past caretaking patterns are a good guide to which parent is best able to care for the child and which parent has the closest emotional tie to the child. They also provide a more objective basis for decision-making, thereby cutting down on litigation and strategic behavior. Most importantly for present purposes, when the standards are more determinate, there is less opportunity for courts to allow unconscious race and gender stereotypes to intrude. . . .

Whatever non-discrimination provisions exist, it is important to realize that ending race and sex discrimination is not simply a question of getting the legal standards right. The law can prohibit race and sex discrimination in a firm and decisive manner, but not be able to recognize either when they occur. Indeed, it is the recognition of discrimination, rather than the commitment to end it, that poses the most significant impediment to its elimination in today's society. This Lecture has tried to show that race and sex present patterns and habits of thinking that are similar in some ways and different in others—looking at them together may help to break up those patterns and enable society to better recognize the ways in which race and sex should not matter, but do.

4. RELIGION

Kendall v. Kendall

Supreme Judicial Court of Massachusetts, 1997.
426 Mass. 238, 687 N.E.2d 1228.

■ LYNCH, JUSTICE.

This appeal arises out of a judgment of divorce nisi issued on August 20, 1996. Jeffrey P. Kendall, the defendant, appeals from provisions of the divorce judgment and a temporary order issued after Barbara Zeitler Kendall, the plaintiff, filed a complaint against him in the Probate Court for contempt of the divorce judgment. The plaintiff also filed a cross appeal, requesting an award of attorney's fees and reversal of the joint custody order and disposition of the marital home. We granted the defendant's application for direct appellate review.

1. *Factual background.*

The parties professed to hold different religious beliefs when they were married in 1988, the plaintiff being Jewish, and the defendant, Catholic. The parties' fundamental religious differences would be unremarkable but for their controversial effect on their three minor children[4] caught in the crossfire generated by their parents. Before the parties were married, they discussed the religious upbringing of any children, and agreed that children would be raised in the Jewish faith.[5]

In 1991, the defendant became a member of the Boston Church of Christ, a fundamentalist Christian faith. The defendant believes in Jesus Christ and that those who do not accept the Boston Church of Christ faith are "damned to go to hell" where there will be "weeping and gnashing of teeth." The defendant testified that he would like his children to accept Jesus Christ and that he "will never stop trying to save his children."

4. The children are Ariel (born October 10, 1988), Moriah (born May 19, 1991), and Rebekah (born April 21, 1993).

5. The majority of courts adhere to the view that predivorce agreements are unconstitutionally unenforceable. See C.P. Kindregan & M.L. Inker, Family Law and Practice § 20.5, at 647 (2d ed.1996). We note, however, that the judge found the children had primary familiarity with the Jewish faith. The judge concluded the children had a "Jewish identity" based on evidence that: the parties were married in a traditional Jewish wedding ceremony; Ariel was circumcised in accordance with Jewish tradition; both Moriah and Rebekah had traditional Jewish naming ceremonies; the parties agreed the children would attend a Jewish school; and all three children are so enrolled.

The parties' divergent views polarized in 1994 when the plaintiff adopted Orthodox Judaism.[6] Ariel also began studying and adhering to principles of Orthodox Judaism. Soon after the parties' beliefs drifted to opposite doctrinal extremes, the plaintiff filed for divorce in November, 1994, based on an irretrievable breakdown of the marriage, pursuant to G.L. c. 208, § 1B.

2. *The court proceedings.*

At the outset the plaintiff sought to limit the children's exposure to the defendant's religion, and the defendant objected to any limitation on his ability to share his religious beliefs with the children. On October 18, 1995, the judge granted the plaintiff's request for the appointment of a guardian ad litem (GAL) to "address the inter-religious conflict between the parties in particular."

In Felton v. Felton, 383 Mass. 232, 233, 418 N.E.2d 606 (1981), this court addressed the question of accommodating diverse religious practices of parents, living apart, in the upbringing of minor children. The court held that the overriding goal in any such inquiry is to serve the best interests of the children even where "the attainment of that purpose . . . involve[s] some limitation of the liberties of one or other of the parents." Id. at 233, 418 N.E.2d 606.

The judge found it substantially damaging to the children to leave each parent free to expose the children, as he or she wishes, to his or her religion. The resulting judgment of divorce contained the following paragraphs:[9]

> "5. *RESTRICTIONS UPON RELIGIOUS EXPOSURE:* Each parent shall be entitled to share his/her religious beliefs with the children with restrictions as follows: neither may indoctrinate the children in a manner which substantially promotes their . . . alienation from either parent or their rejection of either parent. The [defendant] shall not take the children to his church (whether to church services or Sunday School or church educational programs); nor engage them in prayer or bible study if it promotes rejection rather than acceptance, of their mother or their own Jewish self-identity. The [defendant] shall not share his religious beliefs with the children if those beliefs cause the children significant emotional distress or worry about their mother or about themselves. Thus, for example, [the defendant] may have pictures of Jesus Christ hanging on the walls of his residence, and that will not serve as any basis for restricting his visitation with his children. But, [the defendant] may not take the children to religious services where they receive the message that adults or children who do not accept Jesus Christ as their lord and savior are destined to burn in hell. By way of further example, [the defendant] may not shave off [Ariel's] payes. This provision shall not be construed so as to prevent [the defendant] from having the children with him at events involving family traditions at Christmas and Easter.
>
> "In the event that there is a disagreement between the parents as to whether one or more of the children could be exposed to the religious belief(s) of [the defendant] *without* substantial negative impact upon their emotional health, the parents shall engage the services of Michael

6. Orthodox Judaism is considered the most strictly doctrinal of the three Jewish movements (Reform, Conservative, and Orthodox).

9. The judgment also ordered that the plaintiff retain sole physical custody of the children, and awarded the parties joint legal custody. . . .

Goldberg, Ph.D., to act as G.A.L. investigator/evaluator on such issues and disputes. The fee of Dr. Goldberg shall be shared equally by the parties. In the event that Dr. Goldberg is unable to serve in this capacity, then the parties shall agree upon an alternate child psychologist, or an alternate shall be selected by the Court. . . .

"6. *EXPLANATION TO CHILDREN.* Neither party shall initially discuss with the children the terms and conditions of this Judgment. Within two (2) days of the date of receipt of this Judgment, the Plaintiff shall contact the Court-appointed Guardian Ad Litem, Dr. Michael Goldberg, to arrange for a meeting with the children. Dr. Goldberg shall explain to the children, in a developmentally appropriate manner, the Court's decision, with the goal being to help the children understand that they are being raised in the way they are because the Court believes that it is in their best interest. It is intended by the Court that this intervention may help the children avoid blaming themselves."

The defendant argues in this appeal that the judge's findings did not demonstrate "substantial harm" to the children so as to warrant the limitations imposed on his liberty interest in educating his children in the tenets of his religion. He challenges both the judge's factual findings of harm and the legal conclusions based on that evidence.

. . .

4. *Analysis.* . . .

The determinative issue is whether the harm found to exist in this case to be so substantial so as to warrant a limitation on the defendant's religious freedom. In Felton v. Felton, this court suggested that a "likely source [ ]" of proof of substantial harm "by implication" could be derived from testimony as to the child's general demeanor, attitude, school work, appetite, health or outlook. The court also opined that the "wholly uncorroborated testimony" of a parent was insufficient to demonstrate harm. By implication, the court suggested that a plaintiff should consult "church, school, medical or psychiatric authorities" to support a charge that a child has been harmed by exposure to the parent's religious beliefs. Id. Moreover, the court specifically recommended the appointment of "a qualified investigator whether called a guardian (or some other title) who would look into the facts, render a report, and be subject to examination by the parties." Id.

Other States have struggled to define what constitutes substantial harm. Very few have actually ruled that substantial harm had been demonstrated.

We adhere to the line of cases requiring clear evidence of substantial harm. Application of the strict requirements in those cases comports with the protections of religious freedoms historically preserved under the Massachusetts Constitution.

The harm found to exist in this case presents more than the generalized fears criticized in Felton v. Felton, supra. The judge afforded substantial weight to the GAL's report.[16] The judge considered the report so "comprehensive" that it should be considered in its entirety on any appellate review. Among the factors the judge cited to support her conclusion that substantial harm to the children had been demonstrated are the following findings:

16. The GAL's report was based on interviews with the parents, the children, and the children's teachers, psychological tests, and observations of the children interacting with both parents.

"20. I find that, in early 1995, the [defendant] threatened to cut the fringe off Ariel's tzitzitz if he did not tuck it inside his pants. This greatly upset Ariel and the [plaintiff], and the [defendant] later apologized.

"21. I also find that, in the summer of 1995, the [defendant] cut off Ariel's payes. I do not find credible the [defendant's] explanation that he did so at Ariel's request.

. . .

"24. I find that the Boston Church of Christ services to which [the defendant] has taken his children have included teachings that those who do not accept the Boston Church of Christ faith are damned to go to hell where there will be 'weeping and gnashing of teeth.'

"25. I find that the oldest child, Ari, has drawn from the above teaching the conclusion that [the plaintiff] may go to hell, and that this causes him substantial worry and upset.

. . .

"56. [The defendant's] behavior toward his children fosters negative and distorted images of the Jewish culture. [The defendant] insists that all individuals who do not accept his beliefs about life and existence are sinners who are destined to tortuous punishment. [The defendant] opposes his children being taught the history of the Holocaust. Further, [the defendant's] cutting off of Ari's religiously meaningful side burns (payes), and his threats to cut off his clothing fringes (tzitzitz) show that he does not refrain from inducing guilt in the child for having the beliefs that he does.

"57. I find that Ari has a strong Jewish self-identity. I am persuaded by the report of the G.A.L. that Ari 'clearly identified himself and his siblings as being Jewish and provided a rationale based on Jewish law for his belief that he is Jewish,' and that the child's 'behavior in which he ascribes his Jewish identity to Jewish law and theology is indicative of his attainment of a formal self-identification of himself as a Jew.' Indeed, [the defendant] himself reluctantly concedes that if asked, Ari would unquestionably say he is Jewish.

"58. [The defendant] understands that Ari perceives himself as Jewish, and that having a Jewish identity is akin to having an ethnic identity. But the matter goes further. Ari perceives his Jewishness as being part of his 'soul.' For Ari, efforts to convince him that his religion is wrong are logically equated with convincing him that his 'soul' is damaged or inadequate. . . .

"59. I credit the G.A.L.'s report and testimony that Ari 'may experience choosing a religion as choosing between his parents, a task that is likely to cause him significant emotional distress.' In fact, the G.A.L. specifically concludes, and I credit his conclusion, that the children are now in a position where they are perilously close to being forced to choose between their parents, and to reject one.

"60. I find, based upon the G.A.L.'s report as well as his testimony, that the oldest child Ari' . . . is emotionally distressed by the conflict between his strong desire for affection and approval from [the defendant] and his desire to maintain his Jewish religious practice," and that as a direct result" . . . there has been a decline in his motivation and academic performance.'

. . .

"62. I find that Ari is understandably uncomfortable and unhappy when he 'has to do the stuff [he's] not supposed to do on Shabbas', and that precisely as the G.A.L. indicates, Ari then has the no-win dilemma of pleasing and obeying [the defendant] (while displeasing and disobeying [the plaintiff] and his own internalized beliefs about how the world is 'supposed' to function on the Sabbath) or the reverse. Poor Ari: he told [the defendant] that he 'wants to celebrate the Sabbath and not do stuff that I'm not supposed to do', and [the defendant's] response was 'we'll discuss that with the lawyers.'

. . .

"64. I credit the G.A.L.'s report that 'Moriah is experiencing emotional distress related to the parental conflict . . .' I find that Moriah has a very solid understanding of who she is and who her family is: 'I'm not Christian. I'm Jewish. Mom is Jewish. My dad is Christian. My brother is Jewish and my sister is Jewish.' Moriah's straightforward description is comfortable and age-appropriate. More importantly, it is accurate. And most important of all, it shows that she can tolerate the knowledge of her parents' religious differences.

. . .

"66. I find, based upon the G.A.L.'s report that Rebekah is likely to experience '. . . a sense of not belonging in her own home' by '. . . anything that serves to promote her identity as fundamentally different from that of her mother and siblings.' I find this would be substantially to her detriment.

"67. I credit the report of the G.A.L. that 'should the children come to accept the religious beliefs that [the defendant] reports he wants them to accept, they are likely to come to view their mother negatively and as a person who will be punished for her sins . . .' resulting in a '. . . negative impact on their relationship with their mother . . . and difficulty accepting guidance and nurturance from her.' I find this would be to the children's substantial detriment.

"68. For children of tender years (and it seems to me that this likely means at least up to age 12), I find directly contradictory messages from trusted adults to be solidly contrary to their best interests."

Whether the harm found to exist amounts to the "substantial harm" required to justify interference with the defendant's liberty interest is a close question, especially because there is considerable value in "frequent and continuing contact" between the child and both parents, and "contact with the parents' separate religious preferences." Felton v. Felton, supra at 234, 418 N.E.2d 606. In this regard the judge ruled:

"There is surface appeal to the [defendant's] argument that the [plaintiff] has not met her burden of establishing substantial present harm to the children from exposure to [the defendant's] religious beliefs and practices, for the G.A.L. found only a few instances of concrete present harm to the children. I am mindful that the G.A.L. has not found current damage to the children so severe that it has caused them to suffer a psychotic break, or to have a 'formal psychiatric diagno-

> sis'.... The case law does not require the court to wait for formal psychiatric breakdown and the evidence paints a strong picture of the reasonably projected course if the children continue to be caught in the cross-fire of their parents' religious difference: [the defendant's] religion may alienate the children from their custodial parent (she is bad, she will burn in hell), and may diminish their own sense of self-worth and self-identity (Jews are bad, Jews will burn in hell). At minimum they will be called upon to 'choose' between their parents, in itself a detrimental result. The G.A.L. predicts damaging consequences of the children's exposure to two vastly different, and on some points directly contradictory religious views. 'Sometimes ... a diversity of religious experience is itself a sound stimulant for a child ... the question that comes to the courts is whether, in particular circumstances, such exposures are disturbing a child to its substantial injury, physical or emotional, and will have a like harmful tendency for the future.' (*Felton,* [*supra*] at 234–235, 418 N.E.2d 606). Applying that standard to the facts of this particular case, I see substantial evidence of current and imminent harm, to these 7, 5, and 3–year-old children."

In balancing these conflicting interests, fully aware of the complexities and nuances involved, we conclude that the judge's findings support her order in paragraph 5 of the judgment.

Where, as here, the judge has found demonstrable evidence of substantial harm to the children, we reject the defendant's arguments that the divorce judgment burdens his right to practice religion under the free exercise clauses of the Massachusetts and United States Constitution. ...

Judgment affirmed.

5. The Child's Preference

McMillen v. McMillen

Supreme Court of Pennsylvania, 1992.
602 A.2d 845, 529 Pa. 198.

■ Larsen, Justice.

Facts

Appellant Vaughn S. McMillen (father) appeals from an order of the Superior Court, vacating the July 22, 1988 child custody order in his favor and reinstating the order of July 31, 1987, which continued primary custody in appellee Carolyn F. Shemo, formerly Carolyn F. McMillen (mother). We reverse.

The record shows that the parties were married on May 2, 1975 and that their son Emmett was born on September 30, 1977. The parties were subsequently divorced in the state of Wyoming on September 25, 1981. At the time of the divorce, the Wyoming court awarded primary custody of Emmett to the mother, subject only to the reasonable visitation of the father.

In March of 1982, the father instituted an action in the Court of Common Pleas of Indiana County, Pennsylvania, seeking partial custody of Emmett. On April 27, 1982, the court awarded general custody of Emmett to the mother with the right of visitation in the father. The court limited the father's visitation to alternating weekends and holidays, one day every other week and two weeks during the summer.

Over the next six years, the father sought modification of the custody order four times and the mother one time. Each time, the Court of Common

Pleas significantly expanded the father's visitation rights. From 1986 on, Emmett repeatedly and steadfastly expressed his preference to live with his father. Finally, on July 22, 1988, the Court of Common Pleas awarded general custody of Emmett to the father. The court opined that:

> . . . Emmett's best interests will be served most appropriately by placing him in the custody of his father because of Emmett's desire to live with his father as well as the fact that each home is a suitable environment for Emmett.

(Trial Court Opinion, Earley, P.J., p. 3).

On appeal, the Superior Court vacated the July 22, 1988 custody order and reinstated the previous order of July 31, 1987. In doing so, the Superior Court determined that: 1) the record failed to present any circumstances warranting a change in custody; and 2) the child's best interests would not be served by changing custody merely because the child wished it.

Our paramount concern in child custody cases is the best interest of the child. A custody order is modifiable without proof of a substantial change in circumstances where such a modification is in the best interests of the child. Therefore, contrary to the holding of the Superior Court, the father is not obliged to demonstrate a substantial change in circumstances in order to have the court entertain his motion to modify the existing custody order. To be successful, the father need only show that the modification is in Emmett's best interest.

The father argues that the Superior Court, in determining Emmett's best interests, usurped the function of the trial court by ignoring the trial court's factual findings and also failed to give proper weight to Emmett's steadfast desire to live with his father. The scope of review of an appellate court reviewing a child custody order is of the broadest type; the appellate court is not bound by the deductions or inferences made by the trial court from its findings of fact, nor must the reviewing court accept a finding that has no competent evidence to support it. However, this broad scope of review does not vest in the reviewing court the duty or the privilege of making its own independent determination. Thus, an appellate court is empowered to determine whether the trial court's incontrovertible factual findings support its factual conclusions, but it may not interfere with those conclusions unless they are unreasonable in view of the trial court's factual findings; and thus, represent a gross abuse of discretion.

Having reviewed the previous custody orders in this case, the trial court concluded that both the home of the mother and that of the father were equally acceptable. The trial court, therefore, was forced to look at other factors in making its decision. The only testimony taken at the most recent custody hearing was that of the child, Emmett, who was then almost 11 years old. Emmett testified that he preferred to live with his father.

Although the express wishes of a child are not controlling in custody decisions, such wishes do constitute an important factor that must be carefully considered in determining the child's best interest. The child's preference must be based on good reasons, and the child's maturity and intelligence must be considered. The weight to be given a child's testimony as to his preference can best be determined by the judge before whom the child appears.

Our review of the record shows that Emmett's preference to live with his father is supported by more than sufficient good reasons. Emmett testified that his stepfather frightens, upsets and threatens him, and his mother does nothing to prevent this mistreatment. He testified that he does not get along with either his mother or his stepfather, and that he gets along well with his stepmother. His testimony also revealed that his mother and stepfather leave him alone after school and that, even though his father and stepmother work, he is never left alone when he is at his father's home for the summer. Emmett also stated that his mother interferes with his sporting and farming activities and refuses even to watch him play ball.[1] Thus, we find that Emmett's steadfast wish to live with his father was properly considered, and we find no abuse of discretion in the amount of weight afforded that preference.

Nor do we find an abuse of discretion in the trial court's conclusion that Emmett's best interests would be served more appropriately by placing him in his father's custody. The record supports the trial court's finding that both households were equally suitable. This being so, Emmett's expressed preference to live with his father could not but tip the evidentiary scale in favor of his father. Thus, the trial court's conclusion that it would be in Emmett's best interest to modify the prior custody order by transferring primary custody from the mother to the father is supported by the record, and we find no gross abuse of discretion by the trial court in awarding primary custody to the father.

Accordingly, we reverse the order of the Superior Court. . . .

NOTES

1. Should a child who is the subject of a custody battle be asked his or her preference? The growing trend toward recognizing the rights of children might suggest that the right answer is yes. Certainly in a situation where the parents are equally fit to assume custody, and both want custody, then the temptation to maximize happiness by allowing the child's preference to control seems almost irresistible. Turning to the child's preference may be a way to avoid this agony as much as it is an objective way to decide what is best for the child. How is a child to know, for example, which parent is more "fit"? The parent who is more permissive may be better liked, but is not necessarily the "better" parent. In addition, even if a child prefers one parent to another, it may place a terrible responsibility on the shoulders of the child to be asked to reveal that preference to his parents—or to the world.

One way of at least reducing the burden assumed by the child would be to make his preference only one factor in the court's decision, and to make this clear to the child.

2. Should all children be consulted or only children above a particular age? The Uniform Probate Code, § 5-206 gives a minor of 14 or more years the right to "nominate" his guardian unless his choice is "clearly contrary to the best interest of the minor." Would a test of maturity be preferable to this kind of chronological test?

3. Who should ask the child and where? Consider the caution of Anna Freud on having the judge question, even in the privacy of the judge's chamber:

> What each [child] has to contribute to the picture is limited inevitably to what they know about themselves. To face up to one's real emotions and to probe into one's real motives is not a capacity which we expect to find in children. On the contrary, children of all ages have a natural tendency to deceive themselves about their motivations, to rationalize their actions, and to shy back from full

1. The trial court deemed this interference sufficiently detrimental to the child's social growth and development to warrant an explicit directive in the custody order that the mother make Emmett available for these activities whenever she has physical custody of him.

> awareness of their feelings, especially where conflicts of loyalty come into question. To pierce through these defenses demands more than usual skill from the investigator. Verbal and non-verbal communications (attitudes, behavior) have to be scrutinized, assessed, and translated into their underlying meaning.

Joseph Goldstein & Jay Katz, The Family and the Law 262 (1965).

4. Even if it is decided that the preference of the child should be given some weight, the question remains whether the "best interests" of the child should be viewed from a long-term or a short-term perspective. The conditions that make a person happy at age seven may have adverse consequences at age thirty. Should the judge decide by thinking what the child as an adult looking back will think? How should a judge weigh happiness at one age against happiness at another age? See generally Robert Mookin, Child Custody Adjudication: Judicial Functions in the Face of Indeterminacy, 39 Law and Contemp Problems 226 (1975).

6. Reliance on Mental Health Experts

K.J.B. v. C.M.B.

Court of Appeals of Missouri, Eastern District, Division Two, 1989.
779 S.W.2d 36.

■ KAROHL. J.

Husband-father appeals from modification of divorce decree which terminated his rights of visitation and temporary custody with the parties' two minor children. ... In 1987, mother withheld father's custody and visitation rights. She alleged the children, now ages seven and eight, were being physically, psychologically and sexually abused during their visits with father or his parents. Mother instituted a motion to modify by petitioning the trial court for modification of custody order.

... On October 27, 1987, by agreement of the parties the hearing was suspended and ordered continued until January 22, 1988. The court ordered, pending further hearing, that the parties undergo counseling with a therapist, to be selected by mutual agreement of the parties. Father was ordered to undergo separate, individual counseling preparatory to joint counseling with his two children. The joint counseling was to commence when the therapist deemed it reasonably safe for the children. The parties, pursuant to the consent order, stipulated in open court that the therapist's written report would be admissible in future proceedings on the pending motions.

After only two sessions, the therapist decided any contact between the father and the children would be dangerous. The therapist discontinued the sessions because he felt father was simply showing up for therapy and not really working to cure the problems.

The hearing resumed on April 21, 1988. The court issued findings of fact and law, and awarded mother sole custody of the two children and terminated any further contact between father and the two children.

Father's principal complaint is there was no substantial evidence to support modification of the decree awarding sole custody to mother or to terminate all contact between father and children ... Specifically, father contends the trial court's fifth and sixth findings of fact are erroneous. In the court's fifth finding of fact the court found father refused to cooperate in the psychological evaluation process and indicated an unwillingness to comply with court orders. The sixth finding of fact was father intentionally undermined the mother's authority as primary custodian and did not intend to change this behavior.

... Father also contended he was prejudiced in preparation for trial by unequal access to the children for purposes of medical and psychological evaluation.

. . .

The testimony which supports the trial court's custody findings and order is substantial. Mother offered testimony from three witnesses concerning the effect of joint custody and the relationship currently existing between the children, father and paternal grandparents. Dr. Joel Ray, a clinical psychologist diagnosed the children as being emotionally disturbed and found their behavior to be consistent with abuse but he could not say abuse was the cause of the disturbance in these children. Dr. A.E. Daniel, a physician and psychiatrist, testified the children had been subjected to physical abuse by their grandfather, grandmother and father in the environment in Montgomery County. His conclusions were based upon facts reported to be several years old and he was not aware of any current physical abuse beyond suspicion. He refused to recommend father not be allowed to see the children. When asked about visitation rights he responded, "Certainly,", "no problem [with that]." Dr. Ann Dell Duncan, a clinical psychologist, testified the boys gave descriptive indication that they had been traumatized at the hands of both the father and the grandparents. She suggested supervised visitation followed by unsupervised visitation for the father only, none for his parents.

Dr. Corrales and Dr. Ro–Trock evaluated father, mother, children, stepfather, and paternal grandparents. Both recommended mother be given primary custody of the children. Even father's expert witness psychologist, Dr. James Hall, testified: "there's a lot of anxiety in the boys ... there's something wrong in the relationship between them and their father and grandparents on father's side." This evidence was sufficient to support the award of sole custody to the mother. We cannot say the trial court abused its discretion and we defer to the trial court and its opportunity to judge the credibility of the witnesses. Rule 73.01; *C.J.(S.) R. v. G.D.S., 701 S.W.2d 165, 167 (Mo. App. 1985).*

. . .

Father contends he did not have the same opportunity as mother to obtain expert testimony. Father claims he was prejudiced because he was unable to develop evidence of the children's inter-relationship with him and the paternal grandparents. Father claims this prejudiced his ability to prepare and develop his case.

The Rules allow the court to order the mother to submit the children to physical or mental examinations. Rule 60.01 RSMo 1986. Here the court did not abuse its discretion by denying father's requests for examination. The court found father, both before and after the dissolution, physically and psychologically abused his children. Father's requests for physical examination of the children were honored in part. Mother testified the children had received bruises during their visits with their father. Father requested physical examinations in September 1987, although he had not been allowed unsupervised visitation with the children after May, 1987. Any evidence of bruises would have disappeared by September. Hence, the request came too late to support a claim of error directed to the relief the court denied.

In October, 1987, at father's request a psychologist, Dr. James Hall, met with the children, mother, father, paternal grandparents, and mother's husband. Although Dr. Hall testified he did not know if it would be dangerous for the children to see their father or paternal grandparents, he did say there is "something wrong" in the relationship between the children and their father and paternal grandparents. Dr. Hall recommended the court not sever the relationship between the children and father. Father also chose Dr. Bill Graham, a psychologist, jointly with mother in connection with an agreement between the parties and pursuant to the court's order. Dr. Graham testified it was dangerous for the children to have further contact with their father and paternal grandparents. The children saw psychologists, Dr. Ramon Corrales and Dr. Larry Ro–Trock, during the interim agreement. These doctors recommended mother be given custody. They did not oppose children's "safe contact" with father. Father had three opportunities to have the children psychologically evaluated, while the mother had expert testimony from four witnesses: Dr. Joel Ray, Dr. A.E. Daniel, Dr. Ann Duncan and Dr. Bill Graham.

The record reflects each expert found, at a minimum, the children, father and paternal grandparents had an abnormal relationship and more counseling was needed. The welfare of the children is the court's primary concern. Father had already been accused of physical and psychological abuse of the children. Also, Dr. Graham testified that in his opinion the children have seen enough professional people and forcing the children to see more professionals would be detrimental to the children. After considering the number of experts each party was able to obtain, the testimony of the experts, and the welfare of the children, we find the trial court did not err in denying father's motion for additional discovery.

. . .

We next review the complete termination of father's visitation rights with the minor children . . .

There was general agreement by the psychologists who testified at the hearing, that reestablishing a father's relationship with his children is a desirable goal. Dr. Hall, father's expert witness, testified "the father not seeing the kids anymore would be the worst outcome." No expert testified specifically that visitation at the home of the children would be detrimental.

The trial court agreed some form of visitation by the father was in the children's best interest provided the visitation would not endanger the children's physical health or impair their emotional development. This was the purpose of the consent order of October 27, 1987 . . .

The temporary consent order of October 27, 1987 provided for father to receive counseling to reestablish visitation and insure that father's visits would not endanger the children's physical health or impair their emotional stability. The parties mutually agreed upon Dr. Graham as the therapist . . .

Father attended both counseling sessions scheduled with Dr. Graham, and has not refused to attend any other sessions. However, no further sessions were scheduled, because Dr. Graham felt the father was uncooperative. However, Dr. Graham testified concerning father, "generally he was friendly towards me. There was no behavior of animosity or any anger outbursts, [he] appeared to want to be cooperative with me during both sessions."

Dr. Graham's reason for asserting father was uncooperative, was that he was merely showing up for therapy but not working on problems honestly, and was unwilling to admit any of the allegations against him or his parents. Significantly, these counseling sessions took place while the modification motions were pending, albeit suspended.

The third condition in the temporary consent order of October 27, 1987, which provided for counseling of father and others and for eventual visitation was: "The parties stipulate in open court that the therapist's written report shall be admissible in future proceedings on the pending motions."

In effect, Dr. Graham required the father, as a precondition to seeing his children, to confess to child abuse and testify that his parents had physically and sexually abused the children, even though these allegations were at issue in the pending case. Further, many of the alleged abusive acts by the grandparents could only have occurred while the father was in Germany. Consequently, father had no personal knowledge and could not admit that these acts occurred. Moreover, the trial court subsequently found the allegations against the grandparents to be unproven.

... Dr. Graham's impressions and conclusions are not conclusive on the matter of visitation. Dr. Graham assumed the allegations made against father and paternal grandparents were true. When asked whether he would reevaluate and change his opinion if some of the assumed facts were not true, Dr. Graham replied, "I don't know." Significantly, the court found many of the allegations unproven.

. . .

Father has not refused to comply with a single court order to date, and has complied with those orders issued. Also, subsequent to the counseling sessions, father testified he would do whatever he had to do concerning supervised visitation.

Dr. Graham was asked what change would have to take place in father in order for beneficial contacts to be possible between the father and the minor children. Graham responded that father would have to come, internally, to an awareness of his behavior, accept that damage has been done, and be willing to work on these problems honestly. Given the fact that the therapist selected pursuant to the consent order, Dr. Graham felt the ultimate issues in dispute had to be discussed before safe contact could occur between the father and children, it appears that counseling was attempted prematurely.

We affirm the modification decree in all respects except the denial of visitation of father with his children and they with him. We remand solely for an order allowing visitation as determined by the court.

7. Counsel for the Child

Schult v. Schult

Supreme Court of Connecticut, 1997.
241 Conn. 767, 699 A.2d 134.

■ Borden, Associate Justice.

The sole issue in this ... appeal is whether an attorney representing a minor child in connection with a custody dispute may advocate a position that is contrary to that of the child's guardian ad litem. The plaintiff, Cheryl Schult, brought this dissolution of marriage action against the defendant,

Jeffrey Scot Schult, seeking, inter alia, custody of their only child. The child's maternal grandmother, Joan Radin, intervened in the dissolution action pursuant to General Statutes § 46b–57. The trial court appointed both an attorney and a guardian ad litem for the child. The guardian ad litem appeals from the judgment of the Appellate Court, which affirmed the judgment of the trial court granting sole custody to the intervenor and visitation rights to the plaintiff and the defendant.... The plaintiff and the defendant were married on February 14, 1986. Their only child was born approximately two and one-half years later, and has a history of emotional, psychological and developmental problems. On March 7, 1991, the plaintiff brought the present dissolution action against the defendant seeking, inter alia, custody of their child. The defendant filed a cross complaint in which he, too, sought custody of the child.

On April 18, 1991, the defendant moved out of the family home. On that same date, Steve Norman moved into the family home as a boarder. The plaintiff and Norman have resided together since that time and now have plans to marry. On August 16, 1991, upon motion by the defendant, the trial court, Jones, J., appointed Colette Griffin as the child's attorney.

The following additional facts are set forth in the Appellate Court opinion. "On the evening of November 19, 1991, Norman was baby-sitting while the plaintiff, a licensed nurse practitioner, was at work. The child was three years old at the time. Norman testified that about five minutes after the child had gone to bed, he came out of the bedroom and was crying. Norman observed that the child had a mark above his eye and treated the injury with an ice pack. After fifteen to twenty minutes, the child stopped crying and went back to bed. The following morning, Norman noticed that the child was limping and would not put any pressure on his leg. When the plaintiff returned home at 7:30 a.m., Norman told her that 'we've got a problem.'

"The plaintiff called Karen Laugel, their pediatrician, who was in her office in Bridgeport. The plaintiff and Norman took the child in the plaintiff's car to Laugel's office. After examining the child, Laugel stated that 'it looks like a broken leg.' Feeling that the child's injury was 'very worrisome for the possibility of abuse' and that the child's injury could not 'be explained by falling out of the bed,' Laugel instructed the plaintiff and Norman to bring the child to Bridgeport Hospital where the child could be treated for his injury and where an investigation would be initiated for child abuse. Laugel also told the plaintiff and Norman that she would meet them at the hospital shortly.'

"The plaintiff and Norman then took the child to the University of Connecticut Health Center, John Dempsey Hospital (Dempsey Hospital), where the child was admitted on November 20, 1991. After approximately two hours at the hospital, Norman told the plaintiff that he had to go home and feed the animals and left the hospital. After remaining at home for approximately two hours, Norman then drove the plaintiff's car to Stratford, where he checked into a Days Inn at about 8:30 p.m. The following day, November 21, Norman drove around New York City and returned to the Days Inn in Stratford for the evening. On November 22, Norman drove to the Boston area and checked into a motel in Devon, Massachusetts. On November 23, three days after he had left the hospital, Norman returned to Dempsey Hospital. The doctors at Dempsey Hospital did not conclude that the child had been abused and released the child to the plaintiff on November 25. The child's discharge diagnosis stated that he had suffered a fractured leg."

"At the request of Laugel, the department of children and family services [department] conducted an investigation for abuse. After meeting with the child, the plaintiff, Norman, and several doctors at Dempsey Hospital, [the department] concluded that the origin of the child's injury was unknown and that abuse could not be confirmed."

On January 3, 1992, Radin intervened in the dissolution action, and the trial court, Sequino, J., ordered that temporary joint custody be awarded to the plaintiff and the intervenor, with physical residence with the intervenor. The child has resided with the intervenor since January 3, 1992. On December 4, 1992, upon motion by the plaintiff, the trial court, Jones, J., appointed Elizabeth Gleason as the child's guardian ad litem.

The trial began on November 1, 1993, before Hon. Thomas J. O'Sullivan, judge trial referee. At the trial, the guardian ad litem was called as a witness during the plaintiff's case-in-chief and testified that custody should be awarded to the plaintiff. The guardian ad litem was the only witness, other than the plaintiff and Norman, to testify that the child's safety would not be endangered by awarding custody to the plaintiff. Allen Rubin the family relations officer who conducted a review of the case, testified that it was in the child's best interest that custody be awarded to the intervenor. Sidney Horowitz, the child's and plaintiff's treating psychologist who conducted a court-ordered evaluation of the child, expressed serious concerns for the child's safety in Norman's presence and recommended that custody be awarded to the intervenor. Laugel testified that the child was not safe in the plaintiff's custody. Margaret Kunsch, the child's clinical social worker at the Parent Child Resource Center, testified that it would be detrimental to the child to remove him from the intervenor's custody. Kunsch also testified that the child considered "home" to be with the intervenor and had made "remarkable progress" within the past three months.

The child's attorney did not testify; rather, she participated in the trial by calling witnesses and conducting direct and cross-examination. The guardian ad litem and the plaintiff objected during the trial to the line of questioning by the child's attorney and requested that the trial court order her to ask the witnesses questions prepared by the guardian. The trial court, however, overruled their objections.

At the conclusion of the evidence, the trial court heard final arguments from all of the attorneys in the case, including the child's attorney, who argued that custody should be awarded to the intervenor. Both the plaintiff and the guardian ad litem objected to the closing argument by the child's attorney. The trial court overruled their objections.

The trial court rendered judgment granting sole custody to the intervenor pursuant to General Statutes § 46b–56b,[15] with visitation rights to the plaintiff and the defendant. In its memorandum of decision, the trial court found " 'as a fact that [the child's] leg was broken by [Norman], that [Norman] told [the plaintiff] when she came home what he had done and they both decided to tell the story that [the child's] leg was broken while [he] was alone in the bedroom in bed. When they told [Laugel] they did not know what happened to [the child], [Laugel] told them that she felt there was some abuse involved and that an investigation would be made for child

15. General Statutes § 46b–56b provides: "Presumption re best interest of child to be in custody of parent. In any dispute as to the custody of a minor child involving a parent and a nonparent, there shall be a presumption that it is in the best interest of the child to be in the custody of the parent, which presumption may be rebutted by showing that it would be detrimental to the child to permit the parent to have custody."

abuse. They did not follow the doctor's order to go to Bridgeport Hospital but went eventually to [Dempsey Hospital] in Farmington. [Norman] left that hospital as soon as he could and testified that he wanted to get away, that he did not know what was going to happen to him. Under these circumstances, it is clear that it would not be in the best interest of [the child] for him to be given into [the plaintiff's] custody with [Norman] there, knowing that he got away with breaking [the child's] leg as the court has found and with the opportunity to abuse [the child] further. The court cannot conceive of a situation more detrimental to [the child] than to permit [the plaintiff] to have custody of [the child] now. Under the above circumstances, [the plaintiff] sided with [Norman] against [the child]. She should not be given the opportunity to do that again.' "

In her appeal from the judgment of the trial court to the Appellate Court, the plaintiff claimed, inter alia, that the trial court abused its discretion by allowing the child's attorney to argue against the recommendation of the child's guardian ad litem. The guardian ad litem filed a brief in support of the plaintiff's position, and argued that the trial court's decision to permit the child's attorney to make a recommendation contrary to that of the guardian ad litem prevented a fair trial on the question of custody. The Appellate Court concluded that the trial court did not abuse its discretion in allowing the attorney for the child to offer her recommendation concerning the custody of the child because there was no indication in the record that the attorney's recommendation was without a basis in fact or that the court relied solely on it.

The guardian ad litem filed a petition for certification to appeal from the judgment of the Appellate Court to this court. We granted certification limited to the following issue: "In an action for dissolution of a marriage, if a child is represented by both a guardian ad litem and an attorney, does the attorney for the child have the authority to express an opinion on behalf of the child that differs from the opinion of the guardian ad litem?" After reviewing the record and the parties' briefs, however, we rephrase the issue as follows: "In an action for dissolution of a marriage, if a child is represented by both a guardian ad litem and an attorney, may the trial court allow the child's attorney to advocate a position that is different than that recommended by the guardian ad litem?" We answer the reformulated certified question in the affirmative. Accordingly, we affirm the judgment of the Appellate Court, although we do so on a different rationale.

The certified question presents an issue of first impression for this court. The guardian ad litem, plaintiff and amicus curiae urge us to adopt a bright line rule that prohibits a child's attorney from advocating a position that is contrary to that of the guardian ad litem. They argue that when a child is represented by both an attorney and a guardian ad litem in a custody dispute, the guardian ad litem becomes the attorney's "client," and that, as the client, the guardian ad litem makes the decisions on behalf of the child, and the attorney must advocate those decisions.

Although we recognize the appeal that a bright line rule would have for practitioners, clients and judges alike, we cannot blind ourselves to the fact that custody disputes involving minor children often do not lend themselves to easy, bright line solutions. We reject a rule that would unduly restrict the trial court's ability to receive information that might aid it in determining where the best interests of a child lie. Therefore, we decline to adopt the bright line rule requested by the guardian ad litem, plaintiff and amicus, and, instead, hold that it is within the trial court's discretion to determine, on a case-by-case basis, whether such dual, conflicting advocacy of position is in the best interests of the child.

The guiding principle in determining custody is the best interests of the child. The best interests of the child include the child's interests in sustained growth, development, well-being, and continuity and stability of its environment.

This principle also governs the appointment of counsel for a minor child in a marriage dissolution action. "The court may appoint counsel for any minor child ... if the court deems it to be in the best interests of the child...." General Statutes § 46b–54(a). The appointment of counsel lies firmly within the trial court's discretion in the best interests of the child. Counsel may also be appointed "when the court finds that the custody, care, education, visitation or support of a minor child is in actual controversy...." General Statutes § 56b–54(b). The statute further provides that "[c]ounsel for the child or children shall be heard on all matters pertaining to the interests of any child, including the custody, care, support, education and visitation of the child, so long as the court deems such representation to be in the best interests of the child." General Statutes § 56b–54(c). The purpose of appointing counsel for a minor child in a dissolution action is to ensure independent representation of the child's interests, and such representation must be entrusted to the professional judgment of appointed counsel within the usual constraints applicable to such representation.

The appointment of a guardian ad litem is neither required nor specifically authorized in chapter 815j of the General Statutes, which governs the resolution of custody disputes. The appointment of a guardian ad litem is authorized, however, pursuant to General Statutes § 55a–132(a), which provides that the court may appoint a guardian ad litem for a minor or incompetent "[i]n any proceeding before a court of probate or the Superior Court including the Family Support Magistrate Division...." The appointment of a guardian ad litem lies within the discretion of the trial court. General Statutes § 55a–132(b). Likewise, the guardian ad litem may be removed by the trial court whenever it appears to the court to be in the best interests of the child to do so. General Statutes § 55a–132(f).

Although this court has not previously delineated the exact roles of the attorney for the child and the guardian ad litem, we have recognized the potential for conflict between these roles when both are appointed by the court. See Newman v. Newman, 235 Conn. 82, 101, 663 A.2d 980 (1995) ("there may be instances in which the functions of counsel for minor children differ fundamentally from those of a guardian ad litem"); Knock v. Knock, supra, 224 Conn. at 791, 621 A.2d 267 ("[t]he legislature has not delineated, nor has this court yet been presented with the opportunity to delineate, the obligations and limitations of the role of counsel for a minor child").

. . .

... [W]e conclude that, where the court has appointed both an attorney and a guardian ad litem to represent a child in a dissolution action, the attorney for the child may advocate a position different from that of the guardian ad litem so long as the trial court determines that it is in the best interests of the child to permit such dual, conflicting advocacy. Leaving the determination to the sound discretion of the trial court is particularly important in those difficult cases, such as the present one, in which the child is unable to state a preference directly, there is an allegation of child abuse, and the parties present drastically differing views of the events. In such situations, it may be particularly difficult for the trial court to determine where the best interests of the child lie. To aid the court in its duty to determine the best interests of the child for purposes of custody, it may be helpful to the trial court to hear the contradictory positions of the attorney and the guardian ad litem. The trial court is in the best position to evaluate the child's needs for representation as the case and the evidence unfold.

In the present case, it is important to note the context in which the attorney and the guardian ad litem were appointed. The minor child suffers from emotional, psychological and developmental problems. Custody of the child was initially contested by the plaintiff and the defendant. At the request of the defendant, the court appointed the attorney for the child pursuant to § 56b–54. Following the intervention by Radin, custody became bitterly contested between the plaintiff and the intervenor, with the defendant siding with the intervenor. The custody battle centered largely around whether the child would be safe in the plaintiff's custody in light of allegations of abuse against the plaintiff's live-in boyfriend. At the request of the plaintiff, the court then appointed the guardian ad litem for the child.

During the course of the trial, the trial referee frequently stated that the case was a very difficult one and that he intended to "hear everyone" on the issues. The guardian ad litem was heard on the issues relating to the child's custody. She was called as a witness in the plaintiff's case-in-chief and testified that she saw no danger in the child being in the plaintiff's custody. Furthermore, she was not the only actor to present that position, which was the same as that advocated by the plaintiff. In addition, there was adequate evidence in the record to support the position of the child's attorney that custody should be awarded to the intervenor. Several experts testified that they had serious reservations about returning the child to the plaintiff's care in light of unanswered questions surrounding the incident of alleged abuse. In fact, the trial court specifically found that Norman had broken the child's leg and that the plaintiff had cooperated in the cover-up of that serious abuse. Finally, the position advocated by the child's attorney was the same as that taken by the attorneys for the intervenor and the defendant. In such circumstances, we cannot conclude that the trial court abused its discretion in hearing from the child's attorney and the guardian ad litem, despite their contrary positions, in making its decision regarding the best interests of the child concerning custody.

The guardian ad litem, plaintiff and amicus nonetheless argue that the Connecticut Rules of Professional Conduct require counsel to advocate for the position of the guardian ad litem. In support of this argument, they point to rules 1.2 and 1.14 of the Connecticut Rules of Professional Conduct. Rule 1.2 requires an attorney to abide by a client's decision with respect to the objectives of the representation. Rule 1.14 requires the attorney representing a client under a disability, which includes minority, to maintain a lawyer-client relationship that is as normal as possible. When the client cannot act in his or her own interest, rule 1.14 permits, but does not require, the attorney to seek the appointment of a guardian. The official comment to rule 1.14 provides that, where the client has a legal representative, such as a guardian ad litem, "the lawyer should ordinarily look to the representative for decisions on behalf of the client." Rules of Professional Conduct 1.14, comment (1995). The guardian ad litem argues that, because she was appointed as the legal representative of the child, the child's attorney was ethically bound to follow her recommended position.

Our review of the rules, however, does not lead us ineluctably to the result advocated by the guardian ad litem. At the most, the rules merely recognize that there will be situations in which the positions of the child's attorney and the guardian may differ. At the least, the rules neither contemplate nor answer the problem posed in the present case. Although we agree that ordinarily the attorney should look to the guardian, we do not agree that the rules require such action in every case. This case is one of those unusual situations. There was no evidence that the child's attorney had been unable to determine the child's interests from her review of the expert reports, medical records and school records. Furthermore, the guardian ad litem was appointed by the court at the request of the plaintiff, not at the request of the child's attorney. In light of the trial court's finding that the plaintiff's boyfriend had abused the child, and that the plaintiff had sided with the boyfriend against the safety of the child, we cannot conclude that the attorney for the child should have been prevented from advocating that custody not be awarded to the plaintiff.

The judgment of the Appellate Court is affirmed.

E. Alternative Approaches

1. Tender Years Presumption

Pusey v. Pusey

Supreme Court of Utah, 1986.
728 P.2d 117.

■ Durham.

. . .

The parties were married twelve years and had two sons, aged twelve and nine at the time of trial in 1984 . . .

The trial court conversed with the parties' two minor children in chambers and learned that the older boy expressed a marked preference for living with his father, whereas the younger boy indicated equal attachment to both parents. In spite of recommendations by a social worker that the parties be awarded joint custody and by plaintiff's brother, who had given the family professional counseling, that plaintiff would be the better parent to have custody of both children, the trial court awarded custody of the older boy to defendant and custody of the younger to plaintiff, with reasonable visitation rights in both parties.

. . .

Plaintiff cross-appeals from that portion of the divorce decree awarding custody of the older son of the marriage to defendant and requests that both children be awarded to her. This Court's judicial preference for the mother, reaffirmed in *Nilson v. Nilson, 652 P.2d 1323 (Utah 1982)*, and *Lembach v. Cox, 639 P.2d 197 (Utah 1981)*, is cited in support. We acknowledged in dictum the continued vitality of that preference in *Jorgenson v. Jorgenson, 599 P.2d 510, 511 (Utah 1979)*, "all other things being equal." We believe the time has come to discontinue our support, even in dictum, for the notion of gender-based preferences in child custody cases. A review of the cases cited by plaintiff shows that "all other things" are rarely equal, and therefore this

Court has not treated a direct challenge to the maternal preference rule in over five years. In the unlikely event that a case with absolute equality "of all things" concerning custody is presented to us, the provisions of article IV, section 1 of the Utah Constitution and of the fourteenth amendment of the United States Constitution would preclude us from relying on gender as a determining factor.

Several courts have declared the maternal preference, or "tender years presumption," unconstitutional. *See, e.g., State ex rel. Watts v. Watts, 350 N.Y.S.2d 285, 290 (1973).* . . . Although *Watts* used a strict scrutiny test, it is equally doubtful that the maternal preference can be sustained on an intermediate level of review. This is particularly true when the tender years doctrine is used as a "tie-breaker," as it is in Utah, because in that situation the Court is "denying custody to all fathers who . . . are as capable as the mother. . . . While over inclusiveness [sic] is tolerable at the rational basis level of review, it becomes problematic at the heightened level of scrutiny recognized in gender discrimination cases."

Even ignoring the constitutional infirmities of the maternal preference, the rule lacks validity because it is unnecessary and perpetuates outdated stereotypes. The development of the tender years doctrine was perhaps useful in a society in which fathers traditionally worked outside the home and mothers did not; however, since that pattern is no longer prevalent, particularly in post-separation single-parent households, the tender years doctrine is equally anachronistic. Further, "by arbitrarily applying a presumption in favor of the mother and awarding custody to her on that basis, a court is not truly evaluating what is in the child's best interests."

We believe that the choice in competing child custody claims should instead be based on function-related factors. Prominent among these, though not exclusive, is the identity of the primary caretaker during the marriage. Other factors should include the identity of the parent with greater flexibility to provide personal care for the child and the identity of the parent with whom the child has spent most of his or her time pending custody determination if that period has been lengthy. Another important factor should be the stability of the environment provided by each parent.

In accord with those guidelines, we disavow today those cases that continue to approve, even indirectly, an arbitrary maternal preference, thereby encouraging arguments such as those made by the cross-appellant in this case . . .

Although the trial court in this case found both parties to be fit custodial parents, its ultimate judgment on custody required an assessment of the complex situation before it. The court did not follow the recommendations made by the social worker or the plaintiff's brother. As child custody determination turns on numerous factors, however, that choice was within its discretion. The evidence indicated that the twelve-year-old son manifested a strong preference for his father, which had caused friction and ill feelings between him and his mother. The father also appeared to show a preference for the older son, which fact supports the trial court's decision to split the custody of the children between the parents. Certainly these were factors dictating the course of action taken by the trial court. We find no abuse of discretion in the custody award.

NOTES

1. Did the *Pusey* court weigh all the important arguments in favor of the tender years presumption? In Dividing the Child: Social and Legal Dilemmas of Custody

(1992), Eleanor E. Maccoby and Robert H. Mnookin, report on a study they conducted of more than 1000 divorcing families. Most of the families they studied had fairly traditional family arrangements before the divorce. Although only 30% of the mothers were full-time homemakers, most who worked were employed either part time or for substantially fewer hours than their husbands. In only about 10 percent of the families was the mother the primary breadwinner, and then only because the father was unemployed, often temporarily, not because he was the children's primary caretaker.

Maccoby and Mnookin found that after divorce:

> ... [T]he distribution of outcomes was again heavily weighted toward a traditional pattern of child care. At each of the three times following separation when we interviewed parents, we found that in about 70 percent of the families we studied, the children resided with the mother. Typically the father maintained some contact with the children, often by having them spend one or two nights in his household during a two-week period but sometimes having daytime visits. In about one out of six families, the residential arrangements were more evenly balanced: in these "dual residence" families, the children spent between one-third and one-half of their residential time (defined as overnight stays) with each parent in a typical two-week period....
>
> We suspect that dual residence was somewhat more common in the late 1980s in California than elsewhere in the country.... Even in these dual-residential families, the division of child-rearing responsibilities was not typically 50–50. More often than not, the mother was responsible for doctor's appointments and for buying everyday clothes....
>
> ... The overwhelming majority of mothers indicated that they wished and expected to be the children's primary custodian, and most mothers acted on that desire. Although a surprisingly high percentage of the father we interviewed indicated a preference for some physical custodial arrangement other than mother custody (with or without visitation), few of the fathers actually sought custody through the formal legal process.

Id. at 268–69. Maccoby and Mnookin further report that three quarters of the family experienced no legal conflict. Of those that did, most were resolved through negotiation. Less than 2 percent required formal adjudication. They add that although the law in California no longer includes a tender years presumption, it persists as a "social norm" if not a legal one. In contests between a fit mother and a fit father, they found that mothers usually end up with custody. Id. at 283. Maccoby and Mnookin favor a primary parent standard in order to increase the bargaining position of women and decrease the risk that father use a custody claim as a bargaining chip to reduce economic support, but report that their "research demonstrates that even under the best interests standard, at least where there are reasonably precise support guidelines, there is no evidence that the strategic use of custody conflict is leading to less financial support for women." Id. at 284. They conclude that although they favor a primary parent standard over the best interests standard, "our research findings suggest that the difference between the two standards has probably been substantially exaggerated, and that in actual operation the best interests standard is not fundamentally different." Id.

A study of 238 randomly selected cases in urban Ohio found that approximately thirteen percent of sole and joint custody awards went to men. The study found that the age of the child still plays a significant role in custody determinations; only twenty-three percent of custodial fathers were awarded custody of a child under the age of five. Wendy Reiboldt and Sharon Seiling, Factors Related to Men's Award of Custody, 15 Fam.Adv. 42 (1993).

See generally, Terry Arendell, Fathers & Divorce (1995); Robert E. Emery, Renegotiating Family Relationships: Divorce, Child Custody, and Mediation (1994); Demie Kurz, For Richer, For Poorer: Mothers Confront Divorce (1995).

3. For support of the maternal presumption see Mary Ann Mason, Motherhood v. Equal Treatment, 29 J. Fam. L. 1, 23–26 (1990–91); Ramsay Laing Klaff, The Tender Years Doctrine: A Defense, 70 Cal. L. Rev. 335, 336–37 (1983).

2. PRIMARY CARETAKER PRESUMPTION

Garska v. McCoy

Supreme Court of Appeals of West Virginia, 1981.
167 W.Va. 59, 278 S.E.2d 357.

■ NEELY, JUSTICE:

The appellant, Gwendolyn McCoy, appeals from an order of the Circuit Court of Logan County which gave the custody of her son, Jonathan Conway McCoy, to the appellee, Michael Garska, the natural father. While in many regards this is a confusing case procedurally, since the mother and father were never married, nonetheless it squarely presents the issue of the proper interaction between the 1980 legislative amendment to W.Va.Code, 48–2–15 which eliminates any gender based presumption in awarding custody and our case of J.B. v. A.B., W.Va., 242 S.E.2d 248 (1978) which established a strong maternal presumption with regard to children of tender years.

In February, 1978 the appellant moved from her grandparents' house in Logan County, where she had been raised, to Charlotte, North Carolina to live with her mother. At that time appellant was 15 years old and her mother shared a trailer with appellee, Michael Garska. In March, Gwendolyn McCoy became pregnant by Michael Garska and in June, she returned to her grandparents' home in West Virginia.

The appellant received no support from the appellee during her pregnancy, but after she gave birth to baby Jonathan the appellee sent a package of baby food and diapers. In subsequent months the baby developed a chronic respiratory infection which required hospitalization and considerable medical attention. Gwendolyn's grandfather, Stergil Altizer, a retired coal miner, attempted to have his great-grandson's hospitalization and medical care paid by the United Mine Workers' medical insurance but he was informed that the baby was ineligible unless legally adopted by the Altizers.

In October, 1979 Gwendolyn McCoy signed a consent in which she agreed to the adoption of Jonathan by her grandparents, the Altizers. Upon learning of the adoption plan, the appellee visited the baby for the first time and began sending weekly money orders for $15. The Altizers filed a petition for adoption in the Logan County Circuit Court on 9 November 1979 and on 7 January 1980 the appellee filed a petition for writ of habeas corpus to secure custody of his son.

Both the adoption and the habeas corpus proceedings were consolidated for hearing . . . and the circuit court awarded custody of Jonathan McCoy to the appellee based upon the following findings of fact:

> (a) The petitioner, Michael Garska, is the natural father of the infant child, Jonathan Conway McCoy;
>
> (b) The petitioner, Michael Garska, is better educated than the natural mother and her alleged fiance;
>
> (c) The petitioner, Michael Garska, is more intelligent than the natural mother;

(d) The petitioner, Michael Garska, is better able to provide financial support and maintenance than the natural mother;

(e) The petitioner, Michael Garska, can provide a better social and economic environment than the natural mother;

(f) The petitioner, Michael Garska, has a somewhat better command of the English language than the natural mother;

(g) The petitioner, Michael Garska, has a better appearance and demeanor than the natural mother;

(h) The petitioner, Michael Garska, is very highly motivated in his desire to have custody of the infant child, and the natural mother had previously executed an adoption consent, for said child.

. . .

While the issue of adoption by the Altizers does, indeed, enter into this case, in the final analysis the entire dispute comes down to a custody fight between the natural father and the natural mother. . . .

In the case before us the father, by providing fifteen dollars a week child support, probably showed sufficient parental interest to give him standing to object to an adoption. However, there is no evidence before us to indicate that the mother was an unfit parent and, consequently, no justification for the trial court to remove custody from the primary caretaker parent and vest it in a parent who had had no previous emotional interaction with the child.

. . .

The loss of children is a terrifying specter to concerned and loving parents; however, it is particularly terrifying to the primary caretaker parent who, by virtue of the caretaking function, was closest to the child before the divorce or other proceedings were initiated. While the primary caretaker parent in most cases in West Virginia is still the mother, nonetheless, now that sex roles are becoming more flexible and high-income jobs are opening to women, it is conceivable that the primary caretaker parent may also be the father. If the primary caretaker parent is, indeed, the father, then under W.Va.Code, 48–2–15 [1980] he will be entitled to the alimony and support payments exactly as a woman would be in similar circumstances.

Since the parent who is not the primary caretaker is usually in the superior financial position, the subsequent welfare of the child depends to a substantial degree upon the level of support payments which are awarded in the course of a divorce. Our experience instructs us that uncertainty about the outcome of custody disputes leads to the irresistible temptation to trade the custody of the child in return for lower alimony and child support payments. Since trial court judges generally approve consensual agreements on child support, underlying economic data which bear upon the equity of settlements are seldom investigated at the time an order is entered. While Code, 48–2–15 [1980] speaks in terms of "the best interest of the children" in every case, the one enormously important function of legal rules is to inspire rational and equitable settlements in cases which never reach adversary status in court.

If every controversy which arose in this society required court resolution, the under-staffed judiciary would topple like a house of cards. It is only voluntary compliance with the criminal law and the orderly settlement of private affairs in the civil law which permits the system to function at all. Consequently, anytime a new statute is passed or a new rule of common law developed, both legislators and judges must pay careful attention to interpreting it in a way which is consonant with equity in the area of private settlements.

. . . J.B. v. A.B., supra, attempted to remove from most run-of-the-mill divorce cases the entire issue of child custody. Certainly if we believed from our experience that full-blown hearings on child custody between two fit parents would afford more intelligent child placement than an arbitrary rule, we would not have adopted an arbitrary rule. However, it is emphatically the case that hearings do not enhance justice, particularly since custody fights are highly destructive to the emotional health of children. Furthermore, our mechanical rule was really quite narrowly drawn to apply only to those cases where voluminous evidence would inevitably be unenlightening. We limited the mechanical rule to the custody of children who are too young to formulate an opinion concerning their own custody and, further, we limited it to cases where an initial determination had been made that the mother was, indeed, a fit parent. While in J.B. v. A.B., supra, we expressed ourselves in terms of the traditional maternal preference, the Legislature has instructed us that such a gender based standard is unacceptable. However, we are convinced that the best interests of the children are best served in awarding them to the primary caretaker parent, regardless of sex.

Since trial courts almost always award custody to the primary caretaker parent anyway, establishment of certainty in this regard permits the issues of alimony and support to stand upon their own legs and to be litigated or settled upon the merits of relevant financial criteria, without introducing into the equation the terrifying prospect of loss to the primary caretaker of the children. As we noted in J.B. v. A.B., supra, "empirical findings directly or indirectly relevant to questions for which judges deciding difficult [custody] cases need answers are virtually nonexistent." The 1980 Amendment to Code, 48–2–15 was not intended to disturb our determination that in most instances the issue of child custody between two competent parents cannot be litigated effectively. Its intent was merely to correct the inherent unfairness of establishing a gender-based, maternal presumption which would defeat the just claims of a father if he had, in fact, been the primary caretaker parent.

II

In setting the child custody law in domestic relations cases we are concerned with three practical considerations. First, we are concerned to prevent the issue of custody from being used in an abusive way as a coercive weapon to affect the level of support payments and the outcome of other issues in the underlying divorce proceeding. Where a custody fight emanates from this reprehensible motive the children inevitably become pawns to be sacrificed in what ultimately becomes a very cynical game. Second, in the average divorce proceeding intelligent determination of relative degrees of fitness requires a precision of measurement which is not possible given the tools available to judges. Certainly it is no more reprehensible for judges to admit that they cannot measure minute gradations of psychological capacity between two fit parents than it is for a physicist to concede that it is impossible for him to measure the speed of an electron. Third, there is an urgent need in contemporary divorce law for a legal structure upon which a divorcing couple may rely in reaching a settlement.

While recent statutory changes encourage private ordering of divorce upon the "no-fault" ground of "irreconcilable differences," W.Va.Code, 48–

2–4(a)(10) [1977], our legal structure has not simultaneously been tightened to provide a reliable framework within which the divorcing couple can bargain intelligently. Nowhere is the lack of certainty greater than in child custody. Not very long ago, the courts were often intimately involved with all aspects of a divorce. Even an estranged couple who had reached an amicable settlement had to undergo "play-acting" before the court in order to obtain a divorce. Now, however, when divorces are numerous, easy, and routinely concluded out of court intelligible, reliable rules upon which out-of-court bargaining can be based must be an important consideration in the formulation of our rules.

Since the Legislature has concluded that private ordering by divorcing couples is preferable to judicial ordering, we must insure that each spouse is adequately protected during the out-of-court bargaining. Uncertainty of outcome is very destructive of the position of the primary caretaker parent because he or she will be willing to sacrifice everything else in order to avoid the terrible prospect of losing the child in the unpredictable process of litigation.

This phenomenon may be denominated the "Solomon syndrome," that is that the parent who is most attached to the child will be most willing to accept an inferior bargain. In the court of Solomon, the "harlot" who was willing to give up her child in order to save him from being cleaved in half so that he could be equally divided, was rewarded for her sacrifice, but in the big world out there the sacrificing parent generally loses necessary support or alimony payments. This then must also be compensated for "in the best interests of the children." Moreover, it is likely that the primary caretaker will have less financial security than the nonprimary caretaker and, consequently, will be unable to sustain the expense of custody litigation, requiring as is so often the case these days, the payments for expert psychological witnesses.

Therefore, in the interest of removing the issue of child custody from the type of acrimonious and counter-productive litigation which a procedure inviting exhaustive evidence will inevitably create, we hold today that there is a presumption in favor of the primary caretaker parent, if he or she meets the minimum, objective standard for being a fit parent as articulated in J.B. v. A.B., supra[9] regardless of sex. Therefore, in any custody dispute involving children of tender years it is incumbent upon the circuit court to determine as a threshold question which parent was the primary caretaker parent before the domestic strife giving rise to the proceeding began.

While it is difficult to enumerate all of the factors which will contribute to a conclusion that one or the other parent was the primary caretaker parent, nonetheless, there are certain obvious criteria to which a court must initially look. In establishing which natural or adoptive parent is the primary caretaker, the trial court shall determine which parent has taken primary responsibility for, inter alia, the performance of the following caring and nurturing duties of a parent: (1) preparing and planning of meals; (2) bathing, grooming and dressing; (3) purchasing, cleaning, and care of clothes; (4) medical care, including nursing and trips to physicians; (5) arranging for social interaction among peers after school, i.e. transporting to friends' houses or, for example, to girl or boy scout meetings; (6) arranging alternative care, i.e. babysitting, day-care, etc.; (7) putting child to bed at

9. As we said in J.B. v. A.B., supra, where the primary caretaker fails to provide: emotional support; routine cleanliness; or nourishing food, the presumption shall not apply.

night, attending to child in the middle of the night, waking child in the morning; (8) disciplining, i.e. teaching general manners and toilet training; (9) educating, i.e., religious, cultural, social, etc.; and, (10) teaching elementary skills, i.e., reading, writing and arithmetic.

In those custody disputes where the facts demonstrate that child care and custody were shared in an entirely equal way, then indeed no presumption arises and the court must proceed to inquire further into relative degrees of parental competence. However, where one parent can demonstrate with regard to a child of tender years that he or she is clearly the primary caretaker parent, then the court must further determine only whether the primary caretaker parent is a fit parent. Where the primary caretaker parent achieves the minimum, objective standard of behavior which qualifies him or her as a fit parent, the trial court must award the child to the primary caretaker parent.

Consequently, all of the principles enunciated in J.B. v. A.B., supra, are reaffirmed today except that wherever the words "mother," "maternal," or "maternal preference" are used in that case, some variation of the term "primary caretaker parent," as defined by this case should be substituted. In this regard we should point out that the absolute presumption in favor of a fit primary caretaker parent applies only to children of tender years. Where a child is old enough to formulate an opinion about his or her own custody the trial court is entitled to receive such opinion and accord it such weight as he feels appropriate. When, in the opinion of the trial court, a child old enough to formulate an opinion but under the age of 14 has indicated a justified desire to live with the parent who is not the primary caretaker, the court may award the child to such parent.

. . .

In the case before us it is obvious that the petitioner was the primary caretaker parent before the proceedings under consideration in this case arose, and there is no finding on the part of the trial court judge that she is an unfit parent. In fact, all of the evidence indicates that she mobilized all of the resources at her command, namely the solicitous regard of her grandparents, in the interest of this child and that she went to extraordinary lengths to provide for him adequate medical attention and financial support. While, as the trial court found, the educational and economic position of the father is superior to that of the mother, nonetheless, those factors alone pale in comparison to love, affection, concern, tolerance, and the willingness to sacrifice—factors above which conclusions can be made for the future most intelligently upon a course of conduct in the past. At least with regard to the primary caretaker parent there is a track record to which a court can look and where that parent is fit he or she should be awarded continued custody.

Certainly the record in the case before us does not demonstrate any intent by the mother to abandon the child through permitting him to be adopted by the grandparents; it is well recognized that mothers in penurious circumstances often resort to adoption in order to make the child eligible for social security or union welfare benefits, all of which significantly enhance the child's opportunities in life. Absent an explicit finding of intent to abandon we cannot construe manipulation of the welfare system to direct maximum benefits towards this child as anything other than a solicitous concern for his welfare.

Reversed and remanded.

NOTE

How does the concept of "primary caretaker" differ from the "psychological parent," defined as "one who, on a continuing, day-to-day basis, through interaction, companionship, interplay, and mutuality, fulfills the child's psychological needs?" Joseph Goldstein, Anna Freud and Albert J. Solnit, Beyond the Best Interests of the Child 98 (1978).

As the Rose litigation indicates, in many divorces both parents may be "psychological parents." The term "primary caretaker," by contrast, suggests only one parent qualifies. Is this appropriate?

The court in *Garska* justifies the new presumption as necessary to eliminate the use of custody challenges as a weapon in the economic bargaining between the divorcing couple. But there may be other ways to avoid emotional blackmail, such as clarifying the standards courts will follow in awarding property or alimony, a subject covered in Chapter 5. The primary caretaker presumption appears to operate at the expense of a spouse who works outside the home. Is that fair? Is the quantity of time spent with a child, as opposed to the quality, the best basis for determining custody? A fair basis?

3. JOINT CUSTODY

Squires v. Squires

Supreme Court of Kentucky, 1993.
854 S.W.2d 765.

■ LAMBERT, J.

This Court granted discretionary review to address the proper construction and application of *KRS 403.270(4)*.[17] With its 1980 enactment of the foregoing statute, the General Assembly expressly declared the right of trial courts to grant joint custody to the parents of a child with the only standard being "best interest." Heretofore this Court has not provided any guidance to trial courts in exercise of their broad discretion. As the appropriate use of joint custody is the subject of considerable debate and there appears to be little uniformity among the trial courts of Kentucky in its application, we took review of this case as it contains the elements of the classic dilemma.

Of the parties' four-month marital cohabitation was born a son. Upon commencement of proceedings to dissolve the marriage and the appearance of a dispute over child custody, inter alia, the case was assigned to the Domestic Relations Commissioner who heard extensive testimony and rendered proposed findings of fact and conclusions of law. The Commissioner found that both parties would be good parents who would place the interest of their child first. This, he believed, made them likely candidates for joint custody. However, he also found that the parties were not sufficiently cooperative to accommodate joint custody and recommended that it not be granted. On exceptions to the Commissioner's report, the trial court acknowledged the hostility between the parties, but concluded that this alone did not prevent an award of joint custody. The court emphasized that the

17. "403.270. Custody—Best interests of child shall determine—Joint custody permitted.—(1) The court shall determine custody in accordance with the best interests of the child and equal consideration shall be given to each parent.

* * *

(4) The court may grant joint custody to the child's parents if it is in the best interest of the child."

parties were "good parents" and in reliance on its "policy" to grant joint custody and the statutory standard of the child's best interest, determined that the benefits of joint custody outweighed the detriments. The court also recognized the availability of subsequent custody litigation when joint custody has been granted, and the extreme difficulty of such litigation when sole custody has been granted. Upon the foregoing, judgment was entered granting the parties joint custody.

A divided panel of the Court of Appeals affirmed the trial court. The majority emphasized the positive aspects of joint custody such as shared decision-making, parental involvement in child rearing and encouragement of parental cooperation. It also noted the availability of subsequent litigation if joint custody proved to be unworkable. The dissenting opinion expressed the view that prior to an award of joint custody, the court must be satisfied that the parties possess sufficient maturity to suppress their enmity toward one another and avoid having their personal animosity destabilize the upbringing of the child.

Appellant contends that "overwhelming evidence of discord and lack of cooperation between the parties" renders the judgment awarding joint custody clearly erroneous when measured against the best interest standard. For this contention she relies upon various scholarly articles and decisions from other jurisdictions which appear to support the view that without substantial parental cooperation, joint custody is undesirable. She concludes that "joint custody demands ideal circumstances and exceptional parents to succeed at all. Even with highly committed and motivated parents, joint custody is not for all children." Appellant asks this Court to set standards for trial courts for the exercise of their discretion with respect to joint custody and, in effect, suggests that in the absence of an agreement by the parties, joint custody should not be awarded, and even then, the trial court should be satisfied that the agreement was not procured improperly and that it is appropriate in the circumstances.

Appellee relies up on the statute and points to the absence of any statutory requirement that the parties agree upon joint custody. He relies upon the trial court's broad discretion and observes that if cooperation is declared a prerequisite for joint custody, any party may defeat it by a bad faith refusal to cooperate. He suggests the proper standard is whether the trial court believes from the evidence there is a reasonable likelihood of future cooperation which will redound to the child's best interest.

From the foregoing facts and arguments, the issue which emerges is whether parties who are found to be good parents who will endeavor to place the interest of their child uppermost should be denied joint custody due to their hostility and refusal to cooperate with one another.

At the outset, we must consult the statute. A cursory examination of *KRS 403.270* manifests the overriding consideration that any custody determination be in the best interest of the child. It is equally clear that neither parent is the preferred custodian and the parents' wishes, while appropriate for consideration, are not binding on the trial court. While the focus of this case is on joint custody as authorized in section (4) of *KRS 403.270*, the decision to grant or deny joint custody cannot be determined without reference to the entire Act. As such, the broad array of factors contained in the Act must be considered appropriately prior to a determination of joint custody or sole custody.

We begin with the assumption that it would be in a child's best interest to be reared by two parents who are married to each other. See *KRS*

405.020. With the occurrence of divorce, however, such a circumstance is not possible and trial courts are faced with the task of formulating a custody arrangement which will as nearly as possible replicate the ideal and minimize disruption of the life of the child. As such, and prior to any particularized assessment of the parents and child, joint custody would appear to be the best available solution. In theory, the child would continue to be reared by both parents and have the benefit of shared decision-making with respect to important matters, with neither parent being designated as the primary custodian and the other relegated to a secondary status. Clearly, it was this ideal which motivated the General Assembly to declare that trial courts may grant joint custody, but place it within the context of the entire custody statute, *KRS 403.270*, and limit it by the best interest test.

It is now widely recognized that in many cases, embittered former spouses are unwilling to put aside their animosity and cooperate toward their child's best interest. Often joint custody merely prolongs familial conflict and provides vindictive parties with a convenient weapon to use against one another. Of course, the same is true of a custody and visitation arrangement. As such, some contend that it is better to have a clean break between spouses and award one or the other sole custody to bring about the child's most rapid adjustment to post-divorce circumstances. While the logic of this position is not unappealing, if it were fully applied, the role of the noncustodial parent would be diminished to a point of insignificance.

Even if this Court were so inclined, it is not our prerogative to eradicate the concept of joint custody from the law of Kentucky. The General Assembly has determined that it is viable and it is our duty to apply the statutory framework in a manner which gives effect to legislative intent. From the language used, we believe the General Assembly intended to inform courts of their option to award joint custody in a proper case without mandating its use in any case. Implicit in the authorization to award joint custody is that the court do so after becoming reasonably satisfied that for the child the positive aspects outweigh those which are negative. We see no significant difference between the analysis required with respect to joint custody than the analysis required when the court grants sole custody. In either case, the court must consider all relevant factors and formulate a result which is in the best interest of the child whose custody is at issue.

. . . .

The parties have debated the significance of parental agreement and willingness to cooperate at the time of the custody determination. While we have no doubt of the greater likelihood of successful joint custody when a cooperative spirit prevails, we do not regard it as a condition precedent. To so hold would permit a party who opposes joint custody to dictate the result by his or her own belligerence and would invite contemptuous conduct. . . .

By what standard then should a trial court determine whether joint custody should be granted? Initially, the court must consider those factors set forth in *KRS 403.270(1)*. By application of these, the child whose custody is being litigated is individualized and his or her unique circumstances accounted for. In many cases, appropriate consideration of *KRS 403.270(1)* may reveal the result which would be in the child's best interest. Thereafter, we believe a trial court should look beyond the present and assess the likelihood of future cooperation between the parents. It would be shortsighted to conclude that because parties are antagonistic at the time of their divorce, such antagonism will continue indefinitely. Emotional maturity would appear to be a dependable guide in predicting future behavior. By cooperation we mean willingness to rationally participate in decisions affecting the upbringing of the child. It should not be overlooked that to achieve such cooperation, the trial court may assist the parties by means of its contempt power and its power to modify custody in the event of a bad faith refusal of cooperation.

. . .

The most recent joint custody decision in this jurisdiction is *Chalupa v. Chalupa, Ky.App., 830 S.W.2d 391 (1992),* in which the Court of Appeals reversed the trial court's award of sole custody to the mother. Despite its finding that both parties were "responsible," the trial court nevertheless deprived the father of joint custody due to his frequent absence from home necessitated by his employment. The Chalupa decision made a number of points worthy of repetition here. First, it noted that even when joint custody is awarded, the court may designate where the child shall usually reside, and we declare that the court may make such other orders as are necessary to properly effectuate joint custody. Chalupa also recognized that joint custody envisions shared decision-making and extensive parental involvement in the child's upbringing, and in general serves the child's best interest. Finally, the Court recognized that joint custody may have the effect of encouraging parents to cooperate and stay on their best behavior.

. . .

While we stop short of endorsing the Chalupa preference for joint custody, i.e. "consider joint custody first," we endorse many of the views expressed therein.... [W]hatever one's philosophy may be with respect to joint custody, so long as *KRS 403.270(4)* remains the law of Kentucky, joint custody must be accorded the same dignity as sole custody and trial courts must determine which form would serve the best interest of the child.

... Just as it is impermissible to prefer one parent over the other based on gender, it is now impermissible to prefer sole custody over joint custody. In every case the parties are entitled to an individualized determination of whether joint custody or sole custody serves the child's best interest. ...

In the case at bar, the Court of Appeals recognized that the trial court's use of the term "policy" as justification for the award of joint custody was merely a means of expressing the view that these were good parents who would put the interest of their child first, and would, in time, achieve an acceptable level of cooperation. While this Court is uncomfortable with the application of a "policy" as such implies insufficient analysis under the statute, our review of the orders and judgment of the trial court reveals no failure of painstaking consideration of the case. ...

We affirm.

■ LEIBSON, J. (dissenting).

Respectfully, I dissent.

. . .

... Social science data amassed since the advent of the joint custody experiment some 20 plus years ago studying the effects of joint custody awards demonstrates overwhelmingly that except for "those few, exceptionally mature adults who are able to set aside animosities in cooperating for the benefit of their children," joint custody is not a problem solver, but a pernicious problem causer. The Appellant's Brief cites numerous articles reviewing some of this social science data ...

significance of data

The Majority Opinion acknowledges the existence of this empirical data, and cites no data to the contrary. None is cited to us. Yet the Majority disregards its significance.

A report prepared in February 1983 by the Ad Hoc Committee on Family Dissolution of the Kentucky Psychological Association, entitled "Custody and Visitation Patterns in Children of Divorce," sums up as follows:

> "It should be recognized that joint custody is not a panacea. It requires that the parents have the emotional capacity and the psychological commitment to resolve their differences and engage in communication, cooperation, and compromise. Obviously, it cannot be imposed on a fighting couple as a way of resolving their dispute. It is also not for those who have not thought through its implications.... It should not be used as a 'cop-out' by the court to avoid the careful weighing of all of the variables determining the child's best interests...."

The Trial Commissioner in this case was tuned in to reality. His findings, after a lengthy, video-taped hearing were as follows:

> "... cooperation and communication between the parties is required for an award of joint custody.... In this case, it is obvious to the Court [Commissioner] that the parties cannot agree or cooperate to the extent necessary to accommodate a joint custody award."

The trial court neither heard the evidence nor reviewed the tapes, but awarded joint custody contrary to this finding, stating it was the court's "policy" to "grant joint custody of children whenever possible to do so," and that "the national trend is for joint custody." The trial court was mistaken as to "policy" and the present direction of the "national trend." Neither reason suffices to support a finding in favor of joint custody in this case.

. . .

Before awarding joint custody the trial court should be required to find that these parties are presently emotionally mature adults capable of cooperating and sharing in the decision-making involved in raising this child, not that "hopefully" they will become so. The final order of the trial court in this case is to the contrary:

> "The Court recognizes that this has been another very bitter divorce in which the parties and their attorneys have hotly contested nearly every issue.... Hopefully, after this divorce is finalized, the parties, who are mature individuals and not teenagers, will cooperate with the give and take that is in the best interest of the child." [Emphasis added.]

This is not good enough. Rather than finding what the record shows is in the best interest of the child, it evades the issue.

. . .

For the benefit of the children who must bear the consequences of the problems that will be caused by this decision, I urge the General Assembly to take suitable steps. Joint custody should not be abolished as an available option, because there are cases where such a finding is appropriate. It is, however, only appropriate upon proof that both parents are presently emotionally mature and psychologically suited to the task of sharing custody cooperatively.

NOTE

In their comprehensive study of some 1000 divorcing family, Dividing the Child: Social and Legal Dilemmas of Custody (1992), Eleanor E. Maccoby and Robert H. Mnookin found that:

> joint legal custody had no significant effects on [parental] contact or [child] support, once the initial income differences between custodial groups had been taken into account. Furthermore, it did not increase non-resident fathers' involvement in decision-making. It also had little bearing on parental relations.

Id. at 289. Nonetheless, Maccoby and Mnookin "cautiously" recommend a presumption in favor of joint legal custody explaining:

> we like the affirmation that both mothers and fathers have rights and responsibilities with respect to their children after divorce. Joint legal custody will not make divorced parents equal partners in the lives of their children, but it does affirm the idea that in the eyes of the law fathers should play a continuing role in their children's lives despite the divorce.

Id. at 289.

A survey conducted in 1976 and again in 1981 of a nationally representative sample of children age 11 to 16 whose parents had divorced or separated found that marital disruption effectively destroys the ongoing relationship between children and the biological parents living outside the home in a majority of families. Forty-nine percent had not seen the nonresident parent for more than a year. Only one child in six averaged weekly contact or better. Only a minority had ever slept over at the nonresident father's house. Many had never set foot in the houses of their nonresident fathers.

The relationships typically grew worse over time. The children saw the absent parent an average of 7.4 days a month in the first two years after separation, but only twice a month thereafter. After 10 years, 74 percent said they never saw that parent. The researchers also found that:

> ... [C]hildren with fathers living outside the home are decidedly more discontent with their paternal relationship than those residing with their father. More than half say that they do not get all the affection they need, and nearly as many say they are only fairly close or not close at all to their father. Outside fathers are also faulted for not making clear and consistent rules and for not being firm enough.

Frank F. Furstenberg Jr. and Christine W. Nord, Parenting Apart: Patterns of Childrearing After Marital Disruption, J. of Marriage and the Family 893 (Nov. 1985).

Consider Jana B. Singer and Reynolds, A Dissent of Joint Custody, 47 Md.L.Rev. 497 (1988), arguing that court-imposed joint custody arrangements are an easy way out for judges who are afraid of making tough decisions about custody awards. Problems arise when children's best interests are sidelined in favor of judicial expedience or equitable results between parents. The authors advocate more widespread use of the "primary caretaker preference" adopted in Minnesota and West Virginia.

4. PAST DIVISION OF PARENTAL RESPONSIBILITY

Young v. Hector

Court of Appeal of Florida, Third District, 1999 (en banc).
740 So.2d 1153.

■ GREEN, J.

Upon our rehearing en banc of this cause, we withdraw the prior panel opinion issued on June 24, 1998 and substitute the following opinion in its stead.

The former husband/father (Robert Young) appeals from the final judgment of dissolution of marriage. We affirm the trial court's decision designating the former wife/mother (Alice Hector) as the primary custodial parent of the two minor children but reverse and remand the court's determination as to rehabilitative alimony, distribution of the parties' assets and liabilities and attorney's fees for further proceedings.

The father's main contention on this appeal is that the trial court abused its discretion when it awarded custody of the minor children to the mother. We do not agree. After laboriously reviewing all of the record evidence in this case, we conclude that there was substantial competent evidence to support the trial court's discretionary call in this regard. Thus, there is no basis for us to overturn the lower court's decision.

As we see it, the child custody issue in this case, with all its attendant notoriety, centers only around our standard of review as an appellate court. The simple issue for our consideration is whether the trial court abused its discretion when it determined that the best interests of the two minor children dictated that their mother be designated their primary custodial parent.

At the outset, it is important to emphasize that both the mother and father are very loving and capable parents. Nobody disputes this fact, which alone made the trial court's determination all the more difficult. What then tilted the scales in favor of awarding custody to the mother? The father suggests that it was gender bias. The record evidence, however, simply does not support this suggestion.

. . .

At the time of their marriage in 1982, both the father and mother were successful professionals in New Mexico. He was an architectural designer with his own home design firm as well as an entrepreneur with a publishing company. She was an attorney in private practice at her own firm. Their marriage was a second for both. He had no children from his first marriage. She had custody of her two minor children (now grown) from her first marriage which she successfully reared while simultaneously juggling the demands of her law practice.

. . .

Hector and Young became the parents of two daughters born in 1985 and 1988. After the birth of their children, both parents continued to work outside of the home and pursued their respective professional endeavors with the assistance of a live-in nanny, au pair, or housekeeper. As typical working parents, they would both arrive home between the hours of 5:30 and 6:00 each evening. Both contributed to and shared in the household expenditures at all times.

Sometime in late 1987, the father's business ventures began to suffer certain financial reversals and the mother became bored with her practice in New Mexico. Both parties agreed to relocate to Miami. Although there is a complete conflict in the record between the parties as to who broached the subject of the couple's relocation to Miami and the circumstances under which they would relocate in terms of their respective careers, it is significant that neither of these parties ever testified that they ever agreed or expected the mother to pursue her legal career while the father remained at home as the full-time caregiver to their minor children. To the contrary, the father actively pursued job leads in the Miami area prior to the couple's relocation.

In June 1989, the mother and her two minor daughters arrived in Miami first. During that summer, she studied for and took the Florida Bar exam and landed a position with a mid-sized law firm. The father stayed behind in New Mexico until October 1989 in order to complete the construction of a new house and to remodel the couple's New Mexico home in order to enhance its resale potential.

After the father's move to Miami in the fall of 1989, he studied for and passed the Florida contractor's examination. Thereafter, during the spring and summer of 1990, the father spent his time repairing the couple's first marital residence in Miami. Thereafter, he renovated the home which ultimately became the couple's second marital residence. It is significant to point out at this juncture, that it is undisputed that from the time the minor children were brought to Miami in 1989 until the fall of 1993, the needs of the minor children were attended to by a live-in housekeeper when they were not in school during the day and by the mother upon her arrival from work in the evenings.

After the father's renovations to the couple's second Miami residence were completed and the family moved in, the mother testified that she began to have serious discussions (which eventually escalated into arguments) about the father's need to find gainful employment. Although the mother was earning a very decent income as an attorney at the time, it was undisputed that this family was operating with a negative cash flow.

Rather than pursue gainful employment to financially assist the household and his minor children, the father turned his attentions elsewhere. During the remainder of 1990 through 1993, the father left the state and was frequently away from the mother and minor children for months at a time. During this time, he returned to New Mexico to attend to lingering matters involving his prior businesses there and to make preparations for an upcoming treasure hunt. He also visited his sick brother in Arkansas and later handled his brother's estate matters upon his brother's demise. During this time, the father spent approximately fourteen months away from his family pursuing buried gold in New Mexico on a treasure hunt. The minor children were continuously being cared for by the housekeeper/baby-sitter during the day and the mother after work. The father saw his family during this fourteen month period once every five weeks and according to the mother, only at her insistence and pursuant to her arrangements for such family reunions.

When the father finally returned to South Florida, in the fall of 1993, the mother had accepted a partnership position with a large Florida law firm at a salary of approximately $300,000 annually. Even with the mother's salary increase, the family remained steep in debt. At that time, the couple no longer had a live-in nanny or baby-sitter for the children. The children were in a public school full-time between the hours of 8:30 a.m. and 2:00–3:00 p.m. The mother had employed a housekeeper ("Hattie") who came to the house each weekday between the hours of noon and 8:00 p.m. to clean, pickup and baby-sit the children after school. The mother's time with the children during the weekdays consisted of her awakening, dressing, and having breakfast with them prior to transporting them to school, and spending the early evening hours with them prior to their bedtime. The mother engaged in activities with the children on a full-time basis on the weekends. When the children became ill or distressed during the middle of the night, the mother was always the parent they looked to for assistance or solace.

. . .

Approximately one month after the father's return to the household in 1993, the mother asked the father for a divorce because of his continued refusal to seek gainful employment and due to his extramarital affair in New Mexico. It must be re-emphasized that at no time did the mother and father have any mutually expressed or tacit agreement for the father to remain unemployed. The father candidly conceded as much at trial. Consequently, this case simply did not involve the typical scenario where two spouses, by mutual agreement, agreed for one to remain at home to care for the children and the other spouse to work outside of the home.

. . .

Once the mother announced to the father that she wanted a divorce, the father began to spend less of his time away from Miami. Although he steadfastly refused to make any efforts to obtain employment, he did become more involved in the activities of his two daughters, who by that time, were 8 and 5. Since both girls were in school full-time at this time, the father's involvement with the girls' activities occurred primarily Mondays through Fridays between the hours of 3:00 p.m. and 6:30 p.m., prior to the mother's arrival from work. Upon the mother's arrival at the home, the father generally absented himself.

. . .

The father nevertheless maintained that he was the "primary caretaker" or "Mr. Mom" of these two children in the three years preceding this dissolution proceeding. The trial court viewed this contention with some degree of skepticism as it was entitled. The trial court's skepticism or disbelief was not at all unreasonable, given the father's admission that the nanny, Hattie, had taken care of these children in large part during the afternoon hours until their mother's arrival at home. The father's concession is what prompted the court to ultimately make inquiry as to why the father did not seek employment or alternatively, why there was a need for a full-time nanny:

. . .

[Father's attorney]: Who picks the kids up?

[Father]: Either Hattie or I. Typically, it's me. If I am tied up, whether it's a meeting or whatever, or if I go somewhere like your office, way up in North Miami Beach, and I don't get back in time and I thought I would, I can call Hattie and say, "Hattie, please pick up the children." She does. She picks them up frequently.

[The Court]: Is Hattie there five days a week?

[Father]: Yes sir. She comes at noon every day. She cleans the house in the afternoons. She prepares the dinners. The kids eat. We eat. I eat with the children every day typically at 6:30. She cleans up after that.

She'll draw a bath for Avery and she leaves at eight o'clock in the evening five days a week.

[The Court]: Maybe I'm missing something. Why don't you get a job.

[Father]: Well, because my background is architecture. That's my degree, but when I graduated, they did not have computers. Today, it's computer dominated and I'm computer illiterate.

. . .

I've gone on interviews. They like me. They like what I have to offer but their offices are basically all computerized.

Previously, because of the number of hours Ms. Hector worked, I filled in. Ms. Hector has a secretary that handles her whole life at the office and in a sense I was the secretary that handled her whole life at home and took care of the children.

[The Court]: But you've got a nanny doing that.

[Father]: No sir, I don't believe you can buy parents. Nannies can pick up. They can drop off.

[The Court]: Why [sic] do you need the nanny for, if you're there doing it?

[Father]: She cooks. She cleans. I could do a lot of that. Typically, people that have incomes of over a quarter of a million dollars or $300,000 can afford the luxury of having help, hired help.

I am not the kind of person that sits around and watches soap operas. I try to do meaningful, worthwhile things.

. . .

Contrary to the father's suggestion on appeal, this inquiry by the court is not evidence of gender bias. Given the undisputed large financial indebtedness of this couple, the trial court's inquiry about the need to employ a full-time nanny was both logical and practical under these circumstances and certainly could have also been appropriately posed to the mother if she had been recalcitrant about seeking gainful employment to assist the family's financial situation.

. . .

Apart from this evidence, the court also had the report and recommendations of the guardian ad litem upon which to rely. In recommending that the mother be named the primary custodial parent, the guardian ad litem cited three factors, all of which we find are supported by competent substantial evidence in the record. First of all, the guardian noted that the mother had been the more economically stable of the two parents throughout the marriage. We do not believe that the guardian gave the mother the edge simply because she earned a large salary. We believe, that what the guardian was attempting to convey was that the mother had shown a proclivity to remain steadily employed, unlike the father who unilaterally removed himself from the job market, although he was employable and the family needed the additional income. The trial court concluded that the father was "where he is largely because of his own choice." . . . Given a choice between the mother, who maintained constant steady employment throughout the marriage to support the children (regardless of the amount of her income), and the father who unilaterally and steadfastly refused to do the same, the trial court's designation of the mother as custodial parent cannot be deemed an abuse of discretion.

. . .

The second factor relied upon by the guardian ad litem in recommending that the mother be declared the primary custodial parent was the fact that the mother had been a constant factor and dominant influence in the children's lives and the father had not. The guardian ad litem observed:

> There have been times in the children's life [sic] when Bob has been, for whatever reasons, away from the home for substantial periods of time and Alice has been the dominant influence.
>
> More recently, while she has been working, he has been available at home more hours of the day than she has been, but over a continuum of time, I believe that her presence has been a more steady presence in the sense of available almost the same time for the kids throughout the relationship, whereas Bob has been intensely absent and intensely present.

In its determination as to the best interests of the minor children, the trial court obviously deemed it more important to assess the children's time spent with each of the parents throughout the course of the marriage and not merely focus on the years immediately preceding the announcement of the dissolution action. That is, the trial court, in an effort to maintain continuity, could have legitimately determined that the children's best interests dictate that they remain with the parent who had continuously been there to care for their needs throughout their young lives rather than the parent who had devoted a substantial amount of time with them perhaps only when it was convenient and/or opportunistic to do so. The record evidence clearly supports the trial court's conclusion that the mother had been the constant parent throughout the children's lives. Thus, there was no basis for the panel to overturn the trial court's finding in this regard.

The last factor cited by the guardian ad litem, which tilted the scale in favor of the mother, was the mother's superior ability to control her anger around the children. The guardian ad litem testified that he personally witnessed one of the father's outbursts of anger in the presence of the children. For that reason, the guardian, who is also a retired circuit court judge, went so far as to recommend that the father receive anger control counseling.

Given this substantial competent evidence in the record, we cannot conclude that the trial court abused its discretion when it awarded custody of the minor children to their mother. Nor can we conclude that the court's determination was impermissibly influenced by gender bias against the father.

As long as the trial court's decision is supported by substantial competent evidence and is not based upon legally impermissible factors such as gender bias, it must be affirmed on appeal. For this reason, we affirm the order awarding primary residential custody of the minor children to the mother. However, on remand, the trial court should grant the father liberal and frequent access to the children.

. . .

■ SCHWARTZ, C.J. (dissenting).

I remain convinced by the panel decision and by the dissents of Judge Nesbitt and Judge Goderich that the trial court's "award" of the children's primary physical residence to the mother is unsupported by any cognizable, equitable consideration presented by the record. As the panel opinion, which has not in my view been successfully challenged by any of the contrary briefs or opinions, demonstrates, the children's parents, who know and care most about their welfare, had themselves established an arrangement prior to the dissolution as a part of which, upon any fair assessment, the father was the primary caretaker. As everyone agrees, under that regime, if not because of it, their girls have turned out to be well-behaved, well-adjusted, and accomplished young women who love both their parents: just what we all devoutly wish for and from our children. There is simply no reason for a court to tamper with what has worked so well. See Principles of the Law of Family Dissolution: Analysis and Recommendations (Am. Law Inst. 1998) (Tentative Draft No. 3, Part I) § 2.09(1).[2] This is not only because it is almost always better to preserve a known good rather than to risk what the unknown future may bring, but, much more important, because the children are themselves entitled to stability in their lives and routine which would be compromised by any purposeless change in their caregiver. In many areas, the law properly recognizes the undesirability of disrupting the children's circumstances any more than is already necessarily required by their parents' separation and divorce. § 61.13(3)(d), Fla. Stat. (1995). See Mize v. Mize, 621 So. 2d 417 (Fla. 1993) (relocation of custodial parent); Pino v. Pino, 418 So. 2d 311 (Fla. 3d DCA 1982) (importance of children's remaining in home). This principle finds special application in the rule that modifications of the custody provisions of a final judgment may be made only when there has been a change of circumstances adversely affecting the welfare of the children. . . . When, as here, the children have manifestly benefitted from an arrangement established before the judgment, the same rule should apply.

. . .

(1) Unless otherwise resolved by agreement of the parents . . . or unless manifestly harmful to the child, the court should allocate custodial responsibility so that the proportion of custodial time the child spends with each parent approximates the proportion of time each parent spent performing caretaking functions for the child prior to the parents' separation.

No change in circumstances

. . .

What happens when that rule is not applied is illustrated by the result in this very case, in which it was necessary below and has been found necessary on appeal to resort to other, inadmissible, factors to justify the so-called exercise of discretion by the trial court and the affirmance of that result by this one.

. . .

In my opinion, there is no question whatever that the result below was dictated by the gender of the competing parties. It is usually extremely difficult to gauge the underlying motivations of any human being and one resists even more the assignment of an unworthy or impermissible reason to any judge's exercise of her judicial functions. This case, however, permits no other conclusion. I believe that this is shown by contemplating a situation in which the genders of the hard working and high earning lawyer and the stay at home architect were reversed, but everything else remained the same. The male attorney's claim for custody would have been virtually laughed out of court, and there is no realistic possibility that the mother architect would have actually "lost her children." (The fact, so heavily emphasized by members of the majority, that the hypothetical mother architect might have sought employment after the dissolution, as usually occurs, and that her time with the children would have therefore diminished, would have made no

2. § 2.09 Allocation of Custodial Responsibility

difference either.) It is, at best, naive in the extreme to suggest, let alone find, that the result below was not dictated by the evil of gender bias.

. . .

By rejecting the obvious but unacceptable in its search for a basis for the result below, the majority has, in my opinion, relied upon something even worse. In the end, after a meticulous inquiry into the father's long past and non-parental conduct which few mortals could withstand, it bases its determination that the discretion of the trial court was properly exercised upon the belief that the record shows (or that the trial court might have properly believed) that Mr. Young is less sincere, less well motivated, less admirable and generally a worse person and a worse parent than Ms. Hector. As I might do myself, one may agree with this assessment of the parties while profoundly disagreeing, as I certainly do, with the idea that any such consideration is a proper basis for decision-making in this field.

It is of course true, as the majority repeatedly emphasizes, that a "custody" decision is one within the discretion of the trial court. But judicial discretion may properly be exercised only on the basis of factors which are legally pertinent to the issue involved.... In this area, that issue is the children's best interests. Its resolution, in turn, cannot be based on a subjective assessment of the worth of the contending parties so long as, as was conclusively demonstrated in this case, the conduct and character traits referred to have not impacted upon the children. We had, I thought, come a long way from the time when a parent could be denied her parental rights—or, more properly stated, when the children could be deprived of their rights to having only their interests considered—merely because a judge may disapprove of her standards of conduct, much less of her character. Apparently, I was mistaken.

. . .

■ Goderich, J. (dissenting):

It is apparent that the trial court abused its discretion by awarding primary residential custody of the minor children to the parent who has been working long hours as a senior litigation partner in one of Miami's top law firms as opposed to the parent who has not worked outside of the home for the three years preceding the filing of the dissolution action.

The majority opinion focuses on the fact that the parties did not mutually agree that the father would stay at home to care for the children. Although it may be true that the mother did not expressly agree, the record demonstrates that the mother nonetheless acquiesced to this arrangement by allowing it to continue for three years. For example, although the parties had "separated," the mother permitted the husband to live in the marital home and to continue his role as a stay-at-home parent. Moreover, there is no doubt that the mother benefited from this arrangement (and possibly that is why she allowed it to continue). As a result of this caretaking arrangement, the mother was free to dedicate herself to her legal career by working extremely long hours without having to worry about whether the minor children's emotional needs were being met. Also, the record indicates that the children also benefited from their father's role as the primary caretaker since he was actively involved in their school and after-school activities.

. . .

Further, I believe that gender played a role in the trial court's decision, and continues to play a role in this Court's decision. At one point, the trial court, while questioning the father as to the nanny's role, stated to the father: "Maybe I'm missing something. Why don't you get a job." Shortly thereafter, the trial court also stated: "Why [sic] do you need the nanny for, if you're there doing it?"

. . .

I do not agree with the majority's observation that these statements had nothing to do with gender bias, but rather was a result of the parties' financial condition. During the trial court's exchange with the husband, there is nothing that would indicate that the trial court was concerned with the parties' financial condition. Further, I find it extremely hard to believe that if the roles were reversed any trial judge would question a mother's lack of employment or the employment of a nanny when the father earns over $300,000 per year. Moreover, the record indicates that it was the mother, not the father, who employed the nanny.

The majority opinion also suggests that the father should have obtained gainful employment in order to financially assist the household and minor children in light of the parties' financial condition. The record clearly demonstrates that with the husband's present skills, he did not have the ability to earn a substantial amount of money. Further, this was not a family in which the working parent was earning $30,000 and any additional sums earned by the other parent would have been helpful to provide the children with basic necessities such as food, clothing, and shelter. The record clearly establishes that the minor children's basic necessities were more than taken care of. There are certain things that money cannot buy and that a nanny cannot provide, such as the attention of caring parents. Once again, I do not believe that if the roles were reversed (a father who earns over $300,000 per year and a non-working mother), the majority would have suggested that the children would have been better off if the mother would have attained employment when her earning potential is limited and the father already makes over $300,000 per year. Instead, the majority would have probably suggested that the father restructure his debt, sell assets, and/or cut down on expenses so that the mother could continue the caretaking role that was established during the marriage.

The majority opinion also addresses the three "determinative factors" that the guardian ad litem looked at in recommending that the mother be named the primary residential parent. First, the guardian focused on the fact that the mother has been more economically stable throughout the marriage. Once again, if the roles were reversed, I believe that the guardian ad litem would not have considered economical stability as a "determinative factor." Further, in light of the child support guidelines, a parent's financial resources should never be considered as a "determinative factor" in deciding which parent should be awarded primary residential custody of the minor children.

The second "determinative factor" was that the mother has been "the more constant factor throughout the entire relationship." The guardian ad litem focused on the fact that the father had been "away from the home for substantial periods of time. . . ." I feel that it is important to explain why the father had been away from the home. First, when the parties decided to move to Miami, the father stayed in New Mexico for approximately three months in order to move the family's possessions to Miami and to make improvements to the marital home so that the parties could sell the home at its highest possible price. Second, the husband, was away for three to four weeks to be with his ill brother, who died shortly after he arrived, and to help settle his brother's estate. Finally, the father was in New Mexico from June 1992 to September 1993 in order to direct a treasure hunt project. The majority relies on the "treasure hunt" to make it appear as if the treasure hunt was a crazy or weird notion. However, what the majority has failed to state is that it may not have been so strange since the mother's parents and trial counsel also invested in this project. Therefore, the reasons for the father's absence from the home were valid. Further, the fact that the father had been away from the family should not be a "determinative factor" when taking into consideration that the father has been the primary caretaker since the fall of 1993.

Finally, the third determinative factor was that the mother "controls her anger better around the kids." The guardian ad litem testified that the father "would say things in the presence of the children that indicated to me his anger and his displeasure at what he perceives to be the financial inequities of the situation. . . ." I agree with the guardian ad litem that being able to control anger is an important factor in deciding child custody issues. However, the father's anger was based on the "financial inequities of the situation," a problem that should be completely resolved based on the majority's decision to reverse and remand all financial determinations made by the trial court, including the insufficient award of alimony to the father and the inequitable distribution of the marital assets and liabilities.

. . .

NOTES

1. Would the decision in this case have been the same if the mother were the architect and the father the lawyer? Would the court have inquired of the mother, "Maybe I'm missing something. Why don't you get a job?"

2. One interpretation of the facts is that the father in *Hector* became more involved with the children once a divorce began to seem likely. If that is so, should this reduce the weight the court gives to the father's caregiving activities?

American Law Institute, Principles of the Law of Family Dissolution

(2002).

§ 2.08 Allocation of Custodial Responsibility

(1) Unless otherwise resolved by agreement of the parents . . . , the court should allocate custodial responsibility so that the proportion of custodial time the child spends with each parent approximates the proportion of time each parent spent performing caretaking functions for the child prior to the parents' separation or, if the parents never lived together, before the filing of the action, except to the extent . . . necessary to achieve one or more of the following objectives:

(a) to permit the child to have a relationship with each parent which, in the case of a legal parent or a parent by estoppel who has performed a reasonable share of parenting functions, should be not less than a presumptive amount of custodial time set by a uniform rule of statewide application;

(b) to accommodate the firm and reasonable preferences of a child who has reached a specific age, set by a uniform rule of statewide application;

(c) to keep siblings together when the court finds that doing so is necessary to their welfare;

. . .

(f) to avoid an allocation of custodial responsibility that would be extremely impractical or that would interfere substantially with the child's need for stability in light of economic, physical, or other circumstances, including the distance between the parents' residences, the cost and difficulty of transporting the child, each parent's and the child's daily schedules, and the ability of the parents to cooperate in the arrangement;

. . .

(h) to avoid substantial and almost certain harm to the child.

COMMENTS:

a. In general. This section states the criteria for allocating custodial responsibility between parents when they have not reached their own agreement about this allocation. These criteria also establish the bargaining context for parents seeking agreement.

Custodial responsibility refers to physical control of and access to the child, or what traditionally has been called child custody. This term refers to the child's living arrangements, including with whom the child lives and when, and any periods of time during which another person is scheduled by the court to have caretaking responsibility for the child . . .

b. Rationale for reliance on past caretaking. The ideal standard for determining a child's custodial arrangements is one that both yields predictable and easily adjudicated results and also consistently serves the child's best interests. While the best-interests-of-the-child test may appear well suited to this objective, the test is too subjective to produce predictable results. Its unpredictability encourages strategic bargaining and prolonged litigation. The indeterminacy of the test also draws the court into comparisons between parenting styles and values that are matters of parental autonomy not appropriate for judicial resolution.

The allocation of custodial responsibility presumed in Paragraph (1) yields more predictable and more easily adjudicated results, thereby advancing the best interests of children in most cases without infringing on parental autonomy. It assumes that the division of past caretaking functions correlates well with other factors associated with the child's best interests, such as the quality of each parent's emotional attachment to the child and the parents' respective parenting abilities. It requires factfinding that is less likely than the traditional best-interests test to require expert testimony about such matters as the child's emotional state or developmental needs, the parents' relative abilities, and the strength of their emotional relationships to the child. Avoiding expert testimony is desirable because such testimony, within an adversarial context, tends to focus on the weaknesses of each parent and thus undermines the spirit of cooperation and compromise necessary to successful post-divorce custodial arrangements; therapists are better used in the divorce context to assist parents in making plans to deal constructively with each other and their children at separation.

Some parents will disagree over how caretaking roles were previously divided, making the past division of caretaking functions itself a potential litigation issue. The difficulties in applying the standard, however, must be evaluated in light of the available alternatives. While each parent's share of past caretaking will in some cases be disputed, these functions encompass specific tasks and responsibilities about which concrete evidence is available and thus offer greater determinacy than more qualitative standards, such as parental competence, the strength of the parent-child emotional bond or—as the general standard simply puts it—the child's best interests. These qualitative criteria are future-oriented and highly subjective, whereas how the parents divided caretaking responsibilities in the past is a concrete question of historical fact, like other questions courts are accustomed to resolving.

§ 2.09 Allocation of Significant Decisionmaking Responsibility

(1) Unless otherwise resolved by agreement of the parents . . . the court should allocate responsibility for making significant life decisions on behalf of the child, including decisions regarding the child's education and health care, to one parent or to two parents jointly, in accordance with the child's best interests, in light of the following:

(a) the allocation of custodial responsibility under § 2.08;

(b) the level of each parent's participation in past decisionmaking on behalf of the child;

(c) the wishes of the parents;

(d) the level of ability and cooperation the parents have demonstrated in past decisionmaking on behalf of the child;

. . .

(2) The court should presume that an allocation of decisionmaking responsibility jointly to each legal parent or parent by estoppel who has been exercising a reasonable share of parenting functions is in the child's best interests. The presumption is overcome if there is a history of domestic violence or child abuse, or if it is shown that joint allocation of decisionmaking responsibility is not in the child's best interests.

. . .

COMMENTS:

a. In general. . . . Section 2.09 sets forth rules for allocating decisionmaking responsibility when the parents have not already done so in an agreement that has been accepted by the court. Decisionmaking responsibility . . . refers to authority to make decisions with respect to significant areas in the child's life. The most common decisionmaking issues covered by this section are education and health care, but other issues may arise, such as permission to enlist in the military, drive a car, work, participate in school sports, and sign a contract.

NOTES

1. The ALI Principles' focus on the parties' prior division of parental responsibilities bears some resemblance to the primary caretaker presumption. It is important, however, to appreciate the difference. The primary caretaker presumption is used to determine which parent will be designated the custodian, with a right of physical custody superior to that of the noncustodian, and a right of legal custody—the authority to make major decisions regarding the child—equal to or greater than that of the noncustodian.

By contrast, the ALI Principles deliberately avoid the terms "custodian" and "noncustodian," because these terms imply that there is a winner and a loser in the custody proceeding. Instead, § 2.08 seeks to allocate shares of "custodial responsibility"—physical custody—in accordance with the preexisting pattern. Consistent with the Principles' ostensibly non-adversarial focus, § 2.09 presumes that joint "decision-making responsibility"—legal custody—is in the best interest of the child.

Section 2.05 of the Principles also requires the parents to submit a parenting plan that sets forth a schedule of custodial responsibility and an allocation of decisionmaking responsibility with respect to significant matters likely to arise. Two commentators suggest that "the trend is clearly in the direction of increased use of parenting plans." Barbara Handschu & Mary Kay Kisthardt, Parenting Plans, National Law Journal, October 3, 2003, at 21.

2. In In re Custody of Kali, 439 Mass. 834, 792 N.E.2d 635 (2003), a Massachusetts court upheld the award of legal custody to the mother, despite the father's contention that he had spent proportionally more time caring for the child prior to the termination of the relationship. The court discussed ALI § 2.08, as reflected in G.L. c. 209C § 10(a), explaining, "It cautions against rearranging a child's living arrangements in an attempt to achieve some optimum from all the available permutations and combinations of custody and visitation, when it is generally wiser and safer not to meddle in arrangements that are already serving the child's needs ... Stability is itself of enormous benefit to a child, and any unnecessary tampering with the status quo simply increases the risk of harm to the child." 439 Mass. 834, 843. See also Rubano v. DiCenzo, 759 A.2d 959 (R.I. 2000), citing the 2000 ALI Principles in support of enforcing visitation as specified by the parties' pre-existing written agreement.

5. Random Selection

Robert Mnookin, Child-Custody Adjudication: Judicial Functions in the Face of Indeterminacy

39 Law and Contemporary Problems 226, 289–91 (1975).

. . .

An inquiry about what is best for a child often yields indeterminate results because of the problems of having adequate information, making the necessary predictions, and finding an integrated set of values by which to choose. But some custody cases may still be comparatively easy to decide. While there is no consensus about what is best for a child, there is much consensus about what is very bad (e.g., physical abuse); some short-term predictions about human behavior can be reliably made (e.g., chronic alcoholism or psychosis is difficult quickly to modify). Asking which alternative is in the best interests of a child may have a rather clear-cut answer in situations where one claimant exposes the child to substantial risks of immediate harm and the other claimant already has a substantial personal relationship with the child and poses no such risk. In a private dispute between two parents, for example, if a judge could predict that one parent's conduct would seriously endanger the child's health, it would not be difficult to conclude that the child's expected utility would be higher if he went with the other parent, whose conduct did not, even without the necessity of defining utility carefully. More generally, where one alternative plainly risks irreversible effects on the child that are bad and the other does not, there is no need to make longer-term predictions or more complicated psychological evaluations of what is likely to happen to the child's personality.

But to be easy, a case must involve only one claimant who is well known to the child and whose conduct does not endanger the child. If there are two such claimants or none, difficult choices remain. Most custody disputes pose difficult choices.

. . .

Assuming that an "intimate" acceptable to both parents cannot be found to make an individualized decision, would not a random process of decision be fairer and more efficient than adjudication under a best-interests principle? Individualized adjudication means that the result will often turn on a largely intuitive evaluation based on unspoken values and unproven predictions. We would more frankly acknowledge both our ignorance and the presumed equality of the natural parents were we to flip a coin. Whether one had a separate flip for each child or one flip for all the children, the process would certainly be cheaper and quicker. It would avoid the pain associated with an adversary proceeding that requires an open exploration of the intimate aspects of family life and an ultimate judgment that one parent is preferable to the other. And it might have beneficial effects on private negotiations.[254]

Resolving a custody dispute by state-administered coin-flip would probably be viewed as unacceptable by most in our society. Perhaps this reaction reflects an abiding faith, despite the absence of an empirical basis for it, that letting a judge choose produces better results for the child. Alternatively, flipping a coin might be unacceptable for some because it represents an abdication of the search for wisdom. While judgments about what is best for the child may be currently beyond our capacity in many cases, this need not be true in fifty years. Movement towards better judgments implies, however, that judges and decision-makers as a group learn from the process of decision. In the absence of systematic feedback, this is not likely. Indeed, adopting a coin-flip now means neither that at a time when more were known and a consensus existed an adjudicatory system might not be adopted, nor that efforts to discover an adjudicatory standard would cease.

Deciding a child's future by flipping a coin might be viewed as callous. Is it more callous, however, than drafting for the military by lottery? In the same way that a lottery is a social affirmation of equality among those upon whom the government might impose the risks of war, a coin-flip would be a government affirmation of the equality of the parents. In a custody case, however, a coin-flip also symbolically abdicates government responsibility for the child and symbolically denies the importance of human differences and distinctiveness. Moreover, flipping a coin would deprive the parents of a process and a forum where their anger and aspirations might be expressed.

254. The effect on negotiation would depend on each parent's risk preferences and on how much each wanted the child. Because each parent would face a 50 percent chance of losing, this might encourage private compromise if both wanted the child and were very risk-averse. But because a coin-flip would be less painful than an adversary proceeding the threat of holding out for such a resolution might be more frequently and credibly used than the threat of litigation is today by a party who did not much want the child but who was bargaining for advantage with regard to other elements of the marriage dissolution. To avoid these bargaining problems, the state might insist that the coin-flip occur at the time of the marriage. Through a state-supervised random process, one of the parents could then be designated as the parent who would have custody (absent a showing of neglect) if the parents should later separate and be unable themselves to decide who should have custody. For children of unmarried parents, the rule of maternal preference might be kept. The winner of the coin-flip would, of course, have an enormous negotiating advantage. It is interesting to speculate whether such a rule would affect the loser's emotional commitment to the child or willingness to stay married to avoid losing custody of the child.

In all, these symbolic and participatory values of adjudication would be lost by a random process.

While forceful arguments can be made in favor of the abandonment of adjudication and the adoption of an openly random process, the repulsion many would probably feel towards this suggestion may reflect an intuitive appreciation of the importance of the educational, participatory, and symbolic values of adjudication as a mode of dispute settlement. Adjudication under the indeterminate best-interests principle may yield something close to a random pattern of outcomes, while at the same time serving these values, affirming parental equality, and expressing a social concern for the child. Insofar as judges as a group may have value preferences that systematically bias the process and make the pattern less than random, these value preferences may reflect widespread values that have not been acknowledged openly in the form of legal rules.

. . .

Jon Elster, Solomonic Judgments: Against the Best Interest of the Child

54 U. Chi. L. Rev. 1, 39–43 (1986).

. . .

Robert Mnookin's argument that coin flipping [to determine custody when both parents are fit] would deprive the parents of a forum where their angers and aspirations might be expressed does not seem well-founded. Social psychology research does not confirm the view that aggression can be relieved by being expressed, through some form of catharsis. If anything, acting out leads to more aggression. Nor do I agree with Mnookin's contention that symbolic and participatory values of adjudication would be lost in a random choice mechanism. One could imagine a cointossing procedure coming to symbolize the equal worth of the parents, as well as the child's right to a speedy decision. It may well be true that "[l]aw, after all, is for the happiness of men, and some men will always be happier with the appearance of justice"[253]—happier, presumably, than with the reality of justice. A legal procedure is not viable if it strongly offends the sense of justice of a large part of the population, whatever else might be said for it. Yet if there *is* something to be said for it, one ought to think seriously about how it could be implemented, perhaps gradually, partially, or optionally, in ways that would not give offense. The cart of procedural justice should not be set before the horse of substantive justice.

Many people seem to think the proposal is inhuman, frivolous, or both. They argue that a decision with such far-reaching consequences must be made by appeal to reason and argument, not by an arbitrary choice. Coin tossing may be acceptable in trivial decisions, but not in matters of such momentous importance. On the other hand, it has been argued that "[r]andom selection is most favoured when the outcome is either of very *small* or very *great* importance to the recipients." This may well be so. Examples of randomly made decisions of great importance to the recipients include draft lotteries, random allocation of kidney machines, and choices by lot of

253. Coons, Approaches to Court–Imposed Compromise—The Uses of Doubt and Reason, 58 Nw. Univ. L. Rev. 750, 771 (1964).

persons to be thrown overboard in an overcrowded life boat or to be eaten by the other passengers.

One central rationale for randomization in these cases seems to be that random choice is appropriate when other criteria would force us to compare the intrinsic worth of persons. This argument also applies to custody decisions. Although the best interest analysis ostensibly scrutinizes the mother and the father only with respect to their fitness for custody, it is easily understood as a judgment on their worth more generally. But the essential point is that randomizing in custody decisions recommends itself because it has good consequences for a person other than the potential recipients—for the child.

In sum: tossing a coin to decide custody disputes shares the advantages of any automatic decision rule, in minimizing the harm done to children by protracted litigation. With regard to parents, it appeals to intuitions about equal treatment and equal worth, whereas it can violate rights-based and needs-based considerations. It shares a drawback with the best interest principle, in creating uncertainty about the final outcome ... [As a result,] the more risk-averse parent, usually the one for whom the child matters most, is punished by loss of bargaining power over other matters.

NOTE

Consider the argument of Professor Carl Schneider that critics of the best interests standard have overlooked the advantages of vesting some discretion in custody decisionmakers:

> Discretion can lead to better decisions because they can be tailored to the particular circumstances of each case. Discretion gives the decisionmaker flexibility to do justice. It does so not just by allowing a decisionmaker to heed all the individual facts that ought to affect a decision but that could not be listed by rules. It also does so by allowing a decisionmaker to see over time how well a decision worked and to adjust future decisions accordingly. Discretion may also conduce to better decisions by discouraging overly bureaucratic ways of thinking, since they often are born of too rigid an insistence on writing elaborate rules and on following them with too mechanical a regularity. Finally, endowing decisionmakers with discretion may make their jobs more interesting and more powerful and thus more attractive to able people.
>
> Discretion has within its fold another, subtler advantage. Discretion sometimes permits the decisionmaker to conceal the basis for his ruling. In custody decisions, for example, a choice commonly must be made between two parents, both of whom have virtues, both of whom have faults, and both of whom will (or should) continue to see their child. It may unnecessarily damage the loser's feelings (and his feelings for his child) to point out to him his faults and the other parent's virtues. This may be true even where the choice involves no moral judgements about the parties. For instance, a parent might not like to hear detailed all the reasons he was not a child's "psychological parent."

Discretion, Rules and Law: Child Custody and the UMDA's Best–Interest Standard, 89 Mich.L.Rev. 2215, 2247–48. Schneider concludes "it is worth considering the possibility that, at its best, the present system provides as reasonable a framework for balancing the advantages of rules and discretion as we are likely to find." Id. at 2291.

F. Modification

In theory, most courts will modify a custody decision only if there is a "substantial change in circumstances." If this exception were construed narrowly to mean proof sufficient to declare the child neglected there would be little incentive to challenge most custody decisions once made. Some courts, however, have construed the modification standard rather loosely, so that parents who lose the initial custody decision can fairly easily find a basis for relitigating the issue, particularly in a different jurisdiction. Although the laudable desire to provide the "best" possible home for children may have created this body of law, consider whether the pursuit of the "best" may be self-defeating in some instances because of the disruption resulting from a change in custody.

1. Change in Circumstances

Uniform Marriage and Divorce Act

SECTION 409. Modification

(a) No motion to modify a custody decree may be made earlier than 2 years after its date, unless the court permits it to be made on the basis of affidavits that there is reason to believe the child's present environment may endanger seriously his physical, mental, moral, or emotional health.

(b) If a court of this State has jurisdiction pursuant to the Uniform Child Custody Jurisdiction Act, the court shall not modify a prior custody decree unless it finds, upon the basis of facts that have arisen since the prior decree or that were unknown to the court at the time of entry of the prior decree, that a change has occurred in the circumstances of the child or his custodian, and that the modification is necessary to serve the best interest of the child. In applying these standards the court shall retain the custodian appointed pursuant to the prior decree unless:

(1) the custodian agrees to the modification;

(2) the child has been integrated into the family of the petitioner with consent of the custodian; or

(3) the child's present environment endangers seriously his physical, mental, moral, or emotional health, and the harm likely to be caused by a change of environment is outweighed by its advantages to him.

(c) Attorney fees and costs shall be assessed against a party seeking modification if the court finds that the modification action is vexatious and constitutes harassment.

COMMENT

Most experts who have spoken to the problems of post-divorce adjustment of children believe that insuring the decree's finality is more important than determining which parent should be the custodian. This section is designed to maximize finality (and thus assure continuity for the child) without jeopardizing the child's interest. Because any emergency which poses an immediate threat to the child's physical safety usually can be handled by the juvenile court, subsection (a) prohibits modification petitions until at least two years have passed following the initial decree, with a "safety valve" for emergency situations. To discourage the noncustodial parent who tries to punish a former spouse by frequent motions to modify, the subsection includes a two-year waiting period following each modification decree. During that two-year period, a contestant can get a hearing only if he can make an initial showing, by affidavit only, that there is some greater urgency for the change than that the child's "best interest" requires it. During the two-year period the judge should deny a motion to modify, without a hearing, unless the moving party carries the onerous burden of showing that the child's present environment may endanger his physical, mental, moral, or emotional health.

Subsection (b) in effect asserts a presumption that the present custodian is entitled to continue as the child's custodian. It does authorize modifications which serve the child's "best interest;" but this standard is to be applied under the principle that modification should be made only in three situations: where the custodian agrees to the change; where the child, although formally in the custody of one parent, has in fact been integrated into the family of the petitioning parent (to avoid encouraging noncustodial kidnapping, this ground requires the consent of the custodial parent); or where the noncustodial parent can prove both that the child's present environment is dangerous to physical, mental, moral, or emotional health and that the risks of harm from change of environment are outweighed by the advantage of such a change to the child. The last phrase of subsection (b)(3) is especially important because it compels attention to the real issue in modification cases. Any change in the child's environment may have an adverse effect, even if the noncustodial parent would better serve the child's interest. Subsection (b)(3) focuses the issue clearly and demands that presentation of evidence relevant to the resolution of that issue.

Hassenstab v. Hassenstab

Nebraska Court of Appeals, 1997.
6 Neb.App. 13, 570 N.W.2d 368.

■ Body, Judge.

Thomas Kelly Hassenstab appeals from an order entered by the Douglas County District Court denying his application to modify custody from Carol Marie Hassenstab to him. For the reasons set forth herein, we affirm the order of the district court.

Facts

Thomas and Carol were married on September 13, 1986. One child was born of this marriage, Jacqueline A. Hassenstab, on March 28, 1986. On May 24, 1990, the Douglas County District Court entered an order dissolving the parties' marriage and awarding custody of Jacqueline to Carol with reasonable rights of visitation to Thomas.

On June 13, 1995, Thomas filed an "Application to Modify Decree of Dissolution of Marriage" requesting, among other things, that the court modify the prior custody determination by awarding custody of Jacqueline to Thomas. Carol filed an answer which generally denied the allegations contained in Thomas' application to modify and also filed a cross-petition requesting an increase in child support and attorney fees.

A trial on the application to modify and Carol's cross-petition was held on March 22, 1996. The evidence adduced at trial established that following the parties' divorce, Carol had been involved in a homosexual relationship. Additionally, Thomas testified to Carol's alleged suicide attempts which he contends occurred prior to and during the marriage. Carol testified that she attempted suicide on one occasion which was 7 years prior to the modification hearing and prior to the time that the dissolution decree became final. In describing the suicide attempt, Carol stated she "fell" out of a car traveling approximately 40 miles per hour. Additionally, the evidence did establish that Carol has sought counseling for several reasons, including her confusion over her sexual identity, but that she was not in counseling at the time of the modification hearing.

The trial judge met with Jacqueline in the court's chambers prior to submission of the case for determination. During the meeting, Jacqueline expressed a desire to remain in her mother's custody.

The district court subsequently entered an order dismissing Thomas' application to modify, modifying the original dissolution decree to increase Thomas' child support obligation, and awarding Carol $1,250 in attorney fees. Thomas timely appealed to this court regarding the dismissal of his application to modify.

On appeal, Thomas contends that the district court erred in finding that no substantial and material change in circumstances had taken place since the entry of the dissolution decree showing that Carol was unfit to retain custody of Jacqueline or that Jacqueline's best interests required a modification of her custody to Thomas. Thomas does not appeal the court's order increasing his child support obligation or the award of attorney fees.

. . .

Thomas contends that the district court erred in finding that no substantial and material change in circumstances had taken place since the entry of the dissolution decree that showed that Carol was unfit to retain custody of Jacqueline or that Jacqueline's best interests required a modification of her custody to Thomas.

Ordinarily, custody of a minor child will not be modified unless there has been a material change of circumstances showing that the custodial parent is unfit or that the best interests of the minor child require such action. Smith–Helstrom v. Yonker, 249 Neb. 449, 544 N.W. 2d 93 (1986); Krohn v. Krohn, 217 Neb. 158, 347 N.W. 2d 869 (1984). The party seeking modification of child custody bears the burden of showing that a material change in circumstances has occurred.

In determining a child's best interests in custody and visitation matters, Neb. Rev. Stat. § 42–364(2) (Cum. Supp. 1994), provides that the factors to be considered shall include, but not be limited to, the following:

(a) The relationship of the minor child to each parent prior to the commencement of the action or any subsequent hearing;

(b) The desires and wishes of the minor child if of an age of comprehension regardless of chronological age, when such desires and wishes are based on sound reasoning;

(c) The general health, welfare, and social behavior of the minor child; and

(d) Credible evidence of abuse inflicted on any family or household member.

Additionally, a court may consider other factors in determining a child's best interests in custody matters, including the moral fitness of the child's parents and the parents' sexual conduct. Helgenberger v. Helgenberger, 209 Neb. 184, 306 N.W.2d 867 (1981). However, the best interests of the minor child remain the court's paramount concern in deciding custody issues. Smith–Helstrom, supra.

First, we address Thomas' contentions that Carol is an unfit mother by reason of her alleged suicide attempts, alcohol consumption, and other psychological difficulties as well as her failure to provide a stable home environment.

"In cases of this nature, it appears to us that in determining whether the custody of a minor child should be changed, the evidence of the custodial parent's behavior during the year or so before the hearing on the motion to modify is of more significance than the behavior prior to that time. What we are interested in is the best interests of the child now and in the immediate future, and how the custodial parent is behaving now is therefore of greater significance than past behavior when attempting to determine the best interests of the child." Kennedy v. Kennedy, 221 Neb. 724, 727–28, 380 N.W.2d 300, 303 (1986) (quoting Riddle v. Riddle, 221 Neb. 109, 375 N.W.2d 143 (1985)).

The evidence was that a suicide attempt occurred 7 years prior to the modification hearing and prior to the time that the dissolution decree became final in which Carol "fell" out of a car traveling approximately 40 miles per hour. Additionally, the evidence did establish that Carol has sought counseling for several reasons, including her confusion over her sexual identity, but that she was not in counseling at the time of the modification hearing.

With regard to Carol's alcohol consumption and throwing loud parties, the record contains no evidence that Jacqueline has ever observed Carol in an intoxicated state or that Carol's alcohol consumption has adversely affected Jacqueline or endangered the child in any way. Furthermore, although Carol and Jacqueline have changed residences approximately four times and Carol has had several different roommates since the divorce decree was entered in 1990, there is no evidence that the change of residences has been harmful to Jacqueline. To the contrary, Carol testified that each move resulted in improved living conditions and that Jacqueline has never had to change schools because of the moves. Thus, based upon the evidence, Thomas has not shown that the above factors were a material change in circumstances requiring a change of custody.

Second, we address Thomas' concerns over the effect that Carol's homosexuality has on Jacqueline. The Nebraska Supreme Court has repeatedly held, albeit not in the context of a homosexual relationship, that a parent's sexual activity is insufficient to establish a material change in circumstances justifying a change in custody absent a showing that the minor child or children were exposed to such activity or were adversely affected or damaged by reason of such activity. Smith–Helstrom, supra; Kennedy, supra; Krohn, supra (where there was no showing that children were exposed to sexual activity or otherwise damaged, mother could retain custody of children). Thus, the issue is whether this rule is to be applied in the context of a homosexual parent.

The South Dakota Supreme Court, in Van Driel v. Van Driel, 525 N.W.2d 37 (S.D. 1994), held that a custodial parent's homosexual relationship does not render that parent unfit or require an award of custody to the other parent absent a showing that the custodial parent's conduct has had some harmful effect on the children and that a change of custody is in the child's or children's best interests. We agree that sexual activity by a parent, whether it is heterosexual or homosexual, is governed by the rule that to establish a material change in circumstances justifying a change in custody there must be a showing that the minor child or children were exposed to such activity or were adversely affected or damaged by reason of such activity and that a change of custody is in the child or children's best interests.

In some cases, courts of other jurisdictions have denied custody and liberal visitation to a homosexual parent. However, these cases involved situations where the children have been exposed to the parent's homosexual activity or where, for other reasons, placing the children in the homosexual parent's custody was not in the children's best interests. For example, in Hall v. Hall, 95 Mich. App. 614, 615, 291 N.W.2d 143, 144 (1980), the appellate court affirmed the trial court's placement of the minor children with the father rather than with the homosexual mother where the evidence established that, given a conflict, the mother would "unquestionably choose the [homosexual] relationship over the children."

In In re Marriage of Wiarda, 505 N.W.2d 506, 508 (Iowa App. 1993), the appellate court affirmed the trial court's grant of custody of the minor child to the father where "it appears from the record that [the mother's] relationship with her [female] friend has not had a calming effect upon either the children or upon the difficult problems of the breakup of this marriage" and "it is certain that [the mother's] friend's presence in this matter has caused twelve-year-old Sarah certain anxieties and, from Sarah's viewpoint, has contributed to the continued breakdown of the relationship between [the mother and father]."

. . .

The case at bar is distinguishable from the aforementioned cases because, although there was evidence that Carol and her partner would engage in sexual activity at times when Jacqueline was in Carol's residence and that Jacqueline was generally aware of her mother's homosexual relationship, there was no showing that the daughter was directly exposed to the sexual activity or that she was in any way harmed by the homosexual relationship between Carol and her partner. Because the evidence in the case at bar simply does not establish any harmful effect on Jacqueline because of Carol's homosexual relationship, there has been no showing of a material change of circumstances.

Furthermore, the evidence does not establish that Jacqueline's best interests require a change of custody. At the trial, Jacqueline was described as a happy, self-assured, and confident child. Thomas characterized Jacqueline as "a very loving, fun, special daughter." He further stated that she is "very, very happy, very joyful, very spirited." Other witnesses testified that Jacqueline is dressed in clean clothes which are appropriate for the weather, she is well-kept, and her hair is combed. The record further reflects that Jacqueline is a "B" student and has few discipline problems.

. . .

In sum, Thomas has failed to meet his burden of proving a material change of circumstances necessitating a change of Jacqueline's custody. Therefore, the order of the district court is affirmed.

NOTE

Hassenstab involved a modification of custody rather than an initial award. If the challenged actions had occurred before the initial custody hearing, would the mother have won?

Wetch v. Wetch

Supreme Court of North Dakota, 1995.
539 N.W.2d 309.

■ SANDSTROM, JUSTICE.

Cheryl Wetch appealed in this divorce case from a Second Amended Judgment, dated October 21, 1994, changing custody of the parties' two minor daughters from Cheryl Wetch to their father, Kirk Wetch. Because the trial court erred in refusing to consider custody-related evidence predating an April 5, 1994, Amended Judgment and Decree, we reverse and remand to redetermine custody.

I

Cheryl and Kirk Wetch were married in 1987. Their daughter Cassandra was born in 1989, and their daughter Kaley Anne was born in 1991. The parties were divorced on March 12, 1993, and by stipulated agreement Cheryl Wetch received custody of Cassandra and Kaley Anne, and Kirk Wetch received liberal visitation rights. About one year later, a dispute arose when Cheryl Wetch wanted to move with the children to Tennessee. Kirk Wetch objected to the move and sought physical custody of the girls. The matter was resolved by stipulated agreement, and an amended judgment was entered on April 5, 1994, permitting Cheryl Wetch to retain custody of the children but restricting her to reside within 60 miles of Fargo–Moorhead.

During the summer of 1994, Cheryl Wetch, without permission of Kirk Wetch or the trial court, moved with the children to Tennessee. Kirk Wetch filed a motion for change of custody. In deciding the motion, the trial court specifically stated it would not consider any evidence of the parties' activities or conduct prior to the April 5, 1994 amended judgment. After conducting an evidentiary hearing on September 7 and 8, 1994, the court granted the motion, awarding Kirk Wetch physical custody of the girls. Cheryl Wetch appealed.

. . .

The dispositive issue Cheryl Wetch raises on appeal is whether the trial court erred in refusing to consider custody evidence relating to conduct and events occurring before the April 5, 1994 judgment. When a trial court makes an original award of custody between parents in a divorce proceeding, it must determine the single issue of what is in the child's best interests. When the court considers a request to modify an original custody award, however, it must determine two issues: (1) whether there has been a significant change of circumstances since entry of the original divorce decree and custody award; and, if so, (2) whether the changed circumstances require in the best interests of the child custody be modified.

During oral argument, Cheryl Wetch conceded her change of residence to Tennessee constituted a significant change of circumstances. She claims the change of circumstances, however, does not justify a change of custody, because prior to the divorce Kirk Wetch perpetrated domestic violence toward Cheryl Wetch and the girls, raising a presumption against Kirk Wetch getting custody. Kirk Wetch responds res judicata precludes the trial court from considering parties' pre-divorce conduct. Alternatively, Kirk Wetch asserts the trial court should have considered evidence of Cheryl's pre-divorce misconduct, including physical abuse of Kirk Wetch and neglect of the children.

The trial court has broad discretion on evidentiary matters. On appeal, we will not overturn a trial court's decision admitting or excluding evidence on relevancy grounds unless the trial court has abused its discretion. A trial court also has substantial discretion in custody matters, providing the court evaluates all factors affecting the children's best interests and welfare . . .

Kirk Wetch asserts the doctrine of res judicata precluded the trial court from considering custody-related evidence predating the April 5, 1994 amended judgment. . . . Under res judicata principles, it is inappropriate to rehash issues which were tried or could have been tried by the court in prior proceedings. The doctrine, however, should be applied as fairness and justice require but should not be applied so rigidly as to defeat the ends of justice or to work an injustice. The doctrine should not be strictly applied to preclude the trial court from hearing for the first time relevant custody-related evidence bearing on considerations of what is in a child's best interests. Under proper circumstances custody issues, although decided in the original divorce action, may be reexamined and a court order modified in the continuing jurisdiction of the trial court.

We have not previously decided whether it is error in a change of custody proceeding for a trial court to refuse to consider evidence of relevant custody factors occurring prior to entry of the original custody decree. There is, however, substantial persuasive authority from other courts that when the original custody decree is entered upon default or based upon a stipulation of the parties, a trial court errs by refusing to consider pre-divorce conduct on the change-of-custody issue. *See, e.g., Wilson v. Wilson, 408 So.2d 114, 116 (Ala. Civ. App. 1981)* cert. denied, *Ex Parte Wilson, 408 So. 2d. 117 (1982).* In Wilson, at 116, the Alabama Court of Civil Appeals reversed the trial court's denial of the ex-husband's petition for change of custody and remanded for a new trial on the custody issue:

> "Appellant's first contention is that the trial court erred in refusing to hear evidence concerning the wife's predivorce misconduct. Appellant sought unsuccessfully to introduce testimony at trial of the mother's immoral conduct prior to the divorce as a ground on which to justify modification of the custody decree. Although facts disclosed to the court and considered by it in fashioning the original custody decree cannot be 'rehashed' in a subsequent modification proceeding, facts existing at the time of the original divorce decree but not disclosed at that time may be considered by the court in a subsequent modification proceeding, even though these facts do not relate to a change of circumstances subsequent to the original divorce decree. . . .
>
> "The provisions of the original divorce decree were, in the present case, based upon the stipulations and agreement of the parties. Apparently, no testimony concerning the child custody issue was offered. Under such circumstances, facts relating to the parties' pre-divorce conduct should be considered by the trial court in a modification proceeding. . . . The trial court's refusal to admit any evidence concerning the parties' prior conduct is clearly error. Accordingly, the trial court's decree must be reversed."

Similar to the circumstances in Wilson, the original custody award in this case was based upon agreement by the parties with no apparent attempt by the trial court to determine the factual underpinning of the custody agreement. The original decree was then amended on April 5, 1994, based upon another stipulation of the parties and without evidentiary hearing or fact-finding by the trial court. Consequently, the custody issue was not litigated until the September 1994 evidentiary hearing. We agree with the Wilson rationale. In deciding a change of custody motion, if the previous custody placement was based upon the parties' stipulation and not by consideration of the evidence and court made findings, the trial court must consider all relevant evidence, including pre-divorce conduct and activities, in making a considered and appropriate custody decision in the best interests of the children. [**10] Here, evidence of the parties' conduct and activities predating the April 5, 1994 judgment is relevant to the court's evaluation of what is in the children's best interests. Because the prior custody decisions in this case were based on stipulation of the parties, not upon evidence introduced in a contested proceeding and not by considered fact finding of the court, we conclude the trial court should have considered custody-related evidence of factors predating the April 5, 1994 Amended Judgment and Decree. Although the trial court attempted to resolve the custody issue in the children's best interests, it was hampered in that task by not admitting the prior custody-related evidence. We conclude the court's exclusion of that evidence was an abuse of discretion.

Rose v. Rose Revisited: The Court Changes Its Position

June 6, 1989.

■ SANGSTER, J. This case had its origin late in 1984 when the Dissolution Petition was first filed. The temporary custody hearing consumed seven trial days and saw the presentation of an impressive array of expert witnesses. This Court at that time indicated a reluctance to grant custody to the father because of what might be termed an arrogant, overprotective and super critical attitude. However, the mother showed some observable residual effects from her suicide attempt (jumping from an eighth story window) and subsequent medical treatment. This court noted that because of some fear and uncertainty as to the mother's ability to care for an almost two year old child, the father would continue as the primary custodian. The mother, however, was granted extensive and exclusive visitation privileges, something she had been denied since her hospitalization a year previous.

Trial on the dissolution itself covered nine trial days in mid-June of 1985. By stipulation the Court was urged to read all notes and exhibits from the January hearing and authorized to consider them at the June dissolution trial. In return counsel agreed to present only evidence which had not been given in the earlier hearing. In effect, the trial lasted 16 full days. Literally dozens of expert witnesses testified, many being flown in from the East Coast and other distant points.

The Court was persuaded that the father's attitude had not changed but the mother's condition had improved substantially. Accordingly, the mother was granted permanent custody. In the decree, the father was given frequent and liberal visitation rights. In retrospect, this may have had the effect of causing some emotional damage to the child, as will be later pointed out.

The continuing saga of the Rose case resumed in November of 1988, with the mother filing a request to eliminate some of the authorized visitation periods. By January 1989, the father had by affidavit and motion resisted the mother's modification motion and filed for a change of custody to himself.

The motions were heard for 14 trial days in April 1989. Again, a number of expert witnesses testified. In substance, the evidence covered two periods since the decree: a time when the mother lived in an apartment in her parents' home, and later when she found her own residence in Northwest Seattle.

The Court finds that the testimony is overwhelming that there has been a substantial change of circumstances since the 1985 Decree. Whatever the custody arrangements are to be, the visitation schedule must be changed to restrict the out of custody parent's visitation rights. It is obvious that there has been an excess of shifting the child from one parent to the other.

The change in circumstances found here is sufficient to bring the Court back into the arena of a custody decision. Some general conclusions as they apply to the parents and child may be relevant here. The child may have some emotional depression at times, he has suffered some possibility of a lowered growth rate, and may have a problem with proper sexual identification. The mother has undergone some emotional traumas since leaving her parents' home for her own apartment, has at times been too dependent on her child and at other times has given him more independence than may have been necessary. The father has mellowed some in his previous poor attitudes, possibly because of his remarriage, has sometimes exhibited poor judgment during the visitation transfers with his ex-wife and has continued to be somewhat overprotective and reactionary.

Having found that the circumstances have substantially changed, the Court now turns to the difficult decision as to which parent is better suited to be the primary custodian and which would be the least detrimental alternative for the child. While our judicial terminology calls for an "award" of custody, this Court cautions the parties that any grant of custody is not an "award" but a responsibility and an awesome obligation. This child has become an emotional pawn between two well meaning parents. He has suffered damage because they could not trust each other and often resorted to tactics of inflicting emotional pain on the other. Without a shadow of a doubt, both parents have, at times, put the child's best interests aside for their own purposes in "getting back" at the other.

Unfortunately, a decision of this kind must be based upon what one or the other parent has done to demonstrate in some small way their disqualification to be the primary custodian. On the brighter side, both parents have shown their love for the child and for the most part been good parents.

As to the child, Jason, the Court has little concern as to his rate of growth. I assume that will accelerate after a decision in this case, if it is somehow connected to something other than simply being the offspring of small parents who themselves come from a long line of small people. I also assume that his diagnosed depression, unhappiness and mood swings can be improved in time, given a better visitation schedule and more consistency in authority figures.

I do find that Jason is emotionally unstable and depressed beyond that to be expected from a child his age. It appears that this condition resulted in large part from frequent contact with two parents who gave their love in vastly differing ways.

After leaving her parents' home for her own apartment, Ms. Rose's emotional stability suffered. She became inclined toward periods of wide emotional swings. At times she would become enraged. Though this was probably not directed at Jason in a physical sense, he did have to experience it. She sometimes sank into depression, at other times acted more like the child's friend than mother, and then could swing into an aggressive mood. It is apparent that while she lived with her parents and when they later visited at her apartment she was able to keep her moods at a consistent level and react normally. Without their steadying influence she became unstable. I think Jason suffered from this inconsistency as much as from the frequent visitations.

The Court finds that the father was more consistent in his parenting of Jason. While he appeared to retain some of his arrogant, overprotective and super-critical attitudes, he has moderated. He is now somewhat established both in his profession and his new marital life. Above all, he has been a good father to Jason on a consistent basis.

Generally, courts give great weight to the primary custodian in motions to modify custody. It is generally thought that continuity of care, stability and psychological parenthood go hand in hand with the in-custody parent. These factors deserve less weight here, however, because of the frequent visitations and the history of the relationship. There is less continuity to be disturbed, little stability and no single psychological parent.

There would be little point to an extensive discussion of each of the numerous points raised by the parties. Suffice it to say, that I have had the opportunity to listen to tens of thousands of words, view hundreds of pages of exhibits, and sit through three hearings covering about thirty full trial days. While the testimony at the 1985 hearings cannot be considered as directly bearing on this instant custody decision, it does lend an important factor by demonstrating changes and causal relationships. I have had the opportunity to compare now with then and see the changes and growth or regression made by the parents and child.

The Court concludes that Jason's best interests lie with his father as primary custodian. He is more stable and offers Jason the best chance to make progress toward normalcy.

As mentioned earlier, the frequent and liberal visitation schedule has been a problem not only to Jason but also to his parents as they confront each other. Accordingly, the Court will set visitation as follows: 30 days in the summer with 30 days notice; one weekend a month (5 p.m. Friday until 5 p.m. Sunday); in alternating fashion: 5 p.m. the day before until 5 p.m. the day of Jason's birthday, Thanksgiving and New Years; and each Mother's Day.

Because of the present difference in the income-producing abilities of the parents, there will be no provision for child support. In that these motions were brought on behalf of Jason and in their roles as parents, no costs or attorney fees will be awarded.

NOTE

An excellent overview of modification is Joan G. Wexler, Rethinking the Modification of Child Custody Decrees, 94 Yale L.J. 757 (1985). In addition to summarizing social science data that suggest custody modifications can be damaging to the emotional needs of the children, Professor Wexler raises constitutional objections to most custody modifications:

> First, the justification for the state's initial intrusion—that the parents could not agree on custody—no longer applies. No decision is being thrust upon the courts; custody has already been allocated, and the matter between the two parents no longer stands in equilibrium. The state may not, simply because a divorce once took place, rely upon a "shattered family" rationale forever to justify its intervention and continuing jurisdiction over the new family unit. . . . The implications of a rule that authorizes the state to have continuing jurisdiction over [the estimated one third of this nation's children who will during their minority experience the divorce of their parents] based on a change of circumstances or best interests standard are Orwellian. Under the traditional standard of custody modification, the behavior of the custodial parent is examined under a microscope, with the noncustodial parent and the family court in the role of Big

> Brother. Has she nurtured her child sufficiently in a manner acceptable to the court? Has she done anything else that in the court's eye constitutes less than acceptable parenting? . . . Any rule of law that puts the government in a position to oversee the most private of matters and sensitive of interests raises serious constitutional questions.

94 Yale L.J. at 817.

2. RELOCATION

Baures v. Lewis

Supreme Court of New Jersey, 2001.
167 N.J. 91, 770 A.2d 214.

■ LONG, J.

Ideally, after a divorce, parents cooperate and remain in close proximity to each other to provide access and succor to their children. But that ideal is not always the reality. In our global economy, relocation for employment purposes is common. On a personal level, people remarry and move away. Noncustodial parents may relocate to pursue other interests regardless of the strength of the bond they have developed with their children. Custodial parents may do so only with the consent of the former spouse. Otherwise, a court application is required.

Inevitably, upon objection by a noncustodial parent, there is a clash between the custodial parent's interest in self-determination and the noncustodial parent's interest in the companionship of the child. There is rarely an easy answer or even an entirely satisfactory one when a noncustodial parent objects. If the removal is denied, the custodial parent may be embittered by the assault on his or her autonomy. If it is granted, the noncustodial parent may live with the abiding belief that his or her connection to the child has been lost forever.

Courts throughout the country, grappling with the issue of relocation, have not developed a uniform approach. Some use a presumption against removal as their point of departure; others use a presumption in favor of removal; still others presume nothing, but rely on a classic best-interests analysis.

We have struggled to accommodate the interests of parents and children in a removal situation in our prior cases. In so doing, we have developed something of a hybrid scheme. Although it is not based upon a presumption in favor of the custodial parent, it does recognize the identity of the interests of the custodial parent and the child, and, as a result, accords particular respect to the custodial parent's right to seek happiness and fulfillment. At the same time, it emphasizes the importance of the noncustodial parent's relationship with the child by guaranteeing regular communication and contact of a nature and quality to sustain that relationship. Further, it incorporates a variation on a best interests analysis by requiring proof that the child will not suffer from the move.

We revisit the issue in this appeal, not only to resolve the matter before us, but because of what we perceive as confusion among the bench, Bar, and litigants over the legal standards that should apply in addressing a removal application, and particularly over what role visitation plays in the calculus.

. . .

Carita Baures (Baures), a native of Wisconsin married Steven Lewis (Lewis), a native of Iowa and an officer in the United States Navy, on October 5, 1985, in Rothschild, Wisconsin. Their only child, Jeremy, was born on June 24, 1990. During the marriage, the couple lived in the various locations in which the Navy billeted them. In 1994, they moved to New Jersey when Lewis was stationed in Leonardo.

At age two, Jeremy began to exhibit developmental difficulties. By 1994, Jeremy, then aged four, was diagnosed with Pervasive Developmental Disorder (PDD), a form of autism. Over the next few years, through trial and error, the parents arranged an effective therapeutic and educational regimen for Jeremy through a combination of public school and the Douglass College Outreach Program.

In 1995, recognizing that their financial resources were being taxed to the limit, Baures and Lewis discussed moving to Wisconsin. Baures' parents live in Wisconsin and are retired school teachers who offered to help care for Jeremy while Baures and Lewis worked. According to both parties, the couple planned to move to Wisconsin after Lewis was discharged from the Navy in 1998. In anticipation of the discharge, Baures' parents sold their home in Schofield, Wisconsin and moved to Galesville because, according to them, it was a short distance to the Chileda Institute (Chileda), a Program for autistic children. Lewis flew to Wisconsin to research job opportunities.

In 1996, escalating marital discord brought the case to court. Lewis sought custody of Jeremy because he believed that Baures was going to remove the child to Wisconsin. One day before the hearing, Baures filed a complaint for divorce alleging extreme cruelty. In response to Lewis's application for custody, Baures denied that she had any intention of moving Jeremy out of New Jersey. The parties then entered into a consent order that provided for custody and visitation and restrained both parties from leaving New Jersey with Jeremy. Baures and Lewis separated in late 1996. In April 1997, Baures filed an amended complaint for divorce requesting permission to relocate to Wisconsin. A three-day trial was held to resolve the issue.

At trial, Baures claimed that she should be allowed to relocate to Wisconsin because the parties had limited funds and could no longer afford to live in New Jersey without the help of her parents. Without a vehicle (Lewis had taken the family car), Baures had no way to get Jeremy to his special programming or to his doctors. Moreover, because Jeremy is a child with special needs, he could not be admitted to regular day care. Baures testified that in Wisconsin, her parents would be able to provide child care and shelter for her and Jeremy so that she could work.

. . .

The trial court denied the removal. Although acknowledging that Baures had a good faith reason to move (financial and emotional stability and caregiving by her parents), the court held that the move would adversely affect Lewis' visitation with Jeremy; that Lewis could not visit regularly or relocate because of his Navy service; and that he does not have the financial resources to travel back and forth to Wisconsin. Further, the court held that Baures had not provided sufficient evidence that the educational opportunities for Jeremy in Wisconsin are comparable to that which he was receiving in New Jersey. Accordingly, the court held it was not in Jeremy's "best interests" to move to Wisconsin.

After being denied permission to remove Jeremy from New Jersey, Baures moved for reconsideration.

. . .

[After hearing additional evidence], the trial court affirmed its denial of Baures' motion. In so doing, the court stated that Baures was required to prove "the prospective advantages" of the move and that she had failed to do so. The court reaffirmed the conclusion that Baures' motion was made in good faith but noted that Jeremy is doing well in New Jersey; that the proximity of both parents is important to a special needs' child; and that there was insufficient evidence adduced to show that Lewis could obtain employment in Wisconsin at a location near Jeremy. Most importantly, in denying removal, the court relied on the fact that Baures did not provide adequate evidence of the comparability of educational and therapeutic facilities available to Jeremy in Wisconsin.

The Appellate Division affirmed the ruling in an unpublished decision. We granted certification.

. . .

Historically, courts throughout the country have disfavored removal of a child from the jurisdiction after divorce. Some courts continue to adhere to that view and apply a presumption against removal based on the notion that it will necessarily destroy the relationship between the noncustodial parent and the child.

Recently, however, many courts have reassessed the burden cast on custodial parents who desire to relocate with their children. Reasons for the change include the geographic mobility of the United States population and post-divorce demands. For example, within four years of separation and divorce about one-fourth of mothers with custody move to a new location. In addition, one in five Americans overall changes his or her residence each year.

That the ability to communicate over long distances has been revolutionized during the years since the first removal cases is also undeniable. Computers, technology and competitive long-distance rates, among other things, essentially have changed the way people connect with each other when they are apart.

Most importantly, social science research links a positive outcome for children of divorce with the welfare of the primary custodian and the stability and happiness within that newly formed post-divorce household . . .

The child's quality of life and style of life are provided by the custodial parent. That the interests of the child are closely interwoven with those of the custodial parent is consistent with psychological studies of children of divorced or separated parents. One researcher has concluded that of all factors related to the child's way of coping with loss [of a parent because of divorce or death], the role of the home parent seemed most central. Some years after the divorce or death, the well-being of the child appeared closely related to the well-being of the homeparent.

Other investigators have found that there is an increased emotional dependence on the custodial parent after divorce and that children of all ages "were in trouble" when the home parent-child relationship was affected by stress on the home-parent, such as "loneliness and discouragement." Since that time, social science research has uniformly confirmed the simple principle that, in general, what is good for the custodial parent is good for the child.

To be sure, the research also affirms the importance of a loving and supportive relationship between the noncustodial parent and the child. What it does not confirm is that there is any connection between the duration and frequency of visits and the quality of the relationship of the child and the noncustodial parent ... According to scholars, so long as the child has regular communication and contact with the noncustodial parent that is extensive enough to sustain their relationship, the child's interests are served. In short, a happy, productive, supportive custodial household along with a loving, sustaining relationship with the noncustodial parent are what is necessary to the adjustment of a child of divorce.

As a result of all those factors, many courts have significantly eased the burden on custodial parents in removal cases.

. . .

Those cases embody the growing trend in the law easing restrictions on the custodial parent's right to relocate with the children and recognizing the identity of interest of the custodial parent and child.

. . .

[T]he template for a removal case [is as follows] ... [T]he moving party ultimately bears a two-pronged burden of proving a good faith reason for the move and that the child will not suffer from it. In terms of the burden of going forward, the party seeking to move, who has had an opportunity to contemplate the issues, should initially produce evidence to establish prima facie that (1) there is a good faith reason for the move and (2) that the move will not be inimical to the child's interests. Included within that prima facie case should be a visitation proposal. By prima facie is meant evidence that, if unrebutted, would sustain a judgment in the proponent's favor.

The initial burden of the moving party is not a particularly onerous one. It will be met, for example, by a custodial parent who shows that he is seeking to move closer to a large extended family that can help him raise his child; that the child will have educational, health and leisure opportunities at least equal to that which is available here, and that he has thought out a visitation schedule that will allow the child to maintain his or her relationship with the noncustodial parent. If, for some reason, the custodial parent fails to produce evidence on the issues to which we have referred, the noncustodial parent will have no duty to go forward and a judgment denying removal should be entered.

Once that prima facie case has been adduced, however, the burden of going forward devolves upon the noncustodial parent who must produce evidence opposing the move as either not in good faith or inimical to the child's interest. She might, for example, challenge the move as pretextual and show that the custodial parent's past actions reveal a desire to stymie her relationship with the child, thus bearing on good faith. She might also offer proof that the move will take the child away from a large extended family that is a mainstay in a child's life. Alternatively, she could adduce evidence that educational, avocational or health care available in the new location are inadequate for the child's particular needs. She might also proffer evidence that because of her work schedule, neither relocation nor reasonable visitation is possible, and that those circumstances will cause the child to suffer.... The burden is on the noncustodial parent to produce evidence, not just that visitation will change, but that the change will negatively affect the child.

. . .

It goes without saying that a noncustodial parent who is lackadaisical or sporadic in his or her visitation ordinarily will be unable to prevail in a removal case. That is not by way of retaliation for past inadequacies but because he or she will not be able to show that particularized harm will occur from removal.

After the noncustodial parent has gone forward, the moving party may rest or adduce additional evidence regarding the noncustodial parent's motives, the visitation scheme or any other matter bearing on the application. The trial court must then apply the burden of proof and the standards to which we have previously adverted.

. . .

As we have indicated, in order for Baures to prevail on her removal application the trial judge must be satisfied that she has a good faith reason for the move and that Jeremy will not suffer from it. Because there was confusion at trial over the details of the standard, and because, with the passage of time, the evidence adduced in the earlier proceedings may have changed, we reverse and remand for further proceedings consistent with this opinion.

NOTE

On remand in the *Baures* case, the parties reached a settlement. Mr. Lewis consented to his wife and son's relocation to Wisconsin, and then moved there himself. Conversation with Veronica Davis, counsel for Ms. Baures (November 17, 2005).

Sanford Braver, Ira Ellman, & William Fabricius, Relocation of Children After Divorce and Children's Best Interests: New Evidence and Legal Considerations

17 J. Fam. Psychol. 206 (2003).

. . .

Discussion

Continuing policy debates over the best rules for deciding relocation disputes have been hampered by a lack of direct data on the long-term impact of parental moves on children of divorce. The present study begins to close this information gap. It provides a window into the relative outcomes for children whose parents move more than one hour's drive away from one another after their divorce. It does so by comparing families in which neither parent ever moved away with families, in which either the mother or the father moved with the child, as well as to families in which either parent moved without the child (who remained with the nonmoving parent). We evaluated the young adult child's outcomes on 14 variables representing financial and emotional support from parents, personal distress and adjustment, social relations, substance abuse, and physical health. . . . We acknowledge, of course, that findings from such a sample may misrepresent the long-term effect of relocation in a more general sample of divorced families [since] . . . a college sample is likely to include those who were least negatively affected by relocation.

We find a preponderance of negative effects associated with parental moves by either mother or father, with or without the child, as compared with divorced families in which neither parent moved away. On 11 of the 14 variables, there were significant (or in one case, near significant . . .) differences. As compared with divorced families in which neither parent moved, students from families in which one parent moved received less financial support from their parents [even after correcting for differences in current financial condition], worried more about that support, felt more hostility in their interpersonal relations, suffered more distress related to their parents' divorce, perceived their parents less favorably as sources of emotional support and as role models, believed the quality of their parents' relations with each other to be worse, and rated themselves less favorably on their general physical health, their general life satisfaction, and their personal and emotional adjustment. In some cases, the differences, although significant, are relatively modest. But in other cases they seem substantial. The students whose divorced parents had moved received, on average, considerably less financial help from their parents for their college expenses. They also rated the distant parent (mother or father) considerably less favorably as a source of emotional support, without regard to whether the distance arose from their move away from that parent or from that parent's move away from them.

In the great majority of these relocating families (82%), the move separated the child from the father, because either the mother moved away with the child or the father moved away alone. . . . [T]he effects are remarkably similar in these two cases. The only exceptions are worry about college expenses (where greater deficits are associated with father moving), hostility (where greater deficits are associated with the father moving for girls), and general global health (where greater deficits are associated with the mother moving for girls). The less common cases (18%) in which the child and mother were separated, either because the child moved with the father or the mother moved alone, similarly appear to have deficits compared with the nonmoving group.

. . .

The data also suggest potentially important physical health implications. The children of divorced parents who moved showed less favorable scores on several variables (hostility, parents getting along, inner turmoil and distress, parent support, and current global health) that may suggest future health problems for them.

. . .

Limitations and Interpretation

Although these data are far more on point in evaluating relocation policies than any previously considered by courts, they are of course correlational, not causal. So whereas the data tell us that a variety of poor outcomes are associated with post divorce parental moves, they cannot establish with anything near certainty that the moves are a contributing cause. It is certainly possible, if not likely, for example, that various preexisting (or self-selection) factors are responsible both for the parents' moving and for the child's diminished outcomes. Preexisting factors that could plausibly play this role include a low level of functioning for one or both parents, the inability of one or both parents to put the child's needs ahead of his or her own, and high levels of premove conflict between the parents.

. . .

In the absence of ... longitudinal data, one must consider several alternative explanations for our results: (a) that moving per se tends to be harmful for children, (b) that families with characteristics that are harmful for children also tend to move, or (c) that both (a) and (b) are true.... Note that the data do appear to exclude what might otherwise seem an additional alternative, that divorced parents who are inclined to move away from one another are not, on average, more risky for their children than other divorced families, and that the parental move improves the children's situation. Had this possibility been valid, the moving groups would have had superior outcomes rather than inferior ones found. The final possibility is excluded whether one focuses on parental moves in general or looks separately at moves by custodial parents or noncustodial parents.

That exclusion offers some help to policymakers in this area. General data on average effects cannot decide individual cases, of course. But the data can help the rulemaker, judicial or legislative, because it suggests that courts would be mistaken to assume, in the absence of contrary evidence, that children benefit from moving with their custodial parent to a new location that is distant from their other parent whenever the custodial parent wants to make the move. Putting the point in legal terminology, the burden of persuasion in relocation disputes, on the question of whether the move is in the child's interests, should probably lie with the custodial parent who decides to relocate rather than with the objecting parent. Decisions like Baures v. Lewis (2001) and In re the Marriage of Burgess (1996) reach the opposite conclusion because they appear to accept the proposition that children are aided by any move that their custodial parent believes desirable....

Alternative (c) appears to us the most likely explanation of the data. In any event, it seems more likely than alternative (b) (that selection accounts for all of the poorer outcomes experienced by children whose divorced parents move), because of the repeated associations found, in a variety of contexts, between the amount of time spent with the noncustodial parent and the quality of the parent-adult child relationship ... And it has been found that the less children saw their father while growing up, the less fathers contributed to college expenses [citation omitted] and the less close were the fathers' relationships with their adult children [citations omitted]. Finally, students report that both they and their divorced fathers generally want more time together [citation omitted]. The overall pattern thus seems consistent with a causal model in which custodial parent moves, even those made for good reasons, thwart the long-term relationship with the parent left behind, which in turn will in some respects impair the child.

Ultimately, however, our data cannot establish with certainty that moves cause children substantial harm. They do allow us to say, however, that there is no empirical basis on which to justify a legal presumption that a move by a custodial parent to a destination she plausibly believes will improve her life will necessarily confer benefits on the children she takes with her.

Implications for Application and Public Policy

... [T]he primary tool available to courts that believe that a proposed move is not in the child's interests is the strategic use of a conditional change of custody order. [Such an order order primary custody changed if the custodial parent chooses to relocate, thus creating a deterrent to relocation.] Such orders have disadvantages. They are of no value in restraining moves by noncustodial parents, which appear from our data generally as harmful to the child as custodial parent moves and their use may seem . . . inconsistent with the prevailing view that nonconsensual changes in primary custody are disfavored . . . [unless] needed to protect the child from some demonstrable detriment in the existing custodial arrangement.

. . .

Yet perhaps our data suggest a reconsideration. . . . From the perspective of the child's interests, there may be real value in discouraging moves by custodial parents, at least in cases in which the child enjoys a good relationship with the other parent and the move is not prompted by the need to otherwise remove the child from a detrimental environment.

NOTE

1. In In re the Marriage of LaMusga, 32 Cal.4th 1072, 12 Cal.Rptr.3d 356 88 P.3d 81 (2004), the California Supreme Court held that, contrary to several lower court opinions, its prior decision in In re Marriage of Burgess, 13 Cal.4th 25, 51 Cal. Rptr.2d 444, 913 P.2d 473 (1996), does not establish a presumption that a custodial parent who desires to relocate may do so as long as the request is made in good faith and the move will not be detrimental to the child. The Court said that a judge faced with a relocation request must consider all factors relevant to the best interest of the child, such as the child's interest in the stability and continuity of the custodial arrangement, the distance of the proposed move, the child's age and relationship with both parents, the parents' relationship, and the reasons for the move. The Court remanded to the court of appeals with instructions to affirm the trial court's decision to transfer custody to the father if the mother moved to Ohio. That decision was based on evaluation of the impact of the move on the children's relationship with their father, as well as several other considerations.

2. How might the standard that a court adopts for reviewing a request for relocation affect the parties' negotiation over custody at the time of divorce? If the parties enter into an agreement that establishes the circumstances under which the custodian can relocate, or that prohibits relocation without the non-custodian's consent, what standard of review should the court employ when reviewing a request to enforce the agreement?

G. VISITATION

Uniform Marriage and Divorce Act

SECTION 407. Visitation

(a) A parent not granted custody of the child is entitled to reasonable visitation rights unless the court finds, after a hearing, that visitation would endanger seriously the child's physical, mental, moral, or emotional health.

(b) The court may modify an order granting or denying visitation rights whenever modification would serve the best interest of the child; but the court shall not restrict a parent's visitation rights unless it finds that the visitation would endanger seriously the child's physical, mental, moral, or emotional health.

COMMENT

With two important exceptions, this section states the traditional rule for visitation rights. The general rule implies a "best interest of the child" standard. Although the judge should never compel the noncustodjal parent to visit the child, visitation rights should be arranged to an extent and in a fashion which suits the child's interest rather than the interest of either the custodial or noncustodial parent. The empirical data on post-divorce living arrangements suggests that, if the judge can arrange visitation with a minimum of contest, most parties will eventually reach an accommodation and the bitterness accompanying the divorce will gradually fade. The section does make clear, however, that the judge must hold a hearing and make an extraordinary finding to deprive the noncustodial parent of all visitation rights. To preclude visitation completely, the judge must find that visitation would endanger "seriously the child's physical, mental, moral, or emotional health." These words are intended to mesh with other uniform legislation. See Uniform Juvenile Court Act, Section 47. Although the standard is necessarily somewhat vague, it was deliberately chosen to indicate its stringency when compared to the "best interest" standard traditionally applied to this problem. The special standard was chosen to prevent the denial of visitation to noncustodial parent on the basis of moral judgments about parental behavior which have no relevance to the parent's interest in or capacity to maintain a close and benign relationship to the child. The same onerous standard is applicable when the custodial parent tries to have the noncustodial parent's visitation privileges restricted or eliminated.

Eldridge v. Eldridge

Supreme Court of Tennessee, Eastern Section, at Knoxville, 2001.
42 S.W.3d 82.

■ JANICE M. HOLDER.

We granted review of this child visitation case to determine whether the trial court abused its discretion in ordering unrestricted overnight visitation with the mother. The Court of Appeals held that the trial court had abused its discretion and imposed restrictions prohibiting the presence of the mother's lesbian partner during overnight visitation. We hold that the record does not support a finding of an abuse of discretion. Accordingly, we reverse the judgment of the Court of Appeals.

BACKGROUND

Anthony and Julia Eldridge were divorced in 1992. The couple agreed to joint custody of their minor daughters, Andrea and Taylor, who were ages eight and nine respectively. Two years later, a dispute arose regarding Ms. Eldridge's visitation rights. Ms. Eldridge, who is engaged in a live-in homosexual relationship with Lisa Franklin, moved the court to establish a visitation schedule. In response, Mr. Eldridge moved for sole custody of the children.

In July 1995, the Court awarded sole custody of the children to Mr. Eldridge. The court also appointed a Special Master, Dr. James Granger, Head of the East Tennessee University Division of Child and Adolescent Psychiatry, to counsel the parties and their children and make recommendations to the court regarding visitation. Dr. Granger's written final report and testimony reflected that counseling was unsuccessful. An agreement as to visitation was not reached.

Upon Mr. Eldridge's motion, the trial court appointed a guardian ad litem ("GAL") for both children. The GAL concluded that regular visitation with the mother was essential and recommended regular visitation with standard visitation every other weekend. The first few weekend visitations were recommended to be limited to Saturday morning through Sunday evening and eventually to be extended to Friday through Sunday.

In September 1996, the trial court ordered overnight visitation with Taylor every other Saturday night through Sunday. Eight months later, Ms. Eldridge moved the court to extend Taylor's overnight visitation to include Friday nights, holidays and summer vacation. Ms. Eldridge also moved that another Special Master be appointed. Mr. Eldridge opposed expanding Ms. Eldridge's visitation rights.

In September 1997, the trial court approved an agreement reached by the parties. The agreement provided for a visitation schedule and appointment of Dr. Judy Millington, a counselor at Church Circle Counseling Center, as Special Master. The court's order provided that Dr. Millington's written recommendations were to take effect immediately without further order of the court. Dr. Millington recommended to the court that Ms. Eldridge's overnight visitation be expanded. Various disputes regarding visitation continued.

A hearing was held in October 1998 to resolve the visitation issue. In November 1998, the trial court entered an order adopting Dr. Millington's recommendations and permitting Ms. Eldridge unrestricted overnight visitation with Taylor. The Court of Appeals reversed, finding that the trial court abused its discretion in failing to prohibit Taylor's overnight visitation with Ms. Eldridge while Ms. Franklin was present in the home. One judge dissented. We granted review.

ANALYSIS

. . .

In reviewing the trial court's visitation order for an abuse of discretion, the child's welfare is given "paramount consideration," and "the right of the noncustodial parent to reasonable visitation is clearly favored." Nevertheless, the noncustodial parent's visitation "may be limited, or eliminated, if there is definite evidence that to permit . . . the right would jeopardize the child, in either a physical or moral sense."

Under the abuse of discretion standard, a trial court's ruling "will be upheld so long as reasonable minds can disagree as to propriety of the decision made." *State v. Scott, 33 S.W.3d 746, 752 (Tenn. 2000)*. . . .

Mr. Eldridge challenges the trial court's visitation order on grounds that Ms. Franklin should not be present during Taylor's overnight visitation with Ms. Eldridge. The Court of Appeals held that "the trial court abused its discretion by not prohibiting Ms. Franklin's presence during the court-ordered overnight visitation." To cure this abuse of discretion, it modified the trial court's visitation order by prohibiting Lisa Franklin's presence during Taylor's overnight visitation with her mother.

The Court of Appeals' opinion makes clear that the court did "not rely on the fact that Ms. Eldridge is a lesbian" in modifying the trial court's order. The court fails to state, however, what it did rely upon. The Court of

Appeals did not identify any legal or factual error by the trial court that might constitute an abuse of discretion. It also failed to establish how the ordered modification would cure the trial court's supposed error. The court offered that "the courts of Tennessee commonly place reasonable restrictions on the visitation rights of heterosexual parents who engage in sexual activity with partners with whom they are not married." Mere observation that restrictions have been imposed in past cases does nothing, however, to reveal why the trial court in this case abused its discretion in permitting unrestricted overnight visitation.

The Court of Appeals cited *Dailey v. Dailey, 635 S.W.2d 391 (Tenn. Ct. App. 1982),* as having "addressed the issue raised by Mr. Eldridge." In Dailey, the Court of Appeals upheld the trial court's decision to modify a custody order to shift custody from the mother, a homosexual, to the father. The court also, sua sponte, modified the trial court's visitation order to prohibit the visitation in the home where the mother lived with her lesbian partner or from having the child in the presence of any lesbian partner.

. . .

The record in Dailey established that the noncustodial parent engaged in overt, lascivious, sexual conduct in the presence of her five-year-old, mentally and physically handicapped child. Certainly, this is the type of "definite evidence" that unrestricted visitation "would jeopardize the child, in either a physical or moral sense" that might constitute a finding of an abuse of discretion.

. . .

The Court of Appeals in this case held that "the facts of this case do not rise to the level of harmful behavior displayed by the mother in Dailey." This statement indicates either: (1) that the court held Dailey to be inapplicable; or (2) that the court found at least some conduct by Ms. Eldridge similar to that in Dailey. The court's recitation of the facts shows no conduct by Ms. Eldridge that might arguably be construed as similar to that of the mother in Dailey, and our independent review of the record reveals none. The only similarity between this case and Dailey is that the mother is homosexual. As the Court of Appeals affirmatively stated that it did not rely on Ms. Eldridge's homosexuality in modifying the trial court's order, we can only infer that the Court of Appeals found Dailey to be completely irrelevant to this case. We agree.

The Court of Appeals' failure to state a basis for its decision leaves us little insight as to what facts in the record show the trial court abused its discretion. Our own review of the record shows that Ms. Eldridge and Ms. Franklin offered substantial testimony regarding their relationship and living arrangement. At the time of the hearing, they had been together for nearly five years. They live in the same home but had slept in separate bedrooms for three months prior to the hearing. Ms. Franklin provides all the financial support for the home. Ms. Eldridge is not a lessor of the home. They have a monogamous relationship but have not been sexually intimate in over a year. Ms. Franklin characterized them as "best friends, roommates." They make no expression of "physical emotion or physical contact" when Taylor is in the home. Taylor has her own bedroom in the home. Ms. Franklin testified that she had a good relationship with Taylor.

Mr. Eldridge and his wife, Chantal Eldridge, testified that unrestricted overnight visitation has a deleterious effect on Taylor. Mr. Eldridge testified that allowing Ms. Franklin to be present during overnight visitation would set a bad example for Taylor. He tries to teach Taylor to live by the Bible and that unmarried persons should not cohabit. He also testified that Taylor, based on her own sense of morality, believed that homosexuality and extramarital relationships were wrong. He testified that Taylor does not want Ms. Franklin present during visitation and that Taylor has many questions about Ms. Eldridge's and Ms. Franklin's relationship. Mr. Eldridge did not believe that Taylor would be physically harmed during overnight visitation. He was, however, concerned about her emotional well-being.

Chantal Eldridge testified that Taylor is visibly upset before leaving to spend the night with her mother. She was unsure what produced Taylor's response but opined that Taylor might miss her, Mr. Eldridge, and their children. Ms. Eldridge, however, testified that Taylor refuses to come into her house only until Taylor is certain her father has left. Then, Taylor enters the home and is very comfortable, eating and playing normally. As the time to return to her father approaches, however, Taylor paces, cries, and worries. Taylor makes efforts to hide the fact that she has eaten or enjoyed herself at Ms. Eldridge's home. Larry Davis, Ms. Eldridge's brother-in-law, offered testimony that supported this contention. He stated that during one of his family's visits with Ms. Eldridge, Taylor was playing outside with him and his children and acting normally. In the last hour before Mr. Eldridge came to pick her up, however, Taylor became withdrawn, refused to come outside, and would not associate with anyone in the home.

Dr. Millington testified that Taylor wants to love and please both of her parents. This conflict causes Taylor to lie to her father about having fun while visiting with her mother. Dr. Millington had observed no adverse or detrimental effects on Taylor resulting from overnight visitation with Ms. Eldridge in Ms. Franklin's presence. Dr. Millington stated, however, that Taylor has admitted to being somewhat uncomfortable during overnight visitation in Ms. Franklin's presence. Dr. Millington observed that Taylor's behavior around Ms. Eldridge was very positive and opined that increased visitation would further encourage their relationship.

In her June 30, 1997 report, Dr. Millington suggested that Taylor's overnight visitation every other weekend should be extended from one night to two. Dr. Millington expressed in an addendum to her report that interaction with Lisa appears (from videotapes viewed) to have no deleterious effects on Taylor at present. Does seeing Lisa and Julie together make a difference for the children for the future? . . . Although Taylor most likely will have difficulty with her mother's orientation in the future, I don't know whether it will make a difference having had Lisa there versus not there. Taylor seems comfortable with Lisa now.

In that same document, Dr. Millington opined that "on the continuum the best for Taylor . . . would be to have visitation without Lisa present, because the sexual orientation and modeling behavior issues become less obvious and so less of an issue parent-to-child in the future than it otherwise might be."

In her deposition of June 30, 1997, Dr. Millington stated that although overnight visits generally might be stressful for a child, she was not sure that Ms. Franklin was the source of Taylor's stress. Upon question about what would be the "ideal situation" regarding visitation, she testified that "the very best situation, which would probably be for the girls to see [Ms. Eldridge] just completely by herself, but I don't know how practical that is."

At the October 1998 hearing, Dr. Millington ultimately was noncommittal on the issue of overnight visits.

. . .

The trial court evaluated and resolved this competing testimony and held that overnight visitation without restriction was appropriate. Mr. Eldridge claims on appeal that prohibiting overnight visitation while Ms. Franklin is present is a reasonable way to resolve his concerns and would constitute a minimal inconvenience to Ms. Eldridge. His argument, however, is one to be made in the trial court, not on appeal.

It is not the function of appellate courts to tweak a visitation order in the hopes of achieving a more reasonable result than the trial court. Appellate courts correct errors. When no error in the trial court's ruling is evident from the record, the trial court's ruling must stand. . . . Reversal should not result simply because the appellate court found a "better" resolution.

there must be an error

. . .

As a general proposition, we agree that in an appropriate case a trial court may impose restrictions on a child's overnight visitation in the presence of non-spouses. The procedural posture of the case at bar is markedly different. In this case, the appellate court, in spite of the deference to which the trial court is entitled, has displaced the trial court's ruling and imposed a restriction that was considered and rejected by the trial court. Justification for that action must be found in the record and, preferably, be developed in the appellate court's opinion. We find no justification in this record.

. . .

The record does not show that Taylor is in moral crisis because of Ms. Franklin's presence during overnight visitation. At most, it appears that Taylor, like many children of divorce, is caught in the crossfire of parental acrimony. It is argued as a general proposition of morality that a parent's unwed love interest should not be present during overnight visitation with the child. A trial court's acceptance of that proposition, taking into account all the facts and circumstances, may give rise to a reasonable conclusion that overnight visitation should be restricted. Nevertheless, that proposition does not in all cases foreclose the possibility of the trial court reaching a reasonable alternative conclusion. In the absence of any evidence of harm beyond the mere unsubstantiated predictions of a vying parent, the trial court's ruling in this case cannot be said to be unreasonable. The evidence adduced in this case supports a reasonable conclusion that unrestricted overnight visitation was in Taylor's best interests. Accordingly, on this record, there was no abuse of discretion by the trial court.

NOTE

The Court of Special Appeals of Maryland found that a lower court "abused its discretion" when it denied overnight visitation rights to a gay man. See North v. North, 102 Md.App. 1, 16, 648 A.2d 1025, 1033 (1994). The court reasoned that the lower court imposed a baseless restriction by allowing the father to visit his children only during the day and not at night when there was no evidence in the record that the children would be any more or less likely to witness "'events or functions' espousing a homosexual lifestyle" at any given time period. See id. at 16, 648 A.2d at 1033. The court did not, however, go so far as to say that a gay father should have unrestricted visitation. Rather, it remanded for further proceedings so that an order consistent with the evidence could be generated. See id. at 17, 648 A. 2d 1033.

Zummo v. Zummo

Superior Court of Pennsylvania, 1990.
394 Pa.Super. 30, 574 A.2d 1130.

■ Kelly, J:

In this case we are asked to determine whether an order prohibiting a father from taking his children to religious services "contrary to the Jewish faith" during periods of lawful custody or visitation violated the father's constitutional rights, or constituted an abuse of discretion. We find that, under the facts of the instant case, the father's constitutional rights were violated, the trial court's discretion was abused, and the restriction challenged cannot be sustained. We vacate the restriction imposed.

We are also called upon to determine whether the father may be directed to present the children at Synagogue for Sunday School during his periods of weekend visitation. We affirm this part of the trial court's order.

The facts and procedural history of the case were set forth by the trial court in its opinion as follows:

> Pamela S. Zummo (mother) and David S. Zummo (father) were married on December 17, 1978, separated August 1987, and divorced April 19, 1988. Three children were born of this marriage, namely Adam, age eight; Rachael, age four; and Daniel, age three. Mother was raised a Jew and has actively practiced her faith since childhood. Father was raised Roman Catholic but had attended Catholic services only sporadically. Prior to their marriage, mother and father discussed their religious differences and agreed that any children would be raised in the Jewish faith.
>
> During the marriage, the Zummo family participated fully in the life of the Jewish faith and community. They became members of the Norristown Community Jewish Center in 1983, celebrated Sabbath every Friday night and attended all of the high holiday services as well. In addition, mother and father participated in a social couples' group at their Synagogue and joined B'nai B'rith. All three of the children were formally given Hebrew names.
>
> Before the parties separated, the children attended no religious services outside the Jewish faith. Adam will begin preparing for his Bar Mitzvah this fall. Customary instruction would require attendance at two classes each week after school, participation in Saturday services and attendance at Sunday School. This training will culminate in Adam's Bar Mitzvah at age thirteen. Rachael will begin her formal Jewish education and training this fall at Sunday School.
>
> Since separation, father has refused to arrange for Adam's attendance to Sunday School while exercising visitation rights on alternate weekends. Father also wishes to take the children to *occasional* Roman Catholic services as he sees fit. Father suggests the children would benefit from a bi-cultural upbringing and should therefore be exposed to the religion of each parent. Mother opposes visitation by father to the extent it disrupts the formal Jewish training of the children. She further opposes exposing the children to a second religion which would confuse and disorient them. Mother filed a divorce complaint on July 6, 1987, which included a count seeking confirmation of her custody of the children. The parties have since agreed to share legal custody. They have also agreed that Mother should have primary physical custody subject so

father's partial physical custody on alternating weekends, as well as certain holidays and vacation periods. To this end, the parties submitted a Stipulation and Agreement setting forth the nature and timing of father's partial physical custody. By virtue of the agreement, the hearing and this Court's Order concerned itself only with the issues of to what extent father should be obligated to see to the attendance of the children at Jewish services during his visitation periods and whether father should be permitted to take the children to Roman Catholic services to the extent he attends on his visitation weekends. Subsequent to hearing, it was determined that Adam's Saturday classes could be made up during the week so as not to interfere with father's visitation....

. . .

The trial court applied the best interests standard to the facts presented, and concluded that restrictions upon the father's right to expose his children to his religious beliefs were permissible and appropriate. ...

Pro–Divorce Religious Training Agreements

. . .

[The court held that the agreement between the parents regarding the children's religious training was unenforceable] ... We note that the authorities establish several persuasive grounds upon which to deny legal effect to such agreements:

1) such agreements are generally too vague to demonstrate a meeting of minds, or to provide an adequate basis for objective enforcement;
2) enforcement of such an agreement would promote a particular religion, serve little or no secular purpose, and would excessively entangle the courts in religious matters; and,
3) enforcement would be contrary to a public policy embodied in the First Establishment and Free Exercise Clauses (as well as their state equivalents) that parents be free to doubt, question, and change their beliefs, and that they be free to instruct their children in accordance with those beliefs.

. . .

Perceived Probability of Harmful Effects From Exposure to "Inconsistent" Religions

The trial court's principal justification [for prohibiting the father from taking the children to Catholic services] was the perceived risk of harm to the children arising from their exposure to Catholicism. The trial court concluded that, "to expose the children to a competing religion after so assiduously grounding them in the tenets of Judaism would unfairly confuse and disorient them and quite possibly vitiate the benefits flowing from either religion."

The vast majority of courts addressing this issue, ... have concluded that each parent must be free to provide religious exposure and instruction, as that parent sees fit, during any and all period of legal custody or visitation without restriction, unless the challenged beliefs or conduct of the parent are demonstrated to present a substantial threat of present or future, physical or emotional harm to the child in absence of the proposed restriction. We find the reasoning expressed in these cases to be persuasive, and adopt the standard stated above as applicable in this Commonwealth.

Applying this standard, courts have rejected speculation by parents and by experts as to potential future emotional harm to a *particular* child based upon the assumption that such exposure is *generally* harmful. Likewise, parental attributions of current child disturbances or distress as the result of a religious conflict, rather than the divorce generally or other causes, have similarly been rejected.

. . .

We hold that in order to justify restrictions upon parent's rights to inculcate religious beliefs in their children, the party seeking the restriction must demonstrate by competent evidence that the belief or practice of the party to be restricted actually presents a substantial threat of present or future physical or emotional harm to the particular child or children involved in absence of the proposed restriction, and that the restriction is the least intrusive means adequate to prevent the specified harm. Because the evidence presented in this case was wholly insufficient to meet this standard, Clause 6 of the Order of May 6. 1988, forbidding the father to take his children to religious services "contrary to the Jewish faith," must be vacated.

Obligations to Take Children to Religious Services

The trial court found "little if any" distinction between prohibiting the father's affirmative act of taking his children to Catholic services and its direction that the father present the children at the Synagogue for Sunday School. We, on the other hand, find a material and controlling distinction; and consequently, affirm that part of the order requiring the father to present his children at the Synagogue for Sunday School.

Both parents have rights to inculcate religious beliefs in their children. Accordingly, the trial court may constitutionally accommodate the mother's rights with a directive of the type imposed here, which essentially carves out a time period each Sunday during which the mother has the right to custody and control of the children.

. . .

While such provisions generally may be affirmed if they do not otherwise restrict the inculcation of religious beliefs, doubts, or disbeliefs by either parent, we emphasize the constitutional prerequisite of "benign neutrality" towards *both* parent's religious viewpoints. If, for example, the court entered an order which granted a Christian parent custody or visitation on all Christian holy days, but denied similar custody or visitation to the other parent on his or her Jewish holy days (without an adequate basis to encroach on the parent's right to expose the child to that parent's religious viewpoint as described supra), such a provision might constitute an impermissible restriction on religious and parental rights, and a violation of the Establishment Clause, albeit an indirect one.

On the other hand, a parent's right to inculcate religious beliefs in his or her child would not provide a compelling reason to justify the denial of the other parent's right to maintain a meaningful parental relationship with his or her children. If the court must choose between meaningful visitation and the full benefits of a desired program of religious indoctrination, the religious indoctrination must yield to the greater interest in preserving the parent-child relationship.

Here, despite the father's argument to the contrary, we find that adequate accommodation of the father's visitation right was made. The

Saturday religion classes desired by the mother will be made up on weeknights. Moreover, the mother has indicated willingness to allow the father reasonable weeknight visitation to compensate for the portion of Sunday taken up by the mother's chosen religious indoctrination for her children. The mother's cooperation on this point is noteworthy and commendable.

We find Clause 5 of the order directing the father to present the children at Synagogue for Sunday School to be severable and distinguishable from Clause 6 which forbids the father to take the children to religious services contrary to the Jewish faith. We affirm Clause 5 of the order.

Troxel v. Granville

Supreme Court of the United States, 2000.
530 U.S. 57, 120 S.Ct. 2054, 147 L.Ed.2d 49.

■ O'CONNOR, J., announced the judgment of the Court and delivered an opinion, in which THE CHIEF JUSTICE, JUSTICE GINSBURG, and JUSTICE BREYER join.

Section 26.10.160(3) of the Revised Code of Washington permits "any person" to petition a superior court for visitation rights "at any time," and authorizes that court to grant such visitation rights whenever "visitation may serve the best interest of the child." Petitioners Jenifer and Gary Troxel petitioned a Washington Superior Court for the right to visit their grandchildren, Isabelle and Natalie Troxel. Respondent Tommie Granville, the mother of Isabelle and Natalie, opposed the petition. The case ultimately reached the Washington Supreme Court, which held that § 26.10.160(3) unconstitutionally interferes with the fundamental right of parents to rear their children.

. . .

Tommie Granville and Brad Troxel shared a relationship that ended in June 1991. The two never married, but they had two daughters, Isabelle and Natalie. Jenifer and Gary Troxel are Brad's parents, and thus the paternal grandparents of Isabelle and Natalie. After Tommie and Brad separated in 1991, Brad lived with his parents and regularly brought his daughters to his parents' home for weekend visitation. Brad committed suicide in May 1993. Although the Troxels at first continued to see Isabelle and Natalie on a regular basis after their son's death, Tommie Granville informed the Troxels in October 1993 that she wished to limit their visitation with her daughters to one short visit per month.

In December 1993, the Troxels commenced the present action by filing, in the Washington Superior Court for Skagit County, a petition to obtain visitation rights with Isabelle and Natalie. The Troxels filed their petition under two Washington statutes, Wash. Rev. Code §§ 26.09.240 and 26.10.160(3) (1994). Only the latter statute is at issue in this case. Section 26.10.160(3) provides: "Any person may petition the court for visitation rights at any time including, but not limited to, custody proceedings. The court may order visitation rights for any person when visitation may serve the best interest of the child whether or not there has been any change of circumstances." At trial, the Troxels requested two weekends of overnight visitation per month and two weeks of visitation each summer. Granville did not oppose visitation altogether, but instead asked the court to order one day of visitation per month with no overnight stay. In 1995, the Superior Court issued an oral ruling and entered a visitation decree ordering visitation one weekend per month, one week during the summer, and four hours on both of the petitioning grandparents' birthdays.

Granville appealed, during which time she married Kelly Wynn. Before addressing the merits of Granville's appeal, the Washington Court of Appeals remanded the case to the Superior Court for entry of written findings of fact and conclusions of law. On remand, the Superior Court found that visitation was in Isabelle and Natalie's best interests:

"The Petitioners [the Troxels] are part of a large, central, loving family, all located in thisarea, and the Petitioners can provide opportunities for the children in the areas of cousins and music.

". . . The court took into consideration all factors regarding the best interest of the children and considered all the testimony before it. The children would be benefitted from spending quality time with the Petitioners, provided that that time is balanced with time with the childrens' [sic] nuclear family. The court finds that the childrens' [sic] best interests are served by spending time with their mother and stepfather's other six children." App. 70a.

Approximately nine months after the Superior Court entered its order on remand, Granville's husband formally adopted Isabelle and Natalie.

The Washington Court of Appeals reversed the lower court's visitation order and dismissed the Troxels' petition for visitation, holding that nonparents lack standing to seek visitation under § 26.10.160(3) unless a custody action is pending. In the Court of Appeals' view, that limitation on nonparental visitation actions was "consistent with the constitutional restrictions on state interference with parents' fundamental liberty interest in the care, custody, and management of their children." . . .

The Washington Supreme Court granted the Troxels' petition for review and, after consolidating their case with two other visitation cases, affirmed. The court disagreed with the Court of Appeals' decision on the statutory issue and found that the plain language of § 26.10.160(3) gave the Troxels standing to seek visitation, irrespective of whether a custody action was pending. The Washington Supreme Court nevertheless agreed with the Court of Appeals' ultimate conclusion that the Troxels could not obtain visitation of Isabelle and Natalie pursuant to § 26.10.160(3). The court rested its decision on the Federal Constitution, holding that § 26.10.160(3) unconstitutionally infringes on the fundamental right of parents to rear their children. In the court's view, there were at least two problems with the nonparental visitation statute. First, according to the Washington Supreme Court, the Constitution permits a State to interfere with the right of parents to rear their children only to prevent harm or potential harm to a child. Section 26.10.160(3) fails that standard because it requires no threshold showing of harm. Second, by allowing " 'any person' to petition for forced visitation of a child at 'any time' with the only requirement being that the visitation serve the best interest of the child," the Washington visitation statute sweeps too broadly. Id. at 20, 969 P.2d at 30. "It is not within the province of the state to make significant decisions concerning the custody of children merely because it could make a 'better' decision." Ibid., 969 P.2d at 31. The Washington Supreme Court held that "parents have a right to limit visitation of their children with third persons," and that between parents and judges, "the parents should be the ones to choose whether to expose their children to certain people or ideas." Four justices dissented from the Washington Supreme Court's holding on the constitutionality of the statute.

We granted certiorari, 527 U.S. 1069 (1999), and now affirm the judgment.

. . .

The liberty interest at issue in this case—the interest of parents in the care, custody, and control of their children—is perhaps the oldest of the fundamental liberty interests recognized by this Court.

. . .

In subsequent cases also, we have recognized the fundamental right of parents to make decisions concerning the care, custody, and control of their children.

. . .

Section 26.10.160(3), as applied to Granville and her family in this case, unconstitutionally infringes on that fundamental parental right. The Washington nonparental visitation statute is breathtakingly broad. According to the statute's text, "any person may petition the court for visitation rights at any time," and the court may grant such visitation rights whenever "visitation may serve the best interest of the child." § 26.10.160(3) (emphases added). That language effectively permits any third party seeking visitation to subject any decision by a parent concerning visitation of the parent's children to state-court review. Once the visitation petition has been filed in court and the matter is placed before a judge, a parent's decision that visitation would not be in the child's best interest is accorded no deference. Section 26.10.160(3) contains no requirement that a court accord the parent's decision any presumption of validity or any weight whatsoever. Instead, the Washington statute places the best-interest determination solely in the hands of the judge. Should the judge disagree with the parent's estimation of the child's best interests, the judge's view necessarily prevails. Thus, in practical effect, in the State of Washington a court can disregard and overturn any decision by a fit custodial parent concerning visitation whenever a third party affected by the decision files a visitation petition, based solely on the judge's determination of the child's best interests.

. . .

The problem here is not that the Washington Superior Court intervened, but that when it did so, it gave no special weight at all to Granville's determination of her daughters' best interests.

. . .

The judge's comments suggest that he presumed the grandparents' request should be granted unless the children would be "impacted adversely." In effect, the judge placed on Granville, the fit custodial parent, the burden of disproving that visitation would be in the best interest of her daughters. The judge reiterated moments later: "I think [visitation with the Troxels] would be in the best interest of the children and I haven't been shown it is not in [the] best interest of the children." Id. at 214.

The decisional framework employed by the Superior Court directly contravened the traditional presumption that a fit parent will act in the best interest of his or her child. See Parham, supra, at 602. In that respect, the court's presumption failed to provide any protection for Granville's fundamental constitutional right to make decisions concerning the rearing of her own daughters.

. . .

In an ideal world, parents might always seek to cultivate the bonds between grandparents and their grandchildren. Needless to say, however, our world is far from perfect, and in it the decision whether such an intergenerational relationship would be beneficial in any specific case is for the parent to make in the first instance. And, if a fit parent's decision of the kind at issue here becomes subject to judicial review, the court must accord at least some special weight to the parent's own determination.

. . .

Because we rest our decision on the sweeping breadth of § 26.10.160(3) and the application of that broad, unlimited power in this case, we do not consider the primary constitutional question passed on by the Washington Supreme Court—whether the Due Process Clause requires all nonparental visitation statutes to include a showing of harm or potential harm to the child as a condition precedent to granting visitation. We do not, and need not, define today the precise scope of the parental due process right in the visitation context.

. . .

■ Souter, J., concurring in the judgment.

I concur in the judgment affirming the decision of the Supreme Court of Washington, whose facial invalidation of its own state statute is consistent with this Court's prior cases addressing the substantive interests at stake. I would say no more. The issues that might well be presented by reviewing a decision addressing the specific application of the state statute by the trial court, are not before us and do not call for turning any fresh furrows in the "treacherous field" of substantive due process.

The Supreme Court of Washington invalidated its state statute based on the text of the statute alone, not its application to any particular case. Its ruling rested on two independently sufficient grounds: the failure of the statute to require harm to the child to justify a disputed visitation order, and the statute's authorization of "any person" at "any time" to petition and to receive visitation rights subject only to a free-ranging best-interests-of-the-child standard. I see no error in the second reason, that because the state statute authorizes any person at any time to request (and a judge to award) visitation rights, subject only to the State's particular best-interests standard, the state statute sweeps too broadly and is unconstitutional on its face. Consequently, there is no need to decide whether harm is required or to consider the precise scope of the parent's right or its necessary protections.

■ Thomas, J., concurring in the judgment.

I write separately to note that neither party has argued that our substantive due process cases were wrongly decided and that the original understanding of the Due Process Clause precludes judicial enforcement of unenumerated rights under that constitutional provision. As a result, I express no view on the merits of this matter, and I understand the plurality as well to leave the resolution of that issue for another day.

■ Stevens, J., dissenting.

The Court today wisely declines to endorse either the holding or the reasoning of the Supreme Court of Washington. In my opinion, the Court would have been even wiser to deny certiorari. Given the problematic character of the trial court's decision and the uniqueness of the Washington statute, there was no pressing need to review a State Supreme Court decision that merely requires the state legislature to draft a better statute.

Having decided to address the merits, however, the Court should begin by recognizing that the State Supreme Court rendered a federal constitutional judgment holding a state law invalid on its face. In light of that judgment, I believe that we should confront the federal questions presented directly. For the Washington statute is not made facially invalid either because it may be invoked by too many hypothetical plaintiffs, or because it leaves open the possibility that someone may be permitted to sustain a relationship with a child without having to prove that serious harm to the child would otherwise result.

. . .

The second key aspect of the Washington Supreme Court's holding—that the Federal Constitution requires a showing of actual or potential "harm" to the child before a court may order visitation continued over a parent's objections—finds no support in this Court's case law. While, as the Court recognizes, the Federal Constitution certainly protects the parent-child relationship from arbitrary impairment by the State, we have never held that the parent's liberty interest in this relationship is so inflexible as to establish a rigid constitutional shield, protecting every arbitrary parental decision from any challenge absent a threshold finding of harm. The presumption that parental decisions generally serve the best interests of their children is sound, and clearly in the normal case the parent's interest is paramount. But even a fit parent is capable of treating a child like a mere possession.

. . .

Cases like this do not present a bipolar struggle between the parents and the State over who has final authority to determine what is in a child's best interests. There is at a minimum a third individual, whose interests are implicated in every case to which the statute applies—the child.

It has become standard practice in our substantive due process jurisprudence to begin our analysis with an identification of the "fundamental" liberty interests implicated by the challenged state action. My colleagues are of course correct to recognize that the right of a parent to maintain a relationship with his or her child is among the interests included most often in the constellation of liberties protected through the Fourteenth Amendment. Our cases leave no doubt that parents have a fundamental liberty interest in caring for and guiding their children, and a corresponding privacy interest—absent exceptional circumstances—in doing so without the undue interference of strangers to them and to their child.

Despite this Court's repeated recognition of these significant parental liberty interests, these interests have never been seen to be without limits. In Lehr v. Robertson, 463 U.S. 248, 77 L. Ed. 2d 614, 103 S.Ct. 2985 (1983), for example, this Court held that a putative biological father who had never established an actual relationship with his child did not have a constitutional right to notice of his child's adoption by the man who had married the child's mother. As this Court had recognized in an earlier case, a parent's liberty interests " 'do not spring full-blown from the biological connection between parent and child. They require relationships more enduring.' "

. . .

A parent's rights with respect to her child have thus never been regarded as absolute, but rather are limited by the existence of an actual, developed relationship with a child, and are tied to the presence or absence of some embodiment of family. These limitations have arisen, not simply out of the definition of parenthood itself, but because of this Court's assumption that a parent's interests in a child must be balanced against the State's long-recognized interests as parens patriae.

While this Court has not yet had occasion to elucidate the nature of a child's liberty interests in preserving established familial or family-like bonds, it seems to me extremely likely that, to the extent parents and families have fundamental liberty interests in preserving such intimate relationships, so, too, do children have these interests, and so, too, must their interests be balanced in the equation ... The constitutional protection against arbitrary state interference with parental rights should not be extended to prevent the States from protecting children against the arbitrary exercise of parental authority that is not in fact motivated by an interest in the welfare of the child.

. . .

This is not, of course, to suggest that a child's liberty interest in maintaining contact with a particular individual is to be treated invariably as on a par with that child's parents' contrary interests. Because our substantive due process case law includes a strong presumption that a parent will act in the best interest of her child, it would be necessary, were the state appellate courts actually to confront a challenge to the statute as applied, to consider whether the trial court's assessment of the "best interest of the child" incorporated that presumption.

But presumptions notwithstanding, we should recognize that there may be circumstances in which a child has a stronger interest at stake than mere protection from serious harm caused by the termination of visitation by a "person" other than a parent. The almost infinite variety of family relationships that pervade our ever-changing society strongly counsel against the creation by this Court of a constitutional rule that treats a biological parent's liberty interest in the care and supervision of her child as an isolated right that may be exercised arbitrarily. It is indisputably the business of the States, rather than a federal court employing a national standard, to assess in the first instance the relative importance of the conflicting interests that give rise to disputes such as this. Far from guaranteeing that parents' interests will be trammeled in the sweep of cases arising under the statute, the Washington law merely gives an individual—with whom a child may have an established relationship—the procedural right to ask the State to act as arbiter, through the entirely well-known best-interests standard, between the parent's protected interests and the child's. It seems clear to me that the Due Process Clause of the Fourteenth Amendment leaves room for States to consider the impact on a child of possibly arbitrary parental decisions that neither serve nor are motivated by the best interests of the child.

. . .

■ SCALIA, J., dissenting.

In my view, a right of parents to direct the upbringing of their children is among the "unalienable Rights" with which the Declaration of Independence proclaims "all Men ... are endowed by their Creator." And in my view that right is also among the "other [rights] retained by the people" which the Ninth Amendment says the Constitution's enumeration of rights "shall not be construed to deny or disparage." The Declaration of Independence, however, is not a legal prescription conferring powers upon the courts; and the Constitution's refusal to "deny or disparage" other rights is far removed from affirming any one of them, and even farther removed from authorizing judges to identify what they might be, and to enforce the judges' list against laws duly enacted by the people. Consequently, while I would think it entirely compatible with the commitment to representative democracy set forth in the founding documents to argue, in legislative chambers or in electoral campaigns, that the state has *no power* to interfere with parents' authority over the rearing of their children, I do not believe that the power which the Constitution confers upon me *as a judge* entitles me to deny legal effect to laws that (in my view) infringe upon what is (in my view) that unenumerated right.

Only three holdings of this Court rest in whole or in part upon a substantive constitutional right of parents to direct the upbringing of their children—two of them from an era rich in substantive due process holdings that have since been repudiated. See *Meyer v. Nebraska, 262 U.S. 390, 399 (1923); Pierce v. Society of Sisters, 268 U.S. 510, 534–535(1925); Wisconsin v. Yoder, 406 U.S. 205, 232–233 (1972).* The sheer diversity of today's opinions persuades me that the theory of unenumerated parental rights underlying these three cases has small claim to *stare decisis* protection. A legal principle that can be thought to produce such diverse outcomes in the relatively simple case before us here is not a legal principle that has induced substantial reliance. While I would not now overrule those earlier cases (that has not been urged), neither would I extend the theory upon which they rested to this new context.

Judicial vindication of "parental rights" under a Constitution that does not even mention them requires (as JUSTICE KENNEDY's opinion rightly points out) not only a judicially crafted definition of parents, but also—unless, as no one believes, the parental rights are to be absolute—judicially approved assessments of "harm to the child" and judicially defined gradations of other persons (grandparents, extended family, adoptive family in an adoption later found to be invalid, long-term guardians, etc.) who may have some claim against the wishes of the parents. If we embrace this unenumerated right, I think it obvious—whether we affirm or reverse the judgment here, or remand as JUSTICE STEVENS or JUSTICE KENNEDY would do—that we will be ushering in a new regime of judicially prescribed, and federally prescribed, family law. I have no reason to believe that federal judges will be better at this than state legislatures; and state legislatures have the great advantages of doing harm in a more circumscribed area, of being able to correct their mistakes in a flash, and of being removable by the people.

For these reasons, I would reverse the judgment below.

■ Kennedy, J., dissenting.

The Supreme Court of Washington has determined that petitioners Jenifer and Gary Troxel have standing under state law to seek court-ordered visitation with their grandchildren, notwithstanding the objections of the children's parent, respondent Tommie Granville.

. . .

After acknowledging this statutory right to sue for visitation, the State Supreme Court invalidated the statute as violative of the United States Constitution, because it interfered with a parent's right to raise his or her child free from unwarranted interference. Although parts of the court's decision may be open to differing interpretations, it seems to be agreed that the court invalidated the statute on its face, ruling it a nullity.

The first flaw the State Supreme Court found in the statute is that it allows an award of visitation to a non-parent without a finding that harm to the child would result if visitation were withheld; and the second is that the statute allows any person to seek visitation at any time. In my view the first theory is too broad to be correct, as it appears to contemplate that the best interests of the child standard may not be applied in any visitation case. I acknowledge the distinct possibility that visitation cases may arise where, considering the absence of other protection for the parent under state laws and procedures, the best interests of the child standard would give insufficient protection to the parent's constitutional right to raise the child without undue intervention by the state; but it is quite a different matter to say, as I understand the Supreme Court of Washington to have said, that a harm to the child standard is required in every instance.

Given the error I see in the State Supreme Court's central conclusion that the best interests of the child standard is never appropriate in third-party visitation cases, that court should have the first opportunity to reconsider this case. I would remand the case to the state court for further proceedings. If it then found the statute has been applied in an unconstitutional manner because the best interests of the child standard gives insufficient protection to a parent under the circumstances of this case, or if it again declared the statute a nullity because the statute seems to allow any person at all to seek visitation at any time, the decision would present other issues which may or may not warrant further review in this Court. These include not only the protection the Constitution gives parents against state-ordered visitation but also the extent to which federal rules for facial challenges to statutes control in state courts. These matters, however, should await some further case. The judgment now under review should be vacated and remanded on the sole ground that the harm ruling that was so central to the Supreme Court of Washington's decision was error, given its broad formulation.

Turning to the question whether harm to the child must be the controlling standard in every visitation proceeding, there is a beginning point that commands general, perhaps unanimous, agreement in our separate opinions: As our case law has developed, the custodial parent has a constitutional right to determine, without undue interference by the state, how best to raise, nurture, and educate the child. The parental right stems from the liberty protected by the Due Process Clause of the Fourteenth Amendment. . . .

The State Supreme Court sought to give content to the parent's right by announcing a categorical rule that third parties who seek visitation must always prove the denial of visitation would harm the child. . . .

While it might be argued as an abstract matter that in some sense the child is always harmed if his or her best interests are not considered, the law of domestic relations, as it has evolved to this point, treats as distinct the two standards, one harm to the child and the other the best interests of the child. The judgment of the Supreme Court of Washington rests on that assumption, and I, too, shall assume that there are real and consequential differences between the two standards.

On the question whether one standard must always take precedence over the other in order to protect the right of the parent or parents, "our Nation's history, legal traditions, and practices" do not give us clear or definitive answers. *Washington v. Glucksberg, 521 U.S. 702, 721 (1997).* The consensus among courts and commentators is that at least through the 19th century there was no legal right of visitation; court-ordered visitation appears to be a 20th-century phenomenon. . . .

To say that third parties have had no historical right to petition for visitation does not necessarily imply, as the Supreme Court of Washington concluded, that a parent has a constitutional right to prevent visitation in all cases not involving harm ... The State Supreme Court's conclusion that the Constitution forbids the application of the best interests of the child standard in any visitation proceeding, however, appears to rest upon assumptions the Constitution does not require.

My principal concern is that the holding seems to proceed from the assumption that the parent or parents who resist visitation have always been the child's primary caregivers and that the third parties who seek visitation have no legitimate and established relationship with the child. That idea, in turn, appears influenced by the concept that the conventional nuclear family ought to establish the visitation standard for every domestic relations case. As we all know, this is simply not the structure or prevailing condition in many households. For many boys and girls a traditional family with two or even one permanent and caring parent is simply not the reality of their childhood. This may be so whether their childhood has been marked by tragedy or filled with considerable happiness and fulfillment.

Cases are sure to arise—perhaps a substantial number of cases—in which a third party, by acting in a caregiving role over a significant period of time, has developed a relationship with a child which is not necessarily subject to absolute parental veto. Some pre-existing relationships, then, serve to identify persons who have a strong attachment to the child with the concomitant motivation to act in a responsible way to ensure the child's welfare. As the State Supreme Court was correct to acknowledge, those relationships can be so enduring that "in certain circumstances where a child has enjoyed a substantial relationship with a third person, arbitrarily depriving the child of the relationship could cause severe psychological harm to the child," and harm to the adult may also ensue. In the design and elaboration of their visitation laws, States may be entitled to consider that certain relationships are such that to avoid the risk of harm, a best interests standard can be employed by their domestic relations courts in some circumstances.

. . .

In light of the inconclusive historical record and case law, as well as the almost universal adoption of the best interests standard for visitation disputes, I would be hard pressed to conclude the right to be free of such review in all cases is itself " 'implicit in the concept of ordered liberty.' " In my view, it would be more appropriate to conclude that the constitutionality of the application of the best interests standard depends on more specific factors. In short, a fit parent's right vis-a-vis a complete stranger is one thing;

her right vis-a-vis another parent or a *de facto* parent may be another. The protection the Constitution requires, then, must be elaborated with care, using the discipline and instruction of the case law system. We must keep in mind that family courts in the 50 States confront these factual variations each day, and are best situated to consider the unpredictable, yet inevitable, issues that arise.

. . .

It should suffice in this case to reverse the holding of the State Supreme Court that the application of the best interests of the child standard is always unconstitutional in third-party visitation cases. Whether, under the circumstances of this case, the order requiring visitation over the objection of this fit parent violated the Constitution ought to be reserved for further proceedings. Because of its sweeping ruling requiring the harm to the child standard, the Supreme Court of Washington did not have the occasion to address the specific visitation order the Troxels obtained. More specific guidance should await a case in which a State's highest court has considered all of the facts in the course of elaborating the protection afforded to parents by the laws of the State and by the Constitution itself. . . .

In my view the judgment under review should be vacated and the case remanded for further proceedings.

NOTE

An analysis of state court decisions construing state grandparent visitation statutes in light of Troxel concludes that courts

> have been ... reluctant to declare these statutes unconstitutional. For the most part ... state courts either have endeavored to interpret their states' statutes to be facially constitutional or have held that specific applications of the statutes failed to meet the Troxel standard. To reach these results, some courts have construed the statutes to be stricter than written. Other courts have emphasized the ways in which their states' laws are distinguishable from the broadly sweeping Washington statute.

Kristine L. Roberts, State Court Applications of Troxel v. Granville and the Courts' Reluctance to Declare Grandparent Visitation Statutes Unconstitutional, 41 Fam. Ct. Rev. 14, 15 (2003) (footnote omitted).

The element of a grandparent visitation scheme most often deemed essential to constitutionality is the presumption that a fit parent's decision concerning visitation is in the best interest of the child. See, e.g., Santi v. Santi, 633 N.W.2d 312 (Iowa 2001); State Department of Social and Rehabilitation Services v. Paillet, 270 Kan. 646, 16 P.3d 962 (2001); Lulay v. Lulay, 193 Ill.2d 455, 250 Ill.Dec. 758, 739 N.E.2d 521 (2000).

H. STEPPARENTS

Kinnard v. Kinnard

Supreme Court of Alaska, 2002.
43 P.3d 150.

■ FABE, CHIEF JUSTICE.

I. INTRODUCTION

This case arises out of the divorce of Bernard and Debra Kinnard. The superior court awarded shared custody of Kristine Kinnard to Bernard, her father, and Debra, her stepmother. Because the trial court did not err in finding that Debra is the psychological parent of Kristine, and that removal of Debra from Kristine's life would be detrimental to the child, we affirm the award of shared custody. We also affirm the trial court's order directing Bernard to either reinstate Debra to his health insurance policy or pay for her surgery out of his share of his pension.

II. FACTS AND PROCEEDINGS

A. Factual History

Bernard and Debra Kinnard were married on October 25, 1993. There were no children born of the marriage. However, during the marriage, Bernard's two children from previous relationships—Brandon, born September 19, 1982, and Kristine, born November 11, 1988—resided with Bernard and Debra. Bernard is a nutritional cook at a hospital and Debra is a licensed foster parent who cares for disabled children. Bernard and Debra separated in November 1999.

. . .

B. Procedural History

When Bernard filed for divorce in January 2000, Debra maintained that she stood *in loco parentis* to both Brandon and Kristine and requested primary physical custody of Brandon and joint physical custody of Kristine. Superior Court Judge Ralph R. Beistline issued a standing order and preliminary injunction for domestic relations actions that restrained the parties from disposing of marital property.

Superior Court Judge Richard D. Savell ordered a custody investigation. The custody investigator quickly determined that Brandon would not be part of the investigation because he would be eighteen years of age before the investigation was complete. The custody investigator ultimately concluded that Debra was the psychological parent of Kristine and recommended that the parties share legal and physical custody of Kristine. The custody investigator recommended that this shared custody consist of alternating weeks with each parent.

Bernard took the position at trial that he should have sole custody and that Debra should have no visitation with Kristine. He claimed that pursuant to the United States Supreme Court's recent decision in *Troxel v. Granville*,[3] Debra bore the burden of proving that Bernard is an unfit parent in order to maintain her claim to custody.

After a three-day trial in December 2000, the trial court found the evidence to be "overwhelming," even "uncontradicted," that Debra holds the place of a mother in Kristine's life. The trial court awarded the parties shared custody

. . .

Bernard appeals the award of shared custody. . . .

. . .

3. 530 U.S. 57 (2000).

III. STANDARD OF REVIEW

. . . We will reverse a trial court's custody determination only if we are convinced that the trial court has abused its discretion or that controlling findings of fact are clearly erroneous.

. . .

IV. DISCUSSION

A. The Finding that Debra Is the Psychological Parent of Kristine Is Not Clearly Erroneous.

The trial court found that Debra had become Kristine's psychological parent. After concluding "that Debra Kinnard holds a place in [Kristine's] life that is of equal or even greater importance than a natural mother," the trial court added that "if this were a contest between two natural parents . . . [Bernard] would be stripped of custody of this child." The trial court further emphasized: "Not only by a preponderance of the evidence, not by clear and convincing evidence, but this court finds beyond any reasonable doubt that removal of Debra Kinnard from [Kristine's] life would be devastating to [her]."

. . .

Many witnesses at trial testified to Debra's status as a psychological parent of Kristine. Kristine had lived with Bernard and Debra from the time that she was in kindergarten, and Bernard admitted that Debra and Kristine "had bonded together" from the beginning of their relationship. Two expert witnesses as well as the custody investigator testified that Debra and Kristine's relationship was that of parent and child; indeed, the custody investigator concluded that Debra was a psychological parent to both Kristine and Brandon. There is ample evidence in the record to support the trial court's finding that Debra was Kristine's psychological parent, and that finding is not clearly erroneous.

B. The Trial Court Applied the Proper Legal Standard.

Bernard maintains that even if Debra is the psychological parent of Kristine, the trial court applied an improper standard to determine custody. Bernard contends that the trial court applied the "best interests" test, when it should have applied the "detrimental to the welfare of the child" test. The former, he argues, only applies when the custody dispute is between two biological parents, while the latter applies when the dispute is between a parent and a third party.

But Bernard appears to have misunderstood the trial court's actions and findings. . . . The trial court explicitly recognized the distinction between the "best interests" and "detriment" standards when it stated that "if this were a contest between two natural parents, and the actions and behaviors of the parties were as they are here, [Bernard] would be stripped of custody of this child." The court then found "beyond any reasonable doubt that removal of Debra Kinnard from [Kristine's] life would be devastating to the child" and "would cause severe and irreparable harm."

We discussed the proper standard for determining custody between a biological parent and a third party in *Turner v. Pannick*.[13] We concluded that parental custody is preferable and only to be refused where "it clearly would

13. 540 P.2d 1051 (Alaska 1975).

be detrimental to the child."[14] The child's biological parent must be awarded custody unless the trial court determines that the parent is unfit, has abandoned the child, or that the welfare of the child requires that a non-parent receive custody. Even in custody disputes between parents and stepparents, the best interests standard is rejected in favor of the *Turner* parental preference. Therefore, the *Turner* standard is the proper standard for this case.

Here, although the trial court did not specifically refer to *Turner*, it did emphasize that removing Debra from Kristine's life altogether would "cause severe and likely irreparable harm" to Kristine. As we recognized in *Buness v. Gillen*, "severing the bond between the psychological parent and the child may well be clearly detrimental to the child's welfare."[16] Thus, the trial court properly examined both the extent of the strong emotional bond between Debra and Kristine and the question of whether severing that bond would be detrimental to Kristine. . . . The trial court thus properly applied the *Turner* standard.

C. The Trial Court's Analysis Does Not Conflict with *Troxel v. Granville*.

Bernard next argues that even if the trial court properly applied the *in loco parentis* doctrine of *Carter* and *Buness*, that doctrine "has been modified" by *Troxel v. Granville*.[17] He explains that "[i]n essence, a portion of *AS 25.24.150(a)* has been found unconstitutional by the United States Supreme Court." In *Troxel*, the Supreme Court ruled that Washington's grandparent visitation statute was unconstitutional as applied. Bernard relies on *Troxel* to challenge the constitutionality of *AS 25.24.150(a)*, which contemplates orders providing "for visitation by a grandparent or other person if that is in the best interests of the child." But *AS 25.24.150(a)* did not form the basis for the trial court's ruling in this case, and, therefore, its constitutionality is not properly before us in this appeal. As noted above, the trial court did not rely on the best interests standard, instead implicitly employing the tests of *Carter v. Brodrick* and *Turner v. Pannick* to determine that Debra is Kristine's psychological parent and that loss of this parent-child bond would have a devastating effect on Kristine. And *Troxel* involved neither a claim of psychological parenthood nor a determination that depriving the child of a psychological parent would negatively affect the welfare of the child. Therefore, the trial court's ruling does not run afoul of the holding in *Troxel*.

. . .

V. CONCLUSION

For the foregoing reasons, the decision of the trial court is AFFIRMED in all respects.

Simons by & Through Simons v. Gisvold

Supreme Court of North Dakota, 1994.
519 N.W.2d 585.

■ SANDSTROM, JUSTICE.

For as long as she could remember, 9-year-old Jessica Simons, her father Bruce, and his wife Debra had lived together as a family. While Bruce

14. Id. at 1054.

16. 781 P.2d 985, 989 n. 8 (Alaska 1989).

17. 530 U.S. 57 (2000).

worked at his job, Debra stayed home and cared for Jessica. In 1993, Bruce died of cancer.

Both Debra Simons, Jessica's "psychological parent," and Joelle Gisvold, Jessica's natural mother, divorced from Bruce shortly after the birth, sought custody. The guardian ad litem recommended Jessica's best interests would be served if she continued to live with Debra.

The district court found the natural mother, although having given up custody of Jessica, had maintained a loving, caring relationship with Jessica. The district court found both the natural mother and the "psychological parent" to be good and decent people: morally fit; able to meet Jessica's physical, emotional and educational needs; and capable and disposed to give her love, affection and guidance.

The district court concluded Joelle Gisvold should be given custody of Jessica because the natural parent has a paramount right to custody when the child would not sustain serious harm or detriment.

Debra Simons appeals, urging, in the exceptional circumstances where there is a "psychological parent," the best interests of the child should prevail, with no preference for a natural parent.

Concluding the district court applied the correct law, we affirm.

I

Jessica was born in July 1983. When Jessica's natural father, Bruce Simons, and Joelle were divorced in May 1984, Bruce was awarded custody of Jessica and Joelle was granted liberal visitation privileges. In 1986, Bruce married Debra, and they resided in Fargo with Jessica until Bruce died from cancer in 1993. Joelle also remarried, and she currently resides with her husband in Galesburg. Bruce left no will or other document expressing his preference as to Jessica's custody after his death.

Joelle filed a motion requesting the district court award her custody of Jessica. Joelle alleged Bruce's death constituted a material change in circumstances and she, as Jessica's natural mother, is entitled to custody of Jessica. Debra responded she is entitled to custody of Jessica because she had become Jessica's psychological parent during the nearly eight years she, Bruce, and Jessica lived together as a family.

In addition to finding both Debra and Joelle to be fit, able and willing to be good parents, the district court made the following findings of fact. Both Debra and Joelle could provide a permanent family unit, and a stable, satisfactory environment. Joelle had exercised her visitation rights and maintained a good relationship with Jessica. Jessica, who had not been asked for nor expressed a preference, expressed love and affection for each, referring to both as "mom." Jessica will not sustain serious harm or detriment to her welfare if she is removed from her home in Fargo and placed in Joelle's custody.

The trial court awarded Joelle custody of Jessica with visitation rights for Debra. Debra then filed this appeal.

. . . In matters of child custody, the district court is vested substantial discretion. On appeal, the district court's custody decision fact finding will not be set aside unless it is clearly erroneous. . . .

II

Parents generally have the right to the custody and companionship of their children superior to that of any other person. This right is not absolute. We recently noted, "parental rights do not spring full-blown from the biological connection between parent and child. They require relationships more enduring." Parental rights may be forfeited because of unfitness or abandonment....

When a psychological parent and a natural parent each seek a court ordered award of custody, the natural parent's paramount right to custody prevails unless the court finds it in the child's best interest to award custody to the psychological parent to prevent serious harm or detriment to the welfare of the child.

The circumstances of this case are distinguishable from those cases where custody has been awarded to a psychological parent, rather than the natural parent. Unlike here, the children in those cases had not established a significant bond or relationship with the natural parent. Also, there was evidence in those cases the children would suffer serious harm or detriment if they were removed from the home of the psychological parent and placed with the natural parent. Here, Jessica has a close relationship and strong bond with her natural mother, and there is no evidence Jessica will suffer harm or detriment by being placed in Joelle's custody. Both natural and psychological parent are good people who are fit, willing, and able to parent. Under the facts of this case, we are not convinced the trial court's custody disposition is clearly erroneous.

Quinn v. Mouw–Quinn

Supreme Court of South Dakota, 1996.
552 N.W.2d 843.

■ GILBERTSON, JUSTICE.

Tamara S. Quinn (Tamara) appeals the provisions of a divorce decree granting Patrick G. Quinn (Patrick) visitation privileges with one of her children, Samantha, and obligating Patrick to pay child support for that child. We affirm.

FACTS

The facts of this case are not in dispute and are submitted under an agreed statement of the record. The parties were married in 1984 and divorced in 1986. No children were born of this first marriage. On November 15, 1988, Tamara gave birth to a daughter, Samantha. Patrick is not the father of Samantha. The parties remarried in 1989 and two children were subsequently born during the second marriage, Jacob (dob 5–25–90) and Connor (dob 8–8–91).

After the first divorce, when Tamara became pregnant with Samantha, she asked Patrick for help although he was not the father. Patrick attended child birth classes and supported Tamara. Upon remarriage in 1989, Patrick accepted Samantha as his own child. To this day, Samantha knows none of the circumstances of her heritage. Patrick has cared for Samantha as a dependent and carries her on his insurance policies. Samantha refers to Patrick as "Daddy" and he is the only father she has ever known. In short, the circuit court found that Patrick and Samantha have established a parent-child relationship.

On November 4, 1993, Patrick served Tamara with a summons and a complaint for divorce in which he sought custody of all three children. Tamara answered and counterclaimed for custody of the children. The divorce was tried before the circuit court and, on November 15, 1994, the court entered its findings of fact, conclusions of law and judgment and decree of divorce. Custody of the children was awarded to Tamara subject to Patrick's rights of reasonable visitation. The trial court found that it would be in the best interests of Tamara's children for Patrick to have visitation with Samantha. Patrick was granted visitation with Samantha on the same schedule as his visitation with the other children. The circuit court also found that Patrick should pay child support to Tamara for the support of Samantha as well as Jacob and Connor. The divorce decree was accordingly entered and this appeal followed.

ISSUE ONE

Did the circuit court err in granting Patrick visitation privileges with Samantha?

The crux of this issue is whether there is authority for the circuit court to authorize this type of visitation. Patrick argues that such authorization exists as set forth in *SDCL 25–4–45*:

> In an action for divorce, the court may, before or after judgment, give such direction for the custody, care, and education *of the children of the marriage* as may seem necessary or proper, and may at any time vacate or modify the same. In awarding the custody of a child, the court shall be guided by consideration of what appears to be *for the best interests of the child in respect to the child's temporal and mental and moral welfare* ... (emphasis added).

. . .

We have held that the right of visitation derives from the right of custody. *Cooper v. Merkel, 470 N.W.2d 253, 255 (SD 1991).* However the legislature has clearly noted that one concept is not synonymous with the other.

SDCL 25–4–45 does not support Patrick's argument. That statute authorizes a divorce court to apply the best interests standard to custody and visitation disputes over "children of the marriage." However, Samantha is not one of the "children of the marriage" between *Patrick and Tamara.* Thus that statute is inapplicable.

. . .

Tamara relies upon *Cooper* and *Matter of Guardianship of Sedelmeier* as authority for her argument that a step-parent has no visitation rights. Both *Cooper* and *Sedelmeier* are premised upon the rationale that, absent extraordinary circumstances, no visitation can be granted to a non-parent against the wishes of the natural parent absent a showing of unfitness on the part of the parent. However, here, the issue is not one of parental fitness, but, rather, what is in the children's welfare. It is also a question of visitation rather than permanent custody. The question of visitation has no more to do with any claim of unfitness of Tamara as a custodial parent than all the other divorce proceedings in this state where visitation is routinely granted to the non-custodial parent. In the end, Tamara retains the custody of all three children regardless of the outcome of this appeal.

The circuit court has already made a finding that it is in the best interests of Jacob and Connor that they exercise regular visitation with Patrick. Tamara has not appealed this finding. More importantly, the circuit court also made the following finding: "it would be in the best interest of Samantha *as well as Jacob and Connor* for the Plaintiff to have visitation with Samantha on the same schedule that Plaintiff has visitation with the two boys." (emphasis added).

"Extraordinary circumstances," recognized in *Sedelmeier* as an independent basis for allowing step-parent visitation, denotes far more than a simple showing that visitation would be in the best interests of the child. The facts before us satisfy this heavier burden. This case is a clear departure from the customary dynamics of a step-parent and step-child relationship. Significantly, there is no indication that Samantha's biological father has ever had any contact with her whatsoever. Patrick is the only father Samantha has known in her seven years of life. She refers to him as "Daddy." Their relationship is that of a father and daughter in all respects except for that of biology. The impact of preventing Samantha from having contact with the only father she has ever known is likely to be devastating. This is especially true when her half-siblings (whom she believes to be full siblings) will be permitted to regularly visit with Patrick.

In the normal visitation case, it would be appropriate that all the "children of the marriage" should visit the non-custodial parent at the same time as it is in their best interests to do so. Here, no argument is made, nor can it be made under the facts of this case, to justify that it would be anything but extremely detrimental to the welfare of all three children to exclude Samantha from this family contact. As such, to now affirm court-ordered visitation for two of the children and forbid it for the third, devastates Jacob and Connor as well as Samantha.

Courts in their role of "parens patriae" have the right and obligation to protect children from the sometimes selfish and destructive actions of divorcing parents. The interests of the three children here are far more important than any petty dispute between parents and step-parents. If, as we have often said, siblings' welfare and best interests are served by being together in custody arrangements, then it follows that remaining together in visitation will probably also serve those interests, especially where the children are so close in age....

This is not to be seen as advancing the interests of the step-father at the expense of the natural mother. It is a continued recognition that the temporal, mental and moral welfare of children are paramount. This strikes the proper balance between a natural parent's custodial rights to his or her child and the child's personal welfare. Children come first. If the circuit court concludes it is in all three children's welfare in these exceptional circumstances to go on visitation together, then it should be so ordered.

. . .

■ AMUNDSON, JUSTICE (dissenting).

I respectfully dissent. It is undisputed that Patrick is not the natural or adoptive parent of Samantha.

In *Cooper v. Merkel, 470 N.W.2d 253 (SD 1991)*, this court squarely addressed the issue of the visitation rights of a nonparent. In *Cooper*, a couple lived together for seven years, however, they never married. The couple separated and, during the course of the protection order proceedings, the plaintiff sought visitation privileges with the defendant's minor child. The plaintiff alleged that he had assumed part of the responsibility for raising the child, that he had become a de facto parent to the child and, therefore, he should be granted the opportunity to visit the child. The trial court dismissed the plaintiffs request and the plaintiff appealed. We affirmed, stating:

> This court has not spoken directly to the issue of the visitation rights of a nonparent. However, "the right of visitation derives from the right of custody and is controlled by the same legal principles." This court *has* spoken to the custodial rights of nonparents.
>
> Before a parent's right to custody over his or her own children will be disturbed in favor of a nonparent a clear showing against the parent of "gross misconduct or unfitness, or of other extraordinary circumstances affecting the welfare of the child" is required, and an award cannot be made to [nonparents] simply because they may be better custodians.
>
> It follows that in order to grant a nonparent visitation rights with a minor child over the wishes of a parent, a clear showing against the parent of gross misconduct, unfitness or other extraordinary circumstances affecting the welfare of the child is required.

Cooper, 470 N.W.2d at 255–56 (citations omitted) (emphasis in original).

. . .

In this instance, there has also been no clear showing of unfitness with regard to Tamara. Therefore, the trial court erred in awarding Patrick visitation privileges with Tamara's child.

I. Unmarried Persons

1. Fathers

Stanley v. Illinois

Supreme Court of the United States, 1972.
405 U.S. 645, 92 S.Ct. 1208, 31 L.Ed.2d 551.

■ MR. JUSTICE WHITE delivered the opinion of the Court.

Joan Stanley lived with Peter Stanley intermittently for 18 years, during which time they had three children. When Joan Stanley died, Peter Stanley lost not only her but also his children. Under Illinois law, the children of unwed fathers become wards of the State upon the death of the mother. Accordingly, upon Joan Stanley's death, in a dependency proceeding instituted by the State of Illinois, Stanley's children were declared wards of the State and placed with court-appointed guardians. Stanley appealed, claiming that he had never been shown to be an unfit parent and that since married fathers and unwed mothers could not be deprived of their children without such a showing, he had been deprived of the equal protection of the laws guaranteed him by the Fourteenth Amendment.

. . .

[W]e are faced with a dependency statute that empowers state officials to circumvent neglect proceedings on the theory that an unwed father is not a "parent" whose existing relationship with his children must be considered. "Parents," says the State, "means the father and mother of a legitimate child, or the survivor of them, or the natural mother of an illegitimate child, and includes any adoptive parent," Ill. Rev. Stat., c. 37, § 701–14, but the term does not include unwed fathers.

Under Illinois law, therefore, while the children of all parents can be taken from them in neglect proceedings, that is only after notice, hearing, and proof of such unfitness as a parent as amounts to neglect, an unwed father is uniquely subject to the more simplistic dependency proceeding. By use of this proceeding, the State, on showing that the father was not married to the mother, need not prove unfitness in fact, because it is presumed at law. Thus, the unwed father's claim of parental qualification is avoided as "irrelevant."

. . .

The private interest here, that of a man in the children he has sired and raised, undeniably warrants deference and, absent a powerful countervailing interest, protection. It is plain that the interest of a parent in the companionship, care, custody, and management of his or her children "come[s] to this Court with a momentum for respect lacking when appeal is made to liberties which derive merely from shifting economic arrangements." *Kovacs v. Cooper, 336 U.S. 77, 95 (1949)* (Frankfurter, J., concurring).

The Court has frequently emphasized the importance of the family. The rights to conceive and to raise one's children have been deemed "essential," *Meyer v. Nebraska, 262 U.S. 390, 399 (1923),* "basic civil rights of man," *Skinner v. Oklahoma, 316 U.S. 535, 541 (1942),* and "rights far more precious ... than property rights," *May v. Anderson, 345 U.S. 528, 533 (1953).* "It is cardinal with us that the custody, care and nurture of the child reside first in the parents, whose primary function and freedom include preparation for obligations the state can neither supply nor hinder." *Prince v. Massachusetts, 321 U.S. 158, 166 (1944).* The integrity of the family unit has found protection in the Due Process Clause of the Fourteenth Amendment, *Meyer v. Nebraska, supra, at 399,* the Equal Protection Clause of the Fourteenth Amendment, *Skinner v. Oklahoma, supra, at 541,* and the Ninth Amendment, *Griswold v. Connecticut, 381 U.S. 479, 496 (1965)* (Goldberg, J., concurring).

Nor has the law refused to recognize those family relationships unlegitimized by a marriage ceremony. The Court has declared unconstitutional a state statute denying natural, but illegitimate, children a wrongful-death action for the death of their mother, emphasizing that such children cannot be denied the right of other children because familial bonds in such cases were often as warm, enduring, and important as those arising within a more formally organized family unit. *Levy v. Louisiana, 391 U.S. 68, 71–72 (1968).* "To say that the test of equal protection should be the 'legal' rather than the biological relationship is to avoid the issue. For the Equal Protection Clause necessarily limits the authority of a State to draw such 'legal' lines as it chooses." *Glona v. American Guarantee Co., 391 U.S. 73, 75–76 (1968).*

These authorities make it clear that, at the least, Stanley's interest in retaining custody of his children is cognizable and substantial.

For its part, the State has made its interest quite plain: Illinois has declared that the aim of the Juvenile Court Act is to protect "the moral, emotional, mental, and physical welfare of the minor and the best interests of the community" and to "strengthen the minor's family ties whenever possible, removing him from the custody of his parents only when his welfare or safety or the protection of the public cannot be adequately safeguarded without removal...." Ill. Rev. Stat., c. 37, § 701–2. These are legitimate interests, well within the power of the State to implement. We do not question the assertion that neglectful parents may be separated from their children.

But we are here not asked to evaluate the legitimacy of the state ends, rather, to determine whether the means used to achieve these ends are constitutionally defensible. What is the state interest in separating children from fathers without a hearing designed to determine whether the father is unfit in a particular disputed case? We observe that the State registers no gain towards its declared goals when it separates children from the custody of fit parents. Indeed, if Stanley is a fit father, the State spites its own articulated goals when it needlessly separates him from his family.

. . .

It may be, as the State insists, that most unmarried fathers are unsuitable and neglectful parents. It may also be that Stanley is such a parent and that his children should be placed in other hands. But all unmarried fathers are not in this category; some are wholly suited to have custody of their children. This much the State readily concedes, and nothing in this record indicates that Stanley is or has been a neglectful father who has not cared for his children. Given the opportunity to make his case, Stanley may have been seen to be deserving of custody of his offspring. Had this been so, the State's statutory policy would have been furthered by leaving custody in him.

. . .

[I]t may be argued that unmarried fathers are so seldom fit that Illinois need not undergo the administrative inconvenience of inquiry in any case, including Stanley's. The establishment of prompt efficacious procedures to achieve legitimate state ends is a proper state interest worthy of cognizance in constitutional adjudication. But the Constitution recognizes higher values than speed and efficiency. Indeed, one might fairly say of the Bill of Rights in general, and the Due Process Clause in particular, that they were designed to protect the fragile values of a vulnerable citizenry from the overbearing concern for efficiency and efficacy that may characterize praiseworthy government officials no less, and perhaps more, than mediocre ones.

. . .

Procedure by presumption is always cheaper and easier than individualized determination. But when, as here, the procedure forecloses the determinative issues of competence and care, when it explicitly disdains present realities in deference to past formalities, it needlessly risks running roughshod over the important interests of both parent and child. It therefore cannot stand.

. . .

The State of Illinois assumes custody of the children of married parents, divorced parents, and unmarried mothers only after a hearing and proof of neglect. The children of unmarried fathers, however, are declared dependent children without a hearing on parental fitness and without proof of neglect. Stanley's claim in the state courts and here is that failure to afford him a hearing on his parental qualifications while extending it to other parents denied him equal protection of the laws. We have concluded that all Illinois parents are constitutionally entitled to a hearing on their fitness before their children are removed from their custody. It follows that denying such a hearing to Stanley and those like him while granting it to other Illinois parents is inescapably contrary to the Equal Protection Clause.

Lehr v. Robertson

Supreme Court of the United States, 1983.
463 U.S. 248, 103 S.Ct. 2985, 77 L.Ed.2d 614.

■ JUSTICE STEVENS delivered the opinion of the Court.

The question presented is whether New York has sufficiently protected an unmarried father's inchoate relationship with a child whom he has never supported and rarely seen in the two years since her birth. The appellant, Jonathan Lehr, claims that the Due Process and Equal Protection Clauses of the Fourteenth Amendment, as interpreted in *Stanley v. Illinois, 405 U.S. 645 (1972),* and *Caban v. Mohammed, 441 U.S. 380 (1979),* give him an absolute right to notice and an opportunity to be heard before the child may be adopted. We disagree.

Jessica M. was born out of wedlock on November 9, 1976. Her mother, Lorraine Robertson, married Richard Robertson eight months after Jessica's birth. On December 21, 1978, when Jessica was over two years old, the Robertsons filed an adoption petition in the Family Court of Ulster County, New York. The court heard their testimony and received a favorable report from the Ulster County Department of Social Services. On March 7, 1979, the court entered an order of adoption. In this proceeding, appellant contends that the adoption order is invalid because he, Jessica's putative father, was not given advance notice of the adoption proceeding.

. . .

The State of New York maintains a "putative father registry." A man who files with that registry demonstrates his intent to claim paternity of a child born out of wedlock and is therefore entitled to receive notice of any proceeding to adopt that child. Before entering Jessica's adoption order, the Ulster County Family Court had the putative father registry examined. Although appellant claims to be Jessica's natural father, he had not entered his name in the registry.

In addition to the persons whose names are listed on the putative father registry, New York law requires that notice of an adoption proceeding be given to several other classes of possible fathers of children born out of wedlock—those who have been adjudicated to be the father, those who have been identified as the father on the child's birth certificate, those who live openly with the child and the child's mother and who hold themselves out to be the father, those who have been identified as the father by the mother in a sworn written statement, and those who were married to the child's mother before the child was six months old.[5] Appellant admittedly was not a member

5. At the time Jessica's adoption order was entered, *N. Y. Dom. Rel. Law §§ 111–a (2)* and (3) (McKinney 1977 and Supp. 1982–1983) provided:

"2. Persons entitled to notice, pursuant to subdivision one of this section, shall include:

"(a) any person adjudicated by a court in this state to be the father of the child;

"(b) any person adjudicated by a court of another state or territory of the United States to be the father of the child, when a certified copy of the court order has been filed with the putative father registry, pursuant to section three hundred seventy-two-c of the social services law;

"(c) any person who has timely filed an unrevoked notice of intent to claim paternity

of any of those classes. He had lived with appellee prior to Jessica's birth and visited her in the hospital when Jessica was born, but his name does not appear on Jessica's birth certificate. He did not live with appellee or Jessica after Jessica's birth, he has never provided them with any financial support, and he has never offered to marry appellee. Nevertheless, he contends that the following special circumstances gave him a constitutional right to notice and a hearing before Jessica was adopted.

On January 30, 1979, one month after the adoption proceeding was commenced in Ulster County, appellant filed a "visitation and paternity petition" in the Westchester County Family Court. In that petition, he asked for a determination of paternity, an order of support, and reasonable visitation privileges with Jessica. Notice of that proceeding was served on appellee on February 22, 1979. Four days later appellee's attorney informed the Ulster County Court that appellant had commenced a paternity proceeding in Westchester County; the Ulster County judge then entered an order staying appellant's paternity proceeding until he could rule on a motion to change the venue of that proceeding to Ulster County. On March 3, 1979, appellant received notice of the change of venue motion and, for the first time, learned that an adoption proceeding was pending in Ulster County.

On March 7, 1979, appellant's attorney telephoned the Ulster County judge to inform him that he planned to seek a stay of the adoption proceeding pending the determination of the paternity petition. In that telephone conversation, the judge advised the lawyer that he had already signed the adoption order earlier that day. According to appellant's attorney, the judge stated that he was aware of the pending paternity petition but did not believe he was required to give notice to appellant prior to the entry of the order of adoption.

Thereafter, the Family Court in Westchester County granted appellee's motion to dismiss the paternity petition, holding that the putative father's right to seek paternity "must be deemed severed so long as an order of adoption exists." Appellant did not appeal from that dismissal. On June 22, 1979, appellant filed a petition to vacate the order of adoption on the ground that it was obtained by fraud and in violation of his constitutional rights. The Ulster County Family Court received written and oral argument on the question whether it had "dropped the ball" by approving the adoption without giving appellant advance notice. After deliberating for several months, it denied the petition, explaining its decision in a thorough written opinion.

The Appellate Division of the Supreme Court affirmed.... One justice dissented on the ground that the filing of the paternity proceeding should

of the child, pursuant to section three hundred seventy-two of the social services law;

"(d) any person who is recorded on the child's birth certificate as the child's father;

"(e) any person who is openly living with the child and the child's mother at the time the proceeding is initiated and who is holding himself out to be the child's father;

"(f) any person who has been identified as the child's father by the mother in written, sworn statement; and

"(g) any person who was married to the child's mother within six months subsequent to the birth of the child and prior to the execution of a surrender instrument or the initiation of a proceeding pursuant to section three hundred eighty-four-b of the social services law.

"3. The sole purpose of notice under this section shall be to enable the person served pursuant to subdivision two to present evidence to the court relevant to the best interests of the child."

have been viewed as the statutory equivalent of filing a notice of intent to claim paternity with the putative father registry.

. . .

The New York Court of Appeals also affirmed by a divided vote. The majority . . . addressed what it described as the only contention of substance advanced by appellant: that it was an abuse of discretion to enter the adoption order without requiring that notice be given to appellant. The court observed that the primary purpose of the notice provision of § 111–a was to enable the person served to provide the court with evidence concerning the best interest of the child, and that appellant had made no tender indicating any ability to provide any particular or special information relevant to Jessica's best interest. Considering the record as a whole, and acknowledging that it might have been prudent to give notice, the court concluded that the Family Court had not abused its discretion either when it entered the order without notice or when it denied appellant's petition to reopen the proceedings. The dissenting judges concluded that the Family Court had abused its discretion, both when it entered the order without notice and when it refused to reopen the proceedings.

Appellant has now invoked our appellate jurisdiction. He offers two alternative grounds for holding the New York statutory scheme unconstitutional. First, he contends that a putative father's actual or potential relationship with a child born out of wedlock is an interest in liberty which may not be destroyed without due process of law; he argues therefore that he had a constitutional right to prior notice and an opportunity to be heard before he was deprived of that interest. Second, he contends that the gender-based classification in the statute, which both denied him the right to consent to Jessica's adoption and accorded him fewer procedural rights than her mother, violated the Equal Protection Clause.

The Due Process Claim.

. . .

This Court has examined the extent to which a natural father's biological relationship with his child receives protection under the Due Process Clause in precisely three cases: *Stanley v. Illinois, 405 U.S. 645 (1972), Quilloin v. Walcott, 434 U.S. 246 (1978),* and *Caban v. Mohammed, 441 U.S. 380 (1979).*

. . .

Quilloin involved the constitutionality of a Georgia statute that authorized the adoption, over the objection of the natural father, of a child born out of wedlock. The father in that case had never legitimated the child. It was only after the mother had remarried and her new husband had filed an adoption petition that the natural father sought visitation rights and filed a petition for legitimation. The trial court found adoption by the new husband to be in the child's best interests, and we unanimously held that action to be consistent with the Due Process Clause.

Caban involved the conflicting claims of two natural parents who had maintained joint custody of their children from the time of their birth until they were respectively two and four years old. The father challenged the validity of an order authorizing the mother's new husband to adopt the children; he relied on both the Equal Protection Clause and the Due Process Clause. Because this Court upheld his equal protection claim, the majority did not address his due process challenge. The comments on the latter claim by the four dissenting Justices are nevertheless instructive, because they identify the clear distinction between a mere biological relationship and an actual relationship of parental responsibility.

Justice Stewart correctly observed:

"Even if it be assumed that each married parent after divorce has some substantive due process right to maintain his or her parental relationship, it by no means follows that each unwed parent has any such right. *Parental rights do not spring full-blown from the biological connection between parent and child. They require relationships more enduring.*" *441 U.S., at 397* (emphasis added).

. . .

The difference between the developed parent-child relationship that was implicated in *Stanley* and *Caban*, and the potential relationship involved in *Quilloin* and this case, is both clear and significant. When an unwed father demonstrates a full commitment to the responsibilities of parenthood by "[coming] forward to participate in the rearing of his child," *Caban, 441 U.S., at 392,* his interest in personal contact with his child acquires substantial protection under the Due Process Clause. At that point it may be said that he "[acts] as a father toward his children." *Id., at 389, n. 7.* But the mere existence of a biological link does not merit equivalent constitutional protection. The actions of judges neither create nor sever genetic bonds. "[The] importance of the familial relationship, to the individuals involved and to the society, stems from the emotional attachments that derive from the intimacy of daily association, and from the role it plays in '[promoting] a way of life' through the instruction of children . . . as well as from the fact of blood relationship." *Smith v. Organization of Foster Families for Equality and Reform, 431 U.S. 816, 844 (1977)* (quoting *Wisconsin v. Yoder, 406 U.S. 205, 231–233 (1972)).*

. . .

The significance of the biological connection is that it offers the natural father an opportunity that no other male possesses to develop a relationship with his offspring. If he grasps that opportunity and accepts some measure of responsibility for the child's future, he may enjoy the blessings of the parent-child relationship and make uniquely valuable contributions to the child's development.[18] If he fails to do so, the Federal Constitution will not automatically compel a State to listen to his opinion of where the child's best interests lie.

In this case, we are not assessing the constitutional adequacy of New York's procedures for terminating a developed relationship. Appellant has never had any significant custodial, personal, or financial relationship with Jessica, and he did not seek to establish a legal tie until after she was two years old.[19] We are concerned only with whether New York has adequately protected his opportunity to form such a relationship.

. . .

18. Of course, we need not take sides in the ongoing debate among family psychologists over the relative weight to be accorded biological ties and psychological ties, in order to recognize that a natural father who has played a substantial role in rearing his child has a greater claim to constitutional protection than a mere biological parent. New York's statutory scheme reflects these differences, guaranteeing notice to any putative father who is living openly with the child, and providing putative fathers who have never developed a relationship with the child the opportunity to receive notice simply by mailing a postcard to the putative father registry.

19. This case happens to involve an adoption by the husband of the natural mother, but we do not believe the natural father

The most effective protection of the putative father's opportunity to develop a relationship with his child is provided by the laws that authorize formal marriage and govern its consequences. But the availability of that protection is, of course, dependent on the will of both parents of the child. Thus, New York has adopted a special statutory scheme to protect the unmarried father's interest in assuming a responsible role in the future of his child.

After this Court's decision in *Stanley*, the New York Legislature appointed a special commission to recommend legislation that would accommodate both the interests of biological fathers in their children and the children's interest in prompt and certain adoption procedures. The commission recommended, and the legislature enacted, a statutory adoption scheme that automatically provides notice to seven categories of putative fathers who are likely to have assumed some responsibility for the care of their natural children. If this scheme were likely to omit many responsible fathers, and if qualification for notice were beyond the control of an interested putative father, it might be thought procedurally inadequate. Yet, as all of the New York courts that reviewed this matter observed, the right to receive notice was completely within appellant's control. By mailing a postcard to the putative father registry, he could have guaranteed that he would receive notice of any proceedings to adopt Jessica. The possibility that he may have failed to do so because of his ignorance of the law cannot be a sufficient reason for criticizing the law itself. The New York Legislature concluded that a more open-ended notice requirement would merely complicate the adoption process, threaten the privacy interests of unwed mothers, create the risk of unnecessary controversy, and impair the desired finality of adoption decrees. Regardless of whether we would have done likewise if we were legislators instead of judges, we surely cannot characterize the State's conclusion as arbitrary.

. . .

Appellant argues, however, that even if the putative father's opportunity to establish a relationship with an illegitimate child is adequately protected by the New York statutory scheme in the normal case, he was nevertheless entitled to special notice because the court and the mother knew that he had filed an affiliation proceeding in another court. This argument amounts to nothing more than an indirect attack on the notice provisions of the New York statute. The legitimate state interests in facilitating the adoption of young children and having the adoption proceeding completed expeditiously that underlie the entire statutory scheme also justify a trial judge's determination to require all interested parties to adhere precisely to the procedural requirements of the statute. The Constitution does not require either a trial judge or a litigant to give special notice to nonparties who are presumptively capable of asserting and protecting their own rights. Since the

has any greater right to object to such an adoption than to an adoption by two total strangers. If anything, the balance of equities tips the opposite way in a case such as this. In denying the putative father relief in *Quilloin v. Walcott, 434 U.S. 246 (1978),* we made an observation equally applicable here:

> "Nor is this a case in which the proposed adoption would place the child with a new set of parents with whom the child had never before lived. Rather, the result of the adoption in this case is to give full recognition to a family unit already in existence, a result desired by all concerned, except appellant. Whatever might be required in other situations, we cannot say that the State was required in this situation to find anything more than that the adoption, and denial of legitimation, were in the 'best interests of the child.'" *Id., at 255.*

New York statutes adequately protected appellant's inchoate interest in establishing a relationship with Jessica, we find no merit in the claim that his constitutional rights were offended because the Family Court strictly complied with the notice provisions of the statute.

The Equal Protection Claim.

. . .

The legislation at issue in this case, is intended to establish procedures for adoptions. Those procedures are designed to promote the best interests of the child, to protect the rights of interested third parties, and to ensure promptness and finality. To serve those ends, the legislation guarantees to certain people the right to veto an adoption and the right to prior notice of any adoption proceeding. The mother of an illegitimate child is always within that favored class, but only certain putative fathers are included. Appellant contends that the gender-based distinction is invidious.

. . .

As we have already explained, the existence or nonexistence of a substantial relationship between parent and child is a relevant criterion in evaluating both the rights of the parent and the best interests of the child.... Because appellant, like the father in *Quilloin*, has never established a substantial relationship with his daughter, the New York statutes at issue in this case did not operate to deny appellant equal protection.

We have held that these statutes may not constitutionally be applied in that class of cases where the mother and father are in fact similarly situated with regard to their relationship with the child. In *Caban v. Mohammed, 441 U.S. 380 (1979),* the Court held that it violated the Equal Protection Clause to grant the mother a veto over the adoption of a 4–year-old girl and a 6–year-old boy, but not to grant a veto to their father, who had admitted paternity and had participated in the rearing of the children. The Court made it clear, however, that if the father had not "come forward to participate in the rearing of his child, nothing in the Equal Protection Clause [would] [preclude] the State from withholding from him the privilege of vetoing the adoption of that child."

. . .

Jessica's parents are not like the parents involved in *Caban*. Whereas appellee had a continuous custodial responsibility for Jessica, appellant never established any custodial, personal, or financial relationship with her. If one parent has an established custodial relationship with the child and the other parent has either abandoned or never established a relationship, the Equal Protection Clause does not prevent a State from according the two parents different legal rights.

. . .

■ Justice White, with whom Justice Marshall and Justice Blackmun join, dissenting.

The question in this case is whether the State may, consistent with the Due Process Clause, deny notice and an opportunity to be heard in an adoption proceeding to a putative father when the State has actual notice of his existence, whereabouts, and interest in the child.

. . .

According to Lehr, he and Jessica's mother met in 1971 and began living together in 1974. The couple cohabited for approximately two years, until Jessica's birth in 1976. Throughout the pregnancy and after the birth, Lorraine acknowledged to friends and relatives that Lehr was Jessica's father; Lorraine told Lehr that she had reported to the New York State Department of Social Services that he was the father. Lehr visited Lorraine and Jessica in the hospital every day during Lorraine's confinement. According to Lehr, from the time Lorraine was discharged from the hospital until August 1978, she concealed her whereabouts from him. During this time Lehr never ceased his efforts to locate Lorraine and Jessica and achieved sporadic success until August 1977, after which time he was unable to locate them at all. On those occasions when he did determine Lorraine's location, he visited with her and her children to the extent she was willing to permit it. When Lehr, with the aid of a detective agency, located Lorraine and Jessica in August 1978, Lorraine was already married to Mr. Robertson. Lehr asserts that at this time he offered to provide financial assistance and to set up a trust fund for Jessica, but that Lorraine refused. Lorraine threatened Lehr with arrest unless he stayed away and refused to permit him to see Jessica. Thereafter Lehr retained counsel who wrote to Lorraine in early December 1978, requesting that she permit Lehr to visit Jessica and threatening legal action on Lehr's behalf. On December 21, 1978, perhaps as a response to Lehr's threatened legal action, appellees commenced the adoption action at issue here.

. . .

Lehr's version of the "facts" paints a far different picture than that portrayed by the majority. The majority's recitation, that "[appellant] has never had any significant custodial, personal, or financial relationship with Jessica, and he did not seek to establish a legal tie until after she was two years old," obviously does not tell the whole story. Appellant has never been afforded an opportunity to present his case. The legitimation proceeding he instituted was first stayed, and then dismissed, on appellees' motions. Nor could appellant establish his interest during the adoption proceedings, for it is the failure to provide Lehr notice and an opportunity to be heard there that is at issue here. We cannot fairly make a judgment based on the quality or substance of a relationship without a complete and developed factual record. This case requires us to assume that Lehr's allegations are true—that but for the actions of the child's mother there would have been the kind of significant relationship that the majority concedes is entitled to the full panoply of procedural due process protections.

. . .

I reject the peculiar notion that the only significance of the biological connection between father and child is that "it offers the natural father an opportunity that no other male possesses to develop a relationship with his offspring." A "mere biological relationship" is not as unimportant in determining the nature of liberty interests as the majority suggests.

"[The] usual understanding of 'family' implies biological relationships, and most decisions treating the relation between parent and child have stressed this element." The "biological connection" is itself a relationship that creates a protected interest. Thus the "nature" of the interest is the parent-child relationship; how well developed that relationship has become goes to its "weight," not its "nature." Whether Lehr's interest is entitled to constitutional protection does not entail a searching inquiry into the quality of the relationship but a simple determination of the *fact* that the relationship exists—a fact that even the majority agrees must be assumed to be established.

Beyond that, however, because there is no established factual basis on which to proceed, it is quite untenable to conclude that a putative father's interest in his child is lacking in substance, that the father in effect has abandoned the child, or ultimately that the father's interest is not entitled to the same minimum procedural protections as the interests of other putative fathers. Any analysis of the adequacy of the notice in this case must be conducted on the assumption that the interest involved here is as strong as that of *any* putative father. That is not to say that due process requires actual notice to every putative father or that adoptive parents or the State must conduct an exhaustive search of records or an intensive investigation before a final adoption order may be entered. The procedures adopted by the State, however, must at least represent a reasonable effort to determine the identity of the putative father and to give him adequate notice.

In this case, of course, there was no question about either the identity or the location of the putative father. The mother knew exactly who he was and both she and the court entering the order of adoption knew precisely where he was and how to give him actual notice that his parental rights were about to be terminated by an adoption order.[5] Lehr was entitled to due process, and the right to be heard is one of the fundamentals of that right, which " 'has little reality or worth unless one is informed that the matter is pending and can choose for himself whether to appear or default, acquiesce or contest.' "

. . .

The State asserts that any problem in this respect is overcome by the seventh category of putative fathers to whom notice must be given, namely, those fathers who have identified themselves in the putative fathers' register maintained by the State. Since Lehr did not take advantage of this device to make his interest known, the State contends, he was not entitled to notice and a hearing even though his identity, location, and interest were known to the adoption court prior to entry of the adoption order. I have difficulty with this position. First, it represents a grudging and crabbed approach to due process. The State is quite willing to give notice and a hearing to putative fathers who have made themselves known by resorting to the putative fathers' register. It makes little sense to me to deny notice and hearing to a father who has not placed his name in the register but who has unmistakably identified himself by filing suit to establish his paternity and has notified the adoption court of his action and his interest. I thus need not question the statutory scheme on its face. Even assuming that Lehr would have been foreclosed if his failure to utilize the register had somehow disadvantaged the State, he effectively made himself known by other means, and it is the

5. Absent special circumstances, there is no bar to requiring the mother of an illegitimate child to divulge the name of the father when the proceedings at issue involve the permanent termination of the father's rights. Likewise, there is no reason not to require such identification when it is the spouse of the custodial parent who seeks to adopt the child. Indeed, the State now requires the mother to provide the identity of the father if she applies for financial benefits under the Aid to Families with Dependent Children Program. See n. 2, *supra*. The State's obligation to provide notice to persons before their interests are permanently terminated cannot be a lesser concern than its obligation to assure that state funds are not expended when there exists a person upon whom the financial responsibility should fall.

sheerest formalism to deny him a hearing because he informed the State in the wrong manner.

. . .

Because in my view the failure to provide Lehr with notice and an opportunity to be heard violated rights guaranteed him by the Due Process Clause, I need not address the question whether § 111–a violates the Equal Protection Clause by discriminating between categories of unwed fathers or by discriminating on the basis of gender.

NOTE

Stanley held that legal status—as a husband or an adoptive parent—cannot serve as the criterion for recognizing a father's rights and obligations. *Lehr* held that biology alone, without meaningful involvement, is not sufficient to bestow such rights and obligations. The next logical question is whether meaningful involvement alone, without status as husband or adoptive parent and without a biological tie to the child, can be the basis for recognizing a paternal interest. The next section considers this issue as it has arisen in the course of adjudicating the rights of unmarried couples.

2. Couples

V.C. v. M.J.B.

Supreme Court of New Jersey, 2000.
163 N.J. 200, 748 A.2d 539.

■ Long, J.

In this case, we are called on to determine what legal standard applies to a third party's claim to joint custody and visitation of her former domestic partner's biological children, with whom she lived in a familial setting and in respect of whom she claims to have functioned as a psychological parent. Although the case arises in the context of a lesbian couple, the standard we enunciate is applicable to all persons who have willingly, and with the approval of the legal parent, undertaken the duties of a parent to a child not related by blood or adoption.

. . .

. . . V.C. and M.J.B., who are lesbians, met in 1992 and began dating on July 4, 1993. On July 9, 1993, M.J.B. went to see a fertility specialist to begin artificial insemination procedures. . . . She had been planning to be artificially inseminated since late 1980. According to M.J.B., she made the final decision to become pregnant independently and before beginning her relationship with V.C. Two individuals who knew M.J.B. before she began dating V.C., confirmed that M.J.B. had been planning to become pregnant through artificial insemination for years prior to the beginning of the parties' relationship.

According to V.C., early in their relationship, the two discussed having children. However, V.C. did not become aware of M.J.B.'s visits with the specialist and her decision to have a baby by artificial insemination until September 1993. In fact, the doctor's records of M.J.B.'s first appointment indicate that M.J.B. was single and that she "desires children."

Nonetheless, V.C. claimed that the parties jointly decided to have children and that she and M.J.B. jointly researched and decided which sperm donor they should use. M.J.B. acknowledged that she consulted V.C. on the issue but maintained that she individually made the final choice about which sperm donor to use.

Between November 1993 and February 1994, M.J.B. underwent several insemination procedures. V.C. attended at least two of those sessions. In December 1993, V.C. moved into M.J.B.'s apartment. Two months later, on February 7, 1994, the doctor informed M.J.B. that she was pregnant. M.J.B. called V.C. at work to tell her the good news. Eventually, M.J.B. was informed that she was having twins.

During M.J.B.'s pregnancy, both M.J.B. and V.C. prepared for the birth of the twins by attending pre-natal and Lamaze classes. In April 1994, the parties moved to a larger apartment to accommodate the pending births. V.C. contended that during that time they jointly decided on the children's names. M.J.B. admitted consulting V.C., but maintained that she made the final decision regarding names.

The children were born on September 29, 1994. V.C. took M.J.B. to the hospital and she was present in the delivery room at the birth of the children. At the hospital, the nurses and staff treated V.C. as if she were a mother. Immediately following the birth, the nurses gave one child to M.J.B. to hold and the other to V.C., and took pictures of the four of them together. After the children were born, M.J.B. took a three-month maternity leave and V.C. took a three-week vacation.

The parties opened joint bank accounts for their household expenses, and prepared wills, powers of attorney, and named each other as the beneficiary for their respective life insurance policies. At some point, the parties also opened savings accounts for the children, and named V.C. as custodian for one account and M.J.B. as custodian for the other.

The parties also decided to have the children call M.J.B. "Mommy" and V.C. "Meema." M.J.B. conceded that she referred to V.C. as a "mother" of the children. In addition, M.J.B. supported the notion, both publicly and privately, that during the twenty-three months after the children were born, the parties and the children functioned as a family unit.

. . .

M.J.B. agreed that both parties cared for the children but insisted that she made substantive decisions regarding their lives. For instance, M.J.B. maintained that she independently researched and made the final decisions regarding the children's pediatrician and day care center. V.C. countered that she was equally involved in all decision-making regarding the children. Specifically, V.C. claimed that she participated in choosing a day care center for the children, and it is clear that M.J.B. brought V.C. to visit the center she selected prior to making a final decision.

M.J.B. acknowledged that V.C. assumed substantial responsibility for the children, but maintained that V.C. was a mere helper and not a co-parent. However, according to V.C., she acted as a co-parent to the children and had equal parenting responsibility. Indeed, M.J.B. listed V.C. as the "other mother" on the children's pediatrician and day care registration forms. M.J.B. also gave V.C. medical power of attorney over the children.

A number of witnesses testified about their observations of the parties' relationship and V.C.'s role in the children's lives. V.C.'s mother testified that M.J.B. told her that V.C. and M.J.B. would be co-parents to the children and that the parties made a joint decision to have children. In addition, she observed that M.J.B., V.C. and the children functioned as a family. Likewise, L.M., a co-worker and friend of M.J.B., testified that she spent time with the parties before, during and after M.J.B.'s pregnancy, and that she regarded the parties as equal co-parents to the children.

Another co-worker and friend of M.J.B., D.B., also testified that V.C. was a co-parent to the children.... However, another witness, A.R., indicated that V.C. was minimally involved in taking care of the children, but acknowledged that V.C. had an important role in the twins' lives. Testifying for M.J.B., both A.R. and M.I. stated that they regarded M.J.B. as the children's primary caretaker.

Together the parties purchased a home in February 1995. Later that year, V.C. asked M.J.B. to marry her, and M.J.B. accepted. In July 1995, the parties held a commitment ceremony where they were "married." At the ceremony, V.C., M.J.B. and the twins were blessed as a "family."

. . .

During their relationship, the couple discussed both changing the twins' surname to a hyphenated form of the women's names and the possibility of V.C. adopting the children. M.J.B. testified that the parties considered adoption and in June 1996 consulted an attorney on the subject. M.J.B. paid a two thousand dollar retainer, and the attorney advised the parties to get letters from family and friends indicating that the parties and the twins functioned as a family. The parties never actually attempted to get the letters or proceed with the adoption. V.C. alleged that M.J.B. was willing to go through with the adoption even after the parties split.

Just two months later, in August 1996, M.J.B. ended the relationship. The parties then took turns living in the house with the children until November 1996. In December 1996, V.C. moved out. M.J.B. permitted V.C. to visit with the children until May 1997. During that time, V.C. spent approximately every other weekend with the children, and contributed money toward the household expenses.

In May 1997, M.J.B. went away on business and left the children with V.C. for two weeks. However, later that month, M.J.B. refused to continue V.C.'s visitation with the children, and at some point, M.J.B. stopped accepting V.C.'s money. M.J.B. asserted that she did not want to continue the children's contact with V.C. because she believed that V.C. was not properly caring for the children, and that the children were suffering distress from continued contact with V.C. Both parties became involved with new partners after the dissolution of their relationship. Eventually, V.C. filed this complaint for joint legal custody.

. . .

The trial court denied V.C.'s applications for joint legal custody and visitation because it concluded that she failed to establish that the bonded relationship she enjoyed with the children had risen to the level of psychological or de facto parenthood. In so doing, the court gave significant weight to the fact that the decision to have children was M.J.B.'s, and not a joint decision between M.J.B. and V.C.

Finding that V.C. did not qualify as a psychological parent to the children, the trial court opined that it would "only be able to consider [V.C.'s] petition for custody if [she] was able [to] prove [M.J.B.] to be an unfit parent." Because V.C. did not allege that M.J.B. was an unfit parent, the trial court held that V.C. lacked standing to petition for joint legal custody.

The court also denied V.C.'s application for visitation, determining that even a step-parent would not be granted such visitation except for equitable reasons, not present here. Further, it resolved that visitation was not in the children's best interests because M.J.B. harbored animosity toward V.C. that would "inevitably pass[] along to the children." According to the trial court, the case might have been different had V.C. "enjoyed a longer and more irreplaceable relationship with the children. . . ." Upon the entry of judgment, V.C. appealed.

On March 5, 1999, an Appellate Division panel decided the case in three separate opinions. Judge Stern authored the majority opinion, which affirmed the denial of V.C.'s application for joint legal custody but reversed the denial of her petition for visitation [and remanded for proceedings to establish a visitation schedule]. In so doing, the court concluded that V.C. had established a parent-like relationship and "stood in the shoes of a parent." The majority analyzed the case under the best interests of the child standard, and, based on the record before it, determined that joint legal custody was not in the best interests of the children. The trial court's judgment denying V.C.'s petition for joint custody was affirmed.

As to visitation, although recognizing that animosity between the parties is an important factor in the best interests test, the majority concluded that M.J.B. cannot deprive V.C. or the twins of visitation simply because M.J.B. harbors negative feelings toward V.C. Relying on the experts' testimony, the majority concluded that V.C.'s continued contact with the children is in their best interests; therefore, it reversed the judgment denying V.C.'s petition for visitation and remanded for proceedings to establish a visitation schedule.

. . .

An order for visitation was established on March 26, 1999. Both M.J.B. and V.C. appealed as of right from the dissents discussed above. M.J.B. also moved for a stay.

Thereafter, we denied M.J.B.'s stay motion and accelerated the appeals.

. . .

On appeal, M.J.B. argues that we lack subject matter jurisdiction to consider V.C.'s custody and visitation claims because the legislative scheme and the common law do not recognize her rights; that V.C. lacks standing to claim custody and visitation because she has not asserted parental unfitness; that V.C.'s application intrudes on M.J.B.'s basic liberty interest in raising her children as she sees fit; that protection of the children from serious harm is the only basis for governmental intervention into her private life with her children; that she has an absolute right to decide with whom her children will associate; that V.C. was the equivalent of a nanny whose status deserves no special acknowledgment; that she did not give consent to V.C.'s role as a "parent"; and finally that the Appellate Division erred in substituting its fact-finding for that of the trial court.

V.C. counters that she qualifies as a parent under *N.J.S.A. 9:2–13(f)*; that she is a psychological parent[3] of the twins thus justifying the invocation of the court's parens patriae power to sustain that relationship; that in such circumstances the best interests test applies; and, on her cross-appeal, that

3. The terms psychological parent, de facto parent, and functional parent are used interchangeably in this opinion to reflect their use in the various cases, statutes, and articles cited. Psychological parent is the preferred term.

denial of joint legal custody was erroneous because of her status as a de facto parent.

. . .

There are no statutes explicitly addressing whether a former unmarried domestic partner has standing to seek custody and visitation with her former partner's biological children. That is not to say, however, that the current statutory scheme dealing with issues of custody and visitation does not provide some guiding principles. *N.J.S.A. 9:2–3* prescribes:

When the parents of a minor child live separately, or are about to do so, the Superior Court, in an action brought by either parent, shall have the same power to make judgments or orders concerning care, custody, education and maintenance as concerning a child whose parents are divorced....

Further, *N.J.S.A. 9:2–4* provides, in part, that the Legislature finds and declares that it is in the public policy of this State to assure minor children of frequent and continuing contact with both parents after the parents have separated or dissolved their marriage and that it is in the public interest to encourage parents to share the rights and responsibilities of child rearing in order to effect this policy. In any proceeding involving the custody of a minor child, the rights of both parents shall be equal....

By that scheme, the Legislature has expressed the view that children should not generally be denied continuing contact with parents after the relationship between the parties ends.

N.J.S.A. 9:2–13(f) provides that "the word 'parent,' when not otherwise described by the context, means a natural parent or parent by previous adoption." M.J.B. argues that because V.C. is not a natural or adoptive parent, we lack jurisdiction to consider her claims. That is an incomplete interpretation of the Act. Although the statutory definition of parent focuses on natural and adoptive parents, it also includes the phrase, "when not otherwise described by the context." That language evinces a legislative intent to leave open the possibility that individuals other than natural or adoptive parents may qualify as "parents," depending on the circumstances.[4]

. . .

By including the words "when not otherwise described by the context" in the statute, the Legislature obviously envisioned a case where the specific relationship between a child and a person not specifically denominated by the statute would qualify as "parental" under the scheme of Title 9. Although the Legislature may not have considered the precise case before us, it is hard to imagine what it could have had in mind in adding the "context" language other than a situation such as this, in which a person not related to a child by blood or adoption has stood in a parental role vis-a-vis the child ...

. . .

Separate and apart from the statute, M.J.B. contends that there is no legal precedent for this action by V.C. She asserts, correctly, that a legal

4. We note that all fifty states, to one extent or another, grant statutory standing to third parties to petition for custody and/or visitation of the biological or adoptive children of others. Those statutes reveal a full spectrum of approaches [ranging from permitting petitions only by blood relatives to permitting them third parties without regard to blood relationship].

parent has a fundamental right to the care, custody and nurturance of his or her child. Various constitutional provisions have been cited as the source of that right, which is deeply imbedded in our collective consciousness and traditions. In general, however, the right of a legal parent to the care and custody of his or her child derives from the notion of privacy. According to M.J.B., that right entitles her to absolute preference over V.C. in connection with custody and visitation of the twins. She argues that V.C., a stranger, has no standing to bring this action. We disagree.

The right of parents to the care and custody of their children is not absolute. For example, a legal parent's fundamental right to custody and control of a child may be infringed upon by the state if the parent endangers the health or safety of the child. Likewise, if there is a showing of unfitness, abandonment or gross misconduct, a parent's right to custody of her child may be usurped.

According to M.J.B., because there is no allegation by V.C. of unfitness, abandonment or gross misconduct, there is no reason advanced to interfere with any of her constitutional prerogatives. What she elides from consideration, however, is the "exceptional circumstances" category (occasionally denominated as extraordinary circumstances) that has been recognized as an alternative basis for a third party to seek custody and visitation of another person's child. The "exceptional circumstances" category contemplates the intervention of the Court in the exercise of its parens patriae power to protect a child.

Subsumed within that category is the subset known as the psychological parent cases in which a third party has stepped in to assume the role of the legal parent who has been unable or unwilling to undertake the obligations of parenthood.

. . .

At the heart of the psychological parent cases is a recognition that children have a strong interest in maintaining the ties that connect them to adults who love and provide for them. That interest, for constitutional as well as social purposes, lies in the emotional bonds that develop between family members as a result of shared daily life.

. . .

To be sure, prior cases in New Jersey have arisen in the context of a third party taking over the role of an unwilling, absent or incapacitated parent. The question presented here is different; V.C. did not step into M.J.B.'s shoes, but labored alongside her in their family. However, because we view this issue as falling broadly within the contours we have previously described, and because V.C. invokes the "exceptional circumstances" doctrine based on her claim to be a psychological parent to the twins, she has standing to maintain this action separate and apart from the statute.

. . .

The next issue we confront is how a party may establish that he or she has, in fact, become a psychological parent to the child of a fit and involved legal parent. That is a question which many of our sister states have attempted to answer. Some have enacted statutes to address the subject by deconstructing psychological parenthood to its fundamental elements, including: the substantial nature of the relationship between the third party and the child, whether or not the third party and the child actually lived together, and whether the unrelated third party had previously provided financial support for the child.

. . .

The most thoughtful and inclusive definition of de facto parenthood is the test enunciated in *Custody of H.S.H.-K., 533 N.W.2d 419, 421 (Wis. 1995)* . . . It addresses the main fears and concerns both legislatures and courts have advanced when addressing the notion of psychological parenthood. Under that test, to demonstrate the existence of the petitioner's parent-like relationship with the child, the petitioner must prove four elements: (1) that the biological or adoptive parent consented to, and fostered, the petitioner's formation and establishment of a parent-like relationship with the child; (2) that the petitioner and the child lived together in the same household; (3) that the petitioner assumed the obligations of parenthood by taking significant responsibility for the child's care, education and development, including contributing towards the child's support, without expectation of financial compensation [a petitioner's contribution to a child's support need not be monetary]; and (4) that the petitioner has been in a parental role for a length of time sufficient to have established with the child a bonded, dependent relationship parental in nature.

. . .

Prong one is critical because it makes the biological or adoptive parent a participant in the creation of the psychological parent's relationship with the child. Without such a requirement, a paid nanny or babysitter could theoretically qualify for parental status. To avoid that result, in order for a third party to be deemed a psychological parent, the legal parent must have fostered the formation of the parental relationship between the third party and the child. By fostered is meant that the legal parent ceded over to the third party a measure of parental authority and autonomy and granted to that third party rights and duties vis-a-vis the child that the third party's status would not otherwise warrant. Ordinarily, a relationship based on payment by the legal parent to the third party will not qualify.

The requirement of cooperation by the legal parent is critical because it places control within his or her hands. That parent has the absolute ability to maintain a zone of autonomous privacy for herself and her child. However, if she wishes to maintain that zone of privacy she cannot invite a third party to function as a parent to her child and cannot cede over to that third party parental authority the exercise of which may create a profound bond with the child.

. . . [A] psychological parent-child relationship that is voluntarily created by the legally recognized parent may not be unilaterally terminated after the relationship between the adults ends. Although the intent of the legally recognized parent is critical to the psychological parent analysis, the focus is on that party's intent during the formation and pendency of the parent-child relationship. The reason is that the ending of the relationship between the legal parent and the third party does not end the bond that the legal parent fostered and that actually developed between the child and the psychological parent. Thus, the right of the legal parent [does] not extend to erasing a relationship between her partner and her child which she voluntarily created and actively fostered simply because after the party's separation she regretted having done so. . . .

Concerning the remaining prongs of the H.S.H.-K. test, we accept Wisconsin's formulation with these additional comments. The third prong, a finding that a third party assumed the obligations of parenthood, is not contingent on financial contributions made by the third party. Financial contribution may be considered but should not be given inordinate weight when determining whether a third party has assumed the obligations of parenthood. Obviously, as we have indicated, the assumption of a parental role is much more complex than mere financial support. It is determined by the nature, quality, and extent of the functions undertaken by the third party and the response of the child to that nurturance.

. . .

... [T]he fourth prong is most important because it requires the existence of a parent-child bond. A necessary corollary is that the third party must have functioned as a parent for a long enough time that such a bond has developed. What is crucial here is not the amount of time but the nature of the relationship. How much time is necessary will turn on the facts of each case including an assessment of exactly what functions the putative parent performed, as well as at what period and stage of the child's life and development such actions were taken. Most importantly, a determination will have to be made about the actuality and strength of the parent-child bond. Generally, that will require expert testimony.

The standards to which we have referred will govern all cases in which a third party asserts psychological parent status as a basis for a custody or visitation action regarding the child of a legal parent, with whom the third party has lived in a familial setting.

. . .

This opinion should not be viewed as an incursion on the general right of a fit legal parent to raise his or her child without outside interference. What we have addressed here is a specific set of circumstances involving the volitional choice of a legal parent to cede a measure of parental authority to a third party; to allow that party to function as a parent in the day-to-day life of the child; and to foster the forging of a parental bond between the third party and the child. In such circumstances, the legal parent has created a family with the third party and the child, and has invited the third party into the otherwise inviolable realm of family privacy.

. . .

Once a third party has been determined to be a psychological parent to a child, under the previously described standards, he or she stands in parity with the legal parent. Custody and visitation issues between them are to be determined on a best interests standard . . .

Visitation, however, will be the presumptive rule, subject to the considerations set forth in *N.J.S.A. 9:2-4*, as would be the case if two natural parents were in conflict. As we said in *Beck v. Beck, 432 A.2d 63 (1981)*, visitation rights are almost "invariably" granted to the non-custodial parent. Indeed, "the denial of visitation rights is such an extraordinary proscription that it should be invoked only in those exceptional cases where it clearly and convincingly appears that the granting of visitation will cause physical or emotional harm to the children or where it is demonstrated that the parent is unfit." Once the parent-child bond is forged, the rights and duties of the parties should be crafted to reflect that reality.

. . .

. . . [T]he issue is whether V.C. should be granted joint legal custody and visitation. As we have stated, the best interests standard applies and the factors set forth in *N.J.S.A. 9:2–4* come into play. Under that statute V.C. and M.J.B. are essentially equal. Each appears to be a fully capable, loving parent committed to the safety and welfare of the twins. Although there is animosity between V.C. and M.J.B., that is not a determinant of whether V.C. can continue in the children's lives.

We note that V.C. is not seeking joint physical custody, but joint legal custody for decision making. However, due to the pendency of this case, V.C. has not been involved in the decision-making for the twins for nearly four years. To interject her into the decisional realm at this point would be unnecessarily disruptive for all involved. We will not, therefore, order joint legal custody in this case.

Visitation, however, is another matter. V.C. and the twins have been visiting during nearly all of the four years since V.C. parted company from M.J.B. Continued visitation in those circumstances is presumed. Nothing suggests that V.C. should be precluded from continuing to see the children on a regular basis. Indeed, it is clear that continued regular visitation is in the twins' best interests because V.C. is their psychological parent. We thus affirm the judgment of the Appellate Division.

. . .

Third parties who live in familial circumstances with a child and his or her legal parent may achieve, with the consent of the legal parent, a psychological parent status vis-a-vis a child. Fundamental to a finding of the existence of that status is that a parent-child bond has been created. That bond cannot be unilaterally terminated by the legal parent. When there is a conflict over custody and visitation between the legal parent and a psychological parent, the legal paradigm is that of two legal parents and the standard to be applied is the best interests of the child.

Titchenal v. Dexter

Supreme Court of Vermont, 1997.
166 Vt. 373, 693 A.2d 682.

■ ALLEN, C.J.

. . .

The dispute arose after the breakup of a relationship between two women who had both participated in raising a child adopted by only one of them . . . In 1985, plaintiff Chris Titchenal and defendant Diane Dexter began an intimate relationship. They purchased a home together, held joint bank accounts, and jointly owned their automobiles. They both contributed financially to their household, and each regarded the other as a life partner.

At some point, the parties decided to have a child. When their attempts to conceive via a sperm donor failed, they decided to adopt a child. In July 1991, defendant adopted a newborn baby girl, who was named Sarah Ruth Dexter–Titchenal. The parties held themselves out to Sarah and all others as her parents. The child called one parent "Mama Chris" and the other parent "Mama Di." For the first three and one-half years of Sarah's life, until the parties' separation, plaintiff cared for the child approximately 65% of the time. Plaintiff did not seek to adopt Sarah because the parties believed that the then-current adoption statute would not allow both of them to do so.

Eventually, the parties' relationship faltered, and by November 1994 defendant had moved out of the couple's home, taking Sarah with her. For the first five months following the parties' separation, Sarah stayed with plaintiff between Wednesday afternoons and Friday evenings. By the spring of 1995, however, defendant had severely curtailed plaintiff's contact with Sarah and had refused plaintiff's offer of financial assistance.

In October 1995, plaintiff filed a complaint requesting that the superior court exercise its equitable jurisdiction to establish and enforce regular, unsupervised parent-child contact between her and Sarah. The court granted defendant's motion to dismiss, refusing to recognize a cause of action for parent-child contact absent a common-law or statutory basis for the claim. On appeal, plaintiff argues that the superior court has equitable jurisdiction under the state's parens patriae authority to consider her complaint, and that both public policy and the doctrines of in loco parentis and de facto parenthood allow the court to exercise its equitable authority in cases such as this. An organization called the Gay & Lesbian Advocates & Defenders (GLAD) makes essentially the same arguments in its amicus curiae brief.

Plaintiff urges us to grant "nontraditional" family members access to the courts by recognizing the legal rights of de facto parents. According to plaintiff, the state's parens patriae power to protect the best interests of children permits the superior court to adjudicate disputes over parent-child contact outside the context of a statutory proceeding. Thus, under the scheme advocated by plaintiff and amicus curiae, the family court would adjudicate disputes concerning parental rights and responsibilities and parent-child contact within the parameters and criteria set forth in [statutes]. . . . while the superior court would exert its equitable powers to consider such disputes arising outside these statutory proceedings.

We find no legal basis for plaintiff's proposal. Courts cannot exert equitable powers unless they first have jurisdiction over the subject matter and parties. *See Perry v. Superior Court of Kern County, 166 Cal. Rptr. 583, 584 (Ct. App. 1980)* (visitation rights may be awarded to nonparents only in proceeding in which court otherwise has jurisdiction over issue of custody). Equity generally has no jurisdiction over imperfect rights arising from moral rather than legal obligations; not every perceived injustice is actionable in equity—only those violating a recognized legal right. A court of equity does not create rights, but rather determines whether legal rights exist and, if so, whether it is proper and just to enforce those rights. In short, a court may exert its equitable powers to grant appropriate relief only when a judicially cognizable right exists, and no adequate legal remedy is available.

The issue, then, is whether there is any underlying legal basis for plaintiff's cause of action that would allow the superior court to apply its equitable powers to adjudicate her claim. Courts may exert equitable powers based upon common-law, statutory, or constitutional rights, or upon judicial acknowledgement of public-policy considerations establishing an as-yet-unrecognized legal right.

Here, we find no legal basis from any of the above sources for plaintiff's claimed right to parent-child contact in her capacity as an equitable or de facto parent. Notwithstanding plaintiff's claims to the contrary, there is no common-law history of Vermont courts interfering with the rights and responsibilities of fit parents absent statutory authority to do so. Although there is some support for the proposition that state courts have equity jurisdiction under their parens patriae power to adjudicate custody matters, such authority is generally invoked in the context of dependency or neglect petitions. Invoking equity jurisdiction under these circumstances was a narrow exception to the general common-law rule that parents had the right to the custody, control, and services of their minor children free from governmental interference.

With one possible minor exception, the custody-related cases cited by plaintiff and amicus curiae involve decisions made within the context of statutory proceedings. From early on, Vermont courts intervened in custody matters concerning fit parents only under the authority of divorce statutes originating from the eighteenth century, and later nonsupport and separation statutes.

. . .

Plaintiff acknowledges that no specific statutory or constitutional provisions require the superior court to assume jurisdiction over her claim, but she argues that public policy compels such a result, given her status as Sarah's de facto parent. We do not agree. The superior court's refusal to extend its jurisdiction here does not create circumstances "cruel or shocking to the average [person's] conception of justice." *Payne, 520 A.2d at 588.* Persons affected by this decision can protect their interests. Through marriage or adoption, heterosexual couples may assure that nonbiological partners will be able to petition the court regarding parental rights and responsibilities or parent-child contact in the event a relationship ends. Nonbiological partners in same-sex relationships can gain similar assurances through adoption.

In this case, plaintiff contends that she did not attempt to adopt Sarah at the time defendant did because the parties believed that Vermont's then-current adoption laws would not permit it. See *15 V.S.A. § 431* (repealed 1996) ("A person or husband and wife together . . . may adopt any other person. . . ."). The language of the statute, however, certainly did not preclude plaintiff from seeking to adopt Sarah; indeed, as of December 1991, when Sarah was only five months old, at least one Vermont probate court had allowed the female partner of a child's adoptive mother to adopt the child as a second parent. Further, in June 1993, more than a year before plaintiff alleges that the parties' relationship ended, this Court construed the earlier adoption statute as allowing a biological mother's female partner to adopt the mother's child without the mother having to terminate her parental rights.[5]

In 1996, the Legislature enacted a new adoption statute . . . allowing unmarried adoptive partners to petition the family court regarding parental rights and responsibilities or parent-child contact. Thus, same-sex couples may participate in child-rearing and have recourse to the courts in the event a custody or visitation dispute results from the breakup of a relationship.

Nor do other public-policy considerations compel the conclusion that courts should intervene to consider whether third parties claiming a parent-like relationship ought to be given parent-child contact with the children of

5. According to the dissent, we should not presume that the parties were aware of judicial decisions that would have permitted both of them to adopt Sarah. We do not presume the parties' knowledge of any judicial or statutory law; rather, we suggest that plaintiff should have at least attempted to adopt Sarah before seeking equitable relief based on her alleged perceived lack of a legal remedy. Equity will not aid those who fail to take advantage of a remedy available at law. If plaintiff wanted to adopt Sarah, she should have attempted to do so . . .

fit parents. Indeed, many courts and commentators have noted the potential dangers of forcing parents to defend third-party visitation claims.

. . .

[J]urisdiction should not rest upon a test that in effect would examine the merits of visitation or custody petitions on a case-by-case basis. In reality, such a fact-based test would not be a threshold jurisdictional test, but rather would require a full-blown evidentiary hearing in most cases. Thus, any such test would not prevent parents from having to defend themselves against the merits of petitions brought by a potentially wide range of third parties claiming a parent-like relationship with their child.

Plaintiff scoffs at the notion that various relatives, foster parents, and even day-care providers could seek visitation through court intervention, but the cases we have reviewed suggest that the possibilities are virtually limitless. See *In re Hood, 847 P.2d 1300, 1301 (Kan. 1993)* (day-care provider claiming right to visitation based on best interest of child and existence of substantial relationship between herself and child); *L. v. G., 497 A.2d 215, 219, 222 (N.J. Super. Ct. Ch. Div. 1985)* (applying its inherent equitable powers, court concluded that adult siblings have right to visit minor siblings, subject to best interests of minors); *Bessette v. Saratoga County Comm'r, 619 N.Y.S.2d 359, 359 (App. Div. 1994)* (petition for visitation by former foster parents). Further, as some courts have noted, third parties could abuse the process by seeking visitation to continue an unwanted relationship or otherwise harass the legal parents. See *Hood, 847 P.2d at 1304* (danger of parents being harassed by third-party visitation petitions is policy consideration that weighs against expanding classes of persons who may seek visitation).

. . .

We recognize that, in this age of the disintegrating nuclear family, there are public-policy considerations that favor allowing third parties claiming a parent-like relationship to seek court-compelled parent-child contact. In our view, however, these considerations are not so clear and compelling that they require us to acknowledge that de facto parents have a legally cognizable right to parent-child contact, thereby allowing the superior court to employ its equitable powers to adjudicate their claims. Given the complex social and practical ramifications of expanding the classes of persons entitled to assert parental rights by seeking custody or visitation, the Legislature is better equipped to deal with the problem. Deference to the Legislature is particularly appropriate in this arena because the laws pertaining to parental rights and responsibilities and parent-child contact have been developed over time solely through legislative enactment or judicial construction of legislative enactments.

For the reasons stated, we concur with the superior court's conclusion that it was without authority to consider plaintiff's petition for visitation. We decline to judicially create a right of unrelated third-party visitation actionable in superior court pursuant to the court's equitable powers and subject only to the court's discretion—a right that would exist above and beyond the circumscribed rights granted by the Legislature. Were we to do so, we would establish, in effect, a two-tiered system in which persons who could not bring their visitation and custody petitions in statutory proceedings before the family court would turn to the superior court for relief. The Legislature did not contemplate such a system, and the law does not compel it.

NOTE

1. In *Titchenal,* the court noted that the claimant had not availed herself of the opportunity under Vermont law to adopt the child. Should a person's claim for parental status be automatically denied if that person is able to adopt the child of his or her companion but does not do so? What if the state provides couples the option of registering as domestic partners and they do not do so?

2. An increasing number of courts that have considered the issue have been willing to recognize parental rights for persons who do not meet statutory definitions of "parent." *See, e.g.*, In re Carvin, 122 P.3d 161 (Wash. 2005); C.E.W v. D.E.W., 845 A.2d 1146 (Me. 2004); In re Interest of E.L.M.C., 100 P.3d 546 (Colo Ct. App. 2004), *cert. denied*, 2004 WL 2377164; In re Parentage of A.B., 818 N.E.2d 126 (Ind. Ct. App. 2004); In re Bonfield, 97 Ohio St.3d 387, 780 N.E.2d 241 (2002); T.B. v. L.R.M., 567 Pa. 222, 786 A.2d 913 (2001); Rubano v. DiCenzo, 759 A.2d 959 (R.I. 2000); E.N.O. v. L.M.M., 429 Mass. 824, 711 N.E.2d 886 (1999); Holtzman v. Knott, 193 Wis.2d 649, 533 N.W.2d 419 (1995); A.C. v. C.B., 113 N.M. 581, 829 P.2d 660 (App.), *cert. denied*, 113 N.M. 449, 827 P.2d 837 (1992).

Some states, however, have refused to do so. *See, e.g.*, In re Thompson, 11 S.W.3d 913 (Tenn. Ct. App. 1999); Kazmierazak v. Query, 736 So.2d 106 (Fla. Ct. App. 1999); In re Alison D., 77 N.Y.2d 651, 569 N.Y.S.2d 586, 572 N.E.2d 27 (1991).

3. Chapter 7, Section D discusses in more detail some of the issues that arise in determining when a person may be recognized as the parent of a child who has been conceived through the use of reproductive technology.

American Law Institute, Principles of the Law of Family Dissolution: Analysis and Recommendations

SELECTED SECTIONS AND COMMENTS.

CHAPTER 2
THE ALLOCATION OF CUSTODIAL AND DECISIONMAKING RESPONSIBILITY FOR CHILDREN

TOPIC 1
SCOPE OBJECTIVES, DEFINITIONS, AND PARTIES

§ 203. Definitions

For purposes of this Chapter, the following definitions apply.

(1) Unless otherwise specified, a *parent* is either a legal parent, a parent by estoppel, or a de facto parent.

(a) A *legal parent* is an individual who is defined as a parent under other state law.

(b) A *parent by estoppel* is an individual who, though not a legal parent,

(i) is obligated to pay child support . . . or

(ii) lived with the child for at least two years and

(A) over that period had a reasonable, good faith belief that he was the child's biological father, based on marriage to the mother or on the actions or representations of the mother, and fully accepted parental responsibilities consistent with that belief, and

(B) if some time thereafter that belief no longer existed, continued to make reasonable, good-faith efforts to accept responsibilities as the child's father; or

(iii) lived with the child since the child's birth, holding out and accepting full and permanent responsibilities as parent, as part of a prior co-parenting agreement with the child's legal parent (or, if there are two legal parents, both parents) to raise a child together each with full parental rights and responsibilities, when the court finds that recognition of the individual as a parent is in the child's best interests; or

(iv) lived with the child for at least two years, holding out and accepting full and permanent responsibilities as a parent, pursuant to an agreement with the child's parent (or, if there are two legal parents, both parents), when the court finds that recognition of the individual as a parent is in the child's best interests.

(c) A *de facto parent* is an individual other than a legal parent or a parent by estoppel who, for a significant period of time not less than two years,

(i) lived with the child and,

(ii) for reasons primarily other than financial compensation, and with the agreement of a legal parent to form a parent-child relationship, or as a result of a complete failure or inability of any legal parent to perform caretaking functions,

(A) regularly performed a majority of the caretaking functions for the child, or

(B) regularly performed a share of caretaking functions at least as great as that of the parent with whom the child primarily lived.

. . .

(5) *Caretaking functions* are tasks that involve interaction with the child or that direct, arrange, and supervise the interaction and care provided by others. Caretaking functions include but are not limited to all of the following:

(a) satisfying the nutritional needs of the child, managing the child's bedtime and wake-up routines, caring for the child when sick or injured, being attentive to the child's personal hygiene needs including washing, grooming, and dressing, playing with the child and arranging for recreation, protecting the child's physical safety, and providing transportation;

(b) directing the child's various developmental needs, including the acquisition of motor and language skills, toilet training, self-confidence, and maturation;

(c) providing discipline, giving instruction in manners, assigning and supervising chores, and performing other tasks that attend to the child's needs for behavioral control and self-restraint;

(d) arranging for the child's education, including remedial or special services appropriate to the child's needs and interests, communicating with teachers and counselors, and supervising homework;

(e) helping the child to develop and maintain appropriate interpersonal relationships with peers, siblings, and other family members;

(f) arranging for health-care providers, medical follow-up, and home health care;

(g) providing moral and ethical guidance;

(h) arranging alternative care by a family member, babysitter, or other child-care provider or facility, including investigation of alternatives, communication with providers, and supervision of care.

COMMENTS

. . .

C. De facto parent. . . . The requirements for becoming a de facto parent are strict, to avoid unnecessary and inappropriate intrusion into the relationships between legal parents and their children. The individual must have lived with the child for a significant period of time (not less than two years), and acted in the role of a parent for reasons primarily other than financial compensation. The legal parent or parents must have agreed to the arrangement, or it must have arisen because of a complete failure or inability of any legal parent to perform caretaking functions. In addition, the individual must have functioned as a parent either by (a) having performed the majority of caretaking functions for the child, or (b) having performed a share of caretaking functions that is equal to or greater than the share assumed by the legal parent with whom the child primarily lives.

. . .

TOPIC 5
ALLOCATIONS OF RESPONSIBILITY TO INDIVIDUALS OTHER THAN LEGAL PARENTS

§ 2.18. Allocations of Responsibility to Individuals Other Than Legal Parents

(1) The court should allocate responsibility to a legal parent, a parent by estoppel, or a de facto parent. . . . in accordance with the same standards [set forth in other sections of the Principles], except that

(a) it should not allocate the majority of custodial responsibility to a de facto parent over the objection of a legal parent or a parent by estoppel who is fit and willing to assume the majority of custodial responsibility unless

(i) the legal parent or parent by estoppel has not been performing a reasonable share of parenting functions . . . or

(ii) the available alternatives would cause harm to the child; and

(b) it should limit or deny an allocation otherwise to be made if, in light of the number of other individuals to be allocated responsibility, the allocation would be impractical in light of the objectives of this Chapter.

J. JURISDICTION

1. INTERSTATE CUSTODY DISPUTES

An increasingly mobile population in the United States enhances the likelihood that more than one state may be asked to decide matters concerning custody and visitation. The Full Faith and Credit Clause of the U.S. Constitution requires states to give full faith and credit to, among other things, the final judgments of other states. Custody decrees, however, are *not* regarded as final judgments because the state court issuing the decree retains jurisdiction to modify it in the best interest of the child until he or she is 18. The Parental Kidnapping Prevention Act (PKPA) is a federal statute that addresses that problem by requiring that states give full faith and credit to the custody decrees of other states.

If there is no outstanding custody decree from another state, a court must determine if it has jurisdiction to entertain a custody petition. The first effort to clarify when state courts have custody jurisdiction and should exercise it was the 1968 Uniform Child Custody Jurisdiction Act (UCCJA), a model act that was adopted in some version in all fifty states and the District of Columbia. The UCCJA provides two essential bases for the exercise of state court custody jurisdiction. The first is *home state* jurisdiction. This exists when: (1) a child has lived with a parental figure for at least six months before the custody proceeding OR (2) a child has moved from his or her home state within the last six months AND one parent still lives in that state.

For instance, Jason lives with mother and father for seven years in Alabama. His mother and father separate, and Jason and his mother move to Tennessee. Three months later, the father initiates a custody action in Alabama. Alabama has home state jurisdiction because Jason has moved from it within the last six months AND his father still lives there.

The second basis for jurisdiction under the UCCJA is when a child and a parent have a "significant connection" with a state AND there is "substantial evidence" in that state with respect to the appropriate care for the child.For instance, Jane lives with her mother and father in Ohio for five years. Her parents split up and she and her mother move to Wisconsin for four months, Indiana for three months and Florida for three months. Jane's mother has a job in Florida and Jane has enrolled in school there and is taking dance classes after school. Jane's father continues to live in Ohio.

No state court in this instance is authorized to exercise home state jurisdiction, because Jane has been gone from Ohio for more than six months and has not lived in another state for six months.

Do Jane and her mother have a "significant connection" to Florida? If her mother's job and Jane's schooling are intended to be permanent, they may. Is there "substantial evidence" available in Florida about the appropriate care for Jane? There could be, since a Florida court might be in a position to evaluate Jane's education and caregiving arrangements, and her mother's schedule. Jane's father, however, might argue that Jane still has a significant connection to Ohio since he lives there, and his claim would be even stronger if, for instance, either or both sets of grandparents lived in Ohio. Such information also could suggest that substantial evidence about the best custody arrangement for Jane is available in Ohio.

Finally, suppose that the facts in the second scenario are the same, except that Jane has moved with her mother from Ohio to Florida within the last six months. Ohio can exercise home state jurisdiction, but Florida also might have a plausible claim that it has jurisdiction on the basis of the significant connection/substantial evidence test. Which state should exercise jurisdiction? The UCCJA provides no explicit answer to this question.

In part to address this uncertainty, the Uniform Child Custody Jurisdiction and Enforcement Act (UCCJEA) was promulgated in 1997. The

UCCJEA, CJEA, adopted in over thirty states, preserves the two main bases for jurisdiction contained in the UCCJA. It provides, however, that a court with home state jurisdiction has priority over a court with jurisdiction based on significant connections and substantial evidence with respect to initial custody determinations. UCCJEA § 201. The PKPA contains this same preference. If a court learns that a custody proceeding has been initiated in another state with jurisdiction under the Act, it must stay its own proceeding and confer with the other state. Unless the other state determines that the court that has contacted it is a more appropriate forum, the latter court must dismiss its proceeding. UCCJEA § 206.

Chaddick v. Monopoli

Supreme Court of Florida, 1998.
714 So.2d 1007.

■ OVERTON, JUSTICE.

... Petitioner, Karen Chaddick, and respondent, Joseph Monopoli, divorced in Massachusetts in 1988, and Chaddick was awarded custody of their two minor children by a Massachusetts court. Subsequently, Chaddick and the children moved to Florida, and Monopoli moved to Virginia. Under the terms of the Massachusetts decree, Monopoli was entitled to summer visitation with the children.

In July 1993, Chaddick sent the children from Florida to Virginia for visitation during July and August. On August 10, 1993, Monopoli filed a custody petition in Virginia alleging, in part, that: (1) Chaddick had custody of the children pursuant to an order of the court of Massachusetts; (2) Monopoli had had visitation with the children for the three weeks prior to the filing of the petition; (3) Monopoli was to return the children to Florida on August 6, 1993, by airplane; (4) United Airlines had refused to allow the children to travel without Chaddick's address in Florida; (5) Chaddick had refused and continued to refuse to provide her address to Monopoli or to the Charlottesville police; and (6) Chaddick was pregnant and living with a man to whom she was not married. A custody order was entered in Virginia that same month awarding custody to Monopoli.

After that action was filed, Chaddick retained a Virginia attorney to represent her to contest the Virginia court's jurisdiction to hear Monopoli's custody petition. In her memorandum of law contesting jurisdiction, she asserted that, under the UCCJA and the Federal Parental Kidnapping Prevention Act (FPKPA), Virginia did not have jurisdiction over this matter. Apparently, subsequent proceedings ensued in Virginia and the Virginia court ruled against Chaddick in March 1995.... Chaddick assert[s] ... that the Virginia tribunal has failed to make determinations and exercise jurisdiction in accordance with [the UCCJA and FPKPA]."

In April 1995, which was almost two years after the Virginia proceeding was initiated, Chaddick filed a petition in Florida seeking enforcement of the Massachusetts decree. The Florida trial judge, following a telephone call to the Virginia court in which he "communicated" with the Virginia judge, dismissed the petition. The Florida judge made a note of that communication, which is part of the record in this proceeding. The Florida trial judge stated in his order of dismissal that he had discussed the case with the Virginia judge and that the Virginia judge "has heard all of the matters raised by petitioner, Karen Chaddick, as late as March 3, 1995, and she ruled against the petitioner on them." The trial judge also determined that he did not have jurisdiction of this case under the UCCJA and must defer to Virginia.

On appeal, a divided Fifth District Court of Appeal affirmed, in an *en banc opinion, concluding that "[t]he record affirmatively shows the Florida trial court acted in conformity with the dictates and objectives of the UCCJA in finding that the Virginia court properly assumed jurisdiction and considered the issues Chaddick wishes to raise in Florida." Chaddick, 677 So.2d at 348.*

The UCCJA was first promulgated by the National Commissioners on Uniform State Laws in 1968. Since that time, all fifty states, the District of Columbia, and the Virgin Islands have adopted the UCCJA. . . .

The UCCJA sets out nine purposes consistent with its overall policy of bringing order to interstate custody disputes. 9 U.L.A. 123–24. As indicated by those purposes, the UCCJA attempts, in part, to avoid relitigation of custody decisions of other states in this state. In giving effect to the purpose of the UCCJA, under section 61.1314, a Florida court must defer to a court in another state in a custody dispute if, at the time a petition was filed in Florida, a similar proceeding was pending in a court of another state exercising jurisdiction in substantial conformity with the UCCJA. That section provides as follows:

> (1) A court of this state shall not exercise its jurisdiction under this act if, at the time the petition is filed, a proceeding concerning the custody of the child was pending in a court of another state exercising jurisdiction substantially in conformity with this act, unless the proceeding is stayed by the court of the other state because this state is a more appropriate forum or for other reasons.
>
> . . .
>
> (3) If the court is informed during the course of the proceeding that a proceeding concerning the custody of the child was pending in another state before the court assumed jurisdiction, it shall stay the proceeding and communicate with the court in which the other proceeding is pending, to the end that the issue may be litigated in the more appropriate forum and that information be exchanged in accordance with s.s. 61.134–61.1346. If a court of this state has made a custody decree before being informed of a pending proceeding in a court of another state, it shall immediately inform that court of the fact. If the court is informed that a proceeding was commenced in another state after it assumed jurisdiction, it shall likewise inform the other court to the end that the issues may be litigated in the more appropriate forum.

(Emphasis added.)

Under section 61.1314(3), a Florida trial judge must, upon learning that a proceeding concerning the custody of a child was pending in another state before the Florida court assumed jurisdiction, "stay the proceeding and communicate with the court in which the other proceeding is pending." This mandated communication is for the purpose of avoiding jurisdictional conflicts. See Stock v. Stock, 677 So.2d 1341 (Fla. 4th DCA 1996). As noted by the court in Stock, "Only if the courts cannot agree on the most appropriate forum does the priority-of-filing principle enunciated in subsection 61.1314(1) require that the dispute be litigated in the first court to exercise jurisdiction substantially in conformity with the UCCJA." 677 So.2d at 1346. Similarly, under section 61.1316, a court having jurisdiction under the

UCCJA may decline to exercise its jurisdiction if it finds that it is an inconvenient forum to make a custody determination under the circumstances of a case and that a court of another state is a more appropriate forum. § 61.1316(1), Fla. Stat. (1997).

. . .

Under these principles, the trial judge in this case did exactly what was required of him by initiating contact with the Virginia court to determine the status of the Virginia litigation, to determine whether Florida was the appropriate forum for resolving this custody issue, and to determine whether a forum was available to the parties to resolve the issue of custody. According to Chaddick, however, the trial court erred in conducting the telephone call to the Virginia court out of her presence and off the record and in failing to conduct a full evidentiary hearing as to whether the Virginia court exercised its jurisdiction substantially in conformity with the UCCJA, as required by the First District Court of Appeal's decision in *Walt v. Walt, 574 So.2d 205 (Fla. 1st DCA 1991).*

By asking Florida to enforce the Massachusetts judgment, Chaddick is clearly seeking to have the Florida court overrule the Virginia court's determination of jurisdiction and to reconsider the Virginia court's determination of custody. The very fact that Chaddick filed the Florida action only a month after the Virginia court ruled against her is evidence of Chaddick's seeking a "second bite at the apple." Such conduct is clearly contrary to the basic philosophy of the UCCJA and requires the type of relitigation that the UCCJA was intended to prevent. As previously stated, one of the purposes of the UCCJA is to avoid relitigation of custody decisions of other states in this state. The UCCJA clearly was not designed to give litigants a second avenue for seeking review of an adverse decision by a trial court of another state in which all parties participated. As noted by Judge Harris in his specially concurring opinion in the district court's decision in this case:

. . .

> If the mother wished to challenge the authority of the Virginia courts to hear this issue without submitting herself to the jurisdiction of the Virginia courts, she should have filed her petition to domesticate and enforce the Massachusetts judgment in Florida. Then the assigned judges, pursuant to the UCCJA, would determine which state should proceed. Indeed that is a primary function of the UCCJA. In our case, the mother did not come to the Florida courts until the Virginia court had not only, with her full participation, ruled on the issue of jurisdiction but also had awarded custody of the children to the father. This was too late.

. . .

> ... Having lost this issue in a forum in which she voluntarily appeared, Judge Baker was correct in not giving her a second bite of the apple.

Chaddick, 677 So.2d at 349–350. We fully agree with this analysis. As indicated by Chaddick's petition to the district court in this case, she "fully participated" in the Virginia proceeding. Chaddick appears to be asking this Court to require an evidentiary hearing regarding the telephone conversation between the Florida judge and the Virginia judge in which they discussed the status of the Virginia case and Virginia's jurisdiction. Apparently, Chaddick's request would allow her to question the Virginia judge and place that judge in the untenable position of having to be a witness to explain the basis of her determination that the Virginia court had properly exercised jurisdiction.

. . .

The First District's opinion in *Walt* does require that an evidentiary hearing be conducted to determine whether a sister court exercised its jurisdiction in substantial conformity with the UCCJA. However, the court in Walt was considering this issue under section 61.1328, which involves the enforcement of an out-of-state decree. The enforcement of the Virginia decree is not at issue here. To clarify this issue, however, we hold that the determination of whether an evidentiary hearing must be conducted regarding the issue of another state's appropriate exercise of jurisdiction is within the discretion of the trial judge, depending upon the facts of the particular case before the court. Consequently, we disapprove Walt to the extent it is inconsistent with our finding here.

In this case, the father lived in Virginia; the children were with him for summer visitation; and he alleged that the mother would not cooperate in providing information to enable him to return the children to Florida. The mother contested jurisdiction and fully participated in the Virginia proceeding. Then, one month after an adverse decision by the Virginia court, she filed the instant petition. Under these circumstances, we conclude that the trial judge properly dismissed Chaddick's petition.

. . .

We do believe that in the future parties should be given an opportunity to be present when a Florida judge and the judge of a sister state communicate[8] or that a record of that conversation must be made.... [T]he record on appeal must be sufficient to allow the appellate court to properly review the trial judge's decision of whether the sister state exercised its jurisdiction "substantially in conformity" with UCCJA. This does not mean, however, that the parties may examine the judge of the sister state; the communication is to be strictly between the judges for the purpose of determining the status of the case in the sister state and to examine the basis for jurisdiction in that state.

In summary, we conclude that the trial judge appropriately dismissed Chaddick's petition under the circumstances of this case. To ensure that future cases are not jeopardized by an inadequate record on this issue, we hold, prospectively, that: (1) the parties must be given the opportunity to be present during a Florida judge's conversation with a judge of a sister court but the parties may not participate in that conversation; and (2) the Florida judge must explicitly set forth in the record the reasons for the judge's finding that the sister state was or was not exercising its jurisdiction in substantial conformity with UCCJA.

Accordingly, we disapprove Walt and those parts of the district court's opinion in this case that are inconsistent with this opinion but we approve the result of the district court's decision in this case.

It is so ordered.

Thompson v. Thompson

United States Supreme Court, 1988.
484 U.S. 174, 108 S.Ct. 513, 98 L.Ed.2d 512.

■ JUSTICE MARSHALL delivered the opinion of the Court.

We granted certiorari in this case to determine whether the Parental Kidnaping Prevention Act of 1980, 28 U.S.C. § 1738A, furnishes an implied

8. The parties, of course, could be present by telephone.

cause of action in federal court to determine which of two conflicting state custody decisions is valid.

. . .

The Parental Kidnaping Prevention Act (PKPA or Act) imposes a duty on the States to enforce a child custody determination entered by a court of a sister State if the determination is consistent with the provisions of the Act. In order for a state court's custody decree to be consistent with the provisions of the Act, the State must have jurisdiction under its own local law and one of five conditions set out in § 1738A(c)(2) must be met.... Once a State exercises jurisdiction consistently with the provisions of the Act, no other State may exercise concurrent jurisdiction over the custody dispute, § 1738A(g), even if it would have been empowered to take jurisdiction in the first instance,[2] and all States must accord full faith and credit to the first State's ensuing custody decree.

As the legislative scheme suggests, and as Congress explicitly specified, one of the chief purposes of the PKPA is to "avoid jurisdictional competition and conflict between State courts." This case arises out of a jurisdictional stalemate that came to pass notwithstanding the strictures of the Act. In July 1978, respondent Susan Clay (then Susan Thompson) filed a petition in Los Angeles Superior Court asking the court to dissolve her marriage to petitioner David Thompson and seeking custody of the couple's infant son, Matthew. The court initially awarded the parents joint custody of Matthew, but that arrangement became infeasible when respondent decided to move from California to Louisiana to take a job. The court then entered an order providing that respondent would have sole custody of Matthew once she left for Louisiana. This state of affairs was to remain in effect until the court investigator submitted a report on custody, after which the court intended to make a more studied custody determination.

Respondent and Matthew moved to Louisiana in December of 1980. Three months later, respondent filed a petition in Louisiana state court for enforcement of the California custody decree, judgment of custody, and modification of petitioner's visitation privileges. By order dated April 7, 1981, the Louisiana court granted the petition and awarded sole custody of Matthew to respondent. Two months later, however, the California court, having received and reviewed its investigator's report, entered an order awarding sole custody of Matthew to petitioner. Thus arose the current impasse.

In August 1983, petitioner brought this action in the District Court for the Central District of California. Petitioner requested an order declaring the Louisiana decree invalid and the California decree valid, and enjoining the enforcement of the Louisiana decree. Petitioner did not attempt to enforce the California decree in a Louisiana state court before he filed suit in federal court. The District Court granted respondent's motion to dismiss the complaint for lack of subject matter and personal jurisdiction. The Court of Appeals for the Ninth Circuit affirmed.... We granted certiorari, 479 U.S. 1063 (1987), and we now affirm.

. . .

2. The sole exception to this constraint occurs where the first State either has lost jurisdiction or has declined to exercise continuing jurisdiction. See § 1738A(f).

In determining whether to infer a private cause of action from a federal statute, our focal point is Congress' intent in enacting the statute. As guides to discerning that intent, we have relied on the four factors set out in Cort v. Ash, see 422 U.S. 66, 78 (1975), along with other tools of statutory construction. Our focus on congressional intent does not mean that we require evidence that Members of Congress, in enacting the statute, actually had in mind the creation of a private cause of action. The implied cause of action doctrine would be a virtual dead letter were it limited to correcting drafting errors when Congress simply forgot to codify its evident intention to provide a cause of action. Rather, as an implied cause of action doctrine suggests, "the legislative history of a statute that does not expressly create or deny a private remedy will typically be equally silent or ambiguous on the question." We therefore have recognized that Congress' "intent may appear implicitly in the language or structure of the statute, or in the circumstances of its enactment." ... In this case, the essential predicate for implication of a private remedy plainly does not exist. None of the factors that have guided our inquiry in this difficult area points in favor of inferring a private cause of action. Indeed, the context, language, and legislative history of the PKPA all point sharply away from the remedy petitioner urges us to infer.

We examine initially the context of the PKPA with an eye toward determining Congress' perception of the law that it was shaping or reshaping. At the time Congress passed the PKPA, custody orders held a peculiar status under the full faith and credit doctrine, which requires each State to give effect to the judicial proceedings of other States, see U.S. Const., Art. IV, § 1; 28 U.S.C. § 1738. The anomaly traces to the fact that custody orders characteristically are subject to modification as required by the best interests of the child. As a consequence, some courts doubted whether custody orders were sufficiently "final" to trigger full faith and credit requirements, and this Court had declined expressly to settle the question. Even if custody orders were subject to full faith and credit requirements, the Full Faith and Credit Clause obliges States only to accord the same force to judgments as would be accorded by the courts of the State in which the judgment was entered. Because courts entering custody orders generally retain the power to modify them, courts in other States were no less entitled to change the terms of custody according to their own views of the child's best interest. For these reasons, a parent who lost a custody battle in one State had an incentive to kidnap the child and move to another State to relitigate the issue. This circumstance contributed to widespread jurisdictional deadlocks like this one, and more importantly, to a national epidemic of parental kidnaping. At the time the PKPA was enacted, sponsors of the Act estimated that between 25,000 and 100,000 children were kidnaped by parents who had been unable to obtain custody in a legal forum.

A number of States joined in an effort to avoid these jurisdictional conflicts by adopting the Uniform Child Custody Jurisdiction Act (UCCJA), 9 U.L.A. §§ 1–28 (1979). ... The project foundered, however, because a number of States refused to enact the UCCJA while others enacted it with modifications. In the absence of uniform national standards for allocating and enforcing custody determinations, noncustodial parents still had reason to snatch their children and petition the courts of any of a number of haven States for sole custody.

The context of the PKPA therefore suggests that the principal problem Congress was seeking to remedy was the inapplicability of full faith and credit requirements to custody determinations. Statements made when the Act was introduced in Congress forcefully confirm that suggestion. The sponsors and supporters of the Act continually indicated that the purpose of the PKPA was to provide for nationwide enforcement of custody orders made in accordance with the terms of the UCCJA. As Deputy Attorney General Michel testified:

. . .

"In essence [the PKPA] would impose on States a Federal duty, under enumerated standards derived from the UCCJA, to give full faith and credit to the custody decrees of other States. Such legislation would, in effect, amount to Federal adoption of key provisions of the UCCJA for all States and would eliminate the incentive for one parent to remove a minor child to another jurisdiction." PKPA Joint Hearing 48.

The significance of Congress' full faith and credit approach to the problem of child snatching is that the Full Faith and Credit Clause, in either its constitutional or statutory incarnations, does not give rise to an implied federal cause of action. Rather, the clause "only prescribes a rule by which courts, Federal and state, are to be guided when a question arises in the progress of a pending suit as to the faith and credit to be given by the court to the public acts, records, and judicial proceedings of a State other than that in which the court is sitting." Because Congress' chief aim in enacting the PKPA was to extend the requirements of the Full Faith and Credit Clause to custody determinations, the Act is most naturally construed to furnish a rule of decision for courts to use in adjudicating custody disputes and not to create an entirely new cause of action. It thus is not compatible with the purpose and context of the legislative scheme to infer a private cause of action. See Cort v. Ash, 422 U.S. at 78.

The language and placement of the statute reinforce this conclusion. The PKPA, 28 U.S.C. § 1738A, is an addendum to the full faith and credit statute, 28 U.S.C. § 1738. This fact alone is strong proof that the Act is intended to have the same operative effect as the full faith and credit statute.... As for the language of the Act, it is addressed entirely to States and state courts. Unlike statutes that explicitly confer a right on a specified class of persons, the PKPA is a mandate directed to state courts to respect the custody decrees of sister States....

Finally, the legislative history of the PKPA provides unusually clear indication that Congress did not intend the federal courts to play the enforcement role that petitioner urges.

. . .

In sum, the context, language, and history of the PKPA together make out a conclusive case against inferring a cause of action in federal court to determine which of two conflicting state custody decrees is valid. Against this impressive evidence, petitioner relies primarily on the argument that failure to infer a cause of action would render the PKPA nugatory. We note, as a preliminary response, that ultimate review remains available in this Court for truly intractable jurisdictional deadlocks. In addition, the unspoken presumption in petitioner's argument is that the States are either unable or unwilling to enforce the provisions of the Act. This is a presumption we are not prepared, and more importantly, Congress was not prepared, to indulge. State courts faithfully administer the Full Faith and Credit Clause every day; now that Congress has extended full faith and credit requirements to child custody orders, we can think of no reason why the courts' administration of federal law in custody disputes will be any less vigilant. Should state courts prove as obstinate as petitioner predicts, Congress may choose to revisit the issue. But any more radical approach to the problem will have to await further legislative action; we "will not engraft a remedy on a statute, no matter how salutary, that Congress did not intend to provide." The judgment of the Court of Appeals is affirmed.

It is so ordered.

2. INTERNATIONAL CUSTODY DISPUTES

Ohlander v. Larson

United States Court of Appeals, Tenth Circuit, 1997.
114 F.3d 1531.

■ BRORBY, CIRCUIT JUDGE.

Ms. Ohlander appeals the United States District Court for the District of Utah's judgment denying her petition for the return of her daughter Julia to Sweden under the Hague Convention, ordering Julia's return to Utah, denying her two motions to withdraw and dismiss her petition, denying her motions to stay enforcement of the judgment, and a subsequent judgment denying her Fed.R.Civ.P. 60(b) motion to set aside the judgment. Applying the standards under Fed.R.Civ.P. 41(a)(2) in the Hague Convention context, we determine the district court abused its discretion in denying the motion to dismiss. We reverse and remand to the district court with instructions to dismiss Ms. Ohlander's petition.

I. BACKGROUND

The Hague Convention on the Civil Aspects of International Child Abduction (the "Convention"), as implemented by both the United States Congress through the International Child Abduction Remedies Act, 42 U.S.C. §§ 11601–11610 (1994), and Sweden, was adopted by the signatory nations "to protect children internationally from the harmful effects of their wrongful removal or retention and to establish procedures to ensure their prompt return to the State of their habitual residence." The Convention is meant to provide for a child's prompt return once it has been established the child has been "wrongfully removed" to or retained in any affiliated state.

Under the Convention, a removal or retention is "wrongful" if:

a. it is in breach of rights of custody attributed to a person, an institution or any other body, either jointly or alone, under the law of the State in which the child was habitually resident immediately before the removal or retention; and

b. at the time of removal or retention those rights were actually exercised, either jointly or alone, or would have been so exercised but for removal or retention.

Once a removal is deemed "wrongful," "the authority concerned shall order the return of the child." However, the Convention provides for several exceptions to return if the person opposing return can show any of the following: 1) the person requesting return was not, at the time of the retention or removal, actually exercising custody rights or had consented to or subsequently acquiesced in the removal or retention; 2) the return of the child would result in grave risk of physical or psychological harm to the child; 3) the return of the child "would not be permitted by the fundamental principles of the requested State relating to the protection of human rights and fundamental freedoms"; or 4) the proceeding was commenced more than one year after the abduction and the child has become settled in the new environment.

II. FACTS

Ms. Ohlander, a Swedish citizen, and Mr. Larson, a United States citizen, were married in Utah in 1989. In August 1990, their daughter Julia was born in Provo, Utah. During the Christmas holiday season of 1990–91, when Julia was five months old, the entire family traveled to Sweden to visit Ms. Ohlander's family with the intent to return to their Utah home in January 1991. After arriving in Sweden, Ms. Ohlander decided to remain in Sweden with Julia; Ms. Ohlander went into hiding with her daughter and severed contact with her husband. Mr. Larson returned to Utah alone in mid-January 1991.

By April 1991, Mr. Larson had reestablished contact with Ms. Ohlander. In June 1991, with Julia now almost a year old, Ms. Ohlander returned to Utah to be with Mr. Larson. Ms. Ohlander and Julia remained with Mr. Larson for seven months. On January 13, 1992, Ms. Ohlander returned with Julia to Sweden without Mr. Larson's consent.

By November 1993,[2] Julia had resided continuously in Sweden for almost two years, and was a little over three years old. Mr. Larson returned to Sweden with his new wife to see Julia, and during one visitation, applied the law of "grab and run" taking Julia back to Utah without Ms. Ohlander's consent. In January 1994, Ms. Ohlander filed a petition seeking her daughter's return pursuant to the Hague Convention in the United States District Court for the District of Utah. Ms. Ohlander also secured an ex parte Order for Issuance of Warrant in Lieu of Writ of Habeas Corpus from the district court, directing peace officers to take Julia into protective custody and to release her to Ms. Ohlander, but prohibiting Ms. Ohlander from removing Julia from Utah pending further order. Mr. Larson delivered Julia to Ms. Ohlander on January 30, 1994, and on February 1, 1994, Ms. Ohlander disobeyed the court's order and applied her own version of the law of "grab and run" by returning to Sweden with Julia.

In August 1994, shortly after Julia's fourth birthday, the district court entered an order finding Ms. Ohlander in contempt and directing her to return Julia to the United States within thirty days. Ms. Ohlander failed to comply. Two months later, in October 1994, following Ms. Ohlander's and Julia's return to Sweden, Mr. Larson filed a Convention application for Julia's return with the United States Central Authority, which was forwarded to Sweden's Central Authority. Ms. Ohlander then filed a motion, pursuant to Fed.R.Civ.P. 41(a)(2), to dismiss her district court petition, based, in part, on the Convention's art. 12, which authorizes a judicial authority to stay or dismiss the application or judicial proceedings seeking a child's return.[4] Hague Convention, art. 12, 51 Fed.Reg. at 10499. In January 1995, prior to the hearing on Ms. Ohlander's motion, Mr. Larson petitioned the Sweden

2. Between January 1992 and November 1993, Ms. Ohlander and Mr. Larson were participating in divorce and custody proceedings taking place in Sweden.

4. Specifically, the Convention's art. 12 states:

> Where the judicial or administrative authority in the requested State has reason to believe that the child has been taken to another state, it may stay the proceedings, or dismiss the application for the return of the child.

Hague Convention, art. 12, 51 Fed.Reg. at 10499.

court pursuant to the Convention for Julia's return on the ground Ms. Ohlander had "wrongfully removed" her from Utah.

The United States district court conducted a hearing on Ms. Ohlander's motion to dismiss. During that hearing, the United States district court was informed of Mr. Larson's Hague Convention proceeding in Sweden. The district court denied the motion to dismiss solely on the basis of Ms. Ohlander's contempt of its order not to remove Julia from Utah. Ms. Ohlander later orally renewed her motion to dismiss, which the district court denied on the same grounds.

The district court conducted a bench trial on Ms. Ohlander's Hague Convention petition to determine the issues of habitual residence and wrongful removal pursuant to the Convention. However, neither Ms. Ohlander nor Julia was present for the hearing, nor did they testify by other means.... Ultimately, the district court found Julia was at all times a "habitual resident" of Utah, and as such, Ms. Ohlander's retention of Julia in Sweden in 1991, and her removals of Julia from Utah in 1992 and 1994 were all "wrongful" under the Convention. Accordingly, the district court ordered Julia's immediate return to Utah and requested the aid of the Contracting States in achieving that goal.

Following the United States district court's decision, the Sweden courts held hearings to determine the merits of Mr. Larson's petition. Both Mr. Larson and Ms. Ohlander were present during the Sweden court proceeding. The Sweden Supreme Administrative Court held Julia's habitual residence changed from Utah to Sweden after she had lived in Sweden for twelve months following the January 1992 abduction—a decision directly in conflict with the United States district court's holding.

Once the Sweden court had made its ruling, Ms. Ohlander filed a motion to stay enforcement of the United States district court's order, and a motion to set aside the United States' judgment under Fed.R.Civ.P. 60(b). The United States district court denied the motions, again solely on the basis of Ms. Ohlander's contempt. We are presented, therefore, with two international decisions standing in direct conflict, and it is this contradiction we attempt to resolve for both the present case and for future cases.

III. DISCUSSION

This case presents issues novel to this court, and according to our research, novel to this country. Our aim is to provide courts with guidance in future similar cases, namely, where two civil actions under the Hague Convention on the Civil Aspects of International Child Abductions are filed in disparate courts due to a child's removal from the court of first jurisdiction. Also, our aim is to give meaning to the Convention's intended purpose of discouraging parents from fleeing with their children in search of a favorable decision. Notably, we are faced not only with issues of the proper interpretation of bare text in the form of the Hague Convention treaty, but also with the plight of a now six-year-old girl to whom the law of "grab and run" repeatedly has been applied.

We therefore must examine the following competing interests of: the district court ensuring compliance with its orders; the procedural conduct of the parties; and most important, the Convention's intent and our duty to see that intent justly carried out.

. . .

IV. MOTION TO DISMISS

Even though Ms. Ohlander appeals several of the district court's rulings, our decision on the motion to dismiss pursuant to Fed.R.Civ.P. 41(a)(2) is dispositive. Thus, we need not address the remaining issues. We therefore turn our focus to whether the district court abused its discretion in denying Ms. Ohlander's motion to dismiss pursuant to Fed.R.Civ.P. 41(a)(2).

. . .

B. *Relevant Factors Considered Under 41(a)(2)/Standard of Review*

Once a defendant files an answer, as was the case here, a plaintiff may voluntarily dismiss an action only upon order of the court. Fed.R.Civ.P. 41(a)(2). We review the district court's decision to deny a voluntary dismissal under such conditions for abuse of discretion. Absent "legal prejudice" to the defendant, the district court normally should grant such a dismissal. The parameters of what constitutes "legal prejudice" are not entirely clear, but relevant factors the district court should consider include: the opposing party's effort and expense in preparing for trial; excessive delay and lack of diligence on the part of the movant; insufficient explanation of the need for a dismissal; and the present stage of litigation. Each factor need not be resolved in favor of the moving party for dismissal to be appropriate, nor need each factor be resolved in favor of the opposing party for denial of the motion to be proper.

The above list of factors is by no means exclusive. Any other relevant factors should come into the district court's equation. In fact, in the context of this Hague Convention proceeding, the district court was impressed with a duty to exercise its discretion by carefully appraising any additional factors unique to the context of this case, including the interests in comity, uniform interpretation of the Convention and the importance of giving import to the Hague Convention's intended purpose as relevant to the motion to dismiss.

. . .

In sum, the district court was obligated to consider the novelty of the circumstances surrounding this case. Instead, the court did not consider the merits of Ms. Ohlander's motion due exclusively to her contumacious conduct. It is true Ms. Ohlander blatantly violated the court's orders and absconded to Sweden with Julia in tow. We refuse to condone such conduct. However, neither can we condone a court ignoring its duty to consider the merits of a motion to dismiss simply because a party has violated its orders. Whether a motion to dismiss under Rule 41(a)(2) may be granted is a matter initially left to the district court's discretion, but such discretion does not excuse a court's failure to exercise any discretion, nor does it save an unpermitted exercise of discretion from reversal.... We believe the district court's decision to deny Ms. Ohlander's motion solely on the grounds of her contempt and without considering any additional circumstances, amounts to a failure to exercise discretion, and is, consequently, an abuse of that discretion.

C. *Merits of Ms. Ohlander's 41(a)(2) Motion*

1. Traditional Factors

Although the district court's failure to apply the correct legal standard could serve as a basis for remand, in the interest of efficiency and judicial economy, and in the interest of providing immediate guidance as to the most appropriate direction of this case in light of the Convention's purpose, we turn to the merits of Ms. Ohlander's motion to dismiss....

a. Proper Interpretation of the Hague Convention's Procedures

When the district court considered whether Ms. Ohlander's removal of Julia from Utah was wrongful, it misconstrued the Convention's contemplated procedures. According to the Convention, once a petition is filed, a court should consider only whether a respondent's removals of a child are wrongful. *See Hague Convention, arts. 3, 12, 51 Fed.Reg. at 10498, 10499, 42 U.S.C. § 11603(b), (e).* Here, antithetic to the Convention's intent as a whole, the court considered whether the petitioner's removals of the child were wrongful.

. . .

b. Intent of the Hague Convention

Failing to grant the motion to dismiss where a second duplicative action has been filed in a different country would potentially render the Hague Convention meaningless. Part of the Convention's intent is "to ensure that rights of custody and of access under the law of one Contracting State are effectively respected in other Contracting States." Hague Convention, art. 1(b), 51 Fed.Reg. at 10498. Prior to the Convention, when faced with an unfavorable custody decision, a parent would flee to another country in search of a custody decision in his or her favor. This would often result in two conflicting custody decisions without guidance as to which country's custody decision had preference. The Hague Convention was drafted with the intent to remove forever the incentive for a parent to flee across borders to obtain a favorable ruling. Under the Convention, a child is to be expediently returned to his or her state of habitual residence "so that a court there can examine the merits of the custody dispute and award custody in the child's best interests." Pub. Notice 957, 51 Fed.Reg. at 10505. As a result, the Convention was meant, in part, to lend priority to the custody determination hailing from the child's state of habitual residence.

While the Convention proceedings in this case certainly have not achieved this intended result, a refusal to dismiss this action only exacerbates the problem. By failing to dismiss the United States action we would allow to stand two conflicting decisions regarding Julia's state of habitual residence, which could very well require a Hague Convention to determine which Hague Convention determination is valid. This, of course, is absurd. By dismissing this action, we instead require these and future litigants to choose which jurisdiction will determine a child's state of habitual residence, thereby salvaging what we can of the Convention's intended purpose.

Failing to grant the motion to dismiss also could create a new incentive for parents to flee Hague Convention proceedings in the hope of obtaining a second, more favorable Convention determination in another country. We then would be left to solve the riddle of which competing ruling in each case is valid. This is a task we refuse to acquire. Rather, we believe the parties' interests would be best represented and judicial resources best spent if parents engaged in this type international custody battle are required to resolve their dispute in one jurisdiction or the other. Holding Mr. Larson and future litigants to one jurisdiction gives import to the Convention's intended meaning.

We REVERSE the district court and REMAND with instructions to dismiss the petition without prejudice.

Silverman v. Silverman

United States Court of Appeals, Eighth Circuit, 2003.
338 F.3d 886.

■ BEAM, CIRCUIT JUDGE.

Robert Silverman (Robert) appeals the district court's rulings on his claim under the Hague Convention on the Civil Aspects of International Child Abduction.... Because we find that the children's habitual residence was Israel at the time of their removal and that there is no grave risk of harm to the children if they are returned to Israel, we reverse the district court.

I. BACKGROUND

According to the facts found by the district court, Robert Silverman and Julie Hechter (Julie) met in Israel in 1988 and married in Seattle, Washington, in 1989. They moved throughout the United States and had two children, Sam and Jacob. The family lived in Plymouth, Minnesota, until their move to Israel in late July of 1999. Both Robert and Julie testified in the district court that the move to Israel was Julie's idea and that she was the one pushing for the family to make the move. They sold their Minnesota home in January of 1999, Robert applied for and made Aliyah (immigration) to Israel, and the family moved all of their possessions and their family pets to Israel. While both Robert and Julie set the move up to be permanent, Julie stated in the district court that she was torn about the move, but went ahead with it as a final effort to reconcile the couple's failing marriage.

Both Robert and Julie obtained employment in Israel. The family lived with relatives in Israel until November 1999, when they rented an apartment and signed a one-year lease. In October 1999, Julie flew to the United States to file for bankruptcy in Minnesota. Julie returned to Israel later that month to discover that Robert had obtained a Tzav Ikuv (restraining order), which prevented her from leaving Israel, and that he had put the children's passports and birth certificates in his father's safe deposit box. Robert told her at this point that he knew about the affair she had been having with a man from Massachusetts. Robert cancelled the restraining order on November 3, 1999, after they decided to try to reconcile their marriage. Robert testified in the district court that he would not have allowed Julie to leave Israel *with the children* at any point between October 1999 and June 2000. During this time, Julie stated that Robert threatened her, used force against her and attempted to coerce her. In January 2000, Julie and Robert returned to Minnesota without the children to complete bankruptcy proceedings and they both stated, under oath, that their permanent address was Plymouth, Minnesota. Both of them subsequently returned to Israel. In April 2000, Robert and Julie signed and filed a joint United States income tax form for 1999, which listed their address as Plymouth, Minnesota.

While in Israel, Sam enrolled in an elementary school and Jacob enrolled in preschool. They made friends, learned to speak Hebrew and did well in school. Sam participated in extracurricular activities at his school. During this time, Julie counseled with an Israeli attorney and was told she would probably not get custody of the children through the Israeli Rabbinical court if she separated from Robert in Israel.

At the end of June 2000, Robert allowed Julie to leave Israel with the two children for what she represented would be a summer trip to the United States. She purchased round-trip tickets with the return trip scheduled for

August 30, 2000. At the airport before their departure, Robert threatened Julie, apparently because of his continuing concern that she would not return to Israel with the children, a fear soon realized. She testified that it was at that moment at the airport that she decided not to return to Israel. Julie filed for legal separation from Robert and for custody of the two children in Minnesota state court on August 10, 2000. Robert was served summons in Israel. Robert immediately moved for dismissal of the action, arguing that the state court lacked authority to hear the custody issues because there had not yet been the necessary determinations of "wrongful removal and retention" and "habitual residence" as mandated by the Hague Convention and ICARA, determinations designed to establish whether Israel or the United States had jurisdiction to hear a child custody case.

The record reveals that on August 24, 2000, fourteen days after Julie's Minnesota action had been commenced, Robert filed in Israel a "Request for Return of Abducted Children" with the National Center for Missing and Exploited Children (NCMEC), pursuant to the Hague Convention. On September 22, 2000, a NCMEC agent contacted Robert's Israeli attorney and requested that the attorney obtain a determination from the Israeli courts as to whether Julie had wrongfully removed or retained the children within the meaning of the Hague Convention. Some time shortly thereafter, Robert filed a Hague Convention petition in Israel seeking such a determination. In addition to filing the Israeli action, Robert filed a Hague petition on October 5, 2000, in the United States District Court for the District of Minnesota seeking return of the children to Israel under the Convention.

On October 17, 2000, although on notice of Robert's Hague filings, a state court referee issued an interlocutory administrative order granting Julie temporary custody of the children. Armed with this temporary order, Julie testified that in February 2001 she decided to move with the two children to Massachusetts to live with her paramour. They subsequently moved.

. . . On November 16, 2000, while both the state custody and federal Hague matters were pending in various courts in the United States, the Israeli court ruled that Israel was the place of habitual residence of Sam and Jacob as defined in the Convention and that Julie's failure to return them to Israel was prima facie evidence of wrongful retention of the children in violation of the Convention. . . . On May 4, 2001, the Minnesota trial court entered a final judgment awarding full child custody to Julie, child support from Robert and attorney fees to Julie. While this order specifically stated that the court was on notice of pending Hague Convention litigation, the court decided the custody issues anyway, applying only Minnesota law. The state court determined neither the "habitual residence" of the children nor the issue of "wrongful removal or retention" as required by and defined in the Hague Convention and ICARA. Indeed, it was not asked to do so. The court, in awarding Julie custody and child support, found that Minnesota was the children's "home state" as referenced in *Minnesota Statutes § 518D.102*. In *section 518D.102(h)*, "home state" is defined as "the state in which a child lived with a parent . . . for at least six consecutive months immediately before the commencement of a child custody proceeding. . . . A period of temporary absence . . . is part of the period." . . .

On May 9, 2002, the federal district court ruled in favor of Julie on Robert's Hague Convention claim, finding that Minnesota was the "habitual residence" of the children and, alternatively, that even if Israel was their habitual residence, that there was a grave risk in returning the children to Israel under the Article 13(b) exception to the Convention.[13]

II. DISCUSSION

. . .

B. Standard of Review

Having determined that the district court had jurisdiction to decide the Hague Convention issues, we now consider which standard of review we should apply in this appeal. Both parties agree that the "grave risk of harm" determination should be reviewed de novo. The conflict arises regarding the standard of review for the district court's habitual residence determination.

This court has not yet articulated a standard of review for habitual residence determinations under the Hague Convention. Julie and the dissent argue that the habitual residence determination is one of fact, to be reviewed for clear error. We disagree, being more persuaded by the Ninth and Third Circuits, which have determined that habitual residence determinations raise mixed questions of fact and law and therefore should be reviewed de novo. . . .

. . . It is imperative that parents be able to assess the status of the law on habitual residence and wrongful removal and retention. If habitual residence is treated as a purely factual matter, to be decided by an individual judge in individual circumstances unique to each case, parents will never be able to guess, let alone determine, whether they are at risk of losing custody by allowing their children to visit overseas or in allowing them to make international trips with an estranged spouse. With such uncertainty, parents experiencing marital difficulties will be less likely to allow children to travel with one parent and less likely to allow children to maintain relationships with families in other countries. Congress must have intended that there be enough consistency in these cases to prevent such a result. Indeed, we find it difficult to believe that American legislators intended to launch American citizens into such unchartable waters. Thus, we think it is not only the correct conclusion that habitual residence be a legal determination subject to de novo review, we also think it is the correct policy conclusion under the language of the Hague Convention and ICARA.

C. Habitual Residence

. . . [T]he district court concluded that, despite the intent present at the time of the move to Israel and the outward appearance of a permanent move, Julie's unilateral desire to return to the United States, coupled with the alleged abuse from October 1999, eliminated the settled intent necessary to establish habitual residence. The district court erred.

The court should have looked at the habitual residence of the Silverman children at the time Julie removed them from Israel, keeping in mind that they could only have one habitual residence. The court should have determined the degree of settled purpose from the children's perspective, including the family's change in geography along with their personal possessions and pets, the passage of time, the family abandoning its prior residence and

13. The court found that the habitual residence of the children had never changed to Israel, but remained in Minnesota the entire time. The law is clear that wrongful removal from a country does not change a child's Hague Convention habitual residence. *Feder v. Evans–Feder, 63 F.3d 217, 222 (3d Cir. 1995).* Therefore, if the children's habitual residence changed when they moved to Israel, it did not change back when Julie removed them back to Minnesota.

selling the house, the application for and securing of benefits only available to Israeli immigrants, the children's enrollment in school, and, to some degree, both parents' intentions at the time of the move to Israel. Fairly assessing these facts, there is only one acceptable legal conclusion regarding the children's habitual residence: they were habitual residents of Israel.

. . . For these reasons, we find that the children's habitual residence is in Israel and that Robert has met his burden of presenting a prima facie case under the Convention.

D. Grave Risk of Harm

The district court found that even if the children's habitual residence is in Israel, they need not be returned to Israel because they will face a "grave risk of physical harm" there. The district court reached this conclusion, in part, because the violence in Israel makes it a "zone of war," which is dangerous for the children. *Id.*

The "grave risk of physical or psychological harm" defense is an affirmative defense under Article 13(b) of the Convention that Julie must prove with clear and convincing evidence. [T]his court [has] held that in order to apply the Article 13(b) exception, the court would need to cite specific evidence of potential harm to the individual children. There are two types of grave risk that are appropriate under Article 13(b): sending a child to a "zone of war, famine, or disease," or in cases of serious abuse or neglect.

The district court found that the current situation in Israel constitutes a "zone of war," warranting application of the "grave risk" exception. In *Freier v. Freier, 969 F. Supp. 436, 443 (E.D. Mich. 1996)*, the district court found that Israel in 1996 was not a "zone of war" under Article 13(b). In so finding, the court determined that the fighting was fifteen to ninety minutes from the children's home, no schools were closed, businesses were open, and the mother was able to travel to and from the country. *Id.* No subsequent case has found that Israel is a "zone of war" under the Convention. In fact, there does not appear to be another case that finds any country a "zone of war" under the Convention. Nor does the district court cite any evidence that these children are in any more specific danger living in Israel than they were when their mother voluntarily moved them there in 1999. Rather, the evidence centered on general regional violence, such as suicide bombers, that threaten everyone in Israel. This is not sufficient to establish a "zone of war" which puts the children in "grave risk of physical or psychological harm" under the Convention.

Additionally, the district court erred in taking into account the "fact that Sam and Jacob are settled in their new environment." A removing parent "must not be allowed to abduct a child and then—when brought to court—complain that the child has grown used to the surroundings to which they were abducted."

Israel is not a "zone of war" as meant by the Convention and, therefore, Julie has not met her burden of proving that a grave risk of harm exists. As no other exception applies, the district court erred in denying Robert's Hague petition.

III. CONCLUSION

For the reasons stated above, we reverse the district court. Israel is the habitual residence of the Silverman children and Julie wrongfully removed the children from their habitual residence. The Convention requires us to return wrongfully removed children to their habitual residence, unless specific, limited exceptions apply. No exceptions to the Hague Convention apply, and the Minnesota court's custody determination cannot be used to prevent us from returning the children to Israel. Israel is the proper forum for a custody determination. We remand for entry of an order that the Silverman children be returned to Israel for a custody determination in the Israeli courts.

. . .

■ HEANEY, CIRCUIT JUDGE, with whom MCMILLIAN, MURPHY, and BYE, CIRCUIT JUDGES, join dissenting.

. . .

B. Affirmative Defenses to Removal

I next come to the question of whether Samuel and Jacob should be returned to Israel if it is their habitual residence. Article 13 of the Hague Convention provides:

> The judicial or administrative authority of the requested State is not bound to order the return of the child if the person, institution or other body which opposes its return establishes that—
>
> there is a grave risk that his or her return would expose the child to physical or psychological harm or otherwise place the child in an intolerable situation.

Here, the district court held that even if it had determined that Israel was the habitual residence of Samuel and Jacob, it found in the alternative "that their return to Israel would pose a grave risk of physical harm or otherwise place them in an intolerable situation." The district court noted that in *Freier v. Freier, 969 F. Supp. 436 (E.D. Mich. 1996)*, evidence of unrest in Israel was insufficient to establish the grave risk defense. The district court went on to say that it did not agree with Freier's conclusion in this case because:

> Significant differences exist between the violence occurring at the time Freir [sic] was decided and the violence occurring in Israel today. Unlike before, the violence has permeated areas that were previously unaffected by the conflict. Furthermore, the type of violence, through suicide bombings, has placed civilians, including children, at much greater risk. The level and intensity of violence occurring in Israel today thus goes well beyond "some unrest" described in Freier. In the Court's view, the current situation in Israel meets the "zone of war" standard contemplated by the Sixth Circuit in Friedrich.

The majority rejects these findings, and instead resolves that Israel is not a zone of war as meant by the Convention. While I agree with this conclusion, neither the district court nor this court have answered the question of whether returning the children to Israel, given its current conditions, may cause them to suffer psychological harm. In my view, the fact that the specific area in which Samuel and Jacob would live is not a zone of war, still does not answer the question of whether they will be psychologically harmed because of the situation that currently exists in Israel.[26] More-

26. On this point, I believe it particularly relevant to reference a lengthy letter written by Samuel to the district court. In it, he expressed his concern about returning to Israel, and made clear that he was worried about his own and his brother's safety if they were forced back. As this is direct evidence of the psychological harm Samuel would suffer if returned, I believe it proper for the district court to consider the letter for that purpose.

over, it would clearly be harmful for the children to be removed from the United States and their mother, or each other, after spending the great majority of their lives here. Therefore, I believe we have no alternative but to remand to the district court to determine whether Samuel and Jacob will be subjected to psychological harm if they are separately or collectively removed from their mother's home in the United States and forced to return to Israel.

K. Enforcement

Wolf v. Wolf

Supreme Court of Iowa, 2005.
690 N.W.2d 887.

■ Larson, Justice.

. . .

I. Facts and Prior Proceedings.

Timothy Wolf and his former wife, Joan, have been embroiled in a bitter tug-of-war in Arizona and Iowa courts over the physical care of Ashley. Ashley, born in 1985, is now an adult, but the battle continues. The parties divorced in 1990, and the court awarded sole legal custody and primary physical care to Joan. In 1993 the court modified the decree by granting the parties joint legal custody and primary physical care to Timothy. In 1998 the district court modified the decree, retaining joint legal custody but granting primary physical care to Joan. Timothy appealed, and the court of appeals reversed, reaffirming physical care in Timothy. By this time, Ashley had moved to Arizona with Joan, and Joan petitioned an Arizona court to award her primary care. The Arizona court refused.

In August 2000, eleven months after the court of appeals ordered that physical care be returned to Timothy, Ashley was still not returned to Iowa. Timothy obtained a writ of habeas corpus in Iowa and went to Arizona to retrieve Ashley. He brought her back to Iowa, and she lived with him for approximately a month and a half. However, on October 8, 2000, when Ashley was fifteen, she left Timothy's home and flew to Arizona. On November 8, 2000, Joan petitioned an Arizona court to award her temporary physical custody, but the Arizona court refused, ruling that Iowa retained jurisdiction.

On November 14, 2000, Joan filed a petition in Iowa to modify the decree, and she and Ashley came to Iowa to testify . . .

[The trial court issued an order that "all parties are to remain in the State of Iowa, and will be personally present for the remainder of these proceedings. In setting a hearing for a show-cause hearing, the court asked Joan if she understood the order to remain and Iowa, to which Joan replied "Yes, I do."]

Joan did not stay in Iowa as promised, but immediately left for Arizona with Ashley. In an order of December 27, 2000, the district court denied Joan's modification petition and confirmed Timothy's right to custody.

In May 2002 Timothy filed this suit for damages, based on [*Wood v. Wood*, 338 N.W.2d 123 (Iowa 1983)] and *Restatement (Second) of Torts section 700* (1977). At the trial, Timothy introduced the evidence outlined above, and the court took judicial notice of the court files in the prior cases between the parties. Joan did not appear for the hearing and produced no evidence. Her lawyer, however, appeared for her and moved to dismiss the suit for failure to establish a prima facie case of tortious interference. The court denied the motion.

In *Wood* we recognized the tort claim of intentional interference with custody and stated the rule:

> "One who, with knowledge that the parent does not consent, abducts or otherwise compels or induces a minor child to leave a parent legally entitled to its custody or not to return to the parent after it has been left him, is subject to liability to the parent."

338 N.W.2d at 124 (quoting *Restatement (Second) of Torts § 700*). A similar cause of action is now codified at *Iowa Code section 710.9* (2001), although this was not a basis for the trial court's ruling and, in fact, was not raised at trial or on appeal until oral arguments.

. . .

To establish a claim of tortious interference with custody, a plaintiff must show (1) the plaintiff has a legal right to establish or maintain a parental or custodial relationship with his or her minor child; (2) the defendant took some action or affirmative effort to abduct the child or to compel or induce the child to leave the plaintiff's custody; (3) the abducting, compelling, or inducing was willful; and (4) the abducting, compelling, or inducing was done with notice or knowledge that the child had a parent whose rights were thereby invaded and who did not consent. *See* 67A C.J.S. *Parent and Child* § 322, at 409 (2002).

II. The Issues.

The defendant argues: (1) the plaintiff's evidence is insufficient to establish a prima facie case of tortious interference, specifically with respect to any active conduct to entice Ashley away from her father; (2) there was insufficient evidence of willful and wanton conduct to support a claim for punitive damages; (3) the punitive damages award was excessive. . . .

The defendant's appeal brief also argues that Timothy could not sue for intentional interference because the parties have joint legal custody. *See Restatement (Second) of Torts § 700* cmt. c ("When the parents are by law jointly entitled to the custody and earnings of the child, no action can be brought against one of the parents who abducts or induces the child to leave the other."). . . . [W]e hold that "primary physical care" under *Iowa Code sections 598.1(7)* and *598.41(5)* is a sufficient basis for maintaining the cause of action, even if the parties have "joint legal custody" under *Iowa Code sections 598.1(3)* and *598.41(2), (4)*. To be consistent with the wording of the Restatement, we use "custody" in this case to refer to primary physical care.

. . .

V. Punitive–Damage Award.

A. *Are punitive damages recoverable in this case?* In *Wood* we recognized a plaintiff's right to punitive damages in tortious-interference cases and noted the public policy considerations underlying that right. . . . Also, the legislature has put its stamp of approval on punitive damages in similar cases in *Iowa Code section 710.9*. We reaffirm the holding in *Wood* that punitive damages may be recovered.

B. *Merits.* We review an award of punitive damages for correction of errors at law. *Jones v. Lake Park Care Ctr., Inc., 569 N.W.2d 369, 378 (Iowa 1997).* Punitive damages are only appropriate when a tort is committed with "either actual or legal malice." *Id.* . . . Under *Iowa Code section 668A.1(1)(a),* the plaintiff must show "by a preponderance of clear, convincing, and satisfactory evidence" that the defendant's conduct "constituted willful and wanton disregard for the rights or safety of another." "Thus, merely objectionable conduct is insufficient . . . To receive punitive damages, plaintiff must offer evidence of defendant's persistent course of conduct to show that the defendant acted with no care and with disregard to the consequences of those acts." *Hockenberg Equip. Co. v. Hockenberg's Equip. & Supply Co., 510 N.W.2d 153, 156 (Iowa 1993)* (citation omitted).

We reject Joan's argument that she was only acting as a good mother by providing Ashley with a protective environment. The court found affirmative acts by her, as outlined above, that demonstrated willful and wanton conduct. Joan kept Ashley for nearly three years after Timothy was awarded physical care. During the short period Timothy did have physical care, Joan provided Ashley with the means to run away—showing a disregard for Timothy's custodial rights and the emotional harm he would likely suffer. When Joan returned to Iowa to seek a modification of physical placement, she disobeyed direct orders from the judge and took Ashley back to Arizona before the proceeding ended. She thereby showed not only a lack of concern for Timothy's custodial rights, but also displayed a complete disregard for the Iowa legal system. In fact, she has defied Iowa court orders for three years. We believe that clear, convincing, and satisfactory evidence supports the district court's finding of willful and wanton conduct warranting punitive damages.

C. *Was the punitive-damage award excessive?* Joan argues that the amount of punitive damages—$25,000—violates the *Due Process Clause of the Fourteenth Amendment* because it is "grossly excessive. . . ."

The Supreme Court has stated that an appellate court reviewing a punitive-damage award for excessiveness should consider three "guideposts." *BMW of N. Am., Inc. v. Gore, 517 U.S. 559, 574–75 (1996).* These guideposts are:

> (1) the degree of reprehensibility of the defendant's misconduct; (2) the disparity between the actual or potential harm suffered by the plaintiff and the punitive damages award; and (3) the difference between the punitive damages awarded by the [trier of fact] and the civil penalties authorized or imposed in comparable cases.

. . .

2. *Disparity between actual or potential harm and the punitive-damage award.* Joan's argument emphasizes the disparity between the district court's actual-damage award (one dollar) and its punitive-damage award ($25,000). In this case, Timothy specifically asked for only one dollar to remove any appearance to Ashley that he was motivated by money. His actual damages award is therefore not an accurate indicator of the actual harm caused by the defendant.

. . .

In this case, the harm done to the plaintiff clearly exceeded the amount of compensatory damages awarded because the plaintiff waived all amounts over one dollar. Although the amount of compensatory damages awarded was nominal, the actual harm to the plaintiff was substantial. We need not attempt to quantify the potential damages that could have been allowed here. Suffice it to say that the deprivation of a parent's relationship with a child, over several years, with the attendant costs such as attorney fees spawned by the defendant's contumacious conduct are sufficient potential damages to make the award of $25,000 in punitive damages well within constitutional parameters.

. . .

[W]e conclude the district court's punitive-damage award was not "grossly excessive" and, therefore, did not violate Joan's due process rights.

NOTE

Courts have held that damages are not available as a remedy for interference with the noncustodian's visitation rights, on the ground that recognition of such a right might create a weapon that would escalate conflict between the parties. *See, e.g.*, Cosner v. Ridinger, 882 P.2d 1243 (Wyo. 1994).

United States v. Amer

United States Court of Appeals, Second Circuit, 1997.
110 F.3d 873.

■ JON O. NEWMAN, CHIEF JUDGE.

This appeal concerns several issues arising from a conviction for violation of the International Parental Kidnapping Crime Act ("IPKCA" or "the Act"), 18 U.S.C. § 1204. The IPKCA bars a parent from removing a child from the United States or retaining outside the United States a child who has been in the United States, with the intent to obstruct the other parent's right to physical custody. We have not previously considered this statute. The specific questions raised are (i) whether the IPKCA is unconstitutionally vague, (ii) whether it is overbroad in intruding upon the free exercise of religion, (iii) whether it incorporates the affirmative defenses found in the Hague Convention on the Civil Aspects of International Parental Child Abduction ("Hague Convention"), (iv) whether the sentencing court properly imposed, as a condition of the convicted defendant's term of supervised release, a requirement that the defendant return the still-retained children to the United States, and (v) whether the sentencing court properly applied a three-level enhancement for substantial interference with the administration of justice.

These issues of first impression arise on an appeal by Ahmed Amer from the March 14, 1996, judgment of the District Court for the Eastern District of New York (Carol Bagley Amon, Judge), convicting him, after a jury trial, of one count of international parental kidnapping in violation of the IPKCA and sentencing him to twenty-four months' imprisonment and a one-year term of supervised release with the special condition that he effect the return of the abducted children to the United States. We affirm.

Background

Ahmed Amer ("Ahmed") and Mona Amer ("Mona"), Egyptian citizens and adherents of the Islamic faith, were married in Egypt in 1980. Four years later, while still in Egypt, Mona gave birth to the couple's first child, a boy named Amachmud. In 1985, Ahmed, seeking employment, left his wife and newborn son in Egypt and moved to the United States. Ahmed eventually settled in Queens, New York.

In 1987, Mona and Amachmud joined Ahmed in Queens. Mona stayed home to take care of the child while Ahmed worked as a cook in various diners in the city. In 1989, the couple had another child, a girl named Maha. In 1991, the couple's third child, a son named Omar, was born.

The two children born in the United States, Maha and Omar, became American citizens upon their birth. In 1991, Ahmed became a naturalized United States citizen, though he continued to retain his Egyptian citizenship. Mona obtained permanent resident alien status in this country the following year. Also in 1992, the entire Amer family returned to Egypt for a one-month visit, which was the only time that anyone in the family returned to Egypt prior to the episode on which the indictment is based.

During the early 1990s, the Amers' marriage began to deteriorate. Ahmed and Mona quarreled frequently over Ahmed's bigamous marriage to another woman, Mona's decision to work outside the home, and her decision to apply for welfare. Ahmed regularly abused Mona both verbally and physically. In April 1994, Mona asked Ahmed to leave the family apartment. He obliged and moved into a friend's apartment. The couple did not, however, divorce or become legally separated. The three children remained with Mona at the Queens home. No formal custody arrangement was made. Ahmed visited the children whenever he wished, usually once each week. During this period, Mona supported herself with public assistance and loans from friends.

Although he was no longer living in the family home, Ahmed continued to abuse Mona when he saw her. He also began to try to persuade her to move back to Egypt with him, suggesting that the children would receive a better education there and that the family would benefit from living among close relatives. Although Mona at one point appeared to agree, she eventually told Ahmed that neither she nor the children would return to Egypt. Ahmed threatened to kill Mona for her refusal, but she would not agree to leave the United States or to allow him to take the children from this country.

On January 27, 1995, Ahmed came to the family apartment in Queens to have dinner with Mona and the children. After dinner, Mona left the house to do some shopping. When she returned two hours later, Ahmed and the children were gone. The next morning Mona learned that Ahmed had taken the children to Egypt. Mona has not seen her children since that time.

Records from Egypt Air showed that on the evening of January 27th, Ahmed and the three children boarded a flight from JFK Airport to Egypt. After arriving in Egypt, Ahmed took the children to his mother's home, which is about ten minutes from the home of Mona's parents. The children visited with Mona's parents a few days after their arrival in Egypt. Amachmud, Maha, and Omar continue to reside in Egypt with Ahmed's mother.

In February 1995, Mona filed a complaint in Queens Family Court seeking custody of the children. The court awarded her full legal custody of the three children and issued a warrant for Ahmed's arrest. At around the same time, Ahmed obtained an order from an Egyptian court compelling Mona to return to the "conjugal home" in Egypt. After Mona failed to return to Egypt within three months, the Egyptian court in May 1995 awarded Ahmed custody of the three children. Additionally, Mona no longer has custody rights to twelve-year-old Amachmud under Egyptian law, which provides that a mother loses all rights to her male child when he reaches the age of ten.

In June 1995 Ahmed left the children in his mother's care and returned to the United States. He was apprehended the following month in New Jersey. The eventual indictment, issued in the Eastern District of New York, charged that "[o]n or about and between January 27, 1995 and August 4, 1995, ... the defendant Ahmed Amer did knowingly and intentionally remove and retain children who had been in the United States, to wit [Amachmud] Amer, Maha Amer and Omar Amer, outside the United States with the intent to obstruct the lawful exercise of parental rights," in violation of the IPKCA. Ahmed was convicted by a jury on the sole count of the indictment. Judge Amon imposed a sentence of twenty-four months' imprisonment and a one-year term of supervised release, with the special condition that Ahmed effect the return of the three children to the United States. At the time of this appeal, the children remain in Egypt.

Discussion

The IPKCA was enacted in December 1993, but has apparently been sparingly used. We have found no published decision of a federal court construing this statute. The IPKCA provides, in relevant part:

(a) Whoever removes a child from the United States or retains a child (who has been in the United States) outside the United States with intent to obstruct the lawful exercise of parental rights shall be fined under this title or imprisoned not more than 3 years, or both.

(b) As used in this section—

(1) the term "child" means a person who has not attained the age of 16 years; and

(2) the term "parental rights," with respect to a child, means the right to physical custody of the child—

(A) whether joint or sole (and includes visiting rights); and

(B) whether arising by operation of law, court order, or legally binding agreement of the parties.

18 U.S.C. § 1204.

. . .

III. Incorporation of Hague Convention Defenses

Ahmed contends that the District Court erred when it refused to permit him to argue in his defense that he was justified in removing and retaining the children in Egypt under the Hague Convention. The Convention, he asserts, affords him a defense where "there is a grave risk that [the children's] return would expose the child[ren] to physical or psychological harm or otherwise place the child[ren] in an intolerable situation." This risk, he argues, arises from Mona's allegedly neglectful care. Ahmed also contends that the Hague Convention allows him to argue in his defense that the children's return would not be "permitted by the fundamental principles of [Egyptian law] relating to the protection of human rights and fundamental freedoms," which allegedly do not permit Muslim children to be denied their right to an Islamic upbringing. Hague Convention, Arts. 13(b) & 20. The District Court denied Ahmed's request because it found that the three affirmative defenses specifically set forth in section 1204(c) of the Act are the only ones available to a defendant facing an IPKCA prosecution:

(c) It shall be an affirmative defense under this section that—

(1) the defendant acted within the provisions of a valid court order granting the defendant legal custody or visitation rights and that order was obtained pursuant to the Uniform Child Custody Jurisdiction Act and was in effect at the time of the offense;

(2) the defendant was fleeing an incidence or pattern of domestic violence;

(3) the defendant had physical custody of the child pursuant to a court order granting legal custody or visitation rights and failed to return the child as a result of circumstances beyond the defendant's control, and the defendant notified or made reasonable attempts to notify the other parent or lawful custodian of the child of such circumstances within 24 hours after the visitation period had expired and returned the child as soon as possible.

18 U.S.C. § 1204(c). Since Ahmed did not qualify under any of these subsections, the Court ruled that he could not argue that he was justified in removing and retaining the children because, among other things, Mona was a poor parent or because Egyptian human rights laws protected the right of Islamic children to a proper religious education.

. . .

The Hague Convention, which was drafted in 1980 and, as of May 1995, had been ratified by forty-one nations, was adopted in order "to protect children internationally from the harmful effects of their wrongful removal or retention and to establish procedures to ensure their prompt return to the State of their habitual residence, as well as to secure protection for rights of access." Hague Convention, preamble. It created a previously unavailable civil remedy for the return of abducted children, whereby the left-behind parent can request the designated "Central Authority" of the state in which the abducted child is retained to locate the child, institute proceedings to effect its return, assist in administrative technicalities, and generally aid in the amicable resolution of the kidnapping situation.

. . .

Because the Convention does not apply when children habitually resident in the United States (and who are often American citizens) are abducted from this country and retained in a non-contracting country, the perception arose that something was needed to deter parents from removing and retaining their children in these "safe haven" countries, and thus to close the gap left open by the unfortunate fact that few countries have signed on to the Convention. As the IPKCA's legislative history shows, it was against this backdrop that the Act was enacted:

> There is an international civil mechanism relating to these cases, the Hague Convention . . . , for which Congress passed implementing legislation in 1988. As a result of this convention, the signatories will recognize the custody decrees of other signatories, thereby facilitating the return of abducted children. However, most countries are not signatories to the Convention, thus leaving individual countries to take whatever legal unilateral action they can to obtain the return of abducted children.
>
> Creating a federal felony offense responds to these problems. . . .

House Report at 3, 1993 U.S.C.C.A.N. at 2421 (emphasis added). Nonetheless, Congress continued to believe that the civil mechanism of the Hague Convention, when available, was the preferred route for resolving the complex and difficult problems surrounding international child abductions. It thus provided a "Sense of Congress" resolution to accompany the Act:

> It is the sense of the Congress that, inasmuch as use of the procedures under the Hague Convention ... has resulted in the return of many children, those procedures, in circumstances in which they are applicable, should be the option of first choice for a parent who seeks the return of a child who has been removed from the parent.

Pub.L. No. 103–173, § 2(b), 107 Stat.1998 (1993) (emphasis added).... In that spirit, section 1204(d) of the IPKCA provides that the Act "does not detract from the Hague Convention." 18 U.S.C. § 1204(d).

Construing the IPKCA against this background, we conclude that rejecting Hague Convention defenses in Ahmed's prosecution does not "detract from" the Convention. In the first place, Egypt, the country to which the Amer children have been removed and in which they are currently being retained, is not a signatory to the Convention. Second, because the civil mechanism of the Convention is therefore unavailable to Mona to effect the return of her children, the United States' criminal prosecution of Ahmed for the abduction and retention of the children under the IPKCA cannot in any way "detract from" the Hague Convention within the meaning of section 1204(d), and, indeed, perfectly fulfills the "enforcement-gap-closing" function for which the IPKCA was partially enacted. Although it might be a close question whether a defendant should be permitted to raise Hague Convention defenses when, for instance, there is a parallel or ongoing civil proceeding under the Convention and its implementing legislation, we do not need to decide that question in this case. The District Court acted properly in restricting Ahmed to the three available affirmative defenses found in section 1204(c) of the Act.

IV. Special Condition of Supervised Release

Ahmed next objects to the District Court's imposition of the following special condition of supervised release: "[T]he defendant [must] effect the return of the children to the United States to Mona Amer." He contends that (a) the District Court exceeded its authority under the Sentencing Guidelines provisions concerning appropriate conditions of supervised release, (b) this condition is inconsistent with the Sentencing Commission's intent that the abducting parent not be punished for the length or duration of his retention of the children, (c) re-imprisonment following a violation of the condition would constitute double jeopardy, (d) the condition is impossible to meet, and (e) the condition violates the Egyptian court order granting Ahmed custody over the children. We discuss each objection in turn.

(a) *Guidelines limitations.* Ahmed contends that the "return" condition exceeds the sentencing court's authority under 18 U.S.C. § 3583 and U.S.S.G. § 5D1.3(b). Although sentencing courts have "broad discretion to tailor conditions of supervised release to the goals and purposes outlined in § 5D1.3(b)," this provision does not provide sentencing courts with "untrammelled discretion" in this regard. Specifically, section 5D1.3(b) provides:

> The court may impose other conditions of supervised release, to the extent that such conditions are reasonably related to (1) the nature and circumstances of the offense and the history and characteristics of the defendant, and (2) the need for the sentence imposed to afford adequate

> deterrence to criminal conduct, to protect the public from further crimes of the defendant, and to provide the defendant with needed educational or vocational training, medical care, or other correctional treatment in the most effective manner.

This Circuit has ruled that "despite the continuous use of the ... conjunctive 'and' in § 5D1.3(b), taking into account the authorizing statutes, a condition may be imposed if it is reasonably related to any one or more of the specified factors."

The "return" condition is obviously closely related to "the nature and circumstances of the offense" of child abduction and "the history and characteristics" of Ahmed. Indeed, it is difficult to imagine a condition more closely tailored to the crime and the criminal in question than this one. Moreover, the requirement that Ahmed return the children serves the goal of general deterrence. As the District Court put it,

> It seems that often in cases such as this, a vindictive parent may be willing to possibly face a modest prison term in order to keep the children from the spouse. But if the parent recognizes that the Court has a legal mechanism to additionally order the return of the children, then recognizing that may well serve as an additional deterrent.

The condition also serves the function of specific deterrence. It deters Ahmed both from committing the offense of the unlawful retention of the children in Egypt after his release from prison, and from attempting to kidnap his children again after they have been returned to the United States.

. . .

(e) *Conflict with Egyptian order.*

. . .

Conclusion

The judgment of the District Court is affirmed.

Hendrickson v. Hendrickson

Supreme Court of North Dakota, 2000.
603 N.W.2d 896.

■ MARING, JUSTICE.

. . .

Diane and Mark Hendrickson married in 1980 and purchased a home in Jamestown. Diane lived in Jamestown with their four children. Mark lived and worked in Dickinson, but lived with Diane and the children on weekends, holidays and vacations. The couple divorced in 1995. Diane received custody of the children and Mark was granted visitation. In the original decree, the trial court found the children were attached to their lives in Jamestown and had developed a warmer and more secure relationship with their mother than with their father, due substantially to the long-distance living arrangement.... The trial court issued a visitation schedule allowing Mark visitation two weekends per month and at Christmas. We affirmed the child custody award in Hendrickson I....

On October 1, 1997, Mark filed a motion for change of custody asserting Diane was alienating the children from him. He filed the motion after disputes arose over visitation, which went unresolved despite the trial court's modification of the visitation order. Several months before Mark's motion of October 1, the trial court appointed Karen Mueller as guardian ad litem and directed her to evaluate the Hendrickson family. According to the report Mueller submitted, Diane believed herself completely blameless in the breakdown of her marriage and the ensuing child custody dispute. She considered herself the children's sole caregiver and asserted she was "unaware of any parenting skills Mark might possess." Diane admitted to Mueller that she hung up on Mark when he called and until he gave her $20,000 she would continue to do so. Mueller also reported on several occasions assistance from police officers was required to complete a visitation exchange; at one exchange, Diane's son-in-law verbally attacked Mueller, and at a second, one of the children obstinately dared her to "try to make me go." Mueller explained Mark's relationship with the children had been tenuous from the beginning because of his absence from the family home, and that Diane's alienating behavior was causing additional, harmful estrangement between Mark and the children. In an order dated December 9, 1997, the trial court awarded custody of the children to Stutsman County and ordered the family into therapy.

Stutsman County, however, declined to take custody of the Hendrickson children. On February 24, 1998, the trial court issued another order, in which the court stated, "this is the most outrageous case that I have seen since I began law school twenty-five years ago." The court also stated:

> by deed and innuendo, Diane rewards the children's rejection of their father making this perhaps the worst case of alienation syndrome in the history of the United States.... Her statement on the stand that she has "tried and tried" to encourage visitation is patently ridiculous.

The court expressed a desire to send Diane to jail for her failure to comply with court orders, yet was concerned this would harm the children. Rather, the court ordered Mark's child support payments to be placed in escrow. The order also stated Mark should continue to have reasonable visitation, but did not grant Mark custody because the relationship between the children and their father had been so poisoned.

We reviewed that order upon Diane's appeal and Mark's cross-appeal in *Hendrickson II.* We concluded the trial court erroneously ordered the child support to be placed in escrow as a sanction against Diane. We noted as an alternative remedy, the court could find her in contempt and impose a jail sentence. As to Mark's assertion the trial court should change custody, we explained "evidence of alienation or persistent frustration can be relevant factors" in a trial court's assessment of whether there has been a significant change of circumstances following an initial custody determination. We then stated:

> we recognize methods other than a change of custody should be used initially to remedy a parent's misbehavior ... we also recognize that, after exhausting other remedies, a change in custody may be the only method to correct the damage of a particularly stubborn and defiant custodial parent. If the alternative remedies fail, the district court should consider a change of custody.

Just before the Hendrickson II appeal, Mark filed another motion to change custody on April 9, 1998, with a supporting affidavit by the guardian ad litem, Karen Mueller.

. . .

On April 26, 1999, Judge Hilden issued an order, first denying Diane's motion for change of venue and then turning to consideration of our remand. In its order, the court found Diane had frustrated visitation between Mark and the children and had attempted to alienate the children from their father. The court concluded there had been a significant change of circumstances following the original child custody determination. The court then stated:

> This Court has exhausted remedies available to correct Diane Hendrickson's misbehavior. Diane Hendrickson has proven to be a stubborn and defiant custodial parent and the only option yet available is to change custody. Moreover, I find that it is in the best interest of the children that custody be changed and, therefore, I grant immediate custody of the Hendrickson children to their father, Mark Hendrickson.

In addition, the trial court ordered that Diane have no visitation for one year after the custody transfer and required her to submit to counseling with a counselor chosen by Mark. Diane appeals from this order.

. . .

Diane . . . argues the change of custody to Mark was clearly erroneous because it was unsupported by the evidence. We disagree. When a trial court entertains a motion to change custody of children of divorced spouses, the judge must determine two issues: whether or not there has been a significant change in circumstances since the original divorce decree and custody award and, if so, whether or not those changed circumstances compel or require a change in custody to foster the best interests of the child. The party seeking modification bears the burden of showing a change of custody is required. A trial court's decision to modify custody is a finding of fact subject to the clearly erroneous standard of review. A finding of fact is clearly erroneous if it is induced by an erroneous view of the law, if there is no evidence to support it, or if it is clear to the reviewing court that a mistake has been made.

In the order of April 26, 1999, the trial court expressly concluded both elements required for a change of custody existed: the circumstances significantly changed after the original child custody award and the changed circumstances required a change in custody in the best interests of the children. Supporting these conclusions were the trial court's findings that Diane frustrated both the original and subsequent visitation orders and attempted to alienate the children from their father. Specifically, the court noted Diane's removal of the children from the home at scheduled visitation times, her refusal to allow Mark to take the children for visitation, and her refusal to make visitation arrangements. Testimony from the record supports these findings, as does the guardian ad litem's report, which states Diane's alienating behavior was "indicative of an unhealthy parental figure." Further, the court noted Diane had numerous opportunities to change her behavior and failed to do so.

[W]e have held that "frustration of visitation does not alone constitute a sufficient change in circumstances to warrant a change in custody," and a court should first resort to a more rigid visitation schedule, rather than change custody. However, we also explained [that] visitation problems may justify a change in custody when a court finds such problems have worked against a child's best interests. In addition, in Hendrickson II, we stated that, though other methods should be used initially to remedy misbehavior by a parent, "after exhausting other remedies, a change in custody may be the only method to correct the damage of a particularly stubborn and defiant custodial parent." Finally, we note the Legislature has expressly recognized frustration of visitation may require a change of custody. Under *N.D.C.C. § 14–09–06.6(5)*, a trial court may not change custody within two years after the date of entry of a custody order. This time limit does not apply, however, if the trial court finds both that a modification is necessary to serve the best interest of the child and also that there has been a "persistent and willful denial or interference with visitation." The next subsection allows the trial court to modify custody before the two year period expires upon a finding that a change is necessary for the child's best interest and that the child's environment "may endanger the child's physical or emotional health or impair the child's emotional development." *N.D.C.C. § 14–09–06.6(5)(b)*. Thus the legislature considers persistent frustration of visitation and the emotional and physical endangerment of children to be in the same behavioral class and accords the same remedy.

While the trial court did not expressly find Diane's persistent frustration of visitation worked against the best interests of her children, we can discern the rationale for the court's conclusion from inference and deduction, so we need not remand for the court to clarify its finding. The trial court's findings make it clear the children were deprived of contact with their father by Diane's withholding visitation rights. The right of the children to visitation is presumed to be in their best interests.

Farmer v. Farmer

Court of Appeals of Indiana, Fifth District, 2000.
735 N.E.2d 285.

■ BARNES, JUDGE.

. . .

Facts

Farmer and his former wife, Susan Farmer n/k/a/ Susan Feliciano, have a thirteen-year-old daughter. Feliciano has custody of the child. On July 1, 1999, the parties appeared on all pending matters, including Feliciano's Petition for Rule to Show Cause for failing to pay child support and Farmer's Petition to Modify Visitation. A few weeks later, the trial court entered a contempt citation and visitation order.

. . .

Analysis

Farmer contends that portions of the trial court's amended order are erroneous because it intermingles the issues of visitation [and] child support. Specifically, Farmer contends that the trial court abused its discretion by conditioning his visitation rights upon the payment of child support.... Farmer also argues that the trial court abused its discretion because it threatens to revoke his suspended sentence, which was imposed for failing to pay child support, if he does not comply with visitation.

. . .

The problems with the amended order are two-fold. First, the trial court impermissibly conditions Farmer's visitation rights upon the payment of child support. This court has held numerous times that a parent may not interfere with visitation when the non-custodial parent fails to pay support. Similarly, we have held that a parent may not withhold child support payments even though the other parent interferes with visitation rights. The facts of these cases are somewhat distinguishable because they involve situations where one parent withheld child support when the other parent refused to permit visitation or where one parent withheld visitation when the other parent failed to pay support. None of those cases address a situation where the court threatened to terminate visitation rights if a parent did not pay child support. Despite these distinctions, however, the underlying principle espoused by those cases is still applicable to the case before us. Visitation rights and child support are separate issues, not to be commingled. A court cannot condition visitation upon the payment of child support if a custodial parent is not entitled to do so.

In so holding, we do not dispute the trial court's use of discretion in visitation matters and recognize its authority to restrict or terminate visitation rights of a parent under certain circumstances. *Indiana Code Section 31–17–4–2* states:

> The court may modify an order granting or denying visitation rights whenever modification would serve the best interests of the child. However, a court shall not restrict a parent's rights unless the court finds that the visitation might endanger the child's physical health or significantly impair the child's emotional development.

Here, the trial court stated in its findings that "in the event that [Farmer] fails to . . . pay all sums required by this Order for current support . . . the Court finds that any further visitation by [Farmer] would endanger the child's physical health or significantly impair the child's emotional development and will vacate its Order with respect to visitation." However, the trial court provides no other findings or rationale to support its conclusion that the failure to pay child support would cause further visitation to endanger the child's physical health or significantly impair her emotional development. Notwithstanding the trial court's statutory authority to restrict or terminate visitation altogether upon a showing that the visitation endangers the child or impairs her emotional development, no such showing was made by the trial court in its amended order. Although we do not condone a non-custodial parent's failure to pay child support, visitation rights cannot be "automatically" terminated as a result of this failure. Consequently, the trial court improperly restricted Farmer's visitation rights by conditioning them upon the continued payment of support without the proper showing with respect to the physical and emotional well-being of the child.

Second, the trial court threatens to revoke Farmer's suspended sentence, which was ordered for failing to pay child support, if he does not continue visitation with his daughter. In particular, the trial court suspended Farmer's 180–day sentence as long as he "diligently schedules and exercises visitation" and "continues to visit with the parties' child without again terminating regular visitation."

We recognize that it is within the discretion of the trial court to hold an individual in contempt for willfully disobeying a court order. We also acknowledge that contempt is available to assist in the enforcement of child support orders and judgments, which is why the trial court held Farmer in contempt here. However, the trial court's amended order goes beyond its original contempt citation for Farmer's failure to pay support and even beyond its threat to revoke his suspended sentence if he fails to make all of his future child support payments. The trial court's threat with respect to

Farmer's suspended sentence crosses into the realm of his visitation rights. We find no authority or policy permitting the trial court to make this leap.

Indiana has long recognized that the right of parents to visit their children is a sacred and precious privilege that should be enjoyed by non-custodial parents. Numerous cases have examined the trial court's discretion to find a parent in contempt for failing to comply with visitation orders. In those cases, the parent who failed to comply with the order was interfering with the other parent's ability to exercise visitation rights. In other words, those cases involve one parent's frustration of the other's visitation rights.

Unlike those cases, however, the case before us presents an unusual situation in which we are faced with a trial court's attempt to force a parent to visit a child and threat to imprison him for failing to do so. Although parents clearly have a statutory duty to support their children, no such duty requires them to visit or maintain a relationship with their children if they choose not to do so. The statute governing visitation states, "A parent not granted custody of the child is entitled to reasonable visitation rights. . . ." *Ind. Code § 31–17–4–1*. As the statute states, visitation is an entitlement to the non-custodial parent, not an obligation. Farmer contends that "If a person chooses not to exercise [his] privilege or entitlement, [he] should not be sanctioned." Although we find it disturbing that a parent would not want to visit his child, we are forced to agree with Farmer's proposition, particularly in this case where the suspended sentence was originally imposed for failing to pay child support. Not only are child support and visitation separate issues that should not be commingled, but we do not believe that a parent should be forced to visit his child under threat of imprisonment.[2]

Conclusion

Although we understand the trial court's attempt to coerce Farmer into complying with the visitation and child support terms set forth in the amended order in an effort to safeguard the well-being of the parties' daughter, we believe it is improper for the trial court to intermingle Farmer's visitation rights with his obligation to pay child support and attorney fees. We reverse the trial court's amended order to the extent it conditions visitation rights and the suspended sentence upon the payment of the attorney fee judgment. We further reverse the amended order to the extent it conditions Farmer's visitation upon his payment of support and to the extent it conditions his suspended sentence on his continued exercise of visitation with his daughter. In all other respects, we affirm the amended order and remand for further proceedings consistent with this opinion.

2. We note, however, that Farmer's failure to exercise his visitation may result in the curtailment and ultimately the termination of the visitation to protect the well-being of the child.

CHAPTER 6

PROPERTY, ALIMONY, AND CHILD SUPPORT AWARDS

Modern divorce law generally seeks to distribute assets fairly between divorcing spouses and, with the exception of child support, send them on their separate ways without further financial entanglement. Courts therefore are commonly encouraged to use property division to settle the parties' financial affairs, and to award alimony only if this is infeasible.

Most states require courts to divide property "equitably" and typically list a set of factors that courts may take into account in doing so. Judges are not limited to these factors, however, nor are they instructed about how much weight to give to each. Some common law states permit the court to distribute all property of the spouses, however and whenever it was acquired. Others exclude from distribution certain specifically defined categories of separate property, and treat the rest as marital property to be divided equitably. In drawing this distinction, common law states follow the practice in community property states at the time of divorce.

Most couples, however, have little or no property available to divide at divorce. This creates a challenge for courts that attempt to make equitable economic arrangements at divorce.

One response has been to increase the amount of property deemed marital, rather than individual, in order to maximize the amount available for distribution between the parties. This has required courts in some cases to push the boundaries of property law in an effort to recognize a financial entitlement. Doing so has expanded the amount of assets available for distribution in some cases, but there are limits on property law's ability to accommodate dependent spouses' claims at divorce.

As a practical matter, therefore, awarding alimony is the most common response to the typical dearth of marital assets available for distribution at divorce. This has led to efforts to formulate a coherent theory of obligation for a practice that has never had one. As the section on alimony discusses, courts awarding alimony rarely have articulated any explicit bases for their awards. If alimony is to serve as the major vehicle for achieving financial justice between divorcing spouses, however, we should identify guiding principles so that courts can act more consistently and predictably in making these awards.

In practice, the line between property and alimony awards can become blurred. A court may conclude that a divorcing spouse has an entitlement to a certain share of assets regardless of future need. This is consistent with the idea of a traditional property interest. The spouse who must provide these assets, however, may be able to do so only over time in the form of periodic payments. In this sense, the entitlement resembles an alimony award. Furthermore, courts attempting to do financial justice between the parties may look to both tangible assets and future earnings as sources for accomplishing this objective.

Finally, statutes governing child support, prompted by the federal government, have moved toward greater restraints on the discretion of judges. Although states vary in the theories of obligation that they adopt, each has established guidelines that specify the presumptive amount of child support that must be awarded. Judges must justify any departure from these guidelines.

As you read the material in this Chapter, take note of the implicit principles that animate statutes and court decisions dealing with property division, alimony, and child support. Ask yourself if it is possible to formulate a coherent and explicit foundation for each.

A. PROPERTY DIVISION

1. EQUITABLE DISTRIBUTION

Uniform Marriage and Divorce Act

Section 307. Disposition of Property: Alternative A

(a) In a proceeding for dissolution of a marriage [or] legal separation . . . the court, without regard to marital misconduct, shall, and in a proceeding for legal separation may, finally equitably apportion between the parties the property and assets belonging to either or both however and whenever acquired, and whether the title thereto is in the name of the husband or wife or both. In making apportionment the court shall consider the duration of the marriage, any prior marriage of either party, any antenuptial agreement of the parties, the age, health, station, occupation, amount and sources of income, vocational skills, employability, estate, liabilities, and needs of each of the parties, custodial provisions, whether the apportionment is in lieu of or in addition to maintenance, and the opportunity of each for future acquisition of capital assets and income. The court shall also consider the contribution or dissipation of each party in the acquisition, preservation, depreciation, or appreciation in value of the respective estates, and as the contribution of a spouse as a homemaker or to the family unit.

Section 307. Disposition of Property: Alternative B

In a proceeding for dissolution of the marriage [or] legal separation . . . the court shall assign each spouse's separate property to that spouse. It also shall divide community property, without regard to marital misconduct, in just proportions after considering all relevant factors including:

(1) contribution of each spouse to acquisition of the marital property, including contribution of a spouse as homemaker;

(2) value of the property set apart to each spouse;

(3) duration of the marriage; and

(4) economic circumstances of each spouse when the division of property is to become effective, including the desirability of awarding the family home or the right to live therein for a reasonable period to the spouse having custody of any children.

COMMENT

Alternative A, which is the alternative recommended generally for adoption, proceeds upon the principle that all the property of the spouses, however acquired, should be regarded as assets of the married couple, available for distribution among them, upon consideration of the various factors enumerated in subsection (a).

. . .

Alternative B was included because a number of Commissioners from community property states represented that their jurisdictions would not wish to substitute, for their own systems, the great hotchpot of assets created by Alternative A, preferring to adhere to the distinction between community property and separate property, and providing for the distribution of that property alone . . .

NOTE

Alternative B of UMDA § 307 was adopted to reflect the practice in community property states of distinguishing between individual and marital property at divorce. The majority of common law states, however, also follow this practice. The ALI Principles that follow do so as well.

American Law Institute, Principles of the Law of Family Dissolution

Section 4.03. Definition of Marital and Separate Property

(1) Property acquired during marriage is marital property, except as otherwise expressly provided in this Chapter.

(2) Inheritances, including bequests and devises, and gifts from third parties, are the separate property of the acquiring spouse even if acquired during marriage.

(3) Property received in exchange for separate property is separate property even if acquired during marriage.

. . .

(6) Property acquired during a relationship between the spouses that immediately preceded their marriage, and which was a domestic-partner relationship as defined by § 6.03, is treated as if it were acquired during the marriage.

COMMENTS

a. Rationale for distinguishing marital from separate property. Section 4.03 distinguishes marital from separate property because the allocation rules applied to each classification are different. In applying different allocation rules to each class of property, these Principles follow both the majority of American states and the predominant view of commentators. The alternative, sometimes called a "hotchpot" system, in principle applies the same equitable-distribution principles to all property, regardless of the time or mode of its acquisition.

The majority view reflects a widespread consensus that marriage alone should not affect the ownership interest that each spouse has over property possessed prior to the marriage or received after the marriage by gift or inheritance. In contrast, the law of nearly every state reflects the view that marriage alone is sufficient to support a spousal claim of shared ownership at divorce to property earned by marital labor (labor performed during marriage by a spouse).

. . .

A system that classifies property necessarily creates an opportunity for the parties to dispute an item's proper classification. The corresponding benefit, as compared to a hotchpot system, is that classifying property as marital or separate allows for more certain allocation rules. . . . Hotchpot systems . . . employ allocation rules that rely heavily on trial-judge discretion to divide the property "equitably." Their advantage in eliminating disputes over the characterization of property is thus outweighed by the added potential for disputes over the property's allocation.

Section 4.05. Enhancement of Separate Property by Marital Labor

(1) A portion of any increase in the value of separate property is marital property whenever either spouse has devoted substantial time during marriage to the property's management or preservation.

(2) The increase in value of separate property over the course of the marriage is measured by the difference between the market value of the property when acquired, or at the beginning of the marriage, if later, and the market value of the property when sold, or at the end of the marriage, if sooner.

(3) The portion of the increase in value that is marital property under Paragraph (1) is the difference between the actual amount by which the property has increased in value, and the amount by which capital of the same value would have increased over the same time period if invested in assets of relative safety requiring little management.

COMMENT

a. General. A fundamental principle of community-property law followed today in most common-law jurisdictions is that the fruits of labor performed during marriage by either spouse ("marital labor") belong to the marital community, and are not the separate property of the laboring spouse. When marital labor is applied to separate capital, and the separate capital appreciates, the principles of marital-property law require an apportionment between the appreciation attributable to the marital labor, which is marital property, and the appreciation attributable to the separate capital itself, which remains the separate property of the spousal owner of the capital. Such an apportionment is required, for example, when the separate-property owner of a business works in that business during the marriage, and the business appreciates in value. Apportionment is also required when the labor of one spouse yields appreciation in the separate property of the other spouse. In both cases, the appreciation attributable to marital labor is shared by both spouses.

. . .

b. Allocation method. Existing cases generally divide between two allocation methods. One method, akin to a *quantum meruit* approach, values the labor input by reference to prevailing compensation rates, and attributes all remaining gain to capital. The other method values the capital input by reference to ordinary rates of return, and attributes all the remaining gain to labor....

Paragraph (3) follows the cases that value the capital's contribution to the gain by reference to prevailing rates of return, attributing all remaining gain to marital labor. This classification rule allocates any surplus that may arise to the marital community, rather than to the separate estate. The rule is consistent with the commonly accepted principle that when separate and marital property are irreversibly commingled, the entire amount is treated as marital rather than separate. When the marital property is divided equally between the spouses, this rule divides the surplus equally between them as well.

Illustration:

1. Alex runs a small contracting business at the time of his marriage to Betty. The business is thus Alex's separate property. He continues to work at the business during their marriage. When they divorce five years later, it has increased in value from $10,000 to $50,000. Because Alex has devoted substantial labor during marriage to the management of his separate-property business, a portion of its increased value is marital property. To calculate the marital-property portion of the $40,000 gain, the court first determines the return that would have been obtained during the same time period from an investment of $10,000 in "assets of relative safety requiring little or no management." In this jurisdiction, the benchmark normally employed to implement this standard is the return on 10-year Treasury bonds. By referring to interest rates prevailing at that time, the court determines that $10,000 invested in 10-year Treasury bonds at the commencement of Betty's and Alex's marriage would have yielded $4,700 by the time of their dissolution. Alex's original $10,000, plus this $4,700 return, is his separate property. The remaining $35,300 ($40,000 minus $4,700) is marital property to be divided between the spouses under [another section of the Principles] . . .

2. DISTINGUISHING MARITAL FROM SEPARATE PROPERTY

Innerbichler v. Innerbichler

Court of Special Appeals of Maryland, 2000.
132 Md.App. 207, 752 A.2d 291.

■ HOLLANDER, J.

This appeal arises from the dissolution of the marriage of Nicholas R. Innerbichler, appellant, and Carole Jean Innerbichler, appellee. After more than fourteen years of marriage, the parties were granted a divorce by the Circuit Court for Prince George's County, pursuant to an order dated July 27, 1998, and modified on January 13, 1999. Two aspects of the court's orders are at the heart of this appeal: 1) the monetary award to appellee, in the amount of $2,581,864.75, which was based, in part, on the court's determination that the appreciation in value of appellant's 51% ownership interest in Technical and Management Services Corporation ("TAMSCO") constituted marital property; and 2) the court's award to appellee of monthly alimony of $8000.00 for five years, followed by indefinite monthly alimony of $6,000.00.

Appellant noted a timely appeal to this Court, posing several questions for our consideration, which we have rephrased slightly:

... Did the trial court err in granting the monetary award to appellee by improperly finding that the increase in value in TAMSCO was marital property?

. . .

The parties were married on January 21, 1984, when Mr. Innerbichler (the "Husband") was 41 years old and appellee (the "Wife") was 33. Although appellant had been married twice before, it was appellee's first marriage. The parties have one child, Michelle Nicole, who was born on May 1, 1986. Appellant also has three adult children from prior marriages.

In 1995, after eleven years of marriage, the Husband moved out of the marital home. On September 12, 1995, he filed a Complaint for Limited Divorce, and the Wife filed a countersuit, seeking an absolute divorce on the ground of adultery. Her suit was later amended in court to include a two year separation as an additional ground for divorce.

. . .

At the time of trial, appellant was 55 years old and resided with his paramour in a home that he purchased for about $600,000.00 and financed with a mortgage and a loan from his business. Appellee was a 47–year-old high school graduate who had completed one semester of college. The trial culminated in a divorce based on the parties' separation of two years....

In October 1982, more than one year prior to the parties' marriage, appellant co-founded TAMSCO with his friend and colleague, William Bilawa. At the time, appellant was employed by Lockheed Corporation, and remained employed there until June 1983; in the evenings, appellant worked for TAMSCO. The company provides technical and management services to agencies of the federal government and to the private sector in various disciplines, including program management, integrated logistics support, software development, and data management. At the relevant time, appellant owned 51% of TAMSCO and Bilawa owned a 49% interest in the company.

When TAMSCO was founded, appellant was married to Barbara Innerbichler ("Barbara"). In 1983, as part of his divorce settlement with Barbara, appellant claimed that he waived his interest in the home that they occupied, allegedly worth about $300,000.00, in exchange for Barbara's agreement to waive her claim to TAMSCO, which appellant contends was worth at least as much as the home.

In June 1983, about six months before appellant's marriage to appellee, appellant submitted an application on behalf of TAMSCO to the United States Small Business Administration ("SBA") to obtain "8(a) certification." According to appellant, who is an Hispanic American, the "8(a) program" was established during the Nixon years to assist small businesses owned and controlled by socially and economically disadvantaged persons.

. . .

Appellee insists that TAMSCO was in its "embryonic stages" when the parties were first married. Ample evidence was presented at trial showing that TAMSCO was in its fledgling stage of development at the time of the marriage.

. . .

On April 14, 1984, some 83 days after the parties' marriage, TAMSCO obtained the desired 8(a) certification. It is undisputed that the 8(a) program enabled TAMSCO to obtain lucrative sole source government contracts, the first of which was awarded to TAMSCO in September 1984. TAMSCO grew rapidly after the award of the 8(a) certification. For fiscal year 1983, the company reported approximately $52,000.00 in revenues, and $188,000.00 in revenues for fiscal year 1984. By the end of fiscal year 1992, TAMSCO had been awarded contracts totaling $356,439,719. For 1995, TAMSCO generated revenues of $46 million and employed over 500 people. In 1996, TAMSCO earned $47,000,000.00 in revenues, followed by $51,000,000.00 for fiscal year 1997.

From 1984 through 1989, approximately 85% of TAMSCO's work related to 8(a) contracts, and from 1989 until 1993, approximately 75% of TAMSCO's work derived from those contracts. When TAMSCO left the SBA's 8(a) program in 1993, it had already received approximately $356,000,000.00 in 8(a) revenue. By the time of the divorce trial, however, TAMSCO was no longer eligible to participate in the SBA's 8(a) program, although it still had residual 8(a) business. According to appellant, because TAMSCO could no longer "pursue contracts in a non-competitive marketplace," its business position had declined. Nevertheless, at the time of trial, appellant was earning in excess of $650,000.00 in annual salary.

Although appellant concedes that most of TAMSCO's lucrative contracts were obtained and performed after his marriage to appellee, he maintains that neither TAMSCO nor the post-marriage appreciation in the company's value constituted marital property. He argues that the company was created before the marriage and its success was directly linked to an Army contract awarded prior to the marriage. Appellant points out that, in October 1993, while the 8(a) application was still pending, TAMSCO was notified that it had "won" a non–8(a) contract with the Army, worth in excess of one million dollars. Thus, he claims that over 97% of TAMSCO's government contracts were "traceable to contracts won at the company's inception and prior to the marriage." ... Although the Army contract was "awarded" on January 1, 1984, shortly before the parties' marriage, performance of the Army contract did not begin until the summer of 1984, after the parties were married.

. . .

On July 27, 1998, the court ... granted a monetary award to the Wife in the amount of $2,880,000.00 [in addition to alimony].

The monetary award was based largely on the court's determination as to TAMSCO's value. The court expressly indicated that it found the testimony of the Wife's expert as to TAMSCO's value "more persuasive" than appellant's expert. Based on the opinion of the Wife's expert, the court concluded that TAMSCO had a fair market value of $8.3 million. The court also determined that appellant's 51% ownership interest in TAMSCO was worth $4,233,000.00, and that appellant's pre-marital interest in TAMSCO was worth $153,000.00.

Additionally, the court found that the post-marriage "increase in value of TAMSCO is marital," and that "the Husband's share (51%) of the increased value of TAMSCO stock is marital," because TAMSCO's "success is attributable to a large degree to the work efforts of the Husband throughout the marriage." The court explained: "He was the president of the company and was more responsible for the mission and rating of TAMSCO than his partner. He made the ultimate decisions on the contracts and was actively involved in making presentations to the early contracting parties which generated the value of TAMSCO." The judge also relied on an informal action of TAMSCO's Board of Directors in July 1988, which acknowledged that "without [appellant] and his personal efforts, the contracts, the past corporate growth and financial stability would not have been realized by the corporation." Further, the court observed that TAMSCO earned less than $60,000.00 before the marriage, and that most of the "contracts which formed the basis of TAMSCO's value were entered into after the marriage."

. . .

Following post-trial motions, the court entered a revised order on January 28, 1999, in which it concluded that the total marital value of TAMSCO was $4,080,000.00. Further, it determined that the total value of marital assets, including TAMSCO, equaled $5,576,280.50. Exclusive of TAMSCO, the court found that appellee had $74,653.00 in property titled to her, appellant had property worth $1,367,991.50 titled to him, and the parties had $53,636.00 in joint property. After awarding appellee $104,804.50 as her share of appellant's pension, the court recalculated the monetary award and reduced it to $2,581,864.75. The court then ordered appellant to make full payment of that sum over a five year period, without interest. Of that sum, $430,310.79 was due by July 27, 1999 . . .

Title 8 of the Family Law Article of the Maryland Code provides for the equitable distribution of marital property. " 'Marital Property' means the property, however titled, acquired by 1 or both parties during the marriage." *F.L. § 8–201(e)(1)*. Pursuant to *F.L. § 8–201(e)(3)*, marital property does not include property that is:

(i) acquired before the marriage;

(ii) acquired by inheritance or gift from a third party;

(iii) excluded by valid agreement; or

(iv) directly traceable to any of these sources.

Property that is initially non-marital can become marital, however. Moreover, the party who asserts a marital interest in property bears the burden of producing evidence as to the identity of the property. Conversely, "the party seeking to demonstrate that particular property acquired during the marriage is nonmarital must trace the property to a nonmarital source." If a property interest cannot be traced to a nonmarital source, it is considered marital property.

. . .

When a party petitions for a monetary award, the trial court must first follow a three-step procedure. First, for each disputed item of property, the court must determine whether it is marital or nonmarital. Second, the court must determine the value of all marital property. Third, the court must decide if the division of marital property according to title will be unfair; if so, the court *may* make a monetary award to rectify any inequity "created by the way in which property acquired during marriage happened to be titled." In doing so, the court must consider the statutory factors contained in *F.L. § 8–205(b)*. [These are:]

(1) the contributions, monetary and nonmonetary, of each party to the well-being of the family;

(2) the value of all property interests of each party;

(3) the economic circumstances of each party at the time the award is to be made;

(4) the circumstances that contributed to the estrangement of the parties;

(5) the duration of the marriage;

(6) the age of each party;

(7) the physical and mental condition of each party;

(8) how and when specific marital property or interest in the pension, retirement, profit sharing, or deferred compensation plan, was acquired, including the effort expended by each party in accumulating the marital property or the interest in the pension, retirement, profit sharing, or deferred compensation plan, or both;

(9) the contribution by either party of property described in § 8-201(e)(3) of this subtitle to the acquisition of real property held by the parties as tenants by the entirety;

(10) any award of alimony and any award or other provision that the court has made with respect to family use personal property or the family home; and

(11) any other factor that the court considers necessary or appropriate to consider in order to arrive at a fair and equitable monetary award or transfer of an interest in the pension, retirement, profit sharing, or deferred compensation plan, or both.

. . .

As we previously observed, appellant contends that the court erred in finding that TAMSCO constituted marital property. He argues that "TAMSCO was brought into the marriage as an established, flourishing non-marital asset. By the time the parties married, the ground work had already been laid to make TAMSCO a success." In addition, the Husband quarrels with the court's decision to attribute the appreciation of TAMSCO solely to his efforts. He maintains that TAMSCO's growth was the result of the efforts of many people as well as several other factors, such as the thriving defense industry. In his view, "this is a classic case of being in the right place at the right time." Moreover, appellant complains that the court should not have treated 51% of the appreciation as marital property, merely because he owned 51% of the company. Appellant asserts that the court was required to ascertain the precise portion of TAMSCO's increase in value for which appellant was responsible, and that only the portion attributable to his work efforts could qualify as marital property.

The court was not clearly erroneous in rejecting appellant's claim that TAMSCO was entirely non-marital property. Although it is undisputed that TAMSCO was created before the marriage, the evidence that we summarized earlier supported the court's conclusion that TAMSCO's value soared after the marriage. For example, when TAMSCO submitted its application for SBA 8(a) certification in June 1983, it had only completed a $13,000.00 contract and a $6,000.00 contract, and a $131,000.00 contract was in progress. Moreover, TAMSCO owned little in the way of tangible property. At the time of the marriage, the business had only two full-time employees and operated from Bilawa's kitchen. TAMSCO received its 8(a) certification after the marriage, and all of the 8(a) contracts were performed during the marriage. By the time TAMSCO graduated from the SBA Section 8(a) program in 1993, it had received over $356,000,000.00 in Section 8(a) revenue, placing it among the top 10 such firms nationally.

Appellant also challenges the court's decision to treat all of the appreciation as marital property. He relies on the court's own acknowledgment that appellant was merely responsible, "to a large degree" (and thus not entirely), for the increased value. On the other hand, appellant also seems to suggest that the court miscalculated the monetary award, because it did not find that all of the appreciation was marital property.

We are of the view that the court found that all of TAMSCO's appreciation constituted marital property, and it attributed all of the appreciation to appellant's work efforts. After comparing the financial status of TAMSCO before and after the marriage, the court focused on the extent of appellant's role in the corporation and his work efforts on behalf of TAMSCO, concluding that "*the increase* in value of TAMSCO is marital. . . ." (Emphasis added). Significantly, the court did not qualify its statement by saying words to the effect that *some* of the increase or *part* of the increase in value is marital. The common sense construction of the court's pronouncement is that it determined that *all* of the appreciation was marital.

Moreover, notwithstanding the court's statement that appellant was responsible "to a large degree" for TAMSCO's success, we are satisfied that the court did not err, on the record before it, when it attributed all of the appreciation to appellant's efforts for purposes of calculating the monetary award. It follows that the court did not err by failing to assign a specific percentage of responsibility to appellant in achieving that corporate growth.

. . .

. . . [W]e pause to question whether the court truly could have ascertained, with either genuine accuracy, mathematical certainty, or scientific precision, the exact extent to which appellant's efforts led to TAMSCO's success. Although we acknowledge that it is rare for one person singularly to wear all hats in the operation of a complex, technical, multi-million dollar business enterprise such as TAMSCO, one person can function in a capacity critical to a company's growth and development. Here, the court was clearly satisfied from the evidence that appellant was the driving force in TAMSCO's huge financial growth. It is equally apparent that, because of appellant's vital and instrumental role in TAMSCO's success, the court did not assign to appellant an arbitrary percentage of responsibility for the increased corporate value.

In determining the marital or non-marital character of disputed property that has its origins as non-marital property, the cases distinguish between passive ownership and increases in value resulting from the active efforts of the owner-spouse. In *Mount v. Mount, 476 A.2d 1175 (1984),* we recognized that there are various ways in which property that increases in value may become marital. We said:

Property can produce other property in many different ways. In some instances, it may require active intervention and management by the owner or some assistance by the owner's spouse; in other instances, non-marital property can accrete or produce income without any effort at all on the part of the owner or the owner's spouse. In either case, all, some, or none of the income or accretion generated by or from the initial property may be used for family purposes.

. . .

... [W]e are satisfied that the record clearly supports the court's decision to treat all of TAMSCO's appreciation as marital; TAMSCO's value soared after the marriage, while the Husband was at the helm and shepherded TAMSCO's growth. Despite the Husband's assertion that the corporate success resulted from the efforts of others and from a variety of factors not related to his skills, such as "the expanding defense industry during the Reagan administration ..." the court, as fact-finder, was not compelled to accept appellant's version of events.

Although the trial court attributed the entire appreciation to appellant's efforts, appellant only owned 51% of TAMSCO. Therefore, the court properly concluded that only 51% of that appreciation, corresponding to appellant's ownership interest, constituted marital property for purposes of a monetary award. After subtracting the premarital value of TAMSCO ($153,000.00), the court multiplied the value of TAMSCO by 51% to determine the value of appellant's ownership interest in the company. The court then allocated half of that value (i.e., 1/2 of 51% of the appreciation) to the Wife's monetary award.

. . .

In this case, the court considered the statutory factors under *F.L. § 8–205(b)* in fashioning the monetary award. For example, the judge also found that appellant "was responsible for the estrangement of the parties by committing adultery during the marriage and later deserting [appellee]." In addition, the court considered that appellant had "spent large amounts of marital property during the separation on his life style and gambling." Moreover, the court was mindful that appellant had invested a substantial amount of marital funds in SeaMats and TRAMS, even though the court did not include these investments as marital property. Under the circumstances of this case, we perceive neither error nor abuse of discretion by the court in evenly dividing the marital portion of TAMSCO.

Thomas v. Thomas

Supreme Court of Georgia, 1989.
259 Ga. 73, 377 S.E.2d 666.

■ HUNT, JUSTICE

This granted discretionary appeal presents another version of the challenge facing factfinders, whether judge or jury, in deciding how to classify as marital or non-marital certain property which has characteristics of both. The subject of this particular inquiry involves the proceeds from the sale of the marital home and from the sale of stock in the company which employed the husband. The house was in the wife's name and had been purchased by her shortly before the marriage but marital funds had reduced the mortgage debt against the house. The stock was purchased during the marriage as the result of stock options obtained by the husband before the marriage. The stock was paid for by a combination of separate and marital funds. The trial judge awarded the wife almost all the proceeds from the sale of the house and awarded her what amounted to one-half the proceeds of the stock sale, conceded by the court to be, in part, separate property of the husband. This was done in order to restore to her a portion of sums which she had given to the husband before the marriage. The husband appeals and we affirm in part and reverse and remand in part.

The wife was a successful sales representative for a computer company in Florida when, in 1979, she met the husband, who was her regional manager in Atlanta. As their relationship developed the husband left his family and moved into a condominium. From June 1981 until the marriage in July 1983, the wife gave the husband almost $39,000 so that he could meet his increased obligations resulting from the separation from his family. In the summer of 1982, the wife terminated her employment from the computer company and moved to Atlanta. She and the husband located a house under construction and decided to purchase it. The actual purchase was made by the wife. In round figures, she met the $260,000 sales price by a down payment of $75,000 and a first mortgage of $185,000. A month after they separated in November of 1986, the house was sold for $351,000. Thus the house appreciated in value during the marriage in the amount of about $91,000. Through monthly payments, made mostly during the marriage, the mortgage was reduced from $185,000 to $177,000 at the time of the sale. The monthly payments between November 15, 1982, the date of purchase, to the date of the marriage in July 1983, were made by the wife.

In 1981 and 1982, the husband had earned stock options as part of his employment compensation. The options were exercised during the marriage at times when the value of the stock was less than its value immediately prior to the marriage. The stock was purchased with a combination of marital funds, a loan from his father, and a loan against his life-insurance policies. The stock was sold prior to the divorce and a profit in excess of $30,000 was realized.

The parties separated in November 1986.

THE STOCK

With respect to the proceeds from the sale of the stock and the connection between those proceeds and the cash advanced by the wife to the husband before the marriage, the court had this to say:

> [T]hose contributions [by the wife] would have been, had they been made during the marriage, treated as marital assets. They would have been a contribution to or investment in the relationship.
>
> However, since the wife contributed $38,967 to the Husband prior to their marriage, then the equitable and rational approach would be to cause an equal amount in non-marital assets of Mr. Thomas to be treated as martial assets since they were expended for his benefit and to satisfy his legal obligations. Therefore, $38,967 of his non-marital assets would be treated as a marital asset for purposes of distribution.
>
> The stock [shares] were premarital assets to the extent that [there] were loans that permitted the purchase of those assets, particularly when those loans were made against non-marital assets such as the cash surrender value of the insurance policies or their loan values. . . . To the extent that marital assets were used in exercising [the stock] option, that would subject the proceeds of such stock sale to that equitable division. *In any event, because of the consumption of $38,967 premaritally, for the benefit of Mr. Thomas, then of those total stock sales, $38,967 would be subject to equitable division.* (Emphasis supplied.)

The husband argues that to the extent the stock proceeds were non-marital assets they would not be subject to equitable division. We agree. In order to divide marital property on an equitable basis, two things must be done. First, the property must be classified as either marital or non-marital. Second, the *marital* property must be divided, not necessarily equally, but equitably under the principles elucidated in the classifying of property as either marital or non-marital is not a discretionary function but is based on legal principles. The second part, the division of marital property itself, is of course discretionary based on a consideration of various equitable factors. The court was not permitted to treat a portion of the husband's separate property as marital property in order to satisfy his perception of the equities of the case. In doing so, he in effect imposed an equitable trust upon those funds to the extent of the wife's premarital contribution. We will remand this issue to the trial court so that the marital aspect of the stock proceeds may be set aside for distribution. The court may then divide those marital proceeds as it sees fit based upon the usual equitable criteria.

THE HOUSE

The husband argues that all the appreciation and value of the house which occurred during the marriage should have been classified as marital property and be subject to equitable division. He concedes that the wife brought the house into the marriage as her separate property and that she was entitled to all of the value in the house apart from its appreciation during the marriage.[2]

The net appreciation in the house amounted to $90,905. The trial court found that in addition to the down payment both parties had reduced the loan balance $7,265, and that the total equity paid by both parties was $82,623. Of the $7,265 reduction in debt which had been occasioned by the monthly mortgage payments, he figured that $1,017 had been paid by the wife and $6,393 were paid out of marital assets. His order then stated:

> A ratio of $6,393 to $82,623 (total equity paid) works out to seven percent of the payments on the equity being marital. Therefore, seven percent of the appreciation of $90,905 is subject to marital distribution as a marital asset, which works out to $12,756. That is a marital asset subject to equitable division.

The method of division utilized by the trial court is referred to as the "source of funds" rule. In *Harper v. Harper*, 294 Md. 54, 448 A.2d 916 (1982), the Court of Appeals of Maryland made a detailed survey of its sister states to determine the appropriate method, under equitable division, of a marital home brought as separate property to the marriage, but paid for, at least in part, from joint funds. It found that some states follow an "inception of title" theory, where the status of property as separate or marital is fixed at the time it is acquired and, despite later contributions by the other spouse, remains separate; some follow a "source of funds," where the property is considered both separate and marital in proportion to the contributions (monetary or otherwise) separately and jointly provided; and others follow a "transmutation of property" theory, where separate property is converted to marital property whenever there is any contribution of marital property. The

2. We are willing to adopt the husband's concession for the purposes of this opinion. However, had there been no market appreciation of the house during the marriage, the marital unit would have still been entitled to have the principal reduction occurring during the marriage set aside as marital property under the "source of funds" rule which we discuss infra.

Maryland court analyzed each treatment with an eye toward developing its own policy on equitable division of this sort of property and adopted the "source of funds" rule. That rule holds that:

[A] spouse contributing nonmarital property is entitled to an interest in the property in the ratio of the nonmarital investment to the total nonmarital and marital investment in the property. The remaining property is characterized as marital property and its value is subject to equitable distribution. Thus, the spouse who contributed nonmarital funds, and the marital unit that contributed marital funds each receive a proportionate and fair return on their investment.

Harper v. Harper supra, 448 A.2d at 929.

. . .

Concerning appreciation, if the house is thought of not as a single unit but as two monetary units, one separate and one marital, the analysis is simplified. The wife brought to the marriage a monetary contribution of approximately $76,000. During the marriage the marital unit contributed $6,000. In this case each sum appreciated by the same rate as a result of market forces. The marital unit's share of the appreciation would be figured by the same method as that adopted by the trial judge. The source of funds rule is a reliable method for classifying property of this sort and is consistent with the purpose behind the doctrine of equitable division of property. This purpose is to assure that property accumulated during the marriage be fairly distributed between the parties while at the same time preserving separate property for the benefit of the spouse to whom it belongs.

. . .

The husband argues that the entire appreciation in value of the parties' interest in the house resulted from their joint efforts to maintain and pay for it. This argument is not supported by the evidence. The parties' payments reduced the principal debt and were responsible for the resulting increase in equity caused by that reduction. The only material cause for the remaining appreciation ($90,000) was outside market forces. The trial court's division of the proceeds from the sale of the home was . . . not error.

3. Dividing Property Equitably

Ferguson v. Ferguson

Mississippi Supreme Court, En Banc, 1994.
639 So.2d 921.

■ Prather, Presiding Justice, for the Court:

. . . This Court has been in a transitory state regarding the division of marital assets. Our prior law adhered to a system of returning property to the spouse in whom title was held (separate property method); however, recent opinions have eroded adherence to that method of division. This Court has "long recognized that, incident to a divorce, the chancery court has authority, where the equities so suggest, to order a fair division of property accumulated through the joint contributions and efforts of the parties." With this opinion, this Court adopts guidelines for application of the equitable distribution method of division of marital assets.

Billy Ferguson, Sr., (Billy), appeals from a final judgment of divorce entered on November 12, 1991, by the Chancery Court of Newton County awarding a divorce to Linda Ferguson, (Linda), on the ground of adultery and denying Billy's counterclaim for divorce filed on the basis of habitual cruel and inhuman treatment. The Court affirms the granting of a divorce to the wife, together with custody and support of the minor child. With adoption of guidelines to aid chancellors in division of marital property under the equitable property division method, this Court reverses the award of marital assets and remands to the chancery court to re-evaluate the marital division in light of these guidelines.

States have devised various methods to divide marital assets at divorce, and approaches have usually followed one of three systems. According to Stephen J. Brake, Equitable Distribution vs. Fixed Rules: Marital Property Reform and the Uniform Marital Property Act, 23 B.C.L.Rev., 761, 762 (1982), the separate property system, the equitable distribution system, and a system of fixed rules (community property) are the three systems reflected in American jurisprudence.

. . .

Our separate property system at times resulted in unjust distributions, especially involving cases of a traditional family where most property was titled in the husband, leaving a traditional housewife and mother with nothing but a claim for alimony, which often proved unenforceable. In a family where both spouses worked, but the husband's resources were devoted to investments while the wife's earnings were devoted to paying the family expenses or vice versa, the same unfair results ensued.

The flaw of the separate property system, however, is not merely that it will occasionally ignore the financial contributions of the non-titleholding spouse. The system ... is also unable to take account of a spouse's non-financial contribution. In the case of many traditional housewives such non-financial contributions are often considerable. Thus, to allow a system of property division to ignore non-financial contributions is to create a likelihood of unjust division of property.

The non-monetary contributions of a traditional housewife have been acknowledged by this Court, and to some extent, case law has helped lessen the unfairness to a traditional housewife in the division of marital property.

. . .

[T]hrough an evolution of case law, this Court has abandoned the title theory method of distribution of marital assets and evolved into an equitable distribution system.[4]

. . .

... Given the development of domestic relations law, this Court recognizes the need for guidelines to aid chancellors in their adjudication of marital property division. ... Although this listing is not exclusive, this Court suggests the chancery courts consider the following guidelines, where applicable, when attempting to effect an equitable division of marital property:

4. While the issue can be simply stated, it is impossible to give a precise definition to the phrase "equitable distribution." Basically, the doctrine refers to the authority of the courts to award property legally owned by one spouse to the other spouse, and recognizes that a non-working spouse's efforts contribute to the acquisition of the marital estate. Under the equitable distribution system, the marriage is viewed as a partnership with both spouses contributing to the marital estate in the manner which they have chosen.

1. Substantial contribution to the accumulation of the property. Factors to be considered in determining contribution are as follows:

a. Direct or indirect economic contribution to the acquisition of the property;

b. Contribution to the stability and harmony of the marital and family relationships as measured by quality, quantity of time spent on family duties and duration of the marriage; and

c. Contribution to the education, training or other accomplishment bearing on the earning power of the spouse accumulating the assets.

2. The degree to which each spouse has expended, withdrawn or otherwise disposed of marital assets and any prior distribution of such assets by agreement, decree or otherwise.

3. The market value and the emotional value of the assets subject to distribution.

4. The value of assets not ordinarily, absent equitable factors to the contrary, subject to such distribution, such as property brought to the marriage by the parties and property acquired by inheritance or inter vivos gift by or to an individual spouse;

5. Tax and other economic consequences, and contractual or legal consequences to third parties, of the proposed distribution;

6. The extent to which property division may, with equity to both parties, be utilized to eliminate periodic payments and other potential sources of future friction between the parties;

7. The needs of the parties for financial security with due regard to the combination of assets, income and earning capacity; and,

8. Any other factor which in equity should be considered.

. . .

Facts

Linda Ferguson, age 44, and Billy Cleveland Ferguson, Sr., age 48, were married on April 15, 1967, and separated on May 13, 1991. Two children were born of this marriage. When the complaint for divorce was filed on May 21, 1991, the parties' daughter, Tamatha Ferguson, was 23 years of age and emancipated. Their son, Billy Cleveland Ferguson, Jr. (Bubba), was 14 years old and resided in the home with his parents in Chunky, Newton County, Mississippi.

During their 24 years of marriage, Linda worked both as a homemaker and as a cosmetologist/beautician. Billy, employed by South Central Bell as a cable repair technician for 24 years, installed and maintained local telephone service in the Chunky, Mississippi, area.

On May 21, 1991, Linda filed for divorce on the grounds of adultery and requested permanent custody of Bubba. Billy denied the adultery charge and counterclaimed for divorce based on habitual cruel and inhuman treatment. Billy also sought custody of his son, alleging that Bubba had expressed a desire to live with his father, and arguing that the court should respect the wishes of the child. No allegations were made that Linda was not a fit, suitable or proper parent to have custody of the child.

The chancellor denied Billy's request for divorce and awarded Linda: (1) a divorce on the ground of adultery; (2) custody of Bubba and $300.00 a month in child support; (3) the marital home and its contents together with four acres of land comprising the homestead, title to the marital home to be divested from Billy and vested in Linda, debt free; (4) one-half interest in Billy's pension plan, stock ownership plan, and savings and security plan; (5) periodic alimony in the amount of $400.00 per month and lump sum alimony in the sum of $30,000.00 to be paid at the rate of $10,000.00 annually beginning on January 1, 1992; (6) attorney fees in the amount of $5,000.00; (7) health insurance through Bell South for as long "as the law allows," and (8) a lien on any and all property owned by Billy to secure the payments ordered by the chancellor.

... Billy appeals all adjudications of the Court.

. . .

Billy contends the chancellor lacked the authority to order him to convey, free of all encumbrances, his one-half interest in the jointly owned four acres on which the marital home was situated. Billy argues that Linda did not seek ownership; rather, she only sought permanent, exclusive use and possession of the residence together with all its contents.

"We have long recognized that, incident to a divorce, the Chancery Court has authority, where the equities so suggest, to order a fair division of property accumulated through the joint contributions and efforts of the parties." Brown v. Brown, 574 So.2d 688, 690 (Miss.1990). In Draper, 627 So.2d at 305, this Court held that the chancery court has authority to effect the divesting of title to real estate to achieve an equitable distribution of marital assets. This is a matter committed to the discretion and conscience of the court, having in mind all of the equities and other relevant facts and circumstances. Moreover, the Chancery Court "has the authority to order an equitable division of jointly accumulated property and in doing so to look behind the formal state of title." Johnson v. Johnson, 550 So.2d 416, 420 (Miss.1989).

"A spouse who has made a material contribution toward the acquisition of property which is titled in the name of the other may claim an equitable interest in such jointly accumulated property incident to a divorce proceeding." Jones v. Jones, 532 So.2d 574, 580 (Miss.1988) (citing Watts v. Watts, 466 So.2d 889 (Miss.1985); Chrismond v. Chrismond, 211 Miss. 746, 52 So.2d 624 (1951)). See also Brendel v. Brendel, 566 So.2d 1269, 1273 (Miss.1990), where this court affirmed the lower court's decision ordering a husband to convey to his wife one-half interest in a home titled only in the husband's name.

This Court pointed out in Jones that recent cases had wrestled with the definition of "contribution" within the context of the acquisition of assets. Nevertheless, we said that "[i]f 'contribution' toward the acquisition of assets is proven by a divorcing party, then the court has the authority to divide these 'jointly' accumulated assets." Jones, 532 So.2d at 580.

In this case, the property was not titled solely in Billy's name, but titled to both Billy and Linda. Moreover, both parties requested, inter alia, an equitable division of the parties' jointly accumulated property. Although it is true that Linda requested in her complaint "the permanent exclusive use and possession" of the marital home together with its contents minus Billy's personal items, it is also noted that she sought a division of the marital assets.

This Court holds that under existing case law the chancellor was within his authority to order Billy to effect a transfer of title to Linda to the marital home and the surrounding four acres to accomplish an equitable division. Linda, we note, was divested of her undivided one-half interest in the adjoining 33 acres of jointly owned and accumulated real property, which was awarded to Billy. It is noted that Billy was also granted ownership of all farm equipment, a leasehold interest on farm property, a cattle operation, and his 100 shares of stock in a mobile home park. Nonetheless, this issue is remanded for consideration together with the other assets subject to equitable division, such division to be guided by the factors promulgated today.

Postema v. Postema

Michigan Court of Appeals, 1991.
189 Mich.App. 89, 471 N.W.2d 912.

■ MAHER, PRESIDING JUDGE.

The defendant appeals and the plaintiff cross appeals from the property distribution provisions of a February 3, 1989, judgment of divorce. The primary issue concerns the valuation of defendant's law degree and whether the trial court erred in finding the law degree to be a marital asset. We affirm in part and remand.

Plaintiff and defendant were married on August 11, 1984. At the time of their marriage, defendant was employed as a cost accountant and plaintiff was working as a licensed practical nurse and attending school in pursuit of an associate's degree in nursing so that she could become a registered nurse. It was the plan of the parties when they married that defendant would enroll in law school and that plaintiff would postpone her schooling and work full-time to support them while defendant attended school. Accordingly, shortly after the marriage, the parties moved from Grand Rapids to the Detroit area, where they stayed from September 1984 until May 1987 while defendant attended Wayne State University Law School. In furtherance of the parties' plan, plaintiff obtained a full-time job at an area hospital, earning approximately $53,000 during the period defendant was in law school. Plaintiff also assumed the primary responsibility of maintaining the household, doing all cooking and cleaning, and running all errands. Though defendant did not work at all during his first year in law school, he later worked as a law clerk, full-time during the summers following his first and second years in law school and then part-time during his second and part of his third years. In all, defendant earned approximately $12,000 from clerking. The parties' earnings were used primarily for their support, while defendant's education was financed mostly through student loans totaling $15,000.

Defendant proved to be a successful law student and wrote for the school's law review. After defendant graduated in May 1987, the parties moved back to the Grand Rapids area, where defendant accepted a position as an associate attorney with a local law firm at a starting annual salary of $41,000. The following September, plaintiff resumed classes in pursuit of her associate's degree in nursing. In November 1987, however, the parties separated. Despite the separation, plaintiff continued her classes and eventually received her associate's degree in May 1988, although she had to support herself during that period by working full-time at a local hospital.

. . .

The trial court found that the breakdown of the marriage was primarily the fault of defendant, and announced it had considered this fact in its property distribution. After awarding each of the parties their respective automobiles, the trial court awarded plaintiff specific household goods and bank funds totaling $5,000, while awarding defendant specific goods and funds totaling $3,000. Defendant was also held solely responsible for repayment of $14,000 in student loans. Finally, the trial court determined that defendant's law degree was a marital asset subject to distribution. The court valued the degree at $80,000, and awarded plaintiff, as her share of the degree, $32,000 on the basis that this amount would equalize the parties' respective distributive shares. The court ordered this obligation to be paid off in monthly installments of $371.55 or more, at seven percent interest, until fully paid. The court did not award either party alimony.

Defendant now appeals and plaintiff cross appeals as of right. . . .

The goal of a trial court with respect to the division of the marital estate is a fair and equitable distribution under all of the circumstances. The division is not governed by any rigid rules or mathematical formula and need not be equal. The primary question is what is fair. On review, this Court is required to accept the trial court's factual findings unless those findings are clearly erroneous.

I. THE LAW DEGREE

Panels of this Court have expressed different views concerning the treatment, characterization, and valuation of an advanced degree in a divorce situation. Nevertheless, most panels have agreed that *fairness* dictates that a spouse who did not earn an advanced degree be compensated whenever the advanced degree is the end product of a *concerted family effort* involving mutual sacrifice and effort by both spouses.

. . .

A. The Concerted Family Effort.

. . . [T]he concept "concerted family effort" stresses the fact that it is not the existence of an advanced degree itself that gives rise to an equitable claim for compensation, but rather the fact of the degree being the end product of the mutual sacrifice, effort, and contribution of both parties as part of a larger, long-range plan intended to benefit the family as a whole. The concept is premised, in part, on the fact that the attainment of an advanced degree is a prolonged undertaking involving considerable expenditure of time, effort, and money, as well as other sacrifices. Where such an undertaking is pursued as part of a concerted family effort, both spouses expect to be compensated for their respective sacrifices, efforts, and contributions by eventually sharing in the fruits of the degree. Where, however, the parties' relationship ends in divorce, such a sharing is impossible. Although the degree holder will always have the degree to show for the efforts, the nonstudent spouse is left with nothing. Therefore, a remedy consistent with fairness and equity requires that an attempt be made to at least return financially to the nonstudent spouse the value of what that spouse contributed toward attainment of the degree.

Generally, the existence of a concerted family effort will be reflected in many ways. For instance, it is reflected not only through a spouse's tangible efforts and financial contributions associated with working and supporting the mate while the mate pursues the advanced degree, but also through other intangible, nonpecuniary efforts and contributions, such as where a spouse increases the share of the daily tasks, child-rearing responsibilities, or other details of household and family management undertaken in order to provide the mate with the necessary time and energy to study and attend classes. A concerted family effort is also exemplified by the fact that both spouses typically share in the emotional and psychological burdens of the educational experience. For the nonstudent spouse, these burdens may be experienced either directly, such as through the presence of increased tension within the household, or indirectly, such as where the spouse shares vicariously in the stress of the educational experience. Finally, the attainment of an advanced degree during marriage is usually accompanied by considerable sacrifice on the part of both spouses. For the nonstudent spouse, such sacrifice may be reflected by a change in life style during the educational process, the availability of less time to pursue personal interests, or even a decision to either give up or temporarily postpone one's own educational or career pursuits as part of the larger, long-range plan designed to benefit the family as a whole.

Turning now to the instant case, the facts show that plaintiff temporarily postponed her pursuit of an associate's degree in nursing, moved with defendant to the Detroit area so that he could attend law school, and then worked full-time to support herself and defendant while defendant attended classes. This was all done as part of a larger plan to benefit both parties as a whole. Plaintiff, in addition to being the primary financial provider while defendant attended school, wherein she accounted for approximately eighty percent of the parties' total financial support, also bore primary responsibility for the daily household tasks. Moreover, the stress of the law school experience was certainly experienced by both parties, as reflected by the fact that defendant repeatedly blamed his inappropriate behavior toward plaintiff on the stress of law school, and by plaintiff's testimony explaining that her whole life revolved around her trying not to agitate defendant.

We conclude, therefore, that defendant's law degree was clearly the end product of a concerted family effort giving rise to an equitable claim for compensation in favor of plaintiff in recognition of her unrewarded sacrifices, efforts, and contributions toward attainment of the degree.

B. Characterization of a Claim for Compensation Involving an Advanced Degree

Despite the common recognition among panels of this Court that a spouse who did not obtain an advanced degree should be compensated whenever the degree is the end product of a concerted family effort, panels are in disagreement over the appropriate manner in which a claim for compensation should be considered. While some panels have characterized an advanced degree as a marital asset subject to property division, other panels have held that an advanced degree is more properly considered as a factor in awarding alimony.

After reviewing the various decisions addressing the issue and taking into consideration the underlying principles upon which an award of compensation for an advanced degree is premised, we reject the view holding that an advanced degree is more properly considered as a factor in awarding alimony.

. . .

In rejecting the alimony approach, we first recognize that the basic purpose of paying alimony is to assist in the other spouse's support. Unlike alimony, however, the principles underlying an award of compensation based on the attainment of an advanced degree are neither rooted in nor based on notions of support. Rather, as noted previously, entitlement to compensation stems from the recognition that where a degree is the end product of a concerted family effort, fairness and equity will not permit the degree holder to reap the benefits of the degree without compensating the other spouse for unrewarded sacrifices, efforts, and contributions toward attainment of the degree. Thus, where a concerted family effort is involved, a spouse's entitlement to compensation constitutes a recognized right; it is not dependent upon factors related to the need for support. Therefore, we do not find that an award of alimony is the appropriate means for awarding compensation.

Moreover . . . an award in terms of alimony may unfairly jeopardize a spouse's recognized right to compensation because a trial court has broad discretion in deciding whether to grant alimony, because an award of alimony is dependent on factors different from those related to the division of marital property, and because, pursuant to M.C.L. § 552.13; M.S.A. § 25.93, alimony may be terminated if the spouse receiving it remarries. Regarding this latter observation, we agree with the panel in *Lewis,* 181 Mich.App. p. 6, 448 N.W.2d 735, which stated: "Because the value of an advanced degree does not 'evaporate' upon the nondegree-earning spouse's remarriage, we do not find an award of alimony a satisfactory method of recognizing that spouse's efforts toward earning the degree." Furthermore, we note that it is often the case that a nonstudent spouse will already have demonstrated the ability of self-support by virtue of having supported the degree-earning spouse through graduate school. While such fact would ordinarily militate against an award of alimony, we do not believe it should operate to deprive the nonstudent spouse of a recognized right to be compensated for unrewarded sacrifices, efforts, and contributions toward attainment of the degree.

Finally, contrary to the observations in *Graham,* supra, we do not believe that the consideration of an advanced degree when making the property distribution would be improper merely because a degree cannot be characterized as "property" in the classic sense. Rather, we agree with *Woodworth,* 126 Mich.App. p. 263, 337 N.W.2d 332, that "whether or not an advanced degree can physically or metaphysically be defined as 'property' is beside the point[;] [c]ourts must instead focus on the most equitable solution to dissolving the marriage and dividing among the respective parties what they have."

. . .

We conclude, therefore, that where an advanced degree is the end product of a concerted family effort, involving the mutual sacrifice, effort, and contribution of both spouses, there arises a "marital asset" subject to distribution, wherein the interest of the nonstudent spouse consists of an "equitable claim" regarding the degree.

C. Valuation

. . .

Woodworth, supra, 126 Mich.App. pp. 268–269, 337 N.W.2d 332, discussed two methods of compensating a nonstudent spouse for an interest in an advanced degree: (1) awarding a percentage share of the present value of the future earnings attributable to the degree, or (2) restitution. The first method focuses on the degree's present value by attempting to estimate what the person holding the degree is likely to make in a particular job market and subtracting therefrom what that person would probably have earned without the degree. According to *Woodworth,* the nonstudent spouse should then be awarded a percentage share of this value after considering (1) the length of the marriage after the degree was obtained, (2) the sources and extent of financial support given to the degreeholder during the years in school, and (3) the overall division of the parties' marital property. The second method is less involved, because it focuses on the cost of obtaining the degree.

In this case, plaintiff presented an expert who, using the present value method discussed in *Woodworth,* valued defendant's law degree at $230,000.... Using essentially the same formula, but with modifications to the underlying assumptions, defendant presented his own valuations of $15,000, $46,000, and $79,500. The trial court ultimately valued defendant's law degree at $80,000, and then, after determining that the remainder of the property distribution resulted in plaintiff receiving a net amount of $5,000, but defendant having a deficit of $11,000, awarded plaintiff $32,000 as her share of the degree, noting that such an award would equalize the parties' respective distributive shares.

It is difficult to tell from the record how the trial court arrived at its initial $80,000 valuation figure. Further, while we certainly agree that plaintiff is entitled to be compensated for her unrewarded sacrifices, efforts, and contributions toward the attainment of defendant's law degree, our review of the record reveals that the trial court's ultimate award of $32,000 failed to account for several relevant and applicable considerations. Accordingly, we conclude that the appropriate remedy in this case is to remand to the trial court for revaluation of plaintiff's "equitable claim" in light of this opinion. On remand, we do not believe that the present value method discussed in *Woodworth,* and purportedly used by plaintiff's expert, is an appropriate means by which to evaluate plaintiff's equitable claim involving the degree. Such a method emphasizes the notion that a nonstudent spouse possesses some sort of pecuniary interest in the degree itself. We believe such a notion misconstrues the underlying premise upon which an award of compensation involving an advanced degree is based. As we have attempted to explain throughout this opinion, an award of compensation is premised upon equitable considerations, wherein the goal is to attempt to financially return to the nonstudent spouse what that spouse contributed toward attainment of the degree. Because such an award is not premised upon the notion that a nonstudent spouse possesses an interest in the degree itself, we do not believe the actual value of the degree is a relevant consideration. In this respect, we agree with the following observations made in *Krause,* supra, 177 Mich.App. pp. 197–198, 441 N.W.2d 66: "The trial court must focus solely on what is necessary to compensate defendant for the burdens on her or the sacrifices made by her so that plaintiff could pursue his degree."

. . .

[W]e emphasize that the focus of an award involving an advanced degree is not to reimburse the nonstudent spouse for "loss of expectations" over what the degree might potentially have produced, but to reimburse that spouse for unrewarded sacrifices, efforts, and contributions toward attainment of the degree on the ground that it would be equitable to do so *in view of the fact* that that spouse will not be sharing in the fruits of the degree.

. . .

In our view, any valuation of a nonstudent spouse's equitable claim involving an advanced degree involves a two-step analysis. First, an examination of the sacrifices, efforts, and contributions of the nonstudent spouse toward attainment of the degree. Second, given such sacrifices, efforts, and contributions, a determination of what remedy or means of compensation would most equitably compensate the nonstudent spouse under the facts of the case. In this regard, we agree with *Woodworth* that the length of the marriage after the degree was obtained, the sources and extent of financial support given to the degree holder during the years in school, and the overall division of the parties' marital property are all relevant considerations in valuing a nonstudent spouse's equitable claim involving an advanced degree upon divorce.

Where, for instance, the parties remain married for a substantial period of time after an advanced degree is obtained, fairness suggests that the value of an equitable claim would not be as great, inasmuch as the nonstudent spouse will already have been rewarded, in part, for efforts contributed by virtue of having already shared, in part, in the fruits of the degree. Similarly, where the extent of support or assistance provided by the nonstudent spouse, financial or otherwise, is not significant, or where such assistance comes primarily from outside sources for which the nonstudent spouse was not responsible or is not liable, fairness and equity would also suggest that the value of an equitable claim would not be as great.

Furthermore, an equitable remedy may be exemplified in different ways. For example, as this Court recognized in *Krause,* supra, 177 Mich.App. pp. 197–198, 441 N.W.2d 66: "[I]f [the nonstudent spouse] wishes to pursue [an] education or take other similar steps to improve . . . employability or income earning potential, it is reasonable and equitable to require the [degree-holding spouse] to assist . . . in those endeavors." Thus, in this type of situation, an award consistent with fairness and equity would be one which requires the degree-earning spouse to provide assistance, in the form of financial support, equivalent to that provided by the nonstudent spouse during the marriage.

Where, however, a nonstudent spouse does not wish to further pursue an education, then perhaps equity would best be served by an award reimbursing the spouse for the amount of financial assistance provided toward attainment of the degree, while also recognizing the other intangible, nonpecuniary sacrifices made and efforts expended.

Ultimately, however, the goal is to arrive at a remedy which, consistent with fairness and equity, will compensate the nonstudent spouse for unrewarded sacrifices, efforts, and contributions toward the degree. Thus, in reviewing such a claim on appeal, the ultimate inquiry is whether the remedy or decision of the trial court was a fair and equitable one under the facts of the case, given the sacrifices, efforts, and contributions of the nonstudent spouse toward the degree.

We note in this case that the parties separated shortly after defendant attained his law degree. Thus, plaintiff received little reward, if any, for her sacrifices, efforts, and contributions toward defendant's degree. Further, while defendant did contribute some financial support during the degree-earning period, it was plaintiff who accounted for the vast majority of it, approximately eighty percent. Moreover, while defendant certainly worked hard in obtaining his degree, it is abundantly clear from the record that plaintiff's nonpecuniary efforts and contributions toward the degree were indeed significant also, and that she certainly endured many hardships and sacrifices as a result of her participation in the law school experience. We also note that while plaintiff did ultimately further her own career objectives in the manner she chose, she was required to do so on her own and did not have nearly the same benefits, financial or otherwise, that defendant had while he attended school. Defendant was, however, primarily responsible for the actual cost of his education, which was financed mostly through student loans for which he remains solely responsible. These are just some of the factors which were not discussed by the trial court, but yet are relevant to the valuation of plaintiff's equitable claim involving the degree. Therefore, these factors shall be considered by the trial court on remand.

After valuing plaintiff's equitable claim, the trial court may order that the amount determined to be due be payable in monthly installments over a fixed period of time. . . . Finally, we believe it would be in order to allow the parties the opportunity to present new evidence on the issue of valuation in light of this opinion.

. . .

NOTE

The holding of the court in *Postema* represents the minority position. Courts in a majority of states have held that educational degrees do not constitute marital property. For example, in In re Marriage of Graham, 194 Colo. 429, 574 P.2d 75 (1978), the court held that the husband's degree in business administration was not marital property, despite the fact that he obtained the degree while his wife was earning approximately seventy percent of the marital income.

Elkus v. Elkus

Supreme Court of New York, Appellate Division, 1st Dept. 1991.
169 A.D.2d 134, 572 N.Y.S.2d 901.

In this matrimonial action, the plaintiff, Frederica von Stade Elkus, moved for an order determining, prior to trial, whether her career and/or celebrity status constituted marital property subject to equitable distribution. The parties have already stipulated to mutual judgments of divorce terminating their 17–year marriage and to joint custody of their two minor children. The trial on the remaining economic issues has been stayed pending the outcome of this appeal from the order of the Supreme Court, which had determined that the enhanced value of the plaintiff's career and/or celebrity status was not marital property subject to equitable distribution. Contrary to the conclusion reached by the Supreme Court, we find that to the extent the defendant's contributions and efforts led to an increase in the value of the plaintiff's career, this appreciation was a product of the marital partnership, and, therefore, marital property subject to equitable distribution.

At the time of her marriage to the defendant on February 9, 1973, the plaintiff had just embarked on her career, performing minor roles with the Metropolitan Opera Company. During the course of the marriage, the plaintiff's career succeeded dramatically and her income rose accordingly. In the first year of the marriage, she earned $2,250. In 1989, she earned $621,878. She is now a celebrated artist with the Metropolitan Opera, as well as an international recording artist, concert and television performer. She has garnered numerous awards, and has performed for the President of the United States.

During the marriage, the defendant traveled with the plaintiff throughout the world, attending and critiquing her performances and rehearsals, and photographed her for album covers and magazine articles. The defendant was also the plaintiff's voice coach and teacher for 10 years of the marriage. He states that he sacrificed his own career as a singer and teacher to devote himself to the plaintiff's career and to the lives of their young children, and that his efforts enabled the plaintiff to become one of the most celebrated opera singers in the world. Since the plaintiff's career and/or celebrity status increased in value during the marriage due in part to his contributions, the defendant contends that he is entitled to equitable distribution of this marital property.

The Supreme Court disagreed, refusing to extend the holding in *O'Brien v O'Brien (66 NY2d 576)* in which the Court of Appeals determined that a medical license constituted marital property subject to equitable distribution, to the plaintiff's career as an opera singer. The court found that since the defendant enjoyed a substantial life-style during the marriage and since he would be sufficiently compensated through distribution of the parties' other assets, the plaintiff's career was not marital property.

. . .

The plaintiff maintains that since her career and celebrity status are not licensed, are not entities which are owned like a business, nor are protected interests which are subject to due process of law, they are not marital property. In our view, neither the Domestic Relations Law, nor relevant case law, allows for such a limited interpretation of the term marital property.

Domestic Relations Law § 236(B)(1)(c) broadly defines marital property as property acquired during the marriage "regardless of the form in which title is held". In enacting the Equitable Distribution Law, the Legislature created a radical change in the traditional method of distributing property upon the dissolution of a marriage. By broadly defining the term "marital property," it intended to give effect to the "economic partnership" concept of the marriage relationship. It then left it to the courts to determine what interests constitute marital property.

Things of value acquired during marriage are marital property even though they may fall outside the scope of traditional property concepts. The statutory definition of marital property does not mandate that it be an asset with an exchange value or be salable, assignable or transferable. The property may be tangible or intangible

Medical licenses have been held to enhance the earning capacity of their holders, so as to enable the other spouse who made direct or indirect contributions to their acquisition, to share their value as part of equitable distribution. A Medical Board certification, a law degree, an accounting degree, a podiatry practice, the licensing and certification of a physician's assistant, a Masters degree in teaching, and a fellowship in the Society of Actuaries have also been held to constitute marital property.

Although the plaintiff's career, unlike that of the husband in *O'Brien (supra)*, is not licensed, the *O'Brien* court did not restrict its holding to professions requiring a license or degree. In reaching its conclusion that a medical license constitutes marital property, the *O'Brien* court referred to the language contained in *Domestic Relations Law § 236* which provides that in making an equitable distribution of marital property, "the court shall consider:

"(6) any equitable claim to, interest in, or direct or indirect contribution made to the acquisition of such marital property by the party not having title, including joint efforts or expenditures and contributions and services as a spouse, parent, wage earner and homemaker, and to the career or career potential of the other party [and]

(*Domestic Relations Law* § *236*[B][5][d][6] [emphasis added]).

The court also cited section 236[B][5][e] which provides that where, equitable distribution of marital property is appropriate, but "the distribution of an interest in a business, corporation or profession would be contrary to law", the court shall make a distributive award in lieu of an actual distribution of the property.

The Court of Appeals' analysis of the statute is equally applicable here. "The words mean exactly what they say: that an interest in a profession or professional career potential is marital property which may be represented by direct or indirect contributions of the non-title-holding spouse, including financial contributions and nonfinancial contributions made by caring for the home and family" *(O'Brien v. O'Brien, supra, at 584)*. Nothing in the statute or the *O'Brien* decision supports the plaintiff's contention that her career and/or celebrity status are not marital property. The purpose behind the enactment of the legislation was to prevent inequities which previously occurred upon the dissolution of a marriage. Any attempt to limit marital property to professions which are licensed would only serve to discriminate against the spouses of those engaged in other areas of employment. Such a distinction would fail to carry out the premise upon which equitable distribution is based, i.e., that a marriage is an economic partnership to which both parties contribute, as spouse, parent, wage earner or homemaker.

. . .

[T]here is tremendous potential for financial gain from the commercial exploitation of famous personalities. While the plaintiff insists that she will never be asked to endorse a product, this is simply speculation. More and more opportunities have presented themselves to her as her fame increased. They will continue to present themselves to her as she continues to advance in her career. The career of the plaintiff is unique, in that she has risen to the top in a field where success is rarely achieved.

. . .

We agree with the courts that have considered the issue, that the enhanced skills of an artist such as the plaintiff, albeit growing from an innate talent, which have enabled her to become an exceptional earner, may be valued as marital property subject to equitable distribution.

The plaintiff additionally contends that her career is not marital property because she had already become successful prior to her marriage to the defendant. As noted, *supra*, during the first year of marriage, the plaintiff earned $2,250. By 1989, her earnings had increased more than 275 fold. Further, in *Price v. Price (supra*, at 11), the Court of Appeals held that "under the Equitable Distribution Law an increase in the value of separate property of one spouse, occurring during the marriage and prior to the commencement of matrimonial proceedings, which is due in part to the indirect contributions or efforts of the other spouse as homemaker and parent, should be considered marital property." In this case, it cannot be overlooked that the defendant's contributions to plaintiff's career were direct and concrete, going far beyond child care and the like, which he also provided.

While it is true that the plaintiff was born with talent, and, while she had already been hired by the Metropolitan Opera at the time of her marriage to the defendant, her career, at this time, was only in the initial stages of development. During the course of the marriage, the defendant's active involvement in the plaintiff's career, in teaching, coaching, and critiquing her, as well as in caring for their children, clearly contributed to the increase in its value. Accordingly, to the extent the appreciation in the plaintiff's career was due to the defendant's efforts and contributions, this appreciation constitutes marital property.

In sum, we find that it is the nature and extent of the contribution by the spouse seeking equitable distribution, rather than the nature of the career, whether licensed or otherwise, that should determine the status of the enterprise as marital property.

NOTE

The courts in both *Postema* and *Elkus* concluded that one spouse who helps the other enhance his or her earning power has a property interest in the income resulting from that enhancement. Why, then, did each court calculate the value of that interest differently? Which is more consistent with the concept of enhanced earning power as property?

4. FINANCIAL MISCONDUCT

Siegel v. Siegel

Superior Court of New Jersey, Chancery Division, 1990.
241 N.J.Super. 12, 574 A.2d 54.

■ BERMAN, J.S.C.

A question of *res nova* confronts this court: do casino gambling losses ($227,850) incurred pre-complaint, but when the marriage was irreparably fractured, fall within the matrimonial "pot" as a credit to distributable assets, or does it equate with a "dissipation" of funds to be borne solely by the one who placed the family treasury at risk?

This court-one of equity-elects to chart the latter course: the debt belongs to the gambler, without offset or credit; and this court shall hereafter elaborate on the equities, generally, and the facts of this case, specifically, which require this result.

Given the absence of similar authority in this jurisdiction, this court's attention is drawn to the Texas case of *Reaney vs. Reaney, 505 S.W.2d 338 (Tex.Ct.App.1974)*. There, the allegations centered on a spouse "squandering" $53,000, all or part of it, gambling in Puerto Rico. The Texas Court of Appeals appropriately opined that the "admitted dissipation ... was presumptively fraudulent." *Id. at 340.*

An Illinois appellate court reached a similar result when a litigant "withdrew a substantial portion of the joint account" and then used it "for a purpose unrelated to the marriage, at a time that the marriage was under going an irreconcilable breakdown." *Klingberg v. Klingberg, 386 N.E.2d 517, 521 (1979).*

In dividing marital property the New Jersey Supreme Court has also stated:

> Financial dishonesty or financial unfairness between the spouses, or overreaching also can be material. [*Mahoney vs. Mahoney, 91 N.J. 488, 502, 453 A.2d 527 (1982)*].

And finally, this court finds some measure of guidance in the statutorily (*N.J.S.A. 2A:34–23.1*) mandated factors of equitable distribution, specifically paragraph "i" which provides:

The contribution of each party to the acquisition, *dissipation*, preservation, depreciation, or appreciation in the amount or value of the marital property.... [Emphasis supplied]

In view of the foregoing, all equities compel the result set forth hereinabove, removing from judicial consideration an area of "liability" too ripe for potential mischief. And as set forth hereinbelow, the specific facts of this case dictate the inexorability of this conclusion.

Defendant's gambling "indebtedness" is evidenced by a note from him to a closely-held corporation of which he is an equal one-third shareholder. Of consuming curiosity are the following facts:

a. all alleged losses were sustained when the marriage had already deteriorated to a terminal level, and some of those losses would have occurred when the parties were actually separated;

b. the note was executed July 23, 1987—ten days *after* the complaint for divorce was filed, purportedly for "losses" which had already been sustained;

c. the note, payable on "demand" has never been "called," and in the defendant's best case scenario, one-third is virtually payable to himself;

d. on September 1, 1989 this court denied defendant's application to compel plaintiff to execute a joint income tax return for the 1988 calendar year. Defendant, with full knowledge of that ruling, then forged plaintiff's signature to the return.

While this court fully respects defendant's right to arrange his finances to minimize his tax liability, forging his wife's signature to gain that end patently crossed the line between legitimate tax avoidance and illegitimate tax evasion. In the process he manifested inexcusable contempt for this court, and bankrupted his own credibility, aside from the discursive explanation at trial elevating incredulity to an art form. This court is constrained to further add that its orders, constructed solely of pen to paper, possess only as much vitality as either the willingness of litigants to adhere to them, or this court's willingness to take appropriate measures if they don't. Anything less perpetuates an unfortunate myth that the Family Court is oftentimes too impotent or too timid to deal decisively and firmly with litigants who pervert the judicial process with impunity.

In conclusion, requiring defendant to fully assume the gambling indebtedness not only places the parties where they belong, but also where they positioned themselves, especially since this court is unconvinced of the actuality of the alleged losses, or plaintiff's knowledge of them assuming its occurrence.

NOTE

Forty-one states authorize taking economic misconduct into account in dividing property at divorce. Charts, Chart 5: Property Division, 38 Fam. L.Q. 809, 813 (2005).

5. PENSIONS AND OTHER DEFERRED INCOME

Laing v. Laing

Supreme Court of Alaska, 1987.
741 P.2d 649.

■ COMPTON, J.

This appeal challenges a marital property division. . . . We affirm the trial court's findings and conclusions except with regard to its disposition of the husband's nonvested pension, which we conclude cannot be presently divided. We remand the case with instructions that the trial court redetermine the property division in a manner consistent with this opinion.

Kenneth and Marla Laing were married on November 16, 1964. At the time of the marriage, Marla lived in her own furnished home, the equity in which was approximately $15,000. She also had benefits from her first husband's death which amounted to approximately $10,000 and a two-year old car worth approximately $500. Throughout their twenty-year marriage, Marla was responsible for most of the housework and child care, even during approximately ten years she was employed outside the home.

Kenneth apparently had no substantial assets at the time of the marriage. He was employed all but a few months during the marriage.

At the time of divorce, Marla was 49 years old and employed as a dental office receptionist/clerk. She earned $18,750 gross income the year before trial. Kenneth was 50 years old and had been employed at Union Chemicals (now UNOCAL) for seven and a half years. The trial court found that he had earned approximately $40,000 by August 1985; his income in 1984 was $61,471.43.

The parties stipulated to the value of most of the marital assets. The only items in dispute were certain household goods not at issue in this appeal.

. . .

The trial court awarded Kenneth his pension with a present value of $27,000 and awarded Marla offsetting marital assets. Kenneth challenges the award on the grounds that there was insufficient evidence to support the $27,000 figure and that Marla's share should not have been awarded in a lump sum. We first address the issue whether the trial court properly characterized Kenneth's nonvested pension as marital property.

. . .

Alaska follows the majority rule that "vested" pension and retirement benefits are subject to division by a divorce court. Annotation, Pension or Retirement Benefits as Subject to Award or Division by Court in Settlement of Property Rights Between Spouses, 94 A.L.R.3d 176, 182. Whether the majority rule can also be applied with regard to Kenneth's *nonvested*[8] pension rights is a question of first impression in Alaska. Jurisdictions are split on this

8. The term "nonvested" is used here to mean that if Kenneth's employment were to terminate immediately he would be entitled to no future retirement or pension benefits. The term is not used, as some courts have done, to indicate merely that the pension rights have not matured. When a pension or retirement benefits plan is vested but not matured, an employee is absolutely entitled to benefits, though he is not entitled to actual payments until some future date.

issue. Those in which nonvested pensions are held not to be divisible marital property rely primarily on the notion that such interests are too speculative and cannot be said to constitute a property right. See, e.g., Wilson v. Wilson, 409 N.E.2d 1169, 1178 (Ind.App.1980); Ratcliff v. Ratcliff, 586 S.W.2d 292, 293 (Ky.App.1979). . . .

The trend, however, is to consider pensions as marital property regardless of whether they have vested.

Supporting this trend is the reasoning that the contingent nature of a nonvested pension presents simply a valuation problem, not bearing on the non-employee spouse's entitlement to a just share of the marital assets. Pension benefits are generally viewed as deferred compensation for services rendered and the employee spouse's right thereto is a contractual right. Johnson v. Johnson, 131 Ariz. 38, 638 P.2d 705, 708 (1981); [In re Marriage of] Brown, 126 Cal.Rptr. at 637, 544 P.2d at 565. "The fact that a contractual right is contingent upon future events does not degrade that right to an expectancy." Brown, 126 Cal.Rptr. at n. 8, 544 P.2d at 566 n. 8.

One commentator provides another persuasive reason for characterizing even nonvested pensions as divisible marital assets:

> The non-employee spouse's contribution to the pension asset is exactly the same whether the pension be labeled a mere *expectancy,* or a *contingent future interest.*

L. Golden, Equitable Distribution of Property 172 (1983) (emphasis in original).

We are persuaded that the contingencies that may prevent the employee spouse from ever collecting his or her nonvested pension should not bar the non-employee spouse from recovering a share if the pension is in fact paid out. Indeed, a contrary rule would frustrate the statutory command that Alaska courts effect a "just division of the marital assets." AS 25.24.160(a)(4). This obviously requires that the trial court consider the financial circumstances of each party. It would be wholly inconsistent with this policy to ignore the existence of so substantial an asset as a party's pension rights. In this regard, we adopt the rule representing the current trend and recognize nonvested pension rights as a marital asset.

The trial court assigned a present value of $27,000 to Kenneth's pension, awarded it to him and awarded Marla offsetting assets. Kenneth asserts that there was insufficient evidence to support the present value figure adopted by the trial court. . . .

Courts have used two primary methods of valuing and dividing pension benefits, whether vested or nonvested, upon divorce: the present value approach and the reserved jurisdiction approach.[9]

In the present value approach, a court faced with a nonvested pension factors the contingencies to collection into a "reduced to present value" calculation. A similar reduction to present value can easily be obtained for a vested pension. The court determines a fraction of the present value representing the marital contribution to the accrued pension benefits. The numerator of this fraction is the number of years the pension has accrued during the marriage; the denominator is the total number of years during which the

9. A third possible method of division is to award the non-employee spouse a percentage of the employee spouse's contribution to the plan plus interest. We reject this method because it ignores employer contributions which, to the extent they were made during marriage, ought to be considered a marital asset.

employee spouse's pension has accrued.[11] Once this calculation is complete, the court may award the pension interest to the employee spouse and give the non-employee spouse an offsetting amount of other assets.

Citing the goal that a property settlement should provide a final resolution of a divorcing couple's financial affairs, a number of courts have stated that the present value approach is preferred where a present value can be attached to the pension and where there exist other marital assets sufficient to satisfy the non-employee spouse's claim without undue hardship on the employee spouse.

We nonetheless find this method unacceptable. Since the non-employee spouse receives his or her share in a lump sum at the time of the divorce, the method unfairly places all risk of possible forfeiture on the employee spouse. While the probability of forfeiture is supposedly factored in to reduce the present value amount determined at the time of the divorce, it is clear that the non-employee spouse has taken only a reduction in the amount of the award whereas the employee spouse loses the entire amount awarded to the non-employee spouse in the event of forfeiture. We find this approach to be inherently unfair.

In the other scheme used by the courts for valuation and division of a pension, the reserved jurisdiction approach, the trial court retains jurisdiction and orders the employee spouse to pay to the former spouse a fraction of each pension payment actually received.[12] This scheme more evenly allocates the risk of forfeiture between the parties, although it also runs counter to our expressed preference for finalizing a couple's financial affairs as soon as possible.

However, reserving jurisdiction does not necessarily mean that a protracted pay-out to the former spouse will follow vesting. Once vesting occurs, that portion of the pension which is marital property can be calculated as of the time of the divorce. The non-employee spouse's share of this figure may, in appropriate cases, be payable in a lump sum or in installments which do not particularly have to be keyed to the time that the pension benefits are actually received.

We are persuaded that reserving jurisdiction more closely parallels the societal goals of retirement benefits generally—that is, to provide financial security to participants. A present lump sum award to the non-employee spouse calculated on a pension which has not vested does not necessarily promote this purpose. The fact is that nonvested pensions are sometimes forfeited, often for reasons which properly should be within the power of the employee to decide, and sometimes for reasons which are entirely beyond the control of the employee. There is no reliable way to factor the contingency of forfeiture into a present value calculation. Thus, we are willing to accept a degree of continued financial entanglement insofar as that may be necessary to effect a just division of nonvested pension rights.

We adopt the following approach for dividing nonvested pension rights after divorce. First, because the nonvested pension may, by definition, be forfeited in its entirety, it should not be considered when the trial court makes the initial property division at the time of the divorce. If and when

11. In this case, Kenneth's entire term of employment with UNOCAL occurred during the marriage.

12. This court recently adopted a variation on this method in a case in which the employee spouse could have begun collecting benefits but desired to continue working. We simply ordered him to pay his wife a monthly amount equivalent to what she would have received if he retired. *Morlan,* 720 P.2d at 498.

the employee spouse's pension rights vest and if the parties are unable to reach an agreement on their own, the non-employee spouse may at any time thereafter seek an order dividing the pension. This is to be done in the same manner as if the pension had been vested at the time of the divorce. Realistically, there is such a variety of pension plan designs that it is impossible to develop any one detailed formula that will produce an equitable result in every instance. Once the pension has vested, the trial court can determine whether the present value or the retained jurisdiction approach is appropriate in a given case and adapt that approach to the specific circumstances presented.

As one possible resolution, we direct the trial court on remand to investigate the applicability of the Retirement Equity Act of 1984 (REACT), Pub.L. No. 98–397, 98 Stat. 1426 (1984). REACT applies to retirement benefit plans covered by the Employee Retirement Income Security Act of 1974 (ERISA), Pub.L. No. 93–406, 88 Stat. 829 (1974). The record does not indicate whether Kenneth's UNOCAL pension was such a plan. Under REACT, a "qualified domestic relations order" (QDRO) can be filed with the administrator of the employee spouse's pension plan. 29 U.S.C. 1056(d)(3). If and when the employee spouse's pension vests and matures, the plan administrator makes appropriate payments directly to the non-employee former spouse in accordance with the QDRO. 29 U.S.C. 1056(d)(3)(A).

REACT thus solves the problem of continuing financial entanglement between former spouses. Moreover, because payments are made directly by the plan, the non-employee spouse is sure to receive the payments to which he or she is entitled.[13] In certain circumstances, REACT allows the non-employee spouse to convert his or her share of the benefits to pay status independently of the employee spouse. 29 U.S.C. § 1056(d)(3)(E).[14]

We reverse and remand for a reevaluation of Kenneth's nonvested pension. If Kenneth's UNOCAL plan is not covered by ERISA, we direct the trial court to retain jurisdiction so that an appropriate division may be made if and when Kenneth's pension becomes vested.

Niroo v. Niroo

Court of Appeals of Maryland, 1988.
313 Md. 226, 545 A.2d 35.

■ Murphy, Chief Judge.

The question presented is whether anticipated renewal commissions on insurance policies sold by a spouse during marriage but accruing after dissolution of the marriage are "marital property" within the meaning of the Property Disposition in Divorce and Annulment Act (the Act).

. . .

13. It is important to note that REACT affects only the method by which a non-employee spouse may *collect* ERISA pension benefits. The fact and amount of his or her entitlement to the former spouse's pension is determined by state law. 29 U.S.C. § 1056(d)(3)(B).

14. Similar provisions for direct payment of retirement benefits to employees' former spouses exist with regard to military and federal civil service retirement benefit plans. . . .

It thus appears that only in rare circumstances would the QDRO solution be unavailable.

The appellant, David Niroo (the husband) contests a monetary award to the wife imposed pursuant to a divorce decree of the Circuit Court for Montgomery County (Messitte, J.). In particular, he challenges the determination of the trial judge that future renewal commissions accruing on insurance policies sold by him or his agents during the marriage were marital property.

The couple was married in 1977. In 1978, the husband began work as an insurance salesman for Pennsylvania Life Insurance Company (Penn Life); pursuant to contract, he received commissions on individual policies sold. In 1980, he became a branch manager and entered into agency manager agreements with Penn Life and the Executive Fund Life Insurance Company. Under these agreements, the husband shared in the profits (and the losses) of the company as determined by specific "office codes," or blocks of insurance, assigned to agents under him and for whom he was responsible. The husband was entitled under the agreements to receive income derived from net profits generated if and when insurance policies coming under his office codes were renewed, provided that certain conditions in the agency manager agreements were satisfied. In particular, the contracts included, *inter alia*, a covenant not to compete, an exclusivity clause, and a required renewal volume. The agreement specified that the husband's "proportional share of the Agency profits shall be vested in him even if he is permanently and totally disabled, or after his death in his heirs and assigns."

At trial, both parties presented expert testimony as to the present day value of these renewal commissions after expenses were deducted, *i.e.*, what the husband could expect to receive from the renewal policies. This valuation was based on industry "persistency rates," explained by the husband's expert witness as "the portion of the premiums that are in force in one year that renew and hence are paid and are still in force in the following year." This expert included only those renewal commission profits on policies sold during the marriage.

The trial judge determined that the husband's interest in the renewal income constituted marital property. He accepted the valuation testimony of the husband's expert and found the present discounted profit value of the renewal commissions to be $410,000. The court also took into account various "advances" made to the husband by the insurance companies which were chargeable against renewal commissions. Under the agreements, these advances were considered as loans, repayable on demand. At the time of trial, the husband was indebted to the companies in the amount of $267,000. In assessing the proper amount to be awarded to the wife, the trial judge determined that although the renewal income was marital property, the husband's $267,000 debt was not marital debt, but instead was to be taken into account as an "economic circumstance." The court arrived at a final monetary award of $200,000; in doing so, it considered various statutory factors, including the economic circumstances of the parties.

The husband appealed. We granted certiorari prior to consideration of the appeal by the Court of Special Appeals to consider the important question involved in the case.

. . .

The husband first challenges the trial judge's determination that renewal commissions on policies sold during the marriage are marital property. He asserts that due to the speculative and contingent nature of these commissions, they are not within the definition of marital property, as contemplated by the legislature in § 8–201(e). Furthermore, he argues that as it is necessary for him to "work" and nurture these accounts through activities performed after the marriage was dissolved, the income thereby derived is not "acquired" during the marriage. Thus, he contends, classification of renewal commissions as marital property would improperly give his former wife the fruits of his future efforts and would penalize him if the renewal commissions were not actually realized.

. . .

When analyzed under the principles set forth in our cases, we think it clear that contractually vested rights in renewal commissions are a type of property interest encompassed within the definition of marital property under § 8–201(e). That an insurance agent has a vested right in commissions on renewal premiums when provided for by contract is well settled. This contractual right was clearly established in the husband's agency contract whereby Penn Life agreed to pay him a stipulated percentage of renewal premiums collected in the future. Indeed, this right to renewal premiums cannot be terminated unilaterally by the company, but instead would require an affirmative surrender by the agent to forfeit the future commissions due.

In this case, the agency contract provided that should the husband die or become disabled, his right to receive the renewal commissions, as well as his heirs' right thereto, would not be affected. We note also that under the agency agreements the husband's right to the renewal commission was assignable with the prior written consent of the company. . . . Thus, considering the legal attributes of a contractual right to renewal commissions, the husband's right amounts to more than a "mere expectancy," or a "mere historical possibility of gain" as he alternatively characterizes it.

The husband claims that after the dissolution of the marriage, he must continue to "service" his accounts after their initial procurement if he is to realize the renewal commissions. He thereby seeks to distinguish his situation from that involving pension benefits. We are not persuaded by his argument. The husband's primary effort was expended in acquiring the original policies. Evidence at trial showed that on a national average, 72% of the existing policies will be automatically renewed after the first year; 82% will be renewed after the second year; and 88% will be renewed thereafter. The husband nevertheless maintains that he must satisfy certain conditions not present with pension benefits, thus rendering his right to the commissions only a tenuous property interest. Specifically, he refers to the covenant in the agency agreements not to compete and to certain requirements as to renewal volume, the violation or nonattainment of which could result in forfeiture or diminishment of his commissions. He also asserts that uncertainties inherent in renewals, such as customer preferences, economic conditions, and agency turnover, render the renewal commissions too speculative for valuation. While we recognize these concerns, we do not find these conditions so onerous, and the contingencies so uncertain, as to make the contractual right to renewal commissions beyond valuation, particularly when the insurance industry itself assigns a value to them based on statistical persistency rates.

. . .

[T]he claim to renewal commissions is not the type of right that is uniquely personal to the holder, as in a personal injury claim or a professional degree. Instead, it is the type of work-related income encompassing a part of the compensation package developed during the marriage by one of the spouses that each could have justifiably relied upon to provide for their economic future. As such, it is a vested right, a valuable asset not separable from the original policies sold during the marriage, and thus properly a part of the couple's shared assets during marriage. This determination, we think, is consistent with the declared policy of the Marital Property Act, as set forth in the Act's preamble, "that marriage is a union between a man and a woman having equal rights under the law." Plainly, this policy recognizes the nonmonetary contributions made by the wife in this case in accumulating the assets. Finally, in so holding, we note that we must construe the Act liberally to effectuate its broad remedial purpose.

The husband next argues that the advances received by him as a loan from Penn Life should have reduced the present value of the future commissions in valuing marital property. In support of his position, the husband asserts that he borrowed the money against the profits from the anticipated renewal commissions to finance his agency operation; and that the debt therefore was an encumbrance upon the renewal income to be paid to him in the future. The wife, on the other hand, argues that the husband did not use the advances for the purpose of acquiring renewal commissions but rather for family expenses, including high personal expenditures of his own to support a lavish life style. The wife suggests that the husband's annual income, particularly in the later years of his agency business, was sufficiently high that no need existed to borrow money from Penn Life to meet the expenses of his branch manager operation.

. . .

In the instant matter the advances drawn by Mr. Niroo against future insurance commissions are repayable on demand. If called, the debt can be set off by Penn Life against future commissions. The debt, in economic effect, is an encumbrance on the future commissions which reduces their present value. The trial judge therefore erred in not subtracting the debt of $267,000 from the value of the renewal income.

NOTE

In Mansell v. Mansell, 490 U.S. 581 (1989), the Supreme Court held that the federal Uniformed Services Former Spouses Protection Act does not authorize state courts to treat as marital property at divorce military retirement pay waived by the retiree in order to receive veterans' disability benefits.

B. Alimony

Historically, alimony appears to have rested on practical considerations rather than a clear conceptual foundation. In an era in which there was no inclination to reconsider title-based property division, divorcing men received most assets of the marriage. Alimony served as a way to mitigate the harsh effects. In addition, when a wife was the "innocent" party at divorce, alimony served to prevent a "guilty" husband from avoiding his support responsibilities by breaching the marital contract.

The movement away from a title-based property regime and the emergence of no-fault divorce deprived alimony of these implicit conceptual justifications. The result is that alimony is a practice that is in search of a theory. Consider how each of the readings in this section purports to respond to this challenge.

1. STANDARDS

Uniform Marriage and Divorce Act

Section 308. Maintenance

(a) In a proceeding for dissolution of marriage, legal separation, or maintenance following a decree of dissolution of the marriage by a court which lacked personal jurisdiction over the absent spouse, the court may grant a maintenance order for either spouse, only if it finds that the spouse seeking maintenance:

(1) lacks sufficient property to provide for his reasonable needs; and

(2) is unable to support himself through appropriate employment or is the custodian of a child whose condition or circumstances make it appropriate that the custodian not be required to seek employment outside the home.

(b) The maintenance order shall be in amounts and for periods of time the court deems just, without regard to marital misconduct, and after considering all relevant factors including:

(1) the financial resources of the party seeking maintenance, including marital property apportioned to him, his ability to meet his needs independently, and the extent to which a provision for support of a child living with the party includes a sum for that party as custodian;

(2) the time necessary to acquire sufficient education or training to enable the party seeking maintenance to find appropriate employment;

(3) the standard of living established during the marriage;

(4) the duration of the marriage;

(5) the age and the physical and emotional condition of the spouse seeking maintenance; and

(6) the ability of the spouse from whom maintenance is sought to meet his needs while meeting those of the spouse seeking maintenance.

COMMENT

. . . The dual intention of this section and Section 307 is to encourage the court to provide for the financial needs of the spouses by property disposition rather than by an award of maintenance. Only if the available property is insufficient for the purpose and if the spouse who seeks maintenance is unable to secure employment appropriate to his skills and interests or is occupied with child care may an award of maintenance be ordered. Assuming that an award of maintenance is appropriate under subsection 308(a), the standards for setting the amount of the award are set forth in subsection 308(b). Here, as in Section 307, the court is expressly admonished not to consider the misconduct of a spouse during the marriage. Instead, the court should consider the factors relevant to the issue of maintenance, including those listed in subdivisions (1)-(6).

NOTE

UMDA § 308(b) directs the court to determine an alimony award "without regard to marital misconduct." Some twenty-five states, however, include marital fault as a factor in alimony decisions. Chart, Chart 1: Alimony/Support Factors, 38 Fam. L.Q. 809, 809 (2005).

In re Marriage of Wilson

Court of Appeal of California, 1988.
201 Cal.App.3d 913, 247 Cal.Rptr. 522.

■ HADEN, ASSOCIATE JUSTICE

Elma Wilson appeals an order terminating her spousal support after 58 months following a 70-month marriage. Having found her permanently disabled and her former husband able to pay continued support, the trial court weighed the length and nature of the marriage, and the duration of spousal support payments and ruled husband no longer had the legal obligation to support his former spouse. Because we find no abuse of discretion, we affirm the order.

Thomas and Elma Wilson (Tom and Elma) were married in May 1976 and separated in March 1982, after 70 months. Elma was injured in a fall two years before separation. As a result of her injuries or subsequent infection following dental work, she could no longer work as a bartender. In 1983 her doctor believed her neurologic deficit would remain permanent but recommended some rehabilitation to enable her to pursue work which would not require verbalization. A clinical psychologist opined Elma suffered brain damage which left her "lacking in social judgment, common sense, and social intelligence." The psychologist felt Elma would probably not succeed where she had to make decisions using common sense.

In the November 1983 stipulated interlocutory judgment, Tom received, inter alia, his Navy pension and a Volkswagen while Elma took the house, a Jaguar automobile, and spousal support of $500 per month for two years plus medical insurance coverage for the same period.

. . . In December 1985 the trial court extended the $500 per month spousal support for one year. . . .

In September 1986 Elma once again sought continuing spousal support, claiming she was still unemployed and neither rehabilitated nor capable of rehabilitation. She continued to receive $436 per month in social security benefits. . . . In October 1986 Tom declared he earned over $2,200 per month in salary plus over $1,000 in Navy retirement.

At a hearing on the support issue in December 1986 Tom argued Elma should not be entitled to lifetime support from him based on a 70-month marriage. The court found Tom, age 46, had the earning capacity to continue to make support payments and Elma, age 48, had a need for such payments because she was both disabled and could not regain her previous income earning status. The court considered the length of the marriage (70 months) and the length of the spousal support period (58 months). The court then stated, "My question . . . that I'm faced with is at what point in time does the obligation to assist Mrs. Wilson become one of society's as distinguished from an obligation that is Mr. Wilson's, and I find that it is society's at this point in time." The court continued support for four months and then terminated it.

A promise to "love, honor and cherish as long as we both shall live" is in fact easily and frequently revocable today. It is lamentable that many decide to live together without benefit of such vows and many who take them soon forget them. However, we are concerned here with legal, not moral, obligations. We are asked to decide whether following a childless marriage of short duration it was an abuse of discretion to terminate spousal support even though the supported spouse was permanently disabled.

Wide discretion is vested in the trial court in determining the amount and duration of spousal support . . . Thus, an appellate court must act with cautious judicial restraint in reviewing these orders.

Here the trial court exercised discretion along legal lines in that it followed Civil Code section 4801 which provides for spousal support in any amount and for any period just and reasonable, provided the trial court in making the award considers all of the following circumstances: (1) the earning capacity of each spouse; (2) the needs of each party; (3) the obligations and assets of each party; (4) the duration of the marriage; (5) the ability of the supported spouse to engage in gainful employment without detriment to dependent children in his or her custody; (6) the age or health of the parties; (7) the standard of living of the parties; and (8) other factors which the court deems just and equitable.

The record reflects the trial court weighed each of these eight factors before exercising discretion to terminate support. Tom had the earning capacity to continue to make support payments. Elma had virtually no marketable skills and could not regain her previous income earning status as a bartender which was about $600 per month plus tips. Elma's psychologist believed she could not succeed in any job which required common sense because of her brain damage. This was not a marriage in which Elma's present or future earning capacity was impaired by periods of unemployment incurred to permit her to attend to domestic duties. The parties were in their 40's when they married and, the court noted, had already established their lives. While Elma already had adult children, there were no children of this marriage. There was no evidence Elma had contributed to the attainment of Tom's career. Since he was retired from the military at the time support was awarded, and the marriage lasted only 70 months, his military career must have been completed or substantially completed when the couple married. The court found Elma had a need for support because she was disabled and could not regain her previous income earning status. The court reviewed the obligations and assets of each party, the length of the marriage and duration of the support period. Finally, the court balanced the equities and decided under these circumstances the obligation to assist Elma should shift from Tom to society.

. . .

Elma contends it was an abuse of discretion to terminate spousal support where there was no present evidence of her ability to be self-supporting. She includes medical coverage in her support claim and we treat them together here. Specifically, Elma argues the trial court failed to comply with *In re Marriage of Morrison* (1978) 20 Cal.3d 437, 143 Cal.Rptr. 139, 573 P.2d 41, in terminating support. *Morrison*, however, concerned a lengthy marriage of 28 years during which wife at husband's insistence devoted her time principally to maintaining the home and raising two children. In this context a trial court should not "burn its bridges" and fail to retain jurisdiction over support unless the record indicates the supported spouse will be able adequately to meet his or her financial needs at the time of termination. As previously discussed, the instant case deals with neither a lengthy marriage nor a typical "displaced homemaker." At the time of this short marriage Elma was a middle aged bartender with adult children. Her lifestyle was established. On separation both parties stipulated to support for a fixed term. . . .

Further, this is not a case in which the trial court terminated support to encourage the supported spouse to seek employment. The court recognized both the grievous and permanent nature of Elma's disability. It was beyond the court's power to render her self-supporting.

"In short-term marriages spousal support will most usually be ordered where the needs of minor children or the employment circumstances of the supported spouse require spousal support until the supported spouse can readjust to single status." (*In re Marriage of Prietsch & Calhoun*, (1987) 190 Cal.App.3d 645, 663, 235 Cal.Rptr. 587.)

Neither minor children nor any reasonable likelihood of employment readjustment was present here.

Elma attempts to demonstrate self-support is the key to termination of jurisdiction over spousal support even in short marriages. Tom suggests duration of the marriage is paramount. While we understand why each seeks to emphasize that factor most favorable to his or her argument, this approach misses the forest for the trees.

. . .

While no one will dispute Elma's tragic disability, the clear trend is for trial courts to consider the totality of circumstances as required by section 4801. Self-support and length of marriage are each but one of eight important factors. Each must be balanced in light of the others. This rule applies even where a permanently disabled spouse may be denied support after a short marriage.

Once the trial court logically and reasonably applies section 4801, all that remains for the appellate court is a review for potential abuse of discretion. Because the trial court carefully weighed all eight factors, the decision to terminate support including medical coverage was not an abuse of discretion given the totality of circumstances.

The order is affirmed.

Clapp v. Clapp

Supreme Court of Vermont, 1994.
163 Vt. 15, 653 A.2d 72.

■ DOOLEY, J.

Defendant, Michael Clapp, appeals a decision of the Chittenden Family Court in the divorce action between him and his former wife, Elizabeth Clapp, challenging both property and maintenance orders contained therein. We [affirm the court's maintenance order].

The parties were married in 1967 following defendant's first year of law school. When defendant graduated in 1969, the parties returned to Vermont and he began his legal practice that continues to this day. The parties' son was born in 1970 and their daughter in 1972. Plaintiff remained home to care for the children full time until 1975, at which time she began pursuing her master's degree in education. In 1977, having received her degree, plaintiff began work as a junior high school guidance counselor. In 1981, she became a high school guidance counselor and has continued in that job to the present. In 1987, after twenty years of marriage, the parties separated.

Plaintiff filed for divorce in 1989. In 1991, her annual income before taxes was $45,237; defendant's annual income before taxes was $137,600.

The parties were divorced by final order of the Chittenden Family Court entered in February 1993. At that time, both parties were forty-eight years old. The court found that the parties' assets totalled $1,257,577, and their liabilities $498,773. Finding that the merits of the situation favored plaintiff wife slightly, the court ordered the parties' assets to be split 60% to wife and 40% to husband. . . .

The court ordered defendant to pay maintenance and set the amount temporarily at $2,000 per month. Thereafter, it required a calculation of maintenance based on an equalization of the parties' after-tax income from June 1987 to the date of the divorce. . . . Once calculated, the base maintenance amount would be adjusted annually based on changes in the Consumer Price Index.

. . .

We can combine defendant's first three arguments for purposes of analysis. Relying on 15 V.S.A. § 752(a), defendant argues that the court could not award maintenance unless plaintiff's reasonable needs are not met by her income, including the income available from any assets awarded to her. In this case, defendant argues, plaintiff's reasonable needs were met by her income, and no maintenance should have been awarded. Alternatively, he claims that any maintenance award cannot exceed the amount necessary to enable the obligee to meet her reasonable needs. Specifically, he argues that the family court has no discretion to increase the award above that reasonably needed in order to compensate her for past contributions as a homemaker because the statute does not allow for restitutionary or compensatory awards based on past events. In this case, he claims the award clearly exceeded the amount reasonably needed even if an award of some maintenance was appropriate.

. . . The argument specifically emphasizes § 752(a)(1) which requires a threshold finding that the prospective obligee lacks income or property to meet "reasonable needs." In defendant's view, the court must first determine reasonable need without regard to the income available during the marriage, or the obligor's current income, and award maintenance only if this need is not met by the obligee's nonmaintenance income and property.

Defendant's argument involves an overly narrow reading of § 752(a)(1). The statute is based on a concept of relative, not absolute, need. In *Downs v. Downs*, 166, 574 A.2d 156, 159 (Vt. 1990), we went further and held that the term "reasonable needs" allowed the court "to balance equities whenever the financial contributions of one spouse enable the other spouse to enhance his or her future earning capacity." We have also held that one purpose of maintenance under § 752(a) is to compensate a homemaker for contributions to family well-being not otherwise recognized in the property distribution.

We do not have to plunge deeply into the detail of plaintiff's post-separation needs to affirm the award of maintenance in this case. According to the findings, the parties were living on an after-tax income of approximately $130,000 per year and spending most of it. Of this, about $33,000 is attributable to plaintiff. Both parties had attained maximum vocational skills and employability. Defendant's earning capacity should, however, grow at a faster rate as he approaches retirement.

It is clear given the differences in income that plaintiff would not maintain the standard of living realized during the marriage on her share of the marital income. The court found that plaintiff needed an additional amount of approximately $1,000 per month to meet reasonable expenses. At trial, defendant apparently agreed that plaintiff's income was inadequate to cover legitimate expenses but calculated the shortfall at $775 per month. In light of the standard of living of the parties, the court acted within its discretion in awarding maintenance in this case.

On a similar theory, defendant attacks the amount of maintenance awarded. As indicated above, the court found that the deficit in plaintiff's income to pay expenses amounted to about $1,000 per month. It also recognized that plaintiff had made a significant nonmonetary contribution to the marriage as a homemaker, and had reduced her earnings over the years because of this contribution. For the dual purpose of avoiding "an adverse economic impact upon the plaintiff" and compensating her for her nonmonetary contributions during the marriage, the court ordered such permanent maintenance as would equalize after-tax income, as calculated over the period from the date of separation to the date of divorce. Maintenance is not to be eliminated or reduced because plaintiff cohabits with another person or remarries. The amount is not adjusted on a regular basis because of changes in either party's income, although it is adjusted for inflation.

At the outset, we point out that the family court has broad discretion in determining the amount of maintenance, and we will reverse only if there is no reasonable basis to support the award. See *Delozier v. Delozier*, 640 A.2d 55, 57 (1994). In determining the amount of maintenance to award, the court must consider all relevant factors, including seven statutory factors. Most of the statutory factors figured into the family court's decision, including the ability of the obligee to meet her needs without maintenance, the standard of living established during the marriage, the duration of the marriage, the age and physical and emotional condition of each spouse, and the ability of the obligor to meet reasonable needs while paying maintenance. The award was tailored to maintain for plaintiff the standard of living during the marriage. As discussed above, it was clear that plaintiff was unable to maintain this standard on her income alone. This objective was supported by the length of the marriage, twenty-five years. It is also supported in this lengthy marriage by the need to compensate plaintiff for homemaker contributions to family well-being not otherwise recognized in the financial awards.

It is important to recognize the difference between the income equalization approach of this award and the approach we rejected in *Delozier*. In *Delozier*, the income equalization award was prospective and permanent so each spouse was to receive half of their joint income for the remainder of their lives. On facts somewhat similar to those here, involving a wife with good employment opportunities, we held that permanent income equalization may "wind up being punitive rather than compensatory." *Delozier*, 640 A.2d at 60.

Here, income equalization was used as a method to calculate an appropriate monthly maintenance award, but the amount of the award will not change in the future because of changes in the income of either of the parties. In light of the court's conclusion that the gap between the income of the parties would grow over time, this award equalized income for only a year, with defendant keeping an increasing share of the combined income in the future. We believe the award equalized income for "an appropriate period of time."

Defendant attacks the award because it gives to plaintiff an income higher than her reasonable needs. Even if this were true, the statute does not prohibit such a result because the obligee's need is only one of the factors to be considered. It is not true because need here should also be viewed in relation to the standard of living established during the marriage, another statutory factor. The main objective of the award was to maintain that standard of living for plaintiff.

Defendant also attacks the award as based in part on a theory of restitution for past homemaker contributions, a basis not authorized by § 752(b). This basis was explicitly recognized in [*Klein v. Klein*, 150 Vt. 466, 474, 555 A.2d 382, 387 (1988)] a recognition that has been reaffirmed in a number of cases. We see no reason to abandon that recognition here.

Related to this attack is defendant's claim that consideration of this factor was not warranted because there was no evidence of the extent of the contribution. The court found that plaintiff delayed her education and entry into the job market in order to raise the parties' children while they were infants. Thereafter, the parties jointly decided that plaintiff should work in a school system, rather than in other employment with higher remuneration, in order to care for the children and manage the home. This also enabled her to stay in the home during the summer. In comparison, defendant consistently put in night and weekend hours at his law office.

Homemaker contributions are, by their nature, nonmonetary so they cannot be quantified or put into a monetary formula to specify their impact on the ultimate maintenance award. The court's characterization of these contributions as "significant . . . over many years" is probably as specific as is possible. The ultimate weighing process is judgmental, which is part of the reason that we accord the trial court discretion in performing it. We find no error in the application of the nonmonetary contribution factor.

In summary, we hold that the family court acted within its discretion in awarding permanent maintenance to plaintiff, and the amount is also within its discretion.

Alicia Brokars Kelly, Rehabilitating Partnership Marriage as a Theory of Wealth Distribution at Divorce: In Recognition of a Shared Life

19 Wis. Women's L.J. 141 (2004).

. . .

II. The Partnership Ideal and its Origins in Family Law

A. The Basic Marital Partnership Concept

Consider the possible answers that might be offered by a person who knows nothing about legal doctrines in family law if we asked the question: what do you think it means to say that marriage is a partnership? Predictably, a common response would emphasize extensive sharing between spouses. A common cultural understanding of the concept is that partnership marriage means working together and sharing your life in a multitude of ways with your partner. Joint labor ("working together") and sharing more generally are central. . . .

The principles of joint labor and pervasive sharing that are core to the cultural meaning of partnership are paralleled in modern family law theory.

It is overwhelmingly the cultural meaning of the term that has been (at least rhetorically) embraced in contemporary law governing marriage and divorce.... In law, partnership theory views marriage as a sharing venture and specifically recognizes that both spouses make vital financial and non-financial contributions. Non-financial contributions are said to be fully credited, so that a spouse who provides home labor, such as a spouse who stays at home to provide care for children, has provided valuable resources to the family just as the spouse who provides income from the paid labor market has. Joint spousal efforts mean that assets are jointly, not individually, owned. As a result, upon divorce, the assets produced by the efforts of either spouse belong to the marital partnership. Each spouse is entitled to share in the marital estate because each participated in its acquisition. Under this view, economic resources are apportioned not based on need or status, but because they have been jointly earned.

. . .

C. The Integration of Partnership Marriage into Contemporary Law

The integration of partnership theory in contemporary law is most strongly evidenced in the structure of modern marital property systems themselves.... [C]ommunity property principles of joint ownership were adopted (although "vesting" only upon divorce) when common law states created "equitable distribution" systems that recognize "marital" property as the product of joint spousal efforts to which each spouse has a claim upon divorce, regardless of title. Contribution—that each person contributes a different but valuable set of benefits for the good of the marriage as a whole—is today a central basis for sharing accumulated wealth at divorce.

. . .

Equitable distribution systems have made their reliance on partnership principles explicit:

> the function of equitable distribution is to recognize that when the marriage ends, each of the spouses, based on the totality of the contribution made to it, has a stake in and a right to a share of the family assets accumulated while it endured, not because that share is needed but because those assets represent the capital product of what was essentially a partnership entity.[7]

Non-economic contributions, traditionally made by wives, make up a critical component of partnership ideology:

> [Equitable distribution] gives recognition to the essential supportive role played by the wife in the home, acknowledging that as homemaker, wife and mother she should clearly be entitled to a share of family assets accumulated during the marriage. Thus the division of property upon divorce is responsive to the concept that marriage is a shared enterprise, a joint undertaking, that in many ways it is akin to a partnership.[8]

. . .

III. Current Constructions of Partnership Theory and its Limitations

Although contemporary marital property systems have widely adopted the rhetoric of partnership marriage, many of its current constructions in law are distortions or only partial, and therefore incomplete, applications of its

7. Gibbons v. Gibbons, 415 A.2d 1174, 1177 (N.J. Super. Ct. App. Div. 1980).

8. *Id.* at 177–78 (quoting Rothman v. Rothman, 320 A.2d 496, 501 (N.J. 1974)).

underlying principles. In some instances, legal decision makers reject the logic of the theory altogether, betraying its basic principles. This section describes the limitations of current constructions of partnership. . . .

. . .

D. The Results of Measuring Contribution: Devaluation of Women's Work

. . . [M]odern divorce law has generally not adopted a rule of equal division of marital wealth that partnership theory logically supports. There is also typically no clear guidance in family law statutes about how to define "property." In the absence of a bright line rule, courts have authority to consider various factors that need not be accorded any particular weight in their decision—judges can do this as they see fit with very little meaningful appellate review. . . . Of particular relevance here, almost unfettered judicial discretion has opened the door for courts to betray partnership's core values of joint contribution and equality, which the law "on the books" purports to embrace. Judges, empowered to measure contribution, have (whether consciously or not) systematically devalued the contributions of women, particularly home labor. Statutory requirements to consider homemaker contributions have not been effective. . . .

1. The Non-Contribution Conclusion in Career Asset Cases

Courts sometimes nominally recognize that a spouse who has supported the other spouse who is pursuing a professional degree has contributed something of value. But overwhelmingly, in the end, the supporting spouse's contributions are deemed unworthy of financial recognition and thus are viewed as worthless . . . [T]his phenomenon is gendered; the titled spouse is almost always the husband and the supporting spouse who is denied an earned right to share in the asset is almost always the wife.

An examination of the leading cases that deny human capital property status reveals that amidst the usual explanations that career assets are not property is another rationale: the titled spouse independently earned the enhancements to his career. The Graham case from Colorado is typical and provides what has become a recurring theme: "An advanced degree is a cumulative product of many years of previous education, combined with diligence and hard work. It may not be acquired by the mere expenditure of money. It is simply an intellectual achievement that may potentially assist in the future acquisition of property." Similarly, a degree has been described as "a personal achievement of the holder" which, if valued in divorce based on cost would "fail to consider the scholastic efforts and acumen of the degree holder." These comments reveal a conclusion that the degree was achieved independently by the diligence, hard work and intellectual capacity of the titled spouse. While this is, no doubt, part of how the degree was earned, since it was acquired during marriage, that effort was not a solitary one. Just as with the house and the pension, the supporting spouse worked alongside the enhanced spouse contributing her own diligence, hard work and intellect to the asset's acquisition. When faced with the challenge that the supporting spouse has also made an important contribution, the "individual achievement response" has, at times, been made even more explicit: "the contribution made by one spouse to another spouse's advanced degree plays only a small part in the overall achievement."

. . .

The conclusion that a career asset is a solitary rather than joint accomplishment ... starkly rejects core partnership principles that each spouse provides a set of different, but equally meaningful contributions to the marital estate. This stance is inconsistent with prevalent American societal norms that view marriage as a sharing relationship and their reflection in law via partnership marriage ... This approach systematically devalues the contributions made by wives.

A closer examination is revealing. The conclusion in nearly all career asset cases is that the supporting spouse has made, at best, only minimal contributions. But what of the facts of the cases that suggest quite the opposite? Case after case describes the supporting spouse as having sacrificed much, including forgone income of the enhanced spouse, or her own career, and, as having contributed extensive resources for the good of the family unit, including direct economic support for education, food and shelter, homemaking services and primary care for children.... While it is not surprising that the marketplace (which has long disadvantaged women) does not value these marital investments, it is appalling that modern marital law adopts this same view. Of course, a view of marriage as a partnership that recognizes the equal dignity and value of each spouse's contribution to the marriage would lead to an opposite conclusion: that earning capacity enhanced during marriage is jointly acquired and therefore jointly owned.

. . .

E. The Impracticable Task of Measuring Contribution

Under modern marital property regimes, legal decision makers face an impracticable task. In the absence of bright line rules, among a list of other factors, judges are asked to identify the respective contributions of each spouse over the length of the marriage and then determine their relative value. How can any person get an accurate view inside a marriage that lasted perhaps many, many years to retrospectively account for the breadth, kinds, and relative value of the innumerable contributions each spouse makes to a marriage?

. . .

Even assuming we could identify discrete contributions, how do you compare and value things like changing diapers against mowing the lawn? As Lee Starnes asks:

> Does ten hours of vacuumuing equal ten hours of watching a little league baseball game? Ten hours of cleaning bathrooms? Ten hours of helping children with homework? Ten hours of painting a bedroom? And what of the husband who was a more efficient grocery shopper than his wife, or the wife who more efficiently vacuumed the house?

. . .

The law does not need to measure contribution in this way. Contributions can be legally recognized and protected by granting an entitlement to wealth without undertaking a strict cost-benefit analysis. Partnership theory does not require the retrospective accounting that modern law sometimes reflects. Although contribution is a core concept, so is equality. The theory assumes that each partner has made valuable contributions to the marriage and thus supports the conclusion of equal ownership.

Aside from the factual premise of equal contribution, ... an assumption of equality is pragmatic because contributions in marriage cannot sensibly be reconstructed and accounted for. Attractive for other reasons as well, an equality norm would relieve legal decision makers of this unworkable responsibility.

F. The Misguided Search for a Direct Causal Link

Current applications of partnership theory further distort the model's principles when legal decision makers search for a direct causal link between one spouse's conduct and a particular increase in wealth. At times, courts raise the question of whether a spouse's labor in fact contributes to the increased value of a particular asset.... [T]he Connecticut Supreme Court [has] observed, "on the whole, a degree of any kind results primarily from the efforts of the student who earns it. Financial and emotional support are important, as are homemaker services, but they bear no logical relation to the value of the resulting degree." The court seems troubled by the lack of evidence of a direct causal link between her work and creation of the asset. Did her labor in the home and her financial and emotional support really "cause" the husband's success? ...

. . .

... [P]artnership marriage casts off the need for this link. Partnership marriage is holistic as it recognizes the many, variable, contributions by each spouse to the marriage generally, rather than to particularized assets of the marriage. [In many cases, a] wife's labor contribute[s] to the shared goal of raising children and [her husband's] labor contribute[s] to the family's economic support. Because of this sharing conduct, partnership principles attribute his labor to her and vice versa—and thus provide an entitlement to all wealth the marriage produced. There is no need to link her specific conduct to show it produced an asset; as long as the asset is marital, it is assumed that the effort to produce it was joint.

. . .

H. The Need for a Clearer Structure for Partnership Marriage

As this discussion suggests, partnership marriage in its current form can rightly be accused of being amorphous beyond its general principles. What counts as property is undefined. There is wide disagreement displayed among judges as to what the term "contribution" actually means. Even when directed to count domestic labors as valuable contributions, it is often disregarded or undervalued because there are no rules stated about how much weight to accord home labor. Identifying and valuing the array of possible contributions spouses make to a marriage is exceedingly difficult. These ambiguities have provided much opportunity for the concept of partnership marriage to be distorted and manipulated when applied.... [R]econstructed and clarified, [however,] the ideal still has much to offer in shaping our thinking about financial allocations at divorce.

IV. Reconstructing Partnership: Recognizing the Centrality of Interdependence in Marriage

. . .

B. Reconstructing Contribution

... [M]odern law has disregarded and distorted partnership theory in crucial ways. This section offers a clearer structure for the theory and means to rehabilitate and reinforce its core components in modern divorce law. In thinking about and applying partnership ideology, much of my focus in this part is on earning power rather than traditional forms of property because human capital is the most important kind of property for most people and has been largely ignored in modern divorce law. . . . I argue here that sharing a life together as partners importantly shapes the economic status of each partner as they exit the relationship and thus justifies wealth sharing at divorce. . . .

1. Rethinking "Causation"

. . .

a. Presuming Joint Causation if Economic Benefits or Losses are Acquired During Marriage

. . . [P]artnership theory . . . concludes that whatever wealth is produced during marriage is the product of the partners' joint labor, even if the kind of labor each spouse performs is different. This joint acquisition norm is based on sharing and interdependent behavior thought to characterize marriage. We don't look for a direct link with traditional property, like a bank account. Instead, we assume accumulated wealth was produced from a host of efforts and decisions by the spouses as to which resources to consume and which to save and invest in. This joint allocation of resources is the basis for sharing its results. For the same reason, the direct link question is the wrong one when thinking about an earnings stream. Under the theory of marriage as a partnership, as long as wealth (whatever its form) is produced during marriage, it is jointly owned. In fact, divorce law readily treats earnings received during marriage as jointly owned without the need for any showing that her labor contributed to his wages (or vice versa).

. . .

b. Assuming Spouses' Economic Circumstances are Caused in Part By Marital Conduct

i. Some Examples of the Consequences of Sharing a Life

Consider [a scenario in which the husband is a dentist and his wife a hygienist]. [T]he spouses share a life for 23 years and at the end of the marriage she earns $22,000 from her employment and he $110,000 from his. It is entirely reasonable to assume that sharing a life as a couple powerfully influenced the path of both spouses' lives. Specifically, a logical conclusion is that an influential reason for why she is, at the end of the marriage, still a hygienist is because within the context of the parties' marriage, that role contributed to the couple's joint welfare. She is a hygienist because that is what made sense for the couple's lives together and likewise, enhancing his profession as a dentist also made sense in the context of their marriage. We can be reasonably confident of this because . . . research demonstrates that spouses generally think of themselves as a unit (although, of course there is not a complete unity of interest) and make major decisions accordingly. The marriage then, although surely not the only factor, nonetheless shaped each partner's life in crucial ways and pervasively contributed to the financial situation each faces at divorce.

. . .

. . . [I]n crucial ways, conduct in marriage [thus] creates the financial situation each spouse confronts at divorce. Accordingly, we need to reconstruct our thinking about "causation" in partnership marriage. Specifically, the law should assume that the economic circumstances faced by each spouse are, in important part, caused by conduct and choices made jointly in marriage. The theory of partnership marriage then demands that there should be shared (not widely disparate) results while the results endure. . . .

. . .

2. Conceptualizing Contribution Broadly

. . . Current applications of contribution often fail to recognize that each spouse has contributed to the marriage as a whole, and instead focus on particularized, discrete assets produced during marriage. Also, consciously or not, judges tend to recognize and value financial additions and market labor rather than non-financial and home-based contributions. The notion of contribution then must be made purposefully explicit.

. . . First (consistent with the original tenets of partnership theory) contribution must be understood to include a host of benefits and sacrifices given by spousal partners to the marriage as a whole. As a result, searching for a direct causal link between one spouse's specific conduct and a particular addition to wealth is inappropriate because it fails to recognize collaborative roles in marriage—that each spouse is contributing to the marriage in their own way, and in many cases, in very different ways than the other spouse. Instead, because both spouses have contributed, partnership marriage assumes that any benefits (or disadvantages) that stem from marriage were jointly produced.

[Second], home-based contributions and market-based contributions must both be recognized as valuable to the family's joint welfare by giving rise to a legal entitlement (a property right) to share in whatever wealth is produced during marriage. Absent a legal entitlement, some contributions can wrongly be ignored. And, as I will argue below, home labor and market labor should be treated as equally valuable. [Third], spouses contribute not only to the acquisition of traditional property such as a house and a bank account, but they pervasively invest in and contribute to career development and enhanced earning power (often primarily in one spouse), which is just another form of wealth that is particularly important in modern families. Contribution then must give rise to an entitlement to property whatever its form, including enhanced earning power. Partnership marriage thus provides a basis for claims to income sharing (alimony) in addition to traditional property.

. . .

In order to implement these clarified partnership principles, the law must provide sufficient guidance to legal decision makers and limit the opportunities for bias and distortion. The next part suggests some possibilities for accomplishing these goals.

3. Presuming Equal Contribution in Marriage

. . . A presumption of contribution within marriage and that the marriage crucially shaped each spouse's economic status would clarify the basis for mutual entitlements to wealth at divorce and would justly extend the application of partnership theory to income streams as well as traditional property.

But should we assume equal contribution? Unequal contribution? Or should we leave the issue to the adversarial process and let divorcing spouses and judges decide on a case-by-case basis who contributed more and how (which is more or less what happens now). Unfettered discretion in evaluating contribution has in many cases already resulted in adverse results for wives. In the professional degree cases . . . allowing individual judges to determine the extent and value of women's contributions to their husband's market success consistently results in the untenable conclusion that women's contributions have little or no value. This suggests that leaving the contribution question to the adversarial process is too risky, for women in particular. A strong presumption of contribution would limit the potential for bias and also provide much needed consistency and predictability in legal results.

A presumption of equal division is desirable and appropriate for a number of reasons. Importantly, a recognition in law that both spouses make contributions that are equally valuable emphasizes the equal human dignity of each person in the marriage. Specifically, home labor should be accorded equal status to market labor, emphasizing that work at home—disproportionately performed by women—must be accorded the same respect and value within marriage as market work. Equality then, is more than just a method of division; it has both real and symbolic power.

. . .

Next, equal division is desirable because, as a practical matter, it is very difficult to get an accurate and reliable record of the various kinds and qualities of contributions each partner makes over the length of a marriage. . . . It would be . . . difficult to come up with general agreement on an inclusive list of all the varying kinds of contributions spouses make to a marriage. By way of example, I have not seen described or included in housework or "family" work studies the chore of managing technology (the computer; understanding and implementing software; the digital camera etc.) that in modern times takes up a portion of time in some families' lives (the ones privileged enough to be able to afford them). In addition to the problem of identifying contributions, there is the impossible dilemma of valuing them. How can we possibly quantify and qualify things like emotional support? Inevitable and undoubtedly pervasive flaws would result. The likely unreliability of this process and lack of consensus on how to go about it argues strongly against doing it.

Lastly, the most important reason for an equal contribution presumption is that it appears that identifying and measuring contributions is antithetical to the way most families structure their relationships.

. . .

The work of sociologist Steven Nock provides insight as to how married couples perceive and experience their relationship and why they generally avoid "bookkeeping." He found in repeated studies that when wives were asked about "the obvious imbalance in the performance of household tasks, the large majority of wives see it as fair." Professor Nock at first expressed disbelief, but in his interviews with such women he found an explanation: "true, some women embrace very traditional sexist beliefs and accept them as legitimate. But more commonly, the unbalanced division of tasks was understood as a temporary situation that would be balanced in the future." He believes "that married couples experience their relationships as a sequence of turn-taking." Marriages do not exist in the present, Nock observes, but are experienced with a strong sense of the past and the future. The relationship is organized in a way that "involves complex assumptions about give-and-take, benefits, and costs, over an entire shared past and an imagined shared future." This results in an "idiosyncratic economy of exchange," that relies on "intimate, subjective, and private constructions of meaning by couples." It appears that couples view fairness relative to the entirety of the relationship and that most couples view the allocation of resources in their ongoing marriage as fair.

It appears that married couples themselves do not precisely count and measure individual contributions and instead accept their collaborative roles as generally equitable. The focus is on mutuality of contribution and a generalized sense of reciprocity appears to be enough to satisfy most spouses. As the best approximation we have for doing equity then, a presumption of equality would most closely correspond to the dominant understandings and perspectives of spousal partners about relative contributions in marriage.

. . .

C. Implications for a Wealth Distribution Scheme Based on a Broadly Constructed Marital Partnership Theory

... What might a wealth distribution scheme that embraces these concepts look like? Here, I will suggest a broad-brush outline of core rules as a starting point.

What should be considered "marital wealth" to which the parties have a claim? Partnership theory dictates that any asset that has been affected by marital conduct ought to be included. Clearly, traditional assets that have accumulated during marriage should be divisible, based on a presumption of mutual contribution to the marriage. Modern property regimes already reflect this principle of partnership marriage. Additionally, ... human capital, the most important kind of wealth for most families, must be recognized as property. Here, current law betrays the partnership ideal and wrongly excludes these assets.

Next, does the partnership ideal support the usual distinction in contemporary law between marital property and separate property? That depends on whether the separate assets have been affected by marital conduct or whether marital assets and conduct have been affected by the existence of separate property. To the extent that separate property has been influenced by the marriage or has itself influenced marital conduct, then these effects should be shared at divorce.

. . .

How should property be divided at divorce? As I have suggested, the law should presume equal contribution by spousal partners to the marriage. This, in turn, supports a presumption of equal division of marital wealth. Recall that interdependent behavior in marriage predictably has a significant affect on the spouses' respective earning capacities as well as on the accumulation of traditional assets. Accordingly, the presumption of equal division must apply to spousal claims to share income in addition to other property.

However, devising a sensible methodology for sharing the effects of marriage on human capital is a difficult challenge. Because of its nature, human capital investments cannot be accurately disaggregated. Additionally, measuring human capital losses that occur either because market skills and experience are diminished during marriage or because they are not "grown" during marriage by new and increasing investments in market work would require wholly unfounded and unreliable speculations about who the spouses would have become if they had never married or had children.

. . .

... Taking into account the nature of conduct in marriage, the best we can do is come up with a sensible compromise for identifying and dividing the impact of changes in human capital that predictably occur during marriage.

Thus, ... I support the adoption of income sharing for a period of time after divorce.... [A]n entitlement to share income acknowledges that marriage merges spouses' economic lives and has long lasting economic consequences, particularly on earning power. Moreover, sharing income is also consistent with the expectations couples commonly have when they arrange their life together. For the same reasons that underpin the equal division of traditional property, income sharing for the relevant period must also be equal.

How long should income be shared? In formulating specific rules, there are a number of appealing proposals already in the literature that, in important ways, the theory of partnership marriage would support. Jana Singer, who has also supported the partnership approach to marriage, suggests one year of income sharing for every two years of marriage. Similarly, the ALI Principles advocate a fractional approach to income sharing related to marital duration. Although a rough compromise of many variables, I endorse this kind of an approach because it takes into account both increases and losses in earning capacity and shares the financial benefits and burdens that accrue from sharing a life together . . . At the same time, the rule of one for two or a similar fraction of marital length recognizes that marital decisions strongly shape respective financial outcomes at divorce, but that the marriage is not completely responsible.

. . . As I have suggested, in terms of methodology for implementing partnership theory, I recommend a formulaic approach rather than a case by case approach to wealth division . . . I believe clear rules that are fairly easy to apply, enhance predictability, and minimize costs are best.

. . .

V. Conclusion

Although current constructions of partnership marriage have been problematic and at times betray the very principles the theory intends to recognize, the core substantive values behind the ideal aptly capture a common societal understanding of the operation and meaning of marriage . . . [A]doption of particular roles in marriage are neither encouraged nor discouraged. Partnership marriage simply accepts as equal whatever roles the spouses choose for themselves. More broadly, sharing and commitment, values thought to be important to families, are recognized and encouraged. For these reasons, once rehabilitated to fully recognize and implement its core values of sharing, interdependence, and joint contribution, partnership marriage continues to be a persuasive theory for a wealth distribution system at divorce.

NOTE

1. Do you agree that partnership theory as Professor Kelly describes it reflects the expectations of most married couples?

2. Is it possible to subscribe to partnership theory without accepting the claim that human capital is a marital asset?

American Law Institute, Principles of the Law of Family Dissolution

Section 5.04. Compensation for Loss of Marital Living Standard

(1) A person married to someone with significantly greater wealth or earning capacity is entitled at dissolution to compensation for a portion of

the loss in the standard of living he or she would otherwise experience, when the marriage was of sufficient duration that equity requires that some portion of the loss be treated as the spouses' joint responsibility.

(2) Entitlement to an award under this section should be determined by a rule of statewide application under which a presumption of entitlement arises in marriages of specified duration and spousal-income disparity.

(3) The value of the award made under this section should be determined by a rule of statewide application that sets a presumptive award of periodic payments calculated by applying a specified percentage to the difference between the incomes the spouses are expected to have after dissolution. This percentage is referred to in this Chapter as the durational factor, and should increase with the duration of the marriage until it reaches a maximum value set by the rule.

COMMENTS

a. In general. This section recognizes the less affluent spouse's loss of his or her expectation of continuing to enjoy a standard of living that has been sustained by the other spouse's income. The traditional rule of alimony, developed in the context of gender-bound marital roles and a wife fully dependent upon her husband for financial support, in principle based her award on the amount necessary to maintain her at the marital living standard, so long as the divorce was not her fault. In practice, awards rarely allowed the former wife to maintain the marital living standard, because the combined income of both spouses is typically insufficient to maintain both of their post-dissolution households at the living standard they were able to maintain when together. Most studies have in fact found that no alimony award is made at all, in the large majority of divorce cases. On the other hand, alimony awards are more common after dissolution of a long-term marriage in which one spouse was a homemaker, and some recent decisions reaffirm the traditional rule of support at the marital living standard in such situations. It is the long-term homemaker in particular who is covered by this section, which provides compensation to the claimant married more than a set number of years whose expected income at divorce is much less than her spouse's. . . .

Illustration:

1. A provision establishing the presumptions required by Paragraphs (2) and (3) might read as follows:

A presumption arises that a spouse is entitled to an award under this section whenever that spouse has been married five years or more to a person whose income at dissolution is expected to be at least 25 percent greater than the claimant's. The presumptive award shall equal the difference in the spouses' expected incomes at dissolution, multiplied by the appropriate durational factor. The durational factor is equal to the years of marriage multiplied by .01, but shall in no case exceed .4.

Under the illustrative provision, the maximum durational factor would be reached after 40 years of marriage, since .01 × 40 = .4. If, at that time, Spouse A's expected monthly income were $5,000, and Spouse B's were $3,000, the award would equal .4 × $2,000, or $800 per month, leaving Spouse A with $4,200 monthly and providing Spouse B with $3,800 monthly. If Spouse A earned $3,000 and Spouse B could only be expected to earn $1,000 monthly after dissolution, the award would still equal .4 × $2,000, or $800, leaving A with $2,200 and

B with $1,800. These awards would be proportionately less for marriages of shorter duration.

. . .

b. Difficulties with the contract and contribution rationales. The factors of marital duration and relative spousal income have long been recognized in alimony cases. There is more agreement on their importance, however, than on the reason for their importance. This Comment considers two commonly mentioned rationales upon which these Principles do not rely, while Comment c explores the rationale upon which it does.

Contract analogies are sometimes relied upon to explain alimony awards to the long-time homemaker. Expectation is the standard measure of contract damages, and contract principles therefore seem a likely rationale for compensating the homemaker for her lost expectation of sharing in the earnings of her spouse. The difficulty is that contract principles allow an expectation award only against a party in breach. But the law does not require an alimony claimant to show that the other spouse breached, nor would such a requirement be consistent with modern no-fault principles. Furthermore, fault assessments, if made, would sometimes place the homemaker in breach rather than her spouse. Finally, a conventional contract rationale would require describing the spousal relation in exchange terms that seem inapt because the parties define their relation by its nonfinancial aspects even though financial sharing is an important part of it. Spouses pool their financial affairs as part of a more general expectation of a shared life in which they have emotional and personal obligations as well as financial ones.

. . .

Some cases explain the traditional alimony award to the long-term home-maker as recognition of the earning-capacity loss the homemaker incurs. To the extent that loss is associated with having been the primary caretaker of the couple's children, these Principles provide compensation in § 5.05, rendering further claims under this section duplicative. A further rationale must therefore explain the claims of the long-term homemaker under this section. One reason sometimes suggested is that the homemaker's efforts contributed to the other spouse's earning capacity, thereby creating a post-divorce entitlement to share in it. This factual claim is undoubtedly accurate in some cases, but not all. Because there are many cases in which the facts would not suggest that the claimant contributed to the potential obligor's earning capacity, this rationale would leave many awards unexplained, under both these Principles and existing law.

. . .

c. Relationships as a source of obligation for the differential risk of marriage. Despite the conceptual difficulties with the contract and contribution rationales, the cases reflect an enduring intuition that the homemaker in a long-term marriage has some claim on the other spouse's post-divorce income. That intuition does not depend on any assumption that the parties made explicit promises to one another, but on the belief that the relationship itself gives rise to obligations. Anglo-American legal traditions, individualistic as they are, recognize duties between relative strangers that arise from even fleeting interactions in which one person's behavior affects another. Further duties may be owed those with whom one has a more established relationship. . . . They emerge from entry into the relationship itself, whether or not the parties expressly adopt them. The relationship of husband and wife is of this kind, but more so. Its effects may accrete slowly, but with great impact as the spouses' lives become entwined over time.

In understanding the nature of the obligation that arises in the long-term marriage, it is useful to think first about the traditional homemaker wife, as perhaps the clearest case, and so this Comment will often refer to her. That wife has more at risk, financially, from the dissolution of a long-term marriage than does her breadwinner spouse. The observation is not limited to full-time homemakers but applies equally to anyone economically dependent on his or her spouse, which typically includes part-time home-makers who are also employed but who each earn much less than their spouse. The marital dissolution may leave both spouses financially less well off, but whenever the spouses have significantly different earning capacities, the loss for the lower-earning spouse will be much greater than for the other. Under this section, when there is such an income differential, and the marriage exceeds some minimum duration, there will usually be a remedy in favor of the lower-earning spouse in an amount that is proportional to both the income differential and the marital duration.

The remedy is proportional to the marital duration because the obligations recognized under this section do not arise from the marriage ceremony alone, but develop over time as the parties' lives become entwined.

. . .

d. Establishing entitlement through statewide rules establishing presumptions. Paragraph (2) requires a rule of statewide application under which a presumption of entitlement arises when spousal-income disparity and marital duration each exceed a value specified in the rule. Paragraph (2) does not itself specify those values. Within bounds, the rulemaker's choice is more a matter of pragmatic accommodation than basic principle, but a choice must be made in the rule to ensure predictable and consistent results. The bounds within which the choice should be made are suggested by the rationale underlying this section. It would be inappropriate for the rule to presume a remedy in marriages of four years' duration, or with spousal-income disparities at dissolution of 10 percent. Such a duration is ordinarily too short to establish shared responsibility, and such an income disparity is too small for the loss to have social significance. It would be equally inappropriate if the rule did not presume a remedy at the dissolution of marriages of 10 years' duration with income disparities at dissolution of 25 percent.

. . .

Section 5.05. Compensation for Primary Caretaker's Residual Loss in Earnings Capacity

(1) A spouse should be entitled at dissolution to compensation for the earning-capacity loss arising from his or her disproportionate share during marriage of the care of the marital children, or of the children of either spouse.

(2) Entitlement to an award under this section should be determined by a rule of statewide application under which a presumption of entitlement arises at the dissolution of a marriage in which

(a) there are or have been marital children, or children of either spouse;

(b) while under the age of majority the children have lived with the claimant (or with both spouses, when the claim is against the stepparent of the children), for a minimum period specified in the rule; and

(c) the claimant's earning capacity at dissolution is substantially less than that of the other spouse.

(3) A presumption of entitlement governs in the absence of a determination by the trial court that the claimant did not provide substantially more than half of the total care that both spouses together provided for the children.

(4) The value of an award under this section should be determined by a rule of statewide application under which a presumption arises that the award shall require a set of periodic payments in an amount calculated by applying a percentage, called the *child-care durational factor*, to the difference between the incomes the spouses are expected to have at dissolution.

(a) The rule of statewide application should specify a value for the child-care durational factor that increases with the duration of the *child-care period*, which is the period during which the claimant provided significantly more than half of the total care that both spouses together provided for the children.

(b) The child-care period equals the entire period during which minor children of the marriage, or of the spouse against whom the claim is made, lived in the same household as the claimant, unless a shorter period is established by the evidence. In the case of stepchildren of the spouse against whom the claim is made, the child-care period equals the entire period during which the minor children lived in the same household as both spouses, unless a shorter period is established by the evidence.

(5) A claimant may be entitled to both an award under this section and an award under § 5.04, but in no case shall the combined value of the child-care durational factor, and the durational factor employed to determine the presumed award under § 5.04, exceed the maximum value allowed for the § 5.04 durational factor alone.

. . .

COMMENTS

a. Compensation for residual loss of earning capacity. This section compensates a spouse whose earning capacity at divorce is less than it would have been had he or she not been the primary caretaker of the couple's children during their marriage. A parent who assumes the responsibilities of primary caretaker of the marital children often limits his or her market labor during this period, and this limitation typically results in a residual loss in earning capacity that continues after the children no longer require close parental supervision. This cost is ordinarily incurred in the expectation that the marriage will endure and the primary caretaker will continue to share in the income of the other parent. The arrangement reflects a division of labor in which one parent fulfills most of the couple's joint responsibility for the care of their children while the other fulfills most of their joint responsibility for the family's financial support. Many married couples find this traditional division of labor convenient. If they divorce, however, the primary caretaker will bear the arrangement's entire financial cost. This result is inappropriate because the cost of raising the couple's children is their joint responsibility. This section ensures that the loss is shared.

. . .

d. Presumption of entitlement: the problem of establishing the existence and size of a compensable loss. While the presumption of entitlement arising under Paragraph (2) is rebutted by evidence that the claimant did not provide a disproportionate share of the parental child care (Paragraph (3)), the inference that child-care responsibilities adversely affected the claimant's earning capacity is not rebuttable. The reasons are partly pragmatic, and arise from the difficulty of establishing what an individual's earning capacity would have been had the individual made different life choices years earlier.

Economic studies demonstrate that responsibility for the care of children ordinarily has a significant continuing impact on parental earning capacity. This effect is not limited to parents who withdraw from full-time employment. It is also observed among primary caretakers who continue full-time market labor. Yet, while group data can establish this fact as a general matter, it is often difficult to show in the particular case. And even where the fact of loss may be clear enough, its size often cannot be established because of the speculation inherent in comparing the actual facts with the hypothetical facts that would have developed had the parties behaved differently years earlier. Requiring specific proof of loss would therefore result in the frequent rejection of claims that are in fact meritorious.

Illustration:

2. At the time of the dissolution of their 10–year marriage, Maria and Tony have two children. Maria worked as a retail clerk prior to the birth, seven years ago, of her first child. She has not worked in the market since that time. When she left her employment, she was earning $1,100 monthly at a department store that went out of business four years ago. Some of her former coworkers were hired by the company that took over the store, and a few still work there, one in a supervisory position. In this case, it probably is not possible to establish what Maria's earning capacity would have been if she had not cared for children, and thus not possible to establish the extent to which, if at all, it is lower today than it might have been. Under § 5.05, however, Maria need not establish such facts to make out a valid claim, as she can rely upon the relevant presumptions.

. . .

e. Measuring the claim.

. . .

Under Paragraph (4) of this section, the value of the award is presumed to equal the difference in the spouse's expected post-dissolution earnings, multiplied by the child-care durational factor. A rule of statewide application must specify a formula for setting the child-care durational factor, which increases with the duration of the marriage. The term of the award, set under § 5.06, is for a period of time equal to a percentage (also specified in a rule of statewide application) of the child-care period. The resulting rule is similar to that in § 5.04, facilitating the coordination of awards under both sections.

Illustration:

5. A and B marry in 1980, have their first child in 1983, their second child in 1987, and seek dissolution of their marriage in 1993. At the time of dissolution, A, a plumber, earns $5,000 monthly. B, who has a degree from a junior college, has in recent years worked part-time as a teacher's aide in a nursery school and could probably obtain regular employment that would pay $750 monthly. Up to the time of dissolution, the spouses have always maintained a joint household with their children. A presumption arises that B is entitled to an award under this section because there are marital children, the children have lived in the same household with B for 10 years (exceeding the minimum period specified in the governing statute in their state), and B's earning capacity at dissolution is substantially less than A's.

The governing rule in the state provides that the child-care durational factor equals .015 multiplied by the child-care period. In this case, the child-care durational factor is therefore equal to .015 multiplied by 10, or .15. A is therefore entitled to an award under this section of monthly payments equal to (.15) ($4,250), or $637.50. The governing state rule also provides that the duration of an award of periodic payments under this section shall equal the child-care period multiplied by .5. Under this section, B is therefore entitled to an award of $637.50 a month for five years, or to another award different in duration and amount but of equivalent value (see § 5.10).

. . .

It will be common for successful claimants under this section to have claims under § 5.04 as well. Paragraph (5) of this section allows such combined claims, but also provides that the combined award cannot exceed the value of the maximum award permitted for § 5.04 alone, which is the value that the § 5.04 award would have if the claimant qualified for the largest durational factor permitted under the state-law provisions implementing § 5.04.

NOTE

In In re Marriage of Meyer, 239 Wis.2d 731, 620 N.W.2d 382 (2000), the court held that a wife's contributions toward her husband's acquisition of an undergraduate and medical degree during the seven years they lived together before marriage could be taken into account in calculating an alimony award of $1,700 for eight years. The court acknowledged that consideration of contributions only during the four years in which the couple were married would result in a maintenance award for a briefer duration, but concluded that the state alimony statute authorized taking premarital contributions into account. The dissent argued that the trial court had jurisdiction over the couple under the statute based only on their desire to dissolve their marriage, and thus was not authorized to consider premarital contributions.

2. MODIFICATION

Uniform Marriage and Divorce Act

Section 316. Modification and Termination of Provisions for Maintenance, Support, and Property Disposition

(a) ... [The provisions of any decree respecting maintenance or support may be modified only as to installments accruing subsequent to the motion for modification and only upon a showing of changed circumstances so substantial and continuing as to make the terms unconscionable. The provisions as to property disposition may not be revoked or modified, unless the court finds the existence of conditions that justify the reopening of a judgment under the laws of this state.

(b) Unless otherwise agreed in writing or expressly provided in the decree, the obligation to pay future maintenance is terminated upon the death of either party or the remarriage of the party receiving maintenance.

(c) Unless otherwise agreed in writing or expressly provided in the decree, provisions for the support of a child are terminated by emancipation of the child but not by the death of a parent obligated to support the child. When a parent obligated to pay support dies, the amount of support may be modified, revoked, or commuted to a lump sum payment, to the extent just and appropriate in the circumstances.

COMMENT

Except where the decree, incorporating the agreement of the parties, provides to the contrary [see Section 306(f)], future installments may be modified, but the person seeking modification must show that circumstances have changed since the date of the original order so that the order is unconscionable at the time the motion is made and will continue to be unconscionable unless modified. This strict standard is intended to discourage repeated or insubstantial motions for modification. In accordance with presently existing law, the provisions of the decree respecting property disposition may not be altered unless the judgment itself can be reopened for fraud or otherwise under the laws of the state. There is no intention to change this law. If the judgment was rendered by another state, normal full faith and credit law would allow it to be reopened in the forum state if it can be reopened under the laws of the rendering state.

Graham v. Graham

Court of Appeals of the District of Columbia, 1991.
597 A.2d 355.

■ PER CURIAM

This is an appeal from an order modifying an award of alimony and child support. At issue is whether an increase in the non-custodial parent's ability to pay can, by itself, constitute a material change in circumstances sufficient to justify an increase in support. We conclude that it can and reverse the order of the trial court.

In March 1982, after twenty years of marriage, the parties divorced. Pursuant to the divorce decree, Mr. Graham was ordered to pay Mrs. Graham alimony of $250 per week and child support of $375 per week ($125 for each of their three children); in addition, he was to pay half the monthly mortgage on the marital home and all private school tuition for the children. At about the time the judgment of absolute divorce was entered, Mr. Graham signed a new contract with his employer which provided for significant salary increases. Mr. Graham had been earning approximately $100,000 in salary in 1981; under the new contract, his salary was to be raised to $185,000 in 1982; $210,000 in 1983; $230,000 in 1984; and $255,000 in 1985. In August 1982, after negotiations between the parties about increasing support payments in light of these salary increases had broken down, Mrs. Graham filed a Motion to Enforce Agreement or in the Alternative for Increased Alimony and Child Support.

On July 27, 1984, after a three-day evidentiary hearing, the trial court issued a Memorandum Opinion and Order in which it held, inter alia, that an increase in the non-custodial parent's income, no matter how great, was, by itself, an insufficient basis upon which to modify a support order. Relying on Sheridan v. Sheridan, 267 A.2d 343 (D.C.1970), the trial judge stated that in order to prove a "material change in circumstances" sufficient to justify an increase in support, Mrs. Graham was required to demonstrate that the needs of herself and her children had increased since the original support order was entered; only after this threshold showing was made would Mr. Graham's increased ability to pay be taken into account. Nonetheless, the trial court found that there had been a modest increase in the needs of Mrs. Graham and the children and that Mr. Graham had the financial resources to contribute toward meeting those needs. The court thus increased Mr. Graham's child support obligation $15 per week per child to $140 per week per child. In addition, the court ordered that the alimony paid to Mrs. Graham be increased from $250 to $350 per week; however, as Mrs. Graham was at the time attending law school part-time and was expected to complete her studies in the spring of 1986, the court ordered that the alimony be decreased to $200 per week beginning in September 1986. Mrs. Graham was also awarded $1,000 in attorney's fees.

Mrs. Graham, supported by amicus, asserts that the trial court applied an incorrect legal standard in modifying the original support order and thus unfairly limited the amount of the increase. She contends that an increase in the non-custodial parent's ability to pay can, by itself, provide a proper basis for an increase in support, beyond or without any proven increase in the needs of the children or the other spouse. We agree.

. . .

An original support order may be modified only upon a showing that there has been a material change in the circumstances of the parties.[5] Hamilton v. Hamilton, supra note 5, 247 A.2d at 422. In Hamilton, we stated that a material change in circumstances can be "a change which affects either the [parent's] ability to pay or the needs of the minor children," and we have reiterated this disjunctive standard in several subsequent decisions.

. . .

... [W]e cannot find that the procedure followed by the trial court comported with the standard for modification set forth in Hamilton. Hamilton and its progeny make clear that a material change in either the parent's income or in the needs of the children and the other spouse may be the basis for modification of the support order. By insisting that there could be no increase in support without a commensurate increase in the needs of Mrs. Graham and the children, the trial court effectively nullified the first prong of this standard.

Nor do we see any reason to apply a different standard where the parent's income increased and where it is decreased. To adopt such a distinction would mean that children would have to bear the burden of a lowered standard of living when their parent's income declined but could

5. A motion for modification of support, therefore, is not to be used as a pretense to relitigate the equities of the prior decree. Tennyson v. Tennyson, 381 A.2d 264, 266 (D.C. 1977); Hamilton v. Hamilton, 247 A.2d 421, 423 (D.C.1968).

not share the benefit when that parent's resources grew—a situation for which we perceive little, if any, sensible justification.

Furthermore, we think it proper that a material increase in the non-custodial parent's income can be the basis for an increase in child support. Although spouses may divorce, the children's legal relationship with both parents continues, and "the children's station in life should not therefore be fixed forever to their parents' station in life at the time of the divorce." We think it appropriate that a trial court may act to ensure that where there is a material increase in non-custodial parents' financial resources, that these parents do not increase their own standard of living without also ensuring that their children live as well as they.

We note finally that the considerations which go into an award of alimony differ somewhat from those which determine child support. In this jurisdiction, parents, for example, have "an unqualified obligation to contribute to the support of their children." By contrast, an award of alimony to a former spouse is a matter left to the discretion of the trial court, and considerations other than a pure calculus of need and ability to pay (such as the length of marriage and the age of the parties) enter into the initial decision. While we may assume that in the vast majority of cases, the relationship between spouses does not survive after divorce to the same degree that the parent-child relationship does, by law the decree granting alimony, just as does the decree providing for child support, remains open for modification. A former spouse seeking an increase in alimony bears the burden of showing that an increase is justified. There must be "a showing of a substantial and material change in the conditions and circumstances of the involved parties since the entry of the decree." A modification of alimony "must reflect changed needs or changed financial resources" (as opposed to "offensive" conduct on the part of the receiving spouse). While it may deter marriage, or divorce, or both, to contemplate that the increase in the income of one divorced spouse, standing alone, will provide justification for an increase in support payments to the receiving spouse, a blanket rule precluding spouses from sharing in the increased resources of their former partners would be unacceptable. It may be, for example, that the spouse receiving support has contributed during the marriage so as to be partly or wholly responsible for the other spouse's subsequent income. Or, at the time of the divorce, there may have been insufficient resources for both spouses to maintain their previous standard of living, and the subsequent increase in the income of the spouse paying support might be used to meet the pre-existing, though previously unmet, financial needs of the other spouse. In short, there may be circumstances, though unusual, in which it may be appropriate for the trial court to award increased alimony where only the income of the paying spouse, and not the needs of the receiving spouse, have increased. In any event, this is a matter for the trial court, marshalling the facts pursuant to correct legal standards.

Therefore, we reverse the trial court's order modifying the prior alimony and support orders and remand for further consideration in light of this opinion. . . .

NOTES

1. In Misinonile v. Misinonile, 35 Conn.App. 228, 645 A.2d 1024 (1994), the court reduced from $175 per week to $100 per week the alimony payments of a sixty-eight year-old ex-husband with a thyroid condition and a hearing disability who voluntarily retired. The court held that the ex-husband's voluntary retirement was a reasonable change of circumstances warranting a reduction in his alimony obligation because of his advanced age and his serious health problems.

2. What if a parent is unable to pay child support because of his or her religious belief? Consider Hunt v. Hunt, 162 Vt. 423, 648 A.2d 843 (1994). The father belonged to the Northeast Kingdom Community Church. Members of the church lead an ascetic, communal existence. They eschew all personal possessions and work for the benefit of the community, often in one of the church-run business enterprises that offer goods to the public and provide income to the church. In return the church provides housing and living necessities to the members. The mother had earlier left the community with their children. The state brought suit against Hunt seeking an order for child support. He was ordered to pay $50 per month. On appeal, the Vermont Supreme Court upheld the order, but refused to enforce it by contempt.

D'Ascanio v. D'Ascanio

Supreme Court of Connecticut, 1996.
237 Conn. 481, 678 A.2d 469.

■ BERDON, JUSTICE.

In this appeal, the plaintiff seeks to reverse the judgment of the trial court for failing to modify an alimony award in accordance with the terms of a settlement agreement entered into between the parties that was incorporated by reference into the original decree dissolving their marriage. The defendant cross appeals, claiming that there was insufficient evidence to support the trial court's modification of the alimony award. The parties appealed to the Appellate Court, and we transferred both appeals to this court . . . We reverse the judgment of the trial court.

The marriage between the plaintiff, Joseph D'Ascanio, and the defendant, Mary Louise D'Ascanio, was dissolved on January 9, 1986. Pursuant to the decree of dissolution, the plaintiff, inter alia, was ordered "to pay the defendant as alimony the sum of $900.00 per week for so long as she lives and remains unmarried." Subsequently, the parties returned to court on numerous occasions regarding various issues pertaining to the dissolution of their marriage, including several motions to modify the alimony award. Ultimately, on August 21, 1990, the parties entered into a written settlement agreement that modified a number of the terms of the dissolution judgment (modification agreement). Following a hearing at which the parties acknowledged their understanding of the modification agreement's terms and consequences, the trial court approved the agreement, finding that it was fair and equitable. . . . Pursuant to § 46b–66, the court ordered that the modification agreement be incorporated in the original dissolution decree.

The pertinent paragraph of the modification agreement provides: "That effective on [August] 25, 1990, the plaintiff shall pay alimony to the defendant of $700 per week; said alimony shall be paid for nine years and four months (507 weeks). Said alimony shall terminate upon the expiration of nine years and four months (507 weeks) and shall not be modifiable by either party in terms of duration or amount *except that in the event that the defendant remarries or cohabitates, as defined by statute, the alimony shall be reduced by one half ($350)*. Further it is understood that if and when the defendant obtains gainful employment, regardless of the amount she earns, that such income shall not be a basis for a reduction in child support by the plaintiff which shall otherwise not be subject to any restriction as to modifiability other than usual statutory and common law criteria." (Emphasis added.)

On May 23, 1994, alleging that the defendant was cohabiting with Dean Griffin, the plaintiff moved, pursuant to the terms of the modification agreement, to have his weekly alimony payment reduced by $350. The trial court, after a hearing on the motion, found that the defendant was in fact cohabiting with Griffin. Notwithstanding its finding, however, the trial court refused to apply the terms of the modification agreement that would have reduced the plaintiff's alimony payment by $350. Instead, the court reduced the alimony award by only $100 per week, obligating the plaintiff to pay $600 per week.

The parties do not contest the fact that the modification agreement defines "cohabitation" by reference to General Statutes § 46b–86(b). Section 46b–86(b), known as the "cohabitation statute," provides in pertinent part that a court may "modify such judgment and suspend, reduce or terminate the payment of periodic alimony upon a showing that the party receiving the periodic alimony is living with another person under circumstances which the court finds should result in the modification . . . of alimony because the living arrangements cause such a change of circumstances as to alter the financial needs of that party." Therefore, in order to find that the defendant was cohabiting with Griffin, as defined by statute, the plaintiff had to prove that (1) the defendant was living with Griffin, and (2) the living arrangement with Griffin caused a change of circumstances so as to alter the financial needs of the defendant.

"[T]he General Assembly chose the broader language of 'living with another person' rather than 'cohabitation.'" Whether an individual is "living with another person" is a fact specific determination. In this case, the trial court found that, because Griffin slept at the defendant's house seven nights a week, was identified by the defendant's children as their stepfather, and traveled with the defendant and her children, the defendant and Griffin were "living together." The defendant does not challenge that finding.

Having found that the defendant was cohabiting with Griffin, as defined in § 46b–86(b), the trial court held that to enforce the terms of the modification agreement and reduce the plaintiff's weekly alimony payment by $350, when the defendant's financial needs were altered by only $100 per week due to her living arrangement with Griffin, would be inequitable and would amount to a penalty. Consequently, the trial court refused to apply the terms of the modification agreement and, sua sponte, reduced the defendant's weekly alimony by $100 retroactive to October 1, 1993.

This deviation from the terms of the modification agreement by the trial court was improper. The only issue raised before the court was whether the defendant was cohabiting with Griffin within the meaning of § 46b–86(b). Both the parties and the trial court agreed that, according to the modification agreement, once a finding of cohabitation was made, the alimony award would be reduced by one half. At the commencement of the hearing on the plaintiff's motion for modification, the issues before the court were delineated as evidenced by the following colloquy between the court and counsel:

"The Court: Let me just use a few minutes here to talk a little bit about the case here. Do you understand the agreement to have the effect of limiting the court's statutory discretion in the sense that if I find that there is cohabitation under the statute . . . it would be an automatic reduction by one half; is that your understanding of the agreement?

"[Michael Beebe, trial counsel for the plaintiff]: Yes, I do, Your Honor, and there is a case that supports [that result], *Mihalyak v. Mihalyak,* 30 Conn.App. 516, 620 A.2d 1327 (1993).

"The Court: All right. Attorney Murrett, is that your thought on—

"[Kathleen Murrett, trial counsel for the defendant]: I don't know that I agree with Mr. Beebe's interpretation of that case, but yes, I would agree with that.

"The Court: Under the facts of this case ... I'm being asked to find whether under the statute I find cohabitation, and ... you have an agreement which removes ... the court's discretion [as to the] type of modification that would be appropriate. Here you've agreed that in the event of cohabitation [alimony] ... would be reduced by one half.... So I just wanted to see if you shared my thought on that."

We agree that the sole issue to be resolved by the trial court, as framed by the parties, was whether there was cohabitation. Once that question had been answered in the affirmative the court should have enforced the terms of the modification agreement entered into by the parties and approved by the court.

The judgment is reversed and the case is remanded with direction to render judgment reducing the plaintiff's weekly alimony payment, in accordance with the terms of the modification agreement, from $700 to $350, retroactive to October 1, 1993.

C. Divorce Awards and Gender Roles

As we have seen, courts making financial awards at divorce attempt to do justice between the two spouses. This process occurs, however, against a larger social background in which gender often shapes the current financial condition and future prospects of the parties. To put it bluntly, the traditional division of labor within households often leaves the husband in better financial shape than the wife at the time of divorce. To what extent do legal rules reflect, or reinforce, assumptions about the division of labor within a marriage? Should these rules take such considerations into account? If so, should they try to create incentives for any particular arrangement? The next reading discusses some of these issues.

June Carbone and Margaret Brinig, Rethinking Marriage: Feminist Ideology, Economic Change, and Divorce Reform

65 Tulane Law Review 953, 954, 957–961, 988–1010 (1991).

. . .

Once a state has precluded consideration of marital misconduct [at divorce], the law of civil obligation ... helps to define the interests that remain.... [W]hile contract and tort remedies depend on a determination of breach of contract or breach of duty, restitution does not. Contract and tort require such a determination in order to justify imposition of one party's loss upon the other. Restitution requires only that one party gain at the other's expense in circumstances in which it would be unjust to allow retention of the gain without payment. Within marriage, restitution is therefore possible whenever the divorce separates gains and losses that would otherwise be shared. Economists observe that the decision to provide compensation—that is, to reach a legal conclusion that retention of the benefit is unjust rather than a conclusion that the benefit has been gratuitously rendered—involves a decision to encourage these forms of exchange.

Translated into the language of civil obligation, the existing divorce system has largely rejected contract and tort, expectation and reliance, in favor of restitution. Marriage as a lifelong commitment is gone, with expanding protection for particular exchanges made while the marriage lasted....

In considering the different visions of the family, it is useful to start with what we will call the "traditionalist" view, that is, a defense of the relatively traditional pattern of gender responsibilities that prevailed during the latter part of the nineteenth and first half of the twentieth century. The traditionalists argue that men and women *should* continue to perform different roles within marriage, that these gender differences make women more economically vulnerable to divorce than men, and that, when divorce is common, women will continue to devote their energies to childrearing and homemaking only if these contributions are protected. The traditionalists favor a contract approach that protects the expectation interest of the non-breaching party in order to encourage specialization within the family and to deter breaches or "shirking" of marital obligations. They therefore decry the elimination of fault from divorce, and favor relatively generous financial settlements for non-breaching wives.

. . .

Herma Hill Kay, writing from a "liberal feminist" perspective, takes the position most diametrically opposed to that of the Chicago School economists. Concerned about equality rather than efficiency, Kay argues that women will never be equal with men so long as they continue to "make choices that will be economically disabling for women, thereby perpetuating their traditional financial dependence upon men and contributing to their inequality with men at divorce". Kay further observes that:

> since ... Anglo–American family law has traditionally reflected the social division of function by sex within marriage, it will be necessary to withdraw existing legal supports for that arrangement as a cultural norm. No sweeping new legal reforms of marriage and divorce will be required, however, to achieve this end. It will be enough, I think, to continue the present trend begun in the nineteenth century toward the emancipation of married women, and implemented more recently by gender-neutral family laws, as well as the current emphasis on sharing principles in marital property law.

Kay concludes that the law, far from encouraging specialization in gender roles, should discourage it. She agrees with [traditionalists] that the most effective way to encourage women's economic independence is to fail to compensate choices that lead to economic marginalization. She therefore opposes the reintroduction of fault in any form, and by implication, contract-based awards, both because she wishes to discourage women from pursuing the traditional homemaking role and because of concern that even if fault-based awards produced higher settlements for women, that outcome might not be "worth the cost of perpetuating the blackmail and other abuses that accompanied the fault system." Kay is equivocal on the subject of restitution-based awards, favoring compensation for the lost career opportunities of older dependent homemakers while opposing support for women who make "economically disabling" choices in the future. Identifying child-care responsibilities as the major source of continued sexual inequality, Kay believes that men should be encouraged to share responsibility for the rearing of their children, receiving joint custody upon divorce and remaining emotionally and financially involved thereafter. She believes that if this is accomplished, the "large disparity between men's and women's household standard of living [after divorce] . . . should be greatly reduced" and "the trend begun in California toward eliminating fault from all aspects of marital dissolution can continue to work itself out without the risk of financial harm to dependent women and children."

Taken to its logical conclusion, Kay's analysis suggests that the appropriate response to women's dependence on their husbands' incomes is less, not more, financial support upon divorce. In order to dismantle the gendered division of labor within the family, Kay argues that the marital bargain, at least the traditional one that exchanges male support for female services, should not be enforceable. Her analysis further implies that compensation for lost career opportunities, at least for modern women who make choices that are "economically disabling," should also be limited. In states that preclude consideration of fault, lost career opportunities are emerging as the primary basis for spousal support. Compensation for those lost opportunities, however, sanctions the very choices of which Kay so strongly disapproves: namely, decisions by modern women to forego substantial career opportunities in order to contribute to the care of their children or their husband's careers. Kay issues no call for a reduction in divorce awards, but such a call is unnecessary. Her endorsement, albeit qualified, of the present divorce system, which [has been described as] a system of transitional awards that falls far short of compensating the career sacrifices modern women are continuing to make, has much the same effect.

Kay's central premise is that in order to achieve equality, men and women need to make the same choices. Women need to join men in the pursuit of careers; men need to join women in caring for their children. "Cultural feminists" or "feminists of difference," influenced by the ideology of Carol Gilligan and the sociology of Lenore Weitzman, question whether women *should* make the same decisions as men and oppose laws that penalize women's different choices. Mary O'Connell, . . . poses the challenge directly:

> [The] issue is this: the vast majority of American women live what can only be fairly described as a feminine lifestyle. They undertake the major—and sometimes sole—responsibility for rearing children, and interrupt or scale down their participation in the paid labor force in order to do so. At divorce, however, this lifestyle choice is either minimized (equality theory) or treated as deviant (victim theory). A woman is either told that she must accept the consequences of her choice and go on, or her husband is ordered to "repair" part of the "damage" his wife has suffered, so that she can be fully self-supporting (that is, function like a man) in the future.

O'Connell further notes:

> If our model for the correct post divorce result is equal lifestyles, and if we begin to recognize that it is not only years absent from the labor force but also the presence of children which compromise one's ability to earn a living at paid work, we may begin to move toward a model which insists that the parent who devotes herself to childrearing must not end up in a worse position than the one who devotes himself to the labor force. . . . We need a new model, a model which does not treat the uncompensated rearing of children as aberrant, a model which sees women as women, but does not rush either to protect or to penalize them on that basis.

O'Connell reaches the "unpopular conclusion" that women will continue to be more likely than men to compromise labor force participation in order to rear their children and that, rather than dissuade them, the childrearing role must be made "less economically perilous." To do so, O'Connell advocates "an augmented role for alimony in the middle-class divorces of the future."

While O'Connell may disagree with Kay about the desired extent of women's contributions to childrearing, she shares her rejection of a fault standard as a way to secure greater economic security for women.

. . .

To be effective in achieving O'Connell's objectives, any new system must encourage women's economic independence without penalizing their devotion to their children. O'Connell herself sets forth no specific suggestions, but other writers propose two broad categories of reform. The first, which we will call restitution based, would formalize and expand the existing trend toward basing divorce awards on the gains and losses of the marriage. This approach, pioneered by Joan Krauskopf and recently set forth in a different form by Ira Ellman, declares that compensation is due any time a marriage ends with one spouse retaining a benefit at the other spouse's expense. If, for example, the wife accepts a lower paying job to be able to spend more time with the children, the couple has, in effect, decided to finance their childrearing efforts through the wife's foregone income. At divorce, both parents will retain the benefit of having had children or of having raised them in a particular way, but only the wife will bear the cost. Similarly, if one spouse finances the other's medical education and the divorce occurs shortly after graduation, the doctor will reap the entire benefit of an investment the couple jointly undertook and paid for. In both cases, an adjustment will be due that goes beyond more conventional provisions for property division or spousal support. Krauskopf identifies a strong trend toward the adoption of this rationale as the primary purpose of support awards.

O'Connell, while viewing these proposals as improvements over the earlier reforms, is nonetheless dissatisfied because restitution awards still place a premium on labor market investments rather than domestic investments. She observes that such proposals reserve their greatest benefits for women who abandon established careers and concludes:

> The theory seems incapable of capturing the subtler effects of the adoption of a feminine lifestyle. It does not, for example, address the fact that the wife may well have chosen her earlier work with an eye to interrupted or reduced labor force participation during her childrearing years. Flexibility may have outweighed remuneration or potential for advancement as a value to be maximized in choosing a job. No formulation of human capital theory captures the impact of this choice. Yet, by ignoring it, the model is, in effect, applying a masculine template to a feminine lifestyle, the contours of which it does not even begin to discern.

While O'Connell's feminine lifestyle does not involve the lifelong separation of home and market, it does embrace decisions, with lifelong consequences, to value family above individual advancement. O'Connell insists on protection not just for well-educated women who delay childrearing long enough to establish careers, but for women who marry young and invest less in their education and in the acquisition of marketable skills than in their search for a suitable mate. She objects not to these choices, but to the economic powerlessness that comes with them.

O'Connell accordingly sees more promise in the recent efforts to use a partnership model to equalize post-divorce standards of living. Jana Singer, writing after O'Connell, proposes that each ex-spouse would be entitled to an equal share of the couple's combined income for a set number of years after the formal dissolution of their marriage. The time period for this post-divorce sharing would depend upon the length of the marriage. I would propose, as a starting point, one year of post-divorce income sharing for each two years of marriage.

. . .

While the justifications advanced for the partnership model are conventional ones, the symbolic consequences are quite different from those of the other models. Partnership proponents will not satisfy the traditionalists because they refuse to embrace what Becker calls "the sharp sexual division of labor in all societies between the market and the household sectors" or the lifetime commitment necessary, in Becker's view, to make that division possible. At the same time, the partnership approach eschews the liberals' insistence that women be encouraged to look to their own careers rather than to their husbands as the primary source of financial security. Rather, because these models reserve their greatest benefits for the marriages with the greatest income disparity and do so independently of any actual contribution made, the proposals validate not just decisions to value children over individual advancement, but marriage over career, and the search for a financially attractive mate over investment in one's own earning capacity. Partnership models, in their effort to make women's choices less disabling, also make the traditional role more comfortable.

CONCLUSION

A. Breaking the Impasse: The Role of Children

. . .

The central premise of the liberal feminist critique of the relationships between men and women is that women's childrearing role stands in the way of full equality. Victor Fuchs argues, however, that it is not the fact that women raise children, but the fact "that, on average, women have a stronger demand for children than men do, and have more concern for children after they are born," that creates the disadvantage. Fuchs observes:

> Suppose women were better than men at producing and caring for children but had no particular desire to do so, while it was the men who wanted the children and cared more about their welfare. We would probably still see the same division of labor we see now, but men would have to pay dearly for women's services. The present hierarchy of power would be reversed.

Instead, women, on average, are more willing than men to sacrifice their own well-being to have children and to protect the interests of their children. The result is that men individually and society generally are able to have children at a lower price than the price they would have to pay if women's preferences were the same as men's.

The liberal feminist strategy of withdrawing support for the maternal childrearing role is aimed at changing these preferences. While the liberal ideal may be shared parenting, the immediate effect of higher divorce rates and low divorce awards is to convince women that they make sacrifices for their children at their own peril. Later marriages and fewer middle-class children are predictable consequences of that strategy. When combined with ... cutbacks in the resources available for poorer families, the result is a dramatically increasing percentage of American children raised in poverty, with a concomitant effect on their performance and well-being. Yet all of the demographic data indicate that the demand for relatively well-educated workers will be increasing in the future.

If the result of this strategy is to persuade women to value children less, then men who want children of their own may have to give up more to have them. Or there may simply be fewer children. At that point, society generally should have a greater interest in encouraging investment in children, mandating more generous parental leave, subsidizing child care, providing tax breaks, increasing educational resources, and otherwise assisting child-care providers. Or the United States could meet its labor force demands by selectively increasing immigration.

Whichever result occurs, the price for children will be higher. But women will no longer pay such a disproportionate share of the price. In the interim, however, women and their children will bear the major burden of the transition. For the liberal strategy to succeed, the disparity between men and women's preferences for children must change. They are more likely to change if society withdraws its support for the traditional maternal role....

Cultural feminists, however much they may agree that the greater value women place on children is the source of women's lack of power, applaud such values. They are unwilling to encourage women to value children less or to pay a penalty for refusing to do so. For cultural feminists, therefore, greater protection for the childrearing role is essential. The challenge for these feminists is to persuade society to do so without perpetuating women's dependence, economic or psychological, on men.

These divisions in feminist theory ... are unnecessarily accentuated by the exclusive focus on divorcing husbands and wives. The historical source of protection for childrearing has been marriages that lock women into unequal relationships with their husbands. To the extent that modern proposals continue to tie support for the childrearing role to the husband's income and the length of the marriage, they risk perpetuating women's dependence. A more radical strategy may be a child-centered approach that separates support for childrearing from marital roles and insists on greater recognition of both the societal and the individual responsibility for children. Such a strategy would emphasize: (1) increased societal support for day care, parental leave, education, nutrition, medical care, and other subsidies that directly benefit children and their primary caretakers; (2) allocation of property and post-divorce income for the children's benefit before the spouse's individual claims are considered; and (3) recognition of the parents' continuing responsibility for, and benefit from, children as a primary basis for divorce adjustments. While these principles can be combined with other approaches, and while they cannot and should not provide the exclusive basis for the financial allocations made upon divorce, we believe that emphasis on children and childrearing will do more to advance a feminist perspective than any examination limited to the relationship between husband and wife.

D. SUMMARY: FINANCIAL AWARDS TO DIVORCING SPOUSES

We've now reviewed various approaches to dividing property and awarding alimony at divorce. Despite the fact that property and alimony formally are two distinct bases for awards, in practice the line between the two can become blurred. Courts seeking to divide a couple's wealth fairly must confront the fact that most spouses have relatively little property available to distribute at divorce. Doing justice between the parties thus may require providing entitlements both to tangible assets and to a future stream of payments. These may resemble property and alimony, respectively. Essentially, however, the court is seeking to fashion a combination of entitlements that will achieve a fair distribution of wealth between the parties.

This leads naturally to the question: what principle should guide this attempt to do economic justice at divorce? From the preceding material in this Chapter, we can extract at least five possibilities: need, status, rehabilitation, contribution, and partnership. In addition, any entitlement could be reduced, or even eliminated, because of marital fault.

If we examine the principles closely, we will see that each leads us in a different direction—sometimes dramatically so. Furthermore, if we examine the factors that courts are instructed to consider in decisions about property division and alimony, we will see that those factors instruct courts to rely on different principles. These statutes therefore point judges simultaneously in different directions. As you read the material below, consider whether we should attempt to use a single principle to guide financial awards at divorce. If so, what should it be? If not, how should a court reconcile several principles that would lead to different outcomes?

1. NEED

As the ALI Principles point out, the need principle can be interpreted in different ways. One is to use the standard of living during the marriage as the benchmark. The other is to refer to some minimum level at which a spouse is able to meet basic needs. Historically, of course, need was most closely associated with the award of alimony. This suggests that the second, more restrictive, interpretation of the principle is likely to prevail in most cases.

Reliance on need as the organizing principle in divorce awards therefore would lead to relatively modest awards that do not attempt to redress any imbalance in economic prospects between the spouses. Furthermore, entitlement to post-divorce payments would end once the recipient were able to meet her needs without alimony. This could occur, for instance, through more gainful employment or remarriage. A major advantage of the need principle from a social standpoint is that it makes the ex-spouse, rather than taxpayers, pay for the support of the recipient. At the same time, reliance on need requires an explanation of why responsibility should be assigned to an ex-spouse, rather than society as a whole, especially in relatively brief marriages. In addition, the need principle can foster the ongoing dependence of one ex-spouse on another for an indefinite time after divorce.

2. STATUS

The status principle would require that the court ensure that a less affluent spouse enjoy the same standard of living that he or she had during the marriage. This principle is expressed most explicitly in § 5.04 of the ALI Principles, which provides that in lengthy marriages the law should recognize the less affluent spouse's "expectation of continuing to enjoy a standard of living that has been sustained by the other spouse's income." The ALI envisions the status principle as benefiting primarily the long-time homemaker whose income at divorce is considerably less than that of her spouse. In theory, however, status could be used as the basis for an award in any divorce.

One possible appeal of the status principle is that it vindicates the notion that marriage is a serious commitment in which the parties pledge to take one another "for richer or poorer." With respect to long marriages in particular, it reflects the idea that, as the Comment to ALI § 5.04 puts it, "[t]o leave the financially dependent spouse in a long marriage without a remedy would facilitate exploitation of the trusting spouse and discourage domestic investment by the nervous one."

On the other hand, an award based on the status principle resembles an award of expectation damages for breach of contract, which leaves the financially dependent spouse in the same position as she would occupy had the marital contract continued in force. In an era of no-fault divorce, however, is it appropriate to conceptualize divorce as a breach of contract? Furthermore, with nearly half of marriages ending in divorce, can any spouse claim a reasonable expectation that his or her marriage will continue indefinitely? Finally, perhaps more relevant in briefer marriages, might reliance on the status principle result in what an economist would call "moral hazard?" That is, would it make a financially dependent spouse indifferent between continuing the marriage or seeking a divorce–thus actually undermining marital commitment?

3. Rehabilitation

One goal of divorce awards might be to enable the financially dependent spouse to acquire sufficient earning capacity to support herself. If "sufficient" earning capacity is defined as enough to meet basic needs, this principle is similar to the need principle. Enabling the recipient to obtain additional education or training, however, often may result an increase in earning power that provides more than mere subsistence.

The rehabilitation principle also differs from the need principle in that its implicit premise is that support should be for a temporary, rather than indefinite, period of time. If earning capacity is defined more expansively as enough to sustain the marital standard of living, rehabilitation resembles the status principle. In this case, rehabilitation still would reflect the assumption that support should be temporary, but the period of time would be longer than if earning capacity were defined in terms of basic needs.

Rehabilitation is appealing in its effort to ensure that spouses are at least able to be self-supporting after divorce. It also is consistent with the "clean break" philosophy in that it attempts to obviate the need for ongoing financial duties after divorce. In some cases, however, a spouse charged with a financial obligation may claim that the marriage is not responsible for the other spouse's low earning capacity. In that instance, the argument goes, it's unfair to require the higher-earning spouse to compensate the other spouse for her own failure to enhance her earning power. Potential recipients also may criticize the rehabilitation principle for not taking into account all the contributions and sacrifices of a spouse during marriage. For these critics, striving to satisfy the "clean break" objective is unrealistic and unfair.

4. Contribution

The contribution principle reflects the idea that the spouses pool their efforts during the marriage for their mutual benefit. On this view, when the marriage ends each spouse has earned certain benefits to which he or she is entitled. Financial awards at divorce thus should seek to compensate spouses for their efforts, regardless of need. Alimony should end only when the entitlement is paid off.

As the readings suggest, there are different ways to determine compensation under the contribution principle.

a. RESTITUTION

Restitution attempts to return to the spouse what she contributed to the marriage. The court in *Postema* adopts this approach, when it says that an award should "compensate the nonstudent spouse for unrewarded sacrifices, efforts, and contributions toward the degree." A court might, for instance, calculate the market value of domestic services actually performed by the spouse, as well as the amount of earnings she contributed to the household.

One drawback of restitution is that many of the services performed in the home have been traditionally undervalued by the job market. The result might be an unrealistically low estimate of the value of the domestic contributions that a spouse has made. The duration of the marriage also will affect the calculation. On the one hand, the longer the marriage, the greater the contributions that the spouse has made. At the same time, however, the spouse has received benefits from those contributions in the form of enjoyment of the marital standard of living. As the court in *Postema* said, for instance, when parties remain married for a substantial time after one of them obtains a degree, "the nonstudent spouse will already have been rewarded, in part, for efforts contributed by virtue of having already shared, in part, in the fruits of the degree."

b. COMPENSATION FOR FORGONE OPPORTUNITIES

We might conceptualize a spouse's contributions not only as the services and income that she has provided, but as the opportunity to enhance her earning power that she has forgone. One way to compute this is to determine what the spouse's earning capacity would be had she stayed full-time in the labor market during the marriage. Subtracting her actual earning power at divorce from this figure, discounted to present value, would represent her reduction in earning power as a result of the marriage.

A major difficulty with this approach is that it may require excessive speculation. If the spouse failed to complete her education, for instance, it may be extremely hard to determine what her earning power would have been. Would she have completed college? Law school? Would she have been first in her class? It is hard to know how life might have been different if a person had not married, much less to determine the economic consequences of each of the different paths she may have taken.

As we have seen, ALI § 5.05 attempts to compensate a spouse for lost earning power while avoiding the need for such speculation. It adopts a conclusive presumption that a spouse who has been the primary caregiver for children during marriage has suffered a reduction in earning power. It presumes that the amount of that reduction is the difference in earning capacity between the two spouses at divorce. The ALI Principles acknowledge that, among other things, this approach is intended to preserve incentives for one spouse to assume the main responsibility for childrearing. Some may argue, however, that the price of avoiding speculation and creating incentives is a willingness to accept unfair awards in a certain percentage of cases.

c. RETURN ON INVESTMENT

Another way to value a spouse's contributions is to determine whether they have enhanced the earning power of the other spouse. A marriage in which one spouse works to support both of them and to put the other spouse through school is an example of this scenario. In such cases, the present value of the difference in lifetime earnings made possible by these contributions should be shared between the divorcing spouses. As the *Elkus* case illustrates, this approach need not be confined to the acquisition of a degree, but to any enhancement of earning power. A return on investment approach focuses on compensating the spouse for the gain that she expected from her contributions, rather than the amount that she has expended.

While it may resemble the status principle, the return on investment principle bases compensation not simply on entry into marriage, but on the existence of identifiable contributions that one spouse made to enhance the earning capacity of the other. At the same time, it may produce the same result in many cases, depending on how demanding a causal link is required for recovery.

Determining what is a fair share is a major uncertainty with this approach. How should the contribution by the supporting spouse be compared to the effort of the spouse who works in the job market? Furthermore, how feasible is it to calculate future earnings that are attributable to a degree? If there is no degree involved, how plausible is it to posit that certain career moves during marriage will result in a specific amount of future earnings? Does an award based on this principle effectively prevent the obligated spouse from ever taking a less remunerative job for personal reasons?

5. PARTNERSHIP

In a general sense, the contribution principle rests on a broader principle of marriage as a partnership. As the excerpt from Professor Kelly suggests, however, attempting to identify and quantify spousal contributions may not fully express the partnership ideal. She suggests that this ideal requires that all assets acquired during marriage be divided equally, on the ground that this best reflects widely-held understandings of what marriage involves. In addition, this principle avoids the need to engage in speculative calculations, and values equally the contributions that each spouse makes regardless of the form that they take.

Professor Kelly argues that treating an increase in earning power as an asset acquired during marriage is most faithful to the partnership principle. It is at least analytically possible, however, to distinguish the selection of a distribution principle from the determination of what constitutes a marital asset. Even if enhanced earning power is not treated as an asset, however, the partnership principle may still require some income-sharing through alimony payments for a period of time after divorce.

The partnership principle offers a relatively straightforward approach that probably resonates with many people. For those wary of introducing economic rhetoric into family matters, the principle has the advantage of not highlighting the implicit exchange of resources between spouses that occurs during marriage. If there have been disproportionate sacrifices by one spouse, however, the partnership approach does not attempt to identify and compensate that spouse for them. The framework of economics, as unromantic as it may seem, thus sometimes can be useful because it clarifies when there has been unequal exchange between the partners.

Take note that the five principles often are mutually exclusive. For instance, a woman who was married for only six weeks, but who contacted a disabling disease might be entitled to a fairly large sum of alimony under the need principle, but little under the contribution principle.

Now that we have identified several possible principles on which to base financial awards at divorce, consider the factors that property division and alimony statutes instruct a court to take into account. Under both alternatives of UMDA § 307, for instance, in dividing property the first factor listed is the *contribution of each spouse to acquiring marital property, including the provision of homemaker services*. This factor reflects the contribution principle, but does not specify which approach to contribution the court should take.

The second factor is *the value of each spouse's separate property*. This could lead the judge to rely on any of the principles. The judge might attempt to divide marital property so that combined separate and marital property ensured that each spouse would be able to meet basic needs; that each spouse would be able to approximate the marital standard of living; that the financially dependent spouse received enough to rehabilitate her earning power; that each spouse received compensation for the contributions that he or she made to the acquisition of marital assets; or that all marital property be divided equally, which might or might not include increased earning power.

The third factor, *the duration of the marriage*, seems most relevant under the status principle. As the ALI suggests, the longer the marriage, the fairer it seems that a spouse should not lose the standard of living to which he or she has become accustomed. In addition, a court could treat the length of the marriage as relevant in determining the extent to which a spouse has been compensated for her contributions by enjoying an enhanced marital standard of living.

Finally, directing the court to consider *the economic circumstances of each spouse* appears to direct the judge to focus on relative, rather than absolute, financial condition. This suggests reliance on either the contribution or partnership principle. The contribution principle would attempt to ensure that neither spouse would enjoy an unfair gain or suffer an unfair loss from participation in the marriage. The partnership principle would lead the court to divide property so that the economic circumstances of the spouses were equivalent.

If we turn to the list of factors relevant to alimony, we see the same mixture of principles. UMDA § 308, for instance, conditions alimony on a finding that a spouse *lacks sufficient property to provide for reasonable needs,* and is *unable to support herself through employment* or is the custodian of a child and work outside the home is infeasible. This signals that need is a prerequisite for receipt of alimony, based on a standard of basic necessities.

If this prerequisite is satisfied, the statute lists six factors that a court may consider. The first is *the financial resources of the party seeking* alimony, her *ability to meet her needs independently*, and the extent to which a provision for support of a child living with the party includes *a sum for that party as custodian.*

This factor asks the court to consider just how needy the spouse is. What resources does she have to meet her needs on her own, taking into account those needs that may arise because she has custody of a child? The second factor is the time necessary for the spouse to acquire enough *education or training to obtain appropriate employment*. This factor reflects reliance on the rehabilitation principle. The third factor, *the standard of living during the marriage*, suggests that the judge should rely on the status principle in making an alimony award.

The fourth principle is *the duration of the marriage*. As under the property division statute, this factor is relevant under the status principle, and also may be taken into account under the contribution principle in determining whether a spouse has been compensated during the marriage for his or her contributions. The *age and physical and emotional condition* of the spouse directs attention to need. Finally, the ability of the obligor spouse to meet his needs indicates that any financial awards should be limited to those that do not jeopardize basic necessities for the obligor.

Faced with factors that point to so many different principles, with no guidance on which should have priority, what's a judge to do? Should we be concerned that there seems to be no overarching principle that governs divorce awards? On the one hand, one might argue that justice is not a unitary concept, but requires flexible reliance on multiple considerations. A certain amount of unpredictability is the price we pay for being able to tailor compensation to the circumstances of divorcing spouses. On the other hand, is it really plausible to contend that such a system reflects the rule of law, as opposed to virtually unfettered judicial discretion? Can we at least identify a smaller number of principles on which there is consensus, so as to provide more consistency and predictability? As this section should make clear, that task requires not only that we ask what we want from divorce, but what it means to be married.

E. UNMARRIED PARTNERS

Marvin v. Marvin

Supreme Court of California, 1976.
18 Cal.3d 660, 134 Cal.Rptr. 815, 557 P.2d 106.

■ TOBRINER, JUSTICE.

During the past 15 years, there has been a substantial increase in the number of couples living together without marrying. Such non-marital relationships lead to legal controversy when one partner dies or the couple separates. . . .

. . .

In the instant case plaintiff and defendant lived together for seven years without marrying; all property acquired during this period was taken in defendant's name. When plaintiff sued to enforce a contract under which she was entitled to half the property and to support payments, the trial court granted judgment on the pleadings for defendant, thus leaving him with all property accumulated by the couple during their relationship. . . .

Since the trial court rendered judgment for defendant on the pleadings, we must accept the allegations of plaintiff's complaint as true, determining whether such allegations state, or can be amended to state, a cause of action. . . .

Plaintiff avers that in October of 1964 she and defendant "entered into an oral agreement" that while "the parties lived together they would combine their efforts and earnings and would share equally any and all property accumulated as a result of their efforts whether individual or combined." Furthermore, they agreed to "hold themselves out to the general public as husband and wife" and that "plaintiff would further render her services as a companion, homemaker, housekeeper and cook to . . . defendant."

Shortly thereafter plaintiff agreed to "give up her lucrative career as an entertainer [and] singer" in order to "devote her full time to defendant . . . as a companion, homemaker, housekeeper and cook;" in return defendant agreed to "provide for all of plaintiff's financial support and needs for the rest of her life."

Plaintiff alleges that she lived with defendant from October of 1964 through May of 1970 and fulfilled her obligations under the agreement. During this period the parties as a result of their efforts and earnings acquired in defendant's name substantial real and personal property, including motion picture rights worth over $1 million. In May of 1970, however, defendant compelled plaintiff to leave his household. He continued to support plaintiff until November of 1971, but thereafter refused to provide further support.

. . .

. . . Although that court did not specify the ground for its conclusion that plaintiff's contractual allegations stated no cause of action, defendant offers some four theories. . . .

Defendant first and principally relies on the contention that the alleged contract is so closely related to the supposed "immoral" character of the relationship between plaintiff and himself that the enforcement of the contract would violate public policy. He points to cases asserting that a contract between nonmarital partners is unenforceable if it is "involved in" an illicit relationship. . . . A review of the numerous California decisions concerning contracts between nonmarital partners, however, reveals that the courts have not employed such broad and uncertain standards to strike down contracts. . . .

. . .

Although the past decisions hover over the issue in the somewhat wispy form of the figures of a Chagall painting, we can abstract from those decisions a clear and simple rule. The fact that a man and woman live together without marriage, and engage in a sexual relationship, does not in itself invalidate agreements between them relating to their earnings, property, or expenses. Neither is such an agreement invalid merely because the parties may have contemplated the creation or continuation of a nonmarital relationship when they entered into it. Agreements between nonmarital partners fail only to the extent that they rest upon a consideration of meretricious sexual services. Thus the rule asserted by defendant, that a contract fails if it is "involved in" or made "in contemplation" of a nonmarital relationship, cannot be reconciled with the decisions.

The . . . cases cited by defendant which have *declined* to enforce contracts between nonmarital partners involved consideration that was expressly founded upon an illicit sexual service. In Hill v. Estate of Westbrook, 95 Cal.App.2d 599, 213 P.2d 727, the woman promised to keep house for the man, to live with him as man and wife, and to bear his children; the man promised to provide for her in his will, but died without doing so. Reversing a judgment for the woman based on the reasonable value of her services, the Court of Appeal stated that "the action is predicated upon a claim which seeks, among other things, the reasonable value of living with decedent in meretricious relationship and bearing him two children. . . . The law does not award compensation for living with a man as a concubine and bearing him children. . . . As the judgment is, at least in part, for the value of the claimed services for which recovery cannot be had, it must be reversed." (95 Cal.App.2d at p. 603, 213 P.2d at p. 730.) Upon retrial, the trial court found that it could not sever the contract and place an independent value upon the legitimate services performed by claimant. We therefore affirmed a judgment for the estate.

In the only other cited decision refusing to enforce a contract, Updeck v. Samuel (1954), 123 Cal.App.2d 264, 266 P.2d 822, the contract "was based on the consideration that the parties live together as husband and wife." Viewing the contract as calling for adultery, the court held it illegal. The decisions in the *Hill* and *Updeck* cases thus demonstrate that a contract between nonmarital partners, even if expressly made in contemplation of a common living arrangement, is invalid only if sexual acts form an inseparable part of the consideration for the agreement. In sum, a court will not enforce a contract for the pooling of property and earnings if it is explicitly and inseparably based upon services as a paramour. The Court of Appeal opinion in *Hill*, however, indicates that even if sexual services are part of the contractual consideration, any *severable* portion of the contract supported by independent consideration will still be enforced.

The principle that a contract between nonmarital partners will be enforced unless expressly and inseparably based upon an illicit consideration of sexual services not only represents the distillation of the decisional law, but also offers a far more precise and workable standard than that advocated by the defendant. . . .

Similarly, . . . a standard which inquires whether an agreement is "involved" in or "contemplates" a nonmarital relationship is vague and unworkable. Virtually all agreements between nonmarital partners can be said to be "involved" in some sense in the fact of their mutual sexual relationship, or to "contemplate" the existence of that relationship. Thus defendant's proposed standards, if taken literally, might invalidate all agreements between nonmarital partners, a result no one favors. Moreover, those standards offer no basis to distinguish between valid and invalid agreements. By looking not to such uncertain tests, but only to the consideration underlying the agreement, we provide the parties and the courts with a practical guide to determine when an agreement between nonmarital partners should be enforced.

. . .

In summary, we base our opinion on the principle that adults who voluntarily live together and engage in sexual relations are nonetheless as competent as any other persons to contract respecting their earnings and property rights. Of course, they cannot lawfully contract to pay for the performance of sexual services, for such a contract is, in essence, an agreement for prostitution and unlawful for that reason. But . . . so long as the agreement does not rest upon illicit meretricious consideration, the parties may order their economic affairs as they choose, and no policy precludes the courts from enforcing such agreements.

In the present instance, plaintiff alleges that the parties agreed to pool their earnings, that they contracted to share equally in all property acquired, and that defendant agreed to support plaintiff. The terms of the contract as alleged do not rest upon any unlawful consideration. We therefore conclude that the complaint furnishes a suitable basis upon which the trial court can render declaratory relief. The trial court consequently erred in granting defendant's motion for judgment on the pleadings.

. . .

As we have noted, both causes of action in plaintiff's complaint allege an express contract; neither assert any basis for relief independent from the contract. In In re Marriage of Cary, [34 Cal.App.3d 345, 109 Cal.Rptr. 862 (1973),] however, the Court of Appeal held that, in view of the policy of the Family Law Act, property accumulated by nonmarital partners in an actual family relationship should be divided equally.... Although our conclusion that plaintiff's complaint states a cause of action based on an express contract alone compels us to reverse the judgment for defendant, resolution of the *Cary* issue will serve both to guide the parties upon retrial and to resolve a conflict presently manifest in published Court of appeal decisions.

. . .

... The classic opinion on this subject is Vallera v. Vallera, [21 Cal.2d 681, 134 P.2d 761 (1943)]. Speaking for a four-member majority, Justice Traynor posed the question: "whether a woman living with a man as his wife but with no genuine belief that she is legally married to him acquires by reason of cohabitation alone the rights of a co-tenant in his earnings and accumulations during the period of their relationship." Citing Flanagan v. Capital Nat. Bank (1931) 213 Cal. 664, 3 P.2d 307 which held that a nonmarital "wife" could not claim that her husband's estate was community property, the majority answered that question "in the negative." ...

. . .

Consequently, when the issue of the rights of a nonmarital partner reached this court in Keene v. Keene (1962) 57 Cal.2d 657, 21 Cal.Rptr. 593, 371 P.2d 329, the claimant forwent reliance upon theories of contract implied in law or fact. Asserting that she had worked on her partner's ranch and that her labor had enhanced its value, she confined her cause of action to the claim that the court should impress a resulting trust on the property derived from the sale of the ranch. The court limited its opinion accordingly, rejecting her argument on the ground that the rendition of services gives rise to a resulting trust only when the services aid in acquisition of the property, not in its subsequent improvement. ...

This failure of the courts to recognize an action by a nonmarital partner based upon implied contract, or to grant an equitable remedy, contrasts with the judicial treatment of the putative spouse. Prior to the enactment of the Family Law Act, no statute granted rights to a putative spouse. The courts accordingly fashioned a variety of remedies by judicial decision. Some cases permitted the putative spouse to recover half the property on a theory that the conduct of the parties implied an agreement of partnership or joint venture. Others permitted the spouse to recover the reasonable value of rendered services, less the value of support received. Finally, decisions affirmed the power of a court to employ equitable principles to achieve a fair division of property acquired during putative marriage.

Thus in summary, the cases prior to Cary exhibited a schizophrenic inconsistency. By enforcing an express contract between nonmarital partners unless it rested upon an unlawful consideration, the courts applied a common law principle as to contracts. Yet the courts disregarded the common law principle that holds that implied contracts can arise from the conduct of the parties.

. . .

Justice Curtis noted this inconsistency in his dissenting opinion in Vallera, pointing out that "if an express agreement will be enforced, there is no legal or just reason why an implied agreement to share the property cannot be enforced." . . .

Still another inconsistency in the prior cases arises from their treatment of property accumulated through joint effort. To the extent that a partner has contributed *funds* or *property,* the cases held that the partner obtains a proportionate share in the acquisition, despite the lack of legal standing of the relationship. Yet courts have refused to recognize just such an interest based upon the contribution of *services.* As Justice Curtis points out "Unless it can be argued that a woman's services as cook, housekeeper, and homemaker are valueless, it would seem logical that if, when she contributes money to the purchase of property, her interest will be protected, then when she contributes her services in the home, her interest in property accumulated should be protected."

Thus as of 1973, the time of filing of In re Marriage of Cary, the cases apparently held that a nonmarital partner who rendered services in the absence of express contract could assert no right to property acquired during the relationship. The facts of *Cary* demonstrated the unfairness of that rule.

Janet and Paul Cary had lived together, unmarried, for more than eight years. They held themselves out to friends and family as husband and wife, reared four children, purchased a home and other property, obtained credit, filed joint income tax returns, and otherwise conducted themselves as though they were married. Paul worked outside the home, and Janet generally cared for the house and children.

In 1971 Paul petitioned for "nullity of the marriage." Following a hearing on that petition, the trial court awarded Janet half the property acquired during the relationship, although all such property was traceable to Paul's earnings. The Court of Appeal affirmed the award.

. . .

If *Cary* is interpreted as holding that the Family Law Act requires an equal division of property accumulated in nonmarital "actual family relationships," then we agree . . . that *Cary* distends the act. No language in the Family Law Act addresses the property rights of nonmarital partners, and nothing in the legislative history of the act suggests that the Legislature considered that subject. The delineation of the rights of nonmarital partners before 1970 had been fixed entirely by judicial decision; we see no reason to believe that the Legislature, by enacting the Family Law Act, intended to change that state of affairs.

But although we reject the reasoning of *Cary* . . . we share the perception . . . that the application of former precedent in the factual setting of those cases would work an unfair distribution of the property accumulated by the couple.

. . .

The principal reason why the pre-*Cary* decisions result in an unfair distribution of property inheres in the court's refusal to permit a nonmarital partner to assert rights based upon accepted principles of implied contract or equity. We have examined the reasons advanced to justify this denial of relief, and find that none have merit.

First, we note that the cases denying relief do not rest their refusal upon any theory of "punishing" a "guilty" partner. Indeed, to the extent that denial of relief "punishes" one partner, it necessarily rewards the other by permitting him to retain a disproportionate amount of the property. Concepts of "guilt" thus cannot justify an unequal division of property between two equally "guilty" persons.

Other reasons advanced in the decisions fare no better. The principal argument seems to be that "[e]quitable considerations arising from the reasonable expectation of . . . benefits attending the statute of marriage . . . are not present [in a nonmarital relationship]." But, although parties to a nonmarital relationship obviously cannot have based any expectations upon the belief that they were married, other expectations and equitable considerations remain. The parties may well expect that property will be divided in accord with the parties' own tacit understanding and that in the absence of such understanding the courts will fairly apportion property accumulated through mutual effort. We need not treat nonmarital partners as putatively married persons in order to apply principles of implied contract, or extend equitable remedies; we need to treat them only as we do any other unmarried persons.

The remaining arguments advanced from time to time to deny remedies to the nonmarital partners are of less moment. There is no more reason to presume that services are contributed as a gift than to presume that funds are contributed as a gift; in any event the better approach is to presume, as Justice Peters suggested, "that the parties intend to deal fairly with each other."

The argument that granting remedies to the nonmarital partners would discourage marriage must fail; as *Cary* pointed out, "with equal or greater force the point might be made that the pre–1970 rule was calculated to cause the income producing partner to avoid marriage and thus retain the benefit of all of his or her accumulated earnings." Although we recognize the well-established public policy to foster and promote the institution of marriage, perpetuation of judicial rules which result in an inequitable distribution of property accumulated during a nonmarital relationship is neither a just nor an effective way of carrying out that policy.

In summary, we believe that the prevalence of nonmarital relationships in modern society and the social acceptance of them, marks this as a time when our courts should by no means apply the doctrine of the unlawfulness of the so-called meretricious relationship to the instant case. As we have explained, the nonenforceability of agreements expressly providing for meretricious conduct rested upon the fact that such conduct, as the word suggests, pertained to and encompassed prostitution. To equate the nonmarital relationship of today to such a subject matter is to do violence to an accepted and wholly different practice.

We are aware that many young couples live together without the solemnization of marriage, in order to make sure that they can successfully later undertake marriage. This trial period, preliminary to marriage, serves as some assurance that the marriage will not subsequently end in dissolution to the harm of both parties. We are aware, as we have stated, of the pervasiveness of nonmarital relationships in other situations.

The mores of the society have indeed changed so radically in regard to cohabitation that we cannot impose a standard based on alleged moral considerations that have apparently been so widely abandoned by so many. Lest we be misunderstood, however, we take this occasion to point out that the structure of society itself largely depends upon the institution of marriage, and nothing we have said in this opinion should be taken to derogate from that institution. The joining of the man and woman in marriage is at once the most socially productive and individually fulfilling relationship that one can enjoy in the course of a lifetime.

We conclude that the judicial barriers that may stand in the way of a policy based upon the fulfillment of the reasonable expectations of the parties to a nonmarital relationship should be removed. As we have explained, the courts now hold that express agreements will be enforced unless they rest on an unlawful meretricious consideration. We add that in the absence of an express agreement, the courts may look to a variety of other remedies in order to protect the parties' lawful expectations.[24]

The courts may inquire into the conduct of the parties to determine whether that conduct demonstrates an implied contract or implied agreement of partnership or joint venture or some other tacit understanding between the parties. The courts may, when appropriate, employ principles of constructive trust or resulting trust. Finally, a nonmarital partner may recover in quantum meruit for the reasonable value of household services rendered less the reasonable value of support received if he can show that he rendered services with the expectation of monetary reward.

Since we have determined that plaintiff's complaint states a cause of action for breach of an express contract, and, as we have explained, can be amended to state a cause of action independent of allegations of express contract,[26] we must conclude that the trial court erred in granting defendant a judgment on the pleadings.

The judgment is reversed and the cause remanded for further proceedings consistent with the views expressed herein.

NOTES

1. On remand, plaintiff Michelle Marvin was awarded $104,000 for "her economic rehabilitation." This award was reversed on appeal, Marvin v. Marvin, 122 Cal. App.3d 871, 176 Cal.Rptr. 555 (2d Dist.1981), on the grounds that:

24. We do not seek to resurrect the doctrine of common law marriage, which was abolished in California by statute in 1895. Thus we do not hold that plaintiff and defendant were "married," nor do we extend to plaintiff the rights which the Family Law Act grants valid or putative spouses; we hold only that she has the same rights to enforce contracts and to assert her equitable interest in property acquired through her effort as does any other unmarried person.

26. We do not pass upon the question whether, in the absence of an express or implied contractual obligation, a party to a nonmarital relationship is entitled to support payments from the other party after the relationship terminates.

> the trial court . . . expressly found that defendant never had any obligation to pay plaintiff . . . for her maintenance and that the defendant had not been unjustly enriched by reason of the relationship or its termination. . . . Id. at 876, 176 Cal.Rptr. at 558.

2. Compare David Chambers, The "Legalization" of the Family: Toward a Policy of Supportive Neutrality, 18 Mich. J. L. Reform 805, 826 (1985):

> [T]he California court would have been wiser to have fashioned a less expansive rule. It should have announced that, in cases of disputes between unmarried partners who are separating, courts are to honor express agreements if, but only if, they are in writing and that courts are neither to recognize implied contracts nor to create new equitable remedies. I regret that such a rule would prevent courts from giving relief to persons who make serious oral agreements and rely on them, and to persons, usually women, who have no formal agreement but who work for many years raising children, accumulate no assets in their own name, and come to regard themselves as in the same position as a married person. Despite this, a rule limiting judicial relief to written agreements would have the virtue of curtailing courts' opportunities to reframe the terms of private relationships and would reduce the number of acrimonious family disputes aired in public. . . .

with Harry Prince, Public Policy Limitations on Cohabitation Agreements: Unruly Horse or Circus Pony?, 70 Minn.L.Rev. 163, 207–208 (1985):

> [C]ohabitants should be allowed to prove an implied-in-fact agreement. Although it can hardly be doubted that cohabitants do not expect a weekly paycheck for their homemaking services, it is equally obvious that the parties do not expect the party contributing such services to derive nothing from their efforts. Some benefit or consideration, other than emotional satisfaction, is almost certainly contemplated by both parties in return for the pooling of their resources and concentration of their efforts. There may be, of course, some instances when both parties understand that a rendered service is gratuitous, but the cohabitants should at least have the opportunity to prove the contrary.

3. Under Marvin, support agreements between cohabitants are enforceable. Moreover, such support agreements are enforceable against an estate when one of the parties to the agreement dies. In Byrne v. Laura, 52 Cal.App.4th 1054, 60 Cal. Rptr.2d 908 (1997), the plaintiff sued the estate of the man with whom she had cohabited. On behalf of the estate, the administratrix contended that the alleged Marvin agreement between the plaintiff and the deceased man was void for uncertainty and thus was unenforceable. Relying primarily on the abundant testimony to the contrary of the plaintiff and of neighbors sympathetic to the plaintiff, the court disagreed.

Norton v. Hoyt

U.S. District Court for the District of Rhode Island, 2003.
278 F.Supp.2d 214.

■ LAGUEU J.

This matter is before the Court on Defendant's Motion for Summary Judgment. . . . The disputed claims arise out of an adulterous twenty-three year relationship between Plaintiff and Defendant, during which time Defendant allegedly maintained that he would terminate his marriage, marry Plaintiff, and support her for the rest of her life. After close examination of the record and existing case law, this Court concludes that Defendant's Motion for Summary Judgment should be granted.

. . . On or about July 24, 1974, Plaintiff Gail M. Norton ("Norton" or "Plaintiff"), a Rhode Island resident, met Defendant Russell L. Hoyt ("Hoyt" or "Defendant"), a Connecticut resident, through mutual acquaintances. At that time Hoyt represented to Norton that he was divorced; in reality he was (and still is) married. Believing Hoyt was single, Norton initiated a relationship with him. Shortly thereafter, when it became apparent to Norton that he actually was married, Hoyt told Norton that he was getting a divorce. Moreover, on or about January 5, 1975, Hoyt told Norton that he had moved out of the marital residence, leading her to believe once again that he was getting a divorce. However, Hoyt was not in the process of getting a divorce when he made these statements to Norton. Because of those alleged continuing misrepresentations over many years, Norton continued to maintain a relationship with Hoyt, which lasted for twenty-three years in all.

When the pair began dating Norton was employed as an elementary school teacher in the Bristol, Rhode Island school system, a position she held for a number of years. Allegedly in reliance upon Hoyt's repeated promises to divorce his wife and marry her, Norton resigned that position in 1980. Norton asserts that at Hoyt's insistence and in reliance on his promises, she resigned in order to be available to travel with him around the world.

The couple maintained a lavish lifestyle. Hoyt was part of the Newport, Rhode Island yachting crowd. Several times a year, they traveled together to destinations such as the Bahamas, London, and Block Island. In addition to bearing all travel and entertainment expenses, Hoyt provided Norton with material benefits and financial support. Specifically, Hoyt would pay rent on an apartment that they shared in Vermont, buy and maintain her automobiles, and make payments toward the maintenance of a condominium they shared in Newport. Periodically, the couple would also discuss plans for their contemplated wedding. According to Norton, but for Hoyt's oft-repeated promises to divorce his wife, marry Norton, and support her for the rest of her life, she would have ended the relationship.

Alas, in life, all good things must come to an end and on or about March 11, 1998, Hoyt ended his relationship with Norton, explaining that he "needed space." Norton was understandably shaken by the news. Not long after, she reported experiencing nervousness and anxiety, frequently crying, feeling depressed and vulnerable, being unable to stay home alone, and having suicidal thoughts. Additionally, Norton reported "not being able to resume work and possibly not being able to commit to another relationship, perhaps ever." Head and stomach aches, vomiting and weight loss also allegedly ensued.

Norton sought medical attention to help her deal with the maladies allegedly occasioned by the split with Hoyt. . . . Hoyt did provide financial support for two years after the break-up in an amount in excess of $80,000.00.

Norton avers that at the time of the break-up Hoyt also promised her that he was going to put $100,000.00 in her bank account and set up a trust that would take care of her for life. Allegedly, Hoyt told Norton that, in order to protect her interests, and to fulfill these promises, he had written a letter to an attorney, David McOsker, evidencing his intentions. Several months after the split, Hoyt allegedly reaffirmed his promise to support Norton and assured her that he would not renege on it, stating, "I know my responsibilities." Subsequently, Norton contacted attorney McOsker and discovered that the letter never existed.

Nearly four months after the break-up, Norton, in a letter to attorney Matthew Callaghan, expressed a desire to reconcile with Hoyt. However, on March 3, 2001, realizing that reconciliation was not a viable option, Norton did the next best thing: she sued him. . . . Remaining for disposition [is, *inter* alia,] the promissory estoppel claim contained in Count I. [This] claim [is] the subject of Defendant's Motion for Summary Judgment.

. . .

IV. Promissory Estoppel

In Rhode Island, a promissory estoppel claim requires: "1) A clear and unambiguous promise; 2) Reasonable and justifiable reliance upon the promise; and 3) Detriment to the promisee, caused by his or her reliance on the promise."

Norton avers that she relied to her detriment upon Hoyt's promise to divorce his wife, marry Norton and provide lifetime support to Norton. Alternatively, she frames the promise by Hoyt as one to provide lifetime support to her regardless of whether he divorced his wife or not. At oral argument Plaintiff's counsel represented that the latter promise, that Hoyt would take care of Norton for life, was the one on which she was basing her claim.

A. Clear and Unambiguous Promise

. . . Even viewed most favorably to the Plaintiff, the record fails to reveal a clear, unconditional, and unambiguous promise. . . . [A]t the hearing on this motion, counsel argued that Hoyt had simply promised to take care of Norton for life. However, there can be many interpretations of the phrase, "take care of for life." It could refer to care in a social, emotional, or financial context. As other courts have recognized, this is certainly not a clear and unambiguous promise. . . .

By belatedly couching Hoyt's promise as one simply to take care of her for life, Norton actually undermines her claim, because she has represented in her answers to Defendant's Interrogatories that she would not have remained in the relationship if he had not promised to get divorced. Thus, any reliance on her part is definitively linked to Hoyt's promise to marry her, not simply the promise that Hoyt would support her for life. Thereby, she interwines Hoyt's marital status back into the alleged promise.

B. Reasonable and Justifiable Reliance

Even assuming, arguendo, that there was a clear and unambiguous promise, Norton's reliance upon that promise was unreasonable. Though the couple had discussions about their life together and even discussed potential wedding plans, Plaintiff knew that Hoyt was married, and that he spent time at the marital domicile with his wife and children. Norton and Hoyt never openly associated as husband and wife, their friends and family knew that they were not married and they did not exclusively cohabitate. Furthermore, Norton knew that Hoyt had lied in the past, was in an adulterous relationship, and apparently had made little effort to fulfill the terms of the promise. Whatever detriment she suffered occurred with full knowledge that she was relying upon an adulterer; the law will not insure the decision to repose her confidence there. Reliance upon an unclear and ambiguous promise made by an apparently unreliable man was imprudent.

C. Detrimental Reliance

. . . Norton claims that she, in reliance on Hoyt's promises and, in fact, at his insistence, left gainful employment as a school teacher. She also claims that she gave up the opportunity to marry and have children at a younger age, and did not attempt to achieve her own financial security. Once again, however, Norton has stated that she remained in the relationship based solely upon Hoyt's promise to get a divorce. It is not clear that she relied to her detriment based on a promise for lifetime support. Any detrimental reliance flowed from the promise to remain together.

In any event, whatever form her reliance took, it is insufficient to overcome the other fatal flaws in her claim. Any promise for support that Hoyt made prior to the March 11, 1998 break-up is ambiguous at best, and, considering the source, was not a reasonable basis upon which to ground reliance. Sometime between year one and year twenty-three of the affair, it should have become clear to Norton that her reliance on Hoyt's promise to divorce his wife and marry her was misplaced

... The doctrine of estoppel "... has no application to a contract or instrument which is void because it violates an express mandate of the law or the dictates of public policy." The public policy in favor of marriage militates against recognizing support claims arising from adulterous relationships. "The institution of marriage is so firmly established in the mores of Anglo-American society [that] agreements believed to be, 'in derogation of marriage' are held to be against public welfare and illegal." 15 Arthur Linton Corbin, Corbin on Contracts, § 1474 at 537 (1962). Therefore, an agreement in furtherance of facilitating divorce proceedings is illegal and contrary to public policy....

Moreover, permitting a promissory estoppel claim based on a promise by Hoyt to divorce his wife, marry Norton and provide her with lifetime support would amount to re-instituting the breach of promise to marry claim that has already been dismissed....

Here, Norton is essentially clothing a palimony claim in other robes. Rhode Island, however, has not recognized palimony as a cause of action and the Rhode Island Supreme Court has shown no inclination to do so ... Norton is seeking enforcement of a promise for future support payments: in a word, palimony. There was no property sharing agreement between Norton and Hoyt; no express agreement of any kind, merely an alleged, ambiguous promise to provide support.

Conclusion

For the foregoing reasons, the Court hereby grants Defendant's Motion for Summary Judgment....

American Law Institute, Principles of the Law of Family Dissolution

Section 6.03. Determination That Persons Are Domestic Partners

(1) For the purpose of defining relationships to which this Chapter applies, domestic partners are two persons of the same or opposite sex, not married to one another, who for a significant period of time share a primary residence and a life together as a couple.

(2) Persons are domestic partners when they have maintained a common household, as defined in Paragraph (4), with their common child, as defined in Paragraph (5), for a continuous period that equals or exceeds a duration, called the cohabitation parenting period, set in a rule of statewide application.

(3) Persons not related by blood or adoption are presumed to be domestic partners when they have maintained a common household, as defined in Paragraph (4), for a continuous period that equals or exceeds a duration, called the cohabitation period, set in a rule of statewide application. The presumption is rebuttable by evidence that the parties did not share life together as a couple, as defined by Paragraph (7).

(4) Persons maintain a common household when they share a primary residence only with each other and family members; or when, if they share a household with other unrelated persons, they act jointly, rather than as individuals, with respect to management of the household.

(5) Persons have a common child when each is either the child's legal parent or parent by estoppel. . . .

. . .

(7) Whether persons share a life together as a couple is determined by reference to all the circumstances, including:

(a) the oral or written statements or promises made to one another, or representations jointly made to third parties, regarding their relationship;

(b) the extent to which the parties intermingled their finances;

(c) the extent to which their relationship fostered the parties' economic interdependence, or the economic dependence of one party upon the other;

(d) the extent to which the parties engaged in conduct and assumed specialized or collaborative roles in furtherance of their life together;

(e) the extent to which the relationship wrought change in the life of either or both parties;

(f) the extent to which the parties acknowledged responsibilities to each other, as by naming the other the beneficiary of life insurance or of a testamentary instrument, or as eligible to receive benefits under an employee-benefit plan;

(g) the extent to which the parties' relationship was treated by the parties as qualitatively distinct from the relationship either party had with any other person;

(h) the emotional or physical intimacy of the parties' relationship;

(i) the parties' community reputation as a couple;

(j) the parties' participation in a commitment ceremony or registration as a domestic partnership;

(k) the parties' participation in a void or voidable marriage that, under applicable law, does not give rise to the economic incidents of marriage;

(*l*) the parties' procreation of, adoption of, or joint assumption of parental functions toward a child;

(m) the parties' maintenance of a common household, as defined by Paragraph (4).

COMMENTS

. . .

b. This section's relationship to existing law. In the United States, courts generally rely on contract law when they conclude that cohabiting parties may acquire financial obligations to one another that survive their relationship. The great majority of jurisdictions recognize express contracts, and only a handful of them require that the contract be written rather than oral. Jurisdictions split on whether to recognize implied contracts. Those that do recognize implied contracts differ in their inclination to infer contractual undertakings from any given set of facts. Some courts reach much further than others. In doing so, they appear to vindicate an equitable rather than a contractual principle. That is, having concluded that a particular set of facts demands a remedy, they may stretch ordinary contract principles to fit the remedy within a contractual rubric. This result is not surprising. Parties may share their lives for many years without having any clear agreement, express or implied, that sets out the financial consequences of terminating their relationship. To find such an agreement may therefore require filling many gaps with terms that flow more from the court's sense of fairness than from any mutual intentions inferable from the parties' conduct.

This section approaches the matter in a more straightforward manner. It identifies the circumstances that would typically lead such a court to find a contract, and defines those circumstances as giving rise to a domestic partnership. Remedies then follow unless the parties have made an enforceable contract to the contrary. In formulating a rubric combining expansive notions of contract with equitable remedies, one court observed that it is appropriate in these cases to presume "that the parties intend to deal fairly with each other." This suggests that, as in marriage, in the ordinary case the law should provide remedies at the dissolution of a domestic partnership that will ensure an equitable allocation of accumulated property and of the financial losses arising from the termination of the relationship. The result, in comparison with a narrow contract approach, is a system that places the burden of showing a contract on the party wishing to avoid such fairness-based remedies, rather than imposing it on the party seeking to claim them.

This section thus does not require, as a predicate to finding the existence of a domestic partnership, that the parties had an implied or express agreement, or even that the facts meet the standard requirements of a quantum meruit claim. It instead relies, as do the marriage laws, on a status classification: property claims and support obligations presumptively arise between persons who qualify as domestic partners, as they do between legal spouses, without inquiry into each couple's particular arrangement, except as the presumption is itself overcome by contract. This approach reflects a judgment that it is usually just to apply to both groups the property and support rules applicable to divorcing spouses, that individualized inquiries are usually impractical or unduly burdensome, and that it therefore makes more sense to require parties to contract out of these property and support rules than to contract into them. This approach, of course, demands careful attention to the factors required to establish a couple's status as domestic partners.

. . .

Section 6.06. Compensatory Payments

(1) Except as otherwise provided in this section,

(a) a domestic partner is entitled to compensatory payments on the same basis as a spouse under Chapter 5, and

(b) wherever a rule implementing a Chapter 5 principle makes the duration of the marriage a relevant factor, the application of that principle in this Chapter should instead employ the duration of the domestic-partnership period. . . .

(2) No claim arises under this section against a domestic partner who is neither a legal parent nor a parent by estoppel . . . of a child whose care provides the basis of the claim.

COMMENTS

. . .

b. Limitations on claims under this section. Paragraph (2) does not extend the application of 5.05 to claims by a domestic partner based upon the care of a child who is not a child of the other partner. By contrast, section 5.05 does permit claims by a married person for the care of a child who is not also the child of the other spouse, so long as the spouses shared a residence with each other and the child during the relevant child-care period. The rationale for recognizing this claim in the context of marriage depends in part upon the law's recognition of a stepparent's duty to support a child living with him during his marriage to the parent. There is no similar child-support duty for a person who lives in a nonmarital relationship with a child and that child's parent.

F. CHILD SUPPORT

1. STANDARDS

The federal government shapes state child support programs through conditions placed on its payments to states under the Aid to Families with Dependent Children program. The 1984 Child Support Amendments required states as a condition of receiving AFDC assistance to establish numerical guidelines on which to rely in determining child support obligations. These guidelines were to be advisory, rather than binding. Four years later, the 1988 Family Support Act required that the guidelines serve as rebuttable presumptions of the appropriate amount of child support. Judges may deviate from the guidelines only upon a written finding that applying them would be inequitable.

The Advisory Panel on Child Support Guidelines of the U.S. Office of Child Support Enforcement has recommended that states follow eight general principles in developing their guidelines:

(1) Both parents share legal responsibility for supporting their children. The economic responsibility should be divided in proportion to their available income.

(2) The subsistence needs of each parent should be taken into account in setting child support, but in virtually no event should the child support obligation be set at zero.

(3) Child support must cover a child's basic needs as a first priority, but, to the extent either parent enjoys a higher than subsistence level standard of living, the child is entitled to share the benefit of that improved standard.

(4) Each child of a given parent has an equal right to share in that parent's income, subject to factors such as age of the child, income of each parent, income of current spouses, and the presence of other dependents.

(5) Each child is entitled to determination of support without respect to the marital status of the parents at the time of the child's birth. Consequently, any guideline should be equally applicable to determining child support related to paternity determinations, separations, and divorces.

(6) Application of a guideline should be sexually non-discriminatory. Specifically, it should be applied without regard to the gender of the custodial parent.

(7) A guideline should not create extraneous negative effects on the major life decisions of either parent. In particular, the guideline should avoid creating economic disincentives for remarriage or labor force participation.

(8) A guideline should encourage the involvement of both parents in the child's upbringing. It should take into account the financial support provided directly by parents in shared physical custody or extended visitation arrangements, recognizing that even a fifty percent sharing of physical custody does not necessarily obviate the child support obligation.

U.S. Department of Health and Human Services, Office of Child Support Enforcement, Development of Guidelines for Child Support Orders 1–4 (1987). In addition, the panel endorsed either of two approaches to guidelines: (1) the Income Shares Model, which is based on the principle that the child should receive the same proportion of parental income that he or she would have received if the parents lived together; and (2) the Delaware Melson Formula, developed by Judge Elwood Melson, Jr., of Delaware.

Under the Income Shares Model, a basic child support obligation is computed based on the combined income of the parents (replicating total income in an intact household). This basic obligation is then pro-rated in proportion to each parent's income. Pro-rated shares of child care and extraordinary medical expenses are added to each parent's basic obligation.

The Melson Formula defines levels of basic, or subsistence, needs for parents and children. It provides that parents are entitled to support themselves at a basic level before having the formula applied. This reserve is usually set at $450 per month (less if living with others). Any additional income beyond the basic level for parents must be applied first in the form of child support to meet any of the child's basic needs, including child care costs and extraordinary medical expenses. The usual amount is $180 for the first child, $135 per month for each of the second and third, and $90 per month for each of the fourth, fifth and sixth. When income is sufficient to cover the basic needs of the parents and all dependents, a portion of remaining parental income is allocated to additional child support (15 percent for the first child, 10 percent for each of the second and third, 5 percent for the fourth, fifth, and sixth).

Both formulas can be adjusted to account for joint and split custody, or for obligations to dependents living with the obligor.

Although no two states have identical systems, every state has now adopted child support guidelines. As of November 2004, 33 states[10] used the

10. Alabama, Arizona, California, Colorado, Connecticut, Florida, Idaho, Indiana, Kansas, Kentucky, Louisiana, Maine, Maryland, Michigan, Missouri, Nebraska, New Jer-

Income Shares model to calculate child support guidelines. American Bar Association Section of Family Law, *Tables Summarizing the Law in the Fifty States*, http://www.abanet.org/family/familylaw/tables.html; ALA. R. JUD. ADMIN. 32. The next most favored approach was the "percentage of income" model which bases payments on a percentage of the nonresident parent's income only. This model was used by 15 jurisdictions.[11] American Bar Association Section of Family Law, *supra*.

The Melson Formula, often considered the most sophisticated model, was used by Delaware, Hawaii, and Montana. Jo Michelle Beld & Len Biernat, *Federal Intent for State Child Support Guidelines: Income Shares, Cost Shares, and the Realities of Shared Parenting*, 37 FAM. L.Q. 165, 167 n.18 (2003). For discussion of the pitfalls and advantages of various child support models see Andrea H. Beller & John W. Graham, Child Support and Children's Poverty—A Review of Small Change: the Economics of Child Support (1993); Charlotte L. Allen, Federalization of Child Support: Twenty Years and Counting, 73 Mich.B.J. 660 (1994); J. Thomas Oldham, The Appropriate Child Support Award When the Noncustodial Parent Earns Less Than the Custodial Parent, 31 Hous.L.Rev. (1994).

Uniform Marriage and Divorce Act

Section 309. Child Support

In a proceeding for dissolution of marriage, legal separation, maintenance, or child support, the court may order either or both parents owing a duty of support to a child to pay an amount reasonable or necessary for his support, without regard to marital misconduct, after considering all relevant factors including:

(1) the financial resources of the child;

(2) the financial resources of the custodial parent;

(3) the standard of living the child would have enjoyed had the marriage not been dissolved;

(4) the physical and emotional condition of the child and his educational needs; and

(5) the financial resources and needs of the noncustodial parent.

Schmidt v. Schmidt

Supreme Court of South Dakota, 1989.
444 N.W.2d 367.

■ SABERS, JUSTICE.

Mother appeals a change in custody of the eldest of three boys to Father. Father appeals the requirement that he pay $250 monthly child support for two boys.

sey, New Mexico, New York, North Carolina, Ohio, Oklahoma, Oregon, Pennsylvania, Rhode Island, South Carolina, South Dakota, Utah, Vermont, Virginia, Washington, West Virginia, and Wyoming.

11. Alaska, Arkansas, District of Columbia, Georgia, Illinois, Iowa, Massachusetts, Minnesota, Mississippi, Nevada, New Hampshire, North Dakota, Tennessee, Texas, and Wisconsin.

Father and Mother were divorced on July 13, 1984. They had three children during the marriage; David, Randy, and Michael. By stipulation, Father and Mother agreed that Mother would receive custody of the three boys. Custody was not contested at the divorce hearing, and Father appeared without counsel. Mother presented evidence in the form of testimony and exhibits. The trial court awarded custody of the three boys to Mother. As provided in the stipulation, Father was ordered to pay $375 monthly child support.

Following the divorce, Father continued to farm near Flandreau, South Dakota. Mother lived in Brookings, South Dakota, where she worked at Minnesota Mining & Manufacturing (3M). On June 3, 1988, Father made a motion to modify the child custody and support provisions in the divorce decree. Father requested custody of the oldest, David, and that all three boys be permitted to reside with him during the summer months. The motion further requested that child support obligations be modified accordingly. A hearing was held on the motion on July 25, 1988.

David was fourteen at the time of the hearing. Father introduced evidence showing that David enjoyed the farm and preferred to live with Father. On the farm, David did chores and repair work on an old car. According to Father's testimony, Randy, age eleven, and Michael, age nine, also enjoyed the farm.

. . .

On September 12, 1988, the trial court amended the original divorce decree and gave Father custody of David. The decree was also modified to permit all three boys to live with Father during the summer months, with the exception of three weeks when all three would be with Mother. Father's monthly child support was reduced to $250 and reduced further to $125 during the summer months when all three boys stay with Father. Mother appeals the custody change and denial of attorney fees. Father appeals the amount of child support. We affirm the change of custody and denial of attorney fees and reverse and remand on child support.

. . .

After granting Father custody of David, the court modified Father's monthly child support obligation. The court determined Father's child support under the guidelines in SDCL 25-7-7 by cancelling out one child with each parent, leaving Mother with an additional child. The court then considered Father's child support for one child under the guidelines. Father's net monthly income at the time of the hearing was $1,250. Accordingly, the court set Father's monthly child support at $250. Father claims this was error. He claims that the court should have compared the amount of child support Father would pay for two children under the guidelines against the amount of child support Mother would pay for one child and subtract the difference to determine Father's support.

We agree with Father in part. SDCL 25-7-7 provides that "The child support obligation shall be established in accordance with the obligor's net income and number of children affected[.]" Following the change of custody, Father was obligated to pay support for two children based on his net monthly income of $1,250. Mother was obligated to pay support for one child based on her net monthly income of $1,582. Since Mother's net monthly income exceeded Father's, her child support obligation for one nearly cancels out Father's child support obligation for two under the guidelines.[12] Mother argues that such a formula may lead to absurd results.[13] However, SDCL 25–7–7 does not permit deviation from the guidelines absent specific findings. Thus, the trial court erred in its calculation of child support. We reverse and remand for the trial court to reconsider child support in accordance with this opinion. We note, however, this may provide inadequate support for the boys. Father's farm occupation provides certain necessities, such as housing, utilities, transportation, etc. which would otherwise be personal expenses. On remand, the trial court may look to the record and make additional specific findings which may support deviations from the child support guidelines and provide adequate support.

Affirmed in part, reversed and remanded in part.

. . .

■ HENDERSON, JUSTICE (concurring in result in part, dissenting in part).

On the change of custody issue, I concur in the result. . . .

As one peruses and ponders upon the majority's child support dissertation, one fancies a trip with Alice through Wonderland. Wonderland is the world of child support, resulting from this State's charting a course, thrusting rigidity upon trial courts, in an effort to follow the United States Congress, which required no such mandated rigidity. The rigidity of the guidelines turns logic on its head.

In the past I have sought, through numerous writings, to academically advance that judges cannot decide child support by formulas and tables. When tables are used, judgment flees. As I have written in the past, judges are not "schedule-automatons." Peterson v. Peterson, 434 N.W.2d 732, 739–741 (S.D.1989) (Henderson, J., concurring in part, concurring in result in part). In my previous writings, I have argued that the abuse of discretion test is not only the primary but solid scope of review test—not whether the guidelines have or have not been followed in the particular set of facts before the trial judge. We are substituting, with these guidelines and decisions thereunder, at least to date, something of inferior value. If we in the law are substituting a new concept, it should be something of greater value. We should continue to consider the needs of the child, the ability to pay by the parent, and, essentially, the trial judge's abuse or non-abuse of his discretion in setting child support. In doing so, we, in the judiciary, retain our independence; we also vault a known, Equity, forged through the centuries in jurisprudence, over an unknown substitute of legislative dogmatism.

. . .

Presently, the states are in fear so the guidelines are born. In time, this mechanical jurisprudence shall disappear because of its despisement by those

12. Under the guidelines, Father's obligation for two children with his net monthly income of $1,250 would be between $360 to $390 monthly. Mother's obligation for one child with her net monthly income of $1,582 would be at least $330 monthly. Subtracting the difference, Father would owe child support of approximately $30 to $60 monthly.

13. Assume a mother with custody of five children and a net monthly income of $1,500, and father with a net monthly income of $1,000. Father would pay approximately $350 per month child support to the mother under the guidelines. However, if the father were to gain custody of one child he would no longer pay any child support for the four children in mother's custody. In fact, the mother would be required to pay $20 per month for support of the one child in the father's custody. While such a result appears inequitable, such a result *is* required under the current guidelines in the absence of specific findings supporting deviations. In this context, it is important to note that the guidelines in SDCL 25–7–7 have been replaced with new guidelines effective July 1, 1989.

who are called upon to administer them. A bond, now established to create these guidelines, is created by a chain of governmental obligation. Fear is the cement which holds the chain unbroken. Unquestionably, many prisoners of this chain will be held captive until reason and courage overcome fear and fad.

... [T]he federal Child Support Enforcement Amendments of 1984 (Pub.L. No. 98–378) required States to establish guidelines, but Congress provided that the guidelines "need not be binding upon such judges or other officials." 42 U.S.C. § 667(b). On October 13, 1988, Congress changed its mandate by deleting the quoted wording and substituted the following:

> There shall be a rebuttable presumption, in any judicial or administrative proceeding for the award of child support, that the amount of the award which would result from the guidelines is the correct amount of child support to be awarded. A written finding or specific finding on the record that the application of the guidelines would be unjust or inappropriate in a particular case as determined under criteria established by the State, shall be sufficient to rebut the presumption in that case.

Pub.L. 100–485, Title I, Subtitle A, § 103, 102 Stat. 2346 (1988) (effective October 13, 1989). Deviation from the guidelines, where their application is unjust, is apt, as trial courts in these cases are sitting in equity. Do we see some sunshine of common sense beginning to evolve?

The 1989 State Legislature, in extensively revising SDCL ch. 25–7, has now provided, effective July 1, 1989, that deviation from that chapter's guidelines may be made, *inter alia,* for "any financial condition of either parent which would make application of the schedule inequitable." The way appears open, under the new law, for any trial court of this State to return to adjudication of child support issues based "on the realities of the domestic situation before it" as in State ex rel. Larsgaard v. Larsgaard, 298 N.W.2d 381, 384 (S.D.1980). May the sunshine illuminate the Lady of Equity.

Under the rules of equity, I would affirm the trial court's award of child support on the ground that there was no abuse of discretion. The majority opinion, while reversing the trial court's award for failure to strictly follow guidelines, simultaneously instructs the trial court to sift through the record seeking an excuse to deviate from the guidelines noting, at footnote 3, the absurdity of such guidelines.

NOTE

Although it seems appropriate to hold both parents responsible for supporting children, it is not easy to determine what share each should pay. Surely taking care of a child is a form of support. Particularly if the child is young, requiring payments in cash rather than in kind by a custodial parent could seriously undermine the quality of care received by the child. This is not to suggest that custodial parents should be forced to stay at home to care for their own children, but is it not poor public policy to penalize them for making such a choice?

Should a custodial parent be penalized for failing to earn up to his or her theoretical "capacity"? On the one hand the noncustodial parent should not have to pay for the custodial parent's laziness, but on the other, failure to recognize parenting as labor (and as a form of child support) seems equally wrong. A reasonable compromise might be to compute the amount of time actually devoted to parenting by the custodial parent (taking into account the age and needs of the child(ren)) and then deduct that amount from the hours available for outside work in computing the earning "capacity" of the custodial parent.

Alternatively, courts might be wise to eschew policing the decision of a custodial parent to work or how much to work by awarding child support according to a formula that reduces the contribution of the noncustodial parent by some appropriate fraction of the custodial parent's actual increase in income since the divorce. A dollar for dollar reduction would mean there was no incentive for the custodial parent to work. A lesser reduction (50%? 25%?) would provide an incentive, but would still leave the custodial parent the option of devoting time to the care of the child.

In re Marriage of Bush

Illinois Appellate Court, 1989.
191 Ill.App.3d 249, 138 Ill.Dec. 423, 547 N.E.2d 590.

■ JUSTICE LUND delivered the opinion of the court:

This appeal follows the dissolution of the marriage of the parties, doctors Vanessa Bush and Garry Turner, on January 21, 1985....

. . .

The parties, both physicians, were married in 1982. Petitioner, now 33 years old, began her medical career as an emergency room physician at Brokaw Hospital in Normal, Illinois. Respondent, a 34-year-old anesthesiologist, began his medical career at Anesthesia Associates, a medical partnership in Bloomington, Illinois. He is now a partner there.

The parties have one child, Alan V. Turner, born October 10, 1984. Petitioner testified respondent physically and mentally abused her before and during her pregnancy. The parties separated eight days after Alan's birth. Petitioner lived with her parents in Chicago during her six weeks of maternity leave and returned to the parties' home in Bloomington in early December 1984. She and respondent lived in the marital home until January 18, 1985, but never reconciled. The petitioner filed for dissolution in Livingston County on December 12, 1984. The circuit court of Livingston County entered the decree of dissolution of marriage on January 21, 1985, on the ground of mental cruelty.

Petitioner continued to work as an emergency room physician at various hospitals in central and northern Illinois. In May 1986, petitioner married Lawrence Webster, also a physician. She and Alan moved to Dr. Webster's home in Decatur in June 1986. Various babysitters, some of them live-ins, cared for Alan while petitioner worked part time at Brokaw Hospital in Normal. In May of 1987, petitioner, Lawrence Webster, and a third party purchased Decatur Urgent Care Center. Petitioner began working at the Decatur Urgent Care Center in October 1987. She is still employed there, and her monthly gross salary is $7,200 per month. Dr. Webster's gross salary is also $7,200 per month.

Respondent continues to work for Anesthesia Associates. His estimated gross salary for 1987 was approximately $299,739, or $24,978 per month. Respondent has not remarried.

. . .

The court entered its final order on September 20, 1988. The court awarded joint custody, physical custody to remain with petitioner during the school year. During the school year, Alan will visit his father on alternate weekends and will live with his father for approximately two months each summer. During summer visitation, petitioner has absolutely no visitation rights. This visitation schedule will begin when the child enters kindergarten. Until then, the visitation schedule established under the temporary order remains in effect. The court ordered respondent to obtain a $100,000 life insurance policy "to guarantee payment of child support" and to name as beneficiary the trust he had been directed to establish for temporary child support arrearages. The court ordered respondent to establish a trust fund on behalf of the child of $18,767. This amount included temporary child support arrearages, the CD, and monies in the trust fund respondent had already established pursuant to the temporary order.

Respondent is to pay $800 per month from Anesthesia Associates directly to petitioner for child support. He is to continue to contribute to the trust fund according to the following formula: "Respondent's payments into the trust fund shall be in an amount equal to 20% of his net income as defined by statute less the cost of the $100,000 life insurance policy premium . . . and the $800 per month cash support payments to petitioner. . . ." The court found respondent in contempt of court for failing to pay $225 in temporary child support between March and June of 1988. Respondent was sentenced to seven days in jail, but could purge himself by paying $225 immediately to petitioner. . . .

. . .

. . . Respondent argues the child support award is excessive because it is far more than the amount necessary to meet the child's reasonable and necessary support needs, particularly in light of each parent's separate abilities to financially care for the child. Petitioner argues the award is insufficient because, according to her calculations, $800 per month is only 6% of respondent's monthly net income.

. . .

The trial court's overall award of 20% of respondent's net income was excessive for a child of such tender years and, as such, constituted an abuse of discretion. Additionally, the use of a trust as a reservoir for that portion of the 20% not directly paid to petitioner was improper. The trial court believed respondent should not be required to pay 20% of his net income directly to petitioner. There is testimony that respondent's net monthly income is approximately $13,000, or $156,000 annually. An award of 20% of respondent's income is approximately $30,000 per year, or more than the average income of most Americans. We have great reservation about finding one four-year-old boy entitled to such a sum. Presumably, the trial court felt the same and devised the formula involving the $800 monthly cash payment, the life insurance policy, and the trust, in order to moderate the cash amount paid for support but yet comply with the guideline figure. We now hold that where the individual incomes of both parents are more than sufficient to provide the reasonable needs of the parties' children, taking into account the life-style the children would have absent the dissolution, the court is justified in setting a figure below the guideline amount.

The court must clearly state the basis for setting a figure below the guidelines, as required by the statute. However, a reasonable basis exists where both parties have more than enough income to provide for a child, and an award of 20% of the noncustodial parent's income exceeds the bounds of anything the child can reasonably need or desire. Certainly, there will be instances where a high child support figure will be warranted. If the situation involved high medical expenses or, when the boy gets older, he is sent to an expensive, private grammar school, a child support figure approaching 20% of respondent's income might be justified. This is not such a case. There is no evidence of unmet needs, and the arguments of both parties devolve into a dispute over life-style.

Our courts have recognized that in fixing child support, or in modifying child support, a court must consider the standard of living the child would have enjoyed absent parental separation and marital dissolution. Despite the requirement that a court consider a child's station in life, the courts are not required to automatically open the door to a windfall for children where one or both parents have large incomes. A large income does not necessarily trigger an extravagant life-style or the accumulation of a trust fund. A large increase in income will not necessarily result in an equal change in one's life-style. There are other rational options for an individual with a large income than just conspicuous consumption. The wealthy person may prefer personal frugality, or the enrichment of others through charitable giving, or simply deferring income through tax-delay investments, in order to build an estate. Keeping in mind the fact that this case involves incomes for both mother and father which are far above average, we know of no rule of law requiring excessive child support so that the child (or the custodial parent) can diminish the accumulation of an estate by the noncustodial parent. We are not required to equate large incomes with lavish life-styles. Neither are the courts required to provide opulence and excess as an award for child support simply because it exists for one of the parties.

In the instant case, petitioner's argument for a 20% award is centered on respondent's income. The evidence in the record of the typical expenditures for Alan tend to support an award closer to the $800 figure set by the court. In sum, the court has the leeway to set an award below the guideline figure in a case such as this. Alan's needs are provided for, and then some. Nevertheless, the noncustodial parent must provide support for his child. The court must accommodate the reasonable needs of the child with the available means of the parents. The Act was not intended to create windfalls but, rather, adequate support payments for the upbringing of the children. We remand this issue to the trial court for determination of a reasonable specific monthly support amount.

. . .

NOTES

1. On remand to the trial court, Garry Turner was ordered to pay child support of $800 per month. In re Marriage of Bush, No. 86D–656 (McClean County Circuit Court 1990).

2. The Illinois statute relied upon by the trial court in its original support award provides in relevant part:

> (a) In a proceeding for dissolution of marriage . . . the court may order either or both parents owing a duty of support to a child of the marriage to pay an amount reasonable and necessary for his support, without regard to marital misconduct. The duty of support owed to a minor child includes the obligation to provide for the reasonable and necessary physical, mental, and emotional health needs of the child.
>
> (1) The Court shall determine the minimum amount of support by using the following guidelines:

Number of Children	Percent of Supporting Party's Net Income
1	20%
2	25%
3	32%
4	40%
5	45%
6 or more	50%

(2) The above guidelines shall be applied in each case unless the court, after considering evidence presented on all relevant factors, finds a reason for deviating from the guidelines. Relevant factors may include but are not limited to:

(a) the financial resources of the child;

(b) the financial resources and needs of the custodial parent;

(c) the standard of living the child would have enjoyed had the marriage not been dissolved;

(d) the physical and emotional condition of the child, and his educational needs; and

(e) the financial resources and needs of the non-custodial parent.

705 Ill.Comp.Stat. 5/505 (West 1992).

3. Unexercised stock options have been held to constitute part of "gross income" for purposes of calculating child support obligations. Murray v. Murray, 128 Ohio App.3d 662, 716 N.E.2d 288 (1999).

4. Unlike alimony payments, child support payments are not deductible by the payor spouse. The tax code attempts to prevent spouses from manipulating the label assigned to payments for tax purposes by providing that if any divorce obligation is reducible upon a contingency "relating to a child," it will be treated as child support and not alimony. IRS Code § 71(a)(2)(A).

Solomon v. Findley

Supreme Court of Arizona, 1991.
167 Ariz. 409, 808 P.2d 294.

■ CAMERON, J.

Defendant, Lloyd Talbott Findley (Findley), petitioned for review of the court of appeals' opinion allowing plaintiffs, Wilma Cornell Solomon and Adrienne Michelle Findley (Solomon), to pursue their claim for post-majority educational support in contract, rather than by enforcement of the dissolution decree.

. . .

On January 8, 1976, Solomon and Findley filed a joint petition for dissolution of marriage. The petition, which the parties filed *in propria persona,* contained the following provision:

> Husband also agrees to provide educational funds to the best of his ability for said minor child through college or until child reaches age of 25 whichever comes first.

On January 30, 1976, at a hearing with Findley absent, the decree was entered by default. The divorce court approved the agreement, including the educational support provision, and incorporated it into the decree.

Solomon first sought to enforce the decree by filing an order to show cause, alleging failure to provide educational funds to Adrienne, their daughter, as the decree required. The divorce court denied the relief requested because Adrienne was beyond the age of minority and the court therefore lacked jurisdiction. Solomon then filed a breach of contract action.

The trial court granted Findley's motion to dismiss, finding that "the doctrine of merger applied in the judgment and that plaintiffs' claim stemmed from the judgment."

Solomon appealed arguing that there had been no merger because there was no language showing an intent to merge and no finding by the court or order pursuant to statute.

Findley argued that any agreement between the parties was merged into the dissolution decree. He urged that the obligation to perform the agreement ended when Adrienne reached majority because the divorce court, in a dissolution action, lacks jurisdiction to adjudicate the question of liability for child support beyond the age of majority.

. . .

Several states have addressed this issue and have reached different solutions. In a leading case from the Tennessee Supreme Court, a property settlement agreement imposed an obligation upon the husband to pay all future educational expenses of the children beyond the high school level. Penland v. Penland, 521 S.W.2d 222, 223 (Tenn.1975). As such, the agreement constituted a contractual obligation outside the scope of the legal duty of support during minority. The Tennessee Supreme Court stated:

> Paragraph 2(c) of the contractual agreement between the Penlands makes no reference, direct or indirect, to age, minority or majority. It imposes an obligation to pay all future educational expenses beyond high school level. Being without any limitation, it necessarily envisioned continuance of the obligation beyond age 21, the age of majority at the time the agreement was entered into.
>
> We hold that paragraph 2(c) is a contractual obligation outside the scope of the legal duty of support during minority, and retained its contractual nature, although incorporated in the final decree of divorce. Mrs. Penland or the daughters are entitled to enforce said obligation by the obtaining of a money judgment, from time to time, as the obligation matures, and for the enforcement thereof by execution as provided by law.

Similarly, the Arkansas Supreme Court noted that when a husband entered into an improvident agreement, this was not grounds for relief and the agreement could be independently enforceable in a court of law. Armstrong v. Armstrong, 454 S.W.2d 660, 663 (1970). In *Armstrong,* the husband agreed to pay alimony to the wife for life or until she remarried, and to provide support for the daughter for so long as she was enrolled in school and not employed. The court could not have ordered these provisions and, therefore, the parties must have made a separate and independently enforceable contract.

The Georgia Supreme Court, taking another approach, allowed a wife to enforce a post-majority support agreement by contempt. McClain v. McClain, 221 S.E.2d 561, 563–64 (1975). In *McClain,* a husband agreed to provide child support until each child reached 21, and further agreed to provide a college education for each child. The court found significant differences between a decree rendered under the law and a contract entered into between husband and wife, which is incorporated into a decree. The court stated that "[w]here parties separate and by contract, as here, settle the right of their minor children for support and maintenance and such contract is approved by the trial judge and made part of a final divorce decree, the trial court will enforce the contract as made by them."

In Gaddis v. Gaddis, 314 N.E.2d 627 (1974) an Illinois appeals court took a similar position. The settlement agreement in *Gaddis* provided that the husband would continue child support payments past majority if the children were attending college, and that the husband would be responsible for tuition, books, and board. The court refused to allow the husband to modify the decree, thereby relieving himself of this obligation. The court noted that the husband was not attempting to relieve himself of his support obligation when he entered into the property settlement agreement, but rather that he contracted to do more than the law required. The court noted further that in divorce proceedings the parties often will promise whatever they can in order to obtain a divorce, and then later try to scale down these promises. The court in *Gaddis* stated that "when the parties voluntarily enter into a property settlement whereby each gives consideration for the promises of the other, the resulting contract will be enforced by the trial court." The agreement is enforced to provide stability in negotiations between the parties, and to prevent one party from being penalized due to the other party's failure to comply.

Although respectable authority allows a court to enforce an agreement for post-majority support by way of contempt in the divorce court, we believe that the better rule is the contract for post-majority support should be enforced in a separate contract action. We reach this conclusion because the divorce court only has jurisdiction to enforce child support provisions until the child reaches majority. See A.R.S. § 25–320 and 327; Young v. Burkholder, 690 P.2d 134 (Ct.App.1984). Because the divorce court did not have authority to enforce the post-majority educational support provision, that portion of the contract did not merge into the dissolution decree, but rather retained its independent nature enforceable as a contract claim.

. . .

The court of appeals' decision is approved, and the case is remanded to the trial court for proceedings consistent with this opinion.

NOTES

1. Divorcing parents often negotiate a contract to cover post-secondary education expenses. Enforcing them can be difficult. In Hawkins v. Gilbo, 663 A.2d 9 (1995), the Supreme Judicial Court of Maine held that a promisee mother's failure to join her college student child (who was the third party donee beneficiary of a tuition contract) severely limited the damages she could recover from her ex-husband. The court explained the dilemma as follows:

> If the promisee has no economic interest in the performance, as in many cases involving gift promises, the ordinary remedy for breach of contract is an inadequate remedy, since only nominal damages can be recovered. Thus without joining Keith, Nancy could have brought an action for specific enforcement of the contract and for her actual damages, but not for damages suffered by Keith. Moreover, absent a showing that she was obligated to pay for Keith's education, her actual damages would be limited to nominal damages. Id. at 11.

See also Noble v. Fisher, 126 Idaho 885, 894 P.2d 118 (1995), (declaring that children and not their mother have standing as third party beneficiaries to enforce the tuition provision in a property settlement); Mattocks v. Matus, 266 Ga. 346, 466 S.E.2d 840 (1996) (holding father's contractual obligation to support college student ceased when child left school and did not resume when the child decided to enroll again).

2. In Stanton v. Stanton, 421 U.S. 7 (1975), a father had agreed to pay child support for his son and daughter until both reached their "majority." The Supreme

Court held that the relevant Utah statute (which provided that minority lasts until twenty-one for males but only eighteen for females) violated the Equal Protection Clause, explaining:

> If a specified age of minority is required for the boy in order to assure him parental support while he attains his education and training, so, too, it is for girls. To distinguish between the two is self-serving: if the female is not to be supported so long as the male, she hardly can be expected to attend school as long as he does, and bringing her education to an end earlier coincides with the role-typing society has long imposed.

On remand, an award of child support for the daughter was granted by the trial court but overturned on appeal to the Utah Supreme Court, 552 P.2d 112 (Utah 1976). This Utah decision was voided by the Supreme Court, 429 U.S. 501 (1977), for failure to deal with the discrimination issue presented by the case. On remand, the Supreme Court of Utah decided that both males and females would be considered emancipated at age eighteen. 564 P.2d 303 (Utah 1977).

Curtis v. Kline

Supreme Court of Pennsylvania, 1995.
542 Pa. 249, 666 A.2d 265.

■ Zappala, Justice

In *Blue v. Blue*, 532 Pa. 521, 616 A.2d 628 (1992), we declined to recognize a duty requiring a parent to provide college educational support because no such legal duty had been imposed by the General Assembly or developed by our case law. As a result of our *Blue* decision, the legislature promulgated Act 62 of 1993. Section 3 of the Act states:

> (a) General rule.—. . . a court may order either or both parents who are separated, divorced, unmarried or otherwise subject to an existing support obligation to provide equitably for educational costs of their child whether an application for this support is made before or after the child has reached 18 years of age.

23 Pa.C.S. § 4327(a).

The issue now before us is whether the Act violates the equal protection clause of the Fourteenth Amendment of the United States Constitution. [footnote omitted] The Court of Common Pleas of Chester County held that it did, resulting in this direct appeal.

The relevant facts are not in dispute. Appellee is the father of Jason, Amber and Rebecca. On July 12, 1991, an order of court for support was entered on behalf of Appellee's children. On March 2, 1993, Appellee filed a petition to terminate his support obligation as to Amber, a student at Kutztown University, and Jason, a student at West Chester University. After Act 62 was promulgated, Appellee was granted leave to include a constitutional challenge to the Act as a basis for seeking relief from post-secondary educational support.

. . .

The equal protection clause of the Fourteenth Amendment of the United States Constitution in pertinent part provides: "No State shall . . . deprive any person of life, liberty, or property, without due process of law; nor deny to any person within its jurisdiction the equal protection of the laws."

. . .

. . . Act 62 must be upheld if there exists any rational basis for the prescribed classification. It is in this context that we review the Act's creation of a duty, and more significantly a legal mechanism for enforcement of that duty, limited to situations of separated, divorced, or unmarried parents and their children.

In applying the rational basis test, we have adopted a two-step analysis. First, we must determine whether the challenged statute seeks to promote any legitimate state interest or public value. If so, we must next determine whether the classification adopted in the legislation is reasonably related to accomplishing that articulated state interest or interests.

The preamble to Act 62 sets forth the legislature's intention "to codify the decision of the Superior Court in the case of *Ulmer v. Sommerville* . . . and the subsequent line of cases interpreting *Ulmer* prior to the decision of the Pennsylvania Supreme Court in *Blue v. Blue*. . . ." (Citations omitted). It also states:

> Further, the General Assembly finds that it has a rational and legitimate governmental interest in requiring some parental financial assistance for a higher education for children of parents who are separated, divorced, unmarried or otherwise subject to an existing support obligation.

This latter statement begs the question of whether the legislature actually has a legitimate interest in treating children of separated, divorced, or unmarried parents differently than children of married parents with respect to the costs of post-secondary education.

. . .

Act 62 classifies young adults according to the marital status of their parents, establishing for one group an action to obtain a benefit enforceable by court order that is not available to the other group. The relevant category under consideration is children in need of funds for a post-secondary education. The Act divides these persons, similarly situated with respect to their need for assistance, into groups according to the marital status of their parents, i.e., children of divorced/separated/never-married parents and children of intact families.

It will not do to argue that this classification is rationally related to the legitimate governmental purpose of obviating difficulties encountered by those in non-intact families who want parental financial assistance for post-secondary education, because such a statement of the governmental purpose assumes the validity of the classification. Recognizing that within the category of young adults in need of financial help to attend college there are some having a parent or parents unwilling to provide such help, the question remains whether the authority of the state may be selectively applied to empower only those from non-intact families to compel such help. We hold that it may not. In the absence of an entitlement on the part of any individual to post-secondary education, or a generally applicable requirement that parents assist their adult children in obtaining such an education, [footnote omitted] we perceive no rational basis for the state government to provide only certain adult citizens with legal means to overcome the difficulties they encounter in pursuing that end.

It is not inconceivable that in today's society a divorced parent, e.g., a father, could have two children, one born of a first marriage and not residing with him and the other born of a second marriage and still residing with him. Under Act 62, such a father could be required to provide post-secondary educational support for the first child but not the second, even to the extent that the second child would be required to forego a college education. Further, a child over the age of 18, of a woman whose husband had died would have no action against the mother to recover costs of a post-secondary education, but a child over the age of 18, of a woman who never married, who married and divorced, or even who was only separated from her husband when he died would be able to maintain such an action. These are but two examples demonstrating the arbitrariness of the classification adopted in Act 62.

In *LeClair v. LeClair*, 137 N.H. 213, 624 A.2d 1350 (1993), the New Hampshire Supreme Court was faced with the issue of the constitutionality of a state statute regarding post-secondary educational support. Initially, it must be noted that the Court decided this appeal based upon the New Hampshire constitution even though the appellant contended that the statute denied him equal protection under both the federal and state constitution.

The underlying premise upon which the New Hampshire Supreme Court undertook its constitutional analysis of the post-secondary educational support scheme was that the legislation created two classifications: married parents and divorced parents. The object of the legislation was to protect children of divorced parents from being unjustly deprived of opportunities they would otherwise have had if their parents had not divorced. The statute was promulgated to ensure that children of divorced families are not deprived of educational opportunities solely because their families are no longer intact. The result is a heightened judicial involvement in the financial and personal lives of divorced families with children that is not necessary with intact families with children. The New Hampshire Supreme Court concluded that because of the unique problems of divorced families, the legislature could rationally conclude that absent judicial involvement, children of divorced families may be less likely than children of intact families to receive post-secondary educational support from both parents.

With all due respect to our sister state, we must reject the New Hampshire Supreme Court's analysis in *LeClair*. The discriminatory classification adopted by our legislature is not focused on the parents but rather the children. The question is whether similarly situated young adults, i.e. those in need of financial assistance, may be treated differently.

Ultimately, we can conceive of no rational reason why those similarly situated with respect to needing funds for college education, should be treated unequally. Accordingly, we agree with the common pleas court and conclude that Act 62 is unconstitutional. . . .

■ Montemuro, Justice, dissenting

I must dissent.

As the Majority correctly points out, the rational basis test to determine whether a statute is constitutional requires, first, a determination of whether the challenged legislation seeks to promote any legitimate state interest. It must then be decided whether the statute bears a reasonable relationship to the intended objective. . . . The Majority challenges not merely the means of execution, but the legitimacy of the government interest which the statute is expressly designed to promote.

Act 62 is directed at furthering the education of the citizens of this Commonwealth. It operates on the assumption that divorce necessarily involves a disadvantage to the children of broken families, and is intended to assure that children who are thus disadvantaged by the divorce or separation of their parents are not deprived of the opportunity to acquire post secondary school education. In effect, it attempts to maintain the children of divorce in the same position they would have been in had their parents' marriage remained intact. The Act is not intended to, nor does it, place a premium on the rights of children of divorce while devaluing the same rights for children from intact marriage. It merely recognizes that, in general, divorce has a deleterious effect upon children, which should, insofar as is possible, be redressed. Thus while constitutional principles permit this intended result, a "difference in fact or opinion" recognized by the Legislature as within its purview, the Majority has declared that, at least for college age children, the distinction between the children of broken families and those of intact families simply does not exist.

In rejecting the authenticity of the premise underlying the statute, the Majority also challenges the validity of the legislative interest. It contends that the expressed intention of the statute "will not do" because the Legislature actually has no legitimate interest in treating children of broken marriages differently than children of intact marriages. The Majority theorizes that since the children of intact families may be no less in need of funds for purposes of higher education, they are situated similarly to children of divorced or separated parents, and any distinction between them is inconsequential.

. . .

It has also been widely acknowledged that among the negative effects of divorce on children are those which concern higher education. . . . Whether because they lose concern for their children's welfare, or out of animosity toward the custodial parent, non-custodial parents frequently become reluctant to provide financial support for any purpose, but are particularly determined to avoid the costs of a college education. Then the custodial parent, who typically has less money than the non-custodial parent, most often becomes the de facto bearer of most, if not all, of the burden of educational expenses, even where the non-custodial parent possesses both resources and background which would inure to the child's benefit were the parents still married. Such parents, are, in addition, even less inclined to assist with the educational expenses of daughters than of sons.

The courts addressing the issue have uniformly decided that equal protection is not offended by an attempt to equalize the disparate situation faced by children of divorce. Only the means are different. Those facing challenges to a statutory provision have all found that the differences between married and divorced parents establishes the necessity to discriminate between the classes. Others, in examining judge-made law found an extended dependency justified court intervention. They all, however, delegated to the court the authority to determine the propriety of an award.

In *LeClair v. LeClair*, 137 N.H. 213, 624 A.2d 1350 (1993), the New Hampshire Supreme Court recognized and addressed the very concerns toward which Act 62 is directed—the disadvantage wrought on children by divorce of their parents, and the necessity for court intervention to protect them from the consequences of this disadvantage. The New Hampshire statute, RSA 458:20, codified decisions in which the New Hampshire Supreme Court had recognized the jurisdiction of the superior court to order divorced parents, consistent with their means, to contribute toward the educational expenses of their college age children. Challengers of the statute bore the burden of showing that the court had committed an abuse of discretion, and that the order was "improper and unfair." The equal protection argument focused on the parents, finding them similarly situated with respect to the issue. However, the Majority here states that because the focus of Act 62 is the treatment of children, the marital status of their parents is irrelevant.

This argument is specious, since any child support legislation necessarily involves the marital status of the parents. Intact families do not suffer intervention by the courts unless their children are abused or neglected. Recognition of the need for legislative or judicial action to require support for children of broken families is irrefutable, as the continuing governmental efforts to improve collection of support attest. It is unrealistic to conclude, as the Majority does, that merely because children are in need of funds for college rather than subsistence, the effect of their parents marital status has magically altered, and that enforcement of an obligation is no longer necessary.

What must be remembered, and what the Majority fails to explore, is that Act 62 does not make mandatory the directive to pay child support for college. Section 4327(e) lists standards to assist the court in determining whether or not support is appropriate. Unless these criteria are, in the estimation of the court, met by the parties, no liability exists.

The problem lies with the nature of the liability, which is, quite simply, a moral duty, circumstantially prescribed. Under Act 62, it is owed only by parents who are subject to an existing support obligation, that is, they have acknowledged either voluntarily through contract, or involuntarily through the necessity of court order that a financial responsibility to pay for their children's upkeep exists. The court has thus already become involved to the extent of entering an order, or there exists another legal mechanism, e.g., separation agreement, through which enforcement can be accomplished and contribution monitored. In intact families, absent abuse or neglect, no such initial intervention has occurred, and the court has no forum in which to enforce a duty imposed on these parents. Moreover, limitations have been placed on the ability to control children's education by legislative fiat. Thus intervention in the form of a statute requiring parents of an intact marriage to finance their children's college education would indeed infringe upon the constitutional/privacy right of the parties.

While it does not necessarily follow that in all cases children of divorce are deprived of parental support for college, or that the reverse is true and all children of intact families are provided with the necessary encouragement and finances, children whose parents are still married most often continue to receive support past majority. [footnote omitted] Equal protection does not demand that every permutation be addressed separately, what is sought is equality not uniformity.

2. MODIFICATION

Ainsworth v. Ainsworth

Supreme Court of Vermont, 1990.
154 Vt. 103, 574 A.2d 772.

■ DOOLEY, JUSTICE.

This action for modification of child support calls upon us to interpret Vermont's recently enacted child support guidelines law, 15 V.S.A. §§ 650–663. Specifically at issue is whether expenses for a second family should enter into the determination of child support for the preexisting family. Although the trial court decided that defendant, Reginald Ainsworth, did not have a duty to support his stepson under 15 V.S.A. § 296, it held, pursuant to § 659, that a child support order based on the guidelines sought by plaintiff, Julie Ann Ainsworth, on her behalf and on behalf of the two children of the parties, would be inequitable and ordered him to pay them less than what would be required under the guidelines. Plaintiff appealed and we reverse and remand.

The parties were divorced on April 30, 1986. They stipulated then that defendant was to pay child support in the amount of $35 per week for each of their two children for a total of $70 per week. Mr. Ainsworth remarried on August 15, 1987, and established a new home with his wife and her son at that time. On September 21, 1987, plaintiff filed a motion for modification pursuant to 15 V.S.A. § 660,[1] seeking increased support in an amount to be determined under the guidelines mandated by the statute that was effective on April 1, 1987.

. . .

In order to fully and logically analyze the issues presented by plaintiff's appeal, we will recategorize the issues from those used by the trial court into three questions: (1) whether the trial court may deviate from child support amounts calculated under the guidelines when defendant is supporting children in a second family; (2) if the answer to the first question is yes, whether the power to deviate applies if the children in the second family are stepchildren and not natural children; and (3) if the answer to the first two questions is yes, whether the actual order in this case was within the discretion of the trial court.

. . .

In Vermont, the guideline amounts are established by rule of the Secretary of Human Services. Under the guideline regulations, a basic support amount for the children is derived from tables based solely on the total gross income of the parents and the number of children. See 15 V.S.A. § 653(1) ("Basic support obligation" defined as guideline amount unless court finds that amount inequitable and establishes a different amount). The next step is to calculate a "total support obligation" by adding expenditures in two categories to the basic support amount: (1) the amount of child care costs reasonably incurred by a parent as a result of employment or employment related education; and (2) extraordinary medical or education expenses. Once the total support obligation is calculated, the amount is divided between the parents "in proportion to their respective gross incomes." In this calculation, as well as in the derivation of the basic support amount from the tables, a broad definition of gross income is used. There are, however, three exclusions from income in reaching the "gross incomes" recognized by the statute: (1) the amount of "preexisting spousal maintenance or child support obligations actually paid;" (2) amounts received from means tested

1. Section 660 provides in part:

(a) On motion of either parent . . . and upon a showing of a real, substantial and unanticipated change of circumstances, the court may annul, vary or modify a child support order, whether or not the order is based upon a stipulation or agreement.

(b) A child support order, including an order in effect prior to adoption of the support guideline, which varies more than 15 percent from the amounts required to be paid under the support guideline, shall be considered a real, substantial and unanticipated change of circumstances.

public assistance programs; and (3) the actual cost of providing adequate health insurance coverage for the involved children.

Except as set forth above, the actual expenditures of the parents are not relevant to the guideline calculation. Thus, the guideline calculation for a noncustodial parent with a large mortgage payment would be the same as for a noncustodial parent with a low rent payment as long as both have the same income.

The total support obligation calculated under the guideline is "presumed to be the amount of child support needed," upon which the noncustodial parent's obligation is calculated. However, if the court finds that a child support order based on the guidelines "would be inequitable," the court may establish support after considering all relevant factors. The statute contains a noninclusive list of factors to be considered.

The first question we face is whether the trial court can find an order based on the guidelines "inequitable" because of the expenses of supporting another child when the support obligation for that other child did not preexist the one for the child or children included in the guideline calculation. We believe that the trial court has this power.

We start with the wording chosen by the Legislature to describe when the court should deviate from the guidelines. The term "equitable" normally means "[j]ust; conformable to the principles of justice and right." Black's Law Dictionary 482 (5th ed. 1979). Thus, the use of the term "inequitable" must give the trial court authority to look at whether a guideline-based amount is just under the circumstances.

While the wording chosen by the Legislature makes clear that it intended to give trial courts discretion to ensure support awards are just, this is an area where we must be careful to define the nature and scope of that discretion so that it is not used to create inequity or to undermine the standardization that the Legislature intended. If we allow the trial courts to consider any variation in the needs of the children or the living situation or expenses of the parents, we would return to the preguideline law where a wide range of support amounts was permissible in almost every case. In short, the "escape valve" of § 659 would eat up the rule and destroy the predictability of amounts and the maintenance of the standard of living of the children that are the desired results of a guideline system.

Our examination of the statutory scheme demonstrates, however, that this case involves the type of situation where the Legislature intended that the court exercise discretion consistent with the policies of the act. That intent is demonstrated by the exclusion from gross income of certain support payments. While the drafting is not a model of clarity, we conclude that the exclusion covers amounts being paid pursuant to preexisting support orders.

It is important to analyze what is covered by the exclusion and what is not. First, as we construe the legislative intent, it requires that there be an actual support order. Second, it requires that the order, not merely the obligation, be preexisting at the time the calculation is made. Third, it requires that payments be made on the order.

The limits of the second requirement are particularly important. It shows that the Legislature was primarily concerned about the timing of the orders. If a noncustodial parent is subject to two child support orders, the amount paid under the first order is always deductible under § 653(5)(E)(i) from that parent's income in determining the amount of the second order, even though the child covered by the second order might have been born before the child covered by the first order.

There are practical reasons why the Legislature created a rule allowing a parent to deduct the expenses of other support obligations only in limited circumstances. They are explained in People in Interest of C.D., 767 P.2d at 811–12, in describing the identical Colorado rule:

> Inherent in the statutory scheme is a legislative recognition that child support obligations which have been previously imposed by a court have been determined to be both necessary and reasonable in amount in proper judicial proceedings. Non-ordered support obligations, on the other hand, have not been judicially scrutinized either as to their necessity or their reasonableness, and the General Assembly accordingly has not provided for automatic income adjustments based upon those obligations, whether or not they are actually paid.

. . .

It would be unfair, however, to consider amounts paid under existing support obligations only when they are the subject of court orders. By allowing consideration of payments made to discharge support obligations in instances where they have been scrutinized by a court and can be fit within mathematical formulas and allowing courts to deviate from support amounts calculated under the guidelines when such amounts are "inequitable," the Legislature must have intended that the courts use their discretion to consider the expenses connected with second families. The use of discretion in this area prevents the guideline system from being wholly arbitrary.

In reaching the conclusion that the court could consider the expenses of supporting other families under § 659, we also rely on the fact that the courts in Colorado, the state with a guideline system closest to that adopted in Vermont,[3] have reached the same conclusion. The Colorado courts have held that support obligations to other dependents may be evaluated in determining the extent to which a deviation from the guidelines is necessary to avoid an "inequitable" support order. . . .

For the above reasons, we answer the first question in this case in the affirmative. The trial court may, under § 659, find that calculating a support order based on the guidelines would be inequitable because of a parent's expenses in supporting other dependents.

The second question is whether the court's discretion under § 659 extends to situations where the expenses are for the support of a second wife and a stepchild. . . .

The trial court found no obligation of support in this case because the statutory support obligation of stepparents is limited to situations where the financial resources of the natural parents are inadequate to provide the child with a reasonable subsistence. . . . Although the stepparent support statute, 15 V.S.A. § 296, contains the language cited, it also states that the duty it imposes is "coextensive" with the duty to support a natural child. Therefore,

3. Colorado and Vermont use an income-share approach to setting guidelines. See Robert Williams, Guidelines for Setting Levels of Child Support Orders, 21 Fam.L.Q. at 291. As noted earlier, Colorado has adopted an exclusion from income for the amount of preexisting child support obligations actually paid. Colorado also allows a deviation from the guidelines where their application would be inequitable. See Colo.Rev.Stat.Ann. § 14–10–115(3)(a).

we disagree with the trial court and find that the statute creates a general obligation of support. . . .

Neither the trial court nor the parties have raised any question about the defendant's obligation to support his second wife. The general obligation to support spouses extends to defendant's second spouse. See 15 V.S.A. § 291.

Having decided that the trial court could find the application of the guidelines to be inequitable in this case, we must address whether the court properly exercised its discretion in setting a support amount. We emphasize here that the fact that the court finds the application of guidelines to be "inequitable" in a particular case does not mean that it must automatically order a substantially lower support amount . . . The use of § 659 means only that the special circumstances of the case make it inappropriate to determine a support amount based *solely* on the mathematical calculations involved in the guidelines. Instead, the court must consider all "relevant factors," including eight specific ones itemized in the statute. It may be that an evaluation of these factors will lead to a support award as high as that calculated under the guidelines.

It is particularly important to emphasize that consideration of a case under § 659 does not necessarily mean a lower support amount in second-family cases. We have held that a change in financial circumstances "resulting from a deliberate and voluntary act, absent a sufficient reason for the sacrificing of income," will not support a modification of a child support order.

The voluntary nature of second-family obligations is not the only consideration in establishing the child support order under § 659. . . . We agree with the trial court in this case that the financial resources of the new spouse of the parent is also a relevant consideration. A parent should not be able to rely on second-family expenses without consideration of second-family income and resources.

We have held with respect to the custody statute, when the Legislature itemized certain factors to be considered in determining parental rights and responsibilities, that the court's findings must show that it took each of the statutory factors into consideration. . . .

The findings and conclusions here are incomplete and much too sketchy to meet the above requirements. The court had evidence from both parties on their income and expenses. The evidence from the defendant showed a high level of consumer debt connected with the purchase of a house and furnishings for his new family. Although the court found that defendant's new spouse had "financial resources as represented by her education and former work experience," it apparently considered her to have no potential income when it set the support amount. In any event, the court never specified how, based on the evidence and its findings, it arrived at the figure of $90 per week as the new child support amount. Nor can we conclude that the court considered all the factors specified in § 659(a)(1)–(8) and considered the extent to which the defendant's expenses were voluntarily incurred in the face of his obligation to the children of his first marriage.

Because the findings and conclusions do not specify the reasons for the amount of support awarded and show consideration of the statutory factors, we must reverse and remand for a new hearing.

■ MORSE, JUSTICE, dissenting.

. . .

In adopting the new child support statute, the legislature stated its purpose as follows:

> The legislature . . . finds and declares as public policy that parents have the responsibility to provide child support and that child support orders should reflect the true costs of raising children and approximate insofar as possible *the standard of living the child would have enjoyed had the marriage not been dissolved*.

15 V.S.A. § 650 (emphasis added). . . . The priority is clear. Children come first. Their living standard should not drop "insofar as possible."

. . .

While I agree with most of what is said in the Court's opinion, I do not construe § 659, which permits deviations from the guidelines "[i]f the court finds that a child support order based on the support guidelines would be inequitable," to allow a deviation on this record. The Court's holding today will lead to irrational results, rendering the child support law less effective and fair; indeed, it undermines the explicit purpose of the legislation. If defendant's new house and furnishings came before his children, he would *not* be honoring his "responsibility to provide child support [where] child support orders should reflect the true costs of raising children," § 650, and the children's needs would *not* be met by "the parents in proportion to their respective gross incomes," § 656.

In light of the legislation as a whole and its evident purpose, § 659 must be given a more narrow reading. The trial court's discretion to deviate from the legislative scheme is constrained. The determination of inequitability cannot be supported by the sorts of facts already considered in arriving at the support guideline figure. As stated above, that figure depends on what parents "ordinarily spend on their children," an amount that necessarily reflects their other ordinary expenses. The legislature therefore did not intend that ordinary expenses incurred by the noncustodial parent could support a finding that a guideline-based order would be inequitable. Only *extraordinary* expenses can justify a departure from the guidelines. This record reveals no extraordinary expenses. What they might be should be left to subsequent cases.

. . .

I am not of the view that defendant has no obligation to support his stepson. I would hold only that any such obligation must not be subtracted from his gross income in calculating the guideline child support figure. In this sense defendant's obligation to his stepchild is no different than his obligation to pay taxes. He may have a legal duty to pay both, but neither enters into the calculation of his child support obligation under the statutory guidelines.

It may be useful to compare the situation of a parent who is subject to a child support order stemming from a *former* marriage. In such a case, the earlier child support obligations, if actually paid, may reduce the parent's obligations to the children of the second marriage under the new statutory framework. See 15 V.S.A. § 653(5)(E)(i). Children of the second marriage receive diminished support relative to children of the first marriage. The legislature had to choose where to place the inevitable hardship—all things being equal—resulting from the assumption of second-family responsibilities. It chose to keep child support, as dictated by the guidelines in the usual case, intact for children who were already the beneficiaries of a child support order. This is as it should be. The decision to assume added familial responsibilities should include an evaluation of the added cost, without factoring in a reduction in support to children of the divorce to help finance the second family. In short, the Court's decision today reduces the cost equation at the expense of children of divorce.

I would not fashion a per se rule. Expenses for children in a second family in some instances might well warrant a departure from the guidelines. It is not necessary to broaden discretion under § 659(a)'s inequitability standard, however, to, in the words of the Court, "prevent[ ] the guideline system from being wholly arbitrary." . . .

. . .

Under today's ruling, determination of child support is subject in large measure to the vagaries of individual judgment as to what is fair, given all the facts and circumstances of each case. The guidelines, however, are designed to give child support determinations a measure of predictability and equality and to reduce litigation. They are intended to ensure that like cases will be treated alike by judges who do not think alike in this area of subjective value judgments. If the guidelines are circumvented under the "equitable" rubric of § 659(a), we will return to the inequities, waste and drain of preguideline litigation. Exceptions to the guidelines should not be based on a judge's opinion of the fairness of the guidelines per se or upon voluntary undertakings by a party to establish and support a second family with funds that would otherwise go to support existing children. This policy may not appear romantic, but it reflects the pragmatic belief that new obligations should not be created or assumed at the expense of existing ones.

Accordingly, I would reverse and remand for an order setting child support at $141 per week.

Little v. Little

Supreme Court of Arizona, 1999.
193 Ariz. 518, 975 P.2d 108.

■ McGregor, Justice.

In this opinion, we consider the standard courts should apply in determining whether a non-custodial parent's voluntary decision to leave his or her employment to become a full-time student constitutes a sufficient change in circumstances to warrant a downward modification of the parent's child support obligation.

The parties divorced in November 1995. The court ordered appellant Billy L. Little, Jr., an Air Force lieutenant, to pay $1,186 per month for the support of his two young children. In August 1996, appellant resigned his commission in the Air Force, a position that paid $48,000 in yearly salary plus benefits, and chose to enroll as a full-time student at Arizona State University College of Law rather than to seek employment.

Upon leaving the Air Force, appellant petitioned the court to reduce his child support obligation to $239 per month. The trial court concluded that appellant had failed to prove a substantial and continuing change of circumstances in accordance with Arizona Revised Statutes (A.R.S.) §§ 25–327.A and 25–503.F, and denied his request for modification. The trial court specifically found that appellant voluntarily left his employment to further his own ambition; that he failed to consider the needs of his children when he made that decision; and that to reduce his child support obligation would be to his children's immediate detriment and their previously established needs. The trial court did reduce appellant's child support obligation to $972 per month on the ground that appellee Lisa L. Little had acquired a higher paying job.

The court of appeals, applying a good faith test to determine whether appellant acted reasonably in voluntarily leaving his employment, held that the trial court abused its discretion in finding that appellant's decision to terminate his employment and pursue a law degree was unreasonable. Because we hold that a court, rather than rely upon a good faith test, must balance a number of factors to determine whether to modify a child support order to reflect a substantial and continuing change of circumstances, we vacate the opinion of the court of appeals and affirm the decision of the trial court.

The decision to modify an award of child support rests within the sound discretion of the trial court and, absent an abuse of that discretion, will not be disturbed on appeal.

Arizona's law governing modification of child support orders, codified at A.R.S. §§ 25–327.A and 25–503.F, states that a court should modify a child support order only if a parent shows a substantial, continuing change of circumstances. Guidelines adopted by this court provide procedural guidance in applying the substantive law. According to the Guidelines, when a parent is unemployed or working below his or her full earning potential, a trial court calculating the appropriate child support payment may impute income to that parent, up to full earning capacity, if the parent's earnings are reduced voluntarily and not for reasonable cause. The Guidelines also state that the trial court may elect not to impute income to a parent if he or she is enrolled in reasonable occupational training that will establish basic skills or is reasonably calculated to enhance earning capacity. Significantly, both the governing statute and the Guidelines recognize that a parent's child support obligation is paramount to all other financial obligations, and that a parent has a legal duty to support his or her biological and adopted children.

A number of other jurisdictions have considered the issue that confronts us. Courts in sister jurisdictions have applied one of three tests to determine whether to modify a child support order when a parent voluntarily terminates his or her employment. The first of these tests, the good faith test, "considers the actual earnings of a party rather than his earning capacity, so long as" he or she acted in good faith and not "primarily for the purpose of avoiding a support obligation" when he or she terminated employment. The second test, designated the strict rule test, "disregards any income reduction produced by voluntary conduct and ... looks at the earning capacity of a party in fashioning a support obligation." The third test, referred to as the intermediate test, balances various factors to determine "whether to use actual income or earning capacity in making a support determination." Each of the tests evidences its own strengths and weaknesses, and each reflects the public policy of its adopting jurisdiction.

Other jurisdictions have detected three fundamental flaws in the good faith test, which assigns the highest value to the obligor parent's individual freedom of choice. First, the test erroneously "assumes that a divorced or separated party to a support proceeding will continue to make decisions in the best overall interest of the family unit," when often, in fact, the party will not. Second, the test fails to attach sufficient importance to a parent's existing obligation to support his or her children. As one court explained, the good faith test allows a parent to be "free to retire, take a vow of poverty, write poetry, or hawk roses in an airport, if he or she sees fit," provided only that his or her motivation for acting is not to shirk a child support obligation. Third, once the party seeking a downward modification provides a seemingly good faith reason for leaving employment, the burden of proof often shifts to the party opposing the reduction to then show that the reason given is merely a sham. Even if the burden of proof does not shift, the trial court is still left with the difficult task of evaluating a party's subjective motivation. While all those factors influence our decision to reject the good faith test, we regard the primary shortcoming of the good faith test as being its focus upon the parent's motivation for leaving employment rather than upon the parent's responsibility to his or her children and the effect of the parent's decision on the best interests of the children.

The strict rule test also contains a fatal flaw. This test is too inflexible because it considers only one factor, the parent's earning capacity, in determining whether to modify a child support order when a parent voluntarily leaves employment. We decline to adopt the strict rule test because it allows no consideration of the parent's individual freedom or of the economic benefits that can result to both parent and children from additional training or education.

We reject both these extreme approaches and instead adopt an intermediate balancing test that considers a number of factors. . . .

Arizona law prescribes that "the obligation to pay child support is primary and other financial obligations are secondary." A.R.S. § 25–501.C. Thus, the paramount factor a trial court must consider in determining whether a voluntary change in employment constitutes a substantial and continuing change in circumstances sufficient to justify a child support modification is the financial impact of the parent's decision on the child or children the support order protects. If a reduction in child support due to a non-custodial parent's voluntary decision to change his or her employment status places a child in financial peril, then the court generally should not permit a downward modification.

In many instances, the impact on the children will not be so severe as to place the children in peril. In those circumstances, courts must consider the overall reasonableness of a parent's voluntary decision to terminate employment and return to school. The answers to several questions will provide relevant information. The court should ask whether the parent's current educational level and physical capacity provide him or her with the ability to find suitable work in the marketplace. If so, the decision to leave employment is less reasonable. In contrast, answers to other questions make the parent's decision to leave employment more reasonable. If the additional training is likely to increase the parent's earning potential, the decision is more likely to be found reasonable. The court should also consider the length of the parent's proposed educational program, because it matters whether the children are young enough to benefit from the parent's increased future income. The court also should inquire whether the parent is able to finance his or her child support obligation while in school through other resources such as student loans or part-time employment. Finally, the court should consider whether the parent's decision is made in good faith, as a decision to forego employment and return to school usually will not be reasonable or made in good faith if the parent acts to avoid a child support obligation.

. . .

We believe the balancing test described above comports not only with Arizona's public policy, but also with a national policy trend that favors strictly enforcing child support obligations.

. . .

Applying the balancing test to the facts involved here, we conclude that the trial court did not abuse its discretion when it refused appellant's request for a downward modification of his child support obligation. First, the negative impact of the requested reduction on appellant's children, had the trial court granted it, would have been substantial. The trial court found that such a reduction "would be to the children's immediate detriment and their previously established needs." The record also reveals that appellee earns only $1,040 per month in salary. This income places the Little family well below the 1998 federal poverty level. Without their father's support, appellant's children would face significant economic hardship. Second, appellant holds Bachelor of Arts and Master of Business Administration degrees. Appellant, by asking the trial court to assume he will earn more money when he completes law school than he could have earned in the private business sector, invited the court to engage in speculation. Therefore, while appellant's children are young enough to benefit from any increased income their father earns, the speculative nature of the increase justified giving this factor minimal weight. Third, the record does not reflect that appellant, upon leaving the Air Force, even attempted to obtain suitable employment in the Phoenix metropolitan area that would have allowed him to be close to his children and fulfill his financial obligations to them. Fourth, appellant has been able to finance his law school education and most of his child support obligation through student loans. Nothing in the record suggests that appellant is unable to obtain part-time employment to fulfill the remainder of his child support obligation. Finally, the trial court specifically found that appellant failed to act in good faith and instead endeavored to further his own ambition when he chose to forego employment and become a full-time student. Thus, the trial court did not abuse its discretion when it determined that appellant failed to act in his children's best interests when he voluntarily left full-time employment to enroll in law school.

We realize that the "responsibilities of begetting a family many times raise havoc with dreams. Nevertheless, the duty [to support one's children] persists, with full authority in the State to enforce it." We therefore vacate the opinion of the court of appeals and affirm the decision of the trial court.

Bender v. Bender

Superior Court of Pennsylvania, 1982.
297 Pa.Super. 461, 444 A.2d 124.

Appellant Kenneth Bender seeks review of an order indefinitely suspending appellee Theresa Bender's obligation to provide support for their nine-year-old daughter, Heather Christina Bender. . . .

At the time of the hearing below, the parties were in the process of getting a divorce. Mr. Bender had been awarded permanent custody of Heather, the parties' only child. He initiated support proceedings against

Mrs. Bender in December, 1978. The court conducted a full hearing during which the parties presented evidence of their respective earning capacities. On April 16, 1979, the court entered an order directing Mrs. Bender to pay support for Heather in the amount of $25.00 per week effective retroactively to December 4, 1978, the date the complaint was filed. Because Mrs. Bender was approximately eight months pregnant at the time of the hearing, the support order was made effective only until January 22, 1979[16] at which time it was suspended until six weeks following the birth of her baby. The order provided that following the six week hiatus, the payments were to be resumed at the weekly rate of $16, plus $4 per week towards arrearages. No appeal was taken from this order and appellee has made no payments thereon.

Nicole Ginning Brown was born on May 13, 1979. Mr. Bender is not the father of this child. According to the terms of the original order, Mrs. Bender's obligation to pay support for Heather would have recommenced on June 26, 1979. Mrs. Bender made a decision at some point not to return to work after Nicole's birth but rather to remain at home to care for her new baby. On November 9, 1979, she filed a petition to suspend the support order. Mr. Bender then filed a petition seeking to have Mrs. Bender held in contempt for failing to pay pursuant to the order. Following a hearing on both petitions, the court, on April 19, 1980, entered an order suspending indefinitely Mrs. Bender's obligation to pay support for Heather. The court based its decision upon a finding that Mrs. Bender was entitled to remain home to nurture Nicole.

The parties, as well as the court below, concluded that the outcome of the case depended upon a determination of whether the "nurturing parent doctrine" established by this court in Commonwealth ex rel. Wasiolek v. Wasiolek, 251 Pa.Super. 108, 380 A.2d 400 (1977) applies in this case. In *Wasiolek,* the lower court ordered a mother of three minor children to seek employment so that she could contribute to the support and maintenance of the children. The mother, who had primary custody of the children, felt that her presence in the home was more important to the children than the money she would be able to contribute if she was gainfully employed. We agreed and reversed the order, thus carving out an exception to the general rule that a mother has an obligation of support measured not by her actual earnings but rather by her earning capacity. We stated in *Wasiolek* that:

> [T]he purpose of a support order is the furtherance of the welfare and best interests of the child for whom it is entered. Obviously, a court cannot ignore the substantial nonmonetary contributions made by a non-working spouse. It would surely be ironic if by its support order a court were to dictate that a parent desert a home where very young children were present when the very purpose of the order is to guarantee the welfare of those same children. Such an order would ignore the importance of the nurture and attention of the parent in whose custody the children have been entrusted and would elevate financial well-being over emotional well-being.

. . .

We believe the lower court's interpretation of *Wasiolek* is erroneous. We did not there establish an absolute rule that an earning capacity can not be

16. Mrs. Bender, due to her pregnancy, had left her job as a licensed practical nurse on January 22, 1979.

imputed to a parent who chooses to stay home with a minor child. Rather, we held that a court should *consider* a parent's desire to stay home to nurture minor children and, in appropriate cases, excuse such nurturing parent from contributing support payments. This court has always recognized that:

"No two support cases are ever alike. Circumstances, although similar in some respect, may differ materially in other respects. It is for the court to consider all the circumstances. It is difficult for an appellate court to state rules equally applicable to all cases."

In fact, we clearly stated in *Wasiolek* that we were *not* promulgating an absolute rule:

Of course, a court is not strictly bound by the nurturing parent's assertion that the best interest of the child is served by the parent's presence in the home. It is for the court to determine the child's best interest. But the court must balance several factors before it can expect the nurturing parent to seek employment. Among those factors are the age and maturity of the child; the availability and adequacy of others who might assist the custodian-parent; the adequacy of available financial resources if the custodian-parent does remain in the home. We underscore that, *while not dispositive,* the custodian-parent's perception that the welfare of the child is served by having a parent at home is to be accorded significant weight in the court's calculation of its support order.

The court below failed to consider the factors discussed in *Wasiolek.* In fact the court sustained objections to questions asked by Mrs. Bender's counsel in an attempt to elicit information as to Mr. Bender's ability to support Heather on his earnings alone. The court held that evidence of Mr. Bender's earnings was not relevant to the issue of whether Mrs. Bender's support obligation should be suspended. On the contrary, Mr. Bender's ability to support Heather is, according to *Wasiolek,* a major factor to be considered in determining whether Mrs. Bender should be permitted to remain at home with Nicole. Therefore the court on remand should consider this evidence. It should also consider Nicole's age and "the availability and adequacy" of people who might assist Mrs. Bender in caring for Nicole should Mrs. Bender be required to return to work in order to provide support for Heather. In addition to these factors which are specifically enunciated in *Wasiolek,* the court on remand may wish to consider the fact that the child to be "nurtured" is not the subject of the support order, although we do not feel that this fact necessarily removes this case from the application of the "nurturing parent doctrine."

3. STEPPARENTS

Miller v. Miller

Supreme Court of New Jersey, 1984.
97 N.J. 154, 478 A.2d 351.

■ GARIBALDI, J.

Today we must decide whether a stepparent can be equitably estopped from denying the duty to provide child support for minor stepchildren after divorcing their natural parent. If equitable estoppel does apply to stepparents' situation, we must also decide what evidence must be presented to establish a cause of action for child support.

Gladys Miller married Jay Miller on December 16, 1972. No children were born of their marriage. During the couple's marriage Gladys' two daughters by her prior marriage lived with the Millers. Gladys and Jay separated on December 12, 1979. In February, 1980, Gladys filed a Verified Complaint seeking dissolution of the Millers' marriage. Although Jay was not the natural or adoptive father of Gladys' daughters, Gladys sought child support from Jay for her children. In her complaint, she alleged that by his actions, Jay had induced the girls to rely on him as their natural father, to their emotional and financial detriment. By so doing, he had prevented and cut off the girls' relationship with their natural father. Therefore, she claimed he was equitably estopped from denying a duty to pay child support. Jay claimed that although he stood *in loco parentis* to the children during his marriage, he was merely their stepfather and any legal relationship he had with the children terminated with his divorce from their mother.

The trial court agreed with Gladys. It held that Jay was equitably estopped from denying his duty to support the girls, and required him to pay child support of $75 per week per child. The trial court based its holding primarily on the concept of "emotional bonding." Jay, by his actions, had knowingly and intentionally fostered a *bona fide* parental relationship with the girls, so that in their minds he became their father. Therefore, he could not avoid the financial obligations flowing from that relationship.

The Appellate Division affirmed the trial court's judgment, primarily because it found that Jay had actively interfered with the normal relationship between the girls and their natural father to the girls' emotional and financial detriment. We granted certification.

We conclude that in appropriate cases *pendente lite* and permanent support obligations may be imposed on a stepparent on the basis of equitable estoppel. In this case, we hold that the facts established at trial are sufficient to impose a *pendente lite* award but are not sufficient to indicate whether a permanent support obligation should be imposed. We therefore reverse and remand this case to the trial court for further findings of fact and a determination consistent with this opinion.

Prior to her marriage to Jay, Gladys was married to Ralph Febre. Two children were born of that marriage: Michelle, born July, 1963, and Suzette, born July, 1966. Shortly after Suzette's birth in 1966, Gladys separated from Ralph; she divorced him in 1969.

The essential facts concerning Ralph's support of his children are undisputed. Although there was no support provision in the divorce agreement, Ralph continued to support Gladys and the children after the couple's separation until he went to prison on a narcotics charge in 1968. Immediately before going to prison, Ralph gave Gladys $5,000 for the support of his daughters. While he was in prison and after he was released, he continued to express his concern for his children.

[Gladys married Jay in 1972, while Ralph was in prison. During the Millers' marriage, Jay developed a loving relationship with the two girls and supported them financially.]

The Appellate Division found from the testimony, and for the purpose of this appeal we find, that

> upon Ralph's release from jail he attempted to visit his children but defendant [Jay] strenously opposed any visitation and, in fact, prohibited it. He rejected all offers of Ralph to contribute to the support of his

children and tore up a check tendered for that purpose. Ralph desisted from further attempts at visitation or payment of support.

Jay contends that the loving relationship he developed with the girls was not sufficient to impose a financial obligation on him to continue to support the girls after his separation from their mother. He claims that upon the termination of his marriage to their mother, his financial obligation to the girls ceased.

New Jersey has no statutory requirement imposing a duty of support on a stepparent for his or her spouse's children by a former marriage. Nor did the common law impose a legal obligation on a stepparent to support the children of his or her spouse by another party. Such an obligation arises by a voluntary assumption on the part of the stepparent to support the children. This *in loco parentis* relationship exists when a stepparent receives a child into the family home under circumstances giving rise to a presumption that he or she will assume responsibility to maintain, rear, and educate the child. The relationship, however,

> exists only so long as the parties thereto, namely the surrogate parent and/or the child, desire that it exist. In that regard, the *in loco parentis* status differs from natural parenthood or adoption. The latter two permanently affix rights and duties, while the former affixed rights and duties temporary in nature.

Thus, in most cases, when a stepparent who stands *in loco parentis* to a stepchild divorces that child's natural parent, the *in loco parentis* relationship is deemed terminated and any obligation of support the stepparent has assumed terminates.

Despite the general rule that an *in loco parentis* relationship terminates upon the intent of the stepparent, courts in certain cases have held that a stepparent's duty to support a spouse's children extends beyond the dissolution of their marriage. In most of these cases the courts have relied on principles of equitable estoppel or implied contract to impose a continuing obligation of child support on a stepparent after he or she divorces the children's natural parent.

The burden of proof of a claim based on principles of equitable estoppel is clearly on the party asserting estoppel. To establish a claim of equitable estoppel, the claiming party must show that the alleged conduct was done, or representation was made, intentionally or under such circumstances that it was both natural and probable that it would induce action. Further, the conduct must be relied on, and the relying party must act so as to change his or her position to his or her detriment.

. . .

Today, we decide that in appropriate cases, a permanent support obligation may be imposed on a stepparent on the basis of equitable estoppel, but that this doctrine should be applied with caution. Voluntary support by a stepparent should not be discouraged.

It is essential, however, that, in the interim period between the spouse's separation and the trial court's decision on permanent child support, the children have a source of support. We therefore find that if, in a motion for *pendente lite* child support, the natural parent demonstrates that he or she is not receiving support for the children from their other natural parent and establishes by affidavit that the stepparent's conduct actively interfered with the children's support by their natural parent, so that *pendente lite* support may not be obtained from the natural parent, the children should be awarded *pendente lite* support from the stepparent. By permitting a spouse to get interim support for the children, we alleviate any immediate hardship to the children caused by the breakup of a marriage in which a stepparent is the sole or major source of support for the family. Such interim support order should remain in force until circumstances justify a modification of the Order or the court makes its final determination.

To be entitled to permanent child support, Gladys, as the party alleging equitable estoppel, has the burden to prove that Jay's conduct established the three prerequisites to equitable estoppel—representation, reliance, and detriment. We recognize that there can be many forms of misrepresentation. We do not agree with those courts that have held that for equitable estoppel to apply the children must believe that the stepparent is their natural parent. Such a requirement would unduly limit this cause of action to those cases in which the stepparent appeared on the scene when the children were infants. We do believe, however, that for equitable estoppel to apply the stepparent must have made some representation of support to either the children or the natural parent as to his or her responsibilities in his or her relationship with them.

With respect to the reliance element of equitable estoppel Gladys contends that Jay's actions induced the girls to rely on him emotionally and financially, while he deliberately alienated the children from their natural father's emotional and financial support. It is undisputed that Jay, while living with Gladys, developed a loving relationship with the girls, and that the girls relied on him for emotional support. However, no court has ever applied equitable estoppel to force a husband to support the children of his divorced spouse merely because he developed a close relationship with the children, nurtured them into a family unit with himself as the father, and had the children call him "daddy." We decline to be the first to set such a precedent.

We specifically determine that the development of "emotional bonding" as set forth by the trial court is not sufficient to invoke the doctrine of equitable estoppel in stepparent cases. As stated previously, to hold otherwise would create enormous policy difficulties. A stepparent who tried to create a warm family atmosphere with his or her stepchildren would be penalized by being forced to pay support for them in the event of a divorce. At the same time, a stepparent who refused to have anything to do with his or her stepchildren beyond supporting them would be rewarded by not having to pay support in the event of a divorce.

To prove equitable estoppel, the custodial parent has the burden to establish not only representation of support and reliance but also detriment, *i.e.*, that the children will suffer future financial detriment as a result of the stepparent's representation or conduct that caused the children to be cut off from their natural parent's financial support. Matrimonial cases are extremely fact-sensitive because each case involves a unique set of interpersonal relationships. The burden of establishing economic detriment depends on the facts of the particular case.

For example, at the final hearing if the custodial parent demonstrates that he or she (1) does not know the whereabouts of the natural parent; (2) cannot locate the other natural parent; or (3) cannot secure jurisdiction over the natural parent for valid legal reasons, and that the natural parent's unavailability is due to the actions of the stepparent, a trial court could hold that the stepparent is equitably estopped from denying his or her duty to support the children.

If, as in the present case, the wife knows where the natural father is, she has the burden to bring him before the court and to seek child support from him. Once in court the burden is on the natural father to show why he should not, in equity, be required to pay child support for his children. If the court finds that the natural father should not be required to pay child support due to the stepfather's conduct, the natural father having relied thereon and having placed himself in such a position that he is unable to meet that obligation, the stepparent should be responsible for the children's continued support. This, of course, is subject to modification or change whenever the natural father can meet his obligation. We have, in countless situations, recognized that changed circumstances should be reflected in changed obligations regardless of earlier commitments.

We emphasize, however, that the natural parent should always be considered the primary recourse for child support because society and its current laws assume that the natural parent will support his or her child. It is only when a stepparent by his or her conduct actively interferes with the children's support from their natural parent that he or she may be equitably estopped from denying his or her duty to support the children.... If a stepparent marries a divorced parent who is not receiving any child support, or if during their marriage the natural parent stops paying child support without interference from the stepparent, the stepparent does not thereby inherit the permanent support obligations of the nonpaying natural parent. The stepparent must take positive action interfering with the natural parent's support obligation to be bound. Further, if the stepparent paid *pendente lite* or permanent support, he or she may have a claim for reimbursement against the natural parent.

In applying this rule to the present case, the trial court must decide whether the two girls, both of whom were in their late teens when this action arose, incurred any detriment as to their *future* support by their previous reliance on their stepfather for support. To decide that the girls have incurred such detriment, the court must find that Jay's conduct interfered with Ralph's present duty to support them.

In concluding this issue, we hold that in appropriate cases, the doctrine of equitable estoppel may be invoked to impose on a stepparent the duty to support a stepchild after a divorce from the child's natural parent. But we admonish that the doctrine be invoked cautiously. Here, Jay should be required to pay child support during the pendency of this litigation since Gladys has satisfied the requirements that we have set down for a motion for *pendente lite* child support. However, to obtain permanent support Gladys must prove at the trial that the facts support the application of the equitable estoppel doctrine. We therefore reverse the Appellate Division's judgment and remand to the trial court for a determination of the facts necessary to decide this issue in accordance with this opinion.

. . .

■ Handler, J. *(Concurring in part and dissenting in part).*

Equity may insist that a stepfather accept a continuing obligation to support his minor stepchildren upon the termination by divorce of his marriage to their mother. I firmly believe that this is an appropriate case to recognize that defendant be required, under principles of equitable estoppel, to continue to provide child support for his minor stepchildren. In my opinion, the record discloses sufficient facts to call for the imposition of such an obligation. I would therefore affirm the judgment of the Appellate Division.

Equitable estoppel is a doctrine that is designed to bring an uniquely individualized controversy to a just and fair disposition, taking into account the special and particular relationship and course of dealing between the parties. The doctrine, well understood in its classic definition, requires of one party a representation, and of the other party expected, consequential, and detrimental reliance. [citations omitted] Equitable estoppel may be appropriate in any equitable cause of action or defense. In this case, its application is especially compelling because children are involved. Consequently, the doctrine, in this setting, requires a somewhat broader conceptualization.

In the matrimonial context, when the rights and interests of innocent children are at stake, we should consider in applying the doctrine of equitable estoppel whether there was a course of conduct that, in its cumulative impact, was tantamount to a representation made by one party with the expectation that other persons would rely on this conduct, and whether, as a natural and probable consequence, such persons did in fact reasonably rely, resulting in a detriment to them. That detriment—the disadvantage or change of position—can occur because of the actor's subsequent repudiation of his or her conduct and disavowal of the expectations engendered by that conduct.

. . .

In this case, the gravamen of plaintiff's complaint is, and the evidence presented shows, that by a pronounced and purposeful course of conduct, defendant induced his stepdaughters to rely on him as their father and as their sole source of paternal sustenance and support. Further, in so doing, he frustrated and cut off the girls' relationship with their natural father. There is little question that when defendant terminated his marriage and ended his familial relationship with his wife and his stepdaughters, he left the children at a substantial financial disadvantage. In effect, he repudiated his prior course of conduct and disavowed the expectations he himself created. I am satisfied that the record meets plaintiff's evidential burden to demonstrate that defendant equitably should be estopped from disclaiming a continuing duty to support these children.

. . .

I agree with the Court that the love between defendant and the stepchildren is not the pivotal consideration. The gist of the equitable cause of action here is rooted in the fact that defendant affirmatively established himself as the sole or primary supporter of the family and zealously deprived his stepchildren of the support they were otherwise entitled to secure from their natural father. Nevertheless, parental love may be a relevant factor to be weighed in making the equitable assessment. Thus, if this emotional bonding with the stepfather has contributed to or exacerbated the alienation of the children from their natural father and, as important, has served to discourage the natural father from maintaining a full parental relationship with his own children, it may have a material bearing on his failure to support his children.

Here, it is undisputed that throughout the seven years that plaintiff and defendant lived together, defendant developed a loving relationship with the two girls.

. . .

In sum, I would find that when a stepparent walks away from his marital family, regardless of spousal fault, after a marriage characterized by a course of conduct on his part that has resulted in the cutting off of financial assistance from the natural parent, the stepparent should remain provisionally responsible for the family's continued support. The responsibility is provisional because, as a matrimonial obligation, it is of course subject to modification or change. Changed circumstances may always be addressed by changing obligations, regardless of how fair these were when first imposed. The support obligation, equitably imposed on the stepfather in this case, need not endure indefinitely and does not eliminate or supersede the natural father's legal obligation to support his own children. Therefore, either party should be required, or given the opportunity, to assert this obligation against the natural father. The trial court should be vested with the discretion to determine the circumstances under which it would be appropriate or necessary to shift the responsibility for child support to the natural father. However, unless and until the natural father can be brought back into the picture, equitable estoppel should prevent the stepfather from passing the buck—literally. In no event should the stepchildren be left holding an empty bag.

NOTE

Miller reflects the general consensus on the obligations of a stepparent for child support. *See, e.g.*, In the Matter of Glaude & Fogg, 151 N.H. 273, 855 A.2d 494 (2004); W. v. W., 256 Conn. 657, 779 A.2d 716 (2001).

4. UNMARRIED PARTNERS

Johnson v. Louis

Supreme Court of Iowa, 2002.
654 N.W.2d 886.

■ CARTER, JUSTICE.

Debbie Johnson, the mother of Jared Johnson, appealed from a denial of her request to modify the child support obligation of Jared's father, Michael Louis, to include a postsecondary educational subsidy for Jared. Debbie and Michael had never married. The court of appeals, although acknowledging that Jared, who would soon be eighteen, had no statutory or common-law right to continued child support after attaining that age, concluded that a refusal to grant him a postsecondary educational subsidy would amount to a denial of equal protection of the law. As a result, it reversed the district court's judgment and ordered that a subsidy be exacted from Michael. After reviewing the record and considering the arguments presented, we vacate the decision of the court of appeals and affirm the judgment of the district court.

Debbie gave birth to Jared on November 3, 1982. In February of 1984 the child support recovery unit, acting on behalf of Debbie, sought and obtained a finding of paternity and a support order against Michael pursuant to Iowa Code section 252A.3(2) (1983).

[Section 252A provides that non-spouse child obligor spouses are required to pay a fair and reasonable amount of support for a child or children under eighteen years old. The court explained that this section has never authorized child support for postsecondary education. By contrast, Section

598 of the Iowa code provides that a court may order child support payments to fund postsecondary education for children whose parents have divorced.]

... In May 2000 Debbie petitioned for a modification of the support order to include a postsecondary educational subsidy. The district court denied that request on February 6, 2001. Other facts that are of significance in deciding the appeal will be discussed in connection with our consideration of the legal issues presented....

The court of appeals concluded that, because support decrees entered in proceedings under Iowa Code chapter 598 allow the court to provide a postsecondary educational subsidy for a child attending college, it is a denial of equal protection of the law to deny the same opportunity for a child whose support obligation is adjudicated under statutes other than chapter 598. Michael urges that the court of appeals' conclusion on that issue is flawed.

The primary basis for the court of appeals' decision was its conclusion that the statutory scheme discriminated against illegitimate children because only children whose parents are married have their support obligation adjudicated under chapter 598. As support for striking down this perceived discrimination, the court of appeals relied on Levy v. Louisiana, 391 U.S. 68 (1968), wherein the Court held that it was a denial of equal protection under the Fourteenth Amendment to the federal constitution for the State of Louisiana to fail to provide the same right of recovery for wrongful death of a parent to illegitimate children as was provided to legitimate children. A similar result, also involving the State of Louisiana, was reached in Weber v. Aetna Casualty & Surety Co., 406 U.S. 164, 169 (1972) (failure to provide identical workers' compensation benefits to legitimate and illegitimate children of a worker killed on the job deemed denial of equal protection).

Because the court of appeals decided the issue under the federal constitution, we consider it in the same manner. We note, however, that we usually deem the federal and state Equal Protection Clauses to be identical in scope, import, and purpose....

Unless a suspect class or a fundamental right is involved, any classification made by the legislature need only have a rational basis. In applying this standard, we apply a rational-basis test in determining the validity of the statutory classifications that are assailed here.

We conclude that the discrimination against illegitimate children that was perceived by the court of appeals is not well-founded.... [T]here is no invidious discrimination between the rights of children whose parents dissolve their marriages under chapter 598 and those for whom support is determined under chapter 252A....

For purposes of an equal protection analysis, Jared's lack of entitlement to a postsecondary educational subsidy is not only similar to the situation of other child-support obligees whose rights are established pursuant to chapter 252A, it is also similar to the situation of children whose parents continue to be married to each other. The class of children who do enjoy the right to seek a postsecondary educational subsidy, i.e., children whose parents are or have been divorced, present a situation different from the classes of children who do not enjoy that entitlement.

As we recognized in In re Marriage of Vrban, 293 N.W.2d 198, 202 (Iowa 1980), the benefited class of children have had the attributes of a legally recognized parental relationship taken from them by court decree.

The educational benefit is a quid pro quo for the loss of stability resulting from divorce. Children like Jared, whose parents never sought State involvement to formalize or dissolve their relationships, are not similarly situated. They cannot claim the loss of stability such change in status brings. And, while they may rightfully claim a similarly vulnerable status insofar as furthering their education, we deem the classification drawn by the legislature to be rational, not arbitrary, and thus not constitutionally infirm.

We have considered all issues presented and conclude that the decision of the court of appeals should be vacated. The judgment of the district court is affirmed.

G. JURISDICTION

1. DIVISIBLE DIVORCE

Vanderbilt v. Vanderbilt

Supreme Court of the United States, 1957.
354 U.S. 416, 77 S.Ct. 1360, 1 L.Ed.2d 1456.

■ JUSTICE BLACK delivered the opinion of the Court.

Cornelius Vanderbilt, Jr., petitioner, and Patricia Vanderbilt, respondent, were married in 1948. They separated in 1952 while living in California. The wife moved to New York where she has resided since February 1953. In March of that year the husband filed suit for divorce in Nevada. This proceeding culminated, in June 1953, with a decree of final divorce which provided that both husband and wife were "freed and released from the bonds of matrimony and all the duties and obligations thereof...."[1] The wife was not served with process in Nevada and did not appear before the divorce court.

In April 1954, Mrs. Vanderbilt instituted an action in a New York court praying for separation from petitioner and for alimony. The New York court did not have personal jurisdiction over him, but in order to satisfy his obligations, if any, to Mrs. Vanderbilt, it sequestered his property within the State. He appeared specially and, among other defenses to the action, contended that the Full Faith and Credit Clause of the United States Constitution compelled the New York court to treat the Nevada divorce as having ended the marriage and as having destroyed any duty of support which he owed the respondent. While the New York court found the Nevada decree valid and held that it had effectively dissolved the marriage, it nevertheless entered an order, under § 1170–b of the New York Civil Practice Act, directing petitioner to make designated support payments to respondent. The New York Court of Appeals upheld the support order. Petitioner then applied to this Court for certiorari contending that § 1170–b, as applied, is unconstitutional because it contravenes the Full Faith and Credit Clause....

In *Estin v. Estin, 334 U.S. 541,* this Court decided that a Nevada divorce court, which had no personal jurisdiction over the wife, had no power to terminate a husband's obligation to provide her support as required in a

1. It seems clear that in Nevada the effect of this decree was to put an end to the husband's duty to support the wife—provided, of course, that the Nevada courts had power to do this.

pre-existing New York separation decree. The factor which distinguishes the present case from *Estin* is that here the wife's right to support had not been reduced to judgment prior to the husband's *ex parte* divorce. In our opinion this difference is not material on the question before us. Since the wife was not subject to its jurisdiction, the Nevada divorce court had no power to extinguish any right which she had under the law of New York to financial support from her husband. It has long been the constitutional rule that a court cannot adjudicate a personal claim or obligation unless it has jurisdiction over the person of the defendant. Here, the Nevada divorce court was as powerless to cut off the wife's support right as it would have been to order the husband to pay alimony if the wife had brought the divorce action and he had not been subject to the divorce court's jurisdiction. Therefore, the Nevada decree, to the extent it purported to affect the wife's right to support, was void and the Full Faith and Credit Clause did not obligate New York to give it recognition.

. . .

NOTE

One of the difficult issues left unresolved by the opinion in Vanderbilt is what law governs the property rights of the stay-at-home spouse, that of the domicile at the time of divorce, or of the forum (if the two are different). The generally accepted view is that the determining law if that of the stay-at-home spouse's domicile at the time of divorce. See Loeb v. Loeb, 4 N.Y.2d 542, 176 N.Y.S.2d 590, 152 N.E.2d 36 (1958); Lewis v. Lewis, 49 Cal.2d 389, 317 P.2d 987 (1957); see generally Note, Long–Arm Jurisdiction in Alimony and Custody Cases, 73 Colum. L. Rev. 289, 293 (1975). Compare Manfrini v. Manfrini, 136 N.J.Super. 390, 346 A.2d 430 (App.Div. 1975), where the court held that full faith and credit would be granted to a decision of the New York Supreme Court granting the husband a divorce because of the wife's adultery, and denying alimony to the wife because of her misconduct. The wife had moved into their summer home in New Jersey, where she was served personally with notice of the New York action. Apparently in an effort to avail herself of the more favorable New Jersey law she chose to default in the New York action.

2. LONG-ARM JURISDICTION

Kulko v. Superior Court of California

United States Supreme Court, 1978.
436 U.S. 84, 98 S.Ct. 1690, 56 L.Ed.2d 132.

■ JUSTICE MARSHALL delivered the opinion of the Court.

The issue before us is whether, in this action for child support, the California state courts may exercise in personam jurisdiction over a nonresident, nondomiciliary parent of minor children domiciled within the State. For reasons set forth below, we hold that the exercise of such jurisdiction would violate the Due Process Clause of the Fourteenth Amendment.

Appellant Ezra Kulko married appellee Sharon Kulko Horn in 1959, during appellant's three-day stopover in California en route from a military base in Texas to a tour of duty in Korea. At the time of this marriage, both parties were domiciled in and residents of New York State. Immediately following the marriage, Sharon Kulko returned to New York, as did appellant after his tour of duty. Their first child, Darwin, was born to the Kulkos in New York in 1961, and a year later their second child, Ilsa, was born, also in New York. The Kulkos and their two children resided together as a family in New York City continuously until March 1972, when the Kulkos separated.

Following the separation, Sharon Kulko moved to San Francisco, Cal. A written separation agreement was drawn up in New York; in September 1972, Sharon Kulko flew to New York City in order to sign this agreement. The agreement provided, inter alia, that the children would remain with their father during the school year but would spend their Christmas, Easter, and summer vacations with their mother. While Sharon Kulko waived any claim for her own support or maintenance, Ezra Kulko agreed to pay his wife $3,000 per year in child support for the periods when the children were in her care, custody, and control. Immediately after execution of the separation agreement, Sharon Kulko flew to Haiti and procured a divorce there; the divorce decree incorporated the terms of the agreement. She then returned to California, where she remarried and took the name Horn.

The children resided with appellant during the school year and with their mother on vacations, as provided by the separation agreement, until December 1973. At this time, just before Ilsa was to leave New York to spend Christmas vacation with her mother, she told her father that she wanted to remain in California after her vacation. Appellant bought his daughter a one-way plane ticket, and Ilsa left, taking her clothing with her. Ilsa then commenced living in California with her mother during the school year and spending vacations with her father. In January 1976, appellant's other child, Darwin, called his mother from New York and advised her that he wanted to live with her in California. Unbeknownst to appellant, appellee Horn sent a plane ticket to her son, which he used to fly to California where he took up residence with his mother and sister.

Less than one month after Darwin's arrival in California, appellee Horn commenced this action against appellant in the California Superior Court. She sought to establish the Haitian divorce decree as a California judgment; to modify the judgment so as to award her full custody of the children; and to increase appellant's child-support obligations.

Appellant appeared specially and moved to quash service of the summons on the ground that he was not a resident of California and lacked sufficient "minimum contacts" with the State under International Shoe Co. v. Washington, 326 U.S. 310, 316 (1945), to warrant the State's assertion of personal jurisdiction over him.

The trial court summarily denied the motion to quash, and appellant sought review in the California Court of Appeal by petition for a writ of mandate. Appellant did not contest the court's jurisdiction for purposes of the custody determination, but, with respect to the claim for increased support, he renewed his argument that the California courts lacked personal jurisdiction over him. The appellate court affirmed the denial of appellant's motion to quash, reasoning that, by consenting to his children's living in California, appellant had "caused an effect in [the] state" warranting the exercise of jurisdiction over him. 133 Cal. Rptr. 627, 628 (1976).

The California Supreme Court granted appellant's petition for review, and in a 4–2 decision sustained the rulings of the lower state courts.

. . .

The Due Process Clause of the Fourteenth Amendment operates as a limitation on the jurisdiction of state courts to enter judgments affecting rights or interests of nonresident defendants. It has long been the rule that a valid judgment imposing a personal obligation or duty in favor of the plaintiff may be entered only by a court having jurisdiction over the person of the defendant. The existence of personal jurisdiction, in turn, depends upon the presence of reasonable notice to the defendant that an action has been brought, and a sufficient connection between the defendant and the forum State to make it fair to require defense of the action in the forum. In this case, appellant does not dispute the adequacy of the notice that he received, but contends that his connection with the State of California is too attenuated, under the standards implicit in the Due Process Clause of the Constitution, to justify imposing upon him the burden and inconvenience of defense in California.

The parties are in agreement that the constitutional standard for determining whether the State may enter a binding judgment against appellant here is that set forth in this Court's opinion in International Shoe Co. v. Washington, supra: that a defendant "have certain minimum contacts with [the forum State] such that the maintenance of the suit does not offend 'traditional notions of fair play and substantial justice.'" While the interests of the forum State and of the plaintiff in proceeding with the cause in the plaintiff's forum of choice are, of course, to be considered, an essential criterion in all cases is whether the "quality and nature" of the defendant's activity is such that it is "reasonable" and "fair" to require him to conduct his defense in that State.

. . . [W]e believe that the California Supreme Court's application of the minimum-contacts test in this case represents an unwarranted extension of International Shoe and would, if sustained, sanction a result that is neither fair, just, nor reasonable.

. . .

The "purposeful act" that the California Supreme Court believed . . . warrant[ed] the exercise of personal jurisdiction over appellant in California was his "actively and fully [consenting] to Ilsa living in California for the school year . . . and . . . [sending] her to California for that purpose." We cannot accept the proposition that appellant's acquiescence in Ilsa's desire to live with her mother conferred jurisdiction over appellant in the California courts in this action. A father who agrees, in the interests of family harmony and his children's preferences, to allow them to spend more time in California than was required under a separation agreement can hardly be said to have "purposefully availed himself" of the "benefits and protections" of California's laws.

Nor can we agree with the assertion of the court below that the exercise of in personam jurisdiction here was warranted by the financial benefit appellant derived from his daughter's presence in California for nine months of the year. This argument rests on the premise that, while appellant's liability for support payments remained unchanged, his yearly expenses for supporting the child in New York decreased. But this circumstance, even if true, does not support California's assertion of jurisdiction here. Any diminution in appellant's household costs resulted, not from the child's presence in California, but rather from her absence from appellant's home. . . . Any ultimate financial advantage to appellant thus results not from the child's presence in California, but from appellee's failure earlier to seek an increase in payments under the separation agreement. The argument below to the contrary, in our view, confuses the question of appellant's liability with that of the proper forum in which to determine that liability.

. . .

The circumstances in this case clearly render "unreasonable" California's assertion of personal jurisdiction. There is no claim that appellant has visited physical injury on either property or persons within the State of California. The cause of action herein asserted arises, not from the defendant's commercial transactions in interstate commerce, but rather from his personal, domestic relations. It thus cannot be said that appellant has sought a commercial benefit from solicitation of business from a resident of California that could reasonably render him liable to suit in state court; appellant's activities cannot fairly be analogized to an insurer's sending an insurance contract and premium notices into the State to an insured resident of the State. Furthermore, the controversy between the parties arises from a separation that occurred in the State of New York; appellee Horn seeks modification of a contract that was negotiated in New York and that she flew to New York to sign.... [T]he instant action involves an agreement that was entered into with virtually no connection with the forum State.

Finally, basic considerations of fairness point decisively in favor of appellant's State of domicile as the proper forum for adjudication of this case, whatever the merits of appellee's underlying claim. It is appellant who has remained in the State of the marital domicile, whereas it is appellee who has moved across the continent. Appellant has at all times resided in New York State, and, until the separation and appellee's move to California, his entire family resided there as well. As noted above, appellant did no more than acquiesce in the stated preference of one of his children to live with her mother in California. This single act is surely not one that a reasonable parent would expect to result in the substantial financial burden and personal strain of litigating a child-support suit in a forum 3,000 miles away, and we therefore see no basis on which it can be said that appellant could reasonably have anticipated being "haled before a [California] court." To make jurisdiction in a case such as this turn on whether appellant bought his daughter her ticket or instead unsuccessfully sought to prevent her departure would impose an unreasonable burden on family relations, and one wholly unjustified by the "quality and nature" of appellant's activities in or relating to the State of California.

. . .

... [T]he mere act of sending a child to California to live with her mother is not a commercial act and connotes no intent to obtain or expectancy of receiving a corresponding benefit in the State that would make fair the assertion of that State's judicial jurisdiction.

Accordingly, we conclude that the appellant's motion to quash service, on the ground of lack of personal jurisdiction, was erroneously denied by the California courts. The judgment of the California Supreme Court is, therefore,

Reversed.

Comment, Personal Jurisdiction and Child Support: Establishing the Parent–Child Relationship as Minimum Contacts

89 Calif. L. Rev. 1125 (2001).

. . .

B. Aftermath of Kulko: Interpreting and Enacting Long-Arm Statutes Based on "Purposeful Availment"

The Court's holding in Kulko not only impacted the authority of state courts to assert jurisdiction over nonresident parents under existing long-arm statutes, but severely limited how legislatures could approach the problem in the future. Because the parent-child relationship was not a relevant basis for asserting jurisdiction, purposeful availment became the focus of courts and legislatures seeking to hold nonresident parents responsible for the financial support of their minor children. Accordingly, state courts struggled to find purposeful availment by analogizing the child support obligation to obligations arising out of relationships based on contractual arrangements or tortious conduct. In addition, legislatures enacted new long-arm statutes incorporating acts of purposeful availment considered to be especially relevant in the context of child support actions. Despite these efforts, courts and legislatures continue to struggle as they are forced to disregard the parent-child relationship in favor of finding some act of purposeful availment in order to navigate the barriers created by Kulko. Indeed, upon closer examination, these efforts confirm that the rule announced in Kulko is untenable and ought tobe overruled.

1. Lower Courts Struggling to Find Purposeful Availment under Existing Long–Arm Statutes

State legislatures authorize the exercise of state power over nonresidents by enacting long-arm statutes. Thus, all assertions of personal jurisdiction must satisfy the forum state's long-arm statute and comport with due process. While many states authorize their courts to exercise personal jurisdiction over nonresident defendants on any basis that is constitutionally permissible, others allow courts to assert jurisdiction based on specific acts or circumstances, such as tortious conduct by a nonresident defendant causing injury within the state. Following Kulko, courts attempted to assert jurisdiction over nonresident parents under both types of long-arm statutes by identifying various acts of purposeful availment related to the parent-child relationship.

Long-arm statutes based on specific acts or circumstances typically allow states to assert jurisdiction based on a nonresident's business transactions or tortious conduct. Although these statutes were designed to protect state citizens in interstate business transactions and to allow recovery for physical injuries resulting from torts committed by nonresidents, following Kulko courts employed "judicial creativity" in extending these provisions to child support actions. Unfortunately, because an existing divorce decree or child support order is required to assert jurisdiction under these statutes, this approach is limited in its ability to address the problems created by Kulko in establishing child support orders in cases involving a nonresident parent.

Under "transacting business" long-arm statutes, courts typically assert jurisdiction based on the existence of a separation or divorce agreement with a "substantial connection" to the forum state. Relying on the separation or divorce agreement, the court is able to treat the dispute as a contract case from which the support obligation arises. This approach obscures the real significance of the dispute as being primarily concerned with the activities of the nonresident parent as opposed to an obligation arising out of the parent-child relationship. Moreover, it is only available to resident parents whose divorce or separation agreement has been entered into in the forum state. It does nothing to aid parents who have left the state of marital domicile, as in Kulko.

Courts have also relied on "tortious conduct" long-arm statutes in asserting personal jurisdiction over nonresident parents. Some courts have construed "tortious conduct" provisions broadly to include failure to support a minor child. For example, in In re Custody of Miller, the Washington Supreme Court held that "the failure of a parent to support his or her children constitutes a tort" within the meaning of the long-arm statute. Unfortunately, this case is an exception to the rule. Most courts require an existing support order before finding that the nonresident defendant is in violation of a duty or has engaged in tortious conduct, reasoning that in the absence of a valid court order no duty has been violated because no support amount has been set. As a result, long-arm statutes based on tortious conduct can usually only be used to enforce existing orders.

In addition to their limited applicability, "tortious conduct" long-arm statutes can take a variety of forms, introducing unnecessary confusion into a court's analysis. Some statutes explicitly include tortious acts that occur outside the forum state but have effects inside the state. Others limit their application to torts occurring within the forum state. Still others distinguish between acts and omissions occurring both within and without the forum state. As a result, in determining whether they may assert personal jurisdiction over a nonresident parent in a particular case, courts may have to determine where the failure to support occurs. In addition, they may be required to decide whether the failure to support is an act or an omission. While the custodial parent is likely to argue that the failure to support is an act occurring in the child's state of residence, the nonresident parent is likely to argue that it is an omission occurring in the nonresident parent's state of residence. Thus, before courts can even consider the child support obligation at issue, they must spend considerable time and effort in working through the above intricacies of long-arm statutes based on tortious conduct.

Both "transacting business" and "tortious conduct" long-arm statutes are of limited use to courts seeking to assert personal jurisdiction over a nonresident parent. Unless the nonresident parent has entered into a divorce agreement in the forum state, there is no act of purposeful availment. Likewise, even if a court is willing to find that the nonresident parent's failure to support the child constitutes an act of purposeful availment, it is of limited use unless there is an existing child support order. In addition to the limited applicability of these long-arm statutes, both approaches focus on the nonresident parent's activities to the total exclusion of the parent-child relationship. The obligation to financially support one's child does not arise out of the activities of a nonresident parent in relation to the state in which the child resides. The parent-child relationship is the source of that obligation and should be the focus of the court's inquiry.

At the other end of the spectrum, some states enact long-arm statutes allowing state courts to assert jurisdiction on any basis not inconsistent with the demands of due process. Kulko's extension of the purposeful availment requirement to child support actions also severely limited the reach of long-arm statutes authorizing the exercise of jurisdiction "on any basis not inconsistent with the Constitution of this state of or the United States." By its holding, Kulko required courts to disregard the parent-child relationship. Thus, even courts presumably given the greatest degree of latitude in asserting jurisdiction were limited by Kulko.

2. Limiting Legislative Efforts to Respond to Issues of Personal Jurisdiction in the Context of Child Support Actions

The holding in Kulko not only served as a barrier to courts asserting personal jurisdiction under existing long-arm statutes, but also dictated how legislatures could approach the problem in the future. While courts have struggled to find acts of purposeful availment comparable to a breach of contract or tortious conduct, legislatures have endeavored to enact new long-arm statutes specifically designed to confer jurisdiction based on activities held to constitute minimum contacts in actions for child support. However, despite these efforts Kulko's purposeful availment requirement remains a barrier to real change.

These specialized statutes do offer some benefit over traditional long-arm statutes in that they clearly indicate the legislature's intent to assert jurisdiction over nonresident parents in child support actions. However, courts are still forced to disregard the parent-child relationship in assessing minimum contacts. Instead, courts must find some act of purposeful availment by analyzing issues such as whether a child is present in the forum state as a result of the actions of the defendant or whether the defendant engaged in sexual intercourse in the state that may have resulted in the conception of the child who is the subject of the child support action.

One act of purposeful availment identified in these specialized long-arm statutes is where the child resides in the forum state because of the acts or directives of the nonresident parent. In Franklin v. Commonwealth, a case in which a mother and her two children had relocated to Virginia after the nonresident defendant abused and finally expelled them from their home, a Virginia appellate court held that it could assert personal jurisdiction over the nonresident father because the children had become residents of Virginia "as a result of his acts." Although the defendant did not contest the fact that he had abused and expelled his family from their home, he argued that he had not purposefully availed himself of the benefits and protections of the forum state because he had not specifically directed them to relocate to Virginia. The court dismissed this argument, stating that to allow [a] husband to escape his support obligations merely because he failed to dictate the specific destination when he ordered his family to leave the marital home would frustrate the purpose of the legislature . . . to create an economical and expedient means of enforcing support orders for parties located in different states.

The court distinguished cases in which other courts declined to exercise jurisdiction over nonresident fathers under similar long-arm provisions by stating that in each of those cases "the children resided in [the forum state] after their mother chose to move out of state without any urging from their fathers."

This distinction has no basis in reality and is an example of why forcing courts to show purposeful availment in the context of an action for child support is inappropriate. As dictated by Kulko, unless a court can point to some act of purposeful availment, there can be no basis for finding minimum contacts. Under this logic, it is significantly more difficult for a mother who leaves an abusive husband of her own volition, as opposed to being ordered out of the home by her abuser, to obtain personal jurisdiction over him should she and her children move to another state.

A nonresident parent's act of sexual intercourse in the forum state, where the act may have resulted in conception of a child who is the subject of the action, is another act of purposeful availment often identified in specialized long-arm statutes. In Phillips v. Fallen, a Missouri appellate court upheld the validity of a support order issued by a Washington court asserting personal jurisdiction over a nonresident defendant where he had "not overcome adequately [the resident mother's] averment that the couple had sexual intercourse in Washington which may have resulted in their child's conception." The defendant father acknowledged visiting Washington with the plaintiff mother around Thanksgiving 1982, but contended that he "did not remember" having sexual intercourse and that "the child's conception could not have occurred during the couple's visit to Washington."

Relying on a medical dictionary and the mother's medical records, the court held that the Washington court had not erred in asserting personal jurisdiction over the nonresident father:

"While the medical records suggest that the child was born prematurely by approximately three weeks, these records were not authenticated, and [defendant] did not present any medical testimony supporting his interpretation of them. We discern no basis for concluding that the decision erred in rejecting Phillips' interpretation. The child was born 271 days after Thanksgiving 1982. A normal gestational period is 280 days, but a range of 250 to 310 days is not abnormal."

In struggling to find some act of purposeful availment, rather than focusing on the parent-child relationship and the child support obligation arising from it, the court spent the majority of its opinion analyzing the definition of a normal gestational period.

The Phillips case is yet another example of how requiring purposeful availment in the context of actions for child support can distort the true nature of the child support obligation and require courts to engage in meaningless analysis. When and where a nonresident parent engaged in sexual intercourse is a private matter and should be irrelevant in child support actions once paternity has been established. Thus, even under long-arm statutes specifically designed to confer jurisdiction in child support actions, Kulko's focus on purposeful availment obscures the real significance of the child support obligation. Courts and legislatures are forced to spend time analyzing the nonresident parent's activities in relation to the forum state, rather than focusing on the parent-child relationship as the source of the obligation.

3. UNIFORM INTERSTATE FAMILY SUPPORT ACT

Child Support Enforcement v. Brenckle

Supreme Judicial Court of Massachusetts, 1997.
424 Mass. 214, 675 N.E.2d 390.

■ MARSHALL, JUSTICE.

This case raises questions about the relationship between successive Massachusetts statutes for the interstate enforcement of child support orders. The child support enforcement division of Alaska brings the action on behalf of Alaska resident Carol A. Brenckle (Carol Brenckle) to collect unpaid child support payments from her former husband, Joseph J. Brenckle, Jr. (Brenckle), a resident of Marshfield. On appeal, Brenckle challenges findings of the District Court entered against him in the amount of $107,365 as determined under a 1991 judgment of the Alaska Superior Court (Alaska court) and enforced by the court below. We affirm the judgment and remand this matter to the District Court, where it shall be transferred to the Probate and Family Court Department for such other proceedings as may be necessary to enforce the judgment.

We summarize the pertinent facts. The couple was married on December 19, 1964, in California. In 1971, they moved to Alaska, where they had one child, Joseph J. Brenckle, III (son), who was born on July 16, 1974. In May, 1978, they filed a joint petition for divorce which was granted by the Alaska court on July 17, 1978.

Under the terms of the divorce agreement Carol Brenckle retained custody of their son, and Brenckle agreed to pay $500 each month for child support. The divorce agreement provided that child support would terminate when their son reached the age of majority, and that the expenses for the child's education (preparatory school, college, and graduate school) would be shared jointly by both parents. The divorce agreement also provided for visitation arrangements between Brenckle and his son.

Soon after the divorce—the record is not specific—and in any event by January, 1979, Brenckle moved to Massachusetts, while Carol Brenckle remained in Alaska with their son. Brenckle made the required child support payments for several months only. It is undisputed that Brenckle made no child support payments after December, 1979. He stopped all payments at that time, he says, because one support payment sent to Carol Brenckle at her home address was returned to him marked "unclaimed," and he "assumed" either that she would contact him with a new address, or that "she no longer intended to accept the checks because of a changed and improved financial position." Brenckle apparently made no effort to determine whether his "assumption" was correct, or whether his support payments could be sent to an alternative address, such as the post office box mailing address listed by Carol Brenckle in the divorce agreement. According to Carol Brenckle, Brenckle had no communication with their son after May, 1979. Because she was financially able to support their son with her own earnings, she did not pursue enforcement of the delinquent child support obligations until their son prepared to go to college.

In 1991, when their son turned seventeen years old and began to make plans to enter college, Carol Brenckle filed an action in the Alaska court to recover the child support arrearages owed to her because she could not afford to support him in college.[4] Brenckle was provided notice of those proceedings and an opportunity to be heard, but he did not enter an appearance or contest the proceedings. On December 19, 1991, the Alaska court entered judgment against Brenckle in the amount of $75,000, with interest. He has not challenged the validity of that judgment.

On June 30, 1992, Carol Brenckle filed a petition in Alaska under the Uniform Reciprocal Enforcement of Support Act (URESA), Alaska Stat. §§ 25.25.010–25.25.100 (since repealed), seeking to establish an enforcement order in Massachusetts, Brenckle's home State. The Alaska court certified the petition on September 18, 1992, and ordered it transmitted to the child support enforcement division of the Massachusetts Department of Revenue (department).

The petition was entered in the Brockton District Court on June 8, 1993, and an order of notice was issued by that court to Brenckle and served on him in hand. On December 9, 1993, Brenckle filed his answer to the petition, and on March 4, 1994, he filed a motion to dismiss or for summary judgment. The District Court denied his motion on March 16, 1994.

4. Alaska law provides that unpaid periodic child support payments are judgments that become vested when each payment becomes due, Alaska Stat. § 25.27.225 (Michie 1996), and further provides for procedures for the collection of the past due payments by obtaining a judgment in the amount owed. Alaska Stat. § 25.27.226 (Michie 1996).

On November 16, 1994, the District Court judge conducted a hearing on the merits of the case; no testimony was received and, by agreement of the parties, the matter was submitted on memoranda and affidavits. On February 10, 1995, the judge found Brenckle liable in the amount of $107,365, the amount of the 1991 Alaska judgment with interest. Brenckle appealed. We transferred his appeal here on our own motion.

This case reaches us in unusual circumstances. URESA, codified at G.L. c. 273A, this Commonwealth's previous statutory mechanism for issuing, modifying and enforcing interstate child support orders, was repealed on February 10, 1995, the same date that the judgment entered in the District Court. At the same time URESA was replaced by the Uniform Interstate Family Support Act (UIFSA), codified at G.L. c. 209D, inserted by St.1995, c. 5, § 87. We consider first which law applies to this appeal.

UIFSA was approved by the National Conference of Commissioners on Uniform State Laws in 1992, and has since been adopted by twenty-six States, including Alaska and Massachusetts. It was developed to improve the two prior uniform laws concerning enforcement of family support orders, URESA and the Revised Uniform Reciprocal Enforcement of Support Act (RURESA). UIFSA aims to cure the problem of conflicting support orders entered by multiple courts, and provides for the exercise of continuing, exclusive jurisdiction by one tribunal over support orders. Under UIFSA, once one court enters a support order, no other court may modify that order for as long as the obligee, obligor, or child for whose benefit the order is entered continues to reside within the jurisdiction of that court unless each party consents in writing to another jurisdiction.

. . .

It was the express intention of the Legislature that UIFSA be applied retrospectively; its provisions govern any URESA action that is "pending or was previously adjudicated." It is also clear that UIFSA, like its predecessor URESA, does not create a duty of support, but rather provides the procedural framework for enforcing one State's support order in another jurisdiction. As a remedial statute, and one not affecting substantive rights, it is proper that UIFSA should be applied retroactively. We recognize that there are limitations to the extent to which even procedural or remedial statutes will operate retroactively. We have examined Brenckle's claims under both UIFSA and URESA; because we conclude that none of his substantive rights is impaired by proceeding under either statute, it is particularly appropriate to apply UIFSA retroactively in this case.

We turn now to consider whether the Alaska judgment against Brenckle can be enforced under UIFSA. We begin by recognizing that under UIFSA the Alaska court had jurisdiction over Brenckle to issue its 1991 judgment. The son is a resident of Alaska, and Brenckle resided with him in that State from his birth in 1974 until Brenckle moved to Massachusetts. Under UIFSA personal jurisdiction may be exercised by a State tribunal if an individual resided with a child in that State. Moreover, as we noted before, Brenckle has never contested the validity of the Alaska judgment and does not do so now.

Brenckle argues that before it could enforce the Alaska judgment the District Court was required to make an independent finding that he owed a duty of support to his son. No independent finding is required. Under UIFSA a support order issued by a tribunal of another State may be registered in a tribunal of the Commonwealth ("responding tribunal," § 1–

101[17]) for enforcement. The Alaska judgment is just such an order. The procedure for registration is set forth in G.L. c. 209D, § 6–602. Carol Brenckle and the child support enforcement division of Alaska have complied with all of the UIFSA registration requirements, and provided all of the information required to register the Alaska support order in Massachusetts. Once registered, the Alaska order is enforceable in the same manner, and is subject to the same procedures, as an order issued by a Massachusetts court. UIFSA requires no de novo or independent review by a Massachusetts court whether Brenckle owes a duty of support to his son. Indeed, requiring an independent finding of a duty of support when an Alaska court has already made that determination would impede and frustrate the purpose of UIFSA.

Under UIFSA, a party contesting the validity or enforcement of a registered order or seeking to vacate the registration, has the burden of proving one or more of the defenses specifically provided by G.L. c. 209D, § 6–607.[14] Brenckle has not articulated his claims as "defenses" under UIFSA. Nevertheless, we have reviewed all of the claims that he has made, both in the court below and on appeal, as well as the record supporting such claims, and conclude that none of his claims is sufficient to constitute a valid defense under UIFSA. The Alaska child support order must be enforced.

While we hold that UIFSA is the statute applicable to these proceedings, we shall review each of Brenckle's claims under URESA. We do so because it is arguable that some of the claims he makes under URESA could be viewed as defenses under UIFSA. Moreover, had URESA precluded enforcement of the Alaska judgment, it is arguable that the application of UIFSA to this appeal could have affected Brenckle's substantive rights. We conclude that his claims under URESA also lack merit and that the District Court was correct in finding that the Alaska judgment could be enforced under URESA.

We turn first to consider again his argument that the District Court was required to make an independent finding that he had an existing duty of support at the time of the Massachusetts proceedings because URESA, unlike UIFSA, did require such a finding. For several independent and sufficient reasons the court below was correct to conclude that Brenckle did owe a duty of support that could be enforced in Massachusetts under URESA. First, URESA defined a duty of support as "any duty of support imposed by law, or by any court order, decree or judgement." The court order obtained by Carol Brenckle in Alaska itself constituted a duty of support, and the District Court could have so found. Moreover, Brenckle's interpretation of his divorce agreement is unpersuasive. The Alaska judgment was obtained by Carol Brenckle before their son reached the age of majority, and there was no requirement under URESA that the child remain a minor while the custodial parent pursued the father for delinquent support payments. In addition, the divorce agreement specifically provided that Brenckle would contribute to his son's college and graduate school expenses, and it was for this very purpose that Carol Brenckle was seeking support.

Brenckle next maintains that the District Court could not find him liable because URESA did not provide explicitly for the payment of child support

14. These defenses are: "(1) the issuing tribunal lacked personal jurisdiction over the contesting party; (2) the order was obtained by fraud; (3) the order has been vacated, suspended, or modified by a later order; (4) the issuing tribunal has stayed the order pending appeal; (5) there is a defense under the law of the commonwealth to the remedy sought; (6) full or partial payment has been made; or (7) the statute of limitations . . . precludes enforcement of some or all of the arrearages." G.L. c. 209D, § 6–607(*a*).

arrearages. We do not agree. URESA provided that the responding State, here Massachusetts, "may order the respondent to furnish support *or reimbursement therefor*" when presented with a child support judgment of another State (emphasis supplied). To pay for their son's college expenses Carol Brenckle sought "reimbursement" for the support that she had provided to him over many years in the absence of all support from his father. Although URESA does not use the word "arrearages," there is nothing talismanic about that term and Carol Brenckle was fully entitled to invoke URESA to obtain reimbursement for the support she alone had provided to their son. Moreover, while URESA was in effect, the Legislature established a child support enforcement division within the department, which was authorized to institute collection procedures for "all arrearages" that had accrued against child support payments owed pursuant to a judgment or support order, including URESA orders. The Legislature would not have granted such authority to the department if it did not intend to compel payment of arrearages sought under URESA.

Brenckle next argues that because Alaska did not provide any support to Carol Brenckle it had no standing to bring this action. He relies on § 5 of URESA, G.L. c. 273A, § 5, now repealed, which provided that "[w]henever any state or political division thereof has furnished support to an obligee it shall have the same right to commence proceedings under this chapter. . . ." While URESA conferred on a State the ability to collect payments it had made, such payments are not a condition precedent for the right of the State to bring an action against a delinquent parent. Massachusetts has a strong interest in ensuring that child support payments are made by the responsible parent. Absent a specific statutory exception we decline to conclude that the Legislature intended to create any barrier to the collection of support payments. Alaska was authorized to pursue this action on behalf of Carol Brenckle.

Finally, Brenckle argues that, because Carol Brenckle declined to request the assistance of the Alaska child support enforcement division at the time the marriage was dissolved, she is precluded from seeking its assistance now. His argument finds no support in the language of the statute, and we are aware of no holding to that effect.

In addition to his claims under URESA, Brenckle argues that his former wife is barred by laches from pursuing him for unpaid child support obligations because she "slumbered on her rights" for thirteen years, made no attempt to contact him for support payments, and because she "consciously chose to forfeit" her rights to collect child support payments from him. We disagree. Because Brenckle's failure to make child support payments became vested as judgments by operation of law, the defense of laches is not available to him. Moreover, for more than fifteen years Brenckle has failed absolutely to fulfil the duties that he owes to his son. Even now Brenckle attempts to relieve himself of all of his responsibilities to his son, including the payment for his son's college education to which he agreed at the time of the divorce. We decline to hold that a child forfeits the protection of one parent because the custodial parent does not take immediate measures to enforce delinquent child support obligations.

We affirm the judgment of the District Court. The case is remanded to the District Court where it shall be transferred to the Probate and Family Court Department for such other proceedings as may be necessary to enforce the judgment.

So ordered.

NOTE

The Uniform Interstate Family Support Act (UIFSA) was approved by the National Conference of Commissioners on Uniform State Laws in 1992. By 2000, all fifty states and the District of Columbia had adopted the UIFSA.

H. CHILD SUPPORT ENFORCEMENT

According to a survey conducted in 2002 by the U.S. Bureau of the Census there were 11.3 million mothers with children under 21 years of age whose fathers were not present in the household. Only 63 percent (7.1 million) of these 11.3 million women had been awarded child support payments as of the survey date. Of the 11.3 million women awarded child support, 6.2 million were due to receive child support payments for their children in 2002. Of these 6.2 million, only 45.4 percent received the full amount due; 29.3 percent received partial payment, and 37 percent received nothing at all. (Current Population Reports, Consumer Income and Poverty, Series P–60, No. 225, Custodial Mothers and Fathers and their Child Support: 2001, October 2003).

Two years earlier, there were 11.5 million mothers with children under 21 years of age whose fathers were not present in the household. Of these women, 7.2 million (62.2 percent) had been awarded child support; and 6.1 million were due to receive payments for their children in 2000. Of the 6.1 million mothers, 45.9 percent received the full amount; 28.7 percent received partial payment, and 37.8 received nothing at all. *Id.*

For all the women in the Census survey who received some child support in 2002, the average amount of the total payment was $5,138. In 2000, the average amount was $5,101. *Id.*

Nationally, child support payments due for 2001, as reported to the Bureau of the Census, amounted to $31.9 billion. The total child support payments received for 2001 was reported to be only $19.8 billion, a shortfall of $12.1 billion or 62.1 percent. In addition to the difference between the amount of child support due and the amount paid, there is also the problem of the adequacy of award levels, both initially and over time.

In FY 1986, the Office of Child Support Enforcement began collecting information on the dollar amount of support owed by non-custodial parents and received by custodial parents whose cases are being handled through State Child Support Enforcement agencies. All 54 States and jurisdictions now report accounts receivable information on the cases handled through State agencies.

The accounts receivable data reported by 54 States and jurisdictions indicate that $28 billion in current child support was due in Fiscal Year 2004. Some !6.5 billion, or 59%, of this amount was collected and distributed. United States Department of Health, Education, and Welfare, Office of Child Support Enforcement, Child Support Enforcement, FY 2004, Preliminary Report.

Children deserve and need emotional and financial support from both their parents. Many custodial parents require assistance in establishing and enforcing support obligations owed to their children. Non-payment will continue to be a severe problem until society ensures that parents support their children and until all units of government, with the necessary vigor, enforce child support obligations. The material below discusses some of the measures that have been adopted to increase compliance with child support responsibilities.

Eunique v. Powell

U.S. Court of Appeals for the Ninth Circuit, 2002.
302 F.3d 971.

■ FERNANDEZ, CIRCUIT JUDGE.

Eudene Eunique was denied a passport because she was severely in arrears on her child support payments. She brought an action for declaratory and injunctive relief on the theory that the statute and regulation authorizing that denial were unconstitutional. The district granted summary judgment against her, and she appealed. We affirm.

When Eunique's marriage was dissolved, her husband was awarded custody of the children, and she was ordered to pay child support. She failed to pay the ordered amounts, and by 1998 she was in arrears in an amount over $20,000. Thereafter, the arrearage continued to grow. Despite the fact that she is unable or unwilling to pay her child support obligations, she desires to travel internationally for both business and pleasure, including visiting a sister in Mexico.

Eunique applied for a passport, but by that time California had certified to the Secretary of Health and Human Services that she owed "arrearages of child support in an amount exceeding $5,000." 42 U.S.C. § 652(k).... The Secretary of Health and Human Services received that certification and was required by law to transmit it "to the Secretary of State for action." That was accomplished here. The law then directed that "the Secretary of State shall, upon certification ... refuse to issue a passport to" the individual in question. 42 U.S.C. § 652(k)(2). The regulations adopted by the Secretary of State track the statutory language....

As a result of the statutory and regulatory requirements, Eunique was denied a passport. In her view, that denial was unconstitutional, so this action ensued. The district court ruled against her and she appeals.

Eunique argues that there is an insufficient connection between her breach of the duty to pay for the support of her children, and the government's interference with her right to international travel. Thus, she argues, her constitutional rights have been violated. We disagree.

Eunique asserts that she has a constitutional right to international travel, which is so fundamental that it can be restricted for only the most important reasons, and by a narrowly tailored statute. It is undoubtedly true that there is a constitutional right to international travel. However, as the Supreme Court has said, "the right of international travel has been considered to be no more than an aspect of the liberty protected by the Due Process Clause of the Fifth Amendment. As such this right, the Court has held, can be regulated within the bounds of due process." In that respect, it differs from "the constitutional right of interstate travel [which] is virtually unqualified." The difference means that we do not apply strict scrutiny to restrictions on international travel rights that do not implicate First Amendment concerns.

At an early point in the development of Supreme Court jurisprudence in this area, the Court seemed to suggest that restrictions upon travel must be looked upon with a jaded eye. However, it was then dealing with a law which touched on First Amendment concerns because it keyed on mere association. The Court has not been as troubled in cases which do not directly involve those concerns. Rather, as I see it, the Court has suggested that rational basis review should be applied.

When confronted with legislation which denied Supplemental Security Income benefits to people who were outside of the country, the Court commented that legislation which was said to infringe the right to international travel was "not to be judged by the same standard applied to laws that penalized the right to interstate travel." "It is enough," said the Court, "if the provision is rationally based." I recognize that because the SSI statute did not directly regulate passports, Califano is not directly applicable here, but it indicates that the Court does not apply the restrictive form of review advocated by Eunique. . . .

In Freedom to Travel Campaign v. Newcomb, 82 F.3d 1431, 1439 (9th Cir. 1996), we held that, "given the lesser importance of ... freedom to travel abroad, the Government need only advance a rational, or at most an important, reason for imposing the ban." The District of Columbia Circuit has read the Supreme Court tea leaves in the same way. As it has noted, "international travel is no more than an aspect of liberty that is subject to reasonable government regulation within the bounds of due process, whereas interstate travel is a fundamental right subject to a more exacting standard." Hutchins v. Dist. of Columbia, 188 F.3d 531, 537 (D.C. Cir. 1999). Because, as I see it, rational basis review is the proper standard, the statute is constitutional if there is a " 'reasonable fit' between governmental purpose ... and the means chosen to advance that purpose". . . .

The statute easily passes that test. There can be no doubt that the failure of parents to support their children is recognized by our society as a serious offense against morals and welfare. It "is in violation of important social duties [and is] subversive of good order." It is the very kind of problem that the legislature can address. . . . Moreover, the economic problems caused by parents who fail to provide support for their children are both well known and widespread. They can be exacerbated when the non-paying parent is out of the state, as, of course, a parent traveling internationally must be. Indeed, even within the United States itself, the problem is serious. . . . [I]nternational travel by what our society often calls "deadbeat parents" presents even more difficulties because the United States cannot easily reach them once they have left the country.

All of this not only illustrates the rationality of Congress's goal, but also demonstrates its rational connection to the passport denial in question. Surely it makes sense to assure that those who do not pay their child support obligations remain within the country, where they can be reached by our processes in an at least relatively easy way. Notably, even when the Court iterated the constitutional right to travel in Kent, 357 U.S. at 127, it, without disapproval, took notice of a long-standing policy of denying passports to those who were "trying to escape the toils of the law" or "engaging in conduct which would violate the laws of the United States." A person who fails to pay child support may well attempt to escape the toils of the law by going abroad, and may even be violating the laws of the United States.

Moreover, if a parent, like Eunique, truly wishes to partake of the joys and benefits of international travel, § 652(k) does have the effect of focusing that person's mind on a more important concern—the need to support one's children first. It doubtless encourages parents to do their duty to family. In short, the statute passes rational basis review with flying colors. The Second Circuit, by the way, agrees with our conclusion.

Eunique has failed to live up to a most basic civic and even moral responsibility: the provision of support to her own children. Yet she has brought this action because she feels that her right to the pleasures and benefits of international travel has been improperly curtailed. Unfortunately for her, Congress has decreed that her duties to her children must take precedence over her international travel plans. It has ordered her priorities for her.

We hold that, without violating Eunique's Fifth Amendment freedom to travel internationally, Congress (and the State Department) can refuse to let her have a passport as long as she remains in substantial arrears on her child support obligations.

■ KLEINFELD, CIRCUIT JUDGE, dissenting.

I respectfully dissent.

Judge Fernandez's opinion would hold that "rational basis review is the proper standard" for testing restrictions on a person's right to leave the United States. The right to leave one's country is too important to be subject to abridgment on so permissive a standard. The practical effect of consigning the right to travel to this lowly category of constitutional protection is to grant Congress plenary power to restrict it....

In this case, unlike those in which the Supreme Court has upheld restrictions on travel, the government has not offered a foreign policy or national security justification for the restriction, the government has not narrowly tailored the restriction to its purpose, and the apparent purpose of the restriction is to penalize past misconduct rather than to restrict travel as such. Thus the travel ban in this case is unconstitutional under controlling Supreme Court precedent. That Court can revise its approach if it so decides, but we can't.

The right to leave is among the most important of all human rights.... Magna Carta established that subjects had a right to leave the kingdom and return. The exceptions to the right to travel abroad in Magna Carta were for "those imprisoned or outlawed" and for "a short period in time of war," a public policy reason relating to national security.... In Europe in the 1930s and 1940s, for many citizens emigration or not meant life or death.

Ms. Eunique got caught by part of the "deadbeat dads" law, and cannot get a passport, because she has not been paying her ex-husband the $175 per month per child in child support that she agreed to pay when she divorced him. She was then in law school and "had thought that all lawyers earned a lot of money," but "things have not turned out as I expected." She has earned negligible net income from her law practice. She says that a Peruvian-American friend has invited her to go to Peru to meet relatives who have a law firm there, and has suggested that her trip "could open up opportunities for the law firm to hire me when they need legal work in California." Ms. Eunique is plainly derelict in her duty to pay child support, and was properly denied a passport, if the statute and regulation are constitutional.

The Supreme Court has dealt with three kinds of interference with the right to travel abroad: bans on travel by specific classes of persons; bans on travel to specific countries; and residency requirements for government benefits that incidentally burden persons who travel abroad. The Court has held that incidental burdens on permitted travel need only have a rational basis, but has subjected restrictions on travel itself to much greater scrutiny. The Court has not formally stated the constitutional test, but its elements are clear. Travel restrictions must be justified by an important or compelling government interest and must be narrowly tailored to that end. Travel bans aimed at specific individuals or classes of individuals must be more narrowly tailored than bans aimed at specific countries.

The statute and regulation in this case impose a direct restriction on travel, rather than an incidental burden, and must meet a higher standard of scrutiny than rational basis. They do not restrict travel to a specific country or region for reasons of national security or foreign policy. . . . Instead, they restrict travel by a specific class of people from their own country. The Supreme Court has upheld such restrictions when a person's activities threaten national security or foreign policy, and has suggested that bans on travel by people "participating in illegal conduct, trying to escape the toils of the law, promoting passport frauds, or otherwise engaging in conduct which would violate the laws of the United States" would also be proper. Had Eunique been held in contempt and ordered to stay in the United States and purge it, she might be "trying to escape the toils of the law" by traveling abroad. But the statute and regulation in this case only require that she be a debtor, not a fugitive, and so far as the record shows, that is all she is. . . .

Judge Fernandez's opinion suggests that "it makes sense to assure that those who do not pay their child support obligations remain within the country." But the statute and regulation do not do require people to remain within the country. Someone fleeing the country to avoid collection attempts may flee to Mexico, Canada, and a number of other countries without a passport. . . .

The passport ban is also overbroad because . . . it does not take into account individual reasons that might support a passport. For example, travel abroad would, in some businesses (importing) and some lines of professional work, be necessary to earning the money with which the parent would be able to pay child support. And it does not allow for considerations that would bear on the risk of a person traveling abroad to evade child support obligations. Were it tailored to avoiding such flight, then posting of security, owning assets fixed in the United States, or having a job or business in the United States could be considered in determining whether to issue a passport, just as they would be in a bail application.

If Ms. Eunique were a murderer who had done her time, she could get a passport. But a person delinquent in paying child support is punished by denial of a passport. All debtors should pay their debts. Debts for child support have special moral force. But that does not justify tossing away a constitutional liberty so important that it has been a constant of Anglo–American law since Magna Carta, and of civilized thought since Plato.

[T]he right to leave one's country is a very important guarantor of freedom (and in some countries, of life). That right is too important to let the government take it away as punishment to advance a government policy just because it is important. . . .

The scheme upheld does not provide a carefully tailored means of enforcing important legal objectives, just an unrelated and ineffective burden on an arbitrarily selected subset of people who don't do what they're supposed to do. Our liberty matters too much for that.

Wisconsin v. Oakley

Supreme Court of Wisconsin, 2001.
245 Wis.2d 447, 629 N.W.2d 200

■ WILCOX, J.

. . . [W]e must decide whether as a condition of probation, a father of nine children, who has intentionally refused to pay child support, can be required to avoid having another child, unless he shows that he can support that child and his current children. We conclude that in light of Oakley's ongoing victimization of his nine children and extraordinarily troubling record manifesting his disregard for the law, this anomalous condition—imposed on a convicted felon facing the far more restrictive and punitive sanction of prison—is not overly broad and is reasonably related to Oakley's rehabilitation. Simply put, because Oakley was convicted of intentionally refusing to pay child support—a felony in Wisconsin—and could have been imprisoned for six years, which would have eliminated his right to procreate altogether during those six years, this probation condition, which infringes on his right to procreate during his term of probation, is not invalid under these facts. Accordingly, we hold that the circuit court did not erroneously exercise its discretion....

David Oakley (Oakley), the petitioner, was initially charged with intentionally refusing to pay child support for his nine children he has fathered with four different women. The State subsequently charged Oakley with seven counts of intentionally refusing to provide child support as a repeat offender. His repeat offender status stemmed from intimidating two witnesses in a child abuse case—where one of the victims was his own child....

Oakley then entered into another plea agreement in which he agreed to enter a no contest plea to three counts of intentionally refusing to support his children and have the other four counts read-in for sentencing.... At sentencing ... [t]he State noted that during the relevant time period, Oakley had paid no child support and that there were arrears in excess of $25,000. Highlighting Oakley's consistent and willful disregard for the law and his obligations to his children, the State argued that Oakley should be sentenced to six years in prison consecutive to his three-year sentence in Sheboygan County. Oakley, in turn, asked for the opportunity to maintain full-time employment, provide for his children, and make serious payment towards his arrears.

... Judge Hazlewood ... recognized that "if Mr. Oakley goes to prison, he's not going to be in a position to pay any meaningful support for these children." Therefore, even though Judge Hazlewood acknowledged that Oakley's "defaults, are obvious, consistent, and inexcusable," he decided against sentencing Oakley to six years in prison consecutive to his three-year sentence in Sheboygan County, as the State had advocated. Instead, Judge Hazlewood sentenced Oakley to three years in prison on the first count, imposed and stayed an eight-year term on the two other counts, and imposed a five-year term of probation consecutive to his incarceration. Judge Hazlewood then imposed the condition at issue here: while on probation, Oakley cannot have any more children unless he demonstrates that he had the ability to support them and that he is supporting the children he already had. After sentencing, Oakley filed for postconviction relief contesting this condition and the State's withdrawal from the first plea agreement.

In a per curiam opinion, the court of appeals ... found that the condition placed on Oakley was not overly broad and that it was reasonable.... Oakley petitioned this court for review, which we granted.

... Refusal to pay child support by so-called "deadbeat parents" has fostered a crisis with devastating implications for our children. Of those single parent households with established child support awards or orders, approximately one-third did not receive any payment while another one-third received only partial payment. For example, in 1997, out of $26,400,000,000 awarded by a court order to custodial mothers, only $15,800,000,000 was actually paid, amounting to a deficit of $10,600,000,000.

. . .

In view of the suffering children must endure when their noncustodial parent intentionally refuses to pay child support, it is not surprising that the legislature has attached severe sanctions to this crime. Wis. Stat. § 948.22(2). This statute makes it a Class E felony for any person "who intentionally fails for 120 or more consecutive days to provide spousal, grandchild or child support which the person knows or reasonably should know the person is legally obligated to provide. . . ." A Class E felony is punishable with "a fine not to exceed $10,000 or imprisonment not to exceed 2 years, or both." Wis. Stat. § 939.50(3)(e). The legislature has amended this statute so that intentionally refusing to pay child support is now punishable by up to five years in prison. See Wis. Stat. § 939.50(3)(e) (1999–2000). . . .

[A] judge may decide to forgo the severe punitive sanction of incarceration and address the violation with the less restrictive alternative of probation coupled with specific conditions. Wisconsin Stat. § 973.09(1)(a) provides:

> If a person is convicted of a crime, the court, by order, may withhold sentence or impose sentence under s. 973.15 and stay its execution, and in either case place the person on probation to the department for a stated period, stating in the order the reasons therefor. The court may impose any conditions which appear to be reasonable and appropriate.

The statute, then, grants a circuit court judge broad discretion in fashioning a convicted individual's conditions of probation. . . . [W]hen a judge allows a convicted individual to escape a prison sentence and enjoy the relative freedom of probation, he or she must take reasonable judicial measures to protect society and potential victims from future wrongdoing. To that end—along with the goal of rehabilitation—the legislature has seen fit to grant circuit court judges broad discretion in setting the terms of probation.

. . .

Given his knowledge of Oakley's past conduct, Judge Hazlewood was prepared to fashion a sentence that would address Oakley's ongoing refusal to face his obligations to his nine children as required by law.

In doing so, Judge Hazlewood asserted that some prison time coupled with conditional probation might convince Oakley to stop victimizing his children. With probation, Judge Hazlewood sought to rehabilitate Oakley while protecting society and potential victims—Oakley's own children—from future wrongdoing. The conditions were designed to assist Oakley in conforming his conduct to the law. In Wisconsin, as expressed in Wis. Stat. § 948.22(2), we have condemned unequivocally intentional refusal to pay child support and allow for the severe sanction of prison to be imposed on offenders. Here, the judge fashioned a condition that was tailored to that particular crime, but avoided the more severe punitive alternative of the full statutory prison term through the rehabilitative tool of probation. At the same time, Judge Hazlewood sought to protect the victims of Oakley's crimes—Oakley's nine children.

But Oakley argues that the condition imposed by Judge Hazlewood violates his constitutional right to procreate. This court, in accord with the

United States Supreme Court, has previously recognized the fundamental liberty interest of a citizen to choose whether or not to procreate. Accordingly, Oakley argues that the condition here warrants strict scrutiny. That is, it must be narrowly tailored to serve a compelling state interest. Although Oakley concedes, as he must, that the State's interest in requiring parents to support their children is compelling, he argues that the means employed here is not narrowly tailored to serve that compelling interest because Oakley's "right to procreate is not restricted but in fact eliminated." According to Oakley, his right to procreate is eliminated because he "probably never will have the ability to support" his children. Therefore, if he exercises his fundamental right to procreate while on probation, his probation will be revoked and he will face the stayed term of eight years in prison.

While Oakley's argument might well carry the day if he had not intentionally refused to pay child support, it is well-established that convicted individuals do not enjoy the same degree of liberty as citizens who have not violated the law. We emphatically reject the novel idea that Oakley, who was convicted of intentionally failing to pay child support, has an absolute right to refuse to support his current nine children and any future children that he procreates, thereby adding more child victims to the list. . . .

Furthermore, Oakley fails to note that incarceration, by its very nature, deprives a convicted individual of the fundamental right to be free from physical restraint, which in turn encompasses and restricts other fundamental rights, such as the right to procreate. Therefore, given that a convicted felon does not stand in the same position as someone who has not been convicted of a crime, we have previously stated that "conditions of probation may impinge upon constitutional rights as long as they are not overly broad and are reasonably related to the person's rehabilitation."

Applying the relevant standard here, we find that the condition is not overly broad because it does not eliminate Oakley's ability to exercise his constitutional right to procreate. He can satisfy the condition of probation by making efforts to support his children as required by law. Judge Hazlewood placed no limit on the number of children Oakley could have. Instead, the requirement is that Oakley acknowledge the requirements of the law and support his present and any future children. If Oakley decides to continue his present course of conduct—intentionally refusing to pay child support—he will face eight years in prison regardless of how many children he has. Furthermore, this condition will expire at the end of his term of probation. He may then decide to have more children, but of course, if he continues to intentionally refuse to support his children, the State could charge him again under § 948.22(2). Rather, because Oakley can satisfy this condition by not intentionally refusing to support his current nine children and any future children as required by the law, we find that the condition is narrowly tailored to serve the State's compelling interest of having parents support their children. It is also narrowly tailored to serve the State's compelling interest in rehabilitating Oakley through probation rather than prison. The alternative to probation with conditions—incarceration for eight years—would have further victimized his children. And it is undoubtedly much broader than this conditional impingement on his procreative freedom for it would deprive him of his fundamental right to be free from physical restraint. Simply stated, Judge Hazlewood preserved much of Oakley's liberty by imposing probation with conditions rather than the more punitive option of imprisonment.

Moreover, the condition is reasonably related to the goal of rehabilitation. A condition is reasonably related to the goal of rehabilitation if it assists the convicted individual in conforming his or her conduct to the law. Here, Oakley was convicted of intentionally refusing to support his children. The condition at bar will prevent him from adding victims if he continues to intentionally refuse to support his children. As the State argues, the condition essentially bans Oakley from violating the law again. Future violations of the law would be detrimental to Oakley's rehabilitation, which necessitates preventing him from continuing to disregard its dictates. Accordingly, this condition is reasonably related to his rehabilitation because it will assist Oakley in conforming his conduct to the law.

. . .

In conclusion, based on the atypical facts presented by this case, the Constitution does not shield Oakley—whose record evidences consistent disregard for the law and ongoing victimization of his own nine children—from this unique probation condition where he has intentionally refused to support his children. Under the exceptional factors presented by this case, the probation condition is not overbroad and it is reasonably related to the probationary goal of rehabilitation. Indeed, this condition is narrowly tailored to serve the compelling state interest of requiring parents to support their children as well as rehabilitating those convicted of crimes. Moreover, this condition will assist Oakley in conforming his conduct to the law and is therefore reasonably related to his rehabilitation. . . .

■ SYKES, J., DISSENTING:

Can the State criminalize the birth of a child to a convicted felon who is likely to be unwilling or unable to adequately support the child financially? That is essentially the crux of the circuit court order in this case, or at least its apparent practical effect.

I agree with the majority opinion that because Oakley is a convicted felon, infringements on his constitutional rights are evaluated differently than infringements on the rights of those who have not been convicted of crimes. The majority opinion has identified the applicable test: "conditions of probation may impinge upon constitutional rights as long as they are not overly broad and are reasonably related to [the probationer's] rehabilitation."

Oakley has fathered nine children by four different women and has consistently failed to support them. He is more than $25,000 in arrears on his support orders, and his pattern of nonsupport is intentional. He is criminally irresponsible, and his children suffer for it. The State's interest in collecting child support for his children is substantial, as is the State's interest in preventing further arrearages.

Under these circumstances, the "no more children" probation condition certainly appears to be reasonably related to Oakley's rehabilitation. No one seems to believe that Oakley will ever be able to bring his arrearages up to date, much less keep current. Adding another child would only make matters worse.

Even under these extreme circumstances, however, and even in light of the State's strong interest in protecting against further victimization of these children, a court-ordered prohibition of procreation without State permission is overly broad.

In Zablocki v. Redhail, 434 U.S. 374, 376 (1978), the United States Supreme Court struck down a Wisconsin statute that prohibited the issuance of a marriage license without court approval to anyone with a court-ordered child support obligation. Under the statute, court approval to marry could not be granted unless the marriage applicant proved compliance with the support obligation, and further, that the children covered by the support order were not, and were not likely to become, public charges. The Supreme Court found the statute to be an unconstitutional infringement on the right to marry, because less restrictive means could achieve the state's objective of protecting the interests of children entitled to financial support from non-custodial parents. The Court applied an equal protection analysis, invalidating the statute because it was not "closely tailored" to effectuate the State's interests.

While I recognize that the constitutional tests are somewhat different, Zablocki is otherwise closely analogous to this case. Here, as in Zablocki, there are less restrictive means available to achieve the State's objectives short of encumbering what everyone agrees is a fundamental human right.... [T]he circuit court can order Oakley to maintain full-time employment—or even two jobs—as a condition of probation, and to execute a wage assignment to pay off his child support arrearages and satisfy his ongoing support obligations. His tax refunds can be intercepted annually. Liens can be placed on his personal property, and he can be found in civil contempt. He can be criminally prosecuted for any additional intentional failures to support his children, present or future. His probation can be revoked if he fails to maintain employment and make support payments. Granted, Oakley's arrearages are so great, and his history so troublesome, that these means may not ultimately be completely successful in achieving the State's objective of collecting child support. But the same was true in Zablocki, and the Supreme Court nevertheless found the statute in that case unconstitutional. I reach the same conclusion here....

Although Oakley is a convicted felon and therefore may constitutionally be subjected to limitations on the fundamental human liberties the rest of us freely enjoy, he cannot constitutionally be banned from having further children without court permission. In light of available alternatives to achieve the State's significant and laudable objective of collecting past and future child support for these children, who are entitled to and need it, this condition of probation is an overly broad encumbrance on Oakley's right to procreate, and therefore cannot stand. Accordingly, I respectfully dissent.

Hicks v. Feiock

Supreme Court of the United States, 1988.
485 U.S. 624, 108 S.Ct. 1423, 99 L.Ed.2d 721.

■ JUSTICE WHITE delivered the opinion of the Court.

. . .

On January 19, 1976, a California state court entered an order requiring respondent, Phillip Feiock, to begin making monthly payments to his ex-wife for the support of their three children. Over the next six years, respondent only sporadically complied with the order, and by December 1982 he had discontinued paying child support altogether. His ex-wife sought to enforce the support orders. On June 22, 1984, a hearing was held in California state court on her petition for ongoing support payments and for payment of the arrearage due her. The court examined respondent's financial situation and ordered him to begin paying $150 per month commencing on July 1, 1984. The court reserved jurisdiction over the matter for the purpose of determining the arrearages and reviewing respondent's financial condition.

Respondent apparently made two monthly payments but paid nothing for the next nine months. He was then served with an order to show cause why he should not be held in contempt on nine counts of failure to make the monthly payments ordered by the court. At a hearing on August 9, 1985, petitioner made out a *prima facie* case of contempt against respondent by establishing the existence of a valid court order, respondent's knowledge of the order, and respondent's failure to comply with the order. Respondent defended by arguing that he was unable to pay support during the months in question. This argument was partially successful, but respondent was adjudged to be in contempt on five of the nine counts. He was sentenced to five days in jail on each count, to be served consecutively, for a total of 25 days. This sentence was suspended, however, and respondent was placed on probation for three years. As one of the conditions of his probation, he was ordered once again to make support payments of $150 per month. As another condition of his probation, he was ordered, starting the following month, to begin repaying $50 per month on his accumulated arrearage, which was determined to total $1650.

At the hearing, respondent had objected to the application of Cal.Civ. Proc.Code Ann. § 1209.5 (1982) against him, claiming that it was unconstitutional under the Due Process Clause of the Federal Constitution because it shifts to the defendant the burden of proving inability to comply with the order, which is an element of the crime of contempt. This objection was rejected, and he renewed it on appeal. The intermediate state appellate court agreed with respondent and annulled the contempt order.... The California Supreme Court denied review, but we granted certiorari.

. . .

The question of how a court determines whether to classify the relief imposed in a given proceeding as civil or criminal in nature, for the purposes of applying the Due Process Clause and other provisions of the Constitution, is one of long standing, and its principles have been settled at least in their broad outlines for many decades. When a State's proceedings are involved, state law provides strong guidance about whether or not the State is exercising its authority "in a nonpunitive, noncriminal manner," and one who challenges the State's classification of the relief imposed as "civil" or "criminal" may be required to show "the clearest proof" that it is not correct as a matter of federal law. Nonetheless, if such a challenge is substantiated, then the labels affixed either to the proceeding or to the relief imposed under state law are not controlling and will not be allowed to defeat the applicable protections of federal constitutional law. This is particularly so in the codified laws of contempt, where the "civil" and "criminal" labels of the law have become increasingly blurred.

Instead, the critical features are the substance of the proceeding and the character of the relief that the proceeding will afford. "If it is for civil contempt the punishment is remedial, and for the benefit of the complainant. But if it is for criminal contempt the sentence is punitive, to vindicate the authority of the court." The character of the relief imposed is thus ascertainable by applying a few straightforward rules. If the relief provided is a sentence of imprisonment, it is remedial if "the defendant stands committed unless and until he performs the affirmative act required by the court's order," and is punitive if "the sentence is limited to imprisonment for a definite period." Id., at 442. If the relief provided is a fine, it is remedial when it is paid to the complainant, and punitive when it is paid to the court, though a fine that would be payable to the court is also remedial when the defendant can avoid paying the fine simply by performing the affirmative act required by the court's order. These distinctions lead up to the fundamental proposition that criminal penalties may not be imposed on someone who has not been afforded the protections that the Constitution requires of such criminal proceedings, including the requirement that the offense be proved beyond a reasonable doubt.

. . .

The distinction between relief that is civil in nature and relief that is criminal in nature has been repeated and followed in many cases. An unconditional penalty is criminal in nature because it is "solely and exclusively punitive in character." Penfield Co. v. SEC, 330 U.S. 585, 593 (1947). A conditional penalty, by contrast, is civil because it is specifically designed to compel the doing of some act. "One who is fined, unless by a day certain he [does the act ordered], has it in his power to avoid any penalty. And those who are imprisoned until they obey the order, 'carry the keys of their prison in their own pockets.' "

. . .

The proper classification of the relief imposed in respondent's contempt proceeding is dispositive of this case. As interpreted by the state court here, § 1209.5 requires respondent to carry the burden of persuasion on an element of the offense, by showing his inability to comply with the court's order to make the required payments. If applied in a criminal proceeding, such a statute would violate the Due Process Clause because it would undercut the State's burden to prove guilt beyond a reasonable doubt. If applied in a civil proceeding, however, this particular statute would be constitutionally valid.

The state court found the contempt proceeding to be "quasi-criminal" in nature without discussing the point. There were strong indications that the proceeding was intended to be criminal in nature, such as the notice sent to respondent, which clearly labeled the proceeding as "criminal in nature." Though significant, these facts are not dispositive of the issue before us, for if the trial court had imposed only civil coercive remedies, as surely it was authorized to do, then it would be improper to invalidate that result merely because the Due Process Clause, as applied in *criminal* proceedings, was not satisfied. It also bears emphasis that the purposes underlying this proceeding were wholly ambiguous. Respondent was charged with violating nine discrete prior court orders, and the proceeding may have been intended primarily to vindicate the court's authority in the face of his defiance. On the other hand, as often is true when court orders are violated, these charges were part of an ongoing battle to force respondent to conform his conduct to the terms of those orders, and of future orders as well.

Applying the traditional rules for classifying the relief imposed in a given proceeding requires the further resolution of one factual question about the nature of the relief in this case. Respondent was charged with nine separate counts of contempt, and was convicted on five of those counts, all of which arose from his failure to comply with orders to make payments in past months. He was sentenced to five days in jail on each of the five counts, for a total of 25 days, but his jail sentence was suspended and he was placed on probation for three years. If this were all, then the relief afforded would be criminal in nature. But this is not all. One of the conditions of respondent's probation was that he begin making payments on his accumulated arrearage, and that he continue making these payments at the rate of $50 per month. At that rate, all of the arrearage would be paid before respondent completed his probation period. Not only did the order therefore contemplate that respondent would be required to purge himself of his past violations, but it expressly states that "[i]f any two payments are missed, whether consecutive or not, the entire balance shall become due and payable." Order of the California Superior Court for Orange County (Aug. 9, 1985), App. 39. What is unclear is whether the ultimate satisfaction of these accumulated prior payments would have purged the determinate sentence imposed on respondent. Since this aspect of the proceeding will vary as a factual matter from one case to another, depending on the precise disposition entered by the trial court, and since the trial court did not specify this aspect of its disposition in this case, it is not surprising that neither party was able to offer a satisfactory explanation of this point at argument. If the relief imposed here is in fact a determinate sentence with a purge clause, then it is civil in nature.

The state court did not pass on this issue because of its erroneous view that it was enough simply to aver that this proceeding is considered "quasi-criminal" as a matter of state law.... In these circumstances, the proper course for this Court is to vacate the judgment below and remand for further consideration of § 1209.5 free from the compulsion of an erroneous view of federal law. If on remand it is found that respondent would purge his sentence by paying his arrearage, then this proceeding is civil in nature and there was no need for the state court to reinterpret its statute to avoid conflict with the Due Process Clause.

We therefore vacate the judgment below and remand for further proceedings consistent with this opinion.

It is so ordered.

NOTE

On remand, the appellate court held that contempt proceedings against the father were criminal in nature. The court also held that the statute did not create a presumption of ability to pay child support. In re Feiock, 215 Cal.App.3d 141, 263 Cal.Rptr. 437 (1989).

United States v. Bongiorno

United States Court of Appeals, First Circuit, 1997.
106 F.3d 1027.

■ SELYA, CIRCUIT JUDGE.

This [case] revolves around the constitutionality of the Child Support Recovery Act (CSRA), 18 U.S.C. § 228 (1994).... [W]e reject the defendant's challenge to his criminal conviction and sentence, holding, among other things, that Congress did not exceed the bounds of its constitutional power in enacting the CSRA.

. . .

In October 1990 a Georgia state court entered a decree ending Sandra Taylor's marriage to defendant-appellant Frank P. Bongiorno, granting Taylor custody of the couple's minor daughter, and directing Bongiorno (a physician specializing in bariatric surgery) to pay $5,000 per month in child support. Shortly thereafter, mother and daughter repaired to Massachusetts. When Bongiorno subsequently sought to modify the child support award, Taylor counterclaimed on the ground that Bongiorno had failed to make the payments stipulated in the original decree. In September 1992 the Georgia court found Bongiorno in contempt for failing to pay upward of $75,000 in mandated child support and directed that he be incarcerated until he had purged the contempt. Bongiorno avoided immurement only because he had accepted a position in Michigan and the contempt order did not operate extraterritorially.

Once in Michigan, Bongiorno made sporadic payments of child support despite the fact that his new post paid $200,000 per year. In March 1993 a Michigan state court domesticated the Georgia support order and authorized garnishment of Bongiorno's wages to satisfy the accumulated arrearage. Soon thereafter, Bongiorno quit his job and paid only $500 a month in child support from June to December 1993. In early 1994 Bongiorno went to work for the State of Michigan. That May a Michigan state court issued an order enforcing the Georgia support award to the extent of $300 per week. Bongiorno failed to satisfy even this modest impost.

Approximately one year later . . . the United States charged Bongiorno with violating the CSRA. Because Bongiorno's minor daughter has resided continuously in Massachusetts from 1990 forward (albeit with her grandmother for much of that time), the government preferred charges in that district. Bongiorno moved unsuccessfully to dismiss the indictment on the ground that the CSRA represents an unconstitutional exercise of Congress' power under the Commerce Clause. At an ensuing bench trial, the district court determined that Bongiorno had possessed the ability to pay $5,000 monthly in the 1992–1993 time frame, but that he had chosen not to do so. Consequently, the court found Bongiorno guilty of willful failure to pay child support and sentenced him to five years of probation. As a condition of probation, the court imposed a work-release arrangement, directing Bongiorno to spend up to twelve hours per day in the custody of the Bureau of Prisons for the first year of his probation. As a further condition, the court ordered restitution in the sum of $220,000 (a figure approximating the total arrearage then outstanding).

Not content with its apparent victory, the government commenced a civil proceeding under the FDCPA as a means of enforcing the restitutionary order. After some procedural wrangling, the court granted the government's motion to attach Bongiorno's wages and disburse the proceeds.

Bongiorno filed timely appeals in both cases, and we heard the appeals in tandem. We now affirm the conviction and sentence in the criminal case, but reverse the judgment in the civil case.

Bongiorno challenges his conviction principally on the ground that the CSRA is an unconstitutional exercise of Congress' authority under the Commerce Clause. . . .

In 1992 Congress focused on the importance of financial support from non-custodial parents as a means of combatting the growing poverty of single-parent families. The House Judiciary Committee observed that of $16.3 billion in child support payments due in 1989, only $11.2 billion was paid, leaving a shortfall of approximately $5 billion to be offset largely through government assistance. The Committee concluded that "the annual deficit in child support payments remains unacceptably high," especially "in interstate collection cases, where enforcement of support is particularly difficult." To illustrate this point, the Committee noted that one-third of all uncollected child support obligations involved non-custodial fathers living out of state and that roughly fifty-seven percent of the custodial parents in such situations received support payments "occasionally, seldom or never."

Because Congress doubted the states' ability efficaciously to enforce support orders beyond their own borders, (recognizing that "interstate extradition and enforcement in fact remains a tedious, cumbersome and slow method of collection"), it devised a federal solution hoping that the new law—the CSRA—would prevent delinquent parents from "mak[ing] a mockery of State law by fleeing across State lines to avoid enforcement actions by State courts and child support agencies." 138 Cong. Rec. H7324, H7326 (daily ed. Aug. 4, 1992) (statement of Rep. Hyde). In final form the statute makes willful failure "to pay a past due support obligation with respect to a child who resides in another State" a federal crime. 18 U.S.C. § 228(a). A "past due support obligation" is an amount determined under a state court order that either has remained unpaid for more than one year or is greater than $5,000. The law subjects violators to a panoply of punishments, including imprisonment, fines, and restitution.

The Commerce Clause bestows upon Congress the power, *inter alia,* to "regulate Commerce . . . among the several States." The appellant claims that the CSRA—which in his case has the effect of regulating the nonpayment of Georgia-imposed child support obligations owed by a Michigan resident to a child domiciled in Massachusetts—does not fall within the ambit of this constitutional grant. The Supreme Court has identified three general categories of activity that lawfully can be regulated under the Commerce Clause: (1) activities that involve use of the channels of interstate commerce, (2) activities that implicate the instrumentalities of interstate commerce (including persons or things in interstate commerce), and (3) activities that have a substantial relation to, or substantially affect, interstate commerce.

While the CSRA is likely supportable under more than one of these rubrics, we believe that its validity is most easily demonstrated in terms of the second class of activities. In other words, because paying court-ordered child support occurs in interstate commerce when the obligated parent and the dependent child reside in different states, the underlying support obligation is subject to regulation under the Commerce Clause.

. . .

As the Court explained in United States v. Shubert, 348 U.S. 222 (1955), commerce exists where there is a "continuous and indivisible stream of intercourse among the states" involving the transmission of money and communications.

This definition fits the economic realities incident to child support orders involving a parent in one state and a child in another. Because compliance with such support orders requires the regular movement of money and communications across state lines, such transactions fall within the scope of permissibly regulated intercourse. It follows inexorably that Congress lawfully can pass legislation designed to prevent the frustration of such interstate transactions.

The CSRA is such a law. It regulates the nonpayment of interstate child support obligations. Because child support orders that require a parent in one state to make payments to a person in another state are functionally equivalent to interstate contracts, such obligations are "things" in interstate commerce. Thus, it is appropriate for Congress to enact legislation that will prevent their nonfulfillment. On this basis, the CSRA is a valid exercise of congressional power under the Commerce Clause.

. . .

[Appellant] posits that uncollected support payments have too tenuous an impact on interstate commerce to justify the exercise of congressional authority. This argument relies heavily on *Lopez,* a case in which the Court struck down the Gun–Free School Zones Act (GFSZA), 18 U.S.C. § 922(q)(1)(A), which criminalized the possession of firearms in local school zones. Holding that Congress exceeded its power under the Commerce Clause when it enacted the statute, the Court reasoned that gun possession in a local school zone is not economic activity of a type that substantially affects interstate commerce. *See Lopez,* 514 U.S. 549, 115 S.Ct. at 1634. *Lopez* is inapposite here. The *Lopez* majority considered only the third, "affecting interstate commerce," branch of Commerce Clause authority, dismissing the first two bases as patently inapplicable. Here, however, we have no occasion to decide whether unpaid child support substantially affects interstate commerce; we instead uphold the CSRA under the second Commerce Clause category because it regulates things (namely, payment obligations) in interstate commerce.

There is another, more basic reason why *Lopez* does not assist the appellant's cause. The concerns articulated by the *Lopez* Court simply are not implicated by the CSRA. The *Lopez* Court observed that the GFSZA by its terms had no relation to any sort of economic enterprise, and that neither the statute nor its legislative history contained express congressional findings purporting to show the regulated activity's effects on interstate commerce. In contrast, the CSRA relates to economic transactions, and the enacting Congress made explicit, well-documented findings regarding the economic effect of unpaid child support upon interstate commerce. In the same vein, the Lopez Court made much of the fact that the GFSZA contained no jurisdictional element to forge a link between the regulated activity and interstate commerce. Such an element is conspicuously present here, for the CSRA by its terms provides that jurisdiction will attach only if child support obligations cross state lines. We have found the presence of such a jurisdictional element to be a powerful argument for distinguishing *Lopez* in other cases, and it is equally potent here.

. . .

Bongiorno next claims that the CSRA violates the Tenth Amendment (and, in the bargain, tramples principles of federalism and comity). This claim hinges on his contention that the CSRA falls beyond Congress' competence because it concerns domestic relations (an area traditionally within the states' domain). We reject the claim out of hand.

The Tenth Amendment declares that "powers not delegated to the United States by the Constitution, nor prohibited by it to the States, are reserved to the States respectively, or to the people." The amendment is not applicable to situations in which Congress properly exercises its authority under an enumerated constitutional power. Inasmuch as Congress passed the CSRA pursuant to the valid exercise of such an enumerated power (the power to regulate interstate commerce), that tenet governs here.

What is more, a Tenth Amendment attack on a federal statute cannot succeed without three ingredients: (1) the statute must regulate the "States as States," (2) it must concern attributes of state sovereignty, and (3) it must be of such a nature that compliance with it would impair a state's ability "to structure integral operations in areas of traditional governmental functions." The CSRA passes this test with flying colors. It does not interfere with state law. To the contrary, the CSRA comes into play only after a state court issues a child support order, and it does not authorize a federal court to revise the underlying decree. Because Congress succeeded in drafting the CSRA "to strengthen, not to supplant, State enforcement efforts," 138 Cong. Rec. at H7326 (statement of Rep. Hyde), the law withstands Tenth Amendment scrutiny.

NOTE

Four other federal appeals courts have upheld the Child Support Recovery Act against challenges that it exceeds Congress' authority under the Commerce Clause. See United States v. Parker, 108 F.3d 28 (3d Cir.1997); United States v. Bailey, 115 F.3d 1222 (5th Cir.1997); United States v. Crawford, 115 F.3d 1397 (8th Cir.1997); United States v. Sage, 92 F.3d 101 (2d Cir. 1996). The Sixth Circuit has held the Act unconstitutional as a violation of the Commerce Clause. See United States v. Faasse, 227 F.3d 660 (6th Cir. 2000).

The Second Circuit has ruled that a custodial parent does not have an implied private right of action against a noncustodial parent under the CSRA. See Salahuddin v. Alaji, 232 F.3d 305 (2d Cir.2000).

I. The Separation Agreement

A large percentage of divorces involve separation agreements between the parties. These agreements are submitted to the court and often incorporated into the divorce decree. Separation agreements are entered into in contemplation of divorce, and thus differ from pre-marital contracts that purport to determine the consequences if the couple ever divorces. As the excerpt from Mnookin & Kornhauser at the beginning of Chapter 4 indicates, the separation agreement reflects "bargaining in the shadow of the law"—that is, the parties' negotiations are shaped by expectations of what a court will do if they do not reach a settlement. As you read the material in this section, consider whether courts should review separation agreements as they do any other contract, or whether divorce should prompt more searching judicial review. Consider also the extent to which couples should be able by contract to preclude courts from retaining jurisdiction to entertain later requests for modification of the custody and financial arrangements made at the time of divorce.

Uniform Marriage and Divorce Act

SECTION 306. Separation Agreement

(a) To promote amicable settlement of disputes between parties to a marriage attendant upon their separation or the dissolution of their marriage, the parties may enter into a written separation agreement containing provisions for disposition of any property owned by either of them, maintenance of either of them, and support, custody, and visitation of their children.

(b) In a proceeding for dissolution of marriage or for legal separation, the terms of the separation agreement, except those providing for the support, custody, and visitation of children, are binding upon the court unless it finds, after considering the economic circumstances of the parties and any other relevant evidence produced by the parties, on their own motion or on request of the court, that the separation agreement is unconscionable.

(c) If the court finds the separation agreement unconscionable, it may request the parties to submit a revised separation agreement or may make orders for the disposition of property, maintenance, and support.

(d) If the court finds that the separation agreement is not unconscionable as to disposition of property or maintenance, and not unsatisfactory as to support:

> (1) unless the separation agreement provides to the contrary, its terms shall be set forth in the decree of dissolution or legal separation and the parties shall be ordered to perform them, or
>
> (2) if the separation agreement provides that its terms shall not be set forth in the decree, the decree shall identify the separation agreement and state that the court has found the terms not unconscionable.

(e) Terms of the agreement set forth in the decree are enforceable by all remedies available for enforcement of a judgment, including contempt, and are enforceable as contract terms.

(f) Except for terms concerning the support, custody, or visitation of children, the decree may expressly preclude or limit modification of terms set forth in the decree if the separation agreement so provides. Otherwise, terms of a separation agreement set forth in the decree are automatically modified by modification of the decree.

COMMENT

An important aspect of the effort to reduce the adversary trappings of marital dissolution is the attempt, made by Section 306, to encourage the parties to reach an amicable disposition of the financial and other incidents of their marriage. This section entirely reverses the older view that property settlement agreements are against public policy because they tend to promote divorce. Rather, when a marriage has broken down irretrievably, public policy will be served by allowing the parties to plan their future by agreeing upon a disposition of their property, their maintenance, and the support, custody, and visitation of their children.

Subsection (b) undergirds the freedom allowed the parties by making clear that the terms of the agreement respecting maintenance and property disposition are binding upon the court unless those terms are found to be unconscionable. The standard of unconscionability is used in commercial law, where its meaning includes protection against one-sidedness, oppression, or unfair surprise and in contract law. It has been used in cases respecting divorce settlements or awards. Hence the act does not introduce a novel standard unknown to the law. In the context of negotiations between spouses as to the financial incidents of their marriage, the standard includes protection against overreaching, concealment of assets, and sharp dealing not consistent with, the obligations of marital partners to deal fairly with each other.

In order to determine whether the agreement is unconscionable, the court may look to the economic circumstances of the parties resulting from the agreement, and any other relevant evidence such as the conditions under which the agreement was made, including the knowledge of the other party. If the court finds the agreement not unconscionable, its terms respecting property division and maintenance may not be altered by the court at the hearing.

The terms of the agreement respecting support, custody, and visitation of children are not binding upon the court even if these terms are not unconscionable. The court should perform its duty to provide for the children by careful examination of the agreement as to these terms in light of the standards established by Section 309 for support and by Part IV for custody and visitation.

Subsection (c) envisages that, if the court finds the agreement unconscionable, it will afford the parties the opportunity to negotiate further. If they are unable to arrive at an agreement that is not unconscionable, the court, on motion of either party, may decide the issues of property disposition, support, and maintenance in light of the standards established in Sections 307 through 309. The court's power to make orders for the custody and visitation of the children is set forth in Part IV.

Subsection (d) permits the parties, in drawing the separation agreement, to choose whether its terms shall or shall not be set forth in the decree. In the former event, the provisions of subsection (e), making these terms enforceable through the remedies available for the enforcement of a judgment, but retaining also the enforceability of them as contract terms, apply. . . . There still remains a place for agreements the terms of which are not set forth in the decree, if the parties prefer that it retain the status of a private contract, only. In this instance, the remedies for the enforcement of a judgment will not be available, but the court's determination, in the decree, that the terms are not unconscionable, under the ordinary rules of res adjudicata, will prevent a later successful claim of unconscionability. Such an agreement, unless its terms expressly so permit, will not be modifiable as to economic matters. Other subjects, relating to the children, by subsection (b) do not bind the Court.

Subsection (f) allows the parties to agree that their provisions as to maintenance and property division will not be modifiable or can be modified only in accordance with the terms of the agreement, even though those terms are included in the decree. If the court finds that these are not unconscionable, it may include them in its decree. The effect of including in the decree a provision precluding or limiting modification of the terms respecting maintenance or property division is to make the decree nonmodifiable or modifiable only in the limited way as to those terms. Subsection (f) thus permits the parties to agree that their future arrangements may not be altered except in accord with their agreement. Such an agreement maximizes the advantages of careful future planning and eliminates uncertainties based on the fear of subsequent motions to increase or decrease the obligations of the parties. However, as stated in the subsection, this does not apply to provisions for the support, custody, or visitation of children.

. . .

Duffy v. Duffy

Court of Appeals of the District of Columbia, 2005.
881 A.2d 630

■ Ruiz, Associate Judge.

Appellant challenges the trial court's enforcement of the parties' separation agreement as part of its Judgment of Absolute Divorce. The trial court found that the agreement, which was contained in a letter signed by both parties, was complete and unambiguous on its face, and that the parties had demonstrated an intention to be bound by it. Consequently, the trial court found that the agreement is an enforceable contract, and required appellant to provide appellee with an accounting of the child support that was in arrears under the terms of the separation agreement, pay the outstanding amount within thirty days, and continue to pay child support in the amount provided for in the separation agreement. Finding no error in the trial court's judgment, we affirm.

The parties were married in Grand Rapids, Michigan on December 29, 1977. They adopted a daughter, born on September 19, 1995, who began residing with them on September 21, 1995. In 1998, appellant decided he wanted to separate from his wife. During their separation, the parties worked together to sell their marital home, divide the proceeds, pay their various debts, and distribute their personal property.

. . .

In an effort to save time and attorney's fees, the parties negotiated an agreement on the terms of their divorce, which the appellee reduced to writing in the form of a letter addressed to her attorney, whom the parties agreed would then prepare a formal agreement incorporating the terms they agreed upon for review by appellant's lawyer.... On May 12, 2001, both parties read over the letter drafted by appellee and signed it (hereinafter referred to as the "Letter").

Soon after, counsel for appellee prepared a Marital Settlement Agreement (hereinafter referred to as the "Draft Agreement") incorporating the terms set out in the Letter, and sent it to appellant on May 23, 2001.[11] Although appellant did not execute the Draft Agreement, the parties abided by the terms set out in the Letter from May 2001, when the Letter was signed, until November 2002, when appellant unilaterally reduced his child support payment from the $5000 per month provided for in the Letter, to $2000 per month.

. . .

The law in this jurisdiction encourages the use of separation agreements to settle the financial affairs of spouses who intend to divorce. This policy is based on the notion that the parties are in a better position than the court to determine what is fair and reasonable in their circumstances. In the absence of fraud, duress, concealment or overreaching, a separation agreement is presumptively valid and binding no matter how ill-advised a party may have been in executing it.

. . .

During trial and on appeal appellant has expressed concern that the Letter does not address what would happen to his child support obligation in the event he lost his job, or had other financial constraints. Although provision for future contingencies could well have been part of the parties'

11. It appears that appellant was not represented by counsel at the time. In her letter to appellant enclosing the Draft Agreement, appellee's counsel advised appellant that she did not represent him and that he had a right to be represented by an attorney and should consult one if he had any questions or concerns about the Draft Agreement she had prepared.

agreement,[12] it is not a necessary component for enforceability because, to be complete, a contract need only be sufficiently definite so that the parties can be reasonably certain as to how they are to perform. However, even without an express provision in the Letter for modification of child support to take into account changes in appellant's financial situation, appellant would not be precluded from seeking relief from the court should a change in his circumstances adversely affect his ability to pay child support.

The standard for granting a modification to child support specified in a settlement agreement depends on whether the agreement was merged into the court's judgment, or incorporated by reference. The trial court has limited authority to alter a child support provision in a separation agreement that is incorporated, but not merged, into an order of divorce, due to the "presumption that 'a child support agreement negotiated between two parents is adequate to meet the child's foreseeable needs, and that at the time of the agreement the best interests of the child were a paramount consideration.'" A trial court may modify such an agreement only upon a showing of "(1) a change in circumstances which was unforeseen at the time the agreement was entered and (2) that the change is both substantial and material to the welfare and best interests of the children." "However, a change in the parents' financial circumstances alone 'cannot provide the basis for modifying a contract between the parties.'" As a result, a trial court may increase a child support payment provided in a settlement agreement if there arises an unforeseen change in circumstances that is substantial and material to the interests of the child, but it may not decrease such a child support agreement simply because the payor's financial circumstances have declined, or the child support payment subsequently proves to exceed the child's needs.

> Thus while a court may find that a child support agreement does not provide a sufficient amount of money to meet a party's legal obligation to support and may order a larger sum to be paid . . . it may not modify such an agreement by reducing the agreed upon amount to the minimum the law would impose in the absence of an agreement, or to any sum different from that provided for in the agreement.

Lanahan, 317 A.2d at 525 (citing Blumenthal v. Blumenthal, 155 A.2d 525, 526–27 (D.C. 1959)). In order to have the court reduce the child support provided in a settlement agreement incorporated by the court, a payor would therefore have to avail himself of a contract theory that would relieve him of the burden of such performance, e.g., contract defenses such as "fraud, duress, concealment, or overreaching," "frustration of performance" either due to "strict impossibility," or "impracticability due to extreme or unreasonable difficulty or expense." Thus, if the appellant were to become unexpectedly disabled and, as a result, his finances suffered significantly, the court could reduce or excuse the child support obligation only if it were impossible or impracticable for appellant to make child support payments at the stipulated amount.

Where a settlement agreement is merged into the trial court's order, on the other hand, the binding force of the amount of child support is not based on the contractual obligation arising from an agreement between the parties, but on the authority of the court's order. The court's order is guided

12. We note, for example, that the Letter states that "Joan would also like a clause that states that amount [of child support] will be adjusted annually to reflect the then current Consumer Price Index." This statement reflects that although some contingencies were considered, the parties did not incorporate them in their agreement.

by the child support guidelines established by statute. Consequently, where a settlement agreement on child support is merged into the court's order, the court has discretion to modify its own order based on a showing by either party of a material change in the circumstances of either the child or the parents. A parent seeking relief from an onerous child support payment need then only show a "substantial or material change of circumstances," that would support a significantly different amount of child support under the guidelines. D.C. Code § 16–916.01 (*o*)(3) (establishing presumption that modification is warranted if current circumstances would vary child support "by 15% or more" under the guidelines).

A settlement agreement is merged, and not merely incorporated into a court order, where "the agreement was adopted by the court as its own determination of the proper disposition of the rights and property between the parties." The trial court's order in this case did not make an independent assessment of the needs of the child, but only determined the enforceability of the terms contained in the Letter. The Letter, for its part, did not specify how the parties wanted the court to treat their agreement in the order granting the divorce. We note, however, that in ordering that "the plaintiff shall pay child support in accordance with the May 12, 2001 letter agreement," the court also required that the amount of child support be "adjusted in accordance with the consumer price index," an adjustment that had not been agreed to in the Letter. See supra note 12. Thus, there is a question whether the trial court in this case merged the settlement agreement into its order, or incorporated it by reference.

Though other jurisdictions have enunciated criteria for determining whether a settlement agreement has been merged or incorporated into an order of divorce, we have not had occasion to do so thus far. Nor do we need to decide it at the present juncture in this case, as appellant is not presently claiming a change in circumstances as a basis for modification. We note, moreover, appellee's concession in her brief and at oral argument that the standard for merged agreements would apply in this case were appellant to claim at some future date that changes in his employment situation, income, or other responsibilities require modification of his child support obligation under the trial court's order.[13] Although the trial court would not necessarily be bound by the parties' interpretation of its order, their agreement on the standard for modification of child support would be an important, if not definitive, consideration.

The record in this case shows a serious, sustained effort by mature adults seeking to come to a reasonable agreement about their property and, most important, their continuing responsibility to and relationship with their child. Appellant may now regret that he entered into an agreement without first seeking the advice of counsel, or he may think, after the passage of time, that he should not have agreed to the terms contained in the Letter. These doubts do not negate that the Letter is complete as to the essential terms of the parties' divorce, and that appellant's course of conduct for over a year—from signing the Letter, to abiding by its terms, to stating in his e-mail communications his desire that any formalized agreement incorporate the terms in the Letter—demonstrates his intent to be bound by the conditions set forth in that agreement.

13. Contrary to appellee's representations on appeal, the Draft Agreement prepared by appellee's counsel provided that it would not be merged into the court's order, and the appellee's counter-complaint similarly requested that the Letter be incorporated, but not merged, into the judgment of divorce.

For the foregoing reasons the trial court's Judgment of Absolute Divorce enforcing the terms of the separation agreement is affirmed.

Toni v. Toni

Supreme Court of North Dakota, 2001.
2001 ND 193, 636 N.W.2d 396.

■ VandeWalle, C.J.

Sheila A. Toni appealed from an order denying her motion to modify a divorce decree under N.D.C.C. § 14-05-24. In the motion Sheila Toni asked the trial court to modify a spousal support award granted in a divorce judgment which incorporated her agreement with Conrad R. Toni to divest the court of jurisdiction to modify the amount and term of spousal support set forth in the agreement. We conclude the parties' agreement, which was found by the court in the divorce action to be "fair, just and equitable," is enforceable under North Dakota law and divested the court of jurisdiction to modify the spousal support award. We therefore affirm.

Conrad and Sheila Toni were married from July 9, 1971, until May 10, 1999. The couple had three children during the marriage, and one of them was a minor at the time of the divorce. Both parties are employed in Fargo: Conrad as a urologist, and Sheila as a clerk at Barnes & Noble Bookstore.

Before their divorce was granted, the parties entered into a "Custody and Property Settlement Agreement" which comprehensively addressed all divorce issues. The agreement stated that, although Conrad had been represented by counsel, Sheila "has not been represented by counsel and has been informed that Maureen Holman does not represent her interests in this matter but has not sought such independent counsel and enters into this custody and property settlement agreement of her own free will." The agreement also stated, "both parties agree that each has made a full disclosure to the other of all assets and liabilities and is satisfied that this custody and property settlement agreement is fair and equitable," and "each party has entered into this custody and property settlement agreement intending it to be a full and final settlement of all claims of every kind, nature, and description which either party may have or claim to have, now or in the future, against the other and, except as is expressly provided herein to the contrary, each is released from all further liability of any kind, nature or description whatsoever to the other."

The agreement provided for "joint physical custody" of the couple's minor daughter, who was expected to graduate from high school in May 1999. The agreement divided the parties' real property, stocks and retirement accounts, but did not disclose the value of those assets. The agreement also contained the following provision on spousal support:

> Commencing May 1, 1999, Conrad shall pay to Sheila the sum of $5,000 per month as and for spousal support. Said payments will continue on the first day of each month thereafter until the death of either party, Sheila's remarriage, or until the payment due on April 1, 2002 has been made. It is intended that the spousal support payable to Sheila shall be included in Sheila's gross income for income tax purposes and shall be deductible by Conrad. The court shall be divested of jurisdiction to modify in any manner whatsoever the amount and term of the spousal support awarded to Sheila immediately upon entry of the judgment and

decree herein. The court shall retain jurisdiction to enforce Conrad's obligation to pay spousal support to Sheila.

At the divorce hearing, Conrad appeared with his attorney, but Sheila, who had admitted service of the summons and complaint, did not personally appear. The trial court granted the divorce and, finding the parties' agreement to be "a fair, just and equitable settlement," incorporated its provisions into the divorce decree.

In November 2000, Sheila moved under N.D.C.C. § 14–05–24 to modify the spousal support award. Sheila claimed in an affidavit that Conrad earned $14,000 per month in "take-home pay" when they married and she believed he continued to earn a "similar" amount per month, while she earns $1,000 per month working full-time as a clerk at Barnes & Noble Bookstore. Sheila further alleged, although income from assets she received in the divorce had paid her about $2,700 per month, the "return on those assets this year has been almost nothing." Sheila estimated her monthly expenses to be $5,340, and said her accountant informed her she could convert a retirement account into an annuity producing $2,000 per month in additional income, but she is "afraid to convert this to an annuity because I believe I need it for my retirement." Sheila claimed she has a "neurological condition" that causes her trouble sleeping, and she stayed home with the children during her marriage to Conrad rather than pursuing her own career. Sheila also stated:

> I met Bob Boman after I separated from my husband. I had agreed to a reduced three-year term for spousal support because Dr. Boman was in his residency following medical school. Once he finished, we had agreed that he would pay the family expenses. Conrad and I had decided to divorce in August and I met Bob in October. Bob and I planned to marry after the divorce. Bob and I are no longer together and I do not receive any money from him.

The parties agreed to submit to the trial court the sole issue whether the provision of the parties' agreement divesting the court of jurisdiction to modify spousal support was valid under North Dakota law, and to stay any proceedings on the merits of the motion to modify the spousal support award. The trial court dismissed Sheila's motion, ruling "the parties entered into a binding contract which was incorporated into the judgment and ... the court now lacks jurisdiction to modify spousal support."

We assume, for purposes of argument only, that Sheila's claims of lowered investment yields and a failed relationship are sufficient to constitute a material change of circumstances to support a motion to modify spousal support.... The legal question in this case is whether the parties' divorce stipulation regarding spousal support can divest the trial court of its statutory authority to modify the amount and duration of support....

Under N.D.C.C. § 14–05–24, the trial court generally retains continuing jurisdiction to modify spousal support, child support, and child custody upon a showing of changed circumstances.... This Court has construed the statute, however, to not allow a trial court continuing jurisdiction to modify a final property distribution, ... and we have held when a trial court makes no initial award of spousal support and fails to expressly reserve jurisdiction over the issue, the court subsequently lacks jurisdiction to award spousal support.... Sheila argues N.D.C.C. § 14–05–24 gives a trial court the unconditional right to modify a spousal support award, regardless of any agreement by divorcing parties purporting to divest the court of that power.

We encourage peaceful settlements of disputes in divorce matters.... It is the promotion of the strong public policy favoring prompt and peaceful resolution of divorce disputes that generates a judicial bias in favor of the adoption of a stipulated agreement of the parties.... We have also noted a person may waive "all rights and privileges to which a person is legally entitled, whether secured by contract, conferred by statute, or guaranteed by the constitution, provided such rights and privileges rest in the individual who has waived them and are intended for his benefit." ...

In line with these principles, this Court has held a trial court has continuing jurisdiction to modify child support notwithstanding parental divorce settlement agreements prohibiting or limiting the court's modification powers, because the right to child support belongs to the child rather than to the parent, rendering such agreements violative of public policy and invalid.... On the other hand, we have encouraged spousal support awards based on agreements between the divorcing parties, and noted those agreements "should be changed only with great reluctance by the trial court." ... Although this Court has often said a spousal support award based on an agreement between the parties can be modified upon a showing of material change of circumstances, ... we have not been confronted with a contractual settlement clause, adopted by the trial court and incorporated into the divorce decree, attempting to divest the court of its continuing jurisdiction to modify the amount and term of the spousal support award.

Jurisdictions differ over their treatment of agreements between divorcing couples seeking to limit a court's ability to modify spousal support arrangements.... Some jurisdictions, by statute, specifically allow parties to enter into nonmodifiable spousal support agreements.... Other jurisdictions, by statute, specifically prohibit nonmodifiable spousal support agreements....

Several jurisdictions, by judicial decision, have allowed contractual waivers of the right to seek spousal support modification.... Other jurisdictions, through court decisions, have disallowed contractual waivers of the right to seek modification of spousal support....

We think the reasoning of the current trend of jurisdictions which allow divorcing couples to agree to make spousal support nonmodifiable is persuasive.

This result is consistent with our prior caselaw on spousal support. In [*Becker*, 262 N.W.2d 478, 484 (N.D. 1978)], this Court held, unless a trial court makes an initial award of spousal support or expressly reserves jurisdiction over the issue, the court lacks jurisdiction under N.D.C.C. § 14–05–24 to subsequently modify its decision and award spousal support. The original divorce decree in Becker stated, " 'neither party shall pay alimony to the other,' " and that language was incorporated from the parties' stipulation and property settlement agreement found to be "fair and equitable" by the trial court. *Id.* at 480, 484. This Court ruled the contract provision was unambiguous, and the "parties are bound by their contract provision for no alimony even if the court is not." *Id.* at 484. We see no valid distinction between a stipulation to waive all spousal support at the time of the initial divorce decree and a waiver of future modification. If a spouse can waive all right to spousal support, it logically follows that a spouse can waive the right to modification....

Section 14–05–24, N.D.C.C., does not expressly prohibit nonmodification agreements. If the legislature intended to prevent parties from entering into nonmodifiable spousal support agreements, it could have expressly prohibited them.... We recognize there can be no waiver of statutory rights if the waiver would be against public policy.... However, we do not believe allowing parties to agree that spousal support is nonmodifiable violates the public policy of this state.

Our case law invalidating parental divorce stipulations prohibiting or limiting a court's modification powers over child support is governed by public policy principles entirely different from those present when reviewing an agreement concerning spousal support. While a spousal support agreement "serves primarily to determine the interests of the contracting parties themselves," a child support agreement "directly affects the interests of the children of the marriage, who have the most at stake as a result of such an agreement but who have the least ability to protect their interests." ... "Put simply, the parties to a [spousal support] agreement are both grown-ups, free to bargain with their own legal rights." ... Freedom to contract on terms not specifically prohibited by statute ... is the major public policy question presented here.

Permitting parties to determine the future modifiability of their spousal support agreements maximizes the advantages of careful future planning and eliminates uncertainties based on the fear of subsequent motions to increase or decrease the obligations of the parties. In [*Staple v. Staple*, 616 N.W.2d 219, 228 (Mich. App. 2000)], the court relied on public policy reasons identified by the American Academy of Matrimonial Lawyers (AAML) for validating agreements to waive future modification of spousal support awards:

> The AAML comments that "recognizing and enforcing" the parties' waiver of modification "does no violence to public policy, and is consistent with the reasonable expectancy interests of the parties." The AAML also offers five public policy reasons why courts should enforce duly executed nonmodifiable alimony arrangements: (1) Nonmodifiable agreements enable parties to structure package settlements, in which alimony, asset divisions, attorney fees, postsecondary tuition for children, and related matters are all coordinated in a single, mutually acceptable agreement; (2) finality of divorce provisions allows predictability for parties planning their postdivorce lives; (3) finality fosters judicial economy; (4) finality and predictability lower the cost of divorce for both parties; (5) enforcing agreed-upon provisions for alimony will encourage increased compliance with agreements by parties who know that their agreements can and will be enforced by the court.

(footnote omitted)....

Nullifying waivers of future spousal support modifications would discourage the settlement of divorce cases, ... contrary to our public policy favoring peaceful settlements of disputes in divorce matters.... We conclude agreements by divorcing parties to make spousal support nonmodifiable and which are adopted by the trial court do not violate N.D.C.C. § 14–05–24 or public policy.

The parties' agreement in this case is not ambiguous, but is clear and unequivocal: "The court shall be divested of jurisdiction to modify in any manner whatsoever the amount and term of the spousal support awarded to Sheila immediately upon entry of the judgment and decree herein." Similar stipulations have been enforced in other jurisdictions.... Sheila acknowledged full disclosure of assets and liabilities; Conrad's attorney did not represent her, she did not obtain counsel, and entered into the agreement "of her own free will;" and the agreement is "fair and equitable" and is intended "to be a full and final settlement of all claims of every kind . . ." The divorce court found the agreement to be "a fair, just and equitable settlement" of the parties' divorce action and incorporated the provisions of the agreement into the divorce decree. We conclude the trial court correctly ruled it had no jurisdiction under N.D.C.C. § 14–05–24 to entertain Sheila's motion to modify the spousal support award.

. . .

■ MARING, J., dissenting.

. . . The principle of finality has never applied to spousal support or child support. If parties need finality and freedom to agree to a definitive spousal support, then we should not modify their agreement for any reason. Parties, however, should not be able to bind themselves in advance to an amount and duration regardless of what circumstances arise because the right to seek modification of a judgment for spousal support is not only given for the protection of persons obligated to pay and the persons who are entitled to support, but also for the benefit of society. If a spouse becomes destitute, then society will bear the burden of support.

Sidden v. Mailman

Court of Appeals of North Carolina, 2000.
137 N.C.App. 669, 529 S.E.2d 266.

■ GREENE, J.

Judy Ann Sidden (Plaintiff) appeals from an order and judgment upholding the validity of a "Contract of Separation and Property Settlement" (the Agreement) between Plaintiff and Richard Bernard Mailman (Defendant) (collectively, the parties).

. . .

The parties separated on or about 15 August 1996, at which time Defendant moved out of the marital home. At that time Plaintiff told Defendant she was "tired of fighting," he could "have it all," and to "draw up what [he thought was] fair" and she would sign it. Defendant prepared a listing of the parties' assets and liabilities, which did not include Defendant's North Carolina State Employees' Retirement Account (State Retirement Account), worth $158,100.00. Defendant testified this was an inadvertent omission.

On 1 September 1996, the parties met, reviewed, and discussed the listing, and then signed a one-page informal document which outlined the terms of a separation agreement. On 9 September 1996, Defendant retained attorney Wayne Hadler (Hadler) to prepare a final separation agreement, the Agreement at issue in this case. The Agreement formalized the terms of the one-page informal agreement the parties had previously signed, and the Agreement was executed and acknowledged before a notary by the parties on 10 September 1996 at Hadler's office.

At trial, Hadler who holds a Master's degree in Social Work and previously worked for twelve years as a social worker for the Alamance County Mental Health Department, testified he did not see anything about Plaintiff's appearance, demeanor, or behavior that would indicate she was confused or lacked the capacity to enter into the Agreement. Hadler informed Plaintiff he was representing Defendant and could not give her any legal advice, and he encouraged her to have the Agreement reviewed by separate counsel. Hadler explained to Plaintiff she could take as much time as she needed to review the Agreement, and he left her in the conference room of his office to allow her time to review the Agreement in privacy. Although Plaintiff was in regular consultation with her business attorneys and an accountant from July 1996 to October 1996, she chose not to have an attorney review the Agreement.

After the parties executed the Agreement, Plaintiff directed Defendant to immediately take her to a bank so she could receive the funds due her under the terms of the Agreement. Defendant followed Plaintiff's directions, and the parties have fully performed and complied with the terms of the Agreement.

Defendant testified at trial that several months after the Agreement's execution he came across a statement of his State Retirement Account. Realizing he had inadvertently omitted the State Retirement Account from his listing of assets and from the Agreement, Defendant telephoned Plaintiff to inquire whether she wanted to discuss the State Retirement Account and whether any adjustment should be made to the Agreement. Defendant testified Plaintiff responded she was "going to get more out of [him] than that," and their conversation ended.

Plaintiff testified at trial that she was suffering from hypo-mania and was psychotic and out of touch with reality from the spring of 1996 throughout the events surrounding the execution of the Agreement until her 20 January 1997 admittance into the UNC Memorial Hospital, where she was placed under a suicide watch. In April of 1995, Plaintiff was seeing a psychiatrist, Thomas N. Stephenson, M.D. (Dr. Stephenson), as an individual patient. Dr. Stephenson diagnosed Plaintiff as suffering from depression and anxiety and prescribed an anti-depressant, Zoloft, for Plaintiff. In May of 1996, before the execution of the Agreement, Dr. Stephenson saw Plaintiff for the last time. Dr. Stephenson found Plaintiff was "continuing to do well," but the problems with her husband were continuing.

Dr. Stephenson testified Zoloft can induce hypo-mania. Plaintiff's expert in psychiatry, Jeffrey J. Fahs, M.D. (Dr. Fahs), defined hypo-mania as a psychiatric condition that is a milder form of mania which is marked by grandiosity, a decreased need for sleep, loquaciousness, and involvement in activities that have a high potential for painful consequences like foolish business investments or buying sprees. Dr. Stephenson saw Plaintiff again on 13 September 1996, and at that time, he thought her judgement was impaired but she was not manic.

Dr. Fahs testified he examined Plaintiff on 10 March 1997 and reviewed her records and summary of treatment. Dr. Fahs opined Plaintiff had exhibited symptoms of a mood disorder that included depression, mania, and hypo-mania. Dr. Fahs testified Plaintiff "may have had a cognitive understanding" she was signing the Agreement, but she could not truly appreciate the consequences of signing it. Dr. Fahs also stated Zoloft can cause mania or hypo-mania, and mania impairs judgement.

. . .

The issues are whether: (I) the evidence supports the trial court's finding that Plaintiff's "mental state ... was not ... impaired" at the time the Agreement was executed; (II) the evidence supports the trial court's findings that Plaintiff signed the Agreement "of her own free and voluntary will ... without ... coercion"; [and] (III) Plaintiff alleged and offered evidence of fraud as a basis to set aside the Agreement....

Separation and/or property settlement agreements are contracts and as such are subject to recission on the grounds of (1) lack of mental capacity, (2) mistake, (3) fraud, (4) duress, or (5) undue influence.... Furthermore, these contracts are not enforceable if their terms are unconscionable....

A claim for fraud may be based "on an affirmative misrepresentation of a material fact or a failure to disclose a material fact relating to a transaction which the parties had a duty to disclose." ... A duty to disclose arises where: (1) "a fiduciary relationship exists between the parties to the transaction"; (2) there is no fiduciary relationship and "a party has taken affirmative steps to conceal material facts from the other"; and (3) there is no fiduciary relationship and "one party has knowledge of a latent defect in the subject matter of the negotiations about which the other party is both ignorant and unable to discover through reasonable diligence." ... A husband and wife, unless they have separated and become adversaries negotiating over the terms of a separation and/or property settlement agreement, are in a fiduciary relationship....

A claim that an agreement is unconscionable "requires a determination that the agreement is both substantively and procedurally unconscionable." ... Procedural deficiencies involve "bargaining naughtiness," ... "such as deception or a refusal to bargain over contract terms," 8 Samuel Williston, *A Treatise on the Law of Contracts* § 18:10, at 57 (Richard A. Lord ed., 4th ed. 1998). The failure of a husband and/or a wife to accurately disclose his or her assets and debts in negotiating a separation and/or a property agreement can constitute procedural unconscionability, even if the failure to disclose does not constitute fraud.... Substantive unconscionability involves the "inequality of the bargain." ...

CONTRACT CLAIMS

Mental Capacity

Plaintiff first argues she was mentally incompetent at the time she signed the Agreement, and the trial court thus erred in refusing to rescind the Agreement on this basis. We disagree.

. . .

The record to this Court reveals conflicting evidence regarding Plaintiff's mental state at the time she executed the Agreement: there is evidence Plaintiff did not have the capacity to enter into a contract because she was under a drug induced mania that impaired her judgement; there is also evidence Plaintiff had the capacity to contract; Hadler did not see anything about Plaintiff's behavior or appearance which would indicate she lacked the capacity to contract at the Agreement's execution; and Dr. Dawkins did not notice any signs that Plaintiff was mentally impaired shortly after the Agreement was executed. Furthermore, Plaintiff directed Defendant take her to a bank so she could receive the money due her under the Agreement, thus, demonstrating she understood the nature of the act she was engaged in and its consequences.

The trial court resolved this conflict of evidence in favor of Defendant, and thus, did not err in refusing to rescind the Agreement on the ground of Plaintiff's lack of capacity to contract.

Undue Influence

Plaintiff argues the Agreement must be rescinded because Defendant exercised undue influence over her decision to sign the Agreement. We disagree.

. . .

The parties executed an informal agreement two weeks after their separation and the formal Agreement was executed two weeks later. At the time of the formal execution, Plaintiff was told by Defendant's attorney she could have an attorney review the Agreement before she signed it and she was given time to review the Agreement, in private, in Hadler's office. Plaintiff chose to sign the Agreement without the advice of an attorney, even though she had a business attorney and an accountant who regularly represented her in her psychotherapy practice. The trial court, thus, did not err in refusing to rescind the Agreement on the ground of undue influence.

Fraud

The trial court found Plaintiff "did not plead ... breach of fiduciary duty in her Complaint nor did she offer any evidence of same."

. . .

Plaintiff offered evidence that she and her husband, the Defendant, soon after separating and before their divorce, informally agreed to the distribution of their marital assets and debts. This informal agreement was reduced to writing by Defendant's attorney and was signed by both parties. At some point after the execution of the Agreement, Plaintiff learned Defendant had failed to disclose the existence of his State Retirement Account, having a value of $158,100.00.

This evidence is some evidence Defendant failed to disclose a material fact to Plaintiff at a time when the parties were in a fiduciary relationship. The trial court, thus, erred in finding Plaintiff had not presented "any evidence" of a breach of a fiduciary relationship.

Because the trial court found Plaintiff had not alleged breach of fiduciary duty and had not offered any evidence on this issue, that court made no findings or conclusions on this issue. This was error and remand must be had to the trial court. On remand, the trial court must enter findings and conclusions, based on the evidence in this record, on the breach of fiduciary duty issue.

. . .

Kelley v. Kelley

Supreme Court of Virginia, 1994.
248 Va. 295, 449 S.E.2d 55.

■ Stephenson, J.

In this appeal, we decide (1) whether a provision of a property settlement agreement, which was ratified, affirmed, and incorporated by reference into a divorce decree, is void and, if so, (2) whether the decree may be attacked and vacated after it has become final.

On April 29, 1985, David Allen Kelley (Husband) and Marilyn Gibson Kelley (Wife) executed a property settlement agreement (the Agreement).

On September 23, 1985, the trial court (the Circuit Court of the City of Roanoke) entered a divorce decree which ratified, affirmed, and incorporated by reference the Agreement.

The Agreement contained the following provision:

> The parties hereto agree, in consideration of Husband relinquishing all of his equity in the jointly-owned marital home, that Husband shall never be responsible for payment of child support. The [Wife] covenants and agrees never to file a petition in any Court requesting that [Husband] be placed under a child support Order because [Wife] has accepted all of [Husband's] equity in lieu of requesting child support.
>
> In the event [Wife] should ever petition any Court of competent jurisdiction for support and maintenance of [the children], and should a Court grant any such child support award, the said [Wife] hereby covenants and agrees to pay directly to [Husband], any amount of support that he is directed to pay to any party. In other words, [Wife] is agreeing to hold harmless [Husband] from the payment of any amount of child support, regardless of the circumstances under which he is paying same.

Pursuant to the Agreement, the Husband conveyed his equity in the marital home, valued at $40,000, to the Wife. For approximately six years thereafter, the Husband paid nothing toward the support of his children; the Wife, alone, supported them.

In late 1990, the Husband petitioned the trial court for definite periods of visitation with his children, and the Wife petitioned the court to require the Husband to pay child support. The Husband countered with a motion requesting the court to order the Wife to reimburse him for any amount of child support he was required to pay.

The trial court ordered the Husband to pay support and denied the Husband's motion, ruling that the indemnification and reimbursement provision of the Agreement was null and void. The Husband appealed from the trial court's judgment to the Court of Appeals. The Husband did not challenge the ordered child support, but contended that the trial court erred in holding that the indemnification and reimbursement provision of the Agreement was void and unenforceable.

The Court of Appeals, upon rehearing en banc, reversed the trial court's judgment, concluding that the trial court lacked jurisdiction to alter the terms of the Agreement or decree. . . . We awarded the Wife an appeal from the judgment of the Court of Appeals, concluding that the case involves a matter of significant precedential value. . . .

Both parents owe a duty of support to their minor children. . . . A divorce court retains continuing jurisdiction to change or modify its decree relating to the maintenance and support of minor children. . . . Consequently, parents cannot contract away their children's rights to support nor can a court be precluded by agreement from exercising its power to decree child support. . . .

In the present case, the parties agreed that the "Husband shall never be responsible for payment of child support." The Wife agreed "never to file a petition in any court" requesting support for the children. The Wife covenanted that, if a court ordered the Husband to pay child support, she would reimburse the Husband for all sums paid by him. She further agreed to hold the Husband harmless for any amount of child support he was required to pay.

Clearly, the parties contracted away the Husband's legal duty to support his children and, in effect, placed upon the Wife the sole duty of support. Additionally, the Wife's ability to contribute to the support of the children was adversely affected. Thus, the children's rights to receive support from both parents were substantially abridged, and the court's power to decree support was diminished. We hold, therefore, that the challenged provision of the Agreement is null and void because it is violative of clearly established law.

Next, we consider whether the trial court had jurisdiction to declare the provision null and void. The Court of Appeals ruled that the trial court lacked jurisdiction. Citing Rule 1:1, the Court of Appeals held that "after the expiration of twenty-one days immediately following the entry of the 1985 divorce decree, except to modify the amount of child support, the trial court lacked jurisdiction to alter the terms of the [Agreement] or the decree." *Kelley*, 435 S.E.2d at 422.

The Court of Appeals relied largely upon Rook v. Rook, 233 Va. 92, 353 S.E.2d 756 (1987). In *Rook*, a married couple executed a property settlement agreement prior to the filing of a suit for divorce. Thereafter, the agreement was ratified, affirmed, and incorporated by reference into a divorce decree. In a subsequent contempt proceeding for failure to comply with the terms of the decree, the husband contended that the agreement was void as against public policy, asserting that its purpose was to facilitate a divorce. We held, in *Rook*, that the challenge to the agreement's validity should have been made before the divorce decree was entered or within 21 days thereafter.

The present case is distinguishable from *Rook* because it involves the rights of children to support and maintenance. These rights, as previously noted, cannot be impinged by contract, and any contract purporting to do so is facially illegal and void.

In the present case, the subject provision of the Agreement was ratified, affirmed, and incorporated by reference into the divorce decree and, therefore, "shall be deemed for all purposes to be a term of the decree." Code § 20–109.1. Consequently, that portion of the decree that relates to the void provision is, itself, void.

It is firmly established that a void judgment may be attacked and vacated in any court at any time, directly or collaterally.... Therefore, the trial court had jurisdiction to declare the provision void and unenforceable.

Accordingly, we will reverse the judgment of the Court of Appeals, affirm the trial court's ruling, and enter final judgment for the Wife.

J. ALTERNATIVE DISPUTE RESOLUTION

1. ARBITRATION

Kelm v. Kelm

Supreme Court of Ohio, 2001.
92 Ohio St.3d 223, 749 N.E.2d 299.

■ OPINION: SWEENEY, SR., J.:

On October 1, 1993, the Franklin County Court of Common Pleas, Division of Domestic Relations, granted appellant, Russell A. Kelm, and appellee, Amy K. Kelm, a judgment of divorce. The judgment incorporated the parties' shared parenting plan, which provided, *inter alia*, that any future disputes between the parties regarding child custody or visitation would be submitted to arbitration.

On May 10, 1999, appellee filed in the domestic relations court a motion to modify or terminate the shared parenting plan. Appellant responded by filing a motion to stay proceedings on appellee's motion and to compel arbitration pursuant to the shared parenting plan. On June 25, 1999, the trial court issued a judgment entry overruling appellant's motion. The trial court concluded that, under Ohio law, matters relating to child custody are not subject to arbitration.

Appellant appealed the trial court's decision to the Tenth District Court of Appeals, arguing that the trial court erred in failing to enforce the arbitration agreement. The court of appeals . . . affirmed the judgment of the trial court, holding that the use of arbitration to resolve child custody or visitation disputes conflicts with the duty of the domestic relations courts to protect the best interests of children. The court of appeals further held that appellee has not, by virtue of her being a party to the shared parenting plan, waived her right to challenge the arbitration clause. The court of appeals also concluded that appellee's challenge is not barred under the doctrine of *res judicata*. . . .

We are asked to decide whether, in a domestic relations case, matters relating to child custody and visitation may be resolved through arbitration. For the reasons that follow, we hold that these matters cannot be resolved through arbitration. Only the courts are empowered to resolve disputes relating to child custody and visitation.

The parties' divorce has a long and convoluted history. . . . In *Kelm I*, we were asked to decide whether an arbitration clause in the parties' antenuptial agreement was enforceable as to matters relating to spousal and child support. We held that these support matters could be made subject to an agreement to arbitrate. In so holding, we recognized that, under the doctrine of *parens patriae*, courts are entrusted to protect the best interests of children. We concluded, however, that permitting parents to arbitrate child support does not interfere with the judicial protection of the best interests of children. In short, we saw "no valid reason why the arbitration process should not be available in the area of child support; the advantages of arbitration in domestic disputes outweigh any disadvantages." Appellant urges us to extend our holding in *Kelm I* to allow matters of child custody and visitation to be resolved through arbitration. We decline to do so.

While we recognize the important impact that monetary support can have upon a child's life, we believe that custody and visitation have a much greater impact upon the child in terms of both the child's daily life and his or her long-term development. Custody and visitation have the potential to affect countless aspects of a child's life, including the child's relationships with his or her parents, the child's relationships with extended family, the child's social and cultural upbringing, and even, in some unfortunate cases, the child's physical and emotional security. More than support determinations, " 'determinations of custody go to the very core of the child's welfare and best interests.' " "The process of arbitration, useful when the mundane matter of the amount of support is in issue, is less so when the delicate balancing of the factors composing the best interests of a child is at issue." *Nestel v. Nestel (1972), 331 N.Y.S.2d 241, 243.* For this reason, we are less inclined than we were in *Kelm I* to permit arbitration to encroach upon the trial court's traditional role as *parens patriae*.

As appellant points out, there are decisions from a number of jurisdictions upholding the use of arbitration to settle disputes over child custody and visitation. Typically, these decisions protect the courts' role as *parens patriae* by making the arbitrator's decision subject to *de novo* review and modification by the courts. While this approach preserves the court's role as *parens patriae*, we believe that, ultimately, it advances neither the children's best interests nor the basic goals underlying arbitration.

A two-stage procedure consisting of an arbitrator's decision followed by *de novo* judicial review "is certain to be wasteful of time and expense and result in a duplication of effort." *Nestel,* 331 N.Y.S.2d at 243. . . .

The protracted two-stage process adopted by some courts also frustrates the very goals underlying arbitration. " 'Arbitration is favored because it provides the parties thereto with a relatively expeditious and economical means of resolving a dispute . . . [and] '. . . has the additional advantage of unburdening crowded court dockets.' " A two-stage process consisting of both arbitration and judicial review achieves none of these goals.

Furthermore, "if an issue is to be arbitrated, the expectation [of the parties] is that an award will not be disturbed." *De novo* review destroys this expectation. Thus, there is an inevitable tension between the court's traditional responsibility to protect the best interests of children and the parties' expectation that an arbitration award will be final.

Appellant argues that because the shared parenting plan contained an agreement to arbitrate any future custody and visitation disputes, and because this agreement was, by consent of both parties, incorporated into the trial court's judgment of divorce, appellee could not subsequently challenge the arbitration agreement. Essentially, appellant argues that by agreeing to arbitrate custody and visitation matters, appellee has waived her right to challenge the agreement. We disagree.

The law permits parties to voluntarily waive a number of important legal rights, and in the interest of finality, courts are usually quite reluctant to relieve parties of the consequences of these choices. However, a waiver of rights will be recognized only when the waiver does not violate public policy. A fundamental flaw in appellant's argument is its assumption that arbitration of custody and visitation matters does not violate public policy. We have already concluded, for the reasons set forth above, that it does.

To hold that appellee has waived her right to challenge the arbitration agreement and to permit arbitration of the parties' child custody and visitation disputes would prevent the trial court from fulfilling its role as *parens patriae*. Because this is contrary to public policy, we conclude that appellee has not, by virtue of her acquiescence to the original shared parenting plan, waived her right to challenge that plan's provision for arbitration of custody and visitation matters.

There is an even more fundamental flaw in appellant's waiver analysis. With respect to matters of custody and visitation, the central focus is not, as appellant suggests, the rights of the parents but is, rather, the best interests of the children. The duty owed by the courts to children under the doctrine of *parens patriae* cannot be severed by agreement of the parties. It stands to reason that "if parents cannot bind the court by an agreement affecting the interests of their children, they cannot bind the court by agreeing to let someone else, an arbitrator, make such a decision for them." . . .

Finally, appellant argues that because appellee could have mounted a challenge to the arbitration clause in a previous action, she is now barred from bringing this challenge under the doctrine of *res judicata*. This argument, too, lacks merit.

. . .

In many states, including Ohio, an allocation of custody and visitation rights remains subject to future modification by the trial court. For this reason, a number of courts have held that the doctrine of *res judicata* should not be applied strictly in cases involving child custody and visitation. We find these decisions persuasive.

In Ohio, the authority of the domestic relations courts to modify their own custody and visitation orders is found in *R.C. 3109.04* . . . Thus, as a practical matter, a custody and visitation order is never absolutely final. This fact makes application of *res judicata* impractical. The very purpose of *res judicata* is to deter the repeated litigation of resolved issues, thereby ensuring finality in judgments and the conservation of judicial resources. However, in the area of custody and visitation, we sacrifice finality and some of our limited judicial resources in order to secure a higher value—the best interests of children.

Hence, appellee's failure to challenge the arbitration clause in the previous divorce action could not deprive the trial court of jurisdiction to consider appellee's subsequent motion to modify or terminate the shared parenting plan. The trial court has a continuing responsibility under *R.C. 3109.04(B)(1)* and (E)(1)(a) to protect the best interests of the children. As we have already held, the parties' agreement to arbitrate custody and visitation disputes impermissibly interferes with the court's ability to carry out this responsibility. The doctrine of *res judicata*, like the doctrine of waiver, cannot be relied upon to enforce this otherwise unenforceable agreement.

For the foregoing reasons, we hold that in a domestic relations case, matters of child custody and parental visitation are not subject to arbitration. The authority to resolve disputes over custody and visitation rests exclusively with the courts. Any agreement to the contrary is void and unenforceable.

■ MOYER, C.J., concurring.

I concur in the majority decision with the observation that it is confined to arbitration and does not apply to agreements reached regarding visitation and custody through the process of mediation.

2. MEDIATION

Ben Barlow, Divorce Child Custody Mediation: In Order to Form a More Perfect Disunion?

52 Clev. St. L. Rev. 499 (2004–05).

I. INTRODUCTION

The adversarial process serves a much needed purpose in American society. Its roots are deep and its usage pervasive. It has become so ingrained in our culture that many are unwilling to discuss possible problems inherent in the system and changes needed to solve those problems.

Nowhere are these problems more apparent than in the sphere of family law. With divorce rates growing in the past fifty years, people have increasingly turned a critical eye toward the system that divorcing parties traverse. The psychological effect of divorce on the parties involved has been widely studied, and frequently counseling is recommended by the family courts involved. Divorcing parties can often proceed in life without close interaction with the other party if there are no children of the marriage; however, a divorce in which children are involved presents an entirely different dynamic. Although the legal system is intended to be a means through which parties can terminate often traumatic relationships, many suggest that some of the trauma suffered in the divorce process is due in part to the process itself, the adversarial pitting of parties against each other in a zero sum game.

Attempts have been made in several states to implement statutes providing for methods of lessening the traumatic effect of the adversarial process. Those statutes often establish a framework of counseling and Alternative Dispute Resolution ("ADR") that courts can use to soften the process and reach more mutually beneficial resolutions to conflict.

ADR has increasingly come into use as an effective way to handle disputes of all types. One part of ADR is the use of mediation to facilitate resolution of the conflict by the parties themselves. The use of mediation has garnered wide support in disputes of all degrees, from neighborhood squabbles to dispute resolution amongst international actors. Many states have implemented mediation provisions in their family law code. Some states have suggested mediation at the discretion of the court while others have mandated its use.

In family law, however, the use of mediation runs into its strongest opposition. Many suggest that family, namely divorce, disputes are multilayered and that mediation potentially harms parties involved by heightening imbalances of power, by encouraging manipulation, by coercing parties, by not allowing parties to avail themselves of their legal rights and by not developing agreements that fully reflect the realities of the relationships involved.

Such a backdrop frames the especially pressing problem of the use of mediation in divorce child custody actions. Proponents of mediation suggest that nowhere are the effects of adversarial divorce proceedings more damaging and, thus, nowhere is mediation more needed. Opponents counter that the seriousness of the situation makes the potential harms of mediation all the more pronounced. The truth lies somewhere in the middle and should serve as a basis for the examination of mediation in divorce custody proceedings throughout the nation.

It is evident that typical adversarial divorces are especially damaging to children involved. That factor alone should force us to search for other methods of dissolving unions and resolving child custody in the wake of such dissolutions. Mediation is one viable alternative....

Mediation is not appropriate in all situations, and the concerns of mediation opponents must be weighed carefully. Courts should deliberate carefully as to whether the use of mediation is appropriate in situations where there has been domestic violence. Mediators should be specially trained and meet objective standards to ensure that imbalances of power do not provide opportunities for manipulation. All agreements reached in such cases should be carefully reviewed by courts to ensure that concerns regarding power imbalances are addressed. Codifying those concerns within a mandatory mediation and counseling statute could significantly impact the divorce process, making way for agreements and freeing the court docket at best, and encouraging an atmosphere of communication that will hopefully extend past the dissolution into the post-divorce child-rearing phase at worst.

II. THE DEVELOPMENT OF ALTERNATIVE DISPUTE RESOLUTION, SPECIFICALLY MEDIATION, IN THE LEGAL ARENA

. . .

B. Mediation

As opposed to arbitration, where "the parties present the dispute to a selected decision-maker or a panel of decision-makers, usually with the expertise in the subject of litigation. . . . [where parties form] binding, non-binding, or advisory [agreements] with very limited grounds for appeal," mediation focuses on facilitated interaction between the parties. Given the use of mediation in both legal and non-legal contexts, it is important to define how the term is used within a primarily legal context. In construing a Minnesota statute that used but did not define "mediation," the Minnesota Supreme Court defined mediation as "[a] forum in which an impartial person, the mediator, facilitates communication between parties to promote conciliation, settlement, or understanding among them." Others view mediation as "the process by which the participants, together with the assistance of a neutral person or persons, systematically isolate disputed issues in order to develop options, consider alternatives, and reach a consensual settlement that will accommodate their needs."

. . .

Proponents of [what is called] transformative mediation focus on the inherent benefit of the process itself, and, regardless of specific outcomes, the ability of the process to "[enable parties] to approach their current problem, as well as later problems" in healthier ways. Proponents of transformative mediation also find that the process "enhances the dignity of those in conflict," and thus is helpful in situations where parties come to mediation with differing degrees of power.

While transformative mediation focuses on the benefits conferred by the process itself regardless of specific outcomes, outcome-oriented mediation focuses on the outcomes of mediations to determine the value of the process in particular situations. In advocating the use of mediation, outcome-oriented mediators focus on high statistical success rates and the docket-clearing benefits that have accompanied the use of mediation in civil disputes. Such emphasis on the "efficiency incentives" of mediation supports the use of mediation in conflicts that are potentially more easily resolved than others. . . .

Because the docket-clearing feature is a primary objective, mediation is often not advocated for disputes likely to come back before the court, either for additional review or because the issue is not likely to be solved by mediation, because mediation would serve as an *additional* step in such situations, not a reduced step.

Areas in which the two mediation motives overlap are obvious. In many civil disputes, where the success rate of mediation is high, the use of mediation accomplishes the goals of proponents of transformative mediation and outcome-oriented mediation: The dockets are cleared *and* parties benefit from the process. In areas of the law dominated by complicated issues and high emotions, the best example being divorce child custody cases, however, transformative mediation advocates would argue that the process of mediation is nowhere more needed. Outcome-oriented mediators would counter that there is little need to use the process because often more effort is required than would be used if the matter were to stay in the adversarial process.

. . .

III. THE USE OF MEDIATION IN DIVORCE CHILD CUSTODY CASES

. . .

A. Mediation's Slow Emergence in Divorce Child Custody

. . .

As divorce rates in the United States rose dramatically in the latter half of the twentieth century, people involved with family law, both legal professionals and mental health professionals began voicing concerns that the divorce process was far too "black and white" in handling marital dissolutions involving child custody. Proponents of mediation argue that there is a need for an empowering process that addresses the needs of the parties and not merely the superficial issues separating them.... In civil disputes, it is often possible for parties to get their judgment and get out, to achieve some sort of closure in their situations and then cut off relations, to some degree, with each other....

Family law is [different] and the adversarial zero sum game approach is potentially devastating. In child custody disputes, it is usually not in the best interests of the child to have parties cut off contact; likewise, regardless of which party wins or loses in the adversarial system, the end result is that a common child gets a winning parent and a losing parent.... Researchers cite many reasons for the harmful effect the adversarial process is thought to have on parties involved in a divorce. Those "adversarial feelings are thought to spring from three sources:" (1) the use of third parties in negotiating (attorneys, etc.); (2) the nature of the adversarial process itself, the practice of taking two opposing views and using a fact-finder to determine which is more or less correct; and, (3) the fact that parties have little say in the actual development of solutions to the problem, that their role is more or less to present facts.

The negative effects of divorce on child development are well-established; however, what portion of those effects are due to the basic separation aspect of the divorce and what portion may be due to the adversarial relationship that is often cultivated by the legal system is not as well-established. Children of different ages are, naturally, impacted by divorce in different ways, from bedwetting in preschoolers to the inability of older teens to form healthy relationships. Four major causes of stress for children of divorcing parents are (1) the family they have always known will be different; (2) loss of attachment; (3) fear of abandonment; and, (4) hostility between the parents. While the first three causes are endemic to the divorce process itself, the fourth, the effect of the hostile relationship between divorcing parties on the children, is one that the mediation process attempts to eliminate....

IV. A QUESTION OF POWER: CONCERNS REGARDING POWER IMBALANCES IN DIVORCE MEDIATION

A primary concern of opponents of divorce and custody mediation is that it does not adequately deal with imbalances of power that are often immersed throughout the domestic dispute. Divorce mediation "tends to bring to the bargaining table unbalanced pairs, typically a husband with a high degree of power, and a wife who possesses a relatively low degree of power." If that indeed [is] representative of parties taking part in divorce mediation, the problems presented are clear. Mediation focuses on a facilitated dialogue that ideally culminates in an agreement between the parties. If parties start from drastically unequal levels of power, the mediation process could, instead of facilitating agreement, further limit the power of the already-powerless spouse. "A mediator may be deceived into allowing, and even contributing to, the unconscionable exploitation of the weaker spouse by the dominant spouse." Courts examining questions of tremendous imbalances of power have posited that mediation might be less suited to balance the power of the parties than the adversarial system.

Many recognize that imbalances in power [also] run throughout the adversarial process. In fact, an "apparent weakness of the adversary system is that it assumes that parties bring equal skill and power, in the form of an attorney and economic support, to bear upon the case." When parties take part in that process and are not of equal skill and economic support, there is no mechanism present to balance the scales.

. . .

A. Power Imbalances in Situations Involving Domestic Violence

Basic inequities in the relative power of divorcing spouses are a fundamental concern to those opposed to the use of mediation in divorce and child custody situations. Opponents to mediation argue that divorcing parties typically include a relatively powerless woman and a powerful man. They further argue that in such a situation, mediation helps further silence the woman by introducing a "fair" process into an unfair relationship. In such cases it is posited that the woman is not provided with the opportunity to fully air her position; a position that would be available in litigation.

In addition to those questions regarding the power structure present in the marital relationship, the far more specific concerns relating to the balance of power in relationships involving domestic violence are pressing. It is often stated that the issue of whether mediation is appropriate in situations where domestic violence has occurred is one of the most controversial areas of family law. The fact that one in three women will suffer violence at the hands of an intimate, and that 5% of all violence against men is at the hands of an intimate, leads to the conclusion that at least a large percentage of divorce cases will involve domestic violence.

It has become widely recognized that domestic violence is often a factor in cases involving child-protection. That realization has come as judges become more aware of the common underlying elements in domestic disputes.

. . .

. . . If mediation's main aim is to foster a better relationship between the parties, is it possible to do so in cases involving violence without causing potential harm to the victimized party? Though ADR is used in other cases involving violence, namely restorative justice, in those cases the heavy hand of the state is looming over or clamped down on the violent offender.

With regard to balances of power and domestic violence, states have taken different approaches in their attempts to implement mediation programs. All of those approaches provide valuable lessons to those contemplating such statutes.

V. MEDIATION CODE PROVISIONS IN THE SEVERAL STATES

A. The State Systems

Thirty-eight states currently have statutes establishing some sort of mediation framework for use in divorce cases ... Those states, however, differ greatly in how rigidly they construct that framework. Some states have mandatory mediation statutes while others have a process through which courts can refer parties to mediation in the court's discretion. The following section provides a brief examination of a representative portion of those state systems.

1. California

... California led all states in implementing a mandatory mediation statute covering all custody issues stemming out of a divorce. California continues to have the most rigid of all mediation statutes. The Code provides that:

> Domestic violence cases shall be handled by Family Court Services in accordance with a separate written protocol approved by the Judicial Council. The Judicial Council shall adopt guidelines for services, other than services provided under this Chapter, that counties may offer to parents who have been unable to resolve their disputes. These services may include, but are not limited to, parent education programs, booklets, videotapes, or referrals to additional community resources.

California understands its mediation statute to be focused on three primary goals: "(1) to reduce acrimony between the parties; (2) to develop an agreement assuring the child close and continuing contact with both parents that is in the best interest of the child; and (3) to effect a settlement of the issue of visitation rights of all parties that is in the best interest of the child." To further those goals, California has attempted to create a system that is applicable in all situations, not simply the cases where there are no exigencies involving violence.

California's code does not contain a "domestic violence escape clause" as do many state mediation statutes; instead, the Judicial Council's written protocol states that, in cases involving domestic violence, the mediators shall meet with the parties at separate times and locations. By so providing, California has attempted to address balance of power and violence concerns while still avoiding, at least in the early stages of the proceedings, the adversarial process. California courts have recognized the legislature's intent to further "mediated, private resolutions" while affirming that normal legal rights remain when the mediation process fails to reach a result.

The California system is by far the most thorough in its use of mediation. That is appropriate given the early introduction of the act and the ability of the California Legislature, along with family law practitioners, to analyze the effectiveness of the earlier versions of the act and make appropriate changes when needed. Such a development process might indicate that it is best for states to implement a program and then tailor it as needed. Most states, however, are unwilling to take that initial leap.

2. Delaware

Delaware also has a mandatory mediation statute for all issues relating to custody, support, or visitation; however, Delaware specifically provides that "family court mediation conferences shall be prohibited in any child custody or visitation proceeding in which [one] of the parties has been found by a court, whether in that proceeding or in some other proceeding, to have committed an act of domestic violence." Delaware's statute also differs from California's in that the mediation is scheduled as a pre-trial mediation conference with a court staff mediator primarily to "attempt amicable settlement of all unresolved issues." Issues involving child custody are handled in the same way.

The Delaware code includes provisions for additional "courses" for parents involved in divorce actions. Courts may require parents to attend certified parenting courses prior to the finalization of their divorce as well as more intensive courses if either parent has a history of domestic violence. Components of many state statutes that work in tandem with the state's mediation laws are counseling statutes that encourage counseling or, as is the case in Delaware, parental education in divorce actions.

Delaware's system, in making specific provisions for parenting courses, codifies an understanding of the importance of ongoing parental responsibilities. Although the Delaware code provisions differ markedly from those in California, they provide for a system that attempts to deal with the complex issues involved in divorce child custody cases.

3. Florida

The Florida code provides that circuit courts may implement mediation programs. In those circuits where a mediation scheme has been developed, the code provides that courts shall refer all contested family matters, particularly custody disputes, to mediation. In Florida, state law details the mediation process more fully than other state mediation statutes. The statute defines family law mediation broadly, including "disputes between married or unmarried persons that arise before or after the rendition of a judgment involving dissolution of marriage, property division, shared or sole parental responsibility, visitation, or child support." While other states tailor their code provisions especially for custody, visitation, and support issues, Florida includes all issues involved in the divorce proceeding in its statute.

In providing for court-referred mediation, Florida's meditation statute also contemplates situations involving abuse. Florida statute provides that, upon motion or request by a party, a court shall not refer a case to mediation "if it finds that there has been a history of domestic violence that would compromise the mediation process." To what extent Florida's statute places a burden on parties to prove such a degree of domestic violence, and the effect of that burden, if present, is a concern of some mediators.

. . .

7. North Carolina

In North Carolina, as is the case in a number of states, statute provides for mandatory mediation for child custody and visitation issues in areas where a mediation program has been established. In fact, the intent of the legislature to support mediation was so clear that North Carolina courts have interpreted the statute, although it is in the divorce and alimony area of the code, as not being limited to those areas of the law.

Because North Carolina at this point does not mandate mediation in custody and visitation matters statewide, the statute can be fairly described as a quasi-mandatory statute. Where mediation exists, there it shall be used. North Carolina has also created the following exemption provision:

> For good cause, on the motion of either party or on the court's own motion, the court may waive the mandatory setting . . . of a contested custody or visitation matter for mediation. Good cause may include, but

> is not limited to, the following: a showing of undue hardship to a party; an agreement between the parties for voluntary mediation, subject to court approval; allegations of abuse or neglect of the minor child; allegations of alcoholism, drug abuse, or spouse abuse; or allegations of severe psychological, psychiatric, or emotional problems. A showing by either party that the party resides more than fifty miles from the court shall be considered good cause.

The North Carolina legislature, in establishing the provision, also codified its goals for the mediation statute, stating:

> The purposes of mediation under [the] section include the pursuit of the following goals: (1) To reduce any acrimony that exists between the parties to a dispute involving custody or visitation of a minor child; (2) The development of custody and visitation agreements that are in the child's best interest; (3) To provide the parties with informed choices and, where possible, to give the parties the responsibility for making decisions about child custody and visitation; (4) To provide a structured, confidential, nonadversarial setting that will facilitate the cooperative resolution of custody and visitation disputes and minimize the stress and anxiety to which the parties, and especially the child, are subjected; and (5) To reduce the relitigation of custody and visitation disputes.

. . .

12. Virginia

The Virginia statute does not establish a mandatory mediation framework; instead, it allows courts discretion to refer parties to mediation if they determine the case is suitable for mediation. The statute neither categorically includes nor excludes certain types of cases from consideration for mediation; instead, "in assessing the appropriateness of a referral, the court shall ascertain upon motion of a party whether there is a history of family abuse."

As is the case with California's statute, the Virginia statute also establishes a system through which the costs of mediation are covered. In cases involving custody, visitation, or support, the statute sets a cost of $100 per mediation session to be paid by the Commonwealth.

Virginia, while leading the nation in its advocacy of mediation in other areas of the law, has been hesitant to provide that same advocacy in family law contexts. The success of mediation in other areas, and the desire of the Virginia judiciary for the efficiency impact of mediation might further the use of mediation in such situations. Experts, when examining Virginia's family law mediation provisions find that "divorce mediation and arbitration alternatives to traditional court litigation, however[,] are not feasible for all parties, and both alternatives require a certain amount of mutual agreement between the parties to settle their disputes in a nonadversarial manner."

B. The State Approaches Analyzed

States have taken varied approaches in their efforts to implement mediation programs. Some, such as California, have taken on mediation part and parcel. In those instances, states have determined that the concerns regarding mediation in divorce cases can be addressed within the mediation framework, not by creating special exceptions to mandatory mediation statutes. California's system best demonstrates this approach by requiring mediation in cases involving domestic violence but by conducting the mediation in a different way.

Other states, such as Delaware, have created mandatory mediation statutes that categorically exclude the statute's application to cases involving domestic violence. Such approaches fully appreciate the grave concerns surrounding domestic violence and the potential exacerbation of those problems by the mediation process.

While Delaware and California present different approaches while applying mandatory mediation, some states have implemented discretionary mediation statutes, allowing courts to determine whether mediation is appropriate. Such a case by case determination attempts to address the concerns raised regarding imbalances in power and domestic violence. Still other states, among them Virginia, have shown a strong preference for mediated settlements of other types of cases and have granted judges discretion to order mediation in divorce cases that they deem suitable. Other states have failed to implement either mandatory or discretionary mediation statutes, they, for the most part, remain committed to the use of mediation in other areas yet are caught . . . between knowing that their current systems are failed and fearing the possible downsides supposedly attached to mediation.

. . .

VI. THE FUTURE OF DIVORCE CHILD CUSTODY MEDIATION

A. *Essential Elements Needed to Address Specific Concerns*

The concerns raised by opponents of divorce mediation are not easily dismissed. The questions surrounding balances of power and domestic violence present real hurdles that must be addressed if any systemic changes to the divorce process are to be made. Concerns raised about the use of mediation in divorce cases are amplified when child custody issues are present. Additional concerns are present when determining whether such mediation should be mandatory. The advocates of mandatory mediation statutes argue vigorously that "parties that would not voluntarily mediate may settle in mandatory mediation and be satisfied with the process. Mandatory mediation may increase the mediation's efficiency impact." Others counter that mandatory mediation statutes cannot adequately address the general concerns raised by divorce mediation.

. . .

Any statute establishing such a mediation framework for divorce child custody situations would have to take the following into consideration.

B. *Provisions Regarding Domestic Violence and Unequal Power*

Universally, the state statutes that discuss the use of mediation in family law cases have provisions designed to address the concerns surrounding the issues of domestic violence and disparities in power. The state systems described above show very different approaches to the possibility of mediation in situations involving domestic violence. Clearly, California's system shows attempts to deal with domestic violence within the mediation framework. Delaware categorically prohibits the use of mediation in such situations.

Other states have made domestic violence provisions in their mediation statute. In some, the parties or court can ask to be exempted because of the presence of past violence in the relationship. North Carolina is an example of a state that expands the exemption clause to cover other "good cause reasons," one of which is domestic violence.

The "good cause" provisions are typical of the vast array of statutory schemes falling in the spectrum between California and the "prohibition" states. Most of those states, regardless of whether their statutes establish mandatory mediation or discretionary mediation, have attempted to address the concerns raised by domestic violence by placing the decision of whether mediation is suitable in the hands of the court. This approach to the process also faces numerous opponents. As discussed earlier, some oppose the use of mediation in divorce cases because of the nature of the case. In circumstances where a court has deemed a situation ready for mediation, those opponents would continue to argue that the process of mediation itself fails to protect the interests of the parties, typically the wife.

C. Quality Standards for Divorce Child Custody Mediators

Whatever mediation schemes states develop, it is essential that mediators meet stringent quality standards. That need for standards grows exponentially when factors like those involved in divorce child custody are in play. Virginia is an example of one state that continues to be on the leading edge of mediator certification standards. Within the already-existing statutory mediation framework, provisions are made for certification of mediators. The Virginia statute provides that, in any case referred for mediation, the mediation is "to be conducted by a mediator certified pursuant to guidelines promulgated by the Judicial Council." In order to become a certified mediator for family law cases in Virginia, an applicant must complete a rigorous program including training, observation, and practice. In addition to the basic training requirement for family mediators in Virginia, applicants must also complete specialized training on domestic violence issues. If the discretionary function of the court prior to referral were to be limited, as would be the case if mandatory mediation statutes were developed, even in states with thorough training such as Virginia, more training in how to identify imbalances in power or underlying issues of domestic violence would be essential.

D. Do We Need Mandatory Statutes?

Mandatory statutes are important tools to use in shaping the course of divorce child custody law. At the same time, the discretionary approach provides a funneling system at the court through which, hopefully, divorce cases with the most settlement potential are directed into mediation. That distinction between the mandatory and discretionary approaches to divorce child custody mediation is an important one. With the former, families, regardless of whether they reach an agreement or not, will be forced through a transformative process and hopefully come out on the other side with a healthier "non-relationship" in which to raise a child. If one's concern is primarily about the effect of the adversarial divorce process upon all of the parties involved, especially children, the mandatory approach is preferable. If that approach is taken, it is essential that the process be designed in such a way so as to balance the power of the parties and deal with issues such as violence so that the safety of the parents and children are not sacrificed.

Often, it seems that implementing mandatory mediation statutes in difficult areas of the law will counter the goals of outcome-oriented proponents while supporting the goals of transformative mediators; however, some find that mandatory mediation statutes, in the end, do not achieve the transformative process, instead "adopting the machine like qualities of the court, elevating the importance of settlement and downplaying the role of empowerment and recognition." Such a statement, if correct, might indicate that discretionary statutes are better able to accomplish the goals of mediators; however, the goals accomplished by discretionary mediation are those of efficiency-driven mediators.

The discretionary approach tends to focus on the benefits of efficiency and judicial economy associated with mediation.... By ordering mediation where it is likely to be successful, not only can courts potentially reduce the backlog in their dockets, but also provide a healthier process for the parties involved. Such an approach does not address the transformative goals envisioned by many proponents of mandatory mediation statutes; it merely incidentally effects the parties whose conflicts are less involved. Mediation in such situations still accomplishes the basic goal of avoiding the adversarial process; however, the parties who need most to break free from the adversarial system, those with the most emotionally laced problems, are left in the system.

Crupi v. Crupi

Court of Appeal of Florida, Fifth District, 2001.
784 So.2d 611.

■ PLEUS, JUSTICE.

Margaret Mary Desmond appeals an order which denied her motion to set aside a Mediated Settlement Agreement in a divorce action with her former husband. After denial of her motion, the Mediated Settlement Agreement was incorporated into the Final Judgment of Dissolution of Marriage.

This is a case in which the trial judge arrived at a correct result but for the wrong reasons. The judge based his decision on the rationale and factors enumerated in Casto v. Casto, 508 So. 2d 330 (Fla. 1987). The Supreme Court's opinion in *Casto* notes that there are essentially two separate grounds for invalidating pre-or post-nuptial agreements. The first deals with fraud, duress, coercion, misrepresentation or overreaching. The second is "unfairness," or as it is sometimes called, the "fair and reasonableness challenge." Unfairness involves an agreement which makes an unfair or unreasonable provision for that spouse, given the circumstances of the parties. The trial court, in following *Casto*, found there was a presumption of concealment or a presumed lack of knowledge. It then found the presumption was overcome because Desmond was sufficiently aware of the marital assets and income of the parties. The problem with the rationale of the trial court is that *Casto* involved a post-nuptial agreement. The agreement in this case is a mediated settlement agreement concluded through the expertise of a trained and certified mediator and in the course of a contested dissolution proceeding. The inquiry on a motion to set aside an agreement reached through mediation is limited to whether there was fraud, misrepresentation in discovery, or coercion.

In *Casto*, the parties' post-nuptial agreement preceded by approximately one year the husband's first filing of a dissolution petition. The Mediated Settlement Agreement entered into in the instant case, in contrast, was entered into in the middle of a contested proceeding pursuant to court-ordered mediation. It was not made simply with the possibility of a future dissolution taking place but during the course of the litigation, litigation in which both parties were represented by counsel and in which the usual rules of discovery apply. In such a context, we agree with the statement made by the Fourth District in Petracca v. Petracca, 706 So. 2d 904, 912 (Fla. 4th DCA

1998) that "The *Casto* line of cases . . . logically has no application when the challenging spouse has had the benefit of litigation discovery through independently chosen counsel to learn the full nature and extent of the finances of the other spouse."

Petracca involved a stipulated settlement agreement made in the course of what the court termed "overheated" and "fierce" divorce litigation. The Fourth District in *Petracca* held that the spouse challenging a litigation settlement agreement is limited to showing fraud, misrepresentation or coercion. Inquiry into the "unreasonableness" or "unfairness" of the settlement agreement to either party is not permitted. The same rule should apply regardless of whether the agreement is a stipulated settlement agreement, as in *Petracca,* or a mediated settlement agreement, as in this case. In fact, the reasons for such limitations are even more compelling in the case of a mediated settlement agreement.

Desmond's pleadings allege fraud, misrepresentation, coercion and undue influence. She also alleges the Agreement is "extremely unreasonable" regarding her interests. However, at the evidentiary hearing on her motion to set aside, which was entirely appropriate and necessary, the parties focused on the factors necessary to determine "fairness." Instead of limiting the issues to fraud, misrepresentation in discovery, or coercion, the court combined those grounds with the issue of reasonableness and stated:

> The critical test in determining the validity of the agreement is whether there was fraud or overreaching on one side, or, assuming unreasonableness, whether the challenging spouse did not have adequate knowledge of marital property and income of the parties at the time the agreement was reached.

The trial court ultimately found "insufficient evidence of coercion, undue influence or duress committed by the husband sufficient to justify setting aside the Mediated Settlement Agreement." While this finding of insufficient evidence by the trial court is all that is necessary for an affirmance, we write further because an examination of the hearing transcript may prove helpful in similar cases.

At the evidentiary hearing, and in an apparent effort to show coercion, a friend of Desmond's, who was present during the mediation process, testified that Desmond was under the impression that she had to come to an agreement that day; that Desmond was not in her right mind; and that she was very upset and anxiety-ridden, despite having taken a Xanax pill in the morning and again at lunch. Desmond testified that because she had had a couple of bad anxiety attacks, her doctor had prescribed Xanax to her and that on the day of the mediation, she took three pills even though normally she testified one "pretty much put me to sleep." She admitted, however, on cross-examination, that she remembered signing the mediation agreement, specifically recalling "the pressure I felt to sign it." She went on to testify that nobody unduly influenced her on the day of the mediation, but she had "a clear feeling that I had no options but to end it that day;" she concluded her testimony by recalling further that a hurricane was expected to strike the next day.

The Mediated Settlement Agreement itself provides "that each party has read this Agreement and neither party was subject to fraud or duress prior to or during the execution of this Agreement." The trial court specifically found that no representation was made to Desmond that it was necessary for her to execute the Mediated Settlement Agreement.

We agree with the trial court's finding that three Xanax pills, and anxiety and pressure to settle are insufficient proof of coercion necessary to set aside such an agreement. Otherwise, few, if any, mediated settlement agreements would be enforceable.

On the issues of fraud and misrepresentation in discovery, Desmond contended the husband had intentionally misrepresented the assets and debts in his financial affidavit. Under examination, the husband, in fact, confirmed the inaccuracies and inconsistencies in both his financial affidavit and in a document prepared by his accountant. The trial court, however, noted the wife's financial affidavit also contained inaccuracies and inconsistencies, and then made a finding that the wife had her own separate opinions and understandings of the nature and appropriate value of what she considered to be both marital and non-marital assets. The trial court concluded with a specific finding that Desmond knew about the inaccuracies and inconsistencies in the affidavit of her husband but signed the Mediated Settlement Agreement anyway.

The trial court was correct in its conclusion that the evidence of fraud or misrepresentation in discovery was insufficient. We affirm the trial court's denial of the motion to set aside the mediated settlement agreement.

AFFIRMED.

■ SHARP, JUSTICE, concurring in part, and dissenting in part.

I agree that the evidence of fraud or misrepresentation in the mediation or discovery process, in this case, was not sufficiently established by Margaret Crupi, the former wife. And, I also conclude after reviewing the transcript, that she had sufficient knowledge concerning the marital assets and their values, to bind her to the agreement.[1] Thus I concur that the trial court's denial of the motion to set aside the mediated settlement agreement should be affirmed. However, I disagree that a spouse challenging a mediated settlement agreement should be limited to a showing of fraud, misrepresentation, or coercion. . . .

3. COLLABORATIVE LAWYERING

Pauline H. Tesler, Collaborative Family Law

4 Pepp. Disp. Resol. L.J. 317 (2004).

Introduction:

Since its emergence in 1990 collaborative law has captured the enthusiasm and commitment of a rapidly growing segment of the family law bar across the U.S. and Canada. Given its rapid expansion and the degree of support accorded it by prominent family law judges, many family law attorneys predict that by the second decade of this millennium, collaborative law may establish itself as the normative first resort for resolution of family law disputes. . . .

Because the model has as its core element an agreement that no participants, neither lawyers nor clients, will threaten or resort to court intervention during the pendency of the collaborative work, all efforts take place entirely outside the court system. For that reason, the model has proved readily adaptable across jurisdictional lines, despite sometimes signifi-

1. As the trial judge noted, most of the failure to disclose on the part of Mr. Crupi dealt with matters that would have reduced the value of the assets.

cant differences in substantive and procedural laws from jurisdiction to jurisdiction. By the late 1990's, vigorous communities of collaborative practitioners had formed and begun representing family law clients in California, New Mexico, Arizona, Florida, Georgia, Pennsylvania, New York, Connecticut, Massachusetts, New Hampshire, Ohio, Illinois, Minnesota, Wisconsin, Colorado, Utah, British Columbia, Alberta, and Ontario. Today, the model has expanded to Ireland and the United Kingdom, Austria and Australia.

. . .

Basic Elements of the Collaborative Law Model:

The core element that distinguishes a collaborative law representation from "friendly negotiations" and other lawyer-facilitated efforts to settle divorce-related disputes is that in collaborative law, the representation begins with the clients and lawyers signing a binding agreement (referred to as a "participation agreement" or "collaborative stipulation") that prohibits those lawyers from ever participating in contested court proceedings on behalf of those clients. With that core element, the case is a collaborative law case, and without it, no matter how cordial or cooperative the lawyers and parties may be in their behavior, attitudes and intention to reach agreement, the case is not a collaborative law case. The term "collaborative law" is not just a synonym for "nice," or "cooperative." It refers to a specifically-defined model for dispute resolution, the essential element of which is that the lawyers are disqualified contractually from ever representing those clients against one another in court proceedings.

It is that unique element that gives collaborative law its considerable power to guide clients to acceptable settlements while building vigorous assistance of legal counsel into the heart of the process. Experienced collaborative practitioners who have come to this work from a background as family law litigators believe that in the face of apparent impasses in settlement negotiations, lawyers who are not contractually barred from taking the issue to court tend to decide too quickly that the issue should be taken to a third party for resolution. By temperament, lawyers tend to be impatient and result oriented. Moreover, trial practice is generally the most lucrative work for lawyers. Thus, the reasoning goes, internal and external factors coincide in favor of inducing traditional litigation-matrix lawyers to abort negotiations in the face of impasse where court is an option. In collaborative practice, however, such a decision will terminate the involvement of those lawyers in the case, and for that reason, collaborative lawyers operate within a significant external incentive to remain longer at the negotiating table working with their clients to find a way through the impasse. With the contractual disqualification from going to court, the risk of failure becomes distributed to the lawyers as well as the clients. With this element, lawyers as well as clients are highly motivated by the procedural "carrots and sticks" built into the model to remain at the negotiating table in the face of apparent impasse far longer than in any other mode of lawyer-facilitated family law dispute resolution. This is sometimes expressed as: collaborative practice liberates the problem solver within.

. . .

Collaborative Law Differs Greatly From Conventional Settlement Negotiations

On first hearing about collaborative law, traditional family law attorneys often remark that it's nothing new, "I've been doing it for years, I just don't call it that. After all, I settle more than 90% of my cases." Family law cases do overwhelmingly settle short of a full trial on the merits, but these are settlements fashioned in the shadow of the law, with the [possibility of] litigation shaping the representation from the first attorney-client contact. Often, family law litigators settle cases these cases virtually, if not literally, on the courthouse steps, after expenditure of enormous emotional and financial resources on pendente lite motions and discovery. The settlement may be on the eve of trial, supervised by a settlement conference judge who applies evaluative pressure on parties and counsel in the interests of lightening the court's docket.

The movement of a case from first interview to settlement in this kind of litigation-[oriented] settlement practice is shaped from the start by the limitations and demands inherent in court rules and legal restrictions on the family court's jurisdiction and exercise of discretion. From the start, a "litigation-oriented" attorney excludes from consideration much of what the new client considers most troubling about the divorce situation, because the court lacks the power to make effective orders about wounded feelings and the nagging annoyances that angry or vengeful spouses can inflict upon one another below the threshold of a court's power or willingness to act.

The job of the lawyer in this kind of representation is to shape and pare the facts of the client's situation into a story, a theory of the case that will enable the lawyer to "win big" on the client's behalf. To do this, the lawyer will ignore or deem irrelevant many parts of the client's story, and will emphasize or exaggerate others. From the first interview, the lawyer typically uses leading, closed-ended questions to spot issues that lie within the court's jurisdiction to resolve and develop goals, strategies, and tactics for successful outcomes. Sometimes, custody and support motions are prepared in the course of the first interview, and the client—who may be highly anxious and driven by fear, grief, or other primitive emotion—may be asked to sign inflammatory declarations under penalty of perjury then or soon afterward, for maximum tactical and strategic advantage in the litigation process. "Hurry up and wait" is the normal pace in litigation: hurry to meet arbitrary court deadlines, wait for the court calendar to have space to attend to client needs. Always, the norm of third party judicial resolution is the template that shapes development of goals, sharing of information, advocacy of positions, and pacing of resolution.

. . .

In many ways, the real interests of divorcing parties get lost in the process of bringing a litigation-driven case to settlement. The focus, in these settlements, is on the immediate divorce-related financial and custody provisions of the divorce judgment. Limited or no attention is given to the interests and needs of the post-divorce restructured family, either in the sense of positive planning for healthy long term family restructuring and change, or in the sense of minimizing the destructive impacts of the divorce process itself on economic interests of family members and on possibilities for effective parenting of children after the divorce. In most U.S. jurisdictions, litigated court proceedings and files (including those of cases that ultimately settle) are open to the public and all vestiges of privacy are lost, at the same time that matters formerly decided privately by the couple are handed placed under the control of disinterested and busy professionals.

. . .

The [collaborative] process invites maximum client involvement and control over outcome, while maximizing privacy and creativity. The participation agreements signed at the outset commit all participants to good faith bargaining, voluntary full disclosures, interest-based bargaining, inclusion of relational and long term interests in the identification of clients' goals and strategies. The role of the lawyer is redefined in collaborative practice, as advocate for achieving the long-term enlightened interests of the client, rather than zealous advocate for goals and strategies identified by clients possessed by transient states of diminished capacity associated with the trauma of divorce. The disqualification of all professionals from participation in litigation between these clients has the effect of keeping both lawyers and clients at the negotiating table in the face of apparent impasse much longer than is typically the case in conventional settlement negotiations, where resort to the local judge to resolve impasses is a comfortable and familiar option on the dispute resolution menu that litigation attorneys carry in their mental armory. For collaborative lawyers, deciding to see what the local judge can do with an apparent impasse is identical to a decision to cease participating in the case. Unlike litigation attorneys, collaborative lawyers share the risk of failure in collaboration with their clients. Collaborative lawyers see these features of the collaborative law model as powerful aids to creative conflict resolution—as the means for liberating the effective problem solver trapped within litigating lawyers.

Collaborative Law Resembles But Differs in Important Ways from Mediation

While collaborative law builds upon important conflict resolution skills and understandings developed in the field of mediation, collaborative law differs from mediation in important ways. First and foremost, collaborative lawyers are advocates, not neutrals. They work within all professional ethics and standards of practice for lawyers and are a licensed profession. They owe a primary duty to their own clients. But, this duty is reframed not as the duty to zealously advocate for whatever fear-driven objective the client might grasp for during the course of recovering from loss of a marriage, but rather the duty to work with the client to help him or her achieve the goal nearly all clients say they want—the "good divorce," speedy, economical, respectful, individualized, and protective of children—in a process specifically tailored to help the client be able to realize that goal. This means that collaborative lawyers undertake much more than either a conventional lawyer or a mediator considers to be part of the job description: to educate clients, help them work from positions to interests, remove them from the negotiating table when they are too upset to think clearly, counsel them when they behave in self-defeating or bad faith ways, and assist them to recalibrate back to the high intentions identified at the start of the collaborative retention. Moreover, collaborative lawyers generally agree to protocols for practice whereby they will withdraw from representing a client who hides information, stonewalls, misrepresents, or otherwise misuses the collaborative process.

Where clients in mediation may occupy an uneven playing field, collaborative law builds in advocacy and legal advice into the heart of the process. Where neutral mediators may encounter great difficulty working with clients who subvert the process (whether intentionally or otherwise) while still maintaining neutrality, collaborative lawyers take on as part of their agreed job description the responsibility to work with such clients until they can return to the table willing and able to engage in effective good faith negotiations.

Finally, the structure of the collaborative legal model itself seems to offer more wattage of focused dispute resolution power than is generally available in family law mediation. Family law mediation often takes place as a three-way process, including the two divorcing spouses and one neutral mediator; lawyers for the parties, if they are involved at all, participate from their own offices, not in the mediation room. Even when consulting attorneys for the parties participate directly in the mediation, they participate not as designated conflict resolution professionals working explicitly toward settlement, but rather as conventional legal counsel who provide advice and representation in an adversarial model in which the decision to terminate mediation and take the matter to court is readily available and without built-in disincentives. Only in collaborative practice is the option-generating and negotiating process conducted by two trained legal advocates committed to consensual dispute resolution and skilled in interest-based bargaining who share a commitment to help clients stay on the high road and discover common ground for solutions. Because these advocates, who have every incentive to continue working toward settlement, meet in "real time" around a table with the clients who are expert in the facts and interests associated with the case, and everyone can hear and respond to the ideas of all the other participants in the conversation, the creative "out of the box" lateral thinking power available at the negotiating table to help clients reach agreement is considerably amplified as compared to single-neutral mediation.

Interdisciplinary Collaborative Practice

During the early 1990's, at the same time that lawyers were developing and extending collaborative legal practice, a parallel model called collaborative divorce emerged among a certain segment of mental health professionals experienced working in the court system on the custody battles of high conflict divorcing couples. These psychologists, social workers, and counselors mediated at the courthouse, and conducted the child custody evaluations used in trials and court-annexed settlement conferences to provide recommendations and rationales about which parent was more deserving of custody of the children. These professionals came to see that their evaluation reports, though intended to serve the best interests of children, were further polarizing the already-conflicted parents and decreasing their ability to provide effective post-divorce parenting for children.

... The collaborative law model, developing simultaneously and separately among family law attorneys, was the final component of an approach that now offers integrated virtual professional teams to divorcing spouses in many communities across the U.S. and Canada. These teams include: two collaborative lawyers, two divorce coaches (who must be licensed mental health professionals experienced in divorce work), a child specialist, and a financial neutral. These professionals are trained in the psychodynamics of divorce and healthy family restructuring as well as effective communication skills, conflict resolution skills, and interdisciplinary collaboration.

. . .

Where clients have the intention, but not the emotional or intellectual ability, to work effectively with their collaborative lawyers in legal negotiations, this interdisciplinary model can provide the additional resources needed for couple to realize their intention of having a "good divorce." For such clients, paradoxically, paying to bring in the necessary range of professional resources typically results in a divorce that costs less than it would have if they had been represented solely by collaborative lawyers, without the interdisciplinary team.... Like collaborative lawyers, all interdisciplinary collaborative divorce professionals sign contractual agreements with their clients that bar them from ever participating in contested court proceedings between the parties.

. . .

Research and Research Needs

Among the many areas in which research would be useful would be: tools for screening and identifying clients unlikely to benefit from collaborative dispute resolution services, study of frequency of post-judgment litigation in collaborative settlements as compared to mediated settlements and litigated judgments; study of outcomes for children after collaborative settlements as compared to mediated settlements and litigated judgments; evaluations of the effectiveness of various approaches for training collaborative practitioners; comparative outcomes for clients using interdisciplinary team model vs. using collaborative lawyers alone. Many of the questions that have been asked by researchers with respect to mediation could usefully be asked regarding collaborative practice.

NOTE

Texas was the first state to adopt a statute specifically recognizing and legitimizing collaborative legal practice. *See* $S 6.603 of the Texas Family Code (2001). The Texas statute defines collaborative law as:

> a procedure in which the parties and their counsel agree in writing to use their best efforts and make a good faith attempt to resolve their dissolution of marriage dispute on an agreed basis without resorting to judicial intervention except to have the court approve the settlement agreement, make the legal pronouncements, and sign the orders required by law to effectuate the agreement of the parties as the court determines appropriate. The parties' counsel may not serve as litigation counsel except to ask the court to approve the settlement agreement.

The statute exempts collaborative cases from being subject to "rocket docket" local rules under which cases are assigned early trial dates after divorce petitions are filed.

There is a substantial body of literature on the advantages and disadvantages of the use of mediation in divorce proceedings. *See, e.g.,* Divorce Mediation: Theory and Practice (Jay Folberg & Ann Milne, eds. 1988); Connie Beck & Bruce Sales, A Critical Reappraisal of Divorce Mediation and Policy, 6 Psychol. Pub. Pol'y 989 (2000); Laurel Wheeler, Mandatory Family Mediation and Domestic Violence, 26 S. Ill. U. L.J. 559 (2002); Nancy Ver Steegh, Yes, No, and Maybe: Informed Decision Making About Divorce Mediation in the Presence of Domestic Violence, 9 Wm. & Mary J. of Women & L. 161 (2003); Mary G. Marcus, Walter Marcus, Nancy A. Stillwell, & Neville Doherty, To Mediate or Not to Mediate: Financial Outcomes in Mediated Versus Adversarial Divorces, 17 Mediation Q. 143 (1999); Colleen N. Kotyk, Tearing Down the House: Weakening the Foundations of Divorce Mediation Brick by Brick, 6 Wm. & Mary Bill of Rts. J. 227 (1997); Peter A. Dillon & Robert E. Emery, Divorce Mediation and Resolution of Child Custody Disputes: Long–Term Effects 66 Am. J. Orthopsychiatry 131 (1996).

*

PART II

CHILDREN, PARENTS AND THE STATE

CHAPTER 7

PROCREATION

A. VOLUNTARY LIMITS ON REPRODUCTION

The Supreme Court has held that there is a constitutional right to procreate. See Skinner v. Oklahoma, 316 U.S. 535 (1942). But increasingly attention has focused on the more controversial question of whether there is a right *not* to procreate, or, to put the matter affirmatively, is there a right to control one's own reproductive capacity?

In studying the material in this Chapter, consider what role, if any, should be played by religious or ethical beliefs, concern about population growth, or the principles of equal protection and of free speech in deciding the constitutional issues. Is it better to consider who should be empowered to decide matters of reproduction than to resolve what the outcome should be? In particular, consider the issue of age, a topic that will be explored at greater length in Chapter 9. It may be, for example, that as a matter of policy (and perhaps as a matter of constitutional law as well) a child of ten should have different legal rights in this area than a child of sixteen.

1. ACCESS TO CONTRACEPTIVES AND TO REPRODUCTIVE INFORMATION

Carey v. Population Services International

Supreme Court of the United States, 1977.
431 U.S. 678, 97 S.Ct. 2010, 52 L.Ed.2d 675.

■ JUSTICE BRENNAN delivered the opinion of the Court (Parts I, II, III, and V), together with an opinion (Part IV), in which JUSTICE STEWART, JUSTICE MARSHALL, and JUSTICE BLACKMUN joined.

Under New York Education Law § 6811(8) it is a crime (1) for any person to sell or distribute any contraceptive of any kind to a minor under the age of 16 years; (2) for anyone other than a licensed pharmacist to distribute contraceptives to persons over 16; and (3) for anyone, including licensed pharmacists, to advertise or display contraceptives. . . .

. . .

II

Although "[t]he Constitution does not explicitly mention any right of privacy," the Court has recognized that one aspect of the "liberty" protected by the Due Process Clause of the Fourteenth Amendment is "a right of personal privacy, or a guarantee of certain areas or zones of privacy." Roe v. Wade, [Chapter 2, Section D, 1]. . . . While the outer limits of this aspect of privacy have not been marked by the Court, it is clear that among the decisions that an individual may make without unjustified government interference are personal decisions relating to marriage, Loving v. Virginia,

[Chapter 1, Section A]; procreation, Skinner v. Oklahoma, 316 U.S. 535, 541–542 (1942); contraception, Eisenstadt v. Baird, [Chapter 2, Section D] ...; family relationships, Prince v. Massachusetts, [Chapter 8, Section D]; and child rearing and education, Pierce v. Society of Sisters, [Chapter 8, Section D, 2];....

The decision whether or not to beget or bear a child is at the very heart of this cluster of constitutionally protected choices. ... This is understandable, for in a field that by definition concerns the most intimate of human activities and relationships, decisions whether to accomplish or to prevent conception are among the most private and sensitive. ...

That the constitutionally protected right of privacy extends to an individual's liberty to make choices regarding contraception does not, however, automatically invalidate every state regulation in this area. The business of manufacturing and selling contraceptives may be regulated in ways that do not infringe protected individual choices. And even a burdensome regulation may be validated by a sufficiently compelling state interest. ...

. . .

We consider first the wider restriction on access to contraceptives created by § 6811(8)'s prohibition of the distribution of nonmedical contraceptives to adults except through licensed pharmacists.

Appellants argue that this Court has not accorded a "right of access to contraceptives" the status of a fundamental aspect of personal liberty. They emphasize that Griswold v. Connecticut, [Chapter 2, Section D], struck down a state prohibition of the *use* of contraceptives, and so had no occasion to discuss laws "regulating their manufacture or sale." Eisenstadt v. Baird, *supra*, was decided under the Equal Protection Clause, holding that "whatever the rights of the individual to access to contraceptives may be, the rights must be the same for the unmarried and the married alike." Thus appellants argue that neither case should be treated as reflecting upon the State's power to limit or prohibit distribution of contraceptives to any persons, married or unmarried. ...

The fatal fallacy in this argument is that it overlooks the underlying premise of those decisions that the Constitution protects "the right of the individual ... to be free from unwarranted governmental intrusion into ... the decision whether to bear or beget a child." Eisenstadt v. Baird, *supra*. ... Similarly, Roe v. Wade, *supra*, held that the Constitution protects "a woman's *decision* whether or not to terminate her pregnancy." These decisions put *Griswold* in proper perspective. *Griswold* may no longer be read as holding only that a State may not prohibit a married couple's use of contraceptives. Read in light of its progeny, the teaching of *Griswold* is that the Constitution protects individual decisions in matters of childbearing from unjustified intrusion by the State.

Restrictions on the distribution of contraceptives clearly burden the freedom to make such decisions. A total prohibition against sale of contraceptives, for example, would intrude upon individual decisions in matters of procreation and contraception as harshly as a direct ban on their use. Indeed, in practice, a prohibition against all sales, since more easily and less offensively enforced, might have an even more devastating effect upon the freedom to choose contraception.

. . .

Limiting the distribution of nonprescription contraceptives to licensed pharmacists clearly imposes a significant burden on the right of the individuals to use contraceptives if they choose to do so. . . .

There remains the inquiry whether the provision serves a compelling state interest. . . .

. . . Appellants argue that the limitation of retail sales of nonmedical contraceptives to pharmacists (1) expresses "a proper concern that young people not sell contraceptive products"; (2) "allows purchasers to inquire as to the relative qualities of the varying products and prevents anyone from tampering with them"; and (3) facilitates enforcement of the other provisions of the statute. . . . The first hardly can justify the statute's incursion into constitutionally protected rights, and in any event the statute is obviously not substantially related to any goal of preventing young people from selling contraceptives. Nor is the statute designed to serve as a quality control device. Nothing in the record suggests that pharmacists are particularly qualified to give advice on the merits of different nonmedical contraceptives, or that such advice is more necessary to the purchaser of contraceptive products than to consumers of other nonprescription items. Why pharmacists are better able or more inclined than other retailers to prevent tampering with prepackaged products, or, if they are, why contraceptives are singled out for this special protection, is also unexplained. As to ease of enforcement, the prospect of additional administrative inconvenience has not been thought to justify invasion of fundamental constitutional rights.

IV

A

The District Court also held unconstitutional, as applied to non-prescription contraceptives, the provision of § 6811(8) prohibiting the distribution of contraceptives to those under 16 years of age.[13]

. . . The question of the extent of state power to regulate conduct of minors not constitutionally regulable when committed by adults is a vexing one, perhaps not susceptible to precise answer. . . . Certain principles, however, have been recognized. "Minors, as well as adults, are protected by the Constitution and possess constitutional rights." Planned Parenthood of Central Missouri v. Danforth, [428 U.S. 52 (1976).] . . . On the other hand, we have held in a variety of contexts that "the power of the state to control the conduct of children reaches beyond the scope of its authority over adults." Ginsberg v. New York, [390 U.S. 629 (1968)]. . . .

. . . Planned Parenthood of Central Missouri v. Danforth, *supra*, held that a State "may not impose a blanket provision . . . requiring the consent of a parent or person *in loco parentis* as a condition for abortion of an unmarried minor during the first 12 weeks of her pregnancy." . . .

Since the State may not impose a blanket prohibition, or even a blanket requirement of parental consent, on the choice of a minor to terminate her pregnancy, the constitutionality of a blanket prohibition of the distribution of contraceptives to minors is *a fortiori* foreclosed. The State's interests in protection of the mental and physical health of the pregnant minor, and in protection of potential life are clearly more implicated by the abortion decision than by the decision to use a nonhazardous contraceptive.

13. Subject to an apparent exception for distribution by physicians in the course of their practice.

Appellants argue, however, that significant state interests are served by restricting minors' access to contraceptives, because free availability to minors of contraceptives would lead to increased sexual activity among the young, in violation of the policy of New York to discourage such behavior. The argument is that minors' sexual activity may be deterred by increasing the hazards attendant on it. The same argument, however, would support a ban on abortions for minors, or indeed support a prohibition on abortions, or access to contraceptives, for the unmarried, whose sexual activity is also against the public policy of many States. Yet, in each of these areas, the Court has rejected the argument, noting in Roe v. Wade, that "no court or commentator has taken the argument seriously." . . .

Moreover, there is substantial reason for doubt whether limiting access to contraceptives will in fact substantially discourage early sexual behavior. Appellants themselves conceded in the District Court that "there is no evidence that teenage extramarital sexual activity increases in proportion to the availability of contraceptives," and accordingly offered none, in the District Court or here. Appellees, on the other hand, cite a considerable body of evidence and opinion indicating that there is no such deterrent effect. . . . [We] again confirm the principle that when a State, as here, burdens the exercise of a fundamental right, its attempt to justify that burden as a rational means for the accomplishment of some significant State policy requires more than a bare assertion, based on a conceded complete absence of supporting evidence, that the burden is connected to such a policy.

. . .

V

The District Court's holding that the prohibition of any "advertisement or display" of contraceptives is unconstitutional was clearly correct. Only last Term Virginia State Board of Pharmacy v. Virginia Citizens Consumer Council, 425 U.S. 748 (1976), held that a state may not "completely suppress the dissemination of concededly truthful information about entirely lawful activity," even when that information could be categorized as "commercial speech." . . .

Affirmed.

■ THE CHIEF JUSTICE dissents.

■ JUSTICE WHITE, concurring in part and concurring in the result in part.

I join Parts I, III and V of the Court's opinion and concur in the result with respect to Part IV.

. . .

I concur in the result in Part IV primarily because the State has not demonstrated that the prohibition against distribution of contraceptives to minors measurably contributes to the deterrent purposes which the State advances as justification for the restriction. Again, however, the legality of state laws forbidding premarital intercourse is not at issue here; and, with JUSTICE STEVENS, "I would describe as 'frivolous' appellee's argument that a minor has the constitutional right to put contraceptives to their intended use, notwithstanding the combined objection of both parents and the State."

. . .

■ JUSTICE POWELL, concurring in part and concurring in the judgment.

. . .

... Neither our precedents nor sound principles of constitutional analysis require state legislation to meet the exacting compelling state interest standard whenever it implicates sexual freedom. In my view, those cases make clear that that standard has been invoked only when the state regulation entirely frustrates or heavily burdens the exercise of constitutional rights in this area. This is not to say that other state regulation is free from judicial review. But a test so severe that legislation rarely can meet it should be imposed by courts with deliberate restraint in view of the respect that properly should be accorded legislative judgments.

B

There is also no justification for subjecting restrictions on the sexual activity of the young to heightened judicial review. Under our prior cases, the States have broad latitude to legislate with respect to adolescents. The principle is well settled that "a State may permissibly determine that, at least in some precisely delineated areas, a child ... is not possessed of that full capacity for individual choice" which is essential to the exercise of various constitutionally protected interests. Ginsberg v. New York, 390 U.S. 629, 649–650 (1968) (STEWART, J., concurring in the result). ...

. . .

... It seems clear to me, for example, that the State would further a constitutionally permissible end if it encouraged adolescents to seek the advice and guidance of their parents before deciding whether to engage in sexual intercourse. Planned Parenthood, 421 U.S., at 91 (STEWART, J., concurring). The State justifiably may take note of the psychological pressures that might influence children at a time in their lives when they generally do not possess the maturity necessary to understand and control their responses. Participation in sexual intercourse at an early age may have both physical and psychological consequences. These include the risks of venereal disease and pregnancy, and the less obvious mental and emotional problems that may result from sexual activity by children. Moreover, society has long adhered to the view that sexual intercourse should not be engaged in promiscuously, a judgment that an adolescent may be less likely to heed than an adult.

. . .

A requirement of prior parental consultation is merely one illustration of permissible regulation in this area. As long as parental distribution is permitted, a State should have substantial latitude in regulating the distribution of contraceptives to minors.

. . .

■ JUSTICE STEVENS, concurring in part and concurring in the judgment.

. . .

There are two reasons why I do not join Part IV. First, the holding in Planned Parenthood of Missouri v. Danforth, 428 U.S. 52, 72–75, that a minor's decision to abort her pregnancy may not be conditioned on parental consent, is not dispositive here. The options available to the already pregnant minor are fundamentally different from those available to nonpregnant minors. The former must bear a child unless she aborts; but persons in the latter category can and generally will avoid childbearing by abstention. Consequently, even if I had joined that part of *Planned Parenthood,* I could not agree that the Constitution provides the same measure of protection to the minor's right to use contraceptives as to the pregnant female's right to abort.

Second, I would not leave open the question whether there is a significant state interest in discouraging sexual activity among unmarried persons under 16 years of age. Indeed, I would describe as "frivolous" appellee's argument that a minor has the constitutional right to put contraceptives to their intended use, notwithstanding the combined objection of both parents and the State.

. . .

The State's important interest in the welfare of its young citizens justifies a number of protective measures. See Planned Parenthood of Missouri v. Danforth, 428 U.S. 52, 102 (STEVENS, J.). Such special legislation is premised on the fact that young persons frequently make unwise choices with harmful consequences; the State may properly ameliorate those consequences by providing, for example, that a minor may not be required to honor his bargain. It is almost unprecedented, however, for a State to require that an ill-advised act by a minor give rise to greater risk of irreparable harm than a similar act by an adult.

. . .

■ JUSTICE REHNQUIST, dissenting.

Those who valiantly but vainly defended the heights of Bunker Hill in 1775 made it possible that men such as James Madison might later sit in the first Congress and draft the Bill of Rights to the Constitution. The post-Civil War Congresses which drafted the Civil War Amendments to the Constitution could not have accomplished their task without the blood of brave men on both sides which was shed at Shiloh, Gettysburg, and Cold Harbor. If those responsible for these Amendments, by feats of valor or efforts of draftsmanship, could have lived to know that their efforts had enshrined in the Constitution the right of commercial vendors of contraceptives to peddle them to unmarried minors through such means as window displays and vending machines located in the men's room of truck stops, notwithstanding the considered judgment of the New York Legislature to the contrary, it is not difficult to imagine their reaction.

I do not believe that the cases discussed in the Court's opinion require any such result, but to debate the Court's treatment of the question on a case-by-case basis would concede more validity to the result reached by the Court than I am willing to do. There comes a point when endless and ill-considered extension of principles originally formulated in quite different cases produces such an indefensible result that no logic-chopping can possibly make the fallacy of the result more obvious. The Court here in effect holds that the First and Fourteenth Amendments not only guarantee full and free debate *before* a legislative judgment as to the moral dangers to which minors within the jurisdiction of the State should not be subjected, but goes further and absolutely prevents the representatives of the majority from carrying out such a policy *after* the issues have been fully aired.

No questions of religious belief, compelled allegiance to a secular creed, or decisions on the part of married couples as to procreation, are involved here. New York has simply decided that it wishes to discourage unmarried minors in the 14– to 16–year–age bracket from having promiscuous sexual intercourse with one another. Even the Court would scarcely go so far as to say that this is not a subject with which the New York Legislature may properly concern itself.

That legislature has not chosen to deny to a pregnant woman, after the *fait accompli* of pregnancy, the one remedy which would enable her to terminate an unwanted pregnancy. It has instead sought to deter the conduct which will produce such *faits accomplis*. The majority of New York's citizens are in effect told that however deeply they may be concerned about the problem of promiscuous sex and intercourse among unmarried teenagers, they may not adopt this means of dealing with it. The Court holds that New York may not use its police power to legislate in the interests of its concept of the public morality as it pertains to minors. The Court's denial of a power so fundamental to self-government must, in the long run, prove to be but a temporary departure from a wise and heretofore settled course of adjudication to the contrary. I would reverse the judgment of the District Court.

NOTES

1. Several lower courts have been faced with the question of whether it is constitutional to teach sex education courses to minors in public school. See, e.g., Citizens for Parental Rights v. San Mateo County Board of Education, 51 Cal.App.3d 1, 124 Cal.Rptr. 68 (1975). In upholding sex education courses for students as young as age 10, the court held: "[A]bsent some serious contention of harm to the mental or physical health of the children of this state or to the public safety, peace of order or welfare, a mere personal difference of opinion as to the curriculum which is taught in one public school system does not give rise to a constitutional right in the private citizen to control exposure to knowledge." The California programs permitted parents or guardians to withdraw their children by submitting a written request. Should the same result be reached if student attendance is mandatory? Consider Hopkins v. Hamden Board of Education, 29 Conn.Supp. 397, 289 A.2d 914 (1971).

The Supreme Court of New Jersey in 1982 upheld the constitutionality of a course on family life education that permitted parents to remove their children from objectionable parts of the program. Smith v. Ricci, 89 N.J. 514, 446 A.2d 501 (1982). But see Fields v. Palmdale, 271 F.Supp.2d 1217 (C.D. Cal. 2003) (parents not entitled to relief when their first, third, and fifth grade students were subjected to a sexually explicit survey without informed parental consent); Brown v. Hot, Sexy and Safer Prods., 68 F.3d 525 (1st Cir. 1995) (upholding a high school sex education program that was sexually explicit). The judge noted that although *Pierce* and *Yoder* affirmed a fundamental right for parents to direct the upbringing of their children, they could not dictate the school's curriculum. See also, Note, Parents' Role in Their Children's Sex Education Undermined, 29 Rutgers L.J. 339 (1998); Michael J. Fucci, Educating our Future: An Analysis of Sex Education in the Classroom, 2000 BYU Educ. & L.J. 91.

2. Should a child have the right to attend a sex education course in school even if his parents object? Could the child sue to compel the school to permit him to attend in light of *Carey?*

Rust v. Sullivan

Supreme Court of the United States, 1991.
500 U.S. 173, 111 S.Ct. 1759, 114 L.Ed.2d 233.

■ CHIEF JUSTICE REHNQUIST delivered the opinion of the Court.

These cases concern a facial challenge to Department of Health and Human Services (HHS) regulations which limit the ability of Title X fund recipients to engage in abortion-related activities. The United States Court of Appeals for the Second Circuit upheld the regulations, finding them to be a permissible construction of the statute as well as consistent with the First and Fifth Amendments of the Constitution. . . . We affirm.

In 1970, Congress enacted Title X of the Public Health Service Act (Act), 84 Stat. 1506, as amended, 42 U.S.C. §§ 300–300a–6, which provides federal funding for family-planning services. . . . Grants and contracts under Title X must "be made in accordance with such regulations as the Secretary may promulgate." Section 1008 of the Act, however, provides that "[n]one of the funds appropriated under this subchapter shall be used in programs where abortion is a method of family planning." 42 U.S.C. § 300a–6. . . .

In 1988, the Secretary promulgated new regulations designed to provide " 'clear and operational guidance' to grantees about how to preserve the distinction between Title X programs and abortion as a method of family planning." 53 Fed.Reg. 2923–2924 (1988). . . .

The regulations attach three principal conditions on the grant of federal funds for Title X projects. First, the regulations specify that a "Title X project may not provide counseling concerning the use of abortion as a method of family planning or provide referral for abortion as a method of family planning" . . . even upon specific request.

Second, the regulations broadly prohibit a Title X project from engaging in activities that "encourage, promote or advocate abortion as a method of family planning." Forbidden activities include lobbying for legislation that would increase the availability of abortion as a method of family planning, developing or disseminating materials advocating abortion as a method of family planning, providing speakers to promote abortion as a method of family planning, using legal action to make abortion available in any way as a method of family planning, and paying dues to any group that advocates abortion as a method of family planning as a substantial part of its activities.

Third, the regulations require that Title X projects be organized so that they are "physically and financially separate" from prohibited abortion activities. To be deemed physically and financially separate, "a Title X project must have an objective integrity and independence from prohibited activities. Mere bookkeeping separation of Title X funds from other monies is not sufficient." The regulations provide a list of nonexclusive factors for the Secretary to consider in conducting a case-by-case determination of objective integrity and independence, such as the existence of separate accounting records and separate personnel, and the degree of physical separation of the project from facilities for prohibited activities.

. . .

We begin by pointing out the posture of the cases before us. Petitioners are challenging the *facial* validity of the regulations. Thus, we are concerned only with the question whether, on their face, the regulations are both authorized by the Act, and can be construed in such a manner that they can be applied to a set of individuals without infringing upon constitutionally protected rights. Petitioners face a heavy burden in seeking to have the regulations invalidated as facially unconstitutional. . . .

We turn first to petitioners' contention that the regulations exceed the Secretary's authority under Title X and are arbitrary and capricious. . . .

We need not dwell on the plain language of the statute because we agree with every court to have addressed the issue that the language is ambiguous.

The language of § 1008—that "[n]one of the funds appropriated under this subchapter shall be used in programs where abortion is a method of family planning"—does not speak directly to the issues of counseling, referral, advocacy, or program integrity. If a statute is "silent or ambiguous with respect to the specific issue, the question for the court is whether the agency's answer is based on a permissible construction of the statute."

The Secretary's construction of Title X may not be disturbed as an abuse of discretion if it reflects a plausible construction of the plain language of the statute and does not otherwise conflict with Congress' expressed intent. In determining whether a construction is permissible, "[t]he court need not conclude that the agency construction was the only one it could permissibly have adopted . . . or even the reading the court would have reached if the question initially had arisen in a judicial proceeding." Rather, substantial deference is accorded to the interpretation of the authorizing statute by the agency authorized with administering it.

The broad language of Title X plainly allows the Secretary's construction of the statute. By its own terms, § 1008 prohibits the use of Title X funds "in programs where abortion is a method of family planning." Title X does not define the term "method of family planning," nor does it enumerate what types of medical and counseling services are entitled to Title X funding. Based on the broad directives provided by Congress in Title X in general and § 1008 in particular, we are unable to say that the Secretary's construction of the prohibition in § 1008 to require a ban on counseling, referral, and advocacy within the Title X project, is impermissible.

. . .

When we find, as we do here, that the legislative history is ambiguous and unenlightening on the matters with respect to which the regulations deal, we customarily defer to the expertise of the agency. Petitioners argue, however, that the regulations are entitled to little or no deference because they "reverse a longstanding agency policy that permitted nondirective counseling and referral for abortion," and thus represent a sharp break from the Secretary's prior construction of the statute. . . .

We find that the Secretary amply justified his change of interpretation with a "reasoned analysis." The Secretary explained that the regulations are a result of his determination, in the wake of the critical reports of the General Accounting Office (GAO) and the Office of the Inspector General (OIG), that prior policy failed to implement properly the statute and that it was necessary to provide "clear and operational guidance to grantees to preserve the distinction between Title X programs and abortion as a method of family planning." He also determined that the new regulations are more in keeping with the original intent of the statute, are justified by client experience under the prior policy, and are supported by a shift in attitude against the "elimination of unborn children by abortion." We believe that these justifications are sufficient to support the Secretary's revised approach. Having concluded that the plain language and legislative history are ambiguous as to Congress' intent in enacting Title X, we must defer to the Secretary's permissible construction of the statute.

. . .

Petitioners contend that the regulations violate the First Amendment by impermissibly discriminating based on viewpoint because they prohibit "all discussion about abortion as a lawful option—including counseling, referral, and the provision of neutral and accurate information about ending a pregnancy—while compelling the clinic or counselor to provide information that promotes continuing a pregnancy to term." . . .

. . . In Maher v. Roe, we upheld a state welfare regulation under which Medicaid recipients received payments for services related to childbirth, but not for nontherapeutic abortions. The Court rejected the claim that this unequal subsidization worked a violation of the Constitution. We held that the government may "make a value judgment favoring childbirth over abortion, and . . . implement that judgment by the allocation of public funds." Here the Government is exercising the authority it possesses under *Maher* and *McRae* to subsidize family planning services which will lead to conception and childbirth, and declining to "promote or encourage abortion." The Government can, without violating the Constitution, selectively fund a program to encourage certain activities it believes to be in the public interest, without at the same time funding an alternate program which seeks to deal with the problem in another way. In so doing, the Government has not discriminated on the basis of viewpoint; it has merely chosen to fund one activity to the exclusion of the other. . . .

The challenged regulations . . . are designed to ensure that the limits of the federal program are observed. . . . This is not a case of the Government "suppressing a dangerous idea," but of a prohibition on a project grantee or its employees from engaging in activities outside of its scope.

To hold that the Government unconstitutionally discriminates on the basis of viewpoint when it chooses to fund a program dedicated to advance certain permissible goals, because the program in advancing those goals necessarily discourages alternate goals, would render numerous government programs constitutionally suspect. When Congress established a National Endowment for Democracy to encourage other countries to adopt democratic principles, it was not constitutionally required to fund a program to encourage competing lines of political philosophy such as Communism and Fascism. Petitioners' assertions ultimately boil down to the position that if the government chooses to subsidize one protected right, it must subsidize analogous counterpart rights. But the Court has soundly rejected that proposition. . . .

Petitioners rely heavily on their claim that the regulations would not, in the circumstance of a medical emergency, permit a Title X project to refer a woman whose pregnancy places her life in imminent peril to a provider of abortions or abortion-related services. This case, of course, involves only a facial challenge to the regulations, and we do not have before us any application by the Secretary to a specific fact situation. On their face, we do not read the regulations to bar abortion referral or counseling in such circumstances. Abortion counseling as a "method of family planning" is prohibited, and it does not seem that a medically necessitated abortion in such circumstances would be the equivalent of its use as a "method of family planning." Neither § 1008 nor the specific restrictions of the regulations would apply. Moreover, the regulations themselves contemplate that a Title X project would be permitted to engage in otherwise prohibited abortion-related activity in such circumstances. Section 59.8(a)(2) provides a specific exemption for emergency care and requires Title X recipients "to refer the client immediately to an appropriate provider of emergency medical services." 42 CFR 59.8(a)(2) (1989). Section 59.5(b)(1) also requires Title X projects to provide "necessary referral to other medical facilities when medically indicated."

Petitioners also contend that the restrictions on the subsidization of abortion-related speech contained in the regulations are impermissible because they condition the receipt of a benefit, in this case Title X funding, on the relinquishment of a constitutional right, the right to engage in abortion advocacy and counseling. Relying on Perry v. Sindermann, 408 U.S. 593, 597 (1972), and FCC v. League of Women Voters of Cal., 468 U.S. 364 (1984), petitioners argue that "even though the government may deny [a] ... benefit for any number of reasons, there are some reasons upon which the government may not rely. It may not deny a benefit to a person on a basis that infringes his constitutionally protected interests—especially, his interest in freedom of speech."

Petitioners' reliance on these cases is unavailing, however, because here the government is not denying a benefit to anyone, but is instead simply insisting that public funds be spent for the purposes for which they were authorized. The Secretary's regulations do not force the Title X grantee to give up abortion-related speech; they merely require that the grantee keep such activities separate and distinct from Title X activities. Title X expressly distinguishes between a Title X *grantee* and a Title X *project.* The grantee, which normally is a health care organization, may receive funds from a variety of sources for a variety of purposes. The grantee receives Title X funds, however, for the specific and limited purpose of establishing and operating a Title X project. 42 U.S.C. § 300(a). The regulations govern the scope of the Title X *project's* activities, and leave the grantee unfettered in its other activities. The Title X *grantee* can continue to perform abortions, provide abortion-related services, and engage in abortion advocacy; it simply is required to conduct those activities through programs that are separate and independent from the project that receives Title X funds. 42 CFR 59.9 (1989).

In contrast, our "unconstitutional conditions" cases involve situations in which the government has placed a condition on the *recipient* of the subsidy rather that on a particular program or service, thus effectively prohibiting the recipient from engaging in the protected conduct outside the scope of the federally funded program. ...

. . .

By requiring that the Title X grantee engage in abortion-related activity separately from activity receiving federal funding, Congress has, consistent with our teachings in *League of Women Voters* and *Regan,* not denied it the right to engage in abortion-related activities. Congress has merely refused to fund such activities out of the public fisc, and the Secretary has simply required a certain degree of separation from the Title X project in order to ensure the integrity of the federally funded program.

. . .

This is not to suggest that funding by the Government, even when coupled with the freedom of the fund recipients to speak outside the scope of the Government-funded project, is invariably sufficient to justify government control over the content of expression. For example, this Court has recognized that the existence of a Government "subsidy," in the form of Government-owned property, does not justify the restriction of speech in areas that have "been traditionally open to the public for expressive activity," United States v. Kokinda, 497 U.S. 720, 725 (1990); Hague v. CIO, 307 U.S. 496, 515 (1939) (opinion of Roberts, J.), or have been "expressly dedicated to speech activity." *Kokinda,* supra, 110 S.Ct., at 3119; Perry Education Assn.

v. Perry Local Educators' Assn., 460 U.S. 37, 45 (1983). Similarly, we have recognized that the university is a traditional sphere of free expression so fundamental to the functioning of our society that the Government's ability to control speech within that sphere by means of conditions attached to the expenditure of Government funds is restricted by the vagueness and overbreadth doctrines of the First Amendment, Keyishian v. Board of Regents, 385 U.S. 589, 603, 605–606 (1967). It could be argued by analogy that traditional relationships such as that between doctor and patient should enjoy protection under the First Amendment from government regulation, even when subsidized by the Government. We need not resolve that question here, however, because the Title X program regulations do not significantly impinge upon the doctor-patient relationship. Nothing in them requires a doctor to represent as his own any opinion that he does not in fact hold. Nor is the doctor-patient relationship established by the Title X program sufficiently all-encompassing so as to justify an expectation on the part of the patient of comprehensive medical advice. The program does not provide post-conception medical care, and therefore a doctor's silence with regard to abortion cannot reasonably be thought to mislead a client into thinking that the doctor does not consider abortion an appropriate option for her. The doctor is always free to make clear that advice regarding abortion is simply beyond the scope of the program. In these circumstances, the general rule that the Government may choose not to subsidize speech applies with full force.

We turn now to petitioners' argument that the regulations violate a woman's Fifth Amendment right to choose whether to terminate her pregnancy. . . .

That the regulations do not impermissibly burden a woman's Fifth Amendment rights is evident from the line of cases beginning with *Maher* and *McRae* and culminating in our most recent decision in *Webster*. Just as Congress' refusal to fund abortions in *McRae* left "an indigent woman with at least the same range of choice in deciding whether to obtain a medically necessary abortion as she would have had if Congress had chosen to subsidize no health care costs at all," and "Missouri's refusal to allow public employees to perform abortions in public hospitals leaves a pregnant woman with the same choices as if the State had chosen not to operate any public hospitals," Congress' refusal to fund abortion counseling and advocacy leaves a pregnant woman with the same choices as if the government had chosen not to fund family-planning services at all. The difficulty that a woman encounters when a Title X project does not provide abortion counseling or referral leaves her in no different position than she would have been if the government had not enacted Title X.

In *Webster* we stated that "[h]aving held that the State's refusal [in *Maher*] to fund abortions does not violate *Roe v. Wade,* it strains logic to reach a contrary result for the use of public facilities and employees." It similarly would strain logic, in light of the more extreme restrictions in those cases, to find that the mere decision to exclude abortion-related services from a federally funded *pre-conceptual* family planning program, is unconstitutional.

Petitioners also argue that by impermissibly infringing on the doctor/patient relationship and depriving a Title X client of information concerning abortion as a method of family planning, the regulations violate a woman's Fifth Amendment right to medical self-determination and to make informed medical decisions free of government-imposed harm. They argue that under our decisions in Akron v. Akron Center for Reproductive Health, Inc., 462

U.S. 416 (1983), and Thornburgh v. American College of Obstetricians and Gynecologists, 476 U.S. 747 (1986), the government cannot interfere with a woman's right to make an informed and voluntary choice by placing restrictions on the patient/doctor dialogue.

In *Akron,* we invalidated a city ordinance requiring *all* physicians to make specified statements to the patient prior to performing an abortion in order to ensure that the woman's consent was "truly informed." Similarly, in *Thornburgh,* we struck down a state statute mandating that a list of agencies offering alternatives to abortion and a description of fetal development be provided to *every* woman considering terminating her pregnancy through an abortion. Critical to our decisions in *Akron* and *Thornburgh* to invalidate a governmental intrusion into the patient/doctor dialogue was the fact that the laws in both cases required *all* doctors within their respective jurisdictions to provide *all* pregnant patients contemplating an abortion a litany of information, regardless of whether the patient sought the information or whether the doctor thought the information necessary to the patient's decision. Under the Secretary's regulations, however, a doctor's ability to provide, and a woman's right to receive, information concerning abortion and abortion-related services outside the context of the Title X project remains unfettered. It would undoubtedly be easier for a woman seeking an abortion if she could receive information about abortion from a Title X project, but the Constitution does not require that the Government distort the scope of its mandated program in order to provide that information.

. . .

The Secretary's regulations are a permissible construction of Title X and do not violate either the First or Fifth Amendments to the Constitution. Accordingly, the judgment of the Court of Appeals is

Affirmed.

■ JUSTICE BLACKMUN, with whom JUSTICE MARSHALL joins, with whom JUSTICE STEVENS joins as to Parts II and III, and with whom JUSTICE O'CONNOR joins as to Part I, dissenting.

. . .

Because I conclude that a plainly constitutional construction of § 1008 "is not only 'fairly possible' but entirely reasonable," *Machinists,* 367 U.S., at 750, I would reverse the judgment of the Court of Appeals on this ground without deciding the constitutionality of the Secretary's Regulations.

I also strongly disagree with the majority's disposition of petitioners' constitutional claims....

. . .

It cannot seriously be disputed that the counseling and referral provisions at issue in the present cases constitute content-based regulation of speech. Title X grantees may provide counseling and referral regarding any of a wide range of family planning and other topics, save abortion.

The Regulations are also clearly viewpoint-based. While suppressing speech favorable to abortion with one hand, the Secretary compels anti-abortion speech with the other. For example, the Department of Health and Human Services' own description of the Regulations makes plain that "Title X projects are *required* to facilitate access to prenatal care and social services, including adoption services, that might be needed by the pregnant client to promote her well-being and that of her child, while making it abundantly clear that the project is not permitted to promote abortion by facilitating access to abortion through the referral process." (emphasis added).

Moreover, the Regulations command that a project refer for prenatal care each woman diagnosed as pregnant, irrespective of the woman's expressed desire to continue or terminate her pregnancy. If a client asks directly about abortion, a Title X physician or counselor is required to say, in essence, that the project does not consider abortion to be an appropriate method of family planning. § 59.8(b)(4). Both requirements are antithetical to the First Amendment.

The Regulations pertaining to "advocacy" are even more explicitly viewpoint-based. These provide: "A Title X project may not *encourage, promote or advocate* abortion as a method of family planning." (emphasis added). They explain: "This requirement prohibits actions to *assist* women to obtain abortions or *increase* the availability or accessibility of abortion for family planning purposes." (emphasis added). The Regulations do not, however, proscribe or even regulate anti-abortion advocacy. These are clearly restrictions aimed at the suppression of "dangerous ideas."

Remarkably, the majority concludes that "the Government has not discriminated on the basis of viewpoint; it has merely chosen to fund one activity to the exclusion of another." But the majority's claim that the Regulations merely limit a Title X project's speech to preventive or preconceptional services rings hollow in light of the broad range of non-preventive services that the Regulations authorize Title X projects to provide.[2] By refusing to fund those family-planning projects that advocate abortion *because* they advocate abortion, the Government plainly has targeted a particular viewpoint. The majority's reliance on the fact that the Regulations pertain solely to funding decisions simply begs the question. Clearly, there are some bases upon which government may not rest its decision to fund or not to fund. For example, the Members of the majority surely would agree that government may not base its decision to support an activity upon considerations of race. As demonstrated above, our cases make clear that ideological viewpoint is a similarly repugnant ground upon which to base funding decisions.

The majority's reliance upon *Regan* in this connection is also misplaced. That case stands for the proposition that government has no obligation to subsidize a private party's efforts to petition the legislature regarding its views. Thus, if the challenged Regulations were confined to non-ideological limitations upon the use of Title X funds for lobbying activities, there would exist no violation of the First Amendment. The advocacy Regulations at issue here, however, are not limited to lobbying but extend to all speech having the effect of encouraging, promoting, or advocating abortion as a method of family planning. . . . This type of intrusive, ideologically based regulation of speech goes far beyond the narrow lobbying limitations approved in *Regan,* and cannot be justified simply because it is a condition upon the receipt of a governmental benefit.[3]

2. In addition to requiring referral for prenatal care and adoption services, the Regulations permit general health services such as physical examinations, screening for breast cancer, treatment of gynecological problems, and treatment for sexually transmitted diseases. None of the latter are strictly preventive, preconceptional services.

3. The majority attempts to obscure the breadth of its decision through its curious contention that "the Title X program regulations do not significantly impinge upon the doctor-patient relationship." That the doctor-patient relationship is substantially burdened by a rule prohibiting the dissemination by the physician of pertinent medical information is

The Court concludes that the challenged Regulations do not violate the First Amendment rights of Title X staff members because any limitation of the employees' freedom of expression is simply a consequence of their decision to accept employment at a federally funded project. But it has never been sufficient to justify an otherwise unconstitutional condition upon public employment that the employee may escape the condition by relinquishing his or her job. It is beyond question "that a government may not require an individual to relinquish rights guaranteed him by the First Amendment as a condition of public employment." Abood v. Detroit Board of Education, 431 U.S. 209, 234 (1977), citing Elrod v. Burns, 427 U.S. 347, 357–360 (1976). . . .

The majority attempts to circumvent this principle by emphasizing that Title X physicians and counselors "remain free ... to pursue abortion-related activities when they are not acting under the auspices of the Title X project." "The regulations," the majority explains, "do not in any way restrict the activities of those persons acting as private individuals." Under the majority's reasoning, the First Amendment could be read to tolerate *any* governmental restriction upon an employee's speech so long as that restriction is limited to the funded workplace. This is a dangerous proposition, and one the Court has rightly rejected in the past.

. . .

The Government's articulated interest in distorting the doctor/patient dialogue—ensuring that federal funds are not spent for a purpose outside the scope of the program—falls far short of that necessary to justify the suppression of truthful information and professional medical opinion regarding constitutionally protected conduct. Moreover, the offending Regulation is not narrowly tailored to serve this interest. For example, the governmental interest at stake could be served by imposing rigorous bookkeeping standards to ensure financial separation or adopting content-neutral rules for the balanced dissemination of family-planning and health information. By failing to balance or even to consider the free speech interests claimed by Title X physicians against the Government's asserted interest in suppressing the speech, the Court falters in its duty to implement the protection that the First Amendment clearly provides for this important message.

Finally, it is of no small significance that the speech the Secretary would suppress is truthful information regarding constitutionally protected conduct of vital importance to the listener. . . .

By far the most disturbing aspect of today's ruling is the effect it will have on the Fifth Amendment rights of the women who, supposedly, are beneficiaries of Title X programs. . . .

Until today, the Court has allowed to stand only those restrictions upon reproductive freedom that, while limiting the availability of abortion, have left intact a woman's ability to decide without coercion whether she will

beyond serious dispute. This burden is undiminished by the fact that the relationship at issue here is not an "all-encompassing" one. A woman seeking the services of a Title X clinic has every reason to expect, as do we all, that her physician will not withhold relevant information regarding the very purpose of her visit. To suggest otherwise is to engage in uninformed fantasy. Further, to hold that the doctor-patient relationship is somehow incomplete where a patient lacks the resources to seek comprehensive healthcare from a single provider is to ignore the situation of a vast number of Americans. . . .

continue her pregnancy to term. Today's decision abandons that principle, and with disastrous results.

. . .

■ JUSTICE O'CONNOR, dissenting.

... In this case, we need only tell the Secretary that his regulations are not a reasonable interpretation of the statute; we need not tell Congress that it cannot pass such legislation. If we rule solely on statutory grounds, Congress retains the power to force the constitutional question by legislating more explicitly. It may instead choose to do nothing. That decision should be left to Congress; we should not tell Congress what it cannot do before it has chosen to do it. It is enough in this case to conclude that neither the language nor the history of § 1008 compels the Secretary's interpretation, and that the interpretation raises serious First Amendment concerns. On this basis alone, I would reverse the judgment of the Court of Appeals and invalidate the challenged regulations.

NOTES

1. In Bowen v. Kendrick, 487 U.S. 589 (1988), the Court rejected an Establishment Clause challenge to the facial validity of the Adolescent Family Life Act (AFLA), Pub.L. 97–35, 95 Stat. 578, codified at 42 U.S.C. § 300z et seq. (1982 ed. and Supp. III). AFLA provides grants to public or non-profit organizations or agencies "for services and research in the area of premarital adolescent sexual relations and pregnancy."

The Court noted that religious institutions have never been barred from participating in publicly-sponsored social welfare programs. 487 U.S. at 609. The Court also found that the statute had a legitimate secular purpose—"the elimination or reduction of social and economic problems caused by teenage sexuality, pregnancy and parenthood." 487 U.S. at 603. The Court remanded the question of whether particular AFLA grants might have the constitutionally impermissible primary effect of advancing religion.

2. In 1977 Congress passed the first Hyde Amendment, which prohibited the use of federal money for obtaining an abortion. Since then Congress has regularly placed similar restrictions in appropriations bills such as Title XIX of the Social Security Act, 42 U.S.C. § 1396 (2005). See generally, Julia Lichtman, Restrictive State Abortion Laws: Today's Most Powerful Conscience Clause, 10 Geo. J. Poverty L. & Pol'y 345 (2003).

2. GENETIC SCREENING AND COUNSELING

Kassama v. Magat

Court of Special Appeals of Maryland, 2001.
136 Md.App. 637, 767 A.2d 348.

■ SALMON, J.

In this "wrongful life" case, an infant plaintiff asserts that she would have been better off if she had never been born and that she should have been aborted. This presents a question of first impression in Maryland, viz:

> May a doctor whose negligence caused a mother not to abort her pregnancy be successfully sued for "wrongful life" by a genetically defective child born as a consequence of the doctor's negligence?

We hold that Maryland does not recognize a cause of action for wrongful life and, accordingly, answer that question in the negative.

. . .

On September 19, 1995, a daughter, Ibrion Fatuo Kassama, was born to Millicent Kassama. The delivery was uneventful; unfortunately, however, Ibrion was born with Down's Syndrome. During her pregnancy, Mrs. Kassama was treated by Dr. Aaron H. Magat, a board-certified obstetrician and gynecologist.

Mrs. Kassama, individually and on behalf of Ibrion, filed suit in the Circuit Court for Baltimore County against Dr. Magat, his professional association, and one of his associates. The complaint contained counts for negligence and lack of informed consent. Mrs. Kassama alleged, inter alia, that, but for Dr. Magat's negligence, she would have had an abortion and would not have delivered Ibrion (hereinafter "the wrongful-birth claim"). In her wrongful-birth claim, Mrs. Kassama, individually, claimed economic damages caused by the necessity of raising her genetically defective child.

On behalf of Ibrion, Mrs. Kassama filed a claim for wrongful life based on negligence and lack of informed consent theories. Prior to trial, the court granted the defendants' motion for partial summary judgment as to Ibrion's claim of lack of informed consent.

The case was tried before a jury in the Circuit Court for Baltimore County. At the close of the plaintiff's case, the trial court granted the defendants' motion for judgment as to Ibrion's claim of negligence, as well as Mrs. Kassama's lack of informed consent claim. Thus, only Mrs. Kassama's wrongful-birth claim was considered by the jury.

The jury found that Dr. Magat had breached the applicable standard of care and that the breach was a proximate cause of Mrs. Kassama's injury. The jury also found that Mrs. Kassama was contributorily negligent and that her negligence was a proximate cause of her own injury.

After the trial judge considered and denied Mrs. Kassama's motion for judgment notwithstanding the verdict, and motion for new trial, a timely appeal was filed by Mrs. Kassama, individually and on behalf of Ibrion. The defendants responded by filing a conditional cross-appeal.

. . .

As a result of being afflicted with Down's Syndrome, Ibrion is moderately retarded and has a congenital heart defect. In her wrongful-life claim, Ibrion seeks to recover for emotional pain and suffering, as well as recompense for the medical and educational expenses incurred (and to be incurred) as a consequence of being afflicted with Down's Syndrome.

Maryland, along with most other states, has recognized wrongful-birth suits like the one brought by Mrs. Kassama. Reed v. Campagnolo, 332 Md. 226, 630 A.2d 1145 (1993). As will be seen, however, the vast majority of courts that have considered the matter have rejected wrongful-life claims.

A wrongful-birth claim differs from a wrongful-life claim in that the latter is brought by or on behalf of the disabled child, and the damages claimed are different. See generally Alan J. Belsky, Injury as a Matter of Law: Is this the Answer to the Wrongful Life Dilemma?, 22 U. Balt. L. Rev. 185 (1993). Using traditional negligence analysis, as has been used in other birth-related claims, a wrongful-life action asserts that the defendant/doctor owed a duty—directly or derivatively—to the infant plaintiff. See Hutton

Brown et al., Special Project: Legal Rights and Issues Surrounding Conception, Pregnancy, and Birth, 39 Vand. L. Rev. 597, 750–55, 767 (1986). The gravamen of a wrongful-life action is the assertion that but for the physician's negligence the mother would have had an abortion and the child would never have had to experience the pain and expenses occasioned by injuries and/or diseases that the physician could have foreseen. Because it was not the doctor who caused the defect, this amounts to an assertion on the part of the infant plaintiff, "not that [he or she] should not have been born without defects, but that [he or she] should not have been born at all." Procanik v. Cillo, 478 A.2d 755, 760 (N.J. 1984). The injury complained of in a wrongful-life lawsuit is life itself.

The Supreme Court of Pennsylvania, in Ellis v. Sherman, 515 A.2d 1327, 1329 (Pa. 1986), took the view that wrongful-life claims should be rejected because the plaintiff could not prove a "legal injury." The Court explained:

> Thus an "injury" is a harm that is inflicted upon one person or entity by another. The condition about which the plaintiff complains, a diseased life, was inflicted upon the plaintiff not by any person, but by the plaintiff's genetic constitution. Thus, it may not be said that the plaintiff has suffered a legal injury, for even though his physical and mental condition is unfortunate, and even though this condition presumably would constitute a legal injury if it had been inflicted by some negligent or intentional act of another, in this case, the condition was caused not by another, but by natural processes. It is not, therefore, a legal injury.

The New York Court of Appeals articulated a different reason for rejecting wrongful-life claims when it ruled that such claims should not be allowed because of the impossibility of calculating damages. Becker v. Schwartz, 386 N.E.2d 807 (N.Y. 1978). The Becker Court said:

> Whether it is better never to have been born at all than to have been born with even gross deficiencies is a mystery more properly to be left to the philosophers and the theologians. Surely the law can assert no competence to resolve the issue, particularly in view of the very nearly uniform high value which the law and mankind has placed on human life, rather than its absence. Not only is there to be found no predicate at common law or in statutory enactment for judicial recognition of the birth of a defective child as an injury to the child; the implications of any such proposition are staggering. Would claims be honored, assuming the breach of an identifiable duty, for less than a perfect birth? And by what standards or by whom would perfection be defined?
>
> . . .
>
> Simply put, a cause of action brought on behalf of an infant seeking recovery for wrongful life demands a calculation of damages dependent upon a comparison between the [child's] choice of life in an impaired state and nonexistence. This comparison the law is not equipped to make. Recognition of so novel a cause of action requiring, as it must, creation of a hypothetical formula for the measurement of an infant's damages is best reserved for legislative, rather than judicial, attention.

386 N.E.2d at 812 (emphasis added).

The impossibility of calculating damages is, of course, determinative, because it is a fundamental goal of tort law to put the victim, insofar as it is possible to do so by compensatory damages, in the position that he/she would have been in if the defendant had not been negligent. Tucker v.

Calmar S.S. Corp., 356 F. Supp. 709, 711 (D. Md. 1973). Twenty-three states have rejected wrongful-life claims based on the belief that it would be an impossible task to calculate damages based on a comparison between life in an impaired state and non-existence.

The West Virginia Supreme Court, in James G. v. Caserta, 332 S.E.2d 872 (W. Va. 1985), held that even if the child was injured, his injury was not caused by the physician's negligence and for that reason rejected a wrongful-life claim. Id. at 881.

In Phillips v. United States, 508 F. Supp. 537 (D.S.C. 1980), the Court held that the public policy of South Carolina barred a wrongful-life claim, notwithstanding the Court's finding that neither the speculative nature of the plaintiff's damages or the difficulty of identifying the child's injury would bar the child's recovery. In reaching its decision, the Phillips Court focused on the "'preciousness of human life.'" Other states have adopted the "preciousness of human life" premise as an alternative ground to reject wrongful-life claims. See, e.g., Blake v. Cruz, 698 P.2d at 322; Bruggeman v. Schimke, 718 P.2d at 642; Elliot v. Brown, 361 So. 2d at 548.

In eight states, the Legislature has acted affirmatively to prohibit wrongful-life claims by statute.

The seminal case recognizing a child's right to recover at least some damages in a wrongful-life action is Turpin v. Sortini, 31 Cal. 3d 220, 643 P.2d 954, 182 Cal. Rptr. 337 (Cal. 1982). In the Turpin case, Dr. Adam Sortini examined James and Donna Turpin's daughter (Hope) and advised the parents that Hope's hearing was within normal limits. 643 P.2d at 956. Approximately one year later, the child was correctly diagnosed as being "stone deaf" as a result of a hereditary ailment. Id. In their complaint, the Turpins alleged that if they had known that Hope was deaf they would not have conceived their second child (Joy), who suffered from the same total deafness as did her sister. Id. The Turpins, on behalf of Joy, brought a wrongful-life action in which they sought:

> (1) general damages for being "deprived of the fundamental right of a child to be born as a whole, functional human being without total deafness" and (2) special damages for the "extraordinary expenses for specialized teaching, training and hearing equipment" which she will incur during her lifetime as a result of her hearing impairment.

Id.

The trial court sustained a demurrer to the Turpins' wrongful-life action. Id. On appeal, the defendants/appellees took the position that Joy had suffered "no legally cognizable injury or rationally ascertainable damages as a result of their alleged negligence." 643 P.2d at 960.

In *Turpin*, the California Supreme Court recognized that there was a "critical difference between wrongful-life actions and the ordinary prenatal injury cases." Id. at 961. In the ordinary prenatal injury case, where some negligent act on the part of the defendant injures the fetus, the child would have been born healthy but for the defendant's negligence; however, in a wrongful-birth case, the obvious tragic fact is that plaintiff never had a chance "to be born as a whole, functional human being without total deafness"; if defendants have performed their job properly, [the plaintiff] would not have been born with hearing intact, but—according to the complaint—would not have been at all.

The *Turpin* court observed:

> Because nothing defendants could have done would have given plaintiff an unimpaired life, it appears inconsistent with basic tort principle to view the injury for which defendants are legally responsible solely by reference to plaintiff's present condition without taking into consideration the fact that if defendants had not been negligent she would have not been born at all.

Id.

The court rejected the proposition that impaired life is always preferable to non-life, saying:

> While it thus seems doubtful that a child's claim for general damages should properly be denied on the rationale that the value of impaired life, as a matter of law, always exceeds the value of non-life, we believe that the out-of-state decisions are on sounder ground in holding that—with respect to the child's claim for pain and suffering or other general damages—recovery should be denied because (1) it is simply impossible to determine in any rational or reasonable fashion whether the plaintiff has in fact suffered an injury in being born impaired rather than not being born, and (2) even if it were possible to overcome the first hurdle, it would be impossible to assess general damages in any fair, nonspeculative manner.

Id. at 963.

In reaching this decision, the court quoted from Justice Weintraub's separate opinion in Gleitman v. Cosgrove, 49 N.J. 22, 227 A.2d 689, 711 (N.J. 1967):

> Ultimately, the infant's complaint is that he would be better off not to have been. Man, who knows nothing of death or nothingness, cannot possibly know whether that is so.
>
> We must remember that the choice is not being born with health or being born without it.... Rather the choice is between a worldly existence and none at all.... To recognize a right not to be born is to enter an area in which no one can find his way.

Turpin, 643 P.2d at 963.

After rejecting the infant plaintiff's claim for general damages, the *Turpin* court held that a plaintiff in a wrongful-life cause of action was entitled to recover damages for " 'extraordinary expenses for specialized teaching, training and hearing equipment' " that she would incur during her lifetime because of her deafness. According to the Court, these types of extraordinary expenses stood on a "different footing" than general damages. After observing that parents, in wrongful-birth actions, were permitted to recover medical expenses incurred on behalf of a child born with disability, the Court said:

> Although the parent and child cannot, of course, both recover for the same medical expenses, we believe it would be illogical and anomalous to permit only parents, and not the child, to recover for the cost of the child's own medical care. If such a distinction were established, the afflicted child's receipt of necessary medical expenses might well depend on the wholly fortuitous circumstances of whether the parents are available to sue and recover such damages or whether the medical expenses are incurred at a time when the parents remain legally responsible for providing such care.

Id. at 965. The distinction between general damages and "extraordinary expense" that the Court made was that the latter expenses were "both certain and readily measurable . . . [and] in many instances . . . vital not only to the child's well being but to his or her very survival."

In Siemieniec v. Lutheran Gen. Hosp., 512 N.E.2d 691, (Ill. 1987), the Supreme Court of Illinois puts its finger on the essential flaw in the rationale of the *Turpin* opinion. The Court said:

> In awarding special damages, . . . the *Turpin* court ignored the reasoning that prevented an award of general damages. The problem of establishing the fact of injury was simply passed over, and all discussion focused on the nonspeculative nature of a recovery for extraordinary medical expenses.
>
> 512 N.E.2d at 700.

. . . .

Despite criticism such as those just mentioned, the Washington Supreme Court, in Harbeson v. Parke–Davis, Inc., 656 P.2d 483 (1983), followed, with no deviation, the reasoning of the *Turpin* court and disallowed general damages but allowed the plaintiff in a wrongful-life suit to recover damages covering the medical and educational needs of the child. 656 P.2d at 493.

Likewise, the Supreme Court of New Jersey, in Procanik v. Cillo, 97 N.J. 339, 478 A.2d 755 (1984), also followed the lead of the *Turpin* court and recognized a wrongful-life action but restricted monies recoverable to special damages for extraordinary medical expenses. 478 A.2d at 762. Like the *Harbeson* and *Turpin* courts, the *Procanik* court made "the analytical leap from injury to damages without explanation." Hutton Brown et al., Special Project: Legal Rights & Issues Surrounding Conception, Pregnancy, and Birth, 39 Vand. L. Rev. 597, 759 (1986). The *Procanik* court, however, emphasized policy grounds that were somewhat different from those enunciated in *Turpin* and *Harbeson,* viz:

> Recovery of the cost of extraordinary medical expenses by either the parents or the infant, but not both, is consistent with the principle that the doctor's negligence vitally affects the entire family. Gleitman[v. Cosgrove, 49 N.J. 22, 50, 227 A.2d 689 (1967)] (Jacobs, J., dissenting). As Justice Jacobs stated in *Gleitman*:
>
>> And while logical objection may be advanced to the child's standing and injury, logic is not the determinative factor and should not be permitted to obscure that he has to bear the frightful weight of his abnormality throughout life, and that such compensation as is received from the defendants or either of them should be dedicated primarily to his care and the lessening of his difficulties. Indeed, if this were suitably provided for in the ultimate judgment, the technical presence or absence of the child as an additional party plaintiff would have little significance. [Id.]
>
> Law is more than an exercise in logic, and logical analysis, although essential to a system of ordered justice, should not become [an] instrument of injustice. Whatever logic inheres in permitting parents to recover for the cost of extraordinary medical care incurred by a birth-defective child, but in denying the child's own right to recover those expenses, must yield to the injustice of that result. The right to recover the often crushing burden of extraordinary expenses visited by an act of medical malpractice should not depend on the "wholly [fortuitous]

> circumstance of whether the parents are available to sue." Turpin v. Sortini, supra, 31 Cal. 3d at 238, 643 P.2d at 965, 182 Cal. Rptr. at 348.
>
> The present case proves the point. Here, the parents' claim is barred by the statute of limitations. Does this mean that Peter must forego medical treatment for his blindness, deafness, and retardation? We think not. His claim for the medical expenses attributable to his birth defects is reasonably certain, readily calculable, and of a kind daily determined by judges and juries. We hold that a child or his parents may recover special damages for extraordinary medical expenses incurred during infancy, and that the infant may recover those expenses during his majority.

Procanik, 97 N.J. 339, 478 A.2d 755 at 762.

Judge Schreiver, dissenting in part in *Procanik*, countered:

> It is unfair and unjust to charge the doctors with the infant's medical expenses. The position that the child may recover special damages despite the failure of his underlying theory of wrongful life violates the moral code underlying our system of justice from which the fundamental principles of tort law are derived.

478 A.2d at 772.

We adopt the view accepted by the highest courts of twenty-three of our sister states that have refused to recognize a cause of action for wrongful life because it is an impossible task to calculate damages based on a comparison between life in an impaired state and no life at all. Attempts by the highest courts in California, Washington, and New Jersey to circumvent this problem are unpersuasive.

For the foregoing reasons we hold that the trial judge did not err when he granted the defense motion for judgment as to Ibrion's wrongful-life claim.

Kentucky Sickle Cell Disease Detection Act of 1972

K.R.S. § 402.320.

Every physician examining applicants for a marriage license may obtain an appropriate blood specimen from each applicant and forward same to the Division of Laboratory Services, Cabinet for and Family Services, or to a laboratory approved by the cabinet, to ascertain the existence or nonexistence of sickle cell trait or sickle cell disease, or any other genetically transmitted disease which affects hemoglobin. In the event the laboratory tests indicate that both applicants are carriers of a trait or disease, the physician may provide genetic counseling or refer the applicants to the cabinet or to an agency approved by the cabinet for such counseling.

NOTES

1. Is the Kentucky statute constitutional? Consider the view of Kirstin Raffone in Note: The Human Genome Project: Genetic Screening and the Fundamental Right of Privacy, 26 Hofstra L. Rev. 503 (1997), that mandatory screening and testing violates the Constitution.

2. Several state legislatures have taken steps to ensure that there is a comprehensive system of screening and counseling for hereditary diseases. E.g., N.J. Stat. § 26:5B–4 (2005), provides for not only screening and counseling, but also treatment, education and financial assistance. See also, Lori Andrews and Erin Shaughnessy Zuiker, Ethical, Legal and Social Issues in Genetic Testing for Complex Genetic Diseases, 37 Val. U. L. Rev. 793 (2003). See generally, President's Commission for the Study of Ethical Problems in Medicine and Biomedical and Behavioral Research, Screening and Counseling for Genetic Conditions 42 U.S.C. § 300v (2005).

Compare Jerry Elmer, Human Genomics: Toward a New Paradigm for Equal–Protection Jurisprudence, Part II, 50 R.I. Bar J. 11 (2002):

> For the past century, the core of our equal-protection jurisprudence has been the notion that people *who are similarly situated* should be treated similarly. The basic public-policy predicate of the new genetic nondiscrimination statutes is precisely the opposite: that even people who are clearly, demonstrably not similarly situated should be treated similarly. If a person has the gene for Huntington's disease, cystic fibrosis, or Duchenne's muscular dystrophy, that person is clearly, unequivocally not similarly situated for purposes of health or life insurance with a person who has the gene for none of these conditions. Yet, most of the new genetic nondiscrimination statutes would require us to treat these differently situated people similarly for purposes, at least, of health insurance.

3. Herman Muller, The Guidance of Human Evolution, 3 Perspectives in Biology and Medicine 1, 9 (1959):

> There is evidence from more than one direction that in man at least one person in five, . . . carries a detrimental gene which arose in the immediately preceding generation and that, therefore, this same proportion—one in five—is, typically, prevented by genetic defects from surviving to maturity or (if surviving) from reproducing. This equilibrium holds only when a population is living under conditions that have long prevailed. Modern techniques are so efficacious that, used to the full, they might today (as judged by recent statistics on deaths and births) be able to save for life and for a virtually normal rate of reproduction some nine-tenths of the otherwise genetically doomed 20 per cent. . . . At this rate, . . . there would after about eight generations, or 240 years, be an accumulation of about 100 "genetic deaths" (scattered over many future generations) per 100 persons then living in addition to the regular "load of mutations" that any population would ordinarily carry.

4. Committee of the American Neurological Association, Eugenic Sterilization 56 (1936): "There is nothing to indicate that mental disease and mental defects are increasing, and from this point there is no evidence of a biological deterioration of the race."

5. Consider the recommendations of Linus Pauling, Foreward, Reflections on the New Biology, 15 UCLA L.Rev. 267, 269 (1968):

> If all pairs of sickle-cell-anemia heterozygotes[a] were to refrain from having children, there would be no infants born with this disease. This suffering would then be eliminated.
>
> Should not all young people be tested for heterozygosity in the gene, be given the information as to whether or not they possess the gene, and advised about the consequences of marriage of two possessors of the gene? The test for heterozygosity is an extremely simple one, involving only one drop of blood which is inspected through a microscope. . . . I have suggested that there should be tattooed on the forehead of every young person a symbol showing possession of the sickle cell gene or whatever other similar gene, such as the gene for phenylketonuria, that he has been found to possess in a single dose. If this were done, two young people carrying the same seriously defective gene in single dose

a. [Editors note].

That is, people who have only one sickle cell gene. There are few problems for these carriers, and indeed there is some evidence that they are more resistant to malaria. But if each parent has one gene, there is roughly a 1 in 4 chance that their child will be homozygote which often means a life of suffering and an early death.

would recognize this situation at first sight, and would refrain from falling in love with one another. It is my opinion that legislation along this line, compulsory testing for defective genes before marriage, and some form of public or semi-public display of this possession, should be adopted.

6. Although most states do not recognize wrongful-life suits, a great deal of litigation stems from negligently performed genetic counseling or testing. See, e.g., Molloy v. Meier, 660 N.W.2d 444 (Minn.App.2003), aff'd 679 N.W.2d 711 (Minn.2004) (Mother sought genetic counseling from three doctors, anxious to determine if her older daughter's disorder was genetic, and if so, to determine the chances of a future child also being afflicted. She was negligently counseled that she was not at risk of having another child with the disorder. The court found that the doctors owed her a duty and allowed her malpractice suit). But see, Simmons v. West Covina Medical Clinic, 212 Cal.App.3d 696, 260 Cal.Rptr. 772 (1989) (mother of child born with Down's Syndrome sued doctors for negligently failing to do genetic tests that had only a twenty percent change of determining if the baby had the disorder. The court held that because of the test's proclivity for yielding false negatives, the doctors' failure to administer the test did not amount to negligence).

3. ABORTION

Roe v. Wade

Supreme Court of the United States, 1973.
410 U.S. 113, 93 S.Ct. 705, 35 L.Ed.2d 147.

[The opinion is printed on page 252 supra].

Planned Parenthood v. Casey

Supreme Court of the United States, 1992.
505 U.S. 833, 112 S.Ct. 2791, 120 L.Ed.2d 674.

[The opinion is printed on page 258 supra].

Stenberg v. Carhart

Supreme Court of the United States, 2000.
530 U.S. 914, 120 S.Ct. 2597, 147 L.Ed. 2d 743.

■ JUSTICE BREYER delivered the opinion of the Court.

. . .

Three established principles determine the issue before us. We shall set them forth in the language of the joint opinion in *Casey*. First, before "viability ... the woman has a right to choose to terminate her pregnancy." 505 U.S. at 870 (joint opinion of O'CONNOR, KENNEDY, and SOUTER, JJ.).

. . .

Second, "a law designed to further the State's interest in fetal life which imposes an undue burden on the woman's decision before fetal viability" is unconstitutional. 505 U.S. at 877.

. . .

Third, " 'subsequent to viability, the State in promoting its interest in the potentiality of human life may, if it chooses, regulate, and even proscribe, abortion except where it is necessary, in appropriate medical judgment, for the preservation of the life or health of the mother.'" 505 U.S. at 879.

We apply these principles to a Nebraska law banning "partial birth abortion." The statute reads as follows:

> "No partial birth abortion shall be performed in this state, unless such procedure is necessary to save the life of the mother whose life is endangered by a physical disorder, physical illness, or physical injury, including a life-endangering physical condition caused by or arising from the pregnancy itself."

The statute defines "partial birth abortion" as:

> "an abortion procedure in which the person performing the abortion partially delivers vaginally a living unborn child before killing the unborn child and completing the delivery."

It further defines "partially delivers vaginally a living unborn child before killing the unborn child" to mean

> "deliberately and intentionally delivering into the vagina a living unborn child, or a substantial portion thereof, for the purpose of performing a procedure that the person performing such procedure knows will kill the unborn child and does kill the unborn child."

The law classifies violation of the statute as a "Class III felony" carrying a prison term of up to 20 years, and a fine of up to $25,000. It also provides for the automatic revocation of a doctor's license to practice medicine in Nebraska.

We hold that this statute violates the Constitution.

. . .

The evidence before the trial court, as supported or supplemented in the literature, indicates the following:

1. About 90% of all abortions performed in the United States take place during the first trimester of pregnancy, before 12 weeks of gestational age. During the first trimester, the predominant abortion method is "vacuum aspiration," which involves insertion of a vacuum tube (cannula) into the uterus to evacuate the contents. Such an abortion is typically performed on an outpatient basis under local anesthesia.... As the fetus grows in size, however, the vacuum aspiration method becomes increasingly difficult to use.

2. Approximately 10% of all abortions are performed during the second trimester of pregnancy (12 to 24 weeks).... The most commonly used procedure is called "dilation and evacuation" (D&E). That procedure (together with a modified form of vacuum aspiration used in the early second trimester) accounts for about 95% of all abortions performed from 12 to 20 weeks of gestational age.

3. The AMA Report, adopted by the District Court, describes the process as follows.

Between 13 and 15 weeks of gestation:

> "D&E is similar to vacuum aspiration except that the cervix must be dilated more widely because surgical instruments are used to remove larger pieces of tissue. ... [I]nstruments are inserted through the cervix into the uterus to removal fetal and placental tissue. Because fetal tissue is friable and easily broken, the fetus may not be removed intact. The

walls of the uterus are scraped with a curette to ensure that no tissue remains."

After 15 weeks:

"Because the fetus is larger at this stage of gestation (particularly the head), and because bones are more rigid, dismemberment or other destructive procedures are more likely to be required than at earlier gestational ages to remove fetal and placental tissue."

. . .

There are variations in D&E operative strategy. ... However, the common points are that D&E involves (1) dilation of the cervix; (2) removal of at least some fetal tissue using nonvacuum instruments; and (3) (after the 15th week) the potential need for instrumental disarticulation or dismemberment of the fetus or the collapse of fetal parts to facilitate evacuation from the uterus.

. . .

6. At trial, Dr. Carhart and Dr. Stubblefield described a variation of the D&E procedure, which they referred to as an "intact D&E." Like other versions of the D&E technique, it begins with induced dilation of the cervix. The procedure then involves removing the fetus from the uterus through the cervix "intact," i.e., in one pass, rather than in several passes. It is used after 16 weeks at the earliest, as vacuum aspiration becomes ineffective and the fetal skull becomes too large to pass through the cervix. The intact D&E proceeds in one of two ways, depending on the presentation of the fetus. If the fetus presents head first (a vertex presentation), the doctor collapses the skull; and the doctor then extracts the entire fetus through the cervix. If the fetus presents feet first (a breech presentation), the doctor pulls the fetal body through the cervix, collapses the skull, and extracts the fetus through the cervix. The breech extraction version of the intact D&E is also known commonly as "dilation and extraction," or D&X. ...

9. Dr. Carhart testified he attempts to use the intact D&E procedure during weeks 16 to 20 because (1) it reduces the dangers from sharp bone fragments passing through the cervix, (2) minimizes the number of instrument passes needed for extraction and lessens the likelihood of uterine perforations caused by those instruments, (3) reduces the likelihood of leaving infection-causing fetal and placental tissue in the uterus, and (4) could help to prevent potentially fatal absorption of fetal tissue into the maternal circulation.

. . .

The question before us is whether Nebraska's statute, making criminal the performance of a "partial birth abortion," violates the Federal Constitution, as interpreted in Planned Parenthood of Southeastern Pa. v. Casey, 505 U.S. 833 (1992), and Roe v. Wade, 410 U.S. 113 (1973). We conclude that it does for at least two independent reasons. First, the law lacks any exception " 'for the preservation of the ... health of the mother.' " Second, it "imposes an undue burden on a woman's ability" to choose a D&E abortion, thereby unduly burdening the right to choose abortion itself. We shall discuss each of these reasons in turn.

. . .

The fact that Nebraska's law applies both pre-and postviability aggravates the constitutional problem presented. The State's interest in regulating abortion previability is considerably weaker than postviability. Since the law requires a health exception in order to validate even a postviability abortion regulation, it at a minimum requires the same in respect to previability regulation.

. . .

We shall reiterate in summary form the relevant findings and evidence. On the basis of medical testimony the District Court concluded that "Carhart's D&X procedure is ... safer than the D&E and other abortion procedures used during the relevant gestational period in the 10 to 20 cases a year that present to Dr. Carhart." It found that the D&X procedure permits the fetus to pass through the cervix with a minimum of instrumentation. It thereby

> "reduces operating time, blood loss and risk of infection; reduces complications from bony fragments; reduces instrument-inflicted damage to the uterus and cervix; prevents the most common causes of maternal mortality (DIC and amniotic fluid embolus); and eliminates the possibility of 'horrible complications' arising from retained fetal parts."

. . .

Nebraska, along with supporting amici, replies that these findings are irrelevant, wrong, or applicable only in a tiny number of instances. It says (1) that the D&X procedure is "little-used," (2) by only "a handful of doctors." It argues (3) that D&E and labor induction are at all times "safe alternative procedures."

[P]etitioners' medical expert ... testified (4) that the ban would not increase a woman's risk of several rare abortion complications....

The Association of American Physicians and Surgeons et al., amici supporting Nebraska, argue (5) that elements of the D&X procedure may create special risks. ...

Nebraska further emphasizes (6) that there are no medical studies "establishing the safety of the partial-birth abortion/D&X procedure," and "no medical studies comparing the safety of partial-birth abortion/D&X to other abortion procedures." It points to (7) an American Medical Association policy statement that " 'there does not appear to be any identified situation in which intact D&X is the only appropriate procedure to induce abortion.' " And it points out that the American College of Obstetricians and Gynecologists qualified its statement that D&X "may be the best or most appropriate procedure," by adding that the panel "could identify no circumstances under which [the D&X] procedure ... would be the only option to save the life or preserve the health of the woman."

We find these ... arguments insufficient to demonstrate that Nebraska's law needs no health exception. For one thing, certain of the arguments are beside the point. The D&X procedure's relative rarity (argument (1)) is not highly relevant. The D&X is an infrequently used abortion procedure; but the health exception question is whether protecting women's health requires an exception for those infrequent occasions....

For another thing, the record responds to Nebraska's (and amici's) medically based arguments. In respect to argument (3), for example, the District Court agreed that alternatives, such as D&E and induced labor, are "safe" but found that the D&X method was significantly safer in certain circumstances. In respect to argument (4), the District Court simply relied on different expert testimony—testimony stating that " 'another advantage of the Intact D&E is that it eliminates the risk of embolism of cerebral tissue into the woman's blood stream.' "

In response to amici's argument (5), the American College of Obstetricians and Gynecologists, in its own amici brief, denies that D&X generally poses risks greater than the alternatives. It says that the suggested alternative procedures involve similar or greater risks of cervical and uterine injury, for "D&E procedures, involve similar amounts of dilitation" and "of course childbirth involves even greater cervical dilitation." . . .

We do not quarrel with Nebraska's argument (6), for Nebraska is right. There are no general medical studies documenting comparative safety. . . .

We cannot, however, read the American College of Obstetricians and Gynecologists panel's qualification (that it could not "identify" a circumstance where D&X was the "only" life-or health-preserving option) as if, according to Nebraska's argument (8), it denied the potential health-related need for D&X. That is because the College writes the following in its amici brief:

> "Depending on the physician's skill and experience, the D&X procedure can be the most appropriate abortion procedure for some women in some circumstances.

. . .

The upshot is a District Court finding that D&X significantly obviates health risks in certain circumstances, a highly plausible record-based explanation of why that might be so, a division of opinion among some medical experts over whether D&X is generally safer, and an absence of controlled medical studies that would help answer these medical questions. Given these medically related evidentiary circumstances, we believe the law requires a health exception.

. . .

[T]he division of medical opinion about the matter at most means uncertainty, a factor that signals the presence of risk, not its absence. That division here involves highly qualified knowledgeable experts on both sides of the issue. Where a significant body of medical opinion believes a procedure may bring with it greater safety for some patients and explains the medical reasons supporting that view, we cannot say that the presence of a different view by itself proves the contrary. Rather, the uncertainty means a significant likelihood that those who believe that D&X is a safer abortion method in certain circumstances may turn out to be right. If so, then the absence of a health exception will place women at an unnecessary risk of tragic health consequences. If they are wrong, the exception will simply turn out to have been unnecessary.

In sum, Nebraska has not convinced us that a health exception is "never necessary to preserve the health of women." Rather, a statute that altogether forbids D&X creates a significant health risk. The statute consequently must contain a health exception.

. . .

The Eighth Circuit found the Nebraska statute unconstitutional because, in *Casey's* words, it has the "effect of placing a substantial obstacle in the path of a woman seeking an abortion of a nonviable fetus." It thereby places an "undue burden" upon a woman's right to terminate her pregnancy before viability. Nebraska does not deny that the statute imposes an "undue burden" if it applies to the more commonly used D&E procedure as well as to D&X. And we agree with the Eighth Circuit that it does so apply.

Our earlier discussion of the D&E procedure, shows that it falls within the statutory prohibition. The statute forbids "deliberately and intentionally delivering into the vagina a living unborn child, or a substantial portion thereof, for the purpose of performing a procedure that the person performing such procedure knows will kill the unborn child." We do not understand how one could distinguish, using this language, between D&E (where a foot or arm is drawn through the cervix) and D&X (where the body up to the head is drawn through the cervix). Evidence before the trial court makes clear that D&E will often involve a physician pulling a "substantial portion" of a still living fetus, say, an arm or leg, into the vagina prior to the death of the fetus. Indeed D&E involves dismemberment that commonly occurs only when the fetus meets resistance that restricts the motion of the fetus: "The dismemberment occurs between the traction of . . . [the] instrument and the counter-traction of the internal os of the cervix." And these events often do not occur until after a portion of a living fetus has been pulled into the vagina. . . .

Even if the statute's basic aim is to ban D&X, its language makes clear that it also covers a much broader category of procedures. The language does not track the medical differences between D&E and D&X—though it would have been a simple matter, for example, to provide an exception for the performance of D&E and other abortion procedures. Nor does the statute anywhere suggest that its application turns on whether a portion of the fetus' body is drawn into the vagina as part of a process to extract an intact fetus after collapsing the head as opposed to a process that would dismember the fetus.

. . .

In sum, using this law some present prosecutors and future Attorneys General may choose to pursue physicians who use D&E procedures, the most commonly used method for performing previability second trimester abortions. All those who perform abortion procedures using that method must fear prosecution, conviction, and imprisonment. The result is an undue burden upon a woman's right to make an abortion decision. We must consequently find the statute unconstitutional.

The judgment of the Court of Appeals is

Affirmed.

■ JUSTICE O'CONNOR concurring.

If Nebraska's statute limited its application to the D&X procedure and included an exception for the life and health of the mother, the question presented would be quite different than the one we face today. As we held in *Casey*, an abortion regulation constitutes an undue burden if it "has the purpose or effect of placing a substantial obstacle in the path of a woman seeking an abortion of a nonviable fetus." If there were adequate alternative methods for a woman safely to obtain an abortion before viability, it is unlikely that prohibiting the D&X procedure alone would "amount in practical terms to a substantial obstacle to a woman seeking an abortion." Thus, a ban on partial-birth abortion that only proscribed the D&X method of abortion and that included an exception to preserve the life and health of the mother would be constitutional in my view.

■ Justice Ginsburg, with whom Justice Stevens joins, concurring.

I write separately only to stress that amidst all the emotional uproar caused by an abortion case, we should not lose sight of the character of Nebraska's "partial birth abortion" law. As the Court observes, this law does not save any fetus from destruction, for it targets only "a method of performing abortion." Nor does the statute seek to protect the lives or health of pregnant women. Moreover, as Justice Stevens points out, the most common method of performing previability second trimester abortions is no less distressing or susceptible to gruesome description.

■ Justice Thomas, with whom The Chief Justice and Justice Scalia join, dissenting.

I think it is clear that the Nebraska statute does not prohibit the D&E procedure.

. . .

Starting with the statutory definition of "partial birth abortion," I think it highly doubtful that the statute could be applied to ordinary D&E....

. . .

Having resolved that Nebraska's partial birth abortion statute permits doctors to perform D&E abortions, the question remains whether a State can constitutionally prohibit the partial birth abortion procedure without a health exception. Although the majority and Justice O'Connor purport to rely on the standard articulated in the *Casey* joint opinion in concluding that a State may not, they in fact disregard it entirely.

. . .

There is no question that the State of Nebraska has a valid interest—one not designed to strike at the right itself—in prohibiting partial birth abortion. *Casey* itself noted that States may "express profound respect for the life of the unborn." States may, without a doubt, express this profound respect by prohibiting a procedure that approaches infanticide, and thereby dehumanizes the fetus and trivializes human life. The AMA has recognized that this procedure is "ethically different from other destructive abortion techniques because the fetus, normally twenty weeks or longer in gestation, is killed outside the womb. The 'partial birth' gives the fetus an autonomy which separates it from the right of the woman to choose treatments for her own body." AMA Board of Trustees Factsheet on H. R. 1122 (June 1997), in App. to Brief for Association of American Physicians and Surgeons et al. as Amici Curiae 1. Thirty States have concurred with this view.

Although the description of this procedure set forth above should be sufficient to demonstrate the resemblance between the partial birth abortion procedure and infanticide, the testimony of one nurse who observed a partial birth abortion procedure makes the point even more vividly:

> "The baby's little fingers were clasping and unclasping, and his little feet were kicking. Then the doctor stuck the scissors in the back of his head, and the baby's arms jerked out, like a startle reaction, like a flinch, like a baby does when he thinks he is going to fall.
>
> "The doctor opened up the scissors, stuck a high-powered suction tube into the opening, and sucked the baby's brains out. Now the baby went completely limp." H. R. 1833 Hearing 18 (statement of Brenda Pratt Shafer).

The question whether States have a legitimate interest in banning the procedure does not require additional authority. In a civilized society, the answer is too obvious, and the contrary arguments too offensive to merit further discussion.

. . .

The next question, therefore, is whether the Nebraska statute is unconstitutional because it does not contain an exception that would allow use of the procedure whenever " 'necessary in appropriate medical judgment, for the preservation of the ... health of the mother.' " According to the majority, such a health exception is required here because there is a "division of opinion among some medical experts over whether D&X is generally safer [than D&E], and an absence of controlled medical studies that would help answer these medical questions." In other words, unless a State can conclusively establish that an abortion procedure is no safer than other procedures, the State cannot regulate that procedure without including a health exception. . . .

The majority and Justice O'Connor suggest that their rule is dictated by a straightforward application of *Roe* and *Casey*. But that is simply not true. In *Roe* and *Casey*, the Court stated that the State may "regulate, and even proscribe, abortion except where it is necessary, in appropriate medical judgment, for the preservation of the life or health of the mother." *Casey* said that a health exception must be available if "continuing her pregnancy would constitute a threat" to the woman. Under these cases, if a State seeks to prohibit abortion, even if only temporarily or under particular circumstances, as *Casey* says that it may, the State must make an exception for cases in which the life or health of the mother is endangered by continuing the pregnancy. These cases addressed only the situation in which a woman must obtain an abortion because of some threat to her health from continued pregnancy. But *Roe* and *Casey* say nothing at all about cases in which a physician considers one prohibited method of abortion to be preferable to permissible methods.

. . .

Although *Roe* and *Casey* mandated a health exception for cases in which abortion is "necessary" for a woman's health, the majority concludes that a procedure is "necessary" if it has any comparative health benefits. In other words, according to the majority, so long as a doctor can point to support in the profession for his (or the woman's) preferred procedure, it is "necessary" and the physician is entitled to perform it. . . . But such a health exception requirement eviscerates *Casey's* undue burden standard and imposes unfettered abortion-on-demand. The exception entirely swallows the rule. In effect, no regulation of abortion procedures is permitted because there will always be some support for a procedure and there will always be some doctors who conclude that the procedure is preferable.

. . .

The majority assiduously avoids addressing the actual standard articulated in *Casey*—whether prohibiting partial birth abortion without a health exception poses a substantial obstacle to obtaining an abortion. And for good reason: Such an obstacle does not exist.

. . .

The *Casey* joint opinion makes clear that the Court should not strike down state regulations of abortion based on the fact that some women might face a marginally higher health risk from the regulation. In *Casey*, the Court upheld a 24–hour waiting period even though the Court credited evidence that for some women the delay would, in practice, be much longer than 24 hours, and even though it was undisputed that any delay in obtaining an abortion would impose additional health risks. . . .

The only case in which this Court has overturned a State's attempt to prohibit a particular form of abortion also demonstrates that a marginal increase in health risks is not sufficient to create an undue burden. In Planned Parenthood of Central Mo. v. Danforth, 428 U.S. 52 (1976), the Court struck down a state regulation because the State had outlawed the method of abortion used in 70% of abortions and because alternative methods were, the Court emphasized, "significantly more dangerous and critical" than the prohibited method.

Like the *Casey* 24–hour waiting period, and in contrast to the situation in *Danforth*, any increased health risk to women imposed by the partial birth abortion ban is minimal at most. Of the 5.5% of abortions that occur after 15 weeks (the time after which a partial birth abortion would be possible), the vast majority are performed with a D&E or induction procedure. And, for any woman with a vertex presentation fetus, the vertex presentation form of intact D&E, which presumably shares some of the health benefits of the partial birth abortion procedure but is not covered by the Nebraska statute, is available. Of the remaining women—that is, those women for whom a partial birth abortion procedure would be considered and who have a breech presentation fetus—there is no showing that any one faces a significant health risk from the partial birth abortion ban.

. . .

The majority justifies its result by asserting that a "significant body of medical opinion" supports the view that partial birth abortion may be a safer abortion procedure. I find this assertion puzzling. If there is a "significant body of medical opinion" supporting this procedure, no one in the majority has identified it. In fact, it is uncontested that although this procedure has been used since at least 1992, no formal studies have compared partial birth abortion with other procedures. The majority's conclusion makes sense only if the undue-burden standard is not whether a "significant body of medical opinion," supports the result, but rather, as Justice Ginsburg candidly admits, whether any doctor could reasonably believe that the partial birth abortion procedure would best protect the woman.

Moreover, even if I were to assume credible evidence on both sides of the debate, that fact should resolve the undue-burden question in favor of allowing Nebraska to legislate. Where no one knows whether a regulation of abortion poses any burden at all, the burden surely does not amount to a "substantial obstacle." Under *Casey*, in such a case we should defer to the legislative judgment. We have said:

> "It is precisely where such disagreement exists that legislatures have been afforded the widest latitude in drafting such statutes. . . . When a legislature undertakes to act in areas fraught with medical and scientific uncertainty, legislative options must be especially broad. . . ."

We were reassured repeatedly in *Casey* that not all regulations of abortion are unwarranted and that the States may express profound respect for fetal life. Under *Casey*, the regulation before us today should easily pass constitutional muster. ... [T]oday we are told that 30 States are prohibited from banning one rarely used form of abortion that they believe to border on infanticide. It is clear that the Constitution does not compel this result.

NOTES

1. Is Justice Thomas right that crushing the skull of the fetus when all but its head is in the vagina seems to resemble infanticide in a way that crushing the skull and dismembering the body in utero does not? What kind of evidence can prove or refute this claim?

2. On September 28, 2000, the Food and Drug Administration (FDA) approved mifepristone, or RU–486, for the termination of early pregnancy, defined as 49 days or fewer from the beginning of the last menstrual period. Food and Drug Administration, FDA Approves Mifepristone for the Termination of Early Pregnancy, Press Release, HHS News, Sept. 28, 2000. Mifepristone interferes with a fertilized egg's ability to adhere to the lining of the uterus. It thus differs from the "morning after" pill approved by the FDA in 1998, which can prevent fertilization up to 72 hours after sexual intercourse.

Under the approved treatment regimen, a woman first takes 600 mg. of mifepristone. Two days later she takes 400 mg. of misoprostol, which prompts uterine contractions. She then must return for a follow-up visit approximately 14 days after taking mifepristone to determine whether the pregnancy has been terminated. The pills must be taken in the presence of someone capable of performing a surgical abortion if the drug fails. Women who do not have access to surgical abortions therefore are unlikely to have access to mifepristone. See Jessica Reaves, RU–486 Noel Ushers New Era of Abortion Debate (2000) http://www.time.com/time/nation/article/0,8599,56214,00.html.

Ayotte v. Planned Parenthood

Supreme Court of the United States, 2006.
___ U.S. ___, 126 S.Ct. 961.

[The opinion is printed on page 278 supra.]

4. Voluntary Sterilization

Hathaway v. Worcester City Hospital

United States Court of Appeals, First Circuit, 1973.
475 F.2d 701.

■ Coffin, Chief Judge.

Appellant, who has had twelve pregnancies resulting in eight live offspring, and whose life would be jeopardized by future pregnancies, challenges as unconstitutional the policy of the Worcester City Hospital barring the use of its facilities in connection with any consensual sterilization.

The following facts are established by the record. Appellant, married and 36 years old at the time of the complaint, suffers from high blood pressure and an umbilical hernia which, in addition to the sheer number of past pregnancies, render future pregnancies a risk to her life. Her blood pressure and heavy, irregular menstrual flow render birth control pills, intrauterine devices and other generally reliable contraceptive means either dangerous or ineffective. A therapeutic sterilization has therefore been recommended by her physician. The correctness of this advice is not disputed. In addition, a psychological evaluation revealed that "further pregnancies might represent a sufficiently stressful circumstance to result in her psychological deterioration." Finally, she and her husband, who both work, have a combined yearly income of approximately $7500, which is below the federally defined poverty level for a non-farm family of 10. Although they are insured, through her husband's employment, by Blue Cross and Blue Shield, their policy, while covering the expenses of childbirth, does not cover the expenses of the recommended tubal ligation.

The hospital is a municipal hospital established pursuant to state law, "for the reception of persons requiring relief during temporary sickness." ... The hospital recognizes the right of the appellant, as a resident of Worcester, to in-patient admission for any surgical or other procedure, such as childbirth, which it permits and for the performance of which it has the proper facilities. Although the hospital does not recognize a right of the appellant to have any in-patient procedure done free of its ordinary charges, it would admit her regardless of her financial condition for the performance of any permitted in-patient procedure. The hospital does provide free of charge, through its clinics, both pre-natal and post-partum care for Worcester residents who meet the hospital's income standards. The cost of a tubal ligation, whether performed in conjunction with a childbirth (in which case it is less expensive, painful, and disruptive of the patient's life) or separately, is significantly less at the Worcester City Hospital than at nearby private hospitals.

In June, 1970, the Board of Trustees, following receipt of an opinion by the Assistant City Solicitor of Worcester, formally adopted its preexisting policy barring physicians from utilizing operating room facilities or staff personnel employed in support of those facilities, for the purpose of sterilization. Appellee administrator specifically refused appellant's request that the hospital permit her doctors to perform a tubal ligation at the time of the delivery of her eighth child in April, 1971. Nor was the operation performed after the delivery, despite apparent further requests. In the interim, the instant suit was filed ... seeking declaratory and injunctive relief and damages. ...

. . .

Appellee's principal present argument is that even if it is not in any way impermissible to perform this procedure, the Trustees are free to decide what they will and will not do. Even under the "rational relationship" test applied in Eisenstadt v. Baird, we might have had difficulty in upholding the policy of a complete ban on sterilizations. For here the evidence shows that tubal ligations involve no greater risk than appendectomies, which the hospital regularly performs, and by inference, than the other listed procedures of like complexity which are also performed. In addition, elective surgery, of unspecified risk, is permitted, though not in any sense therapeutic. No special facilities, equipment or staff are required for a ligation.

But it seems clear, after *Roe* and *Doe,* that a fundamental interest is involved, requiring a compelling rationale to justify permitting some hospital surgical procedures and banning another involving no greater risk or demand on staff and facilities. While *Roe* and *Doe* dealt with a woman's decision whether or not to terminate a particular pregnancy, a decision to terminate the possibility of any future pregnancy would seem to embrace all of the factors deemed important by the Court in *Roe* in finding a fundamental interest, but in magnified form, particularly so in this case given the demonstrated danger to appellant's life and the eight existing children.

. . .

In so holding, we are not mandating the city or state to maintain this hospital, or to retain its present size, staff or facilities. The hospital is not required to perform all kinds of nontherapeutic or even all therapeutic surgical procedures. We are merely saying, ... that once the state has undertaken to provide general short-term hospital care, as here, it may not constitutionally draw the line at medically indistinguishable surgical procedures that impinge on fundamental rights. ...

Accordingly, we reverse and remand for entry of an order declaring the Worcester City Hospital's policy against the use of its facilities in conjunction with sterilization operations unconstitutional and enjoining the individual appellees from enforcing the policy in the future. ...

NOTES

1. *Hathaway* involved what might be termed a "therapeutic" sterilization. The court noted that the mother already had eight children, and the birth of any additional children would endanger her life. Does *Hathaway* thus create a right to sterilization that may not be invoked for mere convenience?

2. Until 1969, the American College of Obstetricians and Gynecologists followed the so-called 120 Rule. Before a woman could be sterilized, her age multiplied by the number of children borne had to equal at least 120. Although the rule had no legal force, it was widely followed. Does the rationale of *Hathaway* bar the use of such a formula? See generally, Comment, A Constitutional Evaluation of Statutory and Administrative Impediments to Voluntary Sterilization, 14 J. Fam. L. 67 (1975).

3. In California Medical Association v. Lackner, 124 Cal.App.3d 28, 177 Cal.Rptr. 188 (1981), the California Court of Appeal examined whether the State Department of Health Services could lawfully promulgate regulations establishing procedures for securing informed consent for human sterilization, in light of California's Health and Safety Code Section 1258, which provides:

> No health facility which permits sterilization operations for contraceptive purposes to be performed therein, nor the medical staff of such health facility, shall require the individual upon whom such a sterilization operation is to be performed to meet any special nonmedical qualifications, which are not imposed on individuals seeking other types of operations in the health facility. Such prohibited nonmedical qualifications shall include, but not be limited to, age, marital status, and number of natural children. Nothing in this section shall prohibit requirements relating to the physical or mental condition of the individual or affect the right of the attending physician to counsel or advise his patient as to whether or not sterilization is appropriate. This section shall not affect existing law with respect to individuals below the age of majority.

The plaintiffs challenged the regulations on the ground that they exceeded the regulatory powers of the Department of Health Services over hospitals, arguing that the Department had no authority to regulate professional treatment, including the securing of informed consent. The court held that the regulations reasonably implemented the Department's regulatory authority over unnecessary operations, and did not constitute a decision on a "truly fundamental issue" properly left to the legislature to resolve. The court also rejected the plaintiffs' argument that the regulations were not reasonably necessary because a patient sterilized without informed consent could recover damages for negligence.

4. Is it constitutional for a state or hospital to require spousal consent before performing a sterilization operation? See generally, Murray v. Vandevander, 522 P.2d 302 (Okla. Ct. App. 1974); 73 Pa. D. & C.2d 325 (1975).

5. Sterilization is the method of preventing conception most used by married couples in the United States. Roughly 10.3 million women have undergone sterilization, constituting 16.7% of the female population of child-bearing age; 21.7% of married women and 35.3 of formerly married women have been sterilized. Choice of sterilization by women seems to be linked to socio-economic factors. Women without a high school diploma are more likely to choose sterilization, while women with a college degree are more likely to use the pill. Among all women of child-bearing age, sterilization is second only to the pill as the most widely used form of contraception. Advance Data: From Vital and Health Statistics, CDC, Number 350, Use of Contraception and Use of Family Planning Services in the United States: 1982–2002, December 10, 2004.

6. Consensual sterilization became a much debated issue when groups concerned with increases in the number of babies born addicted to drugs began to offer incentives to women to stop having children. Programs such as Children Requiring A Caring Kommunity (C.R.A.C.K.) offered $200 to drug addicted women who were willing to seek long-term contraception or sterilization. See generally, Jennifer Mott Johnson, Note: Reproductive Ability for Sale, Do I Hear $200?: Private Cash-for Contraception Agreements As an Alternative to Maternal Substance Abuse, 43 Ariz. L. Rev. 205 (2004); M. Morgan, The Payment of Drug Addicts to Increase Their Sterilization Rate is Morally Unjustified and Not Simply "A Fine Balance", Journal of Obstetrics and Gynecology, Bristol: Feb. 2004, Vol. 24, Iss. 2, pg. 119.

B. Rights of the Fetus

In re Baby Boy Doe

Illinois Appellate Court, 1994.
260 Ill.App.3d 392, 198 Ill.Dec. 267, 632 N.E.2d 326.

■ PRESIDING JUSTICE DIVITO delivered the opinion of the court:

This case asks whether an Illinois court can balance whatever rights a fetus may have against the rights of a competent woman to refuse medical advice to obtain a cesarean section for the supposed benefit of her fetus. Following the lead of the Illinois Supreme Court in Stallman v. Youngquist (1988), 531 N.E.2d 355, we hold that no such balancing should be employed, and that a woman's competent choice to refuse medical treatment as invasive as a cesarean section during pregnancy must be honored, even in circumstances where the choice may be harmful to her fetus.

... "Doe" is a married woman who was expecting her first child. She sought and had been receiving regular prenatal care throughout her pregnancy at St. Joseph's Hospital in Chicago. All parties and the court regarded her as mentally competent.

On November 24, 1993, Dr. James Meserow, a board-certified obstetrician/gynecologist an expert in the field of maternal/fetal medicine who is affiliated with the hospital, examined Doe for the first time. A series of tests he ordered performed on her suggested to Meserow that something was wrong with the placenta, and that the approximately 35–week, viable fetus was receiving insufficient oxygen. Meserow recommended immediate delivery by cesarean section, in his opinion the safest option for the fetus or, in the alternative, by induced labor. Informed of his recommendation, Doe told Meserow that, because of her personal religious beliefs, she would not consent to either procedure. Instead, given her abiding faith in God's healing powers, she chose to await natural childbirth. Her husband agreed with her decision.

Doe was examined by Dr. Meserow again on December 8, and by a Dr. Gautier from the University of Illinois at Chicago on Thursday, December 9. After consulting with Gautier, Meserow concluded that the condition of the fetus had worsened. Meserow advised Doe and her husband that due to the insufficient oxygen flow to the fetus, failure to provide an immediate delivery by cesarean section (Meserow no longer recommended inducement as an option) could result in the child being born dead or severely retarded. Doe reiterated her opposition to a cesarean section, based on her personal religious beliefs.

On December 8, 1993, Dr. Meserow and St. Joseph's Hospital contacted the office of the Cook County State's Attorney. That office filed a petition for adjudication of wardship of the fetus on December 9, seeking to invoke the jurisdiction of the Juvenile Court Act and asking that the hospital be appointed custodian of the fetus. The juvenile court judge appointed an assistant public defender as counsel for Doe and her husband....

... [T]he juvenile court judge commenced the hearing on the issue of the circuit court's jurisdiction, and whether an order compelling Doe to submit to surgery should issue. After oral argument from the parties' attorneys, the court ruled that the Juvenile Court Act does not apply to a fetus. The court held, however, that it had equity jurisdiction over the State's petition as a court of general jurisdiction, and denied the public defender's motion to dismiss the State's petition. The State then sought leave to file an amended petition, which was granted, and filed instanter its amended "Petition for Hearing on Whether a Temporary Custodian Can Be Appointed to Consent to a Medical Procedure: To Wit Cesarean Section."

. . .

The hearing then proceeded on the amended petition. The State called Dr. Meserow as its only witness. Meserow testified that he could not ascertain whether the fetus was already injured, or quantify the degree of risk to the fetus from continuing the pregnancy. He indicated that a fetus has some coping mechanisms to deal with decreased oxygen, and that those mechanisms appeared to be functioning. In his expert opinion, the likelihood of injury to the fetus increased on a daily basis, and the chances that the fetus would survive a natural labor were close to zero. On cross-examination, Meserow further testified about the specific medical procedures involved in a cesarean section, and the serious risks and possible side effects to Doe of such procedures. Although he recommended a cesarean section as the safest mode of delivery for the fetus, Meserow was not advocating that the cesarean section be performed over Doe's objection.

Counsel for Doe and her husband called no witnesses, but entered into a stipulation with the State which was accepted by the court: Doe received the recommendation from the physicians, understood the risks and benefits of the proposed procedures and, in consultation with her husband, decided to await natural childbirth.

On December 11, 1993, the court heard closing arguments and then denied the State's petition....

... This court ... affirmed the judgment of the circuit court. In so doing, this court reserved the right to issue an opinion at some future date.

The Public Guardian petitioned the Illinois Supreme Court for leave to appeal. On December 16, 1993, the supreme court denied the petition.... The Supreme Court subsequently denied certiorari. 510 U.S. 1168 (1994).

Doe vaginally delivered an apparently normal and healthy, although somewhat underweight, baby boy on December 29, 1993. The ACLU has since petitioned for the issuance of a written opinion, pointing out that the issue involved is serious and that the situation is likely to arise again, with little time for a circuit court to make an informed judgment. Cognizant of the seriousness of the question presented, and believing that the circuit courts of Illinois require some guidance in this area, this court issues the present opinion.

. . .

It cannot be doubted that a competent person has the right to refuse medical treatment. The Illinois Supreme Court summed up American attitude and law on this issue very well in *In re Estate of Longeway*: "No right is more sacred, or is more carefully guarded by the common law, than the right of every individual to the possession and control of [the individual's] own person, free from all restraint or interference of others, unless by clear and unquestionable authority of law." (In re Estate of Longeway (1989), 133 Ill.2d 33, 44, quoting Union Pacific Ry. Co. v. Botsford (1891), 141 U.S. 250, 251.) Thus, "[e]very human being of adult years and sound mind has a right to determine what shall be done with his [or her] own body; and a surgeon who performs an operation without his [or her] patient's consent commits an assault for which he [or she] is liable in damages." *Longeway,* 133 Ill.2d at 44 (quoting Schloendorff v. Society of New York Hospital (1914), 211 N.Y. 125, 129–30, 105 N.E. 92, 93).

In Illinois the common law protects the right of a competent individual to refuse medical treatment. Moreover, the right "to withhold consent and refuse treatment incorporates all types of medical treatment, including life saving or life sustaining procedures," demonstrating that the right to refuse treatment does not depend upon whether the treatment is perceived as risky or beneficial to the individual. *Longeway,* 133 Ill.2d at 45.

. . .

The Illinois Supreme Court has acknowledged that the state right of privacy protects substantive fundamental rights, such as the right to reproductive autonomy. Further, the court has conceptually linked the right to privacy with the right of bodily integrity. In Stallman v. Youngquist (1988), 125 Ill.2d 267, 275, the supreme court refused to recognize a tort action against a mother for unintentional infliction of prenatal injuries because it would subject the woman's every act while pregnant to state scrutiny, thereby intruding upon her rights to privacy and bodily integrity, and her right to control her own life.

Religious liberty, protected by both federal and Illinois constitutions, similarly requires that a competent adult may refuse medical treatment on religious grounds. In In re Estate of Brooks (1965), 32 Ill.2d 361, 205 N.E.2d 435, the Illinois Supreme Court held that an adult may refuse medical treatment on religious grounds even under circumstances where treatment is required to save the patient's life....

Particularly important to our supreme court's holding in *Stallman* was the recognition that the relationship between a pregnant woman and a fetus is unique, and

> "unlike the relationship between any other plaintiff and defendant. No other plaintiff depends exclusively on any other defendant for everything necessary for life itself. No other defendant must go through biological changes of the most profound type, possibly at the risk of her own life, in order to bring forth an adversary into the world. It is, after all, the whole life of the pregnant woman which impacts upon the development of the fetus.... [I]t is the mother's every waking and sleeping moment which, for better or worse, shapes the prenatal environment which forms the world for the developing fetus. That this is so is not a pregnant woman's fault; it is a fact of life." *Stallman,* 125 Ill.2d at 278–79, 531 N.E.2d 355.

Appreciating the fact that "the circumstances in which each individual woman brings forth life are as varied as the circumstances of each woman's life," the court strongly suggested that there can be no consistent and objective legal standard by which to judge a woman's actions during pregnancy. *Stallman,* 125 Ill.2d at 279, 531 N.E.2d 355.

Applied in the context of compelled medical treatment of pregnant women, the rationale of *Stallman* directs that a woman's right to refuse invasive medical treatment, derived from her rights to privacy, bodily integrity, and religious liberty, is not diminished during pregnancy. The woman retains the same right to refuse invasive treatment, even of lifesaving or other beneficial nature, that she can exercise when she is not pregnant. The potential impact upon the fetus is not legally relevant; to the contrary, the *Stallman* court explicitly rejected the view that the woman's rights can be subordinated to fetal rights. *Stallman,* 125 Ill.2d at 276, 531 N.E.2d 355.

In Illinois a fetus is not treated as only a part of its mother. It has the legal right to begin life with a sound mind and body, assertable against third parties after it has been born alive. This right is not assertable against its mother, however, for the unintentional infliction of prenatal injuries. (*Stallman,* 125 Ill.2d at 280, 531 N.E.2d 355.) A woman is under no duty to guarantee the mental and physical health of her child at birth, and thus cannot be compelled to do or not do anything merely for the benefit of her unborn child. The Public Guardian's argument that this case is distinguishable from *Stallman* because Doe's actions amounted to *intentional* infliction of prenatal injuries is not persuasive.

The court of appeals for the District of Columbia has held that a woman's competent choice regarding medical treatment of her pregnancy must be honored, even under circumstances where the choice may be fatal to the fetus....

Two courts have held otherwise, ordering forced cesarean sections against pregnant women. The Supreme Court of Georgia, in Jefferson v. Griffin Spalding County Hospital Authority (1981), 247 Ga. 86, 274 S.E.2d 457, balanced the rights of the viable fetus against the rights of the mother, and determined that an expectant mother in the last weeks of pregnancy lacks the right of other persons to refuse surgery or other medical treatment if the life of the unborn child is at stake. The Superior Court of the District of Columbia followed the same logic and came to the same conclusion in In re Madyun (D.C.Super.Ct. July 26, 1986), 114 Daily Wash.L.Rptr. 2233, Appendix to In re A.C., 573 A.2d at 1259.

Those decisions, however, are contrary to the rationale of both *Stallman,* the controlling law in this jurisdiction, and *In re A.C.,* [573 A.2d 1255 (D.C. 1990)], which hold that the rights of the fetus should not be balanced against the rights of the mother. Additionally, neither the *Jefferson* nor the *Madyun* court recognized the constitutional dimension of the woman's right to refuse treatment, or the magnitude of that right. The Supreme Judicial Court of Massachusetts, in Taft v. Taft (1983), 388 Mass. 331, 446 N.E.2d 395, when faced with a similar circumstance, vacated a lower court's order compelling a surgical procedure upon a pregnant woman because the lower court failed to recognize the woman's constitutional right to privacy, and the record did not present circumstances so compelling as to override the right to religious freedom for pregnant Jehovah's Witnesses.

The Public Guardian's reliance on Raleigh Fitkin–Paul Morgan Memorial Hospital v. Anderson (1964), 42 N.J. 421, 201 A.2d 537, cert. denied (1964), 377 U.S. 985, is also misplaced. In that case, the Supreme Court of New Jersey held that the unborn child of a woman who did not wish to have blood transfusions because they were against her religious convictions as a Jehovah's Witness was entitled to the law's protection, and an order was entered to ensure a transfusion in the event that the physician in charge determined that one was necessary to save the woman's life or the life of the child. This and other similar blood transfusion cases are inapposite, because they involve a relatively noninvasive and risk-free procedure, as opposed to the massively invasive, risky, and painful cesarean section. Whether such non-invasive procedures are permissible in Illinois, we leave for another case.

Federal constitutional principles prohibiting the balancing of fetal rights against maternal health further bolster a woman's right to refuse a cesarean section. In Thornburgh v. American College of Obstetricians and Gynecologists (1986), 476 U.S. 747, the United States Supreme Court struck down a Pennsylvania statute which required that in cases of post-viability abortions, permitted under state law only when necessary to save the woman's life or health, a physician must use the abortion technique providing the best opportunity for the fetus to be aborted alive. The Supreme Court, finding the statute unconstitutional for requiring a "trade-off" between the woman's health and fetal survival, stressed that the woman's health is always the paramount consideration; any degree of increased risk to the woman's health is unacceptable. *Thornburgh,* 476 U.S. at 769.

A cesarean section, by its nature, presents some additional risks to the woman's health. When the procedure is recommended solely for the benefit of the fetus, the additional risk is particularly evident. It is impossible to say that compelling a cesarean section upon a pregnant woman does not subject her to additional risks—even the circuit court's findings of fact in this case indicate increased risk to Doe. Under *Thornburgh,* then, it appears that a forced cesarean section, undertaken for the benefit of the fetus, cannot pass constitutional muster.

Courts in Illinois and elsewhere have consistently refused to force one person to undergo medical procedures for the purpose of benefiting another person—even where the two persons share a blood relationship, and even where the risk to the first person is perceived to be minimal and the benefit to the second person may be great. The Illinois Supreme Court addressed this issue in Curran v. Bosze (1990), 141 Ill.2d 473, 153 Ill.Dec. 213, 566 N.E.2d 1319, where it refused to compel twin minors to donate bone marrow to a half-sibling, despite the fact that the procedures involved would pose little risk to the twins, and the sibling's life depended on the transplant. Nor would the court compel the minors to undergo even a blood test for the purpose of determining whether they would be compatible donors. If a sibling cannot be forced to donate bone marrow to save a sibling's life, if an incompetent brother cannot be forced to donate a kidney to save the life of his dying sister (In re Pescinski (1975), 67 Wis.2d 4, 226 N.W.2d 180), then surely a mother cannot be forced to undergo a cesarean section to benefit her viable fetus.

The Public Guardian argues that Roe v. Wade (1973), 410 U.S. 113, 163, seems to imply that a viable fetus does have some rights. *Roe,* however, merely stated that, in the context of abortion, the state's interest in the potential life of the fetus becomes compelling at the point of viability, and therefore the state is permitted to prohibit post-viability abortions, except where necessary to preserve the life or health of the woman. The fact that the state may prohibit post-viability pregnancy terminations does not translate into the proposition that the state may intrude upon the woman's right to remain free from unwanted physical invasion of her person when she chooses to carry her pregnancy to term. *Roe* and its progeny, in particular Planned Parenthood of Southeastern Pennsylvania v. Casey (1992), 505 U.S. 833, make it clear that, even in the context of abortion, the state's compelling interest in the potential life of the fetus is insufficient to override the woman's interest in preserving her health.

Courts generally consider four state interests—the preservation of life, the prevention of suicide, the protection of third parties, and the ethical integrity of the medical profession—in considering whether to override competent treatment decisions. None of those state interests justifies overriding Doe's decision here.

The first two interests—the preservation of life and the prevention of suicide—are simply irrelevant here. Although it might be argued that the State has an interest in the preservation of the potential life of the fetus, courts have traditionally examined the refusal of treatment as it impacts upon the preservation of the life of the maker of the decision. The proposed cesarean section was never suggested as necessary, or even useful, to the preservation of Doe's life or health. To the contrary, it would pose greater risk to her. Further, even in cases where the rejected treatment is clearly necessary to sustain life, these factors alone are not sufficiently compelling to outweigh an individual's right to refuse treatment.

Similarly, the third interest—the protection of third parties—is also irrelevant here. The "third parties" referred to in this context are the family members, particularly the children, of the person refusing treatment. Where an individual's decision to refuse treatment will result in orphaning an already-born child, courts have indicated that this is one factor they might consider. At least one court has hinted that, although it would not permit the overriding of a Jehovah's Witness's competent decision to refuse a possibly required blood transfusion subsequent to an accepted cesarean section because the fetus would not be at risk, it might override such a competent decision if it was medically determined that the fetus would be at risk before birth because of the refusal. (Mercy Hospital, Inc. v. Jackson (1985), 62 Md.App. 409, 489 A.2d 1130, vacated (1986), 306 Md. 556, 510 A.2d 562.) Such was also the approach taken in New Jersey in *Anderson,* but, as discussed above, a court's decision regarding a forced transfusion cannot be persuasive in a case involving a forced cesarean section.

The final factor—the ethical integrity of the medical profession—weighs in Doe's favor, rather than that of the State or the Public Guardian. In the ethical opinions and recommendations it has issued, the medical profession strongly supports upholding the pregnant woman's autonomy in medical decision-making. See, e.g., Legal Interventions During Pregnancy: Court Ordered Medical Treatments and Legal Penalties for Potentially Harmful

Behavior by Pregnant Women, 264 J.A.M.A. 2663, 2670 (1990) (cited by Doe, who included a copy in her brief). The American Medical Association's Board of Trustees cautions that the physician's duty is not to dictate the pregnant woman's decision, but to ensure that she is provided with the appropriate information to make an informed decision. If the woman rejects the doctor's recommendation, the appropriate response is not to attempt to force the recommended procedure upon her, but to urge her to seek consultation and counseling from a variety of sources. In this case, then, the actions taken by the medical professionals appear to be inconsistent with the ethical position taken by the profession.

Of not insignificant concern in this case is how a forced cesarean section would be carried out. The Public Guardian specifically opposed any effort to use force or other means to compel Doe to have the surgery; the State also opposed the use of force. Thus, we have been asked to issue an order that no one expects to be carried out. This court, as a simple matter of policy, will not enter an order that is not intended to be enforced.

If such an order were to be carried out, what would be the circumstances? The *In re A.C.* court considered such a question, and concluded that

> "Enforcement could be accomplished only through physical force or its equivalent. A.C. would have to be fastened with restraints to the operating table, or perhaps rendered unconscious by forcibly injecting her with an anesthetic, and then subjected to unwanted major surgery. Such actions would surely give one pause in a civilized society, especially when A.C. had done no wrong." In re A.C., 573 A.2d at 1244, n. 8.

An even more graphic description of what actually happened when a forced cesarean section was carried out may be found in Gallagher, Prenatal Invasions & Interventions: What's Wrong With Fetal Rights, 10 Harvard Women's L.J. 9, 9–10 (1987). We simply cannot envision issuing an order that, if enforced at all, could be enforced only in this fashion.

For all the reasons given above, we affirm the decision of the circuit court.

Affirmed.

NOTE

In In re Fetus Brown v. Darlene Brown, 294 Ill.App.3d 159, 228 Ill.Dec. 525, 689 N.E.2d 397 (1997), the Illinois Appellate Court overturned a lower court decision that had granted temporary custody of a fetus to a court-appointed guardian in order to require the baby's mother to receive a blood transfusion. She had previously refused the transfusion, although doctors had told her that without the transfusion, she and the baby only had a five percent chance of survival. The circuit court appointed a guardian and ordered the mother to have the transfusion. She had to be restrained, but the transfusion was performed and she gave birth to a healthy baby. The Appellate Court heard the case as a matter of unresolved public policy and determined that the lower court's actions were inappropriate. The Court wrote:

> Illinois public policy values the sanctity of life. In re E.G., 133 Ill.2d at 110, 549 N.E.2d at 327. Along with the State's interest in preservation of life, however, must be considered the State's interest in protecting the autonomy of the individual. "The State rarely acts to protect individuals from themselves.... This is consistent with the primary function of the State to preserve and promote liberty and the personal autonomy of the individual."

294 Ill.App.3d 159, 228 Ill.Dec. 525, 689 N.E.2d 397 (1997). See generally, M. Todd Parker, Comment: The Changing of the Guard: The Propriety of Appointing

Guardians for Fetuses. But see Pemberton v. Tallahassee Memorial Regional Medical Center, Inc., 66 F.Supp.2d 1247 (N.D.Fla.1999) (The District Court upheld a lower court decision that forced a woman to have a caesarean against her will, finding that the woman's constitutional rights did not outweigh the state's interests in preserving the life of the unborn child).

State v. McKnight

Supreme Court of South Carolina, 2003.
352 S.C. 635, 576 S.E.2d 168.

■ WALLER, J.

Appellant, Regina McKnight was convicted of homicide by child abuse; she was sentenced to twenty years, suspended upon service of twelve years. We affirm.

On May 15, 1999, McKnight gave birth to a stillborn five-pound baby girl. The baby's gestational age was estimated to be between 34–37 weeks old. An autopsy revealed the presence of benzoylecgonine, a substance which is metabolized by cocaine. The pathologist, Dr. Proctor, testified that the only way for the infant to have the substance present was through cocaine, and that the cocaine had to have come from the mother. Dr. Proctor testified that the baby died one to three days prior to delivery. Dr. Proctor determined the cause of death to be intrauterine fetal demise with mild chorioamnionitis, funisitis and cocaine consumption. He ruled the death a homicide. McKnight was indicted for homicide by child abuse. A first trial ... resulted in a mistrial. At the second trial held May 14–16, 2001, the jury returned a guilty verdict. McKnight was sentenced to twenty years, suspended to service of twelve years....

McKnight asserts the trial court erred in refusing to direct a verdict for her on the grounds that ... there was no evidence of criminal intent.... We disagree. ...

. . .

Under S.C. Code Ann. § 16–3–85(A), a person is guilty of homicide by child abuse if the person "causes the death of a child under the age of eleven while committing child abuse or neglect, and the death occurs under circumstances manifesting an extreme indifference to human life." McKnight claims there is no evidence she acted with extreme indifference to human life as there was no evidence of how likely cocaine is to cause stillbirth, or that she knew the risk that her use of cocaine could result in the stillbirth of her child.

Recently, in State v. Jarrell, 350 S.C. 90, 97, 564 S.E.2d 362, 366 (Ct. App. 2002), the Court of Appeals defined "extreme indifference," as used in the homicide by child abuse statute, stating:

> In this state, indifference in the context of criminal statutes has been compared to the conscious act of disregarding a risk which a person's conduct has created, or a failure to exercise ordinary or due care.... At least one other jurisdiction with a similar statute has found that "[a] person acts 'under circumstances manifesting extreme indifference to the value of human life.' Therefore, we ... hold that in the context of homicide by abuse statutes, extreme indifference is a mental state akin to intent characterized by a deliberate act culminating in death.

Similarly, in reckless homicide cases, we have held that reckless disregard for the safety of others signifies an indifference to the consequences of one's acts. It denotes a conscious failure to exercise due care or ordinary care or a conscious indifference to the rights and safety of others or a reckless disregard thereof.

In Whitner v. State, 492 S.E.2d 777, 782 (1997), cert. denied 523 U.S. 1145 (1998), this Court noted that "although the precise effects of maternal crack use during pregnancy are somewhat unclear, it is well documented and within the realm of public knowledge that such use can cause serious harm to the viable unborn child." Given this common knowledge, Whitner was on notice that her conduct in utilizing cocaine during pregnancy constituted child endangerment....

Here, it is undisputed that McKnight took cocaine on numerous occasions while she was pregnant, that the urine sample taken immediately after she gave birth had very high concentrations of cocaine, and that the baby had benzoylecgonine in its system. The DSS investigator who interviewed McKnight shortly after the birth testified that McKnight admitted she knew she was pregnant and that she had been using cocaine when she could get it, primarily on weekends. Given the fact that it is public knowledge that usage of cocaine is potentially fatal, we find the fact that McKnight took cocaine knowing she was pregnant was sufficient evidence to submit to the jury on whether she acted with extreme indifference to her child's life. Accordingly, the trial court correctly refused a directed verdict.

McKnight next asserts the trial court erred in refusing to dismiss the homicide by child abuse indictment on the grounds that ... b) the homicide by child abuse statute does not apply to the facts of this case and c) the legislature did not intend the statute to apply to fetuses. We disagree....

. . .

McKnight asserts the term "child," as used in the statute, is most naturally read as including only children already born.... In several cases this Court has specifically held that the Legislature's use of the term "child" includes a viable fetus.... [G]iven the language of the statute, and this Court's prior opinions defining a child to include a viable fetus, we find the plain language of the statute does not preclude its application to the present case.

McKnight lastly asserts that the legislative history of [the statute] conclusively demonstrates that it does not apply to unborn children. We find this contention unpersuasive....

There is a presumption that the legislature has knowledge of previous legislation as well as of judicial decisions construing that legislation when later statutes are enacted concerning related subjects. The homicide by child abuse statute was amended in May 2000, some three years after this Court, in Whitner, had specifically held that the term "child" includes a viable fetus. The fact that the legislature was well aware of this Court's opinion in Whitner, yet failed to omit "viable fetus" from the statute's applicability, is persuasive evidence that the legislature did not intend to exempt fetuses from the statute's operation.[5]

5. We granted McKnight's motion to argue against the precedent of Whitner v. State, supra. We adhere to our opinion in Whitner. As did Whitner, McKnight forebodes a "parade of horribles" and points to commentators who object to the prosecution of pregnant women as being contrary to public policy and deterring women from seeking appropriate

... McKnight's conviction and sentence are affirmed.

■ MOORE, J., dissenting.

Once again, I must part company with the majority for condoning the prosecution of a pregnant woman under a statute that could not have been intended for such a purpose. Our abortion statute carries a maximum punishment of two years or a $1,000 fine for the intentional killing of a viable fetus by its mother. In penalizing this conduct, the legislature recognized the unique situation of a feticide by the mother. I do not believe the legislature intended to allow the prosecution of a pregnant woman for homicide by child abuse[,] which provides a disproportionately greater punishment of twenty years to life.

As expressed in my dissent in Whitner v. State, it is for the legislature to determine whether to penalize a pregnant woman's abuse of her own body because of the potential harm to her fetus. It is not the business of this Court to expand the application of a criminal statute to conduct not clearly within its ambit. To the contrary, we are constrained to strictly construe penal statutes in the defendant's favor.

NOTES

1. In Ferguson v. City of Charleston, 532 U.S. 67 (2001), the Supreme Court struck down a state program in South Carolina that used urine samples from pregnant mothers at hospitals for prenatal care to determine if the mothers were using drugs. The results were then given to the police. The Supreme Court determined that the program as designed was an unconstitutional search under the Fourth Amendment, citing in particular the nonconsensual nature of the search as well as the collusion between the hospital and the law enforcement. In his concurrence, Justice Kennedy stated:

> [W]e must accept the premise that the medical profession can adopt acceptable criteria for testing expectant mothers for cocaine use in order to provide prompt and effective counseling to the mother and to take proper medical steps to protect the child. If prosecuting authorities then adopt legitimate procedures to discover this information and prosecution follows, that ought not to invalidate the testing. One of the ironies of the case, then, may be that the program now under review, which gives the cocaine user a second and third chance, might be replaced by some more rigorous system.

2. By 2005, thirty-two states permitted wrongful death actions on the behalf of a viable fetus. See,e.g., Commonwealth v. Morris, 142 S.W.3d 654 (Ky. 2004), Florence v. Town of Plainfield, 48 Conn.Supp. 440, 849 A.2d 7 (2004) and Aka v. Jefferson, 344 Ark. 627, 42 S.W.3d 508 (2001). Fewer states are willing to extend child abuse statutes to protect fetuses. See Wisconsin ex rel. Angela M.W. v. Kruzicki, 209 Wis.2d 112, 561 N.W.2d 729 (1997) and In Matter of J.B.C. v. State, 18 P.3d 342 (Okla. 2001) (the Legislative intent was to protect children, not viable fetuses.)

medical care and/or creating incentives for women to seek abortions to avoid prosecution.

However, not all of the commentaries concerning Whitner have been critical. As noted by [one commentator], although the threat of abortion or lack of prenatal care is real, "the burden placed on pregnant substance abusers is not the burden to get an abortion. Rather, the burden is on the woman to stop using illegal drugs once she has exercised her constitutional decision not to have an abortion.... Once the mother has made the choice to have a child, she must accept the consequences of that choice. One of the consequences of having children is that it creates certain duties and obligations to that child. If a woman does not fulfill those obligations, then the state must step in to prevent harm to the child." Janssen, Fetal Rights and the Prosecution of Women For Using Drugs During Pregnancy, 48 Drake L. Rev. 741 (2000).

3. Consider Ariela R. Dubler, Note: Monitoring Motherhood, 106 Yale L. J. 935, 937 (1996):

> Far from protecting fetuses, ... prosecutions such as Whitner's may actually be harmful to fetal health. Faced with the prospect of criminal liability, for example, many drug-using women will simply avoid prenatal care for fear of detection. Others might chose to abort rather than risk imprisonment.

See generally Schuyler Frautschi, Understanding the Public Health Policies Behind Ferguson, 27 N.Y.U. Rev. L. & Soc. Change 587 (2001–2002); Samantha Weyrauch, Inside the Womb: Interpreting the *Ferguson* Case, 9 Duke J. Gender L. & Pol'y 81 (2002); and Josephine Gittler, The American Drug War, Maternal Substance Abuse and Child Protection: A Commentary, 7 J. Gender Race & Just. 237 (2003).

C. INVOLUNTARY LIMITS ON REPRODUCTION

1. DIRECT RESTRICTIONS

Buck v. Bell

Supreme Court of the United States, 1927.
274 U.S. 200, 47 S.Ct. 584, 71 L.Ed. 1000.

■ HOLMES, J.

This is a writ of error to review a judgment of the Supreme Court of Appeals of the State of Virginia, affirming a judgment of the Circuit Court of Amherst County, by which ... the superintendent of the State Colony for Epileptics and Feeble Minded, was ordered to perform the operation of salpingectomy upon Carrie Buck, the plaintiff, ... for the purpose of making her sterile. ...

Carrie Buck is a feeble minded white woman who was committed to the State Colony above mentioned in due form. She is the daughter of a feeble minded mother in the same institution, and the mother of an illegitimate feeble minded child. She was eighteen years old at the time of the trial of her case in the Circuit Court, in the latter part of 1924. An Act of Virginia, approved March 20, 1924, recites that the health of the patient and the welfare of society may be promoted in certain cases by the sterilization of mental defectives, under careful safeguard, etc.; that the sterilization may be effected in males by vasectomy and in females by salpingectomy, without serious pain or substantial danger to life; that the Commonwealth is supporting in various institutions many defective persons who if now discharged would become a menace but if incapable of procreating might be discharged with safety and become self-supporting with benefit to themselves and to society; and that experience has shown that heredity plays an important part in the transmission of insanity, imbecility, etc. The statute then enacts that whenever the superintendent of certain institutions including the above named State Colony shall be of opinion that it is for the best interests of the patients and of society that an inmate under his care should be sexually sterilized, he may have the operation performed upon any patient afflicted with hereditary forms of insanity, imbecility, etc., on complying with the very careful provisions by which the act protects the patients from possible abuse.

The superintendent first presents a petition to the special board of directors of his hospital or colony, stating the facts and the grounds for his opinion, verified by affidavit. Notice of the petition and of the time and place of the hearing in the institution is to be served upon the inmate and also upon his guardian, and if there is no guardian the superintendent is to apply to the Circuit Court of the County to appoint one. If the inmate is a minor notice also is to be given to his parents if any with a copy of the petition. The board is to see to it that the inmate may attend the hearings if desired by him or his guardian. The evidence is all to be reduced to writing, and after the board has made its order for or against the operation, the superintendent, or the inmate, or his guardian, may appeal to the Circuit Court of the County. The Circuit Court may consider the record of the board and the evidence before it and such other admissible evidence as may be offered, and may affirm, revise, or reverse the order of the board and enter such order as it deems just. Finally any party may apply to the Supreme Court of Appeals, which, if it grants the appeal, is to hear the case upon the record of the trial in the Circuit Court and may enter such order as it thinks the Circuit Court should have entered. There can be no doubt that so far as procedure is concerned the rights of the patient are most carefully considered, and as every step in this case was taken in scrupulous compliance with the statute and after months of observation, there is no doubt that in that respect the plaintiff in error has had due process of law.

The attack is not upon the procedure but upon the substantive law. It seems to be contended that in no circumstances could such an order be justified. It certainly is contended that the order cannot be justified upon the existing grounds. The judgment finds the facts that have been recited and that Carrie Buck "is the probable potential parent of socially inadequate offspring, likewise afflicted, that she may be sexually sterilized without detriment to her general health and that her welfare and that of society will be promoted by her sterilization," and thereupon makes the order. In view of the general declarations of the legislature and the specific findings of the Court, obviously we cannot say as matter of law that the grounds do not exist, and if they exist they justify the result. We have seen more than once that the public welfare may call upon the best citizens for their lives. It would be strange if it could not call upon those who already sap the strength of the State for these lesser sacrifices, often not felt to be such by those concerned, in order to prevent our being swamped with incompetence. It is better for all the world, if instead of waiting to execute degenerate offspring for crime, or to let them starve for their imbecility, society can prevent those who are manifestly unfit from continuing their kind. The principle that sustains compulsory vaccination is broad enough to cover cutting the Fallopian tubes. Three generations of imbeciles are enough.

But, it is said, however it might be if this reasoning were applied generally, it fails when it is confined to the small number who are in the institutions named and is not applied to the multitudes outside. It is the usual last resort of constitutional arguments to point out shortcomings of this sort. But the answer is that the law does all that is needed when it does all that it can, indicates a policy, applies it to all within the lines, and seeks to bring within the lines all similarly situated so far and so fast as its means allow. Of course so far as the operations enable those who otherwise must be kept confined to be returned to the world, and thus open the asylum to others, the equality aimed at will be more nearly reached.

Judgment affirmed.

NOTES

1. Despite Mr. Justice Holmes' assertion in *Buck* that "three generations of imbeciles are enough," there is evidence to suggest that Carrie Buck, her sister Doris, and her daughter Vivian, who was only one month old at the time she was appraised as "mentally defective" by a nurse, were all within the normal range for intelligence. Dr. Roy Nelson, Director of the Lynchburg Hospital, which conducted many sterilization procedures, tracked both Carrie and Doris and discovered that neither would have been considered retarded by contemporary standards. Sandra G. Boodman & Glenn Frankel, Over 7500 Sterilized by Virginia, Wash. Post, Feb. 23, 1980, at A1. Carrie was reportedly an avid reader and lived a full life. *See* Gostin et al., Law, Science, and Medicine 1162 (2005). Vivian died at the age of 7 but was considered a "bright child" by her second grade teachers. Ben Franklin, Sterilization of Teen–Age Woman Haunting Virginia Decades Later, N.Y. Times, March 7, 1980 at A16. For more information on the Buck family history, see Paul Lombardo, Three Generations, No Imbeciles: New Light on Buck v. Bell, 60 N.Y.U.L.REV. 44 (1985).

Consider Alfred Freedman, et al., Modern Synopsis of the Comprehensive Textbook of Psychiatry 312–313 (1972):

> It is estimated that 3 per cent of the U.S. population is mentally retarded, but no precise figures are available. In the preschool years, only about 1 per cent of the population is diagnosed as mentally retarded, since only the severe forms of this disorder are recognized on routine examination. The highest incidence is found in school age children, with the peak at ages 10 to 14, reflecting the close supervision and continuous evaluation of the children's intellectual and social performance in a school setting. The figures drop abruptly after school age, when most of those who were identified as mentally retarded blend into the general population. . . .
>
> The prevailing cultural norms, against which a person is judged on the basis of his performance, rather than his neuropathology may be decisive in defining the degree of social inadequacy: that is, the inability to learn and to adapt to the demands of a society and to be self-sufficient. Thus, persons classified as mentally retarded in our technological, complex society might have been competent and successful in a more primitive and intellectually less demanding environment.

2. In Skinner v. Oklahoma, 316 U.S. 535 (1942), the Supreme Court held unconstitutional a statute that authorized the involuntary sterilization of certain, rather arbitrary, categories of repeat criminals. The Court noted at 541:

> We are dealing here with legislation which involves one of the basic civil rights of man. Marriage and procreation are fundamental to the very existence and survival of the race. The power to sterilize, if exercised, may have subtle, far-reaching and devastating effects. In evil or reckless hands it can cause races or types which are inimical to the dominant group to wither and disappear. There is no redemption for the individual whom the law touches. Any experiment which the State conducts is to his irreparable injury. He is forever deprived of a basic liberty.

How viable is the *Buck* precedent in light of the decision in *Skinner?*

3. It is estimated that more than 70,000 people have been subjected to compulsory sterilization in the United States under statutes similar to the one upheld in Buck v. Bell; the first such statute was passed in Indiana in 1907. Human Betterment Association of America, Summary of United States Sterilization Laws (1957). More than half the states had such legislation by the 1930s. The statutes were made possible by the development in the late nineteenth century of relatively simply surgical techniques for sterilization. For males, vasectomy, a cutting of the vas deferens, was developed to replace the more objectionable process of castration, and for females, salpingectomy, a cutting or tying of the fallopian tubes. The real spur, however, was the growing interest in eugenics, a term coined by Sir Francis Galton, for the study of factors that improve hereditary qualities. Although Galton favored propagation of desirable qualities, or "positive eugenics," many of his contemporaries argued that the improvement of the human race requires the sterilization of defective persons (labeled "negative eugenics"). For a more detailed account of this period, see Phillip R. Reilly, The Surgical Solution: A History of Involuntary Sterilization in the United

States (1991); Daniel Kevles, In the Name of Eugenics: Genetics and the Use of Human Heredity (1985).

4. William T. Vukowich, The Dawning of the Brave New World: Legal, Ethical, and Social Issues of Eugenics, U. Ill. L. F. 189, 198, 199, 222 (1971):

> Certain genetic traits are now identifiable. ... Once traits are identified, however, the problem of selecting the traits to be diminished and propagated remains. ...
>
> In 1935, when Professor Herman Muller was somewhat sympathetic to the cause of Marxism, he listed Lenin and Marx as examples of persons whose genotypes should be propagated. In 1959, after his social views had changed, Muller's list omitted these two and included Einstein, Pasteur, Lincoln and Descartes.
>
> [Although] the state might have the constitutionally required compelling interest to adopt a negative eugenics program, the state's interest in propagating superior qualities is probably not as compelling. A negative eugenics program is designed to diminish suffering and costs occasioned by genetic disease. The goals of positive eugenics are less concrete and less necessary. The disparity of state interest lies in the merit seen in the two programs. The eradication of misery and diminution of illness are clearly good today, but the expansion of intellectual capacity and the development of more robust physiques are not valued as highly. Life can be pleasant and fulfilling without increased intellectual and physical ability, but the suffering, costs, and inconvenience occasioned by genetic diseases often render life unrewarding and unbearable. The difference in state interest in negative and positive eugenics programs may also be explained by the differences in the immediacy of the results of the two programs. Suffering and debility are real, observable phenomena; their diminution has readily comprehendible value. On the other hand, the values of increased intellect and better physique are more difficult to appreciate. Consequently, constitutional doubts face a positive eugenics program which discriminates either against those with superior genetic qualities or against those with inferior and average genetic qualities.

5. An alternative justification for involuntary sterilization statutes is the state's interest in providing children with fit and capable parents. But is it appropriate to conclude that IQ measures the ability to care for children? On this point consider Charles Murdock, Sterilization of the Retarded: A Problem or a Solution, 62 Cal. L.Rev. 917, 928 (1974):

> A program which would use IQ as a basis for determining fitness for parenthood must take into account the imprecision of the testing process and the fact that both functional ability and testing scores can be improved through education and behavior modification. It must consider the possibility of cultural bias in the testing procedure. Moreover, the tests were designed only to measure suitability for placement in an educational program; any correlation to fitness for parenthood would be fortuitous.
>
> There is, however, undoubtedly some relationship between intelligence and fitness for parenthood. For instance, a parent's ability to provide for a child's intellectual growth probably decreases with decreasing IQ. The ability to provide for a child's physical care may be similarly impaired.
>
> These general correlations, however, cannot be pressed too far. Empirical studies have shown that persons with mild or moderate forms of retardation can fulfill the responsibilities of parenthood. If help were needed in particular situations, social agencies might be used to supplement and enrich the home environment so that children of retarded parents could enjoy normal intellectual development. Moreover, persons who are moderately or even severely retarded are often warm and affectionate, and can provide suitable environments for child-raising.

See generally Chapter 10 for discussion of the issue of who is a "fit" parent.

6. May a state adopt means other than sterilization to prevent procreation? Could a state mental institution, for example, include a birth control pill in the daily food intake of all female patients?

Conservatorship of Angela D.

Court of Appeal of California, Fourth Appellate District, Division Two (1999).
70 Cal.App.4th 1410, 83 Cal.Rptr.2d 411.

■ RAMIREZ, P. J.

Angela D., a conservatee, appeals from a probate court order approving the petition filed by respondents Robert D. and Donna D., Angela's parents and coconservators, for an order authorizing the coconservators to give medical consent for Angela's sterilization under Probate Code section 1950 et seq. Angela is a 20-year-old severely developmentally disabled woman, who additionally is subject to epileptic seizures and suffers from diabetes. Following a detailed review of the record, including statements from Angela's doctors, and review of the legislative history and policy of the statutes under which the order was sought, we affirm.

In July 1996, Robert and Donna D. were appointed coconservators of the person and estate of their daughter, Angela. Their letters of conservatorship granted them authority to give consent to medical treatment for Angela, subject to the limitations stated in section 2356. In September 1997, the coconservators filed a petition seeking an order for sterilization of Angela who was then 19 years old. The petition stated that Angela "has been severely mentally retarded since birth; she is autistic, suffers from complex seizure disorders and is diabetic. [Angela] cannot read nor write; she cannot talk, except for speaking simple words like Hello, Goodbye, etc. She cannot mentally determine right from wrong."

The petition went on to state that Angela lived with the coconservators in the family home and that she had never been institutionalized. At that time she was a full-time student in a special education program at Chino High School in San Bernardino County, where she will continue until she is 22 years old. The petition stated that she was under treatment by W. Donald Shields, M.D., of University of California at Los Angeles Children's Hospital, for complex seizure disorders, and by R. Steven Pulverman, D.O., of Chino Medical Group, for diabetes. Angela's estate consisted of public benefits of $590.68 per month, used by the coconservators for Angela's food, clothing, care and medication.

According to the petition, the coconservators had been advised that if Angela were to become pregnant "it would initiate an event of seizures which would result in [her] death, and also the death of the fetus." The coconservators had also been advised that Angela could not be placed on any form of birth control because of the medications she was required to take to control her seizures and her diabetic condition, and that when contraceptive therapy had been tried she had reacted adversely. Attached to the petition were letters from each of Angela's two primary physicians, as well as a letter from a pediatric endocrinologist, detailing the potential risks to Angela of pregnancy, and recommending sterilization.

Also attached was a letter from an obstetrician/gynecologist, Thomas T. Lee, M.D., who had been approached by the coconservators regarding the sterilization surgery. Dr. Lee was recommending a laparoscopic bilateral tubal ligation as the least invasive medical procedure for sterilizing Angela.

This would require a general anesthetic for approximately thirty minutes, would involve tiny incisions, would permit Angela to go home the same day, and would involve minor pain or discomfort for no more than three to five days following the procedure. The coconservators sought to have the procedure performed during Angela's school holidays in December 1997.

At a hearing held October 31, 1997, the court appointed counsel for Angela, and ordered Inland Regional Center to prepare a report pursuant to section 1955. A hearing was scheduled for December 4, 1997.

Counsel who had been appointed by the court to represent Angela filed a report with the court acknowledging his appointment under section 1954, and recognizing his duty under that section to undertake representation with the presumption that Angela opposed the sterilization. However, counsel then enumerated the factors that the coconservators had to establish in order to have the petition granted, and concluded that "Every element necessary to be present can be proved by the [coconservators]," with the one possible exception of the requirement of a showing that Angela was likely to engage in sexual activity. Counsel concluded that "in the absence of continual parental supervision or upon a placement in a residential facility or in school . . . [Angela] could easily engage in sexual activity," and thus "every element required can be proved." Counsel thus elected on behalf of Angela not to oppose the petition.

The required report was submitted by Inland Regional Center to the court on December 4, 1997, as was the report submitted by the court-appointed clinical psychologist who had evaluated Angela on November 18, 1997. The psychologist concluded, "It is my recommendation that the courts strongly consider sterilization in this case." The comprehensive and detailed report prepared by counsel for the Inland Regional Center stated that "Inland Regional Center does not support depriving an individual of any rights or civil liberties, including the right to procreate," but ultimately concluded that the Center "will not object to this Petition for Sterilization."

At the December 4, 1997, hearing, counsel for Angela offered the opinion that even though he was required by statute to presume that his client opposed the petition, "my thought was that if the evidence is overwhelming that it's in her best interest to do it, then I have the authority to say it's in her best interest." The court took the matter under submission.

At the request of the court, counsel for Angela submitted a supplemental report summarizing the special procedure set forth in California Rules of Court, rule 39.8, Appeals in sterilization cases, which provides for automatic appeal of an order authorizing consent to sterilization.

Following the hearing, the court appointed a facilitator, as required by section 1954.5, to try to understand the wishes of Angela and communicate her wishes to the court. In his report, the facilitator stated that he had met with Angela and the coconservators and their respective attorneys, that he had attempted to communicate with Angela, that he had reviewed all the documents, and that "All information available suggests that the sterilization is necessary, and I have found no information to support a conclusion to the contrary." Counsel for Inland Regional Center filed a supplemental report acknowledging review of the psychological evaluation of Angela that had been submitted.

The hearing on the petition was held March 3, 1998. Present were the coconservators and their counsel, counsel for Angela, and the court-appointed facilitator. Angela was not present because she had the flu. There was discussion of section 1956, which requires that the conservatee be present at the hearing "except for reason of medical inability." The court acknowledged that Angela's flu was a temporary illness, but chose to proceed with the hearing on the recommendations of the facilitator, who noted that the court had previously seen Angela and that it was not likely she would participate if she were present, and counsel for Angela who was satisfied that she was medically unable to attend.

Counsel for Angela and for the coconservators had stipulated that the physicians who had submitted the reports to the court would be made available for questioning by telephone at the hearing. Section 1955, subdivision (g), states that "Any person who has written a report received in evidence may be subpoenaed and questioned by any party to the proceedings or by the court and when so called is subject to all rules of evidence including those of legal objections as to the qualifications of expert witnesses." Counsel for Angela acknowledged that he had "very mixed feelings about how to handle the situation," but in view of the fact that these were practicing physicians located in different areas of Southern California, and that the code did not require their presence at the hearing, counsel had settled on the telephone interview procedure. Telephone testimony was from Drs. Shields, Lee, and Pulverman. Angela's father, Robert D., was present and testified.

At the close of the hearing the court issued its ruling, enumerating the elements that were required to be established under section 1958 and concluding that they had been established beyond a reasonable doubt. The court granted the petition, and ordered that the sterilization of Angela was to be accomplished as soon as was practical. The court then issued a stay pending the automatic review by this court. Counsel for Angela submitted a statement of decision, and a formal order was filed May 4, 1998. This appeal, filed on behalf of Angela, followed.

There are no published decisions under section 1950 et seq., the Probate Code chapter dealing with sterilization of those individuals not able to give meaningful consent to the procedure. We therefore will set forth in some detail the showing that is required under the statute, and the evidence that was presented in support of the petition in the present case.

Angela is represented in this appeal by a vigorous advocate who has sought to identify any weakness in the evidence presented, and any failure to comply with the due process requirements of the statute. There are two main arguments made by Angela in this appeal: First, she argues that the evidence is insufficient to support the required findings that she is likely to engage in sexual activity or that supervision is unworkable as an alternative to sterilization; and second, she argues that she was denied equal protection and due process rights when her trial counsel elected not to oppose the petition for sterilization and when the court conducted the trial in Angela's absence, both of which violate specific provisions of the statute.

. . .

The Probate Code chapter on sterilization was enacted in response to the decision of the California Supreme Court in Conservatorship of Valerie N. (1985) 40 Cal. 3d 143 [219 Cal. Rptr. 387, 707 P.2d 760]. At the time that case was decided there was a Probate Code section in place stating that "No ward or conservatee may be sterilized under the provisions of this division." (Former § 2356, subd. (d).) The Supreme Court concluded that by enacting this provision, and contemporaneously repealing Welfare and Institutions

Code section 7254 (establishing procedures for sterilization of patients in state institutions), the Legislature "intended to discontinue the longstanding, but discredited, practice of eugenic sterilization, and to deny guardians and conservators authorization to have the procedure performed on their wards and conservatees."

In *Valerie N.*, however, a majority of the Supreme Court held that "the present statutory scheme denies incompetent developmentally disabled persons rights which are accorded all other persons in violation of state and federal constitutional guarantees of privacy." The court held the statute unconstitutional, but nonetheless affirmed denial of the conservators' petition for authorization to have the sterilization performed in that case because an inadequate showing had been made. The affirmance was "without prejudice to a renewed petition and hearing at which the requisite showing may be made."

Citing the criteria outlined by courts in other jurisdictions, particularly the decision of the Washington Supreme Court in Matter of Guardianship of Hayes (1980) 93 Wn.2d 228 [608 P.2d 635], the California Supreme Court urged the Legislature to "establish criteria and procedural protections governing these applications." . . .

The resulting statutes, which took effect January 1, 1987, and were reenacted without substantive change in 1990, effective July 1, 1991, are at issue in the present case.

The court may authorize the conservator to consent to sterilization only if the court finds that the petitioner has established, *beyond a reasonable doubt*, the existence of the factors set forth in section 1958.[4]

. . .

4. Section 1958 states: "The court may authorize the conservator of a person proposed to be sterilized to consent to the sterilization of that person only if the court finds that the petitioner has established all of the following beyond a reasonable doubt:

"(a) The person named in the petition is incapable of giving consent to sterilization, as defined in Section 1951, and the incapacity is in all likelihood permanent.

"(b) Based on reasonable medical evidence, the individual is fertile and capable of procreation.

"(c) The individual is capable of engaging in, and is likely to engage in sexual activity at the present or in the near future under circumstances likely to result in pregnancy.

"(d) Either of the following:

"(1) The nature and extent of the individual's disability as determined by empirical evidence and not solely on the basis of any standardized test, renders him or her permanently incapable of caring for a child, even with appropriate training and reasonable assistance.

"(2) Due to a medical condition, pregnancy or childbirth would pose a substantially elevated risk to the life of the individual to such a degree that, in the absence of other appropriate methods of contraception, sterilization would be deemed medically necessary for an otherwise nondisabled woman under similar circumstances.

"(e) All less invasive contraceptive methods including supervision are unworkable even with training and assistance, inapplicable, or medically contraindicated. Isolation and segregation shall not be considered as less invasive means of contraception.

"(f) The proposed method of sterilization entails the least invasion of the body of the individual.

"(g) The current state of scientific and medical knowledge does not suggest either (1) that a reversible sterilization procedure or other less drastic contraceptive method will shortly be available, or (2) that science is on the threshold of an advance in the treatment of the individual's disability.

"(h) The person named in the petition has not made a knowing objection to his or her sterilization. For purposes of this

Section 1958, subdivision (c), is the focus of this appeal. . . .

. . . Angela contends that the coconservators failed to establish, under subdivision (c) of section 1958, that Angela "is capable of engaging in, and is likely to engage in sexual activity at the present or in the near future under circumstances likely to result in pregnancy."

Angela does not dispute that the evidence established that she is physically sexually mature. No evidence was presented that Angela was sexually active as of the time of the hearing, and that is not an issue in this appeal. The question is whether there was evidence that she was likely to engage in sexual activity in the future.

The psychological report on Angela stated that Angela is "quite passive and compliant and is highly likely to participate sexually, if asked, due to her low level of intellectual ability and her high level of emotional compliance." On appeal, counsel for Angela acknowledges that Angela is likely to participate in sexual activity if asked, due to her passive nature, but argues that there was no evidence presented to suggest that Angela would be placed in a situation where others would actually take advantage of her passive nature and engage her in sexual activity.

The report prepared by the Inland Regional Center stated that when Angela turns 22 years old, which will happen in June 2000, she will no longer be eligible for continued public education at the high school, but would instead be able to attend a day program. The report went on to state that due to Angela's "potential placement with male consumers attending a day program the parents of [Angela] feel it is in her interest to undergo this sterilization procedure as she is emotionally and medically not capable of rearing a child, and medically is unable to maintain a pregnancy due to the severe nature of her seizure activity." Shedding further light on the potential for sexual activity the report stated that Angela "has lived an extremely sheltered life residing in the parental home, and may not be so sheltered in the future. In the future she will be interacting with peers and persons other than peers in community settings. A review of her case file provides that she has had a history of wandering from a program even under close supervision."

Angela's father testified to his concerns about what will happen when Angela turns 22 and goes into a work program. When asked whether there was a possibility that Angela might be exposed to sexual relations in the future, her father replied, "Well, you know, she's not under our control 24 hours a day." He continued, "I'm rather naive I suppose, but I would like to think that she's protected, but . . . she's with bus drivers and she's at school now and our real concern would be coming forward in the work program where she will be not as supervised as she is today."

Our analysis is complicated by the presence of section 1959, another section in this Chapter, which must be read in conjunction with subdivision (c) of section 1958. Section 1959 states: "The fact that, due to the nature or severity of his or her disability, a person for whom an authorization to

subdivision, an individual may be found to have knowingly objected to his or her sterilization notwithstanding his or her inability to give consent to sterilization as defined in Section 1951. In the case of persons who are nonverbal, have limited verbal ability to communicate, or who rely on alternative modes of communication, the court shall ensure that adequate effort has been made to elicit the actual views of the individual by the facilitator appointed pursuant to Section 1954.5, or by any other person with experience in communicating with developmentally disabled persons who communicate using similar means."

consent to sterilization is sought may be vulnerable to sexual conduct by others that would be deemed unlawful, shall not be considered by the court in determining whether sterilization is to be authorized under this chapter."[5]

As applied to the present case this provision presents a conundrum. Penal Code section 261 states, in relevant part: "(a) Rape is an act of sexual intercourse accomplished with a person not the spouse of the perpetrator . . . : [P] . . . Where a person is incapable, because of a mental disorder or developmental or physical disability, of giving legal consent, and this is known or reasonably should be known to the person committing the act. . . ." The evidence in the present case is that Angela suffers so severely from her disabilities that she would be unable to give legal consent to sexual intercourse, just as she is unable to consent to the sterilization procedure. Under these facts the court was compelled to consider Angela's vulnerability to "sexual conduct by others that would be deemed unlawful" if it was to conclude that she was likely to engage in sexual activity, as it is not clear that Angela could ever engage in sexual activity that would not be deemed unlawful under Penal Code section 261.[6]

The origins of section 1959 are not obvious. The section does not appear in any of the early drafts of the chapter and thus was not available for analysis and comment during the committee process. The Legislature, in enacting the chapter, clearly intended to follow the direction of the California Supreme Court in *Valerie N.* and to enact statutes that would permit sterilization of a conservatee under circumstances that contained the appropriate safeguards. A provision in the chapter that makes it logically impossible for a conservator to make the necessary showing under the chapter is inconsistent with that intent. To the extent the provision thwarts the purpose of the chapter, and thus frustrates compliance with the mandate of *Valerie N.*, it cannot stand.

Moreover, section 1959 suffers from the same infirmity that prompted the court in *Valerie N.* to strike down the statutes prohibiting sterilization of wards or conservatees, namely, that it denies to wards or conservatees the reproductive choices available to individuals who do not suffer from such disabilities. In a case such as the present one, for example, in which there is unrefuted evidence that a pregnancy would very probably cause severe and possibly fatal reactions in Angela due to her existing epileptic and diabetic conditions, and further evidence that Angela's medications might cause severe damage to her fetus during a pregnancy, a woman with the capacity to consent to sterilization would be able to choose that option if she believed that unlawful sexual conduct by others posed a significant threat. Under section 1959, Angela would lack the right to have that same decision made on her behalf.

Although we cannot at present formulate facts under which section 1959 would not undermine the purpose of the statutory scheme, we are reluctant

5. In *In re Wirsing* (1998) 456 Mich. 467 [573 N.W.2d 51, 53], the trial court made a specific finding that "developmentally disabled individuals are frequently the victims of sexual abuse." The Supreme Court of Michigan there held that the probate court had jurisdiction to hear an application by a guardian for authorization to consent to sterilization, and to order such authorization if it determined the procedure was in the best interest of the ward.

6. The issue was discussed in *Estate of C.W.* (1994) 433 Pa.Super. 167 [640 A.2d 427], where the court stated: "In one sense, any sexual intercourse with C.W. would be essentially nonconsensual, since it would appear that she is incompetent to give legally sufficient consent to sexual intercourse. Our reference to voluntary sexual activity is meant to refer to intercourse without force, that is, wherein C.W., for whatever reason, would not attempt to resist." (*Id.*, at p. 434.)

to assert that such facts could not exist. Thus, we limit our holding in the present case to deciding that section 1959 cannot constitutionally be applied to deny Angela's coconservators the authorization to consent to Angela's sterilization.

Even without the limitation imposed by section 1959, however, we must acknowledge that the actual evidence that Angela "is likely to engage in sexual activity" is slim. Nevertheless, in the context of the facts that appear in this case, and the purposes the statute is trying to achieve, we conclude that the evidence of Angela's future sexual activity is sufficient to support the trial court's ruling.

Sufficient evidence to satisfy the statutory requirement on this issue is not an absolute amount, but is instead a legal conclusion. The statute itself, which seeks an evaluation of the likelihood that something will occur in the future, requires a prediction rather than a determination of fact. Here the evidence was that Angela was passive and compliant and that she was "highly likely" to participate sexually if asked to do so. There was also evidence that Angela would be entering a program that had male participants and in which she would be less supervised. There is a very real possibility, under these facts, that Angela would be asked to participate sexually, and a high probability she would participate if asked.

We have enumerated the dangers a pregnancy would hold both to Angela and to her fetus. With such potentially great harm resulting from pregnancy, the required showing of likelihood that Angela would engage in sexual activity resulting in pregnancy is proportionately smaller. We conclude that the coconservators here have made a sufficient showing as to this issue merely by showing a possibility of such activity, and that this element of the statute has been satisfied.

. . .

Our examination of this case has revealed no basis for reversing the decision of the trial court authorizing the coconservators to give consent to sterilization of Angela. We cannot conceive of facts that would be more compelling and proceedings that would have been carried out with more diligence and attention to Angela's interests.

The statutes that we interpret here for the first time are more restrictive than those of other states, and more restrictive even than required by the California Supreme Court in *Valerie N.* The court in *Valerie N.* indicated that the enumerated findings should be established by clear and convincing evidence. This is the standard that has been adopted by several other states as well. In California, however, the Legislature has required evidence beyond a reasonable doubt.

As we evaluate the high hurdle the Legislature has established for ordering authorization under this chapter we should remember the statement of the court in *Valerie N.* that "The state has not asserted an interest in protecting the right of the incompetent to bear children." It is not the state's interest being protected here, but rather the interests of the disabled individual. Thus, while that individual is entitled to vigorous advocacy to assure compliance with the statute, ultimately it is the conservatee who must be served by the statutes. In the present case there was little that could be said in opposition to the petition, and we believe the probate court correctly permitted the coconservators to authorize the procedure. The statute remains to be interpreted under less compelling facts.

The order appealed from is affirmed. Parties to bear their own costs on appeal.

NOTE

In 1973 the Relf sisters of Alabama, age 12 and 14, set off a storm of national publicity when their family revealed that both girls had been sterilized without their consent, or the consent of their parents. See, e.g. Washington Post, June 23, 1973, at 29A. A suit was eventually brought successfully challenging the constitutionality of using federal funds for such sterilizations. See Relf v. Weinberger, 372 F.Supp. 1196 (D.D.C.1974). The district court opinion was overturned on appeal, however, because the challenged federal regulations had been altered in 1974. 565 F.2d 722 (D.C.Cir. 1977).

The current regulations governing federal funds for sterilizations operations prohibit the use of federal funds for the sterilization of institutionalized persons and those declared incompetent by a state or federal court. In addition, the regulations require the informed consent of the patient, that the patient be at least twenty-one years old, and that absent life-threatening emergency, there be at least a thirty-day waiting period (but not more than 180 days) before the physician may perform the procedure. *See* 42 C.F.R. §§ 441.250–441.259 (2005); 42 C.F.R. §§ 50.201–50.210 (2005).

In re Jane A.

Appeals Court of Massachusetts, 1994.
36 Mass.App.Ct. 236, 629 N.E.2d 1337.

■ KASS, J.

Through a petition filed January 28, 1994, for the appointment of a guardian for the ward, the Department of Mental Retardation sought application of the doctrine of substituted judgment for a determination whether Jane, if competent, would choose to terminate her pregnancy by abortion. See Care & Protection of Beth, 412 Mass. 188, 194–195, 587 N.E.2d 1377 (1992); Matter of R.H., 35 Mass. App. Ct. 478, 484–486 (1993). Based on the subsidiary findings of fact of the Probate Court judge who heard the case and our study of the entire record, we decide that Jane would choose to abort her eighteen-and-a-half-week pregnancy. In so doing, we reverse the judgment of the Probate Court judge.[1]

Facts

. . . Jane is a thirty year old woman who, according to the appointed psychologist, has "moderate mental retardation and . . . an adjustment disorder with mixed emotional features." She has an IQ in the mid-fifties and functions mentally at the level of a three to four year old child, although a four year old would have more cognitive energy for problem solving. Dr. Anne Hurley, whom the court had appointed to examine the ward and who met with her three times, illustrated the extent of the ward's disability by remarking that it would take many years to teach the ward to cook an egg. In addition to her mental retardation, the ward since age six has suffered

1. The judge was conscientious in appointing persons who would examine the question from various points of view. He appointed: a temporary guardian with authority concerning medical issues; counsel for Jane; a guardian ad litem "to investigate and report on the substituted judgment question with respect to the abortion"; a guardian ad litem "to oppose a determination that [the ward] if competent, would choose to have an abortion"; and counsel to represent the fetus. See Matter of Moe, 385 Mass. 555, 566–567, 432 N.E.2d 712 (1982). The judge also appointed a psychologist who specialized in the psychiatric aspects of developmental disability to examine and evaluate the ward.

from seizures. Her seizure disorder is alleviated by daily administration of 200 mg. of Tegretol and of Primidone.

The ward's condition is marked by a proclivity to agitated and assaultive behavior. This takes the form of hitting, kicking, scratching, biting, and ripping clothes off. During the course of such eruptions the ward has managed to dislocate a shoulder and wrench the joints of staff members in her special residence who were performing the task of trying to calm her. Generally, such outbursts occur when Jane is frustrated in any way, particularly by a break in her routine, e.g., being prevented when sick with flu from making a customary trip to a doughnut shop. Such was her rage on that occasion that staff required four-point restraint to manage her until she calmed down.

The ward has been in a variety of special care facilities since age sixteen. Since 1986, she has been living in community programs operated by Vinfen Corporation. She resides in an apartment with three other disabled persons, assisted and watched over by around-the-clock staff.[3] Through intensive effort and a very structured program, Vinfen has enabled Jane to make much progress in controlling her aggressive impulses. Such has been the success of the Vinfen program that, within her restricted circumstances, Jane has a pleasurable life which includes trips to local stores, restaurants, a bank, bowling, movies, parks, the public library, museums, and downtown Boston.

As to her pregnancy, the ward does not seem to understand what that condition means. She varyingly acknowledged and denied that there is a "baby inside me" and stated preferences both to "keep the baby inside my belly" and have the "baby stop growing inside my belly." Efforts to determine Jane's preference about having or not having a baby, the judge found, were "fruitless." As well as hearing testimony from Dr. Hurley, the judge conducted an interview of Jane in chambers, with her counsel, a worker from her residence, and a stenographer present.

In the absence of the ward's capability for an expression of preference, see and compare Matter of Moe, 31 Mass. App. Ct. 473, 476–479, 579 N.E.2d 682 (1991), the judge turned to other factors to ascertain the needs and wants of the ward. See Matter of Moe, 385 Mass. at 555, 565–566 (1982). The family offered no guidance regarding, and on her part there was not adherence to—or consciousness of—a religious faith that might offer clues to the ward's inclinations. The temporary guardian, counsel for the ward, and the guardian ad litem for the ward expressed themselves unequivocally that the ward, who had already complained uncomprehendingly of her morning sickness, would not wish to endure the increasing discomforts, pain, and—for her—terror of childbirth. They uniformly urged that the pregnancy be terminated by abortion.

As he approached his ultimate finding, the judge relied principally on the evidence given by Dr. Hurley, whose testimony occupies more than one-third of the transcript of the entire proceedings. Dr. Hurley said that continuing the pregnancy would undo her observed progress that years of intensive behavioral and educational intervention had achieved.[4] Her "very, very strong" opinion was that continuing the pregnancy would be harmful to Jane psychologically. She anticipated an acute and possibly irretrievable

3. Although staff are on duty at all times at the residence, we do not mean to say that Jane is or should be under twenty-four hour surveillance. Obviously, she is not; were she, this case would not have arisen.

4. Dr. Hurley had examined Jane before, in 1985 and 1986.

deterioration in the ward's mental condition were the pregnancy allowed to proceed. Dr. Hurley thought there was nothing positive in going through a pregnancy for this individual. The ward had no tolerance for discomfort and, in the past, had reacted to physical or psychological stress by being violent, throwing herself down, destroying property, and attacking others. An abortion, Dr. Hurley further testified, was also not without risk. The uncomfortable and frightening aspects of that procedure might cause the ward to disintegrate into a psychotic state.

With adverse consequences possible no matter which path was taken, the judge wrote that, "before an invasive procedure is authorized, we cannot presuppose that [the ward], if competent, would disregard the fetus as an important factor in her decision." Accordingly, the judge determined, the ward's "decision, if competent, would be not to consent to an abortion."

It is axiomatic that an appellate court accepts the subsidiary findings of fact of a trial judge unless they are clearly erroneous. To what ultimate legal determination those subsidiary facts add up, however, is a question of law. Here the judge found that Jane expressed no coherent or consistent preferences about her pregnancy and the fetus she is carrying. The judge does not mention any other source of evidence, such as a caretaker, on which to base a conclusion that Jane, if competent, would regard the fetus as an important (or dispositive) factor in her decision. Our canvass of the record turned up no such evidence. Indeed, as we have observed, the temporary guardian for the ward and guardian ad litem for the ward testified that the ward would not understand or tolerate, and would not wish to tolerate, the accelerating physical trials of pregnancy and childbirth.

The judge found that, were the pregnancy to proceed, Jane "would probably become very behaviorally disturbed again" and "would probably act out aggressively against staff and others and in so doing jeopardize her own safety and the well being of the fetus." For purposes of reaching his ultimate conclusion, the judge treats as having equal weight his finding, based on Dr. Hurley's testimony, that Jane would suffer psychological harm if she were to undergo an abortion. When the findings do not justify the ultimate conclusion, an appellate court may examine the record to see if there are elements of uncontested evidence that would assist resolution of the question to be decided. In saying that there was a possibility of adverse consequence from an abortion, Dr. Hurley offered a crucial qualification: the probability of serious and irreversible harm would be "a thousand fold" greater if the ward proceeded with the pregnancy. An abortion, she thought, was susceptible to careful management, which would minimize the trauma to the ward. Following release by the judge of his findings, Dr. Hurley furnished an affidavit in support of a motion for reconsideration[5] stating that if an abortion were performed under general anesthesia, as she had come to understand could be done, the risk of psychological harm to Jane would be greatly reduced.

On the basis of what the judge found and what appears in the record, it follows that the assaults on the ward's fragile mental state from continuation of the pregnancy would be repetitive, for each additional day she is pregnant, and increasing in severity and danger. Normal discomforts of pregnancy such as bladder pressure, an increasingly bulky body,[6] and backache would be felt as unendurable by Jane because she would not fully under-

5. That motion was denied.

6. Historically, Jane had manifested acute anxiety about her physique.

stand their cause or meaning. From what has been found about Jane's reactions to frustration, changes in her diet to conform with wise prenatal practices might be an occasion for violent encounters. Birth labor would be horrifying and dangerous, again because she could not be prepared for what was happening. In comparison to these difficulties, which would be of an accelerating nature, there is the alternative of one occasion of medical intervention, which can be achieved with a minimum of discomfort and the likelihood of much decreased risk to the ward's psychic makeup. By the very nature of her mental impairment, the ward is self-centered and concerned about how she feels physically, but, in exercising judgment on her behalf, we must take her compassionately as we find her. Only in that way can we determine as best we can the ward's wants, needs, and choices. That choice would be to end the pregnancy she did not seek, barely begins to understand, and which will increasingly cause her greater discomfort and pain.

The judgment is reversed. A judgment shall be entered that the temporary guardian may authorize medical intervention to terminate the ward's pregnancy. . . .

People v. Pointer

Court of Appeal, First District, 1984.
151 Cal.App.3d 1128, 199 Cal.Rptr. 357.

■ Kline, Presiding Justice.

Our principal inquiry in this case is whether a woman convicted of the felony of child endangerment (Pen.Code, § 273a, subd. (1)) and found to be in violation of a custody decree (§ 278.5) may, as a condition of probation, be prohibited from conceiving a child. . . .

Appellant, Ruby Pointer, has at all material times been the devoted adherent of a rigorously disciplined macrobiotic diet.[2] She is also the mother of two children, Jamal and Barron, who at the time of trial were, respectively, two and four years of age. Appellant imposed an elaborate macrobiotic regime on both children despite the objections of Barron's father and despite the repeated advice of her physician, Dr. Gilbert Carter, that such diet was inappropriate and unhealthy for young children. Dr. Carter additionally advised appellant that breastfeeding Jamal while she was herself on a macrobiotic diet was hazardous for the infant.

In October 1980, more than a year prior to the trial, Barron's father sought the assistance of Children's Protective Services, a county agency that investigates complaints of child abuse and neglect. Donald Allegri, a social worker with the agency thereupon met with appellant and, after seeing the children, strongly urged her to immediately consult Dr. Lorreta Rao, a pediatrician. Appellant brought Barron to Dr. Rao for examination, but not Jamal. Upon learning that Jamal had not been examined by Dr. Rao, Allegri phoned appellant's regular physician, Dr. Carter, and expressed his deep concern over Jamal's condition.

On November 8, 1980, Dr. Carter spent nearly two hours with appellant and both children. He was shocked when he observed Jamal and stated

2. At trial a macrobiotic diet was described by appellant's physician as follows: "Macrobiotic, as it's usually used, refers to a diet that is pretty much exclusively grains, beans and vegetables, meaning pretty much excluding fruits, deemphasizing salads, deemphasizing or eliminating milk products of all form, yogurt, milk, cheese, cottage cheese and, also, no fish, meat, poultry or eggs. Pretty narrow diet."

"God, Ruby, God, how could you do this? How could you not take care of your baby?" Dr. Carter reiterated the dangers of breastfeeding Jamal while she was on a macrobiotic diet, importuned her to modify her own diet and recommended increased calories and protein for the child. Dr. Carter also urged her to consult Dr. Rao, who, because she was herself a vegetarian, he thought might be able to more strongly influence appellant. Appellant disregarded Dr. Carter's advice and at this time did not consult Dr. Rao.

Two days later Dr. Carter again saw appellant and Jamal and observed that the child remained malnourished and significantly underdeveloped. He again pressed appellant to visit Dr. Rao and she again declined to do so. During a telephone conversation nearly two weeks later, Dr. Carter repeated his warning of the severity of Jamal's condition and urged appellant once more to visit Dr. Rao or, in the alternative, bring the child to a hospital emergency room. Appellant vaguely indicated that she would "take care of things."

When on November 25th appellant finally brought Jamal to Dr. Rao she was informed that the child, who was emaciated, semicomatose, and in a state of shock, was dying and in need of immediate hospitalization. Appellant demurred, telling Dr. Rao that she wanted to consult others and would return later. Appellant resisted hospitalization because she felt Jamal might intravenously be fed "preservatives" and suffer a rash. Dr. Rao thereupon called the police, who arrived in five minutes and ordered Jamal hospitalized at once. As a result of emergency procedures the child's life was saved.

During Jamal's hospitalization, appellant surreptitiously brought him macrobiotic food despite warnings not to do so and continued to breastfeed him even after being told that her milk contained high levels of sodium that endangered the child.

Upon his discharge from the hospital, Jamal was placed in a foster home. While ostensibly visiting him there, appellant abducted the child and fled to Puerto Rico with him and her other son. An agent of the Federal Bureau of Investigation located appellant and the children in a housing project in Rio Piedras, Puerto Rico, on September 29, 1981, and arrested her at that time. The agent testified at trial that appellant's living quarters were rather squalid and that the only foodstuffs he observed were bags of beans, some millet, a few other grains and noodles. After appellant waived her *Miranda* rights, she admitted to the agent that she had abducted Jamal from the foster home. She did so, she stated, because the woman who managed the home fed Jamal eggs and sugar and did not respect his dietary habits. She said Jamal was "getting fat" and that she did not like it.

When the children returned to California it was determined that as a result of diet and maternal neglect Barron was seriously underdeveloped and Jamal had suffered severe growth retardation and permanent neurological damage.

On the facts just briefly described, appellant was found guilty by a jury of violation of Penal Code sections 273a and 278.5. She was thereafter sentenced to five years probation on the conditions that she serve one year in county jail; participate in an appropriate counseling program; not be informed of the permanent whereabouts of Jamal (who was placed in foster care) and have no unsupervised visits with him; have no custody of any children, including her own, without prior court approval; and that she not conceive during the probationary period. Appellant challenges this last condition as an unconstitutional restriction of her fundamental rights to privacy and to procreate.

. . .

The condition of probation prohibiting conception . . . was imposed only after thoughtful consideration by the trial judge, who fully appreciated the extraordinary nature of his action. As he stated at the sentencing hearing, "I have never considered imposing as a condition of probation the requirement that someone not conceive during the period of probation, and I have never considered requiring as a condition of probation that a defendant not have custody of her children without approval by the sentencing court following a hearing, but that's certainly what I intend to do in this case. This is an extremely serious case."

This assessment is supported by the record. The lengthy probation report repeatedly emphasized appellant's denial of responsibility for her actions and inability or unwillingness to alter her conduct, as well as the high likelihood that, if permitted to do so, she would in the future continue to endanger the health and indeed the lives of her children. Though the report expressed the view that appellant's understanding and acceptance of responsibility would not be enhanced by incarceration in prison and did not recommend a state prison term, it did point out that such confinement would at least prevent appellant from "interfering or attempting to interfere in the treatment and special education of her sons and that she will also not become pregnant and endanger another small child in the future."

In this connection, Dr. Barbara O. Murray, a psychologist who examined appellant at the direction of the court, reported that appellant "is extremely reluctant to take any forms of chemicals or medication [and] . . . would not comply with such a requirement if it were imposed. Thus, if required to take birth control pills, for example, it first of all would be extremely difficult to monitor or supervise such a condition, and the likelihood of noncompliance would be inordinately high. Thus, if such an alternative is ultimately considered desirable by the court, it might be more advisable simply to incarcerate her now rather than wait for her to violate probation." Dr. Murray also concluded that "[a]ny new born child to Ms. Pointer would encounter similar risks as those of her previous children." This conclusion is consistent with the views of Dr. Rao, who stated that appellant suffers "an altered state of reality" that can not easily be reformed.

Under [Penal Code section 1203.1] a sentencing court has broad discretion to describe conditions of probation to foster rehabilitation and to protect the public to the end that justice may be done. However, "The discretion granted is not boundless. In the first place, the authority is wholly statutory; the statute furnishes and limits the measure of authority which the court may thus exercise. Secondly, the discretion to impose conditions of probation . . . is further circumscribed by constitutional safeguards. Human liberty is involved."

. . .

At the same time it is recognized that the government may impose conditions of probation which qualify or impinge upon constitutional rights when circumstances inexorably so require.

The validity of the condition of probation with which we are here concerned must first be assessed in terms of its reasonableness. The test of the reasonableness of a condition of probation was in this jurisdiction first prescribed in the landmark case of People v. Dominguez (1967) 256 Cal. App.2d 623, 627, 64 Cal.Rptr. 290:

> A condition of probation will not be held invalid unless it "(1) has no relationship to the crime of which the offender was convicted, (2) relates to conduct which is not in itself criminal, and (3) requires or forbids conduct which is not reasonably related to future criminality". . . .

Applying this test to the facts of the instant case, we conclude that the condition in question is reasonable. Unlike *Dominguez,* where the court found a similar condition invalid because the defendant's future pregnancy was unrelated to the crime of robbery and had no reasonable relation to future criminality, in this unusual case the condition is related to child endangerment, the crime for which appellant was convicted. Although cases in other jurisdictions have concluded that a condition of probation that a defendant not become pregnant has no relation to the crime of child abuse or to future criminality (Rodriguez v. State (1979) Fla.App. 378 So.2d 7; State v. Livingston (1976) 53 Ohio App.2d 195, 372 N.E.2d 1335), those cases relied heavily upon the fact that the abuse could be entirely avoided by removal of any children from the custody of the defendant. This case is distinguishable, however, because of evidence that the harm sought to be prevented by the trial court may occur before birth. Since the record fully supports the trial court's belief that appellant would continue to adhere to a strict macrobiotic diet despite the dangers it presents to any children she might conceive, we cannot say that the condition of probation prohibiting conception is completely unrelated to the crime for which appellant was convicted or to the possibility of future criminality.

Our determination that the condition of probation is reasonably related to the offense of which appellant was convicted and to possible future criminality does not, however, end our inquiry. For where a condition of probation impinges upon the exercise of a fundamental right and is challenged on constitutional grounds we must additionally determine whether the condition is impermissibly overbroad.

There is, of course, no question that the condition imposed in this case infringes the exercise of a fundamental right to privacy protected by both the federal and state constitutions.

Nor is there any question that for this reason the condition must be subjected to special scrutiny to determine whether the restriction is entirely necessary to serve the dual purposes of rehabilitation and public safety.

The challenged condition was apparently not intended to serve any rehabilitative purpose but rather to protect the public by preventing injury to an unborn child. We believe this salutary purpose can adequately be served by alternative restrictions less subversive of appellant's fundamental right to procreate. Such less onerous conditions might include, for example, the requirement that appellant periodically submit to pregnancy testing; and that upon becoming pregnant she be required to follow an intensive prenatal and neonatal treatment program monitored by both the probation officer and by a supervising physician. If appellant bears a child during the period of probation it can be removed from her custody and placed in foster care, as was done with appellant's existing children, if the court then considers such action necessary to protect the infant.

Though at the sentencing hearing the prosecutor claimed that the probation department and the local children's protective services agency lacked the resources for such intensive probation supervision, there is no evidence on this issue before us. Nor does the record or common sense provide any reason to believe it would be any more difficult to determine whether appellant is pregnant for purposes of enforcing prenatal care requirements than it would be to determine whether she is pregnant for purposes of enforcing the condition here challenged. Indeed, in at least one critical respect we believe it would be *less* difficult; and the reason relates to another troublesome aspect of the challenged condition.

Although the trial judge stated at the sentencing hearing that he would not order appellant to have an abortion if she became pregnant, he also stated that "If she violates probation in this case, I would be sending her to prison; I can assure you of that. I expect her to live up to every single, solitary term and condition of probation." This stern admonition doubtless made it apparent to appellant that in the event she became pregnant during the period of probation the surreptitious procuring of an abortion might be the only practical way to avoid going to prison. A condition of probation that might place a defendant in this position, and, if so, be coercive of abortion, is in our view improper.

In any event, the dilemma that might well confront appellant if she conceived in violation of the condition imposed[4] renders it unlikely she would voluntarily reveal any pregnancy. Less restrictive conditions aimed at protecting the child in utero and after birth would not so clearly induce resistance to the disclosure of pregnancy. To this extent, less restrictive alternative conditions would be easier to monitor and enforce and therefore better protect against the harm sought to be avoided by the trial court.

We conclude that the condition of probation prohibiting conception is overbroad, as less restrictive alternatives are available that would feasibly provide the protections the trial court properly believed necessary. In order to provide the trial court an opportunity to devise a specific alternative condition or conditions we reverse only that portion of the judgment prohibiting conception as a condition of probation and remand for resentencing consistent with the views herein expressed. In all other respects the judgment is affirmed.

NOTE

Ruby Pointer bore three more children, at least one of whom was conceived in violation of her probation. The children, daughters aged two through six, were discovered by police in 1991 living with their mother in a squalid apartment filled with garbage, rotting food, and more than thirty marijuana plants. The children were all malnourished and had apparently been hidden from the outside world. None had been taught to speak. Despite repeated reports by neighbors of seeing and hearing Ruby Pointer beat the children, authorities had not intervened. Stacey L. Arthur, The Norplant Prescription: Birth Control, Woman Control, or Crime Control? 40 UCLA L. Rev. 1, 74 (1992); Julie Mertus and Simon Heller, Norplant Meets the New Eugenicists: The Impermissibility of Coerced Contraception, 11 St. Louis U. Pub. L. Rev. 359, 366 (1992).

4. It deserves to be noted that the condition imposed did not include a prohibition on sexual intercourse. As the trial judge stated at the sentencing hearing: "I would never require somebody to have no sexual activity; I don't think that's even suggested." The conceded fact that even the best birth control measures sometimes fail raises the possibility that appellant could conceive despite reasonable precautions to comply with the condition imposed. This might also occur if, as defense counsel pointed out at the time of sentencing, appellant reasonably relied on a sex partner's false representation that he had undergone a vasectomy.

Court-ordered sterilization and castration for sexual offenders and those convicted of child abuse remains a live topic in criminal justice. Although some lower state courts still order these procedures as a condition of reduced sentence or probation, most such orders are either rescinded by the judges or overturned on appeal.

In In re Lacey P., 189 W.Va. 580, 433 S.E.2d 518 (1993), a West Virginia court ordered the state Department of Health and Human Services to sterilize a mother who had her parental rights terminated for child neglect. On appeal, the mother claimed the order was unconstitutional, but the Supreme Court of West Virginia held the issue moot after appellant voluntarily obtained a five-year Norplant contraceptive implant. In dictum, the court indicated that "such an order could not be upheld" absent specific statutory authority. Id. at 588, 433 S.E.2d at 526.

In Trammell v. State, 751 N.E.2d 283 (Ind. App. 2001), an Indiana appeals court overturned a court order that the defendant, guilty of child abuse and refusing to comply with social services requests, not become pregnant while on probation because the order served no rehabilitative purpose and its intended goals could be served by alternative means less restrictive of defendant's fundamental right to privacy and procreation.

2. INDIRECT RESTRICTIONS

International Union, UAW v. Johnson Controls

Supreme Court of the United States, 1991.
499 U.S. 187, 111 S.Ct. 1196, 113 L.Ed.2d 158.

■ JUSTICE BLACKMUN delivered the opinion of the Court.

. . .

Respondent Johnson Controls, Inc., manufactures batteries. In the manufacturing process, the element lead is a primary ingredient. Occupational exposure to lead entails health risks, including the risk of harm to any fetus carried by a female employee.

Before the Civil Rights Act of 1964, 78 Stat. 241, became law, Johnson Controls did not employ any woman in a battery-manufacturing job. In June 1977, however, it announced its first official policy concerning its employment of women in lead-exposure work:

> "[P]rotection of the health of the unborn child is the immediate and direct responsibility of the prospective parents. While the medical profession and the company can support them in the exercise of this responsibility, it cannot assume it for them without simultaneously infringing their rights as persons.
>
> . . .
>
> ".... Since not all women who can become mothers wish to become mothers (or will become mothers), it would appear to be illegal discrimination to treat all who are capable of pregnancy as though they will become pregnant."

Consistent with that view, Johnson Controls "stopped short of excluding women capable of bearing children from lead exposure," but emphasized that a woman who expected to have a child should not choose a job in which she would have such exposure. The company also required a woman who wished to be considered for employment to sign a statement that she had been advised of the risk of having a child while she was exposed to lead. The statement informed the woman that although there was evidence "that women exposed to lead have a higher rate of abortion," this evidence was "not as clear . . . as the relationship between cigarette smoking and cancer," but that it was, "medically speaking, just good sense not to run that risk if you want children and do not want to expose the unborn child to risk, however small. . . ."

Five years later, in 1982, Johnson Controls shifted from a policy of warning to a policy of exclusion. Between 1979 and 1983, eight employees became pregnant while maintaining blood lead levels in excess of 30 micrograms per deciliter. This appeared to be the critical level noted by the Occupational Health and Safety Administration (OSHA) for a worker who was planning to have a family. The company responded by announcing a broad exclusion of women from jobs that exposed them to lead:

> ". . . [I]t is [Johnson Controls'] policy that women who are pregnant or who are capable of bearing children will not be placed into jobs involving lead exposure or which could expose them to lead through the exercise of job bidding, bumping, transfer or promotion rights."

The policy defined "women . . . capable of bearing children" as "[a]ll women except those whose inability to bear children is medically documented." It further stated that an unacceptable work station was one where, "over the past year," an employee had recorded a blood lead level of more than 30 micrograms per deciliter or the work site had yielded an air sample containing a lead level in excess of 30 micrograms per cubic meter.

In April 1984, petitioners filed . . . a class action challenging Johnson Controls' fetal-protection policy as sex discrimination that violated Title VII of the Civil Rights Act of 1964. Among the individual plaintiffs were petitioners Mary Craig, who had chosen to be sterilized in order to avoid losing her job, Elsie Nason, a 50–year–old divorcee, who had suffered a loss in compensation when she was transferred out of a job where she was exposed to lead, and Donald Penney, who had been denied a request for a leave of absence for the purpose of lowering his lead level because he intended to become a father. . . .

The District Court granted summary judgment for defendant-respondent Johnson Controls. . . .

The Court of Appeals for the Seventh Circuit, sitting en banc, affirmed the summary judgment. . . .

. . .

. . . We granted certiorari . . . to address the important and difficult question whether an employer, seeking to protect potential fetuses, may discriminate against women just because of their ability to become pregnant.

. . . Respondent's fetal-protection policy explicitly discriminates against women on the basis of their sex. The policy excludes women with childbearing capacity from lead-exposed jobs and so creates a facial classification based on gender. . . .

. . . The Court of Appeals . . . assumed that because the asserted reason for the sex-based exclusion (protecting women's unconceived offspring) was ostensibly benign, the policy was not sex-based discrimination. That assumption, however, was incorrect.

First, Johnson Controls' policy classifies on the basis of gender and childbearing capacity, rather than fertility alone. Respondent does not seek to protect the unconceived children of all its employees. Despite evidence in the record about the debilitating effect of lead exposure on the male reproductive system, Johnson Controls is concerned only with the harms that may befall the unborn offspring of its female employees. . . . This Court faced a conceptually similar situation in Phillips v. Martin Marietta Corp., 400 U.S. 542 (1971), and found sex discrimination because the policy established "one hiring policy for women and another for men—each having pre-school-age children." . . .

Our conclusion is bolstered by the Pregnancy Discrimination Act of 1978 (PDA), 92 Stat. 2076, 42 U.S.C. § 2000e(k), in which Congress explicitly provided that, for purposes of Title VII, discrimination "on the basis of sex" includes discrimination "because of or on the basis of pregnancy, childbirth, or related medical conditions." "The Pregnancy Discrimination Act has now made clear that, for all Title VII purposes, discrimination based on a woman's pregnancy is, on its face, discrimination because of her sex." Newport News Shipbuilding & Dry Dock Co. v. EEOC, 462 U.S. 669, 684 (1983). In its use of the words "capable of bearing children" in the 1982 policy statement as the criterion for exclusion, Johnson Controls explicitly classifies on the basis of potential for pregnancy. Under the PDA, such a classification must be regarded, for Title VII purposes, in the same light as explicit sex discrimination. Respondent has chosen to treat all its female employees as potentially pregnant; that choice evinces discrimination on the basis of sex.

We concluded above that Johnson Controls' policy is not neutral because it does not apply to the reproductive capacity of the company's male employees in the same way as it applies to that of the females. Moreover, the absence of a malevolent motive does not convert a facially discriminatory policy into a neutral policy with a discriminatory effect. Whether an employment practice involves disparate treatment through explicit facial discrimination does not depend on why the employer discriminates but rather on the explicit terms of the discrimination. . . .

. . .

Under § 703(e)(1) of Title VII, an employer may discriminate on the basis of "religion, sex, or national origin in those certain instances where religion, sex, or national origin is a bona fide occupational qualification [BFOQ] reasonably necessary to the normal operation of that particular business or enterprise." We therefore turn to the question whether Johnson Controls' fetal-protection policy is one of those "certain instances" that come within the BFOQ exception.

The BFOQ defense is written narrowly, and this Court has read it narrowly. . . .

The wording of the BFOQ defense contains several terms of restriction that indicate that the exception reaches only special situations. The statute thus limits the situations in which discrimination is permissible to "certain instances" where sex discrimination is "reasonably necessary" to the "normal operation" of the "particular" business. Each one of these terms—certain, normal, particular—prevents the use of general subjective standards and favors an objective, verifiable requirement. But the most telling term is "occupational"; this indicates that these objective, verifiable requirements must concern job-related skills and aptitudes.

The concurrence defines "occupational" as meaning related to a job. According to the concurrence, any discriminatory requirement imposed by an employer is "job-related" simply because the employer has chosen to make the requirement a condition of employment. In effect, the concurrence argues that sterility may be an occupational qualification for women because Johnson Controls has chosen to require it. This reading of "occupational" renders the word mere surplusage. "Qualification" by itself would encompass an employer's idiosyncratic requirements. By modifying "qualification" with "occupational," Congress narrowed the term to qualifications that affect an employee's ability to do the job.

Johnson Controls argues that its fetal-protection policy falls within the so-called safety exception to the BFOQ. Our cases have stressed that discrimination on the basis of sex because of safety concerns is allowed only in narrow circumstances. In *Dothard v. Rawlinson,* this Court indicated that danger to a woman herself does not justify discrimination. 433 U.S., at 335. We there allowed the employer to hire only male guards in contact areas of maximum-security male penitentiaries only because more was at stake than the "individual woman's decision to weigh and accept the risks of employment." We found sex to be a BFOQ inasmuch as the employment of a female guard would create real risks of safety to others if violence broke out because the guard was a woman. Sex discrimination was tolerated because sex was related to the guard's ability to do the job—maintaining prison security. We also required in *Dothard* a high correlation between sex and ability to perform job functions and refused to allow employers to use sex as a proxy for strength although it might be a fairly accurate one.

Similarly, some courts have approved airlines' layoffs of pregnant flight attendants at different points during the first five months of pregnancy on the ground that the employer's policy was necessary to ensure the safety of passengers. . . .

We considered safety to third parties in Western Airlines, Inc. v. Criswell, [472 U.S. 400 (1985)]. We focused upon "the nature of the flight engineer's tasks," and the "actual capabilities of persons over age 60" in relation to those tasks. Our safety concerns were not independent of the individual's ability to perform the assigned tasks, but rather involved the possibility that, because of age-connected debility, a flight engineer might not properly assist the pilot, and might thereby cause a safety emergency. Furthermore, although we considered the safety of third parties in *Dothard* and *Criswell,* those third parties were indispensable to the particular business at issue. In *Dothard,* the third parties were the inmates; in *Criswell,* the third parties were the passengers on the plane. We stressed that in order to qualify as a BFOQ, a job qualification must relate to the "essence," or to the "central mission of the employer's business."

The concurrence ignores the "essence of the business" test and so concludes that "the safety to fetuses in carrying out the duties of battery manufacturing is as much a legitimate concern as is safety to third parties in guarding prisons (*Dothard*) or flying airplanes (*Criswell*)." By limiting its discussion to cost and safety concerns and rejecting the "essence of the business" test that our case law has established, the concurrence seeks to expand what is now the narrow BFOQ defense. Third-party safety considerations properly entered into the BFOQ analysis in *Dothard* and *Criswell* because they went to the core of the employee's job performance. Moreover, that performance involved the central purpose of the enterprise. *Dothard* ("The essence of a correctional counselor's job is to maintain prison security"); *Criswell,* 472 U.S., at 413 (the central mission of the airline's business was the safe transportation of its passengers). The concurrence attempts to transform this case into one of customer safety. The unconceived fetuses of Johnson Controls' female employees, however, are neither customers nor third parties whose safety is essential to the business of battery manufacturing. No one can disregard the possibility of injury to future children; the BFOQ, however, is not so broad that it transforms this deep social concern into an essential aspect of batterymaking.

Our case law, therefore, makes clear that the safety exception is limited to instances in which sex or pregnancy actually interferes with the employee's ability to perform the job. This approach is consistent with the language of the BFOQ provision itself, for it suggests that permissible distinctions based on sex must relate to ability to perform the duties of the job. Johnson Controls suggests, however, that we expand the exception to allow fetal-protection policies that mandate particular standards for pregnant or fertile women. We decline to do so. Such an expansion contradicts not only the language of the BFOQ and the narrowness of its exception but the plain language and history of the Pregnancy Discrimination Act.

The PDA's amendment to Title VII contains a BFOQ standard of its own: unless pregnant employees differ from others "in their ability or inability to work," they must be "treated the same" as other employees "for all employment-related purposes." 42 U.S.C. § 2000e(k). This language clearly sets forth Congress' remedy for discrimination on the basis of pregnancy and potential pregnancy. Women who are either pregnant or potentially pregnant must be treated like others "similar in their ability . . . to work." In other words, women as capable of doing their jobs as their male counterparts may not be forced to choose between having a child and having a job.

The concurrence asserts that the PDA did not alter the BFOQ defense. The concurrence arrives at this conclusion by ignoring the second clause of the Act which states that "women affected by pregnancy, childbirth, or related medical conditions shall be treated the same for all employment-related purposes . . . as other persons not so affected but similar in their ability or inability to work." 42 U.S.C. § 2000e(k). Until this day, every Member of this Court had acknowledged that "[t]he second clause [of the PDA] could not be clearer: it mandates that pregnant employees 'shall be treated the same for all employment-related purposes' as nonpregnant employees similarly situated with respect to their ability or inability to work." California Federal S. & L. Assn. v. Guerra, 479 U.S. 272, 297 (1987) (WHITE, J., dissenting). The concurrence now seeks to read the second clause out of the Act.

. . .

We have no difficulty concluding that Johnson Controls cannot establish a BFOQ. Fertile women, as far as appears in the record, participate in the manufacture of batteries as efficiently as anyone else. Johnson Controls' professed moral and ethical concerns about the welfare of the next generation do not suffice to establish a BFOQ of female sterility. Decisions about the welfare of future children must be left to the parents who conceive, bear, support, and raise them rather than to the employers who hire those parents. Congress has mandated this choice through Title VII, as amended by the Pregnancy Discrimination Act. Johnson Controls has attempted to exclude women because of their reproductive capacity. Title VII and the PDA simply do not allow a woman's dismissal because of her failure to submit to sterilization.

Nor can concerns about the welfare of the next generation be considered a part of the "essence" of Johnson Controls' business. Judge Easterbrook in this case pertinently observed: "It is word play to say that 'the job' at Johnson [Controls] is to make batteries without risk to fetuses in the same way 'the job' at Western Air Lines is to fly planes without crashing."

Johnson Controls argues that it must exclude all fertile women because it is impossible to tell which women will become pregnant while working with lead. This argument is somewhat academic in light of our conclusion that the company may not exclude fertile women at all; it perhaps is worth noting, however, that Johnson Controls has shown no "factual basis for believing that all or substantially all women would be unable to perform safely and efficiently the duties of the job involved." Weeks v. Southern Bell Tel. & Tel. Co., 408 F.2d 228, 235 (C.A.5 1969), quoted with approval in *Dothard,* 433 U.S., at 333, 97 S.Ct., at 2751. Even on this sparse record, it is apparent that Johnson Controls is concerned about only a small minority of women. Of the eight pregnancies reported among the female employees, it has not been shown that any of the babies have birth defects or other abnormalities. The record does not reveal the birth rate for Johnson Controls' female workers but national statistics show that approximately nine percent of all fertile women become pregnant each year. The birthrate drops to two percent for blue collar workers over age 30. Johnson Controls' fear of prenatal injury, no matter how sincere, does not begin to show that substantially all of its fertile women employees are incapable of doing their jobs.

A word about tort liability and the increased cost of fertile women in the workplace is perhaps necessary. One of the dissenting judges in this case expressed concern about an employer's tort liability and concluded that liability for a potential injury to a fetus is a social cost that Title VII does not require a company to ignore. It is correct to say that Title VII does not prevent the employer from having a conscience. The statute, however, does prevent sex-specific fetal-protection policies. These two aspects of Title VII do not conflict.

More than 40 States currently recognize a right to recover for a prenatal injury based either on negligence or on wrongful death. ... According to Johnson Controls, however, the company complies with the lead standard developed by OSHA and warns its female employees about the damaging effects of lead. It is worth noting that OSHA gave the problem of lead lengthy consideration and concluded that "there is no basis whatsoever for the claim that women of childbearing age should be excluded from the workplace in order to protect the fetus or the course of pregnancy." Instead, OSHA established a series of mandatory protections which, taken together, "should effectively minimize any risk to the fetus and newborn child." Without negligence, it would be difficult for a court to find liability on the part of the employer. If, under general tort principles, Title VII bans sex-specific fetal-protection policies, the employer fully informs the woman of the risk, and the employer has not acted negligently, the basis for holding an employer liable seems remote at best.

. . .

Our holding today that Title VII, as so amended, forbids sex-specific fetal-protection policies is neither remarkable nor unprecedented. Concern for a woman's existing or potential offspring historically has been the excuse for denying women equal employment opportunities. See, e.g., Muller v. Oregon, 208 U.S. 412 (1908). Congress in the PDA prohibited discrimination on the basis of a woman's ability to become pregnant. We do no more than hold that the Pregnancy Discrimination Act means what it says.

It is no more appropriate for the courts than it is for individual employers to decide whether a woman's reproductive role is more important to herself and her family than her economic role. Congress has left this choice to the woman as hers to make.

The judgment of the Court of Appeals is reversed and the case is remanded for further proceedings consistent with this opinion.

It is so ordered.

D. PROBLEMS POSED BY NEW REPRODUCTIVE TECHNIQUES

In re Marriage of Witbeck–Wildhagen

Appellate Court of Illinois, Fourth Division, 1996.
281 Ill.App.3d 502, 217 Ill.Dec. 329, 667 N.E.2d 122.

■ JUSTICE KNECHT delivered the opinion of the court:

Brief

Petitioner, Marcia Witbeck–Wildhagen, filed a petition for dissolution of marriage on January 26, 1994. One issue raised during the dissolution action was whether respondent, Eric Wildhagen, was the legal father of a child conceived by artificial insemination and born during the marriage. The trial court determined respondent is not the legal father of the child because he did not consent to the artificial insemination of petitioner, as required by section 3 of the Illinois Parentage Act (Act) (750 ILCS 40/3 (West 1994)). Petitioner appeals and we affirm.

Petitioner and respondent were married in November 1990. In April 1992, petitioner and respondent consulted with a nurse clinician at Christie Clinic regarding the procedure of artificial insemination. At the consultation, respondent made it clear to petitioner and the nurse he did not want to participate in, nor did he consent to, petitioner's attempts to become pregnant. Petitioner acknowledges at the consultation respondent expressed his desire not to participate in her attempt to have a baby, but alleges respondent said it would be all right if she pursued the pregnancy alone. Whenever respondent had sexual relations with petitioner, he used a condom to prevent pregnancy. Following the initial consultation at Christie Clinic, petitioner underwent seven artificial insemination procedures. Respondent was not informed of this by Christie Clinic or by petitioner.

In approximately October 1993, petitioner became pregnant. In January 1994, she filed a petition for dissolution of marriage. The petition stated no children were born during the marriage but petitioner was pregnant. The complaint alleged petitioner did not have sufficient property and income to provide for her reasonable needs or those of her unborn child. Petitioner sought custody of the unborn child and asked the court to order respondent to pay reasonable sums for her maintenance, support of the unborn child, and prenatal and delivery expenses.

On July 2, 1994, petitioner gave birth to a son, M.W. In September 1994, respondent filed a motion for blood testing, which was allowed. Petitioner's attorney then notified respondent, in a letter dated September 14, 1994, of the seven artificial insemination procedures, the last of which, the letter stated, may have resulted in the conception of M.W. The parties and M.W. underwent blood testing in November 1994. Respondent was conclusively excluded as M.W.'s biological father.

In February 1995, petitioner filed a motion for summary determination of a major issue (motion for summary determination) under section 2–1005(d) of the Illinois Code of Civil Procedure (735 ILCS 5/2–1005(d) (West 1994)). In the motion, petitioner acknowledged respondent was not M.W.'s biological father and had not given his written consent to her artificial insemination. Nonetheless, petitioner asked the court to find respondent to be the legal father of M.W. within the meaning of the Act (750 ILCS 40/3 (West 1994)). The court heard arguments on the motion for summary determination and determined, under its interpretation of section 3 of the Act, respondent is not the legal father of M.W.

Following this ruling, the parties executed a marital settlement agreement which reflected the court's earlier decision and in which they set forth their agreements on the remaining issues. On August 4, 1995, the trial court entered a judgment of dissolution of marriage which incorporated the marital settlement agreement, and entered a final order stating respondent is not the legal father of M.W. Petitioner filed a timely notice of appeal and asks this court to reverse the trial court's determination respondent is not the legal father of M.W.

The issue presented is whether, under section 3 of the Act, the lack of written consent by respondent to petitioner's artificial insemination precludes the establishment of a father-child relationship and the imposition of a support obligation.

Section 3(a) of the Act provides:

> "(a) If, under the supervision of a licensed physician and with the consent of her husband, a wife is inseminated artificially with semen donated by a man not her husband, the husband shall be treated in law as if he were the natural father of a child thereby conceived. The husband's consent must be in writing executed and acknowledged by both the husband and wife. The physician who is to perform the technique shall certify their signatures and the date of the insemination, and file the husband's consent in the medical record where it shall be kept confidential and held by the patient's physician. However, the physician's failure to do so shall not affect the legal relationship between father and child. All papers and records pertaining to the insemination, whether part of the permanent medical record held by the physician or not, are subject to inspection only upon an order of the court for good cause shown." (Emphasis added.) 750 ILCS 40/3(a) (West 1994).

Only one Illinois case has analyzed this provision of the Act. In In re Marriage of Adams, 174 Ill. App. 3d 595, 610–11, 528 N.E.2d 1075, 1084, 124 Ill. Dec. 184 (1988), rev'd on other grounds, 133 Ill. 2d 437, 551 N.E.2d 635, 141 Ill. Dec. 448 (1990), the Second District Appellate Court decided the failure to obtain the husband's written consent does not bar further inquiry into the circumstances surrounding the decision to use the artificial insemination procedure. The court examined the surrounding circumstances in the case and, although the husband had not executed a written consent to his wife's artificial insemination, agreed with the trial court's finding he had manifested his consent by his conduct before, during, and after the pregnancy. *Adams*, 174 Ill. App. 3d at 615, 528 N.E.2d at 1087. The court concluded nothing in section 3 bars the imposition of a support obligation on an estoppel or waiver theory where written consent is not obtained. Thus, the court imposed a support obligation on the husband, who had manifested actual consent to the procedure by his conduct. In *Adams* the court found the husband consented to the procedure. In this case respondent did not consent to the artificial insemination procedure, either in writing or in any other manner.

After the appellate court decision in *Adams*, the Supreme Court of Illinois reviewed the case but, because it determined Florida law was controlling and remanded the case, the court did not render a conclusive interpretation of section 3 of the Act. In re Marriage of Adams, 133 Ill. 2d 437, 551 N.E.2d 635, 141 Ill. Dec. 448 (1990). In a cursory discussion of both section 3 of the Act and the applicable Florida statute, the court stated, "we note that the provision in the Illinois statute that the husband's consent 'must be in writing' could be considered a mandatory requirement for establishing a parent-child relationship pursuant to the statute." (Emphasis added.) *Adams*, 133 Ill. 2d at 444, 551 N.E.2d at 638. The court went on to note:

> "It is not clear whether under either statute the failure to provide written consent will preclude both the establishment of a parent-child relationship and the imposition of a support obligation. It may be the case that a support obligation will be found even in the absence of a parent-child relationship." (Emphasis added.) Adams, 133 Ill. 2d at 445, 551 N.E.2d at 638.

The court in *Adams* was considering only the possible effects of the failure to obtain written consent. It did not indicate the consent requirement could be waived entirely.

Petitioner argues the language of the statute indicates respondent's written consent is not a prerequisite to the establishment of a father-child relationship. Her argument focuses on the following language: "the physician's failure to do so shall not affect the legal relationship between father and child." This language appears immediately after the description of the physician's duties of certifying the signatures of the husband and wife and the date of insemination and filing the husband's consent in the medical record. Petitioner contends, however, the quoted language means "the physician's failure to obtain the consent shall not affect the legal relationship between father and child." The plain language and structure of the statute does not lend itself to such a reading, nor do we believe this interpretation is what the legislature intended.

The first sentence of section 3 of the Act provides, "if, under the supervision of a licensed physician and with the consent of her husband, a wife is inseminated artificially with semen donated by a man not her husband, the husband shall be treated in law as if he were the natural father." The Act then states, "the husband's consent must be in writing." Following these statements is the explanation of what the duties of the physician performing the procedure are in terms of documenting the husband's consent, and the statement which provides, "the physician's failure to do so shall not affect the legal relationship between father and child." This language refers to the physician's failure to certify and document the consent in accordance with the statute and cannot be interpreted as obviating the consent requirement.

We conclude the legislature intended a husband's written consent to be a prerequisite to the establishment of the legal father-child relationship and the imposition of a support obligation. The several provisions in section 3 of the Act which address the consent requirement would be superfluous if the failure to obtain the husband's written consent would not affect the legal status of the individuals involved.

In addition, because the statute requires the physician to certify the date of insemination, we conclude the husband's written consent is required each time his wife is to undergo the procedure. Such a requirement is not burdensome and it leaves no room for confusion on the part of the married couple or the physician regarding whether a consent previously given by the husband is still viable.

On the facts of this case, we need not decide whether the failure to obtain written consent would be an absolute bar to the establishment of a father-child relationship where the conduct of the father otherwise demonstrated his consent to the artificial insemination procedure. Such a situation was present in Adams and has also been addressed by commentators and the courts of other states. See In re Marriage of L.M.S., 105 Wis. 2d 118, 312 N.W.2d 853 (1981); K.S. v. G.S., 182 N.J. Super. 102, 440 A.2d 64 (1981); Note, The Legal Incubation of Artificial Insemination: A Proposal to Amend the Illinois Parentage Act, 18 J. Marshall L. Rev. 797, 799 (1985); Comment, Artificial Human Reproduction: Legal Problems Presented by the Test Tube Baby, 28 Emory L.J. 1045, 1076 (1979); Comment, Artificial Insemination and Surrogate Motherhood—A Nursery Full of Unresolved Questions, 17 Willamette L. Rev. 913, 939 (1981).

Here, there is no evidence of consent by respondent to the artificial insemination procedure, written or otherwise. Petitioner filed for a dissolution of marriage within two or three months of becoming pregnant. She was impregnated by the sperm of a man other than respondent, without respondent's knowledge or consent, and apparently without any intention of raising the child with respondent. In her brief, petitioner admits she underwent the procedure relying on her doctor's written assurance respondent would be legally responsible for her child, even though it was not his wish she have a child. There is no evidence in the record of any contact or interaction between respondent and M.W., and petitioner had M.W.'s last name legally changed to her maiden name. Under the facts of this case, there is no statutory or equitable basis for concluding a father-child relationship exists between respondent and M.W.

Petitioner urges this court to impose a support obligation on respondent, even absent the existence of a father-child relationship, contending any other result would be contrary to public policy. The two primary policy considerations here are (1) M.W.'s right to support, and (2) respondent's right to choose not to be a parent.

Just as a woman has a constitutionally protected right not to bear a child (see Roe v. Wade, 410 U.S. 113 (1973)), a man has the right not to be deemed the parent of a child that he played no part in conceiving. Respondent made a choice not to parent a child. This choice was evidenced by not giving his consent to petitioner or any support to her choice to undergo artificial insemination. Petitioner underwent the procedure unbeknownst to respondent. Respondent was only informed of the manner in which M.W. was conceived after M.W. was born, by his attorney. This is not a case where respondent has changed his mind or is attempting to evade responsibility for his own actions in helping to conceive or encouraging the conception of a child. The facts of this case illustrate, and the trial court correctly determined, it would be inconsistent with public policy to force upon respondent parental obligations which he declined to undertake.

The second policy consideration here is M.W.'s right to support. The main purpose of the policy recognizing a child's right to support is to prevent minors from becoming dependent on the State. The trial court's order demonstrates it considered M.W.'s need for support and found that support would be forthcoming from his mother. The child's right to support cannot be met by requiring a nonparent to fulfill the obligation of a parent. Respondent has no financial obligation to this child.

It is the duty of the court to ensure the rights of the child are adequately protected. In this case, the trial court did so, and the balance it struck between the attendant interests of the parties was appropriate. It would be unjust to impose a support obligation on respondent where no father-child relationship exists between him and M.W. and he did not consent to the artificial insemination procedure. Accordingly, we affirm.

Affirmed.

Elisa B. v. Superior Court

Supreme Court of California, 2005.
37 Cal.4th 108, 33 Cal.Rptr.3d 46, 117 P.3d 660.

■ MORENO, J.

. . .

Brief

In the present action for child support filed by the El Dorado County District Attorney, we conclude that a woman who agreed to raise children with her lesbian partner, supported her partner's artificial insemination using an anonymous donor, and received the resulting twin children into her home and held them out as her own, is the children's parent under the Uniform Parentage Act and has an obligation to support them.

On June 7, 2001, the El Dorado County District Attorney filed a complaint in superior court to establish that Elisa B. is a parent of two-year-old twins Kaia B. and Ry B., who were born to Emily B.,[1] and to order Elisa to pay child support. Elisa filed an answer in which she denied being the children's parent.

A hearing was held at which Elisa testified that she entered into a lesbian relationship with Emily in 1993. They began living together six months later. Elisa obtained a tattoo that read "Emily, por vida," which in Spanish means Emily, for life. They introduced each other to friends as their "partner," exchanged rings, opened a joint bank account, and believed they were in a committed relationship.

Elisa and Emily discussed having children and decided that they both wished to give birth. Because Elisa earned more than twice as much money as Emily, they decided that Emily "would be the stay-at-home mother" and Elisa "would be the primary breadwinner for the family." At a sperm bank, they chose a donor they both would use so the children would "be biological brothers and sisters."

After several unsuccessful attempts, Elisa became pregnant in February 1997. Emily was present when Elisa was inseminated. Emily began the insemination process in June of 1997 and became pregnant in August 1997. Elisa was present when Emily was inseminated and, the next day, Elisa picked up additional sperm at the sperm bank and again inseminated Emily at their home to "make sure she got pregnant." They went to each other's

1. In order to protect the confidentiality of the minors, we will refer to the parties by their first names.

medical appointments during pregnancy and attended child birth classes together so that each could act as a "coach" for the other during birth, including cutting the children's umbilical cords.

Elisa gave birth to Chance in November 1997, and Emily gave birth to Ry and Kaia prematurely in March 1998. Ry had medical problems; he suffered from Down's syndrome, and required heart surgery.

They jointly selected the children's names, joining their surnames with a hyphen to form the children's surname. They each breast fed all of the children. Elisa claimed all three children as her dependents on her tax returns and obtained a life insurance policy on herself naming Emily as the beneficiary so that if "anything happened" to her, all three children would be "cared for." Elisa believed the children would be considered both of their children.

Elisa's parents referred to the twins as their grandchildren and her sister referred to the twins as part of their family and referred to Elisa as their mother. Elisa treated all of the children as hers and told a prospective employer that she had triplets. Elisa and Emily identified themselves as coparents of Ry at an organization arranging care for his Down's syndrome.

Elisa supported the household financially. Emily was not working. Emily testified that she would not have become pregnant if Elisa had not promised to support her financially, but Elisa denied that any financial arrangements were discussed before the birth of the children. Elisa later acknowledged in her testimony, however, that Emily "was going to be an at-home mom for maybe a couple of years and then the kids were going to go into day care and she was going to return to work."

They consulted an attorney regarding adopting "each other's child," but never did so. Nor did they register as domestic partners or execute a written agreement concerning the children. Elisa stated she later reconsidered adoption because she had misgivings about Emily adopting Chance.

Elisa and Emily separated in November 1999. Elisa promised to support Emily and the twins "as much as I possibly could" and initially paid the mortgage payments of approximately $1,500 per month on the house in which Emily and the twins continued to live, as well as other expenses. Emily applied for aid. When they sold the house and Emily and the twins moved into an apartment in November 2000, Elisa paid Emily $1,000 a month. In early 2001, Elisa stated she lost her position as a full-time employee and told Emily she no longer could support her and the twins. At the time of trial, Elisa was earning $95,000 a year.

The superior court rendered a written decision on July 11, 2002, finding that Elisa and Emily had rejected the option of using a private sperm donor because "[t]hey wanted the child to be raised exclusively by them as a couple." The court further found that they intended to create a child and "acted in all respects as a family," adding "that a person who uses reproductive technology is accountable as a de facto legal parent for the support of that child. Legal parentage is not determined exclusively by biology."

The court further found that Elisa was obligated to support the twins under the doctrine of equitable estoppel, finding Emily "agreed to have children with Respondent, and relied on her promise to raise and support her children. She would not have agreed to impregnation but for this agreement and understanding." "The need for the application of this doctrine is underscored by the fact that the decision of Respondent to create a family and desert them has caused the remaining family members to seek county assistance. One child that was created has special needs that will require the remaining parent or the County to be financially responsible of those needs. The child was deprived of the right to have a traditional father to take care of the financial needs of this child. Respondent chose to step in those shoes and assume the role and responsibility of the 'other' parent. This should be her responsibility and not the responsibility of the taxpayer." Elisa was subsequently ordered to pay child support in the amount of $907.50 per child for a total of $1815 per month.

Elisa petitioned the Court of Appeal for a writ of mandate, and the court directed the superior court to vacate its order and dismiss the action, concluding that Elisa had no obligation to pay child support because she was not a parent of the twins within the meaning of the Uniform Parentage Act (Fam. Code, § 7600 et seq.). We granted review.

We must determine whether the Court of Appeal erred in ruling that Elisa could not be a parent of the twins born to her lesbian partner, and thus had no obligation to support them. This question is governed by the Uniform Parentage Act (UPA). (Fam. Code, § 7600 et seq.) The UPA defines the " '[p]arent and child relationship' " as "the legal relationship existing between a child and the child's natural or adoptive parents. . . . The term includes the mother and child relationship and the father and child relationship." (§ 7601.) One purpose of the UPA was to eliminate distinctions based upon whether a child was born into a marriage, and thus was "legitimate," or was born to unmarried parents, and thus was "illegitimate." Johnson v. Calvert (1993) 5 Cal.4th 84, 88 [19 Cal. Rptr. 2d 494, 851 P.2d 776]. Thus, the UPA provides that the parentage of a child does not depend upon " 'the marital status of the parents' " (*Johnson, supra,* at p. 89), stating: "The parent and child relationship extends equally to every child and to every parent, regardless of the marital status of the parents." (§ 7602.)

The UPA contains separate provisions defining who is a "mother" and who is a "father." Section 7610 provides that "[t]he parent and child relationship may be established . . . : [P] (a) Between a child and the natural mother . . . by proof of her having given birth to the child, or under this part." Subdivision (b) of section 7610 states that the parental relationship "[b]etween a child and the natural father . . . may be established under this part."

Section 7611 provides several circumstances in which "[a] man is presumed to be the natural father of a child," including: if he is the husband of the child's mother, is not impotent or sterile, and was cohabiting with her (§ 7540); if he signs a voluntary declaration of paternity stating he is the "biological father of the child" (§ 7574, subd. (b)(6)); and if "[h]e receives the child into his home and openly holds out the child as his natural child" (§ 7611, subd. (d)).

Although, as noted above, the UPA contains separate provisions defining who is a mother and who is a father, it expressly provides that in determining the existence of a mother and child relationship, "[i]nsofar as practicable, the provisions of this part applicable to the father and child relationship apply." (§ 7650.)

The Court of Appeal correctly recognized that, under the UPA, Emily has a parent and child relationship with each of the twins because she gave birth to them. Thus, the Court of Appeal concluded, Emily is the twins' natural mother. Relying upon our statement in Johnson v. Calvert, *supra,* 5 Cal.4th 84, 92, that "for any child California law recognizes only one natural mother," the Court of Appeal reasoned that Elisa, therefore, could not also be the natural mother of the twins and thus "has no legal maternal relationship with the children under the UPA."

The Attorney General, appearing pursuant to section 17406 to "represent the public interest in establishing, modifying, and enforcing support obligations," argues that the Court of Appeal erred, stating: "*Johnson*'s one-natural-mother comment cannot be thoughtlessly interpreted to deprive the children of same-sex couples the same opportunity as other children to two parents and to two sources of child support when only two parties are eligible for parentage." As we shall explain, the Attorney General is correct that our statement in *Johnson* that a child can have "only one natural mother" does not mean that both Elisa and Emily cannot be parents of the twins.

The issue before us in *Johnson* was whether a wife whose ovum was fertilized in vitro by her husband's sperm and implanted in a surrogate mother was the mother of the child so produced, rather than the surrogate. The surrogate claimed that she was the child's mother because she had given birth to the child. No provision of the UPA expressly addresses the parental rights of a woman who, like the wife in *Johnson v. Calvert*, has not given birth to a child, but has a genetic relationship because she supplied the ovum used to impregnate the birth mother. But, as noted above, the UPA does provide that provisions applicable to determining a father and child relationship shall be used to determine a mother and child relationship "[i]nsofar as practicable." Accordingly, we looked to the provisions regarding presumptions of paternity and concluded that "genetic consanguinity" could be the basis for a finding of maternity just as it is for paternity.

We concluded, therefore, that both women—the surrogate who gave birth to the child and the wife who supplied the ovum—had "adduced evidence of a mother and child relationship as contemplated by the Act." Anticipating this result, the American Civil Liberties Union appearing as amicus curiae urged this court to rule that the child, therefore, had two mothers. Because it was undisputed that the husband, who had supplied the semen used to impregnate the surrogate, was the child's father, this would have left the child with three parents. We declined the invitation, stating: "Even though rising divorce rates have made multiple parent arrangements common in our society, we see no compelling reason to recognize such a situation here. The Calverts are the genetic and intending parents of their son and have provided him, by all accounts, with a stable, intact, and nurturing home. To recognize parental rights in a third party with whom the Calvert family has had little contact since shortly after the child's birth would diminish [the wife]'s role as mother." We held instead that "for any child California law recognizes only one natural mother" and proceeded to conclude that the wife, rather than the surrogate, was the child's mother: "We conclude that although the Act recognizes both genetic consanguinity and giving birth as means of establishing a mother and child relationship, when the two means do not coincide in one woman, she who intended to procreate the child—that is, she who intended to bring about the birth of a child that she intended to raise as her own—is the natural mother under California law."

In *Johnson*, therefore, we addressed the situation in which three people claimed to be the child's parents: the husband, who undoubtedly was the child's father, and two women, who presented conflicting claims to being the child's mother. We rejected the suggestion of amicus curiae that both the wife and the surrogate could be the child's mother, stating that a child can have only one mother, but what we considered and rejected in *Johnson* was the argument that a child could have three parents: a father and two mothers.[4] We did not address the question presented in this case of whether a child could have two parents, both of whom are women.[5] The Court of Appeal in the present case erred, therefore, in concluding that our statement in *Johnson* that a child can have only one mother under California law resolved the issue presented in this case. "Language used in any opinion is of course to be understood in the light of the facts and the issue then before the court, and an opinion is not authority for a proposition not therein considered."

We perceive no reason why both parents of a child cannot be women. That result now is possible under the current version of the domestic partnership statutes, which took effect this year. Two women "who have chosen to share one another's lives in an intimate and committed relationship of mutual caring" and have a common residence (§ 297) can file with the Secretary of State a "Declaration of Domestic Partnership" (§ 298). Section 297.5, subdivision (d) provides, in pertinent part: "The rights and obligations of registered domestic partners with respect to a child of either of them shall be the same as those of spouses."

Prior to the effective date of the current domestic partnership statutes, we recognized in an adoption case that a child can have two parents, both of whom are women. In Sharon S. v. Superior Court, *supra*, 31 Cal.4th 417, we upheld a "second parent" adoption in which the mother of a child that had been conceived by means of artificial insemination consented to adoption of the child by the mother's lesbian partner. If both parents of an adopted child can be women, we see no reason why the twins in the present case cannot have two parents, both of whom are women.

Having determined that our decision in *Johnson* does not preclude a child from having two parents both of whom are women and that no reason appears that a child's two parents cannot both be women, we proceed to examine the UPA to determine whether Elisa is a parent to the twins in addition to Emily. As noted above, section 7650 provides that provisions applicable to determining a father and child relationship shall be used to determine a mother and child relationship "insofar as practicable." Johnson v. Calvert, *supra*, 5 Cal.4th 84, 90; see In re Marriage of Buzzanca (1998) 61 Cal.App.4th 1410, 1418 [72 Cal. Rptr. 2d 280] [the declaration in section 7613 that a husband who consents to artificial insemination is "treated in law" as the father of the child applies equally to the wife if a surrogate, rather than the wife, is artificially inseminated, making both the wife and the husband the parents of the child so produced.]

4. We have not decided "whether there exists an overriding legislative policy limiting a child to two parents." Sharon S. v. Superior Court (2003) 31 Cal.4th 417, 427, fn. 6 [2 Cal. Rptr. 3d 699, 73 P.3d 554].

5. The situation is analogous to that in *Sharon S. v. Superior Court, supra,* 31 Cal.4th 417, in which we held that a mother could consent to a "second parent" adoption by her lesbian partner despite our earlier dictum in *Estate of Jobson* (1912) 164 Cal. 312, 317 [128 P. 938], that the "duties of a child cannot be owed to two fathers at one time." We explained that this statement was "uttered in the context of concluding that a birth father who 'by virtue of the adoption proceeding [in that case], ceased to sustain the legal relation of father' could not thereafter inherit the adopted person's estate [citation] . . . , we did not consider the contingency before us today—viz., two parties who voluntarily have waived the benefit of section 8617 in order to effect a second parent adoption, where the natural parent's relationship with the child is not superseded." *Sharon S.*, at p. 430, fn. 7.

Subdivision (d) of section 7611 states that a man is presumed to be the natural father of a child if "[h]e receives the child into his home and openly holds out the child as his natural child." The Court of Appeal in In re Karen C. (2002) 101 Cal.App.4th 932, 938 [124 Cal. Rptr. 2d 677], held that subdivision (d) of section 7611 "should apply equally to women." This conclusion was echoed by the court in In re Salvador M. (2003) 111 Cal.App.4th 1353, 1357 [4 Cal. Rptr. 3d 705], which stated: "Though most of the decisional law has focused on the definition of the presumed father, the legal principles concerning the presumed father apply equally to a woman seeking presumed mother status."[7]

Applying section 7611, subdivision (d), we must determine whether Elisa received the twins into her home and openly held them out as her natural children. There is no doubt that Elisa satisfied the first part of this test; it is undisputed that Elisa received the twins into her home. Our inquiry focuses, therefore, on whether she openly held out the twins as her natural children.

The circumstance that Elisa has no genetic connection to the twins does not necessarily mean that she did not hold out the twins as her "natural" children under section 7611. We held in In re Nicholas H. (2002) 28 Cal.4th 56 [120 Cal. Rptr. 2d 146, 46 P.3d 932] that the presumption under section 7611, subdivision (d), that a man who receives a child into his home and openly holds the child out as his natural child is not necessarily rebutted when he admits he is not the child's biological father.

. . .

The Court of Appeal in *In re Karen C., supra*, 101 Cal.App.4th 932, 938, applied the principles discussed in *Nicholas H.* regarding presumed fathers and concluded that a woman with no biological connection to a child could be a presumed mother under section 7611, subdivision (d). Twelve-year-old Karen C. petitioned for an order determining the existence of a mother and child relationship between her and Leticia C., who had raised her from birth. Leticia admitted she was not Karen's biological mother, explaining that Karen's birth mother had tried unsuccessfully to abort her pregnancy and then agreed to give the child to Leticia. The birth mother falsely told the hospital staff that her name was Leticia C. so that Leticia's name would appear on the child's birth certificate. The birth mother gave Karen to Leticia promptly after the child was born. The juvenile court denied Karen's petition, ruling that Leticia could not be Karen's mother because she had not given birth to her and had no genetic relationship. The Court of Appeal reversed, determining that Leticia was the child's presumed mother under section 7611 because she had taken Karen into her home and raised her as her child. The court remanded the matter to the juvenile court to apply the rule in *Nicholas H.* to determine whether this was " 'an appropriate action' " in which to find the presumption that Leticia was Karen's mother was rebutted by the fact that she had not given birth to her.

We conclude that the present case, like *Nicholas H.* and *Salvador M.*, is not "an appropriate action" in which to rebut the presumption of presumed parenthood with proof that Elisa is not the twins' biological parent. This is generally a matter within the discretion of the superior court, but we need not remand the matter to permit the superior court to exercise its discretion because it would be an abuse of discretion to conclude that the presumption

7. The fact that questions involving the determination of parentage "focus on paternity is likely due to the fact the identity of a child's birth mother is rarely in dispute." In re Karen C., *supra*, 101 Cal.App.4th 932, 936.

may be rebutted in the present case. It is undisputed that Elisa actively consented to, and participated in, the artificial insemination of her partner with the understanding that the resulting child or children would be raised by Emily and her as coparents, and they did act as coparents for a substantial period of time. Elisa received the twins into her home and held them out to the world as her natural children. She gave the twins and the child to whom she had given birth the same surname, which was formed by joining her surname to her partner's. The twins were half siblings to the child to whom Elisa had given birth. She breast fed all three children, claimed all three children as her dependents on her tax returns, and told a prospective employer that she had triplets. Even at the hearing before the superior court, Elisa candidly testified that she considered herself to be the twins' mother.

Declaring that Elisa cannot be the twins' parent and, thus, has no obligation to support them because she is not biologically related to them would produce a result similar to the situation we sought to avoid in *Nicholas H.* of leaving the child fatherless. The twins in the present case have no father because they were conceived by means of artificial insemination using an anonymous semen donor. Rebutting the presumption that Elisa is the twin's parent would leave them with only one parent and would deprive them of the support of their second parent. Because Emily is financially unable to support the twins, the financial burden of supporting the twins would be borne by the county, rather than Elisa.

In establishing a system for a voluntary declaration of paternity in section 7570, the Legislature declared: "There is a compelling state interest in establishing paternity for all children. Establishing paternity is the first step toward a child support award, which, in turn, provides children with equal rights and access to benefits, including, but not limited to, social security, health insurance, survivors' benefits, military benefits, and inheritance rights. . . . "

By recognizing the value of determining paternity, the Legislature implicitly recognized the value of having two parents, rather than one, as a source of both emotional and financial support, especially when the obligation to support the child would otherwise fall to the public.

We observed in dicta in *Nicholas H.* that it would be appropriate to rebut the section 7611 presumption of parentage if "a court decides that the legal rights and obligations of parenthood should devolve upon an unwilling candidate." But we decline to apply our dicta in *Nicholas H.* here, because we did not consider in *Nicholas H.* a situation like that in the present case.

Although Elisa presently is unwilling to accept the obligations of parenthood, this was not always so. She actively assisted Emily in becoming pregnant with the expressed intention of enjoying the rights and accepting the responsibilities of parenting the resulting children. She accepted those obligations and enjoyed those rights for years. Elisa's present unwillingness to accept her parental obligations does not affect her status as the children's mother based upon her conduct during the first years of their lives.

Further, our observation in *Nicholas H.* that the obligations of parenthood should not be forced upon an unwilling candidate who is not biologically related to the child must be understood in light of the circumstances before us in *Nicholas H.* In that case, as noted above, the presumed father met the child's mother when she was pregnant and voluntarily accepted the unborn child as his own. When the child later was removed from the mother's custody, the presumed father was denied custody of the child because he was not the child's biological father.

. . .

In the present case, Elisa did not meet Emily after she was pregnant, but rather was in a committed relationship with her when they decided to have children together. Elisa actively assisted Emily in becoming pregnant, with the understanding that they would raise the resulting children together. Having helped cause the children to be born, and having raised them as her own, Elisa should not be permitted to later abandon the twins simply because her relationship with Emily dissolved.

As we noted in the context of a husband who consented to the artificial insemination of his wife using an anonymous sperm donor, but later denied responsibility for the resulting child: "One who consents to the production of a child cannot create a temporary relation to be assumed and disclaimed at will, but the arrangement must be of such character as to impose an obligation of supporting those for whose existence he is directly responsible." People v. Sorensen (1968) 68 Cal.2d 280, 285 [66 Cal. Rptr. 7, 437 P.2d 495]; see Dunkin v. Boskey (2000) 82 Cal.App.4th 171, 191 [98 Cal. Rptr. 2d 44]. We observed that the "intent of the Legislature obviously was to include every child, legitimate or illegitimate, born or unborn, and enforce the obligation of support against the person who could be determined to be the lawful parent." Further: "a reasonable man who, because of his inability to procreate, actively participates and consents to his wife's artificial insemination in the hope that a child will be produced whom they will treat as their own, knows that such behavior carries with it the legal responsibilities of fatherhood and criminal responsibility for nonsupport. . . . [I]t is safe to assume that without defendant's active participation and consent the child would not have been procreated."

We were careful in *Nicholas H.*, therefore, not to suggest that every man who begins living with a woman when she is pregnant and continues to do so after the child is born necessarily becomes a presumed father of the child, even against his wishes. The Legislature surely did not intend to punish a man like the one in *Nicholas H.* who voluntarily provides support for a child who was conceived before he met the mother, by transforming that act of kindness into a legal obligation.

But our observation in *Nicholas H.* loses its force in a case like the one at bar in which the presumed mother under section 7611, subdivision (d), acted together with the birth mother to cause the child to be conceived. In such circumstances, unlike the situation before us in *Nicholas H.*, we believe the Legislature would have intended to impose upon the presumed father or mother the legal obligation to support the child whom she caused to be born. As stated by amicus curiae the California State Association of Counties, representing all 58 counties in California: "A person who actively participates in bringing children into the world, takes the children into her home and holds them out as her own, and receives and enjoys the benefits of parenthood, should be responsible for the support of those children—regardless of her gender or sexual orientation."

We conclude, therefore, that Elisa is a presumed mother of the twins under section 7611, subdivision (d), because she received the children into her home and openly held them out as her natural children, and that this is not an appropriate action in which to rebut the presumption that Elisa is the twins' parent with proof that she is not the children's biological mother because she actively participated in causing the children to be conceived with the understanding that she would raise the children as her own together with the birth mother, she voluntarily accepted the rights and obligations of parenthood after the children were born, and there are no competing claims to her being the children's second parent.

. . .

The judgment of the Court of Appeal is reversed.

NOTES

1. By 2000, The Uniform Parentage Act had been adopted in nineteen states. Oklahoma has a similar statute. Prompted by the need to cover artificial insemination when no physician is involved, the National Conference of Commissioners on Uniform State Laws in 1988 promulgated a new Uniform Status of Children of Assisted Conception Act. 9B U.L.A. 184 (Supp. 1998). By 2004 it had been adopted in Delaware, Texas, Washington, Wyoming, North Dakota and Virginia. The USCACA establishes a presumption that the husband of a woman who bears a child through assisted conception is the father of the child unless within two years of the birth he begins a court proceeding that determines he did not consent to the conception. In the Act, "assisted conception" is defined to mean:

> pregnancy resulting from (i) fertilizing an egg of a woman with sperm of a man by means other than sexual intercourse or (ii) implanting an embryo....

See generally Bridget Penick, Note, Give the Child a Legal Father: A Plea for Iowa to Adopt a Statute Regulating Artificial Insemination by Anonymous Donor, 83 Iowa L. Rev. 633 (1998).

Illinois, in Mitchell v. Banary, 203 Ill.2d 526, 272 Ill.Dec. 329, 787 N.E.2d 144 (2003), has gone one step further than the UPA by accepting, under common law contract theories, the claim that a man not married to the mother may be recognized as the father if he promises to act as the parent of a child created with his sperm through AID despite the fact that the promise was not in writing.

In Steven S. v. Deborah D., 127 Cal.App.4th 319, 25 Cal.Rptr.3d 482 (2005) the biological father of a child conceived by artificial insemination provided by a licensed physician sued to be declared the child's father. The trial court upheld his claim "based on estoppel" noting that the parents knew each other and had had a sexual relationship prior to the AID, the mother had referred to him as Treavor's father, and Treavor called him "Daddy Steve." The trial court was reversed on appeal. The appellate court based its decision on section 7613 of the California Uniform Parentage Act which provides "there can be no paternity claim from a sperm donor who is not married to the woman who becomes pregnant from the donor's sperm, so long as it was provided to a licensed physician."

2. Richard M. Restak, Premeditated Man (1975), reprinted in Wash. Post, October 12, 1975, at C1.:

> Mark Frankel, Assistant Professor of Political Science at Wayne State University (in 1971) began an investigation into frozen-semen banking in the United States.... To his surprise, Frankel discovered that no standard procedures existed. "While all the banks attempt to match the donor and recipient with respect to their physical characteristics, only about one-third report using some type of intelligence matching.... Some banks took detailed medical and genetic histories of their donors, others did not...."
>
> One thing we can conclude from this is that our attitude toward the contribution of genetic inheritance to human destiny, always a curious one, is now, as with Alice's experience in Wonderland, getting "curiouser and curiouser."

One sperm bank established in California contains deposits from Nobel Prize laureates. Dr. William Shockley, one of the donors, and himself the subject of controversy for his views linking intelligence and heredity, has endorsed the California project's goal of "increasing the people at the top of the population." Nobel Winner Says He Gave Sperm for Women to Bear Gifted Babies, New York Times, Mar. 1, 1981 at A6. It is alleged that George Bernard Shaw once turned down a request from dancer Isadora Duncan to father her child, warning "the child might have my looks and your intelligence."

There is very little regulation of sperm banks. Although there are hundred of sperm banks located throughout the country (about 400 as of 1998), as of 2004 only ten were AATB (American Association of Tissue Banks) accredited. See Gostin et al., Law Science and Medicine 1180 (2005).

In 1992, Dr. Cecil B. Jacobson, an infertility specialist, was convicted on 52 counts of fraud and perjury for artificially inseminating unwitting patients with his own sperm and for telling some that they were pregnant when they were not. It was estimated that he may have fathered as many as 75 children. There were no laws specifically addressing what he did at the time, so he was charged with criminal fraud involving the use of telephones and of the mail. New York Times, March 5, 1992, at A14.

The ability of medical science to preserve sperm for future insemination has also brought dilemmas to court. In Hecht v. Superior Court (Kane), 16 Cal.App.4th 836, 20 Cal.Rptr.2d 275 (1993), decedent's girlfriend sought to stay his estate from destroying decedent's sperm preserved in sperm bank. The Court of Appeals held that artificial insemination of an unmarried woman by her deceased partner did not violate public policy, and the sperm was "property" within the jurisdiction of the probate court. The court further held that the sperm should be distributed by the probate court according to the intent of the decedent as expressed in his will. On appeal from the probate court, the appellate court held that the executor of the will had to act as though no appeal were pending, even though the order was appealable, in order to prevent injury or loss to the person or property of the girlfriend. Kane v. Superior Court (Hecht), 37 Cal.App.4th 1577, 44 Cal.Rptr.2d 578 (1995). Hecht was over forty and expert medical testimony revealed that her chances of getting pregnant had decreased markedly since she turned forty and would decline further with each successive year. Id.

Should a posthumous donor be considered the legal parent of a child conceived using his genetic material? The UPA states that such a child would only belong to the deceased parent if the deceased party had "consented in a record that if assisted reproduction were to occur after death, the deceased individual would be a parent of the child." 9 U.L.A. § 707 (2005). Should the child be allowed to inherit from the deceased's estate? Taking into account advances in technology, what sort of time limitations should be set on provisions such as the one the UPA has adopted?

3. It is estimated that artificial insemination is responsible for more than 30,000 births annually in the United States. N.Y. Times, Oct. 7, 1990, sec. 6, at 23, col. 3.

4. Lillian Atallah, Report from a Test–Tube Baby, New York Times Mag., April 18, 1976, at 16, 48:

> "My parents ... decided to end their marriage after 26 years, and it was at that point that they told me.... At first, I was incredulous that my parents, tradition bound Arab immigrants, had done anything so radical. On second thought, it made perfect sense.... Barren wives were objects of pity and contempt.
>
> . . .
>
> Knowing about my AID origin did nothing to alter my feelings for my family. Instead, I felt grateful for the trouble they had taken to give me life."

In re Baby M.

Supreme Court of New Jersey, 1988.
109 N.J. 396, 537 A.2d 1227.

■ WILENTZ, C.J.

In this matter the Court is asked to determine the validity of a contract that purports to provide a new way of bringing children into a family. For a fee of $10,000, a woman agrees to be artificially inseminated with the semen of another woman's husband; she is to conceive a child, carry it to term, and after its birth surrender it to the natural father and his wife. . . .

We invalidate the surrogacy contract because it conflicts with the law and public policy of this State. While we recognize the depth of the yearning of infertile couples to have their own children, we find the payment of money to a "surrogate" mother illegal, perhaps criminal, and potentially degrading to women. . . .

. . .

In February 1985, William Stern and Mary Beth Whitehead entered into a surrogacy contract. It recited that Stern's wife, Elizabeth, was infertile, that they wanted a child, and that Mrs. Whitehead was willing to provide that child as the mother with Mr. Stern as the father.

The contract provided that through artificial insemination using Mr. Stern's sperm, Mrs. Whitehead would become pregnant, carry the child to term, bear it, deliver it to the Sterns, and thereafter do whatever was necessary to terminate her maternal rights so that Mrs. Stern could thereafter adopt the child. Mrs. Whitehead's husband, Richard,[1] was also a party to the contract; Mrs. Stern was not. Mr. Whitehead promised to do all acts necessary to rebut the presumption of paternity under the Parentage Act. Although Mrs. Stern was not a party to the surrogacy agreement, the contract gave her sole custody of the child in the event of Mr. Stern's death. Mrs. Stern's status as a nonparty to the surrogate parenting agreement presumably was to avoid the application of the baby-selling statute to this arrangement.

Mr. Stern, on his part, agreed to attempt the artificial insemination and to pay Mrs. Whitehead $10,000 after the child's birth, on its delivery to him. In a separate contract, Mr. Stern agreed to pay $7,500 to the Infertility Center of New York ("ICNY"). The Center's advertising campaigns solicit surrogate mothers and encourage infertile couples to consider surrogacy. ICNY arranged for the surrogacy contract by bringing the parties together, explaining the process to them, furnishing the contractual form, and providing legal counsel.

The history of the parties' involvement in this arrangement suggests their good faith. William and Elizabeth Stern were married in July 1974, having met at the University of Michigan, where both were Ph.D candidates. Due to financial considerations and Mrs. Stern's pursuit of a medical degree and residency, they decided to defer starting a family until 1981. Before then, however, Mrs. Stern learned that she might have multiple sclerosis and

1. Subsequent to the trial court proceedings, Mr. and Mrs. Whitehead were divorced, and soon thereafter Mrs. Whitehead remarried. Nevertheless, in the course of this opinion we will make reference almost exclusively to the facts as they existed at the time of trial, the facts on which the decision we now review was reached. We note moreover that Mr. Whitehead remains a party to this dispute. For these reasons, we continue to refer to appellants as Mr. and Mrs. Whitehead.

that the disease in some cases renders pregnancy a serious health risk. Her anxiety appears to have exceeded the actual risk, which current medical authorities assess as minimal. Nonetheless that anxiety was evidently quite real, Mrs. Stern fearing that pregnancy might precipitate blindness, paraplegia, or other forms of debilitation. Based on the perceived risk, the Sterns decided to forego having their own children. The decision had a special significance for Mr. Stern. Most of his family had been destroyed in the Holocaust. As the family's only survivor, he very much wanted to continue his bloodline.

Initially the Sterns considered adoption, but were discouraged by the substantial delay apparently involved and by the potential problem they saw arising from their age and their differing religious backgrounds. They were most eager for some other means to start a family.

The paths of Mrs. Whitehead and the Sterns to surrogacy were similar. Both responded to advertising by ICNY. The Sterns' response, following their inquiries into adoption, was the result of their long-standing decision to have a child. Mrs. Whitehead's response apparently resulted from her sympathy with family members and others who could have no children (she stated that she wanted to give another couple the "gift of life"); she also wanted the $10,000 to help her family.

Both parties, undoubtedly because of their own self-interest, were less sensitive to the implications of the transaction than they might otherwise have been. Mrs. Whitehead, for instance, appears not to have been concerned about whether the Sterns would make good parents for her child; the Sterns, on their part, while conscious of the obvious possibility that surrendering the child might cause grief to Mrs. Whitehead, overcame their qualms because of their desire for a child. At any rate, both the Sterns and Mrs. Whitehead were committed to the arrangement; both thought it right and constructive.

Mrs. Whitehead had reached her decision concerning surrogacy before the Sterns, and had actually been involved as a potential surrogate mother with another couple. After numerous unsuccessful artificial inseminations, that effort was abandoned. Thereafter, the Sterns learned of the Infertility Center, the possibilities of surrogacy, and of Mary Beth Whitehead. The two couples met to discuss the surrogacy arrangement and decided to go forward. On February 6, 1985, Mr. Stern and Mr. and Mrs. Whitehead executed the surrogate parenting agreement. After several artificial inseminations over a period of months, Mrs. Whitehead became pregnant. The pregnancy was uneventful and on March 27, 1986, Baby M was born.

. . . Her birth certificate indicated her name to be Sara Elizabeth Whitehead and her father to be Richard Whitehead. In accordance with Mrs. Whitehead's request, the Sterns visited the hospital unobtrusively to see the newborn child.

Mrs. Whitehead realized, almost from the moment of birth, that she could not part with this child. She had felt a bond with it even during pregnancy. Some indication of the attachment was conveyed to the Sterns at the hospital when they told Mrs. Whitehead what they were going to name the baby. She apparently broke into tears and indicated that she did not know if she could give up the child. She talked about how the baby looked like her daughter, and made it clear that she was experiencing great difficulty with the decision.

Nonetheless, Mrs. Whitehead was, for the moment, true to her word. Despite powerful inclinations to the contrary, she turned her child over to the Sterns on March 30 at the Whiteheads' home.

The Sterns were thrilled with their new child. They had planned extensively for its arrival, far beyond the practical furnishing of a room for her. It was a time of joyful celebration—not just for them but for their friends as well. The Sterns looked forward to raising their daughter, whom they named Melissa. While aware by then that Mrs. Whitehead was undergoing an emotional crisis, they were as yet not cognizant of the depth of that crisis and its implications for their newly-enlarged family.

Later in the evening of March 30, Mrs. Whitehead became deeply disturbed, disconsolate, stricken with unbearable sadness. She had to have her child. She could not eat, sleep, or concentrate on anything other than her need for her baby. The next day she went to the Sterns' home and told them how much she was suffering.

The depth of Mrs. Whitehead's despair surprised and frightened the Sterns. She told them that she could not live without her baby, that she must have her, even if only for one week, that thereafter she would surrender her child. The Sterns, concerned that Mrs. Whitehead might indeed commit suicide, not wanting under any circumstances to risk that, and in any event believing that Mrs. Whitehead would keep her word, turned the child over to her. It was not until four months later, after a series of attempts to regain possession of the child, that Melissa was returned to the Sterns, having been forcibly removed from the home where she was then living with Mr. and Mrs. Whitehead, the home in Florida owned by Mary Beth Whitehead's parents.

The struggle over Baby M began when it became apparent that Mrs. Whitehead could not return the child to Mr. Stern. Due to Mrs. Whitehead's refusal to relinquish the baby, Mr. Stern filed a complaint seeking enforcement of the surrogacy contract. He alleged, accurately, that Mrs. Whitehead had not only refused to comply with the surrogacy contract but had threatened to flee from New Jersey with the child in order to avoid even the possibility of his obtaining custody. The court papers asserted that if Mrs. Whitehead were to be given notice of the application for an order requiring her to relinquish custody, she would, prior to the hearing, leave the state with the baby. And that is precisely what she did. After the order was entered, *ex parte,* the process server, aided by the police, in the presence of the Sterns, entered Mrs. Whitehead's home to execute the order. Mr. Whitehead fled with the child, who had been handed to him through a window while those who came to enforce the order were thrown off balance by a dispute over the child's current name.

The Whiteheads immediately fled to Florida with Baby M. . . .

Eventually the Sterns discovered where the Whiteheads were staying, commenced supplementary proceedings in Florida, and obtained an order requiring the Whiteheads to turn over the child. Police in Florida enforced the order, forcibly removing the child from her grandparents' home. She was soon thereafter brought to New Jersey and turned over to the Sterns. The prior order of the court, issued *ex parte,* awarding custody of the child to the Sterns *pendente lite,* was reaffirmed by the trial court after consideration of the certified representations of the parties (both represented by counsel) concerning the unusual sequence of events that had unfolded. Pending final judgment, Mrs. Whitehead was awarded limited visitation with Baby M.

The Sterns' complaint, in addition to seeking possession and ultimately custody of the child, sought enforcement of the surrogacy contract. Pursuant to the contract, it asked that the child be permanently placed in their custody, that Mrs. Whitehead's parental rights be terminated, and that Mrs. Stern be allowed to adopt the child, i.e., that, for all purposes, Melissa become the Sterns' child.

The trial took thirty-two days over a period of more than two months. [The trial court] held that the surrogacy contract was valid; ordered that Mrs. Whitehead's parental rights be terminated and that sole custody of the child be granted to Mr. Stern; and, after hearing brief testimony from Mrs. Stern, immediately entered an order allowing the adoption of Melissa by Mrs. Stern, all in accordance with the surrogacy contract. Pending the outcome of the appeal, we granted a continuation of visitation to Mrs. Whitehead, although slightly more limited than the visitation allowed during the trial.

. . .

We have concluded that this surrogacy contract is invalid. Our conclusion has two bases: direct conflict with existing statutes and conflict with the public policies of this State, as expressed in its statutory and decisional law.

. . .

(1) Our law prohibits paying or accepting money in connection with any placement of a child for adoption. Violation is a high misdemeanor. Excepted are fees of an approved agency (which must be a non-profit entity) and certain expenses in connection with childbirth.

Considerable care was taken in this case to structure the surrogacy arrangement so as not to violate this prohibition. . . . Nevertheless, it seems clear that the money was paid and accepted in connection with an adoption.

. . . The payment of the $10,000 occurs only on surrender of custody of the child and "completion of the duties and obligations" of Mrs. Whitehead, including termination of her parental rights to facilitate adoption by Mrs. Stern. As for the contention that the Sterns are paying only for services and not for an adoption, we need note only that they would pay nothing in the event the child died before the fourth month of pregnancy, and only $1,000 if the child were stillborn, even though the "services" had been fully rendered. Additionally, one of Mrs. Whitehead's estimated costs, to be assumed by Mr. Stern, was an "Adoption Fee," presumably for Mrs. Whitehead's incidental costs in connection with the adoption.

Mr. Stern knew he was paying for the adoption of a child; Mrs. Whitehead knew she was accepting money so that a child might be adopted; the Infertility Center knew that it was being paid for assisting in the adoption of a child. The actions of all three worked to frustrate the goals of the statute. It strains credulity to claim that these arrangements, touted by those in the surrogacy business as an attractive alternative to the usual route leading to an adoption, really amount to something other than a private placement adoption for money.

. . . The evils inherent in baby bartering are loathsome for a myriad of reasons. The child is sold without regard for whether the purchasers will be suitable parents. N. Baker, Baby Selling: The Scandal of Black Market Adoption (1978). The natural mother does not receive the benefit of counseling and guidance to assist her in making a decision that may affect her for a lifetime. In fact, the monetary incentive to sell her child may, depending on her financial circumstances, make her decision less voluntary.... The negative consequences of baby buying are potentially present in the surrogacy context, especially the potential for placing and adopting a child without regard to the interest of the child or the natural mother.

termination

(2) The termination of Mrs. Whitehead's parental rights, called for by the surrogacy contract and actually ordered by the court, fails to comply with the stringent requirements of New Jersey law. Our law, recognizing the finality of any termination of parental rights, provides for such termination only where there has been a voluntary surrender of a child to an approved agency or to the Division of Youth and Family Services ("DYFS"), accompanied by a formal document acknowledging termination of parental rights, or where there has been a showing of parental abandonment or unfitness. A termination may ordinarily take one of three forms: an action by an approved agency, an action by DYFS, or an action in connection with a private placement adoption. The three are governed by separate statutes, but the standards for termination are substantially the same, except that whereas a written surrender is effective when made to an approved agency or to DYFS, there is no provision for it in the private placement context.

. . .

Our statutes, and the cases interpreting them, leave no doubt that where there has been no written surrender to an approved agency or to DYFS, termination of parental rights will not be granted in this state absent a very strong showing of abandonment or neglect. That showing is required in every context in which termination of parental rights is sought, be it an action by an approved agency, an action by DYFS, or a private placement adoption proceeding, even where the petitioning adoptive parent is, as here, a stepparent.

In this case a termination of parental rights was obtained not by proving the statutory prerequisites but by claiming the benefit of contractual provisions. From all that has been stated above, it is clear that a contractual agreement to abandon one's parental rights, or not to contest a termination action, will not be enforced in our courts. The Legislature would not have so carefully, so consistently, and so substantially restricted termination of parental rights if it had intended to allow termination to be achieved by one short sentence in a contract.

Since the termination was invalid, it follows, as noted above, that adoption of Melissa by Mrs. Stern could not properly be granted.

. . .

The surrogacy contract guarantees permanent separation of the child from one of its natural parents. Our policy, however, has long been that to the extent possible, children should remain with and be brought up by both of their natural parents.... This is not simply some theoretical ideal that in practice has no meaning. The impact of failure to follow that policy is nowhere better shown than in the results of this surrogacy contract. A child, instead of starting off its life with as much peace and security as possible, finds itself immediately in a tug-of-war between contending mother and father.

public policy

The surrogacy contract violates the policy of this State that the rights of natural parents are equal concerning their child, the father's right no greater than the mother's.... The whole purpose and effect of the surrogacy contract was to give the father the exclusive right to the child by destroying the rights of the mother.

The policies expressed in our comprehensive laws governing consent to the surrender of a child, stand in stark contrast to the surrogacy contract and what it implies. Here there is no counseling, independent or otherwise, of the natural mother, no evaluation, no warning.

The only legal advice Mary Beth Whitehead received regarding the surrogacy contract was provided in connection with the contract that she previously entered into with another couple. Mrs. Whitehead's lawyer was referred to her by the Infertility Center, with which he had an agreement to act as counsel for surrogate candidates. His services consisted of spending one hour going through the contract with the Whiteheads, section by section, and answering their questions. Mrs. Whitehead received no further legal advice prior to signing the contract with the Sterns.

Mrs. Whitehead was examined and psychologically evaluated, but if it was for her benefit, the record does not disclose that fact. The Sterns regarded the evaluation as important, particularly in connection with the question of whether she would change her mind. Yet they never asked to see it, and were content with the assumption that the Infertility Center had made an evaluation and had concluded that there was no danger that the surrogate mother would change her mind. From Mrs. Whitehead's point of view, all that she learned from the evaluation was that "she had passed." It is apparent that the profit motive got the better of the Infertility Center. Although the evaluation was made, it was not put to any use, and understandably so, for the psychologist warned that Mrs. Whitehead demonstrated certain traits that might make surrender of the child difficult and that there should be further inquiry into this issue in connection with her surrogacy. To inquire further, however, might have jeopardized the Infertility Center's fee. The record indicates that neither Mrs. Whitehead nor the Sterns were ever told of this fact, a fact that might have ended their surrogacy arrangement.

Under the contract, the natural mother is irrevocably committed before she knows the strength of her bond with her child. She never makes a totally voluntary, informed decision, for quite clearly any decision prior to the baby's birth is, in the most important sense, uninformed, and any decision after that, compelled by a pre-existing contractual commitment, the threat of a lawsuit, and the inducement of a $10,000 payment, is less than totally voluntary. Her interests are of little concern to those who controlled this transaction.

Although the interest of the natural father and adoptive mother is certainly the predominant interest, realistically the *only* interest served, even they are left with less than what public policy requires. They know little about the natural mother, her genetic makeup, and her psychological and medical history. Moreover, not even a superficial attempt is made to determine their awareness of their responsibilities as parents.

Worst of all, however, is the contract's total disregard of the best interests of the child. There is not the slightest suggestion that any inquiry will be made at any time to determine the fitness of the Sterns as custodial parents, of Mrs. Stern as an adoptive parent, their superiority to Mrs. Whitehead, or the effect on the child of not living with her natural mother.

This is the sale of a child, or, at the very least, the sale of a mother's right to her child, the only mitigating factor being that one of the purchasers is the father. Almost every evil that prompted the prohibition of the payment of money in connection with adoptions exists here.

The differences between an adoption and a surrogacy contract should be noted, since it is asserted that the use of money in connection with surrogacy does not pose the risks found where money buys an adoption. Katz, "Surrogate Motherhood and the Baby–Selling Laws," 20 Colum.J.L. & Soc.Probs. 1 (1986).

First, and perhaps most important, all parties concede that it is unlikely that surrogacy will survive without money. Despite the alleged selfless motivation of surrogate mothers, if there is no payment, there will be no surrogates, or very few. That conclusion contrasts with adoption; for obvious reasons, there remains a steady supply, albeit insufficient, despite the prohibitions against payment. The adoption itself, relieving the natural mother of the financial burden of supporting an infant, is the equivalent of payment.

Second, the use of money in adoptions does not *produce* the problem—conception occurs, and usually the birth itself, before illicit funds are offered. With surrogacy, the "problem," if one views it as such, consisting of the purchase of a woman's procreative capacity, at the risk of her life, is caused by and originates with the offer of money.

Third, with the law prohibiting the use of money in connection with adoptions, the built-in financial pressure of the unwanted pregnancy and the consequent support obligation do not lead the mother to the highest paying, ill-suited, adoptive parents. She is just as well off surrendering the child to an approved agency. In surrogacy, the highest bidders will presumably become the adoptive parents regardless of suitability, so long as payment of money is permitted.

Fourth, the mother's consent to surrender her child in adoptions is revocable, even after surrender of the child, unless it be to an approved agency, where by regulation there are protections against an ill-advised surrender. In surrogacy, consent occurs so early that no amount of advice would satisfy the potential mother's need, yet the consent is irrevocable.

The main difference, that the plight of the unwanted pregnancy is unintended while the situation of the surrogate mother is voluntary and intended, is really not significant. Initially, it produces stronger reactions of sympathy for the mother whose pregnancy was unwanted than for the surrogate mother, who "went into this with her eyes wide open." On reflection, however, it appears that the essential evil is the same, taking advantage of a woman's circumstances (the unwanted pregnancy or the need for money) in order to take away her child, the difference being one of degree.

In the scheme contemplated by the surrogacy contract in this case, a middle man, propelled by profit, promotes the sale. Whatever idealism may have motivated any of the participants, the profit motive predominates, permeates, and ultimately governs the transaction. The demand for children is great and the supply small. The availability of contraception, abortion, and the greater willingness of single mothers to bring up their children has led to a shortage of babies offered for adoption. The situation is ripe for the entry of the middleman who will bring some equilibrium into the market by increasing the supply through the use of money.

Intimated, but disputed, is the assertion that surrogacy will be used for the benefit of the rich at the expense of the poor. See, e.g., Radin, "Market Inalienability," 100 Harv.L.Rev. 1849, 1930 (1987). In response it is noted that the Sterns are not rich and the Whiteheads not poor. Nevertheless, it is clear to us that it is unlikely that surrogate mothers will be as proportionately numerous among those women in the top twenty percent income bracket as among those in the bottom twenty percent. Put differently, we doubt that infertile couples in the low-income bracket will find upper income surrogates.

In any event, even in this case one should not pretend that disparate wealth does not play a part simply because the contrast is not the dramatic "rich versus poor." At the time of trial, the Whiteheads' net assets were probably negative—Mrs. Whitehead's own sister was foreclosing on a second mortgage. Their income derived from Mr. Whitehead's labors. Mrs. Whitehead is a homemaker, having previously held part-time jobs. The Sterns are both professionals, she a medical doctor, he a biochemist. Their combined income when both were working was about $89,500 a year and their assets sufficient to pay for the surrogacy contract arrangements.

The point is made that Mrs. Whitehead *agreed* to the surrogacy arrangement, supposedly fully understanding the consequences. Putting aside the issue of how compelling her need for money may have been, and how significant her understanding of the consequences, we suggest that her consent is irrelevant. There are, in a civilized society, some things that money cannot buy. In America, we decided long ago that merely because conduct purchased by money was "voluntary" did not mean that it was good or beyond regulation and prohibition. Employers can no longer buy labor at the lowest price they can bargain for, even though that labor is "voluntary," or buy women's labor for less money than paid to men for the same job, or purchase the agreement of children to perform oppressive labor, or purchase the agreement of workers to subject themselves to unsafe or unhealthful working conditions. There are, in short, values that society deems more important than granting to wealth whatever it can buy, be it labor, love, or life. Whether this principle recommends prohibition of surrogacy, which presumably sometimes results in great satisfaction to all of the parties, is not for us to say. We note here only that, under existing law, the fact that Mrs. Whitehead "agreed" to the arrangement is not dispositive.

The long-term effects of surrogacy contracts are not known, but feared—the impact on the child who learns her life was bought, that she is the offspring of someone who gave birth to her only to obtain money; the impact on the natural mother as the full weight of her isolation is felt along with the full reality of the sale of her body and her child; the impact on the natural father and adoptive mother once they realize the consequences of their conduct. Literature in related areas suggests these are substantial considerations, although, given the newness of surrogacy, there is little information.

The surrogacy contract creates, it is based upon, principles that are directly contrary to the objectives of our laws. It guarantees the separation of a child from its mother; it looks to adoption regardless of suitability; it totally ignores the child; it takes the child from the mother regardless of her wishes and her maternal fitness; and it does all of this, it accomplishes all of its goals, through the use of money.

Beyond that is the potential degradation of some women that may result from this arrangement. In many cases, of course, surrogacy may bring satisfaction, not only to the infertile couple, but to the surrogate mother herself. The fact, however, that many women may not perceive surrogacy negatively but rather see it as an opportunity does not diminish its potential for devastation to other women.

In sum, the harmful consequences of this surrogacy arrangement appear to us all too palpable. In New Jersey the surrogate mother's agreement to sell her child is void. Its irrevocability infects the entire contract, as does the money that purports to buy it.

We have already noted that under our laws termination of parental rights cannot be based on contract, but may be granted only on proof of the statutory requirements. That conclusion was one of the bases for invalidating the surrogacy contract. Although excluding the contract as a basis for parental termination, we did not explicitly deal with the question of whether the statutory bases for termination existed. We do so here.

. . .

Nothing in this record justifies a finding that would allow a court to terminate Mary Beth Whitehead's parental rights under the statutory standard. It is not simply that obviously there was no "intentional abandonment or very substantial neglect of parental duties without a reasonable expectation of reversal of that conduct in the future," 9:3–48c(1), quite the contrary, but furthermore that the trial court never found Mrs. Whitehead an unfit mother and indeed affirmatively stated that Mary Beth Whitehead had been a good mother to her other children.

. . .

The right to procreate, as protected by the Constitution, has been ruled on directly only once by the United States Supreme Court. See Skinner v. Oklahoma, supra, 316 U.S. 535 (forced sterilization of habitual criminals violates equal protection clause of fourteenth amendment). Although Griswold v. Connecticut, supra, 381 U.S. 479, is obviously of a similar class, strictly speaking it involves the right *not* to procreate. The right to procreate very simply is the right to have natural children, whether through sexual intercourse or artificial insemination. It is no more than that. Mr. Stern has not been deprived of that right. Through artificial insemination of Mrs. Whitehead, Baby M is his child. The custody, care, companionship, and nurturing that follow birth are not parts of the right to procreation; they are rights that may also be constitutionally protected, but that involve many considerations other than the right of procreation. To assert that Mr. Stern's right of procreation gives him the right to the custody of Baby M would be to assert that Mrs. Whitehead's right of procreation does *not* give her the right to the custody of Baby M; it would be to assert that the constitutional right of procreation includes within it a constitutionally protected contractual right to destroy someone else's right of procreation.

. . .

Mr. Stern . . . contends that he has been denied equal protection of the laws by the State's statute granting full parental rights to a husband in relation to the child produced, with his consent, by the union of his wife with a sperm donor. The claim really is that of Mrs. Stern. It is that she is in precisely the same position as the husband in the statute: she is presumably infertile, as is the husband in the statute; her spouse by agreement with a third party procreates with the understanding that the child will be the couple's child. The alleged unequal protection is that the understanding is honored in the statute when the husband is the infertile party, but no similar understanding is honored when it is the wife who is infertile.

It is quite obvious that the situations are not parallel. A sperm donor simply cannot be equated with a surrogate mother. The State has more than a sufficient basis to distinguish the two situations—even if the only difference is between the time it takes to provide sperm for artificial insemination and the time invested in a nine-month pregnancy—so as to justify automatically divesting the sperm donor of his parental rights without automatically divesting a surrogate mother. Some basis for an equal protection argument might exist if Mary Beth Whitehead had contributed her egg to be implanted, fertilized or otherwise, in Mrs. Stern, resulting in the latter's pregnancy. That is not the case here, however.

Mrs. Whitehead, on the other hand, asserts a claim that falls within the scope of a recognized fundamental interest protected by the Constitution. As a mother, she claims the right to the companionship of her child. This is a fundamental interest, constitutionally protected. Furthermore, it was taken away from her by the action of the court below. Whether that action under these circumstances would constitute a constitutional deprivation, however, we need not and do not decide. By virtue of our decision Mrs. Whitehead's constitutional complaint—that her parental rights have been unconstitutionally terminated—is moot. . . .

. . . With the surrogacy contract disposed of, the legal framework becomes a dispute between two couples over the custody of a child produced by the artificial insemination of one couple's wife by the other's husband. Under the Parentage Act the claims of the natural father and the natural mother are entitled to equal weight. . . . The applicable rule given these circumstances is clear: the child's best interests determine custody.

. . .

The Whiteheads contend that the award of custody to the Sterns *pendente lite* was erroneous and that the error should not be allowed to affect the final custody decision. . . . The Whiteheads' conclusion is that had the trial court not given initial custody to the Sterns during the litigation, Mrs. Whitehead not only would have demonstrated her perfectly acceptable personality—the general tenor of the opinion of experts was that her personality problems surfaced primarily in crises—but would also have been able to prove better her parental skills along with an even stronger bond than may now exist between her and Baby M. Had she not been limited to custody for four months, she could have proved all of these things much more persuasively through almost two years of custody.

The argument has considerable force. It is of course possible that the trial court was wrong in its initial award of custody. It is also possible that such error, if that is what it was, may have affected the outcome. We disagree with the premise, however, that in determining custody a court should decide what the child's best interests *would be* if some hypothetical state of facts had existed. Rather, we must look to what those best interests *are, today,* even if some of the facts may have resulted in part from legal error. The child's interests come first: we will not punish it for judicial errors, assuming any were made. . . .

There were eleven experts who testified concerning the child's best interests, either directly or in connection with matters related to that issue. Our reading of the record persuades us that the trial court's decision awarding custody to the Sterns (technically to Mr. Stern) should be affirmed since "its findings . . . could reasonably have been reached on sufficient credible evidence present in the record." . . .

Our custody conclusion is based on strongly persuasive testimony contrasting both the family life of the Whiteheads and the Sterns and the personalities and characters of the individuals. The stability of the Whitehead family life was doubtful at the time of trial. Their finances were in serious trouble (foreclosure by Mrs. Whitehead's sister on a second mortgage was in process). Mr. Whitehead's employment, though relatively steady, was always at risk because of his alcoholism, a condition that he seems not to have been able to confront effectively. Mrs. Whitehead had not worked for quite some time, her last two employments having been part-time. One of the Whiteheads' positive attributes was their ability to bring up two children, and apparently well, even in so vulnerable a household. Yet substantial question was raised even about that aspect of their home life. The expert testimony contained criticism of Mrs. Whitehead's handling of her son's educational difficulties. Certain of the experts noted that Mrs. Whitehead perceived herself as omnipotent and omniscient concerning her children. She knew what they were thinking, what they wanted, and she spoke for them. As to Melissa, Mrs. Whitehead expressed the view that she alone knew what that child's cries and sounds meant. Her inconsistent stories about various things engendered grave doubts about her ability to explain honestly and sensitively to Baby M—and at the right time—the nature of her origin. Although faith in professional counseling is not a *sine qua non* of parenting, several experts believed that Mrs. Whitehead's contempt for professional help, especially professional psychological help, coincided with her feelings of omnipotence in a way that could be devastating to a child who most likely will need such help. In short, while love and affection there would be, Baby M's life with the Whiteheads promised to be too closely controlled by Mrs. Whitehead. The prospects for a wholesome independent psychological growth and development would be at serious risk.

The Sterns have no other children, but all indications are that their household and their personalities promise a much more likely foundation for Melissa to grow and thrive. There *is* a track record of sorts—during the one-and-a-half years of custody Baby M has done very well, and the relationship between both Mr. and Mrs. Stern and the baby has become very strong. The household is stable, and likely to remain so. Their finances are more than adequate, their circle of friends supportive, and their marriage happy. Most important, they are loving, giving, nurturing, and open-minded people. They have demonstrated the wish and ability to nurture and protect Melissa, yet at the same time to encourage her independence. Their lack of experience is more than made up for by a willingness to learn and to listen, a willingness that is enhanced by their professional training, especially Mrs. Stern's experience as a pediatrician. They are honest; they can recognize error, deal with it, and learn from it. They will try to determine rationally the best way to cope with problems in their relationship with Melissa. When the time comes to tell her about her origins, they will probably have found a means of doing so that accords with the best interests of Baby M. All in all, Melissa's future appears solid, happy, and promising with them.

Based on all of this we have concluded, independent of the trial court's identical conclusion, that Melissa's best interests call for custody in the Sterns. Our above-mentioned disagreements with the trial court do not, as we have noted, in any way diminish our concurrence with its conclusions. We feel, however, that those disagreements are important enough to be stated. . . .

It seems to us that given her predicament, Mrs. Whitehead was rather harshly judged—both by the trial court and by some of the experts. She was guilty of a breach of contract, and indeed, she did break a very important promise, but we think it is expecting something well beyond normal human capabilities to suggest that this mother should have parted with her newly born infant without a struggle. Other than survival, what stronger force is there? We do not know of, and cannot conceive of, any other case where a perfectly fit mother was expected to surrender her newly born infant, perhaps forever, and was then told she was a bad mother because she did not. We know of no authority suggesting that the moral quality of her act in those circumstances should be judged by referring to a contract made before she became pregnant. We do not countenance, and would never countenance, violating a court order as Mrs. Whitehead did, even a court order that is wrong; but her resistance to an order that she surrender her infant, possibly forever, merits a measure of understanding. We do not find it so clear that her efforts to keep her infant, when measured against the Sterns' efforts to take her away, make one, rather than the other, the wrongdoer. The Sterns suffered, but so did she. And if we go beyond suffering to an evaluation of the human stakes involved in the struggle, how much weight should be given to her nine months of pregnancy, the labor of childbirth, the risk to her life, compared to the payment of money, the anticipation of a child and the donation of sperm?

There has emerged a portrait of Mrs. Whitehead, exposing her children to the media, engaging in negotiations to sell a book, granting interviews that seemed helpful to her, whether hurtful to Baby M or not, that suggests a selfish, grasping woman ready to sacrifice the interests of Baby M and her other children for fame and wealth. That portrait is a half-truth, for while it may accurately reflect what ultimately occurred, its implication, that this is what Mary Beth Whitehead wanted, is totally inaccurate, at least insofar as the record before us is concerned. There is not one word in that record to support a claim that had she been allowed to continue her possession of her newly born infant, Mrs. Whitehead would have ever been heard of again; not one word in the record suggests that her change of mind and her subsequent fight for her child was motivated by anything other than love—whatever complex underlying psychological motivations may have existed.

We have a further concern regarding the trial court's emphasis on the Sterns' interest in Melissa's education as compared to the Whiteheads'. That this difference is a legitimate factor to be considered we have no doubt. But it should not be overlooked that a best-interests test is designed to create not a new member of the intelligentsia but rather a well-integrated person who might reasonably be expected to be happy with life. "Best interests" does not contain within it any idealized lifestyle; the question boils down to a judgment, consisting of many factors, about the likely future happiness of a human being. Stability, love, family happiness, tolerance, and, ultimately, support of independence—all rank much higher in predicting future happiness than the likelihood of a college education. We do not mean to suggest that the trial court would disagree. We simply want to dispel any possible misunderstanding on the issue.

Even allowing for these differences, the facts, the experts' opinions, and the trial court's analysis of both argue strongly in favor of custody in the Sterns. Mary Beth Whitehead's family life, into which Baby M would be placed, was anything but secure—the quality Melissa needs most. And today it may be even less so. Furthermore, the evidence and expert opinion based on it reveal personality characteristics, mentioned above, that might threaten the child's best development. The Sterns promise a secure home, with an understanding relationship that allows nurturing and independent growth to develop together. Although there is no substitute for reading the entire record, including the review of every word of each experts' testimony and reports, a summary of their conclusions is revealing. Six experts testified for Mrs. Whitehead: one favored joint custody, clearly unwarranted in this case; one simply rebutted an opposing expert's claim that Mary Beth Whitehead had a recognized personality disorder; one testified to the adverse impact of separation on *Mrs. Whitehead;* one testified about the evils of adoption and, to him, the probable analogous evils of surrogacy; one spoke only on the question of whether Mrs. Whitehead's consent in the surrogacy agreement was "informed consent"; and one spelled out the strong bond between mother and child. None of them unequivocally stated, or even necessarily implied, an opinion that custody in the Whiteheads was in the best interests of Melissa—the ultimate issue. The Sterns' experts, both well qualified—as were the Whiteheads'—concluded that the best interests of Melissa required custody in Mr. Stern. Most convincingly, the three experts chosen by the court-appointed guardian *ad litem* of Baby M, each clearly free of all bias and interest, unanimously and persuasively recommended custody in the Sterns.

Some comment is required on the initial *ex parte* order awarding custody *pendente lite* to the Sterns (and the continuation of that order after a plenary hearing). The issue, although irrelevant to our disposition of this case, may recur; and when it does, it can be of crucial importance. When father and mother are separated and disagree, at birth, on custody, only in an extreme, truly rare, case should the child be taken from its mother *pendente lite, i.e.*, only in the most unusual case should the child be taken from its mother before the dispute is finally determined by the court on its merits. The probable bond between mother and child, and the child's need, not just the mother's, to strengthen that bond, along with the likelihood, in most cases, of a significantly lesser, if any, bond with the father—all counsel against temporary custody in the father. A substantial showing that the mother's continued custody would threaten the child's health or welfare would seem to be required.

In this case, the trial court, believing that the surrogacy contract might be valid, and faced with the probable flight from the jurisdiction by Mrs. Whitehead and the baby if *any* notice were served, ordered, *ex parte,* an immediate transfer of possession of the child, *i.e.*, it ordered that custody be transferred immediately to Mr. Stern, rather than order Mrs. Whitehead not to leave the State. We have ruled, however, that the surrogacy contract is unenforceable and illegal. It provides no basis for either an *ex parte,* a plenary, an interlocutory, or a final order requiring a mother to surrender custody to a father. Any application by the natural father in a surrogacy dispute for custody pending the outcome of the litigation will henceforth require proof of unfitness, of danger to the child, or the like, of so high a quality and persuasiveness as to make it unlikely that such application will succeed. Absent the required showing, all that a court should do is list the matter for argument on notice to the mother. Even her threats to flee should not suffice to warrant any other relief unless her unfitness is clearly shown. At most, it should result in an order enjoining such flight. The erroneous transfer of custody, as we view it, represents a greater risk to the child than removal to a foreign jurisdiction, unless parental unfitness is clearly proved. Furthermore, we deem it likely that, advised of the law and knowing that her custody cannot seriously be challenged at this stage of the litigation, surrogate mothers will obey any court order to remain in the jurisdiction.

. . . Our reversal of the trial court's order . . . requires delineation of Mrs. Whitehead's rights to visitation. . . . We . . . remand the visitation issue to the trial court for an abbreviated hearing and determination. . . .

We also note the following for the trial court's consideration: First, this is not a divorce case where visitation is almost invariably granted to the non-custodial spouse. To some extent the facts here resemble cases where the non-custodial spouse has had practically no relationship with the child, but it only "resembles" those cases. In the instant case, Mrs. Whitehead spent the first four months of this child's life as her mother and has regularly visited the child since then. Second, she is not only the natural mother, but also the legal mother, and is not to be penalized one iota because of the surrogacy contract. Mrs. Whitehead, as the mother (indeed, as a mother who nurtured her child for its first four months—unquestionably a relevant consideration), is entitled to have her own interest in visitation considered. . . .

In all of this, the trial court should recall the touchstones of visitation: that it is desirable for the child to have contact with both parents; that besides the child's interests, the parents' interests also must be considered; but that when all is said and done, the best interests of the child are paramount.

We have decided that Mrs. Whitehead is entitled to visitation at some point, and that question is not open to the trial court on this remand. . . . It also should be noted that the guardian's recommendation of a five-year delay is most unusual—one might argue that it begins to border on termination. Nevertheless, if the circumstances as further developed by appropriate proofs or as reconsidered on remand clearly call for that suspension under applicable legal principles of visitation, it should be so ordered.

The judgment is affirmed in part, reversed in part, and remanded for further proceedings consistent with this opinion.

■ JUSTICES CLIFFORD, HANDLER, POLLOCK, O'HERN, GARIBALDI and STEIN join in this opinion.

NOTES

1. On remand, a New Jersey Superior Court held that Melissa's best interests would be served by unsupervised, liberal visitation with Mary Beth Whitehead–Gould. In re Baby M., 225 N.J.Super. 267, 542 A.2d 52 (Ch.Div. 1988). In 1994 it was reported that Melissa, who called herself Sassy, was an active eight year old and still very much torn between her two families. She lived most of the year in New Jersey with the Sterns, but spent two days a week and every other weekend in Long Island with Mrs. Whitehead–Gould and her four half siblings. The acrimony between the Sterns and Mrs. Whitehead–Gould showed no signs of abating. Torn Between Two Moms: Baby M 8 Years Later, Redbook, January 1994, at 60.

2. The contracts in the Baby M case provided:

SURROGATE PARENTING AGREEMENT

THIS AGREEMENT is made this 6th day of February, 1985, by and between MARY BETH WHITEHEAD, a married woman (herein referred to as "Surrogate), RICHARD WHITEHEAD, her husband (herein referred to a "Husband"), and WILLIAM STERN, (herein referred to as "Natural Father").

THIS AGREEMENT is made with reference to the following facts:

(1) WILLIAM STERN, Natural Father, is an individual over the age of eighteen (18) years who is desirous of entering into this Agreement.

(2) The sole purpose of this Agreement is to enable WILLIAM STERN and his infertile wife to have a child which is biologically related to WILLIAM STERN.

(3) MARY BETH WHITEHEAD, Surrogate, and RICHARD WHITEHEAD, her husband, are over the age of eighteen (18) years and desirous of entering into this Agreement in consideration of the following:

NOW THEREFORE, in consideration of the mutual promises contained Herein and the intentions of being legally bound hereby, the parties agree as follows:

1. MARY BETH WHITEHEAD, Surrogate, represents that she is capable of conceiving children. MARY BETH WHITEHEAD understands and agrees that in the best interest of the child, she will not form or attempt to form a parent-child relationship with any child or children she may conceive, carry to term and give birth to, pursuant to the provisions of this Agreement, and shall freely surrender custody to WILLIAM STERN, Natural Father, immediately upon birth of the child; and terminate all parental rights to said child pursuant to this Agreement.

2. MARY BETH WHITEHEAD, Surrogate, and RICHARD WHITEHEAD, her husband, have been married since 12/2/73, and RICHARD WHITEHEAD is in agreement with the purposes, intents and provisions of this Agreement and acknowledges that his wife, MARY BETH WHITEHEAD, Surrogate, shall be artificially inseminated pursuant to the provisions of this Agreement. RICHARD WHITEHEAD agrees that in the best interest of the child, he will not form or attempt to form a parent-child relationship with any child or children MARY BETH WHITEHEAD, Surrogate, may conceive by artificial insemination as described herein, and agrees to freely and readily surrender immediate custody of the child to WILLIAM STERN, Natural Father; and terminate his parental rights; RICHARD WHITEHEAD further acknowledges he will do all acts necessary to rebut the presumption of paternity of any offspring conceived and born pursuant to aforementioned agreement as provided by law, including blood testing and/or HLA testing.

3. WILLIAM STERN, Natural Father, does hereby enter into this written contractual Agreement with MARY BETH WHITEHEAD, Surrogate, where MARY BETH WHITEHEAD shall be artificially inseminated with the semen of WILLIAM STERN by a physician. MARY BETH WHITEHEAD, Surrogate, upon becoming pregnant, acknowledges that she will carry said embryo/fetus(s) until delivery. MARY BETH WHITEHEAD, Surrogate, and RICHARD WHITEHEAD, her husband, agree that they will cooperate with any background investigation into the Surrogate's medical, family and personal history and warrants the information to be accurate to the best of their knowledge. MARY BETH WHITEHEAD, Surrogate, and RICHARD WHITEHEAD, her husband, agree to surrender custody of the child to WILLIAM STERN, Natural Father, immediately upon birth, acknowledging that it is the intent of this Agreement in the best interests of the child to do so; as well as institute and cooperate in proceedings to terminate their respective parental rights to said child, and sign any and all necessary affidavits, documents, and the like, in order to further the intent and purposes of this Agreement. It is understood by MARY BETH WHITEHEAD, and RICHARD WHITEHEAD, that the child to be conceived is being done so for the sole purpose of giving said child to WILLIAM STERN, its natural and biological father. MARY BETH WHITEHEAD and RICHARD WHITEHEAD agree to sign all necessary affidavits prior to and after the birth of the child and voluntarily participate in any paternity proceedings necessary to have WILLIAM STERN'S name entered on said child's birth certificate as the natural or biological father.

4. That the consideration for this Agreement, which is compensation for services and expenses, and in no way is to be construed as a fee for termination of parental rights or a payment in exchange for a consent to surrender the child for adoption, in addition to other provisions contained herein, shall be as follows:

(A) $10,000 shall be paid to MARY BETH WHITEHEAD, Surrogate, upon surrender of custody to WILLIAM STERN, the natural and biological father of the child born pursuant to the provisions of this Agreement for surrogate services and expenses in carrying out her obligations under this Agreement;

(B) The consideration to be paid to MARY BETH WHITEHEAD, Surrogate, shall be deposited with the Infertility Center of New York (hereinafter ICNY), the representative of WILLIAM STERN, at the time of the signing of this Agreement, and held in escrow until completion of the duties and obligations of MARY BETH WHITEHEAD, Surrogate, (see Exhibit "A" for a copy of the Escrow Agreement), as herein described.

(C) WILLIAM STERN, Natural Father, shall pay the expenses incurred by MARY BETH WHITEHEAD, Surrogate, pursuant to her pregnancy, more specifically defined as follows:

(1) All medical, hospitalization, and pharmaceutical, laboratory and therapy expenses incurred as a result of MARY BETH WHITEHEAD'S pregnancy, not covered or allowed by her present health and major medical insurance, including all extraordinary medical expenses and all reasonable expenses for treatment of any emotional or mental conditions or problems related to said pregnancy, but in no case shall any such expenses be paid or reimbursed after a period of six (6) months have elapsed since the date of the termination of the pregnancy, and this Agreement specifically excludes any expenses for lost wages or other non-itemized incidentals (see Exhibit "B") related to said pregnancy.

(2) WILLIAM STERN, Natural Father, shall not be responsible for any latent medical expenses occurring six (6) weeks subsequent to the birth of the child, unless the medical problem or abnormality incident thereto was known and treated by a physician prior to the expiration of said six (6) week period and in written notice of the same sent to ICNY, as representative of WILLIAM STERN by certified mail, return receipt requested, advising of this treatment.

(3) WILLIAM STERN, Natural Father, shall be responsible for the total costs of all paternity testing. Such paternity testing may, at the option of WILLIAM STERN, Natural Father, be required prior to release of the surrogate fee from escrow. In the event WILLIAM STERN, Natural Father, is conclusively determined not to be the biological father of the child as a result of an HLA test, this Agreement will be deemed breached and MARY BETH WHITEHEAD, Surrogate, shall not be entitled to any fee. WILLIAM STERN, Natural Father, shall be entitled to reimbursement of all medical and related expenses from MARY BETH WHITEHEAD, Surrogate, and RICHARD WHITEHEAD, her husband.

(4) MARY BETH WHITEHEAD'S reasonable travel expenses incurred at the request of WILLIAM STERN, pursuant to this Agreement.

(5) MARY BETH WHITEHEAD, Surrogate, and RICHARD WHITEHEAD, her husband, understand and agree to assume all risks, including the risk of death, which are incidental to conception, pregnancy, childbirth, including but not limited to, postpartum complications. A copy of said possible risks and/or complications is attached hereto and made a part hereof (see Exhibit "C").

(6) MARY BETH WHITEHEAD, Surrogate, and RICHARD WHITEHEAD, her husband, hereby agree to undergo psychiatric evaluation by JOAN EINWOHNER, a psychiatrist as designated by WILLIAM STERN or an agent thereof. WILLIAM STERN shall pay for the cost of said psychiatric evaluation. MARY BETH WHITEHEAD and RICHARD WHITEHEAD shall sign, prior to their evaluations, a medical release permitting dissemination of the report prepared as a result of said psychiatric evaluations to ICNY or WILLIAM STERN and his wife.

(7) MARY BETH WHITEHEAD, Surrogate, and RICHARD WHITEHEAD, her husband, hereby agree that it is the exclusive and sole right of WILLIAM STERN, Natural Father, to name said child.

(8) "Child" as referred to in this Agreement shall include all children born simultaneously pursuant to the inseminations contemplated herein.

(9) In the event of the death of WILLIAM STERN, prior or subsequent to the birth of said child, it is hereby understood and agreed by MARY BETH WHITEHEAD, Surrogate, and RICHARD WHITEHEAD, her husband, that the child will be placed in the custody of WILLIAM STERN'S wife.

(10) In the event that the child is miscarried prior to the fifth (5th) month of pregnancy, no compensation, as enumerated in paragraph 4(A), shall be paid to MARY BETH WHITEHEAD, Surrogate. However, the expenses enumerated in paragraph 4(C) shall be paid or reimbursed to MARY BETH WHITEHEAD, Surrogate. In the event the child is miscarried, dies or is stillborn subsequent to the fourth (4th) month of pregnancy and said child does not survive, the Surrogate shall receive $1,000.00 in lieu of the compensation enumerated in paragraph 4(A). In the event of a miscarriage or stillbirth as described above, this Agreement shall terminate and neither MARY BETH WHITEHEAD, Surrogate, nor WILLIAM STERN, Natural Father, shall be under any further obligation under this Agreement.

(11) MARY BETH WHITEHEAD, Surrogate, and WILLIAM STERN, Natural Father, shall have undergone complete physical and genetic evaluation, under the direction and supervision of a licensed physician, to determine whether the physical health and well-being of each is satisfactory. Said physical examination shall include testing for venereal diseases, specifically including but not limited to, syphilis, herpes and gonorrhea. Said venereal diseases testing shall be done prior to, but not limited to, each series of inseminations.

(12) In the event that pregnancy has not occurred within a reasonable time, in the opinion of WILLIAM STERN, Natural Father, this Agreement shall terminate by written notice to MARY BETH WHITEHEAD, Surrogate, at the residence provided to the ICNY by the Surrogate, from ICNY, as representative of WILLIAM STERN, Natural Father.

(13) MARY BETH WHITEHEAD, Surrogate, agrees that she will not abort the child conceived except, if in the professional medical opinion of the inseminating physician, such action is necessary for the physical health of MARY BETH WHITEHEAD or the child has been determined by said physician to be physiologically abnormal. MARY BETH WHITEHEAD further agrees, upon the request of said physician to undergo amniocentesis (see Exhibit "D") or similar tests to detect genetic and congenital defects. In the event said test reveals that the fetus is genetically or congenitally abnormal, MARY BETH WHITEHEAD, Surrogate, agrees to abort the fetus upon demand of WILLIAM STERN, Natural Father, in which event, the fee paid to the Surrogate will be in accordance to Paragraph 10. If MARY BETH WHITEHEAD refuses to abort the fetus upon demand of WILLIAM STERN, his obligations as stated in this Agreement shall cease forthwith, except as to obligation of paternity imposed by statute.

(14) Despite the provisions of Paragraph 13, WILLIAM STERN, Natural Father, recognizes that some genetic and congenital abnormalities may not be detected by amniocentesis or other tests, and therefore, if proven to be the biological father of the child, assumes the legal responsibility for any child who may possess genetic or congenital abnormalities. (See Exhibits "E" and "F").

(15) MARY BETH WHITEHEAD, Surrogate, further agrees to adhere to all medical instructions given to her by the inseminating physician as well as her independent obstetrician. MARY BETH WHITEHEAD also agrees not to smoke cigarette, drink alcoholic beverages, use illegal drugs, or take non-prescription medications or prescribed medications without written consent from her physician. MARY BETH WHITEHEAD agrees to follow a prenatal medical examination schedule to consist of no fewer visits then: one visit per month during the first seven (7) months of pregnancy, two visits (each to occur at two-week intervals) during the eighth and ninth month of pregnancy.

(16) MARY BETH WHITEHEAD, Surrogate, agrees to cause RICHARD WHITEHEAD, her husband, to execute a refusal of consent form as annexed hereto as Exhibit "G".

(17) Each party acknowledges that he or she fully understands this Agreement and its legal effect, and that they are signing the same freely and voluntarily and that neither party has any reason to believe that the other(s) did not freely and voluntarily execute said Agreement.

(18) In the event any of the provisions of this Agreement are deemed to be invalid or unenforceable, the same shall be deemed severable from the remainder of this Agreement and shall not cause the invalidity or unenforceability of the remainder of this Agreement. If such provision shall be deemed invalid due to its scope or breadth, then said provision shall be deemed valid to the extent of the scope or breadth permitted by law.

(19) The original of this Agreement, upon execution, shall be retained by the Infertility Center of New York, with photocopies being distributed to MARY BETH WHITEHEAD, Surrogate and WILLIAM STERN, Natural Father, having the same legal effect as the original.

WILLIAM STERN, Natural Father

DATE 2/6/85
STATE OF NEW YORK

We have read the foregoing five pages of this Agreement, and it is our collective intention by affixing our signatures below, to enter into a binding legal obligation.

MARY BETH WHITEHEAD, Surrogate
DATE 1–30–85

RICHARD WHITEHEAD, Surrogate's Husband
DATE 1–30–85

AGREEMENT BETWEEN WILLIAM STERN AND ICNY

THIS AGREEMENT is made this THIRD day of DECEMBER 1984, by and between WILLIAM STERN hereinafter referred to as Natural Father, and the Primary Research Associates of United States, Inc., d/b/a Infertility Center of New York, (hereinafter referred to as "ICNY").

WHEREAS, Natural Father is desirous of taking part in the process of surrogate parenting wherein he will attempt to conceive a child by artificial insemination of a surrogate mother;

WHEREAS, ICNY is a corporation duly organized and existing under the laws of the State of New York for the purpose inter alia of engaging in research, developmental work and design in the areas of surrogate parenting, ovum transfer and in vitro fertilization with implantation in a surrogate; and additionally providing administrative and supportive services for the above; and

WHEREAS, Natural Father is desirous of contracting with ICNY for such services; and

WHEREAS ICNY is desirous of contracting with the Natural Father to provide such services;

NOW THEREFORE, in consideration of the mutual promises contained herein, and with the intentions of being legally bound hereby, the parties mutually agree as follows:

(1) Natural Father hereby contracts with ICNY for the services offered by ICNY and ICNY agrees to contract with the Natural Father to use its best efforts to assist the Natural Father in the selection of a "surrogate mother" as hereinafter defined, it being understood that the final selection of the "surrogate mother" is solely within the discretion of the Natural Father. In addition to assisting the Natural Father in the selection of a "surrogate mother", ICNY shall also provide the services set forth in Exhibit "A" annexed hereto and made a part hereof and these services shall continue until the completion of the duties and obligations of surrogate or until such time as the Natural Father decides not to utilize ICNY's services, provided that the Natural Father is not in breach of this Agreement.

(2) Natural Father agrees and understands that he must enter into an agreement with the selected surrogate mother whereby Natural Father agrees to the process of artificial insemination with the use of his semen for the purpose of impregnating the surrogate mother. Thereafter, the surrogate mother shall give birth to a child

fathered by the Natural Father and voluntarily surrender custody of said child to the Natural Father.

(3) Natural Father hereby agrees to pay ICNY as compensation for the services provided by ICNY the sum of SEVEN THOUSAND FIVE HUNDRED DOLLARS ($7,500.00) incurred by ICNY on behalf of the Natural Father. The Natural Father understands and agrees that said sum is non-refundable. A partial list of costs and expenses is annexed hereto and made a part hereof as Exhibit "B". ICNY shall on a periodic basis bill the Natural Father for the costs and expenses incurred on behalf of the Natural Father.

The Natural Father agrees that ICNY shall act as escrow agent for the fee to be paid by the Natural Father to the selected surrogate mother.

(4) The following list of definitions shall apply throughout this Agreement:

(a) "Child" is defined as all children born simultaneously as a result of the Insemination contemplated by this Agreement.

(b) "Natural Father" is defined as the individual over the age of eighteen (18) who has selected the surrogate mother and whose semen is used in the insemination contemplated herein resulting in the birth of the child.

(c) "Surrogate mother" is defined as a woman over the age of eighteen (18) selected by the Natural Father to be impregnated by the process of artificial insemination with woman of the Natural Father for the purpose of becoming pregnant and giving birth to a child and surrendering the child to the Natural Father.

(5) ICNY agrees to provide the services detailed in Exhibit "A". Said services including the offering, at the option of the Natural Father, of legal representation of the Natural Father in his negotiations and agreement with the surrogate mother. The Natural Father understands and acknowledges that ICNY offers these legal services through the law firm retained by ICNY but, ICNY makes no representations or warranties with respect to matters of law or the legality of surrogate parenting and is not rendering legal services on providing legal advice. However, the Natural Father has the absolute right to seek legal counsel of his own selection in his negotiations and agreement with the selected surrogate mother or her representative. In the event the Natural Father utilizes the legal services of counsel other than the law firm retained by ICNY, all legal fees and cost shall be borne by the Natural Father and such fees and costs shall be in addition to the fees and costs set forth in Paragraph of this Agreement.

(6) Prior to signing this Agreement, each party has been given the opportunity to consult with an attorney of his own choice concerning the terms and legal significance of the Agreement, and the effect which it has upon any and all interests of the parties. Each party acknowledges that he fully understands the Agreement and its legal effect, and that he is signing the same freely and voluntarily and that neither party has any reason to believe that the other did not understand fully the terms and effects of this Agreement, or that he did not freely and voluntarily execute this Agreement.

(7) Natural Father warrants and represents the following to ICNY:

(a) That the Natural Father's semen is of sufficient nature both quantitatively and qualitatively to impregnate the selected surrogate mother.

(b) That the Natural Father is medically free from disease or other hereditary medical problems which could cause injury, defect, or disease to the surrogate mother or child.

(c) That the Natural Father will not make or attempt to make directly or through a representative, a subsequent agreement with the selected surrogate mother or any other surrogates introduced to the Natural Father by ICNY before or at any time after the birth of his child. In the event of a further arrangement with the surrogate for a child is made, the Natural Father agrees to pay to ICNY a second fee in the amount specified in Paragraph 3 of this Agreement.

(8) Natural Father agrees that breach of any of his warranties and representations shall cause this Agreement to immediately terminate but in no way relieve the Natural Father from his obligations under this Agreement. Further, the Natural Father agrees that his warranties and representations shall survive the termination of this Agreement.

(9) Natural Father hereby acknowledges that ICNY makes no representations or warranties with respect to any agreement or understanding which may be reached, or may have been reached, between himself and a prospective "surrogate mother." Natural Father further acknowledges that the nature of any such agreement or understanding as well as all ramifications, obligations and enforcement matters relating thereto are subject which he must seek advice from his attorney.

(10) It is expressly understood that ICNY does not guarantee or warrant that the "surrogate mother" will in fact conceive a child fathered by Natural Father; nor does ICNY guarantee or warrant that if a child is conceived, it will be a healthy child, free from all defects; nor does ICNY guarantee or warrant the "surrogate mother" (and her husband, if applicable) will comply with the terms and provisions of the separate agreement entered into between herself and Natural Father including but not limited to, the "surrogate mother's" refusal to surrender custody of the child upon birth.

(11) Natural Father hereby specifically releases ICNY and its officers, employees agents and representatives from any and all liability and responsibility of any nature whatsoever except willful and gross negligence, which may result from complications, breaches, damages, losses, claims, actions, liabilities, whether actual or asserted of any kind, and all other costs or detriments of any kind, in any way related to or arising from any agreement or understanding between himself and a "surrogate mother" located through the services of ICNY. Moreover, the Natural Father understands the relationship between ICNY and the relationship of the doctors used in connection with insemination, monitoring and any other medical or psychiatric procedure or treatment of the surrogate or of the child is that of an independent contractor and that there is no other relationship between the parties.

(12) This Agreement is binding on each party's respective executors, heirs, assigns and successors.

(13) This Agreement has been drafted, negotiated and executed in New York, New York, and shall be governed by, continued and enforced in accordance with the laws of the State of New York.

(14) In the event any of the provisions of this Agreement are deemed to be invalid or unenforceable, the same shall be deemed severable from the remainder of this Agreement and shall not cause the invalidity or unenforceability of the remainder of this Agreement. If such provision(s) shall be deemed invalid due to its scope or breadth, then said provision(s) shall be deemed valid to the extent of the scope or breadth permitted by law.

2. In R.R. v. M.H., 426 Mass. 501, 689 N.E.2d, 790 (1998), the Supreme Judicial Court of Massachusetts held unenforceable a surrogacy contract similar to the one in Baby M on the ground that it involved the payment of money. The court explained that "[e]liminating any financial reward to a surrogate mother is the only way to assure that no economic pressure will cause a woman, who may well be a member of an economically vulnerable class, to act as a surrogate." 689 N.E.2d at 796. The court added:

> If no compensation is paid beyond pregnancy-related expenses and if the mother is not bound by her consent to the father's custody of the child unless she consents after a suitable period has passed following the child's birth, [our] objections ... would be overcome.... Other conditions might be important in deciding the enforceability of a surrogacy agreement, such as a requirement that (a) the mother's husband give his informed consent to the agreement in advance; (b) the mother be an adult and have had at least one successful pregnancy; (c) the mother, her husband, and the intended parents have been evaluated for the soundness of their judgment and for their capacity to carry out the agreement;

(d) the father's wife be incapable of bearing a child without endangering her health; (e) the intended parents be suitable persons to assume custody of the child; and (f) all parties have the advice of counsel. The mother and father may not, however, make a binding best-interests-of-the-child determination by private agreement. Any custody agreement is subject to a judicial determination of custody based on the best interest of the child.

3. A number of states have passed statutes that bar the enforcement of surrogacy agreements. See A.R.S. § 25–218(A) (2004); D.C. Code § 16–402(a) (2005); Burns Ind. Code Ann. §§ 30–20–1–1, 30–20–1–2; MCLS § 722.855 (2005); NY CLS Dom Rel § 122 (2005); N.D. Cent. Code § 14–18–05 (2005); Utah Code Ann. § 76–7–204 (2005). Others deny enforcement only if the surrogate is compensated. See KRS § 199.590(4) (2004); La. RS § 9:2713 (2005); RRS Neb. § 25–21,200 (2005); Rev. Code Wash. (ARCW) §§ 26.26.230, 26.26.240 (2005). New Hampshire and Virginia place restrictions on who may act as a surrogate and require advance judicial approval of the agreement. See RSA § 168–B; Va. Code Ann. § 20.

4. In J.R. v. Utah, 261 F.Supp.2d 1268 (D.Utah 2003), the Utah law prohibiting the enforcement of surrogacy contracts was found unconstitutional to the extent that it abridged the parental rights of people who were the biological parents as well as the intended parents of a fetus implanted in a surrogate.

In re C.K.G.

Supreme Court of Tennessee, 2005.
173 S.W.3d 714.

■ FRANK F. DROWOTA, III, CHIEF JUSTICE

Charles K. G. and Ms. Cindy C.[2] first met in 1993 while working at Vanderbilt University Medical Center in Nashville. Cindy was a nurse practitioner who managed a department through which Charles, then a medical resident, rotated. Charles and Cindy began dating in 1994. After an initial period of closeness, they maintained for several years an unsteady dating relationship which included an extended period of estrangement.

In 1999, Charles and Cindy not only reunited as an unmarried couple but also soon thereafter began discussing having a child together. By this time Cindy was forty-five years old and Charles was also in his mid-forties. Charles had never had children. He had not grown up in Tennessee, and a December 1999 visit to his birthplace influenced him; he wanted to be a father. Even though Cindy had at least two adult children from prior marriages as well as grandchildren, she was amenable to starting a family with Charles. However, given her age, Cindy was concerned about the viability of her ova, or eggs.

Having decided to have a child, Charles and Cindy pursued *in vitro*[3] fertilization through the Nashville Fertility Center. On May 2, 2000, they jointly executed several agreements with the Fertility Center. Although Charles and Cindy were unmarried, they did not alter the boilerplate language that the Center frequently used in its agreements describing them as "husband" and "wife." Included among these agreements was a "RECIPIENT CONSENT FOR DONATION OF OOCYTES BY ANONYMOUS DONOR" ("Recipient Consent") which describes the fertilization procedure

2. In order to protect the anonymity of the children who are subject to dispute in this case, we refer to them by their initials. For the same reason, we replace the parties' surnames with initials.

3. *In vitro* means "in an artificial environment, referring to a process or reaction occurring therein, as in a test tube or culture media." PDR Medical Dictionary 889 (Marjory Spraycar ed. 1995).

and its risks, waives the right of Charles and Cindy to know the egg donor's identity, and outlines the responsibilities of the parties to the agreement. The Recipient Consent further provides as follows:

> I, Cindy (wife), understand that the child(ren) conceived by this method will not have my genetic material, but will have that of the oocyte [egg] donor and my husband [sic]. However, regardless of the outcome, I will be the mother of any child(ren) born to me as a result of egg donation and hereby accept all the legal responsibilities required of such a parent.

This document was signed by Cindy as "wife" and by Charles as "husband" and was witnessed and signed by a physician who represented that he had fully explained the procedure to Charles and Cindy and had answered all their questions. However, Charles and Cindy executed no other agreements concerning their intentions as to parentage or surrogacy.

Shortly thereafter, Charles paid the Fertility Center $10,000 for the procedure of having two anonymously donated eggs fertilized with Charles's sperm and inserted in Cindy's uterus. Charles intended for them to conceive only one child (presumably two eggs were used to increase the procedure's odds of success). After fertilization, one of the eggs divided, resulting in the development of three embryos. All three embryos flourished; Cindy had become pregnant with triplets.

During Cindy's pregnancy, Charles began residing consistently at Cindy's home. Due to complications with the pregnancy, Cindy took an early leave from her job. When she was placed on bed rest, Charles maintained the household and cooked for her. On February 21, 2001, Cindy gave birth via caesarian section to three children: C.K.G., C.A.G., and C.L.G. Tennessee Department of Health birth certificates for the children identify Charles as the father and Cindy as the mother.

Although Charles had never promised to marry Cindy, he represented that he desired permanence and stability with her. Further, Cindy understood and expected that they would raise the children together as mother and father. In fact, Cindy even sought assurance from Charles that she would not have to rear them by herself. Cindy stayed home with the triplets on maternity leave until June 2001 when she returned to work four days per week. Having set aside money in anticipation of having a child, Charles took a one-year leave of absence (February 2001 to January 2002) from his position as an emergency room physician. For the first several months after the triplets' birth, Charles and Cindy lived together and shared parenting responsibilities. They each provided financially for the children's needs. Further, for some time they had discussed the need for a larger home, and they purchased a house in Brentwood together as tenants in common with the understanding that they would bear the cost equally. Cindy sold her prior residence, and she, Charles, and the triplets moved into the new house in August 2001.

After hiring a nanny, Charles and Cindy's relationship soon deteriorated. Cindy alleged that Charles began cultivating or renewing relationships with several other women; Charles admitted to having sex with another woman during a December 2001 trip to London, England. Cindy further alleged that once their relationship had begun to deteriorate, Charles not only became dramatically less involved with the children, but also began withholding financial support from them. In April 2002, after utility service to their home had been cut off, Cindy filed a petition in the juvenile court of Williamson County to establish parentage and to obtain custody and child support.

In response, Charles argued that because Cindy lacks genetic connection to the children, she fails to qualify as the children's "mother" under Tennessee's domestic relations statutes. Contending that Cindy thus lacks standing as a parent, Charles sought sole and exclusive custody of the triplets. Charles further denied that he had failed to support the children financially and also alleged that Cindy was often absent from home on account of her part-time pursuit of a master's degree in business administration. Cindy conceded that Charles increased his involvement with the children after she filed suit. A pendente lite order required Charles to pay Cindy $3,000 per month for child support. Charles and Cindy continued to live together pending trial.

In anticipation of trial, Charles and Cindy stipulated that: (1) eggs donated by an anonymous third-party female were fertilized with Charles's sperm and implanted in Cindy's uterus; (2) Cindy carried the resulting embryos to term and gave birth to triplets; (3) based on genetic testing, Charles is the biological father of all three children; (4) based on genetic testing, none of the children obtained genetic material from Cindy; and (5) the genetic testing was valid.

After a bench trial, the juvenile court ruled that Cindy had standing to bring a parentage action "as legal mother of these three (3) minor children with all the rights, privileges, and obligations as if she were their biological mother." The juvenile court reasoned that Cindy "is the birth mother and always had the intent to birth these children for herself and [Charles]." Having so decided, the juvenile court addressed the question of custody and support. The court concluded that in light of all the circumstances, Charles and Cindy were both good and caring parents. Based upon their "comparative fitness . . . as that affects the best interests of the minor children," the court awarded joint custody with Cindy designated as the primary custodial parent. The court further ordered certain visitation rights in favor of Charles and required him to continue to pay Cindy child support in the amount of $3,000 per month. Charles appealed as of right.

The Court of Appeals affirmed the judgments of the juvenile court. . . .

We granted Charles's application for permission to appeal.

In this case, an unmarried, heterosexual couple—Charles and Cindy—had children by obtaining eggs donated from an anonymous third-party female, fertilizing the eggs *in vitro* with Charles's sperm, and implanting the fertilized eggs in Cindy's uterus. Even though Cindy had no genetic connection to the three children to whom she eventually gave birth, she and Charles intended to rear the children together as mother and father. When the couple's relationship deteriorated, Cindy filed a parentage action seeking custody and child support from Charles. In response, Charles claimed that Cindy had no standing as a parent because, lacking genetic connection to the children, she failed to qualify as a parent under Tennessee parentage statutes. On this basis, Charles sought sole and exclusive custody. The facts of this case thus present us with a question of first impression in Tennessee: under such circumstances, who as a matter of law is the children's mother? . . .

. . .

"Historically, gestation proved genetic parentage beyond doubt, so it was unnecessary to distinguish between gestational and genetic mothers." However, recent developments in reproductive technology have caused a tectonic shift in the realities which underlie our legal conceptions of parenthood.

> With the technological development of a number of processes of procreation, most notably in vitro fertilization, the conceptive and gestational phases of reproduction can now be separate. Thus, the genetic and gestational mothers of a child are no longer necessarily the same person, which can result in a child having several possible parents. These new reproductive technologies and arrangements give rise to the fundamental question of who should be recognized as the parents of a child born as a result of various parties making distinct contributions to the process of procreation.

Campbell, 77 A.L.R. 5th at 574, § 2[a].

This technological fragmentation of the procreative process, insofar as it includes techniques for egg and sperm donation and preservation, has engendered a bewildering variety of possibilities which are not easily reconciled with our traditional definitions of "mother," "father," and "parent."

> We now live in an era where a child may have as many as five different "parents." These include a sperm donor, an egg donor, a surrogate or gestational host, and two nonbiologically related individuals who intend to raise the child. Indeed, the process of procreation itself has become so fragmented by the variety and combinations of collaborative-reproductive methods that there are a total of sixteen different reproductive combinations, in addition to traditional conception and childbirth.

John Lawrence Hill, What Does It Mean to Be a "Parent"? The Claims of Biology as the Basis for Parental Rights, 66 N.Y.U.L.Rev. 353, 355 (1991). The degree to which current statutory law governs or fails to govern these realities provides the initial framework for our analysis. . . .

The [Tennessee] parentage statutes define "mother" as "the *biological* mother of a child born out of wedlock." Tenn. Code Ann. § 36–2–302(4) (2001) (emphasis added). Similarly, "parent" is defined as "the *biological* mother or *biological* father of a child, regardless of the marital status of the mother and father." Tenn. Code Ann. § 36–2–302(5) (emphasis added). The parentage statutes do not define "biological mother." Consequently, we adduce definitions provided by Tennessee's adoption statutes. Statutes *in pari materia*—that is, statutes relating to the same subject or having a common purpose—are to be construed together. Lyons v. Rasar, 872 S.W.2d 895, 897 (Tenn. 1994).

The adoption statutes define "biological parents" as "the woman and man who *physically or genetically conceived* the child." Tenn. Code Ann. § 36–1–102(10) (2001) (emphasis added). Code section 36–1–102(10) focuses solely on conception, making no reference to giving birth. The verb "conceived" is modified by two disjunctively related adverbs. On the one hand, "physically" is an adverb meaning "in a physical manner" and "in respect to the body," Webster's Third New Int'l Dictionary of the English Language Unabridged 1707, and which thus means in a manner which relates to or stands "in accordance with the laws of nature," id. at 1706 (defining "physical"). As used in the statute, "physically ... conceived" therefore means having caused conception through natural means (coitus) as opposed to artificial means.

On the other hand, "genetically conceived" means having caused conception in a manner pertaining to "genetic makeup and phenomena." Genetic conception thus entails the contribution of one's genes to a child. By providing for genetic conception in addition to physical or natural conception, Code section 36–1–102(10) implicitly accounts for genetic procreation via technological assistance. If practicable, a statute is to be construed so that its component parts are reasonably consistent. Marsh v. Henderson, 221 Tenn. 42, 424 S.W.2d 193, 196 (Tenn. 1968). "Every word used is presumed to have meaning and purpose, and should be given full effect if so doing does not violate the obvious intention of the Legislature." Id.

We agree with the Court of Appeals that Cindy falls outside the statutory scope of the parentage and adoption statutes, which do not expressly control the circumstances of this case. . . .

. . .

. . . [T]he parentage statutes generally fail to contemplate dispute over maternity. For example, the rebuttable presumptions of parentage provided in Tennessee Code Annotated section 36–2–304 (2001) focus exclusively on establishing paternity. See Tenn. Code Ann. § 36–2–304(a) ("A *man* is rebuttably presumed to be the *father* of a child if. . . .") (emphasis added). The statutes also employ the term "mother" in a way that assumes we already know who the "mother" is, see, e.g., Tenn. Code Ann. §§ 36–2–303, 36–2–305(b)(1)(B) (2001), whereas references to "father" include such phrases as "a man claiming to be the child's father," Tenn. Code Ann. § 36–2–305(b)(1)(C), "alleged father," Tenn. Code Ann. § 36–2–305(b)(4), and "putative father," Tenn. Code Ann. § 36–2–318 (2001). Similarly, the statute providing for an order of parentage is concerned solely with the establishment of paternity. See Tenn. Code Ann. § 36–2–311(a) (2001) ("Upon establishing parentage, the court shall make an order declaring the *father* of the child.") (emphasis added). The statutes lack corresponding language concerning the establishment of maternity.

The legislative history of the parentage statutes reinforces our conclusion that they fail to contemplate or to control the circumstances of this case. . . .

. . .

Significantly, the legislative history shows that the current parentage statutes were not designed to control questions of parentage where sperm or egg donation is involved. In response to the observation that the new parentage statutes could potentially allow a sperm donor to file a parentage claim, Mr. Steve Cobb stated as follows:

> I can tell you that the clear intention, discussed intention, of this [bill] was *not* to deal with sperm donors at all. . . . We wanted to put that off for another day. . . . The intent, and it should be stated by the sponsor in a colloquy on the floor if necessary, is not to affect that issue *at all*.

Tape S–Jud. #4 (Tennessee Senate Judiciary Committee May 13, 1997). Concerning the question of maternity where egg donation is involved, the legislative history contains no indication that this matter was ever contemplated as a potential issue.

In sum, we conclude that Tennessee's parentage and related statutes do not provide for or control the circumstances of this case. Contrary to the position taken by the dissent which would restrict the basis for legal maternity to genetic consanguinity alone, we determine that these statutes simply do not apply to all conceivable parentage determinations. In this regard, we agree with the Court of Appeals.

In the absence of express guidance from the legislature, the Court of Appeals looked to case law from other jurisdictions to resolve the dispute of maternity in this case. Among the few jurisdictions which have addressed cases like this one, where a gestational carrier implanted with donated eggs seeks parental status of the resulting children and where legislation does not clearly resolve the matter, two tests for maternity have arisen. Some courts have focused on intent, holding that under such circumstances the intended "mother" is to be deemed the legal mother. See, e.g., Johnson v. Calvert, 5 Cal. 4th 84, 19 Cal. Rptr. 2d 494, 851 P.2d 776 (Cal. 1993); In re Marriage of Buzzanca, 61 Cal. App. 4th 1410, 72 Cal. Rptr.2d 280 (Cal. Ct. App. 1998); McDonald v. McDonald, 196 A.D.2d 7, 608 N.Y.S.2d 477 (N.Y. App. Div. 1994). Other courts have instead focused on genetics and gestation, holding that genetic connection to the children is of paramount importance in determining legal maternity. See, e.g., Culliton v. Beth Israel Deaconess Med. Ctr., 435 Mass. 285, 756 N.E. 2d 1133 (Mass. 2001); Belsito v. Clark, 67 Ohio Misc. 2d 54, 644 N.E.2d 760 (Ohio Ct. Common Pleas 1994).

The intent test has developed primarily in California. In *Johnson*, a married couple was unable to have children naturally because the wife had undergone a hysterectomy, yet the wife could still produce eggs. The couple entered into a surrogacy agreement with a third-party female who agreed to give birth to a child on their behalf in exchange for $10,000 and other consideration. One of the wife's eggs was fertilized with her husband's sperm and was successfully implanted in the surrogate's uterus. However, when the relationship between the couple and the surrogate deteriorated, litigation over maternity and custody ensued. Under California's version of the Uniform Parentage Act, both genetic consanguinity and giving birth were equally cognizable bases for establishing maternity. The Court declined to recognize two legal mothers. In order to break the tie, the California Supreme Court held that when gestation and genetic consanguinity "do not coincide in one woman, she who intended to procreate the child—that is, she who intended to bring about the birth of the child that she intended to raise as her own—is the natural mother under California law." Id. at 782.[8] The Johnson Court justified its holding in part by strongly affirming the validity of surrogacy contracts.

The genetic test has been set forth most thoroughly by the Ohio Court of Common Pleas in *Belsito*. In *Belsito*, a married couple wanted children, and the wife could produce eggs but could not sustain a pregnancy. By agreement, one of the wife's eggs was fertilized with the husband's sperm and then implanted in the uterus of a gestational surrogate (the wife's sister). Without objection from the surrogate, the couple sought a declaratory judgment of maternity and paternity. Like California, Ohio had adopted a version of the Uniform Parentage Act which provided that "maternity can be established by identifying the natural mother through the birth process or by other means, including DNA blood tests," as provided by statute. Id. at 763 (citing Ohio Rev. Code Ann. ch. 3111). Also declining to recognize two legal mothers, the court applied a two-stage analysis for establishing maternity. First, if the male and female genetic providers have not waived parental rights, they must be declared the legal parents. Second, if the female genetic provider has waived her parental rights, then the gestator is the legal

8. The intent test of *Johnson* was adopted with little analysis in *McDonald,* 608 N.Y.S.2d at 480.

mother. On this basis, the court held that the married couple, as the child's genetic progenitors, were the legal parents.

Significantly, Tennessee's statutory framework for establishing maternity differs markedly from the California and Ohio statutes under consideration in *Johnson* and *Belsito.* Compare Tenn. Code Ann. § 36–2–302(4) (defining "mother" as "the biological mother of a child born out of wedlock") and Tenn. Code Ann. § 36–1–102(10) (defining "biological parents" as "the woman and man who physically or genetically conceived the child") with Cal. Civ. Code § 7003(1) (West 1983) ("The parent and child relationship may be established . . . between a child and the natural mother . . . by proof of her having given birth to the child, or under this part."), *repealed by* 1992 Cal. Stat. c. 162 (A.B. 2650), § 4 and Ohio Rev. Code Ann. § 3111.02 (West 1992) ("The parent and child relationship between a child and the child's natural mother may be established by proof of her having given birth to the child or pursuant to [other sections of the Ohio Revised Code]."). Consequently, neither California's intent test nor Ohio's genetic test is strictly apposite to our statutory scheme.

Further, both the intent test and the genetic test suffer from inadequacies. For example, in *Johnson* the California Supreme Court crafted an unnecessarily broad rule which could afford maternal status even to a woman who failed to qualify under either of California's two statutory bases for maternity. According to *Belsito*, the intent formulation of *Johnson* has "discarded both genetics and birth as the primary means of identifying the natural maternal parent," and provides for, "in effect, a private adoption process that is readily subject to all the defects and pressures of such a process." In Tennessee, unlicensed and unregulated adoption is statutorily prohibited and subject to criminal penalties. See Tenn. Code Ann. §§ 36–1–108 to–109 (2001).

However, the genetic test of *Belsito* also has significantly broad implications. In the event that a dispute were to arise between an intended mother who had obtained eggs from a third-party donor and a gestational surrogate in whom the eggs had been implanted, the genetic test would implicitly invalidate any surrogacy agreement. The genetic test could also have practical effects similar to the "adoption-default model" criticized by In re Marriage of Buzzanca, in that an intended "mother" who employs techniques for assisted reproduction including egg donation would by default have to submit to government-controlled adoption procedures to attain a secure legal status as "mother." Policy-wise, the requirement of such regulation may or may not be sound.

Consequently, we decline to adopt either the intent test or the genetic test as a general rule for resolving this case. We thus vacate the adoption of the intent test of Johnson by the courts below.

. . .

Therefore, in resolving this case we focus closely on its particular facts. . . .

We conclude that Tennessee's parentage statutes neither provide for nor contemplate the circumstances of this case, where an unmarried couple has employed techniques for assisted reproduction involving third-party egg donation to produce children for their own benefit and where dispute has arisen over the genetically unrelated gestator's legal status as mother. Although in some jurisdictions courts have fashioned widely applicable tests for maternity where techniques for assisted reproduction are involved, we decline to adopt as a general rule either the intent test or the genetic test. Consequently, we vacate the adoption of the intent test by the courts below.

Instead we affirm on separate and narrower grounds the holding of the courts below that Cindy is the legal mother of the children C.K.G., C.A.G., and C.L.G. with all the rights and responsibilities of parenthood. Our holding in this regard depends on the following factors: (1) prior to the children's birth, both Cindy as gestator and Charles as the genetic father voluntarily demonstrated the bona fide intent that Cindy would be the children's legal mother and agreed that she would accept the legal responsibility as well as the legal rights of parenthood; (2) Cindy became pregnant, carried to term, and gave birth to the children as her own; and (3) this case does not involve a controversy between a gestator and a female genetic progenitor where the genetic and gestative roles have been separated and distributed among two women, nor does this case involve a controversy between a traditional or gestational surrogate and a genetically-unrelated intended mother. In our view, given the far-reaching, profoundly complex, and competing public policy considerations necessarily implicated by the present controversy, crafting a broadly applicable rule for the establishment of maternity where techniques for assisted human reproduction are involved is more appropriately addressed by the Tennessee General Assembly.

Having concluded that Cindy is the children's legal mother, the question of estoppel is moot, and we vacate the holding of the Court of Appeals that Charles is estopped to deny Cindy's maternal status. However, we affirm in full the judgments of the juvenile court and Court of Appeals concerning comparative fitness, custody, child support, and visitation. Costs of this appeal are taxed to the appellant, Charles, for which execution may issue if necessary.

■ ADOLPHO A. BIRCH, JR., dissenting.

Because my views differ from the majority opinion, I respectfully dissent. At the outset, I am convicted that any resolution reached in this case will be temporary only-a stop-gap solution usable for this case alone, pending legislative action, as the law accelerates to catch up with the rapidly evolving technology of reproduction and its consequences. Still, unless our legislature acts, I fear that this *narrowly tailored* solution designed for this specific case will be used as precedent for other cases involving reproductive technology.

My colleagues have, nevertheless, cobbled together a resolution which would appear at first glance to be just and reasonable. But in so doing, they have side-stepped a clear legislative mandate: the statutory definition of "parent."

The operative facts that this case presents are unusual, though not unique. In short, we have a biological father (hereinafter "Dr. G.") and a gestational host (hereinafter "Ms. C.").[2] The children resulting from this procedure have the father's DNA, but have no DNA from the gestational host. Yet, she desires to be declared the children's legal mother and to receive child support from the children's father.

The majority has chosen to use a totality of the circumstances analysis to validate the plaintiff's status in this case. Although the majority declines to adopt either an intent test or a genetic test, they rely heavily upon intent as a primary factor. The intent test has been soundly criticized. Thus, I submit

2. Presumably, the biological mother agreed to surrender her parental rights prior to the children's birth.

that using intent even as just a factor for establishing parentage, is unwieldy, subjective, and questionable. At least three reasons have been noted why a test based on intent should be rejected. These same criticisms also apply when intent is used solely as a factor. First, it is difficult to apply the "*Johnson* test,"[3] an intent test, because proof is hard to ascertain, especially when each party purports an intention to procreate and raise the child. Second, public policy areas of "procreation and parentage, which involve values that are basic to society," are not supported by this test in established areas such as "[the] surrender of parental rights [by agreement], the best interests of children, [and the] stability in the child-parent relationship." Third, this test does not completely recognize the right of the genetic-provider to decide whether or not to exercise fundamental rights-procreation and parental rights. Id. Furthermore, a party's intent may change after conception, through gestation, and after birth.

. . .

The majority also places considerable weight on gestation, noting the historical link between gestation and genetics. Historically, there was no separation between the gestational host and the genetic provider; thus, the gestational host and genetic provider were one in the same. Now, technology has evolved as we can see in the instant case. It is because of this separation we now have this and other disputes regarding parentage. Therefore, because of the technological advances in reproduction I believe the majority's reliance on the historical binding of gestation to genetics is not applicable to this case and should not be used. Furthermore, the majority admits that gestation is conspicuously missing from the statutes. Therefore, we should conspicuously leave gestation out of consideration in determining parentage.

I would resolve this case through genetics. It is scientific, certain, and has found acceptance in several courts that have addressed the issue. Furthermore, it is easier to apply. Moreover, this is the test that our legislature has already ordained by providing that parentage may be established by either biology or adoption. Indeed, "courts have looked at genetics as the primary basis to determine who is the parent" based on the importance of historical precedence and common ancestry.

The plaintiff is, a fortiori, a non-parent, at least as is determined by the statutory definitions of "mother" and "parent" as one who has biological ties to the child(ren). See Tenn. Code Ann. §§ 36–2–302(4), 36–1–102(10), (28), (36) (2001 & Supp. 2004).

By inquiring—"Who is the mother of these children?"—the majority raises the specter of the "motherless child"; that is, the impression has been given that the children will have no mother unless we find a way to confer those rights upon Ms. C. Such is not the case. The children do indeed have a mother. It just happens that the mother's identity here is, as is sometimes the case, unknown. The real question which should have been considered and answered by this court is whether the plaintiff is the children's legal mother. The answer is apparently no.

The majority, in placing Ms. C. on equal legal footing with the children's biological and legal father, Dr. G., in my view, is an exercise of largesse gone too far awry. We are to apply the law, and in the process, we are neither to

3. In Johnson v. Calvert, the intent to procreate test was used by the court by looking at the parties' intentions as embodied in the surrogacy agreement and held that from the outset the genetic mother intended to be the child's mother. 5 Cal. 4th 84, 19 Cal. Rptr. 2d 494, 851 P.2d 776, 782–87 (Cal. 1993).

unduly restrict or expand statutes' coverage. See Premium Fin. Corp. of Am. v. Crump Ins. Servs. of Memphis, Inc., 978 S.W.2d 91, 93 (Tenn. 1998). In my view, the majority reached beyond existing law to produce a palatable result. This overreaching is not necessary in my opinion. Thus, this case should be resolved under the law as it currently exists today. Tennessee statutes do not use gestation or intent to confer parental status, instead genetics, marriage and adoption are the routes available. Therefore, by reviewing and analyzing the Tennessee statutes which are based on biology, Ms. C. is not the parent nor is she the legal mother of the children for purposes of this case, and she has no legal standing to sue for custody or support as a parent. Adoption, nevertheless, remains an option.

. . .

We, as interpreters of the law, not makers of the law, are powerless, in my view, to reach a different resolution. Accordingly, I would reverse the judgment of the Court of Appeals and remand the cause to the trial court where it would proceed as a contest between a parent and a non-parent under settled Tennessee authority.

K.M. v. E.G.

Supreme Court of California, 2005.
37 Cal.4th 130, 33 Cal.Rptr.3d 61, 117 P.3d 673.

■ MORENO, J.

In the present case, we must decide whether a woman who provided ova to her lesbian partner so that the partner could bear children by means of in vitro fertilization is a parent of those children. For the reasons that follow, we conclude that Family Code section 7613, subdivision (b), which provides that a man is not a father if he provides semen to a physician to inseminate a woman who is not his wife, does not apply when a woman provides her ova to impregnate her partner in a lesbian relationship in order to produce children who will be raised in their joint home. Accordingly, when partners in a lesbian relationship decide to produce children in this manner, both the woman who provides her ova and her partner who bears the children are the children's parents.

On March 6, 2001, petitioner K.M.[1] filed a petition to establish a parental relationship with twin five-year-old girls born to respondent E.G., her former lesbian partner. K.M. alleged that she "is the biological parent of the minor children" because "[s]he donated her egg to respondent, the gestational mother of the children." E.G. moved to dismiss the petition on the grounds that, although K.M. and E.G. "were lesbian partners who lived together until this action was filed," K.M. "explicitly donated her ovum under a clear written agreement by which she relinquished any claim to offspring born of her donation."

On April 18, 2001, K.M. filed a motion for custody of and visitation with the twins.

A hearing was held at which E.G. testified that she first considered raising a child before she met K.M., at a time when she did not have a partner. She met K.M. in October 1992 and they became romantically

1. In order to protect the confidentiality of the minors, we will refer to the parties by their initials.

involved in June 1993. E.G. told K.M. that she planned to adopt a baby as a single mother. E.G. applied for adoption in November 1993. K.M. and E.G. began living together in March 1994 and registered as domestic partners in San Francisco.

E.G. visited several fertility clinics in March 1993 to inquire about artificial insemination and she attempted artificial insemination, without success, on 13 occasions from July 1993 through November 1994. K.M. accompanied her to most of these appointments. K.M. testified that she and E.G. planned to raise the child together, while E.G. insisted that, although K.M. was very supportive, E.G. made it clear that her intention was to become "a single parent."

In December 1994, E.G. consulted with Dr. Mary Martin at the fertility practice of the University of California at San Francisco Medical Center (UCSF). E.G.'s first attempts at in vitro fertilization failed because she was unable to produce sufficient ova. In January 1995, Dr. Martin suggested using K.M.'s ova. E.G. then asked K.M. to donate her ova, explaining that she would accept the ova only if K.M. "would really be a donor" and E.G. would "be the mother of any child," adding that she would not even consider permitting K.M. to adopt the child "for at least five years until [she] felt the relationship was stable and would endure." E.G. told K.M. that she "had seen too many lesbian relationships end quickly, and [she] did not want to be in a custody battle." E.G. and K.M. agreed they would not tell anyone that K.M. was the ova donor.

K.M. acknowledged that she agreed not to disclose to anyone that she was the ova donor, but insisted that she only agreed to provide her ova because she and E.G. had agreed to raise the child together. K.M. and E.G. selected the sperm donor together. K.M. denied that E.G. had said she wanted to be a single parent and insisted that she would not have donated her ova had she known E.G. intended to be the sole parent.

On March 8, 1995, K.M. signed a four-page form on UCSF letterhead entitled "Consent Form for Ovum Donor (Known)." The form states that K.M. agrees "to have eggs taken from my ovaries, in order that they may be donated to another woman." After explaining the medical procedures involved, the form states on the third page: "It is understood that I waive any right and relinquish any claim to the donated eggs or any pregnancy or offspring that might result from them. I agree that the recipient may regard the donated eggs and any offspring resulting therefrom as her own children." The following appears on page 4 of the form, above K.M.'s signature and the signature of a witness: "I specifically disclaim and waive any right in or any child that may be conceived as a result of the use of any ovum or egg of mine, and I agree not to attempt to discover the identity of the recipient thereof." E.G. signed a form entitled "Consent Form for Ovum Recipient" that stated, in part: "I acknowledge that the child or children produced by the IVF procedure is and shall be my own legitimate child or children and the heir or heirs of my body with all rights and privileges accompanying such status."

E.G. testified she received these two forms in a letter from UCSF dated February 2, 1995, and discussed the consent forms with K.M. during February and March. E.G. stated she would not have accepted K.M.'s ova if K.M. had not signed the consent form, because E.G. wanted to have a child on her own and believed the consent form "protected" her in this regard.

K.M. testified to the contrary that she first saw the ovum donation consent form 10 minutes before she signed it on March 8, 1995. K.M.

admitted reading the form, but thought parts of the form were "odd" and did not pertain to her, such as the part stating that the donor promised not to discover the identity of the recipient. She did not intend to relinquish her rights and only signed the form so that "we could have children." Despite having signed the form, K.M. "thought [she] was going to be a parent."

Ova were withdrawn from K.M. on April 11, 1995, and embryos were implanted in E.G. on April 13, 1995. K.M. and E.G. told K.M.'s father about the resulting pregnancy by announcing that he was going to be a grandfather. The twins were born on December 7, 1995. The twins' birth certificates listed E.G. as their mother and did not reflect a father's name. As they had agreed, neither E.G. nor K.M. told anyone K.M. had donated the ova, including their friends, family and the twins' pediatrician. Soon after the twins were born, E.G. asked K.M. to marry her, and on Christmas Day, the couple exchanged rings.

Within a month of their birth, E.G. added the twins to her health insurance policy, named them as her beneficiary for all employment benefits, and increased her life insurance with the twins as the beneficiary. K.M. did not do the same.

E.G. referred to her mother, as well as K.M.'s parents, as the twins' grandparents and referred to K.M.'s sister and brother as the twins' aunt and uncle, and K.M.'s nieces as their cousins. Two school forms listed both K.M. and respondent as the twins' parents. The children's nanny testified that both K.M. and E.G. "were the babies' mother."

The relationship between K.M. and E.G. ended in March 2001 and K.M. filed the present action. In September 2001, E.G. and the twins moved to Massachusetts to live with E.G.'s mother.

The superior court granted the motion to dismiss finding, in a statement of decision, "that [K.M.] . . . knowingly, voluntarily and intelligently executed the ovum donor form, thereby acknowledging her understanding that, by the donation of her ova, she was relinquishing and waiving all rights to claim legal parentage of any children who might result from the *in vitro* fertilization and implantation of her ova in a recipient (in this case, a known recipient, her domestic partner [E.G.]). . . . [K.M.]'s testimony on the subject of her execution of the ovum donor form was contradictory and not always credible.

"[K.M.] and [E.G.] agreed prior to the conception of the children that [E.G.] would be the sole parent unless the children were later adopted, and [E.G.] told [K.M.] prior to her ovum donation that she ([E.G.]) would not consider an adoption by [K.M.] until some years later. [E.G.] and [K.M.] agreed in advance of the ovum donation that they would not tell others of [K.M.]'s genetic connection to the children (they also agreed that if and when it became appropriate they would consider how to inform the children); and they abided by this agreement until late 1999.

". . . By voluntarily signing the ovum donation form, [K.M.] was donating genetic material. Her position was analogous to that of a sperm donor, who is treated as a legal stranger to a child if he donates sperm through a licensed physician and surgeon under Family Code section 7613[, subdivision] (b). The Court finds no reason to treat ovum donors as having greater claims to parentage than sperm donors. . . .

"The Court accepts the proposition that a child may have two legal mothers and assumed it to be the law in its analysis of the evidence herein. [P] . . . [P]

"[K.M.]'s claim to 'presumed' parenthood rests upon her contention that she has met the criteria of Family Code section 7611 [, subdivision] (d). . . . [K.M.] . . . has failed to establish either that she received the twins into her home or that she held them out 'as [her] natural child[ren.]' Although [K.M.] *treated* the twins in all regards as though they were her own (and there can be no question but that they are fully bonded to her as such), the children were *received* into the parties' home as [E.G.]'s children and, up until late 1999, both parties scrupulously held confidential [petitioner]'s 'natural,' i.e., in this case, her genetic relationship to the children.

"[E.G.] is not estopped by her conduct. . . . The Court finds that [petitioner] was not misled by any such conduct; that she knew that [respondent] did not intend thereby to confer parental rights upon her. . . ."

The Court of Appeal affirmed the judgment, ruling that K.M. did not qualify as a parent "because substantial evidence supports the trial court's factual finding that *only* E.G. intended to bring about the birth of a child whom she intended to raise as her own." The court observed that "the status of K.M. . . . is consistent with the status of a sperm donor under the [Uniform Parentage Act], i.e., 'treated in law as if he were not the natural father of a child thereby conceived.' " Having concluded that the parties intended at the time of conception that only E.G. would be the child's mother, the court concluded that the parties' actions following the birth did not alter this agreement. The Court of Appeal concluded that if the parties had changed their intentions and wanted K.M. to be a parent, their only option was adoption.

We granted review.

K.M. asserts that she is a parent of the twins because she supplied the ova that were fertilized in vitro and implanted in her lesbian partner, resulting in the birth of the twins. As we will explain, we agree that K.M. is a parent of the twins because she supplied the ova that produced the children, and Family Code section 7613, subdivision (b)[2] (hereafter section 7613(b)), which provides that a man is not a father if he provides semen to a physician to inseminate a woman who is not his wife, does not apply because K.M. supplied her ova to impregnate her lesbian partner in order to produce children who would be raised in their joint home.

The determination of parentage is governed by the Uniform Parentage Act (UPA). (§ 7600 et seq.) As we observe in the companion case of *Elisa B. v. Superior Court*, *supra*, 37 Cal.4th 108, 116, the UPA defines the " 'parent and child relationship[, which] extends equally to every child and to every parent, regardless of the marital status of the parents.' (§ 7602.)"

In Johnson v. Calvert (1993) 5 Cal.4th 84, 87 [19 Cal. Rptr. 2d 494, 851 P.2d 776], we determined that a wife whose ovum was fertilized in vitro by her husband's sperm and implanted in a surrogate mother was the "natural mother" of the child thus produced. We noted that the UPA states that provisions applicable to determining a father and child relationship shall be used to determine a mother and child relationship "insofar as practicable." We relied, therefore, on the provisions in the UPA regarding presumptions of paternity and concluded that "genetic consanguinity" could be the basis for a finding of maternity just as it is for paternity. (Johnson v. Calvert, *supra*, 5 Cal.4th at p. 92; In re Marriage of Buzzanca (1998) 61 Cal.App.4th 1410, 1415 [72 Cal. Rptr. 2d 280].) Under this authority, K.M.'s genetic relationship to the children in the present case constitutes "evidence of a mother

2. Further undesignated statutory references are to the Family Code.

and child relationship as contemplated by the Act." The Court of Appeal in the present case concluded, however, that K.M. was not a parent of the twins, despite her genetic relationship to them, because she had the same status as a sperm donor. Section 7613(b) states: "The donor of semen provided to a licensed physician and surgeon for use in artificial insemination of a woman other than the donor's wife is treated in law as if he were not the natural father of a child thereby conceived." In *Johnson*, we considered the predecessor statute to section 7613(b), former Civil Code section 7005. We did not discuss whether this statute applied to a woman who provides ova used to impregnate another woman, but we observed that "in a true 'egg donation' situation, where a woman gestates and gives birth to a child formed from the egg of another woman with the intent to raise the child as her own, the birth mother is the natural mother under California law." We held that the statute did not apply under the circumstances in *Johnson*, because the husband and wife in *Johnson* did not intend to "donate" their sperm and ova to the surrogate mother, but rather "intended to procreate a child genetically related to them by the only available means."

The circumstances of the present case are not identical to those in *Johnson*, but they are similar in a crucial respect; both the couple in *Johnson* and the couple in the present case intended to produce a child that would be raised in their own home. In *Johnson*, it was clear that the married couple did not intend to "donate" their semen and ova to the surrogate mother, but rather permitted their semen and ova to be used to impregnate the surrogate mother in order to produce a child to be raised by them. In the present case, K.M. contends that she did not intend to donate her ova, but rather provided her ova so that E. G. could give birth to a child to be raised jointly by K.M. and E.G. E.G. hotly contests this, asserting that K.M. donated her ova to E.G., agreeing that E.G. would be the sole parent. It is undisputed, however, that the couple lived together and that they both intended to bring the child into their joint home. Thus, even accepting as true E.G.'s version of the facts (which the superior court did), the present case, like *Johnson*, does not present a "true 'egg donation' " situation. (Johnson v. Calvert, *supra*, 5 Cal.4th 84, 93, fn. 10.) K.M. did not intend to simply donate her ova to E.G., but rather provided her ova to her lesbian partner with whom she was living so that E.G. could give birth to a child that would be raised in their joint home. Even if we assume that the provisions of section 7613(b) apply to women who donate ova, the statute does not apply under the circumstances of the present case. . . .

. . .

As noted *ante*, K.M.'s genetic relationship with the twins constitutes evidence of a mother and child relationship under the UPA (*Johnson v. Calvert, supra*, 5 Cal.4th 84, 92) and, as explained *ante*, section 7613(b) does not apply to exclude K.M. as a parent of the twins. The circumstance that E.G. gave birth to the twins also constitutes evidence of a mother and child relationship. Thus, both K.M. and E.G. are mothers of the twins under the UPA.[6]

It is true we said in *Johnson* that "for any child California law recognizes only one natural mother." But as we explain in the companion case of *Elisa B. v. Superior Court, supra*, 37 Cal.4th 108, this statement in *Johnson* must be

6. Contrary to the suggestion in Justice Werdegar's dissent, we do not consider whether it is in the twins' best interest for the woman who supplied the ova from which they were produced, intending to raise the children in her home, to be declared their natural mother. We simply follow the dictates of the UPA.

understood in light of the issue presented in that case; "our decision in *Johnson* does not preclude a child from having two parents both of whom are women. . . ."

. . .

Justice Werdegar's dissent states that predictability in this area is important, but relying upon a later judicial determination of the intent of the parties, as the dissent suggests, would not provide such predictability. The present case is a good example. Justice Werdegar's dissent concludes that K.M. did not intend to become a parent, because the superior court "found on the basis of conflicting evidence that she did not," noting that "[w]e must defer to the trial court's findings on this point because substantial evidence supports them." Had the superior court reached the opposite conclusion, however, the dissent presumably again would defer to the trial court's findings and reach the opposite conclusion that K.M. is a parent of the twins. Rather than provide predictability, therefore, using the intent test would rest the determination of parentage upon a later judicial determination of intent made years after the birth of the child.

Justice Werdegar's dissent cites Troxel v. Granville (2000) 530 U.S. 57, 65 for the proposition that "We cannot recognize K.M. as a parent without diminishing E.G.'s existing parental rights." The high court's decision in *Troxel* has no application here. Neither K.M.'s nor E.G.'s claim to parentage preceded the other's. K.M.'s claim to be the twins' mother because the twins were produced from her ova is equal to, and arose at the same time as, E.G.'s claim to be the twins' mother because she gave birth to them.

The superior court in the present case found that K.M. signed a waiver form, thereby "relinquishing and waiving all rights to claim legal parentage of any children who might result." But such a waiver does not affect our determination of parentage. Section 7632 provides: "Regardless of its terms, an agreement between an alleged or presumed father and the mother or child does not bar an action under this chapter." (See In re Marriage of Buzzanca, *supra*, 61 Cal.App.4th 1410, 1426 ["It is well established that parents cannot, by agreement, limit or abrogate a child's right to support." (Fn. omitted.)].) A woman who supplies ova to be used to impregnate her lesbian partner, with the understanding that the resulting child will be raised in their joint home, cannot waive her responsibility to support that child. Nor can such a purported waiver effectively cause that woman to relinquish her parental rights.

In light of our conclusion that section 7613(b) does not apply and that K.M. is the twins' parent (together with E.G.), based upon K.M.'s genetic relationship to the twins, we need not, and do not, consider whether K.M. is presumed to be a parent of the twins under section 7611, subdivision (d), which provides that a man is presumed to be a child's father if "[h]e receives the child into his home and openly holds out the child as his natural child."

The judgment of the Court of Appeal is reversed.

■ GEORGE, C. J., BAXTER, J., AND CHIN, J., concurred.

■ KENNARD, J, Dissenting.

Unlike the majority, I would apply the controlling statutes as written. The statutory scheme for determining parentage contains two provisions that resolve K.M.'s claim to be a parent of the twins born to E.G. Under one provision, a man who donates sperm for physician-assisted artificial insemination of a woman to whom he is not married is not the father of the resulting child. (Fam. Code, § 7613, subd. (b).)[1] Under the other provision, rules for determining fatherhood are to be used for determining motherhood "[i]nsofar as practicable." (§ 7650.) Because K.M. donated her ova for physician-assisted artificial insemination and implantation in another woman, and knowingly and voluntarily signed a document declaring her intention *not* to become a parent of any resulting children, she is not a parent of the twins.

. . .

The Court of Appeal held that K.M. had made a voluntary and informed choice to donate her ova to E.G., and that K.M.'s status with respect to any child born as a result of the ova donation was analogous to that of a sperm donor, who, by statute, is treated as if he were not the natural father of any child conceived as a result of the sperm donation. "The donor of semen provided to a licensed physician and surgeon for use in artificial insemination of a woman other than the donor's wife is treated in law as if he were not the natural father of a child thereby conceived." (§ 7613, subd. (b).) By analogy I would apply that statute here. Section 7650 states that "[i]nsofar as practicable" the provisions "applicable" to a father and child relationship are to be used to determine a mother and child relationship.

Here it is "practicable" to treat a woman who donates ova to a licensed physician for in vitro fertilization and implantation in another woman,[3] in the same fashion as a man who donates sperm to a licensed physician for artificial insemination of a woman to whom he is not married. Treating male and female donors alike is not only practicable, but it is also consistent with the trial court's factual finding here that K.M. intended "to donate ova to E.G." so that E.G. would be the sole mother of a child born to her.

. . .

The majority's desire to give the twins a second parent is understandable and laudable. To achieve that worthy goal, however, the majority must rewrite a statute and disregard the intentions that the parties expressed when the twins were conceived. The majority amends the sperm-donor statute by inserting a new provision making a sperm donor the legal father of a child born to a woman artificially inseminated with his sperm whenever the sperm donor and the birth mother "*intended that the resulting child would be raised in their joint home*," even though both the donor and birth mother also intended that the donor *not* be the child's father. Finding nothing in the statutory language or history to support this construction, I reject it. Relying on the plain meaning of the statutory language, and the trial court's findings that both K.M. and E.G. intended that E.G. would be the only parent of any children resulting from the artificial insemination, I would affirm the judgment of the Court of Appeal, which in turn affirmed the trial court, rejecting K.M.'s claim to parentage of the twins born to E.G.

■ WERDEGAR, J., Dissenting.

1. All further statutory references are to the Family Code.

3. K.M. and E.G. were registered in San Francisco as domestic partners in 1995 at the time of the twins' birth. On March 30, 2001, E.G. filed a notice with the Clerk of the City and County of San Francisco dissolving the domestic partnership. As of January 1, 2005, domestic partners who are registered with the California Secretary of State have the same "rights and obligations" to "a child of either of them" as do spouses. (§ 297.5, subd. (d).) Obviously, this new statute has no application here.

The majority determines that the twins who developed from the ova K.M. donated to E.G. have two mothers rather than one. While I disagree, as I shall explain, with that ultimate conclusion, I agree with the majority's premise that a child can have two mothers. Our previous holding that "for any child California law recognizes only one natural mother" (*Johnson v. Calvert* (1993)) 5 Cal.4th 84, 92 [19 Cal. Rptr. 2d 494, 851 P.2d 776] (*Johnson*)) must be understood in the context in which it arose—a married couple who intended to become parents and provided their fertilized ova to a gestational surrogate who did not intend to become a parent—and, thus understood, may properly be limited to cases in which to recognize a second mother would inject an unwanted third parent into an existing family. When, in contrast to *Johnson*, no natural[1] or adoptive father exists, two women who intend to become mothers of the same child may do so either through adoption (Sharon S. v. Superior Court (2003) 31 Cal.4th 417 [2 Cal. Rptr. 3d 699, 73 P.3d 554]) or because both qualify as natural mothers under the Uniform Parentage Act (Fam. Code, § 7600 et seq.) (UPA), one having donated the ovum and the other having given birth).

Precisely because predictability in this area is so important, I cannot agree with the majority that the children in this case do in fact have two mothers. Until today, when one woman has provided the ova and another has given birth, the established rule for determining disputed claims to motherhood was clear: we looked to the intent of the parties. "[I]n a true 'egg donation' situation, where a woman gestates and gives birth to a child formed from the egg of another woman with the intent to raise the child as her own, the birth mother is the natural mother under California law." Contrary to the majority's apparent assumption, to limit *Johnson*'s holding that a child can have only one mother to cases involving existing two-parent families does not require us to abandon *Johnson*'s intent test as the method for determining disputed claims of motherhood arising from the use of reproductive technology. Indeed, we have no other test sufficient to the task.

Furthermore, to apply *Johnson*'s intent test to the facts of this case necessarily leads to the conclusion that E.G. is a mother and K.M. is not. That E.G. intended to become the mother—and the only mother—of the children to whom she gave birth is unquestioned. Whether K.M. for her part also intended to become the children's mother was disputed, but the trial court found on the basis of conflicting evidence that she did not. We must defer to the trial court's findings on this point because substantial evidence supports them. K.M. represented in connection with the ovum donation process, both orally and in writing, that she did not intend to become the children's mother, and consistent with those representations subsequently held the children out to the world as E.G.'s but not her own. Thus constrained by the facts, the majority can justify its conclusion that K.M. is also the children's mother only by changing the law. This the majority does by displacing *Johnson*'s intent test—at least for the purposes of this case—with the following new rule: a woman who has "supplied her ova to impregnate her lesbian partner in order to produce children who would be raised in their joint home" (maj. opn., *ante*, at p. 138; see also *id.*, at pp. 134, 139, 142, 143, 144) is a mother of the resulting children regardless of any preconception manifestations of intent to the contrary.

. . .

1. As when an unmarried woman becomes pregnant through physician-assisted artificial insemination pursuant to Family Code section 7613, subdivision (b).

Perhaps the most serious problem with the majority's new rule is that it threatens to destabilize ovum donation and gestational surrogacy agreements. One important function of *Johnson*'s intent test was to permit persons who made use of reproductive technology to create, before conception, settled and enforceable expectations about who would and would not become parents. *Johnson, supra*, 5 Cal.4th 84, thus gave E.G. a right at the time she conceived to expect that she alone would be the parent of her children—a right the majority now retrospectively abrogates. E.G.'s expectation has a constitutional dimension. (See Troxel v. Granville (2000) 530 U.S. 57, 65 [due process clause protects a parent's fundamental right to make decisions concerning the care, custody and control of her children].) We cannot recognize K.M. as a parent without diminishing E.G.'s existing parental rights. In light of the majority's abrogation of *Johnson* and apparent willingness to ignore preconception manifestations of intent, at least in some cases, women who wish to donate ova without becoming mothers, serve as gestational surrogates without becoming mothers, or accept ovum donations without also accepting the donor as a coparent would be well advised to proceed with the most extreme caution. While the majority purports to limit its holding to cohabiting lesbians, and possibly only to those cohabiting lesbians who are also domestic partners, these limitations, as I have explained, rest on questionable legal grounds and may well not stand the test of time.

. . .

The majority seems to believe that, having concluded the sperm donation statute (Fam. Code, § 7613, subd. (b)) does not apply, one must necessarily conclude that K.M. is the mother of the children who developed from the ova she donated to E.G. This reasoning entails a non sequitur. The statute, when it applies, merely *excludes* someone as a possible parent; it does not *establish* parentage. In order to reach the further conclusion that K.M. is a parent, the majority must entertain a string of questionable assumptions: first, that we would refuse to apply the sperm donation statute (Fam. Code, § 7613, subd. (b), quoted *ante*, at p. 139), despite its plain language, to cut off the parental rights and responsibilities of a man who donates his sperm through a physician to a woman who is not his wife but with whom he lives (maj. opn., *ante*, at pp. 140–142), and, second, that two women who live together and divide between themselves the genetic and gestational aspects of pregnancy must be treated in exactly the same way as the man and woman just posited (*id.*, at p. 141). The latter assumption, in turn, embodies additional, unstated assumptions about the effect of the equal protection clause. But ovum donation, which requires substantial medical and scientific assistance, is not sufficiently like sperm donation, which can easily be accomplished by unassisted laypersons, to require equal treatment under the law for all purposes. Accordingly, to recognize the sperm donation statute's inapplicability does not dispose of this case; it merely leaves us with the same question with which we began, namely, whether K.M. is a second mother of E.G.'s children. Until today, the *Johnson* intent test would have required us to answer the question in the negative. In my view, it still should.

Perhaps the best way to understand today's decision is that we appear to be moving in cases of assisted reproduction from a categorical determination of parentage based on formal, preconception manifestations of intent to a case-by-case approach implicitly motivated at least in part by our intuitions about the children's best interests. We expressly eschewed a best interests approach in *Johnson, supra*, 5 Cal.4th 84, explaining that it "raises the repugnant specter of governmental interference in matters implicating our most fundamental notions of privacy, and confuses concepts of parentage and custody." This case, in which the majority compels E.G. to accept K.M. as an unintended parent to E.G.'s children, in part because of E.G.'s and K.M.'s sexual orientation and the character of their private relationship, shows that *Johnson*'s warning was prescient. Only legislation defining parentage in the context of assisted reproduction is likely to restore predictability and prevent further lapses into the disorder of ad hoc adjudication.

J.B. v. M.B.

Supreme Court of New Jersey, 2001.
170 N.J. 9, 783 A.2d 707.

■ The opinion of the Court was delivered by PORITZ, C.J.

In this case, a divorced couple disagree about the disposition of seven preembryos[1] that remain in storage after the couple, during their marriage, undertook in vitro fertilization procedures. We must first decide whether the husband and wife have entered into an enforceable contract that is now determinative on the disposition issue. If not, we must consider how such conflicts should be resolved by our courts.

Although the reproductive technology to accomplish in vitro fertilization has existed since the 1970s, there is little caselaw to guide us in our inquiry.

J.B. and M.B. were married in February 1992. After J.B. suffered a miscarriage early in the marriage, the couple encountered difficulty conceiving a child and sought medical advice from the Jefferson Center for Women's Specialties. Although M.B. did not have infertility problems, J.B. learned that she had a condition that prevented her from becoming pregnant. On that diagnosis, the couple decided to attempt in vitro fertilization at the Cooper Center for In Vitro Fertilization, P.C. (the Cooper Center).

The in vitro fertilization procedure requires a woman to undergo a series of hormonal injections to stimulate the production of mature oocytes[2] (egg cells or ova). The medication causes the ovaries to release multiple egg cells during a menstrual cycle rather than the single egg normally produced. The egg cells are retrieved from the woman's body and examined by a physician who evaluates their quality for fertilization. Egg cells ready for insemination are then combined with a sperm sample and allowed to incubate for approximately twelve to eighteen hours. Successful fertilization results in a zygote[3] that develops into a four-to eight-cell preembryo. At that stage, the preembryos are either returned to the woman's uterus for implantation or cryopreserved at a temperature of–196 C and stored for possible future use.

A limited number of preembryos are implanted at one time to reduce the risk of a multiple pregnancy. Cryopreservation of unused preembryos reduces, and may eliminate, the need for further ovarian stimulation and egg retrieval, thereby reducing the medical risks and costs associated with

1. A preembryo is a fertilized ovum (egg cell) up to approximately fourteen days old (the point when it implants in the uterus). The American Heritage Stedman's Medical Dictionary 667 (1995). Throughout this opinion, we use the term "preembryo," rather than "embryo," because preembryo is technically descriptive of the cells' stage of development when they are cryopreserved (frozen).

2. Oocytes are cells from which an egg or ovum develops. Id. at 578.

3. A zygote is a fertilized ovum before it undergoes cell division. Id. at 906.

both the hormone regimen and the surgical removal of egg cells from the woman's body. Cryopreservation also permits introduction of the preembryos into the uterus at the optimal time in the natural cycle for pregnancy. Egg cells must be fertilized before undergoing cryopreservation because unfertilized cells are difficult to preserve and, once preserved, are difficult to fertilize.

The Cooper Center's consent form describes the procedure:

> IVF [or in vitro fertilization] will be accomplished in a routine fashion: that is, ovulation induction followed by egg recovery, insemination, fertilization, embryo development and embryo transfer of up to three or four embryos in the stimulated cycle. With the couple's consent, any "extra" embryos beyond three or four will be cryopreserved according to our freezing protocol and stored at −196C. Extra embryos, upon thawing, must meet certain criteria for viability before being considered eligible for transfer. These criteria require that a certain minimum number of cells composing the embryo survive the freeze-thaw process. These extra embryos will be transferred into the woman's uterus in one or more future menstrual cycles for the purpose of establishing a normal pregnancy. The physicians and embryologists on the IVF team will be responsible for determining the appropriate biological conditions and the timing for transfers of cryopreserved embryos.

The consent form also contains language discussing the control and disposition of the preembryos:

> The control and disposition of the embryos belongs to the Patient and her Partner. You will be asked to execute the attached legal statement regarding control and disposition of cryopreserved embryos. The IVF team will not be obligated to proceed with the transfer of any cryopreserved embryos if experience indicates the risks outweigh the benefits.

Before undertaking in vitro fertilization in March 1995, the Cooper Center gave J.B. and M.B. the consent form with an attached agreement for their signatures. The agreement states, in relevant part:

> I, J.B. (patient), and M.B. (partner), agree that all control, direction, and ownership of our tissues will be relinquished to the IVF Program under the following circumstances:

1. A dissolution of our marriage by court order, unless the court specifies who takes control and direction of the tissues....

The in vitro fertilization procedure was carried out in May 1995 and resulted in eleven preembryos. Four were transferred to J.B. and seven were cryopreserved. J.B. became pregnant, either as a result of the procedure or through natural means, and gave birth to the couple's daughter on March 19, 1996. In September 1996, however, the couple separated, and J.B. informed M.B. that she wished to have the remaining preembryos discarded. M.B. did not agree.

J.B. filed a complaint for divorce on November 25, 1996, in which she sought an order from the court "with regard to the eight[4] frozen embryos." In a counterclaim filed on November 24, 1997, M.B. demanded judgment compelling his wife "to allow the (8) eight frozen embryos currently in storage to be implanted or donated to other infertile couples." J.B. filed a motion for summary judgment on the preembryo issue in April 1998

4. As noted above, seven had actually been cryopreserved.

alleging, in a certification filed with the motion, that she had intended to use the preembryos solely within her marriage to M.B. She stated:

> Defendant and I made the decision to attempt conception through in vitro fertilization treatment. Those decisions were made during a time when defendant and I were married and intended to remain married. Defendant and I planned to raise a family together as a married couple. I endured the in vitro process and agreed to preserve the preembryos for our use in the context of an intact family.

J.B. also certified that "there were never any discussions between the Defendant and I regarding the disposition of the frozen embryos should our marriage be dissolved."

M.B., in a cross-motion filed in July 1998, described his understanding very differently. He certified that he and J.B. had agreed prior to undergoing the in vitro fertilization procedure that any unused preembryos would not be destroyed, but would be used by his wife or donated to infertile couples. His certification stated:

> Before we began the I.V.F. treatments, we had many long and serious discussions regarding the process and the moral and ethical repercussions. For me, as a Catholic, the I.V.F. procedure itself posed a dilemma. We discussed this issue extensively and had agreed that no matter what happened the eggs would be either utilized by us or by other infertile couples. In fact, the option to donate [the preembryos] to infertile couples was the Plaintiff's idea. She came up with this idea because she knew of other individuals in her work place who were having trouble conceiving.

M.B.'s mother, father, and sister also certified that on several occasions during family gatherings J.B. had stated her intention to either use or donate the preembryos.

The couple's final judgment of divorce, entered in September 1998, resolved all issues except disposition of the preembryos. Shortly thereafter, the trial court granted J.B.'s motion for summary judgment on that issue. The court found that the reason for the parties' decision to attempt in vitro fertilization—to create a family as a married couple—no longer existed. J.B. and M.B. had become parents and were now divorced. Moreover, M.B. was not infertile and could achieve parenthood in the future through natural means. The court did not accept M.B.'s argument that the parties undertook the in vitro fertilization procedure to "create life," and found no need for further fact finding on the existence of an agreement between them, noting that there was no written contract memorializing the parties' intentions. Because the husband was "fully able to father a child," and because he sought control of the preembryos "merely to donate them to another couple," the court concluded that the wife had "the greater interest and should prevail."

The Appellate Division affirmed. J.B. v. M.B., 331 N.J. Super. 223, 751 A.2d 613 (2000). The court noted the inconsistency between the trial court's finding that "the parties engaged in IVF to create their child within the context of their marriage" and M.B.'s claim that the couple had entered into an agreement to donate or use, and not to destroy, the preembryos. Before the Appellate Division, the husband argued that his constitutional right to procreate had been violated by the ruling of the trial court and sought a remand to establish the parties' understanding regarding the disposition of the preembryos.

The Appellate Division understood this case to "involve an attempt to enforce an alleged agreement to use embryos to create a child." It initially examined that "attempt" in the context of two fundamental rights, "the right to procreate and the right not to procreate," citing Skinner v. Oklahoma, 316 U.S. 535, 541 (1942), and Roe v. Wade, 410 U.S. 113, 152–53 (1973), among other cases. J.B., supra, 331 N.J. Super. at 231–32. The court found that, on the facts presented, the conflict between those rights was "more apparent than real." It observed that destruction of the preembryos would not seriously impair M.B.'s constitutional right to procreate since "he retains the capacity to father children." In contrast, allowing donation or use of the preembryos would impair J.B.'s right not to procreate "even if [she was] relieved of the financial and custodial responsibility for her child" because she would then have been forced to allow strangers to raise that child. In those circumstances, and assuming "that the Fourteenth Amendment applies," the court found no impairment of the husband's constitutional rights.

Nonetheless, the court chose not to decide this case on constitutional grounds. In its view, whether court enforcement of the alleged agreement would constitute state action under the Fourteenth Amendment was unclear, and resolution of the constitutional issue was not necessary to dispose of the litigation. The court concluded "that a contract to procreate is contrary to New Jersey public policy and is unenforceable." In affirming the judgment of the trial court in favor of J.B., the panel considered the parties' views and the trial court's opinion, and determined that destruction of the preembryos was required.

We granted certification, and now modify and affirm the judgment of the Appellate Division.

M.B. contends that the judgment of the court below violated his constitutional rights to procreation and the care and companionship of his children. He also contends that his constitutional rights outweigh J.B.'s right not to procreate because her right to bodily integrity is not implicated, as it would be in a case involving abortion. He asserts that religious convictions regarding preservation of the preembryos, and the State's interest in protecting potential life, take precedence over his former wife's more limited interests. Finally, M.B. argues that the Appellate Division should have enforced the clear agreement between the parties to give the preembryos a chance at life. He believes that his procedural due process rights have been violated because he was not given an opportunity to introduce evidence demonstrating the existence of that agreement, and because summary judgment is inappropriate in a case involving novel issues of fact and law.

J.B. argues that the Appellate Division properly held that any alleged agreement between the parties to use or donate the preembryos would be unenforceable as a matter of public policy. She contends that New Jersey has "long recognized that individuals should not be bound by agreements requiring them to enter into family relationships or [that] seek to regulate personal intimate decisions relating to parenthood and family life." J.B. also argues that in the absence of an express agreement establishing the disposition of the preembryos, a court should not imply that an agreement exists. It is J.B.'s position that requiring use or donation of the preembryos would violate her constitutional right not to procreate. Discarding the preembryos, on the other hand, would not significantly affect M.B.'s right to procreate because he is fertile and capable of fathering another child.

. . .

M.B. contends that he and J.B. entered into an agreement to use or donate the preembryos, and J.B. disputes the existence of any such agreement. As an initial matter, then, we must decide whether this case involves a contract for the disposition of the cryopreserved preembryos resulting from in vitro fertilization. We begin, therefore, with the consent form provided to J.B. and M.B. by the Cooper Center. Cf. Garfinkel v. Morristown Obstetrics & Gynecology, 168 N.J. 124, 135, 773 A.2d 665 (2001) (noting intent expressed in writing controls interpretation of contract); State Troopers Fraternal Assoc. v. State, 149 N.J. 38, 47, 692 A.2d 519 (1997) (noting fundamental canons of contract construction require examination of plain language of contract). That form states, among other things:

> The control and disposition of the embryos belongs to the Patient and her Partner. You will be asked to execute the attached legal statement regarding control and disposition of cryopreserved embryos.

The attachment, executed by J.B. and M.B., provides further detail in respect of the parties' "control and disposition":

> I, J.B. (patient), and M.B. (partner) agree that all control, direction, and ownership of our tissues will be relinquished to the IVF Program under the following circumstances:
>
> 1. A dissolution of our marriage by court order, unless the court specifies who takes control and direction of the tissues, or
>
> 2. In the event of death of both of the above named individuals, or unless provisions are made in a Will, or
>
> 3. When the patient is no longer capable of sustaining a normal pregnancy, however, the couple has the right to keep embryos maintained for up to two years before making a decision [regarding a] "host womb" or
>
> 4. At any time by our/my election which shall be in writing, or
>
> 5. When a patient fails to pay periodic embryo maintenance payment.

The consent form, and more important, the attachment, do not manifest a clear intent by J.B. and M.B. regarding disposition of the preembryos in the event of "[a] dissolution of [their] marriage." Although the attachment indicates that the preembryos "will be relinquished" to the clinic if the parties divorce, it carves out an exception that permits the parties to obtain a court order directing disposition of the preembryos. That reading is consistent with other provisions of the attachment allowing for disposition by a last will and testament "in the event of death," or "by our/my election . . . in writing." Clearly, the thrust of the document signed by J.B. and M.B. is that the Cooper Center obtains control over the preembryos unless the parties choose otherwise in a writing, or unless a court specifically directs otherwise in an order of divorce.

. . .

. . . [T]he parties have agreed that on the dissolution of their marriage the Cooper Center obtains control of the preembryos unless the court specifically makes another determination. Under that provision, the parties have sought another determination from the court.

M.B. asserts, however, that he and J.B. jointly intended another disposition. Because there are no other writings that express the parties' intentions, M.B. asks the Court either to remand for an evidentiary hearing on that issue or to consider his certified statement. In his statement, he claims that before undergoing in vitro fertilization the couple engaged in extensive discussions in which they agreed to use the preembryos themselves or donate them to others. In opposition, J.B. has certified that the parties never discussed the disposition of unused preembryos and that there was no agreement on that issue.

We find no need for a remand to determine the parties' intentions at the time of the in vitro fertilization process. Assuming that it would be possible to enter into a valid agreement at that time irrevocably deciding the disposition of preembryos in circumstances such as we have here, a formal, unambiguous memorialization of the parties' intentions would be required to confirm their joint determination. The parties do not contest the lack of such a writing. We hold, therefore, that J.B. and M.B. never entered into a separate binding contract providing for the disposition of the cryopreserved preembryos now in the possession of the Cooper Center.

In essence, J.B. and M.B. have agreed only that on their divorce the decision in respect of control, and therefore disposition, of their cryopreserved preembryos will be directed by the court. In this area, however, there are few guideposts for decision-making. Advances in medical technology have far outstripped the development of legal principles to resolve the inevitable disputes arising out of the new reproductive opportunities now available. For infertile couples, those opportunities may present the only way to have a biological family. Yet, at the point when a husband and wife decide to begin the in vitro fertilization process, they are unlikely to anticipate divorce or to be concerned about the disposition of preembryos on divorce. As they are both contributors of the genetic material comprising the preembryos, the decision should be theirs to make. See generally Davis v. Davis, 842 S.W.2d 588, 597 (Tenn. 1992) (stating that donors should retain decision-making authority with respect to their preembryos), reh'g granted in part, 1992 Tenn. LEXIS 622, 1992 WL 341632, at 1 (Nov. 23, 1992), and cert. denied, Stowe v. Davis, 507 U.S. 911, 113 S.Ct. 1259, 122 L.Ed. 2d 657 (1993); Carl H. Coleman, Procreative Liberty and Contemporaneous Choice: An Inalienable Rights Approach to Frozen Embryo Disputes, 84 Minn. L. Rev. 55, 83 (1999) ("Because the embryos are the products of the couple's shared procreative activity, any decision to use them should be the result of the couple's mutual choice."); cf. Paul Walter, His, Hers, or Theirs—Custody, Control, and Contracts: Allocating Decisional Authority Over Frozen Embryos, 29 Seton Hall L. Rev. 937, 959–62 (1999) (discussing approaches to disposition of preembryos, including grant of "sole authority to the biological provider(s)").

But what if, as here, the parties disagree. Without guidance from the Legislature, we must consider a means by which courts can engage in a principled review of the issues presented in such cases in order to achieve a just result. Because the claims before us derive, in part, from concepts found in the Federal Constitution and the Constitution of this State, we begin with those concepts.

Both parties ... invoke the right to privacy in support of their respective positions. More specifically, they claim procreational autonomy as a fundamental attribute of the privacy rights guaranteed by both the Federal and New Jersey Constitutions. Their arguments are based on various opinions of the United States Supreme Court that discuss the right to be free from governmental interference with procreational decisions. See Eisenstadt

v. Baird, 405 U.S. 438, 453 (1972); Griswold v. Connecticut, 381 U.S. 479, 485–86 (1965); Skinner v. Oklahoma, 316 U.S. 535, 541 (1942).

In Skinner v. Oklahoma, *supra,* the Court spoke of that most "basic liberty" when rejecting, on equal protection grounds, an Oklahoma statute that required sterilization of certain repeat criminal offenders. "Marriage and procreation," said Justice Douglas, "are fundamental to the very existence and survival of the race." Later, in *Griswold, supra,* and *Eisenstadt, supra,* the Court invalidated statutes restricting use of and access to contraceptives by both married and unmarried couples, stating in *Griswold* that prohibitions on the use of contraceptives unconstitutionally infringe on the sanctity and privacy of the marital relationship, and, in *Eisenstadt,* that "if the right of privacy means anything, it is the right of the individual, married or single, to be free from unwarranted governmental intrusion into matters so fundamentally affecting a person as the decision whether to bear or beget a child."

This Court also has recognized the fundamental nature of procreational rights. In In re Baby M, we considered a custody dispute between a father and a surrogate mother. Although the case involved the enforceability of a surrogacy contract, the father asserted that his right to procreate supported his claim for custody of Baby M. We held that the right to procreate was not implicated by the custody battle, which dealt with parental rights after birth. We observed, however, that "the rights of personal intimacy, of marriage, of sex, of family, of procreation . . . are fundamental rights protected by both the federal and state Constitutions."

Those decisions provide a framework within which disputes over the disposition of preembryos can be resolved. In *Davis, supra,* for example, a divorced couple could not agree on the disposition of their unused, cryopreserved preembryos. The Tennessee Supreme Court balanced the right to procreate of the party seeking to donate the preembryos (the wife), against the right not to procreate of the party seeking destruction of the preembryos (the husband). The court concluded that the husband's right would be significantly affected by unwanted parenthood "with all of its possible financial and psychological consequences." In his case, that burden was the greater because, as a child, he had been separated from his parents after they divorced and his mother suffered a nervous breakdown. Because of his personal experiences, the husband was "vehemently opposed to fathering a child that would not live with both parents."

Against that interest, the court weighed the wife's "burden of knowing that the lengthy IVF procedures she underwent were futile, and that the preembryos to which she contributed genetic material would never become children." Although that burden was not insignificant, the court found that it did not outweigh the father's interest in avoiding procreation. The court held that the scales "ordinarily" would tip in favor of the right not to procreate if the opposing party could become a parent through other reasonable means.

We agree with the Tennessee Supreme Court that "ordinarily, the party wishing to avoid procreation should prevail." Here, the Appellate Division succinctly described the "apparent" conflict between J.B. and M.B.:

> In the present case, the wife's right not to become a parent seemingly conflicts with the husband's right to procreate. The conflict, however, is more apparent than real. Recognition and enforcement of the wife's right would not seriously impair the husband's right to procreate. Though his right to procreate using the wife's egg would be terminated, he retains the capacity to father children.

[*J.B.*, supra, 331 N.J. Super. at 232.]

In other words, M.B.'s right to procreate is not lost if he is denied an opportunity to use or donate the preembryos. M.B. is already a father and is able to become a father to additional children, whether through natural procreation or further in vitro fertilization. In contrast, J.B.'s right not to procreate may be lost through attempted use or through donation of the preembryos. Implantation, if successful, would result in the birth of her biological child and could have life-long emotional and psychological repercussions. See Patricia A. Martin & Martin L. Lagod, The Human Preembryo, the Progenitors, and the State: Toward a Dynamic Theory of Status, Rights, and Research Policy, 5 High Tech. L.J. 257, 290 (1990) (stating that "genetic ties may form a powerful bond ... even if the progenitor is freed from the legal obligations of parenthood"). Her fundamental right not to procreate is irrevocably extinguished if a surrogate mother bears J.B.'s child. We will not force J.B. to become a biological parent against her will.

The court below "concluded that a contract to procreate is contrary to New Jersey public policy and is unenforceable." 331 That determination follows the reasoning of the Massachusetts Supreme Judicial Court in A.Z. v. B.Z., wherein an agreement to compel biological parenthood was deemed unenforceable as a matter of public policy. 431 Mass. 150, 725 N.E.2d 1051, 1057–58 (2000). The Massachusetts court likened enforcement of a contract permitting implantation of preembryos to other contracts to enter into familial relationships that were unenforceable under the laws of Massachusetts, i.e., contracts to marry or to give up a child for adoption prior to the fourth day after birth. In a similar vein, the court previously had refused to enforce a surrogacy contract without a reasonable waiting period during which the surrogate mother could revoke her consent, and a contract to abandon or to prevent marriage. Likewise, the court declined to enforce a contract that required an individual to become a parent.

As the Appellate Division opinion in this case points out, the laws of New Jersey also evince a policy against enforcing private contracts to enter into or terminate familial relationships. New Jersey has, by statute, abolished the cause of action for breach of contract to marry. N.J.S.A. 2A:23–1. Private placement adoptions are disfavored, Sees v. Baber, 74 N.J. 201, 217, 377 A.2d 628 (1977), and may be approved over the objection of a parent only if that parent has failed or is unable to perform "the regular and expected parental functions of care and support of the child." N.J.S.A. 9:3–46; see N.J.S.A. 9:3–48 (stating statutory requirements for private placement adoption).

That public policy also led this Court to conclude in *Baby M*, supra, that a surrogacy contract was unenforceable. We held that public policy prohibited a binding agreement to require a surrogate, there the biological mother, to surrender her parental rights. The contract in Baby M provided for a $10,000 payment to the surrogate for her to be artificially inseminated, carry the child to term, and then, after the child's birth, relinquish parental rights to the father and his wife. The surrogate mother initially surrendered the child to the father, but subsequently reconsidered her decision and fled with Baby M. In an action by the father to enforce the surrogacy contract, we held that the contract conflicted with "(1) laws prohibiting the use of money in connection with adoptions; (2) laws requiring proof of parental unfitness or abandonment before termination of parental rights is ordered or an adoption is granted; and (3) laws that make surrender of custody and consent to adoption revocable in private placement adoptions." Our decision was consistent with the policy expressed earlier in Sees, supra, that consent to terminate parental rights was revocable in all but statutorily approved circumstances.[8]

Enforcement of a contract that would allow the implantation of preembryos at some future date in a case where one party has reconsidered his or her earlier acquiescence raises similar issues. If implantation is successful, that party will have been forced to become a biological parent against his or her will.

We note disagreement on the issue both among legal commentators and in the limited caselaw on the subject. Kass, supra, held that "agreements between progenitors, or gamete donors, regarding disposition of their prezygotes should generally be presumed valid and binding, and enforced in a dispute between them...." The New York court emphasized that such agreements would "avoid costly litigation," "minimize misunderstandings and maximize procreative liberty by reserving to the progenitors the authority to make what is in the first instance a quintessentially personal private decision."[9] Ibid.; see also New York State Task Force on Life and the Law, Executive Summary of Assisted Reproductive Technologies: Analysis and Recommendations for Public Policy (last modified Aug. 1999) <http://www.health.state.ny.us/nysdoh/taskfce/execsum.htm> (stating that "individuals or couples who have excess embryos no longer desired for assisted reproduction have a strong interest in controlling the fate of those embryos"); John A. Robertson, Prior Agreements For Disposition of Frozen Embryos, 51 Ohio St. L.J. 407, 409–18 (1990) (arguing that enforcement of advance directives maximizes reproductive freedom, minimizes disputes, and provides certainty to couples and in vitro fertilization programs); Peter E. Malo, Deciding Custody of Frozen Embryos: Many Eggs Are Frozen But Who Is Chosen?, 3 DePaul J. Health Care L. 307, 332 (2000) (favoring mandatory preembryo disposition agreements). Yet, as discussed above, the Massachusetts Supreme Judicial Court as well as our Appellate Division have declared that when agreements compel procreation over the subsequent objection of one of the parties, those agreements are violative of public policy.

We recognize that persuasive reasons exist for enforcing preembryo disposition agreements. Both the *Kass* and *Davis* decisions pointed out the benefits of enforcing agreements between the parties. See Kass, supra, 696 N.E.2d at 179 (noting "need for clear, consistent principles to guide parties in protecting their interests and resolving their disputes"); *Davis,* supra, 842 S.W.2d at 597 (discussing benefit of guidance to parties undertaking in vitro fertilization procedures). We also recognize that in vitro fertilization is in widespread use, and that there is a need for agreements between the participants and the clinics that perform the procedure. We believe that the

8. Currently, a minority of states have passed legislation addressing in vitro fertilization. See, e.g., Cal. Penal Code § 367g (West 1999) (permitting use of preembryos only pursuant to written consent form); Fla. Stat. ch. 742.17 (1997) (establishing joint decision-making authority regarding disposition of preembryos); La. Rev. Stat. Ann. §§ 9:121 to 9:133 (West 1991) (establishing fertilized human ovum as biological human being that cannot be intentionally destroyed); Okla. Stat. Ann. tit. 10, § 556 (West 2001) (requiring written consent for embryo transfer); Tex. Family Code Ann. § 151.103 (West 1996) (establishing parental rights over child resulting from preembryo).

9. The Supreme Court of Tennessee, in dicta, also stated "that an agreement regarding disposition of any untransferred preembryos in the event of contingencies (such as the death of one or more of the parties, divorce, financial reversals, or abandonment of the program) should be presumed valid and should be enforced as between the progenitors." Davis, supra, 842 S.W.2d at 597.

better rule, and the one we adopt, is to enforce agreements entered into at the time in vitro fertilization is begun, subject to the right of either party to change his or her mind about disposition up to the point of use or destruction of any stored preembryos.

The public policy concerns that underlie limitations on contracts involving family relationships are protected by permitting either party to object at a later date to provisions specifying a disposition of preembryos that that party no longer accepts. Moreover, despite the conditional nature of the disposition provisions, in the large majority of cases the agreements will control, permitting fertility clinics and other like facilities to rely on their terms. Only when a party affirmatively notifies a clinic in writing of a change in intention should the disposition issue be reopened. Principles of fairness dictate that agreements provided by a clinic should be written in plain language, and that a qualified clinic representative should review the terms with the parties prior to execution. Agreements should not be signed in blank, as in *A.Z.*, supra, 725 N.E.2d at 1057, or in a manner suggesting that the parties have not given due consideration to the disposition question. Those and other reasonable safeguards should serve to limit later disputes.

Finally, if there is disagreement as to disposition because one party has reconsidered his or her earlier decision, the interests of both parties must be evaluated. Because ordinarily the party choosing not to become a biological parent will prevail, we do not anticipate increased litigation as a result of our decision. In this case, after having considered that M.B. is a father and is capable of fathering additional children, we have affirmed J.B.'s right to prevent implantation of the preembryos. We express no opinion in respect of a case in which a party who has become infertile seeks use of stored preembryos against the wishes of his or her partner, noting only that the possibility of adoption also may be a consideration, among others, in the court's assessment.

Under the judgment of the Appellate Division, the seven remaining preembryos are to be destroyed. It was represented to us at oral argument, however, that J.B. does not object to their continued storage if M.B. wishes to pay any fees associated with that storage. M.B. must inform the trial court forthwith whether he will do so; otherwise, the preembryos are to be destroyed.

The judgment of the Appellate Division is affirmed as modified.

■ Justices Stein, Coleman, Long, and LaVecchia join in Chief Justice Poritz's opinion.

■ Verniero, J., concurring.

I join in the disposition of this case and in all but one aspect of the Court's opinion. I do not agree with the Court's suggestion, in dicta, that the right to procreate may depend on adoption as a consideration.

I also write to express my view that the same principles that compel the outcome in this case would permit an infertile party to assert his or her right to use a preembryo against the objections of the other party, if such use were the only means of procreation. In that instance, the balance arguably would weigh in favor of the infertile party absent countervailing factors of greater weight. I do not decide that profound question today, and the Court should not decide it or suggest a result, because it is absent from this case.

■ Justice Zazzali joins in this opinion.

NOTES

1. In the case of Davis v. Davis, mentioned in the opinion above, the pre-embryos were later destroyed at the direction of Junior Lewis Davis (the father/sperm donor for the frozen embryos). 7 Embryos Contested in Divorce are Disposed of by Ex-husband, Wash. Post, June 16, 1993, at A18.

2. Use of donated eggs has increased significantly in the United States despite the fact that it costs an average of over $60,000 for each live birth achieved through IVF. Health insurance rarely pays for the procedure, each attempt has only a 25 to 30 percent chance of resulting in a live birth, and even the few states that have statutes requiring full insurance coverage for IVF procedures apply only to married couples. See Gostin et al., Law Science, and Medicine 1188 (2005).

3. Compensation for women who donate eggs is another contentious issue. Usually women are paid between $2000 and $5000 for a donated ovum, but for certain eggs exorbitant prices have been set. In 1999, a couple advertised in the Yale daily newspaper for a donor who would receive $50,000, over ten times the average compensation. The only catch was that the donor had to meet certain criteria: 5′5″ or taller, athletic, 1400+ SAT score, etc. Working from a slightly different angle, photographer Ron Harris (of Playboy fame), in the same year, started up an online egg and sperm auction, listing professional models as prospective donors and pricing gametes for donation starting at about $30,000. See Kenneth Baum, Golden Eggs: Towards the Rational Regulation of Oocyte Donation, 2001 B.Y.U. L.Rev. 107. There is no regulation on contracting to donate sperm or eggs, and in certain rare instances sperm and/or eggs continue to be bought and sold for well beyond the average price.

CHAPTER 8

PARENTS AND CHILDREN

A. THE TRADITIONAL MODEL

Roe v. Doe

Court of Appeals of New York, 1971.
29 N.Y.2d 188, 324 N.Y.S.2d 71, 272 N.E.2d 567.

■ SCILEPPI, JUDGE.

. . .

Petitioner is the court-appointed guardian for a 20-year-old student at the University of Louisville who had been fully and generously supported by her father, a prominent New York attorney, until April of 1970. Afforded the opportunity of attending college away from home, and after living in the college dormitory for a time, the daughter, contrary to the father's prior instructions and without his knowledge, took up residence with a female classmate in an off-campus apartment. Upon learning of this deception, the father cut off all further support and instructed her to return to New York.

Ignoring her father's demands, the daughter sold her automobile (an earlier gift from her father) and elected to finish out the school year, living off the proceeds realized upon the sale, some $1,000. During the following summer, the daughter enrolled in summer courses at the university and upon her return to New York chose to reside with the parents of a female classmate on Long Island. The family situation has been tense and somewhat less than stable. The daughter was three years old when her mother died and her father has remarried several times since, most recently in the spring of 1970. Academically, the daughter fared poorly, and was placed on academic probation during her freshman year; though, on a reduced credit work load, she has managed to improve her academic standing over the past year. She has experimented with drugs (LSD and marijuana), apparently without addiction. The girl has been comfortably maintained, and there is no real question about the father's ability to provide. Tuition payments, approximately $1,000 per semester, for the academic year 1970–71, are long past due and petitioner has commenced this support proceeding, alleging that the respondent has refused and neglected to provide fair and reasonable support.

The Family Court (Midonick, J.), entered two separate orders: a temporary order of support (August 21, 1970), requiring the father to remit a tuition payment for the then pending semester and to provide for reasonable medical, dental, eye and psychiatric care; and a final order of support (November 30, 1970), requiring that the father pay $250 per month in support for the period between December 1, 1970 and October 20, 1971, the daughter's twenty-first birthday. Respondent was found to have willfully failed to comply with the temporary order of support and was committed to jail for 30 days. . . . The order of commitment was stayed pending appeal.

On appeal, the Appellate Division modified the temporary order [and] directed that the father pay only those university and health bills actually rendered prior to November 30, 1970. The final order of November 30, 1970, requiring that the father pay $250 per month in support for the period between December 1, 1970 and October 20, 1971, the daughter's twenty-first birthday, plus tuition payments through the September, 1971 semester, was reversed. . . .

court of appeals

It has always been, and remains a matter of fundamental policy within this State, that a father of a minor child is chargeable with the discipline and support of that child and none would dispute that the obligation cannot be avoided merely because a young enough child is at odds with her parents or has disobeyed their instructions: delinquent behavior of itself, even if unexplained or persistent, does not generally carry with it the termination of the duty of a parent to support.

On the other hand, while the duty to support is a continuing one, the child's right to support and the parent's right to custody and services are reciprocal: the father in return for maintenance and support may establish and impose reasonable regulations for his child. Accordingly, though the question is novel in this State, it has been held, in circumstances such as here, that where by no fault on the parent's part, a child "voluntarily abandons the parent's home for the purpose of seeking its fortune in the world or to avoid parental discipline and restraint [that child] forfeits the claim to support" (67 C.J.S. Parent and Child § 16, p. 699; Stant v. Lamberson, 103 Ind.App. 411, 8 N.E.2d 115; Schmit v. Campbell, 140 Wash. 376, 249 P. 487). To hold otherwise would be to allow, at least in the case before us, a minor of employable age to deliberately flout the legitimate mandates of her father while requiring that the latter support her in her decision to place herself beyond his effective control.

It is the natural right, as well as the legal duty, of a parent to care for, control and protect his child from potential harm, whatever the source and absent a clear showing of misfeasance, abuse or neglect, courts should not interfere with that delicate responsibility. Here, the daughter, asserting her independence, chose to assume a status inconsistent with that of parental control. The Family Court set about establishing its own standards of decorum, and, having determined that those standards were met, sought to substitute its judgment for that of the father. Needless to say, the intrusion was unwarranted.

We do not have before us the case of a father who casts his helpless daughter upon the world, forcing her to fend for herself; nor has the father been arbitrary in his requests that the daughter heed his demands. The obligations of parenthood, under natural and civil law, require of the child " 'submission to reasonable restraint, and demands habits of propriety, obedience, and conformity to domestic discipline' " (Stant v. Lamberson, 103 Ind.App. 411, 416–417, 8 N.E.2d 115, 117, supra). True, a minor, rather than submit to what her father considers to be proper discipline, may be induced to abandon the latter's home; but in so doing, however impatient of parental authority, she cannot enlist the aid of the court in frustrating that authority, reasonably exercised, by requiring that her father accede to her demands and underwrite her chosen lifestyle or as here, run the risk of incarceration.

Nor can we say that the father was unreasonable or capricious in his request that the daughter take up residence in the college dormitory or return to New York. In view of her past derelictions, and, to use the

Appellate Division's words, "the temptations that abound outside," we can only conclude that it was reasonable for her father to decide that it was in her own best interests that she do so. And the fact that the father doggedly persisted in his demands despite similar evils which may have lurked within the campus residence, or psychiatric advice that the daughter live off campus, cannot be said to amount to a showing of misconduct, neglect or abuse which would justify the Family Court's action. The father has the right, in the absence of caprice, misconduct or neglect, to require that the daughter conform to his reasonable demands. Should she disagree, and at her age that is surely her prerogative, she may elect not to comply; but in so doing, she subjects herself to her father's lawful wrath. Where, as here, she abandons her home, she forfeits her right to support.

The order appealed from should be affirmed.

■ JASEN, JUDGE (concurring).

Although I agree with the majority that the Appellate Division order should be affirmed, I would affirm on the ground that under the facts present in this case, Family Court was without power to direct the father to pay $250 per month in support of his daughter.

To view, as the majority does, that the issues in this case . . . are whether the daughter voluntarily abandoned the parent's home, or whether the daughter's conduct was "involuntary" because the father made unreasonable and capricious requests, would require the courts to decide in every instance whether a father's conduct was unreasonable, arbitrary or capricious. It seems to me that this judicial intervention could lead to a perilous adventure upon which the courts of this State have been loath to embark.

It is basic to our law that the court cannot regulate, by its processes, the internal affairs of the home. As we said more than 30 years ago, "[d]ispute [in the family] when it does not involve anything immoral or harmful to the welfare of the child is beyond the reach of the law. The vast majority of matters concerning the upbringing of children must be left to the conscience, patience and self-restraint of father and mother. No end of difficulties would arise should judges try to tell parents how to bring up their children." (People ex rel. Sisson v. Sisson, 271 N.Y. 285, 287, 2 N.E.2d 660, 661).

Certainly, sections 413 and 423 of the Family Court Act do not change this long-standing policy of the law. Rather, it would seem reasonable and consistent with legislative intent that before a support order could be issued, there should be some showing that the "moral, mental and physical conditions are so bad as seriously to affect the health or morals" of the child. (People ex rel. Sisson v. Sisson, supra, 271 N.Y. at pp. 287–288, 2 N.E.2d at p. 661.)

The health and welfare of a child would almost always, of course, be impaired by a parent's unconditional termination of his support. But where a parent discontinues his support because his child is at odds with him, and at the same time he is amenable to resuming his support if the child will follow his instructions, which are not inherently harmful to the child's welfare, surely it cannot be said that a child's moral and temporal well-being would thereby be so aggrieved as to warrant judicial interference.

In my opinion, since in the instant case her father would resume his support of her if she complied with his requests, the daughter did not establish the requisite showing of grave harm to her health and welfare, and, hence, the Appellate Division properly reversed the Family Court's order of support and dismissed petitioner's petition.

. . .

NOTES

1. Is Judge Jasen right to suggest that this case could lead courts down the path of telling parents how to bring up their children? He proposes that potentially serious injury to the "health or morals" of a child should be shown before the courts take jurisdiction over such disputes. Is this a workable standard? Should courts intervene to force a father to support his unmarried pregnant daughter who refuses to give up her baby as he requests? Compare Inhabitants of the Town of Brunswick v. LaPrise, 262 A.2d 366 (Me.1970) (holding father must support daughter).

At common law, child support was considered a moral rather than a legal obligation. Even when the legal nature of the obligation was recognized, most courts would not permit children of intact families to enforce the obligation, presumably guided by the doctrine of family privacy. Cf. McGuire v. McGuire, Chapter 2, Section A. Currently ten states grant children the right to sue for enforcement of a child support order: five states grant this right without limitation, see, e.g., Or. Rev. Stat. § 109.100 (2003); three states require that the right be enforced through a guardian or custodian, see, e.g., Mo. Rev. Stat. § 454.130 (2004); and two states require that the right be enforced by a state agency, see, e.g., Mont. Code Ann. § 40–5–202 (1999).

2. Compare People ex rel. Sisson v. Sisson, 271 N.Y. 285, 2 N.E.2d 660 (1936):

> The family consists of the father, Howard Sisson, the mother, Blanche Sisson, and the daughter, Beverly. They live together at their home in Sherburne, N.Y. Except for the difficulty over the education to be given the child, the family life appears to be much above the average despite the illness which has afflicted the mother. The father, a graduate of Cornell University, has built up a prosperous produce business. The mother had suffered somewhat from arthritis before the marriage, and afterward the condition became progressively worse. As the condition became acute, the father spared no expense or trouble in attempting to effect a cure, sending her to the Mayo Brothers in Rochester, Minn., and other like places; all to no avail. For the past six years the mother has been bedridden. The child, Beverly, is above the average, both physically and mentally.
>
> Disagreement between the parents has arisen over the education of the child. In no way does it appear that the health or welfare of the child is in danger.
>
> In proceedings for the custody of children, the courts have reiterated that their sole point of view is the welfare of the child. The parents of this child are obviously interested only in her welfare. When they realize that for the good of the child it is necessary for them to repress to some extent the natural desire of each to have the child educated solely according to his or her point of view, the remaining sources of difficulty doubtless will disappear.
>
> The court cannot regulate by its processes the internal affairs of the home. Dispute between parents when it does not involve anything immoral or harmful to the welfare of the child is beyond the reach of the law. The vast majority of matters concerning the upbringing of children must be left to the conscience, patience, and self-restraint of father and mother. No end of difficulties would arise should judges try to tell parents how to bring up their children. Only when moral, mental, and physical conditions are so bad as seriously to affect the health or morals of children should the courts be called upon to act.
>
> The writ of habeas corpus must be dismissed.

3. Consider Hugh LaFollette, Licensing Parents, 9 Phil. & Pub. Affairs 182–197 (1980);

Our society normally regulates a certain range of activities; it is illegal to perform these activities unless one has received prior permission to do so. We require automobile operators to have licenses. We forbid people from practicing medicine, law, pharmacy, or psychiatry unless they have satisfied certain licensing requirements.

Society's decision to regulate just these activities is not ad hoc. The decision to restrict admission to certain vocations and to forbid some people from driving is based on an eminently plausible, though not often explicitly formulated, rationale. . . . Imagine a world in which everyone could legally drive a car, in which everyone could legally perform surgery, prescribe medications, dispense drugs, or offer legal advice. Such a world would hardly be desirable.

Consequently, any activity that is potentially harmful to others and requires certain demonstrated competence for its safe performance, is subject to regulation—that is, it is theoretically desirable that we regulate it. If we also have a reliable procedure for determining whether someone has the requisite competence, then the action is not only subject to regulation but ought, all things considered, to be regulated.

It is particularly significant that we license these hazardous activities, even though denying a license to someone can severely inconvenience and even harm that person. . . . [T]he realization that some people are disappointed or inconvenienced does not diminish our conviction that we must regulate occupations or activities that are potentially dangerous to others. Innocent people must be protected even if it means that others cannot pursue activities they deem highly desirable.

Furthermore, we maintain licensing procedures even though our competency tests are sometimes inaccurate. Some people competent to perform the licensed activity (for example, driving a car) will be unable to demonstrate competence (they freeze up on the driver's test). Others may be incompetent, yet pass the test (they are lucky or certain aspects of competence—for example, the sense of responsibility—are not tested). We recognize clearly—or should recognize clearly—that no test will pick out all and only competent drivers, physicians, lawyers, and so on. Mistakes are inevitable. This does not mean we should forget that innocent people may be harmed by faulty regulatory procedures. In fact, if the procedures are sufficiently faulty, we should cease regulating that activity entirely until more reliable tests are available. I only want to emphasize here that tests need not be perfect. Where moderately reliable tests are available, licensing procedures should be used to protect innocent people from incompetents.

These general criteria for regulatory licensing can certainly be applied to parents. First, parenting is an activity potentially very harmful to children. The potential for harm is apparent: each year more than half a million children are physically abused or neglected by their parents. Many millions more are psychologically abused or neglected—not given love, respect, or a sense of self-worth. The results of this maltreatment are obvious. Abused children bear the physical and psychological scars of maltreatment throughout their lives. . . . Therefore, parenting clearly satisfies the first criterion of activities subject to regulation.

The second criterion is also incontestably satisfied. A parent must be competent if he is to avoid harming his children; even greater competence is required if he is to do the "job" well. But not everyone has this minimal competence. Many people lack the knowledge needed to rear children adequately. Many others lack the requisite energy, temperament, or stability. Therefore, child-rearing manifestly satisfies both criteria of activities subject to regulation. In fact, I dare say that parenting is a paradigm of such activities since the potential for harm is so great (both in the extent of harm any one person can suffer and in the number of people potentially harmed) and the need for competence is so evident. Consequently, there is good reason to believe that all parents should be licensed. . . .

Compare Lawrence Frisch, On Licentious Licensing: A Reply to Hugh LaFollette, 11 Phil. and Pub. Affairs 173 (Spring 1982):

> LaFollette is anxious to make sure that parents are competent, just as he is to make sure that his doctor and the driver in the oncoming car are safely capable. He rightly recognizes that we are at risk from incompetent drivers and doctors and, consequently, license their activities. In a leap, or perhaps a lapse, of logic, LaFollette peremptorily concludes that "the very purpose of licensing is just to determine whether people are going to abuse or neglect their children." Thus, without warning, he appears to have shifted the focus of licensing from its traditional purpose of assessing knowledge to the realm of predicting future behavior and confronting issues of negligence and misconduct—areas in which licensing has no historical interest. Clearly, if we can accurately predict that someone will actually abuse a child we can usefully deny a parenting license to that person. There are many other matters in which such divine foreknowledge would be useful, but lacking divinity, we must rely on other methods. LaFollette falls back on statistics. He envisions tests capable of predicting future abusive behavior, while asking us to forgo our own serious doubts about sociologists' ability to prognosticate, because "even if such tests are not available we could undoubtedly develop them." Unlicensable parents can only be "identified" prior to an abusive incident by their mathematical resemblance on psychological or sociological scales to who, at the time the scales were validated, were thought to be guilty of maltreating their children. This is a most unusual approach to licensing, which he justifies by appealing to analogy with traditional licensing procedures. However, it is just wrong to imply that "the very purpose" of, for example, licensing drivers, is to predict which people will have an accident or violate the law. Licensing procedures, as currently employed, are designed to audit present performance, not to predict future practice.

But see Hugh LaFollette, A Reply to Frisch, 11 Phil. and Pub. Affairs 181 (Spring 1982). See also Claudia Mangel, Licensing Parents: How Feasible?, 22 Fam.L.Q. 17 (1988). Cf. Michael J. Sandmire and Michael S. Wald, Licensing Parents—A Response to Claudia Mangel's Proposal, 24 Fam.L.Q. 53 (1990).

B. ENCROACHMENTS ON THE DOCTRINE OF FAMILY PRIVACY

1. CONSTITUTIONAL LAW

Prince v. Massachusetts

Supreme Court of the United States, 1944.
321 U.S. 158, 64 S.Ct. 438, 88 L.Ed. 645.

■ JUSTICE RUTLEDGE delivered the opinion of the Court.

The case brings for review another episode in the conflict between Jehovah's Witnesses and state authority. This time Sarah Prince appeals from convictions for violating Massachusetts' child labor laws, by acts said to be a rightful exercise of her religious convictions.

When the offenses were committed she was the aunt and custodian of Betty M. Simmons, a girl nine years of age. ... Mrs. Prince, living in Brockton, is the mother of two young sons. She also has legal custody of Betty Simmons, who lives with them. The children too are Jehovah's Witnesses and both Mrs. Prince and Betty testified they were ordained ministers. The former was accustomed to go each week on the streets of Brockton to distribute "Watchtower" and "Consolation," according to the usual plan. She had permitted the children to engage in this activity previously, and had been warned against doing so by the school attendance officer, Mr. Perkins. But, until December 18, 1941, she generally did not take them with her at night.

That evening, as Mrs. Prince was preparing to leave her home, the children asked to go. She at first refused. Childlike, they resorted to tears; and, motherlike, she yielded. Arriving downtown, Mrs. Prince permitted the children "to engage in the preaching work with her upon the sidewalks." That is, with specific reference to Betty, she and Mrs. Prince took positions about twenty feet apart near a street intersection. Betty held up in her hand, for passers-by to see, copies of "Watch Tower" and "Consolation." From her shoulder hung the usual canvas magazine bag, on which was printed: "Watchtower and Consolation 54 per copy." No one accepted a copy from Betty that evening and she received no money. Nor did her aunt. But on other occasions, Betty had received funds and given out copies.

Mrs. Prince and Betty remained until 8:45 p.m. A few minutes before this, Mr. Perkins approached Mrs. Prince. A discussion ensued. He inquired and she refused to give Betty's name. However, she stated the child attended the Shaw School. Mr. Perkins referred to his previous warnings and said he would allow five minutes for them to get off the street. Mrs. Prince admitted she supplied Betty with the magazines and said, "[N]either you nor anybody else can stop me. ... This child is exercising her God-given right and her constitutional right to preach the gospel, and no creature has a right to interfere with God's commands." However, Mrs. Prince and Betty departed. She remarked as she went, "I'm not going through this any more. We've been through it time and time again. I'm going home and put the little girl to bed." It may be added that testimony, by Betty, her aunt and others, was offered at the trials, and was excluded, to show that Betty believed it was her religious duty to perform this work and failure would bring condemnation "to everlasting destruction at Armageddon."

... [T]wo claimed liberties are at stake. One is the parent's, to bring up the child in the way he should go, which for appellant means to teach him the tenets and the practices of their faith. The other freedom is the child's, to observe these; and among them is "to preach the gospel ... by public distribution" of "Watchtower" and "Consolation," in conformity with the scripture: "A little child shall lead them."

. . .

The rights of children to exercise their religion, and of parents to give them religious training and to encourage them in the practice of religious belief, as against preponderant sentiment and assertion of state power voicing it, have had recognition here, most recently in West Virginia State Board of Education v. Barnette, 319 U.S. 624. Previously in Pierce v. Society of Sisters, 268 U.S. 510, this Court had sustained the parents' authority to provide religion with secular schooling, and the child's right to receive it, as against the state's requirement of attendance at public schools. And in Meyer v. Nebraska, 262 U.S. 390, children's rights to receive teaching in languages other than the nation's common tongue were guarded against the state's encroachment. It is cardinal with us that the custody, care and nurture of the child reside first in the parents, whose primary function and freedom include preparation for obligations the state can neither supply nor hinder. Pierce v. Society of Sisters, supra. ...

But the family itself is not beyond regulation in the public interest, as against a claim of religious liberty. Reynolds v. United States, 98 U.S. 145; Davis v. Beason, 133 U.S. 333. And neither rights of religion nor rights of parenthood are beyond limitation. Acting to guard the general interest in youth's well being, the state as *parens patriae* may restrict the parent's control by requiring school attendance, regulating or prohibiting the child's labor and in many other ways.[11] Its authority is not nullified merely because the parent grounds his claim to control the child's course of conduct on religion or conscience. Thus, he cannot claim freedom from compulsory vaccination for the child more than for himself on religious grounds.[12] The right to practice religion freely does not include liberty to expose the community or the child to communicable disease or the latter to ill health or death. The catalogue need not be lengthened. It is sufficient to show what indeed appellant hardly disputes, that the state has a wide range of power for limiting parental freedom and authority in things affecting the child's welfare; and that this includes, to some extent, matters of conscience and religious conviction.

. . .

... The case reduces itself therefore to the question whether the presence of the child's guardian puts a limit to the state's power. That fact may lessen the likelihood that some evils the legislation seeks to avert will occur. But it cannot forestall all of them. The zealous though lawful exercise of the right to engage in propagandizing the community, whether in religious, political or other matters, may and at times does create situations difficult enough for adults to cope with and wholly inappropriate for children, especially of tender years, to face. Other harmful possibilities could be stated, of emotional excitement and psychological or physical injury. Parents may be free to become martyrs themselves. But it does not follow they are free, in identical circumstances, to make martyrs of their children before they have reached the age of full and legal discretion when they can make that choice for themselves. Massachusetts has determined that an absolute prohibition, though one limited to streets and public places and to the incidental uses proscribed, is necessary to accomplish its legitimate objectives. Its power to attain them is broad enough to reach these peripheral instances in which the parent's supervision may reduce but cannot eliminate entirely the ill effects of the prohibited conduct. We think that with reference to the public proclaiming of religion, upon the streets and in other similar public places, the power of the state to control the conduct of children reaches beyond the scope of its authority over adults, as is true in the case of other freedoms, and the rightful boundary of its power has not been crossed in this case.

The judgment is

Affirmed.

■ JUSTICE MURPHY, dissenting:

The state, in my opinion, has completely failed to sustain its burden of proving the existence of any grave or immediate danger to any interest which it may lawfully protect. There is no proof that Betty Simmons' mode of worship constituted a serious menace to the public. It was carried on in an orderly, lawful manner at a public street corner. And "one who is rightfully on a street which the state has left open to the public carries with him there as elsewhere the constitutional right to express his views in an orderly fashion. This right extends to the communication of ideas by handbills and

11. Cf. People v. Ewer, 141 N.Y. 129, 36 N.E. 4.

12. Jacobson v. Massachusetts, 197 U.S. 11.

literature as well as by the spoken word." The sidewalk, no less than the cathedral or the evangelist's tent, is a proper place, under the Constitution, for the orderly worship of God. Such use of the streets is as necessary to the Jehovah's Witnesses, the Salvation Army and others who practice religion without benefit of conventional shelters as is the use of the streets for purposes of passage.

It is claimed, however, that such activity was likely to affect adversely the health, morals and welfare of the child. Reference is made in the majority opinion to "the crippling effects of child employment, more especially in public places, and the possible harms arising from other activities subject to all the diverse influences of the street." To the extent that they flow from participation in ordinary commercial activities, these harms are irrelevant to this case. And the bare possibility that such harms might emanate from distribution of religious literature is not, standing alone, sufficient justification for restricting freedom of conscience and religion. Nor can parents or guardians be subjected to criminal liability because of vague possibilities that their religious teachings might cause injury to the child. The evils must be grave, immediate, substantial. Yet there is not the slightest indication in this record, or in sources subject to judicial notice, that children engaged in distributing literature pursuant to their religious beliefs have been or are likely to be subject to any of the harmful "diverse influences of the street." Indeed, if probabilities are to be indulged in, the likelihood is that children engaged in serious religious endeavor are immune from such influences. Gambling, truancy, irregular eating and sleeping habits, and the more serious vices are not consistent with the high moral character ordinarily displayed by children fulfilling religious obligations. Moreover, Jehovah's Witness children invariably make their distributions in groups subject at all times to adult or parental control, as was done in this case. The dangers are thus exceedingly remote, to say the least. And the fact that the zealous exercise of the right to propagandize the community may result in violent or disorderly situations difficult for children to face is no excuse for prohibiting the exercise of that right.

Parham v. J.R.

Supreme Court of the United States, 1979.
442 U.S. 584, 99 S.Ct. 2493, 61 L.Ed.2d 101.

■ CHIEF JUSTICE BURGER delivered the opinion of the Court.

The question presented in this appeal is what process is constitutionally due a minor child whose parents or guardian seek state administered institutional mental health care for the child and specifically whether an adversary proceeding is required prior to or after the commitment.

(a) Appellee,[1] J.R., a child being treated in a Georgia state mental hospital, was a plaintiff in this class-action suit based on 42 U.S.C. § 1983, in the District Court for the Middle District of Georgia. Appellants are the State's Commissioner of the Department of Human Resources, the Director of the Mental Health Division of the Department of Human Resources and the Chief Medical Officer at the hospital where appellee was being treated. Appellee sought a declaratory judgment that Georgia's voluntary commit-

1. Pending our review one of the named plaintiffs before the District Court, J.L., died. Although the individual claim of J.L. is moot, we discuss the facts of this claim because, in part, they form the basis for the District Court's holding.

ment procedures for children under the age of 18 violated the Due Process Clause of the Fourteenth Amendment and requested an injunction against its future enforcement.

. . .

(b) J.L., a plaintiff before the District Court who is now deceased, was admitted in 1970 at the age of six years to Central State Regional Hospital in Milledgeville, Ga. Prior to his admission, J.L. had received out-patient treatment at the hospital for over two months. J.L.'s mother then requested the hospital to admit him indefinitely.

The admitting physician interviewed J.L. and his parents. He learned that J.L.'s natural parents had divorced and his mother had remarried. He also learned that J.L. had been expelled from school because he was uncontrollable. He accepted the parents' representation that the boy had been extremely aggressive and diagnosed the child as having a "hyperkinetic reaction to childhood."

J.L.'s mother and stepfather agreed to participate in family therapy during the time their son was hospitalized. Under this program, J.L. was permitted to go home for short stays. Apparently his behavior during these visits was erratic. After several months the parents requested discontinuance of the program.

In 1972, the child was returned to his mother and stepfather on a furlough basis, i.e., he would live at home but go to school at the hospital. The parents found they were unable to control J.L. to their satisfaction, and this created family stress. Within two months they requested his readmission to Central State. J.L.'s parents relinquished their parental rights to the county in 1974.

Although several hospital employees recommended that J.L. should be placed in a special foster home with "a warm, supportive, truly involved couple," the Department of Family and Children Services was unable to place him in such a setting. On October 24, 1975, J.L. filed this suit requesting an order of the court placing him in a less drastic environment suitable to his needs.

(c) Appellee J.R. was declared a neglected child by the county and removed from his natural parents when he was three years old. He was placed in seven different foster homes in succession prior to his admission to Central State Hospital at the age of seven.

Immediately preceding his hospitalization, J.R. received outpatient treatment at a county mental health center for several months. He then began attending school where he was so disruptive and incorrigible that he could not conform to normal behavior patterns. Because of his abnormal behavior, J.R.'s seventh set of foster parents requested his removal from their home. The Department of Family and Children Services then sought his admission at Central State. The agency provided the hospital with a complete socio-medical history at the time of his admission. In addition, three separate interviews were conducted with J.R. by the admission team of the hospital.

It was determined that he was borderline retarded, and suffered an "unsocialized, aggressive reaction to childhood." It was recommended unanimously that he would "benefit from the structural environment" of the hospital and would "enjoy living and playing with boys of the same age."

J.R.'s progress was re-examined periodically. In addition, unsuccessful efforts were made by the Department of Family and Children Services during his stay at the hospital to place J.R. in various foster homes. On October 24, 1975, J.R. filed this suit requesting an order of the court placing him in a less drastic environment suitable to his needs.

(d) Georgia Code, § 88–503.1 provides for the voluntary admission to a state regional hospital of children such as J.L. and J.R. Under that provision, admission begins with an application for hospitalization signed by a "parent or guardian." Upon application, the superintendent of each hospital is given the power to admit temporarily any child for "observation and diagnosis." If, after observation, the superintendent finds "evidence of mental illness" and that the child is "suitable for treatment" in the hospital, then the child may be admitted "for such period and under such conditions as may be authorized by law."

Georgia's mental health statute also provides for the discharge of voluntary patients. Any child who has been hospitalized for more than five days may be discharged at the request of a parent or guardian. Even without a request for discharge, however, the superintendent of each regional hospital has an affirmative duty to release any child "who has recovered from his mental illness or who has sufficiently improved that the superintendent determines that hospitalization of the patient is no longer desirable."

. . .

The parties agree that our prior holdings have set out a general approach for testing challenged state procedures under a due process claim. Assuming the existence of a protectible property or liberty interest, the Court has required a balancing of a number of factors:

> "First, the private interest that will be affected by the official action; second, the risk of an erroneous deprivation of such interest through the procedures used, and the probable value, if any, of additional or substitute procedural safeguards; and finally, the Government's interest, including the function involved and the fiscal and administrative burdens that the additional or substitute procedural requirement would entail." Mathews v. Eldridge, 424 U.S. 319, 335 (1976). . . .

. . .

Our jurisprudence historically has reflected Western civilization concepts of the family as a unit with broad parental authority over minor children. Our cases have consistently followed that course; our constitutional system long ago rejected any notion that a child is "the mere creature of the State" and, on the contrary, asserted that parents generally "have the right, coupled with the high duty, to recognize and prepare [their children] for additional obligations." Pierce v. Society of Sisters, 268 U.S. 510, 535 (1924). Surely, this includes a "high duty" to recognize symptoms of illness and to seek and follow medical advice. The law's concept of the family rests on a presumption that parents possess what a child lacks in maturity, experience, and capacity for judgment required for making life's difficult decisions. More important, historically it has recognized that natural bonds of affection lead parents to act in the best interests of their children. 1 W. Blackstone, Commentaries *447; J. Kent, Commentaries on American Law *190.

As with so many other legal presumptions, experience and reality may rebut what the law accepts as a starting point; the incidence of child neglect and abuse cases attests to this. That some parents "may at times be acting against the interests of their child" as was stated in Bartley v. Kremens, 402 F.Supp. 1039, 1047–1048 (E.D.Pa.1975), vacated, 431 U.S. 119 (1977), creates a basis for caution, but is hardly a reason to discard wholesale those pages of human experience that teach that parents generally do act in the child's best interests. The statist notion that governmental power should supersede parental authority in all cases because *some* parents abuse and neglect children is repugnant to American tradition.

Nonetheless, we have recognized that a state is not without constitutional control over parental discretion in dealing with children when their physical or mental health is jeopardized. ... Appellees urge that these precedents limiting the traditional rights of parents, if viewed in the context of the liberty interest of the child and the likelihood of parental abuse, require us to hold that the parents' decision to have a child admitted to a mental hospital must be subjected to an exacting constitutional scrutiny, including a formal, adversary, pre-admission hearing.

Appellees' argument, however, sweeps too broadly. Simply because the decision of a parent is not agreeable to a child or because it involves risks does not automatically transfer the power to make that decision from the parents to some agency or officer of the state. The same characterizations can be made for a tonsillectomy, appendectomy or other medical procedure. Most children, even in adolescence, simply are not able to make sound judgments concerning many decisions, including their need for medical care or treatment. Parents can and must make those judgments. Here there is no finding by the District Court of even a single instance of bad faith by any parent of any member of appellees' class. We cannot assume that the result in ... Pierce v. Society of Sisters, would have been different if the children there had announced a preference to learn only English or a preference to go to a public, rather than a church, school. The fact that a child may balk at hospitalization or complain about a parental refusal to provide cosmetic surgery does not diminish the parents' authority to decide what is best for the child. ... Neither state officials nor federal courts are equipped to review such parental decisions.

. . .

In defining the respective rights and prerogatives of the child and parent in the voluntary commitment setting, we conclude that our precedents permit the parents to retain a substantial, if not the dominant, role in the decision, absent a finding of neglect or abuse, and that the traditional presumption that the parents act in the best interest of their child should apply. We also conclude, however, that the child's rights and the nature of the commitment decision are such that parents cannot always have absolute and unreviewable discretion to decide whether to have a child institutionalized. They, of course, retain plenary authority to seek such care for their children, subject to a physician's independent examination and medical judgment.

. . .

We now turn to considerations of what process protects adequately the child's constitutional rights by reducing risks of error without unduly trenching on traditional parental authority and without undercutting "efforts to further the legitimate interests of both the state and the patient that are served by" voluntary commitments. We conclude that the risk of error inherent in the parental decision to have a child institutionalized for mental health care is sufficiently great that some kind of inquiry should be made by a "neutral factfinder" to determine whether the statutory requirements for admission are satisfied. That inquiry must carefully probe the child's background using all available sources, including, but not limited to, parents, schools and other social agencies. Of course, the review must also include an interview with the child. It is necessary that the decisionmaker have the authority to refuse to admit any child who does not satisfy the medical standards for admission. Finally, it is necessary that the child's continuing need for commitment be reviewed periodically by a similarly independent procedure.

We are satisfied that such procedures will protect the child from an erroneous admission decision in a way that neither unduly burdens the states nor inhibits parental decisions to seek state help.

Due process has never been thought to require that the neutral and detached trier of fact be law-trained or a judicial or administrative officer.... Surely, this is the case as to medical decisions, for "neither judges nor administrative hearing officers are better qualified than psychiatrists to render psychiatric judgments." In re Roger S., 19 Cal.3d 921, 941, 569 P.2d 1286, 1299 (1977) (Clark J., dissenting). Thus, a staff physician will suffice, so long as he or she is free to evaluate independently the child's mental and emotional condition and need for treatment.

. . .

It has been suggested that a hearing conducted by someone other than the admitting physician is necessary in order to detect instances where parents are "guilty of railroading their children into asylums" or are using "voluntary commitment procedures in order to sanction behavior of which they disapprove." Ellis, Volunteering Children: Parental Commitment of Minors to Mental Institutions, 62 Calif.L.Rev. 840, 850, 851 (1974). Curiously it seems to be taken for granted that parents who seek to "dump" their children on the state will inevitably be able to conceal their motives and thus deceive the admitting psychiatrists and the other mental health professionals who make and review the admission decision. It is elementary that one early diagnostic inquiry into the cause of an emotional disturbance of a child is an examination into the environment of the child. It is unlikely if not inconceivable that a decision to abandon an emotionally normal, healthy child and thrust him into an institution will be a discrete act leaving no trail of circumstances. Evidence of such conflicts will emerge either in the interviews or from secondary sources. It is unrealistic to believe that trained psychiatrists, skilled in eliciting responses, sorting medically relevant facts and sensing motivational nuances will often be deceived about the family situation surrounding a child's emotional disturbance. Surely a lay, or even law-trained factfinder, would be no more skilled in this process than the professional.

By expressing some confidence in the medical decisionmaking process, we are by no means suggesting it is error free. On occasion parents may initially mislead an admitting physician or a physician may erroneously diagnose the child as needing institutional care either because of negligence or an overabundance of caution. That there may be risks of error in the process affords no rational predicate for holding unconstitutional an entire statutory and administrative scheme that is generally followed in more than 30 states. "[P]rocedural due process rules are shaped by the risk of error inherent in the truthfinding process as applied to the generality of cases, not the rare exceptions." Mathews v. Eldridge, 424 U.S. 319, 344 (1976). In general, we are satisfied that an independent medical decisionmaking process, which includes the thorough psychiatric investigation described earlier followed by additional periodic review of a child's condition, will protect children who should not be admitted; we do not believe the risks of error in that process would be significantly reduced by a more formal, judicial-type hearing. The issue remains whether the Georgia practices, as described in the record before us, comport with these minimum due process requirements.

. . .

We are satisfied that the voluminous record as a whole supports the conclusion that the admissions' staffs of the hospitals have acted in a neutral and detached fashion in making medical judgments in the best interests of the children. The State, through its mental health programs, provides the authority for trained professionals to assist parents in examining, diagnosing and treating emotionally disturbed children, through its hiring practices it provides well staffed and equipped hospitals and—as the District Court found—conscientious public employees to implement the State's beneficent purposes.

Although our review of the record in this case satisfies us that Georgia's general administrative and statutory scheme for the voluntary commitment of children is not *per se* unconstitutional, we cannot decide on this record whether every child in appellees' class received an adequate, independent diagnosis of his emotional condition and need for confinement under the standards announced earlier in this opinion. On remand, the District Court is free to and should consider any individual claims that initial admissions did not meet the standards we have described in this opinion.

. . .

Our discussion [above] was directed at the situation where a child's natural parents request his admission to a state mental hospital. Some members of appellees' class, including J.R., were wards of the State of Georgia at the time of their admission. Obviously their situation differs from those members of the class who have natural parents. While the determination of what process is due varies somewhat when the state, rather than a natural parent, makes the request for commitment, we conclude that the differences in the two situations do not justify requiring different procedures at the time of the child's initial admission to the hospital.

. . .

Reversed and remanded.

NOTE

The California Supreme Court in In re Roger S., 19 Cal.3d 921, 141 Cal.Rptr. 298, 569 P.2d 1286 (1977), held unconstitutional a California commitment statute that was quite similar to the Georgia statute upheld in Parham. The dissenting opinion challenged the holding of the majority that due process requires that counsel be appointed for such minors:

> As the questions present in this proceeding do not involve guilt or innocence, but necessity and availability of treatment, the youngster should be assisted not by a lawyer but by a mental health professional from his own community, having ready access to witnesses and familiarity with community resources.

> The judiciary is developing a messianic image of itself. It is coming to believe that salvation for society's ills lies in adversary hearings. I cannot subscribe to that view.

Does it make sense to have a third decisionmaker (in addition to the parent(s) and the professional staff of the mental institution) in these cases? Should that decisionmaker be a lawyer? What should happen if the parent and the hospital agree the child needs treatment, but the third party disagrees?

Consider In re J.C.G., 144 N.J.Super. 579, 366 A.2d 733 (1976). A mother who had committed her 13–year–old daughter to a mental hospital sought access to her daughter's psychiatric records. The court denied the request, explaining:

> The rule which mandates the appointment of a guardian ad litem [in such cases] is intended not only to prevent the so-called voluntary commitment of a minor by his parent . . . but is also intended to prevent efforts to discharge a child from treatment by a parent who may be acting from motives not in the best interests of the child.

As a noted scholar has cogently observed: "To assume that the family's and patient's interest are always, or nearly always, compatible is to ignore the realities of family strife. At times it is one's family against which one needs the most protection." Nicholas N. Kittrie, The Right to be Different: Deviance and Enforced Therapy, 66, 86 (1971). What qualifications should guardians have in view of the power they are being given?

2. TORT LAW

Goorland v. Continental Insurance and YMCA

Superior Court of Delaware, New Castle, 2003.
2003 WL 22321462.

■ COOCH, JUDGE

The issue before the Court is whether a parent, Defendant Goorland, can be held potentially liable for the alleged negligent supervision of her unemancipated minor child, plaintiff Jacob Goorland, resulting in injury to that child, when the child was unattended for about one to four minutes before being struck by a moving vehicle in the parking lot of a facility he had just exited. Relying on Delaware Supreme Court precedent that offers broad immunity to parents in situations such as this (and treating any arguable factual issues as matters of law to be decided by the Court given the public policy issues concerned), the Court finds that Defendant Goorland cannot be held liable under the circumstances of this case. Accordingly, any action seeking contribution from Defendant Goorland for the injuries sustained by plaintiff Jacob Goorland is barred, and her Motion is therefore GRANTED.

This litigation results from personal injuries sustained by an unemancipated minor, Jacob Goorland (age four at the time of the accident), who is Defendant Goorland's son. On January 5, 2000, Jacob Goorland was struck by a vehicle being driven by defendant Gloria Thomas ("Thomas") while located within the parking lot of a Young Men's Christian Association ("YMCA") facility, also a defendant in this lawsuit. Jacob Goorland, who was unaccompanied by his mother, Defendant Goorland, at the time, had recently exited a building within which YMCA then operated.

. . .

Under its classic formulation, the doctrine of parental immunity prohibits "an unemancipated minor child . . . from suing a parent for damages allegedly caused by parental negligence." In Delaware, the doctrine appears to have been first recognized in the case of Strahorn v. Sears, Roebuck & Co.[123 A.2d 107 (Del. Super. Ct. 1956)].

In its 1960 disposition of McKeon v. Goldstein (and although not specifically discussed in terms of doctrinal underpinnings in the text of its opinion), the Delaware Supreme Court recognized that the parent of an injured minor could commit an independent act of negligence unforeseen by the defendant in a given case, i.e., the act could be a supervening cause of injury, and the defendant would therefore be absolved of any liability for the injury to the minor child. The McKeon Court therefore stated that "the determination of proximate cause is a question . . . for the trier of facts." In the Delaware Supreme Court's 1995 disposition of [Sears Roebuck & Co. v. Huang, 652 A2d. 568] that Court specifically "adhered to that [prior] holding . . . [of McKeon]."

In 1976, the Delaware Supreme Court was faced with an issue of first impression in Williams [v. Williams, 369 A.2d 669], namely "whether an unemancipated child may recover in an action against a parent for injuries caused by the parent's negligent operation of [an] automobile." After observing that the law of parental tort immunity was then "in a state of change in many jurisdictions" the Supreme Court stated that "the judicial trend is now clearly toward a steady erosion of the doctrine by exception and repudiation." In a footnote, the Court then surveyed those jurisdictions that had repudiated the doctrine in whole or in part, and concluded by enumerating six of the "various exceptions" then recognized by other jurisdictions. Included among those exceptions to parental immunity recognized were: 1) suits by emancipated children; 2) suits against the estate of a deceased parent; 3) suits for willful or intentionally inflicted torts; 4) suits for reckless or grossly negligent conduct; 5) suits against a parent acting in the relation of employer; and 6) suits by an unemancipated child against a parent for injury to his property interests. The Williams Court ultimately concluded that "in an action for negligence arising from an automobile accident, brought on behalf of an unemancipated minor child against a parent, the doctrine of parental immunity is not applicable to the extent of the parent's automobile liability insurance coverage; but that, otherwise, the doctrine is applicable in such case." The Court's reasoning was predicated on the fact that "when insurance is involved, the action between parent and child is not truly adversary[] [as] both parties seek recovery from the insurance carrier to create a fund for the child's medical care and support without depleting the family's other assets."

. . .

The Supreme Court appears to have most recently addressed the issue of parental immunity for negligent supervision in its 1995 disposition of the Huang case. That matter reached the Supreme Court after this Court certified an interlocutory appeal based upon a pretrial ruling that it had made, the effect of which was "to preclude reference at trial to the alleged negligent conduct of . . . [the injured minor's] mother." In its certification, this Court expressed concern that the Supreme Court's decision in Beattie [v. Beattie, 630 A.2d 1096 (1993)], "placed the continued viability of Delaware's limited parental immunity doctrine in question" and that its pretrial ruling may have been "deemed to [be in] conflict" with McKeon, supra.

In response to this Court's first expressed concern, the Supreme Court rejected any argument that in light of its abrogation of interspousal immunity in Beattie, the doctrine of parental immunity should likewise be abrogated; instead, the Supreme Court again decided "to adhere to all of [its] prior precedents with regard to the issue of parental immunity." With regard to this Court's second expressed concern, the Supreme Court decided "to adhere to its prior holding in McKeon that evidence of a parent's negligent supervision may be presented to establish that such negligence was a supervening cause of a minor child's personal injury." The Supreme Court therefore reversed this Court's pretrial rulings, which had been contrary to the appellate rulings made by that Court.

With regard to evidence of a parent's negligence as a supervening cause, the Supreme Court in Huang explicitly stated that "in cases where the parental immunity doctrine applies, defendants who decide to assert the parent's negligence as a supervening cause adopt essentially an 'all or nothing' legal strategy." The Supreme Court explained:

> First, where parental control, authority, or discretion is involved, e.g., in potential actions against parents for negligent supervision of their children, the rule of parental immunity is preserved in Delaware and precludes direct claims by a minor child, as well as third-party claims for contribution.
>
> . . .
>
> Second, if the parent's negligence is relevant to the minor child's theory of liability, but not actionable, a defendant may introduce evidence to establish that the parent's negligence was a supervening cause of the minor child's injury.
>
> . . .
>
> Third, if the parent's negligence was a proximate cause but not a supervening cause, the parent's negligence does not provide a basis for reducing full payment to the minor child or the basis for a claim of contribution by any defendant determined to be a tortfeasor, since by definition the parent cannot be a joint tortfeasor.

This last point was arrived at because "the trier of fact may decide that the parent's negligence and the negligence of one or more of the defendants were all proximate causes of the child's injury" a result which would lead to that parent not being liable "since the parent is immune from direct liability or liability for contribution ... [under those circumstances]."

After reviewing the above-cited Supreme Court precedent and the facts of this case, the Court concludes that because Defendant Goorland was exercising parental authority over Jacob Goorland on the day and time that he was injured, and because the arguments made by the parties against its application have all been previously rejected by the Supreme Court, the doctrine of parental immunity applies in this case so that action for contribution cannot be maintained against Defendant Goorland. The parties are free, however, to assert at trial that her actions on the date in question constitute a supervening or superseding cause as to Jacob Goorland's injuries, a result that is in alignment with the above-cited precedent upon which this Court has relied.

. . .

Lastly, YMCA's argument that this Court should abrogate parental immunity because Delaware's jurisprudence on this issue is based upon "outdated theories and thinking" and that "the national trend is to abrogate the doctrine" is an argument that was raised and then rejected by the Supreme Court in the Huang case itself, as reflected by the Court's language that "while the national trend has been toward eroding the doctrine ..." the

Court nonetheless "adhere[s] to all of [its] prior precedents...." The Court will therefore not endorse this argument since it has already been heard and rejected by Delaware's highest court.

NOTES

1. The doctrine of absolute parental tort immunity has all but disappeared in America. In the few states that retain the doctrine, multiple exceptions have severely limited its applicability. Compare Fager v. Hundt, 610 N.E.2d 246 (Ind.1993) (suit against father for sexual abuse not barred by the doctrine of parental tort immunity because of the criminal nature) with Buono v. Scalia, 179 N.J. 131, 843 A.2d 1120 (2004) (doctrine protects father from suit for negligent supervision). See generally, Martin J. Rooney & Colleen M. Rooney, Parental Tort Immunity: Spare the Liability, Spoil the Parent, 25 New Eng. L. Rev. 1161 (1991).

2. Hoverson v. Noker, 60 Wis. 511, 513–14, 19 N.W. 382, 382–83 (1884):

> It will be seen by an examination of the record that it became important for the plaintiffs to connect the father with the acts of his young sons, which the plaintiffs allege caused the injury complained of, and for this purpose the plaintiffs offered evidence tending to prove that the sons had frequently, before the day upon which the accident happened, called abusive names, shouted, and frequently discharged fire-arms when persons were passing the house of the defendants, and that this was often done in the presence of their father. All evidence of this kind was excluded. This, we are inclined to hold, was error. If the father permitted his young sons to shout, use abusive language, and discharge fire-arms at persons who were passing along the highway in front of his house, he permitted that to be done upon his premises which, in its nature, was likely to result in damage to those passing, and when an injury did happen from that cause he was not only morally but legally responsible for the damage done. If a parent permits his very young children to become a source of damage to those who pass the highway in front of his house, he is as much liable for the injury as though he permitted them to erect some frightful or dangerous object near the highway which would frighten passing teams; and in such case he cannot screen himself by saying that he did not in words order the erection to be made. If he made it himself, with the intention to frighten passing teams, he would be responsible for the injury caused by it; and when he permits his irresponsible children to do it he is equally liable, because he has the control of his premises as well as of the children, and is bound to restrain them from causing a dangerous thing to be erected on his premises near the highway; and permitting his young sons to become an object of fright to teams passing, is certainly equally, if not more reprehensible than permitting an inanimate structure to be placed where it would cause such fright. We think the evidence ought to have been admitted in order to connect the father with the acts of the young sons which caused the injury when the plaintiffs were on their way to church in the morning, as well as when on their return from the church in the afternoon.

3. See generally, Rhonda V. Magee Andrews, The Justice of Parental Accountability: Hypothetical Disinterested Citizens and Real Victims' Voices in the Debate Over Expanded Parental Liability, 75 Temp. L. Rev. 375 (2002):

> From a practical standpoint, there are a number of good reasons why parental liability law should be generally reconsidered. Presently, the parents of a minor child are vastly more likely to be held responsible if their child shatters the window of his high school than if the child shatters the skull of his high school teacher. This is because civil liability statutes in most jurisdictions hold parents responsible on a strict liability basis for minor property damage, but much less so for personal injury. And unlike the strict liability approach of most of the civil statutes and federal statutes governing the liability of parents in subsidized housing, prevailing common law doctrine holds that parents are never held strictly liable for personal injuries inflicted by their offspring. Further, courts

often find that parents do not have a duty of due care that would extend to unforeseeable victims of their minor children's torts.

. . .

Common law rules erect high hurdles for those seeking to impose liability on the parents of minors who commit torts. The first hurdle is erected by the longstanding limited liability and parental immunity approaches at common law. Under American common law, neither vicarious nor strict liability flows from the parent-child relationship itself. Contrary to the belief of many, American common law has not imposed vicarious liability on parents for the torts of their minor children, despite some evidence that very early western law indicates a tradition of vicarious parental liability. Instead, contemporary parental liability, to the extent common law immunity is abrogated, typically turns on principles of direct parental negligence, which turns on elements such as consent or ratification, parental neglect, and dangerous instrumentalities, or has tended to require the finding of an agency relationship.

. . .

There is no question that parenting is a verb, an action, the risks of which include foreseeable harm to others. The starting presumption at common law that minor children are themselves one hundred percent responsible for the harm they cause others flies in the face of both community and widespread legislative understandings of parental responsibility for their children until they reach the age of majority. Indeed, it represents an unfair over-allocation of responsibility to an unrepresented group within American society: minor children. At a minimum, liability for the torts of minor children should be the shared responsibility of the minor tortfeasor and his or her parents. Parental liability should be expanded as a means, not only of promoting corrective justice in cases in which children harm others, but also of underscoring the shared nature of the responsibility for the children's wrongs. The legal responsibility for the harm caused by a minor child should be extended beyond the minor himself or herself to encompass those whose decision it was to bring the child with its attendant risks and responsibilities, into the social world, and who are traditionally considered at least partially responsible for the child's conduct and character in its formative years: the parents.

4. The parents of a teenager who stabbed a 13-year-old girl will pay the largest share of the $10 million awarded by a jury to the injured victim and her family. Parents Pay for Son's Crime, Wash. Post, August 21, 2005, at A14. Benjamin White, the son, had a history of aggressive attacks on classmates and his parents knew he carried a knife. The jury foreman reported that the jury held the parents responsible because they found no evidence that the parents had disciplined their son."I'm not saying they're bad parents, but under the law they have certain responsibilities—and at the time, their son was legally a minor," he said. Id.

Popple v. Rose

Supreme Court of Nebraska, 1998.
254 Neb. 1, 573 N.W.2d 765.

■ White, Chief Justice.

This case raises the issue of whether the parents of a minor child have a duty to warn third parties of the child's allegedly known dangerous sexual propensities....

In September 1992, Brian Popple and Maureen Popple hired W.R. to care for their children, Casey and Nicholas. On November 23, while babysitting the children, W.R. physically overpowered Casey and sexually assaulted him, forcibly committing acts of masturbation, fellatio, and sodomy. W.R. did not sexually assault Nicholas, but forced him to witness these events. At the time, W.R. was nearly 13 years old, Nicholas was 9, and Casey was 6.

W.R. was charged with sexual assault in the juvenile court for Phelps County and admitted the charges. The Popples then filed suit in district court and claimed Wayne Rose and Sharon Rose, W.R.'s parents, negligently failed to warn them of W.R.'s allegedly known dangerous sexual propensities. The Popples argued they were not seeking recovery under the parental vicarious liability statute, Neb.Rev.Stat. § 43–801 (Reissue 1993), but, rather, were seeking to hold the Roses liable for their independent negligence in failing to warn the Popples of W.R.'s allegedly known dangerous sexual propensities. In response, the Roses filed a motion for summary judgment.

The district court granted the motion and held that § 43–801 was the Popples' exclusive remedy. The court also held that no independent duty existed upon which to predicate negligence, because Nebraska has not recognized a cause of action based upon parents' failure to warn of their children's known dangerous sexual propensities. The Popples' motion for a new trial was overruled, and they appeal. . . .

The evidence discloses that prior to engaging W.R. as a babysitter, the Popples knew W.R. had a history of physically violent behavior. The record, however, is devoid of any evidence indicating the Roses, the Popples, or any other person was aware W.R. possessed any propensity to commit any acts of sexual assault and/or abuse. In addition, the record is also devoid of any evidence intimating that W.R. even possessed such a habit. In sum, the record is absent any evidence that W.R. demonstrated a history of committing acts of sexual assault and/or abuse or that anyone knew he was prone to such conduct.

. . .

We must initially determine whether § 43–801 abrogates common-law liability and provides the exclusive source of recovery for claimants filing suit based on the intentional acts of children. Section 43–801 provides as follows:

> The parents shall be jointly and severally liable for the willful and intentional infliction of personal injury to any person or destruction of real and personal property occasioned by their minor or unemancipated children residing with them, or placed by them under the care of other persons; Provided, that in the event of personal injuries willfully and intentionally inflicted by such child or children, damages shall be recoverable only to the extent of hospital and medical expenses incurred but not to exceed the sum of one thousand dollars for each occurrence.

. . .

Section 43–801 imposes vicarious liability on parents of children who intentionally inflict personal injury. However, neither the plain meaning of § 43–801 nor the legislative history can be read to abrogate common-law liability. Because there is no language indicating that common-law liability is prohibited or that § 43–801 was intended to be an exclusive remedy, this court will make no such inference. Therefore, reading the statute in a plain, ordinary manner indicates that § 43–801 does not preclude common-law liability.

Having established that § 43–801 does not preclude common-law liability, we must next determine whether a parental duty to warn could exist in the State of Nebraska. This court has imposed a general duty to warn in numerous situations. Schmidt v. Omaha Pub. Power Dist., 245 Neb. 776, 515

N.W.2d 756 (1994) (duty to warn of electrical lines); Lemke v. Metropolitan Utilities Dist., 243 Neb. 633, 502 N.W.2d 80 (1993) (duty to warn of dangerous condition); Anderson v. Transit Auth. of City of Omaha, 241 Neb. 771, 491 N.W.2d 311 (1992) (duty to warn passengers of known dangerous conditions); Maresh v. State, 241 Neb. 496, 489 N.W.2d 298 (1992) (duty to warn traveling public of dangerous condition); Rahmig v. Mosley Machinery Co., 226 Neb. 423, 412 N.W.2d 56 (1987) (duty to warn of defective product). Moreover, this court has also ruled that upon a prospective foster parent's inquiry, the Nebraska Department of Social Services possesses a duty to inform such parent(s) of the known physical and sexual tendencies of prospective foster children. Talle v. Nebraska Dept. of Soc. Servs., 249 Neb. 20, 541 N.W.2d 30 (1995); Anderson/Couvillon v. Nebraska Dept. of Soc. Servs., 248 Neb. 651, 538 N.W.2d 732 (1995); Moore v. State, 245 Neb. 735, 515 N.W.2d 423 (1994). While we have not previously imposed a duty upon parents to warn third parties of their children's known dangerous sexual propensities, given the rulings in the aforementioned cases, we do not believe that imposing a parental duty to warn is an illogical next step in the law in the State of Nebraska.

. . .

The threshold inquiry in any negligence action, including those involving a duty to warn, is whether the defendant owed the plaintiff a duty. Actionable negligence cannot exist if there is no legal duty to protect the plaintiff from injury. A duty is defined as an obligation, to which the law will give recognition and effect, to conform to a particular standard of conduct toward another. Duty is a question of whether the defendant is under any obligation for the benefit of the plaintiff; in negligence cases, the duty is always the same—to conform to the legal standard of reasonable conduct in light of the apparent risk. Determining whether a legal duty exists is a question of law dependent on the facts of a particular situation.

. . .

Restatement (Second) of Torts § 316 at 123–24, states:

> A parent is under a duty to exercise reasonable care so to control his minor child as to prevent it from intentionally harming others or from so conducting itself as to create an unreasonable risk of bodily harm to them, if the parent
>
> (a) knows or has reason to know that he has the ability to control his child, and
>
> (b) knows or should know of the necessity and opportunity for exercising such control.

Thus, the parent-child relationship is recognized as a special relationship which may warrant imposing a duty to warn.

However, those courts specifically adopting a parental duty to warn of children's dangerous propensities have narrowed the duty even further and limited the application thereof to only situations where the parents are aware of the child's known, habitual, dangerous propensity. Eldredge v. Kamp Kachess, 90 Wash.2d 402, 583 P.2d 626 (1978); Cooper v. Meyer, 50 Ill.App.3d 69, 7 Ill.Dec. 916, 365 N.E.2d 201 (1977)....

Many courts have also refused to impose liability in situations where the child was generally incorrigible, heedless, or vicious.

For example, in [Norton v. Payne, 154 Wash. 241, 281 P. 991 (1929)] the guardian ad litem of a 5–year-old child brought suit against the parents of a 7–year-old child who habitually struck smaller children in the face with sticks. The court remanded the cause for a new trial and stated:

> [P]arents are not liable for torts committed by their minor children without participation in the fault by the parent; and it is not enough to make the father liable that he knew that his child was heedless or vicious....

But by the same authority it seems to be stated as a general rule that the parent is liable if he was himself guilty of negligence. He is liable, however, only for his own fault and not that of his child.

While it is also true that the parents did not actually participate in the particular tort here in controversy, they did *know* of the *habit* of their child of striking other children with sticks. They were bound to *know* that was a *habit* liable to cause injury to other children.... No one could be so familiar with the *habit* of a child of that age as the parent, and while the parent cannot be held to the degree of liability of one harboring a vicious dog ... or a wild animal, we think parents should be held responsible and liable for a dangerous *habit* of a child of which they have *knowledge* and take no steps to correct, or restrain. It is that which constitutes the negligence on the part of the parent.

. . .

The record contains no evidence that the Roses, or anyone else, had prior knowledge of any dangerous sexual propensity. Therefore, no duty to warn arose regarding W.R.'s alleged dangerous sexual propensities because the conduct was not a known, habitual propensity.

Even though we now recognize that a parental duty to warn may exist in certain limited situations, irrespective of § 43–801, the district court correctly ruled that the Popples were relegated to the recovery provided in § 43–801 because the facts involved do not present a scenario where a parental duty to warn could have arisen.

AFFIRMED.

Giuliani v. Guiler

Supreme Court of Kentucky, 1997.
951 S.W.2d 318.

■ WINTERSHEIMER, JUSTICE.

. . .

The question presented is whether this Court should overrule previous decisions of this Court and recognize the right of a minor child for the loss of parental consortium.

Mary K. Giuliani, age 33, died during the birth of her fourth child. Her other children were 9, 7 and 3 years of age respectively. Their father filed a claim for wrongful death as administrator, his own claim for loss of consortium and a claim for loss of consortium as next friend for each of the four minor children. The principal wrongful death case is still in the discovery stage at the circuit court level. The trial judge dismissed the claim for loss of consortium of the three minor children in a one-page partial summary judgment. The Court of Appeals affirmed the dismissal but invited this Court to revisit the question of parental consortium. . . .

Dr. Guiler was the obstetrician but was not present at the time of delivery. He instructed the nurses at the hospital to induce labor. After seeing Mary at 6 p.m., the doctor decided he was not needed and left for dinner at the home of a friend. The record indicates that the nurses apparently became more concerned about the situation and unsuccessfully attempted to reach the doctor by numerous calls. Ultimately, Dr. Bennett, an anesthesiologist, an obstetric resident and members of the CODE team, none of whom were familiar with the case, attempted to aid the mother. The mother suffered a cardiac and respiratory collapse shortly after the child's birth and died.

Kentucky currently recognizes loss of consortium claims between husband and wife and the claim of a parent for the loss of the child's affection and companionship upon the death of a child. The question presented here is whether this Court should now recognize a child's loss of parental consortium as well. The Giuliani children through counsel argue that the loss of the parent's love and affection is devastating to any child. Children should be able to bring a loss of consortium claim to recover from the wrongdoer whose negligent acts have caused the harm. Such a cause of action does not currently exist in Kentucky but it should. The loss of consortium is a judge-made common law doctrine which this Court has the power and duty to modify and conform to the changing conditions of our society. When the common law is out of step with the times, this Court has a responsibility to change that law. Development of the common law is a judicial function and should not be confused with the expression of public policy by the legislature.

Kentucky has recognized the changing nature of the parent-child relationship and the importance of children to the family. The legislature has made it the express public policy of the Commonwealth to protect and care for children in a nurturing home. KRS 600.010. It has also recognized the individuality of the child and the value to a family by providing parents a consortium claim for the loss of the love and affection of their child. KRS 411.135. It is a natural development of the common law to recognize the need for a remedy for those children who lose the love and affection of their parents due to the negligence of another. It is necessary for this Court to conform the common law so as to provide a remedy for loss of consortium for children and to decline to "perpetrate an anachronistic and sterile view of the relationship between parents and children." Gallimore v. Children's Hospital Medical Center, Ohio, 67 Ohio St.3d 244, 617 N.E.2d 1052 (1993).

This Court fully understands and appreciates that the trial court and the intermediate appellate court were not at liberty to recognize the loss of parental consortium resulting from the mother's death because of the Brooks [v. Burkeen, 549 S.W.2d 91 (Ky.1977)].

The premise for the Brooks rationale no longer exists. Since 1977, when Brooks was decided, 15 courts and two state legislatures have recognized the claim of children for loss of parental consortium. ... In addition, the state legislatures of Florida and Louisiana have recognized the parental consortium claim by specific statute. Six of the jurisdictions who have recognized the parental consortium claim reversed previous positions denying such claims. See J. Parker, Parental Consortium: Assessing Contours of the New Tort in Town, 64 Miss.L.J. 37 (Fall 1994).

The doctrine of stare decisis does not commit us to the sanctification of ancient fallacy. Stare decisis does not preclude all change. The principle does not require blind imitation of the past or adherence to a rule which is not suited to present conditions. The "ancient fallacy" continued by *Brooks* ... is the view that children do not have identity as individuals and as members of the family separate from their parents. This has never been true and it is long overdue that we recognize the essential personhood of each individual while giving homage and deference to their inclusion in the family. The loss suffered by each child in this case is separate and distinct from the loss of their brothers and sisters and from the loss suffered by their father.

. . .

It is the holding of this Court that Kentucky recognizes the claim of minor children for loss of parental consortium. The proof of such loss and the necessary proof of monetary loss resulting therefrom are factors to be considered by the trier of fact separate from any wrongful death claim pursued under the wrongful death statute. A claim for loss of parental consortium arises from a recognition of the common law as distinguished from statutory law.

Gallimore v. Children's Hospital Medical Center

Supreme Court of Ohio, 1993.
67 Ohio St.3d 244, 617 N.E.2d 1052.

■ DOUGLAS, JUSTICE.

... The question before us is whether the parents of a minor child who is injured by a third-party tortfeasor may recover damages in a derivative action for loss of filial consortium. In this context, loss of "consortium" would include the parent's loss of the services, society, companionship, comfort, love and solace of the injured child. We are convinced that the right to recover for such a loss has existed in Ohio for some time and, today, we expressly recognize that such losses are compensable in Ohio. Accordingly, we affirm the judgment of the court of appeals on this question.

Ohio has long recognized the right of a parent to maintain a derivative action against a third-party tortfeasor who injures the parent's minor child. We have held that the parent may maintain the action for the child's medical expenses, and for the parent's loss of the child's "services." However, none of our cases has specifically limited the parent's right to maintain the derivative action to recovery of losses of only a pecuniary nature.

. . .

The right of a parent to recover for the loss of an injured child's "services" (i.e., labor and earnings) is a common-law right which dates back to a period in history when children were viewed as economic assets, and the child's value to the family was predominantly (if not exclusively) that of a laborer and wage-earner. See generally, Note, Parent's Recovery for Loss of Society and Companionship of Child (1978), 80 W.Va.L.Rev. 340; Love, Tortious Interference with the Parent–Child Relationship: Loss of an Injured Person's Society and Companionship (1976), 51 Ind.L.J. 590; and Shockley v. Prier (1975), 66 Wis.2d 394, 225 N.W.2d 495. At common law, a child was considered to occupy the same status with regard to a parent as a servant occupied with regard to his master. This historical view of the parent-child relationship was fueled by the realities of an economic system where child labor was prevalent, and children represented a significant source of real or potential income to the family unit. Thus, the gist of an action by the parents of an injured child was for monetary losses occasioned by the tortfeasor's conduct. This is no longer the case.

Times have changed and so should the law. Courts and commentators agree that the master-servant analogy to the relationship between parent and child is long overdue for judicial burial. In the vast majority of modern family situations, children can no longer be considered an economic asset to their parents. The present-day economic burdens of raising children, coupled with child labor laws and mandatory school attendance, virtually ensure that recovery for loss of "services" alone will not adequately compensate the parents of an injured child for the true losses they suffer. Indeed, in these modern times, the society, companionship, comfort, love and solace between parents and their child are the essence of that relationship, more so than the "services" a minor child is capable of rendering to his or her parents.

In addition, Ohio's Wrongful Death Act has been amended since this court's decision in *Keaton, supra.* R.C. 2125.02 now specifically permits wrongful death claimants to recover for loss of earning capacity, services and society of the decedent as elements of compensable damage. Thus, in the present day, it would be incongruous to deny parents recovery for loss of the society and companionship of a seriously injured child while recognizing that such losses are compensable in cases involving death.

. . .

Accordingly, we now hold that a parent may recover damages, in a derivative action against a third-party tortfeasor who intentionally or negligently causes physical injury to the parent's minor child, for loss of filial consortium. We further find that "services" are just one aspect of consortium. "Consortium" includes services, society, companionship, comfort, love and solace....

Appellant sets forth a number of policy arguments against recognition of a parental right to pursue recovery for the parent's loss of the society, companionship, love and solace of an injured child. These arguments include the difficulty of measuring damages, the "need" to limit tort liability, the danger of double recovery, and the undesirability of permitting parents to testify in open court as to the diminished value of the parent's relationship with the child. Appellant's arguments are not persuasive.

The difficulty in measuring damages for a parent's loss of filial consortium is no justification for denying the right to pursue the claim. In the case at bar, the losses suffered by Joshua's mother are readily apparent. Joshua has been rendered profoundly deaf, and he and his mother will be unable to enjoy a number of life experiences normally shared between parent and child. Simply because appellee's loss of the consortium of her child is intangible in nature does not mean that the loss is any less real and substantial, or that the loss should go uncompensated. Courts and juries have been called upon to determine damages for loss of spousal consortium for years, and have apparently done so without much difficulty. We have no reason to believe that assessing damages for loss of filial consortium will prove to be any more difficult. We note that pursuant to R.C. 2125.02(B)(3), courts and juries may currently award damages for loss of society as an element of damages in wrongful death cases. We also note that the jury in this case seemingly had little difficulty measuring damages for loss of filial consortium, although the award was "capped" by virtue of former R.C.

2307.43. We concede that money is a poor substitute for the damages appellee has sustained in this case, and that money will not restore Joshua's hearing. However, monetary compensation is currently the best our system of justice has to offer.

As to the "need" to limit liability, appellant suggests that recognizing the right of parents to maintain a claim for loss of filial consortium (in a derivative action already recognized in the law) could eventually lead to the recognition of the right of stepparents, brothers, sisters, aunts, uncles and grandparents, etc., to maintain separate actions for their loss of the consortium of the injured child. Appellant essentially urges that a line must be drawn, and that it should be drawn here. We agree with appellant that a line should be drawn somewhere, and today we hold only that the parents of a minor child may maintain a claim for loss of filial consortium. We make no suggestion that the right does or should extend to a Gilbert and Sullivan cavalcade of "[h]is sisters and his cousins, whom he reckons up by dozens, and his aunts!"[7] The parent-child relationship is unique, and it is particularly deserving of special recognition in the law. As we stated in Williams v. Williams (1975), 44 Ohio St.2d 28, 29, 73 O.O.2d 121, 122, 336 N.E.2d 426, 427, "[i]n our society, the parent-child relationship is special, invoking strong feelings of love and affection."

. . .

Appellant has also expressed concern that permitting recovery for loss of filial consortium in non-fatal injury cases will cause parents to testify in open court to minimize the worth of the parent-child relationship and disparage the "value" of the injured child. However, we do not believe that a parent is likely to proclaim in open court, before a jury and the injured child, that no love or affection exists between parent and child as a result of the tortfeasor's conduct. This would be an unseemly spectacle indeed, and is not likely to happen. Rather, the parent's testimony will more likely be focused on the parent's and child's inability to share in the activities and enjoyment of life experiences normally shared by parents and their children. Such testimony will not degrade the child or minimize the importance of the parent-child relationship in our society.

. . .

Finally, appellant urges that we should refrain from recognizing a common-law rule permitting parents recovery for their loss of the consortium of a child because a number of courts in our sister states have refused to recognize the existence of such an action. Our answer to this contention is twofold. First, and again, we are not creating a new right. We are, at the most, rediscovering a right that has apparently always existed but has never been given full life by *this* court. Second, we are more persuaded by the decisions of those courts which have undertaken to recognize an action for loss of filial consortium, as opposed to those that have taken a contrary view.

. . .

For the foregoing reasons, we affirm the judgment of the court of appeals. We further order that our holdings today be applied only prospectively and, of course, to the case at bar.

7. The Complete Plays of Gilbert and Sullivan (1938) 110, H.M.S. Pinafore, Act I.

NOTE

Loss of parental consortium is recognized as a legitimate tort in many jurisdictions. Although most states have not yet adopted it as a cause of action, legal action, debate, and scholarship in the last decade have pushed this issue to the front of many dockets. See generally Johnny Parker, Parental Consortium: Assessing the Contours of the New Tort in Town, 64 Miss. L.J. 37 (1994) (providing a comprehensive survey of the development of consortium actions across the United States). Courts have also become willing to recognize a loss of consortium when the parent endures a nonfatal injury. See, e.g., Reagan v. Vaughn, 804 S.W.2d 463 (Tex.1990) (allowing parental consortium claim when parent is only injured). Accord Keele v. St. Vincent Hosp., 258 Mont. 158, 852 P.2d 574 (1993); Williams v. Hook, 804 P.2d 1131, (Okla.1990). But see Guenther v. Stollberg, 242 Neb. 415, 495 N.W.2d 286 (1993) (rejecting action for minors based on loss of consortium with nonfatally injured parent); cf. Belcher v. Goins, 184 W.Va. 395, 400 S.E.2d 830 (1990) (barring loss of consortium action on the grounds that an adult child who is not dependent on his parent cannot claim for loss of consortium). Massachusetts has been particularly expansive in the development of this tort. The Supreme Judicial Court allowed an illegitimate child whose father suffered nonfatal injuries before the birth of the child to recover. Angelini v. OMD Corp., 410 Mass. 653, 575 N.E.2d 41 (1991). But see Klaus v. Fox Valley Sys., 259 Kan. 522, 912 P.2d 703 (1996) (rejecting action of minor children against tortfeasor for negligent injury to parent, even though they were indirectly injured themselves).

3. CRIMINAL LAW

Connecticut v. Miranda

Supreme Court of Connecticut, 2005.
274 Conn. 727, 878 A.2d 1118.

PER CURIAM. This case is before us for a third time. See State v. Miranda, 794 A.2d 506, *cert. denied*, 537 U.S. 902 (2002) (*Miranda* II); State v. Miranda, 715 A.2d 680 (1998) (*Miranda* I). The defendant, Santos Miranda, appeals from the trial court's judgment, rendered after remand from the Appellate Court, resentencing him to a total of thirty years imprisonment for his conviction of assault in the first degree in violation of *General Statutes § 53a–59(a)(3)*[5] and risk of injury to a child in violation of General Statutes (Rev. to 1991) § 53–21. ... [I]n a supplemental brief requested by this court, the defendant contends that we should reconsider and reverse our conclusion in *Miranda I* that the defendant could be convicted of assault in the first degree in violation of *§ 3a–59(a)(3)* for failing to protect the victim from physical abuse by her mother.

. . .

... We agree with the defendant ... that we should reconsider and reverse our conclusion in *Miranda I.* We therefore reverse the defendant's conviction of two counts of assault in the first degree in violation of *§ 53a–59(a)(3)* and remand the case to the trial court, first, to dismiss the charges in those counts of the information and, second, for resentencing on the only remaining count on which the defendant stands convicted, risk of injury to a child, in accordance with *Miranda II.*

5. *General Statutes § 53a–59* provides in relevant part: "(a) A person is guilty of assault in the first degree when ... (3) under circumstances evincing an extreme indifference to human life he recklessly engages in conduct which creates a risk of death to another person, and thereby causes serious physical injury to another person...."

The ... facts and procedural history of this case are set forth in our decision in *Miranda II* as follows:

"The defendant commenced living with his girlfriend and her two children in an apartment [in Meriden] in September, 1992. On January 27, 1993, the defendant was twenty-one years old, his girlfriend was sixteen, her son was two, and her daughter, the victim in this case, born on September 21, 1992, was four months old. Although he was not the biological father of either child, the defendant took care of them and considered himself to be their stepfather. He represented himself as such to the people at Meriden Veteran's Memorial Hospital where, on January 27, 1993, the victim was taken for treatment of her injuries following a 911 call by the defendant that the child was choking on milk. Upon examination at the hospital, it was determined that the victim had multiple rib fractures that were approximately two to three weeks old, two skull fractures that were approximately seven to ten days old, a brachial plexus injury to her left arm, a rectal tear that was actively 'oozing blood' and bilateral subconjunctival nasal hemorrhages. On the basis of extensive medical evidence, the trial court determined that the injuries had been sustained on three or more occasions and that none of the injuries had been the result of an accident, a fall, events that took place at the time of the child's birth, cardiopulmonary resuscitation, a blocked air passageway or the child choking on milk." ... [T]he trial court found that the injuries, many of which created a risk of death, had been caused by great and deliberate force.

"The trial court further found in accordance with the medical evidence that, as a result of the nature of these injuries, at the time they were sustained the victim would have screamed inconsolably, and that her injuries would have caused noticeable physical deformities, such as swelling, bruising and poor mobility, and finally, that her intake of food would have been reduced. The court also determined that anyone who saw the child would have had to notice these injuries, the consequent deformities and her reactions. Indeed, the trial court found that the defendant had been aware of the various bruises on her right cheek and the subconjunctival nasal hemorrhages, as well as the swelling of the child's head, that he knew she had suffered a rectal tear, as well as rib fractures posteriorly on the left and right sides, and that he was aware that there existed a substantial and unjustifiable risk that the child was exposed to conduct that created a risk of death. The trial court concluded that despite this knowledge, the defendant 'failed to act to help or aid [the child] by promptly notifying authorities of her injuries, taking her for medical care, removing her from her circumstances and guarding her from future abuses. As a result of his failure to help her, the child was exposed to conduct which created a risk of death to her and the child suffered subsequent serious physical injuries...."

. . .

After careful reconsideration, we have become persuaded that our conclusion in *Miranda I, supra*, 245 Conn. 230, that the defendant could be convicted of assault in the first degree in violation of *§ 53a–59(a)(3)* was clearly wrong and should be overruled. The six justices of this court who agree with this conclusion and join in this opinion do not, however, arrive at that conclusion by employing the same analysis. As a result, the reasoning of these six justices is set forth in the two concurring opinions issued herewith.

The judgment is reversed in part and the case is remanded with direction to dismiss the two counts of the information for assault in the first degree and for resentencing on the one count of risk of injury to a child.

■ BORDEN, J., with whom NORCOTT and PALMER, J., join, concurring.

. . .

The defendant was not the perpetrator of the physical assaults on the victim. The perpetrator was the victim's mother. Id. The defendant, however, who was the boyfriend of the child's mother, "had established a family-like relationship with the mother and her two children ... had voluntarily assumed responsibility for the care and welfare of both children, and ... had considered himself the victim's stepfather...." On the basis of these facts, the court in *Miranda I* concluded that "there existed a common-law duty to protect the victim from her mother's abuse, the breach of which can be the basis of a conviction under *§ 53a–59(a)(3)*." The court's chain of reasoning was that: (1) parents may be criminally liable for assault by inaction, as opposed to action, based on common-law duties to protect their children; (2) recognition by the courts of such a duty and the criminal consequences of its breach is permitted by *General Statutes § 53a–4*; (3) this duty has been recognized as applying, in addition to biological and adoptive parents and legal guardians, to other adults who establish familial relationships with and assume responsibility for the care of a child; (4) there is a continuing demographic trend reflecting a significant increase in nontraditional alternative family arrangements; and (5) to ascribe such a duty to the defendant under the facts of the case would be harmonious with the public policy of preventing children from abuse and with the concomitant general policy underlying *General Statutes § 53–21*, the risk of injury statute that applies to *any* person. Thus, the linchpin of the court's reasoning was that there is a recognized common-law duty of a parent or legal guardian to protect his or her child from abuse, the breach of which may constitute assault under our Penal Code pursuant to *§ 53a–4*; and the defendant, although neither a parent nor legal guardian, was subject to the same duty because he had established a familial relationship with the victim's mother, had assumed the responsibility for the victim's care, and considered himself the victim's stepfather.

In my view, it is not necessary to decide in the present case whether a parent or legal guardian can be held criminally liable under *§ 53a–59(a)(3)* for failing to protect his child from physical abuse by another. I would leave that question to a case that squarely presents it. I conclude, instead, that, assuming without deciding that a parent or legal guardian could be held so liable, a person in the defendant's position—neither a parent nor a legal guardian—may not be so held criminally liable.[6]

. . .

I conclude, therefore, that the defendant cannot, as a matter of law, be convicted of assault in the first degree, and that the judgments of conviction on counts five and ten of the information must reversed, and a judgment of acquittal be rendered on those counts.

■ VERTEFEUILLE, J., with whom, SULLIVAN, C. J., and ZARELLA, J., join, concurring.

. . .

I ... concur with the conclusion set forth in the accompanying per curiam opinion that *Miranda I* must be overruled. I do so because, in my

6. I would leave the criminal liability of the defendant to the risk of injury statute, namely, *§ 53–21*, the applicability of which the defendant has never challenged.

view, a failure to act cannot constitute assault within the meaning of *General Statutes § 53a–59(a)(3).*

. . .

According to common understanding as expressed in dictionary definitions, "assault" is a crime caused by affirmative action. Webster's Third New International Dictionary defines assault as "a violent attack with physical means" and, alternatively, as an attempt or threat to do violence without actually inflicting the violence. Black's Law Dictionary (8th Ed. 2004) further defines assault as "the threat or use of force on another that causes that person to have a reasonable apprehension of imminent harmful or offensive conduct" or "an attempt to commit battery requiring the specific intent to cause physical injury." An accompanying commentary to that definition of assault provides: "In popular language [assault] has always connoted a physical attack. When we say that D assaults V, we have a mental picture of D *attacking* V, by striking or pushing or stabbing him." (Emphasis added.) Id.

. . .

I . . . conclude that there is "nothing in the text of *§ 53a–59(a)(3)*, or its legislative history, to support [the] conclusion that conduct under *§ 53a–59(a)(3)* includes the failure to act." *Miranda I,* (*Berdon, J.*, dissenting).

. . .

The cases from other jurisdictions on which the majority in *Miranda I* relied, and on which the dissent in the present case also relies in part, were dependent on statutes that are not analogous to *§ 53a–59(a)(3)* . . . Although the defendants in [these cases]had failed to help children who were endangered by others, the statutes under which they were charged directly criminalized inaction as well as action. Thus, these cases are not helpful in deciding the present case, which concerns an assault statute that does *not* specifically criminalize inaction.

. . .

■ KATZ, J., dissenting.

. . .

I consider the legislature's failure to act in the face of our interpretation of *§ 53a–59(a)(3)* to be highly significant. Although the issue of whether to extend criminal liability to a particular class of persons based on a duty to act was a matter of common-law adjudication, the issue of whether *§ 53a–59(a)(3)* can be applied to an act of omission as well as commission is a matter of statutory construction. The legislature often has decided to revisit a statute interpreted by this court or to react to a judicial interpretation that the legislature deemed inaccurate. . . .

Accordingly, it is clear that the legislature had the authority to make it evident that it never intended to punish someone under *§ 53a–59(a)(3)* for his failure to act or to prevent harm, after either the *Miranda I* or *Miranda II* decision. Its failure to respond to either of these decisions involving this defendant strongly suggests that our initial determination was proper.

. . .

Turning to the merits of the inquiry, I continue to believe that the defendant in this case properly was convicted of assault in the first degree in violation of *§ 53a–59(a)(3)* because he recklessly engaged in conduct thereby causing serious physical injury in that he failed to act, help or aid the child victim by promptly notifying authorities of her injuries, taking her for medical care, removing her from her circumstances and guarding her from future abuses. As a result of his failure to help her, the child was exposed to conduct that created a risk of death to her, and the child suffered subsequent serious physical injuries. This court set forth the facts the trial court reasonably had found in *Miranda I*. As best as I can determine, nothing has changed in this regard.

. . .

Today, despite the fact that in *Miranda II*, the court essentially reinforced the reasoning that informed the first case involving this defendant, the majority of the court changes its opinion—a plurality determines that even a parent cannot be held liable for reckless assault under *§ 53a–59(a)(3)* for failing to prevent abuse of his or her own child, as discussed in Justice Vertefeuille's concurrence, and another plurality determines that, even if the assault statute contemplates omission by someone with a duty to act, the defendant does not fall within that category under the facts of this case, as discussed in Justice Borden's concurrence ... I venture to guess that a majority of this court would acknowledge that, if a mother, who did not herself inflict any punishment on her child, but allowed her boyfriend to inflict brutal beatings that caused serious physical injury to her infant, were charged with reckless assault, she should be treated no differently than if she had allowed her child to starve nearly to death or wander into traffic and be hit by a vehicle. In either instance, she would have engaged in conduct that constituted a gross deviation from the standard of conduct that any reasonable parent would observe under the circumstances. In either instance, the injury caused by the mother's conduct would have been a foreseeable and natural result of her conduct, thereby making her criminally responsible. The difference in the present case, however, is that it was the mother who inflicted the injuries, and someone other than an adoptive or biological parent who failed to protect the infant.

. . .

Finally, I disagree with my colleagues that the continuing demographic trend, which we first noted in *Miranda I,* that reflects a significant increase in nontraditional alternative family arrangements counsels against the imposition of liability in this case. I do not agree that persons inclined to enter relationships that involve children will consciously decide against such involvement for fear of being held responsible if and when a child is abused or neglected. Because more and more children will be living with or may depend upon adults who do not qualify as a natural or adoptive parent, the fact that we are, at best, affording protection only to those children whose adult caregivers have chosen to have their relationships officially recognized hardly advances the public policy of protecting children from abuse.

Accordingly, I respectfully dissent.

NOTE

See generally Ricki Rhein, Note, Assessing Criminal Liability for the Passive Parent, 9 Cardozo Women's L.J. 627 (2003). Compare V. Paulani Enos, Prosecuting Battered Mothers: State Laws' Failure to Protect Battered Women and Abused Children, 19 Harv. Women's L.J. 236 (1996). For a more detailed examination of child abuse and neglect, see Chapter 10, *infra*.

Diehl v. State

Court of Appeals of Texas, 1985.
698 S.W.2d 712.

■ WARREN, JUSTICE.

The trial court convicted appellants of possession of marijuana and assessed each appellant's punishment at 10 years probation. In their sole ground of error on appeal, appellants allege that the trial court erred in refusing to grant their motion to suppress the evidence. Appellants argue that the search warrant was based on an affidavit which did not show probable cause.

. . .

Appellant argues that the affidavit is not sufficient to show probable cause for several reasons:

1) The informant [the daughter of Barbara Diehl] is 11 years old, she had never given information to the police before, she did not make a sworn statement to the police, and there is no indication as to why the affiant found her information credible or reliable;

2) There is no indication of any independent police investigation to corroborate any details of the informant's information;

3) There is no indication that the informant was capable of recognizing marijuana;

4) No specific details describing the marijuana or its possession are provided in the affidavit, and the conclusory statement that the informant's descriptions to the affidavit "could only be given by someone who observed it" was not sufficient to show facts upon which a finding of probable cause could be made.

. . .

The informant in the affidavit was named, so that there was no need to indicate why her information was believable. She lived at the residence to be searched, so that her ability to observe the contraband was not at issue. We also note that growing marijuana, unlike processed drugs, is easily recognizable, both by its distinctive leaves and odor, and by the secrecy with which it is normally grown and processed. The informant's detailed descriptions given to the affiant would have given the magistrate even more reason to believe that probable cause existed to issue the warrant, but the omission of this information from the affidavit was not fatal. We hold that the trial court did not err in refusing to grant appellants' motion to suppress.

■ LEVY, JUSTICE, dissenting.

. . .

I am not willing, as the majority apparently is, to bypass so readily, or in fact to ignore, the presence and significance of the parent-child relationship in criminal prosecutions. That relationship, and its significance, are not mentioned at all in the court's discussion. Because of this, and the paucity of case law on the subject, I must assume that in the majority's view the parent-child privilege is simply non-existent in legal contemplation, or of little or no consequence in determining whether the motion to suppress should have been sustained.

With this conclusion I disagree and would hold that the motion to suppress should have been granted. We should not ignore the case law, scarce as it may be, emphasizing the significance of the family and expanding the realm of constitutional protection we accord the private sanctuary of family life. Nor should we ignore the social interest in preserving family units and the confidential exchange of information within them. If we are indifferent to such values and interests, it will be at the immediate risk of allowing the growth of State hostility to them. In contrast to the majority's apparent position, I feel that it is necessary to face the relationship issue squarely in order to reach a just and salutary result in this case, because the most serious, intimate, and far-reaching social values are in conflict here, involving the very nature of the relationships between the individual, the family, and the State.[2]

At the outset, it must be observed that appellants did not invoke the parent-child privilege as the basis for their timely filed motion to suppress, but rather alleged generally the lack of probable cause.... Appellants' failure to raise this issue is not dispositive, given the bereft state of the law on parent-child immunity in Texas; it was not, in other words, a *conscious* waiver in the sense of an "intentional relinquishment or abandonment of a *known* right or privilege." Because of the constitutional stature and transcendent social significance of this privilege, I would hold that the trial court's failure to grant appellant's motion to suppress was fundamental error.

Our Texas jurisprudence, like that of many other States, has a gaping hole where some protection of intrafamilial relationships should be. This void is all the more shocking and conspicuous because, not being based upon any specific judicial repudiation of a parent-child privilege, it is so incompatible with our nation's traditions, values, and conscience. It is not too rhetorical to assess the integrity and inviolability of the family unit—and the loyalty, trust, and confidence that normally exist within the parent-child relationship—as "so rooted in the traditions and conscience of our people as to be ranked as fundamental." Snyder v. Massachusetts, 291 U.S. 97, 105 (1934). The family unit itself has been afforded a right of privacy by the United States Supreme Court, and thus is eligible for protection from harmful intrusion by the State that violates that right. See Moore v. City of East Cleveland, 431 U.S. 494 (1977)....

. . .

... Confidential communications between non-spousal family members have not yet, however, been afforded the status of a testimonial privilege. Ex parte Port, 674 S.W.2d 772 (Tex.Crim.1984).

In contrast, confidential communications between spouses, during their marriage and afterwards, have generally been deemed privileged. In Texas, neither spouse may testify over the objection of the other as to confidential communications between them. Either may refuse to testify about confidential communications made to the other. But the privilege may be waived. A party who acquiesces in the admission of testimony concerning these communications waives his privilege to exclude them, and the privilege does not apply to information acquired independently, rather than from the spouse or as a result of the marital relation. And it is well established—and specified in Texas Rules of Evidence 504(d)(1)—that there is no privilege if the communication was made, even partially, to aid anyone to commit, or plan

2. For an innovative and stimulating discussion of this problem, see S. Levinson, Testimonial Privileges and the Preferences of Friendship, 1984 Duke L.J. 631.

to commit, a crime or fraud. In no case of a criminal prosecution may a spouse testify against the other (this is a disqualification, not merely a privilege, codified in Tex.Code Crim.P.Ann. art. 38.11 [Vernon 1979]), except for an offense committed by one spouse against the other, or against their child, or in certain cases of bigamy, incest, interference with child custody, or non-support. Either may be witness *for* the other in a criminal prosecution. Reason would suggest that similar qualifications and exclusions (particularly relating to child abuse or child assault) should doubtless apply to the parent-child privilege, because the family privacy interest intended to be protected is the same in both situations.

. . .

The role of the parents in developing a child's emotional stability, character, and self-image is universally recognized in our society. Erosion of this influence would have a profound effect on the individual child and on our society as a whole. It is essential to the parent-child relationship that the lines of communication between them remain open and, especially, that the child be encouraged to "talk out" his or her problems.

Certain similarities emerge upon examination of the parent-child relationship and the husband-wife relationship. Ideally, the parent-child relationship encompasses many aspects of the marital relationship—mutual love, affection, trust, and intimacy—with the parent providing the emotional guidance and the child relying upon the parent for help and support. Because parental influence is probably the most important factor in a child's development, society has a vital interest in fostering this affectionate and therapeutic relationship between parent and child. As in the marital relationship, optimal parent-child relations cannot exist without a great deal of communication between the two, characterized by a free flow of highly personal information from child to parent. This relationship, unlike the spousal, lasts during the entire lifetime of the parties, and is ongoing from generation to generation, linking the individual to both the past and the future.

Given that the fostering of a confidential parent-child relationship is necessary to the child's development of a positive system of values, and results in an ultimate good to society as a whole, what effect on that relationship would occur if the State could induce or allow children—as in the instant case—or compel their parents to disclose information given to them in a confidential setting? The security and peace of a family are as much jeopardized by the damaging testimony of an 11 year old daughter of a defendant as by that of the spouse. The recent spectacle in the aforementioned *Port* case of the State attempting to force a mother and father to reveal their child's misdeeds, in order to provide evidence for a capital murder prosecution, is shocking to my sense of decency, propriety, and fairness. If the parents refuse to divulge their children's confidences (or vice versa), the alternatives faced by the parents, i.e., the risk of prosecution for contempt or for perjury, could seriously undermine public respect and confidence in our system of justice. Should such a practice be allowed and then encouraged or abused by the State, a monumental violation of individual rights, as well as a destructive impact on the family unit in society, could result. It is inconsistent with the way of life we cherish, and raises the specter of a totalitarian regime, as created by Adolf Hitler and imagined by George Orwell, where systematic government programs attempt to "persuade" young children to inform against their parents. We want no "Hitler Jugend" in the United States, nor do we want the police to behave in a manner which brings the law into disrepute. In either case, the resulting institutional damage to the State may be as socially undesirable as the crime the police combat. The courts should not be placed in a position to say to parents, "Listen to your child at the risk of being compelled to testify about his confidences," nor should the courts require a child to choose between loyalty to his parents and loyalty to the State. This would necessarily require the State to actively punish selflessness and loyalty which are inculcated into children by their families, their churches, and even the State itself, and not only where such values are deemed consistent with the State's purposes. Such considerations would suggest that the parent-child privilege is logically based not only on the confidential nature of specific communications between parent and child, but also upon the *privacy* which is a constitutionally protectable interest of the family in American society.[3]

I conclude, then, that while the State has an important and legitimate goal in ascertaining "the truth" and presenting all relevant evidence before the court in each proceeding, this goal does not supercede the judiciary's primary commitment to justice. Pursuing this commitment, it is our paramount task to accommodate the vital social need for security and stability against the essential rights of the individual. Thus, I do not believe that the State's interest in full disclosure outweighs an individual's right of privacy in communications within the family, nor the family's interest in its integrity and inviolability. This integrity and inviolability spring from the rights of privacy *inherent* in the family relationship itself. No reasonable basis exists for extending a testimonial privilege for confidential communications to spouses who enjoy a dissoluble legal contract, while yet denying a parent or child the right to claim such a privilege to protect communications made within an indissoluble family unit, bonded by blood, affection, loyalty, tradition, and perhaps religious teaching.[5] If the rationale supporting the privilege of a witness/spouse to refuse to testify adversely against his or her spouse in a criminal proceeding, or supporting the right of a defendant/spouse to exclude such testimony of a present or former spouse, serves to prevent the invasion of the harmony and privacy of the marriage relationship itself, then affording the same protection to the parent-child relationship is even more compelling. The "traditional relation of the family" is "a relation as old and as fundamental as our entire civilization." Griswold, 381 U.S. at 496, 85 S.Ct. at 1688.

American jurisprudence has traditionally judged the integrity of the judicial system's protection of individual rights and basic social values to be worth the price of a few guilty defendants slipping through the judicial system. In suggesting that the State should be required to prosecute defendants through other means than by allowing or compelling their family

3. The parent-child relationship does not cease at the stroke of midnight on the last day of the child's 17th year. If the parent-child privilege flows from the constitutional right to privacy inherent in such a relationship, the State is forbidden to create an age barrier to limit that right to the minority of the child or to certain persons within an artificial age bracket. The parent-child relationship, unlike the marital, is not voluntary or subject to dissolution, but is ongoing throughout the lives of both participants.

5. See, for example, Talmudic commentary in Sanhedrin 27b:

What is the implication of the text "The fathers shall not be put to death for the sins of the children?" If it implies the fathers shall be put to death for the *iniquity* of the fathers, that has already been stated (Deut. 24, 16): "every man shall be put to death for his own sin." But the text implies that the fathers shall not be put to death *on the testimony* of the children and the children *on the testimony* of their fathers.

members to testify against them, I hope that this tradition will be continued—and perhaps even enhanced.

I respectfully dissent, and would hold that the motion to suppress should have been sustained because of the parent-child privilege based on the constitutional right of privacy, the Fourth Amendment to the United States Constitution, and articles 18.01(b) and 38.23 of the Texas Code of Criminal Procedure.

NOTES

1. A few courts have recognized a parent-child testimonial privilege. See, e.g., In re Agosto, 553 F.Supp. 1298 (D. Nev.1983); In re A & M, 61 A.D.2d 426, 403 N.Y.S.2d 375 (1978). New York, however, has refused to extend this privilege for children beyond minority. See People v. Hilligas, 175 Misc.2d 842, 670 N.Y.S.2d 744 (Sup. Ct. 1998); People v. Romer, 152 Misc.2d 915, 579 N.Y.S.2d 306 (Sup. Ct. 1998).

2. In 1981, Minnesota provided protection for communications between parents and children by amending Section 595.02 of its statutes to provide:

> A parent or his minor child may not be examined as to any communication made in confidence by the minor to his parent. A communication is confidential if made out of the presence of persons not members of the child's immediate family living in the same household. This exception may be waived by express consent to disclosure by a parent entitled to claim the privilege or by the child who made the communication, or by failure of the child or parent to object when the contents of a communication are demanded. This exception does not apply to a civil action or proceeding by one spouse against the other or by a parent or child against the other, nor to a proceeding to commit either the child or parent to whom the communication was made or to place the person or property or either under the control of another because of his alleged mental or physical condition, nor to a criminal action or proceeding in which the parent is charged with a crime committed against the person or property of the communicating child, the parent's spouse, or a child of either the parent or the parent's spouse, or in which a child is charged with a crime or act of delinquency committed against the person or property of a parent or a child of a parent, nor to an action or proceeding for termination of parental rights, nor any other action or proceeding on a petition alleging child abuse, child neglect, abandonment or nonsupport by a parent.

Idaho also protects parent-child communications. Idaho Code 9–203(7) (2004).

In 1986, Massachusetts enacted legislation that bars children from testifying against their parents in a criminal proceeding unless the victim of the crime is a member of their immediate family who resides in the household. ALM GL ch. 233 § 20 (2005). See generally Maureen P. O'Sullivan, An Examination of the State and Federal Courts' Treatment of the Parent–Child Privilege, 39 Catholic Law. 201 (1999); Catherine J. Ross, Implementing Constitutional Rights for Juveniles: The Parent–Child Privilege in Context, 14 Stan. L. & Pol'y Rev 85 (2003).

3. Compare United States v. Penn, 647 F.2d 876 (9th Cir.1980). Two years of investigation led Seattle police officers to believe that Clara Penn was distributing heroin from her residence. A search warrant was issued. The police found Clara Penn's children, ages 5 to 22 on the premises. After a fruitless half hour search, a police officer asked the youngest child (Reggie, age 5) if he knew where the little balloons (of heroin) were hidden. The officer offered Reggie five dollars if he would show him where. Reggie did. The police dug up 132.9 grams of heroin in a glass jar. Clara Penn was prosecuted for possession with intent to distribute. She moved and won a suppression motion in district court. On appeal, a closely divided Ninth Circuit reversed the district court. Judge Goodwin in dissent argued:

> By offering money to the defendant's five-year old son, the police intruded ... on a family relationship that is highly valued.... At least, the law should not

> unnecessarily make parents and children apprehensive about exchanging information. Nor should the law encourage children to turn against their parents.

647 F.2d at 887.

Judge Fletcher, dissenting from a denial of a rehearing added:

> The majority is on dangerous and frightening ground when it ties the level of constitutional protection to the court's perception of the quality of the Penn family. This invites police to apply an "Ozzie and Harriet" test by which the reasonableness of a search is based in part on the worthiness of the family.

647 F.3d at 890.

4. International Law

In 1989 the United Nations adopted the Convention on the Rights of the Child, G.A. Res. 25, U.N. GAOR, 44th Sess., U.N. Doc. A/RES/44/25. The Convention is a modern adaptation and expansion of previous child-protective treaties. It seeks to further the goals of improving the lives of children by setting forth certain regulations, among them: no child under fifteen can be recruited for armed conflict, compulsory education for children under eighteen irrespective of sex and religion, no capital punishment for minors, and the protection of certain due process rights in the justice system, to name but a few. By 2005, more than one hundred and ninety countries had ratified the Convention. Only two signatories have not: Somalia and the United States.

C. When Parent, Child, and State Disagree

1. Name

Henne v. Wright

United States Court of Appeals, Eighth Circuit, 1990.
904 F.2d 1208.

■ Bright, Senior Circuit Judge.

Defendants Dr. Gregg F. Wright, M.D., Director of the Nebraska Department of Health, and Stanley S. Cooper, Director of the Nebraska Bureau of Vital Statistics, appeal the judgment of the district court granting plaintiffs Debra Henne and Linda Spidell declaratory and injunctive relief from a Nebraska statute that restricts the choice of surnames that can be entered on an infant's birth certificate. Plaintiffs brought this action under 42 U.S.C. § 1983 individually and as next friends to their daughters alleging that Neb.Rev.Stat. § 71–640.01 (1986) unconstitutionally infringes their fundamental fourteenth amendment right to choose surnames for their daughters other than those prescribed. . . .

On April 4, 1985, Debra Henne gave birth to Alicia Renee Henne at a hospital in Lincoln, Nebraska. Following Alicia's birth, Debra completed a birth certificate form at the request of a hospital employee. Debra listed Gary Brinton as the father and entered the name Alicia Renee Brinton in the space provided for the child's name. Brinton, also present at the hospital, completed and signed a paternity form.

At the time of the birth, Debra was still married to Robert Henne. Although Debra and Robert Henne had filed for a divorce prior to Alicia's birth, the decree dissolving the marriage did not become final until after the birth. As a result of her marital status, hospital personnel, acting on instructions from the Department of Health, informed Debra that she could not surname her daughter "Brinton." Debra then filled out a second birth certificate form, entering the child's name as Alicia Renee Henne and leaving blank the space provided for the father's name. Robert Henne has never claimed to be Alicia's father and, pursuant to the divorce decree, pays no child support for her.

Almost three years later, on February 4, 1988, Debra Henne went in person to the Bureau of Vital Statistics of the Nebraska Department of Health and requested that Alicia's surname be changed to Brinton and that Gary Brinton be listed on the birth certificate as the father. Debra produced a signed statement personally acknowledging Gary Brinton as Alicia's biological father. She also presented a signed acknowledgement of paternity from Gary Brinton and a letter from him requesting that the birth certificate be changed. Personnel at the Bureau of Vital Statistics, acting indirectly at the direction of defendants Cooper and Wright, denied Debra's request. Other than her visit to the Bureau of Vital Statistics and this action, Debra has made no attempt to change Alicia's surname.

On June 17, 1988, at St. Elizabeth's Hospital in Lincoln, Nebraska, Linda Spidell gave birth to a daughter, Quintessa Martha Spidell. Linda wished to give Quintessa the surname "McKenzie," the same surname as her other two children, who were born in California. Hospital personnel, acting upon instructions from the Department of Health, informed Linda that Quintessa could not be surnamed McKenzie and that if Linda did not complete the birth certificate form the hospital would enter Quintessa's last name as Spidell. Linda completed the form, entering "Spidell" as Quintessa's surname and leaving blank the space provided for the father's name.

Linda surnamed her other children McKenzie simply because she liked that name and not because of any familial connection. For that reason, and because she wishes all three children to share the same name, she wants Quintessa surnamed McKenzie. Linda was not married at the time of Quintessa's birth or at the time of this action and there has been no judicial determination of paternity. At trial, however, both Linda and Ray Duffer, who lives with Linda and her children, testified that Duffer is Quintessa's biological father. Other than this action, Linda has made no attempt to change Quintessa's surname.

. . .

Defendants contend that the district court erred in holding Neb.Rev. Stat. § 71-640.01[5] unconstitutional....

5. Section 71-640.01 states:

The information pertaining to the name of an infant born in this state and reported on a birth certificate, filled out and filed pursuant to sections 71-601 to 71-648, shall comply with the following:

(1) If the mother was married at the time of either conception or birth of the child, or at any time between conception and birth, the name of such mother's husband shall be entered on the certificate as the father of the child and the surname of the child shall be entered on the certificate as being (a) the same as that of the husband, unless paternity has been determined otherwise by a court of competent jurisdiction, (b) the surname of the mother, (c) the maiden surname of the mother, or (d) the hyphenated surname of both parents;

(2) If the mother was not married at the time of either conception or birth of the child, or at any time between conception and birth, the name of the father shall not be entered on the certificate without the written consent of the mother and the person named as the father, in

Whether there is a fundamental right to give a child a surname at birth with which the child has no legally established parental connection will dictate the appropriate level of constitutional scrutiny for evaluating Neb. Rev.Stat. § 71–640.01. Specifically, if the statute significantly infringes a right deemed fundamental under the fourteenth amendment right of privacy then we must rigorously scrutinize the asserted justifications for the statute. Otherwise, we analyze the statute under the highly deferential rational basis standard of review applicable to most economic and social legislation challenged under the fourteenth amendment.

. . .

In determining whether a right not enumerated in the Constitution qualifies as fundamental, we ask whether the right is "deeply rooted in this Nation's history and tradition,"....

The custom in this country has always been that a child born in lawful wedlock receives the surname of the father at birth.

While some married parents now may wish to give their children the surname of the mother or a hyphenated surname consisting of both parents' surname, and some unmarried mothers may wish to give their children the surname of the father, we can find no American tradition to support the extension of the right of privacy to cover the right of a parent to give a child a surname with which that child has no legally recognized parental connection. Plaintiffs therefore have not asserted a right that is fundamental under the fourteenth amendment right of privacy and Neb.Rev.Stat. § 71–640.01 need only rationally further legitimate state interests to withstand constitutional scrutiny.

The district court in this case held that section 71–640.01 failed to survive even minimal scrutiny. Other federal courts reviewing statutes restricting the choice of surnames have taken similar positions. Sydney v. Pingree, 564 F.Supp. 412, 413 (S.D.Fla.1982); O'Brien v. Tilson, 523 F.Supp. 494, 496 (E.D.N.C.1981); Jech v. Burch, 466 F.Supp. 714, 721 (D.Hawai'i 1979). Nevertheless, for the reasons discussed below, we determine that the Nebraska statute passes minimal scrutiny, i.e., the rational basis test.

A law must be upheld under the rational basis test unless it bears no rational relation to a legitimate state interest. ...

We determine that the law rationally furthers at least three legitimate state interests: the state's interest in promoting the welfare of children, the state's interest in insuring that the names of its citizens are not appropriated for improper purposes and the state's interest in inexpensive and efficient record keeping. Specifically, a reasonable legislature could believe that in most cases a child's welfare is served by bearing a surname possessing a connection with at least one legally verifiable parent. Furthermore, the legislature could reasonably perceive that in the absence of a law such as section 71–640.01, the name of a non-parent could be improperly appropri-

which case and upon the written request of both such parents the surname of the child shall be that of the father or the hyphenated surname of both parents;

(3) In any case in which paternity of a child is determined by a court of competent jurisdiction, the name of the father shall be entered on the certificate in accordance with the finding of the court and the surname of the child may be entered on the certificate the same as the surname of the father;

(4) In all other cases, the surname of the child shall be the legal surname of the mother; and

(5) If the father is not named on the certificate, no other information about the father shall be entered thereon.

ated to achieve a deliberately misleading purpose, such as the creation of a false implication of paternity. Finally, the legislature could reasonably conclude that it is easier and cheaper to verify and index the birth records of a person who has a surname in common with at least one legally verifiable parent. The district court's review of the evidence buttresses this conclusion. Although the Nebraska legislature could perhaps tailor the statute to more closely serve these purposes, we cannot say that section 71–640.01 bears no rational relationship to the state's legitimate interests. We therefore reject plaintiffs' contention that Neb.Rev.Stat. § 71–640.01 unconstitutionally restricts their parental rights.

Accordingly, the district court's judgment is reversed.

■ Arnold, Circuit Judge, concurring in part and dissenting in part.

. . .

A few salient facts are worth repeating. Debra Henne wants to give her daughter the surname of the little girl's father. The father is willing. He has acknowledged his fatherhood. The man to whom Ms. Henne was married when the baby was born has no objection. Linda Spidell wants to name her daughter "McKenzie," which is neither her name nor the name of the child's father. The choice is not so eccentric as it seems, however: Ms. Spidell's two other children are named "McKenzie," and it is quite natural to desire that all of one's three children have the same surname. Again, no one with a personal interest objects. Ray Duffer, the man who lives with Ms. Spidell, is the child's father, and "McKenzie" is fine with him.

The government, in the person of the State of Nebraska, says no to both mothers. The most plausible reason it offers is administrative convenience.[1] Records are easier to keep and use if every person has the surname of "at least one legally verifiable parent." This interest is legitimate, and the statute under challenge is rationally related to it. If the appropriate level of constitutional scrutiny were the rational-basis test, I would agree that the law is valid. But if a fundamental right is at stake, the State must show a compelling interest, which it has wholly failed to do. So the case comes down to this: Do parents have a fundamental right to name their own children?

. . . In the beginning, surnames were unknown. They "were not considered of controlling importance until the reign of Queen Elizabeth, 1558–1603." Note, What's in a Name?, 2 N.Y.L.Rev. 1, 1 (1924). "The surname, in its origin, was not, as a rule, inherited from the father, but was either voluntarily adopted by the son or conferred upon him by his neighbors. . . . " Fundamentally, names were not inherited. They were something people chose for themselves. "There [was] no such thing as the 'legal name' of a person in the sense that he may not lawfully adopt or acquire another. By the common law a man [sic] may name himself, or change his name at will, and this without solemnity or formality of any kind; or he may acquire a name by reputation, general usage or habit." Even after statutes were passed to provide a fixed procedure for changing one's name, the statutes were treated as merely supplementary to the common law. One could use the

1. It is also true, as the Court says, that allowing an unfettered choice of surname could enable parents to imply falsely that someone was the father of the child. In the example I put at the oral argument, I would have an interest in keeping a stranger from naming her child "Richard S. Arnold, Jr.," and the State would have an interest in defending my reputation against such a false implication. Nothing of the kind is involved in the present cases. Moreover, the State might have an interest in the matter if the child's parents could not agree on a surname. Again, no such issue is presented by these cases.

statute if desired, but the old do-it-yourself right simply to assume a new name still existed.

The early tradition, then, did not restrict one's own choice of a surname. You could freely select any name you chose, whether it was your parents' surname or not. "The ancient custom was for the son to adopt a surname at will, regardless of that borne by his father." And even after this custom had fallen into disuse, and people had begun automatically to assume the surnames of their fathers, " 'there [was] nothing in law prohibiting a man from taking another name if he chooses.' " Names were people's own business, not the government's. One's name did not have to be that of a legally recognized parent.

The best example of this tradition I have found is Doe ex dem. Luscombe v. Yates, 5 B. & Ald. 544, 106 Eng.Rep. 1289 (K.B.1822). Luscombe devised his estate to one Manning, provided that within three years he should cause his name "to be altered and changed to my name of Luscombe, by act or acts of Parliament, or some other effectual way for that purpose." In default of the name change, the devise was to be void. Without securing an Act of Parliament or obtaining a license from the King, Manning simply adopted the name of Luscombe and used it for all purposes and exclusively. The Court held the devise was good. Abbott, C.J., said: "A name assumed by the voluntary act of a young man at his outset into life, adopted by all who knew him and by which he is constantly called, becomes for all purposes that occur to my mind as much and effectually his name as if he had obtained an act of Parliament to confer it upon him." 5 B. & Ald. at 556, 106 Eng.Rep. at 1294. Land was serious business to the law of England, and we can be sure that a name change made without governmental sanction, if effective to confirm a devise of land, was effective for all purposes whatsoever.

The cases cited so far on the question of tradition are all rather old; and it may fairly be asked, whether any tradition that once existed still obtains. There is good evidence that the answer is yes. See, e.g., Hauser v. Callaway, 36 F.2d 667, 669 (8th Cir.1929) ("A man's name for all practical and legal purposes is the name by which he is known and called in the community where he lives and is best known."). The most recent case on the point I have found, Walker v. Jackson, 391 F.Supp. 1395, 1402 (E.D.Ark.1975) (three-judge court) (Webster, Henley, and Eisele, JJ.), squarely holds that under the common law of Arkansas—which has not been changed by statute—a person can change his name at will in the absence of fraud.

So far as the choice of one's own name is concerned, then, it seems well established that the tradition, still extant, is a complete absence of statutory prohibition. Certainly there is no pattern of positive law denying such a right of self-determination. I take it that the Court would concede that there is a fundamental right to choose one's own name. There is no "societal tradition of enacting laws *denying* [this] interest," Michael H. v. Gerald D., 491 U.S. 110 (1989) (plurality opinion) (emphasis in original), and that seems to be the standard that has recently attracted more votes than any other on the Supreme Court.

This Court, however, phrases the question more narrowly: is there a tradition supporting "the right of a parent to give a child a surname with which that child has no legally recognized parental connection"? I grant that there is no such tradition: what the plaintiffs in this case want to do is unusual. Few parents, no doubt, have done or wanted to do it in the past, and few would want to do it now. But, by the same token, there is no solid tradition of legislation denying any such right, and under *Michael H.*, that is the relevant question. In the absence of any tradition either way on the precise point, we should look, I submit, to the tradition we do have. People may choose or change their own names without leave of government. It is only a small step to extend the same right to their children's names. Children are, during infancy anyway, simply legal extensions of their parents for many purposes.

So I would hold that the right asserted here is fundamental, and that the State has no interest compelling enough to override it in the circumstances of this case. In attempting to do so, the State intrudes intolerably into what should be a private decision, one of the basic liberties of the citizen. I respectfully dissent from the judgment of reversal.

NOTE

Much of the recent litigation on the subject of naming children has involved divorced parents or children born out of wedlock. See, e.g., In re D.K.W., Jr. v. J.L.B., 807 P.2d 1222 (Colo.App.1990) (best interest of child born out of wedlock served by denying motion by father to change child's surname from mother's to his); Howard ex rel. Bailey v. Bailey, 343 Ill.App.3d 1201, 279 Ill.Dec. 201, 799 N.E.2d 1004 (2003)(not in the best interest of child to keep father's surname after divorce when father not an active part of child's life); Magiera v. Luera, 106 Nev. 775, 802 P.2d 6 (1990) (in the best interest of child born out of wedlock to keep the surname of the parent she lives with); Acevedo v. Burley, 994 P.2d 389 (1999) (in the best interest of child of divorced parents to keep father's surname). See generally Lisa Kelly, Divining the Deep and Inscrutable: Toward a Gender–Neutral, Child–Centered Approach to Child Name Change Proceedings, 99 W. Va. L. Rev. 1 (1996).

2. EDUCATION

State sponsored schools were the first serious intrusion into the right of parents to rear their own children. In 1647, the Colony of Massachusetts provided:

> It being one chief project of that old deluder Satan to keep men from the knowledge of the Scriptures, [i]t is so at least the true sense and meaning therefore ordered, that every township in this jurisdiction, after the Lord both increased them to the number of fifty householders, shall then forthwith appoint one within their town to teach all such children as shall resort to him to write and read. . . .[1]

"[Since the Old Deluder Act was passed, states] first offered and later forced schooling on ever larger numbers of individuals for ever longer periods.

"Initially this effort was focused on poor children. In 1787 Benjamin Rush proposed a plan for a system of free schools for the poor children of Philadelphia. By 1804, Washington, D.C., had established such a school system for its poor children with Thomas Jefferson as its first school board president.

"For children who were not poor, the primary responsibility remained for a time with their parents. As late as 1827 Kent observed: 'During the minority of the child ... the parent is absolutely bound to provide reasonably for his maintenance and education; and he may be sued for necessaries furnished, and schooling given to a child, under just and reasonable circum-

1. Reprinted in I Children and Youth in America 81 (1970).

stance.' This obligation was not without its rewards: 'In consequence of obligation of the father to provide for the maintenance, and, in some qualified degree, for the education of his infant children, he is entitled to the custody of their persons, and to the value of their labor and services.'

"[The] common school doctrine soon spread to include schools for all children, not just the poor. The first publicly-funded high school was established in 1821. By 1890 about 7 percent of the 14 to 17–year–olds were enrolled; by 1930, 51 percent of that age group were in high school.

"By the 1880's the rationale for providing education focused less on moral or spiritual fulfillment and more on maintaining the social order:

> 'The accumulation of riches in this country, brought about by the rapidity of industrial and commercial movements, tends to devote the sweat and lives of many to the few. If the elevation of the masses does not keep pace with this materialistic progress, misery and demoralization will increase in proportion to the augmentation of production. Communism and Socialism will then claim to be heard.... Nothing less than the State can check the prevalence of the revolutionary ideas and the assailment of social and proprietary rights.... Shall she establish a network of police force? This is the weakest and most unworthy of all remedies. ... The first step of the State should be to get possession of the minds of men; get control of their ideas.... This can be accomplished by a system of uniform, well-organized and liberally supported public schools.... The power of education, rightly conducted, is almost omnipotent. It will make useful peaceable citizens out of ninety percent of the worst children who fall under its influence.'[21]

"It was also at this point that the shift from voluntary to compulsory schooling took place, encouraged by a desire to Americanize the flood of immigrants:

> 'It is largely through immigration that the number of ignorant, vagrant, and criminal youth has recently multiplied to an extent truly alarming in some of our cities. Their depravity is sometimes defiant and their resistance to moral suasion is obstinate. When personal effort and persuasion and organized benevolence have utterly failed, let the law take them in hand, first to the public schools, and if there incorrigibly, then to the Reform School."[22]

"Initially, the compulsory education laws allowed parents, a range of choice in schooling. The 1874 New York law, for example, specified that children aged 8–14 could attend some public or private school for at least fourteen weeks a year, or be instructed at home for the same period in spelling, reading, writing, English grammar, geography, and arithmetic. By 1909, however, the state required regular attendance of children aged 7–16 at a public school conducted in English, or equivalent instruction by a competent teacher for the same number of hours."[a]

Today all states require children to attend school for 9 or more years. As the next cases confirm, few exceptions have been made to this general rule.

21. J.E. Seaman, High School and the State, Journal of Proceedings of the National Education Association 155 (1885).

22. B.G. Northrop, Report of the Secretary of the Board of Education of the State of Connecticut, 1872.

a. Judith Areen, Alternative Schools: Better Guardians than Family or State? 81 U. Chi. School Review 175 (1973).

Pierce v. Society of Sisters

Supreme Court of the United States, 1925.
268 U.S. 510, 45 S.Ct. 571, 69 L.Ed. 1070.

■ JUSTICE MCREYNOLDS delivered the opinion of the Court.

. . .

The challenged Act, effective September 1, 1926, requires every parent, guardian or other person having control or charge or custody of a child between eight and sixteen years to send him "to a public school for the period of time a public school shall be held during the current year" in the district where the child resides; and failure so to do is declared a misdemeanor. There are exemptions—not specially important here—for children who are not normal, or who have completed the eighth grade, or who reside at considerable distances from any public school, or whose parents or guardians hold special permits from the County Superintendent. The manifest purpose is to compel general attendance at public schools by normal children, between eight and sixteen, who have not completed the eighth grade. And without doubt enforcement of the statute would seriously impair, perhaps destroy, the profitable features of appellees' business and greatly diminish the value of their property.

Appellee, the Society of Sisters, is an Oregon corporation, organized in 1880, with power to care for orphans, educate and instruct the youth, establish and maintain academies or schools, and acquire necessary real and personal property. . . .

. . .

Appellee, Hill Military Academy, is a private corporation organized in 1908 under the laws of Oregon, engaged in owning, operating and conducting for profit an elementary, college preparatory and military training school for boys between the ages of five and twenty-one years. . . .

No question is raised concerning the power of the State reasonably to regulate all schools, to inspect, supervise, and examine them, their teachers and pupils; to require that all children of proper age attend some school, that teachers shall be of good moral character and patriotic disposition, that certain studies plainly essential to good citizenship must be taught, and that nothing be taught which is manifestly inimical to the public welfare.

The inevitable practical result of enforcing the Act under consideration would be destruction of appellees' primary schools, and perhaps all other private primary schools for normal children within the State of Oregon. These parties are engaged in a kind of undertaking not inherently harmful, but long regarded as useful and meritorious. Certainly there is nothing in the present records to indicate that they have failed to discharge their obligations to patrons, students or the State. And there are no peculiar circumstances or present emergencies which demand extraordinary measures relative to primary education.

Under the doctrine of Meyer v. Nebraska, 262 U.S. 390, we think it entirely plain that the Act of 1922 unreasonably interferes with the liberty of parents and guardians to direct the upbringing and education of children under their control. As often heretofore pointed out, rights guaranteed by the Constitution may not be abridged by legislation which has no reasonable relation to some purpose within the competency of the State. The fundamental theory of liberty upon which all governments in this Union repose excludes any general power of the State to standardize its children by forcing them to accept instruction from public teachers only. The child is not the mere creature of the State; those who nurture him and direct his destiny have the right, coupled with the high duty, to recognize and prepare him for additional obligations.

Appellees are corporations and therefore, it is said, they cannot claim for themselves the liberty which the Fourteenth Amendment guarantees. Accepted in the proper sense, this is true. But they have business and property for which they claim protection. These are threatened with destruction through the unwarranted compulsion which appellants are exercising over present and prospective patrons of their schools. And this court has gone very far to protect against loss threatened by such action.

The courts of the State have not construed the Act, and we must determine its meaning for ourselves. Evidently it was expected to have general application and cannot be construed as though merely intended to amend the charters of certain private corporations, as in Berea College v. Kentucky, 211 U.S. 45. No argument in favor of such view has been advanced.

Generally it is entirely true, as urged by counsel, that no person in any business has such an interest in possible customers as to enable him to restrain exercise of proper power of the State upon the ground that he will be deprived of patronage. But the injunctions here sought are not against the exercise of any proper power. Plaintiffs asked protection against arbitrary, unreasonable and unlawful interference with their patrons and the consequent destruction of their business and property....

The suits were not premature. The injury to appellees was present and very real, not a mere possibility in the remote future. If no relief had been possible prior to the effective date of the Act, the injury would have become irreparable. Prevention of impending injury by unlawful action is a well recognized function of courts of equity.

The decrees below are

Affirmed.

NOTE

Is Pierce v. Society of Sisters a First Amendment "freedom of religion" case? Compare School Dist. of Abington v. Schempp, 374 U.S. 203 (1963) (Brennan, J., concurring) (Pierce decided no first amendment question) with id. at 312 (Stewart, J. dissenting) (Pierce was based ultimately on recognition of the free exercise claim involved.) See generally Stephen Arons, The Separation of School and State: Pierce Reconsidered, 46 Harv.Educ.Rev. 76 (1976).

Justice McReynolds also authored Meyer v. Nebraska, 262 U.S. 390 (1923), which he cited in *Pierce* to support "the liberty of parents and guardians to direct the upbringing and education of children under their control." *Meyer* considered a Nebraska statute prohibiting instruction in foreign languages before the eighth grade. The Supreme Court found the restriction an invalid burden on the rights of teachers to work and families to raise their children. The purpose of these statutes was summarized by Justice McReynolds in *Meyer:*

> It is said the purpose of the legislation was to promote civic development by inhibiting training and education of the immature in foreign tongues and ideals before they could learn English and acquire American ideals; and "that the English language should be and become the mother tongue of all children reared in this State." It is also affirmed that the foreign born population is very

> large, that certain communities commonly use foreign words, follow foreign leaders, move in a foreign atmosphere, and that the children are thereby hindered from becoming citizens of the most useful type and the public safety is imperiled.
>
> That the State may do much, go very far, indeed, in order to improve the quality of its citizens, physically, mentally and morally, is clear; but the individual has certain fundamental rights which must be respected. The protection of the Constitution extends to all, to those who speak other languages as well as to those born with English on the tongue. Perhaps it would be highly advantageous if all had ready understanding of our ordinary speech, but this cannot be coerced by methods which conflict with the Constitution—a desirable end cannot be promoted by prohibited means.

Would the Supreme Court reach the same result today in Pierce and Meyer? On what grounds?

Mozert v. Hawkins County Board of Education

United States Court of Appeals, Sixth Circuit, 1987.
827 F.2d 1058.

■ Lively, Chief Judge.

This case arose under the Free Exercise Clause of the First Amendment, made applicable to the states by the Fourteenth Amendment. The district court held that a public school requirement that all students in grades one through eight use a prescribed set of reading textbooks violated the constitutional rights of objecting parents and students. The district court entered an injunction which required the schools to excuse objecting students from participating in reading classes where the textbooks are used and awarded the plaintiff parents more than $50,000 damages.

Early in 1983 the Hawkins County, Tennessee Board of Education adopted the Holt, Rinehart and Winston basic reading series (the Holt series) for use in grades 1–8 of the public schools of the county. . . .

The plaintiff Vicki Frost is the mother of four children, three of whom were students in Hawkins County public schools in 1983. At the beginning of the 1983–84 school year Mrs. Frost read a story in a daughter's sixth grade reader that involved mental telepathy. Mrs. Frost, who describes herself as a "born again Christian," has a religious objection to any teaching about mental telepathy. Reading further, she found additional themes in the reader to which she had religious objections. After discussing her objections with other parents, Mrs. Frost talked with the principal of Church Hill Middle School and obtained an agreement for an alternative reading program for students whose parents objected to the assigned Holt reader. The students who elected the alternative program left their classrooms during the reading sessions and worked on assignments from an older textbook series in available office or library areas. Other students in two elementary schools were excused from reading the Holt books.

In November 1983 the Hawkins County School Board voted unanimously to eliminate all alternative reading programs and require every student in the public schools to attend classes using the Holt series. Thereafter the plaintiff students refused to read the Holt series or attend reading classes where the series was being used. The children of several of the plaintiffs were suspended for brief periods for this refusal. Most of the plaintiff students were ultimately taught at home, or attended religious schools, or transferred to public schools outside Hawkins County. One student returned to school because his family was unable to afford alternate schooling. Even after the board's order, two students were allowed some accommodation, in that the teacher either excused them from reading the Holt stories, or specifically noted on worksheets that the student was not required to believe the stories.

On December 2, 1983, the plaintiffs, consisting of seven families—14 parents and 17 children—filed this action pursuant to 42 U.S.C. § 1983. In their complaint the plaintiffs asserted that they have sincere religious beliefs which are contrary to the values taught or inculcated by the reading textbooks and that it is a violation of the religious beliefs and convictions of the plaintiff students to be required to read the books and a violation of the religious beliefs of the plaintiff parents to permit their children to read the books. The plaintiffs sought to hold the defendants liable because "forcing the student-plaintiffs to read school books which teach or inculcate values in violation of their religious beliefs and convictions is a clear violation of their rights to the free exercise of religion protected by the First and Fourteenth Amendments to the United States Constitution."

. . .

Vicki Frost was the first witness for the plaintiffs and she presented the most complete explanation of the plaintiffs' position. The plaintiffs do not belong to a single church or denomination, but all consider themselves born again Christians. Mrs. Frost testified that the word of God as found in the Christian Bible "is the totality of my beliefs." There was evidence that other members of their churches, and even their pastors, do not agree with their position in this case.

Mrs. Frost testified that she had spent more than 200 hours reviewing the Holt series and had found numerous passages that offended her religious beliefs. She stated that the offending materials fell into seventeen categories which she listed. These ranged from such familiar concerns of fundamentalist Christians as evolution and "secular humanism" to less familiar themes such as "futuristic supernaturalism," pacifism, magic and false views of death.

In her lengthy testimony Mrs. Frost identified passages from stories and poems used in the Holt series that fell into each category. Illustrative is her first category, futuristic supernaturalism, which she defined as teaching "Man As God." Passages that she found offensive described Leonardo da Vinci as the human with a creative mind that "came closest to the divine touch." Similarly, she felt that a passage entitled "Seeing Beneath the Surface" related to an occult theme, by describing the use of imagination as a vehicle for seeing things not discernible through our physical eyes. She interpreted a poem, "Look at Anything," as presenting the idea that by using imagination a child can become part of anything and thus understand it better. Mrs. Frost testified that it is an "occult practice" for children to use imagination beyond the limitation of scriptural authority. She testified that the story that alerted her to the problem with the reading series fell into the category of futuristic supernaturalism. Entitled "A Visit to Mars," the story portrays thought transfer and telepathy in such a way that "it could be considered a scientific concept," according to this witness. This theme appears in the testimony of several witnesses, i.e., the materials objected to "could" be interpreted in a manner repugnant to their religious beliefs.

Mrs. Frost described objectionable passages from other categories in much the same way. Describing evolution as a teaching that there is no God, she identified 24 passages that she considered to have evolution as a theme. She admitted that the textbooks contained a disclaimer that evolution is a theory, not a proven scientific fact. Nevertheless, she felt that references to evolution were so pervasive and presented in such a factual manner as to render the disclaimer meaningless. After describing her objection to passages that encourage children to make moral judgments about whether it is right or wrong to kill animals, the witness stated, "I thought they would be learning to read, to have good English and grammar, and to be able to do other subject work." Asked by plaintiffs' attorney to define her objection to the text books, Mrs. Frost replied:

> Very basically, I object to the Holt, Rhinehart [sic] Winston series as a whole, what the message is as a whole. There are some contents which are objectionable by themselves, but my most withstanding [sic] objection would be to the series as a whole.

Another witness for the plaintiffs was Bob Mozert, father of a middle school and an elementary school student in the Hawkins County system. His testimony echoed that of Vicki Frost in large part, though his answers to questions tended to be much less expansive. He also found objectionable passages in the readers that dealt with magic, role reversal or role elimination, particularly biographical material about women who have been recognized for achievements outside their homes, and emphasis on one world or a planetary society. Both witnesses testified under cross-examination that the plaintiff parents objected to passages that expose their children to other forms of religion and to the feelings, attitudes and values of other students that contradict the plaintiffs' religious views without a statement that the other views are incorrect and that the plaintiffs' views are the correct ones.

The district court held that the plaintiffs' free exercise rights have been burdened because their "religious beliefs compel them to refrain from exposure to the Holt series." ...

. . .

The first question to be decided is whether a governmental requirement that a person be exposed to ideas he or she finds objectionable on religious grounds constitutes a burden on the free exercise of that person's religion as forbidden by the First Amendment.... The plaintiffs did not produce a single student or teacher to testify that any student was ever required to affirm his or her belief or disbelief in any idea or practice mentioned in the various stories and passages contained in the Holt series. However, the plaintiffs appeared to assume that materials clearly presented as poetry, fiction and even "make-believe" in the Holt series were presented as facts which the students were required to believe. Nothing in the record supports this assumption.

. . .

... [T]he plaintiffs, in this court, have relied particularly upon three Supreme Court decisions. We find them all distinguishable.

The issue in Torcaso v. Watkins, 367 U.S. 488 (1961), was whether a state could deny public office to a person solely because of the person's refusal to declare a belief in God. Quoting from its earlier decision in Everson v. Board of Education, 330 U.S. 1, 15 (1947), the Court stated:

> "We repeat and reaffirm that neither a State nor the Federal Government can constitutionally force a person 'to profess a belief or disbelief in any religion.' "

Since there was no evidence that the plaintiff students were ever required to profess or deny a religious belief the issue in *Torcaso* simply is not presented by the instant case.

Board of Education v. Barnette, 319 U.S. 624 (1943), grew out of a school board rule that required all schools to make a salute to the flag and a pledge of allegiance a regular part of their daily program.... It is abundantly clear that the exposure to materials in the Holt series did not compel the plaintiffs to "declare a belief," "communicate by word and sign [their] acceptance" of the ideas presented, or make an "affirmation of a belief and an attitude of mind." ...

. . .

The plaintiffs appear to contend that the element of compulsion was supplied by the requirement of class participation in the reading exercises. As we have pointed out earlier, there is no proof in the record that any plaintiff student was required to engage in role play, make up magic chants, read aloud or engage in the activity of haggling. In fact, the Director of Education for the State of Tennessee testified that most teachers do not adhere to the suggestions in the teachers' manuals and a teacher for 11 years in the Hawkins County system stated that she looks at the lesson plans in the teachers' editions, but "does her own thing." Being exposed to other students performing these acts might be offensive to the plaintiffs, but it does not constitute the compulsion described in the Supreme Court cases, where the objector was required to affirm or deny a religious belief or engage or refrain from engaging in a practice contrary to sincerely held religious beliefs.

The third Supreme Court decision relied upon by the plaintiffs is the only one that might be read to support the proposition that requiring mere exposure to materials that offend one's religious beliefs creates an unconstitutional burden on the free exercise of religion. Wisconsin v. Yoder, 406 U.S. 205 (1972). However, *Yoder* rested on such a singular set of facts that we do not believe it can be held to announce a general rule that exposure without compulsion to act, believe, affirm or deny creates an unconstitutional burden.

... The parents in Yoder were required to send their children to some school that prepared them for life in the outside world, or face official sanctions. The parents in the present case want their children to acquire all the skills required to live in modern society. They also want to have them excused from exposure to some ideas they find offensive. Tennessee offers two options to accommodate this latter desire. The plaintiff parents can either send their children to church schools or private schools, as many of them have done, or teach them at home. Tennessee law prohibits any state interference in the education process of church schools:

> The state board of education and local boards of education are prohibited from regulating the selection of faculty or textbooks or the establishment of a curriculum in church-related schools.

TCA 49–50–801(b). Similarly the statute permitting home schooling by parents or other teachers prescribes nothing with respect to curriculum or the content of class work.

Yoder was decided in large part on the impossibility of reconciling the goals of public education with the religious requirement of the Amish that their children be prepared for life in a separated community. As the Court noted, the requirement of school attendance to age 16 posed a "very real threat of undermining the Amish community and religious practice as they exist today...." No such threat exists in the present case, and Tennessee's school attendance laws offer several options to those parents who want their children to have the benefit of an education which prepares for life in the modern world without being exposed to ideas which offend their religious beliefs.

. . .

[We hold] that the requirement that public school students study a basal reader series chosen by the school authorities does not create an unconstitutional burden under the Free Exercise Clause when the students are not required to affirm or deny a belief or engage or refrain from engaging in a practice prohibited or required by their religion. There was no evidence that the conduct required of the students was forbidden by their religion. Rather, the witnesses testified that reading the Holt series "could" or "might" lead the students to come to conclusions that were contrary to teachings of their and their parents' religious beliefs. This is not sufficient to establish an unconstitutional burden.

NOTES

1. The Supreme Court denied certiorari in *Mozert,* 484 U.S. 1066 (1988).

In Smith v. Board of School Commissioners of Mobile County, 827 F.2d 684 (11th Cir.1987), the United States Court of Appeals for the Eleventh Circuit overturned a lower court decision that had banned the use of several public school texts about home economics, history, and social studies on the ground that the books advanced the religion of secular humanism. The Eleventh Circuit held that the use of the book did not advance secular humanism or inhibit theistic religion in violation of the establishment clause, even assuming secular humanism is a religion. The Court explained:

> Examination of the contents of the [challenged passages] in the context of the books as a whole and the undisputably nonreligious purpose sought to be achieved by their use, reveals that the message conveyed is not one of endorsement of secular humanism or any religion. Rather, the message conveyed is one of a governmental attempt to instill in Alabama public school children such values as independent thought, tolerance of diverse views, self-respect, maturity, self-reliance and logical decision-making. This is an entirely appropriate secular effect. Indeed, one of the major objectives of public education is the "inculcat[ion of] fundamental values necessary to the maintenance of a democratic political system."

827 F.2d at 692.

Vicki Frost, one of the parents involved in the Mozert suit, later sought to teach her child reading from a book of her own choice on the child's school campus. She would come to the campus each day, remove her child from class, conduct a reading lesson on the campus or in the family car and then return the child to the classroom. Mrs. Frost was arrested for trespass on school grounds following her refusal to leave school premises in response to the principal's request. She brought suit against the school board, on the basis of false imprisonment and malicious prosecution. The court held for the Hawkins County School Board. Frost v. Hawkins County Board of Education, 851 F.2d 822 (6th Cir.1988).

2. Compare Stephens v. Bongart, 15 N.J.Misc. 80, 189 A. 131 (1937) (home instruction provided by parents found to violate compulsory education law) with State v. Massa, 95 N.J.Super. 382, 231 A.2d 252 (1967) (prosecution failed to show beyond a reasonable doubt that home instruction provided by parents did not satisfy compulsory education law). Cf. Davis v. Page, 385 F.Supp. 395 (D.N.H.1974) (children may not be excused from classes using audio-visual equipment for education purposes because of the religious beliefs of their parents, but may from classes using equipment for entertainment purposes).

See also State v. Rice, 204 Neb. 732, 285 N.W.2d 223 (1979) (children are not neglected because parents taught them at home in violation of compulsory attendance laws); Matter of Franz, 55 A.D.2d 424, 390 N.Y.S.2d 940 (1977) (instruction given by mother at home was not an acceptable substitute for public school instruction because it did not conform in hours and subject matter to requirements of state education laws).

In recent years more parents have resorted to schooling their children at home as an alternative to schools that either provide unsatisfactory results or adopt curricula that fail to reflect the values of the parents. Many estimate that more than one million children receive instruction at home. See Judith G. McMullen, Behind Closed Doors: Should States Regulate Homeschooling? 54 S.C. L. Rev. 75 (2002); see also Bruce D. Page, Jr., Note, Changing Our Perspective: How Presumptive Invalidity of Home School Regulations Will Further the State's Interest in an Educated Citizenry, 14 Regent U.L. Rev. 181 (2002).

Zelman v. Simmons–Harris

Supreme Court of the United States, 2002.
536 U.S. 639, 122 S.Ct. 2460, 153 L.Ed.2d 604.

■ CHIEF JUSTICE REHNQUIST delivered the opinion of the court.

The State of Ohio has established a pilot program designed to provide educational choices to families with children who reside in the Cleveland City School District. The question presented is whether this program offends the Establishment Clause of the United States Constitution. We hold that it does not.

There are more than 75,000 children enrolled in the Cleveland City School District. The majority of these children are from low-income and minority families. Few of these families enjoy the means to send their children to any school other than an inner-city public school. For more than a generation, however, Cleveland's public schools have been among the worse performing public schools in the Nation. In 1995, a Federal District Court declared a "crisis of magnitude" and placed the entire Cleveland school district under state control. Shortly thereafter, the state auditor found that Cleveland's public schools were in the midst of a "crisis that is perhaps unprecedented in the history of American education." The district had failed to meet any of the 18 state standards for minimal acceptable performance. Only 1 in 10 ninth graders could pass a basic proficiency examination, and students at all levels performed at a dismal rate compared with students in other Ohio public schools. More than two-thirds of high school students either dropped or failed out before graduation. Of those students who managed to reach their senior year, one of every four still failed to graduate. Of those students who did graduate, few could read, write, or compute at levels comparable to their counterparts in other cities.

. . .

The program provides two basic kinds of assistance to parents of children in a covered district. First, the program provides tuition aid for students in kindergarten through third grade, expanding each year through eighth grade, to attend a participating public or private school of their parent's choosing. Second, the program provides tutorial aid for students who choose to remain enrolled in public school.

. . .

We believe that the program challenged here is a program of true private choice, consistent with Mueller [v. Allen, 403 U.S. 388 (1983)], Witters [v. Servs. For Blind, 474 U.S. 481 (1986)], and Zobrest [v. Catalina Foothills School Dist. 509 U.S. 1 (1993)], and thus constitutional. As was true in those cases, the Ohio program is neutral in all respects toward religion. It is part of a general and multifaceted undertaking by the State of Ohio to provide educational opportunities to the children of a failed school district. It confers educational assistance directly to a broad class of individuals defined without reference to religion, i.e., any parent of a school-age child who resides in the Cleveland City School District. The program permits the participation of all schools within the district, religious or nonreligious. Adjacent public schools also may participate and have a financial incentive to do so. Program benefits are available to participating families on neutral terms, with no reference to religion. The only preference stated anywhere in the program is a preference for low-income families, who receive greater assistance and are given priority for admission at participating schools.

There are no "financial incentives" that "skew" the program toward religious schools. Witters, supra, at 487–488. Such incentives "[are] not present . . . where the aid is allocated on the basis of neutral, secular criteria that neither favor nor disfavor religion, and is made available to both religious and secular beneficiaries on a nondiscriminatory basis." The program here in fact creates financial disincentives for religious schools, with private schools receiving only half the government assistance given to community schools and one-third the assistance given to magnet schools. Adjacent public schools, should any choose to accept program students, are also eligible to receive two to three times the state funding of a private religious school. Families too have a financial disincentive to choose a private religious school over other schools. Parents that choose to participate in the scholarship program and then to enroll their children in a private school (religious or nonreligious) must copay a portion of the school's tuition. Families that choose a community school, magnet school, or traditional public school pay nothing. Although such features of the program are not necessary to its constitutionality, they clearly dispel the claim that the program "creates . . . financial incentives for parents to choose a sectarian school." Zobrest, 509 U.S. at 10.

Respondents suggest that even without a financial incentive for parents to choose a religious school, the program creates a "public perception that the State is endorsing religious practices and beliefs." But we have repeatedly recognized that no reasonable observer would think a neutral program of private choice, where state aid reaches religious schools solely as a result of the numerous independent decisions of private individuals, carries with it the imprimatur of government endorsement. The argument is particularly misplaced here since "the reasonable observer in the endorsement inquiry must be deemed aware" of the "history and context" underlying a challenged program. Good News Club v. Milford Central School, 533 U.S. 98, 119, 150 L. Ed. 2d 151, 121 S. Ct. 2093 (2001) (internal quotation marks omitted). See also Capitol Square Review and Advisory Bd. v. Pinette, 515 U.S. 753, 780, 132 L. Ed. 2d 650, 115 S. Ct. 2440 (1995) (O'CONNOR, J., concurring in part and concurring in judgment). Any objective observer familiar with the full history and context of the Ohio program would reasonably view it as one aspect of a broader undertaking to assist poor children in failed schools, not as an endorsement of religious schooling in general.

There also is no evidence that the program fails to provide genuine opportunities for Cleveland parents to select secular educational options for their school-age children. Cleveland schoolchildren enjoy a range of educational choices: They may remain in public school as before, remain in public school with publicly funded tutoring aid, obtain a scholarship and choose a religious school, obtain a scholarship and choose a nonreligious private school, enroll in a community school, or enroll in a magnet school. That 46 of the 56 private schools now participating in the program are religious schools does not condemn it as a violation of the Establishment Clause. The Establishment Clause question is whether Ohio is coercing parents into sending their children to religious schools, and that question must be answered by evaluating all options Ohio provides Cleveland schoolchildren, only one of which is to obtain a program scholarship and then choose a religious school.

Justice Souter speculates that because more private religious schools currently participate in the program, the program itself must somehow discourage the participation of private nonreligious schools. But Cleveland's preponderance of religiously affiliated private schools certainly did not arise as a result of the program; it is a phenomenon common to many American cities. See U.S. Dept. of Ed., National Center for Education Statistics, Private School Universe Survey: 1999–2000, pp. 2–4 (NCES 2001–330, 2001) (hereinafter Private School Universe Survey) (cited in Brief for United States as Amicus Curiae 24). Indeed, by all accounts the program has captured a remarkable cross-section of private schools, religious and nonreligious. It is true that 82% of Cleveland's participating private schools are religious schools, but it is also true that 81% of private schools in Ohio are religious schools. See Brief for State of Florida et al. as Amici Curiae 16 (citing Private School Universe Survey). To attribute constitutional significance to this figure, moreover, would lead to the absurd result that a neutral school-choice program might be permissible in some parts of Ohio, such as Columbus, where a lower percentage of private schools are religious schools, see Ohio Educational Directory (Lodging of Respondents Gatton et al., available in Clerk of Court's case file), and Reply Brief for Petitioners in No. 00–1751, p. 12, n. 1, but not in inner-city Cleveland, where Ohio has deemed such programs most sorely needed, but where the preponderance of religious schools happens to be greater. Cf. Brief for State of Florida et al. as Amici Curiae 17 ("The percentages of sectarian to nonsectarian private schools within Florida's 67 school districts . . . vary from zero to 100 percent"). Likewise, an identical private choice program might be constitutional in some States, such as Maine or Utah, where less than 45% of private schools are religious schools, but not in other States, such as Nebraska or Kansas, where over 90% of private schools are religious schools. Id., at 15–16 (citing Private School Universe Survey).

. . .

In sum, the Ohio program is entirely neutral with respect to religion. It provides benefits directly to a wide spectrum of individuals, defined only by financial need and residence in a particular school district. It permits such individuals to exercise genuine choice among options public and private, secular and religious. The program is therefore a program of true private choice. In keeping with an unbroken line of decisions rejecting challenges to similar programs, we hold that the program does not offend the Establishment Clause.

The judgment of the Court of Appeals is reversed.

NOTE

After *Zelman,* a similar voucher program, the Florida Opportunity Scholarship Program(OSP), was challenged under article I, section 3 of the Florida Constitution. Bush v. Holmes, 886 So.2d 340 (Fla.App.2004). The Florida Appellate Court found the program unconstitutional, distinguishing *Zelman* because of the difference between the State and Federal constitutional provisions. The Florida Constitution establishes a "no-aid" provision, stating that no state money can ever be given to a sectarian institution, either directly or indirectly. For more discussion of the issues involved in school choice see Erwin Chemerinsky, Essay, Separate and Unequal: American Public Education Today, 52 Am. U.L. Rev. 1461 (2003); Steven H. Shiffrin, The First Amendment and the socialization of Children: Compulsory Public Education and Vouchers, 11 Cornell J. L. & Pub. Pol'y 503 (2002).

Cedar Rapids Community School District v. Garret F.

Supreme Court of the United States, 1999.
526 U.S. 66, 119 S.Ct. 992, 143 L.Ed.2d 154.

■ JUSTICE STEVENS delivered the opinion of the court.

The Individuals with Disabilities Education Act (IDEA), 84 Stat. 175, as amended, was enacted, in part, "to assure that all children with disabilities have available to them ... a free appropriate public education which emphasizes special education and related services designed to meet their unique needs." 20 U.S.C. § 1400(c). Consistent with this purpose, the IDEA authorizes federal financial assistance to States that agree to provide disabled children with special education and "related services."

The question presented in this case is whether the definition of "related services" in § 1401(a)(17)[1] requires a public school district in a participating State to provide a ventilator-dependent student with certain nursing services during school hours.

Respondent Garret F. is a friendly, creative, and intelligent young man. When Garret was four years old, his spinal column was severed in a motorcycle accident. Though paralyzed from the neck down, his mental capacities were unaffected. He is able to speak, to control his motorized wheelchair through use of a puff and suck straw, and to operate a computer with a device that responds to head movements. Garret is currently a student in the Cedar Rapids Community School District (District), he attends regular classes in a typical school program, and his academic performance has been a success. Garret is, however, ventilator dependent,[2] and therefore requires a

1. "The term 'related services' means transportation, and such developmental, corrective, and other supportive services (including speech pathology and audiology, psychological services, physical and occupational therapy, recreation, including therapeutic recreation, social work services, counseling services, including rehabilitation counseling, and medical services, except that such medical services shall be for diagnostic and evaluation purposes only) as may be required to assist a child with a disability to benefit from special education, and includes the early identification and assessment of disabling conditions in children." 20 U.S.C. § 1401(a)(17).

2. In his report in this case, the Administrative Law Judge explained that "being ventilator dependent means that [Garret] breathes only with external aids, usually an electric ventilator, and occasionally by some-

responsible individual nearby to attend to certain physical needs while he is in school.[3]

During Garret's early years at school his family provided for his physical care during the school day. When he was in kindergarten, his 18-year-old aunt attended him; in the next four years, his family used settlement proceeds they received after the accident, their insurance, and other resources to employ a licensed practical nurse. In 1993, Garret's mother requested the District to accept financial responsibility for the health care services that Garret requires during the school day. The District denied the request, believing that it was not legally obligated to provide continuous one-on-one nursing services.

Relying on both the IDEA and Iowa law, Garret's mother requested a hearing before the Iowa Department of Education. An Administrative Law Judge (ALJ) received extensive evidence concerning Garret's special needs, the District's treatment of other disabled students, and the assistance provided to other ventilator-dependent children in other parts of the country. In his 47-page report, the ALJ found that the District has about 17,500 students, of whom approximately 2,200 need some form of special education or special services. Although Garret is the only ventilator-dependent student in the District, most of the health care services that he needs are already provided for some other students. "The primary difference between Garret's situation and that of other students is his dependency on his ventilator for life support." The ALJ noted that the parties disagreed over the training or licensure required for the care and supervision of such students, and that those providing such care in other parts of the country ranged from nonlicensed personnel to registered nurses. However, the District did not contend that only a licensed physician could provide the services in question.

The ALJ explained that federal law requires that children with a variety of health impairments be provided with "special education and related services" when their disabilities adversely affect their academic performance, and that such children should be educated to the maximum extent appropriate with children who are not disabled. In addition, the ALJ explained that applicable federal regulations distinguish between "school health services," which are provided by a "qualified school nurse or other qualified person," and "medical services," which are provided by a licensed physician. The District must provide the former, but need not provide the latter (except, of course, those "medical services" that are for diagnostic or evaluation purposes, § 1401(a)(17)). According to the ALJ, the distinction in the regulations does not just depend on "the title of the person providing the service"; instead, the "medical services" exclusion is limited to services that are "in the

one else's manual pumping of an air bag attached to his tracheotomy tube when the ventilator is being maintained. This later procedure is called ambu bagging."

3. "He needs assistance with urinary bladder catheterization once a day, the suctioning of his tracheotomy tube as needed, but at least once every six hours, with food and drink at lunchtime, in getting into a reclining position for five minutes of each hour, and ambu bagging occasionally as needed when the ventilator is checked for proper functioning. He also needs assistance from someone familiar with his ventilator in the event there is a malfunction or electrical problem, and someone who can perform emergency procedures in the event he experiences autonomic hyperreflexia. Autonomic hyperreflexia is an uncontrolled visceral reaction to anxiety or a full bladder. Blood pressure increases, heart rate increases, and flushing and sweating may occur. Garret has not experienced autonomic hyperreflexia frequently in recent years, and it has usually been alleviated by catheterization. He has not ever experienced autonomic hyperreflexia at school. Garret is capable of communicating his needs orally or in another fashion so long as he has not been rendered unable to do so by an extended lack of oxygen."

special training, knowledge, and judgment of a physician to carry out." The ALJ thus concluded that the IDEA required the District to bear financial responsibility for all of the services in dispute, including continuous nursing services.

. . .

The District contends that § 1401(a)(17) does not require it to provide Garret with "continuous one-on-one nursing services" during the school day, even though Garret cannot remain in school without such care. However, the IDEA's definition of "related services," our decision in Irving Independent School Dist. v. Tatro, 468 U.S. 883 (1984), and the overall statutory scheme all support the decision of the Court of Appeals.

The text of the "related services" definition, see n. 1, supra, broadly encompasses those supportive services that "may be required to assist a child with a disability to benefit from special education." As we have already noted, the District does not challenge the Court of Appeals' conclusion that the in-school services at issue are within the covered category of "supportive services." As a general matter, services that enable a disabled child to remain in school during the day provide the student with "the meaningful access to education that Congress envisioned." Tatro, 468 U.S. at 891 ("'Congress sought primarily to make public education available to handicapped children' and 'to make such access meaningful'" (quoting Board of Ed. of Hendrick Hudson Central School Dist., Westchester Cty. v. Rowley, 458 U.S. 176, 192 (1982))).

This general definition of "related services" is illuminated by a parenthetical phrase listing examples of particular services that are included within the statute's coverage. § 1401(a)(17). "Medical services" are enumerated in this list, but such services are limited to those that are "for diagnostic and evaluation purposes." Ibid. The statute does not contain a more specific definition of the "medical services" that are excepted from the coverage of § 1401(a)(17).

The scope of the "medical services" exclusion is not a matter of first impression in this Court. In Tatro we concluded that the Secretary of Education had reasonably determined that the term "medical services" referred only to services that must be performed by a physician, and not to school health services. Accordingly, we held that a specific form of health care (clean intermittent catheterization) that is often, though not always, performed by a nurse is not an excluded medical service. We referenced the likely cost of the services and the competence of school staff as justifications for drawing a line between physician and other service but our endorsement of that line was unmistakable. It is thus settled that the phrase "medical services" in § 1401(a)(17) does not embrace all forms of care that might loosely be described as "medical" in other contexts, such as a claim for an income tax deduction.

The District does not ask us to define the term so broadly. Indeed, the District does not argue that any of the items of care that Garret needs, considered individually, could be excluded from the scope of § 1401(a)(17). It could not make such an argument, considering that one of the services Garret needs (catheterization) was at issue in Tatro, and the others may be provided competently by a school nurse or other trained personnel. As the ALJ concluded, most of the requested services are already provided by the District to other students, and the in-school care necessitated by Garret's ventilator dependency does not demand the training, knowledge, and judgment of a licensed physician. While more extensive, the in-school services Garret needs are no more "medical" than was the care sought in Tatro.

Instead, the District points to the combined and continuous character of the required care, and proposes a test under which the outcome in any particular case would "depend upon a series of factors, such as [1] whether the care is continuous or intermittent, [2] whether existing school health personnel can provide the service, [3] the cost of the service, and [4] the potential consequences if the service is not properly performed."

The District's multi-factor test is not supported by any recognized source of legal authority. The proposed factors can be found in neither the text of the statute nor the regulations that we upheld in Tatro. Moreover, the District offers no explanation why these characteristics make one service any more "medical" than another. The continuous character of certain services associated with Garret's ventilator dependency has no apparent relationship to "medical" services, much less a relationship of equivalence. Continuous services may be more costly and may require additional school personnel, but they are not thereby more "medical." Whatever its imperfections, a rule that limits the medical services exemption to physician services is unquestionably a reasonable and generally workable interpretation of the statute. Absent an elaboration of the statutory terms plainly more convincing than that which we reviewed in Tatro, there is no good reason to depart from settled law.

Finally, the District raises broader concerns about the financial burden that it must bear to provide the services that Garret needs to stay in school. The problem for the District in providing these services is not that its staff cannot be trained to deliver them; the problem, the District contends, is that the existing school health staff cannot meet all of their responsibilities and provide for Garret at the same time.[9] Through its multi-factor test, the District seeks to establish a kind of undue-burden exemption primarily based on the cost of the requested services. The first two factors can be seen as examples of cost-based distinctions: intermittent care is often less expensive than continuous care, and the use of existing personnel is cheaper than hiring additional employees. The third factor—the cost of the service—would then encompass the first two. The relevance of the fourth factor is likewise related to cost because extra care may be necessary if potential consequences are especially serious.

The District may have legitimate financial concerns, but our role in this dispute is to interpret existing law. Defining "related services" in a manner that accommodates the cost concerns Congress may have had, cf. Tatro, 468 U.S. at 892, is altogether different from using cost itself as the definition. Given that § 1401(a)(17) does not employ cost in its definition of "related services" or excluded "medical services," accepting the District's cost-based standard as the sole test for determining the scope of the provision would require us to engage in judicial lawmaking without any guidance from Congress. It would also create some tension with the purposes of the IDEA. The statute may not require public schools to maximize the potential of disabled students commensurate with the opportunities provided to other

9. The District, however, will not necessarily need to hire an additional employee to meet Garret's needs. The District already employs a one-on-one teacher associate (TA) who assists Garret during the school day. At one time, Garret's TA was a licensed practical nurse (LPN). In light of the state Board of Nursing's recent ruling that the District's registered nurses may decide to delegate Garret's care to an LPN, see Brief for United States as Amicus Curiae 9–10 (filed Apr. 22, 1998), the dissent's future-cost estimate is speculative.

children, see Rowley, 458 U.S. at 200; and the potential financial burdens imposed on participating States may be relevant to arriving at a sensible construction of the IDEA, see Tatro, 468 U.S. at 892. But Congress intended "to open the door of public education" to all qualified children and "required participating States to educate handicapped children with nonhandicapped children whenever possible." Rowley, 458 U.S. at 192, 202....

This case is about whether meaningful access to the public schools will be assured, not the level of education that a school must finance once access is attained. It is undisputed that the services at issue must be provided if Garret is to remain in school. Under the statute, our precedent, and the purposes of the IDEA, the District must fund such "related services" in order to help guarantee that students like Garret are integrated into the public schools.

The judgment of the Court of Appeals is accordingly

Affirmed.

3. Health Care

Guardianship of Phillip B.

California Court of Appeal, First District, 1983.
139 Cal.App.3d 407, 188 Cal.Rptr. 781.

■ Racanelli, Presiding Justice.

. . .

On February 23, 1981, respondents Herbert and Patsy H. filed a petition for appointment as guardians of the person and estate of Phillip B., then 14 years of age. Phillip's parents, appellants Warren and Patricia B., appeared in opposition to the petition.

On August 7, 1981, following a 12–day trial, the trial court filed a lengthy memorandum of decision ordering—inter alia—1) the issuance of letters of guardianship to respondents with authority to permit a heart catheterization to be performed on Phillip, and 2) the immediate delivery (by appellants) of Phillip to the Sheriff and Juvenile Authority of Santa Clara County. That same day appellants filed a notice of appeal from both orders followed by a petition to this court for a writ of supersedeas which we summarily denied.

On August 20, 1981, the California Supreme Court granted appellants' petition for hearing, stayed the trial court's order authorizing heart catheterization and retransferred the cause to this court with directions to issue an order to show cause why a writ of supersedeas should not issue.

Meanwhile, on September 24, the trial court filed formal findings of fact and conclusions of law and entered a "final order" confirming issuance of letters of guardianship and authorizing a heart catheterization. A second notice of appeal specifying both orders was thereafter filed by appellants.

On October 19, 1981, we again denied supersedeas in an unpublished opinion.

On November 18, 1981, the California Supreme Court granted a second petition for hearing, issued its writ of supersedeas limited to the trial court's orders of August 7 and September 24 "insofar as they give authority for a heart catheterization upon Phillip B.," and retransferred the cause to this court for determination of the merits of the appeal upon the completed record and full briefing. Thereafter, the matter was duly argued and submitted for decision.

. . .

Phillip B. was born on October 16, 1966, with Down's Syndrome....

Appellants, deeply distraught over Phillip's disability, decided upon institutionalization, a course of action recommended by a state social worker and approved by appellants' pediatrician. A few days later, Phillip was transferred from the hospital to a licensed board and care facility for disabled youngsters. Although the facility was clean, it offered no structured educational or developmental programs and required that all the children (up to 8 years of age) sleep in cribs. Appellants initially visited Phillip frequently; but soon their visits became less frequent and they became more detached from him.

When Phillip was three years old a pediatrician informed appellants that Phillip had a congenital heart defect, a condition afflicting half of Down's Syndrome children. Open heart surgery was suggested when Phillip attained age six. However, appellants took no action to investigate or remedy the suspected medical problem.

After the board and care facility had been sold during the summer of 1971, appellants discovered that the condition of the facility had seriously deteriorated under new management; it had become dirty and cluttered with soiled clothing, and smelled strongly of urine. Phillip was very thin and listless and was being fed watery oatmeal from a bottle. At appellants' request, a state social worker arranged for Phillip's transfer in January, 1972, to We Care, a licensed residential facility for developmentally disabled children located in San Jose, where he remained up to the time of trial.

At that time, the facility—which cared for about 20 children more severely handicapped than Phillip—operated under very limited conditions; it had no programs of education or therapy; the children were not enrolled in outside programs; the facility lacked an outdoor play area; the building was in poor repair; and the kitchen had only a two-burner hot plate used to cook pureed food.

In April 1972, We Care employed Jeanne Haight (later to become program director and assistant administrator of the facility) to organize a volunteer program. Mrs. Haight quickly noticed Phillip's debilitated condition. She found him unusually small and thin for his age (five); he was not toilet trained and wore diapers, still slept in a crib, walked like a toddler, and crawled down stairs only inches high. His speech was limited and mostly unintelligible; his teeth were in poor condition.

Mrs. Haight, who undertook a recruitment program for volunteers, soon recruited respondent Patsy H., who had helped to found a school for children with learning disabilities where Mrs. Haight had once been vice-principal. Mrs. H. began working at We Care on a daily basis. Her husband, respondent Herbert H., and their children, soon joined in the volunteer activities.

Mrs. H., initially assigned to work with Phillip and another child, assisted Phillip in experimenting with basic sensory experiences, improving body coordination, and in overcoming his fear of steps. Mr. H. and one of the H. children helped fence the yard area, put in a lawn, a sandbox, and install some climbing equipment.

Mrs. Haight promptly initiated efforts to enroll Phillip in a preschool program for the fall of 1972, which required parental consent.[4] She contacted Mr. B. who agreed to permit Phillip to participate provided learning aptitude could be demonstrated. Mrs. H. used vocabulary cards to teach Phillip 25 to 50 new words and to comprehend word association. Although Mr. B. failed to appear at the appointed time in order to observe what Phillip had learned, he eventually gave his parental consent enabling Phillip to attend Hope Preschool in October, 1972.

Respondents continued working with Phillip coordinating their efforts with his classroom lessons. Among other things, they concentrated on development of feeding skills and toilet training and Mr. H. and the two eldest children gradually became more involved in the volunteer program.

Phillip subsequently attended a school for the trainable mentally retarded (TMR) where the children are taught basic survival words. They are capable of learning to feed and dress themselves appropriately, doing basic community activities such as shopping, and engaging in recreational activities. There is no attempt to teach them academics, and they are expected to live in sheltered settings as adults. In contrast, children capable of attending classes for the educable mentally retarded (EMR) are taught reading, writing, and simple computation, with the objective of developing independent living skills as adults.

A pattern of physical and emotional detachment from their son was developed by appellants over the next several years. In contrast, during the same period, respondents established a close and caring relationship with Phillip. Beginning in December, 1972, Phillip became a frequent visitor at respondents' home; with appellants' consent, Phillip was permitted to spend weekends with respondents, a practice which continued regularly and often included weekday evenings. At the same time, respondents maintained frequent contact with Phillip at We Care as regular volunteer visitors. Meanwhile, appellants visited Phillip at the facility only a few times a year; however, no overnight home visits occurred until after the underlying litigation ensued.

Respondents played an active role in Phillip's behavioral development and educational training. They consistently supplemented basic skills training given Phillip at We Care.[5]

Phillip was openly accepted as a member of the H. family whom he came to love and trust. He eventually had his own bedroom; he was included in sharing household chores. Mr. H. set up a workbench for Phillip and helped him make simple wooden toys; they attended special Boy Scout meetings together. And Phillip regularly participated in family outings. Phillip referred to the H. residence as "my house." When Phillip began to refer to the H's as "Mom" and "Dad," they initially discouraged the familiar reference, eventually succeeding in persuading Phillip to use the discriminate references "Mama Pat" and "Dada Bert" and "Mama B." and "Daddy

4. Apparently, Phillip had received no formal preschool education for the retarded even though such training programs were available in the community. Expert testimony established that early introduction to preschool training is of vital importance in preparing a retarded child for entry level public education.

5. In addition to their efforts to improve Phillip's communication and reading skills through basic sign language and word association exercises, respondents toilet-trained Phillip and taught him to use eating utensils and to sleep in a regular bed (the latter frequently monitored during the night).

B."[6] Both Mrs. Haight and Phillip's teacher observed significant improvements in Phillip's development and behavior. Phillip had developed, in Mrs. Haight's opinion, "true love and strong [emotional] feelings" for respondents.

Meanwhile, appellants continued to remain physically and emotionally detached from Phillip. The natural parents intellectualized their decision to treat Phillip differently from their other children. Appellants testified that Phillip, whom they felt would always require institutionalization, should not be permitted to form close emotional attachments which—upon inevitable disruption—would traumatize the youngster.

In matters of Phillip's health care needs, appellants manifested a reluctant—if not neglectful—concern. When Dr. Gathman, a pediatric cardiologist, diagnosed a ventricular septal defect[7] in Phillip's heart in early 1973 and recommended catheterization (a medically accepted presurgery procedure to measure pressure and to examine the interior of the heart), appellants refused their consent.

In the spring of 1977, Dr. Gathman again recommended heart catheterization in connection with the anticipated use of general anesthesia during Phillip's major dental surgery. Appellants consented to the preoperative procedure which revealed that the heart defect was surgically correctible with a maximum risk factor of 5 percent. At a conference attended by appellants and Mrs. Haight in June, 1977, Dr. Gathman recommended corrective surgery in order to avoid a progressively deteriorating condition resulting in a "bed-to-chair existence" and the probability of death before the age of 30.[8] Although Dr. Gathman—as requested by Mrs. B.—supplied the name of a parent of Down's Syndrome children with similar heart disease, no contact was ever made. Later that summer, appellants decided—without obtaining an independent medical consultation—against surgery. Appellants' stated reason was that Dr. Gathman had "painted" an inaccurate picture of the situation. They felt that surgery would be merely life-prolonging rather than life-saving, presenting the possibility that they would be unable to care for Phillip during his later years.[9] A few months later, in early 1978, appellants' decision was challenged in a juvenile dependency proceeding initiated by the district attorney on the ground that the withholding of surgery constituted neglect within the meaning of Welfare and Institutions Code section 300, subdivision (b); the juvenile court's dismissal of the action on the basis of inconclusive evidence was ultimately sustained on appeal In re Phillip B. (1979) 92 Cal.App.3d 796, 156 Cal.Rptr. 48, cert. den. sub nom. Bothman v. Warren B. (1980) 445 U.S. 949.

In September, 1978, upon hearing from a staff member of We Care that Phillip had been regularly spending weekends at respondents' home, Mr. B. promptly forbade Phillip's removal from the facility (except for medical purposes and school attendance) and requested the respondents be denied

6. At respondents' suggestion, Mrs. Haight requested a photograph of appellants to show Phillip who his parents were; but appellants failed to provide one.

7. The disease, found in a large number of Down's Syndrome children ... consists of an opening or "hole" between the heart chambers resulting in elevated blood pressure and impairment of vascular functions. The disease can become a progressive, and ultimately fatal, disorder.

8. Dr. Gathman's explicit description of the likely ravages of the disease created anger and distrust on the part of appellants and motivated them to seek other opinions and to independently assess the need for surgery.

9. Oddly, Mr. B. expressed no reluctance in the hypothetical case of surgery for his other two sons if they had the "same problem," justifying the distinction on the basis of Phillip's retardation.

personal visits with Phillip at We Care. Although respondents continued to visit Phillip daily at the facility, the abrupt cessation of home visits produced regressive changes in Phillip's behavior; he began acting out violently when respondents prepared to leave, begging to be taken "home"; he resorted to profanity; he became sullen and withdrawn when respondents were gone; bed-wetting regularly occurred, a recognized symptom of emotional disturbance in children. He began to blame himself for the apparent rejection by respondents; he began playing with matches and on one occasion he set his clothes afire; on another, he rode his tricycle to respondents' residence a few blocks away proclaiming on arrival that he was "home." He continuously pleaded to return home with respondents. Many of the behavioral changes continued to the time of trial.[10]

Appellants unsuccessfully pressed to remove Phillip from We Care notwithstanding the excellent care he was receiving. However, in January, 1981, the regional center monitoring public assistance for residential care and training of the handicapped, consented to Phillip's removal to a suitable alternate facility. Despite an extended search, none could be found which met Phillip's individualized needs. Meanwhile, Phillip continued living at We Care, periodically visiting at appellants' home. But throughout, the strong emotional attachment between Phillip and respondents remained intact.

Evidence established that Phillip, with a recently tested I.Q. score of 57,[11] is a highly functioning Down's Syndrome child capable of learning sufficient basic and employable skills to live independently or semi-independently in a non-institutional setting.

Courts generally may appoint a guardian over the person or estate of a minor "if it appears necessary or convenient." But the right of parents to retain custody of a child is fundamental and may be disturbed " '... only in extreme cases of persons acting in a fashion incompatible with parenthood.' " Accordingly, the Legislature has imposed the stringent requirement that before a court may make an order awarding custody of a child to a nonparent without consent of the parents, "it shall make a finding that an award of custody to a parent would be detrimental to the child and the award to a nonparent is required to serve the best interests of the child." ...[12]

The trial court expressly found that an award of custody to appellants would be harmful to Phillip in light of the psychological or "de facto" parental relationship established between him and respondents. Such relationships have long been recognized in the fields of law and psychology. As Justice Tobriner has cogently observed, "The fact of biological parenthood may incline an adult to feel a strong concern for the welfare of his child, but

10. During a pretrial psychological evaluation, Phillip suddenly recoiled in his chair, hiding his face, in response to the examiner's question how he felt about being unable to visit respondents' home. In the examiner's opinion, such reaction manifested continuing emotional pain in light of the earlier trauma and regressive behavior following termination of home visits.

Contrary to appellants' argument, they were not entitled to be present at the pretrial psychological examination. The need for an accurate report, itself subservient to the interest of an effective examination through a free and open communication exchange, is adequately safeguarded through discovery, cross-examination and production of other expert testimony.

11. A retarded child within an I.Q. range of 55–70 is generally considered as mildly retarded and classified as educable under California school standards.

12. Civil Code section 4600 was enacted in response to the celebrated case of Painter v. Bannister in which the state court awarded custody of a young boy to his grandparents because it disapproved of the father's "Bohemian" lifestyle in California....

it is not an essential condition; a person who assumes the role of parent, raising the child in his own home, may in time acquire an interest in the 'companionship, care, custody and management' of that child.... Persons who assume such responsibility have been characterized by some interested professional observers as 'psychological parents': 'Whether any adult becomes the psychological parent of a child is based ... on day-to-day interaction, companionship, and shared experiences. The role can be fulfilled either by a biological parent or by an adoptive parent or by any other caring adult—but never by an absent, inactive adult, whatever his biological or legal relationship to the child may be.'" (Goldstein, [Freud & Solnit, Beyond the Best Interests of the Child (1973)] p. 19.)

Appellants vigorously challenge the evidence and finding that respondents have become Phillip's de facto or psychological parents since he did not reside with them full-time, as underscored in previous California decisions which have recognized de facto parenthood. They argue that the subjective concept of psychological parenthood, relying on such nebulous factors as "love and affection" is susceptible to abuse and requires the countervailing element of objectivity provided by a showing of the child's long-term residency in the home of the claimed psychological parent.

We disagree. Adoption of the proposed standard would require this court to endorse a novel doctrine of child psychology unsupported either by a demonstrated general acceptance in the field of psychology or by the record before us. Although psychological parenthood is said to result from "day-to-day attention to [the child's] needs for physical care, nourishment, comfort, affection, and stimulation" (Goldstein, supra, p. 17), appellants fail to point to any authority or body of professional opinion that equates daily attention with full-time residency. To the contrary, the record contains uncontradicted expert testimony that while psychological parenthood usually will require residency on a "24–hour basis," it is not an absolute requirement; further, that the frequency and quality of Phillip's weekend visits with respondents, together with the regular weekday visits at We Care, provided an adequate foundation to establish the crucial parent-child relationship.

Nor are we persuaded by appellants' suggested policy considerations concerning the arguably subjective inquiry involved in determining psychological parenthood. Trial fact-finders commonly grapple with elusive subjective legal concepts without aid of "countervailing" objective criteria. ...

Appellants also challenge the sufficiency of the evidence....

The record contains abundant evidence that appellants' retention of custody would cause Phillip profound emotional harm. Notwithstanding Phillip's strong emotional ties with respondents, appellants abruptly foreclosed home visits and set out to end all contact between them. When Phillip's home visits terminated in 1978, he displayed many signs of severe emotional trauma; he appeared depressed and withdrawn and became visibly distressed at being unable to return to "my house," a request he steadily voiced up until trial. He became enuretic, which a psychologist, Dr. Edward Becking, testified indicates emotional stress in children. ...

Our law recognizes that children generally will sustain serious emotional harm when deprived of the emotional benefits flowing from a true parent-child relationship.

There was uncontroverted expert testimony that Phillip would sustain further emotional trauma in the event of total separation from respondents; that testimony indicated that, as with all children, Phillip needs love and affection, and he would be profoundly hurt if he were deprived of the existing psychological parental relationship with respondents in favor of maintaining unity with his biological parents.

Phillip's conduct unmistakably demonstrated that he derived none of the emotional benefits attending a close parental relationship largely as a result of appellants' individualized decision to abandon that traditional supporting role. Dr. Becking testified that no "bonding or attachment" has occurred between Phillip and his biological parents, a result palpably consistent with appellants' view that Phillip had none of the emotional needs uniquely filled by natural parents. We conclude that such substantial evidence adequately supports the finding that parental custody would have resulted in harmful deprivation of these human needs contrary to Phillip's best interests.

. . .

We strongly emphasize, as the trial court correctly concluded, that the fact of detriment *cannot* be proved solely by evidence that the biological parent has elected to institutionalize a handicapped child, or that nonparents are able and willing to offer the child the advantages of their home in lieu of institutional placement. Sound reasons may exist justifying institutionalization of a handicapped child. But the totality of the evidence under review permits of no rational conclusion other than that the detriment caused Phillip, and its possible recurrence, was due not to appellants' choice to institutionalize but their calculated decision to remain emotionally and physically detached—abdicating the conventional role of competent decision-maker in times of demonstrated need—thus effectively depriving him of *any* of the substantial benefits of a true parental relationship. *It is the emotional abandonment of Phillip, not his institutionalization,* which inevitably has created the unusual circumstances which led to the award of limited custody to respondents. We do not question the sincerity of appellants' belief that their approach to Phillip's welfare was in their combined best interests. But the record is replete with substantial and credible evidence supporting the trial court's determination, tested by the standard of clear and convincing proof, that appellants' retention of custody has caused and will continue to cause serious detriment to Phillip and that his best interests will be served through the guardianship award of custody to respondents. In light of such compelling circumstances, no legal basis is shown to disturb that carefully considered determination.

. . .

NOTES

1. After the decision of the Court of Appeal, the parties reached a settlement. Phillip then successfully underwent heart surgery.

When asked why he had resisted the operation, Mr. Becker replied:

> It wasn't in his interest. It was risky. What's the point? It might extend his life for a few years, but for what purpose? He's almost 17 and he's still carrying a teddy bear. Who's going to take care of him when the Heaths are gone?

Mr. Heath reported they have established a financial trust to help Phillip survive after their death, adding that with training, Phillip will in time be able to live in a semi-sheltered environment where he can live and work with other handicapped people. Lindsey, Pact on Custody Leads to Surgery, New York Times, October 10, 1983, at A12.

In February 1985, after full notice to the Beckers, who indicated that they did not object, the Heaths adopted Phillip. Robert Mnookin, The Guardianship of Phillip B.: Jay Spears' Achievement, 40 Stan. L.Rev. 841 (1988). At the time Phillip was eighteen years old. Phillip is still living with the Heaths, who are devoted to him. Phillip goes to school and is learning to read. As part of his school program, Phillip works at the Santa Clara Valley Medical Center where he busses tables in the cafeteria. Phillip's successful heart surgery also allowed him to play sports. Phillip participates in Special Olympics and enjoys bowling, basketball, softball and soccer. "The Heaths are committed to seeing that Phillip develops the skills, discipline, and confidence necessary to hold down a job and lead a productive and largely independent life, notwithstanding his handicap."

2. Some courts have circumvented the requirement of parental consent to medical care for minors by declaring the child "neglected," thereby making him or her a ward of the state. Courts routinely have granted requests for such state intervention when the treatment was both necessary to save a child's life, and was not unduly risky itself. See, e.g., State v. Perricone, 37 N.J. 463, 181 A.2d 751 (1962), cert. denied, 371 U.S. 890 (1962); People ex rel. Wallace v. Labrenz, 411 Ill. 618, 104 N.E.2d 769 (1952), cert. denied 344 U.S. 824 (1952). Is the holding in the Phillip Becker case consistent with the general case law?

3. When the health problem at stake is not life threatening, most courts have refused to intervene to override parental objections. See, e.g., In re Seiferth, 309 N.Y. 80, 127 N.E.2d 820 (1955). But see In re Sampson, 65 Misc.2d 658, 317 N.Y.S.2d 641 (1970), affirmed 29 N.Y.2d 900, 328 N.Y.S.2d 686, 278 N.E.2d 918 (1972). Cf. In re Green, 448 Pa. 338, 292 A.2d 387 (1972) (decision of whether to order operation to correct curvature of the spine of 16 year old boy remanded). On remand, the boy refused the operation. On appeal, this refusal was upheld. 452 Pa. 373, 307 A.2d 279 (1973).

Bowen v. American Hospital Association

Supreme Court of the United States, 1986.
476 U.S. 610, 106 S.Ct. 2101, 90 L.Ed.2d 584.

■ JUSTICE STEVENS announced the judgment of the Court and delivered an opinion, in which JUSTICE MARSHALL, JUSTICE BLACKMUN, and JUSTICE POWELL join.

This case presents the question whether certain regulations governing the provision of health care to handicapped infants are authorized by § 504 of the Rehabilitation Act of 1973. That section provides, in part:

> "No otherwise qualified handicapped individual ... shall, solely by reason of his handicap, be excluded from the participation in, be denied the benefits of, or be subjected to discrimination under any program or activity receiving Federal financial assistance." 87 Stat. 394, 29 U.S.C. § 794.

The American Medical Association, the American Hospital Association, and several other respondents challenge the validity of Final Rules promulgated on January 12, 1984, by the Secretary of the Department of Health and Human Services. These Rules establish "Procedures relating to health care for handicapped infants," and in particular require the posting of informational notices, authorize expedited access to records and expedited compliance actions, and command state child protective services agencies to "prevent instances of unlawful medical neglect of handicapped infants."

The Final Rules represent the Secretary's ultimate response to an April 9, 1982, incident in which the parents of a Bloomington, Indiana, infant with Down's syndrome and other handicaps refused consent to surgery to remove an esophageal obstruction that prevented oral feeding. On April 10, the hospital initiated judicial proceedings to override the parents' decision, but an Indiana trial court, after holding a hearing the same evening, denied the requested relief. On April 12 the court asked the local Child Protection Committee to review its decision. After conducting its own hearing, the Committee found no reason to disagree with the court's ruling.[5] The infant died six days after its birth.

Citing "heightened public concern" in the aftermath of the Bloomington Baby Doe incident, on May 18, 1982, the director of the Department's Office of Civil Rights, in response to a directive from the President, "remind[ed]" health care providers receiving federal financial assistance that newborn infants with handicaps such as Down's syndrome were protected by § 504. 47 Fed.Reg. 26027 (1982).[6]

This notice was followed, on March 7, 1983, by an "Interim Final Rule" contemplating a "vigorous federal role." 48 Fed.Reg. 9630. The Interim Rule required health care providers receiving federal financial assistance to post "in a conspicuous place in each delivery ward, each maternity ward, each pediatric ward, and each nursery, including each intensive care nursery" a notice advising of the applicability of § 504 and the availability of a telephone "hotline" to report suspected violations of the law to HHS. Like the Final Rules, the Interim Rule also provided for expedited compliance actions and expedited access to records and facilities when, "in the judgment of the responsible Department official," immediate action or access was "necessary to protect the life or health of a handicapped individual." The Interim Rule took effect on March 22.

On April 6, 1983, respondents American Hospital Association et al. filed a complaint in the Federal District Court for the Southern District of New York seeking a declaration that the Interim Final Rule was invalid and an injunction against its enforcement. . . .

On July 5, 1983, the Department issued new "Proposed Rules" on which it invited comment. Like the Interim Final Rule, the Proposed Rules required hospitals to post informational notices in conspicuous places and authorized expedited access to records to be followed, if necessary, by expedited compliance action. In a departure from the Interim Final Rule, however, the Proposed Rules required federally assisted state child protective services agencies to utilize their "full authority pursuant to State law to prevent instances of medical neglect of handicapped infants." Mandated procedures mirrored those contained in the Final Rules described above. The preamble and appendix to the Proposed Rules did not acknowledge that hospitals and physicians lack authority to perform treatment to which parents have not given their consent.

5. At the instance of the local prosecutor, the Indiana courts on April 13 held another hearing at which the court concluded that "Baby Doe" had not been neglected under Indiana's Child in Need of Services statute. Additional attempts to seek judicial intervention were rebuffed the same day. On the following day, the Indiana Court of Appeals denied a request for an immediate hearing. In re Infant Doe, No. GU 8204–004A (Monroe County Cir.Ct., Apr. 12, 1982). The Indiana Supreme Court, by a vote of 3 to 1, rejected a petition for a writ of mandamus. State ex rel. Infant Doe v. Baker, No. 482 S 140 (May 27, 1982). The infant died while a stay was being sought in this Court, and we subsequently denied certiorari. Infant Doe v. Bloomington Hospital, 464 U.S. 961 (1983).

6. The notice maintained that hospitals would violate § 504 if they "allow[ed] [an] infant" to remain in their care after "the infant's parents or guardian [had withheld consent to] treatment or nourishment discriminatorily." 47 Fed.Reg. 26027 (1982). The Secretary no longer subscribes to this reading of the statute.

After the period for notice and comment had passed, HHS, on December 30, 1983, promulgated the Final Rules and announced that they would take effect on February 13, 1984. On March 12 of that year respondents American Hospital Association et al. amended their complaint and respondents American Medical Association et al. filed suit to declare the new regulations invalid and to enjoin their enforcement. The actions were consolidated in the Federal District Court for the Southern District of New York, which awarded the requested relief on the authority of the decision of the United States Court of Appeals for the Second Circuit in United States v. University Hospital, 729 F.2d 144 (1984). American Hospital Assn. v. Heckler, 585 F.Supp. 541 (1984). On appeal, the parties agreed that the reasoning of the Court of Appeals in *University Hospital,* if valid, required a judgment against the Government in this case. In accordance with its earlier decision, the Court of Appeals summarily affirmed the District Court. 794 F.2d 676 (1984). Since the judgment here thus rests entirely on the reasoning of *University Hospital,* it is appropriate to examine that case now.

On October 11, 1983, after the Department's Interim Final Rule had been declared invalid but before it had promulgated the Final Rules challenged here, a child with multiple congenital defects known as "Baby Jane Doe" was born in Long Island, New York, and was promptly transferred to University Hospital for corrective surgery. After consulting with physicians and other advisers, the parents decided to forgo corrective surgery that was likely to prolong the child's life, but would not improve many of her handicapping conditions.

On October 16, 1983, an unrelated attorney named Washburn filed suit in the New York Supreme Court, seeking the appointment of a guardian *ad litem* for the infant who would direct the hospital to perform the corrective surgery. The trial court granted that relief on October 20, but was reversed the following day by the Appellate Division which found that the "concededly concerned and loving parents" had "chosen one course of appropriate medical treatment over another" and made an informed decision that was "in the best interest of the infant." On October 28, the New York Court of Appeals affirmed, but on the ground that the trial court should not have entertained a petition to initiate child neglect proceedings by a stranger who had not requested the aid of the responsible state agency.

While the state proceedings were in progress, on October 19, HHS received a complaint from a "private citizen" that Baby Jane Doe was being discriminatorily denied medically indicated treatment. HHS promptly referred this complaint to the New York State Child Protective Service. (The agency investigated the charge of medical neglect and soon thereafter concluded that there was no cause for state intervention.) In the meantime, before the State Child Protective Service could act, HHS on October 22, 1983, made repeated requests of the hospital to make its records available for inspection in order to determine whether the hospital was in compliance with § 504. The hospital refused the requests and advised HHS that the parents had not consented to a release of the records.

Subsequently, on November 2, 1983, the Government filed suit in Federal District Court invoking its general authority to enforce § 504 and 45 C.F.R. § 84.61 (1985), a regulation broadly authorizing access to information necessary to ascertain compliance. The District Court allowed the parents to intervene as defendants, expedited the proceeding, and ruled against the Government. It reasoned that the Government had no right of access to information because the record clearly established that the hospital had not violated the statute. United States v. University Hospital, State Univ. of N.Y. at Stony Brook, 575 F.Supp. 607, 614 (E.D.N.Y.). Since the uncontradicted evidence established that the hospital "ha[d] at all times been willing to perform the surgical procedures in question, if only the parents ... would consent," the hospital "failed to perform the surgical procedures in question, not because Baby Jane Doe [wa]s handicapped, but because her parents ha[d] refused to consent."

The Court of Appeals affirmed....

. . .

The Government did not file a certiorari petition in *University Hospital.* It did, however, seek review of the judgment in this case. We granted certiorari, 472 U.S. 1016 (1985), and we now affirm.

. . .

The Solicitor General is correct that "handicapped individual" as used in § 504 includes an infant who is born with a congenital defect. If such an infant is "otherwise qualified" for benefits under a program or activity receiving federal financial assistance, § 504 protects him from discrimination "solely by reason of his handicap." It follows ... that handicapped infants are entitled to "meaningful access" to medical services provided by hospitals, and that a hospital rule or state policy denying or limiting such access would be subject to challenge under § 504.

However, no such rule or policy is challenged, or indeed has been identified, in this case. Nor does this case, in contrast to the *University Hospital* litigation, involve a claim that any specific individual treatment decision violates § 504. This suit is not an enforcement action, and as a consequence it is not necessary to determine whether § 504 ever applies to individual medical treatment decisions involving handicapped infants. Respondents brought this litigation to challenge the four mandatory components of the Final Rules on their face....

Before examining the Secretary's reasons for issuing the Final Rules, it is essential to understand the pre-existing state-law framework governing the provision of medical care to handicapped infants. In broad outline, state law vests decisional responsibility in the parents, in the first instance, subject to review in exceptional cases by the State acting as *parens patriae.* Prior to the regulatory activity culminating in the Final Rules, the Federal Government was not a participant in the process of making treatment decisions for newborn infants. We presume that this general framework was familiar to Congress when it enacted § 504. It therefore provides an appropriate background for evaluating the Secretary's action in this case.

The Secretary has identified two possible categories of violations of § 504 as justifications for federal oversight of handicapped infant care. First, he contends that a hospital's refusal to furnish a handicapped infant with medically beneficial treatment "solely by reason of his handicap" constitutes unlawful discrimination. Second, he maintains that a hospital's failure to report cases of suspected medical neglect to a state child protective services agency may also violate the statute. We separately consider these two possible bases for the Final Rules.

. . .

In the immediate aftermath of the Bloomington Baby Doe incident, the Secretary apparently proceeded on the assumption that a hospital's statutory duty to provide treatment to handicapped infants was unaffected by the absence of parental consent. He has since abandoned that view. Thus, the preamble to the Final Rules correctly states that when "a non-treatment decision, no matter how discriminatory, is made by parents, rather than by the hospital, section 504 does not mandate that the hospital unilaterally overrule the parental decision and provide treatment notwithstanding the lack of consent." A hospital's withholding of treatment when no parental consent has been given cannot violate § 504, for without the consent of the parents or a surrogate decisionmaker the infant is neither "otherwise qualified" for treatment nor has he been denied care "solely by reason of his handicap." Indeed, it would almost certainly be a tort as a matter of state law to operate on an infant without parental consent. This analysis makes clear that the Government's heavy reliance on the analogy to race-based refusals which violate § 601 of the Civil Rights Act is misplaced. If, pursuant to its normal practice, a hospital refused to operate on a black child whose parents had withheld their consent to treatment, the hospital's refusal would not be based on the race of the child even if it were assumed that the parents based their decision entirely on a mistaken assumption that the race of the child made the operation inappropriate.

Now that the Secretary has acknowledged that a hospital has no statutory treatment obligation in the absence of parental consent, it has become clear that the Final Rules are not needed to prevent hospitals from denying treatment to handicapped infants. The Solicitor General concedes that the administrative record contains no evidence that hospitals have ever refused treatment authorized either by the infant's parents or by a court order. Even the Secretary never seriously maintained that posted notices, "hotlines," and emergency on-site investigations were necessary to process complaints against hospitals that might refuse treatment requested by parents....

The Secretary's belated recognition of the effect of parental nonconsent is important, because the supposed need for federal monitoring of hospitals' treatment decisions rests *entirely* on instances in which parents have refused their consent. Thus, in the Bloomington, Indiana, case that precipitated the Secretary's enforcement efforts in this area, as well as in the *University Hospital* case that provided the basis for the summary affirmance in the case now before us, the hospital's failure to perform the treatment at issue rested on the lack of parental consent. The Secretary's own summaries of these cases establish beyond doubt that the respective hospitals did not withhold medical care on the basis of handicap and therefore did not violate § 504; as a result, they provide no support for his claim that federal regulation is needed in order to forestall comparable cases in the future.

The Secretary's initial failure to recognize that withholding of consent by *parents* does not equate with discriminatory denial of treatment by hospitals likewise undermines the Secretary's findings in the preamble to his proposed rulemaking. In that statement, the Secretary cited four sources in support of the claim that "Section 504 [is] not being uniformly followed." None of the cited examples, however, suggests that recipients of federal financial assistance, as opposed to parents, had withheld medical care on the basis of handicap.[18]

18. The Secretary first cited a 1973 survey by Raymond Duff and A.G.M. Campbell calculating that 14% of deaths in the special nursery of the Yale–New Haven hospital "were related to withholding treatment." 48 Fed.Reg. 30847 (1983). The Secretary's solitary quotation from this study, accurately illustrating the locus of the treatment decisions reviewed by the authors, involved refusal of parental consent:

Notwithstanding the ostensible recognition in the preamble of the effect of parental nonconsent on a hospital's obligation to provide care, in promulgating the Final Rules the Secretary persisted in relying on instances in which parents had refused consent to support his claim that, regardless of its "magnitude," there is sufficient evidence of "illegality" to justify "establishing basic mechanisms to allow for effective enforcement of a clearly applicable statute." ... In addition to the evidence relied on in prior notices, the Secretary included a summary of the 49 "Infant Doe cases" that the Department had processed before December 1, 1983. Curiously, however, by the Secretary's own admission *none* of the 49 cases had "resulted in a finding of discriminatory withholding of medical care." In fact, in the entire list of 49 cases there is no finding that a hospital failed or refused to provide treatment to a handicapped infant for which parental consent had been given.

Notwithstanding this concession, the Secretary "believes three of these cases demonstrate the utility of the procedural mechanisms called for in the final rules." However, these three cases, which supposedly provide the strongest support for federal intervention, fail to disclose any discrimination against handicapped newborns in violation of § 504. For example, in Robinson, Illinois, the Department conducted an on-site investigation when it learned that the "hospital *(at the parents' request)* failed to perform necessary surgery." After "[t]he parents refused consent for surgery," "the hospital referred the matter to state authorities, who accepted custody of the infant and arranged for surgery and adoption," all "in compliance with section 504." The Secretary concluded that "the involvement of the state child protective services agency," at the behest of the hospital, "was the most important element in bringing about corrective surgery for the infant.... Had there been no *governmental* involvement in the case, the outcome might have been much less favorable."[21]

The Secretary's second example illustrates with even greater force the effective and nondiscriminatory functioning of state mechanisms and the consequent lack of support for federal intervention. In Daytona Beach, Florida, the Department's hotline received a complaint of medical neglect of a handicapped infant; immediate contact with the hospital and state agency revealed that "the parents did not consent to surgery" for the infant. Notwithstanding this information, which was confirmed by both the hospital and the state agency, and despite the fact that the state agency had "obtained

" 'An infant with Down's syndrome and intestinal atresia, like the much publicized one at Johns Hopkins Hospital, was not treated *because his parents thought the surgery was wrong for their baby and themselves.* He died several days after birth.' " Ibid. (emphasis added) (Quoting Raymond Duff & A.G.M. Campbell, Moral and Ethical Dilemmas in the Special-Care Nursery, 289 New Eng.J.Med. 890, 891 (1973)).

The Secretary next referred to an incident at Johns Hopkins Hospital which, as the above quotation intimates, also concerned parental refusal of consent. Then followed brief mention of the "Bloomington Baby Doe" incident, in which the parents, as the Secretary now admits, refused consent to treatment despite the hospital's insistence that it be provided. The Secretary's fourth and final example involved "a 1979 death of an infant with Down's syndrome and an intestinal obstruction at the Kapiolani-Children's Medical Center in Honolulu, Hawaii," which again appears to have resulted from "a lack of parental consent."

Generalizing from these examples, the Secretary reported the results of a survey of physician attitudes. He faulted "[t]heir acquiescence in nontreatment of Down's children" which he surmised was "apparently *because of* the handicap represented by Down's syndrome."

21. The preamble repeatedly makes the assumption that evidence showing the need for *governmental* involvement provides a basis for *federal* involvement.

a court order to provide surgery" the day *before* HHS was notified, the Department conducted an on-site investigation. In the third case, in Colorado Springs, Colorado, the Department intervened so soon after birth that "the decisionmaking process was in progress at the time the OCR [Office of Civil Rights] inquiry began," and "it is impossible to say the surgery would not have been provided without this involvement." "However," the Secretary added, "the involvement of OCR and the OCR medical consultant was cooperatively received by the hospital and apparently constructive."

In sum, there is nothing in the administrative record to justify the Secretary's belief that "discriminatory withholding of medical care" in violation of § 504 provides any support for federal regulation: In two of the cases (Robinson, Illinois, and Daytona Beach, Florida), the hospital's refusal was based on the absence of parental consent, but the parents' decision was overridden by state authorities and the operation was performed; in the third case (Colorado Springs, Colorado) it is not clear whether the parents would have given their consent or not, but the corrective surgery was in fact performed.[22]

As a backstop to his manifestly incorrect perception that withholding of treatment in accordance with parental instructions necessitates federal regulation, the Secretary contends that a hospital's failure to report parents' refusals to consent to treatment violates § 504, and that past breaches of this kind justify federal oversight.

By itself, § 504 imposes no duty to report instances of medical neglect—that undertaking derives from state-law reporting obligations or a hospital's

22. Justice White's dissent suggests that regulation of health care providers can be justified on a theory the Secretary did not advance—a supposed need to curtail discriminatory advice by biased physicians. After observing that at least some handicapped infants have not been treated, the dissent identifies physician attitudes as a likely explanation and concludes that mandated informational notices were presumably designed to "foste[r] an awareness by health care professionals of their responsibility not to act in a discriminatory manner with respect to medical treatment decisions for handicapped infants."

The dissent's theory finds no support in the text of the regulation, the reasoning of the Secretary, or the briefs filed on his behalf in this Court. The regulations in general—and the informational notices in particular—do not purport to place any constraints on the advice that physicians may give their patients. Moreover, since it is now clear that parental decisionmaking is not covered by § 504, the dissent's theory rests on the unstated premise that the statute may prevent the giving of advice to do something which § 504 does not itself prohibit. It is hardly obvious that the Rehabilitation Act of 1973 prohibits physicians from "aiding and abetting" a parental decision which parents admittedly have a right to make. And if Congress did intend this counterintuitive result, one might expect an explanation from the Secretary as to how the hotlines and emergency on-site inspections contemplated by the Final Rules square with the constitutional doctrines on regulation, direct or indirect, of speech in general and of decisionmaking by health professionals in particular.

In reality, the Secretary neither found nor implied that physicians' predispositions against treating handicapped infants had resulted in parental refusals to consent to treatment. Indeed, he principally relied on attitudinal surveys for the converse proposition that regulation is necessary because parents refuse consent to treatment and physicians will "acquiesce in parental refus[als] to treat." To the extent *any* theory may be discerned in the Secretary's two-column summary of physician surveys, it is that doctors would not *correct* "bad" parental decisions, not that they were responsible for helping them to make such choices in the first place. Moreover, even if the Secretary had relied on this evidence to insinuate that doctors imposed their own value judgments on parents by lobbying them to refuse consent, he never explains that the parental decisionmaking process is one in which doctors exercise the decisive influence needed to force such results. The Secretary, in short, has not even adumbrated a theory of "discrimination" remotely resembling the one invented by the dissent, and therefore has not made the essential connection between the evidence of physician attitudes and the regulatory choice made here.

own voluntary practice. Although a hospital's selective refusal to report medical neglect of handicapped infants might violate § 504, the Secretary has failed to point to any specific evidence that this has occurred. The 49 actual investigations summarized in the preamble to the Final Rules do not reveal *any* case in which a hospital either failed, or was accused of failing, to make an appropriate report to a state agency. Nor can we accept the Solicitor General's invitation to infer discriminatory nonreporting from the studies cited in the Secretary's proposed rulemaking. Even assuming that cases in which parents have withheld consent to treatment for handicapped infants have gone unreported, that fact alone would not prove that the hospitals involved had discriminated on the basis of handicap rather than simply failed entirely to discharge their state-law reporting obligations, if any, a matter which lies wholly outside the nondiscrimination mandate of § 504.

. . .

The need for a proper evidentiary basis for agency action is especially acute in this case because Congress has failed to indicate, either in the statute or in the legislative history, that it envisioned federal superintendence of treatment decisions traditionally entrusted to state governance. . . .

The administrative record demonstrates that the Secretary has asserted the authority to conduct on-site investigations, to inspect hospital records, and to participate in the decisional process in emergency cases in which there was no colorable basis for believing that a violation of § 504 had occurred or was about to occur. The District Court and the Court of Appeals correctly held that these investigative actions were not authorized by the statute and that the regulations which purport to authorize a continuation of them are invalid.

The judgment of the Court of Appeals is affirmed.

NOTES

1. There is a striking difference between the consistent way courts have ordered life-saving treatment for most *children* over parental objection and the recent heated debate concerning appropriate care for *newborns* with congenital disabilities who need life-saving treatment. Does the difference reflect public sympathy for infanticide—at least when a newborn is seriously handicapped?

2. With the passage of the Child Abuse Amendments of 1984, P.L. 98–457, The Child Abuse Prevention and Treatment Act of 1978 was extended and amended to specifically cover denial of medical treatment to disabled infants. Participating states were required to establish programs or procedures for responding to the reporting of medical neglect including instances of withholding of medically indicated treatment from disabled infants with life threatening conditions.

The term "withholding of medically indicated treatment" is defined as:

> The failure to respond to the infant's life-threatening conditions by providing treatment (including appropriate nutrition, hydration and medication) which, in the treating physician's or physicians' reasonable medical judgment, will be most likely to be effective in ameliorating or correcting all such conditions, except that the term does not include the failure to provide treatment (other than appropriate nutrition, hydration or medication) to an infant when, in the treating physician's or physicians' reasonable medical judgment, (A) the infant is chronically and irreversibly comatose; (B) the provision of such treatment would (i) merely prolong dying, (ii) not be effective in ameliorating or correcting all of the infant's life-threatening conditions, or (iii) otherwise be futile in terms of the

survival of the infant; or (C) the provision of such treatment would be virtually futile in terms of the survival of the infant and the treatment itself under such circumstances would be inhumane.

42 U.S.C. § 5106.

The Conference Report explains at 41:

> The reference to "reasonable medical judgment" of the treating physician or physicians means a medical judgment that would be made by a reasonably prudent physician, knowledgeable about the case and the treatment possibilities with respect to the medical conditions involved.

On April 15, 1985, regulations were promulgated to implement the new legislation. 50 Fed.Reg. 14,878.

3. Consider Raymond Duff and A.G.M. Campbell, Moral and Ethical Dilemmas in the Special–Care Nursery, 289 N.Eng.J.Med. 890 (1973):

> Another problem concerns who decides for a child. It may be acceptable for a person to reject treatment and bring about his own death. But it is quite a different situation when others are doing this for him. We do not know how often families and their physicians will make just decisions for severely handicapped children. Clearly, this issue is central in evaluation of the process of decision making that we have described. But we also ask, if these parties cannot make such decisions justly, who can?
>
> We recognize great variability and often much uncertainty in prognoses and in family capacities to deal with defective newborn infants. We also acknowledge that there are limits of support that society can or will give to assist handicapped persons and their families. Severely deforming conditions that are associated with little or no hope of a functional existence pose painful dilemmas for the laymen and professionals who must decide how to cope with severe handicaps. We believe the burdens of decision making must be borne by families and their professional advisers because they are most familiar with the respective situations. Since families primarily must live with and are most affected by the decisions, it therefore appears that society and the health professions should provide only general guidelines for decision making. Moreover, since variations between situations are so great, and the situations themselves so complex, it follows that much latitude in decision making should be expected and tolerated. Otherwise, the rules of society or the policies most convenient for medical technologists may become cruel masters of human beings instead of their servants.

See generally Stephen Wall et al., Death in the Intensive Care Nursery: Physician Practice of Withdrawing and Withholding Life Support, 99 Pediatrics 64 (1997).

4. Consider also Paul Ramsey, Ethics at the Edges of Life 192–93, 201–03, 212–16, 218–19 (1978):

> Surely there is a distinction to be made between, on the one hand, children permitted to die whose deaths "resulted from pathological conditions in spite of the treatment given" (category 1), and, on the other hand, those permitted to die who simply had severe impairments, usually from congenital disorders (category 2). The latter more than likely died because they were not treated. Of the former alone could it correctly be said, as physicians report nurses saying, "We lost him several weeks ago; isn't it time to quit?" or "For this child, don't you think it's time to turn off your curiosity so you can turn on your kindness?" or that the facilities in which they were treated are "hardly more than *dying* bins." . . . In medical care, we rightly compare treatments in order to decide what is indicated as responsible activity on the part of those who are still living toward those who are now dying. But we ought not to compare and contrast the persons—the patients who are dying—with one another in other respects. We have no moral right to choose that some live and others die, when the medical indications for treatment are the same.
>
> That means that the standard for letting die must be the same for the normal child as for the defective child. If an operation to remove a bowel

obstruction is indicated to save the life of a normal infant, it is also the indicated treatment of a mongoloid infant. The latter is certainly not dying because of Down's syndrome. Like any other child with an obstruction in its intestinal tract, it will starve to death unless an operation is performed to remove the obstruction to permit normal feeding.

Dr. John Lorber of Sheffield, England, is now famous for choosing to let some spina bifida or myelomeningocele babies die while others undergo a series of operations over many years. The latter lead impaired lives, but lives Lorber judges to be worth living. He claims he is able to make this determination on the first day of a baby's life by applying five measurements or tests. Now, I do not think that a series of ordinary treatments—closing the open spine, antibiotics, a contraption to deal with urinary incontinence, and a shunt to prevent hydrocephalus—today adds up to extraordinary medical care, except perhaps in the case of a conscious, competent patient who is able himself to refuse treatment. But the point is that Dr. Lorber does not claim that the infants he chooses to "let die" are now dying, or that to intervene medically only prolongs their dying. Indeed, those babies are heavily sedated. Is the reason for that to keep pain at bay? I doubt it. There is rather some ground for suspicion that, since drowsy babies need to be fed less frequently, the spina bifida babies chosen not to be treated are sedated so that they will begin dying of hunger and slowly sleep away. At least, that would be one way of avoiding the notorious case of allowing a defective infant to starve to death in fifteen days, as was done at Johns Hopkins Hospital a few years ago when a Down's baby was refused an operation to remove its intestinal obstruction. So my first point is clear: the fact that dying patients sometimes need no more attempts to be made to save them ought not to be carelessly applied to the case of defective newborns. Sometimes the neglected infants are not born dying. They are only born defective and in need of help. The question whether no treatment is the indicated treatment cannot legitimately be raised, unless there is special medical reason for saying that treatment might make them worse and in any case could not help. The comparison should be between treatments measured to the need. As God is no respecter of persons of high degree, neither should we be. The proper form of the question to be asked is: Should we not close a wound in a newborn expected to be normal? Should we not provide him with devices correcting his incontinence? Should not physical conditions likely to impair any child's mental capacity be stopped if possible; or if not, subdued?

. . .

There is still another moral aspect of the practice of neglect. This is a question of justice. Some physicians who have reported that they let some babies die (perhaps hasten their dying) also report that they make such life or death decisions not only on the basis of the newborn's medical condition and prognosis, but on the basis of familial, social, and economic factors as well. If the marriage seems to be a strong one, an infant impaired to x degree may be treated, while an infant with the same impairment may not be treated if the marriage seems about to fall apart. Treatment may be given if the parents are wealthy; not, if they are poor. Now, life may be unfair, as John Kennedy said; but to deliberately make medical care a function of inequities that exist at birth is evidently to add injustice to injury and fate.

Wiser and more righteous is the practice of Dr. Chester A. Swinyard of the New York University medical school's rehabilitation center. Upon the presentation to him of a defective newborn, he immediately tries to make clear to the mother the distinction between the question of ultimate custody of the child and questions concerning the care it needs. The mother must consent to operations, of course. But she is asked only to make judgments about the baby's care, while she is working through the problem of whether to accept the defective child as a substitute for her "lost child," i.e., the perfect baby she wanted. In the prism of the case, when the question is, Shall this open spine be closed? Shall a shunt be used to prevent further mental impairment? the mothers can usually answer correctly. In the case of spina bifida babies, Dr. Swinyard also reports very infrequent need of institutionalization or foster parents. That results from concentrating the mother's attention on what medical care requires, and not on lifelong burdens of custody. One must entirely reject the contention of Duff and Campbell that parents, facing the prospect of oppressive burdens of care, are capable of making the most morally sensible decisions about the needs and rights of defective newborns. There is a Jewish teaching to the effect that only disinterested parties may, by even so innocuous a method as prayer, take any action which may lead to premature termination of life. Husband, children, family and those charged with the care of the patient may not pray for death.

One can understand—even appreciate—the motives of a physician who considers an unhappy marriage or family poverty when weighing the tragedy facing one child against that facing another; and rations his help accordingly. Nevertheless, that surely is a species of injustice. Physicians are not appointed to remove all life's tragedy, least of all by lessening medical care now and letting infants die who for social reasons seem fated to have less care in the future than others. That's one way to remove every evening the human debris that has accumulated since morning.

. . .

One could perhaps construct some exceptions to the principle of giving equally vigorous treatment to defective newborns as to normals. . . .

My first thought is a proposed *redescription* of one sort of defective newborn, not logically an "exception"; moreover, it is a hypothetical and moot point, worth mentioning anyway. It is not at all necessary to take an anencephalic baby (born without a brain in its brain chamber) as the demonstration case of a defective newborn that certainly ought not to be treated, and then build up from there other cases of gross defects that should not be treated. . . .

But, for one thing, an anencephalic baby is born dying, and here the morality of letting die clearly applies as it does to a Tay–Sachs baby when it is seized by irreversible degeneration. For another thing, even if it were possible to treat anencephalic babies, this should not be done—but not because they would be the demonstration case in support of a policy of not treating nondying defective newborns. Instead we could and should, consistent with our present understanding of brain life and death, take the definition route in resolving that hypothetical case. Such an infant is "human," of course, in a generic sense; also it is a unique individual of our species. However, it has not been born alive. If we use here at the beginning of life the same physiological signs of the difference between life and death which we use at the end of life, an anencephalic baby does not have the unitary function of major organ systems within which the brain has primacy. That is why they soon "die," as we say. Such infants demonstrate their status by dying, in all senses, rather quickly. So an anencephalic baby, it could be argued, no more enters the human community to claim our care and protection than a patient remains in the human community when his brain death (and consequent heart death and lung death) is only disguised behind a heart-lung machine.

. . .

My second suggestion would be a true exception or qualification attached to our moral duty to treat all defective infants who are not born dying and who, of course, cannot for themselves refuse treatment. If care cannot be conveyed, it need not be extended. A mongoloid can receive care. So can a Tay–Sachs baby while it is dying. For the latter we may choose how it will live while dying. In the case of the former, we can add life to its years. But we face an entirely different issue if there is a sort of birth defect for which there is no therapy and if the suffering infant is in insurmountable pain. In such a suppositive case, care cannot be conveyed. Indeed, in regard to adult patients I have elsewhere argued that those circumstances abolish the moral distinction between only caring for the dying (allowing to die) and directly dispatching them.

So now I must ask, is there a birth defect comparable to insurmountable pain or to such deep and prolonged unconsciousness that places terminal patients beyond the reach of the caring human community? From my limited knowledge of it, I am inclined to say that the Lesch–Nyhan syndrome seems a good candidate for this comparison, and that such a suffering infant *may* be an exception to the foregoing ethical analysis. Not, of course, to the moral rule that if possible we should always treat nondying defective newborns: there is no therapy for Lesch–Nyhan genetic illness. It is rather an exception to the rule that, when attempted remedy fails or there is no available remedy, when instead we should move to affirmative caring and comforting action, there is never any reason for stopping caring actions. From cure to care: but then does care never cease? Such a limit, if there is one, would have to be found in the nature of care itself, not in anything extrinsic. Care itself reaches or posits that limit. The fact that there is no remedy for Lesch–Nyhan disease, for example, would not be a reason for ceasing care. But it did seem to me, in the abstract, that giving palliative comfort could not be effectively conveyed to these babies. That seemed a barrier one runs up against by caring until one *can* care no longer.

Lesch–Nyhan disease is a genetic defect, identified and described in a series of cases in 1964, which is passed on only to male children. Its victims are unable to walk or sit up unassisted; they suffer uncontrollable spasms and mental retardation. Initially, I should say, care can and should always be conveyed to such victims, though as yet there is no cure. When, however, the babies' teeth appear they will gnaw through their lips, gnaw their hands and shoulders; they often bite off a finger and mutilate any part of their bodies they can reach. There they lie, bloody and irremediable. Is this not a close approximation to the supposable case of insurmountable pain which in the terminal adult patient places him beyond human caring action and abolishes the moral significance of the distinction between always continuing to care and direct dispatch? When care cannot be conveyed, it need not be extended.

A pediatrician who read these pages expressed dismay over the idea of ever introducing into the special-care nursery the practice of promoting dying; and he told me something about the human care that can be extended to Lesch–Nyhan babies despite the fact that there is now no curative treatment. If he is correct, then my thought experiment need be pursued no further. At any rate, my remarks on this case are exploratory—an extended question....

. . .

... I want it understood that my understanding of care was and is what might be called (to borrow philosophical terminology) a "role and relations" ethics. It was and is a question of agent morality. The sole question raised was whether there ever comes a time when the care of a human agent (parent, physician) no longer reaches the subject cared for, when the eyes of faith and love no longer see, and it would be fanaticism to think so. If such a time does come, care for the dying would become as aimless as earlier further medical attempts to save or cure that life became purposeless. A gift is not a gift unless received; care is not what we suppose unless received, even if minimally. If not at all, there is no obligation to continue to do the useless. Since mine was and is an ethics of agent agape and, in medical ethics, a strong sense of agent care, I never suggested that one should base moral judgments in any degree upon an evaluation of the patient-subject as such. There was not the slightest suggestion that one should decide first whether the patient-subjects are so overwhelmed by their struggle for existence that they have lost effective capacity for meaningful relationship. No quality-of-life judgments were given entrance; only uselessness of agent care was suggested. These outlooks may seem very similar, but the accent is quite different.

5. In 2005, two doctors in the Netherlands, Eduard Verhagen and Pieter J. J. Sauer of the University Medical Center in Groningen, announced that they had developed guidelines, known as the Groningen protocol, for ending the lives of babies born into what is certain to be "a brief life of grievous suffering." The conditions include the full and informed consent of the parents, the agreement of a team of physicians, and a subsequent review of each case by "an outside legal body" to determine whether the decision was justified. Dr. Verhagen stated that although such actions already occur around the world "we find it unacceptable that it is happening in silence." John Schwartz, When Torment Is Baby's Destiny, Euthanasia Is Defended, N.Y.Times, March 10, 2005, at A3, col. 1.

6. Baby Jane Doe, whose real first name was Keri–Lynn, at age seven was described by her mother as a "happy but also very stubborn child." She was confined to a wheelchair and had to be catheterized four times a day because she could not go to the bathroom on her own. Keri–Lynn's intelligence was between "low-normal" and educable mentally retarded. Sarah Glazer, Born Too Soon, Too Small, Too Sick: Whatever Happened to Baby Doe?, Wash. Post, April 2, 1991, at Z8. Keri–Lynn attended a school for the orthopedically impaired where she was a kindergarten level student. Her mother said in retrospect "we were doing what we felt was right for our daughter.... We just took it one day at a time. The first time I got a reaction smile out of her, we decided to take her home. We loved her, wanted her home. Thank God it worked out the way it did."

Miller v. HCA

Supreme Court of Texas, 2003.
118 S.W.3d 758.

■ JUSTICE ENOCH delivered the opinion of the court:

The narrow question we must decide is whether Texas law recognizes a claim by parents for either battery or negligence because their premature infant, born alive but in distress at only twenty-three weeks of gestation, was provided resuscitative medical treatment by physicians at a hospital without parental consent.

The unfortunate circumstances of this case began in August 1990, when approximately four months before her due date, Karla Miller was admitted to Woman's Hospital of Texas (the "Hospital") in premature labor. An ultrasound revealed that Karla's fetus weighed about 629 grams or 1 1/4 pounds and had a gestational age of approximately twenty-three weeks. Because of the fetus's prematurity, Karla's physicians began administering a drug designed to stop labor.

Karla's physicians subsequently discovered that Karla had an infection that could endanger her life and require them to induce delivery. Dr. Mark Jacobs, Karla's obstetrician, and Dr. Donald Kelley, a neonatologist at the Hospital, informed Karla and her husband, Mark Miller, that if they had to induce delivery, the infant had little chance of being born alive. The physicians also informed the Millers that if the infant was born alive, it would most probably suffer severe impairments, including cerebral palsy, brain hemorrhaging, blindness, lung disease, pulmonary infections, and mental retardation. Mark testified at trial that the physicians told him they had never had such a premature infant live and that anything they did to sustain the infant's life would be guesswork.

After their discussion, Drs. Jacobs and Kelley asked the Millers to decide whether physicians should treat the infant upon birth if they were forced to induce delivery. At approximately noon that day, the Millers informed Drs. Jacob and Kelley that they wanted no heroic measures performed on the infant and they wanted nature to take its course. Mark testified that he understood heroic measures to mean performing resuscitation, chest massage, and using life support machines. Dr. Kelley recorded the Millers' request in Karla's medical notes, and Dr. Jacobs informed the medical staff at the Hospital that no neonatologist would be needed at delivery. Mark then left the Hospital to make funeral arrangements for the infant.

In the meantime, the nursing staff informed other Hospital personnel of Dr. Jacobs' instruction that no neonatologist would be present in the delivery room when the Millers' infant was born. An afternoon of meetings involving Hospital administrators and physicians followed. Between approximately 4:00 p.m. and 4:30 p.m that day, Anna Summerfield, the director of the Hospital's neonatal intensive care unit, and several physicians, including Dr. Jacobs, met with Mark upon his return to the Hospital to further discuss the situation. Mark testified that Ms. Summerfield announced at the meeting that the Hospital had a policy requiring resuscitation of any baby who was born weighing over 500 grams....

[T]he physicians at the meeting testified that they and Hospital administrators agreed only that a neonatologist would be present to evaluate the Millers' infant at birth and decide whether to resuscitate based on the infant's condition at that time. As Dr. Jacobs testified:

> What we finally decided that everyone wanted to do was to not make the call prior to the time we actually saw the baby. Deliver the baby, because you see there was this [question] is the baby really 23 weeks, or is the baby further along, how big is the baby, what are we dealing with. We decided to let the neonatologist make the call by looking directly at the baby at birth.

Another physician who attended the meeting agreed, testifying that to deny any attempts at resuscitation without seeing the infant's condition would be inappropriate and below the standard of care....

Mark testified that, after the meeting, Hospital administrators asked him to sign a consent form allowing resuscitation according to the Hospital's plan, but he refused. Mark further testified that when he asked how he could prevent resuscitation, Hospital administrators told him that he could do so by removing Karla from the Hospital, which was not a viable option given her condition. Dr. Jacobs then noted in Karla's medical charts that a plan for evaluating the infant upon her birth was discussed at that afternoon meeting.

That evening, Karla's condition worsened and her amniotic sac broke. Dr. Jacobs determined that he would have to augment labor so that the infant would be delivered before further complications to Karla's health developed. Dr. Jacobs accordingly stopped administering the drug to Karla that was designed to stop labor, substituting instead a drug designed to augment labor. At 11:30 p.m. that night, Karla delivered a premature female infant weighing 615 grams, which the Millers named Sidney. Sidney's actual gestational age was twenty-three and one-seventh weeks. And she was born alive.

Dr. Otero noted that Sidney had a heart beat, albeit at a rate below that normally found in full-term babies. He further noted that Sidney, although blue in color and limp, gasped for air, spontaneously cried, and grimaced. Dr. Otero also noted that Sidney displayed no dysmorphic features other than being premature. He immediately "bagged" and "intubated" Sidney to oxygenate her blood; he then placed her on ventilation. He explained why:

> Because this baby is alive and this is a baby that has a reasonable chance of living. And again, this is a baby that is not necessarily going to have problems later on. There are babies that survive at this gestational age that—with this birth weight, that later on go on and do well.

Neither Karla nor Mark objected at the time to the treatment provided.

Sidney initially responded well to the treatment, as reflected by her Apgar scores. An Apgar score records five different components of a newborn infant: respiratory effort, heart rate, reflex activity, color, and muscle tone. Each component gets a score of zero, one, or two, with a score of two representing the best condition. Sidney's total Apgar score improved from a three at one minute after birth to a six at five minutes after birth. But at some point during the first few days after birth, Sidney suffered a brain hemorrhage—a complication not uncommon in infants born so prematurely....

[A]s predicted by Karla's physicians, the hemorrhage caused Sidney to suffer severe physical and mental impairments. At the time of trial, Sidney was seven years old and could not walk, talk, feed herself, or sit up on her own. The evidence demonstrated that Sidney was legally blind, suffered from severe mental retardation, cerebral palsy, seizures, and spastic quadriparesis in her limbs. She could not be toilet-trained and required a shunt in her brain to drain fluids that accumulate there and needed care twenty-four hours a day. The evidence further demonstrated that her circumstances will not change.

The Millers ... asserted battery and negligence claims ... against HCA and the Hospital.

The Millers' claims stemmed from their allegations that despite their instructions to the contrary, the Hospital not only resuscitated Sidney but performed experimental procedures and administered experimental drugs, without which, in all reasonable medical probability, Sidney would not have survived ...

The trial court rendered judgment jointly and severally against the HCA defendants on the jury's verdict of $29,400,000 in actual damages for medical expenses, $17,503,066 in prejudgment interest, and $13,500,000 in exemplary damages.

HCA appealed. The court of appeals, with one justice dissenting, reversed and rendered judgment that the Millers take nothing....

We granted the Millers' petition for review to consider this important and difficult matter. In addition to briefing from the parties, we received several amici briefs, some supporting the Millers' position and some supporting HCA's position.

This case requires us to determine the respective roles that parents and healthcare providers play in deciding whether to treat an infant who is born alive but in distress and is so premature that, despite advancements in neonatal intensive care, has a largely uncertain prognosis. Although the parties have cited numerous constitutional provisions, statutes, and cases, we conclude that neither the Texas Legislature nor our case law has addressed this specific situation. We accordingly begin our analysis by focusing on what the existing case law and statutes do address.

Generally speaking, the custody, care, and nurture of an infant resides in the first instance with the parents ... The Texas Legislature has likewise recognized that parents are presumed to be appropriate decision-makers, giving parents the right to consent to their infant's medical care and surgical treatment. A logical corollary of that right, as the court of appeals here recognized, is that parents have the right not to consent to certain medical care for their infant, i.e., parents have the right to refuse certain medical care....

With respect to consent, the requirement that permission be obtained before providing medical treatment is based on the patient's right to receive information adequate for him or her to exercise an informed decision to accept or refuse the treatment. Thus, the general rule in Texas is that a physician who provides treatment without consent commits a battery. But there are exceptions. For example, in Gravis v. Physicians & Surgeons Hospital, this Court acknowledged that "consent will be implied where the patient is unconscious or otherwise unable to give express consent and an immediate operation is necessary to preserve life or health."

In Moss v. Rishworth, the court held that a physician commits a "legal wrong" by operating on a minor without parental consent when there is "an absolute necessity for a prompt operation, but not emergent in the sense that death would likely result immediately upon the failure to perform it." But the court in Moss expressly noted that "it [was] not contended [there] that any real danger would have resulted to the child had time been taken to consult the parent with reference to the operation." Moss therefore implicitly acknowledges that a physician does not commit a legal wrong by operating on a minor without consent when the operation is performed under emergent circumstances—i.e., when death is likely to result immediately upon the failure to perform it.

Moss guides us here. We hold that a physician, who is confronted with emergent circumstances and provides life-sustaining treatment to a minor child, is not liable for not first obtaining consent from the parents. The Millers cite to [three state statutory provisions] as illustrating that implied consent does not arise from an emergency context when a healthcare provider has actual notice of lack of consent. Because these statutes apply when a parent is not present to consent, the Millers suggest that this must mean that emergency services cannot be provided when the parents refuse consent. But that is not so.

Providing treatment to a child under emergent circumstances does not imply consent to treatment despite actual notice of refusal to consent. Rather, it is an exception to the general rule that a physician commits a battery by providing medical treatment without consent. As such, the exception is narrowly circumscribed and arises only in emergent circumstances when there is no time to consult the parents or seek court intervention if the parents withhold consent before death is likely to result to the child. Though in situations of this character, the physician should attempt to secure parental consent if possible, the physician will not be liable under a battery or negligence theory solely for proceeding with the treatment absent consent.

We recognize that the Restatement (Second) of Torts § 892D provides that an individual is not liable for providing emergency treatment without consent if that individual has no reason to believe that the other, if he or she had the opportunity to consent, would decline. But that requirement is inapplicable here because, as we have discussed, the emergent circumstances exception does not imply consent.

Further, the emergent circumstances exception acknowledges that the harm from failing to treat outweighs any harm threatened by the proposed treatment, because the harm from failing to provide life-sustaining treatment under emergent circumstances is death. And as we acknowledged in Nelson v. Krusen, albeit in the different context of a wrongful life claim, it is impossible for the courts to calculate the relative benefits of an impaired life versus no life at all.

Following these guiding principles, we now determine whether the Millers can maintain their battery and negligence claims against HCA. The jury found that the Hospital, through Dr. Otero, treated Sidney without the Millers' consent. The parties do not challenge that finding. Thus, we only address whether the Hospital was required to seek court intervention to overturn the lack of parental consent—which it undisputedly did not do—before Dr. Otero could treat Sidney without committing a battery.

The Millers acknowledge that numerous physicians at trial agreed that, absent an emergency situation, the proper course of action is court intervention when health care providers disagree with parents' refusal to consent to a child's treatment. And the Millers contend that, as a matter of law, no emergency existed that would excuse the Hospital's treatment of Sidney without their consent or a court order overriding their refusal to consent. The Millers point out that before Sidney's birth, Drs. Jacobs and Kelley discussed with them the possibility that Sidney might suffer from the numerous physical and mental infirmities that did, in fact, afflict her. And some eleven hours before Sidney's birth, the Millers indicated that they did not want any heroic measures performed on Sidney. The Millers note that these factors prompted the dissenting justice in the court of appeals to conclude that "anytime a group of doctors and a hospital administration have the luxury of multiple meetings to change the original doctors' medical opinions, without taking a more obvious course of action, there is no medical emergency."

We agree that a physician cannot create emergent circumstances from his or her own delay or inaction and escape liability for proceeding without consent. But the Millers' reasoning fails to recognize that, in this case, the evidence established that Sidney could only be properly evaluated when she was born. Any decision the Millers made before Sidney's birth concerning her treatment at or after her birth would necessarily be based on speculation. Therefore, we reject the Millers' argument that a decision could adequately be made pre-birth that denying all post-birth resuscitative treatment would be in Sidney's best interest. Such a decision could not control whether the circumstances facing Dr. Otero were emergent because it would not have been a fully informed one according to the evidence in this case.

The Millers point out that physicians routinely ask parents to make pre-birth treatment choices for their infants including whether to accept or refuse in utero medical treatment and to continue or terminate a pregnancy. While that may be entirely true, the evidence here established that the time for evaluating Sidney was when she was born. The evidence further reflected that Sidney was born alive but in distress. At that time, Dr. Otero had to make a spilt-second decision on whether to provide life-sustaining treatment. While the Millers were both present in the delivery room, there was simply no time to obtain their consent to treatment or to institute legal proceedings to challenge their withholding of consent, had the Millers done so, without jeopardizing Sidney's life. Thus, although HCA never requested a jury instruction, nor challenged the absence of a jury instruction, on whether Dr. Otero treated Sidney under emergent circumstances, the evidence conclusively established that Dr. Otero was faced with emergent circumstances when he treated Sidney. Those circumstances resulted from not being able to evaluate Sidney until she was born, not because of any delay or inaction by HCA, the Hospital, or Dr. Otero. As HCA's expert testified:

I think the important thing to realize here is the physicians have an obligation both for assessment and treatment, and the physicians fulfilled that obligation in this case by attending the delivery, making immediate assessment and determining that the child was viable. That's an important diagnosis that the physicians—two physicians felt that Sidney had the ability to live outside the womb. Having done so, it is important that life-sustaining treatment be given on an emergent basis where that is essential to the maintenance of life, and that is what was done here. It would be improper not to order that care in [an] emergent . . . situation.

We acknowledge that certain physicians in this case initially asked the Millers to decide whether Sidney should be resuscitated some eleven hours before her birth. And certain physicians and Hospital administrators asked the Millers to consent to the subsequent plan developed to have a neonatologist present at Sidney's delivery to evaluate and possibly treat her. We agree that, whenever possible, obtaining consent in writing to evaluate a premature infant at birth and to render any warranted medical treatment is the best course of action. And physicians and hospitals should always strive to do so. But if such consent is not forthcoming, or is affirmatively denied, we decline to impose liability on a physician solely for providing life-sustaining treatment under emergent circumstances to a new-born infant without that consent. . . .

Dr. Otero provided life-sustaining treatment to Sidney under emergent circumstances as a matter of law. Those circumstances provide an exception to the general rule imposing liability on a physician for providing treatment to a minor child without first obtaining parental consent. Therefore, Dr. Otero did not commit a battery. And HCA cannot be held liable for the Millers' battery and negligence claims. We are not presented with and do not decide the question of whether the rule we have announced applies to adults. We affirm the court of appeals' judgment.

NOTE

In Broadnax v. Gonzalez, 2 N.Y.3d 148, 777 N.Y.S.2d 416, 809 N.E.2d 645 (2004), the New York Court of Appeals held that medical malpractice resulting in miscarriage or stillbirth violates a duty of care to the expectant mother, which may entitle her to damages for emotional distress even in the absence of any independent physical injury to her.

Curran v. Bosze

Supreme Court of Illinois, 1990.
141 Ill.2d 473, 153 Ill.Dec. 213, 566 N.E.2d 1319.

■ JUSTICE CALVO delivered the opinion of the court:

Allison and James Curran are 3–1/2–year–old twins. Their mother is Nancy Curran. The twins have lived with Ms. Curran and their maternal grandmother since their birth on January 27, 1987.

The twins' father is Tamas Bosze. Ms. Curran and Mr. Bosze have never been married. As a result of an action brought by Ms. Curran against Mr. Bosze concerning the paternity of the twins, both Mr. Bosze and the twins underwent a blood test in November of 1987. The blood test confirmed that Mr. Bosze is the father of the twins. On February 16, 1989, Mr. Bosze and Ms. Curran entered into an agreed order (parentage order) establishing a parent-child relationship. The parentage order states that Ms. Curran "shall have the sole care, custody, control and educational responsibility of the minor children." Section B, paragraph 4, of the order provides:

> "In all matters of importance relating to the health, welfare and education of the children, Mother shall consult and confer with Father, with a view toward adopting and following a harmonious policy. Mother shall advise Father of which school the children will attend and both parents shall be given full access to the school records of the children."

Section M of the parentage order provides that the court retain jurisdiction over the parties and subject matter for the purposes of enforcing the agreed order.

Mr. Bosze is the father of three other children: a son, age 23; Jean Pierre Bosze, age 12; and a one-year-old daughter. Ms. Curran is not the mother of any of these children. Each of these children has a different mother. Jean Pierre and the twins are half-siblings. The twins have met Jean Pierre on two occasions. Each meeting lasted approximately two hours.

Jean Pierre is suffering from acute undifferentiated leukemia (AUL), also known as mixed lineage leukemia. Mixed lineage leukemia is a rare form of leukemia which is difficult to treat. Jean Pierre was initially misdiagnosed as having acute lymphocytic leukemia (ALL) in June 1988, in Colombia, South America. Jean Pierre was brought to America in August 1988, and has been treated by Dr. Jong Kwon since that time. Jean Pierre was treated with chemotherapy and went into remission. Jean Pierre experienced a testicular relapse in January 1990, and a bone marrow relapse in mid-June 1990. Dr. Kwon has recommended a bone marrow transplant for Jean Pierre.

Mr. Bosze asked Ms. Curran to consent to a blood test for the twins in order to determine whether the twins were compatible to serve as bone marrow donors for a transplant to Jean Pierre. Mr. Bosze asked Ms. Curran to consent to the twins' undergoing a bone marrow harvesting procedure if the twins were found to be compatible. After consulting with the twins' pediatrician, family members, parents of bone marrow donors and bone marrow donors, Ms. Curran refused to give consent to the twins' undergoing either the blood test or the bone marrow harvesting procedure.

On June 28, 1990, Mr. Bosze filed an emergency petition in the circuit court of Cook County. The petition informed the court that Jean Pierre "suffers from leukemia and urgently requires a [bone] marrow transplant from a compatible donor. Without the transplant he will die in a short period of time, thereby creating an emergency involving life and death." The petition stated that persons usually compatible for serving as donors are parents or siblings of the recipient, and Jean Pierre's father, mother, and older brother had been tested and rejected as compatible donors.

According to the petition, "[t]he only siblings who have potential to be donors and who have not been tested are the children, James and Allison." The petition stated Ms. Curran refused to discuss with Mr. Bosze the matter of submitting the twins to a blood test to determine their compatibility as potential bone marrow donors for Jean Pierre. The petition stated the blood test "is minimally invasive and harmless, and no more difficult than the paternity blood testing which the children have already undergone." According to the petition, there would be no expense involved to Ms. Curran.

In the petition, Mr. Bosze requested the court find a medical emergency to exist and order and direct Ms. Curran to "forthwith produce the parties' minor children ... at Lutheran General Hospital ... for the purpose of compatibility blood testing." Further, Mr. Bosze requested in the petition that "if the children, or either of them, are compatible as donors, that the Court order and direct that [Ms. Curran] produce the children, or whichever one may be compatible, for the purpose of donating bone marrow to their sibling."

The court ordered Mr. Bosze and Ms. Curran to prepare briefs on the court's authority to grant the relief requested, and the cause was continued for presentation of medical testimony until July 2, 1990. Both Ms. Curran and Mr. Bosze testified at the hearing. Mr. Bosze called Dr. Jong Kwon, Jean Pierre's treating physician, and Mr. Steven Epstein, a 48–year–old man who had received a bone marrow transplant from his brother. Ms. Curran called Dr. Frank L. Johnson, a physician who has performed bone marrow transplants for 19 years. After hearing the testimony of the witnesses, and the arguments of counsel for both Ms. Curran and Mr. Bosze, the court ruled on July 18, 1990, that it did not have authority to grant Mr. Bosze's petition.

On July 19, 1990, Mr. Bosze filed a notice of appeal and an emergency motion for direct appeal to this court pursuant to Supreme Court Rule 302(b) (107 Ill.2d R. 302(b)). This court granted Mr. Bosze's motion on July 20, 1990.

On August 9, 1990, counsel for Mr. Bosze and Ms. Curran appeared before this court for oral argument. On August 10, 1990, this court remanded the cause to the circuit court for further proceedings. This court directed Mr. Bosze to make the twins parties-defendants to the cause, and ordered that a guardian *ad litem* be appointed to represent the twins. Mr. Bosze was further directed to make Jean Pierre a party-plaintiff to the cause, and a guardian *ad litem* was ordered to be appointed to represent Jean Pierre. Upon remand, counsel for Mr. Bosze and Ms. Curran, as well as the guardian *ad litem* for Jean Pierre and the guardian *ad litem* for the twins, were to be permitted to present further evidence.

. . .

After hearing the testimony of the witnesses, the arguments of counsel, and the arguments of the guardians *ad litem,* the circuit court denied Mr. Bosze's petition for emergency relief. . . .

Mr. Bosze and the guardian *ad litem* for Jean Pierre strenuously argue that the doctrine of substituted judgment, recognized by this court in In re Estate of Longeway (1989), 133 Ill.2d 33, 139 Ill.Dec. 780, 549 N.E.2d 292, and In re Estate of Greenspan (1990), 137 Ill.2d 1, 146 Ill.Dec. 860, 558 N.E.2d 1194, should be applied in this case to determine whether or not the twins would consent, if they were competent to do so, to the bone marrow donation if they, or either of them, were compatible with Jean Pierre. The doctrine of substituted judgment requires a surrogate decision-maker to "attempt[ ] to establish, with as much accuracy as possible, what decision the patient would make if [the patient] were competent to do so." . . .

. . .

. . . Mr. Bosze argues that the standard of the best interests of the child, traditionally the standard in cases involving minors, may not be used because this court rejected the best-interests standard in *Longeway* and *Greenspan.*

In *Longeway,* however, this court did "not pass[ ] on the viability of the best-interests theory in Illinois, [and] we decline[d] to adopt it in [that] case because we believe[d] the record demonstrate[d] the relevancy of the substituted-judgment theory." Concerning the use of the doctrine of substituted judgment, this court in *Longeway* recognized that "[a] dilemma [exists] . . . when the patient is an infant or life-long incompetent who never could have made a reasoned judgment about his [or her] quality of life." Mr. Bosze argues that this dilemma was resolved by this court in *Longeway* when it stated that "although actual, specific express intent would be helpful and compelling, the same is not necessary for the exercise of substituted judgment by a surrogate."

Immediately following this statement in *Longeway,* however, this court stated: "In this case, Mrs. Longeway's guardian must substitute her judgment for that of Longeway's, based upon other clear and convincing evidence of Longeway's intent." (Emphasis added.) This language addressed the instance where a formerly competent, now incompetent, patient had never "expressed explicit intent regarding [the] type of medical treatment prior to becoming incompetent." This language did not address the dilemma of a guardian substituting the judgment of one who never has been able to make "a reasoned judgment about his [or her] quality of life." In applying the doctrine of substituted judgment, "the key element in deciding to refuse or withdraw artificial sustenance is determining the patient's intent."

Under the doctrine of substituted judgment, a guardian of a formerly competent, now incompetent, person may look to the person's life history, in all of its diverse complexity, to ascertain the intentions and attitudes which the incompetent person once held. There must be clear and convincing evidence that the formerly competent, now incompetent, person had expressed his or her intentions and attitudes with regard to the termination of artificial nutrition and hydration before a guardian may be authorized to exercise, on behalf of the incompetent person, the right of the incompetent person to terminate artificial sustenance.

If the doctrine of substituted judgment were to be applied in this case, the guardian of the 3-1/2-year-old twins would have to substitute his or her judgment for that of the twins, based upon clear and convincing evidence of the twins' intent. Because each twin is only 3-1/2 years of age, neither has yet had the opportunity to develop "actual, specific express intent," or any other form of intent, with regard to serving as a bone marrow donor. We agree with Ms. Curran and the guardian *ad litem* for the twins that it is not possible to determine the intent of a 3-1/2-year-old child with regard to consenting to a bone marrow harvesting procedure by examining the child's personal value system. It is not possible to discover the child's " ' "likely treatment/nontreatment preferences" ' " by examining the child's " ' "philosophical, religious and moral views, life goals, values about the purpose of life and the way it should be lived, and attitudes toward sickness, medical procedures, suffering and death." ' " The twins have not yet developed the power of self-determination and are not yet capable of making an informed, rational decision based upon all the available information concerning the risks and benefits associated with serving as bone marrow donors. There is no evidence by which a guardian may be guided in ascertaining whether these 3½-year-old children, if they were adults, would or would not consent to a bone marrow harvesting procedure for another child, their half-brother whom they have met only twice.

. . .

Neither justice nor reality is served by ordering a 3½-year-old child to submit to a bone marrow harvesting procedure for the benefit of another by a purported application of the doctrine of substituted judgment. Since it is not possible to discover that which does not exist, specifically, whether the 3½

–year–old twins would consent or refuse to consent to the proposed bone marrow harvesting procedure if they were competent, the doctrine of substituted judgment is not relevant and may not be applied in this case.

Several courts from sister jurisdictions have addressed the issue whether the consent of a court, parent or guardian, for the removal of a kidney from an incompetent person for transplantation to a sibling, may be legally effective. . . .

In Strunk v. Strunk (Ky.1969), 445 S.W.2d 145, the Kentucky Court of Appeals, in a 4 to 3 decision, determined that a court of equity had the power to permit a kidney to be removed from a mentally incompetent ward of the State, upon the petition of his committee, his mother, for transplantation into his 28–year–old brother who was dying from a kidney disease. The ward of the State was a 27–year–old man who had the mental capacity of a six-year-old.

The mother petitioned the county court for authority to proceed with the kidney transplant. The county court "found that the operation was necessary, that under the peculiar circumstances of this case it would not only be beneficial to [the ward's brother] but also beneficial to [the ward] because [the ward] was greatly dependent upon [his brother], emotionally and psychologically, and that [the ward's] well-being would be jeopardized more severely by the loss of his brother than by the removal of a kidney."

Testimony before the county court included the ward's psychiatrist who opined that the death of the ward's brother would have "an extremely traumatic effect upon [the ward]." The Department of Mental Health recommended the operation take place, and stressed in its recommendation the importance of the close relationship between the two brothers. Appeal was taken to the circuit court, which adopted the findings of the county court. The circuit court "found that it would be to the best interest of the ward of the state that the procedure be carried out."

The *Strunk* court had before it the recommendation of both of the ward's parents and the Department of Mental Health that the kidney transplant take place. Also before the *Strunk* court was the incompetent person's guardian *ad litem,* who "continually questioned the power of the state to authorize the removal of an organ from the body of an incompetent who is a ward of the state." The *Strunk* court noted that the case before it was unique, and looked to the doctrine of substituted judgment for guidance.

The *Strunk* court stated:

> "The right to act for the incompetent in all cases has become recognized in this country as the doctrine of substituted judgment and is broad enough not only to cover property but also to cover all matters touching on the well-being of the ward. The doctrine has been recognized in American courts since 1844.
>
> 'The "doctrine of substituted judgment,' which apparently found its first expression in the leading English case of Ex parte Whitebread (1816) 2 Meriv 99, 35 Eng Reprint 878 (Ch), supra § 3(a), was amplified in Re Earl of Carysfort (1840) Craig & Ph 76, 41 Eng Reprint 418, where the principle was made to apply to one who was not next of kin of the lunatic but a servant of his who was obliged to retire from his service by reason of age and infirmity. The Lord Chancellor permitted the allowance of an annuity out of the income of the estate of the lunatic earl as a retiring pension to the latter's aged personal servant, although no supporting evidence could be found, the court being "satisfied that the

Earl of Carysfort would have approved if he had been capable of acting himself." ' Annot., 24 A.L.R.3d 863 (1969)."

. . .

In Little v. Little (Tex.Civ.1979), 576 S.W.2d 493, the mother of a 14–year–old mentally incompetent daughter petitioned the court to authorize the mother's consent to the removal of a kidney from her daughter for transplantation into her younger son, who suffered from a kidney disease. The mother had been appointed guardian of her mentally incompetent minor daughter. An attorney *ad litem* was appointed by the court to represent the proposed donor. The attorney *ad litem* argued there was no constitutional or statutory provision empowering the probate court to authorize the removal of an incompetent's kidney for the purpose of benefiting another person.

The mother relied on *Strunk*. The Little court discussed the doctrine of substituted judgment as it was applied in *Strunk*. The *Little* court also discussed two cases where the court refused to authorize a transplant, In re Guardianship of Pescinski (1975), 67 Wis.2d 4, 226 N.W.2d 180, and In re Richardson (La.App.1973), 284 So.2d 185.

The court in *Little* stated:

> "It is clear in transplant cases that courts, whether they use the term 'substituted judgment' or not, will consider the benefits to the donor as a basis for permitting an incompetent to donate an organ. Although in *Strunk* the Kentucky Court discussed the substituted judgment doctrine in some detail, the conclusion of the majority there was based on the benefits that the incompetent donor would derive, rather than on the theory that the incompetent would have consented to the transplant if he were competent. We adopt this approach." *Little,* 576 S.W.2d at 498.

The *Little* court determined that "the testimony ... conclusively establish[ed] the existence of a close relationship between [the proposed donor] and [her brother], a genuine concern by each for the welfare of the other and, at the very least, an awareness by [the proposed donor] of the nature of [her brother's] plight and an awareness of the fact that she is in a position to ameliorate [her brother's] burden." (*Little,* 576 S.W.2d at 498.) Both parents of the incompetent minor consented to the kidney donation; there was no evidence that the incompetent minor had been subjected to family pressure; and there were no medically preferable alternatives to the kidney transplant. The Little court also found that the dangers of the operation were minimal and there was evidence the incompetent minor would not suffer psychological harm. The kidney transplant would probably be substantially beneficial to the proposed recipient, and the trial court's decision was made "only after a full judicial proceeding in which the interests of [the incompetent minor] were championed by an attorney ad litem." (*Little,* 576 S.W.2d at 499.) The *Little* court concluded:

> "Given the presence of all the factors and circumstances outlined above, and limiting our decision to such facts and circumstances, we conclude that the trial court did not exceed its authority by authorizing the participation of [the incompetent minor] in the kidney transplant as a donor, since there is strong evidence to the effect that she will receive substantial psychological benefits from such participation. Nothing in this opinion is to be construed as being applicable to a situation where

the proposed [recipient] is not a parent or sibling of the incompetent." *Little,* 576 S.W.2d at 500.

. . .

In each of the foregoing cases where consent to the kidney transplant was authorized, regardless whether the authority to consent was to be exercised by the court, a parent or a guardian, the key inquiry was the presence or absence of a benefit to the potential donor. Notwithstanding the language used by the courts in reaching their determination that a transplant may or may not occur, the standard by which the determination was made was whether the transplant would be in the best interest of the child or incompetent person.

The primary benefit to the donor in these cases arises from the relationship existing between the donor and recipient. In *Strunk,* the donor lived in a State institution. The recipient was a brother who served as the donor's only connection with the outside world. In . . . *Little,* there was evidence that the sibling relationship between the donor and recipient was close. In each of these cases, both parents had given their consent.

We hold that a parent or guardian may give consent on behalf of a minor daughter or son for the child to donate bone marrow to a sibling, only when to do so would be in the minor's best interest.

Dr. Frank Leonard Johnson, a specialist in treating cancer in children, is the chief of pediatric hematology/oncology at the University of Chicago Medical Center, where he is in charge of the pediatric bone marrow transplant program. Dr. Johnson is also a professor of pediatrics at the University of Chicago. Dr. Johnson has been involved in bone marrow transplantations since 1971. Dr. Johnson's practice consists primarily of treating children who have cancer, including leukemia. Dr. Johnson stated he had participated in at least 500 bone marrow harvesting procedures. . . .

. . .

Concerning the risks to the bone marrow donor, Dr. Johnson testified that while the incidence of risk is not very high, the risk is medically significant. When a 3–1/2–year–old child undergoes a bone marrow harvesting procedure, the child is put under general anesthesia. Special needles are put through the skin into the hip bones at the back on both sides of the child and at the front on both sides. Dr. Johnson testified that in order to obtain the amount of bone marrow which would be necessary for a transplant to Jean Pierre, the bone would have to be punctured 100 separate times.

Dr. Johnson's personal experience was that 100% of matched adult siblings have agreed to donate bone marrow to their siblings. Dr. Johnson testified he was aware that both Jean Pierre's father and mother, and Jean Pierre, have consented to the bone marrow transplant. Further, Dr. Johnson stated that without a bone marrow transplant, he was 99% sure Jean Pierre would die. Assuming the twins were compatible as bone marrow donors, Dr. Johnson testified Jean Pierre would have a 5% chance to live, and "in my own experience I [do] not think he ha[s] a chance." If Jean Pierre were to achieve remission, Dr. Johnson stated that Jean Pierre's chances would be in the range of 10% with a bone marrow transplant.

Dr. Johnson stated that since the twins were 3–1/2–year–old children, they could legally neither give nor refuse consent to the proposed bone marrow transplant. In the absence of legally effective consent, Dr. Johnson would normally turn to the parents.

Dr. Johnson testified he had not and would not harvest bone marrow from a child when a custodial parent of the child did not consent. Dr. Johnson explained he would not do so because:

> "I think the custodial parent has a right to make a decision in a situation where we are putting that child at risk from a surgical procedure that is invasive; and admittedly, it's not a major surgical procedure, the risk from an anesthetic; and admittedly, that risk is small, but there's still a risk there.
>
> And if the parent is that concerned because we have one child who has a very little likelihood of surviving and another child—and they have any [concern] at all that they may lose that child with the procedure, in other words, possibly losing two children, then there's no way in the world that I would force them to be marrow donors."

. . .

The evidence reveals three critical factors which are necessary to a determination that it will be in the best interests of a child to donate bone marrow to a sibling. First, the parent who consents on behalf of the child must be informed of the risks and benefits inherent in the bone marrow harvesting procedure to the child.

Second, there must be emotional support available to the child from the person or persons who take care of the child. The testimony reveals that a child who is to undergo general anesthesia and the bone marrow harvesting procedure needs the emotional support of a person whom the child loves and trusts. A child who is to donate bone marrow is required to go to an unfamiliar place and meet with unfamiliar people. Depending upon the age of the child, he or she may or may not understand what is to happen. The evidence establishes that the presence and emotional support by the child's caretaker is important to ease the fears associated with such an unfamiliar procedure.

Third, there must be an existing, close relationship between the donor and recipient. The evidence clearly shows that there is no physical benefit to a donor child. If there is any benefit to a child who donates bone marrow to a sibling it will be a psychological benefit. According to the evidence, the psychological benefit is not simply one of personal, individual altruism in an abstract theoretical sense, although that may be a factor.

The psychological benefit is grounded firmly in the fact that the donor and recipient are known to each other as family. Only where there is an existing relationship between a healthy child and his or her ill sister or brother may a psychological benefit to the child from donating bone marrow to a sibling realistically be found to exist. The evidence establishes that it is the existing sibling relationship, as well as the potential for a continuing sibling relationship, which forms the context in which it may be determined that it will be in the best interests of the child to undergo a bone marrow harvesting procedure for a sibling.

Both Mr. Bosze and Ms. Curran are informed of the risks inherent in a bone marrow harvesting procedure performed on a child. Mr. Bosze has consulted with Dr. Kwon, Jean Pierre's treating physician. Ms. Curran has consulted with the twins' pediatrician, parents of bone marrow donors, and bone marrow donors. Both Ms. Curran and Mr. Bosze listened to Drs. Johnson, Kwon, Leventhal, Lechtor, Camitta, and Kohrman.

The primary risk to a bone marrow donor is the risk associated with undergoing general anesthesia. The risk of a life-threatening complication occurring from undergoing general anesthesia is 1 in 10,000. As noted by the circuit court, the risks associated with general anesthesia include, but are not limited to, "brain damage as a result of oxygen deprivation, stroke, cardiac arrest and death."

The pain following the harvesting procedure is usually easily controlled with post-operative medication. Although there is a risk of infection at the needle puncture site, this is rare.

Ms. Curran has refused consent on behalf of the twins to the bone marrow transplant because she does not think it is in their best interests to subject them to the risks and pains involved in undergoing general anesthesia and the harvesting procedure. While Ms. Curran is aware that the risks involved in donating bone marrow and undergoing general anesthesia are small, she also is aware that when such risk occurs, it may be life-threatening.

On February 16, 1989, Mr. Bosze and Ms. Curran agreed in the parentage order that Ms. Curran would have sole custody of the twins. Allison and James have lived with Ms. Curran and their maternal grandmother since their birth. Mr. Bosze and Ms. Curran also agreed that Mr. Bosze would have visitation rights with the twins. Until the twins reached the age of five years, Mr. Bosze would have visitation once a week. Ms. Curran was to be present during the visitation.

Between February 16, 1989, and February 14, 1990, Mr. Bosze exercised his visitation rights 15 times. On two of these occasions, Jean Pierre was present. Before Mr. Bosze ever requested Ms. Curran to consent to the twins' donating bone marrow to Jean Pierre, Ms. Curran requested that Mr. Bosze not tell the twins that Jean Pierre was their half-brother. Ms. Curran thought that it would be confusing to the twins to be told that they have two half-brothers and a half-sister, each of whom had a different mother. Mr. Bosze honored this request.

It is a fact that the twins and Jean Pierre share the same biological father. There was no evidence produced, however, to indicate that the twins and Jean Pierre are known to each other as family.

Allison and James would need the emotional support of their primary caregiver if they were to donate bone marrow. The evidence establishes that it would not be in a 3–1/2–year–old child's best interests if he or she were required to go to a hospital and undergo all that is involved with the bone marrow harvesting procedure without the constant reassurance and support by a familiar adult known and trusted by the child.

Not only is Ms. Curran presently the twins' primary caretaker, the evidence establishes she is the only caretaker the twins have ever known. Ms. Curran has refused to consent to the twins' participation in donating bone marrow to Jean Pierre. It appears that Mr. Bosze would be unable to substitute his support for the procedure for that of Ms. Curran because his involvement in the lives of Allison and James has, to this point, been a limited one.

The guardian *ad litem* for the twins recommends that it is not in the best interests of either Allison or James to undergo the proposed bone marrow harvesting procedure in the absence of an existing, close relationship with the recipient, Jean Pierre, and over the objection of their primary caretaker, Ms. Curran. Because the evidence presented supports this recommendation, we agree.

. . .

This court shares the opinion of the circuit court that Jean Pierre's situation "evokes sympathy from all who've heard [it]." No matter how small the hope that a bone marrow transplant will cure Jean Pierre, the fact remains that without the transplant, Jean Pierre will almost certainly die. The sympathy felt by this court, the circuit court, and all those who have learned of Jean Pierre's tragic situation cannot, however, obscure the fact that, under the circumstances presented in the case at bar, it neither would be proper under existing law nor in the best interests of the 3–1/2–year–old twins for the twins to participate in the bone marrow harvesting procedure.

On September 28, 1990, this court entered an order affirming the judgment of the circuit court, with opinion to follow, and now for the foregoing reasons, we reaffirm our previous order. For purposes of computing time limits for any further proceedings, the date of the filing of this opinion shall control.

Circuit court affirmed.

NOTE

Non-therapeutic research on children poses very difficult questions. Some professionals argue that no one can give consent for a child in such a situation. See, e.g., Paul Ramsey, The Patient as Person 17 (1970). Needless to say, this approach would make it impossible to test many drugs for use by children. Compare the position of the Judicial Council of the American Medical Association:

> Consent [may be] given by a legally authorized representative of the subject under circumstances in which an informed and prudent adult would reasonably be expected to volunteer himself or his child as a subject.

Ramsey's position has been challenged by Richard McCormick in Proxy Consent in the Experimentation Situation, 18 Perspectives in Biology and Medicine 2, 13–14 (1974):

> To share in the general effort and burden of health maintenance and disease control is part of our flourishing and growth as humans. To the extent that it is a good for all of us to share this burden, we all *ought* to do so and to the extent that we *ought* to do so, it is reasonable construction or presumption of our wishes to say that we would do so. The reasonableness of this presumption validates vicarious consent.... Concretely, when a particular experiment would involve no discernable risks, no notable pain, no notable inconvenience, and yet holds promise of considerable benefit, should not the child be constructed to wish this in the same way we presume he chooses his own life, because he *ought* to. I believe so.

The way Ramsey and McCormick evaluate particular nontherapeutic actions is not necessarily as far apart as their philosophic explanations might suggest. McCormick, for example, defines "no discernible risk" quite strictly and concludes that parental consent for a kidney transplant from one 3 year old to another is without moral justification. For a more detailed look at the problems of experimenting on children see Lawrence Gostin, Judith Areen, Patricia A. King, Steven Goldberg, and Peter D. Jacobson, Law, Science and Medicine 967–971 (3rd Ed. 2005).

D. THE CHILD BORN OUT OF WEDLOCK

Lalli v. Lalli

Supreme Court of the United States, 1978.
439 U.S. 259, 99 S.Ct. 518, 58 L.Ed.2d 503.

■ JUSTICE POWELL announced the judgment of the Court in an opinion, in which THE CHIEF JUSTICE and JUSTICE STEWART join.

This case presents a challenge to the constitutionality of § 4–1.2 of New York's Estates, Powers, and Trusts Law, which requires illegitimate children who would inherit from their fathers by intestate succession to provide a particular form of proof of paternity. Legitimate children are not subject to the same requirement.

Appellant Robert Lalli claims to be the illegitimate son of Mario Lalli who died intestate on January 7, 1973, in the State of New York. Appellant's mother, who died in 1968, never was married to Mario. After Mario's widow, Rosamond Lalli, was appointed administratrix of her husband's estate, appellant petitioned the Surrogate's Court for Westchester County for a compulsory accounting, claiming that he and his sister Maureen Lalli were entitled to inherit from Mario as his children. Rosamond Lalli opposed the petition. She argued that even if Robert and Maureen were Mario's children, they were not lawful distributees of the estate because they had failed to comply with § 4–1.2, which provides in part:

> "An illegitimate child is the legitimate child of his father so that he and his issue inherit from his father if a court of competent jurisdiction has, during the lifetime of the father, made an order of filiation declaring paternity in a proceeding instituted during the pregnancy of the mother or within two years from the birth of the child."

Appellant conceded that he had not obtained an order of filiation during his putative father's lifetime. He contended, however, that § 4–1.2, by imposing this requirement, discriminated against him on the basis of his illegitimate birth in violation of the Equal Protection Clause of the Fourteenth Amendment. Appellant tendered certain evidence of his relationship with Mario Lalli, including a notarized document in which Lalli, in consenting to appellant's marriage, referred to him as "my son," and several affidavits by persons who stated that Lalli had acknowledged openly and often that Robert and Maureen were his children.

. . .

After reviewing recent decisions of this Court concerning discrimination against illegitimate children . . . the [lower] court ruled that appellant was properly excluded as a distributee of Lalli's estate and therefore lacked status to petition for a compulsory accounting.

On direct appeal the New York Court of Appeals affirmed. . . .

. . .

. . . We now affirm.

. . .

We begin our analysis with Trimble [v. Gordon, 430 U.S. 762 (1977)]. At issue in that case was the constitutionality of an Illinois statute providing that a child born out of wedlock could inherit from his intestate father only if the father had "acknowledged" the child and the child had been legitimated by the intermarriage of the parents. The appellant in *Trimble* was a child born out of wedlock whose father had neither acknowledged her nor married her mother. He had, however, been found to be her father in a judicial decree ordering him to contribute to her support. When the father died intestate, the child was excluded as a distributee because the statutory requirements for inheritance had not been met.

We concluded that the Illinois statute discriminated against illegitimate children in a manner prohibited by the Equal Protection Clause. Although

... classifications based on illegitimacy are not subject to "strict scrutiny," they nevertheless are invalid under the Fourteenth Amendment if they are not substantially related to permissible state interests. Upon examination, we found that the Illinois law failed that test.

Two state interests were proposed which the statute was said to foster: the encouragement of legitimate family relationships and the maintenance of an accurate and efficient method of disposing of an intestate decedent's property. Granting that the State was appropriately concerned with the integrity of the family unit, we viewed the statute as bearing "only the most attenuated relationship to the asserted goal." We again rejected the argument that "persons will shun illicit relations because the offspring may not one day reap the benefits" that would accrue to them were they legitimate. Weber v. Aetna Casualty & Surety Co., 406 U.S. 164, 173 (1972). The statute therefore was not defensible as an incentive to enter legitimate family relationships.

Illinois' interest in safeguarding the orderly disposition of property at death was more relevant to the statutory classification. We recognized that devising "an appropriate legal framework" in the furtherance of that interest "is a matter particularly within the competence of the individual States." An important aspect of that framework is a response to the often difficult problem of proving the paternity of illegitimate children and the related danger of spurious claims against intestate estates. These difficulties, we said, "might justify a more demanding standard for illegitimate children claiming under their fathers' estates than that required either for illegitimate children claiming under their mothers' estates or for legitimate children generally."

Under § 4–1.2, by contrast, the marital status of the parents is irrelevant. The single requirement at issue here is an evidentiary one—that the paternity of the father be declared in a judicial proceeding sometime before his death.[5] The child need not have been legitimated in order to inherit from his father. Had the appellant in Trimble been governed by § 4–1.2, she would have been a distributee of her father's estate.

A related difference between the two provisions pertains to the state interests said to be served by them. The Illinois law was defended, in part, as a means of encouraging legitimate family relationships. No such justification has been offered in support of § 4–1.2. The Court of Appeals disclaimed that the purpose of the statute, "even in small part, was to discourage illegitimacy, to mold human conduct or to set societal norms." The absence in § 4–1.2 of any requirement that the parents intermarry or otherwise legitimate a child born out of wedlock and our review of the legislative history of the statute confirm this view.

Our inquiry, therefore, is focused narrowly. We are asked to decide whether the discrete procedural demands that § 4–1.2 places on illegitimate children bear an evident and substantial relation to the particular state interests this statute is designed to serve.

. . .

5. Section 4–1.2 requires not only that the order of filiation be made during the lifetime of the father, but that the proceeding in which it is sought be commenced "during the pregnancy of the mother or within two years from the birth of the child." ... As the New York Court of Appeals has not passed upon the constitutionality of the two-year limitation, that question is not before us. Our decision today therefore sustains § 4–1.2 under the Equal Protection Clause only with respect to its requirement that a judicial order of filiation be issued during the lifetime of the father of an illegitimate child.

The primary state goal underlying the challenged aspects of § 4–1.2 is to provide for the just and orderly disposition of property at death. We long have recognized that this is an area with which the States have an interest of considerable magnitude. . . .

This interest is directly implicated in paternal inheritance by illegitimate children because of the peculiar problems of proof that are involved. Establishing maternity is seldom difficult. As one New York Surrogate's Court has observed, "the birth of the child is a recorded or registered event usually taking place in the presence of others. In most cases the child remains with the mother and for a time is necessarily reared by her. That the child is the child of a particular woman is rarely difficult to prove." In re Oritz, 60 Misc.2d 756, 761, 303 N.Y.S.2d 806, 812 (1969). Proof of paternity, by contrast, frequently is difficult when the father is not part of a formal family unit. "The putative father often goes his way unconscious of the birth of a child. Even if conscious, he is very often totally unconcerned because of the absence of any ties to the mother. Indeed the mother may not know *who* is responsible for her pregnancy." . . .

Thus, a number of problems arise that counsel against treating illegitimate children identically to all other heirs of an intestate father. These were the subject of a comprehensive study by the Temporary State Commission on the Modernization, Revision and Simplification of the Law of Estates. This group, known as the Bennett Commission, consisted of individuals experienced in the practical problems of estate administration. The Commission issued its report and recommendations to the Legislature in 1965. See Fourth Report of the Temporary State Commission on the Modernization, Revision and Simplification of the Law of Estates, Legis.Doc. No. 19 (1965) (hereinafter Commission Report). The statute now codified as § 4–1.2 was included.

. . .

As the State's interests are substantial, we now consider the means adopted by New York to further these interests. In order to avoid the problems described above, the Commission recommended a requirement designed to ensure the accurate resolution of claims of paternity and to minimize the potential for disruption of estate administration. Accuracy is enhanced by placing paternity disputes in a judicial forum during the lifetime of the father. As the New York Court of Appeals observed in its first opinion in this case, the "availability [of the putative father] should be a substantial factor contributing to the reliability of the fact-finding process." In addition, requiring that the order be issued during the father's lifetime permits a man to defend his reputation against "unjust accusations in paternity claims," which was a secondary purpose of § 4–1.2. Commission Report 266.

The administration of an estate will be facilitated, and the possibility of delay and uncertainty minimized, where the entitlement of an illegitimate child to notice and participation is a matter of judicial record before the administration commences. Fraudulent assertions of paternity will be much less likely to succeed, or even to arise, where the proof is put before a court of law at a time when the putative father is available to respond, rather than first brought to light when the distribution of the assets of an estate is in the offing.[18]

18. In affirming the judgment below, we do not, of course, restrict a State's freedom to require proof of paternity by means other than a judicial decree. Thus a State may pre-

Appellant contends that § 4–1.2, like the statute at issue in *Trimble,* excludes "significant categories of illegitimate children" who could be allowed to inherit "without jeopardizing the orderly settlement" of their intestate fathers' estates. He urges that those in his position—"known" illegitimate children who, despite the absence of an order of filiation obtained during their fathers' lifetimes, can present convincing proof of paternity—cannot rationally be denied inheritance as they post none of the risks § 4–1.2 was intended to minimize.

We do not question that there will be some illegitimate children who would be able to establish their relationship to their deceased fathers without serious disruption of the administration of estates and that, as applied to such individuals § 4–1.2 appears to operate unfairly. But few statutory classifications are entirely free from the criticism that they sometimes produce inequitable results. Our inquiry under the Equal Protection Clause does not focus on the abstract "fairness" of a state law, but on whether the statute's relation to the state interests it is intended to promote is so tenuous that it lacks the rationality contemplated by the Fourteenth Amendment.

The Illinois statute in *Trimble* was constitutionally unacceptable because it effected a total statutory disinheritance of children born out of wedlock who were not legitimated by the subsequent marriage of their parents. The reach of the statute was far in excess of its justifiable purposes. Section 4–1.2 does not share this defect. Inheritance is barred only where there has been a failure to secure evidence of paternity during the father's lifetime in the manner prescribed by the State. This is not a requirement that inevitably disqualifies an unnecessarily large number of children born out of wedlock.

The New York courts have interpreted § 4–1.2 liberally and in such a way as to enhance its utility to both father and children without sacrificing its strength as a procedural prophylactic. For example, a father of illegitimate children who is willing to acknowledge paternity can waive his defenses in a paternity proceeding, . . . or even institute such a proceeding himself.[19] In addition, the courts have excused "technical" failures by illegitimate children to comply with the statute in order to prevent unnecessary injustice. . . .

. . .

Even if, as Justice Brennan believes, § 4–1.2 could have been written somewhat more equitably, it is not the function of a court "to hypothesize independently on the desirability or feasibility of any possible alternative[s]" to the statutory scheme formulated by New York. "These matters of practical judgment and empirical calculation are for [the State]. . . . In the end, the precise accuracy of [the State's] calculations is not a matter of specialized judicial competence; and we have no basis to question their detail beyond the evident consistency and substantiality."

We conclude that the requirement imposed by § 4–1.2 on illegitimate children who would inherit from their fathers is substantially related to the important state interests the statute is intended to promote. We therefore find no violation of the Equal Protection Clause.

scribe any *formal* method of proof, whether it be similar to that provided by § 4–1.2 or some other regularized procedure that would assure the authenticity of the acknowledgment. As we noted in Trimble, 430 U.S., at 772 n. 14, such a procedure would be sufficient to satisfy the State's interests. . . .

19. In addition to making intestate succession possible, of course, a father is always free to provide for his illegitimate child by will.

The judgment of the New York Court of Appeals is

Affirmed.

Clark v. Jeter

Supreme Court of the United States, 1988.
486 U.S. 456, 108 S.Ct. 1910, 100 L.Ed.2d 465.

■ Justice O'Connor delivered the opinion of the Court.

Under Pennsylvania law, an illegitimate child must prove paternity before seeking support from his or her father, and a suit to establish paternity ordinarily must be brought within six years of an illegitimate child's birth. By contrast, a legitimate child may seek support from his or her parents at any time. We granted certiorari to consider the constitutionality of this legislative scheme.

On September 22, 1983, petitioner Cherlyn Clark filed a support complaint in the Allegheny County Court of Common Pleas on behalf of her minor daughter, Tiffany, who was born out of wedlock on June 11, 1973. Clark named respondent Gene Jeter as Tiffany's father. The court ordered blood tests, which showed a 99.3% probability that Jeter is Tiffany's father.

Jeter moved to dismiss the complaint on the ground that it was barred by the 6–year statute of limitations for paternity actions. In her response, Clark contended that this statute is unconstitutional under the Equal Protection and Due Process Clauses of the Fourteenth Amendment....

. . .

In considering whether state legislation violates the Equal Protection Clause of the Fourteenth Amendment, U.S. Const., Amdt. 14, § 1, we apply different levels of scrutiny to different types of classifications. At a minimum, a statutory classification must be rationally related to a legitimate governmental purpose. Classifications based on race or national origin, and classifications affecting fundamental rights, are given the most exacting scrutiny. Between these extremes of rational basis review and strict scrutiny lies a level of intermediate scrutiny, which generally has been applied to discriminatory classifications based on sex or illegitimacy.

To withstand intermediate scrutiny, a statutory classification must be substantially related to an important governmental objective. Consequently we have invalidated classifications that burden illegitimate children for the sake of punishing the illicit relations of their parents, because "visiting this condemnation on the head of an infant is illogical and unjust." Weber v. Aetna Casualty & Surety Co., 406 U.S. 164, 175 (1972). Yet, in the seminal case concerning the child's right to support, this Court acknowledged that it might be appropriate to treat illegitimate children differently in the support context because of "lurking problems with respect to proof of paternity." Gomez v. Perez, 409 U.S. 535, 538 (1973).

This Court has developed a particular framework for evaluating equal protection challenges to statutes of limitations that apply to suits to establish paternity, and thereby limit the ability of illegitimate children to obtain support.

> "First, the period for obtaining support ... must be sufficiently long in duration to present a reasonable opportunity for those with an interest in such children to assert claims on their behalf. Second, any time

limitation placed on that opportunity must be substantially related to the State's interest in avoiding the litigation of stale or fraudulent claims." Mills v. Habluetzel, 456 U.S. 91, 99–100 (1982).

In *Mills,* we held that Texas' 1–year statute of limitations failed both steps of the analysis. We explained that paternity suits typically will be brought by the child's mother, who might not act swiftly amidst the emotional and financial complications of the child's first year. And, it is unlikely that the lapse of a mere 12 months will result in the loss of evidence or appreciably increase the likelihood of fraudulent claims. A concurring opinion in *Mills* explained why statutes of limitations longer than one year also may be unconstitutional. (O'Connor, J., joined by Burger, C.J., Brennan and Blackmun, JJ., and joined as to Part I by Powell, J., concurring). First, the State has a countervailing interest in ensuring that genuine claims for child support are satisfied. Second, the fact that Texas tolled most other causes of action during a child's minority suggested that proof problems do not become overwhelming during this period. Finally, the practical obstacles to filing a claim for support are likely to continue after the first year of the child's life.

In Pickett v. Brown, 462 U.S. 1 (1983), the Court unanimously struck down Tennessee's 2–year statute of limitations for paternity and child support actions brought on behalf of certain illegitimate children. Adhering to the analysis developed in *Mills,* the Court first considered whether two years afforded a reasonable opportunity to bring such suits. The Tennessee statute was relatively more generous than the Texas statute considered in *Mills* because it did not limit actions against a father who had acknowledged his paternity in writing or by furnishing support; nor did it apply if the child was likely to become a public charge. Nevertheless, the Court concluded that the 2–year period was too short in light of the persisting financial and emotional problems that are likely to afflict the child's mother. Proceeding to the second step of the analysis, the Court decided that the 2–year statute of limitations was not substantially related to Tennessee's asserted interest in preventing stale and fraudulent claims. The period during which suit could be brought was only a year longer than the period considered in *Mills,* and this incremental difference would not create substantially greater proof and fraud problems. Furthermore, Tennessee tolled most other actions during a child's minority, and even permitted a support action to be brought on behalf of a child up to 18 years of age if the child was or was likely to become a public charge. Finally, scientific advances in blood testing had alleviated some problems of proof in paternity actions. For these reasons, the Tennessee statute failed to survive heightened scrutiny under the Equal Protection Clause.

In light of this authority, we conclude that Pennsylvania's 6–year statute of limitations violates the Equal Protection Clause. Even six years does not necessarily provide a reasonable opportunity to assert a claim on behalf of an illegitimate child. "The unwillingness of the mother to file a paternity action on behalf of her child, which could stem from her relationship with the natural father or ... from the emotional strain of having an illegitimate child, or even from the desire to avoid community and family disapproval, may continue years after the child is born. The problem may be exacerbated if, as often happens, the mother herself is a minor." *Mills,* supra, at 105, n. 4. (O'Connor, J., concurring). Not all of these difficulties are likely to abate in six years. A mother might realize only belatedly "a loss of income attributable to the need to care for the child," *Pickett,* supra, 462 U.S. at 12. Furthermore, financial difficulties are likely to increase as the child matures and incurs expenses for clothing, school, and medical care. See, e.g., Moore v. McNamara, 40 Conn.Supp. 6, 11–12, 478 A.2d 634, 637 (1984) (invalidating a 3–year statute of limitations). Thus it is questionable whether a State acts reasonably when it requires most paternity and support actions to be brought within six years of an illegitimate child's birth.

We do not rest our decision on this ground, however, for it is not entirely evident that six years would necessarily be an unreasonable limitations period for child support actions involving illegitimate children. We are, however, confident that the 6–year statute of limitations is not substantially related to Pennsylvania's interest in avoiding the litigation of stale or fraudulent claims. In a number of circumstances, Pennsylvania permits the issue of paternity to be litigated more than six years after the birth of an illegitimate child. The statute itself permits a suit to be brought more than six years after the child's birth if it is brought within two years of a support payment made by the father. And in other types of suits, Pennsylvania places no limits on when the issue of paternity may be litigated. For example, the intestacy statute, 20 Pa.Cons.Stat. § 2107(3) (1982), permits a child born out of wedlock to establish paternity as long as "there is clear and convincing evidence that the man was the father of the child." Likewise, no statute of limitations applies to a father's action to establish paternity. Recently, the Pennsylvania Legislature enacted a statute that tolls most other civil actions during a child's minority. 42 Pa.Cons.Stat. § 5533(b) (Supp.1987). In *Pickett* and *Mills,* similar tolling statutes cast doubt on the State's purported interest in avoiding the litigation of stale or fraudulent claims. Pennsylvania's tolling statute has the same implications here.

A more recent indication that Pennsylvania does not consider proof problems insurmountable is the enactment by the Pennsylvania Legislature in 1985 of an 18–year statute of limitations for paternity and support actions. 23 Pa.Cons.Stat. § 4343(b) (1985). To be sure the legislature did not act spontaneously, but rather under the threat of losing some federal funds. Nevertheless, the new statute is a tacit concession that proof problems are not overwhelming. The legislative history of the federal Child Support Enforcement Amendments explains why Congress thought such statutes of limitations are reasonable. Congress adverted to the problem of stale and fraudulent claims, but recognized that increasingly sophisticated tests for genetic markers permit the exclusion of over 99% of those who might be accused of paternity, regardless of the age of the child. H.R.Rep. No. 98–527, p. 38 (1983). This scientific evidence is available throughout the child's minority, and it is an additional reason to doubt that Pennsylvania had a substantial reason for limiting the time within which paternity and support actions could be brought.

We conclude that the Pennsylvania statute does not withstand heightened scrutiny under the Equal Protection Clause.... The judgment of the Superior Court is reversed and the case is remanded for further proceedings not inconsistent with this opinion.

It is so ordered.

NOTE

Paternity litigation has been transformed by advancements in science. Although courts relied on HLA (human leucocyte antigen) tests for several decades to determine the likelihood of paternity, courts often expressed concern that the HLA test was not 100% accurate. See, e.g., Brinkley v. King, 549 Pa. 241, 254, 701 A.2d 176,

182 (1997) (Nigro, J., concurring and dissenting) citing John M. v. Paula T., 524 Pa. 306, 316, 571 A.2d 1380, 1385 (1990), and Smith v. Shaffer, 511 Pa. 421, 515 A.2d 527 (1986).

With the development of DNA testing, accuracy has improved significantly, but there is still the problem of human error. In Las Vegas in 2001, a man spent a year in jail after being wrongly convicted of committing two sexual assaults. Investigators later determined that his DNA sample had been switched with another inmate's. Tom Jackman, Paternity Suit Raises Doubts About DNA Tests, Wash. Post, August 21, 2005 at C1. See generally, Mary R. Anderlik and Mark A. Rothstein, The Genetics Revolution: Conflicts, Challenges and Conundra, 28 Am. J. L. and Med. 215 (2002); Elizabeth Bartholet Guiding Principles for Picking Parents, 27 Harv. Women's L.J. 323 (Spring 2004); Donald Hubin, Daddy Dilemmas: Untangling the Puzzles of Paternity, 12 Cornell J. L. & Pol'y 29 (2003).

People in Interest of S.P.B.

Supreme Court of Colorado, 1982.
651 P.2d 1213.

■ Dubofsky, Justice.

P.D.G., the natural father of S.P.B., appeals a child support order of the El Paso County District Court. P.D.G. questions whether the constitutional rights to due process and equal protection of the laws under the state and federal constitutions are violated by the Uniform Parentage Act (UPA), section 19–6–101, et seq., C.R.S.1973 (1978 Repl.Vol. 8), which imposes the duty of child support upon both parents without according the father a right either to decide that the fetus should be aborted or to later avoid child support obligations by showing that he offered to pay for an abortion. ...

The issue underlying this appeal arose in the course of a proceeding to determine the paternity of and support for S.P.B., a child. The respondent-appellant P.D.G. admitted to paternity of S.P.B. but denied any obligation to support the child. P.D.G. and the child's mother, C.F.B., have never married and are not presently living together. P.D.G. asserts that when C.F.B. informed him that she was pregnant, he responded that he did not want her to have the baby and offered to pay for an abortion. P.D.G. claims that this exchange took place within the first trimester of C.F.B.'s pregnancy. C.F.B. did not agree to an abortion and subsequently gave birth to S.P.B. C.F.B. has had custody of S.P.B. since birth.

... The district court ... ordered P.D.G. to pay child support in the amount of $150 per month and one-half of the birth expenses of the child.

At the outset it is important to point out what is not at issue here. There is no question but that the duty to support a child falls upon both its parents. It is equally clear that this obligation of support extends to all parents, regardless of their marital status. Illegitimate children have the same judicially enforceable right to support as do legitimate children.

The crux of P.D.G.'s equal protection argument is that the UPA, while gender-neutral on its face, operates to deny him equal protection by implicitly accommodating the decision of C.F.B. to carry the fetus to term while ignoring his own express desire that the pregnancy be terminated.

Gender-based distinctions must serve important governmental objectives, and a discriminatory classification must be substantially related to the achievement of those objectives in order to withstand judicial scrutiny under the equal protection clause. Mississippi University for Women v. Hogan, 458

U.S. 718 (1982). The General Assembly articulated the state's objective in promulgating the UPA in section 19-1-102 of the Children's Code, of which the UPA is a part. The objective includes:

> (1)(a) To secure for each child subject to these provisions such care and guidance, preferably in his own home, as will best serve his welfare and the interests of society....

We recognized the importance of the state's interest in promoting the welfare of the child in R. McG. v. J.W., [200 Colo. 345, 615 P.2d 666 (1980)]. The appellant does not dispute the significance of the state's objective.

The state has little choice in the means employed to achieve its objective. The statute's tacit accommodation of the mother's decision not to terminate her pregnancy is the only constitutional course open to the state. A woman has a fundamental right to decide in conjunction with her physician whether to terminate her pregnancy. Roe v. Wade, 410 U.S. 113 (1973). Further, the United States Supreme Court declared in Maher v. Roe, 432 U.S. 464, 472, n. 7 (1977), "A woman has at least an equal right to choose to carry the fetus to term as to choose to abort it." In Planned Parenthood of Missouri v. Danforth, 428 U.S. 52, 69 (1976), the United States Supreme Court ruled that the "state cannot delegate to a spouse a veto power which the state itself is absolutely and totally prohibited from exercising during the first trimester of pregnancy." Here, the equal treatment which appellant seeks could only be achieved by according a father the right to compel the mother of his child to procure an abortion. This result is clearly foreclosed by *Roe, Maher,* and *Danforth.* As the Supreme Court noted in Danforth, 428 U.S. at 71, "The obvious fact is that when the wife and the husband disagree on this decision, the view of only one of the two partners can prevail. Inasmuch as it is the woman who bears the child and who is the more directly and immediately affected by the pregnancy, as between the two, the balance weighs in her favor."

Thus, at no stage does the appellant's right to be free from gender-based classifications outweigh the substantial and legitimate competing interest. The appellant's right is overridden prior to childbirth by the state's interest in protecting C.F.B.'s fundamental right to make decisions relating to her pregnancy, and thereafter by the state's interest in ensuring that children receive adequate support. We find no violation of equal protection in the statutory obligation of both parents to pay child support or in the denial to the appellant of the right to demand the termination of C.F.B.'s pregnancy.

The appellant claims that section 19-6-116 violates due process by creating an irrebuttable presumption that a father should share in the duty of child support.[10] He submits that so long as there existed an unalterable nexus between conception and childbirth, the presumption was valid, but contends that the current availability of legalized abortion creates the possibility of demonstrating that the nexus has been broken. In support of his position that he should not shoulder any of the responsibility for support of S.P.B., the appellant made an offer of proof in district court that he had promised to pay for an abortion within the first trimester of C.F.B.'s pregnancy. The appellant argues that the statute must, consistent with due process considerations, provide him an opportunity to rebut the presumption.

10. Section 19-6-116(5) leaves open the possibility that either parent may demonstrate a financial inability to contribute to child support....

Statutes creating permanent irrebuttable presumptions have long been disfavored under the due process clauses of the Fifth and Fourteenth Amendments to the United States Constitution. Vlandis v. Kline, 412 U.S. 441 (1973). . . .

A statutory presumption can be invalidated only when a two-pronged test is met: when the presumption is not necessarily or universally true and when the state has reasonable alternative means of making the crucial determination. *Vlandis*, 412 U.S. at 452. Because the appellant's challenge to the child support statute fails to satisfy the second element of the *Vlandis* test, we need not examine the first.

The statutory presumption of a shared parental obligation of child support protects three critical interests: the interest of the child in receiving adequate support, the interest of the state in ensuring that children not become its wards, and the interest of the parents in being free from governmental intrusion into the intimate sphere of family life. In view of these critical functions, the state has no "reasonable alternative means of making the crucial determination" that a nexus exists between conception and childbirth. The alternative, which the appellant propounds, is a case-by-case determination of whether the presumed nexus was broken by the father's offer to pay for an abortion, by prior agreement between the parties, by a subsequent "release" of one party's obligation by another, or by any of a multitude of legal theories which ingenious litigants and their lawyers might advance. A judicial inquiry of this nature represents unconscionable governmental interference with privacy rights which the Supreme Court has deemed inviolate.

There are additional untoward consequences which lurk behind the establishment of a rule of law that fathers could avoid the obligation to support their children in the manner suggested by appellant. Once the criteria for proving a firm offer of an abortion had been enunciated, any man could forever escape this duty simply by making the offer in the prescribed manner. Taking this theory to its logical extreme, a woman could similarly avoid her obligation of support by proving that she had made a firm offer to procure an abortion and that the father, by declining it, assumed all responsibility for their child. The statutory presumption that parents who have participated in the conception of a child assume a joint responsibility for that child reflects the well-considered judgment of the legislature as to the only feasible means of achieving legitimate societal goals. The presumption embodied in section 19–6–116 furthers the substantial interests which the state has in protecting the respective rights of children, of parents, and of itself. Therefore, we conclude that the presumption contained in section 19–6–116 does not deny due process to the appellant.

. . .

NOTE

Compare the resolution in In re Pamela P. v. Frank S., 110 Misc.2d 978, 443 N.Y.S.2d 343 (Fam.Ct., New York County 1981), where the court found clear and convincing evidence that petitioner falsely told respondent that she was "on the pill." The court concluded:

> [S]ince it is consistent with the support rulings in this State to give weight to petitioner's deceit ... it is in this court's opinion constitutional to deny her application for child support provided that the basic objective of satisfying the child's fair and reasonable needs can be met. Accordingly, under a reasonable

> and valid accommodation of principles, a support order will be entered against respondent only if petitioner's means are insufficient to answer such need.

110 Misc.2d at 985, 443 N.Y.S.2d at 348. The holding was reversed on appeal, 88 A.D.2d 865, 451 N.Y.S.2d 766 (1982), affirmed 59 N.Y.2d 1, 462 N.Y.S.2d 819, 449 N.E.2d 713 (1983). Accord Hughes v. Hutt, 500 Pa. 209, 455 A.2d 623 (1983); Linda D. v. Fritz C., 38 Wash.App. 288, 687 P.2d 223 (1984). Cf. Stephen K. v. Roni L., 105 Cal.App.3d 640, 164 Cal.Rptr. 618 (1980) (plaintiff cannot sue defendant in tort for birth of child conceived when he relied on her false representation that contraceptive measures had been taken because "claims such as those presented ... arise from conduct so intensely private that the courts should not be asked nor attempt to resolve such claims.")

E. THE EXTENDED FAMILY

Moore v. City of East Cleveland

Supreme Court of the United States, 1977.
431 U.S. 494, 97 S.Ct. 1932, 52 L.Ed.2d 531.

■ JUSTICE POWELL announced the judgment of the Court, and delivered an opinion in which JUSTICE BRENNAN, JUSTICE MARSHALL, and JUSTICE BLACKMUN joined.

East Cleveland's housing ordinance, like many throughout the country, limits occupancy of a dwelling unit to members of a single family. But the ordinance contains an unusual and complicated definitional section that recognizes as a "family" only a few categories of related individuals. § 1341.08.[2] Because her family, living together in her home, fits none of those categories, appellant stands convicted of a criminal offense. The question in this case is whether the ordinance violates the Due Process Clause of the Fourteenth Amendment.

Appellant, Mrs. Inez Moore, lives in her East Cleveland home together with her son, Dale Moore, Sr., and her two grandsons, Dale, Jr., and John Moore, Jr. The two boys are first cousins rather than brothers; we are told that John came to live with his grandmother and with the elder and younger Dale Moores after his mother's death.

In early 1973, Mrs. Moore received a notice of violation from the city, stating that John was an "illegal occupant" and directing her to comply with

2. Section 1341.08 (1966) provides:

" 'Family' means a number of individuals related to the nominal head of the household or to the spouse of the nominal head of the household living as a single housekeeping unit in a single dwelling unit, but limited to the following:

"(a) Husband or wife of the nominal head of the household.

"(b) Unmarried children of the nominal head of the household or of the spouse of the nominal head of the household, provided, however, that such unmarried children have no children residing with them.

"(c) Father or mother of the nominal head of the household or of the spouse of the nominal head of the household.

"(d) Notwithstanding the provisions of subsection (b) hereof, a family may include not more than one dependent married or unmarried child of the nominal head of the household or of the spouse of the nominal head of the household and the spouse and dependent children of such dependent child. For the purpose of this subsection, a dependent person is one who has more than fifty percent of his total support furnished for him by the nominal head of the household and the spouse of the nominal head of the household.

"(e) A family may consist of one individual."

the ordinance. When she failed to remove him from her home, the city filed a criminal charge. Mrs. Moore moved to dismiss, claiming that the ordinance was constitutionally invalid on its face. Her motion was overruled, and upon conviction she was sentenced to five days in jail and a $25 fine. The Ohio Court of Appeals affirmed after giving full consideration to her constitutional claims, and the Ohio Supreme Court denied review. . . .

The city argues that our decision in Village of Belle Terre v. Boraas, 416 U.S. 1 (1974), requires us to sustain the ordinance attacked here.

But [the] ordinance there affected only unrelated individuals. It expressly allowed all who were related by "blood, adoption, or marriage" to live together, and in sustaining the ordinance we were careful to note that it promoted "family needs" and "family values." East Cleveland, in contrast, has chosen to regulate the occupancy of its housing by slicing deeply into the family itself. This is no mere incidental result of the ordinance. On its face it selects certain categories of relatives who may live together and declares that others may not. In particular, it makes a crime of a grandmother's choice to live with her grandson in circumstances like those presented here.

When a city undertakes such intrusive regulation of the family, neither *Belle Terre* nor *Euclid* governs; the usual judicial deference to the legislature is inappropriate. "This Court has long recognized that freedom of personal choice in matters of marriage and family life is one of the liberties protected by the Due Process Clause of the Fourteenth Amendment." A host of cases, tracing their lineage to Meyer v. Nebraska, 262 U.S. 390, 399–401 (1923), and Pierce v. Society of Sisters, 268 U.S. 510, 534–535 (1925), have consistently acknowledged a "private realm of family life which the state cannot enter." Prince v. Massachusetts, 321 U.S. 158, 166 (1944). Of course, the family is not beyond regulation. But when the government intrudes on choices concerning family living arrangements, this Court must examine carefully the importance of the governmental interests advanced and the extent to which they are served by the challenged regulation.

When thus examined, this ordinance cannot survive. The city seeks to justify it as a means of preventing overcrowding, minimizing traffic and parking congestion, and avoiding an undue financial burden on East Cleveland's school system. Although these are legitimate goals, the ordinance before us serves them marginally, at best.[7] For example, the ordinance permits any family consisting only of husband, wife, and unmarried children to live together, even if the family contains a half dozen licensed drivers, each with his or her own car. At the same time it forbids an adult brother and sister to share a household, even if both faithfully use public transportation. The ordinance would permit a grandmother to live with a single dependent son and children, even if his school-age children number a dozen, yet it forces Mrs. Moore to find another dwelling for her grandson John, simply because of the presence of his uncle and cousin in the same household. We need not labor the point. Section 1341.08 has but a tenuous relation to alleviation of the conditions mentioned by the city.

The city would distinguish the cases based on *Meyer* and *Pierce*. It points out that none of them "gives grandmothers any fundamental rights with respect to grandsons," . . . and suggests that any constitutional right to live

7. It is significant that East Cleveland has another ordinance specifically addressed to the problem of overcrowding. Section 1351.03 limits population density directly, tying the maximum permissible occupancy of a dwelling to the habitable floor area. Even if John, Jr., and his father both remain in Mrs. Moore's household, the family stays well within these limits.

together as a family extends only to the nuclear family—essentially a couple and their dependent children.

To be sure, these cases did not expressly consider the family relationship presented here. They were immediately concerned with freedom of choice with respect to childbearing, or with the rights of parents to the custody and companionship of their own children, or with traditional parental authority in matters of child rearing and education. But unless we close our eyes to the basic reasons why certain rights associated with the family have been accorded shelter under the Fourteenth Amendment's Due Process Clause, we cannot avoid applying the force and rationale of these precedents to the family choice involved in this case.

Substantive due process has at times been a treacherous field for this Court. There are risks when the judicial branch gives enhanced protection to certain substantive liberties without the guidance of the more specific provisions of the Bill of Rights. As the history of the *Lochner* era demonstrates, there is reason for concern lest the only limits to such judicial intervention become the predilections of those who happen at the time to be Members of this Court. That history counsels caution and restraint. But it does not counsel abandonment, nor does it require what the city urges here: cutting off any protection of family rights at the first convenient, if arbitrary boundary—the boundary of the nuclear family.

Appropriate limits on substantive due process come not from drawing arbitrary lines but rather from careful "respect for the teachings of history [and] solid recognition of the basic values that underlie our society." Our decisions establish that the Constitution protects the sanctity of the family precisely because the institution of the family is deeply rooted in this Nation's history and tradition. It is through the family that we inculcate and pass down many of our most cherished values, moral and cultural.[13]

Ours is by no means a tradition limited to respect for the bonds uniting the members of the nuclear family. The tradition of uncles, aunts, cousins, and especially grandparents sharing a household along with parents and children has roots equally venerable and equally deserving of constitutional recognition.[14] Over the years millions of our citizens have grown up in just such an environment, and most, surely, have profited from it. Even if conditions of modern society have brought about a decline in extended family households, they have not erased the accumulated wisdom of civilization, gained over the centuries and honored throughout our history, that supports a larger conception of the family. Out of choice, necessity, or a sense of family responsibility, it has been common for close relatives to draw together and participate in the duties and the satisfactions of a common home. Decisions concerning child rearing, which *Yoder, Meyer, Pierce* and other cases have recognized as entitled to constitutional protection, long have been shared with grandparents or other relatives who occupy the same household—indeed who may take on major responsibility for the rearing of the children. Especially in times of adversity, such as the death of a spouse or economic need, the broader family has tended to come together for mutual

13. See generally Wilkinson & White, Constitutional Protection for Personal Lifestyles, 62 Cornell L.Rev. 563, 623–624 (1977).

14. See generally B. Yorburg, The Changing Family (1973); Bronfenbrenner, The Calamitous Decline of the American Family, Wash.Post, Jan. 2, 1977, p. C1. Recent census reports bear out the importance of family patterns other than the prototypical nuclear family. In 1970, 26.5% of all families contained one or more members over 18 years of age, other than the head of household and spouse. . . .

sustenance and to maintain or rebuild a secure home life. This is apparently what happened here.[16]

Whether or not such a household is established because of personal tragedy, the choice of relatives in this degree of kinship to live together may not lightly be denied by the State. *Pierce* struck down an Oregon law requiring all children to attend the State's public schools, holding that the Constitution "excludes any general power of the State to standardize its children by forcing them to accept instruction from public teachers only." By the same token the Constitution prevents East Cleveland from standardizing its children—and its adults—by forcing all to live in certain narrowly defined family patterns.

Reversed.

■ JUSTICE BRENNAN, with whom JUSTICE MARSHALL joins, concurring.

... I write only to underscore the cultural myopia of the arbitrary boundary drawn by the East Cleveland ordinance in the light of the tradition of the American home that has been a feature of our society since our beginning as a Nation—the "tradition" in the plurality's words, "of uncles, aunts, cousins, and especially grandparents sharing a household along with parents and children...." The line drawn by this ordinance displays a depressing insensitivity toward the economic and emotional needs of a very large part of our society.

In today's America, the "nuclear family" is the pattern so often found in much of white suburbia. J. Vander Zanden. Sociology: A Systematic Approach 322 (3d ed. 1975). The Constitution cannot be interpreted, however, to tolerate the imposition by government upon the rest of us of white suburbia's preference in patterns of family living. The "extended family" that provided generations of early Americans with social services and economic and emotional support in times of hardship, and was the beachhead for successive waves of immigrants who populated our cities, remains not merely still a pervasive living pattern, but under the goad of brutal economic necessity, a prominent pattern—virtually a means of survival—for large numbers of the poor and deprived minorities of our society. For them compelled pooling of scant resources requires compelled sharing of a household.

The "extended" form is especially familiar among black families. We may suppose that this reflects the truism that black citizens, like generations of white immigrants before them, have been victims of economic and other disadvantages that would worsen if they were compelled to abandon extended, for nuclear, living patterns. Even in husband and wife households, 13% of black families compared with 3% of white families include relatives under 18 years old, in addition to the couple's own children. In black households whose head is an elderly woman, as in this case, the contrast is even more striking: 48% of such black households, compared with 10% of counterpart white households, include related minor children not offspring of the head of the household.

I do not wish to be understood as implying that East Cleveland's enforcement of its ordinance is motivated by a racially discriminatory purpose: The record of this case would not support that implication. But the

16. We are told that the mother of John Moore, Jr., died when he was less than one year old. He, like uncounted others who have suffered a similar tragedy, then came to live with the grandmother to provide the infant with a substitute for his mother's care and to establish a more normal home environment.

prominence of other than nuclear families among ethnic and racial minority groups, including our black citizens, surely demonstrates that the "extended family" pattern remains a vital tenet of our society. It suffices that in prohibiting this pattern of family living as a means of achieving its objectives, appellee city has chosen a device that deeply intrudes into family associational rights that historically have been central, and today remain central, to a large proportion of our population.

■ JUSTICE STEVENS, concurring in the judgment.

There appears to be no precedent for an ordinance which excludes any of an owner's relatives from the group of persons who may occupy his residence on a permanent basis. Nor does there appear to be any justification for such a restriction of an owner's use of his property. The city has failed totally to explain the need for a rule which would allow a homeowner to have two grandchildren live with her if they are brothers, but not if they are cousins. Since this ordinance has not been shown to have any "substantial relation to the public health, safety, morals, or general welfare" of the city of East Cleveland, and since it cuts so deeply into a fundamental right normally associated with the ownership of residential property—that of an owner to decide who may reside on his or her property—it must fall under the limited standard of review of zoning decisions which this Court preserved in *Euclid*.... Under that standard, East Cleveland's unprecedented ordinance constitutes a taking of property without due process and without just compensation.

For these reasons, I concur in the Court's judgment.

■ JUSTICE STEWART, with whom JUSTICE REHNQUIST joins, dissenting.

. . .

In my view, the appellant's claim that the ordinance in question invades constitutionally protected rights of association and privacy is in large part answered by the *Belle Terre* decision. The argument was made there that a municipality could not zone its land exclusively for single-family occupancy because to do so would interfere with protected rights of privacy or association. We rejected this contention, and held that the ordinance at issue "involve[d] no 'fundamental' right guaranteed by the Constitution, such as ... the right of association, NAACP v. Alabama, 357 U.S. 449; ... or any rights of privacy, cf. Griswold v. Connecticut, 381 U.S. 479; Eisenstadt v. Baird, 405 U.S. 438, 453–454." 416 U.S. at 7–8.

The *Belle Terre* decision thus disposes of the appellant's contentions to the extent they focus not on her blood relationships with her sons and grandsons but on more general notions about the "privacy of the home." Her suggestion that every person has a constitutional right permanently to share his residence with whomever he pleases, and that such choices are "beyond the province of legitimate governmental intrusion," amounts to the same argument that was made and found unpersuasive in *Belle Terre.*

To be sure, the ordinance involved in *Belle Terre* did not prevent blood relatives from occupying the same dwelling, and the Court's decision in that case does not, therefore, foreclose the appellant's arguments based specifically on the ties of kinship present in this case. Nonetheless, I would hold, for the reasons that follow, that the existence of those ties does not elevate either the appellant's claim of associational freedom or her claim of privacy to a level invoking constitutional protection.

To suggest that the biological fact of common ancestry necessarily gives related persons constitutional rights of association superior to those of unrelated persons is to misunderstand the nature of the associational freedoms that the Constitution has been understood to protect. Freedom of association has been constitutionally recognized because it is often indispensable to effectuation of explicit First Amendment guarantees. But the scope of the associational right, until now, at least, has been limited to the constitutional need that created it; obviously not every "association" is for First Amendment purposes or serves to promote the ideological freedom that the First Amendment was designed to protect.

The "association" in this case is not for any purpose relating to the promotion of speech, assembly, the press, or religion. And wherever the outer boundaries of constitutional protection of freedom of association may eventually turn out to be, they surely do not extend to those who assert no interest other than the gratification, convenience, and economy of sharing the same residence.

The appellant is considerably closer to the constitutional mark in asserting that the East Cleveland ordinance intrudes upon "the private realm of family life which the state cannot enter." Prince v. Massachusetts, 321 U.S. 158, 166. Several decisions of the Court have identified specific aspects of what might broadly be termed "private family life" that are constitutionally protected against state interference.

Although the appellant's desire to share a single-dwelling unit also involves "private family life" in a sense, that desire can hardly be equated with any of the interests protected in the cases just cited. The ordinance about which the appellant complains did not impede her choice to have or not to have children, and it did not dictate to her how her own children were to be nurtured and reared. The ordinance clearly does not prevent parents from living together or living with their unemancipated offspring.

But even though the Court's previous cases are not directly in point, the appellant contends that the importance of the "extended family" in American society requires us to hold that her decision to share her residence with her grandsons may not be interfered with by the State. This decision, like the decisions involved in bearing and raising children, is said to be an aspect of "family life" also entitled to substantive protection under the Constitution. Without pausing to inquire how far under this argument an "extended family" might extend, I cannot agree.[7] When the Court has found that the Fourteenth Amendment placed a substantive limitation on a State's power to regulate, it has been in those rare cases in which the personal interests at issue have been deemed " 'implicit in the concept of ordered liberty.' " The interest that the appellant may have in permanently sharing a single kitchen and a suite of contiguous rooms with some of her relatives simply does not rise to that level. To equate this interest with the fundamental decisions to marry and to bear and raise children is to extend the limited substantive contours of the Due Process Clause beyond recognition.

7. The opinion of Justice Powell and Justice Brennan's concurring opinion both emphasize the traditional importance of the extended family in American life. But I fail to understand why it follows that the residents of East Cleveland are constitutionally prevented from following what Justice Brennan calls the "pattern" of "white suburbia," even though that choice may reflect "cultural myopia." In point of fact, East Cleveland is a predominantly Negro community, with a Negro City Manager and City Commission.

NOTE

In *Moore,* the plurality opinion found constitutional protection for the extended family. Does this recognition mean that members of the extended family should be given greater rights in intra-family disputes over such matters as custody disputes, placement of neglected children or visitation claims?

Troxel v. Granville

Supreme Court of the United States, 2000.
530 U.S. 57, 120 S.Ct. 2054, 147 L.Ed.2d 49.

[The opinion is printed on page 621 supra].

Americana Healthcare Center v. Randall

Supreme Court of South Dakota, 1994.
513 N.W.2d 566.

■ AMUNDSON, JUSTICE.

. . .

Appellant Robert Randall (Robert) is the only child of Harry and Juanita Randall. Although he grew up in Aberdeen, Robert has not resided in South Dakota since in 1954. Robert is now a resident of the District of Columbia.

Robert's father died in 1981. Four years after his death, Robert's mother Juanita hired counsel to draft a trust document entitled "Juanita Randall Maintenance Trust Agreement." This irrevocable trust named Juanita as the income beneficiary and Robert as both trustee and residual beneficiary. The trust principal consisted of Juanita's house which was valued at approximately $30,000 and $100,000 in mutual funds. The trust did not grant the trustee authority to invade the principal for the benefit of Juanita. Juanita was ninety-two years old when she executed the trust document in 1985.

Following an accident which required Juanita's hospitalization, Robert came back to Aberdeen and checked into various nursing homes to place his mother. In the fall of 1990, Juanita was admitted to the Arcadia Unit of Americana Healthcare Center (Americana) in Aberdeen, South Dakota. The Arcadia Unit is specifically designed to deal with individuals who possess mental problems such as Alzheimer's disease. Robert completed and signed all the necessary documents under the power of attorney from his mother and made a two-month advance payment to Americana from his mother's checking account. He also listed himself as the person who should be sent the monthly statements from the nursing home.

At that time, in view of Juanita's limited income, Robert discussed the possibility of financial assistance from Medicaid with various Americana personnel. Later that month, Robert completed an application for long-term care medical assistance for Juanita. In November, the South Dakota Department of Social Services (DSS) denied this application because Juanita had not exhausted all of her assets.[1] At the time, Juanita's only assets were the house and mutual funds which had been conveyed to the trust.

1. In the November 30, 1990, letter of denial, Robert was advised as follows: "Therefore, until you can provide the Department with [more detailed financial information], the application will be rejected, and *you will be*

Juanita's bill was two months delinquent at the time Americana learned of the rejected Medicaid application. Americana then contacted Robert about his mother's unpaid bills. Because of Juanita's financial position, Robert, as her legal guardian, filed a Chapter 11 bankruptcy on her behalf in the District of Columbia. The District of Columbia court dismissed this bankruptcy proceeding after Americana refused resolution under bankruptcy. Robert then filed a Chapter 7 bankruptcy petition which was transferred to South Dakota and discharged the Americana bill for Juanita individually and Robert, as her guardian, on October 30, 1991. Meanwhile, Americana filed this suit to collect the unpaid bills.[2]

While Juanita stayed at Americana she received social security payments and income from the trust. While the amount of social security benefits is not shown in this record, Robert estimated that the trust produced about $5000–$6000 income per year. This income was used by Robert to pay legal fees incurred by forming the guardianship, the bankruptcy proceedings and the unsuccessful pursuit of Medicaid benefits.

In June of 1991, Robert was requested to remove his mother from Americana because of the unpaid bills. Despite this request, Juanita remained at Americana until her death on December 8, 1991. At the time of Juanita's death, the unpaid balance for her care was $36,772.30.

Americana notified Robert of his mother's unpaid bills on many occasions. Robert was named as a party to this suit in three capacities: individually, as trustee, and as guardian of the person and estate of Juanita Randall. Americana alleged that Robert had agreed to pay his mother's nursing home bill at the time of her admission to Americana's facility.

Prior to trial, the court granted Robert's motion for summary judgment as to Robert Randall as guardian of the person and estate of Juanita because of the discharge in bankruptcy, but denied summary judgment to Robert Randall individually and as trustee of the Juanita A. Randall Maintenance Trust. At the summary judgment hearing, Americana raised its claim under SDCL 25–7–27 for the first time.[3]

On September 3, 1992, Robert renewed his motion for summary judgment on the additional ground that SDCL 25–7–27 was unconstitutional and requested a continuance. Robert also notified the South Dakota Attorney General that the constitutionality of SDCL 25–7–27 was being challenged. The trial court stated that it was premature to rule on the constitutionality of the statute at that time and denied the continuance.

A court trial was held September 22, 1992. At the conclusion of Americana's case, Robert moved for directed verdict on the grounds that Americana had failed to establish either an oral or written contract to act as guarantor for his mother's nursing home bills. Additionally, Robert requested a directed verdict because Americana failed to submit any evidence regarding his financial ability to pay the nursing home bill pursuant to SDCL 25–7–27. The trial court granted Robert's motion for directed verdict on Americana's claims for liability based on an oral or written contract of

responsible for Private pay to the Nursing facility." (Emphasis added.)

2. During this entire time, Americana cared for Juanita without compensation.

3. SDCL 25–7–27 states:

> Every adult child, having the financial ability so to do shall provide necessary food, clothing, shelter or medical attendance for a parent who is unable to provide for himself; provided that no claim shall be made against such adult child until notice has been given such adult child that his parent is unable to provide for himself, and such adult child shall have refused to provide for his parent.

guarantee. However, the court denied Robert's motion for directed verdict on the SDCL 25–7–27 claim and allowed Americana to orally amend their complaint to include the SDCL 25–7–27 claim. The trial court found in favor of Americana on its SDCL 25–7–27 claim. This appeal followed.

. . .

Was Robert Randall liable for his mother's nursing home bill under SDCL 25–7–27?

. . .

At common law, an adult child was not required to support a parent. Such an obligation could only be created by statute. McCook County v. Kammoss, 7 S.D. 558, 64 N.W. 1123 (1895); 67A C.J.S. "Parent & Child" § 97 (1985). Such statutes trace their beginnings from the Elizabethan Poor Law of 1601 in England. Swoap v. Superior Court, 10 Cal.3d 490, 111 Cal.Rptr. 136, 516 P.2d 840, 848 (1973). South Dakota adopted the current version of SDCL 25–7–27 in 1963.

The North Dakota Supreme Court considered a claim premised on a similar statutory provision in Bismarck Hospital & Deaconesses Home v. Harris, 68 N.D. 374, 280 N.W. 423 (1938). That court stated:

> If the person against whom liability is sought to be established refuses to pay for services rendered, an action may be brought against him by such third party. In such action, the plaintiff must establish the kinship of the parties, the financial ability of the person sought to be charged, the indigence of the person to whom relief was furnished, the reasonable value of the services, and that such relief was an immediate necessity.

Id. 280 N.W. at 426.

SDCL 25–7–27 requires an adult child to provide support only when they have the financial ability to do so. Robert claims that this is constitutionally defective because it is unclear when financial ability is to be determined. However, under the facts of this case, a fair reading of the statute shows that the financial ability of the adult child may be determined at any time there is an outstanding debt which has not been barred by the statute of limitations. This certainly seems appropriate where the parent continues to receive care while the child is in control of, and is expending, the parent's assets which are available to pay the debt.

Although Robert could not pay his mother's bills from his own funds, he certainly had the ability to pay after the trust assets had been distributed to him.[4] At trial, it was proven that Robert had received approximately $100,000 in mutual funds from the maintenance trust at his mother's death. Therefore, under the facts of this case, the trial court was correct in holding Robert liable under SDCL 25–7–27.

Does SDCL 25–7–27 deny Robert Randall equal protection of the law?

Robert claims SDCL 25–7–27 violates equal protection because it discriminates against adult children of indigent parents. The trial court held that it did not. Any legislative act is accorded a presumption in favor of constitutionality and that presumption is not overcome until the act is clearly and unmistakably shown beyond a reasonable doubt to violate fundamental

4. Approximately $30,000 of proceeds from sale of the house have been held in escrow pending disposition of this case.

constitutional principles. Since Robert challenges the constitutionality of the statute, he bears the burden of proving the act unconstitutional.

. . .

Under the rational basis test, South Dakota uses a two-pronged analysis when determining whether a statute violates the constitutional right to equal protection under the laws. Lyons v. Lederle Laboratories, 440 N.W.2d 769, 771 (S.D.1989). First, does the statute set up arbitrary classifications among various persons subject to it and, second, whether there is a rational relationship between the classification and some legitimate legislative purpose.

When applying the first prong of the Lyons test, it is clear that SDCL 25–7–27 does not make an arbitrary classification. Rather, "it is the moral as well as the legal duty in this state, of every child, whether minor or adult, to assist in the support of their indigent aged parents." Tobin v. Bruce, 39 S.D. 64, 67, 162 N.W. 933, 934 (1917) (citing Section 118, Civil Code; McCook County v. Kammoss, 7 S.D. 558, 64 N.W. 1123 (1895)). An adult child is liable under SDCL 25–7–27 upon the same principle that a parent is liable for necessary support furnished to their child. Kammoss, 7 S.D. 558, 64 N.W. 1123.

Much like the plaintiffs in Swoap v. Superior Court of Sacramento County, Robert argues that the only support obligations which are rational are those arising out of a relationship voluntarily entered into. 10 Cal.3d 490, 111 Cal.Rptr. 136, 516 P.2d 840, 851 (1973). For instance, the obligation to support a child or spouse is at least initially voluntary, therefore, it is rationally based. Robert argues that, since children do not voluntarily enter into the relationship with their parents, it is arbitrary to force this obligation upon them. The fact that a child has no choice in the creation of a relationship with its parents does not per se make this an arbitrary classification. The fact that an indigent parent has supported and cared for a child during that child's minority provides an adequate basis for imposing a duty on the child to support that parent.

Robert also claims that this classification is unconstitutional because it is based on wealth. However, economic-based discrimination has been upheld by this court....

It is certainly reasonable to place a duty to support an indigent parent on that parent's adult child because they are direct lineal descendants who have received the support, care, comfort and guidance of that parent during their minority. If a parent does not qualify for public assistance, who is best suited to meet that parent's needs? It can reasonably be concluded that no other person has received a greater benefit from a parent than that parent's child and it logically follows that the adult child should bear the burden of reciprocating on that benefit in the event a parent needs support in their later years. *Swoap,* 516 P.2d at 851. Consequently, this statute does not establish an arbitrary classification.

The second prong of the test requires a rational relationship between this classification and some legitimate state interest. Clearly, this state has a legitimate interest in providing for the welfare and care of elderly citizens. SDCL 25–7–27 prevents a parent from being thrown out on the street when in need of specialized care. Placing this obligation for support on an adult child is as legitimate as those interests recognized by this court in the past when applying the rational basis test. We have found legitimate state interests to exist under constitutional challenges in the support of children,

Feltman, 434 N.W.2d 590; balancing the treatment of debtors and creditors, *Accounts Management, Inc.,* 484 N.W.2d 297; education, Birchfield v. Birchfield, 417 N.W.2d 891 (S.D.1988); public safety, Swanson v. Dept. of Commerce & Regulation, 417 N.W.2d 385 (S.D.1987); preventing the adjudication of stale claims, Janish v. Murtha 285 N.W.2d 708 (S.D.1979); and protecting the citizens from drunk drivers, *State v. Heinrich,* 449 N.W.2d 25 (S.D.1989).

The primary purpose of this statute is to place financial responsibility for indigent parents on their adult children when a parent requires such assistance. Although the legislature repealed similar laws in the past,[5] SDCL 25–7–27 has survived. Therefore, SDCL 25–7–27 serves a legitimate legislative interest, especially under the facts of this case, where indigency was voluntarily created by the trust and there would have been sufficient assets to pay for the parent's care had the trust not been created. Robert has not been denied his right to equal protection under the law.

Does SDCL 25–7–27 deny Robert Randall his right to due process?

Robert argues that SDCL 25–7–27 denies him of the right to due process. In support of his argument, he cites Commonwealth v. Mong, 160 Ohio St. 455, 52 O.O. 340, 117 N.E.2d 32 (1954). *Mong* involved an Ohio resident who was not held responsible for the support of his father, a Pennsylvania resident. However, in *Mong,* the adult child was not liable for his indigent parent because Ohio law prohibited a parent who has abandoned their children to later assert their parental right to support from that child. *Id.* 117 N.E.2d at 33.

Robert, a resident of the District of Columbia, argues that Americana cannot enforce the South Dakota support statute against him because the District of Columbia has repealed its parental support statute. Robert has not been denied due process simply because the District of Columbia does not have a support statute similar to South Dakota's. Unlike the situation in *Mong,* District of Columbia does not prohibit an action for support of a parent, it has simply repealed the vehicle for such action in the District of Columbia.

Robert claims a violation of due process exists because the statute forces a nonresident to pay for a resident parent's expenses. Although Robert is not a resident of South Dakota, he has had numerous contacts with the state. He had a power of attorney pertaining to his mother's checking account in Aberdeen, South Dakota. He later became her legal guardian with her residency in South Dakota. As trustee, he held legal title to a house in South Dakota. He visited his mother on several occasions at Americana in Aberdeen. He also maintained a bankruptcy action in the State of South Dakota as guardian for his mother. With these contacts it is obvious that the South Dakota courts have properly asserted jurisdiction over this matter. Residency or, in this case, the lack thereof does not deprive Robert of due process.

Robert also argues that he was denied due process because he was not given notice that "his parent is unable to provide for herself" as required by SDCL 25–7–27. Where the statute contains a notice provision, failure to provide timely notice precludes any claim against an adult child for support of his parent on a due process basis. SDCL 25–7–27 does not specify the

5. *See* SDCL 25–7–6, Duty of parents and children to support poor person unable to work—Child's promise to pay for necessaries furnished to parent. Repealed by 1991 S.D.Sess.L. ch. 212. *See also* SDCL 25–7–29, Nonsupport of parent by adult child as misdemeanor—Notice required. Repealed by 1986 S.D.Sess.L. ch. 26, § 5.

manner in which notice shall be given. Therefore, it should be assumed that it must be reasonable notice.

In this case, the evidence indicates that Robert had complete control over his mother's financial affairs. He was notified by Americana on several occasions that his mother's bill remained unpaid. As his mother's guardian, it was Robert's responsibility to provide for his mother's needs including her nursing home bills. Robert's assertion that Americana's notices were given to him only as trustee or guardian and never individually does not withstand scrutiny. Robert had sufficient notice even though Americana did not explicitly state that he was responsible for his mother's expenses. Surely, a sophisticated person such as Robert was aware that his mother's bills were delinquent and Americana was not in the business of providing services free of charge. This court concludes he received constitutionally adequate notice.

. . .

Under the circumstances, Americana furnished care to Juanita Randall relying on the representations made by her son, Robert. Therefore, it ought to be able to recover from the child who had control of the purse strings but chose to expend the assets to avoid the bill rather than pay for his mother's required care. Our conclusion is that given its plain and ordinary meaning, this statute is not unconstitutionally vague and was properly applied in this case.

NOTES

1. Roscoe Pound, Individual Interests in the Domestic Relations, 14 Mich.L.Rev. 177, 185 (1916):

> In Roman law the duty of children to support parents in case of need, as a duty of gratitude and piety, was turned from a moral duty into a legal duty during the stage of equity and natural law. From the time of the empire this duty and the corresponding duty of the parent with respect to children, as duties of piety, were enforceable *extra ordinem* as legal duties. The principle of reciprocal duties of support on the part of ascendants and descendants passed from the civil law into the modern codes and is universally recognized in the Roman law world. In the Anglo–American system the court of chancery did not take hold of this subject and it was left to modern legislation which is by no means universal.

2. "[The parents, grandparents, and the children of] everie poore olde blind lame and impotente person, or other poore person not able to worke, beinge of a sufficient abilitie, shall at their owne Chardges relieve and maintain everie suche poore person, in that manner and accordinge to that rate, as by the Justices of the Peace of that Countie where suche sufficient persons dwell, or the greater number of them, at their generall Quarter Sessions shall be assessed; upon paine that everie one of them shall forfeite twenty shillings for everie monthe which they shall faile therein." Jacobus tenBroek, California's Dual System of Family Law: Its Origin, Development, and Present Status, Part I, 16 Stan.L.Rev. 257, 283 (1964) (quoting 43 Eliz. 1, c. 2, § VI (1601)). Similar statutes found ready acceptance in the American colonies. See generally, Stephan A. Riesenfeld, The Formative Era of American Public Assistance Law, 43 Cal.L.Rev. 175 (1955).

3. As of 2005, twenty-nine states had filial responsibility statutes. Many states limit the child's responsibilities to necessities. Some impose criminal penalties for failure to provide support to indigent parents. For more discussion of filial responsibility statutes in America see Shannon Frank Edelstone, Filial Responsibility: Can The Legal Duty to Support Our Parents Be Legally Enforced?, 36 Fam. L. Q. 501 (2002); Seymour Moskowitz, Filial Responsibility Statutes: Legal and Policy Considerations, 9 J.L. & Pol'y 709 (2001).

CHAPTER 9

Growing up in the Law

We often speak of children and adults as if the categories were self-evident, but in fact neither term is particularly precise. Not only is there debate about when a person should be considered to be an adult (at age 18? age 21? upon marriage?) but the meaning of the word "child" is even more uncertain. A child of seventeen years, for example, may have more in common with most adults than with a child of seventeen months.

The law mirrors our confusion on these issues. A person can vote in Oklahoma at age eighteen, but not drink liquor until age 21.[1] A nine year old can be a caddy in Colorado, but must wait until fourteen to pump gas.[2] A person can be a peanut commissioner in Oklahoma at age 25, but must wait until age 30 to be governor of Alabama.[3]

As you study the material in this chapter consider what evidence is deemed relevant by courts in making age distinctions. What other information should they consider? Should age-based distinctions be treated as inherently suspect because they do not take into account the abilities or disabilities of particular individuals?

A. Age Distinctions in Tort Law

Tyler v. Weed

Supreme Court of Michigan, 1938.
285 Mich. 460, 280 N.W. 827.

■ McAllister, Justice.

This is an action for damages for negligence, brought by an infant suitor by his next friend. On September 26, 1935, just before noon, plaintiff, a child six years and eight months old, was returning from school to his home in Battle Creek. He was walking in a westerly direction on the north side of Webber Street, which intersects Meachem Avenue, a north and south street. When plaintiff came to the intersection he stepped from the curb and, it is claimed, looked north, took a step or two and then looked south, and started running diagonally across Meachem Avenue in a northwesterly direction.

Defendant, a woman 65 years old, was driving an automobile on Meachem Avenue proceeding in a northerly direction. She testified that when she reached the intersection she glanced to the sidewalk on the right, but saw no one on the corner; but she states that when she arrived in the middle of the intersection she first saw plaintiff two feet from the curb on the

1. Okla. Const. art. III § 1; 37 Okla. Stat. § 537(A)(1).

2. Colo.Rev.Stat. § 8–12–106; Colo.Rev. Stat. § 8–12–108.

3. 2 Okla. Stat. § 18–53; Ala. Const. art. V § 117.

right. From the time she first saw plaintiff until she applied her brakes, her car travelled approximately 25 feet. The plaintiff was struck by the left fender of defendant's car after he had run in a northeasterly direction a distance of 51 feet, and after he had passed the center line of the street he was trying to cross. As a result of the accident, plaintiff suffered severe and permanent injuries, including fractures and the loss of an eye.

The case was tried before a jury and resulted in a verdict of no cause of action. On appeal the plaintiff claims error on the part of the trial court in submitting to the jury the question of his contributory negligence, because he was under seven years of age.

So presented, [the question is raised] whether infant plaintiff in this case, being under the age of seven years, is conclusively presumed to be incapable of negligence.

On this proposition there is a conflict of authorities between those that hold that the question of an infant's negligence is always to be determined as a question of fact regardless of age, and those that follow the so-called common law rule that an infant under the age of seven years is conclusively presumed to be incapable of negligence.

. . .

This rule was transplanted from the civil law to our common law at an early period. In Austin's Jurisprudence the author, in discussing conclusive presumptions of law, mentions the case of infants under the age of seven years and says: "Here, according to the Roman Law, and according to our own, the infant is presumed juris et de jure incapable of unlawful intention or culpable inadvertence. His incapacity is inferred or presumed from the age wherein he is; and proof to the contrary of that preappointed inference is not admissible by the tribunals." Lectures on Jurisprudence, John Austin, Vol. 1, p. 492 (5th Edition, 1929).

In Blackstone's Commentaries, Bk. IV, Sec. 23, the law of England on the subject is stated as follows: "Under seven years of age, indeed, an infant cannot be guilty of felony, for then a felonious discretion is almost an impossibility; but at eight years old, he may be guilty of a felony."

The author then mentions the case where a boy eight years old was tried for burning two barns and was found guilty, condemned and hanged accordingly. We look upon such a proceeding as barbarous, and find it difficult to believe that such cruelty under the masquerade of law and justice could be accepted in seventeenth century England. The impressive fact, however, is that in such times of pitiless jurisprudence, there was an emphatic recognition that the age of seven was an age of innocence, even though after the age of seven, the child could be executed for a capital crime of which he would have been blameless a twelve-month previously.

How well founded in the experience of countless centuries, and in the observation of philosophers of antiquity this understanding of incapacity and blamelessness of childhood was, is seen in modern thought and the researches of outstanding scholars of recent years. . . .

. . .

. . . In recent times, the studies of Alfred Binet, in France, Hans Gross, in Austria, Jean Piaget, in Switzerland, and Maria Montessori, in Italy, have brought a new light upon the mysterious mind of the child, and have elucidated many of the obscure areas in the understanding of mental development and growth in infancy and adolescence.

What is remarkable in the conclusions arrived at by such research, is the fact that the age of seven years marks a transitional line in the mental development of children. In the copious and rich literature devoted to the subject, there repeatedly recurs the emphasis upon this age as marking the inception of thought and reason, the commencement of exchange of ideas, the beginning of concepts of justice. Authorities hold that this age marks the passage from the period of self-centered speech and thought to verbal understanding and social thought and cooperation. In short, the age of seven years can be said to be the threshold over which a human being passes from the realm of imagination and dream to the world of reality and fact.

Dr. Hans Gross, late Professor of Law of the Universities of Prague and Vienna, former judge of the law courts of Austria, and pre-eminent examining magistrate of Europe, referred to by Dean Wigmore as the scholar who has done more than any other man in modern times to encourage the application of science to judicial proof, says:

. . .

> "We cannot place ourselves at the point of view of the child; it uses indeed the same words as we do, but these words convey to it very different ideas. Further, the child perceives things differently from grown-up people. The conceptions of magnitude, great or small, or pace—fast or slow, of beauty and ugliness, of distance—near or far, are quite different in the child's brain, from in ours; still more so when facts are in question. . . . The horizon of the child being much narrower than ours, a large number of our perceptions are outside the frame within which alone the child can perceive. We know, within certain limits, the extent of this frame. . . . But in many directions we do not know the exact point where its faculty of observation commences or stops. At times we cannot explain how it does not understand something or other, while at other times we are astonished to see it find its bearings easily among matters thought to be well beyond its intelligence." Criminal Investigation, A Practical Text for Magistrates, Police Officers and Lawyers, Hans Gross, London, 1924.[1]

. . .

[We are not] impressed with the argument that the common law rule is unjustifiable because it is arbitrary. There is no unfairness from an arbitrary treatment of the matter when it is considered that the cause of the contributory negligence of the infant can come into consideration only after a determination that the defendant himself was negligent. For if the defendant was not negligent, there can be no recovery, as no one is liable for injuries resulting from the sudden and unexpected act of a child, and if the defendant was negligent he should not be allowed to escape on the ground that an infant who is not fully aware of the consequences of his acts, was also negligent.

The citizen is everywhere hedged about by legal qualifications and disabilities based upon arbitrary rules of age. The law fixes the age of 21

1. See also, The Child's Conception of Causality; The Child's Conception of the World; The Language and Thought of the Child by Jean Piaget; The Development of Intelligence, Alfred Binet and Th. Simon; The Secret of Childhood, Maria Montessori; Huntington Cairns, The Child and the Law, in the New Generation (1930).

years under which infants are not liable upon their contracts; and in spite of varying degrees of intelligence and capacity, the same age is prescribed as a qualification for the right to vote. Infants can choose their own guardians at 14 years of age. The age at which persons can consummate a legal marriage is arbitrarily fixed by law. The age qualifications for election to Congress is 25 years; to the Senate, 30 years; to the Presidency, 35 years. If there is any reason for arbitrary age qualifications or disabilities in law, they would certainly be as capable of justification when used in the protection of little children from the infliction of wrongs, as in any other situations above mentioned.

. . .

The rule contended for by defendant that the contributory negligence of the infant is always a question of fact regardless of his age, has been adopted by the Supreme Court of Massachusetts, and has come to be known as the "Massachusetts Rule." While we have the utmost respect for the distinguished tribunal of that commonwealth, we are constrained to differ with it in our determination of this question for several reasons.

. . .

. . . A recent case holding that infants under the age of seven years are chargeable with contributory negligence, presumably based upon reason and logic, states that modern children of tender years have more opportunities to observe and be aware of danger because of the influence exercised upon them by moving pictures, radio and other modern inventions and conditions. But in our opinion, it cannot be said in view of distinguished authorities who hold contrary views that this is a matter of which a court can take judicial notice. Such statements are not generally accepted. One cannot say arbitrarily that the mental growth, intelligence, awareness, capability, and judgment of a modern child under seven years of age, are more developed because of such external stimuli. It is not agreed that the development of the child mentality depends upon such considerations. As has been stated by one authority, the growth of the child mind will be found to be a progression *in orderly relation to age, from infancy to maturity.*[3] It is said that it is because of his inherent weakness of attention, that the young child falls into many illusions of sense perception; and that in spite of children's tendency to experiment widely, they frequently do not see common objects with which they come in contact, unless such objects are pointed out to them and their most outstanding characteristics noted. Where scientists will not draw a conclusion regarding the behavior of mice, or insects, except after thousands of experiments and observations over a period of years, it seems an essay of some intellectual temerity to assume to know the mysterious and complex factors operating upon the mind of a changing infant, which bring about increased intelligence, awareness, and change of behavior, when such conclusions are arrived at without any evidence whatever. We cannot assume that modern inventions advance the growth of mind or increase the awareness, of the child of tender years. There is as much basis for the belief that such development is directly dependent upon age, in these early years of such swiftly marked changes of physical growth.

This somewhat extensive reference to authorities outside the law, however, is not made for the purpose of establishing a rule but rather to justify and confirm an already established rule that seems to us not only to possess the

3. Infancy and Human Growth, Arnold Gesell.

virtue of approval of times past, but also to be founded upon reason and humane considerations. . . . Above the cruelties and carnage of the centuries, History holds aloft the principle of such blameless early childhood. In civil law, in criminal jurisprudence, in the majority rule of our state jurisdictions in matters relating to negligence, the incapacity of children of a certain age is recognized, whether it be a question of intention or inadvertence; and the long experience of humanity has recognized in matters of education, morals, and mental development, a definite age of transition from carefree infancy to that time when a sense of responsibility is born. To surrender that principle one must depart from the sentiments of the past—not from an archaic rule—but from a vital and considered recognition of a transcendent element of human value. It seems, indeed, a paradox to hold the same child incapable of an act of wrongful intention but at the same time to hold him responsible for passive carefree inattention.

In our determination of this case we follow the common law rule announced by the numerous authorities, entitled to eminent respect, which hold that an infant under seven years of age is incapable of contributory negligence.

. . .

It follows that the action of the trial court in submitting infant plaintiff's contributory negligence to the jury for determination as a question of fact, was reversible error.

. . .

■ Wiest, Chief Justice (concurring in the reversal for exclusion of competent testimony).

I cannot join in the holding that a boy, six years and seven months of age, cannot, under any circumstances, be guilty of contributory negligence as a matter of fact, nor can I subscribe to the statement that: "In Michigan, the common law rule is reaffirmed, and children under the age of seven years are conclusively presumed to be incapable of contributory negligence."

The common law rule with reference to nonresponsibility of children under seven years of age related to criminal acts and ought not, by analogy, because wholly lacking in similarity, be applied to negligence.

. . .

Under a proper instruction the Massachusetts rule is the more sound and the one most likely to insure just result. It does not cast upon the general public any and all risks that may be created by the carelessness of a child. Still it does not go so far as to hold a child to a degree of care not commensurate with its age and experience. Under present day circumstances a child of six is permitted to assume many responsibilities. There is much opportunity for him to observe and thus become cognizant of the necessity for exercising some degree of care. Compulsory school attendance, the radio, the movies, and traffic conditions all tend to have this effect. Under the Illinois rule a child may be guilty of the most flagrant violation of duty and still not be precluded from recovering damages for injuries suffered partly because of such violation. The Massachusetts rule contemplates justice for all parties irrespective of age. Jurors, by virtue of their office, are competent to judge whether or not a child has exercised a degree of care commensurate with its age, capacity, and understanding. The Illinois rule has no basis in sound reason or logic. It is based upon an outworn historical rule of criminal law which refused to acknowledge any capacity on the part of any child under seven years of age to distinguish between right and wrong.

. . .

■ Butzel, Sharpe, and Chandler, JJ., concurred with Wiest, C.J. Potter, Justice (dissenting).

My views were stated in Easton v. Medema, 246 Mich. 130, 224 N.W. 636. They did not prevail. The court announced a rule, supported neither by the canon law, the civil law, the common law, or other law, which excludes intelligence and experience in determining culpability and disregards the rule that everyone is bound to use that degree of care which a reasonably prudent person of like age, intelligence and experience should ordinarily use under like circumstances. A rule that age, not sense; years, not intelligence; length of life, not experience, should govern responsibility for human action is unsound and should be discarded.

NOTES

1. Chief Judge Wiest's position was adopted in Michigan when the majority opinion was overruled in Baker v. Alt, 374 Mich. 492, 132 N.W.2d 614 (1965).

2. Compare *Tyler* with Honeycutt v. Wichita, 247 Kan. 250, 796 P.2d 549 (1990):

> Miller, C.J.
>
> Some states hold that a child under seven is not capable of negligence as a matter of law. This is known as the "Illinois rule." See *Toney v. Mazariegos*, 166 Ill.App.3d 399, 116 Ill.Dec. 820, 519 N.E.2d 1035 (1988). Other courts follow the "Massachusetts rule" and hold that a minor's capability for negligence is a question of fact. See, *e.g.*, Peterson v. Taylor, 316 N.W.2d 869 (Iowa 1982). These courts generally hold that a particular minor's capacity for negligence may be determined by the trial court as a matter of law only if the child is so young or the evidence of incapacity is so overwhelming that reasonable minds could not differ on the matter. For example, the Nevada Supreme Court in *Quillian v. Mathews*, 86 Nev. 200, 203, 467 P.2d 111 (1970), noted that the "numerical weight of authority appears to favor" a rule that a minor's negligence is a fact question and held the trial court did not err in submitting the question of negligence of a six-year-old to the jury. The court rejected the defendant's contention that a six-year-old cannot be negligent as a matter of law.
>
> . . .
>
> The plaintiff argues that a conclusive presumption of incapacity for negligence at an age below seven must be made for reasons of public policy to protect children from losses due to their own immaturity. Plaintiff notes that society uses many arbitrary age cutoffs in society; *i.e.*, for driver's licenses, voter registration, and compulsory school attendance. Defendants reply that such arbitrary ages must be established in areas reaching mass quantities of people, but such efficiency is not needed and counteracts the justice intended to be achieved in tort law. We agree and conclude that public policy is best served by submitting the claimed negligence of individual child plaintiffs for jury determination.
>
> . . .
>
> The "Illinois rule" has not been adopted in this state, and we decline to adopt it. We hold that the adoption of specific ages at which a child is incapable of negligence as a matter of law would not be beneficial or serve justice in Kansas. Rather, we hold that the negligence of a particular child in particular circumstances should be determined by the factfinder in each case, based upon

that degree of care exercised by children of the same age, intelligence, capacity, and experience.

. . .

Compare Tagg v. McGeorge, 155 Pa. 368, 26 A. 671 (1893), which also provides an interesting glimpse of nineteenth century child labor practices:

> DEAN, J. William F. Tagg, a boy past 13 years of age, was employed by defendants in their woolen mill at Darby, Delaware County. He went to work with the consent of and by contract with his father, who worked in the same mill. The boy commenced on 10th October, 1887, piecing at what is known as a "woolen mule." His wages were fixed at two dollars per week. The usual wages of a piecer are about six dollars. There was evidence tending to show that Henry T. Kent, one of defendants, made the contract for employment, and then put the boy in charge of Charles Chadwick, who had been foreman in the mill for many years. Under his directions and control he remained as a piecer at the mule up until the 31st of December, 1887. About 12 o'clock of that day, while cleaning the machine with waste, it being then running, the waste caught in the wheels, his hand was drawn in, and so completely crushed that amputation was necessary. The plaintiff then brought suit to recover damages, averring negligence on part of defendants, which resulted in the injury, (1) in putting a young and inexperienced boy to work at dangerous machinery without explaining to him its character, or warning him of its danger; (2) in directing him, by the foreman, Chadwick, to hurriedly clean the machine while it was running, without informing him of the peculiar danger incident to such work.
>
> The law applicable to the issue is well settled. In the text-books, and, with rare exceptions, in all the adjudicated cases, the rule laid down in substance is: When young persons without experience are employed to work with dangerous machines it is the duty of the employer to give suitable instructions as to the manner of using them, and warning as to the hazard of carelessness in their use. If the employer neglect this duty, or if he give improper instructions, he is responsible for the injury resulting from his neglect of duty. He is not answerable for injury to adults, nor for the injuries to young persons who have had that experience from which knowledge of danger may reasonably be presumed, and that discretion which prompts to care.... There was evidence tending to show that the woolen mule was a dangerous piece of machinery even to the adult workman, and that it was highly dangerous to one attempting to clean it while running. As to whether the boy had received any instructions from the foreman, or had by experience or in any other way acquired a knowledge of the machinery and the danger of attempting to clean it while running, there was conflicting evidence. It was of that character that the jury alone could determine the truth, and it was with proper instructions submitted to them....

3. Consider Laurence Tribe's proposal:

> [A] prohibition against irrebuttable presumptions affecting children in particular might conceivably be derivable simply from the status of children as a group sharing *most* of the characteristics of a discrete and insular minority, while having needs so special as to make the goal of a "child-blind" society quite unthinkable. A halfway constitutional position for children as a "semi-discrete minority," and for childhood as a "semi-suspect classification," could thus take the form of a rule that all age-based lines and all governmental allocations of responsibility or opportunity dependent upon the circumstances of youth are "semi-suspect" in the limited sense that there must be an opportunity, absent strong justification for denying it, for a child to *rebut* any implied or asserted age-based incapacity. Unlike a rule treating age as a fully suspect criterion, which would result in completely invalidating all but the most compellingly justifiable age-based lines, the suggested doctrine would have the effect only of making such lines ordinarily permeable to rebuttal; judicial suspicion would, in effect, focus not on the legislative act of making childhood *relevant*—an act as consistent with genuine concern as with stereotyped contempt—but rather on the act of

making childhood *conclusive*. The doctrine would thus preserve childhood as a legal category, with the concomitant protections typically flowing from such categorization, while creating a way out for the unusually mature, capable, or independent young person. Childhood, Suspect Classifications, and Conclusive Presumptions: Three Linked Riddles, 39 L. Contemp.Probs. 7, 32 (1975).

4. The draft Restatement Third of Torts (2001) provides in chapter 3 section 10:

(a) When the actor is a child, the actor's conduct is negligent if it does not conform to that of a reasonably careful person of the same age, intelligence, and experience; except that

(b) A child who is less than five years of age is incapable of negligence; and

(c) The special rule of Subsection (a) does not apply when the child is engaging in a dangerous activity that is characteristically undertaken by adults.

The comment to the Second Restatement notes that the rule is most often applied to cases involving the contributory negligence of children, although it is equally applicable to child defendants. The comment also rejects the notion of fixed age lines, explaining:

> . . . Some courts have endeavored to lay down fixed rules as to a minimum age below which the child is incapable of being negligent, and a maximum age above which he is to be treated like an adult. Usually these rules have been derived from the old rules of criminal law, by which a child under the age of seven was considered incapable of crime, and one over fourteen was considered to be as capable as an adult. The prevailing view is that in tort cases no such arbitrary limits can be fixed. Undoubtedly there is a minimum age, somewhere in the vicinity of four years, below which negligence can never be found; but with the greater variation in the capacities of children and the situation which might arise, it cannot be fixed definitely for all cases. . . . A child of ten may in one situation have sufficient capacity to appreciate the risk involved in his conduct, and to realize its unreasonable character, but in another situation he may lack the necessary mental capacity or experience to do so; and in the case of another child of ten of different mental capacity or experience a different conclusion may be reached in the same situation.

Martin Harvey, Adolescent Competency and the Refusal of Medical Treatment

13 Health Matrix: Journal of Law–Medicine 297, 298–300 (2003).

Should adolescents be allowed to refuse medical treatment such that death/serious disability will most likely be a consequence of their refusal? Tradition responds with a resounding "No." Given their minor status, adolescents have historically been lumped together with other obvious incompetents—e.g., infants—under the legal rubric of "presumptive decisional incapacity." As of late, while some scholars (hereafter the orthodox camp) continue to uphold a modified version of the traditional doctrine, others (hereafter the radical camp) argue for a diametrically opposed position: 'presumptive decisional capacity' for adolescents. On the latter view, the presumptive competency bar for both consent/refusal of medical treatment should be substantially lowered. Both types of presumptive doctrines share a common procedural virtue: each provides a fairly rigorous "bright line" test to determine whether an adolescent's decision to refuse recommended medical treatment ought to be respected. Unfortunately, however, such procedural virtues, in the present case at least, breed substantive vices. On the one hand, a doctrine of presumptive incapacity problematically excludes, as a priori incompetent, the request of a thoughtful and reflective terminally ill adolescent to forgo further clinical interventions. On the other, a doctrine of presumptive capacity problematically includes, as a priori competent, the decision of a less than reflective otherwise healthy adolescent to refuse life-saving medical treatment.

. . .

Adolescents present the law with a metaphysical quandary—their problematically crepuscular legal existence is implied in philosopher John Locke's apt phrase that "we are born free as we are born rational; not that we actually have the exercise [at birth] of either: age that brings one brings with it the other too." In other words, personhood is a metaphysical process involving a transformation from becoming to being over time that at some interval, for purely practical reasons, e.g., granting the right to vote, must be rendered a legal event that, ceteris paribus, occurs at an arbitrarily fixed point in time (the age of majority). Adolescents, in many times being able to give forceful, rational articulations of their wishes and desires, are markedly different from other legal non-persons such as infants, the profoundly retarded, and the senile. Their quasi-personhood is well reflected in the law, which, observes Elizabeth S. Scott, adopts a "binary classification" scheme: occasionally adolescents count as adults but usually they count as children.[6] On the one hand, adolescents may seek gainful employment, decide (in most states) to quit school at age sixteen, and on occasion, be held criminally responsible for their behavior. On the other, adolescents are prohibited from purchasing alcohol or cigarettes, from voting and serving on a jury, and cannot enter into binding contracts.

In the health care arena a similar "binary classification" system exists. In the vast majority of cases physicians must (on the pain of possible battery charges) obtain parental consent before treating an adolescent. Being shy of the age of legal majority, adolescents are assumed to lack sufficient cognitive and conative maturity to craft autonomous health care choices, therefore being deemed legally incapable of giving genuine informed consent to medical treatment. The ease (and in many cases necessity) of a "bright-line" arbitrary cutoff for such legal practices as serving on a jury, however, is not completely carried over to the domain of medical treatment. Legal exceptions, for both practical and ethical reasons, obtain. From a practical perspective, allowing adolescents an independent right to consent to some types of medical treatment, without their parents' foreknowledge, serves important public policy goals. Thus, in the utilitarian interest of preventing suicide, curbing illicit drug and alcohol abuse and halting the spread of venereal disease, adolescents are allowed to consent to the treatment of mental health disorders, alcohol/drug addiction and STDs without parental approval. Furthermore, by and large on ethical grounds alone, abortion case law carves out an independent realm of qualified adolescent medical decision-making. In a string of related cases the courts have consistently ruled that if a minor seeking an abortion can both demonstrate the ability to understand the risks and benefits of an elective abortion procedure and provide acceptable reasons for terminating her pregnancy then she ought to be viewed as a "mature minor," i.e., as a "child who is capable of understanding the nature and consequences of a particular medical intervention, and of its primary alternatives including non-intervention."[7] In turn, despite their formal mi-

6. Elizabeth S. Scott, The Legal Construction of Adolescence, 29 Hofstra L. Rev. 547, 548 (2000). Scott's primary concern is to preserve a separate, though modified, category of juvenile criminal law. She touches on adolescent healthcare issues only tangentially.

7. [A.M. Capron, The Competence of Children as Self–Deciders in Biomedical Inter-

nor status, such pregnant adolescents are afforded a full legal right to reproductive autonomy, substantively identical to that of their adult pregnant peers. To reason otherwise strikes many jurists as grossly iniquitous. More recently, a number of scholars have argued that sufficiently mature adolescents ought to be granted a right to consent to participate in genetic research and clinical drug trials.

NOTES

1. The debate over the ability of minors to make mature and informed decisions has prompted a great deal of social science literature. Much of the literature analyzes the cognitive and psychosocial development of minors and the effect of this development on their decision-making capacity. See, e.g., Tara L. Kuther, Medical Decision–Making and Minors: Issues of Consent and Assent, Adolescence, Vol. 38, No. 150, Summer 2003. In their article, psychologists Elizabeth Cauffman and Laurence Steinberg argue that in order to understand the weaknesses in a minor's decision-making, we should look not at the cognitive factors but rather at the psychosocial factors that influence young people. They present evidence that the decision-making process at various ages is linked more with these factors than with the physical development of the cognitive abilities. Elizabeth Cauffman & Laurence Steinberg, (Im)maturity of Judgment in Adolescence: Why Adolescents May Be Less Culpable Than Adults, Behav. Sci. Law 18: 741–760 (2000). See also, Laurence Steinberg, Cognitive and Affective Development in Adolescence, 9 Trends in Cognitive Sci. 69 (2000). A challenging by-product of recognizing the mature-minor doctrine within the medical community is the creation of several ethical problems for practitioners. See, Deborah P. Griswold & David B. Griswold, Minors' Rights to Refuse Medical Treatment Requested by Their Parents: Remaining Issues, 12 J. Am. Acad. Nurse Prac. 326 (2000).

2. Consider Goss v. Allen, 70 N.J. 442, 360 A.2d 388 (1976):

Sullivan, J.

This case involves a claim for personal injuries and arises out of a skiing accident which occurred at a ski resort in Vermont. . . .

. . .

Defendant, then 17 years of age, was a beginning skier who had limited cross-country skiing experience but had never attempted a downhill run. Nor had he ever been to Mad River Glen before. Upon arrival, defendant was sent to the beginners' slope. However, instead of riding the mechanical T-bar lift to the top, defendant confined his first run to the lower portion of the slope. He walked a quarter of the way up the hill and started to ski down, successfully completing the comparatively short run of 30 feet or so until he came to the abrupt left turn. In attempting to negotiate the turn, defendant lost control over his momentum and direction. He saw the two girls ahead of him but because of the short distance remaining, his efforts to regain control and his lack of experience, he did not call out until he was almost

ventions, in Who Speaks for the Child: The Problems of Proxy Consent 74 (Willard Gaylin & Ruth Macklin eds., 1982)]. Another legal avenue remains open here: the adolescent in question could be viewed as "partially emancipated" from his parents within the context of health care decision-making instead of a "mature minor" (as noted above). The latter alternative is more to the point in the context of an adolescent making an informed refusal of treatment. Emancipation normally only occurs by commissions/omissions on the part of parents, e.g., a minor becomes emancipated when his/her parents grant permission to serve in the armed forces. As such, the choice to emancipate normally rests in the parents' hands, regardless of adolescent competency. With a "mature minor" doctrine *only* looks to the decision-making capacities of the child in question, i.e., whether or not the minor possesses the cognitive equipment to be a "self-decider." *See id.* at 72–74 (explaining that whether one is deemed a "mature minor" depends on his ability to understand his decision and its implications).

upon the girls. Plaintiff attempted to get out of the way but was unable to do so and was struck and knocked down by defendant.

. . .

The trial court charged the jury that the standard of care applicable in the case was not the same degree of care required of an adult, but rather that degree of care which a reasonably prudent person of that age (defendant was 17 years of age) would have exercised under the same or similar circumstances. Following a side bar conference, the court supplemented its charge with the following:

> "All right. Perhaps I didn't charge as clearly as I thought that I had charged with reference to the duty of a 17 year old. I know that I used the term 17—year—old beginner, and that may lead to some confusion. Let me try to straighten it out. The law imposes on a 17 year old that standard of care that a 17 year old with the experience and background that this 17 year old had. It does not impose any higher or any lower degree of care than can reasonably be expected of a 17 year old with respect to the experience and background that Mr. Allen had in this case."

There was no exception taken to the charge. ... [T]he jury found the defendant not negligent.

... Following briefing of the issue and oral argument thereon, the Appellate Division reversed and remanded for a new trial finding plain error in the charge. ...

. . .

The Appellate Division ... criticized the trial court's application of the standard applicable to children to a 17-year-old person, pointing out that by N.J.S.A. 9:17–B1 et seq. every person in this State 18 or more years of age is deemed to be an adult. The Appellate Division could see little sense in holding an 18-year-old person to one standard of care and applying a lesser standard to one 17 years of age.

However, this problem will exist no matter where the line is drawn, whether it be at 10, 14 or 18 years. Since it has to be drawn somewhere, it is not unreasonable to fix it at the age of legal maturity—now 18 in this State—holding those under that age and capable of negligence to the standard of care required of a reasonable person of like age, intelligence and experience under like circumstances. Prosser, Torts, § 32 at 154–157 (4 Ed.1971). This case, though, must be decided on the basis of the law prior to the effective date of the cited statute. Although there is no decided case in New Jersey fixing the age at which the standard of care governing children no longer controls, 18 years would appear to be the age at which a person should be held to adult responsibility in tort matters. Such is already the case with criminal responsibility—18 being the age at which a person's criminal or anti-social behavior ceases to be regarded as juvenile delinquency and is treated as a criminal or quasi-criminal act, subject to the processes and sanctions normally applicable to adults. The trial court, therefore, charged the jury correctly as to the standard of care applicable to the 17-year-old defendant herein.

. . .

SCHREIBER, J. (DISSENTING).

The standard of care now made generally applicable to minors does not square with reality, nor does its purported application justify the charge given.

. . .

Under the norm adopted this day where the negligence or contributory negligence of an infant between ages 7 and 18 is in issue, his activity or inactivity is to be measured by a reasonable person of the same age, intelligence and experience under similar circumstances unless the activities "are so potentially hazardous as to require that the minor be held to an adult standard of care." There are several inherent difficulties in and inequitable consequences of this rule.

What criteria are to be employed by the jury to ascertain whether an activity is "potentially hazardous"? If a "potentially hazardous" activity is one which results in serious or permanent injury, then almost any activity might fall within that category. The injured person who has lost the sight of an eye resulting from a carelessly thrown dart, or stone, or firecracker, the death caused by a bicycle, or an individual seriously maimed due to an errant skier—all are indisputable proof of "potentially hazardous" activity. The majority prescribes no guideline except to imply that whenever licensing is required, the "potentially hazardous" test is met.[2] But the State does not impose a licensing requirement on all "potentially hazardous" activities and whether one has a license or not is often not relevant in measuring conduct of a reasonably prudent person. Whether the driver of an automobile is licensed, for example, is not relevant in adjudicating if the automobile was being driven in a reasonable prudent manner. . . .

To the injured party, his loss is the same irrespective of the wrongdoer's date of birth and it is inequitable and unjust that a minor should not be expected to exercise the same degree of care as the mythical reasonable and prudent person, at least when engaged in adult activities.[3] The majority's proposition unnecessarily sanctions the imposition of the burden of young people's hazards on innocent victims. Whenever an infant participates in activities in which adults normally engage, the infant should be held to the adult standard of care. Other courts have not hesitated to do so. Minors participating in these activities are mature enough to possess the "discretion and physical capacity consistent with . . . the presumption of adult responsibility . . .". Nelson v. Arrowhead Freight Lines, 99 Utah 129, 104 P.2d 225, 228 (1940).

. . .

The 18-year-old line drawn today is contrary to policies enunciated by the legislature in regulating some aspects of the conduct of minors in relation to others. A 16-year-old juvenile may be tried as an adult for a homicide, treason, offense against the person in an aggressive, violent and willful manner, or for sale and distribution of narcotics. At age 16½, a person may obtain a special learner's permit to drive a car so that a driver's license may be obtained at age 17. At age 13 one may be licensed to operate a boat with an outboard motor. Under this Court's rules a 17-year-old infant may file a verified petition. The 18-year-old line is not consonant with the common law rule that at age 14 an infant is presumed to have the capacity to be guilty of criminal intent. Blackstone's Commentaries, Bk. IV, Sec. 23. The Restatement, Torts 2d, § 283A, Comment (a) refers to the fact that its rule "has seldom been applied to anyone over the age of sixteen" and "is commonly applied to children of tender years."

The 18—year demarcation line ignores the earlier mental development of young people. A few comments from experts in the field of child behavior demonstrate the point.

> . . . [T]he middle-years [6 to 12 plus] a child's growing mastery of symbols and his ever-broadening fund of general knowledge permit him to think in ways that come to approximate those of adults. Indeed, in some areas, the child may know a great deal more than his less educated parents and so be able to think more rationally than they. . . . [L. Stone and J. Church, Childhood and Adolescence at 412–413 (2d ed. 1968)].

. . .

> . . . Hillary Rodman [in "Children Under the Law," 43 Harv.Ed.Rev. 487, 489 (1973)] notes that the law's placement of the dividing line between legal minority

2. No license is required for a motorized bike, but a ten-speed bike can be pedaled at 25 miles per hour on a flat road. The U.S. Consumer Product Safety Commission reports that there are 500 to 1000 fatalities and about 500,000 permanently crippled each year from bicycle mishaps.

3. Dean Shulman acknowledged that "in some situations a minor is fully as competent as a person over twenty-one and should be held to the same standard of conduct." "The Standard of Care Required of Children," 37 Yale L.J. 618 (1928).

> and adult status at the age of eighteen or twenty-one years is "artificial and simplistic" because it obscures the dramatic differences among children of different ages and the striking similarities between older children and adults. That observation seems so sound and obvious that it raises the question of how such differences—and also the resemblance between older children and adults—have come to be obscured? [Skolnick, "The Limits of Childhood: Conceptions of Child Development and Social Context," in Children and the Law (Symposium), 39 Law & Contemp.Prob. 38, 43 (1975)].

Selection of the 16th year is a more reasonable age at which to draw the line for the individual to be held to an adult standard of care irrespective of the activity.

I would adopt a rule that an infant 16 years or over would be held to an adult standard of care and that an infant between ages 7 and 16 would be rebuttably presumed to have the duty to act, while engaged in an adult activity, that is, one in which adults normally or usually engage, as a reasonably prudent person, but that, upon a showing that adult judgmental capacity for that type of activity is not warranted, the subjective-objective criteria of the *Restatement* and adopted by the majority be applied.[6] Application of this rule recognizes the difference between negligence and contributory negligence since the required judgment capacity in foreseeing and avoiding the hazards created by others may be substantially greater than that to be comprehended by one's own acts.[7] If the infant between ages 7 and 16 is found not to have been occupied in an adult activity, the Restatement rule adopted by the majority would be applicable. As to those 16 or over I would apply the adult standard.

B. AGE AND THE CAPACITY TO CONTRACT

Shields v. Gross

New York Court of Appeals, 1983.
58 N.Y.2d 338, 461 N.Y.S.2d 254, 448 N.E.2d 108.

■ SIMONS, J.

The issue on this appeal is whether an infant model may disaffirm a prior unrestricted consent executed on her behalf by her parent and maintain an action pursuant to section 51 of the Civil Rights Law against her photographer for republication of photographs of her. We hold that she may not.

Plaintiff is now a well-known actress. For many years prior to these events she had been a child model and in 1975, when she was 10 years of age, she obtained several modeling jobs with defendant through her agent, the Ford Model Agency. One of the jobs, a series of photographs to be

6. Professor Bohlen suggests that where harm has been intended the infant should be held "to exactly the same extent as for his failure to conform to those standards of conduct which are obligatory upon normal persons." "Liability in Torts of Infants and Insane Persons," 23 Mich.L.Rev. 9, 32 (1924). See Note, "A Proposal for a Modified Standard of Care for the Infant Engaged in an Adult Activity," Ind.L.J. 405 (1967).

7. Shulman, supra fn. 3 commented:

> The standard of conduct to which an infant is to be held when his own liability is in question may properly be quite different from that to which he is to be held when he seeks to recover from an admittedly negligent defendant. It is apparent that different considerations may be involved in these several types of cases. There is a strong policy in favor of protecting children from losses attributable to their immaturity. It would be quite plausible, therefore, for a court to be more lenient toward children whose injuries are attributable, not only to their immaturity, but also to conceded tortious conduct on the part of the defendant, than toward children who are the sole responsible causes of injury to others. [37 Yale L.J. at 619].

financed by Playboy Press, required plaintiff to pose nude in a bathtub. It was intended that these photos would be used in a publication entitled "Portfolio 8" (later renamed "Sugar and Spice"). Before the photographic sessions, plaintiff's mother and legal guardian, Teri Shields, executed two consents in favor of defendant.* After the pictures were taken, they were used not only in "Sugar and Spice" but also, to the knowledge of plaintiff and her mother, in other publications and in a display of larger-than-life photo enlargements in the windows of a store on Fifth Avenue in New York City. Indeed, plaintiff subsequently used the photos in a book that she published about herself and to do so her mother obtained an authorization from defendant to use them. Over the years defendant has also photographed plaintiff for *Penthouse Magazine, New York Magazine* and for advertising by the Courtauldts and Avon companies.

In 1980 plaintiff learned that several of the 1975 photographs had appeared in a French magazine called "Photo" and, disturbed by that publication and by information that defendant intended others, she attempted to buy the negatives. In 1981, she commenced this action in tort and contract seeking compensatory and punitive damages and an injunction permanently enjoining defendant from any further use of the photographs. Special Term . . . ruled that the consents were unrestricted as to time and use and it therefore dismissed plaintiff's complaint. In doing so, however, it granted plaintiff limited relief. On defendant's stipulation it permanently enjoined defendant from using the photographs in "pornographic magazines or publications whose appeal is of a predominantly prurient nature" and it charged him with the duty of policing their use. The Appellate Division, by a divided court, modified the judgment on the law and granted plaintiff a permanent injunction enjoining defendant from using the pictures for purposes of advertising or trade. . . . Since the Appellate Division accepted the trial court's findings that the consents were valid and unrestricted as to time and use, we are presented with only a narrow issue of law concerning the legal effect to be given to the parent's consents.

Historically, New York common law did not recognize a cause of action for invasion of privacy. (Arrington v. New York Times Co., 55 N.Y.2d 433; Roberson v. Rochester Folding Box Co., 171 N.Y. 538). In 1909, however, responding to the *Roberson* decision, the Legislature enacted sections 50 and 51 of the Civil Rights Law. Section 50 is penal and makes it a misdemeanor to use a living person's name, portrait or picture for advertising purposes without prior "written consent". Section 51 is remedial and creates a related civil cause of action on behalf of the injured party permitting relief by injunction or damages. Section 51 of the statute states that the prior "written consent" which will bar the civil action is to be as "above provided", referring to section 50, and section 50, in turn, provides that: "A person, firm or corporation that uses for advertising purposes, or for the purposes of trade, the name, portrait or picture of any living person *without having first*

* The consents provided in pertinent part:

"I hereby give the photographer, his legal representatives, and assigns, those for whom the photographer is acting, and those acting with his permission, or his employees, the right and permission to copyright and/or use, reuse and/or publish, and republish photographic pictures or portraits of me, or in which I may be distorted in character, or form, in conjunction with my own or a fictitious name, or reproductions thereof in color, or black and white made through any media by the photographer at his studio or elsewhere, for any purpose whatsoever; including the use of any printed matter in conjunction therewith.

"I hereby waive any right to inspect or approve the finished photograph or advertising copy or printed matter that may be used in conjunction therewith or to the eventual use that it might be applied."

obtained the written consent of such person, or if a minor of his or her parent or guardian, is guilty of a misdemeanor" (emphasis added).

Thus, whereas in *Roberson*, the infant plaintiff had no cause of action against the advertiser under the common law for using her pictures, the new statute gives a cause of action to those similarly situated unless they have executed a consent or release in writing to the advertiser before use of the photographs. The statute acts to restrict an advertiser's prior unrestrained common-law right to use another's photograph until written consent is obtained. Once written consent is obtained, however, the photograph may be published as permitted by its terms.

Concededly, at common law an infant could disaffirm his written consent or, for that matter, a consent executed by another on his or her behalf. Notwithstanding these rules, it is clear that the Legislature may abrogate an infant's common-law right to disaffirm or, conversely, it may confer upon infants the right to make binding contracts. Where a statute expressly permits a certain class of agreements to be made by infants, that settles the question and makes the agreement valid and enforceable. That is precisely what happened here. The Legislature, by adopting section 51, created a new cause of action and it provided in the statute itself the method for obtaining an infant's consent to avoid liability. Construing the statute strictly, as we must since it is in derogation of the common law, the parent's consent is binding on the infant and no words prohibiting disaffirmance are necessary to effectuate the legislative intent. Inasmuch as the consents in this case complied with the statutory requirements, they were valid and may not be disaffirmed.

Nor do we believe that the consents may be considered void because the parties failed to comply with the provisions of section 3–105 of the General Obligations Law requiring prior court approval of infants' contracts. By its terms, section 3–105 applies only to performing artists; such as actors, musicians, dancers and professional athletes. Moreover, it is apparent by comparing other statutes with it that the Legislature knowingly has differentiated between child performers and child models. Thus, section 3229 (formerly § 3216–c) of the Education Law, which applies to "Child performers", is referred to in section 3–105 (subd. 2, par. a) of the General Obligations Law but section 3230 of the Education Law, which applies to child models, is not. Child models are also recognized as a separate work classification in section 172 (subd. 2, par. f) of the Labor Law. Furthermore, section 3–105 was not designed to expand the rights of infants to disaffirm their contracts . . . but to provide assurance to those required to deal with infants that the infants would not later disaffirm executory contracts to the adult contracting party's disadvantage. Sections 50 and 51 as we interpret them serve the same purpose, to bring certainty to an important industry which necessarily uses minors for its work. This same need for certainty was the impetus behind not only section 3–105 but the various other sections of the General Obligations Law which prohibit disaffirmance of an infant's contract.

Realistically, the procedures of prior court approval set forth in section 3–105, while entirely appropriate and necessary for performing artists and professional athletes, are impractical for a child model who, whether employed regularly or sporadically, works from session to session, sometimes for many different photographers. Moreover, they work for fees which are relatively modest when compared to those received by actors or professional athletes who may be employed by one employer at considerably greater remuneration for a statutorily permissible three-year term. Indeed, the fee in this case was $450, hardly sufficient to warrant the elaborate court proceedings required by section 3–105 or to necessitate a court's determination of what part should be set aside and preserved for the infant's future needs. Nor do we think court approval necessary under the circumstances existing in the normal child model's career. Given the nature of the employment, it is entirely reasonable for the Legislature to substitute the parents' judgment and approval of what is best for their child for that of a court.

It should be noted that plaintiff did not contend that the photographs were obscene or pornographic. Her only complaint was that she was embarrassed because "they [the photographs] are not me now." The trial court specifically found that the photographs were not pornographic and it enjoined use of them in pornographic publications. Thus, there is no need to discuss the unenforceability of certain contracts which violate public policy or to equate an infant's common-law right to disaffirm with that principle, as the dissent apparently does.

. . .

■ Jasen, J. (dissenting). Since I believe that the interests of society and this State in protecting its children must be placed above any concern for trade or commercialism, I am compelled to dissent. . . .

At the outset, it should be made clear that this case does not involve the undoing of a written consent given by a mother to invade her infant daughter's privacy so as to affect *prior* benefits derived by a person relying on the validity of the consent pursuant to sections 50 and 51 of the Civil Rights Law. Rather, what is involved is the right of an infant, now 17 years of age, to disaffirm her mother's consent with respect to future use of a nude photograph taken of her at age 10.

The majority holds, as a matter of law, not only in this case but as to all present and future consents executed by parents on behalf of children pursuant to sections 50 and 51 of the Civil Rights Law, that once a parent consents to the invasion of privacy of a child, the child is forever bound by that consent and may never disaffirm the continued invasion of his or her privacy, even where the continued invasion of the child's privacy may cause the child enormous embarrassment, distress and humiliation.

I find this difficult to accept as a rational rule of law, particularly so when one considers that it has long been the rule in this State that a minor enjoys an almost absolute right to disaffirm a contract entered into either by the minor or by the minor's parent on behalf of the minor and the statute in question does not in any manner abrogate this salutary right.

. . .

. . . [N]othing compels the majority's conclusion that the right to disaffirm a contract was eliminated when the Legislature created a new cause of action for invasion of privacy merely because that statute provided safeguards for the child's privacy by giving the parent the right to grant or withhold consent. When both rights are viewed, as I believe they must be, as protection for the child, logic and policy compels the conclusion that the two rights should exist coextensively. The requirement that a parent consent before the child's privacy can be invaded by commercial interests establishes the parent as the first guardian of the child's interest. But the State retains its long-standing role of *parens patriae* so that if the parent fails to protect the child's interests, the State will intervene and do so. One means of doing so is to allow the child to exercise its right to disaffirm if the child concludes that its parent improvidently consented to the invasion of the child's privacy interests. Given the strong policy concern of the State in the child's best interests, I can only conclude that the Legislature did not intend to abrogate the child's common-law right to disaffirm a contract when it required, by statute, the additional protection of written, parental consent prior to any commercial use of the child's image.

. . .

NOTES

1. Consider Rhonda Gay Hartman, Adolescent Autonomy: Clarifying an Ageless Conundrum, 51 Hastings L.J. 1265 (2000):

. . .

> . . . A quintessential query to a contracts class by a law professor may be as follows: Suppose that a 35–year-old strikes an agreement with a 17–year-old regarding the sale of the elder's red corvette, and in good faith delivers to the younger man the automobile under the terms of the agreement, which stipulates that a payment of $5,000.00 constitutes the bargained-for-exchange. Despite requests and demands, no payment is forthcoming. What result? The classic response is that the 17–year-old would prevail, because an adolescent may disaffirm a contract based on minority status, alone. Moreover, upon reaching 18 years, he may either disaffirm or ratify the contract, although the preferred and prevailing approach is to disallow disaffirmance where the adult contracting party relied on the agreement to her detriment. Adolescents, however, are legally responsible for the reasonable value of necessaries furnished to them. Apparently, adolescents may not bargain away the power of disaffirmance, because the quid pro quo surrender is, itself, subject to disaffirmance.
>
> The rule of disaffirmance or "infancy doctrine" dates back centuries. Comparing adolescents "to those persons laboring under mental incapacity," the Ohio Supreme Court in 1896 invoked the disaffirmance rule to further the "elementary principle that contracting minds must meet and agree upon terms and consideration." Not even an "overwhelming influence on modern contract law" like the Uniform Commercial Code has displaced the disaffirmance rule, which is entrenched in American law.
>
> The power of disaffirmance constitutes both a sword and shield, as it may be used either defensively or offensively, as the case of Monahan v. Friederick illustrates. Brian Monahan agreed to purchase a used car owned by Don Friederick and executed a contract for sale. Under the sale agreement, legal consideration amounted to $1,795, which Brian paid. Brian used the auto for transportation to and from work and for recreation, until it entailed mechanical problems. Brian then sought to disaffirm the contract, return the car, and recover the purchase price, which was refused by the defendant. Invoking the disaffirmance rule, the Wisconsin Appellate Court ruled that Brian was entitled to the return of the purchase price, $1,795.
>
> The rule of disaffirmance may also be characterized as a double-edged sword. The purported empowerment based solely on minority status is, in effect, quite disempowering by presuming that adolescents must be protected against improvident judgments and impaired decisional ability that negates responsibility and accountability. The rule is also rather arbitrary and unjust because it requires a contracting party who bargains in good faith to shoulder the risk of disaffirmance, despite the possibility that the contracting adolescent may be more mature or have business acumen that may equal, or even exceed, that of adults. Moreover, the rule may actually invite contrived overreaching or fraud by an adolescent. . . .

One area of law where the doctrine of infant disaffirmance has changed is in the entertainment industry. California, in particular has developed a strong child entertainment law that often allows minors to create legally binding contracts. See Jessica Krieg, There's No Business Like Show Business: Child Entertainers and the Law, 6 U. Pa. J. Lab. & Emp. L. 429 (2004).

2. If the disaffirmance principle appears overbroad in its protection of minors, what additional reforms would be most appropriate:

(a) applying estoppel after misrepresentation of age?

(b) requiring restoration of consideration or its money equivalent?

(c) removing by statute the power of disaffirmance for most types of contracts (not merely for education loans or insurance contracts)?

(d) eliminating the disaffirmance power altogether?

(e) preserving the power to disaffirm, but making the presumption of incapacity rebuttable for minors over 16?

Does the trend toward lowering the general "age of majority" to 18 rectify most of the problems of disaffirmance?

While disaffirmance is often viewed as a license for minors to dupe unwary businessmen, it may also preclude the possibility of a minor contracting at all. As an attorney, how would you treat a minor who approached you for tax advice on the income from a trust or a possible suit for disaffirmance of a contract knowing that he might attempt to disaffirm your fee?

3. A minor's ability to disaffirm a contract has expanded in some jurisdictions. The Florida Court of Appeals has ruled that a minor who waives the rights to sue an actor for negligence in a contract is not bound by that waiver when the negligent activity causes injury. See Dilallo v. Riding Safely, 687 So.2d 353 (Fla.Dist.Ct.App.1997). Cf. Alexander v. Kendall Cent. Sch. Dist., 221 A.D.2d 898, 634 N.Y.S.2d 318 (1995) (minor allowed to proceed with action against athletic club in spite of liability release that the parents executed in part because he is not bound by such a release).

C. AGE AND PROPERTY RIGHTS

Kreigh v. Cogswell

Supreme Court of Wyoming, 1933.
45 Wyo. 531, 21 P.2d 831.

■ BLUME, JUSTICE.

Action by the plaintiffs for conversion. There was a judgment for the plaintiffs and the defendant appeals.

. . .

The plaintiffs are minors, daughters of Claude Kreigh, of the ages of 18, 16, and 10, respectively. The defendant Bertha Cogswell is a creditor of Claude Kreigh, having obtained judgment against him. An execution was issued on this judgment, and the defendant Thompson, as sheriff of Fremont county, levied upon certain sheep, fifteen head in all, as the property of the judgment debtor, and sold them in part satisfaction of the judgment. Before the sale a notice was served upon him by the plaintiffs, claiming to be the owners of the property in question. But no attention was paid to the notice. Some of the sheep in question were originally owned by one Davidson and one Todd. These sheep were then young. They were "bum lambs," that is to say, lambs which would not follow the flock, and hence were presented to the plaintiffs as a gift, and were fed and raised by them. Some of them thereafter had some lambs, and the sheep in question, levied on and sold by the sheriff, were the sheep originally so given to the plaintiffs or the natural increase and increment thereof. The plaintiffs, minors, lived with their father on a farm, and the sheep were brought up within his household and on the property controlled and occupied by him, and the minors had no other property of their own. The father had some of these sheep assessed in his name for taxation in 1930.

Counsel for appellant argues that the minor children acquired the property in question for the benefit of their father, citing as authority the well-known principle that ordinarily the earnings of minor children belong to the father. But this is not such a case. No earnings are involved, except incidentally. The question is whether the property, acquired as a gift by the children, belongs to the father. We have not been able to find any cases which so hold. There is authority in Louisiana that the usufruct of such property, which, possibly, would include the lambs from the sheep given to the minors, belongs to the father. But that rule has its own peculiar historical setting. It appears to be derived from the Roman law, through the Code Napoleon. Originally, under the Roman law, the oldest male member of an agnatic family, who might be the father, the grandfather, or greatgrandfather, had peculiar paternal power (patria potestas). Unless emancipated, the offspring, with some exceptions in the case of married girls, were absolutely under his control, no matter of what age they might be. All property acquired by them in any manner whatever, whether by earnings, by gift or otherwise, was acquired for him. They were incapable of owning any property of their own. . . .

. . .

The common law took a different path from that of the Roman law. Holdsworth and Pollock and Maitland agree that we have no evidence that the Anglo–Saxons knew an institution at all comparable to the paternal power of the Roman law. While the father had control and custody of his minor children, and could even, in case of necessity, sell them when they had not passed the seventh year his control ceased when they became of age. Bracton states that a minor can acquire property, but he makes the consent of a guardian necessary in connection therewith, which seems to hark back to the Roman law, much of which Bracton copied, and the author mentioned such consent, perhaps, in view of the rule existing in full force prior to Justinian, that an acceptance of an inheritance exposed the person accepting to the danger of the payment of the debts of the inheritance-leaver. Holdsworth makes the unqualified statement that, under the Anglo–Saxon law, "the infant can acquire and own property." He, however, merely cites Pollock and Maitland, and these authorities say: "An infant may well have proprietary rights, even though his father is still alive. Boys and girls often inherit land from their mothers or maternal kinsfolk. In such case the father will usually be holding the land for his life as 'tenant by the law of England,' but the fee will belong to the child. ... What is more there are cases in which the father will have no right at all in the land that his infant son has inherited; the wardship of that land will belong to some lord."

The authors do not explain the meaning of a tenancy by the law of England, and the first portion of the statement quoted seems to intimate that, perhaps, in certain cases, the father would have the usufruct of the land during his lifetime. Indeed, a statement in Coke on Littleton, may bear the construction that, while a father would at times be accountable for the profits of the lands held by a minor, he would not be accountable in other cases; the difference arising out of the difference of the tenure under which the land was held. Mr. Hargrave, in his note to this passage, disputes that it bears this construction, and holds that the father was accountable for the profits in all cases. However that may be, subsequent decisions took the view which Mr. Hargrave takes. In Morgan v. Morgan, 1 Atk. 489, 26 Eng.Repr. 310, decided in 1737, the court said that, "where a person, whether a father or a stranger, enters upon the estate of an infant, and continues the possession, this court will consider such person as entering as guardian to the infant, and will decree an account against him." So in Butler v. Butler, 3 Atk. 58, 26 Eng.Repr. 836, decided in 1743, it was held that a father was not entitled to take any part of the personal estate left to a minor, or the accumulations thereof, for the maintenance of the child. This view was upheld in 1746 in the case of Darley v. Darley, 3 Atk. 399, 26 Eng.Repr. 1929, where the court said that, "where legacies are given to a child by a relation, a father cannot make use of them in the maintenance of such child, but must provide for him out of his own pocket." Blackstone in his Commentaries considers the rule well settled, and lucidly states: "A father has no other power over his son's estate than as his trustee or guardian; for though he may receive the profits during the child's minority, yet he must account for them when he comes of age." . . .

The rule stated by Blackstone is the rule announced in every common-law state in this country which has had occasion to pass upon it. In 46 C.J. 1314, it is said: "As a general rule any property acquired by the child in any way except by its own labor or services belongs to the child, and not to the parent." And a creditor, of course, can have no greater interest therein than a parent. It furthermore goes without saying that a parent cannot deprive a child of its property except pursuant to law, and the fact that in this instance the father had the property in question assessed as his property could not affect the title of the children. . . .

It is also held that a father is not entitled to any extraordinary gain of the child, or to profits arising from a sale, or to rents and profits derived from the occupancy of the child's land. The same principle would apply to the increase of the sheep which were given to the children in the case at bar, for the profits thus arising may be likened to the rents and profits from land or to the interest derived from money. Moreover, the fact that the sheep were kept on the farm occupied by the children's father and under his control could not have the effect of transferring ownership to the latter. . . .

It is true that, ordinarily, the earnings of a minor child, unless waived, belong to the father, and that its labor is to its father's use. But the only labor involved in this case is that which the children incidentally bestowed in raising the sheep given them. That labor, even if belonging to the father, and even if he could not waive it or make a gift of it to the children as against creditors, could not, ipso facto in any event, change the ownership of the property involved herein. The most that defendant could claim in this case would be that she could in some way, by the establishment of a lien or otherwise, reach and appropriate to her own use the value of this labor and of the benefit bestowed by the father upon the sheep by reason of them being on his farm. We need not decide whether the law would authorize this under the circumstances of this case, for the reason that there is no evidence that any value, in money, can be attributed thereto.

The judgment of the district court must accordingly be affirmed, and it is so ordered.

NOTES

1. **Uniform Gifts to Minors Act.** As *Kreigh* makes clear, children may receive gifts of property, but any subsequent contracts they make are subject to the principle of disaffirmance. Consequently, effective management and disposal of their property may require a trust arrangement.

All fifty states and the District of Columbia have adopted the Uniform Gifts to Minors Act. It provides a simple and inexpensive method for making gifts to minors that avoids the complexities of the traditional trust arrangement. These statutes can also be a trap for parents who are unaware of the Act's provisions.

2. **Devises and Bequests.** The original Statute of Wills (1540) permitted minors to devise realty, but an amendment three years later placed the minimum age at 21. See 32 Hen. VIII, c. 1; 34 and 35 Hen. VIII, c. 5, § 14. Devises of personal property, on the other hand, were governed by the civil law standard of age 14 for males and age 12 for females. In the 19th century, England provided by statute for wills of both personalty and realty; today every state has the age for testamentary capacity fixed by statute.

Radakovich v. Radakovich

Superior Court of Pennsylvania, 2004.
2004 PA Super 82, 846 A.2d 709.

■ STEVENS, J.

This is an appeal from the March 12, 2003 order entered in the Court of Common Pleas of Indiana County declaring Appellee Scott R. Radakovich (Son) to be the owner of a PNC brokerage account and remanding certain equitable distribution claims relating to Appellee Richard L. Radakovich ("Husband") and Appellant Bonnie Radakovich ("Wife") to a master for resolution. . . . We affirm.

. . . On December 5, 1997, Wife filed a complaint in divorce averring that Husband and Wife were married on November 23, 1974, and have one child, Son, who was then seventeen years old. Wife sought custody of Son, equitable distribution, spousal support and/or alimony, and possession of the marital residence. On January 29, 1999, a master was appointed to resolve the divorce and economic claims, and Wife listed in her income/expense statement a PNC brokerage account number 57840375 as an asset belonging to Husband/Son.

On May 25, 1999, a hearing was held before the master, and on July 19, 1999, the master filed a report. In the report, the master stated the following regarding the PNC brokerage account at issue:

> Testimony revealed that this account contained approximately $113,000 and according to [Husband] was formed for the purpose of financing the parties' [son's] post secondary education. [Wife] testified that she did not know whose names were originally placed on the account which is titled in the joint names of [Husband] and Son, but that she believed [Wife] and [Husband] were joint owners.
>
> The master finds her testimony not believable because she and [Husband] were sitting at the same desk, executed the documents at the same time, and it is believed that she knew the form of ownership. Yet, now [Wife] wants the Master to believe that she did not.
>
> The Master recommends that this account be turned over to [Son] upon his reaching the age of majority.

The master then recommended that the PNC brokerage account ... be placed in trust for Son, to be given to him when he reaches the age of majority.

On July 23, 1999, Husband filed exceptions to the master's report wherein he alleged that the master ... erred in directing that the PNC brokerage account be placed in trust for Son. ... On July 29, 1999, Wife filed exceptions to the master's report wherein she alleged, *inter alia*, that the master erred in ordering the PNC brokerage account be placed in trust and released to Son when he reached the age of majority, and the master erred in failing to make a recommendation concerning equitable distribution. Wife asserted that the account consisted solely of contributions made from marital funds, the account represented a substantial portion of the marital estate, and she never intended that the entire account would be used for Son's educational purposes.

. . .

Subsequently, on May 8, 2000, the trial court filed an opinion and order denying in part and granting in part the parties' exceptions to the master's report. With regard to the PNC brokerage account at issue, the trial court concluded that the account contained $113,825.00 and that the account was primarily established for Son's education. However, the trial court further concluded that Son's education would cost $48,000.00 only, and that the remaining $65,825.00 was marital property subject to equitable distribution.

. . .

On November 30, 2001, Son filed a petition to intervene pursuant to Pa. R.C.P. 2328 alleging that Son is twenty-one years old, he is an indispensable party to the matter, and he is entitled to the entire PNC brokerage account. By order filed March 1, 2002, the trial court granted Son leave to intervene

Following testimony taken on July 15, 2002, and October 7, 2002, by order and opinion filed on March 12, 2003, the trial court concluded that Son was not barred from asserting his claim as an intervener, and that the PNC brokerage account ... was Son's property under the Pennsylvania Uniform Transfers to Minors Act (PUTMA), 20 Pa. C.S.A. § 5301–5310. In so ruling, the trial court stated, "[t]he parties must carefully note the limited scope of this Court's ruling. The Court holds [Son] is the owner of the account under the UTMA. The Court is not ruling on whether any of the account may be treated as marital property for purposes of ongoing litigation between [Husband and Wife]. ..."

On April 3, 2003, Wife filed an appeal to this Court from the trial court's March 12, 2003 order....

. . .

[She contends] that the trial court erred in concluding the PNC brokerage account was subject to the Pennsylvania Uniform Transfers to Minors Act (PUTMA), 20 Pa. C.S.A. § 5301–5310. Wife contends that ownership of the account should have been analyzed under 23 Pa. C.S.A. §§ 3501 and 3323 of the Pennsylvania Divorce Code since Son failed to prove that the brokerage account was an *inter vivos* gift made to him by Husband and Wife. Wife specifically alleges that she had no intent to gift the entire brokerage account to Son.

In determining that PUTMA was applicable in this case, the trial court stated the following:

> The transfer here meets the requirements of the [P]UTMA. The documents plainly indicate an intent to create a [P]UTMA account and otherwise meet the statutory requirements for [P]UTMA creation. Section 5703(a). The transfer was made only for one minor, and only one person was the custodian. Section 5310. As a result, the transfer is irrevocable, and the custodial property is indefeasibly vested in the minor. Section 5311(b) and 5307(a).

We find no abuse of discretion in this regard.

> When the language of a statute is clear and unambiguous, it is not to be disregarded under the pretext of pursuing the spirit of the statute. Only when the language of the statute is ambiguous does statutory construction become necessary.
>
> The purpose of PUTMA is to provide an inexpensive, easy way for giving property to minors. Section 5304 of PUTMA addresses the irrevocable nature of transfers to PUTMA accounts and provides:
>
> > A person may make a transfer by irrevocable gift to, or the irrevocable exercise of a power of appointment in favor of, a custodian for the benefit of a minor pursuant to Section 5309 (relating to manner of creating custodial property and effecting transfer).
>
> 20 Pa. C.S.A. § 5304. Whatever its source, custodial property that is held pursuant to Section 5304 is the property of the minor child. Section 5309, which addresses the manner of creating custodial property and effecting transfer, provides in relevant part:
>
> (a) Creation of custodial property.-Custodial property is created and a transfer is made whenever:
>
> ... (2) Money is paid or delivered to a broker or financial institution for credit to an account in the name of the transferor, an adult other than the transferor or a trust company, followed in substance by the words:
>
> > 'as custodian for (name of minor) under the Pennsylvania Uniform Transfers to Minors Act.'
>
> 20 Pa. C.S.A. § 5309. The plain meaning of Section 5309(a)(2) indicates that a transfer is made and "custodial property" is created when money is deposited into a brokerage account in the name of the parent as custodian for the minor under PUTMA.
>
> . . .
>
> The plain meaning of Section 5311(b) [of PUTMA] is that a transfer made into the PUTMA account of the minor is irrevocable and the vesting of the custodial property in the minor cannot be undone.
>
> As the above reflects, the relevant PUTMA provisions are unambiguous on their face and they, therefore, must be given effect in accordance with their plain and common meaning. The plain and common meaning of the relevant provisions of PUTMA is that money transferred into a custodial brokerage account is irrevocably the property of the minor child.

Sternlicht v. Sternlicht, 2003 PA Super 95, 822 A.2d 732, 737–738 (Pa. Super. 2003), *appeal granted,* 575 Pa. 499, 837 A.2d 459 (Pa. December 2, 2003) (citations and quotations omitted).

. . . Ronald P. Hunter testified that he is a financial consultant at PNC Investments and that he met with Husband and Wife in April 1996. Mr. Hunter testified he established a UGMA[8] account on behalf of Son, and Husband was the named custodian. Mr. Hunter testified that the application indicated that the account was registered to "Richard Radakovich C/F Scott R. Radakovich, PA UGMA custodian," and that "C/F" indicated the account was a custodian account. Mr. Hunter indicated that Husband and Wife were present when the application was completed, Wife did not object to the creation of the account on behalf of Son, and Wife did not object to Husband being named as the custodian.

Husband testified that in April 1996 he opened a custodial account for Son under the Uniformed Gift to Minors Act, and that Wife was present when the account was opened. Husband testified that both he and Wife agreed to set aside money for Son's education, the funds removed from the brokerage account have been used for Son's education, and Son's education was the purpose of the brokerage account. Husband testified that he was named as the custodian of the brokerage account, and he and Wife discussed the brokerage account. . . . Husband testified that he believed he no longer owned the money when it was placed into the brokerage account. Husband testified that the money deposited into the brokerage account came from the parties' joint checking account, that Wife had knowledge of the deposits, that Wife agreed with the deposits, and that Wife saw the statements. Husband specifically testified that he consulted with Wife before deposits were made and that she was in full, total agreement.

Wife testified that Husband handled the finances, he established bank accounts, and he determined the amount to be deposited into the accounts. Wife testified that Husband did not discuss the brokerage account with her, although she was aware that it was being set up for Son's education. admitted that the brokerage account was set up for Son with Husband as the custodian in a UGMA account. Wife testified she did not know the ramifications of establishing a UGMA account and no one explained such to her. Wife admitted that she knew Husband's role as the custodian was to oversee the account because Son was a minor. Wife testified that she was not aware that she was giving money to Son as a gift when the brokerage account was established.

Wife admitted that she and Husband met with Mr. Hunter in April 1996, that a brokerage account was established for Son's education, and that she believed the account would give her and Husband a better return on their money. Wife admitted that PNC sent statements to the house regarding the brokerage account, but she chose not to read the statements. Wife admitted that she never told Husband that he could not use money from the parties' joint checking account to fund the brokerage account.

Based on all of the aforementioned, we conclude that the trial court properly applied PUTMA in determining whether the brokerage account was the property of Son. By Wife's own admission, the account was specifically set up under PUTMA, Wife knew the account was being established on behalf of Son, and Wife knew Husband was the named custodian. The fact Wife did not know all of the ramifications of establishing an account under PUTMA and that she may not have specifically intended the account to be owned by Son does not require the conclusion PUTMA is inapplicable. See

8. PUTMA is the successor legislation to the Pennsylvania Uniform Gifts to Minors Act (UGMA).

Sternlicht, supra (holding that lack of donative intent of the funds are of no consequence under the principles of PUTMA and ignorance of the law is no excuse). As such, we find Wife's last issue to be meritless.

Affirmed.

D. AGE AND THE FIRST AMENDMENT

Tinker v. Des Moines School District

Supreme Court of the United States, 1969.
393 U.S. 503, 89 S.Ct. 733, 21 L.Ed.2d 731.

■ JUSTICE FORTAS delivered the opinion of the Court.

Petitioner John F. Tinker, 15 years old, and petitioner Christopher Eckhardt, 16 years old, attended high schools in Des Moines, Iowa. Petitioner Mary Beth Tinker, John's sister, was a 13–year-old student in junior high school.

In December 1965, a group of adults and students in Des Moines held a meeting at the Eckhardt home. The group determined to publicize their objections to the hostilities in Vietnam and their support for a truce by wearing black armbands during the holiday season and by fasting on December 16 and New Year's Eve. . . .

The principals of the Des Moines schools became aware of the plan to wear armbands. On December 14, 1965, they met and adopted a policy that any student wearing an armband to school would be asked to remove it, and if he refused he would be suspended until he returned without the armband. Petitioners were aware of the regulation that the school authorities adopted.

On December 16, Mary Beth and Christopher wore black armbands to their schools. John Tinker wore his armband the next day. They were all sent home and suspended from school until they would come back without their armbands. They did not return to school until after the planned period for wearing armbands had expired—that is, until after New Year's Day.

This complaint was filed in the United States District Court by petitioners, through their fathers, under § 1983 of Title 42 of the United States Code. It prayed for an injunction restraining the respondent school officials and the respondent members of the board of directors of the school district from disciplining the petitioners, and it sought nominal damages. After an evidentiary hearing the District Court dismissed the complaint. It upheld the constitutionality of the school authorities' action on the ground that it was reasonable in order to prevent disturbance of school discipline. The court referred to but expressly declined to follow the Fifth Circuit's holding in a similar case that the wearing of symbols like the armbands cannot be prohibited unless it "materially and substantially interfere[s] with the requirements of appropriate discipline in the operation of the school." Burnside v. Byars, 363 F.2d 744, 749 (1966).[1]

1. In *Burnside,* the Fifth Circuit ordered that high school authorities be enjoined from enforcing a regulation forbidding students to wear "freedom buttons." It is instructive that in Blackwell v. Issaquena County Board of Education, 363 F.2d 749 (1966), the same panel on the same day reached the opposite result on different facts. It declined to enjoin enforcement of such a regulation in another high school where the students wearing freedom buttons harassed students who did not wear them and created much disturbance.

On appeal, the Court of Appeals for the Eighth Circuit considered the case *en banc*. The court was equally divided, and the District Court's decision was accordingly affirmed, without opinion. We granted *certiorari*.

. . .

First Amendment rights applied in light of the special characteristics of the school environment, are available to teachers and students. It can hardly be argued that either students or teachers shed their constitutional rights to freedom of speech or expression at the schoolhouse gate. . . .

. . . On the other hand, the Court has repeatedly emphasized the need for affirming the comprehensive authority of the States and of school officials, consistent with fundamental constitutional safeguards, to prescribe and control conduct in the schools. Our problem lies in the area where students in the exercise of First Amendment rights collide with the rules of the school authorities.

The problem posed by the present case does not relate to regulation of the length of skirts or the type of clothing, to hair style, or deportment. It does not concern aggressive, disruptive action or even group demonstrations. Our problem involves direct, primary First Amendment rights akin to "pure speech."

The school officials banned and sought to punish petitioners for a silent, passive expression of opinion, unaccompanied by any disorder or disturbance on the part of petitioners. There is here no evidence whatever of petitioners' interference, actual or nascent, with the schools' work or of collision with the rights of other students to be secure and to be let alone. Accordingly, this case does not concern speech or action that intrudes upon the work of the schools or the rights of other students.

Only a few of the 18,000 students in the school system wore the black armbands. Only five students were suspended for wearing them. There is no indication that the work of the schools or any class was disrupted. Outside the classrooms, a few students made hostile remarks to the children wearing armbands, but there were no threats or acts of violence on school premises.

The District Court concluded that the action of the school authorities was reasonable because it was based upon their fear of a disturbance from the wearing of armbands. But, in our system, undifferentiated fear or apprehension of disturbance is not enough to overcome the right to freedom of expression. Any departure from absolute regimentation may cause trouble. Any variation from the majority's opinion may inspire fear. Any word spoken, in class, in the lunchroom, or on the campus, that deviates from the views of another person may start an argument or cause a disturbance. But our Constitution says we must take this risk, Terminiello v. Chicago, 337 U.S. 1 (1949); and our history says that it is this sort of hazardous freedom—this kind of openness—that is the basis of our national strength and of the independence and vigor of Americans who grow up and live in this relatively permissive, often disputatious, society.

In order for the State in the person of school officials to justify prohibition of a particular expression of opinion, it must be able to show that its action was caused by something more than a mere desire to avoid the discomfort and unpleasantness that always accompany an unpopular viewpoint. Certainly where there is no finding and no showing that engaging in the forbidden conduct would "materially and substantially interfere with the requirements of appropriate discipline in the operation of the school," the prohibition cannot be sustained. Burnside v. Byars, supra, at 749.

In the present case, the District Court made no such finding, and our independent examination of the record fails to yield evidence that the school authorities had reason to anticipate that the wearing of the armbands would substantially interfere with the work of the school or impinge upon the rights of other students. Even an official memorandum prepared after the suspension that listed the reasons for the ban on wearing the armbands made no reference to the anticipation of such disruption.

On the contrary, the action of the school authorities appears to have been based upon an urgent wish to avoid the controversy which might result from the expression, even by the silent symbol of armbands, of opposition to this Nation's part in the conflagration in Vietnam. It is revealing, in this respect, that the meeting at which the school principals decided to issue the contested regulation was called in response to a student's statement to the journalism teacher in one of the schools that he wanted to write an article on Vietnam and have it published in the school paper. (The student was dissuaded.)

It is also relevant that the school authorities did not purport to prohibit the wearing of all symbols of political or controversial significance. The record shows that students in some of the schools wore buttons relating to national political campaigns, and some even wore the Iron Cross, traditionally a symbol of Nazism. The order prohibiting the wearing of armbands did not extend to these. Instead, a particular symbol—black armbands worn to exhibit opposition to this Nation's involvement in Vietnam—was singled out for prohibition. Clearly, the prohibition of expression of one particular opinion, at least without evidence that it is necessary to avoid material and substantial interference with schoolwork or discipline is not constitutionally permissible.

In our system, state-operated schools may not be enclaves of totalitarianism. School officials do not possess absolute authority over their students. Students in school as well as out of school are "persons" under our Constitution. They are possessed of fundamental rights which the State must respect, just as they themselves must respect their obligations to the State. In our system, students may not be regarded as closed-circuit recipients of only that which the State chooses to communicate. They may not be confined to the expression of those sentiments that are officially approved. In the absence of a specific showing of constitutionally valid reasons to regulate their speech, students are entitled to freedom of expression of their views. As Judge Gewin, speaking for the Fifth Circuit, said, school officials cannot suppress "expressions of feelings with which they do not wish to contend." Burnside v. Byars, supra, at 749.

Under our Constitution, free speech is not a right that is given only to be so circumscribed that it exists in principle but not in fact. Freedom of expression would not truly exist if the right could be exercised only in an area that a benevolent government has provided as a safe haven for crackpots. The Constitution says that Congress (and the States) may not abridge the right to free speech. This provision means what it says. We properly read it to permit reasonable regulation of speech-connected activities in carefully restricted circumstances. But we do not confine the permissible exercise of First Amendment rights to a telephone booth or the four corners of a pamphlet, or to supervised and ordained discussion in a school classroom.

Reversed and remanded.

■ JUSTICE BLACK, dissenting.

The Court's holding in this case ushers in what I deem to be an entirely new era in which the power to control pupils by the elected "officials of state supported public schools ..." in the United States is in ultimate effect transferred to the Supreme Court. . . .

. . .

While the record does not show that any of these armband students shouted, used profane language, or were violent in any manner, detailed testimony by some of them shows their armbands caused comments, warnings by other students, the poking of fun at them, and a warning by an older football player that other, nonprotesting students had better let them alone. There is also evidence that a teacher of mathematics had his lesson period practically "wrecked" chiefly by disputes with Mary Beth Tinker, who wore her armband for her "demonstration." Even a casual reading of the record shows that this armband did divert students' minds from their regular lessons, and that talk, comments, etc., made John Tinker "self-conscious" in attending school with his armband. While the absence of obscene remarks or boisterous and loud disorder perhaps justifies the Court's statement that the few armband students did not actually "disrupt" the classwork, I think the record overwhelmingly shows that the armbands did exactly what the elected school officials and principals foresaw they would, that is, took the students' minds off their classwork and diverted them to thoughts about the highly emotional subject of the Vietnam war. And I repeat that if the time has come when pupils of state-supported schools, kindergartens, grammar schools, or high schools, can defy and flout orders of school officials to keep their minds on their own schoolwork, it is the beginning of a new revolutionary era of permissiveness in this country fostered by the judiciary. The next logical step, it appears to me, would be to hold unconstitutional laws that bar pupils under 21 or 18 from voting, or from being elected members of the boards of education.

Change has been said to be truly the law of life but sometimes the old and the tried and true are worth holding. The schools of this Nation have undoubtedly contributed to giving us tranquility and to making us a more law-abiding people. Uncontrolled and uncontrollable liberty is an enemy to domestic peace. We cannot close our eyes to the fact that some of the country's greatest problems are crimes committed by the youth, too many of school age. School discipline, like parental discipline, is an integral and important part of training our children to be good citizens—to be better citizens. Here a very small number of students have crisply and summarily refused to obey a school order designed to give pupils who want to learn the opportunity to do so. One does not need to be a prophet or the son of a prophet to know that after the Court's holding today some students in Iowa schools and indeed in all schools will be ready, able, and willing to defy their teachers on practically all orders. This is the more unfortunate for the schools since groups of students all over the land are already running loose, conducting break-ins, sit-ins, lie-ins, and smash-ins. Many of these student groups, as is all too familiar to all who read the newspapers and watch the television news programs, have already engaged in rioting, property seizures, and destruction. They have picketed schools to force students not to cross their picket lines and have too often violently attacked earnest but frightened students who wanted an education that the pickets did not want them to get. Students engaged in such activities are apparently confident that they know far more about how to operate public school systems than do their parents, teachers, and elected school officials. It is no answer to say that the particular students here have not yet reached such high points in their demands to attend classes in order to exercise their political pressures. Turned loose with lawsuits for damages and injunctions against their teachers as they are here, it is nothing but wishful thinking to imagine that young, immature students will not soon believe it is their right to control the schools rather than the right of the States that collect the taxes to hire the teachers for the benefit of the pupils. This case, therefore, wholly without constitutional reasons in my judgment, subjects all the public schools in the country to the whims and caprices of their loudest-mouthed, but maybe not their brightest, students. I, for one, am not fully persuaded that school pupils are wise enough, even with this Court's expert help from Washington, to run the 23,390 public school systems in our 50 States. I wish, therefore, wholly to disclaim any purpose on my part to hold that the Federal Constitution compels the teachers, parents, and elected school officials to surrender control of the American public school system to public school students. I dissent.

NOTES

1. Compare the position of the Court in Ginsberg v. New York, 390 U.S. 629 (1968). At issue was a New York criminal obscenity statute prohibiting the sale to minors under 17 of material defined to be obscene on the basis of its appeal to minors *whether or not* it would be obscene to adults. Justice Brennan's opinion upheld the statute, explaining:

> ... To be sure, there is no lack of "studies" which purport to demonstrate that obscenity is or is not "a basic factor in improving the ethical and moral development of ... youth...." But the growing consensus of commentators is that "while these studies all agree that a caused link has not been demonstrated, they are equally agreed that a caused link has not been disproved either." We do not demand of legislatures "scientifically certain criteria of legislation."

390 U.S. at 641–42.

Justice Stewart, who concurred in *Tinker*, noted the apparent conflict:

> I cannot share the Court's uncritical assumption that school discipline aside, the First Amendment rights of children are co-extensive with those of adults. Indeed, I had thought the court decided otherwise just last term in *Ginsberg*....

393 U.S. at 515. Can the two be reconciled? See generally Tushnet, Free Expression and the Young Adult: A Constitutional Framework, 1976 U.Ill.L.F. 746.

2. Compare *Ginsberg* with recent attempts to regulate obscenity on the internet. In Reno v. ACLU, 521 U.S. 844 (1997) the Supreme Court struck down Title V of the Telecommunication Act of 1996, also known as the Communications Decency Act of 1996 (CDA). Justice Stevens wrote the majority opinion:

. . .

> ... In this Court, though not in the District Court, the Government asserts that—in addition to its interest in protecting children—its "equally significant" interest in fostering the growth of the Internet provides an independent basis for upholding the constitutionality of the CDA. The Government apparently assumes that the unregulated availability of "indecent" and "patently offensive" material on the Internet is driving countless citizens away from the medium because of the risk of exposing themselves or their children to harmful material.
>
> We find this argument singularly unpersuasive. The dramatic expansion of this new marketplace of ideas contradicts the factual basis of this contention. The record demonstrates that the growth of the Internet has been and continues to be phenomenal. As a matter of constitutional tradition, in the absence of evidence to the contrary, we presume that governmental regulation of the

> content of speech is more likely to interfere with the free exchange of ideas than to encourage it. The interest in encouraging freedom of expression in a democratic society outweighs any theoretical but unproven benefit of censorship.
>
> . . .

521 U.S. at 885. Congress' next attempt at curtailing the obscenity on the internet was the Child Online Protection Act (COPA), 47 U.S.C. § 231. It was struck down in Ashcroft v. ACLU, 542 U.S. 656 (2004). COPA was much less stringent than CDA and was written to meet the standards established in Reno v. ACLU. The majority's invalidation of the Act led Justice Breyer to opine in his dissent:

> . . .
>
> ... After eight years of legislative effort, two statutes, and three Supreme Court cases, the Court sends this case back to the District Court for further proceedings. What proceedings? I have found no offer by either party to present more relevant evidence. What remains to be litigated? I know the Court says that the parties may "introduce further evidence" as to the "relative restrictiveness and effectiveness of alternatives to the statute." But I do not understand what that new evidence might consist of.
>
> Moreover, Congress passed the current statute "[i]n response to the Court's decision in Reno" striking down an earlier statutory effort to deal with the same problem. Congress read Reno with care. It dedicated itself to the task of drafting a statute that would meet each and every criticism of the predecessor statute that this Court set forth in Reno. It incorporated language from the Court's precedents, particularly the Miller standard, virtually verbatim. And it created what it believed was a statute that would protect children from exposure to obscene professional pornography without obstructing adult access to material that the First Amendment protects. See H. R. Rep., at 5 (explaining that the bill was "carefully drafted to respond to the Supreme Court's decision in Reno"); S. Rep., at 2 (same). What else was Congress supposed to do?
>
> I recognize that some Members of the Court, now or in the past, have taken the view that the First Amendment simply does not permit Congress to legislate in this area. See, e.g., Ginzburg, 383 U.S., at 476 (Black, J., dissenting) ("[T]he Federal Government is without any power whatever under the Constitution to put any type of burden on speech and expression of ideas of any kind"). Others believe that the Amendment does not permit Congress to legislate in certain ways, e.g., through the imposition of criminal penalties for obscenity. See, e.g., ante, at 673 (Stevens, J., concurring). There are strong constitutional arguments favoring these views. But the Court itself does not adopt those views. Instead, it finds that the Government has not proved the nonexistence of "less restrictive alternatives." That finding, if appropriate here, is universally appropriate. And if universally appropriate, it denies to Congress, in practice, the legislative leeway that the Court's language seem to promise. If this statute does not pass the Court's "less restrictive alternative" test, what does? If nothing does, then the Court should say so clearly.

542 U.S. at 676.

Hosty v. Carter

United States Court of Appeals for the Seventh Circuit, 2005.
412 F.3d 731.

■ CIRCUIT JUDGE EASTERBROOK delivered the opinion of the Court.

Controversy began to swirl when Jeni Porche became editor in chief of the Innovator, the student newspaper at Governors State University. None of the articles concerned the apostrophe missing from the University's name.

Instead the students tackled meatier fare, such as its decision not to renew the teaching contract of Geoffrey de Laforcade, the paper's faculty adviser.

After articles bearing Margaret Hosty's by-line attacked the integrity of Roger K. Oden, Dean of the College of Arts and Sciences, the University's administration began to take intense interest in the paper. (Here, and in Part II of this opinion as well, we relate matters in the light most favorable to the plaintiffs.) Both Oden and Stuart Fagan (the University's President) issued statements accusing the Innovator of irresponsible and defamatory journalism. When the Innovator declined to accept the administration's view of its duties—in particular, the paper refused to retract factual statements that the administration deemed false, or even to print the administration's responses—Patricia Carter, Dean of Student Affairs and Services, called the Innovator's printer and told it not to print any issues that she had not reviewed and approved in advance. The printer was not willing to take the risk that it would not be paid (the paper relies on student activity funds), and the editorial staff was unwilling to submit to prior review. Publication ceased in November 2000. The paper has since resumed publication under new management; Porche, Hosty, and Steven Barba, another of the paper's reporters, have continued the debate in court, suing the University, all of its trustees, most of its administrators, and several of its staff members for damages under 42 U.S.C. § 1983.

. . .

Hazelwood [School District v. Kuhlmeier, 484 U.S. 260 (1988)] provides our starting point. A high school's principal blocked the student newspaper (which was financed by public funds as part of a journalism class) from publishing articles that the principal thought inappropriate for some of the school's younger students and a potential invasion of others' privacy. When evaluating the students' argument that the principal had violated their right to freedom of speech, the Court first asked whether the paper was a public forum. After giving a negative answer based on the school's established policy of supervising the writing and reviewing the content of each issue, the Court observed that the school's subvention of the paper's costs distinguished the situation from one in which students were speaking independently, as in Tinker v. Des Moines Independent Community School District, 393 U.S. 503 (1969). When a school regulates speech for which it also pays, the Court held, the appropriate question is whether the "actions are reasonably related to legitimate pedagogical concerns." "Legitimate" concerns, the Court stated, include setting "high standards for the student speech that is disseminated under its auspices—standards that may be higher than those demanded by some newspaper publishers or theatrical producers in the 'real' world—and [the school] may refuse to disseminate student speech that does not meet those standards. In addition, a school must be able to take into account the emotional maturity of the intended audience in determining whether to disseminate student speech on potentially sensitive topics, which might range from the existence of Santa Claus in an elementary school setting to the particulars of teenage sexual activity in a high school setting." Shortly after this passage the Court dropped a footnote: "A number of lower federal courts have similarly recognized that educators' decisions with regard to the content of school-sponsored newspapers, dramatic productions, and other expressive activities are entitled to substantial deference. We need not now decide whether the same degree of deference is appropriate with respect to school-sponsored expressive activities at the college and university level."

Picking up on this footnote, plaintiffs argue, and the district court held, that Hazelwood is inapplicable to university newspapers and that post-secondary educators therefore cannot ever insist that student newspapers be submitted for review and approval. Yet this footnote does not even hint at the possibility of an on/off switch: high school papers reviewable, college papers not reviewable. It addresses degrees of deference. Whether some review is possible depends on the answer to the public-forum question, which does not (automatically) vary with the speakers' age. Only when courts need assess the reasonableness of the asserted pedagogical justification in non-public-forum situations does age come into play, and in a way suggested by the passage we have quoted from Hazelwood's text. To the extent that the justification for editorial control depends on the audience's maturity, the difference between high school and university students may be important. (Not that any line could be bright; many high school seniors are older than some college freshmen, and junior colleges are similar to many high schools.) To the extent that the justification depends on other matters—not only the desire to ensure "high standards for the student speech that is disseminated under [the school's] auspices" (the Court particularly mentioned "speech that is . . . ungrammatical, poorly written, inadequately researched, biased or prejudiced, vulgar or profane, or unsuitable for immature audiences", 484 U.S. at 271) but also the goal of dissociating the school from "any position other than neutrality on matters of political controversy", id. at 272—there is no sharp difference between high school and college papers.

The Supreme Court itself has established that age does not control the public-forum question. See generally Symposium: Do Children Have the Same First Amendment Rights As Adults?, 79 Chi.-Kent L. Rev. 3–313 (2004) (including many articles collecting and discussing these decisions). So much is clear not only from decisions such as Tinker, which held that public school students have a right of non-disruptive personal expression on school premises, but also from the decisions concerning the use of school funds and premises for religious expression. See, e.g., Lamb's Chapel v. Center Moriches Union Free School District, 508 U.S. 384 (1993). These decisions hold that no public school, of any level—primary, secondary, or post-secondary—may discriminate against religious speech in a public forum (including classrooms made available to extracurricular activities), or withhold funding that would be available to student groups espousing sectarian views. Good News Club, which dealt with student clubs in an elementary school, deemed dispositive (533 U.S. at 110) a decision about the first amendment rights of college students. Having opened its premises to student clubs, and thus created a limited-purpose public forum, even an elementary school could not supervise or censor the views expressed at a meeting of the Good News Club.

If private speech in a public forum is off-limits to regulation even when that forum is a classroom of an elementary school (the holding of Good News Club) then speech at a non-public forum, and underwritten at public expense, may be open to reasonable regulation even at the college level—or later, as Rust v. Sullivan, 500 U.S. 173 (1991), shows by holding that the federal government may insist that physicians use grant funds only for the kind of speech required by the granting authority. Cf. National Endowment for the Arts v. Finley, 524 U.S. 569 (1998). We hold, therefore, that Hazelwood's framework applies to subsidized student newspapers at colleges as well as elementary and secondary schools. See also Axson–Flynn v. Johnson, 356 F.3d 1277 (10th Cir. 2004) (Hazelwood supplies the framework for evaluating collegiate speech and allows regulation when the speech is connected to the curriculum); Bishop v. Aronov, 926 F.2d 1066 (11th Cir.

1991) (Hazelwood supplies the framework for evaluating collegiate speech and allows regulation when readers might infer the school's approval).

. . .

■ Circuit Judge Evans, (dissenting) [joined] by Circuit Judges Rovner, Wood and Williams.

. . .

If the plaintiffs' allegations are true, this case epitomizes this concern. The Innovator, as opposed to writing merely about football games, actually chose to publish hard-hitting stories. And these articles were critical of the school administration. In response, rather than applauding the young journalists, the University decided to prohibit publication unless a school official reviewed the paper's content before it was printed. Few restrictions on speech seem to run more afoul of basic First Amendment values. First, prior restraints are particularly noxious under the Constitution. See Nebraska Press Ass'n v. Stuart, 427 U.S. 539 (1976) ("prior restraints on speech and publication are the most serious and the least tolerable infringement on First Amendment rights"); Near v. Minnesota, 283 U.S. 697 (1931) ("it has been generally, if not universally, considered that it is the chief purpose of the [First Amendment's free press] guaranty to prevent previous restraints upon publication"). Second, and even more fundamental, as Justice Frankfurter stated (albeit in somewhat dated language) in Baumgartner v. United States, 322 U.S. 665, 673–74 (1944), "one of the prerogatives of American citizenship is the right to criticize public men and measures." College students—voting-age citizens and potential future leaders—should feel free to question, challenge, and criticize government action. Nevertheless, as a result of today's holding, Dean Carter could have censored the Innovator by merely establishing "legitimate pedagogical reasons." This court now gives the green light to school administrators to restrict student speech in a manner inconsistent with the First Amendment.

. . .

Therefore, considering that no court, both before or after Hazelwood, has held that a university may censor a student newspaper, and the only authorities to suggest otherwise are not directly on point, I believe that it was "clearly established" that the University could not deny funding to the school newspaper it found objectionable.

. . .

In conclusion, because I believe that Hazelwood does not apply, no pedagogical concerns can justify suppressing the student speech here. Dean Carter violated clearly established First Amendment law in censoring the student newspaper. I would affirm the judgment of the district court.

NOTE

Hazelwood appears to have marked the beginning of a period in which the rights of students have been eroded. In Vernonia School District 47J v. Acton, 515 U.S. 646 (1995), the Supreme Court overturned a lower court decision that had declared random urinalysis for drug testing of all athletes to be unconstitutional. Lower courts have also upheld some compelled speech. See, e.g., Axson–Flynn v. Xan Johnson, 356 F.3d 1277 (10th Cir. 2004) (a religious student who objected to saying certain words within the context of her acting assignment at the University of Utah had to leave the program over her refusal to perform the script as written). The District Court held for the student and the Court of Appeals reversed. See generally, Andrew Miller, Balancing School Authority and Student Expression, 54 Baylor L. Rev. 623 (2002); Gregory C. Lisby, Resolving the Hazelwood Conundrum: The First Amendment Rights of College Students in Kincaid v. Gibson and Beyond, 7 Comm. L & Pol'y 129 (2002). But see Kincaid v. Gibson, 236 F.3d 342 (6th Cir. 2001) (university administration's confiscation of Kentucky State University yearbooks violated the First Amendment), and Hansen v. Ann Arbor, 293 F.Supp.2d 780 (E.D. Mich. 2003). In *Hansen* the District Court found a violation of the First Amendment when the school prevented the expression of student's opinion that was opposed to the supported view for a school panel. In the words of the court:

> This case presents the ironic, and unfortunate, paradox of a public high school celebrating "diversity" by refusing to permit the presentation to students of an "unwelcomed" viewpoint on the topic of homosexuality and religion, while actively promoting the competing view.

293 F.Supp.2d at 782–783.

Peterson v. Sorlien

Supreme Court of Minnesota, 1980.
299 N.W.2d 123.

■ SHERAN, CHIEF JUSTICE.

This action by plaintiff Susan Jungclaus Peterson for false imprisonment and intentional infliction of emotional distress arises from an effort by her parents, in conjunction with other individuals named as defendants, to prompt her disaffiliation from an organization known as The Way Ministry.

At trial, the Hennepin County District Court directed a verdict in favor of defendant Paul Sorlien, plaintiff's former minister, finding the evidence proffered against him insufficient as a matter of law. The jury returned a verdict exonerating Mr. and Mrs. Jungclaus and the other remaining defendants of the charge of false imprisonment; however, the jury found defendants Veronica Morgel and Kathy Mills liable for intentional infliction of emotional distress, assessing against each of them $1 compensatory damages and $4,000 and $6,000 respectively as punitive damages.

Viewing the evidence in the light most favorable to the prevailing defendants, this case marks the emergence of a new cultural phenomenon: youth-oriented religious or pseudo-religious groups which utilize the techniques of what has been termed "coercive persuasion" or "mind control" to cultivate an uncritical and devoted following. Commentators have used the term "coercive persuasion," originally coined to identify the experience of American prisoners of war during the Korean conflict to describe the cult-induction process. The word "cult" is not used pejoratively but in its dictionary sense to describe an unorthodox system of belief characterized by "[g]reat or excessive devotion or dedication to some person, idea, or thing." Webster's New International Dictionary of the English Language Unabridged 552 (1976). Coercive persuasion is fostered through the creation of a controlled environment that heightens the susceptibility of a subject to suggestion and manipulation through sensory deprivation, physiological depletion, cognitive dissonance, peer pressure, and a clear assertion of authority and dominion. The aftermath of indoctrination is a severe impairment of autonomy and the ability to think independently, which induces a subject's unyielding compliance and the rupture of past connections, affiliations and associations. See generally Delgado, Religious Totalism: Gentle and Ungentle Persuasion under the First Amendment, 51 S.Cal.L.Rev. 1 (1977).

One psychologist characterized the process of cult indoctrination as "psychological kidnapping." Id. at 23.

At the time of the events in question, Susan Jungclaus Peterson was 21 years old. For most of her life, she lived with her family on a farm near Bird Island, Minnesota. In 1973, she graduated with honors from high school, ranking second in her class. She matriculated that fall at Moorhead State College. A dean's list student during her first year, her academic performance declined and her interests narrowed after she joined the local chapter of a group organized internationally and identified locally as The Way of Minnesota, Inc.

The operation of The Way is predicated on the fund-raising activities of its members. The Way's fund-raising strategy centers upon the sale of prerecorded learning programs. Members are instructed to elicit the interest of a group of ten or twelve people and then play for them, at a charge of $85 per participant, a taped introductory course produced by The Way International. Advanced tape courses are then offered to the participants at additional cost, and training sessions are conducted to more fully acquaint recruits with the orientation of the group and the obligations of membership. Recruits must contribute a minimum of 10 percent of their earnings to the organization; to meet the tithe, student members are expected to obtain part-time employment. Members are also required to purchase books and other materials published by the ministry, and are encouraged to make larger financial contributions and to engage in more sustained efforts at solicitation.

By the end of her freshman year, Susan was devoting many hours to The Way, listening to instructional tapes, soliciting new members and assisting in training sessions. As her sophomore year began, Susan committed herself significantly, selling the car her father had given her and working part-time as a waitress to finance her contributions to The Way. Susan spent the following summer in South Dakota, living in conditions described as appalling and overcrowded, while recruiting, raising money and conducting training sessions for The Way.

As her junior year in college drew to a close, the Jungclauses grew increasingly alarmed by the personality changes they witnessed in their daughter; overly tired, unusually pale, distraught and irritable, she exhibited an increasing alienation from family, diminished interest in education and decline in academic performance. The Jungclauses, versed in the literature of youth cults and based on conversations with former members of The Way, concluded that through a calculated process of manipulation and exploitation Susan had been reduced to a condition of psychological bondage.

On May 24, 1976, defendant Norman Jungclaus, father of plaintiff, arrived at Moorhead to pick up Susan following the end of the third college quarter. Instead of returning to their family home, defendant drove with Susan to Minneapolis to the home of Veronica Morgel. Entering the home of Mrs. Morgel, Susan was greeted by Kathy Mills and several young people who wished to discuss Susan's involvement in the ministry. Each of those present had been in some way touched by the cult phenomenon. Kathy Mills, the leader of the group, had treated a number of former cult members, including Veronica Morgel's son. It was Kathy Mills, a self-styled professional deprogrammer, to whom the Jungclauses turned, and intermittently for the next sixteen days, it was in the home of Veronica Morgel that Susan stayed.

The avowed purpose of deprogramming is to break the hold of the cult over the individual through reason and confrontation. Initially, Susan was unwilling to discuss her involvement; she lay curled in a fetal position, in the downstairs bedroom where she first stayed, plugging her ears and crying while her father pleaded with her to listen to what was being said. This behavior persisted for two days during which she intermittently engaged in conversation, at one point screaming hysterically and flailing at her father. But by Wednesday Susan's demeanor had changed completely; she was friendly and vivacious and that night slept in an upstairs bedroom. Susan spent all day Thursday reading and conversing with her father and on Saturday night went roller-skating. On Sunday she played softball at a nearby park, afterwards enjoying a picnic lunch. The next week Susan spent in Columbus, Ohio, flying there with a former cult member who had shared with her the experiences of the previous week. While in Columbus, she spoke every day by telephone to her fiance who, playing tapes and songs from the ministry's headquarters in Minneapolis, begged that she return to the fold. Susan expressed the desire to extricate her fiance from the dominion of the cult.

Susan returned to Minneapolis on June 9. Unable to arrange a controlled meeting so that Susan could see her fiance outside the presence of other members of the ministry, her parents asked that she sign an agreement releasing them from liability for their past weeks' actions. Refusing to do so, Susan stepped outside the Morgel residence with the puppy she had purchased in Ohio, motioned to a passing police car and shortly thereafter was reunited with her fiance in the Minneapolis headquarters of The Way. Following her return to the ministry, she was directed to counsel and initiated the present action.

Plaintiff seeks a judgment notwithstanding the verdict on the issue of false imprisonment, alleging that defendants unlawfully interfered with her personal liberty by words or acts which induced a reasonable apprehension that force would be used against her if she did not otherwise comply. The jury, instructed that an informed and reasoned consent is a defense to an allegation of false imprisonment and that a nonconsensual detention could be deemed consensual if one's behavior so indicated, exonerated defendants with respect to the false imprisonment claim.

The period in question began on Monday, May 24, 1976, and ceased on Wednesday, June 9, 1976, a period of 16 days. The record clearly demonstrates that Susan willingly remained in the company of defendants for at least 13 of those days. During that time she took many excursions into the public sphere, playing softball and picnicking in a city park, roller-skating at a public rink, flying aboard public aircraft and shopping and swimming while relaxing in Ohio. Had Susan desired, manifold opportunities existed for her to alert the authorities of her allegedly unlawful detention; in Minneapolis, two police officers observed at close range the softball game in which she engaged; en route to Ohio, she passed through the security areas of the Twin Cities and Columbus airports in the presence of security guards and uniformed police; in Columbus she transacted business at a bank, went for walks in solitude and was interviewed by an F.B.I. agent who sought assurances of her safety. At no time during the 13–day period did she complain of her treatment or suggest that defendants were holding her against her will. If one is aware of a reasonable means of escape that does not present a danger of bodily or material harm, a restriction is not total and complete and does not constitute unlawful imprisonment. Damages may not be assessed for any period of detention to which one freely consents.

In his summation to the jury, the trial judge instructed that to deem consent a defense to the charge of false imprisonment for the entire period or for any part therein, a preponderance of the evidence must demonstrate that such plaintiff voluntarily consented. The central issue for the jury, then, was whether Susan voluntarily participated in the activities of the first three days. The jury concluded that her behavior constituted a waiver.

We believe the determination to have been consistent with the evidence.

To determine whether the findings of the jury can be supported upon review, the behavior Susan manifested during the initial three days at issue must be considered in light of her actions in the remainder of the period. Because, it is argued, the cult conditioning process induces dramatic and non-consensual change giving rise to a new temporary identity on the part of the individuals whose consent is under examination, Susan's volitional capacity prior to treatment may well have been impaired. Following her readjustment, the evidence suggests that Susan was a different person, "like her old self." As such, the question of Susan's consent becomes a function of time. We therefore deem Susan's subsequent affirmation of defendants' actions dispositive.

In Weiss v. Patrick, 453 F.Supp. 717 (D.R.I.), aff'd, 588 F.2d 818 (1st Cir.1978), cert. denied, 442 U.S. 929 (1979), the federal district court in Rhode Island confronted a situation similar to that which faces us. Plaintiff, a devotee of the Unification Church, brought an action for false imprisonment against individuals hired by her parents to prompt her disassociation from the church. Because plaintiff's mother was dying of cancer, the church authorities permitted her to join her family for the Thanksgiving holiday. Met at the airport by her mother, she testified that she was restrained against her will in the home of one of the defendants and subjected to vituperative attacks against the church until she seized an opportunity to flee. Despite the evidently traumatic experience sustained by plaintiff, the district court found that she failed to demonstrate a meaningful deprivation of personal liberty, reasoning that "any limitation upon personal mobility was not her primary concern." In so reasoning, the court underscored a parental right to advocate freely a point of view to one's child, "be she minor or adult." To assure freedom, the court observed, "the right of every person 'to be left alone' must be placed in the scales with the right of others to communicate."

In light of our examination of the record and rules of construction providing that upon review the evidence must be viewed in a manner most favorable to the prevailing party, we find that a reasonable basis existed for the verdict exonerating defendants of the charge of false imprisonment. ... As such, we hold that when parents, or their agents, acting under the conviction that the judgmental capacity of their adult child is impaired, seek to extricate that child from what they reasonably believe to be a religious or pseudo-religious cult, and the child at some juncture assents to the actions in question, limitations upon the child's mobility do not constitute meaningful deprivations of personal liberty sufficient to support a judgment for false imprisonment.[1] But owing to the threat that deprogramming poses to public order, we do not endorse self-help as a preferred alternative. In fashioning a

1. Plaintiff in her motion for a judgment notwithstanding the verdict stated that she wished to recover only nominal damages against her parents. This court has held that a judgment for defendant will not be reversed on appeal simply to allow a plaintiff to recover nominal damages. Erickson v. Midland Nat'l Bank & Trust Co., 205 Minn. 224, 285 N.W. 611 (1939).

remedy, the First Amendment requires resort to the least restrictive alternative so as to not impinge upon religious belief. . . .[2]

. . .

■ WAHL, JUSTICE (dissenting in part, concurring in part).

I must respectfully dissent. In every generation, parents have viewed their children's religious and political beliefs with alarm and dismay if those beliefs were different from their own. Under the First Amendment, however, adults in our society enjoy freedoms of association and belief. In my view, it is unwise to tamper with those freedoms and with longstanding principles of tort law out of sympathy for parents seeking to help their "misguided" offspring, however well-intentioned and loving their acts may be. Whether or not, as the majority opinion asserts, The Way of Minnesota, Inc. is a "youth-oriented," "pseudo-religious group" which pursues its "fundraising strategy" in such a way as to inflict physical and psychological harm on its members, emphasis on this characterization beclouds the purely legal issues which are presented by this appeal.

The first of those legal issues is whether, as a matter of law, any of the defendants in this case are guilty of false imprisonment of the plaintiff. The elements of the tort of false imprisonment are (1) words or acts by defendant intended to confine plaintiff, (2) actual confinement, and (3) awareness by plaintiff that she is being confined. Any imprisonment "which is not legally justifiable" is false imprisonment, therefore, the fact that the tortfeasor acted in good faith is no defense to a charge of false imprisonment. Thus, although the majority opinion correctly concludes that evidence concerning the activities of The Way and the impact of those activities upon plaintiff may have been relevant to the question of whether defendants acted so willfully and maliciously as to justify an award of punitive damages, such evidence has little bearing on the issue of defendants' liability for false imprisonment.

The unrebutted evidence shows that defendant Norman Jungclaus, the father of the 21-year-old plaintiff in this case, took his adult daughter, kicking and screaming, to a small bedroom in the basement of the Morgel home on Monday, May 23. Norman Jungclaus admitted that she did not go with him willingly. Plaintiff curled up on the bed, plugged her ears, and cried. Defendant Perkins testified that plaintiff screamed and cried and pleaded with several people to let her go, but her pleas were ignored. This situation continued until 3 a.m. Tuesday. At one point that morning, plaintiff flew at her father, and he held her arms around her from the back, in his words, "for maybe a half an hour, until she calmed down again." Plaintiff testified that defendant Mills told her papers had been drafted to commit her to Anoka State Hospital if she continued to refuse to cooperate with the "deprogramming."

In its memorandum accompanying the order denying plaintiff's motion for judgment notwithstanding the verdict, the trial court stated:

> It should be noted that there must be considerable room for doubt concerning that portion of the verdict finding that Norman Jungclaus did not participate in a false imprisonment. The evidence is unrebutted that he picked up his 21-year-old daughter Susan and took her into the

2. While we decline at this time to suggest a particular alternative, we observe that some courts have permitted the creation of temporary guardianships to allow the removal of cult members to therapeutic settings. If the individuals desire, at the end of the conservatorship they may return to the cult. Actions have also been initiated against cult leaders on the basis of criminal liability.

> basement without her permission or consent, and against her will. She remained there several days. However, Plaintiff stated that she was not seeking compensatory damages against her parents, and only $1.00 in punitive damages.
>
> In that light, judgment notwithstanding verdict as to false imprisonment would be of no significance in the matter of compensatory damages. And whether or not Mr. Jungclaus's act was done maliciously or willfully so as to justify $1.00 punitive damages is clearly a matter for determination by the jury; and not the Court. Hence, judgment notwithstanding verdict against Norman Jungclaus as to false imprisonment must be denied. On practical grounds, a new trial will not be ordered for a potential $1.00 recovery in any event.

Thus, the trial court refused to grant judgment against Norman Jungclaus because any damages awarded would be insignificant. However, plaintiff's complaint sought not only money damages but an injunction against further interference with her freedoms of religion, association, and expression. The value to plaintiff of a judgment in her favor, while not monetary, is nevertheless significant.

The majority opinion finds, in plaintiff's behavior during the remainder of the 16-day period of "deprogramming," a reasonable basis for acquitting defendant Jungclaus of the false imprisonment charge for the initial three days, during which time he admittedly held plaintiff against her will. Under this theory, plaintiff's "acquiescence" in the later stages of deprogramming operates as consent which "relates back" to the events of the earlier three days, and constitutes a "waiver" of her claims for those days. Cases cited by the majority do not lend support to this proposition.

. . .

Certainly, parents who disapprove of or disagree with the religious beliefs of their adult offspring are free to exercise their own First Amendment rights in an attempt, by speech and persuasion without physical restraints, to change their adult children's minds. But parents who engage in tortious conduct in their "deprogramming" attempts do so at the risk that the deprogramming will be unsuccessful and the adult children will pursue tort remedies against their parents. To allow parents' "conviction that the judgmental capacity of their [adult] child is impaired [by her religious indoctrination]" to excuse their tortious conduct sets a dangerous precedent.

Here, the evidence clearly supported a verdict against Norman Jungclaus on the false imprisonment claim, and no reasonable basis existed for denying judgment notwithstanding the verdict. The trial court's holding in this regard should be reversed.

. . .

Lastly, I would address plaintiff's claim that the trial court erred in denying her motion to amend her complaint or add a new cause of action. I agree that the motion was properly denied because it was untimely, but I would not conclude, as suggested by footnote 4 of the majority opinion, that defendant parents' attempts to "deprogram" their daughter from her religious beliefs did not constitute a violation of her rights under 42 U.S.C. § 1985(3). Although one federal court has so held, see Weiss v. Patrick, 453 F.Supp. 717, 722 (D.R.I.), aff'd, 588 F.2d 818 (1st Cir.1978), cert. denied, 442 U.S. 929 (1979), a number of courts have reached the contrary conclusion. In Augenti v. Cappellini, 84 F.R.D. 73 (M.D.Pa.1979), for example, defendants' arguments that their attempts to deprogram their son "were motivated solely by parental concern . . . to further his physical and mental health" did not persuade the court that the "invidiously discriminatory animus" necessary for a § 1985(3) action was lacking. Several other cases interpreting the legislative history of § 1985(3) have determined that the protection of the provisions does extend to religious groups. See Jackson v. Associated Hospital Service, 414 F.Supp. 315 (E.D.Pa.1976), aff'd, 549 F.2d 795 (3d Cir.), cert. denied, 434 U.S. 832 (1977); Rankin v. Howard, 457 F.Supp. 70, 74–75 (D.Ariz.1978); cf. Mandelkorn v. Patrick, 359 F.Supp. 692, 697 (D.D.C.1973). In reaching this conclusion, the court in Baer v. Baer, 450 F.Supp. 481, 491 (N.D.Cal.1978) observed:

> While religious status may differ from racial status because it is not a congenital and inalterable trait, membership in a minority religious group, like membership in a minority racial group, has often excited the fear, hatred and irrationality of the majority. Two thousand years of human history compellingly prove that no easier road to martyrdom is found than in adherence to an unpopular religious faith. For these reasons, and because the legislative history does not indicate otherwise, this court concludes that religious discrimination may be encompassed by the terms of § 1985(3).

■ OTIS, JUSTICE (dissenting in part).

I join in the views expressed by Justice Wahl, and particularly take issue with a rule which authorizes what is euphemistically described as "limitations upon the adult child's mobility" whenever a parent, or indeed a stranger acting for a parent, subjectively decides, without the benefit of a professional opinion or judicial intervention, that the adult child's "judgmental capacity" is impaired and that she should be "extricated" from what is deemed to be a religious or pseudo-religious cult.

The rule adopted by the majority states:

> We hold that where parents, or their agents, acting under the conviction that the judgmental capacity of their adult child is impaired, seek to extricate that child from what they reasonably believe to be a religious or pseudo-religious cult, and the child at some juncture assents to the actions in question, limitations upon the child's mobility do not constitute meaningful deprivations of personal liberty sufficient to support a judgment for false imprisonment.

We furnish no guidelines or criteria for what constitutes "impaired judgmental capacity" other than the fact that the adult child has embraced an unorthodox doctrine with a zeal which has given the intervenor cause for alarm, a concern which may be well-founded, ill-founded, or unfounded.

Nor do we specify whether the "cult" must be for a benign or a malevolent purpose. It is enough that the intervenor has reason to believe it is a cult i.e. "an unorthodox system of belief" and that at some juncture during the adult child's involuntary confinement, she "assents," that is to say, yields or surrenders, possibly from exhaustion or fatigue, and possibly for a period only long enough to regain her composure.

If there is any constitutional protection we should be slow to erode it is the right of serious-minded people, young or old, well-adjusted, or maladjusted, to search for religious or philosophical fulfillment in their own way and in their own time without the interference of meddling friends or relatives, however well-intentioned they may be.

At age 21, a daughter is no longer a child. She is an adult. Susan Peterson was not only an adult in 1976 but she was a bright, well-educated adult. For whatever reason, she was experiencing a period of restlessness and insecurity which is by no means uncommon in students of that age. But to hold that for seeking companionship and identity in a group whose proselytizing tactics may well be suspect, she must endure without a remedy the degrading and humiliating treatment she received at the hands of her parents, is, in my opinion, totally at odds with the basic rights of young people to think unorthodox thoughts, join unorthodox groups, and proclaim unorthodox views. I would reverse the denial of recovery as to that cause of action.

NOTE

In Ward v. Connor, 657 F.2d 45 (4th Cir.1981), the Fourth Circuit considered whether Thomas Ward, a 28 year old member of the Unification Church who alleged he was kidnapped and subjected to a deprogramming effort by his parents, could seek redress under 42 U.S.C. § 1985(c) on the ground that a private conspiracy interfered with his religious beliefs. The district court had dismissed the complaint, expressing doubt that § 1985(c) was intended to reach conspiracies motivated by religious rather than racial animus and concluding in any event that the parents were motivated by concern for their son's well-being and thus lacked discriminatory bias.

The Fourth Circuit held that 1985(c) does apply to religious discrimination and that the complaint did sufficiently charge that the parents were motivated by animosity towards the members of the Unification Church. The dismissal of the case was therefore reversed. On January 18, 1982, the Supreme Court denied certiorari, 455 U.S. 907 (1982).

The Connors were destitute because of various other suits arising from their deprogramming activities. After certiorari was denied, the Unification Church agreed to settle on the condition that the Connors produce a financial statement and promise never to interfere with the Church or its members again.

E. AGE AND CRIMINAL LAW

Roper v. Simmons

Supreme Court of the United States, 2005.
543 U.S. 551, 125 S.Ct. 1183, 161 L.Ed.2d 1.

■ KENNEDY, JUSTICE.

This case requires us to address, for the second time in a decade and a half, whether it is permissible under the Eighth and Fourteenth Amendments to the Constitution of the United States to execute a juvenile offender who was older than 15 but younger than 18 when he committed a capital crime. In Stanford v. Kentucky, 492 U.S. 361 (1989), a divided Court rejected the proposition that the Constitution bars capital punishment for juvenile offenders in this age group. We reconsider the question.

At the age of 17, when he was still a junior in high school, Christopher Simmons, the respondent here, committed murder. About nine months later, after he had turned 18, he was tried and sentenced to death. There is little doubt that Simmons was the instigator of the crime. Before its commission Simmons said he wanted to murder someone. In chilling, callous terms he talked about his plan, discussing it for the most part with two friends,

Charles Benjamin and John Tessmer, then aged 15 and 16 respectively. Simmons proposed to commit burglary and murder by breaking and entering, tying up a victim, and throwing the victim off a bridge. Simmons assured his friends they could "get away with it" because they were minors.

. . .

During closing arguments, both the prosecutor and defense counsel addressed Simmons' age, which the trial judge had instructed the jurors they could consider as a mitigating factor. Defense counsel reminded the jurors that juveniles of Simmons' age cannot drink, serve on juries, or even see certain movies, because "the legislatures have wisely decided that individuals of a certain age aren't responsible enough." Defense counsel argued that Simmons' age should make "a huge difference to [the jurors] in deciding just exactly what sort of punishment to make." In rebuttal, the prosecutor gave the following response: "Age, he says. Think about age. Seventeen years old. Isn't that scary? Doesn't that scare you? Mitigating? Quite the contrary I submit. Quite the contrary."

The jury recommended the death penalty after finding the State had proved each of the three aggravating factors submitted to it. Accepting the jury's recommendation, the trial judge imposed the death penalty.

. . .

After these proceedings in Simmons' case had run their course, this Court held that the Eighth and Fourteenth Amendments prohibit the execution of a mentally retarded person. Atkins v. Virginia, 536 U.S. 304 (2002). Simmons filed a new petition for state postconviction relief, arguing that the reasoning of *Atkins* established that the Constitution prohibits the execution of a juvenile who was under 18 when the crime was committed.

The Missouri Supreme Court agreed. State ex rel. Simmons v. Roper, 112 S.W.3d 397 (2003) (en banc). It held that since *Stanford*,

> "a national consensus has developed against the execution of juvenile offenders, as demonstrated by the fact that eighteen states now bar such executions for juveniles, that twelve other states bar executions altogether, that no state has lowered its age of execution below 18 since *Stanford*, that five states have legislatively or by case law raised or established the minimum age at 18, and that the imposition of the juvenile death penalty has become truly unusual over the last decade." 112 S.W.3d, at 399.

On this reasoning it set aside Simmons' death sentence and resentenced him to "life imprisonment without eligibility for probation, parole, or release except by act of the Governor."

We granted certiorari, 540 U.S. 1160 (2004), and now affirm.

. . .

In Thompson v. Oklahoma, 487 U.S. 815 (1988), a plurality of the Court determined that our standards of decency do not permit the execution of any offender under the age of 16 at the time of the crime. *Id.*, at 818–838 (opinion of Stevens, J., joined by Brennan, Marshall, and Blackmun, JJ.). . . .

. . .

The next year, in Stanford v. Kentucky, 492 U.S. 361 (1989), the Court, over a dissenting opinion joined by four Justices, referred to contemporary standards of decency in this country and concluded the Eighth and Fourteenth Amendments did not proscribe the execution of juvenile offenders over 15 but under 18....

. . .

... [W]e now reconsider the issue decided in *Stanford.* The beginning point is a review of objective indicia of consensus, as expressed in particular by the enactments of legislatures that have addressed the question. This data gives us essential instruction. We then must determine, in the exercise of our own independent judgment, whether the death penalty is a disproportionate punishment for juveniles.

. . .

As in *Atkins,* the objective indicia of consensus in this case—the rejection of the juvenile death penalty in the majority of States; the infrequency of its use even where it remains on the books; and the consistency in the trend toward abolition of the practice—provide sufficient evidence that today our society views juveniles, in the words *Atkins* used respecting the mentally retarded, as "categorically less culpable than the average criminal." 536 U.S., at 316.

A majority of States have rejected the imposition of the death penalty on juvenile offenders under 18, and we now hold this is required by the Eighth Amendment.

. . .

Three general differences between juveniles under 18 and adults demonstrate that juvenile offenders cannot with reliability be classified among the worst offenders. First, as any parent knows and as the scientific and sociological studies respondent and his *amici* cite tend to confirm, "[a] lack of maturity and an underdeveloped sense of responsibility are found in youth more often than in adults and are more understandable among the young. These qualities often result in impetuous and ill-considered actions and decisions." *Johnson,* [v. Texas, 509 U.S. 350, 367 (1993)]; see also Eddings, [v. Oklahoma, 455 U.S. 104, 115–116 (1982)] ("Even the normal 16-year-old customarily lacks the maturity of an adult"). It has been noted that "adolescents are overrepresented statistically in virtually every category of reckless behavior." Arnett, Reckless Behavior in Adolescence: A Developmental Perspective, 12 Developmental Review 339 (1992). In recognition of the comparative immaturity and irresponsibility of juveniles, almost every State prohibits those under 18 years of age from voting, serving on juries, or marrying without parental consent.

The second area of difference is that juveniles are more vulnerable or susceptible to negative influences and outside pressures, including peer pressure. *Eddings, supra,* at 115,("[Y]outh is more than a chronological fact. It is a time and condition of life when a person may be most susceptible to influence and to psychological damage"). This is explained in part by the prevailing circumstance that juveniles have less control, or less experience with control, over their own environment. See Steinberg & Scott, Less Guilty by Reason of Adolescence: Developmental Immaturity, Diminished Responsibility, and the Juvenile Death Penalty, 58 Am. Psychologist 1009, 1014 (2003) (hereinafter Steinberg & Scott) ("[A]s legal minors, [juveniles] lack the freedom that adults have to extricate themselves from a criminogenic setting").

The third broad difference is that the character of a juvenile is not as well formed as that of an adult. The personality traits of juveniles are more transitory, less fixed. See generally E. Erikson, Identity: Youth and Crisis (1968).

These differences render suspect any conclusion that a juvenile falls among the worst offenders. The susceptibility of juveniles to immature and irresponsible behavior means "their irresponsible conduct is not as morally reprehensible as that of an adult." *Thompson, supra,* at 835 (plurality opinion). Their own vulnerability and comparative lack of control over their immediate surroundings mean juveniles have a greater claim than adults to be forgiven for failing to escape negative influences in their whole environment. See *Stanford*, 492 U.S., at 395,(Brennan, J., dissenting). The reality that juveniles still struggle to define their identity means it is less supportable to conclude that even a heinous crime committed by a juvenile is evidence of irretrievably depraved character. From a moral standpoint it would be misguided to equate the failings of a minor with those of an adult, for a greater possibility exists that a minor's character deficiencies will be reformed. Indeed, "[t]he relevance of youth as a mitigating factor derives from the fact that the signature qualities of youth are transient; as individuals mature, the impetuousness and recklessness that may dominate in younger years can subside." *Johnson, supra,* at 368; see also Steinberg & Scott 1014 ("For most teens, [risky or antisocial] behaviors are fleeting; they cease with maturity as individual identity becomes settled. Only a relatively small proportion of adolescents who experiment in risky or illegal activities develop entrenched patterns of problem behavior that persist into adulthood").

In *Thompson*, a plurality of the Court recognized the import of these characteristics with respect to juveniles under 16, and relied on them to hold that the Eighth Amendment prohibited the imposition of the death penalty on juveniles below that age. 487 U.S., at 833–838. We conclude the same reasoning applies to all juvenile offenders under 18.

. . .

... The differences between juvenile and adult offenders are too marked and well understood to risk allowing a youthful person to receive the death penalty despite insufficient culpability. An unacceptable likelihood exists that the brutality or cold-blooded nature of any particular crime would overpower mitigating arguments based on youth as a matter of course, even where the juvenile offender's objective immaturity, vulnerability, and lack of true depravity should require a sentence less severe than death. In some cases a defendant's youth may even be counted against him. In this very case, as we noted above, the prosecutor argued Simmons' youth was aggravating rather than mitigating. While this sort of overreaching could be corrected by a particular rule to ensure that the mitigating force of youth is not overlooked, that would not address our larger concerns.

It is difficult even for expert psychologists to differentiate between the juvenile offender whose crime reflects unfortunate yet transient immaturity, and the rare juvenile offender whose crime reflects irreparable corruption. See Steinberg & Scott 1014–1016. As we understand it, this difficulty underlies the rule forbidding psychiatrists from diagnosing any patient under 18 as having antisocial personality disorder, a disorder also referred to as psychopathy or sociopathy, and which is characterized by callousness, cynicism, and contempt for the feelings, rights, and suffering of others. American Psychiatric Association, Diagnostic and Statistical Manual of Mental Disorders 701–706 (4th ed. text rev. 2000); see also Steinberg & Scott 1015.

If trained psychiatrists with the advantage of clinical testing and observation refrain, despite diagnostic expertise, from assessing any juvenile under 18 as having antisocial personality disorder, we conclude that States should refrain from asking jurors to issue a far graver condemnation—that a juvenile offender merits the death penalty. When a juvenile offender commits a heinous crime, the State can exact forfeiture of some of the most basic liberties, but the State cannot extinguish his life and his potential to attain a mature understanding of his own humanity.

. . .

Drawing the line at 18 years of age is subject, of course, to the objections always raised against categorical rules. The qualities that distinguish juveniles from adults do not disappear when an individual turns 18. By the same token, some under 18 have already attained a level of maturity some adults will never reach. For the reasons we have discussed, however, a line must be drawn. The plurality opinion in *Thompson* drew the line at 16. In the intervening years the *Thompson* plurality's conclusion that offenders under 16 may not be executed has not been challenged. The logic of *Thompson* extends to those who are under 18. The age of 18 is the point where society draws the line for many purposes between childhood and adulthood. It is, we conclude, the age at which the line for death eligibility ought to rest.

These considerations mean Stanford v. Kentucky should be deemed no longer controlling on this issue. To the extent *Stanford* was based on review of the objective indicia of consensus that obtained in 1989, it suffices to note that those indicia have changed. It should be observed, furthermore, that the *Stanford* Court should have considered those States that had abandoned the death penalty altogether as part of the consensus against the juvenile death penalty; a State's decision to bar the death penalty altogether of necessity demonstrates a judgment that the death penalty is inappropriate for all offenders, including juveniles. Last, to the extent *Stanford* was based on a rejection of the idea that this Court is required to bring its independent judgment to bear on the proportionality of the death penalty for a particular class of crimes or offenders, it suffices to note that this rejection was inconsistent with prior Eighth Amendment decisions, *Thompson*, 487 U.S., at 833–838 (plurality opinion); *Enmund*, 458 U.S., at 797; *Coker*, 433 U.S., at 597(plurality opinion) . . .

. . .

Our determination that the death penalty is disproportionate punishment for offenders under 18 finds confirmation in the stark reality that the United States is the only country in the world that continues to give official sanction to the juvenile death penalty. This reality does not become controlling, for the task of interpreting the Eighth Amendment remains our responsibility. Yet at least from the time of the Court's decision in *Trop*, the Court has referred to the laws of other countries and to international authorities as instructive for its interpretation of the Eighth Amendment's prohibition of "cruel and unusual punishments." 356 U.S., at 102–103 (plurality opinion) ("The civilized nations of the world are in virtual unanimity that statelessness is not to be imposed as punishment for crime")....

As respondent and a number of *amici* emphasize, Article 37 of the United Nations Convention on the Rights of the Child, which every country in the world has ratified save for the United States and Somalia, contains an express prohibition on capital punishment for crimes committed by juveniles under 18. United Nations Convention on the Rights of the Child, Art. 37, Nov. 20, 1989, 1577 U. N. T. S. 3 (entered into force Sept. 2, 1990)....

Respondent and his *amici* have submitted, and petitioner does not contest, that only seven countries other than the United States have executed juvenile offenders since 1990: Iran, Pakistan, Saudi Arabia, Yemen, Nigeria, the Democratic Republic of Congo, and China. Since then each of these countries has either abolished capital punishment for juveniles or made public disavowal of the practice. In sum, it is fair to say that the United States now stands alone in a world that has turned its face against the juvenile death penalty.

. . .

It is proper that we acknowledge the overwhelming weight of international opinion against the juvenile death penalty, resting in large part on the understanding that the instability and emotional imbalance of young people may often be a factor in the crime. See Brief for Human Rights Committee of the Bar of England and Wales et al. as *Amici Curiae* 10–11. The opinion of the world community, while not controlling our outcome, does provide respected and significant confirmation for our own conclusions.

Over time, from one generation to the next, the Constitution has come to earn the high respect and even, as Madison dared to hope, the veneration of the American people. See The Federalist No. 49, p 314 (C. Rossiter ed. 1961). The document sets forth, and rests upon, innovative principles original to the American experience, such as federalism; a proven balance in political mechanisms through separation of powers; specific guarantees for the accused in criminal cases; and broad provisions to secure individual freedom and preserve human dignity. These doctrines and guarantees are central to the American experience and remain essential to our present-day self-definition and national identity. Not the least of the reasons we honor the Constitution, then, is because we know it to be our own. It does not lessen our fidelity to the Constitution or our pride in its origins to acknowledge that the express affirmation of certain fundamental rights by other nations and peoples simply underscores the centrality of those same rights within our own heritage of freedom.

The Eighth and Fourteenth Amendments forbid imposition of the death penalty on offenders who were under the age of 18 when their crimes were committed. The judgment of the Missouri Supreme Court setting aside the sentence of death imposed upon Christopher Simmons is affirmed.

It is so ordered.

■ Scalia, Justice (dissenting)

In urging approval of a constitution that gave life-tenured judges the power to nullify laws enacted by the people's representatives, Alexander Hamilton assured the citizens of New York that there was little risk in this, since "[t]he judiciary ... ha[s] neither FORCE nor WILL but merely judgment." The Federalist No. 78, p 465 (C. Rossiter ed. 1961). But Hamilton had in mind a traditional judiciary, "bound down by strict rules and precedents which serve to define and point out their duty in every particular case that comes before them." *Id.*, at 471. Bound down, indeed. What a mockery today's opinion makes of Hamilton's expectation, announcing the Court's conclusion that the meaning of our Constitution has changed over the past 15 years—not, mind you, that this Court's decision 15 years ago was *wrong*, but that the Constitution *has changed*. The Court reaches this implausible result by purporting to advert, not to the original meaning of the

Eighth Amendment, but to "the evolving standards of decency" of our national society. It then finds, on the flimsiest of grounds, that a national consensus which could not be perceived in our people's laws barely 15 years ago now solidly exists. Worse still, the Court says in so many words that what our people's laws say about the issue does not, in the last analysis, matter: "[I]n the end our own judgment will be brought to bear on the question of the acceptability of the death penalty under the Eighth Amendment." The Court thus proclaims itself sole arbiter of our Nation's moral standards—and in the course of discharging that awesome responsibility purports to take guidance from the views of foreign courts and legislatures. Because I do not believe that the meaning of our Eighth Amendment, any more than the meaning of other provisions of our Constitution, should be determined by the subjective views of five Members of this Court and like-minded foreigners, I dissent.

. . .

Of course, the real force driving today's decision is not the actions of four state legislatures, but the Court's " ' "own judgment" ' " that murderers younger than 18 can never be as morally culpable as older counterparts. *Ante*, at ___, 161 L. Ed. 2d, at 18 (quoting *Atkins*, 536 U.S., at 312 (in turn quoting *Coker*, 433 U.S., at 597, 53 (plurality opinion))). The Court claims that this usurpation of the role of moral arbiter is simply a "retur[n] to the rul[e] established in decisions predating *Stanford*." That supposed rule—which is reflected solely in dicta and never once in a *holding* that purports to supplant the consensus of the American people with the Justices' views—was repudiated in *Stanford* for the very good reason that it has no foundation in law or logic. If the Eighth Amendment set forth an ordinary rule of law, it would indeed be the role of this Court to say what the law is. But the Court having pronounced that the Eighth Amendment is an ever-changing reflection of "the evolving standards of decency" of our society, it makes no sense for the Justices then to *prescribe* those standards rather than discern them from the practices of our people. On the evolving-standards hypothesis, the only legitimate function of this Court is to identify a moral consensus of the American people. By what conceivable warrant can nine lawyers presume to be the authoritative conscience of the Nation?

. . .

Though the views of our own citizens are essentially irrelevant to the Court's decision today, the views of other countries and the so-called international community take center stage.

The Court begins by noting that "Article 37 of the United Nations Convention on the Rights of the Child, [1577 U. N. T. S. 3, entered into force Sept. 2, 1990], which every country in the world has ratified *save for the United States* and Somalia, contains an express prohibition on capital punishment for crimes committed by juveniles under 18." The Court also discusses the International Covenant on Civil and Political Rights (ICCPR), December 19, 1966, 999 U. N. T. S. 175, which the Senate ratified only subject to a reservation that reads:

> "The United States reserves the right, subject to its Constitutional restraints, to impose capital punishment on any person (other than a pregnant woman) duly convicted under existing or future laws permitting the imposition of capital punishment, including such punishment for crime committed by persons below eighteen years of age." Senate

Committee on Foreign Relations, International Covenant on Civil and Political Rights, S. Exec. Rep. No. 102–23 (1992).

Unless the Court has added to its arsenal the power to join and ratify treaties on behalf of the United States, I cannot see how this evidence favors, rather than refutes, its position. . . .

. . .

It is interesting that whereas the Court is not content to accept what the States of our Federal Union *say*, but insists on inquiring into what they *do* (specifically, whether they in fact *apply* the juvenile death penalty that their laws allow), the Court is quite willing to believe that every foreign nation—of whatever tyrannical political makeup and with however subservient or incompetent a court system—in fact *adheres* to a rule of no death penalty for offenders under 18. Nor does the Court inquire into how many of the countries that have the death penalty, but have forsworn (on paper at least) imposing that penalty on offenders under 18, have what no State of this country can constitutionally have: a *mandatory* death penalty for certain crimes, with no possibility of mitigation by the sentencing authority, for youth or any other reason. I suspect it is most of them. See, *e.g.*, R. Simon & D. Blaskovich, A Comparative Analysis of Capital Punishment: Statutes, Policies, Frequencies, and Public Attitudes the World Over 25, 26, 29 (2002). To forbid the death penalty for juveniles under such a system may be a good idea, but it says nothing about our system, in which the sentencing authority, typically a jury, always can, and almost always does, withhold the death penalty from an under-18 offender except, after considering all the circumstances, in the rare cases where it is warranted. The foreign authorities, in other words, do not even speak to the issue before us here.

More fundamentally, however, the basic premise of the Court's argument—that American law should conform to the laws of the rest of the world—ought to be rejected out of hand. . . .

. . .

NOTE

Debate about the appropriate use of foreign law has divided the Supreme Court and led to a growing body of commentary on the nature of our Constitutional system. See, e.g., Kenneth Anderson, Foreign Law and the U.S. Constitution, 131 Policy Review 33 (June & July 2005); Vicki Jackson, Constitutional Law in an Era of Global Constitutionalism, 119 Harv. L. Rev. 109 [forthcoming Nov.]

Judge Wilkinson, Chief Judge of the United States Court of Appeals for the Fourth Circuit, in a speech delivered to the Federalist Society's 2003 National Lawyers Convention, expressed concern over this new trend of judicial incorporation of international law:

> . . . The Constitution is a distinctive American contribution to human freedom, a freedom that is due in no small measure to self-governance and judicial restraint. If we wish others to embrace those traditions—and I do—we must remain true to them ourselves. Those of us who interpret the Constitution must respect the source from which our authority alone can spring, a governing compact formed over two centuries ago by those who envisioned above all the authority expressed in and through the rule of law by the people of America.

Hon. J. Harvie Wilkinson III, The Use of International Law in Judicial Decisions, 27 Harv. J.L. & Pub. Pol'y 423 (2004).

Much of this debate has focused on the issue of the juvenile death penalty. See generally, Carly Baetz-Stangel, Note: The Role of International Law in the Abolition of the Juvenile Death Penalty in the United States, 16 Fla. J. Int'l L. 955 (2004), Curtis A. Bradley, The Juvenile Death Penalty and International Law, 52 Duke L.J. 485 (2002), and Melissa A. Waters, Mediating Norms and Identity: The Role of Transnational Judicial Dialogue in Creating and Enforcing International Law, 93 Geo. L. J. 487 (2005).

The debate over the juvenile death penalty in turn has focused on the decision-making capacities of minors. In his majority opinion, Justice Kennedy relied primarily on the social science work of Laurence Steinberg and Elizabeth S. Scott, who have written:

> ... First, and most obviously, adolescents' levels of cognitive and psychosocial development are likely to shape their choices, including their criminal choices, in ways that distinguish them from adults and that may undermine competent decision making. Second, because adolescents' decision-making capacities are immature and their autonomy constrained, they are more vulnerable than are adults to the influence of coercive circumstances that mitigate culpability for all persons, such as provocation, duress, or threat. Finally, because adolescents are still in the process of forming their personal identity, their criminal behavior is less likely than that of an adult to reflect bad character. Thus, for each of the sources of mitigation in criminal law, typical adolescents are less culpable than are adults because adolescent criminal conduct is driven by transitory influences that are constitutive of this developmental stage. ...
>
> . . .
>
> ... The available evidence supports the conclusion that, like offenders who are mentally retarded and mentally ill, adolescents are less culpable than typical adults because of diminished decision-making capacity ...

Laurence Steinberg and Elizabeth S. Scott, Less Guilty by Reason of Adolescence: Developmental Immaturity, Diminished Responsibility, and the Juvenile Death Penalty, 58 Am. Psychologist 1009, 1011 (2003).

In his dissent, Justice Scalia pointed to inconsistencies in the amicus curiae briefs of the American Psychological Association (APA). In *Roper* they wrote:

> At ages 16 and 17, adolescents, as a group, are not yet mature in ways that affect their decision-making. Behavioral studies show that late adolescents are less likely to consider alternative courses of action, understand the perspective of others, and restrain impulses. Delinquent, even criminal, behavior is characteristic of many adolescents, often peaking around age 18. Heightened risk-taking is also common. During the same period the brain has not reached adult maturity, particularly in the frontal lobes, which control executive functions of the brain related to decision-making.

Brief for the American Psychological Association, and the Missouri Psychological Association as Amici Curiae Supporting Respondent, 2003 U.S. Briefs 633, 2 (2004). This assessment of minors' decision-making capacity is in stark contrast to the image painted by the APA only fifteen years earlier in their Amicus Curiae brief to the Supreme Court in the abortion case Hodgson v. Minnesota, 497 U.S. 417 (1990):

> [B]y middle adolescence (age 14–1) young people develop abilities similar to adults in reasoning about moral dilemmas, understanding social rules and laws, reasoning about interpersonal relationships and interpersonal problems, and reasoning about custody preference during parental divorce. By middle adolescence most young people develop an adult-like identity and understanding of self. Furthermore, the majority of adolescents do not repudiate parental values, but incorporate them, during their search for autonomy. Thus, by age 14 most adolescents have developed adultlike intellectual and social capacities including specific abilities outlined in the law as necessary for understanding treatment alternatives, considering risks and benefits, and giving legally competent consent.

Brief for Amici Curiae American Psychological Association, et al. in support of appellees, 1988 U.S. Briefs 805, 19–20 (1989). See also, Jon Michael–Foxworth, An Unjust Act: the Schizophrenic State of Maturity and Culpability in Juvenile Justice and Minor Abortion Rights Law, 9 Wm. & Mary J. of Women & L. 495 (2003).

F. EMANCIPATION

Meyer v. Meyer

Court of Appeals of Missouri, Kansas City District, 1973.
493 S.W.2d 42.

■ WASSERSTROM, JUDGE.

Under a 1964 decree of divorce, custody of four children born of the marriage was awarded to the mother, and . . . the father was ordered to pay child support for all four children in a single sum of $260.00 per month. The question [is] . . . what change if any should be made prospectively in the support award because of changed circumstances.

. . .

The fourth child is a daughter, Pamela. She lived with her father from August, 1968 until August, 1969, and then returned to live with her mother. She married in July 1970, and became divorced September 20, 1971, while pregnant.

. . .

. . . The wife appeals from those portions of [a lower court] order which denied future support for Pamela. . . .

. . .

The marriage of Pamela in July, 1970 resulted in her emancipation and operated to terminate the father's obligation of support, even though no action was taken by him for a modification of the decree. The father was unquestionably entitled at that point to apply to the court for a modification of the decree, insofar as the award of support included any element of contribution for this married daughter.

However, the mother contests the right of the father to cast off legal responsibility for Pamela, basing her argument on the fact that Pamela was divorced after the marriage and prior to the father's motion for a reduction in the support award. The mother argues in effect that the emancipation was only temporary in nature and could not last beyond the termination of the marriage by divorce, so that the burden of support was again thrown upon the father. No authority directly in point is cited for this proposition by the mother. The closest authority found on this subject is Rinaldi v. Rinaldi, 94 N.J.Eq. 14, 118 A. 685, l.c. 688, which is contrary to the mother's position. The court there said:

> "Even when an infant, emancipated by marriage, becomes a widow before reaching the age of majority, she does not relapse into pupilage. . . ."

Aside from authority, and strictly upon principle, there is good reason why the burden of support should not be reimposed upon the father. His daughter voluntarily chose a completely new and different family relationship when she took the marriage vows. At that time, her husband assumed legal responsibility for any support which she or any child of the marriage might require. This obligation took the place of and supplanted Pamela's former right to look to her father for necessary support. The divorce did not necessarily terminate the legal obligation by her new husband, and indeed there is no showing on the present record that she did not receive some provision by way of alimony or support for her unborn child. We hold that the divorce did not undo the emancipation which had been accomplished by Pamela's marriage.

. . .

NOTES

1. Other actions that traditionally emancipate a minor include military service, see, e.g., Garrison v. Garrison, 147 S.W.3d 925 (Mo.App.2004) and living apart from parents, see, e.g., Lev v. College of Marin, 22 Cal.App.3d 488, 99 Cal.Rptr. 476 (1971) (nineteen year old residing away from home is emancipated for purpose of establishing local residence to fulfill college admission requirements); But see, Dunson v. Dunson, 769 N.E.2d 1120 (Ind.2002) (parents' attempt to have son emancipated was unsuccessful because, although he had not been under their control since he was 15, he did not support himself). But note that emancipation is used in the limited sense of such things as no longer owing wages to parents. If an emancipated minor is underage according to relevant state law, by contrast, he still will not be permitted to vote, to drink, or to contract for services until he has reached the pertinent statutory age minimum.

2. Not all courts have adopted the view that emancipation, once achieved, is forever. See, e.g., Crimmins v. Crimmins, 192 Misc.2d 290, 745 N.Y.S.2d 686 (2002) (eighteen year old who had supported himself away from parents then returned to his mother's house with unpaid bills. He was held unemancipated and the father was liable for support). See generally, Chadwick N. Gardner Note, Don't Come Cryin' to Daddy! Emancipation of Minors: When is a Parent "Free at Last" From the Obligation of Child Support?, U of Louisville J. of Fam. L. 927 (1994).

In re Sumey

Supreme Court of Washington, En Banc, 1980.
94 Wash.2d 757, 621 P.2d 108.

■ UTTER, CHIEF JUDGE.

This appeal was certified to this court by Division Two of the Court of Appeals to determine whether the residential placement procedures of RCW 13.32 violate due process by authorizing placement of a minor without a prior finding of parental unfitness.

Sheila Marie Sumey, the petitioner at trial, is the daughter of appellants Rolin and Laura Sumey. At the time of trial in August 1978, Sheila was 15 years old. In the years preceding the initiation of this action, a number of problems had developed between Sheila and her parents. The parents set several rules for Sheila's conduct, which she did not always follow. On a number of occasions, Sheila ran away from home. Extensive family counseling was attempted, but was not successful.

In early June 1978, there was again conflict in the home and Mrs. Sumey began to believe that Sheila would once again run away from home. On June 17, Mrs. Sumey called the police to prevent Sheila from running away. The police placed Sheila in a receiving home on that day. The

Department of Social and Health Services (DSHS) began to provide crisis intervention services to the family and on June 20, Mrs. Sumey signed a consent form stating that Sheila should be in receiving care.

The DSHS crisis intervention services did not succeed in reconciling the differences between Sheila and her parents. The DSHS staff concluded that Sheila could not be returned home at that time, and she remained in receiving care. On July 15, Sheila filed a petition for alternative residential placement with the Pierce County Juvenile Court, pursuant to RCW 13.32.020. A hearing on the petition was held, and the juvenile court concluded that: the family was in conflict; prior counseling and crisis intervention had failed to remedy that conflict; the conflict could not be remedied by continued placement in the home; and the reasons for the alternative residential placement were not capricious. The court approved the petition for alternative residential placement and ordered that Sheila be placed in a nonsecure licensed facility. The court provided for rights of visitation for Mr. and Mrs. Sumey. The case was set for review in 6 months to determine what had been accomplished in resolving the conflict and reuniting the family.

Mr. and Mrs. Sumey appealed the juvenile court order and challenged the constitutionality of RCW 13.32, the statutory authority for the order of alternative residential placement.

Under RCW 13.30.020, a child may be taken into limited custody when the parents report the child as a runaway or when a law enforcement officer believes that the child is in circumstances which constitute imminent and substantial danger to the child's physical safety. Once a child has been taken into limited custody, DSHS must offer crisis intervention services to the family. The statutes specify that DSHS must pursue a primary goal of attempting to reconcile the differences between parents and child, and effect the child's return to the family home. If a reconciliation cannot be achieved, then DSHS must find a living situation for the child that is agreeable to both parents and child.

If either the parents or the child do not agree with the current placement, then they or the child can petition the juvenile court under RCW 13.32 for an alternative residential placement. The set of statutes challenged in this case govern the juvenile court procedures for alternative residential placements. The procedures that must be followed in a juvenile court hearing on a petition for alternative residential placement are set forth in RCW 13.32.030–.040. At the conclusion of a hearing, the juvenile court can place the child outside the parental home if it finds by a preponderance of the evidence that the petition is not capricious and that "there is a conflict between the parent and the child that cannot be remedied by counseling, crisis intervention, or continued placement in the parental home." RCW 13.32.040. If the court does order residential placement, then the placement is only temporary and a review hearing must be held every 6 months to approve or disapprove the continuation of the placement. Throughout the 6-month period that the child is in the placement, DSHS must provide appropriate interim services to the child and family with the ultimate goal of reuniting the child and parents.

RCW 13.32 thus establishes a means for providing social services to the family and nurturing the parent-child bond in a situation in which the family conflict, although extremely serious, has not as yet resulted in parental abuse, neglect, or abandonment of the child. The use of the RCW 13.32 procedure is predicated on the existence of family conflict of sufficient magnitude that the parents and child are unable to live in the same home even with the assistance of counseling or other rehabilitative social services. The procedure is founded upon a fundamental policy of preserving the relationship between parents and children. The legislature has specifically "declare[d] that the family unit is a fundamental resource of American life which should be nurtured" and that accordingly, "the family unit should remain intact in the absence of compelling evidence to the contrary." RCW 13.34.020. The RCW 13.32 procedure furthers these goals by requiring the employment of all feasible measures such as counseling and rehabilitative social services prior to removing the child from the home, and requiring the continuation of efforts to unite the family after the child has been removed from the home.

Appellants Mr. and Mrs. Sumey contend that RCW 13.32 violates due process in that it authorizes residential placement of a child outside the parental home even though the parents have not been found to be unfit. Appellants argue that the constitutional right to care, custody and companionship of one's child requires that parents retain custody of their children until the parents have been found to be unfit.

The liberty and privacy protections of the due process clause of the Fourteenth Amendment establish a parental constitutional right to the care, custody and companionship of the child. This constitutionally protected interest of parents has been described as a "sacred right" which is " 'more precious . . . than the right of life itself.' "

The parents' constitutional rights, however, do not afford an absolute protection against State interference with the family relationship. It is now well established that when parental actions or decisions seriously conflict with the physical or mental health of the child, the State has a parens patriae right and responsibility to intervene to protect the child.

. . .

In proceedings for child neglect, abuse, or abandonment, where the potential consequence is termination of parental rights on a temporary or permanent basis, the ultimate nature of the abridgement of parental constitutional rights necessitates an extremely substantial justification.... However, a residential placement under RCW 13.32 does not infringe upon parental rights as severely as does a dependency adjudication or termination of parental rights under RCW 13.34.

[It] does not result in the transfer of any legal rights and duties to the custodians of the child and such a placement cannot serve as a basis for a subsequent termination of parental rights. The full termination of parental rights under RCW 13.34 is certainly more severe than an RCW 13.32 placement, for the termination severs "all rights, powers, privileges, immunities, duties, and obligations, including any rights to custody, control, visitation, or support existing between the child and parent." RCW 13.34.200.

It must be determined, therefore, whether the RCW 13.32 basis for a limited infringement upon parental rights represents a constitutionally adequate balance between the rights and interests of the parents, child, and State. On one side of the balance is the parent's constitutional right to care, custody and companionship of the child. On the other side is the State's constitutionally protected *parens patriae* interest in protecting the physical and mental health of the child. The RCW 13.32 process enables the State to safeguard the mental and emotional health of the child by removing him or her from a situation of family conflict that is so extreme that the parents and child are unable to live together even with the aid of counseling. The procedure also allows the State to protect the physical health of children like the minor in the present case, who are driven by the family conflict to run away from home and expose themselves to the physical dangers that attend running away. The State also has an interest in employing the RCW 13.32 procedure to end family problems and strengthen parent-child relationships. The legislature has declared that "the family unit is a fundamental resource of American life which should be nurtured." RCW 13.34.020. The RCW 13.32 residential placement procedure enables the State to resolve family conflict and nurture the family unit before the problems are so severe as to require the drastic step of terminating parental rights on a temporary or permanent basis.

The interests of the State and child supporting the RCW 13.32 procedure are sufficient to justify the degree of intrusion upon parents' constitutional rights. The interests of the State and child which have been identified are extremely weighty for they concern the welfare and best interests of the child as well as the strengthening of the family unit. The degree of intrusion upon the parents' rights is relatively minor in that the parents retain custody over the child, the placement outside the home is designed to be temporary and to end as soon as the family conflict has been resolved through rehabilitative social services, and the temporary placement outside the home cannot serve as the foundation for a subsequent termination of parental rights. Moreover, the RCW 13.32 procedure can only be invoked if there has already been conflict between the parents and child and it has been determined that this conflict cannot be resolved by less restrictive alternatives such as counseling or crisis intervention services. On balance, the substantial interests of the State and child are sufficient to justify the limited infringement upon the parents' rights.

Accordingly, it must be concluded that appellants' due process challenge to RCW 13.32 is without merit. The ruling of the trial court is affirmed.

■ BRACHTENBACH, JUDGE (dissenting).

The majority sanctions a serious intrusion into the fundamental, constitutionally protected, parent-child relationship. In so doing, the majority approves a statute which is fatally defective because it lacks sufficient criteria to justify such trammeling of parental rights. If the record in this case justifies removal of a child from the family home, it means the Department of Social and Health Services and a recalcitrant juvenile can cause a child to be taken from the home of fit and proper parents whose only "fault" was to try to impose reasonable behavioral standards upon their minor child....

Upon what facts did the court find a "conflict" in this case? The juvenile signed a form petition which alleged in material part: "That said child is in conflict with his/her parents as defined in RCW 13.32 [where it is not defined] as follows: ... that said child refuses to endure the physical and verbal fighting and friction within the home and refuses to return; that counseling has been utilized ...; that said child would like to live with [a named family] or in an alternative foster home." Next: "Said conflict cannot be remedied by counseling, crisis intervention or continued placement in the parental home."

Petitioning juvenile was asked at the court hearing the following:

> Q. Could you please tell us why you believe there is a conflict in that home?
>
> A. I just feel that there's a communication gap there....

That is the sum and substance of the petitioner's testimony upon which she was taken from her parents' custody over their objections.

What standards of conduct had these parents laid down which led to this "lack of communication"? They asked [that] their 15-year-old daughter not use drugs, or associate with those who had furnished drugs, that she not use alcohol, that she not be sexually active, and that she be in at a reasonable hour. Because of the daughter's unwillingness to follow these obviously reasonable standards, the parents are summarily deprived of custody and the best opportunity to resolve these problems within the family.

There was no claim or proof of unfitness or neglect by the parents. There was no claim of proof of any imminent threat of harm or danger to this 15-year-old. The only manifestation of any potential harm to the child was her threat to run away. She had done so once in the past and occasionally stayed over night with friends without permission.

Based upon this skimpy petition and proof, the parents were deprived of custody for a minimum of 6 months (if the "conflict" was not resolved earlier), and possibly for additional periods of 6 months thereafter, following review by the court.

It is interesting to note that in the 1979 amendments the legislature recognized the very points raised in this dissent. Laws of 1979, ch. 155, § 15 (codified as RCW 13.32A.010). It specifically declared that the family unit should remain intact *in the absence of compelling evidence to the contrary*. It provided:

> The legislature finds that within any group of people there exists a need for guidelines for acceptable behavior and that, presumptively, experience and maturity are better qualifications for establishing guidelines beneficial to and protective of individual members and the group as a whole than are youth and inexperience. The legislature further finds that it is the right and responsibility of adults to establish laws for the benefit and protection of the society; and that, in the same manner, the right and responsibility for establishing reasonable guidelines for the family unit belongs to the adults within that unit. The legislature reaffirms its position stated in RCW 13.34.020 that the family unit is the fundamental resource of American life which should be nurtured and that it should remain intact in the absence of compelling evidence to the contrary.

RCW 13.32A.010.

The majority characterizes the alternative residential placement as a minor infringement by the State upon parental rights. I disagree. The child may be removed from the parents' home for an initial period of 6 months. After review, the placement may be extended for additional periods of 6 months each. The balance of a child's minority might well be spent in alternative placement solely because the child refuses to try to cope with reasonable parental controls. Deprivation of the physical presence of the child and therefore deprivation of the in-home opportunity to guide and influence the child during these critical years, is a serious intrusion upon the parents' fundamental right to raise and nurture their offspring.

I would hold that the statute, on its face and as applied in this case, violates the due process rights of the parents. On its face, the statute permits a serious infringement of a fundamental and scrupulously guarded constitutional right without providing adequate safeguards to justify such infringement. As applied, the facts and the findings in this case do not demonstrate a compelling state interest being exercised pursuant to a narrowly-drawn legislative enactment.

NOTES

1. California Emancipation of Minors Act, Cal. Fam. Code §§ 7120–23 (Deering 2005), provides that minors may petition the court for an emancipation decree. Apart from the traditional emancipating acts of marriage and military service, minors of at least 14 may show that they are managing their own financial affairs and are living "separate and apart" from their parents with parental "consent or acquiescence." The court retains the power to deny the decree if it would be in the best interest of the minor. § 7122(a). While California allows a particularly young age of eligibility, other states have enacted similar laws.

When should emancipation be considered in the best interest of a minor? See generally, Tia Wallach, Part Ten, Rights of Children: Statutory Emancipation in California: Privilege or Poverty?, 11 J. Contemp. Legal Issues 669 (2000).

2. In the majority of states, children in foster care are automatically emancipated at the age of eighteen, often having to vacate their foster homes within 24 hours. This issue of the "transition youth" has become the focus of legislative and social work efforts. The Foster Care Independence Act of 1999, 106 P.L. 169, gives states increased federal funding and more flexibility for programs to ready youth in foster care for emancipation and independent living. Most of these young people are still unprepared for full emancipation at eighteen. Consider Michele Benedetto, An Ounce of Prevention: A Foster Youth's Substantive Due Process Right to Proper Preparation for Emancipation, 9 U.C. Davis J. Juv. L. & Pol'y 381, 385 (2005):

> With some exceptions, most youth who "age out" of foster care do so at age 18. For the general population, the age of 18 represents freedom: the right to vote, to join the military, and to enter into contracts. But for foster youth, turning 18 and leaving foster care brings a new array of challenges. Without proper preparation, including a solid education or vocational plan, emancipation can bring unemployment and poverty. Failing to prepare youth for emancipation before the age of 18 results in harm, which often manifests itself after a youth has left foster care. Given the high incarceration and homelessness rates of former foster youth, society's failure to prepare foster youth for the "real world" is creating a new population of young adults in poverty.

See generally, Martha Stark & Gary Stangler, On Their Own: What Happens to Kids When They Age out of the Foster Care System? (2005). For alternatives to the present foster care system see generally, Rethinking Orphanages for the 21st Century (Richard B. McKenzie ed., 1999).

Burt v. Burt

Supreme Court of Mississippi, En Banc, 2001.
841 So.2d 108.

■ COBB, ASSOCIATE JUSTICE.

This is an appeal from a final judgment of the Hinds County Chancery Court, First Judicial District. Less than a year after she reached the age of twenty-one years, Amber Burt (Amber), filed suit against her father, Bruce Burt (Bruce), for child support unpaid since 1989. The chancellor, after hearing testimony from Amber, Bruce and Bruce's former wife, entered an order requiring Bruce to pay Amber $29,795 in back child support plus $13,882 interest. This amount, awarded solely to Amber, included the entire monthly sum ordered for both her and her brother in their parents' 1978 divorce. At the hearing there were numerous, short statements made regarding Bruce's son Todd (Amber's brother), who at the time of the hearing was

25 years old. However, Todd was not a party to this suit and no provision was asked for him, nor made for him when the chancellor granted the entire back child support award to Amber. The method of calculating the amount was determined by Gerald Lee, Ph.D. and stipulated to by the parties. However, Bruce's counsel added a handwritten statement to the stipulation, saying that they did "not admit that we owe anything." Following the chancellor's decision, Bruce timely filed a notice of appeal to this Court. ... Finding no manifest error or abuse of discretion in the decision of the trial court, we affirm.

On December 20, 1978, Bruce and Amber's mother, Gloria Burt, [were] granted a divorce by the Hinds County Chancery Court. Bruce and Gloria had two children at the time of the divorce: Amber, who was born July 10, 1977, and Todd, who was born October 11, 1974. Under the terms of the 1978 divorce decree, Bruce was ordered to pay Gloria $275 per month in child support "for the minor children." There was no mention of any special needs or any special allocation between the children, so the presumption, albeit rebuttable, is that each was entitled to one half of the $275 each month. Varner v. Varner, 588 So. 2d 428, 434 (Miss. 1991)

Gloria died on January 24, 1989. Bruce did not make any child support payments after Gloria's death. Amber lived with her grandparents in Jackson, Mississippi, for several years following the death of her mother. At approximately 16 years of age, Amber began to live in a variety of places, all of which were in the Jackson area. During the summer of 1993 she lived in an apartment with her friend Stephanie and Stephanie's mother. Amber lived with her father for approximately four to six months during 1993 and 1994. Amber testified that she moved out of her father's home because she was uncomfortable with his drinking. Later, she moved in with her boyfriend at the time, where she lived from November, 1995 until July 1996.

. . .

Amber had no contact with her father for the seven years preceding the hearing. Bruce's ex-wife, Tina Nail Burt Price, testified that Bruce did attempt unsuccessfully to contact Amber on several occasions when she lived with her grandparents. Bruce testified that he was willing for his children to live with him when Amber left his home and that after she left he would have still welcomed her back into his home at any time.

During the hearing, Bruce contended that Amber's activities after she moved out of his home served to emancipate her. He pointed to her independent way of life, living with other families, friends and a boyfriend, claiming that those activities effectively emancipated her. As a result, Bruce contends Amber was not due any child support.

. . .

The statute governing emancipation is Miss. Code Ann. § 93–5–23 (Supp.2000) which reads in pertinent part as follows:

> The duty of support of a child terminates upon the emancipation of the child. The court may determine that emancipation has occurred and no other support obligation exists when the child:
>
> (a) Attains the age of twenty-one (21) years, or
>
> (b) Marries, or
>
> (c) Discontinues full-time enrollment in school and obtains full-time employment prior to attaining the age of twenty-one (21) years, or

(d) Voluntarily moves from the home of the custodial parent or guardian and establishes independent living arrangements and obtains full-time employment prior to attaining the age of twenty-one (21) years.

The statutory requirements for emancipation are clearly permissive and not mandatory; the court *may* determine that the child has been emancipated if any of the four factors are satisfied. The amount of support awarded by the chancellor was clearly calculated to cease when Amber reached age twenty-one, thus the first factor is not applicable. The second factor is irrelevant because Amber did not marry. Bruce argues the full-time employment aspect of the third and fourth factors was satisfied, but the record does not validate his argument. The chancellor found that Amber's employment was not full-time until after she reached age twenty-one. The difference in calculations here is not significant. In fact, the difference could at least partially be explained by the chancellor having included in her calculations vacation time or other time that Amber may not have worked. Thus the third and fourth factors were not met since full time employment is a component of both.

Bruce also challenges the chancellor's finding that Amber lived with her boyfriend, for a summer, claiming that the record shows they lived together for nine months. Amber testified the two lived together for four to six months. The chancellor's language may be imprecise but the finding certainly does not rise to the level of contradicting the overwhelming weight of the evidence.

It is significant that Bruce never petitioned the chancery court for a modification of his child support obligations. Bruce merely stopped making payments when Gloria died. The law is unequivocal on this issue. Once a child support payment becomes due, that payment vests in the child. Once the payments are vested, "they cannot be modified or forgiven by the courts." Tanner v. Roland, 598 So. 2d 783, 786 (Miss. 1992); Thurman v. Thurman, 559 So. 2d 1014, 1016–17 (Miss. 1990). Each payment that becomes due and remains unpaid "becomes a 'judgment' against the supporting parent." Tanner, 598 So. 2d at 786; Cunliffe v. Swartzfager, 437 So. 2d 43, 45–46 (Miss. 1983). The only defense thereto is payment. Tanner, 598 So. 2d at 786; Varner, 588 So. 2d at 433. The delinquent parent is liable also for the interest which has accrued on each unpaid support payment from the time it was due. Tanner, 598 So. 2d at 786; Brand v. Brand, 482 So. 2d 236, 238 (Miss. 1986).

Bruce's second reason for challenging the chancellor's order as being against the overwhelming weight of the evidence was the finding that Amber's decision to leave Bruce's home was predicated on his continuous intoxication. Bruce claims the record lacked sufficient evidence for such a finding. However, this issue was addressed in the testimony of Amber, Bruce, and Tina (Bruce's ex-wife). It is perplexing that Bruce now objects to a lack of evidence to justify this finding when it was his counsel who objected to the line of questioning when Amber was queried concerning times when she was around her dad while he was drinking. Bruce's counsel objected stating "we are here for child support, not custody." The objection was sustained. Based on the testimony of Amber, Bruce and his witness, Tina, there was more than sufficient evidence in the record for such a finding by the chancellor.

In reviewing such findings, this Court recognizes that the trial judge, sitting in a bench trial as the trier of fact, has the sole authority for determining the credibility of the witnesses. Hall v. State ex rel. Waller, 247 Miss. 896, 903; 157 So. 2d 781, 784 (1963). "Where there is conflicting evidence we must give great deference to the chancellor's findings." McElhaney v. City of Horn Lake, 501So. 2d 401, 403 (Miss.1987). Bruce's first assignment of error is without merit.

Bruce argues an equitable maxim that "He who comes into equity must come with clean hands." Cole v. Hood, 371 So. 2d 861, 863 (Miss. 1979). Bruce claims Amber did not have "clean hands" because she was unwilling to have a relationship with her father, and she was unwilling to live with him even though he was ready and willing to accept her in his home at any time. In fact, Amber had no contact with Bruce for the seven years preceding the hearing. The parties disagree over whether the lack of contact resulted from a voluntary decision by Amber to avoid her father or whether Bruce's alcohol consumption caused Amber to leave the home and caused her to be uncomfortable around her father. Although in the trial court Bruce did not label his defense the "clean hands doctrine," there was ample testimony of Amber's actions and Bruce's actions before the court.

The chancellor was in the best position to resolve this conflict and did so in favor of Amber. Because Bruce failed to raise the unclean hands defense below, he is procedurally barred from doing so on appeal. However, procedural bar aside, we find no manifest error in the chancellor's ruling in favor of Amber.

Bruce's claims of error have no merit. The chancellor did not abuse her discretion in finding that Bruce owed the back child support payments plus interest. In addition, the chancellor's findings of fact regarding Amber's emancipation were not against the overwhelming weight of the evidence. Therefore, the judgment of the Hinds County Chancery Court is affirmed.

AFFIRMED.

NOTE

The plight of 12-year-old Gregory Kingsley brought national attention to the question of whether children should be allowed to "divorce" their parents. A Florida District Court of Appeal found that Gregory had been neglected and abandoned by his natural mother and ordered that her parental rights be terminated despite her eleventh hour attempt to regain custody of Gregory. Kingsley v. Kingsley, 623 So.2d 780 (Fla.App.1993). The order cleared the way for the adoption of Gregory by his foster parents, George and Lizbeth Russ. Since the adoption, Gregory has taken the name Shawn and worked with his adoptive father in support of children's legal rights. In 1999 they approached Congress urging passage of a Child's Rights Amendment which would give children equal protection under the law. George Russ again made national headlines by representing Kimberly Mays in her suit to terminate the legal rights of her birth parents from whom she had been separated at birth. See Mays v. Twigg, 543 So.2d 241 (Fla. App.1989). In an interview conducted seven years after the bitter lawsuit, Shawn's birth mother, Rachel still expressed hope that he would return to his family. Shawn, however, expressed his desire for her to move on with her life. He now considered his life to be with the Russ family. His case is viewed by many as a turning point in the rights of abused and neglected minors, although some critics fear it marks the beginning of increased state encroachment on parental rights. Gregory K. v. Ralph K.: Children Divorcing their Parents, Landmark Trials of Modern Ethics, (World Almanac Video, 2002). See Irreconcilable Differences: When Children Sue their Parents for Divorce, 32 J.Fam.L. 68 (1993–94).

CHAPTER 10

Child Abuse and Neglect

A. What Should the Standards Be for Intervening Between Parent and Child?

Judith Areen, Intervention Between Parent and Child: A Reappraisal of the State's Role in Child Neglect and Abuse Cases

63 Geo. L.J. 887–889, 894–896, 903–904, 910–912, 917 (1975).

[Each year in the United States thousands of children are] brought into court on the ground that they are being neglected or abused by their parents. Once a court agrees that it has sufficient cause to assume jurisdiction in order to protect a child, there is a high probability that the child will be separated from his family for months or years, or permanently. In addition, the parents may find themselves subjected to criminal prosecution or at least to a succession of police investigators, social work investigators, social case workers, mental health professionals, and court hearings. Despite the disruptive impact this process obviously can have on children and their families, at present there is little consensus about when a court should find that a particular child is neglected or abused. Parents convicted of neglect in one community might never have been brought to court in another. Perhaps the most prevalent characteristic of families charged with neglect is poverty; this raises the troubling possibility that class or cultural bias plays a significant role in decisions to label children neglected or abused, because it is clear that child abuse occurs in families of all income levels.

Just as there is little agreement on when intervention in a particular family is justified, there is little agreement about what forms of intervention are constructive. The predominant approach is to separate parent and child. [Although] separation may protect a child from being beaten by his family, the separation itself may seriously damage the child's emotional health, particularly if the child is shifted from one temporary home to another during the separation.

. . .

II. HISTORY OF NEGLECT INTERVENTION

A. From Tudor Times to the Nineteenth Century

. . . The sixteenth century was a period of economic transition and stress in England, during which bands of "sturdy beggars" began to fill the roads and to terrorize town and country. The number of poor mushroomed to the point that private charities no longer could provide adequate relief. As a result, Parliament began to provide for the relief of the poor and their children on a systematic basis. As early as 1535 a statute provided that "[c]hildren under fourteen years of age, and above five, that live in idleness, and be taken begging, may be put to serve by the governors of cities, towns, etc. to husbandry, or other crafts or labors." In 1601, the Elizabethan Poor Law consolidated similar early legislative efforts into a single, comprehensive program of poor relief that became the model for the next three centuries in the United States as well as England.

The Elizabethan system aided the poor in several ways. It provided for the establishment of tax-supported hospitals and poor houses, or almshouses, to shelter the poor who were too old or too ill to work. The employable poor were compelled to work or sent to houses of correction if they refused to work. Finally, children of the poor were put to work or apprenticed....

It is impossible to determine exactly how many children were separated from their families under this legislation; hundreds were shipped to the American colonies beginning in 1617, and thousands were later impressed into the Merchant Marine. As distasteful as the cavalier separation of children from their parents may seem today, however, the conclusion that the statutes manifested only discriminatory attitudes toward the poor would be mistaken; the apparent harshness was more a product of cost consciousness than of discrimination. According to Professor tenBroek, "[o]nce the public agreed to pay the bill, it acquired a pressing concern about the size of the bill and an active interest in finding methods for reducing it." The system of "binding out" poor children reduced the costs; the children who were bound out could pay for part of their care through their own labor. Similarly, the decision to separate poor children from their families and to put them to work did not necessarily indicate class bias because in this pre-child labor law era most children worked and upper class families of the time frequently sent adolescents to other families for training. Indeed, the poor laws were quite humanitarian in their attempt to provide poor children with proper work attitudes as well as useful skills in an age when no other public education or training was available.

The record of providing skills through apprenticeship, however, apparently was poor almost from the start. "Rogues soon swarmed again," complained Lord Coke in 1624, and the cause allegedly was the failure of the overseers to apprentice children. The Privy Council for a time tried to correct the enforcement problems, but the outbreak of civil war soon made them worse. By mid-century, an increasingly harsh and repressive policy toward the poor emerged. Soon work houses for children were established, in sharp contrast with the earlier benevolent statutory scheme for training.

. . .

B. Reforms of the Nineteenth Century

Neglect proceedings in the nineteenth century continued to be primarily part of the poor relief program, but they gradually were expanded to protect children from parental immorality and abuse. The first state intervention to protect a child from parental abuse occurred in 1874. According to the more dramatic versions of the episode, eight-year-old Mary Ellen Wilson was rescued only through the efforts of the recently formed New York Society for the Prevention of Cruelty to Animals, which argued that children were, after all, members of the animal kingdom. Within a few months the first Society for the Prevention of Cruelty to Children was formed in New York City by Elbridge Gerry, who had argued Mary Wilson's cause.

The Society's records demonstrate that poverty, rather than cruelty, continued to be the major justification for family interventions, despite the organization's professed dedication to protecting children from cruelty. Further, the Society focused on punishing cruel parents rather than on the provision of better environments for children. The Society's efforts facilitated passage of a neglect statute authorizing any New York court that convicted a parent for criminal abuse or neglect to commit their children to an orphanage or to effect any other disposition that was available for pauper children. The new statute focused principally on preventing the exploitation of children for commercial purposes rather than on enhancing their physical or emotional development.

. . .

C. The Modern Era

. . . Two major changes in the goals of neglect enforcement occurred in the beginning of the twentieth century. First, changes in the poor relief system, particularly the development of "mother's aid" and aid to dependent children made it possible for states to stop removing children from parents because of family poverty; for the first time poverty became a defense to rather than a ground for a neglect finding. This new distinction between neglect and destitution is highlighted by a 1930 New York statute which provided that destitute children were to be housed separately from those who were delinquent, neglected, or abandoned. Not until 1962, when poverty in theory became an absolute defense to state intervention in New York, was the change begun in 1922 made complete. The legislature abolished the destitute child category and redefined a neglected child as one "whose parent or other person legally responsible for his care does not adequately supply the child with food, clothing, shelter, education, or medical or surgical care, though financially able or offered financial means to do so." Unfortunately, a second section of the 1962 statute allowed its application to families who were simply poor or unconventional, for neglect was defined also to include "improper guardianship, including lack of moral supervision or guidance." The vagueness of this standard was tempered only slightly by a requirement that the state show that the child "suffers or is likely to suffer serious harm" from the improper guardianship and that the child "required the aid of the court," before the statute could be invoked.

The second major change in neglect practice in the twentieth century was the expansion of the *parens patriae* role of the states to encompass protection of children from emotional as well as physical harm. Often this change was accompanied by a revision of statutes that made parental immorality a basis for state intervention. In New York, for example, impairment of emotional health and impairment of mental or emotional condition were made grounds for intervention in 1970, while "lack of moral supervision" was eliminated. Similarly, in 1963 Idaho authorized intervention where a child was "emotionally maladjusted" or where a child who had been denied proper parental love or affectionate association "behaves unnaturally and unrealistically in relation to normal situations, objects, and other persons."

These changes undoubtedly reflect the influence of both Freud and a growing body of child development specialists, who documented the emotional needs of children and affirmed the importance of being raised in a family. . . .

The preceding survey of past neglect practice demonstrates the basis of the current conceptual dilemma: jurisdiction to protect children from physical and emotional harm was only recently embroidered on a statutory framework originally established to provide work or training for poor children and to minimize welfare costs and fraud. Only with the development of aid to dependent children and the new awareness of the special needs of children did the neglect process cease being primarily a welfare program and become instead the chief public arbiter of acceptable parental behavior. . . .

1. Defining Child Abuse

a. UNDERSTANDING THE BATTERED CHILD SYNDROME

State v. Moorman

Superior Court of New Jersey, Appellate Division, 1996.
286 N.J.Super. 648, 670 A.2d 81.

■ Petrella, P.J.A.D.

A jury convicted defendant Sharon Moorman of second degree manslaughter, *N.J.S.A. 2C:11–4(b)*, as a lesser included offense of a charge of first degree murder of her twenty-two-month-old daughter. . . .

. . .

. . . [T]he jury could well have found the following facts. At about 8:00 a.m. on January 21, 1990, emergency medical technicians (EMTs) arrived at Moorman's residence at 1559 Norris Street in Camden. They observed a toddler, later identified as Labria Moorman, defendant's twenty-two-month-old daughter, lying face up on the living room floor. Her body was described as stiff, her skin cool and cyanotic. She was in cardiac arrest, neither breathing nor having any pulse. Attempts to resuscitate Labria both before and after her transportation to a nearby hospital were unavailing. At the hospital, Dr. Attawell concluded that she had been dead for a considerable length of time and that further attempts at resuscitation were futile.

Upon examination, the doctor noticed multiple bruises about Labria's torso, arms, abdomen, lower belly and chest, as well as a circular, non-healing ulcer on the top of her left foot. She also discovered scarring on Labria's left and right buttocks and on her left inner elbow and lower arm, as well as bruising from the base of her right thumb to her right shoulder. The bruising and scarring appeared to be of varying colorations. Chemical analysis of an incontinent stool found in Labria's diaper revealed blood in her feces, indicating an abnormality in the bowel causing blood to flow into it.

Dr. Attawell concluded that the trauma suffered by the infant was of suspicious origin and queried Moorman about Labria's condition. Moorman indicated that Labria had been suffering from a fever and cold symptoms during the five days before January 21, 1990. In response to the doctor's inquiry about any injury which might have caused the bruising and scarring, Moorman replied that two days earlier Labria had fallen down a flight of stairs, but "seemed okay" after the fall. Moorman also said that Labria had fallen down a flight of stairs about a month earlier and was treated at a different hospital. When the doctor informed Moorman that her daughter had died, she became upset.

The county medical examiner was advised of the doctor's suspicions. The police then went to the hospital to interview Moorman. Moorman, who was not then in custody or under arrest, told the officers that Labria had fallen down the stairs in their home on January 18, but was not taken to the hospital because she did not appear to require medical attention. She also told the police that Labria had fallen down the stairs two or three weeks earlier and was admitted to an emergency room for examination and treatment.

Moorman told the police that she and her live-in boyfriend, Rodney Rogers, had had a heated argument on January 20 about his leaving her residence to socialize later that night. After Rogers left, she fell asleep on the sofa with Labria next to her. Moorman indicated that when she awoke, Labria was not on the sofa but lying on the floor. Although Labria was cold, Moorman said she thought the child had a faint heartbeat. Consequently, she ran to a neighbor's home to telephone the police, which resulted in the EMTs' arrival.

The Assistant County Medical Examiner, Dr. Robert L. Catherman, performed an autopsy on January 21, 1990. Photographs were taken during the autopsy. The examination revealed that blunt force had caused the sheering of the mesentery of Labria's bowel, resulting in a lack of blood flow to the bowel and the eventual failure of the heart. The police were told that the type of injuries that were observed in the autopsy could not have occurred by a fall down stairs.

A follow-up interview was conducted on January 22 with Moorman after she was advised of her Miranda rights. . . . When the officer informed Moorman that Labria's death had been ruled a homicide, Moorman cried and repeated that Labria had twice fallen down the stairs. Moorman also described an incident in which she had picked up Labria by the waist and had shaken her after she had disobeyed an instruction not to leave the sofa because a nearby table had been sprayed with furniture polish. Moorman became upset and spontaneously told the officers that she had neither intended to hurt Labria nor wanted her to die.

Moorman agreed to give the police a tape-recorded statement of what she had just told them, and the police again advised her of her Miranda rights. She repeated her understanding of those rights and gave a recorded statement consistent with her unrecorded statement. Moorman was then charged with and arrested for murder. The statement, as well as the autopsy photographs (converted into slides), were admitted into evidence at trial.

The trial judge held a Rule 104 hearing on the State's request to allow its medical expert to render an opinion as to whether Labria had suffered from the "battered child syndrome" in order to support the admission, as prior acts evidence under *N.J.R.E. 404(b)*, of Moorman's prior abuse of the child. This testimony was allowed. Although the judge conceded that the slides were unsightly, he determined that any explanation of Labria's injuries would be incomplete without relevant pictorial aids. The judge had asked the jurors during voir dire whether they could look at graphic medical photographs without being inflamed, with those responding negatively being excused.

At the hearing, after a thorough voir dire, the court recognized the assistant county medical examiner as an expert in the Battered Child Syndrome (BCS). The doctor stated that BCS, which referred to the physical, mechanical abuse of children, had gained acceptance in the medical community over the past two or three decades, noting that the American Academy of Forensic Sciences and the National Association of Medical Examiners have both recognized BCS. The doctor described the "classic" case of BCS as one in which the victim exhibits multiple injuries of varying ages to the head or abdomen.[4]

Dr. Catherman's testimony before the jury essentially tracked that at the voir dire hearing. He reviewed the various autopsy slides, which showed the extent of the injuries to Labria, including old and new bruises and scars. He explained that the non-healing ulcer on Labria's left foot was a traumatic-type injury. He further attributed the creation of five separate abdominal bruises to blunt force. Likewise, Dr. Catherman diagnosed scarring across both of Labria's buttocks as caused by a healing traumatic injury, rather than diaper rash. The doctor also noted that the interior of the abdominal walls was bruised. The slide of the interior of Labria's chest and abdomen showed where some sixteen inches of mesentery was stripped from the bowel due to the force of a fairly substantial trauma, and how blood had found its way into the child's stool through the tear.

As a result of his autopsy on Labria, Dr. Catherman opined that, to a reasonable degree of medical certainty, the cause of the child's death was multiple injuries to her abdomen, and the manner of death was homicide. Dr. Catherman concluded that blunt force trauma had caused the abdominal injuries to Labria, which tore mesentery from her bowel and started internal bleeding that led to her death. The doctor testified that Labria's abdominal injuries, when viewed in the context of her other injuries and in light of his experience and training, were indicative of BCS. He rejected the hypothesis that the injuries could have been caused by a fall down stairs. He said that, in his more than twenty years of experience, the overwhelming majority of abdominal injuries suffered by children had resulted from abuse, not accidents.

The judge instructed the jury that it could only use the expert testimony of prior injuries as evidence that Labria's death was not caused by a fall down stairs, and not as evidence of any predisposition by Moorman to commit the crime. The judge advised the jury that it was not bound to accept the doctor's testimony as credible evidence as to whether or not Labria's death was accidental. The judge cautioned the jury that even if it concluded that Labria was a victim of BCS, and had died because of repeated physical abuse, it could not return a guilty verdict unless it was convinced beyond a reasonable doubt that Moorman had inflicted the injuries.

Defendant's expert witness, Dr. Louis Roh, the Deputy Chief Medical Examiner of Westchester County, New York, agreed that Labria had died of blunt force trauma to her abdomen. He maintained, however, that Labria's injuries were consistent with Moorman's contention that the child had fallen down stairs. He opined that the injuries about Labria's torso and arms were all approximately three to four days old, which was consistent with the time that Labria had allegedly fallen down the stairs. Based upon his familiarity with BCS, he contradicted Dr. Catherman's testimony by concluding that there was no evidence of BCS in this case because there were no serious head injuries, skeletal injuries, or, in his opinion, bruises of varying ages.

On cross-examination, Dr. Roh conceded that he had not seen Dr. Catherman's autopsy photographs before concluding that Labria had not suffered from BCS. He also admitted abusive parents often use "falling down stairs" as an excuse to conceal abusive conduct.

4. According to Dr. Catherman, the victim frequently presents recently healed skeletal injuries as well. Neither a designated number or type of injury nor a fatality are "required" to reach a finding that a child has suffered from BCS. Dr. Catherman cited to other factors, including the extent and location of external injuries, the formation of a pattern among those injuries, the existence of internal injuries, and the delayed presentment of the child for treatment.

In the jury charge, the judge reiterated his former instructions, including that the BCS evidence could only be used as proof that Labria's death was not accidental.

. . .

For expert testimony to be considered reliable, the proponent of the testimony must demonstrate its general acceptability as scientific evidence. See *State v. Kelly, 97 N.J. 178, 208–209, 478 A.2d 364 (1984).* Kelly explained that a party may prove acceptability through presentation of expert testimony by one within the expert's field or profession, submission of authoritative legal and scientific literature, or citation to judicial opinions. *Id. at 209.*

The trial judge here properly recognized BCS as a valid scientific premise underlying Dr. Catherman's expert opinion. First, Dr. Catherman testified during voir dire that BCS is generally recognized in the medical profession on a multi-disciplinary level. Even Dr. Roh testified at trial that BCS has been a recognized medical condition since the early 1960's. BCS was apparently first coined as an expression by Dr. C. H. Kempe in his seminal article, The Battered–Child Syndrome, *181 JAMA 17 (1962).* Orfinger, Battered Child Syndrome: Evidence of Prior Acts in Disguise, *41 Fla. L. Rev. 345, 346 (1989).* The term was used to "describe a pattern of serious and unexplained manifestations of physical abuse" in children. Ibid. Such manifestations include poor general health, malnutrition, multiple soft tissue injuries, poor skin hygiene, subdural hematoma, and long-bone skeletal fractures in various stages of healing. *Id. at 350.*

Second, there is sufficient, authoritative legal and medical literature to substantiate the conclusion that BCS has been widely accepted in the medical community. Although specific treatises were not discussed during voir dire, Dr. Catherman testified at trial as to specific literature dealing with BCS and the type of abdominal injuries present in this matter.

Third, numerous other jurisdictions have accepted BCS as a reliable scientific premise ...

Even if we determined that the trial judge had improperly recognized BCS as a reliable scientific basis for admission of expert testimony tending to show absence of accident or mistake, and we do not, any such error was harmless. Evidence of prior episodes of child abuse unconnected with the direct cause of the child's death was admissible as proof of absence of accident or mistake. The trial judge here could properly have admitted Dr. Catherman's testimony without regard to the BCS characterization as proof of prior abuse at the hands of Moorman to rebut her contention that Labria had fallen down stairs ...

NOTE

For an overview of child sexual abuse, diagnosis and treatment of the perpetrator, and prevention strategies, see generally, A. Kenneth Fuller, Child Molestation and Pedophilia, 261 J.A.M.A. 602 (1989).

b. ABUSE OR DISCIPLINE?

Chronister v. Brenneman

Superior Court of Pennsylvania, 1999.
742 A.2d 190.

■ BROSKY, J.

This is an appeal from the entry of a Protection From Abuse Order. Appellant raises a single issue, does the Protection From Abuse Act, *23*

Pa.C.S.A. § 6102(a), prohibit a parent from using physical punishment to discipline a child for misconduct? We reverse.

The relevant facts do not appear to be in dispute. On the morning of May 18, 1998, appellant administered corporal punishment to his sixteen-year-old daughter, Cassandra Morrison, in the form of hitting her four or five times with a folded belt across the buttocks after she admitted lying to appellant. Ms. Morrison testified that the strapping was painful and made her cry. After the incident she went to school and later reported the incident to her guidance counselor who refused to take action. Ms. Morrison then called her older half-sister, Shannon Chronister, appellee here, and told her what had happened. Ms. Chronister then contacted CYS and reported the incident. A caseworker for CYS met with Cassandra the next day. However, CYS ultimately refused to intervene because the behavior alleged was not viewed as implicating CYS involvement.

Later on the evening of May 18, 1998, and perhaps prompted by the incident that morning, appellant and his girlfriend were having a discussion with Ms. Morrison on the "rules of the house." Shortly thereafter appellant left the kitchen table and retrieved a pistol from a cupboard, looked at the gun, walked by Ms. Morrison and proceeded upstairs. Appellant testified that he had remembered that he left the gun downstairs and retrieved it, checked to make sure it was unloaded, then took it upstairs to a closet where he stores his firearms. Ms. Morrison testified that she had eye contact with appellant as he walked by.

The next day a Petition for Protection From Abuse was filed and a temporary order was signed on May 20, 1998. . . . [A] full hearing was scheduled for July 15, 1998. At the hearing of July 15, 1998, Ms. Morrison testified to the above facts and also to being frightened and intimidated by the incident as well as by appellant's statements that similar punishment would follow if Ms. Morrison continued to break the rules. Appellant also testified and essentially admitted the relevant facts. Appellant asserted that his actions were solely designed to discipline Cassandra and that he felt it was appropriate and necessary given her history of jumping to various caregivers whenever she did not get her way.[1] On October 8, 1998, the court entered the subject PFA order. The present appeal followed.

Before us is the issue of whether or not appellant's conduct in disciplining/punishing his sixteen year-old daughter falls within the definitions of the Protection from Abuse Act. We conclude that it does not.

We would state initially that nothing in this Opinion should be construed to be an approval or condoning of appellant's choice of discipline. Undoubtedly, many individuals regarded as authorities in child rearing would certainly cringe at appellant's choice of punishment for his sixteen-year-old daughter. On the other hand, neither should this Opinion be construed as disapproving of, or critical of, appellant's conduct. Undoubtedly, many individuals believe in the old adage "spare the rod and spoil the child." The topic is certainly suitable for a barstool or roundtable debate. However, it is not for us to dictate, as a policy matter, how a parent should choose to discipline his or her child.

1. Apparently Ms. Morrison had lived in the homes of her mother, paternal grandmother and appellee in addition to appellant's home.

Further, the trial court's lengthy discussion relating to current viewpoints regarding corporal punishment, while interesting and instructive, is, in our opinion, mostly irrelevant. The fact of relevance is that our law allows a parent to administer corporal punishment. The fact that a father chose to discipline his child through the means of corporal punishment is relevant only to the extent it reflects the motivation for the physical conduct in question. In other words, it is relevant only to reflect appellant's state of mind . . .

While appellant's parental judgment and choice of discipline can certainly be called into question, his motivation appears beyond reproach. That is, there appears to be a lack of any evidence to support the conclusion that appellant's acts were intended to be anything other than punishment for a young woman who the trial court admits "has taxed her father's patience to the limit." Thus it appears clear that the strapping of his daughter across the buttocks, in appellant's mind, constituted "punishment." There is no evidence that it was a malevolent infliction of pain or an attempt to terrorize his daughter, nor did the trial court conclude to the contrary.

Nevertheless, this is not to say that appellant's actions, regardless of innocent intent, cannot amount to "abuse" within the contemplation of the Act. But clearly intent is an important element in the equation. If it had been demonstrated that appellant conducted a sadistic reign of terror upon his daughter strapping her on a frequent basis, we would be inclined to affirm the trial court's disposition. After all, good intentions, regardless of how well founded they are, cannot be an excuse for the frequent infliction of physical or mental pain and/or the terrorizing one's children. In the present case, however, such a factual foundation is absent. What remains is the infliction of a painful, yet otherwise relatively harmless, "good, old fashioned whooping" of appellant's daughter. Thus, the question as we see it is whether or not appellant's conduct constitutes abuse within the meaning of the Act.[3]

"Abuse," as defined in the Act encompasses, in relevant part, attempting to cause or intentional, knowingly or recklessly causing bodily injury or serious bodily injury. *23 Pa.C.S.A. § 6107(a)*. At *18 Pa.C.S.A. § 2301* "bodily injury" is defined as "impairment of physical condition or substantial pain." In the present case, although the strapping of Cassandra, according to her testimony, "was painful and made her cry," there is no indication that it resulted in anything more than a temporary painful condition, which, of course, was its intent. Nor was there any indication that the punishment resulted in any degree of bodily impairment. In fact, Cassandra told Cindy Leik, who works for CYS, that the strapping did not leave any bruises. Consequently, we do not think the conduct in question amounts to "abuse" for purposes of the Act.

We believe the above conclusion is bolstered by *18 Pa.C.S.A. § 509* which, although sounding as a justification defense in the criminal law arena, has been characterized as codifying a parental "privilege" to administer

3. The trial court relies upon *23 Pa. C.S.A. § 6102(a)(1)* in granting the PFA order. This subsection focuses upon causing or intending to cause "bodily injury." The court also interjects commentary regarding appellant's pulling a gun out in front of his daughter, yet did not appear to rely upon subsection (a)(2) in entering its order. *23 Pa.C.S.A. § 6102(a)(2)* targets a person's placing of another in "reasonable fear of imminent serious bodily injury." Although the trial court does not specifically raise this issue we would be disinclined to find that this subsection was met by appellant's actions in retrieving the gun and relocating it upstairs. The action was unaccompanied by any verbal threat and the circumstances certainly do not suggest that appellant was "threatening to shoot his daughter" if she continued to disobey him or was a threat to do so.

corporal punishment. This section allows the use of force upon another under certain circumstances. For our purposes subsection (1) is relevant and provides for the use of force if the actor is a parent and the force is used for the purpose of safeguarding or promoting the welfare of a minor, including the preventing or punishment of his misconduct, where the force is "not designed to cause or known to create a substantial risk of causing death, serious bodily injury, disfigurement, extreme pain, or mental distress or gross degradation." Cases interpreting this provision have stated that parents may use corporal punishment to discipline their children "so long as the force used is not designed or known to create a substantial risk of death, serious bodily injury, disfigurement, extreme pain, or mental distress or gross degradation." *Appeal of E.S., 82 Pa. Commw. 168, 474 A.2d 432 (Pa. Cmwlth. 1984).* Other cases have referred to the parental "privilege" to administer corporal punishment. *See Commonwealth v. Ogin, 373 Pa. Super. 116, 540 A.2d 549 (Pa. Super. 1988).* If the activity found in the present case were viewed as violating the Protection From Abuse Act then a parent could exercise his or her "privilege" only to suffer the rather inconsistently seeming consequence of losing custody of the child or being banished from his or her home. This seems grossly illogical.

For the above reason we reverse the order appealed from.[5]

. . .

Dissent

■ Dissenting Opinion by Orie Melvin.

An accurate review of the record reveals that appellant beat his daughter with a belt severely enough to cause bruising and handled her so that imprints from his fingers remained on her body. On the same day he administered this form of "discipline" and while discussing with Cassandra the house rules, appellant felt the need to remove his gun while in his daughter's presence. Based on these circumstances and the fact that appellant admitted he would administer the same form of punishment again if he deems it is warranted, the trial court granted Cassandra's protection from abuse petition. I believe the evidence warranted the protection from abuse order. Furthermore, because the Majority disregards the trial court's factual findings and credibility determinations and instead, picks and chooses testimony which would support its holding, I dissent . . .

The Majority opines that because there is no indication that Cassandra's punishment resulted in anything more than a temporary painful condition, she is not warranted protection from further beating. Nothing in the statute requires that the pain must be of a continuing nature. The pain must be only be "substantial" in nature. *18 Pa.C.S.A. § 2301.* I believe the Majority should not make light of such pain. I would submit that thrashing a young lady with a belt hard enough to produce bruising and handling her in such a manner as to leave the imprint of a hand on her body would produce a "substantial" amount of pain. The Majority also makes light of appellant's action of retrieving his gun while in his daughter's presence. The trial court was

5. One certainly gets the impression that, in the present case, the PFA law has been injected where it does not belong. Although the issue presented might be an appropriate matter for custody court, there is no indication that the PFA law was meant to be utilized to question a parent's personal choice of discipline except for in the rarest of circumstances where a child's welfare is truly jeopardized by the conduct in question. We are unwilling to essentially label appellant an "abuser" of his child merely because his viewpoints on parenting might be viewed as "old fashioned" and out of favor with today's parenting "experts." If allowed to stand one must wonder where we will head next, will any parent who spanks his child be ripe for having a PFA slapped upon him/her?

disturbed by the appellant's action and found the appearance that appellant created by pulling out his gun was inappropriate. I believe that when this action is viewed in light of the surrounding circumstances, including the fact that appellant had just recently beat her and at that time was discussing his rules with Cassandra, the trial court's concern cannot be dismissed so easily.

I agree that the Protection from Abuse Act was not designed to prevent a parent from using corporal punishment. However, the Act provides a remedy in situations where bodily injury is inflicted intentionally, knowingly, or recklessly on a family or household member ... In this case the punishment Cassandra received, which left lasting imprints on her body goes beyond mere corporal discipline and rises to the level of abuse within the meaning of the Protection from Abuse Act. While I recognize in this Commonwealth parents have a right to inflict corporal punishment on their children, their right to do so is restricted ...

c. RELIGIOUS PRACTICE

Walker v. Superior Court

Supreme Court of California, 1988.
47 Cal.3d 112, 253 Cal.Rptr. 1, 763 P.2d 852.

■ MOSK, JUSTICE.

. . .

Defendant Laurie Grouard Walker is a member of the Church of Christ, Scientist (hereafter the Church). Her four-year-old daughter, Shauntay, fell ill with flu-like symptoms on February 21, 1984, and four days later developed a stiff neck. Consistent with the tenets of her religion, defendant chose to treat the child's illness with prayer rather than medical care. Defendant contacted an accredited Christian Science prayer practitioner who thereafter prayed for Shauntay and visited the child on two occasions. Defendant also engaged a Christian Science nurse who attended Shauntay on February 27 and again on March 6 and 8. Shauntay nevertheless lost weight, grew disoriented and irritable during the last week of her illness, and died on March 9 of acute purulent meningitis after a period of heavy and irregular breathing. During the 17 days she lay ill, the child received no medical treatment.

The People charged defendant with involuntary manslaughter and felony child endangerment based on allegations that her criminal negligence proximately caused Shauntay's death. Defendant moved to dismiss the prosecution on the grounds that her conduct was specifically protected by law....

. . .

I. *Statutory Contentions*

A. *Section 270 as a complete defense to prosecution*

Defendant first contends that the provisions of Penal Code section 270 (hereafter section 270) provide a complete defense to any prosecution based on her treatment of Shauntay's illness with prayer rather than medical care. Section 270 enumerates certain necessities that parents must furnish their children and imposes misdemeanor liability for the failure to do so. As enacted in 1872, the statute provided that "Every parent of any child who willfully omits, without lawful excuse, to perform any duty imposed upon him by law, to furnish necessary food, clothing, shelter, or medical attendance for such child, is guilty of a misdemeanor." The Legislature amended the provision in 1925 by inserting the phrase "or other remedial care" after "medical attendance." The statute was again amended in 1976 to specify that "treatment by spiritual means through prayer alone" constitutes "other remedial care."

. . .

Defendant . . . asserts that the plain language of section 270 requires the extension of its religious exemption to her prosecution. She focuses on the reference in the statute to the provision of "*necessary* clothing, food, shelter or medical attendance, or other remedial care. . . ." (Italics added.) Observing that "necessary" is defined, inter alia, as "absolutely required: essential, indispensable" (Webster's New Internat. Dict. (3d ed. 1961) p. 1511), she contends that there can be no circumstance involving the illness of a child in which the use of prayer in lieu of medicine is unlawful.

It is true that the statute recognizes "other remedial care" as an acceptable substitute for "medical attendance" when care is "necessary"; however, this conclusion does not address the question whether compliance with the terms of section 270 absolves defendant of liability under all other provisions of the Penal Code. . . . We turn to the purpose of section 270.

"Rather than punishment of the neglectful parents, the principal statutory objectives [of section 270] are to secure support of the child and to protect the public from the burden of supporting a child who has a parent able to support him." (People v. Sorensen (1968) 68 Cal.2d 280, 287, 66 Cal.Rptr. 7, 437 P.2d 495.) . . .

. . .

Defendant . . . contends that the 1976 amendment identifying prayer treatment as a form of "other remedial care" was . . . intended to shield Christian Scientists from manslaughter prosecutions. . . .

The historical materials documenting the enactment of Assembly Bill No. 3843 demonstrate that the members of the Legislature were well aware the legislation left open the possibility of manslaughter and child endangerment prosecutions, but simply declined to extend their amendatory efforts beyond section 270. . . .

. . .

The Senate Committee on Judiciary received a four-page analysis of the legislation. Under the heading "Comment" and entirely capitalized, unlike any other portion of the document, were the following questions: "Do the provisions of this bill conflict with section 273a of the Penal Code which makes it a crime for any person to willfully cause or permit a minor under his care or custody to suffer any physical harm or injury? [¶] Might a parent be immune from liability for failure to provide for the health of the child because they [sic] choose treatment by prayer rather than common medical treatment, but incur liability if the child suffers any harm?" (Sen. Com. on Judiciary, Analysis of Assem. Bill No. 3843, supra, capitalization omitted.) As in the Assembly, the Senate committee members chose to disregard the issues raised so prominently in their staff analysis and passed the measure to the full Senate without addressing manslaughter and child endangerment liability. No other reference to sections 192(b) and 273a(1) appears in the historical materials documenting the enactment of Assembly Bill No. 3843.

The ineluctable conclusion we must draw from these materials is that the members of the Legislature were fully conscious of the potential liability remaining under sections 192(b) and 273a(1) for conduct they had legalized with respect to section 270, but simply chose to leave the matter unaddressed. Needless to say, considered silence is an insufficient basis to infer that the Legislature, by amending a misdemeanor, support provision, actually exempted from felony liability all parents who offer prayer alone to a dying child....

B. *Expressions of legislative intent in related statutes*

Defendant next contends that an intent to exempt prayer treatment from conduct within the reach of sections 192(b) and 273a(1) is implied by a number of other civil and criminal measures relating to the provision of prayer in lieu of medical care to children. She first cites a plethora of statutes exempting prayer practitioners and their facilities from medical licensure requirements or variously accommodating individuals who choose to rely on such treatment for their own care. These accommodative provisions, however, evince no legislative sanction of prayer for the treatment of children in life-threatening circumstances.

More useful are statutes dealing with the definition of neglected or abused children for purposes of the state's child welfare services program, the activities of the Office of Child Abuse Prevention, and a criminal provision requiring certain individuals to report instances of suspected child abuse. Utilizing substantially similar language, each of these three statutes provides that children receiving treatment by prayer shall not "for that reason alone" be considered abused or neglected for its purposes. Defendant cites these provisions as evidence that the Legislature does not consider prayer treatment to be a threat to the health of children, and thus that the imposition of criminal liability for the results of its use is inconsistent with legislative intent.

The Attorney General urges a different construction of the statutory language. He contends that the phrase "for that reason *alone*" (italics added) denotes that a child receiving prayer treatment can still fall within the reach of the statutory definitions if the provision of such treatment, coupled with a grave medical condition, combine to pose a serious threat to the physical well-being of the child....

While dependency proceedings are civil rather than criminal, their relevance to our inquiry is plain. Parents possess a profound interest in the custody of their children. The Legislature's willingness to intrude on a parental interest of such magnitude to assure that children receiving prayer treatment are spared serious physical harm certainly evinces no contrary intent with respect to the application of the penal laws, which in significant respects constitute a less intrusive method of advancing the state's paramount interest in the protection of its children.

Defendant's argument by analogy to civil neglect and dependency provisions therefore corroborates rather than refutes our previous determination that the Legislature has created no exemption under sections 192(b) and 273a(1) for parents who are charged with having killed or endangered the lives of their seriously ill children by providing prayer alone in lieu of medical care. The legislative design appears consistent: prayer treatment will be accommodated as an acceptable means of attending to the needs of a child only insofar as serious physical harm or illness is not at risk. When a child's life is placed in danger, we discern no intent to shield parents from the chastening prospect of felony liability.

. . .

II. *Constitutional Defenses*

A. *Free exercise under the First Amendment*

In the absence of a statutory basis to bar defendant's prosecution, we necessarily reach her constitutional claims. Defendant and the Church first contend that her conduct is absolutely protected from criminal liability by the First Amendment to the United States Constitution and article I, section 4, of the California Constitution. We do not agree.

The First Amendment bars government from "prohibiting the free exercise" of religion. Although the clause absolutely protects religious belief, religiously motivated conduct "remains subject to regulation for the protection of society." (Cantwell v. Connecticut (1940) 310 U.S. 296, 303–304.) To determine whether governmental regulation of religious conduct is violative of the First Amendment, the gravity of the state's interest must be balanced against the severity of the religious imposition. If the regulation is justified in view of the balanced interests at stake, the free exercise clause requires that the policy additionally represent the least restrictive alternative available to adequately advance the state's objectives.

Defendant does not dispute the gravity of the governmental interest involved in this case, as well she should not. Imposition of felony liability for endangering or killing an ill child by failing to provide medical care furthers an interest of unparalleled significance: the protection of the very lives of California's children, upon whose "healthy, well-rounded growth . . . into full maturity as citizens" our "democratic society rests, for its continuance. . . ." (Prince v. Massachusetts (1944) 321 U.S. 158, 168.) Balanced against this interest is a religious infringement of significant dimensions. Defendant unquestionably relied on prayer treatment as an article of genuine faith, the restriction of which would seriously impinge on the practice of her religion. We note, however, that resort to medicine does not constitute "sin" for a Christian Scientist, does not subject a church member to stigmatization, does not result in divine retribution, and, according to the Church's amicus curiae brief, is not a matter of church compulsion.

Regardless of the severity of the religious imposition, the governmental interest is plainly adequate to justify its restrictive effect. As the United States Supreme Court stated in Prince v. Massachusetts, 321 U.S. at page 170, "Parents may be free to become martyrs themselves. But it does not follow they are free, in identical circumstances, to make martyrs of their children before they have reached the age of full legal discretion when they can make that choice for themselves." If parents are not at liberty to "martyr" children by taking their labor, it follows a fortiori that they are not at liberty to martyr children by taking their very lives. As the court explained, "The right to practice religion freely does not include liberty to expose the community or child to communicable disease or the latter to ill health or death."

In an attempt to avoid this inexorable conclusion, the Church argues at length over the purportedly pivotal distinction between the governmental compulsion of a religiously objectionable act and the governmental prohibition of a religiously motivated act. Accepting arguendo the force of the distinction, we find that it has no relevance in a case involving an interest of this magnitude. As the court in *Prince* recognized, parents have *no* right to free exercise of religion at the price of a child's life, regardless of the prohibitive or compulsive nature of the governmental infringement. Furthermore, the United States Supreme Court has specifically sustained the compulsion of religiously prohibited conduct for interests no more compelling than here implicated. In Jacobson v. Massachusetts (1905) 197 U.S. 11, 99, the court upheld a law compelling the vaccination of children for communicable diseases in the face of parental religious objections. In United States v. Lee (1982) 455 U.S. 252, 261, the court upheld a law requiring that the Amish violate the tenets of their faith by participating in the Social Security system. And in Gillette v. United States (1971) 401 U.S. 437, 462, the court upheld the government's right to compel certain conscientious objectors to make war despite the religious character of their objections. We see no basis in these precedents for the conclusion that parents may constitutionally insulate themselves from state compulsion so long as their life-threatening religious conduct takes the form of an omission rather than an act.

The imposition of felony liability for failure to seek medical care for a seriously ill child is thus justified by a compelling state interest. To survive a First Amendment challenge, however, the policy must also represent the least restrictive alternative available to the state. Defendant and the Church argue that civil dependency proceedings advance the governmental interest in a far less intrusive manner. This is not evident. First, we have already observed the profoundly intrusive nature of such proceedings; it is not clear that parents would prefer to lose custody of their children pursuant to a disruptive and invasive judicial inquiry than to face privately the prospect of criminal liability. Second, child dependency proceedings advance the governmental interest only when the state learns of a child's illness in time to take protective measures, which quite likely will be the exception rather than the rule: "Under ordinary circumstances, . . . the case of a true believer in faith healing will not even come to the attention of the authorities, unless and until someone dies." (Comment, Religious Beliefs and the Criminal Justice System: Some Problems of the Faith Healer, supra, 8 Loyola L.A.L.Rev. at pp. 403–404.) Finally, the imposition of criminal liability is reserved for the actual loss or endangerment of a child's life and thus is narrowly tailored to those instances when governmental intrusion is absolutely compelled.

We conclude that an adequately effective and less restrictive alternative is not available to further the state's compelling interest in assuring the provision of medical care to gravely ill children whose parents refuse such treatment on religious grounds. Accordingly, the First Amendment and its California equivalent do not bar defendant's criminal prosecution.

. . .

III. *Disposition*

We conclude that the prosecution of defendant for involuntary manslaughter and felony child endangerment violates neither statutory law nor the California or federal Constitution. The judgment of the Court of Appeal is affirmed.

. . .

NOTE

Courts are divided over convicting Christian Scientist parents who have withheld conventional medical treatment from their critically ill children. In Commonwealth v.

Twitchell, 416 Mass. 114, 617 N.E.2d 609 (1993), the Supreme Judicial Court of Massachusetts set aside defendants' conviction for involuntary manslaughter of their child after they relied on spiritual treatment for a bowel condition. On appeal the parents asserted that they had been denied due process when the state refused to allow their affirmative defense of entrapment by estoppel caused by their reliance on the Attorney General's opinion as to whether the spiritual treatment statute would protect them from involuntary manslaughter prosecution. The court held that the record below showed that the defendants were dedicated to helping their son while at the same time seeking to adhere to their religion within the limits of what they were advised the law permitted. Because the issue should have been tried before the jury, the judgment was reversed and a new trial ordered.

In the Matter of Christine M., 157 Misc.2d 4, 595 N.Y.S.2d 606 (Fam.Ct.1992) the court found a child to be neglected when her father, contrary to the public health law mandating vaccination of children, knowingly refused to have her vaccinated against measles in the midst of a measles outbreak. The court held that in order to be afforded an exemption from immunization on spiritual grounds a parent must not only demonstrate a religious belief opposed to inoculation, but must also demonstrate that the belief is sincere and genuine and that it forms the basis for the objection to the vaccination. The court found that in this case the father's objections to the vaccination were rooted in medical and scientific concerns rather than spiritual ones and therefore the exemption did not apply.

The case was never retried. Conversation with Steven Umin, attorney for defendants, October 25, 2005.

Hermanson v. State

Supreme Court of Florida, 1992.
604 So.2d 775.

■ OVERTON, J.

. . .

In this tragic case, Amy Hermanson, the daughter of William and Christine Hermanson, died from untreated juvenile diabetes. The Hermansons, members of the First Church of Christ, Scientist, were charged and convicted of child abuse resulting in third-degree murder for failing to provide Amy with conventional medical treatment. . . .

Statutory History

The statutory provisions are critical to the legal and constitutional issues presented in this case. Florida's child abuse statute, section *827.04(1)–(2), Florida Statutes* (1985), provides:

> (1) Whoever, willfully or by culpable negligence, deprives a child of, or allows a child to be deprived of, necessary food, clothing, shelter, or medical treatment, or who, knowingly or by culpable negligence, permits physical or mental injury to the child, and in so doing causes great bodily harm, permanent disability, or permanent disfigurement to such child, shall be guilty of a felony of the third degree. . . .
>
> (2) Whoever, willfully or by culpable negligence, deprives a child of, or allows a child to be deprived of, necessary food, clothing, shelter, or medical treatment, or who, knowingly or by culpable negligence, permits physical or mental injury to the child, shall be guilty of a misdemeanor of the first degree. . . .

The third-degree murder provision of section *782.04(4), Florida Statutes* (1985), provides that the killing of a human being while engaged in the commission of child abuse constitutes murder in the third degree and is a felony of the second degree. Section 415.503 provides, in part, as follows:

> (1) "Abused or neglected child" means a child whose physical or mental health or welfare is harmed, or threatened with harm, by the acts or omissions of the parent or other person responsible for the child's welfare.
>
> . . .
>
> (7) "Harm" to a child's health or welfare can occur when the parent or other person responsible for the child's welfare:
>
> . . .
>
> (f) Fails to supply the child with adequate food, clothing, shelter, or health care, although financially able to do so or although offered financial or other means to do so; however, a parent or other person responsible for the child's welfare legitimately practicing his religious beliefs, who by reason thereof does not provide specified medical treatment for a child, may not be considered abusive or neglectful for that reason alone, but such an exception does not:
>
> 1. Eliminate the requirement that such a case be reported to the department;
>
> 2. Prevent the department from investigating such a case; or
>
> 3. Preclude a court from ordering, when the health of the child requires it, the provision of medical services by a physician, as defined herein, or treatment by a duly accredited practitioner who relies solely on spiritual means for healing in accordance with the tenets and practices of a well-recognized church or religious organization.
>
> . . .

The religious accommodation provision in section 415.503(7)(f) was initially passed by the legislature in 1975 as section 827.07(2), Florida Statutes (1975), the same chapter that contained the child abuse provision under which the Hermansons were prosecuted. The senate staff analysis of the religious accommodation provision stated that these provisions were "a defense for parents who decline medical treatment for legitimate religious reasons." In 1983, the Division of Statutory Revision moved the above religious accommodation provision from chapter 827 to chapter 415.

Facts

The facts of this case, as stipulated to by the parties in the trial court, are as follows:

> 1. The Defendant, Willie F. Hermanson, is 39 years of age. Mr. Hermanson is married to the Defendant, Christine Hermanson, who is 36 years of age.... Mr. Hermanson is a bank vice President, and Mrs. Hermanson is the director of the Sarasota Fine Arts Academy. Mr. and Mrs. Hermanson have graduate degrees from Grand Valley State College and the University of Michigan, respectively. Neither Mr. nor Mrs. Hermanson has ever been arrested for, or convicted of, a crime.
>
> 2. Mr. and Mrs. Hermanson were married on May 30, 1970. There have been two children born of this marriage: Eric Thomas Hermanson, date of birth 8/26/77 and Amy Kathleen Hermanson (deceased) date of birth 7/16/79.

Facts

3. According to the autopsy report of the Medical Examiner, James C. Wilson, M.D., on September 30, 1986, at approximately 1:55 p.m., Amy Hermanson died. Dr. Wilson found the cause of death to be diabetic ketoacidosis due to juvenile onset diabetes mellitus. Additional autopsy findings of dehydration and weight loss were consistent with the disease process. Dr. Wilson believes that the disease could have been diagnosed by a physician prior to death and, within the bounds of medical probability, Amy's death could have been prevented even up to several hours before her death with proper medical treatment.

4. At the time of Amy's death, the Hermanson family, including William, Christine, Eric and Amy, were regular attenders of the First Church of Christ, Scientist in Sarasota.

5. Christian Scientists believe in healing by spiritual means in accordance with the tenets and practices of the Christian Science Church. William and Christine Hermanson, at all times material to the facts in this case, followed the religious teachings of their church and relied upon Christian Science healing in the care and treatment of Amy Hermanson.

6. On or about September 22, 1986, the Hermansons became aware that something was particularly wrong with Amy Hermanson which they believed to be of an emotional nature. They contacted Thomas Keller, a duly-accredited practitioner of the First Church of Christ, Scientist for consultation and treatment in accordance with the religious tenets and beliefs of the Christian Science Religion. Thomas Keller treated Amy from September 22, 1986 until September 30, 1986.

. . .

8. [Upon returning from a trip to Indianapolis on September 29, 1986,] the Hermansons noticed a worsening of Amy's condition. They decided to seek the assistance of a local Christian Science practitioner . . . on September 29, 1986, the Hermansons contacted one Frederick Hillier, a duly-accredited Christian Science practitioner of the First Church of Christ, Scientist whom they secured as a practitioner for Amy. Thereafter, until Amy's death, Hillier provided treatment for Amy relying solely on spiritual means for healing in accordance with the tenets and practices of the First Church of Christ, Scientist.

9. On Monday, September 29, 1986, William Hermanson had a discussion with Jack Morton, the father of Christine Hermanson, wherein Mr. Morton expressed his concern for the health of Amy and suggested the possibility that Amy had diabetes.

10. . . . [O]n September 30, 1986, Hillier went to the Hermanson home to continue treatment and, due to the fact the Hermansons had been up all night with Amy, suggested that a Christian Science nurse be called to help care for Amy.

11. . . . [O]n Tuesday, September 30, 1986, one Molly Jane Sellers was called to the Hermanson residence to assist in the care of Amy Hermanson. Molly Jane Sellers is recognized as a Christian Science nurse by the First Church of Christ, Scientist and has been so recognized for twenty years.

12. On September 30, 1986 at approximately 11 a.m., William Hermanson was contacted by a counselor from the Department of Health and Rehabilitative Services (Willy Torres) who informed him that they

had received a complaint alleging child abuse of his daughter, Amy Hermanson and that a hearing pursuant to said allegation had been set before the Juvenile Court for 1:30 p.m. Torres further informed Mr. Hermanson that the purpose of the hearing was to determine if medical treatment would be court ordered or if treatment as prescribed by the Christian Science practitioner would be ordered at that time.

13. At approximately 12:30 p.m., Mr. Hermanson left his home and traveled to the Sarasota County Courthouse for the hearing pursuant to the notification from Willy Torres. While at the hearing, at approximately 1:27 p.m., Mr. Hermanson received a telephone call from an individual at the Hermanson home who reported that Amy had "taken a turn for the worse and an ambulance had been called." Such information was related to the Court and an order was entered which required that Amy Hermanson be examined by a licensed medical doctor. When paramedics arrived they found that Amy had died.

The district court summarized the facts presented at trial as follows:

In the month or so before her death Amy was having a marked and dramatic weight loss, that she was almost skeletal in her thinness and this was a big change in her appearance. There were great dark circles under her eyes that had never been there before. Her behavior was very different from the usual; she was lethargic and complaining whereas previously she had been bubbly, vivacious, and outgoing. She was seen lying down on the floor to sleep during the day when accompanying her mother to visit music students and lying down on the floor after school at her mother's fine arts academy. She often complained of not feeling well, that her stomach hurt and that she wasn't sleeping well. She was too tired during the day to participate in gym class at school. There was a bluish tint to her skin. Her breath smelled funny, one observer called it a "fruity" odor.

The pathologist who performed the autopsy testified to Amy's skeletal appearance, that her vertebrae and shoulder blades were prominent and her abdomen distended as if she were undernourished. Her eyes were quite sunken, due to the dehydration, although her parents had told the pathologist that on the day before her death she was drinking a lot of fluids but urinating frequently too. They also told him that they had noticed changes in Amy starting about a month previously. Amy had complained of constipation during the last week of her life but at no time seemed feverish although there was intermittent vomiting. The pathologist opined that the illness was chronic, not acute. According to her parents' talk with the pathologist, Amy seemed incoherent on the evening before her death although the next morning she seemed better. The pathologist also testified that vomiting and dehydration are compatible with flu-like symptoms but these, added to a four-week-long history of weight loss with the more severe conditions reported, would not be indicative of flu.

The evidence and the stipulated facts established that the Hermansons treated Amy in accordance with their Christian Science beliefs. On the day of Amy's death, a Christian Science nurse had been summoned to the home to care for her. The nurse testified that Amy was unresponsive and that, when she began vomiting and her condition worsened, she recommended that an ambulance should be called. The Christian Science practitioner who was present advised the nurse that the church headquarters in Boston should be contacted before an ambulance was called. After placing a call to Boston, an ambulance was summoned.

In its argument to the jury, the State asserted that the Hermansons reliance on Christian Science healing practices under these circumstances constituted culpable negligence. The basis of its argument was that the Hermansons were not legitimately practicing their religious beliefs. Drawing on the evidence that the Christian Science nurse had called an ambulance when Amy began vomiting, the State suggested that the Christian Science Church recognizes conventional medical care and, therefore, the Hermansons had not been legitimately practicing their religious beliefs when they failed to seek medical care before Amy's death. No specific evidence was introduced by either side on the question of when, if at all, the Christian Science faith allows its members to call for medical attention. The Hermansons, on the other hand, argued to the jury that they should not be convicted of a criminal offense because they were "legitimately" practicing their faith in accordance with the accommodation provision of section 415.503(7)(f).

The jury, after one and one-half hours of deliberation, sought the answer to three questions: "(1) As a Christian Scientist do they have a choice to go to a medical doctor if they want to? (2) Or if not, can they call a doctor at a certain point? (3) Do they need permission first?" In response, the court advised the jurors that they must look to the evidence presented during the trial to find the answers. Counsel for both parties had previously agreed to this response by the trial court. The jury found the Hermansons guilty of felony child abuse and third-degree murder, and they were sentenced to four-year suspended prison sentences, with fifteen years' probation, on condition that they provide regular medical examinations and treatment for their surviving children.

On appeal, the district court affirmed, finding that the statutory accommodation section in 415.503(7)(f) applied only to matters contained in chapter 415 and that that provision did not provide any protection from criminal penalties for actual child abuse or neglect in chapters 782 and 827, Florida Statutes (1985). The district court rejected the Hermansons' claim that the evidence did not establish that they had acted willfully or with culpable negligence under the circumstances of this case. The district court agreed with the trial court that, when they returned from Indiana thirty-six hours before My's death and had seen that her condition had worsened, the Hermansons were placed on notice "that their attempts at spiritual treatment were unavailing and [that] it was time to call in medical help." The district court concluded that those facts justified the issue's being submitted to the jury and the verdict finding the Hermansons guilty of culpable negligence. The district court also rejected the Hermansons' claim of a due process violation for lack of notice of when their conduct became criminal. In rejecting this contention, the district court relied on the decision of the California Supreme Court in *Walker v. Superior Court, 763 P.2d 852, 872 (Cal. 1988),* cert. denied, *491 U.S. 905,* in which that court stated:

> "The law is full of instances where a man's fate depends on his estimating rightly, that is, as the jury subsequently estimates it, some matter of degree ... An act causing death may be murder, manslaughter, or misadventure according to the degree of danger attending it by common experience in the circumstances known to the actor." The "matter of degree" that persons relying on prayer treatment must estimate rightly is the point at which their course of conduct becomes criminally negligent. In terms of notice, due process requires no more.

In this appeal, the Hermansons challenge the district court decision on the following four issues: (1) that the Florida Statutes under which they were convicted did not give them fair warning of the consequences of practicing their religious belief and their conviction was, therefore, a denial of due process; (2) that the Hermansons were entitled to a judgment of acquittal because the evidence presented at trial failed to establish culpable negligence beyond a reasonable doubt; (3) that permitting a jury to decide the reasonableness of the Hermansons in following their religious beliefs was a violation of the First Amendment freedom of religion; and (4) that the trial court erred in not granting a mistrial when the prosecutor stated in closing argument that Christian Science recognizes conventional medical treatment, which was not supported by any evidence in the record. We choose to discuss only the first issue because we find that it is dispositive.

Due Process

In asserting that they were denied due process, the Hermansons claim that the statutes failed to give them sufficient notice of when their treatment of their child in accordance with their religious beliefs became criminal. They argue that their position is supported by (1) the fact that it took the district court of appeal nine pages to explain how it arrived at its conclusion that the exemption for spiritual treatment was only part of the civil child abuse statute, not the criminal child abuse statute and (2) the trial court's construing the statute differently, holding that they were protected by the provision of section 415.503(7)(f) to the extent of making it a jury issue.

. . .

The state would have us conclude that the choice of spiritual treatment, which has been put on legal footing equal to that of orthodox medical care by the child neglect statute, can result in a manslaughter indictment, simply because of its outcome. That is unacceptably arbitrary, and a violation of due process.

. . .

In addressing the lack of notice claim, the State relies on the previously quoted statements in the Walker decision, particularly the conclusion that "persons relying on prayer treatment must estimate rightly" to avoid criminal prosecution because "due process requires no more." *Walker, 763 P.2d at 871–72.*

. . .

We disagree with the view of the Supreme Court of California in Walker that, in considering the application of this type of religious accommodation statute, persons relying on the statute and its allowance for prayer as treatment are granted only the opportunity to guess rightly with regard to their utilization of spiritual treatment. In commencing on this type of situation, one author has stated: "By authorizing conduct in one statute, but declaring that same conduct criminal under another statute, the State trapped the Hermansons, who had no fair warning that the State would consider their conduct criminal." We agree.

To say that the statutes in question establish a line of demarcation at which a person of common intelligence would know his or her conduct is or is not criminal ignores the fact that, not only did the judges of both the circuit court and the district court of appeal have difficulty understanding the interrelationship of the statutes in question, but, as indicated by their questions, the jurors also had problems understanding what was required.

In this instance, we conclude that the legislature has failed to clearly indicate the point at which a parent's reliance on his or her religious beliefs in the treatment of his or her children becomes criminal conduct. If the legislature desires to provide for religious accommodation while protecting the children of the state, the legislature must clearly indicate when a parent's conduct becomes criminal. As stated by another commentator: "Whatever choices are made . . . both the policy and the letter of the law should be clear and clearly stated, so that these who believe in healing by prayer rather than medical treatment are aware of the potential liabilities they may incur."

Accordingly, for the reasons expressed, we quash the decision of the district court of appeal and remand this case with directions that the trial court's adjudication of guilt and sentence be vacated and the petitioners discharged.

It is so ordered.

d. POTENTIAL ABUSE

Doe v. O'Brien

U.S. Court of Appeals for the Eleventh Circuit, 2003.
329 F.3d 1286.

■ BLACK, J.

Brief

Appellants John Doe and Jane Doe, individually and on behalf of their three minor children, D.M., N.O., and B.O, appeal the district court's dismissal of their action against Appellee Deborah O'Brien. Their claims arise out of an incident in which O'Brien, an authorized agent of the Florida Department of Children and Family Services (DCF), effected an "emergency" removal of Appellants' children without Appellants' permission and without a court order. Appellants brought this action seeking a declaration that Fla. Stat. § 39.401(1), which purportedly authorized the removal of the children, is unconstitutional both facially and as applied to them....

Facts

On January 18, 2000, DCF officials in St. Augustine, Florida, were informed that T.O., John Doe's nine-year-old niece, had recently reported being abused by John Doe approximately four years earlier, when T.O. was five. T.O., who is deaf, reportedly accused John Doe of making her touch his penis and perform oral sex. DCF officials in St. Augustine investigated the report and discovered that John Doe was residing in Hillsborough County, Florida, with his wife, Jane Doe, and their three minor children, D.M. (age 13), N.O. (age 9), and B.O. (age 6). On January 21, 2000, the St. Augustine office forwarded the report to DCF's Hillsborough County office, where the case was assigned to O'Brien at approximately 12:30 P.M.

Soon after receiving the report, O'Brien commenced an investigation and discovered that John Doe had previously been investigated by DCF in 1995. In the 1995 case, John Doe had been accused of placing his penis in the rectum of a three-year old boy whom Jane Doe was baby-sitting. According to O'Brien, DCF believed the allegation to be true but had not pressed charges due to lack of cooperation from the victim.

O'Brien also discovered during her investigation that John Doe had a criminal record involving crimes of a sexual nature. According to a report she received from the Florida Department of Law Enforcement (FDLE),

John Doe was convicted in 1989 of two counts of lewd and lascivious behavior stemming from an incident in which he exposed and fondled himself in front of children at a school bus stop. The report also indicated that John Doe had previously been charged with solicitation of prostitution and had been accused of, but not charged with, rape.

At approximately 2:10 P.M., O'Brien met with her supervisor, Wanda Rios. Rios recommended sheltering all three of Appellants' children, but advised O'Brien to first contact DCF's legal department. Following Rios' recommendation, O'Brien consulted with DCF legal counsel at approximately 2:45 P.M., and was advised to take the children into custody.

At approximately 3:30 P.M., O'Brien proceeded to D.M.'s school. She interviewed the child and explained that she was going to talk to D.M.'s parents and siblings and "make sure everybody was okay." O'Brien then arranged for D.M. to be taken into custody.... O'Brien proceeded to Appellants' residence alone.... [A]fter explaining that she was there to investigate a report of child abuse, was invited inside by Appellants. O'Brien then proceeded to interview John Doe, Jane Doe, N.O, and B.O....

[A]fter she had interviewed each member of the Doe family, O'Brien concluded the children were in danger of abuse from John Doe. She also concluded that Jane Doe was incapable of protecting the children and that the children would need to be temporarily removed for their safety. The children were subsequently taken to their maternal grandparents' home, where they remained for the night. The following morning, a state judge concluded there was a lack of probable cause to keep the children apart from their parents, and ordered that all three children be immediately returned to Appellants. Appellants subsequently commenced this action.

Section 39.401(1) governs the state's emergency removal of children who are believed to be in danger of child abuse. It provides in pertinent part:

> (1) A child may only be taken into custody:
>
> . . .
>
> (b) By a law enforcement officer, or an authorized agent of the [DCF], if the officer or authorized agent has probable cause to support a finding:
>
> 1. That the child has been abused, neglected, or abandoned, or is suffering from or is in imminent danger of illness or injury as a result of abuse, neglect, or abandonment[.]

Fla. Stat. § 39.401(1). [A hearing must be held no more than 24 hours after the removal. Fla. Stat. § 39.401(3).]

Consistent with § 39.401(1), DCF's policy is to remove a child from a parent or legal guardian without prior judicial authorization when there is probable cause to believe the child has been abused or is in imminent danger of abuse.

Appellants maintain that DCF routinely removes children believed to be in danger of abuse without first attempting to determine whether there is time to obtain a court order before effecting the removal without exacerbating the risk to the child. O'Brien acknowledges that she did not attempt to determine whether there was time to obtain a court order before she removed the Doe children from their parents....

Appellants maintain that § 39.401(1), both facially and as applied, violates their right to due process under the Fourteenth Amendment and their Fourth Amendment right to be free from unlawful search and seizure. . . .

. . .

Appellants' as-applied challenge . . . hinges on their argument that O'Brien's warrantless removal of their children was not actually supported by emergency circumstances and therefore violated due process. The issue boils down to how we define an emergency. Appellants assert an emergency must be defined by reference to the feasibility of obtaining a court order before effecting a removal. Stated differently, they argue that if there is time to obtain a court order without exacerbating the risk to the child, then there can never be an emergency and the state must obtain a court order no matter how emergent the child's circumstances otherwise appear. They would have us craft a rule that reads something like this: Due process requires that a state official obtain a court order prior to removing a suspected victim of child abuse from parental custody, unless: (1) the official has probable cause to believe the child is in imminent danger of abuse; and (2) the official reasonably determines that there is insufficient time to obtain judicial permission before temporarily removing the child.

We are not persuaded that due process demands such an inflexible rule. Aside from our concerns about imposing a new and onerous burden on child welfare agencies, many of which already operate under considerable strain, we do not believe that the single focus of a due process analysis ought to be on the court's schedule. Due process is a flexible concept, and "what procedures due process may require under any given set of circumstances must begin with a determination of the precise nature of the government function involved as well as of the private interest that has been affected by governmental action." In order to properly define the interests at stake and weigh their relative importance, courts should be allowed to consider all relevant circumstances, including the state's reasonableness in responding to a perceived danger as well as the objective nature, likelihood, and immediacy of danger to the child. Having considered all relevant factors, courts may then decide whether an objectively imminent danger justified the state's removal of a child without prior judicial authorization. . . .

Only the Second Circuit seems to have taken a position fully consistent with Appellants' argument. In Tenenbaum v. Williams, a two-to-one panel decision, the court held a social worker could not temporarily remove a child from her parents' custody without prior judicial authorization unless there was probable cause to believe the child was in imminent danger of abuse and the social worker reasonably determined there was insufficient time to obtain a court order before removing the child from danger. 193 F.3d at 596.

In Tenenbaum, an employee of the New York City Child Welfare Administration (CWA) removed five-year-old Sarah Tenenbaum from school several days after Sarah's teacher first reported noticing signs of abuse. CWA officials, without consulting legal counsel, took Sarah into custody for the express purpose of physically examining her to rule out the possibility of abuse. After an examination uncovered no signs of abuse and Sarah was returned home, her parents brought suit against the City and the individual CWA employees responsible for Sarah's removal. Their suit alleged a number of constitutional violations, including a violation of their procedural due process rights based on the removal of their daughter without prior court authorization. The district court granted summary judgment for the defendants on the procedural due process claim, finding Sarah's removal was justified by emergency circumstances.

On appeal, the Second Circuit held the district court erred in failing to specifically consider whether CWA workers had enough time obtain a court order before they removed Sarah. The court reasoned:

> If the danger to the child is not so imminent that there is reasonably sufficient time to seek prior judicial authorization, ex parte or otherwise, for the child's removal, then the circumstances are not emergent; there is no reason to excuse the absence of the judiciary's participation in depriving the parents of the care, custody and management of their child. If, irrespective of whether there is time to obtain a court order, all interventions are effected on an "emergency" basis without judicial process, pre-seizure procedural due process for the parents and their child evaporates.

Consequently, the court held that "it is unconstitutional for state officials to effect a child's removal on an 'emergency' basis where there is reasonable time safely to obtain judicial authorization consistent with the child's safety"....

The dissenting member of the panel in Tenenbaum argued that the unintended consequence of the majority's rule would be to force child welfare workers to always obtain a warrant, tipping the constitutional balance away from the state's paramount interest in protecting children. He explained:

> Every time a child welfare worker has reason to suspect child abuse, she will have to consider (i) whether there is reason to believe the child is in imminent danger (which until now has been all that was required) and (ii) whether there is time to get to court and obtain a court order (the majority's new requirement) as well as (iii) whether a court or jury will second-guess that decision on the basis that more efficient decision-making would have afforded sufficient time to obtain the court order. In terms of litigation, individual liability and damages, an error on the side of removal is risky, while an error on the other side is safe.

We agree that the sole focus should not be whether there is time to obtain a court order. The Second Circuit's holding in Tenenbaum, which seems "so measured and reasonable in the pages of a federal appellate opinion, will work serious harm in an exceptionally sensitive area of state responsibility." As we have previously alluded to, due process is a flexible concept—particularly where the well-being of children is concerned—and deciding what process is due in any given case requires a careful balancing of the interests at stake, including the interests of parents, children, and the state. Those interests may be implicated to varying degrees depending on the facts of an individual case, which will necessarily affect the degree of procedural due process required. This kind of subtle balancing cannot be properly accomplished when courts blunt the inquiry by simply asking whether there was time to get a warrant....

In light of the relevant circumstances in this case, we conclude there is no question but that there was an objectively imminent danger to the Doe children so as to justify O'Brien's temporary removal of the children without prior court authorization. O'Brien received two documented reports of severe sexual abuse involving John Doe, one of which involved a disabled family member and both of which involved extremely young children. She also received a report from the FDLE documenting John Doe's criminal past, including a conviction for lewd and lascivious behavior around children.

Furthermore, the record demonstrates that O'Brien responded reasonably and swiftly as soon as she became aware of the possible danger to the Doe children. This is not a case where a social worker manufactured an emergency in order to circumvent judicial participation. Here, O'Brien investigated diligently and acted almost immediately after the relevant facts came to her attention. At the same time, she did not rush to judgment or react impulsively. Rather, she consulted with both her supervisor and DCF legal counsel before taking steps toward removing the Doe children. Even then, O'Brien did not remove the children until after she interviewed both the parents and children and determined the children were unsafe. In short, while it is almost always possible to criticize an official's conduct in hindsight, we conclude O'Brien's actions in this case were nearly unassailable. We therefore hold O'Brien's warrantless removal of the children did not violate Appellants' right to due process.

2. Defining Child Neglect

a. STANDARD

People v. Carroll

Court of Appeals of New York, 1999.
93 N.Y.2d 564, 693 N.Y.S.2d 498, 715 N.E.2d 500.

■ KAYE, CHIEF JUDGE.

Over the course of several days, three-year-old Shanaya Jones was beaten to death by her father. Defendant, the child's stepmother, witnessed most of the violence, but did not alert the authorities or summon medical assistance until Shanaya was dead. The issue before us is whether the Grand Jury that indicted defendant for endangering the welfare of a child had sufficient evidence that defendant was "legally charged" with the care of Shanaya (Penal Law § 260.10[2]). We conclude that it did, because the evidence supported an inference that defendant was acting as the functional equivalent of Shanaya's parent at the relevant time.

According to evidence presented to the Grand Jury, Shanaya Jones on August 6, 1996 began an extended visit with her father and defendant, his wife. Defendant described herself, during Shanaya's visits, as the child's "mother," "stepmother" and "primary caretaker." Between August 14 and 16, Shanaya's father repeatedly punched the child, threw her into a wall and pushed her onto the floor, apparently because she would not eat. While defendant witnessed her husband inflict most of these beatings and was aware that the child had stopped eating, she did not seek medical attention until late in the evening of August 16, when Shanaya was brought by ambulance to a hospital emergency room. By the time the child arrived at the hospital, she had stopped breathing and had no pulse. After attempts to revive her were unsuccessful, she was pronounced dead.

An autopsy revealed that the cause of death was physical abuse sustained while at defendant's apartment. Shanaya's body was covered with bruises, lacerations, abrasions and hemorrhages. Several of her ribs were fractured and a lung was punctured. The Medical Examiner concluded that the injuries were days old, and that many of them would have been very painful, causing the child to scream and cry. The Examiner also determined that Shanaya was starved and dehydrated.

Defendant was charged with endangering the welfare of a child (Penal Law § 260.10[2]). Prior to trial, she moved to dismiss the indictment. Supreme Court granted the motion on the ground that there was insufficient evidence that defendant was "legally charged"—the statutory standard—with the care or custody of Shanaya. The Appellate Division reversed for two reasons *(244 A.D.2d 104)*. First, the court concluded that because defendant was "legally responsible" for Shanaya's care under section 1012(g) of the Family Court Act, she was also "legally charged" with the child's care under Penal Law § 260.10(2). Second, the court held that defendant was criminally liable because she stood in loco parentis at the time of the crime. We now affirm, solely on the first ground.

Pursuant to Penal Law § 260.10(2), "a parent, guardian or other person legally charged with the care or custody of a child less than eighteen years old" is guilty of endangering the welfare of a child if he or she "fails or refuses to exercise reasonable diligence in the control of such child to prevent [the child] from becoming an 'abused child,' a 'neglected child,' a 'juvenile delinquent' or a 'person in need of supervision,' " as those terms are defined in the Family Court Act. One of the purposes of this statute is to establish "the duty of one parent to protect the child from the other parent" (Donnino, Practice Commentaries, McKinney's Cons Laws of NY, Book 39, Penal Law § 260.10, at 348).

Defendant argues that the proof before the Grand Jury was insufficient to show that she was legally charged with the care or custody of Shanaya, emphasizing that she was not Shanaya's biological mother, legal guardian or contractually hired care-giver. As for defendant's own statements to police that she acted as Shanaya's primary caretaker and mother during Shanaya's visits, defendant argues that they were inadequate to create a duty because they did not indicate that she had assumed all of the obligations of motherhood on a permanent basis. Penal Law § 260.10(2) specifically includes parents and guardians as people who are subject to prosecution. In effect, therefore, defendant argues that "other person legally charged with the care or custody of a child" is limited to people who have contracted to care for or who stand in loco parentis to a child. We conclude that the statutory term is not so narrowly confined.

Because the Penal Law does not describe who constitutes a "person legally charged with the care or custody of a child," defining this term falls to the courts. In discharging this responsibility, we are mindful of the statutory language, the legislative purpose and the Penal Law's directive that its provisions should be "construed according to the fair import of their terms to promote justice and effect the objects of the law" (Penal Law § 5.00).

In order to be "legally charged" with caring for a child, obviously a person must have a responsibility to that child based in law. While Penal Law § 260.10(2) does not specify the circumstances giving rise to such a legal duty, the Family Court Act sets forth numerous duties toward children. Indeed, Penal Law § 260.10(2) complements and supplements various Family Court proceedings in order to accomplish the mutual goal of protecting children from abuse and neglect (*see,* Donnino, Practice Commentaries, McKinney's Cons Laws of NY, Book 39, Penal Law § 260.10, at 348). To promote uniformity, Penal Law § 260.10(2) specifically refers to the Family Court Act in order to define the terms "abused child," "neglected child," "juvenile delinquent" and "person in need of supervision."

The Family Court Act does not use the term "person legally charged," but it defines the similar term "person legally responsible" to include "the child's custodian, guardian [or] any other person responsible for the child's care at the relevant time" (*Family Ct. Act § 1012*[g]). The Family Court Act further specifies that a "custodian" "may include any person continually or at regular intervals found in the same household as the child when the conduct of such person causes or contributes to the abuse or neglect of the child." This definition was specifically meant to include "paramours" (Besharov, Practice Commentaries, McKinney's Cons Laws of NY, Book 29A, *Family Ct. Act § 1012*, at 373).

Pursuant to *Family Court Act § 1012(a)*, a person who is "legally responsible" has a duty to care for a child, and can be named as a respondent in Family Court proceedings for abuse or neglect. In fact, the terms "abused child" and "neglected child," which are incorporated by reference into Penal Law § 260.10(2), are defined with reference to the actions of a parent "or other person legally responsible" (*Family Ct Act § 1012*[e], [f]). Because a person who is "legally responsible" for a child under article 10 of the Family Court Act is obligated to prevent a child in one's care from becoming abused or neglected, such a person is necessarily "legally charged" with the child's care.

In determining whether the evidence before the Grand Jury was legally sufficient to indict defendant, the court "must consider whether the evidence, viewed most favorably to the People, if unexplained and uncontradicted—and deferring all questions as to the weight or quality of the evidence—would warrant conviction" (*People v. Swamp, 84 NY2d 725, 730; see also, CPL 70.10*[1]). Using this standard, the evidence before the Grand Jury established a prima facie case that defendant was legally responsible for Shanaya's care under *Family Court Act § 1012(g)*, and therefore legally charged with Shanaya's care under Penal Law § 260.10(2). Defendant's arguments regarding the actual extent of her involvement with the child might be issues for trial, but are not grounds for dismissal of the indictment.

In *Matter of Yolanda D. (88 NY2d 790, 796)*, this Court held that a person who "acts as the functional equivalent of a parent in a familial or household setting" is a "person legally responsible" for a child's care. By expanding the bounds of who is legally responsible for children beyond the realm of the traditional family and legal guardian, this standard takes into account the modern-day reality that parenting functions are not always performed by a parent. As the case before us illustrates, a person who is not a child's biological parent can play a significant role in rearing the child. Defendant acknowledged that whenever Shanaya visited the apartment she shared with Shanaya's father, she functioned as the child's mother. At the time of Shanaya's death, the three year old had spent 10 consecutive days and nights at defendant's apartment.

It would be incongruous for biological parents and guardians, but not a stepmother who assumes the primary caretaking role during the child's visits, to be liable for endangering the welfare of a child. Indeed, in *People v Wong (81 NY2d 600, 607–608)*, this Court indicated that a paid full-time caretaker can be criminally liable for failing to seek emergency medical aid for a seriously injured child. Thus, as defendant concedes, had the two people present during the beating of Shanaya been custodial caretakers hired by the child's father, their failure to secure medical care for Shanaya could have been the basis of criminal charges. The Legislature could not possibly have intended a hired caretaker to be liable for endangering the welfare of a child, but not a stepmother who functions in that role during the child's extended visits.

Defendant insists that she was not legally charged with Shanaya's care because she could not have been in loco parentis to the child absent a showing that she intended to support and care for her on a permanent basis (*Johnson v Jamaica Hosp., 62 NY2d 523, 529*). It is unnecessary for the People to prove that defendant assumed parental duties on a full-time basis, however, because "whether a person stands in loco parentis to a child is a separate inquiry from whether such a person acts as the functional equivalent of a parent" (*Matter of Yolanda D., supra, 88 NY2d, at 796*). A person may act as the functional equivalent of a parent even though that person assumes only temporary care or custody of the child, so long as the circumstances of the case otherwise warrant such a determination, as they appear to here. This conclusion comports with the requirement that a "person legally responsible" need only be responsible for the child's care "at the relevant time" (*Family Ct Act § 1012*[g]).

Defendant's reliance on *People v. Myers (201 AD2d 855)* and *People v. Goddard (206 AD2d 653)* is misplaced. In *Myers,* "no evidence was presented that defendant, who did not characterize himself as the children's father ... considered the children to be his responsibility or acted in such a way as to demonstrate that he entertained such an attitude" (*People v. Myers, supra, 201 AD2d, at 857*). Similarly, the evidence in *Goddard* established that the defendant "was no more than a casual babysitter" who never "intended or agreed to assume any obligations associated with parenthood of [the decedent] during any of the time periods involved" (*People v. Goddard, supra, 206 AD2d, at 654–655*).

The evidence in those cases stands in sharp contrast to the evidence before the Grand Jury in this case. Viewed most favorably to the People, that evidence, if unexplained and uncontradicted, would warrant conviction of defendant for endangering the welfare of Shanaya Jones, and therefore was legally sufficient to support the indictment.

Accordingly, the order of the Appellate Division should be affirmed.

NOTE

Several state courts have since broadly interpreted their neglect laws. See State ex rel. Children, Youth and Families Dep't v. Shawna C., 137 N.M. 687, 114 P.3d 367 (App.2005) (concluding that phrases "mental disorder or incapacity," "proper parental care," and "risk of serious harm," give adequate notice of proper parental behavior); In re Kenneth J., 352 Ill.App.3d 967, 288 Ill.Dec. 290, 817 N.E.2d 940 (2004) (upholding statute allowing the state to review parental fitness for any nine-month period after an adjudication of neglect); Doe v. Department of Social Services, 71 S.W.3d 648 (Mo.App. E.D. 2002) (concluding that the term "well-being" in a child neglect statute was not unconstitutionally vague); Williams v. Garcetti, 5 Cal.4th 561, 20 Cal.Rptr.2d 341, 853 P.2d 507 (1993) (finding child endangerment statute requiring parents to "exercise reasonable care, supervision, protection and control" is not unconstitutionally vague or overbroad); In re Anthony S., 282 A.D.2d 778, 723 N.Y.S.2d 251 (N.Y.A.D. 3 Dept. 2001) (concluding that the phrase "plan for the future of the child" is not unconstitutionally vague in permanent child neglect statute).

In re Pope

Court of Appeals of North Carolina, 2001.
144 N.C.App. 32, 547 S.E.2d 153.

■ GREENE, JUDGE.

Rachel Emily Pope (Respondent) appeals a judgment filed 9 May 2000 terminating her parental rights as the mother of Eva Leonia Grace Pope (the minor child).

The record shows that on 1 June 1999, the Buncombe County Department of Social Services (DSS) filed a petition, in pertinent part, to terminate the parental rights of Respondent pursuant to N.C. Gen. Stat. § 7A–289.32(2) (neglect) and N.C. Gen. Stat. § 7A–289.32(3) (willfully leaving minor child in foster care for more than 12 months).... Subsequent to the hearings, the trial court made the following pertinent findings of fact:

> 12. That [DSS] initially filed a juvenile petition February 26, 1998, alleging that the minor child was an abused and neglected child. That the allegations of abuse were based on the physical condition of the minor child, who was then 9 months old and had been admitted to Memorial Mission Hospital on February 23, 1998, for failure to thrive. At the time of admittance to the hospital, the minor child weighed only a little over 12 pounds; she was below the 5th percentile for her age; and, presented as a typical 3 month old instead of 9 months old. The minor child could not sit up independently, would not attempt to push herself up if lying on her stomach, had difficulty grasping objects, and she continually held her arms in an upright position at a 90 degree angle.
>
> 13. That the allegations of neglect in the original juvenile petition were that the minor child had not been examined by a pediatrician since her birth but had only seen chiropractors and naturopatic doctors, and that the hospital physicians had ruled out medical reasons for the child's condition, indicating that the cause of the child's condition was the failure of [Respondent] to provide proper care for the child.
>
> 14. That on April 23, 1998, [Respondent] consented to an adjudication of neglect in that the minor child did not receive the proper care and supervision from [Respondent], and did not receive the necessary medical care from [Respondent].
>
> . . .
>
> 18. That ... [Respondent] allowed Ms. Foster [the sister of Respondent,] to bring the minor child back with her to Buncombe County for a visit. That Ms. Foster was extremely concerned about the minor child's condition ... Due to her concerns, Ms. Foster took the minor child to see Dr. Sechlar at Asheville Pediatrics on February 23, 1998, at which time Dr. Sechlar immediately admitted the child to Memorial Mission Hospital for failure to thrive.
>
> . . .
>
> 20. That while the child was hospitalized, the hospital staff was concerned about [Respondent's] behaviors. That the staff attempted to discuss with [Respondent] the child's condition and needs, but [Respondent] would respond by talking about her ([Respondent's]) problems. [Respondent] was never willing to discuss or acknowledge that [the] child was starving to death at the time the child was admitted to the hospital.
>
> 21. That the minor child was starving to death before [Respondent's] eyes. Nevertheless, [Respondent] testified at this hearing that the minor child was fine, healthy, happy, well fed, and reaching all her developmental milestones until Ms. Foster took the child to Buncombe County,

and that the child's problems all began due to the change in her environment. . . .

22. That [DSS] provided many services to [Respondent] to aid her in correcting the conditions which led to the removal of the minor child from her care. [Respondent] has had a psychological evaluation; . . . has participated in and completed parenting classes; and has visited with the child on a regular basis. That [Respondent] has made no progress even with all these services, and even after 21 months [Respondent] is still insisting that it was solely Ms. Foster's fault that the minor child is in the custody of [DSS]. . . .

23. . . . That [Respondent] has a personality disorder with seriously disturbed thinking. Her psychological condition is difficult to change; and change would require that [Respondent] be highly motivated to change; and that she acknowledge her problems and work diligently in therapy to change her thinking. That without effective treatment for her personality disorder, there would be a high risk that [Respondent] would continue to treat the minor child as she has done in the past. That [Respondent] has a very high IQ and is able to function well to meet her own needs.

24. That [Respondent] testified at this hearing that she did not agree with the psychological evaluation; denied that she had any disturbed thinking; denied that she had done anything to place the minor child at risk; testified that the only reason [DSS] had taken custody was due to the fault of Ms. Foster; and testified that the only thing she would change if the [minor] child was returned to her care would be to get the [minor] child a pediatrician. That [Respondent] testified[,] . . . "I've racked my brain trying to figure out" why the minor child was starving to death in February, 1998, but did not know why that had occurred.

25. That [Respondent] has been provided supervised visits twice a week at [DSS]. That these visits were supervised by the social worker, who used these supervised visits to show [Respondent] appropriate child care skills. . . . [Respondent] continued to try [to] feed the [minor] child inappropriately both in the manner she tried to feed her and the food she brought to feed the [minor] child. Even after being told that the [minor] child could have an allergic reaction to strawberries, [Respondent] brought strawberries to feed the [minor] child. Further, [Respondent] continued to place the [minor] child in risky situations; specifically, on one occasion[,] [Respondent] stood on a toddler's chair, placed the minor child on a window sill and let go of the [minor] child. That the room this occurred in had cement floors. That the social worker had to intervene to tell [Respondent] that this was dangerous, but [Respondent] did not appear to care or understand. That the social worker had to instruct [Respondent] to take the [minor] child down from the windowsill.

. . .

31. That it is clear to the court that [Respondent] dearly loves [the minor child], and that [Respondent] has made within the limits of her ability a sincere effort to be reunited with [the minor child] and to comply with court orders. However, there is no evidence at all that with all her efforts [Respondent] is now or will ever be able to provide for [the minor child] in a way that would allow [the minor child] to grow up healthy, happy and well developed; nor is there any evidence that would

> give this court the hope that [Respondent] could in the near future make the changes necessary to allow the [minor] child to be placed back with [Respondent] safely.

The trial court then made the following pertinent conclusion of law:

> 3. That the Court finds by clear, cogent and convincing evidence that grounds exist to terminate the parental rights of [Respondent] pursuant to *N.C.G.S. 7B–1111(a)(1)* in that she has neglected the minor child when the minor child was placed into the custody of [DSS], she has continued to neglect the minor child while the child has been in the custody of [DSS] and it is reasonably probable that she would continue to neglect the minor child if she were returned to her care[.] . . .

The trial court then ordered the termination of Respondent's parental rights . . .

The dispositive issue is whether the trial court's findings of fact support a conclusion of law that there is a probability of repetition of neglect if the minor child were returned to Respondent.

Respondent argues "THE TRIAL COURT ERRED WHEN IT CONCLUDED THAT [Respondent] WOULD CONTINUE TO NEGLECT THE MINOR CHILD WHEN [Respondent] HAD COMPLIED WITH ALL OF THE SERVICES RECOMMENDED AND HAD MADE GOOD PROGRESS IN THERAPY." We disagree.

Neglect . . . is one of the grounds which can support the termination of parental rights. To prove neglect in a termination case, there must be clear and convincing evidence: (1) the juvenile has not, at the time of the termination proceeding, "received proper care, supervision, or discipline from the juvenile's parent . . . or . . . is not provided necessary medical care,"; and (2) the juvenile has sustained "some physical, mental, or emotional impairment . . . or [there is] a substantial risk of such impairment as a consequence of [such] failure." If there is no evidence of neglect at the time of the termination proceedings, however, parental rights may nevertheless be terminated if there is a showing of a past adjudication of neglect and the trial court finds by clear and convincing evidence a probability of repetition of neglect if the juvenile were returned to the parent. Thus, the petitioner need not present evidence of neglect subsequent to the prior adjudication of neglect.

In this case, Respondent did not have custody of the minor child at the time of the termination proceedings. The trial court, therefore, did not make any findings the minor child was neglected at the time of the termination proceedings. The trial court, however, made findings there had been a previous adjudication of neglect in 1998. The 1998 adjudication of neglect was based on findings the minor child "was starving to death" while in Respondent's custody and suffered from "failure to thrive"; "hospital physicians had ruled out medical reasons for the child's condition, indicating that the cause of the child's condition was the failure of [Respondent] to provide proper care for the child"; and Respondent did not seek medical care for the minor child. Although Respondent utilized many services provided by DSS subsequent to the 1998 adjudication of neglect, the trial court found as fact Respondent "made no progress even with all these services" and Respondent "still lacks any understanding of the seriousness of [the] child's condition in February, 1998." The trial court also found as fact that at the time of the termination hearing, Respondent denied that she had done anything to place the minor child at risk; testified that the only reason [DSS] had taken custody was due to the fault of Ms. Foster; and testified that the only thing she would change if the child [were] returned to her care would be to get the child a pediatrician.

Additionally, the trial court found as fact that during Respondent's supervised visitations with the minor child, Respondent continued "to try and feed the [minor] child inappropriately both in the manner she tried to feed her and the food she brought to feed the [minor] child." These findings of fact support a conclusion of law that if the minor child were returned to Respondent's custody, there would be a probability the minor child would not receive proper care from Respondent or proper medical care, and the minor child would sustain physical and/or mental impairment as a result of such failure. It follows that if the minor child were returned to Respondent's custody, there would be a probability of repetition of neglect. Accordingly, the trial court's 9 May 2000 judgment, terminating Respondent's parental rights . . . is affirmed.

Affirmed.

■ Tyson, Judge (dissenting).

I would reverse the order and remand for further proceedings toward reunification, consistent with the minor child's best interest, in light of the overriding purpose of the Juvenile Code toward reunification of a child with the natural parent. . . .

A. Purpose of the Juvenile Code

. . . *G.S. § 7B–100* sets forth the purposes of the Juvenile Code:

> (1) To provide procedures for the hearing of juvenile cases that assure fairness and equity and that protect the constitutional rights of juveniles and parents; (2) To develop a disposition in each juvenile case that reflects consideration of the facts, the needs and limitations of the juvenile, and the strengths and weaknesses of the family; (3) To provide for services for the protection of juveniles by means that respect both the right to family autonomy and the juveniles' needs for safety, continuity, and permanence; and (4) To provide standards for the removal, when necessary, of juveniles from their homes and for the return of juveniles to their homes consistent with preventing the unnecessary or inappropriate separation of juveniles from their parents.

. . .

D. Neglect

I disagree with the majority's opinion that the trial court appropriately terminated respondent's parental rights under *G.S. § 7B–1111(a)(1)*. A prior adjudication of neglect cannot be the sole basis for terminating parental rights.

. . .

Respondent complied with all court orders, and completed all DSS-recommended services in the case plan to prepare her for reunification with her minor child. The trial court found that respondent made "a sincere effort to be reunited with her daughter and to comply with court orders." Both the trial court and DSS found that respondent "dearly loves [the minor child]" and visits her twice a week. . . . The record also reveals that, after completion of the DSS case plan, respondent's ability to care for her minor child improved. DSS submitted a report to the court on 1 June 1998, stating that respondent was nearing completion of parenting classes, and that "during the supervised visitation [respondent] interacts with [the minor child] appropriately and demonstrates appropriate parenting skills."

On 22 September 1998, DSS further reported to the court that respondent was doing well in her DSS-recommended monthly therapy sessions, and that respondent's therapist, Nancy Mercer, "reports that [respondent] is doing well and that she [Mercer] has no concerns." . . .

I would hold that the record does not contain clear, cogent and convincing evidence that respondent would continue to neglect the child at the time of the termination proceeding, and after respondent's completion of all DSS-required services. . . . The essential purpose in interpreting *G.S. § 7B–1111(a)* is to assure "fairness and equity" for both juveniles and parents, and to work toward reunification while preventing the inappropriate separation of juveniles from their natural parents. . . .

E. Willfully Leaving Child in Foster Care

. . . The record does not contain clear, cogent and convincing evidence that respondent failed to show "reasonable progress under the circumstances." To the contrary, the evidence clearly shows that respondent willingly completed all DSS case plan requirements and improved her ability to care for the child.

Moreover, respondent consented to the child's initial placement in non-secure custody with respondent's sister. Respondent regularly visited her child . . . A June 1998 DSS report indicated that respondent had not missed a single session of visitation with her child. Throughout the child's placement with the Fosters, the evidence showed that respondent and Ms. Foster had few discussions, and that their relationship cooled considerably over time. Ms. Foster did not always allow respondent to speak to her child. Ms. Foster also resisted allowing grandparent visitation. Ms. Foster further testified that respondent was upset to learn that the child called the Fosters "Mama" and "Daddy."

The record does not contain clear, cogent and convincing evidence that supports the trial court's conclusion of law that (1) respondent willfully left the child in foster care; and (2) respondent failed to show reasonable progress in her ability to care for the child during the child's placement with DSS . . .

F. Willful Failure to Pay Support

. . .

I cannot agree that the clear, cogent and convincing evidence reveals a *willful* failure to pay support where (1) the record does not establish that respondent was ever under a court order to pay support; (2) Ms. Foster led respondent to believe they were helping respondent with her expenses; and (3) respondent did provide food and clothes to the child while the child was in Foster's care. . . .

In light of the essential aims of the Juvenile Code, I would reverse the trial court's order terminating respondent's parental rights, and remand for further proceedings toward reunification. Accordingly, I respectfully dissent.

b. VIOLENCE IN THE HOUSEHOLD

Nicholson v. Scoppetta

New York Court of Appeals, 2004.
3 N.Y.3d 357, 787 N.Y.S.2d 196, 820 N.E.2d 840.

■ KAYE, CHIEF JUDGE:

In this federal class action, the United States Court of Appeals for the Second Circuit has certified three questions centered on New York's statutory scheme for child protective proceedings. The action is brought on behalf of mothers and their children who were separated because the mother had suffered domestic violence, to which the children were exposed, and the children were for that reason deemed neglected by her.

In April 2000, Sharwline Nicholson, on behalf of herself and her two children, brought an action pursuant to *42 USC § 1983*, against the New York City Administration for Children's Services (ACS). The action was later consolidated with similar complaints by Sharlene Tillet and Ekaete Udoh—the three named plaintiff-mothers. Plaintiffs alleged that ACS, as a matter of policy, removed children from mothers who were victims of domestic violence because, as victims, they "engaged in domestic violence" and that defendants removed and detained children without probable cause and without due process of law. That policy, and its implementation—according to plaintiff-mothers—constituted, among other wrongs, an unlawful interference with their liberty interest in the care and custody of their children in violation of the United States Constitution.

In August 2001, the United States District Court for the Eastern District of New York certified two subclasses: battered custodial parents (Subclass A), and their children (Subclass B). For each plaintiff, at least one ground for removal was that the custodial mother had been assaulted by an intimate partner and failed to protect the child or children from exposure to that domestic violence.

In January 2002, the District Court granted a preliminary injunction, concluding that the City "may not penalize a mother, not otherwise unfit, who is battered by her partner, by separating her from her children; nor may children be separated from the mother, in effect visiting upon them the sins of their mother's batterer."

. . .

The District Court concluded that ACS's practices and policies violated both the substantive due process rights of mothers and children not to be separated by the government unless the parent is unfit to care for the child, and their procedural due process rights. The injunction, in relevant part, "prohibited ACS from carrying out ex parte removals 'solely because the mother is the victim of domestic violence,' or from filing an Article Ten petition seeking removal on that basis."

On appeal, the Second Circuit held that the District Court had not abused its discretion in concluding that ACS's practice of effecting removals based on a parent's failure to prevent his or her child from witnessing domestic violence against the parent amounted to a policy or custom of ACS [and] that in some circumstances the removals may raise serious questions of federal constitutional law.... The Court hesitated, however, before reaching the constitutional questions, believing that resolution of uncertain issues of New York statutory law would avoid, or significantly modify, the substantial federal constitutional issues presented.

Given the strong preference for avoiding unnecessary constitutional adjudication, the importance of child protection to New York State and the integral part New York courts play in the removal process, the Second Circuit, by three certified questions, chose to put the open state statutory law issues to us for resolution. We accepted certification and now proceed to answer those questions.

Certified Question No. 1: Neglect

"Does the definition of a 'neglected child' under *N.Y. Family Ct. Act § 1012(f), (h)* include instances in which the sole allegation of neglect is that the parent or other person legally responsible for the child's care allows the child to witness domestic abuse against the caretaker?"

We understand this question to ask whether a court reviewing an Article 10 petition may find a respondent parent responsible for neglect based on evidence of two facts only: that the parent has been the victim of domestic violence, and that the child has been exposed to that violence. That question must be answered in the negative. Plainly, more is required for a showing of neglect under New York law than the fact that a child was exposed to domestic abuse against the caretaker. Answering the question in the affirmative, moreover, would read an unacceptable presumption into the statute, contrary to its plain language.

Family Court Act § 1012(f) is explicit in identifying the elements that must be shown to support a finding of neglect. As relevant here, it defines a "neglected child" to mean:

> "a child less than eighteen years of age (i) whose physical, mental or emotional condition has been impaired or is in imminent danger of becoming impaired as a result of the failure of his parent or other person legally responsible for his care to exercise a minimum degree of care. . . .
>
> "(B) in providing the child with proper supervision or guardianship, by unreasonably inflicting or allowing to be inflicted harm, or a substantial risk thereof, including the infliction of excessive corporal punishment; or by misusing a drug or drugs; or by misusing alcoholic beverages to the extent that he loses self-control of his actions; or by any other acts of a similarly serious nature requiring the aid of the court."

Thus, a party seeking to establish neglect must show, by a preponderance of the evidence, first, that a child's physical, mental or emotional condition has been impaired or is in imminent danger of becoming impaired and second, that the actual or threatened harm to the child is a consequence of the failure of the parent or caretaker to exercise a minimum degree of care in providing the child with proper supervision or guardianship.

. . .

The first statutory element requires proof of actual (or imminent danger of) physical, emotional or mental impairment to the child. This prerequisite to a finding of neglect ensures that the Family Court, in deciding whether to authorize state intervention, will focus on serious harm or potential harm to the child, not just on what might be deemed undesirable parental behavior. "Imminent danger" reflects the Legislature's judgment that a finding of neglect may be appropriate even when a child has not actually been harmed; "imminent danger of impairment to a child is an independent and separate ground on which a neglect finding may be based." Imminent danger, however, must be near or impending, not merely possible.

In each case, additionally, there must be a link or causal connection between the basis for the neglect petition and the circumstances that allegedly produce the child's impairment or imminent danger of impairment.

. . .

The cases at bar concern, in particular, alleged threats to the child's emotional, or mental, health. The statute specifically defines "impairment of emotional health" and "impairment of mental or emotional condition" to include

> "a state of substantially diminished psychological or intellectual functioning in relation to, but not limited to, such factors as failure to thrive, control of aggressive or self-destructive impulses, ability to think and reason, or acting out or misbehavior, including incorrigibility, ungovernability or habitual truancy"

Under New York law, "such impairment must be clearly attributable to the unwillingness or inability of the respondent to exercise a minimum degree of care toward the child." Here, the Legislature recognized that the source of emotional or mental impairment—unlike physical injury—may be murky, and that it is unjust to fault a parent too readily. The Legislature therefore specified that such impairment be "clearly attributable" to the parent's failure to exercise the requisite degree of care.

Assuming that actual or imminent danger to the child has been shown, "neglect" also requires proof of the parent's failure to exercise a minimum degree of care.

. . .

"Minimum degree of care" is a "baseline of proper care for children that all parents, regardless of lifestyle or social or economic position, must meet."

. . .

Courts must evaluate parental behavior objectively: would a reasonable and prudent parent have so acted, or failed to act, under the circumstances then and there existing met the standard of the reasonable and prudent person in similar circumstances.

. . .

As the Subclass A members point out, for a battered mother—and ultimately for a court—what course of action constitutes a parent's exercise of a "minimum degree of care" may include such considerations as: risks attendant to leaving, if the batterer has threatened to kill her if she does; risks attendant to staying and suffering continued abuse; risks attendant to seeking assistance through government channels, potentially increasing the danger to herself and her children; risks attendant to criminal prosecution against the abuser; and risks attendant to relocation. Whether a particular mother in these circumstances has actually failed to exercise a minimum degree of care is necessarily dependent on facts such as the severity and frequency of the violence, and the resources and options available to her.

Only when a petitioner demonstrates, by a preponderance of evidence, that both elements of *section 1012 (f)* are satisfied may a child be deemed neglected under the statute. When "the sole allegation" is that the mother has been abused and the child has witnessed the abuse, such a showing has not been made. This does not mean, however, that a child can never be "neglected" when living in a household plagued by domestic violence. Conceivably, neglect might be found where a record establishes that, for example, the mother acknowledged that the children knew of repeated domestic violence by her paramour and had reason to be afraid of him, yet nonetheless allowed him several times to return to her home, and lacked awareness of any impact of the violence on the children; or where the children were exposed to regular and continuous extremely violent conduct between their parents, several times requiring official intervention, and where caseworkers testified to the fear and distress the children were experiencing as a result of their long exposure to the violence. In such circumstances, the battered mother is charged with neglect not because she is a victim of domestic violence or because her children witnessed the abuse, but rather because a preponderance of the evidence establishes that the children were actually or imminently harmed by reason of her failure to exercise even minimal care in providing them with proper oversight.

Certified Question No. 2: Removals

Next, we are called upon to focus on removals by ACS, in answering the question:

> "Can the injury or possible injury, if any, that results to a child who has witnessed domestic abuse against a parent or other caretaker constitute 'danger' or 'risk' to the child's 'life or health,' as those terms are defined in the *N.Y. Family Ct. Act §§ 1022, 1024, 1026–1028*?"

. . .

The Circuit Court summarized the policy challenged by plaintiffs and found by the District Court as "the alleged practice of removals based on a theory that allowing one's child to witness ongoing domestic violence is a form of neglect, either simply because such conduct is presumptively neglectful or because in individual circumstances it is shown to threaten the child's physical or emotional health."

It is this policy, viewed in light of the District Court's factual findings, that informs our analysis of Certified Question No. 2. In so doing, we acknowledge the Legislature's expressed goal of "placing increased emphasis on preventive services designed to maintain family relationships rather than responding to children and families in trouble only by removing the child from the family." We further acknowledge the legislative findings, made pursuant to the *Family Protection and Domestic Violence Intervention Act of 1994*, that

> "the corrosive effect of domestic violence is far reaching. The batterer's violence injures children both directly and indirectly. Abuse of a parent is detrimental to children whether or not they are physically abused themselves. Children who witness domestic violence are more likely to experience delayed development, feelings of fear, depression and helplessness and are more likely to become batterers themselves"

These legislative findings represent two fundamental—sometimes conflicting—principles.

. . .

As we concluded in response to Certified Question No. 1, exposing a child to domestic violence is not presumptively neglectful. Not every child exposed to domestic violence is at risk of impairment. A fortiori, exposure of a child to violence is not presumptively ground for removal, and in many instances removal may do more harm to the child than good. *Part 2 of Article 10 of the Family Court Act* sets forth four ways in which a child may be removed from the home in response to an allegation of neglect (or abuse) related to domestic violence: 1) temporary removal with consent; 2) preliminary orders after a petition is filed; 3) preliminary orders before a petition is filed; and 4) emergency removal without a court order. The issue before us is whether emotional harm suffered by a child exposed to domestic violence, where shown, can warrant the trauma of removal under any of these provisions.

The Practice Commentaries state, and we agree, that the sections of Article 10, Part 2 create a "continuum of consent and urgency and mandate a hierarchy of required review" before a child is removed from home.

. . .

Post–Petition Removal

If parental consent cannot be obtained, *section 1027*, at issue here, provides for preliminary orders after the filing of a neglect (or abuse) petition. Thus, according to the statutory continuum, where the circumstances are not so exigent, the agency should bring a petition and seek a hearing prior to removal of the child. In any case involving abuse—or in any case where the child has already been removed without a court order—the Family Court must hold a hearing as soon as practicable after the filing of a petition, to determine whether the child's interests require protection pending a final order of disposition.

. . .

In order to justify a finding of imminent risk to life or health, the agency need not prove that the child has suffered actual injury. Rather, the court engages in a fact-intensive inquiry to determine whether the child's emotional health is at risk.

. . .

The plain language of the section and the legislative history supporting it establish that a blanket presumption favoring removal was never intended. The court must do more than identify the existence of a risk of serious harm. Rather, a court must weigh, in the factual setting before it, whether the imminent risk to the child can be mitigated by reasonable efforts to avoid removal. It must balance that risk against the harm removal might bring, and it must determine factually which course is in the child's best interests.

. . .

Ex Parte Removal by Court Order

If the agency believes that there is insufficient time to file a petition, the next step on the continuum should not be emergency removal, but ex parte removal by court order. [The] Family Court Act provides that the court may enter an order directing the temporary removal of a child from home before the filing of a petition if three factors are met.

First, the parent must be absent or, if present, must have been asked and refused to consent to temporary removal of the child and must have been informed of an intent to apply for an order. Second, the child must appear to suffer from abuse or neglect of a parent or other person legally responsible for the child's care to the extent that immediate removal is necessary to avoid imminent danger to the child's life or health. Third, there must be insufficient time to file a petition and hold a preliminary hearing.

. . .

[T]he court must engage in a fact-finding inquiry into whether the child is at risk and appears to suffer from neglect ... [It] must engage in a balancing test of the imminent risk with the best interests of the child and, where appropriate, the reasonable efforts made to avoid removal or continuing removal . . .

Emergency Removal Without Court Order

Finally, *section 1024* provides for emergency removals without a court order. The section permits removal without a court order and without consent of the parent if there is reasonable cause to believe that the child is in such urgent circumstance or condition that continuing in the home or care of the parent presents an imminent danger to the child's life or health, and there is not enough time to apply for an order under *section 1022*. Thus, emergency removal is appropriate where the danger is so immediate, so urgent that the child's life or safety will be at risk before an ex parte order can be obtained. The standard obviously is a stringent one.

. . .

While we cannot say, for all future time, that the possibility can never exist, in the case of emotional injury—or, even more remotely, the risk of emotional injury—caused by witnessing domestic violence, it must be a rare circumstance in which the time would be so fleeting and the danger so great that emergency removal would be warranted.

Question 3

Certified Question No. 3: Process

Finally, the Second Circuit asks us:

"Does the fact that the child witnessed such abuse suffice to demonstrate that 'removal is necessary,' *N.Y. Family Ct. Act §§ 1022, 1024, 1027*, or that 'removal was in the child's best interests,' *N.Y. Family Ct. Act §§ 1028, 1052(b)(i)(A)*, or must the child protective agency offer additional, particularized evidence to justify removal?"

. . .

All parties maintain, however, and we concur, that under the Family Court Act, there can be no "blanket presumption" favoring removal when a child witnesses domestic violence, and that each case is fact-specific. As demonstrated in our discussion of Certified Question No. 2, when a court orders removal, particularized evidence must exist to justify that determination, including, where appropriate, evidence of efforts made to prevent or eliminate the need for removal and the impact of removal on the child.

Accordingly, the certified questions should be answered in accordance with this Opinion.

c. POTENTIAL NEGLECT

In re M.F. v. Florida Dep't of Children & Families

Supreme Court of Florida, 2000.
770 So.2d 1189.

■ PER CURIAM.

. . .

I. FACTS

Brief

On May 11, 1998, the Florida Department of Children and Families ("DCF") filed in circuit court a verified shelter petition seeking to remove from L.F. her three natural children, K.F. (age 8), M.F. (age 5), and M.F.

(age 3).[1] The circuit court granted the petition and ordered the children placed in the grandparents' care.[2] DCF filed an amended petition for dependency on July 6 alleging that the children had been subjected to abuse and neglect in their home and seeking to have them adjudicated dependent and placed in the temporary legal custody of the grandparents. DCF further alleged that the children were subject to both prospective abuse and neglect because the father, R.F., was a convicted child molester who was currently imprisoned.[3] Only the father challenged the petition,[4] and he challenged it only as to M.F. and M.F.[5]

At the hearing on the petition, the inquiry focused on DCF's allegation that the children were subject to both prospective abuse (i.e., as evidenced by the father's prior conviction for a child sex offense) and prospective neglect (i.e., as evidenced by the father's lengthy prison term).[6] The court ultimately entered an order adjudicating M.F. and M.F. dependent as to the father. The court found by clear and convincing evidence that R.F. was a convicted child molester (i.e., he had committed an attempted capital sexual battery against K.F.), that R.F. was currently incarcerated for fifteen years, and that R.F. was unable to care for the children:

> —The children's father is incarcerated for a conviction of attempted sexual battery by an adult on a victim under the age of twelve.[7] This crime was committed upon the child [K.F.]. [R.F.] is serving a fifteen year sentence. He is unable to care for his children.

The court concluded as follows:

> —The children [M.F.] and [M.F.] are dependent having been at risk of prospective neglect and prospective abuse if placed in the father's care.

The Second District Court of Appeal focused only on the fact that R.F. had been convicted of a child sex offence and found that this conviction,

1. The petition alleged the following: The children are in immediate danger because L.F. has failed to protect them from a batterer, i.e., her paramour; her paramour was arrested May 3 for beating L.F. and battering the three-year-old; her paramour made verbal threats to kill L.F. and the children as he was being arrested; L.F. has refused several times to seek a protective order; she has since moved in with the paramour's family; the paramour has a record of prior arrests for aggravated assault, battery, and theft, and is now incarcerated; the children-for their own safety-should be placed in the custody of the maternal grandparents.

2. The court based its decision on the following reasons:

> —To protect the children.
>
> —To provide an opportunity for the children and the family to agree upon conditions for the children's safe return to the home

3. In its amended petition, DCF made the following allegation in paragraph 4(*l*) under the caption "Abuse/Prospective Abuse Neglect/Prospective Neglect":

> The children's father is incarcerated for a conviction of attempted sexual battery by an adult on a victim under the age of twelve (12). This crime was committed upon the child [K.F.]. [R.F.] is serving a fifteen (15) year sentence. He is unable to care for his children.

4. During the pendency of the petition, the mother left Florida with the paramour and she is not now involved in the present proceeding. (The father in the present proceeding is not the paramour.)

5. R.F. is the natural father of both M.F. and M.F. but not K.F.

6. At the commencement of the hearing, the attorney for DCF stated that the Department was relying solely on a copy of the father's prior conviction for a child sex offense . . .

The father then contested the admissibility of the conviction and argued that the victim in the prior offense, K.F., was not his biological daughter. The court concluded that the certified copy of the conviction, standing alone, was sufficient to establish dependency . . .

7. The information alleged that at some time between June 1995 and September 1996 R.F. "with his sexual organ penetrated or had union with the vagina of K.F." He was adjudicated guilty and sentenced in March 1998.

standing alone, was sufficient to support the trial court's ruling. The court framed the issue narrowly:

> We address only the issue of whether evidence of sexual abuse of one child is sufficient evidence of abuse or neglect of a sibling to support an adjudication of dependency.

In re M.F., 742 So. 2d 490, 491 (Fla. 2d DCA 1999). The court noted that conflict on this issue exists between several of the district courts of appeal:

> In cases involving sexual abuse, the Third District has found the act of sexual abuse of a child sufficient in itself to establish a substantial likelihood of future abuse and neglect of a sibling. However, the Fifth District has required additional evidence of a likelihood that the parent will similarly abuse the other children.

Id. (citation omitted). The court then concluded:

> In this case, the only evidence the Department of Children and Families presented to support an adjudication of dependency as to M.F. and M.F. was a copy of the Father's conviction for sexual abuse of the stepdaughter. We adopt the holding of the Third District that this evidence alone is sufficient to support an adjudication of dependency as to M.F. and M.F.

Id. (emphasis added). The court certified conflict with decisions of the Fifth District on this issue. R.F. contends that the Second and Third Districts are in error. He claims the following: The simple fact that a parent committed a sex act on a child is insufficient by itself to support a final ruling of dependency as to a different child.

II. THE APPLICABLE LAW

In a dependency proceeding, DCF must establish its allegations by "a preponderance of the evidence." A court's final ruling of dependency is a mixed question of law and fact and will be sustained on review if the court applied the correct law and its ruling is supported by competent substantial evidence in the record. Competent substantial evidence is tantamount to legally sufficient evidence. The Legislature has explained that a prime purpose of the Florida Juvenile Justice Act (the "Act") is to guarantee to each child in Florida a safe and supportive home environment:

> § 39.001 Purposes and intent. . . .
>
> (1) The purposes of this Chapter are:
>
> . . .
>
> (b) To provide for the care, safety, and protection of children in an environment that fosters healthy social, emotional, intellectual, and physical development; to ensure secure and safe custody; and to promote the health and well-being of all children under the state's care.

§ 39.001, Fla. Stat. (1997). Coextensive with this purpose is a second equally important goal: Preservation of the family.

> (1) The purposes of this Chapter are:
>
> . . .
>
> (d) To preserve and strengthen the child's family ties whenever possible, removing the child from parental custody only when his or her welfare

> or the safety and protection of the public cannot be adequately safeguarded without such removal....

§ 39.001, Fla. Stat. (1997). The severing of the parent-child bond—even temporarily—is a refuge of last resort for the child. Even though a child's home may be lacking in amenities, the alternative—i.e., removal of the child-oftentimes is more harmful to the child. The benefits of an abiding family life are weighty and well-documented.

The purpose of a dependency proceeding is not to punish the offending parent but to protect and care for a child who has been neglected, abandoned, or abused. See § 39.404(2), Fla. Stat. (1997). The Act defines a dependent child as one who inter alia is at risk of imminent abuse or neglect:

> (11) "Child who is found to be dependent" means a child who, pursuant to this Chapter, is found by the court:
>
> ...
>
> (f) To be at substantial risk of imminent abuse or neglect by the parent or parents or the custodian.

§ 39.01, Fla. Stat. (1997) (emphasis added). "Abuse" and "neglect" are defined as follows:

> (2) "Abuse" means any willful act that results in any physical, mental, or sexual injury that causes or is likely to cause the child's physical, mental, or emotional health to be significantly impaired....
>
> ...
>
> (36) "Neglect" occurs when the parent or legal custodian of a child or, in the absence of a parent or legal custodian, the person primarily responsible for the child's welfare deprives a child of, or allows a child to be deprived of, necessary food, clothing, shelter, or medical treatment or permits a child to live in an environment when such deprivation or environment causes the child's physical, mental, or emotional health to be significantly impaired or to be in danger of being significantly impaired.

§ 39.01, Fla. Stat. (1997).

While this Court has not specifically addressed whether a court can issue an order of dependency based on the abuse or neglect of a different child, we have held that a court can enter an order terminating parental rights based on such grounds:

> We hold that the permanent termination of a parent's rights in one child under circumstances involving abuse or neglect may serve as grounds for permanently severing the parent's rights in a different child.

Padgett v. Department of Health & Rehabilitative Servs., 577 So. 2d 565, 571 (Fla. 1991) (footnote omitted). Unlike the district court ruling in the present case, our ruling in Padgett was based not on any one particular fact but on extensive and wide-ranging evidence of abuse and neglect.

III. THE INSTANT CASE

The narrow question posed in the present case is whether a court can base a final ruling of dependency solely on the fact that the parent committed a sex act on a different child. As noted above, the Second District Court of Appeal in the present case recognized conflict between the Third District and the Fifth District on this issue. See *In re M.F., 742 So. 2d at 491.* Whereas the Third District has held that such an act standing alone is sufficient to support a ruling of dependency, the Fifth District has held that some additional proof of risk to the current child is required. In the present case, the Second District agreed with the Third District and adopted that court's per se rule.

We conclude that the flexible approach taken by the Fifth District, rather than the per se rule adopted by the Second and Third Districts, is more consistent with the plain language of the Act. A simple showing by DCF that a parent committed a sex act on one child does not by itself constitute proof that the parent poses a substantial risk of imminent abuse or neglect to the child's sibling, as required by the statute. See *§ 39.01(11), Fla. Stat.* (1997). While the commission of such an act may be highly relevant, it is not automatically dispositive of the issue of dependency. A court instead should focus on all the circumstances surrounding the petition in each case.

. . . While (contrary to the present district court's ruling) a copy of R.F.'s conviction standing alone would be insufficient to support this order of dependency as to M.F. and M.F., the totality of the circumstances surrounding the petition is legally sufficient to support the order. Under existing law, the fact that R.F. will be incarcerated for a substantial portion of the children's years of minority is a weighty factor on its own.

. . .

■ PARIENTE, J., (specially concurring).

. . .

. . . I am compelled to agree that a conviction for the offense of attempted sexual battery on a minor by an adult is insufficient in itself to establish that the adult's other children should be adjudicated dependent. A court may find that a child who has not actually "been abandoned, abused, or neglected by the child's parents" is nonetheless dependent if that child is "at substantial risk of imminent abuse or neglect by the parent or parents or legal custodian." § 39.01(11)(a), (f), Fla. Stat. (1997). In this case, there is nothing in the record as to the nature or circumstances of the crime for which R.F. was convicted. Likewise, there is nothing in the record that shows how in this case, the fact that R.F. has been convicted of attempted sexual battery of one child puts his children, M.F. and M.F., at substantial risk of sexual abuse from R.F., especially because he is incarcerated and serving a fifteen-year prison sentence. Given this lack of evidence, I agree with the majority's conclusion that although "the commission of such an act may be highly relevant, it is not automatically dispositive of the issue of dependency. A court instead should focus on all the circumstances surrounding the petition in each case." Majority op. at 10–11. Indeed, although it occurred in a termination of parental rights proceeding, this Court has previously explained that it is the totality of the circumstances that must be evaluated in determining the likelihood of prospective abuse of a child based on the past abuse of another child.

I also find it significant that our Legislature has not specifically provided a per se rule that a conviction for a sexual offense against another child shall constitute grounds for an adjudication of dependency or the termination of parental rights. Cf. § 39.464(1)(d), Fla. Stat. (1997) (providing that grounds for termination of parental rights exist when the parent engages in egregious conduct that threatens the life of the child's sibling or results in the sibling's serious bodily injury or death). Moreover, a per se rule where the only evidence is a conviction for a sexual offense involving the child's sibling may raise due process concerns, at least in cases where parental rights are being terminated. Thus, instead of a per se rule, I would suggest the adoption by this Court of a rebuttable presumption of dependency when a parent is convicted of sexual abuse of a minor. This presumption would shift the burden to the parent to present evidence as to why a conviction for the prior sexual abuse of one child would not place the parent's other children at substantial risk for abuse or neglect.

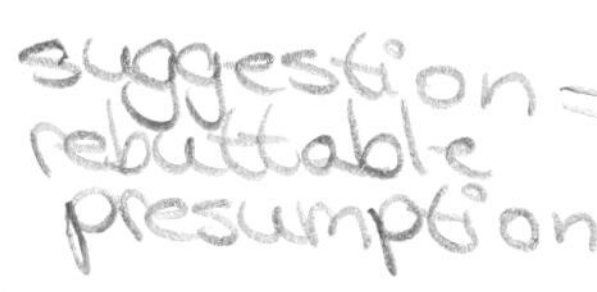

Stecker v. First Commer. Trust Co.

Supreme Court of Arkansas, 1998.
331 Ark. 452, 962 S.W.2d 792.

■ DAVID NEWBERN, JUSTICE.

This is the second appeal concerning the liability of Dr. Rheeta Stecker for the death of her patient, sixteen-month-old Laura Fullbright. First Commercial Trust Company ("First Commercial"), as administrator of the child's estate, sued Dr. Stecker for medical malpractice and for failure to report under the child-abuse-reporting statute, *Ark. Code Ann. §§ 12–12–501* through 12–12–518 (Repl. 1995 and Supp. 1997). In addition to the action on behalf of the estate, First Commercial sued on behalf of several of Laura Fullbright's relatives, individually. It was alleged that Dr. Stecker's failure to report evidence of physical abuse of the child resulted in the child's death. In addition to Dr. Stecker, Mary Ellen Robbins, the child's mother, and Joseph Rank who lived with Ms. Robbins and her child and who was convicted of murdering the child, were named as defendants.

In the first trial, Ms. Robbins was found not liable. Mr. Rank was found liable for damages to Laura Fullbright's halfbrother, but no damages were awarded to the estate. Dr. Stecker was found not liable for civil penalties prescribed under the child-abuse-reporting statute, and she was awarded a directed verdict on the medical malpractice claim because the only medical expert witness sought to be presented by First Commercial was found not to be qualified to testify as to the standard of medical care concerning child abuse in Hot Springs. We reversed and remanded for a new trial on the medical malpractice claim, holding it was error to have excluded the testimony of Dr. Frederick Epstein, the expert medical witness whose testimony First Commercial sought to introduce on behalf of the estate.

In the second trial, a jury verdict resulted in a judgment against Dr. Stecker . . . [S]he contends her motion for a directed verdict should have been granted because there was insufficient evidence that her failure to report the child's condition resulted in the death . . .

At the second trial, there was evidence from which the jury could have concluded the following. Dr. Stecker, a family practitioner, treated Laura Fullbright on several occasions prior to the child's death which occurred on September 12, 1992. On June 12, 1992, Dr. Stecker saw Laura, who was 12 1/2 months old, for a "well baby check-up." Laura was brought to Dr. Stecker by Ms. Robbins, a pharmacist, whom Dr. Stecker regarded as a friend and colleague. She noticed a visible angulation of one of the baby's arms, and she pointed the problem out to Ms. Robbins and to Mr. Rank. An x-ray showed the fracture of two bones in the child's left forearm. Ms.

Robbins and Mr. Rank indicated that they did not know that there was a problem. Dr. Stecker became concerned about the possibility of neglect or abuse. Dr. Stecker referred Laura to Dr. Robert Olive, an orthopedist. After seeing the x-rays as well as the child and her mother, Dr. Olive wrote Dr. Stecker that he did not think that there was any evidence of neglect on the part of the parents.

The letter from Dr. Olive did not totally alleviate Dr. Stecker's suspicions of possible abuse; however, she did not confront Ms. Robbins or Mr. Rank about her suspicions, contact the baby's father, Jim Fullbright, about her suspicions, or report her suspicions to any law enforcement agency. Ms. Robbins did not tell Jim Fullbright about the broken arm because she knew that he would "raise a fuss about it."

On July 9, Dr. Stecker again examined Laura. Her notes reflect that the family had observed that the child was "wobbly" and running into things. Dr. Stecker found that she was better and diagnosed the problem as ataxia or dizziness and concluded that the child had been drinking too much juice. However, she also recognized that the symptoms were consistent with other possibilities, including head trauma.

On July 21, Laura was brought to the clinic with both eyelids swollen, and Ms. Robbins reported that the bruises were a result of the child falling down several stairs. Dr. Stecker was not present and Dr. Stecker's husband, Dr. Elton Stecker, saw the baby. Dr. Elton Stecker's nurse recorded that the child had been nauseated the previous day and had vomited that morning. When she awoke, there was swelling on the right side of the head in the temple area and over the right eye.

On July 22, Dr. Stecker again saw Laura, and she read the record of the July 21 visit. At this time, the child's eyelids were swollen, and Ms. Robbins reported that the child had fallen down several stairs. Ms. Robbins wondered if the swelling of the upper lids could be the result of an allergy or a spider bite, and she stated that Laura had had watery nasal discharge which she felt was due to an allergy. Dr. Stecker wondered why there were new falls when child had been seen in the clinic the day before. Dr. Stecker discussed the possibility of abuse with Ms. Robbins. Ms. Robbins was adamant that abuse was highly unlikely. She stated that her five-year-old son carried Laura around and that he might have dropped her. She also told Dr. Stecker that her boyfriend did not have a temper. Dr. Stecker again considered reporting her suspicions of child abuse to the authorities; however, she did not. She made a conscious decision that there was not enough evidence to put the family in jeopardy of an investigation.

In August, there was an adult guest in Ms. Robbins's home, and nothing happened to the child while he was present. On September 12, 1991, Ms. Robbins returned home from work and found Laura, whom she had left in the care of Mr. Rank, unconscious. She took the child to St. Joseph's Regional Medical Center in Hot Springs. Laura was transported to Arkansas Children's Hospital in Little Rock, where she was later pronounced dead. The medical examiner determined that the cause of death was homicide . . .

2. Proximate Cause

Arkansas Code Ann. § 16–114–206(a) (1987) provides:

In any action for medical injury, the plaintiff shall have the burden of proving:

(1) The degree of skill and learning ordinarily possessed and used by members of the profession of the medical care provider in good standing, engaged in the same type of practice or specialty in the locality in which he practices or in a similar locality;

(2) That the medical care provider failed to act in accordance with that standard; and

(3) That as a proximate result thereof, the injured person suffered injuries which would not otherwise have occurred.

(Emphasis added.)

Causation is ordinarily a fact question for the jury to decide. The law requires more than a mere possibility that certain injuries resulted from negligence; a reasonable probability must be established. *Davis v. Kemp, 252 Ark. 925, 481 S.W.2d 712 (1972).* A plaintiff's proof on the issue of causation must be more than speculation and conjecture. *Hill v. Maxwell, 247 Ark. 811, 448 S.W.2d 9 (1969).* It must be such that reasonable persons might conclude that it is more probable than not that an event was caused by the defendant. *Id.*

Proximate cause may, however, be shown from circumstantial evidence, and such evidence is sufficient to show proximate cause if the facts proved are of such a nature and are so connected and related to each other that the conclusion may be fairly inferred. *Wheeler v. Bennett, 312 Ark. 411, 849 S.W.2d 952 (1991).* The mere fact that other causes intervene between the original act of negligence and the injury for which recovery is sought is not sufficient to relieve the original actor of liability if the injury is the natural and probable consequence of the original negligent act or omission and is such as might reasonably have been foreseen as probable. *State Farm Mut. Auto. Ins. Co. v. Pharr, 305 Ark. 459, 808 S.W.2d 769 (1991).*

Dr. Lander Smith, a witness presented by Dr. Stecker, testified to his opinion that Dr. Stecker had not violated the standard of care required of a family physician in the circumstances presented. On cross-examination, however, he testified, in part, as follows:

> No, sir, I am not an expert in child abuse. But it is correct that in my schooling as a family practitioner and as an emergency room physician I am taught about things to look for in child abuse.... If I have an impression that if someone has abused a child, I certainly would report it. As to whether I would expect the abuser to back off under the bright light of an investigation, I would think so, while there is an investigation hanging over his head. That's why you should report those, because it might save a child's life. More likely than not, I would always hope it would.

Dr. Frederick Epstein, who was presented as First Commercial's witness, testified on cross-examination that in his opinion, "Dr. Stecker should have called Health and Human Services and they would have called the father and everyone else acquainted with this child."

Dr. Stecker argues that the Trial Court erred in denying her motion for a directed verdict because there is no substantial evidence that her conduct was the proximate cause of the death of Laura Fullbright. Dr. Stecker argues that if Dr. Smith's testimony amounts to sufficient evidence of causation, the Administrator has effectively shifted the burden of proof on this element of its cause of action to her. She contends that if it can be presumed that a report of suspected child abuse will more likely than not prevent harm to the victim, she who is allegedly negligent for failing to recognize and report that abuse is put in the position of proving that making such a report would not have made a difference.

There is no presumption involved here. Dr. Epstein testified that Dr. Stecker should have called the Department of Human Services, which would then have notified the father and "everyone acquainted with this child." Dr. Smith informed the jury that such a report could have saved the child's life by exposing the abuser. That opinion was buttressed by the evidence that when there was an outside person in Ms. Robbins's home, the abuse did not occur. Dr. Stecker had the opportunity to rebut that testimony and apparently failed to do so in the eyes of the jury. The issue was one of fact for the jury to decide . . .

NOTE

Since the inception of mandatory reporting laws, the number of child abuse cases reported has seen a sharp increase. Consider Karen Ross, Revealing Confidential Secrets: Will It Save Our Children?, 28 Seton Hall L. Rev. 963, 967–968 (1998):

> Reporting statutes have a twofold purpose: (1) to identify and assist children who have been victims of abuse and (2) to prevent, as well as prosecute, child abuse cases. From 1963 to 1992, the number of cases reported increased from 150,000 to 2.9 million, thus immensely increasing the number of abused and neglected children who received some form of treatment. If states had not enacted laws mandating that certain professionals report child abuse, the majority of reports received by child protective service agencies would not have been made.
>
> One researcher has found that reports of suspected child abuse made by professionals have one of the highest rates of substantiation. Statutes that require professionals to report incidents of suspected abuse may explain the increase in detected abuse. The increase in reporting, however, has not resolved the enormous problem of child abuse. In fact, it is estimated that approximately forty percent of professionals required to report declined to do so in certain circumstances. As a result, a vast number of child abuse cases remains undiscovered.

Professionals often cite confidentiality as a reason for their failure to report. According to Ross, "Professionals invoke two legal principles as a means of escaping the mandatory reporting requirements: (1) their duty to keep certain information confidential; and (2) their privilege not to disclose confidential information. Whether these two principles actually relieve professionals of their duty to disclose suspected child abuse has not yet been resolved." Id. at 968. The confidentiality issues become particularly pronounced when the professional owes a duty of confidentiality to an individual who may be charged with abuse or neglect. Consider Brooke Albrandt, Note: Turning in the Client: Mandatory Child Abuse Reporting Requirements and the Criminal Defense of Battered Women, 81 Tex. L. Rev. 655, 665–6, 668–9 (2002):

> Attorneys who work on domestic violence cases are particularly likely to encounter situations that require reporting because child abuse is often prevalent in domestic violence cases. A national survey of 2000 families in the United States found that approximately fifty percent of men who abused their wives also abused their children, and approximately fifty percent of domestic violence victims lived in homes with children under the age of twelve. Forty-five percent of the mothers of abused children are in fact battered women, and the children of a battered woman are fifteen times more likely to be abused than the children of a mother who is not a victim of domestic violence. Furthermore, children in homes where the mother is battered are more likely to be abused by both parents.
>
> Even if she is not the abuser of the children, a battered woman faces not only criminal prosecution for failure to protect the children from abuse, but also potential termination of the parent-child relationship. For example, the Texas Family Code states:

> The court may order termination of the parent-child relationship if the court finds by clear and convincing evidence ... that the parent has ... knowingly placed or knowingly allowed the child to remain in conditions or surroundings which endanger the physical or emotional well-being of the child ... [or has] engaged in conduct or knowingly placed the child with persons who engaged in conduct which endangers the physical or emotional well-being of the child.
>
> . . .
>
> Because she is often a victim of the abuse herself, a battered woman faces a no-win situation: When mothers stay with a batterer, they and their children may be injured, and mothers run the risk of being held accountable for failure to protect. When mothers leave or attempt to leave the batterer, they frequently face a campaign of harassment from the batterer, great financial insecurity, homelessness, and the risk of serious harm.... Indeed, mothers who leave batterers, as well as mothers who stay, may not appear to be acting in their child's best interest.
>
> This situation is only compounded when a battered woman with abused children seeks legal help for a criminal charge, divorce, or custody matter, and her attorney is required to report her to the authorities if the attorney finds out about the abuse.
>
> . . .
>
> In addition to creating constitutional problems, a mandatory reporting requirement is repugnant to the goals of criminal defense. One of the most important roles of a criminal defense attorney is to guarantee his or her client due process and protection from government abuse. Defense attorneys in particular often see themselves as a client's last line of defense against an abusive government; many would consider a requirement reporting their clients to the government a betrayal of their clients. Jacqueline St. Joan, for example, asserts that "the idea of becoming an informant for the government against one's client [is] an unacceptable violation of the duty of loyalty to the client." An attorney's role is simply not the same as that of a medical worker or a social worker, the most common mandatory reporters. Requiring medical workers to report the suspected abuse of a patient fits well with the purpose of medical workers: to care for the physical and mental health of patients. Similarly, social workers are concerned with the relationships and general well-being of their clients. Attorneys, however, are legal advocates who serve as the legal representatives of their clients. Criminal defense attorneys representing battered women have an assigned role to make use of the law and relevant information about the client's experiences to minimize the impact of criminal charges on the client's life. In many instances, the existence of child abuse is extremely relevant to that task. Mandatory reporting statutes, however, make attorney knowledge of that abuse dangerous, both to the client and to the attorney.

See also State in Interest of CA, 615 So.2d 900 (La.App.1993), in which a mother's parental rights were terminated in part because of her failure to protect her minor child from past and potential future sexual abuse by her spouse. Because of the mother's lack of supervision, her minor child was repeatedly sexually abused by numerous persons. Evidence in the record showed both the mother's lack of sensitivity to this issue and that she blamed her child for the molestation. The court held that to allow custody to remain with the mother would endanger the child's health and moral and emotional well being.

B. EVIDENTIARY ISSUES

Idaho v. Wright

Supreme Court of the United States, 1990.
497 U.S. 805, 110 S.Ct. 3139, 111 L.Ed.2d 638.

■ JUSTICE O'CONNOR delivered the opinion of the Court.

This case requires us to decide whether the admission at trial of certain hearsay statements made by a child declarant to an examining pediatrician violates a defendant's rights under the Confrontation Clause of the Sixth Amendment.

Respondent Laura Lee Wright was jointly charged with Robert L. Giles of two counts of lewd conduct with a minor under 16, in violation of Idaho Code § 18–1508 (1987). The alleged victims were respondent's two daughters, one of whom was 5 ½ and the other 2 ½ years old at the time the crimes were charged.

Respondent and her ex-husband, Louis Wright, the father of the older daughter, had reached an informal agreement whereby each parent would have custody of the older daughter for six consecutive months. The allegations surfaced in November 1986 when the older daughter told Cynthia Goodman, Louis Wright's female companion, that Giles had had sexual intercourse with her while respondent held her down and covered her mouth, and that she had seen respondent and Giles do the same thing to respondent's younger daughter. The younger daughter was living with her parents—respondent and Giles—at the time of the alleged offenses.

Goodman reported the older daughter's disclosures to the police the next day and took the older daughter to the hospital. A medical examination of the older daughter revealed evidence of sexual abuse. One of the examining physicians was Dr. John Jambura, a pediatrician with extensive experience in child abuse cases. Police and welfare officials took the younger daughter into custody that day for protection and investigation. Dr. Jambura examined her the following day and found conditions "strongly suggestive of sexual abuse with vaginal contact," occurring approximately two to three days prior to the examination.

At the joint trial of respondent and Giles, the trial court conducted a *voir dire* examination of the younger daughter, who was three years old at the time of trial, to determine whether she was capable of testifying. The court concluded, and the parties agreed, that the younger daughter was "not capable of communicating to the jury."

At issue in this case is the admission at trial of certain statements made by the younger daughter to Dr. Jambura in response to questions he asked regarding the alleged abuse. Over objection by respondent and Giles, the trial court permitted Dr. Jambura to testify before the jury as follows:

> "Q. [By the prosecutor] Now, calling your attention then to your examination of Kathy Wright on November 10th. What—would you describe any interview dialogue that you had with Kathy at that time? Excuse me, before you get into that, would you lay a setting of where this took place and who else might have been present?
>
> "A. This took place in my office, in my examining room, and, as I recall, I believe previous testimony I said that I recall a female attendant being present, I don't recall her identity.
>
> "I started out with basically, 'Hi, how are you,' you know, 'What did you have for breakfast this morning?' Essentially a few minutes of just sort of chitchat.
>
> "Q. Was there response from Kathy to that first—those first questions?
>
> "A. There was. She started to carry on a very relaxed animated conversation. I then proceeded to just gently start asking questions

about, 'Well, how are things at home,' you know, those sorts. Gently moving into the domestic situation and then moved into four questions in particular, as I reflected in my records, 'Do you play with daddy? Does daddy play with you? Does daddy touch you with his pee-pee? Do you touch his pee-pee?' And again we then established what was meant by pee-pee, it was a generic term for genital area.

"Q. Before you get into that, what was, as best you recollect, what was her response to the question 'Do you play with daddy?'

"A. Yes, we play—I remember her making a comment about yes we play a lot and expanding on that and talking about spending time with daddy.

"Q. And 'Does daddy play with you?' Was there any response?

"A. She responded to that as well, that they played together in a variety of circumstances and, you know, seemed very unaffected by the question.

"Q. And then what did you say and her response?

"A. When I asked her 'Does daddy touch you with his pee-pee,' she did admit to that. When I asked, 'Do you touch his pee-pee,' she did not have any response.

"Q. Excuse me. Did you notice any change in her affect or attitude in that line of questioning?

"A. Yes.

"Q. What did you observe?

"A. She would not—oh, she did not talk any further about that. She would not elucidate what exactly—what kind of touching was taking place, or how it was happening. She did, however, say that daddy does do this with me, but he does it a lot more with my sister than with me.

"Q. And how did she offer that last statement? Was that in response to a question or was that just a volunteered statement?

"A. That was a volunteered statement as I sat and waited for her to respond, again after she sort of clammed-up, and that was the next statement that she made after just allowing some silence to occur." Id., at 121–123.

On cross-examination, Dr. Jambura acknowledged that a picture that he drew during his questioning of the younger daughter had been discarded. Dr. Jambura also stated that although he had dictated notes to summarize the conversation, his notes were not detailed and did not record any changes in the child's affect or attitude.

The trial court admitted these statements under Idaho's residual hearsay exception, which provides in relevant part:

"Rule 803. Hearsay exceptions; availability of declarant immaterial.—The following are not excluded by the hearsay rule, even though the declarant is available as a witness.

. . .

"(24) Other exceptions. A statement not specifically covered by any of the foregoing exceptions but having equivalent circumstantial guarantees of trustworthiness, if the court determines that (A) the statement is offered as evidence of a material fact; (B) the statement is more probative on the point for which it is offered than any other evidence which the proponent can procure through reasonable efforts; and (C) the general purposes of these rules and the interests of justice will best be served by admission of the statement into evidence." Idaho Rule Evid. 803(24).

Respondent and Giles were each convicted of two counts of lewd conduct with a minor under 16 and sentenced to 20 years imprisonment. Each appealed only from the conviction involving the younger daughter. . . .

. . .

We granted certiorari and now affirm.

The Confrontation Clause of the Sixth Amendment, made applicable to the States through the Fourteenth Amendment, provides: "In all criminal prosecutions, the accused shall enjoy the right . . . to be confronted with the witnesses against him."

From the earliest days of our Confrontation Clause jurisprudence, we have consistently held that the Clause does not necessarily prohibit the admission of hearsay statements against a criminal defendant, even though the admission of such statements might be thought to violate the literal terms of the Clause.

Although we have recognized that hearsay rules and the Confrontation Clause are generally designed to protect similar values, we have also been careful not to equate the Confrontation Clause's prohibitions with the general rule prohibiting the admission of hearsay statements. The Confrontation Clause, in other words, bars the admission of some evidence that would otherwise be admissible under an exception to the hearsay rule.

In *Ohio v. Roberts,* we set forth "a general approach" for determining when incriminating statements admissible under an exception to the hearsay rule also meet the requirements of the Confrontation Clause. We noted that the Confrontation Clause "operates in two separate ways to restrict the range of admissible hearsay." "First, in conformance with the Framers' preference for face-to-face accusation, the Sixth Amendment establishes a rule of necessity. In the usual case . . ., the prosecution must either produce or demonstrate the unavailability of, the declarant whose statement it wishes to use against the defendant." Second, once a witness is shown to be unavailable, "his statement is admissible only if it bears adequate 'indicia of reliability.' Reliability can be inferred without more in a case where the evidence falls within a firmly rooted hearsay exception. In other cases, the evidence must be excluded, at least absent a showing of particularized guarantees of trustworthiness."

. . .

Applying the *Roberts* approach to this case, we first note that this case does not raise the question whether, before a child's out-of-court statements are admitted, the Confrontation Clause requires the prosecution to show that a child witness is unavailable at trial—and, if so, what that showing requires. The trial court in this case found that respondent's younger daughter was incapable of communicating with the jury, and defense counsel agreed. The court below neither questioned this finding nor discussed the general requirement of unavailability. For purposes of defending this case, we assume without deciding that, to the extent the unavailability requirement applies in this case, the younger daughter was an unavailable witness within the meaning of the Confrontation Clause.

The crux of the question presented is therefore whether the State, as the proponent of evidence presumptively barred by the hearsay rule and the Confrontation Clause, has carried its burden of proving that the younger daughter's incriminating statements to Dr. Jambura bore sufficient indicia of reliability to withstand scrutiny under the Clause....

We think the Supreme Court of Idaho properly focused on the presumptive unreliability of the out-of-court statements and on the suggestive manner in which Dr. Jambura conducted the interview. Viewing the totality of the circumstances surrounding the younger daughter's responses to Dr. Jambura's questions, we find no special reason for supposing that the incriminating statements were particularly trustworthy. The younger daughter's last statement regarding the abuse of the older daughter, however, presents a closer question. According to Dr. Jambura, the younger daughter "volunteered" that statement "after she sort of clammed-up." Although the spontaneity of the statement and the change in demeanor suggest that the younger daughter was telling the truth when she made the statement, we note that it is possible that "[i]f there is evidence of prior interrogation, prompting, or manipulation by adults, spontaneity may be an inaccurate indicator of trustworthiness." Moreover, the statement was not made under circumstances of reliability comparable to those required, for example, for the admission of excited utterances or statements made for purposes of medical diagnosis or treatment. Given the presumption of inadmissibility accorded accusatory hearsay statements not admitted pursuant to a firmly rooted hearsay exception, we agree with the court below that the State has failed to show that the younger daughter's incriminating statements to the pediatrician possessed sufficient "particularized guarantees of trustworthiness" under the Confrontation Clause to overcome that presumption.

. . .

NOTES

1. The Supreme Court has taken a number of child-assault cases raising the conflict between the Confrontation Clause and the protection of children witnesses. In Coy v. Iowa, 487 U.S. 1012 (1988), for example, the Court overturned a sexual assault conviction that resulted from a trial in which a child witness testified from behind a screen and in which there had been no particularized showing that such a procedure was necessary to avert a risk of harm to the child. In Mayland v. Craig, 497 U.S. 836 (1990), the Court upheld a conviction that resulted from a trial in which a child witness testified via closed circuit television after such a showing of necessity. In White v. Illinois, 502 U.S. 346 (1992), the Court upheld a conviction based on the "spontaneous declaration" and "medical examination" exceptions to the hearsay rule when a four-year-old child was emotionally unable to testify in court.

2. In M.L.B. v. S.L.J., 519 U.S. 102 (1996), the Supreme Court held that a state may not condition appeals from decisions to terminate parental rights on the parent's ability to pay record preparation fees. Such a requirement, the Court said, violated the Due Process and Equal Protection clauses of the Fourteenth Amendment.

Baltimore City Dept. of Social Services v. Bouknight

Supreme Court of the United States, 1990.
493 U.S. 549, 110 S.Ct. 900, 107 L.Ed.2d 992.

■ JUSTICE O'CONNOR delivered the opinion of the Court.

In this action, we must decide whether a mother, the custodian of a child pursuant to a court order, may invoke the Fifth Amendment privilege against self-incrimination to resist an order of the Juvenile Court to produce the child. We hold that she may not.

Petitioner Maurice M. is an abused child. When he was three months old, he was hospitalized with a fractured left femur, and examination revealed several partially healed bone fractures and other indications of severe physical abuse. In the hospital, respondent Bouknight, Maurice's mother, was observed shaking Maurice, dropping him in his crib despite his spica cast, and otherwise handling him in a manner inconsistent with his recovery and continued health. Hospital personnel notified Baltimore City Department of Social Services (BCDSS), of suspected child abuse. In February 1987, BCDSS secured a court order removing Maurice from Bouknight's control and placing him in shelter care. Several months later, the shelter care order was inexplicably modified to return Maurice to Bouknight's custody temporarily. Following a hearing held shortly thereafter, the Juvenile Court declared Maurice to be a "child in need of assistance," thus asserting jurisdiction over Maurice and placing him under BCDSS's continuing oversight. BCDSS agreed that Bouknight could continue as custodian of the child, but only pursuant to extensive conditions set forth in a court-approved protective supervision order. The order required Bouknight to "cooperate with BCDSS," "continue in therapy," participate in parental aid and training programs, and "refrain from physically punishing [Maurice]." The order's terms were "all subject to the further Order of the Court." Bouknight's attorney signed the order, and Bouknight in a separate form set forth her agreement to each term.

Eight months later, fearing for Maurice's safety, BCDSS returned to Juvenile Court. BCDSS caseworkers related that Bouknight would not cooperate with them and had in nearly every respect violated the terms of the protective order. BCDSS stated that Maurice's father had recently died in a shooting incident and that Bouknight, in light of the results of a psychological examination and her history of drug use, could not provide adequate care for the child. On April 20, 1988, the Court granted BCDSS's petition to remove Maurice from Bouknight's control for placement in foster care. BCDSS officials also petitioned for judicial relief from Bouknight's failure to produce Maurice or reveal where he could be found. The petition recounted that on two recent visits by BCDSS officials to Bouknight's home, she had refused to reveal the location of the child or had indicated that the child was with an aunt whom she would not identify. The petition further asserted that inquiries of Bouknight's known relatives had revealed that none of them had recently seen Maurice and that BCDSS had prompted the police to issue a missing persons report and referred the case for investigation by the police homicide division. Also on April 20, the Juvenile Court, upon a hearing on the petition, cited Bouknight for violating the protective custody order and for failing to appear at the hearing. Bouknight had indicated to her attorney that she would appear with the child, but also expressed fear that if she appeared the State would " 'snatch the child.' " The court issued an order to show cause why Bouknight should not be held in civil contempt for failure to produce the child. Expressing concern that Maurice was endangered or perhaps dead, the court issued a bench warrant for Bouknight's appearance.

Maurice was not produced at subsequent hearings. At a hearing one week later, Bouknight claimed that Maurice was with a relative in Dallas. Investigation revealed that the relative had not seen Maurice. The next day, following another hearing at which Bouknight again declined to produce Maurice, the Juvenile Court found Bouknight in contempt for failure to produce the child as ordered. There was and has been no indication that she was unable to comply with the order. The court directed that Bouknight be imprisoned until she "purge[d] herself of contempt by either producing [Maurice] before the court or revealing to the court his exact whereabouts."

. . .

The Fifth Amendment provides that "No person ... shall be compelled in any criminal case to be a witness against himself." U.S. Const., Amdt. 5. The Fifth Amendment's protection "applies only when the accused is compelled to make a *testimonial* communication that is incriminating." The courts below concluded that Bouknight could comply with the order through the unadorned act of producing the child, and we thus address that aspect of the order.... The Fifth Amendment's protection may ... be implicated because the act of complying with the government's demand testifies to the existence, possession, or authenticity of the things produced. But a person may not claim the Amendment's protections based upon the incrimination that may result from the contents or nature of the thing demanded. Bouknight therefore cannot claim the privilege based upon anything that examination of Maurice might reveal, nor can she assert the privilege upon the theory that compliance would assert that the child produced is in fact Maurice (a fact the State could readily establish, rendering any testimony regarding existence or authenticity insufficiently incriminating). Rather, Bouknight claims the benefit of the privilege because the act of production would amount to testimony regarding her control over and possession of Maurice. Although the State could readily introduce evidence of Bouknight's continuing control over the child—e.g., the custody order, testimony of relatives, and Bouknight's own statements to Maryland officials before invoking the privilege—her implicit communication of control over Maurice at the moment of production might aid the State in prosecuting Bouknight.

. . .

The Court has on several occasions recognized that the Fifth Amendment privilege may not be invoked to resist compliance with a regulatory regime constructed to effect the State's public purposes unrelated to the enforcement of its criminal laws.

. . .

Once Maurice was adjudicated a child in need of assistance, his care and safety became the particular object of the State's regulatory interests. Maryland first placed Maurice in shelter care, authorized placement in foster care, and then entrusted responsibility for Maurice's care to Bouknight. By accepting care of Maurice subject to the custodial order's conditions (including requirements that she cooperate with BCDSS, follow a prescribed training regime, and be subject to further court orders), Bouknight submitted to the routine operation of the regulatory system and agreed to hold Maurice in a manner consonant with the State's regulatory interests and subject to inspection by BCDSS.

. . .

We are not called upon to define the precise limitations that may exist upon the State's ability to use the testimonial aspects of Bouknight's act of production in subsequent criminal proceedings. But we note that imposition of such limitations is not foreclosed. The same custodial role that limited the ability to resist the production order may give rise to corresponding limitations upon the direct and indirect use of that testimony. The State's regulatory requirement in the usual case may neither compel incriminating testimony nor aid a criminal prosecution, but the Fifth Amendment protections are not thereby necessarily unavailable to the person who complies with the regulatory requirement after invoking the privilege and subsequently faces prosecution.

The judgment of the Court of Appeals of Maryland is reversed and the cases remanded to that court for further proceedings not inconsistent with this opinion.

So ordered.

NOTE

Jacqueline Bouknight was released from jail on October 31, 1995, after being incarcerated for 7 ½ years for civil contempt, one of the nation's longest sentences for the charge. Bouknight never did reveal the location of her son and claims to have lost track of him during her sentence. Baltimore Circuit Judge David B. Mitchell ordered Bouknight to have no contact with her son. Washington Post, Nov. 11, 1995, at D1.

C. FOSTER CARE

1. "REASONABLE EFFORTS"

The Adoption and Safe Families Act (ASFA), signed into law by President Clinton in 1997, requires that state plans for foster care and adoption assistance make "reasonable efforts . . . to preserve and reunify families (i) prior to the placement of a child in foster care, to prevent or eliminate the need for removing the child from the child's home; and (ii) to make it possible for a child to safely return to the child's home." 42 U.S.C. § 671(a)(15)(B).

In re Eden F.

Supreme Court of Connecticut, 1999.
250 Conn. 674, 741 A.2d 873.

■ PALMER, J.

In this certified appeal, we must decide whether the Appellate Court properly reversed the judgments of the trial court terminating the parental rights of the respondent mother, Ann F., with respect to her two daughters, Eden and Joann. Specifically, we must determine whether the Appellate Court properly concluded that . . . the petitioner, the commissioner of children and families (commissioner), was required to establish by clear and convincing evidence that reasonable efforts were made to reunify Ann F. with Eden and Joann as a predicate to the termination of Ann F.'s parental rights with respect to her two children. We conclude that, contrary to the determination of the Appellate Court, the commissioner was not required to make such a showing under the applicable statutory provisions. We also address two additional claims that Ann F. raised in the Appellate Court but that were not decided by that court, namely, that the trial court improperly:

(1) found that Ann F. had failed to rehabilitate herself; and (2) concluded that the termination of Ann F.'s parental rights was in Eden's best interest. We reject these claims and reverse the judgment of the Appellate Court.

The opinion of the Appellate Court sets forth the following relevant facts. "Ann F. was born in Hartford on February 27, 1959 . . . [and] spent the majority of her childhood in a foster home. In 1975, at the age of fifteen, Ann F. was admitted for psychiatric care to Norwich State Hospital (Norwich). Thereafter, she was admitted to Norwich on several more occasions with one stay lasting for more than one year."

At Norwich, she was diagnosed with chronic undifferentiated schizophrenia and other disorders over the years including bipolar disorder with psychotic features.

"While at Norwich, Ann F. met and married Thomas F. in 1982 and her first child, Eden, was born on July 2, 1988. Eden is a child with special needs. [The department of children and youth services, now the department of children and families (department)] removed Eden from Ann F.'s care when Eden was only five days old, due to Ann F.'s psychiatric state. The court granted temporary custody of Eden to [the department] on July 15, 1988. On September 22, 1989, Eden was committed to the commissioner . . . as a neglected child because of the hospital admission of Ann F. On that date, Ann F. signed expectations that were accepted by the court. Eden remained in foster care until she was nearly three years old.

"Although on January 31, 1991, the court granted [the department's] petition to extend Eden's commitment, Eden began living with [Ann F.] on February 1, 1991. While Eden lived with [Ann F., the department] worked with Ann F. and provided a number of services to her. On June 13, 1991, the [department] filed a petition to revoke Eden's commitment. The court granted [the department's] motion to revoke commitment on August 7, 1991.

"In 1992, [the department] received four referrals concerning Ann F.'s conduct with Eden, including a report of Ann F.'s yelling, shaking and hitting Eden. Another referral, which was made just prior to the birth of Ann F.'s second child, Joann, on September 8, 1992, was from the Manchester police department on July 16, 1992, alleging that '. . . Ann F . . . is a repeated complainant of sexual assault and strange goings on at the home. She claims that Randy M., the [alleged] father of . . . [Joann], sneaks in through the window at about 1:30 a.m. and sexually assaults [her].' That report also stated that she usually slept through it. It also indicated that 'the condition of the apartment is very slovenly with trash and clutter strewn about. The smoke detector was also deactivated due to the removal of the battery.' In a call to [the department], Ann F. reported that her boyfriend, Randy M., would break into her apartment with seven men who sexually harassed her and performed witchcraft techniques on her.

"In March, 1993, [the department] received a referral from the Manchester Memorial Hospital emergency room that Ann F. had walked out of the visitor's lounge leaving Eden, then age four, to care for Joann, then seven months old. At that time, Ann F. was admitted to [that] hospital on a physician's emergency certificate, and [the department] invoked a ninety-six hour hold on both children, who have been cared for in the same foster home ever since. Ann F. was transferred from Manchester Memorial Hospital to Cedarcrest Regional Hospital (Cedarcrest), where she remained until August, 1993. Upon her discharge from Cedarcrest, she began receiving services from the Manchester Memorial Hospital Outpatient Mental Health

Clinic [(clinic)] and the Horizons program [(Horizons)]. Horizons provides services to the psychologically impaired so they can live independently in the community. . . .

"On March 12, 1993, [the department] filed a petition seeking the commitment of Eden and Joann. On that date, the court granted an order of temporary custody of both children to [the department]. On October 21, 1993, the court adjudicated Eden and Joann neglected based on Ann F.'s plea of nolo contendere. The court committed the children to the department for the statutory period. Also on that date, Ann F. signed, and the court entered, a new set of expectations.

"Ann F. was hospitalized three times in 1993 for mental instability. Eden and Joann were taken for weekly visits with Ann F. while she was in Cedarcrest in 1993. Weekly visitation continued after she returned home. Ann F. continued outpatient treatment at [the clinic]. Throughout the remainder of 1993 and into the first six months of 1994, Ann F. stabilized within her limitations and participated in weekly supervised visits with her two children.

"On June 1, 1994, the department developed what it called 'an extensive plan . . . to determine what was in the best interest of [Ann F.'s] children.' This plan was to give [Ann F.] every opportunity to prove her parenting abilities and was to be executed through 'the Exchange Club,' which would supervise the children's visits with Ann F. The length of these visits would be increased from one hour to one and one-half hours for seven weeks. If these visits were successful, a series of unsupervised visits could be scheduled.

"At a department case status conference on July 26, 1994, the consensus opinion was that due to Eden's escalating behaviors she should be thoroughly evaluated by [the] Newington Children's Hospital PEDAL[11] medical program . . . On September 4, 1994, in accordance with the Exchange Club recommendation, four weeks of unsupervised visitation began but there was no mechanism to assess these visits since they were unsupervised. On October 8, 1994, four weeks of overnight visitation began, with an emergency telephone line available if Ann F. needed assistance or had an emergency. These visits again could not be assessed since they were unsupervised. In any event, the children did not show any evidence of physical abuse. In late October, 1994, a decision was made to return Eden to Ann F. on a trial basis for two months to make a final determination of Ann F.'s capabilities of caring for [Eden]. The department's position was: 'If this two month trial was successful then strong consideration would be given to returning the youngest child, Joann, home.' . . .

"Eden was returned to Ann F. on February 27, 1995. Difficulties with the reunification quickly appeared. At the time of Eden's return, PEDAL was in the midst of conducting a comprehensive evaluation of Eden as requested by the department. As part of this evaluation, Eden was seen for the following: pediatric neurology, psychiatry, ophthalmology, audiology, psychology, education and occupational therapy. The testing for this evaluation occurred from December, 1994, through April, 1995. The results of the PEDAL evaluation were not disclosed until after April 19, 1995. The evaluation indicated that Eden 'is diagnosed with Reaction Attachment Disorder compounded by symptoms of depression, behavioral disturbance, including oppositionality and defiance.' The evaluation made a number of suggestions

11. PEDAL is an acronym for program for evaluation of development and learning.

on how to address Eden's needs given her substantial behavioral and emotional issues.

"Upon Eden's return to [Ann F.], Eden did not attend school for almost three weeks. The department was aware, *before* Eden was returned to [Ann F.], that there was a problem with the Manchester board of education in gaining her admission. Nevertheless, the department returned her.

"Additionally, Eden's parent-child therapy with Thomas Spudic, a psychologist who worked with Ann F. and the children, ceased in December, 1994, when he left Connecticut. Therapy was not resumed until sometime in March, 1995, after Eden was returned to Ann F. Moreover, even though the department made arrangements for a parent aide, who came once within the first week or so of Eden's return, neither the new therapist nor the parent aide was in place when Eden was returned.

"A crisis telephone line was put in place when Eden was returned to Ann F. The crisis line, aptly named, had as its apparent purpose to enable rapid communication by Ann F. with department staff. On Sunday, March 12, 1995, Ann F. called the crisis line and stated that she 'needed someone to talk to and Eden had been a little out of control.' Apparently, Ann F. was required to leave this information in a message. Kenneth Crosby, a department social worker, returned Ann F.'s call to the crisis line the following Friday, March 17, 1995, five days later.

"On Tuesday, March 21, 1995, the department removed Eden from [Ann F.'s] home and returned her to foster care. This removal followed an incident that occurred the prior weekend and also was reported to the department. Ann F., who had been caring for Eden without respite for twenty-four hours a day for about three weeks, went to a bingo game in the neighborhood with a female friend. Ann F. left Eden in the care of two men, one of whom Ann F. hardly knew, but who was acquainted with Ann F.'s female friend. The child of Ann F.'s female friend was also there. When Ann F. returned later that evening, there were beer cans strewn about her apartment, the sink was full of dishes, and Eden's bedroom was "trashed." There was no indication, however, that Eden had been harmed in any way.

"The day after the department removed Eden, it received a report of Eden scratching [Ann F.] as well as an anonymous caller who reported hearing Eden cry, 'mommy, don't hit me.' The department replaced Eden in her former foster home. Joann was not returned to Ann F. at all in 1995.

"On April 6, 1995, the parties agreed to, and the court granted, an extension of the [the children's] commitment to the department for the statutory period beginning April 21, 1995. On June 26, 1995, the department filed petitions in the Superior Court, Juvenile Matters, seeking to terminate the parental rights of Ann F., Randy M., the alleged father of Joann, and Thomas F., the father of Eden. Each petition alleged that 'the child has been found in a prior proceeding to have been neglected or uncared for ... [Ann F.] has failed to achieve such degree of personal rehabilitation as would encourage the belief that within a reasonable time, considering the age and needs of the child ... she ... could assume a responsible position in the life of the child.' This ground is alleged to have existed for more than one year. On July 20, 1995, the court accepted Thomas F.'s affidavit of consent to his termination of parental rights as to Eden. The petition concerning Joann was thereafter amended to allege that Randy M. had abandoned Joann, that he failed to rehabilitate and that there was no ongoing parent-child relationship as provided in § 17a–112(b). On July 24, 25, 26, 29 and 30, 1996, a trial was held on both petitions."

Following the trial, the court, citing § 17a–112(b)(2), "found by clear and convincing evidence that the parents have not achieved a useful and constructive role as parents; nor, given the needs of the children, especially Eden, [was] such rehabilitation foreseeable within a reasonable time.... [Upon consideration of each of the seven factors enumerated under § 17a–112(d), the trial court] then proceeded in the dispositional phase to find [by clear and convincing evidence] that the termination of parental rights was in the best interests of the children.

"... Ann F. also filed a 'Motion for Articulation of Decision Terminating Parental Rights of Mother.' The trial court, in articulating its decision, stated, inter alia, that it responded to each of the five specific questions raised [in Ann F.'s motion] including the finding that the department had made reasonable efforts to reunify both Eden and Joann with [Ann F.]. The court concluded that those findings were supported by clear and convincing evidence." (Citation omitted; internal quotation marks omitted.)

On appeal, the Appellate Court concluded that, pursuant to § 17a–112, the trial court was required to find, by clear and convincing evidence, that the department had made reasonable efforts to reunite Eden and Joann with Ann F. The Appellate Court further concluded that the facts did not support such a finding with respect to either child. Consequently, the Appellate Court reversed the trial court's judgment terminating Ann F.'s parental rights with respect to Eden and Joann and remanded the case to the trial court for dismissal of both petitions. On the commissioner's appeal to this court, we reverse the judgment of the Appellate Court.

We first must decide whether the Appellate Court properly determined that the commissioner was required to prove, by clear and convincing evidence, that reasonable efforts were made to reunify Ann F. with her children. The commissioner claims that she was not required to establish that the department had made reasonable reunification efforts because, contrary to the conclusion of the Appellate Court, § 17a–112 contained no such mandate at the time the petitions were filed in this case. Ann F. claims that the Appellate Court properly determined that the commissioner was required to prove reasonable reunification efforts by clear and convincing evidence. Alternatively, Ann F. contends that, even if the commissioner was not required to show that reasonable efforts were made to reunite her with Eden and Joann, the 1995 amendment to § 17a–112; Public Acts 1995, No. 95–238, § 3 (P.A. 95–238);[17] which expressly requires a court to find that the

17. Public Act 95–238, § 3, provides in relevant part: "Section 17a–112 of the general statutes is repealed and the following is substituted in lieu thereof ...

"(b) The superior court upon hearing and notice, as provided in sections 45a–716 and 45a–717, may grant such petition if it finds THAT THE DEPARTMENT OF CHILDREN AND FAMILIES HAS MADE REASONABLE EFFORTS TO REUNIFY THE CHILD WITH THE PARENT AND, upon clear and convincing evidence, that the termination is in the best interest of the child, and that ... with respect to any nonconsenting parent, over an extended period of time, which, except as provided in subsection (c) of this section, shall not be less than one year: (1) The child has been abandoned by the parent in the sense that the parent has failed to maintain a reasonable degree of interest, concern or responsibility as to the welfare of the child; or (2) the parent of a child who has been found by the superior court to have been neglected or uncared for in a prior proceeding has failed to achieve such degree of personal rehabilitation as would encourage the belief that within a reasonable time, considering the age and needs of the child, such parent could assume a responsible position in the life of the child; or (3) the child has been denied, by reason of an act or acts of parental commission or omission, the care, guidance or control necessary for his physical, educational, moral or emotional well-being. Nonaccidental or inadequately explained serious physical injury to a child shall constitute prima facie evidence of acts of parental commission or

department has made reasonable efforts to reunify parent and child, is retroactive and, therefore, applicable to the termination petitions filed in this case. We reject both of Ann F.'s claims and conclude that the commissioner was not required to prove that reasonable efforts were made to reunify Ann F. with her children.

Under § 17a–112, a hearing on a petition to terminate parental rights consists of two phases: the adjudicatory phase and the dispositional phase. During the adjudicatory phase, the trial court must determine whether one or more of the four grounds for termination of parental rights set forth in § 17a–112(b) exists by clear and convincing evidence. ... One of the four predicates for the termination of parental rights under § 17a–112(b) covers the situation in which, over an extended period of time, "the parent of a child who has been found by the superior court to have been neglected or uncared for in a prior proceeding has failed to achieve such degree of personal rehabilitation as would encourage the belief that within a reasonable time, considering the age and needs of the child, such parent could assume a responsible position in the life of the child ..."

If the trial court determines that a statutory ground for termination exists, then it proceeds to the dispositional phase. During the dispositional phase, the trial court must determine whether termination is in the best interests of the child. When the petitions in this case were filed, § 17a–112(d) required that the trial court, in determining whether to terminate parental rights, "consider and ... make written findings regarding" seven separate factors, including: "(1) the timeliness, nature and extent of services offered or provided to the parent and the child by an agency to facilitate the reunion of the child with the parent; [and] (2) whether the department ... has made reasonable efforts to reunite the family pursuant to the federal [Adoption Assistance and] Child Welfare Act of 1980, as amended ..."

The question of whether the commissioner was required to prove that the department had made reasonable efforts to reunify Ann F. with Eden and Joann under the applicable statutory scheme "is a matter of statutory interpretation, which is a matter of law, requiring plenary review.... In interpreting statutes, our analysis is guided by well established principles of statutory construction. Our fundamental objective is to ascertain and give effect to the apparent intent of the legislature.... In seeking to discern that intent, we look to the words of the statute itself, to the legislative history and circumstances surrounding its enactment, to the legislative policy it was designed to implement, and to its relationship to existing legislation and common law principles governing the same general subject matter."

At the time that the petitions were filed in this case, § 17a–112 did not contain any language to suggest that the court could terminate parental rights only upon a finding, by a standard of clear and convincing evidence or otherwise, that the department had made reasonable efforts to reunify parent and child. Rather, pursuant to § 17a–112(b), the trial court was

omission sufficient for the termination of parental rights; or (4) there is no ongoing parent-child relationship, which means the relationship that ordinarily develops as a result of a parent having met on a day to day basis the physical, emotional, moral and educational needs of the child and to allow further time for the establishment or reestablishment of such parent-child relationship would be detrimental to the best interest of the child. THE REQUIREMENT THAT THE DEPARTMENT OF CHILDREN AND FAMILIES HAS MADE REASONABLE EFFORTS TO REUNIFY THE CHILD WITH THE PARENT SHALL NOT APPLY TO TERMINATIONS OF PARENTAL RIGHTS BASED ON CONSENT OR TERMINATIONS OF PARENTAL RIGHTS WHERE SUCH REASONABLE EFFORTS AT REUNIFICATION WERE NOT POSSIBLE...."

authorized to terminate parental rights upon a showing, by clear and convincing evidence, first, that one or more of the four scenarios set forth in § 17a–112(b) had been proven, and second, that the termination of parental rights was in the best interest of the child. Although § 17a–112(d)(1) and (2) mandated that the trial court make written findings regarding the timeliness, nature, extent and reasonableness of the efforts made to reunify parent and child, § 17a–112 contained nothing to indicate that any such finding was a prerequisite to the termination of parental rights. Thus, when the petitions in this case were filed, the factors to be considered under § 17a–112(d) served only to guide the trial court in making its ultimate decision whether to grant the termination petition. Thus, "the fact that the legislature [had interpolated] objective guidelines into the open-ended fact-oriented statutes which govern [parental termination] disputes should not be construed as a predetermined weighing of evidence by the legislature. Where ... the record reveals that the trial court's ultimate conclusions [regarding termination of parental rights] are supported by clear and convincing evidence, we will not reach an opposite conclusion on the basis of any one segment of the many factors considered in a termination proceeding."

The Appellate Court did not expressly articulate its rationale for concluding that the trial court was required to find, as a predicate to the termination of Ann F.'s parental rights, that the commissioner established, clearly and convincingly, that reasonable efforts were made to reunify Ann F. with Eden and Joann. Ann F. claims, however, that the Appellate Court's construction of § 17a–112 is supported by our state's public policy, as expressed by the legislature, "to strengthen the family and to make the home safe for children by enhancing the parental capacity for good child care...."[20] A general statement of public policy underscoring the desirability of maintaining the integrity of the family unit, however, cannot trump the plain and unambiguous language of the statutory provision detailing with specificity the substantive rights of the parties to a termination proceeding. Under § 17a–112(b), the court is authorized to terminate parental rights only in four limited circumstances and, moreover, the court is required to make written findings regarding the seven separate factors set forth in § 17a–112(d), including "the timeliness, nature and extent of services offered or provided to the parent and the child by an agency to facilitate the reunion of the child with the parent" and "whether the department ... has made reasonable efforts to reunite the family pursuant to the federal [Adoption Assistance and] Child Welfare Act of 1980, as amended...." Thus, our interpretation of § 17a–112 as not requiring the commissioner to prove reasonable efforts at reunification does not contravene the public policy declared by the legislature in § 17a–101.

Ann F. also contends that the federal Adoption Assistance and Child Welfare Act of 1980 (act) provides support for her contention that, under § 17a–112, her parental rights could not be terminated absent a showing, by clear and convincing evidence, that the department had made reasonable efforts at reunification. As the Appellate Court has stated, however, "the act ... is an appropriations act and does not apply to individual actions or

20. *General Statutes § 17a–101(a)* provides: "The public policy of this state is: To protect children whose health and welfare may be adversely affected through injury and neglect; to strengthen the family and to make the home safe for children by enhancing the parental capacity for good child care; to provide a temporary or permanent nurturing and safe environment for children when necessary; and for these purposes to require the reporting of suspected child abuse, investigation of such reports by a social agency, and provision of services, where needed, to such child and family."

judicial findings ... but merely sets forth general guidelines for a state's continued eligibility to receive funds for foster care maintenance." The act, therefore, has no bearing on the question of whether, under § 17a–112, the commissioner was required to establish, as a predicate to the termination of Ann F.'s parental rights, that the department had made reasonable efforts to reunite Ann F. with Eden and Joann.

Finally, Ann F. asserts that because principles of due process require proof of the facts that warrant a termination of parental rights by clear and convincing evidence, we must construe § 17a–112(b) as embodying the requirement that the commissioner establish, by clear and convincing evidence, that the department had made reasonable efforts to reunite Ann F. with her two children. We disagree. Proof of reasonable reunification efforts is not a constitutionally mandated prerequisite to granting a petition for the termination of parental rights. The constitutional requirement of proof by clear and convincing evidence applies only to those findings upon which the ultimate decision to terminate parental rights is predicated. Prior to the 1995 amendment of § 17a–112, the reasonableness of the department's efforts at reunification was not one of the factors that the legislature had incorporated in § 17a–112(b) as a prerequisite to termination.

If, prior to 1995, the legislature had intended to condition the termination of parental rights on a finding that reasonable efforts were made to reunify parent with child, it easily could have expressed this intent. Indeed, the legislature manifested just such an intent when, in 1995, it amended § 17a–112 to add the requirement that Ann F. would have us read into the pre-1995 amendment version of the statute. No such legislative directive can be found in the language or history of § 17a–112 as it existed prior to its 1995 amendment. See id. ("absent compelling countervailing reasons, we will not impute to the legislature an intent that is not apparent from the plain statutory language"). Under that statutory provision, the trial court was required to *consider* the efforts the department made to reunify Ann F. with Eden and Joann, and to *make written findings* regarding those efforts, and the trial court did so. For petitions filed before the effective date of the 1995 amendment, however, the commissioner was not required to establish the *reasonableness* of those efforts.

Alternatively, Ann F. claims that P.A. 95–238, which amended § 17a–112(b) by adding the requirement that the department make reasonable efforts to reunify parent and child, applies retroactively.[23] We reject this claim.

"Whether to apply a statute retroactively or prospectively depends upon the intent of the legislature in enacting the statute. ... In order to determine the legislative intent, we utilize well established rules of statutory construction. Our point of departure is *General Statutes § 55–3*, which states: No provision of the general statutes, not previously contained in the statutes of the state, which imposes any new obligation on any person or corporation, shall be construed to have retrospective effect. The obligations referred to in the statute are those of substantive law.... Thus, we have uniformly interpreted § 55–3 as a rule of *presumed* legislative intent that statutes

23. Public Act 95–238 contains no express requirement that reasonable efforts at reunification shall be proven by clear and convincing evidence. The clear and convincing standard, however, is constitutionally mandated. One of the 1996 amendments to § 17a–112; Public Acts 1996, No. 96–246, § 18; expressly provides that the court may grant a termination petition only upon a showing, by clear and convincing evidence, that the department has made reasonable reunification efforts.

affecting *substantive* rights shall apply prospectively only.... This presumption in favor of prospective applicability, however, may be rebutted when the legislature clearly and unequivocally expresses its intent that the legislation shall apply retrospectively.... Where an amendment is intended to clarify the original intent of an earlier statute, it necessarily has retroactive effect.... We generally look to the statutory language and the pertinent legislative history to ascertain whether the legislature intended that the amendment be given retrospective effect."

Neither the language nor the history of P.A. 95–238 contains any indication that the legislature intended that it be applied retroactively. Ann F. contends, however, that the amendment is procedural, rather than substantive and, consequently, we must presume that the legislature intended its retroactive application. Ann F. also claims that the legislative debate on the 1995 amendment indicates that it was intended to clarify the original intent of the earlier statute and, therefore, should be applied retroactively for that reason. In support of her claims, Ann F. relies on several comments made by legislators during the debate on the bill in the House of Representatives.

We disagree with Ann F.'s claims. First, the requirement that the department make reasonable efforts to reunite parent and child affects the substantive rights of the parties to a termination proceeding. The requirement of reunification efforts provides additional substantive protection for any parent who contests a termination action, and places a concomitant burden on the state to take appropriate measures designed to secure reunification of parent and child. Moreover, to the extent that the requirement reflects an important state policy favoring the reunification of parent and child, as Ann F. herself has asserted, the express recognition of that policy in P.A. 95–238 cannot be considered procedural rather than substantive.

Furthermore, P.A. 95–238, which contains five separate sections, also made other substantive changes in the law. For example, §§ 3 and 5 of P.A. 95–238 reduced the time period within which the parental rights with respect to certain children under the age of seven may be terminated. We are especially reluctant to presume that the legislature intended the retroactive application of such provisions, for, as our Appellate Court has stated: "Although the issue of whether parental rights should have been terminated is to be decided by a trial court on the basis of conditions existing at the time of trial ... here is no legislative or decisional mandate allowing a trial court to decide that issue on the basis of statutes existing at the time of trial, but not in effect when the termination petition was filed.... Parents have a constitutionally protected right to raise and care for their children and that protection cannot be diluted by the use of statutory standards enacted subsequent to a petition to terminate that right, absent a counter legislative directive."

Ann F. has provided no evidence, in the legislative history or elsewhere, to suggest that the legislature intended to dilute retroactively a parent's rights under §§ 3 and 5 of P.A. 95–238.

... [W]e conclude that, because P.A. 95–238 effected substantive changes in the law regarding the termination of parental rights, Ann F.'s retroactivity claim must fail.

We turn now to Ann F.'s remaining two claims, namely, that the trial court improperly found that: (1) she had failed to rehabilitate herself in satisfaction of the requirements of § 17a–112(b)(2); and (2) the termination of her parental rights with respect to Eden was in Eden's best interest. We reject both of these claims.

. . .

We first address Ann F.'s claim that the trial court reasonably could not have found that she had failed to achieve such a degree of personal rehabilitation as would encourage the belief that, within a reasonable period of time, she could assume a responsible position with respect to her children's care. We disagree with Ann F.'s contention.

. . .

Our review of the record reveals that the evidence credited by the trial court supports its conclusion that Ann F. had failed to attain a degree of rehabilitation sufficient to warrant the belief that, at some time in the foreseeable future, she would be capable of assuming a responsible position with respect to her children's care. The trial court reasonably relied on the testimony of the three experts, Spudic, Mantell and Sadler, each of whom concluded that, in light of the serious and chronic nature of Ann F.'s mental illness, her future prospects for assuming a responsible parenting role for her children are bleak. Moreover, each of those experts had spent a considerable amount of time evaluating Ann F. and her capacity to reestablish a position of responsibility in the lives of her children. Consequently, the record contains sufficient facts to support their professional opinions.

Ann F. points to certain evidence adduced during the trial tending to establish that, over the years, she has made progress in coping with both her illness and her children. Indeed, the evidence does suggest that Ann F. has achieved a level of stability within her limitations. This fact, coupled with Ann F.'s sincere love for her daughters, evokes genuine sympathy for Ann F. and for her efforts at rehabilitation. Nevertheless, in light of all the evidence, . . . we cannot say that the trial court was clearly erroneous in concluding, by clear and convincing evidence, that Ann F. had failed to reach such a degree of rehabilitation as would encourage the belief that, within a reasonable period of time, she could assume a responsible position in the lives of her children.

Ann F. also claims that the evidence did not support the trial court's finding that termination of her parental rights with respect to Eden was in Eden's best interest. Specifically, Ann F. contends that the termination of a child's relationship with his or her parents cannot be in that child's best interest unless the purpose is to free the child for adoption. Because Eden's foster parents would not commit themselves to adopting Eden, and because there is no guarantee that an alternative adoptive family will be found, Ann F. asserts that the trial court's conclusion that Eden's best interest will be served by the termination of Ann F.'s parental rights was clearly erroneous. We disagree.

Although subsequent adoption is the preferred outcome for a child whose biological parents have had their parental rights terminated, it is not a necessary prerequisite for the termination of parental rights. While long-term stability is critical to a child's future health and development, adoption provides only one option for obtaining such stability. In this case, Eden's foster parents, despite hesitancy about committing themselves to adopting Eden, have indicated a willingness to provide Eden with a permanent foster home, assuming that such a placement is determined to be in Eden's best interest. In light of this testimony, the trial court reasonably could have concluded that the possibility of a permanent placement with Eden's current foster family was preferable to the continuing uncertainty of the status quo.

... [W]e are persuaded that, in light of all the relevant facts and considerations, including Eden's special needs and Ann F.'s demonstrated inability to meet them, Eden's need for permanency and stability, her bond with her foster family and her age, the trial court's conclusion that the commissioner had demonstrated, by clear and convincing evidence, that the termination of Ann F.'s parental rights was in Eden's best interest was not clearly erroneous.

The judgment of the Appellate Court is reversed and the case is remanded to that court with direction to affirm the judgments of the trial court.

In this opinion CALLAHAN, C. J., and BORDEN, J., concurred.

■ MCDONALD, J. (with whom BERDON, J., joins, dissenting).

I would uphold the Appellate Court's decision that: (1) the trial court was required to find, by clear and convincing evidence, that the department of children and families (department) had made reasonable efforts to reunify the respondent mother, Ann F., and her children, Eden and Joann, before terminating Ann F.'s parental rights; and (2) the trial court's determination that such efforts were made was clearly erroneous. I also disagree with part II of the majority opinion, regarding whether Ann F. had rehabilitated herself, and whether the termination of her parental rights with respect to Eden was in Eden's best interest. Accordingly, I dissent.

. . .

The termination of a parent's legal rights is "the complete severance by court order of the legal relationship, with all its rights and responsibilities, between the child and his or her parent." It is, accordingly, a most serious and sensitive judicial action. The United States Supreme Court has recognized that "a natural parent's desire for and right to the companionship, care, custody, and management of his or her children is an interest far more precious than any property right." (Internal quotation marks omitted.) "If the State prevails, it will have worked a unique kind of deprivation.... A parent's interest in the accuracy and justice of the decision to terminate his or her parental status is, therefore, a commanding one." For these reasons, the United States Supreme Court held that "before a State may sever completely and irrevocably the rights of parents in their natural child, due process requires that the State support its allegations by at least clear and convincing evidence." The clear and convincing standard is "necessary to preserve fundamental fairness in a variety of government-initiated proceedings that threaten the individual involved with a significant deprivation of liberty...."

I read *Santosky* to require the department to establish, by at least clear and convincing evidence, the conditions for the termination of parental rights. Under the revision of § 17a–112(d)(2) in effect at the time of trial, the court was required to consider and make written findings regarding whether the department had made reasonable efforts to reunite the family before terminating Ann F.'s parental rights. I would find that the department was required to make such reasonable efforts as a condition of terminating parental rights and that the commissioner was required to prove, by clear and convincing evidence, that those efforts were made. The statute's requirement that the court consider and make written findings regarding such reasonable efforts supports this conclusion. Any civilized and common sense reading of the requirements to forever cut off a parent's relationship with a child dictates this conclusion.

. . .

Moreover, the federal Adoption Assistance and Child Welfare Act of 1980 (federal act) requires the state to facilitate the reunification of the family in order to qualify for federal funding. ... In truth, the department, for years, has complied with the federal act. The department has submitted a plan providing for such efforts, which was approved by the secretary of health and human services, and has accepted the federal funds. Moreover, the department's policy manual, which was in effect in 1995 when the petitions to terminate Ann F.'s parental rights were filed, provides that "[the department] requires that 'reasonable efforts' be made in every case to prevent unnecessary placement or return the child to the family, *as required by federal law*." (Emphasis added.) It is difficult, to say the least, to reconcile the department's determination in the policy manual that federal law requires reasonable efforts and the department's receipt of federal funds—based on compliance with the federal act—with the commissioner's argument in this court.

Finally, I cannot imagine that the citizens of this state, or those of the United States, would countenance the termination of parental rights without a requirement of reasonable efforts on the part of a state agency to attempt to reunify a mother with her daughters. Such a requirement, I believe, is expressed both in the federal and state constitutions and required in a decent society concerned with a mother's most fundamental right to her children. In this case, Ann F., although mentally impaired, loves and wants her children, and she deserves the protection of due process before her rights to her daughters are severed permanently.

Because the majority concludes that the trial court was not required to find, by clear and convincing evidence, that the department had made reasonable efforts to reunify the family, it does not review the trial court's conclusion to that effect. I would affirm the Appellate Court's careful, detailed and proper decision that the trial court's conclusion was not supported by clear and convincing evidence.

As the Appellate Court noted, the department's plan for reunification "lacked planning on a number of critical issues...." Ann F. never was afforded a fair chance to succeed with Eden. When the department reunified Ann F. with Eden on February 27, 1995, Eden's own significant psychological and behavioral needs still were formally being assessed. The department chose not to wait for the results of this assessment, and proceeded with the reunification despite the ongoing evaluation of Eden. Ann F. and her support service providers, i.e., her therapist and department case manager, were not informed of the reunification with Eden until the actual day on which it occurred. The commissioner provided a crisis telephone line for Ann F.; however, when she placed a telephone call to the department, no one returned her call for five days. The department also provided Ann F. with a parent aide, but the aide only visited twice over the course of the month. When Eden returned to live with Ann F., the department had not enrolled Eden in school, and Eden did not have her usual therapeutic services for most of the reunification period. Ann F. was not provided with any respite and, because Eden was not attending school, Ann F. had to care for her, seven days a week, twenty-four hours a day, for three weeks. Ann F. was programmed for failure. The end came when Ann F. went out to play bingo with a friend and left Eden in the care of two people. When the department learned that Eden's bedroom was "trashed" that evening, and that the babysitters had been drinking beer in the apartment, it removed Eden from Ann F.'s care.

The department did not demonstrate any efforts, whatsoever, to reunify Ann F. with her youngest child, Joann, despite the fact that Joann did not share her sister Eden's functional problems and would have been easier to handle.

Because the department did not properly implement the plan to reunify Ann F. with Eden and did not make *any* efforts to reunify Ann F. with Joann, I would affirm the judgment of the Appellate Court reversing the judgments of the trial court and order the trial court to restore Ann F.'s parental rights.

. . .

Accordingly, I respectfully dissent.

2. Termination of Parental Rights

In re Michael B.

Court of Appeals of New York, 1992.
80 N.Y.2d 299, 590 N.Y.S.2d 60, 604 N.E.2d 122.

■ Kaye, J.

This appeal from a custody determination, pitting a child's foster parents against his biological father, centers on the meaning of the statutory term "best interest of the child," and particularly on the weight to be given a child's bonding with his long-time foster family in deciding what placement is in his best interest. The biological father (appellant) on one side, and respondent foster parents (joined by respondent Law Guardian) on the other, each contend that a custody determination in their favor is in the best interest of the child, as that term is used in Social Services Law § 392(6), the statute governing dispositions with respect to children in foster care.

The subject of this protracted battle is Michael B., born July 29, 1985 with a positive toxicology for cocaine. Michael was voluntarily placed in foster care from the hospital by his mother, who was unmarried at the time of the birth and listed no father on the birth certificate. Michael's four siblings were then also in foster care, residing in different homes. At three months, before the identity of his father was known, Michael—needing extraordinary care—was placed in the home of intervenor Maggie W. L., a foster parent certified by respondent Catholic Child Care Society (the agency), and the child remained with the L.'s for more than five years, until December 1990. It is undisputed that the agency initially assured Mrs. L. this was a "preadoptive" placement.

Legal proceedings began in May 1987, after appellant had been identified as Michael's father. The agency sought to terminate the rights of both biological parents and free the child for adoption, alleging that for more than a year following Michael's placement the parents had failed to substantially, continuously or repeatedly maintain contact with Michael and plan for his future, although physically and financially able to do so. Michael's mother (since deceased) never appeared in the proceeding, and a finding of permanent neglect as to her was made in November 1987. Appellant did appear and in September 1987 consented to a finding of permanent neglect, and to committing custody and guardianship to the agency on condition that the children be placed with their two godmothers. That order was later vacated, on appellant's application to withdraw his pleas and obtain custody, because the agency had not in fact placed the children with their godmothers. In late 1987, appellant—a long-time alcohol and substance abuser—entered an 18–month residential drug rehabilitation program and first began to visit Michael.

In August 1988, appellant, the agency and the Law Guardian agreed to reinstatement of the permanent neglect finding, with judgment suspended for 12 months, on condition that appellant: (1) enroll in a program teaching household management and parenting skills; (2) cooperate by attending and complying with the program; (3) remain drug-free, and periodically submit to drug testing, with test results to be delivered to the agency; (4) secure and maintain employment; (5) obtain suitable housing; and (6) submit a plan for the children's care during his working day. The order recited that it was without prejudice to the agency recalendaring the case for a de novo hearing on all allegations of the petition should appellant fail to satisfy the conditions, and otherwise said nothing more of the consequences that would follow on appellant's compliance or noncompliance.

As the 12–month period neared expiration, the agency sought a hearing to help "determine the status and placement of the children." Although appellant was unemployed (he was on public assistance) and had not submitted to drug testing during the year, Family Court at the hearing held October 24, 1989 was satisfied that "there seem[ed] to be substantial compliance" with the conditions of the suspended judgment. . . .

On December 21, 1989, the Law Guardian presented a report indicating that Michael might suffer severe psychological damage if removed from his foster home, and argued for a "best interests" hearing, based on Michael's bonding with the L.'s and, by contrast, his lack of bonding with appellant, who had visited him infrequently. Family Court questioned whether it even had authority for such a hearing, but stayed the order directing Michael's discharge to appellant pending its determination. Michael's siblings, then approximately twelve, eight, seven and six years old, were released to appellant in January and July 1990. Litigation continued as to Michael.

In November 1990, Family Court directed Michael's discharge to appellant, concluding that it was without "authority or jurisdiction" to rehear the issue of custody based on the child's best interest, and indeed that Michael had been wrongfully held in foster care. The court noted, additionally, that the Law Guardian's arguments as to Michael's best interest went to issues of bonding with his temporary custodians rather than appellant's insufficiency as a parent—bonding that had been reinforced by the agency's failure to ensure sufficient contacts with appellant during the proceedings ... The court directed that Michael commence immediate weekend visitation with appellant, with a view to transfer within 60 days. Michael was discharged to appellant in December 1990.

The Appellate Division reversed and remitted for a new hearing and new consideration of Michael's custody, concluding that dismissal of a permanent neglect petition cannot divest Family Court of its continuing jurisdiction over a child until there has been a "best interests" custody disposition *(171 AD2d 790)*. As for the relevance of bonding, the Appellate Division held that, given *Matter of Bennett v. Jeffreys*—referring particularly to Michael's long residence with his foster parents—Family Court should have conducted a hearing to consider issues such as the impact on the child of a change in custody. There having been no question of appellant's fitness, however, the Appellate Division permitted Michael to remain with his father pending the new determination.

On remittal, Family Court heard extensive testimony—including testimony from appellant, the foster parents, the agency (having changed its goal to discharge to appellant), and psychological, psychiatric and social work professionals (who overwhelmingly favored continued foster care over discharge to appellant)—but adhered to its determination that Michael should be released to his father. Family Court found appellant "fit, available and capable of adequately providing for the health, safety and welfare of the subject child, and . . . it is in the child's best interest to be returned to his father."

Again the Appellate Division reversed Family Court's order, this time itself awarding custody to the foster parents under Social Services Law § 392(6)(b), and remitting the matter to a different Family Court Judge solely to determine appellant's visitation rights. Exercising its own authority—as broad as that of the hearing court—to assess the credibility of witnesses and character and temperament of the parents, the court reviewed the evidence and, while pointing up appellant's many deficiencies, significantly stopped short of finding him an unfit parent, as it had the power to do. Rather, the court looked to Michael's lengthy stay and psychological bonding with the foster family, which it felt gave rise to extraordinary circumstances meriting an award of custody to the foster parents. According to the Appellate Division, the evidence "overwhelmingly demonstrate[d] that Michael's foster parents are better able than his natural father to provide for his physical, emotional, and intellectual needs." Since early 1992, Michael has once again resided with the L.'s.

While prolonged, inconclusive proceedings and seesawing custody of a young child—all in the name of Michael's best interest—could not conceivably serve his interest at all, we granted appellant father's motion for leave to appeal, and now reverse the Appellate Division's central holdings. The opinions of Family Court specifying deficiencies of the agency and foster parents, and the opinions of the Appellate Division specifying inadequacies of the biological parent, leave little question that the only blameless person is the child. But rather than assess fault, our review will address the legal standards that have twice divided Family Court and the Appellate Division, hopefully minimizing recurrences, for this child and others, of the tragic scenario now before us.

Analysis

Appellant no longer disputes that Family Court retained jurisdiction to consider the child's best interest in connection with an award of custody even after the finding that he had substantially satisfied the conditions of the suspended judgment. All parties agree with the correctness of the Appellate Division determination that, despite appellant's apparent compliance with the conditions of the suspended judgment, Family Court retained jurisdiction to consider the best interest of the children in foster care until a final order of disposition.

What remains the bone of contention in this Court is the scope of the requisite "best interest" inquiry under Social Services Law § 392(6). Appellant urges that in cases of foster care, so long as the biological parent is not found unfit—and he underscores that neither Family Court nor the Appellate Division found him unfit—"best interest of the child" is only a limited inquiry addressed to whether the child will suffer grievous injury if transferred out of foster care to the biological parent. Respondents, by contrast, maintain that extraordinary circumstances—such as significant bonding with foster parents, after inattention and even admitted neglect by the biological parent—trigger a full inquiry into the more suitable placement as between the biological and foster parents. Subsidiarily, appellant challenges the Appellate Division's outright award of custody to the foster parents, claiming that disposition was beyond the Court's authority under Social Services Law § 392(6).

We conclude, first, that neither party advances the correct "best interest" test in the context of temporary foster care placements, but that appellant's view is more consistent with the statutory scheme than the broad-gauge inquiry advocated by respondents and applied by the Appellate Division. Second, we hold that the award of custody to the foster parents was impermissible as we interpret Social Services Law § 392(6).

The Foster Care Scheme

This being a case of voluntary placement in foster care—a subject controlled by statute—analysis must begin with the legislative scheme, which defines and balances the parties' rights and responsibilities. An understanding of how the system is designed to operate—before the design is complicated, and even subverted, by human actors and practical realities—is essential to resolving the questions before us.

New York's foster care scheme is built around several fundamental social policy choices that have been explicitly declared by the Legislature and are binding on this Court. Under the statute, operating as written, appellant should have received the active support of both the agency in overcoming his parental deficiencies and the foster parents in solidifying his relationship with Michael, and as soon as return to the biological parent proved unrealistic, the child should have been freed for adoption.

A biological parent has a right to the care and custody of a child, superior to that of others, unless the parent has abandoned that right or is proven unfit to assume the duties and privileges of parenthood, even though the State perhaps could find "better" parents. A child is not the parent's property, but neither is a child the property of the State. Looking to the *child's* rights as well as the parents' rights to bring up their own children, the Legislature has found and declared that a child's need to grow up with a "normal family life in a permanent home" is ordinarily best met in the child's "natural home."

Parents in temporary crisis are encouraged to voluntarily place their children in foster care without fear that they will thereby forfeit their parental rights. The State's first obligation is to help the family with services to prevent its break-up, or to reunite the family if the child is out of the home. While a child is in foster care, the State must use diligent efforts to strengthen the relationship between parent and child, and work with the parent to regain custody.

Because of the statutory emphasis on the biological family as best serving a child's long-range needs, the legal rights of foster parents are necessarily limited. Legal custody of a child in foster care remains with the agency that places the child, not with the foster parents. Foster parents enter into this arrangement with the express understanding that the placement is temporary, and that the agency retains the right to remove the child upon notice at any time. As [we have made clear],"foster care custodians must deliver on demand not 16 out of 17 times, but every time, or the usefulness of foster care assignments is destroyed. To the ordinary fears in placing a child in foster care should not be added the concern that the better the foster care custodians the greater the risk that they will assert, out of love and affection grown too deep, an inchoate right to adopt." Foster parents, moreover, have an affirmative obligation—similar to the obligation of the State—to attempt to solidify the relationship between biological parent and child. While foster parents may be heard on custody issues, they have no standing to seek permanent custody absent termination of parental rights.

Fundamental also to the statutory scheme is the preference for providing children with stable, permanent homes as early as possible. "[W]hen it is clear that the natural parent cannot or will not provide a normal family home for the child and when continued foster care is not an appropriate plan for the child, then a permanent alternative home should be sought". Extended foster care is not in the child's best interest, because it deprives a child of a permanent, nurturing family relationship. Where it appears that the child may never be reunited with the biological parents, the responsible agency should institute a proceeding to terminate parental rights and free the child for adoption.

Parental rights may be terminated only upon clear and convincing proof of abandonment, inability to care for the child due to mental illness or retardation, permanent neglect, or severe or repeated child abuse. Of the permissible dispositions in a termination proceeding based on permanent neglect, the Legislature—consistent with its emphasis on the importance of biological ties, yet mindful of the child's need for early stability and permanence—has provided for a suspended judgment, which is a brief grace period designed to prepare the parent to be reunited with the child. Parents found to have permanently neglected a child may be given a second chance, where the court determines it is in the child's best interests, but that opportunity is strictly limited in time. Parents may have up to one year (and a second year only where there are "exceptional circumstances") during which they must comply with terms and conditions meant to ameliorate the difficulty. Noncompliance may lead to revocation of the judgment and termination of parental rights. Compliance may lead to dismissal of the termination petition with the child remaining subject to the jurisdiction of the Family Court until a determination is made as to the child's disposition pursuant to Social Services Law § 392(6).

Where parental rights have not been terminated, Social Services Law § 392 promotes the objectives of stability and permanency by requiring periodic review of foster care placements. The agency having custody must first petition for review after a child has been in continuous foster care for 18 months, and if no change is made, every 24 months thereafter. While foster parents who have been caring for such child for the prior 12 months are entitled to notice, and may also petition for review on their own initiative, a petition under section 392 (captioned "Foster care status; periodic family court review") is not an avenue to permanent custody for foster parents where the child has not been freed for adoption.

Upon such review, the court must consider the appropriateness of the agency's plan for the child, what services have been offered to strengthen and reunite the family, efforts to plan for other modes of care, and other further efforts to promote the child's welfare, and in accordance with the best interest of the child, make one of the following dispositions: (1) continue the child in foster care (which may include continuation with the current foster parents); (2) direct that the child "be returned to the parent, guardian or relative, or [direct] that the child be placed in the custody of a relative or other suitable person or persons"; or (3) require the agency (or foster parents upon the agency's default) to institute a parental rights termination proceeding.

The key element in the court's disposition is the best interest of the child—the statutory term that is at the core of this appeal, and to which we now turn.

"Best Interest" in the Foster Care Scheme

"Best interest(s) of the child" is a term that pervades the law relating to children—appearing innumerable times in the pertinent statutes, judicial decisions and literature—yet eludes ready definition. Two interpretations are advanced, each vigorously advocated.

Appellant would read the best interest standard of Social Services Law § 392(6) narrowly, urging that Family Court should inquire only into whether the biological parent is fit, and whether the child will suffer grievous harm by being returned to the parent. Appellant urges affirmance of the Family Court orders, which (1) defined the contest as one between foster care agency and biological parent, rather than foster parent and biological parent; (2) focused first on "the ability of the father to care for the subject child," and then on whether "the child's emotional health will be so seriously impaired as to require continuance in foster care;" and (3) concluded that appellant was fit, and that Michael would not suffer irreparable emotional harm if returned to him. Wider inquiry, appellant insists, creates an "unwinnable beauty contest" the biological parent will inevitably lose where foster placement has continued for any substantial time.

Respondents take a broader view, urging that because of extraordinary circumstances largely attributable to appellant, the Appellate Division correctly compared him with the foster parents in determining Michael's custody and concluded that the child's best interest was served by the placement that better provided for his physical, emotional and intellectual needs. Respondents rely on *Matter of Bennett v. Jeffreys,* this Court's landmark decision recognizing that a child's prolonged separation from a biological parent may be considered, among other factors, to be extraordinary circumstances permitting the court to inquire into which family situation would be in the child's best interests.

In that *Matter of Bennett v. Jeffreys* concerned an unsupervised private placement, where there was no directly applicable legislation, that case is immediately distinguishable from the matter before us, which is controlled by a detailed statutory scheme. Our analysis must begin at a different point—not whether there are extraordinary circumstances, but what the Legislature intended by the words "best interest of the child" in Social Services Law § 392(6).

Necessarily, we look first to the statute itself. The question is in part answered by Social Services Law § 383 and 384–b, which encourage voluntary placements, with the provision that they will not result in the termination of parental rights so long as the parent is fit. To use the period during which a child lives with a foster family, and emotional ties that naturally eventuate, as a ground for comparing the biological parent with the foster parent undermines the very objective of voluntary foster care as a resource for parents in temporary crisis, who are then at risk of losing their children once a bond arises with the foster families . . .

Absent an explicit legislative directive . . . we are not free to overlook the legislative policies that underlie temporary foster care, including the preeminence of the biological family. Indeed, the legislative history of Social Services Law § 392(5–a), which specifies factors that must be considered in determining the child's best interests, states "this bill clearly advises the Family Court of certain considerations before making an order of disposition. These factors establish a clear policy of exploring all available means of reuniting the child with his family before the Court decides to continue his foster care or to direct a permanent adoptive placement."

We therefore cannot endorse a pure "best interests" hearing, where biological parent and foster parents stand on equal footing and the child's interest is the sole consideration. In cases controlled by Social Services Law § 392(6), analysis of the child's "best interest" must begin not by measuring biological parent against foster parent but by weighing past and continued foster care against discharge to the biological parent, or other relative or suitable person within Social Services Law § 392(6)(b).

While the facts of *Matter of Bennett v. Jeffreys* fell outside the statute, and the Court was unrestrained by legislative prescription in defining the scope of the "best interests" inquiry, principles underlying that decision are also relevant here. It is plainly the case, for example, that a "child may be so long in the custody of the nonparent that, even though there has been no abandonment or persisting neglect by the parent, the psychological trauma of removal is grave enough to threaten destruction of the child," and we cannot discount evidence that a child may have bonded with someone other than the biological parent. In such a case, continued foster care may be appropriate although the parent has not been found unfit.

Under Social Services Law § 392, where a child has not been freed for adoption, the court must determine whether it is nonetheless appropriate to continue foster care temporarily, or whether the child should be permanently discharged to the biological parent (or a relative or "other suitable person"). In determining the best interest of a child in that situation, the fitness of the biological parent must be a primary factor. The court is also statutorily mandated to consider the agency's plan for the child, what services have been offered to strengthen and reunite the family, what reasonable efforts have been made to make it possible for the child to return to the natural home, and if return home is not likely, what efforts have been or should be made to evaluate other options. Finally, the court should consider the more intangible elements relating to the emotional well-being of the child, among them the impact on the child of immediate discharge versus an additional period of foster care.

While it is doubtful whether it could be found to be in the child's best interest to deny the parent's persistent demands for custody simply because it took so long to obtain it legally, neither is a lapse of time necessarily without significance in determining custody. The child's emotional well-being must be part of the equation, parental rights notwithstanding. However, while emotional well-being may encompass bonding to someone other than the biological parent, it includes as well a recognition that, absent termination of parental rights, the nonparent cannot adopt the child, and a child in continued custody with a nonparent remains in legal—and often emotional—limbo.

The Appellate Division, applying an erroneous "best interest" test, seemingly avoided that result when it awarded legal custody to the foster parents. We next turn to why that disposition was improper.

Award of Legal Custody to Foster Parents

The Appellate Division awarded legal custody of Michael to the foster parents pursuant to Social Services Law § 392(6)(b), noting that the statute "permits a court to enter an order of disposition directing, *inter alia,* that a child, whose custody and care have temporarily been transferred to an authorized agency, be placed in the custody of a suitable person or persons." The Court correctly looked to section 392 as the predicate for determining custody, but erroneously relied on paragraph (b) of subdivision (6) in awarding custody to the foster parents.

As set forth above, there are three possible dispositions after foster care review with respect to a child not freed for adoption: continued foster care; release to a parent, guardian, relative or other suitable person; and institution of parental termination proceedings.

As the first dispositional option, paragraph (a) contemplates the continuation of foster care, with the child remaining in the custody of the authorized agency, and the arrangement remaining subject to periodic review. As a result of 1989 amendments, disposition under paragraph (a) can include an order that the child be placed with (or remain with) a particular foster family until the next review. Under the statutory scheme, however, foster care is temporary, contractual and supervised.

Paragraph (b), by contrast, contemplates removal of the child from the foster care system by return to "the parent, guardian or relative, or direct[ion] that the child be placed in the custody of a relative or other suitable person or persons." The 1989 statutory revision added as a permissible disposition the placement of children with relatives or other suitable persons. The purpose of this amendment was to promote family stability by allowing placement with relatives, extended family members or persons like them, as an alternative to foster care.

Plainly, the scheme does not envision also including the foster parents—who were the subject of the amendment to paragraph (a)—as "other suitable persons." Indeed, reading paragraph (b) as the Appellate Division did, to permit removal of the child from foster care and an award of legal custody to the foster parents, exacerbates the legal limbo status. The child is left without a placement looking to the establishment of a permanent parental relationship through adoption, or the prospect of subsequent review of foster care status with the possibility of adoption placement at that time, yet has no realistic chance of return to the biological parent.

The terms of paragraph (c), providing for an order that the agency institute a parental termination proceeding, further buttress the conclusion that foster parents are not included in paragraph (b). Pursuant to paragraph (c), if the court finds reasonable cause to believe there are grounds for termination of parental rights, it may order the responsible agency to institute such proceedings. If the agency fails to do so within 90 days, the foster parents themselves may bring the proceeding, unless the court believes their subsequent petition to adopt would not be approved. Thus, in the statutory scheme the Legislature has provided a means for foster parents to secure a temporary arrangement under paragraph (a) and a permanent arrangement under paragraph (c)—both of which specifically mention foster parents. They are not also implicitly included in paragraph (b), which addresses different interests.

We therefore conclude that the Appellate Division erred in interpreting Social Services Law § 392(6) to permit the award of legal custody to respondent foster parents.

Need for Further Inquiry

We have no occasion to apply the proper legal test to the facts at hand, as the parties urge. New circumstances require remittal to Family Court for an expedited hearing and determination of whether appellant is a fit parent and entitled to custody of Michael.

The Court has been informed that, during the pendency of the appeal, appellant was charged with—and admitted—neglect of the children in his custody (not Michael), and that those children have been removed from his home and are again in the custody of the Commissioner of the Social Services. The neglect petitions allege that appellant abused alcohol and controlled substances including cocaine, and physically abused the children. Orders of fact finding have been entered by Family Court, Queens County, recognizing appellant's admission in open court to "substance abuse, alcohol and cocaine abuse." Moreover, an Order of Protection was entered prohibiting appellant from visiting the children while under the influence of drugs or alcohol.

Appellant's request that we ignore these new developments and simply grant him custody, because matters outside the record cannot be considered by an appellate court, would exalt the procedural rule—important though it is—to a point of absurdity, and "reflect no credit on the judicial process." Indeed, changed circumstances may have particular significance in child custody matters. This Court would therefore take notice of the new facts and allegations to the extent they indicate that the record before us is no longer sufficient for determining appellant's fitness and right to custody of Michael, and remit the matter to Family Court for a new hearing and determination of those issues. The Appellate Division concluded that the hearing should take place before a different Judge of that court, and we see no basis to disturb that determination. Pending the hearing, Michael should physically remain with his current foster parents, but legal custody should be returned to the foster care agency . . .

■ Bellacosa, J. (concurring).

I agree with Judge Kaye's opinion for the Court that Social Services Law § 392(6)(b) cannot be used to award permanent custody to foster parents within that statute's intended operation and integrated structure. I concur in the reversal result in this case solely for that reason, noting additionally that a contrary interpretation of that key provision, as used by the Appellate Division, would have internally contradictory implications in the field of temporary foster child placement. While I prefer an affirmance result because that might more likely conclude the litigation and allow Michael B., the 7 1/2–year-old subject of this custody battle, to get on with his life in a more settled and constructive way, I can discern no principled route to that desirable result without sacrificing the correct application of legal principles and engendering fundamentally troublesome precedential consequences.

This separate concurrence is necessary to express my difference of degree and analytical progression with respect to the best interests analysis and test, as adopted by the Court, for purposes of the remittal of this case and as the controlling guidance for countless other proceedings in the future. I would not relegate *Matter of Bennett v. Jeffreys* essentially to general relevance only, would not limit the beginning of the analysis to the statutory setting, and would allow for appropriate flexibility as to the range and manner of exercising discretion in the application of the best interests test by the Family Courts and Appellate Divisions.

I believe courts, in the fulfillment of the *parens patriae* responsibility of the State, should, as a general operating principle, have an appropriately broad range of power to act in the best interests of children. We agree that the teachings of *Matter of Bennett v. Jeffreys* are still excellent and have served the process and the affected subjects and combatants in custody disputes very well. While the common-law origination in *Bennett* is a distinguishing feature from the instant case, I do not view that aspect as subordinated to or secondary in the use of its wisdom, even in a predominantly statutory setting, where this case originates.... Since the best of *Matter of Bennett v. Jeffreys'* best interest analysis enjoys continued vitality therefore, it should serve as a cogent, coequal common-law building block. In my view, it provides helpful understanding for and intertwined supplementation to the Social Services Law provisions as applied in these extraordinary circumstances, defined in one aspect of *Matter of Bennett v. Jeffreys* as "prolonged separation" of parent and child "for most of the child's life." The child in that case was eight years of age and none of the other serious and disquieting features of this case were apparent there.

The nuances, complexity and variations of human situations make the development and application of the general axiom—best interests of the child—exceedingly difficult. As a matter of degree and perspective, however, the Court's test is concededly more limiting than *Matter of Bennett v. Jeffreys,* and therefore I believe it is more narrow than it should be in this case since I discern no compelling authority for the narrower approach. This 7 1/2–year-old child, born of a long since deceased crack-cocaine mother, has yet to be permanently placed and has suffered a continuing, lengthy, bad trip through the maze of New York's legal system. His father has an extended history of significant substance addiction and other problems, and the child has spent much of his 7 1/2 years with the same foster parents. These graphic circumstances surely present an exceptionally extraordinary and compelling case requiring significant flexibility by the courts in resolving his best interests. On this aspect of the case, therefore, I agree with the Appellate Division in its two decisions in this case, at least with respect to its best interests analysis and handling of this difficult case. On March 18, 1991, it said:

"In view of the extraordinary circumstances present in this case, the Family Court should have conducted a hearing to consider, among other things, the impact that a change of custody will have on the child in view of the bonding which has occurred between Michael and his foster parents, who have raised him since infancy. It is, therefore, necessary to remit this matter for a hearing and a custody determination to be made in accordance with Michael's best interests."

After the proper, broad, "pure" *Matter of Bennett v. Jeffreys*-type best interests hearing was held in Family Court, the Appellate Division on February 24, 1992 added in the order now before us:

"In light of the lengthy period of time during which Michael resided with and psychologically bonded to his foster parents and given the potential for emotional as well as physical harm to Michael should permanent custody be awarded to his natural father, we find that the requisite extraordinary circumstances are present, and conclude that the best interests of this child will be served by allowing him to return to his foster parents.

"In view of the testimony presented during the best interests hearing, this court concludes that Michael's natural father is incapable of giving him the emotional support so vital to his well-being. The testimony presented by Dr. Sullivan and Mr. Falco indicated that an emotional void still existed between Michael and his father despite the eight to nine months during which they resided together prior to the best interests hearing and that this void showed no signs of being bridged."

In sum, I cannot agree that the important and pervasive legal axiom "best interests of the child" is or was meant to be as constricted as it is in the Court's application to this case. The governing phrase and test even in this statutory scheme ought to be as all-encompassing as in *Matter of Bennett v. Jeffreys,* despite the difference in the procedural origin and setting of the two cases. The approach I urge, not unlike that of the Appellate Division in this respect, better serves the objectives of finality and certainty in these matters, more realistically takes into account the widely varying human conditions, and allows the Family Courts to achieve more uniformity and evenness of application of the rules. That is a better way to promote the best interests of this youngster with reasonable finality and the best interests of all others affected by the operation of these rules.

Kingsley v. Kingsley

District Court of Appeal of Florida, 1993.
623 So.2d 780.

■ DIAMANTIS, JUDGE.

Rachel Kingsley, the natural mother of Gregory, a minor child, appeals the trial court's final orders terminating her parental rights based upon findings of abandonment and neglect, and granting the petition for adoption filed by Gregory's foster parents, George and Elizabeth Russ. George Russ, on behalf of Gregory, appeals the trial court's order denying his motion for summary judgment regarding the applicable burden of proof. We affirm the trial court's orders terminating Rachel's parental rights and denying the motion for summary judgment; however, we reverse the trial court's order granting the adoption petition.

On June 25, 1992, Gregory, then 11 years of age, filed in the juvenile division of the circuit court a petition for termination of the parental rights of his natural parents. He separately filed, in the civil division of the circuit court, a complaint for declaration of rights and adoption by his foster parents. This adoption was later transferred to the juvenile division by court order. On July 21, 1992, the trial court ruled that Gregory, as a natural person who had knowledge of the facts alleged, had standing to initiate the action for termination of parental rights. In that order, the trial court implicitly accorded Gregory capacity to file the petition although he was an unemancipated minor. Prior to entering this order, the trial court, noting that there was a distinction between the roles of guardian ad litem and attorney ad litem, appointed one of Gregory's attorneys, Jerri A. Blair, as his attorney ad litem.[2] The trial court made no ruling concerning Gregory's standing to file the adoption petition; however, Gregory's foster parents filed

2. Gregory's foster father, George Russ, later became an additional attorney of record for Gregory. Because the order appointing an attorney ad litem is not challenged on appeal, we do not decide the issue of the propriety of such appointment in a termination of parental rights proceeding.

a petition for adoption on September 3, 1992, with the written consent of Gregory and Gregory's natural father.[3] Between August 11, 1992, and September 11, 1992, four additional petitions for termination of parental rights were filed on behalf of Gregory: the August 11, 1992, petition by George Russ, the foster father; the August 25, 1992, petition by Catherine A. Tucker, Gregory's guardian ad litem; the September 10, 1992, petition by the Department of Health and Rehabilitative Services (HRS); and the September 11, 1992, petition by Elizabeth Russ, the foster mother. On September 17, 1992, Gregory filed an amended petition for termination of parental rights, and on September 18, 1992, Gregory's foster family filed a notice that its members were joining in, and adopting, Gregory's amended petition for termination of parental rights.

This matter proceeded to trial on September 24 and September 25, 1992. The court, over Rachel's objection, tried the termination of parental rights proceeding and the adoption proceeding at the same time pursuant to its earlier order allowing the two cases to travel together. After the various parties had presented their positions, the trial court, orally on the record, terminated Rachel's parental rights. Rachel immediately filed her notice of appeal in open court, contending that the appeal suspends and supersedes the adoption proceeding. The trial court, however, proceeded orally to grant the adoption petition filed by Gregory's foster parents. Subsequently, on October 13, 1992, *nunc pro tunc* to September 25, 1992, the trial court entered a written judgment which terminated Rachel's parental rights and a separate written judgment which granted the adoption.

1. CAPACITY

Rachel contends that the trial court erred in holding that Gregory has the capacity to bring a termination of parental rights proceeding in his own right. Specifically, Rachel argues that the disability of nonage prevents a minor from initiating or maintaining an action for termination of parental rights. We agree.

. . .

Courts historically have recognized that unemancipated minors do not have the legal capacity to initiate legal proceedings in their own names. This historic concept is incorporated into Florida Rule of Civil Procedure 1.210(b). . . .

Although we conclude that the trial court erred in allowing Gregory to file the petition in his own name because Gregory lacked the requisite legal capacity, this error was rendered harmless by the fact that separate petitions for termination of parental rights were filed on behalf of Gregory by the foster father, the guardian ad litem, HRS, and the foster mother.

. . .

4. SIMULTANEOUSLY TRYING TERMINATION AND ADOPTION PROCEEDINGS

Rachel contends that the trial court erred in trying the termination and adoption proceedings simultaneously, arguing that in doing so the trial court violated her rights to procedural due process in that the focus of the proceedings impermissibly shifted from the issues of abandonment and neglect to a comparison of Rachel's parenting skills with those of the

3. Gregory's natural father died during the pendency of this appeal.

potential adoptive parents. More specifically, Rachel argues that this procedure resulted in unduly placing upon her the burden to overcome this comparison, which resulted in an interference with her fundamental liberty interests in Gregory's care, custody, and maintenance as recognized in Santosky v. Kramer, 455 U.S. 745 (1982), and Padgett v. Department of Health & Rehabilitative Services, 577 So.2d 565 (Fla.1991).

We agree with Rachel that trying these two cases simultaneously constituted error and that the better practice would have been to try these cases separately.

. . .

In the instant case, however, this error is harmless for two reasons. First, a great deal of the testimony concerning the relationship between Gregory and his foster parents was admissible in the termination proceeding pursuant to the provisions of section 39.467(2), Florida Statutes (Supp.1992). Although some comparisons were made between the parenting skills of the Russes and Rachel which went beyond the elements of section 39.467(2), the evidence did not emphasize these comparisons. Further, Rachel has not shown that these comparisons became a focal point of the termination proceedings or affected the trial court's decision regarding the determination of the issues of abandonment and neglect. Thus, we hold that trying these two proceedings simultaneously was error, but that such error was harmless in the context of these proceedings.

. . .

5. JURISDICTION OF THE TRIAL COURT TO ENTER JUDGMENT OF ADOPTION

Rachel filed a notice of appeal in open court immediately following the trial court's oral pronouncement terminating her parental rights. The trial court, however, proceeded orally to grant the petition for adoption filed by the foster parents. Subsequently, the trial court entered, and then filed with the clerk, judgments in both the termination and adoption proceedings. These judgments were rendered for appellate purposes when signed and filed. The filing of Rachel's notice of appeal was premature; however, the appeal subsequently matured when the trial court entered and filed its final judgment in the termination proceeding. Consequently, at that point, Rachel was effectively appealing the termination order which the trial court must have logically and legally rendered before it granted the adoption.

Once Rachel's notice of appeal became effective for appellate purposes, her appeal then implicated the provisions of both rule 8.275(a) and section 39.473(3) which respectively provide that the adoption proceedings are superseded and suspended. At that point, the trial court was without subject matter jurisdiction to proceed and clearly erred in granting the foster parents' petition for adoption.

In *In re J.R.G., 1993 Fla. LEXIS 7504, 18 Fla. L. Weekly D1622 (Fla. 2d DCA July 14, 1993),* the second district rejected the argument that this serious procedural error is rendered harmless by the district court's subsequent affirmance of the order terminating parental rights. We agree with the second district's admonition in In re J.R.G. and adopt it as our own:

> ... We are concerned ... that an order of adoption entered prior to an order terminating parental rights could create confusion in the future.

> When an adoption follows a termination proceeding, an order of adoption should not be entered until a written order terminating parental rights has been filed and until it is clear that such order will not be affected by rehearing or appeal. In this case, the petition for adoption has never given the circuit court a legal basis to grant an adoption. That court will not have authority to permit an adoption until this court issues its mandate in the appeal of the order terminating parental rights.
>
> In this case, we hope that the circuit court's serious procedural error will have no great impact upon the children and the several affected adults. If we had been required to reverse the order terminating parental rights, however, the error could have caused serious consequences for these people. We urge all parties involved in adoption proceedings to comply carefully with these important timing requirements.

In re J.R.G., 18 Fla. L. Weekly at D1623 (emphasis in original). Accordingly, we reverse the final judgment granting the adoption and remand that matter to the trial court for further proceedings.

AFFIRMED in part; REVERSED in part; REMANDED for further proceedings.

■ HARRIS, CHIEF JUDGE, concurring in part, dissenting in part:

This rather ordinary termination of parental rights case was transformed into a *cause celebre* by artful representation and the glare of klieg lights. It is the judge's obligation, however, to look beyond the images created by light and shadow and concentrate on the real-life drama being played out on center stage. Florida recognizes no cause of action that permits a child to divorce his parents.

I concur with the majority holding that so long as the parents do nothing to forfeit their fundamental liberty interest in the care, custody and management of their child, no one (including the child) can interfere with that interest. While the child has the right not to be abused, neglected or abandoned, there is no right to change parents simply because the child finds substitutes that he or she likes better or who can provide a better standard of living.

Florida does not recognize "no-fault" termination of parental rights. That is why the focus in a termination case is (and must be), at least in the first analysis, on the alleged misconduct of the biological parent or parents which would authorize termination of parental rights. Termination of parental rights requires a two step analysis. First, did the parents do something that the State has determined to be sufficiently egregious to permit forfeiture of their right to continue as parents (abuse, neglect, abandonment, voluntary consent to adoption)? Unless the answer to this first question is affirmative, the second step in the analysis (the best interest of the child) is unnecessary. Because of the trial strategy employed by the attorneys for the child in this case, the trial court failed to keep these steps separated.

One artful maneuver which attracted the attention of the media (and distracted the court) was the filing of this cause as a declaratory action (along with a standard petition under section 39.461) in the name of the child (as opposed to next friend, etc.) and joining the proposed adoptive parents as parties in interest in the action for declaratory relief. This action for declaratory relief was transferred to the juvenile division and tried with the termination action. Because the court permitted the pleadings to stand, and be tried with the termination proceedings, the focus was shifted to a comparison of this troubled biological mother (a single parent) with the prospective adoptive parents (a lawyer and his wife) to determine which could provide the child a better life. The mother could not win this contest. The alleged misconduct of the biological mother ceased to be an issue independent of (except as a condition precedent to) any consideration of the best interest of the child; instead it became an issue inextricably intertwined with the best interest of the child—and even this issue was improperly influenced by the presence and active participation of the proposed adoptive parents *as parties*—and with the proposed adoptive father acting as one of the child's attorneys.

I concur with the majority that there is sufficient evidence in the record to support the court's finding of abandonment. But I also urge that there is sufficient evidence in the record (and precedent) to support the court had it found no abandonment. That is why I am unable to agree that the numerous errors in this case, and the cumulative effect of them, can be disregarded as merely harmless error.

. . .

... Because the procedural errors may well have affected the outcome of this case, I submit that the mother is entitled to a new hearing on the issue of abandonment under proper pleadings and confronted only by the proper parties.

The mother might lose again. But even if she did, she (and all those who have closely followed this case) would at least know that she lost on a level playing field.

NOTES

1. Gregory ultimately was adopted by his foster parents after the court's decision. Conversation with Catherine A. Tucker, attorney for Guardian ad Litem, October 25, 2005.

2. Consider In re Adoption No. 12612, 353 Md. 209, 725 A.2d 1037 (1999), a dispute over custody of three-year-old Cornilous Pixley between his biological mother, and Laura Blankman who had been his primary care giver since Cornilous was three-and-a-half months old. The lower court awarded custody to the biological mother despite the fact that she had pled guilty to second degree murder for smothering her five-week-old daughter three years before Cornilous was born. The appeals court reversed the lower court decision and remanded with directions to give custody to Ms. Blankman if there were any likelihood of Cornilous being abused or neglected by his biological mother. Judge Cathell concurred in the result but stated that any parent convicted of murdering one of his or her children should be presumed unfit.

3. For other decisions recognizing the need to choose continuity for the child over the rights of biological parents see Ross v. Hoffman, 33 Md.App. 333, 364 A.2d 596 (1976) (mother loses custody of nine-year-old daughter who was entrusted to "babysitter" for two years); In re Petition of New England Home for Little Wanderers, 367 Mass. 631, 328 N.E.2d 854 (1975) (mother loses right to 10 month old child voluntarily placed at birth in care); Bennett v. Jeffreys, 40 N.Y.2d 543, 387 N.Y.S.2d 821, 356 N.E.2d 277 (1976) (mother loses right to eight-year-old child entrusted at birth to former schoolmate); In re John F. (Pa.Ct.Com.Pleas Allegheny Cty. 12/2/76) (mother loses rights to three children who had been in foster care for 6 years). But see In re J. & J.W., 134 Vt. 480, 365 A.2d 521 (1976) (court's reliance on child's need for a psychological parent is error in case where mother's psychological difficulties have prevented her from assuming custody of her children); In re LaRue, 244 Pa.Super. 218, 366 A.2d 1271 (1976) (children voluntarily placed in foster home care for four years must be returned home unless there is proof of "clear necessity" to do otherwise; use of best interests standard was error).

Adoption of Gregory

Supreme Judicial Court of Massachusetts, 2001.
434 Mass. 117, 747 N.E.2d 120.

■ Ireland, J.

This case raises the first impression question whether the Americans with Disabilities Act (ADA), *42 U.S.C. § 12132* (2000), applies to the termination of parental rights proceedings. The parents appeal from a judgment of the juvenile session of the District Court dispensing with their consent to adoption of their son pursuant to *G. L. c. 210, § 3*. . . . The father claims that the judge erred in terminating his parental rights because the Department of Social Services (department) failed to accommodate his disabilities in its provision of services. In addition, the parents assert that the judge erred in finding parental unfitness and refusing to order posttermination and postadoption visits. . . .

1. Background.

The child, whom we call Gregory, was born on March 3, 1997. The hospital staff were concerned immediately that his parents could not care for him. The mother had failed consistently to attend prenatal classes during her pregnancy. After Gregory's birth, she exhibited poor impulse control and an inability to focus on her baby. She admitted to the hospital staff that she did not know what to do with Gregory, would not be able to manage at home, had a bad temper and did not want to hurt him. She referred to Gregory as a "brat," and said such things as, "I don't care about the 'f—ing baby,' " and, "If you [Gregory] give me a wakeup call, I'll kill you." Moreover, while in the hospital, she displayed a lack of concern for personal hygiene and an inability to learn basic caretaking skills, such as diapering and burping. The mother's shortcomings were compounded by the father's inability to provide sufficient support and care to Gregory. Additionally, the parents frequently argued in front of Gregory, and the mother spoke in a loud argumentative voice. Such behavior greatly distressed Gregory, who, due to various medical problems discussed below, is unusually disturbed by loud noises. Based on these concerns, the hospital staff filed a mandated reporter report with the department, alleging that Gregory was at risk of neglect. On March 11, 1997, the department filed a petition in the District Court, alleging that Gregory was in need of care and protection. The department was granted temporary custody on that date, and has retained custody of Gregory since then. The judge subsequently allowed the department's motion to amend the petition to request that the court dispense with the parents' consent to adoption.

To the extent it informs our assessment of the case, we briefly describe Gregory's medical condition. He suffers from complex medical and developmental problems and consequently requires substantial assistance performing daily activities. He is afflicted with global developmental delays and possible mild cerebral palsy. He requires assistance to sit, has tactile hypersensitivity, lacks speech and language development, and exhibits limited spontaneous interaction. He also suffers from cognitive delays, has a short attention span, and engages in a rocking behavior and head shaking when he is not occupied. Due to his difficulty ingesting solid foods, his foster parents must prepare him for meals by massaging his gums, mouth and lips. Gregory's morning routine usually requires up to one and one-half hours of concentrated work on the part of his foster parents. He also needs them to perform thirty minutes of physical therapy on him three time[sic] a day. Gregory will continue to require this therapy, as well as other medical intervention, to address his many needs.

Prior to trial, the department, intending to reunify the family, provided the parents with services designed to improve their parenting skills. As detailed below, the parents did not utilize the services provided by the department to learn to care properly for Gregory. Therefore, after a ten-day trial, the judge entered her findings of fact and conclusions of law: finding the parents currently unfit to care for Gregory; finding him in need of care and protection; committing him to the custody of the department; and dispensing with the need for the parents' consent to adoption.

2. Americans with Disabilities Act.

The father contends that the judge erred in terminating his parental rights,because the department failed reasonably to accommodate his cognitive disorder and attention deficit hyperactivity disorder (ADHD) by providing services designed for these disabilities, in violation of Title II of the ADA, *42 U.S.C. § 12132,* and art. 114 of the Amendments to the Massachusetts Constitution. As discussed below, we conclude that: (1) proceedings to terminate parental rights under *G. L. c. 210, § 3,* do not qualify as "services, programs, or activities" under the ADA, and thus, the ADA may not be raised as a defense to such proceedings; and (2) the ADA, as well as Massachusetts antidiscrimination laws, regulations, and its Constitution require the Department to render services that accommodate the parents' special needs prior to *G. L. c. 210, § 3,* proceedings, which it did in this case.

Congress enacted the ADA "to assure equality of opportunity, full participation, independent living, and economic self-sufficiency" for people with disabilities. *42 U.S.C. § 12101*(a)(8) (2000). The relevant portion of the ADA provides that "no qualified individual with a disability shall, by reason of such disability, be excluded from participation in or denied the benefits of the services, programs, or activities of a public entity, or be subjected to discrimination by any such entity." *42 U.S.C. § 12132.* The ADA requires that the public entity make "reasonable modifications" to allow the person with a disability to receive the services or to participate in the public entity's programs.

Given the novelty of this issue in Massachusetts, we look to other States for guidance. Several courts have recently determined that termination proceedings are not "services, programs or activities" under the ADA, and thus concluded that the ADA may not be raised as a defense to the termination of parental rights. Although at least one court has held that the ADA may constitute an affirmative defense to a termination proceeding, that court ruled that the defense had been waived by the failure to plead it. Other courts have avoided reaching the question by finding on the facts presented that the State agency, through the provision of services designed to meet the parent's special needs, had met any obligations that might be imposed by the ADA.

We conclude that proceedings to terminate parental rights do not constitute "services, programs, or activities" for the purposes of *42 U.S.C. § 12132,* and therefore, the ADA is not a defense to such proceedings. In our view, the parents' rights are secondary to the child's best interests and thus, the proper focus of termination proceedings is the welfare of the child.

Despite the parents' special needs or limited capabilities, "the child is entitled to at least a minimum level of parental care." *People ex rel. T.B., supra at 1224.* See *Adoption of Nicole, 40 Mass. App. Ct. 259, 262, 662 N.E.2d 1058 (1996)* ("the central judgment" concerns whether parent "has the capacity to act as a fit parent"). Although the department is a public entity and therefore subject to the ADA, see *42 U.S.C. § 12131* (2000), "nothing in the ADA suggests that a violation of the statute would interfere with the right of the state to terminate parental rights. To allow the provisions of the ADA to constitute a defense to termination proceedings would improperly elevate the rights of the parent above those of the child." *People ex rel. T.B., supra.* See Petition of the Dep't of Pub. Welfare to Dispense with *Consent to Adoption, 376 Mass. 252, 268–269, 381 N.E.2d 565 (1978)* (under *G. L. c. 210, § 3,* judge's task is to determine [1] whether parents can assume parental responsibility for child; and [2] whether dispensing with parental consent to adoption serves best interests of child). Accordingly, we hold that a parent may not raise violations of the ADA as a defense to a termination of parental rights proceeding.

At the same time, the ADA, as well as Massachusetts anti-discrimination laws, regulations, and our Constitution all require the department to accommodate the parents' special needs in its provision of services prior to a *G. L. c. 210, § 3,* termination proceeding. See *42 U.S.C. § 12131; 110 Code Mass. Regs. §§ 6.01(1),* 6.02 (1998); *G. L. c. 210, § 3*(c)(v) (requires court to consider whether parents "were offered or received services intended to correct the circumstances and refused or were unable to utilize such services on a regular and consistent basis"); *110 Code Mass. Regs. § 1.08* (1998) ("The Department shall make reasonable accommodations to ensure that its services . . . are accessible to all handicapped persons. . . . The Department shall be responsive to issues of handicapping conditions by utilizing social workers who are attuned to the special needs of handicapped persons"); *110 Code Mass. Regs. § 1.09* (1998) ("No applicant for or recipient of Department services shall, on the ground of . . . disability . . . be excluded from participation in, be denied the benefits of, or otherwise be subjected to discrimination in connection with any service, program, or activity administered or provided by the Department"); art. 114 ("No otherwise qualified handicapped individual shall, solely by reason of his handicap, be excluded from the participation in, denied the benefits of, or be subject to discrimination under any program or activity within the Commonwealth").

In this case, the department reasonably accommodated the father's disabilities. As the judge found, the department provided ample services, specifically tailored to meet the father's special needs and designed to improve his parenting skills. The department initially scheduled visitations between the parents and Gregory twice a week, commencing at the time of his removal from them, in order to provide the father an opportunity to bond with Gregory. Unfortunately, the father did not meet this enhanced visitation schedule. To address this problem, the department extended the duration of the visits to three hours, but reduced their frequency to a weekly basis.

The department also accommodated the father by retaining a particular social worker because of her experience working with cognitively limited individuals such as the parents. She was originally assigned to investigate the 51A report and submit an investigation report. In normal circumstances, when the 51B assessment period ended, the case would have been transferred to an assessment worker and then to an ongoing social worker. However, as a direct response to the father's special needs, the department changed its usual practice by keeping her on the case. Moreover, in light of the father's cognitive limitations and need for concrete and repetitive parenting instructions, the social worker sought advice from the Boston Children's Services Association in providing parenting instructions to cognitively limited adults. The social worker then referred the parents to the Catholic Charities' parenting program, which specializes in instructing cognitively limited parents. Thus, in addition to the social worker's parenting instructions, the parents also received education designed for their special needs in these one-on-one parenting classes.

. . . [The father] did not make use of these numerous accommodations. Indeed, he was not present for the entire hour of any of the parenting sessions, nor did he attend any parenting classes at Catholic Charities for the entire month of July, 1998. Although he did attend one session on August 31, 1998, the instructor terminated the sessions shortly thereafter due to the parents' lack of interest. Moreover, the social worker was unable to communicate effectively with Catholic Charities because the father refused to sign the releases necessary for her to discuss his progress with the instructor. She continued to provide three hours of weekly visits between the parents and Gregory, and after witnessing the lack of the parents' progress, sent a letter to the instructor outlining these observations, as well as specific areas for the instructor to cover in the one-on-one parenting sessions. She investigated additional services for the parents, particularly those offered by the Department of Mental Health, but the father did not pursue such services. She also suggested that the parents live in a supervised residential setting with Gregory. The father refused because he did not want to give up his housing or his job. She tried to involve the father in Gregory's medical appointments, with no success. The record clearly shows that the department made substantial efforts to accommodate the father's special needs. That he was unable to develop stronger parenting skills cannot be attributed to the department's alleged failure to provide adequate services.

Finally, we note that a parent must raise a claim of inadequate services in a timely manner so that reasonable accommodations may be made. If a parent believes that the department is not reasonably accommodating a disability, the parent should claim a violation of his rights under either the ADA or other antidiscrimination legislation, either when the parenting plan is adopted, when he receives those services, or shortly thereafter. At that point, the court or the department may address the parent's claim. However, where, as here, a disabled parent fails to make a timely claim that the department is providing inadequate services for his needs, he may not raise noncompliance with the ADA or other antidiscrimination laws for the first time at a termination proceeding.

Here, the father had two possible options to remedy his complaint of inadequate services. He could have pursued his claim that the service plan and other department services failed to address his disabilities through an administrative fair hearing or grievance process. Alternatively, he could have commenced a separate action for discrimination under the ADA. He did neither.

Furthermore, throughout the entire case, the father was represented by counsel, who could have raised this issue at an earlier point in time. . . .

The only indication that the father requested specific services appeared in a letter, dated June 18, 1997, from the father's attorney to the social worker, in which he suggested parenting classes for cognitively limited people at Boston Children's Services.[3] As previously discussed, she took this suggestion and contacted a social worker at Boston Children's Services, who, for various reasons, recommended the parenting classes at Catholic Charities, which the social worker subsequently arranged for the parents to attend. Prior to trial the father never claimed that the classes at Catholic Charities were inadequate. To the contrary, by refusing to sign the release forms, he effectively obviated any discourse with the department about the adequacy of the services for his disabilities.

3. The judge's findings of fact.

The mother and father also argue that the judge's findings are not supported by the evidence and that there is not clear and convincing evidence of parental unfitness. We disagree.

In determining whether to dispense with parental consent to adoption, a judge must "evaluate whether the [parent is] able to assume the duties and responsibilities required of a parent and whether dispensing with the need for parental consent will be in the best interest of the [child]." Because the termination of parental rights is an "extreme step," we require the judge to make specific and detailed findings, demonstrating that close attention has been given the evidence. Subsidiary findings must be supported by a preponderance of the evidence, and none of the findings will be disturbed unless they are clearly erroneous. Substantial deference is given to the judge's assessment of the weight of the evidence and the credibility of witnesses. Taken together, these findings must prove clearly and convincingly that the parents are currently unfit to further the welfare and best interest of the child. . . . *General Laws c. 210, § 3*(c), provides thirteen nonexclusive factors for consideration in these cases.

The department met its burden of clearly and convincingly proving parental unfitness. The judge made ninety detailed findings depicting the parents' history of mental illness and substance abuse, their inability to learn necessary parenting skills, their pattern of neglect of Gregory, their late and missed appointments, their violent arguments and disruptive outbursts, and their failure to utilize the services provided by the department.

Specifically, the judge concluded that both the mother and father suffer from "significant and demonstrable cognitive, mental health and substance abuse histories that make it virtually impossible for them to parent [Gregory] adequately given his significant special needs."[5] Both parents suffer from poor impulse control, and as result, were often agitated in Gregory's presence. The mother sometimes became so upset over minute incidents that she was unable to attend to Gregory's needs. On one occasion, the father, exhibiting an extreme level of frustration and inappropriate behavior, threatened to kill the social worker. Moreover, the parents often engaged in

3. The father also claims that he requested accommodations for his disability by attempting "to find living arrangements that combined parenting instructions with living arrangements." However, the parents ultimately decided that they were not interested in such arrangements.

5. The mother claims that the judge erroneously relied on their mental illness, see *Custody of a Minor, 378 Mass. 712, 722, 393 N.E.2d 379 (1979)*, and substance abuse, see *Adoption of Katharine, 42 Mass. App. Ct. 25, 674 N.E.2d 256 (1997)*, alone in reaching her decision. While the judge considered these factors, she also found that both parents also suffered from "marked cognitive limitations." Furthermore, while the judge acknowledged that "the mere presence of these problems does not imply" parental unfitness, she made concrete findings . . . that the parents could not sufficiently overcome these problems to be able to provide minimally adequate parenting to a child with significant special needs, despite the abundance of services provided by the department. . . .

physically violent arguments, prompting the father to admit, "The cat gets scared. Imagine what a child would do." With the exception of the mother's attending Gregory's circumcision shortly after his birth, the parents have failed to attend any of his medical appointments. This failure is particularly noteworthy in light of the parents' need to comprehend Gregory's numerous medical problems and considerable special needs in order to parent him.

Despite the services provided by the department, the parents failed to learn basic care taking skills, let alone the special care and physical therapy that Gregory requires for his physical and mental condition. During a parenting session the mother admitted that she felt she could not parent Gregory and the father conceded that not only would he feel overwhelmed by the amount of required physical therapy, he "couldn't do the house time," because he "would go nuts." The judge also found that both parents were easily distracted during the parenting classes, and neither could sit through an entire three-hour session.

None of the judge's findings was clearly erroneous. "A finding is clearly erroneous when there is no evidence to support it, or when, 'although there is evidence to support it, the reviewing court on the entire evidence is left with the definite and firm conviction that a mistake has been committed.' " The judge conducted an extensive hearing over ten days, heard the testimony of nine witnesses whose credibility she was in the best position to assess, and reviewed the documentary evidence. Each finding was amply supported in the record.

For these reasons, the judge's findings were not clearly erroneous and her disposition of the case was supported by clear and convincing evidence . . .

4. Postadoption contact.

The parents claim that this case must be remanded to reconsider the judge's refusal to order posttermination and postadoption visits despite their failure to present any argument at trial that such visits would be in the best interest of the child. . . . Although the parents did not raise the issue of postadoption visits at trial, the judge nonetheless addressed it in her decision. She approved the termination of visitation between Gregory and his parents, refused to order postadoption visits, and left the question of Gregory's future contact with the biological parents to the discretion of his adoptive parents,[9] noting that at the time, continued contact did not seem to be in his best interest. . . .

5. Conclusion.

The decree of the District Court is affirmed.

3. Foster Families

Smith, Administrator, New York City Human Resources Administration, et al. v. Organization of Foster Families for Equality & Reform et al.

Supreme Court of the United States, 1977.
431 U.S. 816, 97 S.Ct. 2094, 53 L.Ed.2d 14.

■ BRENNAN, J.

Appellees, individual foster parents and an organization of foster parents, brought this civil rights class action pursuant to *42 U.S.C. § 1983* in the

9. No adoptive family for Gregory has yet been identified.

United States District Court for the Southern District of New York, on their own behalf and on behalf of children for whom they have provided homes for a year or more. They sought declaratory and injunctive relief against New York State and New York City officials, alleging that the procedures governing the removal of foster children from foster homes provided in N.Y. Soc. Serv. Law §§ 383(2) and 400 ... and in 18 N.Y.C.R.R. § 450.14 (1974) violated the Due Process and Equal Protection Clauses of the Fourteenth Amendment ...

A detailed outline of the New York statutory system regulating foster care is a necessary preface to a discussion of the constitutional questions presented.

The expressed central policy of the New York system is that "it is generally desirable for the child to remain with or be returned to the natural parent because the child's need for a normal family life will usually best be met in the natural home, and ... parents are entitled to bring up their own children unless the best interests of the child would be thereby endangered." But the State has opted for foster care as one response to those situations where the natural parents are unable to provide the "positive, nurturing family relationships" and "normal family life in a permanent home" that offer "the best opportunity for children to develop and thrive."

Foster care has been defined as "[a] child welfare service which provides substitute family care for a planned period for a child when his own family cannot care for him for a temporary or extended period, and when adoption is neither desirable nor possible." Child Welfare League of America, Standards for Foster Family Care Service 5 (1959). Thus, the distinctive features of foster care are, first, "that it is care in a *family*, it is noninstitutional substitute care," and, second, "that it is for a *planned* period—either temporary or extended. This is unlike adoptive placement, which implies a *permanent* substitution of one home for another."

Under the New York scheme children may be placed in foster care either by voluntary placement or by court order. Most foster-care placements are voluntary. They occur when physical or mental illness, economic problems, or other family crises make it impossible for natural parents, particularly single parents, to provide a stable home life for their children for some limited period. Resort to such placements is almost compelled when it is not possible in such circumstance to place the child with a relative or friend, or to pay for the services of a homemaker or boarding school.

Voluntary placement requires the signing of a written agreement by the natural parent or guardian, transferring the care and custody of the child to an authorized child welfare agency. Although by statute the terms of such agreements are open to negotiation, it is contended that agencies require execution of standardized forms. The agreement may provide for return of the child to the natural parent at a specified date or upon occurrence of a particular event, and if it does not, the child must be returned by the agency, in the absence of a court order, within 20 days of notice from the parent ...

The New York system divides parental functions among agency, foster parents, and natural parents, and the definitions of the respective roles are often complex and often unclear. The law transfers "care and custody" to the agency, but day-to-day supervision of the child and his activities, and most of the functions ordinarily associated with legal custody, are the responsibility of the foster parent. Nevertheless, agency supervision of the performance of the foster parents takes forms indicating that the foster parent does not have the full authority of a legal custodian. Moreover, the natural parent's placement of the child with the agency does not surrender legal guardianship; the parent retains authority to act with respect to the child in certain circumstances. The natural parent has not only the right but the obligation to visit the foster child and plan for his future; failure of a parent with capacity to fulfill the obligation for more than a year can result in a court order terminating the parent's rights on the ground of neglect.

Children may also enter foster care by court order. The Family Court may order that a child be placed in the custody of an authorized child-care agency after a full adversary judicial hearing under Art. 10 of the New York Family Court Act, if it is found that the child has been abused or neglected by his natural parents. In addition, a minor adjudicated a juvenile delinquent, or "person in need of supervision" may be placed by the court with an agency. The consequences of foster-care placement by court order do not differ substantially from those for children voluntarily placed, except that the parent is not entitled to return of the child on demand pursuant to Soc. Serv. Law § 384–a(2)(a); termination of foster care must then be consented to by the court.

The provisions of the scheme specifically at issue in this litigation come into play when the agency having legal custody determines to remove the foster child from the foster home, either because it has determined that it would be in the child's best interests to transfer him to some other foster home, or to return the child to his natural parents in accordance with the statute or placement agreement. Most children are removed in order to be transferred to another foster home. The procedures by which foster parents may challenge a removal made for that purpose differ somewhat from those where the removal is made to return the child to his natural parent.

Section 383(2) provides that the "authorized agency placing out or boarding [a foster] child . . . may in its discretion remove such child from the home where placed or boarded." Administrative regulations implement this provision. The agency is required, except in emergencies, to notify the foster parents in writing 10 days in advance of any removal. The notice advises the foster parents that if they object to the child's removal they may request a "conference" with the Social Services Department. The department schedules requested conferences within 10 days of the receipt of the request. The foster parent may appear with counsel at the conference, where he will "be advised of the reasons [for the removal of the child] and be afforded an opportunity to submit reasons why the child should not be removed." The official must render a decision in writing within five days after the close of the conference, and send notice of his decision to the foster parents and the agency. The proposed removal is stayed pending the outcome of the conference.

If the child is removed after the conference, the foster parent may appeal to the Department of Social Services for a . . . full adversary administrative hearing, the determination of which is subject to judicial review; however, the removal is not automatically stayed pending the hearing and judicial review.

This statutory and regulatory scheme applies statewide. In addition, regulations promulgated by the New York City Human Resources Administration, Department of Social Services—Special Services for Children (SSC) provide even greater procedural safeguards there. Under SSC Procedure No. 5 (Aug. 5, 1974), in place of or in addition to the conference provided by the state regulations, the foster parents may request a full trial-type hearing *before* the child is removed from their home. This procedure applies, however, only if the child is being transferred to another foster home, and not if the child is being returned to his natural parents. One further preremoval procedural safeguard is available. Under Soc. Serv. Law § 392, the Family Court has jurisdiction to review, on petition of the foster parent or the agency, the status of any child who has been in foster care for 18 months or longer. The foster parents, the natural parents, and all interested agencies are made parties to the proceeding. After hearing, the court may order that foster care be continued, or that the child be returned to his natural parents, or that the agency take steps to free the child for adoption . . .

Foster care of children is a sensitive and emotion-laden subject, and foster-care programs consequently stir strong controversy. The New York regulatory scheme is no exception . . .

From the standpoint of natural parents, such as the appellant intervenors here, foster care has been condemned as a class-based intrusion into the family life of the poor. It is certainly true that the poor resort to foster care more often than other citizens. For example, over 50% of all children in foster care in New York City are from female-headed families receiving Aid to Families with Dependent Children. Minority families are also more likely to turn to foster care; 52.3% of the children in foster care in New York City are black and 25.5% are Puerto Rican. This disproportionate resort to foster care by the poor and victims of discrimination doubtless reflects in part the greater likelihood of disruption of poverty-stricken families. Commentators have also noted, however, that middle-and upper-income families who need temporary care services for their children have the resources to purchase private care. The poor have little choice but to submit to state-supervised child care when family crises strike.

The extent to which supposedly "voluntary" placements are in fact voluntary has been questioned on other grounds as well. For example, it has been said that many "voluntary" placements are in fact coerced by threat of neglect proceedings and are not in fact voluntary in the sense of the product of an informed consent. Studies also suggest that social workers of middle-class backgrounds, perhaps unconsciously, incline to favor continued placement in foster care with a generally higher-status family rather than return the child to his natural family, thus reflecting a bias that treats the natural parents' poverty and lifestyle as prejudicial to the best interests of the child. This accounts, it has been said, for the hostility of agencies to the efforts of natural parents to obtain the return of their children.

Appellee foster parents as well as natural parents question the accuracy of the idealized picture portrayed by New York. They note that children often stay in "temporary" foster care for much longer than contemplated by the theory of the system. The District Court found as a fact that the median time spent in foster care in New York was over four years. Indeed, many children apparently remain in this "limbo" indefinitely. The District Court also found that the longer a child remains in foster care, the more likely it is that he will never leave: "[T]he probability of a foster child being returned to his biological parents declined markedly after the first year in foster care." It is not surprising then that many children, particularly those that enter foster care at a very early age and have little or no contact with their natural parents during extended stays in foster care, often develop deep emotional ties with their foster parents. Yet such ties do not seem to be regarded as obstacles to transfer of the child from one foster placement to another. The record in this case indicates that nearly 60% of the children in foster care in New York City have experienced more than one placement, and about 28% have experienced three or more. The intended stability of the foster-home management is further damaged by the rapid turnover among social work professionals who supervise the foster-care arrangements on behalf of the State. Moreover, even when it is clear that a foster child will not be returned to his natural parents, it is rare that he achieves a stable home life through final termination of parental ties and adoption into a new permanent family.

The parties and *amici* devote much of their discussion to these criticisms of foster care, and we present this summary in the view that some understanding of those criticisms is necessary for a full appreciation of the complex and controversial system with which this lawsuit is concerned. But the issue presented by the case is a narrow one. Arguments asserting the need for reform of New York's statutory scheme are properly addressed to the New York Legislature. The relief sought in this case is entirely procedural. Our task is only to determine whether the District Court correctly held that the present procedures preceding the removal from a foster home of children resident there a year or more are constitutionally inadequate. To that task we now turn.

Our first inquiry is whether appellees have asserted interests within the Fourteenth Amendment's protection of "liberty" and "property." . . .

The appellees' basic contention is that when a child has lived in a foster home for a year or more, a psychological tie is created between the child and the foster parents which constitutes the foster family the true "psychological family" of the child. That family, they argue, has a "liberty interest" in its survival as a family protected by the Fourteenth Amendment. Upon this premise they conclude that the foster child cannot be removed without a prior hearing satisfying due process. . . .

It is, of course, true that "freedom of personal choice in matters of . . . family life is one of the liberties protected by the Due Process Clause of the Fourteenth Amendment." There does exist a "private realm of family life which the state cannot enter," that has been afforded both substantive and procedural protection. But is the relation of foster parent to foster child sufficiently akin to the concept of "family" recognized in our precedents to merit similar protection? Although considerable difficulty has attended the task of defining "family" for purposes of the Due Process Clause, we are not without guides to some of the elements that define the concept of "family" and contribute to its place in our society.

First, the usual understanding of "family" implies biological relationships, and most decisions treating the relation between parent and child have stressed this element . . . A biological relationship is not present in the case of the usual foster family. But biological relationships are not exclusive determination of the existence of a family. The basic foundation of the family in our society, the marriage relationship, is of course not a matter of blood relation. Yet its importance has been strongly emphasized in our cases. . . .

Thus the importance of the familial relationship, to the individuals involved and to the society, stems from the emotional attachments that derive from the intimacy of daily association, and from the role it plays in "promot[ing] a way of life" through the instruction of children, as well as from the fact of blood relationship. No one would seriously dispute that a deeply loving and interdependent relationship between an adult and a child in his or her care may exist even in the absence of blood relationship. At least where a child has been placed in foster care as an infant, has never known his natural parents, and has remained continuously for several years in the care of the same foster parents, it is natural that the foster family should hold the same place in the emotional life of the foster child, and fulfill the same socializing functions, as a natural family. For this reason, we cannot dismiss the foster family as a mere collection of unrelated individuals.

But there are also important distinctions between the foster family and the natural family. First, unlike the earlier cases recognizing a right to family privacy, the State here seeks to interfere, not with a relationship having its origins entirely apart from the power of the State, but rather with a foster family which has its source in state law and contractual arrangements. The individual's freedom to marry and reproduce is "older than the Bill of Rights." Accordingly, unlike the property interests that are also protected by the Fourteenth Amendment, the liberty interest in family privacy has its source, and its contours are ordinarily to be sought, not in state law, but in intrinsic human rights, as they have been understood in "this Nation's history and tradition." Here, however, whatever emotional ties may develop between foster parent and foster child have their origins in an arrangement in which the State has been a partner from the outset.... In this case, the limited recognition accorded to the foster family by the New York statutes and the contracts executed by the foster parents argue against any but the most limited constitutional "liberty" in the foster family.

A second consideration related to this is that ordinarily procedural protection may be afforded to a liberty interest of one person without derogating from the substantive liberty of another. Here, however, such a tension is virtually unavoidable. Under New York law, the natural parent of a foster child in voluntary placement has an absolute right to the return of his child in the absence of a court order obtainable only upon compliance with rigorous substantive and procedural standards, which reflect the constitutional protection accorded the natural family. Moreover, the natural parent initially gave up his child to the State only on the express understanding that the child would be returned in those circumstances. These rights are difficult to reconcile with the liberty interest in the foster family relationship claimed by appellees. It is one thing to say that individuals may acquire a liberty interest against arbitrary governmental interference in the family-like associations into which they have freely entered, even in the absence of biological connection or state-law recognition of the relationship. It is quite another to say that one may acquire such an interest in the face of another's constitutionally recognized liberty interest that derives from blood relationship, state-law sanction, and basic human right—an interest the foster parent has recognized by contract from the outset. Whatever liberty interest might otherwise exist in the foster family as an institution, that interest must be substantially attenuated where the proposed removal from the foster family is to return the child to his natural parents.

As this discussion suggests, appellees' claim to a constitutionally protected liberty interest raises complex and novel questions. It is unnecessary for us to resolve those questions definitively in this case, however, for, like the District Court, we conclude that "narrower grounds exist to support" our reversal. We are persuaded that, even on the assumption that appellees have a protected "liberty interest," the District Court erred in holding that the preremoval procedures presently employed by the State are constitutionally defective.

Where procedural due process must be afforded because a "liberty" or "property" interest is within the Fourteenth Amendment's protection, there must be determined "what process is due" in the particular context. The District Court did not spell out precisely what sort of preremoval hearing would be necessary to meet the constitutional standard, leaving to "the various defendants—state and local officials—the first opportunity to formulate procedures suitable to their own professional needs and compatible with the principles set forth in this opinion." The court's opinion, however, would seem to require at a minimum that in all cases in which removal of a child within the certified class is contemplated, including the situation where the removal is for the purpose of returning the child to his natural parents, a hearing be held automatically, regardless of whether or not the foster parents request a hearing; that the hearing be before an officer who has had no previous contact with the decision to remove the child, and who has authority to order that the child remain with the foster parents; and that the agency, the foster parents, and the natural parents, as well as the child, if he is able intelligently to express his true feelings, and an independent representative of the child's interests, if he is not, be represented and permitted to introduce relevant evidence.

It is true that "[b]efore a person is deprived of a protected interest, he must be afforded opportunity for some kind of a hearing, 'except for extraordinary situations where some valid governmental interest is at stake that justifies postponing the hearing until after the event.' " But the hearing required is only one "appropriate to the nature of the case." "[D]ue process is flexible and calls for such procedural protections as the particular situation demands." Only last Term, the Court held that "identification of the specific dictates of due process generally requires consideration of three distinct factors: First, the private interest that will be affected by the official action; second, the risk of an erroneous deprivation of such interest through the procedures used, and the probable value, if any, of additional or substitute procedural safeguards; and finally, the Government's interest, including the function involved and the fiscal and administrative burdens that the additional or substitute procedural requirement would entail." Consideration of the procedures employed by the State and New York City in light of these three factors requires the conclusion that those procedures satisfy constitutional standards....

First, the court held that the "independent review" administrative proceeding was insufficient because it was only available on the request of the foster parents. In the view of the District Court, the proceeding should be provided as a matter of course, because the interests of the foster parents and those of the child would not necessarily be coextensive, and it could not be assumed that the foster parents would invoke the hearing procedure in every case in which it was in the child's interest to have a hearing. Since the child is unable to request a hearing on his own, automatic review in every case is necessary. We disagree. As previously noted, the constitutional liberty, if any, sought to be protected by the New York procedures is a right of *family* privacy or autonomy, and the basis for recognition of any such interest in the foster family must be that close emotional ties analogous to those between parent and child are established when a child resides for a lengthy period with a foster family. If this is so, necessarily we should expect that the foster parents will seek to continue the relationship to preserve the stability of the family; if they do not request a hearing, it is difficult to see what right or interest of the foster child is protected by holding a hearing to determine whether removal would unduly impair his emotional attachments to a foster parent who does not care enough about the child to contest the removal. . . .

Second, the District Court faulted the city procedure on the ground that participation is limited to the foster parents and the agency, and the natural parent and the child are not made parties to the hearing. This is not fatal in light of the nature of the alleged constitutional interests at stake. When the child's transfer from one foster home to another is pending, the interest arguably requiring protection is that of the foster family, not that of the natural parents. Moreover, the natural parent can generally add little to the accuracy of factfinding concerning the wisdom of such a transfer, since the foster parents and the agency, through its caseworkers, will usually be most knowledgeable about conditions in the foster home. Of course, in those cases where the natural parent does have a special interest in the proposed transfer or particular information that would assist the factfinder, nothing in the city's procedure prevents any party from securing his testimony.

Much the same can be said in response to the District Court's statement:

> "[I]t may be advisable, under certain circumstances, for the agency to appoint an adult representative better to articulate the interests of the child. In making this determination, the agency should carefully consider the child's age, sophistication and ability effectively to communicate his own true feelings."

But nothing in the New York City procedure prevents consultation of the child's wishes, directly or through an adult intermediary. We assume, moreover, that some such consultation would be among the first steps that a rational factfinder, inquiring into the child's best interests, would pursue. Such consultation, however, does not require that the child or an appointed representative must be a party with full adversary powers in all preremoval hearings . . .

As the District Court acknowledged, where delicate judgments concerning "the often ambiguous indices of a child's emotional attachments and psychological development" are involved, we must also consider the possibility that making the decisionmaking process increasingly adversary "might well impede the effort to elicit the sensitive and personal information required," or make the struggle for custody, already often difficult for the child, even more traumatic. In such a situation, there is a value in less formalized hearing procedures . . .

We deal here with issues of unusual delicacy, in an area where professional judgments regarding desirable procedures are constantly and rapidly changing. In such a context, restraint is appropriate on the part of courts called upon to adjudicate whether a particular procedural scheme is adequate under the Constitution. Since we hold that the procedures provided by New York State . . . and by New York City . . . are adequate to protect whatever liberty interests appellees may have, the judgment of the District Court is Reversed.

Wilder v. Bernstein

United States Court of Appeals, Second Circuit, 1988.
848 F.2d 1338.

■ JON O. NEWMAN, CIRCUIT JUDGE:

This appeal challenges the settlement of a class action that effects major changes in the way New York City discharges its obligations to arrange for the care of children requiring placement in institutions and foster homes. Because New York City has historically contracted with religiously affiliated child care agencies to provide placement for most of the children requiring institutional and foster home settings and because New York law provides for religious matching of children and sectarian child care agencies, the lawsuit posed troublesome issues arising under both the Establishment of Religion and the Free Exercise of Religion Clauses of the Constitution. The suit also raised serious issues under the Equal Protection Clause and related statutes arising from alleged inequality of treatment based on the race of the children. The settlement has been achieved between the plaintiffs, representing a class of Black Protestant children, and the defendant municipal officials responsible for the City's child care system (collectively "the City"). The settlement has also been agreed to by a group of private child care agencies, which intervened in the District Court, initially to oppose the settlement. The settlement was opposed in the District Court and now on appeal by a group of administrators of private child care agencies that characterize themselves as "Catholic and Jewish affiliated" agencies. These administrators (hereinafter "the sectarian agencies") were defendants in the District Court but were dismissed as parties when the settlement was approved. Officials of New York State, who were defendants, were dismissed as parties after advising the District Court that they had withdrawn their objections to the settlement.

The appeal, brought by the sectarian agencies, is from the April 28, 1987, judgment of the District Court for the Southern District of New York (Robert J. Ward, Judge), giving final approval to the settlement. The settlement had been initially approved by Judge Ward on October 8, 1986, subject to compliance with four conditions. The final judgment ruled that the conditions had been met....

Under New York law children are "placed" in institutions or foster care homes by one of two procedures. Some are taken away from their parents upon a finding by the Family Court of abuse or neglect, others are voluntarily committed by parents. In both situations the child is placed in the custody of the New York City Commissioner of Social Services. About 17,000 children are currently in placement.

New York City has the option of caring for these children in its own facilities or contracting with private agencies. In pursuance of a long tradition, it has elected to rely heavily on private agencies. At present more than 90% of the children are placed through private agencies. The City contracts with some 60 private agencies. Most of them are religiously affiliated. These agencies place the child either with a foster family or in an institution run by the agency, depending on the child's needs. About 70% of the children are in foster homes. About 90% of the per diem expenses of the children are paid to the agencies from federal, state, and city funds.

The religious matching aspect of New York's child care scheme is set forth in state constitutional and statutory provisions. The State Constitution provides that a child shall be placed "when practicable, in an institution or agency governed by persons, or in the custody of a person, of the same religious persuasion as the child." N.Y. Const. art. 6, § 32 (McKinney 1987). The primary implementing statute provides that a commitment shall be made "when practicable, to an authorized agency under the control of persons of the same religious faith as that of the child." N.Y.Soc.Serv.Law § 373(1) (McKinney 1983). The statute further provides that it shall be applied "so far as consistent with the best interests of the child" and "where practicable ... so as to give effect to the religious wishes" of the parents. In the absence of the parents' expressed wishes, "it shall be presumed that the parent wishes the child to be reared in the religion of the parent."

These religious matching provisions were authoritatively construed by the New York Court of Appeals in 1972. Considering the provisions in the context of an adoption, the Court said that the statutes "place[ ] primary emphasis on the temporal best interests of the child, although the religious preference of the natural parents remains a relevant consideration." "[R]eligion," the Court continued, "is but one of many factors in the placement of a child," and a religious placement, "though desirable, is not mandatory."

The pending litigation, brought initially to challenge the state law provisions regarding religious matching in connection with publicly funded child care placements, was initiated in 1973. ... Wilder v. Sugarman, 385 F.Supp. 1013 (S.D.N.Y.1974) (per curiam) (Wilder I). Since the Court's reasoning bears on issues raised in the pending appeal, it must be set forth, at least briefly.

The Court initially analyzed the Establishment Clause claim under the three-part test of Lemon v. Kurtzman, 403 U.S. 602 (1971).... Viewing the state law provisions for funding and religious matching as part of an integrated scheme, the three-judge court in *Wilder I* concluded that the scheme did not have a solely secular purpose and did have an effect that, "[a]bsent countervailing circumstances, ... could be to impermissibly inculcate religion." However, the Court concluded, such countervailing circumstances arose out of the State's obligation, once it accepted the responsibility for caring for the children in the place of their parents, to enforce the parents' right to determine the religious upbringing of their children, and to assure the children's rights under the Free Exercise Clause. The Court analogized the situation to a state's responsibility to make provision for the religious needs of those in its care in prisons, hospitals, and military establishments. Finally, the Court considered the suggestion that the State could fulfill its obligations toward the parents and the children by placing the children in the care of non-religious agencies and then arranging for the religious needs of the children to be met outside the purview of the child care agencies. That option, the Court believed, would itself encounter Establishment Clause concerns because the State would become "hopelessly entangled in religion." Thus, obviously sensitive to the tension between the Establishment and the Free Exercise Clauses no matter how New York chose to meet the religious needs of children in its care, the Court upheld the statutory scheme on its face and deferred for further proceedings inquiry as to whether the implementation of any aspect of the scheme violated the Constitution.

After the decision in *Wilder I,* discovery ensued, and the complaint was amended several times. Ultimately a fourth amended complaint was filed in 1983, which set forth four claims that awaited trial at the time of the settlement. These were that the City's child care scheme (1) discriminates on the basis of race in that Black children are placed in disproportionately low numbers in Catholic and Jewish agencies, which tend to be the agencies that are better funded and provide higher quality services, (2) discriminates on the basis of religion in that, among other things, Protestant children wait longer for placement and are placed in inferior programs compared with Catholic and Jewish children, (3) involves an excessive entanglement of government with religion that violates the Establishment Clause, and (4) infringes the Free Exercise rights of Protestant children in that, among other things, there are no agencies operated by members of most of the Protestant sects and that Protestant children are chilled in the exercise of their own religion when placed in the care of Catholic and Jewish agencies....

In April 1984 the plaintiffs and the City defendants presented a proposed settlement for approval by the District Court....

The settlement proclaims its purposes to be the assurance of placement of children without racial or religious discrimination and "appropriate" recognition of preferences for religious matching in a manner consistent with federal and state constitutions, statutes, and regulations. These purposes are implemented by an elaborate plan for child placement that requires the City to place children on a first-come, first-served basis, with a preference for religious matching honored only to the extent that it does not give a child greater access to a program appropriate for his needs over other children for whom the program is also appropriate but who earlier became candidates for placement.

The settlement recognizes that its attempt to provide equal opportunities for placement requires some system for determining the relative quality of various agencies that provide the services appropriate for any particular child. To this end, the settlement provides for classification of agencies and programs by one or more expert consultants to be selected by the City with the participation of plaintiffs' counsel and the signatory and nonsignatory agencies.

Once the classification has been made, the City will be required to place a child in the best available program appropriate for the child's needs. If the parents express a preference for a religious matching placement, the City will be required to place the child in the best available program of an agency with the preferred religious affiliation, provided there is a vacancy. If no vacancy exists, the parent then has a three-fold option: (a) having the child wait until there is a vacancy in the best "in-religion" program, (b) having the child placed in the next best "in-religion" program, or (c) having the child placed in the best available "out-of-religion" program. The preference of a child over fourteen is to be given serious consideration. Exceptions to the first-come, first-served principle may be made for "compelling therapeutic reasons."

The settlement also permits an exception from its basic pattern to be made for children whose parents request placement in programs "specially designated" by the City to care for children of religious groups with "adherents whose religious beliefs pervade and determine the entire mode of their lives, regulating it with detail through strictly enforced rules of the religion." The plaintiffs and the City contemplate that the Ohel Children's Home, which provides child care in an Orthodox Jewish setting, would be an agency falling within this category.

In order to meet concerns arising under the Free Exercise Clause, the settlement includes a "religious practices" section imposing requirements upon the City and all contracting agencies. As summarized by the District Court:

> Specifically, each agency would provide "comparable opportunities" for children to practice their own religion and observe religious holidays, would permit but not require children in its care to attend religious or holiday observances on its premises, would not impose religious dietary practices (to the extent practicable) on children who do not wish to

follow them, would provide benefits and privileges to children without regard to religion, and would not convey religious tenets regarding family planning except in the course of providing religious counseling. SSC [Special Services for Children, the City's agency responsible for child placement] would ensure that all children have "meaningful access to the full range of family planning information, services and counseling" through the agency or an outside source or both. Religious symbols would be permitted in children's rooms at their request; agencies would not display "excessive religious symbols."

The settlement is to last for three years after full implementation of the classification system or five years after entry of the stipulation on which the settlement is based, whichever is sooner. This Court granted a partial stay of the final judgment pending appeal, permitting the City to proceed with steps preparatory to implementation of the settlement but deferring those aspects of the settlement that change the placement system.

... The appellants advance essentially four objections to the settlement: (1) that it should not have been approved in the absence of a prima facie case of discrimination because it adopts race-conscious remedies, (2) that it violates New York requirements for religious matching, (3) that it infringes the free exercise rights of the children and their parents, and (4) that it will precipitate excessive entanglement between government and religion in violation of the Establishment Clause.

1. *Lack of evidence to justify race-conscious remedies....*

The basis for the appellants' claim of race-conscious remedies is the requirement that statistics be maintained as to the race and religion of the children placed with each agency. Contrary to the appellants' contention, this requirement is not intended to force each agency to take its proportionate share of each racial and religious group. The statistics serve the entirely permissible purpose of providing a basis for determining whether, despite the nondiscriminatory objectives of the decree, some discrimination is in fact occurring.

Expanding their contention that the settlement adopts a race-conscious remedy, the appellants contend that it will result in reverse discrimination of a type proscribed by cases such as Regents of the University of California v. Bakke, 438 U.S. 265 (1978). Since no quota has been imposed upon any agency to take any prescribed number of children of any particular race or religion, Bakke is not remotely applicable. Appellants' claim of reverse discrimination is in reality only another way of describing the fact that a prohibition against discrimination on the basis of race or religion tends over time to result in a distribution among the relevant entities—here, child care agencies—of members of racial and religious groups approximately proportional to their numbers in the relevant population. It is a perversion of the term to call this "reverse discrimination." To the extent that the appellants are really complaining about the prospect that Catholic and Jewish children might be placed in Catholic and Jewish agencies less frequently than occurred in the past, the claim will be considered subsequently when appellants' Free Exercise Clause contentions are examined.

2. *Violation of New York religious matching requirements.*

... In essence, appellants are contending that the only lawful way to comply with New York's religious matching provisions is to permit each religious agency either to maintain vacancies in its programs to accommodate children seeking in-religion placements or at least, when full, to reject children of other religions and limit its waiting list to children of its own religion. We see nothing in the New York provisions, as construed in *Dickens v. Ernesto,* supra, to support such an interpretation. . . .

3. *Infringement of free exercise rights. . . .*

. . . Appellants do not contend . . . that every child in need of institutional or foster care has a constitutional right to have that care provided by an agency of the child's religion. The context in which this lawsuit arose and has been settled differs significantly from the context of religiously affiliated private education voluntarily selected by parents. It is one thing to recognize the right of parents to choose a religious school for their children as a private alternative to meeting state-imposed educational requirements in public schools. It is quite another matter, however, to suggest that parents who are unable to fulfill their parental obligations, thereby obliging the state to act in their stead, at their request or involuntarily, nonetheless retain a constitutional right to insist that their children receive state-sponsored parenting under the religious auspices preferred by the parents. So long as the state makes reasonable efforts to assure that the religious needs of the children are met during the interval in which the state assumes parental responsibilities, the free exercise rights of the parents and their children are adequately observed.

We agree with the appellants that the first-come, first-served principle is likely to reduce the frequency of in-religion placements, especially with respect to Catholic and Jewish agencies, because preferred agencies will sometimes have no vacancies. This prospect, though doubtless contrary to the preferences of many Catholic and Jewish parents whose children will require placement, is not a denial of their free exercise rights. Indeed, as often happens in litigation arising under the religion clauses of the First Amendment, it is the effort of the settlement to safeguard the children's free exercise rights that encounters the appellants' final objection concerning the Establishment Clause.

4. *Establishment of religion.*

In considering appellants' final contention—that the settlement violates the Establishment Clause—it is worth recalling that this lawsuit was originally brought by plaintiffs who objected on establishment grounds to the basic arrangement whereby New York City purchases child care services from religiously affiliated private agencies. Not surprisingly, the appellant agencies, who wish to continue receiving public funding for their services under the scheme prevailing before the settlement, make no establishment objection to their receipt of public funds. Instead, the appellants contend that the settlement will precipitate a degree of entanglement between government and religious agencies that exceeds the permissible limit of the Establishment Clause. In making this argument, the appellants are obliged to walk a very fine line. They accept the degree of state entanglement with religion that accompanied the funding and placement scheme prior to the settlement. . . . At the same time, the appellants contend that the particular arrangements contemplated by the settlement to assure the protection of the children's free exercise rights require an extra degree of entanglement that is constitutionally impermissible. In essence, appellants say the entanglement that occurred before the settlement was at the allowable limit, but whatever the settlement adds beyond the prior placement scheme goes too far.

. . .

In making our own effort to determine whether the detailed provisions of the settlement overstep the limits of permissible entanglement, we are guided by two related considerations. First, the difference we have previously noted between the contexts of private religious schools and of private religious child care agencies has an important bearing on the entanglement issue. Private religious schools are an option available to parents who choose not to educate their children in public schools. The extent to which government may become entangled in the affairs of those schools in the course of endeavoring to provide financial assistance and other resources has been a continuing concern to the Supreme Court in its effort to enforce the First Amendment precisely because the state's extension of such financial assistance is gratuitous. The state entirely discharges its obligation to the education of children by funding public schools and affording parents the option of paying for religiously affiliated education outside the public schools. In that context, the Supreme Court has drawn the line against impermissible entanglement somewhat rigorously.

In the child care context, however, the state has a responsibility to act for the parents when the parents are unable to discharge their own responsibilities. Yet in exercising its responsibilities the state must take some steps to assure that the religious needs of the children are met. Providing funds or other assistance for this religious component of the parental obligations that the state has assumed is not gratuitous. The state must either concern itself with the children's religious needs directly or provide funds to assure that these needs are met under the auspices of private agencies. There will be some degree of entanglement however the state elects to discharge this responsibility. The entanglement standard cannot be applied as rigorously in this context as in the context of aid to private religious schools.

Second, the considerations that have impelled the Supreme Court to be rigorous in setting entanglement limits in the religious school context have led to a readiness to assess entanglement objections on the basis of what conduct is likely to occur rather than what conduct has in fact occurred.... Since the state was under no obligation to provide any resources in the context of religiously affiliated education, the Court saw no need to accept the risk that provisions that appeared to precipitate excessive entanglement would actually do so in practice. In the context of child care, however, where the state is obliged to act one way or the other to meet religious needs, it is entirely appropriate to accept some risks and assess entanglement primarily on the basis of what occurs in fact, not what is apprehended to occur. Indeed, to assess provisions in this context on the basis of the entanglement that *might* occur runs the unacceptable risk of invalidating some arrangements that would in practice be permissible, with the ultimate result that the state's ability to meet the religious needs of the children for whom it has undertaken to provide care will be seriously impaired. Of course, even in the child care context some arrangements may so inevitably lead to impermissible entanglement that there is no need to await their implementation before recognizing their invalidity. The deficiency of such provisions, however, will normally be readily apparent.

With these considerations in mind, we agree with Judge Ward that the settlement on its face does not exceed an entanglement standard appropriate to the context of state-sponsored child care in substitution of the responsibilities of parents. We acknowledge that some of the provisions pose a risk of excessive entanglement. For example, we are apprehensive about the implementation of paragraph 70(9) of the settlement prohibiting agencies that contract with the City from displaying "excessive" religious symbols. Sensitive to the risk that this provision could be interpreted to lead to an unacceptable degree of intrusion by City officials into the management of the property of religious agencies, Judge Ward wisely narrowed the scope of the provision so that it is enforceable only "where plaintiffs can demonstrate that a religious symbol or aggregation of symbols displayed in the common areas of a child care agency has the effect of impermissibly chilling the Free Exercise rights of children in the agency's care."

Even that narrowed construction, however, does not eliminate the risk of impermissible entanglement in the course of enforcing the provision. Nevertheless, we do not believe the provision is inherently vulnerable, and we believe it prudent to await whatever implementation of the provision may occur, if any. It is by no means certain that the plaintiffs will even attempt to require a detailed measurement of the extent to which religious symbols are displayed, much less precipitate litigation as to whether the display of any particular symbol can be said to be "excessive." In practice, the provision itself may well be only a symbol, reminding the religious agencies that their acceptance of public funds while providing services to children of different religions carries with it an obligation to avoid proselytizing efforts that would make the children feel uncomfortable and unwelcome and that would threaten their rights under the Free Exercise Clause.

. . .

For all of the reasons set forth above, and those more fully elaborated in Judge Ward's opinion, the judgment of the District Court is affirmed.

. . .

NOTE

The stipulation in *Wilder* was limited to ten years. It eventually was dismissed by Marisol A. ex rel. Forbes v. Giuliani, 185 F.R.D. 152 (S.D.N.Y.) (1999), a case based on similar issues and involving some of the same parties. The parties in *Marisol A.* incorporated into the settlement the primary concerns and goals of *Wilder*. The court found that the Agreement "addresse[d] and advance[d] the needs of the Wilder plaintiff class, rendering the continuation of Wilder unnecessary, and dismissed *Wilder*. *Id* at 166." The court also noted that the *Wilder* obligations only affected one aspect of the child welfare system and had proven "difficult to implement within a system with so many other functioning areas." *Id.* For a detailed account of the events surrounding the *Wilder* litigation, see Nina Bernstein, The Lost Children of *Wilder*: The Epic Struggle to Change Foster Care (2002).

4. LIABILITY

DeShaney v. Winnebago County Dept. of Social Services

Supreme Court of the United States, 1989.
489 U.S. 189, 109 S.Ct. 998, 103 L.Ed.2d 249.

■ CHIEF JUSTICE REHNQUIST delivered the opinion of the Court.

The facts of this case are undeniably tragic. Petitioner Joshua DeShaney was born in 1979. In 1980, a Wyoming court granted his parents a divorce and awarded custody of Joshua to his father, Randy DeShaney. The father shortly thereafter moved to Neenah, a city located in Winnebago County, Wisconsin, taking the infant Joshua with him. There he entered into a second marriage, which also ended in divorce.

The Winnebago County authorities first learned that Joshua DeShaney might be a victim of child abuse in January 1982, when his father's second wife complained to the police, at the time of their divorce, that he had previously "hit the boy causing marks and [was] a prime case for child abuse." The Winnebago County Department of Social Services (DSS) interviewed the father, but he denied the accusations, and DSS did not pursue them further. In January 1983, Joshua was admitted to a local hospital with multiple bruises and abrasions. The examining physician suspected child abuse and notified DSS, which immediately obtained an order from a Wisconsin juvenile court placing Joshua in the temporary custody of the hospital. Three days later, the county convened an ad hoc "Child Protection Team"—consisting of a pediatrician, a psychologist, a police detective, the county's lawyer, several DSS caseworkers, and various hospital personnel—to consider Joshua's situation. At this meeting, the Team decided that there was insufficient evidence of child abuse to retain Joshua in the custody of the court. The Team did, however, decide to recommend several measures to protect Joshua, including enrolling him in a preschool program, providing his father with certain counselling services, and encouraging his father's girlfriend to move out of the home. Randy DeShaney entered into a voluntary agreement with DSS in which he promised to cooperate with them in accomplishing these goals.

Based on the recommendation of the Child Protection Team, the juvenile court dismissed the child protection case and returned Joshua to the custody of his father. A month later, emergency room personnel called the DSS caseworker handling Joshua's case to report that he had once again been treated for suspicious injuries. The caseworker concluded that there was no basis for action. For the next six months, the caseworker made monthly visits to the DeShaney home, during which she observed a number of suspicious injuries on Joshua's head; she also noticed that he had not been enrolled in school and that the girlfriend had not moved out. The caseworker dutifully recorded these incidents in her files, along with her continuing suspicions that someone in the DeShaney household was physically abusing Joshua, but she did nothing more. In November 1983, the emergency room notified DSS that Joshua had been treated once again for injuries that they believed to be caused by child abuse. On the caseworker's next two visits to the DeShaney home, she was told that Joshua was too ill to see her. Still DSS took no action.

In March 1984, Randy DeShaney beat 4-year-old Joshua so severely that he fell into a life-threatening coma. Emergency brain surgery revealed a series of hemorrhages caused by traumatic injuries to the head inflicted over a long period of time. Joshua did not die, but he suffered brain damage so severe that he is expected to spend the rest of his life confined to an institution for the profoundly retarded. Randy DeShaney was subsequently tried and convicted of child abuse.

Joshua and his mother brought this action under 42 U.S.C. § 1983 in the United States District Court for the Eastern District of Wisconsin against respondents Winnebago County, its Department of Social Services, and various individual employees of the Department. The complaint alleged that respondents had deprived Joshua of his liberty without due process of law, in violation of his rights under the Fourteenth Amendment, by failing to intervene to protect him against a risk of violence at his father's hands of which they knew or should have known.

The District Court granted summary judgement for respondents.

The Court of Appeals for the Seventh Circuit affirmed.

Because of the inconsistent approaches taken by the lower courts in determining when, if ever, the failure of a state or local governmental entity or its agents to provide an individual with adequate protective services constitutes a violation of the individual's due process rights, and the importance of the issue to the administration of state and local governments, we granted certiorari. We now affirm.

... Petitioners contend that the State deprived Joshua of his liberty interest in "free[dom] from ... unjustified intrusions on personal security," by failing to provide him with adequate protection against his father's violence. The claim is one invoking the substantive rather than procedural component of the Due Process Clause; petitioners do not claim that the State denied Joshua protection without according him appropriate procedural safeguards, but that it was categorically obligated to protect him in these circumstances, see Youngberg v. Romeo, 457 U.S. 307, 309 (1982).

But nothing in the language of the Due Process Clause itself requires the State to protect the life, liberty, and property of its citizens against invasion by private actors. The Clause is phrased as a limitation on the State's power to act, not as a guarantee of certain minimal levels of safety and security. It forbids the State itself to deprive individuals of life, liberty, or property without "due process of law," but its language cannot fairly be extended to impose an affirmative obligation on the State to ensure that those interests do not come to harm through other means.... Its purpose was to protect the people from the State, not to ensure that the State protected them from each other. The Framers were content to leave the extent of governmental obligation in the latter area to the democratic political processes.

. . .

Petitioners contend, however, that even if the Due Process Clause imposes no affirmative obligation on the State to provide the general public with adequate protective services, such a duty may arise out of certain "special relationships" created or assumed by the State with respect to particular individuals. Petitioners argue that such a "special relationship" existed here because the State knew that Joshua faced a special danger of abuse at his father's hands, and specifically proclaimed, by word and by deed, its intention to protect him against that danger. Having actually undertaken to protect Joshua from this danger—which petitioners concede the State played no part in creating—the State acquired an affirmative "duty," enforceable through the Due Process Clause, to do so in a reasonably competent fashion. Its failure to discharge that duty, so the argument goes, was an abuse of governmental power that so "shocks the conscience," Rochin v. California, 342 U.S. 165, 172 (1952), as to constitute a substantive due process violation.

We reject this argument. It is true that in certain limited circumstances the Constitution imposes upon the State affirmative duties of care and protection with respect to particular individuals. In Estelle v. Gamble, 429 U.S. 97 (1976), we recognized that the Eighth Amendment's prohibition against cruel and unusual punishment, made applicable to the States through the Fourteenth Amendment's Due Process Clause, requires the State to provide adequate medical care to incarcerated prisoners. We reasoned that because the prisoner is unable " 'by reason of the deprivation of his liberty [to] care for himself,' " it is only " 'just' " that the State be required to care for him.

In Youngberg v. Romeo, 457 U.S. 307 (1982), we extended this analysis beyond the Eighth Amendment setting, holding that the substantive component of the Fourteenth Amendment's Due Process Clause requires the State to provide involuntarily committed mental patients with such services as are necessary to ensure their "reasonable safety" from themselves and others. Id., at 315, 324 (dicta indicating that the State is also obligated to provide such individuals with "adequate food, shelter, clothing, and medical care"). As we explained, "[i]f it is cruel and unusual punishment to hold convicted criminals in unsafe conditions, it must be unconstitutional [under the Due Process Clause] to confine the involuntarily committed—who may not be punished at all—in unsafe conditions."

But these cases afford petitioners no help. Taken together, they stand only for the proposition that when the State takes a person into its custody and holds him there against his will, the Constitution imposes upon it a corresponding duty to assume some responsibility for his safety and general well-being. The rationale for this principle is simple enough: when the State by the affirmative exercise of its power so restrains an individual's liberty that it renders him unable to care for himself, and at the same time fails to provide for his basic human needs—e.g., food, clothing, shelter, medical care, and reasonable safety—it transgresses the substantive limits on state action set by the Eighth Amendment and the Due Process Clause. The affirmative duty to protect arises not from the State's knowledge of the individual's predicament or from its expressions of intent to help him, but from the limitation which it has imposed on his freedom to act on his own behalf. In the substantive due process analysis, it is the State's affirmative act of restraining the individual's freedom to act on his own behalf—through incarceration, institutionalization, or other similar restraint of personal liberty—which is the "deprivation of liberty" triggering the protections of the Due Process Clause, not its failure to act to protect his liberty interests against harms inflicted by other means.

The *Estelle–Youngberg* analysis simply has no applicability in the present case. Petitioners concede that the harms Joshua suffered did not occur while he was in the State's custody, but while he was in the custody of his natural father, who was in no sense a state actor.[9] While the State may have been aware of the dangers that Joshua faced in the free world, it played no part in their creation, nor did it do anything to render him any more vulnerable to them. That the State once took temporary custody of Joshua does not alter the analysis, for when it returned him to his father's custody, it placed him in no worse position than that in which he would have been had it not acted at all; the State does not become the permanent guarantor of an individual's safety by having once offered him shelter. Under these circumstances, the State had no constitutional duty to protect Joshua.

9. Complaint ¶ 16, App. 6 ("At relevant times to and until March 8, 1984 [the date of the final beating], Joshua DeShaney was in the custody and control of Defendant Randy DeShaney"). Had the State by the affirmative exercise of its power removed Joshua from free society and placed him in a foster home operated by its agents, we might have a situation sufficiently analogous to incarceration or institutionalization to give rise to an affirmative duty to protect. Indeed, several Courts of Appeals have held, by analogy to *Estelle* and *Youngberg*, that the State may be held liable under the Due Process Clause for failing to protect children in foster homes from mistreatment at the hands of their foster parents. See Doe v. New York City Dept. of Social Services, 649 F.2d 134, 141–142 (C.A.2 1981), after remand, 709 F.2d 782, cert. denied sub nom. Catholic Home Bureau v. Doe, 464 U.S. 864 (1983); Taylor ex rel. Walker v. Ledbetter, 818 F.2d 791, 794–797 (C.A.11 1987) (en banc), cert. pending sub nom. Ledbetter v. Taylor, No. 87–521. We express no view on the validity of this analogy, however, as it is not before us in the present case.

It may well be that, by voluntarily undertaking to protect Joshua against a danger it concededly played no part in creating, the State acquired a duty under state tort law to provide him with adequate protection against that danger. See Restatement (Second) of Torts § 323 (1965) (one who undertakes to render services to another may in some circumstances be held liable for doing so in a negligent fashion); see generally W. Keeton, D. Dobbs, R. Keeton, & D. Owen, Prosser and Keeton on the Law of Torts § 56 (5th ed. 1984) (discussing "special relationships" which may give rise to affirmative duties to act under the common law of tort). But the claim here is based on the Due Process Clause of the Fourteenth Amendment, which, as we have said many times, does not transform every tort committed by a state actor into a constitutional violation. A State may, through its courts and legislatures, impose such affirmative duties of care and protection upon its agents as it wishes. But not "all common-law duties owed by government actors were . . . constitutionalized by the Fourteenth Amendment." Because, as explained above, the State had no constitutional duty to protect Joshua against his father's violence, its failure to do so—though calamitous in hindsight—simply does not constitute a violation of the Due Process Clause.

Judges and lawyers, like other humans, are moved by natural sympathy in a case like this to find a way for Joshua and his mother to receive adequate compensation for the grievous harm inflicted upon them. But before yielding to that impulse, it is well to remember once again that the harm was inflicted not by the State of Wisconsin, but by Joshua's father. The most that can be said of the state functionaries in this case is that they stood by and did nothing when suspicious circumstances dictated a more active role for them. In defense of them it must also be said that had they moved too soon to take custody of the son away from the father, they would likely have been met with charges of improperly intruding into the parent-child relationship, charges based on the same Due Process Clause that forms the basis for the present charge of failure to provide adequate protection.

. . .

■ JUSTICE BLACKMUN, dissenting.

Today, the Court purports to be the dispassionate oracle of the law, unmoved by "natural sympathy." But, in this pretense, the Court itself retreats into a sterile formalism which prevents it from recognizing either the facts of the case before it or the legal norms that should apply to those facts. As Justice Brennan demonstrates [in his dissent] the facts here involve not mere passivity, but active state intervention in the life of Joshua DeShaney—intervention that triggered a fundamental duty to aid the boy once the State learned of the severe danger to which he was exposed.

The Court fails to recognize this duty because it attempts to draw a sharp and rigid line between action and inaction. But such formalistic reasoning has no place in the interpretation of the broad and stirring clauses of the Fourteenth Amendment. Indeed, I submit that these clauses were designed, at least in part, to undo the formalistic legal reasoning that infected antebellum jurisprudence, which the late Professor Robert Cover analyzed so effectively in his significant work entitled Justice Accused (1975).

Like the antebellum judges who denied relief to fugitive slaves, the Court today claims that its decision, however harsh, is compelled by existing legal doctrine. On the contrary, the question presented by this case is an open one, and our Fourteenth Amendment precedents may be read more broadly or narrowly depending upon how one chooses to read them. Faced with the choice, I would adopt a "sympathetic" reading, one which comports with dictates of fundamental justice and recognizes that compassion need not be exiled from the province of judging. Cf. A. Stone, Law, Psychiatry, and Morality 262 (1984) ("We will make mistakes if we go forward, but doing nothing can be the worst mistake. What is required of us is moral ambition. Until our composite sketch becomes a true portrait of humanity we must live with our uncertainty; we will grope, we will struggle, and our compassion may be our only guide and comfort").

Poor Joshua! Victim of repeated attacks by an irresponsible, bullying, cowardly, and intemperate father, and abandoned by respondents who placed him in a dangerous predicament and who knew or learned what was going on, and yet did essentially nothing except, as the Court revealingly observes, "dutifully recorded these incidents in [their] files." It is a sad commentary upon American life, and constitutional principles—so full of late of patriotic fervor and proud proclamations about "liberty and justice for all," that this child, Joshua DeShaney, now is assigned to live out the remainder of his life profoundly retarded. Joshua and his mother, as petitioners here, deserve—but now are denied by this Court—the opportunity to have the facts of their case considered in the light of the constitutional protection that 42 U.S.C. § 1983 is meant to provide.

NOTES

1. In May, 1995, United States District Judge Thomas F. Hogan ordered the District of Columbia to relinquish its authority over the $53 million annual program that cares for some 5,000 abused or abandoned children. This decision marked the first time that an American court seized control of an entire child welfare system. Toni Locy, Washington Post, May 23, 1995, at A11. Jerome Miller, a nationally recognized specialist in the care of abused and troubled children, was later selected to be the receiver. Locy, Washington Post, August 12, 1995, at B1.

The receivership ended on June 15, 2001, and responsibility was transferred to a newly-established Cabinet-level Child and Family Services Agency. The Order terminating receivership created a probationary period that will end when the District of Columbia has demonstrated progress on a series of performance measures. *See* Sari Horwitz & Scott Higham, *D.C. Child Welfare Receivership Ends; Williams to Take Over Agency in June,* WASH. POST, May 23, 2001, at B03; see also States News Service, Hearing Statement: Subcommittee on District of Columbia Appropriations, Mar. 10, 2005.

2. For insight into the foster care system, see the District Court's opinion in *LaShawn A. v. Dixon,* 762 F.Supp. 959 (D.D.C.1991). The court described some of the harm to children caused by deficiencies in the District of Columbia's foster care system:

> LaShawn came into custody in September 1986, when she was two-and-a-half years old.... LaShawn was placed in the foster home of a woman in her sixties who had no interest in adopting [her]. She had no contact with her natural family for at least two years after she came into care. During this period, a psychiatrist who examined her discovered potential psychiatric problems and developmental delays.... A psychiatric evaluation ... indicated she may have been experiencing an overuse of physical punishment and perhaps even sexual abuse in her foster home.... Dr. Eist concluded that LaShawn suffered from "Attention Deficit Hyperactivity Disorder," was severely emotionally delayed, and was overwhelmed by stimuli.... [S]he will likely experience four to six exacerbations of depression throughout her adulthood, lasting anywhere from one to four years each. Dr. Eist ... concluded that the mishandling of her case while in custody contributed to her disorders.

> . . . With minor exceptions, Kevin has been in the District's custody in his entire life. . . . Kevin is now 11 years old. He has been in 11 different placements, including foster homes, group homes, residential treatment facilities, and hospitals. . . . Reports . . . indicate that he might not be able to tolerate the intensity of a family setting due to his history of abandonment. Although adoption has been Kevin's planning goal for much of his life, his case has never been referred to the Adoption and Placement Resources Branch. . . . Dr. Clotworthy testified that he believed that the frequent changes in placements were each interpreted by Kevin as being his fault and signifying that something was wrong with him. . . . In Dr. Clotworthy's opinion, Kevin was moved at inappropriate times, was returned to his mother inappropriately, was not prescribed medication early enough (to control his depression and hyperactivity), and was generally not provided with the help he needed to be a success in school or at other endeavors.

762 F.Supp. at 983, 985.

3. In Suter v. Artist M., 503 U.S. 347 (1992), respondent class sought declaratory and injunctive relief against the Illinois Department of Children and Family Services (DCFS) under the Adoption Assistance and Child Welfare Act of 1980, 42 U.S.C. § 620–628, 670–679a. The Act establishes a federal reimbursement program for expenses incurred by States in administering foster care and adoption services. Respondents alleged that DCFS failed to make "reasonable efforts . . . to prevent or eliminate the need for removal of [a] child from his home" as required to qualify for the program. 42 U.S.C. § 671(a)(15). Rejecting the lower courts' finding of an implied cause of action, the Supreme Court held that the "reasonable efforts" requirement is to be enforced by the Secretary of Health and Human Services, and not through private individuals and remedies.

Nichol v. Stass

Supreme Court of Illinois, 2000.
192 Ill.2d 233, 248 Ill.Dec. 931, 735 N.E.2d 582.

■ JUSTICE MILLER.

. . . The plaintiffs alleged that Jonathan, their son, died while in the care of the Stasses, who were acting as Jonathan's foster parents at the time of his death and who were allegedly under the supervision of the Human Enrichment and Developmental Association (HEDA). The plaintiffs sought recovery from the defendants under several different theories. The trial judge dismissed the plaintiffs' action against the Stasses on the ground that it was barred by sovereign immunity. The appellate court affirmed . . .

According to the allegations in the complaint, Jonathan died on June 16, 1995, while at the Stasses' home and in their care, by drowning in a toilet. He was two years old. The plaintiffs sought recovery from each of the defendants under the Wrongful Death Act, the Rights of Married Persons Act, and the Survival Act, alleging that the defendants negligently violated various duties imposed by the common law and by administrative regulations, and, further, that liability was established under the doctrine of *res ipsa loquitur.* The complaint alleged that the Stasses failed to supervise Jonathan, failed to protect him from hazards within the home, failed to provide him with sufficient food and water, and failed to provide him with immediate medical care after the occurrence. The amended complaint described HEDA as an independent licensed child welfare agency that has contracted with the Department of Children and Family Services "to provide supervision, inspections, management, guidance and discipline" to foster parents and foster children. The amended complaint further asserted that HEDA "was in charge of, supervisor of, manager of, and director of" the Stasses. The plaintiffs alleged, among other things, that HEDA negligently failed to supervise the Stasses, failed to ensure that the child was provided with adequate food and water, failed to complete background checks on the Stasses, and failed to place the child in a home "free from observable hazards."

. . . [T]he Stasses moved to dismiss the counts of the amended complaint that were directed against them, arguing that the claims were barred by the doctrines of sovereign immunity and public officials' immunity. Following a hearing, the trial judge stated that he would deny the Stasses' motion. Counsel for the Stasses then advised the trial judge that a pending case in the appellate court raised a similar issue, and the judge said that he would postpone his ruling on the motion until the outcome of the appeal was known. The appellate court soon filed its opinion in the other case, *Griffin v. Fluellen, 283 Ill. App. 3d 1078, 219 Ill. Dec. 167, 670 N.E.2d 845 (1996)*, holding that the foster parent named as a defendant in that action was a state employee and could invoke the protection of the sovereign immunity doctrine. In a later proceeding in the case at bar, the trial judge concluded that he was required to follow *Griffin* and granted the Stasses' motion to dismiss. The trial judge also entered a finding . . . permitting the plaintiffs to appeal immediately from that ruling; the plaintiffs' separate claims against HEDA remained pending in the circuit court of Cook County, and they are not at issue in this appeal.

The appellate court affirmed the circuit court's dismissal order. The appellate court believed that the Stasses should be considered agents of the state and therefore could assert the protection of the sovereign immunity doctrine. The court theorized that the state owed the foster child a nondelegable duty of care and that the state would therefore be vicariously liable for the foster parents' conduct. The court rejected the plaintiffs' contention that the Stasses, even as agents of the state, could still be liable for the Jonathan's death because they owed the child a duty of care that was entirely independent of their status as foster parents . . .

Before this court, the plaintiffs contend that the defendants are neither employees nor agents of the state and therefore cannot avoid suit through the sovereign immunity doctrine. The Stasses, in response, maintain that the lower courts correctly concluded that they are state employees or agents and that the plaintiffs' action against them is one in substance against the State of Illinois, triggering the sovereign immunity doctrine. The Stasses also argue, as an alternative ground in support of the judgments below, that even if they are not protected from suit by sovereign immunity, they may still assert parental immunity as an affirmative defense to the plaintiffs' action. We will consider these contentions in turn.

Article XIII, section 4, of the Illinois Constitution provides, "Except as the General Assembly may provide by law, sovereign immunity in this State is abolished." The legislature has reinstated sovereign immunity. Section 1 of the State Lawsuit Immunity Act reads:

> "Except as provided in the 'Illinois Public Labor Relations Act', enacted by the 83rd General Assembly, or except as provided in 'AN ACT to create the Court of Claims, to prescribe its powers and duties, and to repeal AN ACT herein named', filed July 17, 1945, as amended, the State of Illinois shall not be made a defendant or party in any court."

Section 8(d) of the Court of Claims Act grants the court of claims exclusive jurisdiction over . . . "all claims against the State for damages in cases sounding in tort, if a like cause of action would lie against a private person or corporation in a civil suit."

In *Healy v. Vaupel, 133 Ill. 2d 295, 308, 140 Ill. Dec. 368, 549 N.E.2d 1240 (1990),* this court summarized the scope and effect of the preceding provisions:

> "Whether an action is in fact one against the State, and hence one that must be brought in the Court of Claims, depends not on the formal identification of the parties but rather on the issues involved and the relief sought. Thus, the prohibition 'against making the State of Illinois a party to a suit cannot be evaded by making an action nominally one against the servants or agents of the State when the real claim is against the State of Illinois itself and when the State of Illinois is the party vitally interested.' " Sovereign immunity affords no protection, however, when it is alleged that the State's agent acted in violation of statutory or constitutional law or in excess of his authority, and in those instances an action may be brought in circuit court."

A threshold question in the present appeal is whether the defendants are in fact state employees or agents ... The appellate court has reached conflicting results on the question whether foster parents are either agents or employees of the state. In the present case and in *Griffin v. Fluellen* ... the appellate court concluded that foster parents are state agents or employees and therefore are protected from suit by the doctrine of sovereign immunity. The appellate court reached the opposite result in *Commerce Bank v. Augsburger, 288 Ill. App. 3d 510, 223 Ill. Dec. 872, 680 N.E.2d 822 (1997),* and in *Swanigan v. Smith, 294 Ill. App. 3d 263, 228 Ill. Dec. 578, 689 N.E.2d 637 (1998),* holding in those cases that foster parents are not state agents or employees and therefore cannot assert immunity from suit under the doctrine of sovereign immunity. We conclude in the present case that the defendants have failed to establish that they are state employees or agents.

The Foster Parent Law does not describe foster parents as either employees or agents. Nor are foster parents deemed state employees in any of a variety of statutes relating to state employment. The record in the present case is not entirely clear concerning the relationship among the Stasses, HEDA, and the Department of Children and Family Services. According to the allegations in the complaint, HEDA, an independent child welfare organization, was "in charge of, supervisor of, manager of, and director of" the Stasses as foster parents. Neither side appended to any of their pleadings copies of the contracts between the Department and HEDA and between HEDA and the Stasses. To be sure, it was the defendants' motion to dismiss, and therefore it was their duty to supply a record in support of their motion. In the absence of those documents, and in light of the relevant statutes and the allegations in the plaintiffs' amended complaint, we must conclude that the Stasses were independent contractors rather than employees or agents of the state.

The Stasses argue, however, that, as foster parents, they were subject to a diverse and comprehensive set of requirements concerning their care for foster children. For example, the Department regulates the cleanliness, temperature, and lighting of a foster home. Pets in the home must be inoculated against rabies. Foster parents must develop and rehearse fire evacuation plans. Foster parents must provide a child with closet and dresser space and adequate bedding Meals and discipline are also subject to extensive regulation.

We do not believe that the preceding measures are anything more than licensing requirements or that they serve to establish the defendants' role as state employees or agents. The state licenses a broad range of activities and professions, often in regulations as detailed and encyclopedic as those involved here. The existence of those administrative requirements, however, does not mean that the persons subject to them are state employees or agents.

Nor is state employment established, for purposes of sovereign immunity, through the State Employee Indemnification Act. Section 1(b) of the Indemnification Act provides, "For the purpose of this Act," in pertinent part:

> "The term 'employee' means . . . individuals who serve as foster parents for the Department of Children and Family Services when caring for a Department ward, . . . but does not mean an independent contractor except as provided in this Section."

. . .

Even though the Indemnification Act terms foster parents "employees," we do not believe that the provision must be construed as establishing foster parents' position as state employees for purposes of sovereign immunity. Rather, the preceding definition simply affirms the entitlement of foster parents to indemnification, without also establishing, for other purposes, their status as government employees or agents. As noted, the provision in the Indemnification Act begins with the restrictive phrase "For the purposes of this Act," limiting the scope of the ensuing definition. Moreover, section 1 of the Act expressly recognizes that some independent contractors might be considered "state employees" for purposes of indemnification, but the provision does not purport to alter their status as independent contractors for all other purposes.

The appellate court also believed that sovereign immunity could be invoked in the present case because, whether or not the defendants are deemed state agents or employees, the state owed Jonathan, a ward of the court, a continuing, nondelegable duty of care. The appellate court further believed that the state would be vicariously liable for conduct of the foster parents in violation of that duty.

We do not disagree with the broad proposition that the state owes certain duties to persons whom it places in state-run institutions or even in private care. [Holdings to this effect, however, come in cases involving] actions under section 1983 *(42 U.S.C. § 1983* (1994)) against the state or state officers, and they concern what degree of misconduct must be shown to give rise to public liability for injuries occurring to a state ward while in private custody. Notably, state liability in those circumstances does not extend to state misconduct that is.

The issues raised in the present case are far different from those involved in the cases cited previously. The plaintiffs in this action are not attempting to recover from the state for its decision to place Jonathan with the Stasses, and we do not believe that the state must be considered the real party in interest in this proceeding.

The appellate court below cited section 424 of the Restatement (Second) of Torts in support of its nondelegable duty analysis. Section 424 provides:

> "One who by statute or by administrative regulation is under a duty to provide specified safeguards or precautions for the safety of others is subject to liability to the others for whose protection the duty is imposed for harm caused by the failure of a contractor employed by him to provide such safeguards or precautions."

We do not believe that section 424 is applicable here. Under the circumstances envisioned by section 424, it is the principal in the first instance, and not the independent contractor, who must be required by statute or regulation to provide specified safeguards. In the present case, however, it is the principal—the state—who has imposed these duties on the independent contractor; the administrative regulations pertinent to this case are imposed by the state on foster parents.

The appellate court also cited sections 214 and 251 of the Restatement (Second) of Agency in support of its discussion of this question. Section 214 provides:

> "A master or other principal who is under a duty to provide protection for or to have care used to protect others or their property and who confides the performance of such duty to a servant or other person is subject to such others for harm caused to them by the failure of such agent to perform the duty."

Under section 251, a principal may be liable for physical harm caused by the negligence of a "servant or a non-servant agent: (a) in the performance of an act which the principal is under a duty to have performed with care." Again, although foster parents are required to comply with numerous administrative regulations, we do not find anything that imposes on the state an independent duty to guarantee compliance by foster parents with those provisions. In addition, the hallmark of a nondelegable duty is the right of the principal "to control physical details as to the manner of performance" by the actor. The administrative regulations cited in this case, however, do not go so far.

We agree with the plaintiffs that whatever duty there is to provide placement, to institute procedures, or even to exercise general authority over foster children is not the same as a continuing, nondelegable duty to provide for the care of children placed in foster homes. Moreover, even if a continuing duty can be said to exist, we agree with the plaintiffs' observations that it would pertain to the relationship between the state and the foster children and not to the relationship between the state and foster parents, and that it would not operate to confer sovereign immunity on foster parents.

. . . As a separate ground in support of the judgment below, however, the defendants now contend, for the first time in these proceedings, that they are shielded from liability by the doctrine of parental immunity. They argue that they stand *in loco parentis* in relation to the foster child and that they must therefore enjoy the same protection from liability that a child's biological parents could assert, if the latter had retained custody of the child.

In *Cates v. Cates, 156 Ill. 2d 76, 189 Ill. Dec. 14, 619 N.E.2d 715 (1993),* this court reevaluated the doctrine of parental immunity, abrogating its application in a limited number of circumstances. The child in that case was injured in an automobile collision that occurred as she was riding in a car being driven by her father, and the court concluded that the father was not immune from suit. The court distinguished the child's action in that case from conduct inherent to the parent-child relationship, with respect to which the doctrine of parental immunity survived. The court explained:

> "Thus, under our standard, parental discretion in the provision of care includes maintenance of the family home, medical treatment, and supervision of the child. A child may attempt to sue a parent alleging that the child fell on a wet, freshly mopped floor in the home, but the immunity

would bar such an action because the parent was exercising his discretion in providing and maintaining housing for the child."

Courts in other states are divided on this question, with some jurisdictions allowing the assertion of parental immunity by foster parents and other jurisdictions denying it. We conclude that a limited form of parental immunity should be available in negligence actions against foster parents ... [A]lthough the relationship between foster parents and foster children is not identical with the relationship between biological parents and their children, we believe that it would be anomalous to reject some form of the defense in these circumstances. The rationale identified by the *Cates* court as justifying the retention of some portion of the doctrine—the preservation of parental authority and discipline—is also applicable in the foster parent setting. Although foster parents receive compensation for their role, they exercise a substantial amount of discretion in discipline, supervision, and care, areas in which *Cates* found immunity to be appropriate ...

An analogous situation arises in the educational context. In *Kobylanski v. Chicago Board of Education, 63 Ill. 2d 165, 347 N.E.2d 705 (1976),* this court determined that sections ... of the School Code ... which conferred upon teachers the status of parents or guardians, entitled teachers to a qualified immunity for their actions in supervising and disciplining students ...

We believe that a similar rationale provides further support for our decision to extend a qualified form of parental immunity to foster parents. Like teachers, foster parents receive compensation for their work. Moreover, the relationship between a foster parent and a foster child, like the relationship between a teacher and a student, is not permanent and may even be relatively brief. Yet foster parents, like teachers and biological parents, are responsible for a broad range of decisions affecting the vital interests of the children involved. It would be anomalous to grant a qualified immunity to educators and biological parents but to deny immunity entirely to foster parents, who, in their relationships with their foster children, share many important similarities with the others ...

To be sure, the defendants correctly suggest that the scope of parental immunity in this context must be tempered by the circumstances peculiar to the foster-child relationship. Thus, the defendants acknowledge that parental immunity should not be available when, for example, the underlying conduct resulted in the revocation of a foster parent's license or a finding of neglect, or when it is the subject of a criminal charge. The defendants also suggest that any recognized immunity should not override Department regulations to the contrary. We believe that these are appropriate restrictions on the scope of the immunity in these circumstances.

. . .

The Stasses did not submit any affidavits or other material in support of their dismissal motion, even under the two theories they pursued in the circuit court, so in considering the defense of parental immunity we are necessarily limited to an examination of the amended complaint, and an assessment of whether the allegations in the amended complaint on their face disclose that the action is barred by parental immunity. In light of the procedural posture of this case, we are not prepared at this time to determine whether the plaintiffs' action is completely barred by the doctrine of parental immunity.

. . .

On the present record, we believe that there remains a genuine issue of material fact concerning the Stasses' parental immunity defense. The defendants did not raise this particular theory in the circuit court. Although that omission does not preclude them from now arguing the theory as an alternative ground in support of the ruling below, it does mean that the issues on this point were not shaped as they ordinarily would have been through the adversary process. We therefore believe that the plaintiff should be entitled to plead anew.

For the reasons stated, the judgments of the appellate and circuit courts are reversed, and the cause is remanded to the circuit court for further proceedings.

■ JUSTICE HEIPLE (dissenting).

. . . The majority correctly holds that foster parents are not employees or agents of the state and therefore the Stasses cannot invoke sovereign immunity as a defense to plaintiffs' claims. Regrettably, however, the majority also holds that foster parents enjoy a limited but undefined form of parental immunity which apparently bars some but not all of plaintiffs' claims against the Stasses. I disagree. There are fundamental differences in the relationship between foster parents and foster children and the relationship between a child and his actual parents which preclude extending parental immunity to foster parents . . .

. . . Fundamental differences between a foster parent and an actual parent's relationship with a child militate against extending parental immunity to foster parents. A foster parent is not related to a foster child by blood or adoption. The relationship between a foster parent and a foster child is created exclusively by contract. Foster parents, unlike biological or adoptive parents, receive reimbursement for expenses related to the care of the foster child. *89 Ill. Adm. Code §§ 353.5, 359.4* (1996) (foster parents have "right to receive timely financial reimbursement commensurate with the care needs of the [foster] child"). Moreover, a foster parent's relationship with a foster child is purposely designed to be temporary. When a child is placed in foster care, the state's paramount goal remains to reunite the child with his biological parents. A foster parent is . . . not a foster child's permanent family member and caregiver. The licensing of foster parents, the placement of foster children and the relationship between foster parents and foster children are all extensively regulated by the state. Since foster parents voluntarily assume a contractual duty to provide care and supervision for foster children, they should not be immunized for failure to use reasonable care in the performance of their duties.

The majority states that the primary policy justification for parental immunity—preservation of parental authority and discipline—also applies to foster parents. The extensive regulations governing foster parents' ability to discipline foster children, however, demonstrate that this justification is not viable when applied to foster parents. Foster parents cannot decide for themselves how to discipline foster children; their authority to discipline foster children is strictly circumscribed by regulation. Foster parents, for example, cannot subject foster children to corporal punishment, but they are permitted to assign special or additional chores as a disciplinary measure. Foster parents cannot deprive a foster child of a meal or part of a meal as punishment. Foster parents are permitted to restrict a foster child to his bedroom as punishment, but the bedroom must be unlocked, the foster child can only be confined for a "reasonable" amount of time, and he must be given full access to the bathroom. Foster parents are permitted to withhold a foster child's monthly personal spending money for breaking family rules, but only if the child has been given an oral warning. The State even regulates how much of the foster child's spending money (50%) that the foster parent can withhold for disciplinary reasons. The state places no such restrictions on the authority of biological or adoptive parents to discipline their children.

The majority asserts that " 'exposure to suit for negligence in supervising and disciplining the children in their custody would be a deterrent to the best performance by the foster parents in this regard.' " I have no idea what this means. In any event, the majority has it exactly backwards. Immunizing foster parents from liability eliminates a powerful incentive for ensuring that foster parents adequately perform the duties for which they were hired. The majority's rationale, whatever it means, has little relevance to this case. The Stasses have no more duties to perform as foster parents; they no longer care for Jonathan Nichol. He is dead.

The majority gives great weight to the interest of preserving foster parents' authority to discipline foster children, but the majority fails to consider the foster child's interest in receiving proper care and, if so indicated, compensation for his injuries. Granting parental immunity to the foster parents in this case has the perverse effect of protecting conduct which plaintiffs allege is responsible for severing the only permanent family relationship Jonathan Nichol had, his relationship with his biological parents . . .

Accordingly, I respectfully dissent.

CHAPTER 11

Adoption

A. Historical Background

Jamil Zainaldin, The Emergence of a Modern American Family Law: Child Custody, Adoption, and the Courts, 1796–1851

73 Nw. U. L. Rev. 1038, 1041–45.

Like many aspects of family law, the status of adoption can be traced back through early civilization. Adoption existed in ancient Greece and Rome, in portions of continental Europe that "received" Roman law in the fifteenth century, in the Middle East, in Asia, and in the tribal societies of Africa and Oceania. Adoption in history ordinarily served one or more purposes: preventing the extinction of a bloodline, preserving a sacred descent group, facilitating the generational transfer of a patrimony, providing for ancestral worship, or mending the ties between factious clans or tribes. In each case, the adoption of an individual, most often an adult male, fulfilled some kin, religious, or communal requirement.

Yet, unlike most historical phenomena, the first instance of departure from the traditional model of adoption can be isolated by location, day, and year. On April 2, 1847, the Massachusetts House of Representatives ordered that the Committee on the Judiciary consider the "expediency of providing by law for the adoption of children." On May 13, 1851, the Committee reported to the House "A Bill for the Adoption of Children." There seems to have been little or no opposition. Eleven days later the Massachusetts legislature passed the first general "Act to Provide for the Adoption of Children" in America.[9]

The Massachusetts adoption statute of 1851 was the first *modern* adoption law in history. It is notable for two reasons. First, it contradicted the most fundamental principles of English domestic relations law, and overruled centuries of English precedent and legislation which prohibited the absolute, permanent, and voluntary transfer of parental power to third persons. Second, the traditional status of adoption allocated benefits between

9. Mass.Rev.Stat. ch. 324 (Supp. 1851). Under the novel 1851 Act, child adoption was to proceed by petition in the probate branch of the county court. The petitioners were required to notify and receive the consent of the natural parents to the adoption. If the child's parents or kin were not alive or could not be found, the judge was empowered to appoint some "discreet and suitable person" to act in the proceedings as the child's next friend. If satisfied that the adopters were of "sufficient ability to bring up the child, and furnish suitable nurture and education, having reference to the degree and condition of its parents, and that it is fit and proper that such adoption should take effect," the statute authorized the judge to issue a decree of adoption. The child was to stand toward the adopters as if born to them "in lawful wedlock" for the purposes of legitimacy, custody, support, obedience, inheritance, "and all other legal consequences and incidents of the natural relation of parents and children." All reciprocal rights and obligations between the child and the natural parents were terminated.

the giver and the taker, while the Massachusetts statute distinguished the adoptee as the prime beneficiary. The heart of the adoption transaction became the judicially monitored transfer of rights with the due regard for the *welfare of the child* and the *parental qualifications* of the adopters.

Within the next twenty-five years, more than a score of states would enact some form of adoption law, and in most cases the Massachusetts statute served as the model. Strangely, it would seem, the passage of the first Massachusetts act attracted little public attention. Little or no debate over the issue occurred in the legislature, apparently no social reform movements advocated passage of the law, and, even when the law did appear, few newspapers bothered to take note of the event. And for several years after the passage of the statute, few adopters took advantage of the law. There is, then, no clear explanation for why the legislature passed the law when it did. Nor at first glance would there seem to be any explanation for the casual reception accorded such an apparently radical statute.

The new law may have been part of the larger legislative trend of substituting private enactments with general statutes. Private laws granting divorce, legitimacy, incorporation, and change of name were becoming particularly cumbersome in the 1840s. And there is ample evidence that children throughout the United States were being "adopted" through private acts, especially those concerning change of name . . .

Just why the Massachusetts legislature moved in 1851 may never be known. Perhaps all of these reasons prompted the lawmakers to action. At once they endeavored to protect the child and to endow his standing in the family with status, while conferring upon adopters the rights and duties of parents. The discretionary proceeding in the probate court was perceived as the soundest, most efficient method for effecting adoption.

B. TYPES

Adoption creates a new, legally-recognized parent-child relationship. The child's birth parents must consent to the adoption unless they have been deemed unfit or certain other exceptions apply. In most, although not all, cases, adoption terminates all pre-existing parental rights.

There are two basic types of adoptions: agency adoption and private adoption. Agency adoption involves either a governmental agency or an organization that has been licensed by the government. The latter often are affiliated with churches or other non-governmental social service entities.

In an agency adoption, the birth parents typically relinquish all parental rights to the agency, including the right to place the child themselves for adoption. When the surrender is to a public agency, the child may be placed in foster care for some period of time until suitable adoptive parents are found. The agency investigates potential adoptive parents and maintains a file to which it refers when a child becomes available to adopt. Most agency placements involve children older than infants and children with special needs such as physical disabilities and whose adoption may entitle the adoptive parents to financial assistance from the state.

In private adoptions, the birth parents make a child available to the adoptive parents, often with the aid of an intermediary. In most, but not all, states these intermediaries must be licensed. The major difference between private and agency adoptions is that in private adoptions birth parents are more involved in selection of the adoptive parents. Most adoptions of infants are private adoptions.

As with agency adoptions, the adoptive parents in a private adoption generally must formalize the adoption in a court proceeding. As part of that process, the state must conduct an investigation into the suitability of the adoptive parents. Some observers suggest, however, that agency home study investigations in private placements are not as thorough as those conducted in agency adoptions.

1. Agency Adoption

Florida Department of Children & Families v. Adoption of B.G.J.

Court of Appeal of Florida, Fourth District, 2002.
819 So.2d 984.

■ Stevenson, J.

Appellants, the Department of Children and Families (DCF) and K.W. and M.W., prospective adoptive parents, challenge the final order of consent for adoption filed on December 14, 2001, granting the foster parents, J.M. and G.M., the right to proceed with their adoption of the minor, B.G.J. We reverse because the trial court did not have the authority to place B.G.J. for adoption with the foster parents when that decision was contrary to DCF's appropriate selection of M.W. and K.W. as adoptive parents. In addition, we conclude that there is no competent substantial evidence in the record to support the trial court's finding that DCF orally consented to B.G.J.'s adoptive placement with the foster parents, J.M. and G.M.

B.G.J. was born to a cocaine addicted mother on June 13, 2000, and was thereafter placed in a foster home with J.M. and G.M. Later, DCF filed a Petition for Termination of Parental Rights (TPR) on September 27, 2000, which was issued on January 10, 2001. Pursuant to the TPR order, B.G.J. was placed in the custody of DCF for the purpose of subsequent adoption.

Within a few weeks of placement in the foster home, J.M. and G.M. contacted DCF, expressing interest in adopting B.G.J. DCF adoption unit caseworker, Michelle Foraker, was concerned, however, with J.M. and G.M. proceeding with adoption because of DCF's policy to try to keep siblings together; in March of 2001, Tallahassee residents, K.W. and M.W., finalized their adoption of B.G.J.'s twin brothers.[10]

At a hearing on April 5, 2001, DCF stated that it was exploring other options for the placement of B.G.J., including placement with her siblings. The trial court set a hearing date, asking that Mr. May, a DCF District Administrator, be present to explain DCF's decision. At the hearing, Mr. May stated that he personally preferred placement with J.M. and G.M. because B.G.J. had bonded with them, but that DCF wanted to give due consideration to K.W. and M.W. as well. On August 8, 2001, another hearing was held concerning the adoption of B.G.J. where a DCF adoption supervisor represented to the court that:

10. The twin boys were almost two years old when placed with K.W. and M.W. for adoption in August of 2000. Upon adopting the twins, K.W. and M.W. did not express interest in adopting B.G.J., but DCF wanted to keep that option open, giving them a chance to first adjust to the twins.

> We have a family [the foster parents, J.M. and G.M.] identified that is interested in continuing for permanency for the child. The Department is diligently working on the home study. There was interest of another party that has siblings of the child. The Department recognizes and respects the growing bond with the present care givers. It was a difficult decision. The Department is proceeding with the home study, however, on the present care givers and we hope to have that completed very shortly. We would like, we would be happy if we had a final scheduled, whatever Your Honor's pleasure is.[11]

On September 14, 2001, the parties came before the trial court again in an attempt to finalize B.G.J.'s adoption. This time, DCF stated that it would not place the child with J.M. and G.M. as a permanent placement. Judge Virginia Broome expressed her concern as to why DCF now considered J.M. and G.M. unsuitable and rather preferred K.W. and M.W. as appropriate adoptive parents for B.G.J. DCF stated that it needed more time to conduct a "match staffing" whereby the two families would be considered and rated numerically in several different categories. On September 20, 2001, after the match staffing was completed, DCF gave consent to K.W. and M.W. to adopt B.G.J. On October 29, 2001, B.G.J.'s guardian ad litem filed an objection to DCF's selection of K.W. and M.W. After a hearing was held, Judge Broome decided that it was in B.G.J.'s best interest to stay with J.M. and G.M. because they had bonded. In addition, the trial court found that DCF had previously consented to J.M. and G.M. adopting B.G.J. at the August 8th hearing, and therefore, DCF was estopped from contesting that consent.

The resolution of this case is largely controlled by *C.S. v. S.H., 671 So. 2d 260* (Fla. 4th DCA), *rev. denied, 680 So. 2d 424 (Fla. 1996)*. There, S.D.V–H., a baby girl, was placed in temporary foster care. Subsequently, both the foster parents and the child's biological aunt wished to adopt her. The Department of Health and Rehabilitative Services (now DCF) advised the foster parents of its decision to approve the biological relatives as adoptive parents. The foster parents, however, challenged that decision, alleging that HRS promised them approval as adoptive parents. The trial court concluded that "to remove the child from her 'loving, caring and nurturing environment' would result in psychological stress to the child," and determined that it had authority to grant the foster parents' adoption petition notwithstanding HRS's selection of the biological relatives.

In *C.S.*, this court thoroughly discussed the interplay between the statutory provisions regarding HRS's power to select adoptive parents for children whose parental rights have been terminated and the trial court's overall jurisdiction to entertain adoption petitions, found in Florida Statutes chapters 39 and 63, respectively. Based on that analysis, we concluded that the trial court had no authority to reject an appropriate adoptive placement by HRS, reversed the trial court's final judgment of adoption, and remanded so that the biological relatives could proceed with the adoption. Likewise, we find that the trial court, here, did not have the authority to determine the adoptive placement of B.G.J.

The statutory scheme presumes that DCF is in the best position to determine which family is appropriate for adoption placement, but allows the trial court to review the appropriateness of that selection. DCF performed a match staffing that thoroughly reviewed certain criteria as to which

11. J.M. and G.M. argue on appeal that this statement qualified as consent by DCF to B.G.J.'s adoptive placement with them, and therefore, that DCF was estopped from giving K.W. and M.W. consent to adopt B.G.J.

family would be more suitable for B.G.J. It is DCF's policy to try to keep siblings together, and that policy was given great weight by DCF in its determination that K.W. and M.W. should be the adoptive parents. The trial court's order did not contain any findings that DCF's selection of K.W. and M.W. was inappropriate. Rather, the trial court stated that they were both "fine families" and that "the Court has great admiration for both families." As found in *C.S.*, a trial court cannot interfere with DCF's decision to select an adoptive family "where HRS's selection was appropriate, consonant with its policies and made in an expeditious manner." Furthermore, we find that J.M. and G.M.'s estoppel argument is not well founded. The equivocal statements made by the DCF adoption supervisor at the August 8th hearing did not amount to an oral affirmation of DCF's consent that J.M. and G.M. would be the adoptive parents, and in any event, DCF's consent must be in writing.

Accordingly, we reverse the final order allowing J.M. and G.M. to adopt B.G.J. and remand for further proceedings consistent with this opinion which will allow K.W. and M.W. to proceed with their adoption of B.G.J.

REVERSED and REMANDED.

Vela v. Marywood

Court of Appeals of Texas, Third District, Austin, 2000.
17 S.W.3d 750.

■ Lee Yeakel, J.

This case presents the question of how forthright a licensed child-placing agency must be with an unmarried, expectant mother who seeks its counsel prior to the birth of her child. The child's mother, Corina Vela, is an exemplary young woman who made a mistake. The district court held that the law compels the compounding of her error, terminated her parental rights, and appointed appellee Marywood managing conservator of her child. Corina appeals the district-court judgment.

FACTUAL BACKGROUND

In September 1997, Corina, then nineteen years of age and unmarried, learned she was pregnant. At the time of the district-court trial, Corina, still living with her parents, had completed two years at Austin Community College where she had earned high grades and was planning to attend Southwest Texas State University. Corina is a member of a strong, stable, and supportive family. Her parents have been married for more than twenty-five years and have lived in the same house for over twenty years. They both hold long-term government jobs and are community leaders who volunteer at recreation centers, in political campaigns, and with senior-citizen groups. Corina herself has volunteered at her church, with Big Brothers/Big Sisters, in the neonatal unit at Brackenridge Hospital, and with her eight-year-old sister's Brownie troop. Corina has participated in various school activities and dances with a dance company. There is no evidence that Corina has abused drugs or alcohol or is in any way irresponsible. In fact, all evidence is to the contrary. A state senator and a well-known community activist both testified to the outstanding character of Corina and her family. A neighbor who had lived next to the Velas for over twenty-one years said that Corina is the envy of all the mothers in the neighborhood.

In February 1998, this pregnant young woman sought counseling services from Marywood, a licensed child-placing agency. She met with a Marywood counselor, Aundra Moore, several times in early March.[2] During these meetings, Corina informed Moore that she wanted to place her child for adoption. In Moore's view, Corina was adamant that her child have a future, be in a two-parent family, be safe, and have the security of a family. Moore observed that Corina wanted "the best for her child" and felt that adoption "was the place to go with that." Corina indicated to Moore that her parents could help but she didn't want to burden them. Moore told Corina that "the adoption process is very much at [Corina's] discretion" and that Corina's "wishes and requests" as to what type of family she would place her child with and what type of relationship she would have with her child after adoption would be "considered." At a meeting on March 16, Corina reported to Moore that she had bonded with her unborn child, and Moore noted that Corina "may be grasping the difficulty of her decision."

On March 25, Corina and Moore discussed what Marywood terms an "open adoption," a process by which the birth mother expresses her criteria for adoptive parents.... She also told Moore that "she wanted to visit with the child after the adoption." Moore informed Corina that "her relationship with the adoptive family would establish what type of ongoing relationship [with her child] she would have."

Moore first showed Corina an "Affidavit of Voluntary Relinquishment of Parental Rights" (the "relinquishment affidavit") on March 30.[4] Moore did not discuss the relinquishment affidavit with Corina and did not explain the meaning of the term "irrevocable"; rather, Moore simply "showed her the form" but did not give her a copy to take with her to study....

Corina selected an adoptive couple at her next counseling session with Moore and had a face-to-face meeting with them on April 8. The meeting lasted about an hour. The prospective adoptive parents met all of Corina's criteria and indicated their willingness to comply with post-adoption visits. Throughout Corina's counseling sessions, she and Moore discussed a "shar-

2. Moore describes herself as "a maternity counselor ... responsible for working with birth parents and their families ... in finding options for an unplanned pregnancy."

4. In pertinent part, the relinquishment affidavit reads:

> It is in the best interest of my child that the child be placed for adoption in a suitable home by an agency licensed by the Texas Department of Protective and Regulatory Services to place children for adoption. I therefore designate MARYWOOD, 510 West 26th Street, Austin, Texas, 78705 as managing conservator of the child. I have been informed of my parental rights, powers, duties and privileges. I freely, voluntarily, and permanently give and relinquish to the agency all my parental rights, privileges, powers and duties. I consent to the placement of the child for adoption by this agency.
>
> I fully understand that a lawsuit will be promptly filed in the 126th District Court of Travis County, Texas, to terminate forever the parent-child relationship between me and my child. Termination of the parent-child relationship between me and my child is in the best interest of the child. I understand that by executing this affidavit, I make this termination possible. With this in mind, I hereby declare that this affidavit of relinquishment of parental rights is and shall be final, permanent, and irrevocable. I FULLY UNDERSTAND THAT IF I CHANGE MY MIND AT ANY TIME, I CAN NEVER FORCE THE AGENCY TO DESTROY, REVOKE, OR RETURN THIS AFFIDAVIT AND THAT I CANNOT TAKE BACK OR UNDO THIS AFFIDAVIT IN ANY WAY.
>
> It is in the best interest of my child that this be my last parental act and deed. Not wishing to appear or be cited in the termination suit, I hereby waive the right to issuance, service and return of all process in any suit to terminate the parent-child relationship between me and the child. I agree to termination of the parent-child relationship between the child and me without further notice to me. I FULLY UNDERSTAND THAT I WILL NOT BE INFORMED FURTHER ABOUT THIS SUIT.

ing plan," a standard practice of Marywood. A sharing plan ostensibly allows the birth mother to select the adoptive family, visit her child on a regular basis after the adoption, and exchange letters and pictures. The adoptive parents are aware of the plan prior to placement and agree in writing with Marywood to conform to this arrangement. Significantly, the birth mother does not sign this agreement; thus, neither Marywood nor the adoptive parents enter into any agreement with the birth mother. Marywood admits that aside from advocating that the adoptive parents abide by the plan, Marywood can do nothing if the adoptive parents decide, post-adoption, to disregard it. In fact, the executive director of Marywood admits that the sharing plan is an "empty promise." Clearly, the birth mother has no power to enforce such an agreement. Marywood never discussed the unenforceability of the sharing plan with Corina.

At Corina's last meeting with Moore before her child's birth. . . . Moore . . . discussed the relinquishment affidavit with Corina. Moore read the affidavit to Corina and "talked about each paragraph, what each paragraph means, what it is saying." Moore also asked Corina if she had any questions. Although Moore did not first explain the word "irrevocable," she asked Corina if she knew what it meant. Corina replied that once the relinquishment is signed, it cannot be undone. Moore confirmed that meaning and also told Corina that once she signed the affidavit, she could not "take it back, undo it, or change it."

Corina gave birth to a son on April 24. Moore met with Corina at the hospital on April 26, and Corina signed a temporary foster-care request. Moore told Corina that she "would always be able to visit her baby" and that her baby would always know that Corina was his mother. Corina cried throughout the one-and-one-half-hour visit. Moore scheduled a subsequent meeting with Corina to complete the adoption process. The child was placed in foster care on April 27.

On April 28, Corina and her parents visited Marywood. Before the meeting, Corina was not aware that she was to sign the relinquishment affidavit then and was undecided as to whether she wanted to sign it. During the two-hour meeting, Corina, her parents, and Moore read and discussed the relinquishment affidavit in detail. Eventually, Corina signed the affidavit. During the meeting, and before Corina signed the relinquishment affidavit, Moore told Corina that she would "always be that child's birth mother and that with her sharing plan that she had with the adoptive family that she would have an opportunity to be in that child's life forever"; that she would "always have a relationship with [the adoptive] family and with [her] child"; that requests she made of the adoptive family would be "respected"; that the baby would have "two mothers," "both of whom would have input into his life"; that Corina "would be able to see her son grow up"; and that the birth family would be like the child's extended family. Corina specifically asked what the agency could do to guarantee that she would have continual, post-adoptive visits with the child. Moore responded by "assuring her that . . . the adoptive family has an adoption worker working with them and that they would encourage them to respect what she wished for in terms . . . of sharing and visits. And during their . . . face-to-face visit and even after that, they said that they would respect her wishes in . . . having that sharing plan." Moore repeated to Corina that she would always be a part of the baby's life. According to Corina and her mother, these promises are what convinced Corina to sign the relinquishment affidavit; the promises were "the only reason she signed."

Before the April 28 meeting, Corina did not have a copy of the relinquishment affidavit and did not review it with her parents. Corina was crying when she signed the affidavit, but Moore testified that "it's very common to have tears." Moore asked Corina if signing the relinquishment affidavit "was what she wanted to do" and informed Corina that once she signed it, she "couldn't undo or take it back." Moore never told Corina that signing the relinquishment affidavit meant that she would "never have any legal rights to see [her] child." According to Corina, Moore told her that she would only be "giving up [her] guardianship of [the child]." Corina understood this to mean that she would not be the one "taking care of him and raising him." Corina was not aware and no one informed her that she could have signed a second foster-care agreement to allow herself more time to make the final decision. Moore was the only person who explained the relinquishment affidavit to Corina, and she never told Corina that she could seek legal counsel or another person's opinion. Marywood never revealed to Corina that the relinquishment affidavit could nullify the sharing plan that she believed would allow her a continuing role in her child's life. It is significant that the relinquishment affidavit was never mentioned to Corina until after she and Marywood had devised a sharing plan satisfactory to her. From that point forward, all of Corina's actions and decisions were founded on her belief in and reliance on the sharing plan.

The following day, April 29, Corina asked to visit her child. The same day Marywood filed a petition to terminate Corina's parental rights. On May 1, Corina was allowed to visit her son for one hour at Marywood. Later that day, Corina called Marywood. Exactly what was said in that phone call is disputed. Moore claims that although Corina was crying, in emotional pain, and "having a hard time," Corina never indicated that she wanted to terminate the adoption process. Corina claims that she told Moore that she "wanted [her] baby back" and that she "changed [her] mind." She asked if there was anything she could do, including hiring an attorney. Moore responded that there was nothing that could be done. Corina's mother also called on the afternoon of May 1 and according to Moore, asked if they "could undo the papers" because her daughter was in so much pain. Moore told Corina's mother that the relinquishment was "irrevocable and that it is signed and that there is no way to undo the document." Moore stated that there was nothing "in her conversation with Corina's mother on May 1st that would [have led her] to believe that Corina wanted the baby back" and that the conversation was "about documents." Yet Moore testified at trial that had Marywood known before the child was placed with the adoptive parents that Corina wanted to keep him, Marywood would have returned the child to Corina.

On May 12, an associate judge recommended termination of Corina's parental rights. In spite of the earlier conversations between Marywood, Corina, and Corina's mother, Marywood placed Corina's child with the prospective adoptive parents the day after the associate judge's decision. Corina immediately gave notice that she was appealing the associate judge's termination recommendation to the district court.... Even in the face of this clear and immediate assertion that Corina did not want to give up her child, Marywood continued its efforts to terminate Corina's parental rights.

On June 8, the district court conducted a *de novo* trial. ... The court heard testimony about Corina's stable family situation and unquestioned character. The guardian *ad litem* appointed for the child recommended that termination would *not* be in the best interest of the child and testified that Corina would be a competent parent and the child would be well cared for.

Although initially concerned about Corina's commitment to raising her child, after meeting with Corina the guardian concluded that Corina "impressed [him] as someone who had clearly thought about these things" and wanted to be a mother. Other evidence showed Corina's ability to care for the child: the Velas were building an additional room on their home, had purchased a crib and other necessities, and had arranged health insurance for the child. Corina planned to continue with her schooling while living with her parents. They would all contribute to the child's care, and on days when the family could not provide care, Corina planned to enroll him in the same licensed day-care facility that her younger sister had attended. After hearing this testimony, the district court terminated Corina's parental rights and appointed Marywood managing conservator.

Corina brings this appeal, arguing that (1) there was not clear and convincing evidence that she knowingly and voluntarily executed the relinquishment affidavit, and in fact the evidence shows that she did *not* execute it voluntarily; and (2) there was not clear and convincing evidence that termination of Corina's parental rights was in the best interest of the child....

DISCUSSION

The district court filed findings of facts and conclusions of law.[10]

. . .

II. Termination of Parental Rights

The Family Code provides that the court may order termination of the parent-child relationship if the court finds by clear and convincing evidence: (1) that the parent has: ... (K) executed before or after the suit is filed an unrevoked or irrevocable affidavit of relinquishment of parental rights as provided in this Chapter; ... *and* (2) that termination is in the best interest of the child.

. . .

... Termination proceedings must be strictly scrutinized, and termination statutes are strictly construed in favor of the parent. This oft-chanted mantra emphasizes that we must exercise the utmost care in reviewing the termination of parental rights to be certain that the child's interests are best served and that the parent's rights are acknowledged and protected.

A. Whether the Relinquishment Affidavit was Executed Voluntarily

It is undisputed that Marywood proved by clear and convincing evidence that the relinquishment affidavit was executed in conformity with section 161.001 of the Family Code. However, in her first issue, Corina argues that "no rational trier of fact could find ... that the Affidavit of Relinquishment was executed voluntarily and knowingly, rather than as the result of misrepresentation, fraud, overreaching, and coercion."

10. Two findings are pertinent to this appeal:

6. Corina ... voluntarily executed [the relinquishment affidavit] in accordance with the provisions of the Texas Family Code.

. . .

8. Termination of the parent-child relationship between Corina ... and the child is in the best interest of the child.

The district court concluded, *inter alia*, that "the parent-child relationship between Corina ... and the child should be terminated."

1. Standard of Review

We have held that Corina must carry the burden of proving that she did not voluntarily execute the relinquishment affidavit.

. . .

2. Marywood's Duty to Corina

Corina argues that Marywood affirmatively misrepresented to her facts that induced her to sign the relinquishment affidavit. Specifically, Corina claims that the only reason she signed the relinquishment affidavit was that Marywood led her to believe that she had the right and would continue to play a significant role in her child's life after the adoption, would continue to have conact with her child, and was only giving up guardianship of her child. At the time they were made, these representations were either false or misleading because Marywood knew that Corina would have no legal right to enforce the sharing plan against the adoptive parents. And, because Marywood was in a close relationship with Corina as her counselor, it had a duty to fully disclose that the open-adoption arrangement had no legal effect. Corina also emphasizes that she was never given a copy of the relinquishment affidavit to bring home with her; Marywood never suggested she seek legal advice; and Moore was the only person who ever explained the relinquishment affidavit to her. Thus, Corina insists that she did not voluntarily and knowingly execute the relinquishment affidavit and that she signed only as the result of coercion, misrepresentation, fraud, and overreaching.

. . .

... At common law, the word "fraud" refers to an act, omission, or concealment in breach of a legal duty, trust, or confidence justly imposed, when the breach causes injury to another or the taking of an undue and unconscientious advantage.

. . .

Marywood, by its own admission, is more than an adoption agency. It provides extensive parental-counseling services and advertises these services to the public. Moore testified that she is given the discretion to counsel "openly, objectively, and honestly." Corina, in seeking counseling from Marywood, was reasonably entitled to rely fully and unconditionally on Marywood's representations. We hold that Marywood owed Corina a duty of complete disclosure when discussing adoption procedures, including any proposed post-adoption plan. Complete disclosure encompassed the obligation to tell Corina the entire truth about the ramifications of the sharing plan she had chosen with Marywood's help and to make her fully aware that it lacked legally binding effect. Marywood's duty springs from two sources. First, when Marywood made a partial disclosure to Corina about the post-adoption plan, it assumed the duty to tell the whole truth.... Second, the evidence conclusively establishes that Corina placed special confidence in Moore, who by virtue of the counseling relationship occupied a position of superiority and influence on behalf of Marywood; thus, Moore and Marywood became bound, in equity and good conscience, to act in good faith and with due regard to Corina's interests ...

3. Whether There Is Any Evidence that Corina Voluntarily Signed the Relinquishment Affidavit

... Marywood argues that it discharged any duty it owed Corina and that there is ample evidence that Corina fully understood the relinquishment affidavit and wanted to proceed with the adoption. Marywood points out that Moore read and explained the relinquishment affidavit to Corina on three separate occasions; that Corina and her mother both testified that Corina fully understood the relinquishment affidavit when she signed it; that the relinquishment affidavit itself says it was voluntary; and that after Marywood discussed with Corina her option to parent, Corina still wanted to place the child for adoption.

Although the face of the affidavit reflects it was signed knowingly and voluntarily, we must consider the surrounding circumstances to determine if Corina's signature on the document was procured by misrepresentation, fraud, or the like.... Corina neither signed nor understood the relinquishment affidavit in a vacuum. She signed and understood it in the context of and in reliance on the post-adoption plan that she and Marywood created, a plan that Marywood now admits is an "empty promise." The evidence conclusively establishes that Corina wanted to proceed with the adoption *only* if she could have post-adoption visits with her child; there is no evidence to the contrary.

... Marywood states that it "did not make any guarantees about the [post-adoption] plan." Instead, Marywood merely told Corina that her wishes for post-adoption visits would be "respected" and that Marywood would " 'encourage' the adoptive parents to follow through with the planned relationship with [Corina]."

There is no evidence in the record, however, that Corina was ever told that the post-adoption plan could not be legally enforced. Marywood's words to Corina were at worst deceptive and at best vague.... [I]n counseling Corina, Moore carefully selected her words and minced her explanation of the sharing plan with the result that Corina understood one thing while Moore meant another. Whether the incomplete disclosure was deliberate or inadvertent, it does not satisfy the duty of full disclosure that Marywood owed Corina.

. . .

At the time she signed the affidavit, Corina did not know that the post-adoption plan was unenforceable and thus had no reason to believe that she would not have access to her child. Corina's testimony cannot be considered evidence that the affidavit was signed knowingly and voluntarily because she was testifying about her state of mind *before* she knew that the post-adoption plan was unenforceable.

... We hold that there is no evidence of probative value that supports the district court's finding that Corina voluntarily executed the relinquishment affidavit. Corina has surmounted the first hurdle.

4. Whether Corina Established as a Matter of Law that the Relinquishment Affidavit was Wrongfully Procured

We turn our attention now to [the] second hurdle: Has Corina established as a matter of law that the relinquishment affidavit was procured by fraud, coercion, overreaching, or misrepresentation?

We find no evidence in the record that Corina was compelled by force or threat to sign the relinquishment affidavit. We overrule Corina's issue to the extent that it complains that the affidavit was procured by coercion.

However, we find conclusive evidence in the record that the relinquishment affidavit was wrongfully procured. Considering only Marywood's version of events, we conclude as a matter of law that its statements and omissions to Corina constituted misrepresentation, fraud, or overreaching. Marywood admits that it told Corina that "with her sharing plan ... she would have an opportunity to be in that child's life forever"; that she would "always have a relationship with [the adoptive] family and with [her] child"; that requests she made of the adoptive family would be "respected"; that the baby would have "two mothers," "both of whom would have input into his life"; and that Corina "would be able to see her son grow up." Marywood never told Corina that she would not have any legal right to see her child after she signed the relinquishment affidavit, and even when Corina directly asked if Marywood could guarantee post-adoption visits, Marywood failed to give her a complete answer. Marywood's statements [were] misleading and stop short of complete disclosure. They are half-truths that would lead a reasonable person in Corina's circumstance to believe that she had a continuing right to see her child according to the terms of the sharing plan.... It is undisputed that Corina sought counseling from Marywood to aid her in the difficult decision of whether to keep her child. She was a young woman faced with a life-changing situation. She found comfort in and placed reliance on Marywood's counseling. We need not and do not determine whether Marywood deliberately misled Corina. At a minimum, Marywood's advice and counsel was incomplete. We hold that Corina conclusively established that the relinquishment affidavit was procured by misrepresentation, fraud, or overreaching and therefore was not voluntarily signed. We sustain Corina's first issue and hold that the relinquishment affidavit is void as a matter of law.

B. Best Interest of the Child

Because we have determined that the relinquishment affidavit is void, it is not necessary to decide Corina's second issue, whether there was clear and convincing evidence that termination of her parental rights was in the best interest of the child. We note, however, that without the affidavit, there is scant evidence in the record as to the child's best interest.

. . .

There is no evidence that Corina is an unfit mother or is financially or emotionally unable to care for the needs of her son.

CONCLUSION

In conclusion, we hold that once a child-placing agency undertakes to counsel an expectant mother with regard to her alternatives upon the birth of her child, the agency must provide her with complete information regarding those alternatives. It may not leave the mother to speculate on the consequences of the action upon which she and the agency have agreed. In this particular case, our decision is made difficult because the child is now two years of age and has spent almost his entire life with the prospective adoptive parents. However, any fault lies with the pace of the legal system and not with the mother.

Because we hold that the evidence conclusively establishes that Corina did not voluntarily sign the relinquishment affidavit, we reverse the district court's judgment and render judgment in favor of Corina that her parental rights are not terminated.

Reversed.

Uniform Adoption Act

SECTION 2–405. PROCEDURE FOR EXECUTION OF CONSENT OR RELINQUISHMENT.

. . .

(c) A parent who is a minor is competent to execute a consent or relinquishment if the parent has had access to counseling and has had the advice of a lawyer who is not representing an adoptive parent or the agency to which the parent's child is relinquished.

(d) An individual before whom a consent or relinquishment is signed or confirmed ... shall certify in writing that he or she orally explained the contents and consequences of the consent or relinquishment, and to the best of his or her knowledge or belief, the individual executing the consent or relinquishment:

(1) read or was read the consent or relinquishment and understood it;

(2) signed the consent or relinquishment voluntarily and received or was offered a copy of it;

. . .

(4) received or was offered counseling services and information about adoption; and

(5) if a parent who is a minor, was advised by a lawyer who is not representing an adoptive parent or the agency to which the parent's child is being relinquished, or, if an adult, was informed of the right to have a lawyer who is not representing an adoptive parent or an agency to which the parent's child is being relinquished.

SECTION 2–408. REVOCATION OF CONSENT.

(a) In a direct placement of a minor for adoption by a parent or guardian, a consent is revoked if:

(1) within 192 hours after the birth of the minor, a parent who executed the consent notifies in writing the prospective adoptive parent, or the adoptive parent's lawyer, that the parent revokes the consent, or the parent complies with any other instructions for revocation specified in the consent; or

(2) the individual who executed the consent and the prospective adoptive parent named or described in the consent agree to its revocation.

(b) In a direct placement of a minor for adoption by a parent or guardian, the court shall set aside the consent if the individual who executed the consent establishes:

(1) by clear and convincing evidence, before a decree of adoption is issued, that the consent was obtained by fraud or duress;

. . .

(c) If the consent of an individual who had legal and physical custody of a minor when the minor was placed for adoption or when the consent was executed is revoked, the prospective adoptive parent shall immediately return the minor to the individual's custody and move to dismiss a proceeding for adoption or termination of the individual's parental relationship to the minor. If the minor is not returned immediately, the individual may petition the court named in the consent for appropriate relief. The court shall hear the petition expeditiously.

(d) If the consent of an individual who had legal and physical custody of a minor when the minor was placed for adoption or the consent was executed is set aside under subsection (b)(1), the court shall order the return of the minor to the custody of the individual and dismiss a proceeding for adoption.

2. INDEPENDENT ADOPTION

Matter of Petrie

Supreme Court of Arizona, En Banc, 1987.
154 Ariz. 295, 742 P.2d 796.

■ HOLOHAN, JUSTICE.

This matter comes to us on the objections of the respondent attorney to the findings, conclusions and recommendation of the Disciplinary Commission.

. . .

This matter requires that we answer two questions:

1. Did respondent violate conflict of interest rules by representing multiple clients in an adoption proceeding?

2. If so, is a thirty-day suspension the appropriate sanction?

. . .

The complainants, Gregory and Barbara Pietz (Pietzes) consulted with respondent on July 21, 1981 to express their interest in adopting an infant child. Respondent told the Pietzes that he did not know of any infants available at that time. The Pietzes and respondent agreed that if the Pietzes located a baby for adoption, respondent would represent them in the adoption. The Pietzes paid $30 for this consultation.

The Committee found that shortly before January 26, 1983, the Pietzes received information from a long-time friend, Carolyn Iverson, about a child that would be available for adoption. The Pietzes asked Iverson to make an appointment for respondent to meet with the natural mother, and to inform the respondent specifically that the mother was being referred by the Pietzes. Iverson called respondent, advised him that she had found a baby for the Pietzes, and made an appointment for respondent to meet with the natural mother. The Pietzes had moved to Sierra Vista sometime after their meeting with respondent, so Iverson gave respondent the Pietzes' current address and telephone number in Sierra Vista. She also told him that the Pietzes had become certified by the State of Arizona as acceptable to adopt children.

Respondent testified that he received a call from a woman who advised him of the baby and that "she knew of someone who was interested in an adoption," namely the Pietzes. Respondent claims he did not recognize the Pietzes' name from their visit one and a half years earlier.

The evidence indicates that respondent met with the natural mother and her sister, and he advised them that he had a set of adoptive parents in mind. On January 26, 1983, he wrote to the Pietzes, telling them that he had recently interviewed a woman who intended to place a child for adoption and that the Pietzes' names were given when the interview was arranged. Respondent inquired in the letter whether the Pietzes were interested in the adoption. Respondent received a written response on February 3, 1983, in which the Pietzes stated that they were interested in adopting the child, that they were certified by the State to adopt children, and that they were very hopeful concerning the present situation. The Pietzes' letter disclosed knowledge of facts about the natural mother that respondent had not conveyed to them in his original correspondence. Respondent interpreted the Pietzes' letter as "equivocal" because the Pietzes had questions about the adoption and the fees.

Shortly thereafter, respondent received a phone call from another couple, the Buckmasters, who expressed an interest in adopting a second child. In response to respondent's inquiry on February 18, 1983, the natural mother's sister stated that the mother had no obligation to the Pietzes. At respondent's recommendation, the mother agreed to place the baby with the Buckmasters. The Committee found that respondent recommended placement with the Buckmasters because they were more cooperative than the Pietzes and they were locally situated. In addition, respondent was not "excited" about making two appearances in Cochise County, which may have been necessary if the Pietzes were to adopt the child.

When the Pietzes learned from Iverson that the child was going to another couple, Mr. Pietz called respondent, and respondent advised Mr. Pietz for the first time that he had recommended to the natural mother that the child be placed with someone else. Mr. Pietz told respondent that the Pietzes had referred the child to the respondent and consequently they wanted the child placed with them. Respondent refused to do so. Mr. Pietz then initiated this complaint with the State Bar.

The complaint charged that the respondent violated Disciplinary Rule 5–105(A) and (B), which provides:

> DR 5–105. Refusing to Accept or Continue Employment if the Interests of Another Client May Impair the Independent Professional Judgment of the Lawyer
>
> (A) A lawyer shall decline proffered employment if the exercise of his independent professional judgment in behalf of a client will be or is likely to be adversely affected by the acceptance of the proffered employment.
>
> (B) A lawyer shall not continue multiple employment if the exercise of his independent professional judgment in behalf of a client will be or is likely to be adversely affected by his representation of another client.

It is common for the parties to an independent adoption to retain an attorney to represent their individual interests.[2] The adoption proceeding itself is unusual because generally the parties to the adoption—the natural parents and the adoptive parents—are not in a true adversary relationship.

2. Independent (i.e., non-agency) adoptions are permitted by statute in Arizona. It is not alleged that respondent violated the adoption statute, which provided:

> D. Any attorney licensed to practice in this state may perform legal services in an adoption proceeding if he does not receive any compensation or thing of value, directly or indirectly beyond a reasonable fee, approved by the court, for legal services rendered, which fee shall not include any compensation for participation in the finding, locating or placing a child for adoption or for the finding of adoptive parents.

Usually, both sides in the proceeding have complementary interests and no real negotiating or posturing is necessary; in most cases the natural parents want to find a good home for the baby and need to have the birthing expenses paid, and the adoptive parents want to provide a home for the baby and are willing to pay the expenses. Legal counsel is necessary only to facilitate the exchange and ensure that the legal requirements are met.

Despite the spirit of cooperation often present in an adoption, conflict of interest situations are likely to arise for an attorney involved in the proceedings. First, the interests of potential adoptive parents of the same child are always adverse to one another. In a situation involving independent sets of adoptive parents and only one available child, obviously one set of parents will be disappointed. An attorney cannot simultaneously represent both sets of adoptive parents without compromising his representation of one of them.

Second, and perhaps less apparent, the interests of the adoptive parents may be adverse to the interests of the natural parents. The decision to give the baby up for adoption is often a difficult one to make. The natural parents' attorney has a duty to provide them with counsel about such matters as paternity issues, economic matters, and the legal effect of signing the consent to adopt. Under our statute, the natural parents' consent to the adoption is not valid unless it is given at least 72 hours after the birth of the child. The statute protects the right of the natural parents to withhold a decision on whether to keep the baby until after the baby is born. The attorney must counsel the natural parents on the adoption decision right up until the natural parents consent to the adoption. Clearly, the adoptive parents want the natural parents to consent to the adoption rather than to keep the baby. It is obvious, therefore, that the natural parents' interests may be adverse to the interests of the adoptive parents, and the same attorney cannot represent both parties.

Notwithstanding the foregoing discussion, in some instances an attorney may be able to represent multiple parties in an adoption proceeding. Disciplinary Rule 5–105(C) provides for an exception to the dictates of DR 5–105(A) and (B). It provides that a lawyer may represent multiple clients "if it is obvious that he can adequately represent the interests of each and if each consents to the representation after full disclosure of the possible effect of such representation on the exercise of his independent professional judgment on behalf of each." DR 5–105(C). Under this exception, then, it may be possible for an attorney to represent multiple parties to an adoption, but only after full disclosure and upon consent of the parties. This exception has no application to the current case, however, because there is no evidence that respondent complied with its provisions.

. . .

1. *The Pietzes*

The record contains clear and convincing evidence that respondent became the Pietzes' attorney for handling the adoption. At their initial meeting, respondent agreed to represent the Pietzes if they found a baby to adopt. Clearly, the Pietzes sought out respondent's legal assistance at that time. In referring the pregnant woman through Iverson to respondent for independent placement, the Pietzes had every reason to rely on respondent's original promise that he would represent them in the adoption. Furthermore, the referral of the natural mother by the Pietzes indicates that they understood that the attorney-client relationship with respondent was ongoing. The relationship was not terminated until they wrote to respondent in June 1983, and expressly stated they were discharging him as their attorney.

Even accepting respondent's argument that an attorney-client relationship was subject to the condition that the Pietzes locate a baby, correspondence between the respondent and the Pietzes immediately after respondent's first meeting with the natural mother belies respondent's contention that he did not know that the natural mother had been referred to him by the Pietzes. Respondent's letter to the Pietzes indicated that the person who had made the appointment for the natural mother indicated that the Pietzes might be interested in the adoption. Furthermore, respondent stated in the letter, "I would not expect to have any problem in placing the child but I thought we should write to determine your interest in the placement." The Pietzes unequivocally stated in their response that they were "*very* hopeful" to adopt the baby. In addition, in their letter the Pietzes alluded to circumstances regarding the natural mother which were not communicated to them by respondent in his original letter. If nothing else, respondent surely should have realized from their letter that the Pietzes were involved in the referral of the baby's mother.

. . .

We agree with the Commission's finding that there was an attorney-client relationship between respondent and the Pietzes.

2. *The Buckmasters*

The Commission found that an attorney-client relationship later developed between respondent and the Buckmasters. We agree. Mr. Buckmaster testified that he believed that he and his wife were respondent's clients. They met with respondent regarding the adoption and understood that if the natural mother consented, respondent would perform the adoption for them and they would pay the necessary fees. The fact that respondent never actually performed the adoption of the baby does not nullify the existence of an attorney-client relationship.

3. *The Natural Mother*

Respondent agrees that he and the natural mother had an attorney-client relationship. Although the mother was not liable to respondent for legal fees, clearly the natural mother came to respondent seeking legal advice and she received that advice from respondent.

We find that respondent violated DR 5–105 by representing the Buckmasters in the same matter in which he was already counsel for the Pietzes. Respondent had a duty to advocate for the Pietzes in the adoption proceeding. The natural mother's indication that she was not committed to the Pietzes did not lessen the respondent's duty of loyalty to them. The respondent breached that duty when he accepted proffered employment from the Buckmasters and recommended them as adoptive parents to the natural mother. It is difficult to imagine an action by respondent that would have been more adverse to the Pietzes' interest in the adoption. By accepting employment from the Buckmasters while already representing the Pietzes in the same adoption proceeding without full disclosure and consent, respondent violated DR 5–105(A); by continuing in the simultaneous representation and by ultimately recommending the Buckmasters over the Pietzes, respondent violated DR 5–105(B).

We find that respondent also violated DR 5–105 by representing both the natural mother and the adoptive parents in an adoption proceeding.

Respondent claimed that he always represented the natural mother in adoption proceedings. From his testimony, it appears that his usual custom was to maintain a file of potential adoptive parents from which the natural mother who is his client may select the couple best suited to adopt the baby. We do not expressly prohibit this practice. However, the attorney must take special care to avoid violating the ethical rules regarding representation of multiple clients.

. . .

The ABA standards recommend suspension when an attorney *knows* of a conflict of interest, does not fully disclose to a client the possible effect of that conflict, and causes injury or potential injury to a client. Standard 4.32. The standards recommended only reprimand (censure) when the attorney is *negligent* in determining whether a conflict of interest exists, and causes injury or potential injury to a client. Standard 4.33. From the findings of facts made by the Committee and from our review of the record, it is unclear whether respondent was only negligent in determining a conflict of interest existed or whether he actually knew of the conflict. Respondent testified that his only client was the natural mother. We have determined that both the Pietzes and the Buckmasters were his clients as well. If respondent did not think either the Pietzes or the Buckmasters were his clients, he would not have "known" a conflict of interest existed. However, at a minimum, respondent was negligent in failing to recognize that the potential adoptive parents were his clients and that a conflict existed. Accordingly, we agree with the Local Committee that the appropriate sanction due respondent is censure. We decline to adopt the recommendation of the Disciplinary Commission that respondent be suspended for 30 days because neither the findings of the Local Committee nor our independent review of the record unequivocally reveals that respondent knew the conflict existed. Considering also that respondent has an otherwise flawless record in the almost 30 years he has practiced in Arizona, we find the recommendation of the Commission unduly harsh.

The findings of fact and conclusions of law of the Local Committee are approved. Respondent is censured and assessed costs of $2,225.10.

Diana Lafemina, Note, The Lawyer's Role in the Independent Adoption Process: Parental Consent and Best Interests of the Child

3 Touro L.Rev. 283, 284–88 (1987).

An "independent adoption" is any adoption in which a licensed agency does not participate in placing the child into the adoptive parents' home. Independent adoptions can be performed through the services of a lawyer, physician or a private individual.... In the past, the independent adoption process has often been divided into two categories—the "black market" and the "gray market"—terms with obviously negative connotations. A black market adoption is one in which an intermediary or third party participates solely for his own profit.

The primary criticism of the black market is that profit takes precedence over the child's best interest. In the black market, the newborn is merely a commodity in a market that serves the highest bidder. The adoption may eventually become legal with the help of an experienced attorney. This is difficult, however, because adoptive parents are reluctant to reveal the cost of the transaction to any outsider. In view of the blatant illegalities involved, some adoptive parents may never seek to finalize a legitimate adoption. It is for this reason some states do not permit independent adoptions. Attorneys who have engaged in the black market have tarnished the independent adoption process so that its legitimization will be viewed with suspicion by legislative bodies.

The use of the term "gray market" to describe the independent adoption process is a misnomer. It is not as callous or unscrupulous a process as is the black market. Instead the term refers to private placement—with its primary objective of finding the adoptive child a home. The biological mother's travel, medical, and living expenses, coupled with a reasonable attorney's fee for professional services rendered,[2] justify the high fees paid. The term "gray market" developed because the lack of safeguards in the independent adoption process served as a stepping stone for the black market. This abuse can be attributed to the lack of properly designed legislative restraints.

Even so, agency placement cannot be the sole solution to the independent adoption problem. Agencies often specialize in finding homes for hard to place children—those who are older or mentally or physically handicapped. They are not able to devote their time to placing healthy newborns. One reason for so much specialized placement is that agencies which receive subsidies for foster care are able to absorb the cost.

Independent adoptions have become a much-needed alternative to agency adoptions. This alternative, however, is subject to the criticism that attorneys do not adequately represent the child's best interests. Agencies can employ professional social workers who not only can counsel women with unwanted pregnancies, but evaluate and investigate prospective adoptive parents. While agency homestudy investigations are required in independent adoptions, these investigations are considered to be cursory compared to those performed specifically for the benefit of an agency adoption. . . .

Since adoption agencies cannot satisfy the need for independent adoptions, and because the guidelines in private adoptions are less stringent, it soon becomes the attorney's moral obligation to ensure that the child is placed in a loving and caring home. The attorney becomes more than just a facilitator of the adoption process. An attorney who is unaware of the possibility of detriment to the adoptive child can easily harm the child's best interests.

Attorneys specializing in independent adoptions offer a service both to the couples desiring children and to women with unwanted pregnancies. The lawyer performs customary legal services, provides information about the possible ramifications of the independent adoption process, and also acts as an "adoption consultant."

The independent adoption process is primarily concerned with ensuring that the biological mother relinquishes all rights to the child. This prevents future adverse legal consequences after the child is placed. In a sense, the lawyer's responsibility is to the child. While legally representing only the adoptive parents (the natural mother is often not represented by counsel), the lawyer also undertakes a moral responsibility to the adoptive child he is

2. A legitimate legal fee ranges from $1,500 to $3,000 for intra-state adoptions. Interstate adoptions can cost more.

attempting to place. While the adoption lawyer is not a trained social worker or related professional, the legal services he renders must alert him to the essential role that he plays in the child's future. Any defects in the lawyer's service will adversely affect the child. The most destructive defects occur in execution of the biological parent's consent. The child's life can be disrupted by removal from its adoptive home if the biological mother can successfully revoke her consent. Thus, the lawyer managing the independent adoption serves the child's best interest by ensuring a secure and flawless placement. His moral role is similar to that of a guardian ad litem.

3. Children with Special Needs

Ferdinand v. Department for Children and Their Families

United States District Court, District of Rhode Island, 1991.
768 F.Supp. 401.

■ Pettine, Senior United States District Judge

Litigation in this case began when the plaintiff, Rose Ferdinand's, request for an adoption subsidy under Title IV–E, *42 U.S.C. § 673*(c) was denied by the defendants, Department for Children and Their Families of the State of Rhode Island *et al* ("DCF"), in February of 1990. Ms. Ferdinand adopted her daughter, Nia, a black child, through Children's Friend and Service and DCF. At that time, Ms. Ferdinand was married, lived with her husband in Massachusetts and both she and her husband were employed at Dupont. As of 1990, the situation had changed. The Ferdinands were divorced. Rose Ferdinand received no child support and she was responsible for supporting not only herself and Nia but also a younger child born to the couple during the marriage. The defendants denied the "belated" request for adoption assistance contending that because the Ferdinands were offered and declined such at the time of the adoption, the present request could not even be considered. In other words, Nia Ferdinand's possible entitlement had been waived.

This matter first came before this Court on December 5, 1990 in response to the plaintiff's motion for preliminary injunction. At that time, I reviewed the case and decided to treat the motion as a request for a temporary restraining order ("TRO"). The TRO was granted and the defendants were ordered to "qualify plaintiff for adoption assistance payments and related available benefits, including medical insurance." The parties agreed that the TRO would remain in effect until this Court rendered a further opinion following the receipt of additional briefs. The TRO did not reach the issue of the plaintiff's requested effective date of eligibility. This court ordered payments to commence on December 15, 1990.

Based on the discussion that follows, plaintiff's motion for permanent injunction is now granted. I adopt the terms that were set out in the TRO: defendants shall continue to carry plaintiff as qualified plaintiff for adoption assistance payments and related available benefits, including medical insurance and shall continue to forward payments to the plaintiff. Such assistance shall continue in light of any changing circumstances pursuant to the periodic readjustment provisions of *42 U.S.C. § 673*(a)(3) and the provision of *42 U.S.C. § 673*(a)(4).

I. *Adoption Assistance*

With the Adoption Assistance and Child Welfare Act of 1980, Congress "amended the Social Security Act to make needed improvements in the child welfare and social services programs ... to establish a program of Federal support to encourage adoptions of children with special needs ..." 1980 U.S. Code Cong. and Admin. News at 1450. The subsidized adoption program provides federal matching once a state determines that a child in foster care would be eligible for such. *Id.* at 1450–51. Eligibility turns on whether the child has special needs which tend to discourage adoption. "Each State would be responsible for deciding which factors would ordinarily result in making it difficult to place certain children in adoptive homes." "The determination could be based on such factors as a physical or emotional handicap, the need to place members of a sibling group with a single adoptive family, difficulty in placing children of certain ages or ethnic backgrounds, or similar factors or combinations of factors." *Id.* "If the State determines that adoption assistance is needed, it would be able to offer such assistance to parents who adopt the child, so long as their income does not exceed 125 percent of the median income of a family of four in the State, adjusted to reflect family size." *Id.*[4]

II. *Regulations*

To decide this case, this Court must first determine whether Nia Ferdinand is eligible for federal adoption assistance. This determination, in turn, focuses on *45 C.F.R. § 1356.40(b)(1)*. That section requires that the adoption assistance agreement "be signed and in effect at the time of or prior to the final decree of adoption." The defendants contend that because the Ferdinands did not enter into such an agreement, their right to adoption assistance was waived. Defendants argument, based on various policy inter-

4. The Adoption Assistance Program for children with special needs is set out at *42 U.S.C. § 673*(a)(1)(C) and (c).

42 U.S.C. § 673

(1) Each State with a plan approved under this part shall, directly through the State agency or through another public or nonprofit private agency, make adoption assistance payments pursuant to an adoption assistance agreement in amounts determined under paragraph (2) of this subsection to parents who, after June 17, 1980, adopt a child who—

(C) has been determined by the State, pursuant to subsection (c) of this section, to be a child with special needs.

. . .

(c) Children with special needs

For the purposes of this section, a child shall not be considered a child with special needs unless—

(1) the State has determined that the child cannot or should not be returned to the home of his parents; and

(2) the State had first determined (A) that there exists with respect to the child a specific factor or condition (such as his ethnic background, age, or membership in a minority or sibling group, or the presence of factors such as medical conditions or physical, mental, or emotional handicaps) because of which it is reasonable to conclude that such child cannot be placed with adoptive parents without providing adoption assistance, and (B) that, except where it would be against the best interest of the child because of such factors as the existence of significant emotional ties with prospective adoptive parents while in the care of such parents as a foster child, a reasonable, but unsuccessful, effort has been made to place the child with appropriate adoptive parents without providing adoption assistance under this section.

R.I.G.L. § 15–7–25 is the enabling legislation for the federal matching program. It reads:

> The state shall make funds available through the department for children and their families for special reimbursement to adoptive parents in matters of placement of handicapped or hard to place children. These funds will be disbursed in accordance with the guidelines to be promulgated by the department for children and their families.

pretations issued by the Department of Health and Human Services including ACYF PIQ–83–5 (December 14, 1983), is that "if parents are apprised of the availability of a subsidy, decline such subsidy, and do not enter into *a nominal adoption assistance agreement*, they may not later receive any assistance as the child is no longer eligible as a child with special needs under the Act." Defendants Brief at 8–9 (emphasis added).

When the defendants denied adoption assistance to the Ferdinands in 1990, they noted that the "prior agreement" requirement could be "reviewed if there were extenuating circumstances at the time of the adoption. That is, if a subsidy was not offered, or proper benefits were not explained (i.e., SSI or SSA)." Letter from John Sinapi, Jr., Administrator, DCF (February 19, 1990). However, the defendants stated that with regard to the Ferdinands, "this was not the case."

Defendants contend and plaintiffs concede that there was some minimal discussion about adoption subsidies with the Ferdinands prior to Nia's adoption and that Ms. Ferdinand told Mr. deLong, Assistant Director of Children's Friend and Service, that "she hadn't needed a subsidy at that time." Inter–Office Memo to John Sinapi from Daniel Wheelan, Assistant Administrator, DCF (February 6, 1990). The fact that the discussion was nothing more than a minimal one is supported by a letter from Mr. deLong, dated February 4, 1991, stating that "we have found nothing in our records that indicates that Ms. Ferdinand or Mr. Ferdinand were ever offered a subsidy by our agency, nor any record that they either accepted or rejected an offer." Moreover, in a memorandum from Ted Keenaghan, Chief Social Services Policy and Systems Specialist, Children and Their Families, to Kevin Aucoin, Legal Counsel for the same, dated December 24, 1990, Mr. Keenaghan stated that he was "shocked to tell [Mr. Aucoin] that there is *no* mention in [the] records about a subsidy being offered to this family when the child was first adopted!!!" (emphasis in original). Even if the Ferdinands knew something about the program, the defendants' own interpretation of their mandate allows that if "proper benefits were not explained" the case may be re-opened based on the extenuating circumstances rationale.

What, therefore, would constitute a proper explanation of available benefits? This Court has no doubt that Congress intended to place the burden on the States to promote the adoption assistance program. The Code of Federal Regulations, 42 C.F.R. § 1356.40(f), states that "the State agency must actively seek ways to promote the adoption assistance program." Moreover, the United States Department of Health and Human Services, in Policy Announcement ACYF–PA–83–5, discussing various assistance programs available to adoptive parents stated:

> Because there are many complexities and financial implications for the States as well as the adoptive families, it is important for all parties to discuss all aspects of a combination of SSI and adoption assistance at the time the adoption assistance agreement is negotiated.
>
> . . .
>
> With full knowledge of the SSI and Adoption Assistance programs, the adoptive parents can then make an informed decision about application for or receipt of benefits from either or both programs for which they or the child are eligible. They should be advised, however, that if they decline title IV–E adoption assistance and choose to receive only SSI for the child, and if they do not execute an adoption assistance agreement before the adoption is finalized and do not receive adoption assistance

> payments pursuant to such an agreement, they may not later receive title IV–E adoption assistance payments, the child would no longer meet all of the eligibility requirements as a child with special needs (section 473(c)(2)).

The clear implication is that the state has an affirmative duty to fully explain all available assistance programs so that potential adoptive parents can make an informed decision. The fact that Ms. Ferdinand was never made aware of the fact that even if she did not need a subsidy at that time she might still qualify for nominal assistance that would leave the door open for later recalculation constitutes an extenuating circumstance. Defendants reference to ACYF PA–83–5 (referring to nominal adoption assistance). In fact, the defendants' own procedures regarding adoption subsidies indicate that it is not the adoptive parents' needs, but rather the child's needs that determine eligibility for assistance.[5] Parents, therefore, should not be allowed to waive adoption assistance for their children without full information and knowledge of all possible benefits—present and future.

Reopening of the case, however, does not inevitably lead to the conclusion that the Ferdinands would have qualified for adoption assistance. The defendants argue that regardless of plaintiff's eligibility for federal adoption assistance, applicable federal law did not mandate that states provide Title IV–E adoption assistance subsidies to non-resident adoptive parents. Section 1356.40(3) of 45 C.F.R. states only that "[a] state may make an adoption assistance agreement with adopting parents who reside in another state." Because the defendants' own policies in effect at the time of Nia's adoption were mute on the issue of providing federal subsidies to non-resident parents, defendants contend that they have no obligation to the Ferdinands. Whether such obligation existed or not, however, is eclipsed by the fact that in Daniel Wheelan's memo to John Sinapi of February 6, 1990, he states that "after speaking with Camille Hardiman of Children's Friend and Service, Ted Keenaghan has determined that this child was probably IV–E eligible at the time of adoption." Mr. Keenaghan's statement is not *contrary* to the regulations which clearly allow subsidies for non-resident adoptive parents. My sense is that the residency issue is, as plaintiff contends, a mere post-hoc rationalization. I find that the Ferdinands' out of state residency did not and does not affect their eligibility for the Adoption Assistance Program.

Finally, the fact that Nia's special educational needs were not evident at the time of her adoption does not lead to the conclusion that she was not eligible for Title IV–E assistance as a "hard-to-place" special needs child. According to *42 U.S.C. § 673*(c) race or minority status can enable a child to be classified as a "special needs" child for adoption assistance purposes. Again, Ted Keenaghan's statement comports with this understanding of Nia's eligibility at the time of her adoption.

III. *Conclusion*

In sum, plaintiffs have demonstrated that Nia was eligible for adoption assistance at the time of her adoption and that the Adoption Assistance Program was not adequately explained to the Ferdinands. Such lack of explanation was a violation by the defendants of their affirmative duty to inform clients of the program and provided the extenuating circumstances necessary to allow the reopening of the plaintiff's case and, finally, the grant

5. In R.I. Department for Children and Their Families Adoption Procedures Manual states that a "worker meets with prospective adoptive parents to review the criteria for subsidy and makes them aware it is based on the needs of the child."

of adoption assistance. The permanent injunction requested by the plaintiff is, therefore, granted.

4. STEPPARENT ADOPTION

Uniform Adoption Act Article 4. Adoption of Minor Stepchild by Stepparent

Comment

A stepparent who seeks to adopt a minor stepchild under this article has to deal with fewer as well as somewhat different legal requirements than does an individual who seeks to adopt an unrelated minor. These differences are justified because in the typical stepparent adoption, the minor has been living with the stepparent and the stepparent's spouse (the minor's custodial parent), and the adoption merely formalizes a de facto parent-child relationship.

. . .

Typically, the custodial parent is allowed to retain his or her parental status, the adoptive stepparent acquires the status of a legal parent, and the noncustodial parent's relationship to the child is cut off for most purposes.... For stepfamilies in which a child maintains emotional ties to a noncustodial parent or to the noncustodial parent's family, the traditional approach of completely severing all ties to the noncustodial parent and that parent's family is not necessarily beneficial for the child, and is not always preferred by the parents or the stepparent....

... By allowing post-adoption visitation by noncustodial former parents, siblings, or grandparents, this article may encourage an increase in the number of stepparent adoptions in proportion to the total number of blended families. This would give more children the advantage of living in a household with two legal parents (custodial parent and adoptive stepparent), while not depriving these children of access to their noncustodial parent's family—assuming that such access would not be detrimental to the child. Moreover, if the traditional rule of "complete severance" between adoptive and biological families is subject to some exceptions in the context of stepparent adoptions, it might be possible to avoid the bitterness that is often attendant upon efforts to terminate the rights of noncustodial parents, and more consensual adoptions might result.

. . .

SECTION 4–103. LEGAL CONSEQUENCES OF ADOPTION OF STEPCHILD.

(a) Except as otherwise provided in subsections (b) and (c), the legal consequences of an adoption of a stepchild by a stepparent are the same as [for other adoptions under the Act]

(b) An adoption by a stepparent does not affect:

(1) the relationship between the adoptee and the adoptee's parent who is the adoptive stepparent's spouse or deceased spouse;

(2) an existing court order for visitation or communication with a minor adoptee by an individual related to the adoptee through the parent who is the adoptive stepparent's spouse or deceased spouse; [or]

. . .

(4) A court order or agreement for visitation or communication with a minor adoptee which is approved by the court pursuant to Section 4–113.

. . .

Comment

Although the legal consequences of an adoption of a stepchild are generally the same as [for other adoptions under this Act], this section provides that the rights and duties of the adoptive parent's spouse—i.e., the child's custodial parent—are not terminated by the adoption. The child remains in all respects the child of the adoptive parent's spouse, even if the spouse is deceased, and becomes in all respects the child of the adoptive stepparent.... By contrast, except for child support arrearages, the rights and duties of the child's former noncustodial parent are terminated....

SECTION 4–105. CONTENT OF CONSENT BY STEPPARENT'S SPOUSE.

. . .

(b) A consent ... must state that:

(1) the parent executing the consent has legal and physical custody of the parent's minor child and voluntarily and unequivocally consents to the adoption of the minor by the stepparent;

. . .

SECTION 4–106. CONTENT OF CONSENT BY MINOR'S OTHER PARENT.

. . .

(b) A consent ... must state that:

(1) the parent executing the consent voluntarily and unequivocally consents to the adoption of the minor by the stepparent and the transfer to the stepparent's spouse and the adoptive stepparent of any right the parent executing the consent has to legal or physical custody of the minor;

(2) the parent executing the consent understands and agrees that the adoption will terminate his or her parental relationship to the minor and will terminate any existing court order for custody, visitation, or communication with the minor, but:

. . .

(ii) a court order for visitation or communication with the minor by an individual related to the minor through the minor's other parent, or an agreement or order concerning another individual which is approved by the court ... survives the decree of adoption

. . .

SECTION 4–113. VISITATION AGREEMENT AND ORDER.

(a) Upon the request of the petitioner in a proceeding for adoption of a minor stepchild, the court shall review a written agreement that permits another individual to visit or communicate with the minor after the decree of adoption becomes final, which must be signed by the individual, the petitioner, the petitioner's spouse, the minor if 12 years of age or older, and, if an agency placed the minor for adoption, an authorized employee of the agency.

(b) The court may enter an order approving the agreement only upon determining that the agreement is in the best interest of the minor adoptee.

. . .

(c) In addition to any agreement approved pursuant to subsections (a) and (b), the court may approve the continuation of an existing order or issue a new order permitting the minor adoptee's former parent, grandparent, or sibling to visit or communicate with the minor. . . .

. . .

Comment

This section permits a petitioner in a proceeding to adopt under this article to ask the court to approve an agreement for post-adoption visitation or communication with the adoptee by another individual. . . . Subsection (c) permits an adoptee's former parent (i.e., the noncustodial parent), grandparent, or sibling to seek a court order for post-adoption visitation or communication with the adoptee over the objection of the custodial parent and the adoptive stepparent. The court cannot issue an order unless it . . . determines that, despite the objections, it would be in the best interests of the adoptee.

In the Matter of the Adoption of K.J.B., L.D.B., and R.J.B.

Supreme Court of Kansas, 1998.
265 Kan. 90, 959 P.2d 853.

■ SIX, JUSTICE:

This is . . . stepparent adoption case. The father of three minor children appeals the district court's order granting the stepfather's petition for adoption. The district court found that the father had failed to assume the duties of a parent during the 2 years next preceding the filing of the adoption petition; therefore, his consent to the adoption was not required. The Court of Appeals affirmed. We granted the father's petition for review. . . .

The questions before us are: (1) whether, social security payments for the benefit of the minor children resulting from the father's filing for and receiving disability benefits qualify as credits against the father's liability for child support in a [stepparent] adoption case; and, (2) if they do, was the district court correct in holding that the father's consent was not required because he had "failed or refused to assume the duties of a parent" under [the statute].

The answer is "yes" to the first question and "no" to the second. We reverse the district court and the Court of Appeals.

FACTS

... The stepfather's petition for adoption was filed on November 6, 1995. The [statutory] two-year period is November 6, 1993, to November 6, 1995. At the time the adoption petition was filed, K.J.B. was, 11, L.D.B., 9, and R.J.B., 7.

The facts were set forth in the Court of Appeals opinion:

"The mother and father of K.J.B., L.D.B., and R.J.B. were divorced in 1989. The mother was given residential custody of L.D.B and R.J.B. and the father was given residential custody of K.J.B. This arrangement lasted until May 1989, when all three children began residing with the mother as a result of a child in need of care proceeding regarding K.J.B. The mother married the petitioner/stepfather in May 1991. The mother testified she has lived at the same residence since she remarried.

"Following the divorce, the father was ordered to pay $254 per month in child support for the two children in the mother's custody. The mother never requested a change in the amount of support after all three children were placed in her custody. The mother testified the only check she ever received from the father was one for $98. [The mother received this amount in the month before the June 1996 hearing.]

"In 1991, the father filed for social security disability benefits and the children began receiving a portion of these benefits, which were back-dated to 1990. The father testified it is the advice of his physician that he not seek employment. From 1990, the children received $255 per month in social security benefits.... The mother claimed the benefits were less than what the children should have received because the father claimed parentage of another child in order for that child's mother to receive a portion of the benefits.

"The father exercised regular visitation for approximately 1 year after the children began residing with their mother. On June 29, 1992, the district court entered an order approving the change of custody of all three children to the mother. The court permitted visitation by the father, but due to the father's mental problems, the visitation was to be under the direct supervision of the Pawnee Mental Health Center. The father exercised four supervised visits with the children in the following 3 months.

"On September 23, 1992, the father filed a motion to set specific visitation rights. After filing the motion, the father had a visit with the children for a birthday party, and other visits also took place when the father volunteered his time.... On February 11, 1993, the district court entered an order allowing visitation by the father at his home for 3 hours on alternating weekends, with the visits increasing an hour each visit until a full weekend was allowed. The father exercised his visitation rights under this order until September 1993. On October 20, 1993, the mother filed a motion to alter the father's visitation schedule. The father exercised no visitation or contact with the children from that point on.

"On January 4, 1994, the district court entered an order modifying the father's visitation rights in response to the mother's motion to alter. The father did not appear at the January 4, 1994, hearing. He was granted certain visitation rights, but the judge ordered the visitation stayed until the father appeared and requested the same to be reinstated. However, the court permitted visitation in the mother's home under her supervision. The mother testified the district court stayed the visitation because the father had not visited the children since September and had received two DUI's.

"Approximately a month after the court stayed the father's visitation, he called the mother, and she tried to arrange visitation in her home. The mother testified the father told her that was not correct and hung up the phone. She did not hear from him again. The father has not filed any legal proceedings regarding visitation or custody. The mother indicated the father sent only two of the three children birthday cards in 1994 and 1995. Additionally, the children received Christmas cards in 1994, but nothing for Christmas 1995.

"The father is mentally disabled and suffers from depression and agoraphobia, a fear of strange places with large numbers of people. He acknowledged he takes several medications for his mental illness. He claims that when he takes his medications, he is able to function as a normal person. He stated that shortly after the mother filed the motion to alter visitation in September 1993, he was involuntarily hospitalized in Osawatomie State Hospital from October 1993 through December 1993.

"The father testified he called the stepfather in April 1994 and was told that the children were not his anymore, they were the stepfather's children, and to never call again. The father testified he did not call the children because of the stepfather's command. The father stated that as a result of the inability to see his children, he voluntarily checked himself into Osawatomie State Hospital and then was transferred to Topeka State Hospital from May 1994 to July 1994. When the father was released from the hospital, he was sent to a halfway house in Liberal, Kansas, where he lived from July 1994 through November 1994. Because of a DUI conviction, the father then spent November and December 1994 in the Riley County jail.

. . . At the time of the hearing on whether his consent to the adoption was necessary, the father resided in Topeka in an assisted living home for the mentally ill.

"On November 6, 1995, the stepfather, with the consent of the mother, filed a petition for adoption of the three children. The adoption proceedings were heard before a district magistrate judge. The petition claimed the father's consent was unnecessary because he had failed or refused to assume the duties of a parent for the 2 years prior to the filing of the adoption petition.

"The issue of whether the father's consent was required for the adoption was removed to the district court. The court held an evidentiary hearing on the matter and reviewed briefs submitted by the parties. On August 23, 1996, the court held that within the 2 years previous to the filing of the adoption petition, the father had only nominal and incidental contacts with the children and that the social security benefits the children received were not sufficient to require his consent to the adoption. The court concluded the father had failed to assume his parental responsibilities for the 2-year period and his consent to the adoption was unnecessary. The district court returned the case to the magistrate court for the continuation of the adoption proceedings.

"On September 16, 1996, the magistrate judge granted the stepfather's petition for adoption. On the same day, the father filed a motion to stay the adoption and a notice of appeal concerning the district court's order finding his consent to be unnecessary. On September 20, 1996, the father withdrew the motion for a stay and filed a notice of appeal from the decree of adoption."

DISCUSSION

A prologue to our discussion is formed by five concepts that guide the resolution of [an adoption under] *K.S.A. 59–2136(d)*. . . .

The first concept is our standard of review.

"In an adoption proceeding, the question of whether an individual has failed or refused to assume the duties of a parent for the required period of time is ordinarily a factual one to be determined by the trier of facts upon competent evidence after a full and complete hearing."

We do not weigh the evidence or pass on the credibility of the witnesses. We review the evidence in the light most favorable to the party prevailing below.

. . . The question remains: Is the father's compliance with the court-ordered child support, after he initially signed up for the social security disability, enough to override the almost complete lack of contact by the father with the children during the critical time period?

Our standard of review changes at this point. . . . The district court found that social security disability payments were made to the children. The district court concluded the payments were not sufficient, in and of themselves, to require the father's consent to the adoption. The conclusion follows that the father had not assumed his parental duties. . . .

Second, the fitness of the natural father is not a controlling factor.

Third, the best interests of the child is not a controlling factor.

Fourth, adoption statutes are to be strictly construed in favor of maintaining the rights of a natural parent especially in a *K.S.A. 59–2136(d)* case.

Fifth, when the father is incarcerated and unable to fulfill customary parental duties, the court must decide whether he has pursued the opportunities and options available to carry out such duties to the best of his ability.

. . .

The Social Security Payments

We next consider the district court's determination that the social security payments received by the mother for the benefit of the children based on the father's disability did not rebut the *K.S.A. 59–2136(d)* presumption.

K.S.A. 59–2136(d) is controlling.

"In a stepparent adoption, if a mother consents to the adoption of a child who has a presumed father . . . or who has a father as to whom the child is a legitimate child . . . the consent of such father must be given to the adoption unless such father has failed or refused to assume the duties of a parent for two consecutive years next preceding the filing of the petition for adoption or is incapable of giving such consent. In determining whether a father's consent is required under this subsection, the court may disregard incidental visitations, contacts, communications or contributions. In determining whether the father has failed or refused to assume the duties of a parent for two consecutive years next preceding the filing of the petition for adoption, there shall be a rebuttable presumption that if the father, after having knowledge of the child's birth, has knowingly failed to provide a substantial portion of the child support as required by judicial decree, when financially able to do so, for a period of two years next preceding the filing of the petition for adoption, then such father has failed or refused to assume the duties of a parent.' "

We focus on whether the monthly social security payments qualify as child support.... It is undisputed that the father was ordered to pay $254 per month in child support. Other than the social security payments, the father said he paid some child support but did not have a specific amount and provided no documentation.

. . .

Andler holds that social security payments made to children based on a father's disability constitute a satisfaction of child support payments required by a divorce decree.

We apply the *Andler* rationale to this case.

K.S.A. 59–2136(d) allows the court to disregard incidental visits, contacts, communications, or contributions. The father may rebut the 59–2136(d) presumption that he failed to assume parental duties by showing that he provided a substantial portion of the judicially ordered child support. Here, the father does not directly take issue with the court's finding that his contacts with the children were incidental. He asserts, however, that the social security disability payments received by the mother for the children's support serve to rebut the presumption that he did not assume parental duties. We agree.

While we may disregard incidental visits, contacts, communications, or contributions under a strict construction of *K.S.A. 59–2136(d)*, the father's contributions here were not incidental. "Incidental" has been defined in this context as "casual, of minor importance, insignificant, and of little consequence." At the time of the hearing, the monthly contributions, which were backdated to 1990, were more than the court ordered child support.

. . .

Here, the father has provided financial support for his children—whether it be by accident or design.

Both the district court and the Court of Appeals appeared to focus on *F.A.R.*'s recognition of the "natural and moral duty of a parent to show affection, care and interest toward his or her child." Both courts concluded that the father's financial support was not sufficient to overcome his complete lack of "love and affection" duties.

Under the facts of this case, while there was little or no affection, care, or interest shown to the children, the father did provide a substantial portion of the children's support. The father's consent was therefore necessary for the completion of this stepparent adoption.

Parental Duties Under *K.S.A. 59–2136(d)*

. . .

Because of its ruling that the social security payments were not credits on the child support obligation, the Court of Appeals did not reach the difficult question now before us. The question is: Must the father fail in both the financial and the affection, care, and interest aspects of parenting to fail under *K.S.A. 59–2136(d)* in assuming the duties of a parent?

. . .

[In *In re Adoption of C.R.D.*, *897 P.2d 181 (Kan.* 1995), the] issue was whether the father otherwise failed to assume the duties of a parent, having failed on love and affection. *C.R.D.* reasoned that payment of $1,000 during the 2 years when $4,800 was due plus furnishing an insurance card sent by the father's ex-wife was sufficient.

The *C.R.D.* court said:

"Basic parental rights are fundamental rights protected by the Fourteenth Amendment to the Constitution of the United States. The right to be the legal parent of a child is one of these rights, which cannot be abrogated except for compelling reasons. See *Quilloin v. Walcott, 434 U.S. 246, 54 L. Ed. 2d 511, 98 S. Ct. 549,* reh. denied *435 U.S. 918, 98 S. Ct. 1477, 55 L. Ed. 2d 511 (1979)*. . . .

We agree.

C.R.D. concluded:

"In the instant case, we do not believe the support payments and insurance benefits provided can reasonably be called insubstantial, as we believe that term must be defined in this context. The father's support of his child in this case was certainly not what it should have been. But it was not so insubstantial as to deprive him of his rights of parenthood."

Judge Lewis concurred. He reasoned:

"The evidence indicates without any doubt that the natural father failed to assume the 'love and affection' side of the duties of a parent.

"The other factor of parenthood is a financial one. On this side of the ledger, the absent father's performance is somewhat better. I believe that if we are going to judicially sever parental rights, there must be a failure to assume and perform the duties of a parent on both sides of the ledger. I conclude that under the evidence shown and on the basis of the traditional approach taken to this issue by our Supreme Court, the evidence does not show, as a matter of law, that the noncustodial father in this case failed to assume the duties of a parent insofar as those duties relate to financial obligations."

Our obligation here is to construe *K.S.A. 59–2136(d)* strictly in favor of maintaining the rights of natural parents. By applying a strict construction, we are compelled to reverse the district court and the Court of Appeals. We conclude that as a matter of law, the father here, who has provided a substantial portion of the child support as required by judicial decree has not "failed or refused" to assume the duties of a parent under *K.S.A. 59–2136(d)*.

The effect of our holding is an endorsement of Judge Lewis' concurring opinion in *C.R.D.* To judicially sever parental rights under *K.S.A. 59–2136(d)*, there must be a failure "on both sides of the ledger."

. . .

Reversed.

■ Abbott, J., dissenting:

I am of the opinion the legislature intended that the courts look at the entire picture in determining whether a parent has performed parental duties during the 2 years next preceding the filing of a petition for adoption pursuant to *K.S.A. 59–2136*. I would adopt the reasoning of the majority in the Court of Appeals' decision in this case.

In the Matter of the Adoption of C.D.M.

Supreme Court of Oklahoma, 2001.
39 P.3d 802.

■ KAUGER, J.:

Two issues are presented: 1) whether a father who was denied visitation and who was incarcerated for stalking and assaulting the mother and violating a victim's protective order (VPO) which was entered to protect the child and its mother from the father's acts of violence may rely on court orders to excuse his lack of relationship with the child; and 2) whether sufficient evidence was presented to support a finding that the adoption is in the child's best interests. We hold that: 1) the father may not rely on the existence of court orders to excuse his lack of relationship with the child; and 2) the trial court's determination that the adoption was in the best interests of the child is supported by the evidence.

FACTS

On February 11, 2000, the appellees, Kori Rene Wyman and her husband, David Lee Wyman (collectively Wymans/respectively mother and stepfather), filed a petition for the stepfather to adopt the mother's child (C.D.M./child) without the consent of the appellant, Chad Louis Maxwell (Maxwell/father). In their petition, the Wymans asserted that the father's consent was unnecessary because he had for twelve months of the fourteen months immediately preceding the filing of the petition: 1) wilfully failed to maintain a significant relationship with the child; and 2) wilfully failed, refused, or neglected to contribute to the support of the child in substantial compliance with a court order.

A. Agreed Facts.

The parties jointly stipulated to several facts. On January 8, 1996, the mother gave birth to C.D.M. Maxwell is the biological father of the child. Since July of 1996, Maxwell has had no relationship with C.D.M. On August 2, 1996, a permanent protective order was entered against Maxwell in favor of the mother and the child. The order prohibited any contact or communication between Maxwell and either the mother or the child, with the provision that the order could be modified by an assigned Judge in any domestic proceeding between the parties.[2] Maxwell made no effort to contact the child. Maxwell wrote to the mother, but she took no steps to punish him for his violation of the protective order.

In March of 1997, Maxwell was arrested and charged with criminal trespass on the property of the mother, for felony stalking and repeatedly telephoning the mother, breaking into the mother's apartment and for hiding in her closet, and violating the permanent protective order. He pled

2. The protective order provides in pertinent part:

"... The Defendant is Ordered NOT TO ABUSE, INJURE, ASSAULT, MOLEST, HARASS, THREATEN OR OTHERWISE INTERFERE with the victims.

The Defendant is Ordered NOT TO VISIT OR COMMUNICATE with the Victim.

The Defendant is Ordered TO LEAVE AND STAY AWAY FROM THE RESIDENCE located at where the Plaintiffs reside.

The Defendant is Ordered to CEASE HARASSING the Victims.

The Defendant is Ordered to CEASE STALKING the Victims.

. . .

This Order specifically applies to the minor ... and is subject to any appropriate modification, in writing, which may be made by the assigned judge in any domestic action between the parties."

. . .

guilty to the stalking charges and was sentenced to a five year suspended sentence except for the first three years. On June 4, 1997, Maxwell filed a petition to establish paternity and a request for visitation with the child. On October 29, 1997, a temporary order was entered which denied visitation and ordered child support in the amount of $141.80 per month.

On March 12, 1998, Maxwell plead guilty to additional charges of assault and battery and another violation of the VPO stemming from an incident in which he assaulted and battered the mother in a convenience store parking lot and attempted to take the child forcibly from the mother's car. He was sentenced to one year. He began serving his sentences for his convictions in November of 1998. A decree establishing Maxwell as the father, but denying visitation was filed on December 2, 1999, and child support was set at $125.00 per month. Although he receives between $8.00 and $11.00 a month in wages at the prison, Maxwell has never forwarded any portion of his earning to the mother for child support. However, Maxwell's mother sent a money order dated September 21, 1999, for $160.00, checks for $125.00 on December 13, 1999, and December 29, 1999, respectively which was apparently from the sale of Maxwell's personal property.

I. A FATHER WHO WAS DENIED VISITATION AND WHO WAS INCARCERATED FOR STALKING AND ASSAULTING THE MOTHER AND VIOLATING A PROTECTIVE ORDER WHICH WAS ENTERED TO PROTECT THE CHILD AND ITS MOTHER FROM THE FATHER'S ACTS OF VIOLENCE MAY NOT RELY ON THE EXISTENCE OF COURT ORDERS TO EXCUSE HIS LACK OF RELATIONSHIP WITH THE CHILD.

The Wymans assert that the adoption should proceed without the consent of the natural father because: 1) it is undisputed that Maxwell has had no relationship with the child since the child was six months old; 2) Maxwell wilfully and intentionally through illegal and threatening actions sought to control and intimidate the mother, rather than seek modification of the protective order in an attempt to establish a relationship with the child; 3) Maxwell's conduct was wilful and intentional and he took actions which he knew would have the result of preventing a relationship with his child; and 4) to allow Maxwell to rely on his own illegal and threatening acts toward the mother and the child as a grounds to prevent adoption would violate public policy. Maxwell admits to the violations of the protective order, but characterizes his behavior as a misguided effort to see the child. He argues that his lack of relationship should be excused, not only by the fact that he was involuntarily incarcerated but also by the fact that court orders prohibited him from having any contact with the child.

The law presumes that consent of a child's natural parents is necessary before an adoption may be effected. The exceptions to this presumption are found in *10 O.S. Supp. 1998 § 7505–4.2*. . . . One of the situations in which a nonconsensual adoption may be obtained under § 7505–4.2(H) is if a parent wilfully fails to maintain a significant relationship with the child through visitation or communication for a period of twelve months out of fourteen months immediately preceding the filing of the petition for adoption. The burden is on the party seeking to adopt without consent to prove such adoption is warranted by clear and convincing evidence. Accordingly, the decision of the trial court will not be disturbed unless it fails to rest on clear and convincing evidence.

. . . During the relevant period the father has been incarcerated, denied visitation by a paternity order, and prohibited from contacting the mother and/or the child by a protective order. Because Maxwell relies on his incarceration and the court orders to excuse his lack of relationship with the child and prevent the adoption without his consent, we must decide whether . . . the father's lack of communication and lack of relationship with the child was wilful within the intent of the statute, obviating the necessity of obtaining his consent to the adoption.

We have not previously applied § 7505–4.2(H) in this context—circumstances in which a natural father, through his own fault, has placed himself in a position where he is not permitted by court orders to visit or communicate with his child and maintain a satisfactory relationship. However, in the *Matter of Adoption of V.A.J., 660 P.2d 139 (Okla. 1983),* this Court addressed whether the life imprisonment of a natural father for murder was sufficient *per se* to establish the child's eligibility for adoption without parental consent on the grounds of wilful failure to contribute to the support of the minor child. . . .

In V.A.J., the father's only source of income was a meager monthly stipend from his parents which would be granted or withdrawn at will. The Court held that incarceration alone is not enough to support termination of parental rights. This holding was consistent with the majority view from other jurisdictions. Regarding whether failure to support was wilful and his parental rights could be terminated, the V.A.J. court said:

> "The statutory language of § 60.6(3) is clearly devoid of any explicit legislative intent that imprisonment for any crime or for any duration afford a ground for dispensing with a parents consent. The statute requires wilful failure or refusal to contribute. Imprisonment cannot be equated with wilful failure to contribute to the child's support. . . . The proper inquiry to address in this case is whether the natural parent intentionally incapacitated himself for the purpose of avoiding the duty imposed by law; if so, then imprisonment may constitute justification for dispensing with his consent in the adoption proceeding. The evidence here does not support an inference that the father's commission of a felony, and subsequent incarceration therefore, was for the purpose of avoiding his support obligation. Thus his incapacity to earn income and pay support may not be deemed 'wilful.' "

. . . [A]lthough parental rights may not be terminated solely for a parent's incarceration, parental incarceration and the reason for the incarceration—i.e. the nature of the crime committed as well as the person against whom the criminal act was perpetrated—are relevant to the issue of whether parental consent to an adoption is necessary. The question of intent is to be determined in each case from all of the facts and circumstances.

. . . It is noteworthy that several other courts when faced with non-consensual termination of parental rights have concluded that: 1) the parent's incarceration and the conduct which resulted in incarceration as well as the person against whom the criminal act is committed are factors which may be considered in determining whether parental rights should be terminated; 2) a parent's wilful criminal act and course of conduct can imply a conscious disregard and indifference to the child in respect to parental obligations that a parent owes to a child; and 3) intent is generally an inferred fact determined by conduct within the statutory period combined with relevant conduct both before and after such period.

Parental obligations entail minimal attributes such as: 1) expression of love and affection for the child; 2) expression of personal concern over the health, education and general well-being of the child; 3) the duty to supply necessary food, clothing, and medical care; 4) the duty to provide adequate domicile; and 5) the duty to furnish social and religious guidance. Maxwell was incarcerated for stalking and assaulting the mother and violating a protective order which was entered to protect the child and its mother from his acts of violence. Here, the father clearly never assumed his responsibilities as a parent nor did he attempt to foster a healthy, loving, and supportive relationship with his child. Rather, since the child's birth, he has embarked on intentional acts which evidence a total disregard for the parent-child relationship and the welfare of the child. His conduct which resulted in incarceration was in direct contradiction to basic parental obligations. Maxwell's conscious decisions supply the circumstances for the conclusion that he did not intend to establish or maintain a significant relationship with the child. Consequently, we hold that the father may not rely on the existence of the court orders to excuse his lack of relationship with the child.

Considering all aspects of the father's intentional conduct, the evidence clearly and convincingly establishes that the father wilfully failed to maintain a significant relationship with the child through visitation or communication for a period of twelve consecutive months out of the last fourteen months immediately preceding the filing of the petition for adoption. This situation is obviously within the intention of *10 O.S. Supp. 1998 § 7505–4.2(H)*. The state, through its Legislature, has wide power with respect to the rights of parents over their children which affect the welfare of the child. In order to protect the integrity of the home and natural bond between parent and child, a strict construction of adoption statutes is required. However, the Legislature has provided that parental rights must yield when the welfare of the child so demands. The record establishes that the trial court's determination is supported by the requisite clear and convincing evidence.

II. THE TRIAL COURT'S DETERMINATION THAT THE ADOPTION WAS IN THE BEST INTERESTS OF THE CHILD IS SUPPORTED BY THE EVIDENCE.

In addition to the statutory requirements, this Court has also required that the adoption and termination of parental rights be in the best interests of the child.

. . .

The trial court's finding that the best interests of the child would be served by approving the adoption and maintaining the child's current family unit are supported by the evidence. Consequently, we hold that the trial court did not err in finding that the adoption was in the best interests of the child.

CONCLUSION

Nonconsensual adoption may be obtained under *10 O.S. Supp. 1998 § 7505–4.2(H)* if a parent wilfully fails to maintain a significant relationship with the child through visitation or communication for a period of twelve months out of fourteen month immediately preceding the filing of the petition for adoption.... The decision of the trial court will not be disturbed unless it fails to rest on clear and convincing evidence.

When a parent is incarcerated during the relevant statutory period, the question of intent is to be determined in each case from all of the facts and circumstances including the nature of the crime committed as well as the person against whom the criminal act was perpetrated. A father who was denied visitation and who was incarcerated for stalking and assaulting the mother and violating a protective order which was entered to protect the child and its mother from the father's acts of violence may not rely on the existence of court orders to excuse his lack of relationship with the child. The trial court's determination that the best interests of the child would be served by approving the adoption and maintaining the child's current family unit is supported by the evidence.

COURT OF CIVIL APPEALS OPINION VACATED; TRIAL COURT AFFIRMED.

■ DISSENT: OPALA

The court holds today that neither a father's incarceration nor his previous court-ordered bar of visitation will provide a defense against a mother's complaint of his willful failure to maintain a relationship with his child, a ruling which ... may result in the nonconsensual termination of paternal status. Today's pronouncement is fraught with state and federal constitutional infirmities. Insofar as the court's ruling deprives the father of his interposed defense of lack of willfulness, it denies him unimpeded access to court and due process affordable under the state and federal fundamental charters. There is no indication in the pertinent statute of legislative intent to sanction either complete destruction or even an abridgment of this father's defense based on his lack of willfulness. Today's pronouncement that rules out that defense is arbitrary and impermissible. When a court circumscribes the range of plainly admissible probative facts to show the absence of willfulness, due process is offended. The tone of today's opinion—pronouncing that the father "may not rely on the existence of court orders to excuse his lack of relationship with the child"—denies him full opportunity to explore all available facts that are probative of his lack of willfulness. Today's ruling operates significantly to restrict his access to the courts for establishing a statute-based defense against the mother's termination quest.

. . .

Proceedings to terminate one's recognized family status present matters of grave consequence. Constitutional law surrounds both the marital as well as the parental status with a panoply of protections. Consistently with the obligations imposed by the due process clause, indigent individuals seeking dissolution of a marital bond are entitled to court access at the expense of the government, and parental-status termination decrees are constitutionally infirm unless they be based on clear and convincing proof. A state does not act in a manner consistent with the due process and equal protection clauses, when it conditions, based on the litigant's ability to pay, a parent's access to appellate review of a decree that destroys parental rights.

Parental terminations are, perhaps, the most serious of all status-based bond severance proceedings. Federal due process and equal protection afford safeguards protecting familial associations. Oklahoma also surrounds all access to courts with constitutional shelter. Yet, today's pronouncement severely abridges this father's recognized federal-and state-law shields by fashioning a short-cut to termination that is neither legislatively sanctioned nor cognizable at common law. I hence recede from today's pronouncement because it (a) severely abridges this litigant's statute-based opportunity to defend against the mother's severance quest by demonstrating that one indispensable probative element is absent from the evidence she adduced in the proceeding—that of willful failure "to maintain a significant relationship with a minor through visitation or communication ..." and (2) invites as well as licenses the use of public law's quasi-criminal process regime (victim protection orders) as a designing custodial parent's collateral weapon for orchestrating the destruction of the noncustodial sire's legal status.

5. Open Adoption

Groves v. Clark

Supreme Court of Montana, 1996.
277 Mont. 179, 920 P.2d 981.

■ Trieweiler, Justice.

On July 24, 1995, Debbie Groves petitioned the District Court for the Eighth Judicial District in Cascade County for specific performance of a visitation agreement that she had entered into with Lonn and Loralee Clark. The Clarks filed an objection to Groves' petition and a brief opposing Groves' request for open adoption. On December 21, 1995, the District Court, by agreement of the parties, deemed the Clarks' objection a motion for summary judgment, concluded that the visitation agreement was void from its inception, and denied Groves' petition for specific performance. Groves appeals the District Court's order. We reverse the order of the District Court and remand the matter to that court for further proceedings in accordance with this opinion.

The issue on appeal is whether the District Court erred when it concluded that the visitation agreement executed between the birth mother and the adoptive parents prior to adoption was void as a matter of law.

FACTUAL BACKGROUND

Debbie Groves is the natural mother of Laci Lee Groves Clark. Laci lived with Groves from June 5, 1990, the date of Laci's birth, until approximately January 28, 1994, when Groves signed a document relinquishing custody of Laci to Lutheran Social Services (LSS) and consenting to adoption.

Prior to her relinquishment of Laci, Groves had become acquainted with Lonn and Loralee Clark, who had encouraged Groves to permit them to adopt Laci through LSS. At one of their meetings, the Clarks told Groves that they would agree to an "open adoption" so that Groves could have visitation rights with Laci after the adoption. Groves was adamant that she would not consent to adoption until the Clarks signed a visitation agreement.

On January 11, 1994, the Clarks signed a post-adoption visitation agreement, and on January 14 Groves signed a separate but identical agreement. The agreement provided:

> This agreement pertains to Debbie's desire to have visitation time with Laci Lee Groves (DOB 6–5–90) after Laci is adopted by Lonn and Loralee Clark.
>
> Debbie desires the following:
>
> 1. I hope to be able to give a 2 day notice whenever I'd like have Laci go with me or whenever I'd like to come visit at the Clark home.
> 2. I would like to have telephone contact with Laci and the Clark's [sic] as often as I feel it is necessary.

3. I don't intend to take Laci out of school unless I have to go to Butte for some emergency. If that happens I do need to take Lacy [sic] with me.

The Clarks signed the agreement in the presence of a notary public. Their signatures followed a provision that read: "We, Lonn and Loralee Clark, are willing to honor Debbie Groves' wishes regarding her requests for contact with Laci Lee Groves." Groves signed an identical notarized agreement three days later.

On January 28, 1994, Groves executed a document entitled "Relinquishment and Consent to Adoption." In that document, Groves relinquished Laci to LSS and granted LSS the right to place Laci for adoption. In addition, Groves expressly waived service of any notice of the proceedings for termination of her parental rights and placement of Laci for adoption, and agreed that LSS' executive director would appear at those proceedings as her attorney-in-fact to execute any documents that may have been required and to complete the placement of Laci in a suitable adoptive home. On February 2, 1994, the Eighth Judicial District Court entered an order awarding custody of Laci to LSS and terminating Groves' custodial and parental rights. After the Clarks filed a petition for adoption on September 23, 1994, that court entered a summary decree of adoption. At no time during the adoption proceedings did the Clarks mention their visitation agreement with Groves. As set forth in the "Relinquishment and Consent to Adoption," Groves did not participate in those proceedings.

Groves and the Clarks abided by the terms of the executed visitation agreement until June 5, 1995. On that date, when Groves telephoned the Clarks to make arrangements to visit Laci on her birthday, the Clarks refused and told Groves she could no longer visit her daughter. Prior to that time, the Clarks had allowed Groves to visit Laci on major holidays and on other occasions.

On July 24, 1995, Groves filed a petition requesting specific performance of her visitation agreement with the Clarks. In response, the Clarks filed an objection to Groves' petition and a brief in opposition to Groves' request for open adoption. The parties agreed that the Clarks' objection could be treated as a motion for summary judgment. The District Court denied Groves' motion for specific performance on December 21, 1995. In its order, the court held that the "Relinquishment and Consent to Adoption" constituted the final, controlling agreement by Groves relating to Laci. Because that document did not reserve any visitation and because that document purported to "terminate all [Groves'] parental rights to [Laci], now and forever," the court concluded that Groves had given up all of her parental rights and had no claim for post-adoption visitation. Based on that conclusion, the court held that the parties' visitation agreement was void and unenforceable.

DISCUSSION

Did the District Court err when it held that the visitation agreement executed between Groves and the Clarks prior to adoption was void as a matter of law?

In this case, the District Court treated the matter as appropriate for summary judgment pursuant to Rule 56, M.R.Civ.P. We review a district court's order for summary judgment *de novo* and apply the same evaluation as the district court based on Rule 56, M.R.Civ.P. Rule 56(c), M.R.Civ.P., provides that summary judgment is appropriate when there is no genuine issue of material fact and the moving party is entitled to judgment as a matter of law.

The District Court denied Groves' petition for specific performance on the basis of its determination that Groves had voluntarily given up all of her parental rights to Laci in the "Relinquishment and Consent to Adoption" which she signed on January 28, 1994. The court determined that that document constituted "the final agreement by Groves relating to the child," and concluded that its failure to reserve any visitation within its terms accomplished full termination of the relationship between Groves and Laci. In reaching its conclusion, the court relied on § 40–8–125, MCA, and *In re C.P.* (1986), 221 Mont. 180, 717 P.2d 1093.

Section 40–8–125, MCA, provides in relevant part:

> (1) After the final decree of adoption is entered, the relation of parent and child and all the rights, duties, and other legal consequences of the natural relation of child and parent shall thereafter exist between such adopted child and the adoptive parents adopting such child and the kindred of the adoptive parents.
>
> (2) After the final decree of adoption is entered, the natural parents and the kindred of the natural parents of the adopted child, unless they are the adoptive parents or the spouse of an adoptive parent, shall be relieved of all parental responsibilities for said child and have no rights over such adopted child.

In *In re C.P.*, 221 Mont. at 181, 717 P.2d at 1093, this Court interpreted § 40–8–125, MCA, to preclude visitation rights for the natural parents once a trial court has entered its final decree of adoption. Specifically, we stated:

> This language [of § 40–8–125, MCA] is clear. When parental rights are terminated, the natural parent no longer has *any* rights over the child. *This includes visitation rights.*

In re C.P., 221 Mont. at 183, 717 P.2d at 1095 (underlining added).

In re C.P. is distinguishable from this case, however. First, in *In re C.P.*, although the parties discussed including visitation rights in the final order, there was no indication in the record that the parties reached any agreement on the issue. In contrast, in this case both parties voluntarily signed a notarized agreement which provided the terms of the visitation arrangement. In addition, the Court recognized in *In re C.P.* that the outcome of that case might have been different had there been a statute that provided for visitation after a final adoption decree and had the parties bargained for the right of visitation. In that case, we noted:

> Even if the statutes provided for such a retention of visitation rights, the record in this case contains *no* evidence to support such a finding.... There is no question that appellant disputed SRS obtaining permanent custody. Thus, there is no question of whether she agreed to their custody in exchange for visitation rights.

In this case, the parties did bargain for the right of visitation. In fact, Groves alleges that she agreed to termination of her parental rights and consented to place Laci for adoption only after the Clarks agreed to sign the visitation agreement. Furthermore, since our decision in *In re C.P.*, the Montana Legislature has enacted a statutory provision which recognizes agreements entered into between birth parents and prospective adoptive parents relating to the future conduct of the parties and the adoptive child. Specifically, § 40–8–136, MCA, enacted in 1989, provides in relevant part:

(1) Prior to a hearing under 40–8–109, the birth parents, prospective adoptive parents, and their representatives shall file with the court a report of agreements and disbursements, and they shall serve a copy of the report on the central office of the department.

(2) The report must contain:

(a) *all oral and written agreements between the parties that relate to the future conduct of a party with respect to the child.* If an oral agreement is reported, the substance of the agreement must be contained in the report and a copy of the report must be served on each party to the oral agreement. Copies of all written agreements must be attached to the report.

(Emphasis added.)

Although 40–8–136, MCA, does not specifically reference visitation agreements or agreements for continuing contact, that statute does clearly refer to "the future conduct of a party with respect to the child." If, as this Court determined in *In re C.P.*, the termination of parental rights automatically terminates all rights of the natural parents over the child, then the future conduct of the natural parents with respect to the adoptive child would be irrelevant. Such a construction would render § 40–8–136, MCA, meaningless. It is well established that this Court must give meaning and effect to all statutory provisions, and that a construction which renders a provision meaningless is disfavored. We therefore interpret § 40–8–136, MCA, to provide for the recognition of agreements for post-adoption contact and visitation. That does not, however, end our inquiry.

Section 40–8–136, MCA, provides that prior to a district court hearing for the relinquishment of parental rights and adoptive placement, "the birth parents, prospective adoptive parents, and their representatives shall file with the court a report of agreements and disbursements, and they shall serve a copy of the report on the central office of the department." On appeal, the Clarks contend that Groves had a duty to file a report of the visitation agreement with the court and that her failure to do so waives her right to now object. The Clarks have, however, mistakenly interpreted the statute's requirements. Section 40–8–136, MCA, does not place the burden of filing an agreement solely on the birth parent, but rather provides that "*the birth parents, prospective parents, and their representatives*" share the requirement of filing any such agreement. (Emphasis added.) Furthermore, in this case, Groves had expressly waived her right to participate in the hearing for termination of her rights and adoption of Laci and had appointed LSS' director to act on her behalf. Therefore, it was the duty of both the Clarks, as prospective parents, and the director of LSS, as Groves' representative, to file a report of the executed visitation agreement. Groves should not be penalized for those parties' failure to comply with the requirements of § 40–8–136, MCA. Accordingly, we hold that the failure to file a report of the written visitation agreement does not, of itself, bar Groves' petition for specific performance.

In order to determine the merit of Groves' petition for specific performance, however, we must address a district court's responsibilities once a report of a visitation agreement between the natural parents and prospective adoptive parents has been filed with that court. It is well established that: "It is the policy of the state of Montana to ensure that the best interests of the child are met by adoption proceedings." Section 40–8–114(1), MCA. To that end, "[t]he needs of the child must be the primary focus of adoption proceedings, with full recognition of the interdependent needs and interests of birth parents and adoptive parents." Section 40-8-114(3), MCA. It is therefore essential for a trial court, when it considers a post-adoption visitation agreement, to recognize that that agreement should only be given effect if continued contact between the natural parents and the child is in the child's best interest. If, following a hearing, the district court concludes that such an agreement is in the child's best interest, we conclude that there is no reason that such an agreement should not be enforced by the court.

Our conclusion that natural parents and prospective adoptive parents may contract for post-adoption visitation and that such agreements should be enforced when they are determined to be in the best interest of the child is supported by the case law of other jurisdictions. For example, in *People ex rel. Sibley v. Sheppard* (1981), 54 N.Y.2d 320, 445 N.Y.S.2d 420, 429 N.E.2d 1049, 1052–53, the Court of Appeals of New York concluded that the statutory creation of an adoptive family does not automatically require the complete severance of all further contact with former relatives. Similarly, the Maryland Special Court of Appeals held that the adoptive parent and the natural parent may "enter into any agreement with respect to visitation rights between the child and the natural parent so long as the visitation is in the best interest of the child and public policy does not prevent such visitation." Finally, the Connecticut Supreme Court upheld a visitation agreement that was negotiated in good faith in order to promote the best interest of the child and noted:

> The plaintiff's rights are not premised on an ongoing genetic relationship that somehow survives a termination of parental rights and an adoption. Instead, the plaintiff is asking us to decide whether, as an adult who has an ongoing personal relationship with the child, she may contract with the adopting parents, prior to adoption, for the continued right to visit with the child, so long as that visitation continues to be in the best interest of the child.
>
> . . .
>
> Traditional models of the nuclear family have come, in recent years, to be replaced by various configurations of parents, stepparents, adoptive parents and grandparents. We are not prepared to assume that the welfare of children is best served by a narrow definition of those whom we permit to continue to manifest their deep concern for a child's growth and development.

Michaud v. Wawruck (1988), 209 Conn. 407, 551 A.2d 738, 740–42 (footnotes and citations omitted).

We conclude that birth parents and prospective adoptive parents are free to contract for post-adoption visitation and that trial courts must give effect to such contracts when continued visitation is in the best interest of the child. We further conclude that Groves was not precluded from filing a petition for specific performance of the parties' visitation agreement solely on the basis of the Clarks' failure to file a report of the agreement with the District Court prior to the adoption proceeding. We therefore hold that the District Court erred when it summarily denied Groves' petition for specific performance without a determination of whether continued visitation is in Laci's best interest. Accordingly, we remand this case to the District Court for a hearing on whether enforcement of the visitation agreement between Groves and the Clarks would be in Laci's best interest.

■ TURNAGE, C.J., and GRAY, LEAPHART and NELSON, JJ., concur.

NOTE

The *Groves* case illustrates a recent trend among courts toward greater recognition of open adoption arrangements. But see McLaughlin v. Strickland, 279 S.C. 513, 309 S.E.2d 787 (App.1983) (natural father's execution of a consent to adoption not valid where conditioned upon father retaining visitation with child); Hede v. Gilstrap, 107 P.3d 158 (Wyo.2005) (holding that adoption severs all ties to the biological family, and visitation rights with an adopted grandchild may only be established if one of the biological parents has retained parental rights and the child has been adopted by a stepparent; otherwise, "adoption would be a strange status if the only biological family members cut off from the adoptee were his or her parents."); In re Gregory B., 74 N.Y.2d 77, 544 N.Y.S.2d 535, 542 N.E.2d 1052 (1989). In *Gregory B.*, the New York Court of Appeals upheld the termination of parental rights of a life-sentence prison inmate. As to any continuing visitation, the court stated:

> We express no opinion as to whether such contacts generally would be helpful and appropriate once parental rights have been terminated and the child has been adopted into a new family or whether a court should have the discretionary authority to order such contacts. We note, however, that the "open" adoption concept would appear to be inconsistent with this State's view as expressed by the Legislature that adoption relieves the biological parent "of all parental duties toward and of all responsibilities for" the adoptive child over whom the parent "shall have no rights" (Domestic Relations Law § 117(1)(a); Matter of Best, 66 N.Y.2d 151, 495 N.Y.S.2d 345, 485 N.E.2d 1010). Although adoptive parents are free, at their election, to judicially require such contacts between the adopted child and the child's biological parent, to judicially require such contacts arguably may be seen as threatening the integrity of the adoptive family unit. In any event, "open" adoptions are not presently authorized. If they are to be established, it is the Legislature that more appropriately should be called upon to balance the critical social policy choices and the delicate issues of family relations involved in such a determination.

74 N.Y.2d at 91.

See generally Annette Ruth Appell, Blending Families Through Adoption: Implications for Collaborative Adoption Law and Practice, 75 B.U.L. Rev. 997 (1995); Candace M. Zierdt, Make New Parents But Keep The Old, 69 N.D. L. Rev. 497 (1993); Cynthia E. Cordle, Note: Open Adoption: The Need for Legislative Action, 2 Va. J. Soc. Pol'y & L. 275 (1995); Laurie A. Ames, Open Adoptions: Truth and Consequences, 16 Law & Psychol. Rev. 137, 1992).

Compare the 1994 Uniform Adoption Act:

> Agreements by adoptive parents to permit post-adoption visitation by birth parents or other members of a child's original family are not barred, but neither are they expressly permitted except in the context of stepparent adoptions. In contrast to the deeply divided views of committee members and the Conference as a whole about post-adoption contact in adoptions by nonrelatives, a consensus emerged concerning the importance for adoptive stepchildren to maintain previously established visitation arrangements with families of their noncustodial parent, subject to the agreement of the adoptive and custodial parents and a judicial determination, based on a list of specific factors, that the agreement is in the child's best interests. For all other adoptions, however, the Act contains what appears to be a bright line rule that when a decree of adoption becomes final, "any previous order for visitation or communication with the adoptee terminates." Note, however, that anyone with an existing order for visitation must be given notice of the adoption proceeding, and that the court has authority to request information about the proposed adoption from anyone else who had a previous relationship with the birth parents or adoptee. Most important, perhaps, is that while an adoption terminates "previous orders," the Act contains no prohibitory language with respect to visitation or communication orders that might be issued in some circumstance in the future.

Joan Heifetz Hollinger, The Uniform Adoption Act: Reporter's Ruminations, 30 Fam. L.Q. 345, 372–373 (1996).

6. Equitable Adoption

Lankford v. Wright

Supreme Court of North Carolina, 1997.
347 N.C. 115, 489 S.E.2d 604.

■ Frye, Justice.

The sole issue in this case is whether North Carolina recognizes the doctrine of equitable adoption. We hold that the doctrine should be recognized in this state, and therefore, we reverse the decision of the Court of Appeals.

Plaintiff, Barbara Ann Newton Lankford, was born to Mary M. Winebarger on 15 January 1944. When plaintiff was a child, her natural mother entered into an agreement with her neighbors, Clarence and Lula Newton, whereby the Newtons agreed to adopt and raise plaintiff as their child. Shortly thereafter, plaintiff moved into the Newton residence and became known as Barbara Ann Newton, the only child of Clarence and Lula Newton.

The Newtons held plaintiff out to the public as their own child, and plaintiff was at all times known as Barbara Ann Newton. Plaintiff's school records referred to plaintiff as Barbara Ann Newton and indicated that Clarence and Lula Newton were her parents. Plaintiff's high-school diploma also referred to plaintiff as Barbara Ann Newton. After Clarence Newton died in 1960, the newspaper obituary listed Barbara Ann Newton as his surviving daughter. Later, with Lula Newton's assistance, plaintiff obtained a Social Security card issued to her under the name of Barbara Ann Newton.

After plaintiff joined the Navy, plaintiff and Lula Newton frequently wrote letters to each other. In most of the letters, plaintiff referred to Lula Newton as her mother and Lula Newton referred to plaintiff as her daughter. Lula Newton also established several bank accounts with plaintiff, where Lula Newton deposited money plaintiff sent to her while plaintiff was in the Navy. On several occasions, plaintiff took leaves of absence from work to care for Lula Newton during her illness.

In 1975, Lula Newton prepared a will. When she died in 1994, the will was not accepted for probate because some unknown person had defaced a portion of the will. The will named plaintiff as co-executrix of the estate and made specific bequests to plaintiff. Since the will could not be probated, Lula Newton died intestate.

After Lula Newton's death, plaintiff filed for declaratory judgment seeking a declaration of her rights and status as an heir of the estate of Lula Newton. Defendants, the administrators and named heirs of Lula Newton, filed a motion for summary judgment. The trial court granted defendants' motion. The North Carolina Court of Appeals affirmed the order granting summary judgment, reasoning that plaintiff was not adopted according to N.C.G.S. §§ 48–1 to–38 and that North Carolina does not recognize the doctrine of equitable adoption. This Court granted plaintiff's petition for discretionary review, and we now conclude that the doctrine of equitable adoption should be recognized in North Carolina.

. . .

Equitable adoption is a remedy to "protect the interest of a person who was supposed to have been adopted as a child but whose adoptive parents failed to undertake the legal steps necessary to formally accomplish the adoption." The doctrine is applied in an intestate estate to "give effect to the intent of the decedent to adopt and provide for the child."

. . .

Adoption did not exist at common law and is of purely statutory origin. Equitable adoption, however, does not confer the incidents of formal statutory adoption; rather, it merely confers rights of inheritance upon the foster child in the event of intestacy of the foster parents. In essence, the doctrine invokes the principle that equity regards that as done which ought to be done. The doctrine is not intended to replace statutory requirements or to create the parent-child relationship; it simply recognizes the foster child's right to inherit from the person or persons who contracted to adopt the child and who honored that contract in all respects except through formal statutory procedures. As an equitable matter, where the child in question has faithfully performed the duties of a natural child to the foster parents, that child is entitled to be placed in the position in which he would have been had he been adopted. Likewise, based on principles of estoppel, those claiming under and through the deceased are estopped to assert that the child was not legally adopted or did not occupy the status of an adopted child.

. . .

The elements necessary to establish the existence of an equitable adoption are:

(1) an express or implied agreement to adopt the child,

(2) reliance on that agreement,

(3) performance by the natural parents of the child in giving up custody,

(4) performance by the child in living in the home of the foster parents and acting as their child,

(5) partial performance by the foster parents in taking the child into their home and treating the child as their own, and

(6) the intestacy of the foster parents.

See 2 Am. Jur. 2d Adoption § 54 (1994).

. . .

In this case, the evidence in the record tends to show that the above elements can be satisfied by clear, cogent, and convincing evidence. The record demonstrates that the Newtons agreed to adopt plaintiff; that the Newtons and plaintiff relied on that agreement; that plaintiff's natural mother gave up custody of plaintiff to the Newtons; that plaintiff lived in the Newtons' home, cared for them in their old age, and otherwise acted as their child; that the Newtons treated plaintiff as their child by taking her into their home, giving her their last name, and raising her as their child; and that Mrs. Newton died intestate several years after Mr. Newton died. These facts fit squarely within the parameters of the doctrine of equitable adoption and are indicative of the dilemma the doctrine is intended to remedy.

. . .

The dissent points out that a minority of jurisdictions have declined to recognize the doctrine of equitable adoption. However, we again note that an overwhelming majority of states that have addressed the question have recognized and applied the doctrine. More importantly, it is the unique role of the courts to fashion equitable remedies to protect and promote the principles of equity such as those at issue in this case. We are convinced that acting in an equitable manner in this case does not interfere with the legislative scheme for adoption, contrary to the assertions of the dissent. Recognition of the doctrine of equitable adoption does not create a legal adoption, and therefore does not impair the statutory procedures for adoption.

In conclusion, a decree of equitable adoption should be granted where justice, equity, and good faith require it. The fairness of applying the doctrine once the prerequisite facts have been established is apparent. Accordingly, we reverse the Court of Appeals' decision which affirmed the trial court's entry of summary judgment for defendants and remand to the trial court for further proceedings not inconsistent with this opinion.

REVERSED AND REMANDED.

■ DISSENT: MITCHELL, Chief Justice

In its opinion, the majority for the first time accepts the doctrine of equitable adoption for North Carolina. As applied by the majority in this case, the doctrine results in neither an adoption nor equity. Therefore, although I am convinced the majority is engaged in an honest but unfortunate attempt to do good in the present case, I must dissent.

. . .

One maxim of equity, as the majority explains, is that equity regards as done that which in fairness and good conscience ought to be done. A court's notion of what is good or desirable does not determine what "ought to be done" in applying equity. The maxim of equity upon which the majority relies must yield to other controlling and established rules or maxims. One such maxim is that a court of equity, however benevolent its motives, is "bound by any explicit statute or directly applicable rule of law, regardless of its view of the equities." *Id.* Thus, no equitable remedy may properly be applied to disturb statutorily defined and established rights, such as those rights created by North Carolina statutes controlling intestate succession or those controlling legal adoption.

The North Carolina Intestate Succession Act provides a comprehensive and extensive legislative scheme controlling intestate succession by, through, and from adopted children. *N.C.G.S. § 29–17(a)* provides:

> A child, *adopted in accordance with Chapter 48 of the General Statutes* or in accordance with the applicable law of any other jurisdiction, and the heirs of such child, are entitled by succession to any property by, through and from his adoptive parents and their heirs the same as if he were the natural legitimate child of the adoptive parents.

N.C.G.S. § 29–17(a) (1995) (emphasis added). The extensive scheme created by the legislature is clear and unambiguous. It provides, in pertinent part, that only those children who are adopted *in compliance with chapter 48* or adopted according to the requirements of another jurisdiction are eligible to take by intestate succession. Therefore, the maxim relied upon by the majority may not properly be applied here.

> Equity will not interfere where a statute applies and dictates requirements for relief. Use of equitable principles to trump an apposite statute thus is legally indefensible. The disregard of an unambiguous law based on sympathy is unjustifiable under the rubric of equity.

27A Am. Jur. 2d Equity § 246 (footnotes omitted).

It is well established that "where an extensive legislative scheme governs, it is incumbent upon chancellors to restrain their equity powers." *Id.* The application of the doctrine of equitable adoption by the majority in this case violates this principle of equity requiring greater restraint when dealing with statutory law than when addressing the common law. The majority's application of the doctrine of equitable adoption here negates the rights of other heirs such as defendants which are expressly provided for in the extensive legislative scheme established by the North Carolina Intestate Succession Act. In the instant case, the application of the doctrine of equitable adoption denies other rightful heirs their statutory intestate shares, in effect voiding the intestate succession hierarchy enacted by our legislature. This result is contrary to established maxims of equity.

. . .

Presently, all states recognize a parent-child relationship through adoption if the certain and unambiguous statutory procedures of each specific state are followed. A strong minority of courts that have reviewed the issue have declined to recognize the doctrine of equitable adoption....

. . .

Despite plaintiff's foster parents' verbal acknowledgments and holding plaintiff out as their natural child, they never legally adopted her by complying with the statutory process.... Thus, it is my opinion that this Court should not declare plaintiff to have been "equitably adopted," thereby subrogating the rights of the statutorily determined heirs for purposes of intestate succession.

. . .

In the present case, the controlling maxims of equity clearly require that this Court restrain its equity powers so as not to overrule comprehensive statutory schemes and, thereby, do harm to innocents. For these reasons, I respectfully dissent from the decision of the majority and would affirm the holding of the Court of Appeals which affirmed the order of the trial court.

Chambers v. Chambers

Supreme Court of Georgia, 1990.
260 Ga. 610, 398 S.E.2d 200.

■ FLETCHER, JUSTICE.

Appellant, Pete Carlton Chambers, filed a petition in equity seeking to establish and enforce his right to share in the intestate estate of Ethel Louise Chambers, deceased, contending that the deceased had virtually adopted him and, therefore, appellant was an heir-at-law of the deceased. The petition named both of the natural children of the deceased as defendants. Appellee, Harold Gaines Chambers, was named individually and as administrator of the deceased's estate, while George David Chambers was named individually.

Appellee filed a motion for partial summary judgment accompanied by the affidavit of appellant's natural mother wherein she stated that she had never surrendered her parental rights to appellant, that her parental rights had not been terminated and that she had not given her consent for the deceased to adopt the appellant.

In response, appellant filed the affidavit of the former director of the Clarke County Department of Public Welfare (now the Department of Family and Children's Services) who had been involved with appellant's situation since his infancy. In her affidavit, the former director stated that appellant's natural mother, who at the time of appellant's birth was in a mental institution, had given her consent that a certain Jones County couple, who desired to adopt appellant, be allowed to do so. However, upon discovering that the wife of the couple was terminally ill, the couple turned appellant over to the Jones County Department of Public Welfare. When it was learned that the natural mother of appellant had been a resident of Clarke County prior to her institutionalization, officials of the Jones County Department notified affiant to come get appellant. Affiant did so and appellant was eventually placed in the home of the deceased, who raised appellant from infancy, calling him Pete Carlton Chambers rather than by his given name.

In 1978, a petition was filed in the Clarke County Superior Court seeking to have appellant's name legally changed to Pete Carlton Chambers. The petition specifically stated that the deceased was not adopting appellant. Apparently had the deceased adopted appellant, the deceased would no longer have been eligible to receive a stipend from the Clarke County Department of Family and Children's Services for being appellant's foster parent.

The trial court granted summary judgment to appellee, individually and in his capacity as administrator of the estate of the deceased. Appellant appeals and we affirm.

We sympathize with appellant's plight: born to a woman he has never known while she was confined to a mental institution, placed in the home of the deceased, raised along with the deceased's natural children and even given a new name by the deceased. Yet the fact remains that appellant has not made out a case for virtual adoption.

To establish a cause of action for virtual or equitable adoption in Georgia, one must make "some showing of an agreement between the natural and adoptive parents, performance by the natural parents of the child in giving up custody, performance by the child by living in the home of the adoptive parents, partial performance by the foster parents in taking the child into the home and treating [it] as their child, and . . . the intestacy of the foster parent."

Appellant has failed to show that there was an agreement between his natural mother and the deceased. He has also failed to show that there was performance by his natural mother in giving up custody. His natural mother's affidavit specifically states that she did not consent to the deceased's adopting the appellant, that there was no agreement between her and the deceased for the purpose of carrying out an adoption, and that she received no compensation for an adoption by the deceased of the appellant.

The record contains no proof concerning any official acts taken to terminate the parental rights of appellant's natural mother; nor is there anything in the record to demonstrate that his natural mother gave her permission for an adoption of appellant or for a surrender of custody of appellant to either the Jones County Department of Public Welfare, the Clarke County Department of Public Welfare, the State Department of Public Welfare, or any other state or local agency.

As a result, we hold that the trial court did not err in granting partial summary judgement in favor of the appellee.

Judgment affirmed.

7. A Market for Adoptions?

Richard A. Posner, Sex and Reason

409–416 (1992).

The second big question about adoption is, why is it so heavily regulated rather than being left, like other voluntary transactions, to the free market? And heavily regulated it is in the country—with the results predicted by economics. In most states, only adoption agencies may lawfully supply children for adoption. The agencies are private organizations, most of them nonprofit (often church-sponsored). Many states limit the fees that agencies may charge to the adoptive parents, but the essential regulation is the prohibition against the agencies' "buying" children. Buying is defined in this context as paying the biological mother more than the medical and maintenance costs (food, housing, and so forth) of pregnancy and childbirth. The nonprofit character of most adoption agencies, coupled with regulatory supervision, has generated a cost-plus system of adoption fees, with the result that the limitation on the payment to the biological mother is passed through to, and holds down, the adoption fee. Adoption agencies screen couples applying for a baby, excluding those couples whom the agency considers unfit to raise a child, for example because in the agency's opinion the couple is too old. Applicants who are not screened out often must wait years before the agency has a baby for them to adopt.

Some states permit independent adoption, that is, adoption not arranged through an adoption agency. Usually the arranger is a lawyer or an obstetrician. He is forbidden to charge a fee for the adoption beyond his usual professional fee for such incidental services as drawing up the necessary papers, in the case of a lawyer, or checking the health of the infant, in the case of an obstetrician. Thus, like the adoption agency, the arranger of an independent adoption is forbidden to "buy" children for adoption, defined as before. But because independent adoption is difficult to monitor (much more so than agency adoption), it often operates much as a free market in babies for adoption would, with payments to the biological mothers that exceed the mothers' medical and maintenance costs and that are recouped in high fees charged the adoptive parents. Independent adoption is therefore commonly referred to as the "gray market." Just as gray is a mixture of white and black, so independent adoption is a mixture of lawful adoption and "baby selling," the latter constituting an illegal (black) market.

The term *baby selling*, while inevitable, is misleading. A mother who surrenders her parental rights for a fee is not selling her baby; babies are not chattels, and cannot be bought and sold. She is selling her parental rights. Of course in like vein one might speak of a slaveowner's selling his rights over the slave. But those rights are rights of ownership; a parent's rights, in our society anyway, are not. So, sacrificing vividness to accuracy, I hereby rename "baby selling" "parental-right selling."

One of the best confirmed hypotheses of economics—confirmed daily, in fact, in eastern Europe and the Soviet Union—is that a ceiling on the price that may lawfully be charged for a good or service will created both queues (waiting periods) and a black market, provided, of course, that the ceiling is lower than the free market price (otherwise it is not a real ceiling). This is what we observe in the adoption market today. The price ceiling that results from limiting the amount that may be paid the biological mother to her medical and maintenance expenses has created a shortage of babies for adoption. The consequence is queuing by the clientele of adoption agencies and of other lawful suppliers, and a black market for the bolder demanders.

The imbalance between demand and supply is growing. It is true that advances in the treatment of infertility, which have reduced the number of childless couples, may have offset the rising age of marriage, which has increased the number of childless couples because infertility is a positive function of a woman's age. If so, the demand for children for adoption is not increasing. But the supply is decreasing. For even though the increase in the illegitimacy rate has exceeded the decrease in the birth rate, the resulting net increase in the number of illegitimate births has in turn been exceeded by the increase in the rate at which unmarried mothers decide to retain their child rather than put it up for adoption. There appear to be two reasons for this increase. Women's income has risen, making women less dependent on men to support them and their children and thereby reducing the cost of illegitimacy. And the availability of abortion has reduced the fraction of accidental pregnancies that result in unwanted births.

The diminished supply of babies for adoption, interacting with a demand that is not declining, has exacerbated the effects of the price ceiling. It has increased the queue for babies, increased the number of independent adoptions—may of them black market adoptions—at the expense of the adoption agencies, driven up the black market price of parental rights (to about $25,000 in the case of a healthy white infant, the type of baby most highly valued by the market), and increased the pressures from the adoption agencies for stronger laws against the sale of parental rights and against independent adoptions generally.

The straightforward way to deal with the problems created by a price ceiling is to remove the ceiling. Why has this not been done in the adoption market, now that the declining supply of babies for adoption has made the economic consequences of the price ceiling palpable? Usury laws, which are to lending as adoption law is to adoption, have been phased out for just this reason. The answer most students of adoption would give is that the social costs of a free market in babies for adoption would exceed those of the existing regulated market. All the arguments made in support of this proposition, however, either are bad ones or could easily be met by placing minor restrictions on an otherwise free market.

1. *The rich will snap up all the good babies, and the cost of acquisition will deprive those few middle-income couples fortunate enough to obtain a good baby of the resources they require to raise it properly.* Actually the rich do better under the present system than they would in a free market. The rich have connections, and connections are vital in maneuvering in a regulated system. Wealthy couples always manage to jump to the head of the adoption queue, thereby paying a lower real price—a price that includes the cost of waiting as well as the adoption fee—than the couple of modest means, who must wait years for

their baby. (Granted this comparison ignores the cost to a wealthy person of using his connections.)

It is true that black market prices for adoption are high, though they are only a small fraction of the total cost of raising a child. But they are not a good predictor of what the price would be in a free, unregulated market. For they are high because the seller has to be compensated for bearing the risk of punishment and because illegal sellers incur high costs of operation by virtue of having to conceal their activities from the authorities. Competition among pregnant women to sell their parental rights would drive the price of those rights down to a level only slightly above the medical and maintenance costs of pregnancy. Since those costs are saved by a woman who does not become pregnant, the net additional cost of buying parental rights over an existing baby, versus making a baby, would be slight or even negative—as where a woman having high opportunity costs of pregnancy (maybe she has a high income) buys the parental rights of a woman whose opportunity costs of pregnancy are low.

What is probably true is that most women who sold their parental rights would be less prosperous than the women who bought them. But this means that parental-rights selling would be wealth-equalizing.

2. *The sale of parental rights may be value-maximizing from the standpoint of pregnant women and infertile couples, but it is bad from the standpoint of the children.* Of course the welfare of children as well as that of their natural and adoptive parents should be considered in the design of public policy, since neither set of parents can be relied on in their decision making to weight to child's welfare as highly as the child itself would do, if it could be consulted. Adoption agencies screen adoptive parents in the interest of the children, and this screening would not be an inherent feature of a market in parental rights, just as it is not a feature, at least a systematic feature, of independent adoption. But adoption agencies lack good information about the relative fitness of competing couples seeking children, and many of the rules that such agencies have employed—such as requiring that the adoptive parents be of the same religion as the infant's parents (for it is unrealistic to speak of the infant's religion), or automatically excluding all couples over 40 years of age—make a poor fit with the interests of the child. There is no evidence that children adopted independently—even those obtained through the black market—are less happy or successful or well adjusted than children adopted through agencies, though admittedly the question appears not to have been studied.

3. *What about the danger that pedophiles will buy parental rights over children in order to abuse the children sexually?* . . . [T]his danger cannot be dismissed out of hand. But it can be minimized, perhaps eliminated, by forbidding the sale of rights over children who are no longer infants—say children more than six months old. Very few child abusers have a sexual interest in infants; very few would acquire an infant for the purpose of being able to abuse it five or ten or fifteen years later; and whereas a stepfather usually first encounters his stepchild after the latter has emerged from infancy, when it is too late for the stepfather to be expected to form a parental-type bond that will inhibit incest with the child, the adoptive father ordinarily meets his adopted child when the latter is an infant, and would do so only then if the sale of rights over noninfants was prohibited. The suggested restriction on sale would be a minor curtailment of the market because for reasons discussed earlier there is little demand—little legitimate demand, at least—to adopt children past infancy. Moreover, persons with a criminal record of

child abuse, or even all men not living as part of a heterosexual couple, could be forbidden to buy parental rights.

4. *The sale of a human being in any circumstances and for any reason is morally repulsive, and if permitted could undermine the taboo against slavery.* A variant of this argument, made by Margaret Jane Radin, is that what she naturally terms baby selling promotes "commodification," which is the tendency, characteristic of capitalist societies, to view goods and services as things that can be exchanged in a market. Fair enough, but some of us believe that this and most societies could use more, not less, commodification and a more complete diffusion of the market-oriented ethical values that it promotes. If, for example, clean air were commodified, we would have less air pollution than we do.

A better answer, though, is that baby selling, when viewed as a method of adoption, is not at all like the sale of a person into slavery. The "purchasers" get no more power over the baby than natural parents have over their children. What is sold, in fact, is not the baby but the natural mother's rights to keep the baby—which is why I say that "baby selling" is misnamed. The term misled Radin.

5. *The sale of parental rights will encourage eugenic breeding, altering the human gene pool in potentially harmful ways.* Markets foster innovation; so should we not be concerned that eugenic entrepreneurs will try to breed a race of supermen and superwomen? Too great a disparity among human beings, owing to selective breeding of some, could create differences among persons in physical appearance and in physical and mental ability that would undermine cooperation and foment conflict, exploitation, even genocide, and, much like selective breeding of domestic animals, could introduce harmful mutations or, like incest, reduce genetic diversity. There are three reasons to discount these dangers. The first is that the market is unlikely to attract fertile couples. The second (and related) reason is that most people want their baby, biological or adopted, to be like them, so only Superman and Superwoman will want to have Superbaby. There is a genetic explanation for this preference (which is gene-fooling when the baby is adopted)—the similarity increases the confidence that it is *your* baby, not someone else's—and in addition it reduces the potential for conflicts between parents and child. Third, long before the eugenicists create a master race, biological parents will be improving their babies by surgical intervention in the fertilized ovum.

The more plausible concern with the genetic effects of parental-rights selling is the opposite. The mothers are likely to be drawn from the lower strata of society; and, if poverty and intelligence are negatively related, the IQs of these mothers will be below average, and the average IQ in society will therefore fall, with possible detrimental effects—higher costs of public education, more crime, and so on. But the danger that IQs will fall hardly seems a serious one, even if there is a strong, and genetic rather than environmental, positive correlation between income and IQ. It's not so much that if infertile couples were willing to pay for rights over high-IQ babies, a supply would be forthcoming, for demand would be limited by price. It is that most of the babies who would be obtained n a free market in parental rights are not babies who would be aborted; they are babies who would be retained by unmarried mothers. There probably would be a net increase in the number of babies from this class of mothers, but a small one.

6. *How would parental-rights selling work? Could the buyer return the baby if it was not as healthy and intelligent as the seller had warranted it to be? Does this*

question not show that such a market is simply too bizarre an intellectual construct to deserve serious consideration? Contracts in which the thing contracted over is a human being do present unique difficulties in matters of remedy, although the usual response is to require modification of the remedy rather than abolition of the market. A contract for the exclusive services of a person for a specified period of time is lawful and enforceable—but not by deeming the person a slave of the other party or even by issuing an injunction commanding him to continue working for that party, as distinct from an injunction forbidding him to work for anyone else. Similar adjustments in the normal principles of contract remedies would be necessary if adoption were left to the market. Adjustments are necessary already for cases in which adoptive parents sue the adoption agency or the independent adoption middleman because the baby turns out to be defective. Maybe for the baby's sake the purchaser of parental rights should not be allowed the usual privilege of returning defective merchandise, any more than he should be allowed to destroy it, but should be limited to a remedy in damages against the seller for the breach of whatever warranty of quality the seller may have given. Intermediaries—successors to today's adoption agencies—would spring into existence to guarantee quality to buyers.

What is true is that this program *sounds* fantastic and weird, just as it seems fantastic to imagine these literal "bonus babies" bragging when they grow up of the tremendous prices their parents paid in the baby market, and just as it seems fantastic and sad to imagine what would undoubtedly be the pronounced racial element in baby pricing. The demand for babies for adoption is weaker among blacks than among whites, while the supply of such babies is vastly greater; so the price of acquiring parental rights over black babies would be lower unless white couples considered black babies a close substitute for white ones, which most white couples probably would not, even if white demand for black babies were not artificially depressed by opposition within the black community.

. . .

I have left for last Gary Becker and Kevin Murphy's criticism of parental-rights selling, a criticism of particular importance because it comes from within economics rather than from persons hostile to a market system or ignorant of its workings. They argue that "the universal ban on this practice strongly suggests that the sale of children lowers social utility. Young unmarried women and poor parents who need money are the two groups most likely to sell their children. Some children sold to prosperous families who want them may consider themselves better off than if they had remained with their parents. But even children who would suffer greatly might be sold because they have no way to compensate their parents for keeping them." There actually are two arguments here rather than one. The argument from the universal ban on the practice is logically independent of the argument from the adverse effect on children. For one might think the existence of a universal ban against a practice a good reason for suspecting on Darwinian grounds that the practice was a bad one, even if one could not think of a convincing hypothesis as to why it was bad.

Neither of the arguments persuades me. First, the ban is not universal, even if we ignore Roman and Japanese adult adoptions—straightforward commercial exchanges—on the ground that an adult can protect his interests better than a child can. Not only was there adoption of children as well as adults among the Romans, but money changed hands frequently. And until the seventh century A.D. an Anglo-Saxon father was permitted to sell his child in a case of necessity, provided the child had not yet turned 7. What is true is that the sale of parental rights appears to be rare outside of the United States today (which is one reason the United States is the major importer of babies—from Romania, Korea, and elsewhere). But then adoption is rare outside of the United States, for reasons presumably independent of legal sanctions. As for the ban on such sales in the United States, it is extraordinarily porous, and parental-rights selling is therefore in fact common, to the despair of its critics. Do words speak louder than actions, or actions louder than words? Little effort is made to stamp out the sale of parental rights, so one may question the social commitment to the ban.

Becker and Murphy's second argument appears to envisage the sale of rights over children who are no longer infants. The picture is of parents who have decided they cannot afford to raise their child after all and therefore abandon it, to its intense distress, to strangers. In these circumstances the sale certainly has a serious third-party effect—that is an effect on the child—that the parties to the sale may not take fully into account. This is another reason for forbidding the sale of rights over children who are no longer infants, but it does not touch the sale of rights over infants. Here the only sellers are single mothers; and who can say whether the average infant would (if fully informed) prefer to be raised by an unmarried woman eager to unload it rather than by a couple from a higher social and economic stratum eager to raise it? Any loss of welfare to the child, moreover, would have to be compared to the gain to the transacting parties.

NOTE

Judge Posner's approach has stirred considerable controversy. For criticisms, see, *e.g.*, Jane Mastow Cohen, Posnerism, Pluralism, Pessimism, 67 B.U.L.Rev. 105 (1987); Robin West, Submission, Choice, and Ethics: A Rejoinder to Judge Posner, 99 Harv.L.Rev. 1449 (1986).

C. STANDARDS

1. CHILD'S BEST INTEREST

Sonet v. Unknown Father

Court of Appeals of Tennessee, 1990.
797 S.W.2d 1.

■ CANTRELL, J.

Brief

The appellant, Mary Elisabeth Sonet, appeals the trial court's dismissal of her petition to adopt Joseph Daniel Hasty, and the trial judge's finding that the adoption was not in the child's best interest.

Facts

Joseph Daniel Hasty was born on November 20, 1987 to an unmarried teen-aged daughter of a workman who did odd jobs for Mr. and Mrs. Sonet. The natural mother surrendered the child to Mr. and Mrs. Sonet on November 25, 1987. The Sonets filed a petition to adopt on April 7, 1988. After a hearing in the lower court in August of 1989, the trial judge denied the petition. For the reasons set out below, we affirm the judgment.

FACTS

[Harry and Mary Elisabeth Sonet married in June of 1987. Mrs. Sonet was approximately sixty-five years old at the time of the marriage. Mr. Sonet was sixty-two. In November of 1987, the fourteen-year-old daughter of a man working for Mr. and Mrs. Sonet gave birth to a son, Joseph Daniel Hasty. The Sonets, who had previously discussed adopting a child, persuaded the mother to surrender the child to them. They filed a petition for adoption in April of 1988. Mr. and Mrs. Sonets' relationship became strained, and in February of 1989, Mrs. Sonet and the child had moved out of the home they had previously occupied. The Sonets have not lived together since that time. Mr. Sonet ceased to be a factor in this adoption. The petition has been pursued solely by Mrs. Sonet.]

Wanda Martin, a Protective Service worker assigned to the Sonet case, testified that the Department of Human Services had received five neglect referrals regarding this child. The first referral was received on June 27, 1988, and alleged that this child was not being properly cared for and was being carried awkwardly.... [A] second referral was received from Metro General Hospital on July 7, 1988 asserting that Joseph was a failure to thrive child. The failure to thrive was asserted to be caused by neglect due to a lack of knowledge in properly caring for an infant.

On September 30, 1988, the Department received two referrals alleging that Joseph was being neglected due to no electricity in the home among other concerns. An investigation revealed that although the home was without electricity, Ms. Sonet was making the necessary provisions for Joseph's food and care.

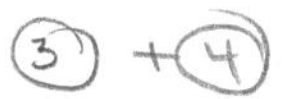

Another referral of neglect was made on January 4, 1989, alleging that Joseph was malnourished and developmentally delayed. An investigation by the Department of Human Services did not substantiate this allegation.

On March 31, 1989, Joseph was removed from the custody of Mrs. Sonet by the State of Florida Department of Health and Human Resources. Mrs. Sonet was in Florida taking care of some of her business interests. She stopped at a roadside park where the child allegedly ran into the road and climbed on the playground equipment unsupervised. When Mrs. Sonet asked a stranger in the park to watch the child for her, some bystanders became concerned and contacted the Florida Department of Human Services. Because of Mrs. Sonet's age, her out of state automobile registration, and the lack of any papers showing her right to custody of the child, the authorities were suspicious that the child was being kidnapped.

From March 31, 1989 until May 11, 1989, Joseph remained in the custody of the Florida Department of Health and Human Services and resided at the Lee County Children's Home. During that period of time Joseph contracted strep throat, scarlet fever, pink eye and ear infections. Joseph was placed in the temporary legal custody of the Tennessee Department of Human Services on May 11, 1989 and subsequently placed in a foster home in Tennessee for about one month until custody was returned to Ms. Sonet by court order on June 26, 1989. Ms. Sonet testified that when he was returned to her, Joseph had two fingernails missing and that one of his toes was raw and bleeding from wearing shoes that were too small and that he had another ear infection.

On June 23, 1989, the Tennessee Department of Human Services had Joseph evaluated at the Vanderbilt Child Development Center by Dr. Anna Baumgaertel. She found that Joseph had been environmentally deprived over a long period of time and that he was developmentally delayed as a result. At eighteen months, she found Joseph to have developed only to the extent of a thirteen month old. She advised against his being returned to the custody of Ms. Sonet.

On the other hand, Dr. Charlene Weisburg, the pediatrician at Metro Nashville General Hospital that treated Joseph for failure to thrive, feels strongly that Ms. Sonet should be allowed to adopt the child and does not attribute Joseph's slow development to environmental deprivation, but to the fact that Joseph's parents are short and small.

Ms. Sonet was evaluated by numerous doctors and social workers prior to the hearing. These evaluations resulted in both negative and positive recommendations. . . .

Wanda Martin and Cindy Holton are the two social counselors from the Tennessee Department of Human Services assigned to the Sonet case. Wanda Martin testified that none of the five neglect referrals received prior to the Florida incident justified removal of Joseph from the Sonets' custody. Moreover, she testified that the Sonets were willing to work with the Department on any problem it found.

. . .

At the conclusion of the proof, the trial court dismissed the adoption petition and awarded custody of Joseph to the Tennessee Department of Human Services in order that Joseph be placed in a stable and permanent environment. The trial court found that due to the lack of Mrs. Sonet's parenting ability with no foreseeable improvement, her age and the child's failure to thrive, it is not in the best interest of Joseph to continue to live with or to be adopted by Mrs. Sonet.

The Standard of Review

. . .

It is well established that the best interest of the child is the paramount consideration in an adoption proceeding. . . . Moreover, when the interest of a child and those of an adult are in conflict, such conflict must be resolved in favor of the child. . . .

There was conflicting evidence presented at trial as to whether it was in the best interest of this child to be adopted by Mrs. Sonet. Mrs. Sonet testified that she loved Joseph and that she had been a good mother to him. There was no dispute that Joseph was bonded to Mrs. Sonet. However, for every positive evaluation of Mrs. Sonet as a parent, there is a negative evaluation to match it.

Mrs. Sonet's age was one factor mentioned by the trial court in its decision to dismiss the adoption petition. Age is a legitimate factor to be considered in adoptions especially if the petitioner could not be expected to be in good health until the child is emancipated. . . . Mrs. Sonet is now approximately seventy years old. Her only help in raising the child would come from the unrelated family living in her home. The child is now almost three. We agree that Mrs. Sonet's age is a factor to be considered. The other factors mentioned by the trial court were a lack of parenting ability with no foreseeable improvement and Joseph's failure to thrive in Ms. Sonet's care.

Our standard of review is "de novo upon the record of the trial court, accompanied by a presumption of the correctness of the finding, unless the preponderance of the evidence is otherwise." . . . Also, the findings of the trial court as to the credibility of the witnesses are entitled to great weight ... After a careful review of the record in this case, we conclude that the judgment of the trial court is supported by a preponderance of the evidence.

2. Race and Ethnicity

Twila L. Perry, The Transracial Adoption Controversy: An Analysis of Discourse and Subordination, 21 N.Y.U. Rev. L. & Soc. Change

33 (1993–94).

Introduction

The debate over transracial adoption is alive and well. After two decades, this topic continues to generate spirited, heated exchanges between those who view transracial placements as positive for both the children and society as a whole and those who view them as injurious to Black children and Black communities.

. . .

I

Overview of Transracial Adoption and the Perspectives on Transracial Adoption

. . .

B. *Colorblind Individualism vs. Color and Community Consciousness*

In my analysis of the transracial adoption controversy, I have uncovered two competing perspectives, liberal colorblind individualism and color and community consciousness. Liberal colorblind individualism has three dominant characteristics. The first is a belief that complete eradication of racism in this country can be achieved. The second is the affirmation of colorblindness as an ideal—that race should not be an important factor in evaluating individuals and that a colorblind society should be our ultimate goal. Finally, the perspective of liberal colorblind individualism emphasizes the individual as the primary unit for the analysis of rights and interests. In many ways, this perspective is grounded in traditional notions of American liberalism.

The perspective I call color and community consciousness is far more pessimistic about the eradication of racism. Instead, it views racism as a pervasive and permanent part of the American landscape. This perspective recognizes that race has a profound influence in the lives of individuals—in terms of both the choices they make and the choices they believe they have. In addition, the color and community consciousness perspective values a multicultural society, which requires the continued existence of diverse cultures within our society. Finally, while colorblind individualism views the individual as the significant unit for the analysis of rights and interests, color and community consciousness also emphasizes the rights and interests of the group with which the individual is identified. This ideological difference stems from a strong belief in the interrelationship between the subordination of a group as a whole and the oppression of the individuals within that group.

. . .

II

Influence of the Perspectives on the Transracial Adoption Controversy

The differing perspectives of colorblind individualism and color and community consciousness shape the transracial adoption controversy in several ways. First, colorblind individualism's focus on the individual accords substantial significance to the right of the individual to make decisions regarding family structure without state interference. In contrast, the color and community consciousness perspective focuses on the struggle of Blacks to make choices to create a meaningful family in light of the oppressive circumstances under which many Black families live.

Second, colorblind individualism minimizes the significance of racial differences between parent and child. In contrast, from the perspective of color and community consciousness such racial differences must be recognized and addressed. Third, for colorblind individualists, the interests of the Black community have little relevance to the discussion of transracial adoption; only the immediate best interests of the individual child are important. The perspective of color and community consciousness also focuses on the needs of the individual child but does so within the context of the Black community's legitimate stake in transracial adoption. The color and community consciousness perspective sees the individual Black child as inextricably linked to the Black community and inevitably identified with that community. Finally, to colorblind individualists, cultural genocide is a nonissue because of the small number of children who are transracially adopted. From the perspective of color and community consciousness, cultural genocide—the potential loss of Black culture—is an issue of great practical and symbolic importance.

. . .

C. *The Question of Cultural Genocide*

The color and community consciousness perspective represents more than mere pessimism about the future of relationships between the races. This complex perspective also embodies the view that multiculturalism, rather than colorblindness, is the desired goal of a nonracist society. Cultural difference is viewed as valuable and worth preserving.

When a minority culture is threatened with eradication, the term cultural genocide is often invoked. Cultural genocide has two connotations. First, a particular practice may constitute a threat to the existence of a group or that group's culture. Given the numbers and fertility rates of Blacks in this country, it seems clear that the transracial adoption of a small number of children poses no serious threat to the existence of Black people or Black culture as a whole and thus does not qualify as cultural genocide under the term's first connotation. But cultural genocide may also refer to the effect of depriving individuals of the experience of their own culture. Transracial adoption clearly poses that threat to the Black children transracially adopted.

. . .

In contrast, advocates of transracial adoption view transracial adoption as an opportunity to enrich cultural exchange between adoptive parents and children. Indeed, it is unlikely that most transracial-adoption supporters would believe they are eradicating or even devaluing the culture from which their adoptive children come. Instead, they might consider themselves as purveyors of multiculturalism. But labelling transracial adoption a cultural exchange oversimplifies a complex issue. Let us suppose, for example, that a

Jewish family in Israel wished to adopt a Palestinian child. Should that child be raised Jewish? Or hypothesize the unlikely situation of a Palestinian family adopting a Jewish child. If the family was willing to raise the child with exposure to Jewish traditions, should the family's own judgment as to the manner of exposure be deemed sufficient to preserve the child's cultural heritage? Is it important to preserve that heritage at all?

The issues raised by such scenarios, of course, are complex. Several researchers on transracial adoption conclude that transracial adoptees have a more positive sense of their racial identity if their families make a conscious effort to affirm the child's cultural heritage. But if children have the right and the need not to be deprived of the everyday experience of their birth culture, what level of exposure is sufficient to prevent a child from being deprived of that culture? Writers from the perspective of colorblind individualism espouse the belief that a white family can provide a Black child with an appropriate cultural experience through exposure to Black culture. Blacks may see this as insulting, suggesting that Black culture is no more than seeing a play with Black actors and a Black theme, reading a book about Jackie Robinson, or occasionally eating some greens and fried chicken. Blacks may view the essence of culture as the day-to-day experience of family life—the reality of living as a Black person in America.

. . .

3. The Pursuit of Equality: Do Black Children Alone Pay the Price?

Some advocates of colorblind individualism claim that Black children who have been transracially adopted grow up to be comfortable in both the Black and the white worlds and view the creation of interracial families as a positive step in the move toward a truly nonracist society. The vision of transracially adopted Black children as pioneers in the creation of a future, nonracist society can easily affirm the subordination of Black children by its willingness to have them bear a disproportionate burden in changing the society.

. . .

Like school desegregation, transracial adoption poses risks to Black children and Black communities. Transracial adoption, however, is not a necessary step for practical or symbolic social progress for Blacks. The emphasis on placing Black children in white homes raises the concern that less emphasis is being placed on strengthening Black homes. Opponents of transracial adoption argue that the key to changing the conditions of Black people lies in strengthening Black communities and families, as opposed to token desegregation into the white world.

Transracial adoption does not constitute true integration. It is essentially a one-way street where Blacks bear the personal weight of the integration process. It is Black children who are placed in environments that are dominated by whites. Leaving aside the question of whether or not this results in actual psychological harm, Black children bear the emotional strains of being the minority "outsider" group in the process of integration.

Although Black children are the victims and not the creators of racism, colorblind individualism selects them to bear any discomforts incurred in the battle against racism. Scholars from the colorblind perspective advocate the adoption of Black children by whites but do not argue that white children should be dispersed and isolated in Black families, schools, or other institutions in Black communities in order to further the goal of integration.

The argument that transracial adoption creates Black children who are comfortable in both worlds suggests that Blacks feel uncomfortable in the white world due to their own deficiencies or deficiencies of their upbringing and not from the overt, painful, discriminatory, and humiliating treatment that Blacks often suffer every day at the hands of whites. Racism exists in this society not because Blacks have not learned to be comfortable in white environments. Rather, Blacks are not comfortable in white environments because of institutionalized and individualized racism. Eradicating racism does not require the creation of Blacks who are comfortable in both white and Black worlds but the creation of whites who are comfortable in the multicultural society that this nation is rapidly becoming.

The willingness to use Black children as agents in the eradication of racism is an interesting twist to the colorblind individualist perspective. In making Black children the creators of a new society, advocates of transracial adoption focus on more than the interests of the individual child. They betray an agenda no less political than the insistence of some Blacks that the interests of the Black community be considered in formulating policies concerning the adoption of Black children.

Petition of R.M.G.

District of Columbia Court of Appeals, 1982.
454 A.2d 776.

■ FERREN, ASSOCIATE JUDGE:

In this case of competing petitions for adoption of a black child, we review a trial court decision granting the petition of the child's black grandparents and denying the petition of her white foster parents. Applying all relevant factors, the trial court found both families suitable to adopt the child, but concluded that the race factor tipped the scales in favor of the black grandparents.

Although race, among other factors, can be relevant in deciding between competing petitions for adoption, the statute expressly incorporating that factor, as well as the trial court's application of it, must survive "strict scrutiny," in order to comport with the equal protection requirement of the Constitution. I conclude that the statute on its face withstands constitutional challenge but that the trial court's application is not sufficiently precise to satisfy the Constitution. The judgment accordingly must be reversed and the case remanded for further proceedings.

. . .

D. was born September 22, 1977, to unwed, teenage, black parents. By that time, her father lived in Cleveland, Ohio; her mother, in Washington, D.C. In early January 1978, D.'s mother decided to give her up for adoption and signed papers relinquishing parental rights. She did not tell the natural father. Nor did she tell his mother and stepfather, appellees R.M.G. and E.M.G.

On January 6, 1978, the Department of Human Resources placed D. with foster parents, appellants J.H. and J.H., who are white. The foster mother realized almost immediately that D. was not healthy. D. was suffering from nausea and diarrhea and, although more than three months old, weighed only 10 pounds. D., moreover, was extremely lethargic and, according to Dr. Robert Ganter, a child psychiatrist, showed signs of mental retardation. During the next year, however, D.'s foster parents nurtured her to good physical and mental health.[1]

On April 26, 1978, a few months after D. came to live with them, J.H. and J.H. filed a petition for adoption. Initially, the Department of Human Resources recommended approval. At the foster mother's insistence, however, the Department notified the child's natural father of the proposed adoption. He objected. His own mother and stepfather, R.M.G. and E.M.G., then filed a petition to adopt D. The natural father consented. The Department of Human Resources studied the grandparents' home and, withdrawing its earlier support of the foster parents' petition, recommended approval of the grandparents' petition.

At the hearing on both petitions beginning on April 27, 1979, the court received the following evidence: The foster parents have four other children—three natural and a fourth, a black male, by adoption. They are a military family, living on a racially integrated military base with racially integrated schools. When asked about the problems of raising a child of another race, the foster mother testified that she and her husband had begun "an affirmative program" with their adopted male child. For example, she had obtained pre-school black history and coloring books for their son. She testified, "I make sure he knows that he's not white. I don't care how long he lives with us, he's black, and he's beautiful, and he's ours."

The child's natural grandmother and her husband also testified at the hearing. The grandmother has eight children (all by a previous marriage) of whom the youngest was 14 at the time of the hearing. She also has nine grandchildren, two of whom reside at her home (one is a few months younger than D.). Although the grandmother is employed outside the home, she testified that she would take a leave of absence to be with the child. Both the grandmother and her husband added that they wanted to raise D., that they were able to care for her, and that they desired to show her their love.

Doris Kirksey, a social worker, testified on behalf of the Department of Human Resources. She recommended D.'s placement with her grandparents "based on the premise that the best place for a child is . . . with blood relatives." Ms. Kirksey discounted any harm that might come to D. from removal from her foster family. She based her assessment, in part, on the advice of her agency psychiatrist, Dr. Frances Welsing.

The trial court asked Dr. Welsing to testify in person. Her position, in a nutshell, was that cross-racial adoption always will be harmful to a child and—at the very least—should be discouraged. She emphasized that a non-white child would encounter particular difficulties in a white home upon reaching adolescence. Dr. Welsing made her recommendation to the Department of Human Resources without having met the J.H. family. Most of Dr. Welsing's testimony concerned the problems of cross-racial adoption in a broad social context.

In response to Dr. Welsing, the foster parents called their own expert, Dr. F. Jay Pepper. He identified several factors germane to adoption. He agreed that race should be considered, but only with respect to the attitudes

1. At the adoption hearing in April 1979, Dr. Ganter testified that D. had "bloomed enormously" and was of "high average to above average intelligence." The trial court concluded: "As a direct result of [the foster parents'] love, affection and special efforts, the child prospered to her present state of good health."

of the particular family petitioning for adoption. Like Dr. Welsing, Dr. Pepper had not met J.H. and J.H.

. . .

The question of race is important. . . . However unpleasant, it would seem that race is a problem which must be considered and should not be ignored or minimized. Conversely, there are not conclusive absolutes to be drawn on the basis of race. It would seem, however, entirely reasonable that as a child grows older the ramifications of this problem would increase. At a later stage, notwithstanding love and affection, severe questions of identity arising from the adoption and race most probably would evolve. In the world at large, as the circle of contacts and routines widens, there are countless adjustments which must be made. Given the circumstances in this case, the child's present status is relatively secure and carefree. The future, in each of its stages—childhood, adolescence, young adulthood, etc.—would likely accentuate these vulnerable points. The Court does not conclude such a family could not sustain itself. Rather the question is, is there not a better alternative? . . . The Court is concerned that, without fault, the H_______s stand to lose a beloved member of their family. However, our test remains the best interest of the child. It is believed that applying all of the factors to be considered, and evaluating the question in terms of past, present and future, that the appropriate alternative is adoption of the child by the G_______ family.

. . .

The cases I have found concerning the use of race in an adoption statute do not discuss whether advancement of a child's best interest is a "compelling" governmental interest. Implicitly, though, the courts treat it as such—and I agree. The critical question, then, is whether the particular use of race, as authorized and applied, is "necessary"—and thus precisely enough "tailored"—to achieve the child's best interest.

A. *Statutory Authorization of the Race Factor*

I turn, first, to statutory authorization. [The relevant statute] does not bar cross-racial adoption, which of course would be fatal. Thus, the racial classification is sustainable, if at all, only because it is one among a number of relevant factors.

. . .

The question thus becomes: whether statutory authority to consider race among the factors relevant to adoption, without preference for the race of any party, can ever be "necessary" for a determination of the child's best interest. Appellants say it cannot be, alleging that the "equal protection doctrine of the Constitution prohibits the use of skin color-defined race as a relevant issue in an adoption." I cannot agree with that unqualified statement.

Whether adopted by parents of their own or another race, adoptees often find it difficult to establish a sense of identity. "Identity," in this context, has at least three components: (1) a sense of "belonging" in a stable family and community; (2) a feeling of self-esteem and confidence; and (3) "survival skills" that enable the child to cope with the world outside the family. One's sense of identity, therefore, includes perceptions of oneself as both an individual and a social being. While adoptive parents' attitudes toward the adoption and their child are not the only influence on that child, these parental attitudes do affect, to a significant extent, whether the child will feel secure and confident in the family and community. Because race may be highly relevant to these parental attitudes,—as the expert witnesses of both parties confirmed—it is relevant to the larger issue of the child's best interest.

I conclude, accordingly, that a significant number of instances where prospects for adoption are evaluated, those who are responsible for a recommendation and decision—social workers from the Department of Human Resources, expert witnesses at trial, and the trial court itself—will not be able to focus adequately on an adoptive child's sense of identity, and thus on the child's best interest, without considering race. Statutory authority for the court to take race into account, therefore, can be critically important in adoption proceedings. When considered among a number of factors, on the basis of evidence, without automatic or presumptive preference for an adoptive parent of a particular race, that criterion does not reflect a "racial slur or stigma" against any group. It is a criterion that markedly contrasts with the impermissible use of race both in facially discriminatory statutes and in facially neutral statutes—some referring to race, others not—masking invidious racial discrimination in the law either as enacted or as administered.

In sum, an inherently suspect, indeed presumptively invalid, racial classification in the adoption statute is, in a constitutional sense, necessary to advance a compelling governmental interest: the best interest of the child. It thus survives strict scrutiny—a result that is unusual, as racial classifications go, but not precluded.

B. *Judicial Application of the Race Factor*

The fact that the adoption statute does not per se reflect an unconstitutional denial of equal protection does not end our inquiry; for although—as a general proposition—the use of race, as one factor, may be necessary to serve the best interest of the child, there also is risk that this classification may be invoked in a racially discriminatory fashion. Thus, there remains the significant question whether the racial classification in the adoption statute, as applied in this particular case, is precisely enough tailored to the child's best interest to survive strict scrutiny, or suffers instead from a more generalized application that possibly reflects invidious discrimination.

. . .

[A] well-intentioned effort to protect a child against community prejudice [is not] a proper justification, in itself, for an adoption decision. This is not to suggest that such concerns motivated the trial court here. The point, rather, is to illustrate that there is a very real risk of misuse—of discriminatory application—of a racial classification in an adoption proceeding. We would be naive simply to ignore that possibility based on the commonly shared hope that times have changed. Thus, where race is a factor for the trial court to consider, appellate review of judicial discretion under the statute must be as exacting as our scrutiny of the statute itself.

. . .

When race is relevant in an adoption contest, the court must make a three-step evaluation: (1) how each family's race is likely to affect the child's development of a sense of identity, including racial identity; (2) how the families compare in this regard; and (3) how significant the racial differences between the families are when all the factors relevant to adoption are considered together.

In taking the first step concerning identity, the court must evaluate the probable effect of each family's race and related attitudes on the child's sense of belonging in the family and community, the child's self-esteem and confidence, and the child's ability to cope with problems outside the family.[22] Relevant questions bearing on one or more of these concerns, for example, would be: To what extent would the family expose the child to others of her own race through the immediate family? Through family friendships? Through the neighborhood? Through school? What other efforts will the family most likely make to foster the child's sense of identity—including racial and cultural identity—and self-esteem? To what extent has the family associated itself with efforts to enhance respect for the child's race and culture? To what extent has the family reflected any prejudice against the race of the child it proposes to adopt?

When the court takes the second step in the analysis—comparing the families—it hardly would be surprising if the answers to these questions favor prospective parents of the same race as the child.[38] But even when that is true, it is also possible that prospective parents of a different race may receive very positive ratings on these questions. If so, the third analytic step—how significant the racial differences are when all relevant factors are taken together—becomes especially important; for in that situation the racial factor may present such a close question that it will not have the significant, perhaps determinative, impact that it would if racial differences between parent and child simply were deemed a wholly negative factor.

. . .

In the present case, the trial court obviously was conscientious and thorough, properly treating race as only one of several relevant considerations. After reviewing the other concerns specified by statute, the court took the first analytic step as to race, beginning with the proposition—for which there was testimonial support—that "race is a problem which . . . should not be ignored or minimized." The court carefully noted, however, that, "[c]onversely, there are not conclusive absolutes to be drawn on the basis of race. . . . The Court is concerned that little medical or scientific attention has been devoted to this problem." But the Court then found that generally "as a child grows older the ramifications of this problem would increase," and "severe questions of identity arising from the adoption and race most probably would evolve." As a consequence, the court concluded that racial differences between parent and child should be weighed as a negative factor in evaluating adoption.[39] The court then announced its decision, preceded by a rhetorical question: "The Court does not conclude such a[n interracial] family could not sustain itself. Rather, the question is, is there not a better alternative?" The Court answered in the affirmative. I understand the court to have concluded that although the other factors, taken together, may have slightly favored the white foster family, or at least given it equal standing to

22. All black children, whether adopted or not, must be taught "survival skills"—that is, ways to cope with discrimination encountered in the world outside the family. To be capable of teaching survival skills, the family itself must be sturdy enough to stand up to any prejudice it may encounter.

38. Thus, contrary to our dissenting colleague's understanding of our opinion, I do not disagree with the proposition that there can be "a preference for intraracial adoption that is supported by evidence."

39. The court was explicit in saying it would not rule out a cross-racial adoption if there were only the one petition at issue.

adopt, the race factor tipped the decision in favor of adoption by D.'s black grandparents.

The trial court ... obviously was careful and concerned and did not necessarily reach an impermissible result. Nonetheless, while correctly beginning with the first analytical step as to race focusing on growth of the child's sense of identity, the court made no specific findings (reflecting the kinds of questions listed above) as to how race would be likely to affect this particular black child growing up, respectively, in the families of J.H. and J.H. and of E.M.G. and R.M.G. Furthermore, aside from reciting facts about the racial makeup of each family, the court did not articulate the comparative analysis required by steps two and three: how the families compare in their respective abilities to accommodate race, and how significant racial differences between the families are when all factors relevant to the adoption are considered together.

. . .

... Accordingly, we must reverse the judgment of the trial court and remand the case for further proceedings consistent with this opinion.

So ordered.

■ MACK, ASSOCIATE JUDGE, concurring:

In joining the disposition ordered by Judge Ferren, I find it necessary to say in my own words what is, and is not, in issue here.

. . .

I think that reversal is required in this case because the trial court, unwittingly, employed the factor of race as an impermissible *presumption.* In Bazemore v. Davis, D.C.App., 394 A.2d 1377 (1978) (en banc), we held that a presumption based upon the sex of a parent has no place in custody proceedings. Similarly, I suggest, a presumption based solely upon the race of competing sets of would-be parents has no place in adoption proceedings. In both instances the court is weighing the best interest of a particular child—an interest in which the human factor of love is paramount. As we noted in *Bazemore,* a "norm is ill suited" for making that determination and it must be made "upon specific evidence relating to that child alone."

■ NEWMAN, CHIEF JUDGE, dissenting:

. . .

The hazards of interracial adoption should not be exaggerated, but neither should they be ignored. An inevitably imprecise prediction about the effects of an interracial placement must be made in the context of all relevant circumstances, including any mitigating efforts by the parents. But *when all other factors are in equipoise,* the *possibility* of an adverse effect, no matter how small or how unlikely, would suffice to permit the trial judge to tip the balance in the direction of the intraracial alternative.

The trial court found as facts that "[a]t a later stage, notwithstanding love and affection, severe questions of identity arising from the adoption and race most probably would evolve. In the world at large, as the circle of contacts and routines widens, there are countless adjustments which must be made." It concluded that the child's interests would probably be better served in the G. family. Given the equal balance of other factors, this conclusion is adequately supported if it is permissible to conclude that there is any potential adverse effect from the interracial alternative. That is indisputably the case here. Accordingly, the result below can be upset only if it is constitutionally impermissible to give any weight whatsoever to adverse effects on the child related to racial differences between herself and her parents.

NOTES

1. Is the court in *R.M.G.* correct in its assessment of the constitutionality of weighing race as one factor in adoption in light of the decision of the Supreme Court in *Palmore v. Sidoti*, 466 U.S. 429 (1984) [Chapter 4, Section B], holding that race may not be the deciding factor in a custody case?

For background to the controversy surrounding transracial adoptions and legal standards for decisionmaking, see generally Elizabeth Bartholet, Where Do Black Children Belong?: The Politics of Race Matching in Adoption, 139 U.Pa.L.Rev. 1163 (1991); Angela T. McCormick, Note, Transracial Adoption: A Critical View of the Court's Present Standards, 28 J.Fam.L. 303 (1989–1990).

2. The three-part approach taken in *R.M.G.* was later criticized by a majority of the D.C. Appellate Court "primarily because it effectuates a sharp departure from the flexible framework developed in our decisions for determining the best interests of the child." In re Adoption of S.A.O., 494 A.2d 1316 (D.C.App.1985). In McLaughlin v. Pernsley, 693 F.Supp. 318, 324 (E.D.Pa.1988), the court explicitly found a compelling governmental interest in considering a child's "racial and cultural needs," but held race could not be the sole factor used in determining placement in a foster home.

In 1996, Congress passed legislation that prohibits states or any other entities that receive federal funds from denying or delaying a child's adoption because of the race, color, or national origin of the child or the person seeking to adopt the child. Pub.L. No. 104–188, Sec. 1808.

R. Richard Banks, The Color of Desire: Fulfilling Adoptive Parents' Racial Preferences Through Discriminatory State Action, 107 YALE L.J. 875

(1998).

. . .

Both supporters and opponents of race matching often assume that putting an end to the practice would make adoption policy colorblind. The race-and-adoption debate, then, is framed as a contest between those who believe that race-conscious state action (race matching) furthers the interests of black children, and those who believe that colorblind state action (transracial adoption) does so. Contrary to the assumptions that underlie the debate, however, race matching is not the only form of race-based state action that structures the adoption process.

Adoption agencies' classification of children on the basis of race facilitates and promotes the exercise of racial preferences by prospective adoptive parents. I term this practice "facilitative accommodation." When engaged in by public agencies, facilitative accommodation, like race matching, is an instance of race-based state action.... Through facilitative accommodation, the state's racial classification promotes the race-based decisionmaking of prospective adoptive parents by framing the choice of a child in terms of race, encouraging parents to consider children based on the ascribed characteristic of race rather than individually. In both cases, a court, in finalizing the adoption, validates the actions of the adoption agency.

As a result of facilitative accommodation policies, most black children in need of adoption are categorically denied, on the basis of race, the opportunity to be considered individually for adoption by the majority of prospective adoptive parents. This could not occur were it not for current policies of facilitative accommodation.

. . .

My proposal is a simple one: Adoption agencies that receive any government funding should not accommodate adoptive parents' racial preferences. Beyond ceasing the classification of children by race in order to facilitate the satisfaction of adoptive parents' racial preferences, adoption agencies should make clear to prospective adoptive parents that their racial preferences are to play no role in the parents' selection of a child to adopt.

My vision of strict nonaccommodation consists of two elements. First, prospective adoptive parents would generally be prohibited from discriminating on the basis of race in their selection of a child to adopt, and birth parents who participate in the selection of adoptive parents would generally be prohibited from discriminating on the basis of race in doing so. Prospective adoptive parents and birth parents would be informed at the outset that the adoption process is not one in which racial discrimination is allowed. Parents would be encouraged to withdraw from the process if they did not think that they could abide by that rule, and adoption agency officials would have the authority to remove parents from the process if they determined that the parents in fact were discriminating on the basis of race. Parents could even be asked to sign a nondiscrimination agreement just as do other parties who do business with or enter a relationship with the government. Admittedly, this approach runs the risk of unintentionally underscoring the importance of race by constantly proclaiming that it must not matter. Nonetheless, the extent to which race currently matters in adoption suggests that mere governmental blindness to race would not decrease its significance.

Second, the general principle of nondiscrimination is qualified by my goal of promoting the maintenance of particular groups in the interest of cultural pluralism. Notwithstanding the law's focus on the rights of individuals and the primacy of the individual rather than the group in liberal political and social theory, our society has an important interest in maintaining cultural diversity. In American society, racial identity for minority groups is linked, though not identical, to a distinctive set of cultural characteristics, a nomos. To the extent the nomos is race-linked, racial minorities would be allowed to choose a child on the basis of race as a means of furthering that nomos. If one embraces cultural pluralism and accepts the inevitability of the state's either suppressing or promoting such communities (given the impossibility of neutrality), then such racially identified choices should be promoted in principle. The claim of contributing to the cultural pluralism of American society through their own race-consciousness is a claim that blacks and other racial minorities, but not whites, can make. The nomos of whiteness as a racial identity is nothing more than a historically generated and self-perpetuated set of privileges, expectations, and entitlements that are implemented through and reflected in the dominant norms, processes, rules, and structure of American society. There is no white race-based culture separate from mainstream American culture. In principle, then, strict nonaccommodation should allow fulfillment of the racial preferences of racial minorities, but not those of whites.

The demands of race politics, however, may make it difficult to enact a policy that allows blacks, but not whites, to choose a child of their own race.

Whites might argue that such an asymmetry is unfair, perhaps even unconstitutional, a conclusion the Supreme Court might adopt as well. Even as it strives to undo the most pernicious race-consciousness, such a policy might itself be decried as a pernicious type of race-based treatment. More debate might ensue about the justice of the asymmetry than about the idea of nonaccommodation itself. If the merits of the policy were obscured by contentious debate about whether groups should be treated differently, I would advise the practical solution of not allowing any expression of same-race preference.

NOTE

For further discussion of Professor Banks' proposal, see Elizabeth Bartholet, Correspondence: Private Race Preferences in Family Formation, 107 Yale L.J. 2351 (1998) and R. Richard Banks, A Response to Elizabeth Bartholet, 107 Yale L.J. 2357 (1998).

Mississippi Band of Choctaw Indians v. Holyfield

Supreme Court of the United States, 1989.
490 U.S. 30, 109 S.Ct. 1597, 104 L.Ed.2d 29.

■ BRENNAN, J.

This appeal requires us to construe the provisions of the Indian Child Welfare Act that establish exclusive tribal jurisdiction over child custody proceedings involving Indian children domiciled on the tribe's reservation.

. . .

The Indian Child Welfare Act of 1978 (ICWA), was the product of rising concern in the mid–1970's over the consequences to Indian children, Indian families, and Indian tribes of abusive child welfare practices that resulted in the separation of large numbers of Indian children from their families and tribes through adoption or foster care placement, usually in non-Indian homes. Senate oversight hearings in 1974 yielded numerous examples, statistical data, and expert testimony documenting what one witness called "[t]he wholesale removal of Indian children from their homes, . . . the most tragic aspect of Indian life today." . . . Studies undertaken by the Association on American Indian Affairs in 1969 and 1974, and presented in the Senate hearings, showed that 25 to 35% of all Indian children had been separated from their families and placed in adoptive families, foster care, or institutions. . . . Adoptive placements counted significantly in this total: in the State of Minnesota, for example, one in eight Indian children under the age of 18 was in an adoptive home, and during the year 1971–1972 nearly one in every four infants under one year of age was placed for adoption. The adoption rate of Indian children was eight times that of non-Indian children. Approximately 90% of the Indian placements were in non-Indian homes. . . . A number of witnesses also testified to the serious adjustment problems encountered by such children during adolescence, as well as the impact of the adoptions on Indian parents and the tribes themselves.

. . .

The congressional findings that were incorporated into the ICWA reflect these sentiments. The Congress found:

"(3) that there is no resource that is more vital to the continued existence and integrity of Indian tribes than their children . . . ;

"(4) that an alarmingly high percentage of Indian families are broken up by the removal, often unwarranted, of their children from them by nontribal public and private agencies and that an alarmingly high percentage of such children are placed in non-Indian foster and adoptive homes and institutions; and

"(5) that the States, exercising their recognized jurisdiction over Indian child custody proceedings through administrative and judicial bodies, have often failed to recognize the essential tribal relations of Indian people and the cultural and social standards prevailing in Indian communities and families." 25 U.S.C. § 1901.

At the heart of the ICWA are its provisions concerning jurisdiction over Indian child custody proceedings. Section 1911 lays out a dual jurisdictional scheme. Section 1911(a) establishes exclusive jurisdiction in the tribal courts for proceedings concerning an Indian child "who resides or is domiciled within the reservation of such tribe," as well as for wards of tribal courts regardless of domicile. Section 1911(b), on the other hand, creates concurrent but presumptively tribal jurisdiction in the case of children not domiciled on the reservation: on petition of either parent or the tribe, state-court proceedings for foster care placement or termination of parental rights are to be transferred to the tribal court, except in cases of "good cause," objection by either parent, or declination of jurisdiction by the tribal court.

Various other provisions of ICWA Title I set procedural and substantive standards for those child custody proceedings that do take place in state court. The procedural safeguards include requirements concerning notice and appointment of counsel; parental and tribal rights of intervention and petition for invalidation of illegal proceedings; procedures governing voluntary consent to termination of parental rights; and a full faith and credit obligation in respect to tribal court decisions. . . . The most important substantive requirement imposed on state courts is that of § 1915(a), which, absent "good cause" to the contrary, mandates that adoptive placements be made preferentially with (1) members of the child's extended family, (2) other members of the same tribe, or (3) other Indian families.

The ICWA thus, in the words of the House Report accompanying it, "seeks to protect the rights of the Indian child as an Indian and the rights of the Indian community and tribe in retaining its children in its society." It does so by establishing "a Federal policy that, where possible, an Indian child should remain in the Indian community," . . . and by making sure that Indian child welfare determinations are not based on "a white, middle-class standard which, in many cases, forecloses placement with [an] Indian family."

. . .

This case involves the status of twin babies, known for our purposes as B. B. and G. B., who were born out of wedlock on December 29, 1985. Their mother, J. B., and father, W. J., were both enrolled members of appellant Mississippi Band of Choctaw Indians (Tribe), and were residents and domiciliaries of the Choctaw Reservation in Neshoba County, Mississippi. J. B. gave birth to the twins in Gulfport, Harrison County, Mississippi, some 200 miles from the reservation. On January 10, 1986, J. B. executed a consent-to-adoption form before the Chancery Court of Harrison County. . . . W. J. signed a similar form. On January 16, appellees Orrey and Vivian Holyfield filed a petition for adoption in the same court . . . and the chancellor issued a Final Decree of Adoption on January 28. . . . Despite the court's apparent awareness of the ICWA, the adoption decree contained no reference to it, nor to the infants' Indian background.

Two months later the Tribe moved in the Chancery Court to vacate the adoption decree on the ground that under the ICWA exclusive jurisdiction was vested in the tribal court . . . On July 14, 1986, the court overruled the motion, holding that the Tribe "never obtained exclusive jurisdiction over the children involved herein. . . ." The court's one-page opinion relied on two facts in reaching that conclusion. The court noted first that the twins' mother "went to some efforts to see that they were born outside the confines of the Choctaw Indian Reservation" and that the parents had promptly arranged for the adoption by the Holyfields. Second, the court stated: "At no time from the birth of these children to the present date have either of them resided on or physically been on the Choctaw Indian Reservation." . . .

The Supreme Court of Mississippi affirmed. . . . It rejected the Tribe's arguments that the state court lacked jurisdiction and that it, in any event, had not applied the standards laid out in the ICWA. The court recognized that the jurisdictional question turned on whether the twins were domiciled on the Choctaw Reservation. . . .

Because of the centrality of the exclusive tribal jurisdiction provision to the overall scheme of the ICWA, as well as the conflict between this decision of the Mississippi Supreme Court and those of several other state courts, we granted plenary review. We now reverse.

. . .

Tribal jurisdiction over Indian child custody proceedings is not a novelty of the ICWA. Indeed, some of the ICWA's jurisdictional provisions have a strong basis in pre-ICWA case law in the federal and state courts. . . . In enacting the ICWA Congress confirmed that, in child custody proceedings involving Indian children domiciled on the reservation, tribal jurisdiction was exclusive as to the States.

. . . The sole issue in this case is, as the Supreme Court of Mississippi recognized, whether the twins were "domiciled" on the reservation.

The meaning of "domicile" in the ICWA is, of course, a matter of Congress' intent. The ICWA itself does not define it. The initial question we must confront is whether there is any reason to believe that Congress intended the ICWA definition of "domicile" to be a matter of state law. . . .

First, and most fundamentally, the purpose of the ICWA gives no reason to believe that Congress intended to rely on state law for the definition of a critical term; quite the contrary. It is clear from the very text of the ICWA, not to mention its legislative history and the hearings that led to its enactment, that Congress was concerned with the rights of Indian families and Indian communities vis-a-vis state authorities. More specifically, its purpose was, in part, to make clear that in certain situations the state courts did *not* have jurisdiction over child custody proceedings. Indeed, the congressional findings that are a part of the statute demonstrate that Congress perceived the States and their courts as partly responsible for the problem it intended to correct. . . . Under these circumstances it is most improbable that Congress would have intended to leave the scope of the statute's key jurisdictional provision subject to definition by state courts as a matter of state law.

Second, Congress could hardly have intended the lack of nationwide uniformity that would result from state-law definitions of domicile. . . .

We therefore think it beyond dispute that Congress intended a uniform federal law of domicile for the ICWA.

It remains to give content to the term "domicile" in the circumstances of the present case. . . . The question before us, therefore, is whether under the ICWA definition of "domicile" such facts suffice to render the twins nondomiciliaries of the reservation.

. . .

"Domicile" is, of course, a concept widely used in both federal and state courts for jurisdiction and conflict-of-laws purposes, and its meaning is generally uncontroverted. . . . "Domicile" is not necessarily synonymous with "residence," . . . and one can reside in one place but be domiciled in another. . . . For adults, domicile is established by physical presence in a place in connection with a certain state of mind concerning one's intent to remain there. . . . One acquires a "domicile of origin" at birth, and that domicile continues until a new one (a "domicile of choice") is acquired. . . . Since most minors are legally incapable of forming the requisite intent to establish a domicile, their domicile is determined by that of their parents. . . . In the case of an illegitimate child, that has traditionally meant the domicile of its mother. . . . Under these principles, it is entirely logical that "[o]n occasion, a child's domicil of origin will be in a place where the child has never been." Restatement § 14, Comment *b*.

It is undisputed in this case that the domicile of the mother (as well as the father) has been, at all relevant times, on the Choctaw Reservation. . . . Thus, it is clear that at their birth the twin babies were also domiciled on the reservation, even though they themselves had never been there. The statement of the Supreme Court of Mississippi that "[a]t no point in time can it be said the twins . . . were domiciled within the territory set aside for the reservation," . . . may be a correct statement of that State's law of domicile, but it is inconsistent with generally accepted doctrine in this country and cannot be what Congress had in mind when it used the term in the ICWA.

Nor can the result be any different simply because the twins were "voluntarily surrendered" by their mother. Tribal jurisdiction under § 1911(a) was not meant to be defeated by the actions of individual members of the tribe, for Congress was concerned not solely about the interests of Indian children and families, but also about the impact on the tribes themselves of the large numbers of Indian children adopted by non-Indians. . . . The numerous prerogatives accorded the tribes through the ICWA's substantive provisions . . . must, accordingly, be seen as a means of protecting not only the interests of individual Indian children and families, but also of the tribes themselves.

. . .

These congressional objectives make clear that a rule of domicile that would permit individual Indian parents to defeat the ICWA's jurisdictional scheme is inconsistent with what Congress intended. . . . The appellees in this case argue strenuously that the twins' mother went to great lengths to give birth off the reservation so that her children could be adopted by the Holyfields. But that was precisely part of Congress' concern. Permitting individual members of the tribe to avoid tribal exclusive jurisdiction by the simple expedient of giving birth off the reservation would, to a large extent, nullify the purpose the ICWA was intended to accomplish. The Supreme Court of Utah expressed this well in its scholarly and sensitive opinion in what has become a leading case on the ICWA:

> . . . The protection of [the tribe's] interest [in its children] is at the core of the ICWA, which recognizes that the tribe has an interest in the child which is distinct from but on a parity with the interest of the parents. This relationship between Indian tribes and Indian children domiciled on the reservation finds no parallel in other ethnic cultures found in the United States. It is a relationship that many non-Indians find difficult to understand and that non-Indian courts are slow to recognize. It is precisely in recognition of this relationship, however, that the ICWA designates the tribal court as the exclusive forum for the determination of custody and adoption matters for reservation-domiciled Indian children, and the preferred forum for nondomiciliary Indian children.

We agree with the Supreme Court of Utah that the law of domicile Congress used in the ICWA cannot be one that permits individual reservation-domiciled tribal members to defeat the tribe's exclusive jurisdiction by the simple expedient of giving birth and placing the child for adoption off the reservation. Since, for purposes of the ICWA, the twin babies in this case were domiciled on the reservation when adoption proceedings were begun, the Choctaw tribal court possessed exclusive jurisdiction pursuant to 25 U.S.C. § 1911(a). The Chancery Court of Harrison County was, accordingly, without jurisdiction to enter a decree of adoption; . . . its decree of January 28, 1986, must be vacated.

We are not unaware that over three years have passed since the twin babies were born and placed in the Holyfield home, and that a court deciding their fate today is not writing on a blank slate in the same way it would have in January 1986. Three years' development of family ties cannot be undone, and a separation at this point would doubtless cause considerable pain.

Whatever feelings we might have as to where the twins should live, however, it is not for us to decide that question. We have been asked to decide the legal question of *who* should make the custody determination concerning these children—not what the outcome of that determination should be. The law places that decision in the hands of the Choctaw tribal court. Had the mandate of the ICWA been followed in 1986, of course, much potential anguish might have been avoided, and in any case the law cannot be applied so as automatically to "reward those who obtain custody, whether lawfully or otherwise, and maintain it during any ensuing (and protracted) litigation." . . . It is not ours to say whether the trauma that might result from removing these children from their adoptive family should outweigh the interest of the Tribe—and perhaps the children themselves—in having them raised as part of the Choctaw community. Rather, "we must defer to the experience, wisdom, and compassion of the [Choctaw] tribal courts to fashion an appropriate remedy." . . .

The judgment of the Supreme Court of Mississippi is reversed, and the case is remanded for further proceedings not inconsistent with this opinion.

■ Justice Stevens, with whom The Chief Justice and Justice Kennedy join, dissenting.

The parents of these twin babies unquestionably expressed their intention to have the state court exercise jurisdiction over them. . . . Indeed,

Appellee Vivian Holyfield appears before us today, urging that she be allowed to retain custody of B. B. and G. B.

Because J. B.'s domicile is on the reservation and the children are eligible for membership in the Tribe, the Court today closes the state courthouse door to her. I agree with the Court that Congress intended a uniform federal law of domicile for the Indian Child Welfare Act of 1978 (ICWA) ..., and that domicile should be defined with reference to the objectives of the congressional scheme.... I cannot agree, however, with the cramped definition the Court gives that term. To preclude parents domiciled on a reservation from deliberately invoking the adoption procedures of state court, the Court gives "domicile" a meaning that Congress could not have intended and distorts the delicate balance between individual rights and group rights recognized by the ICWA.

The ICWA was passed in 1978 in response to congressional findings that "an alarmingly high percentage of Indian families are broken up by the *removal*, often unwarranted, of their children from them by nontribal public and private agencies"

. . .

The Act gives Indian tribes certain rights, not to restrict the rights of parents of Indian children, but to complement and help effect them. The Indian tribe may petition to transfer an action in state court to the tribal court, but the Indian parent may veto the transfer. § 1911(b). The Act provides for a tribal right of notice and intervention in involuntary proceedings but not in voluntary ones. Finally, the tribe may petition the court to set aside a parental termination action upon a showing that the provisions of the ICWA that are designed to protect parents and Indian children have been violated. § 1914.

. . .

Although parents of Indian children are shielded from the exercise of state jurisdiction when they are temporarily off the reservation, the Act also reflects recognition that allowing the tribe to defeat the parents' deliberate choice of jurisdiction would be conducive neither to the best interests of the child nor to the stability and security of Indian tribes and families....

If J. B. and W. J. had established a domicile off the reservation, the state courts would have been required to give effect to their choice of jurisdiction; there should not be a different result when the parents have not changed their own domicile, but have expressed an unequivocal intent to establish a domicile for their children off the reservation. The law of abandonment, as enunciated by the Mississippi Supreme Court in this case, does not defeat, but serves the purposes of, the Act. An abandonment occurs when a parent deserts a child and places the child with another with an intent to relinquish all parental rights and obligations....

When an Indian child is temporarily off the reservation, but has not been abandoned to a person off the reservation, the tribe has an interest in exclusive jurisdiction.... Similarly, when the child is abandoned by one parent to a person off the reservation, the tribe and the other parent domiciled on the reservation may still have an interest in the exercise of exclusive jurisdiction. That interest is protected by the rule that a child abandoned by one parent takes on the domicile of the other. But when an Indian child is deliberately abandoned by both parents to a person off the reservation, no purpose of the ICWA is served by closing the state courthouse door to them. The interests of the parents, the Indian child, and the tribe in preventing the unwarranted removal of Indian children from their families and from the reservation are protected by the Act's substantive and procedural provisions. In addition, if both parents have intentionally invoked the jurisdiction of the state court in an action involving a non-Indian, no interest in tribal self-governance is implicated.

NOTE

On remand, the tribal court determined that the best interest of the child would be served by the children's adoption by the Holyfields.

3. Sexual Orientation

Lofton v. Department of Children and Family Services

U.S. Court of Appeals for the Eleventh Circuit, 2004.
358 F.3d 804.

■ Birch, J.

In this appeal, we decide the states' rights issue of whether Florida Statute § 63.042(3), which prevents adoption by practicing homosexuals, is constitutional as enacted by the Florida legislature and as subsequently enforced. The district court granted summary judgment to Florida over an equal protection and due process challenge by homosexual persons desiring to adopt. We AFFIRM.

I. BACKGROUND

A. The Challenged Florida Statute

Since 1977, Florida's adoption law has contained a codified prohibition on adoption by any "homosexual" person. For purposes of this statute, Florida courts have defined the term "homosexual" as being "limited to applicants who are known to engage in current, voluntary homosexual activity, "thus drawing 'a distinction between homosexual orientation and homosexual activity' " . . .

II. DISCUSSION

. . .

B. The Litigants

Six plaintiffs-appellants bring this case. The first, Steven Lofton, is a registered pediatric nurse who has raised from infancy three Florida foster children, each of whom tested positive for HIV at birth. By all accounts, Lofton's efforts in caring for these children have been exemplary, and his story has been chronicled in dozens of news stories and editorials as well as on national television. We confine our discussion of that story to those facts relevant to the legal issues before us and properly before us in the record. John Doe, also named as a plaintiff-appellant in this litigation, was born on 29 April 1991. Testing positive at birth for HIV and cocaine, Doe immediately entered the Florida foster care system. Shortly thereafter, Children's Home Society, a private agency, placed Doe in foster care with Lofton, who has extensive experience treating HIV patients. At eighteen months, Doe sero-reverted and has since tested HIV negative. In September of 1994,

Lofton filed an application to adopt Doe but refused to answer the application's inquiry about his sexual preference and also failed to disclose Roger Croteau, his cohabitating partner, as a member of his household. After Lofton refused requests from the Department of Children and Families ("DCF") to supply the missing information, his application was rejected pursuant to the homosexual adoption provision....

Two years later, in light of the length of Doe's stay in Lofton's household, DCF offered Lofton the compromise of becoming Doe's legal guardian. This arrangement would have allowed Doe to leave the foster care system and DCF supervision. However, because it would have cost Lofton over $300 a month in lost foster care subsidies and would have jeopardized Doe's Medicaid coverage, Lofton declined the guardianship option unless it was an interim stage toward adoption. Under Florida law, DCF could not accommodate this condition, and the present litigation ensued.

C. Procedural History

Appellants filed suit in the United States District Court for the Southern District of Florida and named as defendants Kathleen A. Kearney and Charles Auslander in their respective official capacities as DCF Secretary and DCF District Administrator for Dade and Monroe Counties. Their complaint alleged that the statute violates appellants' fundamental rights and the principles of equal protection. Jointly, appellants asked the district court to declare Fla. Stat. § 63.042(3) unconstitutional and to enjoin its enforcement. Appellants also sought class certification on behalf of two purported classes: all similarly situated adults and all similarly situated children. The district court denied the request for class certification and granted summary judgment in favor of the state on all counts, thereby upholding the statute. It is from this judgment that appellants now appeal....

II. Discussion

. . .

B. Florida's Adoption Scheme

Under Florida law, "adoption is not a right; it is a statutory privilege." ... In formulating its adoption policies and procedures, the State of Florida acts in the protective and provisional role of in loco parentis for those children who, because of various circumstances, have become wards of the state ... [I]n the adoption context, the state's overriding interest is the best interests of the children whom it is seeking to place with adoptive families....

In short, a person who seeks to adopt is asking the state to conduct an examination into his or her background and to make a determination as to the best interests of a child in need of adoption. In doing so, the state's overriding interest is not providing individuals the opportunity to become parents, but rather identifying those individuals whom it deems most capable of parenting adoptive children and providing them with a secure family environment....

C. Appellants' Due Process Challenges

. . .

2. Fundamental Right to "Private Sexual Intimacy"

Laws that burden the exercise of a fundamental right require strict scrutiny and are sustained only if narrowly tailored to further a compelling government interest. Appellants argue that the Supreme Court's recent decision in Lawrence v. Texas, 539 U.S. 558 (2003), which struck down

Texas's sodomy statute, identified a hitherto unarticulated fundamental right to private sexual intimacy. They contend that the Florida statute, by disallowing adoption to any individual who chooses to engage in homosexual conduct, impermissibly burdens the exercise of this right.

We begin with the threshold question of whether Lawrence identified a new fundamental right to private sexual intimacy. Lawrence's holding was that substantive due process does not permit a state to impose a criminal prohibition on private consensual homosexual conduct. The effect of this holding was to establish a greater respect than previously existed in the law for the right of consenting adults to engage in private sexual conduct. Nowhere, however, did the Court characterize this right as "fundamental."

... We are particularly hesitant to infer a new fundamental liberty interest from an opinion whose language and reasoning are inconsistent with standard fundamental-rights analysis ... Most significant ... is the fact that the Lawrence Court never applied strict scrutiny, the proper standard when fundamental rights are implicated, but instead invalidated the Texas statute on rational-basis grounds, holding that it "furthers no legitimate state interest which can justify its intrusion into the personal and private life of the individual."

We conclude that it is a strained and ultimately incorrect reading of Lawrence to interpret it to announce a new fundamental right....

Moreover, the holding of Lawrence does not control the present case. Apart from the shared homosexuality component, there are marked differences in the facts of the two cases. The Court itself stressed the limited factual situation it was addressing in Lawrence:

> The present case does not involve minors. It does not involve persons who might be injured or coerced or who are situated in relationships where consent might not easily be refused. It does not involve public conduct or prostitution. It does not involve whether the government must give formal recognition to any relationship that homosexual persons seek to enter. The case does involve two adults who, with full and mutual consent from each other, engaged in sexual practices common to a homosexual lifestyle.

Here, the involved actors are not only consenting adults, but minors as well. The relevant state action is not criminal prohibition, but grant of a statutory privilege. And the asserted liberty interest is not the negative right to engage in private conduct without facing criminal sanctions, but the affirmative right to receive official and public recognition. Hence, we conclude that the Lawrence decision cannot be extrapolated to create a right to adopt for homosexual persons.

In re M.M.D.

District of Columbia Court of Appeals, 1995.
662 A.2d 837.

■ Ferren, Associate Judge:

This case presents the question whether, under District of Columbia law, two unmarried persons—in particular, a same-sex couple living together in a committed personal relationship—may adopt a child. If the answer is yes, there is a second question: whether the fact that one member of the couple already has adopted the child creates any impediment to both members' joining in the adoption. We answer the first question "yes," the second question "no." We therefore reverse and remand for issuance of factual findings and, if still indicated, for entry of a decree granting the adoption appellants seek.

I. Facts and Proceedings

We quote the statement of facts from the trial judge's opinion (footnotes omitted):

> Hillary is a healthy, happy, and delightful 2 ½ year-old Black/Hispanic child who was born on August 15, 1991 in the District of Columbia. Hillary's biological mother is a young . . . Black woman who met Bruce and Mark after reading an advertisement that they had placed in a local newspaper. The ad identified the petitioners as a gay couple who were seeking to adopt a child. Bruce and Mark are adult, white, homosexual males who have shared an intimate relationship for almost five years.
>
> At the time she read the newspaper advertisement, the birth mother was several months pregnant and was not on good terms with her mother with whom she then lived. The birth mother, therefore, not only answered the ad, but shortly after meeting the petitioners, she began living with them. Eventually, she delivered Hillary on August 15, 1991. All went as planned when Hillary's mother signed her consent to an adoption of Hillary on September 9, 1991. Bruce filed the first petition to adopt the child on the following day.
>
> The baby's natural mother and Bruce reached an agreement that the mother would continue to have visitation privileges with Hillary, even after the adoption was finalized. These visitation arrangements, however, did not proceed smoothly. Rather, the mother accused Bruce of denying her access to Hillary and eventually she filed a motion to vacate her consent to the adoption. This motion was submitted to this court and was scheduled for a hearing.
>
> After much discussion and several preliminary hearings, the parties reached an accord which they reduced to writing. Essentially, Hillary's mother and Bruce agreed again to permit the mother to visit with Hillary even after a final decree of adoption was issued.
>
> In their discussion with the court about this agreement, the parties expressly stated that they understood that under the District of Columbia law, the natural mother had no enforceable right to visit Hillary after a final decree of adoption was signed because the law in the District of Columbia, as the parties understood it, mandated that upon the signing of the final decree of adoption, all of the mother's rights as a parent would be terminated. No one suggested that this severance of Hillary's mother's rights was waivable. At the parties' request, this court reviewed the agreement and satisfied itself that . . . the mother's decision to reaffirm her consent to the adoption and to withdraw her motion to vacate her consent was voluntarily made. Therefore, since all of the evidence supported a finding that Bruce M. was a suitable person to adopt Hillary, and since Hillary was clearly suitable to be adopted, and because this court found that the adoption was in Hillary's best interest, this court signed the final decree of adoption in favor of Bruce M.[[1]]

1. According to the trial judge, "Hillary's biological father's consent to the adoption was waived after unsuccessful efforts were made to notify him, to locate him, and to secure his consent, *vel non*."

In March 1993, both Bruce M. and Mark D. petitioned to adopt Hillary. In addition, Bruce M. signed his consent to the petition to adopt in favor of himself and Mark D.

The petitioners, Bruce and Mark, are thirty and thirty-five respectively. They are both Catholics who are members of a gay and lesbian religious organization called Dignity. Bruce has a Bachelor's Degree in Electrical Engineering and a Master's Degree in Engineering Computer Science. He currently works as an engineer for a major corporation. Mark has a Bachelor's Degree in Political Science and a Master's Degree in Public Administration. He now works as a Court Administrator in the state of Pennsylvania.

The petitioners own a condominium that they bought jointly and have shared since 1990. They have committed themselves to each other as a family to the extent legally possible, and they seek to raise Hillary together, *whether or not* their joint petition to adopt her is approved. They have, for example, introduced Hillary to, and included here as, a part of both of their extended families. They shared in her baptism at their church. They have enrolled her in a monthly play group arranged by the Gay and Lesbian Parent Coalition of Washington. Hillary is a beneficiary in their wills, insurance policies and other funds.

Hillary appears to be bonded equally well to both Bruce and Mark. She calls Bruce "Daddy" and Mark "Poppy." Bruce cooks most of the meals, while Mark often reads the bedtime stories. They both take Hillary on outings. The Department of Human Services has recommended in favor of their joint petition.

The judge added:

[T]he only issue before the court is a legal one since factually this court is satisfied by all of the evidence that Mark D. is fit and suitable to raise Hillary, even alone, and that this court would conclude on a single petition by Mark D. that it would be in Hillary's best interests to be adopted by him.

The judge then ruled, for reasons explained below, that the adoption statute did not permit Mark to join in Bruce's adoption of Hillary. This appeal followed.

II. Summary of Decision

. . .

1. D.C.Code § 16–302 (1989 Repl.) expressly authorizes adoptions by "[a]ny person," without limitation. It then imposes a restriction on adoption by a spouse of the natural parent (that parent must "consent"), as well as a restriction on adoption by every other married petitioner (the petitioner's spouse must "join[ ] in the petition"). There is no mention of adoptions by unmarried couples. A later provision, D.C.Code § 16–305, refers generally to adoptions by "more than one petitioner," and D.C.Code § 16–312(a) acknowledges the "adopting parent or parents." Finally, D.C.Code § 49–202 (1990 Repl.), which antedates the adoption statute, provides that "[w]ords importing the singular ... shall be held to include the plural" unless that "construction would be unreasonable." These provisions, taken together,

neither assuredly authorize adoptions by unmarried couples nor conclusively preclude them. The court, therefore, must consider this ambiguous statutory language in light of other interpretive criteria.

2. The legislative histories of the 1954 (present) adoption statute and of its 1937 predecessor add little to our understanding of legislative intent except for a significant, unexplained omission: beginning with the 1937 statute, Congress withheld language found in the first (1895) District of Columbia adoption statute limiting adoptions by couples to "husband and wife." After 1895, no committee report or comment from the House or Senate floor addressed "who may adopt." And nothing in the legislative history can be said to exclude adoptions by unmarried couples.

3. Because the statutory language and legislative history of the 1954 statute do not indicate that Congress paid attention to unmarried couples, one way or another, the language in D.C.Code § 16–302 specifying restrictions that apply "if" a petitioner has a "spouse" does not provide a basis for inferring that Congress consciously decided to exclude unmarried couples from eligibility to adopt. According to applicable case law, the *expressio unius* canon of construction (expression of one thing excludes another) only applies when the legislature is aware of the matter excluded.

4. In contrast, the doctrine of "strict construction" would limit adoptions to couples who are married, regardless of whether Congress thought about the matter, simply because the statute refers to married couples and no others. This court, however, has rejected strict construction of the adoption statute in favor of "liberal construction" in other adoption contexts. Moreover, courts in other states have employed liberal construction to allow adoptions by unmarried couples under statutes similar to the District of Columbia statute, in order to further the statute's beneficial purposes. The trial court's adherence to strict construction, therefore, is not easily justified.

. . .

6. Under the circumstances, where the statutory language, legislative history, and other applicable criteria are not dispositive, the controlling interpretive criterion, according to applicable case law, is the court's obligation to effectuate the legislative purpose of the adoption statute. There is no proper way of discerning legislative intent based on how Congress in 1954 would have answered the question whether unmarried couples should be eligible to adopt. This court, therefore, must focus on the general purpose or policy that motivated Congress to pass the adoption statute. There is considerable case law emphasizing that the "paramount concern" of the adoption statute—its central beneficial purpose—is the "best interests of the prospective adoptee." We conclude that this purpose is better served by applying a liberal, inclusionary reading of the statute to the facts presented here, for which there is persuasive decisional precedent; this case and others demonstrate that adoption by an unmarried couple can be in a child's best interests—especially when the alternative would be a child's living in a family with two unmarried parents, only one of whom would be allowed to establish a formal parental relationship.

. . .

The trial judge ruled in an earlier proceeding that Bruce's adoption of Hillary was in the child's best interest. In this case, the judge found that Hillary's adoption by Mark, "even alone," would also be in her best interest. Thus, the judge strongly intimated that Hillary's joint adoption by Bruce and Mark, if legally permissible, would be in Hillary's best interest, since the judge was aware that Hillary has been living with Bruce and Mark together from the time Hillary's mother placed her with them both.

. . .

The proposed adoption by Mark very well may be in Hillary's best interests because it would formalize a parental relationship that she recognizes in fact, and it would assure that both men are equally committed to her. Although both Mark and Bruce currently provide support for Hillary, Mark's joining Bruce in the adoption would guarantee that they both continue to have an ongoing financial responsibility to her. Furthermore, in the event that Mark and Bruce were to separate, Hillary would be assured of legal access to, and support from, both of them.

As Hillary's parent, Mark, like Bruce, would be able to obtain health insurance and other employment-related benefits for her. In addition, Mark, like Bruce, would be allowed to act in Hillary's best interest without challenge to his parental authority by third parties such as doctors, hospitals, day care programs, schools, and camps.

Hillary would be protected in the event Mark died without a will because she would be entitled to inherit from him under the laws of intestate succession. Hillary also would have the right to inherit from Mark's relatives, and she would be eligible for other benefits, such as workers' compensation payments and Social Security benefits upon Mark's unemployment, disability, or death. Hillary, moreover, would have standing to bring a wrongful death action if Mark were accidentally killed, and she could benefit from various statutes and regulations that provide certain rights and privileges for "next of kin" with respect to Mark (in addition to Bruce). Additionally, Mark would have rights relating to Hillary which could inure to her best interests.

The adoption also would protect Hillary in the event of Bruce's death, because Mark would be entitled to presumptive guardianship of Hillary and thus the family unit would not be threatened. If Mark were not Hillary's legal parent in the event Bruce were to die, Mark would have to file an action for custody, guardianship, or adoption to preserve his relationship with Hillary. If contested, this process could be lengthy and costly and could culminate not merely in denial of Mark's petition but, more significantly, in Hillary's losing, in effect, not one but two parents.

Recitation of the foregoing benefits of adoption have revealed what a child, living with an unmarried couple, could lose if only one of two parents-in-fact is allowed to adopt under the law. This reality cannot be ignored. In this connection it is important to emphasize again that, in making the child's "best interests" the "decisive consideration," the statute does not expressly prescribe any limitation on how the family, in the child's "best interests," shall be structured. The focus is on how the child shall best thrive, not on what the particular family format shall look like.

We are satisfied that the paramount statutory purpose—the "best interests" of the adoptee—will be best served, and that no other affected interests protected by the statute will be ill served, by a liberal, inclusive interpretation of D.C.Code § 16–302 that says: unmarried couples, whether same-sex or opposite-sex, who are living together in a committed personal relationship, are eligible to file petitions for adoption under D.C.Code § 16–305. We so hold. We therefore finally can say that it is not "unreasonable" to conclude that D.C.Code § 49–202, as applied to unmarried couples, modifies D.C.Code § 16–302 to say "[a]ny persons" may petition for adoption. Accordingly, adoption petitions by unmarried couples shall be granted or rejected on a case-by-case basis in the best interests of the prospective adoptee (on the assumption that all other statutory requirements are met).

IV. Whether An Adoptive Parent's Relationship With the Child Will Be Cut Off If That Parent's Unmarried Life Partner Is Permitted to Adopt

A. *The "Stepparent Exception"*

The final question is whether, despite the legality of an adoption by an unmarried couple in the best interests of the child, the "legal effects" provision, D.C.Code § 16–312(a)C . . . would cut off Bruce's relationship with Hillary as her adoptive (and thus "natural") parent if Mark's petition to adopt Hillary is granted. This provision has two discernible purposes: (1) to guarantee the adopted child's right of "inheritance and succession" as though that child "had been born to the adopting parent or parents in lawful wedlock," and (2) to "cut off" all rights and duties between the natural parents and the adopted child, including those of inheritance and succession—"except that" no such "rights and relations," including inheritance and succession, shall be altered in any way "when one of the natural parents is the spouse of the adopter."

The specified exception reflects the typical stepparent situation identified in § 16–302. It recognizes that when a natural parent remarries and plans to live with his or her children and new spouse as a family unit, the statutory "cut off" requirement—terminating the birth parent's rights so that the adopting parent and child can begin a new family without interference by the birth parent—does not apply. Indeed, an important goal of adoption, to "strengthen the [ ] family as a social unit," would be frustrated altogether if adoption by a stepparent would terminate the parental relationship between the birth parent and the child with whom both parents plan to live.

The trial court concluded that the cut-off language of § 36–312 is mandatory, not directory, and that its literal limitation to preserving the parental rights of the "spouse" of an adopting stepparent would preclude its use to save Bruce's parental rights if Mark were allowed to adopt Hillary. To the contrary, we do not hesitate to hold that this stepparent exception applies here, even though the natural parent (by adoption), Bruce, is not the "spouse of the adopter," Mark.

In the first place, the stepparent exception easily applies here by analogy; Bruce and Mark are living together in a committed personal relationship, as though married, and are jointly caring for Hillary as their child.

Second, we have held that the particular provisions in 16–302 referring to adoption by a married couple do not foreclose adoption by an unmarried couple. Section 16–312, which announces the "legal effects" of adoption, does not apply unless and until a petitioner qualifies for adoption under 16–302, which prescribes "who may adopt." Accordingly, 16–312 is subject to the fundamental inclusiveness of 16–302. It follows that the stepparent exception—reflecting the married couple example identified in 16–302—cannot be limited exclusively to couples who marry. Were we to limit the exception literally to a stepparent, forcing a cutoff of Bruce's parental rights if Mark were allowed to adopt, we would be interpreting the plain language of the statute in a way that imposes "absurd results" and "obvious injustice," whenever two unmarried persons, one of whom has adopted a child, decide to live together and form a family with that child. If the limitation were literally applied, unmarried couples who simultaneously seek to adopt a child could do so unaffected by the "cut off" provision of 16–312(a), whereas unmarried couples in Bruce's and Mark's situation could not do so—a result that would make no sense whatsoever, and would clearly harm the child if joint adoption were in the child's best interests.

. . .

In light of the logic inherent in the statutory scheme, and given the case law where courts have extended "stepparent" exceptions under "cut off" provisions to cover unmarried, though personally committed, same-sex couples, we are satisfied that § 16–312(a) is no impediment to Bruce's retaining his parental relationship with Hillary upon Mark's adoption of Hillary.

. . .

V. Conclusion

For the foregoing reasons, we conclude that unmarried couples living together in a committed personal relationship, whether of the same sex or of opposite sexes, are eligible to "petition the court for a decree of adoption" under D.C. § 16–302. We further conclude that, when one of the natural parents (by birth or adoption) is living in a committed personal relationship with the prospective adoptive parent, then pursuant to D.C.Code § 16–312(a) "the rights and relation as between adoptee, that natural [including adoptive] parent, and his [or her] parents and collateral relations, including natural rights of inheritance and succession, are in no ways altered."

We therefore reverse and remand the case for further proceedings consistent with this opinion.

So ordered.

■ Steadman, Associate Judge, dissenting:

. . . Here, the statute focuses upon only one circumstance in which a joint adoption may take place; *viz.*, a petition by a married couple where both spouses must join. D.C.Code § 16–302 (1989 Repl.). To that provision, one exception is provided; *viz.*, where either the husband or wife is the natural parent of the prospective adoptee. Where the legislature has concretely provided for a regimen for joint adoption, I think that an expansion of the regimen to other forms of joint adoptions should only be made by the legislature.[2]

. . . I fail to discern any convincing reason why the legislature would target adoptions by married couples, including a mandate of joint adoption, and yet leave completely unmentioned and untrammeled all other forms of joint adoptions, especially by those in a "committed personal relationship"—leaving the latter, for example, free to seek to adopt jointly or not, as they saw fit. Finally, the apparent legislative intent to limit joint adoptions to married couples gleaned from the statute itself would seem to be supported by consideration of the broader background of then extant legislation on related subjects; for example, the distinctions drawn between legitimate and illegitimate children and the criminalization of consensual fornication and sodomy.

NOTES

1. Some other states have provisions that explicitly or indirectly prohibit adoption by homosexuals. Miss. Code Ann. § 93–17–3 (2003), for instance, provides: "Adoption

2. Adoption is a purely statutory matter, not recognized at common law.

by couples of the same gender is prohibited." In Utah, although the state permits single adults to adopt, it prohibits unmarried, cohabitating couples from adopting. *See* UTAH CODE ANN. § 78–30–1 (2002). The law thus prevents gay and lesbian couples from adopting, as such couples cannot get married under Utah law. Oklahoma bars gay and lesbian couples from adopting and recently enacted a law preventing out-of-state same-sex partners from adopting children from Oklahoma and denying recognition of out-of-state adoptions by gay and lesbian couples. *See* 10 OKLA. STAT. ANN. § 7502–1.4 (West 2004) ("[T]his state, any of its agencies, or any court of this state shall not recognize an adoption by more than one individual of the same sex from any other state or foreign jurisdiction."). The Missouri Department of Social Services denied a lesbian's application to become a foster parent, although Missouri law permits any adult to adopt, MO. ANN. STAT. § 453.010 (2003). The Department claimed case law indicated that homosexuals were barred from adopting. Johnston v. Missouri Dep't Soc. Servs., 2005 WL 3465711 (Mo. Cir. Ct. filed May 3, 2005).

Other states do permit adoption by same-sex couples. *See, e.g.*, MASS. CODE REGS. tit. 110 § 1.09 (2005) ("The Department shall not deny to any person the opportunity to become an adoptive or foster parent, on the basis of the ... marital status, sex, sexual orientation ... of the person, or of the child, involved."); VT. STAT. ANN. tit. 15, § 1204 (2004). New Hampshire is the most recent state to repeal discriminatory legislation. In 1999, the New Hampshire legislature passed legislation repealing a 1997 statute which prohibited adoptions by homosexuals.

2. The en banc Pennsylvania Supreme Court has held that a parent's same-sex partner cannot draw on the stepparent exception to avoid the requirement that parental rights be terminated before a non-spouse can adopt the partner's child. In re Adoption of R.B.F., 569 Pa. 269, 803 A.2d 1195 (2002). The court held, however, that state law gives courts discretion to permit adoptions in the best interest of the child when not all statutory conditions have been met, upon a showing of good cause.

D. JURISDICTION

State Ex Rel. Torres v. Mason

Oregon Supreme Court, En Banc, 1993.
315 Or. 386, 848 P.2d 592.

■ PETERSON, JUSTICE.

The questions presented in this mandamus proceeding are whether Oregon's Uniform Child Custody Jurisdiction Act (UCCJA), ORS 109.700 to 109.930, applies to adoption proceedings and, if so, whether that Act confers jurisdiction on an Oregon court under the facts of this case. We conclude that the UCCJA applies to adoption proceedings but that, in this instance, it does not confer jurisdiction on an Oregon court. Accordingly, we order that a peremptory writ of mandamus shall issue, directing the trial court judge to dismiss this adoption proceeding.

Jose Hernandez Torres (father) married Donna Lee Wing (mother) in the state of Washington in 1983. In 1986, a child was born to the couple. In May 1990, father and mother were divorced in Washington. The Superior Court for Cowlitz County entered a Decree of Dissolution of Marriage that awarded custody of child to mother, with reasonable visitation rights to father. Following the divorce, father, mother, and child continued to reside in Washington state.

In July 1991, in Washington state, mother consented to the adoption of child by Douglas and Kathleen Ray, residents of Oregon. In August 1991, the Rays took child to Columbia County Circuit Court of Oregon, the Rays filed a petition to adopt child. On September 24, 1991, the Columbia County Circuit Court Judge (defendant) appointed the Rays as temporary guardians of child. On February 7, 1992, father moved to dismiss the adoption proceeding, arguing that the Oregon court lacked subject-matter jurisdiction. After a hearing, defendant judge denied father's motion to dismiss. Father then filed a petition for an alternative writ of mandamus, which this court granted.

Father contends that whether an Oregon court has jurisdiction over an adoption proceeding is determined by the UCCJA, ORS 109.700 et seq. The UCCJA applies to "a child *custody determination* by initial or modification decree." ORS 109.730(1)(emphasis added). If an adoption proceeding is a "child custody determination," then the UCCJA applies to adoption proceedings.

ORS 109.710 defines "custody determination" and "custody proceeding" as follows:

> "(2) 'Custody determination' means a court decision and court orders and instructions providing for the custody of a child, including visitation rights. 'Custody determination' does not include a decision relating to child support or any other monetary obligation of any person.
>
> "(3) 'Custody proceeding' includes proceedings in which a custody determination is one of several issues, such as an action for divorce or separation, and includes child neglect and dependency proceedings."

The UCCJA does not expressly state whether an adoption proceeding is a "custody determination." However, adoption proceedings invariably result in "court orders and instructions providing for the custody of a child." The purpose of an adoption proceeding is to divest a natural parent of all parental rights, including the right of custody, and to bestow those parental rights, including the right of custody, on the adoptive parent or parents. ORS 109.350 states that, "from the date of the decree the child, to all legal intents and purposes, is the child of the petitioner." In a real sense, an adoption decree is the ultimate "custody determination." Unless adoptions are covered, the stated purposes of the UCCJA are only partially achieved.

The commentary to the uniform act states that the phrase " 'custody proceeding' is to be understood in a broad sense. The term covers habeas corpus actions, guardianship petitions, and *other proceedings* available under general state laws to determine custody." Uniform Child Custody Jurisdiction Act § 2 Comment, 9 ULA 115, 134 (1988) (emphasis added). According to Bodenheimer and Neeley–Kvarme (Professor Bodenheimer was the drafter and reporter for the uniform act), in all cases involving "divorce custody disputes, guardianship, neglect and abuse cases, adoptions, and actions to terminate parental rights, . . . the core question is where and with whom a child should live when something has occurred to disrupt the family." They conclude that the uniform act should be applied to adoption proceedings. A majority of states that have considered the issue, under statutes virtually identical to ours, agree.

In addition, ORS 109.720(2) mandates that the UCCJA "shall be construed to promote the general purposes stated in this section." Many of those general purposes would be promoted by applying the UCCJA to adoption proceedings.

First, "jurisdictional competition and conflict with courts" would be minimized. ORS 109.720(1)(a). For example, an adopting parent may initiate adoption proceedings in one state while, simultaneously, the natural parent seeks modification of a prior custody determination in another state. The question becomes, which state should exercise jurisdiction? This exact scenario arose in Souza v. Superior Court, supra, 238 Cal.Rptr. at 896, where the California court, after applying uniform act principles, declined to exercise jurisdiction over the adoption proceeding, because an Hawaiian court had already exercised jurisdiction over a custody modification proceeding.

This court has recognized the importance of avoiding jurisdictional conflict. Grubs v. Ross, 291 Or. 263, 268–69, 630 P.2d 353 (1981), states:

> "The Act aims to avoid the jurisdictional conflicts and confusions which have resulted in the past by providing, as clearly as possible, for *one* court in *one* state to have major responsibility to determine who is to have custody of a particular child."

Adoption proceedings, like post-divorce custody proceedings, may result in knotty jurisdictional conflicts unless the UCCJA is applied.

Second, applying the UCCJA to adoption proceedings would encourage cooperation with the courts of other states, in order to further the best interests of children. The UCCJA provides that, if an Oregon court "has reason to believe that [custody] proceedings may be pending in another state it shall direct an inquiry to the state court administrator or other appropriate official of the other state." ORS 109.760(2).

Third, applying the UCCJA to adoption proceedings would help ensure that the proceedings take place in the state with the closest connection to the family and in which significant evidence is available.

The UCCJA is a uniform act, adopted as part of a uniform scheme. Its goals include the avoidance of relitigation and multiple litigation of custody decisions and uniform application of the law from one state to the next. In the light of those goals, the language of ORS 109.710(2) . . . the commentary to the uniform act, and considering the purposes for which the UCCJA was enacted, we conclude that the UCCJA applies to adoption proceedings.

We next turn to the question whether, in this adoption proceeding, the UCCJA confers jurisdiction on the Oregon court. . . .

Defendant judge first relies on ORS 109.730(1)(b), which vests Oregon courts with jurisdiction if the child and at least one contestant have a "significant connection" with Oregon *and* substantial evidence exists in Oregon. Whether substantial evidence exists in Oregon is irrelevant, however, if the child does not have a significant connection to this state. The UCCJA does not say when a child's connection to a state becomes "significant." In Grubs v. Ross, supra, this court discussed whether a child had a "significant connection" to Oregon when that child had been abducted in Montana by his natural father and then resided in Oregon for 21 months. Regarding whether "home state" jurisdiction existed under ORS 109.730(1)(a) and "significant connection" jurisdiction existed under ORS 109.730(1)(b), the court stated:

> "Therefore, even in cases involving abduction of over six months in length, where the parent has been in the forum state for six months or longer, jurisdiction would exist under ORS 109.730(1)(a) unless barred by another section of the Act. As a corollary, in such cases jurisdiction would seem to exist, as well, under ORS 109.730(1)(b), for with the passage of time, the abducting parent and the child develop 'a significant connection' with the state. . . ."

In this case, child had lived his whole life in Washington, only to move to Oregon one month before the adoption proceeding was commenced. Under the facts of this case, one month is not a sufficient passage of time to develop a significant connection under ORS 109.730(1)(b). Because child did not have a significant connection to Oregon, we need not inquire whether "substantial evidence concerning the child's present or future care, protection, training, and personal relationships" exists in Oregon. The Oregon circuit court did not have jurisdiction under ORS 109.730(1)(b).

Defendant judge also relies on ORS 109.730(1)(d), which provides for "default jurisdiction" if "[i]t appears that no other state would have jurisdiction under prerequisites substantially in accordance with paragraph (a), (b) or (c) of this subsection." In other words, Oregon may exercise jurisdiction if Washington could not. Washington has adopted the uniform act.... [Its] counterpart to ORS 109.730(1)(a) creates Washington jurisdiction if, within six months before the commencement of the proceeding, a child has lived with a parent for six consecutive months in Washington. This is commonly referred to as "home state" jurisdiction. Here, child had lived his whole life in Washington, until one month before the adoption proceeding. Thus it appears that, under the uniform act, a Washington court would have had "home state" jurisdiction at the time that the petition was filed. Although we have found no Washington appellate decision holding that an adoption proceeding is governed by the Washington version of the uniform act, it appears that a Washington court would have jurisdiction of the adoption proceeding under RCW 26.33.030. Because a Washington court would have had jurisdiction over this adoption proceeding when it was filed, Oregon did not have default jurisdiction under ORS 109.730(1)(d). We conclude that, under the UCCJA, the Oregon circuit court did not have subject-matter jurisdiction over this adoption proceeding. It follows that the adoption proceeding should be dismissed.

NOTE

There have been several efforts to achieve more uniformity in adoption laws, although success has been minimal. For instance, nineteen states have adopted the 1973 version of the Uniform Parentage Act (UPA), which was designed to clarify the legal status of married and unmarried parents in adoption proceedings. A revised version of the UPA was approved by the National Conference of Commissioners on Uniform State Laws (NCCUSL) in 2000. The more recent version has been adopted by only six states. In 1994, the National Conference of Commissioners on Uniform State Laws (NCCUSL) approved a new Uniform Adoption Act. To date it has been enacted only in Vermont.

E. Post-Adoption Issues

1. Agency Liability

McKinney v. State

Supreme Court of Washington, 1998.
134 Wash.2d 388, 950 P.2d 461.

■ Talmadge, Justice.

In a case with very compelling facts, we must decide if Washington recognizes a cause of action for the negligent failure of an adoption placement agency to disclose statutorily-mandated information about the child to prospective adoptive parents. We hold adoptive parents may state a cause of action against an adoption placement agency for the negligent failure to meet the disclosure requirements of RCW 26.33.350 or RCW 26.33.380. We further hold the status of prospective adoptive parent attaches when the child is eligible for adoption under RCW 26.33, and the persons interested in adopting the child have manifested a formal intent to adopt and the adoption placement agency has formally acknowledged the eligibility of such persons to adopt the child.

In the present case, the trial court properly instructed the jury on the duty of the Department of Social and Health Services (DSHS), the adoption placement agency, to disclose information to the McKinneys, on their status as prospective adoptive parents, and on proximate cause. Substantial evidence supported the jury's determination DSHS was negligent, but such negligence was not a proximate cause of damages to the McKinneys. We affirm the trial court's judgment.

. . .

The McKinneys became acquainted with Gabriella (Abby) in 1985 when she was two and a half years old and in foster placement with a friend. For six months to one year, they were Abby's baby-sitters on weekends and when the foster mother was out of town. Through this contact with Abby, the McKinneys knew: Abby had behavior problems including approximately twenty to thirty temper tantrums a day; there were rumors that she had been sexually abused; she was not talking; she did not engage in play like other children her age, nor did she seem to want to jump, climb, or even walk to any length; she was in a special education program; she was receiving speech therapy and physical therapy; she was receiving counseling and treatment at Good Samaritan Mental Health Center (Vicky McKinney accompanied Abby and the foster mother to at least one of these mental health appointments in 1985); Abby had already been in several foster homes and was removed from the biological mother due to neglect; the biological mother "liked to party"; and Abby was developmentally delayed.

Despite Abby's special needs and troubled history, the McKinneys admitted they fell in love with Abby at first sight, and unilaterally decided to adopt Abby before they ever met a caseworker. On October 25, 1985, the McKinneys applied to Catholic Community Services to become foster parents. Although they had decided to adopt Abby, they indicated on the foster application they had not applied to adopt a child.

Abby was placed in the McKinneys' home as a foster child on August 1, 1986. The McKinneys acknowledge this was a foster placement, for which they received regular monthly foster care payments and a special needs allowance from DSHS for Abby because of her developmental problems. In 1986, Vicky McKinney asked a state caseworker to have Abby's medical records forwarded to the family pediatrician, but the records were not sent.

From the time of Abby's foster placement in the McKinneys' home in 1986, until the McKinneys applied to adopt her in 1989, they gained more knowledge of Abby's background and medical/psychological condition. In 1986, Vicky McKinney indicated to a caseworker she understood Abby's biological mother drank heavily while pregnant with Abby. Vicky McKinney also had a copy of a doctor's letter indicating Fetal Alcohol Syndrome (FAS) was a possibility in Abby's case, and stating Abby may have been born prematurely. In a conversation between Abby's developmental disabilities caseworker and Vicky McKinney, the caseworker expressed her concerns regarding Abby's developmental delays and the fact that "we did not have a clear knowledge of what Abby's needs would be or how long the behaviors would continue." Report of Proceedings at 1779. Responding to the caseworker's concern about the McKinneys' decision to adopt Abby in light of these uncertainties, Vicky McKinney "indicated that they were clear with that decision."

The parental rights of Abby's birth parents were terminated in November 1987, freeing Abby for adoption.

In 1988, caseworkers discussed with the McKinneys an array of Abby's problems including possible FAS, sexual abuse, and mental retardation. When the McKinneys filed their adoption application for Abby on August 5, 1988, they also applied for an adoption support subsidy, listing Abby's special needs as hyperactivity, learning disability, and alcohol syndrome. On March 21, 1989, the McKinneys' application for an adoption support subsidy for Abby was accepted by DSHS. A preplacement evaluation or "home study" on the McKinneys, as required by RCW 26.33.190, was completed by April 1990.

On January 9, 1990, the McKinneys received the Child's Medical and Family Background Report from DSHS, which noted Abby's developmental delays and her biological mother's history of alcohol abuse. Vicky McKinney spoke with a nurse at the University of Washington's FAS Clinic on March 28, 1990, regarding Abby; the nurse sent her five articles regarding FAS and FAE (Fetal Alcohol Effect), which Vicky McKinney confirmed she read in April 1990. Through a referral from the UW FAS Clinic, the McKinneys took Abby to a FAS specialist for an evaluation. That doctor concluded Abby had possible FAE. Abby was diagnosed as having FAS in December 1993.

Upon completion of a favorable home study, the Pierce County Superior Court entered a formal decree of adoption on June 19, 1990, placing Abby with the McKinneys.

The McKinneys did not receive all the medical and social records on Abby's birth and upbringing until after the formal adoption. After the adoption, the McKinneys requested and received Madigan Army Medical Center birth records concerning Abby's premature birth. In April 1992, the McKinneys requested and received DSHS's records concerning Abby, which indicated there were questions as early as 1984 that Abby's problems might be attributable to her birth mother's alcohol abuse. Other theories for Abby's problems, such as Downs Syndrome, were also considered in the records. As early as 1984, DSHS records also contained police reports and medical records indicating Abby may have been sexually abused.

The McKinneys filed this action against DSHS in November 1993, alleging negligence, violation of 42 U.S.C. § 1983, and outrage. An amended complaint added causes of action for fraud and breach of contract. The breach of contract claims were dismissed on summary judgment. The fraud claims were dismissed on DSHS's motion at the close of plaintiff's case. The case went to the jury only on the McKinneys' negligence claims.

In conjunction with pretrial motions, the trial court decided the issue of when the McKinneys became prospective adoptive parents. The State argued such status attached only when the McKinneys formally petitioned to adopt and the home study on them was completed. The McKinneys contended the appropriate date was August 1, 1986, the date Abby was first placed in their home. The trial court ruled that when the McKinneys' written application to adopt and request for adoption support assistance was approved by DSHS on March 21, 1989, they became prospective adopting parents, and later so instructed the jury. The jury returned a defense verdict after a month-long trial, finding DSHS negligent, but such negligence was not the proximate cause of damages to the McKinneys. Both parties appealed and we granted direct review. RAP 4.2(a).

. . .

A. Negligent Failure of an Adoption Agency to Disclose Information on a Child to Prospective Adoptive Parents

The McKinneys assert had they known the truth about Abby's developmental and other problems they would not have taken her into their home or adopted her. They claim DSHS's negligent failure to disclose medical and other background information about Abby affected their adoption decision.

The State argues the trial court's recognition of a wrongful adoption claim based on negligence is unprecedented and only causes of action for fraud and intentional misrepresentation in failing to disclose pertinent information about an adoptive child have been recognized in other jurisdictions. The State further contends public policy concerns weigh against creating a cause of action for wrongful adoption based on negligence because adoption agencies should not be required to guarantee the health of the children they place or have the burdensome duty to discover and disclose all health information regarding the child.

The trial court determined the McKinneys' negligence claims survived the State's motions for summary judgment and directed verdict or judgment as a matter of law under CR 50 because a claim for negligent adoption placement, including negligent failure to investigate, locate or disclose information, may be made under RCW 26.33.350. The court ultimately instructed the jury on both RCW 26.33.350 and .380.

Under the current versions of RCW 26.33.350 and .380, DSHS has a duty to timely provide medical and social information regarding the child and the child's birth parents to prospective adoptive parents. The current version of each statute requires a placement agency to make reasonable efforts to obtain background information described in the statute and disclose such information to prospective adoptive parents, but the agency has no further duty to explain or interpret such information. *See* RCW 26.33.350(4) and .380(2).

We believe the Legislature has established the duty owed by adoption placement agencies in RCW 26.33.350 (medical/psychological history) and RCW 26.33.380 (social history). The negligent failure of an adoption placement agency to comply with the statutory disclosure mandate to prospective adoptive parents may result in liability. The scope of the agency's duty is appropriately drawn in those disclosure statutes.

A duty predicated upon a statutory obligation has been recognized in analogous settings by our courts. In *Lesley v. Department of Soc. and Health Servs.*, 273, 921 P.2d 1066 (Wash. App. 1996), *review denied,* 939 P.2d 216 (Wash. 1997), and *Yonker v. State Dep't of Soc. and Health Servs.*, 930 P.2d 958 (Wash. App. 1997), the Court of Appeals upheld a cause of action for negligent investigation against DSHS caseworkers based on RCW 26.44.050

where caseworkers have a statutory duty to investigate possible occurrences of child abuse or neglect.

Similarly, in *Gibbs v. Ernst,* 647 A.2d 882 (Pa. 1994), the Pennsylvania Supreme Court recognized a cause of action for negligent failure to disclose information based on statutory obligations comparable to those imposed by the Washington statutes. The court found Pennsylvania's disclosure statute, which requires an adoption agency to obtain medical history on adoptees and to "deliver such information to the adopting parents or their physician" created a duty to reveal all available nonidentifying information about a child. *Gibbs,* 647 A.2d at 892. The *Gibbs* Court found this duty to be consistent with the intent of the Pennsylvania legislature and recognition of a cause of action based on statute was also consistent with long-standing common law principles.

Aside from the statutory imperative, there are strong public policy grounds for establishing a cause of action for prospective adoptive parents against adoption placement agencies that negligently fail to disclose pertinent information about the child. The *Gibbs* court found the unique relationship of trust and confidence between the agency and the prospective parents supports a disclosure duty[.]

. . .

The special relationship between adoption placement agencies and adopting parents argues strongly for recognition of a cause of action in tort.

In *Mohr v. Commonwealth,* 421 Mass. 147, 653 N.E.2d 1104, 1113 (1995), the Supreme Judicial Court of Massachusetts recognized claims for negligent, as well as intentional, failure to disclose information based on a statutory disclosure duty. The Court concluded public policy ultimately favors recognizing liability for an adoption agency's material misrepresentations of fact regarding the child's history prior to adoption.

. . .

In *Mallette v. Children's Friend and Serv.,* 661 A.2d 67, 73 (R.I.1995), the Rhode Island Supreme Court recognized a claim for negligent misrepresentation despite the fact Rhode Island had no statutory duty to disclose, declaring:

> the need for accurate disclosure becomes more acute when special-needs children are involved. Parents need to be financially and emotionally equipped to provide an atmosphere that is optimally conducive to that special child's growth and development. Although biological parents can assess the risks of having a child by investigating their own genetic backgrounds, adopting parents remain at the mercy of adoption agencies for information, . . . We believe extending the tort of negligent representation to the adoption context will help alleviate some of the artificial uncertainty imposed on a situation inherent with uncertainty.

We are mindful of the concern a broad duty of disclosure could impose an excessive burden on adoption placement agencies who are exerting their best efforts to place children with loving adoptive parents. This concern is particularly acute for special needs children like Abby. But we believe the Legislature understood this concern in limiting the scope of disclosure and confining agency investigative efforts to reasonable efforts in both RCW 26.33.350 and .380.

. . .

We hold the negligent failure of an adoption placement agency to disclose the information required by RCW 26.33.350 or .380 to prospective adoptive parents is actionable. Disclosure of a child's medical/psychological and familial background will not only enable Washington's adoptive parents to obtain timely and appropriate medical care for the child, but it will also enable them to make an intelligent and informed adoption decision.

B. Prospective Adoptive Parents

The duty to disclose under RCW 26.33.350 or .380 attached when the McKinneys became prospective adoptive parents, but the statute does not define the term. The adoption statute only cursorily defines "adoptive parent." RCW 26.33.020(4).

In addressing pretrial motions, the trial court was confronted with several different options for the date upon which the McKinneys became prospective adoptive parents. On the suggestion of the McKinneys' attorney, the trial court considered WAC 388–70–460 as a convenient guidepost in determining when the McKinneys' status changed from foster parents to prospective adoptive parents. WAC 388–70–460, regarding adoption services for families, states in part:

> (1) Department placements:
>
> (a) Applications are accepted from families residing in the state of Washington based upon the anticipated children needing placement;
>
> (b) Upon acceptance of an application, a home study shall be initiated....

The McKinneys' attorney argued the filing of the adoption application on August 5, 1988, changed the McKinneys' from foster parents to prospective adoptive parents. The McKinneys assert on appeal because RCW 26.33.350 requires disclosure of Abby's background information to prospective adoptive parents prior to placement, they should have received Abby's records on August 1, 1986 when Abby was placed in their home. Br. of Appellant at 24.

The State below claimed the McKinneys did not become prospective adopting parents until the home study was completed in April 1990 because a home study was a mandatory condition to any adoption. RCW 26.33.180

The trial court ruled DSHS's obligation to the McKinneys began when the adoption application was signed by DSHS on March 21, 1989, indicating DSHS's acceptance of the McKinneys' application and approval of their request for an adoption subsidy for Abby. Instruction 16 stated: "The McKinneys became prospective adoptive parents on March 21, 1989. The adoption took place June 19, 1990." ...

The trial court correctly determined the disclosure requirements of RCW 26.33.350 or .380 were triggered with DSHS's acceptance of the McKinneys' eligibility to adopt and receive adoption support payments.

... [I]n *In re Dependency of G.C.B.*, 73 Wash.App. 708, 719, 870 P.2d 1037, *review denied*, 124 Wash.2d 1019, 881 P.2d 254 (1994), the Court of Appeals noted in dicta:

> An adoption proceeding is initiated when a "prospective adoptive parent" files a petition for adoption accompanied by a preplacement report. RCW 26.33.150(1), (5). The statute does not define "prospective adoptive parent," nor does it describe the qualifications necessary to become one. Although "[a]ny person who is legally competent and who is eighteen years of age or older may be an adoptive parent," RCW

> 26.33.140(2), it does not follow that every such person is a "prospective adoptive parent" with the right to commence adoption proceedings and obtain placement of a particular child. Rather, we surmise from both common sense and a long line of Supreme Court authority that *it is ordinarily the prerogative of the Department or child-placing agency to designate prospective adoptive parents for a particular child.*

(Emphasis added.) . . . Nevertheless, the Legislature has not provided such a definition. For purposes of the requirements of RCW 26.33.350 and .380, we adopt the essence of the test from *G.C.B.* for prospective adoptive parent, mindful of the fact the Legislature has declined to provide a more comprehensive definition of the term since *G.C.B.* and must be presumed to find the definition satisfactory.

To fairly balance the interests of all persons involved in the adoption relationship—the child, the birth parents, and the prospective adoptive parents—we believe the status of prospective adoptive parents comes into existence only when a child is eligible for adoptive placement. The language in RCW 26.33.350 and .380 references *adoptive* placement, not any out of home placement. The McKinneys knew Abby's placement in their home in 1986 was a foster placement. RCW 26.33.350 and .380 do not mandate disclosure to anyone other than prospective *adoptive* parents, and we decline the McKinneys' invitation to blur the distinction between foster and adoptive parents in light of distinct statutory disclosure provisions for foster and adoptive parents.

Moreover, the McKinneys' argument that prospective adoptive parent status attached before the termination of parental rights as to Abby is flawed in light of strong legislative policy on out of home placements. The Legislature has made a clear policy decision that while the best interests of the child are a paramount concern, where feasible, the family unit should remain intact. Recent legislation reiterates preservation of the family and reunification of a dependent child with his or her parents are goals for dependent children, where feasible. If an out of home placement is necessary, first priority for placement is given to the child's relatives. In this case, Abby's maternal grandmother was interested in adoption, for example. Thus, until termination of parental rights occurs, there is no assurance that adoption is even a likelihood, and we do not believe the status of prospective adoptive parents can attach regarding such a child.

On the other hand, DSHS's bright-line test is at odds with the language of the statute. Rather than requiring disclosure to adoptive parents, the Legislature mandated disclosure to *prospective* adoptive parents, a status which may be achieved before completion of the home study and entry of the decree of adoption, if the placement agency has formally acknowledged the eligibility of particular parents to adopt a particular child. Plainly, prospective adoptive parent status may be achieved by more than one set of potential adoptive parents; DSHS's argument implies only the ultimately successful adoptive parents are entitled to disclosure. This is not consistent with the statutory language.

In summary, for purposes of RCW 26.33.350 and .380, a person interested in adopting a particular child must formally manifest an intent to adopt, ordinarily in writing. When the adoption placement agency then acknowledges the applicant's interest in a particular child by formally manifesting acceptance of the adoptive parents, usually in writing, the status attaches, triggering the agency's duty to disclose information as required by

RCW 26.33.350 and 380. This approach balances the interests of all parties and provides a workable rule.

. . .

In this very difficult case, we are sensitive to the many competing interests associated with Abby's adoption. The McKinneys, to their lasting credit, fell in love with a child affected by substantial developmental and behavioral problems and a very difficult life history. They, and parents like them, are entitled to the information described in RCW 26.33.350 and .380 before making their decision to adopt.

Adoption placement agencies, whether individuals, DSHS, or private agencies, must give prospective adoptive parents needed information about children so the prospective parents can make a wise decision so fundamentally important to them and their adoptive child. The burden of disclosure must not be such that adoptions will be "chilled" by the specter of litigation; placement agencies are not guarantors the adoptive children will have no physical or psychological special needs, or their familial histories are picture perfect. They must only make reasonable efforts to disclose the statutorily-prescribed medical/psychological and social information on adoptive children.

The trial court's recognition of a cause of action for negligent failure to disclose medical and social information required by RCW 26.33.350 and .380, and its ruling as to when prospective adoptive parent status attaches were correct. Substantial evidence supported the jury's verdict on proximate cause. We affirm the judgment on the verdict of the jury.

NOTE

Some states by statute provide for abrogation in certain circumstances. Cal. Fam. Code § 9100 (West 2005) provides:

> (a) If a child adopted pursuant to the law of this state shows evidence of a developmental disability or mental illness as a result of conditions existing before the adoption to an extent that the child cannot be relinquished to an adoption agency on the grounds that the child is considered unadoptable, and of which conditions the adoptive parents or parent had no knowledge or notice before the entry of the decree or order of adoption, a petition setting forth those facts may be filed by the adoptive parents or parent with the court that granted the adoption petition. If these facts are proved to the satisfaction of the court, it may make an order setting aside the order of adoption.
>
> (b) The petition shall be filed within five years after the entering of the decree or order of adoption.
>
> . . .

The California Supreme Court has ruled this statutory mechanism may be used to set aside a decree as to only one of the adopting parents, as well as to both adopting parents. The court stressed that abrogation is not automatic however, and listed several factors it would consider:

> When, as in this case, the joint adopting parents have been separated by divorce and only one of such parents seeks to be relieved of his relationship and obligations toward the child, it is our view that the statute authorizes the setting aside of the decree as to that parent, thus leaving the relationship to continue with respect to the other parent, or as to both parents, should the circumstances warrant such action in the opinion of the court. However the effect of the divorce of the adopting parents is but one of the several factors to be considered by the trial court in the exercise of the broad discretion vested in it by the statute in

> deciding whether to grant the relief sought by the petitioning parent. Other factors include the welfare of the child, the extent, nature, duration and prognosis as to the disability of the child, the degree of dependency, the length of time of the adoption, the bonds of affection or attachment, and should the decree be set aside as to the petitioning parent only, the sources of support for the child which may be available thereafter to the nonpetitioning parent and the ability of that parent to care for the needs of the child.

Department of Soc. Welfare v. Superior Court of Contra Costa Co., 1 Cal.3d 1, 81 Cal.Rptr. 345, 459 P.2d 897, 900 (1969).

2. Adoptee's Right to Know Identity of Biological Parents

Doe v. Sundquist

United States Court of Appeals for the Sixth Circuit, 1997.
106 F.3d 702.

■ Engle, J.

Two birth mothers (Promise Doe and Jane Roe), an adoptive couple (Kimberly C. and Russ C.), and a nonprofit organization licensed by Tennessee as a child-placing agency (Small World Ministries, Inc.) appeal the district court's denial of their motion for a preliminary injunction to block the enforcement of Tennessee's new statute governing the disclosure of adoption records. The plaintiffs allege that the statute violates both the U.S. Constitution and the Tennessee Constitution. We affirm the district court's denial of the preliminary injunction, and on the merits of the case, we dismiss the federal claims and decline to exercise jurisdiction over the state claims.

From 1951 to 1996, sealed adoption records were available in Tennessee only upon court order that disclosure was "in the best interest of the child or of the public." Tenn. Code Ann. § 36–1–131 (repealed). Under a recently enacted statute that was to go into effect July 1, 1996:

> (A) All adoption records . . . shall be made available to the following eligible persons:
>
> > (i) An adopted person . . . who is twenty-one (21) years of age or older . . .;
> >
> > (ii) The legal representative of [such] a person. . . .
>
> (B) Information . . . shall be released . . . only to the parents, siblings, lineal descendants, or lineal ancestors, of the adopted person . . . and only with the express written consent [of] the adopted person. . . .

Id. § 36–1–127(c)(1). The new law also provides for a "contact veto," under which a parent, sibling, spouse, lineal ancestor, or lineal descendant of an adopted person may register to prevent contact by the adopted person. *Id.* § 36–1–128. The contact veto also can prohibit the adopted person from contacting any spouse, sibling, lineal descendant, or lineal ancestor of the person registering the veto. *Id.* § 36–1–130(a)(6)(A)(i). A violator of the contact veto provision is subject to civil and criminal liability. *Id.* § 36–1–132. Before disclosure of the identity of an adopted person's relatives is made, the state "shall conduct a diligent search" for the relatives to give them a chance to register for the veto. *Id.* § 36–1–131. In any event, the relatives of an adopted person can veto only contact, not disclosure of their identities.

* * *

The plaintiffs claim that the new law violates their right of privacy under the United States and Tennessee Constitutions. They argue that the "zone of privacy" established in *Griswold v. Connecticut*, 381 U.S. 479 (1965), now encompasses familial privacy, reproductive privacy, and privacy against disclosure of confidential information and that the new statute violates each of these three. We will consider these theories in turn, but first we note our skepticism that information concerning a birth might be protected from disclosure by the Constitution. A birth is simultaneously an intimate occasion and a public event—the government has long kept records of when, where, and by whom babies are born. Such records have myriad purposes, such as furthering the interest of children in knowing the circumstances of their birth. The Tennessee legislature has resolved a conflict between that interest and the competing interest of some parents in concealing the circumstances of a birth. We are powerless to disturb this resolution unless the Constitution elevates the right to avoid disclosure of adoption records above the right to know the identity of one's parents.

First, the plaintiffs cite *Meyer v. Nebraska*, 262 U.S. 390 (1923), as protecting familial privacy. Dicta in *Meyer* noted that the Due Process Clause guarantees the right to "marry, establish a home and bring up children." Nothing in the Tennessee statute infringes on that right. Under the new scheme, people in Tennessee are still free not only to marry and to raise children, but also to adopt children and to give children up for adoption. We find that if there is a federal constitutional right of familial privacy, it does not extend as far as the plaintiffs would like.

Second, the plaintiffs claim that their right to reproductive privacy, as established in *Roe v. Wade*, 410 U.S. 113 (1973), and its progeny, is violated by the Tennessee statute. The freedom to make decisions about adoption, they argue, is sufficiently analogous to the freedom to decide whether to carry a baby to term to justify an extension of *Roe*. Even should it ultimately be held some day that the right to give up a baby for adoption or to adopt a child is protected by the Constitution, such a right would not be relevant to this case. Because the challenged law does not limit adoptions, cases striking down laws restricting abortions are not analogous. And even assuming that a law placing an undue burden on adoptions might conceivably be held to infringe on privacy rights in the *Roe* realm, much as laws placing "undue burdens" on abortions are unconstitutional under *Planned Parenthood v. Casey*, 505 U.S. 833, 874–79 (1992), § 36–1–127 does not unduly burden the adoption process. Whether it burdens the process at all is the subject of great dispute in two briefs submitted to this court by *amici curiae*. Any burden that does exist is incidental and not "undue." *See Casey*, 505 U.S. at 878 (equating "undue burden" with "substantial obstacle").

Third, the plaintiffs claim that the law violates their right to avoid disclosure of confidential information. They rely on a dictum in *Whalen v. Roe*, 429 U.S. 589 (1977), that describes one type of privacy right as "the individual interest in avoiding disclosure of personal matters." This right has not been fleshed out by the Supreme Court. The plaintiffs' argument that it should be extended to cover this case runs counter to our decisions in *J.P. v. DeSanti*, 653 F.2d 1080 (6th Cir. 1981), and *Doe v. Wigginton*, 21 F.3d 733 (6th Cir. 1994). In *DeSanti*, we read the *Whalen* dicta narrowly, 653 F.2d at 1088–89, and held that "the Constitution does not encompass a general right to nondisclosure of private information." 653 F.2d at 1090. We concluded that no constitutional right was violated by the post-adjudication dissemination of juvenile court records. *Wigginton*, which held that the disclosure of an inmate's HIV status was not unconstitutional, reaffirmed the nonexistence of the right claimed by the plaintiffs here. 21 F.3d at 740. The plaintiffs distinguish these cases by arguing that the information released in each did not implicate fundamental rights. As discussed above, even if a court were someday to recognize adoption-related rights as fundamental, such recognition would not be relevant to this case because the challenged part of the new Tennessee law does not directly regulate when, how, or by whom a child may be adopted.

. . .

The element of public interest also weighs against enjoining enforcement of the Tennessee statute. The statute appears to be a serious attempt to weigh and balance two frequently conflicting interests: the interest of a child adopted at an early age to know who that child's birth parents were, an interest entitled to a good deal of respect and sympathy, and the interest of birth parents in the protection of the integrity of a sound adoption system. It is an issue of peculiar relevance to the primary police functions of the state as reserved to Tennessee under the Tenth Amendment. *See United States v. Lopez*, 514 U.S. 549 (1995). Another aspect of public interest favoring the defendants' position is the interest of comity between states and federal governments, including the interest of the state in having the first opportunity to construe its own constitution and laws.

We are mindful that even when a plaintiff's probability of success on the merits of a claim is not very high, a preliminary injunction may be appropriate if the plaintiff is in serious danger of irreparable harm absent an injunction. Thus we have observed that the degree of likelihood of success that need be shown to support a preliminary injunction varies inversely with the degree of injury the plaintiff might suffer. *Friendship Materials, Inc. v. Michigan Brick, Inc.*, 679 F.2d 100, 105 (6th Cir. 1982). We are particularly sympathetic to the plight of the Roe birth mother, whose identity may be disclosed imminently to her biological child if the statute is upheld. The likelihood of irreparable harm does not, however, control completely; other factors must still be weighed. Here the plaintiffs' ultimate chance of success on their federal claims is so slim as to be entirely ephemeral. We must observe also that the plaintiffs have always had the opportunity to present their state claims to the Tennessee courts, and if there is any danger of loss in their having failed earlier to pursue that avenue, the cause of it lies in their own hands. . . .

For the foregoing reasons, we affirm the district court's denial of the plaintiffs' motion for a preliminary injunction. On the merits of the case, we dismiss the plaintiffs' claims insofar as they rely on federal law, and we decline to exercise supplemental jurisdiction over the claims insofar as they rely on state law. The stay pending appeal is vacated and the case is remanded to the district court for dismissal of the complaint and other proceedings consistent with the decision of this court.

NOTES

1. Legislatures have been more responsive than courts to requests by adopted persons seeking to learn the identity of their parents. Since 1980 the number of states with "mutual consent registry" systems that enable persons involved in adoption to register their willingness to meet has greatly increased. Currently, twenty-two states have mutual consent registries. 2–13A Adoption Law and Practice § 13–A.–01 (Joan Heifetz Hollinger, ed. 2002).

Consider the New York approach:

1. There shall be established in the department an adoption information registry operated by employees of the department specifically designated by the commissioner....

2. The registry shall accept and maintain the verified registration transmitted by an agency [involved in an adoption], or of an adoptee, or of a biological sibling of an adoptee, or of the parents of an adoptee whose consent to the adoption was required at the time of the adoption, or whose signature was required on an instrument of surrender to an authorized agency if such adoptee was born in this state but no sooner than eighteen years after the adoptee's birth, or in the case of registration by a biological sibling of an adoptee, no sooner than the longer of eighteen years after the biological sibling's birth or eighteen years after the adoptee's birth; provided, however, that any person whose registration was accepted may withdraw such registration prior to the release of any identifying information.

3. For the purposes of this section, the term "non-identifying information" shall only include the following information, if known, concerning the parents of an adoptee:

(a) Age of the parents in years, at birth of such adoptee.

(b) Heritage of the parents, which shall include nationality, ethnic background and race.

(c) Education, which shall be the number of years of school completed by the parents at the time of birth of such adoptee.

(d) General physical appearance of the parents at the time of the birth of such adoptee, which shall include height, weight, color of hair, eyes, skin and other information of similar nature.

(e) Religion of parents.

(f) Occupation of parents.

(g) Health history of parents.

(h) Talents, hobbies and special interests of parents.

(i) Facts and circumstances relating to the nature and cause of the adoption.

(j) Name of the authorized agency involved in such adoption.

(k) The existence of any known biological siblings.

(*l*) The number, sex and age, at the time of the adoptee's adoption, of any known biological siblings.

4. Upon acceptance of a registration by an adoptee pursuant to this section, the department shall search the records of the department to determine whether the adoptee's adoption occurred within the state.

(a) If the department determines that the adoption occurred within the state, it shall notify the court wherein the adoption occurred to submit to the department non-identifying information as may be contained in the records of the court and the names of the parents of the adoptee whose consent to the adoption was required at the time of the adoption or whose signature was required on an instrument of surrender to an authorized agency. Notwithstanding any other provision of law to the contrary, the court shall thereupon transmit to the department non-identifying information as may be contained in the records of the court, and the names of the parents of the adoptee whose consent to the adoption was required at the time of the adoption or whose signature was required on an instrument of surrender to an authorized agency. ... The department and/or an authorized agency may restrict the nature of the non-identifying information released pursuant to this section upon a reasonable determination that disclosure of such non-identifying information would not be in the adoptee's, biological sibling's, or parent's best interest.

5. Upon acceptance of a registration pursuant to this section, the department shall search the registry to determine whether the adoptee, any biological sibling of the adoptee, or parents whose consent to the adoption was required is also registered.

(a) If the department determines the adoptee is not in contact with a biological sibling under the age of eighteen and that there is a corresponding registration for the adoptee for each of the parents whose consent to the adoption was required or whose signature was required on an instrument of surrender to an authorized agency, and/or for the biological sibling registrant, it shall notify the court wherein the adoption occurred and the department shall notify all such persons that a corresponding match has been made and request such persons' final consent to the release of identifying information.

(b) If the department determines that there is no corresponding registration for the adoptee for each of the parents whose consent to the adoption was required or whose signature was required on an instrument of surrender to an authorized agency, and/or for a biological sibling of the adoptee, it shall notify the registering person that no corresponding match has been made. The department shall not solicit or request the consent of the non-registered person or persons.

6. Upon receipt of a final consent by the adoptee, and by each of the parents whose consent to the adoption was required or whose signature was required on an instrument of surrender to an authorized agency, and/or by a biological sibling of the adoptee, the department shall, unless the adoptee registrant shall elect otherwise, if an authorized agency was involved in such adoption, release identifying information to such agency; such agency shall thereafter promptly release identifying information to all the registrants.

N.Y.Pub.Health L. § 413–B (Consol. 2000).

2. Compare Humphers v. First Interstate Bank of Oregon, 68 Or.App. 573, 684 P.2d 581 (1984) (holding that a mother may sue the doctor who disclosed identifying birth information to her adopted-out child for "breach of confidential relationship").

. . .

3. Fraud

Joslyn v. Reynolds

Court of Appeals of Ohio, 2001.
2001 WL 1194869.

■ WHITMORE, J.

. . .

Robert B. Joslyn ("Appellant") and Michelle A. Reynolds ("Appellee") married on July 1, 1994. Appellee had three children from a prior marriage. On November 8, 1994, Appellant adopted each of Appellee's three children. The parties divorced on August 14, 1998. Pursuant to the divorce decree, Appellant was ordered to pay child support for each of the three children.

On July 30, 1999, Appellant filed an action under R.C. 3107.16 to vacate the adoption decrees of Appellee's three children on the ground of fraud, and for compensatory damages, including all previously paid child support.

Appellee filed a motion to dismiss, arguing that even if the allegations in Appellant's complaint were true, Appellant failed to state a claim upon which relief can be granted. The trial court found that Appellant's complaint was barred by the one-year statute of limitations found in R.C. 3107.16(B), and that Appellant could not be granted relief because his action endeavors to hold Appellee liable based upon a promise of marriage or upon an obligation dependent upon or growing out of a contract for marriage. The court granted the motion and dismissed the complaint.

From the dismissal of his complaint, Appellant has appealed and has assigned three errors for this Court's review. Appellant has asserted that the trial court erred in granting Appellee's motion to dismiss pursuant to Civ.R. 12(B) (6) because the court: (1) erred in ruling that he was required to file his action within one year of the entry of the adoption decrees; (2) erred in ruling that the one-year statute of limitations began to run in July 1997; and (3) erred in determining that the children's best interests prevented vacating the adoptions.

Appellant's complaint, filed nearly four and a half years after the decrees had been entered, sought vacation of the adoptions on the basis that Appellant had been fraudulently induced to marry Appellee and to adopt her children. Appellant asserts that Appellee's fraud had its origins in the early part of the parties' relationship—a relationship which began when Appellee was hired to care for Appellant, who is a quadriplegic. Appellant asserts that Appellee, who was married and had three children, began to ingratiate herself to Appellant, and began managing his money—which consisted of monthly annuity payments of over $10,000. Eventually, Appellee left her husband and she and her three children moved into Appellant's home. According to the complaint, Appellee immediately started spending large amounts of Appellant's money, and initiated a sexual relationship with him. Appellee told Appellant that she wanted to be married to him, that she, like he, believed marriage was a lifetime commitment, and that she wanted to spend her life with Appellant and her children as one family. Two years after Appellee and her children moved into Appellant's home, the couple married, and shortly thereafter, Appellant adopted Appellee's three children. However, Appellant says that it was not long before Appellee stopped providing Appellant the necessary care, and that she suddenly had no interest in a sexual relationship. She did, however, have a great interest in spending his money.

The relationship rapidly deteriorated. Appellee began engaging in adulterous affairs, and told Appellant's sister that she had married Appellant "only for her children and their security." The relationship became hostile, and Appellant feared for his life. Appellant's family intervened and transported Appellant to the hospital, while Appellee and one man with whom she was having an affair destroyed much of Appellant's property, including the wheelchair ramps at the house. Appellant went to live with his family. Appellee denied Appellant any contact with the children. The parties divorced and Appellant was ordered to pay $2,354.00 per month in child support. Appellant's complaint asserts that because Appellee "connived and plotted to get [him] to marry her and adopt her children and get his money, and falsely represented her intentions for the marriage and subsequent adoptions ... inducing [him] to marry her and adopt her three children[,] ... he has incurred damages including substantial financial damages for child support [.]"

While the allegations, which must be taken as true, are heart-wrenching, the issue, quite simply, is whether R.C. 3107.16(B) permits vacation of an adoption based on the facts as alleged in Appellant's complaint. This Court finds that it does not. We agree with the trial court's conclusion that "the nature of this action is one of the heart ... based upon a promise of marriage or upon an obligation dependent upon, or growing out of, a contract of marriage and [is] not cognizable by law[.]"

R.C. 3107.16(B) provides:

> Subject to the disposition of an appeal, *upon the expiration of one year after an adoption decree is issued, the decree cannot be questioned by any person*, including the petitioner, in any manner or upon any ground, including fraud, misrepresentation, failure to give any required notice, or lack of jurisdiction of the parties or of the subject matter, *unless*, in the case of the adoption of a minor, the petitioner has not taken custody of the minor, or, *in the case of the adoption of a minor by a stepparent, the adoption would not have been granted but for fraud perpetrated by the petitioner or the petitioner's spouse*, or, in the case of the adoption of an adult, the adult had no knowledge of the decree within the one-year period.
>
> (Emphasis added.)

Appellant has contended that the trial court erred in finding that his complaint is barred by the one-year statute of limitations. He has insisted that the language "the [stepparent] adoption would not have been granted but for fraud perpetrated by the.... petitioner's spouse[,]" expressly provides for his claim because "if the Court had known that [Appellee] had married [Appellant] and induced him to adopt her three children only because of his money with no intention of staying married to him, it certainly would not have granted the adoptions."

There is no case law interpreting what "fraud" means in the context of the particular provision "the [stepparent] adoption would not have been granted but for fraud perpetrated by the ... petitioner's spouse[.]" Courts have, however, permitted adoptions to be challenged on the basis of fraud in the general context. In those cases, the fraud has concerned either the consent of the birthparents, or the health or identity of the children.... We see no reason to expand the type of fraud permitted to challenge stepparent adoptions. This Court rejects Appellant's contention that the General Assembly intended to permit all stepparent adoptions to be challenged upon divorce of the adoptive parent(s). We also reject Appellant's assertion that a stepparent adoption can be vacated on the basis of fraud where the fraud goes to misrepresentations concerning the marriage. Therefore, we find that the trial court did not err in dismissing Appellant's complaint.

Because we have determined that Appellant has stated a claim for which there is no relief, this Court need not decide whether the trial court erred in finding that the statute of limitations began to run in July 1997, or whether the best interests of the children prevent vacating the adoption decrees.

In re Petition of Otakar Kirchner

Supreme Court of Illinois, 1995.
164 Ill.2d 468, 208 Ill.Dec. 268, 649 N.E.2d 324.

■ Per Curiam

Otakar Kirchner was granted leave to file with this court a complaint for writ of *habeas corpus* on behalf of his son on November 15, 1994. The petition was premised upon this court's June 16, 1994, opinion invalidating the Does' adoption of Kirchner's son, herein identified as Richard.... The petition requested that this court order the Does to surrender custody of Richard to Kirchner.

. . .

History of the Case

Otakar Kirchner (Otto) and Daniella Janikova, both Czechoslovakian immigrants, started dating in September of 1989 and began living together later that year. Seven months later, Daniella became pregnant. She and Otto continued living together and planned to get married. They obtained two marriage licenses towards this end, though they did not marry prior to the birth of their child, now commonly known as "Baby Richard." Shortly before Richard's birth, Otto returned to his native Czechoslovakia for two weeks to visit a dying relative. While he was away, a relative from Czechoslovakia telephoned Daniella and told her that Otto had resumed a relationship there with a former girlfriend. Distraught upon hearing this report, Daniella tore up their current marriage license, gathered her belongings and moved into a women's shelter because she had nowhere else to go.

[While living at the shelter, and before Otto returned from his trip abroad, Daniella decided to place the baby for adoption, and] the private adoption of not-yet-born Richard was arranged between Daniella and the Does.... At all relevant times, both the Does' lawyer and the Does were fully aware that Daniella knew who the father was and that she intended to tell the father that the child had died at birth....

Rather than insist that Daniella disclose the name of the father so that he could be properly notified and his consent to the adoption procured, the Does and their attorney acquiesced in Daniella's scheme to tell Otto that his child had died at birth, even arranging for Daniella to give birth in a different hospital than she and Otto had originally planned.

. . .

Unsuspecting, Otto returned to Chicago prior to Daniella's due date, whereupon he discovered that Daniella had left him. He learned through friends that she had gone to a women's shelter. He and Daniella then went through a period of reconciliation, during which time she did not inform him that she had arranged to place their child for adoption. When the birth took place on March 16, 1991, Otto's efforts to contact Daniella were rebuffed. He was told by Daniella's friends and relatives that his child had died at birth. We note that Otto and Daniella married in September of 1991.

In the weeks immediately following the birth, Otto, suspicious of the story that his child had died, attempted to discover the truth....

On May 12, 1991, or 57 days after the birth of Richard, Daniella confessed to Otto that she had given birth to a baby boy and had placed him in an adoptive home. At this juncture, Otto commenced his efforts to gain custody of his son.

[In May 1992, the trial court found that Kirchner's consent to Richard's adoption was not necessary because Kirchner was unfit pursuant to section 1(D)(*l*) of the Adoption Act, which provides that an unwed father is unfit where it is found by clear and convincing evidence that he has "failed to demonstrate a reasonable degree of interest, concern or responsibility as to the welfare of a new born child during the first 30 days after its birth." The appeals court affirmed, agreeing that Kirchner was an unfit parent. In addition, the court concentrated its discussion on the best-interests-of-the-child standard.]

... Otto then appealed to this court, which, in a unanimous decision on June 16, 1994, reversed the trial and appellate courts and vacated the adoption, holding that Otto was fit under section 8(a)(1) of the Adoption Act and, thus, that his parental rights had never been properly terminated....

In vacating the adoption, this court noted that a child is not available for adoption until it has been validly determined that the rights of his parents have been properly terminated. As this court held ... when ruling on parental unfitness, a court cannot consider the child's best interests, since the child's welfare is not relevant in judging the fitness of the natural parent. Only after the parent has been found by clear and convincing evidence to be unfit can the court proceed to consider the child's best interests and whether those interests would be served if the child were adopted by the petitioners. Though we note that the best-interests-of-the-child standard is not to be denigrated, we reiterate that this standard is never triggered until after it has been validly determined that a child is available for adoption.

Under Illinois law, parents may be divested of parental rights either through their voluntary consent or involuntarily due to a finding of abuse, abandonment, neglect or unfitness by clear and convincing evidence.... The adoption laws of Illinois ... intentionally place the burden of proof on the adoptive parents. In addition, Illinois law requires a good-faith effort to notify the natural father of the adoption proceedings.... We call this due process of law. In the case at hand, the Does and their lawyer knew that a real father existed whose name the birth mother knew. They also knew that the father, if contacted, would not consent to the adoption....

This court then observed that Otto, as the natural father of Richard, was statutorily entitled to receive notice of the adoption and statutorily required to consent in order for the adoption to be valid, absent a finding of unfitness. Examining the unfitness finding of the trial court, we concluded that the trial court's finding was against the manifest weight of the evidence....

The Does ... did not return Richard to Otto upon the issuance of this court's mandate. Subsequent to this court's opinion vacating the adoption, the General Assembly enacted an amendment to the Adoption Act which specified that it was to take effect immediately and apply to all cases pending at the time of the effective date.... This new legislation ... requires that upon the vacation of an adoption proceeding a custody hearing take place in order to determine who should have custody of the child based upon the child's best interests.

Armed with this new amendment to the Adoption Act, as well as their interpretation of section 601(b)(2) of the Illinois Marriage and Dissolution of Marriage Act ..., the Does then petitioned for a custody hearing in the circuit court of Cook County. Richard's guardian *ad litem* joined that suit on Richard's behalf.

At this juncture, Otto filed the instant petition for writ of *habeas corpus* with our court, in essence arguing that upon the vacatur of Richard's adoption, he was legally vested with Richard's custody and that the Does and Richard's guardian *ad litem* were without standing to seek custody under either the Marriage and Dissolution of Marriage Act or the amendments to the Adoption Act. Insofar as Otto challenged the constitutionality of the Adoption Act, the Illinois Attorney General requested and was granted leave to intervene in support of the constitutionality of the amendment.

... [T]his court concluded that the Does did not legally have standing to request a custody hearing. Consequently, we ordered the writ of *habeas corpus* to issue immediately

. . .

Standing under Section 601(B)(2) of the Illinois Marriage and Dissolution of Marriage Act

Our decision of June 16, 1994, unanimously held that Otto had exhibited sufficient interest in his child during the first 30 days of his life and that the trial court had thus erred in finding him unfit pursuant to section 8(a)(1) of the Adoption Act....

The Does assert that they have standing under section 601(b)(2) of the Marriage and Dissolution of Marriage Act to seek a custody hearing to determine who should have custody of Otto's son now that the adoption has been vacated. We disagree.

. . .

Though our decision is based solely on Illinois law, in determining what role section 601(b)(2) of the Marriage and Dissolution of Marriage Act plays in the instant case we commence with a review of the rights afforded unwed fathers by our Federal Constitution. At stake here is the interest that a natural parent has in the care, custody and control of his or her child, an interest that has long been recognized and afforded constitutional protection....

We find that the rationale underlying the Court's opinions dealing with the rights of unwed fathers thus far suggests that fathers such as Otto, whose parental rights are not properly terminated and who, through deceit, are kept from assuming responsibility for and developing a relationship with their children, are entitled to the same due process rights as fathers who actually are given an opportunity and do develop this relationship. To hold otherwise would be to encourage and reward deceit similar to that which occurred in the instant case.

Moreover, without regard to Federal constitutional jurisprudence, Illinois law requires that Otto be granted the care, custody and control of his son. The Adoption Act ... creates a framework which acknowledges the due process rights of unwed fathers and balances their rights to the care, custody and control of their children with the need to facilitate orderly and final adoptions which are not subject to collateral attack. Toward this end, the Adoption Act provides that where the birth mother is not married to the father, his consent to the adoption is essential except where he has been found unfit by clear and convincing evidence.... Among the statutory factors for finding unfitness, and the one asserted to be applicable to the instant case, is the provision finding unfitness where the father fails to "demonstrate a reasonable degree of interest, concern or responsibility as to the welfare of a new born child during the first 30 days after its birth."

Under the Adoption Act effective at the time this court invalidated the Does' adoption of Richard, an unwed father who was both fit and willing to take on the responsibility of raising his child had a right superior to all others except the birth mother to the care, custody and control of his child.

Moreover, such a fit and willing father had the absolute right to block the adoption of his child, notwithstanding the birth mother's desire to place the child with an adoptive family.... In this manner, the statute safeguards the rights of unwed fathers who come forward and are willing and fit to raise their children.

. . .

Now that the invalid adoption of Richard has been vacated, the Does seek to use the Marriage and Dissolution of Marriage Act to obtain a custody hearing. However, it follows from the Adoption Act that the Does cannot, once an invalid adoption is vacated, attempt to circumvent the rights afforded fathers under the Adoption Act by seeking a custody hearing under the Marriage and Dissolution of Marriage Act, which, unlike the Adoption Act, could result in a father's being divested of his right to the care, custody and control of his child without being found unfit by clear and convincing evidence.

[W]e hold that where an unwed father is fit and willing to develop a relationship with and raise his child, but is prevented from doing so through deceit and an invalid adoption proceeding, that father is entitled to the care, custody and control of his child upon the subsequent vacatur of the invalid adoption. Under these facts, we hold that a section 601(b)(2) hearing under the Marriage and Dissolution of Marriage Act would be improper because it would contravene the safeguards afforded unwed fathers in the Adoption Act.

. . .

The superior rights of the natural parents to the care, custody and control of their child is the law of the land and is also embodied in Illinois statutory law.... Unless a parent consents or is adjudged unfit, a child may not be placed in the custody of a nonparent.... Given that section 601(b)(2) of the Marriage and Dissolution of Marriage Act allows for custody to be vested in a nonparent without first finding unfitness, its application must be narrowly construed to ensure the sanctity of the family and the reciprocal familial rights of parents and their children....

Due Process Rights Of Richard

The final argument raised both by the Does and Richard's guardian *ad litem* is that Richard himself has a liberty interest in the familial relationship he has developed with the Does. In making this argument, the Does and the guardian *ad litem* fail to address the liberty interest Richard may have in being with his natural father. The United States Supreme Court has never decided whether a child has a liberty interest symmetrical with that of a natural parent in maintaining his current relationship.... Attempts to assert such a right on behalf of children who have become psychologically attached to a nonparent have not met with success.... We likewise hold that no such liberty interest exists as regards Richard's psychological attachment to the Does. To hold otherwise would be to overturn the entire jurisprudential history of parental rights in Illinois.

. . .

Conclusion

It would be a grave injustice not only to Otakar Kirchner, but to all mothers, fathers and children, to allow deceit, subterfuge and the erroneous rulings of two lower courts, together with the passage of time resulting from the Does' persistent and intransigent efforts to retain custody of Richard, to inure to the Does' benefit at the expense of the right of Otto and Richard to develop and maintain a family relationship. Moreover, the laws of Illinois, as hereinabove set forth, clearly compel us to order Richard delivered to his father, Otakar Kirchner. Accordingly, we ordered the writ of *habeas corpus* to issue on January 25, 1995, and we hereby reaffirm that order.

. . .

■ Miller, J., dissenting

I do not agree with the majority that we can now conclude, on the evidence before us, that the Does lack standing to request a custody hearing on behalf of the minor child they have unsuccessfully attempted to adopt....

The Does base their right to seek a custody hearing on section 601(b)(2) of the Illinois Marriage and Dissolution of Marriage Act, which provides that a custody hearing may be initiated "by a person other than a parent, by filing a petition for custody of the child in the county in which he is permanently resident or found, but only if he is not in the physical custody of one of his parents." Once the standing requirements of section 601 are satisfied, section 602 directs the court to "determine custody in accordance with the best interest of the child."

The majority concludes that the Does lack standing under section 601(b)(2) to seek a custody hearing on behalf of Baby Richard because the biological father did not voluntarily relinquish custody of the child and because the Does participated in Daniella's deception of Kirchner. In addition, the majority believes that, upon the reversal of an adoption decree, custody of the child involved must automatically vest in a parent whose rights would otherwise have been terminated by the decree.

. . .

The requirement of a voluntary relinquishment of the child by his or her biological parents is intended to discourage child abductions and other illicit self-help measures that would otherwise grant a third party standing pursuant to the literal terms of section 601(b)(2).... This sensible limitation on the availability of relief under that provision is not implicated in the present case, however. Kirchner never had custody of the child to begin with, and therefore he had nothing to relinquish. Indeed, the majority's construction would erect an insuperable bar to the application of these provisions in any case involving an unwed father who is absent at the time of the child's birth and whose parentage is not established prior to the mother's consent for adoption. If one accepts the majority's view that a biological parent must have voluntarily relinquished custody over the child before a nonparent can have standing under section 601(b)(2), then an unwed father who has never had custody will find himself in a more advantageous position than a married father whose conduct could be found to amount to a voluntary relinquishment.

The majority also concludes that standing must be denied to the Does because they took part in Daniella's deception of Kirchner. I agree with the majority's premise that a nonparent seeking standing under section 601(b)(2) must not have acted illicitly in gaining custody of the child. That inquiry, however, raises a number of important factual questions that have not previously been resolved. Indeed, determinations of standing under section

601(b)(2) are fact-intensive inquiries that require consideration of a number of circumstances ... Nonetheless, the majority proceeds to resolve these issues without the benefit of a factual record adequate to support the opinion's conclusions.

. . .

■ McMorrow, J., dissenting:

. . .

Today, by its total failure to recognize the rights of the child who has come to be known as "Baby Richard" and the rights of adoptive parents in the circumstances of this case, the majority grants Otakar Kirchner the unfettered right to remove Richard, almost four years old, from the only home and parents he has known. This ruling is extraordinary and in contravention of Illinois law and constitutional protections: the majority permits Richard to be taken by Kirchner from his home of the past four years, and be placed in the home occupied by a man and woman Richard has never seen or known. Significantly, the transfer into the home of these total strangers to Richard is ordered by the majority without any hearing to determine how and when such transfer should occur, and whether the home into which Richard is being placed is in his best interests. In abdication of its duty to minors, and irrespective of the fact that there has never at any time been a hearing at the trial court level at which a record would be developed, the majority issued the writ of *habeas corpus* to forthwith turn over the child to Kirchner.

The majority today sanctions the placement of this child into a home that is strange to him. The majority permits this transfer, although the court has little knowledge of the fitness of the occupants of that home or of the environment in that home.

. . .

III. Awarding the Writ of *Habeas Corpus* "Forthwith" Violated Richard's Constitutional Rights.

. . .

The majority's summary decision to grant Kirchner's petition for a writ of *habeas corpus* violates Richard's right to procedural due process under the fourteenth amendment of the United States Constitution. [T]he issue of custody is different from the issues of adoption and the improper termination of parental rights. Unlike a termination of parental rights, which is concerned primarily with protecting the rights of parents, a change or modification of an existing custodial relationship is primarily concerned with protecting the child's interest in a healthy, stable environment. Under the Marriage Act and section 20 of the Adoption Act, the Illinois legislature created a constitutionally protected liberty interest in a child's emotional and psychological relationship with nonparent custodians, and has also provided the requisite procedures to prevent the summary or improper severing of this relationship in a way that would be harmful to the child.... By ignoring the child custody procedures provided by the Marriage Act and section 20 of the Adoption Act, the majority has arbitrarily deprived Richard of due process under the law by disregarding the intent of the legislature.

. . .

The granting of Kirchner's writ of *habeas corpus* effectively extinguished Richard's opportunity to receive a best-interests custody hearing. The trial court has jurisdiction under the Marriage Act and section 20 of the Adoption Act to adjudicate Richard's custody. The trial court is also the proper forum to conduct a fact finding hearing that would result in a custody determination in accord with Richard's best interests. Since this court found that Kirchner was a fit parent and that Kirchner's parental rights were improperly terminated, a valid adoption of Richard by the Does cannot be granted absent Kirchner's voluntary termination of his parental rights. [T]he proper termination of parental rights is the necessary prerequisite to granting a valid adoption.

However, in a custody dispute, the best interest of the child is of paramount importance. In dispensing with a custody hearing, the majority has placed the emotional and psychological well-being of a small child in danger.... One of the purposes of a custody hearing is to provide for an orderly change or modification in custody without exposing the child to risk of undue harm. At such a custody hearing, Kirchner's important rights will be considered along with the other relevant factors. The granting of the writ of *habeas corpus* to Kirchner, as the majority has done, ignores the State's valid interest in the psychological and emotional health of its children and unconstitutionally deprives Richard of a best-interests custody hearing, granted to him by the Illinois legislature.

IV. The Right to a Custody Hearing Provided for in the Marriage Act and the Adoption Act Does Not Impinge on Kirchner's Constitutional Right Against State Interference.

. . .

By giving the constitutional protections afforded to a "natural" or "unitary" family to Kirchner, the majority has clouded the central question: Do the custody interests identified in the Marriage Act and the Adoption Act to prevent the summary, arbitrary or wrongful termination of Richard's emotional and psychological ties to the Does unconstitutionally impinge on the rights of Kirchner, the unwed, noncustodial, biological father who lacks any emotional or psychological ties to his offspring? A study of the five cases in which the U.S. Supreme Court has addressed the constitutional rights of unwed biological fathers indicates that Kirchner's rights as a biological father are not impinged upon by the allowance of the custody hearings sanctioned in the Marriage Act and the Adoption Act.

. . .

The majority asserts that the rationale underlying these five Supreme Court opinions entitles Kirchner to the highest degree of constitutional protection available to an unwed biological father because of the alleged deceit in the termination of Kirchner's parental rights.... This assertion is unfounded. The majority fails to understand that the Supreme Court, in these opinions, has afforded a biological father a high degree of due process protection to prevent improper *termination of his parental rights*.... These opinions do not afford the same protection to a biological father in a *custody proceeding*. Kirchner's parental rights were afforded complete protection under due process pursuant to *In re Petition of Doe* (1994), 638 N.E.2d 181, which reinstated Kirchner's improperly terminated parental rights. On the issue of Kirchner's improperly terminated rights, his due process rights have been vindicated. However, neither the United States Constitution nor Illinois law automatically vest custody in a noncustodial, biological father following the recognition of his parental rights. In sum, although Kirchner's right to develop a psychological father-son relationship was vindicated in the prior appeal, the State does not unconstitutionally impinge on that right by limiting or overseeing the way in which this relationship will develop under the circumstances of this case. That is the purpose of a custody determination. Custody will only be granted after a hearing on the child's best interests.

CONCLUSION

In defiance of established Illinois law and the constitutional rights of a small child under this law, the majority has given Kirchner the power to summarily terminate the only family relationship that Richard has ever known.

In denying Richard the protections the State has provided him, the majority places more importance on biology than on the importance of the nurturing, caring, and loving involved in raising a child....

Hopefully, someday children will be given their due process rights under the law, and also be given the same guarantees of their rights as are given to all other citizens. In its wisdom, this court should have examined its thinking, not only in the light of statutes and precedent, but also in the light of reality and human consequences. In both lights this court has failed Baby Richard. Accordingly, I dissent.

NOTE

Uniform Adoption Act § 3–707(d) provides: "A decree of adoption or other order issued under this [Act] is not subject to a challenge begun more than six months after the decree or order is issued. If a challenge is brought by an individual whose parental relationship to an adoptee is terminated by a decree or order under this [Act], the court shall deny the challenge, unless the court finds by clear and convincing evidence that the decree or order is not in the best interest of the adoptee."

The Comment to this section states:

> "Under current law in most States, it is not clear for how long a decree of adoption may be challenged for fraud, undue influence, duress, failure to provide notice, lack of subject matter jurisdiction, or other alleged irregularities or constitutional violations. Some States have specific time limitations for challenging adoption decrees; many simply rely on their general statutes of limitation or on their own version of Federal Rule of Civil Procedure 60(b).
>
> For at least two reasons, this Act, like the Uniform Putative and Unknown Fathers Act (UPUFA) and the Uniform Parentage Act (UPA), provides that any challenge must be brought within six months of the entry of the decree of adoption or other final order under the Act. The first reason is the desire to minimize the risks of serious harm to minor children and their adoptive families which arise if the finality of adoptions and termination orders is not secure. Second, if the procedures of this Act are followed in good faith, there are likely to be very few cases in which a challenge is warranted. Therefore, six months is a sufficient period of time for bringing a challenge.

INDEX

References are to Pages

†